PROFESSIONAL
C# 4 AND .NET 4

INTRODUCTION..LI

▶ **PART I: THE C# LANGUAGE**

CHAPTER 1: .NET Architecture...3
CHAPTER 2: Core C# 23
CHAPTER 3: Objects and Types...65
CHAPTER 4: Inheritance...89
CHAPTER 5: Generics...107
CHAPTER 6: Arrays and Tuples 129
CHAPTER 7: Operators and Casts..151
CHAPTER 8: Delegates, Lambdas, and Events 183
CHAPTER 9: Strings and Regular Expressions 207
CHAPTER 10: Collections 225
CHAPTER 11: Language Integrated Query.....................................267
CHAPTER 12: Dynamic Language Extensions...................................295
CHAPTER 13: Memory Management and Pointers................................307
CHAPTER 14: Reflection..333
CHAPTER 15: Errors and Exceptions 351

▶ **PART II: VISUAL STUDIO**

CHAPTER 16: Visual Studio 2010..373
CHAPTER 17: Deployment..407

▶ **PART III: FOUNDATION**

CHAPTER 18: Assemblies 431
CHAPTER 19: Instrumentation 461
CHAPTER 20: Threads, Tasks, and Synchronization..........................491
CHAPTER 21: Security 545

Continues

CHAPTER 22: Localization 569

CHAPTER 23: System.Transactions 605

CHAPTER 24: Networking 637

CHAPTER 25: Windows Services 667

CHAPTER 26: Interop 695

CHAPTER 27: Core XAML 727

CHAPTER 28: Managed Extensibility Framework 747

CHAPTER 29: Manipulating Files and the Registry 771

▶ **PART IV: DATA**

CHAPTER 30: Core ADO.NET 817

CHAPTER 31: ADO.NET Entity Framework. 861

CHAPTER 32: Data Services 885

CHAPTER 33: Manipulating XML 903

CHAPTER 34: .NET Programming with SQL Server 955

▶ **PART V: PRESENTATION**

CHAPTER 35: Core WPF. 983

CHAPTER 36: Business Applications with WPF. 1035

CHAPTER 37: Creating Documents with WPF 1075

CHAPTER 38: Silverlight. 1095

CHAPTER 39: Windows Forms 1117

CHAPTER 40: Core ASP.NET 1149

CHAPTER 41: ASP.NET Features 1185

CHAPTER 42: ASP.NET Dynamic Data and MVC. 1243

▶ **PART VI: COMMUNICATION**

CHAPTER 43: Windows Communication Foundation. 1279

CHAPTER 44: Windows Workflow Foundation 4 1309

CHAPTER 45: Peer-to-Peer Networking 1339

CHAPTER 46: Message Queuing 1357

CHAPTER 47: Syndication 1387

APPENDIX: Guidelines for Windows 7 and Windows Server 2008 R2 1397

INDEX. **1417**

▶ ONLINE CHAPTERS

CHAPTER 48: Graphics with GDI+ OC1

CHAPTER 49: Visual Studio Tools for Office. OC49

CHAPTER 50: Managed Add-In Framework. OC77

CHAPTER 51: Enterprise Services OC97

CHAPTER 52: Directory Services OC123

CHAPTER 53: C#, Visual Basic, C++/CLI, and F# OC157

CHAPTER 54: .NET Remoting OC191

CHAPTER 55: Web Services with ASP.NET OC233

CHAPTER 56: LINQ to SQL OC255

CHAPTER 57: Windows Workflow Foundation 3.0 . . . . .OC279

PROFESSIONAL

C# 4 and .NET 4

Christian Nagel
Bill Evjen
Jay Glynn
Karli Watson
Morgan Skinner

WILEY

Wiley Publishing, Inc.

Professional C# 4 and .NET 4

Published by
Wiley Publishing, Inc.
10475 Crosspoint Boulevard
Indianapolis, IN 46256
www.wiley.com

Copyright © 2010 by Wiley Publishing, Inc., Indianapolis, Indiana

Published simultaneously in Canada

ISBN: 978-0-470-50225-9

Manufactured in the United States of America

10 9 8 7 6 5 4 3 2 1

For general information on our other products and services please contact our Customer Care Department within the United States at (877) 762-2974, outside the United States at (317) 572-3993 or fax (317) 572-4002.

Wiley also publishes its books in a variety of electronic formats. Some content that appears in print may not be available in electronic books.

Library of Congress Control Number: 2009942439

ABOUT THE AUTHORS

 **CHRISTIAN NAGEL** is a Microsoft Regional Director and Microsoft MVP, an associate of thinktecture, and owner of CN innovation. He is a software architect and developer who offers training and consulting on how to develop Microsoft .NET solutions. He looks back on more than 25 years of software development experience. Christian started his computing career with PDP 11 and VAX/ VMS systems, covering a variety of languages and platforms. Since 2000, when .NET was just a technology preview, he has been working with various .NET technologies to build numerous .NET solutions. With his profound knowledge of Microsoft technologies, he has written numerous .NET books, and is certified as a Microsoft Certified Trainer and Professional Developer. Christian speaks at international conferences such as TechEd and Tech Days, and started INETA Europe to support .NET user groups. You can contact Christian via his web sites, www.cninnovation.com and www.thinktecture.com, and follow his tweets on www.twitter.com/christiannagel.

 **BILL EVJEN** is an active proponent of .NET technologies and community-based learning initiatives for .NET. He has been actively involved with .NET since the first bits were released in 2000. In the same year, Bill founded the St. Louis .NET User Group (www.stlnet.org), one of the world's first such groups. Bill is also the founder and former executive director of the International .NET Association (www.ineta.org), which represents more than 500,000 members worldwide.

Based in St. Louis, Missouri, Bill is an acclaimed author and speaker on ASP.NET and Web Services. He has authored or coauthored more than 20 books including *Professional ASP.NET 4*, *Professional VB 2008*, *ASP.NET Professional Secrets*, *XML Web Services for ASP.NET*, and *Web Services Enhancements: Understanding the WSE for Enterprise Applications* (all published by Wiley). In addition to writing, Bill is a speaker at numerous conferences, including DevConnections, VSLive, and TechEd. Along with these activities, Bill works closely with Microsoft as a Microsoft Regional Director and an MVP.

Bill is the Global Head of Platform Architecture for Thomson Reuters, Lipper, the international news and financial services company (www.thomsonreuters.com). He graduated from Western Washington University in Bellingham, Washington, with a Russian language degree. When he isn't tinkering on the computer, he can usually be found at his summer house in Toivakka, Finland. You can reach Bill on Twitter at @billevjen.

 **JAY GLYNN** is the Principle Architect at PureSafety, a leading provider of results-driven software and information solutions for workforce safety and health. Jay has been developing software for over 25 years and has worked with a variety of languages and technologies including PICK Basic, C, C++, Visual Basic, C# and Java. Jay currently lives in Franklin, Tennessee with his wife and son.

KARLI WATSON is consultant at Infusion Development (www.infusion.com), a technology architect at Boost.net (www.boost.net), and a freelance IT specialist, author, and developer. For the most part, he immerses himself in .NET (in particular C# and lately WPF) and has written numerous books in the field. He specializes in communicating complex ideas in a way that is accessible to anyone with a passion to learn, and spends much of his time playing with new technology to find new things to teach people about.

During those (seemingly few) times where he isn't doing the above, Karli will probably be wishing he was hurtling down a mountain on a snowboard. Or possibly trying to get his novel published. Either way, you'll know him by his brightly colored clothes. You can also find him tweeting online at www.twitter.com/karlequin, and maybe one day he'll get round to making himself a web site.

MORGAN SKINNER began his computing career at a young age on the Sinclair ZX80 at school, where he was underwhelmed by some code a teacher had written and so began programming in assembly language. Since then he's used all sorts of languages and platforms, including VAX Macro Assembler, Pascal, Modula2, Smalltalk, X86 assembly language, PowerBuilder, C/C++, VB, and currently C# (of course). He's been programming in .NET since the PDC release in 2000, and liked it so much he joined Microsoft in 2001. He now works in premier support for developers and spends most of his time assisting customers with C#. You can reach Morgan at www.morganskinner.com.

ABOUT THE TECHNICAL EDITORS

ALEXEI GORKOV is the chief software engineer at EPAM Systems (www.epam.com), a leading software development outsourcing company in Central and Eastern Europe. He has worked with .NET since 2004 and as a front-end developer involved in development of web portals and line-of-business web applications using Microsoft technologies. Over the past four years, he has edited more than a dozen programming books from Wiley Publishing on ASP.NET, Ajax, JavaScript, CSS and XML. He lives in Saratov, Russia.

MITCHEL SELLERS is the CEO of IowaComputerGurus Inc. His extensive experience in software development has lead to a focus on proper architecture, performance, stability, and overall cost effectiveness of delivered solutions. He is the author of *Professional DotNetNuke Module Programming* and many technical articles, and is currently working on his next book, *Visual Studio 2010 and .NET 4 Six-in-One*, scheduled for publication by Wiley in early 2010. He is a regular speaker at user groups and conferences.

Mitchel is a Microsoft C# MVP and a Microsoft Certified Professional, an active participant in the .NET and DotNetNuke development communities, and a DotNetNuke Core Team member. For more information, see his resume at MitchelSellers.com.

CREDITS

ACQUISITIONS EDITOR
Paul Reese

PROJECT EDITOR
Sara Shlaer

DEVELOPMENT EDITOR
Susan Cohen

TECHNICAL EDITORS
Alexei Gorkov
Mitchel Sellers

PRODUCTION EDITOR
Kathleen Wisor

COPY EDITORS
Tricia Liebig
Foxxe Editorial Services

EDITORIAL DIRECTOR
Robyn B. Siesky

EDITORIAL MANAGER
Mary Beth Wakefield

MARKETING MANAGER
David Mayhew

PRODUCTION MANAGER
Tim Tate

VICE PRESIDENT AND EXECUTIVE GROUP PUBLISHER
Richard Swadley

VICE PRESIDENT AND EXECUTIVE PUBLISHER
Barry Pruett

ASSOCIATE PUBLISHER
Jim Minatel

PROJECT COORDINATOR, COVER
Lynsey Stanford

PROOFREADER
Word One New York

INDEXER
Robert Swanson

COVER DESIGNER
Michael E. Trent

COVER IMAGE
© Punchstock/Corbis

ACKNOWLEDGMENTS

THANKS TO ALL AT WILEY for your patience when I started working later on the book than I had expected and planned. Special thanks to Sara Shlaer who was of great support with the time pressure and the change of the Wrox style. Similar to the authors, she worked many weekends to get the book out on time. Many thanks!

—Christian Nagel

THANKS TO SARA SHLAER, Paul Reese, and Jim Minatel for the opportunity to work on such a great book, and to the technical editors, Alexei Gorkov and Mitchel Sellers, for their excellent work. In addition to my co-authors, I would like to thank my family for putting up with all the writing. Thank you Tuija, Sofia, Henri, and Kalle!

—Bill Evjen

I WOULD LIKE TO THANK Sara Shlaer, Paul Reese, and the rest of the team at Wrox for all the help they provided. I would also like to thank my wife and son for putting up with the nights and weekends lost to the computer. They are my inspiration.

—Jay Glynn

THANKS TO ALL AT WILEY for their support and assistance on this project, as well as their understanding and flexibility in dealing with an author who never seems to have enough time to write. Special thanks to Sara Shlaer — one of the best and friendliest editors I've had the pleasure to work with. Also, thanks to friends, family, and work colleagues for understanding why I haven't had time for much socializing lately, and to donna, as always, for all her support and for putting up with all the late nights.

—Karli Watson

CONTENTS

INTRODUCTION   *LI*

PART I: THE C# LANGUAGE

CHAPTER 1: .NET ARCHITECTURE   3

The Relationship of C# to .NET	**3**
The Common Language Runtime	**4**
Platform Independence	4
Performance Improvement	4
Language Interoperability	5
A Closer Look at Intermediate Language	**6**
Support for Object Orientation and Interfaces	7
Distinct Value and Reference Types	8
Strong Data Typing	8
Error Handling with Exceptions	13
Use of Attributes	13
Assemblies	**14**
Private Assemblies	14
Shared Assemblies	15
Reflection	15
Parallel Programming	15
.NET Framework Classes	**16**
Namespaces	**17**
Creating .NET Applications Using C#	**17**
Creating ASP.NET Applications	17
Creating Windows Forms	19
Using the Windows Presentation Foundation (WPF)	19
Windows Controls	19
Windows Services	20
Windows Communication Foundation	20
Windows Workflow Foundation	20
The Role of C# in the .NET Enterprise Architecture	**20**
Summary	**21**

CHAPTER 2: CORE C#   23

Your First C# Program   23
The Code   24
Compiling and Running the Program   24
A Closer Look   25

Variables   26
Initialization of Variables   27
Type Inference   28
Variable Scope   29
Constants   31

Predefined Data Types   31
Value Types and Reference Types   31
CTS Types   33
Predefined Value Types   33
Predefined Reference Types   35

Flow Control   37
Conditional Statements   37
Loops   40
Jump Statements   43

Enumerations   44

Namespaces   45
The using Directive   46
Namespace Aliases   47

The Main() Method   48
Multiple Main() Methods   48
Passing Arguments to Main()   49

More on Compiling C# Files   50

Console I/O   51

Using Comments   53
Internal Comments within the Source Files   53
XML Documentation   53

The C# Preprocessor Directives   55
#define and #undef   55
#if, #elif, #else, and #endif   56
#warning and #error   57
#region and #endregion   57
#line   57
#pragma   58

C# Programming Guidelines   58
Rules for Identifiers   58
Usage Conventions   59

Summary   64

CHAPTER 3: OBJECTS AND TYPES — 65

Classes and Structs — 65
Classes — 66
    Data Members — 66
    Function Members — 67
    readonly Fields — 78
Anonymous Types — 79
Structs — 80
    Structs Are Value Types — 81
    Structs and Inheritance — 82
    Constructors for Structs — 82
Partial Classes — 82
Static Classes — 84
The Object Class — 84
    System.Object Methods — 84
    The ToString() Method — 85
Extension Methods — 86
Summary — 87

CHAPTER 4: INHERITANCE — 89

Types of Inheritance — 89
    Implementation Versus Interface Inheritance — 89
    Multiple Inheritance — 90
    Structs and Classes — 90
Implementation Inheritance — 90
    Virtual Methods — 91
    Hiding Methods — 92
    Calling Base Versions of Functions — 93
    Abstract Classes and Functions — 93
    Sealed Classes and Methods — 94
    Constructors of Derived Classes — 94
Modifiers — 99
    Visibility Modifiers — 99
    Other Modifiers — 99
Interfaces — 100
    Defining and Implementing Interfaces — 101
    Derived Interfaces — 104
Summary — 105

CHAPTER 5: GENERICS   107

Generics Overview   107
Performance   108
Type Safety   109
Binary Code Reuse   109
Code Bloat   109
Naming Guidelines   110
Creating Generic Classes   110
Generics Features   113
Default Values   114
Constraints   114
Inheritance   117
Static Members   117
Generic Interfaces   118
Covariance and Contra-variance   118
Covariance with Generic Interfaces   119
Contra-Variance with Generic Interfaces   120
Generic Structs   121
Generic Methods   123
Generic Methods Example   124
Generic Methods with Constraints   125
Generic Methods with Delegates   126
Generic Methods Specialization   126
Summary   128

CHAPTER 6: ARRAYS AND TUPLES   129

Simple Arrays   129
Array Declaration   129
Array Initialization   130
Accessing Array Elements   130
Using Reference Types   131
Multidimensional Arrays   132
Jagged Arrays   133
Array Class   134
Creating Arrays   134
Copying Arrays   135
Sorting   136
Arrays as Parameters   139
Array Covariance   139
ArraySegment<T>   140
Enumerations   140

IEnumerator Interface   141
foreach Statement   141
yield Statement   142
Tuples   **146**
Structural Comparison   **147**
Summary   **149**

CHAPTER 7: OPERATORS AND CASTS   **151**

Operators   **151**
Operator Shortcuts   153
Operator Precedence   157
Type Safety   **157**
Type Conversions   158
Boxing and Unboxing   161
Comparing Objects for Equality   **162**
Comparing Reference Types for Equality   162
Comparing Value Types for Equality   163
Operator Overloading   **163**
How Operators Work   164
Operator Overloading Example: The Vector Struct   165
Which Operators Can You Overload?   171
User-Defined Casts   **172**
Implementing User-Defined Casts   173
Multiple Casting   179
Summary   **182**

CHAPTER 8: DELEGATES, LAMBDAS, AND EVENTS   **183**

Delegates   **183**
Declaring Delegates   184
Using Delegates   185
Simple Delegate Example   188
Action<T> and Func<T> Delegates   190
BubbleSorter Example   190
Multicast Delegates   193
Anonymous Methods   196
Lambda Expressions   **197**
Parameters   198
Multiple Code Lines   198
Variables Outside of the Lambda Expression   199
Events   **200**

Event Publisher 200

Event Listener 202

Weak Events 203

Summary **205**

CHAPTER 9: STRINGS AND REGULAR EXPRESSIONS 207

Examining System.String **208**

Building Strings 209

StringBuilder Members 211

Format Strings 212

Regular Expressions **217**

Introduction to Regular Expressions 218

The RegularExpressionsPlayaround Example 219

Displaying Results 221

Matches, Groups, and Captures 223

Summary **224**

CHAPTER 10: COLLECTIONS 225

Collection Interfaces and Types **225**

Lists **226**

Creating Lists 228

Read-Only Collections 236

Queue **236**

Stack **240**

Linked List **241**

Sorted List **246**

Dictionaries **248**

Key Type 248

Dictionary Example 250

Lookup 253

Sorted Dictionary 254

Sets **255**

Observable Collection **256**

Bit Arrays **258**

BitArray 258

BitVector32 260

Concurrent Collections **262**

Performance **264**

Summary **266**

CHAPTER 11: LANGUAGE INTEGRATED QUERY   267

LINQ Overview   **267**
Lists and Entities   267
LINQ Query   271
Extension Methods   272
Deferred Query Execution   273
Standard Query Operators   **275**
Filtering   277
Filtering with Index   277
Type Filtering   278
Compound from   278
Sorting   279
Grouping   280
Grouping with Nested Objects   281
Join   282
Set Operations   283
Zip   284
Partitioning   285
Aggregate Operators   286
Conversion   287
Generation Operators   288
Parallel LINQ   **289**
Parallel Queries   289
Partitioners   290
Cancellation   290
Expression Trees   **291**
LINQ Providers   **293**
Summary   **294**

CHAPTER 12: DYNAMIC LANGUAGE EXTENSIONS   295

Dynamic Language Runtime   **295**
The Dynamic Type   **296**
Dynamic Behind the Scenes   297
Hosting the DLR ScriptRuntime   **300**
DynamicObject and ExpandoObject   **302**
DynamicObject   302
ExpandoObject   304
Summary   **305**

CHAPTER 13: MEMORY MANAGEMENT AND POINTERS   307

Memory Management Under the Hood   **307**
Value Data Types   308
Reference Data Types   309
Garbage Collection   311
Freeing Unmanaged Resources   **312**
Destructors   313
The IDisposable Interface   314
Implementing IDisposable and a Destructor   315
Unsafe Code   **317**
Accessing Memory Directly with Pointers   317
Pointer Example: PointerPlayground   325
Using Pointers to Optimize Performance   329
Summary   **332**

CHAPTER 14: REFLECTION   333

Custom Attributes   **334**
Writing Custom Attributes   334
Custom Attribute Example: WhatsNewAttributes   337
Using Reflection   **340**
The System.Type Class   340
The TypeView Example   342
The Assembly Class   344
Completing the WhatsNewAttributes Example   345
Summary   **349**

CHAPTER 15: ERRORS AND EXCEPTIONS   351

Exception Classes   **352**
Catching Exceptions   **353**
Implementing Multiple Catch Blocks   355
Catching Exceptions from Other Code   359
System.Exception Properties   359
What Happens If an Exception Isn't Handled?   360
Nested try Blocks   360
User-Defined Exception Classes   **362**
Catching the User-Defined Exceptions   363
Throwing the User-Defined Exceptions   364
Defining the User-Defined Exception Classes   367
Summary   **369**

PART II: VISUAL STUDIO

CHAPTER 16: VISUAL STUDIO 2010 — 373

Working with Visual Studio 2010 — 373
Creating a Project — 378
Distinguishing Projects from Solutions — 383
Windows Application Code — 386
Exploring and Coding a Project — 386
Building a Project — 394
Debugging Your Code — 398
Refactoring Tools — 401
Multi-Targeting the .NET Framework — 403
WPF, WCF, WF, and More — 404
Building WPF Applications in Visual Studio 2010 — 404
Building WF Applications in Visual Studio 2010 — 405
Summary — 406

CHAPTER 17: DEPLOYMENT — 407

Planning for Deployment — 407
Deployment Options — 408
Deployment Requirements — 408
Deploying the .NET Runtime — 409
Simple Deployment Options — 409
Xcopy Deployment — 410
Xcopy and Web Applications — 411
Publishing a Web Site — 411
Visual Studio 2010 Setup and Deployment Projects — 412
What is Windows Installer? — 412
Creating Installers — 413
ClickOnce — 419
ClickOnce Operation — 419
Publishing a ClickOnce Application — 420
ClickOnce Settings — 420
Application Cache for ClickOnce Files — 421
Application Security — 421
Visual Studio 2010 Editors — 422
File System Editor — 422
Registry Editor — 422
File Types Editor — 423
User Interface Editor — 423

Custom Actions Editor	424
Launch Conditions Editor	426
Summary	**427**

PART III: FOUNDATION

CHAPTER 18: ASSEMBLIES | 431

What Are Assemblies?	**431**
Assembly Features	432
Assembly Structure	432
Assembly Manifests	433
Namespaces, Assemblies, and Components	434
Private and Shared Assemblies	434
Satellite Assemblies	434
Viewing Assemblies	434
Creating Assemblies	**435**
Creating Modules and Assemblies	435
Assembly Attributes	436
Creating and Loading Assemblies Dynamically	438
Application Domains	**441**
Shared Assemblies	**445**
Strong Names	445
Integrity Using Strong Names	446
Global Assembly Cache	446
Creating a Shared Assembly	447
Create a Strong Name	447
Installing the Shared Assembly	448
Using the Shared Assembly	448
Delayed Signing of Assemblies	449
References	450
Native Image Generator	451
Configuring .NET Applications	**452**
Configuration Categories	452
Binding to Assemblies	453
Versioning	**454**
Version Numbers	455
Getting the Version Programmatically	455
Binding to Assembly Versions	456
Publisher Policy Files	457
Runtime Version	458
Summary	**458**

CHAPTER 19: INSTRUMENTATION   461

Code Contracts   461
Preconditions   463
Postconditions   464
Invariants   465
Contracts for Interfaces   465

Tracing   467
Trace Sources   468
Trace Switches   469
Trace Listeners   470
Filters   471
Correlation   472

Event Logging   475
Event-Logging Architecture   476
Event-Logging Classes   477
Creating an Event Source   478
Writing Event Logs   479
Resource Files   479

Performance Monitoring   483
Performance-Monitoring Classes   483
Performance Counter Builder   484
Adding PerformanceCounter Components   486
perfmon.exe   488

Summary   489

CHAPTER 20: THREADS, TASKS, AND SYNCHRONIZATION   491

Overview   492
Asynchronous Delegates   492
Polling   493
Wait Handle   493
Asynchronous Callback   494

The Thread Class   495
Passing Data to Threads   496
Background Threads   497
Thread Priority   498
Controlling Threads   499

Thread Pools   499
Tasks   501
Starting Tasks   501
Continuation Tasks   502

Task Hierarchies 502
Results from Tasks 503
Parallel Class **504**
Looping with the Parallel.For Method 504
Looping with the Parallel.ForEach Method 506
Invoking Multiple Methods with the Parallel.Invoke Method 507
Cancellation Framework **507**
Cancellation of Parallel.For 507
Cancellation of Tasks 509
Threading Issues **510**
Race Condition 510
Deadlock 513
Synchronization **514**
lock Statement and Thread Safety 515
Interlocked 520
Monitor 521
SpinLock 522
WaitHandle 522
Mutex 523
Semaphore 524
Events 526
Barrier 529
ReaderWriterLockSlim 530
Timers **533**
Event-Based Asynchronous Pattern **534**
BackgroundWorker 535
Creating an Event-Based Asynchronous Component 539
Summary **543**

CHAPTER 21: SECURITY **545**

Authentication and Authorization **545**
Identity and Principal 545
Roles 547
Declarative Role-Based Security 547
Client Application Services 548
Encryption **552**
Signature 554
Key Exchange and Secure Transfer 556
Access Control to Resources **558**
Code Access Security **561**
Security Transparency Level 2 562

Permissions 562
Distributing Code Using Certificates **567**
Summary **568**

CHAPTER 22: LOCALIZATION **569**

Namespace System.Globalization **569**
Unicode Issues 570
Cultures and Regions 570
Cultures in Action 574
Sorting 578
Resources **579**
Creating Resource Files 579
Resource File Generator 579
ResourceWriter 580
Using Resource Files 581
The System.Resources Namespace 584
Windows Forms Localization Using Visual Studio **584**
Changing the Culture Programmatically 588
Using Custom Resource Messages 590
Automatic Fallback for Resources 590
Outsourcing Translations 591
Localization with ASP.NET **591**
Localization with WPF **593**
.NET Resources with WPF 594
XAML Resource Dictionaries 594
A Custom Resource Reader **598**
Creating a DatabaseResourceReader 598
Creating a DatabaseResourceSet 600
Creating a DatabaseResourceManager 600
Client Application for DatabaseResourceReader 601
Creating Custom Cultures **601**
Summary **603**

CHAPTER 23: SYSTEM.TRANSACTIONS **605**

Overview **605**
Transaction Phases 606
ACID Properties 607
Database and Entity Classes **607**
Traditional Transactions **609**
ADO.NET Transactions 609

System.EnterpriseServices 610
System.Transactions **611**
Committable Transactions 612
Transaction Promotion 614
Dependent Transactions 616
Ambient Transactions 618
Isolation Level **624**
Custom Resource Managers **626**
Transactional Resources 627
Transactions with Windows 7 and Windows Server 2008 **632**
Summary **635**

CHAPTER 24: NETWORKING **637**

The WebClient Class **638**
Downloading Files 638
Basic WebClient Example 638
Uploading Files 639
WebRequest and WebResponse Classes **640**
Authentication 642
Working with Proxies 642
Asynchronous Page Requests 642
Displaying Output as an HTML Page **643**
Allowing Simple Web Browsing from Your Applications 643
Launching Internet Explorer Instances 645
Giving Your Application More IE-Type Features 645
Printing Using the WebBrowser Control 651
Displaying the Code of a Requested Page 651
The WebRequest and WebResponse Classes Hierarchy 652
Utility Classes **653**
URIs 653
IP Addresses and DNS Names 654
Lower-Level Protocols **656**
Using SmtpClient 657
Using the TCP Classes 658
The TcpSend and TcpReceive Examples 658
TCP Versus UDP 660
The UDP Class 661
The Socket Class 661
Summary **665**

CHAPTER 25: WINDOWS SERVICES   **667**

What Is a Windows Service?   **667**

Windows Services Architecture   **668**

Service Program   668
Service Control Program   670
Service Configuration Program   670
Classes for Windows Services   670

Creating a Windows Service Program   **670**

Creating Core Functionality for the Service   671
QuoteClient Example   673
Windows Service Program   675
Threading and Services   679
Service Installation   679
Installation Program   679

Monitoring and Controlling Windows Services   **683**

MMC Snap-in   683
net.exe Utility   684
sc.exe Utility   684
Visual Studio Server Explorer   684
Writing a Custom Service Controller   684

Troubleshooting and Event Logging   **692**

Summary   **693**

CHAPTER 26: INTEROP   **695**

.NET and COM   **695**

Metadata   696
Freeing Memory   696
Interfaces   697
Method Binding   698
Data Types   698
Registration   698
Threading   699
Error Handling   700
Events   701
Marshaling   701

Using a COM Component from a .NET Client   **702**

Creating a COM Component   702
Creating a Runtime Callable Wrapper   707
Using the RCW   708
Using the COM Server with Dynamic Language Extensions   709

Threading Issues | 710
Adding Connection Points | 710
Using a .NET Component from a COM Client | **712**
COM Callable Wrapper | 713
Creating a .NET Component | 713
Creating a Type Library | 714
COM Interop Attributes | 716
COM Registration | 718
Creating a COM Client Application | 718
Adding Connection Points | 720
Creating a Client with a Sink Object | 721
Platform Invoke | **722**
Summary | **726**

CHAPTER 27: CORE XAML | 727

Overview | **727**
Elements Map to .NET Objects | 728
Using Custom .NET Classes | 729
Properties as Attributes | 730
Properties as Elements | 731
Essential .NET Types | 731
Collections | 731
Constructors | 732
Dependency Properties | **732**
Creating a Dependency Property | 733
Coerce Value Callback | 734
Value Changed Callbacks and Events | 735
Bubbling and Tunneling Events | **736**
Attached Properties | **739**
Markup Extensions | **741**
Creating Custom Markup Extensions | 742
XAML-Defined Markup Extensions | 744
Reading and Writing XAML | **744**
Summary | **745**

CHAPTER 28: MANAGED EXTENSIBILITY FRAMEWORK | 747

MEF Architecture | **747**
Contracts | **754**
Exports | **755**
Exporting Properties and Methods | 759

Exporting Metadata 760

Imports **762**

Lazy Loading of Parts 764

Containers and Export Providers **765**

Catalogs **767**

Summary **769**

CHAPTER 29: MANIPULATING FILES AND THE REGISTRY **771**

Managing the File System **771**

.NET Classes That Represent Files and Folders 772

The Path Class 775

A FileProperties Sample 775

Moving, Copying, and Deleting Files **780**

FilePropertiesAndMovement Sample 780

Looking at the Code for FilePropertiesAndMovement 781

Reading and Writing to Files **784**

Reading a File 784

Writing to a File 786

Streams 787

Buffered Streams 788

Reading and Writing to Binary Files Using FileStream 789

Reading and Writing to Text Files 793

Mapped Memory Files **799**

Reading Drive Information **800**

File Security **802**

Reading ACLs from a File 802

Reading ACLs from a Directory 803

Adding and Removing ACLs from a File 805

Reading and Writing to the Registry **806**

The Registry 806

The .NET Registry Classes 808

Reading and Writing to Isolated Storage **810**

Summary **814**

PART IV: DATA

CHAPTER 30: CORE ADO.NET **817**

ADO.NET Overview **817**

Namespaces 818

Shared Classes 818

Database-Specific Classes 819
Using Database Connections **820**
Managing Connection Strings 821
Using Connections Efficiently 822
Transactions 824
Commands **825**
Executing Commands 826
Calling Stored Procedures 829
Fast Data Access: The Data Reader **832**
Managing Data and Relationships: The DataSet Class **835**
Data Tables 835
Data Relationships 840
Data Constraints 842
XML Schemas: Generating Code with XSD **844**
Populating a DataSet **850**
Populating a DataSet Class with a Data Adapter 850
Populating a DataSet from XML 851
Persisting DataSet Changes **852**
Updating with Data Adapters 852
Writing XML Output 854
Working with ADO.NET **855**
Tiered Development 855
Key Generation with SQL Server 857
Naming Conventions 859
Summary **860**

CHAPTER 31: ADO.NET ENTITY FRAMEWORK **861**

Overview of the ADO.NET Entity Framework **861**
Entity Framework Mapping **862**
Logical Layer 863
Conceptual Layer 864
Mapping Layer 865
Entity Client **866**
Connection String 867
Entity SQL 867
Entities **868**
Object Context **871**
Relationships **873**
Table per Hierarchy 873
Table per Type 874
Lazy, Delayed, and Eager Loading 876

Object Query 876
Updates 879
Object Tracking 880
Change Information 881
Attaching and Detaching Entities 882
Storing Entity Changes 882
LINQ to Entities 883
Summary 884

CHAPTER 32: DATA SERVICES 885

Overview 885
Custom Hosting with CLR Objects 886
CLR Objects 886
Data Model 888
Data Service 889
Hosting the Service 889
Additional Service Operations 890
HTTP Client Application 891
Queries with URLs 893
Using WCF Data Services with the ADO.NET Entity Framework 894
ASP.NET Hosting and EDM 894
.NET Applications Using System.Data.Service.Client 895
Summary 902

CHAPTER 33: MANIPULATING XML 903

XML Standards Support in .NET 904
Introducing the System.Xml Namespace 904
Using System.Xml Classes 905
Reading and Writing Streamed XML 906
Using the XmlReader Class 906
Validating with XmlReader 910
Using the XmlWriter Class 911
Using the DOM in .NET 913
Using the XmlDocument Class 914
Using XPathNavigators 917
The System.Xml.XPath Namespace 917
The System.Xml.Xsl Namespace 922
XML and ADO.NET 927
Converting ADO.NET Data to XML 927
Converting XML to ADO.NET Data 932

Serializing Objects in XML	**934**
Serialization without Source Code Access	940
LINQ to XML and .NET	**942**
Working with Different XML Objects	**943**
XDocument	943
XElement	944
XNamespace	945
XComment	946
XAttribute	947
Using LINQ to Query XML Documents	**948**
Querying Static XML Documents	948
Querying Dynamic XML Documents	949
More Query Techniques for XML Documents	**951**
Reading from an XML Document	951
Writing to an XML Document	952
Summary	**953**

CHAPTER 34: .NET PROGRAMMING WITH SQL SERVER	**955**
.NET Runtime Host	**956**
Microsoft.SqlServer.Server	**957**
User-Defined Types	**958**
Creating UDTs	958
Using UDTs with SQL Server	963
Using UDTs from Client-Side Code	963
User-Defined Aggregates	**964**
Creating User-Defined Aggregates	965
Using User-Defined Aggregates	966
Stored Procedures	**967**
Creating Stored Procedures	967
Using Stored Procedures	968
User-Defined Functions	**969**
Creating User-Defined Functions	969
Using User-Defined Functions	970
Triggers	**970**
Creating Triggers Example	970
Using Triggers	972
XML Data Type	**972**
Tables with XML Data	972
Reading XML Values	973
Query the Data	976
XML Data Modification Language (XML DML)	977

XML Indexes 978
Strongly Typed XML 979
Summary **980**

PART V: PRESENTATION

CHAPTER 35: CORE WPF **983**

Overview **983**
Namespaces 984
Class Hierarchy 985
Shapes **986**
Geometry **988**
Transformation **990**
Brushes **991**
SolidColorBrush 991
LinearGradientBrush 991
RadialGradientBrush 992
DrawingBrush 992
ImageBrush 993
VisualBrush 993
Controls **994**
Simple Controls 994
Content Controls 995
Headered Content Controls 996
Items Controls 998
Headered Items Controls 998
Decoration 998
Layout **999**
StackPanel 999
WrapPanel 1000
Canvas 1000
DockPanel 1001
Grid 1001
Styles and Resources **1003**
Styles 1003
Resources 1004
System Resources 1005
Accessing Resources from Code 1006
Dynamic Resources 1006
Resource Dictionaries 1007
Triggers **1008**

Property Triggers	1008
MultiTrigger	1010
Data Triggers	1010
Templates	**1011**
Control Templates	1012
Data Templates	1014
Styling a ListBox	1016
ItemTemplate	1017
Control Templates for ListBox Elements	1018
Animations	**1020**
Timeline	1020
Non-Linear Animations	1023
Event Triggers	1023
Keyframe Animations	1025
Visual State Manager	**1026**
3-D	**1029**
Model	1030
Cameras	1032
Lights	1032
Rotation	1032
Summary	**1033**

CHAPTER 36: BUSINESS APPLICATIONS WITH WPF   **1035**

Data Binding	**1035**
BooksDemo Application	1036
Binding with XAML	1037
Simple Object Binding	1040
Change Notification	1041
Object Data Provider	1043
List Binding	1045
Master Details Binding	1048
MultiBinding	1048
Priority Binding	1049
Value Conversion	1051
Adding List Items Dynamically	1053
Data Template Selector	1053
Binding to XML	1055
Binding Validation	1057
Commanding	**1061**
Defining Commands	1062
Defining Command Sources	1062

Command Bindings 1063

TreeView **1063**

DataGrid **1067**

Custom Columns 1069

Row Details 1070

Grouping with the DataGrid 1070

Summary **1073**

CHAPTER 37: CREATING DOCUMENTS WITH WPF 1075

Text Elements **1075**

Fonts 1075

TextEffect 1077

Inline 1078

Block 1080

Lists 1081

Tables 1082

Anchor to Blocks 1083

Flow Documents **1085**

Fixed Documents **1086**

XPS Documents **1089**

Printing **1091**

Printing with the PrintDialog 1091

Printing Visuals 1092

Summary **1094**

CHAPTER 38: SILVERLIGHT 1095

Comparing WPF and Silverlight **1095**

Creating a Silverlight Project **1097**

Navigation **1097**

Networking **1102**

Creating an ADO.NET Entity Data Model 1102

Creating a WCF Service for Silverlight Clients 1103

Calling WCF Services 1104

Using WCF Data Services 1107

Using System.Net to Access the Service 1109

Browser Integration **1110**

Calling out to JavaScript 1111

JavaScript Calling Silverlight 1112

Silverlight Out-of-Browser Applications **1113**

Summary **1115**

CHAPTER 39: WINDOWS FORMS — 1117

Creating a Windows Forms Application — 1117
Class Hierarchy — 1122
Control Class — 1122
Size and Location — 1123
Appearance — 1123
User Interaction — 1124
Windows Functionality — 1125
Miscellaneous Functionality — 1125
Standard Controls and Components — 1125
Button — 1125
CheckBox — 1126
RadioButton — 1126
ComboBox, ListBox, and CheckedListBox — 1127
The DataGridView Control — 1128
DateTimePicker — 1135
ErrorProvider — 1135
ImageList — 1136
Label — 1136
ListView — 1136
PictureBox — 1136
ProgressBar — 1137
TextBox, RichTextBox, and MaskedTextBox — 1137
Panel — 1138
FlowLayoutPanel and TableLayoutPanel — 1138
SplitContainer — 1139
TabControl and TabPages — 1139
ToolStrip — 1140
MenuStrip — 1141
ContextMenuStrip — 1141
ToolStripMenuItem — 1141
ToolStripManager — 1141
ToolStripContainer — 1142
Forms — 1142
Form Class — 1142
Multiple Document Interface — 1146
Creating Your Own User Controls — 1147
Summary — 1147

CHAPTER 40: CORE ASP.NET   1149

ASP.NET Introduction   1150
How ASP.NET Files are Processed   1150
Web Sites and Web Applications   1150
State Management in ASP.NET   1151
ASP.NET Web Forms   1151
The ASP.NET Code Model   1154
ASP.NET Server Controls   1155
ADO.NET and Data Binding   1169
Updating the Event-Booking Application   1169
More on Data Binding   1175
Application Configuration   1181
Summary   1182

CHAPTER 41: ASP.NET FEATURES   1185

User and Custom Controls   1186
User Controls   1186
Custom Controls   1192
Master Pages   1195
Accessing Master Page Content from Web Pages   1196
Nested Master Pages   1197
Master Pages in PCSDemoSite   1197
Site Navigation   1198
Adding a Site Map File   1199
Navigating in PCSDemoSite   1200
Security   1201
Adding Forms Authentication Using the Security Setup Wizard   1201
Implementing a Login System   1202
Login Web Server Controls   1203
Securing Directories   1204
Security in PCSDemoSite   1204
Themes   1206
Applying Themes to Pages   1207
Defining Themes   1207
Themes in PCSDemoSite   1208
Web Parts   1210
Web Parts Application Components   1211
Web Parts Example   1212
ASP.NET AJAX   1218
What Is Ajax?   1219

What Is ASP.NET AJAX? 1221
ASP.NET AJAX Web Site Example 1224
ASP.NET AJAX-Enabled Web Site Configuration 1227
Adding ASP.NET AJAX Functionality 1227
Using the AJAX Library 1234
Summary 1242

CHAPTER 42: ASP.NET DYNAMIC DATA AND MVC 1243

Routing 1244
Query String Parameters 1245
Defining Routes 1246
Using Route Parameters 1249
Dynamic Data 1251
Creating Dynamic Data Web Sites 1251
Customizing Dynamic Data Web Sites 1255
Further Development 1259
MVC 1259
What Is MVC? 1260
What Is ASP.NET MVC? 1260
A Simple ASP.NET MVC Application 1261
Customizing ASP.NET MVC Applications 1266
Further Development 1274
Summary 1274

PART VI: COMMUNICATION

CHAPTER 43: WINDOWS COMMUNICATION FOUNDATION 1279

WCF Overview 1279
SOAP 1281
WSDL 1281
REST 1282
JSON 1282
Simple Service and Client 1282
Service Contract 1283
Service Implementation 1284
WCF Service Host and WCF Test Client 1284
Custom Service Host 1287
WCF Client 1288
Diagnostics 1289
Contracts 1291

Data Contract 1291
Versioning 1292
Service Contract 1292
Message Contract 1293
Service Implementation **1294**
Creating a Client Programmatically 1297
Error Handling 1298
Binding **1300**
Hosting **1302**
Custom Hosting 1302
WAS Hosting 1303
Preconfigured Host Classes 1303
Clients **1304**
Duplex Communication **1306**
Summary **1308**

CHAPTER 44: WINDOWS WORKFLOW FOUNDATION 4 **1309**

Hello World **1310**
Activities **1311**
If Activity 1312
InvokeMethod Activity 1313
Parallel Activity 1313
Delay Activity 1314
Pick Activity 1314
Custom Activities **1316**
Activity Validation 1317
Designers 1317
Custom Composite Activities 1319
Workflows **1322**
Arguments and Variables 1322
WorkflowApplication 1323
WorkflowServiceHost 1327
Hosting the Designer 1332
Summary **1337**

CHAPTER 45: PEER-TO-PEER NETWORKING **1339**

Peer-to-Peer Networking Overview **1339**
Client-Server Architecture 1340
P2P Architecture 1340
P2P Architectural Challenges 1341

P2P Terminology 1342
P2P Solutions 1342
Microsoft Windows Peer-to-Peer Networking **1343**
Peer Name Resolution Protocol (PNRP) 1343
People Near Me 1346
Building P2P Applications **1346**
System.Net.PeerToPeer 1347
System.Net.PeerToPeer.Collaboration 1352
Summary **1355**

CHAPTER 46: MESSAGE QUEUING **1357**

Overview **1357**
When to Use Message Queuing 1358
Message Queuing Features 1359
Message Queuing Products **1360**
Message Queuing Architecture **1361**
Messages 1361
Message Queue 1361
Message Queuing Administrative Tools **1362**
Creating Message Queues 1362
Message Queue Properties 1363
Programming Message Queuing **1363**
Creating a Message Queue 1363
Finding a Queue 1364
Opening Known Queues 1365
Sending a Message 1366
Receiving Messages 1368
Course Order Application **1370**
Course Order Class Library 1370
Course Order Message Sender 1371
Sending Priority and Recoverable Messages 1372
Course Order Message Receiver 1373
Receiving Results **1376**
Acknowledgment Queues 1376
Response Queues 1377
Transactional Queues **1377**
Message Queuing with WCF **1378**
Entity Classes with a Data Contract 1379
WCF Service Contract 1380
WCF Message Receiver Application 1380
WCF Message Sender Application 1383

Message Queue Installation   **1384**
Summary   **1385**

CHAPTER 47: SYNDICATION   **1387**

Overview of System.ServiceModel.Syndication   **1387**
Reading Syndication Feeds Sample   **1388**
Offering Syndication Feeds Sample   **1390**
Summary   **1394**

**APPENDIX: GUIDELINES FOR WINDOWS 7
           AND WINDOWS SERVER 2008 R2**   **1397**

INDEX   *1417*

ONLINE CHAPTERS

CHAPTER 48: GRAPHICS WITH GDI+   **OC1**

Understanding Drawing Principles   **OC2**
    GDI and GDI+   OC2
    Drawing Shapes   OC4
    Painting Shapes Using OnPaint()   OC6
    Using the Clipping Region   OC7
Measuring Coordinates and Areas   **OC9**
    Point and PointF   OC9
    Size and SizeF   OC10
    Rectangle and RectangleF   OC11
    Region   OC12
Drawing Scrollable Windows   **OC13**
World, Page, and Device Coordinates   **OC17**
Colors   **OC18**
    Red-Green-Blue Values   OC18
    The Named Colors   OC19
    Graphics Display Modes and the Safety Palette   OC19
    The Safety Palette   OC20
Pens and Brushes   **OC20**
    Brushes   OC21
    Pens   OC21
Drawing Shapes and Lines   **OC22**
Displaying Images   **OC24**
Issues When Manipulating Images   **OC26**
Drawing Text   **OC27**

Simple Text Example   **OC27**

Fonts and Font Families   **OC28**

Enumerating Font Families Example   **OC29**

Editing a Text Document: The CapsEditor Example   **OC31**

The Invalidate() Method   OC35

Calculating Item Sizes and Document Size   OC36

OnPaint()   OC37

Coordinate Transforms   OC39

Responding to User Input   OC40

Printing   **OC43**

Implementing Print and Print Preview   OC44

Summary   **OC48**

CHAPTER 49: VISUAL STUDIO TOOLS FOR OFFICE   **OC49**

VSTO Overview   **OC50**

Project Types   OC50

Project Features   OC52

VSTO Project Fundamentals   **OC53**

Office Object Model   OC53

VSTO Namespaces   OC54

Host Items and Host Controls   OC54

Basic VSTO Project Structure   OC56

The Globals Class   OC58

Event Handling   OC59

Building VSTO Solutions   **OC59**

Managing Application-Level Add-Ins   OC61

Interacting with Applications and Documents   OC62

UI Customization   OC62

Example Application   **OC66**

Summary   **OC75**

CHAPTER 50: MANAGED ADD-IN FRAMEWORK   **OC77**

MAF Architecture   **OC77**

Pipeline   OC78

Discovery   OC79

Activation and Isolation   OC80

Contracts   OC82

Lifetime   OC83

Versioning   OC84

Add-In Sample   **OC84**

Add-In Contract   OC85

Calculator Add-In View   OC86
Calculator Add-In Adapter   OC86
Calculator Add-In   OC88
Calculator Host View   OC89
Calculator Host Adapter   OC89
Calculator Host   OC91
Additional Add-Ins   OC94
Summary   **OC95**

CHAPTER 51: ENTERPRISE SERVICES   **OC97**

Using Enterprise Services   **OC97**
History   OC98
Where to Use Enterprise Services   OC98
Key Features   OC99
Creating a Simple COM+ Application   **OC101**
The ServicedComponent Class   OC101
Assembly Attributes   OC101
Creating the Component   OC102
Deployment   **OC103**
Automatic Deployment   OC103
Manual Deployment   OC104
Creating an Installer Package   OC104
Component Services Explorer   **OC105**
Client Application   **OC106**
Transactions   **OC107**
Transaction Attributes   OC107
Transaction Results   OC108
Sample Application   **OC108**
Entity Classes   OC109
The OrderControl Component   OC111
The OrderData Component   OC111
The OrderLineData Component   OC113
Client Application   OC114
Integrating WCF and Enterprise Services   **OC116**
WCF Service Façade   OC116
Client Application   OC120
Summary   **OC121**

CHAPTER 52: DIRECTORY SERVICES   **OC123**

The Architecture of Active Directory   **OC124**
Active Directory Features   OC124

Active Directory Concepts   OC124
Characteristics of Active Directory Data   OC128
Specifying Schema   OC128
Administration Tools for Active Directory   **OC129**
Active Directory Users and Computers   OC129
ADSI Edit   OC130
Programming Active Directory   **OC131**
Classes in System.DirectoryServices   OC132
Binding to Directory Services   OC132
Cache   OC138
Creating New Objects   OC139
Updating Directory Entries   OC139
Accessing Native ADSI Objects   OC140
Searching in Active Directory   OC141
Searching for User Objects   **OC145**
User Interface   OC145
Get the Schema Naming Context   OC146
Get the Property Names of the User Class   OC146
Search for User Objects   OC147
Account Management   **OC149**
Display User Information   OC150
Create a User   OC150
Reset a Password   OC151
Create a Group   OC151
Add a User to a Group   OC152
Finding Users   OC152
DSML   **OC153**
Classes in System.DirectoryServices.Protocols   OC153
Searching for Active Directory Objects with DSML   OC153
Summary   **OC155**

CHAPTER 53: C#, VISUAL BASIC, C++/CLI, AND F#   **OC157**

Namespaces   **OC158**
Defining Types   **OC159**
Reference Types   OC159
Value Types   OC160
Type Inference   OC161
Interfaces   OC161
Enumerations   OC163
Methods   **OC163**
Method Parameters and Return Types   OC164

Parameter Modifiers | OC165
Constructors | OC166
Properties | OC167
Object Initializers | OC169
Extension Methods | OC169
Static Members | **OC169**
Arrays | **OC170**
Control Statements | **OC171**
if Statement | OC171
Conditional Operator | OC172
switch Statement | OC172
Loops | **OC173**
for Statement | OC173
while and do . . . while Statements | OC174
foreach Statement | OC175
Exception Handling | **OC175**
Inheritance | **OC177**
Access Modifiers | OC177
Keywords | OC178
Resource Management | **OC179**
IDisposable Interface Implementation | OC179
using Statement | OC180
Override Finalize | OC181
Delegates | **OC182**
Events | **OC184**
Generics | **OC186**
LINQ Queries | **OC188**
C++/CLI Mixing Native and Managed Code | **OC188**
C# Specifics | **OC189**
Summary | **OC190**

CHAPTER 54: .NET REMOTING | **OC191**

Why Use .NET Remoting? | **OC191**
.NET Remoting Terms Explained | **OC193**
Client-Side Communication | OC195
Server-Side Communication | OC195
Contexts | **OC196**
Activation | OC197
Attributes and Properties | OC197
Communication Between Contexts | OC197
Remote Objects, Clients, and Servers | **OC197**

Remote Objects   OC198
A Simple Server Application   OC198
A Simple Client Application   OC199
.NET Remoting Architecture   **OC200**
Channels   OC201
Formatters   OC203
ChannelServices and RemotingConfiguration   OC204
Object Activation   OC205
Message Sinks   OC208
Passing Objects in Remote Methods   OC209
Lifetime Management   OC212
Configuration Files   **OC214**
Server Configuration for Well-Known Objects   OC215
Client Configuration for Well-Known Objects   OC216
Server Configuration for Client-Activated Objects   OC217
Client Configuration for Client-Activated Objects   OC217
Server Code Using Configuration Files   OC217
Client Code Using Configuration Files   OC218
Delayed Loading of Client Channels   OC219
Debugging Configuration   OC219
Lifetime Services in Configuration Files   OC220
Formatter Providers   OC220
Hosting Servers in ASP.NET   **OC221**
Classes, Interfaces, and Soapsuds   **OC222**
Interfaces   OC222
Soapsuds   OC222
Asynchronous Remoting   **OC223**
Using Delegates with .NET Remoting   OC223
OneWay Attribute   OC224
Security with .NET Remoting   **OC224**
Remoting and Events   **OC225**
Remote Object   OC226
Event Arguments   OC227
Server   OC228
Server Configuration File   OC228
Event Sink   OC228
Client   OC229
Client Configuration File   OC230
Running Programs   OC230
Call Contexts   **OC231**
Summary   **OC232**

CHAPTER 55: WEB SERVICES WITH ASP.NET   **OC233**

SOAP   **OC234**
WSDL   **OC235**
Web Services   **OC236**
     Exposing Web Services   OC236
     Consuming Web Services   OC239
Extending the Event-Booking Example   **OC242**
     The Event-Booking Web Service   OC242
     The Event-Booking Client   OC246
Exchanging Data Using SOAP Headers   **OC249**
Summary   **OC254**

CHAPTER 56: LINQ TO SQL   **OC255**

LINQ to SQL Using Visual Studio 2010   **OC257**
     Calling the Products Table   OC257
     Adding a LINQ to SQL Class   OC258
     Introducing the O/R Designer   OC258
     Creating the Product Object   OC259
How Objects Map to LINQ Objects   **OC261**
     The DataContext Object   OC262
     The Table<TEntity> Object   OC266
Working Without the O/R Designer   **OC266**
     Creating Your Own Custom Object   OC266
     Querying with Your Custom Object and LINQ   OC267
     Limiting the Columns Called with the Query   OC268
     Working with Column Names   OC269
     Creating Your Own DataContext Object   OC269
Custom Objects and the O/R Designer   **OC271**
Querying the Database   **OC272**
     Using Query Expressions   OC272
     Query Expressions in Detail   OC273
     Filtering Using Expressions   OC273
     Performing Joins   OC274
     Grouping Items   OC275
Stored Procedures   **OC276**
Summary   **OC277**

CHAPTER 57: WINDOWS WORKFLOW FOUNDATION 3.0   **OC279**

Hello World   **OC280**
Activities   **OC281**

IfElseActivity OC281
ParallelActivity OC282
CallExternalMethodActivity OC283
DelayActivity OC283
ListenActivity OC284
Activity Execution Model OC285
Custom Activities **OC285**
Activity Validation OC287
Themes and Designers OC288
ActivityToolboxItem and Icons OC289
Custom Composite Activities OC291
Workflows **OC296**
Sequential Workflows OC297
State Machine Workflows OC297
Passing Parameters to a Workflow OC299
Returning Results from a Workflow OC300
Binding Parameters to Activities OC300
The Workflow Runtime **OC301**
Workflow Services **OC302**
The Persistence Service OC303
The Tracking Service OC305
Custom Services OC306
Integration with Windows Communication Foundation **OC307**
Hosting Workflows **OC309**
The Workflow Designer **OC310**
Moving from WF 3.x to WF 4 **OC311**
Extract Activity Code into Services OC311
Remove Code Activities OC311
Run 3.x and 4 Side by Side OC312
Consider Moving State Machines to Flowcharts OC312
Summary **OC312**

INTRODUCTION

IF WE WERE TO DESCRIBE THE C# LANGUAGE AND ITS ASSOCIATED ENVIRONMENT, the .NET Framework, as the most significant technology for developers around right now, we would not be exaggerating. .NET is designed to provide an environment within which you can develop almost any application to run on Windows, while C# is a programming language that has been designed specifically to work with the .NET Framework. By using C#, you can, for example, write a dynamic web page, a Windows Presentation Foundation application, an XML Web service, a component of a distributed application, a database access component, a classic Windows desktop application, or even a new smart client application that allows for online/offline capabilities. This book covers the .NET Framework 4. If you are coding using any of the prior versions, there may be sections of the book that will not work for you. We try to notify you of items that are new and specific to the .NET Framework 4.

Don't be fooled by the .NET label in the Framework's name and think that this is a purely Internet-focused framework. The NET bit in the name is there to emphasize Microsoft's belief that *distributed applications*, in which the processing is distributed between client and server, are the way forward. It is also important to understand that C# is not just a language for writing Internet or network-aware applications. It provides a means for you to code up almost any type of software or component that you need to write for the Windows platform. Between them, C# and .NET have revolutionized the way that developers write their programs and have made programming on Windows much easier than it has ever been before.

So what's the big deal about .NET and C#?

THE SIGNIFICANCE OF .NET AND C#

To understand the significance of .NET, it is useful to remind ourselves of the nature of many of the Windows technologies that have appeared in the past 18 years or so. Although they may look quite different on the surface, all of the Windows operating systems from Windows 3.1 (introduced in 1992) through Windows 7 and Windows Server 2008 R2 have the same familiar Windows API at their core. As we have progressed through new versions of Windows, huge numbers of new functions have been added to the API, but this has been a process of evolving and extending the API rather than replacing it.

The same can be said for many of the technologies and frameworks that we have used to develop software for Windows. For example, *COM (Component Object Model)* originated as *OLE (Object Linking and Embedding)*. Originally, it was largely a means by which different types of Office documents could be linked, so that you could place a small Excel spreadsheet in your Word document, for example. From that it evolved into COM, *DCOM (Distributed COM)*, and eventually *COM+* — a sophisticated technology that formed the basis of the way almost all components communicated, as well as implementing transactions, messaging services, and object pooling.

Microsoft chose this evolutionary approach to software for the obvious reason that it is concerned about backward compatibility. Over the years, a huge base of third-party software has been written for Windows, and Windows would not have enjoyed the success it has had if every time Microsoft introduced a new technology it broke the existing code base!

Although backward compatibility has been a crucial feature of Windows technologies and one of the strengths of the Windows platform, it does have a big disadvantage. Every time some technology evolves and adds new features, it ends up a bit more complicated than it was before.

It was clear that something had to change. Microsoft could not go on forever extending the same development tools and languages, always making them more and more complex in order to satisfy the conflicting demands of keeping up with the newest hardware and maintaining backward compatibility with what was around when Windows first became popular in the early 1990s. There comes a point where you have to start with a clean slate if you want a simple yet sophisticated set of languages, environments, and developer tools, which makes it easy for developers to write state-of-the-art software.

This fresh start is what C# and .NET were all about in the first incarnation. Roughly speaking, .NET is a framework — an API — for programming on the Windows platform. Along with the .NET Framework, C# is a language that has been designed from scratch to work with .NET, as well as to take advantage of all the progress in developer environments and in our understanding of object-oriented programming principles that have taken place over the past 25 years.

Before we continue, we should make it clear that backward compatibility has not been lost in the process. Existing programs will continue to work, and .NET was designed with the capability to work with existing software. Presently, communication between software components on Windows takes place almost entirely using COM. Taking this into account, the .NET Framework does have the capability to provide wrappers around existing COM components so that .NET components can talk to them.

It is true that you don't need to learn C# in order to write code for .NET. Microsoft has extended C++, and made substantial changes to Visual Basic to turn it into a more powerful language, in order to allow code written in either of these languages to target the .NET environment. These other languages, however, are hampered by the legacy of having evolved over the years rather than having been written from the start with today's technology in mind.

This book will equip you to program in C#, while at the same time provide the necessary background in how the .NET architecture works. We not only cover the fundamentals of the C# language but also go on to give examples of applications that use a variety of related technologies, including database access, dynamic web pages, advanced graphics, and directory access.

ADVANTAGES OF .NET

So far, we've talked in general terms about how great .NET is, but we haven't said much about how it helps to make your life as a developer easier. This section briefly identifies some of the improved features of .NET.

➤ **Object-oriented programming** — Both the .NET Framework and C# are entirely based on object-oriented principles right from the start.

➤ **Good design** — A base class library, which is designed from the ground up in a highly intuitive way.

➤ **Language independence** — With .NET, all of the languages — Visual Basic, C#, and managed C++ — compile to a common *Intermediate Language*. This means that languages are interoperable in a way that has not been seen before.

➤ **Better support for dynamic web pages** — Though Classic ASP offered a lot of flexibility, it was also inefficient because of its use of interpreted scripting languages, and the lack of object-oriented design often resulted in messy ASP code. .NET offers an integrated support for web pages, using ASP. NET. With ASP.NET, code in your pages is compiled and may be written in a .NET-aware high-level language such as C# or Visual Basic 2010. .NET now takes it even further with outstanding support for the latest web technologies such as Ajax and jQuery.

➤ **Efficient data access** — A set of .NET components, collectively known as ADO.NET, provides efficient access to relational databases and a variety of data sources. Components are also available to allow access to the file system, and to directories. In particular, XML support is built into .NET, allowing you to manipulate data, which may be imported from or exported to non-Windows platforms.

➤ **Code sharing** — .NET has completely revamped the way that code is shared between applications, introducing the concept of the *assembly*, which replaces the traditional DLL. Assemblies have formal facilities for versioning, and different versions of assemblies can exist side by side.

➤ **Improved security** — Each assembly can also contain built-in security information that can indicate precisely who or what category of user or process is allowed to call which methods on which classes. This gives you a very fine degree of control over how the assemblies that you deploy can be used.

➤ **Zero-impact installation** — There are two types of assemblies: shared and private. Shared assemblies are common libraries available to all software, whereas private assemblies are intended only for use with particular software. A private assembly is entirely self-contained, so the process of installing it is simple. There are no registry entries; the appropriate files are simply placed in the appropriate folder in the file system.

➤ **Support for Web services** — .NET has fully integrated support for developing Web services as easily as you would develop any other type of application.

➤ **Visual Studio 2010** — .NET comes with a developer environment, Visual Studio 2010, which can cope equally well with C++, C#, and Visual Basic 2010, as well as with ASP.NET or XML code. Visual Studio 2010 integrates all the best features of the respective language-specific environments of all the previous versions of this amazing IDE.

➤ **C#** — C# is a powerful and popular object-oriented language intended for use with .NET.

We look more closely at the benefits of the .NET architecture in Chapter 1, ".NET Architecture."

WHAT'S NEW IN THE .NET FRAMEWORK 4

The first version of the .NET Framework (1.0) was released in 2002 to much enthusiasm. The .NET Framework 2.0 was introduced in 2005 and was considered a major release of the Framework. The .NET Framework 4 is another major release of the product with many outstanding new features.

With each release of the Framework, Microsoft has always tried to ensure that there were minimal breaking changes to code developed. Thus far, Microsoft has been very successful at this goal.

The following section details some of the changes that are new to C# 2010 and the .NET Framework 4.

Dynamic Typing

The world of programming has seen tremendous growth in dynamic languages such as JavaScript, Python, and Ruby. Because of the growing popularity of this type of programming, Microsoft has released a new dynamic typing capability in C#. It is not always possible to know statically what objects might end up being. Instead of using the `object` keyword and making everything of this type, we can now let the Dynamic Language Runtime (DLR) figure this out at runtime.

Using the new dynamic capabilities of C#, you now have a better interoperability story. You are able to interop with various dynamic languages and work with the DOM more easily. It's even simple to work with the Microsoft Office COM APIs now.

In this release of the .NET Framework 4, Microsoft has included the Dynamic Language Runtime. The DLR has been built upon the Common Language Runtime (CLR) to provide the ability to tie together all the dynamic language interactions.

C# provides access to the new DLR through the use of the new `dynamic` keyword. This is a flag to the compiler; whenever this keyword is encountered, the compiler will realize that it is a dynamic invocation and not the typical static invocation.

Optional and Named Parameters

Optional parameters and named parameters have been in Visual Basic for some time but have not been available to C# until the .NET 4 release. Optional parameters allow you to provide default values for some of the parameters of your methods and allow for a type of overloading by the consumer, even if there is only a single method in place to deal with all the variants. Here's an example:

```
public void CreateUser(string firstname, string lastname,
 bool isAdmin, bool isTrialUser)
{

}
```

If you wanted to overload this and have default values for the two `bool` objects, then you could easily have a few more methods that populate these values for the consumer and then make a call to the master method to actually create the user. Now with optional parameters, you are able to do something like this:

```
public void CreateUser(string firstname, string lastname,
 bool isAdmin = false, bool isTrialUser = true)
{

}
```

Looking over this bit of code, the parameters `firstname` and `lastname` do not have a default value set, while `isAdmin` and `isTrailUser` do have default values set. As a consumer of something like this, you are now able to do some of the following:

```
myClass.CreateUser("Bill", "Evjen");
myClass.CreateUser("Bill", "Evjen", true);
myClass.CreateUser("Bill", "Evjen", true, false);
myClass.CreateUser("Bill", "Evjen", isTrailUser: false);
```

The last example makes use of named parameters, which are also a new feature for C# in this release of the .NET Framework. Named parameters will potentially change the way you write your code. This new feature will allow you to make your code easier to read and understand. As an example of this in action, take a look at the `File.Copy()` method of the `System.IO` namespace. Typically, it would be constructed similarly to this:

```
File.Copy(@"C:\myTestFile.txt", @"C:\myOtherFile.txt", true);
```

In this case, this simple method is working with three parameters, but what are the actual items being passed into the `Copy()` method? Unless you know this method backward and forward, it is hard to tell what is going on by just glancing at this method. Using named parameters, you are able to use the parameter name in the code prior to the value being provided, as in the following example:

```
File.Copy(sourceFileName: @"C:\myTestFile.txt",
    destFileName: @"C:\myOtherFile.txt", overwrite: true);
```

Now with the named parameters in place, you can more easily read and understand what is going on with this line of code. Using named parameters makes no difference to the resulting compilation; they are only used in the coding of the application.

Covariance and Contravariance

Covariance and contravariance were included in prior versions of the .NET Framework, but they have been extended in .NET 4 to perform even better when working with generics, delegates, and more. In the prior versions of .NET, you were able to use contravariance with objects and arrays, but, for instance, you were unable to use contravariance with generic interfaces. In .NET 4, you are able to do this.

ASP.NET MVC

ASP.NET MVC is the latest major addition to ASP.NET and has generated a lot of excitement in the development community. ASP.NET MVC supplies you with the means to create ASP.NET using the model-view-controller model that many developers expect. ASP.NET MVC provides developers with testability, flexibility, and maintainability in the applications they build. It is important to remember that ASP.NET MVC is not meant to be a replacement for the ASP.NET everyone knows and loves, but is simply a different way to construct your applications.

This release of ASP.NET allows you to build using this new model. You will find that it is completely built in to the Framework and Visual Studio.

WHERE C# FITS IN

In one sense, C# can be seen as being the same thing to programming languages that .NET is to the Windows environment. Just as Microsoft has been adding more and more features to Windows and the Windows API over the past decade and a half, Visual Basic 2010 and C++ have undergone expansion. Although Visual Basic and C++ have ended up as hugely powerful languages as a result of this, both languages also suffer from problems because of the legacies left over from the way they evolved.

In the case of Visual Basic 6 and earlier versions, the main strength of the language was the fact that it was simple to understand and made many programming tasks easy, largely hiding the details of the Windows API and the COM component infrastructure from the developer. The downside to this was that Visual Basic was never truly object oriented, so that large applications quickly became disorganized and hard to maintain. As well, because Visual Basic's syntax was inherited from early versions of BASIC (which, in turn, was designed to be intuitively simple for beginning programmers to understand, rather than to write large commercial applications), it didn't really lend itself to well-structured or object-oriented programs.

C++, on the other hand, has its roots in the ANSI C++ language definition. It is not completely ANSI-compliant for the simple reason that Microsoft first wrote its C++ compiler before the ANSI definition had become official, but it comes close. Unfortunately, this has led to two problems. First, ANSI C++ has its roots in a decade-old state of technology, and this shows up in a lack of support for modern concepts (such as Unicode strings and generating XML documentation) and for some archaic syntax structures designed for the compilers of yesteryear (such as the separation of declaration from definition of member functions). Second, Microsoft has been simultaneously trying to evolve C++ into a language that is designed for high-performance tasks on Windows, and in order to achieve that, it has been forced to add a huge number of Microsoft-specific keywords as well as various libraries to the language. The result is that on Windows, the language has become a complete mess. Just ask C++ developers how many definitions for a string they can think of: `char*`, `LPTSTR`, `string`, `CString` (MFC version), `CString` (WTL version), `wchar_t*`, `OLECHAR*`, and so on.

Now enter .NET — a completely revolutionary environment that has brought forth new extensions to both languages. Microsoft has gotten around this by adding yet more Microsoft-specific keywords to C++, and by completely revamping Visual Basic to the current Visual Basic 2010, a language that retains some of the basic VB syntax, but that is so different in design from the original VB that it can be considered, for all practical purposes, a new language.

It is in this context that Microsoft has provided developers an alternative — a language designed specifically for .NET, and designed with a clean slate. C# is the result. Officially, Microsoft describes C# as a "simple, modern, object-oriented, and type-safe programming language derived from C and C++." Most independent observers would probably change that to "derived from C, C++, and Java." Such descriptions are technically accurate but do little to convey the beauty or elegance of the language. Syntactically, C# is very similar to both C++ and Java, to such an extent that many keywords are the same, and C# also shares the same block structure with braces ({}) to mark blocks of code and semicolons to separate statements. The first impression of a piece of C# code is that it looks quite like C++ or Java code. Beyond that initial similarity, however, C# is a lot easier to learn than C++, and of comparable difficulty to Java. Its design is more in tune with modern developer tools than both of those other languages, and it has been designed to provide, simultaneously, the ease of use of Visual Basic and the high-performance, low-level memory access of C++, if required. Some of the features of C# are:

➤ Full support for classes and object-oriented programming, including both interface and implementation inheritance, virtual functions, and operator overloading.

➤ A consistent and well-defined set of basic types.

➤ Built-in support for automatic generation of XML documentation.

➤ Automatic cleanup of dynamically allocated memory.

➤ The facility to mark classes or methods with user-defined attributes. This can be useful for documentation and can have some effects on compilation (for example, marking methods to be compiled only in debug builds).

➤ Full access to the .NET base class library, as well as easy access to the Windows API (if you really need it, which will not be very often).

➤ Pointers and direct memory access are available if required, but the language has been designed in such a way that you can work without them in almost all cases.

➤ Support for properties and events in the style of Visual Basic.

➤ Just by changing the compiler options, you can compile either to an executable or to a library of .NET components that can be called up by other code in the same way as ActiveX controls (COM components).

➤ C# can be used to write ASP.NET dynamic web pages and XML Web services.

Most of these statements, it should be pointed out, do also apply to Visual Basic 2010 and Managed C++. The fact that C# is designed from the start to work with .NET, however, means that its support for the features of .NET is both more complete and offered within the context of a more suitable syntax than those of other languages. Although the C# language itself is very similar to Java, there are some improvements; in particular, Java is not designed to work with the .NET environment.

Before leaving the subject, it is important to point out a couple of limitations of C#. The one area the language is not designed for is time-critical or extremely high-performance code — the kind where you really are worried about whether a loop takes 1,000 or 1,050 machine cycles to run through, and you need to clean up your resources the millisecond they are no longer needed. C++ is likely to continue to reign supreme among low-level languages in this area. C# lacks certain key facilities needed for extremely high-performance apps, including the ability to specify inline functions and destructors that are guaranteed to run at particular points in the code. However, the proportions of applications that fall into this category are very low.

WHAT YOU NEED TO WRITE AND RUN C# CODE

The .NET Framework 4 will run on Windows XP, 2003, 7, and the latest Windows Server 2008 R2. In order to write code using .NET, you will need to install the .NET 4 SDK.

In addition, unless you are intending to write your C# code using a text editor or some other third-party developer environment, you will almost certainly also want Visual Studio 2010. The full SDK is not needed to run managed code, but the .NET runtime is needed. You may find you need to distribute the .NET runtime with your code for the benefit of those clients who do not have it already installed.

WHAT THIS BOOK COVERS

This book starts by reviewing the overall architecture of .NET in Chapter 1 in order to give you the background you need to be able to write managed code. After that, the book is divided into a number of sections that cover both the C# language and its application in a variety of areas.

Part I: The C# Language

This section gives a good grounding in the C# language itself. This section doesn't presume knowledge of any particular language, although it does assume you are an experienced programmer. You start by looking at C#'s basic syntax and data types, and then explore the object-oriented features of C# before moving on to look at more advanced C# programming topics.

Part II: Visual Studio

This section looks at the main IDE utilized by C# developers worldwide: Visual Studio 2010. The two chapters in this section look at the best way to use the tool to build applications based on the .NET Framework 4. In addition, this section also focuses on the deployment of your projects.

Part III: Foundation

In this section, you look at the principles of programming in the .NET environment. In particular, you look at security, threading, localization, transactions, how to build Windows services, and how to generate your own libraries as assemblies, among other topics.

Part IV: Data

Here, you look at accessing databases with ADO.NET and LINQ, and at interacting with directories and files. This part also extensively covers support in .NET for XML and on the Windows operating system side, and the .NET features of SQL Server 2008.

Part V: Presentation

This section starts with coverage on building classic Windows applications, which are called *Windows Forms* in .NET. Windows Forms are the thick-client version of applications, and using .NET to build these types of applications is a quick and easy way of accomplishing this task. This section also shows how to build applications based upon the Windows Presentation Foundation and Silverlight, and covers writing components that will run on web sites, serving up web pages. Finally, it includes coverage of the tremendous number of features that ASP.NET and ASP.NET MVC provide.

Part VI: Communication

This section is all about communication. It covers services for platform-independent communication using the Windows Communication Foundation (WCF). With Message Queuing, asynchronous disconnected communication is shown. This section looks at utilizing the Windows Workflow Foundation (WF), as well as peer-to-peer networking, and creating syndication feeds.

Appendix

The book closes with an appendix covering Windows 7 and Windows Server 2008 R2 development.

Online Chapters

Even with such a large book, we can't fit in everything we'd like to tell you about C# and using this language with other .NET technologies, so we've made ten additional chapters available online at www.wrox.com. These chapters include information on a variety of topics: GDI+, which is a technology that is used for building applications that include advanced graphics; .NET Remoting for communication between .NET clients and servers; Enterprise Services for the services in the background; and the Managed Add-In Framework (MAF). Some other big topics found online include VSTO development and working with LINQ to SQL.

CONVENTIONS

To help you get the most from the text and keep track of what's happening, we've used a number of conventions throughout the book.

> *Boxes with a warning icon like this one hold important, not-to-be forgotten information that is directly relevant to the surrounding text.*

> *The pencil icon indicates notes, tips, hints, tricks, or asides to the current discussion.*

As for styles in the text:

➤ We *highlight* new terms and important words when we introduce them.

➤ We show keyboard strokes like this: Ctrl+A.

➤ We show file names, URLs, and code within the text like so: `persistence.properties`.

➤ We present code in two different ways:

```
We use a monofont type with no highlighting for most code examples.
We use bold to emphasize code that's particularly important in the present context or to show
changes from a previous code snippet.
```

SOURCE CODE

As you work through the examples in this book, you may choose either to type in all the code manually or to use the source code files that accompany the book. All of the source code used in this book is available for download at http://www.wrox.com. Once at the site, simply locate the book's title (either by using the Search box or by using one of the title lists) and click the Download Code link on the book's detail page to obtain all the source code for the book.

> *Because many books have similar titles, you may find it easiest to search by ISBN; this book's ISBN is 978-0-470-50225-9.*

Once you download the code, just decompress it with your favorite compression tool. Alternately, you can go to the main Wrox code download page at http://www.wrox.com/dynamic/books/download.aspx to see the code available for this book and all other Wrox books.

ERRATA

We make every effort to ensure that there are no errors in the text or in the code. However, no one is perfect, and mistakes do occur. If you find an error in one of our books, like a spelling mistake or faulty piece of code, we would be very grateful for your feedback. By sending in errata you may save another reader hours of frustration and at the same time you will be helping us provide even higher quality information.

To find the errata page for this book, go to http://www.wrox.com and locate the title using the Search box or one of the title lists. Then, on the book details page, click the Book Errata link. On this page you can view all errata that has been submitted for this book and posted by Wrox editors. A complete book list including links to each book's errata is also available at www.wrox.com/misc-pages/booklist.shtml.

If you don't spot "your" error on the Book Errata page, go to www.wrox.com/contact/techsupport. shtml and complete the form there to send us the error you have found. We'll check the information and, if appropriate, post a message to the book's errata page and fix the problem in subsequent editions of the book.

P2P.WROX.COM

For author and peer discussion, join the P2P forums at p2p.wrox.com. The forums are a Web-based system for you to post messages relating to Wrox books and related technologies and interact with other readers and technology users. The forums offer a subscription feature to e-mail you topics of interest of your choosing when new posts are made to the forums. Wrox authors, editors, other industry experts, and your fellow readers are present on these forums.

At http://p2p.wrox.com you will find a number of different forums that will help you not only as you read this book, but also as you develop your own applications. To join the forums, just follow these steps:

1. Go to p2p.wrox.com and click the Register link.
2. Read the terms of use and click Agree.
3. Complete the required information to join as well as any optional information you wish to provide and click Submit.
4. You will receive an e-mail with information describing how to verify your account and complete the joining process.

 You can read messages in the forums without joining P2P but in order to post your own messages, you must join.

Once you join, you can post new messages and respond to messages other users post. You can read messages at any time on the Web. If you would like to have new messages from a particular forum e-mailed to you, click the Subscribe to this Forum icon by the forum name in the forum listing.

For more information about how to use the Wrox P2P, be sure to read the P2P FAQs for answers to questions about how the forum software works as well as many common questions specific to P2P and Wrox books. To read the FAQs, click the FAQ link on any P2P page.

PART I
The C# Language

▶ **CHAPTER 1:** .NET Architecture

▶ **CHAPTER 2:** Core C#

▶ **CHAPTER 3:** Objects and Types

▶ **CHAPTER 4:** Inheritance

▶ **CHAPTER 5:** Generics

▶ **CHAPTER 6:** Arrays and Tuples

▶ **CHAPTER 7:** Operators and Casts

▶ **CHAPTER 8:** Delegates, Lambdas, and Events

▶ **CHAPTER 9:** Strings and Regular Expressions

▶ **CHAPTER 10:** Collections

▶ **CHAPTER 11:** Language Integrated Query

▶ **CHAPTER 12:** Dynamic Language Extensions

▶ **CHAPTER 13:** Memory Management and Pointers

▶ **CHAPTER 14:** Reflection

▶ **CHAPTER 15:** Errors and Exceptions

.NET Architecture

WHAT'S IN THIS CHAPTER?

➤ Compiling and running code that targets .NET

➤ Advantages of Microsoft Intermediate Language (MSIL)

➤ Value and reference types

➤ Data typing

➤ Understanding error handling and attributes

➤ Assemblies, .NET base classes, and namespaces

Throughout this book, we emphasize that the C# language must be considered in parallel with the .NET Framework, rather than viewed in isolation. The C# compiler specifically targets .NET, which means that all code written in C# will always run within the .NET Framework. This has two important consequences for the C# language:

1. The architecture and methodologies of C# reflect the underlying methodologies of .NET.

2. In many cases, specific language features of C# actually depend on features of .NET, or of the .NET base classes.

Because of this dependence, it is important to gain some understanding of the architecture and methodology of .NET before you begin C# programming. That is the purpose of this chapter.

THE RELATIONSHIP OF C# TO .NET

C# is a relatively new programming language and is significant in two respects:

➤ It is specifically designed and targeted for use with Microsoft's .NET Framework (a feature-rich platform for the development, deployment, and execution of distributed applications).

➤ It is a language based on the modern object-oriented design methodology, and, when designing it, Microsoft learned from the experience of all the other similar languages that have been around since object-oriented principles came to prominence some 20 years ago.

One important thing to make clear is that C# is a language in its own right. Although it is designed to generate code that targets the .NET environment, it is not itself part of .NET. Some features are supported by .NET but not by C#, and you might be surprised to learn that some features of the C# language are not supported by .NET (for example, some instances of operator overloading)!

However, because the C# language is intended for use with .NET, it is important for you to have an understanding of this Framework if you want to develop applications in C# effectively. Therefore, this chapter takes some time to peek underneath the surface of .NET. Let's get started.

THE COMMON LANGUAGE RUNTIME

Central to the .NET Framework is its runtime execution environment, known as the *Common Language Runtime* (CLR) or the *.NET runtime*. Code running under the control of the CLR is often termed *managed code*.

However, before it can be executed by the CLR, any source code that you develop (in C# or some other language) needs to be compiled. Compilation occurs in two steps in .NET:

1. Compilation of source code to Microsoft Intermediate Language (IL).
2. Compilation of IL to platform-specific code by the CLR.

This two-stage compilation process is very important, because the existence of the Microsoft Intermediate Language is the key to providing many of the benefits of .NET.

IL shares with Java byte code the idea that it is a low-level language with a simple syntax (based on numeric codes rather than text), which can be very quickly translated into native machine code. Having this well-defined universal syntax for code has significant advantages: platform independence, performance improvement, and language interoperability.

Platform Independence

First, platform independence means that the same file containing byte code instructions can be placed on any platform; at runtime, the final stage of compilation can then be easily accomplished so that the code will run on that particular platform. In other words, by compiling to IL you obtain platform independence for .NET, in much the same way as compiling to Java byte code gives Java platform independence.

Note that the platform independence of .NET is only theoretical at present because, at the time of writing, a complete implementation of .NET is available only for Windows. However, a partial implementation is available (see, for example, the Mono project, an effort to create an open source implementation of .NET, at www.go-mono.com).

Performance Improvement

Although we previously made comparisons with Java, IL is actually a bit more ambitious than Java byte code. IL is always *Just-in-Time* compiled (known as JIT compilation), whereas Java byte code was often interpreted. One of the disadvantages of Java was that, on execution, the process of translating from Java byte code to native executable resulted in a loss of performance (with the exception of more recent cases, where Java is JIT compiled on certain platforms).

Instead of compiling the entire application in one go (which could lead to a slow startup time), the JIT compiler simply compiles each portion of code as it is called (just in time). When code has been compiled once, the resultant native executable is stored until the application exits so that it does not need to be recompiled the next time that portion of code is run. Microsoft argues that this process is more efficient than compiling the entire application code at the start, because of the likelihood that large portions of any application code will not actually be executed in any given run. Using the JIT compiler, such code will never be compiled.

This explains why we can expect that execution of managed IL code will be almost as fast as executing native machine code. What it does not explain is why Microsoft expects that we will get a performance *improvement*. The reason given for this is that, because the final stage of compilation takes place at runtime, the JIT compiler will know exactly what processor type the program will run on. This means that it can optimize the final executable code to take advantage of any features or particular machine code instructions offered by that particular processor.

Traditional compilers will optimize the code, but they can only perform optimizations that are independent of the particular processor that the code will run on. This is because traditional compilers compile to native executable code before the software is shipped. This means that the compiler does not know what type of processor the code will run on beyond basic generalities, such as that it will be an x86-compatible processor or an Alpha processor.

Language Interoperability

The use of IL not only enables platform independence, it also facilitates *language interoperability*. Simply put, you can compile to IL from one language, and this compiled code should then be interoperable with code that has been compiled to IL from another language.

You are probably now wondering which languages aside from C# are interoperable with .NET; the following sections briefly discuss how some of the other common languages fit into .NET.

Visual Basic 2010

Visual Basic .NET 2002 underwent a complete revamp from Visual Basic 6 to bring it up to date with the first version of the .NET Framework. The Visual Basic language itself had dramatically evolved from VB6, and this meant that VB6 was not a suitable language for running .NET programs. For example, VB6 is heavily integrated into Component Object Model (COM) and works by exposing only event handlers as source code to the developer — most of the background code is not available as source code. Not only that, it does not support implementation inheritance, and the standard data types that Visual Basic 6 uses are incompatible with .NET.

Visual Basic 6 was upgraded to Visual Basic .NET in 2002, and the changes that were made to the language are so extensive you might as well regard Visual Basic as a new language. Existing Visual Basic 6 code does not compile to the present Visual Basic 2010 code (or to Visual Basic .NET 2002, 2003, 2005, and 2008 for that matter). Converting a Visual Basic 6 program to Visual Basic 2010 requires extensive changes to the code. However, Visual Studio 2010 (the upgrade of Visual Studio for use with .NET) can do most of the changes for you. If you attempt to read a Visual Basic 6 project into Visual Studio 2010, it will upgrade the project for you, which means that it will rewrite the Visual Basic 6 source code into Visual Basic 2010 source code. Although this means that the work involved for you is heavily cut down, you will need to check through the new Visual Basic 2010 code to make sure that the project still works as intended because the conversion might not be perfect.

One side effect of this language upgrade is that it is no longer possible to compile Visual Basic 2010 to native executable code. Visual Basic 2010 compiles only to IL, just as C# does. If you need to continue coding in Visual Basic 6, you can do so, but the executable code produced will completely ignore the .NET Framework, and you will need to keep Visual Studio 6 installed if you want to continue to work in this developer environment.

Visual C++ 2010

Visual C++ 6 already had a large number of Microsoft-specific extensions on Windows. With Visual C++ .NET, extensions have been added to support the .NET Framework. This means that existing C++ source code will continue to compile to native executable code without modification. It also means, however, that it will run independently of the .NET runtime. If you want your C++ code to run within the .NET Framework, you can simply add the following line to the beginning of your code:

```
#using <mscorlib.dll>
```

You can also pass the flag /clr to the compiler, which then assumes that you want to compile to managed code, and will hence emit IL instead of native machine code. The interesting thing about C++ is that when you compile to managed code, the compiler can emit IL that contains an embedded native executable. This means that you can mix managed types and unmanaged types in your C++ code. Thus the managed C++ code

```
class MyClass
{
```

defines a plain C++ class, whereas the code

```
ref class MyClass
{
```

gives you a managed class, just as if you had written the class in C# or Visual Basic 2010. The advantage of using managed C++ over C# code is that you can call unmanaged C++ classes from managed C++ code without having to resort to COM interop.

The compiler raises an error if you attempt to use features that are not supported by .NET on managed types (for example, templates or multiple inheritances of classes). You will also find that you need to use nonstandard C++ features when using managed classes.

Because of the freedom that C++ allows in terms of low-level pointer manipulation and so on, the C++ compiler is not able to generate code that will pass the CLR's memory type-safety tests. If it is important that your code be recognized by the CLR as memory type-safe, you will need to write your source code in some other language (such as C# or Visual Basic 2010).

COM and COM+

Technically speaking, COM and COM+ are not technologies targeted at .NET — components based on them cannot be compiled into IL (although it is possible to do so to some degree using managed C++, if the original COM component was written in C++). However, COM+ remains an important tool, because its features are not duplicated in .NET. Also, COM components will still work — and .NET incorporates COM interoperability features that make it possible for managed code to call up COM components and vice versa (this is discussed in Chapter 26, "Interop"). In general, however, you will probably find it more convenient for most purposes to code new components as .NET components, so that you can take advantage of the .NET base classes as well as the other benefits of running as managed code.

A CLOSER LOOK AT INTERMEDIATE LANGUAGE

From what you learned in the previous section, Microsoft Intermediate Language obviously plays a fundamental role in the .NET Framework. It makes sense now to take a closer look at the main features of IL, because any language that targets .NET will logically need to support these characteristics too.

Here are the important features of IL:

- ➤ Object orientation and the use of interfaces
- ➤ Strong distinction between value and reference types
- ➤ Strong data typing
- ➤ Error handling using exceptions
- ➤ Use of attributes

The following sections explore each of these features.

Support for Object Orientation and Interfaces

The language independence of .NET does have some practical limitations. IL is inevitably going to implement some particular programming methodology, which means that languages targeting it need to be compatible with that methodology. The particular route that Microsoft has chosen to follow for IL is that of classic object-oriented programming, with single implementation inheritance of classes.

 If you are unfamiliar with the concepts of object orientation, refer to the Web Download Chapter 53, "C#, Visual Basic, C++/CLI, and F#" for more information.

In addition to classic object-oriented programming, IL also brings in the idea of interfaces, which saw their first implementation under Windows with COM. Interfaces built using .NET produce interfaces that are not the same as COM interfaces. They do not need to support any of the COM infrastructure (for example, they are not derived from IUnknown, and they do not have associated globally unique identifiers, more commonly know as GUIDs). However, they do share with COM interfaces the idea that they provide a contract, and classes that implement a given interface must provide implementations of the methods and properties specified by that interface.

You have now seen that working with .NET means compiling to IL, and that in turn means that you will need to use traditional object-oriented methodologies. However, that alone is not sufficient to give you language interoperability. After all, C++ and Java both use the same object-oriented paradigms, but they are still not regarded as interoperable. We need to look a little more closely at the concept of language interoperability.

So what exactly do we mean by language interoperability?

After all, COM allowed components written in different languages to work together in the sense of calling each other's methods. What was inadequate about that? COM, by virtue of being a binary standard, did allow components to instantiate other components and call methods or properties against them, without worrying about the language in which the respective components were written. To achieve this, however, each object had to be instantiated through the COM runtime, and accessed through an interface. Depending on the threading models of the relative components, there may have been large performance losses associated with marshaling data between apartments or running components or both on different threads. In the extreme case of components hosted as an executable rather than DLL files, separate processes would need to be created to run them. The emphasis was very much that components could talk to each other but only via the COM runtime. In no way with COM did components written in different languages directly communicate with each other, or instantiate instances of each other — it was always done with COM as an intermediary. Not only that, but the COM architecture did not permit implementation inheritance, which meant that it lost many of the advantages of object-oriented programming.

An associated problem was that, when debugging, you would still need to debug components written in different languages independently. It was not possible to step between languages in the debugger. Therefore, what we *really* mean by language interoperability is that classes written in one language should be able to talk directly to classes written in another language. In particular:

➤ A class written in one language can inherit from a class written in another language.

➤ The class can contain an instance of another class, no matter what the languages of the two classes are.

➤ An object can directly call methods against another object written in another language.

➤ Objects (or references to objects) can be passed around between methods.

➤ When calling methods between languages, you can step between the method calls in the debugger, even when this means stepping between source code written in different languages.

This is all quite an ambitious aim, but amazingly, .NET and IL have achieved it. In the case of stepping between methods in the debugger, this facility is really offered by the Visual Studio integrated development environment (IDE) rather than by the CLR itself.

Distinct Value and Reference Types

As with any programming language, IL provides a number of predefined primitive data types. One characteristic of IL, however, is that it makes a strong distinction between value and reference types. *Value types* are those for which a variable directly stores its data, whereas *reference types* are those for which a variable simply stores the address at which the corresponding data can be found.

In C++ terms, using reference types is similar to accessing a variable through a pointer, whereas for Visual Basic, the best analogy for reference types are objects, which in Visual Basic 6 are always accessed through references. IL also lays down specifications about data storage: instances of reference types are always stored in an area of memory known as the *managed heap,* whereas value types are normally stored on the *stack* (although if value types are declared as fields within reference types, they will be stored inline on the heap). Chapter 2, "Core C#," discusses the stack and the heap and how they work.

Strong Data Typing

One very important aspect of IL is that it is based on exceptionally *strong data typing.* That means that all variables are clearly marked as being of a particular, specific data type (there is no room in IL, for example, for the `Variant` data type recognized by Visual Basic and scripting languages). In particular, IL does not normally permit any operations that result in ambiguous data types.

For instance, Visual Basic 6 developers are used to being able to pass variables around without worrying too much about their types, because Visual Basic 6 automatically performs type conversion. C++ developers are used to routinely casting pointers between different types. Being able to perform this kind of operation can be great for performance, but it breaks type safety. Hence, it is permitted only under certain circumstances in some of the languages that compile to managed code. Indeed, pointers (as opposed to references) are permitted only in marked blocks of code in C#, and not at all in Visual Basic (although they are allowed in managed C++). Using pointers in your code causes it to fail the memory type-safety checks performed by the CLR. You should note that some languages compatible with .NET, such as Visual Basic 2010, still allow some laxity in typing, but that it's possible only because the compilers behind the scenes ensure that the type safety is enforced in the emitted IL.

Although enforcing type safety might initially appear to hurt performance, in many cases the benefits gained from the services provided by .NET that rely on type safety far outweigh this performance loss. Such services include the following:

➤ Language interoperability

➤ Garbage collection

➤ Security

➤ Application domains

The following sections take a closer look at why strong data typing is particularly important for these features of .NET.

Strong Data Typing as a Key to Language Interoperability

If a class is to derive from or contains instances of other classes, it needs to know about all the data types used by the other classes. This is why strong data typing is so important. Indeed, it is the absence of any agreed-on system for specifying this information in the past that has always been the real barrier to inheritance and interoperability across languages. This kind of information is simply not present in a standard executable file or DLL.

Suppose that one of the methods of a Visual Basic 2010 class is defined to return an `Integer` — one of the standard data types available in Visual Basic 2010. C# simply does not have any data type of that name. Clearly, you will be able to derive from the class, use this method, and use the return type from C# code, only if the compiler knows how to map Visual Basic 2010s `Integer` type to some known type that is defined in C#. So, how is this problem circumvented in .NET?

Common Type System

This data type problem is solved in .NET using the *Common Type System* (CTS). The CTS defines the predefined data types that are available in IL, so that all languages that target the .NET Framework will produce compiled code that is ultimately based on these types.

For the previous example, Visual Basic 2010s `Integer` is actually a 32-bit signed integer, which maps exactly to the IL type known as `Int32`. Therefore, this will be the data type specified in the IL code. Because the C# compiler is aware of this type, there is no problem. At source code level, C# refers to `Int32` with the keyword `int`, so the compiler will simply treat the Visual Basic 2010 method as if it returned an `int`.

The CTS does not specify merely primitive data types but a rich hierarchy of types, which includes well-defined points in the hierarchy at which code is permitted to define its own types. The hierarchical structure of the CTS reflects the single-inheritance object-oriented methodology of IL, and resembles Figure 1-1.

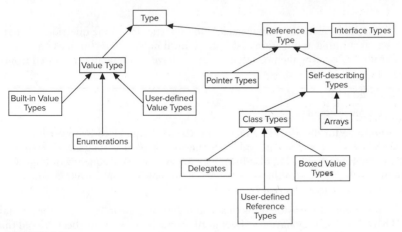

FIGURE 1-1

We will not list all the built-in value types here, because they are covered in detail in Chapter 3, "Objects and Types." In C#, each predefined type is recognized by the compiler maps onto one of the IL built-in types. The same is true in Visual Basic 2010.

Common Language Specification

The *Common Language Specification* (CLS) works with the CTS to ensure language interoperability. The CLS is a set of minimum standards that all compilers targeting .NET must support. Because IL is a very rich language, writers of most compilers will prefer to restrict the capabilities of a given compiler to support only a subset of the facilities offered by IL and the CTS. That is fine, as long as the compiler supports everything that is defined in the CLS.

For example, take case sensitivity. IL is case-sensitive. Developers who work with case-sensitive languages regularly take advantage of the flexibility that this case sensitivity gives them when selecting variable names. Visual Basic 2010, however, is not case-sensitive. The CLS works around this by indicating that CLS-compliant code should not expose any two names that differ only in their case. Therefore, Visual Basic 2010 code can work with CLS-compliant code.

This example shows that the CLS works in two ways.

1. Individual compilers do not have to be powerful enough to support the full features of .NET — this should encourage the development of compilers for other programming languages that target .NET.

2. If you restrict your classes to exposing only CLS-compliant features, then it guarantees that code written in any other compliant language can use your classes.

The beauty of this idea is that the restriction to using CLS-compliant features applies only to public and protected members of classes and public classes. Within the private implementations of your classes, you can write whatever non-CLS code you want, because code in other assemblies (units of managed code; see later in this chapter) cannot access this part of your code anyway.

We will not go into the details of the CLS specifications here. In general, the CLS will not affect your C# code very much because there are very few non-CLS-compliant features of C# anyway.

 It is perfectly acceptable to write non-CLS-compliant code. However, if you do, the compiled IL code is not guaranteed to be fully language interoperable.

Garbage Collection

The *garbage collector* is .NET's answer to memory management and in particular to the question of what to do about reclaiming memory that running applications ask for. Up until now, two techniques have been used on the Windows platform for de-allocating memory that processes have dynamically requested from the system:

➤ Make the application code do it all manually.

➤ Make objects maintain reference counts.

Having the application code responsible for de-allocating memory is the technique used by lower-level, high-performance languages such as C++. It is efficient, and it has the advantage that (in general) resources are never occupied for longer than necessary. The big disadvantage, however, is the frequency of bugs. Code that requests memory also should explicitly inform the system when it no longer requires that memory. However, it is easy to overlook this, resulting in memory leaks.

Although modern developer environments do provide tools to assist in detecting memory leaks, they remain difficult bugs to track down. That's because they have no effect until so much memory has been leaked that Windows refuses to grant any more to the process. By this point, the entire computer may have appreciably slowed down due to the memory demands being made on it.

Maintaining reference counts is favored in COM. The idea is that each COM component maintains a count of how many clients are currently maintaining references to it. When this count falls to zero, the component can destroy itself and free up associated memory and resources. The problem with this is that it still relies on the good behavior of clients to notify the component that they have finished with it. It takes only one client not to do so, and the object sits in memory. In some ways, this is a potentially more serious problem than a simple C++-style memory leak because the COM object may exist in its own process, which means that it will never be removed by the system. (At least with C++ memory leaks, the system can reclaim all memory when the process terminates.)

The .NET runtime relies on the garbage collector instead. The purpose of this program is to clean up memory. The idea is that all dynamically requested memory is allocated on the heap (that is true for all languages, although in the case of .NET, the CLR maintains its own managed heap for .NET applications to use). Every so often, when .NET detects that the managed heap for a given process is becoming full and therefore needs tidying up, it calls the garbage collector. The garbage collector runs through variables currently in scope in your code, examining references to objects stored on the heap to identify which ones are accessible from your code — that is, which objects have references that refer to them. Any objects that are not referred to are deemed to be no longer accessible from your code and can therefore be removed. Java uses a system of garbage collection similar to this.

Garbage collection works in .NET because IL has been designed to facilitate the process. The principle requires that you cannot get references to existing objects other than by copying existing references and that IL be type safe. In this context, what we mean is that if any reference to an object exists, then there is sufficient information in the reference to exactly determine the type of the object.

It would not be possible to use the garbage collection mechanism with a language such as unmanaged C++, for example, because C++ allows pointers to be freely cast between types.

One important aspect of garbage collection is that it is not deterministic. In other words, you cannot guarantee when the garbage collector will be called; it will be called when the CLR decides that it is needed, though it is also possible to override this process and call up the garbage collector in your code.

Look to Chapter 13, "Memory Management and Pointers," for more information on the garbage collection process.

Security

.NET can really excel in terms of complementing the security mechanisms provided by Windows because it can offer code-based security, whereas Windows really offers only role-based security.

Role-based security is based on the identity of the account under which the process is running (that is, who owns and is running the process). *Code-based security,* by contrast, is based on what the code actually does and on how much the code is trusted. Thanks to the strong type safety of IL, the CLR is able to inspect code before running it to determine required security permissions. .NET also offers a mechanism by which code can indicate in advance what security permissions it will require to run.

The importance of code-based security is that it reduces the risks associated with running code of dubious origin (such as code that you have downloaded from the Internet). For example, even if code is running under the administrator account, it is possible to use code-based security to indicate that that code should still not be permitted to perform certain types of operations that the administrator account would normally be allowed to do, such as read or write to environment variables, read or write to the registry, or access the .NET reflection features.

Security issues are covered in more depth in Chapter 21, "Security."

Application Domains

Application domains are an important innovation in .NET and are designed to ease the overhead involved when running applications that need to be isolated from each other but that also need to be able to communicate with each other. The classic example of this is a web server application, which may be simultaneously responding to a number of browser requests. It will, therefore, probably have a number of instances of the component responsible for servicing those requests running simultaneously.

In pre-.NET days, the choice would be between allowing those instances to share a process (with the resultant risk of a problem in one running instance bringing the whole web site down) or isolating those instances in separate processes (with the associated performance overhead).

Up until now, the only means of isolating code has been through processes. When you start a new application, it runs within the context of a process. Windows isolates processes from each other through address spaces. The idea is that each process has available 4GB of virtual memory in which to store its data and executable code (4GB is for 32-bit systems; 64-bit systems use more memory). Windows imposes an extra level of indirection by which this virtual memory maps into a particular area of actual physical memory or disk space. Each process gets a different mapping, with no overlap between the actual physical memories that the blocks of virtual address space map to (see Figure 1-2).

In general, any process is able to access memory only by specifying an address in virtual memory — processes do not have direct access to physical memory. Hence, it is simply impossible for one process to access the memory allocated to another process. This provides an excellent guarantee that any badly behaved code will not be able to damage anything outside of its own address space. (Note that on Windows 95/98, these safeguards are not quite as thorough as they are on Windows NT/2000/XP/2003/Vista/7, so the theoretical possibility exists of applications crashing Windows by writing to inappropriate memory.)

Processes do not just serve as a way to isolate instances of running code from each other. On Windows NT/2000/XP/2003/Vista/7 systems, they also form the unit to which security privileges and permissions are assigned. Each process has its own security token, which indicates to Windows precisely what operations that process is permitted to do.

Although processes are great for security reasons, their big disadvantage is in the area of performance. Often, a number of processes will actually be working together, and therefore need to communicate with each other. The obvious example of this is where a process calls up a COM component, which is an executable and therefore is required to run in its own process. The same thing happens in COM when surrogates are used. Because processes cannot share any memory, a complex marshaling process must be used to copy data between the processes. This results in a very significant performance hit. If you need components to work together and do not want that performance hit, you must use DLL-based components and have everything running in the same address space — with the associated risk that a badly behaved component will bring everything else down.

Application domains are designed as a way of separating components without resulting in the performance problems associated with passing data between processes. The idea is that any one process is divided into a number of application domains. Each application domain roughly corresponds to a single application, and each thread of execution will be running in a particular application domain (see Figure 1-3).

Physical
Memory

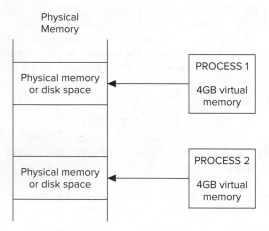

FIGURE 1-2

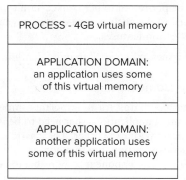

FIGURE 1-3

If different executables are running in the same process space, then they are clearly able to easily share data, because, theoretically, they can directly see each other's data. However, although this is possible in principle, the CLR makes sure that this does not happen in practice by inspecting the code for each running application to ensure that the code cannot stray outside of its own data areas. This looks, at first, like an almost impossible task to pull off — after all, how can you tell what the program is going to do without actually running it?

In fact, it is usually possible to do this because of the strong type safety of the IL. In most cases, unless code is using unsafe features such as pointers, the data types it is using will ensure that memory is not accessed inappropriately. For example, .NET array types perform bounds checking to ensure that no out-of-bounds array operations are permitted. If a running application does need to communicate or share data with other applications running in different application domains, it must do so by calling on .NET's remoting services.

Code that has been verified to check that it cannot access data outside its application domain (other than through the explicit remoting mechanism) is said to be *memory type safe*. Such code can safely be run alongside other type-safe code in different application domains within the same process.

Error Handling with Exceptions

The .NET Framework is designed to facilitate handling of error conditions using the same mechanism, based on exceptions, that is employed by Java and C++. C++ developers should note that because of IL's stronger typing system, there is no performance penalty associated with the use of exceptions with IL in the way that there is in C++. Also, the `finally` block, which has long been on many C++ developers' wish lists, is supported by .NET and by C#.

Exceptions are covered in detail in Chapter 15, "Errors and Exceptions." Briefly, the idea is that certain areas of code are designated as exception handler routines, with each one able to deal with a particular error condition (for example, a file not being found, or being denied permission to perform some operation). These conditions can be defined as narrowly or as widely as you want. The exception architecture ensures that when an error condition occurs, execution can immediately jump to the exception handler routine that is most specifically geared to handle the exception condition in question.

The architecture of exception handling also provides a convenient means to pass an object containing precise details of the exception condition to an exception-handling routine. This object might include an appropriate message for the user and details of exactly where in the code the exception was detected.

Most exception-handling architecture, including the control of program flow when an exception occurs, is handled by the high-level languages (C#, Visual Basic 2010, C++), and is not supported by any special IL commands. C#, for example, handles exceptions using `try{}`, `catch{}`, and `finally{}` blocks of code. (For more details, see Chapter 15.)

What .NET does do, however, is provide the infrastructure to allow compilers that target .NET to support exception handling. In particular, it provides a set of .NET classes that can represent the exceptions, and the language interoperability to allow the thrown exception objects to be interpreted by the exception-handling code, regardless of what language the exception-handling code is written in. This language independence is absent from both the C++ and Java implementations of exception handling, although it is present to a limited extent in the COM mechanism for handling errors, which involves returning error codes from methods and passing error objects around. The fact that exceptions are handled consistently in different languages is a crucial aspect of facilitating multi-language development.

Use of Attributes

Attributes are familiar to developers who use C++ to write COM components (through their use in Microsoft's COM Interface Definition Language [IDL]). The initial idea of an attribute was that it provided extra information concerning some item in the program that could be used by the compiler.

Attributes are supported in .NET — and hence now by C++, C#, and Visual Basic 2010. What is, however, particularly innovative about attributes in .NET is that you can define your own custom attributes in your source code. These user-defined attributes will be placed with the metadata for the corresponding data types or methods. This can be useful for documentation purposes, in which they can be used in conjunction with reflection technology to perform programming tasks based on attributes. In addition, in common with the .NET philosophy of language independence, attributes can be defined in source code in one language and read by code that is written in another language.

Attributes are covered in Chapter 14, "Reflection."

ASSEMBLIES

An *assembly* is the logical unit that contains compiled code targeted at the .NET Framework. Assemblies are not covered in detail in this chapter because they are covered thoroughly in Chapter 18, "Assemblies," but we summarize the main points here.

An assembly is completely self-describing and is a logical rather than a physical unit, which means that it can be stored across more than one file (indeed, dynamic assemblies are stored in memory, not on file at all). If an assembly is stored in more than one file, there will be one main file that contains the entry point and describes the other files in the assembly.

Note that the same assembly structure is used for both executable code and library code. The only real difference is that an executable assembly contains a main program entry point, whereas a library assembly does not.

An important characteristic of assemblies is that they contain metadata that describes the types and methods defined in the corresponding code. An assembly, however, also contains assembly metadata that describes the assembly itself. This assembly metadata, contained in an area known as the *manifest,* allows checks to be made on the version of the assembly, and on its integrity.

 `ildasm`, *a Windows-based utility, can be used to inspect the contents of an assembly, including the manifest and metadata.* `ildasm` *is discussed in Chapter 18.*

The fact that an assembly contains program metadata means that applications or other assemblies that call up code in a given assembly do not need to refer to the registry, or to any other data source, to find out how to use that assembly. This is a significant break from the old COM way of doing things, in which the GUIDs of the components and interfaces had to be obtained from the registry, and in some cases, the details of the methods and properties exposed would need to be read from a type library.

Having data spread out in up to three different locations meant there was the obvious risk of something getting out of synchronization, which would prevent other software from being able to use the component successfully. With assemblies, there is no risk of this happening, because all the metadata is stored with the program executable instructions. Note that even though assemblies are stored across several files, there are still no problems with data going out of synchronization. This is because the file that contains the assembly entry point also stores details of, and a hash of, the contents of the other files, which means that if one of the files gets replaced, or in any way tampered with, this will almost certainly be detected and the assembly will refuse to load.

Assemblies come in two types: *private* and *shared* assemblies.

Private Assemblies

Private assemblies are the simplest type. They normally ship with software and are intended to be used only with that software. The usual scenario in which you will ship private assemblies is when you are supplying an application in the form of an executable and a number of libraries, where the libraries contain code that should be used only with that application.

The system guarantees that private assemblies will not be used by other software because an application may load only private assemblies that are located in the same folder that the main executable is loaded in, or in a subfolder of it.

Because you would normally expect that commercial software would always be installed in its own directory, there is no risk of one software package overwriting, modifying, or accidentally loading private assemblies intended for another package. And, because private assemblies can be used only by the software package that they are intended for, you have much more control over what software uses them. There is, therefore, less need to take security precautions because there is no risk, for example, of some other commercial software overwriting one of your assemblies with some new version of it (apart from software that is designed specifically to perform malicious damage). There are also no problems with name collisions. If classes in your private assembly happen to have the same name as classes in someone else's private assembly, that does not matter, because any given application will be able to see only the one set of private assemblies.

Because a private assembly is entirely self-contained, the process of deploying it is simple. You simply place the appropriate file(s) in the appropriate folder in the file system (no registry entries need to be made). This process is known as *zero impact (xcopy) installation*.

Shared Assemblies

Shared assemblies are intended to be common libraries that any other application can use. Because any other software can access a shared assembly, more precautions need to be taken against the following risks:

➤ Name collisions, where another company's shared assembly implements types that have the same names as those in your shared assembly. Because client code can theoretically have access to both assemblies simultaneously, this could be a serious problem.

➤ The risk of an assembly being overwritten by a different version of the same assembly — the new version is incompatible with some existing client code.

The solution to these problems is placing shared assemblies in a special directory subtree in the file system, known as the *global assembly cache* (GAC). Unlike with private assemblies, this cannot be done by simply copying the assembly into the appropriate folder — it needs to be specifically installed into the cache. This process can be performed by a number of .NET utilities and requires certain checks on the assembly, as well as the set up of a small folder hierarchy within the assembly cache that is used to ensure assembly integrity.

To prevent name collisions, shared assemblies are given a name based on private key cryptography (private assemblies are simply given the same name as their main file name). This name is known as a *strong name*; it is guaranteed to be unique and must be quoted by applications that reference a shared assembly.

Problems associated with the risk of overwriting an assembly are addressed by specifying version information in the assembly manifest and by allowing side-by-side installations.

Reflection

Because assemblies store metadata, including details of all the types and members of these types that are defined in the assembly, it is possible to access this metadata programmatically. Full details of this are given in Chapter 14. This technique, known as reflection, raises interesting possibilities, because it means that managed code can actually examine other managed code, and can even examine itself, to determine information about that code. This is most commonly used to obtain the details of attributes, although you can also use reflection, among other purposes, as an indirect way of instantiating classes or calling methods, given the names of those classes or methods as strings. In this way, you could select classes to instantiate methods to call at runtime, rather than at compile time, based on user input (dynamic binding).

Parallel Programming

The .NET Framework 4 introduces the ability to take advantage of all the dual and quad processors that are out there today. The new parallel computing capabilities provides the means to separate work actions and run these across multiple processors. The new parallel programming APIs that are available now make writing safe multi-threaded code so simple, though it is important to realize that you still need to account for race conditions as well as things such as locks.

The new parallel programming capabilities provide a new Task Parallel Library as well as a PLINQ Execution Engine. Parallel programming is covered in Chapter 20, "Threads, Tasks, and Synchronization."

.NET FRAMEWORK CLASSES

Perhaps one of the biggest benefits of writing managed code, at least from a developer's point of view, is that you get to use the .NET *base class library*. The .NET base classes are a massive collection of managed code classes that allow you to do almost any of the tasks that were previously available through the Windows API. These classes follow the same object model that IL uses, based on single inheritance. This means that you can either instantiate objects of whichever .NET base class is appropriate or derive your own classes from them.

The great thing about the .NET base classes is that they have been designed to be very intuitive and easy to use. For example, to start a thread, you call the `Start()` method of the `Thread` class. To disable a `TextBox`, you set the `Enabled` property of a `TextBox` object to `false`. This approach — though familiar to Visual Basic and Java developers, whose respective libraries are just as easy to use — will be a welcome relief to C++ developers, who for years have had to cope with such API functions as `GetDIBits()`, `RegisterWndClassEx()`, and `IsEqualIID()`, as well as a whole plethora of functions that require Windows handles to be passed around.

However, C++ developers always had easy access to the entire Windows API, unlike Visual Basic 6 and Java developers who were more restricted in terms of the basic operating system functionality that they have access to from their respective languages. What is new about the .NET base classes is that they combine the ease of use that was typical of the Visual Basic and Java libraries with the relatively comprehensive coverage of the Windows API functions. Many features of Windows still are not available through the base classes, and for those you will need to call into the API functions, but in general, these are now confined to the more exotic features. For everyday use, you will probably find the base classes adequate. Moreover, if you do need to call into an API function, .NET offers a so-called *platform-invoke* that ensures data types are correctly converted, so the task is no harder than calling the function directly from C++ code would have been — regardless of whether you are coding in C#, C++, or Visual Basic 2010.

 WinCV, a Windows-based utility, can be used to browse the classes, structs, interfaces, and enums in the base class library. WinCV is discussed in Chapter 16, "Visual Studio 2010."

Although Chapter 3 is nominally dedicated to the subject of base classes, after we have completed our coverage of the syntax of the C# language, most of the rest of this book shows you how to use various classes within the .NET base class library for the .NET Framework 4. That is how comprehensive base classes are. As a rough guide, the areas covered by the .NET 3.5 base classes include the following:

➤ Core features provided by IL (including the primitive data types in the CTS discussed in Chapter 3)

➤ Windows GUI support and controls (see Chapters 39, "Windows Forms," and 35, "Core WPF")

➤ Web Forms (ASP.NET is discussed in Chapters 40, "Core ASP.NET" and 41, "ASP.NET Features")

➤ Data access (ADO.NET; see Chapters 30, "Core ADO.NET" 34, ".NET Programming with SQL Server," and 33, "Manipulating XML")

➤ Directory access (see Chapter 52 on the Web, "Directory Services")

➤ File system and registry access (see Chapter 29, "Manipulating Files and the Registry")

➤ Networking and web browsing (see Chapter 24, "Networking")

➤ .NET attributes and reflection (see Chapter 14)

➤ Access to aspects of the Windows OS (environment variables and so on; see Chapter 21)

➤ COM interoperability (see Chapter 51 on the Web, "Enterprise Services" and Chapter 26)

Incidentally, according to Microsoft sources, a large proportion of the .NET base classes have actually been written in C#!

NAMESPACES

Namespaces are the way that .NET avoids name clashes between classes. They are designed to prevent situations in which you define a class to represent a customer, name your class `Customer`, and then someone else does the same thing (a likely scenario — the proportion of businesses that have customers seems to be quite high).

A namespace is no more than a grouping of data types, but it has the effect that the names of all data types within a namespace are automatically prefixed with the name of the namespace. It is also possible to nest namespaces within each other. For example, most of the general-purpose .NET base classes are in a namespace called `System`. The base class `Array` is in this namespace, so its full name is `System.Array`.

.NET requires all types to be defined in a namespace; for example, you could place your `Customer` class in a namespace called `YourCompanyName`. This class would have the full name `YourCompanyName.Customer`.

 If a namespace is not explicitly supplied, the type will be added to a nameless global namespace.

Microsoft recommends that for most purposes you supply at least two nested namespace names: the first one represents the name of your company, and the second one represents the name of the technology or software package of which the class is a member, such as `YourCompanyName.SalesServices.Customer`. This protects, in most situations, the classes in your application from possible name clashes with classes written by other organizations.

Chapter 2 looks more closely at namespaces.

CREATING .NET APPLICATIONS USING C#

C# can also be used to create console applications: text-only applications that run in a DOS window. You will probably use console applications when unit testing class libraries, and for creating UNIX or Linux daemon processes. More often, however, you will use C# to create applications that use many of the technologies associated with .NET. This section gives you an overview of the different types of applications that you can write in C#.

Creating ASP.NET Applications

The original introduction of ASP.NET 1.0 fundamentally changed the web programming model. ASP.NET 4 is a major release of the product and builds upon its earlier achievements. ASP.NET 4 follows on a series of major revolutionary steps designed to increase your productivity. The primary goal of ASP.NET is to enable you to build powerful, secure, dynamic applications using the least possible amount of code. As this is a C# book, there are many chapters showing you how to use this language to build the latest in web applications.

The following section explores the key features of ASP.NET. For more details, refer to Chapters 40, "Core ASP.NET," 41, "ASP.NET Features," and 42, "ASP.NET MVC."

Features of ASP.NET

First, and perhaps most important, ASP.NET pages are *structured*. That is, each page is effectively a class that inherits from the .NET `System.Web.UI.Page` *class* and can override a set of methods that are evoked during the `Page` object's lifetime. (You can think of these events as page-specific cousins of the `OnApplication_Start` and `OnSession_Start` events that went in the `global.asa` files from the classic

ASP days.) Because you can factor a page's functionality into event handlers with explicit meanings, ASP. NET pages are easier to understand.

Another nice thing about ASP.NET pages is that you can create them in Visual Studio 2010, the same environment in which you create the business logic and data access components that those ASP.NET pages use. A Visual Studio 2010 project, or *solution,* contains all the files associated with an application. Moreover, you can debug your classic ASP pages in the editor as well; in the old days of Visual InterDev, it was often a vexing challenge to configure InterDev and the project's web server to turn debugging on.

For maximum clarity, the ASP.NET code-behind feature lets you take the structured approach even further. ASP.NET allows you to isolate the server-side functionality of a page to a class, compile that class into a DLL with the other pages, and place that DLL into a directory below the HTML portion. A @Page directive at the top of the page associates the file with a class. When a browser requests the page, the web server fires the events in the class in the page's class file.

Last, but not least, ASP.NET is remarkable for its increased performance. Whereas classic ASP pages are interpreted with each page request, the web server caches ASP.NET pages after compilation. This means that subsequent requests of an ASP.NET page execute more quickly than the first.

ASP.NET also makes it easy to write pages that cause forms to be displayed by the browser, which you might use in an intranet environment. The traditional wisdom is that form-based applications offer a richer user interface but are harder to maintain because they run on so many different machines. For this reason, people have relied on form-based applications when rich user interfaces were a necessity and extensive support could be provided to the users.

Web Forms

To make web page construction even easier, Visual Studio 2010 supplies *Web Forms.* They allow you to build ASP.NET pages graphically in the same way that Visual Basic 6 or C++ Builder windows are created; in other words, by dragging controls from a toolbox onto a form, then flipping over to the code aspect of that form and writing event handlers for the controls. When you use C# to create a Web Form, you are creating a C# class that inherits from the Page base class and an ASP.NET page that designates that class as its code-behind. Of course, you do not have to use C# to create a Web Form; you can use Visual Basic 2010 or another .NET-compliant language just as well.

In the past, the difficulty of web development discouraged some teams from attempting it. To succeed in web development, you needed to know so many different technologies, such as VBScript, ASP, DHTML, JavaScript, and so on. By applying the Form concepts to web pages, Web Forms have made web development considerably easier.

Web Server Controls

The controls used to populate a Web Form are not controls in the same sense as ActiveX controls. Rather, they are XML tags in the ASP.NET namespace that the web browser dynamically transforms into HTML and client-side script when a page is requested. Amazingly, the web server is able to render the same server-side control in different ways, producing a transformation appropriate to the requestor's particular web browser. This means that it is now easy to write fairly sophisticated user interfaces for web pages, without worrying about how to ensure that your page will run on any of the available browsers — because Web Forms will take care of that for you.

You can use C# or Visual Basic 2010 to expand the Web Form toolbox. Creating a new server-side control is simply a matter of implementing .NET's System.Web.UI.WebControls.WebControl class.

XML Web Services

Today, HTML pages account for most of the traffic on the World Wide Web. With XML, however, computers have a device-independent format to use for communicating with each other on the Web. In the future, computers may use the Web and XML to communicate information rather than dedicated lines and proprietary formats such as *Electronic Data Interchange* (EDI). XML Web services are designed for a service-oriented Web, in which remote computers provide each other with dynamic information that can be analyzed and reformatted, before final presentation to a user. An XML Web service is an easy way for a computer to expose information to other computers on the Web in the form of XML.

In technical terms, an XML Web service on .NET is an ASP.NET page that returns XML instead of HTML to requesting clients. Such pages have a `code-behind` DLL containing a class that derives from the `WebService` class. The Visual Studio 2010 IDE provides an engine that facilitates web service development.

An organization might choose to use XML Web services for two main reasons. The first reason is that they rely on HTTP; XML Web services can use existing networks (HTTP) as a medium for conveying information. The other is that because XML Web services use XML, the data format is self-describing, nonproprietary, and platform-independent.

Creating Windows Forms

Although C# and .NET are particularly suited to web development, they still offer splendid support for so-called *fat-client* or *thick-client* apps — applications that must be installed on the end user's machine where most of the processing takes place. This support is from *Windows Forms*.

A Windows Form is the .NET answer to a Visual Basic 6 Form. To design a graphical window interface, you just drag controls from a toolbox onto a Windows Form. To determine the window's behavior, you write event-handling routines for the form's controls. A Windows Form project compiles to an executable that must be installed alongside the .NET runtime on the end user's computer. As with other .NET project types, Windows Form projects are supported by both Visual Basic 2010 and C#. Chapter 39, "Windows Forms," examines Windows Forms more closely.

Using the Windows Presentation Foundation (WPF)

One of the newest technologies to hit the block is the *Windows Presentation Foundation* (WPF). WPF makes use of XAML in building applications. XAML stands for Extensible Application Markup Language. This new way of creating applications within a Microsoft environment is something that was introduced in 2006 and is part of the .NET Framework 3.0, 3.5, and 4. This means that to run any WPF application, you need to make sure that the .NET Framework 3.0, 3.5, or 4 is installed on the client machine. WPF applications are available for Windows 7, Windows Vista, Windows XP, Windows Server 2003, and Windows Server 2008 (the only operating systems that allow for the installation of the .NET Framework 3.0, 3.5, or 4).

XAML is the XML declaration that is used to create a form that represents all the visual aspects and behaviors of the WPF application. Though it is possible to work with a WPF application programmatically, WPF is a step in the direction of declarative programming, which the industry is moving to. Declarative programming means that instead of creating objects through programming in a compiled language such as C#, VB, or Java, you declare everything through XML-type programming. Chapter 35, "Core WPF" details how to build these new types of applications using XAML and C#.

Windows Controls

Although Web Forms and Windows Forms are developed in much the same way, you use different kinds of controls to populate them. Web Forms use web server controls, and Windows Forms use *Windows Controls*.

A Windows Control is a lot like an ActiveX control. After a Windows Control is implemented, it compiles to a DLL that must be installed on the client's machine. In fact, the .NET SDK provides a utility that creates a wrapper for ActiveX controls, so that they can be placed on Windows Forms. As is the case with Web Controls, Windows Control creation involves deriving from a particular class: `System.Windows.Forms .Control`.

Windows Services

A Windows Service (originally called an NT Service) is a program designed to run in the background in Windows NT/2000/XP/2003/Vista/7 (but not Windows 9x). Services are useful when you want a program to be running continuously and ready to respond to events without having been explicitly started by the user. A good example is the World Wide Web Service on web servers, which listens for web requests from clients.

It is very easy to write services in C#. .NET Framework base classes are available in the `System .ServiceProcess` namespace that handles many of the boilerplate tasks associated with services. In addition, Visual Studio .NET allows you to create a C# Windows Service project, which uses C# source code for a basic Windows Service. Chapter 25, "Windows Services," explores how to write C# Windows Services.

Windows Communication Foundation

Looking at how you move data and services from one point to another using Microsoft-based technologies, you will find that there are a lot of choices at your disposal. For instance, you can use ASP.NET Web services, .NET Remoting, Enterprise Services, and MSMQ for starters. What technology should you use? Well, it really comes down to what you are trying to achieve, because each technology is better used in a particular situation.

With that in mind, Microsoft brought all these technologies together, and with the release of the .NET Framework 3.0 as well as its inclusion in the .NET Framework 3.5 and 4, you now have a single way to move data — the Windows Communication Foundation (WCF). WCF provides you with the ability to build your service one time and then expose this service in a multitude of ways (under different protocols even) by just making changes within a configuration file. You will find that WCF is a powerful new way of connecting disparate systems. Chapter 43, "Windows Communication Foundation," covers this in detail.

Windows Workflow Foundation

The Windows Workflow Foundation (WF) was really introduced back with the release of the .NET Framework 3.0, but has had a good overhaul that many will find more approachable now. You will find that Visual Studio 2010 has greatly improved as far as working with WF and makes it easier to construct your workflows. You will also find a new flow control, the `Flowchart` class, as well as new activities such as `DoWhile`, `ForEach`, and `ParallelForEach`.

WF is covered in Chapter 44, "Windows Workflow Foundation 4."

THE ROLE OF C# IN THE .NET ENTERPRISE ARCHITECTURE

C# requires the presence of the .NET runtime, and it will probably be a few years before most clients — particularly most home computers — have .NET installed. In the meantime, installing a C# application is likely to mean also installing the .NET redistributable components. Because of that, it is likely that we will see many C# applications first in the enterprise environment. Indeed, C# arguably presents an outstanding opportunity for organizations that are interested in building robust, *n*-tiered client-server applications.

When combined with ADO.NET, C# has the ability to quickly and generically access data stores such as SQL Server and Oracle databases. The returned datasets can easily be manipulated using the ADO.NET object model or LINQ, and automatically render as XML for transport across an office intranet.

After a database schema has been established for a new project, C# presents an excellent medium for implementing a layer of data access objects, each of which could provide insertion, updates, and deletion access to a different database table.

Because it's the first component-based C language, C# is a great language for implementing a business object tier, too. It encapsulates the messy plumbing for intercomponent communication, leaving developers free to focus on gluing their data access objects together in methods that accurately enforce their organizations' business rules. Moreover, with attributes, C# business objects can be outfitted for method-level security checks, object pooling, and JIT activation supplied by COM+ Services. Furthermore, .NET ships with utility programs that allow your new .NET business objects to interface with legacy COM components.

To create an enterprise application with C#, you create a class library project for the data access objects and another for the business objects. While developing, you can use Console projects to test the methods on your classes. Fans of extreme programming can build Console projects that can be executed automatically from batch files to unit test that working code has not been broken.

On a related note, C# and .NET will probably influence the way you physically package your reusable classes. In the past, many developers crammed a multitude of classes into a single physical component because this arrangement made deployment a lot easier; if there was a versioning problem, you knew just where to look. Because deploying .NET enterprise components involves simply copying files into directories, developers can now package their classes into more logical, discrete components without encountering "DLL Hell."

Last, but not least, ASP.NET pages coded in C# constitute an excellent medium for user interfaces. Because ASP.NET pages compile, they execute quickly. Because they can be debugged in the Visual Studio 2010 IDE, they are robust. Because they support full-scale language features such as early binding, inheritance, and modularization, ASP.NET pages coded in C# are tidy and easily maintained.

Seasoned developers acquire a healthy skepticism about strongly hyped new technologies and languages and are reluctant to use new platforms simply because they are urged to. If you are an enterprise developer in an IT department, though, or if you provide application services across the World Wide Web, let us assure you that C# and .NET offer at least four solid benefits, even if some of the more exotic features such as XML Web services and server-side controls don't pan out:

➤ Component conflicts will become infrequent and deployment is easier because different versions of the same component can run side by side on the same machine without conflicting.

➤ Your ASP.NET code will not look like spaghetti code.

➤ You can leverage a lot of the functionality in the .NET base classes.

➤ For applications requiring a Windows Forms user interface, C# makes it very easy to write this kind of application.

Windows Forms have, to some extent, been downplayed due to the advent of Web Forms and Internet-based applications. However, if you or your colleagues lack expertise in JavaScript, ASP, or related technologies, Windows Forms are still a viable option for creating a user interface with speed and ease. Just remember to factor your code so that the user interface logic is separate from the business logic and the data access code. Doing so will allow you to migrate your application to the browser at some point in the future if you need to. In addition, it is likely that Windows Forms will remain the dominant user interface for applications for use in homes and small businesses for a long time to come. In addition to this, the new smart client features of Windows Forms (the ability to easily work in an online/offline mode) will bring a new round of exciting applications.

SUMMARY

This chapter has covered a lot of ground, briefly reviewing important aspects of the .NET Framework and C#'s relationship to it. It started by discussing how all languages that target .NET are compiled into Microsoft Intermediate Language (IL) before this is compiled and executed by the Common Language Runtime (CLR). This chapter also discussed the roles of the following features of .NET in the compilation and execution process:

➤ Assemblies and .NET base classes

➤ COM components

➤ JIT compilation

➤ Application domains

➤ Garbage collection

Figure 1-4 provides an overview of how these features come into play during compilation and execution.

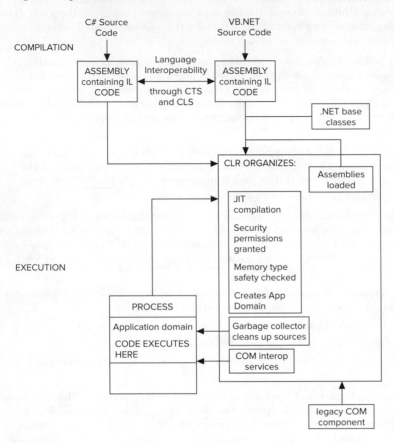

FIGURE 1-4

You learned about the characteristics of IL, particularly its strong data typing and object orientation, and how these characteristics influence the languages that target .NET, including C#. You also learned how the strongly typed nature of IL enables language interoperability, as well as CLR services such as garbage collection and security. There was also a focus on the Common Language Specification (CLS) and the Common Type System (CTS) to help deal with language interoperability.

Finally, you learned how C# could be used as the basis for applications that are built on several .NET technologies, including ASP.NET.

Chapter 2 discusses how to write code in C#.

2

Core C#

WHAT'S IN THIS CHAPTER?

➤ Declaring variables

➤ Initialization and scope of variables

➤ Predefined C# data types

➤ Dictating the flow of execution within a C# program using conditional statements, loops, and jump statements

➤ Enumerations

➤ Namespaces

➤ The `Main()` method

➤ Basic command-line C# compiler options

➤ Using `System.Console` to perform console I/O

➤ Using internal comments and documentation features

➤ Preprocessor directives

➤ Guidelines and conventions for good programming in C#

Now that you understand more about what C# can do, you will want to learn how to use it. This chapter gives you a good start in that direction by providing you with a basic knowledge of the fundamentals of C# programming, which is built on in subsequent chapters. By the end of this chapter, you will know enough C# to write simple programs (though without using inheritance or other object-oriented features, which are covered in later chapters).

YOUR FIRST C# PROGRAM

Let's start by compiling and running the simplest possible C# program — a simple console app consisting of a class that writes a message to the screen.

Later chapters present a number of code samples. The most common technique for writing C# programs is to use Visual Studio 2010 to generate a basic project and add your own code to it. However, because the aim of Part I is to teach the C# language, we are going to keep things simple and avoid relying on Visual Studio 2010 until Chapter 16, "Visual Studio 2010." Instead, we will present the code as simple files that you can type in using any text editor and compile from the command line.

The Code

Type the following into a text editor (such as Notepad), and save it with a `.cs` extension (for example, `First.cs`). The `Main()` method is shown here (for more information, see "The Main Method" section later in this chapter):

Available for download on Wrox.com

```csharp
using System;

namespace Wrox
{
    public class MyFirstClass
    {
        static void Main()
        {
            Console.WriteLine("Hello from Wrox.");
            Console.ReadLine();
            return;
        }
    }
}
```

code snippet First.cs

Compiling and Running the Program

You can compile this program by simply running the C# command-line compiler (`csc.exe`) against the source file, like this:

```
csc First.cs
```

If you want to compile code from the command line using the `csc` command, you should be aware that the .NET command-line tools, including `csc`, are available only if certain environment variables have been set up. Depending on how you installed .NET (and Visual Studio 2010), this may or may not be the case on your machine.

If you do not have the environment variables set up, you have the following two options: The first is to run the batch file `%Microsoft Visual Studio 2010%\Common7\Tools\vsvars32.bat` *from the command prompt before running* `csc`, *where* `%Microsoft Visual Studio 2010%` *is the folder to which Visual Studio 2010 has been installed. The second, and easier, way is to use the Visual Studio 2010 command prompt instead of the usual command prompt window. You will find the Visual Studio 2010 command prompt in the Start menu, under Programs, Microsoft Visual Studio 2010, Visual Studio Tools. It is simply a command prompt window that automatically runs* `vsvars32.bat` *when it opens.*

Compiling the code produces an executable file named `First.exe`, which you can run from the command line or from Windows Explorer like any other executable. Give it a try:

```
csc First.cs
Microsoft (R) Visual C# 2010 Compiler version 4.0.20506.1
Copyright (C) Microsoft Corporation. All rights reserved.

First.exe
Hello from Wrox.
```

A Closer Look

First, a few general comments about C# syntax. In C#, as in other C-style languages, most statements end in a semicolon (`;`) and can continue over multiple lines without needing a continuation character. Statements can be joined into blocks using curly braces (`{}`). Single-line comments begin with two forward slash characters (`//`), and multiline comments begin with a slash and an asterisk (`/*`) and end with the same combination reversed (`*/`). In these aspects, C# is identical to C++ and Java but different from Visual Basic. It is the semicolons and curly braces that give C# code such a different visual appearance from Visual Basic code. If your background is predominantly Visual Basic, take extra care to remember the semicolon at the end of every statement. Omitting this is usually the biggest single cause of compilation errors among developers new to C-style languages. Another thing to remember is that C# is case-sensitive. That means that variables named `myVar` and `MyVar` are two different variables.

The first few lines in the previous code example have to do with *namespaces* (mentioned later in this chapter), which is a way to group together associated classes. The `namespace` keyword declares the namespace your class should be associated with. All code within the braces that follow it is regarded as being within that namespace. The `using` statement specifies a namespace that the compiler should look at to find any classes that are referenced in your code but that aren't defined in the current namespace. This serves the same purpose as the `import` statement in Java and the `using namespace` statement in C++.

```
using System;

namespace Wrox
{
```

The reason for the presence of the `using` statement in the `First.cs` file is that you are going to use a library class, `System.Console`. The `using System` statement allows you to refer to this class simply as `Console` (and similarly for any other classes in the `System` namespace). Without the `using`, we would have to fully qualify the call to the `Console.WriteLine` method like this:

```
System.Console.WriteLine("Hello from Wrox.");
```

The standard `System` namespace is where the most commonly used .NET types reside. It is important to realize that everything you do in C# depends on the .NET base classes. In this case, you are using the `Console` class within the `System` namespace to write to the console window. C# has no built-in keywords of its own for input or output; it is completely reliant on the .NET classes.

 Because almost every C# program uses classes in the `System` namespace, we will assume that a `using System;` statement is present in the file for all code snippets in this chapter.

Next, you declare a class called `MyFirstClass`. However, because it has been placed in a namespace called `Wrox`, the fully qualified name of this class is `Wrox.MyFirstCSharpClass`:

```
class MyFirstCSharpClass
{
```

All C# code must be contained within a class. The class declaration consists of the `class` keyword, followed by the class name and a pair of curly braces. All code associated with the class should be placed between these braces.

Next, you declare a method called `Main()`. Every C# executable (such as console applications, Windows applications, and Windows services) must have an entry point — the `Main()` method (note the capital `M`):

```
public static void Main()
{
```

The method is called when the program is started. This method must return either nothing (`void`) or an integer (`int`). Note the format of method definitions in C#:

```
[modifiers] return_type MethodName([parameters])
{
    // Method body. NB. This code block is pseudo-code.
}
```

Here, the first square brackets represent certain optional keywords. Modifiers are used to specify certain features of the method you are defining, such as where the method can be called from. In this case, you have two modifiers: `public` and `static`. The `public` modifier means that the method can be accessed from anywhere, so it can be called from outside your class. The `static` modifier indicates that the method does not operate on a specific instance of your class and therefore is called without first instantiating the class. This is important because you are creating an executable rather than a class library. You set the return type to `void`, and in the example, you don't include any parameters.

Finally, we come to the code statements themselves:

```
Console.WriteLine("Hello from Wrox.");
Console.ReadLine();
return;
```

In this case, you simply call the `WriteLine()` method of the `System.Console` class to write a line of text to the console window. `WriteLine()` is a `static` method, so you don't need to instantiate a `Console` object before calling it.

`Console.ReadLine()` reads user input. Adding this line forces the application to wait for the carriage return key to be pressed before the application exits, and, in the case of Visual Studio 2010, the console window disappears.

You then call `return` to exit from the method (also, because this is the `Main()` method, you exit the program as well). You specified `void` in your method header, so you don't return any values.

Now that you have had a taste of basic C# syntax, you are ready for more detail. Because it is virtually impossible to write any nontrivial program without *variables*, we will start by looking at variables in C#.

VARIABLES

You declare variables in C# using the following syntax:

```
datatype identifier;
```

For example:

```
int i;
```

This statement declares an `int` named `i`. The compiler won't actually let you use this variable in an expression until you have initialized it with a value.

After it has been declared, you can assign a value to the variable using the assignment operator, `=`:

```
i = 10;
```

You can also declare the variable and initialize its value at the same time:

```
int i = 10;
```

If you declare and initialize more than one variable in a single statement, all of the variables will be of the same data type:

```
int x = 10, y =20;    // x and y are both ints
```

To declare variables of different types, you need to use separate statements. You cannot assign different data types within a multiple variable declaration:

```
int x = 10;
bool y = true;              // Creates a variable that stores true or false
int x = 10, bool y = true;   // This won't compile!
```

Notice the `//` and the text after it in the preceding examples. These are comments. The `//` character sequence tells the compiler to ignore the text that follows on this line because it is for a human to better understand the program and not part of the program itself. We further explain comments in code later in this chapter.

Initialization of Variables

Variable initialization demonstrates an example of C#'s emphasis on safety. Briefly, the C# compiler requires that any variable be initialized with some starting value before you refer to that variable in an operation. Most modern compilers will flag violations of this as a warning, but the ever-vigilant C# compiler treats such violations as errors. This prevents you from unintentionally retrieving junk values from memory that is left over from other programs.

C# has two methods for ensuring that variables are initialized before use:

➤ Variables that are fields in a class or struct, if not initialized explicitly, are by default zeroed out when they are created (classes and structs are discussed later).

➤ Variables that are local to a method must be explicitly initialized in your code prior to any statements in which their values are used. In this case, the initialization doesn't have to happen when the variable is declared, but the compiler will check all possible paths through the method and will flag an error if it detects any possibility of the value of a local variable being used before it is initialized.

For example, you can't do the following in C#:

```
public static int Main()
{
   int d;
   Console.WriteLine(d);   // Can't do this! Need to initialize d before use
   return 0;
}
```

Notice that this code snippet demonstrates defining `Main()` so that it returns an `int` instead of `void`.

When you attempt to compile these lines, you will receive this error message:

```
Use of unassigned local variable 'd'
```

Consider the following statement:

```
Something objSomething;
```

In C#, this line of code would create only a *reference* for a `Something` object, but this reference would not yet actually refer to any object. Any attempt to call a method or property against this variable would result in an error.

Instantiating a reference object in C# requires use of the `new` keyword. You create a reference as shown in the previous example and then point the reference at an object allocated on the heap using the `new` keyword:

```
objSomething = new Something();   // This creates a Something on the heap
```

Type Inference

Type inference makes use of the `var` keyword. The syntax for declaring the variable changes somewhat. The compiler "infers" what type the variable is by what the variable is initialized to. For example,

```
int someNumber = 0;
```

becomes

```
var someNumber = 0;
```

Even though `someNumber` is never declared as being an `int`, the compiler figures this out and `someNumber` is an `int` for as long as it is in scope. Once compiled, the two preceding statements are equal.

Here is a short program to demonstrate:

```csharp
using System;

namespace Wrox
{
  class Program
  {
    static void Main(string[] args)
    {
      var name = "Bugs Bunny";
      var age = 25;
      var isRabbit = true;

      Type nameType = name.GetType();
      Type ageType = age.GetType();
      Type isRabbitType = isRabbit.GetType();

      Console.WriteLine("name is type " + nameType.ToString());
      Console.WriteLine("age is type " + ageType.ToString());
      Console.WriteLine("isRabbit is type " + isRabbitType.ToString());
    }
  }
}
```

code snippet Var.cs

The output from this program is:

```
name is type System.String
age is type System.Int32
isRabbit is type System.Bool
```

There are a few rules that you need to follow:

➤   The variable must be initialized. Otherwise, the compiler doesn't have anything to infer the type from.

➤   The initializer cannot be null.

➤   The initializer must be an expression.

➤   You can't set the initializer to an object unless you create a new object in the initializer.

We examine this more closely in the discussion of anonymous types in Chapter 3, "Objects and Types."

After the variable has been declared and the type inferred, the variable's type cannot be changed. When established, the variable's type follows all the strong typing rules that any other variable type must follow.

Variable Scope

The *scope* of a variable is the region of code from which the variable can be accessed. In general, the scope is determined by the following rules:

➤   A *field* (also known as a member variable) of a class is in scope for as long as its containing class is in scope.

➤   A *local variable* is in scope until a closing brace indicates the end of the block statement or method in which it was declared.

➤   A local variable that is declared in a `for`, `while`, or similar statement is in scope in the body of that loop.

Scope Clashes for Local Variables

It's common in a large program to use the same variable name for different variables in different parts of the program. This is fine as long as the variables are scoped to completely different parts of the program so that there is no possibility for ambiguity. However, bear in mind that local variables with the same name can't be declared twice in the same scope. For example, you can't do this:

```
int x = 20;
// some more code
int x = 30;
```

Consider the following code sample:

```
using System;

namespace Wrox.ProCSharp.Basics
{
    public class ScopeTest
    {
        public static int Main()
        {
            for (int i = 0; i < 10; i++)
            {
                Console.WriteLine(i);
            }   // i goes out of scope here

            // We can declare a variable named i again, because
            // there's no other variable with that name in scope

            for (int i = 9; i >= 0; i--)
            {
                Console.WriteLine(i);
            }   // i goes out of scope here.
            return 0;
        }
    }
}
```

code snippet Scope.cs

This code simply prints out the numbers from 0 to 9, and then back again from 9 to 0, using two `for` loops. The important thing to note is that you declare the variable `i` twice in this code, within the same method. You can do this because `i` is declared in two separate loops, so each `i` variable is local to its own loop.

Here's another example:

```csharp
public static int Main()
{
    int j = 20;
    for (int i = 0; i < 10; i++)
    {
        int j = 30;    // Can't do this—j is still in scope
        Console.WriteLine(j + i);
    }
    return 0;
}
```

code snippet ScopeBad.cs

If you try to compile this, you'll get an error like the following:

```
ScopeTest.cs(12,15): error CS0136: A local variable named 'j' cannot be declared in
this scope because it would give a different meaning to 'j', which is already used
in a 'parent or current' scope to denote something else.
```

This occurs because the variable j, which is defined before the start of the for loop, is still in scope within the for loop, and won't go out of scope until the Main() method has finished executing. Although the second j (the illegal one) is in the loop's scope, that scope is nested within the Main() method's scope. The compiler has no way to distinguish between these two variables, so it won't allow the second one to be declared.

Scope Clashes for Fields and Local Variables

In certain circumstances, however, you can distinguish between two identifiers with the same name (although not the same fully qualified name) and the same scope, and in this case the compiler allows you to declare the second variable. The reason is that C# makes a fundamental distinction between variables that are declared at the type level (fields) and variables that are declared within methods (local variables).

Consider the following code snippet:

```csharp
using System;

namespace Wrox
{
    class ScopeTest2
    {
        static int j = 20;
        public static void Main()
        {
            int j = 30;
            Console.WriteLine(j);
            return;
        }
    }
}
```

code snippet ScopeTest2.cs

This code will compile, even though you have two variables named j in scope within the Main() method: the j that was defined at the class level, and doesn't go out of scope until the class is destroyed (when the Main() method terminates, and the program ends); and the j defined in Main(). In this case, the new variable named j that you declare in the Main() method *hides* the class-level variable with the same name, so when you run this code, the number 30 will be displayed.

However, what if you want to refer to the class-level variable? You can actually refer to fields of a class or struct from outside the object, using the syntax object.fieldname. In the previous example, you are accessing a static field (you look at what this means in the next section) from a static method, so you can't use an instance of the class; you just use the name of the class itself:

```
    ...
    public static void Main()
    {
        int j = 30;
        Console.WriteLine(j);
        Console.WriteLine(ScopeTest2.j);
    }
    ...
```

If you were accessing an instance field (a field that belongs to a specific instance of the class), you would need to use the `this` keyword instead.

Constants

As the name implies, a constant is a variable whose value cannot be changed throughout its lifetime. Prefixing a variable with the `const` keyword when it is declared and initialized designates that variable as a constant:

```
const int a = 100;    // This value cannot be changed.
```

Constants have the following characteristics:

➤ They must be initialized when they are declared, and after a value has been assigned, it can never be overwritten.

➤ The value of a constant must be computable at compile time. Therefore, you can't initialize a constant with a value taken from a variable. If you need to do this, you will need to use a read-only field (this is explained in Chapter 3).

➤ Constants are always implicitly static. However, notice that you don't have to (and, in fact, are not permitted to) include the `static` modifier in the constant declaration.

At least three advantages exist for using constants in your programs:

➤ Constants make your programs easier to read by replacing magic numbers and strings with readable names whose values are easy to understand.

➤ Constants make your programs easier to modify. For example, assume that you have a `SalesTax` constant in one of your C# programs, and that constant is assigned a value of 6 percent. If the sales tax rate changes at a later point in time, you can modify the behavior of all tax calculations simply by assigning a new value to the constant; you don't have to hunt through your code for the value `.06` and change each one, hoping that you will find all of them.

➤ Constants help prevent mistakes in your programs. If you attempt to assign another value to a constant somewhere in your program other than at the point where the constant is declared, the compiler will flag the error.

PREDEFINED DATA TYPES

Now that you have seen how to declare variables and constants, let's take a closer look at the data types available in C#. As you will see, C# is much stricter about the types available and their definitions than some other languages are.

Value Types and Reference Types

Before examining the data types in C#, it is important to understand that C# distinguishes between two categories of data type:

➤ Value types

➤ Reference types

The next few sections look in detail at the syntax for value and reference types. Conceptually, the difference is that a *value type* stores its value directly, whereas a *reference type* stores a reference to the value.

These types are stored in different places in memory; value types are stored in an area known as the *stack,* and reference types are stored in an area known as the *managed heap.* It is important to be aware of whether a type is a value type or a reference type because of the different effect each assignment has. For example, int is a value type, which means that the following statement will result in two locations in memory storing the value 20:

```
// i and j are both of type int
i = 20;
j = i;
```

However, consider the following code. For this code, assume that you have defined a class called Vector. Assume that Vector is a reference type and has an int member variable called Value:

```
Vector x, y;
x = new Vector();
x.Value = 30;    // Value is a field defined in Vector class
y = x;
Console.WriteLine(y.Value);
y.Value = 50;
Console.WriteLine(x.Value);
```

The crucial point to understand is that after executing this code, there is only one Vector object around. x and y both point to the memory location that contains this object. Because x and y are variables of a reference type, declaring each variable simply reserves a reference — it doesn't instantiate an object of the given type. In neither case is an object actually created. To create an object, you have to use the new keyword, as shown. Because x and y refer to the same object, changes made to x will affect y and vice versa. Hence the code will display 30 and then 50.

> *C++ developers should note that this syntax is like a reference, not a pointer. You use the . notation, not ->, to access object members. Syntactically, C# references look more like C++ reference variables. However, behind the superficial syntax, the real similarity is with C++ pointers.*

If a variable is a reference, it is possible to indicate that it does not refer to any object by setting its value to null:

```
y = null;
```

If a reference is set to null, then clearly it is not possible to call any nonstatic member functions or fields against it; doing so would cause an exception to be thrown at runtime.

In C#, basic data types such as bool and long are value types. This means that if you declare a bool variable and assign it the value of another bool variable, you will have two separate bool values in memory. Later, if you change the value of the original bool variable, the value of the second bool variable does not change. These types are copied by value.

In contrast, most of the more complex C# data types, including classes that you yourself declare, are reference types. They are allocated upon the heap, have lifetimes that can span multiple function calls, and can be accessed through one or several aliases. The Common Language Runtime (CLR) implements an elaborate algorithm to track which reference variables are still reachable and which have been orphaned. Periodically, the CLR will destroy orphaned objects and return the memory that they once occupied back to the operating system. This is done by the garbage collector.

C# has been designed this way because high performance is best served by keeping primitive types (such as `int` and `bool`) as value types and larger types that contain many fields (as is usually the case with classes) as reference types. If you want to define your own type as a value type, you should declare it as a struct.

CTS Types

As mentioned in Chapter 1, ".NET Architecture," the basic predefined types recognized by C# are not intrinsic to the language but are part of the .NET Framework. For example, when you declare an `int` in C#, what you are actually declaring is an instance of a .NET struct, `System.Int32`. This may sound like a small point, but it has a profound significance: it means that you are able to treat all the primitive data types syntactically as if they were classes that supported certain methods. For example, to convert an `int i` to a `string`, you can write:

```
string s = i.ToString();
```

It should be emphasized that, behind this syntactical convenience, the types really are stored as primitive types, so there is absolutely no performance cost associated with the idea that the primitive types are notionally represented by .NET structs.

The following sections review the types that are recognized as built-in types in C#. Each type is listed, along with its definition and the name of the corresponding .NET type (CTS type). C# has 15 predefined types, 13 value types, and 2 (`string` and `object`) reference types.

Predefined Value Types

The built-in CTS value types represent primitives, such as integer and floating-point numbers, character, and Boolean types.

Integer Types

C# supports eight predefined integer types, shown in the following table.

NAME	CTS TYPE	DESCRIPTION	RANGE (MIN:MAX)
sbyte	System.SByte	8-bit signed integer	-128:127 (-2^7:2^7-1)
short	System.Int16	16-bit signed integer	-32,768:32,767 (-2^{15}:$2^{15}-1$)
int	System.Int32	32-bit signed integer	-2,147,483,648:2,147,483,647 (-2^{31}:$2^{31}-1$)
long	System.Int64	64-bit signed integer	-9,223,372,036,854,775,808: 9,223,372,036,854,775,807 (-2^{63}:$2^{63}-1$)
byte	System.Byte	8-bit unsigned integer	0:255 (0:2^8-1)
ushort	System.UInt16	16-bit unsigned integer	0:65,535 (0:$2^{16}-1$)
uint	System.UInt32	32-bit unsigned integer	0:4,294,967,295 (0:$2^{32}-1$)
ulong	System.UInt64	64-bit unsigned integer	0:18,446,744,073,709,551,615 (0:$2^{64}-1$)

Some C# types have the same names as C++ and Java types but have different definitions. For example, in C#, an `int` is always a 32-bit signed integer. In C++ an `int` is a signed integer, but the number of bits is platform-dependent (32 bits on Windows). In C#, all data types have been defined in a platform-independent manner to allow for the possible future porting of C# and .NET to other platforms.

A `byte` is the standard 8-bit type for values in the range 0 to 255 inclusive. Be aware that, in keeping with its emphasis on type safety, C# regards the `byte` type and the `char` type as completely distinct, and any programmatic conversions between the two must be explicitly requested. Also be aware that unlike the other types in the integer family, a `byte` type is by default unsigned. Its signed version bears the special name `sbyte`.

With .NET, a `short` is no longer quite so short; it is now 16 bits long. The `int` type is 32 bits long. The `long` type reserves 64 bits for values. All integer-type variables can be assigned values in decimal or in hex notation. The latter requires the `0x` prefix:

```
long x = 0x12ab;
```

If there is any ambiguity about whether an integer is `int`, `uint`, `long`, or `ulong`, it will default to an `int`. To specify which of the other integer types the value should take, you can append one of the following characters to the number:

```
uint ui = 1234U;
long l = 1234L;
ulong ul = 1234UL;
```

You can also use lowercase `u` and `l`, although the latter could be confused with the integer `1` (one).

Floating-Point Types

Although C# provides a plethora of integer data types, it supports floating-point types as well.

NAME	CTS TYPE	DESCRIPTION	SIGNIFICANT FIGURES	RANGE (APPROXIMATE)
float	System.Single	32-bit single-precision floating point	7	$\pm1.5 \times 10^{245}$ to $\pm3.4 \times 10^{38}$
double	System.Double	64-bit double-precision floating point	15/16	$\pm5.0 \times 10^{2324}$ to $\pm1.7 \times 10^{308}$

The `float` data type is for smaller floating-point values, for which less precision is required. The `double` data type is bulkier than the `float` data type but offers twice the precision (15 digits).

If you hard-code a non-integer number (such as 12.3) in your code, the compiler will normally assume that you want the number interpreted as a `double`. If you want to specify that the value is a `float`, you append the character F (or f) to it:

```
float f = 12.3F;
```

The Decimal Type

The `decimal` type represents higher-precision floating-point numbers, as shown in the following table.

NAME	CTS TYPE	DESCRIPTION	SIGNIFICANT FIGURES	RANGE (APPROXIMATE)
decimal	System.Decimal	128-bit high-precision decimal notation	28	$\pm1.0 \times 10^{228}$ to $\pm7.9 \times 10^{28}$

One of the great things about the CTS and C# is the provision of a dedicated `decimal` type for financial calculations. How you use the 28 digits that the decimal type provides is up to you. In other words, you can track smaller dollar amounts with greater accuracy for cents or larger dollar amounts with more rounding in the fractional area. Bear in mind, however, that `decimal` is not implemented under the hood as a primitive type, so using `decimal` will have a performance effect on your calculations.

To specify that your number is a `decimal` type rather than a `double`, `float`, or an integer, you can append the M (or m) character to the value, as shown in the following example:

```
decimal d = 12.30M;
```

The Boolean Type

The C# `bool` type is used to contain Boolean values of either `true` or `false`.

NAME	CTS TYPE	DESCRIPTION	SIGNIFICANT FIGURES	RANGE (APPROXIMATE)
bool	System.Boolean	Represents true or false	NA	true false

You cannot implicitly convert `bool` values to and from integer values. If a variable (or a function return type) is declared as a `bool`, you can only use values of `true` and `false`. You will get an error if you try to use zero for `false` and a non-zero value for `true`.

The Character Type

For storing the value of a single character, C# supports the `char` data type.

NAME	CTS TYPE	VALUES
char	System.Char	Represents a single 16-bit (Unicode) character

Literals of type `char` are signified by being enclosed in single quotation marks, for example `'A'`. If you try to enclose a character in double quotation marks, the compiler will treat this as a string and throw an error.

As well as representing `chars` as character literals, you can represent them with four-digit hex Unicode values (for example `'\u0041'`), as integer values with a cast (for example, `(char)65`), or as hexadecimal values (`'\x0041'`). You can also represent them with an escape sequence, as shown in the following table.

ESCAPE SEQUENCE	CHARACTER
\'	Single quotation mark
\"	Double quotation mark
\\	Backslash
\0	Null
\a	Alert
\b	Backspace
\f	Form feed
\n	Newline
\r	Carriage return
\t	Tab character
\v	Vertical tab

Predefined Reference Types

C# supports two predefined reference types, `object` and `string`, described in the following table.

NAME	CTS TYPE	DESCRIPTION
object	System.Object	The root type. All other types in the CTS are derived (including value types) from object.
string	System.String	Unicode character string

The object Type

Many programming languages and class hierarchies provide a root type, from which all other objects in the hierarchy are derived. C# and .NET are no exception. In C#, the object type is the ultimate parent type from which all other intrinsic and user-defined types are derived. This means that you can use the object type for two purposes:

➤ You can use an object reference to bind to an object of any particular subtype. For example, in Chapter 7, "Operators and Casts," you will see how you can use the object type to box a value object on the stack to move it to the heap. object references are also useful in reflection, when code must manipulate objects whose specific types are unknown.

➤ The object type implements a number of basic, general-purpose methods, which include Equals(), GetHashCode(), GetType(), and ToString(). Responsible user-defined classes may need to provide replacement implementations of some of these methods using an object-oriented technique known as *overriding,* which is discussed in Chapter 4, "Inheritance." When you override ToString(), for example, you equip your class with a method for intelligently providing a string representation of itself. If you don't provide your own implementations for these methods in your classes, the compiler will pick up the implementations in object, which may or may not be correct or sensible in the context of your classes.

We examine the object type in more detail in subsequent chapters.

The string Type

C# recognizes the string keyword, which under the hood is translated to the .NET class, System.String. With it, operations like string concatenation and string copying are a snap:

```
string str1 = "Hello ";
string str2 = "World";
string str3 = str1 + str2; // string concatenation
```

Despite this style of assignment, string is a reference type. Behind the scenes, a string object is allocated on the heap, not the stack, and when you assign one string variable to another string, you get two references to the same string in memory. However, with string there are some differences from the usual behavior for reference types. For example, strings are immutable. Should you make changes to one of these strings, this will create an entirely new string object, leaving the other string unchanged. Consider the following code:

```
using System;

class StringExample
{
    public static int Main()
    {
        string s1 = "a string";
        string s2 = s1;
        Console.WriteLine("s1 is " + s1);
        Console.WriteLine("s2 is " + s2);
        s1 = "another string";
        Console.WriteLine("s1 is now " + s1);
        Console.WriteLine("s2 is now " + s2);
        return 0;
    }
}
```

code snippet StringExample.cs

The output from this is:

```
s1 is a string
s2 is a string
s1 is now another string
s2 is now a string
```

Changing the value of s1 has no effect on s2, contrary to what you'd expect with a reference type! What's happening here is that when s1 is initialized with the value a string, a new string object is allocated on the heap. When s2 is initialized, the reference points to this same object, so s2 also has the value a string. However, when you now change the value of s1, instead of replacing the original value, a new object will be allocated on the heap for the new value. The s2 variable will still point to the original object, so its value is unchanged. Under the hood, this happens as a result of operator overloading, a topic that is explored in Chapter 7. In general, the string class has been implemented so that its semantics follow what you would normally intuitively expect for a string.

String literals are enclosed in double quotation marks ("."); if you attempt to enclose a string in single quotation marks, the compiler will take the value as a char, and throw an error. C# strings can contain the same Unicode and hexadecimal escape sequences as chars. Because these escape sequences start with a backslash, you can't use this character unescaped in a string. Instead, you need to escape it with two backslashes (\\):

```
string filepath = "C:\\ProCSharp\\First.cs";
```

Even if you are confident that you can remember to do this all the time, typing all those double backslashes can prove annoying. Fortunately, C# gives you an alternative. You can prefix a string literal with the at character (@) and all the characters in it will be treated at face value; they won't be interpreted as escape sequences:

```
string filepath = @"C:\ProCSharp\First.cs";
```

This even allows you to include line breaks in your string literals:

```
string jabberwocky = @"'Twas brillig and the slithy toves
Did gyre and gimble in the wabe.";
```

Then the value of jabberwocky would be this:

```
'Twas brillig and the slithy toves
Did gyre and gimble in the wabe.
```

FLOW CONTROL

This section looks at the real nuts and bolts of the language: the statements that allow you to control the *flow* of your program rather than executing every line of code in the order it appears in the program.

Conditional Statements

Conditional statements allow you to branch your code depending on whether certain conditions are met or on the value of an expression. C# has two constructs for branching code — the if statement, which allows you to test whether a specific condition is met, and the switch statement, which allows you to compare an expression with a number of different values.

The if Statement

For conditional branching, C# inherits the C and C++ if.else construct. The syntax should be fairly intuitive for anyone who has done any programming with a procedural language:

```
if (condition)
    statement(s)
else
    statement(s)
```

If more than one statement is to be executed as part of either condition, these statements need to be joined together into a block using curly braces ({ . }). (This also applies to other C# constructs where statements can be joined into a block, such as the `for` and `while` loops):

```
bool isZero;
if (i == 0)
{
    isZero = true;
    Console.WriteLine("i is Zero");
}
else
{
    isZero = false;
    Console.WriteLine("i is Non-zero");
}
```

If you want to, you can use an `if` statement without a final `else` statement. You can also combine `else if` clauses to test for multiple conditions:

```
using System;

namespace Wrox
{
    class MainEntryPoint
    {
        static void Main(string[] args)
        {
            Console.WriteLine("Type in a string");
            string input;
            input = Console.ReadLine();
            if (input == "")
            {
                Console.WriteLine("You typed in an empty string.");
            }
            else if (input.Length < 5)
            {
                Console.WriteLine("The string had less than 5 characters.");
            }
            else if (input.Length < 10)
            {
                Console.WriteLine("The string had at least 5 but less than 10
                    Characters.");
            }
            Console.WriteLine("The string was " + input);
        }
    }
```

code snippet ElseIf.cs

There is no limit to how many `else if`s you can add to an `if` clause.

You'll notice that the previous example declares a string variable called `input`, gets the user to enter text at the command line, feeds this into `input`, and then tests the length of this string variable. The code also shows how easy string manipulation can be in C#. To find the length of `input`, for example, use `input.Length`.

One point to note about `if` is that you don't need to use the braces if there's only one statement in the conditional branch:

```
if (i == 0) Let's add some brackets here.
    Console.WriteLine("i is Zero");         // This will only execute if i == 0
Console.WriteLine("i can be anything");     // Will execute whatever the
                                            // value of i
```

However, for consistency, many programmers prefer to use curly braces whenever they use an `if` statement.

The `if` statements presented also illustrate some of the C# operators that compare values. Note in particular that C# uses == to compare variables for equality. Do not use = for this purpose. A single = is used to assign values.

In C#, the expression in the `if` clause must evaluate to a Boolean. It is not possible to test an integer (returned from a function, say) directly. You have to convert the integer that is returned to a Boolean `true` or `false`, for example, by comparing the value with zero or with `null`:

```
if (DoSomething() != 0)
{
    // Non-zero value returned
}
else
{
    // Returned zero
}
```

The switch Statement

The `switch.case` statement is good for selecting one branch of execution from a set of mutually exclusive ones. It takes the form of a `switch` argument followed by a series of `case` clauses. When the expression in the `switch` argument evaluates to one of the values beside a `case` clause, the code immediately following the `case` clause executes. This is one example where you don't need to use curly braces to join statements into blocks; instead, you mark the end of the code for each case using the `break` statement. You can also include a `default` case in the `switch` statement, which will execute if the expression evaluates to none of the other cases. The following `switch` statement tests the value of the `integerA` variable:

```
switch (integerA)
{
    case 1:
        Console.WriteLine("integerA =1");
        break;
    case 2:
        Console.WriteLine("integerA =2");
        break;
    case 3:
        Console.WriteLine("integerA =3");
        break;
    default:
        Console.WriteLine("integerA is not 1,2, or 3");
        break;
}
```

Note that the case values must be constant expressions; variables are not permitted.

Though the `switch.case` statement should be familiar to C and C++ programmers, C#'s `switch.case` is a bit safer than its C++ equivalent. Specifically, it prohibits fall-through conditions in almost all cases. This means that if a `case` clause is fired early on in the block, later clauses cannot be fired unless you use a `goto` statement to mark that you want them fired, too. The compiler enforces this restriction by flagging every `case` clause that is not equipped with a `break` statement as an error similar to this:

```
Control cannot fall through from one case label ('case 2:') to another
```

Although it is true that fall-through behavior is desirable in a limited number of situations, in the vast majority of cases, it is unintended and results in a logical error that's hard to spot. Isn't it better to code for the norm rather than for the exception?

By getting creative with `goto` statements, however, you can duplicate fall-through functionality in your `switch.cases`. But, if you find yourself really wanting to, you probably should reconsider your approach.

The following code illustrates both how to use `goto` to simulate fall-through, and how messy the resultant code can get:

```
// assume country and language are of type string
switch(country)
{
    case "America":
        CallAmericanOnlyMethod();
        goto case "Britain";
    case "France":
        language = "French";
        break;
    case "Britain":
        language = "English";
        break;
}
```

There is one exception to the no-fall-through rule, however, in that you can fall through from one case to the next if that case is empty. This allows you to treat two or more cases in an identical way (without the need for `goto` statements):

```
switch(country)
{
    case "au":
    case "uk":
    case "us":
        language = "English";
        break;
    case "at":
    case "de":
        language = "German";
        break;
}
```

One intriguing point about the `switch` statement in C# is that the order of the cases doesn't matter — you can even put the `default` case first! As a result, no two cases can be the same. This includes different constants that have the same value, so you can't, for example, do this:

```
// assume country is of type string
const string england = "uk";
const string britain = "uk";
switch(country)
{
    case england:
    case britain:      // This will cause a compilation error.
        language = "English";
        break;
}
```

The previous code also shows another way in which the `switch` statement is different in C# compared to C++: In C#, you are allowed to use a string as the variable being tested.

Loops

C# provides four different loops (`for`, `while`, `do . . . while`, and `foreach`) that allow you to execute a block of code repeatedly until a certain condition is met.

The for Loop

C# `for` loops provide a mechanism for iterating through a loop where you test whether a particular condition holds before you perform another iteration. The syntax is:

```
for (initializer; condition; iterator)
    statement(s)
```

where:

> ➤ The initializer is the expression evaluated before the first loop is executed (usually initializing a local variable as a loop counter).

> ➤ The condition is the expression checked before each new iteration of the loop (this must evaluate to `true` for another iteration to be performed).

> ➤ The iterator is an expression evaluated after each iteration (usually incrementing the loop counter).

The iterations end when the condition evaluates to `false`.

The `for` loop is a so-called pretest loop because the loop condition is evaluated before the loop statements are executed, and so the contents of the loop won't be executed at all if the loop condition is `false`.

The `for` loop is excellent for repeating a statement or a block of statements for a predetermined number of times. The following example is typical of the use of a `for` loop. The following code will write out all the integers from 0 to 99:

```
for (int i = 0; i < 100; i=i+1)    // This is equivalent to
                                   // For i = 0 To 99 in VB.
{
    Console.WriteLine(i);
}
```

Here, you declare an `int` called `i` and initialize it to zero. This will be used as the loop counter. You then immediately test whether it is less than 100. Because this condition evaluates to `true`, you execute the code in the loop, displaying the value 0. You then increment the counter by one, and walk through the process again. Looping ends when `i` reaches 100.

Actually, the way the preceding loop is written isn't quite how you would normally write it. C# has a shorthand for adding 1 to a variable, so instead of `i = i + 1`, you can simply write i++:

```
for (int i = 0; i < 100; i++)
{
    // etc.
    }
```

You can also make use of type inference for the iteration variable `i` in the preceding example. Using type inference the loop construct would be:

```
for (var i = 0; i < 100; i++)
...
```

It's not unusual to nest `for` loops so that an inner loop executes once completely for each iteration of an outer loop. This scheme is typically employed to loop through every element in a rectangular multidimensional array. The outermost loop loops through every row, and the inner loop loops through every column in a particular row. The following code displays rows of numbers. It also uses another `Console` method, `Console.Write()`, which does the same as `Console.WriteLine()` but doesn't send a carriage return to the output.

```
using System;

namespace Wrox
{
    class MainEntryPoint
    {
        static void Main(string[] args)
        {
            // This loop iterates through rows
            for (int i = 0; i < 100; i+=10)
            {
                // This loop iterates through columns
                for (int j = i; j < i + 10; j++)
```

```
        {
            Console.Write(" " + j);
        }
        Console.WriteLine();
    }
  }
 }
}
```

code snippet NestedFor.cs

Although j is an integer, it will be automatically converted to a string so that the concatenation can take place.

The preceding sample results in this output:

```
0   1   2   3   4   5   6   7   8   9
10  11  12  13  14  15  16  17  18  19
20  21  22  23  24  25  26  27  28  29
30  31  32  33  34  35  36  37  38  39
40  41  42  43  44  45  46  47  48  49
50  51  52  53  54  55  56  57  58  59
60  61  62  63  64  65  66  67  68  69
70  71  72  73  74  75  76  77  78  79
80  81  82  83  84  85  86  87  88  89
90  91  92  93  94  95  96  97  98  99
```

Although it is technically possible to evaluate something other than a counter variable in a for loop's test condition, it is certainly not typical. It is also possible to omit one (or even all) of the expressions in the for loop. In such situations, however, you should consider using the while loop.

The while Loop

Like the for loop, while is a pretest loop. The syntax is similar, but while loops take only one expression:

```
while(condition)
    statement(s);
```

Unlike the for loop, the while loop is most often used to repeat a statement or a block of statements for a number of times that is not known before the loop begins. Usually, a statement inside the while loop's body will set a Boolean flag to false on a certain iteration, triggering the end of the loop, as in the following example:

```
bool condition = false;
while (!condition)
{
    // This loop spins until the condition is true.
    DoSomeWork();
    condition = CheckCondition();   // assume CheckCondition() returns a bool
}
```

The do . . . while Loop

The do...while loop is the post-test version of the while loop. This means that the loop's test condition is evaluated after the body of the loop has been executed. Consequently, do...while loops are useful for situations in which a block of statements must be executed at least one time, as in this example:

```
bool condition;
do
{
    // This loop will at least execute once, even if Condition is false.
    MustBeCalledAtLeastOnce();
    condition = CheckCondition();
} while (condition);
```

The foreach Loop

The `foreach` loop allows you to iterate through each item in a collection. For now, we won't worry about exactly what a collection is (it is explained fully in Chapter 10, "Collections"); we will just say that it is an object that represents a list of objects. Technically, to count as a collection, it must support an interface called `IEnumerable`. Examples of collections include C# arrays, the collection classes in the `System .Collection` namespaces, and user-defined collection classes. You can get an idea of the syntax of `foreach` from the following code, if you assume that `arrayOfInts` is (unsurprisingly) an array of `int`s:

```
foreach (int temp in arrayOfInts)
{
    Console.WriteLine(temp);
}
```

Here, `foreach` steps through the array one element at a time. With each element, it places the value of the element in the `int` variable called `temp` and then performs an iteration of the loop.

Here is another situation where type inference can be used. The `foreach` loop would become:

```
foreach (var temp in arrayOfInts)
...
```

`temp` would be inferred to `int` because that is what the collection item type is.

An important point to note with `foreach` is that you can't change the value of the item in the collection (`temp` in the preceding code), so code such as the following will not compile:

```
foreach (int temp in arrayOfInts)
{
    temp++;
    Console.WriteLine(temp);
}
```

If you need to iterate through the items in a collection and change their values, you will need to use a `for` loop instead.

Jump Statements

C# provides a number of statements that allow you to jump immediately to another line in the program. The first of these is, of course, the notorious `goto` statement.

The goto Statement

The `goto` statement allows you to jump directly to another specified line in the program, indicated by a *label* (this is just an identifier followed by a colon):

```
goto Label1;
    Console.WriteLine("This won't be executed");
Label1:
    Console.WriteLine("Continuing execution from here");
```

A couple of restrictions are involved with `goto`. You can't jump into a block of code such as a `for` loop, you can't jump out of a class, and you can't exit a `finally` block after `try.catch` blocks (Chapter 15, "Errors and Exceptions," looks at exception handling with `try.catch.finally`).

The reputation of the `goto` statement probably precedes it, and in most circumstances, its use is sternly frowned upon. In general, it certainly doesn't conform to good object-oriented programming practice.

The break Statement

You have already met the `break` statement briefly — when you used it to exit from a case in a `switch` statement. In fact, `break` can also be used to exit from `for`, `foreach`, `while`, or `do...while` loops. Control will switch to the statement immediately after the end of the loop.

If the statement occurs in a nested loop, control will switch to the end of the innermost loop. If the break occurs outside of a `switch` statement or a loop, a compile-time error will occur.

The continue Statement

The `continue` statement is similar to `break`, and must also be used within a `for`, `foreach`, `while`, or `do...while` loop. However, it exits only from the current iteration of the loop, meaning that execution will restart at the beginning of the next iteration of the loop, rather than outside the loop altogether.

The return Statement

The `return` statement is used to exit a method of a class, returning control to the caller of the method. If the method has a return type, `return` must return a value of this type; otherwise if the method returns `void`, you should use `return` without an expression.

ENUMERATIONS

An *enumeration* is a user-defined integer type. When you declare an enumeration, you specify a set of acceptable values that instances of that enumeration can contain. Not only that, but you can give the values user-friendly names. If, somewhere in your code, you attempt to assign a value that is not in the acceptable set of values to an instance of that enumeration, the compiler will flag an error.

Creating an enumeration can save you a lot of time and headaches in the long run. At least three benefits exist to using enumerations instead of plain integers:

➤ As mentioned, enumerations make your code easier to maintain by helping to ensure that your variables are assigned only legitimate, anticipated values.

➤ Enumerations make your code clearer by allowing you to refer to integer values by descriptive names rather than by obscure "magic" numbers.

➤ Enumerations make your code easier to type, too. When you go to assign a value to an instance of an enumerated type, the Visual Studio .NET IDE will, through IntelliSense, pop up a list box of acceptable values to save you some keystrokes and to remind you of what the possible options are.

You can define an enumeration as follows:

```
public enum TimeOfDay
{
   Morning = 0,
   Afternoon = 1,
   Evening = 2
}
```

In this case, you use an integer value to represent each period of the day in the enumeration. You can now access these values as members of the enumeration. For example, `TimeOfDay.Morning` will return the value 0. You will typically use this enumeration to pass an appropriate value into a method and iterate through the possible values in a `switch` statement:

```
class EnumExample
{
   public static int Main()
   {
      WriteGreeting(TimeOfDay.Morning);
      return 0;
   }

   static void WriteGreeting(TimeOfDay timeOfDay)
   {
      switch(timeOfDay)
```

```
        {
            case TimeOfDay.Morning:
                Console.WriteLine("Good morning!");
                break;
            case TimeOfDay.Afternoon:
                Console.WriteLine("Good afternoon!");
                break;
            case TimeOfDay.Evening:
                Console.WriteLine("Good evening!");
                break;
            default:
                Console.WriteLine("Hello!");
                break;
        }
    }
}
```

The real power of enums in C# is that behind the scenes they are instantiated as structs derived from the base class, System.Enum. This means it is possible to call methods against them to perform some useful tasks. Note that because of the way the .NET Framework is implemented there is no performance loss associated with treating the enums syntactically as structs. In practice, after your code is compiled, enums will exist as primitive types, just like int and float.

You can retrieve the string representation of an enum as in the following example, using the earlier TimeOfDay enum:

```
TimeOfDay time = TimeOfDay.Afternoon;
Console.WriteLine(time.ToString());
```

This will return the string Afternoon.

Alternatively, you can obtain an enum value from a string:

```
TimeOfDay time2 = (TimeOfDay) Enum.Parse(typeof(TimeOfDay), "afternoon", true);
Console.WriteLine((int)time2);
```

This code snippet illustrates both obtaining an enum value from a string and converting to an integer. To convert from a string, you need to use the static Enum.Parse() method, which, as shown, takes three parameters. The first is the type of enum you want to consider. The syntax is the keyword typeof followed by the name of the enum class in brackets. (Chapter 7 explores the typeof operator in more detail.) The second parameter is the string to be converted, and the third parameter is a bool indicating whether you should ignore case when doing the conversion. Finally, note that Enum.Parse() actually returns an object reference — you need to explicitly convert this to the required enum type (this is an example of an unboxing operation). For the preceding code, this returns the value 1 as an object, corresponding to the enum value of TimeOfDay.Afternoon. On converting explicitly to an int, this produces the value 1 again.

Other methods on System.Enum do things such as return the number of values in an enum definition or list the names of the values. Full details are in the MSDN documentation.

NAMESPACES

As you saw earlier in this chapter, namespaces provide a way of organizing related classes and other types. Unlike a file or a component, a namespace is a logical rather than physical grouping. When you define a class in a C# file, you can include it within a namespace definition. Later, when you define another class that performs related work in another file, you can include it within the same namespace, creating a logical grouping that gives an indication to other developers using the classes how they are related and used:

```
namespace CustomerPhoneBookApp
{
    using System;

    public struct Subscriber
```

```
    {
        // Code for struct here...
    }
}
```

Placing a type in a namespace effectively gives that type a long name, consisting of the type's namespace as a series of names separated with periods (.), terminating with the name of the class. In the preceding example, the full name of the Subscriber struct is CustomerPhoneBookApp.Subscriber. This allows distinct classes with the same short name to be used within the same program without ambiguity. This full name is often called the fully qualified name.

You can also nest namespaces within other namespaces, creating a hierarchical structure for your types:

```
namespace Wrox
{
    namespace ProCSharp
    {
        namespace Basics
        {
            class NamespaceExample
            {
                // Code for the class here...
            }
        }
    }
}
```

Each namespace name is composed of the names of the namespaces it resides within, separated with periods, starting with the outermost namespace and ending with its own short name. So the full name for the ProCSharp namespace is Wrox.ProCSharp, and the full name of NamespaceExample class is Wrox.ProCSharp.Basics.NamespaceExample.

You can use this syntax to organize the namespaces in your namespace definitions too, so the previous code could also be written as follows:

```
namespace Wrox.ProCSharp.Basics
{
    class NamespaceExample
    {
        // Code for the class here...
    }
}
```

Note that you are not permitted to declare a multipart namespace nested within another namespace.

Namespaces are not related to assemblies. It is perfectly acceptable to have different namespaces in the same assembly or to define types in the same namespace in different assemblies.

Defining the namespace hierarchy should be planned out prior to the start of a project. Generally the accepted format is CompanyName.ProjectName.SystemSection. So in the previous example, Wrox is the company name, ProCSharp is the project, and in the case of this chapter, Basics is the section.

The using Directive

Obviously, namespaces can grow rather long and tiresome to type, and the ability to indicate a particular class with such specificity may not always be necessary. Fortunately, as noted at the beginning of this chapter, C# allows you to abbreviate a class's full name. To do this, list the class's namespace at the top of the file, prefixed with the using keyword. Throughout the rest of the file, you can refer to the types in the namespace simply by their type names:

```
using System;
using Wrox.ProCSharp;
```

As remarked earlier, virtually all C# source code will have the statement using System; simply because so many useful classes supplied by Microsoft are contained in the System namespace.

If two namespaces referenced by using statements contain a type of the same name, you will need to use the full (or at least a longer) form of the name to ensure that the compiler knows which type is to be accessed. For example, say classes called NamespaceExample exist in both the Wrox.ProCSharp.Basics and Wrox .ProCSharp.OOP namespaces. If you then create a class called Test in the Wrox.ProCSharp namespace, and instantiate one of the NamespaceExample classes in this class, you need to specify which of these two classes you're talking about:

```
using Wrox.ProCSharp.OOP;
using Wrox.ProCSharp.Basics;
namespace Wrox.ProCSharp
{
  class Test
  {
    public static int Main()
    {
      Basics.NamespaceExample nSEx = new Basics.NamespaceExample();
     // do something with the nSEx variable.
      return 0;
    }
  }
}
```

 Because using *statements occur at the top of C# files, in the same place that C and C++ list* #include *statements, it's easy for programmers moving from C++ to C# to confuse namespaces with C++-style header files. Don't make this mistake. The* using *statement does no physical linking between files, and C# has no equivalent to C++ header files.*

Your organization will probably want to spend some time developing a namespace schema so that its developers can quickly locate functionality that they need and so that the names of the organization's homegrown classes won't conflict with those in off-the-shelf class libraries. Guidelines on establishing your own namespace scheme along with other naming recommendations are discussed later in this chapter.

Namespace Aliases

Another use of the using keyword is to assign aliases to classes and namespaces. If you have a very long namespace name that you want to refer to several times in your code but don't want to include in a simple using statement (for example, to avoid type name conflicts), you can assign an alias to the namespace. The syntax for this is as follows:

```
using alias = NamespaceName;
```

The following example (a modified version of the previous example) assigns the alias Introduction to the Wrox.ProCSharp.Basics namespace and uses this to instantiate a NamespaceExample object, which is defined in this namespace. Notice the use of the namespace alias qualifier (::). This forces the search to start with the Introduction namespace alias. If a class called Introduction had been introduced in the same scope, a conflict would happen. The :: operator allows the alias to be referenced even if the conflict exists. The NamespaceExample class has one method, GetNamespace(), which uses the GetType() method exposed by every class to access a Type object representing the class's type. You use this object to return a name of the class's namespace:

```
using System;
using Introduction =  Wrox.ProCSharp.Basics;
```

```
class Test
{
   public static int Main()
   {
      Introduction::NamespaceExample NSEx =
         new Introduction::NamespaceExample();
      Console.WriteLine(NSEx.GetNamespace());
      return 0;
   }
}

namespace Wrox.ProCSharp.Basics
{
   class NamespaceExample
   {
      public string GetNamespace()
      {
         return this.GetType().Namespace;
      }
   }
}
```

THE MAIN() METHOD

As you saw at the start of this chapter, C# programs start execution at a method named `Main()`. This must be a static method of a class (or struct), and must have a return type of either `int` or `void`.

Although it is common to specify the `public` modifier explicitly, because by definition the method must be called from outside the program, it doesn't actually matter what accessibility level you assign to the entry-point method — it will run even if you mark the method as `private`.

Multiple Main() Methods

When a C# console or Windows application is compiled, by default the compiler looks for exactly one `Main()` method in any class matching the signature that was just described and makes that class method the entry point for the program. If there is more than one `Main()` method, the compiler will return an error message. For example, consider the following code called `DoubleMain.cs`:

```
using System;

namespace Wrox
{
   class Client
   {
      public static int Main()
      {
         MathExample.Main();
         return 0;
      }
   }

   class MathExample
   {
      static int Add(int x, int y)
      {
         return x + y;
      }

      public static int Main()
```

```
        {
            int i = Add(5,10);
            Console.WriteLine(i);
            return 0;
        }
    }
}
```

code snippet DoubleMain.cs

This contains two classes, both of which have a `Main()` method. If you try to compile this code in the usual way, you will get the following errors:

```
csc DoubleMain.cs
Microsoft (R) Visual C# 2010 Compiler version 4.0.20506.1
Copyright (C) Microsoft Corporation. All rights reserved.

DoubleMain.cs(7,25): error CS0017: Program
        'DoubleMain.exe' has more than one entry point defined:
        'Wrox.Client.Main()'.  Compile with /main to specify the type that
        contains the entry point.
DoubleMain.cs(21,25): error CS0017: Program
        'DoubleMain.exe' has more than one entry point defined:
        'Wrox.MathExample.Main()'.  Compile with /main to specify the type that
        contains the entry point.
```

However, you can explicitly tell the compiler which of these methods to use as the entry point for the program by using the `/main` switch, together with the full name (including namespace) of the class to which the `Main()` method belongs:

```
csc DoubleMain.cs /main:Wrox.MathExample
```

Passing Arguments to Main()

The examples so far have shown only the `Main()` method without any parameters. However, when the program is invoked, you can get the CLR to pass any command-line arguments to the program by including a parameter. This parameter is a string array, traditionally called `args` (although C# will accept any name). The program can use this array to access any options passed through the command line when the program is started.

The following sample, `ArgsExample.cs`, loops through the string array passed in to the `Main()` method and writes the value of each option to the console window:

```
using System;

namespace Wrox
{
    class ArgsExample
    {
        public static int Main(string[] args)
        {
            for (int i = 0; i < args.Length; i++)
            {
                Console.WriteLine(args[i]);
            }
            return 0;
        }
    }
}
```

code snippet ArgsExample.cs

You can compile this as usual using the command line. When you run the compiled executable, you can pass in arguments after the name of the program, as shown in this example:

```
ArgsExample /a /b /c
/a
/b
/c
```

MORE ON COMPILING C# FILES

You have seen how to compile console applications using `csc.exe`, but what about other types of applications? What if you want to reference a class library? The full set of compilation options for the C# compiler is of course detailed in the MSDN documentation, but we list here the most important options.

To answer the first question, you can specify what type of file you want to create using the `/target` switch, often abbreviated as `/t`. This can be one of those shown in the following table.

OPTION	OUTPUT
`/t:exe`	A console application (the default)
`/t:library`	A class library with a manifest
`/t:module`	A component without a manifest
`/t:winexe`	A Windows application (without a console window)

If you want a nonexecutable file (such as a DLL) to be loadable by the .NET runtime, you must compile it as a library. If you compile a C# file as a module, no assembly will be created. Although modules cannot be loaded by the runtime, they can be compiled into another manifest using the `/addmodule` switch.

Another option we need to mention is `/out`. This allows you to specify the name of the output file produced by the compiler. If the `/out` option isn't specified, the compiler will base the name of the output file on the name of the input C# file, adding an extension according to the target type (for example, `exe` for a Windows or console application or `dll` for a class library). Note that the `/out` and `/t`, or `/target`, options must precede the name of the file you want to compile.

If you want to reference types in assemblies that aren't referenced by default, you can use the `/reference` or `/r` switch, together with the path and filename of the assembly. The following example demonstrates how you can compile a class library and then reference that library in another assembly. It consists of two files:

➤ The class library

➤ A console application, which will call a class in the library

The first file is called `MathLibrary.cs` and contains the code for your DLL. To keep things simple, it contains just one (public) class, `MathLib`, with a single method that adds two `int`s:

```
namespace Wrox
{
    public class MathLib
    {
        public int Add(int x, int y)
        {
            return x + y;
        }
    }
}
```

code snippet MathLibrary.cs

You can compile this C# file into a .NET DLL using the following command:

```
csc /t:library MathLibrary.cs
```

The console application, `MathClient.cs`, will simply instantiate this object and call its `Add()` method, displaying the result in the console window:

```csharp
using System;

namespace Wrox
{
    class Client
    {
        public static void Main()
        {
            MathLib mathObj = new MathLib();
            Console.WriteLine(mathObj.Add(7,8));
        }
    }
}
```

code snippet MathClient.cs

You can compile this code using the `/r` switch to point at or reference the newly compiled DLL:

```
csc MathClient.cs /r:MathLibrary.dll
```

You can then run it as normal just by entering `MathClient` at the command prompt. This displays the number `15` — the result of your addition.

CONSOLE I/O

By this point, you should have a basic familiarity with C#'s data types, as well as some knowledge of how the thread-of-control moves through a program that manipulates those data types. In this chapter, you have also used several of the `Console` class's static methods used for reading and writing data. Because these methods are so useful when writing basic C# programs, this section quickly reviews them in more detail.

To read a line of text from the console window, you use the `Console.ReadLine()` method. This will read an input stream (terminated when the user presses the `Return` key) from the console window and return the input string. There are also two corresponding methods for writing to the console, which you have already used extensively:

➤ `Console.Write()` — Writes the specified value to the console window.

➤ `Console.WriteLine()` — This does the same, but adds a newline character at the end of the output.

Various forms (overloads) of these methods exist for all the predefined types (including `object`), so in most cases you don't have to convert values to strings before you display them.

For example, the following code lets the user input a line of text and displays that text:

```csharp
string s = Console.ReadLine();
Console.WriteLine(s);
```

`Console.WriteLine()` also allows you to display formatted output in a way comparable to C's `printf()` function. To use `WriteLine()` in this way, you pass in a number of parameters. The first is a string containing markers in curly braces where the subsequent parameters will be inserted into the text. Each marker contains a zero-based index for the number of the parameter in the following list. For example, `{0}` represents the first parameter in the list. Consider the following code:

```csharp
int i = 10;
int j = 20;
Console.WriteLine("{0} plus {1} equals {2}", i, j, i + j);
```

This code displays:

```
10 plus 20 equals 30
```

You can also specify a width for the value, and justify the text within that width, using positive values for right-justification and negative values for left-justification. To do this, use the format {n,w}, where n is the parameter index and w is the width value:

```
int i = 940;
int j = 73;
Console.WriteLine(" {0,4}\n+{1,4}\n — \n {2,4}", i, j, i + j);
```

The result of this is:

```
 940
+  73
 ———
1013
```

Finally, you can also add a format string, together with an optional precision value. It is not possible to give a complete list of potential format strings because, as you will see in Chapter 9, "Strings and Regular Expressions," you can define your own format strings. However, the main ones in use for the predefined types are shown in the following table.

STRING	DESCRIPTION
C	Local currency format.
D	Decimal format. Converts an integer to base 10, and pads with leading zeros if a precision specifier is given.
E	Scientific (exponential) format. The precision specifier sets the number of decimal places (6 by default). The case of the format string (e or E) determines the case of the exponential symbol.
F	Fixed-point format; the precision specifier controls the number of decimal places. Zero is acceptable.
G	General format. Uses E or F formatting, depending on which is more compact.
N	Number format. Formats the number with commas as the thousands separators, for example 32,767.44.
P	Percent format.
X	Hexadecimal format. The precision specifier can be used to pad with leading zeros.

Note that the format strings are normally case insensitive, except for e/E.

If you want to use a format string, you should place it immediately after the marker that gives the parameter number and field width, and separate it with a colon. For example, to format a decimal value as currency for the computer's locale, with precision to two decimal places, you would use C2:

```
decimal i = 940.23m;
decimal j = 73.7m;
Console.WriteLine(" {0,9:C2}\n+{1,9:C2}\n — \n {2,9:C2}", i, j, i + j);
```

The output of this in U.S. currency is:

```
   $940.23
+   $73.70
 ————————
 $1,013.93
```

As a final trick, you can also use placeholder characters instead of these format strings to map out formatting. For example:

```
double d = 0.234;
Console.WriteLine("{0:#.00}", d);
```

This displays as `.23`, because the # symbol is ignored if there is no character in that place, and zeros will either be replaced by the character in that position if there is one or be printed as a zero.

USING COMMENTS

The next topic — adding comments to your code — looks very simple on the surface, but can be complex.

Internal Comments within the Source Files

As noted earlier in this chapter, C# uses the traditional C-type single-line (`//...`) and multiline (`/* ... */`) comments:

```
// This is a singleline comment
/* This comment
   spans multiple lines. */
```

Everything in a single-line comment, from the `//` to the end of the line, will be ignored by the compiler, and everything from an opening `/*` to the next `*/` in a multiline comment combination will be ignored. Obviously, you can't include the combination `*/` in any multiline comments, because this will be treated as the end of the comment.

It is actually possible to put multiline comments within a line of code:

```
Console.WriteLine(/* Here's a comment! */ "This will compile.");
```

Use inline comments with care because they can make code hard to read. However, they can be useful when debugging if, say, you temporarily want to try running the code with a different value somewhere:

```
DoSomething(Width, /*Height*/ 100);
```

Comment characters included in string literals are, of course, treated like normal characters:

```
string s = "/* This is just a normal string .*/";
```

XML Documentation

In addition to the C-type comments, illustrated in the preceding section, C# has a very neat feature that we want to highlight: the ability to produce documentation in XML format automatically from special comments. These comments are single-line comments but begin with three slashes (`///`) instead of the usual two. Within these comments, you can place XML tags containing documentation of the types and type members in your code.

The tags in the following table are recognized by the compiler.

TAG	DESCRIPTION
`<c>`	Marks up text within a line as code, for example `<c>int i = 10;</c>`.
`<code>`	Marks multiple lines as code.
`<example>`	Marks up a code example.
`<exception>`	Documents an exception class. (Syntax is verified by the compiler.)
`<include>`	Includes comments from another documentation file. (Syntax is verified by the compiler.)
`<list>`	Inserts a list into the documentation.
`<param>`	Marks up a method parameter. (Syntax is verified by the compiler.)
`<paramref>`	Indicates that a word is a method parameter. (Syntax is verified by the compiler.)
`<permission>`	Documents access to a member. (Syntax is verified by the compiler.)

continues

(continued)

TAG	DESCRIPTION
<remarks>	Adds a description for a member.
<returns>	Documents the return value for a method.
<see>	Provides a cross-reference to another parameter. (Syntax is verified by the compiler.)
<seealso>	Provides a "see also" section in a description. (Syntax is verified by the compiler.)
<summary>	Provides a short summary of a type or member.
<value>	Describes a property.

To see how this works, add some XML comments to the `MathLibrary.cs` file from the previous "More on Compiling C# Files" section. You will add a `<summary>` element for the class and for its `Add()` method, and also a `<returns>` element and two `<param>` elements for the `Add()` method:

```
// MathLib.cs
namespace Wrox
{

    ///<summary>
    ///   Wrox.Math class.
    ///   Provides a method to add two integers.
    ///</summary>
    public class MathLib
    {
        ///<summary>
        ///   The Add method allows us to add two integers.
        ///</summary>
        ///<returns>Result of the addition (int)</returns>
        ///<param name="x">First number to add</param>
        ///<param name="y">Second number to add</param>
        public int Add(int x, int y)
        {
            return x + y;
        }
    }
}
```

The C# compiler can extract the XML elements from the special comments and use them to generate an XML file. To get the compiler to generate the XML documentation for an assembly, you specify the `/doc` option when you compile, together with the name of the file you want to be created:

```
csc /t:library /doc:MathLibrary.xml MathLibrary.cs
```

The compiler will throw an error if the XML comments do not result in a well-formed XML document.

This will generate an XML file named `Math.xml`, which looks like this:

Available for
download on
Wrox.com

```
<?xml version="1.0"?>
<doc>
    <assembly>
        <name>MathLibrary</name>
    </assembly>
    <members>
        <member name="T:Wrox.MathLibrary">
            <summary>
                Wrox.MathLibrary class.
                Provides a method to add two integers.
            </summary>
        </member>
        <member name=
            "M:Wrox.MathLibrary.Add(System.Int32,System.Int32)">
```

```
        <summary>
            The Add method allows us to add two integers.
        </summary>
        <returns>Result of the addition (int)</returns>
        <param name="x">First number to add</param>
        <param name="y">Second number to add</param>
    </member>
  </members>
</doc>
```

code snippet MathLibrary.xml

Notice how the compiler has actually done some work for you; it has created an `<assembly>` element and also added a `<member>` element for each type or member of a type in the file. Each `<member>` element has a name attribute with the full name of the member as its value, prefixed by a letter that indicates whether this is a type (`T:`), field (`F:`), or member (`M:`).

THE C# PREPROCESSOR DIRECTIVES

Besides the usual keywords, most of which you have now encountered, C# also includes a number of commands that are known as *preprocessor directives*. These commands never actually get translated to any commands in your executable code, but instead they affect aspects of the compilation process. For example, you can use preprocessor directives to prevent the compiler from compiling certain portions of your code. You might do this if you are planning to release two versions of the code — a basic version and an enterprise version that will have more features. You could use preprocessor directives to prevent the compiler from compiling code related to the additional features when you are compiling the basic version of the software. Another scenario is that you might have written bits of code that are intended to provide you with debugging information. You probably don't want those portions of code compiled when you actually ship the software.

The preprocessor directives are all distinguished by beginning with the # symbol.

C++ developers will recognize the preprocessor directives as something that plays an important part in C and C++. However, there aren't as many preprocessor directives in C#, and they are not used as often. C# provides other mechanisms, such as custom attributes, that achieve some of the same effects as C++ directives. Also, note that C# doesn't actually have a separate preprocessor in the way that C++ does. The so-called preprocessor directives are actually handled by the compiler. Nevertheless, C# retains the name preprocessor directive because these commands give the impression of a preprocessor.

The next sections briefly cover the purposes of the preprocessor directives.

#define and #undef

`#define` is used like this:

```
#define DEBUG
```

What this does is tell the compiler that a symbol with the given name (in this case `DEBUG`) exists. It is a little bit like declaring a variable, except that this variable doesn't really have a value — it just exists. And this symbol isn't part of your actual code; it exists only for the benefit of the compiler, while the compiler is compiling the code, and has no meaning within the C# code itself.

#undef does the opposite, and removes the definition of a symbol:

```
#undef DEBUG
```

If the symbol doesn't exist in the first place, then #undef has no effect. Similarly, #define has no effect if a symbol already exists.

You need to place any #define and #undef directives at the beginning of the C# source file, before any code that declares any objects to be compiled.

#define isn't much use on its own, but when combined with other preprocessor directives, especially #if, it becomes very powerful.

> *Incidentally, you might notice some changes from the usual C# syntax. Preprocessor directives are not terminated by semicolons and normally constitute the only command on a line. That's because for the preprocessor directives, C# abandons its usual practice of requiring commands to be separated by semicolons. If it sees a preprocessor directive, it assumes that the next command is on the next line.*

#if, #elif, #else, and #endif

These directives inform the compiler whether to compile a block of code. Consider this method:

```
int DoSomeWork(double x)
{
    // do something
#if DEBUG
    Console.WriteLine("x is " + x);
#endif
}
```

This code will compile as normal, except for the Console.WriteLine() method call that is contained inside the #if clause. This line will be executed only if the symbol DEBUG has been defined by a previous #define directive. When the compiler finds the #if directive, it checks to see if the symbol concerned exists and compiles the code inside the #if clause only if the symbol does exist. Otherwise, the compiler simply ignores all the code until it reaches the matching #endif directive. Typical practice is to define the symbol DEBUG while you are debugging and have various bits of debugging-related code inside #if clauses. Then, when you are close to shipping, you simply comment out the #define directive, and all the debugging code miraculously disappears, the size of the executable file gets smaller, and your end users don't get confused by being shown debugging information. (Obviously, you would do more testing to make sure your code still works without DEBUG defined.) This technique is very common in C and C++ programming and is known as *conditional compilation.*

The #elif (=else if) and #else directives can be used in #if blocks and have intuitively obvious meanings. It is also possible to nest #if blocks:

```
#define ENTERPRISE
#define W2K

// further on in the file

#if ENTERPRISE
    // do something
    #if W2K
        // some code that is only relevant to enterprise
        // edition running on W2K
    #endif
#elif PROFESSIONAL
```

```
    // do something else
#else
    // code for the leaner version
#endif
```

 Note that, unlike the situation in C++, using `#if` *is not the only way to compile code conditionally. C# provides an alternative mechanism through the* `Conditional` *attribute, which is explored in Chapter 14, "Reflection."*

`#if` and `#elif` support a limited range of logical operators too, using the operators !, ==, !=, and ||. A symbol is considered to be `true` if it exists and `false` if it doesn't. For example:

```
#if W2K && (ENTERPRISE==false)    // if W2K is defined but ENTERPRISE isn't
```

#warning and #error

Two other very useful preprocessor directives are `#warning` and `#error`. These will respectively cause a warning or an error to be raised when the compiler encounters them. If the compiler sees a `#warning` directive, it will display whatever text appears after the `#warning` to the user, after which compilation continues. If it encounters a `#error` directive, it will display the subsequent text to the user as if it were a compilation error message and then immediately abandon the compilation, so no IL code will be generated.

You can use these directives as checks that you haven't done anything silly with your `#define` statements; you can also use the `#warning` statements to remind yourself to do something:

```
#if DEBUG && RELEASE
    #error "You've defined DEBUG and RELEASE simultaneously!"
#endif

#warning "Don't forget to remove this line before the boss tests the code!"
    Console.WriteLine("*I hate this job.*");
```

#region and #endregion

The `#region` and `#endregion` directives are used to indicate that a certain block of code is to be treated as a single block with a given name, like this:

```
#region Member Field Declarations
    int x;
    double d;
    Currency balance;
#endregion
```

This doesn't look that useful by itself; it doesn't affect the compilation process in any way. However, the real advantage is that these directives are recognized by some editors, including the Visual Studio .NET editor. These editors can use these directives to lay out your code better on the screen. You will see how this works in Chapter 16.

#line

The `#line` directive can be used to alter the filename and line number information that is output by the compiler in warnings and error messages. You probably won't want to use this directive that often. It's most useful when you are coding in conjunction with some other package that alters the code you are typing in before sending it to the compiler. In this situation, line numbers, or perhaps the filenames reported by the compiler, won't match up to the line numbers in the files or the filenames you are editing. The `#line` directive can be used to restore the match. You can also use the syntax `#line default` to restore the line to the default line numbering:

```
#line 164 "Core.cs" // We happen to know this is line 164 in the file
                    // Core.cs, before the intermediate
                    // package mangles it.

// later on

#line default       // restores default line numbering
```

#pragma

The `#pragma` directive can either suppress or restore specific compiler warnings. Unlike command-line options, the `#pragma` directive can be implemented on a class or method level, allowing fine-grained control of what warnings are suppressed and when. The following example disables the "field not used" warning and then restores it after the `MyClass` class compiles:

```
#pragma warning disable 169
public class MyClass
{
    int neverUsedField;
}
#pragma warning restore 169
```

C# PROGRAMMING GUIDELINES

The final section of this chapter supplies the guidelines you need to bear in mind when writing C# programs.

Rules for Identifiers

This section examines the rules governing what names you can use for variables, classes, methods, and so on. Note that the rules presented in this section are not merely guidelines: they are enforced by the C# compiler.

Identifiers are the names you give to variables, to user-defined types such as classes and structs, and to members of these types. Identifiers are case-sensitive, so, for example, variables named `interestRate` and `InterestRate` would be recognized as different variables. Following are a few rules determining what identifiers you can use in C#:

➤   They must begin with a letter or underscore, although they can contain numeric characters.

➤   You can't use C# keywords as identifiers.

The following table lists the C# reserved keywords.

abstract	event	new	struct
as	explicit	null	switch
base	extern	object	this
bool	false	operator	throw
break	finally	out	true
byte	fixed	override	try
case	float	params	typeof
catch	for	private	uint

char	foreach	protected	ulong
checked	goto	public	unchecked
class	if	readonly	unsafe
const	implicit	ref	ushort
continue	in	return	using
decimal	int	sbyte	virtual
default	interface	sealed	volatile
delegate	internal	short	void
do	is	sizeof	while
double	lock	stackalloc	
else	long	static	
enum	namespace	string	

If you need to use one of these words as an identifier (for example, if you are accessing a class written in a different language), you can prefix the identifier with the @ symbol to indicate to the compiler that what follows is to be treated as an identifier, not as a C# keyword (so abstract is not a valid identifier, but @ abstract is).

Finally, identifiers can also contain Unicode characters, specified using the syntax \uXXXX, where XXXX is the four-digit hex code for the Unicode character. The following are some examples of valid identifiers:

➤   Name

➤   Überfluß

➤   _Identifier

➤   \u005fIdentifier

The last two items in this list are identical and interchangeable (because 005f is the Unicode code for the underscore character), so obviously these identifiers couldn't both be declared in the same scope. Note that although syntactically you are allowed to use the underscore character in identifiers, this isn't recommended in most situations. That's because it doesn't follow the guidelines for naming variables that Microsoft has written to ensure that developers use the same conventions, making it easier to read each other's code.

Usage Conventions

In any development language, there usually arise certain traditional programming styles. The styles are not part of the language itself but are conventions concerning, for example, how variables are named or how certain classes, methods, or functions are used. If most developers using that language follow the same conventions, it makes it easier for different developers to understand each other's code — which in turn generally helps program maintainability. Conventions do, however, depend on the language and the environment. For example, C++ developers programming on the Windows platform have traditionally used the prefixes psz or lpsz to indicate strings — char *pszResult; char *lpszMessage; — but on Unix machines it's more common not to use any such prefixes: char *Result; char *Message;.

You'll notice from the sample code in this book that the convention in C# is to name variables without prefixes: string Result; string Message;.

> *The convention by which variable names are prefixed with letters that represent the data type is known as* Hungarian notation. *It means that other developers reading the code can immediately tell from the variable name what data type the variable represents. Hungarian notation is widely regarded as redundant in these days of smart editors and IntelliSense.*

Whereas, with many languages, usage conventions simply evolved as the language was used, with C# and the whole of the .NET Framework, Microsoft has written very comprehensive usage guidelines, which are detailed in the .NET/C# MSDN documentation. This should mean that, right from the start, .NET programs will have a high degree of interoperability in terms of developers being able to understand code. The guidelines have also been developed with the benefit of some 20 years' hindsight in object-oriented programming. Judging by the relevant newsgroups, the guidelines have been carefully thought out and are well received in the developer community. Hence the guidelines are well worth following.

It should be noted, however, that the guidelines are not the same as language specifications. You should try to follow the guidelines when you can. Nevertheless, you won't run into problems if you have a good reason for not doing so — for example, you won't get a compilation error because you don't follow these guidelines. The general rule is that if you don't follow the usage guidelines you must have a convincing reason. Departing from the guidelines should be a positive decision rather than simply not bothering. Also, if you compare the guidelines with the samples in the remainder of this book, you'll notice that in numerous examples we have chosen not to follow the conventions. That's usually because the conventions are designed for much larger programs than our samples, and although they are great if you are writing a complete software package, they are not really suitable for small 20-line standalone programs. In many cases, following the conventions would have made our samples harder, rather than easier, to follow.

The full guidelines for good programming style are quite extensive. This section is confined to describing some of the more important guidelines, as well as the ones most likely to surprise you. If you want to make absolutely certain that your code follows the usage guidelines completely, you will need to refer to the MSDN documentation.

Naming Conventions

One important aspect to making your programs understandable is how you choose to name your items — and that includes naming variables, methods, classes, enumerations, and namespaces.

It is intuitively obvious that your names should reflect the purpose of the item and should not clash with other names. The general philosophy in the .NET Framework is also that the name of a variable should reflect the purpose of that variable instance and not the data type. For example, `height` is a good name for a variable, whereas `integerValue` isn't. However, you will probably feel that that principle is an ideal that is hard to achieve. Particularly when you are dealing with controls, in most cases, you'll probably be happier sticking with variable names such as `confirmationDialog` and `chooseEmployeeListBox`, which do indicate the data type in the name.

The following sections look at some of the things you need to think about when choosing names.

Casing of Names

In many cases you should use *Pascal casing* for names. Pascal casing means that the first letter of each word in a name is capitalized: `EmployeeSalary`, `ConfirmationDialog`, `PlainTextEncoding`. You will notice that essentially all of the names of namespaces, classes, and members in the base classes follow Pascal casing. In particular, the convention of joining words using the underscore character is discouraged. So, you should try not to use names such as `employee_salary`. It has also been common in other languages to use all capitals for names of constants. This is not advised in C# because such names are harder to read — the convention is to use Pascal casing throughout:

```
const int MaximumLength;
```

The only other casing scheme that you are advised to use is *camel casing*. Camel casing is similar to Pascal casing, except that the first letter of the first word in the name is not capitalized: `employeeSalary`, `confirmationDialog`, `plainTextEncoding`. Following are three situations in which you are advised to use camel casing:

➤ For names of all private member fields in types:

```
public int subscriberId;
```

Note, however, that often it is conventional to prefix names of member fields with an underscore:

```
public int _subscriberId;
```

➤ For names of all parameters passed to methods:

```
public void RecordSale(string salesmanName, int quantity);
```

➤ To distinguish items that would otherwise have the same name. A common example is when a property wraps around a field:

```
private string employeeName;


public string EmployeeName
{
    get
    {
        return employeeName;

    }

}
```

If you are doing this, you should always use camel casing for the private member and Pascal casing for the public or protected member, so that other classes that use your code see only names in Pascal case (except for parameter names).

You should also be wary about case sensitivity. C# is case-sensitive, so it is syntactically correct for names in C# to differ only by the case, as in the previous examples. However, you should bear in mind that your assemblies might at some point be called from Visual Basic .NET applications — and *Visual Basic .NET is not case-sensitive*. Hence, if you do use names that differ only by case, it is important to do so only in situations in which both names will never be seen outside your assembly. (The previous example qualifies as okay because camel case is used with the name that is attached to a `private` variable.) Otherwise, you may prevent other code written in Visual Basic .NET from being able to use your assembly correctly.

Name Styles

You should be consistent about your style of names. For example, if one of the methods in a class is called `ShowConfirmationDialog()`, then you should not give another method a name such as `ShowDialogWarning()` or `WarningDialogShow()`. The other method should be called `ShowWarningDialog()`.

Namespace Names

Namespace names are particularly important to design carefully to avoid risk of ending up with the same name for one of your namespaces as someone else's. Remember, namespace names are the *only* way that .NET distinguishes names of objects in shared assemblies. So, if you use the same namespace name for your software package as another package, and both packages get installed on the same computer, there are going to be problems. Because of this, it's almost always a good idea to create a top-level namespace with the name of your company and then nest successive namespaces that narrow down the technology, group, or department you are working in or the name of the package your classes are intended for. Microsoft recommends namespace names that begin with `<CompanyName>.<TechnologyName>` as in these two examples:

```
WeaponsOfDestructionCorp.RayGunControllers
WeaponsOfDestructionCorp.Viruses
```

Names and Keywords

It is important that the names do not clash with any keywords. In fact, if you attempt to name an item in your code with a word that happens to be a C# keyword, you'll almost certainly get a syntax error because the compiler will assume that the name refers to a statement. However, because of the possibility that your classes will be accessed by code written in other languages, it is also important that you don't use names that are keywords in other .NET languages. Generally speaking, C++ keywords are similar to C# keywords, so confusion with C++ is unlikely, and those commonly encountered keywords that are unique to Visual C++ tend to start with two underscore characters. As with C#, C++ keywords are spelled in lowercase, so if you hold to the convention of naming your public classes and members with Pascal-style names, they will always have at least one uppercase letter in their names, and there will be no risk of clashes with C++ keywords. However, you are more likely to have problems with Visual Basic .NET, which has many more keywords than C# does, and being non-case–sensitive means that you cannot rely on Pascal-style names for your classes and methods.

The following table lists the keywords and standard function calls in Visual Basic .NET, which you should avoid, if possible, in whatever case combination, for your public C# classes.

Abs	Do	Loc	RGB
Add	Double	Local	Right
AddHandler	Each	Lock	RmDir
AddressOf	Else	LOF	Rnd
Alias	ElseIf	Log	RTrim
And	Empty	Long	SaveSettings
Ansi	End	Loop	Second
AppActivate	Enum	LTrim	Seek
Append	EOF	Me	Select
As	Erase	Mid	SetAttr
Asc	Err	Minute	SetException
Assembly	Error	MIRR	Shared
Atan	Event	MkDir	Shell
Auto	Exit	Module	Short
Beep	Exp	Month	Sign
Binary	Explicit	MustInherit	Sin
BitAnd	ExternalSource	MustOverride	Single
BitNot	False	MyBase	SLN
BitOr	FileAttr	MyClass	Space
BitXor	FileCopy	Namespace	Spc
Boolean	FileDateTime	New	Split
ByRef	FileLen	Next	Sqrt
Byte	Filter	Not	Static
ByVal	Finally	Nothing	Step
Call	Fix	NotInheritable	Stop
Case	For	NotOverridable	Str
Catch	Format	Now	StrComp

CBool	FreeFile	NPer	StrConv
CByte	Friend	NPV	Strict
CDate	Function	Null	String
CDbl	FV	Object	Structure
CDec	Get	Oct	Sub
ChDir	GetAllSettings	Off	Switch
ChDrive	GetAttr	On	SYD
Choose	GetException	Open	SyncLock
Chr	GetObject	Option	Tab
CInt	GetSetting	Optional	Tan
Class	GetType	Or	Text
Clear	GoTo	Overloads	Then
CLng	Handles	Overridable	Throw
Close	Hex	Overrides	TimeOfDay
Collection	Hour	ParamArray	Timer
Command	If	Pmt	TimeSerial
Compare	Iif	PPmt	TimeValue
Const	Implements	Preserve	To
Const	Implements	Preserve	To
Cos	Imports	Print	Today
CreateObject	In	Private	Trim
CShort	Inherits	Property	Try
CSng	Input	Public	TypeName
CStr	InStr	Put	TypeOf
CurDir	Int	PV	UBound
Date	Integer	QBColor	UCase
DateAdd	Interface	Raise	Unicode
DateDiff	Ipmt	RaiseEvent	Unlock
DatePart	IRR	Randomize	Until
DateSerial	Is	Rate	Val
DateValue	IsArray	Read	Weekday
Day	IsDate	ReadOnly	While
DDB	IsDbNull	ReDim	Width
Decimal	IsNumeric	Remove	With
Declare	Item	RemoveHandler	WithEvents
Default	Kill	Rename	Write
Delegate	Lcase	Replace	WriteOnly
DeleteSetting	Left	Reset	Xor
Dim	Lib	Resume	Year

Use of Properties and Methods

One area that can cause confusion in a class is whether a particular quantity should be represented by a property or a method. The rules here are not hard and fast, but in general, you ought to use a property if something really should look and feel like a variable. (If you're not sure what a property is, see Chapter 3.) This means, among other things, that:

➤ Client code should be able to read its value. Write-only properties are not recommended, so, for example, use a `SetPassword()` method, not a write-only `Password` property.

➤ Reading the value should not take too long. The fact that something is a property usually suggests that reading it will be relatively quick.

➤ Reading the value should not have any observable and unexpected side effect. Further, setting the value of a property should not have any side effect that is not directly related to the property. Setting the width of a dialog box has the obvious effect of changing the appearance of the dialog box on the screen. That's fine, because that's obviously related to the property in question.

➤ It should be possible to set properties in any order. In particular, it is not good practice when setting a property to throw an exception because another related property has not yet been set. For example, to use a class that accesses a database, you need to set `ConnectionString`, `UserName`, and `Password`, then the author of the class should make sure the class is implemented so that the user really can set them in any order.

➤ Successive reads of a property should give the same result. If the value of a property is likely to change unpredictably, you should code it as a method instead. `Speed`, in a class that monitors the motion of an automobile, is not a good candidate for a property. Use a `GetSpeed()` method here; but, `Weight` and `EngineSize` are good candidates for properties because they will not change for a given object.

If the item you are coding satisfies all the preceding criteria, it is probably a good candidate for a property. Otherwise, you should use a method.

Use of Fields

The guidelines are pretty simple here. Fields should almost always be private, except that in some cases it may be acceptable for constant or read-only fields to be public. The reason is that if you make a field public, you may hinder your ability to extend or modify the class in the future.

The previous guidelines should give you a foundation of good practices, and you should also use them in conjunction with a good object-oriented programming style.

A final helpful note to keep in mind is that Microsoft has been fairly careful about being consistent and has followed its own guidelines when writing the .NET base classes. So a very good way to get an intuitive feel for the conventions to follow when writing .NET code is to simply look at the base classes — see how classes, members, and namespaces are named, and how the class hierarchy works. Consistency between the base classes and your classes will help in readability and maintainability.

SUMMARY

This chapter examined some of the basic syntax of C#, covering the areas needed to write simple C# programs. We covered a lot of ground, but much of it will be instantly recognizable to developers who are familiar with any C-style language (or even JavaScript).

You have seen that although C# syntax is similar to C++ and Java syntax, there are many minor differences. You have also seen that in many areas this syntax is combined with facilities to write code very quickly, for example high-quality string handling facilities. C# also has a strongly defined type system, based on a distinction between value and reference types. Chapters 3 and 4 cover the C# object-oriented programming features.

3

Objects and Types

WHAT'S IN THIS CHAPTER?

➤ The differences between classes and structs

➤ Class members

➤ Passing values by value and by reference

➤ Method overloading

➤ Constructors and static constructors

➤ Read-only fields

➤ Partial classes

➤ Static classes

➤ The Object class, from which all other types are derived

So far, you've been introduced to some of the building blocks of the C# language, including variables, data types, and program flow statements, and you have seen a few very short complete programs containing little more than the Main() method. What you haven't really seen yet is how to put all these together to form a longer, complete program. The key to this lies in working with classes — the subject of this chapter. Note that we cover inheritance and features related to inheritance in Chapter 4, "Inheritance."

This chapter introduces the basic syntax associated with classes. However, we assume that you are already familiar with the underlying principles of using classes — for example, that you know what a constructor or a property is. This chapter is largely confined to applying those principles in C# code.

CLASSES AND STRUCTS

Classes and structs are essentially templates from which you can create objects. Each object contains data and has methods to manipulate and access that data. The class defines what data and functionality each particular object (called an *instance*) of that class can contain. For example, if you have a class that represents a customer, it might define fields such as CustomerID, FirstName, LastName, and Address, which you will use to hold information about a particular customer. It might also define functionality that acts upon the data stored in these fields. You can then instantiate an object of this class to represent one specific customer, set the field values for that instance, and use its functionality.

```
class PhoneCustomer
{
    public const string DayOfSendingBill = "Monday";
    public int CustomerID;
    public string FirstName;
    public string LastName;
}
```

Structs differ from classes in the way that they are stored in memory and accessed (classes are reference types stored in the heap; structs are value types stored on the stack), and in some of their features (for example, structs don't support inheritance). You will tend to use structs for smaller data types for performance reasons. In terms of syntax, however, structs look very similar to classes; the main difference is that you use the keyword struct instead of class to declare them. For example, if you wanted all PhoneCustomer instances to be allocated on the stack instead of the managed heap, you could write:

```
struct PhoneCustomerStruct
{
    public const string DayOfSendingBill = "Monday";
    public int CustomerID;
    public string FirstName;
    public string LastName;
}
```

For both classes and structs, you use the keyword new to declare an instance. This keyword creates the object and initializes it; in the following example, the default behavior is to zero out its fields:

```
PhoneCustomer myCustomer = new PhoneCustomer();        // works for a class
PhoneCustomerStruct myCustomer2 = new PhoneCustomerStruct();// works for a struct
```

In most cases, you'll use classes much more often than structs. Therefore, we discuss classes first and then the differences between classes and structs and the specific reasons why you might choose to use a struct instead of a class. Unless otherwise stated, however, you can assume that code presented for a class will work equally well for a struct.

CLASSES

The data and functions within a class are known as the class's *members*. Microsoft's official terminology distinguishes between data members and function members. In addition to these members, classes can contain nested types (such as other classes). Accessibility to the members can be public, protected, internal protected, private, or internal. These are described in detail in Chapter 5, "Generics."

Data Members

Data members are those members that contain the data for the class — fields, constants, and events. Data members can be static. A class member is always an instance member unless it is explicitly declared as static.

Fields are any variables associated with the class. You have already seen fields in use in the PhoneCustomer class in the previous example.

After you have instantiated a PhoneCustomer object, you can then access these fields using the Object. FieldName syntax, as shown in this example:

```
PhoneCustomer Customer1 = new PhoneCustomer();
Customer1.FirstName = "Simon";
```

Constants can be associated with classes in the same way as variables. You declare a constant using the const keyword. If it is declared as public, then it will be accessible from outside the class.

```
class PhoneCustomer
{
    public const string DayOfSendingBill = "Monday";
    public int CustomerID;
    public string FirstName;
    public string LastName;
}
```

Events are class members that allow an object to notify a caller whenever something noteworthy happens, such as a field or property of the class changing, or some form of user interaction occurring. The client can have code, known as an event handler, which reacts to the event. Chapter 8, "Delegates, Lambdas, and Events," looks at events in detail.

Function Members

➤ Function members are those members that provide some functionality for manipulating the data in the class. They include methods, properties, constructors, finalizers, operators, and indexers.

➤ *Methods* are functions that are associated with a particular class. Just as with data members, function members are instance members by default. They can be made static by using the `static` modifier.

➤ *Properties* are sets of functions that can be accessed from the client in a similar way to the public fields of the class. C# provides a specific syntax for implementing read and write properties on your classes, so you don't have use method names that have the words `Get` or `Set` embedded in them. Because there's a dedicated syntax for properties that is distinct from that for normal functions, the illusion of objects as actual things is strengthened for client code.

➤ *Constructors* are special functions that are called automatically when an object is instantiated. They must have the same name as the class to which they belong and cannot have a return type. Constructors are useful for initialization.

➤ *Finalizers* are similar to constructors but are called when the CLR detects that an object is no longer needed. They have the same name as the class, preceded by a tilde (~). It is impossible to predict precisely when a finalizer will be called. Finalizers are discussed in Chapter 13, "Memory Management and Pointers."

➤ *Operators*, at their simplest, are actions such as + or –. When you add two integers, you are, strictly speaking, using the + operator for integers. However, C# also allows you to specify how existing operators will work with your own classes (*operator overloading*). Chapter 7, "Operators and Casts," looks at operators in detail.

➤ *Indexers* allow your objects to be indexed in the same way as an array or collection.

Methods

Note that official C# terminology makes a distinction between functions and methods. In C# terminology, the term "function member" includes not only methods, but also other nondata members of a class or struct. This includes indexers, operators, constructors, destructors, and also — perhaps somewhat surprisingly — properties. These are contrasted with data members: fields, constants, and events.

Declaring Methods

In C#, the definition of a method consists of any method modifiers (such as the method's accessibility), the type of the return value, followed by the name of the method, followed by a list of input arguments enclosed in parentheses, followed by the body of the method enclosed in curly braces:

```
[modifiers] return_type MethodName([parameters])
{
    // Method body
}
```

Each parameter consists of the name of the type of the parameter, and the name by which it can be referenced in the body of the method. Also, if the method returns a value, a return statement must be used with the return value to indicate each exit point. For example:

```
public bool IsSquare(Rectangle rect)
{
    return (rect.Height == rect.Width);
}
```

This code uses one of the .NET base classes, System.Drawing.Rectangle, which represents a rectangle.

If the method doesn't return anything, you specify a return type of void because you can't omit the return type altogether, and if it takes no arguments, you still need to include an empty set of parentheses after the method name. In this case, including a return statement is optional — the method returns automatically when the closing curly brace is reached. You should note that a method can contain as many return statements as required:

```
public bool IsPositive(int value)
{
    if (value < 0)
        return false;
    return true;
}
```

Invoking Methods

The following example, MathTest, illustrates the syntax for definition and instantiation of classes, and definition and invocation of methods. Besides the class that contains the Main() method, it defines a class named MathTest, which contains a couple of methods and a field.

```
using System;

namespace Wrox
{
    class MainEntryPoint
    {
        static void Main()
        {
            // Try calling some static functions.
            Console.WriteLine("Pi is " + MathTest.GetPi());
            int x = MathTest.GetSquareOf(5);
            Console.WriteLine("Square of 5 is " + x);

            // Instantiate at MathTest object
            MathTest math = new MathTest();    // this is C#'s way of
                                               // instantiating a reference type

            // Call nonstatic methods
            math.value = 30;
            Console.WriteLine(
                "Value field of math variable contains " + math.value);
            Console.WriteLine("Square of 30 is " + math.GetSquare());
        }
    }

    // Define a class named MathTest on which we will call a method
    class MathTest
    {
        public int value;

        public int GetSquare()
        {
            return value*value;
```

```
        }

        public static int GetSquareOf(int x)
        {
            return x*x;
        }

        public static double GetPi()
        {
            return 3.14159;
        }
    }
}
```

code snippet MathTest.cs

Running the `MathTest` example produces these results:

```
Pi is 3.14159
Square of 5 is 25
Value field of math variable contains 30
Square of 30 is 900
```

As you can see from the code, the `MathTest` class contains a field that contains a number, as well as a method to find the square of this number. It also contains two static methods, one to return the value of pi and one to find the square of the number passed in as a parameter.

Some features of this class are not really good examples of C# program design. For example, `GetPi()` would usually be implemented as a `const` field, but following good design here would mean using some concepts that we have not yet introduced.

Passing Parameters to Methods

In general, parameters can be passed into methods by reference or by value. When a variable is passed by reference, the called method gets the actual variable — so any changes made to the variable inside the method persist when the method exits. But, when a variable is passed by value, the called method gets an identical copy of the variable — which means any changes made are lost when the method exits. For complex data types, passing by reference is more efficient because of the large amount of data that must be copied when passing by value.

In C#, all parameters are passed by value unless you specifically say otherwise. However, you need to be careful in understanding the implications of this for reference types. Because reference type variables hold only a reference to an object, it is this reference that will be copied, not the object itself. Hence, changes made to the underlying object will persist. Value type variables, in contrast, hold the actual data, so a copy of the data itself will be passed into the method. An `int`, for instance, is passed by value to a method, and any changes that the method makes to the value of that `int` do not change the value of the original `int` object. Conversely, if an array or any other reference type, such as a class, is passed into a method, and the method uses the reference to change a value in that array, the new value is reflected in the original array object.

Here is an example, `ParameterTest.cs`, which demonstrates the following:

```
using System;

namespace Wrox
{
    class ParameterTest
    {
        static void SomeFunction(int[] ints, int i)
        {
            ints[0] = 100;
            i = 100;
```

```
        }

        public static int Main()
        {
            int i = 0;
            int[] ints = { 0, 1, 2, 4, 8 };
            // Display the original values.
            Console.WriteLine("i = " + i);
            Console.WriteLine("ints[0] = " + ints[0]);
            Console.WriteLine("Calling SomeFunction.");

            // After this method returns, ints will be changed,
            // but i will not.
            SomeFunction(ints, i);
            Console.WriteLine("i = " + i);
            Console.WriteLine("ints[0] = " + ints[0]);
            return 0;
        }
    }
}
```

code snippet ParameterTest.cs

The output of this is:

```
ParameterTest.exe
i = 0
ints[0] = 0
Calling SomeFunction...
i = 0
ints[0] = 100
```

Notice how the value of i remains unchanged, but the value changed in ints is also changed in the original array.

The behavior of strings is different again. This is because strings are immutable (if you alter a string's value, you create an entirely new string), so strings don't display the typical reference-type behavior. Any changes made to a string within a method call won't affect the original string. This point is discussed in more detail in Chapter 9, "Strings and Regular Expressions."

ref Parameters

As mentioned, passing variables by value is the default, but you can force value parameters to be passed by reference. To do so, use the ref keyword. If a parameter is passed to a method, and if the input argument for that method is prefixed with the ref keyword, any changes that the method makes to the variable will affect the value of the original object:

```
static void SomeFunction(int[] ints, ref int i)
{
    ints[0] = 100;
    i = 100;      // The change to i will persist after SomeFunction() exits.
}
```

You will also need to add the ref keyword when you invoke the method:

```
SomeFunction(ints, ref i);.
```

Finally, it is also important to understand that C# continues to apply initialization requirements to parameters passed to methods. Any variable must be initialized before it is passed into a method, whether it is passed in by value or by reference.

out Parameters

In C-style languages, it is common for functions to be able to output more than one value from a single routine. This is accomplished using output parameters, by assigning the output values to variables that have been passed to the method by reference. Often, the starting values of the variables that are passed by reference are unimportant. Those values will be overwritten by the function, which may never even look at any previous value.

It would be convenient if you could use the same convention in C#. However, C# requires that variables be initialized with a starting value before they are referenced. Although you could initialize your input variables with meaningless values before passing them into a function that will fill them with real, meaningful ones, this practice seems at best needless and at worst confusing. However, there is a way to short-circuit the C# compiler's insistence on initial values for input arguments.

You do this with the out keyword. When a method's input argument is prefixed with out, that method can be passed a variable that has not been initialized. The variable is passed by reference, so any changes that the method makes to the variable will persist when control returns from the called method. Again, you also need to use the out keyword when you call the method, as well as when you define it:

```
static void SomeFunction(out int i)
{
    i = 100;
}

public static int Main()
{
    int i; // note how i is declared but not initialized.
    SomeFunction(out i);
    Console.WriteLine(i);
    return 0;
}
```

Named Arguments

Typically, parameters need to be passed into a method in the same order that they are defined. Named arguments allow you to pass in parameters in any order. So for the following method:

```
string FullName(string firstName, string lastName)
{
    return firstName + " " + lastName;
}
```

The following method calls will return the same full name:

```
FullName("John", "Doe");
FullName(lastName: "Doe", firstName: "John");
```

If the method has several parameters, you can mix positional and named arguments in the same call.

Optional Arguments

Parameters can also be optional. You must supply a default value for parameters that are optional. The optional parameter(s) must be the last ones defined as well. So the following method declaration would be incorrect:

```
void TestMethod(int optionalNumber = 10, int notOptionalNumber)
{
    System.Console.Write(optionalNumber + notOptionalNumber);
}
```

For this method to work, the optionalNumber parameter would have to be defined last.

Method Overloading

C# supports method overloading — several versions of the method that have different signatures (that is, the same name, but a different number of parameters and/or different parameter data types). To overload methods, you simply declare the methods with the same name but different numbers or types of parameters:

```
class ResultDisplayer
{
    void DisplayResult(string result)
    {
        // implementation
    }

    void DisplayResult(int result)
    {
        // implementation
    }
}
```

If optional parameters won't work for you, then you need to use method overloading to achieve the same effect:

```
class MyClass
{
    int DoSomething(int x)    // want 2nd parameter with default value 10
    {
        DoSomething(x, 10);
    }

    int DoSomething(int x, int y)
    {
        // implementation
    }
}
```

As in any language, method overloading carries with it the potential for subtle runtime bugs if the wrong overload is called. Chapter 4 discusses how to code defensively against these problems. For now, you should know that C# does place some minimum restrictions on the parameters of overloaded methods:

➤   It is not sufficient for two methods to differ only in their return type.

➤   It is not sufficient for two methods to differ only by virtue of a parameter having been declared as `ref` or `out`.

Properties

The idea of a property is that it is a method or pair of methods that is dressed to look like a field. A good example of this is the `Height` property of a Windows Form. Suppose that you have the following code:

```
// mainForm is of type System.Windows.Forms
mainForm.Height = 400;
```

On executing this code, the height of the window will be set to 400, and you will see the window resize on the screen. Syntactically, this code looks like you're setting a field, but in fact you are calling a property accessor that contains code to resize the form.

To define a property in C#, you use the following syntax:

```
public string SomeProperty
{
    get
    {
        return "This is the property value.";
    }
    set
```

```
     {
         // do whatever needs to be done to set the property.
     }
   }
}
```

The `get` accessor takes no parameters and must return the same type as the declared property. You should not specify any explicit parameters for the `set` accessor either, but the compiler assumes it takes one parameter, which is of the same type again, and which is referred to as `value`. As an example, the following code contains a property called `Age`, which sets a field called `age`. In this example, `age` is referred to as the backing variable for the property `Age`.

```
private int age;

public int Age
{
   get
   {
      return age;
   }
   set
   {
      age = value;
   }
}
```

Note the naming convention used here. You take advantage of C#'s case sensitivity by using the same name, Pascal-cased for the public property, and camel-cased for the equivalent private field if there is one. Some developers prefer to use field names that are prefixed by an underscore: _age; this provides an extremely convenient way of identifying fields.

Read-Only and Write-Only Properties

It is possible to create a read-only property by simply omitting the `set` accessor from the property definition. Thus, to make `Name` a read-only property, you would do the following:

```
private string name;

public string Name
{
   get
   {
      return Name;
   }
}
```

It is similarly possible to create a write-only property by omitting the `get` accessor. However, this is regarded as poor programming practice because it could be confusing to authors of client code. In general, it is recommended that if you are tempted to do this, you should use a method instead.

Access Modifiers for Properties

C# does allow the `set` and `get` accessors to have differing access modifiers. This would allow a property to have a public `get` and a private or protected `set`. This can help control how or when a property can be set. In the following code example, notice that the `set` has a private access modifier and the `get` does not have any. In this case, the `get` takes on the access level of the property. One of the accessors must follow the access level of the property. A compile error will be generated if the `get` accessor has the `protected` access level associated with it because that would make both accessors have a different access level from the property.

```
public string Name
{
  get
```

```
  {
    return _name;
  }
  private set
  {
    _name = value;
  }
}
```

Auto-Implemented Properties

If there isn't going to be any logic in the properties `set` and `get`, then auto-implemented properties can be used. Auto-implemented properties implement the backing member variable automatically. The code for the earlier `Age` example would look like this:

```
public string Age {get; set;}
```

The declaration `private int age;` is not needed. The compiler will create this automatically.

By using auto-implemented properties, validation of the property cannot be done at the property set. So in the previous example we could not have checked to see if an invalid age is set. Also, both accessors must be present. So an attempt to make a property read-only would cause an error:

```
public string Age {get;}
```

However, the access level of each accessor can be different. So the following is acceptable:

```
public string Age {get; private set;}
```

A NOTE ABOUT INLINING

Some developers may worry that the previous sections have presented a number of situations in which standard C# coding practices have led to very small functions — for example, accessing a field via a property instead of directly. Is this going to hurt performance because of the overhead of the extra function call? The answer is that there is no need to worry about performance loss from these kinds of programming methodologies in C#. Recall that C# code is compiled to IL, then JIT compiled at runtime to native executable code. The JIT compiler is designed to generate highly optimized code and will ruthlessly inline code as appropriate (in other words, it replaces function calls with inline code). A method or property whose implementation simply calls another method or returns a field will almost certainly be inlined. Note, however, that the decision of where to inline is made entirely by the CLR. There is no way for you to control which methods are inlined by using, for example, some keyword similar to the inline keyword of C++.

Constructors

The syntax for declaring basic constructors is a method that has the same name as the containing class and that does not have any return type:

```
public class MyClass
{
  public MyClass()
  {
  }
  // rest of class definition
```

It's not necessary to provide a constructor for your class. We haven't supplied one for any of the examples so far in this book. In general, if you don't supply any constructor, the compiler will make up a default one for you behind the scenes. It will be a very basic constructor that just initializes all the member fields by zeroing them out (`null` reference for reference types, zero for numeric data types, and false for `bool`s). Often, that will be adequate; if not, you'll need to write your own constructor.

Constructors follow the same rules for overloading as other methods (that is, you can provide as many overloads to the constructor as you want, provided they are clearly different in signature):

```
public MyClass()    // zeroparameter constructor
{
    // construction code
}
public MyClass(int number)    // another overload
{
    // construction code
}
```

Note, however, that if you supply any constructors that take parameters, the compiler will not automatically supply a default one. This is done only if you have not defined any constructors at all. In the following example, because a one-parameter constructor is defined, the compiler assumes that this is the only constructor you want to be available, so it will not implicitly supply any others:

```
public class MyNumber
{
    private int number;
    public MyNumber(int number)
    {
        this.number = number;
    }
}
```

This code also illustrates typical use of the `this` keyword to distinguish member fields from parameters of the same name. If you now try instantiating a `MyNumber` object using a no-parameter constructor, you will get a compilation error:

```
MyNumber numb = new MyNumber();    // causes compilation error
```

We should mention that it is possible to define constructors as private or protected, so that they are invisible to code in unrelated classes too:

```
public class MyNumber
{
    private int number;
    private MyNumber(int number)    // another overload
    {
        this.number = number;
    }
}
```

This example hasn't actually defined any public or even any protected constructors for `MyNumber`. This would actually make it impossible for `MyNumber` to be instantiated by outside code using the `new` operator (though you might write a public static property or method in `MyNumber` that can instantiate the class). This is useful in two situations:

➤ If your class serves only as a container for some static members or properties and therefore should never be instantiated

➤ If you want the class to only ever be instantiated by calling some static member function (this is the so-called class factory approach to object instantiation)

Static Constructors

One novel feature of C# is that it is also possible to write a static no-parameter constructor for a class. Such a constructor will be executed only once, as opposed to the constructors written so far, which are instance constructors that are executed whenever an object of that class is created.

```
class MyClass
{
    static MyClass()
```

```
  {
      // initialization code
  }
  // rest of class definition
}
```

One reason for writing a static constructor is if your class has some static fields or properties that need to be initialized from an external source before the class is first used.

The .NET runtime makes no guarantees about when a static constructor will be executed, so you should not place any code in it that relies on it being executed at a particular time (for example, when an assembly is loaded). Nor is it possible to predict in what order static constructors of different classes will execute. However, what is guaranteed is that the static constructor will run at most once, and that it will be invoked before your code makes any reference to the class. In C#, the static constructor is usually executed immediately before the first call to any member of the class.

Notice that the static constructor does not have any access modifiers. It's never called by any other C# code, but always by the .NET runtime when the class is loaded, so any access modifier such as `public` or `private` would be meaningless. For this same reason, the static constructor can never take any parameters, and there can be only one static constructor for a class. It should also be obvious that a static constructor can access only static members, not instance members, of the class.

Note that it is possible to have a static constructor and a zero-parameter instance constructor defined in the same class. Although the parameter lists are identical, there is no conflict. That's because the static constructor is executed when the class is loaded, but the instance constructor is executed whenever an instance is created — so there won't be any confusion about which constructor gets executed when.

Note that if you have more than one class that has a static constructor, the static constructor that will be executed first is undefined. This means that you should not put any code in a static constructor that depends on other static constructors having been or not having been executed. However, if any static fields have been given default values, these will be allocated before the static constructor is called.

The next example illustrates the use of a static constructor and is based on the idea of a program that has user preferences (which are presumably stored in some configuration file). To keep things simple, we'll assume just one user preference — a quantity called `BackColor`, which might represent the background color to be used in an application. And because we don't want to get into the details of writing code to read data from an external source here, we'll make the assumption that the preference is to have a background color of red on weekdays and green on weekends. All the program will do is display the preference in a console window — but this is enough to see a static constructor at work.

```csharp
namespace Wrox.ProCSharp.StaticConstructorSample
{
    public class UserPreferences
    {
        public static readonly Color BackColor;

        static UserPreferences()
        {
            DateTime now = DateTime.Now;
            if (now.DayOfWeek == DayOfWeek.Saturday
                || now.DayOfWeek == DayOfWeek.Sunday)
                BackColor = Color.Green;
            else
                BackColor = Color.Red;
        }

        private UserPreferences()
        {
        }
    }
}
```

This code shows how the color preference is stored in a static variable, which is initialized in the static constructor. This field is declared as read-only, which means that its value can only be set in a constructor. You learn about read-only fields in more detail later in this chapter. The code uses a few helpful structs that Microsoft has supplied as part of the Framework class library: System.DateTime and System.Drawing. Color. DateTime implements a static property — Now, which returns the current time — and an instance property — DayOfWeek, which works out what day of the week a date-time represents. Color (which is discussed in the online Chapter 48, "Graphics with GDI+") is used to store colors. It implements various static properties, such as Red and Green as used in this example, which returns commonly used colors. To use Color, you need to reference the System.Drawing.dll assembly when compiling, and you must add a using statement for the System.Drawing namespace:

```
using System;
using System.Drawing;
```

You test the static constructor with this code:

```
class MainEntryPoint
{
    static void Main(string[] args)
    {
        Console.WriteLine("User-preferences: BackColor is: " +
                         UserPreferences.BackColor.ToString());
    }
}
```

Compiling and running this code results in this output:

```
User-preferences: BackColor is: Color [Red]
```

Of course if the code is executed during the weekend, your color preference would be Green.

Calling Constructors from Other Constructors

You may sometimes find yourself in the situation where you have several constructors in a class, perhaps to accommodate some optional parameters for which the constructors have some code in common. For example, consider this:

```
class Car
{
    private string description;
    private uint nWheels;
    public Car(string description, uint nWheels)
    {
        this.description = description;
        this.nWheels = nWheels;
    }

    public Car(string description)
    {
        this.description = description;
        this.nWheels = 4;
    }
    // etc.
```

Both constructors initialize the same fields. It would clearly be neater to place all the code in one place. C# has a special syntax known as a *constructor initializer* to allow this:

```
class Car
{
    private string description;
    private uint nWheels;

    public Car(string description, uint nWheels)
    {
        this.description = description;
```

```
        this.nWheels = nWheels;
    }

    public Car(string description): this(description, 4)
    {
    }
    // etc
```

In this context, the `this` keyword simply causes the constructor with the nearest matching parameters to be called. Note that any constructor initializer is executed before the body of the constructor. Say that the following code is run:

```
Car myCar = new Car("Proton Persona");
```

In this example, the two-parameter constructor executes before any code in the body of the one-parameter constructor (though in this particular case, because there is no code in the body of the one-parameter constructor, it makes no difference).

A C# constructor initializer may contain either one call to another constructor in the same class (using the syntax just presented) or one call to a constructor in the immediate base class (using the same syntax, but using the keyword `base` instead of `this`). It is not possible to put more than one call in the initializer.

readonly Fields

The concept of a constant as a variable that contains a value that cannot be changed is something that C# shares with most programming languages. However, constants don't necessarily meet all requirements. On occasion, you may have some variable whose value shouldn't be changed, but where the value is not known until runtime. C# provides another type of variable that is useful in this scenario: the `readonly` field.

The `readonly` keyword gives a bit more flexibility than `const`, allowing for situations in which you might want a field to be constant but also need to carry out some calculations to determine its initial value. The rule is that you can assign values to a `readonly` field inside a constructor, but not anywhere else. It's also possible for a `readonly` field to be an instance rather than a static field, having a different value for each instance of a class. This means that, unlike a `const` field, if you want a `readonly` field to be static, you have to declare it as such.

Suppose that you have an MDI program that edits documents, and, for licensing reasons, you want to restrict the number of documents that can be opened simultaneously. Now assume that you are selling different versions of the software, and it's possible that customers can upgrade their licenses to open more documents simultaneously. Clearly, this means you can't hard-code the maximum number in the source code. You'd probably need a field to represent this maximum number. This field will have to be read in — perhaps from a registry key or some other file storage — each time the program is launched. So your code might look something like this:

```
public class DocumentEditor
{
    public static readonly uint MaxDocuments;

    static DocumentEditor()
    {
        MaxDocuments = DoSomethingToFindOutMaxNumber();
    }
}
```

In this case, the field is static, because the maximum number of documents needs to be stored only once per running instance of the program. This is why it is initialized in the static constructor. If you had an instance `readonly` field, you would initialize it in the instance constructor(s). For example, presumably each document you edit has a creation date, which you wouldn't want to allow the user to change (because that would be rewriting the past!). Note that the field is also public — you don't normally need to make `readonly` fields private, because by definition they cannot be modified externally (the same principle also applies to constants).

As noted earlier, date is represented by the class System.DateTime. The following code uses a System. DateTime constructor that takes three parameters (the year, month, and day of the month — you can find details of this and other DateTime constructors in the MSDN documentation):

```
public class Document
{
    public readonly DateTime CreationDate;

    public Document()
    {
        // Read in creation date from file. Assume result is 1 Jan 2002
        // but in general this can be different for different instances
        // of the class
        CreationDate = new DateTime(2002, 1, 1);
    }
}
```

CreationDate and MaxDocuments in the previous code snippet are treated like any other field, except that because they are read-only, they cannot be assigned outside the constructors:

```
void SomeMethod()
{
    MaxDocuments = 10;    // compilation error here. MaxDocuments is readonly
}
```

It's also worth noting that you don't have to assign a value to a readonly field in a constructor. If you don't do so, it will be left with the default value for its particular data type or whatever value you initialized it to at its declaration. That applies to both static and instance readonly fields.

ANONYMOUS TYPES

Chapter 2, "Core C#" discussed the var keyword in reference to implicitly typed variables. When used with the new keyword, anonymous types can be created. An anonymous type is simply a nameless class that inherits from object. The definition of the class is inferred from the initializer, just as with implicitly typed variables.

If you need an object that contains a person's first, middle, and last name, the declaration would look like this:

```
var captain = new {FirstName = "James", MiddleName = "T", LastName = "Kirk"};
```

This would produce an object with FirstName, MiddleName, and LastName properties. If you were to create another object that looked like this:

```
var doctor = new {FirstName = "Leonard", MiddleName = "", LastName = "McCoy"};
```

the types of captain and doctor are the same. You could set captain = doctor, for example.

If the values that are being set come from another object, then the initializer can be abbreviated. If you already have a class that contains the properties FirstName, MiddleName, and LastName and you have an instance of that class with the instance name person, then the captain object could be initialized like this:

```
var captain = new {person.FirstName, person.MiddleName, person.LastName};
```

The property names from the person object would be projected to the new object named captain. So the object named captain would have the FirstName, MiddleName, and LastName properties.

The actual type name of these new objects is unknown. The compiler "makes up" a name for the type, but only the compiler will ever be able to make use of it. So you can't and shouldn't plan on using any type reflection on the new objects because you will not get consistent results.

STRUCTS

So far, you have seen how classes offer a great way of encapsulating objects in your program. You have also seen how they are stored on the heap in a way that gives you much more flexibility in data lifetime, but with a slight cost in performance. This performance cost is small thanks to the optimizations of managed heaps. However, in some situations all you really need is a small data structure. In this case, a class provides more functionality than you need, and for performance reasons you will probably prefer to use a struct. Look at this example:

```
class Dimensions
{
    public double Length;
    public double Width;
}
```

This code defines a class called `Dimensions`, which simply stores the length and width of an item. Perhaps you're writing a furniture-arranging program to let people experiment with rearranging their furniture on the computer, and you want to store the dimensions of each item of furniture. It looks as though you're breaking the rules of good program design by making the fields public, but the point is that you don't really need all the facilities of a class for this. All you have is two numbers, which you'll find convenient to treat as a pair rather than individually. There is no need for a lot of methods, or for you to be able to inherit from the class, and you certainly don't want to have the .NET runtime go to the trouble of bringing in the heap with all the performance implications, just to store two `doubles`.

As mentioned earlier in this chapter, the only thing you need to change in the code to define a type as a struct instead of a class is to replace the keyword `class` with `struct`:

```
struct Dimensions
{
    public double Length;
    public double Width;
}
```

Defining functions for structs is also exactly the same as defining them for classes. The following code demonstrates a constructor and a property for a struct:

```
struct Dimensions
{
    public double Length;
    public double Width;

    public Dimensions(double length, double width)
    {
        Length=length;
        Width=width;
    }

    public double Diagonal
    {
        get
        {
            return Math.Sqrt(Length*Length + Width*Width);
        }
    }
}
```

Structs are value types, not reference types. This means they are stored either in the stack or inline (if they are part of another object that is stored on the heap) and have the same lifetime restrictions as the simple data types.

➤ Structs do not support inheritance.

➤ There are some differences in the way constructors work for structs. In particular, the compiler always supplies a default no-parameter constructor, which you are not permitted to replace.

➤ With a struct, you can specify how the fields are to be laid out in memory (this is examined in Chapter 14, "Reflection," which covers attributes).

Because structs are really intended to group data items together, you'll sometimes find that most or all of their fields are declared as public. This is, strictly speaking, contrary to the guidelines for writing .NET code — according to Microsoft, fields (other than const fields) should always be private and wrapped by public properties. However, for simple structs, many developers would nevertheless consider public fields to be acceptable programming practice.

The following sections look at some of these differences between structs and classes in more detail.

Structs Are Value Types

Although structs are value types, you can often treat them syntactically in the same way as classes. For example, with the definition of the Dimensions class in the previous section, you could write:

```
Dimensions point = new Dimensions();
point.Length = 3;
point.Width = 6;
```

Note that because structs are value types, the new operator does not work in the same way as it does for classes and other reference types. Instead of allocating memory on the heap, the new operator simply calls the appropriate constructor, according to the parameters passed to it, initializing all fields. Indeed, for structs it is perfectly legal to write:

```
Dimensions point;
point.Length = 3;
point.Width = 6;
```

If Dimensions was a class, this would produce a compilation error, because point would contain an uninitialized reference — an address that points nowhere, so you could not start setting values to its fields. For a struct, however, the variable declaration actually allocates space on the stack for the entire struct, so it's ready to assign values to. Note, however, that the following code would cause a compilation error, with the compiler complaining that you are using an uninitialized variable:

```
Dimensions point;
Double D = point.Length;
```

Structs follow the same rules as any other data type — everything must be initialized before use. A struct is considered fully initialized either when the new operator has been called against it, or when values have been individually assigned to all its fields. And of course, a struct defined as a member field of a class is initialized by being zeroed-out automatically when the containing object is initialized.

The fact that structs are value types will affect performance, though depending on how you use your struct, this can be good or bad. On the positive side, allocating memory for structs is very fast because this takes place inline or on the stack. The same goes for removing structs when they go out of scope. On the negative side, whenever you pass a struct as a parameter or assign a struct to another struct (as in A=B, where A and B are structs), the full contents of the struct are copied, whereas for a class only the reference is copied. This will result in a performance loss that depends on the size of the struct, emphasizing the fact that structs are really intended for small data structures. Note, however, that when passing a struct as a parameter to a method, you can avoid this performance loss by passing it as a ref parameter — in this case, only the address in memory of the struct will be passed in, which is just as fast as passing in a class. If you do this, though, be aware that it means the called method can in principle change the value of the struct.

Structs and Inheritance

Structs are not designed for inheritance. This means that it is not possible to inherit from a struct. The only exception to this is that structs, in common with every other type in C#, derive ultimately from the class System.Object. Hence, structs also have access to the methods of System.Object, and it is even possible to override them in structs — an obvious example would be overriding the ToString() method. The actual inheritance chain for structs is that each struct derives from a class, System.ValueType, which in turn derives from System.Object. ValueType does not add any new members to Object, but provides implementations of some of them that are more suitable for structs. Note that you cannot supply a different base class for a struct: every struct is derived from ValueType.

Constructors for Structs

You can define constructors for structs in exactly the same way that you can for classes, except that you are not permitted to define a constructor that takes no parameters. This may seem nonsensical, and the reason is buried in the implementation of the .NET runtime. Some rare circumstances exist in which the .NET runtime would not be able to call a custom zero-parameter constructor that you have supplied. Microsoft has therefore taken the easy way out and banned zero-parameter constructors for structs in C#.

That said, the default constructor, which initializes all fields to zero values, is always present implicitly, even if you supply other constructors that take parameters. It's also impossible to circumvent the default constructor by supplying initial values for fields. The following code will cause a compile-time error:

```
struct Dimensions
{
    public double Length = 1;      // error. Initial values not allowed
    public double Width = 2;       // error. Initial values not allowed
}
```

Of course, if Dimensions had been declared as a class, this code would have compiled without any problems.

Incidentally, you can supply a Close() or Dispose() method for a struct in the same way you do for a class.

PARTIAL CLASSES

The partial keyword allows the class, struct, method or interface to span across multiple files. Typically, a class will reside entirely in a single file. However, in situations where multiple developers need access to the same class, or more likely in the situation where a code generator of some type is generating part of a class, then having the class in multiple files can be beneficial.

The way that the partial keyword is used is to simply place partial before class, struct, or interface. In the following example, the class TheBigClass resides in two separate source files, BigClassPart1.cs and BigClassPart2.cs:

```
//BigClassPart1.cs
partial class TheBigClass
{
    public void MethodOne()
    {
    }
}

//BigClassPart2.cs
partial class TheBigClass
```

```
    {
        public void MethodTwo()
        {
        }
    }
```

When the project that these two source files are part of is compiled, a single type called `TheBigClass` will be created with two methods, `MethodOne()` and `MethodTwo()`.

If any of the following keywords are used in describing the class, the same must apply to all partials of the same type:

➤ `public`

➤ `private`

➤ `protected`

➤ `internal`

➤ `abstract`

➤ `sealed`

➤ `new`

➤ generic constraints

Nested partials are allowed as long as the `partial` keyword precedes the `class` keyword in the nested type. Attributes, XML comments, interfaces, generic-type parameter attributes, and members will be combined when the partial types are compiled into the type. Given these two source files:

```
//BigClassPart1.cs
[CustomAttribute]
partial class TheBigClass: TheBigBaseClass, IBigClass
{
    public void MethodOne()
    {
    }
}

//BigClassPart2.cs
[AnotherAttribute]
partial class TheBigClass: IOtherBigClass
{
    public void MethodTwo()
    {
    }
}
```

after the compile, the equivalent source file would be:

```
[CustomAttribute]
[AnotherAttribute]
partial class TheBigClass: TheBigBaseClass, IBigClass, IOtherBigClass
{
    public void MethodOne()
    {
    }

    public void MethodTwo()
    {
    }
}
```

STATIC CLASSES

Earlier, this chapter discussed static constructors and how they allowed the initialization of static member variables. If a class contains nothing but static methods and properties, the class itself can become static. A static class is functionally the same as creating a class with a private static constructor. An instance of the class can never be created. By using the `static` keyword, the compiler can help by checking that instance members are never accidentally added to the class. If they are, a compile error happens. This can help guarantee that an instance is never created. The syntax for a static class looks like this:

```
static class StaticUtilities
{
  public static void HelperMethod()
  {
  }
}
```

An object of type `StaticUtilities` is not needed to call the `HelperMethod()`. The type name is used to make the call:

```
StaticUtilities.HelperMethod();
```

THE OBJECT CLASS

As indicated earlier, all .NET classes are ultimately derived from `System.Object`. In fact, if you don't specify a base class when you define a class, the compiler will automatically assume that it derives from `Object`. Because inheritance has not been used in this chapter, every class you have seen here is actually derived from `System.Object`. (As noted earlier, for structs this derivation is indirect — a struct is always derived from `System.ValueType`, which in turn derives from `System.Object`.)

The practical significance of this is that, besides the methods and properties and so on that you define, you also have access to a number of public and protected member methods that have been defined for the `Object` class. These methods are available in all other classes that you define.

System.Object Methods

For the time being, we simply summarize the purpose of each method in the following list, and then, in the next section, we provide more detail about the `ToString()` method in particular.

➤ `ToString()` — A fairly basic, quick-and-easy string representation, use it when you just want a quick idea of the contents of an object, perhaps for debugging purposes. It provides very little choice of how to format the data. For example, dates can, in principle, be expressed in a huge variety of different formats, but `DateTime.ToString()` does not offer you any choice in this regard. If you need a more sophisticated string representation that, for example, takes account of your formatting preferences or of the culture (the locale), then you should implement the `IFormattable` interface (see Chapter 9).

➤ `GetHashCode()` — If objects are placed in a data structure known as a map (also known as a hash table or dictionary), it is used by classes that manipulate these structures to determine where to place an object in the structure. If you intend your class to be used as a key for a dictionary, you will need to override `GetHashCode()`. Some fairly strict requirements exist for how you implement your overload, and you learn about those when you examine dictionaries in Chapter 10, "Collections."

➤ `Equals()` (both versions) and `ReferenceEquals()` — As you'll gather by the existence of three different methods aimed at comparing the equality of objects, the .NET Framework has quite a sophisticated scheme for measuring equality. Subtle differences exist between how these three methods, along with the comparison operator, ==, are intended to be used. Not only that, but restrictions also exist on how you should override the virtual, one-parameter version of `Equals()` if you choose to do so, because certain base classes in the `System.Collections` namespace call the method and expect it to behave in certain ways. You explore the use of these methods in Chapter 7 when you examine operators.

➤ `Finalize()` — Covered in Chapter 13, this method is intended as the nearest that C# has to C++ style destructors and is called when a reference object is garbage collected to clean up resources. The `Object` implementation of `Finalize()` actually does nothing and is ignored by the garbage collector. You will normally override `Finalize()` if an object owns references to unmanaged resources that need to be removed when the object is deleted. The garbage collector cannot do this directly because it only knows about managed resources, so it relies on any finalizers that you supply.

➤ `GetType()` — Returns an instance of a class derived from `System.Type` so this object can provide an extensive range of information about the class of which your object is a member, including base type, methods, properties, and so on. `System.Type` also provides the entry point into .NET's reflection technology. Chapter 14 examines this topic.

➤ `MemberwiseClone()` — The only member of `System.Object` that isn't examined in detail anywhere in the book. There is no need to because it is fairly simple in concept. It simply makes a copy of the object and returns a reference (or in the case of a value type, a boxed reference) to the copy. Note that the copy made is a shallow copy — this means that it copies all the value types in the class. If the class contains any embedded references, then only the references will be copied, not the objects referred to. This method is protected and cannot be called to copy external objects. It is also not virtual, so you cannot override its implementation.

The ToString() Method

You've already encountered `ToString()` in Chapter 2. It provides the most convenient way to get a quick string representation of an object.

For example:

```
int i = 50;
string str = i.ToString();  // returns "-50"
```

Here's another example:

```
enum Colors {Red, Orange, Yellow};
// later on in code...
Colors favoriteColor = Colors.Orange;
string str = favoriteColor.ToString();    // returns "Orange"
```

`Object.ToString()` is actually declared as virtual, and all these examples are taking advantage of the fact that its implementation in the C# predefined data types has been overridden for us to return correct string representations of those types. You might not think that the `Colors` enum counts as a predefined data type. It actually gets implemented as a struct derived from `System.Enum`, and `System.Enum` has a rather clever override of `ToString()` that deals with all the enums you define.

If you don't override `ToString()` in classes that you define, your classes will simply inherit the `System.Object` implementation — which displays the name of the class. If you want `ToString()` to return a string that contains information about the value of objects of your class, you will need to override it. To illustrate this, the following example, `Money`, defines a very simple class, also called `Money`, which represents U.S. currency amounts. `Money` simply acts as a wrapper for the decimal class but supplies a `ToString()` method. Note that this method must be declared as `override` because it is replacing (overriding) the `ToString()` method supplied by `Object`. Chapter 4 discusses overriding in more detail. The complete code for this example is as follows (note that it also illustrates use of properties to wrap fields):

```
using System;

namespace Wrox
{
    class MainEntryPoint
```

```
        {
            static void Main(string[] args)
            {
                Money cash1 = new Money();
                cash1.Amount = 40M;
                Console.WriteLine("cash1.ToString() returns: " + cash1.ToString());
                Console.ReadLine();
            }
        }
        public class Money
        {
            private decimal amount;

            public decimal Amount
            {
                get
                {
                    return amount;
                }
                set
                {
                    amount = value;
                }
            }
            public override string ToString()
            {
                return "$" + Amount.ToString();
            }
        }

    }
```

This example is here just to illustrate syntactical features of C#. C# already has a predefined type to represent currency amounts, `decimal`, so in real life, you wouldn't write a class to duplicate this functionality unless you wanted to add various other methods to it. And in many cases, due to formatting requirements, you'd probably use the `String.Format()` method (which is covered in Chapter 8) rather than `ToString()` to display a currency string.

In the `Main()` method, you first instantiate a `Money` object. The `ToString()` method is then called, which actually executes the override version of the method. Running this code gives the following results:

```
cash1.ToString() returns: $40
```

EXTENSION METHODS

There are many ways to extend a class. If you have the source for the class, then inheritance, which is covered in Chapter 4, is a great way to add functionality to your objects. What if the source code isn't available? Extension methods can help by allowing you to change a class without requiring the source code for the class.

Extension methods are static methods that can appear to be part of a class without actually being in the source code for the class. Let's say that the `Money` class from the previous example needs to have a method `AddToAmount(decimal amountToAdd)`. However, for whatever reason the original source for the assembly cannot be changed directly. All that you have to do is create a static class and add the `AddToAmount` method as a static method. Here is what the code would look like:

```
namespace Wrox
{
    public static class MoneyExtension
    {
        public static void AddToAmount(this Money money, decimal amountToAdd)
```

```
        {
          money.Amount += amountToAdd;
        }
      }
    }
```

Notice the parameters for the `AddToAmount` method. For an extension method, the first parameter is the type that is being extended preceded by the `this` keyword. This is what tells the compiler that this method is part of the `Money` type. In this example, `Money` is the type that is being extended. In the extension method you have access to all the public methods and properties of the type being extended.

In the main program, the `AddToAmount` method appears just as another method. The first parameter doesn't appear, and you do not have to do anything with it. To use the new method, you make the call just like any other method:

```
cash1.AddToAmount(10M);
```

Even though the extension method is static, you use standard instance method syntax. Notice that we called `AddToAmount` using the `cash1` instance variable and not using the type name.

If the extension method has the same name as a method in the class, the extension method will never be called. Any instance methods already in the class take precedence.

SUMMARY

This chapter examined C# syntax for declaring and manipulating objects. You have seen how to declare static and instance fields, properties, methods, and constructors. You have also seen that C# adds some new features not present in the OOP model of some other languages — for example, static constructors provide a means of initializing static fields, whereas structs allow you to define types that do not require the use of the managed heap, which could lead to performance gains. You have also seen how all types in C# derive ultimately from the type `System.Object`, which means that all types start with a basic set of useful methods, including `ToString()`.

We mentioned inheritance a few times throughout this chapter. We examine implementation and interface inheritance in C# in Chapter 4.

Inheritance

WHAT'S IN THIS CHAPTER?

➤ Types of inheritance
➤ Implementing inheritance
➤ Access modifiers
➤ Interfaces

Chapter 3, "Objects and Types," examined how to use individual classes in C#. The focus in that chapter was how to define methods, properties, constructors, and other members of a single class (or a single struct). Although you learned that all classes are ultimately derived from the class System.Object, you did not learn how to create a hierarchy of inherited classes. Inheritance is the subject of this chapter. In this chapter, you see how C# and the .NET Framework handle inheritance.

TYPES OF INHERITANCE

Let's start by reviewing exactly what C# does and does not support as far as inheritance is concerned.

Implementation Versus Interface Inheritance

In object-oriented programming, there are two distinct types of inheritance — implementation inheritance and interface inheritance:

➤ **Implementation inheritance** means that a type derives from a base type, taking all the base type's member fields and functions. With implementation inheritance, a derived type adopts the base type's implementation of each function, unless it is indicated in the definition of the derived type that a function implementation is to be overridden. This type of inheritance is most useful when you need to add functionality to an existing type, or when a number of related types share a significant amount of common functionality.

➤ **Interface inheritance** means that a type inherits only the signatures of the functions and does not inherit any implementations. This type of inheritance is most useful when you want to specify that a type makes certain features available.

C# supports both implementation and interface inheritance. Both are baked into the framework and the language from the ground up, thereby allowing you to decide which to use based on the architecture of the application.

Multiple Inheritance

Some languages such as C++ support what is known as *multiple inheritance,* in which a class derives from more than one other class. The benefits of using multiple inheritance are debatable: On one hand, there is no doubt that it is possible to use multiple inheritance to write extremely sophisticated, yet compact, code, as demonstrated by the C++ ATL library. On the other hand, code that uses multiple implementation inheritance is often difficult to understand and debug (a point that is equally well-demonstrated by the C++ ATL library). As mentioned, making it easy to write robust code was one of the crucial design goals behind the development of C#. Accordingly, C# does not support multiple implementation inheritance. It does, however, allow types to be derived from multiple interfaces — multiple interface inheritance. This means that a C# class can be derived from one other class, and any number of interfaces. Indeed, we can be more precise: Thanks to the presence of `System.Object` as a common base type, every C# class (except for `Object`) has exactly one base class, and may additionally have any number of base interfaces.

Structs and Classes

Chapter 3 distinguishes between structs (value types) and classes (reference types). One restriction of using a struct is that structs do not support inheritance, beyond the fact that every struct is automatically derived from `System.ValueType`. In fact, we should be more careful. It's true that it is not possible to code a type hierarchy of structs; however, it is possible for structs to implement interfaces. In other words, structs don't really support implementation inheritance, but they do support interface inheritance. We can summarize the situation for any types that you define as follows:

➤ **Structs** are always derived from `System.ValueType`. They can also be derived from any number of interfaces.

➤ **Classes** are always derived from one other class of your choosing. They can also be derived from any number of interfaces.

IMPLEMENTATION INHERITANCE

If you want to declare that a class derives from another class, use the following syntax:

```
class MyDerivedClass: MyBaseClass
{
    // functions and data members here
}
```

This syntax is very similar to C++ and Java syntax. However, C++ programmers, who will be used to the concepts of public and private inheritance, should note that C# does not support private inheritance, hence the absence of a public or private qualifier on the base class name. Supporting private inheritance would have complicated the language for very little gain. In practice, private inheritance is used extremely rarely in C++ anyway.

If a class (or a struct) also derives from interfaces, the list of base class and interfaces is separated by commas:

```
public class MyDerivedClass: MyBaseClass, IInterface1, IInterface2
{
        // etc.
}
```

For a struct, the syntax is as follows:

```
public struct MyDerivedStruct: IInterface1, IInterface2
{
        // etc.
}
```

If you do not specify a base class in a class definition, the C# compiler will assume that `System.Object` is the base class. Hence, the following two pieces of code yield the same result:

```csharp
class MyClass: Object  // derives from System.Object
{
    // etc.
}
```

and

```csharp
class MyClass    // derives from System.Object
{
    // etc.
}
```

For the sake of simplicity, the second form is more common.

Because C# supports the `object` keyword, which serves as a pseudonym for the `System.Object` class, you can also write:

```csharp
class MyClass: object   // derives from System.Object
{
    // etc.
}
```

If you want to reference the `Object` class, use the `object` keyword, which is recognized by intelligent editors such as Visual Studio .NET and thus facilitates editing your code.

Virtual Methods

By declaring a base class function as `virtual`, you allow the function to be overridden in any derived classes:

```csharp
class MyBaseClass
{
    public virtual string VirtualMethod()
    {
        return "This method is virtual and defined in MyBaseClass";
    }
}
```

It is also permitted to declare a property as `virtual`. For a virtual or overridden property, the syntax is the same as for a nonvirtual property, with the exception of the keyword `virtual`, which is added to the definition. The syntax looks like this:

```csharp
public virtual string ForeName
{
    get { return foreName;}
    set { foreName = value;}
}
private string foreName;
```

For simplicity, the following discussion focuses mainly on methods, but it applies equally well to properties.

The concepts behind virtual functions in C# are identical to standard OOP concepts. You can override a virtual function in a derived class, and when the method is called, the appropriate method for the type of object is invoked. In C#, functions are not virtual by default but (aside from constructors) can be explicitly declared as `virtual`. This follows the C++ methodology: For performance reasons, functions are not virtual unless indicated. In Java, by contrast, all functions are virtual. C# does differ from C++ syntax, though, because it requires you to declare when a derived class's function overrides another function, using the `override` keyword:

```csharp
class MyDerivedClass: MyBaseClass
{
    public override string VirtualMethod()
```

```
    {
        return "This method is an override defined in MyDerivedClass.";
    }
}
```

This syntax for method overriding removes potential runtime bugs that can easily occur in C++, when a method signature in a derived class unintentionally differs slightly from the base version, resulting in the method failing to override the base version. In C#, this is picked up as a compile-time error because the compiler would see a function marked as override but no base method for it to override.

Neither member fields nor static functions can be declared as virtual. The concept simply wouldn't make sense for any class member other than an instance function member.

Hiding Methods

If a method with the same signature is declared in both base and derived classes, but the methods are not declared as virtual and override, respectively, then the derived class version is said to *hide* the base class version.

In most cases, you would want to override methods rather than hide them. By hiding them you risk calling the wrong method for a given class instance. However, as shown in the following example, C# syntax is designed to ensure that the developer is warned at compile time about this potential problem, thus making it safer to hide methods if that is your intention. This also has versioning benefits for developers of class libraries.

Suppose that you have a class called HisBaseClass:

```
class HisBaseClass
{
    // various members
}
```

At some point in the future, you write a derived class that adds some functionality to HisBaseClass. In particular, you add a method called MyGroovyMethod(), which is not present in the base class:

```
class MyDerivedClass: HisBaseClass
{
    public int MyGroovyMethod()
    {
        // some groovy implementation
        return 0;
    }
}
```

One year later, you decide to extend the functionality of the base class. By coincidence, you add a method that is also called MyGroovyMethod() and that has the same name and signature as yours, but probably doesn't do the same thing. When you compile your code using the new version of the base class, you have a potential clash because your program won't know which method to call. It's all perfectly legal in C#, but because your MyGroovyMethod() is not intended to be related in any way to the base class MyGroovyMethod(), the result is that running this code does not yield the result you want. Fortunately, C# has been designed to cope very well with these types of conflicts.

In these situations, C# generates a compilation warning that reminds you to use the new keyword to declare that you intend to hide a method, like this:

```
class MyDerivedClass: HisBaseClass
{
    public new int MyGroovyMethod()
    {
        // some groovy implementation
        return 0;
    }
}
```

However, because your version of `MyGroovyMethod()` is not declared as `new`, the compiler picks up on the fact that it's hiding a base class method without being instructed to do so and will generate a warning (this applies whether or not you declared `MyGroovyMethod()` as `virtual`). If you want, you can rename your version of the method. This is the recommended course of action because it eliminates future confusion. However, if you decide not to rename your method for whatever reason (for example, if you've published your software as a library for other companies, so you can't change the names of methods), all your existing client code will still run correctly, picking up your version of `MyGroovyMethod()`. This is because any existing code that accesses this method must be done through a reference to `MyDerivedClass` (or a further derived class).

Your existing code cannot access this method through a reference to `HisBaseClass`; it would generate a compilation error when compiled against the earlier version of `HisBaseClass`. The problem can only happen in client code you have yet to write. C# arranges things so that you get a warning that a potential problem might occur in future code — you will need to pay attention to this warning and take care not to attempt to call your version of `MyGroovyMethod()` through any reference to `HisBaseClass` in any future code you add. However, all your existing code will still work fine. It may be a subtle point, but it's quite an impressive example of how C# is able to cope with different versions of classes.

Calling Base Versions of Functions

C# has a special syntax for calling base versions of a method from a derived class: `base.<MethodName>()`. For example, if you want a method in a derived class to return 90 percent of the value returned by the base class method, you can use the following syntax:

```
class CustomerAccount
{
    public virtual decimal CalculatePrice()
    {
        // implementation
        return 0.0M;
    }
}
class GoldAccount: CustomerAccount
{
    public override decimal CalculatePrice()
    {
        return base.CalculatePrice() * 0.9M;
    }
}
```

Note that you can use the `base.<MethodName>()` syntax to call any method in the base class — you don't have to call it from inside an override of the same method.

Abstract Classes and Functions

C# allows both classes and functions to be declared as abstract. An abstract class cannot be instantiated, whereas an abstract function does not have an implementation, and must be overridden in any non-abstract derived class. Obviously, an abstract function is automatically virtual (although you don't need to supply the `virtual` keyword; doing so results in a syntax error). If any class contains any abstract functions, that class is also abstract and must be declared as such:

```
abstract class Building
{
    public abstract decimal CalculateHeatingCost();    // abstract method
}
```

 C++ developers should also note the slightly different terminology. In C++, abstract functions are often described as pure virtual; in the C# world, the only correct term to use is abstract.

Sealed Classes and Methods

C# allows classes and methods to be declared as `sealed`. In the case of a class, this means that you can't inherit from that class. In the case of a method, this means that you can't override that method.

```
sealed class FinalClass
{
    // etc
}
class DerivedClass: FinalClass        // wrong. Will give compilation error
{
    // etc
}
```

The most likely situation in which you'll mark a class or method as `sealed` is if the class or method is internal to the operation of the library, class, or other classes that you are writing, so that you ensure that any attempt to override some of its functionality will lead to instability in the code. You might also mark a class or method as `sealed` for commercial reasons, in order to prevent a third party from extending your classes in a manner that is contrary to the licensing agreements. In general, however, you should be careful about marking a class or member as `sealed` because by doing so you are severely restricting how it can be used. Even if you don't think it would be useful to inherit from a class or override a particular member of it, it's still possible that at some point in the future someone will encounter a situation you hadn't anticipated in which it is useful to do so. The .NET base class library frequently uses sealed classes to make these classes inaccessible to third-party developers who might want to derive their own classes from them. For example, `string` is a sealed class.

Declaring a method as `sealed` serves a similar purpose as for a class:

```
class MyClass: MyClassBase
{
    public sealed override void FinalMethod()
    {
        // etc.
    }
}
class DerivedClass: MyClass
{
    public override void FinalMethod()        // wrong. Will give compilation error
    {
    }
}
```

In order to use the `sealed` keyword on a method or property, it must have first been overridden from a base class. If you do not want a method or property in a base class overridden, then don't mark it as virtual.

Constructors of Derived Classes

Chapter 3 discusses how constructors can be applied to individual classes. An interesting question arises as to what happens when you start defining your own constructors for classes that are part of a hierarchy, inherited from other classes that may also have custom constructors.

Assume that you have not defined any explicit constructors for any of your classes. This means that the compiler supplies default zeroing-out constructors for all your classes. There is actually quite a lot going on under the hood when that happens, but the compiler is able to arrange it so that things work out nicely throughout the class hierarchy and every field in every class gets initialized to whatever its default value is. When you add a constructor of your own, however, you are effectively taking control of construction. This has implications right down through the hierarchy of derived classes, and you have to make sure that you don't inadvertently do anything to prevent construction through the hierarchy from taking place smoothly.

You might be wondering why there is any special problem with derived classes. The reason is that when you create an instance of a derived class, there is actually more than one constructor at work. The constructor of the class you instantiate isn't by itself sufficient to initialize the class — the constructors of the base classes must also be called. That's why we've been talking about construction through the hierarchy.

To see why base class constructors must be called, you're going to develop an example based on a cell phone company called MortimerPhones. The example contains an abstract base class, `GenericCustomer`, which represents any customer. There is also a (non-abstract) class, `Nevermore60Customer`, which represents any customer on a particular rate called the `Nevermore60` rate. All customers have a name, represented by a private field. Under the `Nevermore60` rate, the first few minutes of the customer's call time are charged at a higher rate, necessitating the need for the field `highCostMinutesUsed`, which details how many of these higher-cost minutes each customer has used up. The class definitions look like this:

Available for download on Wrox.com

```
abstract class GenericCustomer
{
    private string name;
    // lots of other methods etc.
}
class Nevermore60Customer: GenericCustomer
{
    private uint highCostMinutesUsed;
    // other methods etc.
}
```

code snippet MortimerPhones.cs

We won't worry about what other methods might be implemented in these classes, because we are concentrating solely on the construction process here. And if you download the sample code for this chapter, you'll find that the class definitions include only the constructors.

Take a look at what happens when you use the new operator to instantiate a `Nevermore60Customer`:

```
GenericCustomer customer = new Nevermore60Customer();
```

Clearly, both of the member fields `name` and `highCostMinutesUsed` must be initialized when `customer` is instantiated. If you don't supply constructors of your own, but rely simply on the default constructors, then you'd expect `name` to be initialized to the `null` reference, and `highCostMinutesUsed` initialized to zero. Let's look in a bit more detail at how this actually happens.

The `highCostMinutesUsed` field presents no problem: the default `Nevermore60Customer` constructor supplied by the compiler will initialize this field to zero.

What about `name`? Looking at the class definitions, it's clear that the `Nevermore60Customer` constructor can't initialize this value. This field is declared as private, which means that derived classes don't have access to it. So, the default `Nevermore60Customer` constructor simply won't know that this field exists. The only code items that have that knowledge are other members of `GenericCustomer`. This means that if `name` is going to be initialized, that'll have to be done by some constructor in `GenericCustomer`. No matter how big your class hierarchy is, this same reasoning applies right down to the ultimate base class, `System.Object`.

Now that you have an understanding of the issues involved, you can look at what actually happens whenever a derived class is instantiated. Assuming that default constructors are used throughout, the compiler first grabs the constructor of the class it is trying to instantiate, in this case `Nevermore60Customer`. The first thing that the default `Nevermore60Customer` constructor does is attempt to run the default constructor for the immediate base class, `GenericCustomer`. The `GenericCustomer` constructor attempts to run the constructor for its immediate base class, `System.Object`. `System.Object` doesn't have any base classes, so its constructor just executes and returns control to the `GenericCustomer` constructor. That constructor now executes, initializing `name` to `null`, before returning control to the `Nevermore60Customer` constructor. That constructor in turn executes, initializing `highCostMinutesUsed` to zero, and exits. At this point, the `Nevermore60Customer` instance has been successfully constructed and initialized.

The net result of all this is that the constructors are called in order of System.Object first, and then progress down the hierarchy until the compiler reaches the class being instantiated. Notice also that in this process, each constructor handles initialization of the fields in its own class. That's how it should normally work, and when you start adding your own constructors you should try to stick to that principle.

Notice the order in which this happens. It's always the base class constructors that get called first. This means that there are no problems with a constructor for a derived class invoking any base class methods, properties, and any other members that it has access to, because it can be confident that the base class has already been constructed and its fields initialized. It also means that if the derived class doesn't like the way that the base class has been initialized, it can change the initial values of the data, provided that it has access to do so. However, good programming practice almost invariably means you'll try to prevent that situation from occurring if you can, and you will trust the base class constructor to deal with its own fields.

Now that you know how the process of construction works, you can start fiddling with it by adding your own constructors.

Adding a Constructor in a Hierarchy

We'll take the easiest case first and see what happens if you simply replace the default constructor somewhere in the hierarchy with another constructor that takes no parameters. Suppose that you decide that you want everyone's name to be initially set to the string "<no name>" instead of to the null reference. You'd modify the code in GenericCustomer like this:

```
public abstract class GenericCustomer
{
    private string name;
    public GenericCustomer()
     : base()  // We could omit this line without affecting the compiled code.
    {
        name = "<no name>";
    }
}
```

Adding this code will work fine. Nevermore60Customer still has its default constructor, so the sequence of events described earlier will proceed as before, except that the compiler will use the custom GenericCustomer constructor instead of generating a default one, so the name field will always be initialized to "<no name>" as required.

Notice that in your constructor you've added a call to the base class constructor before the GenericCustomer constructor is executed, using a syntax similar to that used earlier when we discussed how to get different overloads of constructors to call each other. The only difference is that this time you use the base keyword instead of this to indicate that it's a constructor to the base class rather than a constructor to the current class you want to call. There are no parameters in the brackets after the base keyword — that's important because it means you are not passing any parameters to the base constructor, so the compiler will have to look for a parameterless constructor to call. The result of all this is that the compiler will inject code to call the System.Object constructor, just as would happen by default anyway.

In fact, you can omit that line of code and write the following (as was done for most of the constructors so far in this chapter):

```
public GenericCustomer()
{
    name = "<no name>";
}
```

If the compiler doesn't see any reference to another constructor before the opening curly brace, it assumes that you intended to call the base class constructor; this fits in with the way that default constructors work.

The base and this keywords are the only keywords allowed in the line that calls another constructor. Anything else causes a compilation error. Also note that only one other constructor can be specified.

So far, this code works fine. One way to mess up the progression through the hierarchy of constructors, however, is to declare a constructor as `private`:

```
private GenericCustomer()
{
    name = "<no name>";
}
```

If you try this, you'll find you get an interesting compilation error, which could really throw you if you don't understand how construction down a hierarchy works:

```
'Wrox.ProCSharp.GenericCustomer.GenericCustomer()' is inaccessible due to its protection level
```

The interesting thing is that the error occurs not in the `GenericCustomer` class, but in the derived class, `Nevermore60Customer`. What's happened is that the compiler has tried to generate a default constructor for `Nevermore60Customer` but has not been able to because the default constructor is supposed to invoke the no-parameter `GenericCustomer` constructor. By declaring that constructor as `private`, you've made it inaccessible to the derived class. A similar error occurs if you supply a constructor to `GenericCustomer`, which takes parameters, but at the same time you fail to supply a no-parameter constructor. In this case, the compiler will not generate a default constructor for `GenericCustomer`, so when it tries to generate the default constructors for any derived class, it will again find that it can't because a no-parameter base class constructor is not available. A workaround would be to add your own constructors to the derived classes — even if you don't actually need to do anything in these constructors — so that the compiler doesn't try to generate any default constructors for them.

Now that you have all the theoretical background you need, you're ready to move on to an example of how you can neatly add constructors to a hierarchy of classes. In the next section, you start adding constructors that take parameters to the MortimerPhones example.

Adding Constructors with Parameters to a Hierarchy

You're going to start with a one-parameter constructor for `GenericCustomer`, which specifies that customers can be instantiated only when they supply their names:

```
abstract class GenericCustomer
{
    private string name;
    public GenericCustomer(string name)
    {
        this.name = name;
    }
```

So far, so good. However, as mentioned previously, this will cause a compilation error when the compiler tries to create a default constructor for any derived classes because the default compiler-generated constructors for `Nevermore60Customer` will try to call a no-parameter `GenericCustomer` constructor, and `GenericCustomer` does not possess such a constructor. Therefore, you'll need to supply your own constructors to the derived classes to avoid a compilation error:

```
class Nevermore60Customer: GenericCustomer
{
    private uint highCostMinutesUsed;
    public Nevermore60Customer(string name)
      :   base(name)
    {
    }
```

Now instantiation of `Nevermore60Customer` objects can occur only when a string containing the customer's name is supplied, which is what you want anyway. The interesting thing is what the `Nevermore60Customer` constructor does with this string. Remember that it can't initialize the `name` field itself because it has no access to private fields in its base class. Instead, it passes the name through to the base class for the `GenericCustomer` constructor to handle. It does this by specifying that the base class constructor to be executed first is the one that takes the name as a parameter. Other than that, it doesn't take any action of its own.

Next, you investigate what happens if you have different overloads of the constructor as well as a class hierarchy to deal with. To this end, assume that Nevermore60 customers may have been referred to MortimerPhones by a friend as part of one of those sign-up-a-friend-and-get-a-discount offers. This means that when you construct a `Nevermore60Customer`, you may need to pass in the referrer's name as well. In real life, the constructor would have to do something complicated with the name, such as process the discount, but here you'll just store the referrer's name in another field.

The `Nevermore60Customer` definition will now look like this:

```
class Nevermore60Customer: GenericCustomer
{
    public Nevermore60Customer(string name, string referrerName)
      : base(name)
    {
        this.referrerName = referrerName;
    }

    private string referrerName;
    private uint highCostMinutesUsed;
```

The constructor takes the name and passes it to the `GenericCustomer` constructor for processing. `referrerName` is the variable that is your responsibility here, so the constructor deals with that parameter in its main body.

However, not all `Nevermore60Customers` will have a referrer, so you still need a constructor that doesn't require this parameter (or a constructor that gives you a default value for it). In fact, you will specify that if there is no referrer, then the `referrerName` field should be set to `"<None>"`, using the following one-parameter constructor:

```
public Nevermore60Customer(string name)
  : this(name, "<None>")
{
}
```

You now have all your constructors set up correctly. It's instructive to examine the chain of events that now occurs when you execute a line like this:

```
GenericCustomer customer=new Nevermore60Customer("Arabel Jones");
```

The compiler sees that it needs a one-parameter constructor that takes one string, so the constructor it will identify is the last one that you've defined:

```
public Nevermore60Customer(string Name)
  : this(Name, "<None>")
```

When you instantiate `customer`, this constructor will be called. It immediately transfers control to the corresponding `Nevermore60Customer` two-parameter constructor, passing it the values `"ArabelJones"`, and `"<None>"`. Looking at the code for this constructor, you see that it in turn immediately passes control to the one-parameter `GenericCustomer` constructor, giving it the string `"ArabelJones"`, and in turn that constructor passes control to the `System.Object` default constructor. Only now do the constructors execute. First, the `System.Object` constructor executes. Next comes the `GenericCustomer` constructor, which initializes the name field. Then the `Nevermore60Customer` two-parameter constructor gets control back and sorts out initializing the `referrerName` to `"<None>"`. Finally, the `Nevermore60Customer` one-parameter constructor gets to execute; this constructor doesn't do anything else.

As you can see, this is a very neat and well-designed process. Each constructor handles initialization of the variables that are obviously its responsibility, and, in the process, your class is correctly instantiated and prepared for use. If you follow the same principles when you write your own constructors for your classes, you should find that even the most complex classes get initialized smoothly and without any problems.

MODIFIERS

You have already encountered quite a number of so-called modifiers — keywords that can be applied to a type or to a member. Modifiers can indicate the visibility of a method, such as `public` or `private`, or the nature of an item, such as whether a method is `virtual` or `abstract`. C# has a number of modifiers, and at this point it's worth taking a minute to provide the complete list.

Visibility Modifiers

Visibility modifiers indicate which other code items can view an item.

MODIFIER	APPLIES TO	DESCRIPTION
`public`	Any types or members	The item is visible to any other code.
`protected`	Any member of a type, also any nested type	The item is visible only to any derived type.
`internal`	Any member of a type, also any nested type	The item is visible only within its containing assembly.
`private`	Any types or members	The item is visible only inside the type to which it belongs.
`protected internal`	Any member of a type, also any nested type	The item is visible to any code within its containing assembly and also to any code inside a derived type.

Note that type definitions can be internal or public, depending on whether you want the type to be visible outside its containing assembly.

```
public class MyClass
{
   // etc.
```

You cannot define types as protected, private, or protected internal because these visibility levels would be meaningless for a type contained in a namespace. Hence, these visibilities can be applied only to members. However, you can define nested types (that is, types contained within other types) with these visibilities because in this case the type also has the status of a member. Hence, the following code is correct:

```
public class OuterClass
{
   protected class InnerClass
   {
         // etc.
   }
   // etc.
}
```

If you have a nested type, the inner type is always able to see all members of the outer type. Therefore, with the preceding code, any code inside `InnerClass` always has access to all members of `OuterClass`, even where those members are private.

Other Modifiers

The modifiers in the following table can be applied to members of types and have various uses. A few of these modifiers also make sense when applied to types.

MODIFIER	APPLIES TO	DESCRIPTION
new	Function members	The member hides an inherited member with the same signature.
static	All members	The member does not operate on a specific instance of the class.
virtual	Function members only	The member can be overridden by a derived class.
abstract	Function members only	A virtual member that defines the signature of the member, but doesn't provide an implementation.
override	Function members only	The member overrides an inherited virtual or abstract member.
sealed	Classes, methods, and properties	For classes, the class cannot be inherited from. For properties and methods, the member overrides an inherited virtual member, but cannot be overridden by any members in any derived classes. Must be used in conjunction with override.
extern	Static [DllImport] methods only	The member is implemented externally, in a different language.

INTERFACES

As mentioned earlier, by deriving from an interface, a class is declaring that it implements certain functions. Because not all object-oriented languages support interfaces, this section examines C#'s implementation of interfaces in detail.

This section illustrates interfaces by presenting the complete definition of one of the interfaces that has been predefined by Microsoft — System.IDisposable. IDisposable contains one method, Dispose(), which is intended to be implemented by classes to clean up code:

```
public interface IDisposable
{
    void Dispose();
}
```

This code shows that declaring an interface works syntactically in pretty much the same way as declaring an abstract class. You should be aware, however, that it is not permitted to supply implementations of any of the members of an interface. In general, an interface can only contain declarations of methods, properties, indexers, and events.

You can never instantiate an interface; it contains only the signatures of its members. An interface has neither constructors (how can you construct something that you can't instantiate?) nor fields (because that would imply some internal implementation). An interface definition is also not allowed to contain operator overloads, although that's not because there is any problem with declaring them — there isn't; it is because interfaces are usually intended to be public contracts, and having operator overloads would cause some incompatibility problems with other .NET languages, such as Visual Basic .NET, which do not support operator overloading.

It is also not permitted to declare modifiers on the members in an interface definition. Interface members are always implicitly public, and cannot be declared as virtual or static. That's up to implementing classes to decide. Therefore, it is fine for implementing classes to declare access modifiers, as is done in the example in this section.

For example, take `IDisposable`. If a class wants to declare publicly that it implements the `Dispose()` method, it must implement `IDisposable` — which in C# terms means that the class derives from `IDisposable`.

```
class SomeClass: IDisposable
{
    // This class MUST contain an implementation of the
    // IDisposable.Dispose() method, otherwise
    // you get a compilation error.
    public void Dispose()
    {
        // implementation of Dispose() method
    }
    // rest of class
}
```

In this example, if `SomeClass` derives from `IDisposable` but doesn't contain a `Dispose()` implementation with the exact same signature as defined in `IDisposable`, you get a compilation error because the class would be breaking its agreed-on contract to implement `IDisposable`. Of course, there's no problem for the compiler about a class having a `Dispose()` method but not deriving from `IDisposable`. The problem, then, would be that other code would have no way of recognizing that `SomeClass` has agreed to support the `IDisposable` features.

 IDisposable is a relatively simple interface because it defines only one method. Most interfaces will contain more members.

Defining and Implementing Interfaces

This section illustrates how to define and use interfaces through developing a short program that follows the interface inheritance paradigm. The example is based on bank accounts. Assume that you are writing code that will ultimately allow computerized transfers between bank accounts. And assume for this example that there are many companies that may implement bank accounts, but they have all mutually agreed that any classes that represent bank accounts will implement an interface, `IBankAccount`, which exposes methods to deposit or withdraw money, and a property to return the balance. It is this interface that will allow outside code to recognize the various bank account classes implemented by different bank accounts. Although the aim is to allow the bank accounts to talk to each other to allow transfers of funds between accounts, we won't introduce that feature just yet.

To keep things simple, you will keep all the code for the example in the same source file. Of course, if something like the example were used in real life, you could surmise that the different bank account classes would not only be compiled to different assemblies, but would also be hosted on different machines owned by the different banks. That's all much too complicated for our purposes here. However, to maintain some attempt at realism, you will define different namespaces for the different companies.

To begin, you need to define the `IBankAccount` interface:

```
namespace Wrox.ProCSharp
{
    public interface IBankAccount
    {
        void PayIn(decimal amount);
        bool Withdraw(decimal amount);
        decimal Balance
        {
            get;
        }
    }
}
```

Notice the name of the interface, IBankAccount. It's a convention that an interface name traditionally starts with the letter I, so that you know it's an interface.

> Chapter 2, "Core C#," pointed out that, in most cases, .NET usage guidelines discourage the so-called Hungarian notation in which names are preceded by a letter that indicates the type of object being defined. Interfaces are one of the few exceptions in which Hungarian notation is recommended.

The idea is that you can now write classes that represent bank accounts. These classes don't have to be related to each other in any way; they can be completely different classes. They will, however, all declare that they represent bank accounts by the mere fact that they implement the IBankAccount interface.

Let's start off with the first class, a saver account run by the Royal Bank of Venus:

```csharp
namespace Wrox.ProCSharp.VenusBank
{
    public class SaverAccount: IBankAccount
    {
        private decimal balance;
        public void PayIn(decimal amount)
        {
            balance += amount;
        }
        public bool Withdraw(decimal amount)
        {
            if (balance >= amount)
            {
                balance -= amount;
                return true;
            }
            Console.WriteLine("Withdrawal attempt failed.");
            return false;
        }
        public decimal Balance
        {
            get
            {
                return balance;
            }
        }
        public override string ToString()
        {
            return String.Format("Venus Bank Saver: Balance = {0,6:C}", balance);
        }
    }
}
```

code snippet BankAccounts.cs

It should be pretty obvious what the implementation of this class does. You maintain a private field, balance, and adjust this amount when money is deposited or withdrawn. You display an error message if an attempt to withdraw money fails because there is insufficient money in the account. Notice also that, because you want to keep the code as simple as possible, you are not implementing extra properties, such as the account holder's name! In real life that would be pretty essential information, but for this example it's unnecessarily complicated.

The only really interesting line in this code is the class declaration:

```csharp
public class SaverAccount: IBankAccount
```

You've declared that `SaverAccount` is derived from one interface, `IBankAccount`, and you have not explicitly indicated any other base classes (which of course means that `SaverAccount` is derived directly from `System.Object`). By the way, derivation from interfaces acts completely independently from derivation from classes.

Being derived from `IBankAccount` means that `SaverAccount` gets all the members of `IBankAccount`. But because an interface doesn't actually implement any of its methods, `SaverAccount` must provide its own implementations of all of them. If any implementations are missing, you can rest assured that the compiler will complain. Recall also that the interface just indicates the presence of its members. It's up to the class to decide if it wants any of them to be `virtual` or `abstract` (though `abstract` functions are of course only allowed if the class itself is `abstract`). For this particular example, you don't have any reason to make any of the interface functions virtual.

To illustrate how different classes can implement the same interface, assume that the Planetary Bank of Jupiter also implements a class to represent one of its bank accounts — a Gold Account:

```
namespace Wrox.ProCSharp.JupiterBank
{
    public class GoldAccount: IBankAccount
    {
        // etc
    }
}
```

We won't present details of the `GoldAccount` class here; in the sample code, it's basically identical to the implementation of `SaverAccount`. We stress that `GoldAccount` has no connection with `SaverAccount`, other than they both happen to implement the same interface.

Now that you have your classes, you can test them out. You first need a couple of `using` statements:

```
using System;
using Wrox.ProCSharp;
using Wrox.ProCSharp.VenusBank;
using Wrox.ProCSharp.JupiterBank;
```

Now you need a `Main()` method:

```
namespace Wrox.ProCSharp
{
    class MainEntryPoint
    {
        static void Main()
        {
            IBankAccount venusAccount = new SaverAccount();
            IBankAccount jupiterAccount = new GoldAccount();
            venusAccount.PayIn(200);
            venusAccount.Withdraw(100);
            Console.WriteLine(venusAccount.ToString());
            jupiterAccount.PayIn(500);
            jupiterAccount.Withdraw(600);
            jupiterAccount.Withdraw(100);
            Console.WriteLine(jupiterAccount.ToString());
        }
    }
}
```

This code (which if you download the sample, you can find in the file `BankAccounts.cs`) produces this output:

```
C:> BankAccounts
Venus Bank Saver: Balance = £100.00
Withdrawal attempt failed.
Jupiter Bank Saver: Balance = £400.00
```

The main point to notice about this code is the way that you have declared both your reference variables as `IBankAccount` references. This means that they can point to any instance of any class that implements this interface. However, it also means that you can call only methods that are part of this interface through these references — if you want to call any methods implemented by a class that are not part of the interface, you need to cast the reference to the appropriate type. In the example code, you were able to call `ToString()` (not implemented by `IBankAccount`) without any explicit cast, purely because `ToString()` is a `System.Object` method, so the C# compiler knows that it will be supported by any class (put differently, the cast from any interface to `System.Object` is implicit). Chapter 7, "Operators and Casts," covers the syntax for how to perform casts.

Interface references can in all respects be treated as class references — but the power of an interface reference is that it can refer to any class that implements that interface. For example, this allows you to form arrays of interfaces, where each element of the array is a different class:

```
IBankAccount[] accounts = new IBankAccount[2];
accounts[0] = new SaverAccount();
accounts[1] = new GoldAccount();
```

Note, however, that we'd get a compiler error if we tried something like this:

```
accounts[1] = new SomeOtherClass();     // SomeOtherClass does NOT implement
                                        // IBankAccount: WRONG!!
```

This causes a compilation error similar to this:

```
Cannot implicitly convert type 'Wrox.ProCSharp. SomeOtherClass' to
   'Wrox.ProCSharp.IBankAccount'
```

Derived Interfaces

It's possible for interfaces to inherit from each other in the same way that classes do. This concept is illustrated by defining a new interface, `ITransferBankAccount`, which has the same features as `IBankAccount` but also defines a method to transfer money directly to a different account:

```
namespace Wrox.ProCSharp
{
    public interface ITransferBankAccount: IBankAccount
    {
        bool TransferTo(IBankAccount destination, decimal amount);
    }
}
```

Because `ITransferBankAccount` is derived from `IBankAccount`, it gets all the members of `IBankAccount` as well as its own. That means that any class that implements (derives from) `ITransferBankAccount` must implement all the methods of `IBankAccount`, as well as the new `TransferTo()` method defined in `ITransferBankAccount`. Failure to implement all these methods will result in a compilation error.

Note that the `TransferTo()` method uses an `IBankAccount` interface reference for the destination account. This illustrates the usefulness of interfaces: When implementing and then invoking this method, you don't need to know anything about what type of object you are transferring money to — all you need to know is that this object implements `IBankAccount`.

To illustrate `ITransferBankAccount`, assume that the Planetary Bank of Jupiter also offers a current account. Most of the implementation of the `CurrentAccount` class is identical to the implementations of `SaverAccount` and `GoldAccount` (again, this is just to keep this example simple — that won't normally be the case), so in the following code just the differences are highlighted:

```
public class CurrentAccount: ITransferBankAccount
{
    private decimal balance;
    public void PayIn(decimal amount)
    {
        balance += amount;
    }
```

```csharp
      public bool Withdraw(decimal amount)
      {
         if (balance >= amount)
         {
            balance -= amount;
            return true;
         }
         Console.WriteLine("Withdrawal attempt failed.");
         return false;
      }
      public decimal Balance
      {
         get
         {
            return balance;
         }
      }
      public bool TransferTo(IBankAccount destination, decimal amount)
      {
         bool result;
         result = Withdraw(amount);
         if (result)
         {
            destination.PayIn(amount);
         }
         return result;
      }
      public override string ToString()
      {
          return String.Format("Jupiter Bank Current Account: Balance = {0,6:C}",balance);
      }
   }
```

The class can be demonstrated with this code:

```csharp
static void Main()
{
   IBankAccount venusAccount = new SaverAccount();
   ITransferBankAccount jupiterAccount = new CurrentAccount();
   venusAccount.PayIn(200);
   jupiterAccount.PayIn(500);
   jupiterAccount.TransferTo(venusAccount, 100);
   Console.WriteLine(venusAccount.ToString());
   Console.WriteLine(jupiterAccount.ToString());
}
```

code snippet CurrentAccounts.cs

This code (`CurrentAccounts.cs`) produces the following output, which, as you can verify, shows that the correct amounts have been transferred:

```
C:> CurrentAccount
Venus Bank Saver: Balance = £300.00
Jupiter Bank Current Account: Balance = £400.00
```

SUMMARY

This chapter examined how to code inheritance in C#. You have seen that C# offers rich support for both multiple interface and single implementation inheritance. You have also learned that C# provides a number of useful syntactical constructs designed to assist in making code more robust. These include the `override` keyword, which indicates when a function should override a base function; the `new` keyword, which indicates when a function hides a base function; and rigid rules for constructor initializers that are designed to ensure that constructors are designed to interoperate in a robust manner.

5

Generics

WHAT'S IN THIS CHAPTER?

➤ An overview of generics

➤ Creating generic classes

➤ Features of generic classes

➤ Generic interfaces

➤ Generic structs

➤ Generic methods

Since the release of .NET 2.0, .NET has supported generics. Generics are not just a part of the C# programming language, but are also deeply integrated with the IL (Intermediate Language) code in the assemblies. With generics, you can create classes and methods that are independent of contained types. Instead of writing a number of methods or classes with the same functionality for different types, you can create just one method or class.

Another option to reduce the code is using the `Object` class. However, the `Object` class is not type-safe. Generic classes make use of generic types that are replaced with specific types as needed. This allows for type safety: the compiler complains if a specific type is not supported with the generic class.

Generics are not limited to classes; in this chapter, you also see generics with interfaces and methods. Generics with delegates can be found in Chapter 8, "Delegates, Lambdas, and Events."

GENERICS OVERVIEW

Generics are not a completely new construct; similar concepts exist with other languages. For example, C++ templates have some similarity to generics. However, there's a big difference between C++ templates and .NET generics. With C++ templates, the source code of the template is required when a template is instantiated with a specific type. Unlike C++ templates, generics are not only a construct of the C# language, but are defined with the CLR. This makes it possible to instantiate generics with a specific type in Visual Basic even though the generic class was defined with C#.

The following sections explore the advantages and disadvantages of generics, particularly in regard to:

➤ Performance
➤ Type safety
➤ Binary code reuse
➤ Code bloat
➤ Naming guidelines

Performance

One of the big advantages of generics is performance. In Chapter 10, "Collections," you will see non-generic and generic collection classes from the namespaces `System.Collections` and `System.Collections.Generic`. Using value types with non-generic collection classes results in boxing and unboxing when the value type is converted to a reference type and vice versa.

 Boxing and unboxing is discussed in Chapter 7, "Operators and Casts." Here is just a short refresher about these terms.

Value types are stored on the stack. Reference types are stored on the heap. C# classes are reference types; structs are value types. .NET makes it easy to convert value types to reference types, so you can use a value type everywhere an object (which is a reference type) is needed. For example, an `int` can be assigned to an object. The conversion from a value type to a reference type is known as *boxing*. Boxing happens automatically if a method requires an object as a parameter, and a value type is passed. On the other side, a boxed value type can be converted to a value type by using unboxing. With unboxing, the cast operator is required.

The following example shows the `ArrayList` class from the namespace `System.Collections`. `ArrayList` stores objects; the `Add()` method is defined to require an object as a parameter, and so an integer type is boxed. When the values from an `ArrayList` are read, unboxing occurs when the object is converted to an integer type. This may be obvious with the cast operator that is used to assign the first element of the `ArrayList` collection to the variable i1, but also happens inside the `foreach` statement where the variable i2 of type `int` is accessed:

```
var list = new ArrayList();
list.Add(44);    // boxing — convert a value type to a reference type

int i1 = (int)list[0];    // unboxing — convert a reference type to
                          // a value type

foreach (int i2 in list)
{
    Console.WriteLine(i2);    // unboxing
}
```

Boxing and unboxing are easy to use but have a big performance impact, especially when iterating through many items.

Instead of using objects, the `List<T>` class from the namespace `System.Collections.Generic` allows you to define the type when it is used. In the example here, the generic type of the `List<T>` class is defined as `int`, so the `int` type is used inside the class that is generated dynamically from the JIT compiler. Boxing and unboxing no longer happens:

```
var list = new List<int>();
list.Add(44);    // no boxing — value types are stored in the List<int>

int i1 = list[0];    // no unboxing, no cast needed
```

```
    foreach (int i2 in list)
    {
        Console.WriteLine(i2);
    }
```

Type Safety

Another feature of generics is type safety. As with the ArrayList class, if objects are used, any type can be added to this collection. This example shows adding an integer, a string, and an object of type MyClass to the collection of type ArrayList:

```
var list = new ArrayList();
list.Add(44);
list.Add("mystring");
list.Add(new MyClass());
```

Now if this collection is iterated using the following foreach statement, which iterates using integer elements, the compiler accepts this code. However, because not all elements in the collection can be cast to an int, a runtime exception will occur:

```
foreach (int i in list)
{
    Console.WriteLine(i);
}
```

Errors should be detected as early as possible. With the generic class List<T>, the generic type T defines what types are allowed. With a definition of List<int>, only integer types can be added to the collection. The compiler doesn't compile this code because the Add() method has invalid arguments:

```
var list = new List<int>();
list.Add(44);
list.Add("mystring");    // compile time error
list.Add(new MyClass());    // compile time error
```

Binary Code Reuse

Generics allow better binary code reuse. A generic class can be defined once and can be instantiated with many different types. Unlike C++ templates, it is not necessary to access the source code.

As an example, here the List<T> class from the namespace System.Collections.Generic is instantiated with an int, a string, and a MyClass type:

```
var list = new List<int>();
list.Add(44);

var stringList = new List<string>();
stringList.Add("mystring");

var myClassList = new List<MyClass>();
myClassList.Add(new MyClass());
```

Generic types can be defined in one language and used from any other .NET language.

Code Bloat

How much code is created with generics when instantiating them with different specific types?

Because a generic class definition goes into the assembly, instantiating generic classes with specific types doesn't duplicate these classes in the IL code. However, when the generic classes are compiled by the JIT compiler to native code, a new class for every specific value type is created. Reference types share all the same implementation of the same native class. This is because with reference types, only a 4-byte memory address (with 32-bit systems) is needed within the generic instantiated class to reference a reference type.

Value types are contained within the memory of the generic instantiated class, and because every value type can have different memory requirements, a new class for every value type is instantiated.

Naming Guidelines

If generics are used in the program, it helps when generic types can be distinguished from non-generic types. Here are naming guidelines for generic types:

➤ Generic type names should be prefixed with the letter `T`.

➤ If the generic type can be replaced by any class because there's no special requirement, and only one generic type is used, the character `T` is good as a generic type name:

```
public class List<T> { }

public class LinkedList<T> { }
```

➤ If there's a special requirement for a generic type (for example, it must implement an interface or derive from a base class), or if two or more generic types are used, descriptive names should be used for the type names:

```
public delegate void EventHandler<TEventArgs>(object sender, TEventArgs e);

public delegate TOutput Converter<TInput, TOutput>(TInput from);

public class SortedList<TKey, TValue> { }
```

CREATING GENERIC CLASSES

First start with a normal, non-generic simplified linked list class that can contain objects of any kind, and later convert this class to a generic class.

With a linked list, one element references the next one. So, you must create a class that wraps the object inside the linked list and references the next object. The class `LinkedListNode` contains a property named `Value` that is initialized with the constructor. In addition to that, the `LinkedListNode` class contains references to the next and previous elements in the list that can be accessed from properties.

```
public class LinkedListNode
{
    public LinkedListNode(object value)
    {
        this.Value = value;
    }

    public object Value { get; private set; }

    public LinkedListNode Next { get; internal set; }
    public LinkedListNode Prev { get; internal set; }
}
```

code snippet LinkedListObjects/LinkedListNode.cs

The `LinkedList` class includes `First` and `Last` properties of type `LinkedListNode` that mark the beginning and end of the list. The method `AddLast()` adds a new element to the end of the list. First, an object of type `LinkedListNode` is created. If the list is empty, the `First` and `Last` properties are set to the new element; otherwise, the new element is added as the last element to the list. By implementing the `GetEnumerator()` method, it is possible to iterate through the list with the `foreach` statement. The `GetEnumerator()` method makes use of the `yield` statement for creating an enumerator type.

```
<public class LinkedList: IEnumerable
{
    public LinkedListNode First { get; private set; }
    public LinkedListNode Last { get; private set; }

    public LinkedListNode AddLast(object node)
    {
        var newNode = new LinkedListNode(node);
        if (First == null)
        {
            First = newNode;
            Last = First;
        }
        else
        {
            Last.Next = newNode;
            Last = newNode;
        }
        return newNode;
    }

    public IEnumerator GetEnumerator()
    {
        LinkedListNode current = First;
        while (current != null)
        {
            yield return current.Value;
            current = current.Next;
        }
    }
}
```

code snippet LinkedListObjects/LinkedListNode.cs

The `yield` *statement is explained in Chapter 6, "Arrays and Tuples."*

Now you can use the `LinkedList` class with any type. The following code segment instantiates a new `LinkedList` object and adds two integer types and one string type. As the integer types are converted to an object, boxing occurs as explained earlier. With the `foreach` statement, unboxing happens. In the `foreach` statement the elements from the list are cast to an integer, so with the third element in the list a runtime exception occurs as casting to an `int` fails.

```
var list1 = new LinkedList();
list1.AddLast(2);
list1.AddLast(4);
list1.AddLast("6");

foreach (int i in list1)
{
    Console.WriteLine(i);
}
```

code snippet LinkedListObjects/Program.cs

Now let's make a generic version of the linked list. A generic class is defined similarly to a normal class with the generic type declaration. The generic type can then be used within the class as a field member, or with parameter types of methods. The class `LinkedListNode` is declared with a generic type `T`. The property `Value` is now type `T` instead of `object`; the constructor is changed as well to accept an object of type T. A generic type can also be returned and set, so the properties Next and Prev are now of type LinkedListNode<T>:

```
public class LinkedListNode<T>
{
    public LinkedListNode(T value)
    {
        this.Value = value;
    }

    public T Value { get; private set; }
    public LinkedListNode<T> Next { get; internal set; }
    public LinkedListNode<T> Prev { get; internal set; }
}
```

code snippet LinkedListSample/LinkedListNode.cs

In the following code the class LinkedList is changed to a generic class as well. LinkedList<T> contains LinkedListNode<T> elements. The type T from the LinkedList defines the type T of the properties First and Last. The method AddLast() now accepts a parameter of type T and instantiates an object of LinkedListNode<T>.

Besides the interface IEnumerable, a generic version is also available: IEnumerable<T>. IEnumerable<T> derives from IEnumerable and adds the GetEnumerator() method that returns IEnumerator<T>. LinkedList<T> implements the generic interface IEnumerable<T>.

Enumerations and the interfaces IEnumerable *and* IEnumerator *are discussed in Chapter 6.*

```
public class LinkedList<T>: IEnumerable<T>
{
    public LinkedListNode<T> First { get; private set; }
    public LinkedListNode<T> Last { get; private set; }

    public LinkedListNode<T> AddLast(T node)
    {
        var newNode = new LinkedListNode<T>(node);
        if (First == null)
        {
            First = newNode;
            Last = First;
        }
        else
        {
            Last.Next = newNode;
            Last = newNode;
        }
        return newNode;
    }

    public IEnumerator<T> GetEnumerator()
    {
        LinkedListNode<T> current = First;

        while (current != null)
        {
            yield return current.Value;
            current = current.Next;
```

```
            }
        }

        IEnumerator IEnumerable.GetEnumerator()
        {
            return GetEnumerator();
        }
    }
```

Using the generic `LinkedList<T>`, you can instantiate it with an `int` type, and there's no boxing. Also, you get a compiler error if you don't pass an `int` with the method `AddLast()`. Using the generic `IEnumerable<T>`, the `foreach` statement is also type-safe, and you get a compiler error if that variable in the `foreach` statement is not an `int`:

```
var list2 = new LinkedList<int>();
list2.AddLast(1);
list2.AddLast(3);
list2.AddLast(5);

foreach (int i in list2)
{
    Console.WriteLine(i);
}
```

Similarly, you can use the generic `LinkedList<T>` with a `string` type and pass strings to the `AddLast()` method:

```
var list3 = new LinkedList<string>();
list3.AddLast("2");
list3.AddLast("four");
list3.AddLast("foo");

foreach (string s in list3)
{
    Console.WriteLine(s);
}
```

> *Every class that deals with the object type is a possible candidate for a generic implementation. Also, if classes make use of hierarchies, generics can be very helpful in making casting unnecessary.*

GENERICS FEATURES

When creating generic classes, you might need some more C# keywords. For example, it is not possible to assign `null` to a generic type. In this case, the keyword `default` can be used, as demonstrated in the next section. If the generic type does not require the features of the `Object` class, but you need to invoke some specific methods in the generic class, you can define constraints.

This section discusses the following topics:

➤ Default values

➤ Constraints

➤ Inheritance

➤ Static members

Let's start this example with a generic document manager. The document manager is used to read and write documents from a queue. Start by creating a new Console project named `DocumentManager` and add the class `DocumentManager<T>`. The method `AddDocument()` adds a document to the queue. The read-only property `IsDocumentAvailable` returns true if the queue is not empty:

```
using System;
using System.Collections.Generic;

namespace Wrox.ProCSharp.Generics
{
    public class DocumentManager<T>
    {
        private readonly Queue<T> documentQueue = new Queue<T>();

        public void AddDocument(T doc)
        {
            lock (this)
            {
                documentQueue.Enqueue(doc);
            }
        }

        public bool IsDocumentAvailable
        {
            get { return documentQueue.Count > 0; }
        }
    }
}
```

code snippet DocumentManager/DocumentManager.cs

Default Values

Now you add a `GetDocument()` method to the `DocumentManager<T>` class. Inside this method the type `T` should be assigned to `null`. However, it is not possible to assign `null` to generic types. The reason is that a generic type can also be instantiated as a value type, and `null` is allowed only with reference types. To circumvent this problem, you can use the `default` keyword. With the `default` keyword, `null` is assigned to reference types and 0 is assigned to value types:

```
public T GetDocument()
{
    T doc = default(T);
    lock (this)
    {
        doc = documentQueue.Dequeue();
    }
    return doc;
}
```

The `default` keyword has multiple meanings depending on the context where it is used. The `switch` statement uses a `default` for defining the default case, and with generics `default` is used to initialize generic types either to `null` or 0 depending on if it is a reference or value type.

Constraints

If the generic class needs to invoke some methods from the generic type, you have to add constraints.

With `DocumentManager<T>`, all the titles of the documents should be displayed in the `DisplayAllDocuments()` method. The `Document` class implements the interface `IDocument` with the properties `Title` and `Content`:

```csharp
public interface IDocument
{
    string Title { get; set; }
    string Content { get; set; }
}

public class Document: IDocument
{
    public Document()
    {
    }

    public Document(string title, string content)
    {
        this.Title = title;
        this.Content = content;
    }

    public string Title { get; set; }
    public string Content { get; set; }
}
```

code snippet DocumentManager/Document.cs

For displaying the documents with the `DocumentManager<T>` class, you can cast the type `T` to the interface `IDocument` to display the title:

```csharp
public void DisplayAllDocuments()
{
    foreach (T doc in documentQueue)
    {
        Console.WriteLine(((IDocument)doc).Title);
    }
}
```

code snippet DocumentManager/DocumentManager.cs

The problem is that doing a cast results in a runtime exception if type `T` does not implement the interface `IDocument`. Instead, it would be better to define a constraint with the `DocumentManager<TDocument>` class that the type `TDocument` must implement the interface `IDocument`. To clarify the requirement in the name of the generic type, `T` is changed to `TDocument`. The `where` clause defines the requirement to implement the interface `IDocument`:

```csharp
public class DocumentManager<TDocument>
    where TDocument: IDocument
{
```

This way you can write the `foreach` statement in such a way that the type `TDocument` contains the property `Title`. You get support from Visual Studio IntelliSense and from the compiler:

```csharp
public void DisplayAllDocuments()
{
    foreach (TDocument doc in documentQueue)
    {
        Console.WriteLine(doc.Title);
    }
}
```

In the `Main()` method the `DocumentManager<T>` class is instantiated with the type `Document` that implements the required interface `IDocument`. Then new documents are added and displayed, and one of the documents is retrieved:

```
<static void Main()
{
    var dm = new DocumentManager<Document>();
    dm.AddDocument(new Document("Title A", "Sample A"));
    dm.AddDocument(new Document("Title B", "Sample B"));

    dm.DisplayAllDocuments();

    if (dm.IsDocumentAvailable)
    {
        Document d = dm.GetDocument();
        Console.WriteLine(d.Content);
    }
}
```

code snippet DocumentManager/Program.cs

The `DocumentManager` now works with any class that implements the interface `IDocument`.

In the sample application, you've seen an interface constraint. Generics support several constraint types, indicated in the following table.

CONSTRAINT	DESCRIPTION
where T: struct	With a struct constraint, type T must be a value type.
where T: class	The class constraint indicates that type T must be a reference type.
where T: IFoo	where T: IFoo specifies that type T is required to implement interface IFoo.
where T: Foo	where T: Foo specifies that type T is required to derive from base class Foo.
where T: new()	where T: new() is a constructor constraint and specifies that type T must have a default constructor.
where T1: T2	With constraints it is also possible to specify that type T1 derives from a generic type T2. This constraint is known as *naked type constraint*.

Constructor constraints can only be defined for the default constructor. It is not possible to define a constructor constraint for other constructors.

With a generic type, you can also combine multiple constraints. The constraint `where T: IFoo, new()` with the `MyClass<T>` declaration specifies that type T implements the interface `IFoo` and has a default constructor:

```
public class MyClass<T>
    where T: IFoo, new()
{
    //...
```

One important restriction of the where *clause with C# is that it's not possible to define operators that must be implemented by the generic type. Operators cannot be defined in interfaces. With the* where *clause, it is only possible to define base classes, interfaces, and the default constructor.*

Inheritance

The `LinkedList<T>` class created earlier implements the interface `IEnumerable<out T>`:

```
public class LinkedList<T>: IEnumerable<T>
{
    //...
```

A generic type can implement a generic interface. The same is possible by deriving from a class. A generic class can be derived from a generic base class:

```
public class Base<T>
{
}

public class Derived<T>: Base<T>
{
}
```

The requirement is that the generic types of the interface must be repeated, or the type of the base class must be specified, as in this case:

```
public class Base<T>
{
}

public class Derived<T>: Base<string>
{
}
```

This way, the derived class can be a generic or non-generic class. For example, you can define an abstract generic base class that is implemented with a concrete type in the derived class. This allows you to do specialization for specific types:

```
public abstract class Calc<T>
{
    public abstract T Add(T x, T y);
    public abstract T Sub(T x, T y);
}

public class IntCalc: Calc<int>
{
    public override int Add(int x, int y)
    {
        return x + y;
    }

    public override int Sub(int x, int y)
    {
        return x - y;
    }
}
```

Static Members

Static members of generic classes require special attention. Static members of a generic class are only shared with one instantiation of the class. Let's have a look at one example, where the class `StaticDemo<T>` contains the static field `x`:

```
public class StaticDemo<T>
{
    public static int x;
}
```

Because the class `StaticDemo<T>` is used with both a `string` type and an `int` type, two sets of static fields exist:

```
StaticDemo<string>.x = 4;
StaticDemo<int>.x = 5;
Console.WriteLine(StaticDemo<string>.x);    // writes 4
```

GENERIC INTERFACES

Using generics, you can define interfaces that define methods with generic parameters. In the linked list sample, you've already implemented the interface `IEnumerable<out T>`, which defines a `GetEnumerator()` method to return `IEnumerator<out T>`. .NET offers a lot of generic interfaces for different scenarios; examples include `IComparable<T>`, `ICollection<T>`, and `IExtensibleObject<T>`. Often older, non-generic versions of the same interface exist; for example .NET 1.0 had an `IComparable` interface which was based on objects. `IComparable<in T>` is based on a generic type:

```
public interface IComparable<in T>
{
    int CompareTo(T other);
}
```

The older, non-generic `IComparable` interface requires an object with the `CompareTo()` method. This requires a cast to specific types, such as to the `Person` class for using the `LastName` property:

```
public class Person: IComparable
{
    public int CompareTo(object obj)
    {
        Person other = obj as Person;
        return this.lastname.CompareTo(other.LastName);
    }
//
```

When implementing the generic version, it is no longer necessary to cast the `object` to a `Person`:

```
public class Person: IComparable<Person>
{
    public int CompareTo(Person other)
    {
        return this.LastName.CompareTo(other.LastName);
    }
    //...
```

Covariance and Contra-variance

Previous to .NET 4, generic interfaces were invariant. .NET 4 adds an important extension for generic interfaces and generic delegates with covariance and contra-variance. Covariance and contra-variance are about the conversion of types with argument and return types. For example, can you pass a `Rectangle` to a method that requests a `Shape`? Let's get into examples to see the advantages of these extensions.

With .NET, parameter types are covariant. Assume you have the classes `Shape` and `Rectangle`, and `Rectangle` derives from the `Shape` base class. The `Display()` method is declared to accept an object of the `Shape` type as its parameter:

```
public void Display(Shape o) { }
```

Now you can pass any object that derives from the `Shape` base class. Because `Rectangle` derives from `Shape`, a `Rectangle` fulfills all the requirements of a `Shape` and the compiler accepts this method call:

```
Rectangle r = new Rectangle { Width= 5, Height=2.5};
Display(r);
```

Return types of methods are contra-variant. When a method returns a `Shape` it is not possible to assign it to a `Rectangle` because a `Shape` is not necessarily always a `Rectangle`. The opposite is possible. If a method returns a `Rectangle` as the `GetRectangle()` method,

```
public Rectangle GetRectangle();
```

the result can be assigned to a `Shape`.

```
Shape s = GetRectangle();
```

Before version 4 of the .NET Framework, this behavior was not possible with generics. With C# 4, the language is extended to support covariance and contra-variance with generic interfaces and generic delegates. Let's start by defining a `Shape` base class and a `Rectangle` class:

```
public class Shape
{
    public double Width { get; set; }
    public double Height { get; set; }

    public override string ToString()
    {
        return String.Format("Width: {0}, Height: {1}", Width, Height);
    }
}
```

code snippet Variance/Shape.cs

```
public class Rectangle: Shape
{
}
```

code snippet Variance/Rectangle.cs

Covariance with Generic Interfaces

A generic interface is covariant if the generic type is annotated with the `out` keyword. This also means that type `T` is allowed only with return types. The interface `IIndex` is covariant with type `T` and returns this type from a read-only indexer:

```
public interface IIndex<out T>
{
    T this[int index] { get; }
    int Count { get; }
}
```

code snippet Variance/IIndex.cs

> *If a read-write indexer is used with the IIndex interface, the generic type T is passed to the method and also retrieved from the method. This is not possible with covariance — the generic type must be defined as invariant. Defining the type as invariant is done without* out *and* in *annotations.*

The IIndex<T> interface is implemented with the RectangleCollection class. RectangleCollection defines Rectangle for generic type T:

```csharp
public class RectangleCollection: IIndex<Rectangle>
{
    private Rectangle[] data = new Rectangle[3]
    {
        new Rectangle { Height=2, Width=5},
        new Rectangle { Height=3, Width=7},
        new Rectangle { Height=4.5, Width=2.9}
    };

    public static RectangleCollection GetRectangles()
    {
        return new RectangleCollection();
    }

    public Rectangle this[int index]
    {
        get
        {
            if (index < 0 || index > data.Length)
                throw new ArgumentOutOfRangeException("index");
            return data[index];
        }
    }
    public int Count
    {
        get
        {
            return data.Length;
        }
    }
}
```

code snippet Variance/RectangleCollection.cs

The RectangleCollection.GetRectangles() method returns a RectangleCollection that implements the IIndex<Rectangle> interface, so you can assign the return value to a variable *rectangle* of the IIndex<Rectangle> type. Because the interface is covariant, it is also possible to assign the returned value to a variable of IIndex<Shape>. Shape does not need anything more than a Rectangle has to offer. Using the shapes variable, the indexer from the interface and the Count property are used within the for loop:

```csharp
static void Main()
{
    IIndex<Rectangle> rectangles = RectangleCollection.GetRectangles();
    IIndex<Shape> shapes = rectangles;

    for (int i = 0; i < shapes.Count; i++)
    {
        Console.WriteLine(shapes[i]);
    }
}
```

code snippet Variance/Program.cs

Contra-Variance with Generic Interfaces

A generic interface is contra-variant if the generic type is annotated with the in keyword. This way the interface is only allowed to use generic type T as input to its methods:

```csharp
public interface IDisplay<in T>
{
    void Show(T item);
}
```

code snippet Variance/IDisplay.cs

The `ShapeDisplay` class implements `IDisplay<Shape>` and uses a `Shape` object as an input parameter:

```csharp
public class ShapeDisplay: IDisplay<Shape>
{
    public void Show(Shape s)
    {
        Console.WriteLine("{0} Width: {1}, Height: {2}", s.GetType().Name,
                          s.Width, s.Height);
    }
}
```

code snippet Variance/ShapeDisplay.cs

Creating a new instance of `ShapeDisplay` returns `IDisplay<Shape>`, which is assigned to the `shapeDisplay` variable. Because `IDisplay<T>` is contra-variant, it is possible to assign the result to `IDisplay<Rectangle>` where `Rectangle` derives from `Shape`. This time the methods of the interface only define the generic type as input, and `Rectangle` fulfills all the requirements of a `Shape`:

```csharp
static void Main()
{
    //...

    IDisplay<Shape> shapeDisplay = new ShapeDisplay();
    IDisplay<Rectangle> rectangleDisplay = shapeDisplay;
    rectangleDisplay.Show(rectangles[0]);

}
```

code snippet Variance/Program.cs

GENERIC STRUCTS

Similar to classes, structs can be generic as well. They are very similar to generic classes with the exception of inheritance features. In this section you look at the generic struct `Nullable<T>`, which is defined by the .NET Framework.

An example of a generic struct in the .NET Framework is `Nullable<T>`. A number in a database and a number in a programming language have an important difference in their characteristics, as a number in the database can be `null`. A number in C# cannot be `null`. `Int32` is a struct, and because structs are implemented as value types, they cannot be `null`. The problem exists not only with databases but also with mapping XML data to .NET types.

This difference often causes headaches and a lot of additional work to map the data. One solution is to map numbers from databases and XML files to reference types, because reference types can have a `null` value. However, this also means additional overhead during runtime.

With the structure `Nullable<T>`, this can be easily resolved. The following code segment shows a simplified version of how `Nullable<T>` is defined.

The structure `Nullable<T>` defines a constraint that the generic type `T` needs to be a struct. With classes as generic types, the advantage of low overhead would be gone, and because objects of classes can be null anyway, there's no point in using a class with the `Nullable<T>` type. The only overhead in addition to the `T` type defined by `Nullable<T>` is the `hasValue` Boolean field that defines whether the value is set or `null`. Other than that, the generic struct defines the read-only properties `HasValue` and `Value` and some operator overloads. The operator overload to cast the `Nullable<T>` type to `T` is defined as explicit because it can throw an exception in case `hasValue` is `false`. The operator overload to cast to `Nullable<T>` is defined as implicit because it always succeeds:

```csharp
public struct Nullable<T>
    where T: struct
{
    public Nullable(T value)
    {
        this.hasValue = true;
        this.value = value;
    }
    private bool hasValue;
    public bool HasValue
    {
        get
        {
            return hasValue;
        }
    }

    private T value;
    public T Value
    {
        get
        {
            if (!hasValue)
            {
                throw new InvalidOperationException("no value");
            }
            return value;
        }
    }

    public static explicit operator T(Nullable<T> value)
    {
        return value.Value;
    }
    public static implicit operator Nullable<T>(T value)
    {
        return new Nullable<T>(value);
    }

    public override string ToString()
    {
        if (!HasValue)
            return String.Empty;
        return this.value.ToString();
    }
}
```

In this example, `Nullable<T>` is instantiated with `Nullable<int>`. The variable `x` can now be used as an `int`, assigning values and using operators to do some calculation. This behavior is made possible by casting operators of the `Nullable<T>` type. However, `x` can also be `null`. The `Nullable<T>` properties `HasValue` and `Value` can check whether there is a value, and the value can be accessed:

```csharp
Nullable<int> x;
x = 4;
x += 3;
if (x.HasValue)
{
    int y = x.Value;
}
x = null;
```

Because nullable types are used often, C# has a special syntax for defining variables of this type. Instead of using syntax with the generic structure, the ? operator can be used. In the following example, the variables x1 and x2 are both instances of a nullable int type:

```
Nullable<int> x1;
int? x2;
```

A nullable type can be compared with null and also numbers, as shown. Here, the value of x is compared with null, and if it is not null, it is compared with a value less than 0:

```
int? x = GetNullableType();
if (x == null)
{
    Console.WriteLine("x is null");
}
else if (x < 0)
{
    Console.WriteLine("x is smaller than 0");
}
```

Now that you know how Nullable<T> is defined, let's get into using nullable types. Nullable types can also be used with arithmetic operators. The variable x3 is the sum of the variables x1 and x2. If any of the nullable types have a null value, the result is null:

```
int? x1 = GetNullableType();
int? x2 = GetNullableType();
int? x3 = x1 + x2;
```

 The GetNullableType() *method, which is called here, is just a placeholder for any method that returns a nullable* int. *For testing you can implement it as simply to return* null *or to return any integer value.*

Non-nullable types can be converted to nullable types. With the conversion from a non-nullable type to a nullable type, an implicit conversion is possible where casting is not required. This conversion always succeeds:

```
int y1 = 4;
int? x1 = y1;
```

In the reverse situation, a conversion from a nullable type to a non-nullable type can fail. If the nullable type has a null value and the null value is assigned to a non-nullable type, an exception of type InvalidOperationException is thrown. That's the reason the cast operator is required to do an explicit conversion:

```
int? x1 = GetNullableType();
int y1 = (int)x1;
```

Instead of doing an explicit cast, it is also possible to convert a nullable type to a non-nullable type with the coalescing operator. The coalescing operator uses the syntax ?? to define a default value for the conversion in case the nullable type has a value of null. Here, y1 gets a 0 value if x1 is null:

```
int? x1 = GetNullableType();
int y1 = x1 ?? 0;
```

GENERIC METHODS

In addition to defining generic classes, it is also possible to define generic methods. With a generic method, the generic type is defined with the method declaration. Generic methods can be defined within non-generic classes.

The method `Swap<T>()` defines `T` as a generic type that is used for two arguments and a variable `temp`:

```
void Swap<T>(ref T x, ref T y)
{
    T temp;
    temp = x;
    x = y;
    y = temp;
}
```

A generic method can be invoked by assigning the generic type with the method call:

```
int i = 4;
int j = 5;
Swap<int>(ref i, ref j);
```

However, because the C# compiler can get the type of the parameters by calling the `Swap()` method, it is not required to assign the generic type with the method call. The generic method can be invoked as simply as non-generic methods:

```
int i = 4;
int j = 5;
Swap(ref i, ref j);
```

Generic Methods Example

Here's an example where a generic method is used to accumulate all elements of a collection. To show the features of generic methods, the following `Account` class that contains `Name` and `Balance` properties is used:

```
public class Account
{
    public string Name { get; private set; }
    public decimal Balance { get; private set; }

    public Account(string name, Decimal balance)
    {
        this.Name = name;
        this.Balance = balance;
    }
}
```

code snippet GenericMethods/Account.cs

All the accounts where the balance should be accumulated are added to an accounts list of type `List<Account>`:

```
var accounts = new List<Account>()
{
    new Account("Christian", 1500),
    new Account("Stephanie", 2200),
    new Account("Angela", 1800)
};
```

code snippet GenericMethods/Program.cs

A traditional way to accumulate all `Account` objects is by looping through all `Account` objects with a `foreach` statement, as shown here. Because the `foreach` statement uses the `IEnumerable` interface to iterate the elements of a collection, the argument of the `AccumulateSimple()` method is of type `IEnumerable`. The `foreach` statement works with every object implementing `IEnumerable`. This way, the `AccumulateSimple()` method can be used with all collection classes that implement the interface

`IEnumerable<Account>`. In the implementation of this method, the property `Balance` of the `Account` object is directly accessed:

Available for download on Wrox.com

```
public static class Algorithm
{
    public static decimal AccumulateSimple(IEnumerable<Account> source)
    {
        decimal sum = 0;
        foreach (Account a in source)
        {
            sum += a.Balance;
        }
        return sum;
    }
}
```

code snippet GenericMethods/Algorithm.cs

The `AccumulateSimple()` method is invoked this way:

```
decimal amount = Algorithm.AccumulateSimple(accounts);
```

Generic Methods with Constraints

The problem with the first implementation is that it works only with `Account` objects. This can be avoided by using a generic method.

The second version of the `Accumulate()` method accepts any type that implements the interface `IAccount`. As you've seen earlier with generic classes, generic types can be restricted with the `where` clause. The same clause that is used with generic classes can be used with generic methods. The parameter of the `Accumulate()` method is changed to `IEnumerable<T>`. `IEnumerable<T>` is a generic interface that is implemented by generic collection classes:

Available for download on Wrox.com

```
public static decimal Accumulate<TAccount>(IEnumerable<TAccount> source)
    where TAccount: IAccount
{
    decimal sum = 0;

    foreach (TAccount a in source)
    {
        sum += a.Balance;
    }
    return sum;
}
```

code snippet GenericMethods/Algorithm.cs

The `Account` class is now re-factored to implement the interface `IAccount`:

Available for download on Wrox.com

```
public class Account: IAccount
{
    //...
```

code snippet GenericMethods/Account.cs

The `IAccount` interface defines the read-only properties `Balance` and `Name`:

Available for download on Wrox.com

```
public interface IAccount
{
    decimal Balance { get; }
    string Name { get; }
}
```

code snippet GenericMethods/IAccount.cs

The new `Accumulate()` method can be invoked by defining the `Account` type as generic type parameter:

```
decimal amount = Algorithm.Accumulate<Account>(accounts);
```

code snippet GenericMethods/Program.cs

Because the generic type parameter can be automatically inferred by the compiler from the parameter type of the method, it is valid to invoke the `Accumulate()` method this way:

```
decimal amount = Algorithm.Accumulate(accounts);
```

Generic Methods with Delegates

The requirement for the generic types to implement the interface `IAccount` may be too restrictive. The following example hints at how the `Accumulate()` method can be changed by passing a generic delegate. Chapter 8 gives you all the details about how to work with generic delegates, and how to use Lambda expressions.

This `Accumulate()` method uses two generic parameters, `T1` and `T2`. `T1` is used for the collection-implementing `IEnumerable<T1>` parameter, which is the first one of the method. The second parameter uses the generic delegate `Func<T1, T2, TResult>`. Here, the second and third generic parameters are of the same `T2` type. A method needs to be passed that has two input parameters (`T1` and `T2`) and a return type of `T2`:

```
public static T2 Accumulate<T1, T2>(IEnumerable<T1> source,
                                    Func<T1, T2, T2> action)
{
    T2 sum = default(T2);
    foreach (T1 item in source)
    {
        sum = action(item, sum);
    }
    return sum;
}
```

code snippet GenericMethods/Algorithm.cs

In calling this method, it is necessary to specify the generic parameter types because the compiler cannot infer it automatically. With the first parameter of the method, the `accounts` collection that is assigned is of type `IEnumerable<Account>`. With the second parameter, a Lambda expression is used that defines two parameters of type `Account` and `decimal`, and returns a decimal. This Lambda expression gets invoked for every item by the `Accumulate()` method:

```
decimal amount = Algorithm.Accumulate<Account, decimal>(
                    accounts, (item, sum) => sum += item.Balance);
```

code snippet GenericMethods/Program.cs

Don't scratch your head with this syntax yet. The sample should give you a glimpse about the possible ways to extend the `Accumulate()` method. Chapter 8 gives you all the details about Lambda expressions.

Generic Methods Specialization

Generic methods can be overloaded to define specializations for specific types. This is true for methods with generic parameters as well. The `Foo()` method is defined in two versions. The first accepts a generic parameter; the second one is a specialized version for the `int` parameter. During compile time, the best match is taken. If an int is passed, then the method with the int parameter is selected. With any other parameter type, the compiler chooses the generic version of the method:

```
public class MethodOverloads
{
    public void Foo<T>(T obj)
    {
        Console.WriteLine("Foo<T>(T obj), obj type: {0}", obj.GetType().Name);
    }

    public void Foo(int x)
    {
        Console.WriteLine("Foo(int x)");
    }

    public void Bar<T>(T obj)
    {
        Foo(obj);
    }
}
```

code snippet Specialization/Program.cs

The Foo() method can now be invoked with any parameter type. The sample code passes an int and a string to the method:

```
static void Main()
{
    var test = new MethodOverloads();
    test.Foo(33);
    test.Foo("abc");
}
```

code snippet GenericMethods/Program.cs

Running the program, you can see by the output that the method with the best match is taken:

```
Foo(int x)
Foo<T>(T obj), obj type: String
```

You need to be aware that the method invoked is defined during compile time and not runtime. This can be easily demonstrated by adding a generic Bar() method that invokes the Foo() method, passing the generic parameter value along:

```
public class MethodOverloads
{
    // ...

    public void Bar<T>(T obj)
    {
        Foo(obj);
    }
}
```

The Main() method is now changed to invoke the Bar() method passing an int value:

```
static void Main()
{
    var test = new MethodOverloads();
    test.Bar(44);
}
```

From the output on the console you can see that the generic Foo() method was selected by the Bar() method and not the overload with the int parameter. The reason is that the compiler selects the method that is invoked by the Bar() method during compile time. Because the Bar() method defines a generic parameter, and because there's a `Foo()` method that matches this type, the generic `Foo()` method is called. This is not changed during runtime when an `int` value is passed to the `Bar()` method:

```
Foo<T>(T obj), obj type: Int32
```

SUMMARY

This chapter introduced a very important feature of the CLR: generics. With generic classes you can create type-independent classes, and generic methods allow type-independent methods. Interfaces, structs, and delegates can be created in a generic way as well. Generics make new programming styles possible. You've seen how algorithms, particularly actions and predicates, can be implemented to be used with different classes — and all type-safe. Generic delegates make it possible to decouple algorithms from collections.

You will see more features and uses of generics throughout this book. Chapter 8 introduces delegates that are often implemented as generics; Chapter 10 gives information about generic collection classes; and Chapter 11 ("Language Integrated Query") discusses generic extension methods.

The next chapter demonstrates the use of generic methods with arrays.

6

Arrays and Tuples

WHAT'S IN THIS CHAPTER?

➤ SImple arrays

➤ Multidimensional arrays

➤ Jagged arrays

➤ The `Array` class

➤ Arrays as parameters

➤ Enumerations

➤ Tuples

➤ Structural comparison

If you need to work with multiple objects of the same type, you can use collections (see Chapter 10) and arrays. C# has a special notation to declare, initialize, and use arrays. Behind the scenes, the `Array` class comes into play, which offers several methods to sort and filter the elements inside the array. Using an enumerator, you can iterate through all the elements of the array.

Also, .NET 4 introduces a new type `Tuple` that can be used to combine multiple objects of different types. See the "Tuples" section later in this chapter.

SIMPLE ARRAYS

If you need to use multiple objects of the same type, you can use an array. An *array* is a data structure that contains a number of elements of the same type.

Array Declaration

An array is declared by defining the type of elements inside the array followed by empty brackets and a variable name. For example, an array containing integer elements is declared as this:

```
int[] myArray;
```

Array Initialization

After declaring an array, memory must be allocated to hold all the elements of the array. An array is a reference type, so memory on the heap must be allocated. You do this by initializing the variable of the array using the new operator with the type and the number of elements inside the array. Here you specify the size of the array:

```
myArray = new int[4];
```

 Value and reference types are covered in Chapter 3, "Objects and Types."

With this declaration and initialization, the variable `myArray` references four integer values that are allocated on the managed heap (see Figure 6-1).

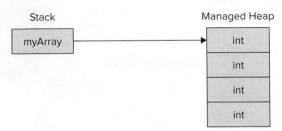

FIGURE 6-1

 The array cannot be resized after the size was specified without copying all elements. If you don't know the number of elements that should be in the array in advance, you can use a collection (see Chapter 10).

Instead of using a separate line to declare and initialize an array, you can use a single line:

```
int[] myArray = new int[4];
```

You can also assign values to every array element using an array initializer. Array initializers can be used only while declaring an array variable, not after the array is declared:

```
int[] myArray = new int[] {4, 7, 11, 2};
```

If you initialize the array using curly brackets, the size of the array can also be left out, because the compiler can count the number of elements itself:

```
int[] myArray = new int[] {4, 7, 11, 2};
```

There's even a shorter form using the C# compiler. Using curly brackets you can write the array declaration and initialization. The code generated from the compiler is the same as in the previous example:

```
int[] myArray = {4, 7, 11, 2};
```

Accessing Array Elements

After an array is declared and initialized, you can access the array elements using an indexer. Arrays only support indexers that have integer parameters.

With the indexer, you pass the element number to access the array. The indexer always starts with a value of 0 for the first element. The highest number you can pass to the indexer is the number of elements minus one, because the index starts at zero. In the following example, the array *myArray* is declared and initialized with four integer values. The elements can be accessed with indexer values 0, 1, 2, and 3.

```
int[] myArray = new int[] {4, 7, 11, 2};
int v1 = myArray[0];   // read first element
int v2 = myArray[1];   // read second element
myArray[3] = 44;       // change fourth element
```

 If you use a wrong indexer value where no element exists, an exception of type `IndexOutOfRangeException` *is thrown.*

If you don't know the number of elements in the array, you can use the `Length` property that is used in this `for` statement:

```
for (int i = 0; i < myArray.Length; i++)
{
    Console.WriteLine(myArray[i]);
}
```

Instead of using a `for` statement to iterate through all elements of the array, you can also use the `foreach` statement:

```
foreach (var val in myArray)
{
    Console.WriteLine(val);
}
```

 The `foreach` *statement makes use of the* `IEnumerable` *and* `IEnumerator` *interfaces, which are discussed later in this chapter.*

Using Reference Types

In addition to being able to declare arrays of predefined types, you can also declare arrays of custom types. Let's start with this `Person` class, the properties `FirstName` and `LastName` using auto-implemented properties, and an override of the `ToString()` method from the `Object` class:

```
public class Person
{
    public string FirstName { get; set; }
    public string LastName { get; set; }

    public override string ToString()
    {
        return String.Format("{0} {1}", FirstName, LastName);
    }
}
```

code snippet Sample1/Person.cs

Declaring an array of two `Person` elements is similar to declaring an array of `int`:

```
Person[] myPersons = new Person[2];
```

However, you must be aware that if the elements in the array are reference types, memory must be allocated for every array element. In case you use an item in the array where no memory was allocated, a `NullReferenceException` is thrown.

 For information about errors and exceptions, see Chapter 15.

You can allocate every element of the array by using an indexer starting from 0:

```
myPersons[0] = new Person { FirstName="Ayrton", LastName="Senna" };
myPersons[1] = new Person { FirstName="Michael", LastName="Schumacher" };
```

Figure 6-2 shows the objects in the managed heap with the `Person` array. `myPersons` is a variable that is stored on the stack. This variable references an array of `Person` elements that is stored on the managed heap. This array has enough space for two references. Every item in the array references a `Person` object that is also stored in the managed heap.

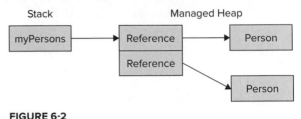

FIGURE 6-2

Similar to the `int` type, you can also use an array initializer with custom types:

```
Person[] myPersons2 =
{
    new Person { FirstName="Ayrton", LastName="Senna"},
    new Person { FirstName="Michael", LastName="Schumacher"}
};
```

MULTIDIMENSIONAL ARRAYS

Ordinary arrays (also known as one-dimensional arrays) are indexed by a single integer. A multidimensional array is indexed by two or more integers.

Figure 6-3 shows the mathematical notation for a two-dimensional array that has three rows and three columns. The first row has the values 1, 2, and 3, and the third row has the values 7, 8, and 9.

$$a = \begin{bmatrix} 1, 2, 3 \\ 4, 5, 6 \\ 7, 8, 9 \end{bmatrix}$$

FIGURE 6-3

Declaring this two-dimensional array with C# is done by putting a comma inside the brackets. The array is initialized by specifying the size of every dimension (also known as rank). Then the array elements can be accessed by using two integers with the indexer:

Available for download on Wrox.com

```
int[,] twodim = new int[3, 3];
twodim[0, 0] = 1;
twodim[0, 1] = 2;
twodim[0, 2] = 3;
twodim[1, 0] = 4;
twodim[1, 1] = 5;
twodim[1, 2] = 6;
twodim[2, 0] = 7;
twodim[2, 1] = 8;
twodim[2, 2] = 9;
```

code snippet Sample1/Program.cs

 You cannot change the rank after declaring an array.

You can also initialize the two-dimensional array by using an array indexer if you know the value for the elements in advance. For the initialization of the array, one outer curly bracket is used, and every row is initialized by using curly brackets inside the outer curly brackets.

```
int[,] twodim = {
                  {1, 2, 3},
                  {4, 5, 6},
                  {7, 8, 9}
                };
```

 When using an array initializer, you must initialize every element of the array. It is not possible to leave the initialization of some values for later.

By using two commas inside the brackets, you can declare a three-dimensional array:

```
int[,,] threedim = {
      { { 1, 2 }, { 3, 4 } },
      { { 5, 6 }, { 7, 8 } },
      { { 9, 10 }, { 11, 12 } }
    };

Console.WriteLine(threedim[0, 1, 1]);
```

JAGGED ARRAYS

A two-dimensional array has a rectangular size (for example, 3 × 3 elements). A jagged array is more flexible in sizing the array. With a jagged array every row can have a different size.

Figure 6-4 contrasts a two-dimensional array that has 3 × 3 elements with a jagged array. The jagged array shown contains three rows where the first row has two elements, the second row has six elements, and the third row has three elements.

Two-Dimensional Array

1	2	3
4	5	6
7	8	9

Jagged Array

1	2				
3	4	5	6	7	8
9	10	11			

FIGURE 6-4

A jagged array is declared by placing one pair of opening and closing brackets after another. With the initialization of the jagged array, only the size that defines the number of rows in the first pair of brackets is set. The second brackets that define the number of elements inside the row are kept empty because every row has a different number of elements. Next, the element number of the rows can be set for every row:

```
int[][] jagged = new int[3][];
jagged[0] = new int[2] { 1, 2 };
jagged[1] = new int[6] { 3, 4, 5, 6, 7, 8 };
jagged[2] = new int[3] { 9, 10, 11 };
```

code snippet Sample1/Program.cs

Iterating through all elements of a jagged array can be done with nested `for` loops. In the outer `for` loop every row is iterated, and the inner `for` loop iterates through every element inside a row.

```
            for (int row = 0; row < jagged.Length; row++)
            {
                for (int element = 0; element < jagged[row].Length; element++)
                {
                    Console.WriteLine("row: {0}, element: {1}, value: {2}",
                        row, element, jagged[row][element]);
                }
            }
```

The outcome of the iteration displays the rows and every element within the rows:

```
row: 0, element: 0, value: 1
row: 0, element: 1, value: 2
row: 1, element: 0, value: 3
row: 1, element: 1, value: 4
row: 1, element: 2, value: 5
row: 1, element: 3, value: 6
row: 1, element: 4, value: 7
row: 1, element: 5, value: 8
row: 2, element: 1, value: 9
row: 2, element: 2, value: 10
row: 2, element: 3, value: 11
```

ARRAY CLASS

Declaring an array with brackets is a C# notation using the `Array` class. Using the C# syntax behind the scenes creates a new class that derives from the abstract base class `Array`. This makes it possible to use methods and properties that are defined with the `Array` class with every C# array. For example, you've already used the `Length` property or iterated through the array by using the `foreach` statement. By doing this, you are using the `GetEnumerator()` method of the `Array` class.

Other properties that are implemented by the `Array` class are `LongLength` for arrays where the number of items doesn't fit within an integer, and `Rank` to get the number of dimensions.

Let's have a look at other members of the `Array` class by getting into various features.

Creating Arrays

The `Array` class is abstract, so you cannot create an array by using a constructor. However, instead of using the C# syntax to create array instances, it is also possible to create arrays by using the static `CreateInstance()` method. This is extremely useful if you don't know the type of elements in advance, because the type can be passed to the `CreateInstance()` method as a `Type` object.

The following example shows how to create an array of type `int` with a size of 5. The first argument of the `CreateInstance()` method requires the type of the elements, and the second argument defines the size. You can set values with the `SetValue()` method and read values with the `GetValue()` method.

Available for download on Wrox.com

```
Array intArray1 = Array.CreateInstance(typeof(int), 5);
for (int i = 0; i < 5; i++)
{
    intArray1.SetValue(33, i);
}

for (int i = 0; i < 5; i++)
{
    Console.WriteLine(intArray1.GetValue(i));
}
```

code snippet Sample1/Program.cs

You can also cast the created array to an array declared as `int[]`:

```
int[] intArray2 = (int[])intArray1;
```

The CreateInstance() method has many overloads to create multidimensional arrays and also to create arrays that are not 0-based. The following example creates a two-dimensional array with 2 × 3 elements. The first dimension is 1-based; the second dimension is 10-based.

```
int[] lengths = { 2, 3 };
int[] lowerBounds = { 1, 10 };
Array racers = Array.CreateInstance(typeof(Person), lengths, lowerBounds);
```

Setting the elements of the array, the SetValue() method accepts indices for every dimension:

```
racers.SetValue(new Person
{
    FirstName = "Alain",
    LastName = "Prost"
}, 1, 10);
racers.SetValue(new Person
{
    FirstName = "Emerson",
    LastName = "Fittipaldi"
}, 1, 11);
racers.SetValue(new Person
{
    FirstName = "Ayrton",
    LastName = "Senna"
}, 1, 12);
racers.SetValue(new Person
{
    FirstName = "Ralf",
    LastName = "Schumacher"
}, 2, 10);
racers.SetValue(new Person
{
    FirstName = "Fernando",
    LastName = "Alonso"
}, 2, 11);
racers.SetValue(new Person
{
    FirstName = "Jenson",
    LastName = "Button"
}, 2, 12);
```

code snippet Sample1/Program.cs

Although the array is not 0-based, you can assign it to a variable with the normal C# notation. You just have to pay attention not to cross the boundaries.

```
Person[,] racers2 = (Person[,])racers;
Person first = racers2[1, 10];
Person last = racers2[2, 12];
```

Copying Arrays

Because arrays are reference types, assigning an array variable to another one just gives you two variables referencing the same array. For copying arrays, the array implements the interface ICloneable. The Clone() method that is defined with this interface creates a shallow copy of the array.

If the elements of the array are value types, as in the following code segment, all values are copied, as you can see in Figure 6-5.

```
int[] intArray1 = {1, 2};
int[] intArray2 = (int[])intArray1.Clone();
```

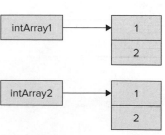

FIGURE 6-5

If the array contains reference types, only the references are copied, not the elements. Figure 6-6 shows the variables *beatles* and *beatlesClone*, where *beatlesClone* is created by calling the `Clone()` method from *beatles*. The `Person` objects that are referenced are the same with *beatles* and *beatlesClone*. If you change a property of an element of *beatlesClone*, you change the same object of *beatles*.

Available for download on Wrox.com

```
Person[] beatles = {
                      new Person { FirstName="John", LastName="Lennon" },
                      new Person { FirstName="Paul", LastName="McCartney" }
                   };
Person[] beatlesClone = (Person[])beatles.Clone();
```

code snippet Sample1/Program.cs

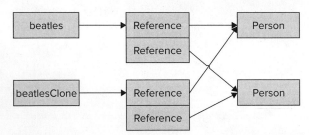

FIGURE 6-6

Instead of using the `Clone()` method, you can use the `Array.Copy()` method, which creates a shallow copy as well. But there's one important difference with `Clone()` and `Copy()`: `Clone()` creates a new array; with `Copy()` you have to pass an existing array with the same rank and enough elements.

 If you need a deep copy of an array containing reference types, you have to iterate the array and create new objects.

Sorting

The `Array` class uses the QuickSort algorithm for sorting the elements in the array. The `Sort()` method requires the interface `IComparable` to be implemented by the elements in the array. Simple types such as `System.String` and `System.Int32` implement `IComparable`, so you can sort elements containing these types.

With the sample program, the array name contains elements of type string, and this array can be sorted:

Available for download on Wrox.com

```
string[] names = {
    "Christina Aguilera",
    "Shakira",
    "Beyonce",
    "Gwen Stefani"
};

Array.Sort(names);

foreach (var name in names)
{
    Console.WriteLine(name);
}
```

code snippet SortingSample/Program.cs

The output of the application shows the sorted result of the array:

```
Beyonce
Christina Aguilera
Gwen Stefani
Shakira
```

If you are using custom classes with the array, you must implement the interface IComparable. This interface defines just one method, CompareTo(), that must return 0 if the objects to compare are equal, a value smaller than 0 if the instance should go before the object from the parameter, and a value larger than 0 if the instance should go after the object from the parameter.

Change the Person class to implement the interface IComparable<Person>. The comparison is done on the value of the LastName. Because the LastName is of type string, and the String class already implements the IComparable interface, with the implementation you can rely on the CompareTo() method of the String class. If the LastName has the same value, the FirstName is compared:

Available for download on Wrox.com

```
public class Person: IComparable<Person>
{
    public int CompareTo(Person other)
    {
        if (other == null) throw new ArgumentNullException("other");

        int result = this.LastName.CompareTo(
                other.LastName);
        if (result == 0)
        {
            result = this.FirstName.CompareTo(
                other.FirstName);
        }
        return result;
    }
    //...
```

code snippet SortingSample/Person.cs

Now it is possible to sort an array of Person objects by the last name:

Available for download on Wrox.com

```
Person[] persons = {
    new Person { FirstName="Damon", LastName="Hill" },
    new Person { FirstName="Niki", LastName="Lauda" },
    new Person { FirstName="Ayrton", LastName="Senna" },
    new Person { FirstName="Graham", LastName="Hill" }
};

Array.Sort(persons);
foreach (var p in persons)
{
    Console.WriteLine(p);
}
```

code snippet SortingSample/Program.cs

Using the sort of the Person class, the output returns the names sorted by the last name:

```
Damon Hill
Graham Hill
Niki Lauda
Ayrton Senna
```

If the Person object should be sorted differently, or if you don't have the option to change the class that is used as an element in the array, you can implement the interface IComparer or IComparer<T>. These interfaces define the method Compare(). One of these interfaces must be implemented by the class that should be compared. The `IComparer` interface is independent of the class to compare. That's why the `Compare()` method defines two arguments that should be compared. The return value is similar to the `CompareTo()` method of the `IComparable` interface.

The class `PersonComparer` implements the `IComparer<Person>` interface to sort `Person` objects either by `firstName` or by `lastName` The enumeration `PersonCompareType` defines the different sorting options that are available with the `PersonComparer`: `FirstName` and `LastName`. How the compare should happen is defined with the constructor of the class `PersonComparer` where a `PersonCompareType` value is set. The `Compare()` method is implemented with a `switch` statement to compare either by `LastName` or by `FirstName`.

```csharp
public enum PersonCompareType
{
    FirstName,
    LastName
}

public class PersonComparer: IComparer<Person>
{
    private PersonCompareType compareType;

    public PersonComparer(PersonCompareType compareType)
    {
        this.compareType = compareType;
    }

    public int Compare(Person x, Person y)
    {
        if (x == null) throw new ArgumentNullException("x");
        if (y == null) throw new ArgumentNullException("y");

        switch (compareType)
        {
            case PersonCompareType.FirstName:
                return x.FirstName.CompareTo(y.FirstName);
            case PersonCompareType.LastName:
                return x.LastName.CompareTo(y.LastName);
            default:
                throw new ArgumentException(
                    "unexpected compare type");
        }
    }
}
```

code snippet SortingSample/PersonComparer.cs

Now you can pass a `PersonComparer` object to the second argument of the `Array.Sort()` method. Here the persons are sorted by first name:

```csharp
Array.Sort(persons,
    new PersonComparer(PersonCompareType.FirstName));
foreach (var p in persons)
{
    Console.WriteLine(p);
}
```

code snippet SortingSample/Program.cs

The `persons` array is now sorted by the first name:

```
Ayrton Senna
Damon Hill
Graham Hill
Niki Lauda
```

 The `Array` *class also offers* `Sort` *methods that require a delegate as an argument. With this argument you can pass a method to do the comparison of two objects instead of relying on the* `IComparable` *or* `IComparer` *interfaces. Chapter 8, "Delegates, Lambdas, and Events," discusses how to use delegates.*

ARRAYS AS PARAMETERS

Arrays can be passed as parameters to methods, and returned from methods. Returning an array, you just have to declare the array as the return type, as shown with the following method `GetPersons()`:

Available for download on Wrox.com

```
static Person[] GetPersons()
{
    return new Person[] {
        new Person { FirstName="Damon", LastName="Hill" },
        new Person { FirstName="Niki", LastName="Lauda" },
        new Person { FirstName="Ayrton", LastName="Senna" },
        new Person { FirstName="Graham", LastName="Hill" }
    };
}
```

code snippet SortingSample/Program.cs

Passing arrays to a method, the array is declared with the parameter, as shown with the method `DisplayPersons()`:

```
static void DisplayPersons(Person[] persons)
{
    //...
```

Array Covariance

With arrays, covariance is supported. This means that an array can be declared as a base type and elements of derived types can be assigned to the elements.

For example, you can declare a parameter of type `object[]` as shown and pass a `Person[]` to it:

```
static void DisplayArray(object[] data)
{
    //...
}
```

 Array covariance is only possible with reference types, not with value types.

Array covariance has an issue that can only resolved with runtime exceptions. If you assign a `Person` *array to an object array, the object array can then be used with anything that derives from the object. The compiler accepts, for example, passing a string to array elements. However, because really a* `Person` *array is referenced by the object array, a runtime exception occurs.*

ArraySegment<T>

The struct `ArraySegment<T>` represents a segment of an array. If parts of an array should be returned from or passed to a method, a segment can be used. Instead of passing the array, offset, and count with separate parameters to a method, you can pass a single parameter with `ArraySegment<T>`. With this structure the information about the segment (the offset and count) is contained within the members of the structure.

The method `SumOfSegments` takes an array of `ArraySegment<int>` elements to calculate the sum of all the integers that are defined with the segments and returns the sum:

```
static int SumOfSegments(ArraySegment<int>[] segments)
{
    int sum = 0;
    foreach (var segment in segments)
    {
        for (int i = segment.Offset; i < segment.Offset +
            segment.Count; i++)
        {
            sum += segment.Array[i];
        }
    }
    return sum;
}
```

code snippet ArraySegmentSample/Program.cs

This method is used by passing an array of segments. The first array element references three elements of `ar1` starting with the first element; the second array element references three elements of `ar2` starting with the fourth element:

```
int[] ar1 = { 1, 4, 5, 11, 13, 18 };
int[] ar2 = { 3, 4, 5, 18, 21, 27, 33 };

var segments = new ArraySegment<int>[2]
{
    new ArraySegment<int>(ar1, 0, 3),
    new ArraySegment<int>(ar2, 3, 3)
};
var sum = SumOfSegments(segments);
```

> *It's important to note that array segments don't copy the elements of the originating array. Instead, the originating array can be accessed through `ArraySegment<T>`. If elements of the array segment are changed, the changes can be seen in the original array.*

ENUMERATIONS

By using the `foreach` statement you can iterate elements of a collection (see Chapter 10) without the need to know the number of elements inside the collection. The `foreach` statement uses an enumerator. Figure 6-7 shows the relationship between the client invoking the `foreach` method and the collection. The array or collection implements the `IEnumerable` interface with the `GetEnumerator()` method. The `GetEnumerator()` method returns an enumerator implementing the IEnumerator interface. The interface IEnumerator then is used by the foreach statement to iterate through the collection.

> *The* GetEnumerator() *method is defined with the interface* IEnumerable. *The foreach statement doesn't really need this interface implemented in the collection class. It's enough to have a method with the name* GetEnumerator() *that returns an object implementing the* IEnumerator *interface.*

IEnumerator Interface

The foreach statement uses the methods and properties of the IEnumerator interface to iterate all elements in a collection. For this, IEnumerator defines the property Current to return the element where the cursor is positioned, and the method MoveNext() to move to the next element of the collection. MoveNext() returns true if there's an element, and false if no more elements are available.

The generic version of this interface IEnumerator<T> derives from the interface IDisposable and thus defines a Dispose() method to clean up resources allocated by the enumerator.

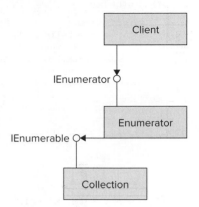

FIGURE 6-7

> *The* IEnumerator *interface also defines the* Reset() *method for COM interoperability. Many .NET enumerators implement this by throwing an exception of type* NotSupportedException.

foreach Statement

The C# foreach statement is not resolved to a foreach statement in the IL code. Instead, the C# compiler converts the foreach statement to methods and properties of the IEnumerator interface. Here's a simple foreach statement to iterate all elements in the persons array and to display them person by person:

```
foreach (var p in persons)
{
    Console.WriteLine(p);
}
```

The foreach statement is resolved to the following code segment. First, the GetEnumerator() method is invoked to get an enumerator for the array. Inside a while loop — as long as MoveNext() returns true — the elements of the array are accessed using the Current property:

```
IEnumerator<Person> enumerator = persons.GetEnumerator();
while (enumerator.MoveNext())
{
    Person p = enumerator.Current;
    Console.WriteLine(p);
}
```

yield Statement

Since the first release of C#, it has been easy to iterate through collections by using the foreach statement. With C# 1.0, it was still a lot of work to create an enumerator. C# 2.0 added the yield statement for creating enumerators easily. The yield return statement returns one element of a collection and moves the position to the next element, and yield break stops the iteration.

The next example shows the implementation of a simple collection using the yield return statement. The class HelloCollection contains the method GetEnumerator(). The implementation of the GetEnumerator() method contains two yield return statements where the strings Hello and World are returned:

```csharp
using System;
using System.Collections;

namespace Wrox.ProCSharp.Arrays
{
    public class HelloCollection
    {
        public IEnumerator<string> GetEnumerator()
        {
            yield return "Hello";
            yield return "World";
        }
    }
}
```

code snippet YieldDemo/Program.cs

> *A method or property that contains yield statements is also known as an iterator block. An iterator block must be declared to return an IEnumerator or IEnumerable interface, or the generic versions of these interfaces. This block may contain multiple yield return or yield break statements; a return statement is not allowed.*

Now it is possible to iterate through the collection using a foreach statement:

```csharp
public void HelloWorld()
{
    var helloCollection = new HelloCollection();
    foreach (var s in helloCollection)
    {
        Console.WriteLine(s);
    }
}
```

With an iterator block the compiler generates a yield type, including a state machine, as shown with the following code segment. The yield type implements the properties and methods of the interfaces IEnumerator and IDisposable. In the sample, you can see the yield type as the inner class Enumerator. The GetEnumerator() method of the outer class instantiates and returns a new yield type. Within the yield type, the variable state defines the current position of the iteration and is changed every time the method MoveNext() is invoked. MoveNext() encapsulates the code of the iterator block and sets the value of the current variable so that the Current property returns an object depending on the position.

```csharp
public class HelloCollection
{
    public IEnumerator GetEnumerator()
    {
        return new Enumerator(0);
    }

    public class Enumerator: IEnumerator<string>, IEnumerator, IDisposable
    {
        private int state;
        private string current;

        public Enumerator(int state)
        {
            this.state = state;
        }
        bool System.Collections.IEnumerator.MoveNext()
        {
            switch (state)
            {
                case 0:
                    current = "Hello";
                    state = 1;
                    return true;
                case 1:
                    current = "World";
                    state = 2;
                    return true;
                case 2:
                    break;
            }

            return false;
        }

        void System.Collections.IEnumerator.Reset()
        {
            throw new NotSupportedException();
        }

        string System.Collections.Generic.IEnumerator<string>.Current
        {
            get
            {
                return current;
            }
        }
        object System.Collections.IEnumerator.Current
        {
            get
            {
                return current;
            }
        }

        void IDisposable.Dispose()
        {
        }
    }
}
```

Remember that the `yield` *statement produces an enumerator, and not just a list that is filled with items. This enumerator is invoked by the* `foreach` *statement. As item by item is accessed from the* `foreach`, *the enumerator is accessed. This makes it possible to iterate through huge amounts of data without reading all the data into memory in one turn.*

Different Ways to Iterate Through Collections

In a slightly larger and more realistic way than the Hello World example, you can use the `yield return` statement to iterate through a collection in different ways. The class `MusicTitles` allows iterating the titles in a default way with the `GetEnumerator()` method, in reverse order with the `Reverse()` method, and to iterate through a subset with the `Subset()` method:

```csharp
public class MusicTitles
{
    string[] names = { "Tubular Bells", "Hergest Ridge", "Ommadawn",
                       "Platinum" };

    public IEnumerator<string> GetEnumerator()
    {
        for (int i = 0; i < 4; i++)
        {
            yield return names[i];
        }
    }

    public IEnumerable<string> Reverse()
    {
        for (int i = 3; i >= 0; i--)
        {
            yield return names[i];
        }
    }

    public IEnumerable<string> Subset(int index, int length)
    {
        for (int i = index; i < index + length; i++)
        {
            yield return names[i];
        }
    }
}
```

code snippet YieldDemo/Program.cs

The default iteration that's supported by a class is the `GetEnumerator()` *method that is defined to return* `IEnumerator`. *Named iterations return* `IEnumerable`.

The client code to iterate through the string array first uses the `GetEnumerator()` method, which you don't have to write in your code because this one is used by default. Then the titles are iterated in reverse, and finally a subset is iterated by passing the index and number of items to iterate to the `Subset()` method:

```csharp
var titles = new MusicTitles();
foreach (var title in titles)
{
    Console.WriteLine(title);
```

```
    }
    Console.WriteLine();

    Console.WriteLine("reverse");
    foreach (var title in titles.Reverse())
    {
        Console.WriteLine(title);
    }
    Console.WriteLine();

    Console.WriteLine("subset");
    foreach (var title in titles.Subset(2, 2))
    {
        Console.WriteLine(title);
    }
```

Returning Enumerators with Yield Return

With the yield statement you can also do more complex things, for example, returning an enumerator from `yield return`.

With the TicTacToe game, players alternate putting a cross or a circle in one of nine fields. These moves are simulated by the `GameMoves` class. The methods `Cross()` and `Circle()` are the iterator blocks for creating iterator types. The variables `cross` and `circle` are set to `Cross()` and `Circle()` inside the constructor of the `GameMoves` class. By setting these fields the methods are not invoked, but they are set to the iterator types that are defined with the iterator blocks. Within the `Cross()` iterator block, information about the move is written to the console and the move number is incremented. If the move number is higher than 8, the iteration ends with `yield break`; otherwise, the enumerator object of the circle yield type is returned with each iteration. The `Circle()` iterator block is very similar to the `Cross()` iterator block; it just returns the cross iterator type with each iteration.

```
public class GameMoves
{
    private IEnumerator cross;
    private IEnumerator circle;

    public GameMoves()
    {
        cross = Cross();
        circle = Circle();
    }

    private int move = 0;
    const int MaxMoves = 9;

    public IEnumerator Cross()
    {
        while (true)
        {
            Console.WriteLine("Cross, move {0}", move);
            if (++move >= MaxMoves)
                yield break;
            yield return circle;
        }
    }

    public IEnumerator Circle()
    {
        while (true)
        {
            Console.WriteLine("Circle, move {0}", move);
            if (++move >= MaxMoves)
```

```
                    yield break;
                yield return cross;
            }
        }
    }
```

code snippet YieldDemo/GameMoves.cs

From the client program, you can use the class `GameMoves` as follows. The first move is set by setting enumerator to the enumerator type returned by `game.Cross()`. In a `while` loop, `enumerator.MoveNext()` is called. The first time this is invoked, the `Cross()` method is called, which returns the other enumerator with a `yield` statement. The returned value can be accessed with the `Current` property and is set to the `enumerator` variable for the next loop:

Available for
download on
Wrox.com

```
var game = new GameMoves();
IEnumerator enumerator = game.Cross();
while (enumerator.MoveNext())
{
    enumerator = enumerator.Current as IEnumerator;
}
```

code snippet YieldDemo/Program.cs

The outcome of this program shows alternating moves until the last move:

```
Cross, move 0
Circle, move 1
Cross, move 2
Circle, move 3
Cross, move 4
Circle, move 5
Cross, move 6
Circle, move 7
Cross, move 8
```

TUPLES

Arrays combine objects of the same type; tuples can combine objects of different types. Tuples have the origin in functional programming languages such as F# where they are used often. With .NET 4, tuples are available with the .NET Framework for all .NET languages.

.NET 4 defines eight generic `Tuple` classes and one static `Tuple` class that act as a factory of tuples. The different generic `Tuple` classes are here for supporting a different number of elements; e.g., `Tuple<T1>` contains one element, `Tuple<T1, T2>` contains two elements, and so on.

The method `Divide()` demonstrates returning a tuple with two members — `Tuple<int, int>`. The parameters of the generic class define the types of the members, which are both integers. The tuple is created with the static `Create()` method of the static `Tuple` class. Again, the generic parameters of the `Create()` method define the type of tuple that is instantiated. The newly created tuple is initialized with the `result` and `reminder` variables to return the result of the division:

Available for
download on
Wrox.com

```
public static Tuple<int, int> Divide(int dividend, int divisor)
{
    int result = dividend / divisor;
    int reminder = dividend % divisor;

    return Tuple.Create<int, int>(result, reminder);
}
```

code snippet TuplesSample/Program.cs

The following code shows invoking the `Divide()` method. The items of the tuple can be accessed with the properties `Item1` and `Item2`:

```
var result = Divide(5, 2);
Console.WriteLine("result of division: {0}, reminder: {1}",
    result.Item1, result.Item2);
```

In case you have more than eight items that should be included in a tuple, you can use the `Tuple` class definition with eight parameters. The last template parameter is named `TRest` to indicate that you must pass a tuple itself. That way you can create tuples with any number of parameters.

To demonstrate this functionality:

```
public class Tuple<T1, T2, T3, T4, T5, T6, T7, TRest>
```

Here, the last template parameter is a tuple type itself, so you can create a tuple with any number of items:

```
var tuple = Tuple.Create<string, string, string, int, int, int, double,
    Tuple<int, int>>(
        "Stephanie", "Alina", "Nagel", 2009, 6, 2, 1.37,
        Tuple.Create<int, int>(52, 3490));
```

STRUCTURAL COMPARISON

Both arrays and tuples implement the interfaces `IStructuralEquatable` and `IStructuralComparable`. These interfaces are new with .NET 4 and not only compare references but the content as well. This interface is implemented explicitly, so it is necessary to cast the arrays and tuples to this interface on use. `IStructuralEquatable` is used to compare whether two tuples or arrays have the same content; `IStructuralComparable` is used to sort tuples or arrays.

With the sample demonstrating `IStructuralEquatable`, the `Person` class implementing the interface `IEquatable` is used. `IEquatable` defines a strongly typed `Equals()` method where the values of the `FirstName` and `LastName` properties are compared:

Available for
download on
Wrox.com

```
public class Person: IEquatable<Person>
{
    public int Id { get; private set; }
    public string FirstName { get; set; }
    public string LastName { get; set; }

    public override string ToString()
    {
        return String.Format("{0}, {1} {2}", Id, FirstName, LastName);
    }

    public override bool Equals(object obj)
    {
        if (obj == null) throw new ArgumentNullException("obj");
        return Equals(obj as Person);
    }

    public override int GetHashCode()
    {
        return Id.GetHashCode();
    }

    public bool Equals(Person other)
    {
        if (other == null) throw new ArgumentNullException("other");

        return this.Id == other.Id && this.FirstName == other.FirstName &&
```

```
                              this.LastName == other.LastName;
                    }
          }
```

Now two arrays containing `Person` items are created. Both arrays contain the same `Person` object with the variable name `janet`, and two different `Person` objects that have the same content. The comparison operator `!=` returns `true` because there are indeed two different arrays referenced from two variable names `persons1` and `persons2`. Because the `Equals()` method with one parameter is not overridden by the `Array` class, the same happens as with the `==` operator to compare the references, and they are not the same:

```
var janet = new Person { FirstName = "Janet", LastName = "Jackson" };
Person[] persons1 = {
                          new Person
                          {
                              FirstName = "Michael",
                              LastName = "Jackson"
                          },
                          janet
                    };
Person[] persons2 = {
                          new Person
                          {
                              FirstName = "Michael",
                              LastName = "Jackson"
                          },
                          janet
                    };
if (persons1 != persons2)
    Console.WriteLine("not the same reference");
```

Invoking the `Equals()` method defined by the `IStructuralEquatable` that is the method with the first parameter of type `object` and the second parameter of type `IEqualityComparer`, you can define how the comparison should be done by passing an object that implements `IEqualityComparer<T>`. A default implementation of the `IEqualityComparer` is done by the `EqualityComparer<T>` class. This implementation checks if the type implements the interface `IEquatable`, and invokes the `IEquatable`. `Equals()` method. If the type does not implement `IEquatable`, the `Equals()` method from the base class `Object` is invoked to do the comparison.

`Person` implements `IEquatable<Person>`, where the content of the objects is compared and the arrays indeed contain the same content:

```
if ((persons1 as IStructuralEquatable).Equals(persons2,
    EqualityComparer<Person>.Default))
{
    Console.WriteLine("the same content");
}
```

You'll see next how the same thing can be done with tuples. Here, two tuple instances are created that have the same content. Of course, because the references `t1` and `t2` reference two different objects, the comparison operator `!=` returns true:

```
var t1 = Tuple.Create<int, string>(1, "Stephanie");
var t2 = Tuple.Create<int, string>(1, "Stephanie");
if (t1 != t2)
    Console.WriteLine("not the same reference to the tuple");
```

The `Tuple<>` class offers two `Equals()` methods: one that is overridden from the `Object` base class with an `object` as parameter, and the second that is defined by the `IStructuralEqualityComparer` interface with `object` and `IEqualityComparer` as parameters. Another tuple can be passed to the first method as shown. This method uses `EqualityComparer<object>.Default` to get an `ObjectEqualityComparer<object>` for the comparison. This way every item of the tuple is compared by invoking the `Object.Equals()` method. If every item returns `true`, the final result of the `Equals()` method is `true`, which is the case here with the same int and string values:

```
if (t1.Equals(t2))
    Console.WriteLine("the same content");
```

You can also create a custom `IEqualityComparer`, as shown with the class `TupleComparer`. This class implements the two methods `Equals()` and `GetHashCode()` of the `IEqualityComparer` interface:

```
class TupleComparer: IEqualityComparer
{
    public new bool Equals(object x, object y)
    {
        return x.Equals(y);
    }

    public int GetHashCode(object obj)
    {
        return obj.GetHashCode();
    }
}
```

code snippet StructuralComparison/Program.cs

> *The implementation of the* `Equals()` *method of the* `IEqualityComparer` *interface requires the new modifier or an implicit interface implementation because the base class* `Object` *defines a static* `Equals()` *method with two parameters as well.*

The `TupleComparer` is used, passing a new instance to the `Equals()` method of the `Tuple<T1, T2>` class. The `Equals()` method of the `Tuple` class invokes the `Equals()` method of the `TupleComparer` for every item to be compared. So with the `Tuple<T1, T2>` class, the `TupleComparer` is invoked two times to check whether all items are equal:

```
if (t1.Equals(t2, new TupleComparer()))
    Console.WriteLine("equals using TupleComparer");
```

SUMMARY

In this chapter, you've seen the C# notation to create and use simple, multidimensional, and jagged arrays. The `Array` class is used behind the scenes of C# arrays, and this way you can invoke properties and methods of this class with array variables.

You've seen how to sort elements in the array by using the `IComparable` and `IComparer` interfaces. You've learned using and creating enumerators, the interfaces `IEnumerable` and `IEnumerator`, and the `yield` statement. You've seen tuples, a new feature of .NET 4.

Moving on, the next chapter focuses on operators and casts.

7

Operators and Casts

WHAT'S IN THIS CHAPTER?

➤ Operators in C#

➤ The idea of equality when dealing with reference and value types

➤ Data conversion between primitive data types

➤ Converting value types to reference types using boxing

➤ Converting between reference types by casting

➤ Overloading the standard operators for custom types

➤ Adding cast operators to custom types

The preceding chapters have covered most of what you need to start writing useful programs using C#. This chapter completes the discussion of the essential language elements and illustrates some powerful aspects of C# that allow you to extend the capabilities of the C# language.

OPERATORS

Although most of C#'s operators should be familiar to C and C++ developers, this section discusses the most important operators for the benefit of new programmers and Visual Basic converts, and sheds light on some of the changes introduced with C#.

C# supports the operators listed in the following table:

CATEGORY	OPERATOR
Arithmetic	+ - * / %
Logical	& | ^ ~ && || !
String concatenation	+
Increment and decrement	++ --
Bit shifting	<< >>
Comparison	== != < > <= >=

continues

(continued)

CATEGORY	OPERATOR
Assignment	= += -= *= /= %= &= |= ^= <<= >>=
Member access (for objects and structs)	.
Indexing (for arrays and indexers)	[]
Cast	()
Conditional (the ternary operator)	?:
Delegate concatenation and removal (discussed in Chapter 8, "Delegates, Lambdas, and Events")	+ -
Object creation	new
Type information	sizeof is typeof as
Overflow exception control	checked unchecked
Indirection and address	[]
Namespace alias qualifier (discussed in Chapter 2, "Core C#")	::
Null coalescing operator	??

Note that four specific operators (sizeof, *, ->, and &, listed in the following table), however, are available only in unsafe code (code that bypasses C#'s type-safety checking), which is discussed in Chapter 13, "Memory Management and Pointers." It is also important to note that the sizeof operator keywords, when used with the very early versions of the .NET Framework 1.0 and 1.1, required the unsafe mode. This is not a requirement since the .NET Framework 2.0 version.

CATEGORY	OPERATOR
Operator keywords	sizeof (for .NET Framework versions 1.0 and 1.1 only)
Operators	* -> &

One of the biggest pitfalls to watch out for when using C# operators is that, as with other C-style languages, C# uses different operators for assignment (=) and comparison (==). For instance, the following statement means *let x equal three*:

```
x = 3;
```

If you now want to compare x to a value, you need to use the double equals sign ==:

```
if (x == 3)
{

}
```

Fortunately, C#'s strict type-safety rules prevent the very common C error where assignment is performed instead of comparison in logical statements. This means that in C# the following statement will generate a compiler error:

```
if (x = 3)
{

}
```

Visual Basic programmers who are accustomed to using the ampersand (&) character to concatenate strings will have to make an adjustment. In C#, the plus sign (+) is used instead for concatenation, whereas the & symbol denotes a bitwise AND between two different integer values. The symbol | allows you to perform a bitwise OR between two integers. Visual Basic programmers also might not recognize the modulus (%)

arithmetic operator. This returns the remainder after division, so, for example, x % 5 returns 2 if x is equal to 7.

You will use few pointers in C#, and, therefore, few indirection operators. More specifically, the only place you will use them is within blocks of unsafe code, because that is the only place in C# where pointers are allowed. Pointers and unsafe code are discussed in Chapter 13.

Operator Shortcuts

The following table shows the full list of shortcut assignment operators available in C#.

SHORTCUT OPERATOR	EQUIVALENT TO
x++, ++x	x = x + 1
x--, --x	x = x - 1
x += y	x = x + y
x -= y	x = x - y
x *= y	x = x * y
x /= y	x = x / y
x %= y	x = x % y
x >>= y	x = x >> y
x <<= y	x = x << y
x &= y	x = x & y
x |= y	x = x | y

You may be wondering why there are two examples each for the ++ increment and the -- decrement operators. Placing the operator *before* the expression is known as a *prefix*, placing the operator *after* the expression is known as a *postfix*, and it is important to note that there is a difference in the way they behave.

The increment and decrement operators can act both as whole expressions and within expressions. When used by themselves, the effect of both the prefix and postfix versions is identical and corresponds to the statement x = x + 1. When used within larger expressions, the prefix operator will increment the value of x *before* the expression is evaluated; in other words, x is incremented and the new value is used in the expression. In contrast, the postfix operator increments the value of x *after* the expression is evaluated — the expression is evaluated using the original value of x. The following example uses the increment operator (++) as an example to demonstrate the difference between the prefix and postfix behavior:

```
int x = 5;

if (++x == 6)  // true - x is incremented to 6 before the evaluation
{
    Console.WriteLine("This will execute");
}

if (x++ == 7) // false - x is incremented to 7 after the evaluation
{
    Console.WriteLine("This won't");
}
```

The first if condition evaluates to true, because x is incremented from 5 to 6 *before* the expression is evaluated. The condition in the second if statement is false, however, because x is incremented to 7 only after the entire expression has been evaluated (while x == 6).

The prefix and postfix operators --x and x-- behave in the same way, but decrement rather than increment the operand.

The other shortcut operators, such as += and -=, require two operands, and are used to modify the value of the first operand by performing an arithmetic, logical, or bitwise operation on it. For example, the next two lines are equivalent:

```
x += 5;
x = x + 5;
```

The following sections look at some of the primary and cast operators that you will frequently use within your C# code.

The Conditional Operator

The conditional operator (?:), also known as the ternary operator, is a shorthand form of the if...else construction. It gets its name from the fact that it involves three operands. It allows you to evaluate a condition, returning one value if that condition is true, or another value if it is false. The syntax is

```
condition ? true_value: false_value
```

Here, *condition* is the Boolean expression to be evaluated, *true_value* is the value that will be returned if *condition* is true, and *false_value* is the value that will be returned otherwise.

When used sparingly, the conditional operator can add a dash of terseness to your programs. It is especially handy for providing one of a couple of arguments to a function that is being invoked. You can use it to quickly convert a Boolean value to a string value of true or false. It is also handy for displaying the correct singular or plural form of a word, for example:

```
int x = 1;
string s = x + " ";
s += (x == 1 ? "man": "men");
Console.WriteLine(s);
```

This code displays 1 man if x is equal to one but will display the correct plural form for any other number. Note, however, that if your output needs to be localized to different languages, you will have to write more sophisticated routines to take into account the different grammatical rules of different languages.

The checked and unchecked Operators

Consider the following code:

```
byte b = 255;
b++;
Console.WriteLine(b.ToString());
```

The byte data type can hold values only in the range 0 to 255, so incrementing the value of b causes an overflow. How the CLR handles this depends on a number of issues, including compiler options, so whenever there's a risk of an unintentional overflow, you need some way of making sure that you get the result you want.

To do this, C# provides the checked and unchecked operators. If you mark a block of code as checked, the CLR will enforce overflow checking, and throw an OverflowException if an overflow occurs. Let's change the code to include the checked operator:

```
byte b = 255;
checked
{
    b++;
}
Console.WriteLine(b.ToString());
```

When you try to run this code, you will get an error message like this:

```
Unhandled Exception: System.OverflowException: Arithmetic operation resulted in an
    overflow at Wrox.ProCSharp.Basics.OverflowTest.Main(String[] args)
```

 You can enforce overflow checking for all unmarked code in your program by specifying the /checked *compiler option.*

If you want to suppress overflow checking, you can mark the code as unchecked:

```
byte b = 255;
unchecked
{
    b++;
}
Console.WriteLine(b.ToString());
```

In this case, no exception will be raised, but you will lose data — because the byte type cannot hold a value of 256, the overflowing bits will be discarded, and your b variable will hold a value of zero (0).

Note that unchecked is the default behavior. The only time you are likely to need to explicitly use the unchecked keyword is if you need a few unchecked lines of code inside a larger block that you have explicitly marked as checked.

The is Operator

The is operator allows you to check whether an object is compatible with a specific type. The phrase "is compatible" means that an object either is of that type or is derived from that type. For example, to check whether a variable is compatible with the object type, you could use the following bit of code:

```
int i = 10;
if (i is object)
{
    Console.WriteLine("i is an object");
}
```

int, like all C# data types, inherits from object; therefore, the expression i is object will evaluate to true in this case, and the appropriate message will be displayed.

The as Operator

The as operator is used to perform explicit type conversions of reference types. If the type being converted is compatible with the specified type, conversion is performed successfully. However, if the types are incompatible, the as operator returns the value null. As shown in the following code, attempting to convert an object reference to a string will return null if the object reference does not actually refer to a string instance:

```
object o1 = "Some String";
object o2 = 5;

string s1 = o1 as string;    // s1 = "Some String"
string s2 = o2 as string;    // s2 = null
```

The as operator allows you to perform a safe type conversion in a single step without the need to first test the type using the is operator and then perform the conversion.

The sizeof Operator

You can determine the size (in bytes) required on the stack by a value type using the sizeof operator:

```
Console.WriteLine(sizeof(int));
```

This will display the number 4, because an `int` is 4 bytes long.

If you are using the `sizeof` operator with complex types (and not primitive types), you will need to block the code within an `unsafe` block as illustrated here:

```
unsafe
{
    Console.WriteLine(sizeof(Customer));
}
```

Chapter 13 looks at unsafe code in more detail.

The typeof Operator

The `typeof` operator returns a `System.Type` object representing a specified type. For example, `typeof(string)` will return a `Type` object representing the `System.String` type. This is useful when you want to use reflection to find information about an object dynamically. Chapter 14, "Reflection," looks at reflection.

Nullable Types and Operators

Looking at the Boolean type, you have a true or false value that you can assign to this type. However, what if you wanted to define the value of the type as undefined? This is where using nullable types can have a distinct value to your applications. If you use nullable types in your programs, you must always consider the effect a `null` value can have when used in conjunction with the various operators. Usually, when using a unary or binary operator with nullable types, the result will be `null` if one or both of the operands is `null`. For example:

```
int? a = null;

int? b = a + 4;      // b = null
int? c = a * 5;      // c = null
```

However, when comparing nullable types, if only one of the operands is `null`, the comparison will always equate to `false`. This means that you cannot assume a condition is `true` just because its opposite is `false`, as often happens in programs using non-nullable types. For example:

```
int? a = null;
int? b = -5;

if (a > = b)
    Console.WriteLine("a > = b");
else
    Console.WriteLine("a < b");
```

> *The possibility of a* `null` *value means that you cannot freely combine nullable and non-nullable types in an expression. This is discussed in the "Type Conversions" section later in this chapter.*

The Null Coalescing Operator

The null coalescing operator (`??`) provides a shorthand mechanism to cater to the possibility of `null` values when working with nullable and reference types. The operator is placed between two operands — the first operand must be a nullable type or reference type, and the second operand must be of the same type as the first or of a type that is implicitly convertible to the type of the first operand. The null coalescing operator evaluates as follows:

➤ If the first operand is not `null`, then the overall expression has the value of the first operand.

➤ If the first operand is `null`, then the overall expression has the value of the second operand.

For example:

```
int? a = null;
int b;

b = a ?? 10;      // b has the value 10
a = 3;
b = a ?? 10;      // b has the value 3
```

If the second operand cannot be implicitly converted to the type of the first operand, a compile-time error is generated.

Operator Precedence

The following table shows the order of precedence of the C# operators. The operators at the top of the table are those with the highest precedence (that is, the ones evaluated first in an expression containing multiple operators).

GROUP	OPERATORS
Primary	`() . [] x++ x-- new typeof sizeof checked unchecked`
Unary	`+ - ! ~ ++x --x and casts`
Multiplication/division	`* / %`
Addition/subtraction	`+ -`
Bitwise shift operators	`<< >>`
Relational	`< ><= >= is as`
Comparison	`== !=`
Bitwise AND	`&`
Bitwise XOR	`^`
Bitwise OR	`|`
Boolean AND	`&&`
Boolean OR	`||`
Conditional operator	`?:`
Assignment	`= += -= *= /= %= &= |= ^= <<= >>= >>>=`

 In complex expressions, you should avoid relying on operator precedence to produce the correct result. Using parentheses to specify the order in which you want operators applied clarifies your code and prevents potential confusion.

TYPE SAFETY

Chapter 1, ".NET Architecture," noted that the Intermediate Language (IL) enforces strong type safety upon its code. Strong typing enables many of the services provided by .NET, including security and language interoperability. As you would expect from a language compiled into IL, C# is also strongly typed. Among other things, this means that data types are not always seamlessly interchangeable. This section looks at conversions between primitive types.

C# also supports conversions between different reference types and allows you to define how data types that you create behave when converted to and from other types. Both of these topics are discussed later in this chapter.

Generics, on the other hand, allow you to avoid some of the most common situations in which you would need to perform type conversions. See Chapter 5, "Generics" and Chapter 10, "Collections," for details.

Type Conversions

Often, you need to convert data from one type to another. Consider the following code:

```
byte value1 = 10;
byte value2 = 23;
byte total;
total = value1 + value2;
Console.WriteLine(total);
```

When you attempt to compile these lines, you get the following error message:

```
Cannot implicitly convert type 'int' to 'byte'
```

The problem here is that when you add 2 bytes together, the result will be returned as an int, not as another byte. This is because a byte can contain only 8 bits of data, so adding 2 bytes together could very easily result in a value that cannot be stored in a single byte. If you do want to store this result in a byte variable, you are going to have to convert it back to a byte. The following sections discuss two conversion mechanisms supported by C# — *implicit* and *explicit*.

Implicit Conversions

Conversion between types can normally be achieved automatically (implicitly) only if you can guarantee that the value is not changed in any way. This is why the previous code failed; by attempting a conversion from an int to a byte, you were potentially losing 3 bytes of data. The compiler is not going to let you do that unless you explicitly tell it that that's what you want to do. If you store the result in a long instead of a byte, however, you will have no problems:

```
byte value1 = 10;
byte value2 = 23;
long total;                 // this will compile fine
total = value1 + value2;
Console.WriteLine(total);
```

Your program has compiled with no errors at this point because a long holds more bytes of data than a byte, so there is no risk of data being lost. In these circumstances, the compiler is happy to make the conversion for you, without your needing to ask for it explicitly.

The following table shows the implicit type conversions supported in C#:

FROM	TO
sbyte	short, int, long, float, double, decimal, BigInteger
byte	short, ushort, int, uint long, ulong, float, double, decimal, BigInteger
short	int, long, float, double, decimal, BigInteger
ushort	int, uint, long, ulong, float, double, decimal, BigInteger
int	long, float double, decimal, BigInteger
uint	long, ulong, float, double, decimal, BigInteger

FROM	TO
`long, ulong`	`float, double, decimal, BigInteger`
`float`	`double, BigInteger`
`char`	`ushort, int, uint, long, ulong, float, double, decimal, BigInteger`

As you would expect, you can perform implicit conversions only from a smaller integer type to a larger one, not from larger to smaller. You can also convert between integers and floating-point values; however, the rules are slightly different here. Though you can convert between types of the same size, such as `int/uint` to `float` and `long/ulong` to `double`, you can also convert from `long/ulong` back to `float`. You might lose 4 bytes of data doing this, but this only means that the value of the `float` you receive will be less precise than if you had used a `double`; this is regarded by the compiler as an acceptable possible error because the magnitude of the value is not affected. You can also assign an unsigned variable to a signed variable as long as the limits of value of the unsigned type fit between the limits of the signed variable.

Nullable types introduce additional considerations when implicitly converting value types:

➤ Nullable types implicitly convert to other nullable types following the conversion rules described for non-nullable types in the previous table; that is, `int?` implicitly converts to `long?`, `float?`, `double?`, and `decimal?`.

➤ Non-nullable types implicitly convert to nullable types according to the conversion rules described in the preceding table; that is, `int` implicitly converts to `long?`, `float?`, `double?`, and `decimal?`.

➤ Nullable types *do not* implicitly convert to non-nullable types; you must perform an explicit conversion as described in the next section. This is because there is the chance a nullable type will have the value `null`, which cannot be represented by a non-nullable type.

Explicit Conversions

Many conversions cannot be implicitly made between types, and the compiler will give you an error if any are attempted. These are some of the conversions that cannot be made implicitly:

➤ `int` to `short` — Data loss is possible.

➤ `int` to `uint` — Data loss is possible.

➤ `uint` to `int` — Data loss is possible.

➤ `float` to `int` — You will lose everything after the decimal point.

➤ Any numeric type to `char` — Data loss is possible.

➤ `decimal` to any numeric type — The decimal type is internally structured differently from both integers and floating-point numbers.

➤ `int?` to `int` — The nullable type may have the value `null`.

However, you can explicitly carry out such conversions using *casts*. When you cast one type to another, you deliberately force the compiler to make the conversion. A cast looks like this:

```
long val = 30000;
int i = (int)val;    // A valid cast. The maximum int is 2147483647
```

You indicate the type to which you are casting by placing its name in parentheses before the value to be converted. If you are familiar with C, this is the typical syntax for casts. If you are familiar with the C++ special cast keywords such as `static_cast`, note that these do not exist in C# and that you have to use the older C-type syntax.

Casting can be a dangerous operation to undertake. Even a simple cast from a `long` to an `int` can cause problems if the value of the original `long` is greater than the maximum value of an `int`:

```
long val = 3000000000;
int i = (int)val;         // An invalid cast. The maximum int is 2147483647
```

In this case, you will not get an error, but you also will not get the result you expect. If you run this code and output the value stored in i, this is what you get:

```
-1294967296
```

It is good practice to assume that an explicit cast will not give the results you expect. As you saw earlier, C# provides a checked operator that you can use to test whether an operation causes an arithmetic overflow. You can use the checked operator to check that a cast is safe and to force the runtime to throw an overflow exception if it is not:

```
long val = 3000000000;
int i = checked((int)val);
```

Bearing in mind that all explicit casts are potentially unsafe, you should take care to include code in your application to deal with possible failures of the casts. Chapter 15, "Errors and Exceptions," introduces structured exception handling using the try and catch statements.

Using casts, you can convert most primitive data types from one type to another; for example, in this code, the value 0.5 is added to price, and the total is cast to an int:

```
double price = 25.30;
int approximatePrice = (int)(price + 0.5);
```

This gives the price rounded to the nearest dollar. However, in this conversion, data is lost — namely, everything after the decimal point. Therefore, such a conversion should never be used if you want to go on to do more calculations using this modified price value. However, it is useful if you want to output the approximate value of a completed or partially completed calculation — if you do not want to bother the user with lots of figures after the decimal point.

This example shows what happens if you convert an unsigned integer into a char:

```
ushort c = 43;
char symbol = (char)c;
Console.WriteLine(symbol);
```

The output is the character that has an ASCII number of 43, the + sign. You can try any kind of conversion you want between the numeric types (including char), and it will work, such as converting a decimal into a char, or vice versa.

Converting between value types is not restricted to isolated variables, as you have seen. You can convert an array element of type double to a struct member variable of type int:

```
struct ItemDetails
{
    public string Description;
    public int ApproxPrice;
}

//..

double[] Prices = { 25.30, 26.20, 27.40, 30.00 };

ItemDetails id;
id.Description = "Hello there.";
id.ApproxPrice = (int)(Prices[0] + 0.5);
```

To convert a nullable type to a non-nullable type or another nullable type where data loss may occur, you must use an explicit cast. This is true even when converting between elements with the same basic underlying type, for example, int? to int or float? to float. This is because the nullable type may have the value null, which cannot be represented by the non-nullable type. As long as an explicit cast between two equivalent non-nullable types is possible, so is the explicit cast between nullable types. However, when casting from a nullable to non-nullable type and the variable has the value null, an InvalidOperationException is thrown. For example:

```
int? a = null;
int  b = (int)a;    // Will throw exception
```

Using explicit casts and a bit of care and attention, you can convert any instance of a simple value type to almost any other. However, there are limitations on what you can do with explicit type conversions — as far as value types are concerned, you can only convert to and from the numeric and char types and enum types. You cannot directly cast Booleans to any other type or vice versa.

If you need to convert between numeric and string, you can use methods provided in the .NET class library. The `Object` class implements a `ToString()` method, which has been overridden in all the .NET predefined types and which returns a string representation of the object:

```
int i = 10;
string s = i.ToString();
```

Similarly, if you need to parse a string to retrieve a numeric or Boolean value, you can use the `Parse()` method supported by all the predefined value types:

```
string s = "100";
int i = int.Parse(s);
Console.WriteLine(i + 50);    // Add 50 to prove it is really an int
```

Note that `Parse()` will register an error by throwing an exception if it is unable to convert the string (for example, if you try to convert the string `Hello` to an integer). Again, exceptions are covered in Chapter 15.

Boxing and Unboxing

In Chapter 2, "Core C#," you learned that all types, both the simple predefined types such as int and char, and the complex types such as classes and structs, derive from the `object` type. This means that you can treat even literal values as though they are objects:

```
string s = 10.ToString();
```

However, you also saw that C# data types are divided into value types, which are allocated on the stack, and reference types, which are allocated on the heap. How does this square with the ability to call methods on an int, if the int is nothing more than a 4-byte value on the stack?

The way C# achieves this is through a bit of magic called *boxing*. Boxing and its counterpart, *unboxing,* allow you to convert value types to reference types and then back to value types. We include this in the section on casting because this is essentially what you are doing — you are casting your value to the `object` type. Boxing is the term used to describe the transformation of a value type to a reference type. Basically, the runtime creates a temporary reference-type box for the object on the heap.

This conversion can occur implicitly, as in the preceding example, but you can also perform it explicitly:

```
int myIntNumber = 20;
object myObject = myIntNumber;
```

Unboxing is the term used to describe the reverse process, where the value of a previously boxed value type is cast back to a value type. We use the term *cast* here, because this has to be done explicitly. The syntax is similar to explicit type conversions already described:

```
int myIntNumber = 20;
object myObject = myIntNumber;          // Box the int
int mySecondNumber = (int)myObject;     // Unbox it back into an int
```

You can only unbox a variable that has previously been boxed. If you execute the last line when `myObject` is not a boxed int, you will get an exception thrown at runtime.

One word of warning: when unboxing, you have to be careful that the receiving value variable has enough room to store all the bytes in the value being unboxed. C#'s ints, for example, are only 32 bits long, so unboxing a `long` value (64 bits) into an int as shown here will result in an `InvalidCastException`:

```
long myLongNumber = 333333423;
object myObject = (object)myLongNumber;
int myIntNumber = (int)myObject;
```

COMPARING OBJECTS FOR EQUALITY

After discussing operators and briefly touching on the equality operator, it is worth considering for a moment what equality means when dealing with instances of classes and structs. Understanding the mechanics of object equality is essential for programming logical expressions and is important when implementing operator overloads and casts, which is the topic of the rest of this chapter.

The mechanisms of object equality are different depending on whether you are comparing reference types (instances of classes) or value types (the primitive data types, instances of structs or enums). The following sections present the equality of reference and value types independently.

Comparing Reference Types for Equality

You might be surprised to learn that System.Object defines three different methods for comparing objects for equality: ReferenceEquals() and two versions of Equals(). Add to this the comparison operator (==), and you actually have four ways of comparing for equality. Some subtle differences exist between the different methods, which are examined next.

The ReferenceEquals() Method

ReferenceEquals() is a static method that tests whether two references refer to the same instance of a class, specifically whether the two references contain the same address in memory. As a static method, it is not possible to override, so the System.Object implementation is what you always have. ReferenceEquals() will always return true if supplied with two references that refer to the same object instance, and false otherwise. It does, however, consider null to be equal to null:

```
SomeClass x, y;
x = new SomeClass();
y = new SomeClass();
bool B1 = ReferenceEquals(null, null);    // returns true
bool B2 = ReferenceEquals(null,x);        // returns false
bool B3 = ReferenceEquals(x, y);          // returns false because x and y
                                          // point to different objects
```

The virtual Equals() Method

The System.Object implementation of the virtual version of Equals() also works by comparing references. However, because this method is virtual, you can override it in your own classes to compare objects by value. In particular, if you intend instances of your class to be used as keys in a dictionary, you will need to override this method to compare values. Otherwise, depending on how you override Object.GetHashCode(), the dictionary class that contains your objects will either not work at all or will work very inefficiently. One point you should note when overriding Equals() is that your override should never throw exceptions. Once again, this is because doing so could cause problems for dictionary classes and possibly certain other .NET base classes that internally call this method.

The static Equals() Method

The static version of Equals() actually does the same thing as the virtual instance version. The difference is that the static version takes two parameters and compares them for equality. This method is able to cope when either of the objects is null, and, therefore, provides an extra safeguard against throwing exceptions if there is a risk that an object might be null. The static overload first checks whether the references it has been passed are null. If they are both null, it returns true (because null is considered to be equal to null). If just one of them is null, it returns false. If both references actually refer to something, it calls the virtual instance version of Equals(). This means that when you override the instance version of Equals(), the effect is as if you were overriding the static version as well.

Comparison Operator (==)

It is best to think of the comparison operator as an intermediate option between strict value comparison and strict reference comparison. In most cases, writing the following means that you are comparing references:

```
bool b = (x == y);   // x, y object references
```

However, it is accepted that there are some classes whose meanings are more intuitive if they are treated as values. In those cases, it is better to override the comparison operator to perform a value comparison. Overriding operators is discussed next, but the obvious example of this is the `System.String` class for which Microsoft has overridden this operator to compare the contents of the strings rather than their references.

Comparing Value Types for Equality

When comparing value types for equality, the same principles hold as for reference types: `ReferenceEquals()` is used to compare references, `Equals()` is intended for value comparisons, and the comparison operator is viewed as an intermediate case. However, the big difference is that value types need to be boxed to be converted to references so that methods can be executed on them. In addition, Microsoft has already overloaded the instance `Equals()` method in the `System.ValueType` class to test equality appropriate to value types. If you call `sA.Equals(sB)` where `sA` and `sB` are instances of some struct, the return value will be `true` or `false`, according to whether `sA` and `sB` contain the same values in all their fields. On the other hand, no overload of `==` is available by default for your own structs. Writing (`sA ==` `sB`) in any expression will result in a compilation error unless you have provided an overload of `==` in your code for the struct in question.

Another point is that `ReferenceEquals()` always returns `false` when applied to value types because, to call this method, the value types need to be boxed into objects. Even if you write the following, you will still get the answer of `false`:

```
bool b = ReferenceEquals(v,v);   // v is a variable of some value type
```

The reason for this is that `v` will be boxed separately when converting each parameter, which means you get different references. Because of this, there really is no reason to call `ReferenceEquals()` to compare value types because it doesn't make much sense.

Although the default override of `Equals()` supplied by `System.ValueType` will almost certainly be adequate for the vast majority of structs that you define, you might want to override it again for your own structs to improve performance. Also, if a value type contains reference types as fields, you might want to override `Equals()` to provide appropriate semantics for these fields because the default override of `Equals()` will simply compare their addresses.

OPERATOR OVERLOADING

This section looks at another type of member that you can define for a class or a struct: the *operator overload*.

Operator overloading is something that will be familiar to C++ developers. However, because the concept will be new to both Java and Visual Basic developers, we explain it here. C++ developers will probably prefer to skip ahead to the main operator overloading example.

The point of operator overloading is that you do not always just want to call methods or properties on objects. Often, you need to do things like adding quantities together, multiplying them, or performing logical operations such as comparing objects. Suppose that you had defined a class that represents a mathematical matrix. Now in the world of math, matrices can be added together and multiplied, just like numbers. Therefore, it is quite plausible that you would want to write code like this:

```
Matrix a, b, c;
// assume a, b and c have been initialized
Matrix d = c * (a + b);
```

By overloading the operators, you can tell the compiler what + and * do when used in conjunction with a `Matrix` object, allowing you to write code like the preceding. If you were coding in a language that did not support operator overloading, you would have to define methods to perform those operations. The result would certainly be less intuitive and would probably look something like this:

```
Matrix d = c.Multiply(a.Add(b));
```

With what you have learned so far, operators like + and * have been strictly for use with the predefined data types, and for good reason: the compiler knows what all the common operators mean for those data types. For example, it knows how to add two `longs` or how to divide one `double` by another `double`, and it can generate the appropriate intermediate language code. When you define your own classes or structs, however, you have to tell the compiler everything: what methods are available to call, what fields to store with each instance, and so on. Similarly, if you want to use operators with your own types, you will have to tell the compiler what the relevant operators mean in the context of that class. The way you do that is by defining overloads for the operators.

The other thing we should stress is that overloading is not concerned just with arithmetic operators. You also need to consider the comparison operators, ==, <, >, !=, >=, and <=. Take the statement `if (a==b)`. For classes, this statement will, by default, compare the references a and b. It tests to see if the references point to the same location in memory, rather than checking to see if the instances actually contain the same data. For the `string` class, this behavior is overridden so that comparing strings really does compare the contents of each string. You might want to do the same for your own classes. For structs, the == operator does not do anything at all by default. Trying to compare two structs to see if they are equal produces a compilation error unless you explicitly overload == to tell the compiler how to perform the comparison.

A large number of situations exist in which being able to overload operators allows you to generate more readable and intuitive code, including:

➤ Almost any mathematical object such as coordinates, vectors, matrices, tensors, functions, and so on. If you are writing a program that does some mathematical or physical modeling, you will almost certainly use classes representing these objects.

➤ Graphics programs that use mathematical or coordinate-related objects when calculating positions on-screen.

➤ A class that represents an amount of money (for example, in a financial program).

➤ A word processing or text analysis program that uses classes representing sentences, clauses, and so on; you might want to use operators to combine sentences (a more sophisticated version of concatenation for strings).

However, there are also many types for which operator overloading would not be relevant. Using operator overloading inappropriately will make code that uses your types far more difficult to understand. For example, multiplying two `DateTime` objects just does not make any sense conceptually.

How Operators Work

To understand how to overload operators, it's quite useful to think about what happens when the compiler encounters an operator. Using the addition operator (+) as an example, suppose that the compiler processes the following lines of code:

```
int myInteger = 3;
uint myUnsignedInt = 2;
double myDouble = 4.0;
long myLong = myInteger + myUnsignedInt;
double myOtherDouble = myDouble + myInteger;
```

What happens when the compiler encounters the following line?

```
long myLong = myInteger + myUnsignedInt;
```

The compiler identifies that it needs to add two integers and assign the result to a `long`. However, the expression `myInteger + myUnsignedInt` is really just an intuitive and convenient syntax for calling a method that adds two numbers together. The method takes two parameters, `myInteger` and `myUnsignedInt`, and returns their sum. Therefore, the compiler does the same thing as it does for any method call — it looks for the best matching overload of the addition operator based on the parameter types — in this case, one that takes two integers. As with normal overloaded methods, the desired return type does not influence the compiler's choice as to which version of a method it calls. As it happens, the overload called in the example takes two `int` parameters and returns an `int`; this return value is subsequently converted to a `long`.

The next line causes the compiler to use a different overload of the addition operator:

```
double myOtherDouble = myDouble + myInteger;
```

In this instance, the parameters are a `double` and an `int`, but there is not an overload of the addition operator that takes this combination of parameters. Instead, the compiler identifies the best matching overload of the addition operator as being the version that takes two `doubles` as its parameters, and it implicitly casts the `int` to a `double`. Adding two `doubles` requires a different process from adding two integers. Floating-point numbers are stored as a mantissa and an exponent. Adding them involves bit-shifting the mantissa of one of the `doubles` so that the two exponents have the same value, adding the mantissas, then shifting the mantissa of the result and adjusting its exponent to maintain the highest possible accuracy in the answer.

Now, you are in a position to see what happens if the compiler finds something like this:

```
Vector vect1, vect2, vect3;
// initialize vect1 and vect2
vect3 = vect1 + vect2;
vect1 = vect1*2;
```

Here, `Vector` is the struct, which is defined in the following section. The compiler will see that it needs to add two `Vector` instances, `vect1` and `vect2`, together. It will look for an overload of the addition operator, which takes two `Vector` instances as its parameters.

If the compiler finds an appropriate overload, it will call up the implementation of that operator. If it cannot find one, it will look to see if there is any other overload for + that it can use as a best match — perhaps something that has two parameters of other data types that can be implicitly converted to `Vector` instances. If the compiler cannot find a suitable overload, it will raise a compilation error, just as it would if it could not find an appropriate overload for any other method call.

Operator Overloading Example: The Vector Struct

This section demonstrates operator overloading through developing a struct named `Vector` that represents a three-dimensional mathematical vector. Do not worry if mathematics is not your strong point — we will keep the vector example very simple. As far as you are concerned, a 3D-vector is just a set of three numbers (`doubles`) that tell you how far something is moving. The variables representing the numbers are called x, y, and z: x tells you how far something moves east, y tells you how far it moves north, and z tells you how far it moves upward (in height). Combine the three numbers and you get the total movement. For example, if x=3.0, y=3.0, and z=1.0 (which you would normally write as (3.0, 3.0, 1.0), you're moving 3 units east, 3 units north, and rising upward by 1 unit.

You can add or multiply vectors by other vectors or by numbers. Incidentally, in this context, we use the term *scalar*, which is math-speak for a simple number — in C# terms that is just a `double`. The significance of addition should be clear. If you move first by the vector (3.0, 3.0, 1.0) then you move by the vector (2.0, -4.0, -4.0), the total amount you have moved can be worked out by adding the two vectors. Adding vectors means adding each component individually, so you get (5.0, -1.0, -3.0). In this context, mathematicians write c=a+b, where a and b are the vectors and c is the resulting vector. You want to be able to use the `Vector` struct the same way.

> *The fact that this example will be developed as a struct rather than a class is not significant. Operator overloading works in the same way for both structs and classes.*

The following is the definition for `Vector` — containing the member fields, constructors, a `ToString()` override so you can easily view the contents of a `Vector`, and, finally, that operator overload:

```
namespace Wrox.ProCSharp.OOCSharp
{
    struct Vector
    {
        public double x, y, z;

        public Vector(double x, double y, double z)
        {
            this.x = x;
            this.y = y;
            this.z = z;
        }

        public Vector(Vector rhs)
        {
            x = rhs.x;
            y = rhs.y;
            z = rhs.z;
        }

        public override string ToString()
        {
            return "( " + x + ", " + y + ", " + z + " )";
        }
```

code download VectorStruct solution

This example has two constructors that require the initial value of the vector to be specified, either by passing in the values of each component or by supplying another `Vector` whose value can be copied. Constructors like the second one that takes a single `Vector` argument are often termed *copy constructors* because they effectively allow you to initialize a class or struct instance by copying another instance. Note that to keep things simple, the fields are left as `public`. We could have made them `private` and written corresponding properties to access them, but it would not have made any difference to the example, other than to make the code longer.

Here is the interesting part of the `Vector` struct — the operator overload that provides support for the addition operator:

```
        public static Vector operator + (Vector lhs, Vector rhs)
        {
            Vector result = new Vector(lhs);
            result.x += rhs.x;
            result.y += rhs.y;
            result.z += rhs.z;

            return result;
        }
    }
}
```

The operator overload is declared in much the same way as a method, except that the `operator` keyword tells the compiler it is actually an operator overload you are defining. The `operator` keyword is followed by the actual symbol for the relevant operator, in this case the addition operator (+). The return type is whatever type you get when you use this operator. Adding two vectors results in a vector, therefore, the return type is also a `Vector`. For this particular override of the addition operator, the return type is the same as the containing class, but that is not necessarily the case, as you will see later in this example. The two parameters are the things you are operating on. For binary operators (those that take two parameters), such as the addition and subtraction operators, the first parameter is the value on the left of the operator, and the second parameter is the value on the right.

> Note that it is convention to name your left-hand parameters `lhs` (for left-hand side) and your right-hand parameters `rhs` (for right-hand side).

C# requires that all operator overloads be declared as `public` and `static`, which means that they are associated with their class or struct, not with a particular instance. Because of this, the body of the operator overload has no access to non-static class members and has no access to the `this` identifier. This is fine because the parameters provide all the input data the operator needs to know to perform its task.

Now that you understand the syntax for the addition operator declaration, you can look at what happens inside the operator:

```
{
    Vector result = new Vector(lhs);
    result.x += rhs.x;
    result.y += rhs.y;
    result.z += rhs.z;

    return result;
}
```

This part of the code is exactly the same as if you were declaring a method, and you should easily be able to convince yourself that this really will return a vector containing the sum of `lhs` and `rhs` as defined. You simply add the members `x`, `y`, and `z` together individually.

Now all you need to do is write some simple code to test the `Vector` struct. Here it is:

```
static void Main()
{
    Vector vect1, vect2, vect3;

    vect1 = new Vector(3.0, 3.0, 1.0);
    vect2 = new Vector(2.0, -4.0, -4.0);
    vect3 = vect1 + vect2;

    Console.WriteLine("vect1 = " + vect1.ToString());
    Console.WriteLine("vect2 = " + vect2.ToString());
    Console.WriteLine("vect3 = " + vect3.ToString());
}
```

Saving this code as `Vectors.cs` and compiling and running it returns this result:

```
vect1 = ( 3, 3, 1 )
vect2 = ( 2, -4, -4 )
vect3 = ( 5, -1, -3 )
```

Adding More Overloads

In addition to adding vectors, you can multiply and subtract them and compare their values. In this section, you develop the `Vector` example further by adding a few more operator overloads. You will not develop the complete set that you'd probably need for a fully functional `Vector` type, but just enough to demonstrate some other aspects of operator overloading. First, you'll overload the multiplication operator to support multiplying vectors by a scalar and multiplying vectors by another vector.

Multiplying a vector by a scalar simply means multiplying each component individually by the scalar: for example, 2 * (1.0, 2.5, 2.0) returns (2.0, 5.0, 4.0). The relevant operator overload looks similar to this:

```
public static Vector operator * (double lhs, Vector rhs)
{
    return new Vector(lhs * rhs.x, lhs * rhs.y, lhs * rhs.z);
}
```

code download VectorStructMoreOverloads.sln

This by itself, however, is not sufficient. If a and b are declared as type Vector, it allows you to write code like this:

```
b = 2 * a;
```

The compiler will implicitly convert the integer 2 to a double to match the operator overload signature. However, code like the following will not compile:

```
b = a * 2;
```

The thing is that the compiler treats operator overloads exactly as method overloads. It examines all the available overloads of a given operator to find the best match. The preceding statement requires the first parameter to be a Vector and the second parameter to be an integer, or something that an integer can be implicitly converted to. You have not provided such an overload. The compiler cannot start swapping the order of parameters, so the fact that you've provided an overload that takes a double followed by a Vector is not sufficient. You need to explicitly define an overload that takes a Vector followed by a double as well. There are two possible ways of implementing this. The first way involves breaking down the vector multiplication operation in the same way that you have done for all operators so far:

```
public static Vector operator * (Vector lhs, double rhs)
{
    return new Vector(rhs * lhs.x, rhs * lhs.y, rhs *lhs.z);
}
```

Given that you have already written code to implement essentially the same operation, however, you might prefer to reuse that code by writing:

```
public static Vector operator * (Vector lhs, double rhs)
{
    return rhs * lhs;
}
```

This code works by effectively telling the compiler that if it sees a multiplication of a Vector by a double, it can simply reverse the parameters and call the other operator overload. The sample code for this chapter uses the second version, because it looks neater and illustrates the idea in action. This version also makes for more maintainable code because it saves duplicating the code to perform the multiplication in two separate overloads.

Next, you need to overload the multiplication operator to support vector multiplication. Mathematics provides a couple of ways of multiplying vectors together, but the one we are interested in here is known as the *dot product* or *inner product,* which actually gives a scalar as a result. That's the reason for this example, to demonstrate that arithmetic operators don't have to return the same type as the class in which they are defined.

In mathematical terms, if you have two vectors (x, y, z) and (X, Y, Z), then the inner product is defined to be the value of x*X + y*Y + z*Z. That might look like a strange way to multiply two things together, but it is actually very useful because it can be used to calculate various other quantities. Certainly, if you ever end up writing code that displays complex 3D graphics, for example using Direct3D or DirectDraw, you will almost certainly find your code needs to work out inner products of vectors quite often as an intermediate step in calculating where to place objects on the screen. What concerns us here is that we want people using your `Vector` to be able to write `double X = a*b` to calculate the inner product of two `Vector` objects (a and b). The relevant overload looks like this:

```
public static double operator * (Vector lhs, Vector rhs)
{
    return lhs.x * rhs.x + lhs.y * rhs.y + lhs.z * rhs.z;
}
```

Now that you understand the arithmetic operators, you can check that they work using a simple test method:

```
static void Main()
{
    // stuff to demonstrate arithmetic operations
    Vector vect1, vect2, vect3;
    vect1 = new Vector(1.0, 1.5, 2.0);
    vect2 = new Vector(0.0, 0.0, -10.0);

    vect3 = vect1 + vect2;

    Console.WriteLine("vect1 = " + vect1);
    Console.WriteLine("vect2 = " + vect2);
    Console.WriteLine("vect3 = vect1 + vect2 = " + vect3);
    Console.WriteLine("2*vect3 = " + 2*vect3);
    vect3 += vect2;

    Console.WriteLine("vect3+=vect2 gives " + vect3);

    vect3 = vect1*2;

    Console.WriteLine("Setting vect3=vect1*2 gives " + vect3);

    double dot = vect1*vect3;

    Console.WriteLine("vect1*vect3 = " + dot);
}
```

Running this code (`Vectors2.cs`) produces the following result:

VECTORS2

```
vect1 = ( 1, 1.5, 2 )
vect2 = ( 0, 0, -10 )
vect3 = vect1 + vect2 = ( 1, 1.5, -8 )
2*vect3 = ( 2, 3, -16 )
vect3+=vect2 gives ( 1, 1.5, -18 )
Setting vect3=vect1*2 gives ( 2, 3, 4 )
vect1*vect3 = 14.5
```

This shows that the operator overloads have given the correct results, but if you look at the test code closely, you might be surprised to notice that it actually used an operator that wasn't overloaded — the addition assignment operator, +=:

```
    vect3 += vect2;

    Console.WriteLine("vect3 += vect2 gives " + vect3);
```

Although += normally counts as a single operator, it can be broken down into two steps: the addition and the assignment. Unlike the C++ language, C# will not actually allow you to overload the = operator, but if you overload +, the compiler will automatically use your overload of + to work out how to perform a += operation. The same principle works for all the assignment operators such as -=, *=, /=, &=, and so on.

Overloading the Comparison Operators

C# has six comparison operators that we introduced earlier in this chapter (see the "Operators" section), and they come in three pairs:

➤ == and !=

➤ > and <

➤ >= and <=

The C# language requires that you overload these operators in pairs. That is, if you overload ==, you must overload != too; otherwise, you get a compiler error. In addition, the comparison operators must return a `bool`. This is the fundamental difference between these operators and the arithmetic operators. The result of adding or subtracting two quantities, for example, can theoretically be any type depending on the quantities. You have already seen that multiplying two `Vector` objects can be implemented to give a scalar. Another example involves the .NET base class `System.DateTime`. It's possible to subtract two `DateTime` instances, but the result is not a `DateTime`; instead it is a `System.TimeSpan` instance. By contrast, it doesn't really make much sense for a comparison to return anything other than a `bool`.

> If you overload == and !=, you must also override the `Equals()` and `GetHashCode()` methods inherited from `System.Object`; otherwise, you'll get a compiler warning. The reasoning is that the `Equals()` method should implement the same kind of equality logic as the == operator.

Apart from these differences, overloading the comparison operators follows the same principles as overloading the arithmetic operators. However, comparing quantities isn't always as simple as you might think. For example, if you simply compare two object references, you will compare the memory address where the objects are stored. This is rarely the desired behavior of a comparison operator, and so you must code the operator to compare the value of the objects and return the appropriate Boolean response. The following example overrides the == and != operators for the `Vector` struct. Here is the implementation of ==:

```
public static bool operator == (Vector lhs, Vector rhs)
{
    if (lhs.x == rhs.x && lhs.y == rhs.y && lhs.z == rhs.z)
        return true;
    else
        return false;
}
```

This approach simply compares two `Vector` objects for equality based on the values of their components. For most structs, that is probably what you will want to do, though in some cases you may need to think carefully about what you mean by equality. For example, if there are embedded classes, should you simply compare whether the references point to the same object (*shallow comparison*) or whether the values of the objects are the same (*deep comparison*)?

A shallow comparison is where the objects point to the same point in memory, whereas deep comparisons are working with values and properties of the object to deem equality. You want to perform equality checks depending on the depth to help you decide what you want to verify.

> Don't be tempted to overload the comparison operator by calling the instance version of the `Equals()` method inherited from `System.Object`. If you do and then an attempt is made to evaluate (objA == objB), when objA happens to be null, you will get an exception as the .NET runtime tries to evaluate null.Equals(objB). Working the other way around (overriding `Equals()` to call the comparison operator) should be safe.

You also need to override the != operator. The simple way to do this is:

```
public static bool operator != (Vector lhs, Vector rhs)
{
    return ! (lhs == rhs);
}
```

As usual, you should quickly check that your override works with some test code. This time you'll define three Vector objects and compare them:

```
static void Main()
{
    Vector vect1, vect2, vect3;

    vect1 = new Vector(3.0, 3.0, -10.0);
    vect2 = new Vector(3.0, 3.0, -10.0);
    vect3 = new Vector(2.0, 3.0, 6.0);

    Console.WriteLine("vect1==vect2 returns  " + (vect1==vect2));
    Console.WriteLine("vect1==vect3 returns  " + (vect1==vect3));
    Console.WriteLine("vect2==vect3 returns  " + (vect2==vect3));

    Console.WriteLine();

    Console.WriteLine("vect1!=vect2 returns  " + (vect1!=vect2));
    Console.WriteLine("vect1!=vect3 returns  " + (vect1!=vect3));
    Console.WriteLine("vect2!=vect3 returns  " + (vect2!=vect3));
}
```

code snippet Vectors3.cs

Compiling this code (the Vectors3.cs sample in the code download) generates the following compiler warning because you haven't overridden Equals() for your Vector. For our purposes here, that does not matter, so we will ignore it.

```
Microsoft (R) Visual C# 2010 Compiler version 4.0.21006.1
for Microsoft (R) .NET Framework version 4.0
Copyright (C) Microsoft Corporation. All rights reserved.


Vectors3.cs(5,11): warning CS0660: 'Wrox.ProCSharp.OOCSharp.Vector' defines
        operator == or operator != but does not override Object.Equals(object o)
Vectors3.cs(5,11): warning CS0661: 'Wrox.ProCSharp.OOCSharp.Vector' defines
        operator == or operator != but does not override Object.GetHashCode()
```

Running the example produces these results at the command line:

VECTORS3

```
vect1==vect2 returns  True
vect1==vect3 returns  False
vect2==vect3 returns  False

vect1!=vect2 returns  False
vect1!=vect3 returns  True
vect2!=vect3 returns  True
```

Which Operators Can You Overload?

It is not possible to overload all the available operators. The operators that you can overload are listed in the following table.

CATEGORY	OPERATORS	RESTRICTIONS
Arithmetic binary	+, *, /, −, %	None.
Arithmetic unary	+, −, ++, −−	None.
Bitwise binary	&, |, ^, <<, >>	None.
Bitwise unary	!, ~true, false	The true and false operators must be overloaded as a pair.
Comparison	==, !=, >=, <=>, <,	Comparison operators must be overloaded in pairs.
Assignment	+=, −=, *=, /=, >>=, <<=, %=, &=, |=, ^=	You cannot explicitly overload these operators; they are overridden implicitly when you override the individual operators such as +, -, %, and so on.
Index	[]	You cannot overload the index operator directly. The indexer member type, discussed in Chapter 2, allows you to support the index operator on your classes and structs.
Cast	()	You cannot overload the cast operator directly. User-defined casts (discussed next) allow you to define custom cast behavior.

USER-DEFINED CASTS

Earlier in this chapter (see the "Explicit Conversions" section), you learned that you can convert values between predefined data types through a process of *casting*. You also saw that C# allows two different types of casts: implicit and explicit. This section looks at these types of casts.

For an explicit cast, you *explicitly* mark the cast in your code by writing the destination data type inside parentheses:

```
int I = 3;
long l = I;              // implicit
short s = (short)I;      // explicit
```

For the predefined data types, explicit casts are required where there is a risk that the cast might fail or some data might be lost. The following are some examples:

➤ When converting from an int to a short, the short might not be large enough to hold the value of the int.

➤ When converting from signed to unsigned data types, incorrect results will be returned if the signed variable holds a negative value.

➤ When converting from floating-point to integer data types, the fractional part of the number will be lost.

➤ When converting from a nullable type to a non-nullable type, a value of null will cause an exception.

By making the cast explicit in your code, C# forces you to affirm that you understand there is a risk of data loss, and therefore presumably you have written your code to take this into account.

Because C# allows you to define your own data types (structs and classes), it follows that you will need the facility to support casts to and from those data types. The mechanism is that you can define a cast as a member operator of one of the relevant classes. Your cast operator must be marked as either implicit or explicit to indicate how you are intending it to be used. The expectation is that you follow the same guidelines as for the predefined casts: if you know that the cast is always safe no matter what the value held by the source variable, then you define it as implicit. If, however, you know there is a risk of something going wrong for certain values — perhaps some loss of data or an exception being thrown — then you should define the cast as `explicit`.

You should define any custom casts you write as explicit if there are any source data values for which the cast will fail or if there is any risk of an exception being thrown.

The syntax for defining a cast is similar to that for overloading operators discussed earlier in this chapter. This is not a coincidence — a cast is regarded as an operator whose effect is to convert from the source type to the destination type. To illustrate the syntax, the following is taken from an example `struct` named `Currency`, which is introduced later in this section:

```
public static implicit operator float (Currency value)
{
    // processing
}
```

The return type of the operator defines the target type of the cast operation, and the single parameter is the source object for the conversion. The cast defined here allows you to implicitly convert the value of a `Currency` into a `float`. Note that if a conversion has been declared as `implicit`, the compiler will permit its use either implicitly or explicitly. If it has been declared as `explicit`, the compiler will only permit it to be used explicitly. In common with other operator overloads, casts must be declared as both `public` and `static`.

C++ developers will notice that this is different from what they are used to with C++, in which casts are instance members of classes.

Implementing User-Defined Casts

This section illustrates the use of implicit and explicit user-defined casts in an example called `SimpleCurrency` (which, as usual, is available in the code download). In this example, you define a struct, `Currency`, which holds a positive USD ($) monetary value. C# provides the `decimal` type for this purpose, but it is possible you will still want to write your own struct or class to represent monetary values if you want to perform sophisticated financial processing and therefore want to implement specific methods on such a class.

The syntax for casting is the same for structs and classes. This example happens to be for a struct, but would work just as well if you declared `Currency` as a class.

Initially, the definition of the `Currency` struct is:

```
struct Currency
{
    public uint Dollars;
    public ushort Cents;

    public Currency(uint dollars, ushort cents)
    {
        this.Dollars = dollars;
        this.Cents = cents;
    }
```

```
public override string ToString()
{
    return string.Format("${0}.{1,-2:00}", Dollars,Cents);
}
}
```

code snippet SimpleCurrency/Program.cs

The use of unsigned data types for the `Dollar` and `Cents` fields ensures that a `Currency` instance can hold only positive values. It is restricted this way to illustrate some points about explicit casts later on. You might want to use a class like this to hold, for example, salary information for employees of a company (people's salaries tend not to be negative!). To keep the class simple, the fields are public, but usually you would make them `private` and define corresponding properties for the dollars and cents.

Start by assuming that you want to be able to convert `Currency` instances to `float` values, where the integer part of the `float` represents the dollars. In other words, you would like to be able to write code like this:

```
Currency balance = new Currency(10,50);
float f = balance; // We want f to be set to 10.5
```

To be able to do this, you need to define a cast. Hence, you add the following to your `Currency` definition:

```
public static implicit operator float (Currency value)
{
    return value.Dollars + (value.Cents/100.0f);
}
```

The preceding cast is implicit. It is a sensible choice in this case because, as should be clear from the definition of `Currency`, any value that can be stored in the currency can also be stored in a `float`. There is no way that anything should ever go wrong in this cast.

 There is a slight cheat here — in fact, when converting a `uint` to a `float`, there can be a loss in precision, but Microsoft has deemed this error sufficiently marginal to count the `uint`-to-`float` cast as implicit.

However, if you have a `float` that you would like to be converted to a `Currency`, the conversion is not guaranteed to work. A `float` can store negative values, which `Currency` instances can't, and a `float` can store numbers of a far higher magnitude than can be stored in the (`uint`) `Dollar` field of `Currency`. Therefore, if a `float` contains an inappropriate value, converting it to a `Currency` could give unpredictable results. Because of this risk, the conversion from `float` to `Currency` should be defined as explicit. Here is the first attempt, which will not give quite the correct results, but it is instructive to examine why:

```
public static explicit operator Currency (float value)
{
    uint dollars = (uint)value;
    ushort cents = (ushort)((value-dollars)*100);
    return new Currency(dollars, cents);
}
```

The following code will now successfully compile:

```
float amount = 45.63f;
Currency amount2 = (Currency)amount;
```

However, the following code, if you tried it, would generate a compilation error, because it attempts to use an explicit cast implicitly:

```
float amount = 45.63f;
Currency amount2 = amount;    // wrong
```

By making the cast explicit, you warn the developer to be careful because data loss might occur. However, as you will soon see, this is not how you want your `Currency` struct to behave. Try writing a test harness and running the sample. Here is the `Main()` method, which instantiates a `Currency` struct and attempts a few conversions. At the start of this code, you write out the value of `balance` in two different ways (this will be needed to illustrate something later in the example):

```
static void Main()
{
    try
    {
        Currency balance = new Currency(50,35);

        Console.WriteLine(balance);
        Console.WriteLine("balance is " + balance);
        Console.WriteLine("balance is (using ToString()) " + balance.ToString());

        float balance2= balance;

        Console.WriteLine("After converting to float, = " + balance2);

        balance = (Currency) balance2;

        Console.WriteLine("After converting back to Currency, = " + balance);
        Console.WriteLine("Now attempt to convert out of range value of " +
                        "-$50.50 to a Currency:");

        checked
        {
            balance = (Currency) (-50.50);
            Console.WriteLine("Result is " + balance.ToString());
        }
    }
    catch(Exception e)
    {
        Console.WriteLine("Exception occurred: " + e.Message);
    }
}
```

Notice that the entire code is placed in a `try` block to catch any exceptions that occur during your casts. In addition, the lines that test converting an out-of-range value to `Currency` are placed in a `checked` block in an attempt to trap negative values. Running this code gives this output:

SIMPLECURRENCY

```
50.35
Balance is $50.35
Balance is (using ToString()) $50.35
After converting to float, = 50.35
After converting back to Currency, = $50.34
Now attempt to convert out of range value of -$100.00 to a Currency:
Result is $4294967246.00
```

This output shows that the code did not quite work as expected. First, converting back from `float` to `Currency` gave a wrong result of $50.34 instead of $50.35. Second, no exception was generated when you tried to convert an obviously out-of-range value.

The first problem is caused by rounding errors. If a cast is used to convert from a `float` to a `uint`, the computer will *truncate* the number rather than *rounding* it. The computer stores numbers in binary rather than decimal, and the fraction 0.35 cannot be exactly represented as a binary fraction (just as 1/3 cannot be represented exactly as a decimal fraction; it comes out as 0.3333 recurring). The computer ends up storing a value very slightly lower than 0.35 that can be represented exactly in binary format. Multiply by 100 and you get a number fractionally less than 35, which is truncated to 34 cents. Clearly, in this situation, such errors caused by truncation are serious, and the way to avoid them is to ensure that some intelligent rounding is performed in numerical conversions instead. Luckily, Microsoft has written a class that will do this: `System.Convert`. The `System.Convert` object contains a large number of static methods to perform various numerical conversions, and the one that we want is `Convert.ToUInt16()`. Note that the extra care taken by the `System.Convert` methods does come at a performance cost. You should use them only when you need them.

Let's examine the second problem — why the expected overflow exception wasn't thrown. The issue here is this: the place where the overflow really occurs isn't actually in the `Main()` routine at all — it is inside the code for the cast operator, which is called from the `Main()` method. The code in this method was not marked as `checked`.

The solution is to ensure that the cast itself is computed in a `checked` context too. With both this change and the fix for the first problem, the revised code for the conversion looks like the following:

```
public static explicit operator Currency (float value)
{
    checked
    {
        uint dollars = (uint)value;
        ushort cents = Convert.ToUInt16((value-dollars)*100);
        return new Currency(dollars, cents);
    }
}
```

Note that you use `Convert.ToUInt16()` to calculate the cents, as described earlier, but you do not use it for calculating the dollar part of the amount. `System.Convert` is not needed when working out the dollar amount because truncating the `float` value is what you want there.

 It is worth noting that the `System.Convert` methods also carry out their own overflow checking. Hence, for the particular case we are considering, there is no need to place the call to `Convert.ToUInt16()` inside the checked context. The checked context is still required, however, for the explicit casting of value to dollars.

You won't see a new set of results with this new `checked` cast just yet because you have some more modifications to make to the `SimpleCurrency` example later in this section.

 If you are defining a cast that will be used very often, and for which performance is at an absolute premium, you may prefer not to do any error checking. That is also a legitimate solution, provided that the behavior of your cast and the lack of error checking are very clearly documented.

Casts Between Classes

The `Currency` example involves only classes that convert to or from `float` — one of the predefined data types. However, it is not necessary to involve any of the simple data types. It is perfectly legitimate to define casts to convert between instances of different structs or classes that you have defined. You need to be aware of a couple of restrictions, however:

➤ You cannot define a cast if one of the classes is derived from the other (these types of casts already exist, as you will see).

➤ The cast must be defined inside the definition of either the source or the destination data type.

To illustrate these requirements, suppose that you have the class hierarchy shown in Figure 7-1.

In other words, classes C and D are indirectly derived from A. In this case, the only legitimate user-defined cast between A, B, C, or D would be to convert between classes C and D, because these classes are not derived from each other. The code to do so might look like this (assuming that you want the casts to be explicit, which is usually the case when defining casts between user-defined classes):

```
public static explicit operator D(C value)
{
    // and so on
}
public static explicit operator C(D value)
{
    // and so on
}
```

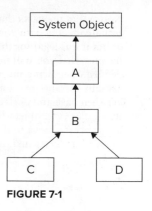

FIGURE 7-1

For each of these casts, you have a choice of where you place the definitions — inside the class definition of C or inside the class definition of D, but not anywhere else. C# requires you to put the definition of a cast inside either the source class (or struct) or the destination class (or struct). A side effect of this is that you cannot define a cast between two classes unless you have access to edit the source code for at least one of them. This is sensible because it prevents third parties from introducing casts into your classes.

After you have defined a cast inside one of the classes, you cannot also define the same cast inside the other class. Obviously, there should be only one cast for each conversion — otherwise, the compiler would not know which one to pick.

Casts Between Base and Derived Classes

To see how these casts work, start by considering the case where the source and destination are both reference types, and consider two classes, MyBase and MyDerived, where MyDerived is derived directly or indirectly from MyBase.

First, from MyDerived to MyBase, it is always possible (assuming the constructors are available) to write:

```
MyDerived derivedObject = new MyDerived();
MyBase baseCopy = derivedObject;
```

In this case, you are casting implicitly from MyDerived to MyBase. This works because of the rule that any reference to a type MyBase is allowed to refer to objects of class MyBase or to objects of anything derived from MyBase. In OO programming, instances of a derived class are, in a real sense, instances of the base class, plus something extra. All the functions and fields defined on the base class are defined in the derived class too.

Alternatively, you can write:

```
MyBase derivedObject = new MyDerived();
MyBase baseObject = new MyBase();
MyDerived derivedCopy1 = (MyDerived) derivedObject;   // OK
MyDerived derivedCopy2 = (MyDerived) baseObject;      // Throws exception
```

This code is perfectly legal C# (in a syntactic sense, that is) and illustrates casting from a base class to a derived class. However, the final statement will throw an exception when executed. When you perform the cast, the object being referred to is examined. Because a base class reference can in principle refer to a derived class instance, it is possible that this object is actually an instance of the derived class that you are attempting to cast to. If that is the case, the cast succeeds, and the derived reference is set to refer to the object. If, however, the object in question is not an instance of the derived class (or of any class derived from it), the cast fails and an exception is thrown.

Notice that the casts that the compiler has supplied, which convert between base and derived class, do not actually do any data conversion on the object in question. All they do is set the new reference to refer to the object if it is legal for that conversion to occur. To that extent, these casts are very different in nature from the ones that you will normally define yourself. For example, in the `SimpleCurrency` example earlier, you defined casts that convert between a `Currency` struct and a `float`. In the `float-to-Currency` cast, you actually instantiated a new `Currency` struct and initialized it with the required values. The predefined casts between base and derived classes do not do this. If you actually want to convert a `MyBase` instance into a real `MyDerived` object with values based on the contents of the `MyBase` instance, you would not be able to use the cast syntax to do this. The most sensible option is usually to define a derived class constructor that takes a base class instance as a parameter and have this constructor perform the relevant initializations:

```
class DerivedClass: BaseClass
{
    public DerivedClass(BaseClass rhs)
    {
        // initialize object from the Base instance
    }
    // etc.
```

Boxing and Unboxing Casts

The previous discussion focused on casting between base and derived classes where both participants were reference types. Similar principles apply when casting value types, although in this case it is not possible to simply copy references — some copying of data must take place.

It is not, of course, possible to derive from structs or primitive value types. Casting between base and derived structs invariably means casting between a primitive type or a struct and `System.Object`. (Theoretically, it is possible to cast between a struct and `System.ValueType`, though it is hard to see why you would want to do this.)

The cast from any struct (or primitive type) to `object` is always available as an implicit cast — because it is a cast from a derived to a base type — and is just the familiar process of *boxing*. For example, with the `Currency` struct:

```
Currency balance = new Currency(40,0);
object baseCopy = balance;
```

When this implicit cast is executed, the contents of `balance` are copied onto the heap into a boxed object, and the `baseCopy` object reference is set to this object. What actually happens behind the scenes is this: When you originally defined the `Currency` struct, the .NET Framework implicitly supplied another (hidden) class, a boxed `Currency` class, which contains all the same fields as the `Currency` struct, but it is a reference type, stored on the heap. This happens whenever you define a value type — whether it is a struct or enum, and similar boxed reference types exist corresponding to all the primitive value types of `int`, `double`, `uint`, and so on. It is not possible, or necessary, to gain direct programmatic access to any of these boxed classes in source code, but they are the objects that are working behind the scenes whenever a value type is cast to `object`. When you implicitly cast `Currency` to `object`, a boxed `Currency` instance gets instantiated and initialized with all the data from the `Currency` struct. In the preceding code, it is this boxed `Currency` instance that `baseCopy` will refer to. By these means, it is possible for casting from derived to base type to work syntactically in the same way for value types as for reference types.

Casting the other way is known as *unboxing*. Just as for casting between a base reference type and a derived reference type, it is an explicit cast because an exception will be thrown if the object being cast is not of the correct type:

```
object derivedObject = new Currency(40,0);
object baseObject = new object();
Currency derivedCopy1 = (Currency)derivedObject;    // OK
Currency derivedCopy2 = (Currency)baseObject;       // Exception thrown
```

This code works in a way similar to the code presented earlier for reference types. Casting `derivedObject` to `Currency` works fine because `derivedObject` actually refers to a boxed `Currency` instance — the cast will be performed by copying the fields out of the boxed `Currency` object into a new `Currency` struct. The second cast fails because `baseObject` does not refer to a boxed `Currency` object.

When using boxing and unboxing, it is important to understand that both processes actually copy the data into the new boxed or unboxed object. Hence, manipulations on the boxed object, for example, will not affect the contents of the original value type.

Multiple Casting

One thing you will have to watch for when you are defining casts is that if the C# compiler is presented with a situation in which no direct cast is available to perform a requested conversion, it will attempt to find a way of combining casts to do the conversion. For example, with the `Currency` struct, suppose the compiler encounters a few lines of code like this:

```
Currency balance = new Currency(10,50);
long amount = (long)balance;
double amountD = balance;
```

You first initialize a `Currency` instance, and then you attempt to convert it to a `long`. The trouble is that you haven't defined the cast to do that. However, this code will still compile successfully. What will happen is that the compiler will realize that you have defined an implicit cast to get from `Currency` to `float`, and the compiler already knows how to explicitly cast a `float` to a `long`. Hence, it will compile that line of code into IL code that converts `balance` first to a `float`, and then converts that result to a `long`. The same thing happens in the final line of the code, when you convert `balance` to a `double`. However, because the cast from `Currency` to `float` and the predefined cast from `float` to `double` are both implicit, you can write this conversion in your code as an implicit cast. If you had preferred, you could have specified the casting route explicitly:

```
Currency balance = new Currency(10,50);
long amount = (long)(float)balance;
double amountD = (double)(float)balance;
```

However, in most cases, this would be seen as needlessly complicating your code. The following code, by contrast, would produce a compilation error:

```
Currency balance = new Currency(10,50);
long amount = balance;
```

The reason is that the best match for the conversion that the compiler can find is still to convert first to `float` then to `long`. The conversion from `float` to `long` needs to be specified explicitly, though.

Not all of this by itself should give you too much trouble. The rules are, after all, fairly intuitive and designed to prevent any data loss from occurring without the developer knowing about it. However, the problem is that if you are not careful when you define your casts, it is possible for the compiler to figure out a path that leads to unexpected results. For example, suppose that it occurs to someone else in the group writing the `Currency` struct that it would be useful to be able to convert a `uint` containing the total number of cents in an amount into a `Currency` (cents, not dollars, because the idea is not to lose the fractions of a dollar). Therefore, this cast might be written to try to achieve this:

```
public static implicit operator Currency (uint value)
{
    return new Currency(value/100u, (ushort)(value%100));
} // Do not do this!
```

Note the u after the first 100 in this code to ensure that `value/100u` is interpreted as a `uint`. If you had written `value/100`, the compiler would have interpreted this as an `int`, not a `uint`.

The code comment `Do not do this` is clearly commented in this code, and here is why. Look at the following code snippet; all it does is convert a `uint` containing 350 into a `Currency` and back again. What do you think `bal2` will contain after executing this?

```
uint bal = 350;
Currency balance = bal;
uint bal2 = (uint)balance;
```

The answer is not 350 but 3! Moreover, it all follows logically. You convert 350 implicitly to a Currency, giving the result balance.Dollars = 3, balance.Cents = 50. Then the compiler does its usual figuring out of the best path for the conversion back. Balance ends up being implicitly converted to a float (value 3.5), and this is converted explicitly to a uint with value 3.

Of course, other instances exist in which converting to another data type and back again causes data loss. For example, converting a float containing 5.8 to an int and back to a float again will lose the fractional part, giving you a result of 5, but there is a slight difference in principle between losing the fractional part of a number and dividing an integer by more than 100. Currency has suddenly become a rather dangerous class that does strange things to integers!

The problem is that there is a conflict between how your casts interpret integers. The casts between Currency and float interpret an integer value of 1 as corresponding to one dollar, but the latest uint-to-Currency cast interprets this value as one cent. This is an example of very poor design. If you want your classes to be easy to use, you should make sure that all your casts behave in a way that is mutually compatible, in the sense that they intuitively give the same results. In this case, the solution is obviously to rewrite the uint-to-Currency cast so that it interprets an integer value of 1 as one dollar:

```
public static implicit operator Currency (uint value)
{
    return new Currency(value, 0);
}
```

Incidentally, you might wonder whether this new cast is necessary at all. The answer is that it could be useful. Without this cast, the only way for the compiler to carry out a uint-to-Currency conversion would be via a float. Converting directly is a lot more efficient in this case, so having this extra cast provides performance benefits, though you need to make sure it gives the same result as via a float, which you have now done. In other situations, you may also find that separately defining casts for different predefined data types allows more conversions to be implicit rather than explicit, though that is not the case here.

A good test of whether your casts are compatible is to ask whether a conversion will give the same results (other than perhaps a loss of accuracy as in float-to-int conversions), regardless of which path it takes. The Currency class provides a good example of this. Look at this code:

```
Currency balance = new Currency(50, 35);
ulong bal = (ulong) balance;
```

At present, there is only one way that the compiler can achieve this conversion: by converting the Currency to a float implicitly, then to a ulong explicitly. The float-to-ulong conversion requires an explicit conversion, but that is fine because you have specified one here.

Suppose, however, that you then added another cast, to convert implicitly from a Currency to a uint. You will actually do this by modifying the Currency struct by adding the casts both to and from uint. This code is available as the SimpleCurrency2 example:

```
public static implicit operator Currency (uint value)
{
    return new Currency(value, 0);
}

public static implicit operator uint (Currency value)
{
    return value.Dollars;
}
```

Now the compiler has another possible route to convert from Currency to ulong: to convert from Currency to uint implicitly, then to ulong implicitly. Which of these two routes will it take? C# has some precise rules about the best route for the compiler if there are several possibilities. (The rules are not detailed in this book, but if you are interested, details are in the MSDN documentation.) The best answer is that you should design your casts so that all routes give the same answer (other than possible loss of precision), in which case it doesn't really matter which one the compiler picks. (As it happens in this case, the compiler picks the `Currency-to-uint-to-ulong` route in preference to `Currency-to-float-to-ulong`.)

To test the `SimpleCurrency2` sample, add this code to the test code for `SimpleCurrency`:

```
try
{
    Currency balance = new Currency(50,35);

    Console.WriteLine(balance);
    Console.WriteLine("balance is " + balance);
    Console.WriteLine("balance is (using ToString()) " + balance.ToString());

    uint balance3 = (uint) balance;

    Console.WriteLine("Converting to uint gives " + balance3);
```

code snippet SimpleCurrency2/Program.cs

Running the sample now gives you these results:

SIMPLECURRENCY2

```
50
balance is $50.35
balance is (using ToString()) $50.35
Converting to uint gives 50
After converting to float, = 50.35
After converting back to Currency, = $50.34
Now attempt to convert out of range value of -$50.50 to a Currency:
Result is $4294967246.00
```

The output shows that the conversion to `uint` has been successful, though as expected, you have lost the cents part of the `Currency` in making this conversion. Casting a negative `float` to `Currency` has also produced the expected overflow exception now that the `float-to-Currency` cast itself defines a `checked` context.

However, the output also demonstrates one last potential problem that you need to be aware of when working with casts. The very first line of output has not displayed the balance correctly, displaying `50` instead of `$50.35`. Consider these lines:

```
Console.WriteLine(balance);
Console.WriteLine("balance is " + balance);
Console.WriteLine("balance is (using ToString()) " + balance.ToString());
```

Only the last two lines correctly display the `Currency` as a string. So what is going on? The problem here is that when you combine casts with method overloads, you get another source of unpredictability. We will look at these lines in reverse order.

The third `Console.WriteLine()` statement explicitly calls the `Currency.ToString()` method, ensuring that the `Currency` is displayed as a string. The second does not do so. However, the string literal `"balance is"` passed to `Console.WriteLine()` makes it clear to the compiler that the parameter is to be interpreted as a string. Hence, the `Currency.ToString()` method will be called implicitly.

The very first `Console.WriteLine()` method, however, simply passes a raw `Currency` struct to `Console.WriteLine()`. Now, `Console.WriteLine()` has many overloads, but none of them takes a `Currency` struct. So the compiler will start fishing around to see what it can cast the `Currency` to in order to make it match up with one of the overloads of `Console.WriteLine()`. As it happens, one of the `Console.WriteLine()` overloads is designed to display `uint`s quickly and efficiently, and it takes a `uint` as a parameter — you have now supplied a cast that converts `Currency` implicitly to `uint`.

In fact, `Console.WriteLine()` has another overload that takes a `double` as a parameter and displays the value of that `double`. If you look closely at the output from the first `SimpleCurrency` example, you will find the very first line of output displayed `Currency` as a `double`, using this overload. In that example, there wasn't a direct cast from `Currency` to `uint`, so the compiler picked `Currency-to-float-to-double` as its preferred way of matching up the available casts to the available `Console.WriteLine()` overloads. However, now that there is a direct cast to `uint` available in `SimpleCurrency2`, the compiler has opted for this route.

The upshot of this is that if you have a method call that takes several overloads, and you attempt to pass it a parameter whose data type doesn't match any of the overloads exactly, then you are forcing the compiler to decide not only what casts to use to perform the data conversion, but which overload, and hence which data conversion, to pick. The compiler always works logically and according to strict rules, but the results may not be what you expected. If there is any doubt, you are better off specifying which cast to use explicitly.

SUMMARY

This chapter looked at the standard operators provided by C#, described the mechanics of object equality, and examined how the compiler converts the standard data types from one to another. It also demonstrated how you can implement custom operator support on your data types using operator overloads. Finally, this chapter looked at a special type of operator overload, the cast operator, which allows you to specify how instances of your types are converted to other data types.

Delegates, Lambdas, and Events

WHAT'S IN THIS CHAPTER?

➤ Delegates

➤ Lambda expressions

➤ Events

Delegates are the .NET version of addresses to methods. Compare this to C++, where function pointers are nothing more than a pointer to a memory location that are not type-safe. You have no idea what a pointer is really pointing to, and items such as parameters and return types are not known. This is completely different with .NET; delegates are type-safe classes that define the return types and types of parameters. The delegate class not only contains a reference to a method, but can hold references to multiple methods.

Lambda expressions are directly related to delegates. When the parameter is a delegate type, you can use a Lambda expression to implement a method that's referenced from the delegate.

This chapter teaches you the basics of delegates and Lambda expressions, and shows you how to implement methods called by delegates with Lambda expressions. It also demonstrates how .NET uses delegates as the means of implementing events.

DELEGATES

Delegates exist for situations in which you want to pass methods around to other methods. To see what that means, consider this line of code:

```
int i = int.Parse("99");
```

You are so used to passing data to methods as parameters, as in this example, that you don't consciously think about it, and for this reason the idea of passing methods around instead of data might sound a little strange. However, there are cases in which you have a method that does something, and rather than operating on data, the method might need to do something that involves invoking another method. To complicate things further, you do not know at compile time what this second method is. That information is available only at runtime and hence will need to be passed in as a parameter to the first method. That might sound confusing but should become clearer with a couple of examples:

Starting threads and tasks — It is possible in C# to tell the computer to start some new sequence of execution in parallel with what it is currently doing. Such a sequence is known as a *thread*, and starting one up is done using the `Start()` method on an instance of one of the base classes, `System.Threading.Thread`. If you tell the computer to start a new sequence of execution, you have to tell it where to start that sequence. You have to supply it with the details of a method in which execution can start. In other words, the constructor of the `Thread` class takes a parameter that defines the method to be invoked by the thread.

➤ **Generic library classes** — Many libraries contain code to perform various standard tasks. It is usually possible for these libraries to be self-contained, in the sense that you know when you write to the library exactly how the task must be performed. However, sometimes the task contains some subtask, which only the individual client code that uses the library knows how to perform. For example, say that you want to write a class that takes an array of objects and sorts them into ascending order. Part of the sorting process involves repeatedly taking two of the objects in the array and comparing them to see which one should come first. If you want to make the class capable of sorting arrays of any object, there is no way that it can tell in advance how to do this comparison. The client code that hands your class the array of objects will also have to tell your class how to do this comparison for the particular objects it wants sorted. The client code has to pass your class details of an appropriate method that can be called and does the comparison.

➤ **Events** — The general idea here is that often you have code that needs to be informed when some event takes place. GUI programming is full of situations similar to this. When the event is raised, the runtime will need to know what method should be executed. This is done by passing the method that handles the event as a parameter to a delegate. This is discussed later in this chapter.

In C and C++, you can just take the address of a function and pass this as a parameter. There's no type safety with C. You can pass any function to a method where a function pointer is required. Unfortunately, this direct approach not only causes some problems with type safety but also neglects the fact that when you are doing object-oriented programming, methods rarely exist in isolation, but usually need to be associated with a class instance before they can be called. As a result of these problems, the .NET Framework does not syntactically permit this direct approach. Instead, if you want to pass methods around, you have to wrap up the details of the method in a new kind of object, a delegate. Delegates quite simply are a special type of object — special in the sense that, whereas all the objects defined up to now contain data, a delegate contains the address of a method, or the address of multiple methods.

Declaring Delegates

When you want to use a class in C#, you do so in two stages. First, you need to define the class — that is, you need to tell the compiler what fields and methods make up the class. Then (unless you are using only static methods), you instantiate an object of that class. With delegates it is the same process. You have to start by defining the delegates you want to use. Defining delegates means telling the compiler what kind of method a delegate of that type will represent. Then, you have to create one or more instances of that delegate. Behind the scenes, the compiler creates a class that represents the delegate.

The syntax for defining delegates looks like this:

```
delegate void IntMethodInvoker(int x);
```

In this case, you have defined a delegate called `IntMethodInvoker`, and you have indicated that each instance of this delegate can hold a reference to a method that takes one `int` parameter and returns `void`. The crucial point to understand about delegates is that they are type-safe. When you define the delegate, you have to give full details of the signature and the return type of the method that it is going to represent.

One good way of understanding delegates is by thinking of a delegate as something that gives a name to a method signature and the return type.

Suppose that you want to define a delegate called `TwoLongsOp` that will represent a method that takes two `long`s as its parameters and returns a `double`. You could do so like this:

```
delegate double TwoLongsOp(long first, long second);
```

Or, to define a delegate that will represent a method that takes no parameters and returns a `string`, you might write this:

```
delegate string GetAString();
```

The syntax is similar to that for a method definition, except that there is no method body and the definition is prefixed with the keyword `delegate`. Because what you are doing here is basically defining a new class, you can define a delegate in any of the same places that you would define a class — that is to say, either inside another class, outside of any class, or in a namespace as a top-level object. Depending on how visible you want your definition to be, and the scope of the delegate, you can apply any of the normal access modifiers to delegate definitions — `public`, `private`, `protected`, and so on:

```
public delegate string GetAString();
```

 We really mean what we say when we describe defining a delegate as defining a new class. Delegates are implemented as classes derived from the class `System.MulticastDelegate`, *which is derived from the base class* `System.Delegate`. *The C# compiler is aware of this class and uses its delegate syntax to shield you from the details of the operation of this class. This is another good example of how C# works in conjunction with the base classes to make programming as easy as possible.*

After you have defined a delegate, you can create an instance of it so that you can use it to store details of a particular method.

 There is an unfortunate problem with terminology here. With classes there are two distinct terms — class, which indicates the broader definition, and object, which means an instance of the class. Unfortunately, with delegates there is only the one term; delegate can refer to both the class and the object. When you create an instance of a delegate, what you have created is also referred to as a delegate. You need to be aware of the context to know which meaning we are using when we talk about delegates.

Using Delegates

The following code snippet demonstrates the use of a delegate. It is a rather long-winded way of calling the `ToString()` method on an `int`:

```
private delegate string GetAString();

static void Main()
{
    int x = 40;
    GetAString firstStringMethod = new GetAString(x.ToString);
    Console.WriteLine("String is {0}", firstStringMethod());
```

```
    // With firstStringMethod initialized to x.ToString(),
    // the above statement is equivalent to saying
    // Console.WriteLine("String is {0}", x.ToString());
}
```

code snippet GetAStringDemo/Program.cs

In this code, you instantiate a delegate of type `GetAString`, and you initialize it so it refers to the `ToString()` method of the integer variable x. Delegates in C# always syntactically take a one-parameter constructor, the parameter being the method to which the delegate will refer. This method must match the signature with which you originally defined the delegate. So in this case, you would get a compilation error if you tried to initialize the variable `firstStringMethod` with any method that did not take any parameters and return a string. Notice that, because `int.ToString()` is an instance method (as opposed to a static one), you need to specify the instance (x) as well as the name of the method to initialize the delegate properly.

The next line actually uses the delegate to display the string. In any code, supplying the name of a delegate instance, followed by brackets containing any parameters, has exactly the same effect as calling the method wrapped by the delegate. Hence, in the preceding code snippet, the `Console.WriteLine()` statement is completely equivalent to the commented-out line.

In fact, supplying brackets to the delegate instance is the same as invoking the `Invoke()` method of the delegate class. Because `firstStringMethod` is a variable of a delegate type, the C# compiler replaces `firstStringMethod()` with `firstStringMethod.Invoke()`:

```
firstStringMethod();
firstStringMethod.Invoke();
```

For less typing, at every place where a delegate instance is needed, you can just pass the name of the address. This is known by the term *delegate inference*. This C# feature works as long as the compiler can resolve the delegate instance to a specific type. The example initialized the variable `firstStringMethod` of type `GetAString` with a new instance of the delegate `GetAString`:

```
GetAString firstStringMethod = new GetAString(x.ToString);
```

You can write the same just by passing the method name with the variable x to the variable `firstStringMethod`:

```
GetAString firstStringMethod = x.ToString;
```

The code that is created by the C# compiler is the same. The compiler detects that a delegate type is required with `firstStringMethod`, so it creates an instance of the delegate type `GetAString` and passes the address of the method with the object x to the constructor.

 Be aware that you can't type the brackets to the method name as `x.ToString()` *and pass it to the delegate variable. This would be an invocation of the method. The invocation of* `x.ToString()` *returns a string object that can't be assigned to the delegate variable. You can only assign the address of a method to the delegate variable.*

Delegate inference can be used any place a delegate instance is required. Delegate inference can also be used with events because events are based on delegates (as you will see later in this chapter).

One feature of delegates is that they are type-safe to the extent that they ensure the signature of the method being called is correct. However, interestingly, they do not care what type of object the method is being called against or even whether the method is a static method or an instance method.

> *An instance of a given delegate can refer to any instance or static method on any object of any type, provided that the signature of the method matches the signature of the delegate.*

To demonstrate this, the following example expands the previous code snippet so that it uses the `firstStringMethod` delegate to call a couple of other methods on another object — an instance method and a static method. For this, you use the `Currency` struct. The `Currency` struct has its own overload of `ToString()` and a static method with the same signature to `GetCurrencyUnit()`. This way the same delegate variable can be used to invoke these methods.

```
struct Currency
{
    public uint Dollars;
    public ushort Cents;

    public Currency(uint dollars, ushort cents)
    {
        this.Dollars = dollars;
        this.Cents = cents;
    }

    public override string ToString()
    {
        return string.Format("${0}.{1,2:00}", Dollars,Cents);
    }

    public static string GetCurrencyUnit()
    {
        return "Dollar";
    }

    public static explicit operator Currency (float value)
    {
        checked
        {
            uint dollars = (uint)value;
            ushort cents = (ushort)((value-dollars)*100);
            return new Currency(dollars, cents);
        }
    }

    public static implicit operator float (Currency value)
    {
        return value.Dollars + (value.Cents/100.0f);
    }

    public static implicit operator Currency (uint value)
    {
        return new Currency(value, 0);
    }

    public static implicit operator uint (Currency value)
    {
        return value.Dollars;
    }
}
```

code snippet GetAStringDemo/Currency.cs

Now you can use your `GetAString` instance as follows:

```
private delegate string GetAString();

static void Main()
{
    int x = 40;
    GetAString firstStringMethod = x.ToString;
    Console.WriteLine("String is {0}", firstStringMethod());

    Currency balance = new Currency(34, 50);

    // firstStringMethod references an instance method
    firstStringMethod = balance.ToString;
    Console.WriteLine("String is {0}", firstStringMethod());

    // firstStringMethod references a static method
    firstStringMethod = new GetAString(Currency.GetCurrencyUnit);
    Console.WriteLine("String is {0}", firstStringMethod());
}
```

This code shows how you can call a method via a delegate and subsequently reassign the delegate to refer to different methods on different instances of classes, even static methods or methods against instances of different types of class, provided that the signature of each method matches the delegate definition.

When you run the application, you get the output from the different methods that are referenced by the delegate:

```
String is 40
String is $34.50
String is Dollar
```

However, you still haven't seen the process of actually passing a delegate to another method. Nor have you actually achieved anything particularly useful yet. It is possible to call the `ToString()` method of `int` and `Currency` objects in a much more straightforward way than using delegates! Unfortunately, the nature of delegates requires a fairly complex example before you can really appreciate their usefulness. The next section presents two delegate examples. The first one simply uses delegates to call a couple of different operations. It illustrates how to pass delegates to methods and how you can use arrays of delegates — although arguably it still doesn't do much that you couldn't do a lot more simply without delegates. Then, a second, much more complex example of a `BubbleSorter` class is presented, which implements a method to sort out arrays of objects into increasing order. This class would be difficult to write without using delegates.

Simple Delegate Example

This example defines a `MathOperations` class that has a couple of static methods to perform two operations on doubles. Then you use delegates to call up these methods. The math class looks like this:

Available for
download on
Wrox.com

```
class MathOperations
{
    public static double MultiplyByTwo(double value)
    {
        return value * 2;
    }

    public static double Square(double value)
    {
        return value * value;
    }
}
```

code snippet SimpleDelegate/MathOperations.cs

You call up these methods like this:

```
using System;

namespace Wrox.ProCSharp.Delegates
{
    delegate double DoubleOp(double x);

    class Program
    {
        static void Main()
        {
            DoubleOp[] operations =
                {
                    MathOperations.MultiplyByTwo,
                    MathOperations.Square
                };

            for (int i=0; i < operations.Length; i++)
            {
                Console.WriteLine("Using operations[{0}]:", i);
                ProcessAndDisplayNumber(operations[i], 2.0);
                ProcessAndDisplayNumber(operations[i], 7.94);
                ProcessAndDisplayNumber(operations[i], 1.414);
                Console.WriteLine();
            }
        }

        static void ProcessAndDisplayNumber(DoubleOp action, double value)
        {
            double result = action(value);
            Console.WriteLine(
                "Value is {0}, result of operation is {1}", value, result);
        }
    }
}
```

code snippet SimpleDelegate/Program.cs

In this code, you instantiate an array of `DoubleOp` delegates (remember that after you have defined a delegate class, you can basically instantiate instances just as you can with normal classes, so putting some into an array is no problem). Each element of the array gets initialized to refer to a different operation implemented by the `MathOperations` class. Then, you loop through the array, applying each operation to three different values. This illustrates one way of using delegates — that you can group methods together into an array using them, so that you can call several methods in a loop.

The key lines in this code are the ones in which you actually pass each delegate to the `ProcessAndDisplayNumber()` method, for example:

```
ProcessAndDisplayNumber(operations[i], 2.0);
```

Here, you are passing in the name of a delegate but without any parameters. Given that `operations[i]` is a delegate, syntactically:

➤ `operations[i]` means the *delegate* (that is, the method represented by the delegate).

➤ `operations[i](2.0)` means *actually call this method, passing in the value in parentheses.*

The `ProcessAndDisplayNumber()` method is defined to take a delegate as its first parameter:

```
static void ProcessAndDisplayNumber(DoubleOp action, double value)
```

Then, when in this method, you call

```
double result = action(value);
```

this actually causes the method that is wrapped up by the `action` delegate instance to be called and its return result stored in `Result`. Running this example gives you the following:

```
SimpleDelegate
Using operations[0]:
Value is 2, result of operation is 4
Value is 7.94, result of operation is 15.88
Value is 1.414, result of operation is 2.828

Using operations[1]:
Value is 2, result of operation is 4
Value is 7.94, result of operation is 63.0436
Value is 1.414, result of operation is 1.999396
```

Action<T> and Func<T> Delegates

Instead of defining a new delegate type with every parameter and return type, you can use the `Action<T>` and `Func<T>` delegates. The generic `Action<T>` delegate is meant to reference a method with `void` return. This delegate class exists in different variants so that you can pass up to 16 different parameter types. The `Action` class without the generic parameter is for calling methods without parameters. `Action<in T>` is to call a method with one parameter, `Action<in T1, in T2>` for a method with two parameters, and `Action<in T1, in T2, in T3, in T4, in T5, in T6, in T7, in T8>` for a method with eight parameters.

The `Func<T>` delegates can be used in a similar manner. `Func<T>` allows you to invoke methods with a return type. Similar to `Action<T>`, `Func<T>` is defined in different variants to pass up to 16 parameter types and a return type. `Func<out TResult>` is the delegate type to invoke a method with a return type and without parameters. `Func<in T, out TResult>` is for a method with one parameter, and `Func<in T1, in T2, in T3, in T4, out TResult>` is for a method with four parameters.

The example in the preceding section declared a delegate with `double` parameter and `double` return type:

```
delegate double DoubleOp(double x);
```

Instead of declaring the custom delegate `DoubleOp` you can use the `Func<in T, out TResult>` delegate. You can declare a variable of the delegate type, or as shown here an array of the delegate type:

```
Func<double, double>[] operations =
    {
        MathOperations.MultiplyByTwo,
        MathOperations.Square
    };
```

and use it with the `ProcessAndDisplayNumber()` method as parameter:

```
static void ProcessAndDisplayNumber(Func<double, double> action,
                                    double value)
{
    double result = action(value);
    Console.WriteLine(
        "Value is {0}, result of operation is {1}", value, result);
}
```

BubbleSorter Example

You are now ready for an example that will show the real usefulness of delegates. You are going to write a class called `BubbleSorter`. This class implements a static method, `Sort()`, which takes as its first parameter an array of objects, and rearranges this array into ascending order. For example, if you were to pass it this array of ints, {0, 5, 6, 2, 1}, it would rearrange this array into {0, 1, 2, 5, 6}.

The bubble-sorting algorithm is a well-known and very simple way of sorting numbers. It is best suited to small sets of numbers, because for larger sets of numbers (more than about 10) far more efficient algorithms are available. It works by repeatedly looping through the array, comparing each pair of numbers and, if necessary, swapping them, so that the largest numbers progressively move to the end of the array. For sorting ints, a method to do a bubble sort might look similar to this:

```
bool swapped = true;
do
{
    swapped = false;
    for (int i = 0; i < sortArray.Length - 1; i++)
    {
        if (sortArray[i] < sortArray[i+1])) // problem with this test
        {
            int temp = sortArray[i];
            sortArray[i] = sortArray[i + 1];
            sortArray[i + 1] = temp;
            swapped = true;
        }
    }
} while (swapped);
```

This is all very well for ints, but you want your Sort() method to be able to sort any object. In other words, if some client code hands you an array of Currency structs or any other class or struct that it may have defined, you need to be able to sort the array. This presents a problem with the line if(sortArray[i] < sortArray[i+1]) in the preceding code, because that requires you to compare two objects on the array to see which one is greater. You can do that for ints, but how are you to do it for some new class that doesn't implement the < operator? The answer is that the client code that knows about the class will have to pass in a delegate wrapping a method that will do the comparison. Also, instead of using an int type for the *temp* variable, a generic Sort() method can be implemented using a generic type.

With a generic Sort<T>() method accepting type T, a comparison method is needed that has two parameters of type T and a return type of type bool for the if comparison. This method can be referenced from a Func<T1, T2, TResult> delegate where T1 and T2 are the same type: Func<T, T, bool>.

This way you give your Sort<T> method this signature:

```
static public void Sort<T>(IList<T> sortArray, Func<T, T, bool> comparison)
```

The documentation for this method states that comparison must refer to a method that takes two arguments, and returns true if the value of the first argument is *smaller than* the second one.

Now you are all set. Here is the definition for the BubbleSorter class:

```
class BubbleSorter
{
    static public void Sort<T>(IList<T> sortArray, Func<T, T, bool> comparison)
    {
        bool swapped = true;
        do
        {
            swapped = false;
            for (int i = 0; i < sortArray.Count - 1; i++)
            {
                if (comparison(sortArray[i+1], sortArray[i]))
                {
                    T temp = sortArray[i];
                    sortArray[i] = sortArray[i + 1];
```

```
                            sortArray[i + 1] = temp;
                        swapped = true;
                    }
                }
            } while (swapped);
        }
    }
```

code snippet BubbleSorter/BubbleSorter.cs

To use this class, you need to define some other class, which you can use to set up an array that needs sorting. For this example, assume that the Mortimer Phones mobile phone company has a list of employees and wants them sorted according to salary. The employees are each represented by an instance of a class, `Employee`, which looks similar to this:

Available for download on Wrox.com

```csharp
class Employee
{
    public Employee(string name, decimal salary)
    {
        this.Name = name;
        this.Salary = salary;
    }

    public string Name { get; private set; }
    public decimal Salary { get; private set; }

    public override string ToString()
    {
        return string.Format("{0}, {1:C}", Name, Salary);
    }

    public static bool CompareSalary(Employee e1, Employee e2)
    {
        return e1.Salary < e2.Salary;
    }
}
```

code snippet BubbleSorter/Employee.cs

Notice that to match the signature of the `Func<T, T, bool>` delegate, you have to define `CompareSalary` in this class as taking two `Employee` references and returning a Boolean. In the implementation the comparison based on salary is performed.

Now you are ready to write some client code to request a sort:

Available for download on Wrox.com

```csharp
using System;

namespace Wrox.ProCSharp.Delegates
{
    class Program
    {
        static void Main()
        {
            Employee[] employees =
            {
                new Employee("Bugs Bunny", 20000),
                new Employee("Elmer Fudd", 10000),
                new Employee("Daffy Duck", 25000),
                new Employee("Wile Coyote", 1000000.38m),
                new Employee("Foghorn Leghorn", 23000),
                new Employee("RoadRunner", 50000)
            };
```

```
                BubbleSorter.Sort(employees, Employee.CompareSalary);

                foreach (var employee in employees)
                {
                    Console.WriteLine(employee);
                }
            }
        }
    }
```

code snippet BubbleSorter/Program.cs

Running this code shows that the `Employees` are correctly sorted according to salary:

```
BubbleSorter
Elmer Fudd, $10,000.00
Bugs Bunny, $20,000.00
Foghorn Leghorn, $23,000.00
Daffy Duck, $25,000.00
RoadRunner, $50,000.00
Wile Coyote, $1,000,000.38
```

Multicast Delegates

So far, each of the delegates you have used wraps just one single method call. Calling the delegate amounts to calling that method. If you want to call more than one method, you need to make an explicit call through a delegate more than once. However, it is possible for a delegate to wrap more than one method. Such a delegate is known as a *multicast delegate*. If a multicast delegate is called, it will successively call each method in order. For this to make sense, the delegate signature should return a `void`; otherwise, you would only get the result of the last method that is invoked by the delegate.

With a `void` return type the `Action<double>` delegate can be used.

```
class Program
{
    static void Main()
    {
        Action<double> operations = MathOperations.MultiplyByTwo;
        operations += MathOperations.Square;
```

code snippet MulticastDelegates/Program.cs

In the earlier example, you wanted to store references to two methods, so you instantiated an array of delegates. Here, you simply add both operations into the same multicast delegate. Multicast delegates recognize the operators + and +=. Alternatively, you can also expand the last two lines of the preceding code, as in this snippet:

```
Action<double> operation1 = MathOperations.MultiplyByTwo;
Action<double> operation2 = MathOperations.Square;
Action<double> operations = operation1 + operation2;
```

Multicast delegates also recognize the operators – and -= to remove method calls from the delegate.

In terms of what's going on under the hood, a multicast delegate is a class derived from System.MulticastDelegate, *which in turn is derived from* System.Delegate. System.MulticastDelegate, *and has additional members to allow chaining of method calls together into a list.*

To illustrate the use of multicast delegates, the following code recasts the `SimpleDelegate` example into a new example, `MulticastDelegate`. Because you now need the delegate to refer to methods that return `void`, you have to rewrite the methods in the `MathOperations` class, so they display their results instead of returning them:

```
class MathOperations
{
    public static void MultiplyByTwo(double value)
    {
        double result = value * 2;
        Console.WriteLine("Multiplying by 2: {0} gives {1}", value, result);
    }

    public static void Square(double value)
    {
        double result = value * value;
        Console.WriteLine("Squaring: {0} gives {1}", value, result);
    }
}
```

code snippet MulticastDelegates/MathOperations.cs

To accommodate this change, you also have to rewrite `ProcessAndDisplayNumber`:

```
static void ProcessAndDisplayNumber(Action<double> action, double value)
{
    Console.WriteLine();
    Console.WriteLine("ProcessAndDisplayNumber called with value = {0}", value);
    action(value);
}
```

Now you can try out your multicast delegate like this:

```
static void Main()
{
    Action<double> operations = MathOperations.MultiplyByTwo;
    operations += MathOperations.Square;

    ProcessAndDisplayNumber(operations, 2.0);
    ProcessAndDisplayNumber(operations, 7.94);
    ProcessAndDisplayNumber(operations, 1.414);
    Console.WriteLine();
}
```

Now, each time `ProcessAndDisplayNumber` is called, it will display a message to say that it has been called. Then the following statement will cause each of the method calls in the `action` delegate instance to be called in succession:

```
    action(value);
```

Running this code produces this result:

```
MulticastDelegate

ProcessAndDisplayNumber called with value = 2
Multiplying by 2: 2 gives 4
Squaring: 2 gives 4

ProcessAndDisplayNumber called with value = 7.94
Multiplying by 2: 7.94 gives 15.88
Squaring: 7.94 gives 63.0436
```

```
ProcessAndDisplayNumber called with value = 1.414
Multiplying by 2: 1.414 gives 2.828
Squaring: 1.414 gives 1.999396
```

If you are using multicast delegates, you should be aware that the order in which methods chained to the same delegate will be called is formally undefined. You should, therefore, avoid writing code that relies on such methods being called in any particular order.

Invoking multiple methods by one delegate might cause an even bigger problem. The multicast delegate contains a collection of delegates to invoke one after the other. If one of the methods invoked by a delegate throws an exception, the complete iteration stops. Have a look at the following MulticastIteration example. Here, the simple delegate Action that returns void without arguments is used. This delegate is meant to invoke the methods One() and Two() that fulfill the parameter and return type requirements of the delegate. Be aware that method One() throws an exception:

```
using System;

namespace Wrox.ProCSharp.Delegates
{
    class Program
    {
        static void One()
        {
            Console.WriteLine("One");
            throw new Exception("Error in one");
        }

        static void Two()
        {
            Console.WriteLine("Two");
        }
```

code snippet MulticastDelegateWithIteration/Program.cs

In the Main() method, delegate d1 is created to reference method One(); next, the address of method Two() is added to the same delegate. d1 is invoked to call both methods. The exception is caught in a try/ catch block.

```
        static void Main()
        {
            Action d1 = One;
            d1 += Two;

            try
            {
                d1();
            }
            catch (Exception)
            {
                Console.WriteLine("Exception caught");
            }
        }
    }
}
```

Only the first method is invoked by the delegate. Because the first method throws an exception, iterating the delegates stops here and method Two() is never invoked. The result might differ because the order of calling the methods is not defined.

```
One
Exception Caught
```

Errors and exceptions are explained in detail in Chapter 15.

In such a scenario, you can avoid the problem by iterating the list on your own. The `Delegate` class defines the method `GetInvocationList()` that returns an array of `Delegate` objects. You can now use this delegate to invoke the methods associated with them directly, catch exceptions, and continue with the next iteration:

```
static void Main()
{
    Action d1 = One;
    d1 += Two;

    Delegate[] delegates = d1.GetInvocationList();
    foreach (Action d in delegates)
    {
        try
        {
            d();
        }
        catch (Exception)
        {
            Console.WriteLine("Exception caught");
        }
    }
}
```

When you run the application with the code changes, you can see that the iteration continues with the next method after the exception is caught:

```
One
Exception caught
Two
```

Anonymous Methods

Up to this point, a method must already exist for the delegate to work (that is, the delegate is defined with the same signature as the method(s) it will be used with). However, there is another way to use delegates — with *anonymous methods*. An anonymous method is a block of code that is used as the parameter for the delegate.

The syntax for defining a delegate with an anonymous method doesn't change. It's when the delegate is instantiated that things change. The following is a very simple console application that shows how using an anonymous method can work:

Available for download on Wrox.com

```
using System;

namespace Wrox.ProCSharp.Delegates
{
    class Program
    {
        static void Main()
        {
            string mid = ", middle part,";

            Func<string, string> anonDel = delegate(string param)
            {
                param += mid;
```

```
            param += " and this was added to the string.";
            return param;
        };
        Console.WriteLine(anonDel("Start of string"));

    }
  }
}
```

code snippet AnonymousMethods/Program.cs

The delegate `Func<string, string>` takes a single string parameter and returns a string. `anonDel` is a variable of this delegate type. Instead of assigning the name of a method to this variable, a simple block of code is used, prefixed by the delegate keyword, followed by a string parameter.

As you can see, the block of code uses a method-level string variable, `mid`, which is defined outside of the anonymous method and adds it to the parameter that was passed in. The code then returns the string value. When the delegate is called, a string is passed in as the parameter and the returned string is output to the console.

The benefit of using anonymous methods is to reduce the amount of code you have to write. You don't have to define a method just to use it with a delegate. This becomes very evident when defining the delegate for an event. (Events are discussed later in this chapter.) This can help reduce the complexity of code, especially where there are several events defined. With anonymous methods, the code does not perform faster. The compiler still defines a method; the method just has an automatically assigned name that you don't need to know.

A couple of rules must be followed when using anonymous methods. You can't have a jump statement (`break`, `goto`, or `continue`) in an anonymous method that has a target outside of the anonymous method. The reverse is also true — a jump statement outside the anonymous method cannot have a target inside the anonymous method.

Unsafe code cannot be accessed inside an anonymous method. Also, `ref` and `out` parameters that are used outside of the anonymous method cannot be accessed. Other variables defined outside of the anonymous method can be used.

If you have to write the same functionality more than once, don't use anonymous methods. In this case, instead of duplicating the code, writing a named method is the preferred way. You only have to write it once and reference it by its name.

Beginning with C# 3.0, you can use Lambda expressions instead of writing anonymous methods.

LAMBDA EXPRESSIONS

Since C# 3.0, you can use a new syntax for assigning code implementation to delegates: *Lambda expressions*. Lambda expressions can be used whenever you have a delegate parameter type. The previous example using anonymous methods is changed here to use a Lambda expression.

The syntax of Lambda expressions is simpler than the syntax of anonymous methods. In a case where a method to be invoked has parameters and you don't need the parameters, the syntax of anonymous methods is simpler, as you don't need to supply parameters in that case.

```
using System;

namespace Wrox.ProCSharp.Delegates
{
  class Program
  {
    static void Main()
    {
      string mid = ", middle part,";

      Func<string, string> lambda = param =>
        {
            param += mid;
            param += " and this was added to the string.";
            return param;
        };

      Console.WriteLine(anonDel("Start of string"));
    }
  }
}
```

code snippet LambdaExpressions/Program.cs

The left side of the Lambda operator => lists the parameters needed. The right side following the Lambda operator defines the implementation of the method that is assigned to the variable `lambda`.

Parameters

With Lambda expressions there are several ways to define parameters. If there's only one parameter, just the name of the parameter is enough. The following Lambda expression uses the parameter named `s`. Because the delegate type defines a `string` parameter, `s` is of type `string`. The implementation invokes the `String.Format()` method to return a string that is finally written to the console when the delegate is invoked: change uppercase TEST.

```
Func<string, string> oneParam = s => String.Format(
            "change uppercase {0}", s.ToUpper());
Console.WriteLine(oneParam("test"));
```

If a delegate uses more than one parameter, you can combine the parameter names inside brackets. Here the parameters *x* and *y* are of type `double` as defined by the `Func<double, double, double>` delegate:

```
Func<double, double, double> twoParams = (x, y) => x * y;
Console.WriteLine(twoParams(3, 2));
```

For convenience, you can add the parameter types to the variable names inside the brackets:

```
Func<double, double, double> twoParamsWithTypes =
    (double x, double y) => x * y;
Console.WriteLine(twoParamsWithTypes(4, 2));
```

Multiple Code Lines

If the Lambda expression consists of a single statement, a method block with curly brackets and a `return` statement is not needed. There's an implicit `return` added by the compiler:

```
Func<double, double> square = x => x * x;
```

It's completely legal to add curly brackets, a `return` statement, and semicolons. Usually it's just easier to read without:

```
Func<double, double> square = x =>
    {
        return x * x;
    }
```

However, if you need multiple statements in the implementation of the Lambda expression, curly brackets and the `return` statement are required:

```
Func<string, string> lambda = param =>
    {
        param += mid;
        param += " and this was added to the string.";
        return param;
    };
```

Variables Outside of the Lambda Expression

With Lambda expressions you can access variables outside the block of the Lambda expression. This is a great feature but can also be very dangerous if not used correctly.

In the example here, a Lambda expression of type `Func<int, int>` requires one `int` parameter and returns an `int`. The parameter for the Lambda expression is defined with the variable x. The implementation also accesses the variable `someVal` that is outside the Lambda expression. As long as you do not think that the Lambda expression creates a new method that is used later when f is invoked, this might not look confusing at all. Looking at this code block the returned value calling f should be the value from x plus 5, but this might not be the case:

```
int someVal = 5;
Func<int, int> f = x => x + someVal;
```

Assuming the variable `someVal` is later changed, and then the Lambda expression invoked, the new value of `someVal` is used. The result here invoking `f(3)` is `10`:

```
someVal = 7;
Console.WriteLine(f(3));
```

In particular, when the Lambda expression is invoked by a separate thread you might not know when the invocation happened and thus what value the outside variable currently has.

Now you might wonder how it is possible at all to access variables outside of the Lambda expression from within the Lambda expression. To understand this, look at what the compiler does when you define a Lambda expression. With the Lambda expression `x => x + someVal`, the compiler creates an anonymous class that has a constructor to pass the outer variable. The constructor depends on how many variables you access from the outside. With this simple example, the constructor accepts an `int`. The anonymous class contains an anonymous method that has the implementation as was defined by the Lambda expression, with the parameters and return type.

```
public class AnonymousClass
{
    private int someVal;
    public AnonymousClass(int someVal)
    {
        this.someVal = someVal;
    }
    public int AnonymousMethod(int x)
    {
        return x + someVal;
    }
}
```

Using the Lambda expression and invoking the method creates an instance of the anonymous class and passes the value of the variable from the time when the call is made.

> *Lambda expressions can be used any place where the type is a delegate. Another use of Lambda expressions is when the type is* Expression *or* Expression<T>. *Here the compiler creates an expression tree. This feature is discussed in Chapter 11, "Language Integrated Query."*

EVENTS

Events are based on delegates and offer a publish/subscribe mechanism to delegates. You can find events everywhere across the framework. In Windows applications, the Button class offers the Click event. This type of event is a delegate. A handler method that is invoked when the Click event is fired needs to be defined, with the parameters as defined by the delegate type.

In the code example shown in this section, events are used to connect CarDealer and Consumer classes. The CarDealer offers an event when a new car arrives. The Consumer class subscribes to the event to get informed when a new car arrives.

Event Publisher

Start with a CarDealer class that offers a subscription based on events. CarDealer defines the event named NewCarInfo of type EventHandler<CarInfoEventArgs> with the event keyword. Inside the method NewCar() the event NewCarInfo is fired:

Available for
download on
Wrox.com

```
using System;

namespace Wrox.ProCSharp.Delegates
{
    public class CarInfoEventArgs: EventArgs
    {
        public CarInfoEventArgs(string car)
        {
            this.Car = car;
        }

        public string Car { get; private set; }
    }

    public class CarDealer
    {
        public event EventHandler<CarInfoEventArgs> NewCarInfo;

        public void NewCar(string car)
        {
            Console.WriteLine("CarDealer, new car {0}", car);
            if (NewCarInfo != null)
            {
                NewCarInfo(this, new CarInfoEventArgs(car));
            }
        }
    }
}
```

code snippet EventsSample/CarDealer.cs

The class CarDealer offers the event NewCarInfo of type EventHandler<CarInfoEventArgs>. As a convention, events typically use methods with two parameters where the first parameter is an object and contains the sender of the event, and the second parameter gives information about the event. The second parameter is different for various event types. .NET 1.0 defined several hundred delegates for events for all different data types. That's no longer necessary with the generic delegate EventHandler<T>. EventHandler<TEventArgs> defines a handler that returns void and accepts two parameters. With EventHandler<TEventArgs>, the first parameter needs to be of type object, and the second parameter is of type T. EventHandler<TEventArgs> also defines a constraint on T; it must derive from the base class EventArgs, which is the case with CarInfoEventArgs:

```
public event EventHandler<CarInfoEventArgs> NewCarInfo;
```

The delegate EventHandler<TEventArgs> is defined as follows:

```
public delegate void EventHandler<TEventArgs>(object sender, TEventArgs e)
    where TEventArgs: EventArgs
```

Defining the event in one line is a C# shorthand notation. The compiler creates a variable of the delegate type EventHandler<CarInfoEventArgs> and adds methods to subscribe and unsubscribe from the delegate. The long form of the shorthand notation is shown next. This is very similar to auto-properties and full properties. With events, the add and remove keywords are used to add and remove a handler to the delegate:

```
private delegate EventHandler<CarInfoEventArgs> newCarInfo;
public event EventHandler<CarInfoEventArgs> NewCarInfo
{
    add
    {
        newCarInfo += value;
    }
    remove
    {
        newCarInfo = value;
    }
}
```

 The long notation to define events is useful if more needs to be done than just adding and removing the event handler, for example, to add synchronization for multiple thread access. The WPF controls make use of the long notation to add bubbling and tunneling functionality with the events. You can read more about event bubbling and tunneling events in Chapter 27, "Core XAML."

The class CarDealer fires the event in the method NewCar. Using NewCarInfo with brackets invokes all the handlers that are subscribed to the event. Remember, as was shown with multicast delegates, the order of the methods invoked is not guaranteed. To have more control over calling the handler methods you can use the Delegate class method GetInvocationList() to access every item in the delegate list and invoke each on its own, as shown earlier.

Before firing the event, it is necessary to check whether the delegate NewCarInfo is not null. If no one subscribed, the delegate is null:

```
public void NewCar(string car)
{
    Console.WriteLine("CarDealer, new car {0}", car);
    if (NewCarInfo != null)
    {
        NewCarInfo(this, new CarInfoEventArgs(car));
    }
}
```

Event Listener

The class `Consumer` is used as the event listener. This class subscribes to the event of the `CarDealer` and defines the method `NewCarIsHere` that in turn fulfills the requirements of the `EventHandler<CarInfoEventArgs>` delegate with parameters of type `object` and `CarInfoEventArgs`:

```csharp
using System;

namespace Wrox.ProCSharp.Delegates
{
    public class Consumer
    {
        private string name;

        public Consumer(string name)
        {
            this.name = name;
        }

        public void NewCarIsHere(object sender, CarInfoEventArgs e)
        {
            Console.WriteLine("{0}: car {1} is new", name, e.Car);
        }
    }
}
```

code snippet EventsSample/Consumer.cs

Now the event publisher and subscriber need to connect. This is done by using the `NewCarInfo` event of the `CarDealer` to create a subscription with `+=`. The consumer *michael* subscribes to the event, then the consumer *nick*, and next *michael* unsubscribes with `-=`:

```csharp
namespace Wrox.ProCSharp.Delegates
{
    class Program
    {
        static void Main()
        {
            var dealer = new CarDealer();

            var michael = new Consumer("Michael");
            dealer.NewCarInfo += michael.NewCarIsHere;

            dealer.NewCar("Mercedes");

            var nick = new Consumer("Nick");
            dealer.NewCarInfo += nick.NewCarIsHere;

            dealer.NewCar("Ferrari");

            dealer.NewCarInfo = michael.NewCarIsHere;

            dealer.NewCar("Toyota");
        }
    }
}
```

code snippet EventsSample/Program.cs

Running the application, a Mercedes arrived and Michael was informed. Because after that Nick registers for the subscription as well, both Michael and Nick are informed about the new Ferrari. Then Michael unsubscribes and only Nick is informed about the Toyota:

```
CarDealer, new car Mercedes
Michael: car Mercedes is new
CarDealer, new car Ferrari
Michael: car Ferrari is new
Nick: car Ferrari is new
CarDealer, new car Toyota
Nick: car Toyota is new
```

Weak Events

With events, the publisher and listener are directly connected. This can be a problem with garbage collection. For example, if a listener is not directly referenced any more, there's still a reference from the publisher. The garbage collector cannot clean up memory from the listener, as the publisher still holds a reference and fires events to the listener.

This strong connection can be resolved by using the weak event pattern and using the WeakEventManager as an intermediate between the publisher and listeners.

The sample from before with the CarDealer as publisher and Consumer as listener is modified in the following section to use the weak event pattern.

Weak Event Manager

To use weak events you need to create a class that derives from WeakEventManager. WeakEventManager is defined in the namespace System.Windows in the assembly WindowsBase.

The class WeakCarInfoEventManager is the weak event manager class that manages the connection between the publisher and listener for the NewCarInfo event. This class implements a singleton pattern so that only one instance is created. The static property CurrentManager creates an object of type WeakCarInfoEventManager if it doesn't exist, and returns a reference to it. WeakCarInfoEventManager. CurrentManager is used to access the singleton object from the WeakCarInfoEventManager.

With the weak event pattern, the weak event manager class needs static methods AddListener() and RemoveListener(). The listener is connected and disconnected to the events of the publisher with these methods instead of using the events from the publisher directly. The listener also needs to implement the interface IWeakEventListener that is shown shortly. With the AddListener() and RemoveListener() methods, methods from the base class WeakEventManager are invoked to add and remove the listeners.

With the WeakCarInfoEventManager class you also need to override the StartListening() and StopListening() methods from the base class. StartListening() is called when the first listener is added, StopListening() when the last listener is removed. StartListening() and StopListening() subscribes and unsubscribes a method from the weak event manager to listen for the event from the publisher. In case the weak event manager class needs to connect to different publisher types, you can check the type information from the source object before doing the cast. The event is then forwarded to the listeners by calling the DeliverEvent() method from the base class, which in turn invokes the method ReceiveWeakEvent() from the IWeakEventListener interface in the listeners:

```
using System.Windows;

namespace Wrox.ProCSharp.Delegates
{
    public class WeakCarInfoEventManager: WeakEventManager
    {
        public static void AddListener(object source, IWeakEventListener listener)
        {
            CurrentManager.ProtectedAddListener(source, listener);
        }

        public static void RemoveListener(object source,
                                          IWeakEventListener listener)
```

```
        {
            CurrentManager.ProtectedRemoveListener(source, listener);
        }

        public static WeakCarInfoEventManager CurrentManager
        {
            get
            {
                WeakCarInfoEventManager manager =
                    GetCurrentManager(typeof(WeakCarInfoEventManager))
                        as WeakCarInfoEventManager;
                if (manager == null)
                {
                    manager = new WeakCarInfoEventManager();
                    SetCurrentManager(typeof(WeakCarInfoEventManager), manager);
                }
                return manager;
            }
        }

        protected override void StartListening(object source)
        {
            (source as CarDealer).NewCarInfo += CarDealer_NewCarInfo;
        }

        void CarDealer_NewCarInfo(object sender, CarInfoEventArgs e)
        {
            DeliverEvent(sender, e);
        }

        protected override void StopListening(object source)
        {
            (source as CarDealer).NewCarInfo = CarDealer_NewCarInfo;
        }
    }
}
```

code snippet WeakEventsSample/WeakCarInfoEventManager.cs

 WPF makes use of the weak event pattern with the event manager classes CollectionChangedEventManager, CurrentChangedEventManager, CurrentChangingEventManager, PropertyChangedEventManager, DataChangedEventManager, *and* LostFocusEventManager.

With the publisher class CarDealer there's no need to change anything. It has the same implementation as before.

Event Listener

The listener needs to be changed to implement the interface IWeakEventListener. This interface defines the method ReceiveWeakEvent() that is called from the weak event manager when the event arrives. In the method implementation the method that should be invoked from the event is invoked, which is NewCarIsHere().

```
using System;
using System.Windows;

namespace Wrox.ProCSharp.Delegates
{
```

```
    public class Consumer: IWeakEventListener
    {
        private string name;

        public Consumer(string name)
        {
            this.name = name;
        }

        public void NewCarIsHere(object sender, CarInfoEventArgs e)
        {
            Console.WriteLine("{0}: car {1} is new", name, e.Car);
        }

        bool IWeakEventListener.ReceiveWeakEvent(Type managerType, object sender,
                                                 EventArgs e)
        {
            NewCarIsHere(sender, e as CarInfoEventArgs);
            return true;
        }
    }
}
```

code snippet WeakEventsSample/Consumer.cs

Inside the Main method where the publisher and listeners are connected, the connection is now done by using the static `AddListener()` and `RemoveListener()` methods from the `WeakCarInfoEvent Manager` class.

Available for
download on
Wrox.com

```
    static void Main()
    {
        var dealer = new CarDealer();

        var michael = new Consumer("Michael");
        WeakCarInfoEventManager.AddListener(dealer, michael);

        dealer.NewCar("Mercedes");

        var nick = new Consumer("Nick");
        WeakCarInfoEventManager.AddListener(dealer, nick);

        dealer.NewCar("Ferrari");

        WeakCarInfoEventManager.RemoveListener(dealer, michael);

        dealer.NewCar("Toyota");
    }
```

code snippet WeakEventsSample/Program.cs

With this additional work of implementing the weak event pattern, the publisher and listeners are no longer strongly connected. When a listener is not referenced anymore, it can be garbage collected.

SUMMARY

This chapter gave you the basics of delegates, Lambda expressions, and events. You learned how to declare a delegate and add methods to the delegate list. You learned how to implement methods called by delegates with Lambda expressions. You also learned the process of declaring event handlers to respond to an event, as well as how to create a custom event and use the patterns for raising the event.

As a .NET developer, you will be using delegates and events extensively, especially when developing Windows applications. Events are the means that the .NET developer has to monitor the various Windows messages that occur while the application is executing. Otherwise, you would have to monitor the WndProc and catch the WM_MOUSEDOWN message instead of getting the mouse Click event for a button.

The use of delegates and events in the design of a large application can reduce dependencies and the coupling of layers. This allows you to develop components that have a higher reusability factor.

Lambda expressions are C# language features on delegates. With these, you can reduce the amount of code you need to write. Lambda expressions are not used only with delegates, as you will see in Chapter 11.

The next chapter goes into the foundation of strings and regular expressions.

Strings and Regular Expressions

WHAT'S IN THIS CHAPTER?

➤ Building strings

➤ Formatting expressions

➤ Using regular expressions

Since the beginning of this book, you have been using strings almost constantly, and might not have realized that the stated mapping that the `string` keyword in C# actually refers to is the `System.String` .NET base class. `System.String` is a very powerful and versatile class, but it is by no means the only string-related class in the .NET armory. This chapter starts by reviewing the features of `System.String` and then looks at some nifty things you can do with strings using some of the other .NET classes — in particular those in the `System.Text` and `System.Text.RegularExpressions` namespaces. This chapter covers the following areas:

➤ **Building strings** — If you're performing repeated modifications on a string, for example, to build up a lengthy string prior to displaying it or passing it to some other method or application, the `String` class can be very inefficient. When you find yourself in this kind of situation, another class, `System.Text.StringBuilder`, is more suitable because it has been designed exactly for this situation.

➤ **Formatting expressions** — This chapter takes a closer look at those formatting expressions that have been used in the `Console.WriteLine()` method throughout the past few chapters. These formatting expressions are processed using a couple of useful interfaces, `IFormatProvider` and `IFormattable`. By implementing these interfaces on your own classes, you can actually define your own formatting sequences so that `Console.WriteLine()` and similar classes will display the values of your classes in whatever way you specify.

➤ **Regular expressions** — .NET also offers some very sophisticated classes that deal with situations in which you need to identify or extract substrings that satisfy certain fairly sophisticated criteria; for example, finding all occurrences within a string where a character or set of characters is repeated, finding all words that begin with "s" and contain at least one "n," or strings that adhere to an employee ID or a Social Security number construction. Although you can write methods to perform this kind of processing using the `String` class, such methods are cumbersome to write. Instead, you will find that some classes, specifically those from `System.Text.RegularExpressions`, are designed to perform this kind of processing.

EXAMINING SYSTEM.STRING

Before digging into the other string classes, this section quickly reviews some of the available methods in the String class itself.

System.String is a class specifically designed to store a string and allow a large number of operations on the string. In addition, due to the importance of this data type, C# has its own keyword and associated syntax to make it particularly easy to manipulate strings using this class.

You can concatenate strings using operator overloads:

```
string message1 = "Hello";  // returns "Hello"
message1 += ", There"; // returns "Hello, There"
string message2 = message1 + "!"; // returns "Hello, There!"
```

C# also allows extraction of a particular character using an indexer-like syntax:

```
string message = "Hello";
char char4 = message[4];   // returns 'o'. Note the string is zero-indexed
```

This enables you to perform such common tasks as replacing characters, removing whitespace, and capitalization. The following table introduces the key methods:

METHOD	PURPOSE
Compare	Compares the contents of strings, taking into account the culture (locale) in assessing equivalence between certain characters.
CompareOrdinal	Same as Compare but doesn't take culture into account.
Concat	Combines separate string instances into a single instance.
CopyTo	Copies a specific number of characters from the selected index to an entirely new instance of an array.
Format	Formats a string containing various values and specifiers for how each value should be formatted.
IndexOf	Locates the first occurrence of a given substring or character in the string.
IndexOfAny	Locates the first occurrence of any one of a set of characters in a string.
Insert	Inserts a string instance into another string instance at a specified index.
Join	Builds a new string by combining an array of strings.
LastIndexOf	Same as IndexOf but finds the last occurrence.
LastIndexOfAny	Same as IndexOfAny but finds the last occurrence.
PadLeft	Pads out the string by adding a specified repeated character to the left side of the string.
PadRight	Pads out the string by adding a specified repeated character to the right side of the string.
Replace	Replaces occurrences of a given character or substring in the string with another character or substring.
Split	Splits the string into an array of substrings; the breaks occur wherever a given character occurs.
Substring	Retrieves the substring starting at a specified position in a string.
ToLower	Converts string to lowercase.
ToUpper	Converts string to uppercase.
Trim	Removes leading and trailing whitespace.

Please note that this table is not comprehensive but is intended to give you an idea of the features offered by strings.

Building Strings

As you have seen, String is an extremely powerful class that implements a large number of very useful methods. However, the String class has a shortcoming that makes it very inefficient for making repeated modifications to a given string — it is actually an *immutable* data type, which means that after you initialize a string object, that string object can never change. The methods and operators that appear to modify the contents of a string actually create new strings, copying across the contents of the old string if necessary. For example, look at the following code:

```
string greetingText = "Hello from all the guys at Wrox Press. ";
greetingText += "We do hope you enjoy this book as much as we enjoyed writing it.";
```

What happens when this code executes is this: first, an object of type System.String is created and initialized to hold the text Hello from all the guys at Wrox Press. (Note the space *after* the period.) When this happens, the .NET runtime allocates just enough memory in the string to hold this text (39 chars), and the variable greetingText is set to refer to this string instance.

In the next line, syntactically it looks like more text is being added onto the string — though it is not. Instead, what happens is that a new string instance is created with just enough memory allocated to store the combined text — that's 103 characters in total. The original text, Hello from all the people at Wrox Press., is copied into this new string instance along with the extra text: We do hope you enjoy this book as much as we enjoyed writing it. Then, the address stored in the variable greetingText is updated, so the variable correctly points to the new String object. The old String object is now unreferenced — there are no variables that refer to it — and so will be removed the next time the garbage collector comes along to clean out any unused objects in your application.

By itself, that does not look too bad, but suppose that you wanted to encode that string by replacing each letter (not the punctuation) with the character that has an ASCII code further on in the alphabet, as part of some extremely simple encryption scheme. This would change the string to Ifmmp gspn bmm uif hvst bu Xspy Qsftt. Xf ep ipqf zpv fokpz uijt cppl bt nvdi bt xf fokpzfe xsjujoh ju. Several ways of doing this exist, but the simplest and (if you are restricting yourself to using the String class) almost certainly the most efficient way is to use the String.Replace() method, which replaces all occurrences of a given substring in a string with another substring. Using Replace(), the code to encode the text looks like this:

```
string greetingText = "Hello from all the guys at Wrox Press. ";
greetingText += "We do hope you enjoy this book as much as we enjoyed writing it.";

for(int i = 'z'; i>= 'a'; i--)
{
    char old1 = (char)i;
    char new1 = (char)(i+1);
    greetingText = greetingText.Replace(old1, new1);
}

for(int i = 'Z'; i>='A'; i--)
{
    char old1 = (char)i;
    char new1 = (char)(i+1);
    greetingText = greetingText.Replace(old1, new1);
}

Console.WriteLine("Encoded:\n" + greetingText);
```

code snippet StringEncoder.cs

For simplicity, this code does not wrap Z to A or z to a. These letters get encoded to
[and {, respectively.

In this example, the `Replace()` method works in a fairly intelligent way, to the extent that it won't actually create a new string unless it actually makes changes to the old string. The original string contained 23 different lowercase characters and 3 different uppercase ones. The `Replace()` method will therefore have allocated a new string 26 times in total, with each new string storing 103 characters. That means that because of the encryption process, there will be string objects capable of storing a combined total of 2,678 characters now sitting on the heap waiting to be garbage-collected! Clearly, if you use strings to do text processing extensively, your applications will run into severe performance problems.

To address this kind of issue, Microsoft has supplied the `System.Text.StringBuilder` class. `StringBuilder` is not as powerful as `String` in terms of the number of methods it supports. The processing you can do on a `StringBuilder` is limited to substitutions and appending or removing text from strings. However, it works in a much more efficient way.

When you construct a string using the `String` class, just enough memory is allocated to hold the string. The `StringBuilder`, however, normally allocates more memory than is actually needed. You, as a developer, have the option to indicate how much memory the `StringBuilder` should allocate, but if you do not, the amount will default to some value that depends on the size of the string that the `StringBuilder` instance is initialized with. The `StringBuilder` class has two main properties:

➤ `Length`, which indicates the length of the string that it actually contains

➤ `Capacity`, which indicates the maximum length of the string in the memory allocation

Any modifications to the string take place within the block of memory assigned to the `StringBuilder` instance, which makes appending substrings and replacing individual characters within strings very efficient. Removing or inserting substrings is inevitably still inefficient because it means that the following part of the string has to be moved. Only if you perform some operation that exceeds the capacity of the string is it necessary to allocate new memory and possibly move the entire contained string. In adding extra capacity, based on our experiments the `StringBuilder` appears to double its capacity if it detects the capacity has been exceeded and no new value for the capacity has been set.

For example, if you use a `StringBuilder` object to construct the original greeting string, you might write this code:

```
StringBuilder greetingBuilder =
    new StringBuilder("Hello from all the guys at Wrox Press. ", 150);
greetingBuilder.AppendFormat("We do hope you enjoy this book as much as we enjoyed
                    writing it");
```

 To use the `StringBuilder` *class, you need a* `System.Text` *reference in your code.*

This code sets an initial capacity of `150` for the `StringBuilder`. It is always a good idea to set some capacity that covers the likely maximum length of a string, to ensure the `StringBuilder` does not need to relocate because its capacity was exceeded. By default, the capacity is set to 16. Theoretically, you can set as large a number as you can pass in an `int`, although the system will probably complain that it does not have enough memory if you actually try to allocate the maximum of two billion characters (this is the theoretical maximum that a `StringBuilder` instance is allowed to contain, in principle).

When the preceding code is executed, it first creates a `StringBuilder` object that looks like Figure 9-1.

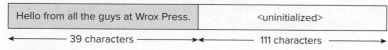

Hello from all the guys at Wrox Press.	<uninitialized>

◄———— 39 characters ————►◄———— 111 characters ————►

FIGURE 9-1

Then, on calling the `AppendFormat()` method, the remaining text is placed in the empty space, without the need for more memory allocation. However, the real efficiency gain from using a `StringBuilder` comes when you are making repeated text substitutions. For example, if you try to encrypt the text in the same way as before, you can perform the entire encryption without allocating any more memory whatsoever:

```
StringBuilder greetingBuilder =
   new StringBuilder("Hello from all the guys at Wrox Press. ", 150);
greetingBuilder.AppendFormat("We do hope you enjoy this book as much as we " +
   "enjoyed writing it");

Console.WriteLine("Not Encoded:\n" + greetingBuilder);

for(int i = 'z'; i>='a'; i--)
{
   char old1 = (char)i;
   char new1 = (char)(i+1);
   greetingBuilder = greetingBuilder.Replace(old1, new1);
}

for(int i = 'Z'; i>='A'; i--)
{
   char old1 = (char)i;
   char new1 = (char)(i+1);
   greetingBuilder = greetingBuilder.Replace(old1, new1);
}

   Console.WriteLine("Encoded:\n" + greetingBuilder);
```

This code uses the `StringBuilder.Replace()` method, which does the same thing as `String.Replace()`, but without copying the string in the process. The total memory allocated to hold strings in the preceding code is 150 characters for the `StringBuilder` instance, as well as the memory allocated during the string operations performed internally in the final `Console.WriteLine()` statement.

Normally, you want to use `StringBuilder` to perform any manipulation of strings and `String` to store or display the final result.

StringBuilder Members

You have seen a demonstration of one constructor of `StringBuilder`, which takes an initial string and capacity as its parameters. There are others. For example, you can supply only a string:

```
StringBuilder sb = new StringBuilder("Hello");
```

Or you can create an empty `StringBuilder` with a given capacity:

```
StringBuilder sb = new StringBuilder(20);
```

Apart from the `Length` and `Capacity` properties, there is a read-only `MaxCapacity` property that indicates the limit to which a given `StringBuilder` instance is allowed to grow. By default, this is given by `int .MaxValue` (roughly two billion, as noted earlier), but you can set this value to something lower when you construct the `StringBuilder` object:

```
// This will both set initial capacity to 100, but the max will be 500.
// Hence, this StringBuilder can never grow to more than 500 characters,
// otherwise it will raise exception if you try to do that.
StringBuilder sb = new StringBuilder(100, 500);
```

You can also explicitly set the capacity at any time, though an exception will be raised if you set it to a value less than the current length of the string or a value that exceeds the maximum capacity:

```
StringBuilder sb = new StringBuilder("Hello");
sb.Capacity = 100;
```

The following table lists the main `StringBuilder` methods.

METHOD	PURPOSE
`Append()`	Appends a string to the current string.
`AppendFormat()`	Appends a string that has been worked out from a format specifier.
`Insert()`	Inserts a substring into the current string.
`Remove()`	Removes characters from the current string.
`Replace()`	Replaces all occurrences of a character with another character or a substring with another substring in the current string.
`ToString()`	Returns the current string cast to a `System.String` object (overridden from `System.Object`).

Several overloads of many of these methods exist.

> `AppendFormat()` *is actually the method that is ultimately called when you call* `Console.WriteLine()`, *which has responsibility for working out what all the format expressions like* `{0:D}` *should be replaced with. This method is examined in the next section.*

There is no cast (either implicit or explicit) from `StringBuilder` to `String`. If you want to output the contents of a `StringBuilder` as a `String`, you must use the `ToString()` method.

Now that you have been introduced to the `StringBuilder` class and have learned some of the ways in which you can use it to increase performance, you should be aware that this class will not always give you the increased performance you are looking for. Basically, the `StringBuilder` class should be used when you are manipulating multiple strings. However, if you are just doing something as simple as concatenating two strings, you will find that `System.String` will be better-performing.

Format Strings

So far, a large number of classes and structs have been written for the code samples presented in this book, and they have normally implemented a `ToString()` method in order to display the contents of a given variable. However, quite often users might want the contents of a variable to be displayed in different, often culture- and locale-dependent ways. The .NET base class, `System.DateTime`, provides the most obvious example of this. For example, you might want to display the same date as 10 June 2010, 10 Jun 2010, 6/10/10 (USA), 10/6/10 (UK), or 10.06.2010 (Germany).

Similarly, the `Vector` struct in Chapter 7, "Operators and Casts," implements the `Vector.ToString()` method to display the vector in the format `(4, 56, 8)`. There is, however, another very common way of writing vectors, in which this vector would appear as `4i + 56j + 8k`. If you want the classes that you write to be user-friendly, they need to support the facility to display their string representations in any of the formats that users are likely to want to use. The .NET runtime defines a standard way in which this should be done: the `IFormattable` interface. Showing how to add this important feature to your classes and structs is the subject of this section.

As you probably know, you need to specify the format in which you want a variable displayed when you call `Console.WriteLine()`. Therefore, this section uses this method as an example, although most of the discussion applies to any situation in which you want to format a string. For example, if you want to display the value of a variable in a list box or text box, you will normally use the `String.Format()` method to obtain the appropriate string representation of the variable. However, the actual format specifiers you use to request a particular format are identical to those passed to `Console.WriteLine()`. Hence, you will focus on `Console.WriteLine()` as an example. You start by examining what actually happens when you supply a format string to a primitive type, and from this, you will see how you can plug format specifiers for your own classes and structs into the process.

Chapter 2, "Core C#," uses format strings in `Console.Write()` and `Console.WriteLine()` like this:

```
double d = 13.45;
int i = 45;
Console.WriteLine("The double is {0,10:E} and the int contains {1}", d, i);
```

The format string itself consists mostly of the text to be displayed, but wherever there is a variable to be formatted, its index in the parameter list appears in braces. You might also include other information inside the braces concerning the format of that item. For example, you can include:

➤ The number of characters to be occupied by the representation of the item, prefixed by a comma. A negative number indicates that the item should be left-justified, whereas a positive number indicates that it should be right-justified. If the item actually occupies more characters than have been requested, it will still appear in full.

➤ A format specifier, preceded by a colon. This indicates how you want the item to be formatted. For example, you can indicate whether you want a number to be formatted as a currency or displayed in scientific notation.

The following table lists the common format specifiers for the numeric types, which were briefly discussed in Chapter 2.

SPECIFIER	APPLIES TO	MEANING	EXAMPLE
C	Numeric types	Locale-specific monetary value	$4834.50 (USA) £4834.50 (UK)
D	Integer types only	General integer	4834
E	Numeric types	Scientific notation	4.834E+003
F	Numeric types	Fixed-point decimal	4384.50
G	Numeric types	General number	4384.5
N	Numeric types	Common locale-specific format for numbers	4,384.50 (UK/USA) 4 384,50 (continental Europe)
P	Numeric types	Percentage notation	432,000.00%
X	Integer types only	Hexadecimal format	1120 (If you want to display 0x1120, you will have to write out the 0x separately)

If you want an integer to be padded with zeros, you can use the format specifier 0 (zero) repeated as many times as the number length is required. For example, the format specifier 0000 will cause 3 to be displayed as 0003, and 99 to be displayed as 0099, and so on.

It is not possible to give a complete list, because other data types can add their own specifiers. Showing how to define your own specifiers for your own classes is the aim of this section.

How the String Is Formatted

As an example of how strings are formatted, if you execute the following statement:

```
Console.WriteLine("The double is {0,10:E} and the int contains {1}", d, i);
```

`Console.WriteLine()` just passes the entire set of parameters to the static method, `String.Format()`. This is the same method that you would call if you wanted to format these values for use in a string to be displayed in a text box, for example. The implementation of the three-parameter overload of `WriteLine()` basically does this:

```
// Likely implementation of Console.WriteLine()

public void WriteLine(string format, object arg0, object arg1)
{
    this.WriteLine(string.Format(this.FormatProvider, format,
        new object[]{arg0, arg1}));
}
```

The one-parameter overload of this method, which is in turn called in the preceding code sample, simply writes out the contents of the string it has been passed, without doing any further formatting on it.

`String.Format()` now needs to construct the final string by replacing each format specifier with a suitable string representation of the corresponding object. However, as you saw earlier, for this process of building up a string you need a `StringBuilder` instance rather than a `string` instance. In this example, a `StringBuilder` instance is created and initialized with the first known portion of the string, the text "The double is". Next, the `StringBuilder.AppendFormat()` method is called, passing in the first format specifier, {0,10:E}, as well as the associated object, `double`, to add the string representation of this object to the string object being constructed. This process continues with `StringBuilder.Append()` and `StringBuilder.AppendFormat()` being called repeatedly until the entire formatted string has been obtained.

Now comes the interesting part: `StringBuilder.AppendFormat()` has to figure out how to format the object. First, it probes the object to find out whether it implements an interface in the `System` namespace called `IFormattable`. You can determine this quite simply by trying to cast an object to this interface and seeing whether the cast succeeds, or by using the C# is keyword. If this test fails, `AppendFormat()` calls the object's `ToString()` method, which all objects either inherit from `System.Object` or override. This is exactly what happens here because none of the classes written so far has implemented this interface. That is why the overrides of `Object.ToString()` have been sufficient to allow the structs and classes from earlier chapters such as `Vector` to get displayed in `Console.WriteLine()` statements.

However, all the predefined primitive numeric types do implement this interface, which means that for those types, and in particular for `double` and `int` in the example, the basic `ToString()` method inherited from `System.Object` will not be called. To understand what happens instead, you need to examine the `IFormattable` interface.

`IFormattable` defines just one method, which is also called `ToString()`. However, this method takes two parameters as opposed to the `System.Object` version, which doesn't take any parameters. The following code shows the definition of `IFormattable`:

```
interface IFormattable
{
    string ToString(string format, IFormatProvider formatProvider);
}
```

The first parameter that this overload of `ToString()` expects is a string that specifies the requested format. In other words, it is the specifier portion of the string that appears inside the braces ({}) in the string originally passed to `Console.WriteLine()` or `String.Format()`. For example, in the example the original statement was:

```
Console.WriteLine("The double is {0,10:E} and the int contains {1}", d, i);
```

Hence, when evaluating the first specifier, {0,10:E}, this overload will be called against the double variable, d, and the first parameter passed to it will be E. StringBuilder.AppendFormat() will pass in here the text that appears after the colon in the appropriate format specifier from the original string.

We won't worry about the second ToString() parameter in this book. It is a reference to an object that implements the IFormatProvider interface. This interface gives further information that ToString() might need to consider when formatting the object, such as culture-specific details (a .NET culture is similar to a Windows locale; if you are formatting currencies or dates, you need this information). If you are calling this ToString() overload directly from your source code, you might want to supply such an object. However, StringBuilder.AppendFormat() passes in null for this parameter. If formatProvider is null, then ToString() is expected to use the culture specified in the system settings.

Getting back to the example, the first item you want to format is a double, for which you are requesting exponential notation, with the format specifier E. The StringBuilder.AppendFormat() method establishes that the double does implement IFormattable, and will therefore call the two-parameter ToString() overload, passing it the string E for the first parameter and null for the second parameter. It is now up to the double's implementation of this method to return the string representation of the double in the appropriate format, taking into account the requested format and the current culture. StringBuilder.AppendFormat() will then sort out padding the returned string with spaces, if necessary, to fill the 10 characters the format string specified.

The next object to be formatted is an int, for which you are not requesting any particular format (the format specifier was simply {1}). With no format requested, StringBuilder.AppendFormat() passes in a null reference for the format string. The two-parameter overload of int.ToString() is expected to respond appropriately. No format has been specifically requested; therefore, it will call the no-parameter ToString() method.

This entire string formatting process is summarized in Figure 9-2.

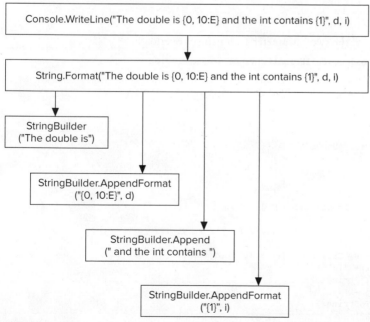

FIGURE 9-2

The FormattableVector Example

Now that you know how format strings are constructed, in this section you extend the Vector example from Chapter 7 so that you can format vectors in a variety of ways. You can download the code for this example from www.wrox.com; the filename is FormattableVector.cs. With your new knowledge of the principles involved now in hand, you will discover that the actual coding is quite simple. All you need to do is implement IFormattable and supply an implementation of the ToString() overload defined by that interface.

The format specifiers you are going to support are:

➤ N — Should be interpreted as a request to supply a quantity known as the Norm of the Vector. This is just the sum of squares of its components, which for mathematics buffs happens to be equal to the square of the length of the Vector, and is usually displayed between double vertical bars, like this: ||34.5||.

➤ VE — Should be interpreted as a request to display each component in scientific format, just as the specifier E applied to a double indicates (2.3E+01, 4.5E+02, 1.0E+00).

➤ IJK — Should be interpreted as a request to display the vector in the form 23i + 450j + 1k.

➤ Anything else should simply return the default representation of the Vector (23, 450, 1.0).

To keep things simple, you are not going to implement any option to display the vector in combined IJK and scientific format. However, you will make sure to test the specifier in a case-insensitive way, so that you allow ijk instead of IJK. Note that it is entirely up to you which strings you use to indicate the format specifiers.

To achieve this, you first modify the declaration of Vector so it implements IFormattable:

```
struct Vector: IFormattable
{
    public double x, y, z;

    // Beginning part of Vector
```

Now you add your implementation of the two-parameter ToString() overload:

```
public string ToString(string format, IFormatProvider formatProvider)
{
    if (format == null)
    {
        return ToString();
    }

    string formatUpper = format.ToUpper();

    switch (formatUpper)
    {
        case "N":
            return "|| " + Norm().ToString() + " ||";
        case "VE":
            return String.Format("( {0:E}, {1:E}, {2:E} )", x, y, z);
        case "IJK":
            StringBuilder sb = new StringBuilder(x.ToString(), 30);
            sb.AppendFormat(" i + ");
            sb.AppendFormat(y.ToString());
            sb.AppendFormat(" j + ");
            sb.AppendFormat(z.ToString());
            sb.AppendFormat(" k");
            return sb.ToString();
        default:
            return ToString();
    }
}
```

That is all you have to do! Notice how you take the precaution of checking whether format is `null` before you call any methods against this parameter — you want this method to be as robust as reasonably possible. The format specifiers for all the primitive types are case-insensitive, so that is the behavior that other developers are going to expect from your class, too. For the format specifier `VE`, you need each component to be formatted in scientific notation, so you just use `String.Format()` again to achieve this. The fields x, y, and z are all `doubles`. For the case of the `IJK` format specifier, there are quite a few substrings to be added to the string, so you use a `StringBuilder` object to improve performance.

For completeness, you also reproduce the no-parameter `ToString()` overload developed earlier:

```
public override string ToString()
{
    return "( " + x + ", " + y + ", " + z + " )";
}
```

Finally, you need to add a `Norm()` method that computes the square (norm) of the vector because you didn't actually supply this method when you developed the `Vector` struct:

```
public double Norm()
{
    return x*x + y*y + z*z;
}
```

Now you can try your formattable vector with some suitable test code:

```
static void Main()
{
    Vector v1 = new Vector(1,32,5);
    Vector v2 = new Vector(845.4, 54.3, -7.8);
    Console.WriteLine("\nIn IJK format,\nv1 is {0,30:IJK}\nv2 is {1,30:IJK}",
                      v1, v2);
    Console.WriteLine("\nIn default format,\nv1 is {0,30}\nv2 is {1,30}", v1, v2);
    Console.WriteLine("\nIn VE format\nv1 is {0,30:VE}\nv2 is {1,30:VE}", v1, v2);
    Console.WriteLine("\nNorms are:\nv1 is {0,20:N}\nv2 is {1,20:N}", v1, v2);
}
```

The result of running this sample is this:

```
FormattableVector
In IJK format,
v1 is                  1 i + 32 j + 5 k
v2 is        845.4 i + 54.3 j + -7.8 k

In default format,
v1 is                    ( 1, 32, 5 )
v2 is          ( 845.4, 54.3, -7.8 )

In VE format
v1 is ( 1.000000E+000, 3.200000E+001, 5.000000E+000 )
v2 is ( 8.454000E+002, 5.430000E+001, -7.800000E+000 )

Norms are:
v1 is              || 1050 ||
v2 is          || 717710.49 ||
```

This shows that your custom specifiers are being picked up correctly.

REGULAR EXPRESSIONS

Regular expressions are part of those small technology areas that are incredibly useful in a wide range of programs, yet rarely used among developers. You can think of regular expressions as a mini-programming language with one specific purpose: to locate substrings within a large string expression. It is not a new technology; it originated in the UNIX environment and is commonly used with the Perl programming language.

Microsoft ported it onto Windows, where up until now it has been used mostly with scripting languages. Today, regular expressions are supported by a number of .NET classes in the namespace `System.Text.RegularExpressions`. You can also find the use of regular expressions in various parts of the .NET Framework. For instance, you will find that they are used within the ASP.NET Validation server controls.

If you are not familiar with the regular expressions language, this section introduces both regular expressions and their related .NET classes. If you are already familiar with regular expressions, you will probably want to just skim through this section to pick out the references to the .NET base classes. You might like to know that the .NET regular expression engine is designed to be mostly compatible with Perl 5 regular expressions, although it has a few extra features.

Introduction to Regular Expressions

The regular expressions language is designed specifically for string processing. It contains two features:

➤ A set of *escape codes* for identifying specific types of characters. You will be familiar with the use of the * character to represent any substring in DOS expressions. (For example, the DOS command `Dir Re*` lists the files with names beginning with `Re`.) Regular expressions use many sequences like this to represent items such as *any one character*, *a word break*, *one optional character*, and so on.

➤ A system for grouping parts of substrings and intermediate results during a search operation.

With regular expressions, you can perform quite sophisticated and high-level operations on strings. For example, you can:

➤ Identify (and perhaps either flag or remove) all repeated words in a string (for example, "The computer books books" to "The computer books")

➤ Convert all words to title case (for example, "this is a Title" to "This Is A Title")

➤ Convert all words longer than three characters to title case (for example, "this is a Title" to "This is a Title")

➤ Ensure that sentences are properly capitalized

➤ Separate the various elements of a URI (for example, given `http://www.wrox.com`, extract the protocol, computer name, file name, and so on)

Of course, all these tasks can be performed in C# using the various methods on `System.String` and `System.Text.StringBuilder`. However, in some cases, this would require writing a fair amount of C# code. If you use regular expressions, this code can normally be compressed to just a couple of lines. Essentially, you instantiate a `System.Text.RegularExpressions.RegEx` object (or, even simpler, invoke a static `RegEx()` method), pass it the string to be processed, and pass in a regular expression (a string containing the instructions in the regular expressions language), and you're done.

A regular expression string looks at first sight rather like a regular string, but interspersed with escape sequences and other characters that have a special meaning. For example, the sequence `\b` indicates the beginning or end of a word (a word boundary), so if you wanted to indicate you were looking for the characters `th` at the beginning of a word, you would search for the regular expression, `\bth` (that is, the sequence word boundary-t-h). If you wanted to search for all occurrences of `th` at the end of a word, you would write `th\b` (the sequence t-h-word boundary). However, regular expressions are much more sophisticated than that and include, for example, facilities to store portions of text that are found in a search operation. This section merely scratches the surface of the power of regular expressions.

 For more on regular expressions, please review the book Beginning Regular Expressions, *Wiley Publishing, 2005 (ISBN 978-0-7645-7489-4).*

Suppose your application needed to convert U.S. phone numbers to an international format. In the United States, the phone numbers have this format: 314-123-1234, which is often written as (314) 123-1234. When converting this national format to an international format you have to include +1 (the country code of the United States) and add brackets around the area code: +1 (314) 123-1234. As find-and-replace operations go, that is not too complicated. It would still require some coding effort if you were going to use the `String` class for this purpose (which would mean that you would have to write your code using the methods available from `System.String`). The regular expressions language allows you to construct a short string that achieves the same result.

This section is intended only as a very simple example, so it concentrates on searching strings to identify certain substrings, not on modifying them.

The RegularExpressionsPlayaround Example

For the rest of this section, you develop a short example, called `RegularExpressionsPlayaround`, that illustrates some of the features of regular expressions and how to use the .NET regular expressions engine in C# by performing and displaying the results of some searches. The text you are going to use as your sample document is an introduction to a Wrox Press book on ASP.NET (*Professional ASP.NET 4: in C# and VB*, Wiley Publishing, 2010, ISBN 978-0-4705-0220-4).

Available for
download on
Wrox.com

```
const string myText =
@"This comprehensive compendium provides a broad and thorough investigation of all
aspects of programming with ASP.NET. Entirely revised and updated for the fourth
release of .NET, this book will give you the information you need to
master ASP.NET and build a dynamic, successful, enterprise Web application.";
```

code snippet RegularExpressionsPlayaround.cs

 This code is valid C# code, despite all the line breaks. It nicely illustrates the utility of verbatim strings that are prefixed by the @ symbol.

This text is referred to as the *input string*. To get your bearings and get used to the regular expressions of .NET classes, you start with a basic plain text search that does not feature any escape sequences or regular expression commands. Suppose that you want to find all occurrences of the string `ion`. This search string is referred to as the *pattern*. Using regular expressions and the `Text` variable declared previously, you could write this:

```
const string pattern = "ion";
MatchCollection myMatches = Regex.Matches(myText, pattern,
                                RegexOptions.IgnoreCase |
                                RegexOptions.ExplicitCapture);

foreach (Match nextMatch in myMatches)
{
    Console.WriteLine(nextMatch.Index);
}
```

This code uses the static method `Matches()` of the `Regex` class in the `System.Text.RegularExpressions` namespace. This method takes as parameters some input text, a pattern, and a set of optional flags taken from the `RegexOptions` enumeration. In this case, you have specified that all searching should be case-insensitive. The other flag, `ExplicitCapture`, modifies the way that the match is collected in a way that, for your purposes, makes the search a bit more efficient — you see why this is later (although it does have other uses that we won't explore here). `Matches()` returns a reference to a `MatchCollection` object. A *match* is the technical term for the results of finding an instance of the pattern in the expression. It is represented by the class `System.Text.RegularExpressions.Match`. Therefore, you return a `MatchCollection` that contains all the matches, each represented by a `Match` object. In the preceding code, you simply iterate over the collection and use the `Index` property of the `Match` class, which returns the index in the input text of where the match was found. Running this code results in three matches. The following table details some of the `RegexOptions` enumerations.

MEMBER NAME	DESCRIPTION
CultureInvariant	Specifies that the culture of the string is ignored.
ExplicitCapture	Modifies the way the match is collected by making sure that valid captures are the ones that are explicitly named.
IgnoreCase	Ignores the case of the string that is input.
IgnorePatternWhitespace	Removes unescaped whitespace from the string and enables comments that are specified with the pound or hash sign.
Multiline	Changes the characters ^ and $ so that they are applied to the beginning and end of each line and not just to the beginning and end of the entire string.
RightToLeft	Causes the inputted string to be read from right to left instead of the default left to right (ideal for some Asian and other languages that are read in this direction).
Singleline	Specifies a single-line mode where the meaning of the dot (.) is changed to match every character.

So far, nothing is new from the preceding example apart from some .NET base classes. However, the power of regular expressions really comes from that pattern string. The reason is that the pattern string does not have to contain only plain text. As hinted earlier, it can also contain what are known as *meta-characters*, which are special characters that give commands, as well as escape sequences, which work in much the same way as C# escape sequences. They are characters preceded by a backslash (\) and have special meanings.

For example, suppose that you wanted to find words beginning with n. You could use the escape sequence \b, which indicates a word boundary (a word boundary is just a point where an alphanumeric character precedes or follows a whitespace character or punctuation symbol). You would write this:

```
const string pattern = @"\bn";
MatchCollection myMatches = Regex.Matches(myText, pattern,
                                RegexOptions.IgnoreCase |
                                RegexOptions.ExplicitCapture);
```

Notice the @ character in front of the string. You want the \b to be passed to the .NET regular expressions engine at runtime — you don't want the backslash intercepted by a well-meaning C# compiler that thinks it's an escape sequence intended for itself! If you want to find words ending with the sequence ion, you write this:

```
const string pattern = @"ion\b";
```

If you want to find all words beginning with the letter a and ending with the sequence ion (which has as its only match the word *application* in the example), you will have to put a bit more thought into your code. You clearly need a pattern that begins with \ba and ends with ion\b, but what goes in the middle? You need to somehow tell the application that between the a and the ion there can be any number of characters as long as none of them are whitespace. In fact, the correct pattern looks like this:

```
const string pattern = @"\ba\S*ion\b";
```

Eventually you will get used to seeing weird sequences of characters like this when working with regular expressions. It actually works quite logically. The escape sequence \S indicates any character that is not a whitespace character. The * is called a *quantifier*. It means that the preceding character can be repeated any number of times, including zero times. The sequence \S* means *any number of characters as long as they are not whitespace characters*. The preceding pattern will, therefore, match any single word that begins with a and ends with ion.

The following table lists some of the main special characters or escape sequences that you can use. It is not comprehensive, but a fuller list is available in the MSDN documentation.

SYMBOL	MEANING	EXAMPLE	MATCHES
^	Beginning of input text	^B	B, but only if first character in text
$	End of input text	X$	X, but only if last character in text
.	Any single character except the newline character (\ )	i.ation	isation, ization
*	Preceding character may be repeated zero or more times	ra*t	rt, rat, raat, raaat, and so on
+	Preceding character may be repeated one or more times	ra+t	rat, raat, raaat and so on, but not rt
?	Preceding character may be repeated zero or one time	ra?t	rt and rat only
\s	Any whitespace character	\sa	[space]a, \ta, \na (\t and \n have the same meanings as in C#)
\S	Any character that isn't whitespace	\SF	aF, rF, cF, but not \tf
\b	Word boundary	ion\b	Any word ending in ion
\B	Any position that isn't a word boundary	\BX\B	Any X in the middle of a word

If you want to search for one of the meta-characters, you can do so by escaping the corresponding character with a backslash. For example, . (a single period) means any single character other than the newline character, whereas \ . means a dot.

You can request a match that contains alternative characters by enclosing them in square brackets. For example, [1|c] means one character that can be either 1 or c. If you wanted to search for any occurrence of the words map or man, you would use the sequence ma[n|p]. Within the square brackets, you can also indicate a range, for example [a-z], to indicate any single lowercase letter, [A-E] to indicate any uppercase letter between A and E (including the letters A and E themselves), or [0-9] to represent a single digit. If you want to search for an integer (that is, a sequence that contains only the characters 0 through 9), you could write [0-9]+.

 The use of the + character indicates there must be at least one such digit, but there may be more than one — so this would match 9, 83, 854, and so on.

Displaying Results

In this section, you code the RegularExpressionsPlayaround example, so you can get a feel for how the regular expressions work.

The core of the example is a method called WriteMatches(), which writes out all the matches from a MatchCollection in a more detailed format. For each match, it displays the index of where the match was found in the input string, the string of the match, and a slightly longer string, which consists of the match plus up to ten surrounding characters from the input text — up to five characters before the match and up to five afterward. (It is fewer than five characters if the match occurred within five characters of the beginning or end of the input text.) In other words, a match on the word messaging that occurs near the end of the input text quoted earlier would display and messaging of d (five characters before and after the match), but a match on the final word `data` would display `g of data.` (only one character after the match), because after that you get to the end of the string. This longer string lets you see more clearly where the regular expression locates the match:

```
static void WriteMatches(string text, MatchCollection matches)
{
    Console.WriteLine("Original text was: \n\n" + text + "\n");
    Console.WriteLine("No. of matches: " + matches.Count);

    foreach (Match nextMatch in matches)
    {
        int index = nextMatch.Index;
        string result = nextMatch.ToString();
        int charsBefore = (index < 5) ? index: 5;
        int fromEnd = text.Length-index-result.Length;
        int charsAfter = (fromEnd < 5) ? fromEnd: 5;
        int charsToDisplay = charsBefore + charsAfter + result.Length;

        Console.WriteLine("Index: {0}, \tString: {1}, \t{2}",
            index, result,
            text.Substring(index-charsBefore, charsToDisplay));
    }
}
```

The bulk of the processing in this method is devoted to the logic of figuring out how many characters in the longer substring it can display without overrunning the beginning or end of the input text. Note that you use another property on the `Match` object, `Value`, which contains the string identified for the match. Other than that, `RegularExpressionsPlayaround` simply contains a number of methods with names such as `Find1`, `Find2`, and so on, which perform some of the searches based on the examples in this section. For example, `Find2` looks for any string that contains `a` at the beginning of a word:

```
static void Find2()
{
    string text = @"This comprehensive compendium provides a broad and thorough
        investigation of all aspects of programming with ASP.NET. Entirely revised and
        updated for the 3.5 Release of .NET, this book will give you the information
        you need to master ASP.NET and build a dynamic, successful, enterprise Web
        application.";
    string pattern = @"\ba";
    MatchCollection matches = Regex.Matches(text, pattern,
        RegexOptions.IgnoreCase);
    WriteMatches(text, matches);
}
```

Along with this comes a simple `Main()` method that you can edit to select one of the `Find<n>()` methods:

```
static void Main()
{
    Find1();
    Console.ReadLine();
}
```

The code also needs to make use of the `RegularExpressions` namespace:

```
using System;
using System.Text.RegularExpressions;
```

Running the example with the `Find2()` method shown previously gives these results:

```
RegularExpressionsPlayaround
Original text was:

This comprehensive compendium provides a broad and thorough investigation of all
aspects of programming with ASP.NET. Entirely revised and updated for the 3.5
```

```
Release of .NET, this book will give you the information you need to master ASP.NET
and build a dynamic, successful, enterprise Web application.

No. of matches: 1
Index: 291,      String: application,      Web application.
```

Matches, Groups, and Captures

One nice feature of regular expressions is that you can group characters. It works the same way as compound statements in C#. In C#, you can group any number of statements by putting them in braces, and the result is treated as one compound statement. In regular expression patterns, you can group any characters (including meta-characters and escape sequences), and the result is treated as a single character. The only difference is that you use parentheses instead of braces. The resultant sequence is known as a *group*.

For example, the pattern (an)+ locates any recurrences of the sequence an. The + quantifier applies only to the previous character, but because you have grouped the characters together, it now applies to repeats of an treated as a unit. This means that if you apply (an)+ to the input text, bananas came to Europe late in the annals of history, the anan from bananas is identified. Yet, if you write an+, the program selects the ann from annals, as well as two separate sequences of an from bananas. The expression (an)+ identifies occurrences of an, anan, ananan, and so on, whereas the expression an+ identifies occurrences of an, ann, annn, and so on.

> *You might wonder why with the preceding example* (an)+ *picks out* anan *from the word banana but doesn't identify either of the two occurrences of* an *from the same word. The rule is that matches must not overlap. If there are a couple of possibilities that would overlap, then by default the longest possible sequence will be matched.*

However, groups are actually more powerful than that. By default, when you form part of the pattern into a group, you are also asking the regular expression engine to remember any matches against just that group, as well as any matches against the entire pattern. In other words, you are treating that group as a pattern to be matched and returned in its own right. This can actually be extremely useful if you want to break up strings into component parts.

For example, URIs have the format <protocol>://<address>:<port>, where the port is optional. An example of this is http://www.wrox.com:4355. Suppose that you want to extract the protocol, the address, and the port from a URI, where you know that there may or may not be whitespace (but no punctuation) immediately following the URI. You could do so using this expression:

```
\b(\S+)://([^:]+)(?::(\S+))?\b
```

Here is how this expression works: First, the leading and trailing \b sequences ensure that you consider only portions of text that are entire words. Within that, the first group, (\S+)://, identifies one or more characters that don't count as whitespace, and that are followed by:// — the http:// at the start of an HTTP URI. The brackets cause the http to be stored as a group. Next, ([^:]+) identifies the string www.wrox.com in the URI. This group will end either when it encounters the end of the word (the closing \b) or a colon (:) as marked by the next group.

The next group identifies the port (:4355). The following ? indicates that this group is optional in the match — if there is no:xxxx, this won't prevent a match from being marked. This is very important because the port number is not always specified in a URI — in fact, it is absent most of the time. However, things are a bit more complicated than that. You want to indicate that the colon might or might not appear too, but you don't want to store this colon in the group. You've achieved this by having two nested groups. The inner (\S+) identifies anything that follows the colon (for example, 4355). The outer group contains the inner group preceded by the colon, and this group in turn is preceded by the sequence ?:. This sequence indicates that the group in question should not be saved (you only want to save `4355`; you don't need `:4355` as well!). Don't get confused by the two colons following each other — the first colon is part of the `?:` sequence that says "don't save this group," and the second is text to be searched for.

If you run this pattern on the following string, you'll get one match: `http://www.wrox.com`.

```
Hey I've just found this amazing URI at
http:// what was it --oh yes http://www.wrox.com
```

Within this match, you will find the three groups just mentioned as well as a fourth group, which represents the match itself. Theoretically, it is possible that each group itself might return no, one, or more than one match. Each of these individual matches is known as a *capture*. So, the first group, (`\S+`), has one capture, `http`. The second group also has one capture (`www.wrox.com`). The third group, however, has no captures, because there is no port number on this URI.

Notice that the string contains a second `http://`. Although this does match up to the first group, it will not be captured by the search because the entire search expression does not match this part of the text.

There isn't space to show examples of C# code that uses groups and captures, but you should know that the .NET `RegularExpressions` classes support groups and captures through classes known as `Group` and `Capture`. Also, the `GroupCollection` and `CaptureCollection` classes represent collections of groups and captures. The `Match` class exposes the `Groups` property, which returns the corresponding `GroupCollection` object. The `Group` class correspondingly implements the `Captures` property, which returns a `CaptureCollection`. The relationship between the objects is shown in Figure 9-3.

You might not want to return a `Group` object every time you just want to group some characters. A fair amount of overhead is involved in instantiating the object, which is not necessary if all you want is to group some characters as part of your search pattern. You can disable this by starting the group with the character sequence `?:` for an individual group, as was done for the URI example, or for all groups by specifying the `RegExOptions.ExplicitCaptures` flag on the `RegEx.Matches()` method, as was done in the earlier examples.

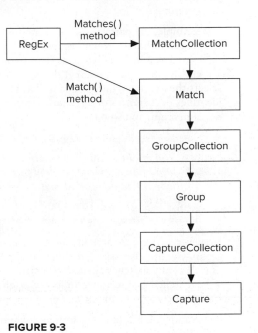

FIGURE 9-3

SUMMARY

You have quite a number of available data types at your disposal when working with the .NET Framework. One of the most used types in your applications (especially applications that focus on the submission and retrieval of data) is the `string` data type. The importance of `string` is the reason that this book has a complete chapter focused on how to use the `string` data type and manipulate it in your applications.

When working with strings in the past, it was quite common to just slice and dice the strings as needed using concatenation. With the .NET Framework, you can use the `StringBuilder` class to accomplish a lot of this task with better performance than before.

Last, but hardly least, advanced string manipulation using regular expressions is an excellent tool to search through and validate your strings.

10

Collections

WHAT'S IN THIS CHAPTER?

➤ Understanding collection interfaces and types

➤ Working with lists, queues, and stacks

➤ Working with linked and sorted lists

➤ Using dictionaries and sets

➤ Using bit arrays and bit vectors

➤ Evaluating performance

In Chapter 6, "Arrays and Tuples," you read about arrays and the interfaces implemented by the `Array` class. The size of arrays is fixed. If the number of elements is dynamic, you should use a collection class.

`List<T>` is a collection class that can be compared to arrays. But there are also other kinds of collections: queues, stacks, linked lists, and dictionaries.

 Version 1 of the .NET Framework included non-generic collection classes such as `ArrayList` and `HashTable`. CLR 2.0 added support for generics and generic collection classes. The focus of this chapter is on the newer group of collection classes and mainly ignores the old ones, as they are rarely needed with new applications.

COLLECTION INTERFACES AND TYPES

Most collection classes can be found in the `System.Collections` and `System.Collections.Generic` namespaces. Generic collection classes are located in the `System.Collections.Generic` namespace. Collection classes that are specialized for a specific type are located in the `System.Collections.Specialized` namespace. Thread-safe collection classes are in the `System.Collections.Concurrent` namespace.

Of course, there are also other ways to group collection classes. Collections can be grouped into lists, collections, and dictionaries based on the interfaces that are implemented by the collection class.

You can read detailed information about the interfaces IEnumerable *and* IEnumerator *in Chapter 6.*

The following table describes interfaces implemented by collections and lists.

INTERFACE	DESCRIPTION
IEnumerable<T>	The interface IEnumerable is required by the foreach statement. This interface defines the method GetEnumerator() which returns an enumerator that implements the IEnumerator interface.
ICollection<T>	ICollection<T> is implemented by generic collection classes. With this you can get the number of items in the collection (Count property), and copy the collection to an array (CopyTo() method). You can also add and remove items from the collection (Add(), Remove(), Clear()).
IList<T>	The IList<T> interface is for lists where elements can be accessed from their position. This interface defines an indexer, as well as ways to insert or remove items from specific positions (Insert(), RemoveAt() methods). IList<T> derives from ICollection<T>.
ISet<T>	The ISet<T> interface is new with .NET 4. This interface is implemented by sets that allow combining different sets to a union, get the intersection of two sets, and check whether two sets overlap. ISet<T> derives from ICollection<T>.
IDictionary<TKey, TValue>	The interface IDictionary<TKey, TValue> is implemented by generic collection classes that have a key and a value. With this interface all the keys and values can be accessed, items can be accessed with an indexer of type key, and items can be added or removed.
ILookup<TKey, TValue>	Similar to the IDictionary<TKey, TValue> interface, lookups have keys and values. However, with lookups the collection can contain multiple values with one key.
IComparer<T>	The interface IComparer<T> is implemented by a comparer and used to sort elements inside a collection with the Compare() method.
IEqualityComparer<T>	IEqualityComparer<T> is implemented by a comparer that can be used for keys in a dictionary. With this interface the objects can be compared for equality. With .NET 4, this interface is also implemented by arrays and tuples.
IProducerConsumerCollection<T>	The interface IProducerConsumerCollection<T> is new with .NET 4 to support new thread-safe collection classes.

LISTS

For dynamic lists, the .NET Framework offers the generic class List<T>. This class implements the IList, ICollection, IEnumerable, IList<T>, ICollection<T>, and IEnumerable<T> interfaces.

The following examples use the members of the class `Racer` as elements to be added to the collection to represent a Formula-1 racer. This class has five properties: `Id`, `FirstName`, `LastName`, `Country`, and the number of `Wins`. With the constructor of the class, the name of the racer and the number of wins can be passed to set the members. The method `ToString()` is overridden to return the name of the racer. The class `Racer` also implements the generic interface `IComparable<T>` for sorting racer elements and `IFormattable`.

```csharp
[Serializable]
public class Racer: IComparable<Racer>, IFormattable
{
    public int Id { get; private set; }
    public string FirstName { get; set; }
    public string LastName { get; set; }
    public string Country { get; set; }
    public int Wins { get; set; }
    public Racer(int id, string firstName, string lastName,
                string country = null, int wins = 0)
    {
        this.Id = id;
        this.FirstName = firstName;
        this.LastName = lastName;
        this.Country = country;
        this.Wins = wins;
    }

    public override string ToString()
    {
        return String.Format("{0} {1}", FirstName, LastName);
    }

    public string ToString(string format, IFormatProvider formatProvider)
    {
        if (format == null) format = "N";
        switch (format.ToUpper())
        {
            case "N": // name
                return ToString();
            case "F": // first name
                return FirstName;
            case "L": // last name
                return LastName;
            case "W": // Wins
                return String.Format("{0}, Wins: {1}", ToString(), Wins);
            case "C": // Country
                return String.Format("{0}, Country: {1}", ToString(), Country);
            case "A": // All
                return String.Format("{0}, {1} Wins: {2}", ToString(), Country,
                                     Wins);
            default:
                throw new FormatException(String.Format(formatProvider,
                    "Format {0} is not supported", format));
        }
    }

    public string ToString(string format)
    {
        return ToString(format, null);
    }

    public int CompareTo(Racer other)
```

```
        {
            int compare = this.LastName.CompareTo(other.LastName);
            if (compare == 0)
                return this.FirstName.CompareTo(other.FirstName);
            return compare;
        }
    }
```

code snippet ListSamples/Racer.cs

Creating Lists

You can create list objects by invoking the default constructor. With the generic class `List<T>`, you must specify the type for the values of the list with the declaration. The code shows how to declare a `List<T>` with `int` and a list with `Racer` elements. `ArrayList` is a non-generic list that accepts any `Object` type for its elements.

Using the default constructor creates an empty list. As soon as elements are added to the list, the capacity of the list is extended to allow four elements. If the fifth element is added, the list is resized to allow eight elements. If eight elements are not enough, the list is resized again to contain 16 elements. With every resize the capacity of the list is doubled.

```
        var intList = new List<int>();
        var racers = new List<Racer>();
```

If the capacity of the list changes, the complete collection is reallocated to a new memory block. With the implementation of `List<T>`, an array of type `T` is used. With reallocation, a new array is created, and `Array.Copy()` copies the elements from the old to the new array. To save time, if you know the number of elements in advance, that should be in the list; you can define the capacity with the constructor. Here a collection with a capacity of 10 elements is created. If the capacity is not large enough for the elements added, the capacity is resized to 20 and 40 elements — doubled again.

```
        List<int> intList = new List<int>(10);
```

You can get and set the capacity of a collection by using the `Capacity` property:

```
        intList.Capacity = 20;
```

The capacity is not the same as the number of elements in the collection. The number of elements in the collection can be read with the `Count` property. Of course, the capacity is always larger or equal to the number of items. As long as no element was added to the list, the count is 0.

```
        Console.WriteLine(intList.Count);
```

If you are finished adding elements to the list and don't want to add any more elements, you can get rid of the unneeded capacity by invoking the `TrimExcess()` method. However, because the relocation takes time, `TrimExcess()` does nothing if the item count is more than 90 percent of capacity.

```
        intList.TrimExcess();
```

Collection Initializers

You can also assign values to collections using collection initializers. The syntax of collection initializers is similar to array initializers, which were explained in Chapter 6. With a collection initializer, values are assigned to the collection within curly brackets at the initialization of the collection:

```
        var intList = new List<int>() {1, 2};
        var stringList = new List<string>() {"one", "two"};
```

Collection initializers are not reflected within the IL code of the compiled assembly. The compiler converts the collection initializer to invoke the Add() *method for every item from the initializer list.*

Adding Elements

You can add elements to the list with the Add() method as shown. The generic instantiated type defines the parameter type of the Add() method.

```
var intList = new List<int>();
intList.Add(1);
intList.Add(2);

var stringList = new List<string>();
stringList.Add("one");
stringList.Add("two");
```

The variable racers is defined as type List<Racer>. With the new operator, a new object of the same type is created. Because the class List<T> was instantiated with the concrete class Racer, now only Racer objects can be added with the Add() method. In the following sample code, five Formula-1 racers are created and added to the collection. The first three are added using the collection initializer, and the last two are added by invoking the Add() method explicitly:

Available for download on Wrox.com

```
var graham = new Racer(7, "Graham", "Hill", "UK", 14);
var emerson = new Racer(13, "Emerson", "Fittipaldi", "Brazil", 14);
var mario = new Racer(16, "Mario", "Andretti", "USA", 12);

var racers = new List<Racer>(20) {graham, emerson, mario};

racers.Add(new Racer(24, "Michael", "Schumacher", "Germany", 91));
racers.Add(new Racer(27, "Mika", "Hakkinen", "Finland", 20));
```

code snippet ListSamples/Program.cs

With the AddRange() method of the List<T> class, you can add multiple elements to the collection at once. The method AddRange() accepts an object of type IEnumerable<T>, so you can also pass an array as shown:

```
racers.AddRange(new Racer[] {
        new Racer(14, "Niki", "Lauda", "Austria", 25),
        new Racer(21, "Alain", "Prost", "France", 51)});
```

The collection initializer can be used only during declaration of the collection. The AddRange() *method can be invoked after the collection is initialized.*

If you know some elements of the collection when instantiating the list, you can also pass any object that implements IEnumerable<T> to the constructor of the class. This is very similar to the AddRange() method:

```
var racers =
    new List<Racer>(new Racer[] {
        new Racer(12, "Jochen", "Rindt", "Austria", 6),
        new Racer(22, "Ayrton", "Senna", "Brazil", 41) });
```

Inserting Elements

You can insert elements at a specified position with the `Insert()` method:

```
racers.Insert(3, new Racer(6, "Phil", "Hill", "USA", 3));
```

The method `InsertRange()` offers the capability to insert a number of elements, similarly to the `AddRange()` method shown earlier.

If the index set is larger than the number of elements in the collection, an exception of type `ArgumentOutOf RangeException` is thrown.

Accessing Elements

All classes that implement the `IList` and `IList<T>` interface offer an indexer, so you can access the elements by using an indexer and passing the item number. The first item can be accessed with an index value 0. By specifying `racers[3]`, you will access the fourth element of the list:

```
Racer r1 = racers[3];
```

Getting the number of elements with the `Count` property, you can do a `for` loop to iterate through every item in the collection, and use the indexer to access every item:

```
for (int i = 0; i < racers.Count; i++)
{
    Console.WriteLine(racers[i]);
}
```

 Indexed access to collection classes is available with `ArrayList`, `StringCollection`, *and* `List<T>`.

Because `List<T>` implements the interface `IEnumerable`, you can iterate through the items in the collection using the `foreach` statement as well:

```
foreach (Racer r in racers)
{
    Console.WriteLine(r);
}
```

 How the `foreach` *statement is resolved by the compiler to make use of the* `IEnumerable` *and* `IEnumerator` *interfaces is explained in Chapter 6.*

Instead of using the `foreach` statement, the `List<T>` class also offers a `ForEach()` method that is declared with an `Action<T>` parameter:

```
public void ForEach(Action<T> action);
```

The implementation of `ForEach()` is shown next. `ForEach()` iterates through every item of the collection and invokes the method that is passed as parameter for every item.

```
public class List<T>: IList<T>
{
    private T[] items;

    //...

    public void ForEach(Action<T> action)
```

```
        {
            if (action == null) throw new ArgumentNullException("action");

            foreach (T item in items)
            {
                action(item);
            }
        }
        //...
    }
```

For passing a method with ForEach, Action<T> is declared as a delegate that defines a method with a void return type and parameter T:

```
public delegate void Action<T>(T obj);
```

With a list of Racer items, the handler for the ForEach() method must be declared with a Racer object as parameter and a void return type:

```
public void ActionHandler(Racer obj);
```

Because one overload of the Console.WriteLine() method accepts Object as parameter, you can pass the address of this method to the ForEach() method, and every racer of the collection is written to the console:

```
racers.ForEach(Console.WriteLine);
```

You can also write a Lambda expression that accepts a Racer object as parameter and does the Console. WriteLine() with the implementation. Here, the format A is used with the ToString() method of the IFormattable interface to display all information about the racer:

```
racers.ForEach(r => Console.WriteLine("{0:A}", r));
```

 Lambda expressions are explained in Chapter 8, "Delegates, Lambdas, and Events."

Removing Elements

You can remove elements by index or pass the item that should be removed. Here, the fourth element is removed by passing 3 to RemoveAt():

```
racers.RemoveAt(3);
```

You can also directly pass a Racer object to the Remove() method to remove this element. Removing by index is faster, because here the collection must be searched for the item to remove. The Remove() method first searches in the collection to get the index of the item with the IndexOf() method, and then uses the index to remove the item. IndexOf() first checks if the item type implements the interface IEquatable<T>. If it does, the Equals() method of this interface is invoked to find the item in the collection that is the same as the one passed to the method. If this interface is not implemented, the Equals() method of the Object class is used to compare the items. The default implementation of the Equals() method in the Object class does a bitwise compare with value types, but compares only references with reference types.

 Chapter 7, "Operators and Casts," explains how you can override the Equals() method.

Here, the racer referenced by the variable graham is removed from the collection. The variable graham was created earlier when the collection was filled. Because the interface IEquatable<T> and the Object. Equals() method are not overridden with the Racer class, you cannot create a new object with the same content as the item that should be removed and pass it to the Remove() method.

```
if (!racers.Remove(graham))
{
    Console.WriteLine(
    "object not found in collection");
}
```

The method RemoveRange() removes a number of items from the collection. The first parameter specifies the index where the removal of items should begin; the second parameter specifies the number of items to be removed.

```
int index = 3;
int count = 5;
racers.RemoveRange(index, count);
```

To remove all items with some specific characteristics from the collection, you can use the RemoveAll() method. This method uses the Predicate<T> parameter when searching for elements, which is discussed next. For removing all elements from the collection, use the Clear() method defined with the ICollection<T> interface.

Searching

There are different ways to search for elements in the collection. You can get the index to the found item, or the item itself. You can use methods such as IndexOf(), LastIndexOf(), FindIndex(), FindLastIndex(), Find(), and FindLast(). And for just checking if an item exists, the List<T> class offers the Exists() method.

The method IndexOf() requires an object as parameter and returns the index of the item if it is found inside the collection. If the item is not found, –1 is returned. Remember that IndexOf() is using the IEquatable<T> interface to compare the elements.

```
int index1 = racers.IndexOf(mario);
```

With the IndexOf() method, you can also specify that the complete collection should not be searched, but rather specify an index where the search should start and the number of elements that should be iterated for the comparison.

Instead of searching a specific item with the IndexOf() method, you can search for an item that has some specific characteristics that you can define with the FindIndex() method. FindIndex() requires a parameter of type Predicate:

```
public int FindIndex(Predicate<T> match);
```

The Predicate<T> type is a delegate that returns a Boolean value and requires type T as parameter. This delegate can be used similarly to the Action delegate shown earlier with the ForEach() method. If the predicate returns true, there's a match and the element is found. If it returns false, the element is not found and the search continues.

```
public delegate bool Predicate<T>(T obj);
```

With the List<T> class that is using Racer objects for type T, you can pass the address of a method that returns a bool and defines a parameter of type Racer to the FindIndex() method. Finding the first racer of a specific country, you can create the FindCountry class as shown. The FindCountryPredicate() method has the signature and return type defined by the Predicate<T> delegate. The Find() method uses the variable country to search for a country that you can pass with the constructor of the class.

```
public class FindCountry
{
    public FindCountry(string country)
    {
        this.country = country;
    }
    private string country;

    public bool FindCountryPredicate(Racer racer)
    {
        if (racer == null) throw new ArgumentNullException("racer");

        return racer.Country == country;
    }
}
```

With the FindIndex() method, you can create a new instance of the FindCountry() class, pass a country string to the constructor, and pass the address of the Find method. After FindIndex() completes successfully, index2 contains the index of the first item where the Country property of the racer is set to Finland.

```
int index2 = racers.FindIndex(new FindCountry("Finland").
                   FindCountryPredicate);
```

Instead of creating a class with a handler method, you can use a Lambda expression here as well. The result is exactly the same as before. Now the Lambda expression defines the implementation to search for an item where the Country property is set to Finland.

```
int index3 = racers.FindIndex(r => r.Country == "Finland");
```

Similar to the IndexOf() method, with the FindIndex() method, you can also specify the index where the search should start and the count of items that should be iterated through. To do a search for an index beginning from the last element in the collection, you can use the FindLastIndex() method.

The method FindIndex() returns the index of the found item. Instead of getting the index, you can also get directly to the item in the collection. The Find() method requires a parameter of type Predicate<T>, much as the FindIndex() method. The Find() method here is searching for the first racer in the list that has the FirstName property set to Niki. Of course, you can also do a FindLast() to find the last item that fulfills the predicate.

```
Racer racer = racers.Find(r => r.FirstName == "Niki");
```

To get not only one, but all items that fulfill the requirements of a predicate, you can use the FindAll() method. The FindAll() method uses the same Predicate<T> delegate as the Find() and FindIndex() methods. The FindAll() method does not stop when the first item is found but instead iterates through every item in the collection and returns all items where the predicate returns true.

With the FindAll() method invoked here, all racer items are returned where the property Wins is set to more than 20. All racers who won more than 20 races are referenced from the bigWinners list.

```
List<Racer> bigWinners = racers.FindAll(r => r.Wins > 20);
```

Iterating through the variable bigWinners with a foreach statement gives the following result:

```
foreach (Racer r in bigWinners)
{
        Console.WriteLine("{0:A}", r);
}
```

```
Michael Schumacher, Germany Wins: 91
Niki Lauda, Austria Wins: 25
Alain Prost, France Wins: 51
```

The result is not sorted, but this is done next.

Sorting

The List<T> class allows sorting its elements by using the Sort() method. Sort() uses the quick sort algorithm where all elements are compared until the complete list is sorted.

You can use several overloads of the Sort() method. The arguments that can be passed are a generic delegate Comparison<T>, the generic interface IComparer<T>, and a range together with the generic interface IComparer<T>:

```
public void List<T>.Sort();
public void List<T>.Sort(Comparison<T>);
public void List<T>.Sort(IComparer<T>);
public void List<T>.Sort(Int32, Int32, IComparer<T>);
```

Using the Sort() method without arguments is possible only if the elements in the collection implement the interface IComparable.

The class Racer implements the interface IComparable<T> to sort racers by the last name:

```
racers.Sort();
racers.ForEach(Console.WriteLine);
```

If you need to do a sort other than the default supported by the item types, you need to use other techniques, for example passing an object that implements the IComparer<T> interface.

The class RacerComparer implements the interface IComparer<T> for Racer types. This class allows you to sort either by the first name, last name, country, or number of wins. The kind of sort that should be done is defined with the inner enumeration type CompareType. The CompareType is set with the constructor of the class RacerComparer. The interface IComparer<Racer> defines the method Compare that is required for sorting. In the implementation of this method, the CompareTo() method of the string and int types is used.

```
public class RacerComparer: IComparer<Racer>
{
    public enum CompareType
    {
        FirstName,
        LastName,
        Country,
        Wins
    }

    private CompareType compareType;
    public RacerComparer(CompareType compareType)
    {
        this.compareType = compareType;
    }

    public int Compare(Racer x, Racer y)
    {
        if (x == null) throw new ArgumentNullException("x");
        if (y == null) throw new ArgumentNullException("y");

        int result;
        switch (compareType)
        {
            case CompareType.FirstName:
                return x.FirstName.CompareTo(y.FirstName);
            case CompareType.LastName:
                return x.LastName.CompareTo(y.LastName);
            case CompareType.Country:
                if ((result = x.Country.CompareTo(y.Country)) == 0)
                    return x.LastName.CompareTo(y.LastName);
```

```
            else
                return result;
        case CompareType.Wins:
            return x.Wins.CompareTo(y.Wins);
        default:
            throw new ArgumentException("Invalid Compare Type");
        }
    }
}
```

code snippet ListSamples/RacerComparer.cs

An instance of the `RacerComparer` class can now be used with the `Sort()` method. Passing the enumeration `RacerComparer.CompareType.Country` sorts the collection by the property `Country`:

```
racers.Sort(new RacerComparer(RacerComparer.CompareType.Country));
racers.ForEach(Console.WriteLine);
```

Another way to do the sort is by using the overloaded `Sort()` method, which requires a `Comparison<T>` delegate:

```
public void List<T>.Sort(Comparison<T>);
```

`Comparison<T>` is a delegate to a method that has two parameters of type `T` and a return type `int`. If the parameter values are equal, the method must return `0`. If the first parameter is less than the second, a value less than zero must be returned; otherwise, a value greater than zero is returned:

```
public delegate int Comparison<T>(T x, T y);
```

Now you can pass a Lambda expression to the `Sort()` method to do a sort by the number of wins. The two parameters are of type `Racer`, and in the implementation the `Wins` properties are compared by using the `int` method `CompareTo()`. In the implementation, `r2` and `r1` are used in the reverse order, so the number of wins is sorted in descending order. After the method has been invoked, the complete racer list is sorted based on the number of wins of the racer:

```
racers.Sort((r1, r2) => r2.Wins.CompareTo(r1.Wins));
```

You can also reverse the order of a complete collection by invoking the `Reverse()` method.

Type Conversion

With the `List<T>` method `ConvertAll<TOutput>()`, all types of a collection can be converted to a different type. The `ConvertAll<TOutput>()` method uses a `Converter` delegate that is defined like this:

```
public sealed delegate TOutput Converter<TInput, TOutput>(TInput from);
```

The generic types `TInput` and `TOutput` are used with the conversion. `TInput` is the argument of the delegate method, and `TOutput` is the return type.

In this example, all `Racer` types should be converted to `Person` types. Whereas the `Racer` type contains a `firstName`, `lastName`, `country`, and the number of wins, the `Person` type contains just a name. For the conversion, the country of the racer and race wins can be ignored, but the name must be converted:

```
[Serializable]
public class Person
{
    private string name;

    public Person(string name)
    {
        this.name = name;
```

```
        }

        public override string ToString()
        {
            return name;
        }
    }
```

The conversion happens by invoking the `racers.ConvertAll<Person>()` method. The argument of this method is defined as a Lambda expression with an argument of type `Racer` and a `Person` type that is returned. In the implementation of the Lambda expression, a new `Person` object is created and returned. For the `Person` object, the `FirstName` and `LastName` are passed to the constructor:

```
        List<Person> persons =
            racers.ConvertAll<Person>(
                r => new Person(r.FirstName + " " + r.LastName));
```

The result of the conversion is a list containing the converted `Person` objects: `persons` of type `List<Person>`.

Read-Only Collections

After collections are created they are read/write. Of course, they must be read/write; otherwise, you couldn't fill them with any values. However, after the collection is filled, you can create a read-only collection. The `List<T>` collection has the method `AsReadOnly()` that returns an object of type `ReadOnlyCollection<T>`. The class `ReadOnlyCollection<T>` implements the same interfaces as `List<T>`, but all methods and properties that change the collection throw a `NotSupportedException`.

QUEUE

A queue is a collection where elements are processed *first in, first out* (FIFO). The item that is put first in the queue is read first. Examples of queues are standing in the queue at the airport, a human resources queue to process employee applicants, print jobs waiting to be processed in a print queue, and a thread waiting for the CPU in a round-robin fashion. Often, there are queues where the elements processed differ in their priority. For example, in the queue at the airport, business passengers are processed before economy passengers. Here, multiple queues can be used, one queue for every priority. At the airport this can easily be found out, because there are separate check-in queues for business and economy passengers. The same is true for print queues and threads. You can have an array or a list of queues where one item in the array stands for a priority. Within every array item there's a queue, where processing happens with the FIFO principle.

 Later in this chapter, a different implementation with a linked list is used to define a list of priorities.

A queue is implemented with the `Queue<T>` class in the namespace `System.Collections.Generic`. Internally, the `Queue<T>` class is using an array of type `T`, similar to the `List<T>` type. It implements the interfaces `IEnumerable<T>` and `ICollection`, but not `ICollection<T>`. `ICollection<T>` is not implemented because this interface defines `Add()` and `Remove()` methods which shouldn't be available for queues.

The `Queue<T>` class does not implement the interface `IList<T>`, so you cannot access the queue using an indexer. The queue just allows you to add an item to the queue, where the item is put at the end of the queue (with the `Enqueue()` method), and to get items from the head of the queue (with the `Dequeue()` method).

Figure 10-1 shows the items of the queue. The `Enqueue()` method adds items to one end of the queue; the items are read and removed at the other end of the queue with the `Dequeue()` method. Invoking the `Dequeue()` method once more removes the next item from the queue.

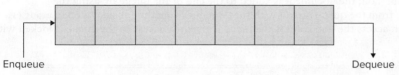

Enqueue   Dequeue

FIGURE 10-1

Methods of the `Queue<T>` class are described in the following table.

SELECTED QUEUE <T> MEMBERS	DESCRIPTION
Count	The property `Count` returns the number of items in the queue.
Enqueue()	The `Enqueue()` method adds an item to the end of the queue.
Dequeue()	The `Dequeue()` method reads and removes an item from the head of the queue. If there are no more items in the queue when the `Dequeue()` method is invoked, an exception of type `InvalidOperationException` is thrown.
Peek()	The `Peek()` method reads an item from the head of the queue but does not remove the item.
TrimExcess()	`TrimExcess()` resizes the capacity of the queue. The `Dequeue()` method removes items from the queue, but it doesn't resize the capacity of the queue. To get rid of the empty items at the beginning of the queue, use the `TrimExcess()` method.

When creating queues, you can use constructors similar to those used with the `List<T>` type. The default constructor creates an empty queue, but you can also use a constructor to specify the capacity. As items are added to the queue, the capacity is increased to hold 4, 8, 16, and 32 items if the capacity is not defined. Similarly to the `List<T>` class, the capacity is always doubled as required. The default constructor of the non-generic `Queue` class is different, because it creates an initial array of 32 empty items. With an overload of the constructor, you can also pass any other collection that implements the `IEnumerable<T>` interface that is copied to the queue.

The sample application that demonstrates the use of the `Queue<T>` class is a document management application. One thread is used to add documents to the queue, and another thread reads documents from the queue and processes them.

The items stored in the queue are of type `Document`. The `Document` class defines a title and content:

Available for
download on
Wrox.com

```csharp
public class Document
{
    public string Title { get; private set; }
    public string Content { get; private set; }

    public Document(string title, string content)
    {
        this.Title = title;
        this.Content = content;
    }
}
```

code snippet QueueSample/Document.cs

The `DocumentManager` class is a thin layer around the `Queue<T>` class. The class `DocumentManager` defines how to handle documents: adding documents to the queue with the `AddDocument()` method, and getting documents from the queue with the `GetDocument()` method.

Inside the `AddDocument()` method, the document is added to the end of the queue by using the `Enqueue()` method. The first document from the queue is read with the `Dequeue()` method inside `GetDocument()`. Because multiple threads can access the `DocumentManager` concurrently, access to the queue is locked with the `lock` statement.

Threading and the `lock` *statement are discussed in Chapter 20, "Threads, Tasks, and Synchronization."*

`IsDocumentAvailable` is a read-only Boolean property that returns `true` if there are documents in the queue, and `false` if not:

```csharp
public class DocumentManager
{
    private readonly Queue<Document> documentQueue = new Queue<Document>();

    public void AddDocument(Document doc)
    {
        lock (this)
        {
            documentQueue.Enqueue(doc);
        }
    }

    public Document GetDocument()
    {
        Document doc = null;
        lock (this)
        {
            doc = documentQueue.Dequeue();
        }
        return doc;
    }

    public bool IsDocumentAvailable
    {
        get
        {
            return documentQueue.Count > 0;
        }
    }
}
```

code snippet QueueSample/DocumentManager.cs

The class `ProcessDocuments` processes documents from the queue in a separate thread. The only method that can be accessed from the outside is `Start()`. In the `Start()` method, a new thread is instantiated. A `ProcessDocuments` object is created for starting the thread, and the `Run()` method is defined as the start method of the thread. `ThreadStart` is a delegate that references the method to be started by the thread. After creating the `Thread` object, the thread is started by calling the method `Thread.Start()`.

With the `Run()` method of the `ProcessDocuments` class, an endless loop is defined. Within this loop, the property `IsDocumentAvailable` is used to see if there is a document in the queue. If there is a document in the queue, the document is taken from the `DocumentManager` and processed. Processing here is writing information only to the console. In a real application, the document could be written to a file, written to the database, or sent across the network:

```
<public class ProcessDocuments
{
    public static void Start(DocumentManager dm)
    {
        new Thread(new ProcessDocuments(dm).Run).Start();
    }

    protected ProcessDocuments(DocumentManager dm)
    {
        documentManager = dm;
    }

    private DocumentManager documentManager;

    protected void Run()
    {
        while (true)
        {
            if (documentManager.IsDocumentAvailable)
            {
                Document doc = documentManager.GetDocument();
                Console.WriteLine("Processing document {0}", doc.Title);
            }
            Thread.Sleep(new Random().Next(20));
        }
    }
}
```

code snippet QueueSample/ProcessDocuments.cs

In the `Main()` method of the application, a `DocumentManager` object is instantiated, and the document processing thread is started. Then 1,000 documents are created and added to the `DocumentManager`:

```
class Program
{
    static void Main()
    {
        var dm = new DocumentManager();

        ProcessDocuments.Start(dm);

        // Create documents and add them to the DocumentManager
        for (int i = 0; i < 1000; i++)
        {
            Document doc = new Document("Doc " + i.ToString(), "content");
            dm.AddDocument(doc);
            Console.WriteLine("Added document {0}", doc.Title);
            Thread.Sleep(new Random().Next(20));
        }
    }
}
```

code snippet QueueSample/Program.cs

When you start the application, the documents are added to and removed from the queue, and you get output similar to the following:

```
Added document Doc 279
Processing document Doc 236
Added document Doc 280
Processing document Doc 237
Added document Doc 281
Processing document Doc 238
Processing document Doc 239
Processing document Doc 240
Processing document Doc 241
Added document Doc 282
Processing document Doc 242
Added document Doc 283
Processing document Doc 243
```

A real-life scenario doing the task described with the sample application can be an application that processes documents received with a Web service.

STACK

A stack is another container that is very similar to the queue. You just use different methods to access the stack. The item that is added last to the stack is read first. The stack is a *last in, first out* (LIFO) container.

Figure 10-2 shows the representation of a stack where the `Push()` method adds an item to the stack, and the `Pop()` method gets the item that was added last.

Similar to the `Queue<T>` class, the `Stack<T>` class implements the interfaces `IEnumerable<T>` and `ICollection`.

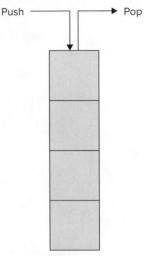

FIGURE 10-2

Members of the `Stack<T>` class are listed in the following table.

SELECTED STACK<T> MEMBERS	DESCRIPTION
Count	The property `Count` returns the number of items in the stack.
Push()	The `Push()` method adds an item on top of the stack.
Pop()	The `Pop()` method removes and returns an item from the top of the stack. If the stack is empty, an exception of type `InvalidOperation Exception` is thrown.
Peek()	The `Peek()` method returns an item from the top of the stack but does not remove the item.
Contains()	The `Contains()` method checks whether an item is in the stack and returns `true` if it is.

In this example, three items are added to the stack with the `Push()` method. With the `foreach` method, all items are iterated using the `IEnumerable` interface. The enumerator of the stack does not remove the items; it just returns item by item:

```
var alphabet = new Stack<char>();
alphabet.Push('A');
alphabet.Push('B');
alphabet.Push('C');

foreach (char item in alphabet)
```

```
        {
            Console.Write(item);
        }
        Console.WriteLine();
```

code snippet StackSample/Program.cs

Because the items are read in order from the last added to the first, the following result is produced:

    CBA

Reading the items with the enumerator does not change the state of the items. With the `Pop()` method, every item that is read is also removed from the stack. This way you can iterate the collection using a `while` loop and verify the `Count` property if items still exist:

```
var alphabet = new Stack<char>();
alphabet.Push('A');
alphabet.Push('B');
alphabet.Push('C');

Console.Write("First iteration: ");
foreach (char item in alphabet)
{
    Console.Write(item);
}
Console.WriteLine();

Console.Write("Second iteration: ");
while (alphabet.Count > 0)
{
    Console.Write(alphabet.Pop());
}
Console.WriteLine();
```

The result gives CBA twice, once for each iteration. After the second iteration, the stack is empty because the second iteration used the `Pop()` method:

    First iteration: CBA
    Second iteration: CBA

LINKED LIST

`LinkedList<T>` is a doubly linked list, where one element references the next and the previous one, as shown in Figure 10-3.

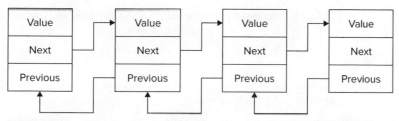

FIGURE 10-3

The advantage of a linked list is that if items are inserted in the middle of a list, the linked list is very fast. When an item is inserted, only the Next reference of the previous item and the Previous reference of the next item must be changed to reference the inserted item. With the List<T> class, when an element is inserted all following elements must be moved.

Of course, there's also a disadvantage with linked lists. Items of linked lists can be accessed only one after the other. It takes a long time to find an item that's somewhere in the middle or at the end of the list.

A linked list cannot just store the items inside the list; together with every item, the linked list must have information about the next and previous items. That's why the LinkedList<T> contains items of type LinkedListNode<T>. With the class LinkedListNode<T>, you can get to the next and previous items in the list. The LinkedListNode<T> class defines the properties List, Next, Previous, and Value. The List property returns the LinkedList<T> object that is associated with the node. Next and Previous are for iterating through the list and accessing the next or previous item. Value returns the item that is associated with the node. Value is of type T.

The LinkedList<T> class itself defines members to access the first (First) and last (Last) item of the list, to insert items at specific positions (AddAfter(), AddBefore(), AddFirst(), AddLast()), to remove items from specific positions (Remove(), RemoveFirst(), RemoveLast()), and to find elements where the search either starts from the begin (Find()) or the end (FindLast()) of the list.

The sample application to demonstrate linked lists uses a linked list together with a list. The linked list contains documents as in the queue example, but the documents have an additional priority associated with them. The documents will be sorted inside the linked list depending on the priority. If multiple documents have the same priority, the elements are sorted according to the time the document was inserted.

Figure 10-4 describes the collections of the sample application. LinkedList<Document> is the linked list containing all the Document objects. The figure shows the title and the priority of the documents. The title indicates when the document was added to the list: The first document added has the title "One", the second document has the title "Two", and so on. You can see that the documents One and Four have the same priority, 8, but because One was added before Four, it is earlier in the list.

When new documents are added to the linked list, they should be added after the last document that has the same priority. The LinkedList<Document> collection contains elements of type LinkedListNode <Document>. The class LinkedListNode<T> adds Next and Previous properties to walk from one node to the next. For referencing such elements, the List<T> is defined as List<LinkedListNode<Document>>. For fast access to the last document of every priority, the collection List<LinkedListNode> contains up to 10 elements, each referencing the last document of every priority. In the upcoming discussion, the reference to the last document of every priority is called the *priority node*.

From the previous example, the Document class is extended to contain the priority. The priority is set with the constructor of the class:

```
public class Document
{
    public string Title { get; private set; }
    public string Content { get; private set; }
    public byte Priority { get; private set; }

    public Document(string title, string content, byte priority = 0)
    {
        this.Title = title;
        this.Content = content;
        this.Priority = priority;
    }
}
```

code snippet LinkedListSample/Document.cs

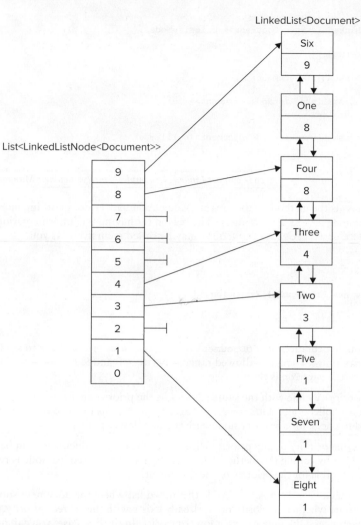

FIGURE 10-4

The heart of the solution is the PriorityDocumentManager class. This class is very easy to use. With the public interface of this class, new Document elements can be added to the linked list, the first document can be retrieved, and for testing purposes it also has a method to display all elements of the collection as they are linked in the list.

The class PriorityDocumentManager contains two collections. The collection of type LinkedList<Document> contains all documents. The collection of type List<LinkedListNode <Document>> contains references of up to 10 elements that are entry points for adding new documents with a specific priority. Both collection variables are initialized with the constructor of the class PriorityDocumentManager. The list collection is also initialized with null:

```
public class PriorityDocumentManager
{
    private readonly LinkedList<Document> documentList;
```

```
// priorities 0.9
private readonly List<LinkedListNode<Document>> priorityNodes;

public PriorityDocumentManager()
{
   documentList = new LinkedList<Document>();

   priorityNodes = new List<LinkedListNode<Document>>(10);
   for (int i = 0; i < 10; i++)
   {
      priorityNodes.Add(new LinkedListNode<Document>(null));
   }
}
```

code snippet LinkedListSample/PriorityDocumentManager.cs

Part of the public interface of the class is the method `AddDocument()`. `AddDocument()` does nothing more than call the private method `AddDocumentToPriorityNode()`. The reason for having the implementation inside a different method is that `AddDocumentToPriorityNode()` may be called recursively, as you will see soon:

```
public void AddDocument(Document d)
{
   if (d == null) throw new ArgumentNullException("d");

   AddDocumentToPriorityNode(d, d.Priority);
}
```

The first action that is done in the implementation of `AddDocumentToPriorityNode()` is a check to see if the priority fits in the allowed priority range. Here, the allowed range is between 0 and 9. If a wrong value is passed, an exception of type `ArgumentException` is thrown.

Next, you check if there's already a priority node with the same priority as the priority that was passed. If there's no such priority node in the list collection, `AddDocumentToPriorityNode()` is invoked recursively with the priority value decremented to check for a priority node with the next lower priority.

If there's no priority node with the same priority or any priority with a lower value, the document can be safely added to the end of the linked list by calling the method `AddLast()`. Also, the linked list node is referenced by the priority node that's responsible for the priority of the document.

If there's an existing priority node, you can get the position inside the linked list where the document should be inserted. Here, you must differentiate whether a priority node already exists with the correct priority, or if there's just a priority node that references a document with a lower priority. In the first case, you can just insert the new document after the position that's referenced by the priority node. Because the priority node always must reference the last document with a specific priority, the reference of the priority node must be set. It gets more complex if just a priority node referencing a document with a lower priority exists. Here, the document must be inserted before all documents with the same priority as the priority node. To get the first document of the same priority, a `while` loop iterates through all linked list nodes, using the `Previous` property, until a linked list node is reached that has a different priority. This way, you know the position where the document must be inserted, and the priority node can be set:

```
private void AddDocumentToPriorityNode(Document doc, int priority)
{
   if (priority > 9 || priority < 0)
      throw new ArgumentException("Priority must be between 0 and 9");

   if (priorityNodes[priority].Value == null)
   {
      --priority;
      if (priority >= 0)
```

```
            {
                // check for the next lower priority
                AddDocumentToPriorityNode(doc, priority);
            }
            else // now no priority node exists with the same priority or lower
                // add the new document to the end
            {
                documentList.AddLast(doc);
                priorityNodes[doc.Priority] = documentList.Last;
            }
            return;
        }
        else // a priority node exists
        {
            LinkedListNode<Document> prioNode = priorityNodes[priority];
            if (priority == doc.Priority)
                // priority node with the same priority exists
            {
                documentList.AddAfter(prioNode, doc);

                // set the priority node to the last document with the same priority
                priorityNodes[doc.Priority] = prioNode.Next;
            }
            else // only priority node with a lower priority exists
            {
                // get the first node of the lower priority
                LinkedListNode<Document> firstPrioNode = prioNode;

                while (firstPrioNode.Previous != null &&
                    firstPrioNode.Previous.Value.Priority == prioNode.Value.Priority)
                {
                    firstPrioNode = prioNode.Previous;
                    prioNode = firstPrioNode;
                }

                documentList.AddBefore(firstPrioNode, doc);

                // set the priority node to the new value
                priorityNodes[doc.Priority] = firstPrioNode.Previous;
            }
        }
    }
}
```

Now only simple methods are left for discussion. `DisplayAllNodes()` just does a `foreach` loop to display the priority and the title of every document to the console.

The method `GetDocument()` returns the first document (the document with the highest priority) from the linked list and removes it from the list:

```
public void DisplayAllNodes()
{
    foreach (Document doc in documentList)
    {
        Console.WriteLine("priority: {0}, title {1}", doc.Priority, doc.Title);
    }
}

// returns the document with the highest priority
// (that's first in the linked list)
public Document GetDocument()
{
    Document doc = documentList.First.Value;
```

```
                documentList.RemoveFirst();
                return doc;
            }
        }
```

In the `Main()` method, the `PriorityDocumentManager` is used to demonstrate its functionality.
Eight new documents with different priorities are added to the linked list, and then the complete list
is displayed:

**Available for
download on
Wrox.com**

```
        static void Main()
        {
            PriorityDocumentManager pdm =  new PriorityDocumentManager();
            pdm.AddDocument(new Document("one", "Sample", 8));
            pdm.AddDocument(new Document("two", "Sample", 3));
            pdm.AddDocument(new Document("three", "Sample", 4));
            pdm.AddDocument(new Document("four", "Sample", 8));
            pdm.AddDocument(new Document("five", "Sample", 1));
            pdm.AddDocument(new Document("six", "Sample", 9));
            pdm.AddDocument(new Document("seven", "Sample", 1));
            pdm.AddDocument(new Document("eight", "Sample", 1));

            pdm.DisplayAllNodes();
        }
```

code snippet LinkedListSample/Program.cs

With the processed result, you can see that the documents are sorted first by the priority and second by
when the document was added:

```
priority: 9, title six
priority: 8, title one
priority: 8, title four
priority: 4, title three
priority: 3, title two
priority: 1, title five
priority: 1, title seven
priority: 1, title eight
```

SORTED LIST

If the collection you need should be sorted based on a key, you can use `SortedList<TKey, TValue>`.
This class sorts the elements based on a key. Not only can you use any type for the value, but also for
the key.

The example creates a sorted list where both the key and the value are of type `string`. The default constructor
creates an empty list, and then two books are added with the `Add()` method. With overloaded constructors,
you can define the capacity of the list and also pass an object that implements the interface `IComparer<TKey>`,
which is used to sort the elements in the list.

The first parameter of the `Add()` method is the key (the book title); the second parameter is the value (the
ISBN number). Instead of using the `Add()` method, you can use the indexer to add elements to the list.
The indexer requires the key as index parameter. If a key already exists, the `Add()` method throws an
exception of type `ArgumentException`. If the same key is used with the indexer, the new value replaces
the old value.

`SortedList<TKey, TValue>` *allows only one value per key. If you need multiple values
per key you can use* `Lookup<TKey, TElement>`.

```
var books = new SortedList<string, string>();
books.Add("C# 2008 Wrox Box", "978-0-470-047205-7");
books.Add("Professional ASP.NET MVC 1.0", "978-0-470-38461-9");

books["Beginning Visual C# 2008"] = "978-0-470-19135-4";
books["Professional C# 2008"] = "978-0-470-19137-6";
```

code snippet SortedListSample/Program.cs

You can iterate through the list by using a `foreach` statement. Elements that are returned by the enumerator are of type `KeyValuePair<TKey, TValue>`, which contains both the key and the value. The key can be accessed with the `Key` property, and the value can be accessed with the `Value` property:

```
foreach (KeyValuePair<string, string> book in books)
{
    Console.WriteLine("{0}, {1}", book.Key, book.Value);
}
```

The iteration displays book titles and ISBN numbers ordered by the key:

```
Beginning Visual C# 2008, 978-0-470-19135-4
C# 2008 Wrox Box, 978-0-470-047205-7
Professional ASP.NET MVC 1.0, 978-0-470-38461-9
Professional C# 2008, 978-0-470-19137-6
```

You can also access the values and keys by using the `Values` and `Keys` properties. The `Values` property returns `IList<TValue>` and the `Keys` property returns `IList<TKey>`, so you can use these properties with a `foreach`:

```
foreach (string isbn in books.Values)
{
    Console.WriteLine(isbn);
}

foreach (string title in books.Keys)
{
    Console.WriteLine(title);
}
```

The first loop displays the values, and next the keys:

```
978-0-470-19135-4
978-0-470-047205-7
978-0-470-38461-9
978-0-470-19137-6
Beginning Visual C# 2008
C# 2008 Wrox Box
Professional ASP.NET MVC 1.0
Professional C# 2008
```

If you try to access an element with an indexer passing a key that does not exist, an exception of type `KeyNotFoundException` is thrown. To avoid that exception you can use the method `ContainsKey()` that returns `true` if the key passed exists in the collection, or you can invoke the method `TryGetValue()` that tries to get the value but doesn't throw an exception if the value is not here:

```
string isbn;
string title = "Professional C# 7.0";
if (!books.TryGetValue(title, out isbn))
{
    Console.WriteLine("{0} not found", title);
}
```

DICTIONARIES

Dictionaries represent a sophisticated data structure that allows you to access an element based on a key. Dictionaries are also known as hash tables or maps. The main feature of dictionaries is fast lookup based on keys. You can also add and remove items freely, a bit like a `List<T>`, but without the performance overhead of having to shift subsequent items in memory.

Figure 10-5 shows a simplified representation of a dictionary. Here `employee-ids` such as B4711 are the keys added to the dictionary. The key is transformed into a hash. With the hash a number is created to associate an index with the values. The index then contains a link to the value. The figure is simplified because it is possible that a single index entry can be associated with multiple values, and the index can be stored as a tree.

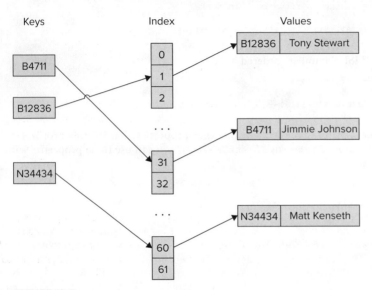

FIGURE 10-5

The .NET Framework offers several dictionary classes. The main class you can use is `Dictionary <TKey, TValue>`.

Key Type

A type that is used as a key in the dictionary must override the method `GetHashCode()` of the `Object` class. Whenever a dictionary class needs to work out where an item should be located, it calls the `GetHashCode()` method. The `int` that is returned by `GetHashCode()` is used by the dictionary to calculate an index of where to place the element. We don't go into this part of the algorithm. What you should know is that it involves prime numbers, so the capacity of a dictionary is a prime number.

The implementation of `GetHashCode()` must satisfy these requirements:

➤　The same object should always return the same value.

➤　Different objects can return the same value.

➤　It should execute as quickly as possible; it must be inexpensive to compute.

➤　It must not throw exceptions.

➤　It should use at least one instance field.

➤ The hash code value should be evenly distributed across the entire range of numbers that an `int` can store.

➤ The hash code should not change during the lifetime of the object.

 A good performance of the dictionary is based on a good implementation of the method `GetHashCode()`.

What's the reason for having hash code values evenly distributed across the range of integers? If two keys return hashes that give the same index, the dictionary class needs to start looking for the nearest available free location to store the second item — and will have to do some searching to retrieve this item later on. This is obviously going to hurt performance, and clearly, if lots of your keys are tending to give the same indexes for where they should be stored, this kind of clash becomes more likely. However, because of the way that Microsoft's part of the algorithm works, this risk is minimized when the calculated hash values are evenly distributed between `int.MinValue` and `int.MaxValue`.

Besides having an implementation of `GetHashCode()`, the key type also must implement the `IEquatable<T>.Equals()` method or override the `Equals()` method from the `Object` class. Because different key objects may return the same hash code, the method `Equals()` is used by the dictionary comparing keys. The dictionary examines if two keys A and B are equal; it invokes `A.Equals(B)`. This means that you must ensure that the following is always true:

If `A.Equals(B)` is true, then `A.GetHashCode()` and `B.GetHashCode()` must always return the same hash code.

This probably seems a fairly subtle point, but it is crucial. If you contrived some way of overriding these methods so that the preceding statement was not always true, a dictionary that uses instances of this class as its keys would simply not work properly. Instead, you'd find funny things happening. For example, you might place an object in the dictionary and then discover that you could never retrieve it, or you might try to retrieve an entry and have the wrong entry returned.

 For this reason, the C# compiler will display a compilation warning if you supply an override for `Equals()` *but don't supply an override for* `GetHashCode()`.

For `System.Object` this condition is true, because `Equals()` simply compares references, and `GetHashCode()` actually returns a hash that is based solely on the address of the object. This means that hash tables based on a key that doesn't override these methods will work correctly. However, the problem with this way of doing things is that keys are regarded as equal only if they are the same object. That means that when you place an object in the dictionary, you then have to hang onto the reference to the key. You can't simply instantiate another key object later with the same value. If you don't override `Equals()` and `GetHashCode()`, the type is not very convenient to use in a dictionary.

Incidentally, `System.String` implements the interface `IEquatable` and overloads `GetHashCode()` appropriately. `Equals()` provides value comparison, and `GetHashCode()` returns a hash based on the value of the string. Strings can be used conveniently as keys in dictionaries.

Number types such as `Int32` also implement the interface `IEquatable` and overload `GetHashCode()`. However, the hash code returned by these types simply maps to the value. If the number you would like to use as a key is not itself distributed around the possible values of an integer, using integers as keys doesn't fulfill the rule of evenly distributing key values to get the best performance. `Int32` is not meant to be used in a dictionary.

If you need to use a key type that does not implement IEquatable and override GetHashCode according to the key values you store in the dictionary, you can create a comparer implementing the interface IEqualityComparer<T>. IEqualityComparer<T> defines the methods GetHashCode() and Equals() with an argument of the object passed, so you can offer an implementation different from the object type itself. An overload of the Dictionary<TKey, TValue> constructor allows passing an object implementing IEqualityComparer<T>. If such an object is assigned to the dictionary, this class is used to generate the hash codes and compare the keys.

Dictionary Example

The dictionary example is a program that sets up a dictionary of employees. The dictionary is indexed by EmployeeId objects, and each item stored in the dictionary is an Employee object that stores details of an employee.

The struct EmployeeId is implemented to define a key to be used in a dictionary. The members of the class are a prefix character and a number for the employee. Both of these variables are read-only and can be initialized only in the constructor. A key within the dictionary shouldn't change, and this way that is guaranteed. The fields are filled within the constructor. The ToString() method is overloaded to get a string representation of the employee ID. As required for a key type, EmployeeId implements the interface IEquatable and overloads the method GetHashCode().

```csharp
[Serializable]
public class EmployeeIdException : Exception
{
    public EmployeeIdException(string message) : base(message)  { }
}


[Serializable]
public struct EmployeeId : IEquatable<EmployeeId>
{
    private readonly char prefix;
    private readonly int number;

    public EmployeeId(string id)
    {
        if (id == null) throw new ArgumentNullException("id");

        prefix = (id.ToUpper())[0];
        int numLength = id.Length  1;
        try
        {
            number = int.Parse(id.Substring(1, numLength > 6 ? 6 : numLength));
        }
        catch (FormatException)
        {
            throw new EmployeeIdException("Invalid EmployeeId format");
        }
    }

    public override string ToString()
    {
        return prefix.ToString() + string.Format("{0,6:000000}", number);
    }

    public override int GetHashCode()
    {
        return (number ^ number << 16) * 0x15051505;
    }

    public bool Equals(EmployeeId other)
```

```
        {
            if (other == null) return false;

            return (prefix == other.prefix && number == other.number);
        }

        public override bool Equals(object obj)
        {
            return Equals((EmployeeId)obj);
        }

        public static bool operator ==(EmployeeId left, EmployeeId right)
        {
            return left.Equals(right);
        }

        public static bool operator !=(EmployeeId left, EmployeeId right)
        {
            return !(left == right);
        }
    }
```

code snippet DictionarySample/EmployeeId.cs

The `Equals()` method that is defined by the `IEquatable<T>` interface compares the values of two `EmployeeId` objects and returns `true` if both values are the same. Instead of implementing the `Equals()` method from the `IEquatable<T>` interface, you can also override the `Equals()` method from the `Object` class:

```
public bool Equals(EmployeeId other)
{
    if (other == null) return false;
    return (prefix == other.prefix && number == other.number);
}
```

With the number variable, a value from 1 to around 190,000 is expected for the employees. This doesn't fill the range of an integer. The algorithm used by `GetHashCode()` shifts the number 16 bits to the left, then does an XOR with the original number, and finally multiplies the result by the hex value 15051505. The hash code is fairly distributed across the range of an integer:

```
public override int GetHashCode()
{
    return (number ^ number << 16) * 0x15051505;
}
```

> *On the Internet, you can find a lot more complex algorithms that have a better distribution across the integer range. You can also use the `GetHashCode()` method of a string to return a hash.*

The `Employee` class is a simple entity class containing the name, salary, and ID of the employee. The constructor initializes all values, and the method `ToString()` returns a string representation of an instance. The implementation of `ToString()` uses a format string to create the string representation for performance reasons:

Available for
download on
Wrox.com

```
[Serializable]
public class Employee
{
    private string name;
    private decimal salary;
```

```
        private readonly EmployeeId id;

        public Employee(EmployeeId id, string name, decimal salary)
        {
            this.id = id;
            this.name = name;
            this.salary = salary;
        }

        public override string ToString()
        {
            return String.Format("{0}: {1, -20} {2:C}",
                    id.ToString(), name, salary);
        }
    }
}
```

code snippet DictionarySample/Employee.cs

In the `Main()` method of the sample application, a new `Dictionary<TKey, TValue>` instance is created, where the key is of type `EmployeeId` and the value is of type `Employee`. The constructor allocates a capacity of 31 elements. Remember, the capacity is based on prime numbers. However, when you assign a value that is not a prime number, you don't need to worry. The `Dictionary<TKey, TValue>` class itself takes the next prime number that follows the integer passed to the constructor to allocate the capacity. The employee objects and IDs are created and added to the dictionary with the `Add()` method. Instead of using the `Add()` method, you can also use the indexer to add keys and values to the dictionary, as shown with the employees Dale and Jeff:

Available for download on Wrox.com

```
        static void Main()
        {
            var employees = new Dictionary<EmployeeId, Employee>(31);

            var idKyle = new EmployeeId("T3755");
            var kyle = new Employee(idKyle, "Kyle Bush", 5443890.00m);
            employees.Add(idKyle, kyle);
            Console.WriteLine(kyle);

            var idCarl = new EmployeeId("F3547");
            var carl = new Employee(idCarl, "Carl Edwards", 5597120.00m);
            employees.Add(idCarl, carl);
            Console.WriteLine(carl);

            var idJimmie = new EmployeeId("C3386");
            var jimmie = new Employee(idJimmie, "Jimmie Johnson", 5024710.00m);
            employees.Add(idJimmie, jimmie);
            Console.WriteLine(jimmie);

            var idDale = new EmployeeId("C3323");
            var dale = new Employee(idDale, "Dale Earnhardt Jr.", 3522740.00m);
            employees[idDale] = dale;
            Console.WriteLine(dale);

            var idJeff = new EmployeeId("C3234");
            var jeff = new Employee(idJeff, "Jeff Burton", 3879540.00m);
            employees[idJeff] = jeff;
            Console.WriteLine(jeff);
```

code snippet DictionarySample/Program.cs

After the entries are added to the dictionary, inside a `while` loop employees are read from the dictionary. The user is asked to enter an employee number to store in the variable `userInput`. The user can exit the application by entering X. If the key is in the dictionary, it is examined with the `TryGetValue()` method of the `Dictionary<TKey, TValue>` class. `TryGetValue()` returns `true` if the key is found and `false` otherwise. If the value is found, the value associated with the key is stored in the employee variable. This value is written to the console.

 You can also use an indexer of the `Dictionary<TKey, TValue>` *class instead of* `TryGetValue()` *to access a value stored in the dictionary. However, if the key is not found, the indexer throws an exception of type* `KeyNotFoundException`.

```
while (true)
{
    Console.Write("Enter employee id (X to exit)> ");
    var userInput = Console.ReadLine();
    userInput = userInput.ToUpper();
    if (userInput == "X") break;

    EmployeeId id;
    try
    {
        id = new EmployeeId(userInput);


        Employee employee;
        if (!employees.TryGetValue(id, out employee))
        {
            Console.WriteLine("Employee with id {0} does not exist",
                              id);
        }
        else
        {
            Console.WriteLine(employee);
        }
    }
    catch (EmployeeIdException ex)
    {
        Console.WriteLine(ex.Message);
    }
}
```

Running the application produces the following output:

```
Enter employee id (X to exit)> C3386
C003386: Jimmie Johnson      ? 5.024.710,00
Enter employee id (X to exit)> F3547
F003547: Carl Edwards        ? 5.597.120,00
Enter employee id (X to exit)> X
Press any key to continue …
```

Lookup

`Dictionary<TKey, TValue>` supports only one value per key. The class `Lookup<TKey, TElement>` resembles a `Dictionary<TKey, TValue>` but maps keys to a collection of values. This class is implemented in the assembly `System.Core` and defined with the namespace `System.Linq`.

`Lookup<TKey, TElement>` cannot be created as a normal dictionary. Instead, you have to invoke the method `ToLookup()` that returns a `Lookup<TKey, TElement>` object. The method `ToLookup()` is an extension method that is available with every class implementing `IEnumerable<T>`. In the following example, a list of `Racer` objects is filled. Because `List<T>` implements `IEnumerable<T>`, the `ToLookup()` method can be invoked on the racers list. This method requires a delegate of type `Func<TSource, TKey>` that defines the selector of the key. Here the racers are selected based on the country by using the Lambda expression `r => r.Country`. The `foreach` loop accesses only the racers from Australia by using the indexer.

> You can read more about extension methods in Chapter 11, "Language Integrated Query." Lambda expressions are explained in Chapter 8.

Available for download on Wrox.com

```
var racers = new List<Racer>();
racers.Add(new Racer("Jacques", "Villeneuve", "Canada", 11));
racers.Add(new Racer("Alan", "Jones", "Australia", 12));
racers.Add(new Racer("Jackie", "Stewart", "United Kingdom", 27));
racers.Add(new Racer("James", "Hunt", "United Kingdom", 10));
racers.Add(new Racer("Jack", "Brabham", "Australia", 14));

var lookupRacers = racers.ToLookup(r => r.Country);

foreach (Racer r in lookupRacers["Australia"])
{
    Console.WriteLine(r);
}
```

code snippet LookupSample/Program.cs

The output shows the racers from Australia:

```
Alan Jones
Jack Brabham
```

Sorted Dictionary

`SortedDictionary<TKey, TValue>` is a binary search tree where the items are sorted based on the key. The key type must implement the interface `IComparable<TKey>`. If the key type is not sortable, you can also create a comparer implementing `IComparer<TKey>` and assign the comparer as a constructor argument of the sorted dictionary.

Earlier in this chapter you read about `SortedList<TKey, TValue>`. `SortedDictionary<TKey, TValue>` and `SortedList<TKey, TValue>` have similar functionalities. But because `SortedList<TKey, TValue>` is implemented as a list that is based on an array and `SortedDictionary<TKey, TValue>` is implemented as a dictionary, the classes have different characteristics:

➤ `SortedList<TKey, TValue>` uses less memory than `SortedDictionary<TKey, TValue>`.

➤ `SortedDictionary<TKey, TValue>` has faster insertion and removal of elements.

➤ When populating the collection with already sorted data, `SortedList<TKey, TValue>` is faster, if capacity changes are not needed.

> `SortedList` *consumes less memory than* `SortedDictionary`. `SortedDictionary` *is faster with inserts and with the removal of unsorted data.*

SETS

A collection that contains only distinct items is known by the term *set*. .NET 4 includes two sets, HashSet<T> and SortedSet<T>, that both implement the interface ISet<T>. HashSet<T> contains an unordered list of distinct items; with SortedSet<T> the list is ordered.

The ISet<T> interface offers methods to create a union of multiple sets, an intersection of sets, or give information if one set is a super- or subset of another.

With the sample code, three new sets of type string are created and filled with Formula-1 cars. The HashSet<T> class implements the ICollection<T> interface. However, the Add() method is implemented explicitly and a different Add() method is offered by the class as you can see here. The Add() method differs by the return type; a Boolean value is returned to give the information if the element was added. If the element was already in the set, it is not added, and false is returned:

Available for download on Wrox.com

```
var companyTeams = new HashSet<string>()
    { "Ferrari", "McLaren", "Toyota", "BMW", "Renault" };
var traditionalTeams = new HashSet<string>()
    { "Ferrari", "McLaren" };
var privateTeams = new HashSet<string>()
    { "Red Bull", "Toro Rosso", "Force India", "Brawn GP" };

if (privateTeams.Add("Williams"))
    Console.WriteLine("Williams added");
if (!companyTeams.Add("McLaren"))
    Console.WriteLine("McLaren was already in this set");
```

code snippet SetSample/Program.cs

The result of these two Add() methods is written to the console:

```
Williams added
McLaren was already in this set
```

The methods IsSubsetOf() and IsSupersetOf() compare a set with a collection that implements the IEnumerable<T> interface and returns a Boolean result. Here, IsSubsetOf() verifies if every element in traditionalTeams is contained in companyTeams, which is the case; IsSupersetOf() verifies whether traditionalTeams has any additional elements compared to companyTeams:

```
if (traditionalTeams.IsSubsetOf(companyTeams))
{
    Console.WriteLine("traditionalTeams is subset of companyTeams");
}

if (companyTeams.IsSupersetOf(traditionalTeams))
{
    Console.WriteLine("companyTeams is a superset of traditionalTeams");
}
```

The output of this verification is shown here:

```
traditionalTeams is a subset of companyTeams
companyTeams is a superset of traditionalTeams
```

Williams is a traditional team as well, and that's why this team is added to the traditionalTeams collection:

```
traditionalTeams.Add("Williams");
if (privateTeams.Overlaps(traditionalTeams))
{
    Console.WriteLine("At least one team is the same with the " +
        "traditional and private teams");
}
```

Because there's an overlap, this is the result:

```
At least one team is the same with the traditional and private teams.
```

The variable `allTeams` that references a new `SortedSet<string>` is filled with a union of `companyTeams`, `privateTeams`, and `traditionalTeams` by calling the `UnionWith()` method:

```
var allTeams = new SortedSet<string>(companyTeams);
allTeams.UnionWith(privateTeams);
allTeams.UnionWith(traditionalTeams);

Console.WriteLine();
Console.WriteLine("all teams");
foreach (var team in allTeams)
{
    Console.WriteLine(team);
}
```

Here all teams are returned, but every team is listed just once because the set contains only unique values. Because the container is a `SortedSet<string>`, the result is ordered:

```
BMW
Brawn GP
Ferrari
Force India
McLaren
Red Bull
Renault
Toro Rosso
Toyota
Williams
```

The method `ExceptWith()` removes all private teams from the `allTeams` set:

```
allTeams.ExceptWith(privateTeams);
Console.WriteLine();
Console.WriteLine("no private team left");
foreach (var team in allTeams)
{
    Console.WriteLine(team);
}
```

The remaining elements in the collection do not contain any private team:

```
BMW
Ferrari
McLaren
Renault
Toyota
```

OBSERVABLE COLLECTION

In case you need information when items in the collection are removed or added, you can use the `ObservableCollection<T>` class. This class was defined for WPF so that the UI gets informed on collection changes, thus this class is defined in the assembly WindowsBase and you need to reference this assembly. The namespace of this class is `System.Collections.ObjectModel`.

`ObservableCollection<T>` derives from the base class `Collection<T>` that can be used to create custom collections and uses `List<T>` internal. From the base class the virtual method `SetItem()` and `RemoveItem()` is overridden to fire the `CollectionChanged` event. Clients of this class can register to this event by using the interface `INotifyCollectionChanged`.

The next sample shows using an `ObservableCollection<string>` where the method `Data_CollectionChanged` is registered to the `CollectionChanged` event. Two items are added to the end — one item is inserted, and one item is removed:

```
var data = new ObservableCollection<string>();
data.CollectionChanged += Data_CollectionChanged;
data.Add("One");
data.Add("Two");
data.Insert(1, "Three");
data.Remove("One");
```

code snippet ObservableCollectionSample/Program.cs

The method `Data_CollectionChanged` receives `NotifyCollectionChangedEventArgs` containing information about the changes of the collection. The `Action` property gives information if an item was added or removed. With removed items, the `OldItems` property is set and lists the removed items. With added items, the `NewItems` property is set and lists the new items:

```
static void Data_CollectionChanged(object sender,
                                   NotifyCollectionChangedEventArgs e)
{
    Console.WriteLine("action: {0}", e.Action.ToString());

    if (e.OldItems != null)
    {
        Console.WriteLine("starting index for old item(s): {0}",
                          e.OldStartingIndex);
        Console.WriteLine("old item(s):");
        foreach (var item in e.OldItems)
        {
            Console.WriteLine(item);
        }
    }
    if (e.NewItems != null)
    {
        Console.WriteLine("starting index for new item(s): {0}",
                          e.NewStartingIndex);
        Console.WriteLine("new item(s): ");
        foreach (var item in e.NewItems)
        {
            Console.WriteLine(item);
        }
    }
    Console.WriteLine();
}
```

Running the application, you can see the output as follows. The first items `One` and `Two` are added to the collection and thus the `Add` action is shown with the index `0` and `1`. The third item `Three` is inserted on position 1 so it shows the action `Add` with index `1`. Finally, the item `One` is removed as shown with action `Remove` and index `0`:

```
action: Add
starting index for new item(s): 0
new item(s):
One

action: Add
starting index for new item(s): 1
new item(s):
Two

action: Add
```

```
starting index for new item(s): 1
new item(s):
Three

action: Remove
starting index for old item(s): 0
old item(s):
One
```

BIT ARRAYS

If you need to deal with a number of bits, you can use the class `BitArray` and the struct `BitVector32`. `BitArray` is located in the namespace `System.Collections`; `BitVector32` is in the namespace `System.Collections.Specialized`. The most important difference between these two types is that `BitArray` is resizable, which is useful if you don't know the number of bits needed in advance, and it can contain a large number of bits. `BitVector32` is stack-based and therefore faster. `BitVector32` contains only 32 bits, which are stored in an integer.

BitArray

The class `BitArray` is a reference type that contains an array of `int`s, where for every 32 bits a new integer is used. Members of this class are explained in the following table:

BITARRAY MEMBERS	DESCRIPTION
Count Length	The get accessor of both `Count` and `Length` return the number of bits in the array. With the `Length` property, you can also define a new size and resize the collection.
Item Get() Set()	You can use an indexer to read and write bits in the array. The indexer is of type `bool`. Instead of using the indexer, you can also use the `Get()` and `Set()` methods to access the bits in the array.
SetAll()	The method `SetAll()` sets the values of all bits according to the parameter passed to the method.
Not()	The method `Not()` generates the inverse of all bits of the array.
And() Or() Xor()	With the methods `And()`, `Or()`, and `Xor()`, you can combine two `BitArray` objects. The `And()` method does a binary AND, where the result bits are set only if the bits from both input arrays are set. The `Or()` method does a binary OR, where the result bits are set if one or both of the input arrays are set. The `Xor()` method is an exclusive OR, where the result is set if only one of the input bits is set.

The helper method `DisplayBits()` iterates through a `BitArray` and displays 1 or 0 to the console, depending on whether or not the bit is set:

Available for download on Wrox.com

```
static void DisplayBits(BitArray bits)
{
    foreach (bool bit in bits)
    {
        Console.Write(bit ? 1: 0);
    }
}
```

code snippet BitArraySample/Program.cs

The example to demonstrate the `BitArray` class creates a bit array with 8 bits, indexed from 0 to 7. The `SetAll()` method sets all 8 bits to `true`. Then the `Set()` method changes bit 1 to `false`. Instead of the `Set` method, you can also use an indexer, as shown with index 5 and 7:

```
var bits1 = new BitArray(8);
bits1.SetAll(true);
bits1.Set(1, false);
bits1[5] = false;
bits1[7] = false;
Console.Write("initialized: ");
DisplayBits(bits1);
Console.WriteLine();
```

This is the displayed result of the initialized bits:

```
initialized: 10111010
```

The `Not()` method generates the inverse of the bits of the `BitArray`:

```
Console.Write(" not ");
DisplayBits(bits1);
bits1.Not();
Console.Write(" = ");
DisplayBits(bits1);
Console.WriteLine();
```

The result of `Not()` is all bits inversed. If the bit was `true`, it is `false`, and if it was `false`, it is `true`:

```
not 10111010 = 01000101
```

Here, a new `BitArray` is created. With the constructor, the variable `bits1` is used to initialize the array, so the new array has the same values. Then the values for bits 0, 1, and 4 are set to different values. Before the `Or()` method is used, the bit arrays `bits1` and `bits2` are displayed. The `Or()` method changes the values of `bits1`:

```
var bits2 = new BitArray(bits1);
bits2[0] = true;
bits2[1] = false;
bits2[4] = true;
DisplayBits(bits1);
Console.Write(" or ");
DisplayBits(bits2);
Console.Write(" = ");
bits1.Or(bits2);
DisplayBits(bits1);
Console.WriteLine();
```

With the `Or()` method, the set bits are taken from both input arrays. In the result, the bit is set if it was set with either the first or the second array:

```
01000101 or 10001101 = 11001101
```

Next, the `And()` method is used to operate on `bits2` and `bits1`:

```
DisplayBits(bits2);
Console.Write(" and ");
DisplayBits(bits1);
Console.Write(" = ");
bits2.And(bits1);
DisplayBits(bits2);
Console.WriteLine();
```

The result of the `And()` method only sets the bits where the bit was set in both input arrays:

```
10001101 and 11001101 = 10001101
```

Finally the Xor() method is used for an exclusive OR:

```
DisplayBits(bits1);
Console.Write(" xor ");
DisplayBits(bits2);
bits1.Xor(bits2);
Console.Write(" = ");
DisplayBits(bits1);
Console.WriteLine();
```

With the Xor() method, the resultant bits are set only if the bit was set either in the first or the second input, but not both:

```
11001101 xor 10001101 = 01000000
```

BitVector32

If you know the number of bits you need in advance, you can use the BitVector32 structure instead of BitArray. BitVector32 is more efficient because it is a value type and stores the bits on the stack inside an integer. With a single integer you have a place for 32 bits. If you need more bits, you can use multiple BitVector32 values or the BitArray. The BitArray can grow as needed; this is not an option with BitVector32.

The next table shows the members of BitVector that are very different from BitArray:

BITVECTOR MEMBERS	DESCRIPTION
Data	The property Data returns the data behind the BitVector32 as integer.
Item	The values for the BitVector32 can be set using an indexer. The indexer is overloaded — you can get and set the values using a mask or a section of type BitVector32.Section.
CreateMask()	CreateMask() is a static method that you can use to create a mask for accessing specific bits in the BitVector32.
CreateSection()	CreateSection() is a static method that you can use to create several sections within the 32 bits.

The sample code creates a BitVector32 with the default constructor, where all 32 bits are initialized to false. Then masks are created to access the bits inside the bit vector. The first call to CreateMask() creates a mask to access the first bit. After CreateMask() is invoked, bit1 has a value of 1. Invoking CreateMask() once more and passing the first mask as a parameter to CreateMask() returns a mask to access the second bit, which is 2. bit3 then has a value of 4 to access bit number 3. bit4 has a value of 8 to access bit number 4.

Then the masks are used with the indexer to access the bits inside the bit vector and set fields accordingly:

Available for download on Wrox.com

```
var bits1 = new BitVector32();
int bit1 = BitVector32.CreateMask();
int bit2 = BitVector32.CreateMask(bit1);
int bit3 = BitVector32.CreateMask(bit2);
int bit4 = BitVector32.CreateMask(bit3);
int bit5 = BitVector32.CreateMask(bit4);

bits1[bit1] = true;
bits1[bit2] = false;
bits1[bit3] = true;
bits1[bit4] = true;
bits1[bit5] = true;
Console.WriteLine(bits1);
```

code snippet BitArraySample/Program.cs

The `BitVector32` has an overridden `ToString()` method that not only displays the name of the class but also 1 or 0 if the bits are set or not, respectively:

```
BitVector32{00000000000000000000000000011101}
```

Instead of creating a mask with the `CreateMask()` method, you can define the mask yourself; you can also set multiple bits at once. The hexadecimal value `abcdef` is the same as the binary value `1010 1011 1100 1101 1110 1111`. All the bits defined with this value are set:

```
bits1[0xabcdef] = true;
Console.WriteLine(bits1);
```

With the output shown you can verify the bits that are set:

```
BitVector32{00000000101010111100110111101111}
```

Separating the 32 bits to different sections can be extremely useful. For example, an IPv4 address is defined as a 4-byte number that is stored inside an integer. You can split the integer by defining four sections. With a multicast IP message, several 32-bit values are used. One of these 32-bit values is separated in these sections: 16 bits for the number of sources, 8 bits for a querier's query interval code, 3 bits for a querier's robustness variable, a 1-bit suppress flag, and 4 bits that are reserved. You can also define your own bit meanings to save memory.

The example simulates receiving the value `0x79abcdef` and passes this value to the constructor of `BitVector32`, so that the bits are set accordingly:

```
int received = 0x79abcdef;


BitVector32 bits2 = new BitVector32(received);
Console.WriteLine(bits2);
```

The bits are shown on the console as initialized:

```
BitVector32{01111001101010111100110111101111}
```

Then six sections are created. The first section requires 12 bits, as defined by the hexadecimal value `0xfff` (12 bits are set); section B requires 8 bits; section C, 4 bits; section D and E, 3 bits; and section F, 2 bits. The first call to `CreateSection()` just receives `0xfff` to allocate the first 12 bits. With the second call to `CreateSection()`, the first section is passed as an argument, so that the next section continues where the first section ended. `CreateSection()` returns a value of type `BitVector32.Section` that contains the offset and the mask for the section.

```
// sections: FF EEE DDD CCCC BBBBBBBB
// AAAAAAAAAAAA
BitVector32.Section sectionA = BitVector32.CreateSection(0xfff);
BitVector32.Section sectionB = BitVector32.CreateSection(0xff, sectionA);
BitVector32.Section sectionC = BitVector32.CreateSection(0xf, sectionB);
BitVector32.Section sectionD = BitVector32.CreateSection(0x7, sectionC);
BitVector32.Section sectionE = BitVector32.CreateSection(0x7, sectionD);
BitVector32.Section sectionF = BitVector32.CreateSection(0x3, sectionE);
```

Passing a `BitVector32.Section` to the indexer of the `BitVector32` returns an int just mapped to the section of the bit vector. Here, a helper method, `IntToBinaryString()`, retrieves a string representation of the int number:

```
Console.WriteLine("Section A: {0}",
                  IntToBinaryString(bits2[sectionA], true));
Console.WriteLine("Section B: {0}",
                  IntToBinaryString(bits2[sectionB], true));
Console.WriteLine("Section C: {0}",
                  IntToBinaryString(bits2[sectionC], true));
Console.WriteLine("Section D: {0}",
                  IntToBinaryString(bits2[sectionD], true));
Console.WriteLine("Section E: {0}",
                  IntToBinaryString(bits2[sectionE], true));
Console.WriteLine("Section F: {0}",
                  IntToBinaryString(bits2[sectionF], true));
```

The method `IntToBinaryString()` receives the bits in an integer and returns a string representation containing 0 and 1. With the implementation, 32 bits of the integer are iterated through. In the iteration, if the bit is set, 1 is appended to the `StringBuilder`; otherwise, 0 is appended. Within the loop, a bit shift happens to check if the next bit is set.

```csharp
static string IntToBinaryString(int bits, bool removeTrailingZero)
{
    var sb = new StringBuilder(32);

    for (int i = 0; i < 32; i++)
    {
        if ((bits & 0x80000000) != 0)
        {
            sb.Append("1");
        }
        else
        {
            sb.Append("0");
        }
        bits = bits << 1;
    }
    string s = sb.ToString();
    if (removeTrailingZero)
    {
        return s.TrimStart('0');
    }
    else
    {
        return s;
    }
}
```

The result displays the bit representation of sections A to F, which you can now verify with the value that was passed into the bit vector:

```
Section A: 110111101111
Section B: 10111100
Section C: 1010
Section D: 1
Section E: 111
Section F: 1
```

CONCURRENT COLLECTIONS

.NET 4 contains the new namespace `System.Collections.Concurrent` with several new thread-safe collection classes. Thread-safe collections are guarded from multiple threads accessing the collections in conflicting ways.

For thread-safe access of collections the interface `IProducerConsumerCollection<T>` is defined. The most important methods of this interface are `TryAdd()` and `TryTake()`. `TryAdd()` tries to add an item to the collection, but this might fail if the collection is locked from adding items. To give this information, the method returns a Boolean value to inform about success or failure. `TryTake()` works the same way to inform the caller about success or failure and returns on success an item from the collection. The following list shows classes from the `System.Collections.Concurrent` namespace and its functionality:

➤ `ConcurrentQueue<T>` — This collection class is implemented with a lock-free algorithm and uses 32 item arrays that are combined in a linked list internally. Methods to access the elements of the queue are `Enqueue()`, `TryDequeue()`, and `TryPeek()`. The naming of these methods is very similar to the methods of `Queue<T>` that you know already, with the difference to the Try prefix where the method call might fail.

Because this class implements the interface `IProducerConsumerCollection<T>`, the methods `TryAdd()` and `TryTake()` just invoke `Enqueue()` and `TryDequeue()`.

➤ `ConcurrentStack<T>` — Very similar to `ConcurrentQueue<T>`, just with other item access methods, `ConcurrentStack<T>` defines the methods `Push()`, `PushRange()`, `TryPeek()`, `TryPop()`, and `TryPopRange()`. Internally this class uses a linked list of its items.

➤ `ConcurrentBag<T>` — This doesn't define any order to add or take items. This class uses a concept to map threads to arrays used internally and thus tries to reduce locks. The methods to access elements are `Add()`, `TryPeek()`, and `TryTake()`.

➤ `ConcurrentDictionary<TKey, TValue>` — This is a thread-safe collection of keys and values. `TryAdd()`, `TryGetValue()`, `TryRemove()`, and `TryUpdate()` are methods to access the members in a non-blocking fashion. Because the items are based on keys and values, `ConcurrentDictionary<TKey, TValue>` does not implement `IProducerConsumerCollection<T>`.

➤ The `ConcurrentXXX` — These collections are thread-safe in a way to return false if an action is not possible with the current state of threads. You always have to check if adding or taking the item was successful before moving on. You can't trust the collection to fulfill the task.

➤ `BlockingCollection<T>` — A collection that blocks and waits until it is possible to do the task by adding or taking the item, `BlockingCollection<T>` offers an interface to add and remove items with the `Add()` and `Take()` methods. These methods block the thread and wait until the task becomes possible.

The `Add()` method has an overload where you also can pass a `CancellationToken`. This token allows cancelling a blocking call.

If you do not want the thread to wait for an endless time, and do not want to cancel the call from the outside, the methods `TryAdd()` and `TryTake()` are offered as well, where you can also specify a timeout value for the maximum amount of time you would like to block the thread and wait before the call should fail.

➤ `BlockingCollection<T>` — This is a decorator to any class implementing the `IProducerConsumer Collection<T>` interface and by default uses `ConcurrentQueue<T>`. With the constructor you can also pass any other class that implements `IProducerConsumerCollection<T>`.

The following code example is a simple demonstration of using the `BlockingCollection<T>` class with multiple threads. One thread is the producer to write items in the collection with the `Add()` method, the other thread is the consumer to take items from the collection with the `Take()` method:

```csharp
var sharedCollection = new BlockingCollection<int>();
var events = new ManualResetEventSlim[2];
var waits = new WaitHandle[2];
for (int i = 0; i < 2; i++)
{
    events[i] = new ManualResetEventSlim(false);
    waits[i] = events[i].WaitHandle;
}


var producer = new Thread(obj =>
{
    var state =
        (Tuple<BlockingCollection<int>, ManualResetEventSlim>)obj;
    var coll = state.Item1;
    var ev = state.Item2;
    var r = new Random();

    for (int i = 0; i < 300; i++)
    {
        coll.Add(r.Next(3000));
```

```
        }
        ev.Set();
    });
    producer.Start(
        Tuple.Create<BlockingCollection<int>, ManualResetEventSlim>(
            sharedCollection, events[0]));

    var consumer = new Thread(obj =>
    {
        var state =
            (Tuple<BlockingCollection<int>, ManualResetEventSlim>)obj;
        var coll = state.Item1;
        var ev = state.Item2;

        for (int i = 0; i < 300; i++)
        {
            int result = coll.Take();
        }
        ev.Set();
    });
    consumer.Start(
        Tuple.Create<BlockingCollection<int>, ManualResetEventSlim>(
            sharedCollection, events[1]));

    if (!WaitHandle.WaitAll(waits))
        Console.WriteLine("wait failed");
    else
        Console.WriteLine("reading/writing finished");
```

code snippet ConcurrentSample/Program.cs

 Using the concurrent collections really gets interesting as soon as multiple threads come into play. This as well as the use of the CancellationToken *is shown in Chapter 20. The next chapter also gives information about using the concurrent collections with Parallel LINQ.*

PERFORMANCE

Many collection classes offer the same functionality as others; for example, SortedList offers nearly the same features as SortedDictionary. However, often there's a big difference in performance. Whereas one collection consumes less memory, the other collection class is faster with retrieval of elements. In the MSDN documentation, you often find performance hints with methods of the collection giving you information about the time the operation represents in *big-O* notation:

```
O(1)
O(log n)
O(n)
```

O(1) means that the time this operation needs is constant no matter how many items are in the collection. For example, the ArrayList has an Add() method with O(1) behavior. No matter how many elements are in the list, it always takes the same time when adding a new element to the end of the list. The Count property gives the number of items, so it is easy to find the end of the list.

O(n) means that for every element in the collection the same amount of additional time is needed. The `Add()` method of `ArrayList` can be an O(n) operation if a reallocation of the collection is required. Changing the capacity causes the copying of the list, and the time for the copy increases linearly with every element.

O(log n) means that the time needed for the operation increases with every element in the collection. But the increase of time for every element is not linear but logarithmic. `SortedDictionary<TKey,TValue>` has O(log n) behavior for inserting operations inside the collection; `SortedList<TKey,TValue>` has O(n) behavior for the same functionality. Here, `SortedDictionary<TKey,TValue>` is a lot faster because it is more efficient to insert elements into a tree structure than into a list.

The following table lists collection classes and their performance for different actions such as adding, inserting, and removing items. Using this table you can select the best collection class for the purpose of your use. The left column lists the collection class. The Add column gives timing information about adding items to the collection. The `List<T>` and the `HashSet<T>` classes define `Add` methods to add items to the collection. With other collection classes, there's a different method to add elements to the collection; for example, the `Stack<T>` class defines a `Push()` method, and the `Queue<T>` class defines an `Enqueue()` method. You can find this information in the table as well.

If there are multiple big-O values in a cell, the reason is that if a collection needs to be resized, resizing takes a while. For example, with the `List<T>` class, adding items needs O(1). If the capacity of the collection is not large enough and the collection needs to be resized, the resize requires O(n) time. The larger the collection is, the longer the resize operation takes. It's best to avoid resizes by setting the capacity of the collection to a value that can hold all elements.

If the cell content is *na*, this means that this operation is *not applicable* with this collection type.

COLLECTION	ADD	INSERT	REMOVE	ITEM	SORT	FIND
`List<T>`	O(1) or O(n) if the collection must be resized	O(n)	O(n)	O(1)	O (n log n), worst case O (n ^ 2)	O(n)
`Stack<T>`	Push(), O(1) or O(n) if the stack must be resized	na	Pop(), O(1)	na	na	na
`Queue<T>`	Enqueue(), O(1) or O(n) if the queue must be resized	na	Dequeue(), O(1)	na	na	na
`HashSet<T>`	O(1) or O(n) if the set must be resized	Add() O(1) or O(n)	O(1)	na	na	na
`SortedSet<T>`	O(1) or O(n) if the set must be resized	Add() O(1) or O(n)	O(1)	na	na	na
`LinkedList<T>`	AddLast() O(1)	Add After() O(1)	O(1)	Na	na	O(n)

continues

(continued)

COLLECTION	ADD	INSERT	REMOVE	ITEM	SORT	FIND
Dictionary \<TKey, TValue\>	O(1) or O(n)	na	O(1)	O(1)	na	na
SortedDictionary \<TKey, TValue\>	O(log n)	na	O(log n)	O(log n)	na	na
SortedList \<TKey, TValue\>	O(n) for unsorted data, O(log n) for end of list, O(n) if resize is needed	na	O(n)	O(log n) to read/ write, O(log n) if the key is in the list, O(n) if the key is not in the list	na	na

SUMMARY

This chapter took a look at working with different kinds of collections. Arrays are fixed in size, but you can use lists for dynamically growing collections. For accessing elements on a first-in, first-out basis, there's a queue, and there's a stack for last-in, first-out operations. Linked lists allow for fast inserting and removing of elements but are slow for searching. With keys and value, you can use dictionaries, which are fast for searching and inserting elements. Sets are for unique items and can be ordered (SortedSet<T>) or not ordered (HashSet<T>). ObservableCollection<T> gives events when items change in the list.

In this chapter, you've seen a lot of interfaces and classes and their use for accessing and sorting collections. You've also seen some specialized collections, such as BitArray and BitVector32, which are optimized for working with a collection of bits.

Chapter 11 gives you details about Language Integrated Query (LINQ).

11

Language Integrated Query

WHAT'S IN THIS CHAPTER?

➤ Traditional queries across objects using `List<T>`
➤ Extension methods
➤ LINQ query operators
➤ Parallel LINQ
➤ Expression trees

LINQ (Language Integrated Query) integrates query syntax inside the C# programming language and makes it possible to access different data sources with the same syntax. LINQ makes this possible by offering an abstraction layer.

This chapter gives you the core foundation of LINQ and the language extensions for C# that make the new features possible.

 For using LINQ across the database you should read Chapter 31, "ADO.NET Entity Framework." To query XML data, read Chapter 33, "Manipulating XML," after reading this chapter.

LINQ OVERVIEW

This chapter starts with a simple LINQ query before diving into the full potential of LINQ. The C# language offers integrated query language that is converted to method calls. This section shows you what the conversion looks like so you can use all the possibilities of LINQ.

Lists and Entities

The LINQ queries in this chapter will be done on a collection containing Formula-1 champions from 1950 to 2008. This data needs to be prepared with entity classes and lists.

For the entities, the type `Racer` is defined. `Racer` defines several properties and an overloaded `ToString()` method to display a racer in a string format. This class implements the interface

`IFormattable` to support different variants of format strings, and the interface `IComparable<Racer>`, which can be used to sort a list of racers based on the `LastName`. For doing more advanced queries, the class `Racer` contains not only single value properties such as `FirstName`, `LastName`, `Wins`, `Country`, and `Starts`, but also multivalue properties such as `Cars` and `Years`. The `Years` property lists all the years of the championship title. Some racers have won more than one title. The `Cars` property is used to list all the cars that have been used by the driver during the title years.

```csharp
using System;
using System.Text;

namespace Wrox.ProCSharp.LINQ
{
    [Serializable]
    public class Racer: IComparable<Racer>, IFormattable
    {
        public Racer(string firstName = null, string lastName = null,
                string country = null, int starts = 0, int wins = 0,
                IEnumerable<int> years = null, IEnumerable<string> cars = null)
        {
            this.FirstName = firstName;
            this.LastName = lastName;
            this.Country = country;
                        this.Starts = starts;
            this.Wins = wins;


            var yearsList = new List<int>();
            foreach (var year in years)
            {
                yearsList.Add(year);
            }
            this.Years = yearsList.ToArray();
            var carList = new List<string>();
            foreach (var car in cars)
            {
                carList.Add(car);
            }
            this.Cars = carList.ToArray();


        }

        public string FirstName {get; set;}
        public string LastName {get; set;}
        public int Wins {get; set;}
        public string Country {get; set;}
        public int Starts {get; set;}
        public string[] Cars { get; private set; }
        public int[] Years { get; private set; }

        public override string ToString()
        {
            return String.Format("{0} {1}", FirstName, LastName);
        }

        public int CompareTo(Racer other)
        {
            if (other == null) throw new ArgumentNullException("other");

            return this.LastName.CompareTo(other.LastName);
```

```
        }

        public string ToString(string format)
        {
            return ToString(format, null);
        }

        public string ToString(string format, IFormatProvider formatProvider)
        {
            switch (format)
            {
                case null:
                case "N":
                    return ToString();
                case "F":
                    return FirstName;
                case "L":
                return LastName;
                case "C":
                    return Country;
                case "S":
                  return Starts.ToString();
                case "W":
                    return Wins.ToString();
                case "A":
                    return String.Format("{0} {1}, {2}; starts: {3}, wins: {4}",
                        FirstName, LastName, Country, Starts, Wins);
                default:
                    throw new FormatException(String.Format(
                        "Format {0} not supported", format));
            }
        }
    }
}
```

code snippet DataLib/Racer.cs

A second entity class is `Team`. This class just contains the name and an array of years for constructor championships.

```
[Serializable]
public class Team
{
    public Team(string name, params int[] years)
    {
        this.Name = name;
        this.Years = years;
    }
    public string Name { get; private set; }
    public int[] Years { get; private set; }
}
```

code snippet DataLib/Team.cs

The class `Formula1` returns a list of racers in the method `GetChampions()`. The list is filled with all Formula-1 champions from the years 1950 to 2008:

```
using System.Collections.Generic;

namespace Wrox.ProCSharp.LINQ
{
    public static class Formula1
```

```
{
    private static List<Racer> racers;

    public static IList<Racer> GetChampions()
    {
        if (racers == null)
        {
            racers = new List<Racer>(40);
            racers.Add(new Racer("Nino", "Farina", "Italy", 33, 5,
                            new int[] { 1950 },
                            new string[] { "Alfa Romeo" }));
            racers.Add(new Racer("Alberto", "Ascari", "Italy", 32, 10,
                            new int[] { 1952, 1953 },
                            new string[] { "Ferrari" }));
            racers.Add(new Racer("Juan Manuel", "Fangio", "Argentina", 51, 24,
                            new int[] { 1951, 1954, 1955, 1956, 1957 },
                            new string[] { "Alfa Romeo", "Maserati",
                                           "Mercedes", "Ferrari" }));
            racers.Add(new Racer("Mike", "Hawthorn", "UK", 45, 3,
                            new int[] { 1958 },
                            new string[] { "Ferrari" }));
            racers.Add(new Racer("Phil", "Hill", "USA", 48, 3,
                            new int[] { 1961 },
                            new string[] { "Ferrari" }));
            racers.Add(new Racer("John", "Surtees", "UK", 111, 6,
                            new int[] { 1964 },
                            new string[] { "Ferrari" }));
            racers.Add(new Racer("Jim", "Clark", "UK", 72, 25,
                            new int[] { 1963, 1965 },
                            new string[] { "Lotus" }));
            racers.Add(new Racer("Jack", "Brabham", "Australia", 125, 14,
                            new int[] { 1959, 1960, 1966 },
                            new string[] { "Cooper", "Brabham" }));
            racers.Add(new Racer("Denny", "Hulme", "New Zealand", 112, 8,
                            new int[] { 1967 },
                            new string[] { "Brabham" }));
            racers.Add(new Racer("Graham", "Hill", "UK", 176, 14,
                            new int[] { 1962, 1968 },
                            new string[] { "BRM", "Lotus" }));
            racers.Add(new Racer("Jochen", "Rindt", "Austria", 60, 6,
                            new int[] { 1970 },
                            new string[] { "Lotus" }));
            racers.Add(new Racer("Jackie", "Stewart", "UK", 99, 27,
                            new int[] { 1969, 1971, 1973 },
                            new string[] { "Matra", "Tyrrell" }));
            //...

        return racers;
        }
    }
}
```

code snippet DataLib/Formula1.cs

Where queries are done across multiple lists, the `GetConstructorChampions()` method that follows returns the list of all constructor championships. Constructor championships have been around since 1958.

```
private static List<Team> teams;
public static IList<Team> GetConstructorChampions()
{
    if (teams == null)
```

```
            {
                teams = new List<Team>()
                {
                    new Team("Vanwall", 1958),
                    new Team("Cooper", 1959, 1960),
                    new Team("Ferrari", 1961, 1964, 1975, 1976, 1977, 1979, 1982,
                            1983, 1999, 2000, 2001, 2002, 2003, 2004, 2007, 2008),
                    new Team("BRM", 1962),
                    new Team("Lotus", 1963, 1965, 1968, 1970, 1972, 1973, 1978),
                    new Team("Brabham", 1966, 1967),
                    new Team("Matra", 1969),
                    new Team("Tyrrell", 1971),
                    new Team("McLaren", 1974, 1984, 1985, 1988, 1989, 1990, 1991,
                            1998),
                    new Team("Williams", 1980, 1981, 1986, 1987, 1992, 1993, 1994,
                            1996, 1997),
                    new Team("Benetton", 1995),
                    new Team("Renault", 2005, 2006 )
                };
            }
            return teams;
        }
```

LINQ Query

Using these prepared lists and entities, you can do a LINQ query, for example, a query to get all world champions from Brazil sorted by the highest number of wins. To accomplish this you could use methods of the List<T> class; e.g. the FindAll() and Sort() methods. However, using LINQ there's a simpler syntax as soon as you're used to it:

Available for
download on
Wrox.com

```
private static void LinqQuery()
{
    var query = from r in Formula1.GetChampions()
                where r.Country == "Brazil"
                orderby r.Wins descending
                select r;

    foreach (Racer r in query)
    {
        Console.WriteLine("{0:A}", r);
    }
}
```

code snippet LINQIntro/Program.cs

The result of this query shows world champions from Brazil ordered:

```
Ayrton Senna, Brazil; starts: 161, wins: 41
Nelson Piquet, Brazil; starts: 204, wins: 23
Emerson Fittipaldi, Brazil; starts: 143, wins: 14
```

The statement

```
from r in Formula1.GetChampions()
where r.Country == "Brazil"
orderby r.Wins descending
select r;
```

is a LINQ query. The clauses from, where, orderby, descending, and select are predefined keywords in this query.

The query expression must begin with a from clause and end with a select or group clause. In between you can optionally use where, orderby, join, let, and additional from clauses.

It is important to note that the variable query *just has the LINQ query assigned to it. The query is not performed by this assignment but rather as soon as the query is accessed using the* foreach *loop. This is discussed in more detail later in the section "Deferred Query Execution."*

Extension Methods

The compiler modifies the LINQ query to invoke methods instead. LINQ offers various extension methods for the IEnumerable<T> interface so you can use the LINQ query across any collection that implements this interface.

Extension methods make it possible to write a method to a class that doesn't offer the method at first. You can also add a method to any class that implements a specific interface, so multiple classes can make use of the same implementation.

For example, wouldn't you like to have a Foo() method with the String class? The String class is sealed, so it is not possible to inherit from this class. You can do an extension method, as shown in the following code:

```
public static class StringExtension
{
    public static void Foo(this string s)
    {
        Console.WriteLine("Foo invoked for {0}", s);
    }
}
```

An *extension method* is defined as a static method where the first parameter defines the type it extends and it is declared in a static class. The Foo() method extends the string class, as is defined with the first parameter. For differentiating extension methods from normal static methods, the extension method also requires the this keyword with the first parameter.

Indeed, it is now possible to use the Foo() method with the string type:

```
string s = "Hello";
s.Foo();
```

The result shows Foo invoked for Hello in the console, because Hello is the string passed to the Foo() method.

This might appear to be breaking object-oriented rules because a new method is defined for a type without changing the type or deriving from it. However, this is not the case. The extension method cannot access private members of the type it extends. Calling an extension method is just a new syntax of invoking a static method. With the string you can get the same result by calling the method Foo() this way:

```
string s = "Hello";
StringExtension.Foo(s);
```

To invoke the static method, write the class name followed by the method name. Extension methods are a different way to invoke static methods. You don't have to supply the name of the class where the static method is defined. Instead, the static method is taken because of the parameter type. You just have to import the namespace that contains the class to get the Foo() extension method in the scope of the String class.

One of the classes that define LINQ extension methods is Enumerable in the namespace System.Linq. You just have to import the namespace to open the scope of the extension methods of this class. A sample implementation of the Where() extension method is shown in the following code. The first parameter of the `Where()` method that includes the `this` keyword is of type `IEnumerable<T>`. This way the `Where()` method can be used with every type that implements `IEnumerable<T>`. A few examples of types that implement this interface are arrays and `List<T>`. The second parameter is a `Func<T, bool>` delegate that references a method that returns a Boolean value and requires a parameter of type `T`. This predicate is invoked within the implementation to examine if the item from the `IEnumerable<T>` source should go into the destination collection. If the method is referenced by the delegate, the `yield return` statement returns the item from the source to the destination:

```
public static IEnumerable<TSource> Where<TSource>(
        this IEnumerable<TSource> source,
        Func<TSource, bool> predicate)
{
    foreach (TSource item in source)
        if (predicate(item))
            yield return item;
}
```

Because `Where()` is implemented as a generic method, it works with any type that is contained in a collection. Any collection implementing `IEnumerable<T>` is supported.

> *The extension methods here are defined in the namespace* `System.Linq` *in the assembly* `System.Core`.

Now it's possible to use the extension methods `Where()`, `OrderByDescending()`, and `Select()` from the class `Enumerable`. Because each of these methods returns `IEnumerable<TSource>`, it is possible to invoke one method after the other by using the previous result. With the arguments of the extension methods, anonymous methods that define the implementation for the delegate parameters are used:

Available for
download on
Wrox.com

```
static void ExtensionMethods()
{
    var champions = new List<Racer>(Formula1.GetChampions());
    IEnumerable<Racer> brazilChampions =
        champions.Where(r => r.Country == "Brazil").
                OrderByDescending(r => r.Wins).
                Select(r => r);

    foreach (Racer r in brazilChampions)
    {
        Console.WriteLine("{0:A}", r);
    }
}
```

code snippet LINQIntro/Program.cs

Deferred Query Execution

When the query expression is defined during runtime, the query does not run. The query runs when the items are iterated.

Let's have a look once more at the extension method `Where()`. This extension method makes use of the `yield return` statement to return the elements where the predicate is true. Because the `yield return` statement is used, the compiler creates an enumerator and returns the items as soon as they are accessed from the enumeration:

```
public static IEnumerable<T> Where<T>(this IEnumerable<T> source,
Func<T, bool> predicate)
{
```

```
        foreach (T item in source)
            if (predicate(item))
                yield return item;
    }
```

This has a very interesting and important effect. With the following example a collection of String elements is created and filled with the name arr. Next, a query is defined to get all names from the collection where the item starts with the letter J. The collection should also be sorted. The iteration does not happen when the query is defined. Instead, the iteration happens with the foreach statement, where all items are iterated. Only one element of the collection fulfills the requirements of the where expression by starting with the letter J: Juan. After the iteration is done and Juan is written to the console, four new names are added to the collection. Then the iteration is done again:

```
var names = new List<string> { "Nino", "Alberto", "Juan", "Mike", "Phil" };

var namesWithJ = from n in names
                 where n.StartsWith("J")
                 orderby n
                 select n;

Console.WriteLine("First iteration");
foreach (string name in namesWithJ)
{
    Console.WriteLine(name);
}
Console.WriteLine();

names.Add("John");
names.Add("Jim");
names.Add("Jack");
names.Add("Denny");

Console.WriteLine("Second iteration");
foreach (string name in namesWithJ)
{
    Console.WriteLine(name);
}
```

Because the iteration does not happen when the query is defined, but it does happen with every foreach, changes can be seen, as the output from the application demonstrates:

```
First iteration
Juan

Second iteration
Jack
Jim
John
Juan
```

Of course, you also must be aware that the extension methods are invoked every time the query is used within an iteration. Most of the time this is very practical, because you can detect changes in the source data. However, there are situations where this is impractical. You can change this behavior by invoking the extension methods ToArray(), ToEnumerable(), ToList(), and the like. In the example, you can see that ToList iterates through the collection immediately and returns a collection implementing IList<string>. The returned list is then iterated through twice; in between iterations, the data source gets new names:

```
var names = new List<string>
                 { "Nino", "Alberto", "Juan", "Mike", "Phil" };
var namesWithJ = (from n in names
```

```
                                 where n.StartsWith("J")
                                 orderby n
                                 select n).ToList();

                Console.WriteLine("First iteration");
                foreach (string name in namesWithJ)
                {
                    Console.WriteLine(name);
                }
                Console.WriteLine();

                names.Add("John");
                names.Add("Jim");
                names.Add("Jack");
                names.Add("Denny");

                Console.WriteLine("Second iteration");
                foreach (string name in namesWithJ)
                {
                    Console.WriteLine(name);
                }
```

In the result, you can see that in between the iterations the output stays the same although the collection values have changed:

```
First iteration
Juan

Second iteration
Juan
```

STANDARD QUERY OPERATORS

`Where`, `OrderByDescending`, and `Select` are only a few of the query operators defined by LINQ. The LINQ query defines a declarative syntax for the most common operators. There are many more query operators available with the `Enumerable` class.

The following table lists the standard query operators defined by the `Enumerable` class:

STANDARD QUERY OPERATORS	DESCRIPTION
`Where OfType<TResult>`	*Filtering* operators define a restriction to the elements returned. With the `Where` query operator you can use a predicate, for example, defined by a Lambda expression that returns a bool. `OfType<TResult>` filters the elements based on the type and returns only the elements of the type `TResult`.
`Select SelectMany`	*Projection* operators are used to transform an object into a new object of a different type. `Select` and `SelectMany` define a projection to select values of the result based on a selector function.
`OrderBy ThenBy OrderByDescending ThenByDescending Reverse`	*Sorting* operators change the order of elements returned. `OrderBy` sorts values in ascending order; `OrderByDescending` sorts values in descending order. `ThenBy` and `ThenByDescending` operators are used for a secondary sort if the first sort gives similar results. `Reverse` reverses the elements in the collection.

continues

(continued)

STANDARD QUERY OPERATORS	DESCRIPTION
Join GroupJoin	*Join* operators are used to combine collections that might not be directly related to each other. With the Join operator a join of two collections based on key selector functions can be done. This is similar to the JOIN you know from SQL. The GroupJoin operator joins two collections and groups the results.
GroupBy ToLookup	*Grouping* operators put the data into groups. The GroupBy operator groups elements with a common key. ToLookup groups the elements by creating a one-to-many dictionary.
Any All Contains	*Quantifier* operators return a Boolean value if elements of the sequence satisfy a specific condition. Any, All, and Contains are quantifier operators. Any determines if any element in the collection satisfies a predicate function; All determines if all elements in the collection satisfy a predicate. Contains checks whether a specific element is in the collection. These operators return a Boolean value.
Take Skip TakeWhile SkipWhile	*Partitioning* operators return a subset of the collection. Take, Skip, TakeWhile, and SkipWhile are partitioning operators. With these, you get a partial result. With Take, you have to specify the number of elements to take from the collection; Skip ignores the specified number of elements and takes the rest. TakeWhile takes the elements as long as a condition is true.
Distinct Union Intersect Except Zip	*Set* operators return a collection set. Distinct removes duplicates from a collection. With the exception of Distinct, the other set operators require two collections. Union returns unique elements that appear in either of the two collections. Intersect returns elements that appear in both collections. Except returns elements that appear in just one collection. Zip is new with .NET 4 and combines two collections into one.
First FirstOrDefault Last LastOrDefault ElementAt ElementAtOrDefault Single SingleOrDefault	*Element* operators return just one element. First returns the first element that satisfies a condition. FirstOrDefault is similar to First, but it returns a default value of the type if the element is not found. Last returns the last element that satisfies a condition. With ElementAt, you specify the position of the element to return. Single returns only the one element that satisfies a condition. If more than one element satisfies the condition, an exception is thrown.
Count Sum Min Max Average Aggregate	*Aggregate* operators compute a single value from a collection. With aggregate operators, you can get the sum of all values, the number of all elements, the element with the lowest or highest value, an average number, and so on.
ToArray AsEnumerable ToList ToDictionary Cast<TResult>	*Conversion* operators convert the collection to an array: IEnumerable, IList, IDictionary, and so on.
Empty Range Repeat	*Generation* operators return a new sequence. The collection is empty using the Empty operator; Range returns a sequence of numbers, and Repeat returns a collection with one repeated value.

The following sections are examples of using these operators.

Filtering

Have a look at some examples for a query.

With the `where` clause, you can combine multiple expressions; for example, get only the racers from Brazil and Austria who won more than 15 races. The result type of the expression passed to the `where` clause just needs to be of type bool:

```
var racers = from r in Formula1.GetChampions()
             where r.Wins > 15 &&
                (r.Country == "Brazil" || r.Country == "Austria")
             select r;

foreach (var r in racers)
{
    Console.WriteLine("{0:A}", r);
}
```

code snippet Enumerablesample/Program.cs

Starting the program with this LINQ query returns Niki Lauda, Nelson Piquet, and Ayrton Senna as shown:

```
Niki Lauda, Austria, Starts: 173, Wins: 25
Nelson Piquet, Brazil, Starts: 204, Wins: 23
Ayrton Senna, Brazil, Starts: 161, Wins: 41
```

Not all queries can be done with the LINQ query. Not all extension methods are mapped to LINQ query clauses. Advanced queries require using extension methods. To better understand complex queries with extension methods, it's good to see how simple queries are mapped. Using the extension methods `Where()` and `Select()` produces a query very similar to the LINQ query done before:

```
var racers = Formula1.GetChampions().
    Where(r => r.Wins > 15 &&
        (r.Country == "Brazil" || r.Country == "Austria")).
    Select(r => r);
```

Filtering with Index

One example where you can't use the LINQ query is an overload of the `Where()` method. With an overload of the `Where()` method you can pass a second parameter that is the index. The index is a counter for every result returned from the filter. You can use the index within the expression to do some calculation based on the index. Here the index is used within the code that is called by the `Where()` extension method to return only racers whose last name starts with A if the index is even:

```
var racers = Formula1.GetChampions().
    Where((r, index) => r.LastName.StartsWith("A") && index % 2 != 0);
foreach (var r in racers)
{
    Console.WriteLine("{0:A}", r);
}
```

All the racers with last names beginning with the letter A are Alberto Ascari, Mario Andretti, and Fernando Alonso. Because Mario Andretti is positioned within an index that is odd, he is not in the result:

```
Alberto Ascari, Italy; starts: 32, wins: 10
Fernando Alonso, Spain; starts: 132, wins: 21
```

Type Filtering

For filtering based on a type you can use the `OfType()` extension method. Here the array data contains both `string` and `int` objects. Using the extension method `OfType()`, passing the string class to the generic parameter returns only the strings from the collection:

```
object[] data = { "one", 2, 3, "four", "five", 6 };
var query = data.OfType<string>();
foreach (var s in query)
{
    Console.WriteLine(s);
}
```

Running this code, the strings one, four, and five are displayed:

```
one
four
five
```

Compound from

If you need to do a filter based on a member of the object that itself is a sequence, you can use a compound `from`. The `Racer` class defines a property `Cars` where `Cars` is a string array. For a filter of all racers who were champions with a Ferrari, you can use the LINQ query as shown. The first `from` clause accesses the `Racer` objects returned from `Formula1.GetChampions()`. The second `from` clause accesses the `Cars` property of the `Racer` class to return all cars of type `string`. Next the cars are used with the `where` clause to filter only the racers who were champions with a Ferrari:

```
var ferrariDrivers = from r in Formula1.GetChampions()
                     from c in r.Cars
                     where c == "Ferrari"
                     orderby r.LastName
                     select r.FirstName + " " + r.LastName;
```

If you are curious about the result of this query, all Formula-1 champions driving a Ferrari are:

```
Alberto Ascari
Juan Manuel Fangio
Mike Hawthorn
Phil Hill
Niki Lauda
Kimi Räikkönen
Jody Scheckter
Michael Schumacher
John Surtees
```

The C# compiler converts a compound `from` clause with a LINQ query to the `SelectMany()` extension method. `SelectMany()` can be used to iterate a sequence of a sequence. The overload of the `SelectMany` method that is used with the example is shown here:

```
public static IEnumerable<TResult> SelectMany<TSource, TCollection, TResult> (
    this IEnumerable<TSource> source,
    Func<TSource,
    IEnumerable<TCollection>> collectionSelector,
    Func<TSource, TCollection, TResult>
    resultSelector);
```

The first parameter is the implicit parameter that receives the sequence of `Racer` objects from the `GetChampions()` method. The second parameter is the `collectionSelector` delegate where the inner sequence is defined. With the Lambda expression `r => r.Cars` the collection of cars should be returned. The third parameter is a delegate that is now invoked for every car and receives the `Racer` and `Car` objects. The Lambda expression creates an anonymous type with a `Racer` and a `Car` property. As a result of this

`SelectMany()` method, the hierarchy of racers and cars is flattened and a collection of new objects of an anonymous type for every car is returned.

This new collection is passed to the `Where()` method so that only the racers driving a Ferrari are filtered. Finally, the `OrderBy()` and `Select()` methods are invoked:

```
var ferrariDrivers = Formula1.GetChampions().
    SelectMany(
        r => r.Cars,
        (r, c) => new { Racer = r, Car = c }).
        Where(r => r.Car == "Ferrari").
        OrderBy(r => r.Racer.LastName).
        Select(r => r.Racer.FirstName + " " + r.Racer.LastName);
```

Resolving the generic `SelectMany()` method to the types that are used here, the types are resolved as follows. In this case the source is of type `Racer`, the filtered collection is a `string` array, and of course the name of the anonymous type that is returned is not known and is shown here as `TResult`:

```
public static IEnumerable<TResult> SelectMany<Racer, string, TResult> (
    this IEnumerable<Racer> source,
    Func<Racer, IEnumerable<string>> collectionSelector,
    Func<Racer, string, TResult> resultSelector);
```

Because the query was just converted from a LINQ query to extension methods, the result is the same as before.

Sorting

For sorting a sequence, the `orderby` clause was used already. Let's review the example from before with the `orderby descending` clause. Here the racers are sorted based on the number of wins as specified by the key selector in descending order:

Available for
download on
Wrox.com

```
var racers = from r in Formula1.GetChampions()
             where r.Country == "Brazil"
             orderby r.Wins descending
             select r;
```

code snippet EnumerableSample/Program.cs

The `orderby` clause is resolved to the `OrderBy()` method, and the `orderby descending` clause is resolved to the `OrderByDescending()` method:

```
var racers = Formula1.GetChampions().
    Where(r => r.Country == "Brazil").
    OrderByDescending(r => r.Wins).
    Select(r => r);
```

The `OrderBy()` and `OrderByDescending()` methods return `IOrderedEnumerable<TSource>`. This interface derives from the interface `IEnumerable<TSource>` but contains an additional method `Create OrderedEnumerable<TSource>()`. This method is used for further ordering of the sequence. If two items are the same based on the key selector, ordering can continue with the `ThenBy()` and `ThenByDescending()` methods. These methods require an `IOrderedEnumerable<TSource>` to work on, but return this interface as well. So, you can add any number of `ThenBy()` and `ThenByDescending()` to sort the collection.

Using the LINQ query you just have to add all the different keys (with commas) for sorting to the `orderby` clause. Here the sort of all racers is done first based on the country, next on the last name, and finally on the first name. The `Take()` extension method that is added to the result of the LINQ query is used to take the first 10 results:

```
var racers = (from r in Formula1.GetChampions()
              orderby r.Country, r.LastName, r.FirstName
              select r).Take(10);
```

The sorted result is shown here:

```
Argentina: Fangio, Juan Manuel
Australia: Brabham, Jack
Australia: Jones, Alan
Austria: Lauda, Niki
Austria: Rindt, Jochen
Brazil: Fittipaldi, Emerson
Brazil: Piquet, Nelson
Brazil: Senna, Ayrton
Canada: Villeneuve, Jacques
Finland: Hakkinen, Mika
```

Doing the same with extension methods makes use of the `OrderBy()` and `ThenBy()` methods:

```
var racers = Formula1.GetChampions().
    OrderBy(r => r.Country).
    ThenBy(r => r.LastName).
    ThenBy(r => r.FirstName).
    Take(10);
```

Grouping

To group query results based on a key value, the `group` clause can be used. Now the Formula-1 champions should be grouped by the country, and the number of champions within a country should be listed. The clause `group r by r.Country into g` groups all the racers based on the `Country` property and defines a new identifier `g` that can be used later to access the group result information. The result from the `group` clause is ordered based on the extension method `Count()` that is applied on the group result, and if the count is the same, the ordering is done based on the key. This is the country because this was the key used for grouping. The `where` clause filters the results based on groups that have at least two items, and the `select` clause creates an anonymous type with `Country` and `Count` properties:

```
var countries = from r in Formula1.GetChampions()
                group r by r.Country into g
                orderby g.Count() descending, g.Key
                where g.Count() >= 2
                select new {
                        Country = g.Key,
                        Count = g.Count()
                    };

foreach (var item in countries)
{
    Console.WriteLine("{0, -10} {1}", item.Country, item.Count);
}
```

The result displays the collection of objects with the `Country` and `Count` property:

```
UK          9
Brazil      3
Australia   2
Austria     2
Finland     2
Italy       2
USA         2
```

Doing the same with extension methods, the `groupby` clause is resolved to the `GroupBy()` method. What's interesting with the declaration of the `GroupBy()` method is that it returns an enumeration of objects implementing the `IGrouping` interface. The `IGrouping` interface defines the `Key` property, so you can access the key of the group after defining the call to this method:

```
public static IEnumerable<IGrouping<TKey, TSource>> GroupBy<TSource, TKey>(
    this IEnumerable<TSource> source, Func<TSource, TKey> keySelector);
```

The `group r by r.Country into g` clause is resolved to `GroupBy(r => r.Country)` and returns the group sequence. The group sequence is first ordered by the `OrderByDecending()` method, then by the `ThenBy()` method. Next the `Where()` and `Select()` methods that you already know are invoked:

```
var countries = Formula1.GetChampions().
    GroupBy(r => r.Country).
    OrderByDescending(g => g.Count()).
    ThenBy(g => g.Key).
    Where(g => g.Count() >= 2).
    Select(g => new { Country = g.Key,
                      Count = g.Count() });
```

Grouping with Nested Objects

If the grouped objects should contain nested sequences, you can do that by changing the anonymous type created by the `select` clause. With this example the returned countries should contain not only the properties for the name of the country and the number of racers, but also a sequence of the names of the racers. This sequence is assigned by using an inner `from`/in clause assigned to the `Racers` property. The inner `from` clause is using the `g` group to get all racers from the group, order them by last name, and create a new string based on the first and last name:

Available for
download on
Wrox.com

```
var countries = from r in Formula1.GetChampions()
                group r by r.Country into g
                orderby g.Count() descending, g.Key
                where g.Count() >= 2
                select new
                {
                    Country = g.Key,
                    Count = g.Count(),
                    Racers = from r1 in g
                             orderby r1.LastName
                             select r1.FirstName + " " + r1.LastName
                };
foreach (var item in countries)
{
    Console.WriteLine("{0, -10} {1}", item.Country, item.Count);
    foreach (var name in item.Racers)
    {
        Console.Write("{0}; ", name);
    }
    Console.WriteLine();
}
```

code snippet EnumerableSample/Program.cs

The output now lists all champions from the specified countries:

```
UK          9
Jim Clark; Lewis Hamilton; Mike Hawthorn; Graham Hill; Damon Hill; James Hunt;
Nigel Mansell; Jackie Stewart; John Surtees;
Brazil      3
Emerson Fittipaldi; Nelson Piquet; Ayrton Senna;
Australia   2
Jack Brabham; Alan Jones;
Austria     2
Niki Lauda; Jochen Rindt;
Finland     3
Mika Hakkinen; Kimi Raikkonen; Keke Rosberg;
Italy       2
Alberto Ascari; Nino Farina;
USA         2
Mario Andretti; Phil Hill;
```

Join

You can use the `join` clause to combine two sources based on specific criteria. But first, let's get two lists that should be joined. With Formula-1, there's a drivers and a constructors championship. The drivers are returned from the method `GetChampions()`, and the constructors are returned from the method `GetConstructorChampions()`. Now it would be interesting to get a list by year where every year lists the driver and the constructor champion.

For doing this, the first two queries for the racers and the teams are defined:

```
var racers = from r in Formula1.GetChampions()
             from y in r.Years
             where y > 2003
             select new
             {
                 Year = y,
                 Name = r.FirstName + " " + r.LastName
             };

var teams = from t in
            Formula1.GetContructorChampions()
            from y in t.Years
            where y > 2003
            select new
            {
                Year = y,
                Name = t.Name
            };
```

Using these two queries, a join is done based on the year of the driver champion and the year of the team champion with the clause `join t in teams on r.Year equals t.Year`. The `select` clause defines a new anonymous type containing `Year`, `Racer`, and `Team` properties:

```
var racersAndTeams =
    from r in racers
    join t in teams on r.Year equals t.Year
    select new
    {
        Year = r.Year,
        Racer = r.Name,
        Team = t.Name
    };
Console.WriteLine("Year  Champion " + "Constructor Title");
foreach (var item in racersAndTeams)
{
    Console.WriteLine("{0}: {1,-20} {2}",
        item.Year, item.Racer, item.Team);
}
```

Of course you can also combine this to one LINQ query, but that's a matter of taste:

```
int year = 2003;
var racersAndTeams =
    from r in
        from r1 in Formula1.GetChampions()
        from yr in r1.Years
        where yr > year
        select new
        {
            Year = yr,
            Name = r1.FirstName + " " + r1.LastName
        }
```

```
            join t in
                from t1 in
                    Formula1.GetConstructorChampions()
                from yt in t1.Years
                where yt > year
                select new
                {
                    Year = yt,
                    Name = t1.Name
                }
            on r.Year equals t.Year
            select new
            {
                Year = r.Year,
                Racer = r.Name,
                Team = t.Name
            };
```

The output displays data from the anonymous type:

```
Year   Champion             Constructor Title
2004   Michael Schumacher   Ferrari
2005   Fernando Alonso      Renault
2006   Fernando Alonso      Renault
2007   Kimi Räikkönen       Ferrari
2008   Lewis Hamilton       Ferrari
```

Set Operations

The extension methods `Distinct()`, `Union()`, `Intersect()`, and `Except()` are set operations. Let's create a sequence of Formula-1 champions driving a Ferrari and another sequence of Formula-1 champions driving a McLaren, and then let's find out if any driver has been a champion driving both of these cars. Of course, that's where the `Intersect()` extension method can help.

First get all champions driving a Ferrari. This is just using a simple LINQ query with a compound `from` to access the property `Cars` that's returning a sequence of string objects:

Available for
download on
Wrox.com

```
var ferrariDrivers = from r in
                         Formula1.GetChampions()
                     from c in r.Cars
                     where c == "Ferrari"
                     orderby r.LastName
                     select r;
```

code snippet EnumerableSample/Program.cs

Now the same query with a different parameter of the `where` clause would be needed to get all McLaren racers. It's not a good idea to write the same query another time. You have one option to create a method where you can pass the parameter `car`:

```
private static IEnumerable<Racer>GetRacersByCar(string car)
{
    return from r in Formula1.GetChampions()
               from c in r.Cars
               where c == car
               orderby r.LastName
               select r;
}
```

However, because the method wouldn't be needed in other places, defining a variable of a delegate type to hold the LINQ query is a good approach. The variable `racersByCar` needs to be of a delegate type that requires a string parameter and returns IEnumerable<Racer>, similar to the method that was implemented before. For doing this, several generic Func<> delegates are defined, so you do not need to declare your own delegate. A Lambda expression is assigned to the variable racersByCar. The left side of the Lambda expression defines a car variable of the type that is the first generic parameter of the Func delegate (a string). The right side defines the LINQ query that uses the parameter with the where clause:

```
Func<string, IEnumerable<Racer>> racersByCar =
    car => from r in Formula1.GetChampions()
           from c in r.Cars
           where c == car
           orderby r.LastName
           select r;
```

Now you can use the Intersect() extension method to get all racers that won the championship with a Ferrari and a McLaren:

```
Console.WriteLine("World champion with Ferrari and McLaren");
foreach (var racer in racersByCar("Ferrari").Intersect(
                       racersByCar("McLaren")))
{
    Console.WriteLine(racer);
}
```

The result is just one racer, Niki Lauda:

```
World champion with Ferrari and McLaren
Niki Lauda
```

> The Set operations compares the objects by invoking the GetHashCode() and Equals() method of the entity class. For custom comparision, you can also pass an object that implements the interface IEqualityComparer<T>. In the sample here, the GetChampions() method always returns the same objects and thus the default comparison works.

Zip

The Zip() method is new with .NET 4 and enables you to merge two related sequences into one with a predicate function.

First, two related sequences are created, both with the same filtering (country Italy) and ordering. For merging this is important, as item 1 from the first collection is merged with item 1 from the second collection, item 2 with item 2, and so on. In case the count of the two sequences is different, Zip() just stops when the end of the smaller collection is reached.

The items in the first collection have a Name property and the items in the second collection have LastName and Starts properties.

Using the Zip() method on the collection racerNames requires the second collection racerNamesAndStarts as the first parameter. The second parameter is of type Func<TFirst, TSecond, TResult>. This parameter is implemented as a Lambda expression and receives the elements of the first collection with the parameter first, and the elements of the second collection with the parameter second. The implementation creates and returns a string containing the Name property of the first element and the Starts property of the second element:

```
var racerNames = from r in Formula1.GetChampions()
                 where r.Country == "Italy"
                 orderby r.Wins descending
                 select new
```

```
                            {
                                Name = r.FirstName + " " + r.LastName
                            };

            var racerNamesAndStarts = from r in Formula1.GetChampions()
                                      where r.Country == "Italy"
                                      orderby r.Wins descending
                                      select new
                                      {
                                          LastName = r.LastName,
                                          Starts = r.Starts
                                      };

            var racers = racerNames.Zip(racerNamesAndStarts,
                    (first, second) => first.Name + ", starts: " + second.Starts);
            foreach (var r in racers)
            {
                Console.WriteLine(r);
            }
```

The result of this merge is shown here:

```
    Alberto Ascari, starts: 32
    Nino Farina, starts: 33
```

Partitioning

Partitioning operations such as the extension methods `Take()` and `Skip()` can be used for easily paging, for example, to display 5 by 5 racers.

With the LINQ query shown here, the extension methods `Skip()` and `Take()` are added to the end of the query. The `Skip()` method first ignores a number of items calculated based on the page size and the actual page number; the `Take()` method then takes a number of items based on the page size:

```
            int pageSize = 5;

            int numberPages = (int)Math.Ceiling(Formula1.GetChampions().Count() /
                    (double)pageSize);

            for (int page = 0; page < numberPages; page++)
            {
                Console.WriteLine("Page {0}", page);

                var racers =
                    (from r in Formula1.GetChampions()
                     orderby r.LastName
                     select r.FirstName + " " + r.LastName).
                    Skip(page * pageSize).Take(pageSize);

                foreach (var name in racers)
                {
                    Console.WriteLine(name);
                }
                Console.WriteLine();
            }
```

Here is the output of the first three pages:

```
    Page 0
    Fernando Alonso
    Mario Andretti
    Alberto Ascari
    Jack Brabham
```

```
Jim Clark

Page 1
Juan Manuel Fangio
Nino Farina
Emerson Fittipaldi
Mika Hakkinen
Lewis Hamilton

Page 2
Mike Hawthorn
Phil Hill
Graham Hill
Damon Hill
Denny Hulme
```

Paging can be extremely useful with Windows or web applications showing the user only a part of the data.

> *An important behavior of this paging mechanism that you will notice: because the query is done with every page, changing the underlying data affects the results. New objects are shown as paging continues. Depending on your scenario this can be advantageous to your application. If this behavior is not what you need, you can do the paging not over the original data source, but by using a cache that maps to the original data.*

With the `TakeWhile()` and `SkipWhile()` extension methods you can also pass a predicate to take or skip items based on the result of the predicate.

Aggregate Operators

The aggregate operators such as `Count()`, `Sum()`, `Min()`, `Max()`, `Average()`, and `Aggregate()` do not return a sequence but a single value instead.

The `Count()` extension method returns the number of items in the collection. Here the `Count()` method is applied to the `Years` property of a `Racer` to filter the racers and return only the ones who won more than three championships:

```
var query = from r in Formula1.GetChampions()
            where r.Years.Count() > 3
            orderby r.Years.Count() descending
            select new
            {
                Name = r.FirstName + " " + r.LastName,
                TimesChampion = r.Years.Count()
            };

foreach (var r in query)
{
    Console.WriteLine("{0} {1}", r.Name, r.TimesChampion);
}
```

The result is shown here:

```
Michael Schumacher 7
Juan Manuel Fangio 5
Alain Prost 4
```

The `Sum()` method summarizes all numbers of a sequence and returns the result. Here, `Sum()` is used to calculate the sum of all race wins for a country. First the racers are grouped based on the country, then with the new anonymous type created, the `Wins` property is assigned to the sum of all wins from a single country:

```
            var countries =
                (from c in
                    from r in Formula1.GetChampions()
                    group r by r.Country into c
                    select new
                    {
                        Country = c.Key,
                        Wins = (from r1 in c
                                select r1.Wins).Sum()
                    }
                    orderby c.Wins descending, c.Country
                    select c).Take(5);

            foreach (var country in countries)
            {
                Console.WriteLine("{0} {1}", country.Country, country.Wins);
            }
```

The most successful countries based on the Formula-1 race champions are as follows:

```
UK 147
Germany 91
Brazil 78
France 51
Finland 42
```

The methods `Min()`, `Max()`, `Average()`, and `Aggregate()` are used in the same way as `Count()` and `Sum()`. `Min()` returns the minimum number of the values in the collection, and `Max()` returns the maximum number. `Average()` calculates the average number. With the `Aggregate()` method you can pass a Lambda expression that should do an aggregation with all the values.

Conversion

In this chapter you've already seen that the query execution is deferred until the items are accessed. Using the query within an iteration, the query is executed. With a conversion operator, the query is executed immediately and you get the result in an array, a list, or a dictionary.

In this example the `ToList()` extension method is invoked to immediately execute the query and get the result into a `List<T>`:

Available for download on Wrox.com

```
            List<Racer> racers =
                (from r in Formula1.GetChampions()
                    where r.Starts > 150
                    orderby r.Starts descending
                    select r).ToList();
            foreach (var racer in racers)
            {
                Console.WriteLine("{0} {0:S}", racer);
            }
```

code snippet EnumerableSample/Program.cs

It's not that simple to just get the returned objects to the list. For example, for fast access from a car to a racer within a collection class, you can use the new class `Lookup<TKey, TElement>`.

> *The* `Dictionary<TKey, TValue>` *supports only a single value for a key. With the class* `Lookup<TKey TElement>` *from the namespace* `System.Linq` *you can have multiple values for a single key. These classes are covered in detail in Chapter 10, "Collections."*

Using the compound `from` query, the sequence of racers and cars is flattened, and an anonymous type with the properties `Car` and `Racer` gets created. With the lookup that is returned, the key should be of type `string` referencing the car, and the value should be of type `Racer`. To make this selection, you can pass a key and an element selector to one overload of the `ToLookup()` method. The key selector references the `Car` property, and the element selector references the `Racer` property:

```
var racers = (from r in Formula1.GetChampions()
              from c in r.Cars
              select new
              {
                  Car = c,
                  Racer = r
              }).ToLookup(cr => cr.Car, cr => cr.Racer);
if (racers.Contains("Williams"))
{
   foreach (var williamsRacer in
      racers["Williams"])
   {
      Console.WriteLine(williamsRacer);
   }
}
```

The result of all "Williams" champions that are accessed using the indexer of the `Lookup` class is shown here:

```
Alan Jones
Keke Rosberg
Nigel Mansell
Alain Prost
Damon Hill
Jacques Villeneuve
```

In case you need to use a LINQ query over an untyped collection, for example the `ArrayList`, you can use the `Cast()` method. With the following sample, an `ArrayList` collection that is based on the `Object` type is filled with `Racer` objects. To make it possible to define a strongly typed query, you can use the `Cast()` method:

```
var list = new System.Collections.ArrayList(Formula1.GetChampions()
        as System.Collections.ICollection);

var query = from r in list.Cast<Racer>()
            where r.Country == "USA"
            orderby r.Wins descending
            select r;
foreach (var racer in query)
{
   Console.WriteLine("{0:A}", racer);
}
```

Generation Operators

The generation operators `Range()`, `Empty()`, and `Repeat()` are not extension methods but normal static methods that return sequences. With LINQ to objects, these methods are available with the `Enumerable` class.

Have you ever needed a range of numbers filled? Nothing is easier than with the `Range()` method. This method receives the start value with the first parameter and the number of items with the second parameter:

```
var values = Enumerable.Range(1, 20);
foreach (var item in values)
{
   Console.Write("{0} ", item);
}
```

```
Console.WriteLine();
```

Of course the result now looks like this:

```
1 2 3 4 5 6 7 8 9 10 11 12 13 14 15 16 17 18 19 20
```

 The Range() *method does not return a collection filled with the values as defined. This method does a deferred query execution similar to the other methods. The method returns a* RangeEnumerator *that just does a* yield *return with the values incremented.*

You can combine the result with other extension methods to get a different result — for example, using the Select() extension method:

```
var values = Enumerable.Range(1, 20).Select(n => n * 3);
```

The Empty() method returns an iterator that does not return values. This can be used for parameters that require a collection where you can pass an empty collection.

The Repeat() method returns an iterator that returns the same value a specific number of times.

PARALLEL LINQ

.NET 4 contains a new class ParallelEnumerable in the System.Linq namespace to split the work of queries across multiple threads. Although the Enumerable class defines extension methods to the IEnumerable<T> interface, most extension methods of the ParallelEnumerable class are extensions for the class ParallelQuery<TSource>. One important exception is the AsParallel() method that extends IEnumerable<TSource> and returns ParallelQuery<TSource>, so a normal collection class can be queried in a parallel manner.

Parallel Queries

To dmonstrate Parallel LINQ, a large collection is needed. With small collections you will not see any effect when the collection fits inside the CPU's cache. In the following code, a large int array is filled with random values:

Available for
download on
Wrox.com

```
const int arraySize = 100000000;
var data = new int[arraySize];
var r = new Random();
for (int i = 0; i < arraySize; i++)
{
    data[i] = r.Next(40);
}
```

code snippet ParallelLinqSample/Program.cs

Now you can use a LINQ query to filter the data and get a sum of the filtered data. The query defines a filter with the where clause to summarize only the items with values < 20, and then the aggregation function sum is invoked. The only difference to the LINQ queries you've seen so far is the call to the AsParallel() method.

```
var sum = (from x in data.AsParallel()
              where x < 20
              select x).Sum();
```

As with the LINQ queries you've seen so far, the compiler changes the syntax to invoke the methods AsParallel(), Where(), Select(), and Sum(). AsParallel() is defined with the ParallelEnumerable class to extend the IEnumerable<T> interface, so it can be called with a simple array. AsParallel()

returns `ParallelQuery<TSource>`. Because of the returned type, the `Where()` method that is chosen by the compiler is `ParallelEnumerable.Where()` instead of `Enumerable.Where()`. In the following code, the `Select()` and `Sum()` methods are from `ParallelEnumerable` as well. In contrast to the implementation of the `Enumerable` class, with the `ParallelEnumerable` class the query is *partitioned* so that multiple threads can work on the query. The array can be split into multiple parts where different threads work on every part to filter the remaining items. After the partitioned work is completed, *merging* needs to take place to get the summary result of all parts.

```
var sum = data.AsParallel().Where(x => x < 20).Select(x => x).Sum();
```

Running this code starts the task manager so you can see that all CPUs of your system are busy. If you remove the `AsParallel()` method, multiple CPUs might not be used. Of course if you do not have multiple CPUs on your system, then don't expect to see an improvement with the parallel version.

Partitioners

The `AsParallel()` method is an extension not only to the `IEnumerable<T>` interface, but also to the `Partitioner` class. With this you can influence the partitions to be created.

The `Partitioner` class is defined with the namespace `System.Collections.Concurrent` and has different variants. The `Create()` method accepts arrays or objects implementing `IList<T>`. Depending on that, as well as on the parameter `loadBalance` that is of type Boolean and available with some overloads of the method, a different partitioner type is returned. For arrays, .NET 4 includes `DynamicPartitionerFor Array<TSource>` and `StaticPartitionerForArray<TSource>` that both derive from the abstract base class `OrderablePartitioner<TSource>`.

The code from the "Parallel Queries" section is changed to manually create a partitioner instead of relying on the default one:

```
var sum = (from x in Partitioner.Create(data, true).AsParallel()
            where x < 20
            select x).Sum();
```

You can also influence the parallelism by invoking the methods `WithExecutionMode()` and `WithDegreeOfParallelism()`. With `WithExecutionMode()` you can pass a value of `ParallelExecutionMode` that can be `Default` or `ForceParallelism`. By default, Parallel LINQ avoids parallelism with high overheads. With the method `WithDegreeOfParallelism()` you can pass an integer value to specify the maximum number of tasks that should run in parallel.

Cancellation

.NET 4 offers a standard way to cancel long-running tasks, and this is also true for Parallel LINQ.

To cancel a long-running query, you can add the method `WithCancellation()` to the query and pass a `CancellationToken` to the parameter. The `CancellationToken` is created from the `CancellationTokenSource`. The query is run in a separate thread where the exception of type `OperationCanceledException` is caught. This exception is fired if the query is cancelled. From the main thread the task can be cancelled by invoking the `Cancel()` method of the `CancellationTokenSource`.

```
var cts = new CancellationTokenSource();

new Thread(() =>
    {
        try
        {
            var sum = (from x in data.AsParallel().
                            WithCancellation(cts.Token)
                        where x < 80
                        select x).Sum();
            Console.WriteLine("query finished, sum: {0}", sum);
```

```
        }
        catch (OperationCanceledException ex)
        {
            Console.WriteLine(ex.Message);
        }
    }).Start();


    Console.WriteLine("query started");
    Console.Write("cancel? ");
    int input = Console.Read();
    if (input == 'Y' || input == 'y')
    {
        // cancel!
        cts.Cancel();
    }
```

 You can read more about cancellation and the `CancellationToken` *in Chapter 20, "Threads, Tasks, and Synchronization."*

EXPRESSION TREES

With LINQ to objects, the extension methods require a delegate type as parameter; this way, a Lambda expression can be assigned to the parameter. Lambda expressions can also be assigned to parameters of type Expression<T>. The C# compiler defines different behavior for Lambda expressions depending on the type. If the type is Expression<T>, the compiler creates an expression tree from the Lambda expression and stores it in the assembly. The expression tree can be analyzed during runtime and optimized for doing the query to the data source.

Let's turn to a query expression that was used previously:

```
var brazilRacers = from r in racers
                   where r.Country == "Brazil"
                   orderby r.Wins
                   select r;
```

code snippet ExpressionTreeSample/Program.cs

This query expression is using the extension methods Where, OrderBy, and Select. The Enumerable class defines the Where() extension method with the delegate type Func<T, bool> as parameter predicate:

```
public static IEnumerable<TSource> Where<TSource>(this IEnumerable<TSource> source,
    Func<TSource, bool> predicate);
```

This way, the Lambda expression is assigned to the predicate. Here, the Lambda expression is similar to an anonymous method, as was explained earlier:

```
Func<Racer, bool> predicate = r => r.Country == "Brazil";
```

The Enumerable class is not the only class to define the Where() extension method. The Where() extension method is also defined by the class Queryable<T>. This class has a different definition of the Where() extension method:

```
public static IQueryable<TSource> Where<TSource>(this IQueryable<TSource> source,
    Expression<Func<TSource, bool>> predicate);
```

Here, the Lambda expression is assigned to the type Expression<T>, which behaves differently:

```
Expression<Func<Racer, bool>> predicate = r => r.Country == "Brazil";
```

Instead of using delegates, the compiler emits an expression tree to the assembly. The expression tree can be read during runtime. Expression trees are built from classes that are derived from the abstract base class `Expression`. The `Expression` class is not the same as `Expression<T>`. Some of the expression classes that inherit from `Expression` are `BinaryExpression`, `ConstantExpression`, `InvocationExpression`, `LambdaExpression`, `NewExpression`, `NewArrayExpression`, `TernaryExpression`, `UnaryExpression`, and so on. The compiler creates an expression tree resulting from the Lambda expression.

For example, the Lambda expression `r.Country == "Brazil"` makes use of `ParameterExpression`, `MemberExpression`, `ConstantExpression`, and `MethodCallExpression` to create a tree and store the tree in the assembly. This tree is then used during runtime to create an optimized query to the underlying data source.

The method `DisplayTree()` is implemented to display an expression tree graphically on the console. Here an `Expression` object can be passed, and depending on the expression type some information about the expression is written to the console. Depending on the type of the expression, `DisplayTree()` is called recursively.

> *With this method not all expression types are dealt with; only the types that are used with the next sample expression.*

```csharp
private static void DisplayTree(int indent, string message,
                               Expression expression)
{
    string output = String.Format("{0} {1} ! NodeType: {2}; Expr: {3} ",
        "".PadLeft(indent, '>'), message, expression.NodeType, expression);

    indent++;
    switch (expression.NodeType)
    {
        case ExpressionType.Lambda:
            Console.WriteLine(output);
            LambdaExpression lambdaExpr = (LambdaExpression)expression;
            foreach (var parameter in lambdaExpr.Parameters)
            {
                DisplayTree(indent, "Parameter", parameter);
            }
            DisplayTree(indent, "Body", lambdaExpr.Body);
            break;
        case ExpressionType.Constant:
            ConstantExpression constExpr = (ConstantExpression)expression;
            Console.WriteLine("{0} Const Value: {1}", output, constExpr.Value);
            break;
        case ExpressionType.Parameter:
            ParameterExpression paramExpr = (ParameterExpression)expression;
            Console.WriteLine("{0} Param Type: {1}", output,
                              paramExpr.Type.Name);
            break;
        case ExpressionType.Equal:
        case ExpressionType.AndAlso:
        case ExpressionType.GreaterThan:
            BinaryExpression binExpr = (BinaryExpression)expression;
            if (binExpr.Method != null)
            {
                Console.WriteLine("{0} Method: {1}", output,
                                  binExpr.Method.Name);
            }
            else
```

```
        {
            Console.WriteLine(output);
        }
        DisplayTree(indent, "Left", binExpr.Left);
        DisplayTree(indent, "Right", binExpr.Right);
        break;
    case ExpressionType.MemberAccess:
        MemberExpression memberExpr = (MemberExpression)expression;
        Console.WriteLine("{0} Member Name: {1}, Type: {2}", output,
            memberExpr.Member.Name, memberExpr.Type.Name);
        DisplayTree(indent, "Member Expr", memberExpr.Expression);
        break;
    default:
        Console.WriteLine();
        Console.WriteLine("{0} {1}", expression.NodeType,
                        expression.Type.Name);
        break;
    }
}
```

The expression that is used for showing the tree is already well known. It's a Lambda expression with a `Racer` parameter, and the body of the expression takes racers from Brazil only if they have won more than six races:

```
Expression<Func<Racer, bool>> expression =
    r => r.Country == "Brazil" && r.Wins > 6;

DisplayTree(0, "Lambda", expression);
```

Let's look at the tree result. As you can see from the output, the Lambda expression consists of a `Parameter` and an `AndAlso` node type. The `AndAlso` node type has an `Equal` node type to the left and a `GreaterThan` node type to the right. The `Equal` node type to the left of the `AndAlso` node type has a `MemberAccess` node type to the left and a `Constant` node type to the right, and so on:

```
Lambda! NodeType: Lambda; Expr: r => ((r.Country == "Brazil")
    AndAlso (r.Wins > 6))
> Parameter! NodeType: Parameter; Expr: r  Param Type: Racer
> Body! NodeType: AndAlso; Expr: ((r.Country == "Brazil")
    AndAlso (r.Wins > 6))
>> Left! NodeType: Equal; Expr: (r.Country == "Brazil")  Method: op_Equality
>>> Left! NodeType: MemberAccess; Expr: r.Country
    Member Name: Country, Type: String
>>>> Member Expr! NodeType: Parameter; Expr: r  Param Type: Racer
>>> Right! NodeType: Constant; Expr: "Brazil" Const Value: Brazil
>> Right! NodeType: GreaterThan; Expr: (r.Wins > 6)
>>> Left! NodeType: MemberAccess; Expr: r.Wins  Member Name: Wins, Type: Int32
>>>> Member Expr! NodeType: Parameter; Expr: r  Param Type: Racer
>>> Right! NodeType: Constant; Expr: 6  Const Value: 6
```

One example where the `Expression<T>` type is used is with the ADO.NET Entity Framework and LINQ to SQL. These technologies define methods with `Expression<T>` parameters. This way the LINQ provider accessing the database can create a runtime-optimized query by reading the expressions to get the data from the database.

LINQ PROVIDERS

.NET 4 includes several LINQ providers. A LINQ provider implements the standard query operators for a specific data source. LINQ providers might implement more extension methods than are defined by LINQ, but the standard operators must at least be implemented. LINQ to XML implements more methods that are particularly useful with XML, for example, the methods `Elements()`, `Descendants()`, and `Ancestors()` are defined by the class `Extensions` in the `System.Xml.Linq` namespace.

The implementation of the LINQ provider is selected based on the namespace and on the type of the first parameter. The namespace of the class that implements the extension methods must be opened, otherwise the extension class is not in scope. The parameter of the `Where()` method that is defined by LINQ to objects and the `Where()` method that is defined by LINQ to SQL is different.

The `Where()` method of LINQ to objects is defined with the `Enumerable` class:

```
public static IEnumerable<TSource> Where<TSource>(this IEnumerable<TSource> source,
    Func<TSource, bool> predicate);
```

Inside the `System.Linq` namespace there's another class that implements the operator `Where`. This implementation is used by LINQ to SQL. You can find the implementation in the class `Queryable`:

```
public static IQueryable<TSource> Where<TSource>(this IQueryable<TSource> source,
    Expression<Func<TSource, bool>> predicate);
```

Both of these classes are implemented in the `System.Core` assembly in the `System.Linq` namespace. How is it defined and what method is used? The Lambda expression is the same no matter whether it is passed with a `Func<TSource, bool>` parameter or with an `Expression<Func<TSource, bool>>` parameter. Just the compiler behaves differently. The selection is done based on the `source` parameter. The method that matches best based on its parameters is chosen by the compiler. The `CreateQuery<T>()` method of the `ObjectContext` class that is defined by ADO.NET Entity Framework returns an `ObjectQuery<T>` object that implements `IQueryable<TSource>`, and thus the Entity Framework uses the `Where()` method of the `Queryable` class.

SUMMARY

In this chapter, you've seen the LINQ query and the language constructs that the query is based on, such as extension methods and Lambda expressions. You've seen the various LINQ query operators not just for filtering and ordering of data sources, but also for partitioning, grouping, doing conversions, joins, and so on.

With Parallel LINQ you've seen how longer queries can easily be parallelized.

Another important concept is the expression tree. Expression trees allow building the query to the data source at runtime because the tree is stored in the assembly. You can read about the great advantages of it in Chapter 31. LINQ is a very in-depth topic, and you should see Chapters 31 and 33 for more information. Other third-party providers are available for download; for example, LINQ to MySQL, LINQ to Amazon, LINQ to Flickr, LINQ to LDAP, and LINQ to SharePoint. No matter what data source you have, with LINQ you can use the same query syntax.

12

Dynamic Language Extensions

WHAT'S IN THIS CHAPTER?

➤ Understanding the Dynamic Language Runtime

➤ The `dynamic` type

➤ The DLR ScriptRuntime

➤ `DynamicObject`

➤ `ExpandoObject`

The growth of languages such as Ruby, Python, and the increased use of JavaScript have intensified interest in dynamic programming. In previous versions of the .NET Framework, the `var` keyword and anonymous methods started C# down the "dynamic" road. In version 4, the `dynamic` type was added. Although C# is still a statically typed language, these additions give it the dynamic capabilities that some developers are looking for.

In this chapter, you'll look at the `dynamic` type and the rules for using it. You'll also see what an implementation of `DynamicObject` looks like and how it can be used.

DYNAMIC LANGUAGE RUNTIME

The dynamic capabilities of C# 4 are part of the Dynamic Language Runtime (DLR). The DLR is a set of services that is added to the CLR to allow the addition of dynamic languages such as Ruby and Python. It also allows C# to take on some of the same dynamic capabilities that these dynamic languages have.

There is a version of the DLR that is open source and resides on the CodePlex web site. This same version is included with the .NET 4 Framework, with some additional support for language implementers.

In the .NET Framework, the DLR is found in the `System.Dynamic` namespace as well as a few additional classes in the `System.Runtime.CompilerServices` namespace.

IronRuby and IronPython, which are open source versions of the Ruby and Python languages, use the DLR. Silverlight also uses the DLR. It's possible to add scripting capabilities to your applications by hosting the DLR. The scripting runtime allows you to pass variables to and from the script.

THE DYNAMIC TYPE

The `dynamic` type allows you to write code that will bypass compile time type checking. The compiler will assume that whatever operation is defined for an object of type `dynamic` is valid. If that operation isn't valid, the error won't be detected until runtime. This is shown in the following example:

```
class Program
{
    static void Main(string[] args)
    {
        var staticPerson = new Person();
        dynamic dynamicPerson = new Person();
        staticPerson.GetFullName("John", "Smith");
        dynamicPerson.GetFullName("John", "Smith");
    }
}

class Person
{
    public string FirstName { get; set; }
    public string LastName { get; set; }
    public string GetFullName()
    {
        return string.Concat(FirstName, " ", LastName);
    }
}
```

This example will not compile because of the call to `staticPerson.GetFullName()`. There isn't a method on the `Person` object that takes two parameters, so the compiler raises the error. If that line of code were to be commented out, the example would compile. If executed, a runtime error would occur. The exception that is raised is `RuntimeBinderException`. The `RuntimeBinder` is the object in the runtime that evaluates the call to see if `Person` really does support the method that was called. This is discussed later in the chapter.

Unlike the `var` keyword, an object that is defined as *dynamic* can change type during runtime. Remember, when the `var` keyword is used, the determination of the object's type is delayed. Once the type is defined, it can't be changed. Not only can you change the type of a dynamic object, you can change it many times. This differs from casting an object from one type to another. When you cast an object you are creating a new object with a different but compatible type. For example, you cannot cast an `int` to a `Person` object. In the following example, you can see that if the object is a dynamic object, you can change it from `int` to `Person`:

Available for download on Wrox.com

```
dynamic dyn;

dyn = 100;
Console.WriteLine(dyn.GetType());
Console.WriteLine(dyn);

dyn = "This is a string";
Console.WriteLine(dyn.GetType());
Console.WriteLine(dyn);

dyn = new Person() { FirstName = "Bugs", LastName = "Bunny" };
Console.WriteLine(dyn.GetType());
Console.WriteLine("{0} {1}", dyn.FirstName, dyn.LastName);
```

code snippet Dynamic\Program.cs

Executing this code would show that the `dyn` object actually changes type from `System.Int32` to `System.String` to `Person`. If `dyn` had been declared as an `int` or `string`, the code would not have compiled.

There are a couple of limitations to the `dynamic` type. A dynamic object does not support extension methods. Anonymous functions (Lambda expressions) also cannot be used as parameters to a dynamic method call, thus LINQ does not work well with dynamic objects. Most LINQ calls are extension methods and Lambda expressions are used as arguments to those extension methods.

Dynamic Behind the Scenes

So what's going on behind the scenes to make this happen? C# is still a statically typed language. That hasn't changed. Take a look at the IL (Intermediate Language) that's generated when the `dynamic` type is used.

First, this is the example C# code that you're looking at:

```
using System;

namespace DeCompile
{
    class Program
    {
        static void Main(string[] args)
        {
            StaticClass staticObject = new StaticClass();
            DynamicClass dynamicObject = new DynamicClass();
            Console.WriteLine(staticObject.IntValue);
            Console.WriteLine(dynamicObject.DynValue);
            Console.ReadLine();
        }
    }

    class StaticClass
    {
        public int IntValue = 100;
    }

    class DynamicClass
    {
        public dynamic DynValue = 100;
    }
}
```

You have two classes, `StaticClass` and `DynamicClass`. `StaticClass` has a single field that returns an int. `DynamicClass` has a single field that returns a `dynamic` object. The `Main` method just creates these objects and prints out the value that the methods return. Simple enough.

Now comment out the references to the `DynamicClass` in `Main` like this:

```
static void Main(string[] args)
{
    StaticClass staticObject = new StaticClass();
    //DynamicClass dynamicObject = new DynamicClass();
    Console.WriteLine(staticObject.IntValue);
    //Console.WriteLine(dynamicObject.DynValue);
    Console.ReadLine();
}
```

Using the `ildasm` tool (discussed in Chapter 18, "Assemblies"), you can look at the IL that is generated for the `Main` method:

```
.method private hidebysig static void  Main(string[] args) cil managed
{
  .entrypoint
  // Code size       26 (0x1a)
  .maxstack  1
```

```
    .locals init ([0] class DeCompile.StaticClass staticObject)
    IL_0000:  nop
    IL_0001:  newobj      instance void DeCompile.StaticClass::.ctor()
    IL_0006:  stloc.0
    IL_0007:  ldloc.0
    IL_0008:  ldfld       int32 DeCompile.StaticClass::IntValue
    IL_000d:  call        void [mscorlib]System.Console::WriteLine(int32)
    IL_0012:  nop
    IL_0013:  call        string [mscorlib]System.Console::ReadLine()
    IL_0018:  pop
    IL_0019:  ret
  } // end of method Program::Main
```

Without going into the details of IL but just looking at this section of code, you can still pretty much tell what's going on. Line 0001, the `StaticClass` constructor, is called. Line 0008 calls the `IntValue` field of `StaticClass`. The next line writes out the value.

Now comment out the `StaticClass` references and uncomment the `DynamicClass` references:

```
static void Main(string[] args)
{
    //StaticClass staticObject = new StaticClass();
    DynamicClass dynamicObject = new DynamicClass();
    Console.WriteLine(staticObject.IntValue);
    //Console.WriteLine(dynamicObject.DynValue);
    Console.ReadLine();
}
```

Compile the application again and this is what gets generated:

```
.method private hidebysig static void  Main(string[] args) cil managed
{
  .entrypoint
  // Code size       121 (0x79)
  .maxstack  9
  .locals init ([0] class DeCompile.DynamicClass dynamicObject,
           [1] class [Microsoft.CSharp]Microsoft.CSharp.RuntimeBinder.CSharpArgumentInfo[]
                CS$0$0000)
    IL_0000:  nop
    IL_0001:  newobj      instance void DeCompile.DynamicClass::.ctor()
    IL_0006:  stloc.0
    IL_0007:  ldsfld      class [System.Core]System.Runtime.CompilerServices.CallSite`1
                          <class [mscorlib]
System.Action`3<class
[System.Core]System.Runtime.CompilerServices.CallSite,class [mscorlib]
System.Type,object>> DeCompile.Program/'<Main>o__SiteContainer0'::'<>p__Site1'
    IL_000c:  brtrue.s    IL_004d
    IL_000e:  ldc.i4.0
    IL_000f:  ldstr       "WriteLine"
    IL_0014:  ldtoken     DeCompile.Program
    IL_0019:  call        class [mscorlib]System.Type [mscorlib]System.Type::GetTypeFromHandle
(valuetype [mscorlib]System.RuntimeTypeHandle)
    IL_001e:  ldnull
    IL_001f:  ldc.i4.2
    IL_0020:  newarr      [Microsoft.CSharp]Microsoft.CSharp.RuntimeBinder.CSharpArgumentInfo
    IL_0025:  stloc.1
    IL_0026:  ldloc.1
    IL_0027:  ldc.i4.0
    IL_0028:  ldc.i4.s    33
    IL_002a:  ldnull
    IL_002b:  newobj      instance void [Microsoft.CSharp]Microsoft.CSharp.RuntimeBinder
.CSharpArgumentInfo::.ctor(valuetype [Microsoft.CSharp]Microsoft.CSharp.RuntimeBinder
.CSharpArgumentInfoFlags,
      string)
    IL_0030:  stelem.ref
```

```
   IL_0031:  ldloc.1
   IL_0032:  ldc.i4.1
   IL_0033:  ldc.i4.0
   IL_0034:  ldnull
   IL_0035:  newobj     instance void [Microsoft.CSharp]Microsoft.CSharp.RuntimeBinder
.CSharpArgumentInfo::.ctor(valuetype [Microsoft.CSharp]Microsoft.CSharp.RuntimeBinder
.CSharpArgumentInfoFlags,

string)
   IL_003a:  stelem.ref
   IL_003b:  ldloc.1
   IL_003c:  newobj     instance void [Microsoft.CSharp]Microsoft.CSharp.RuntimeBinder
.CSharpInvokeMemberBinder::.ctor(valuetype Microsoft.CSharp]Microsoft.CSharp
.RuntimeBinder.CSharpCallFlags,

string,

class [mscorlib]System.Type,

class [mscorlib]System.Collections.Generic.IEnumerable`1
<class [mscorlib]System.Type>,

class [mscorlib]System.Collections.Generic.IEnumerable`1
<class [Microsoft.CSharp]Microsoft.CSharp.RuntimeBinder.CSharpArgumentInfo>)
   IL_0041:  call       class [System.Core]System.Runtime.CompilerServices.CallSite`1
<!0> class [System.Core]System.Runtime.CompilerServices.CallSite`1
<class [mscorlib]System.Action`3
<class [System.Core]System.Runtime.CompilerServices.CallSite,
class [mscorlib]System.Type,object>>::Create(class [System.Core]System.Runtime.CompilerServices
                          .CallSiteBinder)
   IL_0046:  stsfld     class [System.Core]System.Runtime.CompilerServices.CallSite`1
<class [mscorlib]System.Action`3
<class [System.Core]System.Runtime.CompilerServices.CallSite,
class [mscorlib]System.Type,object>> DeCompile.Program/'<Main>o__SiteContainer0'::'<>p__Site1'
   IL_004b:  br.s       IL_004d
   IL_004d:  ldsfld     class [System.Core]System.Runtime.CompilerServices.CallSite`1
<class [mscorlib]System.Action`3
<class [System.Core]System.Runtime.CompilerServices.CallSite,
class [mscorlib]System.Type,object>> DeCompile.Program/'<Main>o__SiteContainer0'::'<>p__Site1'
   IL_0052:  ldfld      !0 class [System.Core]System.Runtime.CompilerServices.CallSite`1
<class [mscorlib]System.Action`3
<class [System.Core]System.Runtime.CompilerServices.CallSite,
class [mscorlib]System.Type,object>>::Target
   IL_0057:  ldsfld     class [System.Core]System.Runtime.CompilerServices.CallSite`1
<class [mscorlib]System.Action`3
<class [System.Core]System.Runtime.CompilerServices.CallSite,
class [mscorlib]System.Type,object>> DeCompile.Program/'<Main>o__SiteContainer0'::'<>p__Site1'
   IL_005c:  ldtoken    [mscorlib]System.Console
   IL_0061:  call       class [mscorlib]System.Type [mscorlib]System.Type::GetTypeFromHandle
(valuetype [mscorlib]System.RuntimeTypeHandle)
   IL_0066:  ldloc.0
   IL_0067:  ldfld      object DeCompile.DynamicClass::DynValue
   IL_006c:  callvirt   instance void class [mscorlib]System.Action`3
             <class [System.Core]System.Runtime.CompilerServices.CallSite, class
             [mscorlib]System.Type,object>::Invoke(!0,!1,!2)
   IL_0071:  nop
   IL_0072:  call       string [mscorlib]System.Console::ReadLine()
   IL_0077:  pop
   IL_0078:  ret
} // end of method Program::Main
```

So it's safe to say that the C# compiler is doing a little extra work to support the dynamic type. Looking at the generated code, you can see references to System.Runtime.CompilerServices.CallSite and System.Runtime.CompilerServices.CallSiteBinder.

The `CallSite` is a type that handles the lookup at runtime. When a call is made on a dynamic object at runtime, something has to go and look at that object to see if the member really exists. The call site caches this information so the lookup doesn't have to be performed repeatedly. Without this process, performance in looping structures would be questionable.

After the `CallSite` does the member lookup, the `CallSiteBinder` is invoked. It takes the information from the call site and generates an expression tree representing the operation the binder is bound to.

There is obviously a lot going on here. Great care has been taken to optimize what would appear to be a very complex operation. It should be obvious that while using the `dynamic` type can be useful, it does come with a price.

HOSTING THE DLR SCRIPTRUNTIME

Imagine being able to add scripting capabilities to an application. Imagine passing values in and out of the script so the application can take advantage of the work that the script does. These are the kind of capabilities that hosting the DLR's ScriptRuntime in your app gives you. Currently, IronPython, IronRuby, and JavaScript are supported as hosted scripting languages.

With the ScriptRuntime, you have the capability of executing snippets of code or a complete script stored in a file. You can select the proper language engine or allow the DLR to figure out which engine. The script can be created in its own app domain or in the current one. Not only can you pass values in and out of the script, but you can call methods on dynamic objects created in the script.

With this amount of flexibility there are countless uses for hosting the ScriptRuntime. The following example demonstrates one way that the ScriptRuntime can be used. Imagine a shopping cart application. One of the requirements is to calculate a discount based on certain criteria. These discounts change often as new sales campaigns are started and completed. There are many ways of handling such a requirement; this example shows how it could be handled using the ScriptRuntime and a little Python scripting.

For simplicity, the example is a Windows client app. It could be part of a larger web application or any other application. Figure 12-1 shows a sample screen for the application.

The application takes the number of items and the total cost of the items and applies a discount based on which radio button is selected. In a real application the system would use a slightly more sophisticated way to determine the discount to apply, but for this example, the radio buttons will work.

FIGURE 12-1

Here is the code that performs the discount:

```
private void button1_Click(object sender, RoutedEventArgs e)
{
    string scriptToUse;
    if (CostRadioButton.IsChecked.Value)
    {
        scriptToUse = "AmountDisc.py";
    }
    else
    {
        scriptToUse = "CountDisc.py";
    }
    ScriptRuntime scriptRuntime = ScriptRuntime.CreateFromConfiguration();
    ScriptEngine pythEng = scriptRuntime.GetEngine("Python");
```

```
    ScriptSource source = pythEng.CreateScriptSourceFromFile(scriptToUse);
    ScriptScope scope = pythEng.CreateScope();
    scope.SetVariable("prodCount", Convert.ToInt32(totalItems.Text));
    scope.SetVariable("amt", Convert.ToDecimal(totalAmt.Text));
    source.Execute(scope);
    label5.Content = scope.GetVariable("retAmt").ToString();
}
```

code snippet Window1.xaml.cs

The first part is just determining which script to apply, `AmountDisc.py` or `CountDisc.py`. `AmountDisc.py` does the discount based on the amount of the purchase:

```
discAmt = .25
retAmt = amt
if amt > 25.00:
   retAmt = amt-(amt*discAmt)
```

The minimum amount needed for a discount to be applied is $25.00. If the amount is less than that, then no discount is applied, otherwise a discount of 25 percent is applied.

`ContDisc.py` applies the discount based on the number of items purchased:

```
discCount = 5
discAmt = .1
retAmt = amt
if prodCount > discCount:
   retAmt = amt-(amt*discAmt)
```

In this Python script, the number of items purchased must be more than 5 for a 10 percent discount to be applied to the total cost.

The next part is getting the ScriptRuntime environment set up. There are four specific steps that are performed, creating the `ScriptRuntime` object, setting the proper `ScriptEngine`, creating the `ScriptSource`, and creating the `ScriptScope`.

The ScriptRuntime object is the starting point or the base for hosting. It has the global state of the hosting environment. The ScriptRuntime is created using the `CreateFromConfiguration` static method. This is what the `app.config` looks like:

```
<configuration>
  <configSections>
    <section
      name="microsoft.scripting"
      type="Microsoft.Scripting.Hosting.Configuration.Section,
          Microsoft.Scripting,
          Version=0.9.6.10,
          Culture=neutral,
          PublicKeyToken=null"
          requirePermission="false" />
  </configSections>

  <microsoft.scripting>
    <languages>
      <language
        names="IronPython;Python;py"
        extensions=".py"
        displayName="IronPython 2.6 Alpha"
        type="IronPython.Runtime.PythonContext,
            IronPython,
            Version=2.6.0.1,
            Culture=neutral,
            PublicKeyToken=null" />
```

```
    </languages>
  </microsoft.scripting>
</configuration>
```

The code defines a section for "microsoft.scripting" and set a couple of properties for the IronPython language engine.

Next, you get a reference to the `ScriptEngine` from the `ScriptRuntime`. In the example, you specify that you want the Python engine, but the `ScriptRuntime` would have been able to determine this on its own because of the `py` extension on the script.

The `ScriptEngine` does the work of executing the script code. There are several methods for executing scripts from files or from snippets of code. The `ScriptEngine` also gives you the `ScriptSource` and `ScriptScope`.

The `ScriptSource` object is what gives you access to the script. It represents the source code of the script. With it you can manipulate the source of the script. Load it from a disk, parse it line by line, and even compile the script into a `CompiledCode` object. This is handy if the same script is executed multiple times.

The `ScriptScope` object is essentially a namespace. To pass a value into or out of a script, you bind a variable to the `ScriptScope`. In the example, you call the `SetVariable` method to pass into the Python script the `prodCount` variable and the `amt` variable. These are the values from the `totalItems` text box and the `totalAmt` text box. The calculated discount is retrieved from the script by using the `GetVariable` method. In this example, the `retAmt` variable has the value you're looking for.

In the `CalcTax` button you look at how to call a method on a Python object. The script `CalcTax.py` is a very simple method that takes an input value, adds 7.5 percent tax, and returns the new value. Here's what the code looks like:

```
def CalcTax(amount):
    return amount*1.075
```

Here is the C# code to call the `CalcTax` method:

```
private void button2_Click(object sender, RoutedEventArgs e)
{
    ScriptRuntime scriptRuntime = ScriptRuntime.CreateFromConfiguration();
    dynamic calcRate = scriptRuntime.UseFile("CalcTax.py");
    label6.Content = calcRate.CalcTax(Convert.ToDecimal(label5.Content)).ToString();
}
```

A very simple process. Again you create the `ScriptRuntime` object using the same configuration settings as before. `calcRate` is a `ScriptScope` object. You defined it as dynamic so you can easily call the `CalcTax` method. This is an example of the how the dynamic type can make life a little easier.

DYNAMICOBJECT AND EXPANDOOBJECT

What if you want to create your own dynamic object? You have a couple of choices for doing that, by deriving from `DynamicObject` or by using `ExpandoObject`. Using `DynamicObject` will be a little more work because you have to override a couple of methods. `ExpandoObject` is a sealed class that is ready to use.

DynamicObject

Consider an object that represents a person. Normally, you would define properties for the first name, middle name, and last name. Now imagine the capability to build that object during runtime, with the system having no prior knowledge of what properties the object may have or what methods the object may support. That's what having a `DynamicObject`-based object can give you. There may be very few times when you need this sort of functionality, but until now, the C# language had no way of accommodating you.

First let's see what the `DynamicObject` looks like:

```
class WroxDynamicObject : DynamicObject
{
    Dictionary<string, object> _dynamicData = new Dictionary<string, object>();

    public override bool TryGetMember(GetMemberBinder binder, out object result)
    {
        bool success = false;
        result = null;
        if (_dynamicData.ContainsKey(binder.Name))
        {
            result = _dynamicData[binder.Name];
            success = true;
        }
        else
        {
            result = "Property Not Found!";
            success = false;
        }
        return success;
    }

    public override bool TrySetMember(SetMemberBinder binder, object value)
    {
        _dynamicData[binder.Name] = value;
        return true;
    }

    public override bool TryInvokeMember(InvokeMemberBinder binder,
                                         object[] args,
                                         out object result)
    {
        dynamic method = _dynamicData[binder.Name];
        result = method((DateTime)args[0]);
        return result != null;
    }

}
```

code snippet Dynamic\Program.cs

In this example, you're overriding three methods: `TrySetMember`, `TryGetMember`, and `TryInvokeMember`.

`TrySetMember` adds the new method, property, or field to the object. In this example, you store the member information in a `Dictionary` object. The `SetMemberBinder` object that is passed into the `TrySetMember` method contains the `Name` property, which is used to identify the element in the `Dictionary`.

The `TryGetMember` retrieves the object stored in the `Dictionary` based on the `GetMemberBinder` `Name` property.

So how are these used? Here is the code that makes use of the new dynamic object just created:

```
dynamic wroxDyn = new WroxDynamicObject();
wroxDyn.FirstName = "Bugs";
wroxDyn.LastName = "Bunny";
Console.WriteLine(wroxDyn.GetType());
Console.WriteLine("{0} {1}", wroxDyn.FirstName, wroxDyn.LastName);
```

Looks simple enough, but where is the call to the methods you overrode? Well, that's where the .NET Framework helps. `DynamicObject` handles the binding for you; all you have to do is reference the properties `FirstName` and `LastName` as if they were there all the time.

What about adding a method? That can be done easily. You can use the same `WroxDynamicObject` and add a `GetTomorrowDate` method on it. It takes a `DateTime` object and returns a date string that is the next day. Here's the code:

```
dynamic wroxDyn = new WroxDynamicObject();
Func<DateTime, string> GetTomorrow = today => today.AddDays(1).ToShortDateString();
wroxDyn.GetTomorrowDate = GetTomorrow;
Console.WriteLine("Tomorrow is {0}", wroxDyn.GetTomorrowDate(DateTime.Now));
```

You create the delegate `GetTomorrow` using `Func<T, TResult>`. The method the delegate represents is the call to `AddDays`. One day is added to the `Date` that is passed in, and a string of that date is returned. The delegate is then set to `GetTomorrowDate` on the `wroxDyn` object. The last line calls the new method, passing in today's date.

Once again the dynamic magic happens and you have an object with a valid method.

ExpandoObject

`ExpandoObject` works similar to the `WroxDynamicObject` created in the previous section. The difference is that you don't have to override any methods, as shown in the following code example:

```
static void DoExpando()
{
    dynamic expObj = new ExpandoObject();
    expObj.FirstName = "Daffy";
    expObj.LastName = "Duck";
    Console.WriteLine(expObj.FirstName + " " + expObj.LastName);
    Func<DateTime, string> GetTomorrow = today => today.AddDays(1).ToShortDateString();
    expObj.GetTomorrowDate = GetTomorrow;
    Console.WriteLine("Tomorrow is {0}", expObj.GetTomorrowDate(DateTime.Now));

    expObj.Friends = new List<Person>();
    expObj.Friends.Add(new Person() { FirstName = "Bob", LastName = "Jones" });
    expObj.Friends.Add(new Person() { FirstName = "Robert", LastName = "Jones" });
    expObj.Friends.Add(new Person() { FirstName = "Bobby", LastName = "Jones" });

    foreach (Person friend in expObj.Friends)
    {
        Console.WriteLine(friend.FirstName + " " + friend.LastName);
    }
}
```

Notice that this code is almost identical to what you did earlier. You add a `FirstName` and `LastName` property, add a `GetTomorrow` function, and do one additional thing—add a collection of `Person` objects as a property of the object.

At first glance, it may seem that this is no different than using the `dynamic` type. Well, there are a couple of subtle differences that are important. First, you can't just create an empty `dynamic` typed object. The `dynamic` type has to have something assigned to it. For example, the following code won't work:

```
dynamic dynObj;
dynObj.FirstName = "Joe";
```

As seen in the previous example, this is possible with `ExpandoObject`.

Second, because the `dynamic` type has to be assigned to, it will report back the type of what was assigned to it if you do a `GetType` call. So if you say assign an `int`, it will report back that it is an `int`. This won't happen with `ExpandoObject` or an object derived from `DynamicObject`.

If you have to control the addition and access of properties in your dynamic object, then deriving from `DynamicObject` is your best choice. With `DynamicObject`, you can use several methods to override and control exactly how the object interacts with the runtime. For other cases, using the `dynamic` type or the `ExpandoObject` may be just what you need.

SUMMARY

This chapter showed you how the new dynamic type can be used. You also saw what the compiler does when it sees a dynamic type. The Dynamic Language Runtime was discussed and you were able to host it in a simple app. You used Python as a way to use the DLR, and executed Python scripts, passing in and out values for the scripts to use. And finally, you created your own dynamic type by deriving a class from `DynamicObject`.

Dynamic development is becoming very popular. It allows you to do things that are very difficult in a statically typed language. The `dynamic` type and the DLR allow C# programmers to make use of some dynamic capabilities.

13

Memory Management and Pointers

WHAT'S IN THIS CHAPTER?

➤ Allocating space on the stack and heap with runtime

➤ Garbage collection

➤ Releasing unmanaged resources using destructors and the `System.IDisposable` interface

➤ The syntax for using pointers in C#

➤ Using pointers to implement high-performance stack-based arrays

This chapter presents various aspects of memory management and memory access. Although the runtime takes much of the responsibility for memory management away from the programmer, it is useful to understand how memory management works and important to know how to work with unmanaged resources efficiently.

A good understanding of memory management and knowledge of the pointer capabilities provided by C# will better enable you to integrate C# code with legacy code and perform efficient memory manipulation in performance-critical systems.

MEMORY MANAGEMENT UNDER THE HOOD

One of the advantages of C# programming is that the programmer does not need to worry about detailed memory management; the garbage collector deals with the problem of memory cleanup on your behalf. The result is that you get something that approximates the efficiency of languages such as C++ without the complexity of having to handle memory management yourself as you do in C++. However, although you do not have to manage memory manually, it still pays to understand what is going on behind the scenes. Understanding how your program manages memory under the covers will only help you increase the speed and performance of your applications. This section looks at what happens in the computer's memory when you allocate variables.

The precise details of many of the topics of this section are not presented here. You should interpret this section as a simplified guide to the general processes rather than as a statement of exact implementation.

Value Data Types

Windows uses a system known as *virtual addressing*, in which the mapping from the memory address seen by your program to the actual location in hardware memory is entirely managed by Windows. The result of this is that each process on a 32-bit processor sees 4GB of available memory, regardless of how much hardware memory you actually have in your computer (on 64-bit processors this number will be greater). This 4GB of memory contains everything that is part of the program, including the executable code, any DLLs loaded by the code, and the contents of all variables used when the program runs. This 4GB of memory is known as the *virtual address space* or *virtual memory*. For convenience, in this chapter, we call it simply *memory*.

Each memory location in the available 4GB is numbered starting from zero. To access a value stored at a particular location in memory, you need to supply the number that represents that memory location. In any compiled high-level language, including C#, Visual Basic, C++, and Java, the compiler converts human-readable variable names into memory addresses that the processor understands.

Somewhere inside a processor's virtual memory is an area known as the *stack*. The stack stores value data types that are not members of objects. In addition, when you call a method, the stack is used to hold a copy of any parameters passed to the method. To understand how the stack works, you need to understand the importance of variable scope in C#. If variable a goes into scope before variable b, then b will always go out of scope first. Look at this code:

```
{
    int a;
    // do something
    {
        int b;
        // do something else
    }
}
```

First, a gets declared. Then, inside the inner code block, b gets declared. Then the inner code block terminates and b goes out of scope, then a goes out of scope. So, the lifetime of b is entirely contained within the lifetime of a. The idea that you always deallocate variables in the reverse order to how you allocate them is crucial to the way the stack works.

You will also notice that b is in a different block of code (defined by a different nesting of curly braces). For this reason, it is contained within a different scope. This is termed as *block scope* or *structure scope*.

You do not know exactly where in the address space the stack is — you don't need to know for C# development. A *stack pointer* (a variable maintained by the operating system) identifies the next free location on the stack. When your program first starts running, the stack pointer will point to just past the end of the block of memory that is reserved for the stack. The stack actually fills downward, from high memory addresses to low addresses. As data is put on the stack, the stack pointer is adjusted accordingly, so it always points to just past the next free location. This is illustrated in Figure 13-1, which shows a stack pointer with a value of 800000 (0xC3500 in hex); the next free location is the address 799999.

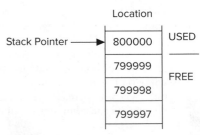

FIGURE 13-1

The following code instructs the compiler that you need space in memory to store an integer and a double, and these memory locations are referred to as nRacingCars and engineSize. The line that declares each variable indicates the point at which you will start requiring access to this variable. The closing curly brace of the block in which the variables are declared identifies the point at which both variables go out of scope:

```
{
    int nRacingCars = 10;
    double engineSize = 3000.0;
    // do calculations;
}
```

Assuming that you use the stack shown in Figure 13-1, when the variable nRacingCars comes into scope and is assigned the value 10, the value 10 is placed in locations 799996 through 799999, the 4 bytes just below the location pointed to by the stack pointer (four bytes because that's how much memory is needed to store an int.) To accommodate this, 4 is subtracted from the value of the stack pointer, so it now points to the location 799996, just after the new first free location (799995).

The next line of code declares the variable engineSize (a double) and initializes it to the value 3000.0. A double occupies 8 bytes, so the value 3000.0 is placed in locations 799988 through 799995 on the stack, and the stack pointer is decremented by 8, so that once again, it points to the location just after the next free location on the stack.

When engineSize goes out of scope, the computer knows that it is no longer needed. Because of the way variable lifetimes are always nested, you can guarantee that, whatever happened while engineSize was in scope, the stack pointer is now pointing to the location where engineSize is stored. To remove engineSize from the stack, the stack pointer is incremented by 8 and it now points to the location immediately after the end of engineSize. At this point in the code, you are at the closing curly brace, so nRacingCars also goes out of scope. The stack pointer is incremented by 4. When another variable comes into scope after engineSize and nRacingCars have been removed from the stack, it overwrites the memory descending from location 799999, where nRacingCars was stored.

If the compiler hits a line such as int i, j, then the order of variables coming into scope looks indeterminate. Both variables are declared at the same time and go out of scope at the same time. In this situation, it does not matter in what order the two variables are removed from memory. The compiler internally always ensures that the one that was put in memory first is removed last, thus preserving the rule about no crossover of variable lifetimes.

Reference Data Types

Although the stack gives very high performance, it is not flexible enough to be used for all variables. The requirement that the lifetimes of variables must be nested is too restrictive for many purposes. Often, you need to use a method to allocate memory for storing data and keeping that data available long after that method has exited. This possibility exists whenever storage space is requested with the new operator — as is the case for all reference types. That is where the *managed heap* comes in.

If you have done any C++ coding that required low-level memory management, you are familiar with the heap. The managed heap is not quite the same as the heap C++ uses; the managed heap works under the control of the garbage collector and provides significant benefits when compared to traditional heaps.

The managed heap (or heap for short) is just another area of memory from the processor's available 4GB. The following code demonstrates how the heap works and how memory is allocated for reference data types:

```
void DoWork()
{
    Customer arabel;
    arabel = new Customer();
    Customer otherCustomer2 = new EnhancedCustomer();
}
```

This code assumes the existence of two classes, `Customer` and `EnhancedCustomer`. The `EnhancedCustomer` class extends the `Customer` class.

First, you declare a `Customer` reference called `arabel`. The space for this is allocated on the stack, but remember that this is only a reference, not an actual `Customer` object. The `arabel` reference takes up 4 bytes, enough space to hold the address at which a `Customer` object will be stored. (You need 4 bytes to represent a memory address as an integer value between 0 and 4GB.)

The next line,

```
arabel = new Customer();
```

does several things. First, it allocates memory on the heap to store a `Customer` object (a real object, not just an address). Then it sets the value of the variable `arabel` to the address of the memory it has allocated to the new `Customer` object. (It also calls the appropriate `Customer()` constructor to initialize the fields in the class instance, but we won't worry about that here.)

The `Customer` instance is not placed on the stack — it is placed on the heap. In this example, you don't know precisely how many bytes a `Customer` object occupies, but assume for the sake of argument that it is 32. These 32 bytes contain the instance fields of `Customer` as well as some information that .NET uses to identify and manage its class instances.

To find a storage location on the heap for the new `Customer` object, the .NET runtime looks through the heap and grabs the first adjacent, unused block of 32 bytes. Again for the sake of argument, assume that this happens to be at address `200000`, and that the `arabel` reference occupied locations `799996` through `799999` on the stack. This means that before instantiating the `arabel` object, the memory content will look similar to Figure 13-2.

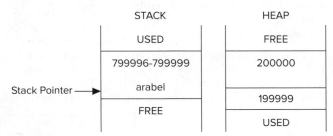

FIGURE 13-2

After allocating the new `Customer` object, the content of memory will look like Figure 13-3. Note that unlike the stack, memory in the heap is allocated upward, so the free space can be found above the used space.

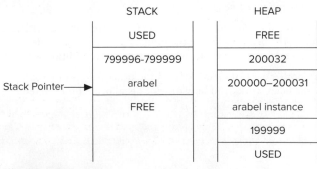

FIGURE 13-3

The next line of code both declares a `Customer` reference and instantiates a `Customer` object. In this instance, space on the stack for the `otherCustomer2` reference is allocated and space for the `mrJones` object is allocated on the heap in a single line of code:

```
Customer otherCustomer2 = new EnhancedCustomer();
```

This line allocates 4 bytes on the stack to hold the `otherCustomer2` reference, stored at locations `799992` through `799995`. The `otherCustomer2` object is allocated space on the heap starting at location `200032`.

It is clear from the example that the process of setting up a reference variable is more complex than that for setting up a value variable, and there is a performance overhead. In fact, the process is somewhat oversimplified here, because the .NET runtime needs to maintain information about the state of the heap, and this information needs to be updated whenever new data is added to the heap. Despite this overhead, you now have a mechanism for allocating variables that is not constrained by the limitations of the stack. By assigning the value of one reference variable to another of the same type, you have two variables that reference the same object in memory. When a reference variable goes out of scope, it is removed from the stack as described in the previous section, but the data for a referenced object is still sitting on the heap. The data will remain on the heap until either the program terminates or the garbage collector removes it, which will happen only when it is no longer referenced by any variables.

That is the power of reference data types, and you will see this feature used extensively in C# code. It means that you have a high degree of control over the lifetime of your data, because it is guaranteed to exist in the heap as long as you are maintaining some reference to it.

Garbage Collection

The previous discussion and diagrams show the managed heap working very much like the stack, to the extent that successive objects are placed next to each other in memory. This means that you can work out where to place the next object by using a heap pointer that indicates the next free memory location, and that is adjusted as you add more objects to the heap. However, things are complicated because the lives of the heap-based objects are not coupled to the scope of the individual stack-based variables that reference them.

When the garbage collector runs, it removes all those objects from the heap that are no longer referenced. Immediately after it has done this, the heap will have objects scattered on it, mixed up with memory that has just been freed (see Figure 13-4).

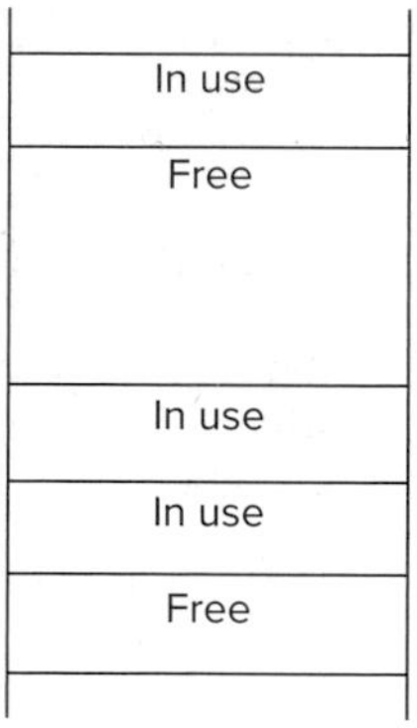

If the managed heap stayed like this, allocating space for new objects would be an awkward process, with the runtime having to search through the heap for a block of memory big enough to store each new object. However, the garbage collector does not leave the heap in this state. As soon as the garbage collector has freed up all the objects it can, it compacts the heap by moving all remaining objects to form one continuous block of memory. This means that the heap can continue working just like the stack, as far as locating where to store new objects. Of course, when the objects are moved about, all the references to those objects need to be updated with the correct new addresses, but the garbage collector handles that too.

FIGURE 13-4

This action of compacting by the garbage collector is where the managed heap really works differently from old, unmanaged heaps. With the managed heap, it is just a question of reading the value of the heap pointer, rather than iterating through a linked list of addresses to find somewhere to put the new data. For this reason, instantiating an object under .NET is much faster. Interestingly, accessing objects tends to be faster too, because the objects are compacted toward the same area of memory on the heap, resulting in less page swapping. Microsoft believes that these performance gains more than compensate for the performance penalty that you get whenever the garbage collector needs to do some work to compact the heap and change all those references to objects it has moved.

Generally, the garbage collector runs when the .NET runtime determines that garbage collection is required. You can force the garbage collector to run at a certain point in your code by calling System.GC.Collect(). *The* System.GC *class is a .NET class that represents the garbage collector, and the* Collect() *method initiates a garbage collection. The* GC *class is intended for rare situations in which you know that it's a good time to call the garbage collector; for example, if you have just de-referenced a large number of objects in your code. However, the logic of the garbage collector does not guarantee that all unreferenced objects will be removed from the heap in a single garbage collection pass.*

When the garbage collector runs, it actually hurts the performance of your application as it is impossible for your application to continue running while the garbage collector finishes its tasks. Use the .NET garbage collector to make this less of a problem, as it is a *generational garbage collector.*

When objects are created, they are placed within the managed heap. The first section of the heap is called the generation 0 section or gen 0. As your new objects are created, they are moved into this section of the heap. Therefore, this is where the youngest objects reside.

Your objects are there until the first collection of objects occurs through the garbage collection process. The objects that remain alive after this cleansing are compacted and then moved to the next section or generational part of the heap — the generation 1 or gen 1 section.

At this point, the generation 0 section is empty, and all new objects are again placed in this section. Older objects that survived the GC (garbage collection) process are found further down in the generation 1 section. This movement of aged items actually occurs one more time. The next collection process that occurs is then repeated. This means that the items that survived the GC process from the generation 1 section are moved to the generation 2 section, and the gen 0 items go to gen 1, again leaving gen 0 open for new objects.

It is interesting to note that a garbage collection will occur when you allocate an item that exceeds the capacity of the generation 0 section or when a GC.Collect() *is called.*

This process greatly improves the performance of your application. It is generally observed that your youngest objects are usually the ones that can be collected and that there are a large number of younger-related objects that might be reclaimed as well. If these objects reside next to each other in the heap, then the garbage collection process will be faster. In addition, the fact that related objects are residing next to each other will also make program execution faster all around.

Another area in the performance realm of garbage collection in .NET is in how the framework deals with larger objects that go onto the heap. Under the covers of .NET, larger objects have their own managed heap, referred to as the Large Object Heap. When objects greater than 85,000 bytes are utilized, they go to this special heap rather than the main heap. Your .NET application doesn't know the difference, as this is all managed for you. The reason for this is that compressing large items in the heap is expensive and therefore isn't done for the objects residing in the Large Object Heap.

FREEING UNMANAGED RESOURCES

The presence of the garbage collector means that you will usually not worry about objects that you no longer need; you will simply allow all references to those objects to go out of scope and allow the garbage collector to free memory as required. However, the garbage collector does not know how to free unmanaged resources (such as file handles, network connections, and database connections). When managed classes encapsulate direct or indirect references to unmanaged resources, you need to make special provisions to ensure that the unmanaged resources are released when an instance of the class is garbage collected.

When defining a class, you can use two mechanisms to automate the freeing of unmanaged resources. These mechanisms are often implemented together because each provides a slightly different approach to the solution of the problem. The mechanisms are:

➤ Declaring a *destructor* (or finalizer) as a member of your class

➤ Implementing the System.IDisposable interface in your class

The following sections discuss each of these mechanisms in turn, and then look at how to implement them together for best effect.

Destructors

You have seen that constructors allow you to specify actions that must take place whenever an instance of a class is created. Conversely, destructors are called before an object is destroyed by the garbage collector. Given this behavior, a destructor would initially seem like a great place to put code to free unmanaged resources and perform a general cleanup. Unfortunately, things are not so straightforward.

 Although we talk about destructors *in C#, in the underlying .NET architecture these are known as* finalizers. *When you define a destructor in C#, what is emitted into the assembly by the compiler is actually a* Finalize() *method. It doesn't affect any of your source code, but you need to be aware of it when examining the content of an assembly.*

The syntax for a destructor will be familiar to C++ developers. It looks like a method, with the same name as the containing class, but prefixed with a tilde (~). It has no return type, and takes no parameters and no access modifiers. Here is an example:

```
class MyClass
{
    ~MyClass()
    {
        // destructor implementation
    }
}
```

When the C# compiler compiles a destructor, it implicitly translates the destructor code to the equivalent of a Finalize() method, which ensures that the Finalize() method of the parent class is executed. The following example shows the C# code equivalent to the Intermediate Language (IL) that the compiler would generate for the ~MyClass destructor:

```
protected override void Finalize()
{
    try
    {
        // destructor implementation
    }
    finally
    {
        base.Finalize();
    }
}
```

As shown, the code implemented in the ~MyClass destructor is wrapped in a try block contained in the Finalize() method. A call to the parent's Finalize() method is ensured by placing the call in a finally block. We discuss try and finally blocks in Chapter 15, "Errors and Exceptions."

Experienced C++ developers make extensive use of destructors, sometimes not only to clean up resources but also to provide debugging information or perform other tasks. C# destructors are used far less than their C++ equivalents. The problem with C# destructors as compared to their C++ counterparts is that they are nondeterministic. When a C++ object is destroyed, its destructor runs immediately. However, because of the way the garbage collector works when using C#, there is no way to know when an object's destructor will actually execute. Hence, you cannot place any code in the destructor that relies on being run at a certain time, and you should not rely on the destructor being called for different class instances in any particular order. When your object is holding scarce and critical resources that need to be freed as soon as possible, you do not want to wait for garbage collection.

Another problem with C# destructors is that the implementation of a destructor delays the final removal of an object from memory. Objects that do not have a destructor are removed from memory in one pass of the garbage collector, but objects that have destructors require two passes to be destroyed: The first pass calls the destructor without removing the object, and the second pass actually deletes the object. In addition, the runtime uses a single thread to execute the Finalize() methods of all objects. If you use destructors frequently, and use them to execute lengthy cleanup tasks, the impact on performance can be noticeable.

The IDisposable Interface

In C#, the recommended alternative to using a destructor is using the System.IDisposable interface. The IDisposable interface defines a pattern (with language-level support) that provides a deterministic mechanism for freeing unmanaged resources and avoids the garbage collector–related problems inherent with destructors. The IDisposable interface declares a single method named Dispose(), which takes no parameters and returns void. Here is an implementation for MyClass:

```
class MyClass: IDisposable
{
    public void Dispose()
    {
        // implementation
    }
}
```

The implementation of Dispose() should explicitly free all unmanaged resources used directly by an object and call Dispose() on any encapsulated objects that also implement the IDisposable interface. In this way, the Dispose() method provides precise control over when unmanaged resources are freed.

Suppose that you have a class named ResourceGobbler, which relies on the use of some external resource and implements IDisposable. If you want to instantiate an instance of this class, use it, and then dispose of it, you could do it like this:

```
ResourceGobbler theInstance = new ResourceGobbler();

// do your processing

theInstance.Dispose();
```

Unfortunately, this code fails to free the resources consumed by theInstance if an exception occurs during processing, so you should write the code as follows using a try block (which is discussed fully in Chapter 15):

```
ResourceGobbler theInstance = null;

try
{
    theInstance = new ResourceGobbler();
```

```
        // do your processing
    }
    finally
    {
        if (theInstance != null)
        {
            theInstance.Dispose();
        }
    }
```

This version ensures that `Dispose()` is always called on `theInstance` and that any resources consumed by it are always freed, even if an exception occurs during processing. However, it would make for confusing code if you always had to repeat such a construct. C# offers a syntax that you can use to guarantee that `Dispose()` will automatically be called against an object that implements `IDisposable` when its reference goes out of scope. The syntax to do this involves the `using` keyword — though now in a very different context, which has nothing to do with namespaces. The following code generates IL code equivalent to the `try` block just shown:

```
using (ResourceGobbler theInstance = new ResourceGobbler())
{
    // do your processing
}
```

The `using` statement, followed in brackets by a reference variable declaration and instantiation, will cause that variable to be scoped to the accompanying statement block. In addition, when that variable goes out of scope, its `Dispose()` method will be called automatically, even if an exception occurs. However, if you are already using `try` blocks to catch other exceptions, it is cleaner and avoids additional code indentation if you avoid the `using` statement and simply call `Dispose()` in the `Finally` clause of the existing `try` block.

 For some classes, the notion of a `Close()` *method is more logical than* `Dispose()`; *for example, when dealing with files or database connections. In these cases, it is common to implement the* `IDisposable` *interface and then implement a separate* `Close()` *method that simply calls* `Dispose()`. *This approach provides clarity in the use of your classes but also supports the* `using` *statement provided by C#.*

Implementing IDisposable and a Destructor

The previous sections discussed two alternatives for freeing unmanaged resources used by the classes you create:

➤   The execution of a destructor is enforced by the runtime but is nondeterministic and places an unacceptable overhead on the runtime because of the way garbage collection works.

➤   The `IDisposable` interface provides a mechanism that allows users of a class to control when resources are freed but requires discipline to ensure that `Dispose()` is called.

In general, the best approach is to implement both mechanisms to gain the benefits of both while overcoming their limitations. You implement `IDisposable` on the assumption that most programmers will call `Dispose()` correctly, but implement a destructor as a safety mechanism in case `Dispose()` is not called. Here is an example of a dual implementation:

```
using System;

public class ResourceHolder: IDisposable
{

    private bool isDisposed = false;
```

```
public void Dispose()
{
    Dispose(true);
    GC.SuppressFinalize(this);
}

protected virtual void Dispose(bool disposing)
{
    if (!isDisposed)
    {
        if (disposing)
        {
            // Cleanup managed objects by calling their
            // Dispose() methods.
        }
        // Cleanup unmanaged objects
    }
    isDisposed = true;
}

~ResourceHolder()
{
    Dispose (false);
}

public void SomeMethod()
{
    // Ensure object not already disposed before execution of any method
    if(isDisposed)
    {
        throw new ObjectDisposedException("ResourceHolder");
    }

    // method implementation...
}
}
```

code snippet ResourceHolder.cs

You can see from this code that there is a second `protected` overload of `Dispose()`, which takes one `bool` parameter — and this is the method that does all the cleaning up. `Dispose(bool)` is called by both the destructor and by `IDisposable.Dispose()`. The point of this approach is to ensure that all cleanup code is in one place.

The parameter passed to `Dispose(bool)` indicates whether `Dispose(bool)` has been invoked by the destructor or by `IDisposable.Dispose()` — `Dispose(bool)` should not be invoked from anywhere else in your code. The idea is this:

➤ If a consumer calls `IDisposable.Dispose()`, that consumer is indicating that all managed and unmanaged resources associated with that object should be cleaned up.

➤ If a destructor has been invoked, all resources still need to be cleaned up. However, in this case, you know that the destructor must have been called by the garbage collector and you should not attempt to access other managed objects because you can no longer be certain of their state. In this situation, the best you can do is clean up the known unmanaged resources and hope that any referenced managed objects also have destructors that will perform their own cleaning up.

The `isDisposed` member variable indicates whether the object has already been disposed of and ensures that you do not try to dispose of member variables more than once. It also allows you to test whether an object has been disposed of before executing any instance methods, as shown in `SomeMethod()`. This simplistic approach is not thread-safe and depends on the caller ensuring that only one thread is calling the method concurrently. Requiring a consumer to enforce synchronization is a reasonable assumption and one that is used repeatedly throughout the .NET class libraries (in the `Collection` classes, for example). Threading and synchronization are discussed in Chapter 20, "Threads, Tasks, and Synchronization."

Finally, `IDisposable.Dispose()` contains a call to the method `System.GC.SuppressFinalize()`. `GC` is the class that represents the garbage collector, and the `SuppressFinalize()` method tells the garbage collector that a class no longer needs to have its destructor called. Because your implementation of `Dispose()` has already done all the cleanup required, there's nothing left for the destructor to do. Calling `SuppressFinalize()` means that the garbage collector will treat that object as if it doesn't have a destructor at all.

UNSAFE CODE

As you have just seen, C# is very good at hiding much of the basic memory management from the developer, thanks to the garbage collector and the use of references. However, sometimes you will want direct access to memory. For example, you might want to access a function in an external (non-.NET) DLL that requires a pointer to be passed as a parameter (as many Windows API functions do), or possibly for performance reasons. This section examines the C# facilities that provide direct access to the content of memory.

Accessing Memory Directly with Pointers

Although we are introducing *pointers* as if they were a new topic, in reality pointers are not new at all. You have been using references freely in your code, and a reference is simply a type-safe pointer. You have already seen how variables that represent objects and arrays actually store the memory address of where the corresponding data (the *referent*) is stored. A pointer is simply a variable that stores the address of something else in the same way as a reference. The difference is that C# does not allow you direct access to the address contained in a reference variable. With a reference, the variable is treated syntactically as if it stores the actual content of the referent.

C# references are designed to make the language simpler to use and to prevent you from inadvertently doing something that corrupts the contents of memory. With a pointer, however, the actual memory address is available to you. This gives you a lot of power to perform new kinds of operations. For example, you can add 4 bytes to the address, so that you can examine or even modify whatever data happens to be stored 4 bytes further on in memory.

The two main reasons for using pointers are:

> ➤ **Backward compatibility** — Despite all the facilities provided by the .NET runtime, it is still possible to call native Windows API functions, and for some operations this may be the only way to accomplish your task. These API functions are generally written in C and often require pointers as parameters. However, in many cases it is possible to write the `DllImport` declaration in a way that avoids use of pointers; for example, by using the `System.IntPtr` class.

> ➤ **Performance** — On those occasions where speed is of the utmost importance, pointers can provide a route to optimized performance. If you know what you are doing, you can ensure that data is accessed or manipulated in the most efficient way. However, be aware that more often than not, there are other areas of your code where you can make the necessary performance improvements without resorting to using pointers. Try using a code profiler to look for the bottlenecks in your code — one comes with Visual Studio.

Low-level memory access comes at a price. The syntax for using pointers is more complex than that for reference types, and pointers are unquestionably more difficult to use correctly. You need good programming skills and an excellent ability to think carefully and logically about what your code is doing to use pointers successfully. If you are not careful, it is very easy to introduce subtle, difficult-to-find bugs into your program when using pointers. For example, it is easy to overwrite other variables, cause stack overflows, access areas of memory that don't store any variables, or even overwrite information about your code that is needed by the .NET runtime, thereby crashing your program.

In addition, if you use pointers your code must be granted a high level of trust by the runtime's code access security mechanism or it will not be allowed to execute. Under the default code access security policy, this is only possible if your code is running on the local machine. If your code must be run from a remote location, such as the Internet, users must grant your code additional permissions for it to work. Unless the users trust you and your code, they are unlikely to grant these permissions. Code access security is discussed more in Chapter 21, "Security."

Despite these issues, pointers remain a very powerful and flexible tool in the writing of efficient code.

 We strongly advise against using pointers unnecessarily because your code will not only be harder to write and debug, but it will also fail the memory type-safety–checks imposed by the CLR, which is discussed in Chapter 1, ".NET Architecture."

Writing Unsafe Code with the unsafe Keyword

As a result of the risks associated with pointers, C# allows the use of pointers only in blocks of code that you have specifically marked for this purpose. The keyword to do this is `unsafe`. You can mark an individual method as being `unsafe` like this:

```
unsafe int GetSomeNumber()
{
    // code that can use pointers
}
```

Any method can be marked as `unsafe`, regardless of what other modifiers have been applied to it (for example, `static` methods or `virtual` methods). In the case of methods, the `unsafe` modifier applies to the method's parameters, allowing you to use pointers as parameters. You can also mark an entire class or struct as `unsafe`, which means that all of its members are assumed unsafe:

```
unsafe class MyClass
{
    // any method in this class can now use pointers
}
```

Similarly, you can mark a member as `unsafe`:

```
class MyClass
{
    unsafe int* pX;    // declaration of a pointer field in a class
}
```

Or you can mark a block of code within a method as `unsafe`:

```
void MyMethod()
{
    // code that doesn't use pointers
    unsafe
    {
        // unsafe code that uses pointers here
    }
    // more 'safe' code that doesn't use pointers
}
```

Note, however, that you cannot mark a local variable by itself as `unsafe`:

```
int MyMethod()
{
    unsafe int *pX;    // WRONG
}
```

If you want to use an unsafe local variable, you need to declare and use it inside a method or block that is unsafe. There is one more step before you can use pointers. The C# compiler rejects unsafe code unless you tell it that your code includes unsafe blocks. The flag to do this is `unsafe`. Hence, to compile a file named `MySource.cs` that contains unsafe blocks (assuming no other compiler options), the command is this:

```
csc /unsafe MySource.cs
```

or this:

```
csc -unsafe MySource.cs
```

If you are using Visual Studio 2005, 2008, or 2010, you will also find the option to compile unsafe code in the Build tab of the project properties window.

Pointer Syntax

After you have marked a block of code as `unsafe`, you can declare a pointer using this syntax:

```
int* pWidth, pHeight;
double* pResult;
byte*[] pFlags;
```

This code declares four variables: `pWidth` and `pHeight` are pointers to integers, `pResult` is a pointer to a `double`, and `pFlags` is an array of pointers to bytes. It is common practice to use the prefix `p` in front of names of pointer variables to indicate that they are pointers. When used in a variable declaration, the symbol `*` indicates that you are declaring a pointer (that is, something that stores the address of a variable of the specified type).

C++ developers should be aware of the syntax difference between C++ and C#. The C# statement `int* pX, pY;` *corresponds to the C++ statement* `int *pX, *pY;`. *In C#, the * symbol is associated with the type rather than the variable name.*

When you have declared variables of pointer types, you can use them in the same way as normal variables, but first you need to learn two more operators:

➤ `&` means *take the address of*, and converts a value data type to a pointer, for example `int` to `*int`. This operator is known as the *address operator*.

➤ `*` means *get the content of this address*, and converts a pointer to a value data type (for example, `*float` to `float`). This operator is known as the *indirection operator* (or sometimes as the *dereference operator*).

You will see from these definitions that `&` and `*` have opposite effects.

*You might be wondering how it is possible to use the symbols & and * in this manner because these symbols also refer to the operators of bitwise AND (&) and multiplication (*). Actually, it is always possible for both you and the compiler to know what is meant in each case because with the new pointer meanings, these symbols always appear as unary operators — they act on only one variable and appear in front of that variable in your code. By contrast, bitwise AND and multiplication are binary operators — they require two operands.*

The following code shows examples of how to use these operators:

```
int x = 10;
int* pX, pY;
pX = &x;
pY = pX;
*pY = 20;
```

You start by declaring an integer, x, with the value 10 followed by two pointers to integers, pX and pY. You then set pX to point to x (that is, you set the content of pX to the address of x). Then you assign the value of pX to pY, so that pY also points to x. Finally, in the statement *pY = 20, you assign the value 20 as the contents of the location pointed to by pY — in effect changing x to 20 because pY happens to point to x. Note that there is no particular connection between the variables pY and x. It is just that at the present time, pY happens to point to the memory location at which x is held.

To get a better understanding of what is going on, consider that the integer x is stored at memory locations 0x12F8C4 through 0x12F8C7 (1243332 to 1243335 in decimal) on the stack (there are four locations because an int occupies 4 bytes). Because the stack allocates memory downward, this means that the variables pX will be stored at locations 0x12F8C0 to 0x12F8C3, and pY will end up at locations 0x12F8BC to 0x12F8BF. Note that pX and pY also occupy 4 bytes each. That is not because an int occupies 4 bytes. It is because on a 32-bit processor you need 4 bytes to store an address. With these addresses, after executing the previous code, the stack will look like Figure 13-5.

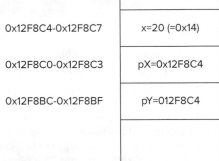

FIGURE 13-5

 Although this process is illustrated with integers, which will be stored consecutively on the stack on a 32-bit processor, this does not happen for all data types. The reason is that 32-bit processors work best when retrieving data from memory in 4-byte chunks. Memory on such machines tends to be divided into 4-byte blocks, and each block is sometimes known under Windows as a DWORD because this was the name of a 32-bit unsigned int *in pre-.NET days. It is most efficient to grab DWORDs from memory — storing data across DWORD boundaries normally results in a hardware performance hit. For this reason, the .NET runtime normally pads out data types so that the memory they occupy is a multiple of 4. For example, a short occupies 2 bytes, but if a short is placed on the stack, the stack pointer will still be decremented by 4, not 2, so that the next variable to go on the stack will still start at a DWORD boundary.*

You can declare a pointer to any value type (that is, any of the predefined types uint, int, byte, and so on, or to a struct). However, it is not possible to declare a pointer to a class or an array; this is because doing so could cause problems for the garbage collector. To work properly, the garbage collector needs to know exactly what class instances have been created on the heap, and where they are, but if your code started manipulating classes using pointers, you could very easily corrupt the information on the heap concerning classes that the .NET runtime maintains for the garbage collector. In this context, any data type that the garbage collector can access is known as a *managed type*. Pointers can only be declared as *unmanaged types* because the garbage collector cannot deal with them.

Casting Pointers to Integer Types

Because a pointer really stores an integer that represents an address, you won't be surprised to know that the address in any pointer can be converted to or from any integer type. Pointer-to-integer-type conversions must be explicit. Implicit conversions are not available for such conversions. For example, it is perfectly legitimate to write the following:

```
int x = 10;
int* pX, pY;
pX = &x;
pY = pX;
*pY = 20;
uint y = (uint)pX;
int* pD = (int*)y;
```

The address held in the pointer pX is cast to a uint and stored in the variable y. You have then cast y back to an int* and stored it in the new variable pD. Hence, now pD also points to the value of x.

The primary reason for casting a pointer value to an integer type is to display it. The Console.Write() and Console.WriteLine() methods do not have any overloads that can take pointers, but will accept and display pointer values that have been cast to integer types:

```
Console.WriteLine("Address is " + pX);     // wrong -- will give a
                                           // compilation error
Console.WriteLine("Address is " + (uint)pX);   // OK
```

You can cast a pointer to any of the integer types. However, because an address occupies 4 bytes on 32-bit systems, casting a pointer to anything other than a uint, long, or ulong is almost certain to lead to overflow errors. (An int causes problems because its range is from roughly –2 billion to 2 billion, whereas an address runs from zero to about 4 billion.) When C# is released for 64-bit processors, an address will occupy 8 bytes. Hence, on such systems, casting a pointer to anything other than ulong is likely to lead to overflow errors. It is also important to be aware that the checked keyword does not apply to conversions involving pointers. For such conversions, exceptions will not be raised when overflows occur, even in a checked context. The .NET runtime assumes that if you are using pointers you know what you are doing, and are not worried about possible overflows.

Casting Between Pointer Types

You can also explicitly convert between pointers pointing to different types. For example:

```
byte aByte = 8;
byte* pByte= &aByte;
double* pDouble = (double*)pByte;
```

This is perfectly legal code, though again, if you try something like this, be careful. In this example, if you look at the double value pointed to by pDouble, you will actually be looking up some memory that contains a byte (aByte), combined with some other memory, and treating it as if this area of memory contained a double, which will not give you a meaningful value. However, you might want to convert between types to implement the equivalent of a C union, or you might want to cast pointers from other types into pointers to sbyte to examine individual bytes of memory.

void Pointers

If you want to maintain a pointer, but do not want to specify what type of data it points to, you can declare it as a pointer to a void:

```
int* pointerToInt;
void* pointerToVoid;
pointerToVoid = (void*)pointerToInt;
```

The main use of this is if you need to call an API function that requires void* parameters. Within the C# language, there isn't a great deal that you can do using void pointers. In particular, the compiler will flag an error if you attempt to dereference a void pointer using the * operator.

Pointer Arithmetic

It is possible to add or subtract integers to and from pointers. However, the compiler is quite clever about how it arranges this. For example, suppose that you have a pointer to an int and you try to add 1 to its value. The compiler will assume that you actually mean you want to look at the memory location following the int, and hence it will increase the value by 4 bytes — the size of an int. If it is a pointer to a double, adding 1 will actually increase the value of the pointer by 8 bytes, the size of a double. Only if the pointer points to a byte or sbyte (1 byte each), will adding 1 to the value of the pointer actually change its value by 1.

You can use the operators +, -, +=, -=, ++, and -- with pointers, with the variable on the right side of these operators being a long or ulong.

 It is not permitted to carry out arithmetic operations on void pointers.

For example, assume these definitions:

```
uint u = 3;
byte b = 8;
double d = 10.0;
uint* pUint= &u;        // size of a uint is 4
byte* pByte = &b;       // size of a byte is 1
double* pDouble = &d;   // size of a double is 8
```

Next, assume the addresses to which these pointers point are:

➤ pUint: 1243332

➤ pByte: 1243328

➤ pDouble: 1243320

Then execute this code:

```
++pUint;                // adds (1*4) = 4 bytes to pUint
pByte -= 3;             // subtracts (3*1) = 3 bytes from pByte
double* pDouble2 = pDouble + 4; // pDouble2 = pDouble + 32 bytes (4*8 bytes)
```

The pointers now contain this:

➤ pUint: 1243336

➤ pByte: 1243325

➤ pDouble2: 1243352

 The general rule is that adding a number X to a pointer to type T with value P gives the result P + X*(sizeof(T)).

 You need to be aware of the previous rule. If successive values of a given type are stored in successive memory locations, pointer addition works very well, allowing you to move pointers between memory locations. If you are dealing with types such as byte or char, though, with sizes not in multiples of 4, successive values will not, by default, be stored in successive memory locations.

You can also subtract one pointer from another pointer, if both pointers point to the same data type. In this case, the result is a `long` whose value is given by the difference between the pointer values divided by the size of the type that they represent:

```
double* pD1 = (double*)1243324;    // note that it is perfectly valid to
                                   // initialize a pointer like this.
double* pD2 = (double*)1243300;
long L = pD1-pD2;                  // gives the result 3 (=24/sizeof(double))
```

The sizeof Operator

This section has been referring to the sizes of various data types. If you need to use the size of a type in your code, you can use the `sizeof` operator, which takes the name of a data type as a parameter and returns the number of bytes occupied by that type. For example:

```
int x = sizeof(double);
```

This will set x to the value 8.

The advantage of using `sizeof` is that you don't have to hard-code data type sizes in your code, making your code more portable. For the predefined data types, `sizeof` returns the following values:

```
sizeof(sbyte) = 1;  sizeof(byte) = 1;
sizeof(short) = 2;  sizeof(ushort) = 2;
sizeof(int) = 4;    sizeof(uint) = 4;
sizeof(long) = 8;   sizeof(ulong) = 8;
sizeof(char) = 2;   sizeof(float) = 4;
sizeof(double) = 8; sizeof(bool) = 1;
```

You can also use `sizeof` for structs that you define yourself, although in that case, the result depends on what fields are in the struct. You cannot use `sizeof` for classes.

Pointers to Structs: The Pointer Member Access Operator

Pointers to structs work in exactly the same way as pointers to the predefined value types. There is, however, one condition — the struct must not contain any reference types. This is due to the restriction mentioned earlier that pointers cannot point to any reference types. To avoid this, the compiler will flag an error if you create a pointer to any struct that contains any reference types.

Suppose that you had a struct defined like this:

```
struct MyStruct
{
    public long X;
    public float F;
}
```

You could define a pointer to it like this:

```
MyStruct* pStruct;
```

Then you could initialize it like this:

```
MyStruct Struct = new MyStruct();
pStruct = &Struct;
```

It is also possible to access member values of a struct through the pointer:

```
(*pStruct).X = 4;
(*pStruct).F = 3.4f;
```

However, this syntax is a bit complex. For this reason, C# defines another operator that allows you to access members of structs through pointers using a simpler syntax. It is known as the *pointer member access operator*, and the symbol is a dash followed by a greater-than sign, so it looks like an arrow: `->`.

C++ developers will recognize the pointer member access operator because C++ uses the same symbol for the same purpose.

Using the pointer member access operator, the previous code can be rewritten:

```
pStruct->X = 4;
pStruct->F = 3.4f;
```

You can also directly set up pointers of the appropriate type to point to fields within a struct:

```
long* pL = &(Struct.X);
float* pF = &(Struct.F);
```

or:

```
long* pL = &(pStruct->X);
float* pF = &(pStruct->F);
```

Pointers to Class Members

As indicated earlier, it is not possible to create pointers to classes. That is because the garbage collector does not maintain any information about pointers, only about references, so creating pointers to classes could cause garbage collection to not work properly.

However, most classes do contain value type members, and you might want to create pointers to them. This is possible but requires a special syntax. For example, suppose that you rewrite the struct from the previous example as a class:

```
class MyClass
{
    public long X;
    public float F;
}
```

Then you might want to create pointers to its fields, X and F, in the same way as you did earlier. Unfortunately, doing so will produce a compilation error:

```
MyClass myObject = new MyClass();
long* pL = &(myObject.X);    // wrong -- compilation error
float* pF = &(myObject.F);   // wrong -- compilation error
```

Although X and F are unmanaged types, they are embedded in an object, which sits on the heap. During garbage collection, the garbage collector might move MyObject to a new location, which would leave pL and pF pointing to the wrong memory addresses. Because of this, the compiler will not let you assign addresses of members of managed types to pointers in this manner.

The solution is to use the fixed keyword, which tells the garbage collector that there may be pointers referencing members of certain objects, so those objects must not be moved. The syntax for using fixed looks like this if you just want to declare one pointer:

```
MyClass myObject = new MyClass();
fixed (long* pObject = &(myObject.X))
{
    // do something
}
```

You define and initialize the pointer variable in the brackets following the keyword fixed. This pointer variable (pObject in the example) is scoped to the fixed block identified by the curly braces. As a result, the garbage collector knows not to move the myObject object while the code inside the fixed block is executing.

If you want to declare more than one pointer, you can place multiple `fixed` statements before the same code block:

```
MyClass myObject = new MyClass();
fixed (long* pX = &(myObject.X))
fixed (float* pF = &(myObject.F))
{
    // do something
}
```

You can nest entire `fixed` blocks if you want to fix several pointers for different periods:

```
MyClass myObject = new MyClass();
fixed (long* pX = &(myObject.X))
{
    // do something with pX
    fixed (float* pF = &(myObject.F))
    {
        // do something else with pF
    }
}
```

You can also initialize several variables within the same `fixed` block, if they are of the same type:

```
MyClass myObject = new MyClass();
MyClass myObject2 = new MyClass();
fixed (long* pX = &(myObject.X), pX2 = &(myObject2.X))
{
    // etc.
}
```

In all these cases, it is immaterial whether the various pointers you are declaring point to fields in the same or different objects or to static fields not associated with any class instance.

Pointer Example: PointerPlayground

This section presents an example that uses pointers. The following code is an example named `PointerPlayground`. It does some simple pointer manipulation and displays the results, allowing you to see what is happening in memory and where variables are stored:

```
using System;

namespace PointerPlayground
{
    class MainEntryPoint
    {
        static unsafe void Main()
        {
            int x=10;
            short y = -1;
            byte y2 = 4;
            double z = 1.5;
            int* pX = &x;
            short* pY = &y;
            double* pZ = &z;

            Console.WriteLine(
                "Address of x is 0x{0:X}, size is {1}, value is {2}",
                (uint)&x, sizeof(int), x);
            Console.WriteLine(
                "Address of y is 0x{0:X}, size is {1}, value is {2}",
                (uint)&y, sizeof(short), y);
            Console.WriteLine(
                "Address of y2 is 0x{0:X}, size is {1}, value is {2}",
```

```
            (uint)&y2, sizeof(byte), y2);
        Console.WriteLine(
          "Address of z is 0x{0:X}, size is {1}, value is {2}",
          (uint)&z, sizeof(double), z);
        Console.WriteLine(
          "Address of pX=&x is 0x{0:X}, size is {1}, value is 0x{2:X}",
          (uint)&pX, sizeof(int*), (uint)pX);
        Console.WriteLine(
          "Address of pY=&y is 0x{0:X}, size is {1}, value is 0x{2:X}",
          (uint)&pY, sizeof(short*), (uint)pY);
        Console.WriteLine(
          "Address of pZ=&z is 0x{0:X}, size is {1}, value is 0x{2:X}",
          (uint)&pZ, sizeof(double*), (uint)pZ);

        *pX = 20;
        Console.WriteLine("After setting *pX, x = {0}", x);
        Console.WriteLine("*pX = {0}", *pX);

        pZ = (double*)pX;
        Console.WriteLine("x treated as a double = {0}", *pZ);

        Console.ReadLine();
      }
    }
  }
```

code snippet PointerPlayground/Program.cs

This code declares four value variables:

➤ An int x

➤ A short y

➤ A byte y2

➤ A double z

It also declares pointers to three of these values: pX, pY, and pZ.

Next, you display the values of these variables as well as their sizes and addresses. Note that in taking the address of pX, pY, and pZ, you are effectively looking at a pointer *to* a pointer — an address of an address of a value. Notice that, in accordance with the usual practice when displaying addresses, you have used the {0:X} format specifier in the Console.WriteLine() commands to ensure that memory addresses are displayed in hexadecimal format.

Finally, you use the pointer pX to change the value of x to 20 and do some pointer casting to see what happens if you try to treat the content of x as if it were a double.

Compiling and running this code results in the following output. This screen output demonstrates the effects of attempting to compile both with and without the /unsafe flag:

```
csc PointerPlayground.cs
Microsoft (R) Visual C# 2010 Compiler version 4.0.21006.1
Copyright (C) Microsoft Corporation. All rights reserved.

PointerPlayground.cs(7,26): error CS0227: Unsafe code may only appear if
       compiling with /unsafe

csc /unsafe PointerPlayground.cs
Microsoft (R) Visual C# 2010 Compiler version 4.0.21006.1
Copyright (C) Microsoft Corporation. All rights reserved.

PointerPlayground
```

```
Address of x is 0x12F4B0, size is 4, value is 10
Address of y is 0x12F4AC, size is 2, value is -1
Address of y2 is 0x12F4A8, size is 1, value is 4
Address of z is 0x12F4A0, size is 8, value is 1.5
Address of pX=&x is 0x12F49C, size is 4, value is 0x12F4B0
Address of pY=&y is 0x12F498, size is 4, value is 0x12F4AC
Address of pZ=&z is 0x12F494, size is 4, value is 0x12F4A0
After setting *pX, x = 20
*pX = 20
x treated as a double = 2.86965129997082E-308
```

Checking through these results confirms the description of how the stack operates presented in the "Memory Management Under the Hood" section earlier in this chapter. It allocates successive variables moving downward in memory. Notice how it also confirms that blocks of memory on the stack are always allocated in multiples of 4 bytes. For example, y is a short (of size 2), and has the (decimal) address 1242284, indicating that the memory locations reserved for it are locations 1242284 through 1242287. If the .NET runtime had been strictly packing up variables next to each other, Y would have occupied just two locations, 1242284 and 1242285.

The next example illustrates pointer arithmetic, as well as pointers to structs and class members. This example is named PointerPlayground2. To start, you define a struct named CurrencyStruct, which represents a currency value as dollars and cents. You also define an equivalent class named CurrencyClass:

```
internal struct CurrencyStruct
{
    public long Dollars;
    public byte Cents;

    public override string ToString()
    {
        return "$" + Dollars + "." + Cents;
    }
}

internal class CurrencyClass
{
    public long Dollars;
    public byte Cents;

    public override string ToString()
    {
        return "$" + Dollars + "." + Cents;
    }
}
```

code download PointerPlayground.sln

Now that you have your struct and class defined, you can apply some pointers to them. Following is the code for the new example. Because the code is fairly long, we will go through it in detail. You start by displaying the size of CurrencyStruct, creating a couple of CurrencyStruct instances and creating some CurrencyStruct pointers. You use the pAmount pointer to initialize the members of the amount1 CurrencyStruct and then display the addresses of your variables:

```
public static unsafe void Main()
{
    Console.WriteLine(
        "Size of CurrencyStruct struct is " + sizeof(CurrencyStruct));
    CurrencyStruct amount1, amount2;
    CurrencyStruct* pAmount = &amount1;
    long* pDollars = &(pAmount->Dollars);
    byte* pCents = &(pAmount->Cents);
```

```
Console.WriteLine("Address of amount1 is 0x{0:X}", (uint)&amount1);
Console.WriteLine("Address of amount2 is 0x{0:X}", (uint)&amount2);
Console.WriteLine("Address of pAmount is 0x{0:X}", (uint)&pAmount);
Console.WriteLine("Address of pDollars is 0x{0:X}", (uint)&pDollars);
Console.WriteLine("Address of pCents is 0x{0:X}", (uint)&pCents);
pAmount->Dollars = 20;
*pCents = 50;
Console.WriteLine("amount1 contains " + amount1);
```

Now you do some pointer manipulation that relies on your knowledge of how the stack works. Due to the order in which the variables were declared, you know that amount2 will be stored at an address immediately below amount1. The sizeof(CurrencyStruct) operator returns 16 (as demonstrated in the screen output coming up), so CurrencyStruct occupies a multiple of 4 bytes. Therefore, after you decrement your currency pointer, it will point to amount2:

```
--pAmount;    // this should get it to point to amount2
Console.WriteLine("amount2 has address 0x{0:X} and contains {1}",
    (uint)pAmount, *pAmount);
```

Notice that when you call Console.WriteLine(), you display the contents of amount2, but you haven't yet initialized it. What gets displayed will be random garbage — whatever happened to be stored at that location in memory before execution of the example. There is an important point here: Normally, the C# compiler would prevent you from using an uninitialized variable, but when you start using pointers, it is very easy to circumvent many of the usual compilation checks. In this case, you have done so because the compiler has no way of knowing that you are actually displaying the contents of amount2. Only you know that, because your knowledge of the stack means that you can tell what the effect of decrementing pAmount will be. Once you start doing pointer arithmetic, you will find that you can access all sorts of variables and memory locations that the compiler would usually stop you from accessing, hence the description of pointer arithmetic as unsafe.

Next, you do some pointer arithmetic on your pCents pointer. pCents currently points to amount1.Cents, but the aim here is to get it to point to amount2.Cents, again using pointer operations instead of directly telling the compiler that's what you want to do. To do this, you need to decrement the address pCents contains by sizeof(Currency):

```
// do some clever casting to get pCents to point to cents
// inside amount2
CurrencyStruct* pTempCurrency = (CurrencyStruct*)pCents;
pCents = (byte*) ( --pTempCurrency );
Console.WriteLine("Address of pCents is now 0x{0:X}", (uint)&pCents);
```

Finally, you use the fixed keyword to create some pointers that point to the fields in a class instance and use these pointers to set the value of this instance. Notice that this is also the first time that you have been able to look at the address of an item stored on the heap rather than the stack:

```
Console.WriteLine("\nNow with classes");
// now try it out with classes
CurrencyClass amount3 = new CurrencyClass();

fixed(long* pDollars2 = &(amount3.Dollars))
fixed(byte* pCents2 = &(amount3.Cents))
{
    Console.WriteLine(
        "amount3.Dollars has address 0x{0:X}", (uint)pDollars2);
    Console.WriteLine(
        "amount3.Cents has address 0x{0:X}", (uint) pCents2);
    *pDollars2 = -100;
    Console.WriteLine("amount3 contains " + amount3);
}
```

Compiling and running this code gives output similar to this:

```
csc /unsafe PointerPlayground2.cs
Microsoft (R) Visual C# 2010 Compiler version 4.0.21006.1
Copyright (C) Microsoft Corporation. All rights reserved.

PointerPlayground2
Size of CurrencyStruct struct is 16
Address of amount1 is 0x12F4A4
Address of amount2 is 0x12F494
Address of pAmount is 0x12F490
Address of pDollars is 0x12F48C
Address of pCents is 0x12F488
amount1 contains $20.50
amount2 has address 0x12F494 and contains $0.0
Address of pCents is now 0x12F488

Now with classes
amount3.Dollars has address 0xA64414
amount3.Cents has address 0xA6441C
amount3 contains $-100.0
```

Notice in this output the uninitialized value of amount2 that is displayed, and notice that the size of the CurrencyStruct struct is 16 — somewhat larger than you would expect given the size of its fields (a long and a byte should total 9 bytes).

Using Pointers to Optimize Performance

Until now, all the examples have been designed to demonstrate the various things that you can do with pointers. We have played around with memory in a way that is probably interesting only to people who like to know what's happening under the hood, but that doesn't really help you write better code. Now you're going to apply your understanding of pointers and see an example of how judicious use of pointers has a significant performance benefit.

Creating Stack-Based Arrays

This section explores one of the main areas in which pointers can be useful: creating high-performance, low-overhead arrays on the stack. As discussed in Chapter 2, "Core C#," C# includes rich support for handling arrays. Although C# makes it very easy to use both 1-dimensional and rectangular or jagged multidimensional arrays, it suffers from the disadvantage that these arrays are actually objects; they are instances of System.Array. This means that the arrays are stored on the heap with all the overhead that this involves. There may be occasions when you need to create a short-lived, high-performance array and don't want the overhead of reference objects. You can do this by using pointers, although as you see in this section, this is easy only for 1-dimensional arrays.

To create a high-performance array, you need to use a new keyword: stackalloc. The stackalloc command instructs the .NET runtime to allocate an amount of memory on the stack. When you call stackalloc, you need to supply it with two pieces of information:

➤ The type of data you want to store

➤ The number of these data items you need to store

For example, to allocate enough memory to store 10 decimal data items, you can write:

```
decimal* pDecimals = stackalloc decimal[10];
```

This command simply allocates the stack memory; it does not attempt to initialize the memory to any default value. This is fine for the purpose of this example because you are creating a high-performance array, and initializing values unnecessarily would hurt performance.

Similarly, to store 20 `double` data items, you write this:

```
double* pDoubles = stackalloc double[20];
```

Although this line of code specifies the number of variables to store as a constant, this can equally be a quantity evaluated at runtime. So, you can write the previous example like this:

```
int size;
size = 20;    // or some other value calculated at run-time
double* pDoubles = stackalloc double[size];
```

You can see from these code snippets that the syntax of `stackalloc` is slightly unusual. It is followed immediately by the name of the data type you want to store (and this must be a value type) and then by the number of items you need space for in square brackets. The number of bytes allocated will be this number multiplied by `sizeof`(data type). The use of square brackets in the preceding code sample suggests an array, which is not too surprising. If you have allocated space for 20 doubles, then what you have is an array of 20 doubles. The simplest type of array that you can have is a block of memory that stores one element after another (see Figure 13-6).

This diagram also shows the pointer returned by `stackalloc`, which is always a pointer to the allocated data type that points to the top of the newly allocated memory block. To use the memory block, you simply dereference the returned pointer. For example, to allocate space for 20 doubles and then set the first element (element 0 of the array) to the value 3.0, write this:

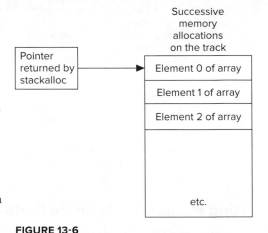

FIGURE 13-6

```
double* pDoubles = stackalloc double [20];
*pDoubles = 3.0;
```

To access the next element of the array, you use pointer arithmetic. As described earlier, if you add 1 to a pointer, its value will be increased by the size of whatever data type it points to. In this case, this will be just enough to take you to the next free memory location in the block that you have allocated. So, you can set the second element of the array (element number 1) to the value 8.4 like this:

```
double* pDoubles = stackalloc double [20];
*pDoubles = 3.0;
*(pDoubles+1) = 8.4;
```

By the same reasoning, you can access the element with index X of the array with the expression `*(pDoubles+X)`.

Effectively, you have a means by which you can access elements of your array, but for general-purpose use, this syntax is too complex. Fortunately, C# defines an alternative syntax using square brackets. C# gives a very precise meaning to square brackets when they are applied to pointers; if the variable p is any pointer type and X is an integer, then the expression `p[X]` is always interpreted by the compiler as meaning `*(p+X)`. This is true for all pointers, not only those initialized using `stackalloc`. With this shorthand notation, you now have a very convenient syntax for accessing your array. In fact, it means that you have exactly the same syntax for accessing 1-dimensional stack-based arrays as you do for accessing heap-based arrays that are represented by the `System.Array` class:

```
double* pDoubles = stackalloc double [20];
pDoubles[0] = 3.0;    // pDoubles[0] is the same as *pDoubles
pDoubles[1] = 8.4;    // pDoubles[1] is the same as *(pDoubles+1)
```

This idea of applying array syntax to pointers is not new. It has been a fundamental part of both the C and the C++ languages ever since those languages were invented. Indeed, C++ developers will recognize the stack-based arrays they can obtain using stackalloc *as being essentially identical to classic stack-based C and C++ arrays. This syntax and the way it links pointers and arrays is one reason why the C language became popular in the 1970s, and the main reason why the use of pointers became such a popular programming technique in C and C++.*

Although your high-performance array can be accessed in the same way as a normal C# array, a word of caution is in order. The following code in C# raises an exception:

```
double[] myDoubleArray = new double [20];
myDoubleArray[50] = 3.0;
```

The exception occurs because you are trying to access an array using an index that is out of bounds; the index is 50, whereas the maximum allowed value is 19. However, if you declare the equivalent array using stackalloc, there is no object wrapped around the array that can perform bounds checking. Hence, the following code will *not* raise an exception:

```
double* pDoubles = stackalloc double [20];
pDoubles[50] = 3.0;
```

In this code, you allocate enough memory to hold 20 doubles. Then you set sizeof(double) memory locations, starting at the location given by the start of this memory + 50*sizeof(double) to hold the double value 3.0. Unfortunately, that memory location is way outside the area of memory that you have allocated for the doubles. There is no knowing what data might be stored at that address. At best, you may have used some currently unused memory, but it is equally possible that you may have just overwritten some locations in the stack that were being used to store other variables or even the return address from the method currently being executed. Once again, you see that the high performance to be gained from pointers comes at a cost; you need to be certain you know what you are doing, or you will get some very strange runtime bugs.

QuickArray Example

Our discussion of pointers ends with a stackalloc example called QuickArray. In this example, the program simply asks users how many elements they want to be allocated for an array. The code then uses stackalloc to allocate an array of longs that size. The elements of this array are populated with the squares of the integers starting with 0 and the results are displayed on the console:

```
using System;

namespace QuickArray
{
    internal class Program
    {
        private static unsafe void Main()
        {
            Console.Write("How big an array do you want? \n> ");
            string userInput = Console.ReadLine();
            uint size = uint.Parse(userInput);

            long* pArray = stackalloc long[(int) size];
            for (int i = 0; i < size; i++)
            {
                pArray[i] = i*i;
            }

            for (int i = 0; i < size; i++)
```

```
          {
              Console.WriteLine("Element {0} = {1}", i, *(pArray + i));
          }

          Console.ReadLine();
      }
   }
}
```

The output from the `QuickArray` example is illustrated in Figure 13-7.

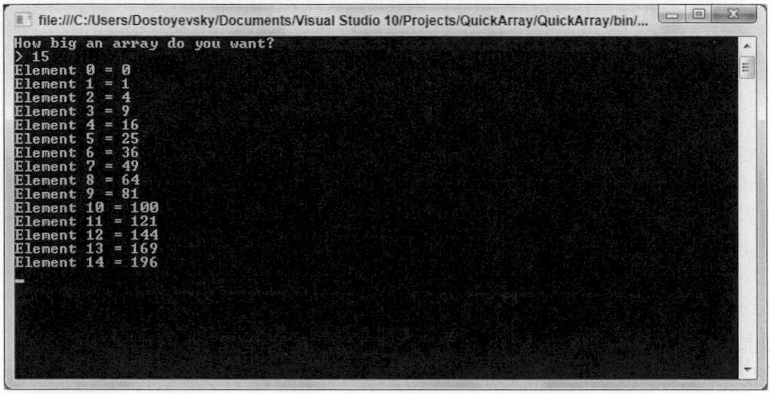

```
file:///C:/Users/Dostoyevsky/Documents/Visual Studio 10/Projects/QuickArray/QuickArray/bin/...
How big an array do you want?
> 15
Element 0 = 0
Element 1 = 1
Element 2 = 4
Element 3 = 9
Element 4 = 16
Element 5 = 25
Element 6 = 36
Element 7 = 49
Element 8 = 64
Element 9 = 81
Element 10 = 100
Element 11 = 121
Element 12 = 144
Element 13 = 169
Element 14 = 196
```

FIGURE 13-7

SUMMARY

Remember, to become a truly proficient C# programmer, you must have a solid understanding of how memory allocation and garbage collection work. This chapter described how the CLR manages and allocates memory on the heap and the stack. It also illustrated how to write classes that free unmanaged resources correctly, and how to use pointers in C#. These are both advanced topics that are poorly understood and often implemented incorrectly by novice programmers.

This chapter should be treated as a companion to what you learn from Chapter 15 on error handling and in Chapter 20 when dealing with threading. The next chapter of this book looks at reflection in C#.

14

Reflection

➤   Using custom attributes

➤   Inspecting the metadata at runtime using reflection

➤   Building access points from classes that enable reflection

This chapter focuses on custom attributes and reflection. *Custom attributes* are mechanisms that allow you to associate custom metadata with program elements. This metadata is created at compile time and embedded in an assembly. *Reflection* is a generic term that describes the ability to inspect and manipulate program elements at runtime. For example, reflection allows you to:

➤   Enumerate the members of a type

➤   Instantiate a new object

➤   Execute the members of an object

➤   Find out information about a type

➤   Find out information about an assembly

➤   Inspect the custom attributes applied to a type

➤   Create and compile a new assembly

This list represents a great deal of functionality and encompasses some of the most powerful and complex capabilities provided by the .NET Framework class library. Although this chapter does not have the space to cover all the capabilities of reflection, it focuses on those elements that you are likely to use most frequently.

To demonstrate custom attributes and reflection, you develop an example based on a company that regularly ships upgrades of its software and wants to have details of these upgrades documented automatically. In the example, you define custom attributes that indicate the date when program elements were last modified, and what changes were made. You then use reflection to develop an application that looks for these attributes in an assembly, and can automatically display all the details about what upgrades have been made to the software since a given date.

Another example in this chapter considers an application that reads from or writes to a database and uses custom attributes as a way of marking which classes and properties correspond to which database tables and columns. By reading these attributes from the assembly at runtime, the program is able to automatically retrieve or write data to the appropriate location in the database, without requiring specific logic for each table or column.

CUSTOM ATTRIBUTES

From this book, you have seen how you can define attributes on various items within your program. These attributes have been defined by Microsoft as part of the .NET Framework class library, and many of them receive special support from the C# compiler. This means that for those particular attributes, the compiler could customize the compilation process in specific ways; for example, laying out a struct in memory according to the details in the StructLayout attributes.

The .NET Framework also allows you to define your own attributes. Clearly, these attributes will not have any effect on the compilation process, because the compiler has no intrinsic awareness of them. However, these attributes will be emitted as metadata in the compiled assembly when they are applied to program elements.

By itself, this metadata might be useful for documentation purposes, but what makes attributes really powerful is that by using reflection, your code can read this metadata and use it to make decisions at runtime. This means that the custom attributes that you define can directly affect how your code runs. For example, custom attributes can be used to enable declarative code access security checks for custom permission classes, to associate information with program elements that can then be used by testing tools, or when developing extensible frameworks that allow the loading of plug-ins or modules.

Writing Custom Attributes

To understand how to write your own custom attributes, it is useful to know what the compiler does when it encounters an element in your code that has a custom attribute applied to it. To take the database example, suppose that you have a C# property declaration that looks like this:

```
[FieldName("SocialSecurityNumber")]
public string SocialSecurityNumber
{
    get {
        // etc.
```

When the C# compiler recognizes that this property has an attribute applied to it (FieldName), it will start by appending the string Attribute to this name, forming the combined name FieldNameAttribute. The compiler will then search all the namespaces in its search path (those namespaces that have been mentioned in a using statement) for a class with the specified name. Note that if you mark an item with an attribute whose name already ends in the string Attribute, the compiler will not add the string to the name a second time; it will leave the attribute name unchanged. Therefore, the preceding code is equivalent to this:

```
[FieldNameAttribute("SocialSecurityNumber")]
public string SocialSecurityNumber
{
    get {
    // etc.
```

The compiler expects to find a class with this name, and it expects this class to be derived directly or indirectly from System.Attribute. The compiler also expects that this class contains information that governs the use of the attribute. In particular, the attribute class needs to specify the following:

- ➤ The types of program elements to which the attribute can be applied (classes, structs, properties, methods, and so on)
- ➤ Whether it is legal for the attribute to be applied more than once to the same program element
- ➤ Whether the attribute, when applied to a class or interface, is inherited by derived classes and interfaces
- ➤ The mandatory and optional parameters the attribute takes

If the compiler cannot find a corresponding attribute class, or if it finds one but the way that you have used that attribute does not match the information in the attribute class, the compiler will raise a compilation error. For example, if the attribute class indicates that the attribute can be applied only to classes, but you have applied it to a struct definition, a compilation error will occur.

To continue with the example, assume that you have defined the `FieldName` attribute like this:

```
[AttributeUsage(AttributeTargets.Property,
    AllowMultiple=false,
    Inherited=false)]
public class FieldNameAttribute: Attribute
{
    private string name;
    public FieldNameAttribute(string name)
    {
        this.name = name;
    }
}
```

The following sections discuss each element of this definition.

AttributeUsage Attribute

The first thing to note is that the attribute class itself is marked with an attribute — the `System .AttributeUsage` attribute. This is an attribute defined by Microsoft for which the C# compiler provides special support. (You could argue that `AttributeUsage` isn't an attribute at all; it is more like a meta-attribute, because it applies only to other attributes, not simply to any class.) The primary purpose of `AttributeUsage` is to identify the types of program elements to which your custom attribute can be applied. This information is given by the first parameter of the `AttributeUsage` attribute — this parameter is mandatory, and is of an enumerated type, `AttributeTargets`. In the previous example, you have indicated that the `FieldName` attribute can be applied only to properties, which is fine, because that is exactly what you have applied it to in the earlier code fragment. The members of the `AttributeTargets` enumeration are:

➤   `All`

➤   `Assembly`

➤   `Class`

➤   `Constructor`

➤   `Delegate`

➤   `Enum`

➤   `Event`

➤   `Field`

➤   `GenericParameter` (.NET 2.0 and higher only)

➤   `Interface`

➤   `Method`

➤   `Module`

➤   `Parameter`

➤   `Property`

➤   `ReturnValue`

➤   `Struct`

This list identifies all the program elements to which you can apply attributes. Note that when applying the attribute to a program element, you place the attribute in square brackets immediately before the element. However, two values in the preceding list do not correspond to any program element: `Assembly` and `Module`. An attribute can be applied to an assembly or module as a whole instead of to an element in your code; in this case the attribute can be placed anywhere in your source code, but needs to be prefixed with the `Assembly` or `Module` keyword:

```
[assembly:SomeAssemblyAttribute(Parameters)]
[module:SomeAssemblyAttribute(Parameters)]
```

When indicating the valid target elements of a custom attribute, you can combine these values using the bitwise OR operator. For example, if you want to indicate that your `FieldName` attribute can be applied to both properties and fields, you would write:

```
[AttributeUsage(AttributeTargets.Property | AttributeTargets.Field,
    AllowMultiple=false,
    Inherited=false)]
public class FieldNameAttribute: Attribute
```

You can also use `AttributeTargets.All` to indicate that your attribute can be applied to all types of program elements. The `AttributeUsage` attribute also contains two other parameters, `AllowMultiple` and `Inherited`. These are specified using the syntax of `<ParameterName>=<ParameterValue>`, instead of simply giving the values for these parameters. These parameters are optional — you can omit them if you want.

The `AllowMultiple` parameter indicates whether an attribute can be applied more than once to the same item. The fact that it is set to `false` here indicates that the compiler should raise an error if it sees something like this:

```
[FieldName("SocialSecurityNumber")]
[FieldName("NationalInsuranceNumber")]
public string SocialSecurityNumber
{

    // etc.
```

If the `Inherited` parameter is set to `true`, an attribute applied to a class or interface will also automatically be applied to all derived classes or interfaces. If the attribute is applied to a method or property, it will automatically apply to any overrides of that method or property, and so on.

Specifying Attribute Parameters

This section examines how you can specify the parameters that your custom attribute takes. The way it works is that when the compiler encounters a statement such as the following,

```
[FieldName("SocialSecurityNumber")]
public string SocialSecurityNumber
{

    // etc.
```

the compiler examines the parameters passed into the attribute — which is a string — and looks for a constructor for the attribute that takes exactly those parameters. If the compiler finds an appropriate constructor, the compiler will emit the specified metadata to the assembly. If the compiler does not find an appropriate constructor, a compilation error occurs. As discussed later in this chapter, reflection involves reading metadata (attributes) from assemblies and instantiating the attribute classes they represent. Because of this, the compiler must ensure that an appropriate constructor exists that will allow the runtime instantiation of the specified attribute.

In the example, you have supplied just one constructor for `FieldNameAttribute`, and this constructor takes one string parameter. Therefore, when applying the `FieldName` attribute to a property, you must supply one string as a parameter, as was done in the preceding sample code.

If you want to allow a choice of what types of parameters should be supplied with an attribute, you can provide different constructor overloads, although normal practice is to supply just one constructor and use properties to define any other optional parameters, as explained next.

Specifying Optional Attribute Parameters

As demonstrated with reference to the `AttributeUsage` attribute, an alternative syntax exists by which optional parameters can be added to an attribute. This syntax involves specifying the names and values of the optional parameters. It works through `public` properties or fields in the `attribute` class. For example, suppose that you modified the definition of the `SocialSecurityNumber` property as follows:

```
[FieldName("SocialSecurityNumber", Comment="This is the primary key field")]
public string SocialSecurityNumber
{

    // etc.
```

In this case, the compiler recognizes the `<ParameterName>=<ParameterValue>` syntax of the second parameter and does not attempt to match this parameter to a `FieldNameAttribute` constructor. Instead, it looks for a `public` property or field (although public fields are not considered good programming practice, so normally you will work with properties) of that name that it can use to set the value of this parameter. If you want the previous code to work, you have to add some code to `FieldNameAttribute`:

```
[AttributeUsage(AttributeTargets.Property,
    AllowMultiple=false,
    Inherited=false)]
public class FieldNameAttribute: Attribute
{
    private string comment;
    public string Comment
    {
        get
        {
            return comment;
        }
        set
        {
            comment = value;
        }
    }

        // etc
}
```

Custom Attribute Example: WhatsNewAttributes

In this section, you start developing the example mentioned at the beginning of the chapter. `WhatsNewAttributes` provides for an attribute that indicates when a program element was last modified. This is a more ambitious code sample than many of the others in that it consists of three separate assemblies:

➤   The `WhatsNewAttributes` assembly, which contains the definitions of the attributes

➤   The `VectorClass` assembly, which contains the code to which the attributes have been applied

➤   The `LookUpWhatsNew` assembly, which contains the project that displays details of items that have changed

Of these, only `LookUpWhatsNew` is a console application of the type that you have used until now. The remaining two assemblies are libraries — they each contain class definitions but no program entry point. For the `VectorClass` assembly, this means that the entry point and test harness class have been removed from the `VectorAsCollection` sample, leaving only the `Vector` class. These classes are represented later in this chapter.

Managing three related assemblies by compiling at the command line is tricky. Although the commands for compiling all these source files are provided separately, you might prefer to edit the code sample (which you can download from the Wrox web site at www.wrox.com) as a combined Visual Studio solution, as discussed in Chapter 16, "Visual Studio 2010." The download includes the required Visual Studio 2010 solution files.

The WhatsNewAttributes Library Assembly

This section starts with the core WhatsNewAttributes assembly. The source code is contained in the file WhatsNewAttributes.cs, which is located in the WhatsNewAttributes project of the WhatsNewAttributes solution in the example code for this chapter. The syntax for doing this is quite simple. At the command line, you supply the flag target:library to the compiler. To compile WhatsNewAttributes, type the following:

```
csc /target:library WhatsNewAttributes.cs
```

The WhatsNewAttributes.cs file defines two attribute classes, LastModifiedAttribute and SupportsWhatsNewAttribute. The attribute LastModifiedAttribute is the attribute that you can use to mark when an item was last modified. It takes two mandatory parameters (parameters that are passed to the constructor): the date of the modification and a string containing a description of the changes. There is also one optional parameter named issues (for which a public property exists), which can be used to describe any outstanding issues for the item.

In practice, you would probably want this attribute to apply to anything. To keep the code simple, its usage is limited here to classes and methods. You will allow it to be applied more than once to the same item (AllowMultiple=true) because an item might be modified more than once, and each modification will have to be marked with a separate attribute instance.

SupportsWhatsNew is a smaller class representing an attribute that doesn't take any parameters. The idea of this attribute is that it is an assembly attribute that is used to mark an assembly for which you are maintaining documentation via the LastModifiedAttribute. This way, the program that will examine this assembly later on knows that the assembly it is reading is one on which you are actually using your automated documentation process. Here is the complete source code for this part of the example:

Available for
download on
Wrox.com

```csharp
using System;

namespace WhatsNewAttributes
{
    [AttributeUsage(
        AttributeTargets.Class | AttributeTargets.Method,
        AllowMultiple=true, Inherited=false)]
    public class LastModifiedAttribute: Attribute
    {
        private readonly DateTime _dateModified;
        private readonly string _changes;

        public LastModifiedAttribute(string dateModified, string changes)
        {
            dateModified = DateTime.Parse(dateModified);
            changes = changes;
        }

        public DateTime DateModified
        {
            get { return dateModified; }
        }

        public string Changes
        {
            get { return changes; }
        }

        public string Issues { get; set; }
```

```
      }

      [AttributeUsage(AttributeTargets.Assembly)]
      public class SupportsWhatsNewAttribute: Attribute
      {
      }
   }
```

code snippet WhatsNewAttributes.cs

This code should be clear with reference to previous descriptions. Notice, however, that we have not bothered to supply `set` accessors to the `Changes` and `DateModified` properties. There is no need for these accessors because you are requiring these parameters to be set in the constructor as mandatory parameters. You need the `get` accessors so that you can read the values of these attributes.

The VectorClass Assembly

Next, you need to use these attributes. To this end, you use a modified version of the earlier `VectorAsCollection` sample. Note that you need to reference the `WhatsNewAttributes` library that you have just created. You also need to indicate the corresponding namespace with a `using` statement so that the compiler can recognize the attributes:

```
using System;
using System.Collections;
using System.Text;
using WhatsNewAttributes;

[assembly: SupportsWhatsNew]
```

In this code, you have also added the line that will mark the assembly itself with the `SupportsWhatsNew` attribute.

Now for the code for the `Vector` class. You are not making any major changes to this class; you only add a couple of `LastModified` attributes to mark out the work that you have done on this class in this chapter. Then `Vector` is defined as a class instead of a struct to simplify the code (of the next iteration of the sample) that displays the attributes. (In the `VectorAsCollection` sample, `Vector` is a struct, but its enumerator is a class. This means that the next iteration of the sample would have had to pick out both classes and structs when looking at the assembly, which would have made the example less straightforward.)

```
namespace VectorClass
{
   [LastModified("14 Feb 2010", "IEnumerable interface implemented " +
      "So Vector can now be treated as a collection")]
   [LastModified("10 Feb 2010", "IFormattable interface implemented " +
      "So Vector now responds to format specifiers N and VE")]
   class Vector: IFormattable, IEnumerable
   {
      public double x, y, z;

      public Vector(double x, double y, double z)
      {
         this.x = x;
         this.y = y;
         this.z = z;
      }

      [LastModified("10 Feb 2010",
                   "Method added in order to provide formatting support")]
      public string ToString(string format, IFormatProvider formatProvider)
      {
         if (format == null)
         {
            return ToString();
         }
```

You also mark the contained `VectorEnumerator` class as new:

```
[LastModified("14 Feb 2010",
                "Class created as part of collection support for Vector")]
private class VectorEnumerator: IEnumerator
{
```

To compile this code from the command line, type the following:

```
csc /target:library /reference:WhatsNewAttributes.dll VectorClass.cs
```

That's as far as you can get with this example for now. You are unable to run anything yet because all you have are two libraries. You will develop the final part of the example, in which you look up and display these attributes, as soon as you have had a look at how reflection works.

USING REFLECTION

In this section, we take a closer look at the `System.Type` class, which lets you access information concerning the definition of any data type. We then discuss the `System.Reflection.Assembly` class, which you can use to access information about an assembly or to load that assembly into your program. Finally, you will combine the code in this section with the code in the previous section to complete the `WhatsNewAttributes` sample.

The System.Type Class

So far you have used the `Type` class only to hold the reference to a type as follows:

```
Type t = typeof(double);
```

Although previously referred to as a class, `Type` is an abstract base class. Whenever you instantiate a `Type` object, you are actually instantiating a class derived from `Type`. `Type` has one derived class corresponding to each actual data type, though in general the derived classes simply provide different overloads of the various `Type` methods and properties that return the correct data for the corresponding data type. They do not generally add new methods or properties. In general, there are three common ways to obtain a `Type` reference that refers to any given type:

1. You can use the C# `typeof` operator as in the preceding code. This operator takes the name of the type (not in quotation marks, however) as a parameter.

2. You can use the `GetType()` method, which all classes inherit from `System.Object`:

   ```
   double d = 10;
   Type t = d.GetType();
   ```

   `GetType()` is called against a variable, rather than taking the name of a type. Note, however, that the `Type` object returned is still associated with only that data type. It does not contain any information that relates to that instance of the type. The `GetType()` method can be useful if you have a reference to an object but are not sure what class that object is actually an instance of.

3. You can call the `static` method of the `Type` class, `GetType()`:

   ```
   Type t = Type.GetType("System.Double");
   ```

`Type` is really the gateway to much of the reflection functionality. It implements a huge number of methods and properties — far too many to provide a comprehensive list here. However, the following subsections should give you some idea of the kinds of things you can do with the `Type` class. Note that the available properties are all read-only; you use `Type` to find out about the data type — you cannot use it to make any modifications to the type!

Type Properties

You can split the properties implemented by `Type` into three categories. First, a number of properties retrieve the strings containing various names associated with the class, as shown in the following table.

PROPERTY	RETURNS
Name	The name of the data type
FullName	The fully qualified name of the data type (including the namespace name)
Namespace	The name of the namespace in which the data type is defined

Second, it is possible to retrieve references to further type objects that represent related classes, as shown in the following table.

PROPERTY	RETURNS TYPE REFERENCE CORRESPONDING TO
BaseType	Immediate base type of this type
UnderlyingSystemType	The type that this type maps to in the .NET runtime (recall that certain .NET base types actually map to specific predefined types recognized by IL)

A number of Boolean properties indicate whether this type is, for example, a class, an enum, and so on. These properties include IsAbstract, IsArray, IsClass, IsEnum, IsInterface, IsPointer, IsPrimitive (one of the predefined primitive data types), IsPublic, IsSealed, and IsValueType. For example, using a primitive data type:

```
Type intType = typeof(int);
Console.WriteLine(intType.IsAbstract);      // writes false
Console.WriteLine(intType.IsClass);         // writes false
Console.WriteLine(intType.IsEnum);          // writes false
Console.WriteLine(intType.IsPrimitive);     // writes true
Console.WriteLine(intType.IsValueType);     // writes true
```

Or using the Vector class:

```
Type vecType = typeof(Vector);
Console.WriteLine(vecType.IsAbstract);      // writes false
Console.WriteLine(vecType.IsClass);         // writes true
Console.WriteLine(vecType.IsEnum);          // writes false
Console.WriteLine(vecType.IsPrimitive);     // writes false
Console.WriteLine(vecType.IsValueType);     // writes false
```

Finally, you can also retrieve a reference to the assembly that the type is defined in. This is returned as a reference to an instance of the System.Reflection.Assembly class, which is examined shortly:

```
Type t = typeof (Vector);
Assembly containingAssembly = new Assembly(t);
```

Methods

Most of the methods of System.Type are used to obtain details of the members of the corresponding data type — the constructors, properties, methods, events, and so on. Quite a large number of methods exist, but they all follow the same pattern. For example, two methods retrieve details of the methods of the data type: GetMethod() and GetMethods(). GetMethod() returns a reference to a System.Reflection.MethodInfo object, which contains details of a method. GetMethods() returns an array of such references. The difference is that GetMethods() returns details of all the methods, whereas GetMethod() returns details of just one method with a specified parameter list. Both methods have overloads that take an extra parameter, a BindingFlags enumerated value that indicates which members should be returned — for example, whether to return public members, instance members, static members, and so on.

For example, the simplest overload of GetMethods() takes no parameters and returns details of all the public methods of the data type:

```
Type t = typeof(double);
MethodInfo[] methods = t.GetMethods();
foreach (MethodInfo nextMethod in methods)
{
    // etc.
    }
```

The member methods of `Type` that follow the same pattern are shown in the following table.

TYPE OF OBJECT RETURNED	METHODS (THE METHOD WITH THE PLURAL NAME RETURNS AN ARRAY)
ConstructorInfo	GetConstructor(), GetConstructors()
EventInfo	GetEvent(), GetEvents()
FieldInfo	GetField(), GetFields()
MemberInfo	GetMember(), GetMembers(), GetDefaultMembers()
MethodInfo	GetMethod(), GetMethods()
PropertyInfo	GetProperty(), GetProperties()

The `GetMember()` and `GetMembers()` methods return details of any or all members of the data type, regardless of whether these members are constructors, properties, methods, and so on.

The TypeView Example

This section demonstrates some of the features of the `Type` class with a short example, `TypeView`, which you can use to list the members of a data type. The example demonstrates how to use `TypeView` for a `double`; however, you can swap this type with any other data type just by changing one line of the code in the sample. `TypeView` displays far more information than can be displayed in a console window, so we're going to take a break from our normal practice and display the output in a message box. Running `TypeView` for a `double` produces the results shown in Figure 14-1.

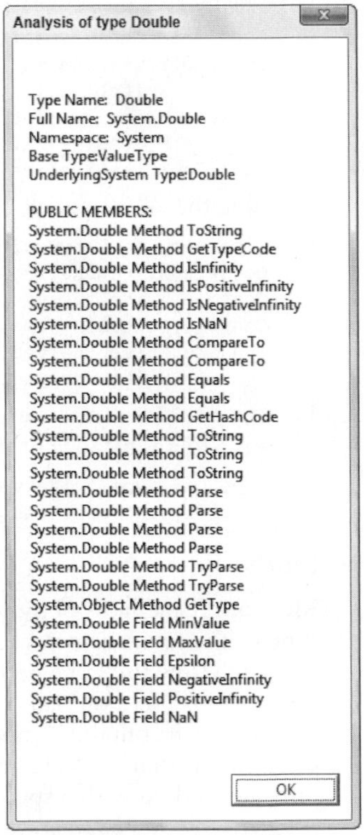

The message box displays the name, full name, and namespace of the data type as well as the name of the underlying type and the base type. Next, it simply iterates through all the public instance members of the data type, displaying for each member the declaring type, the type of member (method, field, and so on), and the name of the member. The *declaring type* is the name of the class that actually declares the type member (for example, `System.Double` if it is defined or overridden in `System.Double`, or the name of the relevant base type if the member is simply inherited from some base class).

`TypeView` does not display signatures of methods because you are retrieving details of all public instance members through `MemberInfo` objects, and information about parameters is not available through a `MemberInfo` object. To retrieve that information, you would need references to `MethodInfo` and other more specific objects, which means that you would need to obtain details of each type of member separately.

`TypeView` does display details of all public instance members, but for doubles, the only ones defined are fields and methods. For this example, you will compile `TypeView` as a console application — there is no problem with displaying a message box from a console application. However, the fact that you are using a message box means that you need to reference the base class assembly `System.Windows.Forms.dll`, which contains the classes in the `System.Windows.Forms` namespace in which the `MessageBox` class that you will

FIGURE 14-1

need is defined. The code for `TypeView` is as follows. To begin, you need to add a few `using` statements:

```
using System;
using System.Reflection;
using System.Text;
using System.Windows.Forms;
```

You need `System.Text` because you will be using a `StringBuilder` object to build up the text to be displayed in the message box, and `System.Windows.Forms` for the message box itself. The entire code is in one class, `MainClass`, which has a couple of `static` methods and one `static` field, a `StringBuilder` instance called `OutputText`, which will be used to build up the text to be displayed in the message box. The main method and class declaration look like this:

```
class MainClass
{
    static StringBuilder OutputText = new StringBuilder();

    static void Main()
    {
        // modify this line to retrieve details of any
        // other data type
        Type t = typeof(double);

        AnalyzeType(t);
        MessageBox.Show(OutputText.ToString(), "Analysis of type "
                                         + t.Name);
        Console.ReadLine();
    }
```

The `Main()` method implementation starts by declaring a `Type` object to represent your chosen data type. You then call a method, `AnalyzeType()`, which extracts the information from the `Type` object and uses it to build up the output text. Finally, you show the output in a message box. Using the `MessageBox` class is fairly intuitive. You just call its `static` `Show()` method, passing it two strings, which will, respectively, be the text in the box and the caption. `AnalyzeType()` is where the bulk of the work is done:

```
static void AnalyzeType(Type t)
{
    AddToOutput("Type Name: " + t.Name);
    AddToOutput("Full Name: " + t.FullName);
    AddToOutput("Namespace: " + t.Namespace);

    Type tBase = t.BaseType;

    if (tBase != null)
    {
        AddToOutput("Base Type:" + tBase.Name);
    }

    Type tUnderlyingSystem = t.UnderlyingSystemType;

    if (tUnderlyingSystem != null)
    {
        AddToOutput("UnderlyingSystem Type:" + tUnderlyingSystem.Name);
    }

    AddToOutput("\nPUBLIC MEMBERS:");
```

```
MemberInfo [] Members = t.GetMembers();

foreach (MemberInfo NextMember in Members)
{
    AddToOutput(NextMember.DeclaringType + " " +
    NextMember.MemberType + " " + NextMember.Name);
}
}
```

You implement the `AnalyzeType()` method by calling various properties of the `Type` object to get the information you need concerning the type names, then call the `GetMembers()` method to get an array of `MemberInfo` objects that you can use to display the details of each member. Note that you use a helper method, `AddToOutput()`, to build up the text to be displayed in the message box:

```
static void AddToOutput(string Text)
{
    OutputText.Append("\n" + Text);
}
```

Compile the `TypeView` assembly using this command:

```
csc /reference:System.Windows.Forms.dll Program.cs
```

The Assembly Class

The `Assembly` class is defined in the `System.Reflection` namespace and provides access to the metadata for a given assembly. It also contains methods to allow you to load and even execute an assembly — assuming that the assembly is an executable. As with the `Type` class, `Assembly` contains a large number of methods and properties — too many to cover here. Instead, this section is confined to covering those methods and properties that you need to get started and that you will use to complete the `WhatsNewAttributes` example.

Before you can do anything with an `Assembly` instance, you need to load the corresponding assembly into the running process. You can do this with either the `static` members `Assembly.Load()` or `Assembly.LoadFrom()`. The difference between these methods is that `Load()` takes the name of the assembly, and the runtime searches in a variety of locations in an attempt to locate the assembly. These locations include the local directory and the global assembly cache. `LoadFrom()` takes the full path name of an assembly and does not attempt to find the assembly in any other location:

```
Assembly assembly1 = Assembly.Load("SomeAssembly");
Assembly assembly2 = Assembly.LoadFrom
    (@"C:\My Projects\Software\SomeOtherAssembly");
```

A number of other overloads of both methods exist, which supply additional security information. After you have loaded an assembly, you can use various properties on it to find out, for example, its full name:

```
string name = assembly1.FullName;
```

Finding Out About Types Defined in an Assembly

One nice feature of the `Assembly` class is that it allows you to obtain details of all the types that are defined in the corresponding assembly. You simply call the `Assembly.GetTypes()` method, which returns an array of `System.Type` references containing details of all the types. You can then manipulate these `Type` references as explained in the previous section:

```
Type[] types = theAssembly.GetTypes();

foreach(Type definedType in types)
{
    DoSomethingWith(definedType);
}
```

Finding Out About Custom Attributes

The methods you use to find out which custom attributes are defined on an assembly or type depend on what type of object the attribute is attached to. If you want to find out what custom attributes are attached to an assembly as a whole, you need to call a `static` method of the `Attribute` class, `GetCustomAttributes()`, passing in a reference to the assembly:

```
Attribute[] definedAttributes =
         Attribute.GetCustomAttributes(assembly1);
         // assembly1 is an Assembly object
```

 This is actually quite significant. You may have wondered why, when you defined custom attributes, you had to go to all the trouble of actually writing classes for them, and why Microsoft hadn't come up with some simpler syntax. Well, the answer is here. The custom attributes do genuinely exist as objects, and when an assembly is loaded you can read in these attribute objects, examine their properties, and call their methods.

`GetCustomAttributes()`, which is used to get assembly attributes, has a few overloads. If you call it without specifying any parameters other than an assembly reference, it will simply return all the custom attributes defined for that assembly. You can also call `GetCustomAttributes()` specifying a second parameter, which is a `Type` object that indicates the attribute class in which you are interested. In this case, `GetCustomAttributes()` returns an array consisting of all the attributes present that are of the specified type.

Note that all attributes are retrieved as plain `Attribute` references. If you want to call any of the methods or properties you defined for your custom attributes, you will need to cast these references explicitly to the relevant custom attribute classes. You can obtain details of custom attributes that are attached to a given data type by calling another overload of `Assembly.GetCustomAttributes()`, this time passing a `Type` reference that describes the type for which you want to retrieve any attached attributes. If you want to obtain attributes that are attached to methods, constructors, fields, and so on, however, you will need to call a `GetCustomAttributes()` method that is a member of one of the classes `MethodInfo`, `ConstructorInfo`, `FieldInfo`, and so on.

If you expect only a single attribute of a given type, you can call the `GetCustomAttribute()` method instead, which returns a single `Attribute` object. You will use `GetCustomAttribute()` in the `WhatsNewAttributes` example to find out whether the `SupportsWhatsNew` attribute is present in the assembly. To do this, you call `GetCustomAttribute()`, passing in a reference to the `WhatsNewAttributes` assembly, and the type of the `SupportsWhatsNewAttribute` attribute. If this attribute is present, you get an `Attribute` instance. If no instances of it are defined in the assembly, you get `null`. And if two or more instances are found, `GetCustomAttribute()` throws a `System` `.Reflection.AmbiguousMatchException`.

```
Attribute supportsAttribute =
         Attribute.GetCustomAttributes(assembly1,
         typeof(SupportsWhatsNewAttribute));
```

Completing the WhatsNewAttributes Example

You now have enough information to complete the `WhatsNewAttributes` example by writing the source code for the final assembly in the sample, the `LookUpWhatsNew` assembly. This part of the application is a console application. However, it needs to reference the other assemblies of `WhatsNewAttributes` and

VectorClass. Although this is going to be a command-line application, you will follow the previous TypeView sample in actually displaying your results in a message box because there is a lot of text output — too much to show in a console window screenshot.

The file is called LookUpWhatsNew.cs, and the command to compile it is:

```
csc /reference:WhatsNewAttributes.dll /reference:VectorClass.dll LookUpWhatsNew.cs
```

In the source code of this file, you first indicate the namespaces you want to infer. System.Text is there because you need to use a StringBuilder object again:

```
using System;
using System.Reflection;
using System.Windows.Forms;
using System.Text;
using WhatsNewAttributes;

namespace LookUpWhatsNew
{
```

The class that contains the main program entry point as well as the other methods is WhatsNewChecker. All the methods you define are in this class, which also has two static fields: outputText, which contains the text as you build it up in preparation for writing it to the message box, and backDateTo, which stores the date you have selected. All modifications made since this date will be displayed. Normally, you would display a dialog box inviting the user to pick this date, but we don't want to get sidetracked into that kind of code. For this reason, backDateTo is hard-coded to a value of 1 Feb 2010. You can easily change this date if you want when you download the code:

```
internal class WhatsNewChecker
{
    private static readonly StringBuilder outputText = new StringBuilder(1000);
    private static DateTime backDateTo = new DateTime(2010, 2, 1);

    static void Main()
    {
        Assembly theAssembly = Assembly.Load("VectorClass");
        Attribute supportsAttribute =
            Attribute.GetCustomAttribute(
                theAssembly, typeof(SupportsWhatsNewAttribute));
        string name = theAssembly.FullName;

        AddToMessage("Assembly: " + name);

        if (supportsAttribute == null)
        {
            AddToMessage(
                "This assembly does not support WhatsNew attributes");
            return;
        }
        else
        {
            AddToMessage("Defined Types:");
        }

        Type[] types = theAssembly.GetTypes();

        foreach(Type definedType in types)
            DisplayTypeInfo(definedType);

        MessageBox.Show(outputText.ToString(),
```

```
            "What\'s New since " + backDateTo.ToLongDateString());
        Console.ReadLine();
    }
```

The `Main()` method first loads the `VectorClass` assembly, and then verifies that it is marked with the `SupportsWhatsNew` attribute. You know `VectorClass` has the `SupportsWhatsNew` attribute applied to it because you have only recently compiled it, but this is a check that would be worth making if users were given a choice of what assembly they wanted to check.

Assuming that all is well, you use the `Assembly.GetTypes()` method to get an array of all the types defined in this assembly, and then loop through them. For each one, you call a method, `DisplayTypeInfo()`, which will add the relevant text, including details of any instances of `LastModifiedAttribute` to the `outputText` field. Finally, you show the message box with the complete text. The `DisplayTypeInfo()` method looks like this:

```
private static void DisplayTypeInfo(Type type)
{
    // make sure we only pick out classes
    if (!(type.IsClass))
    {
        return;
    }

    AddToMessage("\nclass " + type.Name);

    Attribute [] attribs = Attribute.GetCustomAttributes(type);

    if (attribs.Length == 0)
    {
        AddToMessage("No changes to this class\n");
    }
    else
    {
        foreach (Attribute attrib in attribs)
        {
            WriteAttributeInfo(attrib);
        }
    }

    MethodInfo [] methods = type.GetMethods();
    AddToMessage("CHANGES TO METHODS OF THIS CLASS:");

    foreach (MethodInfo nextMethod in methods)
    {
        object [] attribs2 =
            nextMethod.GetCustomAttributes(
                typeof(LastModifiedAttribute), false);

        if (attribs2 != null)
        {
            AddToMessage(
                nextMethod.ReturnType + " " + nextMethod.Name + "()");
            foreach (Attribute nextAttrib in attribs2)
            {
                WriteAttributeInfo(nextAttrib);
            }
        }
    }
}
```

Notice that the first thing you do in this method is check whether the `Type` reference you have been passed actually represents a class. Because, to keep things simple, you have specified that the `LastModified` attribute can be applied only to classes or member methods — you would be wasting your time by doing any processing if the item is not a class (it could be a class, delegate, or enum).

Next, you use the `Attribute.GetCustomAttributes()` method to find out if this class has any `LastModifiedAttribute` instances attached to it. If it does, you add their details to the output text, using a helper method, `WriteAttributeInfo()`.

Finally, you use the `Type.GetMethods()` method to iterate through all the member methods of this data type, and then do the same with each method as you did for the class — check if it has any `LastModifiedAttribute` instances attached to it and, if so, display them using `WriteAttributeInfo()`.

The next bit of code shows the `WriteAttributeInfo()` method, which is responsible for working out what text to display for a given `LastModifiedAttribute` instance. Note that this method is passed an `Attribute` reference, so it needs to cast this to a `LastModifiedAttribute` reference first. After it has done that, it uses the properties that you originally defined for this attribute to retrieve its parameters. It checks that the date of the attribute is sufficiently recent before actually adding it to the text for display:

```
private static void WriteAttributeInfo(Attribute attrib)
{

    LastModifiedAttribute lastModifiedAttrib =
        attrib as LastModifiedAttribute;

    if (lastModifiedAttrib == null)
    {
        return;
    }

    // check that date is in range
    DateTime modifiedDate = lastModifiedAttrib.DateModified;

    if (modifiedDate < backDateTo)
    {
        return;
    }

    AddToMessage(" MODIFIED: " +
        modifiedDate.ToLongDateString() + ":");
    AddToMessage(" " + lastModifiedAttrib.Changes);

    if (lastModifiedAttrib.Issues != null)
    {
        AddToMessage(" Outstanding issues:" +
            lastModifiedAttrib.Issues);
    }
}
```

Finally, here is the helper `AddToMessage()` method:

```
static void AddToMessage(string message)
{
    outputText.Append("\n" + message);
}
}
}
```

Running this code produces the results shown in Figure 14-2.

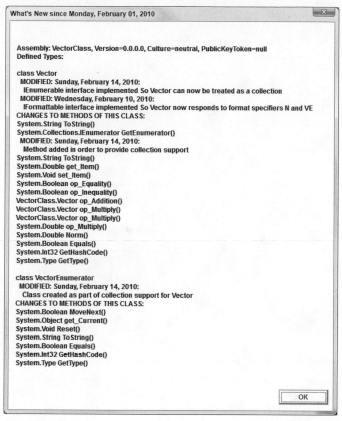

FIGURE 14-2

Notice that when you list the types defined in the VectorClass assembly, you actually pick up two classes: Vector and the embedded VectorEnumerator class. Also notice that because the backDateTo date of 1 Feb is hard-coded in this example, you actually pick up the attributes that are dated 14 Feb (when you added the collection support) but not those dated 10 Feb (when you added the IFormattable interface).

SUMMARY

This chapter did not attempt to cover the entire topic of reflection. Reflection is an extensive subject worthy of a book of its own. Instead, it illustrated the Type and Assembly classes, which are the primary entry points through which you can access the extensive capabilities provided by reflection.

In addition, this chapter demonstrated a specific aspect of reflection that you are likely to use more often than any other — the inspection of custom attributes. You learned how to define and apply your own custom attributes, and how to retrieve information about custom attributes at runtime.

Chapter 15, "Errors and Exceptions," explores exceptions and structured exception handling.

15

Errors and Exceptions

WHAT'S IN THIS CHAPTER?

➤ Looking at the exception classes

➤ Using `try...catch...finally` to capture exceptions

➤ Creating user-defined exceptions

Errors happen, and they are not always caused by the person who coded the application. Sometimes your application will generate an error because of an action that was initiated by the end user of your application or it might be simply due to the environmental context in which your code is running. In any case, you should anticipate errors occurring in your applications and code accordingly.

The .NET Framework has enhanced the ways in which you deal with errors. C#'s mechanism for handling error conditions allows you to provide custom handling for each type of error condition as well as to separate the code that identifies errors from the code that handles them.

By the end of this chapter, you will have a good grasp on advanced exception handling in your C# applications.

No matter how good your coding is, your programs should have the ability to handle any possible errors that may occur. For example, in the middle of some complex processing of your code, you may discover that it doesn't have permission to read a file, or, while it is sending network requests, the network may go down. In such exceptional situations, it is not enough for a method to simply return an appropriate error code — there might be 15 or 20 nested method calls, so what you really want the program to do is jump back up through all those 15 or 20 calls to exit the task completely and take the appropriate counteractions. The C# language has very good facilities to handle this kind of situation, through the mechanism known as *exception handling*.

 If you are a Java or C++ developer you are familiar with the principle of exceptions because these languages handle errors in a similar way to C#. Developers using C++ are sometimes wary of exceptions because of possible C++ performance implications, but this is not the case in C#. Using exceptions in C# code in general does not adversely affect performance. Visual Basic developers will find that working with exceptions in C# is very similar to using exceptions in Visual Basic (except for the syntax differences).

EXCEPTION CLASSES

In C#, an exception is an object created (or *thrown*) when a particular exceptional error condition occurs. This object contains information that should help track down the problem. Although you can create your own exception classes (and you will be doing so later), .NET provides you with many predefined exception classes.

This section provides a quick survey of some of the exceptions available in the .NET base class library. Microsoft has provided a large number of exception classes in .NET — too many to provide a comprehensive list here. The class hierarchy diagram in Figure 15-1 shows a few of these classes, which give you a sense of the general pattern.

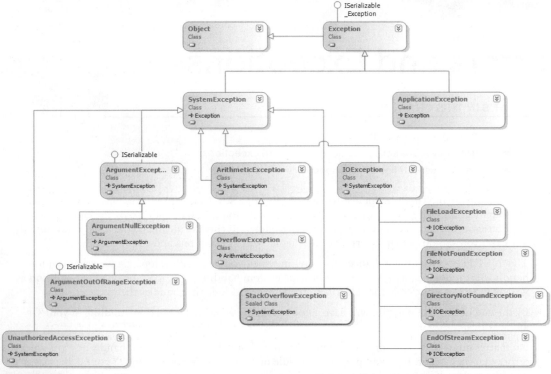

FIGURE 15-1

All the classes in Figure 15-1 are part of the System namespace, except for IOException and the classes derived from IOException, which are part of the namespace System.IO. The System.IO namespace deals with reading and writing data to files. In general, there is no specific namespace for exceptions. Exception classes should be placed in whatever namespace is appropriate to the classes that can generate them — hence IO-related exceptions are in the System.IO namespace. You will find exception classes in quite a few of the base class namespaces.

The generic exception class, System.Exception, is derived from System.Object, as you would expect for a .NET class. In general, you should not throw generic System.Exception objects in your code, because they provide no specifics about the error condition.

Two important classes in the hierarchy are derived from System.Exception:

➤ System.SystemException — This class is for exceptions that are usually thrown by the .NET runtime or that are considered to be of a generic nature and might be thrown by almost any application. For example, StackOverflowException will be thrown by the .NET runtime if it detects the stack is full. However, you might choose to throw ArgumentException or its subclasses in your own code if you detect that a method has been called with inappropriate arguments. Subclasses of `System.SystemException` include classes that represent both fatal and nonfatal errors.

➤ `System.ApplicationException` — This class is important, because it is the intended base for any class of exception defined by third parties. If you define any exceptions covering error conditions unique to your application, you should derive these directly or indirectly from `System.ApplicationException`.

Other exception classes that might come in handy include:

➤ `StackOverflowException` — This exception is thrown when the area of memory allocated to the stack is full. A stack overflow can occur if a method continuously calls itself recursively. This is generally a fatal error, because it prevents your application from doing anything apart from terminating (in which case it is unlikely that even the `finally` block will execute). Trying to handle errors like this yourself is usually pointless; instead, you should get the application to gracefully exit.

➤ `EndOfStreamException` — The usual cause of an `EndOfStreamException` is an attempt to read past the end of a file. A *stream* represents a flow of data between data sources. Streams are covered in detail in Chapter 24, "Networking."

➤ `OverflowException` — An `OverflowException` is what happens if you attempt to cast an `int` containing a value of -40 to a `uint` in a `checked` context.

The other exception classes shown in Figure 15-1 are not discussed here.

The class hierarchy for exceptions is somewhat unusual in that most of these classes do not add any functionality to their respective base classes. However, in the case of exception handling, the common reason for adding inherited classes is to indicate more specific error conditions. There is often no need to override methods or add any new ones (although it is not uncommon to add extra properties that carry extra information about the error condition). For example, you might have a base `ArgumentException` class intended for method calls where inappropriate values are passed in, and an `ArgumentNullException` class derived from it, which is intended to handle a `null` argument if passed.

CATCHING EXCEPTIONS

Given that the .NET Framework includes a selection of predefined base class exception objects, how do you use them in your code to trap error conditions? To deal with possible error conditions in C# code, you will normally divide the relevant part of your program into blocks of three different types:

➤ `try` blocks encapsulate the code that forms part of the normal operation of your program and that might encounter some serious error conditions.

➤ `catch` blocks encapsulate the code that deals with the various error conditions that your code might have encountered by working through any of the code in the accompanying `try` block. This place could also be used for logging errors.

➤ `finally` blocks encapsulate the code that cleans up any resources or takes any other action that you will normally want done at the end of a `try` or `catch` block. It is important to understand that the `finally` block is executed whether or not an exception is thrown. Because the aim is that the `finally` block contains cleanup code that should always be executed, the compiler will flag an error if you place a `return` statement inside a `finally` block. For an example of using the `finally` block, you might close any connections that were opened in the `try` block. It is also important to understand that the `finally` block is completely optional. If you do not have a requirement for any cleanup code (such as disposing or closing any open objects), then there is no need for this block.

So how do these blocks fit together to trap error conditions? Here is how:

1. The execution flow first enters the `try` block.
2. If no errors occur in the `try` block, execution proceeds normally through the block, and when the end of the `try` block is reached, the flow of execution jumps to the `finally` block if one is present

(Step 5). However, if an error does occur within the `try` block, execution jumps to a `catch` block (Step 3).

3. The error condition is handled in the `catch` block.

4. At the end of the `catch` block, execution automatically transfers to the `finally` block if one is present.

5. The `finally` block is executed (if present).

The C# syntax used to bring all this about looks roughly like this:

```
try
{
    // code for normal execution
}
catch
{
    // error handling
}
finally
{
    // clean up
}
```

Actually, a few variations on this theme exist:

➤ You can omit the `finally` block because it is optional.

➤ You can also supply as many `catch` blocks as you want to handle specific types of errors. However, the idea is not to get too carried away and have a huge number of `catch` blocks, because this can hurt the performance of your application.

➤ You can omit the `catch` blocks altogether, in which case the syntax serves not to identify exceptions, but as a way of guaranteeing that code in the `finally` block will be executed when execution leaves the `try` block. This is useful if the `try` block contains several exit points.

So far so good, but the question that has yet to be answered is this: If the code is running in the `try` block, how does it know when to switch to the `catch` block if an error has occurred? If an error is detected, the code does something known as *throwing an exception*. In other words, it instantiates an exception object class and throws it:

```
throw new OverflowException();
```

Here, you have instantiated an exception object of the `OverflowException` class. As soon as the computer encounters a `throw` statement inside a `try` block, it immediately looks for the `catch` block associated with that `try` block. If there is more than one `catch` block associated with the `try` block, it identifies the correct `catch` block by checking which exception class the `catch` block is associated with. For example, when the `OverflowException` object is thrown, execution jumps to the following `catch` block:

```
catch (OverflowException ex)
{
    // exception handling here
}
```

In other words, the computer looks for the `catch` block that indicates a matching exception class instance of the same class (or of a base class).

With this extra information, you can expand the `try` block just demonstrated. Assume, for the sake of argument, that there are two possible serious errors that can occur in the `try` block: an overflow and an array out of bounds. Assume that your code contains two Boolean variables, `Overflow` and `OutOfBounds`, which indicate whether these conditions exist. You have already seen that a predefined exception class exists to indicate overflow (`OverflowException`); similarly, an `IndexOutOfRangeException` class exists to handle an array that is out of bounds.

Now your `try` block looks like this:

```
try
{
    // code for normal execution

    if (Overflow == true)
    {
        throw new OverflowException();
    }

    // more processing

    if (OutOfBounds == true)
    {
        throw new IndexOutOfRangeException();
    }

    // otherwise continue normal execution
}
catch (OverflowException ex)
{
    // error handling for the overflow error condition
}
catch (IndexOutOfRangeException ex)
{
    // error handling for the index out of range error condition
}
finally
{
    // clean up
}
```

So far, this might not look that much different from what you could have done a long time ago if you ever used the Visual Basic 6 `On Error GoTo` statement (with the exception perhaps that the different parts in the code are separated). C#, however, provides a far more powerful and flexible mechanism for error handling.

This is because you can have `throw` statements that are nested in several method calls inside the `try` block, but the same `try` block continues to apply even as execution flow enters these other methods. If the computer encounters a `throw` statement, it immediately goes back up through all the method calls on the stack, looking for the end of the containing `try` block and the start of the appropriate `catch` block. During this process, all the local variables in the intermediate method calls will correctly go out of scope. This makes the `try...catch` architecture well suited to the situation described at the beginning of this section, where the error occurs inside a method call that is nested inside 15 or 20 method calls, and processing has to stop immediately.

As you can probably gather from this discussion, `try` blocks can play a very significant part in controlling the flow of execution of your code. However, it is important to understand that exceptions are intended for exceptional conditions, hence their name. You wouldn't want to use them as a way of controlling when to exit a `do...while` loop.

Implementing Multiple Catch Blocks

The easiest way to see how `try...catch...finally` blocks work in practice is with a couple of examples. The first example is called `SimpleExceptions`. It repeatedly asks the user to type in a number and then displays it. However, for the sake of this example, imagine that the number has to be between 0 and 5; otherwise, the program won't be able to process the number properly. Therefore, you will throw an exception if the user types in anything outside of this range.

The program then continues to ask for more numbers for processing until the user simply presses the Enter key without entering anything.

> *You should note that this code does not provide a good example of when to use exception handling. As already indicated, the idea of exceptions is that they are provided for exceptional circumstances. Users are always typing in silly things, so this situation doesn't really count. Normally, your program will handle incorrect user input by performing an instant check and asking the user to retype the input if there is a problem. However, generating exceptional situations is difficult in a small example that you can read through in a few minutes! So, we will tolerate this bad practice for now to demonstrate how exceptions work. The examples that follow present more realistic situations.*

The code for `SimpleExceptions` looks like this:

```csharp
using System;

namespace Wrox.ProCSharp.AdvancedCSharp
{
    public class MainEntryPoint
    {
        public static void Main()
        {
            while (true)
            {
                try
                {
                    string userInput;

                    Console.Write("Input a number between 0 and 5 " +
                        "(or just hit return to exit)> ");
                    userInput = Console.ReadLine();

                    if (userInput == "")
                    {
                        break;
                    }

                    int index = Convert.ToInt32(userInput);

                    if (index < 0 || index > 5)
                    {
                        throw new IndexOutOfRangeException(
                            "You typed in " + userInput);
                    }

                    Console.WriteLine("Your number was " + index);
                }
                catch (IndexOutOfRangeException ex)
                {
                    Console.WriteLine("Exception: " +
                        "Number should be between 0 and 5. {0}", ex.Message);
                }
                catch (Exception ex)
                {
                    Console.WriteLine(
```

```
                    "An exception was thrown. Message was: {0}", ex.Message);
                }
                finally
                {
                    Console.WriteLine("Thank you");
                }
            }
        }
    }
}
```

code snippet SimpleExceptions.cs

The core of this code is a `while` loop, which continually uses `Console.ReadLine()` to ask for user input. `ReadLine()` returns a string, so your first task is to convert it to an `int` using the `System.Convert.ToInt32()` method. The `System.Convert` class contains various useful methods to perform data conversions and provides an alternative to the `int.Parse()` method. In general, `System.Convert` contains methods to perform various type conversions. Recall that the C# compiler resolves `int` to instances of the `System.Int32` base class.

> *It is also worth pointing out that the parameter passed to the `catch` block is scoped to that `catch` block — which is why you are able to use the same parameter name, ex, in successive `catch` blocks in the preceding code.*

In the preceding example, you also check for an empty string, because this is your condition for exiting the `while` loop. Notice how the `break` statement actually breaks right out of the enclosing `try` block as well as the `while` loop because this is valid behavior. Of course, when execution breaks out of the `try` block, the `Console.WriteLine()` statement in the `finally` block is executed. Although you just display a greeting here, more commonly you will be doing tasks like closing file handles and calling the `Dispose()` method of various objects to perform any cleaning up. After the computer leaves the `finally` block, it simply carries on executing into the next statement that it would have executed had the `finally` block not been present. In the case of this example, though, you iterate back to the start of the `while` loop, and enter the `try` block again (unless the `finally` block was entered as a result of executing the `break` statement in the `while` loop, in which case you simply exit the `while` loop).

Next, you check for your exception condition:

```
if (index < 0 || index > 5)
{
    throw new IndexOutOfRangeException("You typed in " + userInput);
}
```

When throwing an exception, you need to choose what type of exception to throw. Although the class `System.Exception` is available, it is intended only as a base class. It is considered bad programming practice to throw an instance of this class as an exception, because it conveys no information about the nature of the error condition. Instead, the .NET Framework contains many other exception classes that are derived from `System.Exception`. Each of these matches a particular type of exception condition, and you are free to define your own ones as well. The idea is that you give as much information as possible about the particular exception condition by throwing an instance of a class that matches the particular error condition. In the preceding example, `System.IndexOutOfRangeException` is the best choice for the circumstances. `IndexOutOfRangeException` has several constructor overloads. The one chosen in the example takes a string, which describes the error. Alternatively, you might choose to derive your own custom `Exception` object that describes the error condition in the context of your application.

Suppose that the user then types a number that is not between 0 and 5. This will be picked up by the if statement and an IndexOutOfRangeException object will be instantiated and thrown. At this point, the computer will immediately exit the try block and hunt for a catch block that handles IndexOutOfRangeException. The first catch block it encounters is this:

```
catch (IndexOutOfRangeException ex)
{
    Console.WriteLine(
        "Exception: Number should be between 0 and 5. {0}", ex.Message);
}
```

Because this catch block takes a parameter of the appropriate class, the catch block will be passed the exception instance and executed. In this case, you display an error message and the Exception.Message property (which corresponds to the string you passed to the IndexOutOfRangeException's constructor). After executing this catch block, control then switches to the finally block, just as if no exception had occurred.

Notice that in the example, you have also provided another catch block:

```
catch (Exception ex)
{
    Console.WriteLine("An exception was thrown. Message was: {0}", ex.Message);
}
```

This catch block would also be capable of handling an IndexOutOfRangeException if it weren't for the fact that such exceptions will already have been caught by the previous catch block. A reference to a base class can also refer to any instances of classes derived from it, and all exceptions are derived from System.Exception. So why isn't this catch block executed? The answer is that the computer executes only the first suitable catch block it finds from the list of available catch blocks. So why is this second catch block even here? Well, it is not only your code that is covered by the try block. Inside the block, you actually make three separate calls to methods in the System namespace (Console.ReadLine(), Console.Write(), and Convert.ToInt32()), and any of these methods might throw an exception.

If you type in something that is not a number — say a or hello — the Convert.ToInt32() method will throw an exception of the class System.FormatException to indicate that the string passed into ToInt32() is not in a format that can be converted to an int. When this happens, the computer will trace back through the method calls, looking for a handler that can handle this exception. Your first catch block (the one that takes an IndexOutOfRangeException) will not do. The computer then looks at the second catch block. This one will do because FormatException is derived from Exception, so a FormatException instance can be passed in as a parameter here.

The structure of the example is actually fairly typical of a situation with multiple catch blocks. You start with catch blocks that are designed to trap very specific error conditions. Then, you finish with more general blocks that will cover any errors for which you have not written specific error handlers. Indeed, the order of the catch blocks is important. If you had written the previous two blocks in the opposite order, the code would not have compiled, because the second catch block is unreachable (the Exception catch block would catch all exceptions). Therefore, the uppermost catch blocks should be the most granular options available and ending with the most general options.

Now that you have analyzed the code for the example, you can run it. The following output illustrates what happens with different inputs and demonstrates both the IndexOutOfRangeException and the FormatException being thrown:

```
SimpleExceptions
Input a number between 0 and 5 (or just hit return to exit)>4
Your number was 4
Thank you
Input a number between 0 and 5 (or just hit return to exit)>0
Your number was 0
Thank you
Input a number between 0 and 5 (or just hit return to exit)>10
```

```
Exception: Number should be between 0 and 5. You typed in 10
Thank you
Input a number between 0 and 5 (or just hit return to exit)>hello
An exception was thrown. Message was: Input string was not in a correct format.
Thank you
Input a number between 0 and 5 (or just hit return to exit)>
Thank you
```

Catching Exceptions from Other Code

The previous example demonstrates the handling of two exceptions. One of them, IndexOutOfRangeException, was thrown by your own code. The other, FormatException, was thrown from inside one of the base classes. It is very common for code in a library to throw an exception if it detects that some problem has occurred, or if one of the methods has been called inappropriately by being passed the wrong parameters. However, library code rarely attempts to catch exceptions; this is regarded as the responsibility of the client code.

Often, you will find that exceptions are thrown from the base class libraries while you are debugging. The process of debugging to some extent involves determining why exceptions have been thrown and removing the causes. Your aim should be to ensure that by the time the code is actually shipped, exceptions do occur only in very exceptional circumstances, and if possible, are handled in some appropriate way in your code.

System.Exception Properties

The example has illustrated the use of only the Message property of the exception object. However, a number of other properties are available in System.Exception, as shown in the following table.

PROPERTY	DESCRIPTION
Data	This provides you with the ability to add key/value statements to the exception that can be used to supply extra information about the exception.
HelpLink	This is a link to a help file that provides more information about the exception.
InnerException	If this exception was thrown inside a catch block, then InnerException contains the exception object that sent the code into that catch block.
Message	This is text that describes the error condition.
Source	This is the name of the application or object that caused the exception.
StackTrace	This provides details of the method calls on the stack (to help track down the method that threw the exception).
TargetSite	This is a .NET reflection object that describes the method that threw the exception.

Of these properties, StackTrace and TargetSite are supplied automatically by the .NET runtime if a stack trace is available. Source will always be filled in by the .NET runtime as the name of the assembly in which the exception was raised (though you might want to modify the property in your code to give more specific information), whereas Data, Message, HelpLink, and InnerException must be filled in by the code that threw the exception, by setting these properties immediately before throwing the exception. For example, the code to throw an exception might look something like this:

```
if (ErrorCondition == true)
{
    Exception myException = new ClassMyException("Help!!!!");
    myException.Source = "My Application Name";
    myException.HelpLink = "MyHelpFile.txt";
    myException.Data["ErrorDate"] = DateTime.Now;
```

```
        myException.Data.Add("AdditionalInfo", "Contact Bill from the Blue Team");
        throw myException;
}
```

Here, `ClassMyException` is the name of the particular exception class you are throwing. Note that it is common practice for the names of all exception classes to end with `Exception`. Also, note that the `Data` property is assigned in two possible ways.

What Happens If an Exception Isn't Handled?

Sometimes an exception might be thrown, but there might not be a `catch` block in your code that is able to handle that kind of exception. The `SimpleExceptions` example can serve to illustrate this. Suppose, for example, that you omitted the `FormatException` and catch-all `catch` blocks, and supplied only the block that traps an `IndexOutOfRangeException`. In that circumstance, what would happen if a `FormatException` were thrown?

The answer is that the .NET runtime would catch it. Later in this section, you learn how you can nest `try` blocks, and in fact, there is already a nested `try` block behind the scenes in the example. The .NET runtime has effectively placed the entire program inside another huge `try` block — it does this for every .NET program. This `try` block has a `catch` handler that can catch any type of exception. If an exception occurs that your code does not handle, the execution flow will simply pass right out of your program and be trapped by this `catch` block in the .NET runtime. However, the results of this probably will not be what you want. What happens is that the execution of your code will be terminated promptly; the user will see a dialog box that complains that your code has not handled the exception, and that provides any details about the exception the .NET runtime was able to retrieve. At least the exception will have been caught! This is what happened earlier in Chapter 2, "Core C#," in the `Vector` example when the program threw an exception.

In general, if you are writing an executable, try to catch as many exceptions as you reasonably can and handle them in a sensible way. If you are writing a library, it is normally best not to handle exceptions (unless a particular exception represents something wrong in your code that you can handle), but instead, assume that the calling code will handle any errors it encounters. However, you may nevertheless want to catch any Microsoft-defined exceptions, so that you can throw your own exception objects that give more specific information to the client code.

Nested try Blocks

One nice feature of exceptions is that you can nest `try` blocks inside each other, like this:

```
try
{
    // Point A
    try
    {
        // Point B
    }
    catch
    {
        // Point C
    }
    finally
    {
        // clean up
    }
    // Point D
}
catch
```

```
{
    // error handling
}
finally
{
    // clean up
}
```

Although each `try` block is accompanied by only one `catch` block in this example, you could string several `catch` blocks together, too. This section takes a closer look at how nested `try` blocks work.

If an exception is thrown inside the outer `try` block but outside the inner `try` block (points A and D), the situation is no different from any of the scenarios you have seen before: either the exception is caught by the outer `catch` block and the outer `finally` block is executed, or the `finally` block is executed and the .NET runtime handles the exception.

If an exception is thrown in the inner `try` block (point B), and there is a suitable inner `catch` block to handle the exception, then, again, you are in familiar territory: the exception is handled there, and the inner `finally` block is executed before execution resumes inside the outer `try` block (at point D).

Now suppose that an exception occurs in the inner `try` block, but there *isn't* a suitable inner `catch` block to handle it. This time, the inner `finally` block is executed as usual, but then the .NET runtime will have no choice but to leave the entire inner `try` block to search for a suitable exception handler. The next obvious place to look is in the outer `catch` block. If the system finds one here, then that handler will be executed and then the outer `finally` block will be executed. If there is no suitable handler here, the search for one will go on. In this case, it means the outer `finally` block will be executed, and then, because there are no more `catch` blocks, control will be transferred to the .NET runtime. Note that the code beyond point D in the outer `try` block is not executed at any point.

An even more interesting thing happens if an exception is thrown at point C. If the program is at point C, it must be already processing an exception that was thrown at point B. It is quite legitimate to throw another exception from inside a `catch` block. In this case, the exception is treated as if it had been thrown by the outer `try` block, so flow of execution will immediately leave the inner `catch` block, and execute the inner `finally` block, before the system searches the outer `catch` block for a handler. Similarly, if an exception is thrown in the inner `finally` block, control will immediately be transferred to the best appropriate handler, with the search starting at the outer `catch` block.

> It is perfectly legitimate to throw exceptions from `catch` and `finally` blocks.

Although the situation has been shown with just two `try` blocks, the same principles hold no matter how many `try` blocks you nest inside each other. At each stage, the .NET runtime will smoothly transfer control up through the `try` blocks, looking for an appropriate handler. At each stage, as control leaves a `catch` block, any cleanup code in the corresponding `finally` block (if present) will be executed, but no code outside any `finally` block will be run until the correct `catch` handler has been found and run.

The nesting of `try` blocks can also occur between methods themselves. For example, if method A calls method B from within a `try` block, then method B itself has a `try` block within it as well.

You have now seen how having nested `try` blocks can work. The obvious next question is why would you want to do that? There are two reasons:

➤ To modify the type of exception thrown

➤ To enable different types of exception to be handled in different places in your code

Modifying the Type of Exception

Modifying the type of the exception can be useful when the original exception thrown does not adequately describe the problem. What typically happens is that something — possibly the .NET runtime — throws a fairly low-level exception that says something like an overflow occurred (`OverflowException`) or an argument passed to a method was incorrect (a class derived from `ArgumentException`). However, because of the context in which the exception occurred, you will know that this reveals some other underlying problem (for example, an overflow can only happen at that point in your code because a file you have just read contained incorrect data). In that case, the most appropriate thing that your handler for the first exception can do is throw another exception that more accurately describes the problem, so that another `catch` block further along can deal with it more appropriately. In this case, it can also forward the original exception through a property implemented by `System.Exception` called `InnerException`. `InnerException` simply contains a reference to any other related exception that was thrown — in case the ultimate handler routine will need this extra information.

Of course, the situation also exists where an exception occurs inside a `catch` block. For example, you might normally read in some configuration file that contains detailed instructions for handling the error, and it might turn out that this file is not there.

Handling Different Exceptions in Different Places

The second reason for having nested `try` blocks is so that different types of exceptions can be handled at different locations in your code. A good example of this is if you have a loop where various exception conditions can occur. Some of these might be serious enough that you need to abandon the entire loop, whereas others might be less serious and simply require that you abandon that iteration and move on to the next iteration around the loop. You could achieve this by having one `try` block inside the loop, which handles the less serious error conditions, and an outer `try` block outside the loop, which handles the more serious error conditions. You will see how this works in the next exceptions example.

USER-DEFINED EXCEPTION CLASSES

You are now ready to look at a second example that illustrates exceptions. This example, called `SolicitColdCall`, contains two nested `try` blocks and illustrates the practice of defining your own custom exception classes and throwing another exception from inside a `try` block.

This example assumes that a sales company wants to have additional customers on its sales list. The company's sales team is going to phone a list of people to invite them to become customers, a practice known in sales jargon as *cold calling*. To this end, you have a text file available that contains the names of the people to be cold called. The file should be in a well-defined format in which the first line contains the number of people in the file and each subsequent line contains the name of the next person. In other words, a correctly formatted file of names might look like this:

```
4
George Washington
Benedict Arnold
John Adams
Thomas Jefferson
```

This version of cold calling is designed to display the name of the person on the screen (perhaps for the salesperson to read). That is why only names and not phone numbers of the individuals are contained in the file.

For this example, your program will ask the user for the name of the file and will then simply read it in and display the names of people. That sounds like a simple task, but even so, a couple of things can go wrong and require you to abandon the entire procedure:

➤ The user might type the name of a file that does not exist. This will be caught as a `FileNotFound` exception.

➤ The file might not be in the correct format. There are two possible problems here. First, the first line of the file might not be an integer. Second, there might not be as many names in the file as the first line of the file indicates. In both cases, you want to trap this oddity as a custom exception that has been written specially for this purpose, `ColdCallFileFormatException`.

There is something else that can go wrong that, while not causing you to abandon the entire process, will mean that you need to abandon that person and move on to the next person in the file (and therefore will be trapped by an inner `try` block). Some people are spies working for rival sales companies, and obviously, you would not want to let these people know what you are up to by accidentally phoning one of them. Your research has indicated that you can identify who the spies are because their names begin with B. Such people should have been screened out when the data file was first prepared, but just in case any have slipped through, you will need to check each name in the file and throw a `SalesSpyFoundException` if you detect a sales spy. This, of course, is another custom exception object.

Finally, you will implement this example by coding a class, `ColdCallFileReader`, which maintains the connection to the cold-call file and retrieves data from it. You will code this class in a very safe way, which means that its methods will all throw exceptions if they are called inappropriately; for example, if a method that will read a file is called before the file has even been opened. For this purpose, you will write another exception class, `UnexpectedException`.

Catching the User-Defined Exceptions

Let's start with the `Main()` method of the `SolicitColdCall` sample, which catches your user-defined exceptions. Note that you will need to call up file-handling classes in the `System.IO` namespace as well as the `System` namespace.

```
using System;
using System.IO;

namespace Wrox.ProCSharp.AdvancedCSharp
{
    class MainEntryPoint
    {
        static void Main()
        {
            Console.Write("Please type in the name of the file " +
                "containing the names of the people to be cold called > ");
            string fileName = Console.ReadLine();
            ColdCallFileReader peopleToRing = new ColdCallFileReader();

            try
            {
                peopleToRing.Open(fileName);
                for (int i=0; i<peopleToRing.NPeopleToRing; i++)
                {
                    peopleToRing.ProcessNextPerson();
                }
                Console.WriteLine("All callers processed correctly");
            }
            catch(FileNotFoundException)
            {
                Console.WriteLine("The file {0} does not exist", fileName);
            }
            catch(ColdCallFileFormatException ex)
            {
                Console.WriteLine(
                "The file {0} appears to have been corrupted", fileName);
                Console.WriteLine("Details of problem are: {0}", ex.Message);
                if (ex.InnerException != null)
                {
```

```
            Console.WriteLine(
                "Inner exception was: {0}", ex.InnerException.Message);
        }
    }
    catch(Exception ex)
    {
        Console.WriteLine("Exception occurred:\n" + ex.Message);
    }
    finally
    {
        peopleToRing.Dispose();
    }
    Console.ReadLine();
}
}
```

This code is a little more than just a loop to process people from the file. You start by asking the user for the name of the file. Then you instantiate an object of a class called `ColdCallFileReader`, which is defined shortly. The `ColdCallFileReader` class is the class that handles the file reading. Notice that you do this outside the initial `try` block — that's because the variables that you instantiate here need to be available in the subsequent `catch` and `finally` blocks, and if you declared them inside the `try` block they would go out of scope at the closing curly brace of the `try` block, which would not be a good thing.

In the `try` block, you open the file (using the `ColdCallFileReader.Open()` method) and loop over all the people in it. The `ColdCallFileReader.ProcessNextPerson()` method reads in and displays the name of the next person in the file, and the `ColdCallFileReader.NPeopleToRing` property tells you how many people should be in the file (obtained by reading the first line of the file). There are three `catch` blocks: one for `FileNotFoundException`, one for `ColdCallFileFormatException`, and one to trap any other .NET exceptions.

In the case of a `FileNotFoundException`, you display a message to that effect. Notice that in this `catch` block, the exception instance is not actually used at all. This `catch` block is used to illustrate the user-friendliness of the application. Exception objects generally contain technical information that is useful for developers, but not the sort of stuff you want to show to your end users. So in this case, you create a simpler message of your own.

For the `ColdCallFileFormatException` handler, you have done the opposite, and illustrated how to give fuller technical information, including details of the inner exception, if one is present.

Finally, if you catch any other generic exceptions, you display a user-friendly message, instead of letting any such exceptions fall through to the .NET runtime. Note that you have chosen not to handle any other exceptions not derived from `System.Exception`, because you are not calling directly into non-.NET code.

The `finally` block is there to clean up resources. In this case, this means closing any open file — performed by the `ColdCallFileReader.Dispose()` method.

Throwing the User-Defined Exceptions

Now take a look at the definition of the class that handles the file reading and (potentially) throws your user-defined exceptions: `ColdCallFileReader`. Because this class maintains an external file connection, you need to make sure that it is disposed of correctly in accordance with the principles laid down for the disposing of objects in Chapter 4, "Inheritance." Therefore, you derive this class from `IDisposable`.

First, you declare some variables:

```
class ColdCallFileReader: IDisposable
{
    FileStream fs;
    StreamReader sr;
```

```
uint nPeopleToRing;
bool isDisposed = false;
bool isOpen = false;
```

`FileStream` and `StreamReader`, both in the `System.IO` namespace, are the base classes that you will use to read the file. `FileStream` allows you to connect to the file in the first place, whereas `StreamReader` is specially geared up to reading text files and implements a method, `ReadLine()`, which reads a line of text from a file. You look at `StreamReader` more closely in Chapter 29, "Manipulating Files and the Registry," which discusses file handling in depth.

The `isDisposed` field indicates whether the `Dispose()` method has been called. `ColdCallFileReader` is implemented so that after `Dispose()` has been called, it is not permitted to reopen connections and reuse the object. `isOpen` is also used for error checking — in this case, checking whether the `StreamReader` actually connects to an open file.

The process of opening the file and reading in that first line — the one that tells you how many people are in the file — is handled by the `Open()` method:

```
public void Open(string fileName)
{
    if (isDisposed)
        throw new ObjectDisposedException("peopleToRing");

    fs = new FileStream(fileName, FileMode.Open);
    sr = new StreamReader(fs);

    try
    {
        string firstLine = sr.ReadLine();
        nPeopleToRing = uint.Parse(firstLine);
        isOpen = true;
    }
    catch (FormatException ex)
    {
        throw new ColdCallFileFormatException(
            "First line isn\'t an integer", ex);
    }
}
```

code snippet SolicitColdCall.cs

The first thing you do in this method (as with all other `ColdCallFileReader` methods) is check whether the client code has inappropriately called it after the object has been disposed of, and if so, throw a predefined `ObjectDisposedException` object. The `Open()` method checks the `isDisposed` field to see whether `Dispose()` has already been called. Because calling `Dispose()` implies that the caller has now finished with this object, you regard it as an error to attempt to open a new file connection if `Dispose()` has been called.

Next, the method contains the first of two inner `try` blocks. The purpose of this one is to catch any errors resulting from the first line of the file not containing an integer. If that problem arises, the .NET runtime will throw a `FormatException`, which you trap and convert to a more meaningful exception that indicates there is actually a problem with the format of the cold-call file. Note that `System.FormatException` is there to indicate format problems with basic data types, not with files, and so is not a particularly useful exception to pass back to the calling routine in this case. The new exception thrown will be trapped by the outermost `try` block. Because no cleanup is needed here, there is no need for a `finally` block.

If everything is fine, you set the `isOpen` field to `true` to indicate that there is now a valid file connection from which data can be read.

The `ProcessNextPerson()` method also contains an inner `try` block:

```
public void ProcessNextPerson()
{
    if (isDisposed)
    {
        throw new ObjectDisposedException("peopleToRing");
    }

    if (!isOpen)
    {
        throw new UnexpectedException(
            "Attempted to access coldcall file that is not open");
    }

    try
    {
        string name;
        name = sr.ReadLine();
        if (name == null)
            throw new ColdCallFileFormatException("Not enough names");
        if (name[0] == 'B')
        {
            throw new SalesSpyFoundException(name);
        }
        Console.WriteLine(name);
    }
    catch(SalesSpyFoundException ex)
    {
        Console.WriteLine(ex.Message);
    }

    finally
    {
    }
}
```

Two possible problems exist with the file here (assuming that there actually is an open file connection; the `ProcessNextPerson()` method checks this first). First, you might read in the next name and discover that it is a sales spy. If that condition occurs, the exception is trapped by the first of the `catch` blocks in this method. Because that exception has been caught here, inside the loop, it means that execution can subsequently continue in the `Main()` method of the program and the subsequent names in the file will continue to be processed.

A problem might also occur if you try to read the next name and discover that you have already reached the end of the file. The way that the `StreamReader` object's `ReadLine()` method works is if it has gone past the end of the file, it doesn't throw an exception, but simply returns `null`. Therefore, if you find a null string, you know that the format of the file was incorrect because the number in the first line of the file indicated a larger number of names than were actually present in the file. If that happens, you throw a `ColdCallFileFormatException`, which will be caught by the outer exception handler (which will cause the execution to terminate).

Once again, you don't need a `finally` block here because there is no cleanup to do; however, this time an empty `finally` block is included, just to show that you can do so, if you want.

The example is nearly finished. You have just two more members of `ColdCallFileReader` to look at: the `NPeopleToRing` property, which returns the number of people supposed to be in the file, and the `Dispose()` method, which closes an open file. Notice that the `Dispose()` method returns only if it has already been called — this is the recommended way of implementing it. It also checks that there actually is a file stream to close before closing it. This example is shown here to illustrate defensive coding techniques, so that's what you are doing!

```
            public uint NPeopleToRing
            {
                get
                {
                    if (isDisposed)
                    {
                        throw new ObjectDisposedException("peopleToRing");
                    }

                    if (!isOpen)
                    {
                        throw new UnexpectedException(
                            "Attempted to access cold-call file that is not open");
                    }

                    return nPeopleToRing;
                }
            }

            public void Dispose()
            {
                if (isDisposed)
                {
                    return;
                }

                isDisposed = true;
                isOpen = false;

                if (fs != null)
                {
                    fs.Close();
                    fs = null;
                }
            }
```

Defining the User-Defined Exception Classes

Finally, you need to define your own three exception classes. Defining your own exception is quite easy because there are rarely any extra methods to add. It is just a case of implementing a constructor to ensure that the base class constructor is called correctly. Here is the full implementation of `SalesSpyFoundException`:

```
            class SalesSpyFoundException: ApplicationException
            {
                public SalesSpyFoundException(string spyName)
                :   base("Sales spy found, with name " + spyName)
                {
                }

                public SalesSpyFoundException(
                    string spyName, Exception innerException)
                :   base(
                        "Sales spy found with name " + spyName, innerException)
                {
                }
            }
```

code snippet SolicitColdCall.cs

Notice that it is derived from `ApplicationException`, as you would expect for a custom exception. In fact, in practice, you would probably have put in an intermediate class, something like `ColdCallFileException`, derived from `ApplicationException`, and derived both of your exception classes from this class. This ensures that the handling code has that extra-fine degree of control over which exception handler handles each exception. However, to keep the example simple, you will not do that.

You have done one bit of processing in `SalesSpyFoundException`. You have assumed that the message passed into its constructor is just the name of the spy found, so you turn this string into a more meaningful error message. You have also provided two constructors, one that simply takes a message, and one that also takes an inner exception as a parameter. When defining your own exception classes, it is best to include, at a minimum, at least these two constructors (although you will not actually be using the second `SalesSpyFoundException` constructor in this example).

Now for the `ColdCallFileFormatException`. This follows the same principles as the previous exception, except that you don't do any processing on the message:

```
class ColdCallFileFormatException: ApplicationException
{
    public ColdCallFileFormatException(string message)
    :   base(message)
    {
    }

    public ColdCallFileFormatException(
        string message, Exception innerException)
    :   base(message, innerException)
    {
    }
}
```

And finally, `UnexpectedException`, which looks much the same as `ColdCallFileFormatException`:

```
class UnexpectedException: ApplicationException
{
    public UnexpectedException(string message)
    :   base(message)
    {
    }

    public UnexpectedException(string message, Exception innerException)
    :   base(message, innerException)
    {
    }
}
```

Now you are ready to test the program. First, try the `people.txt` file; the contents are defined here:

```
4
George Washington
Benedict Arnold
John Adams
Thomas Jefferson
```

This has four names (which match the number given in the first line of the file), including one spy. Then try the following `people2.txt` file, which has an obvious formatting error:

```
49
George Washington
Benedict Arnold
John Adams
Thomas Jefferson
```

Finally, try the example but specify the name of a file that does not exist, say, `people3.txt`. Running the program three times for the three filenames gives these results:

```
SolicitColdCall
Please type in the name of the file containing the names of the people to be cold
   called > people.txt
George Washington
Sales spy found, with name Benedict Arnold
John Adams
Thomas Jefferson
All callers processed correctly


SolicitColdCall
Please type in the name of the file containing the names of the people to be cold
   called > people2.txt
George Washington
Sales spy found, with name Benedict Arnold
John Adams
Thomas Jefferson
The file people2.txt appears to have been corrupted.
Details of the problem are: Not enough names


SolicitColdCall
Please type in the name of the file containing the names of the people to be cold
   called > people3.txt
The file people3.txt does not exist.
```

In the end, this application shows you a number of different ways in which you can handle the errors and exceptions that you might find in your own applications.

SUMMARY

This chapter examined the rich mechanism C# has for dealing with error conditions through exceptions. You are not limited to the generic error codes that could be output from your code; instead, you have the ability to go in and uniquely handle the most granular of error conditions. Sometimes these error conditions are provided to you through the .NET Framework itself, but at other times, you might want to go in and code your own error conditions as illustrated in this chapter. In either case, you have many ways of protecting the workflow of your applications from unnecessary and dangerous faults.

The next chapter allows you to take a lot of what you learned so far in this book and works at implementing these lessons within the .NET developers IDE — Visual Studio 2010.

PART II
Visual Studio

▶ **CHAPTER 16:** Visual Studio 2010

▶ **CHAPTER 17:** Deployment

16

Visual Studio 2010

WHAT'S IN THIS CHAPTER?

➤ Using Visual Studio 2010

➤ Refactoring with Visual Studio

➤ Visual Studio 2010's multi-targeting capabilities

➤ Working with the technologies WPF, WCF, WF, and more.

At this point, you should be familiar with the C# language and almost ready to move on to the applied sections of the book, which cover how to use C# to program a variety of applications. Before doing that, however, you need to examine how you can use Visual Studio and some of the features provided by the .NET environment to get the best from your programs.

This chapter explains what programming in the .NET environment means in practice. It covers Visual Studio, the main development environment in which you will write, compile, debug, and optimize your C# programs, and provides guidelines for writing good applications. Visual Studio is the main IDE used for everything from writing Web Forms, Windows Forms, Windows Presentation Foundation (WPF) applications, and even Silverlight applications to XML Web services, and more. For more details on Windows Forms and how to write user interface code, see Chapter 39, "Windows Forms."

This chapter also explores what it takes to build applications that are targeted at the .NET Framework 4. Working with Visual Studio 2010 will provide you the ability to work with the latest application types, such as WPF, the Windows Communication Foundation (WCF), and the Windows Workflow Foundation (WF), directly.

WORKING WITH VISUAL STUDIO 2010

Visual Studio 2010 is a fully integrated development environment. It is designed to make the process of writing your code, debugging it, and compiling it to an assembly to be shipped as easy as possible. What this means is that Visual Studio gives you a very sophisticated multiple-document-interface application in which you can do just about everything related to developing your code. It offers these features:

➤ **Text editor** — Using this editor, you can write your C# (as well as Visual Basic 2010 and Visual C++) code. This text editor is quite sophisticated. For example, as you type, it automatically lays out your code by indenting lines, matching start and end brackets of code blocks, and color-coding keywords. It also performs some syntax checks as you type, and it underlines code that causes compilation errors, also known as design-time debugging. In addition, it features IntelliSense, which automatically displays the names of classes, fields, or methods as you begin to type them. As you start typing parameters to methods, it will also show you the parameter lists for the available overloads. Figure 16-1 shows the IntelliSense feature in action with one of the .NET base classes, `ListBox`.

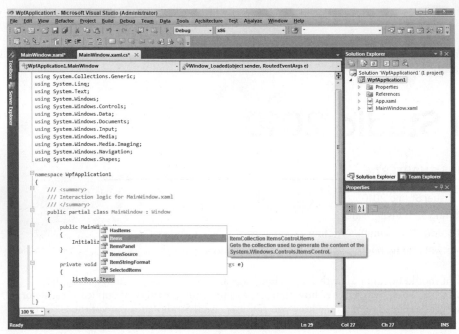

FIGURE 16-1

 By pressing Ctrl+Space, you can bring back the IntelliSense list box if you need it or if for any reason it is not visible.

➤ **Design view editor** — This editor enables you to place user-interface and data-access controls in your project; Visual Studio automatically adds the necessary C# code to your source files to instantiate these controls in your project. (This is possible because all .NET controls are instances of particular base classes.)

➤ **Supporting windows** — These windows allow you to view and modify aspects of your project, such as the classes in your source code, as well as the available properties (and their startup values) for Windows Forms and Web Forms classes. You can also use these windows to specify compilation options, such as which assemblies your code needs to reference.

➤ **The ability to compile from within the environment** — Instead of needing to run the C# compiler from the command line, you can simply select a menu option to compile the project, and Visual Studio will call the compiler for you and pass all the relevant command-line parameters to the compiler, detailing such things as which assemblies to reference and what type of assembly you want to be emitted (executable or library `.dll`, for example). If you want, it can also run the compiled executable for you so that you can see whether it runs satisfactorily. You can even choose between different build configurations (for example, a release or debug build).

➤ **Integrated debugger** — It is in the nature of programming that your code will not run correctly the first time you try it. Or the second time. Or the third time. Visual Studio seamlessly links up to a debugger for you, allowing you to set breakpoints and watches on variables from within the environment.

➤ **Integrated MSDN help** — Visual Studio enables you to access the MSDN documentation from within the IDE. For example, if you are not sure of the meaning of a keyword while using the text editor, simply select the keyword and press the F1 key, and Visual Studio will access MSDN to show you related topics. Similarly, if you are not sure what a certain compilation error means, you can bring up the documentation for that error by selecting the error message and pressing F1.

➤ **Access to other programs** — Visual Studio can also access a number of other utilities that allow you to examine and modify aspects of your computer or network, without your having to leave the developer environment. With the tools available, you can check running services and database connections, look directly into your SQL Server tables, and even browse the Web using an Internet Explorer window.

If you have developed previously using C++ or Visual Basic, you will already be familiar with the relevant Visual Studio 6 version of the IDE, and many of the features in the preceding list will not be new to you. What is new in Visual Studio is that it combines all the features that were previously available across all Visual Studio 6 development environments. This means that regardless of what language you used in Visual Studio 6, you will find some new features in Visual Studio. For example, in the older Visual Basic environment, you could not compile separate debug and release builds. If you are coming to C# from a background of C++, though, then much of the support for data access and the ability to drop controls into your application with a click of the mouse, which has long been part of the Visual Basic developer's experience, will be new to you.

 C++ developers will miss two Visual Studio 6 features in Visual Studio 2010: edit-and-continue debugging and an integrated profiler. Visual Studio 2010 also does not include a full profiler application. Instead, you will find a number of .NET classes that assist with profiling in the System.Diagnostics *namespace. The perfmon profiling tool is available from the command line (just type perfmon) and has a number of new .NET-related performance monitors.*

Whatever your background, you will find that the overall look of the Visual Studio 2010 developer environment has changed since the days of Visual Studio 6 to accommodate the new features, the single cross-language IDE, and the integration with .NET. There are new menu and toolbar options, and many of the existing ones from Visual Studio 6 have been renamed. Therefore, you will need to spend some time familiarizing yourself with the layout and commands available in Visual Studio 2010.

The differences between Visual Studio 2008 and Visual Studio 2010 are a few nice additions that facilitate working in Visual Studio 2010. Probably the biggest change to Visual Studio this time around is that the entire editor was rebuilt on the .NET Framework 4 and makes use of the Microsoft Extensibility Framework (MEF) as well as WPF. Visual Studio 2010 includes the ability to target specific versions of the .NET Framework (including the .NET Framework versions 2.0, 3.0, 3.5, or 4), JavaScript IntelliSense support, and outstanding abilities to work with CSS. You will also find built-in features that allow you to build ASP.NET AJAX applications as well as applications using some of the newest technical capabilities coming out of Microsoft, including the WCF, WF, and WPF.

One of the biggest items to notice with your installation of Visual Studio 2010 is that this rebuilt IDE works with the .NET Framework 4. In fact, when you install Visual Studio 2010, you will also be installing the .NET Framework 4 if it isn't already installed. Like Visual Studio 2005/2008, this new IDE, Visual Studio 2010, is not built to work with version 1.0 or 1.1 of the .NET Framework, which means that if you still want to develop 1.0 or 1.1 applications, you will want to keep Visual Studio 2002 or 2003, respectively, installed on your machine. Installing Visual Studio 2010 installs a complete and new copy of Visual Studio and does not upgrade the previous Visual Studio 2002, 2003, 2005, or 2008 IDEs. The four copies of Visual Studio will then run side by side on your machine if required.

Note that if you attempt to open your Visual Studio 2002 to 2008 projects using Visual Studio 2010, the IDE will warn you that your solution will be upgraded to Visual Studio 2010 if you continue by popping up the Visual Studio Conversion Wizard (see Figure 16-2).

FIGURE 16-2

The Upgrade Wizard has been dramatically improved since Visual Studio 2003 to this one provided by Visual Studio 2010. This wizard can make backup copies of the solutions prior to backing it up (see Figure 16-3), and it can also back up solutions that are contained within source control.

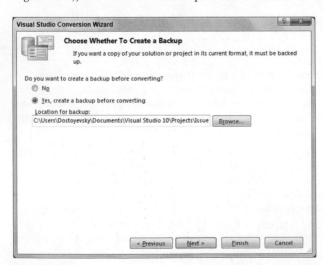

FIGURE 16-3

It is also possible to have Visual Studio generate a conversion report for you in the conversion process's final step. The report will then be viewable directly in the document window of Visual Studio. This report is illustrated (done with a simple conversion) in Figure 16-4.

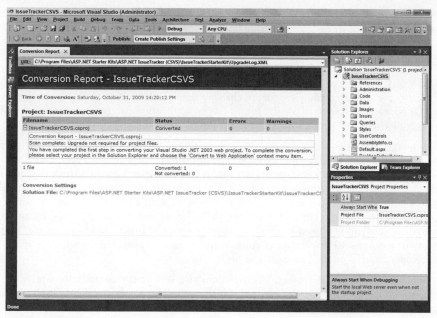

FIGURE 16-4

Because this is a professional-level book, it does not look in detail at every feature or menu option available in Visual Studio 2010. Surely, you will be able to find your way around the IDE. The real aim of this Visual Studio coverage is to ensure that you are sufficiently familiar with the concepts involved when building and debugging a C# application that you can make the most of working with Visual Studio 2010. Figure 16-5 shows what your screen might look like when working in Visual Studio 2010. (Note that because the appearance of Visual Studio is highly customizable, the windows might not be in the same locations, or different windows might be visible when you launch this development environment.)

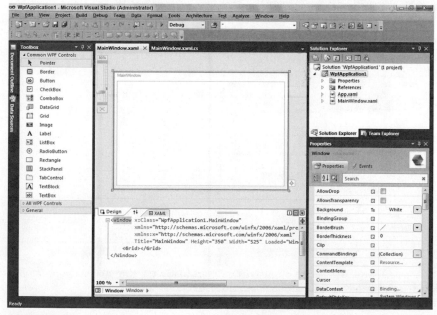

FIGURE 16-5

The following sections walk you through the process of creating, coding, and debugging a project, showing what Visual Studio can do to help you at each stage.

Creating a Project

Once you have installed Visual Studio 2010, you will want to start your first project. With Visual Studio, you rarely start with a blank file and then add C# code, in the way that you have been doing in the previous chapters in this book. (Of course, the option of asking for an empty application project is there if you really do want to start writing your code from scratch or if you are going to create a solution that will contain a number of projects.)

Instead, the idea is that you tell Visual Studio roughly what type of project you want to create, and it will generate the files and C# code that provide a framework for that type of project. You then work by adding your code to this outline. For example, if you want to build a Windows GUI-interface-based application (or, in .NET terminology, a Windows Form), Visual Studio will start you off with a file containing C# source code that creates a basic form. This form is capable of talking to Windows and receiving events. It can be maximized, minimized, or resized; all you need to do is add the controls and functionality you want. If your application is intended to be a command-line utility (a console application), Visual Studio will give you a basic namespace, class, and a `Main()` method to start you off.

Last, but hardly least, when you create your project, Visual Studio also sets up the compilation options that you are likely to supply to the C# compiler — whether it is to compile to a command-line application, a library, or a WPF application. It will also tell the compiler which base class libraries you will need to reference (a WPF GUI application will need to reference many of the WPF-related libraries; a console application probably will not). Of course, you can modify all these settings as you are editing, if you need to.

The first time you start Visual Studio, you will be presented with a blank IDE (see Figure 16-6). The Start Page contains various links to useful web sites and enables you to open existing projects or start a new project altogether.

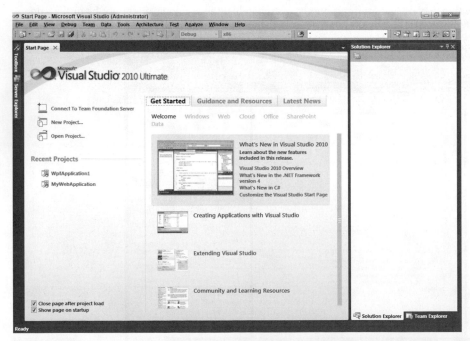

FIGURE 16-6

Figure 16-6 shows the type of Start Page you get after you have used Visual Studio 2010; it includes a list of the most recently edited projects. You can just click one of these projects to open it again.

Selecting a Project Type

You can create a new project by selecting File ⇨ New Project from the Visual Studio menu. From there you will get the New Project dialog box (see Figure 16-7) — and your first inkling of the variety of different projects you can create.

Using this dialog box, you effectively select the initial framework files and code you want Visual Studio to generate for you, the type of compilation options you want, and the compiler you want to compile your code with — either the C# 2010, Visual Basic 2010, or C++ 2010 compiler. You can immediately see the language integration that Microsoft has promised for .NET at work here! This particular example uses a C# console application.

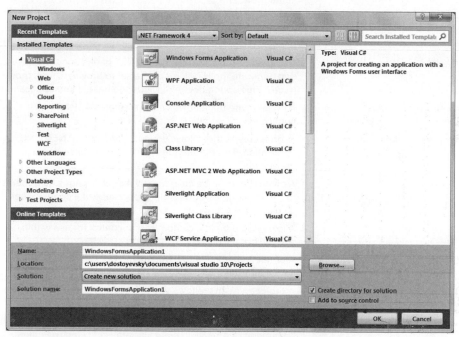

FIGURE 16-7

 We do not have space to cover all the various options for different types of projects here. On the C++ side, all the old C++ project types are there — MFC application, ATL project, and so on. On the Visual Basic side, the options have changed somewhat. For example, you can create a Visual Basic command-line application (Console Application), a .NET component (Class Library), a Windows Forms control (Windows Forms Control Library), and more. However, you cannot create an old-style COM-based control (the .NET control is intended to replace such ActiveX controls).

The following table lists all the options that are available to you under the Visual C# Projects. Note that some other, more specialized C# template projects are available under the Other Projects option.

IF YOU CHOOSE . . .	YOU GET THE C# CODE AND COMPILATION OPTIONS TO GENERATE . . .
Windows Forms Application	A basic empty form that responds to events.
Class Library	A .NET class that can be called up by other code.
WPF Application	A basic empty form that responds to events. Although the project type is similar to the Windows Forms Application project type (Windows Forms), this Windows Application project type allows you to build an XAML-based smart client solution.
WPF Browser Application	Quite similar to the Windows Application for WPF, this variant allows you to build an XAML-based application that is targeted at the browser.
ASP.NET Web Application	An ASP.NET-based web site: ASP.NET pages and C# classes that generate the HTML response sent to browsers from those pages. This option includes a base demo application.
Empty ASP.NET Web Application	An ASP.NET-based web site: ASP.NET pages and C# classes that generate the HTML response set to browsers from those pages. This option doesn't include the base demo application.
ASP.NET MVC 2 Web Application	A project type that allows you to create an ASP.NET MVC application.
ASP.NET MVC2 Empty Web Application	A project type that allows you to create an ASP.NET MVC application. This option doesn't include the base demo application.
ASP.NET Server Control	A control that can be called up by ASP.NET pages, to generate the HTML code that gives the appearance of a control when displayed on a browser.
ASP.NET AJAX Server Control	Allows you to build a custom server control for use within ASP.NET applications.
ASP.NET AJAX Server Control Extender	A project type that allows you to create extenders for ASP.NET server controls.
ASP.NET Dynamic Data Linq to SQL Web Application	A project type that allows you to build an ASP.NET that will take advantage of ASP.NET Dynamic Data using Linq to SQL.
ASP.NET Dynamic Data Entities Web Application	A project type that allows you to build an ASP.NET that will take advantage of ASP.NET Dynamic Data using Linq to Entities.
Silverlight Application	A project type that allows you to create a Silverlight application.
Silverlight Navigation Application	A project type that allows you to create a Silverlight application. This application starts with a core Silverlight application that can be extended for your personal needs.
Silverlight Class Library	A project type that allows you to create a Silverlight class library.
WPF Custom Control Library	A custom control that can be used in a Windows Presentation Foundation application.
WPF User Control Library	A user control library built using the Windows Presentation Foundation.
Windows Forms Control Library	A project for creating controls to use in Windows Forms applications.

IF YOU CHOOSE . . .	YOU GET THE C# CODE AND COMPILATION OPTIONS TO GENERATE . . .
Syndication Service Library	A WCF project that allows you to build and expose a syndication service.
Console Application	An application that runs at the command-line prompt, or in a console window.
WCF Service Application	A project type for Windows Communication Foundation services.
Windows Service	A service that runs in the background on a Windows operating system.
Enable Windows Azure Tools	Allows you to load Azure-based tools for cloud computing solutions.
Reports Application	A project for creating an application with a Windows user interface and a report.
Crystal Reports Application	A project for creating a C# application with a Windows user interface and a sample Crystal Report.
Activity Designer Library	A project that provides an Activity Designer template for working with Windows Workflow.
Activity Library	A project that provides a blank Workflow Activity Library. This project provides for creating a library of activities that can later be reused as building blocks in workflows.
Workflow Console Application	A project that provides a basic console application to use with Windows Workflow.
WCF Service Library	A project that provides for creating a WCF service class library (`.dll`) that has endpoints controlled via XML configuration files.
WCF Workflow Service Application	A project type that allows you to create a WCF-based distributed communication applications that make use of Windows Workflow.
Office	A series of projects that are aimed at building applications or add-ins targeted at the Microsoft Office applications (Word, Excel, PowerPoint, InfoPath, Outlook, Visio, and SharePoint).

As mentioned, this is not a full list of the .NET Framework 4 projects, but it is a good start. The big additions to this project table are the latest projects that are aimed at the WPF, the WCF, and the WF. You will find chapters covering these new capabilities later in this book. Be sure to look at Chapter 35, "Core WPF," Chapter 43, "Windows Communication Foundation," and Chapter 44, "Windows Workflow Foundation 4."

You will also notice that new project templates are available because of the ability to search online for templates through the New Project dialog.

Reviewing the Newly Created Console Project

When you click OK after selecting the Console Application option, Visual Studio gives you a couple of files, including a source code file, `Program.cs`, which contains the initial framework code. Figure 16-8 shows what code Visual Studio has written for you.

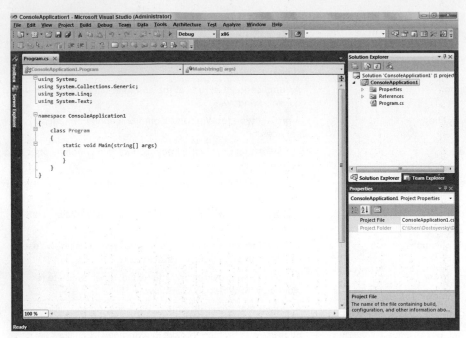

FIGURE 16-8

As you can see, you have a C# program that does not do anything yet but contains the basic items required in any C# executable program: a namespace and a class that contains the `Main()` method, which is the program's entry point. (Strictly speaking, the namespace is not necessary, but it would be very bad programming practice not to declare one.) This code is all ready to compile and run, which you can do immediately by pressing the F5 key or by selecting the Debug menu and choosing Start. However, before you do that, add the following line of code — to make your application actually do something!

```
static void Main(string[] args)
{
    Console.WriteLine("Hello from all the authors of Professional C#");
}
```

If you compile and run the project, you will see a console window that stays onscreen barely long enough to read the message. The reason this happens is that Visual Studio, remembering the settings you specified when you created the project, arranged for it to be compiled and run as a console application. Windows then realizes that it has to run a console application but does not have a console window to run it from. Therefore, Windows creates a console window and runs the program. As soon as the program exits, Windows recognizes that it does not need the console window anymore and promptly removes it. That is all very logical but does not help you very much if you actually want to look at the output from your project!

A good way to prevent this problem is to insert the following line just before the `Main()` method returns in your code:

```
static void Main(string[] args)
{
    Console.WriteLine("Hello from all the folks at Wrox Press");
    Console.ReadLine();
}
```

That way, your code will run, display its output, and come across the `Console.ReadLine()` statement, at which point it will wait for you to press the Return (or Enter) key before the program exits. This means that the console window will hang around until you press Return.

Note that all this is only an issue for console applications that you test run from Visual Studio — if you are writing a Windows Presentation Foundation or Windows Forms application, the window displayed by the application will automatically remain onscreen until you exit it. Similarly, if you run a console application from the command-line prompt, you will not have any problems with the window disappearing.

Viewing Other Project Files

The `Program.cs` source code file is not the only file that Visual Studio has created for you. Looking in the folder in which you asked Visual Studio to create your project, you will see not just the C# file but also a complete directory structure that looks like the one shown in Figure 16-9.

The two folders, `bin` and `obj`, store compiled and intermediate files. Subfolders of `obj` hold various temporary or intermediate files; subfolders of `bin` hold the compiled assemblies.

 Traditionally, Visual Basic developers would simply write the code and then run it. Before shipping, the code would then need to be compiled into an executable; Visual Basic tended to hide the process of compilation when debugging. In C#, it is more explicit: to run the code, you have to compile (or build) it first, which means that an assembly must be created somewhere.

You will also find a `Properties` folder that holds the `AssemblyInfo.cs` file. The remaining files in the project's main folder, `ConsoleApplication1`, are there for Visual Studio's benefit. They contain information about the project (for example, the files it contains) so that Visual Studio knows how to have the project compiled and how to read it in the next time you open the project.

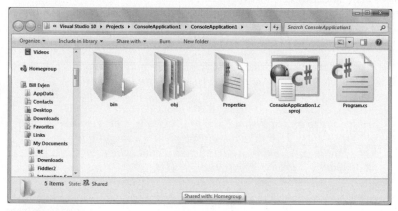

FIGURE 16-9

Distinguishing Projects from Solutions

One important distinction you must understand is that between a project and a solution:

➤ A *project* is a set of all the source code files and resources that will compile into a single assembly (or in some cases, a single module). For example, a project might be a class library or a Windows GUI application.

➤ A *solution* is the set of all the projects that make up a particular software package (application).

To understand this distinction, look at what happens when you ship a project — the project consists of more than one assembly. For example, you might have a user interface, custom controls, and other components that ship as libraries of the parts of the application. You might even have a different user interface for administrators. Each of these parts of the application might be contained in a separate assembly, and hence, they are regarded by Visual Studio as separate projects. However, it is quite likely that you will be coding these projects in parallel and in conjunction with each other. Thus, it is quite useful to be able to edit them all as one single unit in Visual Studio. Visual Studio allows this by regarding all the projects as forming one solution and by treating the solution as the unit that it reads in and allows you to work on.

Up until now, we have been loosely talking about creating a console project. In fact, in the example you are working on, Visual Studio has actually created a solution for you — although this particular solution contains just one project. You can see the situation in a window in Visual Studio known as the Solution Explorer (see Figure 16-10), which contains a tree structure that defines your solution.

Figure 16-10 shows that the project contains your source file, `Program.cs`, as well as another C# source file, `AssemblyInfo.cs` (found in the `Properties` folder), which allows you to provide information that describes the assembly as well as the ability to specify versioning information. (You look at this file in detail in Chapter 18, "Assemblies.") The Solution Explorer also indicates the assemblies that your project references according to namespace. You can see this by expanding the `References` folder in the Solution Explorer.

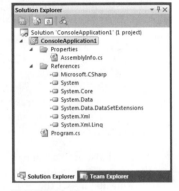

If you have not changed any of the default settings in Visual Studio, you will probably find the Solution Explorer in the top-right corner of your screen. If you cannot see it, just go to the View menu and select Solution Explorer.

The solution is described by a file with the extension `.sln` — in this example, it is `ConsoleApplication1.sln`. The project is described by various other files in the project's main folder. If you attempt to edit these

FIGURE 16-10

files using Notepad, you will find that they are mostly plain-text files, and, in accordance with the principle that .NET and .NET tools rely on open standards wherever possible, they are mostly in XML format.

 C++ developers will recognize that a Visual Studio solution corresponds to an old Visual C++ project workspace (stored in a `.dsw` file), and a Visual Studio project corresponds to an old C++ project (`.dsp` file). By contrast, Visual Basic developers will recognize that a solution corresponds to an old Visual Basic project group (`.vbg` file), and the .NET project corresponds to an old Visual Basic project (`.vbp` file). Visual Studio differs from the old Visual Basic IDE in that it always creates a solution for you automatically. In Visual Studio 6, Visual Basic developers would get a project; however, they would need to request a project group from the IDE separately.

Adding Another Project to the Solution

As you work through the following sections, you will see how Visual Studio works with Windows applications as well as with console applications. To that end, you create a Windows project called `BasicForm` that you will add to your current solution, `ConsoleApplication1`.

 This means that you will end up with a solution containing a Windows application and a console application. That is not a very common scenario — you are more likely to have one application and a number of libraries — but it allows you to see more code! You might, however, create a solution like this if, for example, you are writing a utility that you want to run either as a Windows application or as a command-line utility.

You can create the new project in two ways. You can select New Project from the File menu (as you have done already) or you can select Add ⇨ New Project from the File menu. If you select New Project from the File menu, this will bring up the familiar Add New Project dialog box; this time, however, you will notice that Visual Studio wants to create the new project in the preexisting `ConsoleApplication1` project location (see Figure 16-11).

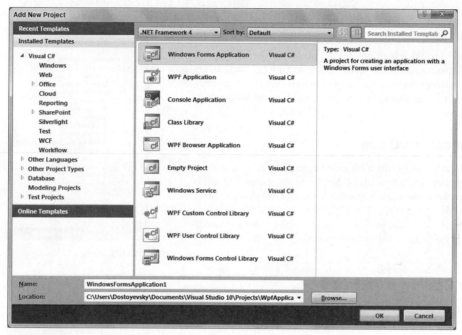

FIGURE 16-11

If you select this option, a new project is added so that the `ConsoleApplication1` solution now contains a console application and a Windows application.

In accordance with the language independence of Visual Studio, the new project does not need to be a C# project. It is perfectly acceptable to put a C# project, a Visual Basic project, and a C++ project in the same solution. However, we will stick with C# here because this is a C# book!

Of course, this means that `ConsoleApplication1` is not really an appropriate name for the solution anymore! To change the name, you can right-click the name of the solution and select Rename from the context menu. Call the new solution `DemoSolution`. The Solution Explorer window now looks like Figure 16-12.

You can see from this that Visual Studio has made your newly added Windows project automatically reference some of the extra base classes that are important for Windows Forms functionality.

You will notice if you look in Windows Explorer that the name of the solution file has changed to `DemoSolution.sln`. In general, if you want to rename any files, the Solution Explorer window is the best place to do so, because Visual Studio will then automatically update any references to that file in the other project files. If you rename files using just Windows Explorer, you might break the solution because Visual Studio will not be able to locate all the files it needs to read into the IDE. You will then need to manually edit the project and solution files to update the file references.

Setting the Startup Project

Bear in mind that if you have multiple projects in a solution, only one of them can be run at a time! When you compile the solution, all the projects in it will be compiled. However, you must specify which one you want Visual Studio to start running when you press F5 or select Start. If you have one executable and several libraries that it calls, this will clearly be the executable. In this case, where you have two independent executables in the project, you would simply need to debug each in turn.

You can tell Visual Studio which project to run by right-clicking that project in the Solution Explorer window and selecting Set as Startup Project from the context menu. You can tell which one is the current startup project — it is the one that appears in bold in the Solution Explorer window (`ConsoleApplication1` in Figure 16-12).

Windows Application Code

A Windows application contains a lot more code right from the start than a console application when Visual Studio first creates it. That is because creating a window is an intrinsically more complex process. Chapter 39, "Windows Forms," discusses the code for a Windows application in detail. For now, look at the code in the `Form1` class in the `WindowsApplication1` project to see for yourself how much is auto-generated.

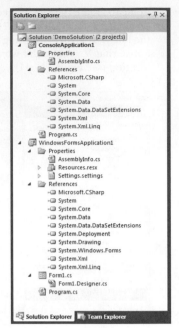

FIGURE 16-12

Exploring and Coding a Project

This section looks at the features that Visual Studio provides to help you add code to your project.

The Folding Editor

One really exciting feature of Visual Studio is its use of a folding editor as its default code editor.

Figure 16-13 shows the code for the console application that you generated earlier. Notice those little minus signs on the left-hand side of the window. These signs mark the points where the editor assumes that a new block of code (or documentation comment) begins. You can click these icons to close up the view of the corresponding block of code just as you would close a node in a tree control (see Figure 16-14).

```
Program.cs  ×

ConsoleApplication1.Program                              Main(string[] args)

  1  using System;
  2  using System.Collections.Generic;
  3  using System.Linq;
  4  using System.Text;
  5
  6  namespace ConsoleApplication1
  7  {
  8      class Program
  9      {
 10          static void Main(string[] args)
 11          {
 12              Console.WriteLine("Hello from all the authors of Professional C#");
 13              Console.ReadLine();
 14          }
 15      }
 16  }
 17

100 %
```

FIGURE 16-13

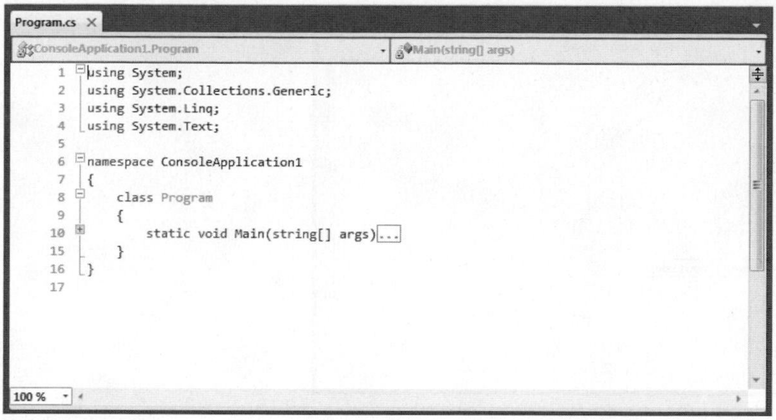

FIGURE 16-14

This means that while you are editing you can focus on just the areas of code you want to look at, and you can hide the bits of code you are not interested in working with at that moment. If you do not like the way the editor has chosen to block off your code, you can indicate your own blocks of collapsing code with the C# preprocessor directives, #region and #endregion, which were examined earlier in the book. For example, to collapse the code inside the Main() method, you would add the code shown in Figure 16-15.

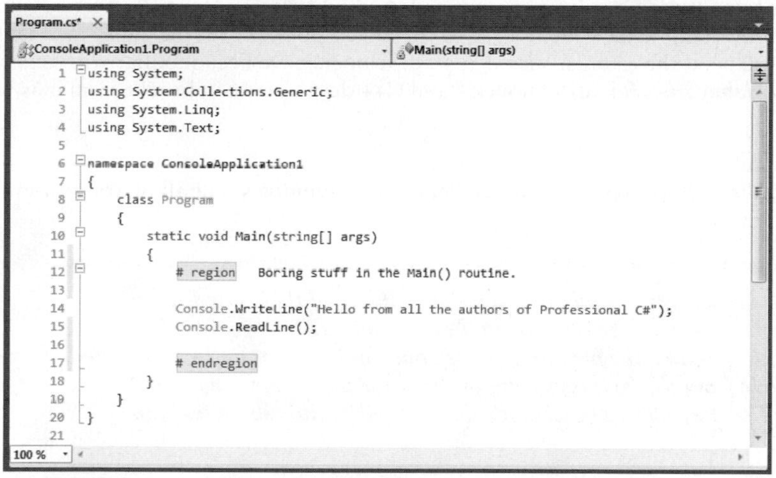

FIGURE 16-15

The code editor will automatically detect the #region block and place a new minus sign by the #region directive, as shown in Figure 16-15, allowing you to close the region. Enclosing this code in a region means that you can get the editor to close the block of code (see Figure 16-16), marking the area with the comment you specified in the #region directive. The compiler, however, ignores the directives and compiles the Main() method as normal.

```
Program.cs*  ✕
ConsoleApplication1.Program                    ▾  Main(string[] args)                ▾
 1  using System;
 2  using System.Collections.Generic;
 3  using System.Linq;
 4  using System.Text;
 5
 6  namespace ConsoleApplication1
 7  {
 8      class Program
 9      {
10          static void Main(string[] args)
11          {
12              Boring stuff in the Main() routine.
18          }
19      }
20  }
21
100 %  ▾  ◂                                                        ▸
```

FIGURE 16-16

In addition to the folding editor feature, Visual Studio's code editor brings across all the familiar functionality from Visual Studio 6. In particular, it features IntelliSense, which not only saves you typing but also ensures that you use the correct parameters. C++ developers will notice that the Visual Studio IntelliSense feature is a bit more robust than the Visual Studio 6 version and works more quickly. You will also notice that IntelliSense has been improved since Visual Studio 2005. It is now smarter in that it remembers your preferred choices and starts with one of these choices instead of starting directly at the beginning of the sometimes rather lengthy lists that IntelliSense can now provide.

The code editor also performs some syntax checking on your code and underlines most syntax errors with a short wavy line, even before you compile the code. Hovering the mouse pointer over the underlined text brings up a small box telling you what the error is. Visual Basic developers have been familiar with this feature, known as *design-time debugging,* for years; now C# and C++ developers can benefit from it as well.

Other Windows

In addition to the code editor, Visual Studio provides a number of other windows that allow you to view your project from different points of view.

> *The rest of this section describes several other windows. If one of these windows is not visible on your screen, you can select it from the View menu. To show the design view and code editor, right-click the file name in the Solution Explorer and select View Designer or View Code from the context menu, or select the item from the toolbar at the top of the Solution Explorer. The design view and code editor share the same tabbed window.*

The Design View Window

If you are designing a user interface application, such as a Windows application, Windows control library, or an ASP.NET application, you will use the Design View window. This window presents a visual overview of what your form will look like. You normally use the Design View window in conjunction with a window known as the toolbox. The toolbox contains a large number of .NET components that you can drag onto your program (see Figure 16-17).

Visual Studio 2010 provides a toolbox with a large number of components that are available for your development purposes. The categories of components available through the toolbox depend, to some extent, on the type of project you are editing — for example, you will get a far wider range when you are editing the `WindowsFormsApplication1` project in the `DemoSolution` solution than you will when you are editing the `ConsoleApplication1` project. The most important ranges of items available include the following:

➤ **Data** — Classes that allow you to connect to data sources and manage the data they contain. Here, you will find components for working with Microsoft SQL Server, Oracle, and any OleDb data source.

➤ **Windows Forms Controls (labeled as Common Controls)** — Classes that represent visual controls such as text boxes, list boxes, or tree views for working with thick-client applications.

➤ **Web Forms Controls (labeled as Standard)** — Classes that basically do the same thing as Windows controls but work in the context of web browsers, and that work by sending HTML output to simulate the controls to the browser. (You will see this only when working with ASP.NET applications.)

➤ **Components** — Miscellaneous .NET classes that perform various useful tasks on your machine, such as connecting to directory services or to the event log.

You can also add your own custom categories to the toolbox by right-clicking any category and selecting Add Tab from the context menu. You can also place other tools in the toolbox by selecting Choose Items from the same context menu — this is particularly useful for adding your favorite COM components and ActiveX controls, which are not present in the toolbox by default. If you add a COM control, you can still click to place it in your project just as you would with a .NET control. Visual Studio automatically adds all the required COM interoperability code to allow your project to call up the control. In this case, what is actually added to your project is a .NET control that Visual Studio creates behind the scenes and that acts as a wrapper for your COM control.

FIGURE 16-17

To see how the toolbox works, place a text box in your basic form project. You simply click the `TextBox` control contained within the toolbox and then click again to place it in the form in the design view (or if you prefer, you can simply drag and drop the control directly onto the design surface). Now the design view looks like Figure 16-18, showing roughly what `WindowsFormsApplication1` will look like if you compile and run it.

If you look at the code view of your form, you can see that Visual Studio 2010 does not add the code that instantiates a `TextBox` object to go on the form directly as it did in the early versions of the IDE. Instead, you will need to expand the plus sign next to `Form1.cs` in the Visual Studio Solution Explorer. Here, you will find a file that is dedicated to the design of the form and the controls that are placed on the form — `Form1.Designer.cs`. In this class file, you will find a new member variable in the `Form1` class:

```
partial class Form1
{
    private System.Windows.Forms.TextBox textBox1;
```

There is also some code to initialize it in the method, `InitializeComponent()`, which is called from the Form1 constructor:

```
/// <summary>
/// Required method for Designer support — do not modify
/// the contents of this method with the code editor.
/// </summary>
private void InitializeComponent()
{
        this.textBox1 = new System.Windows.Forms.TextBox();
        this.SuspendLayout();
        //
        // textBox1
        //
        this.textBox1.Location = new System.Drawing.Point(0, 0);
        this.textBox1.Name = "textBox1";
        this.textBox1.Size = new System.Drawing.Size(100, 20);
        this.textBox1.TabIndex = 0;
        //
        // Form1
        //
        this.AutoScaleDimensions = new System.Drawing.SizeF(6F, 13F);
        this.AutoScaleMode = System.Windows.Forms.AutoScaleMode.Font;
        this.ClientSize = new System.Drawing.Size(284, 265);
        this.Controls.Add(this.textBox1);
        this.Name = "Form1";
        this.Text = "Form1";
        this.ResumeLayout(false);
        this.PerformLayout();

}
```

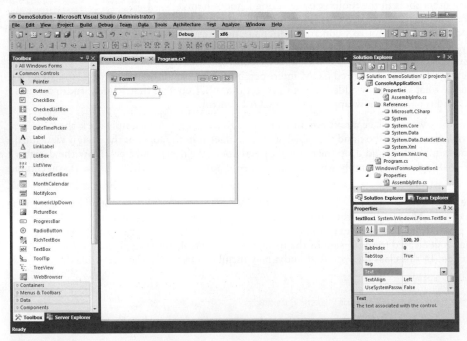

FIGURE 16-18

In one sense, there is no difference between the code editor and the design view; they simply present different views of the same code. What actually happened when you clicked to add the TextBox to the design view is that the editor placed the preceding extra code in your C# source file for you. The design view simply reflects this change because Visual Studio is able to read your source code and determine from it what controls should be around when the application starts up. This is a fundamental shift from the old Visual Basic way of looking at things, in which everything was based around the visual design. Now, your C# source code is what fundamentally controls your application, and the design view is just a different way of viewing the source code. Incidentally, if you do write any Visual Basic 2010 code with Visual Studio, you will find the same principles at work.

If you had wanted to, you could have worked the other way around. If you had manually added the same code to your C# source files, Visual Studio would have automatically detected from the code that your application contained a TextBox control and would have shown it in the design view at the designated position. It is best to add these controls visually, and let Visual Studio handle the initial code generation — it is a lot quicker and less error-prone to click the mouse button a couple of times than to type a few lines of code!

Another reason for adding these controls visually is that, to recognize that they are there, Visual Studio does need the relevant code to conform to certain criteria — and code that you write by hand might not do so. In particular, you will notice that the InitializeComponent() method that contains the code to initialize the TextBox is commented to warn you against modifying it. That is because this is the method that Visual Studio looks at to determine what controls are around when your application starts up. If you create and define a control somewhere else in your code, Visual Studio will not be aware of it, and you will not be able to edit it in the design view or in certain other useful windows.

In fact, despite the warnings, you can modify the code in InitializeComponent(), provided that you are careful. There is generally no harm in changing the values of some of the properties, for example, so that a control displays different text or so that it is a different size. In practice, the developer studio is pretty robust when it comes to working around any other code you place in this method. Just be aware that if you make too many changes to InitializeComponent(), you do run the risk that Visual Studio will not recognize some of your controls. We should stress that this will not affect your application in any way whatsoever when it is compiled, but it might disable some of the editing features of Visual Studio for those controls. Hence, if you want to add any other substantial initialization, it is probably better to do so in the Form1 constructor or in some other method.

The Properties Window

This is another window that has its origins in the old Visual Basic IDE. You know from the first part of the book that .NET classes can implement properties. In fact, as you will discover when building Windows Forms (see Chapter 39), the .NET base classes that represent forms and controls have a lot of properties that define their action or appearance — properties such as Width, Height, Enabled (whether the user can type input to the control), and Text (the text displayed by the control) — and Visual Studio knows about many of these properties. The Properties window, shown in Figure 16-19, appears and allows you to edit the initial values of most of these properties for the controls that Visual Studio has been able to detect by reading your source code.

The Properties window can also show events. You can view events for what you are focused on in the IDE or selected in the drop-down list box directly in the Properties window by clicking the icon that looks like a lightning bolt at the top of the window.

At the top of the Properties window is a list box that allows you to select which control you want to view. In the example in this chapter, you have selected `Form1`, the main form class for your `WindowsFormsApplication1` project, and have edited the text to "Basic Form — Hello!" If you now check the source code, you can see that what you have actually done is edit the source code — using a friendlier user interface:

```
this.AutoScaleDimensions = new System.Drawing.SizeF(6F, 13F);
this.AutoScaleMode = System.Windows.Forms.AutoScaleMode.Font;
this.ClientSize = new System.Drawing.Size(284, 265);
this.Controls.Add(this.textBox1);
this.Name = "Form1";
this.Text = "Basic Form — Hello";
this.ResumeLayout(false);
this.PerformLayout();
```

Not all the properties shown in the Properties window are explicitly mentioned in your source code. For those that are not, Visual Studio will display the default values that were set when the form was created and that are set when the form is actually initialized. Obviously, if you change a value for one of these properties in the Properties window, a statement explicitly setting that property will magically appear in your source code — and vice versa. It is interesting to note that if a property is changed from its original value, this property will then appear in bold type within the list box of the Properties window. Sometimes double-clicking the property in the Properties window returns the value to its original value.

The Properties window provides a convenient way to get a broad overview of the appearance and properties of a particular control or window.

FIGURE 16-19

 It is interesting to note that the Properties window is implemented as a `System.Windows.Forms.PropertyGrid` *instance, which will internally use the reflection technology described in Chapter 14, "Reflection," to identify the properties and property values to display.*

The Class View Window

Unlike the Properties window, the Class View window, shown in Figure 16-20, owes its origins to the C++ (and J++) developer environments. The class view is not actually treated by Visual Studio as a window in its own right — rather it is an additional tab in the Solution Explorer window. By default, the class view will not even appear in the Visual Studio Solution Explorer. To invoke the class view, select View ➪ Class View. The class view (see Figure 16-20) shows the hierarchy of the namespaces and classes in your code. It gives you a tree view that you can expand to see which namespaces contain what classes and what classes contain what members.

A nice feature of the class view is that if you right-click the name of any item for which you have access to the source code, then the context menu features the Go To Definition option, which takes you to the definition of the item in the code editor. Alternatively, you can do this by double-clicking the item in class view (or, indeed, by right-clicking the item you want in the source code editor and choosing the same option from the resulting context menu). The context menu also gives you the option to add a field, method, property, or indexer to a class. This means that you specify the details of the relevant member in a dialog box, and the code is added for you. This might not be that useful for fields or methods, which can be quickly added to your code; however, you might find this feature helpful for properties and indexers, where it can save you quite a bit of typing.

The Object Browser Window

One important aspect of programming in the .NET environment is being able to find out what methods and other code items are available in the base classes and any other libraries that you are referencing from your assembly. This feature is available through a window called the Object Browser. You can access this window by selecting Object Browser from the View menu in Visual Studio 2010.

The Object Browser window is quite similar to the Class View window in that it displays a tree view that gives the class structure of your application, allowing you to inspect the members of each class. The user interface is slightly different in that it displays class members in a separate pane rather than in the tree view itself. The real difference is that it lets you look at not just the namespaces and classes in your project but also the ones in all the assemblies referenced by the project. Figure 16-21 shows the Object Browser viewing the `SystemException` class from the .NET base classes.

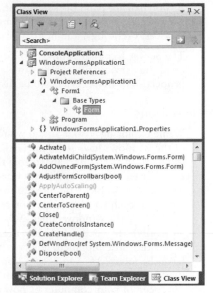

FIGURE 16-20

One note of caution with the Object Browser is that it groups classes by the assembly in which they are located first and by namespace second. Unfortunately, because namespaces for the base classes are often spread across several assemblies, this means you might have trouble locating a particular class unless you know what assembly it is in.

The Object Browser is there to view .NET objects. If for any reason you want to investigate installed COM objects, you will find that the OLEView tool previously used in the C++ IDE is still available — it is located in the folder `C:\Program Files\Microsoft SDKs\Windows\v6.0A\bin` along with several other similar utilities.

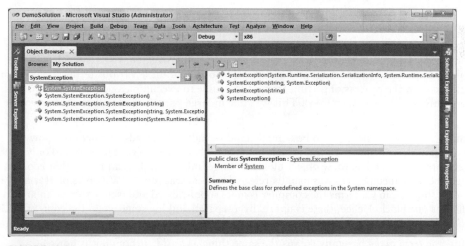

FIGURE 16-21

The Server Explorer Window

You can use the Server Explorer window, shown in Figure 16-22, to find out about aspects of the computers in your network while coding.

As you can see from the screenshot, among the things you can access through the Server Explorer are database connections, information about services, event logs, and more.

The Server Explorer is linked to the Properties window so that if you open the Services node, for example, and click a particular service, the properties of that service will be displayed in the Properties window.

Pin Buttons

While exploring Visual Studio, you might have noticed that many of the windows have some interesting functionality more reminiscent of toolbars. In particular, apart from the code editor, they can all be docked. Another feature of them is that when they are docked, they have an extra icon that looks like a pin next to the minimize button in the top-right corner of each window. This icon really does act like a pin — it can be used to pin the windows open. When they are pinned (the pin is displayed vertically), they behave just like the regular windows that you are used to.

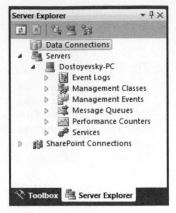

FIGURE 16-22

When they are unpinned, however (the pin is displayed horizontally), they remain open only as long as they have the focus. As soon as they lose the focus (because you clicked or moved your mouse somewhere else), they smoothly retreat into the main border around the entire Visual Studio application. (You can also feel the speed of your computer by how quickly or slowly they open and close.)

Pinning and unpinning windows provides another way of making the best use of the limited space on your screen. It has not really been seen a great deal in Windows before, though a few third-party applications, such as PaintShop Pro, have used similar concepts. Pinned windows have, however, been around on many UNIX-based systems for quite a while.

Building a Project

Visual Studio is not only about coding your projects. It is actually an IDE that manages the full lifecycle of your project including the building or compiling of your solutions. This section examines the options that Visual Studio gives you for building your project.

Building, Compiling, and Making

Before examining the various build options, it is important to clarify some terminology. You will often see three different terms used in connection with the process of getting from your source code to some sort of executable code: compiling, building, and making. The origin of these various terms comes from the fact that until recently, the process of getting from source code to executable code involved more than one step (and this is still the case in C++). This was due in large part to the number of source files in a program.

In C++, for example, each source file needs to be compiled individually. This leads to what are known as object files, each containing something like executable code, but where each object file relates to only one source file. To generate an executable, these object files need to be linked together, a process that is officially known as linking. The combined process was usually referred to — at least on the Windows platform — as building your code. However, in C# terms the compiler is more sophisticated and is able to read in and treat all your source files as one block. Hence, there is not really a separate linking stage, so in the context of C#, the terms *compile* and *build* are used interchangeably.

In addition to this, the term *make* basically means the same thing as *build,* although it is not really used in the context of C#. The term originated on old mainframe systems on which, when a project was composed of many source files, a separate file would be written that contained instructions to the compiler on how to build a project — which files to include and what libraries to link to and so on. This file was generally known as a make file and is still quite standard on UNIX systems. Make files are not normally needed on Windows, although you can still write them (or get Visual Studio to generate them) if you need to.

Debugging and Release Builds

The idea of having separate builds is very familiar to C++ developers, and to a lesser degree, to those with a Visual Basic background. The point here is that when you are debugging, you typically want your executable to behave differently from when you are ready to ship the software. When you are ready to ship your software, you want the size of the executable to be as small as possible and the executable itself to be as fast as possible. Unfortunately, these requirements are not compatible with your needs when you are debugging code, as explained in the following sections.

Optimization

High performance is achieved partly by the compiler doing many optimizations on the code. This means that the compiler actively looks at your source code as it is compiling to identify places where it can modify the precise details of what you are doing in a way that does not change the overall effect, but that makes things more efficient. For example, if the compiler encountered the following source code:

```
double InchesToCm(double Ins)
{
    return Ins*2.54;
}

// later on in the code

Y = InchesToCm(X);
```

it might replace it with this:

```
Y = X * 2.54;
```

Or it might replace this code:

```
{
    string Message = "Hi";
    Console.WriteLine(Message);
}
```

with this:

```
Console.WriteLine("Hi");
```

By doing so, it bypasses having to declare an unnecessary object reference in the process.

It is not possible to exactly pin down what optimizations the C# compiler does — nor whether the two previous examples actually would occur with any particular example — because those kinds of details are not documented. (Chances are that for managed languages such as C#, the previous optimizations would occur at JIT compilation time, not when the C# compiler compiles source code to assembly.) For obvious commercial reasons, companies that write compilers are usually quite reluctant to give too many details about the tricks that their compilers use. We should stress that optimizations do not affect your source code — they affect only the contents of the executable code. However, the previous examples should give you a good idea of what to expect from optimizations.

The problem is that although optimizations like the previous ones help a great deal in making your code run faster, they are not that helpful for debugging. Suppose that, in the first example, you want to set a breakpoint inside the InchesToCm() method to see what is going on in there. How can you possibly do that if the executable code does not actually have an InchesToCm() method because the compiler has removed it? Moreover, how can you set a watch on the Message variable when that does not exist in the compiled code either?

Debugger Symbols

When you are debugging, you often have to look at values of variables, and you will specify them by their source code names. The trouble is that executable code generally does not contain those names — the compiler replaces the names with memory addresses. .NET has modified this situation somewhat to the extent that certain items in assemblies are stored with their names, but this is only true of a small minority of items — such as public classes and methods — and those names will still be removed when the assembly is JIT-compiled. Asking the debugger to tell you what the value is in the variable called `HeightInInches` is not going to get you very far if, when the debugger examines the executable code, it sees only addresses and no reference to the name `HeightInInches` anywhere. Therefore, to debug properly, you need to have extra debugging information made available in the executable. This information includes, among other things, names of variables and line information that allows the debugger to match up which executable machine assembly language instructions correspond to your original source code instructions. You will not, however, want that information in a release build, both for commercial reasons (debugging information makes it a lot easier for other people to disassemble your code) and because it increases the size of the executable.

Extra Source Code Debugging Commands

A related issue is that quite often while you are debugging there will be extra lines in your code to display crucial debugging-related information. Obviously, you want the relevant commands removed entirely from the executable before you ship the software. You could do this manually, but wouldn't it be so much easier if you could simply mark those statements in some way so that the compiler ignores them when it is compiling your code to be shipped? You've already seen in the first part of the book how this can be done in C# by defining a suitable processor symbol, and possibly using this in conjunction with the `Conditional` attribute, giving you what is known as *conditional compilation.*

What all these factors add up to is that you need to compile almost all commercial software in a slightly different way when debugging than in the final product that is shipped. Visual Studio is able to consider this because, as you have already seen, it stores details of all the options that it is supposed to pass to the compiler when it has your code compiled. All that Visual Studio has to do to support different types of builds is to store more than one set of such details. The different sets of build information are referred to as configurations. When you create a project, Visual Studio automatically gives you two configurations, called Debug and Release:

➤　The Debug configuration commonly specifies that no optimizations are to take place, extra debugging information is to be present in the executable, and the compiler is to assume that the debug preprocessor symbol `Debug` is present unless it is explicitly `#undefined` in the source code.

➤　The Release configuration specifies that the compiler should optimize the compilation, that there should be no extra debugging information in the executable, and that the compiler should not assume that any particular preprocessor symbol is present.

You can define your own configurations as well. You might want to do this, for example, if you want to set up professional-level builds and enterprise-level builds so that you can ship two versions of the software. In the past, because of issues concerning the Unicode character encodings being supported on Windows NT but not on Windows 95, it was common for C++ projects to feature a Unicode configuration and an MBCS (multi-byte character set) configuration.

Selecting a Configuration

One obvious question is that, because Visual Studio stores details of more than one configuration, how does it determine which one to use when arranging for a project to be built? The answer is that there is always an active configuration, which is the configuration that will be used when you ask Visual Studio to build a project. (Note that configurations are set for each project rather than for each solution.)

By default, when you create a project, the Debug configuration is the active configuration. You can change which configuration is the active one by clicking the Build menu option and selecting the Configuration Manager item. It is also available through a drop-down menu in the main Visual Studio toolbar.

Editing Configurations

In addition to choosing the active configuration, you can also examine and edit the configurations. To do this, you select the relevant project in the Solution Explorer and then select the Properties from the Project menu. This brings up a very sophisticated dialog box. (Alternatively, you can access the same dialog box by right-clicking the name of the project in the Solution Explorer and then selecting Properties from the context menu.)

This dialog contains a tree view, which allows you to select many different general areas to examine or edit. We do not have space to show all of these areas, but we will show a couple of the most important ones.

Figure 16-23 shows a tabbed view of the available properties for a particular application. This screenshot shows the general application settings for the `ConsoleApplication1` project that you created earlier in the chapter.

Among the points to note are that you can select the name of the assembly as well as the type of assembly to be generated. The options here are Console Application, Windows Application, and Class Library. Of course, you can change the assembly type if you want. (Though arguably, if you want, you might wonder why you did not pick the correct project type at the time that you asked Visual Studio to generate the project for you in the first place!)

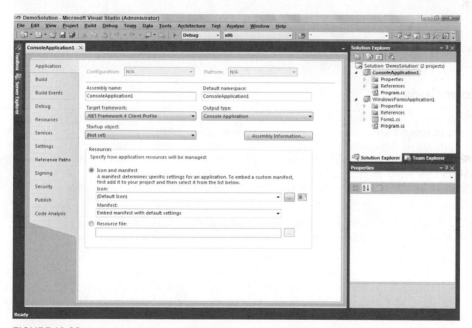

FIGURE 16-23

Figure 16-24 shows the build configuration properties. You will notice that a list box near the top of the dialog box allows you to specify which configuration you want to look at. You can see — in the case of the Debug configuration — that the compiler assumes that the DEBUG and TRACE preprocessor symbols have been defined. In addition, the code is not optimized and extra debugging information is generated.

In general, it is not that often that you will need to adjust the configuration settings. However, if you ever do need to use them, you now know the difference between the available configuration properties.

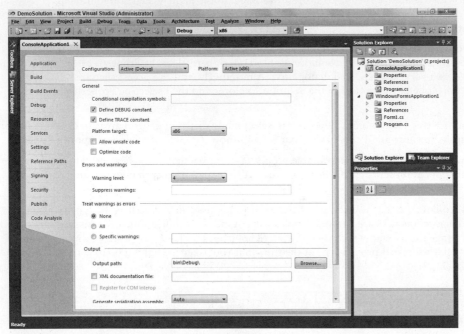

FIGURE 16-24

Debugging Your Code

After the long discussion about building and build configurations, you might be surprised to learn that this chapter is not going to spend a great deal of time discussing debugging itself. The reason for that is that the principles and the process of debugging — setting breakpoints and examining the values of variables — is not really significantly different in Visual Studio from any of the various Visual Studio 6 IDEs. Instead, this section briefly reviews the features offered by Visual Studio, focusing on those areas that might be new to some developers. It also discusses how to deal with exceptions, because these can cause problems during debugging.

In C#, as in pre-.NET languages, the main technique involved in debugging is simply setting breakpoints and using them to examine what is going on in your code at a certain point in its execution.

Breakpoints

You can set breakpoints from Visual Studio on any line of your code that is actually executed. The simplest way is to click the line in the code editor, within the shaded area toward the far left of the document window (or press the F9 key when the appropriate line is selected). This sets up a breakpoint on that particular line, which causes execution to break and control to be transferred to the debugger as soon as that line is reached in the execution process. As in previous versions of Visual Studio, a breakpoint is indicated by a large circle to the left of the line in the code editor. Visual Studio also highlights the line by displaying the text and background in a different color. Clicking the circle again removes the breakpoint.

If breaking every time at a particular line is not adequate for your particular problem, you can also set conditional breakpoints. To do this, select Debug ➪ Windows ➪ Breakpoints. This brings up a dialog box asking you for details of the breakpoint you want to set. Among the options available, you can:

➤ Specify that execution should break only after the breakpoint has been passed a certain number of times.

➤ Specify that the breakpoint should come into effect only every so many times that the line is reached, for example, every 20th time that a line is executed. (This is useful when debugging large loops.)

➤ Set the breakpoints relative to a variable rather than to an instruction. In this case, the value of the variable will be monitored and the breakpoints will be triggered whenever the value of this variable changes. You might find, however, that using this option slows down your code considerably. Checking whether the value of a variable has changed after every instruction adds a lot of processor time.

Watches

After a breakpoint has been hit, you will usually want to investigate the values of variables. The simplest way to do this is to hover the mouse cursor over the name of the variable in the code editor. This causes a little box that shows the value of that variable to pop up, which can also be expanded to greater detail. This is shown in Figure 16-25.

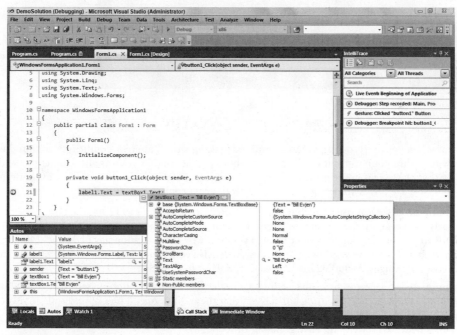

FIGURE 16-25

However, you might also prefer to use the Autos window to examine the contents of variables. The Autos window (shown in Figure 16-26) is a tabbed window that appears only when the program is running under the debugger. If you do not see it, try selecting Debug ➪ Windows ➪ Autos.

Variables that are classes or structs are shown with a + icon next to them, which you can click to expand the variable and see the values of its fields.

The three tabs to this window are each designed to monitor different variables:

➤ **Autos** monitors the last few variables that have been accessed as the program was executing.

➤ **Locals** monitors variables that are accessible in the method currently being executed.

➤ **Watch** monitors any variables that you have explicitly specified by typing their names into the Watch window.

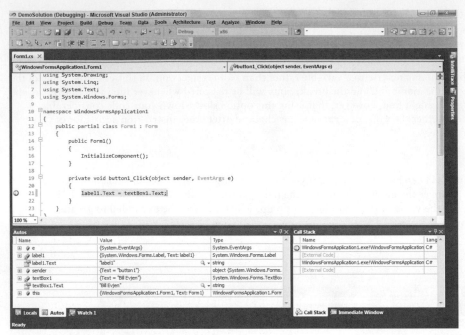

FIGURE 16-26

Exceptions

Exceptions are great when you ship your application and for making sure that error conditions are handled in an appropriate way within your application. Used well, they can ensure that your application copes with difficulties well and that the user is never presented with a technical dialog box. Unfortunately, exceptions are not so great when you are trying to debug your application. The problem is twofold:

➤ If an exception occurs when you are debugging, you often do not want it to be handled automatically — especially if automatically handling it means retiring gracefully and terminating execution! Rather, you want the debugger to help you find why the exception has occurred. Of course, the trouble is that if you have written good, robust, defensive code, your program will automatically handle almost anything — including the bugs that you want to detect!

➤ If an exception occurs that you have not written a handler for, the .NET runtime will still go off looking for a handler. However, by the time it discovers that there is not one, it will have terminated your program. There will not be a call stack left, and you will not be able to look at the values of any of your variables because they will all have gone out of scope.

Of course, you can set breakpoints in your catch blocks, but that often does not help very much because when the catch block is reached, flow of execution will, by definition, have exited the corresponding try block. That means that the variables you probably wanted to examine the values of to figure out what has gone wrong will have gone out of scope. You will not even be able to look at the stack trace to find what method was being executed when the throw statement occurred — because control will have left that method. Setting the breakpoints at the throw statement will of course solve this, except that if you are coding defensively, there will be many throw statements in your code. How can you tell which one is the one that threw the exception?

In fact, Visual Studio provides a very neat answer to all of this. If you look into the main Debug menu, you will find a menu item called Exceptions. This item opens the Exceptions dialog box (see Figure 16-27), which allows you to specify what happens when an exception is thrown. You can choose to continue execution or to stop and start debugging — in which case execution stops and the debugger steps in at the throw statement itself.

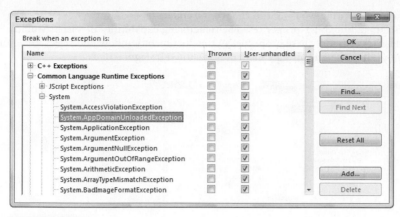

FIGURE 16-27

What makes this a really powerful tool is that you can customize the behavior according to which class of exception is thrown. For example, in Figure 16-27, we have told Visual Studio to break into the debugger whenever it encounters any exception thrown by a .NET base class, but not to break into the debugger if the exception is an `AppDomainUnloadedException`.

Visual Studio knows about all the exception classes available in the .NET base classes, and about quite a few exceptions that can be thrown outside the .NET environment. Visual Studio is not automatically aware of your own custom exception classes that you write, but you can manually add your exception classes to the list and thereby specify which of your exceptions should cause execution to stop immediately. To do this, just click the Add button (which is enabled when you have selected a top-level node from the tree) and type in the name of your exception class.

REFACTORING TOOLS

Many developers develop their applications first for functionality and then, once the functionality is in place, they *rework* their applications to make them more manageable and more readable. This is called *refactoring*. Refactoring is the process of reworking code for readability, performance, providing type safety, and lining applications up to better adhere to standard OO (object-oriented) programming practices.

For this reason, the C# environment of Visual Studio 2010 includes a set of refactoring tools. You can find these tools under the Refactoring option in the Visual Studio menu. To show this in action, create a new class called `Car` in Visual Studio:

```
using System;
using System.Collections.Generic;
using System.Text;

namespace ConsoleApplication1
{
    public class Car
    {
        public string _color;
        public string _doors;

        public int Go()
        {
            int speedMph = 100;
            return speedMph;
        }
    }
}
```

Now, suppose that in the idea of refactoring, you want to change the code a bit so that the `color` and the `door` variables are encapsulated in public .NET properties. The refactoring capabilities of Visual Studio 2010 allow you to simply right-click either of these properties in the document window and select Refactor ⇨ Encapsulate Field. This will pull up the Encapsulate Field dialog shown in Figure 16-28.

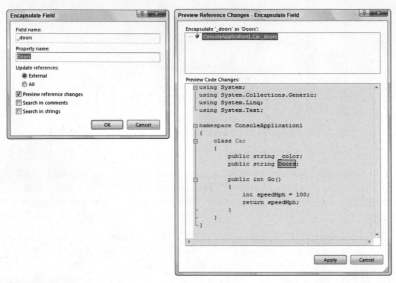

FIGURE 16-28

From this dialog, you can provide the name of the property and click the OK button. This will turn the selected public field into a private field, while also encapsulating the field in a public .NET property. After you click OK, the code will be reworked into the following (after redoing both fields):

```
namespace ConsoleApplication1
{
    public class Car
    {
        private string _color;

        public string Color
        {
            get { return _color; }
            set { _color = value; }
        }
        private string _doors;

        public string Doors
        {
            get { return _doors; }
            set { _doors = value; }
        }

        public int Go()
        {
            int speedMph = 100;
            return speedMph;
        }
    }
}
```

As you can see, these wizards make it quite simple to refactor your code not just on one page but also for an entire application. Also included are the capabilities to do the following:

➤ Rename method names, local variables, fields, and more

➤ Extract methods from a selection of code

➤ Extract interfaces based on a set of existing type members

➤ Promote local variables to parameters

➤ Rename or reorder parameters

You will find the refactoring capabilities provided by Visual Studio 2010 a great way to get the cleaner, more readable, better-structured code that you are looking for.

MULTI-TARGETING THE .NET FRAMEWORK

Visual Studio 2010 allows you to target the version of the .NET Framework that you want to work with. When you open the New Project dialog and get ready to create a new project, you will notice that there is a drop-down list in the upper-right corner of the dialog that allows you to pick the version of the framework that you are interested in using. This dialog is presented in Figure 16-29.

From this figure, you can see that the drop-down list provides you with the ability to target the .NET Frameworks 2.0, 3.0, 3.5, and 4. When you use the upgrade dialog to upgrade a Visual Studio 2008 solution to Visual Studio 2010, it is important to understand that you are only upgrading the solution to *use* Visual Studio 2010 and that you are not upgrading your project to the .NET Framework 4. Your project will stay on the framework version you were using, but now, you will be able use the new Visual Studio 2010 to work on your project.

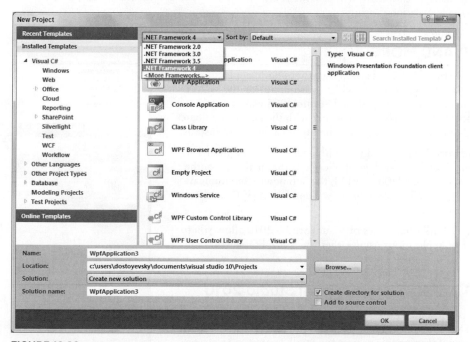

FIGURE 16-29

If you want to change the version of the framework the solution is using, right-click the project and select the properties of the solution. If you are working with an ASP.NET project, you will get a dialog as shown in Figure 16-30.

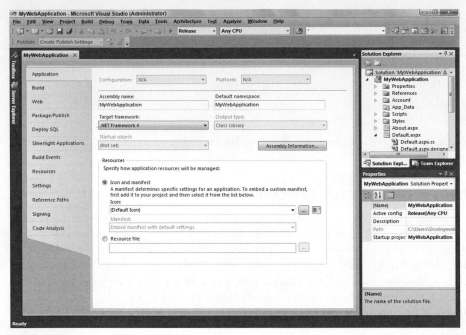

FIGURE 16-30

From this dialog, the Application tab will provide you with the ability to change the version of the framework that the application is using.

WPF, WCF, WF, AND MORE

By default, Visual Studio 2005 did not allow you to build applications targeted at the .NET Framework 3.0, which was out during the VS2005 lifetime. The default installation of Visual Studio 2005 was targeted only at the .NET Framework 2.0. To start working with the new technologies targeted at the .NET Framework 3.0, you had to do a few extra installs.

The .NET Framework 3.0 provided you with access to a class library for building application types such as applications that make use of the Windows Presentation Foundation (WPF), the Windows Communication Foundation (WCF), the Windows Workflow Foundation (WF), and Windows CardSpace.

The targeted framework capabilities of Visual Studio 2010 allow you to build these types of applications using either the .NET Framework 3.0, 3.5, or 4.

Building WPF Applications in Visual Studio 2010

One good example of some of the capabilities that the .NET Framework 4 brings to Visual Studio is the WPF Application project type (found in the Windows category). Selecting this project type will create a `MainWindow.xaml` and `MainWindow.xaml.cs` file for you to work from. Everything that is created by default with this project type in the Solution Explorer is presented in Figure 16-31 (shown here with a searchable Properties dialog).

FIGURE 16-31

Right away, you will notice options available to you in Visual Studio 2010 in the document window. The default view of the document window after creating this project is presented in Figure 16-32.

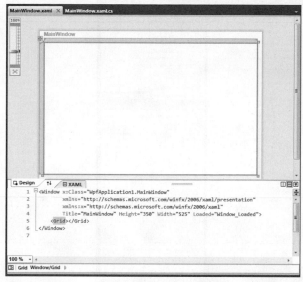

FIGURE 16-32

The document window has two views — a design view and an XAML view. Making changes in the design view will make the appropriate changes in the XAML view, and vice versa. As with traditional Windows Forms applications, WPF applications also include the ability to use controls that are contained within Visual Studio's toolbox. This toolbox of controls is presented in Figure 16-33.

Building WF Applications in Visual Studio 2010

Another dramatically different application style (when it comes to building the application from within Visual Studio) is the Windows Workflow application type. For an example of this, select the Workflow Console Application project type from the Workflow section of the New Project dialog. This will create a console application as illustrated here with a view of the Solution Explorer (see Figure 16-34).

You will notice when building applications that make use of the Windows Workflow Foundation that there is a heavy dependency on the design view. Looking closely at the workflow (see Figure 16-35), you can see that it is made up of multiple sequential steps and even includes actions based on conditions (such as an `if-else` statement).

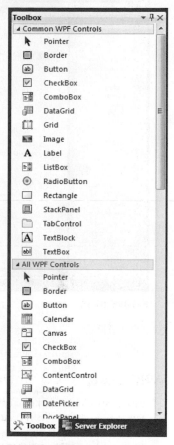

FIGURE 16-33

FIGURE 16-34

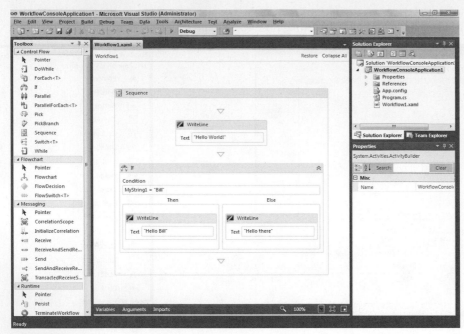

FIGURE 16-35

SUMMARY

This chapter explored one of the most important programming tools in the .NET environment — Visual Studio 2010. The bulk of the chapter examined how this tool facilitates writing code in C# (and C++ and Visual Basic).

Visual Studio 2010 is one of the easiest development environments to work with in the programming world. You will find that Visual Studio makes Rapid Application Development (RAD) easy to achieve, but at the same time, you can dig deep into the mechanics of how your applications are created. This chapter focused on using Visual Studio for everything from refactoring to multi-targeting to reading in Visual Studio 6 projects to debugging. It also covered many of the windows available to Visual Studio.

This chapter also looked at some of the latest projects available to you through the .NET Framework 4. These project types focused on the Windows Presentation Foundation, the Windows Communication Foundation, and the Windows Workflow Foundation.

Chapter 17 presents the deployment situation in detail.

17

Deployment

WHAT'S IN THIS CHAPTER?

➤ Deployment requirements
➤ Simple deployment scenarios
➤ WIndows Installer-based projects
➤ ClickOnce technology

The development process does not end when the source code is compiled and the testing is complete. At that stage, the job of getting the application into the user's hands begins. Whether it's an ASP.NET application, a smart client application, or an application built using the Compact Framework, the software must be deployed to a target environment. The .NET Framework has made deployment much easier than it was in the past. The pains of registering COM components and writing new hives to the registry are all gone.

This chapter looks at the options that are available for application deployment, both from an ASP.NET perspective and from the smart client perspective.

PLANNING FOR DEPLOYMENT

Often, deployment is an afterthought in the development process that can lead to nasty, if not costly, surprises. To avoid grief in deployment scenarios, you should plan the deployment process during the initial design stage. Any special deployment considerations — such as server capacity, desktop security, or where assemblies will be loaded from — should be built into the design from the start, resulting in a much smoother deployment process.

Another issue that you should address early in the development process is the environment in which to test the deployment. Whereas unit testing of application code and of deployment options can be done on the developer's system, the deployment must be tested in an environment that resembles the target system. This is important to eliminate the dependencies that don't exist on a targeted computer. An example of this might be a third-party library that has been installed on the developer's computer early in the project. The target computer might not have this library on it. It can be easy to forget to include it in the deployment package. Testing on the developer's system would not uncover the error because the library already exists. Documenting dependencies can help to eliminate this potential problem.

Deployment processes can be complex for a large application. Planning for the deployment can save time and effort when the deployment process is implemented.

Choosing the proper deployment option must be done with the same care and planning as any other aspect of the system being developed. Choosing the wrong option will make the process of getting the software into the users' hands difficult and frustrating.

Deployment Options

This section provides an overview of the deployment options that are available to .NET developers. Most of these options are discussed in greater detail later in this chapter.

➤ **Xcopy** — The xcopy utility lets you copy an assembly or group of assemblies to an application folder, cutting down on your development time. Because assemblies are self-discovering (that is, the metadata that describes the assembly is included in the assembly), you do not need to register anything in the registry.

Each assembly keeps track of what other assemblies it requires to execute. By default, the assembly looks in the current application folder for the dependencies. The process of moving (or probing) assemblies to other folders is discussed later in this chapter.

➤ **Publishing web sites** — When a web site is published, the entire site is compiled and then copied to a specified location. As a result of precompiling, all source code is removed from the final output and all compile errors can be found and dealt with.

➤ **Deployment projects** — Visual Studio 2010 has the capability to create setup programs for an application. There are four options based on Microsoft Windows Installer technology:

➤ Creating merge modules,

➤ Creating a setup for client applications,

➤ Creating a setup for web applications, and

➤ Creating a setup for Smart Device-based (Compact Framework) applications.

The ability to create cab files is also available. Deployment projects offer a great deal of flexibility and customization for the setup process. One of these deployment options will be useful for larger applications.

➤ **ClickOnce technology** — The ClickOnce technology offers a way to build self-updating Windows-based applications. ClickOnce allows an application to be published to a web site, file share, or even a CD. As updates and new builds are made to the application, they can be published to the same location or site by the development team. As the application is used by the end user, it checks the location to see if an update is available. If there is, an update is attempted.

Deployment Requirements

It is instructive to look at the runtime requirements of a .NET-based application. The CLR has certain requirements on the target platform before any managed application can execute.

The first requirement that must be met is the operating system. Currently, the following operating systems can run .NET-based applications:

➤ Windows XP SP3

➤ Windows Vista SP1

➤ Windows 7

The following server platforms are supported:

➤   Windows 2003 Server Family SP2

➤   Windows 2008 Server Family (Server Core Role not supported)

The following architectures are supported:

➤   x86

➤   x64

➤   ia64 (some features not supported)

Other requirements are Windows Internet Explorer version 5.01 or later, MDAC version 2.8 or later (if the application is designed to access data), and Internet Information Services (IIS) for ASP.NET applications.

You also must consider hardware requirements when deploying .NET applications. The minimum hardware requirements for both the client and the server are a Pentium 400 MHz and 96 MB RAM

For best performance, increase the amount of RAM — the more RAM the better your .NET application runs. This is especially true for server applications.

Deploying the .NET Runtime

When an application is developed using .NET, there is a dependency on the .NET runtime. This may seem rather obvious, but sometimes the obvious can be overlooked. The following table shows the version number and the filename that would have to be distributed:

.NET VERSION	FILENAME
2.0.50727.42	dotnetfx.exe
3.0.4506.30	dotnetfx3.exe (includes x86 and x64)
3.5.21022.8	dotnetfx35.exe (includes x86, x64, and ia64)
4.0.0.0	dotnetfx40.exe (includes x86, x64, and ia64)

SIMPLE DEPLOYMENT OPTIONS

If deployment is part of an application's original design considerations, deployment can be as simple as copying a set of files to the target computer. For a web application, it can be a simple menu choice in Visual Studio 2010. This section discusses these simple deployment scenarios.

To see how the various deployment options are set up, you must have an application to deploy. The sample download at www.wrox.com contains four projects:

➤   ClientWinForms

➤   ClientWPF

➤   WebClient

➤   AppSupport

ClientWinForms and ClientWPF are smart client applications using WinForms and WPF, respectively. WebClient is a simple web app. AppSupport is a class library that contains one simple class that returns a string with the current date and time.

The sample applications use AppSupport to fill a label with a string containing the current date. To use the examples, first load and build AppSupport. Then, in each of the other applications, set a reference to the newly built AppSupport.dll.

Here is the code for the `AppSupport` assembly:

```csharp
using System;
using System.Collections.Generic;
using System.Linq;
using System.Text;

namespace AppSupport
{
    public class DateService
    {
        public string GetLongDateInfoString()
        {
            return string.Concat("Today's date is ", DateTime.Now.ToLongDateString());
        }

        public string GetShortDateInfoString()
        {
            return string.Concat("Today's date is ", DateTime.Now.ToShortDateString());
        }
    }
}
```

code snippet Dateservice.cs

This simple assembly suffices to demonstrate the deployment options available to you.

Xcopy Deployment

Xcopy deployment is a term used for the process of copying a set of files to a folder on the target machine and then executing the application on the client. The term comes from the DOS command `xcopy.exe`. Regardless of the number of assemblies, if the files are copied into the same folder, the application will execute — rendering the task of editing the configuration settings or registry obsolete.

To see how an xcopy deployment works, execute the following steps:

1. Open the `ClientWinForms` solution (`ClientWinForms.sln`) that is part of the sample download file.

2. Change the target to Release and do a full compile.

3. Use either My Computer or File Explorer to navigate to the project folder `\ClientWinForms\bin\Release` and double-click `ClientWinForms.exe` to run the application.

4. Click the button to see the current date displayed in the two textboxes. This verifies that the application functions properly. Of course, this folder is where Visual Studio placed the output, so you would expect the application to work.

5. Create a new folder and call it `ClientWinFormsTest`. Copy the two files from the release folder to this new folder and then delete the release folder. Again, double-click the `ClientWinForms.exe` file to verify that it's working.

That's all there is to it; xcopy deployment provides the ability to deploy a fully functional application simply by copying the assemblies to the target machine. Just because the example that is used here is simple does not mean that this process cannot work for more complex applications. There really is no limit to the size or number of assemblies that can be deployed using this method. The reason that you might not want to use xcopy deployment is the ability to place assemblies in the Global Assembly Cache (GAC) or the ability to add icons to the Start menu. Also, if your application still relies on a COM library of some type, you will not be able to register the COM components easily.

Xcopy and Web Applications

Xcopy deployment can also work with web applications with the exception of the folder structure. You must establish the virtual directory of your web application and configure the proper user rights. This process is generally accomplished with the IIS administration tool.

After the virtual directory is set up, the web application files can be copied to the virtual directory. Copying a web application's files can be a bit tricky. A couple of configuration files, as well as the images that the pages might be using, need to be accounted for.

Publishing a Web Site

Another deployment option for web projects is to publish the web site. Publishing a web site will precompile the entire site and place the compiled version into a specified location. The location can be a file share, FTP location, or any other location that can be accessed via HTTP. The compilation process strips all source code from the assemblies and creates the DLLs for deployment. This also includes the markup contained in the .ASPX source files. Instead of containing the normal markup, the .ASPX files contain a pointer to an assembly. Each .ASPX file relates to an assembly. This process works regardless of the model: code-behind or single file.

The advantages of publishing a web site are speed and security. Speed is enhanced because all the assemblies are already compiled. Otherwise, the first time a page is accessed there is a delay while the page and dependent code is compiled and cached. The security is enhanced because the source code is not deployed. Also, because everything is precompiled before deployment all compilation errors will be found.

You publish a web site from the Build - Publish menu choice. In the Publish Method drop-down menu, you can choose MSDeploy Publish, FTP, or file system. The FTP option will ask for the FTP address as well as any login credentials that will be needed. The file system option will ask for the path to the target location. The MSDeploy Publish option is the interesting option.

You can define many properties for the deployment of your web site from the Package and Publish tab of the project properties page. You can define what files should be included, including debug information. Database information from the Deploy Sql tab can be included. This information includes connection strings, schema information and database script options.

You can also select packaging options from here. A zip file that contains everything you need to install your web site will be generated. Along with the zip file, three other files will be generated:

➤ `projectname.deploy.cmd` — A command file used by MSDeploy to install the web site.

➤ `projectname.SetParameters.xml` — An XML file that contains different parameters to pass to the Web Deployment Tool. This can be used to deploy to different servers or in different environments.

➤ `projectname.SourceManifest.xml` — Settings used by Visual Studio 2010 to create the package.

Projectname is the name of your project that is being packaged. Packages can be deployed using Visual Studio or by MSBuild.

VISUAL STUDIO 2010 SETUP AND DEPLOYMENT PROJECTS

Xcopy deployment can be easy to use, but there are times when the lack of functionality becomes an issue. To overcome this shortcoming, Visual Studio 2010 has six installer project types. Four of these options are based on the Windows Installer technology. The following table lists the project types.

PROJECT TYPE	DESCRIPTION
Setup Project	Used for the installation of client applications, middle-tier applications, and applications that run as a Windows Service.
Web Setup Project	Used for the installation of web-based applications.
Merge Module Project	Creates `.msm` merge modules that can be used with other Windows Installer-based setup applications.
CAB Project	Creates `.cab` files for distribution through older deployment technologies.
Setup Wizard	Aids in the creation of a deployment project.
Smart Device CAB Project	CAB project for Pocket PC, Smartphone, and other CE-based applications.

Setup and Web Setup Projects are very similar. The key difference is that with Web Setup the project is deployed to a virtual directory on a web server, whereas with Setup Project it is deployed to a folder structure. Both project types are based on Windows Installer and have all the features of a Windows Installer-based setup program.

Merge Module Project is generally used when you have created a component or library of functionality that is included in a number of deployment projects. By creating a merge module, you can set any configuration items specific to the component and without having to worry about them in the creation of the main deployment project.

The Cab Project type simply creates `.cab` files for the application. `.cab` files are used by older installation technologies as well as some web-based installation processes. The Setup Wizard project type steps through the process of creating a deployment project, asking specific questions along the way.

The following sections discuss how to create each of these deployment projects, what settings and properties can be changed, and what customization you can add.

What is Windows Installer?

Windows Installer is a service that manages the installation, update, repair, and removal of applications on most Windows operating systems. It is part of Windows ME, Windows 2000, Windows XP, Windows Vista, and Windows 7, and is available for Windows 95, Windows 98, and Windows NT 4.0. The current version of Windows Installer is 4.5.

Windows Installer tracks the installation of applications in a database. When an application has to be uninstalled, you can easily track and remove the registry settings that were added, the files that were copied to the hard drive, and the desktop and Start menu icons that were added. If a particular file is still referenced by another application, the installer leaves it on the hard drive so that the other application doesn't break. The database also makes it possible to perform repairs. If a registry setting or a DLL associated with an application becomes corrupt or is accidentally deleted, you can repair the installation. During a repair, the installer reads the database from the last install and replicates that installation.

The deployment projects in Visual Studio 2010 give you the ability to create a Windows Installation package. The deployment projects give you access to most of what you will need to do to install a given application. However, if you need even more control, check out the Windows Installer SDK, which is part of the Platform SDK — it contains documentation on creating custom installation packages for your application. The following sections deal with creating these installation packages using the Visual Studio 2010 deployment projects.

Creating Installers

Creating installation packages for client applications or for web applications is not that difficult. One of the first tasks is to identify all the external resources your application requires, including configuration files, COM components, third-party libraries, and controls and images. Including a list of dependencies in the project documentation was discussed earlier. This is where having that documentation can prove to be very useful. Visual Studio 2010 can do a reasonable job of interrogating an assembly and retrieving the dependencies for it, but you still have to audit the findings to make sure that nothing is missing.

Another concern might be when in the overall process the install package is created. If you have an automated build process set up, you can include the building of the installation package upon a successful build of the project. Automating the process greatly reduces the chance for errors in what can be a time-consuming and complicated process for large projects.

What you can do is to include the deployment project with the project solution. The Solution Property Pages dialog box has a setting for Configuration Properties. You can use this setting to select the projects that will be included for your various build configurations. If you select the Build check box under Release builds but not for the Debug builds, the installation package will be created only when you are creating a release build. This is the process used in the following examples. Figure 17-1 shows the Solution Property Pages dialog box of the `ClientWPF` solution. Notice that the Debug configuration is displayed and that the Build check box is unchecked for the setup project.

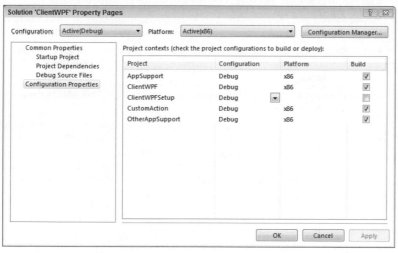

FIGURE 17-1

Simple Client Application

In the following example, you create an installer for the `ClientWinForms` solution (which is included in the sample download, together with the completed installer projects). This will show how having the installer project in a separate solution works. Later we'll take a look at the `ClientWPF` which has the installer project in the same solution.

Before you get started creating the deployment project, make sure that you have a release build of the application that will be deployed.

Next, create a new project in Visual Studio 2010. In the New Project dialog box, select Setup and Deployment Projects on the left. On the right, select Setup Project and assign it a name of your choice (for example, `ClientWinFormsSetup`).

In the Solution Explorer window, click the project and then the Properties window. You will see a list of properties. These properties are displayed during the setup of your application. Some of these properties are also displayed in the Add/Remove Programs Control Panel applet. Because most of these properties are visible to users during the installation process (or when they are looking at your installation in Add or Remove Programs), setting them correctly adds a professional touch to your application.

The list of properties is important, especially if your application will be deployed commercially. The following table describes the properties and the values that you should enter:

PROJECT PROPERTY	DESCRIPTION
AddRemoveProgramsIcon	The icon that appears in the Add/Remove dialog box.
Author	The author of the application. Generally this property setting is the same as the manufacturer. It displays on the Summary page of the Properties dialog of the `msi` package, as well as the Contact field of the SupportInfo page on the Add/Remove dialog box.
Description	A freeform text field that describes the application or component that is being installed. This information is displayed on the Summary page of the Properties dialog of the `msi` package, as well as the Comment field of the SupportInfo page on the Add/Remove dialog box.
DetectNewerInstalled Version	A Boolean value that, when set to `true`, checks to see if a newer version of the application is already installed. If so, the installation process will stop.
InstallAllUsers	Boolean value that, when set to `true`, will install that application for all users of the computer. If set to `false`, only the current user will have access.
Keywords	Keywords that can be used to search for the `.msi` file on the target computer. This information is displayed on the Summary page of the Properties dialog box of the `msi` package.
Localization	The locale used for string resources and registry settings. This affects the user interface of the installer.
Manufacturer	Name of the company that manufactured the application or component. Typically, this is the same information as specified in the `Author` property. This information is displayed on the Summary page of the Properties dialog box of the `msi` package as well as the Publisher field of the SupportInfo page in the Add/Remove dialog box. It is used as part of the default installation path of the application.
ManufacturerURL	The URL for a web site that relates to the application or component being installed.
PostBuildEvent	A command that is executed after the build ends.
PreBuildEvent	A command that is executed before the build begins.
ProductCode	A string GUID that is unique to this application or component. Windows Installer uses this property to identify the application for subsequent upgrades or installs.
ProductName	A name that describes the application. Used as the description of an application in the Add/Remove dialog box as well as part of the default install path: `C:\Program Files\Manufacturer\ProductName`.
RemovePrevious- Versions	Boolean value that, if set to `true`, will check for a previous version of the application. If yes, the uninstall function of the previous version is called before installation continues. This property uses `ProductCode` and `UpgradeCode` to determine if uninstall should occur. `UpgradeCode` should be the same; `ProductCode` should be different.
RunPostBuildEvent	When the `PostBuildEvent` should be run. Options are On successful build or Always.

PROJECT PROPERTY	DESCRIPTION
SearchPath	A string that represents the search path for dependent assemblies, files, or merge modules. Used when the installer package is built on the development machine.
Subject	Additional information regarding the application. This information is displayed on the Summary page of the Properties dialog box of the msi package.
SupportPhone	A phone number for support of the application or component. This information is displayed in the Support Information field of the SupportInfo page on the Add/Remove dialog box.
SupportURL	A URL for support of the application or component. This information is displayed in the Support Information field of the SupportInfo page in the Add/Remove dialog box.
TargetPlatform	Supports the 32- or 64-bit versions of Windows.
Title	The title of the installer. This is displayed on the Summary page of the Properties dialog box of the msi package.
UpgradeCode	A string GUID that represents a shared identifier of different versions of the same application. The UpgradeCode should not change for different versions or different language versions of the application. Used by DetectNewerInstalledVersion and RemovePreviousVersion.
Version	The version number of the installer, .cab file, or merge module. Note that this is not the version of the application being installed.

After you have set the properties, you can start to add assemblies. In this example, the only assembly you have to add is the main executable (ClientWinForms.exe). To do this, you can either right-click the project in the Solution Explorer or select Add from the Project menu. You have four options:

➤ Project Output — You explore this option in the next example.

➤ File — This is used for adding a readme text file or any other file that is not part of the build process.

➤ Merge Module — A merge module that was created separately.

➤ Assembly — Use this option to select an assembly that is part of the installation.

Choose Assembly for this example. You will be presented with the Component Selector dialog box, which resembles the dialog box you use for adding references to a project. Browse to the \bin\release folder of your application. Select ClientWinForms.exe and click OK in the Component Selector dialog box. You can now see ClientWinForms.exe listed in the Solution Explorer of the deployment project. In the Detected Dependencies section, you can see that Visual Studio interrogated ClientWinForms.exe to find the assemblies on which it depends; in this case, AppSupport.dll is included automatically. You would continue this process until all the assemblies in your application are accounted for in the Solution Explorer of the deployment project.

Next, you have to determine where the assemblies will be deployed. By default, the File System editor is displayed in Visual Studio 2010. The File System editor is split into two panes: the left pane shows the hierarchical structure of the file system on the target machine; the right pane provides a detail view of the selected folder. The folder names might not be what you expect to see, but keep in mind that these are for the target machine. For example, the folder labeled User's Programs Menu maps to the folder on the target client that contains the user's Program Menu. This will vary depending on the version of Windows being used.

You can add other folders at this point, either special folders or a custom folder. To add a special folder, make sure that File System on Target Machine is highlighted in the left pane, and select Action menu on the main menu. The Add Special Folder menu choice provides a list of folders that can be added. For example, if you want to add a folder under the Application folder, you can select the Application Folder folder in the left pane of the editor and then select the Action menu. This time, there will be an Add menu that enables you to create the new folder. Rename the new folder and it will be created for you on the target machine.

One of the special folders that you might want to add is a folder for the GAC. `AppSupport.dll` can be installed to the GAC if it is used by several different applications. To add an assembly to the GAC, it does have to have a strong name. The process for adding the assembly to the GAC is to add the GAC from the Special Folder menu as described previously and then drag the assembly that you want in the GAC from the current folder to the Global Assembly Cache folder. If you try to do this with an assembly that is not strongly named, the deployment project will not compile.

If you select Application Folder, you see on the right pane that the assemblies that you added are automatically added to the Application folder. You can move the assemblies to other folders, but keep in mind that the assemblies have to be able to find each other. (For more details on probing, see Chapter 18, "Assemblies.")

If you want to add a shortcut to the application on the user's desktop or to the Start menu, drag the items to the appropriate folders. To create a desktop shortcut, go to the Application folder. On the right side of the editor select the application. Go to the Action menu and select the Create Shortcut item to create a shortcut to the application. After the shortcut is created, drag it to the User's Desktop folder. Now when the application is installed, the shortcut will appear on the desktop. Typically, it is up to the user to decide if he or she wants a desktop shortcut to the application.

The process of asking the user for input and taking conditional steps is explored later in this chapter. The same process can be followed to create an item in the Start menu. Also, if you look at the properties for the shortcut that you just created, you will see that you can configure the basic shortcut properties such as Arguments and what icon to use. The application icon is the default icon.

Before you build the deployment project, you might have to check some project properties. If you select Project menu, then ClientWinFormsSetup Properties, you will see the project Property Pages dialog box. These are properties that are specific to a current configuration. After selecting the configuration in the Configuration drop-down, you can change the properties listed in the following table.

PROPERTY	DESCRIPTION
Output filename	The name of the .msi or .msm file that is generated when the project is compiled.
Package files	This property enables you to specify how the files are packaged. Your options are:
	As loose uncompressed files — All the deployment files are stored in the same directory as the .msi file.
	In setup file — Files are packaged in the .msi file (default setting).
	In cabinet file(s) — Files are in one or more .cab files in the same directory. When this is selected the CAB file size option becomes available.
Prerequisites URL	Allows you to specify where prerequisites such as the .NET Framework or Windows Installer can be found. Clicking the Settings button will display a dialog that has a list of items such as Windows Installer 4.5, the .NET Framework, and SQL Express 2008. There is also an option for choosing where the prerequisites can be downloaded from.
Compression	This specifies the compression style for the files included. Your options are:
	Optimized for speed — Larger files but faster installation time (default setting).
	Optimized for size — Smaller files but slower installation time.
	None — No compression applied.
CAB size	This is enabled when the Package file setting is set to In CAB files. Unlimited creates one single CAB file; custom allows you to set the maximum size for each .cab file.
Authenticode signature	When this is checked, the deployment project output is signed using Authenticode; the default setting is unchecked.

After you have set the project properties, you should be able to build the deployment project and create the setup for the `ClientWinForms` application. After you build the project, you can test the installation by right-clicking the project name in the Solution Explorer. This lets you access an Install and Uninstall choice in the context menu. If you have done everything correctly, you should be able to install and uninstall `ClientWinForms` successfully.

Same Solution Project

The previous example works well for creating a deployment package, but it does have a couple of downsides. For example, what happens when a new assembly is added to the original application? The deployment project will not automatically recognize any changes; you will have to add the new assemblies and verify that any new dependencies are covered. In smaller applications (like the example), this isn't that big of a deal.

However, when you're dealing with an application that contains dozens or maybe hundreds of assemblies, this can become quite tedious to maintain. Visual Studio 2010 has a simple way of resolving this potential headache. Include the deployment project in your application's solution. You can then capture the output of the main project as your deployment assemblies. You can look at the `ClientWPF` as an example.

Open the `ClientWPF` solution in Visual Studio 2010. Add a new project using Solution Explorer. Select Deployment and Setup Projects and then select Setup Project, following the steps outlined in the previous section. You can name this project `ClientWPFSetup`. In the previous example, you added the assemblies by selecting Add ⇨ Assemblies from the Project menu. This time, select Add ⇨ Project Output from the Project menu. This opens the Add Project Output Group dialog box (see Figure 17-2).

The top part of the dialog box has a drop-down list box that shows all the projects in the current solution. Select the main startup project. Then select the items that you want to include in your project from the following list. Your options are Documentation, Primary output, Localized resources, Debug symbols, Content files, and Source files.

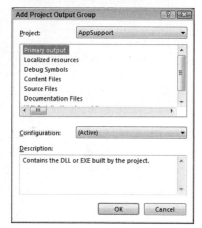

First, select Primary Output. This includes the output and all dependencies when the application is built. Another drop-down list box lists the valid configurations: Debug and Release, plus any custom configurations you might have added. This also determines what outputs are picked up. For deployment, you will most likely want to use the Release configuration.

After you make these selections, a new item is added to your deployment project in Solution Explorer. The name of the item is Primary output from `ClientWPF` (`Release .NET`). You will also see the file `AppSupport.dll` listed under the dependencies. As before, no need to search for the dependent assemblies.

FIGURE 17-2

At this point, all the various project properties discussed in the previous section still apply. You can change the Name, Manufacturer, `.cab` file size, and other properties. After setting the properties, do a release build of the solution and test the installation. Everything should work as expected.

To see the advantage of adding the deployment package to the applications solution, add a new project to the solution. In the example it is called `OtherAppSupport`. In it is a simple test method that returns the string "This is the message." Set a reference in `ClientWPF` to the newly added project, and do another release build of the solution. You should see that the deployment project picked up the new assembly without you having to do anything. You can also right-click the Detected Dependencies section of the installer project and select Refresh Dependencies. If you had been using a standalone deployment project, the newly added project would not have been picked up.

Simple Web Application

Creating an installation package for a web application is not that different from creating a client install package. The download examples include a `WebClient` that also utilizes the `AppSupport.dll` assembly. You can create the deployment project the same way that the client deployment projects are created, either standalone or in the same solution. In this example, the deployment project is built in the same solution.

Start the `WebClient` solution and add a new deployment and setup project. This time, be sure to choose Web Setup Project in the Templates window. If you look at the properties view for the project, you will see that all the same properties exist for web applications that existed for client applications. The only addition is `RestartWWWService`. This is a Boolean value that will restart IIS during the install. If you're using ASP. NET components and not replacing any ATL or ISAPI DLLs, you shouldn't have to do this.

If you look at the File System editor, you will notice that there is only one folder. The Web Application folder will be your virtual directory. By default, the name of the directory is the name of the deployment project, and it is located below the web root directory. The following table explains the properties that can be set from the installer. The properties discussed in the previous section are not included.

PROPERTY	DESCRIPTION
AllowDirectoryBrowsing	A Boolean value that, if `true`, allows an HTML listing of the files and subfolders of the virtual directory. Maps to the Directory browsing property of IIS.
AllowReadAccess	A Boolean value that, if `true`, allows users to read or download files. Maps to the Read property of IIS.
AllowScriptSourceAccess	A Boolean value that, if `true`, allows users to access source code, including scripts. Maps to Script source access in IIS.
AllowWriteAccess	A Boolean value that, if `true`, allows users to change content in write-enabled files. Maps to the Write property of IIS.
ApplicationProtection	Determines the protection level of applications that are run on the server. The valid values are: Low — Applications run in the same process as web services. Medium — Applications run in same process but not the same as web services. High — Application runs in its own process. Maps to the Application Protection property in IIS. Has no effect if the `IsApplication` property is `false`.
AppMappings	A list of application names and document or data files that are associated with the applications. Maps to the Application Mappings property of IIS.
Condition	A Windows Installer condition that must be met for the item to be installed.
DefaultDocument	The default or startup document when the user first browses to the site.
ExecutePermissions	The level of permissions that a user has to execute applications. The valid values are: None — Only static content can be accessed. ScriptsOnly — Only scripts can be accessed. Includes ASP. ScriptsAndExecutables — Any files can be accessed. Maps to Execute Permissions in IIS.
Index	Boolean value that, if `true`, would allow indexing of the content for Microsoft Indexing Service. Maps to the Index this resource property of IIS.

PROPERTY	DESCRIPTION
IsApplication	Boolean value that, if `true`, instructs IIS to create the application root for the folder.
LogVisits	Boolean value that, if `true`, logs visits to the web site in a log file. Maps to the Log Visits property of IIS.
Property	The named property that can be accessed at installation time.
VirtualDirectory	The virtual directory for the application. This is relative to the web server.

You might notice that most of these properties are properties of IIS and can be set in the IIS Administrator tool. So, the logical assumption is that to set these properties in the installer, the installer will need to run with administrator privileges. The settings made here can compromise security, so the changes should be well documented.

Other than these properties, the process of creating the deployment package is very similar to the previous client example. The main difference between the two projects is the ability to modify IIS from the installation process. As you can see, you have a great deal of control over the IIS environment.

Client from Web Server

Another installation scenario is either running the install program from a web site or actually running the application from a web site. Both of these are attractive options if you must deploy an application to a large number of users. By deploying from a web site, you eliminate the need for a distribution medium such as CD-ROMs, DVDs, or even floppy disks. By running the application from a web site or even a network share, you eliminate the need to distribute a setup program at all.

Running an installer from a web site is fairly simple. You use the Web Bootstrapper project compile option. You will be asked to provide the URL of the setup folder. This is the folder in which the setup program is going to look for the `.msi` and other files necessary for the setup to work. After you set this option and compile the deployment package, you can copy it to the web site that you specify in the Setup folder URL property. At this point, when the user navigates to the folder, she will be able to either run the setup or download it and then run it. In both instances, the user must be able to connect to the same site to finish the installation.

CLICKONCE

ClickOnce is a deployment technology that allows applications to be self-updating. Applications are published to a file share, web site, or media such as a CD. When published, ClickOnce apps can be automatically updated with minimal user input.

ClickOnce also solves the security permission problem. Normally, to install an application the user needs Administrative rights. With ClickOnce, a user can install and run an application with only the absolute minimum permissions required to run the application.

ClickOnce Operation

ClickOnce applications have two XML-based manifest files associated with them. One is the application manifest, and the other is the deployment manifest. These two files describe everything that is required to deploy an application.

The application manifest contains information about the application such as permissions required, assemblies to include, and other dependencies. The deployment manifest is about the deployment of the app. Items such as the location of the application manifest are contained in the deployment manifest. The complete schemas for the manifests are in the .NET SDK documentation.

ClickOnce has some limitations. Assemblies cannot be added to the GAC, for example. The following table compares ClickOnce and Windows Installer.

FEATURE	CLICKONCE	WINDOWS INSTALLER
Application installation location	ClickOnce application cache	Program Files folder
Install for multiple users	No	Yes
Install shared files	No	Yes
Install drivers	No	Yes
Install to the GAC	No	Yes
Add application to the Startup group	No	Yes
Add application to the Favorites menu	No	Yes
Register file types	No	Yes
Access registry	No. The HKLM can be accessed with Full Trust permissions.	Yes
Binary patching of files	Yes	No
Install assemblies on demand	Yes	No

Some situations certainly exist where using Windows Installer is clearly a better choice, however, ClickOnce can be used for a large number of applications.

Publishing a ClickOnce Application

Everything that ClickOnce needs to know is contained in the two manifest files. The process of publishing an application for ClickOnce deployment is simply generating the manifests and placing the files in the proper location. The manifest files can be generated in Visual Studio 2010. There is also a command-line tool (mage.exe) and a version with a GUI (mageUI.exe).

You can create the manifest files in Visual Studio 2010 in two ways. At the bottom of the Publish tab on the Project Properties dialog are two buttons. One is the Publish Wizard and the other is Publish Now. The Publish Wizard asks several questions about the deployment of the application and then generates the manifest files and copies all the needed files to the deployment location. The Publish Now button uses the values that have been set in the Publish tab to create the manifest files and copies the files to the deployment location.

To use the command-line tool, mage.exe, the values for the various ClickOnce properties must be passed in. Manifest files can be both created and updated using mage.exe. Typing **mage.exe -help** at the command prompt gives the syntax for passing in the values required.

The GUI version of mage.exe (mageUI.exe) is similar in appearance to the Publish tab in Visual Studio 2010. An application and deployment manifest file can be created and updated using the GUI tool.

ClickOnce applications appear in the Add/Remove Control Panel applet just as any other installed application. One big difference is that the user is presented with the choice of either uninstalling the application or rolling back to the previous version. ClickOnce keeps the previous version in the ClickOnce application cache.

ClickOnce Settings

Several properties are available for both manifest files. The most important property is where the application should be deployed from. The dependencies for the application must be specified. The Publish tab has an Application Files button that shows a dialog for entering all the assemblies required by the application. The Prerequisite button displays a list of common prerequisites that can be installed along with the application. You have the choice of installing the prerequisites from the same location that the application is being published to or optionally having the prerequisites installed from the vendor's web site.

The Update button displays a dialog that has the information about how the application should be updated. As new versions of an application are made available, ClickOnce can be used to update the application. Options include to check for updates every time the application starts or to check in the background. If the background option is selected, a specified period of time between checks can be entered. Options for allowing the user to be able to decline or accept the update are available. This can be used to force an update in the background so that the user is never aware that the update is occurring. The next time the application is run, the new version will be used instead of the older version. A separate location for the update files can be used as well. This way the original installation package can be located in one location and installed for new users, and all the updates can be staged in another location.

The application can be set up so that it will run in either online or offline mode. In offline mode the application can be run from the Start menu and acts as if it were installed using the Windows Installer. Online mode means that the application will run only if the installation folder is available.

Application Cache for ClickOnce Files

Applications distributed with ClickOnce are not installed in the Program Files folder. Instead, they are placed in an application cache that resides in the Local Settings folder under the current user's Documents and Settings folder. Controlling this aspect of the deployment means that multiple versions of an application can reside on the client PC at the same time. If the application is set to run online, every version that the user has accessed is retained. For applications that are set to run locally, the current and previous versions are retained.

Because of this, it is a very simple process to roll back a ClickOnce application to its previous version. If the user goes to the Add/Remove Programs Control Panel applet, the dialog presented will contain the choice of removing the ClickOnce application or rolling back to the previous version. An Administrator can change the manifest file to point to the previous version. If the administrator does this, the next time the user runs that application, a check will be made for an update. Instead of finding new assemblies to deploy, the application will restore the previous version without any interaction from the user.

Application Security

Applications deployed over the Internet or an intranet have a lower security or trust setting than applications that have been installed to the local drive. For example, by default, if an application is launched or deployed from the Internet it is in the Internet Security Zone. This means that it cannot access the file system, among other things. If the application is installed from a file share, it will run in the Intranet Zone.

If your ClickOnce application requires a higher level of trust than the default, the user will be prompted to grant the permissions required for the application to run. These permissions are set in the trustInfo element of the application manifest. Only the permissions asked for in this setting will be granted. So, if an application asks for file access permissions, Full Trust will not be granted, only the specific permissions requested.

Another option is to use Trusted Application Deployment. Trusted Application Deployment is a way to grant permissions on an enterprise-wide basis without having to prompt the user. A trust license issuer is identified to each client machine. This is done with public key cryptography. Typically, an organization will have only one issuer. It is important to keep the private key for the issuer in a safe, secure location.

A trust license is requested from the issuer. The level of trust that is being requested is part of the trust license configuration. A public key used to sign the application must also be supplied to the license issuer. The license created contains the public key used to sign the application and the public key of the license issuer. This trust license is then embedded in the deployment manifest. The last step is to sign the deployment manifest with your own key pair. The application is now ready to deploy.

When the client opens the deployment manifest the Trust Manager will determine if the ClickOnce application has been given a higher trust. The issuer license is looked at first. If it is valid, the public key in the license is compared to the public key that was used to sign the application. If these match, the application is granted the requested permissions.

VISUAL STUDIO 2010 EDITORS

The installation processes discussed so far are very powerful and can do quite a bit. But there is much more that you can control in the installation process. For example, you can use the various editors in Visual Studio 2010 to build conditional installations or add registry keys and custom dialog boxes. The `SampleClientSetupSolution` example has all these advanced options enabled.

File System Editor

The File System editor enables you to specify where in the target the various files and assemblies that make up the application will be deployed. By default, a standard set of deployment folders is displayed. You can add any number of custom and special folders with the editor. This is also where you would add desktop and Start menu shortcuts to the application. Any file that must be part of the deployment must be referenced in the File System editor.

Registry Editor

The Registry editor allows you to add keys and data to the registry. When the editor is first displayed, a standard set of main keys is displayed:

➤ HKEY_CLASSES_ROOT

➤ HKEY_CURRENT_USER

➤ HKEY_LOCAL_MACHINE

➤ HKEY_USERS

HKEY_CURRENT_USER and HKEY_LOCAL_MACHINE contain additional entries in the Software/[Manufacturer] key where Manufacturer is the information you entered in the `Manufacturer` property of the deployment project.

To add additional keys and values, highlight one of the main keys on the left side of the editor. Select Action from the main menu and then select New. Select the key or the value type that you want to add. Repeat this step until you have all the registry settings that you want. If you select the Registry on Target Machine item on the left pane and then select the Action menu, you will see an Import option, which enables you to import an already defined `*.reg` file.

To create a default value for a key you must first enter a value for the key, and then select the value name in the right or value pane. Select Rename from the File menu and delete the name. Press Enter and the value name is replaced with (Default).

You can also set some properties for the subkeys and values in the editor. The only one that hasn't been discussed already is the `DeleteAtUninstall` property. A well-designed application should remove all keys that have been added by the application at uninstall time. The default setting is not to delete the keys.

One thing to keep in mind is that the preferred method for maintaining application settings is to use XML-based configuration files. These files offer a great deal more flexibility and are much easier to restore and back up than registry entries.

File Types Editor

The File Types editor is used to establish associations between files and applications. For example, when you double-click a file with the `.doc` extension, the file is opened in Word. You can create these same associations for your application.

To add an association, execute the following steps:

1. Select File Types on Target Machine from the Action menu.

2. Then select Add File Type. In the properties window, you can now set the name of the association.

3. In the `Extension` property, add the file extension that should be associated with the application. Do not enter the periods; you can separate multiple extensions with a semicolon, like this: **ex1;ex2**.

4. In the Command property, select the Ellipsis button.

5. Now, select the file (typically an executable) that you want to associate with the specified file types. Keep in mind that any one extension should be associated with only one application.

By default, the editor shows &Open as the Document Action. You can add others. The order in which the actions appear in the editor is the order in which they will appear in the context menu when the user right-clicks the file type. Keep in mind that the first item is always the default action. You can set the `Arguments` property for the actions. This is the command-line argument used to start the application.

User Interface Editor

Sometimes you might want to ask the user for more information during the installation process. The User Interface editor is used to specify properties for a set of predefined dialog boxes. The editor is separated into two sections, Install and Admin. One is for the standard installation and the other is used for an administrator's installation. Each section is broken up into three subsections: Start, Progress, and End. These subsections represent the three basic stages of the installation process (see Figure 17-3).

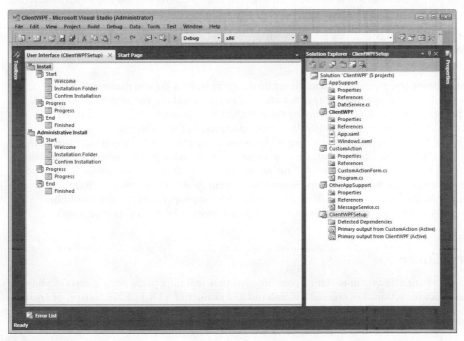

FIGURE 17-3

The following table lists the types of dialog boxes that you can add to the project.

DIALOG BOX	DESCRIPTION
Check Boxes	Contains up to four check boxes. Each check box has a `Label`, `Value`, and `Visible` property.
Confirm Installation	Gives the user the ability to confirm the various settings before installation takes place.
Customer Information	Has edit fields for the collection name, organization name, and serial number. Organization name and serial number are optional.
Finished	Displayed at the end of the setup process.
Installation Address	For web applications, displays a dialog box so that users can choose an alternative installation URL.
Installation Folder	For client applications, displays a dialog box so that users can select an alternative installation folder.
License Agreement	Displays the license agreement that is located in a file specified by the `LicenseFile` property.
Progress	Displays a progress indicator during the installation process that shows the current installation status.
Radio Buttons	Contains up to four radio buttons. Each radio button has a `Label` and `Value` property.
Read Me	Shows the readme information contained in the file specified by the `ReadMe` property.
Register User	Executes an application that will guide the user through the registration process. This application must be supplied in the setup project.
Splash	Displays a bitmap image.
Text Boxes	Contains up to four text box fields. Each text box has a `Label`, `Value`, and `Visible` property.
Welcome	Contains two properties: the `WelcomeText` property and the `CopyrightWarning`. Both are string properties.

Each of these dialog boxes also contains a property for setting the banner bitmap, and most have a property for banner text. You can also change the order in which the dialog boxes appear by dragging them up or down in the editor window.

Now that you can capture some of this information, the question is, how do you make use of it? This is where the `Condition` property that appears on most of the objects in the project comes in. The `Condition` property must evaluate to true for the installation step to proceed. For example, say the installation comes with three optional installation components. In this case, you would add a dialog box with three check boxes. The dialog should be somewhere after the Welcome and before the Confirm Installation dialog box. Change the `Label` property of each check box to describe the action. The first action could be "Install Component A," the second could be "Install Component B," and so on. In the File System editor, select the file that represents Component A. Assuming that the name of the check box on the dialog box is CHECKBOXA1, the `Condition` property of the file would be CHECKBOXA1=Checked — that is, if CHECKBOXA1 is checked, install the file; otherwise, don't install it.

Custom Actions Editor

The Custom Actions editor allows you to define custom steps that will take place during certain phases of the installation. Custom actions are created beforehand and consist of a DLL, EXE, script, or Installer class. The action would contain special steps to perform that can't be defined in the standard deployment project. The actions will be performed at four specific points in the deployment. When the editor is first started, you will see the four points in the project (see Figure 17-4):

➤ Install — Actions will be executed at the end of the installation phase.

➤ Commit — Actions will be executed after the installation has finished and no errors have been recorded.

➤ Rollback — Actions occur after the rollback phase has completed.

➤ Uninstall — Actions occur after uninstall has completed.

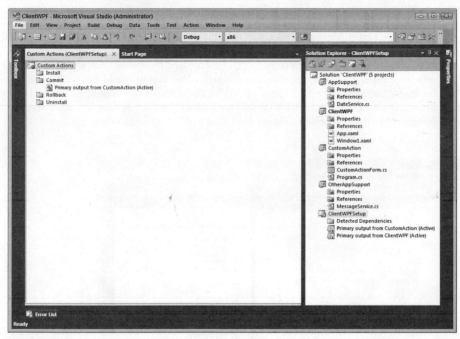

FIGURE 17-4

To add an action, you first select the phase of the installation in which you want the action to occur. Select the Add Custom Action menu option from the Action menu to open the File System dialog box. This means that the component that contains the action must be part of the deployment project. Because it will be executing on the target machine it has to be deployed; therefore, it should be listed in the File System editor.

After you have added the action, you can select one or more of the properties listed in the following table.

ARGUMENTS	COMMAND-LINE ARGUMENTS
Condition	A Windows Installer condition that must be evaluated and result in true for the action to execute.
CustomDataAction	Custom data that will be available to the action.
EntryPoint	The entry point for the custom DLL that contains the action. If the action is contained in an executable, this property does not apply.
InstallerClass	A Boolean value that, if true, specifies that the action is a .NET `ProjectInstaller` class.
Name	Name of the action. Defaults to the filename of the action.
SourcePath	The path to action on the development machine.

Because the action is code that you develop outside the deployment project, you have the freedom to add just about anything that adds a professional touch to your application. The thing to remember is that such an action happens after the phase it is associated with is complete. If you select the Install phase, the action will not execute until after the install phase has completed. If you want to make determinations before the process, you will want to create a launch condition.

Launch Conditions Editor

The Launch Conditions editor allows you to specify that certain conditions must be met before installation can continue. Launch conditions are organized into types of conditions. The basic launch conditions are File Search, Registry Search, and Windows Installer Search. When the editor is first started you see two groups (see Figure 17-5): Search Target Machine and Launch Conditions. Typically, a search is conducted, and, based on the success or failure of that search, a condition is executed. This happens by setting the `Property` property of the search. The `Property` property can be accessed by the installation process. It can be checked in the `Condition` property of other actions, for example. You can also add a launch condition in the editor. In this condition, you set the `Condition` property to the value of the `Property` property in the search. In the condition, you can specify a URL that will download the file, registry key, or installer component that was being searched for. Notice in Figure 17-5 that a .NET Framework condition is added by default.

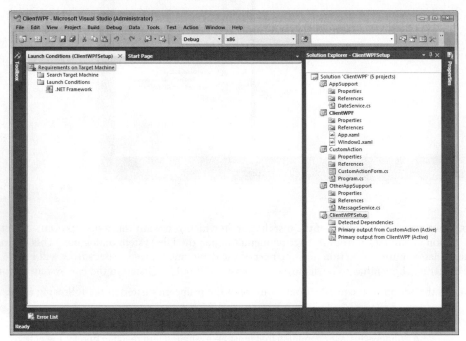

FIGURE 17-5

File Search will search for a file or type of file. You can set many different file-related properties that determine how files are searched, including filename, folder location, various date values, version information, and size. You can also set the number of subfolders that are searched.

Registry Search allows you to search for keys and values. It also allows you to set the root key for searching.

Windows Installer Search looks for the specified Installer component. The search is conducted by GUID.

The Launch Conditions editor provides two prepackaged launch conditions: the .NET Framework Launch Condition, which allows you to search for a specific version of the runtime, and a search for a specific version of MDAC, which uses the registry search to find the relevant MDAC registry entries.

SUMMARY

Deploying software has become difficult for developers of desktop software. As web sites have grown more complex, the deployment of server-based software has become more difficult. This chapter looked at the options and capabilities that Visual Studio 2010 and version 3.5 of the .NET Framework provide to help make deployment easier and less error-prone.

After reading this chapter, you should be able to create a deployment package that resolves almost any deployment issue that you might have. Client applications can be deployed locally or via the Internet or an intranet. The extensive features of deployment projects and the ways that deployment projects can be configured were covered. You can also use no-touch deployment and ClickOnce to deploy applications. The security features of ClickOnce will make this a secure and efficient way of deploying client applications. Using deployment projects to install web applications can make the process of configuring IIS much easier as well. Publishing a web site provides the added benefit of precompiling the application.

PART III
Foundation

▶ **CHAPTER 18:** Assemblies

▶ **CHAPTER 19:** Instrumentation

▶ **CHAPTER 20:** Threads, Tasks, and Synchronization

▶ **CHAPTER 21:** Security

▶ **CHAPTER 22:** Localization

▶ **CHAPTER 23:** System.Transactions

▶ **CHAPTER 24:** Networking

▶ **CHAPTER 25:** Windows Services

▶ **CHAPTER 26:** Interop

▶ **CHAPTER 27:** Core XAML

▶ **CHAPTER 28:** Managed Extensibility Framework

▶ **CHAPTER 29:** Manipulating Files and the Registry

18

Assemblies

WHAT'S IN THIS CHAPTER?

➤   An overview of assemblies
➤   Creating assemblies
➤   Using application domains
➤   Sharing assemblies
➤   Versioning

An *assembly* is the .NET term for a deployment and configuration unit. This chapter discusses exactly what assemblies are, how they can be applied, and why they are such a useful feature.

This chapter teaches you how to create assemblies dynamically, how to load assemblies into appdomains, and how to share assemblies between different applications. The chapter also covers versioning, which is an important aspect of sharing assemblies.

WHAT ARE ASSEMBLIES?

Assemblies are the deployment units of .NET applications. .NET applications consist of one or more assemblies. .NET executables with the usual extension EXE or DLL are known by the term *assembly*. What's the difference between an assembly and a native DLL or EXE? Although they both have the same file extension, .NET assemblies include metadata that describes all the types that are defined in the assembly with information about its members — methods, properties, events, and fields.

The metadata of .NET assemblies also provides information about the files that belong to the assembly, version information, and the exact information about assemblies that are used. .NET assemblies are the answer to the DLL hell we've seen previously with native DLLs.

Assemblies are self-describing installation units, consisting of one or more files. One assembly could be a single DLL or EXE that includes metadata, or it can be made of different files, for example, resource files, modules, and an EXE.

Assemblies can be private or shared. With simple .NET applications, using just private assemblies is the best way to work. No special management, registration, versioning, and so on is needed with private assemblies. The only application that could have version problems with private assemblies is your own application. Other applications are not influenced because they have their own copies of the assemblies. The private components you use within your application are installed at the same time as the application itself. Private assemblies are located in the same directory as the application or subdirectories thereof. This way you shouldn't have any versioning problems with the application. No other application will ever overwrite your private assemblies. Of course, it is still a good idea to use version numbers for private assemblies, too. This helps a lot with code changes, but it's not a requirement of .NET.

With shared assemblies, several applications can use the same assembly and have a dependency on it. Shared assemblies reduce the need for disk and memory space. With shared assemblies, many rules must be fulfilled — a shared assembly must have a version number and a unique name, and usually it's installed in the *global assembly cache* (GAC). The GAC allows you to share different versions of the same assembly on a system.

Assembly Features

The assembly features can be summarized as follows:

➤ Assemblies are *self-describing*. It's no longer necessary to pay attention to registry keys for apartments, to get the type library from some other place, and so on. Assemblies include metadata that describes the assembly. The metadata includes the types exported from the assembly and a manifest; the next section describes the function of a manifest.

➤ *Version dependencies* are recorded inside an assembly manifest. Storing the version of any referenced assemblies in the manifest makes it possible to easily find deployment faults because of wrong versions available. The version of the referenced assembly that will be used can be configured by the developer and the system administrator. Later in this chapter, you learn which version policies are available and how they work.

➤ Assemblies can be loaded *side by side*. Beginning with Windows 2000, you have a side-by-side feature where different versions of the same DLL can be used on a system. Did you ever check the directory `<windows>\winsxs`? .NET allows different versions of the same assembly to be used inside a single process! How is this useful? If assembly A references version 1 of the shared assembly `Shared`, and assembly B uses version 2 of the shared assembly `Shared`, and you are using both assembly A and B, you need both versions of the shared assembly `Shared` in your application — and with .NET both versions are loaded and used. The .NET 4 runtime even allows multiple CLR versions (2 and 4) inside one process. This allows, for example, loading plugins with different CLR requirements. While there's no direct .NET way to communicate between objects in different CLR versions inside one process, you can use other techniques, for example COM.

➤ Application isolation is ensured by using *application domains*. With application domains a number of applications can run independently inside a single process. Faults in one application cannot directly affect other applications inside the same process.

➤ Installation can be as easy as copying the files that belong to an assembly. An xcopy can be enough. This feature is named *ClickOnce deployment*. However, there are cases in which ClickOnce deployment cannot be applied, and a normal Windows installation is required. Deployment of applications is discussed in Chapter 17, "Deployment."

Assembly Structure

An assembly consists of assembly metadata describing the complete assembly, type metadata describing the exported types and methods, MSIL code, and resources. All these parts can be inside of one file or spread across several files.

In the first example (see Figure 18-1), the assembly metadata, type metadata, MSIL code, and resources are all in one file — `Component.dll`. The assembly consists of a single file.

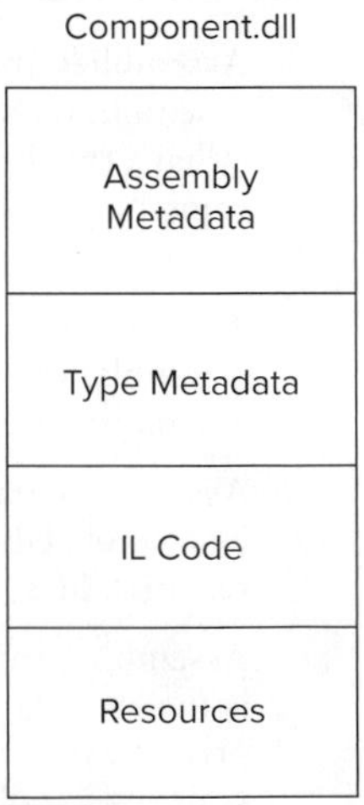

Component.dll

| Assembly Metadata |
| Type Metadata |
| IL Code |
| Resources |

FIGURE 18-1

The second example shows a single assembly spread across three files (see Figure 18-2). `Component.dll` has assembly metadata, type metadata, and MSIL code, but no resources. The assembly uses a picture from `picture.jpeg` that is not embedded inside `Component.dll`, but is referenced from within the assembly metadata. The assembly metadata also references a module called `util.netmodule`, which itself includes only type metadata and MSIL code for a class. A module has no assembly metadata; thus, the module itself has no version information. It also cannot be installed separately. All three files in this example make up a single assembly; the assembly is the installation unit. It would also be possible to put the manifest in a different file.

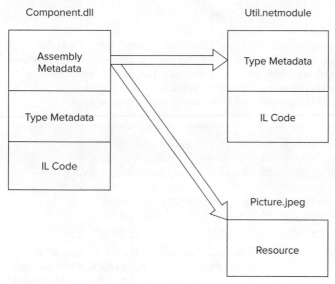

FIGURE 18-2

Assembly Manifests

An important part of an assembly is a *manifest,* which is part of the metadata. It describes the assembly with all the information that's needed to reference it and lists all its dependencies. The parts of the manifest are as follows:

➤ **Identity** — Name, version, culture, and public key.

➤ **A list of files** — Files belonging to this assembly. A single assembly must have at least one file but may contain a number of files.

➤ **A list of referenced assemblies** — All assemblies used from the assembly are documented inside the manifest. This reference information includes the version number and the public key, which is used to uniquely identify assemblies. The public key is discussed later in this chapter.

➤ **A set of permission requests** — These are the permissions needed to run this assembly. You can find more information about permissions in Chapter 21, "Security."

➤ **Exported types** — These are included if they are defined within a module and the module is referenced from the assembly; otherwise, they are not part of the manifest. A module is a unit of reuse. The type description is stored as metadata inside the assembly. You can get the structures and classes with the properties and methods from the metadata. This replaces the type library that was used with COM to describe the types. For the use of COM clients, it's easy to generate a type library from the manifest. The reflection mechanism uses the information about the exported types for late binding to classes. See Chapter 14, "Reflection," for more information about reflection.

Namespaces, Assemblies, and Components

You might be a little bit confused by the meanings of namespaces, types, assemblies, and components. How does a namespace fit into the assembly concept? The namespace is completely independent of an assembly. You can have different namespaces in a single assembly, but the same namespace can be spread across assemblies. The namespace is just an extension of the type name — it belongs to the name of the type.

For example, the assemblies `mscorlib` and `system` contain the namespace `System.Threading` among many other namespaces. Although the assemblies contain the same namespaces, you will not find the same class names.

Private and Shared Assemblies

Assemblies can be shared or private. A *private assembly* is found either in the same directory as the application, or within one of its subdirectories. With a private assembly, it's not necessary to think about naming conflicts with other classes or versioning problems. The assemblies that are referenced during the build process are copied to the application directory. Private assemblies are the usual way to build assemblies, especially when applications and components are built within the same company.

> *Although it is still possible to have naming conflicts with private assemblies (multiple private assemblies may be part of the application and they could have conflicts, or a name in a private assembly might conflict with a name in a shared assembly used by the application), naming conflicts are greatly reduced. If you find you'll be using multiple private assemblies or working with shared assemblies in other applications, it's a good idea to utilize well-named namespaces and types to minimize naming conflicts.*

When using *shared assemblies,* you have to be aware of some rules. The assembly must be unique and, therefore, must also have a unique name, called a *strong name.* Part of the strong name is a mandatory version number. Shared assemblies will mostly be used when a vendor, different from that of the application, builds the component, or when a large application is split into subprojects. Also, some technologies, such as .NET Enterprise Services, require shared assemblies in specific scenarios.

Satellite Assemblies

A satellite assembly is an assembly that only contains resources. This is extremely useful for localization. Because an assembly has a culture associated, the resource manager looks for satellite assemblies containing the resources of a specific culture.

> *You can read more about satellite assemblies in Chapter 22, "Localization."*

Viewing Assemblies

You can view assemblies by using the command-line utility `ildasm`, the MSIL disassembler. You can open an assembly by starting `ildasm` from the command line with the assembly as an argument or by selecting the File⇨Open menu.

Figure 18-3 shows `ildasm` opening the example that you will build a little later in the chapter, `SharedDemo.dll`. `ildasm` shows the manifest and the `SharedDemo` type in the `Wrox.ProCSharp.Assemblies` namespace. When you open the manifest, you can see the version number and the assembly attributes, as well as the referenced assemblies and their versions. You can see the MSIL code by opening the methods of the class.

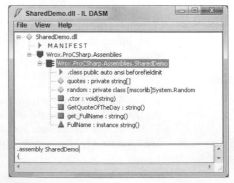

FIGURE 18-3

In addition to using ildasm, *the .NET Reflector is another great tool to use to analyze assemblies. The .NET Reflector allows type and member search, and call and callee graphs, and decompiles IL code to C#, C++, or Visual Basic. You can download this tool from* www.redgate.com/products/reflector.

CREATING ASSEMBLIES

Now that you know what assemblies are, it is time to build some. Of course, you have already built assemblies in previous chapters, because a .NET executable counts as an assembly. This section looks at special options for assemblies.

Creating Modules and Assemblies

All C# project types in Visual Studio create an assembly. Whether you choose a DLL or EXE project type, an assembly is always created. With the command-line C# compiler csc, it's also possible to create modules. A module is a DLL without assembly attributes (so it's not an assembly, but it can be added to assemblies at a later time). The command:

```
csc /target:module hello.cs
```

creates a module hello.netmodule. You can view this module using ildasm.

A module also has a manifest, but there is no .assembly entry inside the manifest (except for the external assemblies that are referenced) because a module has no assembly attributes. It's not possible to configure versions or permissions with modules; that can be done only at the assembly scope. You can find references to assemblies in the manifest of the module. With the /addmodule option of csc, it's possible to add modules to existing assemblies.

To compare modules to assemblies, create a simple class A and compile it by using the following command:

```
csc /target:module A.cs
```

The compiler generates the file A.netmodule, which doesn't include assembly information (as you can see using ildasm to look at the manifest information). The manifest of the module shows the referenced assembly mscorlib and the .module entry in Figure 18-4.

Next, create an assembly B, which includes the module A.netmodule. It's not necessary to have a source file to generate this assembly. The command to build the assembly is:

FIGURE 18-4

```
csc /target:library /addmodule:A.netmodule /out:B.dll
```

Looking at the assembly using ildasm, you can find only a manifest. In the manifest, the assembly mscorlib is referenced. Next, you see the assembly section with a hash algorithm and the version. The number of the algorithm defines the type of the algorithm that was used to create the hash code of the assembly. When creating an assembly programmatically it is possible to select the algorithm. Part of the manifest is a list of all modules belonging to the assembly. In Figure 18-5 you see .file A.netmodule, which belongs to the assembly. Classes exported from modules are part of the assembly manifest; classes exported from the assembly itself are not.

What's the purpose of modules? Modules can be used for faster startup of assemblies because not all types are inside a single file. The modules are loaded only when needed. Another reason to use modules is if you want to create an assembly with more than one programming language. One module could be written using Visual Basic, another module could be written using C#, and these two modules could be included in a single assembly.

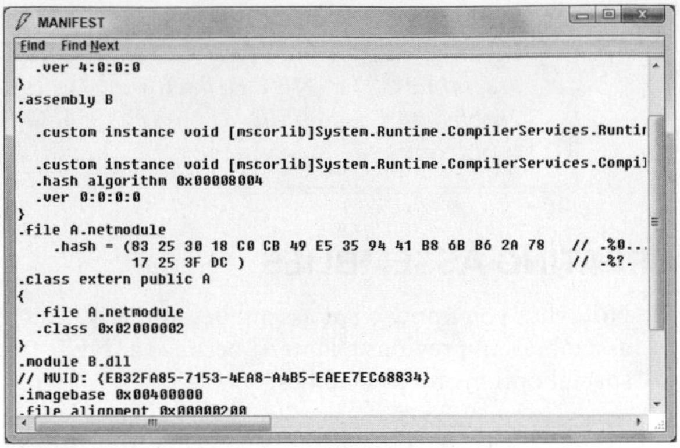

FIGURE 18-5

Assembly Attributes

When creating a Visual Studio project, the source file `AssemblyInfo.cs` is generated automatically. You can find this file below Properties in Solution Explorer. You can use the normal source code editor to configure the assembly attributes in this file. This is the file generated from the project template:

```
using System.Reflection;
using System.Runtime.CompilerServices;
using System.Runtime.InteropServices;
//
// General Information about an assembly is controlled through the following
// set of attributes. Change these attribute values to modify the information
// associated with an assembly.
//
[assembly: AssemblyTitle("DomainTest")]
[assembly: AssemblyDescription("")]
[assembly: AssemblyConfiguration("")]
[assembly: AssemblyCompany("")]
[assembly: AssemblyProduct("DomainTest")]
[assembly: AssemblyCopyright("Copyright @ 2010")]
[assembly: AssemblyTrademark("")]
[assembly: AssemblyCulture("")]

// Setting ComVisible to false makes the types in this assembly not visible
// to COM components.  If you need to access a type in this assembly from
// COM, set the ComVisible attribute to true on that type.
[assembly: ComVisible(false)]

// The following GUID is for the ID of the typelib if this project is exposed
// to COM
[assembly: Guid("ae0acc2c-0daf-4bb0-84a3-f9f6ac48bfe9")]


//
// Version information for an assembly consists of the following four
// values:
//
//      Major Version
//      Minor Version
//      Build Number
//      Revision
//
[assembly: AssemblyVersion("1.0.0.0")]
[assembly: AssemblyFileVersion("1.0.0.0")]
```

This file is used for configuration of the assembly manifest. The compiler reads the assembly attributes to inject the specific information into the manifest.

The `assembly:` prefix with the attribute marks an assembly-level attribute. Assembly-level attributes are, in contrast to the other attributes, not attached to a specific language element. The arguments that can be used for the assembly attribute are classes of the namespaces `System.Reflection`, `System.Runtime` `.CompilerServices`, and `System.Runtime.InteropServices`.

 You can read more about attributes and how to create and use custom attributes in Chapter 14.

The following table contains a list of assembly attributes defined within the `System.Reflection` namespace.

ASSEMBLY ATTRIBUTE	DESCRIPTION
`AssemblyCompany`	Specifies the company name.
`AssemblyConfiguration`	Specifies build information such as retail or debugging information.
`AssemblyCopyright` and `AssemblyTrademark`	Hold the copyright and trademark information.
`AssemblyDefaultAlias`	Can be used if the assembly name is not easily readable (such as a GUID when the assembly name is created dynamically). With this attribute an alias name can be specified.
`AssemblyDescription`	Describes the assembly or the product. Looking at the properties of the executable file this value shows up as Comments.
`AssemblyProduct`	Specifies the name of the product where the assembly belongs.
`AssemblyTitle`	Used to give the assembly a friendly name. The friendly name can include spaces. With the file properties you can see this value as Description.
`AssemblyCulture`	Defines the culture of the assembly. This attribute is important for satellite assemblies.
`AssemblyInformationalVersion`	This attribute isn't used for version checking when assemblies are referenced; it is for information only. It is very useful to specify the version of an application that uses multiple assemblies. Opening the properties of the executable you can see this value as the Product Version.
`AssemblyVersion`	This attribute gives the version number of the assembly. Versioning is discussed later in this chapter.
`AssemblyFileVersion`	This attribute defines the version of the file. The value shows up with the Windows file properties dialog, but it doesn't have any influence on the .NET behavior.

Here's an example of how these attributes might be configured:

```
[assembly: AssemblyTitle("Professional C#")]
[assembly: AssemblyDescription("Sample Application")]
[assembly: AssemblyConfiguration("Retail version")]
[assembly: AssemblyCompany("Wrox Press")]
[assembly: AssemblyProduct("Wrox Professional Series")]
[assembly: AssemblyCopyright("Copyright (C) Wrox Press 2010")]
[assembly: AssemblyTrademark("Wrox is a registered trademark of " +
    "John Wiley & Sons, Inc.")]
[assembly: AssemblyCulture("")]

[assembly: AssemblyVersion("1.0.0.0")]
[assembly: AssemblyFileVersion("1.0.0.0")]
```

With Visual Studio 2010, you can configure these attributes with the project properties, Application settings, and Assembly Information, as you can see in Figure 18-6.

Creating and Loading Assemblies Dynamically

During development time, you add a reference to an assembly so that it gets included with the assembly references, and the types of the assembly are available to the compiler. During runtime the referenced assembly is loaded as soon as a type of the assembly is instantiated or a method of the type is used. Instead of using this automatic behavior, you can also load assemblies programmatically. To load assemblies programmatically, you can use the class `Assembly` with the static method `Load()`. This method is overloaded where you can pass the name of the assembly using `AssemblyName`, the name of the assembly, or a byte array.

FIGURE 18-6

It is also possible to create an assembly on the fly, as shown with the next example. This sample demonstrates how C# code can be entered in a text box, a new assembly is dynamically created by starting the C# compiler, and the compiled code is invoked.

To compile C# code dynamically, you can use the class `CSharpCodeProvider` from the namespace `Microsoft.CSharp`. Using this class, you can compile code and generate assemblies from a DOM tree, from a file, and from source code.

The UI of the application is created by using WPF. You can see the design view of the UI in Figure 18-7. The window is made up of a `TextBox` to enter C# code, a `Button`, and a `TextBlock` WPF control that spans all columns of the last row to display the result, as shown in Figure 18-7.

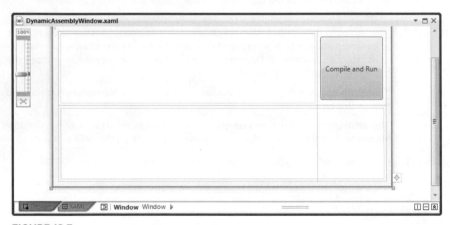

FIGURE 18-7

To dynamically compile and run C# code, the class `CodeDriver` defines the method `CompileAndRun()`. This method compiles the code from the text box and starts the generated method.

```
using System;
using System.CodeDom.Compiler;
using System.IO;
using System.Reflection;
using System.Text;
```

```csharp
using Microsoft.CSharp;

namespace Wrox.ProCSharp.Assemblies
{

    public class CodeDriver
    {
        private string prefix =
            "using System;" +
            "public static class Driver" +
            "{" +
            "   public static void Run()" +
            "   {";

        private string postfix =
            "   }" +
            "}";


        public string CompileAndRun(string input, out bool hasError)
        {
            hasError = false;
            string returnData = null;

            CompilerResults results = null;
            using (var provider = new CSharpCodeProvider())
            {
                var options = new CompilerParameters();
                options.GenerateInMemory = true;

                var sb = new StringBuilder();
                sb.Append(prefix);
                sb.Append(input);
                sb.Append(postfix);

                results = provider.CompileAssemblyFromSource(
                        options, sb.ToString());
            }

            if (results.Errors.HasErrors)
            {
                hasError = true;
                var errorMessage = new StringBuilder();
                foreach (CompilerError error in results.Errors)
                {
                    errorMessage.AppendFormat("{0} {1}", error.Line,
                            error.ErrorText);
                }
                returnData = errorMessage.ToString();
            }
            else
            {
                TextWriter temp = Console.Out;
                var writer = new StringWriter();
                Console.SetOut(writer);
                Type driverType = results.CompiledAssembly.GetType("Driver");

                driverType.InvokeMember("Run", BindingFlags.InvokeMethod |
                        BindingFlags.Static | BindingFlags.Public,
                        null, null, null);
```

```
            Console.SetOut(temp);

            returnData = writer.ToString();
        }

        return returnData;
    }
}
}
```

The method `CompileAndRun()` requires a string input parameter where one or multiple lines of C# code can be passed. Because every method that is called must be included in a method and a class, the variables `prefix` and `postfix` define the structure of the dynamically created class `Driver` and the method `Run()` that surround the code from the parameter. Using a `StringBuilder`, the `prefix`, `postfix`, and the code from the `input` variable are merged to create a complete class that can be compiled. Using this resultant string, the code is compiled with the `CSharpCodeProvider` class. The method `CompileAssemblyFromSource()` dynamically creates an assembly. Because this assembly is just needed in memory, the compiler parameter option `GenerateInMemory` is set.

If the source code that was passed contains some errors, these will show up in the `Errors` collection of `CompilerResults`. The errors are returned with the return data, and the variable `hasError` is set to `true`.

If the source code compiles successfully, the `Run()` method of the new `Driver` class is invoked. The invocation of this method is done using reflection. From the newly compiled assembly that can be accessed using `CompilerResults.CompiledType`, the new class `Driver` is referenced by the `driverType` variable. Then the `InvokeMember()` method of the `Type` class is used to invoke the method `Run()`. Because this method is defined as a public static method, the `BindingFlags` must be set accordingly. To see a result of the program that is written to the console, the console is redirected to a `StringWriter` to finally return the complete output of the program with the `returnData` variable.

 Running the code with the `InvokeMember()` method makes use of .NET reflection. Reflection is discussed in Chapter 14.

The `Click` event of the WPF button is connected to the `Compile_Click()` method where the `CodeDriver` class is instantiated, and the `CompileAndRun()` method is invoked. The input is taken from the `TextBox` named `textCode`, and the result is written to the `TextBlock` `textOutput`.

Available for
download on
Wrox.com

```
        private void Compile_Click(object sender, RoutedEventArgs e)
        {
            var driver = new CodeDriver ();
            bool isError;
            textOutput.Text = driver.CompileAndRun(textCode.Text, out isError);
            if (isError)
            {
                textOutput.Background = Brushes.Red;
            }
        }
```

Now you can start the application; enter C# code in the `TextBox` as shown in Figure 18-8, and compile and run the code.

The program as written so far has the disadvantage that every time you click the Compile and Run button, a new assembly is created and loaded, and the program always needs more and more memory. You cannot unload an assembly from the application. To unload assemblies, application domains are needed.

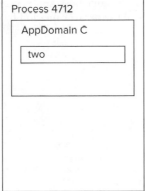

FIGURE 18-8

APPLICATION DOMAINS

Before .NET, processes were used as isolation boundaries, with every process having its private virtual memory; an application running in one process could not write to the memory of another application and thereby crash the other application. The process was used as an isolation and security boundary between applications. With the .NET architecture, you have a new boundary for applications: *application domains*. With managed IL code, the runtime can ensure that access to the memory of another application inside a single process can't happen. Multiple applications can run in a single process within multiple application domains (see Figure 18-9).

An assembly is loaded into an application domain. In Figure 18-9, you can see process 4711 with two application domains. In application domain A, objects one and two are instantiated, object one in assembly one, and object two in assembly two. The second application domain in process 4711 has an instance one. To minimize memory consumption, the code of assemblies is only loaded once into an application domain. Instance and static members are not shared among application domains. It's not possible to directly access objects within another application domain; a proxy is needed instead. So in Figure 18-9, the object one in application domain B cannot directly access the objects one or two in application domain A without a proxy.

```
Process 4711
  ┌─────────────────────┐
  │ AppDomain A         │
  │   ┌─────────────┐   │
  │   │ one         │   │
  │   └─────────────┘   │
  │   ┌─────────────┐   │
  │   │ two         │   │
  │   └─────────────┘   │
  └─────────────────────┘
  ┌─────────────────────┐
  │ AppDomain B         │
  │   ┌─────────────┐   │
  │   │ one         │   │
  │   └─────────────┘   │
  └─────────────────────┘

Process 4712
  ┌─────────────────────┐
  │ AppDomain C         │
  │   ┌─────────────┐   │
  │   │ two         │   │
  │   └─────────────┘   │
  └─────────────────────┘
```

FIGURE 18-9

The `AppDomain` class is used to create and terminate application domains, load and unload assemblies and types, and enumerate assemblies and threads in a domain. In this section, you program a small example to see application domains in action.

First, create a C# console application called `AssemblyA`. In the `Main()` method add a `Console.WriteLine()` so that you can see when this method is called. In addition, add the class `Demo` with a constructor with two `int` values as arguments, which will be used to create instances with the `AppDomain` class. The `AssemblyA.exe` assembly will be loaded from the second application that will be created:

```csharp
using System;

namespace Wrox.ProCSharp.Assemblies
{
    public class Demo
    {
        public Demo(int val1, int val2)
        {
            Console.WriteLine("Constructor with the values {0}, {1}" +
                    " in domain {2} called", val1, val2,
                    AppDomain.CurrentDomain.FriendlyName);
        }
    }

    class Program
    {
        static void Main()
        {
            Console.WriteLine("Main in domain {0} called",
                    AppDomain.CurrentDomain.FriendlyName);
        }
    }
}
```

code snippet AssemblyA/Program.cs

Running the application produces this output:

```
Main in domain AssemblyA.exe called.
```

The second project you create is again a C# console application: `DomainTest`. First, display the name of the current domain using the property `FriendlyName` of the `AppDomain` class. With the `CreateDomain()` method, a new application domain with the friendly name `New AppDomain` is created. Next, load the assembly `AssemblyA` into the new domain and call the `Main()` method by calling `ExecuteAssembly()`:

```csharp
using System;
using System.Reflection;

namespace Wrox.ProCSharp.Assemblies
{
    class Program
    {
        static void Main()
        {
            AppDomain currentDomain = AppDomain.CurrentDomain;
            Console.WriteLine(currentDomain.FriendlyName);
            AppDomain secondDomain = AppDomain.CreateDomain("New AppDomain");
            secondDomain.ExecuteAssembly("AssemblyA.exe");
        }
    }
}
```

code snippet DomainTest/Program.cs

Before starting the program `DomainTest.exe`, reference the assembly `AssemblyA.exe` with the `DomainTest` project. Referencing the assembly with Visual Studio 2010 copies the assembly to the project directory, so that the assembly can be found. If the assembly cannot be found, a `System.IO.FileNotFoundException` exception is thrown.

When `DomainTest.exe` is run, you get the following console output. `DomainTest.exe` is the friendly name of the first application domain. The second line is the output of the newly loaded assembly in the New

AppDomain. With a process viewer, you will not see the process `AssemblyA.exe` executing because there's no new process created. `AssemblyA` is loaded into the process `DomainTest.exe`.

```
DomainTest.exe
Main in domain New AppDomain called
```

Instead of calling the `Main()` method in the newly loaded assembly, you can also create a new instance. In the following example, replace the `ExecuteAssembly()` method with a `CreateInstance()`. The first argument is the name of the assembly, `AssemblyA`. The second argument defines the type that should be instantiated: `Wrox.ProCSharp.Assemblies.AppDomains.Demo`. The third argument, `true`, means that case is ignored. `System.Reflection.BindingFlags.CreateInstance` is a binding flag enumeration value to specify that the constructor should be called:

Available for
download on
Wrox.com

```
AppDomain secondDomain = AppDomain.CreateDomain("New AppDomain");
// secondDomain.ExecuteAssembly("AssemblyA.exe");
secondDomain.CreateInstance("AssemblyA", "Wrox.ProCSharp.Assemblies.Demo",
    true, BindingFlags.CreateInstance, null, new object[] {7, 3},
    null, null);
```

code snippet DomainTest/Program.cs

The results of a successful run of the application are as follows:

```
DomainTest.exe
Constructor with the values 7, 3 in domain New AppDomain called
```

Now you have seen how to create and call application domains. In runtime hosts, application domains are created automatically. ASP.NET creates an application domain for each web application that runs on a web server. Internet Explorer creates application domains in which managed controls will run. For applications, it can be useful to create application domains if you want to unload an assembly. You can unload assemblies only by terminating an application domain.

 Application domains are an extremely useful construct if assemblies are loaded dynamically, and the requirement exists to unload assemblies after use. Within the primary application domain, it is not possible to get rid of loaded assemblies. However, it is possible to end application domains where all assemblies loaded just within the application domain are cleaned from the memory.

With this knowledge about application domains, it is now possible to change the WPF program created earlier. The new class `CodeDriverInAppDomain` creates a new application domain using `AppDomain.CreateDomain`. Inside this new application domain, the class `CodeDriver` is instantiated using `CreateInstanceAndUnwrap()`. Using the `CodeDriver` instance, the `CompileAndRun()` method is invoked before the new app-domain is unloaded again.

Available for
download on
Wrox.com

```
using System;
using System.Runtime.Remoting;

namespace Wrox.ProCSharp.Assemblies
{
    public class CodeDriverInAppDomain
    {
        public string CompileAndRun(string code, out bool hasError)
        {
            AppDomain codeDomain = AppDomain.CreateDomain("CodeDriver");

            CodeDriver codeDriver = (CodeDriver)
```

```
                    codeDomain.CreateInstanceAndUnwrap("DynamicAssembly",
                        "Wrox.ProCSharp.Assemblies.CodeDriver");

            string result = codeDriver.CompileAndRun(code, out hasError);

            AppDomain.Unload(codeDomain);

            return result;
        }
    }
}
```

code snippet DynamicAssembly/CodeDriverInAppDomain.cs

 The class `CodeDriver` *itself now is used both in the main app-domain and in the new app-domain, that's why it is not possible to get rid of the code that this class is using. If you would like to do that, you can define an interface that is implemented by the* `CodeDriver` *and just use the interface in the main app-domain. However, here this is not an issue because there's only the need to get rid of the dynamically created assembly with the* `Driver` *class.*

To access the class `CodeDriver` from a different app-domain, the class `CodeDriver` must derive from the base class `MarshalByRefObject`. Only classes that derive from this base type can be accessed across another app-domain. In the main app-domain, a proxy is instantiated to invoke the methods of this class across an inter-appdomain channel.

```
using System;
using System.CodeDom.Compiler;
using System.IO;
using System.Reflection;
using System.Text;
using Microsoft.CSharp;

namespace Wrox.ProCSharp.Assemblies
{

    public class CodeDriver: MarshalByRefObject
    {
```

code snippet DynamicAssembly/CodeDriver.cs

The `Compile_Click()` event handler can now be changed to use the `CodeDriverInAppDomain` class instead of the `CodeDriver` class:

```
        private void Compile_Click(object sender, RoutedEventArgs e)
        {
            var driver = new CodeDriverInAppDomain();
            bool isError;
            textOutput.Text = driver.CompileAndRun(textCode.Text, out isError);
            if (isError)
            {
                textOutput.Background = Brushes.Red;
            }
        }
```

code snippet DynamicAssembly/DynamicAssemblyWindow.xaml.cs

Now you can click the Compile and Run button of the application any number of times, and the generated assembly is always unloaded.

You can see the loaded assemblies in an app-domain with the GetAssemblies() *method of the* AppDomain *class.*

SHARED ASSEMBLIES

Assemblies can be isolated for use by a single application — not sharing an assembly is the default. When using shared assemblies there are specific requirements that must be followed.

This section explores all that's needed for sharing assemblies. Strong names are required for uniquely identifying a share assembly. Strong names are created by signing the assembly. This section also explains the process of delayed signing. Shared assemblies are typically installed into the global assembly cache (GAC). You will read about how to use the GAC.

Strong Names

The goals for a shared assembly name are that it must be globally unique and it must be possible to protect the name. At no time can any other person create an assembly using the same name.

COM solved the first problem by using a globally unique identifier (GUID). The second problem, however, still existed because anyone could steal the GUID and create a different object with the same identifier. Both problems are solved with *strong names* of .NET assemblies.

A strong name is made of these items:

➤ The *name* of the assembly itself.

➤ A *version number*. This allows it to use different versions of the same assembly at the same time. Different versions can also work side by side and can be loaded concurrently inside the same process.

➤ A *public key* guarantees that the strong name is unique. It also guarantees that a referenced assembly cannot be replaced from a different source.

➤ A *culture*. Cultures are discussed in Chapter 22.

 A shared assembly must have a strong name to uniquely identify the assembly.

A strong name is a simple text name accompanied by a version number, a public key, and a culture. You wouldn't create a new public key with every assembly, but you'd have one in your company, so the key uniquely identifies your company's assemblies.

However, this key cannot be used as a trust key. Assemblies can carry Authenticode signatures to build up a trust. The key for the Authenticode signature can be a different one from the key used for the strong name.

 For development purposes, a different public key can be used and later be exchanged easily with the real key. This feature is discussed later in the section "Delayed Signing of Assemblies."

To uniquely identify the assemblies in your companies, a useful namespace hierarchy should be used to name your classes. Here is a simple example showing how to organize namespaces: Wrox Press can use the major namespace Wrox for its classes and namespaces. In the hierarchy below the namespace, the namespaces must be organized so that all classes are unique. Every chapter of this book uses a different namespace of the form Wrox.ProCSharp.<Chapter>; this chapter uses Wrox.ProCSharp.Assemblies. So, if there is a class Hello in two different chapters, there's no conflict because of different namespaces. Utility classes that are used across different books can go into the namespace `Wrox.Utilities`.

A company name commonly used as the first part of the namespace is not necessarily unique, so something more must be used to build a strong name. For this the public key is used. Because of the public/private key principle in strong names, no one without access to your private key can destructively create an assembly that could be unintentionally called by the client.

Integrity Using Strong Names

A public/private key pair must be used to create a shared component. The compiler writes the public key to the manifest, creates a hash of all files that belong to the assembly, and signs the hash with the private key, which is not stored within the assembly. It is then guaranteed that no one can change your assembly. The signature can be verified with the public key.

During development, the client assembly must reference the shared assembly. The compiler writes the public key of the referenced assembly to the manifest of the client assembly. To reduce storage, it is not the public key that is written to the manifest of the client assembly, but a public key token. The public key token consists of the last 8 bytes of a hash of the public key and is unique.

At runtime, during loading of the shared assembly (or at install time if the client is installed using the native image generator), the hash of the shared component assembly can be verified by using the public key stored inside the client assembly. Only the owner of the private key can change the shared component assembly. There is no way a component `Math` that was created by vendor A and referenced from a client can be replaced by a component from a hacker. Only the owner of the private key can replace the shared component with a new version. Integrity is guaranteed insofar as the shared assembly comes from the expected publisher.

Figure 18-10 shows a shared component with a public key referenced by a client assembly that has a public key token of the shared assembly inside the manifest.

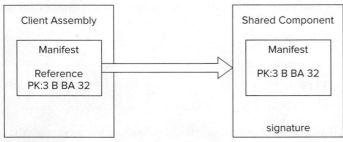

FIGURE 18-10

Global Assembly Cache

The *global assembly cache* (GAC) is, as the name implies, a cache for globally available assemblies. Most shared assemblies are installed inside this cache; otherwise, a shared directory (also on a server) can be used.

The GAC is located in the directory `<windows>\assembly`. Inside this directory, you can find multiple GACxxx directories and a `NativeImages_<runtime version>` directory. The GACxxx directories contain shared assemblies. `GAC_MSIL` contains the assemblies with pure .NET code; `GAC_32` contains the assemblies that are specific to a 32-bit platform. On a 64-bit system, you can also find the directory `GAC_64` with assemblies specific for 64 bit. The directory GAC is for backward compatibility with .NET 1.0 and 1.1. In the directory `NativeImages_ <runtime version>`, you can find the assemblies compiled to native code. If you go deeper in the directory structure, you will find directory names that are similar to the assembly names, and below that, a version directory and the assemblies themselves. This allows the installation of different versions of the same assembly.

`gacutil.exe` is a utility to install, uninstall, and list assemblies using the command line. The following list explains some of the `gacutil` options:

➤ `gacutil /l` lists all assemblies from the assembly cache.

➤ `gacutil /i mydll` installs the shared assembly `mydll` into the assembly cache. With the option `/f` you can force the installation to the GAC even if the assembly is already installed. This is useful if you changed the assembly but didn't change the version number.

➤ `gacutil /u mydll` uninstalls the assembly `mydll`.

 For production you should use an installer program to install shared assemblies to the GAC. Deployment is covered in Chapter 17.

Creating a Shared Assembly

In the next example, you create a shared assembly and a client that uses it.

Creating shared assemblies is not much different from creating private assemblies. Create a simple Visual C# class library project with the name `SharedDemo`. Change the namespace to `Wrox.ProCSharp.Assemblies` and the class name to `SharedDemo`. Enter the following code. In the constructor of the class, all lines of a file are read into an array. The name of the file is passed as an argument to the constructor. The method `GetQuoteOfTheDay()` just returns a random string of the array.

Available for download on Wrox.com

```
using System;
using System.IO;

namespace Wrox.ProCSharp.Assemblies
{
    public class SharedDemo
    {
        private string[] quotes;
        private Random random;

        public SharedDemo(string filename)
        {
            quotes = File.ReadAllLines(filename);
            random = new Random();
        }

        public string GetQuoteOfTheDay()
        {
            int index = random.Next(1, quotes.Length);
            return quotes[index];
        }
    }
}
```

code snippet SharedDemo/SharedDemo.cs

Create a Strong Name

A strong name is needed to share this assembly. You can create such a name with the *strong name tool* (sn):

```
sn -k mykey.snk
```

The strong name utility generates and writes a public/private key pair, and writes this pair to a file; here the file is `mykey.snk`.

With Visual Studio 2010, you can sign the assembly with the project properties by selecting the Signing tab, as shown in Figure 18-11. You can also create keys with this tool. However, you should not create a key file for every project. Just a few keys for the complete company can be used instead. It is useful to create different keys depending on security requirements (see Chapter 21).

Setting the signing option with Visual Studio adds the /keyfile option to the compiler setting. Visual Studio also allows you to create a keyfile that is secured with a password. Such a file has the file extension .pfx (see Figure 18-11).

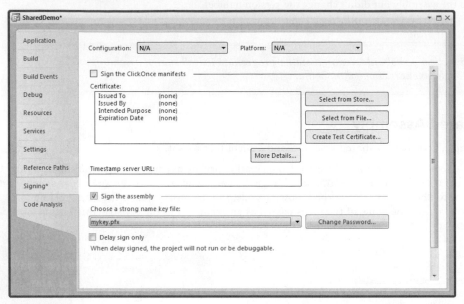

FIGURE 18-11

After rebuilding, the public key can be found inside the manifest. You can verify this using ildasm, as shown in Figure 18-12.

Installing the Shared Assembly

With a public key in the assembly, you can now install it in the global assembly cache using the global assembly cache tool gacutil with the /i option. The /f option forces you to write the assembly to the GAC, even if it is already there.

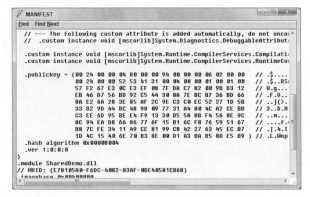

FIGURE 18-12

```
gacutil /i SharedDemo.dll /f
```

Then you can use the Global Assembly Cache Viewer or gacutil /l SharedDemo to check the version of the shared assembly and see if it is successfully installed.

Using the Shared Assembly

To use the shared assembly, create a C# console application called Client. Change the name of the namespace to Wrox.ProCSharp.Assemblies. The shared assembly can be referenced in the same way as a private assembly: by using the Project → Add Reference menu.

> *With shared assemblies the reference property* Copy Local *can be set to* false. *This way the assembly is not copied to the directory of the output files but will be loaded from the GAC instead.*

Add the file `quotes.txt` to the project items, and set the property `Copy to Output Directory` to `Copy if newer`.

Here's the code for the `Client` application:

```csharp
using System;
namespace Wrox.ProCSharp.Assemblies
{
    class Program
    {
        static void Main()
        {
            var quotes = new SharedDemo("Quotes.txt");
            for (int i=0; i < 3; i++)
            {
                Console.WriteLine(quotes.GetQuoteOfTheDay());
                Console.WriteLine();
            }
        }
    }
}
```

code snippet Client/Program.cs

Looking at the manifest in the client assembly using `ildasm` (see Figure 18-13), you can see the reference to the shared assembly SharedDemo: `.assembly extern SharedDemo`. Part of this referenced information is the version number, discussed next, and the token of the public key.

The token of the public key can also be seen within the shared assembly using the strong name utility: `sn –T` shows the token of the public key in the assembly, and `sn –Tp` shows the token and the public key. Pay attention to the use of the uppercase T!

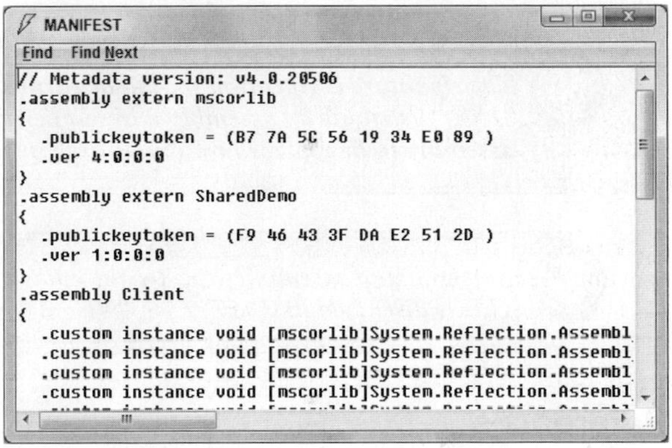

FIGURE 18-13

The result of your program with a sample quotes file is shown here:

```
"We don't like their sound. And guitar music is on the way out." — Decca Recording,
Co., in rejecting the Beatles, 1962

"The ordinary 'horseless carriage' is at present a luxury for the wealthy; and
although its price will probably fall in the future, it will never come into as
common use as the bicycle." — The Literary Digest, 1889

"Landing and moving around the moon offers so many serious problems for human
beings that it may take science another 200 years to lick them", Lord Kelvin
(1824-1907)
```

Delayed Signing of Assemblies

The private key of a company should be safely stored. Most companies don't give all developers access to the private key; only a few security people have it. That's why the signature of an assembly can be added at a later date, such as before distribution. When the assembly attribute `AssemblyDelaySign` is set to true, no signature is stored in the assembly, but enough free space is reserved so that it can be added later. Without using a key, you cannot test the assembly and install it in the GAC; however, you can use a temporary key for testing purposes, and replace this key with the real company key later.

The following steps are required to delay signing of assemblies:

1. Create a public/private key pair with the strong name utility `sn`. The generated file `mykey.snk` includes both the public and private keys.

   `sn -k mykey.snk`

2. Extract the public key to make it available to developers. The option `-p` extracts the public key of the keyfile. The file `mykeypub.snk` only holds the public key.

   `sn -p mykey.snk mykeypub.snk`

   All developers in the company can use this keyfile `mykeypub.snk` and compile the assembly with the `/delaysign+` option. This way the signature is not added to the assembly, but it can be added afterward. In Visual Studio 2010, the delay sign option can be set with a check box in the Signing settings.

3. Turn off the verification of the signature, because the assembly doesn't have a signature:

   `sn -Vr SharedDemo.dll`

4. Before distribution the assembly can be re-signed with the `sn` utility. Use the `-R` option to re-sign previously signed or delayed signed assemblies. Re-signing of the assembly can be done by the person who does the deployment package for the application and has access to the private key that is used for distribution.

   `sn -R MyAssembly.dll mykey.snk`

 The signature verification should be turned off only during the development process. Never distribute an assembly without verification, because it would be possible for this assembly to be replaced by a malicious one.

 Re-signing of assemblies can be automated by defining the tasks in an MSBuild file. This is discussed in Chapter 16, "Visual Studio 2010."

References

Assemblies in the GAC can have references associated with them. These references are responsible for the fact that a cached assembly cannot be deleted if it is still needed by an application. For example, if a shared assembly is installed by a Microsoft installer package (`.msi` file), it can only be deleted by uninstalling the application, not by deleting it directly from the GAC. Trying to delete the assembly from the GAC results in the error message "`Assembly <name> could not be uninstalled because it is required by other applications.`"

A reference to the assembly can be set by using the `gacutil` utility with the option `/r`. The option `/r` requires a reference type, a reference ID, and a description. The type of the reference can be one of three options: `UNINSTALL_KEY`, `FILEPATH`, or `OPAQUE`. `UNINSTALL_KEY` is used by MSI when a registry key is defined that is also needed for the uninstallation. A directory can be specified with `FILEPATH`. A useful directory would be the root directory of the application. The `OPAQUE` reference type allows you to set any type of reference.

The command line

`gacutil /i shareddemo.dll /r FILEPATH c:\ProCSharp\Assemblies\Client "Shared Demo"`

installs the assembly `shareddemo` in the GAC with a reference to the directory of the client application. Another installation of the same assembly can happen with a different path, or an `OPAQUE` ID like in this command line:

`gacutil /i shareddemo.dll /r OPAQUE 4711 "Opaque installation"`

Now, the assembly is in the GAC only once, but it has two references. To delete the assembly from the GAC, both references must be removed:

```
gacutil /u shareddemo /r OPAQUE 4711 "Opaque installation"
gacutil /u shareddemo /r FILEPATH c:\ProCSharp\Assemblies\Client "Shared Demo"
```

> *To remove a shared assembly, the option /u requires the assembly name without the file extension DLL. On the contrary, the option /i to install a shared assembly requires the complete filename including the file extension.*

> *Chapter 17 deals with deployment of assemblies, where the reference count is being dealt with in an MSI package.*

Native Image Generator

With the native image generator, Ngen.exe, you can compile the IL code to native code at installation time. This way the program can start faster because the compilation during runtime is no longer necessary. Comparing precompiled assemblies to assemblies where the JIT compiler needs to run is not different from a performance view after the IL code is compiled. The only improvement you get with the native image generator is that the application starts faster because there's no need to run JIT. Reducing the startup time of the application might be enough reason for using the native image generator. In case you create a native image from the executable, you should also create native images from all the DLLs that are loaded by the executable. Otherwise, the JIT compiler still needs to run.

The ngen utility installs the native image in the native image cache. The physical directory of the native image cache is <windows>\assembly\NativeImages<RuntimeVersion>.

With ngen install myassembly, you can compile the MSIL code to native code and install it into the native image cache. This should be done from an installation program if you would like to put the assembly in the native image cache.

With ngen, you can also display all assemblies from the native image cache with the option display. If you add an assembly name to the display option, you get the information about all installed versions of this assembly and the assemblies that are dependent on the native assembly:

```
C:\>ngen display System.AddIn
Microsoft (R) CLR Native Image Generator - Version 4.0.21006.1
Copyright (c) Microsoft Corporation.  All rights reserved.

NGEN Roots:

System.AddIn, Version=3.5.0.0, Culture=Neutral, PublicKeyToken=b77a5c561934e089,
 processorArchitecture=msil
System.AddIn, Version=4.0.0.0, Culture=neutral, PublicKeyToken=b77a5c561934e089


NGEN Roots that depend on "System.AddIn":

C:\Program Files (x86)\Common Files\Microsoft Shared\VSTA\Pipeline.v10.0\
AddInSideAdapters\Microsoft.VisualStudio.Tools.Applications.AddInAdapter.v9.0.dll
C:\Program Files (x86)\Common Files\Microsoft Shared\VSTA\Pipeline.v10.0\
AddInSideAdapters\Microsoft.VisualStudio.Tools.Office.AddInAdapter.v9.0.dll
 . . .
```

If the security of the system changes, it's not sure if the native image has the security requirements it needs for running the application. This is why the native images become invalid with a system configuration change. With the command ngen update, all native images are rebuilt to include the new configurations.

Installing .NET 4 also installs the Native Runtime Optimization Service. This service can be used to defer compilation of native images and regenerates native images that have been invalidated.

The command `ngen install myassembly /queue` can be used by an installation program to defer compilation of `myassembly` to a native image using the Native Image Service. `ngen update /queue` regenerates all native images that have been invalidated. With the `ngen queue` options `pause`, `continue`, and `status` you can control the service and get status information.

 You might ask why the native images cannot be created on the developer system, and you just distribute the native image to the production system. The reason is that the native image generator takes care of the CPU that is installed with the target system and compiles the code optimized for the CPU type. During installation of the application, the CPU is known.

CONFIGURING .NET APPLICATIONS

COM components are used in the registry to configure components. Configuration of .NET applications is done by using configuration files. With registry configurations, an xcopy deployment is not possible. Configuration files can simply be copied. The configuration files use XML syntax to specify startup and runtime settings for applications.

This section explores the following:

➤ What you can configure using the XML base configuration files

➤ How you can redirect a strongly named referenced assembly to a different version

➤ How you can specify the directory of assemblies to find private assemblies in subdirectories and shared assemblies in common directories or on a server

Configuration Categories

The configuration can be grouped into these categories:

➤ **Startup settings** enable you to specify the version of the required runtime. It's possible that different versions of the runtime could be installed on the same system. The version of the runtime can be specified with the `<startup>` element.

➤ **Runtime settings** enable you to specify how garbage collection is performed by the runtime and how the binding to assemblies works. You can also specify the version policy and the code base with these settings. You take a more detailed look into the runtime settings later in this chapter.

➤ **WCF settings** are used to configure applications using WCF. You deal with these configurations in Chapter 43, "Windows Communication Foundation."

➤ **Security settings** are introduced in Chapter 21 and configuration for cryptography and permissions is done there.

These settings can be provided in three types of configuration files:

➤ **Application configuration files** include specific settings for an application, such as binding information to assemblies, configuration for remote objects, and so on. Such a configuration file is placed into the same directory as the executable; it has the same name as the executable with a `.config` extension appended. ASP.NET configuration files are named `web.config`.

➤ **Machine configuration files** are used for system-wide configurations. You can also specify assembly binding and remoting configurations here. During a binding process, the machine configuration file is consulted before the application configuration file. The application configuration can override settings from the machine configuration. The application configuration file should be the preferred place for application-specific settings so that the machine configuration file stays smaller and more manageable. A machine configuration file is located in `%runtime_install_path%\config\Machine.config`.

➤ **Publisher policy files** can be used by a component creator to specify that a shared assembly is compatible with older versions. If a new assembly version just fixes a bug of a shared component, it is not necessary to put application configuration files in every application directory that uses this component; the publisher can mark it as compatible by adding a publisher policy file instead. In case the component doesn't work with all applications, it is possible to override the publisher policy setting in an application configuration file. In contrast to the other configuration files, publisher policy files are stored in the GAC.

How are these configuration files used? How a client finds an assembly (also called *binding*) depends on whether the assembly is private or shared. Private assemblies must be in the directory of the application or in a subdirectory thereof. A process called *probing* is used to find such an assembly. If the assembly doesn't have a strong name, the version number is not used with probing.

Shared assemblies can be installed in the GAC or placed in a directory, on a network share, or on a web site. You specify such a directory with the configuration of the `codeBase` shortly. The public key, version, and culture are all important aspects when binding to a shared assembly. The reference of the required assembly is recorded in the manifest of the client assembly, including the name, the version, and the public key token. All configuration files are checked to apply the correct version policy. The GAC and code bases specified in the configuration files are checked, followed by the application directories, and probing rules are then applied.

Binding to Assemblies

You've already seen how to install a shared assembly to the GAC. Instead of installing a shared assembly to the GAC, you can configure a specific shared directory by using configuration files. This feature can be used if you want to make the shared components available on a server. Another possible scenario arises if you want to share an assembly between your applications, but you don't want to make it publicly available in the GAC, so you put it into a shared directory instead.

There are two ways to find the correct directory for an assembly: the `codeBase` element in an XML configuration file, or through probing. The `codeBase` configuration is available only for shared assemblies, and probing is done for private assemblies.

<codeBase>

The `<codeBase>` can be configured with an application configuration file. The following application configuration file redirects the search for the assembly `SharedDemo` to load it from the network:

```xml
<?xml version="1.0" encoding="utf-8" ?>
<configuration>
  <runtime>
    <assemblyBinding xmlns="urn:schemas-microsoft-com:asm.v1">
      <dependentAssembly>
        <assemblyIdentity name="SharedDemo" culture="neutral"
              publicKeyToken="f946433fdae2512d" />
        <codeBase version="1.0.0.0"
              href="http://www.christiannagel.com/WroxUtils/SharedDemo.dll" />
      </dependentAssembly>
    </assemblyBinding>
  </runtime>
</configuration>
```

The `<codeBase>` element has the attributes `version` and `href`. With `version`, the original referenced version of the assembly must be specified. With `href`, you can define the directory from which the assembly should be loaded. In the example, a path using the HTTP protocol is used. A directory on a local system or a share is specified by using `href="file://C:/WroxUtils/SharedDemo.dll"`.

<probing>

When the `<codeBase>` is not configured and the assembly is not stored in the GAC, the runtime tries to find an assembly through probing. The .NET runtime tries to find assemblies with either a `.dll` or an `.exe` file extension in the application directory or in one of its subdirectories that has the same name as the assembly searched for. If the assembly is not found here, the search continues. You can configure search directories with the `<probing>` element in the `<runtime>` section of application configuration files. This XML configuration can also be done easily by selecting the properties of the application with the .NET Framework Configuration tool. You can configure the directories where the probing should occur by using the search path in the .NET Framework configuration.

The XML file produced has these entries:

```
<?xml version="1.0" encoding="utf-8" ?>
<configuration>
    <runtime>
        <assemblyBinding xmlns="urn:schemas-microsoft-com:asm.v1">
            <probing privatePath="bin;utils;" />
        </assemblyBinding>
    </runtime>
</configuration>
```

The `<probing>` element has just a single required attribute: `privatePath`. This application configuration file tells the runtime that assemblies should be searched for in the base directory of the application, followed by the `bin` and the `util` directory. Both directories are subdirectories of the application base directory. It's not possible to reference a private assembly outside the application base directory or a subdirectory thereof. An assembly outside of the application base directory must have a shared name and can be referenced using the `<codeBase>` element, as you saw earlier.

VERSIONING

For private assemblies, versioning is not important because the referenced assemblies are copied with the client. The client uses the assembly it has in its private directories.

This is, however, different for shared assemblies. This section looks at the traditional problems that can occur with sharing. With shared components, more than one client application can use the same component. The new version can break existing clients when updating a shared component with a newer version. You can't stop shipping new versions because new features will be requested and introduced with new versions of existing components. You can try to program carefully to be backward compatible, but that's not always possible.

A solution to this dilemma could be an architecture that allows installation of different versions of shared components, with clients using the version that they referenced during the build process. This solves a lot of problems but not all of them. What happens if you detect a bug in a component that's referenced from the client? You would like to update this component and make sure that the client uses the new version instead of the version that was referenced during the build process.

Therefore, depending on the type in the fix of the new version, you sometimes want to use a newer version, and you also want to use the older referenced version. The .NET architecture enables both scenarios.

In .NET, the original referenced assembly is used by default. You can redirect the reference to a different version by using configuration files. Versioning plays a key role in the binding architecture — how the client gets the right assembly where the components live.

Version Numbers

Assemblies have a four-part version number, for example, 1.1.400.3300. The parts are
`<Major>.<Minor>.<Build>.<Revision>`.

How these numbers are used depends on your application configuration.

> *A good policy is to change the major or minor number on changes incompatible with
> the previous version, but just the build or revision number with compatible changes.
> This way, it can be assumed that redirecting an assembly to a new version where just
> the build and revision have changed is safe.*

With Visual Studio 2010, you can define the version number of the assembly with the assembly information
in the project settings. The project settings write the assembly attribute `[AssemblyVersion]` to the file
`AssemblyInfo.cs`:

```
[assembly: AssemblyVersion("1.0.0.0")]
```

Instead of defining all four version numbers, you can also place an asterisk in the third or fourth place:

```
[assembly: AssemblyVersion("1.0.*")]
```

With this setting, the first two numbers specify the major and minor version, and the asterisk (*) means that
the build and revision numbers are auto-generated. The build number is the number of days since January
1, 2000, and the revision is the number of seconds since midnight divided by two. Though the automatic
versioning might help during development time, before shipping it is a good practice to define a specific
version number.

This version is stored in the `.assembly` section of the manifest.

Referencing the assembly in the client application stores the version of the referenced assembly in the
manifest of the client application.

Getting the Version Programmatically

To make it possible to check the version of the assembly that is used from the client application, add
the read-only property `FullName` to the `SharedDemo` class created earlier to return the strong name of the
assembly. For easy use of the `Assembly` class, you have to import the `System.Reflection` namespace:

Available for
download on
Wrox.com

```
public string FullName
{
    get
    {
        return Assembly.GetExecutingAssembly().FullName;
    }
}
```

code snippet SharedDemo/SharedDemo.cs

The `FullName` property of the `Assembly` class holds the name of the class, the version, the locality, and the
public key token, as you see in the following output, when calling `FullName` in your client application.

In the client application, just add a call to `FullName` in the `Main()` method after creating the shared
component:

Available for
download on
Wrox.com

```
static void Main()
{
    var quotes = new SharedDemo("Quotes.txt");
    Console.WriteLine(quotes.FullName);
```

code snippet Client/Program.cs

Be sure to register the new version of the shared assembly SharedDemo again in the GAC, using gacutil. If the referenced version cannot be found, you will get a System.IO.FileLoadException, because the binding to the correct assembly failed.

With a successful run, you can see the full name of the referenced assembly:

```
SharedDemo, Version=1.0.0.0, Culture=neutral, PublicKeyToken= f946433fdae2512d
```

This client program can now be used to test different configurations of this shared component.

Binding to Assembly Versions

With a configuration file, you can specify that the binding should happen to a different version of a shared assembly. Assume that you create a new version of the shared assembly SharedDemo with major and minor versions 1.1. Maybe you don't want to rebuild the client but just want the new version of the assembly to be used with the existing client instead. This is useful in cases where either a bug is fixed with the shared assembly or you just want to get rid of the old version because the new version is compatible.

By running gacutil.exe, you can see that the versions 1.0.0.0 and 1.0.3300.0 are installed for the SharedDemo assembly:

```
> gacutil -l SharedDemo

Microsoft (R) .NET Global Assembly Cache Utility.  Version 4.0.21006.1
Copyright (c) Microsoft Corporation.  All rights reserved.

The Global Assembly Cache contains the following assemblies:
    SharedDemo, Version=1.0.0.0, Culture=neutral, PublicKeyToken=f946433fdae2512d,
  processorArchitecture=x86
    SharedDemo, Version=1.0.3300.0, Culture=neutral, PublicKeyToken=f946433fdae251
2d, processorArchitecture=x86

Number of items = 2
```

Figure 18-14 shows the manifest of the client application where the client references version 1.0.0.0 of the assembly SharedDemo.

Now, again, an application configuration file is needed. As before, the assembly that is redirected needs to be specified with the <assemblyIdentity> element. This element identifies the assembly using the name, culture, and public key token. For a redirect to a different version, the <bindingRedirect> element is used. The oldVersion attribute specifies what version of the assembly should be redirected to a new version. With oldVersion you can specify a range like the one shown that all assemblies from version 1.0.0.0 to 1.0.3300.0 should be redirected. The new version is specified with the newVersion attribute.

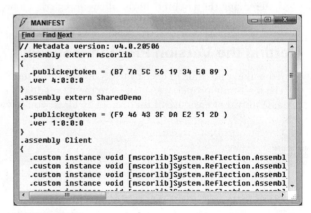

FIGURE 18-14

Available for download on Wrox.com

```
<?xml version="1.0" encoding="utf-8" ?>
<configuration>
    <runtime>
        <assemblyBinding xmlns="urn:schemas-microsoft-com:asm.v1">
            <dependentAssembly>
                <assemblyIdentity name="SharedDemo" culture="neutral"
                    publicKeyToken="f946433fdae2512d" />
                <bindingRedirect oldVersion="1.0.0.0-1.0.3300.0"
                    newVersion="1.0.3300.0" />
            </dependentAssembly>
```

```
            </assemblyBinding>
        </runtime>
    </configuration>
```

code snippet Client/App.config

Publisher Policy Files

Using assemblies shared from the GAC allows you to use publisher policies to override versioning issues. Assume that you have an assembly used by some applications. What can be done if a critical bug is found in the shared assembly? You have seen that it is not necessary to rebuild all the applications that use this shared assembly, because you can use configuration files to redirect to the new version of this shared assembly. Maybe you don't know all the applications that use this shared assembly, but you want to get the bug fix to all of them. In that case, you can create publisher policy files to redirect all applications to the new version of the shared assembly.

 Publisher policy files apply only to shared assemblies installed in the GAC.

To set up publisher policies, you have to do the following:

➤ Create a publisher policy file

➤ Create a publisher policy assembly

➤ Add the publisher policy assembly to the GAC

Create a Publisher Policy File

A publisher policy file is an XML file that redirects an existing version or version range to a new version. The syntax used here is the same as that used for application configuration files, so you can use the file you created earlier to redirect the old versions 1.0.0.0 through 1.0.3300.0 to the new version 1.0.3300.0.

Rename the previously created file to `mypolicy.config` to use it as a publisher policy file.

Create a Publisher Policy Assembly

To associate the publisher policy file with the shared assembly, it is necessary to create a publisher policy assembly and to put it into the GAC. The tool that can be used to create such files is the assembly linker `al`. The option `/linkresource` adds the publisher policy file to the generated assembly. The name of the generated assembly must start with policy, followed by the major and minor version number of the assembly that should be redirected, and the filename of the shared assembly. In this case the publisher policy assembly must be named `policy.1.0.SharedDemo.dll` to redirect the assemblies `SharedDemo` with the major version 1 and minor version 0. The key that must be added to this publisher key with the option `/keyfile` is the same key that was used to sign the shared assembly `SharedDemo` to guarantee that the version redirection is from the same publisher.

```
al /linkresource:mypolicy.config /out:policy.1.0.SharedDemo.dll
/keyfile:.\.\mykey.snk
```

Add the Publisher Policy Assembly to the GAC

The publisher policy assembly can now be added to the GAC with the utility `gacutil`:

```
gacutil -i policy.1.0.SharedDemo.dll
```

Do not forget the `-f` option if the same policy file was already published. Now remove the application configuration file that was placed in the directory of the client application and start the client application. Although the client assembly references 1.0.0.0, you use the new version 1.0.3300.0 of the shared assembly because of the publisher policy.

Overriding Publisher Policies

With a publisher policy, the publisher of the shared assembly guarantees that a new version of the assembly is compatible with the old version. As you know, from changes of traditional DLLs, such guarantees don't always hold. Maybe all except one application is working with the new shared assembly. To fix the one application that has a problem with the new release, the publisher policy can be overridden by using an application configuration file.

You can disable the publisher policy by adding the XML element `<publisherPolicy>` with the attribute `apply="no"`.

Available for download on Wrox.com

```xml
<?xml version="1.0" encoding="utf-8" ?>
<configuration>
  <runtime>
    <assemblyBinding xmlns="urn:schemas-microsoft-com:asm.v1">
      <dependentAssembly>
        <assemblyIdentity name="SharedDemo" culture="neutral"
            publicKeyToken="f946433fdae2512d" />
        <publisherPolicy apply="no" />
      </dependentAssembly>
    </assemblyBinding>
  </runtime>
</configuration>
```

code snippet Client/App.config

By disabling the publisher policy, you can configure different version redirection in the application configuration file.

Runtime Version

Installing and using multiple versions is not only possible with assemblies but also with the .NET runtime (CLR). The versions 1.0, 1.1, 2.0, and 4.0 (and later versions) of the CLR can be installed on the same operating system side by side. Visual Studio 2010 targets applications running on CLR 2.0 with .NET 2.0, 3.0, and 3.5 and CLR 4.0 with .NET 4.

If the application is built with CLR 2.0, it might run without changes on a system where only CLR version 4.0 is installed. The reverse is not true, if the application is built with CLR 4.0, it cannot run on a system where only CLR 2.0 is installed.

In an application configuration file, it's not just possible to redirect versions of referenced assemblies; you can also define the required version of the runtime. You can specify the version that's required for the application in an application configuration file. The element `<supportedRuntime>` marks the runtime versions that are supported by the application. The order of `<supportedRuntime>` elements defines the preference if multiple runtime versions are available on the system. The configuration here prefers the .NET 4 runtime and also supports 2.0. Remember, for this to be possible, the application must be built with the target framework .NET 2.0, 3.0 or 3.5.

```xml
<?xml version="1.0"?>
<configuration>
  <startup>
    <supportedRuntime version="v4.0.21006" />
    <supportedRuntime version="v2.0.50727" />
  </startup>
</configuration>
```

SUMMARY

Assemblies are the new installation unit for the .NET platform. Microsoft learned from problems with previous architectures and did a complete redesign to avoid the old problems. This chapter discussed the features of assemblies: they are self-describing, and no type library and registry information is needed.

Version dependencies are exactly recorded so that with assemblies, the DLL hell of old DLLs no longer exists. Because of these features, development, deployment, and administration have become a lot easier.

You learned the differences between private and shared assemblies and saw how shared assemblies can be created. With private assemblies, you don't have to pay attention to uniqueness and versioning issues because these assemblies are copied and only used by a single application. Sharing assemblies requires you to use a key for uniqueness and to define the version. You looked at the GAC, which can be used as an intelligent store for shared assemblies.

You can have faster application startups by using the native image generator. With this the JIT compiler does not need to run because the native code is created during installation time.

You looked at overriding versioning issues to use a version of an assembly different from the one that was used during development; this is done through publisher policies and application configuration files. Finally, you learned how probing works with private assemblies.

The chapter also discussed loading assemblies dynamically and creating assemblies during runtime. If you want to get more information on this, you should read about the plugin model of .NET 4 in Chapter 28, "Managed Extensibility Framework." To use a plugin model with the advantage of app-domains, see coverage of the `System.Addin` namespace in Chapter 50, "Add-Ins."

19

Instrumentation

WHAT'S IN THIS CHAPTER?

➤ Code contracts
➤ Tracing
➤ Event logging
➤ Performance monitoring

This chapter helps you to get live information about your running application to find the issues that your application might have during production or to monitor resources needed to adapt earlier to higher user loads. This is where the namespace `System.Diagnostics` comes into play.

One way to mark errors in your application, of course, is by throwing exceptions. However, an application might not fail that badly, but still not behave as expected. The application might be running well on most systems, but might have a problem on a few. On the live system, you can change the log behavior by changing a configuration value and get detailed live information about what's going on in the application. This can be done with *tracing*.

If there are problems with applications, the system administrator needs to be informed. With the Event Viewer, the system administrator can both interactively monitor problems with applications and be informed about specific events that happen by adding subscriptions. The *event-logging* mechanism allows you to write information about the application.

To analyze resources needed from applications, monitor applications with specified time intervals, and plan for a different application distribution or the extension of system resources, the system administrator can use the Performance Monitor. You can write live data from your application by using *performance counts*.

New in .NET 4 are classes that offer design-by-contract in the namespace `System.Diagnostics .Contracts`. With these classes, you can define preconditions, postconditions, and invariants that can be checked during runtime but also with a static contract analyzer.

This chapter explains these facilities and demonstrates how you can use them from your applications.

CODE CONTRACTS

Design-by-contracts is an idea from the Eiffel programming language. Now .NET 4 includes classes for static and runtime checks of code within the namespace `System.Diagnostics.Contracts` that can be used by all .NET languages.

With this functionality you can define preconditions, postconditions, and invariants within a method. The preconditions lists what requirements the parameters must fulfill, the postconditions define the requirements on returned data, and the invariants define the requirements of variables within the method itself.

Contract information can be compiled both into the debug and the release code. It is also possible to define a separate contract assembly, and many checks can also be made statically without running the application. You can also define contracts on interfaces that cause the implementations of the interface to fulfill the contracts. Contract tools can rewrite the assembly to inject contract checks within the code for runtime checks, check the contracts during compile time, and add contract information to the generated XML documentation.

Figure 19-1 shows the project properties for the code contracts in Visual Studio 2010. Here, you can define what level of runtime checking should be done, indicate if assert dialogs should be opened on contract failures, and configure static checking. Setting the Perform Runtime Contract Checking to Full defines the symbol CONTRACTS_FULL. Because many of the contract methods are annotated with the attribute [Conditional("CONTRACTS_FULL")], all runtime checks are only done with this setting.

FIGURE 19-1

 To work with code contracts you can use classes that are available with .NET 4 in the namespace System.Diagnostics.Contracts. *However, there's no tool included with Visual Studio 2010. You need to download an extension to Visual Studio from Microsoft DevLabs:* http://msdn.microsoft.com/en-us/devlabs/dd491992.aspx. *For static analysis with this tool, the Visual Studio Team System is required; for runtime analysis, Visual Studio Standard edition is enough.*

Code contracts are defined with the Contract class. All contract requirements that you define in a method, no matter if they are preconditions or postconditions, must be placed at the beginning of the method. You can also assign a global event handler to the event `ContractFailed` that is invoked for every failed contract during runtime. Invoking `SetHandled()` with the `ContractFailedEventArgs` parameter e stops the standard behavior of failures that would throw an exception.

Available for download on Wrox.com

```
Contract.ContractFailed += (sender, e) =>
{
    Console.WriteLine(e.Message);
    e.SetHandled();
};
```

code snippet CodeContractsSamples/Program.cs

Preconditions

Preconditions check the parameters that are passed to a method. `Requires()` and `Requires<TException>()` are preconditions that can be defined with the `Contract` class. With the `Requires()` method, a Boolean value must be passed, and an optional message string with the second parameter that is shown when the condition does not succeed. The following sample requires that the argument *min* be lower than or equal to the argument *max*.

Available for download on Wrox.com

```
static void MinMax(int min, int max)
{
    Contract.Requires(min <= max);
    //...
}
```

code snippet CodeContractsSamples/Program.cs

The following contract throws an `ArgumentNullException` if the argument o is null. The exception is not thrown if an event handler that sets the `ContractFailed` event to `handled`. Also, if the Assert on Contract Failure is configured, `Trace.Assert()` is done to stop the program instead of throwing the exception defined.

```
static void Preconditions(object o)
{
    Contract.Requires<ArgumentNullException>(o != null,
        "Preconditions, o may not be null");
    //...
```

`Requires<TException>()` is not annotated with the attribute `[Conditional("CONTRACTS_FULL")]`, and it also doesn't have a condition on the DEBUG symbol, so this runtime check is done in any case. `Requires<TException>()` throws the defined exception if the condition is not fulfilled.

With a lot of legacy code, arguments are often checked with `if` statements and throw an exception if a condition is not fulfilled. With code contracts, it is not necessary to rewrite the verification; just add one line of code:

```
static void PrecondtionsWithLegacyCode(object o)
{
    if (o == null) throw new ArgumentNullException("o");
    Contract.EndContractBlock();
```

The `EndContractBlock()` defines that the preceding code should be handled as a contract. If other contract statements are used as well, the `EndContractBlock()` is not necessary.

For checking collections that are used as arguments, the `Contract` class offers `Exists()` and `ForAll()` methods. `ForAll()` checks every item in the collection if the condition succeeds. In the example, it is checked if every item in the collection has a value smaller than 12. With the `Exists()` method, it is checked if any one element in the collection succeeds the condition.

```
static void ArrayTest(int[] data)
{
    Contract.Requires(Contract.ForAll(data, i => i < 12));
```

Both the methods `Exists()` and `ForAll()` have an overload where you can pass two integers, *fromInclusive* and *toExclusive*, instead of `IEnumerable<T>`. A range from the numbers (excluding *toExclusive*) is passed to the delegate `Predicate<int>` defined with the third parameter. `Exists()` and `ForAll()` can be used with preconditions, postconditions, and also invariants.

Postconditions

Postconditions define guarantees about shared data and return values after the method has completed. Although they define some guarantees on return values, they must be written at the beginning of a method; all contract requirements must be at the beginning of the method.

`Ensures()` and `EnsuresOnThrow<TException>()` are postconditions. The following contract ensures that the variable `sharedState` is lower than 6 at the end of the method. The value can change in between.

```
private static int sharedState = 5;
static void Postcondition()
{
    Contract.Ensures(sharedState < 6);
    sharedState = 9;
    Console.WriteLine("change sharedState invariant {0}", sharedState);
    sharedState = 3;
    Console.WriteLine("before returning change it to a valid value {0}",
                      sharedState);
}
```

code snippet CodeContractsSamples/Program.cs

With `EnsuresOnThrow<TException>()`, it is guaranteed that a shared state succeeds a condition if a specified exception is thrown.

To guarantee a return value, the special value `Result<T>` can be used with an `Ensures()` contract. Here, the result is of type `int` as is also defined with the generic type `T` for the `Result()` method. The `Ensures()` contract guarantees that the *return* value is lower than 6.

```
static int ReturnValue()
{
    Contract.Ensures(Contract.Result<int>() < 6);
    return 3;
}
```

You can also compare a value to an old value. This is done with the `OldValue<T>()` method that returns the original value on method entry for the variable passed. The following ensures that the contract defines that the result returned (`Contract.Result<int>()`) is larger than the old value from the argument *x* (`Contract.OldValue<int>(x)`).

```
static int ReturnLargerThanInput(int x)
{
    Contract.Ensures(Contract.Result<int>() > Contract.OldValue<int>(x));
    return x + 3;
}
```

If a method returns values with the `out` modifier instead of just with the `return` statement, conditions can be defined with `ValueAtReturn()`. The following contract defines that the *x* variable must be larger than 5 and smaller than 20 on return, and with the *y* variable modulo 5 must equal 0 on return.

```
static void OutParameters(out int x, out int y)
{
    Contract.Ensures(Contract.ValueAtReturn<int>(out x) > 5 &&
                     Contract.ValueAtReturn<int>(out x) < 20);
    Contract.Ensures(Contract.ValueAtReturn<int>(out y) % 5 == 0);
    x = 8;
    y = 10;
}
```

Invariants

Invariants define contracts for variables during the method lifetime. `Contract.Requires()` defines input requirements, `Contract.Ensures()` defines requirements on method end. `Contract.Invariant()` defines conditions that must succeed during the whole lifetime of the method.

Available for download on Wrox.com

```
static void Invariant(ref int x)
{
    Contract.Invariant(x > 5);
    x = 3;
    Console.WriteLine("invariant value: {0}", x);
    x = 9;
}
```

code snippet CodeContractsSamples/Program.cs

Contracts for Interfaces

With interfaces you can define methods, properties, and events that a class that derives from the interface must implement. With the interface declaration you cannot define how the interface must be implemented. Now this is possible using code contracts.

Take a look at the following interface. The interface `IPerson` defines `FirstName`, `LastName`, and `Age` properties, and the method `ChangeName()`. What's special with this interface is just the attribute `ContractClass`. This attribute is applied to the interface `IPerson` and defines that the `PersonContract` class is used as the code contract for this interface.

Available for download on Wrox.com

```
[ContractClass(typeof(PersonContract))]
public interface IPerson
{
    string FirstName { get; set; }
    string LastName { get; set; }
    int Age { get; set; }
    void ChangeName(string firstName, string lastName);
}
```

code snippet CodeContractsSamples/IPerson.cs

The class `PersonContract` implements the interface `IPerson` and defines code contracts for all the members. The attribute `PureAttribute` means that the method or property may not change state of a class instance. This is defined with the `get` accessors of the properties but can also be defined with all methods that are not allowed to change state. The `FirstName` and `LastName` `get` accessors also define that the result must be a string with `Contract.Result()`. The `get` accessor of the `Age` property defines a postcondition and ensures that the returned value is between 0 and 120. The `set` accessor of the `FirstName` and `LastName` properties requires that the value passed is not null. The `set` accessor of the `Age` property defines a precondition that the passed value is between 0 and 120.

Available for download on Wrox.com

```
[ContractClassFor(typeof(IPerson))]
public sealed class PersonContract : IPerson
{
    string IPerson.FirstName
    {
        [Pure] get { return Contract.Result<String>(); }
        set { Contract.Requires(value != null); }
    }
    string IPerson.LastName
    {
        [Pure] get { return Contract.Result<String>(); }
        set { Contract.Requires(value != null); }
    }
```

```
      int IPerson.Age
      {
          [Pure]
          get
          {
              Contract.Ensures(Contract.Result<int>() >= 0 &&
                               Contract.Result<int>() < 121);
              return Contract.Result<int>();
          }
          set
          {
              Contract.Requires(value >= 0 && value < 121);
          }
      }
      void IPerson.ChangeName(string firstName, string lastName)
      {
          Contract.Requires(firstName != null);
          Contract.Requires(lastName != null);
      }
  }
```

code snippet CodeContractsSamples/PersonContract.cs

Now a class implementing the IPerson interface must fulfill all the contract requirements. The class Person is a simple implementation of the interface that fulfills the contract.

```
  public class Person : IPerson
  {
      public Person(string firstName, string lastName)
      {
          this.FirstName = firstName;
          this.LastName = lastName;
      }

      public string FirstName { get; private set; }
      public string LastName { get; private set; }
      public int Age { get; set; }


      public void ChangeName(string firstName, string lastName)
      {
          this.FirstName = firstName;
          this.LastName = lastName;
      }
  }
```

code snippet CodeContractsSamples/Person.cs

When using the class Person, the contract must also be fulfilled. For example, it's not allowed to assign null to a property:

```
      var p = new Person { FirstName = "Tom", LastName = null }; // contract error
```

code snippet CodeContractsSamples/Program.cs

It's also not allowed to assign an invalid value to the Age property:

```
      var p = new Person { FirstName = "Tom", LastName = "Turbo" };
      p.Age = 133;  // contract error
```

TRACING

With tracing, you can see messages from the running application. To get information about a running application, you can start the application in the debugger. During debugging, you can walk through the application step by step and set breakpoints at specific lines and when you reach specific conditions. The problem with debugging is that a program with release code can behave differently from a program with debug code. For example, while the program is stopping at a breakpoint, other threads of the application are suspended as well. Also, with a release build, the compiler-generated output is optimized and, thus, different effects can occur. There is a need to have information from a release build as well. Trace messages are written with both debug and release code.

A scenario showing how tracing helps is described here. After an application is deployed, it runs on one system without problems, while on another system intermediate problems occur. When you turn on verbose tracing, the system with the problems gives you detailed information about what's happening inside the application. The system that is running without problems has tracing configured just for error messages redirected to the Windows event log system. Critical errors are seen by the system administrator. The overhead of tracing is very small, because you configure a trace level only when needed.

The tracing architecture has four major parts:

➤ The *source* is the originator of the trace information. You use the source to send trace messages.

➤ The *switch* defines the level of information to log. For example, you can request just error information or detailed verbose information.

➤ Trace *listeners* define where the trace messages should be written to.

➤ Listeners can have *filters* attached. The filter defines what trace messages should be written by the listener. This way, you can have different listeners for the same source that write different levels of information.

Figure 19-2 shows the major classes for tracing and how they are connected, in a Visual Studio class diagram. The `TraceSource` uses a switch to define what information to log. The `TraceSource` has a `TraceListenerCollection` associated with it, which trace messages are forwarded to. The collection consists of `TraceListener` objects, and every listener has a `TraceFilter` connected.

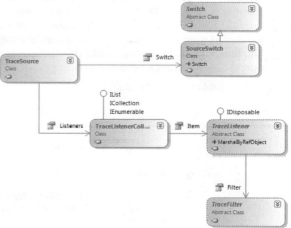

FIGURE 19-2

 Several .NET technologies make use of trace sources that you just need to turn on to see what's going on. For example, WPF defines sources among others with the names `System.Windows.Data`, `System.Windows.RoutedEvent`, `System.Windows.Markup`, `System.Windows.Media.Animation`. *However, with WPF, you need to turn tracing on not only by configuring listeners but also by setting within the registry key* `HKEY_CURRENT_USER\Software\MicrosoftTracing\WPF` *a new* DWORD *to the name* `ManagedTracing` *and the value 1.*

Classes from the `System.Net` *namespace use the trace source* `System.Net`; *WCF uses the trace sources* `System.ServiceModel` *and* `System.ServiceModel.MessageLogging`. *WCF tracing is discussed in Chapter 43, "Windows Communication Foundation."*

Trace Sources

You can write trace messages with the `TraceSource` class. Tracing requires the `Trace` flag of the compiler settings. With a Visual Studio project, the `Trace` flag is set by default with debug and release builds, but you can change it through the `Build` properties of the project.

 The `TraceSource` class is more difficult to use compared to the `Trace` class writing trace messages, but it provides more options.

To write trace messages, you need to create a new `TraceSource` instance. In the constructor, the name of the trace source is defined. The method `TraceInformation()` writes an information message to the trace output. Instead of just writing informational messages, the `TraceEvent()` method requires an enumeration value of type `TraceEventType` to define the type of the trace message. `TraceEventType.Error` specifies the message as an error message. You can define it with a trace switch to see only error messages. The second argument of the `TraceEvent()` method requires an identifier. The ID can be used within the application itself. For example, you can use id 1 for entering a method and id 2 for exiting a method. The method `TraceEvent()` is overloaded, so the `TraceEventType` and the ID are the only required parameters. Using the third parameter of an overloaded method, you can pass the message written to the trace. `TraceEvent()` also supports passing a format string with any number of parameters in the same way as `Console.WriteLine()`. `TraceInformation()` does nothing more than invoke `TraceEvent()` with an identifier of 0. `TraceInformation()` is just a simplified version of `TraceEvent()`. With the `TraceData()` method, you can pass any object, for example, an exception instance, instead of a message. To make sure that data is written by the listeners and does not stay in memory, you need to do a `Flush()`. If the source is no longer needed, you can invoke the `Close()` method that closes all listeners associated with the trace source. `Close()` does a `Flush()` as well.

Available for download on Wrox.com

```
public class Program
{
    internal static TraceSource trace =
        new TraceSource("Wrox.ProCSharp.Instrumentation");

    static void TraceSourceDemo1()
    {
        trace.TraceInformation("Info message");

        trace.TraceEvent(TraceEventType.Error, 3, "Error message");
        trace.TraceData(TraceEventType.Information, 2, "data1", 4, 5);
        trace.Flush();
        trace.Close();
    }
```

code snippet TracingDemo/Program.cs

 You can use different trace sources within your application. It makes sense to define different sources for different libraries, so that you can turn on different trace levels for different parts of your application. To use a trace source, you need to know its name. A commonly used name for the trace source is the same name as the assembly name.

The `TraceEventType` enumeration that is passed as an argument to the `TraceEvent()` method defines the following levels to specify the severity of the problem: `Verbose`, `Information`, `Warning`, `Error`, and `Critical`. `Critical` defines a fatal error or application crash; `Error` defines a recoverable error. Trace messages at the `Verbose` level give you detailed debugging information. `TraceEventType` also defines action levels `Start`, `Stop`, `Suspend`, and `Resume`. These levels define timely events inside a logical operation.

The code, as it is written now, does not display any trace message because the switch associated with the trace source is turned off.

Trace Switches

To enable or disable trace messages, you can configure a trace switch. Trace switches are classes that are derived from the abstract base class `Switch`. Derived classes are `BooleanSwitch`, `TraceSwitch`, and `SourceSwitch`. The class `BooleanSwitch` can be turned on and off, and the other two classes provide a range level. One range is defined by the `SourceLevels` enumeration. To configure trace switches, you must know the values associated with the `SourceLevels` enumeration. `SourceLevels` defines the values `Off`, `Error`, `Warning`, `Info`, and `Verbose`.

You can associate a trace switch programmatically by setting the `Switch` property of the `TraceSource`. Here, the switch associated is of type `SourceSwitch`, has the name `Wrox.ProCSharp.Instrumentation`, and has the level `Verbose`:

Available for download on Wrox.com

```
internal static SourceSwitch traceSwitch =
    new SourceSwitch("Wrox.ProCSharp.Instrumentation")
        { Level = SourceLevels.Verbose };
internal static TraceSource trace =
    new TraceSource("Wrox.ProCSharp.Instrumentation")
        { Switch = traceSwitch };
```

code snippet TracingDemo/Program.cs

Setting the level to `Verbose` means that all trace messages should be written. If you set the value to `Error`, only error messages should show up. Setting the value to `Information` means that error, warning, and info messages are shown. By writing the trace messages once more, you can see the messages while running the debugger in the Output window.

Usually, you would want to change the switch level, not by recompiling the application, but instead by changing the configuration. The trace source can be configured in the application configuration file. Tracing is configured within the `<system.diagnostics>` element. The trace source is defined with the `<source>` element as a child element of `<sources>`. The name of the source in the configuration file must exactly match the name of the source in the program code. Here, the trace source has a switch of type `System.Diagnostics.SourceSwitch` associated with the name `MySourceSwitch`. The switch itself is defined within the `<switches>` section, and the level of the switch is set to `verbose`.

Available for download on Wrox.com

```
<?xml version="1.0" encoding="utf-8" ?>
<configuration>
  <system.diagnostics>
    <sources>
      <source name="Wrox.ProCSharp.Instrumentation" switchName="MySourceSwitch"
          switchType="System.Diagnostics.SourceSwitch" />
    </sources>
    <switches>
      <add name="MySourceSwitch" value="Verbose"/>
    </switches>
  </system.diagnostics>
</configuration>
```

code snippet TracingDemo/App.config

Now, you can change the trace level just by changing the configuration file without the need to recompile the code. After the configuration file is changed, you must restart the application.

Currently, trace messages are written to just the Output window of Visual Studio while you are running it in a debug session. Adding trace listeners changes this.

Trace Listeners

By default, trace information is written to the Output window of the Visual Studio debugger. Just by changing the application's configuration, you can redirect the trace output to different locations.

Where the tracing results should be written to is defined by trace listeners. A trace listener is derived from the abstract base class `TraceListener`. NET comes with several trace listeners to write the trace events to different targets. For file-based trace listeners, the base class `TextWriterTraceListener` is used, along with the derived classes `XmlWriterTraceListener` to write to XML files and `DelimitedListTraceListener` to write to delimited files. Writing to the event log is done with either the `EventLogTraceListener` or the `EventProviderTraceListener`. `EventProviderTraceListener` uses the event file format that is new since Windows Vista. You can also combine web tracing with `System.Diagnostics` tracing and use the `WebPageTraceListener` to write `System.Diagnostics` tracing to the Web trace file, `trace.axd`.

.NET Framework delivers many listeners to which trace information can be written. In case the listeners don't fulfill your requirements, you can create a custom listener by deriving a class from the base class `TraceListener`. With a custom listener, you can, for example, write trace information to a Web service, write messages to your mobile phone, and so on. I guess it's not that interesting to receive hundreds of messages on your phone in your spare time. And with verbose tracing this can become really expensive.

You can configure a trace listener programmatically by creating a listener object and assigning it to the `Listeners` property of the `TraceSource` class. However, usually it is more interesting to just change a configuration to define a different listener.

You can configure listeners as child elements of the `<source>` element. With the listener, you define the type of the listener class and use `initializeData` to specify where the output of the listener should go. The configuration here defines the `XmlWriterTraceListener` to write to the file `demotrace.xml`, and the `DelimitedListTraceListener` to write to the file `demotrace.txt`:

```xml
<?xml version="1.0" encoding="utf-8" ?>
<configuration>
  <system.diagnostics>
    <sources>
      <source name="Wrox.ProCSharp.Tracing" switchName="MySourceSwitch"
          switchType="System.Diagnostics.SourceSwitch">
        <listeners>
          <add name="xmlListener"
              type="System.Diagnostics.XmlWriterTraceListener"
              traceOutputOptions="None"
              initializeData="c:/logs/mytrace.xml" />

          <add name="delimitedListener" delimiter=":"
              type="System.Diagnostics.DelimitedListTraceListener"
              traceOutputOptions="DateTime, ProcessId"
              initializeData="c:/logs/mytrace.txt" />
        </listeners>
      </source>
    </sources>
    <switches>
      <add name="MySourceSwitch" value="Verbose"/>
    </switches>
  </system.diagnostics>
</configuration>
```

code snippet TracingDemo/App.config

With the listener, you can also specify what additional information should be written to the trace log. This information is defined with the `traceOutputOptions` XML attribute and is defined by the `TraceOptions` enumeration. The enumeration defines `Callstack`, `DateTime`, `LogicalOperationStack`, `ProcessId`, `ThreadId`, and `None`. The information needed can be added with comma separation to the `traceOutputOptions` XML attribute, as shown with the delimited trace listener.

The delimited file output from the `DelimitedListTraceListener`, including the process ID and date/time, is shown here:

```
"Wrox.ProCSharp.Instrumentation":Information:0:"Info message"::
    5288:""::"2009-10-11T10:35:55.8479950Z"::
"Wrox.ProCSharp.Instrumentation":Error:3:"Error message"::5288:""::
    "2009-10-11T10:35:55.8509257Z"::
"Wrox.ProCSharp.Instrumentation":Information:2::
    "data1","4","5":5288:""::"2009-10-11T10:35:55.8519026Z"::
```

The XML output from the `XmlWriterTraceListener` always contains the name of the computer, the process ID, the thread ID, the message, the time created, the source, and the activity ID. Other fields, such as the call stack, logical operation stack, and timestamp, depend on the trace output options.

 You can use the `XmlDocument` and `XPathNavigator` classes to analyze the content from the XML file. These classes are covered in Chapter 33, "Manipulating XML."

If a listener should be used by multiple trace sources, you can add the listener configuration to the element `<sharedListeners>`, which is independent of the trace source. The name of the listener that is configured with a shared listener must be referenced from the listeners of the trace source:

Available for download on Wrox.com

```xml
<?xml version="1.0" encoding="utf-8" ?>
<configuration>
  <system.diagnostics>
    <sources>
      <source name="Wrox.ProCSharp.Tracing" switchName="MySourceSwitch"
          switchType="System.Diagnostics.SourceSwitch">
        <listeners>
          <add name="xmlListener"
              type="System.Diagnostics.XmlWriterTraceListener"
              traceOutputOptions="None"
              initializeData="c:/logs/mytrace.xml" />
          <add name="delimitedListener" />
        </listeners>
      </source>
    </sources>
    <sharedListeners>
      <add  name="delimitedListener" delimiter=":"
          type="System.Diagnostics.DelimitedListTraceListener"
          traceOutputOptions="DateTime, ProcessId"
          initializeData="c:/logs/mytrace.txt" />
    </sharedListeners>
    <switches>
      <add name="MySourceSwitch" value="Verbose"/>
    </switches>
  </system.diagnostics>
</configuration>
```

code snippet TracingDemo/app.config

Filters

Every listener has a `Filter` property that defines whether the listener should write the trace message. For example, multiple listeners can be used with the same trace source. One of the listeners writes verbose messages to a log file, and another listener writes error messages to the event log. Before a listener writes a trace message, it invokes the `ShouldTrace()` method of the associated filter object to decide if the trace message should be written.

A filter is a class that is derived from the abstract base class `TraceFilter`. .NET 4 offers two filter implementations: `SourceFilter` and `EventTypeFilter`. With the source filter, you can specify that trace messages are to be written only from specific sources. The event type filter is an extension of the switch functionality. With a switch, it is possible to define, according to the trace severity level, if the event source should forward the trace message to the listeners. If the trace message is forwarded, the listener now can use the filter to decide if the message should be written.

The changed configuration now defines that the delimited listener should write trace messages only if the severity level is of type warning or higher, because of the defined `EventTypeFilter`. The XML listener specifies a `SourceFilter` and accepts trace messages only from the source `Wrox.ProCSharp.Tracing`. If you have a large number of sources defined to write trace messages to the same listener, you can change the configuration for the listener to concentrate on trace messages from a specific source.

```xml
<?xml version="1.0" encoding="utf-8" ?>
<configuration>
  <system.diagnostics>
    <sources>
      <source name="Wrox.ProCSharp.Tracing" switchName="MySourceSwitch"
          switchType="System.Diagnostics.SourceSwitch">
        <listeners>
          <add name="xmlListener" />
          <add name="delimitedListener" />
        </listeners>
      </source>
    </sources>
    <sharedListeners>
        <add name="delimitedListener" delimiter=":"
            type="System.Diagnostics.DelimitedListTraceListener"
            traceOutputOptions="DateTime, ProcessId"
            initializeData="c:/logs/mytrace.txt">
          <filter type="System.Diagnostics.EventTypeFilter"
              initializeData="Warning" />
        </add>
        <add name="xmlListener"
            type="System.Diagnostics.XmlWriterTraceListener"
            traceOutputOptions="None"
            initializeData="c:/logs/mytrace.xml">
          <filter type="System.Diagnostics.SourceFilter"
              initializeData="Wrox.ProCSharp.Instrumentation" />
        </add>
    </sharedListeners>
    <switches>
      <add name="MySourceSwitch" value="Verbose"/>
    </switches>
  </system.diagnostics>
</configuration>
```

code snippet TracingDemo/App.config

The tracing architecture can be extended. Just as you can write a custom listener derived from the base class `TraceListener`, you can create a custom filter derived from `TraceFilter`. With that capability, you can create a filter that specifies to write trace messages, for example, depending on the time, depending on an exception that occurred lately, or depending on the weather.

Correlation

With trace logs, you can see the relation of different methods in several ways. To see the call stack of the trace events, just a configuration is needed to track the call stack with the XML listener. You can also define a logical call stack that can be shown in the log messages. And you can define activities to map trace messages.

To show the call stack and the logical call stack with the trace messages, the `XmlWriterTraceListener` can be configured to the corresponding `traceOuputOptions`. The MSDN documentation gives details on all the other options you can configure for tracing with this listener.

```
<sharedListeners>
  <add name="xmlListener" type="System.Diagnostics.XmlWriterTraceListener"
       traceOutputOptions="LogicalOperationStack, Callstack"
       initializeData="c:/logs/mytrace.xml">
  </add>
</sharedListeners>
```

code snippet TracingDemo/App.config

To see correlation and logical call stack in action, in the Main method a new activity ID is assigned to the `CorrelationManager` by setting the `ActivityID` property. Events of type `TraceEventType.Start` and `TraceEventType.Stop` are done at the beginning and end of the `Main` method. Also, a logical operation named "Main" is started and stopped with the `StartLogicalOperation()` and `StopLogicalOperation()` methods.

```
static void Main()
{
    // start a new activity
    if (Trace.CorrelationManager.ActivityId == Guid.Empty)
    {
        Guid newGuid = Guid.NewGuid();
        Trace.CorrelationManager.ActivityId = newGuid;
    }
    trace.TraceEvent(TraceEventType.Start, 0, "Main started");

    // start a logical operation
    Trace.CorrelationManager.StartLogicalOperation("Main");

    TraceSourceDemo1();
    StartActivityA();
    Trace.CorrelationManager.StopLogicalOperation();
    Thread.Sleep(3000);
    trace.TraceEvent(TraceEventType.Stop, 0, "Main stopped");
}
```

code snippet TracingDemo/Program.cs

The method `StartActivityA()` that is called from within the `Main()` method creates a new activity by setting the `ActivityId` of the `CorrelationManager` to a new GUID. Before the activity stops, the `ActivityId` of the `CorrelationManager` is reset to the previous value. This method invokes the `Foo()` method and creates a new task with the `Task.Factory.StartNew()` method. This task is created so that you can see how different threads are displayed in a trace viewer.

 Tasks are explained in Chapter 20, "Threads, Tasks, and Synchronization."

```
private static void StartActivityA()
{
    Guid oldGuid = Trace.CorrelationManager.ActivityId;
    Guid newActivityId = Guid.NewGuid();
    Trace.CorrelationManager.ActivityId = newActivityId;

    Trace.CorrelationManager.StartLogicalOperation("StartActivityA");

    trace.TraceEvent(TraceEventType.Verbose, 0,
                     "starting Foo in StartNewActivity");
    Foo();

    trace.TraceEvent(TraceEventType.Verbose, 0,
```

```
                          "starting a new task");
         Task.Factory.StartNew(WorkForATask);

         Trace.CorrelationManager.StopLogicalOperation();
         Trace.CorrelationManager.ActivityId = oldGuid;
     }
```

The `Foo()` method that is started from within the `StartActivityA()` method starts a new logical operation. The logical operation `Foo` is started within the `StartActivityA` logical operation.

```
         private static void Foo()
         {
             Trace.CorrelationManager.StartLogicalOperation("Foo operation");

             trace.TraceEvent(TraceEventType.Verbose, 0, "running Foo");

             Trace.CorrelationManager.StopLogicalOperation();
         }
```

The task that is created from within the `StartActivityA()` method runs the method `WorkForATask()`. Here, just simple trace events with start and stop information, and verbose information, are written to the trace.

```
         private static void WorkForATask()
         {
             trace.TraceEvent(TraceEventType.Start, 0, "WorkForATask started");

             trace.TraceEvent(TraceEventType.Verbose, 0, "running WorkForATask");

             trace.TraceEvent(TraceEventType.Stop, 0, "WorkForATask completed");
         }
```

To analyze the trace information, the tool Service Trace Viewer, `svctraceviewer.exe`, can be started. This tool is mainly used to analyze WCF traces, but it can also be used to analyze any trace that is written with the `XmlWriterTraceListener`. Figure 19-3 shows the activities in the Activity screen, and each activity shows the events in the right screen. When you select an event you can set the display to show the complete message in XML or in a formatted view. In the formatted view, basic information, application data, the logical operation stack, and the call stack are nicely formatted.

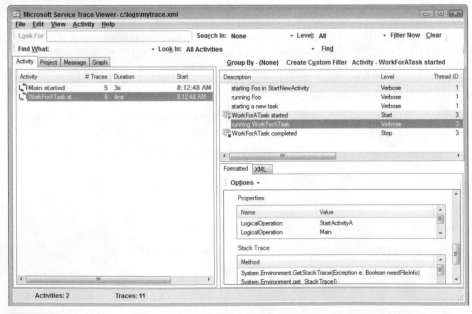

FIGURE 19-3

Figure 19-4 shows the graph view, where different processes or threads can be selected to be displayed in separate swimlanes. As a new thread is created with the `TaskFactory` class, a second swimlane shows up selecting the thread view.

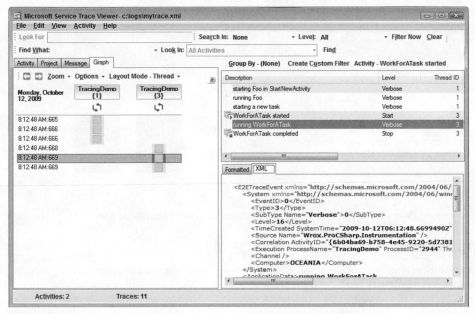

FIGURE 19-4

EVENT LOGGING

The system administrator uses the Event Viewer to get critical messages on the health of the system and applications and also information messages. You should write error messages from your application to the event log so that the information can be read with the Event Viewer.

Trace messages can be written to the event log if you configure the `EventLogTraceListener` class. The `EventLogTraceListener` has an `EventLog` object associated with it to write the event log entries. You can also use the `EventLog` class directly to write and read event logs.

In this section, you explore the following:

➤ Event-logging architecture

➤ Classes for event logging from the `System.Diagnostics` namespace

➤ Adding event logging to services and to other application types

➤ Creating an event log listener with the `EnableRaisingEvents` property of the `EventLog` class

➤ Use a resource file to define messages

Figure 19-5 shows an example of a log entry from a failed access with Distributed COM.

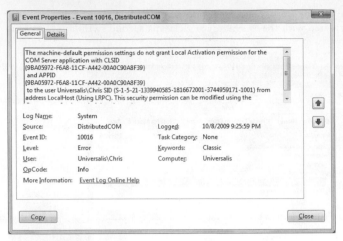

FIGURE 19-5

For custom event logging, you can use classes from the `System.Diagnostics` namespace.

Event-Logging Architecture

The event log information is stored in several log files. The most important ones are application, security, and system. Looking at the registry configuration of the event log service, you will notice several entries under `HKEY_LOCAL_MACHINE\System\CurrentControlSet\Services\Eventlog` with configurations pointing to the specific files. The system log file is used from the system and device drivers. Applications and services write to the application log. The security log is a read-only log for applications. The auditing feature of the operating system uses the security log. Every application can also create a custom category and log file to write event log entries there. For example, this is done by Media Center.

You can read these events by using the administrative tool Event Viewer. The Event Viewer can be started directly from the Server Explorer of Visual Studio by right-clicking the Event Logs item and selecting the Launch Event Viewer entry from the context menu. The Event Viewer is shown in Figure 19-6.

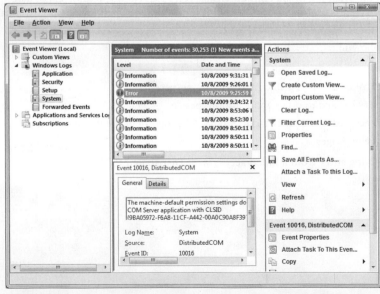

FIGURE 19-6

In the event log, you can see this information:

➤ **Type** — The type can be Information, Warning, or Error. Information is an infrequent successful operation; Warning is a problem that is not immediately significant; and Error is a major problem. Additional types are FailureAudit and SuccessAudit, but these types are used only for the security log.

➤ **Date** — Date and Time show the day and time that the event occurred.

➤ **Source** — The Source is the name of the software that logs the event. The source for the application log is configured in this registry key:

```
HKEY_LOCAL_MACHINE\System\CurrentControlSet\Services\Eventlog\Application\
[ApplicationName]
```

Within this key, the value `EventMessageFile` is configured to point to a resource DLL that holds error messages.

➤ **Event ID** — The Event identifier specifies a particular event message.

➤ **Category** — A Category can be defined so that event logs can be filtered when using the Event Viewer. Categories can be defined by an event source.

Event-Logging Classes

For writing event logs, two different Windows APIs exist. One API that is available since Windows Vista is wrapped by classes in the namespace `System.Diagnostics.Eventing`, the other wrapper classes are in the `System.Diagnostics` namespace.

The `System.Diagnostics` namespace has the following classes for event logging, which are shown in the following table.

CLASS	DESCRIPTION
EventLog	With the `EventLog` class, you can read and write entries in the event log, and establish applications as event sources.
EventLogEntry	The `EventLogEntry` class represents a single entry in the event log. With the `EventLogEntryCollection`, you can iterate through `EventLogEntry` items.
EventLogInstaller	The `EventLogInstaller` class is the installer for an `EventLog` component. `EventLogInstaller` calls `EventLog.CreateEventSource()` to create an event source.
EventLogTraceListener	With the help of the `EventLogTraceListener`, traces can be written to the event log. This class implements the abstract class `TraceListener`.

The heart of event logging is in the `EventLog` class. The members of this class are explained in the following table.

EVENTLOG MEMBERS	DESCRIPTION
Entries	With the `Entries` property, you can read event logs. `Entries` returns an `EventLogEntryCollection` that contains `EventLogEntry` objects holding information about the events. There is no need to invoke a `Read()` method. The collection is filled as soon as you access this property.
Log	Specify the log for reading or writing event logs with the `Log` property.
LogDisplayName	`LogDisplayName` is a read-only property that returns the display name of the log.
MachineName	With the `MachineName`, you can specify the system on which to read or write log entries.

continues

(continued)

EVENTLOG MEMBERS	DESCRIPTION
Source	The Source property specifies the source of the event entries to write.
CreateEventSource()	The CreateEventSource() creates a new event source and a new log file, if a new log file is specified with this method.
DeleteEventSource()	To get rid of an event source, you can invoke DeleteEventSource().
SourceExists()	Before creating an event source, you can verify if the source already exists by using this element.
WriteEntry() WriteEvent()	Write event log entries with either the WriteEntry() or WriteEvent() method. WriteEntry() is simpler, because you just need to pass a string. WriteEvent() is more flexible, because you can use message files that are independent of the application and that support localization.
Clear()	The Clear() method removes all entries from an event log.
Delete()	The Delete() method deletes a complete event log.

Creating an Event Source

Before writing events, you must create an event source. You can use either the CreateEventSource() method of the EventLog class or the class EventLogInstaller. Because you need administrative privileges when creating an event source, an installation program would be best for defining the new source.

 Chapter 17, "Deployment," explains how to create installation programs.

The following sample verifies that an event log source named EventLogDemoApp already exists. If it doesn't exist, an object of type EventSourceCreationData is instantiated that defines the source name EventLogDemoApp and the log name ProCSharpLog. Here, all events of this source are written to the ProCSharpLog event log. The default is the application log.

Available for download on Wrox.com

```csharp
string logName = "ProCSharpLog";
string sourceName = "EventLogDemoApp";

if (!EventLog.SourceExists(sourceName))
{
    var eventSourceData = new EventSourceCreationData(sourceName,
        logName);

    EventLog.CreateEventSource(eventSourceData);
}
```

code snippet EventLogDemo/Program.cs

The name of the event source is an identifier of the application that writes the events. For the system administrator reading the log, the information helps in identifying the event log entries to map them to application categories. Examples of names for event log sources are LoadPerf for the performance monitor, MSSQLSERVER for Microsoft SQL Server, MsiInstaller for the Windows Installer, Winlogon, Tcpip, Time-Service, and so on.

Setting the name Application for the event log writes event log entries to the application log. You can also create your own log by specifying a different application log name. Log files are located in the directory <windows>\System32\WinEvt\Logs.

With the `EventSourceCreationData`, you can also specify several more characteristics for the event log, as shown in the following table.

EVENTSOURCECREATIONDATA	DESCRIPTION
Source	The property `Source` gets or sets the name of the event source.
LogName	`LogName` defines the log where event log entries are written. The default is the application log.
MachineName	With `MachineName`, you can define the system to read or write log entries.
CategoryResourceFile	With the `CategoryResourceFile` property, you can define a resource file for categories. Categories can be used for an easier filtering of event log entries within a single source.
CategoryCount	The `CategoryCount` property defines the number of categories in the category resource file.
MessageResourceFile	Instead of specifying that the message should be written to the event log in the program that writes the events, messages can be defined in a resource file that is assigned to the `MessageResourceFile` property. Messages from the resource file are localizable.
ParameterResourceFile	Messages in a resource file can have parameters. The parameters can be replaced by strings defined in a resource file that is assigned to the `ParameterResourceFile` property.

Writing Event Logs

For writing event log entries, you can use the `WriteEntry()` or `WriteEvent()` methods of the `EventLog` class. The `EventLog` class has both a static and an instance method `WriteEntry()`. The static method `WriteEntry()` requires a parameter of the source. The source can also be set with the constructor of the `EventLog` class. Here in the constructor, the log name, the local machine, and the event source name are defined. Next, three event log entries are written with the message as the first parameter of the `WriteEntry()` method. `WriteEntry()` is overloaded. The second parameter you can assign is an enumeration of type `EventLogEntryType`. With `EventLogEntryType`, you can define the severity of the event log entry. Possible values are `Information`, `Warning`, and `Error`, and for auditing `SuccessAudit` and `FailureAudit`. Depending on the type, different icons are shown in the Event Viewer. With the third parameter, you can specify an application-specific event ID that can be used by the application itself. In addition to that, you can also pass application-specific binary data and a category.

Available for download on Wrox.com

```
using (var log = new EventLog(logName, ".", sourceName))
{
    log.WriteEntry("Message 1");
    log.WriteEntry("Message 2", EventLogEntryType.Warning);
    log.WriteEntry("Message 3", EventLogEntryType.Information, 33);
}
```

code snippet EventLogDemo/Program.cs

Resource Files

Instead of defining the messages for the event log in the C# code and passing it to the `WriteEntry()` method, you can create a *message resource file*, define messages in the resource file, and pass message identifiers to the `WriteEvent()` method. Resource files also support localization.

Message resource files are native resource files that have nothing in common with .NET resource files. .NET resource files are covered in Chapter 22, "Localization."

A message file is a text file with the mc *file extension. The syntax that this file uses to define messages is very strict. The sample file* EventLogMessages.mc *contains four categories followed by event messages. Every message has an ID that can be used by the application writing event entries. Parameters that can be passed from the application are defined with* % *syntax in the message text.*

For the exact syntax of message files, check the MSDN documentation for Message Text Files.

```
; // EventLogDemoMessages.mc
; // *********************************************************

; // - Event categories -
; // Categories must be numbered consecutively starting at 1.
; // *********************************************************

MessageId=0x1
Severity=Success
SymbolicName=INSTALL_CATEGORY
Language=English
Installation
.

MessageId=0x2
Severity=Success
SymbolicName=DATA_CATEGORY
Language=English
Database Query
.

MessageId=0x3
Severity=Success
SymbolicName=UPDATE_CATEGORY
Language=English
Data Update
.

MessageId=0x4
Severity=Success
SymbolicName=NETWORK_CATEGORY
Language=English
Network Communication
.

; // - Event messages -
; // ******************************

MessageId = 1000
Severity = Success
Facility = Application
SymbolicName = MSG_CONNECT_1000
```

```
Language=English
Connection successful.
.


MessageId = 1001
Severity = Error
Facility = Application
SymbolicName = MSG_CONNECT_FAILED_1001
Language=English
Could not connect to server %1.
.


MessageId = 1002
Severity = Error
Facility = Application
SymbolicName = MSG_DB_UPDATE_1002
Language=English
Database update failed.
.


MessageId = 1003
Severity = Success
Facility = Application
SymbolicName = APP_UPDATE
Language=English
Application %%5002 updated.
.


; // — Event log display name -
; // ******************************************************


MessageId = 5001
Severity = Success
Facility = Application
SymbolicName = EVENT_LOG_DISPLAY_NAME_MSGID
Language=English
Professional C# Sample Event Log
.


; // — Event message parameters -
; //       Language independent insertion strings
; // ******************************************************


MessageId = 5002
Severity = Success
Facility = Application
SymbolicName = EVENT_LOG_SERVICE_NAME_MSGID
Language=English
EventLogDemo.EXE
.
```

code snippet EventLogDemo/EventLogDemoMessages.mc

Use the Messages Compiler, `mc.exe`, to create a binary message file. The command `mc -s`
`EventLogDemoMessages.mc` compiles the source file containing the messages to a messages file with the
`.bin` extension and the file `Messages.rc`, which contains a reference to the binary message file:

```
mc -s EventLogDemoMessages.mc
```

Next, you must use the Resource Compiler, `rc.exe`. The command `rc EventLogDemoMessages.rc` creates the resource file `EventLogDemoMessages.RES`:

```
rc EventLogDemoMessages.rc
```

With the linker, you can bind the binary message file `EventLogDemoMessages.RES` to a native DLL:

```
link /DLL /SUBSYSTEM:WINDOWS /NOENTRY /MACHINE:x86 EventLogDemoMessages.RES
```

Now, you can register an event source that defines the resource files as shown in the following code. First, a check is done to see if the event source named `EventLogDemoApp` exists. If the event log must be created because it does not exist, the next check verifies that the resource file is available. Some samples in the MSDN documentation demonstrate writing the message file to the `<windows>\system32` directory, but you shouldn't do that. Copy the message DLL to a program-specific directory that you can get with the `SpecialFolder` enumeration value `ProgramFiles`. If you need to share the messages file among multiple applications, you can put it into `Environment.SpecialFolder.CommonProgramFiles`.

If the file exists, a new object of type `EventSourceCreationData` is instantiated. In the constructor, the name of the source and the name of the log are defined. You use the properties `CategoryResourceFile`, `MessageResourceFile`, and `ParameterResourceFile` to define a reference to the resource file. After the event source is created, you can find the information on the resource files in the registry with the event source. The method `CreateEventSource` registers the new event source and log file. Finally, the method `RegisterDisplayName()` from the `EventLog` class specifies the name of the log as it is displayed in the Event Viewer. The ID 5001 is taken from the message file.

> *If you want to delete a previously created event source, you can do so with* `EventLog.DeleteEventSource(sourceName)`. *To delete a log, you can invoke* `EventLog.Delete(logName)`.

```csharp
string logName = "ProCSharpLog";
string sourceName = "EventLogDemoApp";
string resourceFile = Environment.GetFolderPath(
        Environment.SpecialFolder.ProgramFiles) +
        @"\procsharp\EventLogDemoMessages.dll";

if (!EventLog.SourceExists(sourceName))
{
    if (!File.Exists(resourceFile))
    {
        Console.WriteLine("Message resource file does not exist");
        return;
    }

    var eventSource = new EventSourceCreationData(sourceName, logName);

    eventSource.CategoryResourceFile = resourceFile;
    eventSource.CategoryCount = 4;
    eventSource.MessageResourceFile = resourceFile;
    eventSource.ParameterResourceFile = resourceFile;

    EventLog.CreateEventSource(eventSource);
}
else
{
    logName = EventLog.LogNameFromSourceName(sourceName, ".");
}
```

```
var evLog = new EventLog(logName, ".", sourceName);
evLog.RegisterDisplayName(resourceFile, 5001);
```

code snippet EventLogDemo/Program.cs

Now, you can use the `WriteEvent()` method instead of `WriteEntry()` to write the event log entry.
`WriteEvent()` requires an object of type `EventInstance` as parameter. With the `EventInstance`, you
can assign the message ID, the category, and the severity of type `EventLogEntryType`. In addition to the
`EventInstance` parameter, `WriteEvent()` accepts parameters for messages that have parameters and
binary data in the form of a byte array.

```
using (var log = new EventLog(logName, ".", sourceName))
{
    var info1 = new EventInstance(1000, 4,
        EventLogEntryType.Information);

    log.WriteEvent(info1);
    var info2 = new EventInstance(1001, 4,
        EventLogEntryType.Error);
    log.WriteEvent(info2, "avalon");

    var info3 = new EventInstance(1002, 3,
        EventLogEntryType.Error);
    byte[] addionalInfo = { 1, 2, 3 };
    log.WriteEvent(info3, addionalInfo);
}
```

 For the message identifiers, it is useful to define a class with const *values that provide
a more meaningful name for the identifiers in the application.*

You can read the event log entries with the Event Viewer.

PERFORMANCE MONITORING

Performance monitoring can be used to get information about the normal behavior of applications. Performance
monitoring is a great tool that helps you understand the workload of the system and observe changes and trends,
particularly in applications running on the server.

Microsoft Windows has many performance objects, such as `System`, `Memory`, `Objects`, `Process`,
`Processor`, `Thread`, `Cache`, and so on. Each of these objects has many counts to monitor. For example,
with the `Process` object, the user time, handle count, page faults, thread count, and so on can be monitored
for all processes or for specific process instances. Some applications, such as SQL Server, also add
application-specific objects.

Performance-Monitoring Classes

The `System.Diagnostics` namespace provides these classes for performance monitoring:

➤ `PerformanceCounter` can be used both to monitor counts and to write counts. New performance
   categories can also be created with this class.

➤ `PerformanceCounterCategory` enables you to step through all existing categories, as well as create
   new ones. You can programmatically get all the counters in a category.

➤ `PerformanceCounterInstaller` is used for the installation of performance counters. Its use is
   similar to that of the `EventLogInstaller` discussed previously.

Performance Counter Builder

The sample application PerformanceCounterDemo is a simple Windows application with just two buttons to demonstrate writing performance counts. With the handler of one button, a performance counter category is registered; with the handler of the other button, a performance counter value is written. In a similar way to the sample application, you can add performance counters to a Windows Service (see Chapter 25, "Windows Services"), to a network application (see Chapter 24, "Networking"), or to any other application from that you would like to receive live counts.

Using Visual Studio, you can create a new performance counter category by selecting the performance counters in the Server Explorer and by selecting the menu entry Create New Category on the context menu. This launches the Performance Counter Builder (see Figure 19-7).

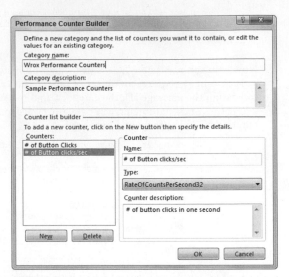

FIGURE 19-7

 To create a performance counter category with Visual Studio, Visual Studio must be started in elevated mode.

Set the name of the performance counter category to `Wrox Performance Counters`. The following table shows all performance counters of the quote service.

NAME	DESCRIPTION	TYPE
# of button clicks	Total # of button clicks	`NumberOfItems32`
# of button clicks/sec	# of button clicks in one second	`RateOfCountsPerSecond32`
# of mouse move events	Total # of mouse move events	`NumberOfItems32`
# of mouse move events/sec	# of mouse move events in one second	`RateOfCountsPerSecond32`

The Performance Counter Builder writes the configuration to the performance database. This can also be done dynamically by using the `Create()` method of the `PerformanceCounterCategory` class in the `System.Diagnostics` namespace. An installer for other systems can easily be added later using Visual Studio.

The following code snippet shows how a performance category can be added programmatically. With the tool from Visual Studio, you can only create a global performance category that doesn't have different values for different processes of running applications. Creating a performance category programmatically allows you to monitor performance counts from different applications, which is also done here.

First, a `const` for the category name is defined, as well as `SortedList<TKey, TValue>`, which contains the names of the performance counts:

```
private const string perfomanceCounterCategoryName = "Wrox Performance Counters";
private SortedList<string, Tuple<string, string>> perfCountNames;
```

code snippet PerformanceCounterDemo/MainWindow.xaml.cs

The list of the `perfCountNames` variable is filled in within the method `InitializePerformanceCountNames()`. The value of the sorted list is defined as `Tuple<string, string>` to define both the name and the description of the performance counter.

```
private void InitializePerfomanceCountNames()
{
    perfCountNames = new SortedList<string, Tuple<string, string>>();
    perfCountNames.Add("clickCount",
        Tuple.Create("# of button Clicks", "Total # of button clicks"));
    perfCountNames.Add("clickSec",
        Tuple.Create("# of button clicks/sec",
                     "# of mouse button clicks in one second"));
    perfCountNames.Add("mouseCount",
        Tuple.Create("# of mouse move events",
                     "Total # of mouse move events"));
    perfCountNames.Add("mouseSec",
        Tuple.Create("# of mouse move events/sec",
                     "# of mouse move events in one second"));
}
```

code snippet PerformanceCounterDemo/MainWindow.xaml.cs

The performance counter category is created next, in the method `OnRegisterCounts`. After a check to verify that the category does not already exist, an array of `CounterCreationData` is created that is filled with the types and names of the performance counts. Next, `PerformanceCounterCategory.Create()` creates the new category. `PerformanceCounterCategoryType.MultiInstance` defines that the counts are not global but that different values for different instances can exist.

```
private void OnRegisterCounts(object sender, RoutedEventArgs e)
{
    if (!PerformanceCounterCategory.Exists(
        perfomanceCounterCategoryName))
    {

        var counterCreationData = new CounterCreationData[4];
        counterCreationData[0] = new CounterCreationData
        {
            CounterName = perfCountNames["clickCount"].Item1,
            CounterType = PerformanceCounterType.NumberOfItems32,
            CounterHelp = perfCountNames["clickCount"].Item2
        };
        counterCreationData[1] = new CounterCreationData
        {
            CounterName = perfCountNames["clickSec"].Item1,
            CounterType = PerformanceCounterType.RateOfCountsPerSecond32,
            CounterHelp = perfCountNames["clickSec"].Item2,
        };
        counterCreationData[2] = new CounterCreationData
        {
            CounterName = perfCountNames["mouseCount"].Item1,
            CounterType = PerformanceCounterType.NumberOfItems32,
            CounterHelp = perfCountNames["mouseCount"].Item2,
        };
        counterCreationData[3] = new CounterCreationData
        {
            CounterName = perfCountNames["mouseSec"].Item1,
            CounterType = PerformanceCounterType.RateOfCountsPerSecond32,
            CounterHelp = perfCountNames["mouseSec"].Item2,
        };
```

```
var counters =
    new CounterCreationDataCollection(counterCreationData);

var category = PerformanceCounterCategory.Create(
    perfomanceCounterCategoryName,
    "Sample Counters for Professional C#",
    PerformanceCounterCategoryType.MultiInstance,
    counters);

MessageBox.Show(String.Format(
                "category {0} successfully created",
                category.CategoryName));
}
```

code snippet PerformanceCounterDemo/MainWindow.xaml.cs

Adding PerformanceCounter Components

With Windows Forms or Windows Service applications, you can add PerformanceCounter components from the toolbox or from the Server Explorer with drag and drop to the designer surface.

With WPF applications that's not possible. However, it's not a lot of work to define the performance counters manually, as this is done with the method InitializePerformanceCounts(). Here, the CategoryName for all performance counts is set from the const string performanceCounterCategoryName; the CounterName is set from the sorted list. Because the application writes performance counts, the ReadOnly property must be set to false. When writing an application that just reads performance counts for display purposes, you can use the default value of the ReadOnly property, which is true. The InstanceName of the PerformanceCounter object is set to an application name. If the counters are configured to be global counts, the InstanceName may not be set.

```
private PerformanceCounter performanceCounterButtonClicks;
private PerformanceCounter performanceCounterButtonClicksPerSec;
private PerformanceCounter performanceCounterMouseMoveEvents;
private PerformanceCounter performanceCounterMouseMoveEventsPerSec;

private void InitializePerformanceCounts()
{
    performanceCounterButtonClicks = new PerformanceCounter
    {
        CategoryName = perfomanceCounterCategoryName,
        CounterName = perfCountNames["clickCount"].Item1,
        ReadOnly = false,
        MachineName = ".",
        InstanceLifetime = PerformanceCounterInstanceLifetime.Process,
        InstanceName = this.instanceName
    };
    performanceCounterButtonClicksPerSec = new PerformanceCounter
    {
        CategoryName = perfomanceCounterCategoryName,
        CounterName = perfCountNames["clickSec"].Item1,
        ReadOnly = false,
        MachineName = ".",
        InstanceLifetime = PerformanceCounterInstanceLifetime.Process,
        InstanceName = this.instanceName
    };
    performanceCounterMouseMoveEvents = new PerformanceCounter
    {
        CategoryName = perfomanceCounterCategoryName,
        CounterName =  perfCountNames["mouseCount"].Item1,
```

```
                        ReadOnly = false,
                        MachineName = ".",
                        InstanceLifetime = PerformanceCounterInstanceLifetime.Process,
                        InstanceName = this.instanceName
                    };
                performanceCounterMouseMoveEventsPerSec = new PerformanceCounter
                    {
                        CategoryName = perfomanceCounterCategoryName,
                        CounterName =  perfCountNames["mouseSec"].Item1,
                        ReadOnly = false,
                        MachineName = ".",
                        InstanceLifetime = PerformanceCounterInstanceLifetime.Process,
                        InstanceName = this.instanceName
                    };
            }
```

code snippet PerformanceCounterDemo/MainWindow.xaml.cs

For the calculation of the performance values, you need to add the fields `clickCountPerSec` and `mouseMoveCountPerSec`:

```
    public partial class MainWindow : Window
    {
        // Performance monitoring counter values
        private int clickCountPerSec = 0;
        private int mouseMoveCountPerSec = 0;
```

Add an event handler to the `Click` event of the button and an event handler to the `MouseMove` event to the button, and add the following code to the handlers:

```
    private void OnButtonClick(object sender, RoutedEventArgs e)
    {
        this.performanceCounterButtonClicks.Increment();
        this.clickCountPerSec++;
    }

    private void OnMouseMove(object sender, MouseEventArgs e)
    {

        this.performanceCounterMouseMoveEvents.Increment();
        this.mouseMoveCountPerSec++;
    }
```

The `Increment()` method of the `PerformanceCounter` object increments the counter by one. If you need to increment the counter by more than one, for example, to add information about a byte count sent or received, you can use the `IncrementBy()` method. For the performance counts that show the value in seconds, just the two variables, `clickCountPerSec` and `mouseMovePerSec`, are incremented.

To show updated values every second, add a `DispatcherTimer` to the members of the `MainWindow`:

```
    private DispatcherTimer timer;
```

This timer is configured and started in the constructor. The `DispatcherTimer` class is a timer from the namespace `System.Windows.Threading`. For other than WPF applications, you can use other timers that are discussed in Chapter 20, "Threads, Tasks, and Synchronization." The code that is invoked by the timer is defined with an anonymous method.

```
    public MainWindow()
    {
        InitializeComponent();
        InitializePerfomanceCountNames();
        InitializePerformanceCounts();
        if (PerformanceCounterCategory.Exists(perfomanceCounterCategoryName))
```

```
            {
                buttonCount.IsEnabled = true;
                timer = new DispatcherTimer(TimeSpan.FromSeconds(1),
                    DispatcherPriority.Background,
                    delegate
                    {
                        this.performanceCounterButtonClicksPerSec.RawValue =
                            this.clickCountPerSec;
                        this.clickCountPerSec = 0;
                        this.performanceCounterMouseMoveEventsPerSec.RawValue =
                            this.mouseMoveCountPerSec;
                        this.mouseMoveCountPerSec = 0;
                    },
                    Dispatcher.CurrentDispatcher);
                timer.Start();
            }
        }
```

perfmon.exe

Now you can monitor the application. You can start the Performance Monitor from the Administrative Tools. Within the Performance Monitor, click the + button in the toolbar; there, you can add performance counts. Wrox Performance Counters shows up as a performance object. All the counters that have been configured appear in the counter list, as shown in Figure 19-8.

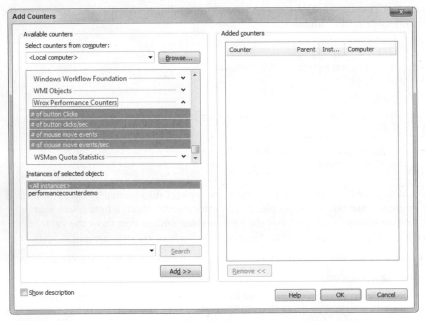

FIGURE 19-8

After you have added the counters to the performance monitor, you can see the actual values of the service over time (see Figure 19-9). Using this performance tool, you can also create log files to analyze the performance at a later time.

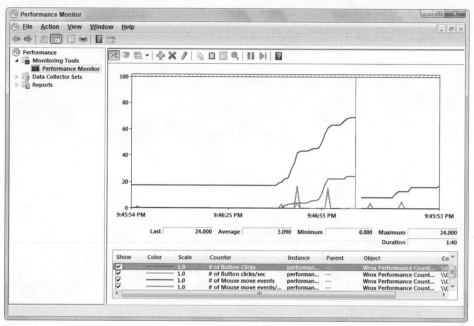

FIGURE 19-9

SUMMARY

In this chapter, you have seen tracing and logging facilities that can help you find intermediate problems in your applications. You should plan early, building these features into your applications. This will help you avoid many troubleshooting problems later.

With tracing, you can write debugging messages to an application that can also be used for the final product delivered. If there are problems, you can turn tracing on by changing configuration values, and find the issues.

Event logging provides information to the system administrator to help find some of the critical issues with the application. Performance monitoring helps in analyzing the load from applications and in planning in advance for resources that might be required.

In the next chapter you learn all about writing multithreaded applications.

20

Threads, Tasks, and Synchronization

WHAT'S IN THIS CHAPTER?

- ➤ An overview of threading
- ➤ Lightweight threading using delegates
- ➤ `Thread` class and thread pools
- ➤ Tasks
- ➤ `Parallel` class
- ➤ Cancellation framework
- ➤ Threading issues
- ➤ Synchronization techniques
- ➤ Timers
- ➤ Event-based asynchronous pattern

There are several reasons for using threading. Suppose that you are making a network call from an application that might take some time. You don't want to stall the user interface and just let the user wait until the response is returned from the server. The user could perform some other actions in the meantime or even cancel the request that was sent to the server. Using threads can help.

For all activities that require a wait — for example, because of file, database, or network access — a new thread can be started to fulfill other tasks at the same time. Even if you have only processing-intensive tasks to do, threading can help. Multiple threads of a single process can run on different CPUs, or, nowadays, on different cores of a multiple-core CPU, at the same time.

You must be aware of some issues when running multiple threads, however. Because they can run during the same time, you can easily get into problems if the threads access the same data. You must implement synchronization mechanisms.

This chapter provides the foundation you will need when programming applications with multiple threads.

OVERVIEW

A thread is an independent stream of instructions in a program. All your C# programs up to this point have one entry point — the `Main()` method. Execution starts with the first statement in the `Main()` method and continues until that method returns.

This program structure is all very well for programs in which there is one identifiable sequence of tasks, but often a program needs to do more than one thing at the same time. Threads are important both for client-side and for server-side applications. While you type C# code in the Visual Studio editor, the code is analyzed to underline missing semicolons or other syntax errors. This is done by a background thread. The same thing is done by the spell checker in Microsoft Word. One thread is waiting for input from the user, while the other does some background research. A third thread can store the written data in an interim file, while another one downloads some additional data from the Internet.

In an application that is running on the server, one thread, the listener thread, waits for a request from a client. As soon as the request comes in, the request is forwarded to a separate worker thread, which continues the communication with the client. The listener thread immediately comes back to get the next request from the next client.

A process contains resources, such as Window handles, handles to the file system, or other kernel objects. Every process has virtual memory allocated. A process contains at least one thread. The operating system schedules threads. A thread has a priority, a program counter for the program location where it is actually processing, and a stack in which to store its local variables. Every thread has its own stack, but the memory for the program code and the heap are shared among all threads of a single process. This makes communication among threads of one process fast — the same virtual memory is addressed by all threads of a process. However, this also makes things difficult because multiple threads can change the same memory location.

A process manages resources, which include virtual memory and Window handles, and contains at least one thread. A thread is required to run the program.

ASYNCHRONOUS DELEGATES

A simple way to create a thread is by defining a delegate and invoking the delegate asynchronously. In Chapter 8, "Delegates, Lambdas, and Events," you saw delegates as type-safe references to methods. The `Delegate` class also supports invoking the methods asynchronously. Behind the scenes, the `Delegate` class creates a thread that fulfills the task.

The delegate uses a thread pool for asynchronous tasks. Thread pools are discussed later in this chapter.

To demonstrate the asynchronous features of delegates, start with a method that takes a while to complete. The method `TakesAWhile()` needs at least the number of milliseconds passed with the second argument to finish because of the `Thread.Sleep()` method:

```
static int TakesAWhile(int data, int ms)
{
    Console.WriteLine("TakesAWhile started");
    Thread.Sleep(ms);
    Console.WriteLine("TakesAWhile completed");
    return ++data;
}
```

code snippet AsyncDelegate/Program.cs

To invoke this method from a delegate, a delegate with the same parameter and return types must be defined, as shown by the delegate `TakesAWhileDelegate`:

```
public delegate int TakesAWhileDelegate(int data, int ms);
```

Now you can use different techniques, invoking the delegate asynchronously and having the result returned.

Polling

One technique is to poll and check if the delegate has already finished its work. The created `delegate` class provides the method `BeginInvoke()`, where you can pass the input parameters defined with the delegate type. `BeginInvoke()` always has two additional parameters of type `AsyncCallback` and `object`, which are discussed later. What's important now is the return type, `BeginInvoke(): IAsyncResult`. With `IAsyncResult`, you can get information about the delegate, and also verify if the delegate has already finished its work, as is done with the `IsCompleted` property. The main thread of the program continues the `while` loop as long as the delegate hasn't completed its work.

```
static void Main()
{
    // synchronous method call
    // TakesAWhile(1, 3000);

    // asynchronous by using a delegate
    TakesAWhileDelegate d1 = TakesAWhile;

    IAsyncResult ar = d1.BeginInvoke(1, 3000, null, null);
    while (!ar.IsCompleted)
    {
        // doing something else in the main thread
        Console.Write(".");
        Thread.Sleep(50);
    }
    int result = d1.EndInvoke(ar);
    Console.WriteLine("result: {0}", result);
}
```

code snippet Async Delegate/Program.cs

When you run the application, you can see the main thread and the thread of the delegate running concurrently, and the main thread stops looping after the delegate thread completes:

```
.TakesAWhile started
..TakesAWhile completed
result: 2
```

Instead of examining if the delegate is completed, you can just invoke the `EndInvoke()` method of the delegate type after you are finished with the work that can be done by the main thread. `EndInvoke()` itself waits until the delegate has completed its work.

> *If you don't wait for the delegate to complete its work and end the main thread before the delegate is finished, the thread of the delegate will be stopped.*

Wait Handle

Another way to wait for the result from the asynchronous delegate is by using the wait handle that is associated with `IAsyncResult`. You can access the wait handle with the `AsyncWaitHandle` property. This property returns an object of type `WaitHandle`, where you can wait for the delegate thread to finish its work. The method `WaitOne()` accepts a timeout with the optional first parameter, where you can define the maximum time you want to wait; here, it is set to 50 milliseconds. If a timeout occurs, `WaitOne()` returns `false` and the `while` loop continues. If the wait is successful, the `while` loop is exited with a break, and the result is received with the delegate `EndInvoke()` method. From the UI standpoint the result is similar to the previous sample; just the wait is done in a different manner.

```
static void Main()
{
    TakesAWhileDelegate d1 = TakesAWhile;

    IAsyncResult ar = d1.BeginInvoke(1, 3000, null, null);
    while (true)
    {
        Console.Write(".");
        if (ar.AsyncWaitHandle.WaitOne(50, false))
        {
            Console.WriteLine("Can get the result now");
            break;
        }
    }
    int result = d1.EndInvoke(ar);
    Console.WriteLine("result: {0}", result);
}
```

 You can read more information about wait handles later in the "Synchronization" section of this chapter.

Asynchronous Callback

The third version of waiting for the result from the delegate uses an asynchronous callback. With the third parameter of `BeginInvoke()`, you can pass a method that fulfills the requirements of the `AsyncCallback` delegate. The `AsyncCallback` delegate defines a parameter of `IAsyncResult` and a `void` return type. Here, the address of the method `TakesAWhileCompleted` is assigned to the third parameter, which fulfills the requirements of the `AsyncCallback` delegate. For the last parameter, you can pass any object for accessing it from the callback method. It is useful to pass the delegate instance itself, so the callback method can use it to get the result of the asynchronous method.

The method `TakesAWhileCompleted()` is invoked as soon as the delegate `TakesAWhileDelegate` has completed its work. There is no need to wait for a result inside the main thread. However, you may not end the main thread before the work of the delegate threads is finished, unless you don't have a problem with delegate threads stopping when the main thread ends.

Available for download on Wrox.com

```
static void Main()
{
    TakesAWhileDelegate d1 = TakesAWhile;

    d1.BeginInvoke(1, 3000, TakesAWhileCompleted, d1);
    for (int i = 0; i < 100; i++)
    {
        Console.Write(".");
        Thread.Sleep(50);
    }
}
```

code snippet Async Delegate/Program.cs

The method `TakesAWhileCompleted()` is defined with the parameter and return type specified by the `AsyncCallback` delegate. The last parameter passed with the `BeginInvoke()` method can be read here by using `ar.AsyncState`. With the `TakesAWhileDelegate`, you can invoke the `EndInvoke` method to get the result.

```
static void TakesAWhileCompleted(IAsyncResult ar)
{
    if (ar == null) throw new ArgumentNullException("ar");

    TakesAWhileDelegate d1 = ar.AsyncState as TakesAWhileDelegate;
    Trace.Assert(d1 != null, "Invalid object type");

    int result = d1.EndInvoke(ar);
    Console.WriteLine("result: {0}", result);
}
```

 With a callback method, you need to pay attention to the fact that this method is invoked from the thread of the delegate and not from the main thread.

Instead of defining a separate method and passing it to the `BeginInvoke()` method, Lambda expressions can be used. The parameter `ar` is of type `IAsyncResult`. With the implementation, there is no need to assign a value to the last parameter of the `BeginInvoke()` method because the Lambda expression can directly access variable `d1` that is in the outer scope. However, the implementation block of the Lambda expression is still invoked from the thread of the delegate, which might not be clear immediately when defining the method this way.

```
static void Main()
{
    TakesAWhileDelegate d1 = TakesAWhile;
    d1.BeginInvoke(1, 3000,
        ar =>
        {
            int result = d1.EndInvoke(ar);
            Console.WriteLine("result: {0}", result);
        },
        null);
    for (int i = 0; i < 100; i++)
    {
        Console.Write(".");
        Thread.Sleep(50);
    }
}
```

The programming model and all of these options with asynchronous delegates — polling, wait handles, and asynchronous callbacks — are not only available with delegates. The same programming model — this is the asynchronous pattern — can be found in various places in the .NET Framework. For example, you can send an HTTP Web request asynchronously with the `BeginGetResponse()` method of the `HttpWebRequest` class. You can send an asynchronous request to the database with the `BeginExecuteReader()` of the `SqlCommand` class. The parameters are similar to those of the `BeginInvoke()` class of the delegate, and you can use the same mechanisms to get the result.

 `HttpWebRequest` *is covered in Chapter 24, "Networking," and* `SqlCommand` *is discussed in Chapter 30, "Core ADO.NET."*

Instead of using the delegate for creating threads, you can create threads with the `Thread` class, which is covered in the next section.

THE THREAD CLASS

With the `Thread` class, you can create and control threads. The code here is a very simple example of creating and starting a new thread. The constructor of the `Thread` class is overloaded to accept a delegate parameter of type `ThreadStart` or `ParameterizedThreadStart`. The `ThreadStart` delegate defines a method with a void return type and without arguments. After the `Thread` object is created, you can start the thread with the `Start()` method:

```csharp
using System;
using System.Threading;

namespace Wrox.ProCSharp.Threading
{
    class Program
    {
        static void Main()
        {
            var t1 = new Thread(ThreadMain);
            t1.Start();
            Console.WriteLine("This is the main thread.");
        }

        static void ThreadMain()
        {
            Console.WriteLine("Running in a thread.");
        }
    }
}
```

code snippet ThreadSamples/Program.cs

When you run the application, you get the output of the two threads:

```
This is the main thread.
Running in a thread.
```

There is no guarantee as to what output comes first. Threads are scheduled by the operating system; which thread comes first can be different each time.

You have seen how a Lambda expression can be used with an asynchronous delegate. You can use it with the `Thread` class as well by passing the implementation of the thread method to the argument of the `Thread` constructor:

```csharp
using System;
using System.Threading;

namespace Wrox.ProCSharp.Threading
{
    class Program
    {
        static void Main()
        {
            var t1 = new Thread(() => Console.WriteLine("running in a thread, id: {0}",
                                    Thread.CurrentThread.ManagedThreadId));
            t1.Start();
            Console.WriteLine("This is the main thread, id: {0}",
                            Thread.CurrentThread.ManagedThreadId);
        }
    }
}
```

With the output of the application, now you can also see the thread name and ID:

```
This is the main thread, id: 1
Running in a thread, id: 3.
```

Passing Data to Threads

There are two ways to pass some data to a thread. You can either use the `Thread` constructor with the `ParameterizedThreadStart` delegate, or you can create a custom class and define the method of the thread as an instance method so that you can initialize data of the instance before starting the thread.

For passing data to a thread, a class or struct that holds the data is needed. Here, the struct `Data` containing a string is defined, but you can pass any object you want:

```
public struct Data
{
    public string Message;
}
```

code snippet ThreadSamples/Program.cs

If the `ParameterizedThreadStart` delegate is used, the entry point of the thread must have a parameter of type object and a void return type. The object can be cast to what it is, and here the message is written to the console:

```
static void ThreadMainWithParameters(object o)
{
    Data d = (Data)o;
    Console.WriteLine("Running in a thread, received {0}", d.Message);
}
```

With the constructor of the `Thread` class, you can assign the new entry point `ThreadMainWithParameters` and invoke the `Start()` method, passing the variable `d`:

```
static void Main()
{
    var d = new Data { Message = "Info" };
    var t2 = new Thread(ThreadMainWithParameters);
    t2.Start(d);
}
```

Another way to pass data to the new thread is to define a class (see the class `MyThread`), where you define the fields that are needed as well as the main method of the thread as an instance method of the class:

```
public class MyThread
{
    private string data;

    public MyThread(string data)
    {
        this.data = data;
    }

    public void ThreadMain()
    {
        Console.WriteLine("Running in a thread, data: {0}", data);
    }
}
```

This way, you can create an object of `MyThread` and pass the object and the method `ThreadMain()` to the constructor of the `Thread` class. The thread can access the data.

```
var obj = new MyThread("info");
var t3 = new Thread(obj.ThreadMain);
t3.Start();
```

Background Threads

The process of the application keeps running as long as at least one foreground thread is running. If more than one foreground thread is running and the `Main()` method ends, the process of the application remains active until all foreground threads finish their work.

A thread you create with the `Thread` class, by default, is a foreground thread. Thread pool threads are always background threads.

When you create a thread with the `Thread` class, you can define whether it should be a foreground or background thread by setting the property `IsBackground`. The `Main()` method sets the `IsBackground` property of the thread `t1` to `false` (which is the default). After starting the new thread, the main thread just writes an end message to the console. The new thread writes a start and an end message, and in between it sleeps for 3 seconds. The 3 seconds provide a good chance for the main thread to finish before the new thread completes its work.

Available for
download on
Wrox.com

```
class Program
{
    static void Main()
    {
        var t1 = new Thread(ThreadMain)
            { Name = "MyNewThread", IsBackground = false };
        t1.Start();
        Console.WriteLine("Main thread ending now.");
    }

    static void ThreadMain()
    {
        Console.WriteLine("Thread {0} started", Thread.CurrentThread.Name);
        Thread.Sleep(3000);
        Console.WriteLine("Thread {0} completed", Thread.CurrentThread.Name);
    }
}
```

code snippet ThreadSamples/Program.cs

When you start the application, you will still see the completion message written to the console, although the main thread completed its work earlier. The reason is that the new thread is a foreground thread as well.

```
Main thread ending now.
Thread MyNewThread1 started
Thread MyNewThread1 completed
```

If you change the `IsBackground` property used to start the new thread to `true`, the result shown at the console is different. You can have the same result as shown here — the start message of the new thread is shown but never the end message. You might not see the start message either, if the thread was prematurely ended before it had a chance to kick off.

```
Main thread ending now.
Thread MyNewThread1 started
```

Background threads are very useful for background tasks. For example, when you close the Word application, it doesn't make sense for the spell checker to keep its process running. The spell checker thread can be killed when the application is closed. However, the thread organizing the Outlook message store should remain active until it is finished, even if Outlook is closed.

Thread Priority

You have learned that the operating system schedules threads. You have had a chance to influence the scheduling by assigning a priority to the thread.

Before changing the priority, you must understand the thread scheduler. The operating system schedules threads based on a priority, and the thread with the highest priority is scheduled to run in the CPU. A thread stops running and gives up the CPU if it waits for a resource. There are several reasons why a thread must wait; for example, in response to a sleep instruction, while waiting for disk I/O to complete, while waiting for a network packet to arrive, and so on. If the thread does not give up the CPU on its own, it is preempted by the thread scheduler. If a thread does have a *time quantum,* it can use the CPU continuously. If there are multiple threads running with the same priority waiting to get the CPU, the thread scheduler uses a *round-robin* scheduling principle to give the CPU to one thread after another. If a thread is preempted, it goes last to the queue.

The time quantum and round-robin principles are used only if multiple threads are running at the same priority. The priority is dynamic. If a thread is CPU-intensive (requires the CPU continuously without waiting for resources), the priority is lowered to the level of the base priority that is defined with the thread. If a thread is waiting for a resource, the thread gets a priority boost and the priority is increased. Because of the boost, there is a good chance that the thread gets the CPU the next time that the wait ends.

With the Thread class, you can influence the base priority of the thread by setting the Priority property. The Priority property requires a value that is defined by the ThreadPriority enumeration. The levels defined are Highest, AboveNormal, Normal, BelowNormal, and Lowest.

Be careful when giving a thread a higher priority, because this may decrease the chance for other threads to run. You can change the priority for a short time if necessary.

Controlling Threads

The thread is created by invoking the Start() method of a Thread object. However, after invoking the Start() method, the new thread is still not in the Running state, but in the Unstarted state. The thread changes to the Running state as soon as the operating system thread scheduler selects the thread to run. You can read the current state of a thread by reading the property Thread.ThreadState.

With the Thread.Sleep() method, a thread goes into the WaitSleepJoin state and waits until it is woken up again after the time span defined with the Sleep() method has elapsed.

To stop another thread, you can invoke the method Thread.Abort(). When this method is called, an exception of type ThreadAbortException is thrown in the thread that receives the abort. With a handler to catch this exception, the thread can do some cleanup before it ends. The thread also has a chance to continue running after receiving the ThreadAbortException as a result of invoking Thread.ResetAbort(). The state of the thread receiving the abort request changes from AbortRequested to the Aborted state if the thread does not reset the abort.

If you need to wait for a thread to end, you can invoke the Thread.Join() method. Thread.Join() blocks the current thread and sets it to the WaitSleepJoin state until the thread that is joined is completed.

THREAD POOLS

Creating threads takes time. When you have different short tasks to do, you can create a number of threads in advance and send requests as they should be done. It would be nice if this number increased as more threads were needed and decreased as needed to release resources.

There is no need to create such a list on your own. The list is managed by the ThreadPool class. This class increases and decreases the number of threads in the pool as they are needed, up to the maximum number of threads. The maximum number of threads in a pool is configurable. With a dual-core CPU, the default number is set to 1,023 worker threads and 1,000 I/O threads. You can specify the minimum number of threads that should be started immediately when the pool is created and the maximum number of threads that are available in the pool. If there are more jobs to process, and the maximum number of threads in the pool has already been reached, the newest jobs are queued and must wait for a thread to complete its work.

The following sample application first reads the maximum number of worker and I/O threads and writes this information to the console. Then, in a for loop, the method JobForAThread() is assigned to a thread from the thread pool by invoking the method ThreadPool.QueueUserWorkItem() and passing a delegate of type WaitCallback. The thread pool receives this request and selects one of the threads from the pool to invoke the method. If the pool is not already running, the pool is created and the first thread is started. If the pool is already running and one thread is free to do the task, the job is forwarded to that thread.

```
using System;
using System.Threading;

namespace Wrox.ProCSharp.Threading
{
    class Program
    {
        static void Main()
        {
            int nWorkerThreads;
            int nCompletionPortThreads;
            ThreadPool.GetMaxThreads(out nWorkerThreads, out nCompletionPortThreads);
            Console.WriteLine("Max worker threads: {0}, " +
                              "I/O completion threads: {1}",
                              nWorkerThreads, nCompletionPortThreads);

            for (int i = 0; i < 5; i++)
            {
                ThreadPool.QueueUserWorkItem(JobForAThread);
            }
            Thread.Sleep(3000);
        }

        static void JobForAThread(object state)
        {
            for (int i = 0; i < 3; i++)
            {
                Console.WriteLine("loop {0}, running inside pooled thread {1}",
                    i, Thread.CurrentThread.ManagedThreadId);
                Thread.Sleep(50);
            }
        }
    }
}
```

code snippet ThreadPoolSamples/Program.cs

When you run the application, you can see that 50 worker threads are possible with the current settings. The five jobs are processed by just two pooled threads. Your experience may be different, and you can also change the sleep time with the job and the number of jobs to process to get very different results.

```
Max worker threads: 1023, I/O completion threads: 1000
loop 0, running inside pooled thread 4
loop 0, running inside pooled thread 3
loop 1, running inside pooled thread 4
loop 1, running inside pooled thread 3
loop 2, running inside pooled thread 4
loop 2, running inside pooled thread 3
loop 0, running inside pooled thread 4
loop 0, running inside pooled thread 3
loop 1, running inside pooled thread 4
loop 1, running inside pooled thread 3
loop 2, running inside pooled thread 4
loop 2, running inside pooled thread 3
loop 0, running inside pooled thread 4
loop 1, running inside pooled thread 4
loop 2, running inside pooled thread 4
```

Thread pools are very easy to use. However, there are some restrictions:

➤ All thread pool threads are background threads. If all foreground threads of a process are finished, all background threads are stopped. You cannot change a pooled thread to a foreground thread.

➤ You cannot set the priority or name of a pooled thread.

➤ For COM objects, all pooled threads are multithreaded apartment (MTA) threads. Many COM objects require a single-threaded apartment (STA) thread.

➤ Use pooled threads only for a short task. If a thread should run all the time (for example, the spell-checker thread of Word), create a thread with the Thread class.

TASKS

.NET 4 includes the new namespace System.Threading.Tasks, which contains classes to abstract threading functionality. Behind the scenes, ThreadPool is used. A *task* represents some unit of work that should be done. This unit of work can run in a separate thread; and it is also possible to start a task in a synchronized manner, which results in a wait for the calling thread. With tasks, you have an abstraction layer but also a lot of control over the underlying threads.

Tasks allow much more flexibility in organizing the work you need to do. For example, you can define continuation work — what should be done after a task is complete. This can be differentiated whether the task was successful or not. Also, you can organize tasks in a hierarchy. For example, a parent task can create new children tasks. This can create a dependency, so that canceling a parent task also cancels its child tasks.

Starting Tasks

To start a task, you can use either the TaskFactory or the constructor of the Task and the Start() method. The Task constructor just gives you more flexibility in creating the task.

When starting a task, an instance of the Task class can be created and the code that should run can be assigned, with an Action or Action<object> delegate, with either no parameters or one object parameter. This is similar to what you saw with the Thread class. Here, a method is defined without a parameter. In the implementation, the ID of the task is written to the console.

Available for download on Wrox.com

```
static void TaskMethod()
{
    Console.WriteLine("running in a task");
    Console.WriteLine("Task id: {0}", Task.CurrentId);
}
```

code snippet TaskSamples/Program.cs

In the previous code, you can see different ways to start a new task. The first way is with an instantiated TaskFactory, where the method TaskMethod is passed to the StartNew() method, and the task is immediately started. The second approach uses the constructor of the Task class. When the Task object is instantiated, the task does not run immediately. Instead, it is given the status Created. The task is then started by calling the Start() method of the Task class. With the Task class, instead of invoking the Start() method, you can invoke the RunSynchronously() method. This way, the task is started as well, but it is running in the current thread of the caller, and the caller needs to wait until the task finishes. By default, the task runs asynchronously.

```
// using task factory
TaskFactory tf = new TaskFactory();
Task t1 = tf.StartNew(TaskMethod);

// using the task factory via a task
Task t2 = Task.Factory.StartNew(TaskMethod);

// using Task constructor
Task t3 = new Task(TaskMethod);
t3.Start();
```

With both the Task constructor and the StartNew() method of the TaskFactory, you can pass values from the enumeration TaskCreationOptions. Setting the option LongRunning, you can inform the task scheduler that the task takes a long time, so the scheduler will more likely use a new thread. If the task should be attached to the parent task and, thus, should be canceled if the parent were canceled, set the option `AttachToParent`. The value `PreferFairness` means that the scheduler should take first tasks that are already waiting. That's not the default case if a task is created within another task. If tasks create additional work using child tasks, child tasks are preferred to other tasks. They are not waiting last in the thread pool queue for the work to be done. If these tasks should be handled in a fair manner to all other tasks, set the option to `PreferFairness`.

```
Task t4 = new Task(TaskMethod, TaskCreationOptions.PreferFairness);
t4.Start();
```

Continuation Tasks

With tasks, you can specify that after a task is finished another specific task should start to run, for example, a new task that uses a result from the previous one or that should do some cleanup if the previous task failed.

Whereas the task handler has either no parameter or one object parameter, the continuation handler has a parameter of type `Task`. Here, you can access information about the originating task.

Available for
download on
Wrox.com

```
static void DoOnFirst()
{
    Console.WriteLine("doing some task {0}", Task.CurrentId);
    Thread.Sleep(3000);
}

static void DoOnSecond(Task t)
{
    Console.WriteLine("task {0} finished", t.Id);
    Console.WriteLine("this task id {0}", Task.CurrentId);
    Console.WriteLine("do some cleanup");
    Thread.Sleep(3000);
}
```

code snippet TaskSamples/Program.cs

A continuation task is defined by invoking the `ContinueWith` method on a task. You could also use the `TaskFactory` for this. `t1.OnContinueWith(DoOnSecond)` means that a new task invoking the method `DoOnSecond()` should be started as soon as the task `t1` is finished. You can start multiple tasks when one task is finished, and a continuation task can also have another continuation task, as this example demonstrates.

```
Task t1 = new Task(DoOnFirst);
Task t2 = t1.ContinueWith(DoOnSecond);
Task t3 = t1.ContinueWith(DoOnSecond);
Task t4 = t2.ContinueWith(DoOnSecond);
```

The continuation tasks so far were always started when the previous task was finished, no matter how the previous task was finished. With values from `TaskContinuationOptions`, you can define that a continuation task should only start if the originating task was successful (or faulted). Some of the possible values are `OnlyOnFaulted`, `NotOnFaulted`, `OnlyOnCanceled`, `NotOnCanceled`, and `OnlyOnRanToCompletion`.

```
Task t5 = t1.ContinueWith(DoOnError,
                          TaskContinuationOptions.OnlyOnFaulted);
```

Task Hierarchies

With task continuations, one task is started after another. Tasks can also form a hierarchy. When a task itself starts a new task, a parent/child hierarchy is started.

In the code snippet that follows, within the task of the parent, a new task is created. The code to create a child task is the same as creating a parent task. The only difference is that the task is created from within another task.

```
static void ParentAndChild()
{
    var parent = new Task(ParentTask);
    parent.Start();
    Thread.Sleep(2000);
    Console.WriteLine(parent.Status);
    Thread.Sleep(4000);
    Console.WriteLine(parent.Status);

}
static void ParentTask()
{
    Console.WriteLine("task id {0}", Task.CurrentId);
    var child = new Task(ChildTask);
    child.Start();
    Thread.Sleep(1000);
    Console.WriteLine("parent started child");
}
static void ChildTask()
{
    Console.WriteLine("child");
    Thread.Sleep(5000);
    Console.WriteLine("child finished");
}
```

code snippet TaskSamples/Program.cs

If the parent task is finished before the child task, the status of the parent task is shown as WaitingForChildrenToComplete. The parent task is completed with the status RanToCompletion as soon as all children are completed as well. Of course, this is not valid if the parent creates a task with the TaskCreationOption DetachedFromParent.

Canceling a parent task also cancels the children. The cancellation framework is discussed later in this chapter.

Results from Tasks

When a task is finished, it can write some stateful information to a shared object. Such a shared object must be thread-safe. Another option is to use a task that returns a result. With the generic version of the Task class, it is possible to define the type that is returned with a task that returns a result.

A method that is invoked by a task to return a result can be declared with any return type. The example method TaskWithResult returns two int values with the help of a Tuple. The input of the method can be void or of type object, as shown here.

```
static Tuple<int, int> TaskWithResult(object division)
{
    Tuple<int, int> div = (Tuple<int, int>)division;
    int result = div.Item1 / div.Item2;
    int reminder = div.Item1 % div.Item2;
    Console.WriteLine("task creates a result...");

    return Tuple.Create<int, int>(result, reminder);
}
```

code snippet TaskSamples/Program.cs

Tuples are explained in Chapter 6, "Arrays and Tuples."

When defining a task to invoke the method `TaskWithResult`, the generic class `Task<TResult>` is used. The generic parameter defines the return type. With the constructor, the method is passed to the `Func` delegate, and the second parameter defines the input value. Because this task needs two input values in the `object` parameter, a tuple is created as well. Next, the task is started. The `Result` property of the `Task` instance `t1` blocks and waits until the task is completed. Upon task completion, the `Result` property contains the result from the task.

```
var t1 = new Task<Tuple<int,int>>(TaskWithResult,
                                  Tuple.Create<int, int>(8, 3));
t1.Start();
Console.WriteLine(t1.Result);
t1.Wait();
Console.WriteLine("result from task: {0} {1}", t1.Result.Item1,
                 t1.Result.Item2);
```

PARALLEL CLASS

Another abstraction of threads that is new with .NET 4 is the `Parallel` class. This class defines static methods for a parallel `for` and `foreach`. With the language defined for `for` and `foreach`, the loop is run from one thread. The `Parallel` class uses multiple tasks and, thus, multiple threads for this job.

While the `Parallel.For()` and `Parallel.ForEach()` methods invoke the same method several times, `Parallel.Invoke()` allows invoking different methods concurrently.

Looping with the Parallel.For Method

The `Parallel.For()` method is similar to the C# `for` loop statement to do a task a number of times. With the `Parallel.For()`, the iterations run in parallel. The order of iteration is not defined.

With the `For()` method, the first two parameters define the start and end of the loop. The sample has the iterations from 0 to 9. The third parameter is an `Action<int>` delegate. The integer parameter is the iteration of the loop that is passed to the method referenced by the delegate. The return type of `Parallel.For()` is the struct `ParallelLoopResult`, which provides information if the loop is completed.

Available for download on Wrox.com

```
ParallelLoopResult result =
    Parallel.For(0, 10, i =>
    {
        Console.WriteLine("{0}, task: {1}, thread: {2}", i,
            Task.CurrentId, Thread.CurrentThread.ManagedThreadId);
        Thread.Sleep(10);
    });
Console.WriteLine(result.IsCompleted);
```

code snippet ParallelSamples/Program.cs

In the body of the `Parallel.For()`, the index, task identifier, and thread identifier are written to the console. As you can see from this output, the order is not guaranteed. This run of the program had the order 0-5-1-6-2... with three tasks and three threads.

```
0, task: 1, thread: 1
5, task: 2, thread: 3
1, task: 3, thread: 4
6, task: 2, thread: 3
2, task: 1, thread: 1
4, task: 3, thread: 4
7, task: 2, thread: 3
3, task: 1, thread: 1
```

```
8, task: 3, thread: 4
9, task: 3, thread: 4
True
```

You can also break the `Parallel.For()` early. A method overload of the `For()` method accepts a third parameter of type `Action<int, ParallelLoopState>`. By defining a method with these parameters, you can influence the outcome of the loop by invoking the `Break()` or `Stop()` methods of the `ParallelLoopState`.

Remember, the order of iterations is not defined.

```
ParallelLoopResult result =
    Parallel.For(10, 40, (int i, ParallelLoopState pls) =>
        {
            Console.WriteLine("i: {0} task {1}", i, Task.CurrentId);
            Thread.Sleep(10);
            if (i > 15)
                pls.Break();
        });
    Console.WriteLine(result.IsCompleted);
    Console.WriteLine("lowest break iteration: {0}",
                result.LowestBreakIteration);
```

This run of the application demonstrates that the iteration breaks up with a value higher than 15, but other tasks can simultaneously run and tasks with other values can run. With the help of the `LowestBreakIteration` property, you can decide to ignore results from other tasks.

```
10 task 1
25 task 2
11 task 1
13 task 3
12 task 1
14 task 3
16 task 1
15 task 3
False
lowest break iteration: 16
```

`Parallel.For()` might use several threads to do the loops. If you need an initialization that should be done with every thread, you can use the `Parallel.For<TLocal>()` method. The generic version of the `For` method accepts — besides the `from` and `to` values — three delegate parameters. The first parameter is of type `Func<TLocal>`. Because the example here uses a string for `TLocal`, the method needs to be defined as `Func<string>`, a method returning a `string`. This method is invoked only once for each thread that is used to do the iterations.

The second delegate parameter defines the delegate for the body. In the example, the parameter is of type `Func<int, ParallelLoopState, string, string>`. The first parameter is the loop iteration; the second parameter, `ParallelLoopState`, allows for stopping the loop, as you saw earlier. With the third parameter, the body method receives the value that is returned from the init method. The body method also needs to return a value of the type that was defined with the generic `For` parameter.

The last parameter of the `For()` method specifies a delegate, `Action<TLocal>`; in the example, a string is received. This method again is called only once for each thread; this is a thread exit method.

```
Parallel.For<string>(0, 20,
    () =>
    {
        // invoked once for each thread
        Console.WriteLine("init thread {0}, task {1}",
            Thread.CurrentThread.ManagedThreadId, Task.CurrentId);
        return String.Format("t{0}",
            Thread.CurrentThread.ManagedThreadId);
    },
    (i, pls, str1) =>
```

```
    {
        // invoked for each member
        Console.WriteLine("body i {0} str1 {1} thread {2} task {3}", i, str1,
            Thread.CurrentThread.ManagedThreadId,
            Task.CurrentId);
        Thread.Sleep(10);
        return String.Format("i {0}", i);

    },
    (str1) =>
    {
        // final action on each thread
        Console.WriteLine("finally {0}", str1);
    });
```

The result of one time running this program is shown here:

```
init thread 1, task 1
body i 0 str1 t1 thread 1 task 1
body i 1 str1 i 0 thread 1 task 1
init thread 3, task 2
body i 10 str1 t3 thread 3 task 2
init thread 4, task 3
body i 3 str1 t4 thread 4 task 3
body i 2 str1 i 1 thread 1 task 1
body i 11 str1 i 10 thread 3 task 2
body i 4 str1 i 3 thread 4 task 3
body i 6 str1 i 2 thread 1 task 1
body i 12 str1 i 11 thread 3 task 2
body i 5 str1 i 4 thread 4 task 3
body i 7 str1 i 6 thread 1 task 1
body i 13 str1 i 12 thread 3 task 2
body i 17 str1 i 5 thread 4 task 3
body i 8 str1 i 7 thread 1 task 1
body i 14 str1 i 13 thread 3 task 2
body i 9 str1 i 8 thread 1 task 1
body i 18 str1 i 17 thread 4 task 3
body i 15 str1 i 14 thread 3 task 2
body i 19 str1 i 18 thread 4 task 3
finally i 9
body i 16 str1 i 15 thread 3 task 2
finally i 19
finally i 16
```

Looping with the Parallel.ForEach Method

Parallel.ForEach iterates through a collection implementing IEnumerable in a way similar to the foreach statement, but in an asynchronous manner. Again, the order is not guaranteed.

```
string[] data = {"zero", "one", "two", "three", "four",
                 "five", "six", "seven", "eight", "nine",
                 "ten", "eleven", "twelve"};

ParallelLoopResult result =
    Parallel.ForEach<string>(data, s =>
        {
            Console.WriteLine(s);
        });
```

code snippet ParallelSamples/Program.cs

If you need to break up the loop, you can use an overload of the `ForEach()` method with a `ParallelLoopState` parameter. You can do this in the same way as with the `For()` method you saw earlier. An overload of the `ForEach()` method can also be used to access an indexer to get the iteration number as shown.

```
Parallel.ForEach<string>(data,
    (s, pls, 1) =>
    {
        Console.WriteLine("{0} {1}", s, 1);

    });
```

Invoking Multiple Methods with the Parallel.Invoke Method

If multiple tasks should run in parallel, you can use the `Parallel.Invoke()` method. `Parallel.Invoke()` allows the passing of an array of `Action` delegates, where you can assign methods that should run. The sample code passes the `Foo` and `Bar` methods to be invoked in parallel.

```
static void ParallelInvoke()
{
    Parallel.Invoke(Foo, Bar);
}

static void Foo()
{
    Console.WriteLine("foo");
}

static void Bar()
{
    Console.WriteLine("bar");
}
```

code snippet ParallelSamples/Program.cs

CANCELLATION FRAMEWORK

.NET 4 includes a new cancellation framework to allow the canceling of long-running tasks in a standard manner. Every blocking call should support this mechanism. As of today, of course, not every blocking call implements this new technology, but more and more are doing so. Among the technologies that offer this mechanism already are tasks, concurrent collection classes, and Parallel LINQ, as well as several synchronization mechanisms.

The cancellation framework is based on cooperative behavior; it is not forceful. A long-running task checks if it is canceled and returns control.

A method that supports cancellation accepts a `CancellationToken` parameter. This class defines the property `IsCancellationRequested`, where a long operation can check if it should abort. Other ways for a long operation to check for cancellation are to use a `WaitHandle` property that is signaled when the token is canceled, or to use the `Register()` method. The `Register()` method accepts parameters of type `Action` and `ICancelableOperation`. The method that is referenced by the `Action` delegate is invoked when the token is canceled. This is similar to the `ICancelableOperation`, where the `Cancel()` method of an object implementing this interface is invoked when the cancellation is done.

Cancellation of Parallel.For

Let's start with a simple example using the `Parallel.For()` method. The `Parallel` class provides overloads for the `For()` method, where you can pass parameter of type `ParallelOptions`. With the `ParallelOptions`, you can pass a `CancellationToken`. The `CancellationToken` is generated by creating a `CancellationTokenSource`. `CancellationTokenSource` implements the interface `ICancelableOperation` and, thus, can be registered with the `CancellationToken` and allows cancellation with the `Cancel()` method. To cancel the parallel loop, a new task is created to invoke the `Cancel()` method of the `CancellationTokenSource` after 500 milliseconds.

Within the implementation of the `For()` loop, the `Parallel` class verifies the outcome of the `CancellationToken` and cancels the operation. Upon cancellation, the `For()` method throws an exception of type `OperationCanceledException`, which is caught in the example. With the `CancellationToken`, it is possible to register for information when the cancellation is done. This is accomplished by calling the `Register()` method and passing a delegate that is invoked on cancellation.

Available for
download on
Wrox.com

```
var cts = new CancellationTokenSource();
cts.Token.Register(() =>
    Console.WriteLine("*** token canceled"));

// start a task that sends a cancel after 500 ms
new Task(() =>
    {
        Thread.Sleep(500);
        cts.Cancel(false);
    }).Start();

try
{
    ParallelLoopResult result =
        Parallel.For(0, 100,
            new ParallelOptions()
            {
                CancellationToken = cts.Token,
            },
            x =>
            {
                Console.WriteLine("loop {0} started", x);
                int sum = 0;
                for (int i = 0; i < 100; i++)
                {
                    Thread.Sleep(2);
                    sum += i;
                }
                Console.WriteLine("loop {0} finished", x);
            });
}
catch (OperationCanceledException ex)
{
    Console.WriteLine(ex.Message);
}
```

code snippet CancellationSamples/Program.cs

When running the application, you will get output similar to the following. Iteration 0, 1, 25, 26, 50, 51, 75, and 76 were all started. This is on a system with a quad-core CPU. With the cancellation, all other iterations were canceled before starting. The iterations that were started are allowed to finish because cancellation is always done in a cooperative way so as to avoid the risk of resource leaks when iterations are canceled somewhere in between.

```
loop 0 started
loop 50 started
loop 25 started
loop 75 started
loop 50 finished
```

```
loop 25 finished
loop 0 finished
loop 1 started
loop 26 started
loop 51 started
loop 75 finished
loop 76 started
** token canceled
loop 1 finished
loop 51 finished
loop 26 finished
loop 76 finished
The operation was canceled.
```

Cancellation of Tasks

The same cancellation pattern is used with tasks. First, a new `CancellationTokenSource` is created. If you need just one cancellation token, you can use a default one by accessing `Task.Factory.CancellationToken`. Then, similar to the previous code, a new task is created that sends a cancel request to this `cancellationSource` by invoking the `Cancel()` method after 500 milliseconds. The task doing the major work within a loop receives the cancellation token via the `TaskFactory` object. The cancellation token is assigned to the `TaskFactory` by setting it in the constructor. This cancellation token is used by the task to check if cancellation is requested by checking the `IsCancellationRequested` property of the `CancellationToken`.

Available for download on Wrox.com

```
var cts = new CancellationTokenSource();
cts.Token.Register(() =>
    Console.WriteLine("*** task canceled"));


// start a task that sends a cancel to the
// cts after 500 ms
Task.Factory.StartNew(() =>
{
    Thread.Sleep(500);
    cts.Cancel();
});

var factory = new TaskFactory(cancellationSource.Token);
Task t1 = factory.StartNew(new Action<object>(f =>
    {
        Console.WriteLine("in task");
        for (int i = 0; i < 20; i++)
        {
            Thread.Sleep(100);
            CancellationToken ct = (f as TaskFactory).CancellationToken;
            if (ct.IsCancellationRequested)
            {
                Console.WriteLine("canceling was requested, " +
                    "canceling from within the task");
                ct.ThrowIfCancellationRequested();
                break;
            }
            Console.WriteLine("in loop");
        }
        Console.WriteLine("task finished without cancellation");
    }), factory, cts.Token);

try
{
```

```
        t1.Wait();
    }
    catch (Exception ex)
    {
        Console.WriteLine("exception: {0}, {1}", ex.GetType().Name,
            ex.Message);
        if (ex.InnerException != null)
            Console.WriteLine("inner exception: {0}, {1}",
                              ex.InnerException.GetType().Name,
                              ex.InnerException.Message);
    }
    Console.WriteLine("status of the task: {0}", t1.Status);
```

code snippet CancellationSamples/Program.cs

When running the application, you can see that the task starts, runs for a few loops, and gets the cancellation request. The task is canceled and throws a `TaskCanceledException`, which is initiated from the method call `ThrowIfCancellationRequested()`. With the caller waiting for the task, you can see that the exception `AggregateException` is caught and contains the inner exception `TaskCanceledException`. This is used for a hierarchy of cancellations, for example, if you run a `Parallel.For` within a task that is canceled as well. The final status of the task is `Canceled`.

```
in task
in loop
in loop
in loop
in loop
*** task canceled
canceling was requested, canceling from within the task
exception AggregateException, One or more errors occurred.
inner exception TaskCanceledException, A task was canceled.
status of the task: Canceled
```

THREADING ISSUES

Programming with multiple threads is not easy. When starting multiple threads that access the same data, you can get intermittent problems that are hard to find. This is the same if you use tasks, Parallel LINQ, or the `Parallel` class. To avoid getting into trouble, you must pay attention to synchronization issues and the problems that can happen with multiple threads. We discuss two in particular next: race conditions and deadlocks.

Race Condition

A race condition can occur if two or more threads access the same objects and access to the shared state is not synchronized.

To demonstrate a race condition, the class `StateObject`, with an int field and the method `ChangeState`, is defined. In the implementation of `ChangeState`, the state variable is verified to see if it contains 5; if it does, the value is incremented. `Trace.Assert` is the next statement, which immediately verifies that state now contains the value 6.

After incrementing by 1 a variable that contains the value 5, you might expect that the variable now has the value 6. But this is not necessarily the case. For example, if one thread has just completed the `if (state == 5)` statement, it might be preempted and the scheduler run another thread. The second thread now goes into the `if` body and, because the state still has the value 5, the state is incremented by 1 to 6. The first thread is now scheduled again, and in the next statement the state is incremented to 7. This is when the race condition occurs and the assert message is shown.

```
public class StateObject
{
    private int state = 5;

    public void ChangeState(int loop)
    {
        if (state == 5)
        {
            state++;
            Trace.Assert(state == 6, "Race condition occurred after " +
                loop + " loops");
        }
        state = 5;
    }
}
```

code snippet ThreadingIssues/SampleTask.cs

Let's verify this by defining a method for a task. The method `RaceCondition()` of the class `SampleTask` gets a `StateObject` as a parameter. Inside an endless `while` loop, the `ChangeState()` method is invoked. The variable `i` is used just to show the loop number in the assert message:

```
public class SampleTask
{
    public void RaceCondition(object o)
    {
        Trace.Assert(o is StateObject, "o must be of type StateObject");
        StateObject state = o as StateObject;

        int i = 0;
        while (true)
        {
            state.ChangeState(i++);
        }
    }
}
```

code snippet ThreadingIssues/SampleTask.cs

In the `Main()` method of the program, a new `StateObject` is created that is shared among all the tasks. `Task` objects are created by passing the address of `RaceCondition` with an object of type `SampleThread` in the constructor of the `Task` class. The task is then started with the `Start()` method, passing the state object. The main thread then sleeps for 10 seconds, assuming in that time that the race condition will occur.

```
static void Main()
{
    var state = new StateObject();
    for (int i = 0; i < 20; i++)
    {
        new Task(new SampleTask().RaceCondition, state).Start();
    }
    Thread.Sleep(10000);
}
```

code snippet ThreadingIssues/SampleTask.cs

When you start the program, you will get race conditions. How long it takes until the first race condition happens depends on your system and whether you build the program as a release or debug build. With a release build, the problem will happen more often because the code is optimized. If you have multiple CPUs in your system or dual/quad-core CPUs, where multiple threads can run concurrently, the problem will also occur more often than with a single-core CPU. The problem will occur with a single-core CPU because thread scheduling is preemptive, but not that often.

Figure 20-1 shows an assertion of the program, where the race condition occurred after 75,069 loops. You can start the application multiple times, and you will always get different results.

You can avoid the problem by locking the shared object. You can do this inside the thread by locking the variable state, which is shared among the threads, with the `lock` statement as shown. Only one thread can be inside the lock block for the state object. Because this object is shared among all threads, a thread must wait at the lock if another thread has the lock for state. As soon as the lock is accepted, the thread owns the lock and gives it up with the end of the lock block. If every thread changing the object referenced with the state variable is using a lock, the race condition no longer occurs.

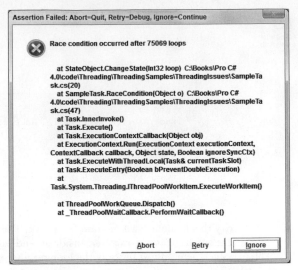

FIGURE 20-1

Available for download on Wrox.com

```csharp
public class SampleTask
{
    public void RaceCondition(object o)
    {
        Trace.Assert(o is StateObject, "o must be of type StateObject");
        StateObject state = o as StateObject;

        int i = 0;
        while (true)
        {
            lock (state)  // no race condition with this lock
            {
                state.ChangeState(i++);
            }
        }
    }
}
```

code snippet ThreadingIssues/SampleTask.cs

Instead of performing the lock when using the shared object, you can make the shared object thread-safe. Here, the `ChangeState()` method contains a `lock` statement. Because you cannot lock the state variable itself (only reference types can be used for a lock), the variable `sync` of type `object` is defined and used with the `lock` statement. If a lock is done using the same synchronization object every time the value state is changed, race conditions no longer happen.

Available for download on Wrox.com

```csharp
public class StateObject
{
    private int state = 5;
    private object sync = new object();

    public void ChangeState(int loop)
    {
        lock (sync)
        {
            if (state == 5)
            {
```

```
                    state++;
                    Trace.Assert(state == 6, "Race condition occurred after " +
                            loop + " loops");
                }
                state = 5;
            }
        }
    }
```

Deadlock

Too much locking can get you in trouble as well. In a deadlock, at least two threads halt and wait for each other to release a lock. As both threads wait for each other, a deadlock occurs and the threads wait endlessly.

To demonstrate deadlocks, two objects of type `StateObject` are instantiated and passed with the constructor of the `SampleTask` class. Two tasks are created: one task running the method `Deadlock1()` and the other task running the method `Deadlock2()`:

```
var state1 = new StateObject();
var state2 = new StateObject();
new Task(new SampleTask(state1, state2).Deadlock1).Start();
new Task(new SampleTask(state1, state2).Deadlock2).Start();
```

The methods `Deadlock1()` and `Deadlock2()` now change the state of two objects: s1 and s2. That's why two locks are generated. The method `Deadlock1()` first does a lock for s1 and next for s2. The method `Deadlock2()` first does a lock for s2 and then for s1. Now, it may happen from time to time that the lock for s1 in `Deadlock1()` is resolved. Next, a thread switch occurs, and `Deadlock2()` starts to run and gets the lock for s2. The second thread now waits for the lock of s1. Because it needs to wait, the thread scheduler schedules the first thread again, which now waits for s2. Both threads now wait and don't release the lock as long as the lock block is not ended. This is a typical deadlock.

```
public class SampleThread
{
    public SampleThread(StateObject s1, StateObject s2)
    {
        this.s1 = s1;
        this.s2 = s2;
    }

    private StateObject s1;
    private StateObject s2;

    public void Deadlock1()
    {
        int i = 0;
        while (true)
        {
            lock (s1)
            {
                lock (s2)
                {
                    s1.ChangeState(1);
                    s2.ChangeState(i++);
                    Console.WriteLine("still running, {0}", i);
                }
            }
        }
    }
```

```
        }

        public void Deadlock2()
        {
            int i = 0;
            while (true)
            {
                lock (s2)
                {
                    lock (s1)
                    {
                        s1.ChangeState(i);
                        s2.ChangeState(i++);
                        Console.WriteLine("still running, {0}", i);
                    }
                }
            }
        }
    }
```

code snippet ThreadingIssues/SampleTask.cs

As a result, the program will run a number of loops and will soon be unresponsive. The message still running is just written a few times to the console. Again, how soon the problem happens depends on your system configuration, and the result will differ from time to time.

With Visual Studio 2010, you can run the program in debug mode, click the Break All button, and open the Parallel Tasks window (see Figure 20-2). Here, you can see that the threads are in the status Waiting-Deadlocked.

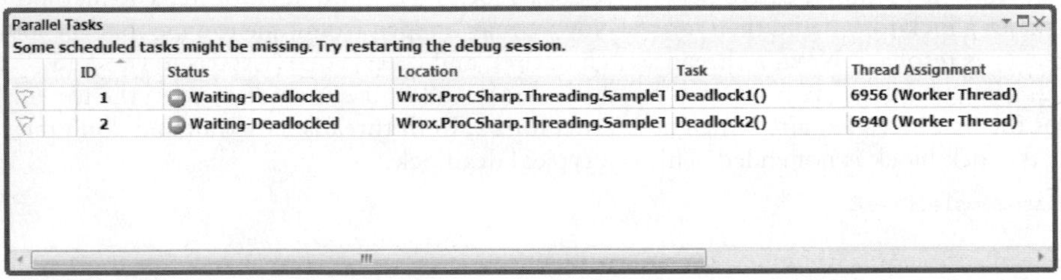

	ID	Status	Location	Task	Thread Assignment
	1	Waiting-Deadlocked	Wrox.ProCSharp.Threading.Sample1	Deadlock1()	6956 (Worker Thread)
	2	Waiting-Deadlocked	Wrox.ProCSharp.Threading.Sample1	Deadlock2()	6940 (Worker Thread)

Parallel Tasks
Some scheduled tasks might be missing. Try restarting the debug session.

FIGURE 20-2

The problem of deadlocks is not always as obvious as it is here. One thread locks s1 and then s2; the other thread locks s2 and then s1. You just need to change the order so that both threads perform the locks in the same order. However, the locks might be hidden deeply inside a method. You can prevent this problem by designing a good lock order from the beginning in the architecture of the application, and also by defining timeouts for the locks, which we show in the next section.

SYNCHRONIZATION

It is best to avoid synchronization issues by not sharing data between threads. Of course, this is not always possible. If data sharing is necessary, you must use synchronization techniques so that only one thread at a time accesses and changes shared state. Remember the synchronization issues with race conditions and deadlocks. If you don't pay attention to these issues, the reason for problems in applications is hard to find because threading issues occur only from time to time.

This section discusses synchronization technologies that you can use with multiple threads:

➤ lock statement

➤ Interlocked class

- ➤ Monitor class
- ➤ SpinLock struct
- ➤ WaitHandle class
- ➤ Mutex class
- ➤ Semaphore class
- ➤ Events classes
- ➤ Barrier class
- ➤ ReaderWriterLockSlim class

lock, Interlocked, and Monitor can be used for synchronization within a process. The classes Mutex, Event, SemaphoreSlim, and ReaderWriterLockSlim also offer synchronization among threads of multiple processes.

lock Statement and Thread Safety

C# has its own keyword for the synchronization of multiple threads: the lock statement. The lock statement is an easy way to hold for a lock and release it.

Before adding lock statements, let's go into another race condition. The class SharedState demonstrates using shared state between threads and keeps an integer value:

```
public class SharedState
{
    public int State { get; set; }
}
```

code snippet SynchronizationSamples/SharedState.cs

The class Job contains the method DoTheJob(), which is the entry point for a new task. With the implementation, the State of SharedState is incremented 50,000 times. The variable sharedState is initialized in the constructor of this class.

```
public class Job
{
    SharedState sharedState;
    public Job(SharedState sharedState)
    {
        this.sharedState = sharedState;
    }
    public void DoTheJob()
    {
        for (int i = 0; i < 50000; i++)
        {
            sharedState.State += 1;
        }
    }
}
```

code snippet SynchronizationSamples/Job.cs

In the Main() method, a SharedState object is created and passed to the constructor of 20 Task objects. All tasks are started. After starting the tasks, the Main() method does another loop to wait until every one of the 20 tasks is completed. After the tasks are completed, the summarized value of the shared state is written to the console. Having 50,000 loops and 20 tasks, a value of 1,000,000 could be expected. Often, however, this is not the case.

```
class Program
{
    static void Main()
    {
        int numTasks = 20;
        var state = new SharedState();
        var tasks = new Task[numTasks];

        for (int i = 0; i < numTasks; i++)
        {
            tasks[i] = new Task(new Job(state).DoTheJob);
            tasks[i].Start();
        }

        for (int i = 0; i < numTasks; i++)
        {
            tasks[i].Wait();
        }
        Console.WriteLine("summarized {0}", state.State);
    }
}
```

code snippet SynchronizationSamples/Program.cs

Results received from multiple runs of the application are as shown here:

```
summarized 785895
summarized 776131
summarized 774400
summarized 871286
```

The behavior is different every time, but none of the results are correct. You get big differences between debug and release builds, and according to the types of CPUs that you are using. If you change the loop count for smaller values, you will get correct values many times — but not every time. The application is small enough to see the problem easily; the reason for such a problem can be hard to find in a large application.

You must add synchronization to this program. This can be done with the `lock` keyword.

The object's being defined with the `lock` statement means that you wait to get the lock for the specified object. You can pass only a reference type. Locking a value type would just lock a copy, and this wouldn't make any sense. Anyway, the C# compiler provides an error if value types are used with the `lock` statement. As soon as the lock is granted — only one thread gets the lock — the block of the `lock` statement can run. At the end of the `lock` statement block, the lock for the object is released, and another thread waiting for the lock can be granted access to it.

```
lock (obj)
{
    // synchronized region
}
```

To lock static members, you can place the lock on the type object:

```
lock (typeof(StaticClass))
{
}
```

You can make the instance members of a class thread-safe by using the `lock` keyword. This way, only one thread at a time can access the methods `DoThis()` and `DoThat()` for the same instance.

```
public class Demo
{
    public void DoThis()
    {
```

```
      lock (this)
      {
          // only one thread at a time can access the DoThis and DoThat methods
      }
   }
   public void DoThat()
   {
      lock (this)
      {
      }
   }
}
```

However, because the object of the instance can also be used for synchronized access from the outside, and you can't control this from the class itself, you can apply the SyncRoot pattern. With the SyncRoot pattern, a private object named syncRoot is created, and this object is used with the lock statements:

```
public class Demo
{
   private object syncRoot = new object();

   public void DoThis()
   {
      lock (syncRoot)
      {
          // only one thread at a time can access the DoThis and DoThat methods
      }
   }
   public void DoThat()
   {
      lock (syncRoot)
      {
      }
   }
}
```

Using locks costs time and is not always needed. You can create two versions of a class: a synchronized and a nonsynchronized version. This is demonstrated here by changing the class Demo. The class Demo itself is not synchronized, as you can see in the implementation of the DoThis() and DoThat() methods. The class also defines the IsSynchronized property, where the client can get information about the synchronization option of the class. To make a synchronized variant of the class, the static method Synchronized() can be used to pass a nonsynchronized object, and this method returns an object of type SynchronizedDemo. SynchronizedDemo is implemented as an inner class that is derived from the base class Demo and overrides the virtual members of the base class. The overridden members make use of the SyncRoot pattern.

```
public class Demo
{
   private class SynchronizedDemo: Demo
   {
      private object syncRoot = new object();
      private Demo d;

      public SynchronizedDemo(Demo d)
      {
         this.d = d;
      }

      public override bool IsSynchronized
      {
         get { return true; }
      }
```

```
        public override void DoThis()
        {
            lock (syncRoot)
            {
                d.DoThis();
            }
        }

        public override void DoThat()
        {
            lock (syncRoot)
            {
                d.DoThat();
            }
        }
    }

    public virtual bool IsSynchronized
    {
        get { return false; }
    }

    public static Demo Synchronized(Demo d)
    {
        if (!d.IsSynchronized)
        {
            return new SynchronizedDemo(d);
        }
        return d;
    }

    public virtual void DoThis()
    {
    }

    public virtual void DoThat()
    {
    }
}
```

You must bear in mind that, when using the `SynchronizedDemo` class, only methods are synchronized. There is no synchronization for invoking two members of this class.

Let's change the `SharedState` class that was not synchronized at first to use the SyncRoot pattern now. If you try to make the `SharedState` class thread-safe by locking access to the properties with the SyncRoot pattern, you still get the race condition shown earlier in the "Race Condition" section.

```
public class SharedState
{
    private int state = 0;
    private object syncRoot = new object();

    public int State // there's still a race condition,
                     // don't do this!
    {
        get { lock (syncRoot) {return state; }}
        set { lock (syncRoot) {state = value; }}
    }
}
```

code snippet SynchronizationSamples/SharedState.cs

The thread invoking the `DoTheJob()` method is accessing the `get` accessor of the `SharedState` class to get the current value of the state, and then the `get` accessor sets the new value for the state. In between calling the `get` and the `set` accessor, the object is not locked, and another thread can be the interim value.

```
public void DoTheJob()
{
    for (int i = 0; i < 50000; i++)
    {
        sharedState.State += 1;
    }
}
```

code snippet SynchronizationSamples/Job.cs

So, it is better to leave the `SharedState` class as it was earlier without thread safety:

```
public class SharedState
{
    public int State { get; set; }
}
```

code snippet SynchronizationSamples/SharedState.cs

And to add the `lock` statement where it belongs, inside the method `DoTheJob()`:

```
public void DoTheJob()
{
    for (int i = 0; i < 50000; i++)
    {
        lock (sharedState)
        {
            sharedState.State += 1;
        }
    }
}
```

code snippet SynchronizationSamples/Job.cs

This way, the results of the application are always as expected:

```
summarized 1000000
```

 Using the `lock` statement in one place does not mean that all other threads accessing the object are waiting. You have to explicitly use synchronization with every thread accessing the shared state.

Of course, you can also change the design of the `SharedState` class and offer incrementing as an atomic operation. This is a design question — what should be an atomic functionality of the class?

```
public class SharedState
{
    private int state = 0;
    private object syncRoot = new object();

    public int State
    {
        get { return state; }
    }

    public int IncrementState()
    {
```

```
        lock (syncRoot)
        {
            return ++state;
        }
    }
}
```

code snippet SynchronizationSamples/SharedState.cs

There is, however, a faster way to lock the increment of the state, as shown next.

Interlocked

The `Interlocked` class is used to make simple statements for variables atomic. `i++` is not thread-safe. `i++` consists of getting a value from the memory, incrementing the value by 1, and storing the value back in memory. These operations can be interrupted by the thread scheduler. The `Interlocked` class provides methods for incrementing, decrementing, exchanging, and reading values in a thread-safe manner.

Using the `Interlocked` class is much faster than other synchronization techniques. However, you can use it only for simple synchronization issues.

For example, instead of using the `lock` statement to lock access to the variable `someState` when setting it to a new value, in case it is null, you can use the `Interlocked` class, which is faster:

```
lock (this)
{
    if (someState == null)
    {
        someState = newState;
    }
}
```

code snippet SynchronizationSamples/SharedState.cs

The faster version with the same functionality uses the `Interlocked.CompareExchange()` method:

```
Interlocked.CompareExchange<SomeState>(ref someState,
        newState, null);
```

And instead of performing incrementing inside a `lock` statement:

```
public int State
{
    get
    {
        lock (this)
        {
            return ++state;
        }
    }
}
```

You can use `Interlocked.Increment()`, which is faster:

```
public int State
{
    get
    {
        return Interlocked.Increment(ref state);
    }
}
```

Monitor

The C# compiler resolves the `lock` statement to use the `Monitor` class. The following `lock` statement:

```
lock (obj)
{
    // synchronized region for obj
}
```

is resolved to invoking the `Enter()` method, which waits until the thread gets the lock of the object. Only one thread at a time may be the owner of the object lock. As soon as the lock is resolved, the thread can enter the synchronized section. The `Exit()` method of the `Monitor` class releases the lock. The compiler puts the `Exit()` method into a `finally` handler of a `try` block so that the lock is also released if an exception is thrown.

 `try/finally` *is covered in Chapter 15, "Errors and Exceptions."*

Available for
download on
Wrox.com

```
Monitor.Enter(obj);
try
{
    // synchronized region for obj
}
finally
{
    Monitor.Exit(obj);
}
```

code snippet SynchronizationSamples/Program.cs

The `Monitor` class has a big advantage compared to the `lock` statement of C#: you can add a timeout value for waiting to get the lock. So instead of endlessly waiting to get the lock, you can use the `TryEnter()` method, where you can pass a timeout value that defines the maximum amount of time to wait to get the lock. If the lock for `obj` is acquired, `TryEnter()` sets the Boolean ref parameter to `true` and performs synchronized access to the state guarded by the object `obj`. If `obj` is locked for more than 500 milliseconds by another thread, `TryEnter()` sets the variable `lockTaken` to `false`, and the thread does not wait any longer but is used to do something else. Maybe at a later time, the thread can try to acquire the lock once more.

```
bool lockTaken = false;
Monitor.TryEnter(obj, 500, ref lockTaken);
if (lockTaken)
{
    try
    {
        // acquired the lock
        // synchronized region for obj
    }
    finally
    {
        Monitor.Exit(obj);
    }

}
else
{
    // didn't get the lock, do something else
}
```

SpinLock

The SpinLock struct is new with .NET 4. If the overhead on object-based lock objects (Monitor) would be too high because of garbage collection, SpinLock can be used. SpinLock is useful if you have a high number of locks (for example, for every node in a list) and hold times are always extremely short. You should avoid holding more than one SpinLock and don't call anything that might block.

Other than the architectural differences, SpinLock is very similar in usage to the Monitor class. Acquiring the lock is done with Enter() or TryEnter() and releasing the lock with Exit(). SpinLock also offers properties to provide information if it is currently locked: IsHeld and IsHeldByCurrentThread.

 Be careful when passing SpinLock instances around. Because SpinLock is defined as a struct, assigning one variable to another creates a copy. Always pass SpinLock instances by reference.

WaitHandle

WaitHandle is an abstract base class that you can use to wait for a signal to be set. There are different things you can wait for, because WaitHandle is a base class and some classes are derived from it.

When describing asynchronous delegates earlier in this chapter, the WaitHandle was already in use. The method BeginInvoke() of the asynchronous delegate returns an object that implements the interface IAsyncResult. Using IAsyncResult, you can access a WaitHandle with the property AsyncWaitHandle. When you invoke the method WaitOne(), the thread waits until a signal is received that is associated with the wait handle.

Available for download on Wrox.com

```
static void Main()
{
    TakesAWhileDelegate d1 = TakesAWhile;

    IAsyncResult ar = d1.BeginInvoke(1, 3000, null, null);
    while (true)
    {
        Console.Write(".");
        if (ar.AsyncWaitHandle.WaitOne(50, false))
        {
            Console.WriteLine("Can get the result now");
            break;
        }
    }
    int result = d1.EndInvoke(ar);
    Console.WriteLine("result: {0}", result);
}
```

code snippet AsyncDelegate/Program.cs

With WaitHandle, you can wait for one signal to occur (WaitOne()), multiple objects that all must be signaled (WaitAll()), or one of multiple objects (WaitAny()). WaitAll and WaitAny are static members of the WaitHandle class and accept an array of WaitHandle parameter.

WaitHandle has a SafeWaitHandle property, where you can assign a native handle to an operating system resource and wait for that handle. For example, you can assign a SafeFileHandle to wait for a file I/O operation to complete, or a custom SafeTransactionHandle as shown in Chapter 23, "System.Transactions."

The classes `Mutex`, `EventWaitHandle`, and `Semaphore` are derived from the base class `WaitHandle`, so you can use all of these with waits.

Mutex

`Mutex` (mutual exclusion) is one of the classes of the .NET Framework that offers synchronization across multiple processes. It is very similar to the `Monitor` class in that there is just one owner. Just one thread can get a lock on the mutex and access the synchronized code regions that are secured by the mutex.

With the constructor of the `Mutex` class, you can define if the mutex should initially be owned by the calling thread, define a name for the mutex, and get the information if the mutex already exists. In the sample code, the third parameter is defined as an `out` parameter to receive a Boolean value if the mutex was newly created. If the value returned is `false`, the mutex was already defined. The mutex might be defined in a different process, because a mutex with a name is known to the operating system and is shared among different processes. If there is no name assigned to the mutex, the mutex is unnamed and not shared among different processes.

```
bool createdNew;
Mutex mutex = new Mutex(false, "ProCSharpMutex", out createdNew);
```

To open an existing mutex, you can also use the method `Mutex.OpenExisting()`, which doesn't require the same .NET privileges as creating the mutex with the constructor.

Because the `Mutex` class derives from the base class `WaitHandle`, you can do a `WaitOne()` to acquire the mutex lock and be the owner of the mutex during that time. The mutex is released by invoking the `ReleaseMutex()` method.

```
if (mutex.WaitOne())
{
    try
    {
        // synchronized region
    }
    finally
    {
        mutex.ReleaseMutex();
    }
}
else
{
    // some problem happened while waiting
}
```

Because a named mutex is known system-wide, you can use it to keep an application from being started twice. In the following Windows Forms application, the constructor of the `Mutex` object is invoked. Then, it is verified if the mutex with the name `SingletonWinAppMutex` exists already. If it does, the application exits.

```
static class Program
{
    [STAThread]
    static void Main()
    {
        bool createdNew;
        Mutex mutex = new Mutex(false, "SingletonWinAppMutex",
                                out createdNew);
        if (!createdNew)
        {
            MessageBox.Show("You can only start one instance " +
                            "of the application");
            Application.Exit();
            return;
```

```
        }
        Application.EnableVisualStyles();
        Application.SetCompatibleTextRenderingDefault(false);
        Application.Run(new Form1());
    }
}
```

Semaphore

A semaphore is very similar to a mutex, but, in contrast, the semaphore can be used by multiple threads at once. A semaphore is a counting mutex, meaning that with a semaphore you can define the number of threads that are allowed to access the resource guarded by the semaphore simultaneously. This can be used if you have several of the resources available and can allow only a specific number of threads access to the resource. For example, say that you want to access physical I/O ports on the system and there are three ports available. So, three threads can access the I/O ports simultaneously, but the fourth thread needs to wait until the resource is released by one of the other threads.

.NET 4 gives you two classes with semaphore functionality: `Semaphore` and `SemaphoreSlim`. `Semaphore` can be named, use system-wide resources, and allow synchronization between different processes. `SemaphoreSlim` is lightweight version that is optimized for shorter wait times.

In the sample application, in the `Main()` method six threads are created and one semaphore with a count of 4. In the constructor of the `Semaphore` class, you can define the count for the number of locks that can be acquired with the semaphore (the second parameter) and the number of locks that are free initially (the first parameter). If the first parameter has a lower value than the second parameter, the difference between the values defines the already allocated semaphore count. As with the mutex, you can also assign a name to the semaphore to share it among different processes. Here, no name is defined with the semaphore, so it is used only within this process. After the `SemaphoreSlim` object is created, six threads are started, and they all get the same semaphore.

```
using System;
using System.Threading;
using System.Diagnostics;

namespace Wrox.ProCSharp.Threading
{
    class Program
    {
        static void Main()
        {
            int threadCount = 6;
            int semaphoreCount = 4;
            var semaphore = new SemaphoreSlim(semaphoreCount, semaphoreCount);
            var threads = new Thread[threadCount];

            for (int i = 0; i < threadCount; i++)
            {
                threads[i] = new Thread(ThreadMain);
                threads[i].Start(semaphore);
            }

            for (int i = 0; i < threadCount; i++)
            {
                threads[i].Join();
            }
            Console.WriteLine("All threads finished");
        }
```

code snippet Semaphore/Program.cs

In the thread's main method, `ThreadMain()`, the thread does a `WaitOne()` to lock the semaphore. Remember, the semaphore has a count of 4, so four threads can acquire the lock. Thread 5 must wait and, here, the timeout of 600 milliseconds is defined as the maximum wait time. If the lock cannot be acquired after the wait time, the thread writes a message to the console and repeats the wait in a loop. As soon as the lock is made, the thread writes a message to the console, sleeps for some time, and releases the lock. Again, with the release of the lock it is important that the resource be released in all cases. That's why the `Release()` method of the `Semaphore` class is invoked in a `finally` handler.

```csharp
static void ThreadMain(object o)
{
    SemaphoreSlim semaphore = o as SemaphoreSlim;
    Trace.Assert(semaphore != null, "o must be a Semaphore type");
    bool isCompleted = false;
    while (!isCompleted)
    {
        if (semaphore.Wait(600))
        {
            try
            {
                Console.WriteLine("Thread {0} locks the semaphore",
                    Thread.CurrentThread.ManagedThreadId);
                Thread.Sleep(2000);
            }
            finally
            {
                semaphore.Release();
                Console.WriteLine("Thread {0} releases the semaphore",
                    Thread.CurrentThread.ManagedThreadId);
                isCompleted = true;
            }
        }
        else
        {
            Console.WriteLine("Timeout for thread {0}; wait again",
                Thread.CurrentThread.ManagedThreadId);
        }
    }
}
```

When you run the application, you can indeed see that, with four threads, the lock is made immediately. The threads with IDs 7 and 8 must wait. The wait continues in the loop until one of the other threads releases the semaphore.

```
Thread 3 locks the semaphore
Thread 4 locks the semaphore
Thread 5 locks the semaphore
Thread 6 locks the semaphore
Timeout for thread 8; wait again
Timeout for thread 7; wait again
Timeout for thread 8; wait again
Timeout for thread 7; wait again
Timeout for thread 7; wait again
Timeout for thread 8; wait again
Thread 3 releases the semaphore
Thread 8 locks the semaphore
Thread 4 releases the semaphore
Thread 7 locks the semaphore
Thread 5 releases the semaphore
Thread 6 releases the semaphore
Thread 8 releases the semaphore
Thread 7 releases the semaphore
All threads finished
```

Events

Events are the next of the system-wide synchronization resources. For using system events from managed code, the .NET Framework offers the classes ManualResetEvent, AutoResetEvent, ManualResetEventSlim, and CountdownEvent in the namespace System.Threading. ManualResetEventSlim and CountdownEvent are new with .NET 4.

 The event *keyword from C# that was covered in Chapter 8 has nothing to do with the event classes from the namespace* System.Threading. *The* event *keyword is based on delegates; however, both event classes are .NET wrappers to the system-wide native event resource for synchronization.*

You can use events to inform other tasks that some data is present, something is completed, and so on. An event can be signaled or not signaled. A task can wait for the event to be in a signaled state with the help of the WaitHandle class, which was already discussed.

A ManualResetEventSlim is signaled by invoking the Set() method and turned back to a nonsignaled state with the Reset() method. If multiple threads are waiting for an event to be signaled, and the Set() method is invoked, then all threads waiting are released. Also, if a thread just invokes the WaitOne() method, but the event is already signaled, the waiting thread can continue immediately.

An AutoResetEvent is also signaled by invoking the Set() method. It is also possible to set it back to a nonsignaled state with the Reset() method. However, if a thread is waiting for an auto-reset event to be signaled, the event is automatically changed into a nonsignaled state when the wait state of the first thread is finished. This way, if multiple threads are waiting for the event to be set, only one thread is released from its wait state. It is not the thread that has been waiting the longest for the event to be signaled, but the thread waiting with the highest priority.

To demonstrate events with the ManualResetEventSlim class, the class Calculator defines the method Calculation(), which is the entry point for a task. With this method, the task receives input data for calculation and writes the result to the variable result that can be accessed from the Result property. As soon as the result is completed (after a random amount of time), the event is signaled by invoking the Set() method of the ManualResetEventSlim.

Available for download on Wrox.com

```
public class Calculator
{
    private ManualResetEventSlim mEvent;

    public int Result { get; private set; }

    public Calculator(ManualResetEventSlim ev)
    {
        this.mEvent = ev;
    }

    public void Calculation(object obj)
    {
        Tuple<int, int> data = (Tuple<int, int>)obj;
        Console.WriteLine("Task {0} starts calculation", Task.Current.Id);
        Thread.Sleep(new Random().Next(3000));
        Result = data.Item1 + data.Item2;

        // signal the event-completed!
        Console.WriteLine("Task {0} is ready", Task.Current.Id);
        mEvent.Set();
    }
}
```

code snippet EventSample/Program.cs

The Main() method of the program defines arrays of four ManualResetEventSlim objects and four Calculator objects. Every Calculator is initialized in the constructor with a ManualResetEventSlim object, so that every task gets its own event object to signal when it is completed. Now the TaskFactory class is used to have different tasks running the calculation.

```
class Program
{
    static void Main()
    {
        const int taskCount = 4;

        var mEvents = new ManualResetEventSlim[taskCount];
        var waitHandles = new WaitHandle[taskCount];
        var calcs = new Calculator[taskCount];

        TaskFactory taskFactory = new TaskFactory();
        for (int i = 0; i < taskCount; i++)
        {
            mEvents[i] = new ManualResetEventSlim(false);
            waitHandles[i] = mEvents[i].WaitHandle;
            calcs[i] = new Calculator(mEvents[i]);

            taskFactory.StartNew(calcs[i].Calculation, Tuple.Create(i + 1, i + 3));
        }
        //...
```

The WaitHandle class is now used to wait for any one of the events in the array. WaitAny() waits until any one of the events is signaled. In contrast to ManualResetEvent, ManualResetEventSlim does not derive from WaitHandle. That's why a separate collection of WaitHandle objects is kept that is filled from the WaitHandle property of the ManualResetEventSlim class. WaitAny() returns an index value that provides information about the event that was signaled. The returned value matches the index of the event array that is passed to WaitAny(). Using this index the information from the signaled event can be read:

```
        for (int i = 0; i < taskCount; i++)
        {
            int index = WaitHandle.WaitAny(mEvents);
            if (index == WaitHandle.WaitTimeout)
            {
                Console.WriteLine("Timeout!!");
            }
            else
            {
                mEvents[index].Reset();
                Console.WriteLine("finished task for {0}, result: {1}",
                            index, calcs[index].Result);
            }
        }
    }
}
```

code snippet EventSample/Program.cs

When starting the application, you can see the threads doing the calculation and setting the event to inform the main thread that it can read the result. At random times, depending on whether the build is a debug or release build and on your hardware, you might see different orders and also a different number of threads from the pool performing tasks. Here, thread 4 was reused from the pool for doing two tasks because it was fast enough to finish the calculation first:

```
Task 1 starts calculation
Task 2 starts calculation
Task 2 is ready
Task 3 starts calculation
```

```
finished task for 0, result: 4
Task 4 starts calculation
Task 3 is ready
finished task for 2, result: 8
Task 1 is ready
finished task for 1, result: 6
Thread 4 is ready
finished task for 3, result: 10
```

In a scenario like this, to fork some work into multiple tasks and later join the result, the new `CountdownEvent` class can be very useful. Instead of creating a separate event object for every task, you need to create just one. `CountdownEvent` defines an initial number for all the tasks that set the event, and after the count is reached, the `CountdownEvent` is signaled.

The `Calculator` class is modified to use the `CountdownEvent` instead of the `ManualResetEvent`. Instead of setting the signal with the `Set()` method, `CountdownEvent` defines the `Signal()` method.

```csharp
public class Calculator
{
    private CountdownEvent cEvent;

    public int Result { get; private set; }

    public Calculator(CountdownEvent ev)
    {
        this.cEvent = ev;
    }

    public void Calculation(object obj)
    {
        Tuple<int, int> data = (Tuple<int, int>)obj;
        Console.WriteLine("Task {0} starts calculation", Task.Current.Id);
        Thread.Sleep(new Random().Next(3000));
        Result = data.Item1 + data.Item2;

        // signal the event-completed!
        Console.WriteLine("Task {0} is ready", Task.Current.Id);
        cEvent.Signal();
    }
}
```

code snippet EventSample/Calculator.cs

The `Main()` method can now be simplified so that it's just necessary to wait for the single event. If you don't deal with the results separately as it was done before, this new edition might be all that's needed.

```csharp
const int taskCount = 4;
var cEvent = new CountdownEvent(taskCount);
var calcs = new Calculator[taskCount];

var taskFactory = new TaskFactory();
for (int i = 0; i < taskCount; i++)
{
    calcs[i] = new Calculator(cEvent);

    taskFactory.StartNew(calcs[i].Calculation,
                         Tuple.Create(i + 1, i + 3));
}

cEvent.Wait();
Console.WriteLine("all finished");
```

```
        for (int i = 0; i < taskCount; i++)
        {
            Console.WriteLine("task for {0}, result: {1}", i, calcs[i].Result);
        }
```

code snippet EventSample/Program.cs

Barrier

For synchronization, .NET 4 offers the new Barrier class. Barrier is great for a scenario where work is forked into multiple tasks, and the work needs to be joined afterward. Barrier is used for participants need to be synchronized. While the job is active, additional participants can be added dynamically, for example, child tasks that are created from a parent task. Participants can wait until the work is done by all the other participants before continuing.

The sample application uses a collection containing 2,000,000 strings. Multiple tasks are used to iterate through the collection and count the number of strings starting with a, b, c, and so on.

The method FillData() creates a collection and fills it with random strings.

```
        public static IEnumerable<string> FillData(int size)
        {
            List<string> data = new List<string>(size);
            Random r = new Random();
            for (int i = 0; i < size; i++)
            {
                data.Add(GetString(r));
            }
            return data;
        }
        private static string GetString(Random r)
        {
            StringBuilder sb = new StringBuilder(6);
            for (int i = 0; i < 6; i++)
            {
                sb.Append((char)(r.Next(26) + 97));
            }
            return sb.ToString();
        }
```

code snippet BarrierSample/Program.cs

The CalculationInTask() method defines the job that's done by a task. With the parameter, a tuple containing four items is received. The third parameter is a reference to the Barrier instance. When the job is done by the task, the task removes itself from the barrier with the RemoveParticipant() method.

```
        static int[] CalculationInTask(object p)
        {
            var p1 = p as Tuple<int, int, Barrier, List<string>>;
            Barrier barrier = p1.Item3;
            List<string> data = p1.Item4;

            int start = p1.Item1 * p1.Item2;
            int end = start + p1.Item2;
            Console.WriteLine("Task {0}: partition from {1} to {2}",
                    Task.Current.Id, start, end);
            int[] charCount = new int[26];
            for (int j = start; j < end; j++)
            {
                char c = data[j][0];
                charCount[c - 97]++;
```

```
        }
        Console.WriteLine("Calculation completed from task {0}. {1} " +
                "times a, {2} times z", Task.Current.Id, charCount[0],
                charCount[25]);

        barrier.RemoveParticipant();
        Console.WriteLine("Task {0} removed from barrier, " +
                "remaining participants {1}", Task.Current.Id,
                barrier.ParticipantsRemaining);
        return charCount;
    }
```

With the `Main()` method, a `Barrier` instance is created. In the constructor, you can specify the number of participants. In the sample, this number is 3 because there are two created tasks, and the `Main()` method itself is a participant as well. Using a `TaskFactory`, two tasks are created to fork the iteration through the collection into two parts. After starting the tasks, using `SignalAndWait()`, the main method signals its completion and waits until all remaining participants either signal the completion or remove themselves as participants from the barrier. As soon as all participants are ready, the results from the tasks are taken and zipped together with the `Zip()` extension method.

```
        static void Main()
        {
            const int numberTasks = 2;
            const int partitionSize = 1000000;
            var data = new List<string>(FillData(partitionSize * numberTasks));

            var barrier = new Barrier(numberTasks + 1);

            var taskFactory = new TaskFactory();
            var tasks = new Task<int[]>[numberTasks];
            for (int i = 0; i < participants; i++)
            {
                tasks[i] = taskFactory.StartNew<int[]>(CalculationInTask,
                    Tuple.Create(i, partitionSize, barrier, data));
            }

            barrier.SignalAndWait();
            var resultCollection = tasks[0].Result.Zip(tasks[1].Result, (c1, c2) =
                {
                    return c1 + c2;
                });

            char ch = 'a';
            int sum = 0;
            foreach (var x in resultCollection)
            {
                Console.WriteLine("{0}, count: {1}", ch++, x);
                sum += x;
            }

            Console.WriteLine("main finished {0}", sum);
            Console.WriteLine("remaining {0}", barrier.ParticipantsRemaining);

        }
```

ReaderWriterLockSlim

For a locking mechanism to allow multiple readers, but just one writer, for a resource, the class `ReaderWriterLockSlim` can be used. This class offers a locking functionality in which multiple readers can access the resource if no writer locked it, and only a single writer can lock the resource.

The `ReaderWriterLockSlim` class has properties to acquire a read lock that are blocking and nonblocking, such as `EnterReadLock()` and `TryEnterReadLock()`, and to acquire a write lock with `EnterWriteLock()` and `TryEnterWriteLock()`. If a task reads first and writes afterward, it can acquire an upgradable read lock with `EnterUpgradableReadLock()` or `TryEnterUpgradableReadLock()`. With this lock, the write lock can be acquired without releasing the read lock.

Several properties of this class offer information about the held locks, for example, `CurrentReadCount`, `WaitingReadCount`, `WaitingUpgradableReadCount`, and `WaitingWriteCount`.

The sample program creates a collection containing six items and a `ReaderWriterLockSlim` object. The method `ReaderMethod()` acquires a read lock to read all items of the list and write them to the console. The method `WriterMethod()` tries to acquire a write lock to change all values of the collection. In the `Main()` method, six threads are started that invoke either the method `ReaderMethod()` or the method `WriterMethod()`.

```csharp
using System;
using System.Collections.Generic;
using System.Threading;
using System.Threading.Tasks;

namespace Wrox.ProCSharp.Threading
{
    class Program
    {
        private static List<int> items = new List<int>() { 0, 1, 2, 3, 4, 5};
        private static ReaderWriterLockSlim rwl =
            new ReaderWriterLockSlim(LockRecursionPolicy.SupportsRecursion);

        static void ReaderMethod(object reader)
        {
            try
            {
                rwl.EnterReadLock();

                for (int i = 0; i < items.Count; i++)
                {
                    Console.WriteLine("reader {0}, loop: {1}, item: {2}",
                        reader, i, items[i]);
                    Thread.Sleep(40);
                }
            }
            finally
            {
                rwl.ExitReadLock();
            }
        }

        static void WriterMethod(object writer)
        {
            try
            {
                while (!rwl.TryEnterWriteLock(50))
                {
                    Console.WriteLine("Writer {0} waiting for the write lock",
                        writer);
                    Console.WriteLine("current reader count: {0}",
                        rwl.CurrentReadCount);
                }
                Console.WriteLine("Writer {0} acquired the lock", writer);
                for (int i = 0; i < items.Count; i++)
                {
```

```
            items[i]++;
            Thread.Sleep(50);
        }
        Console.WriteLine("Writer {0} finished", writer);
    }
    finally
    {
        rwl.ExitWriteLock();
    }
}

static void Main()
{
    var taskFactory = new TaskFactory(TaskCreationOptions.LongRunning,
        TaskContinuationOptions.None);
    var tasks = new Task[6];
    tasks[0] = taskFactory.StartNew(WriterMethod, 1);
    tasks[1] = taskFactory.StartNew(ReaderMethod, 1);
    tasks[2] = taskFactory.StartNew(ReaderMethod, 2);
    tasks[3] = taskFactory.StartNew(WriterMethod, 2);
    tasks[4] = taskFactory.StartNew(ReaderMethod, 3);
    tasks[5] = taskFactory.StartNew(ReaderMethod, 4);

    for (int i = 0; i < 6; i++)
    {
        tasks[i].Wait();
    }
}
}
}
```

code snippet ReaderWriterSample/Program.cs

With a run of the application here, the first writer gets the lock first. The second writer and all readers need to wait. Next, the readers can work concurrently, while the second writer still waits for the resource.

```
Writer 1 acquired the lock
Writer 2 waiting for the write lock
current reader count: 0
Writer 2 waiting for the write lock
current reader count: 0
Writer 2 waiting for the write lock
current reader count: 0
Writer 2 waiting for the write lock
current reader count: 0
Writer 1 finished
reader 4, loop: 0, item: 1
reader 1, loop: 0, item: 1
Writer 2 waiting for the write lock
current reader count: 4
reader 2, loop: 0, item: 1
reader 3, loop: 0, item: 1
reader 4, loop: 1, item: 2
reader 1, loop: 1, item: 2
reader 3, loop: 1, item: 2
reader 2, loop: 1, item: 2
Writer 2 waiting for the write lock
current reader count: 4
reader 4, loop: 2, item: 3
reader 1, loop: 2, item: 3
reader 2, loop: 2, item: 3
reader 3, loop: 2, item: 3
```

```
Writer 2 waiting for the write lock
current reader count: 4
reader 4, loop: 3, item: 4
reader 1, loop: 3, item: 4
reader 2, loop: 3, item: 4
reader 3, loop: 3, item: 4
reader 4, loop: 4, item: 5
reader 1, loop: 4, item: 5
Writer 2 waiting for the write lock
current reader count: 4
reader 2, loop: 4, item: 5
reader 3, loop: 4, item: 5
reader 4, loop: 5, item: 6
reader 1, loop: 5, item: 6
reader 2, loop: 5, item: 6
reader 3, loop: 5, item: 6
Writer 2 waiting for the write lock
current reader count: 4
Writer 2 acquired the lock
Writer 2 finished
```

TIMERS

The .NET Framework offers several `Timer` classes that can be used to invoke a method after some time interval. The following table lists the `Timer` classes and their namespaces, as well as their functionality.

NAMESPACE	DESCRIPTION
System.Threading	The `Timer` class from the `System.Threading` namespace offers core functionality. In the constructor, you can pass a delegate that should be invoked at the time interval specified.
System.Timers	The `Timer` class from the `System.Timers` namespace is a component, because it derives from the `Component` base class. So, you can drag and drop it from the toolbox to the design surface of a server application such as a Windows service. This `Timer` class uses `System.Threading.Timer` but provides an event-based mechanism instead of a delegate.
System.Windows.Forms	With the `Timer` classes from the namespaces `System.Threading` and `System.Timers`, the callback or event methods are invoked from a different thread than the calling thread. Windows Forms controls are bound to the creator thread. Calling back into this thread is done by the `Timer` class from the `System.Windows.Forms` namespace.
System.Web.UI	The `Timer` from the `System.Web.UI` namespace is an AJAX Extension that can be used with web pages.
System.Windows.Threading	The `DispatcherTimer` class from the `System.Windows.Threading` namespace is used by WPF applications. `DispatcherTimer` runs on the UI thread.

Using the `System.Threading.Timer` class, you can pass the method to be invoked as the first parameter in the constructor. This method must fulfill the requirements of the `TimerCallback` delegate, which defines a void return type and an `object` parameter. With the second parameter, you can pass any object, which is then received with the object argument in the callback method. For example, you can pass an `Event` object to signal the caller. The third parameter specifies the time span during which the callback should be invoked the first time. With the last parameter, you specify the repeating interval for the callback. If the timer should fire only once, set the fourth parameter to the value –1.

If the time interval should be changed after creating the `Timer` object, you can pass new values with the `Change()` method.

```
private static void ThreadingTimer()
{
    var t1 = new System.Threading.Timer(
        TimeAction, null, TimeSpan.FromSeconds(2),
        TimeSpan.FromSeconds(3));

    Thread.Sleep(15000);

    t1.Dispose();
}

static void TimeAction(object o)
{
    Console.WriteLine("System.Threading.Timer {0:T}", DateTime.Now);
}
```

code snippet TimerSample/Program.cs

The constructor of the `Timer` class from the `System.Timers` namespace requires just a time interval. The method that should be invoked after the interval is specified by the `Elapsed` event. This event requires a delegate of type `ElapsedEventHandler`, which requires object and `ElapsedEventArgs` parameters, as you can see with the `TimeAction` method. The `AutoReset` property specifies whether the timer should be fired repeatedly. If you set this property to `false`, the event is fired only once. Calling the `Start` method enables the timer to fire the events. Instead of calling the `Start` method, you can set the `Enabled` property to `true`. Behind the scenes `Start()` does nothing else. The `Stop()` method sets the `Enabled` property to `false` to stop the timer.

```
private static void TimersTimer()
{
    var t1 = new System.Timers.Timer(1000);
    t1.AutoReset = true;
    t1.Elapsed += TimeAction;
    t1.Start();
    Thread.Sleep(10000);
    t1.Stop();

    t1.Dispose();
}

static void TimeAction(object sender, System.Timers.ElapsedEventArgs e)
{
    Console.WriteLine("System.Timers.Timer {0:T}", e.SignalTime );
}
```

EVENT-BASED ASYNCHRONOUS PATTERN

Earlier in this chapter, you saw the asynchronous pattern based on the `IAsyncResult` interface. With an asynchronous callback, the callback thread is different from the calling thread. Using Windows Forms or WPF, this is a problem, because Windows Forms and WPF controls are bound to a single thread. With every control, you can invoke methods only from the thread that created the control. This also means that if you have a background thread, you cannot directly access the UI controls from this thread.

The only methods with Windows Forms controls that you can invoke from a different thread than the creator thread are `Invoke()`, `BeginInvoke()`, `EndInvoke()`, and the property `InvokeRequired`. `BeginInvoke()` and `EndInvoke()` are asynchronous variants of `Invoke()`. These methods switch to the creator thread to invoke the method that is assigned to a delegate parameter that you can pass to these methods. Using these methods is not that easy, which is why beginning with .NET 2.0 a new component, together with a new asynchronous pattern, was added: the event-based asynchronous pattern.

With the event-based asynchronous pattern, the asynchronous component offers a method with the suffix `Async`; for example, the synchronous method `DoATask()` has the name `DoATaskAsync()` in the asynchronous version. To get the result information, the component also needs to define an event that has the suffix `Completed`, for example, `DoATaskCompleted`. While the action happening in the `DoATaskAsync()` method is running in a background thread, the event `DoATaskCompleted` is fired in the same thread as the caller.

With the event-based asynchronous pattern, the asynchronous component optionally can support cancellation and information about progress. For cancellation, the method should have the name `CancelAsync()`, and for progress information, an event with the suffix `ProgressChanged`, for example, `DoATaskProgressChanged`, is provided.

BackgroundWorker

The `BackgroundWorker` class is one implementation of the asynchronous event pattern. The method `RunWorkerAsync()` starts the method that is associated with the `DoWork` event asynchronously. As soon as the work is done, the event `RunWorkerCompleted` is fired. The names used here are in complete conformance with the event-based asynchronous pattern naming explained earlier.

The `BackgroundWorker` might also support cancellation if the property `WorkerSupportsCancellation` is set to `true`. In that case, the work can be canceled by invoking the `CancelAsync` method. However, the job that is done needs to check for the `CancellationPending` property to verify if it should stop its work. Similar to the new cancellation framework, the `BackgroundWorker` supports cooperative cancellation.

Displaying progress information, the `BackgroundWorker` also does a useful job. The property `WorkerReportsProgress` provides information if the task at work returns progress information. If that's the case, the `ProgressChanged` event can be assigned to receive information about progress changes. The job that does the work needs to report progress by calling the method `ReportProgress()` with the percentage of completed information.

 Another class that implements the asynchronous event pattern is the component `WebClient` *in the* `System.Net` *namespace. This class uses the* `WebRequest` *and* `WebResponse` *classes but provides an easier-to-use interface. The* `WebRequest` *and* `WebResponse` *classes also offer asynchronous programming, but here it is based on the asynchronous pattern with the* `IAsyncResult` *interface.*

The sample application demonstrates the use of the `BackgroundWorker` control in a WPF application by doing a task that takes some time. Create a new WPF application, and add three `Label` controls, three `TextBox` controls, two `Button` controls, and one `ProgressBar` to the window, as you can see for the running application in Figure 20-3.

Configure the properties of the controls as listed in the following table.

FIGURE 20-3

CONTROL	PROPERTY AND EVENTS	VALUE
Label	Content	X:
TextBox	x:Name	textX
Label	Content	Y:
TextBox	x:Name	textY

continues

(continued)

CONTROL	PROPERTY AND EVENTS	VALUE
Label	Content	Result:
TextBox	x:Name	textResult
Button	x:Name	buttonCalculate
	Text	Calculate
	Click	OnCalculate
Button	x:Name	buttonCancel
	Text	Cancel
	IsEnabled	False
	Click	OnCancel
ProgressBar	x:Name	progressBar

Within the code-behind, add a `BackgroundWorker` object to the `BackgroundWorkerWindow` and assign the event `DoWork` to the `OnDoWork()` method. For the `BackgroundWorker` class, you need to import the namespace `System.ComponentModel`.

```csharp
public partial class BackgroundWorkerWindow : Window
{
    private BackgroundWorker backgroundWorker;

    public BackgroundWorkerWindow()
    {
        InitializeComponent();
        backgroundWorker = new BackgroundWorker();
        backgroundWorker.DoWork += OnDoWork;
```

code snippet BackgroundWorkersSample/Window1.xaml.cs

The method `OnCalculate()` is the event handler for the `Click` event from the `Button` control named `buttonCalculate`. In the implementation, `buttonCalculate` is disabled, so the user cannot click the button again until the calculation is completed. To start the `BackgroundWorker`, invoke the method `RunWorkerAsync()`. The `BackgroundWorker` uses a thread pool thread to do the calculation. `RunWorkerAsync()` requires the input parameters, which are passed to the handler that is assigned to the `DoWork` event.

```csharp
private void OnCalculate(object sender, RoutedEventArgs e)
{
    this.buttonCalculate.IsEnabled = false;
    this.textResult.Text = String.Empty;
    this.buttonCancel.IsEnabled = true;
    this.progressBar.Value = 0;

    backgroundWorker.RunWorkerAsync(Tuple.Create<int.Parse(textX.Text),
        int.Parse(textY.Text)));
}
```

The method `OnDoWork()` is connected to the `DoWork` event of the `BackgroundWorker` control. With the `DoWorkEventArgs`, the input parameters are received with the property `Argument`. The implementation simulates functionality that takes some time with a sleep time of 5 seconds. After sleeping, the result of the calculation is written to the `Result` property of `DoEventArgs`. If you add the calculation and sleep time to the `OnCalculate()` method instead, the Windows application is blocked from user input while this is active. However, here a separate thread is used, and the user interface is still active.

```
private void OnDoWork(object sender, DoWorkEventArgs e)
{
    var t = e.Argument as Tuple<int, int>;

    Thread.Sleep(5000);
    e.Result = t.Item1 + t.Item2;
}
```

After `OnDoWork` is completed, the background worker fires the `RunWorkerCompleted` event. The method `OnWorkCompleted()` is associated with this event. Here, the result is received from the `Result` property of the `RunWorkerCompletedEventArgs` parameter, and this result is written to the result `TextBox` control. When firing the event, the `BackgroundWorker` control changes control to the creator thread, so there is no need to use the `Invoke` methods of the WPF controls, and you can invoke properties and methods of UI controls directly.

```
private void OnWorkCompleted(object sender,
                             RunWorkerCompletedEventArgs e)
{
    this.textResult.Text = e.Result.ToString();

    this.buttonCalculate.IsEnabled = true;
    this.buttonCancel.IsEnabled = false;
}
```

Now, you can test the application and see that the calculation runs independently of the UI thread, the UI is still active, and the window can be moved around. However, the cancel and progress bar functionality still needs implementation.

Enable Cancel

To enable the cancel functionality to stop the thread's progress while it is running, you must set the `BackgroundWorker` property `WorkerSupportsCancellation` to true. Next, you have to implement the `OnCancel` handler that is connected to the `Click` event of the control `buttonCancel`. The `BackgroundWorker` control has the `CancelAsync()` method to cancel an asynchronous task that is going on.

Available for download on Wrox.com

```
private void OnCancel(object sender, RoutedEventArgs e)
{
    backgroundWorker.CancelAsync();
}
```

code snippet BackgroundWorkersSample/Window1.xaml.cs

The asynchronous task is not canceled automatically. In the `OnDoWork()` handler that does the asynchronous task, you must change the implementation to examine the `CancellationPending` property of the `BackgroundWorker` control. This property is set as soon as `CancelAsync()` is invoked. If a cancellation is pending, set the `Cancel` property of `DoWorkEventArgs` to true and exit the handler.

```
private void OnDoWork(object sender, DoWorkEventArgs e)
{
    var t = e.Argument as Tuple<int, int>;

    for (int i = 0; i < 10; i++)
    {
        Thread.Sleep(500);

        if (backgroundWorker.CancellationPending)
        {
            e.Cancel = true;
            return;
        }
    }

    e.Result = t.Item1 + t.Item2;
}
```

The completion handler `OnWorkCompleted()` is invoked if the asynchronous method has completed successfully or if it was canceled. If it was canceled, you cannot access the `Result` property, because this throws an `InvalidOperationException` with the information that the operation has been canceled. So, you have to check the `Cancelled` property of `RunWorkerCompletedEventArgs` and behave accordingly.

```
private void OnWorkCompleted(object sender,
                             RunWorkerCompletedEventArgs e)
{
    if (e.Cancelled)
    {
        this.textResult.Text = "Cancelled";
    }
    else
    {
        this.textResult.Text = e.Result.ToString();
    }
    this.buttonCalculate.IsEnabled = true;
    this.buttonCancel.IsEnabled = false;
}
```

Running the application once more, you can cancel the asynchronous progress from the user interface.

Enable Progress

To get progress information to the user interface, you must set the `BackgroundWorker` property `WorkerReportsProgress` to true.

With the `OnDoWork` method, you can report the progress to the `BackgroundWorker` control with the `ReportProgress()` method:

Available for download on Wrox.com

```
private void OnDoWork(object sender, DoWorkEventArgs e)
{
    var t = e.Argument as Tuple<int, int>;

    for (int i = 0; i < 10; i++)
    {
        Thread.Sleep(500);
        backgroundWorker.ReportProgress(i * 10);
        if (backgroundWorker.CancellationPending)
        {
            e.Cancel = true;
            return;
        }
    }

    e.Result = t.Item1 + t.Item2;
}
```

code snippet BackgroundWorkersSample/Window1.xaml.cs

The method `ReportProgress()` fires the `ProgressChanged` event of the `BackgroundWorker` control. This event changes the control to the UI thread.

Add the method `OnProgressChanged()` to the `ProgressChanged` event, and in the implementation set a new value to the progress bar control that is received from the property `ProgressPercentage` of `ProgressChangedEventArgs`:

```
private void OnProgressChanged(object sender, ProgressChangedEventArgs e)
{
    this.progressBar.Value = e.ProgressPercentage;
}
```

In the `OnWorkCompleted()` event handler, the progress bar finally is set to the 100% value:

```
    private void OnWorkCompleted(object sender, RunWorkerCompletedEventArgs e)
    {
        if (e.Cancelled)
        {
            this.textBoxResult.Text = "Canceled";
        }
        else
        {
            this.textBoxResult.Text = e.Result.ToString();
        }
        this.buttonCalculate.Enabled = true;
        this.buttonCancel.Enabled = false;
        this.progressBar.Value = 100;
    }
```

Creating an Event-Based Asynchronous Component

To create a custom component that supports the event-based asynchronous pattern, more work needs to be done. To demonstrate this with a simple scenario, the class `AsyncComponent` just returns a converted input string after a time span, as you can see with the synchronous method `LongTask()`. To offer asynchronous support, the public interface provides the asynchronous method `LongTaskAsync()` and the event `LongTaskCompleted`. This event is of type `EventHandler<LongTaskCompletedEventArgs>`, which defines the parameter types `object` and `LongTaskCompletedEventArgs`. `LongTaskCompletedEventArgs` is a type created later where the caller can read the result of the asynchronous operation.

In addition, some helper methods such as `DoLongTask` and `CompletionMethod` are needed; these are discussed next.

```
using System;
using System.Collections.Generic;
using System.ComponentModel;
using System.Threading;

namespace Wrox.ProCSharp.Threading
{
    public delegate void LongTaskCompletedEventHandler(object sender,
        LongTaskCompletedEventArgs e);

    public partial class AsyncComponent: Component
    {
        private Dictionary<object, AsyncOperation> userStateDictionary =
            new Dictionary<object, AsyncOperation>();
        private SendOrPostCallback onCompletedDelegate;

        public event EventHandler<LongTaskCompletedEventArgs> LongTaskCompleted;

        public AsyncComponent()
        {
            InitializeComponent();
            InitializeDelegates();
        }

        public AsyncComponent(IContainer container)
        {
            container.Add(this);

            InitializeComponent();
            InitializeDelegates();
        }

        private void InitializeDelegates()
```

```
        {
            onCompletedDelegate = LongTaskCompletion;
        }

        public string LongTask(string input)
        {
            Console.WriteLine("LongTask started");
            Thread.Sleep(5000);
            Console.WriteLine("LongTask finished");
            return input.ToUpper();
        }

        public void LongTaskAsync(string input, object taskId)
        {
            //.
        }

        private void LongTaskCompletion(object operationState)
        {
            //.
        }

        protected void OnLongTaskCompleted(LongTaskCompletedEventArgs e)
        {
            //.
        }

        // running in a background thread
        private void DoLongTask(string input, AsyncOperation asyncOp)
        {
            //.
        }

        private void CompletionMethod(string output, Exception ex,
                bool cancelled, AsyncOperation asyncOp)
        {
            //.
        }
    }

    public class LongTaskCompletedEventArgs: AsyncCompletedEventArgs
    {
        //.
    }
}
```

code snippet AsyncComponent/AsyncComponent.cs

The method LongTaskAsync needs to start the synchronous operation asynchronously. If the component allows starting the asynchronous task several times concurrently, the client needs to have an option to map the different results to the tasks started. This is why the second parameter of LongTaskAsync requires a taskId that can be used by the client to map the results. Of course, inside the component itself the task ID needs to be remembered to map the results. .NET provides the class AsyncOperationManager to create AsyncOperationObjects to help keep track of the state of operations. The class AsyncOperationManager has one method, CreateOperation(), where a task identifier can be passed, and an AsyncOperation object is returned. This operation is kept as an item in the dictionary userStateDictionary that was created earlier.

Then, a delegate of type Action<string, AsyncOperation> is created, and the method DoLongTask is assigned to that delegate instance. BeginInvoke() is the method of the delegate used to start the method DoLongTask() asynchronously, using a thread from the thread pool. The parameters needed with this delegate are all input parameters from the caller plus the `AsyncOperation` parameter for getting the status and mapping the result of the operation.

```
public void LongTaskAsync(string input, object taskId)
{
    AsyncOperation asyncOp = AsyncOperationManager.CreateOperation(taskId);

    lock (userStateDictionary)
    {
        if (userStateDictionary.ContainsKey(taskId))
            throw new ArgumentException("taskId must be unique", "taskId");

        userStateDictionary[taskId] = asyncOp;
    }

    Action<string, Asyncoperation> longTaskDelegate = DoLongTask;
    longTaskDelegate.BeginInvoke(input, asyncOp, null, null);
}
```

The method `DoLongTask()` is now called asynchronously by using the delegate. The synchronous method `LongTask()` can now be invoked to get the output value.

Because an exception that might happen inside the synchronous method should not just blow up the background thread, any exception is caught and remembered with the variable e of type `Exception`. Finally, the `CompletionMethod()` is invoked to inform the caller about the result.

```
// running in a background thread
private void DoLongTask(string input, AsyncOperation asyncOp)
{
    Exception e = null;
    string output = null;
    try
    {
        output = LongTask(input);
    }
    catch (Exception ex)
    {
        e = ex;
    }

    this.CompletionMethod(output, e, false, asyncOp);
}
```

With the implementation of the `CompletionMethod`, the `userStateDictionary` is cleaned up as the operation is removed. The `PostOperationCompleted()` method of the `AsyncOperation` object ends the lifetime of the asynchronous operation and informs the caller, using the `onCompletedDelegate` method. This method ensures that the delegate is invoked on the thread as needed for the application type. To get information to the caller, an object of type `LongTaskCompletedEventArgs` is created and passed to the method `PostOperationCompleted()`.

```
private void CompletionMethod(string output, Exception ex,
    bool cancelled, AsyncOperation asyncOp)
{
    lock (userStateDictionary)
    {
        userStateDictionary.Remove(asyncOp.UserSuppliedState);
    }

    // results of the operation
    asyncOp.PostOperationCompleted(onCompletedDelegate,
        new LongTaskCompletedEventArgs(output, ex, cancelled,
            asyncOp.UserSuppliedState));
}
```

For passing information to the caller, the class LongTaskCompletedEventArgs derives from the base class AsyncCompletedEventArgs and adds a property containing output information. In the constructor, the base constructor is invoked to pass exception, cancellation, and user state information.

```
public class LongTaskCompletedEventArgs: AsyncCompletedEventArgs
{
    public LongTaskCompletedEventArgs(string output, Exception e,
                                      bool cancelled, object state)
       : base(e, cancelled, state)
    {
       this.output = output;
    }

    private string output;

    public string Output
    {
       get
       {
          RaiseExceptionIfNecessary();
          return output;
       }
    }
}
```

The method asyncOp.PostOperationCompleted() uses the onCompletedDelegate. This delegate was initialized to reference the method LongTaskCompletion. LongTaskCompletion needs to fulfill the parameter requirements of the SendOrPostCallbackDelegate. The implementation just casts the parameter to LongTaskCompletedEventArgs, which was the type of the object that was passed to the PostOperationCompleted method, and calls the method OnLongTaskCompleted.

```
private void LongTaskCompletion(object operationState)
{
    var e = operationState as LongTaskCompletedEventArgs;

    OnLongTaskCompleted(e);
}
```

OnLongTaskCompleted then just fires the event LongTaskCompleted to return the LongTaskCompletedEventArgs to the caller.

```
protected void OnLongTaskCompleted(LongTaskCompletedEventArgs e)
{
    if (LongTaskCompleted != null)
    {
        LongTaskCompleted(this, e);
    }
}
```

After creating the component, it is really easy to use it. The event LongTaskCompleted is assigned to the method Comp_LongTaskCompleted, and the method LongTaskAsync() is invoked. With a simple console application, you will see that the event handler Comp_LongTaskCompleted is called from a thread different from the main thread. (This is different from Windows Forms applications, as you will see in the code that follows.)

```
static void Main()
{
    Console.WriteLine("Main thread: {0}",
          Thread.CurrentThread.ManagedThreadId);

    AsyncComponent comp = new AsyncComponent();
    comp.LongTaskCompleted += Comp_LongTaskCompleted;
```

```
    comp.LongTaskAsync("input", 33);

    Console.ReadLine();
}

static void Comp_LongTaskCompleted(object sender,
    LongTaskCompletedEventArgs e)
{
    Console.WriteLine("completed, result: {0}, thread: {1}", e.Output,
        Thread.CurrentThread.ManagedThreadId);
}
```

code snippet AsyncComponent/Program.cs

With a Windows Forms application the `SynchronizationContext` is set to `WindowsFormsSynchronizationContext` — that's why the event handler code is invoked in the same thread:

```
WindowsFormsSynchronizationContext syncContext =
    new WindowsFormsSynchronizationContext();
SynchronizationContext.SetSynchronizationContext(syncContext);
```

SUMMARY

This chapter explored how to code applications that use multiple threads using the `System.Threading` namespace and multiple tasks using the `System.Threading.Tasks` namespace. Using multithreading in your applications takes careful planning. Too many threads can cause resource issues, and not enough threads can cause your application to seem sluggish and to perform poorly. With tasks, you get an abstraction to threads. This abstraction helps you not to create too many threads because threads are reused from a pool.

You've seen various ways to create multiple threads such as using the delegate, timers, a `ThreadPool`, and the `Thread` class. Various synchronization techniques have been explored, such as a simple `lock` statement, as well as the `Monitor`, `Semaphore`, and `Event` classes. You've seen how to program the asynchronous pattern with the `IAsyncResult` interface and the event-based asynchronous pattern.

The `System.Threading` namespace in the .NET Framework gives you multiple ways to manipulate threads; however, this does not mean that the .NET Framework handles all the difficult tasks of multithreading for you. You need to consider thread priority and synchronization issues. This chapter discussed these issues and how to code for them in your C# applications. It also looked at the problems associated with deadlocks and race conditions.

Just remember that if you are going to use multithreading in your C# applications, careful planning needs to be a major part of your efforts.

Here are some final guidelines regarding threading:

➤ Try to keep synchronization requirements to a minimum. Synchronization is complex and blocks threads. You can avoid it if you try to avoid sharing state. Of course, this is not always possible.

➤ Static members of a class should be thread-safe. Usually, this is the case with classes in the .NET Framework.

➤ Instance state does not need to be thread-safe. For best performance, synchronization is better used outside of the class where it is needed, and not with every member of the class. Instance members of .NET Framework classes usually are not thread-safe. In the MSDN library, you can find this information documented for every class of the Framework in the Thread Safety section.

The next chapter gives information on another core .NET topic: security.

21

Security

WHAT'S IN THIS CHAPTER?

➤ Authentication and authorization

➤ Cryptography

➤ Access control to resources

➤ Code access security

Security has several key elements that you need to consider in making your applications secure. One is the user of the application. Is it really the user, or someone posing as the user, who is accessing the application? How can this user be trusted? As you will see in this chapter, the user first needs to be authenticated, and then authorization occurs to verify if the user is allowed to use the requested resources.

What about data that is stored or sent across the network? Is it possible that someone accesses this data, for example, by using a network sniffer? Encryption of data is important here. Some technologies, such as Windows Communication Foundation (WCF) provide encryption capabilities by simple configuration, so you can see what's done behind the scenes.

Yet another aspect is the application itself. What if the application is hosted by a web provider? How is the application restricted from doing harm to the server?

This chapter explores the features available in .NET to help you manage security, and shows you how .NET protects you from malicious code, how to administer security policies, and how to access the security subsystem programmatically.

AUTHENTICATION AND AUTHORIZATION

Two fundamental pillars of security are authentication and authorization. *Authentication* is the process of identifying the user, and *authorization* occurs afterward to verify if the identified user is allowed to access a specific resource.

Identity and Principal

You can identify the user running the application by using an *identity*. The WindowsIdentity class represents a Windows user. If you don't identify the user with a Windows account, you can use other classes that implement the interface IIdentity. With this interface you have access to the name of the user, information about whether the user is authenticated, and the authentication type.

A *principal* is an object that contains the identity of the user and the roles that the user belongs to. The interface IPrincipal defines the property Identity, which returns an IIdentity object, and the method IsInRole with which you can verify that the user is a member of a specific role. A *role* is a collection of users who have the same security permissions, and it is the unit of administration for users. Roles can be Windows groups or just a collection of strings that you define.

The principal classes available with .NET are WindowsPrincipal and GenericPrincipal. You can also create a custom principal class that implements the interface IPrincipal.

In the following example, you create a console application that provides access to the principal in an application that, in turn, enables you to access the underlying Windows account. You need to import the System.Security.Principal and System.Threading namespaces. First, you must specify that .NET should automatically hook up the principal with the underlying Windows account. This must be done because .NET does not automatically populate the thread's CurrentPrincipal property for security reasons. You can do it like this:

Available for download on Wrox.com

```csharp
using System;
using System.Security.Principal;
using System.Threading;

namespace Wrox.ProCSharp.Security
{
    class Program
    {
        static void Main()
        {
AppDomain.CurrentDomain.SetPrincipalPolicy(PrincipalPolicy.WindowsPrincipal);
```

code snippet WindowsPrincipal/Program.cs

It is possible to use WindowsIdentity.GetCurrent() to access the Windows account details; however, that method is best used when you are going to look at the principal only once. If you want to access the principal a number of times, it is more efficient to set the policy so that the current thread provides access to the principal for you. If you use the SetPrincipalPolicy method, it is specified that the principal in the current thread should hold a WindowsIdentity object. All identity classes, such as WindowsIdentity, implement the IIdentity interface. The interface contains three properties (AuthenticationType, IsAuthenticated, and Name) for all derived identity classes to implement.

Add code to access the principal's properties from the Thread object:

```csharp
WindowsPrincipal principal =
    (WindowsPrincipal)Thread.CurrentPrincipal;
WindowsIdentity identity = (WindowsIdentity)principal.Identity;
Console.WriteLine("IdentityType: " + identity.ToString());
Console.WriteLine("Name: {0}", identity.Name);
Console.WriteLine("'Users'?: {0} ",
                    principal.IsInRole(WindowsBuiltInRole.User));
Console.WriteLine("'Administrators'? {0}",
        principal.IsInRole(WindowsBuiltInRole.Administrator));
Console.WriteLine("Authenticated: {0}", identity.IsAuthenticated);
Console.WriteLine("AuthType: {0}", identity.AuthenticationType);
Console.WriteLine("Anonymous? {0}", identity.IsAnonymous);
Console.WriteLine("Token: {0}", identity.Token);
        }
    }
}
```

The output from this console application looks similar to the following lines; it will vary according to your machine's configuration and the roles associated with the account under which you are signed in:

```
IdentityType:System.Security.Principal.WindowsIdentity
Name: farabove\christian
'Users'? True
'Administrators'? False
Authenticated: True
AuthType: NTLM
Anonymous? False
Token: 416
```

It is enormously beneficial to be able to easily access details about the current users and their roles. With this information, you can make decisions about what actions should be permitted or denied. The ability to make use of roles and Windows user groups provides the added benefit that administration can be done by using standard user administration tools, and you can usually avoid altering the code when user roles change. The following section looks at roles in more detail.

Roles

Role-based security is especially useful in situations in which access to resources is an issue. A primary example is the finance industry, in which employees' roles define what information they can access and what actions they can perform.

Role-based security is also ideal for use in conjunction with Windows accounts, or a custom user directory to manage access to web-based resources. For example, a web site could restrict access to its content until a user registers with the site, and then additionally provide access to special content only, if the user is a paying subscriber. In many ways, ASP.NET makes role-based security easier because much of the code is based on the server.

For example, to implement a Web service that requires authentication, you could use the account subsystem of Windows and write the web method in such a way that it ensures the user is a member of a specific Windows user group before allowing access to the method's functionality.

Imagine a scenario with an intranet application that relies on Windows accounts. The system has a group called `Manager` and one called `Assistant`; users are assigned to these groups according to their role within the organization. Say that the application contains a feature that displays information about employees that should be accessed only by users in the `Managers` group. You can easily use code that checks whether the current user is a member of the `Managers` group and whether he is permitted or denied access.

However, if you decide later to rearrange the account groups and to introduce a group called `Personnel` that also has access to employee details, you will have a problem. You will need to go through all the code and update it to include rules for this new group.

A better solution would be to create a permission called something like `ReadEmployeeDetails` and assign it to groups where necessary. If the code applies a check for the `ReadEmployeeDetails` permission, updating the application to allow those in the `Personnel` group access to employee details is simply a matter of creating the group, placing the users in it, and assigning the `ReadEmployeeDetails` permission.

Declarative Role-Based Security

Just as with code access security, you can implement role-based security requests ("the user must be in the Administrators group") using imperative requests by calling the `IsInRole()` method from the `IPrincipal` class, or using attributes. You can state permission requirements declaratively at the class or method level using the `[PrincipalPermission]` attribute:

```
using System;
using System.Security;
using System.Security.Principal;
using System.Security.Permissions;
```

```
namespace Wrox.ProCSharp.Security
{
    class Program
    {
        static void Main()
        {
            AppDomain.CurrentDomain.SetPrincipalPolicy(
                PrincipalPolicy.WindowsPrincipal);
            try
            {
                ShowMessage();
            }
            catch (SecurityException exception)
            {
                Console.WriteLine("Security exception caught ({0})", exception.Message);
                Console.WriteLine("The current principal must be in the local"
                                    + "Users group");
            }
        }

        [PrincipalPermission(SecurityAction.Demand, Role = "BUILTIN\\Users")]
        static void ShowMessage()
        {
            Console.WriteLine("The current principal is logged in locally ");
            Console.WriteLine("(member of the local Users group)");
        }
    }
}
```

code snippet RoleBasedSecurity/Program.cs

The ShowMessage() method will throw an exception unless you execute the application in the context of a user in the Windows local Users group. For a web application, the account under which the ASP.NET code is running must be in the group, although in a "real-world" example you would certainly avoid adding this account to the administrators group!

If you run the preceding code using an account in the local Users group, the output will look like this:

```
The current principal is logged in locally
(member of the local Users group)
```

Client Application Services

Visual Studio makes it easy to use authentication services that previously have been built for ASP.NET web applications. With this service, it is possible to use the same authentication mechanism with both Windows and web applications. This is a provider model that is primarily based on the classes Membership and Roles in the namespace System.Web.Security. With the Membership class you can validate, create, delete, and find users; change the password; and do other things related to users. With the Roles class you can add and delete roles, get the roles for a user, and change roles for a user. Where the roles and users are stored depends on the provider. The ActiveDirectoryMembershipProvider accesses users and roles in the Active Directory; the SqlMembershipProvider uses a SQL Server database. With .NET 4 these providers exist for client application services ClientFormsAuthenticationMembershipProvider and ClientWindowsAuthenticationMembershipProvider.

Next, you use client application services with Forms authentication. To do this, first you need to start an application server, and then you can use this service from Windows Forms or Windows Presentation Foundation (WPF).

Application Services

For using client application services, you can create an ASP.NET Web service project that offers application services.

With the project a membership provider is needed. You can use an existing one, but you can also easily create a custom provider. The sample code here defines the class `SampleMembershipProvider`, which is derived from the base class `MembershipProvider`. `MembershipProvider` is defined in the namespace `System.Web.Security` in the assembly `System.Web.ApplicationServices`. You must override all abstract methods from the base class. For login, the only implementation needed is the method `ValidateUser`. All other methods can throw a `NotSupportedException`, as shown with the property `ApplicationName`. The sample code here uses a `Dictionary<string, string>` that contains usernames and passwords. Of course, you can change it to your own implementation, for example, to read username and password from the database.

```csharp
using System;
using System.Collections.Generic;
using System.Collections.Specialized;
using System.Web.Security;

namespace Wrox.ProCSharp.Security
{
    public class SampleMembershipProvider: MembershipProvider
    {
        private Dictionary<string, string> users = new Dictionary<string, string>();
        internal static string ManagerUserName = "Manager".ToLowerInvariant();
        internal static string EmployeeUserName = "Employee".ToLowerInvariant();

        public override void Initialize(string name, NameValueCollection config)
        {
            users = new Dictionary<string, string>();
            users.Add(ManagerUserName, "secret@Pa$$w0rd");
            users.Add(EmployeeUserName, "s0me@Secret");

            base.Initialize(name, config);
        }

        public override string ApplicationName
        {
            get
            {
                throw new NotImplementedException();
            }
            set
            {
                throw new NotImplementedException();
            }
        }

        // override abstract Membership members
        // ...

        public override bool ValidateUser(string username, string password)
        {
            if (users.ContainsKey(username.ToLowerInvariant()))
            {
                return password.Equals(users[username.ToLowerInvariant()]);
            }
            return false;
        }
    }
}
```

code snippet AppServices/SampleMembershipProvider.cs

For using roles, you also need to implement a role provider. The class `SampleRoleProvider` derives from the base class `RoleProvider` and implements the methods `GetRolesForUser()` and `IsUserInRole()`:

Available for
download on
Wrox.com

```csharp
using System;
using System.Collections.Specialized;
using System.Web.Security;

namespace Wrox.ProCSharp.Security
{
    public class SampleRoleProvider: RoleProvider
    {
        internal static string ManagerRoleName = "Manager".ToLowerInvariant();
        internal static string EmployeeRoleName = "Employee".ToLowerInvariant();

        public override void Initialize(string name, NameValueCollection config)
        {
            base.Initialize(name, config);
        }

        public override void AddUsersToRoles(string[] usernames,
                string[] roleNames)
        {
            throw new NotImplementedException();
        }

        // override abstract RoleProvider members
        // ...

        public override string[] GetRolesForUser(string username)
        {
            if (string.Compare(username,
                SampleMembershipProvider.ManagerUserName, true) == 0)
            {
                return new string[] { ManagerRoleName };
            }
            else if (string.Compare(username,
                    SampleMembershipProvider.EmployeeUserName, true) == 0)
            {
                return new string[] { EmployeeRoleName };
            }
            else
            {
                return new string[0];
            }
        }

        public override bool IsUserInRole(string username, string roleName)
        {
            string[] roles = GetRolesForUser(username);
            foreach (var role in roles)
            {
                if (string.Compare(role, roleName, true) == 0)
                {
                    return true;
                }
            }
            return false;
        }
    }
}
```

code snippet AppServices/SampleRoleProvider.cs

Authentication services must be configured in the `Web.config` file. On the production system, it would be useful from a security standpoint to configure SSL with the server hosting application services.

Available for
download on
Wrox.com

```
<system.web.extensions>
  <scripting>
    <webServices>
      <authenticationService enabled="true" requireSSL="false"/>
      <roleService enabled="true"/>
    </webServices>
  </scripting>
</system.web.extensions>
```

code snippet AppServices/web.config

Within the `<system.web>` section, the `membership` and `roleManager` elements must be configured to reference the classes that implement the membership and role provider:

```
<system.web>
  <membership defaultProvider="SampleMembershipProvider">
    <providers>
      <add name="SampleMembershipProvider"
           type="Wrox.ProCSharp.Security.SampleMembershipProvider"/>
    </providers>
  </membership>
  <roleManager enabled="true" defaultProvider="SampleRoleProvider">
    <providers>
      <add name="SampleRoleProvider"
           type="Wrox.ProCSharp.Security.SampleRoleProvider"/>
    </providers>
  </roleManager>
```

For debugging, you can assign a port number and virtual path with the Web tab of project properties. The sample application uses the port 55555 and the virtual path `/AppServices`. If you use different values, you need to change the configuration of the client application accordingly.

Now the application service can be used from a client application.

Client Application

With the client application, WPF is used. Visual Studio has a project setting named Services that allows the use of client application services. Here, you can set Forms authentication and the location of the authentication and roles service to the address defined previously: `http://localhost:55555/AppServices`. All that's done from this project configuration is to reference the assemblies `System.Web` and `System.Web.Extensions`, and change the application's configuration file to configure membership and role providers that use the classes `ClientAuthenticationMembershipProvider` and `ClientRoleProvider` and the address of the Web service that is used by these providers.

Available for
download on
Wrox.com

```
<?xml version="1.0" encoding="utf-8"?>
<configuration>
  <system.web>
    <membership defaultProvider="ClientAuthenticationMembershipProvider">
      <providers>
        <add name="ClientAuthenticationMembershipProvider"
             type="System.Web.ClientServices.Providers,
             ClientFormsAuthenticationMembershipProvider,
             System.Web.Extensions, Version=4.0.0.0, Culture=neutral,
             PublicKeyToken=31bf3856ad364e35" serviceUri=
"http://localhost:55555/AppServices/Authentication_JSON_AppService.axd" />
      </providers>
    </membership>
    <roleManager defaultProvider="ClientRoleProvider" enabled="true">
      <providers>
```

```
              <add name="ClientRoleProvider"
                  type="System.Web.ClientServices.Providers.ClientRoleProvider,
                  System.Web.Extensions, Version=4.0.0.0, Culture=neutral,
                  PublicKeyToken=31bf3856ad364e35" serviceUri=
                  "http://localhost:55555/AppServices/Role_JSON_AppService.axd"
                  cacheTimeout="86400" />
          </providers>
        </roleManager>
      </system.web>
    </configuration>
```

code snippet AuthenticationServices/app.config

The Windows application just uses `Label`, `TextBox`, `PasswordBox`, and `Button` controls, as shown in Figure 21-1. The `Label` with the content User Validated shows up only when the logon is successful.

The handler of the `Button.Click` event invokes the `ValidateUser()` method of the `Membership` class. Because of the configured provider `ClientAuthenticationMembershipProvider`, the provider in turn invokes the Web service and calls the method `ValidateUser()` of the `SampleMembershipProvider` class to verify a successful logon. With success, the Label `labelValidatedInfo` is made visible; otherwise, a message box pops up:

Available for download on Wrox.com

```csharp
private void OnLogin(object sender, RoutedEventArgs e)
{
    try
    {
        if (Membership.ValidateUser(textUsername.Text,
            textPassword.Password))
        {
            // user validated!
            labelValidatedInfo.Visibility = Visibility.Visible;
        }
        else
        {
            MessageBox.Show("Username or password not valid",
                    "Client Authentication Services", MessageBoxButton.OK,
                    MessageBoxImage.Warning);
        }
    }
    catch (WebException ex)
    {
        MessageBox.Show(ex.Message, "Client Application Services",
                MessageBoxButton.OK, MessageBoxImage.Error);
    }
}
```

FIGURE 21-1

Figure showing the Client Application Services window with Username "Manager", Password field filled, a Login button, and "User Validated" text.

code snippet AuthenticationServices/MainWindow.xaml.cs

ENCRYPTION

Confidential data should be secured so that it cannot be read by unprivileged users. This is valid both for data that is sent across the network, or stored data. You can encrypt such data with symmetric or asymmetric encryption keys.

With a symmetric key, the same key can be used for encryption and decryption. With asymmetric encryption, different keys are used for encryption and decryption: a public and a private key. Something encrypted using a public key can be decrypted with the corresponding private key. This also works the other way around: something encrypted using a private key can be decrypted by using the corresponding public key, but not the private key.

Public and private keys are always created as a pair. The public key can be made available to everybody, and it can even be put on a web site, but the private key must be safely locked away. Following are some examples where these public and private keys are used to explain encryption.

If Alice sends a message to Bob (see Figure 21-2), and Alice wants to make sure that no one else but Bob can read the message, she uses Bob's public key. The message is encrypted using Bob's public key. Bob opens the message and can decrypt it using his secretly stored private key. This key exchange guarantees that no one but Bob can read Alice's message.

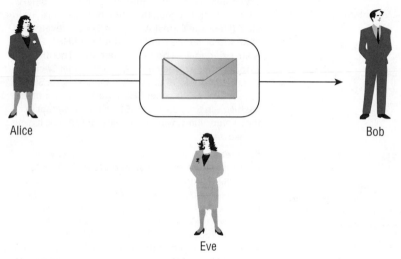

Alice

Bob

Eve

FIGURE 21-2

There is one problem left: Bob can't be sure that the mail comes from Alice. Eve can use Bob's public key to encrypt messages sent to Bob and pretend to be Alice. We can extend this principle using public/private keys. Let's start again with Alice sending a message to Bob. Before Alice encrypts the message using Bob's public key, she adds her signature and encrypts the signature using her own private key. Then she encrypts the mail using Bob's public key. Therefore, it is guaranteed that no one else but Bob can read the mail. When Bob decrypts the message, he detects an encrypted signature. The signature can be decrypted using Alice's public key. For Bob, it is not a problem to access Alice's public key because the key is public. After decrypting the signature, Bob can be sure that it was Alice who sent the message.

The encryption and decryption algorithms using symmetric keys are a lot faster than those using asymmetric keys. The problem with symmetric keys is that the keys must be exchanged in a safe manner. With network communication, one way to do this is by using asymmetric keys first for the key exchange and then symmetric keys for encryption of the data that is sent across the wire.

With the .NET Framework, you find classes for encryption in the namespace `System.Security` `.Cryptography`. Several symmetric and asymmetric algorithms are implemented. You can find algorithm classes for many different purposes. Some of the classes added in .NET 3.5 have a `Cng` prefix or suffix. Cng is short for *Cryptography Next Generation,* which can be used since Windows Vista and Windows Server 2008. This API makes it possible to write a program independently of the algorithm by using a provider-based model. If you are targeting Windows Server 2003 as well, you need to pay attention to what encryption classes to use.

The following table lists encryption classes from the namespace `System.Security.Cryptography` and their purposes. The classes without a `Cng`, `Managed`, or `CryptoServiceProvider` suffix are abstract base classes, such as `MD5`. The `Managed` suffix means that this algorithm is implemented with managed code; other classes might wrap native Windows API calls. The suffix `CryptoServiceProvider` is used with classes that implement the abstract base class. The `Cng` suffix is used with classes that make use of the new Cryptography CNG API.

CATEGORY	CLASSES	DESCRIPTION
Hash	MD5, MD5Cng SHA1, SHA1Managed, SHA1Cng SHA256, SHA256Managed, SHA256Cng SHA384, SHA384Managed, SHA384Cng SHA512, SHA512Managed, SHA512Cng	The purpose of hash algorithms is to create a fixed-length hash value from binary strings of arbitrary length. These algorithms are used with digital signatures and for data integrity. If the same binary string is hashed again, the same hash result is returned. MD5 (Message Digest Algorithm 5) was developed at RSA Laboratories and is faster than SHA1. SHA1 is stronger against brute force attacks. The SHA algorithms were designed by the National Security Agency (NSA). MD5 uses a 128-bit hash size; SHA1 uses 160 bits. The other SHA algorithms contain the hash size in the name. SHA512 is the strongest of these algorithms; with a hash size of 512 bits; it is also the slowest.
Symmetric	DES, DESCryptoServiceProvider TripleDES, TripleDESCryptoServiceProvider Aes, AesCryptoServiceProvider, AesManaged RC2, RC2CryptoServiceProvider Rijandel, RijandelManaged	Symmetric key algorithms use the same key for encryption and decryption of data. DES (Data Encryption Standard) is now considered insecure because it uses just 56 bits for the key size and can be broken in less than 24 hours. Triple-DES is the successor to DES and has a key length of 168 bits, but the effective security it provides is only 112 bit. AES (Advanced Encryption Standard) has a key size of 128, 192, or 256 bits. Rijandel is very similar to AES; it just has more options with the key size. AES is an encryption standard adopted by the U.S. government.
Asymmetric	DSA, DSACryptoServiceProvider ECDsa, ECDsaCng ECDiffieHellman, ECDiffieHellmanCng RSA, RSACryptoServiceProvider	Asymmetric algorithms use different keys for encryption and decryption. RSA (Rivest, Shamir, Adleman) was the first algorithm used for signing as well as encryption. This algorithm is widely used in e-commerce protocols. DSA (Digital Signature Algorithm) is a United States Federal Government standard for digital signatures. ECDSA (Elliptic Curve DSA) and ECDiffieHellman use algorithms based on elliptic curve groups. These algorithms are more secure with shorter key sizes. For example, having a key size of 1024 bits for DSA is similar in security to 160 bits for ECDSA. As a result, ECDSA is much faster. ECDiffieHellman is an algorithm used to exchange private keys in a secure way over a public channel.

Let's get into examples of how these algorithms can be used programmatically.

Signature

The first example demonstrates a signature using the ECDSA algorithm for signing. Alice creates a signature that is encrypted with her private key and can be accessed using her public key. This way, it is guaranteed that the signature is from Alice.

First, take a look at the major steps in the `Main()` method: Alice's keys are created, and the string `"Alice"` is signed and finally verified if the signature is really from Alice by using the public key. The message that is signed is converted to a byte array by using the `Encoding` class. To write the encrypted signature to the console, the byte array that contains the signature is converted to a string with the method `Convert.ToBase64String()`.

Never convert encrypted data to a string using the `Encoding` *class. The* `Encoding` *class verifies and converts invalid values that are not allowed with Unicode, and thus converting the string back to a byte array yields a different result.*

Available for download on Wrox.com

```csharp
using System;
using System.Security.Cryptography;
using System.Text;

namespace Wrox.ProCSharp.Security
{
    class Program
    {
        internal static CngKey aliceKeySignature;
        internal static byte[] alicePubKeyBlob;

        static void Main()
        {
            CreateKeys();

            byte[] aliceData = Encoding.UTF8.GetBytes("Alice");
            byte[] aliceSignature = CreateSignature(aliceData, aliceKeySignature);
            Console.WriteLine("Alice created signature: {0}",
                Convert.ToBase64String(aliceSignature));

            if (VerifySignature(aliceData, aliceSignature, alicePubKeyBlob))
            {
                Console.WriteLine("Alice signature verified successfully");
            }
        }
    }
```

Code snippet SigningDemo/Program.cs

`CreateKeys()` is the method that creates a new key pair for Alice. This key pair is stored in a static field, so it can be accessed from the other methods. The `Create()` method of `CngKey` gets the algorithm as an argument to define a key pair for the algorithm. With the `Export()` method, the public key of the key pair is exported. This public key can be given to Bob for the verification of the signature. Alice keeps the private key. Instead of creating a key pair with the `CngKey` class, you can open existing keys that are stored in the key store. Usually Alice would have a certificate containing a key pair in her private store, and the store could be accessed with `CngKey.Open()`.

```csharp
        static void CreateKeys()
        {
            aliceKeySignature = CngKey.Create(CngAlgorithm.ECDsaP256);
            alicePubKeyBlob = aliceKeySignature.Export(CngKeyBlobFormat.GenericPublicBlob);
        }
```

With the key pair, Alice can create the signature using the `ECDsaCng` class. The constructor of this class receives the `CngKey` from Alice that contains both the public and private key. The private key is used, signing the data with the `SignData()` method.

```csharp
        static byte[] CreateSignature(byte[] data, CngKey key)
        {
            var signingAlg = new ECDsaCng(key);
```

```
            byte[] signature = signingAlg.SignData(data);
            signingAlg.Clear();

            return signature;
        }
```

For verification if the signature was really from Alice, Bob checks the signature by using the public key from Alice. The byte array containing the public key blob can be imported to a `CngKey` object with the static `Import()` method. The `ECDsaCng` class is then used to verify the signature by invoking `VerifyData()`.

```
        static bool VerifySignature(byte[] data, byte[] signature, byte[] pubKey)
        {
            bool retValue = false;
            using (CngKey key = CngKey.Import(pubKey, CngKeyBlobFormat.GenericPublicBlob))
            {
                var signingAlg = new ECDsaCng(key);
                retValue = signingAlg.VerifyData(data, signature);
                signingAlg.Clear();
            }
            return retValue;
        }
    }
}
```

Key Exchange and Secure Transfer

Let's get into a more complex example to exchange a symmetric key for a secure transfer by using the Diffie Hellman algorithm. In the `Main()` method, you can see the main functionality. Alice creates an encrypted message and sends the encrypted message to Bob. Before that, key pairs are created for Alice and Bob. Bob gets access only to Alice's public key, and Alice gets access only to Bob's public key.

```
using System;
using System.IO;
using System.Security.Cryptography;
using System.Text;

namespace Wrox.ProCSharp.Security
{
    class Program
    {
        static CngKey aliceKey;
        static CngKey bobKey;
        static byte[] alicePubKeyBlob;
        static byte[] bobPubKeyBlob;

        static void Main()
        {
            CreateKeys();
            byte[] encrytpedData = AliceSendsData("secret message");
            BobReceivesData(encrytpedData);

        }
```

code snippet SecureTransfer/Program.cs

In the implementation of the `CreateKeys()` method, keys are created to be used with the EC Diffie Hellman 256 algorithm.

```
        private static void CreateKeys()
        {
            aliceKey = CngKey.Create(CngAlgorithm.ECDiffieHellmanP256);
            bobKey = CngKey.Create(CngAlgorithm.ECDiffieHellmanP256);
```

```
        alicePubKeyBlob = aliceKey.Export(CngKeyBlobFormat.EccPublicBlob);
        bobPubKeyBlob = bobKey.Export(CngKeyBlobFormat.EccPublicBlob);
    }
```

In the method `AliceSendsData()`, the string that contains text characters is converted to a byte array by using the `Encoding` class. An `ECDiffieHellmanCng` object is created and initialized with the key pair from Alice. Alice creates a symmetric key by using her key pair and the public key from Bob calling the method `DeriveKeyMaterial()`. The returned symmetric key is used with the symmetric algorithm AES to encrypt the data. `AesCryptoServiceProvider` requires the key and an initialization vector (IV). The IV is generated dynamically from the method `GenerateIV()`. The symmetric key is exchanged with the help of the EC Diffie Hellman algorithm, but the IV must also be exchanged. From the security standpoint, it is okay to transfer the IV unencrypted across the network — just the key exchange must be secured. The IV is stored first as content in the memory stream, followed by the encrypted data where the `CryptoStream` class uses the `encryptor` created by the `AesCryptoServiceProvider` class. Before the encrypted data is accessed from the memory stream, the crypto stream must be closed. Otherwise, end bits would be missing from the encrypted data.

```
        private static byte[] AliceSendsData(string message)
        {
            Console.WriteLine("Alice sends message: {0}", message);
            byte[] rawData = Encoding.UTF8.GetBytes(message);
            byte[] encryptedData = null;

            using (var aliceAlgorithm = new ECDiffieHellmanCng(aliceKey))
            using (CngKey bobPubKey = CngKey.Import(bobPubKeyBlob,
                CngKeyBlobFormat.EccPublicBlob))
            {
                byte[] symmKey = aliceAlgorithm.DeriveKeyMaterial(bobPubKey);
                Console.WriteLine("Alice creates this symmetric key with " +
                    "Bobs public key information: {0}",
                    Convert.ToBase64String(symmKey));

                var aes = new AesCryptoServiceProvider();
                aes.Key = symmKey;
                aes.GenerateIV();
                using (ICryptoTransform encryptor = aes.CreateEncryptor())
                using (MemoryStream ms = new MemoryStream())
                {
                    // create CryptoStream and encrypt data to send
                    var cs = new CryptoStream(ms, encryptor, CryptoStreamMode.Write);

                    // write initialization vector not encrypted
                    ms.Write(aes.IV, 0, aes.IV.Length);
                    cs.Write(rawData, 0, rawData.Length);
                    cs.Close();
                    encryptedData = ms.ToArray();
                }
                aes.Clear();
            }
            Console.WriteLine("Alice: message is encrypted: {0}",
                Convert.ToBase64String(encryptedData));;
            Console.WriteLine();
            return encryptedData;
        }
```

Bob receives encrypted data in the argument of the method `BobReceivesData()`. First, the unencrypted initialization vector must be read. The `BlockSize` property of the class `AesCryptoServiceProvider` returns the number of bits for a block. The number of bytes can be calculated by doing a divide by 8, and the fastest way to do this is by doing a bit shift of 3 bits. Shifting by 1 bit is a division by 2, 2 bits by 4, and 3 bits by 8. With the `for` loop, the first bytes of the raw bytes that contain the IV unencrypted are written to the array `iv`. Next, an `ECDiffieHellmanCng` object is instantiated with the key pair from Bob. Using the public key from Alice, the symmetric key is returned from the method `DeriveKeyMaterial()`.

Comparing the symmetric keys created from Alice and Bob shows that the same key value gets created. Using this symmetric key and the initialization vector, the message from Alice can be decrypted with the `AesCryptoServiceProvider` class.

```
private static void BobReceivesData(byte[] encryptedData)
{
    Console.WriteLine("Bob receives encrypted data");
    byte[] rawData = null;

    var aes = new AesCryptoServiceProvider();

    int nBytes = aes.BlockSize  3;
    byte[] iv = new byte[nBytes];
    for (int i = 0; i < iv.Length; i++)
        iv[i] = encryptedData[i];

    using (var bobAlgorithm = new ECDiffieHellmanCng(bobKey))
    using (CngKey alicePubKey = CngKey.Import(alicePubKeyBlob,
        CngKeyBlobFormat.EccPublicBlob))
    {
        byte[] symmKey = bobAlgorithm.DeriveKeyMaterial(alicePubKey);
        Console.WriteLine("Bob creates this symmetric key with " +
            "Alices public key information: {0}",
            Convert.ToBase64String(symmKey));

        aes.Key = symmKey;
        aes.IV = iv;

        using (ICryptoTransform decryptor = aes.CreateDecryptor())
        using (MemoryStream ms = new MemoryStream())
        {
            var cs = new CryptoStream(ms, decryptor, CryptoStreamMode.Write);
            cs.Write(encryptedData, nBytes, encryptedData.Length - nBytes);
            cs.Close();

            rawData = ms.ToArray();

            Console.WriteLine("Bob decrypts message to: {0}",
                Encoding.UTF8.GetString(rawData));
        }
        aes.Clear();
    }
}
```

When you run the application, you can see output similar to the following on the console. The message from Alice is encrypted, and decrypted by Bob with the securely exchanged symmetric key.

```
Alice sends message: secret message
Alice creates this symmetric key with Bobs public key information:
5NWat8AemzFCYo1IIae9S3Vn4AXyai4aL8ATFo41vbw=
Alice: message is encrypted: 3C5U9CpYxnoFTk3Ew2V0T5Po0Jgryc5R7Te8ztau5N0=

Bob receives encrypted message
Bob creates this symmetric key with Alices public key information:
5NWat8AemzFCYo1IIae9S3Vn4AXyai4aL8ATFo41vbw=
Bob decrypts message to: secret message
```

ACCESS CONTROL TO RESOURCES

With the operating system, resources such as files and registry keys, as well as handles of a named pipe, are secured by using an access control list. Figure 21-3 shows the structure of how this maps. The resource has a security descriptor associated. The security descriptor contains information about the owner of the resource and references two access control lists: a discretionary access control list (DACL) and a system access control list (SACL). The DACL defines who has access or no access; the SACL defines audit rules for security event logging. An ACL contains a list of access control entries (ACE). The ACE contains a type, a security identifier, and rights. With the DACL, the ACE can be of type access allowed or access denied. Some of the rights that you can set and get with a file are create, read, write, delete, modify, change permissions, and take ownership.

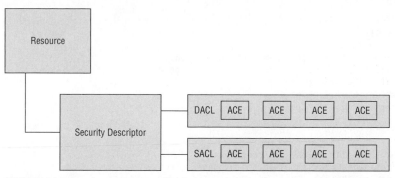

FIGURE 21-3

The classes to read and modify access control are located in the namespace `System.Security .AccessControl`. The following program demonstrates reading the access control list from a file.

The `FileStream` class defines the `GetAccessControl()` method, which returns a `FileSecurity` object. `FileSecurity` is the .NET class that represents a security descriptor for files. `FileSecurity` derives from the base classes `ObjectSecurity`, `CommonObjectSecurity`, `NativeObjectSecurity`, and `FileSystemSecurity`. Other classes that represent a security descriptor are `CryptoKeySecurity`, `EventWaitHandleSecurity`, `MutexSecurity`, `RegistrySecurity`, `SemaphoreSecurity`, `PipeSecurity`, and `ActiveDirectorySecurity`. All of these objects can be secured using an access control list. In general, the corresponding .NET class defines the method `GetAccessControl` to return the corresponding security class; for example, the `Mutex.GetAccessControl()` method returns a `MutexSecurity`, and the `PipeStream.GetAccessControl()` method returns a `PipeSecurity`.

The `FileSecurity` class defines methods to read and change the DACL and SACL. The method `GetAccessRules()` returns the DACL in the form of the class `AuthorizationRuleCollection`. To access the SACL, you can use the method `GetAuditRules()`.

With the method `GetAccessRules()`, you can define if inherited access rules, and not only access rules directly defined with the object, should be used. The last parameter defines the type of the security identifier that should be returned. This type must derive from the base class `IdentityReference`. Possible types are `NTAccount` and `SecurityIdentifier`. Both of these classes represent users or groups; the `NTAccount` class finds the security object by its name and the `SecurityIdentifier` class finds the security object by a unique security identifier.

The returned `AuthorizationRuleCollection` contains `AuthorizationRule` objects. The `AuthorizationRule` is the .NET representation of an ACE. With the sample here, a file is accessed, so the `AuthorizationRule` can be cast to a `FileSystemAccessRule`. With ACEs of other resources, different .NET representations exist, such as `MutexAccessRule` and `PipeAccessRule`. With the `FileSystemAccessRule` class, the properties `AccessControlType`, `FileSystemRights`, and `IdentityReference` return information about the ACE.

```
using System;
using System.IO;
using System.Security.AccessControl;
using System.Security.Principal;
```

```
namespace Wrox.ProCSharp.Security
{
    class Program
    {
        static void Main(string[] args)
        {
            string filename = null;
            if (args.Length == 0)
                return;

            filename = args[0];

            FileStream stream = File.Open(filename, FileMode.Open);
            FileSecurity securityDescriptor = stream.GetAccessControl();
            AuthorizationRuleCollection rules =
                    securityDescriptor.GetAccessRules(true, true,
                        typeof(NTAccount));

            foreach (AuthorizationRule rule in rules)
            {
                var fileRule = rule as FileSystemAccessRule;
                Console.WriteLine("Access type: {0}", fileRule.AccessControlType);
                Console.WriteLine("Rights: {0}", fileRule.FileSystemRights);
                Console.WriteLine("Identity: {0}",
                        fileRule.IdentityReference.Value);
                Console.WriteLine();
            }
        }
    }
}
```

code snippet FileAccessControl/Program.cs

By running the application and passing a filename, you can see the access control list for the file. The output shown here lists full control to Administrators and System, modification rights to authenticated users, and read and execute rights to all users belonging to the group Users:

```
Access type: Allow
Rights: FullControl
Identity: BUILTIN\Administrators

Access type: Allow
Rights: FullControl
Identity: NT AUTHORITY\SYSTEM

Access type: Allow
Rights: Modify, Synchronize
Identity: NT AUTHORITY\Authenticated Users

Access type: Allow
Rights: ReadAndExecute, Synchronize
Identity: BUILTIN\Users
```

Setting access rights is very similar to reading access rights. To set access rights, several resource classes that can be secured offer the SetAccessControl() and ModifyAccessControl() methods. The sample code here modifies the access control list of a file by invoking the SetAccessControl() method from the File class. To this method a FileSecurity object is passed. The FileSecurity object is filled with FileSystemAccessRule objects. The access rules listed here deny write access to the Sales group, give read access to the Everyone group, and give full control to the Developers group.

This program runs on your system only if the Windows groups Sales and Developers are defined. You can change the program to use groups that are available in your environment.

```
private static void WriteAcl(string filename)
{
    var salesIdentity = new NTAccount("Sales");
    var developersIdentity = new NTAccount("Developers");
    var everyOneIdentity = new NTAccount("Everyone");

    var salesAce = new FileSystemAccessRule(salesIdentity, FileSystemRights.Write,
                                    AccessControlType.Deny);
    var everyoneAce = new FileSystemAccessRule(everyOneIdentity,
                                        FileSystemRights.Read,
                                        AccessControlType.Allow);
    var developersAce = new FileSystemAccessRule(developersIdentity,
                                        FileSystemRights.FullControl,
                                        AccessControlType.Allow);

    var securityDescriptor = new FileSecurity();
    securityDescriptor.SetAccessRule(everyoneAce);
    securityDescriptor.SetAccessRule(developersAce);
    securityDescriptor.SetAccessRule(salesAce);

    File.SetAccessControl(filename, securityDescriptor);
}
```

You can verify the access rules by opening the Properties window and selecting a file in the Windows Explorer. Selecting the Security tab lists the access control list.

CODE ACCESS SECURITY

What is the importance of code access security? With role-based security, you can define what the user is allowed to do. Code access security defines what the code is allowed to do. .NET 4 simplifies this model by removing the complex policy configuration that existed up to .NET 3.5 and adding the security transparency level 2. Security transparency level existed before, but Level 2 is new with .NET 4. Security transparency makes a distinction between code that is allowed to do privileged calls (such as calling native code) and code that is not allowed to do so. The code is grouped into three categories:

➤ **Security-critical** code can run any code. This code cannot be called by transparent code.

➤ **Safe-critical** code can be called by transparent code. Security verifications are done with this code.

➤ **Transparent** code is very limited in what it can do. This code is allowed to run in a specified permission set and it runs in a sandbox. It cannot contain unsafe or unverifiable code, and cannot call security critical code.

If you write Windows applications, the restricted code permissions do not apply. Applications running on the desktop have full trust privileges and can contain any code. Sandboxing is used with Silverlight applications as well as ASP.NET applications that are hosted from a web provider, or with custom functionality, such as running add-ins with the Managed Add-In Framework.

The Managed Add-In Framework is explained in Chapter 50, available on the book's web site.

Security Transparency Level 2

You can annotate an assembly with the attribute `SecurityRules` and set the `SecurityRuleSet.Level2` for applying the new level with .NET 4. (This is the default with .NET 4.) For backward compatibility, set it to `Level1`.

```
[assembly: SecurityRules(SecurityRuleSet.Level2)]
```

If you set the attribute `SecurityTransparent`, the complete assembly will not do anything privileged or unsafe. This assembly can only call other transparent code or safe-critical code. This attribute can be applied only to the complete assembly.

```
[assembly: SecurityTransparent()]
```

The attribute `AllowPartiallyTrustedCallers` is somewhere between transparent and the other categories. With this attribute, the code defaults to transparent, but individual types or members can have other attributes:

```
[assembly: AllowPartiallyTrustedCallers()]
```

If none of these attributes are applied, the code is security critical. However, you can apply the attribute `SecuritySafeCritical` to individual types and members to make them callable from transparent code:

```
[assembly: SecurityCritical()]
```

Permissions

If code runs inside a sandbox, the sandbox can define what the code is allowed to do by defining .NET permissions. While the full trust applies to applications running on the desktop, applications running in a sandbox are only allowed to do the actions that are defined by the permissions that the host is giving to the sandbox. You can also define permissions for an application domain that is started from a desktop application. This is done with the Sandbox API.

 Application domains are discussed in Chapter 18, "Assemblies."

Permissions refer to the actions that each code group is allowed to perform (or prevented from performing). For example, permissions include "read files from the file system," "write to the Active Directory," and "use sockets to open network connections." Several predefined permissions exist, but you can also create your own permissions.

.NET permissions are independent of operating system permissions. .NET permissions are just verified by the CLR. An assembly demands a permission for a specific operation (for example, the `File` class demands the `FileIOPermission`), and the CLR verifies that the assembly has the permission granted so that it can continue.

There is a very fine-grained list of permissions that you can apply to an assembly or request from code. The following list shows a few of the code access permissions provided by the CLR; as you can see, you have great control of what code is or is not permitted to do:

➤   `DirectoryServicesPermission` controls the ability to access Active Directory through the `System.DirectoryServices` classes.

➤   `DnsPermission` controls the ability to use the TCP/IP Domain Name System (DNS).

➤   `EnvironmentPermission` controls the ability to read and write environment variables.

➤   `EventLogPermission` controls the ability to read and write to the event log.

➤ `FileDialogPermission` controls the ability to access files that have been selected by the user in the Open dialog box. This permission is commonly used when `FileIOPermission` is not granted to allow limited access to files.

➤ `FileIOPermission` controls the ability to work with files (reading, writing, and appending to files, as well as creating, altering, and accessing folders).

➤ `IsolatedStorageFilePermission` controls the ability to access private virtual file systems.

➤ `IsolatedStoragePermission` controls the ability to access isolated storage; storage that is associated with an individual user and with some aspect of the code's identity. Isolated storage is discussed in Chapter 29, "Manipulating Files and the Registry."

➤ `MessageQueuePermission` controls the ability to use message queues through the Microsoft Message Queue.

➤ `PerformanceCounterPermission` controls the ability to make use of performance counters.

➤ `PrintingPermission` controls the ability to print.

➤ `ReflectionPermission` controls the ability to discover information about a type at runtime by using `System.Reflection`.

➤ `RegistryPermission` controls the ability to read, write, create, or delete registry keys and values.

➤ `SecurityPermission` controls the ability to execute, assert permissions, call into unmanaged code, skip verification, and other rights.

➤ `ServiceControllerPermission` controls the ability to control Windows services.

➤ `SocketPermission` controls the ability to make or accept TCP/IP connections on a network transport address.

➤ `SQLClientPermission` controls the ability to access SQL Server databases with the .NET data provider for SQL Server.

➤ `UIPermission` controls the ability to access the user interface.

➤ `WebPermission` controls the ability to make or accept connections to or from the Web.

With each of these permission classes, it is often possible to specify an even deeper level of granularity; for example, the `DirectoryServicesPermission` allows you to differentiate between read and write access, and it also allows you to define which entries in the directory services are allowed or denied access.

Permission Sets

Permission sets are collections of permissions. With permission sets, it is not necessary to apply every single permission to code; permissions are grouped into permission sets. For example, an assembly that has FullTrust permissions has full access to all resources. With intranet permissions, the assembly is restricted; that is, it is not allowed to write to the file system other than using the isolated storage. You can create a custom permission set that includes required permissions.

By assigning the permission to code groups, there is no need to deal with every single permission. Instead, the permissions are applied in blocks, which is why .NET has the concept of permission sets. These are lists of code access permissions grouped into a named set. The following list explains the seven named permission sets you get out of the box:

➤ **FullTrust** means no permission restrictions.

➤ **SkipVerification** means that verification is not done.

➤ **Execution** grants the ability to run, but not to access, any protected resources.

➤ **Nothing** grants no permissions and prevents the code from executing.

➤ **LocalIntranet** specifies a subset of the full set of permissions. For example, file IO is restricted to read access on the share where the assembly originates. With .NET 3.5 and earlier editions (before .NET 3.5 SP1) this permission set was used when an application was running from a network share.

➤ **Internet** specifies the default policy for code of unknown origin. This is the most restrictive policy listed. For example, code executing in this permission set has no file IO capability, cannot read or write event logs, and cannot read or write environment variables.

➤ **Everything** grants all the permissions that are listed under this set, except the permission to skip code verification. The administrator can alter any of the permissions in this permission set. This is useful when the default policy needs to be tighter.

 Note that you can change the definitions of only the Everything permission set — the other sets are fixed and cannot be changed. Of course, you can also create your own permission set.

Demanding Permissions Programmatically

An assembly can demand permissions declaratively or programmatically. The following code snippet demonstrates how permissions can be demanded with the method `DemandFileIOPermissions()`. If you import the namespace `System.Security.Permissions`, you can check for permissions by creating a `FileIOPermission` object, and calling its `Demand()` method. This verifies if the caller of the method, here the caller of the method `DemandFileIOPermissions`, has the required permissions. In case the `Demand()` method fails, an exception of type `SecurityException` is thrown. It's okay not to catch the exception and let it be handled by the caller.

```
using System;
using System.Security;
using System.Security.Permissions;

[assembly: AllowPartiallyTrustedCallers()]

namespace Wrox.ProCSharp.Security
{
    [SecuritySafeCritical]
    public class DemandPermissions
    {
        public void DemandFileIOPermissions(string path)
        {
            var fileIOPermission = new FileIOPermission(PermissionState.Unrestricted);
            fileIOPermission.Demand();

            //...
        }
    }
}
```

code snippet DemandPermissionDemo/DemandPermissions.cs

`FileIOPermission` is contained within the `System.Security.Permissions` namespace, which is home to the full set of permissions and also provides classes for declarative permission attributes and enumerations for the parameters that are used to create permissions objects (for example, creating a `FileIOPermission` specifying whether read-only or full access is needed).

To catch exceptions thrown by the CLR when code attempts to act contrary to its granted permissions, you can catch the exception of the type `SecurityException`, which provides access to a number of useful pieces of information, including a human-readable stack trace (`SecurityException.StackTrace`) and a reference to the method that threw the exception (`SecurityException.TargetSite`). `SecurityException` even provides you with the `SecurityException.PermissionType` property, which returns the type of `Permission` object that caused the security exception to occur.

If you just use the .NET classes for file I/O you don't have to demand the `FileIOPermission` yourself as this is demanded by the .NET classes doing file I/O. However, you need to make the demand yourself if you wrap native API calls such as `CreateFileTransacted()`. Also, you can use this mechanism to demand custom permissions from the caller.

Using the Sandbox API to Host Unprivileged Code

By default, with a desktop application, the application has full trust. Using the Sandbox API, you can create an app-domain that doesn't have full trust.

To see the Sandbox API in action, first create a C# library project named RequireFileIOPermissionsDemo. This library contains the class `RequirePermissionsDemo` with the method `RequireFilePermissions()`. This method returns `true` or `false`, depending on whether the code has file permissions. With the implementation of this code, the `File` class creates a file where the path is passed with the argument variable `path`. In case writing the file fails, an exception of type `SecurityException` is thrown. The `File` class checks for the `FileIOSecurity` as you saw earlier with the DemandPermissonDemo sample. If the security check fails, a `SecurityException` is thrown by the `Demand()` method of the `FileIOSecurity` class. Here, the `SecurityException` is caught to return `false` from the `RequireFilePermissions()` method.

```csharp
using System;
using System.IO;
using System.Security;

[assembly: AllowPartiallyTrustedCallers()]

namespace Wrox.ProCSharp.Security
{
    [SecuritySafeCritical]
    public class RequirePermissionsDemo : MarshalByRefObject
    {
        public bool RequireFilePermissions(string path)
        {
            bool accessAllowed = true;

            try
            {
                StreamWriter writer = File.CreateText(path);
                writer.WriteLine("written successfully");
                writer.Close();
            }
            catch (SecurityException)
            {
                accessAllowed = false;
            }

            return accessAllowed;
        }
    }
}
```

code snippet RequireFileIOPermissionsDemo/RequirePermissionsDemo.cs

The hosting application where the Sandbox API is used is the project AppDomainHost that is a simple C# console application. The Sandbox API is an overload of the `AppDomain.CreateDomain()` method that creates a new app-domain in a sandbox. This method requires four parameters including the name of the app-domain, the evidence that is taken from the current app-domain, the `AppDomainSetup` information, and a permission set. The permission set that is created only contains `SecurityPermission` with the flag `SecurityPermissionFlag.Execution` so that the code is allowed to execute — nothing more. In the new sandboxed app-domain, the object of type `DemandPermissions` in the assembly `DemandPermission` is instantiated.

Calling across app-domains requires .NET Remoting. That's why the class `RequirePermissionsDemo` needs to derive from the base class `MarshalByRefObject`. Unwrapping the returned `ObjectHandle` returns a transparent proxy to the object in the other app-domain to invoke the method `RequireFilePermissions()`.

 You can read about .NET Remoting in Chapter 54, available online.

Available for download on Wrox.com

```csharp
using System;
using System.Runtime.Remoting;
using System.Security;
using System.Security.Permissions;

namespace Wrox.ProCSharp.Security
{
    class Program
    {
        static void Main()
        {
            PermissionSet permSet = new PermissionSet(PermissionState.None);
            permSet.AddPermission(new SecurityPermission(
                SecurityPermissionFlag.Execution));

            AppDomainSetup setup = AppDomain.CurrentDomain.SetupInformation;
            AppDomain newDomain = AppDomain.CreateDomain(
                "Sandboxed domain", AppDomain.CurrentDomain.Evidence, setup, permSet);
            ObjectHandle oh = newDomain.CreateInstance("RequireFileIOPermissionsDemo",
                                "Wrox.ProCSharp.Security.RequirePermissionsDemo");
            object o = oh.Unwrap();
            var io = o as RequirePermissionsDemo;
            string path = @"c:\temp\file.txt";
            Console.WriteLine("has {0}permissions to write to {1}",
                                io.RequireFilePermissions(path) ? null : "no ",
                                path);
        }
    }
}
```

code snippet AppDomainHost/Program.cs

Running the application you can see the result that the called assembly doesn't have permissions to create the file. If you add the `FileIOPermissionSet` to the permission set of the created appdomain as shown with the following code change, writing the file succeeds.

```csharp
PermissionSet permSet = new PermissionSet(PermissionState.None);
permSet.AddPermission(new SecurityPermission(
    SecurityPermissionFlag.Execution));
permSet.AddPermission(new FileIOPermission(
    FileIOPermissionAccess.AllAccess, "c:/temp"));
```

Implicit Permissions

When permissions are granted, there is often an implicit statement that you are also granted other permissions. For example, if you assign the `FileIOPermission` for `C:\`, there is an implicit assumption that there is also access to its subdirectories.

To check whether a granted permission implicitly brings another permission as a subset, you can do this:

Available for download on Wrox.com

```csharp
class Program
{
    static void Main()
```

```
    {
        CodeAccessPermission permissionA =
            new FileIOPermission(FileIOPermissionAccess.AllAccess, @"C:\");
        CodeAccessPermission permissionB =
            new FileIOPermission(FileIOPermissionAccess.Read, @"C:\temp");
        if (permissionB.IsSubsetOf(permissionA))
        {
            Console.WriteLine("PermissionB is a subset of PermissionA");
        }
    }
}
```

code snippet ImplicitPermissions/Program.cs

The output looks like this:

```
PermissionB is a subset of PermissionA
```

DISTRIBUTING CODE USING CERTIFICATES

You can make use of digital certificates and sign assemblies so that consumers of the software can verify the identity of the software publisher. Depending on where the application is used, certificates may be required. For example, with ClickOnce the user installing the application can verify the certificate to trust the publisher. Using Windows Error Reporting, Microsoft uses the certificate to find out which vendor to map to the error report.

 ClickOnce is explained in Chapter 17, "Deployment." Windows Error Reporting is discussed in Appendix A, "Guidelines for Windows 7 and Windows Server 2008 R2."

In a commercial environment, you would obtain a certificate from a company such as Verisign or Thawte. The advantage of buying a certificate from a supplier instead of creating your own is that it provides a high level of trust in the authenticity of the certificate; the supplier acts as a trusted third party. For test purposes, however, .NET includes a command-line utility you can use to create a test certificate. The process of creating certificates and using them for publishing software is complex, but we walk through a simple example in this section.

The example code is for a fictitious company called ABC Corporation. The company's software product (simple.exe) should be trusted. First, create a test certificate by typing the following command:

```
makecert -sv abckey.pvk -r -n "CN=ABC Corporation" abccorptest.cer
```

The command creates a test certificate under the name ABC Corporation and saves it to a file called abccorptest.cer. The -sv abckey.pvk argument creates a key file to store the private key. When creating the key file, you are asked for a password that you should remember.

After creating the certificate, you can create a software publisher test certificate with the Software Publisher Certificate Test tool (Cert2spc.exe):

```
>cert2spc abccorptest.cer abccorptest.spc
```

With a certificate that is stored in an spc file and the key file that is stored in a pvk file, you can create a pfx file that contains both with the pvk2pfx utility:

```
>pvk2pfx -pvk abckey.pvk -spc abccorptest.spc -pfx abccorptest.pfx
```

Now the assembly can be signed with the signtool.exe utility. The sign option is used for signing, -f specifies the certificate in the pfx file, and -v is for verbose output:

```
>signtool sign -f abccorptest.pfx -v simple.exe
```

To establish trust for the certificate, install it with the Trusted Root Certification Authorities and the Trusted Publishers using the Certificate Manager `certmgr` or the MMC snap-in Certificates. Then you can verify the successful signing with the `signtool`:

```
>signtool verify -v -a simple.exe
```

SUMMARY

This chapter covered several aspects of security with .NET applications. Authentication and authorization with role-based security allow you to decide in the application which users are allowed to access application features. Users are represented by identities and principals, classes that implement the interface `IIdentity` and `IPrincipal`. Role verification can be done within the code but also in a simple way using attributes.

Cryptography was shown to demonstrate signing and encrypting of data, to exchange keys in a secure way. .NET offers several cryptography algorithms offering both symmetric and asymmetric algorithms.

With access control lists, you have also seen how to read and modify access to operating system resources such as files. Programming ACLs is done in ways similar to the programming of secure pipes, registry keys, Active Directory entries, and many other operating system resources.

If your applications are used in different regions and with different languages, in the next chapter you can read about globalization and localization features of .NET.

22

Localization

WHAT'S IN THIS CHAPTER?

➤ Using classes that represent cultures and regions

➤ Globalization of applications

➤ Localization of applications

NASA's Mars Climate Orbiter was lost on September 23, 1999, at a cost of $125 million, because one engineering team used metric units, while another one used inches for a key spacecraft operation. When writing applications for international distribution, different cultures and regions must be kept in mind.

Different cultures have diverging calendars and use different number and date formats. Also, sorting strings may lead to various results because the order of A–Z is defined differently based on the culture. To make applications fit for global markets, you have to globalize and localize them.

This chapter covers the globalization and localization of .NET applications. *Globalization* is about internationalizing applications: preparing applications for international markets. With globalization, the application supports number and date formats that vary depending on culture, calendars, and so on. *Localization* is about translating applications for specific cultures. For translations of strings, you can use resources such .NET resources or WPF resource dictionaries.

.NET supports the globalization and localization of Windows and Web applications. To globalize an application, you can use classes from the namespace `System.Globalization`; to localize an application, you can use resources that are supported by the namespace `System.Resources`.

NAMESPACE SYSTEM.GLOBALIZATION

The `System.Globalization` namespace holds all the culture and region classes necessary to support different date formats, different number formats, and even different calendars that are represented in classes such as `GregorianCalendar`, `HebrewCalendar`, `JapaneseCalendar`, and so on. By using these classes, you can display different representations according to the user's locale.

This section looks at the following issues and considerations with using the `System.Globalization` namespace:

➤ Unicode issues

➤ Cultures and regions

➤ An example showing all cultures and their characteristics

➤ Sorting

Unicode Issues

A Unicode character has 16 bits, so there is room for 65,536 characters. Is this enough for all languages currently used in information technology? In the case of the Chinese language, for example, more than 80,000 characters are needed. However, Unicode has been designed to deal with this issue. With Unicode you have to differentiate between base characters and combining characters. You can add multiple combining characters to a base character to build up a single display character or a text element.

Take, for example, the Icelandic character Ogonek. Ogonek can be combined by using the base character 0x006F (Latin small letter o) and the combining characters 0x0328 (combining Ogonek) and 0x0304 (combining Macron) as shown in Figure 22-1. Combining characters are defined within ranges from 0x0300 to 0x0345. For American and European markets, predefined characters exist to facilitate dealing with special characters. The character Ogonek is also defined by the predefined character 0x01ED.

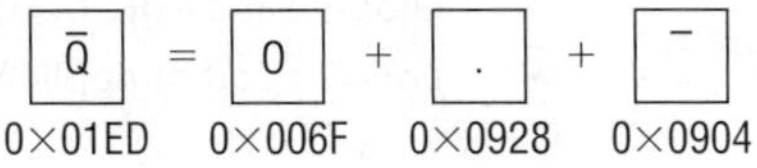

For Asian markets, where more than 80,000 characters are necessary for Chinese alone, such predefined characters do not exist. In Asian languages, you always have to deal with combining characters. The problem is getting the right number of display characters or text elements, and getting to the base characters instead of the combined characters. The namespace `System.Globalization` offers the class `StringInfo`, which you can use to deal with this issue.

ǭ = o + . + ‾

0×01ED   0×006F   0×0928   0×0904

FIGURE 22-1

The following table lists the static methods of the class `StringInfo` that help in dealing with combined characters.

METHOD	DESCRIPTION
GetNextTextElement()	Returns the first text element (base character and all combining characters) of a specified string
GetTextElementEnumerator()	Returns a `TextElementEnumerator` object that allows iterating all text elements of a string
ParseCombiningCharacters()	Returns an integer array referencing all base characters of a string

A single display character can contain multiple Unicode characters. To address this issue, when you write applications that support international markets, don't use the data type `char`; *use* `string` *instead. A string can hold a text element that contains both base characters and combining characters, whereas a* `char` *cannot.*

Cultures and Regions

The world is divided into multiple cultures and regions, and applications have to be aware of these cultural and regional differences. A culture is a set of preferences based on a user's language and cultural habits. RFC 1766 (`www.ietf.org/rfc/rfc1766.txt`) defines culture names that are used worldwide, depending on a language and a country or region. Some examples are en-AU, en-CA, en-GB, and en-US for the English language in Australia, Canada, the United Kingdom, and the United States, respectively.

Possibly the most important class in the System.Globalization namespace is CultureInfo. CultureInfo represents a culture and defines calendars, formatting of numbers and dates, and sorting strings used with the culture.

The class RegionInfo represents regional settings (such as the currency) and shows whether the region is using the metric system. Some regions can use multiple languages. One example is the region of Spain, which has Basque (eu-ES), Catalan (ca-ES), Spanish (es-ES), and Galician (gl-ES) cultures. Similar to one region having multiple languages, one language can be spoken in different regions; for example, Spanish is spoken in Mexico, Spain, Guatemala, Argentina, and Peru, to name only a few countries.

Later in this chapter, you see a sample application that demonstrates these characteristics of cultures and regions.

Specific, Neutral, and Invariant Cultures

When using cultures in the .NET Framework, you have to differentiate between three types: *specific, neutral*, and *invariant* cultures.

A specific culture is associated with a real, existing culture defined with RFC 1766, as you saw in the preceding section. A specific culture can be mapped to a neutral culture. For example, de is the neutral culture of the specific cultures de-AT, de-DE, de-CH, and others. de is shorthand for the German language (Deutsch); AT, DE, and CH are shorthand for the countries Austria, Germany, and Switzerland, respectively.

When translating applications, it is typically not necessary to do translations for every region; not much difference exists between the German language in the countries Austria and Germany. Instead of using specific cultures, you can use a neutral culture to localize applications.

The invariant culture is independent of a real culture. When storing formatted numbers or dates in files, or sending them across a network to a server, using a culture that is independent of any user settings is the best option.

Figure 22-2 shows how the culture types relate to each other.

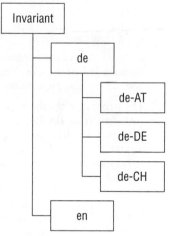

FIGURE 22-2

CurrentCulture and CurrentUICulture

When you set cultures, you need to differentiate between a culture for the user interface and a culture for the number and date formats. Cultures are associated with a thread, and with these two culture types, two culture settings can be applied to a thread. The Thread class has the properties CurrentCulture and CurrentUICulture. The property CurrentCulture is for setting the culture that is used with formatting and sort options, whereas the property CurrentUICulture is used for the language of the user interface.

Users can change the default setting of the CurrentCulture by using the Regional and Language options in the Windows Control Panel (see Figure 22-3). With this configuration, it is also possible to change the default number, the time, and the date format for the culture.

The CurrentUICulture does not depend on this configuration. The CurrentUICulture setting depends on the language of the operating system. There is one exception, though: If a multi-language user interface (MUI) is installed with Windows 7, Windows Vista or Windows XP, it is possible to change the language of the user interface with the regional configuration, and this influences the property CurrentUICulture.

These settings make a very good default, and in many cases, there is no need to change the default behavior. If the culture should be changed, you can easily do this by changing both cultures of the thread to, say, the Spanish culture, as shown in this code snippet:

```
System.Globalization.CultureInfo ci = new
    System.Globalization.CultureInfo("es-ES");
System.Threading.Thread.CurrentThread.CurrentCulture = ci;
System.Threading.Thread.CurrentThread.CurrentUICulture = ci;
```

Now that you know about setting the culture, the following sections discuss number and date formatting, which are influenced by the `CurrentCulture` setting.

Number Formatting

The number structures `Int16`, `Int32`, `Int64`, and so on in the `System` namespace have an overloaded `ToString()` method. This method can be used to create a different representation of the number, depending on the locale. For the `Int32` structure, `ToString()` is overloaded with these four versions:

```
public string ToString();
public string ToString(IFormatProvider);
public string ToString(string);
public string ToString(string,
IFormatProvider);
```

`ToString()` without arguments returns a string without format options. You can also pass a string and a class that implements `IFormatProvider`.

The string specifies the format of the representation. The format can be a standard numeric formatting string or a picture numeric formatting string. For standard numeric formatting,

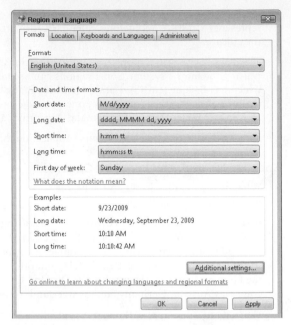

FIGURE 22-3

strings are predefined in which `C` specifies the currency notation, `D` creates a decimal output, `E` creates scientific output, `F` creates fixed-point output, `G` creates general output, `N` creates number output, and `X` creates hexadecimal output. With a picture numeric formatting string, it is possible to specify the number of digits, section and group separators, percent notation, and so on. The picture numeric format string `###,###` means two 3-digit blocks separated by a group separator.

The `IFormatProvider` interface is implemented by the `NumberFormatInfo`, `DateTimeFormatInfo`, and `CultureInfo` classes. This interface defines a single method, `GetFormat()`, that returns a format object.

`NumberFormatInfo` can be used to define custom formats for numbers. With the default constructor of `NumberFormatInfo`, a culture-independent or invariant object is created. Using the properties of `NumberFormatInfo`, it is possible to change all the formatting options, such as a positive sign, a percent symbol, a number group separator, a currency symbol, and a lot more. A read-only culture-independent `NumberFormatInfo` object is returned from the static property `InvariantInfo`. A `NumberFormatInfo` object in which the format values are based on the `CultureInfo` of the current thread is returned from the static property `CurrentInfo`.

To create the next example, you can start with a simple console project. In this code, the first example shows a number displayed in the format of the culture of the thread (here: English-US, the setting of the operating system). The second example uses the `ToString()` method with the `IFormatProvider` argument. `CultureInfo` implements `IFormatProvider`, so create a `CultureInfo` object using the French culture. The third example changes the culture of the thread. The culture is changed to German by using the property `CurrentCulture` of the `Thread` instance:

```
using System;
using System.Globalization;
using System.Threading;

namespace NumberAndDateFormatting
{
    class Program
```

```
    {
        static void Main(string[] args)
        {
            NumberFormatDemo();
        }

        private static void NumberFormatDemo()
        {
            int val = 1234567890;

            // culture of the current thread
            Console.WriteLine(val.ToString("N"));

            // use IFormatProvider
            Console.WriteLine(val.ToString("N", new CultureInfo("fr-FR")));

            // change the culture of the thread
            Thread.CurrentThread.CurrentCulture = new CultureInfo("de-DE");
            Console.WriteLine(val.ToString("N"));
        }
    }
}
```

code snippet NumberAndDateFormatting/Program.cs

The output is shown here. You can compare the different outputs for U.S. English, French, and German, respectively.

```
1,234,567,890.00
1 234 567 890,00
1.234.567.890,00
```

Date Formatting

The same support for numbers is available for dates. The `DateTime` structure has some methods for date-to-string conversions. The public instance methods `ToLongDateString()`, `ToLongTimeString()`, `ToShortDateString()`, and `ToShortTimeString()` create string representations using the current culture. You can use the `ToString()` method to assign a different culture:

```
public string ToString();
public string ToString(IFormatProvider);
public string ToString(string);
public string ToString(string, IFormatProvider);
```

With the string argument of the `ToString()` method, you can specify a predefined format character or a custom format string for converting the date to a string. The class `DateTimeFormatInfo` specifies the possible values. With `DateTimeFormatInfo`, the case of the format strings has a different meaning. `D` defines a long date format, `d` a short date format. Other examples of possible formats are `ddd` for the abbreviated day of the week, `dddd` for the full day of the week, `yyyy` for the year, `T` for a long time, and `t` for a short time format. With the `IFormatProvider` argument, you can specify the culture. Using an overloaded method without the `IFormatProvider` argument implies that the culture of the current thread is used:

```
DateTime d = new DateTime(2009, 06, 02);

// current culture
Console.WriteLine(d.ToLongDateString());

// use IFormatProvider
Console.WriteLine(d.ToString("D", new CultureInfo("fr-FR")));

// use culture of thread
CultureInfo ci = Thread.CurrentThread.CurrentCulture;
Console.WriteLine("{0}: {1}", ci.ToString(), d.ToString("D"));
```

```
ci = new CultureInfo("es-ES");
Thread.CurrentThread.CurrentCulture = ci;
Console.WriteLine("{0}: {1}", ci.ToString(), d.ToString("D"));
```

The output of this example program shows `ToLongDateString()` with the current culture of the thread, a French version where a `CultureInfo` instance is passed to the `ToString()` method, and a Spanish version where the `CurrentCulture` property of the thread is changed to es-ES:

```
Tuesday, June 02, 2009
mardi 2 juin 2009
en-US: Tuesday, June 02, 2009
es-ES: martes, 02 de junio de 2009
```

Cultures in Action

To see all cultures in action, you can use a sample Windows Presentation Foundation (WPF) application that lists all cultures and demonstrates different characteristics of culture properties. Figure 22-4 shows the user interface of the application in the Visual Studio 2010 WPF Designer.

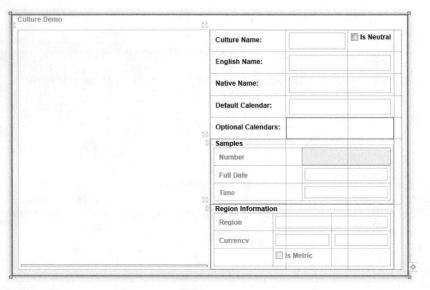

FIGURE 22-4

During initialization of the application, all available cultures are added to the tree view control that is placed on the left side of the application. This initialization happens in the method `AddCulturesToTree()`, which is called in the constructor of the `Window` class `CultureDemoWindow`:

```
public CultureDemoWindow()
{
    InitializeComponent();

    AddCulturesToTree();
}
```

code snippet CultureDemo/MainWindow.xaml.cs

In the method `AddCulturesToTree()`, you get all cultures from the static method `CultureInfo` `.GetCultures()`. Passing `CultureTypes.AllCultures` to this method returns an unsorted array of all available cultures. The array is sorted using a Lambda expression that is passed to the `Comparison` delegate of the second argument of the `Array.Sort()` method. Next, in the `foreach` loop, every single culture is added to the tree view. A `TreeViewItem` object is created for every single culture because the WPF `TreeView` class uses `TreeViewItem` objects for display. The `Tag` property of the `TreeViewItem` object is set to the `CultureInfo` object, so that you can access the `CultureInfo` object at a later time from within the tree.

Where the `TreeViewItem` is added inside the tree depends on the culture type. If the culture does not have a parent culture, it is added to the root nodes of the tree. To find parent cultures, all cultures are remembered inside a dictionary. Recall Chapter 10, "Collections," for more information about dictionaries and Chapter 8, "Delegates, Lambdas, and Events," for Lambda expressions.

```
// add all cultures to the tree view
public void AddCulturesToTree()
{
    var culturesByName = new Dictionary<string, TreeViewItem>();

    // get all cultures
    var cultures = CultureInfo.GetCultures(CultureTypes.AllCultures);
    Array.Sort(cultures, (c1, c2) = c1.Name.CompareTo(c2.Name));

    var nodes = new TreeViewItem[cultures.Length];

    int i = 0;
    foreach (var ci in cultures)
    {
        nodes[i] = new TreeViewItem();
        nodes[i].Header = ci.DisplayName;
        nodes[i].Tag = ci;
        culturesByName.Add(ci.Name, nodes[i]);

        TreeViewItem parent;
        if (!String.IsNullOrEmpty(ci.Parent.Name) &&
            culturesByName.TryGetValue(ci.Parent.Name, out parent))
        {
            parent.Items.Add(nodes[i]);
        }
        else
        {
            treeCultures.Items.Add(nodes[i]);
        }
        i++;
    }
}
```

When the user selects a node inside the tree, the handler of the `SelectedItemChanged` event of the `TreeView` will be called. Here the handler is implemented in the method `TreeCultures_SelectedItemChanged()`. Within this method, all fields are cleared by calling the method `ClearTextFields()` before you get the `CultureInfo` object from the tree by selecting the `Tag` property of the `TreeViewItem`. Then some text fields are set using the properties `Name`, `NativeName`, and `EnglishName` of the `CultureInfo` object. If the `CultureInfo` is a neutral culture that can be queried with the `IsNeutralCulture` property, the corresponding check box will be set:

```
private void TreeCultures_SelectedItemChanged(object sender,
                RoutedPropertyChangedEventArgs<object> e)
{
    ClearTextFields();

    // get CultureInfo object from tree
    CultureInfo ci = (CultureInfo)((TreeViewItem)e.NewValue).Tag;

    textCultureName.Text = ci.Name;
    textNativeName.Text = ci.NativeName;
    textEnglishName.Text = ci.EnglishName;

    checkIsNeutral.IsChecked = ci.IsNeutralCulture;
```

Next you get the calendar information about the culture. The `Calendar` property of the `CultureInfo` class returns the default `Calendar` object for the specific culture. Because the `Calendar` class doesn't have a property to tell its name, you use the `ToString()` method of the base class to get the name of the class, and remove the namespace of this string to be displayed in the text field `textCalendar`.

Because a single culture might support multiple calendars, the `OptionalCalendars` property returns an array of additional supported `Calendar` objects. These optional calendars are displayed in the list box `listCalendars`. The `GregorianCalendar` class that derives from `Calendar` has an additional property called `CalendarType` that lists the type of the Gregorian calendar. This type can be a value of the enumeration `GregorianCalendarTypes`: `Arabic`, `MiddleEastFrench`, `TransliteratedFrench`, `USEnglish`, or `Localized`, depending on the culture. With Gregorian calendars, the type is also displayed in the list box:

```
// default calendar
textCalendar.Text = ci.Calendar.ToString().
                        Remove(0, 21).Replace("Calendar", "");

// fill optional calendars
listCalendars.Items.Clear();
foreach (Calendar optCal in ci.OptionalCalendars)
{
    StringBuilder calName = new StringBuilder(50);
    calName.Append(optCal.ToString());
    calName.Remove(0, 21);
    calName.Replace("Calendar", "");

    // for GregorianCalendar add type information
    GregorianCalendar gregCal = optCal as GregorianCalendar;
    if (gregCal != null)
    {
        calName.AppendFormat(" {0}", gregCal.CalendarType.ToString());
    }
    listCalendars.Items.Add(calName.ToString());
}
```

code snippet CultureDemo/MainWindow.xaml.cs

Next, you check whether the culture is a specific culture (not a neutral culture) by using `!ci` `.IsNeutralCulture` in an `if` statement. The method `ShowSamples()` displays number and date samples. This method is implemented in the next code section. The method `ShowRegionInformation()` is used to display some information about the region. With the invariant culture, you can display only number and date samples, but no region information. The invariant culture is not related to any real language, and therefore it is not associated with a region:

```
// display number and date samples
if (!ci.IsNeutralCulture)
{
    groupSamples.IsEnabled = true;
    ShowSamples(ci);

    // invariant culture doesn't have a region
    if (String.Compare(ci.ThreeLetterISOLanguageName, "IVL", true) == 0)
    {
        groupRegion.IsEnabled = false;
    }
    else
    {
        groupRegion.IsEnabled = true;
        ShowRegionInformation(ci.Name);
    }
}
else // neutral culture: no region, no number/date formatting
```

```
                {
                    groupSamples.IsEnabled = false;
                    groupRegion.IsEnabled = false;
                }
            }
```

To show some localized sample numbers and dates, the selected object of type `CultureInfo` is passed with the `IFormatProvider` argument of the `ToString()` method:

```
private void ShowSamples(CultureInfo ci)
{
    double number = 9876543.21;
    textSampleNumber.Text = number.ToString("N", ci);

    DateTime today = DateTime.Today;
    textSampleDate.Text = today.ToString("D", ci);

    DateTime now = DateTime.Now;
    textSampleTime.Text = now.ToString("T", ci);
}
```

To display the information associated with a `RegionInfo` object, in the method `ShowRegionInformation()` a `RegionInfo` object is constructed, passing the selected culture identifier. Then you access the `DisplayName`, `CurrencySymbol`, `ISOCurrencySymbol`, and `IsMetric` properties to display this information:

```
private void ShowRegionInformation(string culture)
{
    var ri = new RegionInfo(culture);
    textRegion.Text = ri.DisplayName;
    textCurrency.Text = ri.CurrencySymbol;
    textCurrencyISO.Text = ri.ISOCurrencySymbol;
    checkIsMetric.IsChecked = ri.IsMetric;
}
```

When you start the application, you can see all available cultures in the tree view, and selecting a culture lists the cultural characteristics, as shown in Figure 22-5.

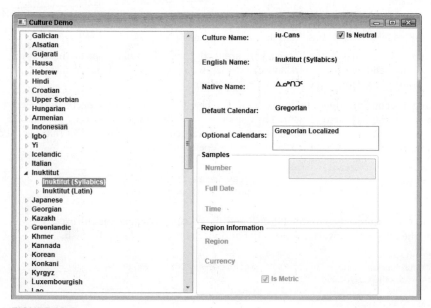

FIGURE 22-5

Sorting

Sorting strings is dependent on the culture. Some cultures have different sorting orders. One example is Finnish, where the characters V and W are treated the same. The algorithms that compare strings for sorting by default use a culture-sensitive sort, in which the sort is dependent on the culture.

To demonstrate this behavior with a Finnish sort, the following code creates a small sample console application where some U.S. states are stored unsorted inside an array. You are going to use classes from the namespaces `System.Collections.Generic`, `System.Threading`, and `System.Globalization`, so these namespaces must be declared. The method `DisplayNames()` shown here is used to display all elements of an array or of a collection on the console:

```
static void DisplayNames(string title, IEnumerable<string> e)
{
    Console.WriteLine(title);
    foreach (string s in e)
        Console.Write(s + "-");
    Console.WriteLine();
    Console.WriteLine();
}
```

code snippet SortingDemo/Program.cs

In the `Main()` method, after creating the array with some of the U.S. states, the thread property `CurrentCulture` is set to the Finnish culture, so that the following `Array.Sort()` uses the Finnish sort order. Calling the method `DisplayNames()` displays all the states on the console:

```
static void Main()
{
    string[] names = {"Alabama", "Texas", "Washington",
                      "Virginia", "Wisconsin", "Wyoming",
                      "Kentucky", "Missouri", "Utah", "Hawaii",
                      "Kansas", "Louisiana", "Alaska", "Arizona"};

    Thread.CurrentThread.CurrentCulture =
        new CultureInfo("fi-FI");

    Array.Sort(names);
    DisplayNames("Sorted using the Finnish culture", names);
```

After the first display of some U.S. states in the Finnish sort order, the array is sorted once again. If you want to have a sort that is independent of the users' culture, which would be useful when the sorted array is sent to a server or stored somewhere, you can use the invariant culture.

You can do this by passing a second argument to `Array.Sort()`. The `Sort()` method expects an object implementing `IComparer` with the second argument. The `Comparer` class from the `System.Collections` namespace implements `IComparer`. `Comparer.DefaultInvariant` returns a `Comparer` object that uses the invariant culture for comparing the array values for a culture-independent sort:

```
    // sort using the invariant culture
    Array.Sort(names, System.Collections.Comparer.DefaultInvariant);
    DisplayNames("Sorted using the invariant culture", names);
}
```

The program output shows different sorts with the Finnish and the culture-independent cultures: Virginia goes before Washington when using the invariant sort order and vice versa when using Finnish.

```
Sorted using the Finnish culture
Alabama-Alaska-Arizona-Hawaii-Kansas-Kentucky-Louisiana-Missouri-Texas-Utah-
Washington-Virginia-Wisconsin-Wyoming -

Sorted using the invariant culture
Alabama-Alaska-Arizona-Hawaii-Kansas-Kentucky-Louisiana-Missouri-Texas-Utah-
Virginia-Washington-Wisconsin-Wyoming -
```

> *If sorting a collection should be independent of a culture, the collection must be sorted with the invariant culture. This can be particularly useful when sending the sort result to a server or storing it inside a file.*

In addition to a locale-dependent formatting and measurement system, text and pictures may differ depending on the culture. This is where resources come into play.

RESOURCES

Resources such as pictures or string tables can be put into resource files or satellite assemblies. Such resources can be very helpful when localizing applications, and .NET has built-in support to search for localized resources.

Before you see how to use resources to localize applications, the next sections discuss how resources can be created and read without looking at language aspects.

Creating Resource Files

Resource files can contain items such as pictures and string tables. A resource file is created by using either a normal text file or a `.resX` file that uses XML. This section starts with a simple text file.

A resource that embeds a string table can be created by using a normal text file. The text file just assigns strings to keys. The key is the name that can be used from a program to get the value. Spaces are allowed in both keys and values.

This example shows a simple string table in the file `Wrox.ProCSharp.Localization.MyResources.txt`:

Available for download on Wrox.com

```
Title = Professional C#
Chapter = Localization
Author = Christian Nagel
Publisher = Wrox Press
```

code snippet Resources/Wrox.ProCSharp.Localization.MyResources.txt

> *When saving text files with Unicode characters, you must save the file with the proper encoding. Select the Unicode encoding with the Save dialog.*

Resource File Generator

The Resource File Generator (`Resgen.exe`) utility can be used to create a resource file out of `Wrox.ProCSharp.Localization.MyResources.txt`. Typing the following line:

```
resgen Wrox.ProCSharp.Localization.MyResources.txt
```

creates the file `Wrox.ProCSharp.Localization.MyResources.resources`. The resulting resource file can either be added to an assembly as an external file or embedded into the DLL or EXE. Resgen also supports the creation of XML-based `.resX` resource files. One easy way to build an XML file is by using Resgen itself:

```
resgen Wrox.ProCSharp.Localization.MyResources.txt Wrox.ProCSharp.Localization.MyResources.resX
```

This command creates the XML resource file `Wrox.ProCSharp.LocalizationMyResources.resX`. You see how to work with XML resource files in the section "Windows Forms Localization Using Visual Studio" later in this chapter.

Resgen supports strongly typed resources. A strongly typed resource is represented by a class that accesses the resource. The class can be created with the /str option of the Resgen utility:

```
resgen /str:C#,Wrox.ProCSharp.Localization,MyResources,MyResources.cs
Wrox.ProCSharp.Localization.MyResources.resX
```

With the option /str, the language, namespace, class name, and the filename for the source code are defined in that order.

The Resgen utility does not support adding pictures. With the .NET Framework SDK samples, you get a ResXGen sample with the tutorials. With ResXGen, it is possible to reference pictures in a .resX file. Adding pictures can also be done programmatically by using the ResourceWriter or ResXResourceWriter classes, as you will see next.

ResourceWriter

Instead of using the Resgen utility to build resource files, it's a simple task to write a program to create resources. The class ResourceWriter from the namespace System.Resources can be used to write binary resource files; ResXResourceWriter writes XML-based resource files. Both of these classes support pictures and any other object that is serializable. When you use the class ResXResourceWriter, the assembly System.Windows.Forms must be referenced.

In the following code example, you create a ResXResourceWriter object, *rw*, using a constructor with the filename Demo.resx. After creating an instance, you can add a number of resources of up to 2GB in total size by using the AddResource() method of the ResXResourceWriter class. The first argument of AddResource() specifies the name of the resource, and the second argument specifies the value. A picture resource can be added using an instance of the Image class. To use the Image class, you have to reference the assembly System.Drawing. You also add the using directive to open the namespace System.Drawing.

Create an Image object by opening the file logo.gif. You will have to copy the picture to the directory of the executable or specify the full path to the picture in the method argument of Image.ToFile(). The using statement specifies that the image resource should automatically be disposed of at the end of the using block. Additional simple string resources are added to the ResXResourceWriter object. The Close() method of the ResXResourceWriter class automatically calls ResXResourceWriter.Generate() to finally write the resources to the file Demo.resx:

Available for
download on
Wrox.com

```csharp
using System;
using System.Resources;
using System.Drawing;

class Program
{
    static void Main()
    {
        var rw = new ResXResourceWriter("Demo.resx");
        using (Image image = Image.FromFile("logo.gif"))
        {
            rw.AddResource("WroxLogo", image);
            rw.AddResource("Title", "Professional C#");
            rw.AddResource("Chapter", "Localization");
            rw.AddResource("Author", "Christian Nagel");
            rw.AddResource("Publisher", "Wrox Press");
            rw.Close();
        }
    }
}
```

code snippet CreateResource/Program.cs

Starting this small program creates the resource file Demo.resx, which embeds the image logo.gif. In the next example, the resources will be used with a Windows application.

Using Resource Files

You can add resource files to assemblies with the command-line C# compiler csc.exe by using the /resource option, or directly with Visual Studio. To see how resource files can be used with Visual Studio, create a Console application and name it ResourceDemo.

Use the context menu of the Solution Explorer (Add ⇨ Existing Item) to add the previously created resource file Demo.resx to this project. By default, Build Action of this resource is set to Embedded Resource so that this resource is embedded into the output assembly.

In the project settings (Application ⇨ Assembly information), set the Neutral Language setting of the application to the main language, for example, English (United States), as shown in Figure 22-6. Changing this setting adds the attribute [NeutralResourceLanguageAttribute] to the file assemblyinfo.cs, as you can see here:

```
[assembly: NeutralResourcesLanguageAttribute("en-US")]
```

Setting this option gives a performance improvement with the ResourceManager because it more quickly finds the resources for en-US that are also used as a default fallback. With this attribute, you can also specify the location of the default resource by using the second parameter with the constructor. With the enumeration UltimateResourceFallbackLocation, you can specify that the default resource is to be stored in the main assembly or in a satellite assembly (values MainAssembly and Satellite).

After building the project, you can check the generated assembly with ildasm to see the attribute .mresource in the manifest (see Figure 22-7). .mresource declares the name for the resource in the assembly. If .mresource is declared as public (as in the example), the resource is exported from the assembly and can be used from classes in other assemblies. .mresource private means that the resource is not exported and is available only within the assembly.

FIGURE 22-6

To access the embedded resource, use the ResourceManager class from the System .Resources namespace. You can pass the assembly that has the resources as an argument to the constructor of the ResourceManager class. In this example, the resources are embedded in the executing assembly, so pass the result of Assembly.GetExecutingAssembly() as the second argument. The first argument is the root name of the resources. The root name consists of the namespace, with the name of the resource file but without the resources extension. As you saw earlier, ildasm shows the name. All you have to do is remove the file

FIGURE 22-7

extension resources from the name shown. You can also get the name programmatically by using the GetManifestResourceNames() method of the System.Reflection.Assembly class:

Available for
download on
Wrox.com

```
using System;
using System.Drawing;
using System.Reflection;
using System.Resources;
```

```
namespace Wrox.ProCSharp.Localization
{
    class Program
    {
        static void Main()
        {
            var rm = new ResourceManager("Wrox.ProCSharp.Localization.Demo",
                                          Assembly.GetExecutingAssembly());
```

code snippet ResourceDemo/Program.cs

Using the `ResourceManager` instance `rm`, you can get all the resources by specifying the key to the methods `GetObject()` and `GetString()`:

```
Console.WriteLine(rm.GetString("Title"));
Console.WriteLine(rm.GetString("Chapter"));
Console.WriteLine(rm.GetString("Author"));
using (Image logo = (Image)rm.GetObject("WroxLogo"))
{
    logo.Save("logo.bmp");
}
```

With strongly typed resources, the code written earlier can be simplified; there is no need to instantiate the `ResourceManager` and access the resources using indexers. Instead, the names of the resources are accessed with properties:

```
private static void StronglyTypedResources()
{
    Console.WriteLine(Demo.Title);
    Console.WriteLine(Demo.Chapter);
    Console.WriteLine(Demo.Author);
    using (Bitmap logo = Demo.WroxLogo)
    {
        logo.Save("logo.bmp");
    }
}
```

To create a strongly typed resource with the Managed Resources Editor, the Access Modifier can be reset from No Code Generation to Public or Internal. With Public, the generated class has a public access modifier and is available from other assemblies. With Internal, the generated class has an internal access modifier and can only be accessed from within the assembly.

When you set this option, the class `Demo` (it has the same name as the resource) is created. This class has static properties for all the resources to provide a strongly typed resource name. With the implementation of the static properties, a `ResourceManager` object is used that is instantiated on first access and then cached:

```
//------------------------------------------------------------------------------
// <auto-generated>
//     This code was generated by a tool.
//     Runtime Version:4.0.21006.1
//
//     Changes to this file may cause incorrect behavior and will be lost if
//     the code is regenerated.
// </auto-generated>
//------------------------------------------------------------------------------

namespace Wrox.ProCSharp.Localization {
    using System;
```

```
/// <summary>
///   A strongly-typed resource class, for looking up localized strings, etc.
/// </summary>
// This class was auto-generated by the StronglyTypedResourceBuilder
// class via a tool like ResGen or Visual Studio.
// To add or remove a member, edit your .ResX file then rerun ResGen
// with the /str option, or rebuild your VS project.
[global::System.CodeDom.Compiler.GeneratedCodeAttribute(
   "System.Resources.Tools.StronglyTypedResourceBuilder", "4.0.0.0")]
[global::System.Diagnostics.DebuggerNonUserCodeAttribute()]
[global::System.Runtime.CompilerServices.CompilerGeneratedAttribute()]
internal class Demo {

    private static global::System.Resources.ResourceManager resourceMan;

    private static global::System.Globalization.CultureInfo resourceCulture;

    [global::System.Diagnostics.CodeAnalysis.SuppressMessageAttribute(
        "Microsoft.Performance", "CA1811:AvoidUncalledPrivateCode")]
    internal Demo() {
    }

    /// <summary>
    ///   Returns the cached ResourceManager instance used by this class.
    /// </summary>
    [global::System.ComponentModel.EditorBrowsableAttribute(
        global::System.ComponentModel.EditorBrowsableState.Advanced)]
    internal static global::System.Resources.ResourceManager ResourceManager {
        get {
            if (object.ReferenceEquals(resourceMan, null)) {
                global::System.Resources.ResourceManager temp =
                    new global::System.Resources.ResourceManager(
                        "Wrox.ProCSharp.Localization.Demo", typeof(Demo).Assembly);
                resourceMan = temp;
            }
            return resourceMan;
        }
    }

    /// <summary>
    ///   Overrides the current thread's CurrentUICulture property for all
    ///   resource lookups using this strongly typed resource class.
    /// </summary>
    [global::System.ComponentModel.EditorBrowsableAttribute(
        global::System.ComponentModel.EditorBrowsableState.Advanced)]
    internal static global::System.Globalization.CultureInfo Culture {
        get {
            return resourceCulture;
        }
        set {
            resourceCulture = value;
        }
    }

    /// <summary>
    ///   Looks up a localized string similar to Chapter.
    /// </summary>
    internal static string Chapter {
        get {
            return ResourceManager.GetString("Chapter", resourceCulture);
```

```
            }
        }

        //...

        internal static System.Drawing.Bitmap WroxLogo {
            get {
                object obj = ResourceManager.GetObject("WroxLogo", resourceCulture);
                return ((System.Drawing.Bitmap)(obj));
            }
        }
    }
}
```

code snippet ResourceDemo/Demo.Designer.cs

The System.Resources Namespace

Before moving on to the next example, this section concludes with a review of the classes contained in the System.Resources namespace that deal with resources:

➤ The ResourceManager class can be used to get resources for the current culture from assemblies or resource files. Using the ResourceManager, you can also get a ResourceSet for a particular culture.

➤ A ResourceSet represents the resources for a particular culture. When a ResourceSet instance is created, it enumerates over a class, implementing the interface IResourceReader, and it stores all resources in a Hashtable.

➤ The interface IResourceReader is used from the ResourceSet to enumerate resources. The class ResourceReader implements this interface.

➤ The class ResourceWriter is used to create a resource file. ResourceWriter implements the interface IResourceWriter.

➤ ResXResourceSet, ResXResourceReader, and ResXResourceWriter are similar to ResourceSet, ResourceReader, and ResourceWriter; however, they are used to create an XML-based resource file, .resX, instead of a binary file. You can use ResXFileRef to make a link to a resource instead of embedding it inside an XML file.

➤ The namespace System.Resources.Tools contains the class StronglyTypedResourceBuilder to create a class from a resource.

WINDOWS FORMS LOCALIZATION USING VISUAL STUDIO

In this section, you create a simple Windows Forms application that shows how to use Visual Studio 2010 for localization. This application does not use complex Windows Forms and does not have any real inner functionality because the key feature it is intended to demonstrate here is localization. In the automatically generated source code, change the namespace to Wrox.ProCSharp.Localization and the class name to BookOfTheDayForm. The namespace is not only changed in the source file BookOfTheDayForm.cs but also in the project settings, so that all generated resource files will get this namespace, too. You can change the namespace for all new items that are created by selecting Common Properties from the Project ⇨ Properties menu.

 Windows Forms applications are covered in more detail in Chapter 39, "Windows Forms."

To show some issues with localization, this program has a picture, some text, a date, and a number. The picture shows a flag that is also localized. Figure 22-8 shows this form of the application as seen in the Windows Forms Designer.

The following table lists the values for the `Name` and `Text` properties of the Windows Forms elements.

NAME	TEXT
labelBookOfTheDay	Book of the day
labelItemsSold	Books sold
textDate	Date
textTitle	Professional C#
textItemsSold	30000
pictureFlag	

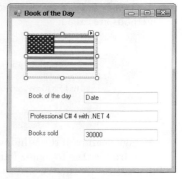

FIGURE 22-8

In addition to this form, you might want a message box that displays a welcome message; this message might change depending on the current time of day. This example demonstrates that the localization for dynamically created dialogs must be done differently. In the method `WelcomeMessage()`, display a message box using `MessageBox.Show()`. Call the method `WelcomeMessage()` in the constructor of the form class `BookOfTheDayForm`, before the call to `InitializeComponent()`.

Here is the code for the method `WelcomeMessage()`:

```
public void WelcomeMessage()
{
    DateTime now = DateTime.Now;
    string message;
    if (now.Hour <= 12)
    {
        message = "Good Morning";
    }
    else if (now.Hour <= 19)
    {
        message = "Good Afternoon";
    }
    else
    {
        message = "Good Evening";
    }
    MessageBox.Show(String.Format("{0}\nThis is a localization sample",
        message));
}
```

The number and date in the form should be set by using formatting options. Add a new method, `SetDateAndNumber()`, to set the values with the format option. In a real application, these values could be received from a Web service or a database, but this example is just concentrating on localization. The date is formatted using the D option (to display the long date name). The number is displayed using the picture number format string ###,###,###, where # represents a digit and ", " is the group separator.

Available for download on Wrox.com

```
public void SetDateAndNumber()
{
    DateTime today = DateTime.Today;
    textDate.Text = today.ToString("D");
    int itemsSold = 327444;
    textItemsSold.Text = itemsSold.ToString("###,###,###");
}
```

code snippet BookOfTheDay/Demo.BookOfTheDayForm.cs

In the constructor of the `BookOfTheDayForm` class, both the `WelcomeMessage()` and `SetDateAndNumber()` methods are called:

```
public BookOfTheDayForm()
{
    WelcomeMessage();

    InitializeComponent();

    SetDateAndNumber();
}
```

A magic feature of the Windows Forms Designer is started when you set the `Localizable` property of the form from `false` to `true`. This results in the creation of an XML-based resource file for the dialog box that stores all resource strings, properties (including the location and size of Windows Forms elements), embedded pictures, and so on. In addition, the implementation of the `InitializeComponent()` method is changed; an instance of the class `System.Resources.ResourceManager` is created, and to get to the values and positions of the text fields and pictures, the `GetObject()` method is used instead of writing the values directly into the code. `GetObject()` uses the `CurrentUICulture` property of the current thread for finding the correct localization of the resources.

Here is part of `InitializeComponent()` from the file `BookOfTheDayForm.Designer.cs` before the `Localizable` property is set to `true`, where all properties of `textboxTitle` are set:

```
private void InitializeComponent()
{
    //...
    this.textTitle = new System.Windows.Forms.TextBox();
    //
    // textTitle
    //
    this.textTitle.Anchor = ((System.Windows.Forms.AnchorStyles)
        (((System.Windows.Forms.AnchorStyles.Top
            | System.Windows.Forms.AnchorStyles.Left)
            | System.Windows.Forms.AnchorStyles.Right)));
    this.textTitle.Location = new System.Drawing.Point(29, 164);
    this.textTitle.Name = "textTitle";
    this.textTitle.Size = new System.Drawing.Size(231, 20);
    this.textTitle.TabIndex = 3;
```

The code for the `IntializeComponent()` method is automatically changed by setting the `Localizable` property to `true`:

Available for download on Wrox.com

```
private void InitializeComponent()
{
    System.ComponentModel.ComponentResourceManager resources =
        new System.ComponentModel.ComponentResourceManager(
            typeof(BookOfTheDayForm));
    //...
    this.textTitle = new System.Windows.Forms.TextBox();
    //
    // textTitle
    //
    resources.ApplyResources(this.textTitle, "textTitle");
    this.textTitle.Name = "textTitle";
```

code snippet BookOfTheDay/Demo.BookOfTheDayForm.Designer.cs

Where does the resource manager get the data from? When the `Localizable` property is set to `true`, the resource file `BookOfTheDay.resX` is generated. In this file, you can find the scheme of the XML resource, followed by all elements in the form: `Type`, `Text`, `Location`, `TabIndex`, and so on.

The class `ComponentResourceManager` is derived from `ResourceManager` and offers the method `ApplyResources()`. With `ApplyResources()`, the resources that are defined with the second argument are applied to the object in the first argument.

The following XML segment shows a few of the properties of `textBoxTitle`: the `Location` property has a value of `29, 164`; the `Size` property has a value of `231, 20`; the `Text` property is set to `Professional C# 4 with .NET 4`; and so on. For every value, the type of the value is stored as well. For example, the `Location` property is of type `System.Drawing.Point`, and this class can be found in the assembly `System.Drawing`.

Why are the locations and sizes stored in this XML file? With translations, many strings have completely different sizes and no longer fit into the original positions. When the locations and sizes are all stored inside the resource file, everything that is needed for localization is stored in these files, separate from the C# code:

```xml
<data name="textTitle.Anchor" type=
    "System.Windows.Forms.AnchorStyles, System.Windows.Forms">
  <value>Top, Left, Right</value>
</data>
<data name="textTitle.Location" type="System.Drawing.Point, System.Drawing">
  <value>29, 164</value>
</data>
<data name="textTitle.Size" type="System.Drawing.Size, System.Drawing">
  <value>231, 20</value>
</data>
<data name="textTitle.TabIndex" type="System.Int32, mscorlib">
  <value>3</value>
</data>
<data name="textTitle.Text" xml:space="preserve">
  <value>Professional C# 4 with .NET 4</value>
</data>
<data name="&gt;&gt;textTitle.Name" xml:space="preserve">
  <value>textTitle</value>
</data>
<data name="&gt;&gt;textTitle.Type" xml:space="preserve">
  <value>System.Windows.Forms.TextBox, System.Windows.Forms, Version=4.0.0.0,
         Culture=neutral, PublicKeyToken=b77a5c561934e089</value>
</data>
<data name="&gt;&gt;textTitle.Parent" xml:space="preserve">
  <value>$this</value>
</data>
<data name="&gt;&gt;textTitle.ZOrder" xml:space="preserve">
  <value>2</value>
</data>
```

code snippet BookOfTheDay/BookOfTheDayForm.resx

When changing some of these resource values, it is not necessary to work directly with the XML code. You can change these resources directly in the Visual Studio Designer. Whenever you change the `Language` property of the form and the properties of some form elements, a new resource file is generated for the specified language. Create a German version of the form by setting the `Language` property to German, and a French version by setting the `Language` property to French. For every language, you get a resource file with the changed properties: in this case, `BookOfTheDayForm.de.resX` and `BookOfTheDayForm.fr.resX`.

The following table shows the changes needed for the German version.

GERMAN NAME	VALUE
`$this.Text` (title of the form)	Buch des Tages
`labelItemsSold.Text`	Bücher verkauft:
`labelBookOfTheDay.Text`	Buch des Tages:

The following table lists the changes for the French version.

FRENCH NAME	VALUE
$this.Text (title of the form)	Le livre du jour
labelItemsSold.Text	Des livres vendus:
labelBookOfTheDay.Text	Le livre du jour:

By default, images are not moved to satellite assemblies. However, in the sample application, the flag should be different depending on the country. To achieve this, you have to add the image of the American flag to the file `Resources.resx`. You can find this file in the Properties section of the Visual Studio Solution Explorer. With the resource editor, select the Images category, as shown in Figure 22-9, and add the file `americanflag.bmp`. To make localization with images possible, the image must have the same name in all languages. Here, the image in the file `Resources.resx` has the name Flag. You can rename the image in the properties

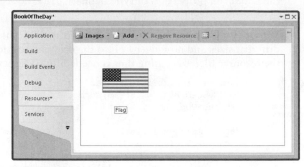

FIGURE 22-9

editor. Within the properties editor, you can also change whether the image should be linked or embedded. For best performance with resources, images are linked by default. With linked images, the image file must be delivered together with the application. If you want to embed the image within the assembly, you can change the `Persistence` property to `Embedded`.

The localized versions of the flags can be added by copying the file `Resource.resx` to `Resource.de.resx` and `Resource.fr.resx` and replacing the flags with `GermanFlag.bmp` and `FranceFlag.bmp`. Because a strongly typed resource class is needed only with the neutral resource, the property `CustomTool` can be cleared with the resource files of all specific languages.

Compiling the project now creates a *satellite assembly* for each language. Inside the debug directory (or the release, depending on your active configuration), language subdirectories like `de` and `fr` are created. In such a subdirectory, you will find the file `BookOfTheDay.resources.dll`. Such a file is a satellite assembly that includes only localized resources. Opening this assembly with `ildasm`, you see a manifest with the embedded resources and a defined locale. The assembly has the locale `de` in the assembly attributes, so it can be found in the `de` subdirectory. You can also see the name of the resource with `.mresource`; it is prefixed with the namespace name `Wrox.ProCSharp.Localization`, followed by the class name `BookOfTheDayForm` and the language code `de`.

Changing the Culture Programmatically

After translating the resources and building the satellite assemblies, you will get the correct translations according to the configured culture for the user. The welcome message is not translated at this time. This needs to be done in a different way, as you'll see shortly.

In addition to the system configuration, it should be possible to send the language code as a command-line argument to your application for testing purposes. The `BookOfTheDayForm` constructor is changed to allow the passing of a culture string and the setting of the culture according to this string. A `CultureInfo` instance is created to pass it to the `CurrentCulture` and `CurrentUICulture` properties of the current thread. Remember that the `CurrentCulture` is used for formatting, and the `CurrentUICulture` is used for loading resources.

```
public BookOfTheDayForm(string culture)
{
    if (!String.IsNullOrEmpty(culture))
    {
        CultureInfo ci = new CultureInfo(culture);
        // set culture for formatting
        Thread.CurrentThread.CurrentCulture = ci;
        // set culture for resources
        Thread.CurrentThread.CurrentUICulture = ci;
    }

    WelcomeMessage();

    InitializeComponent();
    SetDateAndNumber();
}
```

code snippet BookOfTheDay/BookOfTheDayForm.cs

The `BookOfTheDayForm` is instantiated in the `Main()` method, which can be found in the file `Program.cs`. In this method, you pass the culture string to the `BookOfTheDayForm` constructor:

```
[STAThread]
static void Main(string[] args)
{
    string culture = String.Empty;
    if (args.Length == 1)
    {
        culture = args[0];
    }

    Application.EnableVisualStyles();
    Application.SetCompatibleTextRenderingDefault(false);
    Application.Run(new BookOfTheDayForm(culture));
}
```

code snippet BookOfTheDay/Program.cs

Now you can start the application by using command-line options. With the running application, you can see that the formatting options and the resources that were generated from the Windows Forms Designer show up. Figures 22-10 and 22-11 show two localizations in which the application is started with the command-line options `de-DE` and `fr-FR`, respectively.

There is still a problem with the welcome message box: the strings are hard-coded inside the program. Because these strings are not properties of elements inside the form, the Forms Designer does not extract XML resources as it does from the properties for Windows controls when changing the `Localizable` property of the form. You have to change this code yourself.

FIGURE 22-10

FIGURE 22-11

Using Custom Resource Messages

For the welcome message, you have to translate the hard-coded strings. The following table shows the translations for German and French. You can write custom resource messages directly in the file Resources .resx and the language-specific derivations. Of course, you can also create a new resource file.

NAME	ENGLISH	GERMAN	FRENCH
GoodMorning	Good Morning	Guten Morgen	Bonjour
GoodAfternoon	Good Afternoon	Guten Tag	Bonjour
GoodEvening	Good Evening	Guten Abend	Bonsoir
Message1	This is a localization sample.	Das ist ein Beispiel mit Lokalisierung.	C'est un exemple avec la localisation.

The source code of the method WelcomeMessage() must also be changed to use the resources. With strongly typed resources, there is no need to instantiate the ResourceManager class. Instead, the properties of the strongly typed resource can be used:

Available for download on Wrox.com

```
public static void WelcomeMessage()
{
    DateTime now = DateTime.Now;
    string message;
    if (now.Hour <= 12)
    {
        message = Properties.Resources.GoodMorning;
    }
    else if (now.Hour <= 19)
    {
        message = Properties.Resources.GoodAfternoon;
    }
    else
    {
        message = Properties.Resources.GoodEvening;
    }
    MessageBox.Show(String.Format("{0}\n{1}", message,
        Properties.Resources.Message1);
}
```

code snippet BookOfTheDay/BookOfTheDayForm.cs

When the program is started using English, German, or French, you will get the message box with the appropriate language.

Automatic Fallback for Resources

For the French and German versions in the example, all the resources are located inside the satellite assemblies. If you are not using these versions, then all the values of labels or text boxes are changed; this is not a problem at all. You must have only the values that will change in the satellite assembly; the other values will be taken from the parent assembly. For example, for de-AT (Austria), you could change the value for the *Good Afternoon* resource to *Grüß Gott* while leaving the other values intact. During runtime, when looking for the value of the resource *Good Morning*, which is not located in the de-AT satellite assembly, the parent assembly would be searched. The parent for de-AT is de. In cases where the de assembly does not have this resource either, the value would be searched for in the parent assembly of de, the neutral assembly. The neutral assembly does not have a culture code.

Keep in mind that with the culture code of the main assembly you shouldn't define any culture!

Outsourcing Translations

It is an easy task to outsource translations using resource files. It is not necessary to install Visual Studio to translate resource files; a simple XML editor will suffice. The disadvantage of using an XML editor is that there is no real chance to rearrange Windows Forms elements and change the sizes if the translated text does not fit into the original borders of a label or button. Using a Windows Forms Designer to do translations is a natural choice.

Microsoft provides a tool as part of the .NET Framework SDK that fulfills all these requirements: the Windows Resource Localization Editor, `winres.exe` (see Figure 22-12). Users working with this tool do not need access to the C# source files; only binary or XML-based resource files are needed for translations. After these translations are completed, you can import the resource files to the Visual Studio project to build satellite assemblies.

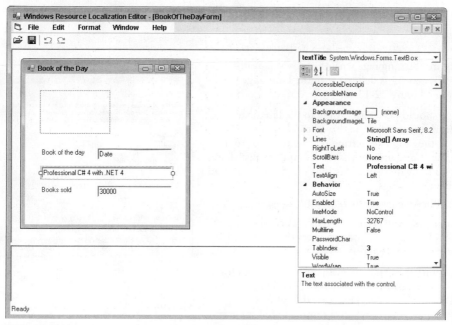

FIGURE 22-12

If you don't want your translation bureau to change the sizes and locations of labels and buttons, and they cannot deal with XML files, you can send a simple text-based file. With the command-line utility `resgen .exe`, you can create a text file from an XML file:

```
resgen myresource.resX myresource.txt
```

And after you have received the translation from the translation bureau, you can create an XML file from the returned text file. Remember to add the culture name to the filename:

```
resgen myresource.es.txt myresource.es.resX
```

LOCALIZATION WITH ASP.NET

With ASP.NET applications, localization happens in a similar way to Windows applications. Chapter 40, "Core ASP.NET," discusses the functionality of ASP.NET applications; this section discusses the localization issues of ASP.NET applications. ASP.NET 4 and Visual Studio 2010 have many features to support localization. The basic concepts of localization and globalization are the same as discussed before. However, some specific issues are associated with ASP.NET.

As you have already learned, with ASP.NET you have to differentiate between the user interface culture and the culture used for formatting. Both of these cultures can be defined on a web and page level, as well as programmatically.

To be independent of the web server's operating system, the culture and user interface culture can be defined with the `<globalization>` element in the configuration file `web.config`:

```
<configuration>
   <system.web>
      <globalization culture="en-US" uiCulture="en-US" />
   </system.web>
</configuration>
```

code snippet WebApplication/Web.config

If the configuration should be different for specific web pages, the `Page` directive allows you to assign the culture:

```
<%Page Language="C#" Culture="en-US" UICulture="en-US" %>
```

The user can configure the language with the browser. With Internet Explorer, this setting is defined with the Language Preference options (see Figure 22-13).

If the page language should be set according to the language setting of the client, the culture of the thread can be set programmatically to the language setting that is received from the client. ASP.NET has an automatic setting that does just that. Setting the culture to the value `Auto` sets the culture of the thread according to the client's settings.

FIGURE 22-13

```
<%Page Language="C#" Culture="Auto" UICulture="Auto" %>
```

In dealing with resources, ASP.NET differentiates resources that are used for the complete web site and resources that are needed only within a page.

If a resource is used within a page, you can create resources for the page by selecting the Visual Studio menu Tools ⇨ Generate Local Resource in the design view. This way, the subdirectory `App_LocalResources` is created, where a resource file for every page is stored. These resources can be localized similarly to the way they are in Windows applications. The association between the web controls and the local resource files is achieved by using a `meta:resourcekey` attribute, as shown here with the ASP.NET `Label` control. `Label1Resource1` is the name of the resource that can be changed in the local resource file:

```
<asp:Label ID="Label1" Runat="server" Text="English Text"
   meta:resourcekey="Label1Resource1"></asp:Label>
```

code snippet WebApplication/MultiLanguage.aspx

For the resources that should be shared between multiple pages, you have to create an ASP.NET folder, `Appl_GlobalResources`. In this directory, you can add resource files, for example, `Messages.resx` with its resources. To associate the web controls with these resources, you can use Expressions in the property editor. Clicking the Expressions button opens the Expressions dialog (see Figure 22-14). Here, you can select the expression type Resources, set the name of the `ClassKey` (which is the name of the resource file — here, a strongly typed resource file is generated), and the name of the `ResourceKey`, which is the name of the resource.

In the ASPX file, you can see the association to the resource with the binding expressions syntax `<%$:`

```
<asp:Label ID="Label2" Runat="server"
    Text="<%$ Resources:Messages, String1 %>">
</asp:Label>
```

LOCALIZATION WITH WPF

Visual Studio 2010 still does not have great support
for the localization of WPF applications. However,
you do not have to wait until the next version to
localize your WPF application. WPF has localization
support built-in. With WPF, you need to decide
between different options: You can use .NET
resources similar to what you've done with Windows
Forms and ASP.NET applications, but you can also
use an XAML (XML for Applications Markup
Language) resource dictionary.

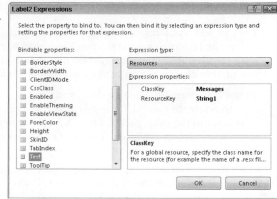

FIGURE 22-14

These options are discussed next. You can read more
about WPF and XAML in Chapters 35, "Core WPF," and 36, "Business Applications with WPF."

To demonstrate the use of resources with a WPF application, create a simple WPF application containing
just one button, as shown in Figure 22-15.

FIGURE 22-15

The XAML code for this application is shown here:

```xml
<Window x:Class="Wrox.ProCSharp.Localization.MainWindow"
    xmlns="http://schemas.microsoft.com/winfx/2006/xaml/presentation"
    xmlns:x="http://schemas.microsoft.com/winfx/2006/xaml"
    Title="WPF Sample" Height="240" Width="500">
  <Grid>
    <Button Name="button1" Margin="30,20,30,20" Click="Button_Click"
        Content="English Button" />
  </Grid>
</Window>
```

code snippet WPFApplicationUsingResources/MainWindow.xaml

With the handler code for the `Click` event of the button, just a message box containing a sample message
pops up:

```csharp
private void Button_Click(object sender, RoutedEventArgs e)
{
    MessageBox.Show("English Message");
}
```

.NET Resources with WPF

You can add .NET resources to a WPF application similar to the way you do with other applications. Define the resources named `Button1Text` and `Button1Message` in the file `Resources.resx`. By default this resource file has an `Internal` access modifier to create the `Resources` class. To use it from within XAML, you need to change this to `Public` within the Managed Resources Editor.

To use the generated resource class, you need to change the XAML code. Add an XML namespace alias to reference the .NET namespace `Wrox.ProCSharp.Localization.Properties` as shown. Here, the alias is set to the value `props`. From XAML elements, properties of this class can be used with the `x:Static` markup extension. The `Content` property of the `Button` is set to the `Button1Text` property of the `Resources` class.

```xml
<Window x:Class="Wrox.ProCSharp.Localization.Window1"
    xmlns="http://schemas.microsoft.com/winfx/2006/xaml/presentation"
    xmlns:x="http://schemas.microsoft.com/winfx/2006/xaml"
    xmlns:props="clr-namespace:Wrox.ProCSharp.Localization.Properties"
    Title="WPF Sample" Height="300" Width="300">
  <Grid>
    <Button Name="button1" Margin="30,20,30,20" Click="Button_Click"
        Content="{x:Static props:Resources.Button1Text}" />
  </Grid>
</Window>
```

code snippet WPFApplicationUsingResources/MainWindow.xaml

To use the .NET resource from code-behind, you can just access the `Button1Message` property directly in the same way you did with Windows Forms applications:

```csharp
private void Button_Click(object sender, RoutedEventArgs e)
{
    MessageBox.Show(Properties.Resources.Button1Message);
}
```

Now the resources can be localized in the same way as you've done before.

The advantages of using .NET resources for localization of WPF applications are:

➤ .NET resources can be easily managed.

➤ x:Static bindings are checked by the compiler.

Of course, there are also disadvantages:

➤ You need to add the x:Static bindings to the XAML file, and there's no designer support for this.

➤ Binding is done to the generated resource classes that use the `ResourceManager`. You would need to do some additional plumbing to support other resource managers, such as the `DatabaseResourceManager`, which is discussed later in this chapter.

➤ There's no type-converter support that can be used with other XAML elements.

XAML Resource Dictionaries

Instead of using .NET resources for localization of WPF applications, you can work directly with XAML to create localized content. This has its own advantages and disadvantages. The steps for a localization process can be described by these actions:

➤ Create a satellite assembly from the main content.

➤ Use resource dictionaries for localizable content.

➤ Add x:Uid attributes to elements that should be localized.

➤ Extract localization content from an assembly.

➤ Translate the content.

➤ Create satellite assemblies for every language.

These steps are described in the following sections.

Create Satellite Assemblies

When compiling a WPF application, the XAML code is compiled to a binary format, BAML, that is stored into an assembly. To move the BAML code from the main assembly to a separate satellite assembly, you can change the `.csproj` build file and add a `<UICulture>` element as shown as a child to the `<PropertyGroup>` element. The culture, here `en-US`, defines the default culture of the project. Building the project with this build setting creates a subdirectory en-US and creates a satellite assembly containing BAML code for the default language.

```
<UICulture>en-US</UICulture>
```

code snippet WPFApplicationUsingXAMLDictionaries/WPFApplicationUsingXAMLDictionaries.csproj

> *The easiest way to modify the project settings that are not available from the UI is to unload the project by selecting the project in the Solution Explorer and select Unload Project from the context menu, and next click Edit project-file from the context menu. After the project file is changed, the project can be loaded again.*

Separating the BAML into a satellite assembly, you should also apply the `NeutralResourcesLanguage` attribute and supply the resource fallback location to a satellite assembly. If you decide to keep BAML in the main assembly (by not defining the `<UICulture>` to the `.csproj` file), the `UltimateResourceFallbackLocation` should be set to `MainAssembly`.

```
[assembly: NeutralResourcesLanguage("en-US",
UltimateResourceFallbackLocation.Satellite)]
```

code snippet WPFApplicationUsingXAMLDictionaries/AssemblyInfo.cs

Add a Resource Dictionary

For code-behind content that needs to be localized, a resource dictionary can be added. Using XAML, you can define resources within the `<ResourceDictionary>` element as shown. With Visual Studio, you can create a new resource dictionary by adding a new resource dictionary item and defining the filename. In the example here, the resource dictionary contains one string item. To get access to the `String` type from the `System` namespace, an XML namespace alias needs to be defined. Here, the alias `system` is set to the clr-namespace `System` in the assembly `mscorlib`. The string that is defined can be accessed with the key `message1`. This resource dictionary is defined in the file `LocalizedStrings.xaml`.

```
<ResourceDictionary
    xmlns="http://schemas.microsoft.com/winfx/2006/xaml/presentation"
    xmlns:x="http://schemas.microsoft.com/winfx/2006/xaml"
    xmlns:system="clr-namespace:System;assembly=mscorlib">
  <system:String x:Key="Message1">English Message</system:String>
</ResourceDictionary>
```

code snippet WPFApplicationUsingXAMLDictionaries/LocalizationStrings.xaml

To have the resource dictionary available with the application, it must be added to the resources. If the resource dictionary is required only within a window or just within a specific WPF element, it can be added to the resources collection of the specific window or WPF element. If the same resource dictionary is needed by multiple windows, it can be added to the file `App.xaml` within the `<Application>` element, and thus be available to the complete application. Here, the resource dictionary is added within the resources of the main window:

```
<Window.Resources>
    <ResourceDictionary>
        <ResourceDictionary.MergedDictionaries>
            <ResourceDictionary Source="LocalizationStrings.xaml" />
        </ResourceDictionary.MergedDictionaries>
            </ResourceDictionary>
        </Window.Resources>
```

code snippet WPFApplicationUsingXAMLDictionaries/MainWindow.xaml

To use the XAML resource dictionary from code behind, you can use the indexer of the `Resources` property, the `FindResource()` method or the `TryFindResource()` method. Because the resource is defined with the window, the indexer of the `Resources` property of the `Window` class can be used to access the resource. `FindResource()` does a hierarchical search for a resource. If you use the `FindResource()` method of the `Button`, and if it is not found with the `Button` resources, then resources are searched in the `Grid`. If the resource is not there, a lookup to the `Window` resources is done before the `Application` resources are consulted.

```
private void Button_Click(object sender, RoutedEventArgs e)
{
    MessageBox.Show(this.Resources["Message1"] as string);
    MessageBox.Show(this.FindResource("Message1") as string);
}
```

code snippet WPFApplicationUsingXAMLDictionaries/MainWindow.xaml.cs

Uid Attributes for Localization

With the custom resource dictionary file, the text from the code that should be localized can be referenced. For localizing XAML code with WPF elements, the `x:Uid` attribute is used as a unique identifier for the elements that need localization. You don't have to apply this attribute manually to the XAML content; instead, you can use the `msbuild` command with this option:

```
msbuild /t:updateuid
```

When you call this command in the directory where the project file is located, the XAML files of the project are modified to add an `x:Uid` attribute with a unique identifier to every element. If the control already has a `Name` or `x:Name` attribute applied, the `x:Uid` has the same value; otherwise, a new value is generated. The same XAML that was shown before now has the new attributes applied:

```
<Window x:Uid="Window_1"
        x:Class="WPFApplicationUsingXAMLDictionaries.MainWindow"
        xmlns="http://schemas.microsoft.com/winfx/2006/xaml/presentation"
        xmlns:x="http://schemas.microsoft.com/winfx/2006/xaml"
        Title="Main Window" Height="240" Width="500">
    <Window.Resources>
        <ResourceDictionary x:Uid="ResourceDictionary_1">
            <ResourceDictionary.MergedDictionaries>
                <ResourceDictionary x:Uid="ResourceDictionary_2"
                                    Source="LocalizationStrings.xaml" />
            </ResourceDictionary.MergedDictionaries>
        </ResourceDictionary>
    </Window.Resources>
    <Grid x:Uid="Grid_1">
        <Button x:Uid="button1" Name="button1" Margin="30,20,30,20" Click="Button_Click"
            Content="English Button" />
    </Grid>
</Window>
```

If you change the XAML file after `x:Uid` attributes have been added, you can verify correctness of the `x:Uid` attributes with the option `/t:checkuid`.

Now you can compile the project to create BAML code containing the `x:Uid` attributes and use a tool to extract this information.

LocBaml Tool for Localization

Compiling the project creates a satellite assembly containing the BAML code. From this satellite assembly, you can extract the content that needs to be localized with classes from the `System.Windows.Markup.Localizer` namespace. With the Windows SDK, you will find the sample program LocBaml. This program can be used to extract localization content from BAML. You need to copy the executable, the satellite assembly with the default content, and `LocBaml.exe` to one directory and start the sample program to produce a `.csv` file with the localization content:

```
LocBaml /parse WPFApplicationUsingXAMLDictionaries.resources.dll /out: trans.csv
```

 To use the LocBaml with a WPF application that is built with .NET 4, the tool also must be built with .NET 4 or a newer version. If you have an old version of the LocBaml tool that was built with .NET 2.0, it cannot load the .NET 4 assemblies. The Windows SDK contains the source of the tool, so you can rebuild it with the newest version of .NET.

You can use Microsoft Excel to open the `.csv` file and translate its content. An extract from the `.csv` file that lists the content of the button and the message from the resource dictionary is shown here:

```
WPFandXAMLResources.g.en-US.resources:localizationstrings.baml,
system:String_1:System.String.$Content,None,True,True,,English Message
WPFandXAMLResources.g.en-US.resources:window1.baml,
button1:System.Windows.Controls.ContentControl.Content,Button,True,True,,
English Button
```

This file contains these fields:

➤ Name of the BAML

➤ The identifier of the resource

➤ The category of the resource that gives the type of the content

➤ A Boolean value if the resource is visible for translation (readable)

➤ A Boolean value if the resource can be modified for the translation (modifiable)

➤ Localization comments

➤ The value of the resource

After localization of the resource, you can create a new directory for the new language (for example, `de` for German). The directory structure follows the same convention that was shown earlier in this chapter with satellite assemblies. With the LocBaml tool, you can create satellite assemblies with the translated content:

```
LocBaml /generate WPFandXAMLResources.resources.dll /trans:trans_de.csv
        /out: ./de /cul:de-DE
```

Now the same rules for setting the culture of the thread and finding satellite assemblies that were shown with Windows Forms applications apply here.

As you've seen, it's quite a chore to do the localization with XAML dictionaries. This is one of the disadvantages. Luckily it's not necessary to do this day by day. What are the advantages?

➤ You can delay the localization process within the XAML file until the application is completed. There's no special markup or resource-mapping syntax needed. The localization process can be separated from the development process.

➤ Using XAML resource dictionaries is very efficient at runtime.

➤ Localization can be done easily with a CSV editor.

The disadvantages are:

➤ LocBaml is an unsupported tool found in the samples of the SDK.

➤ Localization is a one-time process. It's hard to make changes to the localization.

A CUSTOM RESOURCE READER

With the resource readers that are part of .NET Framework 4, you can read resources from resource files and satellite assemblies. If you want to put the resources into a different store (such as a database), you can use a custom resource reader to read these resources.

To use a custom resource reader, you also need to create a custom resource set and a custom resource manager. Doing this is not a difficult task, however, because you can derive the custom classes from existing classes.

For the sample application, you need to create a simple database with just one table for storing messages that has one column for every supported language. The following table lists the columns and their corresponding values.

KEY	DEFAULT	DE	ES	FR	IT
Welcome	Welcome	Willkommen	Bienvenido	Bienvenue	Benvenuto
GoodMorning	Good morning	Guten Morgen	Buenos díaz	Bonjour	Buona mattina
GoodEvening	Good evening	Guten Abend	Buenos noches	Bonsoir	Buona sera
ThankYou	Thank you	Danke	Gracias	Merci	Grazie
Goodbye	Goodbye	Auf Wiedersehen	Adiós	Au revoir	Arrivederci

For the custom resource reader, you create a component library with three classes. The classes are `DatabaseResourceReader`, `DatabaseResourceSet`, and `DatabaseResourceManager`.

Creating a DatabaseResourceReader

With the class `DatabaseResourceReader`, you define two fields: the connection string that is needed to access the database and the language that should be returned by the reader. These fields are filled inside the constructor of this class. The field `language` is set to the name of the culture that is passed with the `CultureInfo` object to the constructor:

Available for download on Wrox.com

```
public class DatabaseResourceReader: IResourceReader
{
    private string connectionString;
    private string language;

    public DatabaseResourceReader(string connectionString,
        CultureInfo culture)
    {
        this.connectionString = connectionString;
        this.language = culture.Name;
    }
```

code snippet DatabaseResourceReader/DatabaseResourceReader.cs

A resource reader has to implement the interface `IResourceReader`. This interface defines the methods `Close()` and `GetEnumerator()` to return an `IDictionaryEnumerator` that returns keys and values for the resources. In the implementation of `GetEnumerator()`, create a `Hashtable` where all keys and values for a specific language are stored. Next, you can use the `SqlConnection` class in the namespace `System.Data.SqlClient` to access the database in SQL Server. `Connection.CreateCommand()` creates a `SqlCommand()` object that you use to specify the SQL `SELECT` statement to access the data in the database. If the language is set to `de`, the `SELECT` statement is `SELECT [key], [de] FROM Messages`. Then you use a `SqlDataReader` object to read all values from the database and put them into a `Hashtable`. Finally, the enumerator of the `Hashtable` is returned.

 For more information about accessing data with ADO.NET, see Chapter 30, "Core ADO.NET."

```
public System.Collections.IDictionaryEnumerator GetEnumerator()
{
    Dictionary<string, string> dict = new Dictionary<string, string>();

    SqlConnection connection = new SqlConnection(connectionString);
    SqlCommand command = connection.CreateCommand();
    if (String.IsNullOrEmpty(language))
        language = "Default";

    command.CommandText = "SELECT [key], [" + language + "] " +
                          "FROM Messages";

    try
    {
        connection.Open();

        SqlDataReader reader = command.ExecuteReader();
        while (reader.Read())
        {
            if (reader.GetValue(1) != System.DBNull.Value)
            {
                dict.Add(reader.GetString(0).Trim(), reader.GetString(1));
            }
        }

        reader.Close();
    }
    catch (SqlException ex)
    {
        if (ex.Number != 207)  // ignore missing columns in the database
            throw;             // rethrow all other exceptions
    }
    finally
    {
        connection.Close();
    }
    return dict.GetEnumerator();
}

public void Close()
{
}
```

Because the interface `IResourceReader` is derived from `IEnumerable` and `IDisposable`, the methods `GetEnumerator()`, which returns an `IEnumerator` interface, and `Dispose()` must be implemented, too:

```
IEnumerator IEnumerable.GetEnumerator()
{
    return this.GetEnumerator();
}

void IDisposable.Dispose()
{
}
```

Creating a DatabaseResourceSet

The class `DatabaseResourceSet` can use nearly all implementations of the base class `ResourceSet`. You just need a different constructor that initializes the base class with your own resource reader, `DatabaseResourceReader`. The constructor of `ResourceSet` allows passing an object by implementing `IResourceReader`; this requirement is fulfilled by `DatabaseResourceReader`:

Available for
download on
Wrox.com

```
public class DatabaseResourceSet: ResourceSet
{
    internal DatabaseResourceSet(string connectionString, CultureInfo culture)
        : base(new DatabaseResourceReader(connectionString, culture))
    {
    }

    public override Type GetDefaultReader()
    {
        return typeof(DatabaseResourceReader);
    }
}
```

code snippet DatabaseResourceReader/DatabaseResourceSet.cs

Creating a DatabaseResourceManager

The third class you have to create is the custom resource manager. `DatabaseResourceManager` is derived from the class `ResourceManager`, and you only have to implement a new constructor and override the method `InternalGetResourceSet()`.

In the constructor, create a new `Dictionary<string, DatabaseResourceSet>` to store all queried resource sets and set it into the field `ResourceSets` defined by the base class:

Available for
download on
Wrox.com

```
public class DatabaseResourceManager: ResourceManager
{
    private string connectionString;
    private Dictionary<string, DatabaseResourceSet> resourceSets;

    public DatabaseResourceManager(string connectionString)
    {
        this.connectionString = connectionString;
        resourceSets = new Dictionary<string, DatabaseResourceSet>();
    }
```

code snippet DatabaseResourceReader/DatabaseResourceManager.cs

The methods of the `ResourceManager` class that you can use to access resources (such as `GetString()` and `GetObject()`) invoke the method `InternalGetResourceSet()` to access a resource set where the appropriate values can be returned.

In the implementation of `InternalGetResourceSet()`, check first if the resource set for the culture queried for a resource is already in the hash table; if it already exists, return it to the caller. If the resource set is not available, create a new `DatabaseResourceSet` object with the queried culture, add it to the dictionary, and return it to the caller:

```
protected override ResourceSet InternalGetResourceSet(
    CultureInfo culture, bool createIfNotExists, bool tryParents)
{
    DatabaseResourceSet rs = null;

    if (resourceSets.ContainsKey(culture.Name))
    {
        rs = resourceSets[culture.Name];
    }
    else
    {
        rs = new DatabaseResourceSet(connectionString, culture);
        resourceSets.Add(culture.Name, rs);
    }
    return rs;
}
```

Client Application for DatabaseResourceReader

The way the class `ResourceManager` is used from the client application here does not differ much from the previous use of the `ResourceManager` class. The only difference is that the custom class `DatabaseResourceManager` is used instead of the class `ResourceManager`. The following code snippet demonstrates how you can use your own resource manager.

A new `DatabaseResourceManager` object is created by passing the database connection string to the constructor. Then, you can invoke the `GetString()` method that is implemented in the base class as you did earlier, passing the key and an optional object of type `CultureInfo` to specify a culture. In turn, you get a resource value from the database because this resource manager is using the classes `DatabaseResourceSet` and `DatabaseResourceReader`.

Available for
download on
Wrox.com

```
var rm = new DatabaseResourceManager(
        @"server=(local)\sqlexpress;database=LocalizationDemo;" +
        "trusted_connection=true");

string spanishWelcome = rm.GetString("Welcome", new CultureInfo("es-ES"));
string italianThankyou = rm.GetString("ThankYou", new CultureInfo("it"));
string threadDefaultGoodMorning = rm.GetString("GoodMorning");
```

code snippet DatabaseResourceReaderClient/Program.cs

CREATING CUSTOM CULTURES

Over time, more and more languages have become supported by the .NET Framework. However, not all languages of the world are available with .NET. You can create a custom culture. Some examples of when creating custom cultures can be useful are to support a minority within a region or to create subcultures for different dialects.

Custom cultures and regions can be created with the class `CultureAndRegionInfoBuilder` in the namespace `System.Globalization`. This class is located in the assembly `sysglobl`.

> *Because the* sysglobl *assembly is not in the .NET Framework 4 Client Profile, you have to set the Target Framework with the project settings for .NET Framework 4 to reference it.*

With the constructor of the class CultureAndRegionInfoBuilder, you can pass the culture's name. The second argument of the constructor requires an enumeration of type CultureAndRegionModifiers. This enumeration allows one of three values: Neutral for a neutral culture, Replacement if an existing Framework culture should be replaced, or None.

After the CultureAndRegionInfoBuilder object is instantiated, you can configure the culture by setting properties. With the properties of this class, you can define all the cultural and regional information such as name, calendar, number format, metric information, and so on. If the culture should be based on existing cultures and regions, you can set the properties of the instance using the methods LoadDataFromCultureInfo() and LoadDataFromRegionInfo(), and change the values that are different by setting the properties afterward.

Calling the method Register() registers the new culture with the operating system. Indeed, you can find the file that describes the culture in the directory <windows>\Globalization. Look for files with the extension .nlp.

```csharp
using System;
using System.Globalization;

namespace CustomCultures
{
    class Program
    {
        static void Main()
        {
            try
            {
                // Create a Styria culture
                var styria = new CultureAndRegionInfoBuilder("de-AT-ST",
                                    CultureAndRegionModifiers.None);
                var cultureParent = new CultureInfo("de-AT");
                styria.LoadDataFromCultureInfo(cultureParent);
                styria.LoadDataFromRegionInfo(new RegionInfo("AT"));
                styria.Parent = cultureParent;
                styria.RegionNativeName = "Steiermark";
                styria.RegionEnglishName = "Styria";
                styria.CultureEnglishName = "Styria (Austria)";
                styria.CultureNativeName = "Steirisch";

                styria.Register();
            }
            catch (UnauthorizedAccessException ex)
            {
                Console.WriteLine(ex.Message);
            }


        }
    }
}
```

code snippet CustomCultures/Program.cs

Because registering custom languages on the system requires administrative privileges, an application manifest file is required that specifies the requested execution rights. In the project properties, the manifest file needs to be set in the Application settings.

Available for download on Wrox.com

```xml
<?xml version="1.0" encoding="utf-8"?>
<asmv1:assembly manifestVersion="1.0" xmlns="urn:schemas-microsoft-com:asm.v1"
xmlsn:asmv1="urn:schemas-microsoft-com:asm.v1" xmlns:asmv2="urn:schemas-microsoft-
com:asm.v2" xmlns:xsi="http://www.w3.org/2001/XMLSchema-instance">
  <assemblyIdentity version="1.0.0.0" name="MyApplication.app"/>
  <trustInfo xmlns="urn:schemas-microsoft-com:asm.v2">
    <security>
      <requestedPrivileges xmlns="urn:schemas-microsoft-com:asm.v3">
        <requestedExecutionLevel level="requireAdministrator" uiAccess="false" />
      </requestedPrivileges>
    </security>
  </trustInfo>
</asmv1:assembly>
```

code snippet CustomCultures/app.manifest

The newly created culture can now be used like other cultures:

```csharp
var ci = new CultureInfo("de-AT-ST");
Thread.CurrentThread.CurrentCulture = ci;
Thread.CurrentThread.CurrentUICulture = ci;
```

You can use the culture for formatting and also for resources. If you start the Cultures in Action application that was written earlier in this chapter again, you can see the custom culture as well.

SUMMARY

This chapter discussed the globalization and localization of .NET applications.

In the context of globalization of applications, you learned about using the namespace `System .Globalization` to format culture-dependent numbers and dates. Furthermore, you learned that sorting strings by default depends on the culture, and you used the invariant culture for a culture-independent sort. Using the `CultureAndRegionInfoBuilder` class, you've learned how to create a custom culture.

Localization of applications is accomplished by using resources. Resources can be packed into files, satellite assemblies, or a custom store such as a database. The classes used with localization are in the namespace `System.Resources`. For reading resources from other places, such as satellite assemblies or resource files, you can create a custom resource reader.

You have seen how to localize Windows Forms, WPF, and ASP.NET applications. Besides all that, you've learned some important vocabulary in different languages.

The next chapter provides information about a completely different topic — transactions. Don't expect that transactions will only be useful with databases. In addition to database transactions, the chapter gives you information on memory-based transactional resources and a transactional file system.

23

System.Transactions

WHAT'S IN THIS CHAPTER?

➤ Transaction phases and ACID properties

➤ Traditional transactions

➤ Committable transactions

➤ Transaction promotions

➤ Dependent transactions

➤ Ambient transactions

➤ Transaction isolation levels

➤ Custom resource managers

➤ Transactions with Windows 7 and Windows Server 2008

All or nothing — this is the main characteristic of a transaction. When writing a few records, either all are written, or everything will be undone. If there is even one failure when writing one record, all the other things that are done within the transaction will be rolled back.

Transactions are commonly used with databases, but with classes from the namespace System.Transactions, you can also perform transactions on volatile or in-memory-based objects such as a list of objects. With a list that supports transactions, if an object is added or removed and the transaction fails, the list action is automatically undone. Writing to a memory-based list can be done in the same transaction as writing to a database.

Since Windows Vista, the file system and registry also get transactional support. Writing a file and making changes within the registry supports transactions.

OVERVIEW

What are transactions? Think about ordering a book from a web site. The book-ordering process removes the book you want to buy from stock and puts it in your order box, and the cost of your book is charged to your credit card. With these two actions, either both actions should complete successfully or neither of these actions should happen. If there is a failure when getting the book from stock, the credit card should not be charged. Transactions address such scenarios.

The most common use of transactions is writing or updating data within the database. Transactions can also be performed when writing a message to a message queue, or writing data to a file or the registry. Multiple actions can be part of a single transaction.

> System.Messaging *is discussed in Chapter 46, "Message Queuing."*

Figure 23-1 shows the main actors in a transaction. Transactions are managed and coordinated by the transaction manager, and a resource manager manages every resource that influences the outcome of the transaction. The transaction manager communicates with resource managers to define the outcome of the transaction.

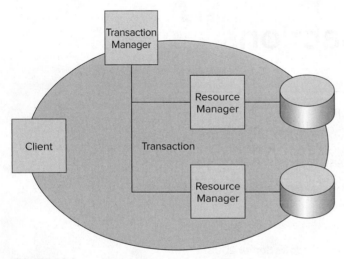

FIGURE 23-1

Transaction Phases

The timely phases of a transaction are the *active, preparing,* and *committing* phases:

➤ **Active phase** — During the active phase, the transaction is created. Resource managers that manage the transaction for resources can enlist with the transaction.

➤ **Preparing phase** — During the preparing phase, every resource manager can define the outcome of the transaction. This phase starts when the creator of the transaction sends a commit to end the transaction. The transaction manager sends a *Prepare* message to all resource managers. If the resource manager can produce the transaction outcome successfully, it sends a *Prepared* message to the transaction manager. Resource managers can abort the transaction if they fail to prepare by forcing a rollback with the transaction manager by sending a *Rollback* message. After the Prepared message is sent, the resource managers must guarantee to finish the work successfully in the committing phase. To make this possible, durable resource managers must write a log with the information from the prepared state, so that they can continue from there in case of, for example, a power failure between the prepared and committing phases.

➤ **Committing phase** — The committing phase begins when all resource managers have prepared successfully. This is when the *Prepared* message is received from all resource managers. Then the transaction manager can complete the work by sending a *Commit* message to all participants. The resource managers can now finish the work on the transaction and return a *Committed* message.

ACID Properties

A transaction has specific requirements; for example, a transaction must result in a valid state, even if the server has a power failure. The characteristics of transactions can be defined by the term ACID. *ACID* is a four-letter acronym for *atomicity, consistency, isolation,* and *durability*:

➤ **Atomicity** — Represents one unit of work. With a transaction, either the complete unit of work succeeds or nothing is changed.

➤ **Consistency** — The state before the transaction was started and after the transaction is completed must be valid. During the transaction, the state may have interim values.

➤ **Isolation** — Means that transactions that happen concurrently are isolated from the state, which is changed during a transaction. Transaction A cannot see the interim state of transaction B until the transaction is completed.

➤ **Durability** — After the transaction is completed, it must be stored in a durable way. This means that if the power goes down or the server crashes, the state must be recovered at reboot.

Not every transaction requires all four ACID properties. For example, a memory-based transaction (for example, writing an entry into a list) does not need to be durable. Also, a complete isolation from the outside is not always required, as we discuss later with transaction isolation levels.

DATABASE AND ENTITY CLASSES

The sample database `CourseManagement` that is used with the transactions in this chapter is defined by the structure from Figure 23-2. The table `Courses` contains information about courses: course number and title. The table `CourseDates` contains the date of specific courses and is linked to the `Courses` table. The table `Students` contains information about persons attending a course. The table `CourseAttendees` is the link between `Students` and `CourseDates`. It defines which student is attending what course.

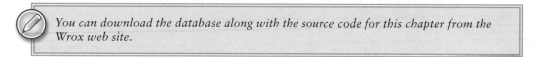

You can download the database along with the source code for this chapter from the Wrox web site.

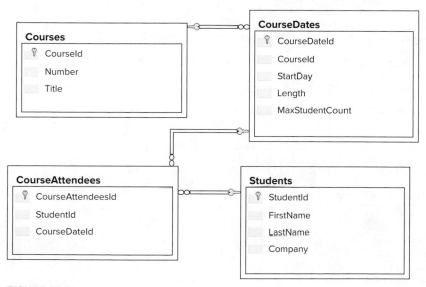

FIGURE 23-2

The sample applications in this chapter use a library with entity and data access classes. The class `Student` contains properties to define a student; for example, `FirstName`, `LastName`, and `Company`:

```csharp
using System;

namespace Wrox.ProCSharp.Transactions
{
    [Serializable]
    public class Student
    {
        public string FirstName { get; set; }
        public string LastName { get; set; }
        public string Company { get; set; }
        public int Id { get; set; }

        public override string ToString()
        {
            return String.Format("{0} {1}", FirstName, LastName);
        }
    }
}
```

code snippet DataLib/Student.cs

Adding student information to the database is done in the method `AddStudent()` of the class `StudentData`. Here, an ADO.NET connection is created to connect to the SQL Server database, the `SqlCommand` object defines the SQL statement, and the command is executed by invoking `ExecuteNonQuery()`:

```csharp
using System;
using System.Collections.Generic;
using System.Data;
using System.Data.SqlClient;
using System.Transactions;

namespace Wrox.ProCSharp.Transactions
{
    public class StudentData
    {
        public void AddStudent(Student student)
        {
            var connection = new SqlConnection(
                Properties.Settings.Default.CourseManagementConnectionString);
            connection.Open();
            try
            {
                SqlCommand command = connection.CreateCommand();

                command.CommandText = "INSERT INTO Students " +
                    "(FirstName, LastName, Company) VALUES " +
                    "(@FirstName, @LastName, @Company)";
                command.Parameters.AddWithValue("@FirstName", student.FirstName);
                command.Parameters.AddWithValue("@LastName", student.LastName);
                command.Parameters.AddWithValue("@Company", student.Company);

                command.ExecuteNonQuery();
            }
            finally
            {
                connection.Close();
            }
        }
    }
}
```

code snippet DataLib/StudentData.cs

ADO.NET is covered in detail in Chapter 30, "Core ADO.NET."

TRADITIONAL TRANSACTIONS

Before `System.Transaction` was released, you could create transactions directly with ADO.NET, or you could do transactions with the help of components, attributes, and the COM+ runtime, which is covered in the namespace `System.EnterpriseServices`. To show you how the new transaction model compares to the traditional ways of working with transactions, we present a short look at how ADO.NET transactions and transactions with Enterprise Services are done.

ADO.NET Transactions

Let's start with traditional ADO.NET transactions. If you don't create transactions manually, there is a single transaction with every SQL statement. If multiple statements need to participate with the same transaction, however, you must create a transaction manually to achieve this.

The following code segment shows how to work with ADO.NET transactions. The `SqlConnection` class defines the method `BeginTransaction()`, which returns an object of type `SqlTransaction`. This transaction object must then be associated with every command that participates with the transaction. To associate a command with a transaction, set the `Transaction` property of the `SqlCommand` class to the `SqlTransaction` instance. For the transaction to be successful, you must invoke the `Commit()` method of the `SqlTransaction` object. If there is an error, you have to invoke the `Rollback()` method, and every change is undone. You can check for an error with the help of a try/catch and do the rollback inside the catch:

```csharp
using System;
using System.Data.SqlClient;
using System.Diagnostics;

namespace Wrox.ProCSharp.Transactions
{
    public class CourseData
    {
        public void AddCourse(Course course)
        {
            var connection = new SqlConnection(
                Properties.Settings.Default.CourseManagementConnectionString);
            SqlCommand courseCommand = connection.CreateCommand();
            courseCommand.CommandText =
                "INSERT INTO Courses (Number, Title) VALUES (@Number, @Title)";
            connection.Open();
            SqlTransaction tx = connection.BeginTransaction();

            try
            {
                courseCommand.Transaction = tx;

                courseCommand.Parameters.AddWithValue("@Number", course.Number);
                courseCommand.Parameters.AddWithValue("@Title", course.Title);
                courseCommand.ExecuteNonQuery();

                tx.Commit();
            }
            catch (Exception ex)
            {
```

```
                    Trace.WriteLine("Error: " + ex.Message);
                    tx.Rollback();
                }
                finally
                {
                    connection.Close();
                }
            }
        }
    }
```

If you have multiple commands that should run in the same transaction, every command must be associated with the transaction. Because the transaction is associated with a connection, every one of these commands must also be associated with the same connection instance. ADO.NET transactions do not support transactions across multiple connections; it is always a local transaction associated with one connection.

When you create an object persistence model using multiple objects, for example, classes `Course` and `CourseDate`, which should be persisted inside one transaction, it gets very difficult using ADO.NET transactions. Here, it is necessary to pass the transaction to all the objects participating in the same transaction.

 ADO.NET transactions are not distributed transactions. In ADO.NET transactions, it is difficult to have multiple objects working on the same transaction.

System.EnterpriseServices

With Enterprise Services, you get a lot of services for free. One of them is automatic transactions. Using transactions with `System.EnterpriseServices` has the advantage that it is not necessary to deal with transactions explicitly; transactions are automatically created by the runtime. You just have to add the attribute `[Transaction]` with the transactional requirements to the class. The `[AutoComplete]` attribute marks the method to automatically set the status bit for the transaction: if the method succeeds, the success bit is set, so the transaction can commit. If an exception happens, the transaction is aborted:

```csharp
using System;
using System.Data.SqlClient;
using System.EnterpriseServices;
using System.Diagnostics;

namespace Wrox.ProCSharp.Transactions
{
    [Transaction(TransactionOption.Required)]
    public class CourseData: ServicedComponent
    {
        [AutoComplete]
        public void AddCourse(Course course)
        {
            var connection = new SqlConnection(
                    Properties.Settings.Default.CourseManagementConnectionString);
            SqlCommand courseCommand = connection.CreateCommand();
            courseCommand.CommandText =
                    "INSERT INTO Courses (Number, Title) VALUES (@Number, @Title)";
            connection.Open();
            try
            {
                courseCommand.Parameters.AddWithValue("@Number", course.Number);
                courseCommand.Parameters.AddWithValue("@Title", course.Title);
                courseCommand.ExecuteNonQuery();
```

```
        }
        finally
        {
            connection.Close();
        }
    }
  }
}
```

A big advantage of creating transactions with `System.EnterpriseServices` is that multiple objects can easily run within the same transaction, and transactions are automatically enlisted. The disadvantages are that it requires the COM+ hosting model, and the class using the features of this technology must be derived from the base class `ServicedComponent`.

 Enterprise Services and using COM+ transactional services are covered in the downloadable Chapter 51, "Enterprise Services."

SYSTEM.TRANSACTIONS

The namespace `System.Transactions` became available with .NET 2.0 and brings a modern transaction programming model to .NET applications.

This namespace offers a few dependent `TransactionXXX` classes. `Transaction` is the base class of all transaction classes and defines properties, methods, and events available with all transaction classes. `CommittableTransaction` is the only transaction class that supports committing. This class has a `Commit()` method; all other transaction classes can do only a rollback. The class `DependentTransaction` is used with transactions that are dependent on another transaction. A dependent transaction can depend on a transaction created from the committable transaction. Then the dependent transaction adds to the outcome of the committable transaction whether or not it is successful. The class `SubordinateTransaction` is used in conjunction with the Distributed Transaction Coordinator (DTC). This class represents a transaction that is not a root transaction but can be managed by the DTC.

The following table describes the properties and methods of the `Transaction` class.

TRANSACTION CLASS MEMBER	DESCRIPTION
Current	The property `Current` is a static property without the need to have an instance. `Transaction.Current` returns an ambient transaction if one exists. Ambient transactions are discussed later in this chapter.
IsolationLevel	The `IsolationLevel` property returns an object of type `IsolationLevel`. `IsolationLevel` is an enumeration that defines what access other transactions have to the interim results of the transaction. This affects the *I* in ACID; not all transactions are isolated.
TransactionInformation	The `TransactionInformation` property returns a `TransactionInformation` object. `TransactionInformation` gives you information about the current state of the transaction, the time when the transaction was created, and transaction identifiers.
EnlistVolatile() EnlistDurable() EnlistPromotableSinglePhase()	With the enlist methods `EnlistVolatile()`, `EnlistDurable()`, and `EnlistPromotableSinglePhase()`, you can enlist custom resource managers that participate with the transaction.
Rollback()	With the `Rollback()` method, you can abort a transaction and undo everything to set all results to the state before the transaction.

continues

(continued)

TRANSACTION CLASS MEMBER	DESCRIPTION
DependentClone()	With the DependentClone() method, you can create a transaction that depends on the current transaction.
TransactionCompleted	TransactionCompleted is an event that is fired when the transaction is completed — either successfully or unsuccessfully. With an event handler object of type TransactionCompletedEventHandler, you get access to the Transaction object and can read its status.

For demonstrating the features of System.Transaction, the class Utilities inside a separate assembly offers some static methods. The method AbortTx() returns true or false depending on the input from the user. The method DisplayTransactionInformation() gets a TransactionInformation object as parameter and displays all the information from the transaction: creation time, status, local, and distributed identifiers:

Available for download on Wrox.com

```csharp
public static class Utilities
{
    public static bool AbortTx()
    {
        Console.Write("Abort the Transaction (y/n)?");
        return Console.ReadLine() == "y";
    }

    public static void DisplayTransactionInformation(string title,
            TransactionInformation ti)
    {
        if (ti != null)
        {
            Console.WriteLine(title);

            Console.WriteLine("Creation Time: {0:T}", ti.CreationTime);
            Console.WriteLine("Status: {0}", ti.Status);
            Console.WriteLine("Local ID: {0}", ti.LocalIdentifier);
            Console.WriteLine("Distributed ID: {0}", ti.DistributedIdentifier);
            Console.WriteLine();
        }
    }
}
```

code snippet Utilities/Utilities.cs

Committable Transactions

The Transaction class cannot be committed programmatically; it does not have a method to commit the transaction. The base class Transaction just supports aborting the transaction. The only transaction class that supports a commit is the class CommittableTransaction.

With ADO.NET, a transaction can be enlisted with the connection. To make this possible, an AddStudent() method is added to the class StudentData that accepts a System.Transactions.Transaction object as second parameter. The object tx is enlisted with the connection by calling the method EnlistTransaction of the SqlConnection class. This way, the ADO.NET connection is associated with the transaction:

Available for download on Wrox.com

```csharp
public void AddStudent(Student student, Transaction tx)
{
    var connection = new SqlConnection(
            Properties.Settings.Default.CourseManagementConnectionString);
    connection.Open();
```

```
                        try
                        {
                            if (tx != null)
                                connection.EnlistTransaction(tx);
                            SqlCommand command = connection.CreateCommand();

                            command.CommandText = "INSERT INTO Students (FirstName, " +
                                    "LastName, Company)" +
                                    "VALUES (@FirstName, @LastName, @Company)";
                            command.Parameters.AddWithValue("@FirstName", student.FirstName);
                            command.Parameters.AddWithValue("@LastName", student.LastName);
                            command.Parameters.AddWithValue("@Company", student.Company);

                            command.ExecuteNonQuery();
                        }
                        finally
                        {
                            connection.Close();
                        }
                }
```

code snippet DataLib/StudentData.cs

In the `CommittableTransaction()` method of the console application TransactionSamples, first a transaction of type `CommittableTransaction` is created, and information is shown on the console. Then a `Student` object is created, and this object is written to the database from the `AddStudent()` method. If you verify the record in the database from outside the transaction, you cannot see the student added until the transaction is completed. In case the transaction fails, there is a rollback, and the student is not written to the database.

After the `AddStudent()` method is invoked, the helper method `Utilities.AbortTx()` is called to ask if the transaction should be aborted. If the user aborts, an exception of type `ApplicationException` is thrown and, in the catch block, a rollback with the transaction is done by calling the method `Rollback()` of the `Transaction` class. The record is not written to the database. If the user does not abort, the `Commit()` method commits the transaction, and the final state of the transaction is committed:

```
static void CommittableTransaction()
{
    var tx = new CommittableTransaction();
    Utilities.DisplayTransactionInformation("TX created",
            tx.TransactionInformation);

    try
    {
        var s1 = new Student
        {
            FirstName = "Jörg",
            LastName = "Neumann",
            Company = "thinktecture"
        };
        var db = new StudentData();
        db.AddStudent(s1, tx);

        if (Utilities.AbortTx())
        {
            throw new ApplicationException("transaction abort");
        }

        tx.Commit();
    }
    catch (Exception ex)
```

```
        {
            Console.WriteLine(ex.Message);
            Console.WriteLine();
            tx.Rollback();
        }

        Utilities.DisplayTransactionInformation("TX completed",
            tx.TransactionInformation);

    }
```

code snippet TransactionSamples/Program.cs

Here, you can see the output of the application where the transaction is active and has a local identifier. The output of the application that follows shows the result with the user choice to abort the transaction. After the transaction is finished, you can see the aborted state:

```
TX created
Creation Time: 7:30:49 PM
Status: Active
Local ID: bdcf1cdc-a67e-4ccc-9a5c-cbdfe0fe9177:1
Distributed ID: 00000000-0000-0000-0000-000000000000

Abort the Transaction (y/n)? y
Transaction abort

TX completed
Creation Time: 7:30:49 PM
Status: Aborted
Local ID: bdcf1cdc-a67e-4ccc-9a5c-cbdfe0fe9177:1
Distributed ID: 00000000-0000-0000-0000-000000000000
```

With the second output of the application that you can see here, the transaction is not aborted by the user. The transaction has the status committed, and the data is written to the database:

```
TX Created
Creation Time: 7:33:04 PM
Status: Active
Local ID: 708bda71-fa24-46a9-86b4-18b83120f6af:1
Distributed ID: 00000000-0000-0000-0000-000000000000

Abort the Transaction (y/n)? n

TX completed
Creation Time: 7:33:04 PM
Status: Committed
Local ID: 708bda71-fa24-46a9-86b4-18b83120f6af:1
Distributed ID: 00000000-0000-0000-0000-000000000000
```

Transaction Promotion

`System.Transactions` supports promotable transactions. Depending on the resources that participate with the transaction, either a local or a distributed transaction is created. SQL Server 2005 and 2008 support promotable transactions. So far you have seen only local transactions. With all previous samples, the distributed transaction ID was always set to 0, and only the local ID was assigned. With a resource that does not support promotable transactions, a distributed transaction is created. If multiple resources are added to the transaction, the transaction may start with a local transaction and promote to a distributed transaction as required. Such a promotion happens when multiple SQL Server database connections are added to the transaction. The transaction starts as a local transaction and then is promoted to a distributed transaction.

The console application is now changed in that a second student is added by using the same transaction object tx. Because every AddStudent() method opens a new connection, two connections are associated with the transaction after the second student is added:

```
static void TransactionPromotion()
{
    var tx = new CommittableTransaction();
    Utilities.DisplayTransactionInformation("TX created",
        tx.TransactionInformation);

    try
    {
        var s1 = new Student
        {
            FirstName = "Jörg",
            LastName = "Neumann",
            Company = "thinktecture"
        };
        var db = new StudentData();
        db.AddStudent(s1, tx);

        var s2 = new Student
        {
            FirstName = "Richard",
            LastName = "Blewett",
            Company = "thinktecture"
        };
        db.AddStudent(s2, tx);

        Utilities.DisplayTransactionInformation("2nd connection enlisted",
            tx.TransactionInformation);

        if (Utilities.AbortTx())
        {
            throw new ApplicationException("transaction abort");
        }

        tx.Commit();
    }
    catch (Exception ex)
    {
        Console.WriteLine(ex.Message);
        Console.WriteLine();
        tx.Rollback();
    }

    Utilities.DisplayTransactionInformation("TX finished",
        tx.TransactionInformation);
}
```

code snippet TransactionSamples/Program.cs

Running the application now, you can see that with the first student added the distributed identifier is 0, but with the second student added the transaction was promoted, so a distributed identifier is associated with the transaction:

```
TX created
Creation Time: 7:56:24 PM
Status: Active
Local ID: 0d2f5ada-32aa-40eb-b9d7-cc6aa9a2a554:1
Distributed ID: 00000000-0000-0000-0000-000000000000

2nd connection enlisted
```

```
Creation Time: 7:56:24 PM
Status: Active
Local ID: 0d2f5ada-32aa-40eb-b9d7-cc6aa9a2a554:1
Distributed ID: 501abd91-e512-47f3-95d5-f0488743293d

Abort the Transaction (y/n)?
```

Transaction promotion requires the DTC to be started. If promoting transactions fails with your system, verify that the DTC service is started. Starting the Component Services MMC snap-in, you can see the actual status of all DTC transactions running on your system.

By selecting Transaction List on the tree view, you can see all active transactions. In Figure 23-3, you can see that there is a transaction active with the same distributed identifier as was shown with the console output earlier. If you verify the output on your system, make sure that the transaction has a timeout and aborts in case the timeout is reached. After the timeout, you cannot see the transaction in the transaction list anymore. You can also verify the transaction statistics with the same tool. Transaction Statistics shows the number of committed and aborted transactions.

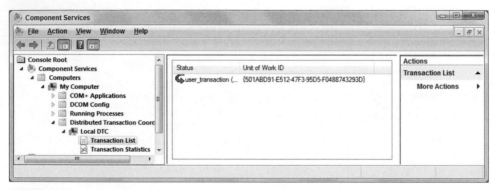

FIGURE 23-3

Dependent Transactions

With dependent transactions, you can influence one transaction from multiple threads. A dependent transaction depends on another transaction and influences the outcome of the transaction.

The sample application DependentTransactions creates a dependent transaction for a new thread. The method TxThread() is the method of the new thread where a DependentTransaction object is passed as a parameter. Information about the dependent transaction is shown with the helper method DisplayTransactionInformation(). Before the thread exits, the Complete() method of the dependent transaction is invoked to define the outcome of the transaction. A dependent transaction can define the outcome of the transaction by calling either the Complete() or Rollback() method. The Complete() method sets the success bit. If the root transaction finishes, and if all dependent transactions have set the success bit to true, the transaction commits. If any of the dependent transactions set the abort bit by invoking the Rollback() method, the complete transaction aborts:

Available for download on Wrox.com

```
static void TxThread(object obj)
{
    DependentTransaction tx = obj as DependentTransaction;
    Utilities.DisplayTransactionInformation("Dependent Transaction",
        tx.TransactionInformation);

    Thread.Sleep(3000);
```

```
            tx.Complete();

            Utilities.DisplayTransactionInformation("Dependent TX Complete",
                tx.TransactionInformation);
        }
```

code snippet TransactionSamples/Program.cs

With the `DependentTransaction()` method, first a root transaction is created by instantiating the class `CommittableTransaction`, and the transaction information is shown. Next, the method `tx.DependentClone()` creates a dependent transaction. This dependent transaction is passed to the method `TxThread()` that is defined as the entry point of a new thread.

The method `DependentClone()` requires an argument of type `DependentCloneOption`, which is an enumeration with the values `BlockCommitUntilComplete` and `RollbackIfNotComplete`. This option is important if the root transaction completes before the dependent transaction. Setting the option to `RollbackIfNotComplete`, the transaction aborts if the dependent transaction didn't invoke the `Complete()` method before the `Commit()` method of the root transaction. Setting the option to `BlockCommitUntilComplete`, the method `Commit()` waits until the outcome is defined by all dependent transactions.

Next, the `Commit()` method of the `CommittableTransaction` class is invoked if the user does not abort the transaction.

Chapter 20, "Threads, Tasks, and Synchronization," covers threading.

```
static void DependentTransaction()
{
    var tx = new CommittableTransaction();
    Utilities.DisplayTransactionInformation("Root TX created",
        tx.TransactionInformation);

    try
    {
        new Thread(TxThread).Start(tx.DependentClone(
            DependentCloneOption.BlockCommitUntilComplete));

        if (Utilities.AbortTx())
        {
            throw new ApplicationException("transaction abort");
        }

        tx.Commit();
    }
    catch (Exception ex)
    {
        Console.WriteLine(ex.Message);
        tx.Rollback();
    }

    Utilities.DisplayTransactionInformation("TX finished",
        tx.TransactionInformation);
}
```

code snippet TransactionSamples/Program.cs

With the output of the application, you can see the root transaction with its identifier. Because of the option `DependentCloneOption.BlockCommitUntilComplete`, the root transaction waits in the `Commit()` method until the outcome of the dependent transaction is defined. As soon as the dependent transaction is finished, the transaction is committed:

```
Root TX created
Creation Time: 8:35:25 PM
Status: Active
Local ID: 50126e07-cd28-4e0f-a21f-a81a8e14a1a8:1
Distributed ID: 00000000-0000-0000-0000-0000000000

Abort the Transaction (y/n)? n

Dependent Transaction
Creation Time: 8:35:25 PM
Status: Active
Local ID: 50126e07-cd28-4e0f-a21f-a81a8e14a1a8:1
Distributed ID: 00000000-0000-0000-0000-0000000000

Dependent TX Complete
Root TX finished
Creation Time: 8:35:25 PM
Status: Committed
Local ID: 50126e07-cd28-4e0f-a21f-a81a8e14a1a8:1
Distributed ID: 00000000-0000-0000-0000-0000000000

Creation Time: 8:35:25 PM
Status: Committed
Local ID: 50126e07-cd28-4e0f-a21f-a81a8e14a1a8:1
Distributed ID: 00000000-0000-0000-0000-0000000000
```

Ambient Transactions

The really big advantage of `System.Transactions` is the ambient transactions feature. With ambient transactions, there is no need to manually enlist a connection with a transaction; this is done automatically from the resources supporting ambient transactions.

An ambient transaction is associated with the current thread. You can get and set the ambient transaction with the static property `Transaction.Current`. APIs supporting ambient transactions check this property to get an ambient transaction and enlist with the transaction. ADO.NET connections support ambient transactions.

You can create a `CommittableTransaction` object and assign it to the property `Transaction.Current` to initialize the ambient transaction. Another way to create ambient transactions is with the `TransactionScope` class. The constructor of the `TransactionScope` creates an ambient transaction.

Important methods of the `TransactionScope` are the `Complete()` and the `Dispose()` methods. The `Complete()` method sets the happy bit for the scope, and the `Dispose()` method finishes the scope and commits or rolls back the transaction if the scope is a root scope.

Because the `TransactionScope` class implements the `IDisposable` interface, you can define the scope with the `using` statement. The default constructor creates a new transaction. Immediately after creating the `TransactionScope` instance, the transaction is accessed with the get accessor of the property `Transaction.Current` to display the transaction information on the console.

To get the information when the transaction is completed, the method `OnTransactionCompleted()` is set to the `TransactionCompleted` event of the ambient transaction.

Then a new `Student` object is created and written to the database by calling the `StudentData.AddStudent()` method. With ambient transactions, it is no longer necessary to pass a `Transaction` object to this method because the `SqlConnection` class supports ambient transactions and automatically enlists it with the connection. Then the `Complete()` method of the `TransactionScope` class sets the success bit. With the end of the `using` statement, the `TransactionScope` is disposed, and a commit is done. If the `Complete()` method is not invoked, the `Dispose()` method aborts the transaction.

> *If an ADO.NET connection should not enlist with an ambient transaction, you can set the value* `Enlist=false` *with the connection string.*

Available for
download on
Wrox.com

```csharp
static void TransactionScope()
{
    using (var scope = new TransactionScope())
    {
        Transaction.Current.TransactionCompleted +=
            OnTransactionCompleted;

        Utilities.DisplayTransactionInformation("Ambient TX created",
            Transaction.Current.TransactionInformation);

        var s1 = new Student
        {
            FirstName = "Ingo",
            LastName = "Rammer",
            Company = "thinktecture"
        };
        var db = new StudentData();
        db.AddStudent(s1);

        if (!Utilities.AbortTx())
            scope.Complete();
        else
            Console.WriteLine("transaction will be aborted");

    } // scope.Dispose()
}

static void OnTransactionCompleted(object sender, TransactionEventArgs e)
{
    Utilities.DisplayTransactionInformation("TX completed",
        e.Transaction.TransactionInformation);
}
```

code snippet TransactionSamples/Program.cs

Running the application, you can see an active ambient transaction after an instance of the `TransactionScope` class is created. The last output of the application is the output from the `TransactionCompleted` event handler to display the finished transaction state:

```
Ambient TX created
Creation Time: 9:55:40 PM
Status: Active
Local ID: a06df6fb-7266-435e-b90e-f024f1d6966e:1
Distributed ID: 00000000-0000-0000-0000-000000000000

Abort the Transaction (y/n)? n

TX completed
Creation Time: 9:55:40 PM
Status: Committed
Local ID: a06df6fb-7266-435e-b90e-f024f1d6966e:1
Distributed ID: 00000000-0000-0000-0000-000000000000
```

Nested Scopes with Ambient Transactions

With the `TransactionScope` class you can also nest scopes. The nested scope can be directly inside the scope or within a method that is invoked from a scope. A nested scope can use the same transaction as the outer scope, suppress the transaction, or create a new transaction that is independent from the outer scope. The requirement for the scope is defined with a `TransactionScopeOption` enumeration that is passed to the constructor of the `TransactionScope` class.

The values available with the `TransactionScopeOption` enumeration and their functionality are described in the following table:

TRANSACTIONSCOPEOPTION MEMBER	DESCRIPTION
Required	`Required` defines that the scope requires a transaction. If the outer scope already contains an ambient transaction, the inner scope uses the existing transaction. If an ambient transaction does not exist, a new transaction is created.
	If both scopes share the same transaction, every scope influences the outcome of the transaction. Only if all scopes set the success bit can the transaction commit. If one scope does not invoke the `Complete()` method before the root scope is disposed of, the transaction is aborted.
RequiresNew	`RequiresNew` always creates a new transaction. If the outer scope already defines a transaction, the transaction from the inner scope is completely independent. Both transactions can commit or abort independently.
Suppress	With `Suppress`, the scope does not contain an ambient transaction, whether or not the outer scope contains a transaction.

The next sample defines two scopes, in which the inner scope is configured to require a new transaction with the option `TransactionScopeOption.RequiresNew`:

Available for
download on
Wrox.com

```
using (var scope = new TransactionScope())
{
    Transaction.Current.TransactionCompleted +=
        OnTransactionCompleted;

    Utilities.DisplayTransactionInformation("Ambient TX created",
        Transaction.Current.TransactionInformation);

    using (var scope2 =
        new TransactionScope(TransactionScopeOption.RequiresNew))
    {
        Transaction.Current.TransactionCompleted +=
            OnTransactionCompleted;

        Utilities.DisplayTransactionInformation(
            "Inner Transaction Scope",
            Transaction.Current.TransactionInformation);

        scope2.Complete();
    }
    scope.Complete();
}
```

code snippet TransactionSamples/Program.cs

Running the application, you can see that both scopes have different transaction identifiers, although the same thread is used. Having one thread with different ambient transactions because of different scopes, the transaction identifier differs in the last number following the GUID.

A GUID is a globally unique identifier consisting of a 128-bit unique value.

```
Ambient TX created
Creation Time: 11:01:09 PM
Status: Active
Local ID: 54ac1276-5c2d-4159-84ab-36b0217c9c84:1
Distributed ID: 00000000-0000-0000-0000-0000000000

Inner Transaction Scope
Creation Time: 11:01:09 PM
Status: Active
Local ID: 54ac1276-5c2d-4159-84ab-36b0217c9c84:2
Distributed ID: 00000000-0000-0000-0000-0000000000

TX completed
Creation Time: 11:01:09 PM
Status: Committed
Local ID: 54ac1276-5c2d-4159-84ab-36b0217c9c84:2
Distributed ID: 00000000-0000-0000-0000-0000000000

TX completed
Creation Time: 11:01:09 PM
Status: Committed
Local ID: 54ac1276-5c2d-4159-84ab-36b0217c9c84:1
Distributed ID: 00000000-0000-0000-0000-0000000000
```

If you change the inner scope to the setting `TransactionScopeOption.Required`, you will find that both scopes are using the same transaction, and both scopes influence the outcome of the transaction.

Multithreading with Ambient Transactions

If multiple threads should use the same ambient transaction, you need to do some extra work. An ambient transaction is bound to a thread, so if a new thread is created, it does not have the ambient transaction from the starter thread.

This behavior is demonstrated in the next example. In the `Main()` method, a `TransactionScope` is created. Within this transaction scope, a new thread is started. The main method of the new thread `ThreadMethod()` creates a new transaction scope. With the creation of the scope, no parameters are passed, and therefore, the default option `TransactionScopeOption.Required` gets into play. If an ambient transaction exists, the existing transaction is used. If there is no ambient transaction, a new transaction is created:

```csharp
using System;
using System.Threading;
using System.Transactions;

namespace Wrox.ProCSharp.Transactions
{
    class Program
    {
        static void Main()
        {
            try
            {
                using (var scope = new TransactionScope())
                {
                    Transaction.Current.TransactionCompleted +=
                        TransactionCompleted;

                    Utilities.DisplayTransactionInformation("Main thread TX",
```

```
                    Transaction.Current.TransactionInformation);

            new Thread(ThreadMethod).Start();

            scope.Complete();
        }
    }
    catch (TransactionAbortedException ex)
    {
        Console.WriteLine("Main—Transaction was aborted, {0}",
                        ex.Message);
    }
}

static void TransactionCompleted(object sender, TransactionEventArgs e)
{
    Utilities.DisplayTransactionInformation("TX completed",
        e.Transaction.TransactionInformation);
}

static void ThreadMethod(object dependentTx)
{
    try
    {
        using (var scope = new TransactionScope())
        {
            Transaction.Current.TransactionCompleted +=
                TransactionCompleted;

            Utilities.DisplayTransactionInformation("Thread TX",
                Transaction.Current.TransactionInformation);
            scope.Complete();
        }
    }
    catch (TransactionAbortedException ex)
    {
        Console.WriteLine("ThreadMethod—Transaction was aborted, {0}",
            ex.Message);
    }
}
}
}
```

code snippet MultithreadingAmbientTx/Program.cs

As you start the application, you can see that the transactions from the two threads are completely independent. The transaction from the new thread has a different transaction ID. The transaction ID differs by the last number after the GUID in the same way as you have seen with nested scopes when the nested scope required a new transaction:

```
Main thread TX
Creation Time: 21:41:25
Status: Active
Local ID: f1e736ae-84ab-4540-b71e-3de272ffc476:1
Distributed ID: 00000000-0000-0000-0000-000000000000

TX completed
Creation Time: 21:41:25
Status: Committed
Local ID: f1e736ae-84ab-4540-b71e-3de272ffc476:1
Distributed ID: 00000000-0000-0000-0000-000000000000

Thread TX
```

```
Creation Time: 21:41:25
Status: Active
Local ID: f1e736ae-84ab-4540-b71e-3de272ffc476:2
Distributed ID: 00000000-0000-0000-0000-000000000000

TX completed
Creation Time: 21:41:25
Status: Committed
Local ID: f1e736ae-84ab-4540-b71e-3de272ffc476:2
Distributed ID: 00000000-0000-0000-0000-000000000000
```

To use the same ambient transaction in another thread, you need the help of dependent transactions. Now, the sample is changed to pass a dependent transaction to the new thread. The dependent transaction is created from the ambient transaction by calling the `DependentClone()` method on the ambient transaction. With this method, the setting `DependentCloneOption.BlockCommitUntilComplete` is set so that the calling thread waits until the new thread is completed before committing the transaction:

```csharp
class Program
{
    static void Main()
    {
        try
        {
            using (var scope = new TransactionScope())
            {
                Transaction.Current.TransactionCompleted +=
                    TransactionCompleted;

                Utilities.DisplayTransactionInformation("Main thread TX",
                    Transaction.Current.TransactionInformation);

                new Thread(ThreadMethod).Start(
                    Transaction.Current.DependentClone(
                    DependentCloneOption.BlockCommitUntilComplete));

                scope.Complete();
            }
        }
        catch (TransactionAbortedException ex)
        {
            Console.WriteLine("Main—Transaction was aborted, {0}",
                        ex.Message);
        }
    }
```

In the method of the thread, the dependent transaction that is passed is assigned to the ambient transaction by using the set accessor of the `Transaction.Current` property. Now the transaction scope is using the same transaction by using the dependent transaction. When you are finished using the dependent transaction, you need to invoke the `Complete()` method of the `DependentTransaction` object:

```csharp
static void ThreadMethod(object dependentTx)
{
    DependentTransaction dTx = dependentTx as DependentTransaction;

    try
    {
        Transaction.Current = dTx;

        using (var scope = new TransactionScope())
        {
            Transaction.Current.TransactionCompleted +=
                TransactionCompleted;

            Utilities.DisplayTransactionInformation("Thread TX",
```

```
                    Transaction.Current.TransactionInformation);
                scope.Complete();
            }
        }
        catch (TransactionAbortedException ex)
        {
            Console.WriteLine("ThreadMethod — Transaction was aborted, {0}",
                ex.Message);
        }
        finally
        {
            if (dTx != null)
            {
                dTx.Complete();
            }
        }
    }

    static void TransactionCompleted(object sender, TransactionEventArgs e)
    {
        Utilities.DisplayTransactionInformation("TX completed",
            e.Transaction.TransactionInformation);
    }
}
```

Running the application now, you can see that the main thread and the newly created thread are using, and influencing, the same transaction. The transaction listed by the threads has the same identifier. If with one thread the success bit is not set by calling the `Complete()` method, the complete transaction aborts:

```
Main thread TX
Creation Time: 23:00:57
Status: Active
Local ID: 2fb1b54d-61f5-4d4e-a55e-f4a9e04778be:1
Distributed ID: 00000000-0000-0000-0000-000000000000

Thread TX
Creation Time: 23:00:57
Status: Active
Local ID: 2fb1b54d-61f5-4d4e-a55e-f4a9e04778be:1
Distributed ID: 00000000-0000-0000-0000-000000000000

TX completed
Creation Time: 23:00:57
Status: Committed
Local ID: 2fb1b54d-61f5-4d4e-a55e-f4a9e04778be:1
Distributed ID: 00000000-0000-0000-0000-000000000000

TX completed
Creation Time: 23:00:57
Status: Committed
Local ID: 2fb1b54d-61f5-4d4e-a55e-f4a9e04778be:1
Distributed ID: 00000000-0000-0000-0000-000000000000
```

ISOLATION LEVEL

At the beginning of this chapter, you see the ACID properties used to describe transactions. The letter *I* (Isolation) in *ACID* is not always fully required. For performance reasons, you might reduce isolation requirements, but you must be aware of the issues that you will encounter if you change the isolation level.

The problems that you can encounter if you don't completely isolate the scope outside the transaction can be divided into three categories:

➤ **Dirty reads** — Another transaction can read records that are changed within the transaction. Because the data that is changed within the transaction might roll back to its original state, reading this intermediate state from another transaction is considered "dirty" — the data has not been committed. You can avoid this by locking the records to be changed.

➤ **Nonrepeatable reads** — When data is read inside a transaction, and while the transaction is running, another transaction changes the same records. If the record is read once more inside the transaction, the result is different — nonrepeatable. You can avoid this by locking the read records.

➤ **Phantom reads** — When a range of data is read, for example, with a WHERE clause. Another transaction can add a new record that belongs to the range that is read within the transaction. A new read with the same WHERE clause returns a different number of rows. Phantom reads can be a specific problem when doing an UPDATE of a range of rows. For example, UPDATE Addresses SET Zip=4711 WHERE (Zip=2315) updates the ZIP code of all records from 2315 to 4711. After doing the update, there may still be records with a ZIP code of 2315 if another user added a new record with ZIP 2315 while the update was running. You can avoid this by doing a range lock.

When defining the isolation requirements, you can set the isolation level. This is set with an IsolationLevel enumeration that is configured when the transaction is created (either with the constructor of the CommittableTransaction class or with the constructor of the TransactionScope class). The IsolationLevel defines the locking behavior. The next table lists the values of the IsolationLevel enumeration.

ISOLATION LEVEL	DESCRIPTION
ReadUncommitted	With ReadUncommitted, transactions are not isolated from each other. With this level, there is no wait for locked records from other transactions. This way, uncommitted data can be read from other transactions — dirty reads. This level is usually used just for reading records where it does not matter if you read interim changes (for example, reports).
ReadCommitted	ReadCommitted waits for records with a write-lock from other transactions. This way, a dirty read cannot happen. This level sets a read-lock for the current record read and a write-lock for the records being written until the transaction is completed. Reading a sequence of records, with every new record that is read, the prior record is unlocked. That's why nonrepeatable reads can happen.
RepeatableRead	RepeatableRead holds the lock for the records read until the transaction is completed. This way, the problem of nonrepeatable reads is avoided. Phantom reads can still occur.
Serializable	Serializable holds a range lock. While the transaction is running, it is not possible to add a new record that belongs to the same range from which the data is being read.
Snapshot	The isolation level Snapshot is possible only with SQL Server 2005 and later versions. This level reduces the locks as modified rows are copied. This way, other transactions can still read the old data without the need to wait for an unlock.
Unspecified	The level Unspecified indicates that the provider is using an isolation level value that is different from the values defined by the IsolationLevel enumeration.
Chaos	The level Chaos is similar to ReadUncommitted, but in addition to performing the actions of the ReadUncommitted value, Chaos does not lock updated records.

The next table gives you a summary of the problems that can occur as a result of setting the most commonly used transaction isolation levels.

ISOLATION LEVEL	DIRTY READS	NONREPEATABLE READS	PHANTOM READS
Read Uncommitted	Y	Y	Y
Read Committed	N	Y	Y
Repeatable Read	N	N	Y
Serializable	N	N	N

The following code segment shows how the isolation level can be set with the `TransactionScope` class. With the constructor of `TransactionScope`, you can set the `TransactionScopeOption` that was discussed earlier and the `TransactionOptions`. The `TransactionOptions` class allows you to define the `IsolationLevel` and the `Timeout`:

```
var options = new TransactionOptions();
options.IsolationLevel = IsolationLevel.ReadUncommitted;
options.Timeout = TimeSpan.FromSeconds(90);
using (TransactionScope scope =
    new TransactionScope(TransactionScopeOption.Required,
    options))
{
    // Read data without waiting for locks from other transactions,
    // dirty reads are possible.
}
```

CUSTOM RESOURCE MANAGERS

One of the biggest advantages of the new transaction model is that it is relatively easy to create custom resource managers that participate in the transaction. A resource manager does not manage only durable resources but can also manage volatile or in-memory resources — for example, a simple `int` and a generic list.

Figure 23-4 shows the relationship between a resource manager and transaction classes. The resource manager implements the interface `IEnlistmentNotification` that defines the methods `Prepare()`, `InDoubt()`, `Commit()`, and `Rollback()`. The resource manager implements this interface to manage transactions for a resource. To be part of a transaction, the resource manager must enlist with the `Transaction` class. Volatile resource managers invoke the method `EnlistVolatile()`; durable resource managers invoke `EnlistDurable()`. Depending on the transaction's outcome, the transaction manager invokes the methods from the interface `IEnlistmentNotification` with the resource manager.

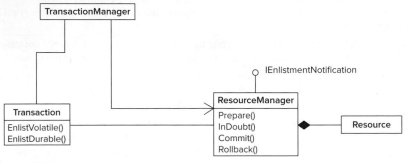

FIGURE 23-4

The next table explains the methods of the `IEnlistmentNotification` interface that you must implement with resource managers. As you review the table, recall the active, prepared, and committing phases explained earlier in this chapter in the "Transaction Phases" section.

IENLISTMENTNOTIFICATION MEMBER	DESCRIPTION
Prepare()	The transaction manager invokes the Prepare() method for preparation of the transaction. The resource manager completes the preparation by invoking the Prepared() method of the PreparingEnlistment parameter, which is passed to the Prepare() method. If the work cannot be done successfully, the resource manager informs the transaction manager by invoking the method ForceRollback(). A durable resource manager must write a log so that it can finish the transaction successfully after the prepare phase.
Commit()	When all resource managers have successfully prepared for the transaction, the transaction manager invokes the Commit() method. The resource manager can now complete the work to make it visible outside the transaction and invoke the Done() method of the Enlistment parameter.
Rollback()	If one of the resources could not successfully prepare for the transaction, the transaction manager invokes the Rollback() method with all resource managers. After the state is returned to the state prior to the transaction, the resource manager invokes the Done() method of the Enlistment parameter.
InDoubt()	If there is a problem after the transaction manager invokes the Commit() method (and the resources don't return completion information with the Done() method), the transaction manager invokes the InDoubt() method.

Transactional Resources

A transactional resource must keep the live value and a temporary value. The live value is read from outside the transaction and defines the valid state when the transaction rolls back. The temporary value defines the valid state of the transaction when the transaction commits.

To make non-transactional types transactional, the generic sample class Transactional<T> wraps a non-generic type, so you can use it like this:

```
Transactional<int> txInt = new Transactional<int>();
Transactional<string> txString = new Transactional<string>();
```

Let's look at the implementation of the class Transactional<T>. The live value of the managed resource has the variable liveValue; the temporary value that is associated with a transaction is stored within the ResourceManager<T>. The variable enlistedTransaction is associated with the ambient transaction if there is one:

Available for
download on
Wrox.com

```
using System.Diagnostics;
Insert IconMargin     [FILENAME]
using System.Transactions;

namespace Wrox.ProCSharp.Transactions
{
    public partial class Transactional<T>
    {
        private T liveValue;
        private ResourceManager<T> enlistment;
        private Transaction enlistedTransaction;
```

code snippet CustomResource/Transactional.cs

With the Transactional constructor, the live value is set to the variable liveValue. If the constructor is invoked from within an ambient transaction, the GetEnlistment() helper method is invoked. GetEnlistment() first checks if there is an ambient transaction and asserts if there is none. If the transaction is not already enlisted, the ResourceManager<T> helper class is instantiated, and the resource manager is enlisted with the transaction by invoking the method EnlistVolatile(). Also, the variable enlistedTransaction is set to the ambient transaction.

If the ambient transaction is different from the enlisted transaction, an exception is thrown. The implementation does not support changing the same value from within two different transactions. If you have this requirement, you can create a lock and wait for the lock to be released from one transaction before changing it within another transaction:

```
public Transactional(T value)
{
    if (Transaction.Current == null)
    {
        this.liveValue = value;
    }
    else
    {
        this.liveValue = default(T);
        GetEnlistment().Value = value;
    }
}

public Transactional()
    : this(default(T)) {}

private ResourceManager<T> GetEnlistment()
{
    Transaction tx = Transaction.Current;
    Trace.Assert(tx != null, "Must be invoked with ambient transaction");

    if (enlistedTransaction == null)
    {
        enlistment = new ResourceManager<T>(this, tx);
        tx.EnlistVolatile(enlistment, EnlistmentOptions.None);
        enlistedTransaction = tx;
        return enlistment;
    }
    else if (enlistedTransaction == Transaction.Current)
    {
        return enlistment;
    }
    else
    {
        throw new TransactionException(
            "This class only supports enlisting with one transaction");
    }
}
```

The property `Value` returns the value of the contained class and sets it. However, with transactions, you cannot just set and return the `liveValue` variable. This would be the case only if the object were outside a transaction. To make the code more readable, the property `Value` uses the methods `GetValue()` and `SetValue()` in the implementation:

```
public T Value
{
    get { return GetValue(); }
    set { SetValue(value); }
}
```

The method `GetValue()` checks if an ambient transaction exists. If one doesn't exist, the `liveValue` is returned. If there is an ambient transaction, the `GetEnlistment()` method shown earlier returns the resource manager, and with the `Value` property, the temporary value for the contained object within the transaction is returned.

The method SetValue() is very similar to GetValue(); the difference is that it changes the live or temporary value:

```
protected virtual T GetValue()
{
    if (Transaction.Current == null)
    {
        return liveValue;
    }
    else
    {
        return GetEnlistment().Value;
    }
}

protected virtual void SetValue(T value)
{
    if (Transaction.Current == null)
    {
        liveValue = value;
    }
    else
    {
        GetEnlistment().Value = value;
    }
}
```

The Commit() and Rollback() methods that are implemented in the class Transactional<T> are invoked from the resource manager. The Commit() method sets the live value from the temporary value received with the first argument and nullifies the variable enlistedTransaction as the transaction is completed. With the Rollback() method, the transaction is completed as well, but here the temporary value is ignored, and the live value is kept in use:

```
internal void Commit(T value, Transaction tx)
{
    liveValue = value;
    enlistedTransaction = null;
}

internal void Rollback(Transaction tx)
{
    enlistedTransaction = null;
}
}
```

Because the resource manager that is used by the class Transactional<T> is used only within the Transactional<T> class itself, it is implemented as an inner class. With the constructor, the parent variable is set to have an association with the transactional wrapper class. The temporary value used within the transaction is copied from the live value. Remember the isolation requirements with transactions:

```
using System;
using System.Diagnostics;
using System.IO;
using System.Runtime.Serialization.Formatters.Binary;
using System.Transactions;

namespace Wrox.ProCSharp.Transactions
{
    public partial class Transactional<T>
    {
        internal class ResourceManager<T1>: IEnlistmentNotification
        {
            private Transactional<T1> parent;
```

```
private Transaction currentTransaction;

internal ResourceManager(Transactional<T1> parent, Transaction tx)
{
    this.parent = parent;
    Value = DeepCopy(parent.liveValue);
    currentTransaction = tx;
}

public T1 Value { get; set; }
```

code snippet CustomResource/ResourceManager.cs

Because the temporary value may change within the transaction, the live value of the wrapper class may not be changed within the transaction. When creating a copy with some classes, it is possible to invoke the `Clone()` method that is defined with the `ICloneable` interface. However, as the `Clone()` method is defined, it allows implementations to create either a shallow or a deep copy. If type `T` contains reference types and implements a shallow copy, changing the temporary value would also change the original value. This would be in conflict with the isolation and consistency features of transactions. Here, a deep copy is required.

To do a deep copy, the method `DeepCopy()` serializes and deserializes the object to and from a stream. Because in C# 4 it is not possible to define a constraint to the type `T` indicating that serialization is required, the static constructor of the class `Transactional<T>` checks if the type is serializable by checking the property `IsSerializable` of the `Type` object.

```
static ResourceManager()
{
    Type t = typeof(T1);
    Trace.Assert(t.IsSerializable, "Type " + t.Name +
        " is not serializable");
}

private T1 DeepCopy(T1 value)
{
    using (MemoryStream stream = new MemoryStream())
    {
        BinaryFormatter formatter = new BinaryFormatter();
        formatter.Serialize(stream, value);
        stream.Flush();
        stream.Seek(0, SeekOrigin.Begin);

        return (T1)formatter.Deserialize(stream);
    }
}
```

The interface `IEnlistmentNotification` is implemented by the class `ResourceManager<T>`. This is the requirement for enlisting with transactions.

The implementation of the `Prepare()` method just answers by invoking `Prepared()` with `preparingEnlistment`. There should not be a problem assigning the temporary value to the live value, so the `Prepare()` method succeeds. With the implementation of the `Commit()` method, the `Commit()` method of the parent is invoked, where the variable `liveValue` is set to the value of the `ResourceManager` that is used within the transaction. The `Rollback()` method just completes the work and leaves the live value where it was. With a volatile resource, there is not a lot you can do in the `InDoubt()` method. Writing a log entry could be useful:

```
public void Prepare(PreparingEnlistment preparingEnlistment)
{
    preparingEnlistment.Prepared();
}
```

```
            public void Commit(Enlistment enlistment)
            {
                parent.Commit(Value, currentTransaction);
                enlistment.Done();
            }

            public void Rollback(Enlistment enlistment)
            {
                parent.Rollback(currentTransaction);
                enlistment.Done();
            }

            public void InDoubt(Enlistment enlistment)
            {
                enlistment.Done();
            }
        }
    }
}
```

The class `Transactional<T>` can now be used to make non-transactional classes transactional — for example, `int` and `string` but also more complex classes such as `Student` — as long as the type is serializable:

```
using System;
using System.Transactions;

namespace Wrox.ProCSharp.Transactions
{
    class Program
    {
        static void Main()
        {
            var intVal = new Transactional<int>(1);
            var student1 = new Transactional<Student>(new Student());
            student1.Value.FirstName = "Andrew";
            student1.Value.LastName = "Wilson";

            Console.WriteLine("before the transaction, value: {0}",
                intVal.Value);
            Console.WriteLine("before the transaction, student: {0}",
                student1.Value);

            using (var scope = new TransactionScope())
            {
                intVal.Value = 2;
                Console.WriteLine("inside transaction, value: {0}", intVal.Value);

                student1.Value.FirstName = "Ten";
                student1.Value.LastName = "SixtyNine";

                if (!Utilities.AbortTx())
                    scope.Complete();
            }
            Console.WriteLine("outside of transaction, value: {0}",
                intVal.Value);
            Console.WriteLine("outside of transaction, student: {0}",
                student1.Value);
        }
    }
}
```

code snippet CustomResource/Program.cs

The following console output shows a run of the application with a committed transaction:

```
before the transaction, value: 1
before the transaction: student: Andrew Wilson
inside transaction, value: 2

Abort the Transaction (y/n)? n

outside of transaction, value: 2
outside of transaction, student: Ten SixtyNine
```

TRANSACTIONS WITH WINDOWS 7 AND WINDOWS SERVER 2008

You can write a custom durable resource manager that works with the `File` and `Registry` classes. A file-based durable resource manager can copy the original file and write changes to the temporary file inside a temporary directory to make the changes persistent. When committing the transaction, the original file is replaced by the temporary file. Writing custom durable resource managers for files and the registry is no longer necessary since Windows Vista and Windows Server 2008. With these and follow-on operating systems, native transactions with the file system and with the registry are supported. For this, there are new API calls such as `CreateFileTransacted()`, `CreateHardLinkTransacted()`, `CreateSymbolicLinkTransacted()`, `CopyFileTransacted()`, and so on. What these API calls have in common is that they require a handle to a transaction passed as an argument; they do not support ambient transactions. The transactional API calls are not available from .NET 4, but you can create a custom wrapper by using `Platform Invoke`.

> `Platform Invoke` *is discussed in more detail in Chapter 26, "Interop"*

The sample application wraps the native method `CreateFileTransacted()` for creating transactional file streams from .NET applications.

When invoking native methods, the parameters of the native methods must be mapped to .NET data types. Because of security issues, the base class `SafeHandle` is used to map a native `HANDLE` type. `SafeHandle` is an abstract type that wraps operating system handles and supports critical finalization of handle resources. Depending on the allowed values of a handle, the derived classes `SafeHandleMinusOneIsInvalid` and `SafeHandleZeroOrMinusOneIsInvalid` can be used to wrap native handles. `SafeFileHandle` itself derives from `SafeHandleZeroOrMinusOneIsInvalid`. To map a handle to a transaction, the class `SafeTransactionHandle` is defined:

```csharp
using System;
using System.Runtime.Versioning;
using System.Security.Permissions;
using Microsoft.Win32.SafeHandles;

namespace Wrox.ProCSharp.Transactions
{
    [SecurityPermission(SecurityAction.LinkDemand, UnmanagedCode = true)]
    internal sealed class SafeTransactionHandle: SafeHandleZeroOrMinusOneIsInvalid
    {
        private SafeTransactionHandle()
            : base(true) { }

        public SafeTransactionHandle(IntPtr preexistingHandle, bool ownsHandle)
            : base(ownsHandle)
        {
```

```
            SetHandle(preexistingHandle);
        }

        [ResourceExposure(ResourceScope.Machine)]
        [ResourceConsumption(ResourceScope.Machine)]
        protected override bool ReleaseHandle()
        {
            return NativeMethods.CloseHandle(handle);
        }
    }
}
```

code snippet FileSystemTransactions/SafeTransactionHandle.cs

All native methods used from .NET are defined with the class `NativeMethods` shown here. With the sample, the native APIs needed are `CreateFileTransacted()` and `CloseHandle()`, which are defined as static members of the class. The methods are declared extern because there is no C# implementation. Instead, the implementation is found in the native DLL as defined by the attribute `DllImport`. Both of these methods can be found in the native DLL `Kernel32.dll`. With the method declaration, the parameters defined with the Windows API call are mapped to .NET data types. The parameter `txHandle` represents a handle to a transaction and is of the previously defined type `SafeTransactionHandle`:

```
using System;
using System.Runtime.ConstrainedExecution;
using System.Runtime.InteropServices;
using System.Runtime.Versioning;
using Microsoft.Win32.SafeHandles;

namespace Wrox.ProCSharp.Transactions
{
    internal static class NativeMethods
    {
        [DllImport("Kernel32.dll", CallingConvention = CallingConvention.StdCall,
                CharSet = CharSet.Unicode)]
        internal static extern SafeFileHandle CreateFileTransacted(
            String lpFileName,
            uint dwDesiredAccess,
            uint dwShareMode,
            IntPtr lpSecurityAttributes,
            uint dwCreationDisposition,
            int dwFlagsAndAttributes,
            IntPtr hTemplateFile,
            SafeTransactionHandle txHandle,
            IntPtr miniVersion,
            IntPtr extendedParameter);

        [DllImport("Kernel32.dll", SetLastError = true)]
        [ResourceExposure(ResourceScope.Machine)]
        [ReliabilityContract(Consistency.WillNotCorruptState, Cer.Success)]
        [return: MarshalAs(UnmanagedType.Bool)]
        internal static extern bool CloseHandle(IntPtr handle);

    }
}
```

code snippet FileSystemTransactions/NativeMethods.cs

The interface `IKernelTransaction` is used to get a transaction handle and pass it to the transacted Windows API calls. This is a COM interface and must be wrapped to .NET by using COM interop attributes as shown. The attribute GUID must have exactly the identifier as it is used here with the interface definition, because this is the identifier used with the definition of the COM interface:

```
using System;
using System.Runtime.InteropServices;

namespace Wrox.ProCSharp.Transactions
{
    [ComImport]
    [Guid("79427A2B-F895-40e0-BE79-B57DC82ED231")]
    [InterfaceType(ComInterfaceType.InterfaceIsIUnknown)]
    internal interface IKernelTransaction
    {
        void GetHandle(out SafeTransactionHandle ktmHandle);
    }
}
```

code snippet FileSystemTransactions/IKernelTransaction.cs

Finally, the class `TransactedFile` is the class that will be used by .NET applications. This class defines the method `GetTransactedFileStream()` that requires a filename as parameter and returns a `System.IO.FileStream`. The returned stream is a normal .NET stream; it just references a transacted file.

With the implementation, `TransactionInterop.GetDtcTransaction()` creates an interface pointer of the `IKernelTransaction` to the ambient transaction that is passed as an argument to `GetDtcTransaction()`. Using the interface `IKernelTransaction`, the handle of type `SafeTransactionHandle` is created. This handle is then passed to the wrapped API called `NativeMethods.CreateFileTransacted()`. With the returned file handle, a new `FileStream` instance is created and returned to the caller:

```
using System;
using System.IO;
using System.Security.Permissions;
using System.Transactions;
using Microsoft.Win32.SafeHandles;

namespace Wrox.ProCSharp.Transactions
{
    public static class TransactedFile
    {
        internal const short FILE_ATTRIBUTE_NORMAL = 0x80;
        internal const short INVALID_HANDLE_VALUE = -1;
        internal const uint GENERIC_READ = 0x80000000;
        internal const uint GENERIC_WRITE = 0x40000000;
        internal const uint CREATE_NEW = 1;
        internal const uint CREATE_ALWAYS = 2;
        internal const uint OPEN_EXISTING = 3;

        [FileIOPermission(SecurityAction.Demand, Unrestricted=true)]
        public static FileStream GetTransactedFileStream(string fileName)
        {
            IKernelTransaction ktx = (IKernelTransaction)
                TransactionInterop.GetDtcTransaction(Transaction.Current);

            SafeTransactionHandle txHandle;
            ktx.GetHandle(out txHandle);

            SafeFileHandle fileHandle = NativeMethods.CreateFileTransacted(
                fileName, GENERIC_WRITE, 0,
                IntPtr.Zero, CREATE_ALWAYS, FILE_ATTRIBUTE_NORMAL,
                IntPtr.Zero,
```

```
                        txHandle, IntPtr.Zero, IntPtr.Zero);

            return new FileStream(fileHandle, FileAccess.Write);
        }
    }
}
```

code snippet FileSystemTransactions/TransactedFile.cs

Now it is very easy to use the transactional API from .NET code. You can create an ambient transaction with the `TransactionScope` class and use the `TransactedFile` class within the context of the ambient transaction scope. If the transaction is aborted, the file is not written. If the transaction is committed, you can find the file in the temp directory:

Available for
download on
Wrox.com

```
using System;
using System.IO;
using System.Transactions;

namespace Wrox.ProCSharp.Transactions
{
    class Program
    {
        static void Main()
        {
            using (var scope = new TransactionScope())
            {
                FileStream stream = TransactedFile.GetTransactedFileStream(
                    "sample.txt");

                var writer = new StreamWriter(stream);
                writer.WriteLine("Write a transactional file");
                writer.Close();

                if (!Utilities.AbortTx())
                    scope.Complete();
            }
        }
    }
}
```

code snippet Windows7Transactions/Program.cs

Now you can use databases, volatile resources, and files within the same transaction.

SUMMARY

In this chapter, you learned the attributes of transactions and how you can create and manage transactions with the classes from the `System.Transactions` namespace.

Transactions are described with ACID properties: atomicity, consistency, isolation, and durability. Not all these properties are always required, as you have seen with volatile resources that don't support durability but have isolation options.

The easiest way to deal with transactions is by creating ambient transactions and using the `TransactionScope` class. Ambient transactions are very useful working with the ADO.NET data adapter and the ADO.NET Entity Framework, where usually you do not open and close database connections explicitly. ADO.NET is covered in Chapter 30, "Core ADO.NET." Entity Framework is explained in Chapter 31, "ADO.NET Entity Framework."

Using the same transaction across multiple threads, you can use the `DependentTransaction` class to create a dependency on another transaction. By enlisting a resource manager that implements the interface `IEnlistmentNotification`, you can create custom resources that participate with transactions.

Finally, you have seen how to use Windows 7 and Windows Server 2008 transactions with the .NET Framework and C#.

With .NET Enterprise Services, you can create automatic transactions that make use of `System.Transactions`. You can read about this technology in the online Chapter 51, "Enterprise Services."

In the next chapter, you can learn how to create a Windows service that can be automatically started when the operating system boots. Transactions can be useful within a service as well.

24

Networking

WHAT'S IN THIS CHAPTER?

➤ Downloading files from the Web

➤ Using the WebBrowser control in a Windows Forms application

➤ Manipulating IP addresses and performing DNS lookups

➤ Socket programming with TCP, UDP, and socket classes

This chapter takes a fairly practical approach, mixing examples with a discussion of the relevant theory and networking concepts as appropriate. This chapter is not a guide to computer networking but an introduction to using the .NET Framework for network communication.

You will learn how to use the `WebBrowser` control in a Windows Forms environment. You will also learn how the `WebBrowser` control can make some specific Internet access tasks easier to accomplish. However, the chapter starts with the simplest case, sending a request to a server and storing the information sent back in the response.

This chapter covers facilities provided through the .NET base classes for using various network protocols, particularly HTTP and TCP, to access networks and the Internet as a client. We cover some of the lower-level means of getting at these protocols through the .NET Framework. You will also find other means of communicating via these items using technologies, such as the Windows Communication Foundation (WCF), covered in Chapter 43.

The two namespaces of most interest for networking are `System.Net` and `System.Net.Sockets`. The `System.Net` namespace is generally concerned with higher-level operations, for example, downloading and uploading files, and making web requests using HTTP and other protocols, whereas `System.Net .Sockets` contains classes to perform lower-level operations. You will find these classes useful when you want to work directly with sockets or protocols, such as TCP/IP. The methods in these classes closely mimic the Windows socket (Winsock) API functions derived from the Berkeley sockets interface. You will also find that some of the objects that this chapter works with are found in the `System.IO` namespace.

Chapters 40 through 42 discuss how you can use C# to write powerful, efficient, and dynamic web pages using ASP.NET. For the most part, the clients accessing ASP.NET pages will be users running Internet Explorer or other web browsers such as Opera or Firefox. However, you might want to add web-browsing features to your own application, or you might need your applications to programmatically obtain information from a web site. In this latter case, it is usually better for the site to implement a web service. However, when you are accessing public Internet sites, you might not have any control over how the site is implemented.

THE WEBCLIENT CLASS

If you only want to request a file from a particular URI (Uniform Resource Identifier), then you will find that the easiest .NET class to use is `System.Net.WebClient`. This is an extremely high-level class designed to perform basic operations with only one or two commands. The .NET Framework currently supports URIs beginning with the `http:`, `https:`, and `file:` identifiers.

> *It is worth noting that the term URL (Uniform Resource Locator) is no longer in use in new technical specifications, and URI (Uniform Resource Identifier) is now preferred. URI has roughly the same meaning as URL, but is a bit more general because URI does not imply you are using one of the familiar protocols, such as HTTP or FTP.*

Downloading Files

Two methods are available for downloading a file using `WebClient`. The method you choose depends on how you want to process the file's contents. If you simply want to save the file to disk, then you use the `DownloadFile()` method. This method takes two parameters: the URI of the file and a location (path and filename) to save the requested data:

```
WebClient Client = new WebClient();
Client.DownloadFile("http://www.reuters.com/", "ReutersHomepage.htm");
```

More commonly, your application will want to process the data retrieved in response from the web site. To do this, use the `OpenRead()` method, which returns a `Stream` reference that you can then use to retrieve the data into memory:

```
WebClient Client = new WebClient();
Stream strm = Client.OpenRead("http://www.reuters.com/");
```

Basic WebClient Example

The first example demonstrates the `WebClient.OpenRead()` method. You will display the contents of the downloaded page in a `ListBox` control. To begin, create a new project as a standard C# Windows Forms application and add a `ListBox` called `listBox1` with the docking property set to `DockStyle.Fill`. At the beginning of the file, you need to add the `System.Net` and `System.IO` namespaces references to your list of using directives. You then make the following changes to the constructor of the main form:

```
public Form1()
{
    InitializeComponent();
    WebClient client = new WebClient();
    Stream strm = client.OpenRead("http://www.reuters.com");
    StreamReader sr = new StreamReader(strm);
    string line;

    while ( (line=sr.ReadLine()) != null )
    {
        listBox1.Items.Add(line);
    }

    strm.Close();
}
```

code download BasicWebClient.sln

In this example, you connect a `StreamReader` class from the `System.IO` namespace to the network stream. This allows you to obtain data from the stream as text through the use of higher-level methods, such as `ReadLine()`. This is an excellent example of the point made in Chapter 29, "Manipulating Files and the Registry," about the benefits of abstracting data movement into the concept of a stream.

Figure 24-1 shows the results of running this sample code.

FIGURE 24-1

The `WebClient` class also has an `OpenWrite()` method. This method returns a writable stream for you to send data to a URI. You can also specify the method used to send the data to the host; the default method is POST. The following code snippet assumes a writable directory named `accept` on the local machine. The code will create a file in the directory with the name `newfile.txt` and the contents `Hello World`:

```
WebClient webClient = new WebClient();
Stream stream = webClient.OpenWrite("http://localhost/accept/newfile.txt", "PUT");
StreamWriter streamWriter = new StreamWriter(stream);
streamWriter.WriteLine("Hello World");
streamWriter.Close();
```

Uploading Files

The `WebClient` class also features `UploadFile()` and `UploadData()` methods. You use these methods when you need to post an HTML form or to upload an entire file. `UploadFile()` uploads a file to a specified location given the local filename, whereas `UploadData()` uploads binary data supplied as an array of bytes to the specified URI (there is also a `DownloadData()` method for retrieving an array of bytes from a URI):

```
WebClient client = new WebClient();
client.UploadFile("http://www.ourwebsite.com/NewFile.htm",
                  "C:\\WebSiteFiles\\NewFile.htm");
byte[] image;
// code to initialize image so it contains all the binary data for
// some jpg file
client.UploadData("http://www.ourwebsite.com/NewFile.jpg", image);
```

Although the WebClient class is very simple to use, it has very limited features. In particular, you cannot use it to supply authentication credentials — a particular problem with uploading data is that not many sites will accept uploaded files without authentication! It is possible to add header information to requests and to examine any headers in the response, but only in a very generic sense — there is no specific support for any one protocol. This is because WebClient is a very general-purpose class designed to work with any protocol for sending a request and receiving a response (such as HTTP or FTP). It cannot handle any features specific to any one protocol, such as cookies, which are specific to HTTP. To take advantage of these features, you need to use a family of classes based on two other classes in the System.Net namespace: WebRequest and WebResponse.

WEBREQUEST AND WEBRESPONSE CLASSES

The WebRequest class represents the request for information to send to a particular URI. The URI is passed as a parameter to the Create() method. A WebResponse represents the data you retrieve from the server. By calling the WebRequest.GetResponse() method, you actually send the request to the web server and create a WebResponse object to examine the return data. As with the WebClient object, you can obtain a stream to represent the data, but in this case you use the WebResponse.GetResponseStream() method.

This section briefly discusses a few of the other areas supported by WebRequest, WebResponse, and other related classes.

You start off by downloading a web page using these classes, which is the same example as before, but using WebRequest and WebResponse. In the process, you uncover the class hierarchy involved, and then see how to take advantage of extra HTTP features that are supported by this hierarchy.

The following code shows the modifications you need to make to the BasicWebClient sample to use the WebRequest and WebResponse classes:

```
public Form1()
{
    InitializeComponent();

    WebRequest wrq = WebRequest.Create("http://www.reuters.com");
    WebResponse wrs = wrq.GetResponse();
    Stream strm = wrs.GetResponseStream();
    StreamReader sr = new StreamReader(strm);
    string line;

    while ( (line = sr.ReadLine()) != null)
    {
        listBox1.Items.Add(line);
    }

    strm.Close();
}
```

In the code example, you start by instantiating an object representing a web request. You don't do this using a constructor, but instead call the static method WebRequest.Create(). As you learn in more detail later in this chapter (see "The Web Request and Web Response Hierarchy" section), the WebRequest class is part of a hierarchy of classes supporting different network protocols. To receive a reference to the correct object for the request type, a factory mechanism is in place. The WebRequest.Create() method will create the appropriate object for the given protocol.

An important part of the HTTP protocol is the ability to send extensive header information with both request and response streams. This information can include cookies and the details of the particular browser sending the request (the user agent). As you would expect, the .NET Framework provides full support for accessing the most significant data. The WebRequest and WebResponse classes provide some support for reading the header information. However, two derived classes provide additional HTTP-specific information: `HttpWebRequest` and `HttpWebResponse`.

As you will see in more detail later in the section "The WebRequest and WebResponse Classes Hierarchy," creating a `WebRequest` with an HTTP URI results in an `HttpWebRequest` object instance. Because `HttpWebRequest` is derived from `WebRequest`, you can use the new instance whenever a `WebRequest` is required. In addition, you can cast the instance to an `HttpWebRequest` reference and access properties specific to the HTTP protocol. Likewise, the `GetResponse()` method call will actually return an `HttpWebResponse` instance as a `WebResponse` reference when dealing with HTTP. Again, you can perform a simple cast to access the HTTP-specific features.

You can examine a few of the header properties by adding the following code before the `GetResponse()` method call:

```
WebRequest wrq = WebRequest.Create("http://www.reuters.com");
HttpWebRequest hwrq = (HttpWebRequest)wrq;
listBox1.Items.Add("Request Timeout (ms) = " + wrq.Timeout);
listBox1.Items.Add("Request Keep Alive = " + hwrq.KeepAlive);
listBox1.Items.Add("Request AllowAutoRedirect = " + hwrq.AllowAutoRedirect);
```

The `Timeout` property is specified in milliseconds, and the default value is `100,000`. You can set the `Timeout` property to control how long the `WebRequest` object will wait for the response before throwing a `WebException`. You can check the `WebException.Status` property to view the reason for an exception. This enumeration includes status codes for timeouts, connection failures, protocol errors, and more.

The `KeepAlive` property is a specific extension to the HTTP protocol, so you access this property through an `HttpWebRequest` reference. `KeepAlive` allows multiple requests to use the same connection, saving time in closing and reopening connections on subsequent requests. The default value for this property is `true`.

The `AllowAutoRedirect` property is also specific to the `HttpWebRequest` class. Use this property to control whether the web request should automatically follow redirection responses from the web server. Again, the default value is `true`. If you want to allow only a limited number of redirections, then set the `MaximumAutomaticRedirections` property of the `HttpWebRequest` to the desired number.

Although the request and response classes expose most of the important headers as properties, you can also use the `Headers` property itself to view the entire collection of headers. Add the following code after the `GetResponse()` method call to place all the headers in the `ListBox` control:

```
WebRequest wrq = WebRequest.Create("http://www.reuters.com");
WebResponse wrs = wrq.GetResponse();
WebHeaderCollection whc = wrs.Headers;

for(int i = 0; i < whc.Count; i++)
{
    listBox1.Items.Add(string.Format("Header {0}: {1}",
        whc.GetKey(i), whc[i]));
}
```

This example code produces the list of headers shown in Figure 24-2.

FIGURE 24-2

Authentication

Another property in the `WebRequest` class is the `Credentials` property. If you need authentication credentials to accompany your request, then you can create an instance of the `NetworkCredential` class (also from the `System.Net` namespace) with a username and password. You can place the following code *before* the call to `GetResponse()`:

```
NetworkCredential myCred = new NetworkCredential("myusername", "mypassword");
wrq.Credentials = myCred;
```

Working with Proxies

You will find in enterprises that many firms must deal with a proxy server to make any type of HTTP or FTP request. Many times, the proxy server, which routes all the organization's requests and responses, uses some form of security (usually a username and a password). For your applications that use the `WebClient` or the `WebRequest` objects, you might need to take these proxy servers into account. As with the preceding `NetworkCredential` object, you are going to want to use the `WebProxy` object *before* you make a call to make the actual request:

```
WebProxy wp = new WebProxy("192.168.1.100", true);
wp.Credentials = new NetworkCredential("user1", "user1Password");
WebRequest wrq = WebRequest.Create("http://www.reuters.com");
wrq.Proxy = wp;
WebResponse wrs = wrq.GetResponse();
```

If you also require a designation of the user's domain in addition to its credentials, then you would use a different signature on the `NetworkCredential` instantiation:

```
WebProxy wp = new WebProxy("192.168.1.100", true);
wp.Credentials = new NetworkCredential("user1", "user1Password", "myDomain");
WebRequest wrq = WebRequest.Create("http://www.reuters.com");
wrq.Proxy = wp;
WebResponse wrs = wrq.GetResponse();
```

Asynchronous Page Requests

An additional feature of the `WebRequest` class is the ability to request pages asynchronously. This feature is significant because there can be quite a long delay between sending a request to a host and receiving the response. Methods such as `WebClient.DownloadData()` and `WebRequest.GetResponse()` will not return until the response from the server is complete. You might not want your application frozen due to a long period of inactivity, and in such scenarios it is better to use the `BeginGetResponse()` and `EndGetResponse()` methods. `BeginGetResponse()` works asynchronously and returns almost immediately. Under the covers, the runtime will asynchronously manage a background thread to retrieve the response from the server. Instead of returning a `WebResponse` object, `BeginGetResponse()` returns an object implementing the `IAsyncResult` interface. With this interface, you can poll or wait for the response to become available and then invoke `EndGetResponse()` to gather the results.

You can also pass a callback delegate into the `BeginGetResponse()` method. The target of a callback delegate is a method returning `void` and accepting an `IAsyncResult` reference as a parameter. When the worker thread is finished gathering the response, the runtime invokes the callback delegate to inform you of the completed work. As shown in the following code, calling `EndGetResponse()` in the callback method allows you to retrieve the `WebResponse` object:

```
public Form1()
{
    InitializeComponent();
    WebRequest wrq = WebRequest.Create("http://www.reuters.com");
```

```
        wrq.BeginGetResponse(new AsyncCallback(OnResponse), wrq);
    }

    protected static void OnResponse(IAsyncResult ar)
    {
        WebRequest wrq = (WebRequest)ar.AsyncState;
        WebResponse wrs = wrq.EndGetResponse(ar);
        // read the response...
    }
```

Notice that you can retrieve the original `WebRequest` object by passing the object as the second parameter to `BeginGetResponse()`. The second parameter is an object reference known as the state parameter. During the callback method, you can retrieve the same state object using the `AsyncState` property of `IAsyncResult`.

DISPLAYING OUTPUT AS AN HTML PAGE

The examples so far in this chapter show how the .NET base classes make it very easy to download and process data from the Internet. However, so far you have displayed files only as plain text. Quite often, you will want to view an HTML file in an Internet Explorer-style interface in which the rendered HTML allows you to see what the web document actually looks like. Unfortunately, there is no .NET version of Microsoft's Internet Explorer, but that does not mean that you cannot easily accomplish this task.

Before the release of the .NET Framework 2.0, you could make reference to a Component Object Model (COM) object that was an encapsulation of Internet Explorer and use the .NET-interop capabilities to have aspects of your application work as a browser. Now, since the release of the .NET Framework 2.0, you can use the built-in `WebBrowser` control available for your Windows Forms applications.

The `WebBrowser` control encapsulates the COM object even further for you and makes the tasks that were once more complicated, even easier. In addition to the `WebBrowser` control, another option is to use the programmatic ability to call up Internet Explorer instances from your code.

When not using the new `WebBrowser` control, you can programmatically start an Internet Explorer process and navigate to a web page using the `Process` class in the `System.Diagnostics` namespace:

```
Process myProcess = new Process();
myProcess.StartInfo.FileName = "iexplore.exe";
myProcess.StartInfo.Arguments = "http://www.wrox.com";
myProcess.Start();
```

However, the preceding code launches Internet Explorer as a separate window. Your application has no connection to the new window and therefore cannot control the browser.

Using the new `WebBrowser` control, however, allows you to display and control the browser as an integrated part of your application. The new `WebBrowser` control is quite sophisticated, featuring a large number of methods, properties, and events.

Allowing Simple Web Browsing from Your Applications

For the sake of simplicity, start by creating a Windows Forms application that simply has a `TextBox` control and a `WebBrowser` control. You will build the application so that the end user will simply enter a URL into the text box and press Enter, and the `WebBrowser` control will do all the work of fetching the web page and displaying the resulting document.

In Visual Studio 2010 Designer, your application should look like Figure 24-3.

With this application, when the end user types a URL and presses Enter, this key press will register with the application. Then the WebBrowser control will go off to retrieve the requested page, subsequently displaying it in the control itself.

FIGURE 24-3

The code behind this application is illustrated here:

```csharp
using System;
using System.Windows.Forms;

namespace Browser
{
    partial class Form1: Form
    {
        public Form1()
        {
            InitializeComponent();
        }

        private void textBox1_KeyPress(object sender, KeyPressEventArgs e)
        {
            if (e.KeyChar == (char)13)
            {
                webBrowser1.Navigate(textBox1.Text);
            }
        }
    }
}
```

code download Browser.sln

From this example, you can see that each key press that the end user makes in the text box is captured by the textBox1_KeyPress event. If the character input is a carriage return (a press of the Enter key, which is (char)13), then you take action with the WebBrowser control. Using the WebBrowser control's Navigate method, you specify the URL (as a string) using the textBox1.Text property. The end result is shown in Figure 24-4.

FIGURE 24-4

Launching Internet Explorer Instances

It might be that you are not interested in hosting a browser inside your application, as shown in the previous section, but instead are only interested in allowing the user to find your web site in a typical browser (for example, by clicking a link inside your application). For an example of this task, create a Windows Forms application that has a `LinkLabel` control on it. For instance, you can have a form that has a `LinkLabel` control on it that states "Visit our company web site!"

When you have this control in place, use the following code to launch your company's web site in an independent browser as opposed to directly being in the form of your application:

```
private void linkLabel1_LinkClicked(object sender, LinkLabelLinkClickedEventArgs e)
{
    WebBrowser wb = new WebBrowser();
    wb.Navigate("http://www.wrox.com", true);
}
```

In this example, when the `LinkLabel` control is clicked by the user, a new instance of the `WebBrowser` class is created. Then, using the `WebBrowser` class's `Navigate()` method, the code specifies the location of the web page as well as a Boolean value that specifies whether this endpoint should be opened within the Windows Forms application (a `false` value) or from within an independent browser (using a `true` value). By default, this is set to `false`. With the preceding construct, when the end user clicks the link found in the Windows application, a browser instance will be instantiated, and the Wrox web site at www.wrox.com will be launched.

Giving Your Application More IE-Type Features

In the previous example, in which you used the `WebBrowser` control directly in the Windows Forms application, you may notice that when you click on the links contained in the page, the text within the `TextBox` control is not updated to show the URL of the exact location where you are in the browsing process. You can fix this by listening for events coming from the `WebBrowser` control and adding handlers to the control.

Updating the form's title with the title of the HTML page is easy. You just need to use the `Navigated` event and update the `Text` property of the form:

```
private void webBrowser1_Navigated(object sender, EventArgs e)
{
    this.Text = webBrowser1.DocumentTitle.ToString();
}
```

In this case, when the `WebBrowser` control moves onto another page, the `Navigated` event will fire, and this will cause the form's title to change to the title of the page being viewed. In some instances when working with pages on the Web, even though you have typed in a specific address, you are going to be redirected to another page altogether. You are most likely going to want to reflect this in the textbox (address bar) of the form; to do this, you change the form's text box based on the complete URL of the page being viewed. To accomplish this task, you can use the `WebBrowser` control's `Navigated` event as well:

```
private void webBrowser1_Navigated(object sender, WebBrowserNavigatedEventArgs e)
{
    textBox1.Text = webBrowser1.Url.ToString();
    this.Text = webBrowser1.DocumentTitle.ToString();
}
```

In this case, when the requested page has finished downloading in the `WebBrowser` control, the `Navigated` event is fired. In your case, you simply update the `Text` value of the `textBox1` control to the URL of the page. This means that after a page is loaded in the `WebBrowser` control's HTML container, and if the URL changes in this process (for instance, if there is a redirect), then the new URL will be shown in the text box. If you employ these steps and navigate to the Wrox web site (www.wrox.com), then you will notice that the page's URL will immediately change to www.wrox.com/WileyCDA/. This process also means that if the end user clicks one of the links contained within the HTML view, then the URL of the newly requested page will also be shown in the text box.

Now if you run the application with the preceding changes in place, you will find that the form's title and address bar work as they do in Microsoft's Internet Explorer, as demonstrated in Figure 24-5.

FIGURE 24-5

The next step is to create an IE-like toolbar that will allow the end user to control the WebBrowser control a little better. This means that you will incorporate buttons such as Back, Forward, Stop, Home, and Refresh.

Rather than using the ToolBar control, you will just add a set of Button controls at the top of the form where you currently have the address bar. Add five buttons to the top of the control, as illustrated in Figure 24-6.

In this example, the text on the button face is changed to indicate the function of the button. Of course, you can even go as far as to use a screen capture utility to "borrow" button images from IE and use those. The buttons should be named buttonBack, buttonForward, buttonStop, buttonRefresh, and buttonHome. To get the resizing to work properly, make sure that you set the Anchor property of the three buttons on the right to Top, Right.

On startup, buttonBack, buttonForward, and buttonStop should be disabled because there is no point to the buttons if there is no initial page loaded in the WebBrowser control. You will later tell the application when to enable and disable the Back and Forward buttons yourself, depending on where the user is in the page stack. In addition, when a page is being loaded, you will need to enable the Stop button — but also, you will need to disable the Stop button when the page has finished being loaded. You will also have a Submit button on the page that will allow for the submission of the URL being requested.

FIGURE 24-6

First, however, you will add the functionality behind the buttons. The WebBrowser class itself has all the methods that you need, so this is all very straightforward:

```
using System;
using System.Windows.Forms;

namespace Browser
{
    partial class Form1: Form
    {
        public Form1()
        {
            InitializeComponent();
        }

        private void textBox1_KeyPress(object sender, KeyPressEventArgs e)
        {
```

```csharp
        if (e.KeyChar == (char)13)
        {
            webBrowser1.Navigate(textBox1.Text);
        }
    }

    private void webBrowser1_Navigated(object sender,
        WebBrowserNavigatedEventArgs e)
    {
        textBox1.Text = webBrowser1.Url.ToString();
        this.Text = webBrowser1.DocumentTitle.ToString();
    }

    private void Form1_Load(object sender, EventArgs e)
    {
        buttonBack.Enabled = false;
        buttonForward.Enabled = false;
        buttonStop.Enabled = false;

        this.webBrowser1.CanGoBackChanged +=
            new EventHandler(webBrowser1_CanGoBackChanged);
        this.webBrowser1.CanGoForwardChanged +=
            new EventHandler(webBrowser1_CanGoForwardChanged);
        this.webBrowser1.DocumentTitleChanged +=
            new EventHandler(webBrowser1_DocumentTitleChanged);
    }

    private void buttonBack_Click(object sender, EventArgs e)
    {
        webBrowser1.GoBack();
        textBox1.Text = webBrowser1.Url.ToString();
    }

    private void buttonForward_Click(object sender, EventArgs e)
    {
        webBrowser1.GoForward();
        textBox1.Text = webBrowser1.Url.ToString();
    }

    private void buttonStop_Click(object sender, EventArgs e)
    {
        webBrowser1.Stop();
    }

    private void buttonHome_Click(object sender, EventArgs e)
    {
        webBrowser1.GoHome();
        textBox1.Text = webBrowser1.Url.ToString();
    }

    private void buttonRefresh_Click(object sender, EventArgs e)
    {
        webBrowser1.Refresh();
    }

    private void buttonSubmit_Click(object sender, EventArgs e)
    {
        webBrowser1.Navigate(textBox1.Text);
    }
```

```
private void webBrowser1_Navigating(object sender,
    WebBrowserNavigatingEventArgs e)
{
    buttonStop.Enabled = true;
}

private void webBrowser1_DocumentCompleted(object sender,
    WebBrowserDocumentCompletedEventArgs e)
{
    buttonStop.Enabled = false;
    if (webBrowser1.CanGoBack)
    {
        buttonBack.Enabled = true;
    }
    else
    {
        buttonBack.Enabled = false;
    }
    if (webBrowser1.CanGoForward)
    {
        buttonForward.Enabled = true;
    }
    else
    {
        buttonForward.Enabled = false;
    }
}
}
}
```

code download Browser.sln

Many different activities are going on in this example because there are so many options for the end user when using this application. For each of the button-click events, there is a specific `WebBrowser` class method assigned as the action to initiate. For instance, for the Back button on the form, you simply use the `WebBrowser` control's `GoBack()` method; for the Forward button you have the `GoForward()` method; and for the others, you have methods such as `Stop()`, `Refresh()`, and `GoHome()`. This makes it fairly simple and straightforward to create a toolbar that will give you action similar to that of Microsoft's Internet Explorer.

When the form is first loaded, the `Form1_Load` event disables the appropriate buttons. From there, the end user can enter a URL into the text box and click the Submit button to have the application retrieve the desired page.

To manage the enabling and disabling of the buttons, you must key in to a couple of events. As mentioned before, whenever downloading begins, you need to enable the Stop button. For this, you simply added an event handler for the `Navigating` event to enable the Stop button:

```
private void webBrowser1_Navigating(object sender,
    WebBrowserNavigatingEventArgs e)
{
    buttonStop.Enabled = true;
}
```

Then, the Stop button is again disabled when the document has finished loading:

```
private void webBrowser1_DocumentCompleted(object sender,
    WebBrowserDocumentCompletedEventArgs e)
{
    buttonStop.Enabled = false;
}
```

Enabling and disabling the appropriate Back and Forward buttons really depends on the ability to go backward or forward in the page stack. This is achieved by using both the CanGoForwardChanged() and the CanGoBackChanged() events:

```
private void webBrowser1_CanGoBackChanged(object sender, EventArgs e)
{
    if (webBrowser1.CanGoBack)
    {
        buttonBack.Enabled = true;
    }
    else
    {
        buttonBack.Enabled = false;
    }
}

private void webBrowser1_CanGoForwardChanged(object sender, EventArgs e)
{
    if (webBrowser1.CanGoForward)
    {
        buttonForward.Enabled = true;
    }
    else
    {
        buttonForward.Enabled = false;
    }
}
```

Run the project now, visit a web page, and click through a few links. You should also be able to use the toolbar to enhance your browsing experience. The end product is shown in Figure 24-7.

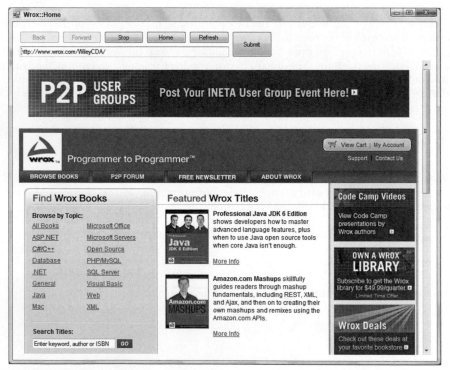

FIGURE 24-7

Printing Using the WebBrowser Control

Not only can users use the `WebBrowser` control to view pages and documents, but they can also use the control to send these pages and documents to the printer for printing. To print the page or document being viewed in the control, simply use the following construct:

```
webBrowser1.Print();
```

As before, you do not need to view the page or document to print it. For instance, you can use the `WebBrowser` class to load an HTML document and print it without even displaying the loaded document. This can be accomplished as shown here:

```
WebBrowser wb = new WebBrowser();
wb.Navigate("http://www.wrox.com");
wb.Print();
```

Displaying the Code of a Requested Page

In the beginning of this chapter, you used the `WebRequest` and the `Stream` classes to get at a remote page to display the code of the requested page. You used this code to accomplish this task:

```
public Form1()
{
    InitializeComponent();
    System.Net.WebClient Client = new WebClient();
    Stream strm = Client.OpenRead("http://www.reuters.com");
    StreamReader sr = new StreamReader(strm);
    string line;

    while ( (line=sr.ReadLine()) != null )
    {
        listBox1.Items.Add(line);
    }

    strm.Close();
}
```

Now, however, with the introduction of the `WebBrowser` control, it is quite easy to accomplish the same results. To accomplish this, change the browser application that you have been working on thus far in this chapter. To make this change, simply add a single line to the `Document_Completed` event, as illustrated here:

```
private void webBrowser1_DocumentCompleted(object sender,
    WebBrowserDocumentCompletedEventArgs e)
{
    buttonStop.Enabled = false;
    textBox2.Text = webBrowser1.DocumentText;
}
```

In the application itself, add another `TextBox` control below the `WebBrowser` control. The idea is that when the end user requests a page, you display not only the visual aspect of the page but also the code for the page, in the `TextBox` control. The code of the page is displayed simply by using the `DocumentText` property of the `WebBrowser` control, which will give you the entire page's content as a `String`. The other option is to get the contents of the page as a `Stream` using the `DocumentStream` property. The end result of adding the second `TextBox` to display the contents of the page as a `String` is shown in Figure 24-8.

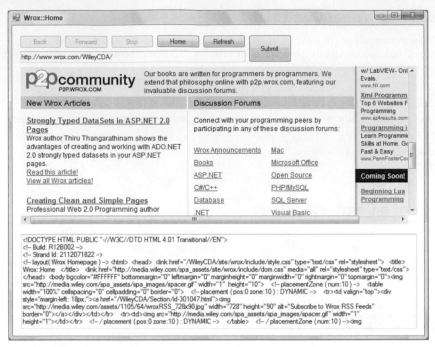

FIGURE 24-8

The WebRequest and WebResponse Classes Hierarchy

In this section, you take a closer look at the underlying architecture of the `WebRequest` and `WebResponse` classes.

Figure 24-9 illustrates the inheritance hierarchy of the classes involved.

The hierarchy contains more than just the two classes that you have used in your code. You should also know that the `WebRequest` and `WebResponse` classes are both abstract and cannot be instantiated. These base classes provide general functionality for dealing with web requests and responses independent of the protocol used for a given operation. Requests are made using a particular protocol (HTTP, FTP, SMTP, and so on), and a derived class written for the given protocol will handle the request. Microsoft refers to this scheme as *pluggable protocols*.

Remember in the code that you examined earlier in the "WebRequest and WebResponse Classes" section, your variables are defined as references to the base classes. However, `WebRequest.Create()` actually gives you an `HttpWebRequest` object, and the `GetResponse()` method actually returns an `HttpWebResponse` object. This factory-based mechanism hides many of the details from the client code, allowing support for a wide variety of protocols from the same code base.

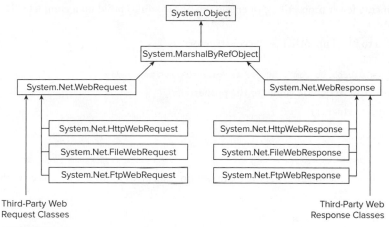

FIGURE 24-9

The fact that you need an object specifically capable of dealing with the HTTP protocol is clear from the URI that you supply to WebRequest.Create(). WebRequest.Create() examines the protocol specifier in the URI to instantiate and return an object of the appropriate class. This keeps your code free from having to know anything about the derived classes or specific protocol used. When you need to access specific features of a protocol, you might need the properties and methods of the derived class, in which case you can cast your WebRequest or WebResponse reference to the derived class.

With this architecture, you should be able to send requests using any of the common protocols. However, Microsoft currently provides derived classes to cover only the HTTP, HTTPS, FTP, and FILE protocols. The FTP option is the latest option provided by the .NET Framework (ever since the release of the .NET Framework 2.0). If you want to utilize other protocols, for example SMTP, then you need to use the Windows Communication Foundation, revert to using the Windows API, or use the SmtpClient object.

UTILITY CLASSES

This section covers a couple of utility classes to make web programming easier when dealing with URIs and IP addresses.

URIs

Uri and UriBuilder are two classes in the System (not System.Net) namespace, and they are both intended to represent a URI. UriBuilder allows you to build a URI given the strings for the component parts, and the Uri class allows you to parse, combine, and compare URIs.

For the Uri class, the constructor requires a completed URI string:

```
Uri MSPage = new

  Uri("http://www.Microsoft.com/SomeFolder/SomeFile.htm?Order=true");
```

The class exposes a large number of read-only properties. A Uri object is not intended to be modified after it has been constructed:

```
string Query = MSPage.Query;                  // ?Order=true;
string AbsolutePath = MSPage.AbsolutePath;    // /SomeFolder/SomeFile.htm
string Scheme = MSPage.Scheme;                // http
int Port = MSPage.Port;                       // 80 (the default for http)
string Host = MSPage.Host;                    // www.microsoft.com
bool IsDefaultPort = MSPage.IsDefaultPort;    // true since 80 is default
```

`UriBuilder`, however, implements fewer properties, just enough to allow you to build up a complete URI. These properties are read-write.

You can supply the components to build up a URI to the constructor:

```
UriBuilder MSPage = new
    UriBuilder("http", "www.microsoft.com", 80, "SomeFolder/SomeFile.htm");
```

Or, you can build the components by assigning values to the properties:

```
UriBuilder MSPage = new UriBuilder();
MSPage.Scheme ="http";
MSPage.Host = "www.microsoft.com";
MSPage.Port = 80;
MSPage.Path = "SomeFolder/SomeFile.htm";
```

After you have completed initializing the `UriBuilder`, you can obtain the corresponding `Uri` object with the `Uri` property:

```
Uri CompletedUri = MSPage.Uri;
```

IP Addresses and DNS Names

On the Internet, you identify servers as well as clients by IP address or host name (also referred to as a DNS name). Generally speaking, the host name is the human-friendly name that you type in a web browser window, such as `www.wrox.com` or `www.microsoft.com`. An IP address is the identifier computers use to identify each other. IP addresses are the identifiers used to ensure that web requests and responses reach the appropriate machines. It is even possible for a computer to have more than one IP address.

Today, IP addresses are typically a 32-bit value. An example of a 32-bit IP address is 192.168.1.100. This format of IP address is referred to as Internet Protocol version 4. Because there are now so many computers and other devices vying for a spot on the Internet, a newer type of address was developed — Internet Protocol version 6. IPv6 provides a 64-bit IP address. IPv6 can potentially provide a maximum number of about 3×10^{28} unique addresses. You will find that the .NET Framework allows your applications to work with both IPv4 and IPv6.

For host names to work, you must first send a network request to translate the host name into an IP address, a task carried out by one or more DNS servers.

A DNS server stores a table mapping host names to IP addresses for all the computers it knows about, as well as the IP addresses of other DNS servers to look up the host names it does not know about. Your local computer should always know about at least one DNS server. Network administrators configure this information when a computer is set up.

Before sending out a request, your computer will first ask the DNS server to tell it the IP address corresponding to the host name you have typed in. When it is armed with the correct IP address, the computer can address the request and send it over the network. All this work normally happens behind the scenes while the user is browsing the Web.

.NET Classes for IP Addresses

The .NET Framework supplies a number of classes that are able to assist with the process of looking up IP addresses and finding information about host computers.

IPAddress

`IPAddress` represents an IP address. The address itself is available as the `GetAddressBytes` property and may be converted to a dotted decimal format with the `ToString()` method. `IPAddress` also implements a static `Parse()` method, which effectively performs the reverse conversion of `ToString()` — converting from a dotted decimal string to an `IPAddress`:

```
IPAddress ipAddress = IPAddress.Parse("234.56.78.9");
byte[] address = ipAddress.GetAddressBytes();
string ipString = ipAddress.ToString();
```

In this example, the `byte` integer `address` is assigned a binary representation of the IP address, and the string `ipString` is assigned the text `"234.56.78.9"`.

`IPAddress` also provides a number of constant static fields to return special addresses. For example, the `Loopback` address allows a machine to send messages to itself, whereas the `Broadcast` address allows multicasting to the local network:

```
// The following line will set loopback to "127.0.0.1".
// the loopback address indicates the local host.
string loopback = IPAddress.Loopback.ToString();

// The following line will set broadcast address to "255.255.255.255".
// the broadcast address is used to send a message to all machines on
// the local network.
string broadcast = IPAddress.Broadcast.ToString();
```

IPHostEntry

The `IPHostEntry` class encapsulates information relating to a particular host computer. This class makes the host name available via the `HostName` property (which returns a string), and the `AddressList` property returns an array of `IPAddress` objects. You are going to use the `IPHostEntry` class in the next example: `DNSLookupResolver`.

Dns

The `Dns` class is able to communicate with your default DNS server to retrieve IP addresses. The two important (static) methods are `Resolve()`, which uses the DNS server to obtain the details of a host with a given host name, and `GetHostByAddress()`, which also returns details of the host but this time using the IP address. Both methods return an `IPHostEntry` object:

```
IPHostEntry wroxHost = Dns.Resolve("www.wrox.com");
IPHostEntry wroxHostCopy = Dns.GetHostByAddress("208.215.179.178");
```

In this code, both `IPHostEntry` objects will contain details of the Wrox.com servers.

The `Dns` class differs from the `IPAddress` and `IPHostEntry` classes because it has the ability to actually communicate with servers to obtain information. In contrast, `IPAddress` and `IPHostEntry` are more along the lines of simple data structures with convenient properties to allow access to the underlying data.

The DnsLookup Example

The DNS and IP-related classes are illustrated with an example that looks up DNS names: `DnsLookup` (see Figure 24-10).

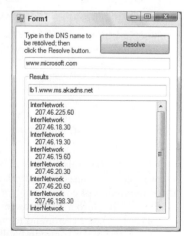

This sample application simply invites the user to type in a DNS name using the main text box. When the user clicks the Resolve button, the sample uses the `Dns.Resolve()` method to retrieve an `IPHostEntry` reference and display the host name and IP addresses. Note how the host name displayed may be different from the name typed in. This can occur if one DNS name (`www.microsoft.com`) simply acts as a proxy for another DNS name (`1b1.www.ms.akadns.net`).

The `DnsLookup` application is a standard C# Windows application. The controls are added as shown in Figure 24-10, giving them the names `txtBoxInput`, `btnResolve`, `txtBoxHostName`, and `listBoxIPs`, respectively. Then, you simply add the following method to the `Form1` class as the event handler for the `buttonResolve Click` event:

FIGURE 24-10

```
void btnResolve_Click (object sender, EventArgs e)
{
    try
    {
        IPHostEntry iphost = Dns.GetHostEntry(txtBoxInput.Text);
```

```
            foreach (IPAddress ip in iphost.AddressList)
            {
                string ipaddress = ip.AddressFamily.ToString();
                listBoxIPs.Items.Add(ipaddress);
                listBoxIPs.Items.Add(" " + ip.ToString());
            }
            txtBoxHostName.Text = iphost.HostName;
        }
        catch(Exception ex)
        {
            MessageBox.Show("Unable to process the request because " +
                "the following problem occurred:\n" +
                 ex.Message, "Exception occurred");
        }
    }
}
```

Notice that in this code you are careful to trap any exceptions. An exception might occur if the user types an invalid DNS name or if the network is down.

After retrieving the `IPHostEntry` instance, you use the `AddressList` property to obtain an array containing the IP addresses, which you then iterate through with a `foreach` loop. For each entry, you display the IP address as an integer and as a string, using the `IPAddress.AddressFamily.ToString()` method.

LOWER-LEVEL PROTOCOLS

This section briefly discusses some of the .NET classes used to communicate at a lower level.

The `System.Net.Sockets` namespace contains the relevant classes. These classes, for example, allow you to directly send out TCP network requests or to listen to TCP network requests on a particular port. The following table explains the main classes:

CLASS	PURPOSE
Socket	Deals with managing connections. Classes such as `WebRequest`, `TcpClient`, and `UdpClient` use this class internally.
NetworkStream	Derived from Stream. Represents a stream of data from the network.
SmtpClient	Enables you to send messages (mail) through the Simple Mail Transfer Protocol.
TcpClient	Enables you to create and use TCP connections.
TcpListener	Enables you to listen for incoming TCP connection requests.
UdpClient	Enables you to create connections for UDP clients. (UDP is an alternative protocol to TCP but is much less widely used, mostly on local networks.)

Network communications work on several different levels. The classes you have seen in this chapter so far work at the highest level — the level at which specific commands are processed. It is probably easiest to understand this concept if you think of file transfer using FTP. Although today's GUI applications hide many of the FTP details, it was not so long ago when you executed FTP from a command-line prompt. In this environment, you explicitly typed commands to send to the server for downloading, uploading, and listing files.

FTP is not the only high-level protocol relying on textual commands. HTTP, SMTP, POP, and other protocols are based on a similar type of behavior. Again, many of the modern graphical tools hide the transmission of commands from the user, so you are generally not aware of them. For example, when you type a URL into a web browser, and the web request goes off to a server, the browser is actually sending a (plain-text) GET command to the server, which fulfills a similar purpose as the FTP get command. It can also send a POST command, which indicates that the browser has attached other data to the request.

These protocols, however, are not sufficient by themselves to achieve communication between computers. Even if both the client and the server understand, for example, the HTTP protocol, it will still not be possible for them to understand each other unless there is also agreement on exactly how to transmit the characters — what binary format will be used? Moreover, getting down to the lowest level, what voltages will be used to represent 0s and 1s in the binary data? Because there are so many items to configure and agree upon, developers and hardware engineers in the networking field often refer to a *protocol stack*. When you list all the various protocols and mechanisms required for communication between two hosts, you create a protocol stack with high-level protocols on the top and low-level protocols on the bottom. This approach results in a modular and layered approach to achieving efficient communication.

Luckily, for most development work, you do not need to go far down the stack or work with voltage levels. If you are writing code that requires efficient communication between computers, then it's not unusual to write code that works directly at the level of sending binary data packets between computers. This is the realm of protocols such as TCP, and Microsoft has supplied a number of classes that allow you to conveniently work with binary data at this level.

Using SmtpClient

The SmtpClient object allows you to send mail messages through the Simple Mail Transfer Protocol. A simple sample of using the SmtpClient object is illustrated here:

```
SmtpClient sc = new SmtpClient("mail.mySmtpHost.com");
sc.Send("evjen@yahoo.com", "editor@wrox.com",
   "The latest chapter", "Here is the latest.");
```

In its simplest form, you work from an instance of the SmtpClient object. In this case, the instantiation also provided the host of the SMTP server that is used to send the mail messages over the Internet. You could have also achieved the same task by using the Host property:

```
SmtpClient sc = new SmtpClient();
sc.Host = "mail.mySmtpHost.com";
sc.Send("evjen@yahoo.com", "editor@wrox.com",
   "The latest chapter", "Here is the latest.");
```

When you have the SmtpClient in place, it is simply a matter of calling the Send() method and providing the From address, the To address, and the Subject, followed by the Body of the mail message.

In many cases, you will have mail messages that are more complex than this. To work with this possibility, you can also pass in a MailMessage object into the Send() method:

```
SmtpClient sc = new SmtpClient();
sc.Host = "mail.mySmtpHost.com";
MailMessage mm = new MailMessage();
mm.Sender = new MailAddress("evjen@yahoo.com", "Bill Evjen");
mm.To.Add(new MailAddress("editor@wrox.com", "Paul Reese"));
mm.To.Add(new MailAddress("marketing@wrox.com", "Wrox Marketing"));
mm.CC.Add(new MailAddress("publisher@wrox.com", "Barry Pruett"));
mm.Subject = "The latest chapter";
mm.Body = "<b>Here you can put a long message</b>";
mm.IsBodyHtml = true;
mm.Priority = MailPriority.High;
sc.Send(mm);
```

Using MailMessage allows you to really fine-tune how you build your mail messages. You are able to send HTML messages, add as many To and CC recipients as you wish, change the message priority, work with the message encodings, and add attachments. The ability to add attachments is defined in the following code snippet:

```
SmtpClient sc = new SmtpClient();
sc.Host = "mail.mySmtpHost.com";
MailMessage mm = new MailMessage();
mm.Sender = new MailAddress("evjen@yahoo.com", "Bill Evjen");
```

```
mm.To.Add(new MailAddress("editor@wrox.com", "Paul Reese"));
mm.To.Add(new MailAddress("marketing@wrox.com", "Wrox Marketing"));
mm.CC.Add(new MailAddress("publisher@wrox.com", "Barry Pruett"));
mm.Subject = "The latest chapter";
mm.Body = "<b>Here you can put a long message</b>";
mm.IsBodyHtml = true;
mm.Priority = MailPriority.High;
Attachment att = new Attachment("myExcelResults.zip",
    MediaTypeNames.Application.Zip);
mm.Attachments.Add(att);
sc.Send(mm);
```

In this case, an `Attachment` object is created and added using the `Add()` method to the `MailMessage` object before the `Send()` method is called.

Using the TCP Classes

The Transmission Control Protocol (TCP) classes offer simple methods for connecting and sending data between two endpoints. An endpoint is the combination of an IP address and a port number. Existing protocols have well-defined port numbers, for example, HTTP uses port 80, whereas SMTP uses port 25. The Internet Assigned Numbers Authority, IANA, (`www.iana.org`) assigns port numbers to these well-known services. Unless you are implementing a well-known service, you will want to select a port number larger than 1,024.

TCP traffic makes up the majority of traffic on the Internet today. TCP is often the protocol of choice because it offers guaranteed delivery, error correction, and buffering. The `TcpClient` class encapsulates a TCP connection and provides a number of properties to regulate the connection, including buffering, buffer size, and timeouts. Reading and writing is accomplished by requesting a `NetworkStream` object via the `GetStream()` method.

The `TcpListener` class listens for incoming TCP connections with the `Start()` method. When a connection request arrives, you can use the `AcceptSocket()` method to return a socket for communication with the remote machine, or use the `AcceptTcpClient()` method to use a higher-level `TcpClient` object for communication. The easiest way to see how the `TcpListener` and `TcpClient` classes work together is to work through an example.

The TcpSend and TcpReceive Examples

To demonstrate how these classes work, you need to build two applications. Figure 24-11 shows the first application, `TcpSend`. This application opens a TCP connection to a server and sends the C# source code for itself.

FIGURE 24-11

Once again, you create a C# Windows application. The form consists of two text boxes (`txtHost` and `txtPort`) for the host name and port, respectively, as well as a button (`btnSend`) to click and start a connection. First, you ensure that you include the relevant namespaces:

```
using System;
using System.IO;
using System.Net.Sockets;
using System.Windows.Forms;
```

The following code shows the event handler for the button's `Click` event:

```
private void btnSend_Click(object sender, System.EventArgs e)
{
    TcpClient tcpClient = new TcpClient(txtHost.Text, Int32.Parse(txtPort.Text));
```

```
    NetworkStream ns = tcpClient.GetStream();
    FileStream fs = File.Open("form1.cs", FileMode.Open);

    int data = fs.ReadByte();

    while(data != -1)
    {
        ns.WriteByte((byte)data);
        data = fs.ReadByte();
    }

    fs.Close();
    ns.Close();
    tcpClient.Close();
}
```

This example creates the `TcpClient` using a host name and a port number. Alternatively, if you have an instance of the `IPEndPoint` class, then you can pass the instance to the `TcpClient` constructor. After retrieving an instance of the `NetworkStream` class, you open the source code file and begin to read bytes. As with many of the binary streams, you need to check for the end of the stream by comparing the return value of the `ReadByte()` method to `-1`. After your loop has read all the bytes and sent them along to the network stream, you must close all the open files, connections, and streams.

On the other side of the connection, the `TcpReceive` application displays the received file after the transmission is finished (see Figure 24-12).

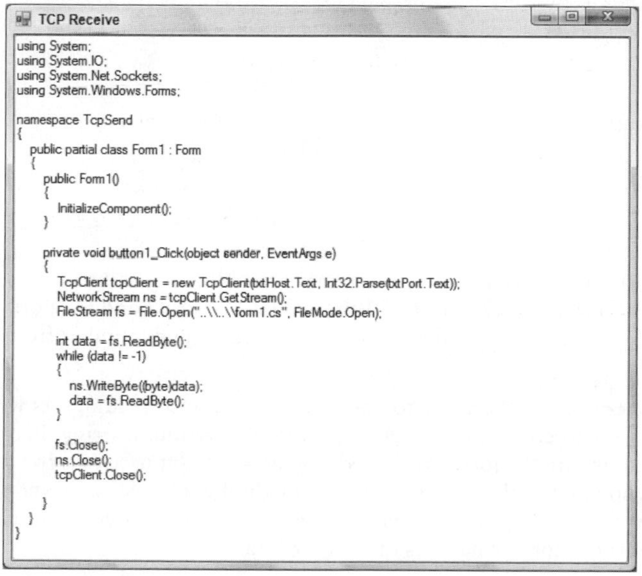

FIGURE 24-12

The form consists of a single `TextBox` control named `txtDisplay`. The `TcpReceive` application uses a `TcpListener` to wait for the incoming connection. To prevent freezing the application interface, you use a background thread to wait for and then read from the connection. Thus, you need to include the `System.Threading` namespace as well these other namespaces:

```
using System;
using System.IO;
```

```
using System.Net;
using System.Net.Sockets;
using System.Threading;
using System.Windows.Forms;
```

Inside the form's constructor, you spin up a background thread:

```
public Form1()
{
    InitializeComponent();
    Thread thread = new Thread(new ThreadStart(Listen));
    thread.Start();
}
```

The remaining important code is this:

```
public void Listen()
{
    IPAddress localAddr = IPAddress.Parse("127.0.0.1");
    Int32 port = 2112;
    TcpListener tcpListener = new TcpListener(localAddr, port);
    tcpListener.Start();

    TcpClient tcpClient = tcpListener.AcceptTcpClient();

    NetworkStream ns = tcpClient.GetStream();
    StreamReader sr = new StreamReader(ns);
    string result = sr.ReadToEnd();
    Invoke(new UpdateDisplayDelegate(UpdateDisplay),new object[] {result} );
    tcpClient.Close();
    tcpListener.Stop();
}

public void UpdateDisplay(string text)
{
    txtDisplay.Text= text;
}

protected delegate void UpdateDisplayDelegate(string text);
```

The thread begins execution in the `Listen()` method and allows you to make the blocking call to `AcceptTcpClient()` without halting the interface. Notice that the IP address (`127.0.0.1`) and the port number (`2112`) are hard-coded into the application, so you will need to enter the same port number from the client application.

You use the `TcpClient` object returned by `AcceptTcpClient()` to open a new stream for reading. As with the earlier example, you create a `StreamReader` to convert the incoming network data into a string. Before you close the client and stop the listener, you update the form's text box. You do not want to access the text box directly from your background thread, so you use the form's `Invoke()` method with a delegate and pass the result string as the first element in an array of `object` parameters. `Invoke()` ensures that your call is correctly marshaled into the thread that owns the control handles in the user interface.

TCP Versus UDP

The other protocol covered in this section is UDP (User Datagram Protocol). UDP is a simple protocol with few features and little overhead. Developers often use UDP in applications where the speed and performance requirements outweigh the reliability needs, for example, video streaming. In contrast, TCP offers a number of features to confirm the delivery of data. TCP provides error correction and retransmission in the case of lost or corrupted packets. Last, but hardly least, TCP buffers incoming and outgoing data and also guarantees that a sequence of packets scrambled in transmission is reassembled before delivery to the application. Even with the extra overhead, TCP is the most widely used protocol across the Internet because of its high reliability.

The UDP Class

As you might expect, the UdpClient class features a smaller and simpler interface than TcpClient. This reflects the relatively simpler nature of the protocol. Although both TCP and UDP classes use a socket underneath the covers, the UdpClient class does not contain a method to return a network stream for reading and writing. Instead, the member function Send() accepts an array of bytes as a parameter, and the Receive() function returns an array of bytes. Also, because UDP is a connectionless protocol, you can wait to specify the endpoint for the communication as a parameter to the Send() and Receive() methods, instead of specifying it earlier in a constructor or Connect() method. You can also change the endpoint on each subsequent send or receive.

The following code fragment uses the UdpClient class to send a message to an echo service. A server with an echo service running accepts TCP or UDP connections on port 7. The echo service simply echoes any data sent to the server back to the client. This service is useful for diagnostics and testing, although many system administrators disable echo services for security reasons:

```
using System;
using System.Text;
using System.Net;
using System.Net.Sockets;
namespace Wrox.ProCSharp.InternetAccess.UdpExample
{

    class Class1
    {
        [STAThread]
        static void Main(string[] args)
        {
            UdpClient udpClient = new UdpClient();
            string sendMsg = "Hello Echo Server";
            byte [] sendBytes = Encoding.ASCII.GetBytes(sendMsg);
            udpClient.Send(sendBytes, sendBytes.Length, "SomeEchoServer.net", 7);
            IPEndPoint endPoint = new IPEndPoint(0,0);
            byte [] rcvBytes = udpClient.Receive(ref endPoint);
            string rcvMessage = Encoding.ASCII.GetString(rcvBytes,
                                                         0,
                                                         rcvBytes.Length);
            // should print out "Hello Echo Server"
            Console.WriteLine(rcvMessage);
        }
    }
}
```

You make heavy use of the Encoding.ASCII class to translate strings into arrays of byte and vice versa. Also note that you pass an IPEndPoint by reference into the Receive() method. Because UDP is not a connection-oriented protocol, each call to Receive() might pick up data from a different endpoint, so Receive() populates this parameter with the IP address and port of the sending host.

Both UdpClient and TcpClient offer a layer of abstraction over the lowest of the low-level classes: the Socket.

The Socket Class

The Socket class offers the highest level of control in network programming. One of the easiest ways to demonstrate the class is to rewrite the TcpReceive application with the Socket class. The updated Listen() method is listed in this example:

```
public void Listen()
{
    Socket listener = new Socket(AddressFamily.InterNetwork,
```

```
                                            SocketType.Stream,
                                            ProtocolType.Tcp);
        listener.Bind(new IPEndPoint(IPAddress.Any, 2112));
        listener.Listen(0);
        Socket socket = listener.Accept();
        Stream netStream = new NetworkStream(socket);
        StreamReader reader = new StreamReader(netStream);

        string result = reader.ReadToEnd();
        Invoke(new UpdateDisplayDelegate(UpdateDisplay),
                new object[] {result} );
        socket.Close();
        listener.Close();
    }
```

The Socket class requires a few more lines of code to complete the same task. For starters, the constructor arguments need to specify an IP addressing scheme for a streaming socket with the TCP protocol. These arguments are just one of the many combinations available to the Socket class. The TcpClient class can configure these settings for you. You then bind the listener socket to a port and begin to listen for incoming connections. When an incoming request arrives, you can use the Accept() method to create a new socket to handle the connection. You ultimately attach a StreamReader instance to the socket to read the incoming data, in much the same fashion as before.

The Socket class also contains a number of methods for asynchronously accepting, connecting, sending, and receiving. You can use these methods with callback delegates in the same way you used the asynchronous page requests with the WebRequest class. If you really need to dig into the internals of the socket, the GetSocketOption() and SetSocketOption() methods are available. These methods allow you to see and configure options, including timeout, time-to-live, and other low-level options. Next, this chapter looks at another example of using sockets.

Building a Server Console Application

Looking further into the Socket class, the next example creates a console application that acts as a server for incoming socket requests. From there, a second example will be created in parallel (another console application), which sends a message to the server console application.

The first application you will build is the console application that acts as a server. This application will open a socket on a specific TCP port and listen for any incoming messages. The code for this console application is presented in its entirety here:

```
using System;
using System.Net;
using System.Net.Sockets;
using System.Text;

namespace SocketConsole
{
    class Program
    {
        static void Main()
        {
            Console.WriteLine("Starting: Creating Socket object");
            Socket listener = new Socket(AddressFamily.InterNetwork,
                                    SocketType.Stream,
                                    ProtocolType.Tcp);
            listener.Bind(new IPEndPoint(IPAddress.Any, 2112));
            listener.Listen(10);

            while (true)
            {
                Console.WriteLine("Waiting for connection on port 2112");
```

```
                    Socket socket = listener.Accept();
                    string receivedValue = string.Empty;

                    while (true)
                    {
                        byte[] receivedBytes = new byte[1024];
                        int numBytes = socket.Receive(receivedBytes);
                        Console.WriteLine("Receiving .");
                        receivedValue += Encoding.ASCII.GetString(receivedBytes,
                                             0, numBytes);
                        if (receivedValue.IndexOf("[FINAL]") > -1)
                        {
                            break;
                        }
                    }

                    Console.WriteLine("Received value: {0}", receivedValue);
                    string replyValue = "Message successfully received.";
                    byte[] replyMessage = Encoding.ASCII.GetBytes(replyValue);
                    socket.Send(replyMessage);
                    socket.Shutdown(SocketShutdown.Both);
                    socket.Close();
                }
                listener.Close();
            }
        }
    }
```

This example sets up a socket using the `Socket` class. The socket created uses the TCP protocol and is set up to receive incoming messages from any IP address using port 2112. Values that come in through the open socket are written to the console screen. This consuming application will continue to receive bytes until the `[FINAL]` string is received. This `[FINAL]` string signifies the end of the incoming message, and the message can then be interpreted.

After the end of the message is received from a client, a reply message is sent to the same client. From there, the socket is closed using the `Close()` method, and the console application will continue to stay up until a new message is received.

Building the Client Application

The next step is to build a client application that will send a message to the first console application. The client will be able to send any message that it wants to the server console application as long as it follows some rules that were established by this application. The first of these rules is that the server console application is listening only on a particular protocol. In the case of this server application, it is listening using the TCP protocol. The other rule is that the server application is listening only on a particular port — in this case, port 2112. The last rule is that in any message that is being sent, the last bits of the message need to end with the string `[FINAL]`.

The following client console application follows all these rules:

```
using System;
using System.Net;
using System.Net.Sockets;
using System.Text;

namespace SocketConsoleClient
{
    class Program
    {
        static void Main()
        {
```

```
            byte[] receivedBytes = new byte[1024];
            IPHostEntry ipHost = Dns.Resolve("127.0.0.1");
            IPAddress ipAddress = ipHost.AddressList[0];
            IPEndPoint ipEndPoint = new IPEndPoint(ipAddress, 2112);
            Console.WriteLine("Starting: Creating Socket object");

            Socket sender = new Socket(AddressFamily.InterNetwork,
                                       SocketType.Stream,
                                       ProtocolType.Tcp);
            sender.Connect(ipEndPoint);
            Console.WriteLine("Successfully connected to {0}",
                    sender.RemoteEndPoint);
            string sendingMessage = "Hello World Socket Test";
            Console.WriteLine("Creating message: Hello World Socket Test");
            byte[] forwardMessage = Encoding.ASCII.GetBytes(sendingMessage
                + "[FINAL]");
            sender.Send(forwardMessage);
            int totalBytesReceived = sender.Receive(receivedBytes);
            Console.WriteLine("Message provided from server: {0}",
                          Encoding.ASCII.GetString(receivedBytes,
                          0, totalBytesReceived));
            sender.Shutdown(SocketShutdown.Both);
            sender.Close();
            Console.ReadLine();
        }
    }
}
```

In this example, an IPEndPoint object is created using the IP address of *localhost* as well as using port 2112 as required by the server console application. In this case, a socket is created and the Connect() method is called. After the socket is opened and connected to the server console application socket instance, a string of text is sent to the server application using the Send() method. Because the server application is going to return a message, the Receive() method is used to grab this message (placing it in a byte array). From there, the byte array is converted into a string and displayed in the console application before the socket is shut down.

Running this application will produce the results presented in Figure 24-13.

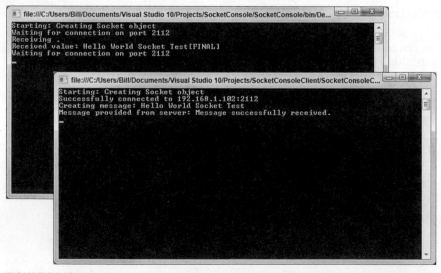

FIGURE 24-13

Reviewing the two console applications in the figure, you can see that the server application opens and awaits incoming messages. The incoming message is sent from the client application, and the string sent is then displayed by the server application. The server application waits for other messages to come in, even after the first message is received and displayed. You can see this for yourself by shutting down the client application and re-running the application. You will then see that the server application again displays the message received.

SUMMARY

In this chapter, you reviewed the .NET Framework classes available in the `System.Net` namespace for communication across networks. You have seen some of the .NET base classes that deal with opening client connections on the network and Internet, and how to send requests to and receive responses from servers (the most obvious use of this being to receive HTML pages). By taking advantage of the `WebBrowser` control in .NET 4, you can easily make use of Internet Explorer from your desktop applications.

As a rule of thumb, when programming with classes in the `System.Net` namespace, you should always try to use the most generic class possible. For instance, using the `TcpClient` class instead of the `Socket` class isolates your code from many of the lower-level socket details. Moving one step higher, the `WebRequest` class allows you to take advantage of the pluggable protocol architecture of the .NET Framework. Your code will be ready to take advantage of new application-level protocols as Microsoft and other third-party developers introduce new functionality.

Finally, you learned how to use the asynchronous capabilities in the networking classes, which give a Windows Forms application the professional touch of a responsive user interface.

Now you move on to learning about Windows Services.

25

Windows Services

WHAT'S IN THIS CHAPTER?

➤ The architecture of a Windows Service

➤ Windows Services installation programs

➤ Windows Services control programs

➤ Troubleshooting Windows Services

Windows Services are programs that can be started automatically at boot time without the need for anyone to log on to the machine. The following section explains the architecture of Windows Services. The rest of the chapter shows you how to create, monitor, control, and troubleshoot your Windows Services.

WHAT IS A WINDOWS SERVICE?

Windows Services are applications that can be automatically started when the operating system boots. These applications can run without having an interactive user logged on to the system and do some processing in the background.

For example, on a Windows Server, system networking services should be accessible from the client without a user logging on to the server. And on the client system, services allow you to get a new software version from the Internet or to do some file cleanup on the local disk.

You can configure a Windows Service to run from a specially configured user account or from the system user account — a user account that has even more privileges than that of the system administrator.

 Unless otherwise noted, when we refer to a service, we are referring to a Windows Service.

Here are a few examples of services:

➤ Simple TCP/IP Services is a service program that hosts some small TCP/IP servers: echo, daytime, quote, and others.

➤ World Wide Web Publishing Service is the service of the Internet Information Server (IIS).

➤ Event Log is a service to log messages to the event log system.

➤ Windows Search is a service that creates indexes of data on the disk.

You can use the Services administration tool, shown in Figure 25-1, to see all the services on a system. This program can be found with the Administrative Tools.

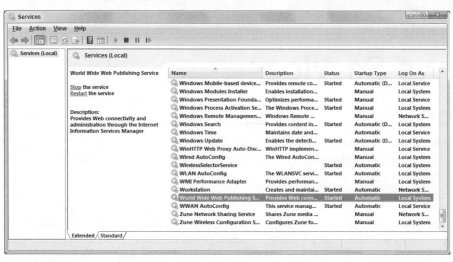

FIGURE 25-1

WINDOWS SERVICES ARCHITECTURE

Three program types are necessary to operate a Windows Service:

➤ A service program

➤ A service control program

➤ A service configuration program

The *service program* itself provides the actual functionality you are looking for. With a *service control* program, it is possible to send control requests to a service, such as start, stop, pause, and continue. With a *service configuration* program, a service can be installed; it is copied to the file system, written into the registry, and configured as a service. Although .NET components can be installed simply with an xcopy — because they don't need to write information to the registry — installation for services requires registry configuration. A service configuration program can also be used to change the configuration of that service at a later point.

These three ingredients of a Windows Service are discussed in the following subsections.

Service Program

Before looking at the .NET implementation of a service, let's explore, from an independent point of view, what the Windows architecture of services looks like and what the inner functionality of a service is.

The service program implements the functionality of the service. It needs three parts:

➤ A main function

➤ A service-main function

➤ A handler

Before discussing these parts, we need to quickly introduce you to the *Service Control Manager (SCM)*. The SCM plays an important role for services — sending requests to your service to start and to stop it.

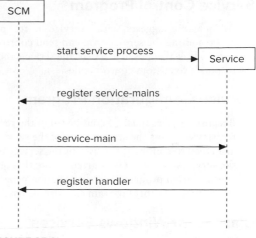

FIGURE 25-2

Service Control Manager

The SCM is the part of the operating system that communicates with the service. Figure 25-2 illustrates how this communication works with a sequence diagram.

At boot time, each process for which a service is set to start automatically is started, and so the main function of this process is called. The service has the responsibility of registering the service-main function for each of its services. The main function is the entry point of the service program, and in this function the entry points for the service-main functions must be registered with the SCM.

Main Function, Service-Main, and Handlers

The main function of the service is the normal entry point of a program, the `Main()` method. The main function of the service might register more than one service-main function. The *service-main* function contains the actual functionality of the service. The service must register a service-main function for each service it provides. A service program can provide a lot of services in a single program; for example, `<windows>\system32\services.exe` is the service program that includes Alerter, Application Management, Computer Browser, and DHCP Client, among other items.

The SCM now calls the service-main function for each service that should be started. One important task of the service-main function is to register a handler with the SCM.

The *handler* function is the third part of a service program. The handler must respond to events from the SCM. Services can be stopped, suspended, and resumed, and the handler must react to these events.

After a handler has been registered with the SCM, the service control program can post requests to the SCM to stop, suspend, and resume the service. The service control program is independent of the SCM and the service itself. The operating system contains many service control programs, for example, the MMC Services snap-in that you saw earlier. You can also write your own service control program; a good example of this is the SQL Server Configuration Manager shown in Figure 25-3.

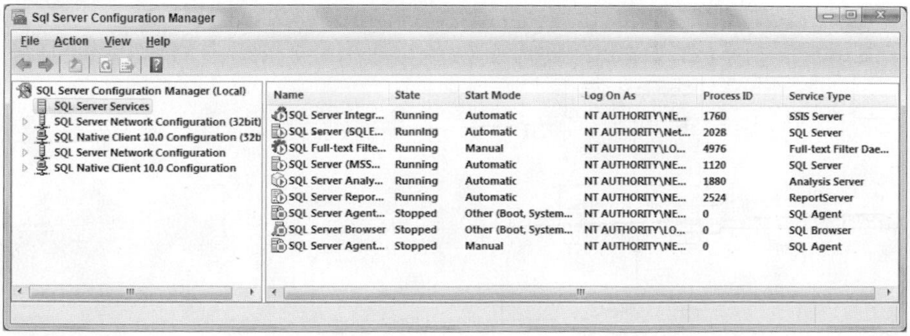

FIGURE 25-3

Service Control Program

As the name suggests, with a service control program, you can control the service. For stopping, suspending, and resuming the service, you can send control codes to the service, and the handler should react to these events. It is also possible to ask the service about the actual status and to implement a custom handler that responds to custom control codes.

Service Configuration Program

Because services must be configured in the registry, you can't use xcopy installation with services. The registry contains the startup type of the service, which can be set to automatic, manual, or disabled. You also need to configure the user of the service program and dependencies of the service — for example, the services that must be started before this one can start. All these configurations are made within a service configuration program. The installation program can use the service configuration program to configure the service, but this program can also be used at a later time to change service configuration parameters.

Classes for Windows Services

In the .NET Framework, you can find service classes in the `System.ServiceProcess` namespace that implement the three parts of a service:

➤ You must inherit from the `ServiceBase` class to implement a service. The `ServiceBase` class is used to register the service and to answer start and stop requests.

➤ The `ServiceController` class is used to implement a service control program. With this class, you can send requests to services.

➤ The `ServiceProcessInstaller` and `ServiceInstaller` classes are, as their names suggest, classes to install and configure service programs.

Now you are ready to create a new service.

CREATING A WINDOWS SERVICE PROGRAM

The service that you create in this chapter hosts a quote server. With every request that is made from a client, the quote server returns a random quote from a quote file. The first part of the solution uses three assemblies, one for the client and two for the server. Figure 25-4 gives an overview of the solution. The assembly `QuoteServer` holds the actual functionality. The service reads the quote file in a memory cache, and answers requests for quotes with the help of a socket server. The `QuoteClient` is a WPF rich-client application. This application creates a client socket to communicate with the `QuoteServer`. The third assembly is the actual service. The `QuoteService` starts and stops the `QuoteServer`; the service controls the server.

Before creating the service part of your program, create a simple socket server in an extra C# class library that will be used from your service process.

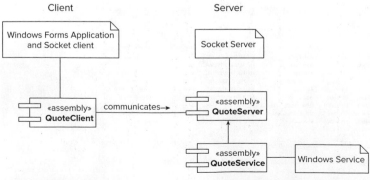

FIGURE 25-4

Creating Core Functionality for the Service

You can build any functionality in a Windows Service, such as scanning for files to do a backup or a virus check or starting a WCF server. However, all service programs share some similarities. The program must be able to start (and to return to the caller), stop, and suspend. This section looks at such an implementation using a socket server.

With Windows 7, the Simple TCP/IP Services can be installed as part of the Windows components. Part of the Simple TCP/IP Services is a "quote of the day," or qotd, TCP/IP server. This simple service listens to port 17 and answers every request with a random message from the file `<windir>\system32\drivers\etc\quotes`. With the sample service, a similar server will be built. The sample server returns a Unicode string, in contrast to the good-old qotd server that returns an ASCII string.

First, create a Class Library called `QuoteServer` and implement the code for the server. The following walks through the source code of your `QuoteServer` class in the file `QuoteServer.cs`:

```csharp
using System;
using System.Collections.Generic;
using System.Diagnostics;
using System.IO;
using System.Linq;
using System.Net;
using System.Net.Sockets;
using System.Text;
using System.Threading;

namespace Wrox.ProCSharp.WinServices
{
    public class QuoteServer
    {
        private TcpListener listener;
        private int port;
        private string filename;
        private List<string> quotes;
        private Random random;
        private Thread listenerThread;
```

code snippet QuoteServer/QuoteServer.cs

The constructor `QuoteServer()` is overloaded so that a filename and a port can be passed to the call. The constructor where just the file name is passed uses the default port 7890 for the server. The default constructor defines the default filename for the quotes as `quotes.txt`:

```csharp
public QuoteServer()
    : this ("quotes.txt")
{
}
public QuoteServer(string filename)
    : this(filename, 7890)
{
}
public QuoteServer(string filename, int port)
{
    this.filename = filename;
    this.port = port;
}
```

`ReadQuotes()` is a helper method that reads all the quotes from a file that was specified in the constructor. All the quotes are added to the `List<string>` quotes. In addition, you are creating an instance of the `Random` class that will be used to return random quotes:

```
protected void ReadQuotes()
{
    quotes = File.ReadAllLines(filename).ToList();
    random = new Random();
}
```

Another helper method is `GetRandomQuoteOfTheDay()`. This method returns a random quote from the quotes collection:

```
protected string GetRandomQuoteOfTheDay()
{
    int index = random.Next(0, quotes.Count);
    return quotes[index];
}
```

In the `Start()` method, the complete file containing the quotes is read in the `List<string>` quotes by using the helper method `ReadQuotes()`. After this, a new thread is started, which immediately calls the `ListenerThread()` method — similarly to the `TcpReceive` example in Chapter 24, "Networking."

Here a thread is used because the `Start()` method cannot block and wait for a client; it must return immediately to the caller (SCM). The SCM would assume that the start failed if the method didn't return to the caller in a timely fashion (30 seconds). The listener thread is set as a background thread so that the application can exit without stopping this thread. The `Name` property of the thread is set because this helps with debugging, as the name will show up in the debugger:

```
public void Start()
{
    ReadQuotes();
    listenerThread = new Thread(ListenerThread);
    listenerThread.IsBackground = true;
    listenerThread.Name = "Listener";
    listenerThread.Start();
}
```

The thread function `ListenerThread()` creates a `TcpListener` instance. The `AcceptSocket()` method waits for a client to connect. As soon as a client connects, `AcceptSocket()` returns with a socket associated with the client. Next, `GetRandomQuoteOfTheDay()` is called to send the returned random quote to the client using `socket.Send()`:

```
protected void ListenerThread()
{
    try
    {
        IPAddress ipAddress = IPAddress.Parse("127.0.0.1");
        listener = new TcpListener(ipAddress, port);
        listener.Start();
        while (true)
        {
            Socket clientSocket = listener.AcceptSocket();
            string message = GetRandomQuoteOfTheDay();
            UnicodeEncoding encoder = new UnicodeEncoding();
            byte[] buffer = encoder.GetBytes(message);
            clientSocket.Send(buffer, buffer.Length, 0);
            clientSocket.Close();
        }
    }
    catch (SocketException ex)
```

```
            {
                Trace.TraceError(String.Format("QuoteServer {0}", ex.Message));
            }
        }
    }
```

In addition to the `Start()` method, the following methods are needed to control the service: `Stop()`, `Suspend()`, and `Resume()`:

```
        public void Stop()
        {
            listener.Stop();
        }
        public void Suspend()
        {
            listener.Stop();
        }
        public void Resume()
        {
            Start();
        }
```

Another method that will be publicly available is `RefreshQuotes()`. If the file containing the quotes changes, the file is re-read with this method:

```
        public void RefreshQuotes()
        {
            ReadQuotes();
        }
    }
}
```

Before building a service around the server, it is useful to build a test program that creates just an instance of the `QuoteServer` and calls `Start()`. This way, you can test the functionality without the need to handle service-specific issues. This test server must be started manually, and you can easily walk through the code with a debugger.

The test program is a C# console application, `TestQuoteServer`. You need to reference the assembly of the `QuoteServer` class. The file containing the quotes must be copied to the directory `c:\ProCSharp\` `Services` (or you must change the argument in the constructor to specify where you have copied the file). After calling the constructor, the `Start()` method of the `QuoteServer` instance is called. `Start()` returns immediately after having created a thread, so the console application keeps running until `Return` is pressed:

```
static void Main()
{
    var qs = new QuoteServer("quotes.txt", 4567);
    qs.Start();
    Console.WriteLine("Hit return to exit");
    Console.ReadLine();
    qs.Stop();
}
```

code snippet TestQuoteServer/Program.cs

Note that `QuoteServer` will be running on port 4567 on localhost using this program — you will have to use these settings in the client later.

QuoteClient Example

The client is a simple WPF Windows application in which you can request quotes from the server. This application uses the `TcpClient` class to connect to the running server, and receives the returned message, displaying it in a text box. The user interface just contains a `Button` and a `TextBox`. The `Button` has the Click event assigned to the method OnGetQuote and the TextBox has the x:Name property set to textQuote.

Server and port information to connect to the server is configured with settings of the application. You can add settings with the Settings tab inside the properties of the project (see Figure 25-5). Here, you can define the ServerName and PortNumber settings, and define some default values. From here, with the Scope set to User, the settings go into a user-specific configuration file, and every user of the application can have different settings. This Settings feature of Visual Studio also creates a Settings class so that the settings can be read and written with a strongly typed class.

Name	Type	Scope	Value
ServerName	string	User	localhost
PortNumber	int	User	4567

FIGURE 25-5

You need to add the following using directives to your code:

```
using System;
using System.Net.Sockets;
using System.Text;
using System.Windows;
using System.Windows.Input;
```

code snippet QuoteClient/MainWindow.xaml.cs

The major functionality of the client lies in the handler for the click event of the Get Quote button:

```
protected void OnGetQuote(object sender, RoutedEventArgs e)
{
    const int bufferSize = 1024;
    Cursor currentCursor = this.Cursor;
    this.Cursor = Cursors.Wait;

    string serverName = Properties.Settings.Default.ServerName;
    int port = Properties.Settings.Default.PortNumber;

    var client = new TcpClient();
    NetworkStream stream = null;
    try
    {
        client.Connect(serverName, port);
        stream = client.GetStream();
        byte[] buffer = new byte[bufferSize];
        int received = stream.Read(buffer, 0, bufferSize);
        if (received <= 0)
        {
            return;
        }
        textQuote.Text = Encoding.Unicode.GetString(buffer).Trim('\0');
    }
    catch (SocketException ex)
    {
        MessageBox.Show(ex.Message, "Error Quote of the day",
                MessageBoxButton.OK, MessageBoxImage.Error);
    }
    finally
    {
        if (stream != null)
        {
            stream.Close();
        }
```

```
        if (client.Connected)
        {
            client.Close();
        }
    }
    this.Cursor = currentCursor;
}
```

After starting the test server and this Windows application client, you can test the functionality. Figure 25-6 shows a successful run of this application.

Next, you implement the service functionality in the server. The program is already running, so what else do you need? Well, the server program should be automatically started at boot time without anyone logged on to the system. You want to control this by using service control programs.

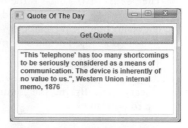

FIGURE 25-6

Windows Service Program

Using the new project template for C# Windows Services, you can now start to create a Windows Service program. For the new service, use the name QuoteService.

After you click the OK button to create the Windows Service program, you see the Designer surface. However, you can't insert any UI components because the application cannot directly display anything on the screen. The Designer surface is used later in this chapter to add other components, such as installation objects, performance counters, and event logging.

Selecting the properties of this service opens up the Properties editor window, where you can configure the following values:

➤ AutoLog specifies that events are automatically written to the event log for starting and stopping the service.

➤ CanPauseAndContinue, CanShutdown, and CanStop specify pause, continue, shut down, and stop requests.

➤ ServiceName is the name of the service written to the registry and is used to control the service.

➤ CanHandleSessionChangeEvent defines whether the service can handle change events from a terminal server session.

➤ CanHandlePowerEvent is a very useful option for services running on a laptop or mobile devices. If this option is enabled, the service can react to low-power events and change the behavior of the service accordingly. Examples of power events include battery low, power status change (because of a switch from or to A/C power), and change to suspend.

> *The default service name is* Service1, *regardless of what the project is called. You can install only one Service1 service. If you get installation errors during your testing process, you might already have installed one Service1 service. Therefore, make sure that you change the name of the service with the Properties editor to a more suitable name at the beginning of the service development.*

Changing these properties with the Properties editor sets the values of your ServiceBase-derived class in the InitalizeComponent() method. You already know this method from Windows Forms applications. It is used in a similar way with services.

A wizard generates the code, but change the filename to `QuoteService.cs`, the name of the namespace to `Wrox.ProCSharp.WinServices`, and the class name to `QuoteService`. The code of the service is discussed in detail shortly.

The ServiceBase Class

The `ServiceBase` class is the base class for all Windows Services developed with the .NET Framework. The class `QuoteService` is derived from `ServiceBase`; this class communicates with the SCM using an undocumented helper class, `System.ServiceProcess.NativeMethods`, which is just a wrapper class to the Win32 API calls. The class is internal, so it cannot be used in your code.

The sequence diagram in Figure 25-7 shows the interaction of the SCM, the class `QuoteService`, and the classes from the `System.ServiceProcess` namespace. In the sequence diagram, you can see the lifelines of objects vertically and the communication going on horizontally. The communication is time-ordered from top to bottom.

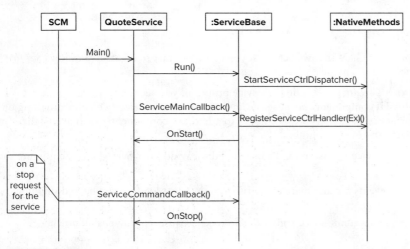

FIGURE 25-7

The SCM starts the process of a service that should be started. At startup, the `Main()` method is called. In the `Main()` method of the sample service, the `Run()` method of the base class `ServiceBase` is called. `Run()` registers the method `ServiceMainCallback()` using `NativeMethods.StartServiceCtrlDispatcher()` in the SCM and writes an entry to the event log.

Next, the SCM calls the registered method `ServiceMainCallback()` in the service program. `ServiceMainCallback()` itself registers the handler in the SCM using `NativeMethods.RegisterService CtrlHandler[Ex]()` and sets the status of the service in the SCM. Then the `OnStart()` method is called. In `OnStart()`, you need to implement the startup code. If `OnStart()` is successful, the string "Service started successfully" is written to the event log.

The handler is implemented in the `ServiceCommandCallback()` method. The SCM calls this method when changes are requested from the service. The `ServiceCommandCallback()` method routes the requests further to `OnPause()`, `OnContinue()`, `OnStop()`, `OnCustomCommand()`, and `OnPowerEvent()`.

Main Function

This section looks into the application template–generated main function of the service process. In the main function, an array of `ServiceBase` classes, `ServicesToRun`, is declared. One instance of the `QuoteService` class is created and passed as the first element to the `ServicesToRun` array. If more than one service should run inside this service process, it is necessary to add more instances of the specific service classes to the array. This array is then passed to the static `Run()` method of the `ServiceBase` class. With the `Run()` method of `ServiceBase`, you are giving the SCM references to the entry points of your services. The main thread of your service process is now blocked and waits for the service to terminate.

Here is the automatically generated code:

Available for
download on
Wrox.com

```
/// <summary>
/// The main entry point for the application.
/// </summary>
static void Main()
{
    ServiceBase[] ServicesToRun;
    ServicesToRun = new ServiceBase[]
    {
        new QuoteService()
    };
    ServiceBase.Run(ServicesToRun);
}
```

code snippet QuoteService/Program.cs

If there is only a single service in the process, the array can be removed; the `Run()` method accepts a single object derived from the class `ServiceBase`, so the `Main()` method can be reduced to this:

```
ServiceBase.Run(new QuoteService());
```

The service program `Services.exe` includes multiple services. If you have a similar service, where more than one service is running in a single process in which you must initialize some shared state for multiple services, the shared initialization must be done before the `Run()` method. With the `Run()` method, the main thread is blocked until the service process is stopped, and any following instructions would not be reached before the end of the service.

The initialization shouldn't take longer than 30 seconds. If the initialization code were to take longer than this, the SCM would assume that the service startup failed. You need to take into account the slowest machines where this service should run within the 30-second limit. If the initialization takes longer, you could start the initialization in a different thread so that the main thread calls `Run()` in time. An event object can then be used to signal that the thread has completed its work.

Service Start

At service start, the `OnStart()` method is called. In this method, you can start the previously created socket server. You must reference the `QuoteServer` assembly for the use of the `QuoteService`. The thread calling `OnStart()` cannot be blocked; this method must return to the caller, which is the `ServiceMainCallback()` method of the `ServiceBase` class. The `ServiceBase` class registers the handler and informs the SCM that the service started successfully after calling `OnStart()`:

Available for
download on
Wrox.com

```
protected override void OnStart(string[] args)
{
    quoteServer = new QuoteServer(
        Path.Combine(AppDomain.CurrentDomain.BaseDirectory, "quotes.txt"),
        5678);
    quoteServer.Start();
}
```

code snippet QuoteService/QuoteService.cs

The `quoteServer` variable is declared as a private member in the class:

```
namespace Wrox.ProCSharp.WinServices
{
    public partial class QuoteService: ServiceBase
    {
        private QuoteServer quoteServer;
```

Handler Methods

When the service is stopped, the `OnStop()` method is called. You should stop the service functionality in this method:

```
protected override void OnStop()
{
    quoteServer.Stop();
}
```

In addition to `OnStart()` and `OnStop()`, you can override the following handlers in the service class:

➤ `OnPause()` is called when the service should be paused.

➤ `OnContinue()` is called when the service should return to normal operation after being paused. To make it possible for the overridden methods `OnPause()` and `OnContinue()` to be called, the `CanPauseAndContinue` property must be set to `true`.

➤ `OnShutdown()` is called when Windows is undergoing system shutdown. Normally, the behavior of this method should be similar to the `OnStop()` implementation; if more time is needed for a shutdown, you can request additional time. Similarly to `OnPause()` and `OnContinue()`, a property must be set to enable this behavior: `CanShutdown` must be set to `true`.

➤ `OnPowerEvent()` is called when the power status of the system changes. The information about the change of the power status is in the argument of type `PowerBroadcastStatus`. `PowerBroadcastStatus` is an enumeration with values such as `Battery Low` and `PowerStatusChange`. Here, you will also get information if the system would like to suspend (`QuerySuspend`), where you can approve or deny the suspend. You can read more about power events later in this chapter.

➤ `OnCustomCommand()` is a handler that can serve custom commands that are sent by a service control program. The method signature of `OnCustomCommand()` has an int argument where you get the custom command number. The value can be in the range from 128 to 256; values below 128 are system-reserved values. In your service, you are re-reading the quotes file with the custom command 128:

```
protected override void OnPause()
{
    quoteServer.Suspend();
}

protected override void OnContinue()
{
    quoteServer.Resume();
}

public const int commandRefresh = 128;
protected override void OnCustomCommand(int command)
{
    switch (command)
    {
        case commandRefresh:
            quoteServer.RefreshQuotes();
            break;

        default:
```

```
                    break;
            }
        }
```

Threading and Services

As stated earlier in this chapter, the SCM assumes that the service failed if the initialization takes too long. To deal with this, you need to create a thread.

The `OnStart()` method in your service class must return in time. If you call a blocking method such as `AcceptSocket()` from the `TcpListener` class, you need to start a thread for doing this. With a networking server that deals with multiple clients, a thread pool is also very useful. `AcceptSocket()` should receive the call and hand the processing off to another thread from the pool. This way, no one waits for the execution of code and the system seems responsive.

Service Installation

A service must be configured in the registry. All services can be found in `HKEY_LOCAL_MACHINE\System\CurrentControlSet\Services`. You can view the registry entries by using `regedit`. The type of the service, display name, path to the executable, startup configuration, and so on, are all found here. Figure 25-8 shows the registry configuration of the W3SVC service.

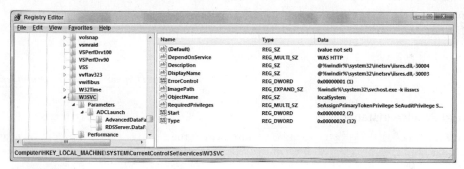

FIGURE 25-8

This configuration can be done by using the installer classes from the `System.ServiceProcess` namespace, as discussed in the following section.

Installation Program

You can add an installation program to the service by switching to the design view with Visual Studio and then selecting the Add Installer option from the context menu. With this option, a new `ProjectInstaller` class is created, and a `ServiceInstaller` and a `ServiceProcessInstaller` instance are created.

Figure 25-9 shows the class diagram of the installer classes for services.

With this diagram in mind, let's go through the source code in the file `ProjectInstaller.cs` that was created with the Add Installer option.

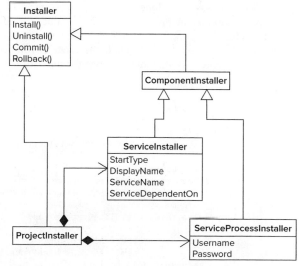

FIGURE 25-9

The Installer Class

The class `ProjectInstaller` is derived from `System.Configuration.Install.Installer`. This is the base class for all custom installers. With the `Installer` class, it is possible to build transaction-based installations. With a transaction-based installation, it is possible to roll back to the previous state if the installation fails, and any changes made by this installation up to that point will be undone. As you can see in Figure 25-9, the `Installer` class has `Install()`, `Uninstall()`, `Commit()`, and `Rollback()` methods, and they are called from installation programs.

The attribute `[RunInstaller(true)]` means that the class `ProjectInstaller` should be invoked when installing an assembly. Custom action installers, as well as `installutil.exe` (which is used later in this chapter), check for this attribute.

`InitializeComponent()` is called inside the constructor of the `ProjectInstaller` class:

Available for download on Wrox.com

```
using System.ComponentModel;
using System.Configuration.Install;

namespace Wrox.ProCSharp.WinServices
{
    [RunInstaller(true)]
    public partial class ProjectInstaller: Installer
    {
        public ProjectInstaller()
        {
            InitializeComponent();
        }
    }
}
```

code snippet QuoteService/ ProjectInstaller.cs

Process Installer and Service Installer

Within the implementation of `InitializeComponent()`, instances of the `ServiceProcessInstaller` class and the `ServiceInstaller` class are created. Both of these classes derive from the `ComponentInstaller` class, which itself derives from `Installer`.

Classes derived from `ComponentInstaller` can be used with an installation process. Remember that a service process can include more than one service. The `ServiceProcessInstaller` class is used for the configuration of the process that defines values for all services in this process, and the `ServiceInstaller` class is for the configuration of the service, so one instance of `ServiceInstaller` is required for each service. If three services are inside the process, you need to add `ServiceInstaller` objects — three `ServiceInstaller` instances are needed in that case:

Available for download on Wrox.com

```
partial class ProjectInstaller
{
    /// <summary>
    /// Required designer variable.
    /// </summary>
    private System.ComponentModel.IContainer components = null;

    /// <summary>
    /// Required method for Designer supportdo not modify
    /// the contents of this method with the code editor.
    /// </summary>
    private void InitializeComponent()
    {
        this.serviceProcessInstaller1 =
                new System.ServiceProcess.ServiceProcessInstaller();
        this.serviceInstaller1 =
```

- Creating a Windows Service Program | **681**

```
                new System.ServiceProcess.ServiceInstaller();
    //
    // serviceProcessInstaller1
    //
    this.serviceProcessInstaller1.Password = null;
    this.serviceProcessInstaller1.Username = null;
    //
    // serviceInstaller1
    //
    this.serviceInstaller1.ServiceName = "QuoteService";
    //
    // ProjectInstaller
    //
    this.Installers.AddRange(
        new System.Configuration.Install.Installer[]
          {this.serviceProcessInstaller1,
            this.serviceInstaller1});
    }

    private System.ServiceProcess.ServiceProcessInstaller
                serviceProcessInstaller1;
    private System.ServiceProcess.ServiceInstaller serviceInstaller1;

  }
```

code snippet QuoteService/ProjectInstaller.Designer.cs

`ServiceProcessInstaller` installs an executable that implements the class `ServiceBase`
. `ServiceProcessInstaller` has properties for the complete process. The following table explains the
properties shared by all the services inside the process.

PROPERTY	DESCRIPTION
Username, Password	Indicates the user account under which the service runs if the `Account` property is set to `ServiceAccount.User`.
Account	With this property, you can specify the account type of the service.
HelpText	`HelpText` is a read-only property that returns the help text for setting the username and password.

The process that is used to run the service can be specified with the `Account` property of the
`ServiceProcessInstaller` class using the `ServiceAccount` enumeration. The following table explains
the different values of the `Account` property.

VALUE	MEANING
LocalSystem	Setting this value specifies that the service uses a highly privileged user account on the local system, and acts as the computer on the network.
NetworkService	Similarly to `LocalSystem`, this value specifies that the computer's credentials are passed to remote servers, but unlike `LocalSystem`, such a service acts as a non-privileged user on the local system. As the name implies, this account should be used only for services that need resources from the network.
LocalService	This account type presents anonymous credentials to any remote server and has the same privileges locally as `NetworkService`.
User	Setting the `Account` property to `ServiceAccount.User` means that you can define the account that should be used from the service.

`ServiceInstaller` is the class needed for every service; it has the following properties for each service inside a process: `StartType`, `DisplayName`, `ServiceName`, and `ServicesDependentOn`, as described in the following table.

PROPERTY	DESCRIPTION
StartType	The `StartType` property indicates whether the service is manually or automatically started. Possible values are `ServiceStartMode.Automatic`, `ServiceStartMode.Manual`, and `ServiceStartMode.Disabled`. With `ServiceStartMode.Disabled`, the service cannot be started. This option is useful for services that shouldn't be started on a system. You might want to set the option to `Disabled` if, for example, a required hardware controller is not available.
DelayedAutoStart	This property is ignored if the `StartType` is not set to `Automatic`. Here you can specify if the service should not be started immediately when the system boots but afterwards. This feature for Windows Services is new with .NET 4 and supported by the operating system since Windows Vista.
DisplayName	`DisplayName` is the friendly name of the service that is displayed to the user. This name is also used by management tools that control and monitor the service.
ServiceName	`ServiceName` is the name of the service. This value must be identical to the `ServiceName` property of the `ServiceBase` class in the service program. This name associates the configuration of the `ServiceInstaller` to the required service program.
ServicesDependentOn	Specifies an array of services that must be started before this service can be started. When the service is started, all these dependent services are started automatically, and then your service will start.

If you change the name of the service in the `ServiceBase`-derived class, be sure to also change the `ServiceName` property in the `ServiceInstaller` object!

In the testing phases, set `StartType` to `Manual`. This way, if you can't stop the service (for example, when it has a bug), you still have the possibility to reboot the system. But if you have `StartType` set to `Automatic`, the service would be started automatically with the reboot! You can change this configuration at a later time when you are sure that it works.

The ServiceInstallerDialog Class

Another installer class in the `System.ServiceProcess.Design` namespace is `ServiceInstallerDialog`. This class can be used if you want the System Administrator to enter the account that should be used by the service by assigning the username and password during the installation.

If you set the `Account` property of the class `ServiceProcessInstaller` to `ServiceAccount.User` and the `Username` and `Password` properties to `null`, you will see the Set Service Login dialog box at installation time (see Figure 25-10). You can also cancel the installation at this point.

Set Service Login	
Username:	
Password:	
Confirm password:	
	OK Cancel

FIGURE 25-10

installutil

After adding the installer classes to the project, you can use the `installutil.exe` utility to install and uninstall the service. This utility can be used to install any assembly that has an `Installer` class. The `installutil.exe` utility calls the method `Install()` of the class that derives from the `Installer` class for installation, and `Uninstall()` for the *uninstallation*.

The command-line inputs for the installation and uninstallation of our service are as follows:

```
installutil quoteservice.exe
installutil /u quoteservice.exe
```

 If the installation fails, be sure to check the installation log files, `InstallUtil.` `InstallLog` *and* `<servicename>.InstallLog`. *Often, you can find very useful information, such as "The specified service already exists."*

Client

After the service has been successfully installed, you can start the service manually from the Services MMC (see the next section for further details), and then you can start the client application.

MONITORING AND CONTROLLING WINDOWS SERVICES

To monitor and control Windows Services, you can use the Services Microsoft Management Console (MMC) snap-in that is part of the Computer Management administration tool. Every Windows system also has a command-line utility, `net.exe`, which allows you to control services. Another Windows command-line utility is `sc.exe`. This utility has much more functionality than `net.exe`. You can also control services directly from the Visual Studio Server Explorer. In this section, you also create a small Windows application that makes use of the `System.ServiceProcess.ServiceController` class to monitor and control services.

MMC Snap-in

Using the Services snap-in to the MMC, you can view the status of all services (see Figure 25-11). It is also possible to send control requests to services to stop, enable, or disable them, as well as to change their configuration. The Services snap-in is a service control program as well as a service configuration program.

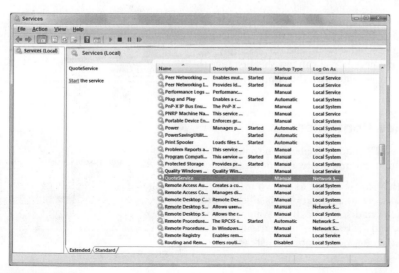

FIGURE 25-11

When you double-click QuoteService, you get the
Properties dialog box shown in Figure 25-12. This dialog
box enables you to view the service name, the description,
the path to the executable, the startup type, and the
status. The service is currently started. The account for
the service process can be changed with the Log On tab in
this dialog box.

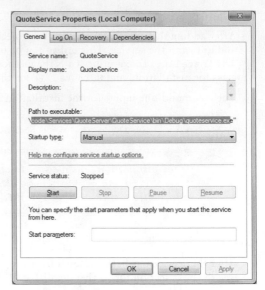

FIGURE 25-12

net.exe Utility

The Services snap-in is easy to use, but the system
administrator cannot automate it because it is not usable
within an administrative script. Controlling services with
a tool that can be automated with a script, you can use the
command-line utility net.exe. The net start command
shows all running services, net start servicename
starts a service, and net stop servicename sends a stop
request to the service. It is also possible to pause and to
continue a service with net pause and net continue
(only if the service allows it, of course).

sc.exe Utility

Another little-known utility delivered as part of the operating system is sc.exe. This is a great tool to play
with services. Much more can be done with sc.exe than with the net.exe utility. With sc.exe, you can
check the actual status of a service, or configure, remove, and add services. This tool also facilitates the
deinstallation of the service, if it fails to function correctly.

Visual Studio Server Explorer

You can also control services using the Server Explorer within Visual Studio by selecting Services. The
Services item is listed in the tree view with the first element Servers; below that you can find the name of
your computer, and below that there's the Services item. By selecting a service and opening the context
menu, you can start or stop a service. This context menu can also be used to add a ServiceController
class to the project.

To control a specific service in your application, drag and drop a service from the Server Explorer to the
Designer: a ServiceController instance is added to the application. The properties of this object are
automatically set to access the selected service, and the assembly
System.ServiceProcess is referenced. You can use this instance to
control a service in the same way you can with the application that you
develop in the next section.

Writing a Custom Service Controller

In this section, you create a small Windows application that uses the
ServiceController class to monitor and control Windows Services.

Create a WPF application with a user interface as shown in
Figure 25-13. The main window of this application has a list box to
show all services, four text boxes to display the display name, status,
type, and name of the service, and six buttons. Four buttons are used
to send control events, one button for a refresh of the list, and one
button to exit the application.

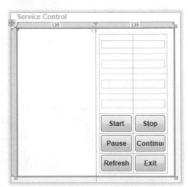

FIGURE 25-13

You can read more about WPF in Chapter 35, "Core WPF."

Monitoring the Service

With the `ServiceController` class, you can get the information about each service. The following table shows the properties of the `ServiceController` class.

PROPERTY	DESCRIPTION
CanPauseAndContinue	Returns true if pause and continue requests can be sent to the service.
CanShutdown	Returns true if the service has a handler for a system shutdown.
CanStop	Returns true if the service is stoppable.
DependentServices	Returns a collection of dependent services. If the service is stopped, then all dependent services are stopped beforehand.
ServicesDependentOn	Returns a collection of the services that this service depends on.
DisplayName	Specifies the name that should be displayed for this service.
MachineName	Specifies the name of the machine that the service runs on.
ServiceName	Specifies the name of the service.
ServiceType	Specifies the type of the service. The service can be run inside a shared process where more than one service uses the same process (Win32ShareProcess), or run in such a way that there is just one service in a process (Win32OwnProcess). If the service can interact with the desktop, the type is InteractiveProcess.
Status	Specifies the status of the service. The status can be running, stopped, paused, or in some intermediate mode such as start pending, stop pending, and so on. The status values are defined in the enumeration ServiceControllerStatus.

In the sample application, the properties `DisplayName`, `ServiceName`, `ServiceType`, and `Status` are used to display the service information. Also, `CanPauseAndContinue` and `CanStop` are used to enable or disable the Pause, Continue, and Stop buttons.

To get all the needed information for the user interface, the class `ServiceControllerInfo` is created. This class can be used for data binding and offers status information, the name of the service, the service type, and the information about which buttons to control the service should be enabled or disabled.

Because the class `System.ServiceProcess.ServiceController` *is used, you must reference the assembly* `System.ServiceProcess`.

`ServiceControllerInfo` contains an embedded `ServiceController` that is set with the constructor of the `ServiceControllerInfo` class. There is also a read-only property `Controller` to access the embedded `ServiceController`:

```csharp
public class ServiceControllerInfo
{
    private readonly ServiceController controller;

    public ServiceControllerInfo(ServiceController controller)
    {
        this.controller = controller;
    }

    public ServiceController Controller
    {
        get { return controller; }
    }
```

code snippet ServiceControl/ServiceControllerInfo.cs

To display current information about the service, the `ServiceControllerInfo` class has the read-only properties `DisplayName`, `ServiceName`, `ServiceTypeName`, and `ServiceStatusName`. The implementation of the properties `DisplayName` and `ServiceName` just accesses the properties `DisplayName` and `ServiceName` of the underlying `ServiceController` class. With the implementation of the properties `ServiceTypeName` and `ServiceStatusName`, more work is done — the status and type of the service cannot be returned that easily because a string should be displayed instead of a number, which is what the `ServiceController` class returns. The property `ServiceTypeName` returns a string that represents the type of the service. The `ServiceType` you get from the property `ServiceController` `.ServiceType` represents a set of flags that can be combined by using the bitwise OR operator. The `InteractiveProcess` bit can be set together with `Win32OwnProcess` and `Win32ShareProcess`. So, first it is checked if the `InteractiveProcess` bit is set before continuing to check for the other values. With services, the string returned will be "`Win32 Service Process`" or "`Win32 Shared Process`":

```csharp
public string ServiceTypeName
{
    get
    {
        ServiceType type = controller.ServiceType;
        string serviceTypeName = "";
        if ((type & ServiceType.InteractiveProcess) != 0)
        {
            serviceTypeName = "Interactive ";
            type -= ServiceType.InteractiveProcess;
        }
        switch (type)
        {
            case ServiceType.Adapter:
                serviceTypeName += "Adapter";
                break;

            case ServiceType.FileSystemDriver:
            case ServiceType.KernelDriver:
            case ServiceType.RecognizerDriver:
                serviceTypeName += "Driver";
                break;

            case ServiceType.Win32OwnProcess:
                serviceTypeName += "Win32 Service Process";
                break;

            case ServiceType.Win32ShareProcess:
```

```
                    serviceTypeName += "Win32 Shared Process";
                    break;

                default:
                    serviceTypeName += "unknown type " + type.ToString();
                    break;
            }
            return serviceTypeName;
        }
    }

    public string ServiceStatusName
    {
        get
        {
            switch (controller.Status)
            {
                case ServiceControllerStatus.ContinuePending:
                    return "Continue Pending";
                case ServiceControllerStatus.Paused:
                    return "Paused";
                case ServiceControllerStatus.PausePending:
                    return "Pause Pending";
                case ServiceControllerStatus.StartPending:
                    return "Start Pending";
                case ServiceControllerStatus.Running:
                    return "Running";
                case ServiceControllerStatus.Stopped:
                    return "Stopped";
                case ServiceControllerStatus.StopPending:
                    return "Stop Pending";
                default:
                    return "Unknown status";
            }
        }
    }

    public string DisplayName
    {
        get { return controller.DisplayName; }
    }

    public string ServiceName
    {
        get { return controller.ServiceName; }
    }
```

The ServiceControllerInfo class has some more properties to enable the Start, Stop, Pause, and Continue buttons: EnableStart, EnableStop, EnablePause, and EnableContinue. These properties return a Boolean value according to the current status of the service:

```
    public bool EnableStart
    {
        get
        {
            return controller.Status == ServiceControllerStatus.Stopped;
        }
    }

    public bool EnableStop
    {
        get
        {
```

```
            return controller.Status == ServiceControllerStatus.Running;
        }
    }

    public bool EnablePause
    {
        get
        {
            return controller.Status == ServiceControllerStatus.Running &&
                controller.CanPauseAndContinue;
        }
    }

    public bool EnableContinue
    {
        get
        {
            return controller.Status == ServiceControllerStatus.Paused;
        }
    }
}
```

In the `ServiceControlWindow` class, the method `RefreshServiceList()` gets all the services using `ServiceController.GetServices()` for display in the list box. The `GetServices()` method returns an array of `ServiceController` instances representing all Windows Services installed on the operating system. The `ServiceController` class also has the static method `GetDevices()` that returns a `ServiceController` array representing all device drivers. The returned array is sorted with the help of the generic `Array.Sort()` method. The sort is done by the `DisplayName` as is defined with the Lambda expression that is passed to the `Sort()` method. Using `Array.ConvertAll()`, the `ServiceController` instances are converted to the type `ServiceControllerInfo`. Here, a Lambda expression is passed that invokes the `ServiceControllerInfo` constructor for every `ServiceController` object. Last, the `ServiceControllerInfo` array is assigned to the `DataContext` property of the window for data binding:

```
protected void RefreshServiceList()
{
    ServiceController[] services = ServiceController.GetServices();

    Array.Sort(services, (s1, s2) =>
                s1.DisplayName.CompareTo(s2.DisplayName));

    this.DataContext =
        Array.ConvertAll(services, controller =>
            new ServicesControllerInfo(controller));
}
```

code snippet ServiceControl/ServiceControlWindow.xaml.cs

The method `RefreshServiceList()` to get all the services in the list box is called within the constructor of the class `ServiceControlWindow`. The constructor also defines the event handler for the `Click` event of the buttons:

```
public ServiceControlWindow()
{
    InitializeComponent();

    RefreshServiceList();
}
```

Now, you can define the XAML code to bind the information to the controls.

First, a `DataTemplate` is defined for the information that is shown inside the `ListBox`. The `ListBox` will contain a `Label` where the `Content` is bound to the `DisplayName` property of the data source. As you bind an array of `ServiceControllerInfo` objects, the property `DisplayName` is defined with the `ServiceControllerInfo` class:

Available for download on Wrox.com

```xml
<Window.Resources>
  <DataTemplate x:Key="listTemplate">
    <Label Content="{Binding Path=DisplayName}"/>
  </DataTemplate>
</Window.Resources>
```

code snippet ServiceControl/ServiceControlWindow.xaml

The `ListBox` that is placed in the left side of the Window sets the `ItemsSource` property to `{Binding}`. This way, the data that is shown in the list is received from the `DataContext` property that was set in the `RefreshServiceList()` method. The `ItemTemplate` property references the resource `listTemplate` that is defined with the `DataTemplate` shown earlier. The property `IsSynchronizedWithCurrentItem` is set to `True` so that the `TextBox` and `Button` controls that are inside the same Window are bound to the current item that is selected with the `ListBox`:

```xml
<ListBox Grid.Row="0" Grid.Column="0" HorizontalAlignment="Left"
    Name="listBoxServices" VerticalAlignment="Top"
    ItemsSource="{Binding}"
    ItemTemplate="{StaticResource listTemplate}"
    IsSynchronizedWithCurrentItem="True">
</ListBox>
```

With the `TextBlock` controls, the `Text` property is bound to the corresponding property of the `ServiceControllerInfo` instance. Whether the `Button` controls are enabled or disabled is also defined from the data binding by binding the `IsEnabled` property to the corresponding properties of the `ServiceControllerInfo` instance that return a Boolean value:

```xml
<TextBlock Grid.Row="0" Grid.ColumnSpan="2" Name="textDisplayName"
    Text="{Binding Path=DisplayName, Mode=OneTime}" />
<TextBlock Grid.Row="1" Grid.ColumnSpan="2" Name="textStatus"
    Text="{Binding Path=ServiceStatusName, Mode=OneTime}" />
<TextBlock Grid.Row="2" Grid.ColumnSpan="2" Name="textType"
    Text="{Binding Path=ServiceTypeName, Mode=OneTime}" />
<TextBlock Grid.Row="3" Grid.ColumnSpan="2" Name="textName"
    Text="{Binding Path=ServiceName, Mode=OneTime}" />
<Button Grid.Row="4" Grid.Column="0" Name="buttonStart" Content="Start"
    IsEnabled="{Binding Path=EnableStart, Mode=OneTime}"
    Click="OnServiceCommand" />
<Button Grid.Row="4" Grid.Column="1" Name="buttonStop" Content="Stop"
    IsEnabled="{Binding Path=EnableStop, Mode=OneTime}"
    Click="OnServiceCommand" />
<Button Grid.Row="5" Grid.Column="0" Name="buttonPause" Content="Pause"
    IsEnabled="{Binding Path=EnablePause, Mode=OneTime}"
    Click="OnServiceCommand" />
<Button Grid.Row="5" Grid.Column="1" Name="buttonContinue"
    Content="Continue" IsEnabled="{Binding Path=EnableContinue,
    Mode=OneTime}" Click="OnServiceCommand" />
<Button Grid.Row="6" Grid.Column="0" Name="buttonRefresh" Content="Refresh"
    Click="OnRefresh" />
<Button Grid.Row="6" Grid.Column="1" Name="buttonExit"
    Content="Exit" Click="OnExit" />
```

Controlling the Service

With the `ServiceController` class, you can also send control requests to the service. The following table explains the methods that can be applied.

METHOD	DESCRIPTION
`Start()`	`Start()` tells the SCM that the service should be started. In the example service program, `OnStart()` is called.
`Stop()`	`Stop()` calls `OnStop()` in the example service program with the help of the SCM if the property `CanStop` is `true` in the service class.
`Pause()`	`Pause()` calls `OnPause()` if the property `CanPauseAndContinue` is `true`.
`Continue()`	`Continue()` calls `OnContinue()` if the property `CanPauseAndContinue` is `true`.
`ExecuteCommand()`	With `ExecuteCommand()`, it is possible to send a custom command to the service.

The following code controls the services. Because the code for starting, stopping, suspending, and pausing is similar, only one handler is used for the four buttons:

```csharp
protected void OnServiceCommand(object sender, RoutedEventArgs e)
{
    Cursor oldCursor = this.Cursor;
    try
    {
        this.Cursor = Cursors.Wait;
        ServiceControllerInfo si =
                (ServiceControllerInfo)listBoxServices.SelectedItem;
        if (sender == this.buttonStart)
        {
            si.Controller.Start();
            si.Controller.WaitForStatus(ServiceControllerStatus.Running,
                TimeSpan.FromSeconds(10));
        }
        else if (sender == this.buttonStop)
        {
            si.Controller.Stop();
            si.Controller.WaitForStatus(ServiceControllerStatus.Stopped,
                TimeSpan.FromSeconds(10));
        }
        else if (sender == this.buttonPause)
        {
            si.Controller.Pause();
            si.Controller.WaitForStatus(ServiceControllerStatus.Paused,
                TimeSpan.FromSeconds(10));
        }
        else if (sender == this.buttonContinue)
        {
            si.Controller.Continue();
            si.Controller.WaitForStatus(ServiceControllerStatus.Running,
                TimeSpan.FromSeconds(10));
        }
        int index = listBoxServices.SelectedIndex;
        RefreshServiceList();
        listBoxServices.SelectedIndex = index;
    }
    catch (System.ServiceProcess.TimeoutException ex)
```

```
        {
            MessageBox.Show(ex.Message, "Timout Service Controller",
                MessageBoxButton.OK, MessageBoxImage.Error);
        }
        catch (InvalidOperationException ex)
        {
            MessageBox.Show(String.Format("{0} {1}", ex.Message,
                ex.InnerException != null ? ex.InnerException.Message :
                                            String.Empty),
                MessageBoxButton.OK, MessageBoxImage.Error);
        }
        finally
        {
            this.Cursor = oldCursor;
        }
    }

    protected void OnExit(object sender, RoutedEventArgs e)
    {
        Application.Current.Shutdown();
    }

    protected void OnRefresh_Click(object sender, RoutedEventArgs e)
    {
        RefreshServiceList();
    }
```

code snippet ServiceControl/ServiceControlWindow.xaml.cs

Because the action of controlling the services can take some time, the cursor is switched to the wait cursor in the first statement. Then a ServiceController method is called depending on the pressed button. With the WaitForStatus() method, you are waiting to check that the service changes the status to the requested value, but you only wait 10 seconds maximum. After this time, the information in the ListBox is refreshed, and the same service as before is selected. The new status of this service is then displayed.

Because the application requires administrative privileges, as most services require that for starting and stopping, an application manifest with the requestedExecutionLevel set to requireAdministrator is added to the project:

Available for
download on
Wrox.com

```
<?xml version="1.0" encoding="utf-8"?>
<asmv1:assembly manifestVersion="1.0"
    xmlns="urn:schemas-microsoft-com:asm.v1"
    xmlns:asmv1="urn:schemas-microsoft-com:asm.v1"
    xmlns:asmv2="urn:schemas-microsoft-com:asm.v2"
    xmlns:xsi="http://www.w3.org/2001/XMLSchema-instance">
  <assemblyIdentity version="1.0.0.0" name="MyApplication.app"/>
  <trustInfo xmlns="urn:schemas-microsoft-com:asm.v2">
    <security>
      <requestedPrivileges xmlns="urn:schemas-microsoft-com:asm.v3">
        <requestedExecutionLevel level="requireAdministrator" uiAccess="false" />
      </requestedPrivileges>
    </security>
  </trustInfo>
</asmv1:assembly>
```

code snippet ServiceControl/app.manifest

Figure 25-14 shows the completed, running application.

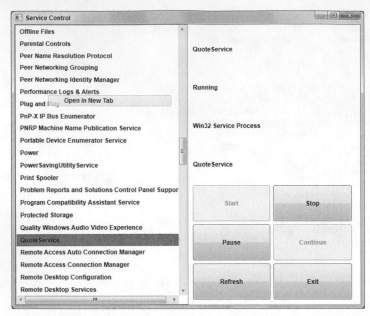

FIGURE 25-14

TROUBLESHOOTING AND EVENT LOGGING

Troubleshooting services is different from troubleshooting normal applications. This section touches on some service issues, problems specific to interactive services, and event logging.

The best way to start building a service is to create an assembly with the functionality you want and a test client, before the service is actually created. Here, you can do normal debugging and error handling. As soon as the application is running, you can build a service by using this assembly. Of course, there might still be problems with the service:

➤ Don't display errors in a message box from the service (except for interactive services that are running on the client system). Instead, use the event logging service to write errors to the event log. Of course, in the client application that uses the service, you can display a message box to inform the user about errors.

➤ The service cannot be started from within a debugger, but a debugger can be attached to the running service process. Open the solution with the source code of the service and set breakpoints. From the Visual Studio Debug menu, select Processes and attach the running process of the service.

➤ The Performance Monitor can be used to monitor the activity of services. You can add your own performance objects to the service. This can add some useful information for debugging. For example, with the Quote service, you could set up an object to give the total number of quotes returned, the time it takes to initialize, and so on.

Services can report errors and other information by adding events to the event log. A service class derived from `ServiceBase` automatically logs events when the `AutoLog` property is set to `true`. The `ServiceBase` class checks this property and writes a log entry at start, stop, pause, and continue requests.

Figure 25-15 shows an example of a log entry from a service.

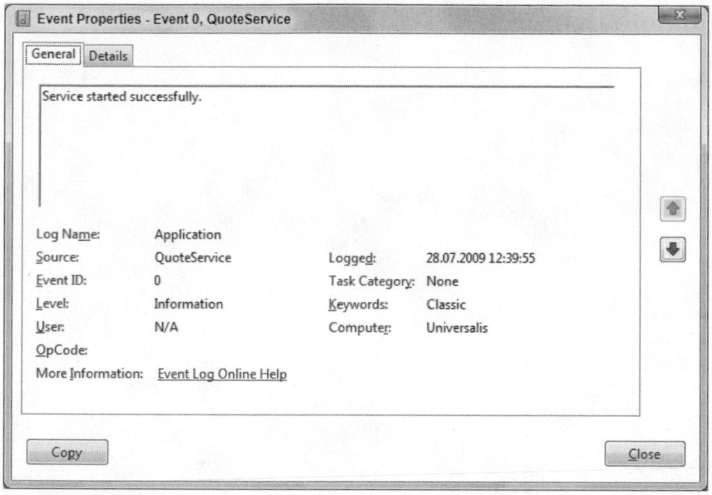

FIGURE 25-15

> *You can read more about event logging and how to write custom events in Chapter 19, "Instrumentation."*

SUMMARY

In this chapter, you have seen the architecture of Windows Services and how you can create them with the .NET Framework. Applications can start automatically at boot time with Windows Services, and you can use a privileged system account as the user of the service. Windows Services are built from a main function, a service-main function, and a handler, and you've seen other relevant programs in regard to Windows Services, such as a service control program and a service installation program.

The .NET Framework has great support for Windows Services. All the plumbing code that is necessary for building, controlling, and installing services is built into the .NET Framework classes in the `System.ServiceProcess` namespace. By deriving a class from `ServiceBase`, you can override methods that are invoked when the service is paused, resumed, or stopped. For installation of services, the classes `ServiceProcessInstaller` and `ServiceInstaller` deal with all registry configurations needed for services. You can also control and monitor services by using `ServiceController`.

The next chapter gives you information about interop with native code. Behind the scenes, many .NET classes make use of native code. For example, the `ServiceBase` class wraps the Windows API `CreateService()`. With the next chapter, you learn how to use native methods and COM objects from your own classes.

26

Interop

WHAT'S IN THIS CHAPTER?

➤ COM and .NET technologies

➤ Using COM objects from within .NET applications

➤ Using .NET components from within COM clients

➤ Platform invoke for Invoking native methods

If you have Windows programs written prior to .NET, you probably don't have the time and resources to rewrite everything for .NET. Sometimes rewriting code is useful for refactoring or rethinking the application architecture. A rewrite can also help with productivity in the long term, when adding new features is easier to do with the new technology. However, there is no reason to rewrite old code just because a new technology is available. You might have thousands of lines of existing, running code, which would require too much effort to rewrite just to move it into the managed environment.

The same applies to Microsoft. With the namespace System.DirectoryServices, Microsoft hasn't rewritten the COM objects accessing the hierarchical data store; the classes inside this namespace are wrappers accessing the ADSI COM objects instead. The same thing happens with System.Data.OleDb, where the OLE DB providers that are used by classes from this namespace do have quite complex COM interfaces.

The same issue may apply to your own solutions. If you have existing COM objects that should be used from .NET applications, or the other way around, if you want to write .NET components that should be used in old COM clients, this chapter is a starter for using COM interoperability (or *interop*).

If you don't have existing COM components you want to integrate with your application, or old COM clients that should use some .NET components, you can skip this chapter.

Like all other chapters, you can download the sample code for this chapter from the Wrox web site at www.wrox.com.

.NET AND COM

COM is the predecessor technology to .NET. COM defines a component model where components can be written in different programming languages. A component written with C++ can be used from a Visual Basic client. Components can also be used locally inside a process, across processes, or across the network. Does this sound familiar? Of course, .NET has similar goals. However, the way in which these goals are achieved is different. The COM concepts became more and more complex to use and turned out not to be extensible enough. .NET fulfills goals similar to those of COM but introduces new concepts to make your job easier.

Even today, when using COM interop the prerequisite is to know COM. It doesn't matter if .NET components are used by COM clients or if COM components are used by .NET applications — you must know COM. So, this section compares COM and .NET functionality.

If you already have a good grasp of COM technologies, this section may refresh your COM knowledge. Otherwise, it introduces you to the concepts of COM — that now, using .NET, you happily don't have to deal with anymore in your daily work. However, all the problems that came with COM still apply when COM technology is integrated into .NET applications.

COM and .NET do have many similar concepts, with very different approaches to using them, including:

➤ Metadata
➤ Freeing memory
➤ Interfaces
➤ Method binding
➤ Data types
➤ Registration
➤ Threading
➤ Error handling
➤ Event handling

These concepts, plus the marshaling mechanism, are covered in the following sections.

Metadata

With COM, all information about the component is stored inside the type library. The type library includes information such as names and IDs of interfaces, methods, and arguments. With .NET, all this information can be found inside the assembly itself, as you saw in Chapter 14, "Reflection," and Chapter 18, "Assemblies." The problem with COM is that the type library is not extensible. With C++, IDL (Interface Definition Language) files have been used to describe the interfaces and methods. Some of the IDL modifiers cannot be found inside the type library, because Visual Basic (and the Visual Basic team was responsible for the type library) couldn't use these IDL modifiers. With .NET, this problem doesn't exist because the .NET metadata is extensible using custom attributes.

As a result of this behavior, some COM components have a type library and others don't. When no type library is available, a C++ header file can be used that describes the interfaces and methods. With .NET, it is easier to use COM components that do have a type library, but it is also possible to use COM components without a type library. In that case, it is necessary to redefine the COM interface by using C# code.

Freeing Memory

With .NET, memory is released by the garbage collector. This is completely different with COM. COM relies on reference counts.

The interface IUnknown, which is the interface that is required to be implemented by every COM object, offers three methods. Two of these methods are related to reference counts. The method AddRef() must be called by the client if another interface pointer is needed; this method increments the reference count. The method Release() decrements the reference count, and if the resulting reference count is 0, the object destroys itself to free the memory.

Interfaces

Interfaces are the heart of COM. They distinguish between a contract used between the client and the object, and the implementation. The interface (the contract) defines the methods that are offered by the component and that can be used by the client. With .NET, interfaces play an important part, too.

COM distinguishes among three interface types: *custom*, *dispatch*, and *dual* interfaces.

Custom Interfaces

Custom interfaces derive from the interface IUnknown. A custom interface defines the order of the methods in a *virtual table* (*vtable*), so that the client can access the methods of the interface directly. This also means that the client needs to know the vtable during development time, because binding to the methods happens by using memory addresses. As a result, custom interfaces cannot be used by scripting clients. Figure 26-1 shows the vtable of the custom interface IMath, which provides the methods Add() and Sub() in addition to the methods of the IUnknown interface.

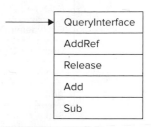

FIGURE 26-1

Dispatch Interfaces

Because a scripting client (and earlier Visual Basic clients) doesn't support custom interfaces, a different interface type is needed. With dispatch interfaces, the interface available for the client is always the IDispatch interface. IDispatch derives from IUnknown and offers four methods in addition to the IUnknown methods. The two most important methods are GetIDsOfNames() and Invoke(). As shown in Figure 26-2, with a dispatch interface two tables are needed. The first one maps the method or property name to a dispatch ID; the second one maps the dispatch ID to the implementation of the method or property.

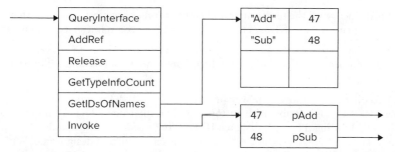

FIGURE 26-2

When the client invokes a method in the component, it first calls the method GetIDsOfNames(), passing the name of the method it wants to call. GetIDsOfNames() makes a lookup into the name-to-ID table to return the dispatch ID. This ID is used by the client to call the Invoke() method.

 Usually, the two tables for the IDispatch interface are stored inside the type library, but this is not a requirement, and some components have the tables in other places.

Dual Interfaces

As you can imagine, on one hand, dispatch interfaces are a lot slower than custom interfaces. On the other hand, custom interfaces cannot be used by scripting clients. A dual interface can solve this dilemma. As you can see in Figure 26-3, a dual interface is derived from IDispatch but provides the additional methods of the interface directly in the vtable. Scripting clients can use the IDispatch interface to invoke the Add and Sub methods, whereas clients aware of the vtable can call the Add and Sub methods directly.

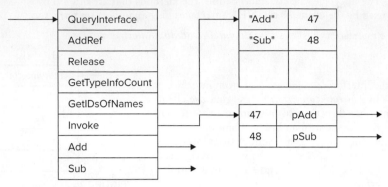

FIGURE 26-3

Casting and QueryInterface

If a .NET class implements multiple interfaces, casts can be done to get one interface or another. With COM, the interface IUnknown offers a similar mechanism with the method QueryInterface(). As discussed in the previous section, the interface IUnknown is the base interface of every interface, so QueryInterface() is available anyway.

Method Binding

How a client maps to a method is defined with the terms *early* and *late binding*. Late binding means that the method to invoke is looked for during runtime. .NET uses the System.Reflection namespace to make this possible (see Chapter 14).

COM uses the IDispatch interface discussed earlier for late binding. Late binding is possible with dispatch and dual interfaces.

With COM, early binding has two different options. One way of early binding, also known as vtable binding, is to use the vtable directly — this is possible with custom and dual interfaces. The second option for early binding is also known as ID binding. Here the dispatch ID is stored inside the client code, so during runtime only a call to Invoke() is necessary. GetIdsOfNames() is called during design time. With such clients, it is important to remember that the dispatch ID must not be changed.

Data Types

For dual and dispatch interfaces, the data types that can be used with COM are restricted to a list of automation-compatible data types. The Invoke() method of the IDispatch interface accepts an array of VARIANT data types. The VARIANT is a union of many different data types, such as BYTE, SHORT, LONG, FLOAT, DOUBLE, BSTR, IUnknown*, IDispatch*, and so on. VARIANTs have been easy to use from Visual Basic, but it was complex to use them from C++. .NET has the Object class instead of VARIANTs.

With custom interfaces, all data types available with C++ can be used with COM. However, this also restricts the clients that can use this component to certain programming languages.

Registration

.NET distinguishes between private and shared assemblies, as discussed in Chapter 18. With COM, all components are globally available through a registry configuration.

All COM objects have a unique identifier that consists of a 128-bit number and is also known as class ID (CLSID). The COM API call to create COM objects, CoCreateInstance(), just looks into the registry to find the CLSID and the path to the DLL or EXE to load the DLL or launch the EXE and instantiate the component.

Because such a 128-bit number cannot be easily remembered, many COM objects also have a ProgID. The ProgID is an easy-to-remember name, such as Excel.Application, that just maps to the CLSID.

In addition to the CLSID, COM objects also have a unique identifier for each interface (IID) and for the type library (typelib ID).

Information in the registry is discussed in more detail later in the chapter.

Threading

COM uses apartment models to relieve the programmer of having to deal with threading issues. However, this also adds some more complexity. Different apartment types have been added with different releases of the operating system. This section discusses the single-threaded apartment and the multithreaded apartment.

 Threading with .NET is discussed in Chapter 20, "Threads, Tasks, and Synchronization."

Single-Threaded Apartment

The *single-threaded apartment (STA)* was introduced with Windows NT 3.51. With an STA, only one thread (the thread that created the instance) is allowed to access the component. However, it is legal to have multiple STAs inside one process, as shown in Figure 26-4.

In this figure, the inner rectangles with the lollipop represent COM components. Components and threads (curved arrows) are surrounded by apartments. The outer rectangle represents a process.

With STAs, there's no need to protect instance variables from multiple-thread access, because this protection is provided by a COM facility, and only one thread accesses the component.

A COM object that is not programmed with thread safety marks the requirements for an STA in the registry with the registry key ThreadingModel set to Apartment.

Multithreaded Apartment

Windows NT 4.0 introduced the concept of a *multithreaded apartment (MTA)*. With an MTA, multiple threads can access the component simultaneously. Figure 26-5 shows a process with one MTA and two STAs.

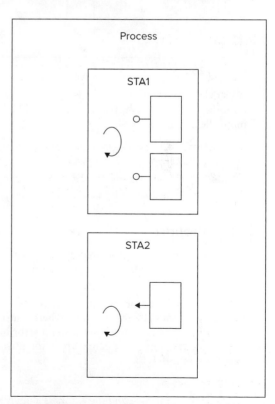

FIGURE 26-4

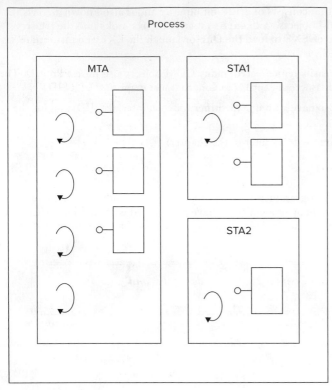

FIGURE 26-5

A COM object programmed with thread safety in mind marks the requirement for an MTA in the registry with the key `ThreadingModel` set to `Free`. The value `Both` is used for thread-safe COM objects that don't mind the apartment type.

 Visual Basic 6.0 didn't offer support for multithreaded apartments. If you're using COM objects that have been developed with VB6 that's an important issue to know.

Error Handling

With .NET, errors are generated by throwing exceptions. With the older COM technology, errors are defined by returning HRESULT values with the methods. An HRESULT value of S_OK means that the method was successful.

If a more detailed error message is offered by the COM component, the COM component implements the interface ISupportErrorInfo, where not only an error message but also a link to a help file and the source of the error are returned with an error information object on the return of the method. Objects that implement ISupportErrorInfo are automatically mapped to more detailed error information with an exception in .NET.

 How to trace and log errors is discussed in Chapter 19, "Instrumentation."

Events

.NET offers a callback mechanism with the C# keywords `event` and `delegate` (see Chapter 8, "Delegates, Lambdas, and Events").

Figure 26-6 shows the COM event-handling architecture. With COM events, the component has to implement the interface `IConnectionPointContainer` and one or more connection point objects (CPOs) that implement the interface `IConnectionPoint`. The component also defines an outgoing interface — `ICompletedEvents` in Figure 26-6 — that is invoked by the CPO. The client must implement this outgoing interface in the sink object, which itself is a COM object. During runtime, the client queries the server for the interface `IConnectionPointContainer`. With the help of this interface, the client asks for a CPO with the method `FindConnectionPoint()` to get a pointer to `IConnectionPoint` returned. This interface pointer is used by the client to call the `Advise()` method, where a pointer to the sink object is passed to the server. In turn, the component can invoke methods inside the sink object of the client.

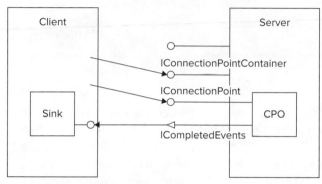

FIGURE 26-6

Later in this chapter, you learn how the .NET events and the COM events can be mapped so that COM events can be handled by a .NET client and vice versa.

Marshaling

Data passed from .NET to the COM component and the other way around must be converted to the corresponding representation. This mechanism is also known as *marshaling*. What happens here depends on the data type of the data that is passed: You have to differentiate between blittable and nonblittable data types.

Blittable data types have a common representation with both .NET and COM, and no conversion is needed. Simple data types such as `byte`, `short`, `int`, `long`, and classes and arrays that only contain these simple data types belong to the blittable data types. Arrays must be one-dimensional to be blittable.

A conversion is needed with *nonblittable* data types. The following table lists some of the nonblittable COM data types with their .NET-related data types. Nonblittable types have a higher overhead because of the conversion.

COM DATA TYPE	.NET DATA TYPE
`SAFEARRAY`	`Array`
`VARIANT`	`Object`
`BSTR`	`String`
`IUnknown*, IDispatch*`	`Object`

USING A COM COMPONENT FROM A .NET CLIENT

To see how a .NET application can use a COM component, you first have to create a COM component. Creating COM components is not possible with C# or Visual Basic 2010; you need either Visual Basic 6.0 or C++ (or any other language that supports COM). This chapter uses the Active Template Library (ATL) and C++ with Visual Studio 2010.

Here we will start creating a simple COM component and use this from a runtime callable wrapper (RCW). We will also use the component with the new C# 4 dynamic language extensions. Threading issues are discussed, and finally COM connection points are mapped to .NET events.

 A short note about building COM components with Visual Basic 9.0 and C#: With Visual Basic 10.0 and C# it is possible to build .NET components that can be used as COM objects by using a wrapper that is the real COM component. It would make no sense for a .NET component that is wrapped from a COM component to be used by a .NET client with COM interop.

Because this is not a COM book, it does not discuss all aspects of the code but only what you need to build the sample.

Creating a COM Component

To create a COM component with ATL and C++, create a new ATL Project. You can find the ATL Project Wizard within the Visual C++ Projects group when you select File New Project. Set the name to COMServer. With the Application Settings, select Dynamic Link Library and click Finish.

 Because a build step registers the COM component in the registry, which requires admin privileges, Visual Studio should be started in elevated mode to write ATL COM objects.

The ATL Project Wizard just creates the foundation for the server. A COM object is still needed. Add a class in Solution Explorer and select ATL Simple Object. In the dialog that starts up, enter COMDemo in the Short name field. The other fields will be filled in automatically, but change the interface name to `IWelcome` and the ProgID to `COMServer.COMDemo` (see Figure 26-7). Click Finish to create the stub code for the class and the interface.

The COM component offers two interfaces, so that you can see how `QueryInterface()` is mapped from .NET, and just three simple methods, so that you can see how the interaction takes place. In class view, select the interface `IWelcome` and add the method `Greeting()` (see Figure 26-8) with these parameters:

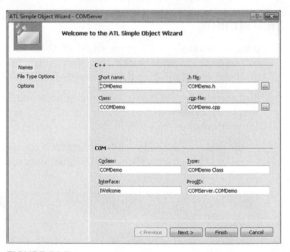

FIGURE 26-7

```
HRESULT Greeting([in] BSTR name, [out, retval] BSTR* message);
```

FIGURE 26-8

The IDL file COMServer.idl defines the interface for COM. Your wizard-generated code from the file COMServer.idl should look similar to the following code. The unique identifiers (uuids) will differ. The interface IWelcome defines the Greeting() method. The brackets before the keyword interface define some attributes for the interface. uuid defines the interface ID and dual marks the type of the interface:

Available for download on Wrox.com

```
[
    object,
    uuid(EB1E5898-4DAB-4184-92E2-BBD8F9341AFD),
    dual,
    nonextensible,
    pointer_default(unique)
]
interface IWelcome : IDispatch{
    [id(1)] HRESULT Greeting([in] BSTR name, [out,retval] BSTR* message);
};
```

code snippet COMServer/COMServer.idl

The IDL file also defines the content of the type library, which is the COM object (coclass) that implements the interface IWelcome:

```
[
    uuid(8C123EAE-F567-421F-ACBE-E11F89909160),
    version(1.0),
]
library COMServerLib
{
    importlib("stdole2.tlb");
    [
        uuid(ACB04E72-EB08-4D4A-91D3-34A5DB55D4B4)
    ]
    coclass COMDemo
    {
        [default] interface IWelcome;
    };
};
```

With custom attributes, it is possible to change the name of the class and interfaces that are generated by a .NET wrapper class. You just have to add the attribute custom *with the identifier* 0F21F359-AB84-41e8-9A78-36D110E6D2F9, *and the name under which it should appear within .NET.*

Add the custom attribute with the same identifier and the name Wrox.ProCSharp.Interop.Server .IWelcome to the header section of the IWelcome interface. Add the same attribute with a corresponding name to the coclass COMDemo:

```
[
    object,
    uuid(EB1E5898-4DAB-4184-92E2-BBD8F9341AFD),
    dual,
    nonextensible,
    helpstring("IWelcome Interface"),
    pointer_default(unique),
    custom(0F21F359-AB84-41e8-9A78-36D110E6D2F9,
    "Wrox.ProCSharp.Interop.Server.IWelcome")
]
interface IWelcome : IDispatch{
    [id(1)] HRESULT Greeting([in] BSTR name, [out,retval] BSTR* message);
};
[
    uuid(8C123EAE-F567-421F-ACBE-E11F89909160),
    version(1.0),
]
library COMServerLib
{
    importlib("stdole2.tlb");
    [
        uuid(ACB04E72-EB08-4D4A-91D3-34A5DB55D4B4),
        helpstring("COMDemo Class"),
        custom(0F21F359-AB84-41e8-9A78-36D110E6D2F9,
        "Wrox.ProCSharp.Interop.Server.COMDemo")
    ]
    coclass COMDemo
    {
        [default] interface IWelcome;
    };
};
```

Now add a second interface to the file COMServer.idl. You can copy the header section of the IWelcome interface to the header section of the new IMath interface, but be sure to change the unique identifier that is defined with the uuid keyword. You can generate such an ID with the guidgen utility. The interface IMath offers the methods Add() and Sub():

```
// IMath
[
    object,
    uuid(2158751B-896E-461d-9012-EF1680BE0628),
    dual,
    nonextensible,
    helpstring("IMath Interface"),
    pointer_default(unique),
    custom(0F21F359-AB84-41e8-9A78-36D110E6D2F9,
    "Wrox.ProCSharp.Interop.Server.IMath")
]
interface IMath: IDispatch
{
```

```
[id(1)] HRESULT Add([in] LONG val1, [in] LONG val2,
                    [out, retval] LONG* result);
[id(2)] HRESULT Sub([in] LONG val1, [in] LONG val2,
                    [out, retval] LONG* result);
};
```

The coclass COMDemo must also be changed so that it implements both the interfaces IWelcome and Math. The IWelcome interface is the default interface:

```
importlib("stdole2.tlb");
[
    uuid(ACB04E72-EB08-4D4A-91D3-34A5DB55D4B4),
    helpstring("COMDemo Class"),
    custom(0F21F359-AB84-41e8-9A78-36D110E6D2F9,
    "Wrox.ProCSharp.Interop.Server.COMDemo")
]
coclass COMDemo
{
    [default] interface IWelcome;
    interface IMath;
};
```

Now, you can set the focus away from the IDL file toward the C++ code. In the file COMDemo.h, you can find the class definition of the COM object. The class CCOMDemo uses multiple inheritances to derive from the template classes CComObjectRootEx, CComCoClass, and IDisplatchImpl. The CComObjectRootEx class offers an implementation of the IUnknown interface functionality such as implementation of the AddRef() and Release() methods. The CComCoClass class creates a factory that instantiates objects of the template argument, which here is CComDemo. IDispatchImpl offers an implementation of the methods from the IDispatch interface.

With the macros that are surrounded by BEGIN_COM_MAP and END_COM_MAP, a map is created to define all the COM interfaces that are implemented by the COM class. This map is used by the implementation of the QueryInterface method.

Available for download on Wrox.com

```
class ATL_NO_VTABLE CCOMDemo:
    public CComObjectRootEx<CComSingleThreadModel>,
    public CComCoClass<CCOMDemo, &CLSID_COMDemo>,
    public IDispatchImpl<IWelcome, &IID_IWelcome, &LIBID_COMServerLib,
        /*wMajor =*/ 1, /*wMinor =*/ 0>
{
public:
    CCOMDemo()
    {
    }


DECLARE_REGISTRY_RESOURCEID(IDR_COMDEMO)


BEGIN_COM_MAP(CCOMDemo)
    COM_INTERFACE_ENTRY(IWelcome)
    COM_INTERFACE_ENTRY(IDispatch)
END_COM_MAP()


    DECLARE_PROTECT_FINAL_CONSTRUCT()

    HRESULT FinalConstruct()
    {
        return S_OK;
    }

    void FinalRelease()
    {
```

```
    }

public:
    STDMETHOD(Greeting)(BSTR name, BSTR* message);
};

OBJECT_ENTRY_AUTO(__uuidof(COMDemo), CCOMDemo)
```

code snippet COMServer/COMDemo.h

With this class definition, you have to add the second interface, IMath, as well as the methods that are defined with the IMath interface:

```
class ATL_NO_VTABLE CCOMDemo:
    public CComObjectRootEx<CComSingleThreadModel>,
    public CComCoClass<CCOMDemo, &CLSID_COMDemo>,
    public IDispatchImpl<IWelcome, &IID_IWelcome, &LIBID_COMServerLib,
        /*wMajor =*/ 1, /*wMinor =*/ 0>
 public IDispatchImpl<IMath, &IID_IMath, &LIBID_COMServerLib, 1, 0>
{
public:
    CCOMDemo()
    {
    }

DECLARE_REGISTRY_RESOURCEID(IDR_COMDEMO)


BEGIN_COM_MAP(CCOMDemo)
    COM_INTERFACE_ENTRY(IWelcome)
    COM_INTERFACE_ENTRY(IMath)
    COM_INTERFACE_ENTRY2(IDispatch, IWelcome)
END_COM_MAP()


    DECLARE_PROTECT_FINAL_CONSTRUCT()

    HRESULT FinalConstruct()
    {
        return S_OK;
    }

    void FinalRelease()
    {
    }

public:
    STDMETHOD(Greeting)(BSTR name, BSTR* message);
    STDMETHOD(Add)(long val1, long val2, long* result);
    STDMETHOD(Sub)(long val1, long val2, long* result);
};

OBJECT_ENTRY_AUTO(__uuidof(COMDemo), CCOMDemo)
```

Now, you can implement the three methods in the file COMDemo.cpp with the following code. The CComBSTR is an ATL class that makes it easier to deal with BSTRs. In the Greeting() method, only a welcome message is returned, which adds the name passed in the first argument to the message that is returned. The Add() method just does a simple addition of two values, and the Sub() method does a subtraction and returns the result:

```
STDMETHODIMP CCOMDemo::Greeting(BSTR name, BSTR* message)
{
    CComBSTR tmp("Welcome, ");
    tmp.Append(name);
```

```
    *message = tmp;
    return S_OK;
}

STDMETHODIMP CCOMDemo::Add(LONG val1, LONG val2, LONG* result)
{
    *result = val1 + val2;
    return S_OK;
}

STDMETHODIMP CCOMDemo::Sub(LONG val1, LONG val2, LONG* result)
{
    *result = val1 - val2;
    return S_OK;
}
```

code snippet COMServer/COMDemo.cpp

Now, you can build the component. The build process also configures the component in the registry.

Creating a Runtime Callable Wrapper

You can now use the COM component from within .NET. To make this possible, you must create a runtime callable wrapper (RCW). Using the RCW, the .NET client sees a .NET object instead of the COM component; there is no need to deal with the COM characteristics because this is done by the wrapper. An RCW hides the `IUnknown` and `IDispatch` interfaces (see Figure 26-9) and deals itself with the reference counts of the COM object.

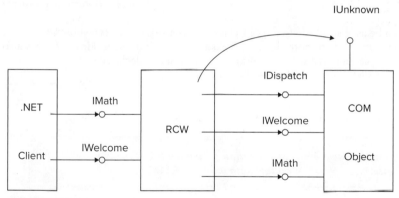

FIGURE 26-9

The RCW can be created by using the command-line utility `tlbimp` or by using Visual Studio. Starting the command

```
tlbimp COMServer.dll /out:Interop.COMServer.dll
```

creates the file `Interop.COMServer.dll`, which contains a .NET assembly with the wrapper class. In this generated assembly, you can find the namespace `COMWrapper` with the class `CCOMDemoClass` and the interfaces `CCOMDemo`, `IMath`, and `IWelcome`. The name of the namespace can be changed by using options of the `tlbimp` utility. The option `/namespace` allows you to specify a different namespace, and with `/asmversion` you can define the version number of the assembly.

 Another important option of this command-line utility is `/keyfile`, which is used for assigning a strong name to the generated assembly. Strong names are discussed in Chapter 18.

An RCW can also be created by using Visual Studio. To create a simple sample application, create a C# console project. In Solution Explorer, add a reference to the COM server by selecting the COM tab in the Add Reference dialog, and scroll down to the entry `COMServer 1.0 Type Library`. Here are listed all COM objects that are configured in the registry. Selecting a COM component from the list creates an RCW class. With Visual Studio 2010, this wrapper class can be created in the main assembly of the project by setting the property `Embed Interop Types` to true, which is the default. Setting it to `false` creates a separate interop assembly that needs to be deployed with the application.

Using the RCW

After creating the wrapper class, you can write the code for the application to instantiate and access the component. Because of the custom attributes in the C++ file, the generated namespace of the RCW class is `Wrox.ProCSharp.COMInterop.Server`. Add this namespace, as well as the namespace `System.Runtime.InteropServices`, to the declarations. From the namespace `System.Runtime.InteropServices`, the `Marshal` class will be used to release the COM object:

Available for download on Wrox.com

```
using System;
using System.Runtime.InteropServices;
using Wrox.ProCSharp.Interop.Server;

namespace Wrox.ProCSharp.Interop.Client
{
    class Program
    {
        [STAThread]
        static void Main()
        {
```

code snippet DotnetClient/Program.cs

Now, the COM component can be used similarly to a .NET class. `obj` is a variable of type `COMDemo`. `COMDemo` is a .NET interface that offers the methods of both the `IWelcome` and `IMath` interfaces. However, it is also possible to cast to a specific interface such as `IWelcome`. With a variable that is declared as type `IWelcome`, the method `Greeting()` can be called.

```
var obj = new COMDemo();
IWelcome welcome = obj;
Console.WriteLine(welcome.Greeting("Stephanie"));
```

 Although `COMDemo` is an interface, you can instantiate new objects of type `COMDemo`. Contrary to normal interfaces, you can do this with wrapped COM interfaces.

If the object — as in this case — offers multiple interfaces, a variable of the other interface can be declared, and by using a simple assignment with the cast operator, the wrapper class does a `QueryInterface()` with the COM object to return the second interface pointer. With the I `Math` variable, the methods of the `IMath` interface can be called.

```
IMath math;
math = (IMath)welcome;
int x = math.Add(4, 5);
Console.WriteLine(x);
```

If the COM object should be released before the garbage collector cleans up the object, the static method `Marshal.ReleaseComObject()` invokes the `Release()` method of the component, so that the component can destroy itself and free up memory:

```
            Marshal.ReleaseComObject(math);
        }
    }
}
```

Earlier you learned that the COM object is released as soon as the reference count is 0.
`Marshal.ReleaseComObject()` *decrements the reference count by 1 by invoking the*
`Release()` *method. Because the RCW does just one call to* `AddRef()` *to increment
the reference count, a single call to* `Marshal.ReleaseComObject()` *is enough to release
the object no matter how many references to the RCW you keep.*

After releasing the COM object using `Marshal.ReleaseComObject()`, you may not use any variable that references the object. In the example, the COM object is released by using the variable `math`. The variable `welcome`, which references the same object, cannot be used after releasing the object. Otherwise, you will get an exception of type `InvalidComObjectException`.

*Releasing COM objects when they are no longer needed is extremely important. COM
objects make use of the native memory heap, whereas .NET objects make use of the
managed memory heap. The garbage collector only deals with managed memory.*

As you can see, with a runtime callable wrapper, a COM component can be used similarly to a .NET object.

Using the COM Server with Dynamic Language Extensions

C# 4 includes an extension for using dynamic languages from C#. This is also an advantage for using COM servers that offer the `IDispatch` interface. As you read earlier in the "Dispatch Interfaces" section, this interface is resolved at runtime with the methods `GetIdsOfNames()` and `Invoke()`. With the `dynamic` keyword and the help of a COM binder that is used behind the scenes, the COM component can be called without creating an RCW object.

Declaring a variable of type `dynamic` and assigning a COM object to it uses the COM binder, and you can invoke the methods of the default interface as shown. Creating an instance of the COM object without using an RCW can be done by getting the `Type` object using `Type.GetTypeFromProgID()`, and instantiating the COM object with the `Activator.CreateInstance()` method. You just don't get IntelliSense with the dynamic keyword, but can use the optional parameters that are very common with COM:

```csharp
using System;

namespace Wrox.ProCSharp.Interop
{
    class Program
    {
        static void Main()
        {
            Type t = Type.GetTypeFromProgID("COMServer.COMDemo");
            dynamic o = Activator.CreateInstance(t);
            Console.WriteLine(o.Greeting("Angela"));
        }
    }
}
```

code snippet DynamicDotnetClient/Program.cs

*The dynamic language extensions of C# are explained in Chapter 12, "Dynamic
Language Extensions."*

Threading Issues

As discussed earlier in this chapter, a COM component marks the apartment (STA or MTA) it wants to live in, based on whether or not it is implemented as thread-safe. However, the thread has to join an apartment. What apartment the thread should join can be defined with the [STAThread] and [MTAThread] attributes, which can be applied to the Main() method of an application. The attribute [STAThread] means that the thread joins an STA, whereas the attribute [MTAThread] means that the thread joins an MTA. Joining an MTA is the default if no attribute is applied.

It is also possible to set the apartment state programmatically with the ApartmentState property of the Thread class. The ApartmentState property allows you to set a value from the ApartmentState enumeration. ApartmentState has the possible values STA and MTA (and Unknown if it wasn't set). Be aware that the apartment state of a thread can be set only once. If it is set a second time, the second setting is ignored.

> *What happens if the thread chooses a different apartment from the apartments supported by the component? The correct apartment for the COM component is created automatically by the COM runtime. Yet, the performance decreases if the apartment boundaries are crossed while calling the methods of a component.*

Adding Connection Points

To see how COM events can be handled in a .NET application, the COM component must be extended. First, you have to add another interface to the interface definition file COMDemo.idl. The interface _ICompletedEvents is implemented by the client, which is the .NET application, and called by the component. In this example, the method Completed() is called by the component when the calculation is ready. Such an interface is also known as an outgoing interface. An outgoing interface must be either a dispatch or a custom interface. Dispatch interfaces are supported by all clients. The custom attribute with the ID 0F21F359-AB84-41e8-9A78-36D110E6D2F9 defines the name of the interface that will be created in the RCW. The outgoing interface must also be written to the interfaces supported by the component inside the coclass section, and marked as a source interface:

```
library COMServerLib
{
    importlib("stdole2.tlb");

    [
        uuid(5CFF102B-0961-4EC6-8BB4-759A3AB6EF48),
        helpstring("_ICompletedEvents Interface"),
        custom(0F21F359-AB84-41e8-9A78-36D110E6D2F9,
          "Wrox.ProCSharp.COMInterop.Server.ICompletedEvents"),
    ]
    dispinterface _ICompletedEvents
    {
        properties:
        methods:
            [id(1)] void Completed(void);
    };

    [
        uuid(ACB04E72-EB08-4D4A-91D3-34A5DB55D4B4),
        helpstring("COMDemo Class")
        custom(0F21F359-AB84-41e8-9A78-36D110E6D2F9,
          "Wrox.ProCSharp.COMInterop.Server.COMDemo"),
    ]
```

```
coclass COMDemo
{
    [default] interface IWelcome;
    interface IMath;
    [default, source] dispinterface _ICompletedEvents;
};
```

code snippet COMServer/COMServer.idl

You can use a wizard to create an implementation that fires the event back to the client. Open the class view, select the class CComDemo, open the context menu, and select Add ➪ Add Connection Point . . . to start the Implement Connection Point Wizard (see Figure 26-10). Select the source interface ICompletedEvents for implementation with the connection point.

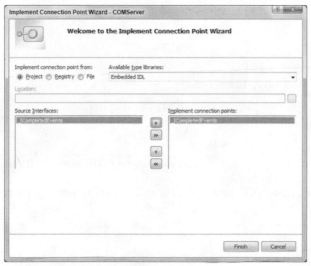

FIGURE 26-10

The wizard creates the proxy class CProxy_ICompletedEvents to fire the events to the client. Also, the class CCOMDemo is changed. The class now inherits from IConnectionPointContainerImpl and the proxy class. The interface IConnectionPointContainer is added to the interface map, and a connection point map is added to the source interface _ICompletedEvents.

Available for
download on
Wrox.com

```
class ATL_NO_VTABLE CCOMDemo:
    public CComObjectRootEx<CComSingleThreadModel>,
    public CComCoClass<CCOMDemo, &CLSID_COMDemo>,
    public IDispatchImpl<IWelcome, &IID_IWelcome, &LIBID_COMServerLib,
        /*wMajor =*/ 1, /*wMinor =*/ 0>,
    public IDispatchImpl<IMath, &IID_IMath, &LIBID_COMServerLib, 1, 0>,
    public IConnectionPointContainerImpl<CCOMDemo>,
    public CProxy_ICompletedEvents<CCOMDemo>
{
public:

//.

BEGIN_COM_MAP(CCOMDemo)
    COM_INTERFACE_ENTRY(IWelcome)
    COM_INTERFACE_ENTRY(IMath)
    COM_INTERFACE_ENTRY2(IDispatch, IWelcome)
    COM_INTERFACE_ENTRY(IConnectionPointContainer)
END_COM_MAP()
```

```
//.

public:
    BEGIN_CONNECTION_POINT_MAP(CCOMDemo)
        CONNECTION_POINT_ENTRY(__uuidof(_ICompletedEvents))
    END_CONNECTION_POINT_MAP()
};
```

code snippet COMServer/COMDemo.h

Finally, the method `Fire_Completed()` from the proxy class can be called inside the methods `Add()` and `Sub()` in the file `COMDemo.cpp`:

Available for
download on
Wrox.com

```
STDMETHODIMP CCOMDemo::Add(LONG val1, LONG val2, LONG* result)
{
    *result = val1 + val2;
    Fire_Completed();
    return S_OK;
}

STDMETHODIMP CCOMDemo::Sub(LONG val1, LONG val2, LONG* result)
{
    *result = val1 - val2;
    Fire_Completed();
    return S_OK;
}
```

code snippet COMServer/COMDemo.cpp

After rebuilding the COM DLL, you can change the .NET client to use these COM events just like a normal .NET event:

Available for
download on
Wrox.com

```
static void Main()
{
    COMDemo obj = new COMDemo();

    IWelcome welcome = obj;
    Console.WriteLine(welcome.Greeting("Stephanie"));

    obj.Completed += () => Console.WriteLine("Calculation completed");

    IMath math = (IMath)welcome;
    int result = math.Add(3, 5);
    Console.WriteLine(result);

    Marshal.ReleaseComObject(math);
}
```

code snippet DotnetClient/Program.cs

As you can see, the RCW offers automatic mapping from COM events to .NET events. COM events can be used similarly to .NET events in a .NET client.

USING A .NET COMPONENT FROM A COM CLIENT

So far, you have seen how to access a COM component from a .NET client. Equally interesting is to find a solution for accessing .NET components on an old COM client that is using Visual Basic 6.0, or C++ with MFC (Microsoft Foundation Classes), or ATL.

In this section, a COM object is defined with .NET code that is used by a COM client with the help of a COM callable wrapper (CCW). By using the object from a COM client, you will see how to create a type library from the .NET assembly, use different .NET attributes to specify COM interop behaviors, and register the .NET assembly as a COM component. Then, a COM client with C++ is created to use the CCW. Finally, the .NET component is expanded to offer COM connection points.

COM Callable Wrapper

If you want to access a COM component with a .NET client, you have to work with an RCW. To access a .NET component from a COM client application, you must use a CCW. Figure 26-11 shows the CCW that wraps a .NET class, and offers COM interfaces that a COM client expects to use. The CCW offers interfaces such as `IUnknown`, `IDispatch`, and others. It also offers interfaces such as `IConnectionPointContainer` and `IConnectionPoint` for events. Of course, the CCW also offers the custom interfaces that are defined by the .NET class such as `IWelcome` and `IMath`. A COM client gets what it expects from a COM object — although a .NET component operates behind the scenes. The wrapper deals with methods such as `AddRef()`, `Release()`, and `QueryInterface()` from the `IUnknown` interface, whereas in the .NET object you can count on the garbage collector without the need to deal with reference counts.

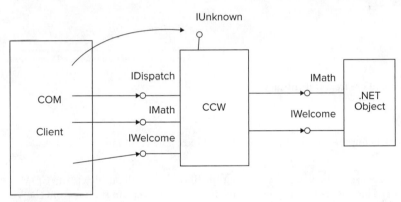

FIGURE 26-11

Creating a .NET Component

In the following example, you build the same functionality into a .NET class that you have previously built into a COM component. Start by creating a C# class library, and name it `DotNetServer`. Then add the interfaces `IWelcome` and `IMath`, and the class `DotNetComponent` that implements these interfaces. The attribute `ComVisible(true)` makes the class and interfaces available for COM:

```csharp
using System;
using System.Runtime.InteropServices;

namespace Wrox.ProCSharp.Interop.Server
{
    [ComVisible(true)]
    public interface IWelcome
    {
        string Greeting(string name);
    }

    [ComVisible(true)]
    public interface IMath
    {
        int Add(int val1, int val2);
        int Sub(int val1, int val2);
```

```
    }

    [ComVisible(true)]
    public class DotnetComponent: IWelcome, IMath
    {
        public DotnetComponent()
        {
        }

        public string Greeting(string name)
        {
            return "Hello " + name;
        }

        public int Add(int val1, int val2)
        {
            return val1 + val2;
        }

        public int Sub(int val1, int val2)
        {
            return val1 - val2;
        }
    }
}
```

code snippet DotnetServer/DotnetServer.cs

After building the project, you can create a type library.

Creating a Type Library

A type library can be created by using the command-line utility tlbexp. The command

```
tlbexp DotnetServer.dll
```

creates the type library DotnetServer.tlb. You can view the type library with the utility *OLE/COM Object Viewer* oleview32.exe. This tool is part of the Microsoft SDK, and you can start it from the Visual Studio 2010 Command Prompt. Select File ➪ View TypeLib to open the type library. Now you can see the interface definition that is very similar to the interfaces created with the COM server earlier.

The name of the type library is created from the name of the assembly. The header of the type library also defines the full name of the assembly in a custom attribute, and all the interfaces are forward-declared before they are defined.

```
// Generated .IDL file (by the OLE/COM Object Viewer)
//
// typelib filename: DotnetServer.tlb

[
  uuid(14F7A17A-B97D-41DA-B3E1-B6025F188FAD),
  version(1.0),
  custom(90883F05-3D28-11D2-8F17-00A0C9A6186D, "DotnetServer, Version=1.0.0.0,
        Culture=neutral, PublicKeyToken=null")
]
library DotnetServer
{
    // TLib :      // TLib : mscorlib.dll : {BED7F4EA-1A96-11D2-8F08-00A0C9A6186D}
    importlib("mscorlib.tlb");
    // TLib : OLE Automation : {00020430-0000-0000-c260-000000000046}
    importlib("stdole2.tlb");

    // Forward declare all types defined in this typelib
```

```
        interface IWelcome;
        interface IMath;
        interface _DotnetComponent;
```

In the following generated code, you can see that the interfaces IWelcome and IMath are defined as COM dual interfaces. You can see all methods that have been declared in the C# code are listed here in the type library definition. The parameters changed; the .NET types are mapped to COM types (for example, from the String class to the BSTR type), and the signature is changed, so that a HRESULT is returned. Because the interfaces are dual, dispatch IDs are also generated:

```
    [
        odl,
        uuid(6AE7CB9C-7471-3B6A-9E13-51C2294266F0),
        version(1.0),
        dual,
        oleautomation,
        custom(0F21F359-AB84-41E8-9A78-36D110E6D2F9,
            "Wrox.ProCSharp.Interop.Server.IWelcome")
    ]
    interface IWelcome : IDispatch {
        [id(0x60020000)]
        HRESULT Greeting(
                    [in] BSTR name,
                    [out, retval] BSTR* pRetVal);
    };

    [
        odl,
        uuid(AED00E6F-3A60-3EB8-B974-1556096350CB),
        version(1.0),
        dual,
        oleautomation,
        custom(0F21F359-AB84-41E8-9A78-36D110E6D2F9,
            "Wrox.ProCSharp.Interop.Server.IMath")

    ]
    interface IMath : IDispatch {
        [id(0x60020000)]
        HRESULT Add(
                    [in] long val1,
                    [in] long val2,
                    [out, retval] long* pRetVal);
        [id(0x60020001)]
        HRESULT Sub(
                    [in] long val1,
                    [in] long val2,
                    [out, retval] long* pRetVal);
    };
```

The coclass section marks the COM object itself. The uuid in the header is the CLSID used to instantiate the object. The class DotnetComponent supports the interfaces _DotnetComponent, _Object, IWelcome, and IMath. _Object is defined in the file mscorlib.tlb included in an earlier code section and offers the methods of the base class Object. The default interface of the component is _DotnetComponent, which is defined after the coclass section as a dispatch interface. In the interface declaration, it is marked as dual, but because no methods are included, it is a dispatch interface. With this interface, it is possible to access all methods of the component using late binding:

```
    [
        uuid(2F1E78D4-1147-33AC-9233-C0F51121DAAA),
        version(1.0),
        custom(0F21F359-AB84-41E8-9A78-36D110E6D2F9,
            "Wrox.ProCSharp.Interop.Server.DotnetComponent")
```

```
    ]
    coclass DotnetComponent {
        [default] interface _DotnetComponent;
        interface _Object;
        interface IWelcome;
        interface IMath;
    };

    [
        odl,
        uuid(2B36C1BF-61F7-3E84-87B2-EAB52144046D),
        hidden,
        dual,
        oleautomation,
        custom(0F21F359-AB84-41E8-9A78-36D110E6D2F9,
                "Wrox.ProCSharp.Interop.Server.DotnetComponent")

    ]
    interface _DotnetComponent : IDispatch {
    };
};
```

There are quite a few defaults for generating the type library. However, often it is advantageous to change some of the default .NET to COM mappings. This can be done with several attributes in the System. Runtime.InteropServices namespaces.

COM Interop Attributes

Applying attributes from the namespace System.Runtime.InteropServices to classes, interfaces, or methods allows you to change the implementation of the CCW. The following table lists these attributes and their descriptions.

ATTRIBUTE	DESCRIPTION
Guid	This attribute can be assigned to the assembly, interfaces, and classes. Using the Guid as an assembly attribute defines the type-library ID, applying it to interfaces defines the interface ID (IID), and setting the attribute to a class defines the class ID (CLSID). The unique IDs that must be defined with this attribute can be created with the utility guidgen. The CLSID and type-library IDs are changed automatically with every build. If you don't want to change them with every build, you can fix this by using this attribute. The IID is changed only if the signature of the interface changes; for example, if a method is added or removed, or some parameters are changed. Because with COM the IID should change with every new version of this interface, this is a very good default behavior, and usually there's no need to apply the IID with the Guid attribute. The only time you want to apply a fixed IID for an interface is when the .NET interface is an exact representation of an existing COM interface, and the COM client already expects this identifier.
ProgId	This attribute can be applied to a class to specify what name should be used when the object is configured in the registry.
ComVisible	With the Assembly Information settings of the Project properties you can configure if all the types of the assembly should be visible by COM. By default this setting is false which is a good default that makes it necessary to explicitly mark the classes, interfaces, and delegates with the ComVisible attribute to create a COM representation. In case the default setting is changed to make all types visible by COM, you can set that ComVisible attribute to false for the types where a COM representation should not be created.

ATTRIBUTE	DESCRIPTION
InterfaceType	This attribute, if set to a `ComInterfaceType` enumeration value, enables you to modify the default dual interface type that is created for .NET interfaces. `ComInterfaceType` has the values `InterfaceIsDual`, `InterfaceIsIDispatch`, and `InterfaceIsIUnknown`. If you want to apply a custom interface type to a .NET interface, set the attribute like this: `InterfaceType(ComInterfaceType .InterfaceIsIUnknown)`.
ClassInterface	This attribute enables you to modify the default dispatch interface that is created for a class. `ClassInterface` accepts an argument of a `ClassInterfaceType` enumeration. The possible values are `AutoDispatch`, `AutoDual`, and `None`. In the previous example, you have seen that the default is `AutoDispatch`, because a dispatch interface is created. If the class should only be accessible by the defined interfaces, apply the attribute `ClassInterface(ClassInterfaceType.None)` to the class.
DispId	This attribute can be used with dual and dispatch interfaces to define the `DispId` of methods and properties.
In Out	COM allows the specification of attributes for parameter types if the parameter should be sent to the component `In`, from the component to the client `Out`, or in both directions `In, Out`.
Optional	Parameters of COM methods may be optional. Parameters that should be optional can be marked with the `Optional` attribute.

Now, you can change the C# code to specify a dual interface type for the `IWelcome` interface and a custom interface type for the `IMath` interface. With the class `DotnetComponent`, the attribute `ClassInterface` with the argument `ClassInterfaceType.None` specifies that no separate COM interface will be generated. The attributes `ProgId` and `Guid` specify a ProgID and a GUID:

```csharp
[InterfaceType(ComInterfaceType.InterfaceIsDual)]
[ComVisible(true)]
public interface IWelcome
{
    [DispId(60040)]
    string Greeting(string name);
}

[InterfaceType(ComInterfaceType.InterfaceIsIUnknown)]
[ComVisible(true)]
public interface IMath
{
  int Add(int val1, int val2);
  int Sub(int val1, int val2);
}

[ClassInterface(ClassInterfaceType.None)]
[ProgId("Wrox.DotnetComponent")]
[Guid("77839717-40DD-4876-8297-35B98A8402C7")]
[ComVisible(true)]
public class DotnetComponent: IWelcome, IMath
{
   public DotnetComponent()
   {
   }
```

code snippet DotnetServer/DotnetServer.cs

Rebuilding the class library and the type library changes the interface definition. You can verify this with `OleView.exe`. `IWelcome` is now a dual interface, `IMath` a custom interface that derives from `IUnknown` instead of `IDispatch`, and the `coclass` section no longer has a `_DotnetComponent` interface.

COM Registration

Before the .NET component can be used as a COM object, it is necessary to configure it in the registry. Also, if you don't want to copy the assembly into the same directory as the client application, it is necessary to install the assembly in the global assembly cache. The global assembly cache itself is discussed in Chapter 18.

To install the assembly in the global assembly cache, you must sign it with a strong name (using Visual Studio 2010, you can define a strong name in properties of the solution). Then you can register the assembly in the global assembly cache:

```
gacutil -i DotnetServer.dll
```

Now, you can use the regasm utility to configure the component inside the registry. The option /tlb extracts the type library and also configures the type library in the registry:

```
regasm DotnetServer.dll /tlb
```

The information for the .NET component that is written to the registry is as follows. The All COM configuration is in the hive HKEY_CLASSES_ROOT (HKCR). The key of the ProgID (in this example, it is Wrox.DotnetComponent) is written directly to this hive, along with the CLSID.

The key HKCR\CLSID\{CLSID}\InProcServer32 has the following entries:

➤ mscoree.dll — mscoree.dll represents the CCW. This is a real COM object that is responsible for hosting the .NET component. This COM object accesses the .NET component to offer COM behavior for the client. The file mscoree.dll is loaded and instantiated from the client via the normal COM instantiation mechanism.

➤ ThreadingModel=Both — This is an attribute of the mscoree.dll COM object. This component is programmed in a way that offers support both for STA and MTA.

➤ Assembly=DotnetServer, Version=1.0.0.0, Culture=neutral, PublicKeyToken=5cd57c9 3b4d9c41a — The value of the Assembly stores the assembly full name, including the version number and the public key token, so that the assembly can be uniquely identified. The assembly registered here will be loaded by mscoree.dll.

➤ Class=Wrox.ProCSharp.Interop.Server.DotnetComponent — The name of the class will also be used by mscoree.dll. This is the class that will be instantiated.

➤ RuntimeVersion=v4.0.20826 — The registry entry RuntimeVersion specifies the version of the .NET runtime that will be used to host the .NET assembly.

In addition to the configurations shown here, all the interfaces and the type library are configured with their identifiers, too.

Creating a COM Client Application

Now, it's time to create a COM client. Start by creating a simple C++ Win32 Console application project, and name it COMClient. You can leave the default options selected and click Finish in the Project Wizard.

At the beginning of the file COMClient.cpp, add a preprocessor command to include the <iostream> header file and to import the type library that you created for the .NET component. The import statement creates a "smart pointer" class that makes it easier to deal with COM objects. During a build process, the import statement creates .tlh and .tli files that you can find in the debug directory of your project, which includes the smart pointer class. Then add using namespace directives to open the namespace std that will be used for writing output messages to the console, and the namespace DotnetComponent that is created inside the smart pointer class:

Available for download on Wrox.com

```
// COMClient.cpp: Defines the entry point for the console application.
//

#include "stdafx.h"
#include <iostream>
```

```
#import "./DotNetComponent/bin/debug/DotnetServer.tlb" named_guids

using namespace std;
using namespace DotnetComponent;
```

code snippet COMClient/COMClient.cpp

In the `_tmain()` method, the first thing to do before any other COM call is the initialization of COM with the API call `CoInitialize()`. `CoInitialize()` creates and enters an STA for the thread. The variable `spWelcome` is of type `IWelcomePtr`, which is a smart pointer. The smart pointer method `CreateInstance()` accepts the ProgID as an argument to create the COM object by using the COM API `CoCreateInstance()`. The operator `->` is overridden with the smart pointer, so that you can invoke the methods of the COM object such as `Greeting()`:

```
int _tmain(int argc, _TCHAR* argv[])
{
  HRESULT hr;
  hr = CoInitialize(NULL);

  try
  {
    IWelcomePtr spWelcome;

    // CoCreateInstance()
    hr = spWelcome.CreateInstance("Wrox.DotnetComponent");

    cout << spWelcome->Greeting("Bill") << endl;
```

The second interface supported by your .NET component is `IMath`, and there is also a smart pointer that wraps the COM interface: `IMathPtr`. You can directly assign one smart pointer to another as in `spMath = spWelcome;`. In the implementation of the smart pointer (the = operator is overridden), the `QueryInterface()` method is called. With a reference to the `IMath` interface, you can call the `Add()` method.

```
    IMathPtr spMath;
    spMath = spWelcome;    // QueryInterface()

    long result = spMath->Add(4, 5);
    cout << "result:" << result << endl;
  }
```

If an `HRESULT` error value is returned by the COM object (this is done by the CCW that returns `HRESULT` errors if the .NET component generates exceptions), the smart pointer wraps the `HRESULT` errors and generates `_com_error` exceptions instead. Errors are handled in the `catch` block. At the end of the program, the COM DLLs are closed and unloaded using `CoUninitialize()`:

```
  catch (_com_error& e)
  {
    cout << e.ErrorMessage() << endl;
  }

  CoUninitialize();
  return 0;
}
```

Now you can run the application, and you will get outputs from the `Greeting()` and the `Add()` methods to the console. You can also try to debug into the smart pointer class, where you can see the COM API calls directly.

> *If you get an exception stating that the component cannot be found, check if the same version of the assembly that is configured in the registry is installed in the global assembly cache.*

Adding Connection Points

Adding support for COM events to the .NET components requires some changes to the implementation of your .NET class. Offering COM events is not a simple matter of using the `event` and `delegate` keywords; it is necessary to add some more COM interop attributes.

First, you have to add an interface to the .NET project: `IMathEvents`. This interface is the source or outgoing interface for the component, and will be implemented by the `sink` object in the client. A source interface must be either a dispatch or a custom interface. A scripting client supports only dispatch interfaces. Dispatch interfaces are usually preferred as source interfaces:

Available for download on Wrox.com

```
[InterfaceType(ComInterfaceType.InterfaceIsIDispatch)]
[ComVisible(true)]
public interface IMathEvents
{
    [DispId(46200)]
    void CalculationCompleted();
}
```

code snippet DotnetServer/DotnetServer.cs

With the class `DotnetComponent`, a source interface must be specified. This can be done with the attribute `[ComSourceInterfaces]`. Add the attribute `[ComSourceInterfaces]`, and specify the outgoing interface declared earlier. You can add more than one source interface with different constructors of the attribute class; however, the only client language that supports more than one source interface is C++. Visual Basic 6.0 clients support only one source interface.

```
[ClassInterface(ClassInterfaceType.None)]
[ProgId("Wrox.DotnetComponent")]
[Guid("77839717-40DD-4876-8297-35B98A8402C7")]
[ComSourceInterfaces(typeof(IMathEvents))]
[ComVisible(true)]
public class DotnetComponent : IWelcome, IMath
{
    public DotnetComponent()
    {
    }
```

Inside the class `DotnetComponent`, you have to declare an event for every method of the source interface. The type of the method must be the name of the delegate, and the name of the event must be exactly the same as the name of the method inside the source interface. You can add the event calls to the `Add()` and `Sub()` methods. This step is the normal .NET way to invoke events, as discussed in Chapter 8.

```
    public event Action CalculationCompleted;

    public int Add(int val1, int val2)
    {
        int result = val1 + val2;
        if (CalculationCompleted != null)
            CalculationCompleted();
        return result;
    }

    public int Sub(int val1, int val2)
    {
        int result = val1 - val2;
        if (CalculationCompleted != null)
            CalculationCompleted();
        return result;
    }
}
```

> *The name of the event must be the same as the name of the method inside the source interface. Otherwise, the events cannot be mapped for COM clients.*

Creating a Client with a Sink Object

After you've built and registered the .NET assembly and installed it into the global assembly cache, you can build a client application by using the event sources. Implementing a callback or sink object that implements the IDispatch interface was — using Visual Basic 6.0 — just a matter of adding the With Events keyword, very similar to how Visual Basic deals with .NET events today. It's more work with C++, but here the Active Template Library helps.

Open the C++ Console application created in the section "Creating a COM Client Application" and add the following includes to the file stdafx.h:

Available for
download on
Wrox.com

```
#include <atlbase.h>
extern CComModule _Module;
#include <atlcom.h>
```

code snippet COMClient/stdafx.h

The file stdafx.cpp requires an include of the ATL implementation file atlimpl.cpp:

Available for
download on
Wrox.com

```
#include <atlimpl.cpp>
```

code snippet COMClient/stdafx.cpp

Add the new class CEventHandler to the file COMClient.cpp. This class contains the implementation of the IDispatch interface to be called by the component. The implementation of the IDispatch interface is done by the base class IDispEventImpl. This class reads the type library to match the dispatch IDs of the methods and the parameters to the methods of the class. The template parameters of the class IDispatchEventImpl requires an ID of the sink object (here the ID 4 is used), the class that implements the callback methods (CEventHandler), the interface ID of the callback interface (DIID_IMathEvents), the ID of the type library (LIBID_DotnetComponent), and the version number of the type library. You can find the named IDs DIID_IMathEvents and LIBID_DotnetComponent in the file dotnetcomponent.tlh that was created from the #import statement.

The sink map that is surrounded by BEGIN_SINK_MAP and END_SINK_MAP defines the methods that are implemented by the sink object. SINK_ENTRY_EX maps the method OnCalcCompleted to the dispatch ID 46200. This dispatch ID was defined with the method CalculationCompleted of the IMathEvents interface in the .NET component.

Available for
download on
Wrox.com

```cpp
class CEventHandler: public IDispEventImpl<4, CEventHandler,
      &DIID_IMathEvents, &LIBID_DotnetComponent, 1, 0>
{
public:
    BEGIN_SINK_MAP(CEventHandler)
        SINK_ENTRY_EX(4, DIID_IMathEvents, 46200, OnCalcCompleted)
    END_SINK_MAP()

    HRESULT __stdcall OnCalcCompleted()
    {
        cout << "calculation completed" << endl;
        return S_OK;
    }
};
```

code snippet COMClient/COMClient.cpp

The main method now needs a change to advise the component of the existence of the event sink object, so that the component can call back into the sink. This can be done with the method `DispEventAdvise()` of the `CEventHandler` class by passing an `IUnknown` interface pointer. The method `DispEventUnadvise()` unregisters the sink object again.

```cpp
int _tmain(int argc, _TCHAR* argv[])
{
    HRESULT hr;
    hr = CoInitialize(NULL);

    try
    {
        IWelcomePtr spWelcome;
        hr = spWelcome.CreateInstance("Wrox.DotnetComponent");

        IUnknownPtr spUnknown = spWelcome;


        cout << spWelcome->Greeting("Bill") << endl;

        CEventHandler* eventHandler = new CEventHandler();
        hr = eventHandler->DispEventAdvise(spUnknown);


        IMathPtr spMath;
        spMath = spWelcome;    // QueryInterface()

        long result = spMath->Add(4, 5);
        cout << "result:" << result << endl;

        eventHandler->DispEventUnadvise(spWelcome.GetInterfacePtr());
        delete eventHandler;
    }
    catch (_com_error& e)
    {
        cout << e.ErrorMessage() << endl;
    }

    CoUninitialize();
    return 0;
}
```

PLATFORM INVOKE

Not all the features of Windows API calls are available from the .NET Framework. This is not only true for old Windows API calls but also for very new features from Windows 7 or Windows Server 2008 R2. Maybe you've written some DLLs that export unmanaged methods, and you would like to use them from C# as well.

 You can read about specific features of Windows 7 and Windows Server 2008 R2 in Appendix A, "Guidelines for Windows 7 and Windows Server 2008 R2."

To reuse an unmanaged library that doesn't contain COM objects, just exported functions, platform invoke (p/invoke) can be used. With p/invoke, the CLR loads the DLL that includes the function that should be called and marshals the parameters.

To use the unmanaged function, first you have to find out the name of the function as it is exported. You can do this by using the `dumpbin` tool with the `/exports` option.

For example, the command

```
dumpbin /exports c:\windows\system32\kernel32.dll | more
```

lists all exported functions from the DLL `kernel32.dll`. In the example, you use the `CreateHardLink()` Windows API function to create a hard link to an existing file. With this API call, you can have several filenames that reference the same file as long as the filenames are on just one hard disk. This API call is not available from .NET Framework 4, so platform invoke must be used.

To call a native function, you have to define a C# external method with the same number of arguments, and the argument types that are defined with the unmanaged method must have mapped types with managed code.

The Windows API call `CreateHardLink()` has this definition in C++:

```
BOOL CreateHardLink(
    LPCTSTR lpFileName,
    LPCTSTR lpExistingFileName,
    LPSECURITY_ATTRIBUTES lpSecurityAttributes);
```

Now, this definition must be mapped to .NET data types. The return type is a `BOOL` with unmanaged code; this simply maps to the `bool` data type. `LPCTSTR` defines a `long` pointer to a `const` string. The Windows API uses the Hungarian naming convention for the data type. LP is a `long` pointer, C a const, and STR is a null-terminated string. The T marks the type as a generic type, and the type is either resolved to `LPCSTR` (an ANSI string) or `LPWSTR` (a wide Unicode string), depending on the compiler's settings. C strings map to the .NET type `String`. `LPSECURITY_ATTRIBUTES`, which is a long pointer to a struct of type `SECURITY_ATTRIBUTES`. Because you can pass `NULL` to this argument, mapping this type to `IntPtr` is okay. The C# declaration of this method must be marked with the `extern` modifier, because there's no implementation of this method within the C# code. Instead, the implementation of this method is found in the DLL `kernel32.dll`, which is referenced with the attribute `[DllImport]`. Because the return type of the .NET declaration `CreateHardLink()` is of type `bool`, and the native method `CreateHardLink()` returns a `BOOL`, some additional clarification is useful. Because there are different Boolean data types with C++ (for example the native `bool` and the Windows-defined `BOOL`, which have different values), the attribute `[MarshalAs]` specifies to what native type the .NET type `bool` should map.

```
[DllImport("kernel32.dll", SetLastError="true",
           EntryPoint="CreateHardLink", CharSet=CharSet.Unicode)]
[return: MarshalAs(UnmanagedType.Bool)]
public static extern bool CreateHardLink(string newFileName,
                                         string existingFilename,
                                         IntPtr securityAttributes);
```

 The web site http://www.pinvoke.net *and the tool P/Invoke Interop Assistant, which can be downloaded from* http://www.codeplex.com, *are very helpful with the conversion from native to managed code.*

The settings that you can specify with the attribute `[DllImport]` are listed in the following table.

DLLIMPORT PROPERTY OR FIELD	DESCRIPTION
EntryPoint	You can give the C# declaration of the function a different name than it has with the unmanaged library. The name of the method in the unmanaged library is defined in the field EntryPoint.
CallingConvention	Depending on the compiler or compiler settings that were used to compile the unmanaged function, different calling conventions can be used. The calling convention defines how the parameters are dealt with and where to put them on the stack. You can define the calling convention by setting an enumerable value. The Windows API usually uses the StdCall calling convention on the Windows operating system, and it uses the Cdecl calling convention on Windows CE. Setting the value to CallingConvention.Winapi works for the Windows API in both the Windows and the Windows CE environments.
CharSet	String parameters can be either ANSI or Unicode. With the CharSet setting, you can define how strings are managed. Possible values that are defined with the CharSet enumeration are Ansi, Unicode, and Auto. CharSet.Auto uses Unicode on the Windows NT platform, and ANSI on Windows 98 and Windows ME.
SetLastError	If the unmanaged function sets an error by using the Windows API SetLastError, you can set the SetLastError field to true. This way, you can read the error number afterward by using Marshal .GetLastWin32Error().

To make the CreateHardLink() method easier to use from a .NET environment, you should follow these guidelines:

➤   Create an internal class named NativeMethods that wraps the platform invoke method calls.

➤   Create a public class to offer the native method functionality to .NET applications.

➤   Use security attributes to mark the required security.

In the sample code, the public method CreateHardLink() in the class FileUtility is the method that can be used by .NET applications. This method has the filename arguments reversed compared to the native Windows API method CreateHardLink(). The first argument is the name of the existing file, and the second argument is the name of the new file. This is similar to other classes in the Framework; for example, File.Copy(). Because the third argument used to pass the security attributes for the new filename is not used with this implementation, the public method has just two parameters. The return type is changed as well. Instead of returning an error by returning the value false, an exception is thrown. In case of an error, the unmanaged method CreateHardLink() sets the error number with the unmanaged API SetLastError(). To read this value from .NET, the [DllImport] field SetLastError is set to true. Within the managed method CreateHardLink(), the error number is read by calling Marshal. GetLastWin32Error(). To create an error message from this number, the Win32Exception class from the namespace System.ComponentModel is used. This class accepts an error number with the constructor, and returns a localized error message. In case of an error, an exception of type IOException is thrown, which has an inner exception of type Win32Exception. The public method CreateHardLink() has the FileIOPermission attribute applied to check if the caller has the necessary permission. You can read more about .NET security in Chapter 21, "Security."

Available for
download on
Wrox.com

```
using System;
using System.ComponentModel;
using System.IO;
using System.Runtime.InteropServices;
using System.Security;
using System.Security.Permissions;
```

```
namespace Wrox.ProCSharp.Interop
{
    [SecurityCritical]
    internal static class NativeMethods
    {
        [DllImport("kernel32.dll", SetLastError = true,
            EntryPoint = "CreateHardLinkW", CharSet = CharSet.Unicode)]
        [return: MarshalAs(UnmanagedType.Bool)]
        private static extern bool CreateHardLink(
            [In, MarshalAs(UnmanagedType.LPWStr)] string newFileName,
            [In, MarshalAs(UnmanagedType.LPWStr)] string existingFileName,
            IntPtr securityAttributes);


        internal static void CreateHardLink(string oldFileName,
                                            string newFileName)
        {
            if (!CreateHardLink(newFileName, oldFileName, IntPtr.Zero))
            {
                var ex = new Win32Exception(Marshal.GetLastWin32Error());
                throw new IOException(ex.Message, ex);
            }
        }
    }

    public static class FileUtility
    {
        [FileIOPermission(SecurityAction.LinkDemand, Unrestricted = true)]
        public static void CreateHardLink(string oldFileName,
                                          string newFileName)
        {
            NativeMethods.CreateHardLink(oldFileName, newFileName);
        }
    }
}
```

code snippet PInvokeSample/NativeMethods.cs

This class can now be used to create hard links very easily. If the file passed with the first argument of the program does not exist, you will get an exception with the message "The system cannot find the file specified." If the file exists, you get a new filename referencing the original file. You can easily verify this by changing text in one file; it will show up in the other file as well.

```
using System;
using System.IO;

namespace Wrox.ProCSharp.Interop
{
    class Program
    {
        static void Main(string[] args)
        {
            if (args.Length != 2)
            {
                Console.WriteLine("usage: PInvokeSample " +
                            "existingfilename newfilename");
                return;
            }
            try
            {
                FileUtility.CreateHardLink(args[0], args[1]);
            }
            catch (IOException ex)
            {
```

```
                    Console.WriteLine(ex.Message);
            }

        }
    }
}
```

With native method calls, often you have to use Window handles. A Window handle is a 32-bit value where, depending on the handle types, some values are not allowed. With .NET 1.0 for handles, usually the `IntPtr` structure was used because you can set every possible 32-bit value with this structure. However, with some handle types, this led to security problems and possible threading race conditions and leaked handles with the finalization phase. That's why .NET 2.0 introduced the `SafeHandle` class. The class `SafeHandle` is an abstract base class for every Windows handle. Derived classes inside the `Microsoft.Win32.SafeHandles` namespace are `SafeHandleZeroOrMinusOneIsInvalid` and `SafeHandleMinusOneIsInvalid`. As the name indicates, these classes do not accept invalid 0 or –1 values. Further derived handle types are `SafeFileHandle`, `SafeWaitHandle`, `SafeNCryptHandle`, and `SafePipeHandle`, which can be used by the specific Windows API calls.

For example, to map the Windows API `CreateFile()`, you can use this declaration to return a `SafeFileHandle`. Of course, usually you could use the .NET classes `File` and `FileInfo` instead.

```
[DllImport("Kernel32.dll", SetLastError = true,
            CharSet = CharSet.Unicode)]
internal static extern SafeFileHandle CreateFile(
    string fileName,
    [MarshalAs(UnmanagedType.U4)] FileAccess fileAccess,
    [MarshalAs(UnmanagedType.U4)] FileShare fileShare,
    IntPtr securityAttributes,
    [MarshalAs(UnmanagedType.U4)] FileMode creationDisposition,
    int flags,
    SafeFileHandle template);
```

 In Chapter 23, "System.Transactions," you saw how to create a custom `SafeHandle`
class to work with the transacted file API from Windows 7.

SUMMARY

In this chapter, you have seen how the different generations of COM and .NET applications can interact. Instead of rewriting applications and components, a COM component can be used from a .NET application just like a .NET class. The tool that makes this possible is `tlbimp`, which creates a runtime callable wrapper (RCW) that hides the COM object behind a .NET façade.

Likewise, `tlbexp` creates a type library from a .NET component that is used by the COM callable wrapper (CCW). The CCW hides the .NET component behind a COM façade. Using .NET classes as COM components makes it necessary to use some attributes from the namespace `System.Runtime.InteropServices` to define specific COM characteristics that are needed by the COM client.

With platform invoke, you've seen how native methods can be invoked using C#. Platform invoke requires redefining the native method with C# and .NET data types. After defining the mapping, you can invoke the native method as if it were a C# method. Another option for doing interop would be to use the technology It Just Works (IJW) with C++/CLI. You can read information about C++/CLI in Chapter 53, "C#, Visual Basic, C++/CLI, and F#."

27

Core XAML

WHAT'S IN THIS CHAPTER?

- ➤ XAML syntax
- ➤ Dependency properties
- ➤ Markup extensions
- ➤ Loading XAML dynamically

When writing a .NET application, usually C# is not the only syntax you need to know. If you write Windows Presentation Foundation (WPF) applications, use Windows Workflow Foundation (WF), create XPS documents, or write Silverlight applications, you also need XAML. XAML (eXtensible Application Markup Language) is a declarative XML syntax that's usually needed with these applications.

This chapter gives you more information on the syntax of XAML and extensibility mechanisms that are available with this markup language.

OVERVIEW

XAML code is declared using textual XML. You can use designers to create XAML code or write XAML code by hand. Visual Studio contains designers to write XAML code for WPF, Silverlight, or WF. Other tools are also available to create XAML such as Microsoft Expression Design and Microsoft Expression Blend.

XAML is used with several technologies, but there are differences among the various technologies. With the XML namespace http://schemas.microsoft.com/winfx/2006/xaml/presentation, which is mapped as the default with WPF applications, WPF extensions to XAML are defined. WPF makes use of dependency properties, attached properties, and several WPF-specific markup extensions. WF 4 uses the XML namespace http://schemas.microsoft.com/netfx/2009/xaml/activities for the definition of the Workflow activities. The XML namespace http://schemas.microsoft.com/winfx/2006/xaml usually is mapped to the x prefix and defines features that are common to all XAML vocabularies.

A XAML element usually maps to a .NET class. That's not a strict requirement, but that's usually the case. With Silverlight 1.0, .NET was not available with the plugin and the XAML code was interpreted and could be accessed programmatically just with JavaScript. This changed since Silverlight 2.0, where a smaller version of the .NET Framework is part of the Silverlight plugin. With WPF, every XAML element has a class behind it. That's also the case with Windows Workflow Foundation, for example, the `DoWhile` XAML element is a looping activity backed by the `DoWhile` class in the namespace `System.Activities.Statements`. The `Button` XAML element is the same as the `Button` class in the `System.Windows.Controls` namespace.

It's also possible to use custom .NET classes within XML by mapping the .NET namespace to an XML alias, which is explained later. With .NET 4, XAML gets syntax enhancements, and this version is known as XAML 2009. The first version of XAML is XAML 2006, which is defined in the XML namespace `http://schemas.microsoft.com/winfx/2006/xaml/presentation`. The new version of XAML supports enhancements, like generics within XAML code. However, the WPF and WF designers available with the release of Visual Studio 2010 are still based on XAML 2006. You can use XAML 2009 by using it directly from within your applications to load XAML. This chapter gives you the information on changes of XAML 2009.

What happens with XAML code on a build process? To compile a WPF project, MSBuild tasks are defined in the assembly `PresentationBuildTasks`, named `MarkupCompilePass1` and `MarkupCompilePass2`. These MSBuild tasks create a binary representation of the markup code named BAML (Binary Application Markup Language) that is added to the .NET resources of an assembly. During runtime the binary representation is used.

Reading and writing XAML and BAML can be done with readers and writers. In the namespace `System.Xaml`, classes for core XAML features, such as abstract `XamlReader` and `XamlWriter` classes, and concrete implementations to read and write objects and XAML XML formats are available. The namespace `System.Windows.Markup` also contains some features that are available for all technologies using XAML from the assembly `System.Xaml`. Classes from this namespace that are found in the assembly `PresentationFramework` are WPF-specific extensions. For example, there you can find other `XamlReader` and `XamlWriter` classes that are optimized for WPF features.

Let's get into the syntax of XAML next.

Elements Map to .NET Objects

As mentioned in the last section, usually a XAML element maps to a .NET class. Let's start with creating a `Button` object inside a `Window` programmatically with a C# console project. To compile the following code where a `Button` object is instantiated with the `Content` property set to a string, a `Window` is defined with `Title` and `Content` properties set, and the assemblies `PresentationFramework`, `PresentationCore`, `WindowsBase` and `System.Xaml` need to be referenced.

Available for
download on
Wrox.com

```csharp
using System;
using System.Windows;
using System.Windows.Controls;

namespace Wrox.ProCSharp.XAML
{
    class Program
    {
        [STAThread]
        static void Main()
        {
            var b = new Button
            {
                Content = "Click Me!"
            };
            var w = new Window
            {
                Title = "Code Demo",
                Content = b
            };
```

```
                var app = new Application();
                app.Run(w);
            }
        }
    }
```

A similar UI can be created by using XAML code. As before, a `Window` element is created that contains a `Button` element. The `Window` element has the `Title` attribute set in addition to its content.

Available for download on Wrox.com

```xml
<Window x:Class="Wrox.ProCSharp.XAML.MainWindow"
        xmlns="http://schemas.microsoft.com/winfx/2006/xaml/presentation"
        xmlns:x="http://schemas.microsoft.com/winfx/2006/xaml"
        Title="XAML Demo" Height="350" Width="525">
    <Button Content="Click Me!" />
</Window>
```

Of course, the `Application` instance from before is missing. This can be defined with XAML as well. In the `Application` element, the `StartupUri` attribute is set, which links to the XAML file that contains the main window.

Available for download on Wrox.com

```xml
<Application x:Class="Wrox.ProCSharp.XAML.App"
             xmlns="http://schemas.microsoft.com/winfx/2006/xaml/presentation"
             xmlns:x="http://schemas.microsoft.com/winfx/2006/xaml"
             StartupUri="MainWindow.xaml">
    <Application.Resources>
    </Application.Resources>
</Application>
```

Using Custom .NET Classes

To use custom .NET classes within XAML code, only the .NET namespace needs to be declared within XAML, and an XML alias must be defined. To demonstrate this, a simple `Person` class with the `FirstName` and `LastName` properties is defined as shown.

Available for download on Wrox.com

```csharp
namespace Wrox.ProCSharp.XAML
{
    public class Person
    {
        public string FirstName { get; set; }
        public string LastName { get; set; }

        public override string ToString()
        {
            return string.Format("{0} {1}", FirstName, LastName);
        }
    }
}
```

In XAML, an XML namespace alias named `local` is defined that maps to the .NET namespace `Wrox.ProCSharp.XAML`. Now it's possible to use all classes from this namespace with the alias. In the XAML code a `ListBox` is added that contains items of type Person. Using XAML attributes, the values of the properties `FirstName` and `LastName` are set. When you run the application, the output of the `ToString()` method is shown inside the `ListBox`.

Available for
download on
Wrox.com

```xml
<Window x:Class="Wrox.ProCSharp.XAML.MainWindow"
        xmlns="http://schemas.microsoft.com/winfx/2006/xaml/presentation"
        xmlns:x="http://schemas.microsoft.com/winfx/2006/xaml"
        xmlns:local="clr-namespace:Wrox.ProCSharp.XAML"
        Title="XAML Demo" Height="350" Width="525">
    <StackPanel>
        <Button Content="Click Me!" />
        <ListBox>
            <local:Person FirstName="Stephanie" LastName="Nagel" />
            <local:Person FirstName="Angela" LastName="Schoeberl" />
        </ListBox>
    </StackPanel>
</Window>
```

code snippet XAMLIntro/MainWindow.xaml

 If the .NET namespace is not in the same assembly as the XAML code, the assembly name must also be included with the XML namespace alias, for example, `xmlns:local="clr-namespace:Wrox.ProCSharp.XAML;assembly=XAMLIntro"`.

To map a .NET namespace to an XML namespace, you can use the assembly attribute `XmlnsDefinition`. One argument of this attribute defines the XML namespace, the other the .NET namespace. Using this attribute, it is also possible to map multiple .NET namespaces to a single XML namespace.

Available for
download on
Wrox.com

```csharp
[assembly: XmlnsDefinition("http://www.wrox.covm/Schemas/2010",
"Wrox.ProCSharp.XAML")]
```

code snippet DemoLib/AssemblyInfo.cs

With this attribute in place, the namespace declaration in the XAML code can be changed to map to the XML namespace.

```xml
<Window x:Class="Wrox.ProCSharp.XAML.MainWindow"
        xmlns="http://schemas.microsoft.com/winfx/2006/xaml/presentation"
        xmlns:x="http://schemas.microsoft.com/winfx/2006/xaml"
        xmlns:local="http://www.wrox.com/Schemas/2010"
        Title="XAML Demo" Height="350" Width="525">
    <StackPanel>
        <Button Content="Click Me!" />
        <ListBox>
            <local:Person FirstName="Stephanie" LastName="Nagel" />
            <local:Person FirstName="Angela" LastName="Schoeberl" />
        </ListBox>
    </StackPanel>
</Window>
```

Properties as Attributes

Properties can be set as attributes as long as the property type can be represented as a string or there is a conversion from a string to the property type. The following code snippet sets the `Content` and `Background` property of the `Button` element with attributes. The `Content` property is of type `object` and thus also accepts a string. The `Background` property is of type `Brush`. The `Brush` type defines the `BrushConverter` class as a converter type with the attribute `TypeConverter` with which the class is annotated. `BrushConverter` uses a list of colors to return a `SolidColorBrush` from the `ConvertFromString()` method.

Available for
download on
Wrox.com

```xml
<Button Content="Click Me!" Background="LightGoldenrodYellow" />
```

code snippet XAMLSyntax/MainWindow.xaml

A type converter derives from the base class TypeConverter *in the* System. ComponentModel *namespace. The type of the class that needs conversion defines the type converter with the* TypeConverter *attribute. WPF uses many type converters to convert XML attributes to a specific type.* ColorConverter, FontFamilyConverter, PathFigureCollectionConverter, ThicknessConverter, GeometryConverter *are just a few of a large number of type converters.*

Properties as Elements

It's always also possible to use the element syntax to supply the value for properties. The Background property of the Button class can be set with the child element Button.Background. This way more complex brushes can be applied to this property, for example, a LinearGradientBrush, as shown in the example.

When setting the content in the sample, neither the Content attribute nor a Button.Content element is used to write the content; instead, the content is written directly as a child value to the Button element. That's possible because with a base class of the Button class (ContentControl), the ContentProperty attribute is applied, which marks the Content property as a ContentProperty: [ContentProperty ("Content")]. With such a marked property, the value of the property can be written as child element.

Available for download on Wrox.com

```
<Button>
    Click Me!
    <Button.Background>
        <LinearGradientBrush StartPoint="0.5,0.0" EndPoint="0.5, 1.0">
            <GradientStop Offset="0" Color="Yellow" />
            <GradientStop Offset="0.3" Color="Orange" />
            <GradientStop Offset="0.7" Color="Red" />
            <GradientStop Offset="1" Color="DarkRed" />
        </LinearGradientBrush>
    </Button.Background>
</Button>
```

code snippet XAMLSyntax/MainWindow.xaml

Essential .NET Types

In XAML 2006, core .NET types need to be referenced from an XML namespace like all other .NET classes, for example, the String with the sys alias, as shown here:

```
<sys:String xmlns:sys="clr-namespace:System;assembly=mscorlib">Simple String</sys:String>
```

XAML 2009 defines types such as String, Boolean, Object, Decimal, Double, Int32 and others with the x alias.

```
<x:String>Simple String</x:String>
```

Collections

In the ListBox that contains Person elements, you've already seen a collection within XAML. In the ListBox, the items have been directly defined as child elements. Also, the LinearGradientBrush contained a collection of GradientStop elements. This is possible because the base class ItemsControl has the attribute ContentProperty set to the Items property of the class, and the GradientBrush base class sets the attribute ContentProperty to GradientStops.

A longer version that defines the background by directly setting the `GradientStops` property and defining the `GradientStopCollection` element as its child is shown here:

```
<Button Click="OnButtonClick">
    Click Me!
    <Button.Background>
        <LinearGradientBrush StartPoint="0.5,0.0" EndPoint="0.5, 1.0">
            <LinearGradientBrush.GradientStops>
                <GradientStopCollection>
                    <GradientStop Offset="0" Color="Yellow" />
                    <GradientStop Offset="0.3" Color="Orange" />
                    <GradientStop Offset="0.7" Color="Red" />
                    <GradientStop Offset="1" Color="DarkRed" />
                </GradientStopCollection>
            </LinearGradientBrush.GradientStops>
        </LinearGradientBrush>
    </Button.Background>
</Button>
```

code snippet XAMLSyntax/MainWindow.xaml

To define an array, the `x:Array` extension can be used. The `x:Array` extension has a `Type` property where you can specify the type of the items of the array.

```
<x:Array Type="local:Person">
    <local:Person FirstName="Stephanie" LastName="Nagel" />
    <local:Person FirstName="Angela" LastName="Schoeberl" />
</x:Array>
```

XAML 2006 does not support generics, so to use a generic collection class from XAML you need to define a non-generic class that derives from the generic class and use the non-generic class instead. In XAML 2009, generics are directly supported in XAML with the `x:TypeArguments` to define the generic type, as shown here with `ObservableCollection<T>`.

```
<ObservableCollection x:TypeArguments="local:Person">
    <local:Person FirstName="Stephanie" LastName="Nagel" />
    <local:Person FirstName="Angela" LastName="Schoeberl" />
</ObservableCollection>
```

Constructors

If a class doesn't have a default constructor, it cannot be used with XAML 2006. With XAML 2009, you can use `x:Arguments` to invoke a constructor with parameters. Here is the `Person` class instantiated with a constructor that requires two `String` arguments.

```
<local:Person>
    <x:Arguments>
        <x:String>Stephanie</x:String>
        <x:String>Nagel</x:String>
    </x:Arguments>
</local:Person>
```

DEPENDENCY PROPERTIES

WPF uses dependency properties for data binding, animations, property change notification, styling, and so forth. For data binding, the property of the UI element that is bound to the source of a .NET property must be a dependency property.

From the outside, a dependency property looks like a normal .NET property. However, with a normal .NET property you usually also define the data member that is accessed by the `get` and `set` accessors of the property.

```
private int val;
public int Value
{
    get
    {
        return val;
    }
    set
    {
        val = value;
    }
}
```

That's not the case with dependency properties. A dependency property usually has a `get` and `set` accessor of a property as well. With the implementation of the `get` and `set` accessors, the methods `GetValue()` and `SetValue()` are invoked. `GetValue()` and `SetValue()` are members of the base class `DependencyObject`, which also gives you a requirement for dependency objects — that they must be implemented in a class that derives from `DependencyObject`.

With a dependency property, the data member is kept inside an internal collection that is managed by the base class and only allocates data if the value is changed. With unchanged values, the data can be shared between different instances or also base classes. The `GetValue` and `SetValue` methods require a `DependencyProperty` argument. This argument is defined by a static member of the class that has the same name as the property appended to the term `Property`. With the property `Value`, the static member has the name `ValueProperty`. `DependencyProperty.Register()` is a helper method that registers the property in the dependency property system. In this code snippet the `Register` method is used with three arguments to define the name of the property, the type of the property, and the type of the owner that is the class `MyDependencyObject`.

Available for download on Wrox.com

```
public int Value
{
    get { return (int)GetValue(ValueProperty); }
    set { SetValue(ValueProperty, value); }
}

public static readonly DependencyProperty ValueProperty =
    DependencyProperty.Register("Value", typeof(int), typeof(MyDependencyObject));
```

code snippet DependencyObjectDemo/MyDependencyObject.cs

Creating a Dependency Property

Let's look at a sample that defines not one but three dependency properties. The class `MyDependencyObject` defines the dependency properties `Value`, `Minimum`, and `Maximum`. All of these properties are dependency properties that are registered with the method `DependencyProperty.Register()`. The methods `GetValue()` and `SetValue()` are members of the base class `DependencyObject`. For the `Minimum` and `Maximum` properties, default values are defined that can be set with the `DependencyProperty.Register()` method and a fourth argument to set the `PropertyMetadata`. Using a constructor with one parameter, `PropertyMetadata`, the `Minimum` property is set to `0`, and the `Maximum` property is set to `100`.

Available for download on Wrox.com

```
using System;
using System.Windows;

namespace Wrox.ProCSharp.XAML
{
    class MyDependencyObject : DependencyObject
    {
        public int Value
        {
            get { return (int)GetValue(ValueProperty); }
```

```
            set { SetValue(ValueProperty, value); }
        }

        public static readonly DependencyProperty ValueProperty =
            DependencyProperty.Register("Value", typeof(int), typeof(MyDependencyObject));

        public int Minimum
        {
            get { return (int)GetValue(MinimumProperty); }
            set { SetValue(MinimumProperty, value); }
        }

        public static readonly DependencyProperty MinimumProperty =
            DependencyProperty.Register("Minimum", typeof(int), typeof(MyDependencyObject),
                                new PropertyMetadata(0));

        public int Maximum
        {
            get { return (int)GetValue(MaximumProperty); }
            set { SetValue(MaximumProperty, value); }
        }

        public static readonly DependencyProperty MaximumProperty =
            DependencyProperty.Register("Maximum", typeof(int), typeof(MyDependencyObject),
                                new PropertyMetadata(100));
    }
}
```

code snippet DependencyObjectDemo/MyDependencyObject.cs

> *Within the* get *and* set *property accessors you may not do more than just calling the* GetValue() *and* SetValue() *methods. Using the dependency properties, the property values can be accessed from the outside with the* GetValue() *and* SetValue() *methods, which is also done from WPF, and thus, the strongly-typed property accessors might not be invoked at all. They are just here for convenience for custom code.*

Coerce Value Callback

Dependency properties support coercion. With coercion, the value of the property can be checked to see if it is valid, for example, that it falls within a valid range. That's why the Minimum and Maximum properties are included in the sample. Now the registration of the Value property is changed to pass the event handler method CoerceValue() to the constructor of PropertyMetadata, which is passed as an argument to the DependencyProperty.Register() method. The CoerceValue() method is now invoked with every change of the property value from the implementation of the SetValue() method. Within CoerceValue(), the set value is checked to see if it falls within the range between the minimum and maximum, and the value is set accordingly if this is not the case.

```
using System;
using System.Windows;

namespace Wrox.ProCSharp.XAML
{
    class MyDependencyObject : DependencyObject
    {
        public int Value
        {
            get { return (int)GetValue(ValueProperty); }
```

```
            set { SetValue(ValueProperty, value); }
        }

        public static readonly DependencyProperty ValueProperty =DependencyProperty.
            Register("Value", typeof(int), typeof(MyDependencyObject));new PropertyMetadata
            (0, null, CoerceValue));

        public int Minimum
        {
            get { return (int)GetValue(MinimumProperty); }
            set { SetValue(MinimumProperty, value); }
        }

        public static readonly DependencyProperty MinimumProperty =
            DependencyProperty.Register("Minimum", typeof(int), typeof(MyDependencyObject),
                                new PropertyMetadata(0));

        public int Maximum
        {
            get { return (int)GetValue(MaximumProperty); }
            set { SetValue(MaximumProperty, value); }
        }

        public static readonly DependencyProperty MaximumProperty =
            DependencyProperty.Register("Maximum", typeof(int), typeof(MyDependencyObject),
                                new PropertyMetadata(100));

        private static object CoerceValue(DependencyObject element, object value)
        {
            int newValue = (int)value;
            MyDependencyObject control = (MyDependencyObject)element;

            newValue = Math.Max(control.Minimum, Math.Min(control.Maximum, newValue));
            return newValue;
        }
    }
}
```

code snippet DependencyObjectDemo/MyDependencyObject.cs

Value Changed Callbacks and Events

To get some information on value changes, dependency properties also support value change callbacks.
You can add a DependencyPropertyChanged event handler to the DependencyProperty.Register()
method that is invoked when the property value changes. In the sample code, the handler method
OnValueChanged() is assigned to the PropertyChangedCallback to the PropertyMetadata object.
In the OnValueChanged method, you can access the old and new values of the property with the
DependencyPropertyChangedEventArgs() argument.

```
using System;
using System.Windows;

namespace Wrox.ProCSharp.XAML
{
    class MyDependencyObject : DependencyObject
    {
        public int Value
        {
            get { return (int)GetValue(ValueProperty); }
            set { SetValue(ValueProperty, value); }
        }
```

```
public static readonly DependencyProperty ValueProperty =
    DependencyProperty.Register("Value", typeof(int), typeof(MyDependencyObject),
    new PropertyMetadata(0, OnValueChanged, CoerceValue));

//...

private static void OnValueChanged(DependencyObject obj,
                                    DependencyPropertyChangedEventArgs args)
{
    int oldValue = (int)args.OldValue;
    int newValue = (int)args.NewValue;
    //...
}
}
}
```

code snippet DependencyObjectDemo/MyDependencyObject.cs

BUBBLING AND TUNNELING EVENTS

Elements can be contained in elements. With XAML and WPF, you can define that a Button contains a ListBox; the ListBox contains items that are Button controls again. When you click on an inner control, the event should go all the way to the outside. WPF supports bubbling and tunneling events. Often these events are used in pairs. The PreviewMouseMove event is a tunneling event that tunnels from the outside to the inside. MouseMove follows the PreviewMouseMove event and is a bubbling event that bubbles from the inside to the outside.

 Core information about .NET events is explained in Chapter 8, "Delegates, Lambdas, and Events."

To demonstrate bubbling, the following XAML code contains four Button controls where the surrounding StackPanel defines an event handler for the Button.Click event named OnOuterButtonClick(). button2 contains a ListBox that has two Button controls as its children and the Click event handler OnButton2(). Both of the inner buttons also have an event handler associated with the Click event.

Available for
download on
Wrox.com

```
<Window x:Class=" Wrox.ProCSharp.XAML.MainWindow"
        xmlns="http://schemas.microsoft.com/winfx/2006/xaml/presentation"
        xmlns:x="http://schemas.microsoft.com/winfx/2006/xaml"
        Title="MainWindow" Height="350" Width="525">
    <StackPanel x:Name="stackPanel1" Button.Click="OnOuterButtonClick">
        <Button x:Name="button1" Content="Button 1" Margin="5" />
        <Button x:Name="button2" Margin="5" Click="OnButton2" >
            <ListBox x:Name="listBox1">
                <Button x:Name="innerButton1" Content="Inner Button 1" Margin="4"
                        Padding="4" Click="OnInner1" />
                <Button x:Name="innerButton2" Content="Inner Button 2" Margin="4"
                        Padding="4" Click="OnInner2" />
            </ListBox>
        </Button>
        <ListBox ItemsSource="{Binding}" />
    </StackPanel>
</Window>
```

code snippet BubbleDemo/MainWindow.xaml

The event handler methods are implemented in the code-behind. The second argument of the handler methods is of type RoutedEventArgs, which provides information about the Source of the event and the OriginalSource. When you click button1, the handler method OnOuterButtonClick() is invoked, although there's no Click event directly associated with this button; the event is bubbled to the container element. Source and OriginalSource is button1 in that case. If you click on button2 first, the event handler OnButton2() is invoked, followed by OnOuterButtonClick(). The handler OnButton2() changes the Source property, so with OnOuterButtonClick() you can see a different Source than in the handler before. The Source property of an event can be changed, but the OriginalSource is readonly. Clicking the button innerButton1 invokes the OnInner1() event handler followed by OnButton2() and by OnOuterButtonClick(). The event bubbles. When you click innerButton2 only the handler OnInner2() is invoked because the Handled property there is set to true. Bubbling stops here.

```csharp
using System;
using System.Collections.ObjectModel;
using System.Windows;

namespace BubbleDemo
{
    public partial class MainWindow : Window
    {
        private ObservableCollection<string> messages = new ObservableCollection<string>();
        public MainWindow()
        {
            InitializeComponent();
            this.DataContext = messages;
        }

        private void AddMessage(string message, object sender, RoutedEventArgs e)
        {
            messages.Add(String.Format("{0}, sender: {1}; source: {2}; original source: {3}",
                message, (sender as FrameworkElement).Name,
                (e.Source as FrameworkElement).Name,
                (e.OriginalSource as FrameworkElement).Name));
        }

        private void OnOuterButtonClick(object sender, RoutedEventArgs e)
        {
            AddMessage("outer event", sender, e);
        }

        private void OnInner1(object sender, RoutedEventArgs e)
        {
            AddMessage("inner1", sender, e);
        }

        private void OnInner2(object sender, RoutedEventArgs e)
        {
            AddMessage("inner2", sender, e);
            e.Handled = true;
        }

        private void OnButton2(object sender, RoutedEventArgs e)
        {
            AddMessage("button2", sender, e);
            e.Source = sender;
        }
    }
}
```

code snippet BubbleDemo/MainWindow.xaml.cs

Changing the source and also changing the event type is very common. For example, the Button *class reacts to the mouse down and up events, handles these, and creates a button click event instead.*

If the implementation of different handlers is very similar (for example, multiple buttons in a container), writing just one event handler bubbling is very beneficial. In the implementation, you just need to differentiate the sender or source.

How can you define bubbling and tunneling events in custom classes? The MyDependencyObject is changed to support an event on a value change. For bubbling and tunneling event support, the class must now derive from UIElement instead of DependencyObject because this class defines AddHandler() and RemoveHandler() methods for events.

To let the caller of the MyDependencyObject receive information on value changes, the class defines the ValueChanged event. The event is declared with explicit add and remove handlers, where the AddHandler() and RemoveHandler() methods of the base class are invoked. The AddHandler() and RemoveHandler() methods require a type RoutedEvent and the delegate as parameters. The routed event named ValueChangedEvent is declared very similarly to a dependency property. It is declared as a static member and registered by calling the method EventManager.RegisterRoutedEvent(). This method requires the name of the event, the routing strategy (which can be Bubble, Tunnel, and Direct), the type of the handler, and the type of the owner class. The EventManager class also gives you the capability to register static events and get information about the events registered.

```csharp
using System;
using System.Windows;

namespace Wrox.ProCSharp.XAML
{
    class MyDependencyObject : UIElement
    {
        public int Value
        {
            get { return (int)GetValue(ValueProperty); }
            set { SetValue(ValueProperty, value); }
        }

        public static readonly DependencyProperty ValueProperty =
            DependencyProperty.Register("Value", typeof(int), typeof(MyDependencyObject),
            new PropertyMetadata(0, OnValueChanged, CoerceValue));

        //...

        private static void OnValueChanged(DependencyObject obj,
                                           DependencyPropertyChangedEventArgs args)
        {
            MyDependencyObject control = (MyDependencyObject)obj;

            RoutedPropertyChangedEventArgs<int> e = new RoutedPropertyChangedEventArgs<int>(
                    (int)args.OldValue, (int)args.NewValue, ValueChangedEvent);
            control.OnValueChanged(e);
        }

        public static readonly RoutedEvent ValueChangedEvent =
            EventManager.RegisterRoutedEvent("ValueChanged", RoutingStrategy.Bubble,
                typeof(RoutedPropertyChangedEventHandler<int>), typeof(MyDependencyObject));
```

```
        public event RoutedPropertyChangedEventHandler<int> ValueChanged
        {
            add
            {
                AddHandler(ValueChangedEvent, value);
            }
            remove
            {
                RemoveHandler(ValueChangedEvent, value);
            }
        }

        protected virtual void OnValueChanged(RoutedPropertyChangedEventArgs<int> args)
        {
            RaiseEvent(args);
        }
    }
}
```

code snippet DependencyObjectDemo/MyDependencyObject.cs

Now you can use this with bubbling functionality in the same way that you've seen it used before with the button click event.

ATTACHED PROPERTIES

Dependency properties are properties available with a specific type. With an attached property, you can define properties for other types. Some container controls define attached properties for their children; for example, if the DockPanel control is used, a Dock property is available for its children. The Grid control defines Row and Column properties.

The code snippet below demonstrates how this looks in XAML. The Button class doesn't have the property Dock, but it's attached from the DockPanel.

```
<DockPanel>
    <Button Content="Top" DockPanel.Dock="Top" Background="Yellow" />
    <Button Content="Left" DockPanel.Dock="Left" Background="Blue" />
</DockPanel>
```

Attached properties can be defined very similarly to dependency properties, as you can see in the next sample. The class that defines the attached properties must derive from the base class DependencyObject and defines a normal property, where the get and set accessors invoke the methods GetValue() and SetValue() of the base class. This is where the similarities end. Instead of invoking the method Register() with the DependencyProperty class, now RegisterAttached() is invoked. RegisterAttached() registers an attached property that is now available with every element.

```
using System.Windows;

namespace Wrox.ProCSharp.XAML
{
    class MyAttachedPropertyProvider : DependencyObject
    {
        public int MyProperty
        {
            get { return (int)GetValue(MyPropertyProperty); }
            set { SetValue(MyPropertyProperty, value); }
        }

        public static readonly DependencyProperty MyPropertyProperty =
            DependencyProperty.RegisterAttached("MyProperty", typeof(int),
                typeof(MyAttachedPropertyProvider));
```

```
        public static void SetMyProperty(UIElement element, int value)
        {
            element.SetValue(MyPropertyProperty, value);
        }

        public static int GetMyProperty(UIElement element)
        {
            return (int)element.GetValue(MyPropertyProperty);
        }
    }
}
```

code snippet AttachedPropertyDemo/MyAttachedPropertyProvider.cs

 It seems like `DockPanel.Dock` *can only be added to elements within a* `DockPanel`. *In reality, attached properties can be added to any element. However, no one would use this property value. The* `DockPanel` *is aware of this property and reads it from its child elements to arrange them.*

In the XAML code, the attached property can now be attached to any elements. The second `Button` control, named `button2`, has the property `MyAttachedPropertyProvider.MyProperty` attached to it and the value 5 assigned.

```xml
<Window x:Class="Wrox.ProCSharp.XAML.MainWindow"
        xmlns="http://schemas.microsoft.com/winfx/2006/xaml/presentation"
        xmlns:x="http://schemas.microsoft.com/winfx/2006/xaml"
        xmlns:local="clr-namespace:Wrox.ProCSharp.XAML"
        Title="MainWindow" Height="350" Width="525">
    <Grid x:Name="grid1">
        <Grid.RowDefinitions>
            <RowDefinition Height="Auto" />
            <RowDefinition Height="Auto" />
            <RowDefinition Height="*" />
        </Grid.RowDefinitions>

        <Button Grid.Row="0" x:Name="button1" Content="Button 1" />
        <Button Grid.Row="1" x:Name="button2" Content="Button 2"
                local:MyAttachedPropertyProvider.MyProperty="5" />

        <ListBox Grid.Row="2" x:Name="list1" />
    </Grid>
</Window>
```

code snippet AttachedPropertyDemo/MainWindow.xaml

Doing the same in code-behind it is necessary to invoke the static method `SetMyProperty()` of the class `MyAttachedPropertyProvider`. It's not possible to extend the class `Button` with a property. The method `SetProperty()` gets a `UIElement` instance that should be extended by the property and the value. In the code snippet, the property is attached to `button1` and the value is set to 44.

The `foreach` loop that follows the property setting retrieves the values from the attached properties from all child elements of the `Grid` element `grid1`. Retrieving the values is done with the `GetProperty()` method of the class `MyAttachedPropertyProvider`. This is done from the `DockPanel` and the `Grid` control to retrieve the settings from its children to arrange them.

```
using System;
using System.Windows;

namespace Wrox.ProCSharp.XAML
```

```
{
    public partial class MainWindow : Window
    {
        public MainWindow()
        {
            InitializeComponent();

            MyAttachedPropertyProvider.SetMyProperty(button1, 44);

            foreach (object item in LogicalTreeHelper.GetChildren(grid1))
            {
                FrameworkElement e = item as FrameworkElement;
                if (e != null)
                    list1.Items.Add(String.Format("{0}: {1}", e.Name,
                        MyAttachedPropertyProvider.GetMyProperty(e)));
            }
        }
    }
}
```

code snippet AttachedPropertyDemo/MainWindow.xaml.cs

 There are some mechanisms available to extend classes at a later time. Extension methods can be used to extend any class with methods. Extension methods only support extending classes with methods, not properties. Extension methods are explained in Chapter 3, "Objects and Types." The ExpandoObject *class allows the extension of types with methods and properties. To use this feature, the class must derive from* ExpandoObject. ExpandoObject *and dynamic types are explained in Chapter 12, "Dynamic Language Extensions."*

 Chapters 35 and 36 show many different attached properties in action, for example attached properties from container controls such as Canvas, DockPanel, Grid, *but also the* ErrorTemplate *property from the* Validation *class.*

MARKUP EXTENSIONS

With markup extensions you can extend XAML, with either element or attribute syntax. If an XML attribute contains curly brackets, that's a sign of a markup extension. Often markup extensions with attributes are used as shorthand notation instead of using elements.

One example of such a markup extension is StaticResourceExtension, which finds resources. Here's a resource of a linear gradient brush with the key gradientBrush1.

```
<Window.Resources>
    <LinearGradientBrush x:Key="gradientBrush1" StartPoint="0.5,0.0" EndPoint="0.5, 1.0">
        <GradientStop Offset="0" Color="Yellow" />
        <GradientStop Offset="0.3" Color="Orange" />
        <GradientStop Offset="0.7" Color="Red" />
        <GradientStop Offset="1" Color="DarkRed" />
    </LinearGradientBrush>
</Window.Resources>
```

code snippet MarkupExtensionDemo/MainWindow.xaml

This resource can be referenced by using the `StaticResourceExtension` with attribute syntax to set the `Background` property of a `TextBlock`. Attribute syntax is defined by curly brackets and the name of the extension class without the `Extension` postfix.

```
<TextBlock Text="Test" Background="{StaticResource gradientBrush1}" />
```

The longer form of the attribute shorthand notation uses element syntax, as the next code snippet demonstrates. `StaticResourceExtension` is defined as a child element of the `TextBlock.Background` element. The property `ResourceKey` is set with an attribute to `gradientBrush1`. In the previous example, the resource key is not set with the property `ResourceKey` (which would be possible as well) but with a constructor overload where the resource key can be set.

```
<TextBlock Text="Test">
    <TextBlock.Background>
        <StaticResourceExtension ResourceKey="gradientBrush1" />
    </TextBlock.Background>
</TextBlock>
```

Creating Custom Markup Extensions

A markup extension is created by defining a class that derives from the base class `MarkupExtension`. Most markup extensions have the `Extension` postfix (this naming convention is similar to the `Attribute` postfix with attributes, which you can read about in Chapter 14, "Reflection"). With a custom markup extension, you only need to override the method `ProvideValue()`, which returns the value from the extension. The type that is returned is annotated to the class with the attribute `MarkupExtensionReturnType`. With the method `ProvideValue`, an `IServiceProvider` object is passed. With this interface you can query for different services, such as `IProvideValueTarget` or `IXamlTypeResolver`. `IProvideValueTarget` can be used to access the control and property where the markup extension is applied to with the `TargetObject` and `TargetProperty` properties. `IXamlTypeResolver` can be used to resolve XAML element names to CLR objects. The custom markup extension class `CalculatorExtension` defines the properties `X` and `Y` of type `double` and an `Operation` property that is defined by an enumeration. Depending on the value of the `Operation` property, different calculations are done on the `X` and `Y` input properties, and a string is returned.

Available for
download on
Wrox.com

```csharp
using System;
using System.Windows;
using System.Windows.Markup;

namespace Wrox.ProCSharp.XAML
{
    public enum Operation
    {
        Add,
        Subtract,
        Multiply,
        Divide
    }

    [MarkupExtensionReturnType(typeof(string))]
    public class CalculatorExtension : MarkupExtension
    {
        public CalculatorExtension()
        {

        }

        public double X { get; set; }
        public double Y { get; set; }

        public Operation Operation { get; set; }
```

```csharp
public override object ProvideValue(IServiceProvider serviceProvider)
{
    IProvideValueTarget provideValue =
        serviceProvider.GetService(typeof(IProvideValueTarget))
                                as IProvideValueTarget;
    if (provideValue != null)
    {
        var host = provideValue.TargetObject as FrameworkElement;
        var prop = provideValue.TargetProperty as DependencyProperty;
    }

    double result = 0;
    switch (Operation)
    {
        case Operation.Add:
            result = X + Y;
            break;
        case Operation.Subtract:
            result = X - Y;
            break;
        case Operation.Multiply:
            result = X * Y;
            break;
        case Operation.Divide:
            result = X / Y;
            break;
        default:
            throw new ArgumentException("invalid operation");
    }

    return result.ToString();
}
}
}
```

code snippet MarkupExtensionDemo/CalculatorExtension.cs

The markup extension can now be used with an attribute syntax in the first TextBlock to add the values 3 and 4, or with the element syntax with the second TextBlock.

```xml
<Window x:Class="Wrox.ProCSharp.XAML.MainWindow"
        xmlns="http://schemas.microsoft.com/winfx/2006/xaml/presentation"
        xmlns:x="http://schemas.microsoft.com/winfx/2006/xaml"
        xmlns:local="clr-namespace:Wrox.ProCSharp.XAML"
        Title="MainWindow" Height="350" Width="525">
    <StackPanel>
        <TextBlock Text="{local:Calculator Operation=Add, X=3, Y=4}" />
        <TextBlock>
            <TextBlock.Text>
                <local:CalculatorExtension>
                    <local:CalculatorExtension.Operation>
                        <local:Operation>Multiply</local:Operation>
                     </local:CalculatorExtension.Operation>
                    <local:CalculatorExtension.X>7</local:CalculatorExtension.X>
                    <local:CalculatorExtension.Y>11</local:CalculatorExtension.Y>
                </local:CalculatorExtension>
            </TextBlock.Text>
        </TextBlock>
    </StackPanel>
</Window>
```

code snippet MarkupExtensionDemo/MainWindow.xaml

XAML-Defined Markup Extensions

Markup extensions provide a lot of capabilities. And indeed XAML-defined markup extensions have already been used in this chapter. x:Array, which was shown in the "Collections" section, is defined as the markup extension class ArrayExtension. With this markup extension, using the attribute syntax is not possible because it would be difficult to define a list of elements.

Other markup extensions that are defined with XAML are the TypeExtension (x:Type), which returns the type based on string input; NullExtension (x:Null), which can be used to set values to null in XAML; and StaticExtension (x:Static) to invoke static members of a class.

WPF, WF, and WCF define markup extensions that are specific to these technologies. WPF uses markup extensions to access resources, for data binding, and color conversion; WF uses markup extensions with activities; and WCF defines markup extensions for endpoint definitions.

READING AND WRITING XAML

Several APIs exist for reading and writing XAML. There are high-level APIs that are easy to use but have less functionality and low-level APIs with more features. Technology-specific APIs that make use of specific WPF or WF features are also available. XAML can be read from a textual XML form, from BAML, or from object trees, and written to XML or object trees.

Generic high-level APIs are available in the namespace System.Xaml. The class XamlServices allows loading, parsing, saving, and transforming XAML. XamlServices.Load() can load XAML code from a file, a stream, or a reader, or by using a XamlReader object. XamlReader (in the namespace System.Xaml) is an abstract base class that has several concrete implementations. XamlObjectReader reads an object tree, XamlXmlReader reads XAML from an XML file, Baml2006Reader reads the binary form of XAML. XamlDebuggerXmlReader from the namespace System.Activities.Debugger is a special reader for WF with special debugging support.

When passing XAML code in a string to XamlServices, the Parse() method can be used. XamlServices. Save() can be used to save XAML code. With the Save() method you can use similar data sources as with the Load() method. The object passed can be saved to a string, a stream, a TextWriter, a XamlWriter, or an XmlWriter. XamlWriter is an abstract base class. Classes that derive from XamlWriter are XamlObjectWriter and XamlXmlWriter. In the release of .NET 4, there's no writer for BAML code, but it is expected to have a BAML writer available at a later time.

When converting XAML from one format in another, you can use XamlServices.Transform(). With the Transform method, you pass a XamlReader and a XamlWriter so that you can convert any format that is supported by specific readers and writers.

Instead of using the high-level API XamlServices class, you can use generic low-level APIs directly, which means using specific XamlReader and XamlWriter classes. With a reader, you can read node by node from a XAML tree with the Read() method.

The generic XamlServices class doesn't support specific WPF features such as dependency properties or freezable objects. To read and write WPF XAML, you can use the classes XamlReader and XamlWriter from the namespace System.Windows.Markup that is defined in the assembly PresentationFramework and thus has access to the WPF features. The names of these classes might be confusing, as the same class names are used with classes from different namespaces. System.Xaml.XamlReader is the abstract base class for readers; System.Windows.Markup.XamlReader is the WPF class to read XAML. This can be even more confusing when using the Load method of the WPF XamlReader class that accepts a System.Xaml .XamlReader as argument.

An optimized version to read XAML for WF is WorkflowXamlServices in the namespace System.Activities. This class is used to create dynamic activities during runtime.

Dynamic activities and Windows Workflow Foundation 4 are explained in Chapter 44, "Windows Workflow Foundation 4."

A simple example to load XAML dynamically from a file to create an object tree and to attach the object tree to a container element, such as a `StackPanel`, is shown here.

```
FileStream stream = File.OpenRead("Demo1.xaml");
object tree = System.Windows.Markup.XamlReader.Load(stream);

container1.Children.Add(tree as UIElement);
```

SUMMARY

In this chapter, you've seen the core functionality of XAML and some specific characteristics such as dependency properties, attached properties, and markup extensions. You have seen the extensibility of XAML, which serves as the base for other technologies such as WPF and WF. In other chapters that make use of XAML, you can see a lot of different uses for these XAML characteristics.

You can read more about XAML and see XAML in action in a lot of chapters in this book. In particular, you should read Chapters 35 and 36 for WPF, Chapter 37 for XPS, Chapter 38 for Silverlight, and Chapter 44 for Windows Workflow Foundation.

The next chapter is about MEF, the Managed Extensibility Framework.

28

Managed Extensibility Framework

WHAT'S IN THIS CHAPTER?

➤ Architecture of the Managed Extensibility Framework

➤ Contracts

➤ Exports and imports of parts

➤ Containers used by hosting applications

➤ Catalogs for finding parts

Add-ins (or plugins) allow you to add functionality to an application at a later time. You can create a hosting application that gains more and more functionality over time — such functionality might be written by your team of developers, but different vendors can also extend your application by creating add-ins.

Today, add-ins are used with many different applications, such as Internet Explorer and Visual Studio. Internet Explorer is a hosting application that offers an add-in framework that is used by many companies to provide extensions when viewing web pages. The Shockwave Flash Object allows you to view web pages with Flash content. The Google toolbar offers specific Google features that can be accessed quickly from Internet Explorer. Visual Studio also has an add-in model that allows you to extend Visual Studio with different levels of extensions.

For your custom applications, it has always been possible to create an add-in model to dynamically load and use functionality from assemblies. However, all the issues with finding and using add-ins need to be resolved. This task can be accomplished automatically using the Managed Extensibility Framework.

The major namespace that is covered in this chapter is `System.ComponentModel.Composition`.

MEF ARCHITECTURE

The .NET 4 Framework offers two technologies for writing flexible applications that load add-ins dynamically. One technology is the Managed Extensibility Framework (MEF), which is covered in this chapter. Another technology that has been available since .NET 3.5 is the Managed Add-in

Framework (MAF), which is covered in the downloadable Chapter 50, "Managed Add-In Framework." MAF uses a pipeline for communication between the add-in and the host application that makes the development process more complex but also offers separation of add-ins via appdomains or even different processes. In that regard, MEF is the simpler of these two technologies. MAF and MEF can be combined to get the advantage of each (but also doubles the work).

MEF is built up with parts and containers, as shown in Figure 28-1. A container finds parts from a catalog. The catalog finds parts within an assembly or a directory. The container connects imports to exports and, thus, makes parts available to the hosting application.

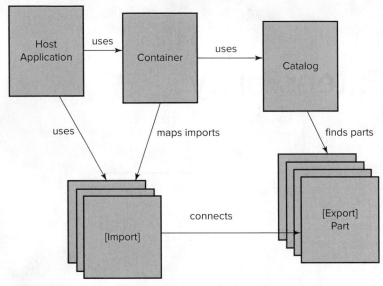

FIGURE 28-1

Here's the full picture of how parts are loaded. Parts are found within a catalog. The catalog uses exports to find its parts. An export provider accesses the catalog to offer the exports from the catalog. Multiple export providers can be connected in chains for customizing exports, for example, with a custom export provider to only allow parts for specific users or roles. The container uses export providers to connect imports to exports and is itself an export provider.

MEF consists of three large categories: classes for hosting, primitives, and classes for the attribute-based mechanism. Hosting classes include catalogs and containers. Primitive classes can be used as base classes to extend the MEF architecture to use other techniques to connect exports and imports. And of course, the classes that make up the implementation of the attribute-based mechanism with reflection, such as the Export and Import attributes, and classes that offer extension methods make it easier to work with attribute-based parts are also part of MEF.

The MEF implementation is based on attributes that mark what parts should be exported and map these to the imports. However, the technology is flexible and allows for other mechanisms to be implemented by using the abstract base class ComposablePart *and extension methods with reflection-based mechanisms from the class* ReflectionModelServices. *This architecture can be extended to derive classes from* ComposablePart *and provide additional extension methods that retrieve information from add-ins via other mechanisms.*

Let's start with a simple example to demonstrate the MEF architecture. The hosting application can dynamically load add-ins. With MEF, an add-in is referred to as a *part*. Parts are defined as *exports* and are loaded into a container that *imports* parts. The container finds parts by using a catalog. The catalog lists parts.

In this example, a simple Console application that is the host is created to host calculator-add-ins from a library. To create independence from the host and the calculator add-in, three assemblies are required. One assembly, SimpleContract, holds the contracts that are used by both the add-in assembly and the hosting executable. The add-in assembly SimpleCalculator implements the contract defined by the contract assembly. The host uses the contract assembly to invoke the add-in.

The contracts in the assembly SimpleContract are defined by two interfaces, ICalculator and IOperation. The ICalculator interface defines the methods GetOperations() and Operate(). The GetOperations() method returns a list of all operations that the add-in calculator supports, and with the Operate() method an operation is invoked. This interface is flexible in that the calculator can support different operations. If the interface defined Add() and Subtract() methods instead of the flexible Operate() method, a new version of the interface would be required to support Divide() and Multiply() methods. With the ICalculator interface as it is defined in this example, however, the calculator can offer any number of operations with any number of operands.

```
using System.Collections.Generic;

namespace Wrox.ProCSharp.MEF
{
    public interface ICalculator
    {
        IList<IOperation> GetOperations();
        double Operate(IOperation operation, double[] operands);
    }
}
```

code snippet SimpleContract/ICalculator.cs

The ICalculator interface uses the IOperation interface to return the list of operations and to invoke an operation. The IOperation interface defines the read-only properties Name and NumberOperands.

```
namespace Wrox.ProCSharp.MEF
{
    public interface IOperation
    {
        string Name { get; }
        int NumberOperands { get; }
    }
}
```

code snippet SimpleContract/IOperation.cs

The SimpleContract assembly doesn't require any reference to MEF assemblies. Only simple .NET interfaces are contained within it.

The Add-in assembly SimpleCalculator contains classes that implement the interfaces defined by the contracts. The class Operation implements the interface IOperation. This class contains just two properties as defined by the interface. The interface defines get accessors of the properties; internal set accessors are used to set the properties from within the assembly.

```
namespace Wrox.ProCSharp.MEF
{
    public class Operation : IOperation
    {
        public string Name { get; internal set; }
```

```
            public int NumberOperands { get; internal set; }
        }
    }
```

code snippet SimpleCalculator/Operation.cs

The `Calculator` class provides the functionality of this add-in by implementing the `ICalculator` interface. The `Calculator` class is exported as a part as defined by the `Export` attribute. This attribute is defined in the `System.ComponentModel.Composition` namespace in the `System.ComponentModel.Composition` assembly.

```
using System;
using System.Collections.Generic;
using System.ComponentModel.Composition;

namespace Wrox.ProCSharp.MEF
{
    [Export(typeof(ICalculator))]
    public class Calculator : ICalculator
    {
        public IList<IOperation> GetOperations()
        {
            return new List<IOperation>()
            {
                new Operation { Name="+", NumberOperands=2},
                new Operation { Name="-", NumberOperands=2},
                new Operation { Name="/", NumberOperands=2},
                new Operation { Name="*", NumberOperands=2}
            };
        }

        public double Operate(IOperation operation, double[] operands)
        {
            double result = 0;
            switch (operation.Name)
            {
                case "+":
                    result = operands[0] + operands[1];
                    break;
                case "-":
                    result = operands[0] - operands[1];
                    break;
                case "/":
                    result = operands[0] / operands[1];
                    break;
                case "*":
                    result = operands[0] * operands[1];
                    break;
                default:
                    throw new InvalidOperationException(
                        String.Format("invalid operation {0}", operation.Name));
            }
            return result;
        }
    }
}
```

code snippet SimpleCalculator/Calculator.cs

The hosting application is a simple console application. The add-in uses an `Export` attribute to define what is exported; with the hosting application, the `Import` attribute defines what is used. Here, the `Import` attribute annotates the `Calculator` property that sets and gets an object implementing `ICalculator`. So, any calculator add-in that implements this interface can be used here.

```
using System;
using System.Collections.Generic;
using System.ComponentModel.Composition;
using System.ComponentModel.Composition.Hosting;
using Wrox.ProCSharp.MEF.Properties;

namespace Wrox.ProCSharp.MEF
{
    class Program
    {
        [Import]
        public ICalculator Calculator { get; set; }
```

code snippet SimpleHost/Program.cs

In the entry method `Main()` of the console application, a new instance of the `Program` class is created, and then the `Run()` method is invoked. In the `Run()` method, a `DirectoryCatalog` is created that is initialized with the `AddInDirectory`, which is configured in the application configuration file. `Settings.Default.AddInDirectory` makes use of the project property `Settings` to use a strongly typed class to access a custom configuration.

The `CompositionContainer` class is a repository of parts. This container is initialized with the `DirectoryCatalog` to get the parts from the directory that is served by this catalog. `ComposeParts()` is an extension method that extends the class `CompositionContainer` and is defined with the class `AttributedModelServices`. This method requires parts with an `Import` attribute passed with the arguments. Because the `Program` class has an `Import` attribute with the property `Calculator`, the instance of the `Program` class can be passed to this method. With the implementation for the imports, exports are searched and mapped. After a successful call of this method, exports mapped to the imports can be used. If not all imports can be mapped to exports, an exception of type `ChangeRejectedException` is thrown, which is caught to write the error message and to exit from the `Run()` method.

```
static void Main()
{
    var p = new Program();
    p.Run();
}

public void Run()
{
    var catalog = new DirectoryCatalog(Settings.Default.AddInDirectory);
    var container = new CompositionContainer(catalog);
    try
    {
        container.ComposeParts(this);
    }
    catch (ChangeRejectedException ex)
    {
        Console.WriteLine(ex.Message);
        return;
    }
}
```

With the `Calculator` property, the methods from the interface `ICalculator` can be used. `GetOperations()` invokes the methods of the previously created add-in, which returns four operations. After asking the user what operation should be invoked and asking for the operand values, the add-in method `Operate()` is called.

```
var operations = Calculator.GetOperations();
var operationsDict = new SortedList<string, IOperation>();
```

```
            foreach (var item in operations)
            {
                Console.WriteLine("Name: {0}, number operands: {1}", item.Name,
                                  item.NumberOperands);
                operationsDict.Add(item.Name, item);
            }
            Console.WriteLine();
            string selectedOp = null;
            do
            {
                try
                {
                    Console.Write("Operation? ");
                    selectedOp = Console.ReadLine();
                    if (selectedOp.ToLower() == "exit" ||
                        !operationsDict.ContainsKey(selectedOp))
                        continue;

                    var operation = operationsDict[selectedOp];
                    double[] operands = new double[operation.NumberOperands];
                    for (int i = 0; i < operation.NumberOperands; i++)
                    {
                        Console.Write("\t operand {0}? ", i + 1);
                        string selectedOperand = Console.ReadLine();
                        operands[i] = double.Parse(selectedOperand);
                    }
                    Console.WriteLine("calling calculator");
                    double result = Calculator.Operate(operation, operands);
                    Console.WriteLine("result: {0}", result);
                }
                catch (FormatException ex)
                {
                    Console.WriteLine(ex.Message);
                    Console.WriteLine();
                    continue;
                }
            } while (selectedOp != "exit");
        }
    }
}
```

The output of one sample run of the application is shown here:

```
Name: +, number operands: 2
Name: -, number operands: 2
Name: /, number operands: 2
Name: *, number operands: 2

Operation? +
        operand 1? 3
        operand 2? 5
calling calculator
result: 8
Operation? -
        operand 1? 7
        operand 2? 2
calling calculator
result: 5
Operation? exit
```

Without recompiling the host application, it is possible to use a completely different add-in library. The assembly AdvCalculator defines a different implementation for the Calculator class to offer more operations. This calculator can be used in place of the other one by copying the assembly to the directory that is specified by the `DirectoryCatalog` in the hosting application.

```csharp
using System;
using System.Collections.Generic;
using System.ComponentModel.Composition;

namespace Wrox.ProCSharp.MEF
{
    [Export(typeof(ICalculator))]
    public class Calculator : ICalculator
    {
        public IList<IOperation> GetOperations()
        {
            return new List<IOperation>()
            {
                new Operation { Name="+", NumberOperands=2},
                new Operation { Name="-", NumberOperands=2},
                new Operation { Name="/", NumberOperands=2},
                new Operation { Name="*", NumberOperands=2},
                new Operation { Name="%", NumberOperands=2},
                new Operation { Name="++", NumberOperands=1},
                new Operation { Name="--", NumberOperands=1}
            };
        }

        public double Operate(IOperation operation, double[] operands)
        {
            double result = 0;
            switch (operation.Name)
            {
                case "+":
                    result = operands[0] + operands[1];
                    break;
                case "-":
                    result = operands[0] - operands[1];
                    break;
                case "/":
                    result = operands[0] / operands[1];
                    break;
                case "*":
                    result = operands[0] * operands[1];
                    break;
                case "%":
                    result = operands[0] % operands[1];
                    break;
                case "++":
                    result = ++operands[0];
                    break;
                case "--":
                    result = --operands[0];
                    break;
                default:
                    throw new InvalidOperationException(
                        String.Format("invalid operation {0}", operation.Name));
            }
            return result;
        }
    }
}
```

code snippet AdvCalculator/Calculator.cs

Now you've seen imports, exports, and catalogs from the MEF architecture. Let's get into the details and different options of MEF by using a WPF application to host add-ins.

CONTRACTS

The following sample application extends the first one. The hosting application is a WPF application that loads calculator add-ins for calculation functionality and other add-ins that bring their own user interface into the host.

 To get more information on writing WPF applications, you can read Chapter 35, "Core WPF," and Chapter 36, "Business Applications with WPF."

For the calculation, the same contracts that were defined earlier are used: `ICalculator` and `IOperation`. Another contract is `ICalculatorExtension`. This interface defines the `Title` and `Description` properties that can be used by the hosting application. The method `GetUI()` returns a `FrameworkElement` that allows the add-in to return any WPF element that derives from `FrameworkElement` to be shown as the user interface within the host.

```csharp
using System.Windows;

namespace Wrox.ProCSharp.MEF
{
    public interface ICalculatorExtension
    {
        string Title { get; }
        string Description { get; }

        FrameworkElement GetUI();
    }
}
```

code snippet CalculatorContract/ICalculatorExtension.cs

.NET interfaces make a good contract between the hosting application and the add-in. If the interface is defined in a separate assembly, as with the `CalculatorContract` assembly, the hosting application and the add-in don't have a direct dependency. Instead, the hosting application and the add-in just reference the contract assembly.

From a MEF standpoint, an interface contract is not required at all. The contract can be a simple string. To avoid conflicts with other contracts, the name of the string should contain a namespace name, for example, `Wrox.ProCSharp.MEF.SampleContract`, as shown in the following code snippet. Here, the class `Foo` is exported by using the `Export` attribute and a string passed to the attribute instead of the interface.

```csharp
[Export("Wrox.ProCSharp.MEF.SampleContract")]
public class Foo
{
    public string Bar()
    {
        return "Foo.Bar";
    }
}
```

The problem with using a contract as a string is that the methods, properties, and events provided by the type are not strongly defined. Either the caller needs a reference to the type `Foo` to use it, or .NET reflection can be used to access its members. The C# 4 `dynamic` keyword makes reflection easier to use and can be very helpful in such scenarios.

The hosting application can use the `dynamic` type to import a contract with the name `Wrox.ProCSharp.MEF.SampleContract`:

```
[Import("Wrox.ProCSharp.MEF.SampleContract")]
public dynamic Foo { get; set; }
```

With the `dynamic` keyword, the `Foo` property can now be used to access the `Bar()` method directly. The call to this method is resolved during runtime:

```
string s = Foo.Bar();
```

 The `dynamic` *type is explained in Chapter 12, "Dynamic Language Extensions."*

Contract names and interfaces can also be used in conjunction to define that the contract is used only if both the interface and the contract name are the same. This way, you can use the same interface for different contracts.

EXPORTS

In the previous example, you saw the part `SimpleCalculator`, which exports the type `Calculator` with all its methods and properties. The following example contains the `SimpleCalculator` as well, with the same implementation that was shown previously. Another part that is used here is a WPF User Control library named `TemperatureConversion` that defines a user interface, as shown in Figure 28-2. This control provides conversion between Celsius, Fahrenheit, and Kelvin scales. With the first and second combo box, the conversion source and target can be selected. The `Calculate` button starts the calculation to do the conversion.

FIGURE 28-2

The user control has a simple implementation for temperature conversion. The enumeration `TempConversionType` defines the different conversions that are possible with that control. The enumeration values are shown in the two combo boxes by setting the `DataContext` property of the user control in the constructor.

The method `ToCelsiusFrom()` converts the argument *t* from its original value to Celsius. The temperature source type is defined with the second argument `TempConversionType`. The method `FromCelsiusTo()` converts a Celsius value to the selected temperature scale. The method `OnCalculate()` is the handler of the `Button.Click` event and invokes the `ToCelsiusFrom()` and `FromCelsiusTo()` methods to do the conversion according to the user's selected conversion type.

```csharp
using System;
using System.Windows;
using System.Windows.Controls;

namespace Wrox.ProCSharp.MEF
{
    public enum TempConversionType
    {
        Celsius,
        Fahrenheit,
        Kelvin
    }

    public partial class TemperatureConversion : UserControl
```

```
    {
        public TemperatureConversion()
        {
            InitializeComponent();
            this.DataContext = Enum.GetNames(typeof(TempConversionType));
        }

        private double ToCelsiusFrom(double t, TempConversionType conv)
        {
            switch (conv)
            {
                case TempConversionType.Celsius:
                    return t;
                case TempConversionType.Fahrenheit:
                    return (t - 32) / 1.8;
                case TempConversionType.Kelvin:
                    return (t - 273.15);
                default:
                    throw new ArgumentException("invalid enumeration value");
            }
        }

        private double FromCelsiusTo(double t, TempConversionType conv)
        {
            switch (conv)
            {
                case TempConversionType.Celsius:
                    return t;
                case TempConversionType.Fahrenheit:
                    return (t * 1.8) + 32;
                case TempConversionType.Kelvin:
                    return t + 273.15;
                default:
                    throw new ArgumentException("invalid enumeration value");
            }
        }

        private void OnCalculate(object sender, System.Windows.RoutedEventArgs e)
        {
            try
            {
                TempConversionType from;
                TempConversionType to;
                if (Enum.TryParse<TempConversionType>(
                        (string)comboFrom.SelectedValue, out from) &&
                    Enum.TryParse<TempConversionType>(
                        (string)comboTo.SelectedValue, out to))
                {
                    double result = FromCelsiusTo(
                        ToCelsiusFrom(double.Parse(textInput.Text), from), to);
                    textOutput.Text = result.ToString();
                }

            }
            catch (FormatException ex)
            {
                MessageBox.Show(ex.Message);
            }
        }
    }
}
```

code snippet TemperatureConversion/TemperatureConversion.xaml.cs

So far, this control is just a simple WPF user control. To create a MEF part, the class `TemperatureCalculatorExtension` is exported by using the `Export` attribute. The class implements the interface `ICalculatorExtension`, offering `Title` and `Description` information, and returning the `UserControl TemperatureConversion` from the `GetUI()` method.

```csharp
using System.ComponentModel.Composition;
using System.Windows;

namespace Wrox.ProCSharp.MEF
{
    [Export(typeof(ICalculatorExtension))]
    public class TemperatureCalculatorExtension : ICalculatorExtension
    {
        public string Title
        {
            get { return "Temperature Conversion"; }
        }

        public string Description
        {
            get { return "Convert Celsius to Fahrenheit and " +
                        "Fahrenheit to Celsius"; }
        }

        public FrameworkElement GetUI()
        {
            return new TemperatureConversion();
        }
    }
}
```

code snippet TemperatureConversion/TemperatureCalculatorExtension.cs

Another user control that implements the interface `ICalculatorExtension` is `FuelEconomy`. With this control either miles per gallon or liters per 100 km can be calculated.

```csharp
using System.Collections.Generic;
using System.Windows;
using System.Windows.Controls;

namespace Wrox.ProCSharp.MEF
{
    public partial class FuelEconomyUC : UserControl
    {
        private List<FuelEconomyType> fuelEcoTypes;

        public FuelEconomyUC()
        {
            InitializeComponent();
            InitializeFuelEcoTypes();
        }

        private void InitializeFuelEcoTypes()
        {
            var t1 = new FuelEconomyType
            {
                Id = "lpk",
                Text = "L/100 km",
                DistanceText = "Distance (kilometers)",
                FuelText = "Fuel used (liters)"
            };
            var t2 = new FuelEconomyType
```

```
            {
                Id = "mpg",
                Text = "Miles per gallon",
                DistanceText = "Distance (miles)",
                FuelText = "Fuel used (gallons)"
            };
            fuelEcoTypes = new List<FuelEconomyType>() { t1, t2 };
            this.DataContext = fuelEcoTypes;
        }

        private void OnCalculate(object sender, RoutedEventArgs e)
        {
            double fuel = double.Parse(textFuel.Text);
            double distance = double.Parse(textDistance.Text);
            FuelEconomyType ecoType = comboFuelEco.SelectedItem as FuelEconomyType;
            double result = 0;
            switch (ecoType.Id)
            {
                case "lpk":
                    result = fuel / (distance / 100);
                    break;
                case "mpg":
                    result = distance / fuel;
                    break;
                default:
                    break;
            }
            this.textResult.Text = result.ToString();
        }
    }
}
```

code snippet FuelEconomy/FuelEconomyUC.xaml.cs

Again, the interface ICalculatorExtension is implemented and exported with the Export attribute:

```
using System.ComponentModel.Composition;
using System.Windows;

namespace Wrox.ProCSharp.MEF
{
    [Export(typeof(ICalculatorExtension))]
    public class FuelCalculatorExtension : ICalculatorExtension
    {
        public string Title
        {
            get { return "Fuel Economy"; }
        }

        public string Description
        {
            get { return "Calculate fuel economy"; }
        }

        public FrameworkElement GetUI()
        {
            return new FuelEconomyUC();
        }
    }
}
```

code snippet FuelEconomy/FuelCalculatorExtension.cs

Before continuing the WPF calculator example to import the user controls, let's take a look at what other options you have with exports. With exports you can not only export complete types but also properties and methods, and also add metadata information to the exports.

Exporting Properties and Methods

Instead of exporting complete classes with properties, methods, and events, it is possible to export just properties or methods. Exporting properties makes it possible to use classes that you don't have under control by adding the Export attribute to them (for example, classes from the .NET Framework or third-party libraries). For this, you just have to define a property of this specific type and export the property.

Exporting methods allows for a finer control than with types. The caller doesn't need to know about the type. Methods are exported with the help of delegates. The following code snippet defines the Add() and Subtract() methods with exports. The type of the export is the delegate Func<double, double, double>, which is a delegate that accepts two double parameters and a double return type. For methods without return types, the Action<T> delegate can be used.

 You can read about the Func<T> *and* Action<T> *delegates in Chapter 8, "Delegates, Lambdas, and Events."*

Available for
download on
Wrox.com

```
using System;
using System.ComponentModel.Composition;

namespace Wrox.ProCSharp.MEF
{
    public class Operations
    {
        [Export("Add", typeof(Func<double, double, double>))]
        public double Add(double x, double y)
        {
            return x + y;
        }

        [Export("Subtract", typeof(Func<double, double, double>))]
        public double Subtract(double x, double y)
        {
            return x - y;
        }
    }
}
```

code snippet Operations/Operations.cs

The exported methods are imported from the SimpleCalculator add-in. A part itself can use other parts. For using the exported methods, delegates are declared with the attribute Import. This attribute contains the same name and the delegate type that was declared with the export.

 SimpleCalculator *itself is a part that exports the* ICalculator *interface and consists of parts that are imported.*

Available for
download on
Wrox.com

```
[Export(typeof(ICalculator))]
public class Calculator : ICalculator
{
    [Import("Add", typeof(Func<double, double, double>))]
    public Func<double, double, double> Add { get; set; }
```

```
[Import("Subtract", typeof(Func<double, double, double>))]
public Func<double, double, double> Subtract { get; set; }
```

code snippet SimpleCalculator/Calculator.cs

The imported methods that are represented by the `Add` and `Subtract` delegates are invoked via these delegates in the `Operate()` method.

```
public double Operate(IOperation operation, double[] operands)
{
    double result = 0;
    switch (operation.Name)
    {
        case "+":
            result = Add(operands[0], operands[1]);
            break;
        case "-":
            result = Subtract(operands[0], operands[1]);
            break;
        case "/":
            result = operands[0] / operands[1];
            break;
        case "*":
            result = operands[0] * operands[1];
            break;
        default:
            throw new InvalidOperationException(
                String.Format("invalid operation {0}", operation.Name));
    }
    return result;
}
```

code snippet SimpleCalculator/Calculator.cs

Exporting Metadata

With exports, you can also attach metadata information. Metadata allows you to add information in addition to a name and a type. This can be used to add capability information and decide on the import side which of the exports should be used.

The exported `Add()` method is now changed to add speed capabilities with the attribute `ExportMetadata`:

```
[Export("Add", typeof(Func<double, double, double>))]
[ExportMetadata("speed", "fast")]
public double Add(double x, double y)
{
    return x + y;
}
```

code snippet Operations/Operation.cs

To have the option to choose from another implementation of the `Add()` method, another method with different speed capabilities but the same delegate type and name is implemented:

```
public class Operations2
{
    [Export("Add", typeof(Func<double, double, double>))]
    [ExportMetadata("speed", "slow")]
    public double Add(double x, double y)
    {
```

```
            Thread.Sleep(3000);
            return x + y;
        }
    }
```

Because there is more than one exported `Add` method available, the import definition must be changed. The attribute `ImportMany` is used if more than one export of the same name and type is available. This attribute is applied to an array or `IEnumeration<T>` interface. `ImportMany` is explained with more detail in the next section. For accessing metadata, an array of `Lazy<T, TMetadata>` can be used. The class `Lazy<T>` is new in .NET 4 and is used to support lazy initialization of types on first use. `Lazy<T, TMetadata>` derives from `Lazy<T>` and supports, in addition to the base class, access to metadata information with the `Metadata` property. In the sample, the method is referenced by the delegate `Func<double, double, double>`, which is the first generic parameter of `Lazy<T, TMetadata>`. The second generic parameter is `IDictionary<string, object>` for the metadata collection. The `ExportMetadata` attribute can be used multiple times to add more than one capability, and always consists of a key of type string and a value of type object.

Available for download on Wrox.com

```
[ImportMany("Add", typeof(Func<double, double, double>))]
public Lazy<Func<double, double, double>, IDictionary<string, object>>[]
        AddMethods { get; set; }

//[Import("Add", typeof(Func<double, double, double>))]
//public Func<double, double, double> Add { get; set; }
```

The call to the `Add` method is now changed to iterate through the collection of `Lazy<Func<double, double, double>, IDictionary<string, object>>` elements. With the `Metadata` property, the key for the capability is checked; if the speed capability has the value `fast`, the operation is invoked by using the `Value` property of `Lazy<T>` to get to the delegate:

```
case "+":
    // result = Add(operands[0], operands[1]);
    foreach (var addMethod in AddMethods)
    {
        if (addMethod.Metadata.ContainsKey("speed") &&
                (string)addMethod.Metadata["speed"] == "fast")
            result = addMethod.Value(operands[0], operands[1]);
    }
    // result = operands[0] + operands[1];
    break;
```

Instead of using the attribute `ExportMetadata`, you can create a custom export attribute class that derives from `ExportAttribute`. The class `SpeedExportAttribute` defines an additional `Speed` property that is of type `Speed`:

Available for download on Wrox.com

```
using System;
using System.ComponentModel.Composition;

namespace Wrox.ProCSharp.MEF
{
    public enum Speed
    {
        Fast,
        Slow
    }

    [MetadataAttribute]
    [AttributeUsage(AttributeTargets.Method | AttributeTargets.Class)]
    public class SpeedExportAttribute : ExportAttribute
```

```
        {
            public SpeedExportAttribute(string contractName, Type contractType)
                : base(contractName, contractType) { }

            public Speed Speed { get; set; }
        }
    }
```

code snippet CalculatorUtils/ExportAttribute.cs

> *To get more information about how to create custom attributes, read Chapter 14, "Reflection."*

With the exported `Add()` method, now the `SpeedExport` attribute can be used instead of the `Export` and `ExportMetadata` attributes:

Available for download on Wrox.com

```
[SpeedExport("Add", typeof(Func<double, double, double>), Speed=Speed.Fast)]
public double Add(double x, double y)
{
    return x + y;
}
```

code snippet Operations/Operations.cs

For the import, an interface with all the metadata is required. This makes it possible to access the strongly typed capabilities. The capabilities that are defined by the attribute `SpeedExport` are just the speed. The interface `ISpeedCapabilities` defines the property `Speed` by using the same enumeration type `Speed` that was used with the `SpeedExport` attribute:

Available for download on Wrox.com

```
namespace Wrox.ProCSharp.MEF
{
    public interface ISpeedCapabilities
    {
        Speed Speed { get; }
    }
}
```

code snippet CalculatorUtils/ISpeedCapabilities.cs

Now it's possible to change the definition of the import by using the interface `ISpeedCapabilities` instead of the dictionary defined earlier:

Available for download on Wrox.com

```
[ImportMany("Add", typeof(Func<double, double, double>))]
public Lazy<Func<double, double, double>, ISpeedCapabilities>[]
        AddMethods { get; set; }
```

code snippet SimpleCalculator/Calculator.cs

Using the imports, the `Speed` property of the interface, `ISpeedCapability`, can now be used directly:

```
        foreach (var addMethod in AddMethods)
        {
            if (addMethod.Metadata.Speed == Speed.Fast)
                result = addMethod.Value(operands[0], operands[1]);
        }
```

IMPORTS

Now let's get into using the WPF User Controls with a WPF hosting application. The design view of the hosting application is shown in Figure 28-3. The application WPFCalculator is a WPF application that loads the functional calculator add-in, which implements the interfaces `ICalculator` and `IOperation`, and add-ins with user interfaces that implement the interface ICalculatorExtension. To connect to the exports of the parts, you need imports.

An import connects to an export. When using exported parts, an import is needed to make the connection. With the Import attribute, it's possible to connect to a single export. If more than one add-in should be loaded, the ImportMany attribute is required and needs to be defined as an array type or IEnumerable<T>. Because the hosting calculator application allows many calculator extensions that implement the interface ICalculatorExtension to be loaded,

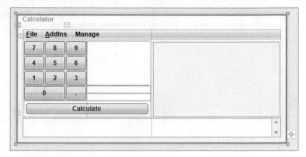

FIGURE 28-3

the class CalculatorExtensionImport defines the property CalculatorExtensions of type IEnumerable <ICalculatorExtension> to access all the calculator extension parts.

Available for download on Wrox.com

```csharp
using System.Collections.Generic;
using System.ComponentModel.Composition;

namespace Wrox.ProCSharp.MEF
{
    public class CalculatorExtensionImport
    {
        [ImportMany(AllowRecomposition=true)]
        public IEnumerable<ICalculatorExtension> CalculatorExtensions { get; set; }
    }
}
```

code snippet WPFCalculator/CalculatorExtensionImport.cs

The Import and ImportMany attributes allow the use of ContractName and ContractType to map the import to an export. Other properties that can be set with these attributes are AllowRecomposition and RequiredCreationPolicy. AllowRecomposition allows dynamic mapping to new exports while the application is running, and also the unloading of exports. With RequiredCreationPolicy, you can choose if the parts should be shared (CreationPolicy.Shared) or not shared (CreationPolicy.NonShared) between requestors, or if the policy should be defined by the container (CreationPolicy.Any).

To see that all imports are successful, the interface IPartImportsSatisfiedNotification can be implemented. This interface just defines a single method, OnImportsSatisfed(), that is called when all imports of the class are successful. In the CalculatorImport class, the method fires an ImportsSatisfied event:

Available for download on Wrox.com

```csharp
using System;
using System.ComponentModel.Composition;
using System.Windows.Controls;

namespace Wrox.ProCSharp.MEF
{
    public class CalculatorImport : IPartImportsSatisfiedNotification
    {
        public event EventHandler<ImportEventArgs> ImportsSatisfied;

        [Import(typeof(ICalculator))]
        public ICalculator Calculator { get; set; }

        public void OnImportsSatisfied()
        {
            if (ImportsSatisfied != null)
```

```
                    ImportsSatisfied(this, new ImportEventArgs {
                        StatusMessage = "ICalculator import successful" });
                }
            }
        }
```

The event of the `CalculatorImport` is connected to an event handler on creation of the `CalculatorImport` to write a message to a `TextBlock` for displaying status information:

```
private void InitializeContainer()
{
    var catalog = new DirectoryCatalog(
                            Properties.Settings.Default.AddInDirectory);
    container = new CompositionContainer(catalog);
    calcImport = new CalculatorImport();
    calcImport.ImportsSatisfied += (sender, e) =>
        {
            textStatus.Text += String.Format("{0}\n", e.StatusMessage);
        };
    container.ComposeParts(calcImport);

    InitializeOperations();
}
```

Lazy Loading of Parts

By default, parts are loaded from the container, for example, by calling the extension method `ComposeParts()` on the `CompositionContainer`. With the help of the `Lazy<T>` class, the parts can be loaded on first access. The type `Lazy<T>` allows the late instantiation of any type `T` and defines the properties `IsValueCreated` and `Value`. `IsValueCreated` is a Boolean that returns the information if the contained type `T` is already instantiated. `Value` initializes the contained type `T` on first access and returns the instance.

The import of an add-in can be declared to be of type `Lazy<T>`, as shown in the `Lazy<ICalculator>` example.

```
[Import(typeof(ICalculator))]
public Lazy<ICalculator> Calculator { get; set; }
```

Calling the imported property also requires some changes to access the `Value` property of the `Lazy<T>` type. `calcImport` is a variable of type `CalculatorImport`. The `Calculator` property returns `Lazy<ICalculator>`. The `Value` property instantiates the imported type lazily and returns the `ICalculator` interface, where now the `GetOperations()` method can be invoked to get all supported operations from the calculator add-in.

```
private void InitializeOperations()
{
    Contract.Requires(calcImport != null);
    Contract.Requires(calcImport.Calculator != null);

    var operators = calcImport.Calculator.Value.GetOperations();
    foreach (var op in operators)
    {
        var b = new Button();
        b.Width = 40;
```

```
            b.Height = 30;
            b.Content = op.Name;
            b.Margin = new Thickness(2);
            b.Padding = new Thickness(4);
            b.Tag = op;
            b.Click += new RoutedEventHandler(DefineOperation);
            listOperators.Items.Add(b);
        }
    }
```

code snippet WPFCalculator/MainWindow.xaml.cs

CONTAINERS AND EXPORT PROVIDERS

The import of parts happens with help of a container. The types for hosting parts are defined in the namespace System.ComponentModel.Composition.Hosting. The class CompositionContainer is the container for parts. In the constructor of this class, multiple ExportProvider objects can be assigned, as well as a ComposablePartCatalog. Catalogs are sources of parts and are discussed in the next section. Export providers allow you to access all exports programmatically with overloaded GetExport<T>() methods. An export provider is used to access the catalog, and the CompositionContainer itself is an export provider. This makes it possible to nest containers in other containers.

Parts are loaded when the Compose() method is invoked (if they are not lazy loaded). So far, we've always used the ComposePart() method, as shown in the InitializeContainer() method:

```
private void InitializeContainer()
{
    catalog = new DirectoryCatalog(
                    Properties.Settings.Default.AddInDirectory);
    container = new CompositionContainer(catalog);
    calcImport = new CalculatorImport();
    calcImport.ImportsSatisfied += (sender, e) =>
        {
            textStatus.Text += String.Format("{0}\n", e.StatusMessage);
        };
    container.ComposeParts(calcImport);

    InitializeOperations();
}
```

code snippet WPFCalculator/MainWindow.xaml.cs

ComposePart() is an extension method defined with the class AttributedModelServices. This class provides methods that use attributes and .NET reflection to access part information and add parts to the container. Instead of using this extension method, the Compose() method of CompositionContainer can be used. The Compose() method works with the class CompositionBatch. A CompostionBatch can be used to define which parts should be added and which parts should be removed from the container. The methods AddPart() and RemovePart() have overloads where either an attributed part can be added (calcImport is an instance of the CalculatorImport class and contains Import attributes) or a part that derives from the base class ComposablePart.

```
var batch = new CompositionBatch();
batch.AddPart(calcImport);
container.Compose(batch);
```

The hosting application WPFCalculator loads two different kinds of parts. The first part implements the ICalculator interface and is loaded in the InitializeContainer method shown previously. The parts that implement the interface ICalculatorExtension are loaded in the RefreshExtensions method. Container.ComposeParts gets the import from the CalculatorExtensionImport class and connects it to all available exports from the catalog. Because here multiple add-ins are dynamically loaded (the user can select the add-in to use), the Menu control is dynamically extended. The application iterates through all the calculator extensions, and a new MenuItem is created for each extension. The header of the MenuItem control contains a Label with the Title property of the extension and a CheckBox. The CheckBox will later be used to remove the export dynamically. The ToolTip property of the MenuItem is set to the Description property of the extender control. The Tag property is set to the extender control itself, which makes it easy to get to the extender control when the menu item is selected. The Click event of the MenuItem is set to the method ShowAddIn(). This method invokes the GetUI() method of the extender control for displaying the control within a new TabItem of a TabControl.

```csharp
private void RefreshExensions()
{
    catalog.Refresh();
    calcExtensionImport = new CalculatorExtensionImport();
    calcExtensionImport.ImportsSatisfied += (sender, e) =>
        {
            this.textStatus.Text += String.Format("{0}\n", e.StatusMessage);
        };

    container.ComposeParts(calcExtensionImport);
    menuAddins.Items.Clear();
    foreach (var extension in calcExtensionImport.CalculatorExtensions)
    {
        var menuItemHeader = new StackPanel { Orientation = Orientation.Horizontal };
        menuItemHeader.Children.Add(new Label { Content = extension.Title });
        var menuCheck = new CheckBox { IsChecked = true };
        menuItemHeader.Children.Add(menuCheck);

        var menuItem = new MenuItem {
                                        Header = menuItemHeader,
                                        ToolTip = extension.Description,
                                        Tag = extension
                                    };
        menuCheck.Tag = menuItem;
        menuItem.Click += ShowAddIn;
        menuAddins.Items.Add(menuItem);
    }
}

private void ShowAddIn(object sender, RoutedEventArgs e)
{
    var mi = e.Source as MenuItem;
    var ext = mi.Tag as ICalculatorExtension;
    FrameworkElement uiControl = ext.GetUI();
    var headerPanel = new StackPanel { Orientation = Orientation.Horizontal };
    headerPanel.Children.Add(new Label { Content = ext.Title });
    var closeButton = new Button { Content = "X" };
    var ti = new TabItem { Header = headerPanel, Content = uiControl };
    closeButton.Click += delegate
        {
            tabExtensions.Items.Remove(ti);
        };
    headerPanel.Children.Add(closeButton);

    tabExtensions.SelectedIndex = tabExtensions.Items.Add(ti);
}
```

code snippet WPFCalculator/MainWindow.xaml.cs

To remove exports dynamically, the `Unchecked` event is set in the `CheckBox` control that's within the `MenuItem` header. The `ICalculatorExtension` can be accessed from the `Tag` property of the `MenuItem` control because it was set in the previous code snippet. To remove a part from the container, a `CompositeBatch` object must be created that contains parts for removal. The `RemovePart()` method of the `CompositeBatch` class requires a `ComposablePart` object; there's no overload for attributed objects. With the help of the class `AttributedModelServices` from an attributed object, a `ComposablePart` can be created with the `CreatePart()` method. The `CompositonBatch` is then passed to the `Compose()` method of the `CompositionContainer` to remove the part from it:

```
menuCheck.Unchecked += (sender1, e1) =>
    {
        MenuItem mi = (sender1 as CheckBox).Tag as MenuItem;
        ICalculatorExtension ext = mi.Tag as ICalculatorExtension;
        ComposablePart part =
                AttributedModelServices.CreatePart(ext);
        var batch = new CompositionBatch();
        batch.RemovePart(part);
        container.Compose(batch);
        MenuItem parentMenu = mi.Parent as MenuItem;
        parentMenu.Items.Remove(mi);
    };
```

 Removing parts is only possible if the `AllowRecomposition` *property of the* `Import` *attribute is set to* true.

With an export provider, you can get information on exports added and removed by implementing a handler to the `ExportsChanged` event. The parameter e of type `ExportsChangedEventArgs` contains a list of added exports and removed exports that are written to a `TextBlock` control:

```
var container = new CompositionContainer(catalog);
container.ExportsChanged += (sender, e) =>
    {
        var sb = new StringBuilder();

        foreach (var item in e.AddedExports)
        {
            sb.AppendFormat("added export {0}\n", item.ContractName);
        }
        foreach (var item in e.RemovedExports)
        {
            sb.AppendFormat("removed export {0}\n", item.ContractName);
        }
        this.textStatus.Text += sb.ToString();
    };
```

CATALOGS

A catalog defines where MEF searches for requested parts. The sample application uses a `DirectoryCatalog` to load the assemblies with parts from a specified directory. With the `DirectoryCatalog`, you can get change information with the `Changed` event and iterate through all added and removed definitions. The `DirectoryCatalog` does not itself register to file system changes. Instead, you need to invoke the `Refresh()` method of the `DirectoryCatalog`, and if changes were made since the last read, the `Changing` and `Changed` events are fired.

```
private void InitializeContainer()
{
    catalog = new DirectoryCatalog(Properties.Settings.Default.AddInDirectory);
    container = new CompositionContainer(catalog);
```

```
        catalog.Changed += (sender, e) =>
        {
                var sb = new StringBuilder();

                foreach (var definition in e.AddedDefinitions)
                {
                        foreach (var metadata in definition.Metadata)
                        {
                                sb.AppendFormat(
                                        "added definition with metadata - key: {0}, " +
                                        "value: {1}\n", metadata.Key, metadata.Value);
                        }
                }

                foreach (var definition in e.RemovedDefinitions)
                {
                        foreach (var metadata in definition.Metadata)
                        {
                                sb.AppendFormat(
                                        "removed definition with metadata - key: {0}, " +
                                        "value: {1}\n", metadata.Key, metadata.Value);
                        }
                }
                this.textStatus.Text += sb.ToString();
        };
        //...
```

code snippet WPFCalculator/MainWindow.xaml.cs

 To get immediate notification of new add-ins loaded to a directory, you can use the System.IO.FileSystemWatcher *to register for changes on the add-in directory, and invoke the* Refresh *method of the* DirectoryCatalog *with the* Changed *event of the* FileSystemWatcher.

The CompositionContainer just needs a ComposablePartCatalog to find parts. DirectoryCatalog derives from ComposablePartCatalog. Other catalogs are AssemblyCatalog, TypeCatalog, and AggregateCatalog. Let's compare all these catalogs:

➤ The DirectoryCatalog searches parts within a directory.

➤ The AssemblyCatalog searches for parts directly within a referenced assembly. Contrary to the DirectoryCatalog, where assemblies might change in the directory during runtime, the AssemblyCatalog is immutable and parts cannot change.

➤ The TypeCatalog searches for imports within a list of types. IEnumerable<Type> can be passed to the constructor of this catalog.

➤ The AggregateCatalog is a catalog of catalogs. This catalog can be created from multiple ComposablePartCatalog objects and searches in all these catalogs. For example, you can create an AssemblyCatalog to search for imports within an assembly, two DirectoryCatalog objects to search in two different directories, and an AggregateCatalog that combines the three catalogs for import searches.

When running the sample application (see Figure 28-4), the SimpleCalculator add-in is loaded, and you can do some calculations with operations supported by the add-in. From the AddIns menu, you can start add-ins that implement the interface ICalculatorExtender and see the user interface from these add-ins in the tab control. Information about exports and changes in the directory catalog is shown with the status information at the bottom. You can also remove an `ICalculatorExtender` add-in from the add-in directory (while the application is not running), copy the add-in to the directory while the application is running, and do a refresh of the add-ins to see the new add-ins during runtime.

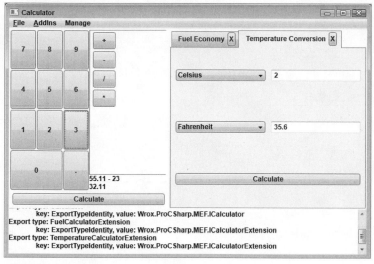

FIGURE 28-4

SUMMARY

In this chapter, you read about a new technology in .NET 4: MEF. The MEF implementation uses attributes to find and connect add-ins. You saw how add-ins can be created and loaded and the possibilities for using interfaces or methods with exports. You learned how catalogs can be used to find add-ins dynamically and how to use containers to map imports to exports.

This book has another chapter on add-ins: online Chapter 50 is about MAF, which offers a better separation between hosts and add-ins via separate appdomains and separate processes, but also has a higher development cost.

The next chapter is on reading and writing files, directories, and the registry.

29

Manipulating Files and the Registry

WHAT'S IN THIS CHAPTER?

➤ Exploring the directory structure

➤ Moving, copying, and deleting files and folders

➤ Reading and writing text in files

➤ Reading and writing keys in the registry

➤ Reading and writing to isolated storage

This chapter examines how to perform tasks involving reading from and writing to files and the C# system registry. Microsoft has provided very intuitive object models covering these areas, and in this chapter, you learn how to use .NET base classes to perform the listed tasks. In the case of file system operations, the relevant classes are almost all found in the `System.IO` namespace, whereas registry operations are dealt with by classes in the `Microsoft.Win32` namespace.

> *The .NET base classes also include a number of classes and interfaces in the* `System` `.Runtime.Serialization` *namespace concerned with serialization — that is, the process of converting data (for example, the contents of a document) into a stream of bytes for storage. This chapter does not focus on these classes; it focuses on the classes that give you direct access to files.*

Note that security is particularly important when modifying either files or registry entries. Security is covered entirely in Chapter 21, "Security." In this chapter, however, we assume that you have sufficient access rights to run all the examples that modify files or registry entries, which should be the case if you are running from an account with administrator privileges.

MANAGING THE FILE SYSTEM

The classes that are used to browse around the file system and perform operations such as moving, copying, and deleting files are shown in Figure 29-1.

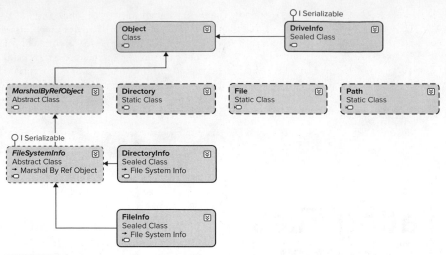

FIGURE 29-1

The following list explains the function of these classes:

➤ `System.MarshalByRefObject` — This is the base object class for .NET classes that are remotable; it permits marshaling of data between application domains. The rest of the items in this list are part of the `System.IO` namespace.

➤ `FileSystemInfo` — This is the base class that represents any file system object.

➤ `FileInfo` and `File` — These classes represent a file on the file system.

➤ `DirectoryInfo` and `Directory` — These classes represent a folder on the file system.

➤ `Path` — This class contains static members that you can use to manipulate pathnames.

➤ `DriveInfo` — This class provides properties and methods that provide information on a selected drive.

> *In Windows, the objects that contain files and that are used to organize the file system are termed folders. For example, in the path* `C:\My Documents\ReadMe.txt`, `ReadMe.txt` *is a file and* `My Documents` *is a folder. Folder is a very Windows-specific term: on virtually every other operating system the term directory is used in place of folder, and in accordance with Microsoft's goal to design .NET as a platform-independent technology, the corresponding .NET base classes are called* `Directory` *and* `DirectoryInfo`. *However, due to the potential for confusion with LDAP directories (as discussed in the online Chapter 52, "Directory Services"), and because this is a Windows book, we'll stick to the term folder in this discussion.*

.NET Classes That Represent Files and Folders

You will notice from the previous list that two classes are used to represent a folder and two classes are used to represent a file. Which one of these classes you use depends largely on how many times you need to access that folder or file:

➤ `Directory` and `File` contain only static methods and are never instantiated. You use these classes by supplying the path to the appropriate file system object whenever you call a member method. If you want to do only one operation on a folder or file, using these classes is more efficient because it saves the overhead of instantiating a .NET class.

➤ `DirectoryInfo` and `FileInfo` implement roughly the same public methods as `Directory` and `File`, as well as some public properties and constructors, but they are stateful and the members of these classes are not static. You need to instantiate these classes before each instance is associated with a particular folder or file. This means that these classes are more efficient if you are performing multiple operations using the same object. That's because they read in the authentication and other information for the appropriate file system object on construction, and then do not need to read that information again, no matter how many methods you call against each object (class instance). In comparison, the corresponding stateless classes need to check the details of the file or folder again with every method you call.

In this section, you are mostly using the `FileInfo` and `DirectoryInfo` classes, but it so happens that many (though not all) of the methods called are also implemented by `File` and `Directory` (although in those cases these methods require an extra parameter — the pathname of the file system object; also, a couple of the methods have slightly different names). For example:

```
FileInfo myFile = new FileInfo(@"C:\Program Files\My Program\ReadMe.txt");
myFile.CopyTo(@"D:\Copies\ReadMe.txt");
```

has the same effect as:

```
File.Copy(@"C:\Program Files\My Program\ReadMe.txt", @"D:\Copies\ReadMe.txt");
```

The first code snippet takes slightly longer to execute because of the need to instantiate a `FileInfo` object, `myFile`, but it leaves `myFile` ready for you to perform further actions on the same file. By using the second example, there is no need to instantiate an object to copy the file.

You can instantiate a `FileInfo` or `DirectoryInfo` class by passing to the constructor a string containing the path to the corresponding file system object. You have just seen the process for a file. For a folder, the code looks similar:

```
DirectoryInfo myFolder = new DirectoryInfo(@"C:\Program Files");
```

If the path represents an object that does not exist, an exception will not be thrown at construction, but will instead be thrown the first time that you call a method that actually requires the corresponding file system object to be there. You can find out whether the object exists and is of the appropriate type by checking the `Exists` property, which is implemented by both of these classes:

```
FileInfo test = new FileInfo(@"C:\Windows");
Console.WriteLine(test.Exists.ToString());
```

Note that for this property to return `true`, the corresponding file system object must be of the appropriate type. In other words, if you instantiate a `FileInfo` object supplying the path of a folder, or you instantiate a `DirectoryInfo` object, giving it the path of a file, `Exists` will have the value `false`. Most of the properties and methods of these objects will return a value if possible — they won't necessarily throw an exception just because the wrong type of object has been called, unless they are asked to do something that really is impossible. For example, the preceding code snippet might first display `false` (because `C:\Windows` is a folder). However, it still displays the time the folder was created because a folder still has that information. But if you tried to open the folder as if it were a file, using the `FileInfo.Open()` method, you'd get an exception.

After you have established whether the corresponding file system object exists, you can (if you are using the `FileInfo` or `DirectoryInfo` class) find out information about it using the properties in the following table.

PROPERTY	DESCRIPTION
`CreationTime`	Time in which the file or folder was created
`DirectoryName` (`FileInfo` only)	Full pathname of the containing folder
`Parent` (`DirectoryInfo` only)	The parent directory of a specified subdirectory
`Exists`	Whether a file or folder exists
`Extension`	Extension of the file; it returns blank for folders
`FullName`	Full pathname of the file or folder

continues

(continued)

PROPERTY	DESCRIPTION
LastAccessTime	Time the file or folder was last accessed
LastWriteTime	Time the file or folder was last modified
Name	Name of the file or folder
Root (DirectoryInfo only)	The root portion of the path
Length (FileInfo only)	The size of the file in bytes

You can also perform actions on the file system object using the methods in the following table.

METHOD	PURPOSE
Create()	Creates a folder or empty file of the given name. For a FileInfo this also returns a stream object to let you write to the file. (Streams are covered later in this chapter.)
Delete()	Deletes the file or folder. For folders, there is an option for the Delete to be recursive.
MoveTo()	Moves and/or renames the file or folder.
CopyTo()	(FileInfo only) Copies the file. Note that there is no copy method for folders. If you are copying complete directory trees you will need to individually copy each file and create new folders corresponding to the old folders.
GetDirectories()	(DirectoryInfo only) Returns an array of DirectoryInfo objects representing all folders contained in this folder.
GetFiles()	(DirectoryInfo only) Returns an array of FileInfo objects representing all files contained in this folder.
GetFileSystemInfos()	(DirectoryInfo only) Returns FileInfo and DirectoryInfo objects representing all objects contained in this folder, as an array of FileSystemInfo references.

Note that these tables list the main properties and methods and are not intended to be exhaustive.

The preceding tables do not list most of the properties or methods that allow you to write to or read the data in files. This is actually done using stream objects, which are covered later in this chapter. FileInfo *also implements a number of methods —* Open(), OpenRead(), OpenText(), OpenWrite(), Create(), *and* CreateText() *— that return stream objects for this purpose.*

Interestingly, the creation time, last access time, and last write time are all writable:

```
// displays the creation time of a file,
// then changes it and displays it again
FileInfo test = new FileInfo(@"C:\MyFile.txt");
Console.WriteLine(test.Exists.ToString());
Console.WriteLine(test.CreationTime.ToString());
test.CreationTime = new DateTime(2010, 1, 1, 7, 30, 0);
Console.WriteLine(test.CreationTime.ToString());
```

Running this application produces results similar to the following:

```
True
2/5/2009 2:59:32 PM
1/1/2010 7:30:00 AM
```

Being able to manually modify these properties might seem strange at first, but it can be quite useful. For example, if you have a program that effectively modifies a file by simply reading it in, deleting it, and creating a new file with the new contents, you would probably want to modify the creation date to match the original creation date of the old file.

The Path Class

The `Path` class is not a class that you would instantiate. Rather, it exposes some static methods that make operations on pathnames easier. For example, suppose that you want to display the full pathname for a file, `ReadMe.txt`, in the folder `C:\My Documents`. You could find the path to the file using the following code:

```
Console.WriteLine(Path.Combine(@"C:\My Documents", "ReadMe.txt"));
```

Using the `Path` class is a lot easier than using separation symbols manually, especially because the `Path` class is aware of different formats for pathnames on different operating systems. At the time of this writing, Windows is the only operating system supported by .NET. However, if .NET is ported to UNIX, `Path` would be able to cope with UNIX paths, in which case /, rather than \, would be used as a separator in pathnames. `Path.Combine()` is the method of this class that you are likely to use most often, but `Path` also implements other methods that supply information about the path or the required format for it.

Some of the static fields available to the `Path` class include the following:

PROPERTY	DESCRIPTION
AltDirectorySeparatorChar	Provides a platform-agnostic way to specify an alternative character to separate directory levels. in Windows, a / symbol is used, whereas in UNIX, a \ symbol is used.
DirectorySeparatorChar	Provides a platform-agnostic way to specify a character to separate directory levels. In Windows, a / symbol is used, whereas in UNIX, a \ symbol is used.
PathSeparator	Provides a platform-agnostic way to specify path strings which divide environmental variables. The default value of this setting is a semicolon.
VolumeSeparatorChar	Provides a platform-agnostic way to specify a volume separator. The default value of this setting is a colon.

The following example illustrates how to browse directories and view the properties of files.

A FileProperties Sample

This section presents a sample C# application called `FileProperties`. This application presents a simple user interface that allows you to browse the file system and view the creation time, last access time, last write time, and size of files. (You can download the sample code for this application from the Wrox web site at www.wrox.com.)

The `FileProperties` application works like this. You type in the name of a folder or file in the main text box at the top of the window and click the Display button. If you type in the path to a folder, its contents are listed in the list boxes. If you type in the path to a file, its details are displayed in the text boxes at the bottom of the form and the contents of its parent folder are displayed in the list boxes. Figure 29-2 shows the `FileProperties` sample application in action.

The user can very easily navigate around the file system by clicking any folder in the right-hand list box to move down to that folder or by clicking the Up button to move up to the parent folder. Figure 29-2 shows the contents of my User folder. The user can also select a file by clicking its name in the list box. This displays the file's properties in the text boxes at the bottom of the application (see Figure 29-3).

FIGURE 29-2

FIGURE 29-3

Note that if you want to, you can also display the creation time, last access time, and last modification time for folders using the `DirectoryInfo` property. You display these properties only for a selected file to keep things simple.

You create the project as a standard C# Windows application in Visual Studio 2010. Add the various text boxes and the list box from the Windows Forms area of the toolbox. You also renamed the controls with the more intuitive names of textBoxInput, textBoxFolder, buttonDisplay, buttonUp, listBoxFiles, listBoxFolders, textBoxFileName, textBoxCreationTime, textBoxLastAccessTime, textBoxLastWriteTime, and textBoxFileSize.

Next, you need to indicate that you will be using the System.IO namespace:

```
using System;
using System.IO;
using System.Windows.Forms;
```

You need to do this for all the file-system-related examples in this chapter, but this part of the code will not be explicitly shown in the remaining examples. You then add a member field to the main form:

```
public partial class Form1: Form
{
    private string currentFolderPath;
```

code download FileProperties.sln

currentFolderPath stores the path of the folder whose contents are displayed in the list boxes.

Next, you need to add event handlers for the user-generated events. The possible user inputs are:

➤ User clicks the Display button — You need to determine whether what the user has typed in the main text box is the path to a file or folder. If it is a folder, you list the files and subfolders of this folder in the list boxes. If it is a file, you still do this for the folder containing that file, but you also display the file properties in the lower text boxes.

➤ User clicks a filename in the Files list box — You display the properties of this file in the lower text boxes.

➤ User clicks a folder name in the Folders list box — You clear all the controls and then display the contents of this subfolder in the list boxes.

➤ User clicks the Up button — You clear all the controls and then display the contents of the parent of the currently selected folder.

Before you see the code for the event handlers, here is the code for the methods that do all the work. First, you need to clear the contents of all the controls. This method is fairly self-explanatory:

```
protected void ClearAllFields()
{
    listBoxFolders.Items.Clear();
    listBoxFiles.Items.Clear();
    textBoxFolder.Text = "";
    textBoxFileName.Text = "";
    textBoxCreationTime.Text = "";
    textBoxLastAccessTime.Text = "";
    textBoxLastWriteTime.Text = "";
    textBoxFileSize.Text = "";
}
```

code download FileProperties.sln

Next, you define a method, DisplayFileInfo(), that handles the process of displaying the information for a given file in the text boxes. This method takes one parameter, the full pathname of the file as a String, and works by creating a FileInfo object based on this path:

```
protected void DisplayFileInfo(string fileFullName)
{
    FileInfo theFile = new FileInfo(fileFullName);

    if (!theFile.Exists)
```

```
    {
        throw new FileNotFoundException("File not found: " + fileFullName);
    }

    textBoxFileName.Text = theFile.Name;
    textBoxCreationTime.Text = theFile.CreationTime.ToLongTimeString();
    textBoxLastAccessTime.Text = theFile.LastAccessTime.ToLongDateString();
    textBoxLastWriteTime.Text = theFile.LastWriteTime.ToLongDateString();
    textBoxFileSize.Text = theFile.Length.ToString() + " bytes";
}
```

code download FileProperties.sln

Note that you take the precaution of throwing an exception if there are any problems locating a file at the specified location. The exception itself will be handled in the calling routine (one of the event handlers). Finally, you define a method, `DisplayFolderList()`, which displays the contents of a given folder in the two list boxes. The full pathname of the folder is passed in as a parameter to this method:

Available for download on Wrox.com

```
protected void DisplayFolderList(string folderFullName)
{
    DirectoryInfo theFolder = new DirectoryInfo(folderFullName);

    if (!theFolder.Exists)
    {
        throw new DirectoryNotFoundException("Folder not found: " + folderFullName);
    }

    ClearAllFields();
    textBoxFolder.Text = theFolder.FullName;
    currentFolderPath = theFolder.FullName;

    // list all subfolders in folder
    foreach(DirectoryInfo nextFolder in theFolder.GetDirectories())
        listBoxFolders.Items.Add(nextFolder.Name);

    // list all files in folder
    foreach(FileInfo nextFile in theFolder.GetFiles())
        listBoxFiles.Items.Add(nextFile.Name);
}
```

code download FileProperties.sln

Next, you examine the event handlers. The event handler that manages the event that is triggered when the user clicks the Display button is the most complex because it needs to handle three different possibilities for the text the user enters in the text box. For instance, it could be the pathname of a folder, the pathname of a file, or neither of these:

Available for download on Wrox.com

```
protected void OnDisplayButtonClick(object sender, EventArgs e)
{
    try
    {
        string folderPath = textBoxInput.Text;
        DirectoryInfo theFolder = new DirectoryInfo(folderPath);

        if (theFolder.Exists)
        {
            DisplayFolderList(theFolder.FullName);
            return;
        }

        FileInfo theFile = new FileInfo(folderPath);
```

```
            if (theFile.Exists)
            {
                DisplayFolderList(theFile.Directory.FullName);
                int index = listBoxFiles.Items.IndexOf(theFile.Name);
                listBoxFiles.SetSelected(index, true);
                return;
            }

            throw new FileNotFoundException("There is no file or folder with "
                                    + "this name: " + textBoxInput.Text);
        }
        catch(Exception ex)
        {
            MessageBox.Show(ex.Message);
        }
    }
```

code download FileProperties.sln

In this code, you establish if the supplied text represents a folder or file by instantiating `DirectoryInfo` and `FileInfo` instances and examining the `Exists` property of each object. If neither exists, you throw an exception. If it's a folder, you call `DisplayFolderList()` to populate the list boxes. If it's a file, you need to populate the list boxes and sort out the text boxes that display the file properties. You handle this case by first populating the list boxes. You then programmatically select the appropriate filename in the Files list box. This has exactly the same effect as if the user had selected that item — it raises the item-selected event. You can then simply exit the current event handler, knowing that the selected item event handler will immediately be called to display the file properties.

The following code is the event handler that is called when an item in the Files list box is selected, either by the user or, as indicated previously, programmatically. It simply constructs the full pathname of the selected file, and passes it to the `DisplayFileInfo()` method presented earlier:

```
protected void OnListBoxFilesSelected(object sender, EventArgs e)
{
    try
    {
        string selectedString = listBoxFiles.SelectedItem.ToString();
        string fullFileName = Path.Combine(currentFolderPath, selectedString);
        DisplayFileInfo(fullFileName);
    }
    catch(Exception ex)
    {
        MessageBox.Show(ex.Message);
    }
}
```

code download FileProperties.sln

The event handler for the selection of a folder in the Folders list box is implemented in a very similar way, except that in this case you call `DisplayFolderList()` to update the contents of the list boxes:

```
protected void OnListBoxFoldersSelected(object sender, EventArgs e)
{
    try
    {
        string selectedString = listBoxFolders.SelectedItem.ToString();
        string fullPathName = Path.Combine(currentFolderPath, selectedString);
        DisplayFolderList(fullPathName);
    }
    catch(Exception ex)
```

```
        {
            MessageBox.Show(ex.Message);
        }
    }
}
```

code download FileProperties.sln

Finally, when the Up button is clicked, `DisplayFolderList()` must also be called, except that this time you need to obtain the path of the parent of the folder currently being displayed. This is done with the `FileInfo.DirectoryName` property, which returns the parent folder path:

Available for download on Wrox.com

```
protected void OnUpButtonClick(object sender, EventArgs e)
{
    try
    {
        string folderPath = new FileInfo(currentFolderPath).DirectoryName;
        DisplayFolderList(folderPath);
    }
    catch(Exception ex)
    {
        MessageBox.Show(ex.Message);
    }
}
```

code download FileProperties.sln

MOVING, COPYING, AND DELETING FILES

As mentioned, moving and deleting files or folders is done by the `MoveTo()` and `Delete()` methods of the `FileInfo` and `DirectoryInfo` classes. The equivalent methods on the `File` and `Directory` classes are `Move()` and `Delete()`. The `FileInfo` and `File` classes also implement the methods `CopyTo()` and `Copy()`, respectively. However, no methods exist to copy complete folders — you need to do that by copying each file in the folder.

Using all these methods is quite intuitive — you can find detailed descriptions in the SDK documentation. This section illustrates their use for the particular cases of calling the static `Move()`, `Copy()`, and `Delete()` methods on the `File` class. To do this, you will build on the previous `FileProperties` example and call its iteration `FilePropertiesAndMovement`. This example will have the extra feature that whenever the properties of a file are displayed, the application gives you the option of deleting that file or moving or copying the file to another location.

FIGURE 29-4

FilePropertiesAndMovement Sample

Figure 29-4 shows the user interface of the new sample application.

As you can see, `FilePropertiesAndMovement` is similar in appearance to `FileProperties`, except for the group of three buttons and a text box at the bottom of the window. These controls are enabled only when the example is actually displaying the properties of a file; at all other times, they are disabled. The existing controls are also squashed up a bit to stop the main form from getting too big. When the properties of a selected file are displayed, `FilePropertiesAndMovement` automatically places the full pathname of that file in the bottom text box for the user to edit. Users can then click any of the buttons to perform the appropriate operation. When they do, a message box is displayed that confirms the action taken by the user (see Figure 29-5).

FIGURE 29-5

When the user clicks the Yes button, the action is initiated. There are some actions in the form that the user can take that will then cause the display to be incorrect. For instance, if the user moves or deletes a file, you obviously cannot continue to display the contents of that file in the same location. In addition, if you change the name of a file in the same folder, your display will also be out of date. In these cases, `FilePropertiesAndMovement` resets its controls to display only the folder where the file resides after the file operation.

Looking at the Code for FilePropertiesAndMovement

To code this process, you need to add the relevant controls, as well as their event handlers, to the code for the `FileProperties` sample. The new controls are given the names `buttonDelete`, `buttonCopyTo`, `buttonMoveTo`, and `textBoxNewPath`.

First, look at the event handler that is called when the user clicks the Delete button:

Available for download on Wrox.com

```
protected void OnDeleteButtonClick(object sender, EventArgs e)
{
    try
    {
        string filePath = Path.Combine(currentFolderPath,
                                    textBoxFileName.Text);
        string query = "Really delete the file\n" + filePath + y?";
        if (MessageBox.Show(query,
            "Delete File?", MessageBoxButtons.YesNo) == DialogResult.Yes)
        {
            File.Delete(filePath);
            DisplayFolderList(currentFolderPath);
        }
    }
    catch(Exception ex)
    {
        MessageBox.Show("Unable to delete file. The following exception"
                        + " occurred:\n" + ex.Message, "Failed");
    }
}
```

code download FilePropertiesAndMovement.sln

The code for this method is contained in a `try` block because of the obvious risk of an exception being thrown if, for example, you don't have permission to delete the file, or the file is moved by another process after it has been displayed but before the user presses the Delete button. You construct the path of the file to be deleted from the `CurrentParentPath` field, which contains the path of the parent folder, and the text in the `textBoxFileName` text box, which contains the name of the file.

The methods to move and copy the file are structured in a very similar manner:

Available for download on Wrox.com

```
protected void OnMoveButtonClick(object sender, EventArgs e)
{
    try
    {
        string filePath = Path.Combine(currentFolderPath,
                                    textBoxFileName.Text);
```

```
            string query = "Really move the file\n" + filePath + "\nto "
                               + textBoxNewPath.Text + "?";
            if (MessageBox.Show(query,
                "Move File?", MessageBoxButtons.YesNo) == DialogResult.Yes)
            {
                File.Move(filePath, textBoxNewPath.Text);
                DisplayFolderList(currentFolderPath);
            }
        }
        catch(Exception ex)
        {
            MessageBox.Show("Unable to move file. The following exception"
                              + " occurred:\n" + ex.Message, "Failed");
        }
    }

    protected void OnCopyButtonClick(object sender, EventArgs e)
    {
        try
        {
            string filePath = Path.Combine(currentFolderPath,
                                        textBoxFileName.Text);
            string query = "Really copy the file\n" + filePath + "\nto "
                               + textBoxNewPath.Text + "?";
            if (MessageBox.Show(query,
                "Copy File?", MessageBoxButtons.YesNo) == DialogResult.Yes)
            {
                File.Copy(filePath, textBoxNewPath.Text);
                DisplayFolderList(currentFolderPath);
            }
        }
        catch(Exception ex)
        {
            MessageBox.Show("Unable to copy file. The following exception"
                              + " occurred:\n" + ex.Message, "Failed");
        }
    }
```

code download FilePropertiesAndMovement.sln

You are not quite done. You also need to make sure that the new buttons and text box are enabled and disabled at the appropriate times. To enable them when you are displaying the contents of a file, you add the following code to `DisplayFileInfo()`:

```
    protected void DisplayFileInfo(string fileFullName)
    {
        FileInfo theFile = new FileInfo(fileFullName);

        if (!theFile.Exists)
        {
            throw new FileNotFoundException("File not found: " + fileFullName);
        }

        textBoxFileName.Text = theFile.Name;
        textBoxCreationTime.Text = theFile.CreationTime.ToLongTimeString();
        textBoxLastAccessTime.Text = theFile.LastAccessTime.ToLongDateString();
        textBoxLastWriteTime.Text = theFile.LastWriteTime.ToLongDateString();
        textBoxFileSize.Text = theFile.Length.ToString() + " bytes";

        // enable move, copy, delete buttons
        textBoxNewPath.Text = theFile.FullName;
        textBoxNewPath.Enabled = true;
```

```
        buttonCopyTo.Enabled = true;
        buttonDelete.Enabled = true;
        buttonMoveTo.Enabled = true;
    }
```

You also need to make one change to `DisplayFolderList`:

```
protected void DisplayFolderList(string folderFullName)
{
    DirectoryInfo theFolder = new DirectoryInfo(folderFullName);

    if (!theFolder.Exists)
    {
        throw new DirectoryNotFoundException("Folder not found: " + folderFullName);
    }

    ClearAllFields();
    DisableMoveFeatures();
    textBoxFolder.Text = theFolder.FullName;
    currentFolderPath = theFolder.FullName;

    // list all subfolders in folder
    foreach(DirectoryInfo nextFolder in theFolder.GetDirectories())
        listBoxFolders.Items.Add(NextFolder.Name);

    // list all files in folder
    foreach(FileInfo nextFile in theFolder.GetFiles())
        listBoxFiles.Items.Add(NextFile.Name);
}
```

`DisableMoveFeatures` is a small utility function that disables the new controls:

```
void DisableMoveFeatures()
{
    textBoxNewPath.Text = "";
    textBoxNewPath.Enabled = false;
    buttonCopyTo.Enabled = false;
    buttonDelete.Enabled = false;
    buttonMoveTo.Enabled = false;
}
```

You also need to add extra code to `ClearAllFields()` to clear the extra text box:

```
protected void ClearAllFields()
{
    listBoxFolders.Items.Clear();
    listBoxFiles.Items.Clear();
    textBoxFolder.Text = "";
    textBoxFileName.Text = "";
    textBoxCreationTime.Text = "";
    textBoxLastAccessTime.Text = "";
    textBoxLastWriteTime.Text = "";
    textBoxFileSize.Text = "";
    textBoxNewPath.Text = "";
}
```

The next section takes a look at reading and writing to files.

READING AND WRITING TO FILES

Reading and writing to files is in principle very simple; however, it is not done through the `DirectoryInfo` or `FileInfo` objects. Instead, using the .NET Framework 4, you can do it through the `File` object. Later in this chapter, you see how to accomplish this using a number of other classes that represent a generic concept called a *stream*.

Before .NET Framework 2.0, it took a bit of wrangling to read and write to files. It was possible using the available classes from the framework, but it was not that straightforward. The .NET Framework 2.0 has expanded the `File` class to make it as simple as just one line of code to read or write to a file. This same functionality is also available in .NET Framework 4.

Reading a File

For an example of reading a file, create a Windows Forms application that contains a regular text box, a button, and a multiline text box. In the end, your form should appear similar to Figure 29-6.

FIGURE 29-6

The idea of this form is that the end user will enter the path of a specific file in the first text box and click the Read button. From there, the application will read the specified file and display the file's contents in the multiline text box. This is illustrated in the following code example:

```
using System;
using System.IO;
using System.Windows.Forms;

namespace ReadingFiles
{
    public partial class Form1: Form
    {
        public Form1()
        {
```

```
            InitializeComponent();
        }

        private void button1_Click(object sender, EventArgs e)
        {
            textBox2.Text = File.ReadAllText(textBox1.Text);
        }
    }
}
```

code download ReadingFiles.sln

In building this example, the first step is to add the `using` statement to bring in the `System.IO` namespace. From there, simply use the `button1_Click` event for the Send button on the form to populate the text box with what comes back from the file. You can now access the file's contents by using the `File. ReadAllText()` method. As you can see, you can read files with a single statement. The `ReadAllText()` method opens the specified file, reads the contents, and then closes the file. The return value of the `ReadAllText()` method is a string containing the entire contents of the file specified. The result would be something similar to what is shown in Figure 29-7.

FIGURE 29-7

The `File.ReadAllText()` signature shown in the preceding example is of the following construction:

```
File.ReadAllText(FilePath);
```

The other option is to also specify the encoding of the file being read:

```
File.ReadAllText(FilePath, Encoding);
```

Using this signature allows you to specify the encoding to use when opening and reading the contents of the file. Therefore, this means that you could do something like the following:

```
File.ReadAllText(textBox1.Text, Encoding.ASCII);
```

Some of the other options for opening and working with files include using the `ReadAllBytes()` and the `ReadAllLines()` methods. The `ReadAllBytes()` method allows you to open a binary file and read the contents into a byte array. The `ReadAllText()` method shown earlier gives you the entire contents of the specified file in a single string instance. You might not be interested in this, but instead might be interested in working with what comes back from the file in a line-by-line fashion. In this case, you should use the `ReadAllLines()` method because it allows for this kind of functionality and will return a string array for you to work with.

Writing to a File

Besides making reading from files an extremely simple process under the .NET Framework umbrella, the base class library has made writing to files just as easy. Just as the base class library (BCL) gives you the `ReadAllText()`, `ReadAllLines()`, and `ReadAllBytes()` methods to read files in a few different ways, it gives you the `WriteAllText()`, `WriteAllBytes()`, and `WriteAllLines()` methods to write files.

For an example of how to write to a file, use the same Windows Forms application, but use the multiline text box in the form to input data into a file. The code for the `button1_Click` event handler should appear as shown here:

```
private void button1_Click(object sender, EventArgs e)
{
    File.WriteAllText(textBox1.Text, textBox2.Text);
}
```

Build and start the form, type `C:\Testing.txt` in the first text box, type some random content in the second text box, and then click the button. Nothing will happen visually, but if you look in your root C: drive, you will see the `Testing.txt` file with the content you specified.

The `WriteAllText()` method went to the specified location, created a new text file, and provided the specified contents to the file before saving and closing the file. Not bad for just one line of code!

If you run the application again, and specify the same file (`Testing.txt`) but with some new content, pressing the button again will cause the application to perform the same task. This time though, the new content is not added to the previous content you specified — instead, the new content completely overrides the previous content. In fact, `WriteAllText()`, `WriteAllBytes()`, and `WriteAllLines()` all override any previous files, so you must be careful when using these methods.

The `WriteAllText()` method in the previous example uses the following signature:

```
File.WriteAllText(FilePath, Contents)
```

You can also specify the encoding of the new file:

```
File.WriteAllText(FilePath, Contents, Encoding)
```

The `WriteAllBytes()` method allows you to write content to a file using a byte array, and the `WriteAllLines()` method allows you to write a string array to a file. An example of this is illustrated in the following event handler:

```
private void button1_Click(object sender, EventArgs e)
{
    string[] movies =
        {"Grease",
         "Close Encounters of the Third Kind",
         "The Day After Tomorrow"};

    File.WriteAllLines(@"C:\Testing.txt", movies);
}
```

Now clicking the button for such an application will give you a `Testing.txt` file with the following contents:

```
Grease
Close Encounters of the Third Kind
The Day After Tomorrow
```

The `WriteAllLines()` method writes out the string array with each array item taking its own line in the file.

Because data may be written not only to disk but to other places as well (such as to named pipes or to memory), it is also important to understand how to deal with file I/O in .NET using streams as a means of moving file contents around. This is shown in the following section.

Streams

The idea of a stream has been around for a very long time. A stream is an object used to transfer data. The data can be transferred in one of two directions:

> ➤ If the data is being transferred from some outside source into your program, it is called *reading* from the stream.

> ➤ If the data is being transferred from your program to some outside source, it is called *writing* to the stream.

Very often, the outside source will be a file, but that is not always the case. Other possibilities include:

> ➤ Reading or writing data on the network using some network protocol, where the intention is for this data to be picked up by or sent from another computer

> ➤ Reading or writing to a named pipe

> ➤ Reading or writing to an area of memory

Of these examples, Microsoft has supplied a .NET base class for writing to or reading from memory, the `System.IO.MemoryStream` object. The `System.Net.Sockets.NetworkStream` object handles network data. There are no base stream classes for writing to or reading from pipes, but there is a generic stream class, `System.IO.Stream`, from which you would inherit if you wanted to write such a class. `Stream` does not make any assumptions about the nature of the external data source.

The outside source might even be a variable within your own code. This might sound paradoxical, but the technique of using streams to transmit data between variables can be a useful trick for converting data between data types. The C language used something similar — the `sprintf` function — to convert between integer data types and strings or to format strings.

The advantage of having a separate object for the transfer of data, rather than using the `FileInfo` or `DirectoryInfo` classes to do this, is that separating the concept of transferring data from the particular data source makes it easier to swap data sources. Stream objects themselves contain a lot of generic code that concerns the movement of data between outside sources and variables in your code. By keeping this code separate from any concept of a particular data source, you make it easier for this code to be reused (through inheritance) in different circumstances. For example, the `StringReader` and `StringWriter` classes are part of the same inheritance tree as two classes that you will be using later on to read and write text files. The classes will almost certainly share a substantial amount of code behind the scenes.

Figure 29-8 illustrates the actual hierarchy of stream-related classes in the `System.IO` namespace.

As far as reading and writing files, the classes that concern us most are:

> ➤ `FileStream` — This class is intended for reading and writing binary data in a binary file. However, you can also use it to read from or write to any file.

> ➤ `StreamReader` and `StreamWriter` — These classes are designed specifically for reading from and writing to text files.

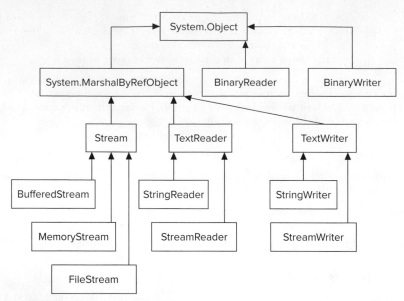

FIGURE 29-8

You might also find the `BinaryReader` and `BinaryWriter` classes useful, although they are not used in the examples here. These classes do not actually implement streams themselves, but they are able to provide wrappers around other stream objects. `BinaryReader` and `BinaryWriter` provide extra formatting of binary data, which allows you to directly read or write the contents of C# variables to or from the relevant stream. Think of the `BinaryReader` and `BinaryWriter` as sitting between the stream and your code, providing extra formatting (see Figure 29-9).

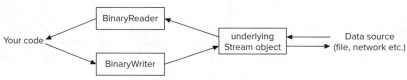

FIGURE 29-9

The difference between using these classes and directly using the underlying stream objects is that a basic stream works in bytes. For example, suppose that as part of the process of saving some document you want to write the contents of a variable of type `long` to a binary file. Each `long` occupies 8 bytes, and if you used an ordinary binary stream, you would have to explicitly write each of those 8 bytes of memory.

In C# code, you would have to perform some bitwise operations to extract each of those 8 bytes from the `long` value. Using a `BinaryWriter` instance, you can encapsulate the entire operation in an overload of the `BinaryWriter.Write()` method, which takes a `long` as a parameter, and which will place those 8 bytes into the stream (and if the stream is directed to a file, into the file). A corresponding `BinaryReader.Read()` method will extract 8 bytes from the stream and recover the value of the `long`. For more information on the `BinaryReader` and `BinaryWriter` classes, refer to the SDK documentation.

Buffered Streams

For performance reasons, when you read or write to or from a file, the output is buffered. This means that if your program asks for the next 2 bytes of a file stream, and the stream passes the request on to Windows, then Windows will not connect to the file system and then locate and read the file off the disk, just to get

2 bytes. Instead, Windows will retrieve a large block of the file at one time and store this block in an area of memory known as a *buffer*. Subsequent requests for data from the stream are satisfied from the buffer until the buffer runs out, at which point, Windows grabs another block of data from the file.

Writing to files works in the same way. For files, this is done automatically by the operating system, but you might have to write a stream class to read from some other device that is not buffered. If so, you can derive your class from `BufferedStream`, which implements a buffer itself. (Note, however, that `BufferedStream` is not designed for the situation in which an application frequently alternates between reading and writing data.)

Reading and Writing to Binary Files Using FileStream

Reading and writing to and from binary files can be done using the `FileStream` class. (Note that if you are working with the .NET Framework 1.x, this will most likely be the case.)

The FileStream Class

A `FileStream` instance is used to read or write data to or from a file. To construct a `FileStream`, you need four pieces of information:

1. The *file* you want to access.
2. The *mode*, which indicates how you want to open the file. For example, are you intending to create a new file or open an existing file? And if you are opening an existing file, should any write operations be interpreted as overwriting the contents of the file or appending to the file?
3. The *access*, which indicates how you want to access the file. For example, do you want to read from or write to the file or do both?
4. The *share* access, which specifies whether you want exclusive access to the file. Or, are you willing to have other streams access the file simultaneously? If so, should other streams have access to read the file, to write to it, or to do both?

The first of these pieces of information is usually represented by a string that contains the full pathname of the file, and this chapter considers only those constructors that require a string here. Besides those constructors, however, some additional ones take an old Windows-API-style Windows handle to a file instead. The remaining three pieces of information are represented by three .NET enumerations called `FileMode`, `FileAccess`, and `FileShare`. The values of these enumerations are listed in the following table and are self-explanatory.

ENUMERATION	VALUES
FileMode	Append, Create, CreateNew, Open, OpenOrCreate, or Truncate
FileAccess	Read, ReadWrite, or Write
FileShare	Delete, Inheritable, None, Read, ReadWrite, or Write

Note that in the case of `FileMode`, exceptions can be thrown if you request a mode that is inconsistent with the existing status of the file. `Append`, `Open`, and `Truncate` will throw an exception if the file does not already exist, and `CreateNew` will throw an exception if it does. `Create` and `OpenOrCreate` will cope with either scenario, but `Create` will delete any existing file to replace it with a new, initially empty, one. The `FileAccess` and `FileShare` enumerations are bitwise flags, so values can be combined with the C# bitwise OR operator, `|`.

There are a large number of constructors for the `FileStream`. The three simplest ones work as follows:

```
// creates file with read-write access and allows other streams read access
FileStream fs = new FileStream(@"C:\C# Projects\Project.doc",
                FileMode.Create);
// as above, but we only get write access to the file
```

```
FileStream fs2 = new FileStream(@"C:\C# Projects\Project2.doc",
                    FileMode.Create, FileAccess.Write);
// as above but other streams don't get access to the file while
// fs3 is open
FileStream fs3 = new FileStream(@"C:\C# Projects\Project3.doc",
                    FileMode.Create, FileAccess.Write, FileShare.None);
```

As this code reveals, the overloads of these constructors have the effect of providing default values of `FileAccess.ReadWrite` and `FileShare.Read` to the third and fourth parameters depending upon the `FileMode` value. It is also possible to create a file stream from a `FileInfo` instance in various ways:

```
FileInfo myFile4 = new FileInfo(@"C:\C# Projects\Project4.doc");
FileStream fs4 = myFile4.OpenRead();
FileInfo myFile5= new FileInfo(@"C:\C# Projects\Project5doc");
FileStream fs5 = myFile5.OpenWrite();
FileInfo myFile6= new FileInfo(@"C:\C# Projects\Project6doc");
FileStream fs6 = myFile6.Open(FileMode.Append, FileAccess.Write,
                    FileShare.None);
FileInfo myFile7 = new FileInfo(@"C:\C# Projects\Project7.doc");
FileStream fs7 = myFile7.Create();
```

`FileInfo.OpenRead()` supplies a stream that gives you read-only access to an existing file, whereas `FileInfo.OpenWrite()` gives you read-write access. `FileInfo.Open()` allows you to specify the mode, access, and file share parameters explicitly.

Of course, after you have finished with a stream, you should close it:

```
fs.Close();
```

Closing the stream frees up the resources associated with it and allows other applications to set up streams to the same file. This action also flushes the buffer. In between opening and closing the stream, you should read data from it and/or write data to it. `FileStream` implements a number of methods to do this.

`ReadByte()` is the simplest way of reading data. It grabs 1 byte from the stream and casts the result to an `int` that has a value between 0 and 255. If you have reached the end of the stream, it returns -1:

```
int NextByte = fs.ReadByte();
```

If you prefer to read a number of bytes at a time, you can call the `Read()` method, which reads a specified number of bytes into an array. `Read()` returns the number of bytes actually read — if this value is zero, you know that you are at the end of the stream. Here is an example where you read into a byte array called `ByteArray`:

```
int nBytesRead = fs.Read(ByteArray, 0, nBytes);
```

The second parameter to `Read()` is an offset, which you can use to request that the `Read` operation start populating the array at some element other than the first. The third parameter is the number of bytes to read into the array.

If you want to write data to a file, two parallel methods are available, `WriteByte()` and `Write()`. `WriteByte()` writes a single byte to the stream:

```
byte NextByte = 100;
fs.WriteByte(NextByte);
```

`Write()`, however, writes out an array of bytes. For instance, if you initialized the `ByteArray` mentioned before with some values, you could use the following code to write out the first `nBytes` of the array:

```
fs.Write(ByteArray, 0, nBytes);
```

As with `Read()`, the second parameter allows you to start writing from some point other than the beginning of the array. Both `WriteByte()` and `Write()` return `void`.

In addition to these methods, `FileStream` implements various other methods and properties related to bookkeeping tasks such as determining how many bytes are in the stream, locking the stream, or flushing the buffer. These other methods are not usually required for basic reading and writing, but if you need them, full details are in the SDK documentation.

BinaryFileReader Sample

The use of the `FileStream` class is illustrated by writing a sample, `BinaryFileReader`, which reads in and displays any file. Create the project in Visual Studio 2010 as a Windows application. It has one menu item, which brings up a standard `OpenFileDialog` asking what file to read in and then displays the file as binary code. As you are reading in binary files, you need to be able to display nonprintable characters. You will do this by displaying each byte of the file individually, showing 16 bytes on each line of a multiline text box. If the byte represents a printable ASCII character, you will display that character; otherwise, you will display the value of the byte in a hexadecimal format. In either case, you pad out the displayed text with spaces so that each byte displayed occupies four columns; this way, the bytes line up nicely under each other.

Figure 29-10 shows what the `BinaryFileReader` application looks like when viewing a text file. (Because `BinaryFileReader` can view any file, it is quite possible to use it on text files as well as binary ones.) In this case, the application has read in a basic ASP.NET page (`.aspx`).

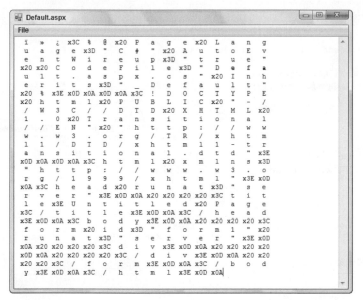

FIGURE 29-10

Clearly, this format is more suited for looking at the values of individual bytes than for displaying text! Later in this chapter, when you develop a sample that is specifically designed to read text files, you will see what this file really says. The advantage of this sample is that you can look at the contents of any file.

This sample does not demonstrate writing to files because you don't want to get bogged down in the complexities of trying to translate the contents of a text box as the one shown in Figure 29-10 into a binary stream! You see how to write to files later when you develop a sample that can read or write, but only to and from text files.

Here is the code used to get these results. First, you need to make sure that you have brought in the `System.IO` namespace through the use of the `using` statement:

```
using System.IO;
```

Next, you add a couple of fields to the main form class — one representing the file dialog and a string that gives the path of the file currently being viewed:

```
partial class Form1: Form
{
    private readonly OpenFileDialog chooseOpenFileDialog =
        new OpenFileDialog();
    private string chosenFile;
```

code download BinaryFileReader.sln

You also need to add some standard Windows Forms code to deal with the handlers for the menu and the file dialog:

```
public Form1()
{
    InitializeComponent();
    menuFileOpen.Click += OnFileOpen;
    chooseOpenFileDialog.FileOk += OnOpenFileDialogOK;
}

void OnFileOpen(object Sender, EventArgs e)
{
    chooseOpenFileDialog.ShowDialog();
}

void OnOpenFileDialogOK(object Sender, CancelEventArgs e)
{
    chosenFile = chooseOpenFileDialog.FileName;
    this.Text = Path.GetFileName(chosenFile);
    DisplayFile();
}
```

code download BinaryFileReader.sln

As this code demonstrates, when the user clicks OK to select a file in the file dialog, you call the `DisplayFile()` method, which does the work of reading in the selected file:

```
void DisplayFile()
{
    int nCols = 16;
    FileStream inStream = new FileStream(chosenFile, FileMode.Open,
                                                  FileAccess.Read);

    long nBytesToRead = inStream.Length;
    if (nBytesToRead > 65536/4)
        nBytesToRead = 65536/4;

    int nLines = (int)(nBytesToRead/nCols) + 1;
    string [] lines = new string[nLines];
    int nBytesRead = 0;

    for (int i=0; i<nLines; i++)
    {
        StringBuilder nextLine = new StringBuilder();
        nextLine.Capacity = 4*nCols;

        for (int j = 0; j<nCols; j++)
        {
            int nextByte = inStream.ReadByte();
            nBytesRead++;
            if (nextByte < 0 || nBytesRead > 65536)
                break;
            char nextChar = (char)nextByte;
```

```
        if (nextChar < 16)
            nextLine.Append(" x0" + string.Format("{0,1:X}",
                                                    (int)nextChar));
        else if
            (char.IsLetterOrDigit(nextChar) ||
                            char.IsPunctuation(nextChar))
            nextLine.Append("  " + nextChar + " ");
        else
            nextLine.Append(" x" + string.Format("{0,2:X}",
                                    (int)nextChar));
    }
    lines[i] = nextLine.ToString();
}
inStream.Close();
this.textBoxContents.Lines = lines;
}
```

code download BinaryFileReader.sln

There is quite a lot going on in this method, so here is the breakdown. You instantiate a `FileStream` object for the selected file, which specifies that you want to open an existing file for reading. You then work out how many bytes there are to read in and how many lines should be displayed. The number of bytes will normally be the number of bytes in the file. This example limits the display of the contents in the textbox control to a maximum of only 65,536 characters — with the chosen display format, you are displaying four characters for every byte in the file.

 You might want to look up the `RichTextBox` class in the `System.Windows.Forms` namespace. `RichTextBox` is similar to a text box, but has many more advanced formatting facilities. `TextBox` is used here to keep the example simple and focused on the process of reading in files.

The bulk of the method is given to two nested `for` loops that construct each line of text to be displayed. You use a `StringBuilder` class to construct each line for performance reasons: you are appending suitable text for each byte to the string that represents each line 16 times. If on each occasion you allocate a new string and take a copy of the half-constructed line, you are not only going to be spending a lot of time allocating strings but will also be wasting a lot of memory on the heap. Notice that the definition of *printable* characters is anything that is a letter, digit, or punctuation, as indicated by the relevant static `System.Char` methods. You exclude any character with a value less than 16 from the printable list, however; this means that you will trap the carriage return (13) and line feed (10) as binary characters (a multiline text box isn't able to display these characters properly if they occur individually within a line).

Furthermore, using the Properties window, you change the Font property for the text box to a fixed-width font. In this case, you choose `Courier New 9pt regular` and set the text box to have vertical and horizontal scrollbars.

Upon completion, you close the stream and set the contents of the text box to the array of strings that you have built up.

Reading and Writing to Text Files

Theoretically, it is perfectly possible to use the `FileStream` class to read in and display text files. You have, after all, just done that. The format in which the `Default.aspx` file is displayed in the preceding sample is not particularly user-friendly, but that has nothing to do with any intrinsic problem with the `FileStream` class, only with how you choose to display the results in the text box.

Having said that, if you know that a particular file contains text, you will usually find it more convenient to read and write it using the `StreamReader` and `StreamWriter` classes instead of the `FileStream` class. That is because these classes work at a slightly higher level and are specifically geared to reading and writing text. The methods that they implement are able to automatically detect convenient points to stop reading text, based on the contents of the stream. In particular:

➤ These classes implement methods to read or write one line of text at a time, `StreamReader` `.ReadLine()` and `StreamWriter.WriteLine()`. In the case of reading, this means that the stream will automatically determine for you where the next carriage return is and stop reading at that point. In the case of writing, it means that the stream will automatically append the carriage return–line feed combination to the text that it writes out.

➤ By using the `StreamReader` and `StreamWriter` classes, you don't need to worry about the encoding (the text format) used in the file. Possible encodings include ASCII (1 byte for each character), or any of the Unicode-based formats, Unicode, UTF7, UTF8, and UTF32. Text files on Windows 9x systems are always in ASCII because Windows 9x does not support Unicode; however, because Windows NT, 2000, XP, 2003, Vista, Windows Server 2008, and Windows 7 all support Unicode, text files might theoretically contain Unicode, UTF7, UTF8, or UTF32 data instead of ASCII data. The convention is that if the file is in ASCII format, it will simply contain the text. If it is in any Unicode format, this will be indicated by the first 2 or 3 bytes of the file, which are set to particular combinations of values to indicate the format used in the file.

These bytes are known as the *byte code markers*. When you open a file using any of the standard Windows applications, such as Notepad or WordPad, you do not need to worry about this because these applications are aware of the different encoding methods and will automatically read the file correctly. This is also true for the `StreamReader` class, which correctly reads in a file in any of these formats, and the `StreamWriter` class is capable of formatting the text it writes out using whatever encoding technique you request. If you want to read in and display a text file using the `FileStream` class, however, you need to handle this yourself.

The StreamReader Class

`StreamReader` is used to read text files. Constructing a `StreamReader` is in some ways easier than constructing a `FileStream` instance because some of the `FileStream` options are not required when using `StreamReader`. In particular, the mode and access types are not relevant to `StreamReader` because the only thing you can do with a `StreamReader` is read! Furthermore, there is no direct option to specify the sharing permissions. However, there are a couple of new options:

➤ You need to specify what to do about the different encoding methods. You can instruct the `StreamReader` to examine the byte code markers in the beginning of the file to determine the encoding method, or you can simply tell the `StreamReader` to assume that the file uses a specified encoding method.

➤ Instead of supplying a filename to be read from, you can supply a reference to another stream.

This last option deserves a bit more discussion because it illustrates another advantage of basing the model for reading and writing data on the concept of streams. Because the `StreamReader` works at a relatively high level, you might find it useful if you have another stream that is there to read data from some other source, but you would like to use the facilities provided by `StreamReader` to process that other stream as if it contained text. You can do so by simply passing the output from this stream to a `StreamReader`. In this way, `StreamReader` can be used to read and process data from any data source — not only files. This is essentially the situation discussed earlier with regard to the `BinaryReader` class. However, in this book you only use `StreamReader` to connect directly to files.

The result of these possibilities is that `StreamReader` has a large number of constructors. Not only that, but there is another `FileInfo` method that returns a `StreamReader` reference: `OpenText()`. The following just illustrates some of the constructors.

The simplest constructor takes just a filename. This `StreamReader` examines the byte order marks to determine the encoding:

```
StreamReader sr = new StreamReader(@"C:\My Documents\ReadMe.txt");
```

Alternatively, you can specify that UTF8 encoding should be assumed:

```
StreamReader sr = new StreamReader(@"C:\My Documents\ReadMe.txt",
                                   Encoding.UTF8);
```

You specify the encoding by using one of several properties on a class, `System.Text.Encoding`. This class is an abstract base class, from which a number of classes are derived and which implements methods that actually perform the text encoding. Each property returns an instance of the appropriate class, and the possible properties you can use are here:

➤ `ASCII`

➤ `Unicode`

➤ `UTF7`

➤ `UTF8`

➤ `UTF32`

➤ `BigEndianUnicode`

The following example demonstrates how to hook up a `StreamReader` to a `FileStream`. The advantage of this is that you can specify whether to create the file and the share permissions, which you cannot do if you directly attach a `StreamReader` to the file:

```
FileStream fs = new FileStream(@"C:\My Documents\ReadMe.txt",
                    FileMode.Open, FileAccess.Read, FileShare.None);
StreamReader sr = new StreamReader(fs);
```

For this example, you specify that the `StreamReader` will look for byte code markers to determine the encoding method used, as it will do in the following examples, in which the `StreamReader` is obtained from a `FileInfo` instance:

```
FileInfo myFile = new FileInfo(@"C:\My Documents\ReadMe.txt");
StreamReader sr = myFile.OpenText();
```

Just as with a `FileStream`, you should always close a `StreamReader` after use. Failure to do so will result in the file remaining locked to other processes (unless you used a `FileStream` to construct the `StreamReader` and specified `FileShare.ShareReadWrite`):

```
sr.Close();
```

Now that you have gone to the trouble of instantiating a `StreamReader`, you can do something with it. As with the `FileStream`, you will simply see the various ways to read data, and the other, less commonly used `StreamReader` methods are left to the SDK documentation.

Possibly the easiest method to use is `ReadLine()`, which keeps reading until it gets to the end of a line. It does not include the carriage return–line feed combination that marks the end of the line in the returned string:

```
string nextLine = sr.ReadLine();
```

Alternatively, you can grab the entire remainder of the file (or strictly, the remainder of the stream) in one string:

```
string restOfStream = sr.ReadToEnd();
```

You can read a single character:

```
int nextChar = sr.Read();
```

This overload of `Read()` casts the returned character to an `int`. This is so that it has the option of returning a value of `-1` if the end of the stream has been reached.

Finally, you can read a given number of characters into an array, with an offset:

```
// to read 100 characters in.

int nChars = 100;
char [] charArray = new char[nChars];
int nCharsRead = sr.Read(charArray, 0, nChars);
```

nCharsRead will be less than nChars if you have requested to read more characters than are left in the file.

The StreamWriter Class

This works in the same way as the StreamReader, except that you can use StreamWriter only to write to a file (or to another stream). Possibilities for constructing a StreamWriter include this:

```
StreamWriter sw = new StreamWriter(@"C:\My Documents\ReadMe.txt");
```

This will use UTF8 encoding, which is regarded by .NET as the default encoding method. If you want, you can specify alternative encoding:

```
StreamWriter sw = new StreamWriter(@"C:\My Documents\ReadMe.txt", true,
    Encoding.ASCII);
```

In this constructor, the second parameter is a Boolean that indicates whether the file should be opened for appending. There is, oddly, no constructor that takes only a filename and an encoding class.

Of course, you may want to hook up StreamWriter to a file stream to give you more control over the options for opening the file:

```
FileStream fs = new FileStream(@"C:\My Documents\ReadMe.txt",
    FileMode.CreateNew, FileAccess.Write, FileShare.Read);
StreamWriter sw = new StreamWriter(fs);
```

FileStream does not implement any methods that return a StreamWriter class.

Alternatively, if you want to create a new file and start writing data to it, you will find this sequence useful:

```
FileInfo myFile = new FileInfo(@"C:\My Documents\NewFile.txt");
StreamWriter sw = myFile.CreateText();
```

Just as with all other stream classes, it is important to close a StreamWriter class when you are finished with it:

```
sw.Close();
```

Writing to the stream is done using any of 17 overloads of StreamWriter.Write(). The simplest writes out a string:

```
string nextLine = "Groovy Line";
sw.Write(nextLine);
```

It is also possible to write out a single character:

```
char nextChar = 'a';
sw.Write(nextChar);
```

And an array of characters:

```
char [] charArray = new char[100];

// initialize these characters

sw.Write(charArray);
```

It is even possible to write out a portion of an array of characters:

```
int nCharsToWrite = 50;
int startAtLocation = 25;
char [] charArray = new char[100];
```

```
        // initialize these characters

        sw.Write(charArray, startAtLocation, nCharsToWrite);
```

ReadWriteText Sample

The `ReadWriteText` sample displays the use of the `StreamReader` and `StreamWriter` classes. It is similar to the earlier `ReadBinaryFile` sample, but it assumes that the file to be read in is a text file and displays it as such. It is also capable of saving the file (with any modifications you have made to the text in the text box). It will save any file in Unicode format.

The screenshot in Figure 29-11 shows `ReadWriteText` displaying the same `Default.aspx` file that you used earlier. This time, however, you are able to read the contents a bit more easily!

We don't cover the details of adding the event handlers for the Open File dialog box, because they are basically the same as in the earlier `BinaryFileReader` sample. As with that sample, opening a new file causes the `DisplayFile()` method to be called. The only real difference between this sample and the previous one is the implementation of `DisplayFile` as well as that you now have the option to save a file. This is represented by another menu option, Save. The handler for this option calls another method you have added to the code, `SaveFile()`. (Note that the new file always overwrites the original file; this sample does not have an option to write to a different file.)

FIGURE 29-11

You look at `SaveFile()` first because it is the simplest function. You simply write each line of the text box, in turn, to a `StreamWriter` stream, relying on the `StreamReader.WriteLine()` method to append the trailing carriage return and line feed to the end of each line:

```
void SaveFile()
{
    StreamWriter sw = new StreamWriter(chosenFile, false, Encoding.Unicode);

    foreach (string line in textBoxContents.Lines)
        sw.WriteLine(line);

    sw.Close();
}
```

code download ReadWriteText.sln

`chosenFile` is a string field of the main form, which contains the name of the file you have read in (just as for the previous example). Notice that you specify Unicode encoding when you open the stream. If you want to write files in some other format, you simply need to change the value of this parameter. The second parameter to this constructor is set to `true` to append to a file, but you do not in this case. The encoding must be set at construction time for a `StreamWriter`. It is subsequently available as a read-only property, `Encoding`.

Now you examine how files are read in. The process of reading in is complicated by the fact that you don't know how many lines it is going to contain until you have read in the file. For example, you don't know how many `(char)13(char)10` sequences are in the file because `char(13)char(10)` is the carriage return–line feed combination that occurs at the end of a line. You solve this problem by initially reading the file into an instance of the `StringCollection` class, which is in the `System.Collections.Specialized` namespace. This class is designed to hold a set of strings that can be dynamically expanded. It implements two methods that you will be interested in: `Add()`, which adds a string to the collection, and `CopyTo()`, which copies the string collection into a normal array (a `System.Array` instance). Each element of the `StringCollection` object holds one line of the file.

The `DisplayFile()` method calls another method, `ReadFileIntoStringCollection()`, which actually reads in the file. After doing this, you now know how many lines there are, so you are in a position to copy the `StringCollection` into a normal, fixed-size array and feed it into the text box. Because only the references to the strings, not the strings themselves, are copied when you actually make the copy, the process is reasonably efficient:

```
void DisplayFile()
{
    StringCollection linesCollection = ReadFileIntoStringCollection();
    string [] linesArray = new string[linesCollection.Count];
    linesCollection.CopyTo(linesArray, 0);
    this.textBoxContents.Lines = linesArray;
}
```

code download ReadWriteText.sln

The second parameter of `StringCollection.CopyTo()` indicates the index within the destination array of where you want the collection to start.

Now you examine the `ReadFileIntoStringCollection()` method. You use a `StreamReader` to read in each line. The main complication here is the need to count the characters read in to make sure that you do not exceed the capacity of the text box:

```
StringCollection ReadFileIntoStringCollection()
{
    const int MaxBytes = 65536;
    StreamReader sr = new StreamReader(chosenFile);
    StringCollection result = new StringCollection();
    int nBytesRead = 0;
    string nextLine;
    while ( (nextLine = sr.ReadLine()) != null)
    {
        nBytesRead += nextLine.Length;
        if (nBytesRead > MaxBytes)
            break;
        result.Add(nextLine);
    }
    sr.Close();
    return result;
}
```

code download ReadWriteText.sln

That completes the code for this sample.

If you run `ReadWriteText`, read in the `Default.aspx` file, and then save it, the file will be in Unicode format. You would not be able to tell this from any of the usual Windows applications. Notepad, WordPad, and even the `ReadWriteText` example will still read the file in and display it correctly under most versions of Windows, although, because Windows 9x doesn't support Unicode, applications like Notepad won't be able to understand the Unicode file on those platforms. (If you download the example from the Wrox Press web site at `www.wrox.com`, you can try this!) However, if you try to display the file again using the earlier `BinaryFileReader` sample, you can see the difference immediately, as shown in Figure 29-12. The two initial bytes that indicate the file is in Unicode format are visible, and thereafter you see that every character is represented by 2 bytes. This last fact is obvious because the high-order byte of every character in this particular file is zero, so every second byte in this file now displays x00.

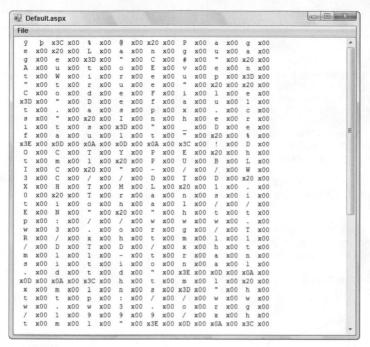

FIGURE 29-12

MAPPED-MEMORY FILES

If you have been working your entire coding life with only managed code, then mapped-memory files might be a brand new concept. .NET Framework 4 now supplies mapped-memory files as part of your toolkit for building applications with the introduction of the `System.IO.MemoryMappedFiles` namespace.

It is always possible to use the concept of mapped-memory files by doing some P/Invokes to the underlying Windows APIs, but now with the introduction of the `System.IO.MemoryMappedFiles` namespace, you can work with managed code rather than operating in the cumbersome P/Invoke world.

Mapped-memory files and the use of this namespace are ideal when your application requires frequent or random access to files. Using this approach allows you to load part or all of the file into a segment of virtual memory, which then appears to your application as if this file is contained within the primary memory for the application.

Interestingly, you can use this file in memory as a shared resource among more than one process. Prior to this, you might have been using Windows Communication Foundation (WCF) or Named Pipes to communicate a shared resource between multiple processes, but now you can share a mapped-memory file between processes using a shared name.

To work with mapped-memory files, you have to work with a couple of objects. The first is a mapped-memory file instance that loads the file. The second is an accessor object. The following code writes to the mapped-memory file object and then reads from it. You also see that the write is also happening when the object is disposed:

```
using System;
using System.IO.MemoryMappedFiles;
using System.Text;

namespace MappedMemoryFiles
```

```
{
    class Program
    {
        static void Main(string[] args)
        {
            using (var mmFile= MemoryMappedFile.CreateFromFile(
                @"C:\Users\Bill\Document\Visual Studio 10\Projects\
                MappedMemoryFiles\MappedMemoryFiles\TextFile1.txt",
                System.IO.FileMode.Create, "fileHandle", 1024 * 1024))
            {
                string valueToWrite = "Written to the mapped-memory file on " +
                    DateTime.Now.ToString();
                var myAccessor = mmFile.CreateViewAccessor();

                myAccessor.WriteArray<byte>(0,
                    Encoding.ASCII.GetBytes(valueToWrite), 0,
                    valueToWrite.Length);

                var readOut = new byte[valueToWrite.Length];
                myAccessor.ReadArray<byte>(0, readOut, 0, readOut.Length);
                var finalValue = Encoding.ASCII.GetString(readOut);

                Console.WriteLine("Message: " + finalValue);
                Console.ReadLine();
            }
        }
    }
}
```

code download MappedMemoryFiles.sln

In this case, a mapped-memory file is created from a physical file using the `CreateFromFile()` method. In addition to a mapped-memory file, you then need to create an accessor object to this mapping. That is done using the following:

```
var myAccessor = mmFile.CreateViewAccessor();
```

After the accessor is in place, you can then write or read to this mapped-memory location as shown in the code example.

It is also possible to create multiple accessors to the same mapped-memory location as shown here:

```
var myAccessor1 = mmFile.CreateViewAccessor();
var myAccessor2 = mmFile.CreateViewAccessor();
```

READING DRIVE INFORMATION

In addition to working with files and directories, the .NET Framework includes the ability to read information from a specified drive. This is done using the `DriveInfo` class. The `DriveInfo` class can perform a scan of a system to provide a list of available drives and then can dig in deeper, providing you with tons of details about any of the drives.

For an example of using the `DriveInfo` class, create a simple Windows Form that will list all the available drives on a computer and then provide details on a user-selected drive. Your Windows Form will consist of a simple `ListBox` and should look like Figure 29-13.

When you have the form all set, the code consists of two events — one for when the form loads and another for when the end user makes a drive selection in the list box. The code for this form is shown here:

FIGURE 29-13

```csharp
using System;
using System.IO;
using System.Windows.Forms;

namespace DriveViewer
{
    public partial class Form1: Form
    {
        public Form1()
        {
            InitializeComponent();
        }

        private void Form1_Load(object sender, EventArgs e)
        {
            DriveInfo[] di = DriveInfo.GetDrives();

            foreach (DriveInfo itemDrive in di)
            {
                listBox1.Items.Add(itemDrive.Name);
            }
        }

        private void listBox1_SelectedIndexChanged(object sender, EventArgs e)
        {
            DriveInfo di = new DriveInfo(listBox1.SelectedItem.ToString());

            MessageBox.Show("Available Free Space: "
                + di.AvailableFreeSpace + "\n" +
                "Drive Format: " + di.DriveFormat + "\n" +
                "Drive Type: " + di.DriveType + "\n" +
                "Is Ready: " + di.IsReady + "\n" +
                "Name: " + di.Name + "\n" +
                "Root Directory: " + di.RootDirectory + "\n" +
                "ToString() Value: " + di + "\n" +
                "Total Free Space: " + di.TotalFreeSpace + "\n" +
                "Total Size: " + di.TotalSize + "\n" +
                "Volume Label: " + di.VolumeLabel, di.Name +
                " DRIVE INFO");
        }
    }
}
```

code download DriveViewer.sln

The first step is to bring in the System.IO namespace with the using keyword. Within the Form1_Load event, you use the DriveInfo class to get a list of all the available drives on the system. This is done using an array of DriveInfo objects and populating this array with the DriveInfo.GetDrives() method. Then using a foreach loop, you are able to iterate through each drive found and populate the list box with the results. This produces something similar to what is shown in Figure 29-14.

This form allows the end user to select one of the drives in the list. After a drive is selected, a message box appears that contains details about that drive. As you can see in Figure 29-14, I have six drives on my current computer. Selecting a couple of these drives produces the message boxes collectively shown in Figure 29-15.

FIGURE 29-14

FIGURE 29-15

From here, you can see that these message boxes provide details about three entirely different drives. The first, drive C:\, is my hard drive, as the message box shows its drive type as `Fixed`. The second drive, drive D:\, is my CD/DVD drive. The third drive, drive F:\, is my USB pen and is labeled with a `Removable` drive type.

FILE SECURITY

When the .NET Framework 1.0/1.1 was first introduced, it didn't come with a way to easily access and work access control lists (ACLs) for files, directories, and registry keys. To do such things at that time usually meant some work with COM interop, thus also requiring a more advanced programming knowledge of working with ACLs.

This has considerably changed after the release of the .NET Framework 2.0 came out. This made the process of working with ACLs considerably easier with a namespace — `System.Security.AccessControl`. With this namespace, it is now possible to manipulate security settings for files, registry keys, network shares, Active Directory objects, and more.

Reading ACLs from a File

For an example of working with `System.Security.AccessControl`, this section looks at working with the ACLs for both files and directories. It starts by looking at how you would review the ACLs for a particular file. This example is accomplished in a console application and is illustrated here:

Available for download on Wrox.com

```
using System;
using System.IO;
using System.Security.AccessControl;
using System.Security.Principal;

namespace ReadingACLs
{
    internal class Program
    {
        private static string myFilePath;

        private static void Main()
        {
            Console.Write("Provide full file path: ");
            myFilePath = Console.ReadLine();

            try
            {
                using (FileStream myFile =
                    new FileStream(myFilePath, FileMode.Open, FileAccess.Read))
```

```
        {
            FileSecurity fileSec = myFile.GetAccessControl();

            foreach (FileSystemAccessRule fileRule in
                fileSec.GetAccessRules(true, true,
                    typeof (NTAccount)))
            {
                Console.WriteLine("{0} {1} {2} access for {3}",
                    myFilePath,
                    fileRule.AccessControlType ==
                    AccessControlType.Allow
                        ? "provides": "denies",
                        fileRule.FileSystemRights,
                        fileRule.IdentityReference);
            }
        }
    }
    catch
    {
        Console.WriteLine("Incorrect file path given!");
    }

    Console.ReadLine();
    }
  }
}
```

code download ReadingACLs.sln

For this example to work, the first step is to refer to the System.Security.AccessControl namespace. This will give you access to the FileSecurity and the FileSystemAccessRule classes later in the program.

After the specified file is retrieved and placed in a FileStream object, the ACLs of the file are grabbed using the GetAccessControl() method now found on the File object. This information from the GetAccessControl() method is then placed in a FileSecurity class. This class has access rights to the referenced item. Each individual access right is then represented by a FileSystemAccessRule object. That is why a foreach loop is used to iterate through all the access rights found in the created FileSecurity object.

Running this example with a simple text file in the root directory produces something similar to the following results:

```
Provide full file path: C:\Sample.txt
C:\Sample.txt provides FullControl access for BUILTIN\Administrators
C:\Sample.txt provides FullControl access for NT AUTHORITY\SYSTEM
C:\Sample.txt provides ReadAndExecute, Synchronize access for BUILTIN\Users
C:\Sample.txt provides Modify, Sychronize access for
    NT AUTHORITY\Authenticated Users
```

The next section presents reading ACLs from a directory instead of a file.

Reading ACLs from a Directory

Reading ACL information about a directory instead of an actual file is not much different from the preceding example. The code for this is illustrated in the following example:

Available for
download on
Wrox.com

```
using System;
using System.IO;
using System.Security.AccessControl;
```

```
using System.Security.Principal;

namespace ConsoleApplication1
{
    internal class Program
    {
        private static string mentionedDir;

        private static void Main()
        {
            Console.Write("Provide full directory path: ");
            mentionedDir = Console.ReadLine();

            try
            {
                DirectoryInfo myDir = new DirectoryInfo(mentionedDir);

                if (myDir.Exists)
                {
                    DirectorySecurity myDirSec = myDir.GetAccessControl();

                    foreach (FileSystemAccessRule fileRule in
                        myDirSec.GetAccessRules(true, true,
                                             typeof (NTAccount)))
                    {
                        Console.WriteLine("{0} {1} {2} access for {3}",
                            mentionedDir, fileRule.AccessControlType ==
                            AccessControlType.Allow
                            ? "provides": "denies",
                            fileRule.FileSystemRights,
                            fileRule.IdentityReference);
                    }
                }
            }
            catch
            {
                Console.WriteLine("Incorrect directory provided!");
            }

            Console.ReadLine();
        }
    }
}
```

code download ReadingACLsFromDirectory.sln

The big difference with this example is that it uses the `DirectoryInfo` class, which now also includes
the `GetAccessControl()` method to pull information about the directory's ACLs. Running this example
produces the following results when using Windows 7:

```
Provide full directory path: C:\Test
C:\Test provides FullControl access for BUILTIN\Administrators
C:\Test provides 268435456 access for BUILTIN\Administrators
C:\Test provides FullControl access for NT AUTHORITY\SYSTEM
C:\Test provides 268435456 access for NT AUTHORITY\SYSTEM
C:\Test provides ReadAndExecute, Synchronize access for BUILTIN\Users
C:\Test provides Modify, Synchronize access for
        NT AUTHORITY\Authenticated Users
C:\Test provides -536805376 access for NT AUTHORITY\Authenticated Users
```

The final thing you will look at when working with ACLs is using the new `System.Security`
`.AccessControl` namespace to add and remove items to and from a file's ACL.

Adding and Removing ACLs from a File

It is also possible to manipulate the ACLs of a resource using the same objects that were used in the previous examples. The following code example changes a previous code example where a file's ACL information was read. Here, the ACLs are read for a specified file, changed, and then read again:

```
try
{
    using (FileStream myFile = new FileStream(myFilePath,
        FileMode.Open, FileAccess.ReadWrite))
    {
        FileSecurity fileSec = myFile.GetAccessControl();

        Console.WriteLine("ACL list before modification:");

        foreach (FileSystemAccessRule fileRule in
            fileSec.GetAccessRules(true, true,
             typeof(System.Security.Principal.NTAccount)))
        {
            Console.WriteLine("{0} {1} {2} access for {3}", myFilePath,
                fileRule.AccessControlType == AccessControlType.Allow ?
                "provides": "denies",
                fileRule.FileSystemRights,
                fileRule.IdentityReference);
        }

        Console.WriteLine();
        Console.WriteLine("ACL list after modification:");

        FileSystemAccessRule newRule = new FileSystemAccessRule(
            new System.Security.Principal.NTAccount(@"PUSHKIN\Tuija"),
            FileSystemRights.FullControl,
            AccessControlType.Allow);

        fileSec.AddAccessRule(newRule);
        File.SetAccessControl(myFilePath, fileSec);

        foreach (FileSystemAccessRule fileRule in
            fileSec.GetAccessRules(true, true,
             typeof(System.Security.Principal.NTAccount)))
        {
            Console.WriteLine("{0} {1} {2} access for {3}", myFilePath,
                fileRule.AccessControlType == AccessControlType.Allow ?
                "provides": "denies",
                fileRule.FileSystemRights,
                fileRule.IdentityReference);
        }
    }
}
```

In this case, a new access rule is added to the file's ACL. This is done by using the `FileSystemAccessRule` object. The `FileSystemAccessRule` class is an abstraction access control entry (ACE) instance. The ACE defines the user account to use, the type of access that this user account can deal with, and whether or not to allow or deny this access. In creating a new instance of this object, a new `NTAccount` is created and given `Full Control` to the file. Even though a new `NTAccount` is created, it must still reference an existing user. Then the `AddAccessRule` method of the `FileSecurity` class is used to assign the new rule. From there, the `FileSecurity` object reference is used to set the access control to the file in question using the `SetAccessControl()` method of the `File` class.

Next, the file's ACL is listed again. The following is an example of what the preceding code could produce:

```
Provide full file path: C:\Users\Bill\Sample.txt
ACL list before modification:
C:\Sample.txt provides FullControl access for NT AUTHORITY\SYSTEM
C:\Sample.txt provides FullControl access for BUILTIN\Administrators
C:\Sample.txt provides FullControl access for PUSHKIN\Bill

ACL list after modification:
C:\Sample.txt provides FullControl access for PUSHKIN\Tuija
C:\Sample.txt provides FullControl access for NT AUTHORITY\SYSTEM
C:\Sample.txt provides FullControl access for BUILTIN\Administrators
C:\Sample.txt provides FullControl access for PUSHKIN\Bill
```

To remove a rule from the ACL list, there is really not much that needs to be done to the code. From the previous code example, you simply need to change the line

```
fileSec.AddAccessRule(newRule);
```

to the following to remove the rule that was just added:

```
fileSec.RemoveAccessRule(newRule);
```

READING AND WRITING TO THE REGISTRY

In all versions of Windows since Windows 95, the registry has been the central repository for all configuration information relating to Windows setup, user preferences, and installed software and devices. Almost all commercial software these days uses the registry to store information about itself, and COM components must place information about themselves in the registry in order to be called by clients. The .NET Framework and its accompanying concept of zero-impact installation has slightly reduced the significance of the registry for applications in the sense that assemblies are entirely self-contained; no information about particular assemblies needs to be placed in the registry, even for shared assemblies. In addition, the .NET Framework has brought the concept of isolated storage — applications can store information that is particular to each user in files — and .NET Framework ensures that data is stored separately for each user registered on a machine.

The fact that applications can now be installed using the Windows Installer also frees developers from some of the direct manipulation of the registry that used to be involved in installing applications. However, despite this, the possibility exists that if you distribute any complete application, your application will use the registry to store information about its configuration. For instance, if you want your application to show up in the Add/Remove Programs dialog box in the Control Panel, this will involve appropriate registry entries. You may also need to use the registry for backward compatibility with legacy code.

As you would expect from a library as comprehensive as the .NET library, it includes classes that give you access to the registry. Two classes are concerned with the registry, and both are in the `Microsoft.Win32` namespace. The classes are `Registry` and `RegistryKey`. Before you examine these classes, the following section briefly reviews the structure of the registry itself.

The Registry

The registry has a hierarchical structure much like that of the file system. The usual way to view or modify the contents of the registry is with one of two utilities: `regedit` or `regedt32`. Of these, `regedit` comes standard with all versions of Windows since Windows 95. `regedt32` comes with Windows NT and Windows 2000; it is less user-friendly than `regedit`, but allows access to security information that `regedit` is unable to view. Windows Server 2003 has merged `regedit` and `regedt32` into a single new editor simply called `regedit`. For the discussion here, you will use `regedit` from Windows 7, which you can launch by typing **regedit** in the Run dialog or at the command prompt.

Figure 29-16 shows what you get when you launch `regedit` for the first time.

`regedit` has a tree view/list view-style user interface similar to Windows Explorer, which matches the hierarchical structure of the registry itself. However, you will see some key differences shortly.

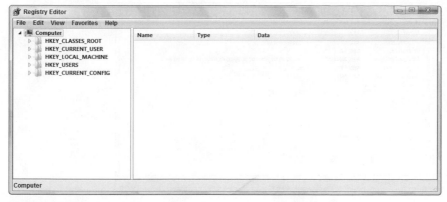

FIGURE 29-16

In a file system, the topmost-level nodes can be thought of as being the partitions on your disks, `C:\`, `D:\`, and so on. In the registry, the equivalent to a partition is the *registry hive*. It is not possible to change the existing hives — they are fixed, and there are seven of them, although only five are actually visible through `regedit`:

➤ `HKEY_CLASSES_ROOT` (HKCR) contains details of types of files on the system (`.txt`, `.doc`, and so on) and which applications are able to open files of each type. It also contains registration information for all COM components (this latter area is usually the largest single area of the registry because Windows, these days, comes with a huge number of COM components).

➤ `HKEY_CURRENT_USER` (HKCU) contains details of user preferences for the user currently logged on to the machine locally. These settings include desktop settings, environment variables, network and printer connections, and other settings that define the user operating environment of the user.

➤ `HKEY_LOCAL_MACHINE` (HKLM) is a huge hive that contains details of all software and hardware installed on the machine. These settings are not user-specific but are for all users that log on to the machine. This hive also includes the HKCR hive; HKCR is actually not really an independent hive in its own right but is simply a convenient mapping onto the registry key `HKLM/SOFTWARE/Classes`.

➤ `HKEY_USERS` (HKUSR) contains details of user preferences for all users. As you might guess, it also contains the HKCU hive, which is simply a mapping onto one of the keys in `HKEY_USERS`.

➤ `HKEY_CURRENT_CONFIG` (HKCF) contains details of hardware on the machine.

The remaining two keys contain information that is temporary and that changes frequently:

➤ `HKEY_DYN_DATA` is a general container for any volatile data that needs to be stored somewhere in the registry.

➤ `HKEY_PERFORMANCE_DATA` contains information concerning the performance of running applications.

Within the hives is a tree structure of registry *keys*. Each key is in many ways analogous to a folder or file on the file system. However, there is one very important difference. The file system distinguishes between files (which are there to contain data) and folders (which are primarily there to contain other files or folders), but in the registry there are only keys. A key may contain both data and other keys.

If a key contains data, it will be presented as a series of values. Each value will have an associated name, data type, and data. In addition, a key can have a default value, which is unnamed.

You can see this structure by using `regedit` to examine registry keys. Figure 29-17 shows the contents of the key `HKCU\Control Panel\Appearance`, which contains the details of the chosen color scheme of the currently logged-in user. `regedit` shows which key is being examined by displaying it with an open folder icon in the tree view.

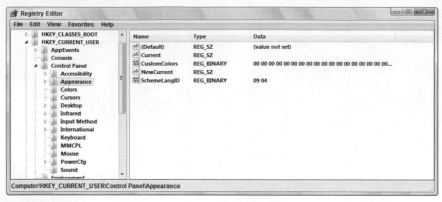

FIGURE 29-17

The `HKCU\Control Panel\Appearance` key has three named values set, although the default value does not contain any data. The column in the screenshot marked Type details the data type of each value. Registry entries can be formatted as one of three data types:

➤ `REG_SZ` (which roughly corresponds to a .NET string instance; the matching is not exact because the registry data types are not .NET data types)

➤ `REG_DWORD` (corresponds roughly to `uint`)

➤ `REG_BINARY` (array of bytes)

An application that stores data in the registry will do so by creating a number of registry keys, usually under the key `HKLM\Software\<CompanyName>`. Note that it is not necessary for these keys to contain any data. Sometimes the very fact that a key exists provides the data that an application needs.

The .NET Registry Classes

Access to the registry is available through two classes in the `Microsoft.Win32` namespace: `Registry` and `RegistryKey`. A `RegistryKey` instance represents a registry key. This class implements methods to browse child keys, to create new keys, or to read or modify the values in the key — in other words, to do everything you would normally want to do with a registry key, including setting the security levels for the key. `RegistryKey` will be the class you use for much of your work with the registry. `Registry`, by contrast, is a class that allows for singular access to registry keys for simple operations. Another role of the `Registry` class is simply to provide you with `RegistryKey` instances that represent the top-level keys, the different hives, to enable you to navigate the registry. `Registry` provides these instances through static properties, and there are seven of them called, respectively, `ClassesRoot`, `CurrentConfig`, `CurrentUser`, `DynData`, `LocalMachine`, `PerformanceData`, and `Users`. It should be obvious which property corresponds to which hive.

So, for example, to obtain a `RegistryKey` instance that represents the `HKLM` key, you would write:

```
RegistryKey hklm = Registry.LocalMachine;
```

The process of obtaining a reference to a `RegistryKey` object is known as opening the key.

Although you might expect that the methods exposed by `RegistryKey` would be similar to those implemented by `DirectoryInfo`, given that the registry has a similar hierarchical structure to the file system, this actually isn't the case. Often, the way that you access the registry is different from the way that you would use files and folders, and `RegistryKey` implements methods that reflect this.

The most obvious difference is in how you open a registry key at a given location in the registry. The `Registry` class does not have any public constructor that you can use, nor does it have any methods that let you go directly to a key, given its name. Instead, you are expected to browse down to that key from the top of the relevant hive. If you want to instantiate a `RegistryKey` object, the only way is to start off with the appropriate static property of `Registry`, and work down from there. So, for example, if you want to read some data in the `HKLM/Software/Microsoft` key, you would get a reference to it like this:

```
RegistryKey hklm = Registry.LocalMachine;
RegistryKey hkSoftware = hklm.OpenSubKey("Software");
RegistryKey hkMicrosoft = hkSoftware.OpenSubKey("Microsoft");
```

A registry key accessed in this way will give you read-only access. If you want to write to the key (that includes writing to its values or creating or deleting direct children of it), you need to use another override to `OpenSubKey`, which takes a second parameter, of type `bool`, that indicates whether you want read-write access to the key. For example, if you want to be able to modify the `Microsoft` key (and assuming that you are a system administrator with permission to do this), you would write this:

```
RegistryKey hklm = Registry.LocalMachine;
RegistryKey hkSoftware = hklm.OpenSubKey("Software");
RegistryKey hkMicrosoft = hkSoftware.OpenSubKey("Microsoft", true);
```

Incidentally, because this key contains information used by Microsoft's applications, in most cases you probably shouldn't be modifying this particular key.

The `OpenSubKey()` method is the one you call if you are expecting the key to be present. If the key isn't there, it returns a `null` reference. If you want to create a key, you should use the `CreateSubKey()` method (which automatically gives you read-write access to the key through the reference returned):

```
RegistryKey hklm = Registry.LocalMachine;
RegistryKey hkSoftware = hklm.OpenSubKey("Software");
RegistryKey hkMine = hkSoftware.CreateSubKey("MyOwnSoftware");
```

The way that `CreateSubKey()` works is quite interesting. It creates the key if it does not already exist, but if it does exist, it quietly returns a `RegistryKey` instance that represents the existing key. The reason for the method behaving in this manner has to do with how you normally use the registry. The registry, overall, contains long-term data such as configuration information for Windows and for various applications. It is not very common, therefore, that you find yourself in a situation where you need to explicitly create a key.

What is much more common is that your application needs to make sure that some data is present in the registry — in other words, create the relevant keys if they do not already exist, but do nothing if they do. `CreateSubKey()` fills that need perfectly. Unlike the situation with `FileInfo.Open()`, for example, there is no chance with `CreateSubKey()` of accidentally removing any data. If deleting registry keys is your intention, you will need to call the `RegistryKey.DeleteSubKey()` method. This makes sense given the importance of the registry to Windows. The last thing you want is to completely break Windows accidentally by deleting a couple of important keys while you are debugging your C# registry calls!

After you have located the registry key you want to read or modify, you can use the `SetValue()` or `GetValue()` methods to set or get at the data in it. Both of these methods take a string giving the name of the value as a parameter, and `SetValue()` requires an additional object reference containing details of the value. Because the parameter is defined as an object reference, it can actually be a reference to any class you want. `SetValue()` will decide from the type of class actually supplied whether to set the value as a `REG_SZ`, `REG_DWORD` or `REG_BINARY` value. For example:

```
RegistryKey hkMine = HkSoftware.CreateSubKey("MyOwnSoftware");
hkMine.SetValue("MyStringValue", "Hello World");
hkMine.SetValue("MyIntValue", 20);
```

This code sets the key with two values: `MyStringValue` will be of type `REG_SZ`, and `MyIntValue` will be of type `REG_DWORD`. These are the only two types you will consider here and use in the example presented later.

RegistryKey.GetValue() works in much the same way. It is defined to return an object reference, which means that it is free to actually return a string reference if it detects the value is of type REG_SZ, and an int if that value is of type REG_DWORD:

```
string stringValue = (string)hkMine.GetValue("MyStringValue");
int intValue = (int)hkMine.GetValue("MyIntValue");
```

Finally, after you have finished reading or modifying the data, close the key:

```
hkMine.Close();
```

RegistryKey implements a large number of methods and properties. The following table lists the most useful properties.

PROPERTY	DESCRIPTION
Name	Name of the key (read-only)
SubKeyCount	The number of children of this key
ValueCount	How many values the key contains

The following table lists the most useful methods.

METHOD	PURPOSE
Close()	Closes the key.
CreateSubKey()	Creates a subkey of a given name (or opens it if it already exists).
DeleteSubKey()	Deletes a given subkey.
DeleteSubKeyTree()	Recursively deletes a subkey and all its children.
DeleteValue()	Removes a named value from a key.
GetAccessControl()	Returns the ACL for a specified registry key. This method was added in .NET Framework 2.0.
GetSubKeyNames()	Returns an array of strings containing the names of the subkeys.
GetValue()	Returns a named value.
GetValueKind()	Returns a named value whose registry data type is to be retrieved. This method was added in .NET Framework 2.0.
GetValueNames()	Returns an array of strings containing the names of all the values of the key.
OpenSubKey()	Returns a reference to a RegistryKey instance that represents a given subkey.
SetAccessControl()	Allows you to apply an ACL to a specified registry key.
SetValue()	Sets a named value.

READING AND WRITING TO ISOLATED STORAGE

In addition to being able to read and write to and from the registry, another option is reading and writing values to and from what is called *isolated storage*. If you are having issues writing to the registry or to disk in general, then isolated storage is where you should turn. You can use isolated storage to store application state or user settings quite easily.

Think of isolated storage as a virtual disk where you can save items that can be shared only by the application that created them, or with other application instances. There are two types of access types for isolated storage. The first is user and assembly.

When accessing isolated storage by user and assembly, there is a single storage location on the machine, which is accessible via multiple application instances. Access is guaranteed through the user identity and the application (or assembly) identity. Figure 29-18 shows this.

This means that you can have multiple instances of the same application all working from the same store.

The second type of access for isolated storage is user, assembly, and domain. In this case, each application instance works off its own isolation store. This is detailed in Figure 29-19.

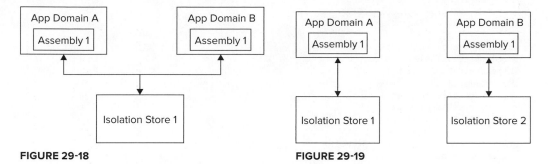

FIGURE 29-18   **FIGURE 29-19**

In this case, each application instance works off its own store, and the settings that each application instance records are related only to itself. This is a more fine-grained approach to isolated storage.

For an example of using isolated storage from a Windows Forms application (although you can use this from an ASP.NET application just as well), you can use the `ReadSettings()` and `SaveSettings()` methods shown next to read and write values to isolated storage as opposed to maybe doing the same directly in the registry.

 It is important to note that the only code shown here is for the `ReadSettings()` *and* `SaveSettings()` *methods. There is more code to the application, and you can see the rest in the download code file in the sample titled* `SelfPlacingWindow`.

To start, you need to rework the `SaveSettings()` method. For this next bit of code to work, you need to add the following using directives:

```
using System.IO;
using System.IO.IsolatedStorage;
using System.Text;
```

The `SaveSettings()` method is detailed in the following code example:

```
void SaveSettings()
{
    IsolatedStorageFile storFile = IsolatedStorageFile.GetUserStoreForDomain();
    IsolatedStorageFileStream storStream = new
        IsolatedStorageFileStream("SelfPlacingWindow.xml",

        FileMode.Create, FileAccess.Write);

    System.Xml.XmlTextWriter writer = new
        System.Xml.XmlTextWriter(storStream, Encoding.UTF8);
    writer.Formatting = System.Xml.Formatting.Indented;

    writer.WriteStartDocument();
    writer.WriteStartElement("Settings");

    writer.WriteStartElement("BackColor");
    writer.WriteValue(BackColor.ToKnownColor().ToString());
    writer.WriteEndElement();
```

```
        writer.WriteStartElement("Red");
        writer.WriteValue(BackColor.R);
        writer.WriteEndElement();

        writer.WriteStartElement("Green");
        writer.WriteValue(BackColor.G);
        writer.WriteEndElement();

        writer.WriteStartElement("Blue");
        writer.WriteValue(BackColor.B);
        writer.WriteEndElement();

        writer.WriteStartElement("Width");
        writer.WriteValue(Width);
        writer.WriteEndElement();

        writer.WriteStartElement("Height");
        writer.WriteValue(Height);
        writer.WriteEndElement();

        writer.WriteStartElement("X");
        writer.WriteValue(DesktopLocation.X);
        writer.WriteEndElement();

        writer.WriteStartElement("Y");
        writer.WriteValue(DesktopLocation.Y);
        writer.WriteEndElement();

        writer.WriteStartElement("WindowState");
        writer.WriteValue(WindowState.ToString());
        writer.WriteEndElement();

        writer.WriteEndElement();

        writer.Flush();
        writer.Close();

        storStream.Close();
        storFile.Close();
    }
```

It is a bit more code than you might be used to when working with the registry, but that is mainly due to the code required to build the XML document placed in isolated storage. The first important thing happening with this code is presented here:

```
        IsolatedStorageFile storFile = IsolatedStorageFile.GetUserStoreForDomain();
        IsolatedStorageFileStream storStream = new
            IsolatedStorageFileStream("SelfPlacingWindow.xml",
            FileMode.Create, FileAccess.Write);
```

Here, an instance of an `IsolatedStorageFile` is created using a user, assembly, and domain type of access. A stream is created using the `IsolatedStorageFileStream` object, which creates the virtual `SelfPlacingWindow.xml` file.

From there, an `XmlTextWriter` object is created to build the XML document and the XML contents are written to the `IsolatedStorageFileStream` object instance:

```
        System.Xml.XmlTextWriter writer = new
            System.Xml.XmlTextWriter(storStream, Encoding.UTF8);
```

After the `XmlTextWriter` object is created, all the values are written to the XML document node by node. When everything is written to the XML document, everything is closed and is stored in the isolated storage.

Reading from the storage is done through the `ReadSettings()` method. This method is presented in the following code example:

```
bool ReadSettings()
{
    IsolatedStorageFile storFile = IsolatedStorageFile.GetUserStoreForDomain();
    string[] userFiles = storFile.GetFileNames("SelfPlacingWindow.xml");

    foreach (string userFile in userFiles)
    {
        if(userFile == "SelfPlacingWindow.xml")
        {
            listBoxMessages.Items.Add("Successfully opened file " +
                                      userFile.ToString());

            StreamReader storStream =
                new StreamReader(new IsolatedStorageFileStream("SelfPlacingWindow.xml",
                FileMode.Open, storFile));
            System.Xml.XmlTextReader reader = new
                System.Xml.XmlTextReader(storStream);

            int redComponent = 0;
            int greenComponent = 0;
            int blueComponent = 0;

            int X = 0;
            int Y = 0;

            while (reader.Read())
            {
                switch (reader.Name)
                {
                    case "Red":
                        redComponent = int.Parse(reader.ReadString());
                        break;
                    case "Green":
                        greenComponent = int.Parse(reader.ReadString());
                        break;
                    case "Blue":
                        blueComponent = int.Parse(reader.ReadString());
                        break;
                    case "X":
                        X = int.Parse(reader.ReadString());
                        break;
                    case "Y":
                        Y = int.Parse(reader.ReadString());
                        break;
                    case "Width":
                        this.Width = int.Parse(reader.ReadString());
                        break;
                    case "Height":
                        this.Height = int.Parse(reader.ReadString());
                        break;
                    case "WindowState":
                        this.WindowState = (FormWindowState)FormWindowState.Parse
                            (WindowState.GetType(), reader.ReadString());
                        break;
                    default:
                        break;
                }
            }
```

```
            this.BackColor =
                Color.FromArgb(redComponent, greenComponent, blueComponent);
            this.DesktopLocation = new Point(X, Y);

            listBoxMessages.Items.Add("Background color: " + BackColor.Name);
            listBoxMessages.Items.Add("Desktop location: " +
                DesktopLocation.ToString());
            listBoxMessages.Items.Add("Size: " + new Size(Width, Height).ToString());
            listBoxMessages.Items.Add("Window State: " + WindowState.ToString());

            storStream.Close();
            storFile.Close();
        }
    }
    return true;
}
```

Using the `GetFileNames()` method, the `SelfPlacingWindow.xml` document is pulled from the isolated storage and then placed into a stream and parsed using the `XmlTextReader` object:

```
IsolatedStorageFile storFile = IsolatedStorageFile.GetUserStoreForDomain();
string[] userFiles = storFile.GetFileNames("SelfPlacingWindow.xml");

foreach (string userFile in userFiles)
{
    if(userFile == "SelfPlacingWindow.xml")
    {
        listBoxMessages.Items.Add("Successfully opened file " +
                        userFile.ToString());

        StreamReader storStream =
            new StreamReader(new IsolatedStorageFileStream("SelfPlacingWindow.xml",
            FileMode.Open, storFile));
```

After the XML document is contained within the `IsolatedStorageFileStream` object, it is parsed using the `XmlTextReader` object:

```
System.Xml.XmlTextReader reader = new
    System.Xml.XmlTextReader(storStream);
```

After, it is pulled from the stream via the `XmlTextReader`. The element values are then pushed back into the application. You will then find — just as was accomplished in the `SelfPlacingWindow` sample that used the registry to record and retrieve application state values — that using isolated storage is just as effective as working with the registry. The application remembers the color, size, and position just as before.

SUMMARY

In this chapter, you examined how to use the .NET base classes to access the file system and registry from your C# code. You have seen that in both cases the base classes expose simple, but powerful, object models that make it very simple to perform almost any kind of action in these areas. For the file system, these actions are copying files; moving, creating, and deleting files and folders; and reading and writing both binary and text files. For the registry, these are creating, modifying, or reading keys.

This chapter also reviewed isolated storage and how to use this from your applications to store them in the application state.

This chapter assumed that you were running your code from an account that has sufficient access rights to do whatever the code needs to do. Obviously, the question of security is an important one, and it is discussed in Chapter 21.

PART IV
Data

▶ **CHAPTER 30:** Core ADO.NET

▶ **CHAPTER 31:** ADO.NET Entity Framework

▶ **CHAPTER 32:** Data Services

▶ **CHAPTER 33:** Manipulating XML

▶ **CHAPTER 34:** .NET Programming with SQL Server

30

Core ADO.NET

WHAT'S IN THIS CHAPTER?

➤ Connecting to the database

➤ Executing commands

➤ Calling stored procedures

➤ The ADO.NET object model

➤ Using XML and XML schemas

This chapter discusses how to access data from your C# programs using ADO.NET. It shows you how to use the `SqlConnection` and `OleDbConnection` classes to connect to and disconnect from the database. You learn the various command object options and see how commands can be used for each of the options presented by the `Sql` and `OleDB` classes, how to call stored procedures with command objects, and how the results of those stored procedures can be integrated into the data cached on the client. The ADO.NET object model is significantly different from the objects available with ADO. The `DataSet`, `DataTable`, `DataRow`, and `DataColumn` classes are discussed as well as the relationships between tables and constraints that are part of `DataSet`. The class hierarchy has changed significantly since the release of the .NET Framework 2.0, and some of these changes are also described. Finally, you examine the XML framework on which ADO.NET is built.

The chapter begins with a brief tour of ADO.NET.

ADO.NET OVERVIEW

ADO.NET is more than just a thin veneer over some existing API. The similarity to ADO is fairly minimal — the classes and methods of accessing data are quite a bit different.

ADO (ActiveX Data Objects) is a library of COM components that has had many incarnations over the past few years. ADO consists primarily of the `Connection`, `Command`, `Recordset`, and `Field` objects. Using ADO, a connection is opened to the database, and some data is selected and placed into a record set consisting of fields; that data is then manipulated and updated on the server, and the connection is closed. ADO also introduced a so-called disconnected record set, which is used when keeping the connection open for long periods of time is not desirable.

There were several problems that ADO did not address satisfactorily, most notably the unwieldiness (in physical size) of a disconnected record set. This support was more necessary than ever with the evolution of web-centric computing, so a fresh approach was required. Upgrading to ADO.NET from ADO should not be too difficult because there are some similarities between the two. What's more, if you are using SQL Server, there is a fantastic set of managed classes that are tuned to squeeze maximum performance out of the database. This alone should be reason enough to migrate to ADO.NET.

ADO.NET ships with three database client namespaces: one for SQL Server, another for Open Database Connectivity (ODBC) data sources, and a third for any database exposed through OLE DB. If your database of choice is not SQL Server, use the OLE DB route unless you have no other choice than to use ODBC. If you are using Oracle as your database, you can visit the Oracle .NET Developer site and get their .NET provider, ODP.NET at `www.oracle.com/technology/tech/windows/odpnet/index.html`.

Namespaces

All of the examples in this chapter access data in one way or another. The namespaces in the following table expose the classes and interfaces used in .NET data access.

NAMESPACE	BRIEF DESCRIPTION
`System.Data`	All generic data access classes
`System.Data.Common`	Classes shared (or overridden) by individual data providers
`System.DataE.EntityClient`	Entity Framework classes
`System.Data.Linq.SqlClient`	LINQ to SQL provider classes
`System.Data.Odbc`	ODBC provider classes
`System.Data.OleDb`	OLE DB provider classes
`System.Data.ProviderBase`	New base classes and connection factory classes
`System.Data.Sql`	New generic interfaces and classes for SQL Server data access
`System.Data.SqlClient`	SQL Server provider classes
`System.Data.SqlTypes`	SQL Server data types

The main classes in ADO.NET are listed in the following subsections.

Shared Classes

ADO.NET contains a number of classes that are used regardless of whether you are using the SQL Server classes or the OLE DB classes. The following table lists the classes contained in the `System.Data` namespace.

CLASS	DESCRIPTION
`DataSet`	This object is designed for disconnected use and can contain a set of `DataTables` and relationships between these tables.
`DataTable`	A container of data that consists of one or more `DataColumns` and, when populated, will have one or more `DataRows` containing data.
`DataRow`	A number of values, akin to a row from a database table or a row from a spreadsheet.
`DataColumn`	This object contains the definition of a column, such as the name and data type.
`DataRelation`	A link between two `DataTable` classes within a `DataSet` class; used for foreign key and master/detail relationships.
`Constraint`	This class defines a rule for a `DataColumn` class (or set of data columns), such as unique values.

The following table lists the classes found in the `System.Data.Common` namespace.

CLASS	DESCRIPTION
`DataColumnMapping`	Maps the name of a column from the database to the name of a column within a `DataTable`.
`DataTableMapping`	Maps a table name from the database to a `DataTable` within a `DataSet`.

Database-Specific Classes

In addition to the shared classes introduced in the previous section, ADO.NET contains a number of database-specific classes. These classes implement a set of standard interfaces defined within the `System.Data` namespace, allowing the classes to be used in a generic manner if necessary. For example, both the `SqlConnection` and `OleDbConnection` classes derive from the `DbConnection` class, which implements the `IDbConnection` interface. The following table lists the database-specific classes.

CLASSES	DESCRIPTION
`SqlCommand`, `OleDbCommand`, and `ODBCCommand`	Used as wrappers for SQL statements or stored procedure calls. Examples for the `SqlCommand` class are shown later in the chapter.
`SqlCommandBuilder`, `OleDbCommandBuilder`, and `ODBCCommandBuilder`	Used to generate SQL commands (such as `INSERT`, `UPDATE`, and `DELETE` statements) from a `SELECT` statement.
`SqlConnection`, `OleDbConnection`, and `ODBCConnection`	Used to connect to the database and is similar to an ADO connection. Examples are shown later in the chapter.
`SqlDataAdapter`, `OleDbDataAdapter`, and `ODBCDataAdapter`	Used to hold `select`, `insert`, `update`, and `delete` commands, which are then used to populate a `DataSet` and update the database. Examples of the `SqlDataAdapter` are presented in this chapter.
`SqlDataReader`, `OleDbDataReader`, and `ODBCDataReader`	Used as a forward-only, connected data reader. Some examples of the `SqlDataReader` are shown in this chapter.
`SqlParameter`, `OleDbParameter`, and `ODBCParameter`	Used to define a parameter to a stored procedure. Examples of how to use the `SqlParameter` class are shown in this chapter.
`SqlTransaction`, `OleDbTransaction`, and `ODBCTransaction`	Used for a database transaction, wrapped in an object.

The most important feature of the ADO.NET classes is that they are designed to work in a disconnected manner, which is important in today's highly web-centric world. It is now common practice to architect a service (such as an online bookshop) to connect to a server, retrieve some data, and then work on that data on the client before reconnecting and passing the data back for processing. The disconnected nature of ADO.NET enables this type of behavior.

Classic ADO 2.1 introduced the disconnected record set, which permits data to be retrieved from a database, passed to the client for processing, and then reattached to the server. This used to be cumbersome to use because disconnected behavior was not part of the original design. The ADO.NET classes are different — in all but one case (the `[provider]DataReader`), they are designed for use offline from the database.

The classes and interfaces used for data access in the .NET Framework are introduced in the course of this chapter. The focus is mainly on the SQL classes used when connecting to the database because the Framework SDK samples install a SQL Server Express database (SQL Server). In most cases, the OLE DB and ODBC classes mimic the SQL code exactly.

USING DATABASE CONNECTIONS

To access the database, you need to provide connection parameters, such as the machine that the database is running on and possibly your login credentials. Anyone who has worked with ADO will be familiar with the .NET connection classes: `OleDbConnection` and `SqlConnection`. Figure 30-1 shows two of the connection classes and includes the class hierarchy.

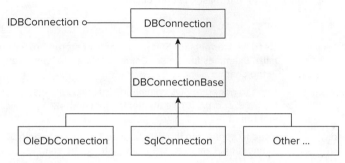

FIGURE 30-1

The examples in this chapter use the Northwind database, which you can find online. The following code snippet illustrates how to create, open, and close a connection to the Northwind database:

```
using System.Data.SqlClient;

string source = "server=(local);" +
                "integrated security=SSPI;" +
                "database=Northwind";
SqlConnection conn = new SqlConnection(source);
conn.Open();

// Do something useful

conn.Close();
```

The connection string should be very familiar to you if you have used ADO or OLE DB before — indeed, you should be able to cut and paste from your old code if you use the `OleDb` provider. In the example connection string, the parameters used are as follows (the parameters are delimited by a semicolon in the connection string):

➤ `server=(local)` — This denotes the database server to connect to. SQL Server permits a number of separate database server instances to be running on the same machine, and here you are connecting to the default SQL Server instance. If you are using SQL Express, change the server part to `server=./sqlexpress`.

➤ `integrated security=SSPI` — This uses Windows Authentication to connect to the database, which is highly recommended over using a username and password within the source code.

➤ `database=Northwind` — This describes the database instance to connect to; each SQL Server process can expose several database instances.

In case you forget the format of database connection strings (as many of us do now and then), the following URL is very handy: www.connectionstrings.com.

The example opens a database connection using the defined connection string and then closes that connection. Once the connection has been opened, you can issue commands against the data source, and when you are finished, the connection can be closed.

SQL Server has another mode of authentication — it can use Windows-integrated security, so that the credentials supplied at logon are passed to SQL Server. This is accomplished by removing the uid and pwd portions of the connection string, and adding in Integrated Security=SSPI.

In the download code available for this chapter, you will find the file login.cs, which simplifies the examples in this chapter. It is linked to all the sample code and includes database connection information used for the examples; you can alter this to supply your own server name, user, and password as appropriate. This, by default, uses Windows-integrated security; however, you can change the username and password as appropriate.

Managing Connection Strings

In the initial release of .NET, it was up to the developer to manage the database connection strings, which was often done by storing a connection string in the application configuration file or, more commonly, hard-coded somewhere within the application itself.

Beginning with .NET 2.0, you have a predefined way to store connection strings, and even use database connections in a type-agnostic manner — for example, it is now possible to write an application and then plug in various database providers, all without altering the main application.

To define a database connection string, you should use the <connectionStrings> section of the configuration file. Here, you can specify a name for the connection and the actual database connection string parameters; in addition, you can also specify the provider for this connection type. Here is an example:

Available for download on Wrox.com

```
<configuration>
  ...
  <connectionStrings>
    <add name="Northwind"
         providerName="System.Data.SqlClient"
         connectionString="server=(local);integrated security=SSPI;database=Northwind" />
  </connectionStrings>
</configuration>
```

code download Connection String Example.txt

You use this same connection string in the other examples in this chapter.

Once the database connection information has been defined within the configuration file, you then need to utilize this within the application. You will most likely want to create a method such as the following to retrieve a database connection based on the name of the connection:

Available for download on Wrox.com

```
private DbConnection GetDatabaseConnection ( string name )
{
  ConnectionStringSettings settings =
    ConfigurationManager.ConnectionStrings[name];

  DbProviderFactory factory = DbProviderFactories.GetFactory
    ( settings.ProviderName );
```

```
      DbConnection conn = factory.CreateConnection ( );
      conn.ConnectionString = settings.ConnectionString;

      return conn;
}
```

code download GetDatabaseConnection.txt

This code reads the named connection string section (using the `ConnectionStringSettings` class), and then requests a provider factory from the base `DbProviderFactories` class. This uses the `ProviderName` property, which was set to `"System.Data.SqlClient"` in the application configuration file. You might be wondering how this maps to the actual factory class used to generate a database connection for SQL Server — in this case, it should utilize the `SqlClientFactory` class from `System.Data.SqlClient`. You will need to add a reference to the `System.Configuration` assembly in order to resolve the `ConfigurationManager` class used in the preceding code.

This may seem like a lot of unnecessary work to obtain a database connection, and indeed it is if your application is never going to run on any other database than the one it was designed for. If, however, you use the preceding factory method and also use the generic Db* classes (such as `DbConnection`, `DbCommand`, and `DbDataReader`), you will future-proof the application, and any move in the future to another database system will be fairly simple.

Using Connections Efficiently

In general, when using scarce resources in .NET, such as database connections, windows, or graphics objects, it is good practice to ensure that each resource is closed after use. Although the designers of .NET have implemented automatic garbage collection, which will tidy up eventually, it is necessary to release resources as early as possible to avoid starvation of resources.

This is all too apparent when writing code that accesses a database because keeping a connection open for slightly longer than necessary can affect other sessions. In extreme circumstances, not closing a connection can lock other users out of an entire set of tables, hurting application performance considerably. Closing database connections should be considered mandatory, so this section shows how to structure your code to minimize the risk of leaving a resource open.

You have two main ways to ensure that database connections and the like are released after use. These are explained in the following sections.

Option One: try . . . catch . . . finally

The first option to ensure that resources are cleaned up is to use `try...catch...finally` blocks, and ensure that you close any open connections within the `finally` block. Here is a short example:

```
try
{
   // Open the connection
   conn.Open();
   // Do something useful
}
catch ( SqlException ex )
{
   // Log the exception
}
finally
{
   // Ensure that the connection is freed
   conn.Close ( );
}
```

Within the `finally` block, you can release any resources you have used. The only trouble with this method is that you have to ensure that you close the connection — it is all too easy to forget to add the `finally` clause, so something less prone to vagaries in coding style might be worthwhile.

In addition, you might find that you open a number of resources (say two database connections and a file) within a given method, so the cascade of `try...catch...finally` blocks can sometimes become less easy to read. There is, however, another way to guarantee resource cleanup — the `using` statement.

Option Two: The using Block Statement

During development of C#, the debate on how .NET uses nondeterministic destruction became very heated.

In C++, as soon as an object went out of scope, its destructor would be automatically called. This was great news for designers of resource-based classes because the destructor was the ideal place to close the resource if the user had forgotten to do so. A C++ destructor is called whenever an object goes out of scope — so, for instance, if an exception were raised and not caught, all destructors would be called.

With C# and the other managed languages, there is no concept of automatic, deterministic destruction. Instead, there is the garbage collector, which disposes of resources at some point in the future. What makes this nondeterministic is that you have little say over when this process actually happens. Forgetting to close a database connection could cause all sorts of problems for a .NET executable. Luckily, help is at hand. The following code demonstrates how to use the `using` clause to ensure that objects that implement the `IDisposable` interface (see Chapter 13, "Memory Management and Pointers") are cleared up immediately after the block exits:

```
string source = "server=(local);" +
                "integrated security=SSPI;" +
                "database=Northwind";

using ( SqlConnection conn = new SqlConnection ( source ) )
{
   // Open the connection
   conn.Open ( );

   // Do something useful
}
```

In this instance, the `using` clause ensures that the database connection is closed, regardless of how the block is exited.

Looking at the IL code for the `Dispose()` method of the connection classes, you can see that all of them check the current state of the connection object and, if it is open, will call the `Close()` method. A great tool for browsing .NET assemblies is Reflector (available at www.red-gate.com/products/reflector/). This tool permits you to view the IL code for any .NET method and will also reverse-engineer the IL into C# source code, so you can easily see what a given method is doing.

When programming, you should use at least one of these methods, and probably both. Wherever you acquire resources, it is good practice to use the `using` statement; even though we all mean to write the `Close()` statement, sometimes we forget, and in the face of exceptions the `using` clause does the right thing. There is no substitute for good exception handling either, so in most instances, it is best to use both methods together, as in the following example:

```
try
{
   using (SqlConnection conn = new SqlConnection ( source ))
   {
      // Open the connection
      conn.Open ( );

      // Do something useful
```

```
        // Close it myself
        conn.Close ( );
    }
}
catch (SqlException e)
{
    // Log the exception
}
```

Note that this example called `Close()`, which is not strictly necessary, because the `using` clause will ensure that this is done anyway. However, you should ensure that any resources such as this are released as soon as possible — you might have more code in the rest of the block, and there is no point locking a resource unnecessarily.

In addition, if an exception is raised within the `using` block, the `IDisposable.Dispose` method will be called on the resource guarded by the `using` clause, which in this example ensures that the database connection is always closed. This produces easier-to-read code than having to ensure you close a connection within an exception clause. You might also note that the exception is defined as a `SqlException` rather than the catch-all `Exception` type — always try to catch as specific an exception as possible and let all others that are not explicitly handled rise up the execution stack. You really should only catch this exception if your specific data class can handle the error and do something with it.

In conclusion, if you are writing a class that wraps a resource, whatever that resource may be, always implement the `IDisposable` interface to close the resource. That way anyone coding with your class can use the `using()` statement and guarantee that the resource will be cleared up.

Transactions

Often when there is more than one update to be made to the database, these updates must be performed within the scope of a transaction. It is common in code to find a transaction object being passed around to many methods that update the database; however, since the release of the .NET Framework 2.0, the `TransactionScope` class has been available. This class is found within the `System.Transactions` assembly. This vastly simplifies writing transactional code because you can compose several transactional methods within a transaction scope, and the transaction will flow to each of these methods as necessary.

The following sequence of code initiates a transaction on a SQL Server connection:

```
string source = "server=(local);" +
                "integrated security=SSPI;" +
                "database=Northwind";

using (TransactionScope scope = new
   TransactionScope(TransactionScopeOption.Required))
{
    using (SqlConnection conn = new SqlConnection(source))
    {
        // Do something in SQL
        .

        // Then mark complete
        scope.Complete();
    }
}
```

Here, the transaction is explicitly marked as complete by using the `scope.Complete()` method. In the absence of this call, the transaction will be rolled back so that no changes are made to the database.

When you use a transaction scope, you can optionally choose the isolation level for commands executed within that transaction. The level determines how changes made in one database session are viewed by another. Not all database engines support all of the four levels presented in the following table.

ISOLATION LEVEL	DESCRIPTION
ReadCommitted	The default for SQL Server. This level ensures that data written by one transaction will be accessible in a second transaction only after the first transaction is committed.
ReadUncommitted	This permits your transaction to read data within the database, even data that has not yet been committed by another transaction. For example, if two users were accessing the same database, and the first inserted some data without concluding the transaction (by means of a Commit or Rollback), the second user with his or her isolation level set to ReadUncommitted could read the data.
RepeatableRead	This level, which extends the ReadCommitted level, ensures that if the same statement is issued within the transaction, regardless of other potential updates made to the database, the same data will always be returned. This level does require extra locks to be held on the data, which could adversely affect performance. This level guarantees that, for each row in the initial query, no changes can be made to that data. It does, however, permit "phantom" rows to show up — these are completely new rows that another transaction might have inserted while your transaction was running.
Serializable	This is the most "exclusive" transaction level, which in effect serializes access to data within the database. With this isolation level, phantom rows can never show up, so a SQL statement issued within a serializable transaction will always retrieve the same data. The negative performance impact of a Serializable transaction should not be underestimated — if you don't absolutely need to use this level of isolation, stay away from it.

The SQL Server default isolation level, ReadCommitted, is a good compromise between data coherence and data availability because fewer locks are required on data than in RepeatableRead or Serializable modes. However, situations exist where the isolation level should be increased, and so within .NET you can simply begin a transaction with a different level from the default. There are no fixed rules as to which levels to pick — that comes with experience.

 If you are currently using a database that does not support transactions, it is well worth changing to a database that does. Once I was working as a trusted employee and had been given complete access to the bug database. I typed what I thought was delete from bug where id=99999, *but in fact had typed a < rather than an =. I deleted the entire database of bugs (except the one I wanted to!). Luckily for me, our IS team backed up the database on a nightly basis and we could restore this, but a rollback command would have been much easier.*

COMMANDS

The "Using Database Connections" section briefly touched on the idea of issuing commands against a database. A command is, in its simplest form, a string of text containing SQL statements that is to be issued to the database. A command could also be a stored procedure, or the name of a table that will return all columns and all rows from that table (in other words, a SELECT *-style clause).

A command can be constructed by passing the SQL clause as a parameter to the constructor of the Command class, as shown in this example:

```
string source = "server=(local);" +
                "integrated security=SSPI;" +
                "database=Northwind";
string select = "SELECT ContactName,CompanyName FROM Customers";
SqlConnection conn = new SqlConnection(source);
conn.Open();
SqlCommand cmd = new SqlCommand(select, conn);
```

The `<provider>Command` classes have a property called `CommandType`, which is used to define whether the command is a SQL clause, a call to a stored procedure, or a full table statement (which simply selects all columns and rows from a given table). The following table summarizes the `CommandType` enumeration.

COMMANDTYPE	EXAMPLE
Text (default)	`String select = "SELECT ContactName FROM Customers";SqlCommand cmd = new SqlCommand(select, conn);`
StoredProcedure	`SqlCommand cmd = new SqlCommand("CustOrderHist", conn);cmd .CommandType = CommandType.StoredProcedure;cmd.Parameters .AddWithValue("@CustomerID", "QUICK");`
TableDirect	`OleDbCommand cmd = new OleDbCommand("Categories", conn);cmd .CommandType = CommandType.TableDirect;`

When executing a stored procedure, it might be necessary to pass parameters to that procedure. The previous example sets the `@CustomerID` parameter directly, although there are other ways of setting the parameter value, which you look at later in this chapter. Note that since .NET 2.0, the `AddWithValue()` method is included in the command parameters collection — and the `Add(name, value)` member was attributed as `Obsolete`. If you have used this original method of constructing parameters for calling a stored procedure, you will receive compiler warnings when you recompile your code. We suggest altering your code now because Microsoft will most likely remove the older method in a subsequent release of .NET.

> The `TableDirect` *command type is valid only for the* `OleDb` *provider; other providers will throw an exception if you attempt to use this command type with them.*

Executing Commands

After you have defined the command, you need to execute it. A number of ways exist to issue the statement, depending on what you expect to be returned (if anything) from that command. The `<provider>Command` classes provide the following execute methods:

➤ `ExecuteNonQuery()` — Executes the command but does not return any output

➤ `ExecuteReader()` — Executes the command and returns a typed `IDataReader`

➤ `ExecuteScalar()` — Executes the command and returns the value from the first column of the first row of any result set

In addition to these methods, the `SqlCommand` class exposes the following method:

➤ `ExecuteXmlReader()` — Executes the command and returns an `XmlReader` object, which can be used to traverse the XML fragment returned from the database

ExecuteNonQuery()

The `ExecuteNonQuery()` method is commonly used for UPDATE, INSERT, or DELETE statements, where the only returned value is the number of records affected. This method can, however, return results if you call a stored procedure that has output parameters:

Available for
download on
Wrox.com

```
using System;
using System.Data.SqlClient;

public class ExecuteNonQueryExample
{
    public static void Main(string[] args)
    {
        string source = "server=(local);" +
                        "integrated security=SSPI;" +
                        "database=Northwind";
        string select = "UPDATE Customers " +
                        "SET ContactName = 'Bob' " +
```

```
                        "WHERE ContactName = 'Bill'";
         SqlConnection  conn = new SqlConnection(source);
         conn.Open();
         SqlCommand cmd = new SqlCommand(select, conn);
         int rowsReturned = cmd.ExecuteNonQuery();
         Console.WriteLine("{0} rows returned.", rowsReturned);
         conn.Close();
      }
   }
```

code download GetDatabaseConnection.txt

`ExecuteNonQuery()` returns the number of rows affected by the command as an `int`.

ExecuteReader()

The `ExecuteReader()` method executes the command and returns a typed data reader object, depending on the provider in use. The object returned can be used to iterate through the record(s) returned, as shown in the following code:

Available for download on Wrox.com

```
using System;
using System.Data.SqlClient;

public class ExecuteReaderExample
{
   public static void Main(string[] args)
   {
      string source = "server=(local);" +
                      "integrated security=SSPI;" +
                      "database=Northwind";
      string select = "SELECT ContactName,CompanyName FROM Customers";
      SqlConnection conn = new SqlConnection(source);
      conn.Open();
      SqlCommand cmd = new SqlCommand(select, conn);
      SqlDataReader reader = cmd.ExecuteReader();
      while(reader.Read())
      {
         Console.WriteLine("Contact: {0,-20} Company: {1}",
                            reader[0], reader[1]);
      }
   }
}
```

code download ExecuteReaderExample.cs

Figure 30-2 shows the output of this code.

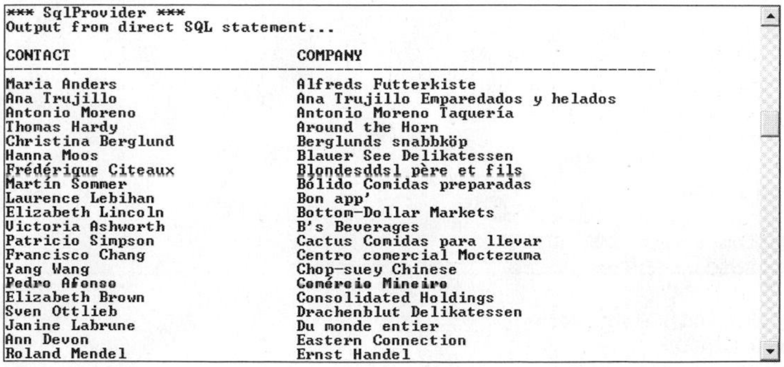

FIGURE 30-2

The `<provider>DataReader` objects are discussed later in this chapter.

ExecuteScalar()

On many occasions, it is necessary to return a single result from a SQL statement, such as the count of records in a given table, or the current date/time on the server. The `ExecuteScalar()` method can be used in such situations:

```csharp
using System;
using System.Data.SqlClient;

public class ExecuteScalarExample
{
    public static void Main(string[] args)
    {
        string source = "server=(local);" +
                        "integrated security=SSPI;" +
                        "database=Northwind";
        string select = "SELECT COUNT(*) FROM Customers";
        SqlConnection conn = new SqlConnection(source);
        conn.Open();
        SqlCommand cmd = new SqlCommand(select, conn);
        object o = cmd.ExecuteScalar();
        Console.WriteLine(o);
    }
}
```

code download ExecuteReaderExample.cs

The method returns an object, which you can cast to the appropriate type if required. If the SQL you are calling returns only one column, it is preferable to use `ExecuteScalar()` over any other method of retrieving that column. That also applies to stored procedures that return a single value.

ExecuteXmlReader() (SqlClient Provider Only)

As its name implies, the `ExecuteXmlReader()` method executes the command and returns an `XmlReader` object to the caller. SQL Server permits a SQL `SELECT` statement to be extended with a `FOR XML` clause. This clause can take one of three options:

➤ `FOR XML AUTO` — Builds a tree based on the tables in the `FROM` clause

➤ `FOR XML RAW` — Maps result set rows to elements, with columns mapped to attributes

➤ `FOR XML EXPLICIT` — Requires that you specify the shape of the XML tree to be returned

For this example, use `AUTO`:

```csharp
using System;
using System.Data.SqlClient;
using System.Xml;

public class ExecuteXmlReaderExample
{
    public static void Main(string[] args)
    {
        string source = "server=(local);" +
                        "integrated security=SSPI;" +
                        "database=Northwind";
        string select = "SELECT ContactName,CompanyName " +
                        "FROM Customers FOR XML AUTO";
        SqlConnection conn = new SqlConnection(source);
        conn.Open();
        SqlCommand cmd = new SqlCommand(select, conn);
        XmlReader xr = cmd.ExecuteXmlReader();
        xr.Read();
        string data;
        do
```

```
        {
            data = xr.ReadOuterXml();
            if (!string.IsNullOrEmpty(data))
                Console.WriteLine(data);
        } while (!string.IsNullOrEmpty(data));
        conn.Close();
    }
}
```

code download ExecuteReaderExample.cs

Note that you have to import the `System.Xml` namespace in order to output the returned XML. This namespace and further XML capabilities of .NET Framework are explored in more detail in Chapter 33, "Manipulating XML." Here, you include the `FOR XML AUTO` clause in the SQL statement, then call the `ExecuteXmlReader()` method. Figure 30-3 shows the output of this code.

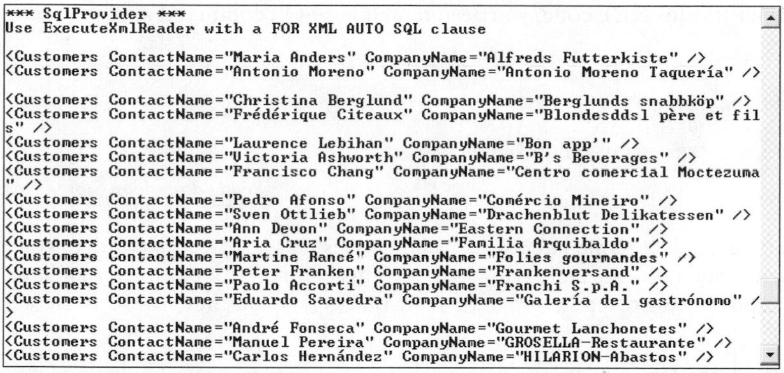

```
*** SqlProvider ***
Use ExecuteXmlReader with a FOR XML AUTO SQL clause

<Customers ContactName="Maria Anders" CompanyName="Alfreds Futterkiste" />
<Customers ContactName="Antonio Moreno" CompanyName="Antonio Moreno Taquería" />

<Customers ContactName="Christina Berglund" CompanyName="Berglunds snabbköp" />
<Customers ContactName="Frédérique Citeaux" CompanyName="Blondesddsl père et fil
s" />
<Customers ContactName="Laurence Lebihan" CompanyName="Bon app'" />
<Customers ContactName="Victoria Ashworth" CompanyName="B's Beverages" />
<Customers ContactName="Francisco Chang" CompanyName="Centro comercial Moctezuma
" />
<Customers ContactName="Pedro Afonso" CompanyName="Comércio Mineiro" />
<Customers ContactName="Sven Ottlieb" CompanyName="Drachenblut Delikatessen" />
<Customers ContactName="Ann Devon" CompanyName="Eastern Connection" />
<Customers ContactName="Aria Cruz" CompanyName="Familia Arquibaldo" />
<Customers ContactName="Martine Rancé" CompanyName="Folies gourmandes" />
<Customers ContactName="Peter Franken" CompanyName="Frankenversand" />
<Customers ContactName="Paolo Accorti" CompanyName="Franchi S.p.A." />
<Customers ContactName="Eduardo Saavedra" CompanyName="Galería del gastrónomo" /
<Customers ContactName="André Fonseca" CompanyName="Gourmet Lanchonetes" />
<Customers ContactName="Manuel Pereira" CompanyName="GROSELLA-Restaurante" />
<Customers ContactName="Carlos Hernández" CompanyName="HILARION-Abastos" />
```

FIGURE 30-3

In the SQL clause, you specified `FROM Customers`, so an element of type `Customers` is shown in the output. To this are added attributes, one for each column selected from the database. This builds up an XML fragment for each row selected from the database.

Calling Stored Procedures

Calling a stored procedure with a command object is just a matter of defining the name of the stored procedure, adding a definition for each parameter of the procedure, and then executing the command with one of the methods presented in the previous section.

To make the examples in this section more useful, a set of stored procedures has been defined that can be used to insert, update, and delete records from the `Region` table in the Northwind sample database. Despite its small size, this is a good candidate to choose for the example because it can be used to define examples for each of the types of stored procedures you will commonly write.

Calling a Stored Procedure That Returns Nothing

The simplest example of calling a stored procedure is one that returns nothing to the caller. Two such procedures are defined in the following two subsections: one for updating a preexisting `Region` record and one for deleting a given `Region` record.

Record Update

Updating a `Region` record is fairly trivial because there is only one column that can be modified (assuming primary keys cannot be updated). You can type these examples directly into the SQL Server Query

Analyzer, or run the `StoredProcs.sql` file that is part of the downloadable code for this chapter. This file installs each of the stored procedures in this section:

```
CREATE PROCEDURE RegionUpdate (@RegionID INTEGER,
                               @RegionDescription NCHAR(50)) AS

    SET NOCOUNT OFF
    UPDATE Region
        SET RegionDescription = @RegionDescription
        WHERE RegionID = @RegionID
GO
```

code download StoredProcs.sql

An update command on a more real-world table might need to reselect and return the updated record in its entirety. This stored procedure takes two input parameters (`@RegionID` and `@RegionDescription`), and issues an `UPDATE` statement against the database.

To run this stored procedure from within .NET code, you need to define a SQL command and execute it:

```
SqlCommand cmd = new SqlCommand("RegionUpdate", conn);

cmd.CommandType = CommandType.StoredProcedure;
cmd.Parameters.AddWithValue ( "@RegionID", 23 );
cmd.Parameters.AddWithValue ( "@RegionDescription", "Something" );
```

code download StoredProcs.sql

This code creates a new `SqlCommand` object named `aCommand`, and defines it as a stored procedure. You then add each parameter in turn, using the `AddWithValue` method. This constructs a parameter and also sets its value — you can also manually construct `SqlParameter` instances and add these to the `Parameters` collection if appropriate.

The stored procedure takes two parameters: the unique primary key of the `Region` record being updated and the new description to be given to this record. After the command has been created, it can be executed by issuing the following command:

```
cmd.ExecuteNonQuery();
```

Because the procedure returns nothing, `ExecuteNonQuery()` will suffice. Command parameters can be set directly, using the `AddWithValue()` method, or by constructing `SqlParameter` instances. Note that the parameter collection is indexable by position or parameter name.

Record Deletion

The next stored procedure required is one that can be used to delete a `Region` record from the database:

```
CREATE PROCEDURE RegionDelete (@RegionID INTEGER) AS
    SET NOCOUNT OFF
    DELETE FROM Region
    WHERE        RegionID = @RegionID
GO
```

code download StoredProcs.sql

This procedure requires only the primary key value of the record. The code uses a `SqlCommand` object to call this stored procedure as follows:

```
SqlCommand cmd = new SqlCommand("RegionDelete", conn);
cmd.CommandType = CommandType.StoredProcedure;
cmd.Parameters.Add(new SqlParameter("@RegionID", SqlDbType.Int, 0,
                                    "RegionID"));
cmd.UpdatedRowSource = UpdateRowSource.None;
```

code download StoredProcs.cs

This command accepts only a single parameter, as shown in the following code, which will execute the `RegionDelete` stored procedure; here, you see an example of setting the parameter by name. If you have many similar calls to make to the same stored procedure, constructing `SqlParameter` instances and setting the values as in the following code may lead to better performance than reconstructing the entire `SqlCommand` for each call.

```
cmd.Parameters["@RegionID"].Value= 999;
cmd.ExecuteNonQuery();
```

Calling a Stored Procedure That Returns Output Parameters

Both of the previous examples execute stored procedures that return nothing. If a stored procedure includes output parameters, these need to be defined within the .NET client so that they can be filled when the procedure returns. The following example shows how to insert a record into the database and return the primary key of that record to the caller.

Record Insertion

The `Region` table consists of only a primary key (`RegionID`) and description field (`RegionDescription`). To insert a record, this numeric primary key must be generated, and then a new row needs to be inserted into the database. The primary key generation in this example has been simplified by creating one within the stored procedure. The method used is exceedingly crude, which is why there is a section on key generation later in this chapter. For now, this primitive example suffices:

Available for download on Wrox.com

```
CREATE PROCEDURE RegionInsert(@RegionDescription NCHAR(50),
                             @RegionID INTEGER OUTPUT)AS
    SET NOCOUNT OFF
    SELECT @RegionID = MAX(RegionID)+ 1
    FROM Region
    INSERT INTO Region(RegionID, RegionDescription)
    VALUES(@RegionID, @RegionDescription)
GO
```

code download StoredProcs.sql

The insert procedure creates a new `Region` record. Because the primary key value is generated by the database itself, this value is returned as an output parameter from the procedure (`@RegionID`). This is sufficient for this simple example, but for a more complex table (especially one with default values), it is more common not to use output parameters, and instead select the entire inserted row and return this to the caller. The .NET classes can cope with either scenario.

Available for download on Wrox.com

```
SqlCommand  cmd = new SqlCommand("RegionInsert", conn);
cmd.CommandType = CommandType.StoredProcedure;
cmd.Parameters.Add(new SqlParameter("@RegionDescription",
                                    SqlDbType.NChar,
                                    50,
                                    "RegionDescription"));
cmd.Parameters.Add(new SqlParameter("@RegionID",
                                    SqlDbType.Int,
                                    0,
                                    ParameterDirection.Output,
                                    false,
                                    0,
                                    0,
                                    "RegionID",
                                    DataRowVersion.Default,
                                    null));
cmd.UpdatedRowSource = UpdateRowSource.OutputParameters;
```

code download StoredProcs.cs

Here, the definition of the parameters is much more complex. The second parameter, `@RegionID`, is defined to include its parameter direction, which in this example is `Output`. In addition to this flag, on the last line of the code, the `UpdateRowSource` enumeration is used to indicate that data will be returned from this stored procedure via output parameters. This flag is mainly used when issuing stored procedure calls from a `DataTable` (which is discussed later in this chapter).

Calling this stored procedure is similar to the previous examples, except in this instance the output parameter is read after executing the procedure:

```
cmd.Parameters["@RegionDescription"].Value = "South West";
cmd.ExecuteNonQuery();
int newRegionID = (int) cmd.Parameters["@RegionID"].Value;
```

After executing the command, the value of the `@RegionID` parameter is read and cast to an integer. A shorthand version of the preceding is the `ExecuteScalar()` method, which will return (as an object) the first value returned from the stored procedure.

You might be wondering what to do if the stored procedure you call returns output parameters and a set of rows. In this instance, define the parameters as appropriate, and rather than calling `ExecuteNonQuery()`, call one of the other methods (such as `ExecuteReader()`) that will permit you to traverse any record(s) returned.

FAST DATA ACCESS: THE DATA READER

A data reader is the simplest and fastest way of selecting some data from a data source, but it is also the least capable. You cannot directly instantiate a data reader object — an instance is returned from the appropriate database's command object (such as `SqlCommand`) after having called the `ExecuteReader()` method.

The following code demonstrates how to select data from the `Customers` table in the Northwind database. The example connects to the database, selects a number of records, loops through these selected records, and outputs them to the console.

This example uses the OLE DB provider as a brief respite from the SQL provider. In most cases, the classes have a one-to-one correspondence with their `SqlClient` cousins; for example, there is the `OleDbConnection` object, which is similar to the `SqlConnection` object used in the previous examples.

To execute commands against an OLE DB data source, the `OleDbCommand` class is used. The following code shows an example of executing a simple SQL statement and reading the records by returning an `OleDbDataReader` object.

Note the second `using` directive, which makes the `OleDb` classes available:

```
using System;
using System.Data.OleDb;
```

Most of the data providers currently available are shipped within the same assembly, so it is only necessary to reference the `System.Data.dll` assembly to import all classes used in this section.

```
public class DataReaderExample
{
    public static void Main(string[] args)
    {
        string source = "Provider=SQLOLEDB;" +
                        "server=(local);" +
                        "integrated security=SSPI;" +
                        "database=northwind";
        string select = "SELECT ContactName,CompanyName FROM Customers";
        OleDbConnection conn = new OleDbConnection(source);
        conn.Open();
```

```
        OleDbCommand cmd = new OleDbCommand(select, conn);
        OleDbDataReader aReader = cmd.ExecuteReader();
        while(aReader.Read())
            Console.WriteLine("'{0}' from {1}",
                              aReader.GetString(0), aReader.GetString(1));
        aReader.Close();
        conn.Close();
    }
}
```

code download DataReaderExample.cs

The preceding code includes many familiar aspects of C# already covered in this chapter. To compile the example, issue the following command:

```
csc /t:exe /debug+ DataReaderExample.cs /r:System.Data.dll
```

The following code from the previous example creates a new OLE DB .NET database connection, based on the source connection string:

```
OleDbConnection conn = new OleDbConnection(source);
conn.Open();
OleDbCommand cmd = new OleDbCommand(select, conn);
```

The third line creates a new OleDbCommand object, based on a particular SELECT statement, and the database connection to be used when the command is executed. When you have a valid command, you need to execute it, which returns an initialized OleDbDataReader:

```
OleDbDataReader aReader = cmd.ExecuteReader();
```

An OleDbDataReader is a forward-only "connected" reader. In other words, you can only traverse the records returned in one direction, and the database connection used is kept open until the data reader has been closed.

 An OleDbDataReader keeps the database connection open until it is explicitly closed.

The OleDbDataReader class cannot be instantiated directly — it is always returned by a call to the ExecuteReader() method of the OleDbCommand class. Once you have an open data reader, there are various ways to access the data contained within the reader.

When the OleDbDataReader object is closed (via an explicit call to Close(), or the object being garbage collected), the underlying connection may also be closed, depending on which of the ExecuteReader() methods is called. If you call ExecuteReader() and pass CommandBehavior.CloseConnection, you can force the connection to be closed when the reader is closed.

The OleDbDataReader class has an indexer that permits access (although not type-safe access) to any field using the familiar array style syntax:

```
    object o = aReader[0];
or
    object o = aReader["CategoryID"];
```

Assuming that the CategoryID field was the first in the SELECT statement used to populate the reader, these two lines are functionally equivalent, although the second is slower than the first; to verify this, a test application was written that performed a million iterations of accessing the same column from an open data reader, just to get some numbers that were big enough to read. You probably don't read the same column a million times in a tight loop, but every (micro) second counts, so you should write code that is as optimal as possible.

As an aside, the numeric indexer took on average 0.09 seconds for the million accesses, and the textual one 0.63 seconds. The reason for this difference is that the textual method looks up the column number internally from the schema and then accesses it using its ordinal. If you know this information beforehand, you can do a better job of accessing the data.

So, should you use the numeric indexer? Maybe, but there is a better way. In addition to the indexers just presented, `OleDbDataReader` has a set of type-safe methods that can be used to read columns. These are fairly self-explanatory, and all begin with `Get`. There are methods to read most types of data, such as `GetInt32`, `GetFloat`, `GetGuid`, and so on.

The million iterations using `GetInt32` took 0.06 seconds. The overhead in the numeric indexer is incurred while getting the data type, calling the same code as `GetInt32`, then boxing (and in this instance unboxing) an integer. So, if you know the schema beforehand, are willing to use cryptic numbers instead of column names, and can be bothered to use a type-safe function for each and every column access, you stand to gain somewhere in the region of a tenfold speed increase over using a textual column name (when selecting those million copies of the same column).

Needless to say, there is a tradeoff between maintainability and speed. If you must use numeric indexers, define constants within class scope for each of the columns that you will be accessing. The preceding code can be used to select data from any OLE DB database; however, there are a number of SQL Server–specific classes that can be used with the obvious portability tradeoff.

The following example is the same as the previous one, except that in this instance the OLE DB provider and all references to OLE DB classes have been replaced with their SQL counterparts. The example is located in the `04_DataReaderSql` directory:

```
using System;
using System.Data.SqlClient;

public class DataReaderSql
{
    public static int Main(string[] args)
    {
        string source = "server=(local);" +
                        "integrated security=SSPI;" +
                        "database=northwind";
        string select = "SELECT ContactName,CompanyName FROM Customers";
        SqlConnection conn = new SqlConnection(source);
        conn.Open();
        SqlCommand cmd = new SqlCommand(select, conn);
        SqlDataReader aReader = cmd.ExecuteReader();
        while(aReader.Read())
            Console.WriteLine("'{0}' from {1}", aReader.GetString(0),
                                aReader.GetString(1));
        aReader.Close();
        conn.Close();
        return 0;
    }
}
```

code download DataReaderSql.cs

Notice the difference? If you're typing this, do a global replace on `OleDb` with `Sql`, change the data source string, and recompile. It's that easy!

The same performance tests were run on the indexers for the SQL provider, and this time the numeric indexers were both exactly the same at 0.13 seconds for the million accesses, and the string-based indexer ran at about 0.65 seconds.

MANAGING DATA AND RELATIONSHIPS: THE DATASET CLASS

The DataSet class has been designed as an offline container of data. It has no notion of database connections. In fact, the data held within a DataSet does not necessarily need to have come from a database — it could just as easily be records from a CSV file, an XML file, or points read from a measuring device.

A DataSet class consists of a set of data tables, each of which will have a set of data columns and data rows (see Figure 30-4). In addition to defining the data, you can also define *links* between tables within the DataSet class. One common scenario would be defining a parent-child relationship (commonly known as master/detail). One record in a table (say Order) links to many records in another table (say Order_Details). This relationship can be defined and navigated within the DataSet.

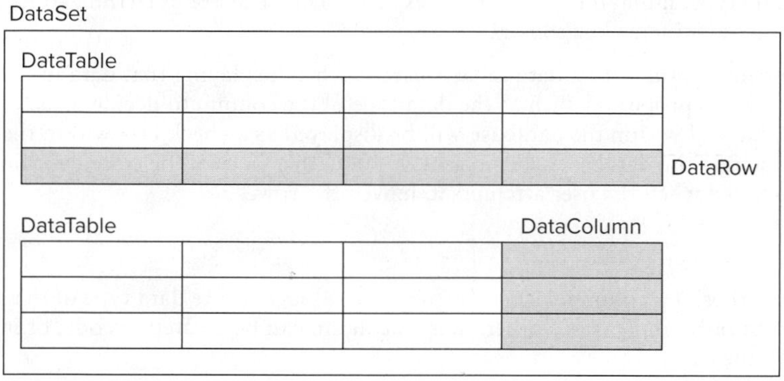

DataSet

```
DataTable



                                                            DataRow


DataTable                              DataColumn

```

FIGURE 30-4

It is important to remember that basically, the DataSet class is an in-memory database that includes all the tables, relationships, and constraints. The following sections describe the classes that are used with a DataSet class.

Data Tables

A data table is very similar to a physical database table — it consists of a set of columns with particular properties and might have zero or more rows of data. A data table might also define a primary key, which can be one or more columns, and might also contain constraints on columns. The generic term for this information used throughout the rest of the chapter is *schema*.

Several ways exist to define the schema for a particular data table (and indeed the DataSet class as a whole). These are discussed after introducing data columns and data rows. Figure 30-5 shows some of the objects that are accessible through the data table.

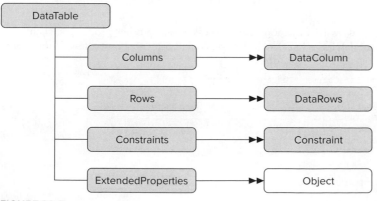

FIGURE 30-5

A `DataTable` object (and also a `DataColumn`) can have an arbitrary number of extended properties associated with it. This collection can be populated with any user-defined information pertaining to the object. For example, a given column might have an input mask used to validate the contents of that column — a typical example is the U.S. Social Security number. Extended properties are especially useful when the data is constructed within a middle tier and returned to the client for some processing. You could, for example, store validation criteria (such as `min` and `max`) for numeric columns in extended properties and use this in the UI tier when validating user input.

When a data table has been populated — by selecting data from a database, reading data from a file, or manually populating within code — the `Rows` collection will contain this retrieved data.

The `Columns` collection contains `DataColumn` instances that have been added to this table. These define the schema of the data, such as the data type, nullability, default values, and so on. The `Constraints` collection can be populated with either unique or primary key constraints.

One example of where the schema information for a data table is used is when displaying that data in a `DataGrid`. The `DataGrid` control uses properties such as the data type of the column to decide what control to use for that column. A bit field within the database will be displayed as a check box within the `DataGrid`. If a column is defined within the database schema as NOT NULL, this fact will be stored within the `DataColumn` so that it can be tested when the user attempts to move off a row.

Data Columns

A `DataColumn` object defines properties of a column within the `DataTable`, such as the data type of that column, whether the column is read-only, and various other facts. A column can be created in code, or it can be automatically generated by the runtime.

When creating a column, it is also useful to give it a name; otherwise, the runtime will generate a name for you in the form `Column`*n* where *n* is an incrementing number.

The data type of the column can be set either by supplying it in the constructor or by setting the `DataType` property. Once you have loaded data into a data table you cannot alter the type of a column — you will just receive an `ArgumentException`.

Data columns can be created to hold the following .NET Framework data types:

Boolean	Decimal
Int64	TimeSpan
Byte	Double
Sbyte	UInt16
Char	Int16
Single	UInt32
DateTime	Int32
String	UInt64

Once it is created, the next thing to do with a `DataColumn` object is to set up other properties, such as the nullability of the column or the default value. The following code fragment shows a few of the more common options that can be set on a `DataColumn` object:

```
DataColumn customerID = new DataColumn("CustomerID", typeof(int));
customerID.AllowDBNull = false;
customerID.ReadOnly = false;
customerID.AutoIncrement = true;
customerID.AutoIncrementSeed = 1000;
DataColumn name = new DataColumn("Name", typeof(string));
name.AllowDBNull = false;
name.Unique = true;
```

The following table shows the properties that can be set on a `DataColumn` object.

PROPERTY	DESCRIPTION
AllowDBNull	If `true`, permits the column to be set to `DBNull`.
AutoIncrement	Defines that this column value is automatically generated as an incrementing number.
AutoIncrementSeed	Defines the initial seed value for an `AutoIncrement` column.
AutoIncrementStep	Defines the step between automatically generated column values, with a default of one.
Caption	Can be used for displaying the name of the column onscreen.
ColumnMapping	Defines how a column is mapped into XML when a `DataSet` class is saved by calling `DataSet.WriteXml`.
ColumnName	The name of the column; this is auto-generated by the runtime if not set in the constructor.
DataType	Defines the `System.Type` value of the column.
DefaultValue	Can define a default value for a column.
Expression	Defines the expression to be used in a computed column.

Data Rows

This class makes up the other part of the `DataTable` class. The columns within a data table are defined in terms of the `DataColumn` class. The actual data within the table is accessed by using the `DataRow` object. The following example shows how to access rows within a data table. First, the connection details:

```
string source = "server=(local);" +
                " integrated security=SSPI;" +
                "database=northwind";
string select = "SELECT ContactName,CompanyName FROM Customers";
SqlConnection  conn = new SqlConnection(source);
```

The following code introduces the `SqlDataAdapter` class, which is used to place data into a `DataSet` class. `SqlDataAdapter` issues the SQL clause and fills a table in the `DataSet` class called `Customers` with the output of the following query. (For more details on the `SqlDataAdapter` class, see the section "Populating a DataSet" later in this chapter.)

```
SqlDataAdapter da = new SqlDataAdapter(select, conn);
DataSet ds = new DataSet();
da.Fill(ds, "Customers");
```

In the following code, you might notice the use of the `DataRow` indexer to access values from within that row. The value for a given column can be retrieved by using one of the several overloaded indexers. These permit you to retrieve a value knowing the column number, name, or `DataColumn`:

```
foreach(DataRow row in ds.Tables["Customers"].Rows)
   Console.WriteLine("'{0}' from {1}", row[0],row[1]);
```

One of the most appealing aspects of `DataRow` is that it is versioned. This permits you to receive various values for a given column in a particular row. The versions are described in the following table.

DATAROW VERSION VALUE	DESCRIPTION
Current	The value existing at present within the column. If no edit has occurred, this will be the same as the original value. If an edit (or edits) has occurred, the value will be the last valid value entered.
Default	The default value (in other words, any default set up for the column).
Original	The value of the column when originally selected from the database. If the `DataRow`'s `AcceptChanges()` method is called, this value will update to the `Current` value.
Proposed	When changes are in progress for a row, it is possible to retrieve this modified value. If you call `BeginEdit()` on the row and make changes, each column will have a proposed value until either `EndEdit()` or `CancelEdit()` is called.

The version of a given column could be used in many ways. One example is when updating rows within the database, in which instance it is common to issue a SQL statement such as the following:

```
UPDATE Products
SET    Name = Column.Current
WHERE  ProductID = xxx
AND    Name = Column.Original;
```

Obviously, this code would never compile, but it shows one use for original and current values of a column within a row.

To retrieve a versioned value from the `DataRow` indexer, use one of the indexer methods that accepts a `DataRowVersion` value as a parameter. The following snippet shows how to obtain all values of each column in a `DataTable` object:

```
foreach (DataRow row in ds.Tables["Customers"].Rows )
{
  foreach ( DataColumn dc in ds.Tables["Customers"].Columns )
  {
    Console.WriteLine ("{0} Current  = {1}", dc.ColumnName,
                                  row[dc,DataRowVersion.Current]);
    Console.WriteLine ("     Default  = {0}", row[dc,DataRowVersion.Default]);
    Console.WriteLine ("     Original = {0}",
                       row[dc,DataRowVersion.Original]);
  }
}
```

The whole row has a state flag called `RowState`, which can be used to determine what operation is needed on the row when it is persisted back to the database. The `RowState` property is set to keep track of all the changes made to the `DataTable`, such as adding new rows, deleting existing rows, and changing columns within the table. When the data is reconciled with the database, the row state flag is used to determine what SQL operations should occur. The following table provides an overview of the flags that are defined by the `DataRowState` enumeration.

DATAROWSTATE VALUE	DESCRIPTION
Added	Indicates that the row has been newly added to a `DataTable`'s `Rows` collection. All rows created on the client are set to this value and will ultimately issue SQL `INSERT` statements when reconciled with the database.
Deleted	Indicates that the row has been marked as deleted from the `DataTable` by means of the `DataRow.Delete()` method. The row still exists within the `DataTable` but will not normally be viewable onscreen (unless a `DataView` has been explicitly set up). `DataViews` are discussed in the next chapter. Rows marked as deleted in the `DataTable` will be deleted from the database when reconciled.
Detached	Indicates that a row is in this state immediately after it is created, and can also be returned to this state by calling `DataRow.Remove()`. A detached row is not considered to be part of any data table, thus no SQL for rows in this state will be issued.
Modified	Indicates that a row will be `Modified` if the value in any column has been changed.
Unchanged	Indicates that the row has not been changed since the last call to `AcceptChanges()`.

The state of the row depends also on what methods have been called on the row. The `AcceptChanges()` method is generally called after successfully updating the data source (that is, after persisting changes to the database).

The most common way to alter data in a `DataRow` is to use the indexer; however, if you have a number of changes to make, you also need to consider the `BeginEdit()` and `EndEdit()` methods.

When an alteration is made to a column within a `DataRow`, the `ColumnChanging` event is raised on the row's `DataTable`. This permits you to override the `ProposedValue` property of the `DataColumnChangeEventArgs` class and change it as required. This is one way of performing some data validation on column values. If you call `BeginEdit()` before making changes, the `ColumnChanging` event will not be raised. This permits you to make multiple changes and then call `EndEdit()` to persist these changes. If you want to revert to the original values, call `CancelEdit()`.

A `DataRow` can be linked in some way to other rows of data. This permits the creation of navigable links between rows, which is common in master/detail scenarios. The `DataRow` contains a `GetChildRows()` method that will return an array of associated rows from another table in the same `DataSet` as the current row. These are discussed in the "Data Relationships" section later in this chapter.

Schema Generation

You can create the schema for a `DataTable` in three ways:

➤ Let the runtime do it for you.

➤ Write code to create the table(s).

➤ Use the XML schema generator.

The following sections describe these three alternatives.

Runtime Schema Generation

The `DataRow` example shown earlier presented the following code for selecting data from a database and populating a `DataSet` class:

```
SqlDataAdapter da = new SqlDataAdapter(select, conn);
DataSet ds = new DataSet();
da.Fill(ds, "Customers");
```

This is obviously easy to use, but it has a few drawbacks as well. For example, you have to make do with the default column names, which might work for you, but in certain instances, you might want to rename a physical database column (say `PKID`) to something more user-friendly.

You could naturally alias columns within your SQL clause, as in `SELECT PID AS PersonID FROM PersonTable`; it's best to not rename columns within SQL, though, because a column only really needs to have a "pretty" name onscreen.

Another potential problem with automated `DataTable`/`DataColumn` generation is that you have no control over the column types that the runtime chooses for your data. It does a fairly good job of deciding the correct data type for you, but as usual there are instances where you need more control. For example, you might have defined an enumerated type for a given column to simplify user code written against your class. If you accept the default column types that the runtime generates, the column will likely be an integer with a 32-bit range, as opposed to an `enum` with your predefined options.

Last, and probably most problematic, is that when using automated table generation, you have no type-safe access to the data within the `DataTable` — you are at the mercy of indexers, which return instances of `object` rather than derived data types. If you like sprinkling your code with typecast expressions, skip the following sections.

Hand-Coded Schema

Generating the code to create a `DataTable`, replete with associated `DataColumns`, is fairly easy. The examples within this section access the `Products` table from the Northwind database, shown in Figure 30-6.

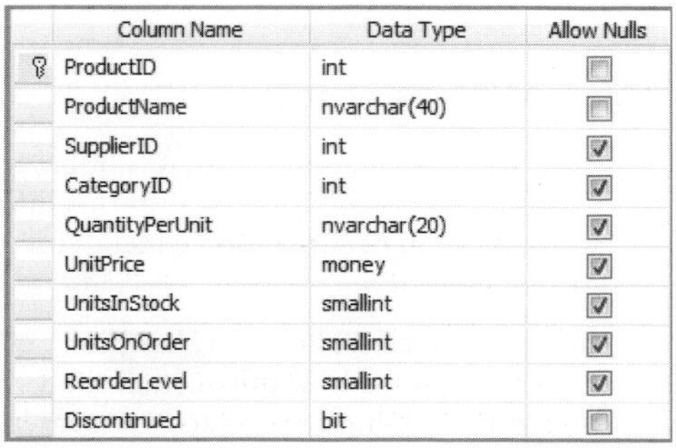

	Column Name	Data Type	Allow Nulls
🔑	ProductID	int	☐
	ProductName	nvarchar(40)	☐
	SupplierID	int	☑
	CategoryID	int	☑
	QuantityPerUnit	nvarchar(20)	☑
	UnitPrice	money	☑
	UnitsInStock	smallint	☑
	UnitsOnOrder	smallint	☑
	ReorderLevel	smallint	☑
	Discontinued	bit	☐

FIGURE 30-6

The following code manufactures a `DataTable`, which corresponds to the schema shown in Figure 30-6 (but does not cover the nullability of columns):

```
public static void ManufactureProductDataTable(DataSet ds)
{
    DataTable    products = new DataTable("Products");
    products.Columns.Add(new DataColumn("ProductID", typeof(int)));
    products.Columns.Add(new DataColumn("ProductName", typeof(string)));
    products.Columns.Add(new DataColumn("SupplierID", typeof(int)));
    products.Columns.Add(new DataColumn("CategoryID", typeof(int)));
    products.Columns.Add(new DataColumn("QuantityPerUnit", typeof(string)));
    products.Columns.Add(new DataColumn("UnitPrice", typeof(decimal)));
    products.Columns.Add(new DataColumn("UnitsInStock", typeof(short)));
    products.Columns.Add(new DataColumn("UnitsOnOrder", typeof(short)));
    products.Columns.Add(new DataColumn("ReorderLevel", typeof(short)));
    products.Columns.Add(new DataColumn("Discontinued", typeof(bool)));
    ds.Tables.Add(products);
}
```

code download ManufacturedDataSet.cs

You can alter the code in the `DataRow` example to use this newly generated table definition as follows:

```
string source = "server=(local);" +
                "integrated security=sspi;" +
                "database=Northwind";
string select = "SELECT * FROM Products";
SqlConnection conn = new SqlConnection(source);
SqlDataAdapter cmd = new SqlDataAdapter(select, conn);
DataSet ds = new DataSet();
ManufactureProductDataTable(ds);
cmd.Fill(ds, "Products");
foreach(DataRow row in ds.Tables["Products"].Rows)
    Console.WriteLine("'{0}' from {1}", row[0], row[1]);
```

The `ManufactureProductDataTable()` method creates a new `DataTable`, adds each column in turn, and finally appends this to the list of tables within the `DataSet`. The `DataSet` has an indexer that takes the name of the table and returns that `DataTable` to the caller.

The previous example is still not really type-safe because indexers are being used on columns to retrieve the data. What would be better is a class (or set of classes) derived from `DataSet`, `DataTable`, and `DataRow` that defines type-safe accessors for tables, rows, and columns. You can generate this code yourself; it is not particularly tedious and you end up with truly type-safe data access classes.

If you don't like generating these type-safe classes yourself, help is at hand. The .NET Framework includes support for the third method listed at the start of this section: using XML schemas to define a `DataSet` class, a `DataTable` class, and the other classes that we have described here. (For more details on this method, see the section "XML Schemas: Generating Code with XSD" later in this chapter.)

Data Relationships

When writing an application, it is often necessary to obtain and cache various tables of information. The `DataSet` class is the container for this information. With regular OLE DB, it was necessary to provide a strange SQL dialect to enforce hierarchical data relationships, and the provider itself was not without its own subtle quirks.

The `DataSet` class, however, has been designed from the start to establish relationships between data tables with ease. The code in this section shows how to generate data manually and populate two tables with data. So, if you don't have access to SQL Server or the Northwind database, you can run this example anyway:

```
DataSet ds = new DataSet("Relationships");
ds.Tables.Add(CreateBuildingTable());
ds.Tables.Add(CreateRoomTable());
ds.Relations.Add("Rooms",
                 ds.Tables["Building"].Columns["BuildingID"],
                 ds.Tables["Room"].Columns["BuildingID"]);
```

code download DataRelationships.cs

The tables used in this example are shown in Figure 30-7. They contain a primary key and name field, with the Room table having BuildingID as a foreign key.

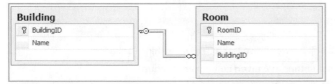

FIGURE 30-7

These tables have been kept deliberately simple. The following code shows how to iterate through the rows in the Building table and traverse the relationship to list all of the child rows from the Room table:

```
foreach(DataRow theBuilding in ds.Tables["Building"].Rows)
{
    DataRow[] children = theBuilding.GetChildRows("Rooms");
    int roomCount = children.Length;
    Console.WriteLine("Building {0} contains {1} room{2}",
                      theBuilding["Name"],
                      roomCount,
                      roomCount > 1 ? "s": "");
    // Loop through the rooms
    foreach(DataRow theRoom in children)
        Console.WriteLine("Room: {0}", theRoom["Name"]);
}
```

The key difference between the DataSet class and the old-style hierarchical Recordset object is in the way the relationship is presented. In a hierarchical Recordset object, the relationship was presented as a pseudo-column within the row. This column itself was a Recordset object that could be iterated through. Under ADO.NET, however, a relationship is traversed simply by calling the GetChildRows() method:

```
DataRow[] children = theBuilding.GetChildRows("Rooms");
```

This method has a number of forms, but the preceding simple example uses just the name of the relationship to traverse between parent and child rows. It returns an array of rows that can be updated as appropriate by using the indexers, as shown in earlier examples.

What's more interesting with data relationships is that they can be traversed both ways. Not only can you go from a parent to the child rows, but you can also find a parent row (or rows) from a child record simply by using the ParentRelations property on the DataTable class. This property returns a DataRelationCollection, which can be indexed by using the [] array syntax (for example, ParentRelations["Rooms"]), or as an alternative, the GetParentRows() method can be called, as shown here:

```
foreach(DataRow theRoom in ds.Tables["Room"].Rows)
{
    DataRow[] parents = theRoom.GetParentRows("Rooms");
    foreach(DataRow theBuilding in parents)
        Console.WriteLine("Room {0} is contained in building {1}",
                          theRoom["Name"],
                          theBuilding["Name"]);
}
```

Two methods with various overrides are available for retrieving the parent row(s): `GetParentRows()` (which returns an array of zero or more rows) and `GetParentRow()` (which retrieves a single parent row given a relationship).

Data Constraints

Changing the data type of columns created on the client is not the only thing a `DataTable` is good for. ADO.NET permits you to create a set of constraints on a column (or columns), which are then used to enforce rules within the data.

The following table lists the constraint types that are currently supported by the runtime, embodied as classes in the `System.Data` namespace.

CONSTRAINT	DESCRIPTION
ForeignKeyConstraint	Enforces a link between two `DataTables` within a `DataSet`.
UniqueConstraint	Ensures that entries in a given column are unique.

Setting a Primary Key

As is common with a table in a relational database, you can supply a primary key, which can be based on one or more columns from the `DataTable`.

The following code creates a primary key for the `Products` table, whose schema was constructed by hand earlier. Note that a primary key on a table is just one form of constraint. When a primary key is added to a `DataTable`, the runtime also generates a unique constraint over the key column(s). This is because there isn't actually a constraint type of `PrimaryKey` — a primary key is simply a unique constraint over one or more columns.

```
public static void ManufacturePrimaryKey(DataTable dt)
{
    DataColumn[] pk = new DataColumn[1];
    pk[0] = dt.Columns["ProductID"];
    dt.PrimaryKey = pk;
}
```

code download ManufacturedDataSet.cs

Because a primary key can contain several columns, it is typed as an array of `DataColumns`. A table's primary key can be set to those columns simply by assigning an array of columns to the property.

To check the constraints for a table, you can iterate through the `ConstraintCollection`. For the auto-generated constraint produced by the preceding code, the name of the constraint is `Constraint1`. That's not a very useful name, so to avoid this problem it is always best to create the constraint in code first, then define which column(s) make up the primary key.

The following code names the constraint before creating the primary key:

```
DataColumn[] pk = new DataColumn[1];
pk[0] = dt.Columns["ProductID"];
dt.Constraints.Add(new UniqueConstraint("PK_Products", pk[0]));
dt.PrimaryKey = pk;
```

Unique constraints can be applied to as many columns as you want.

Setting a Foreign Key

In addition to unique constraints, a `DataTable` class can also contain foreign key constraints. These are primarily used to enforce master/detail relationships but can also be used to replicate columns between tables if you set up the constraint correctly. A master/detail relationship is one where there is commonly one parent record (say an order) and many child records (order lines), linked by the primary key of the parent record.

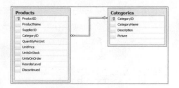

FIGURE 30-8

A foreign key constraint can operate only over tables within the same DataSet, so the following example uses the Categories table from the Northwind database (shown in Figure 30-8), and assigns a constraint between it and the Products table.

The first step is to generate a new data table for the Categories table:

```
DataTable categories = new DataTable("Categories");
categories.Columns.Add(new DataColumn("CategoryID", typeof(int)));
categories.Columns.Add(new DataColumn("CategoryName", typeof(string)));
categories.Columns.Add(new DataColumn("Description", typeof(string)));
categories.Constraints.Add(new UniqueConstraint("PK_Categories",
                           categories.Columns["CategoryID"]));
categories.PrimaryKey = new DataColumn[1]
                        {categories.Columns["CategoryID"]};
```

The last line of this code creates the primary key for the Categories table. The primary key in this instance is a single column; however, it is possible to generate a key over multiple columns using the array syntax shown.

Then the constraint can be created between the two tables:

```
DataColumn parent = ds.Tables["Categories"].Columns["CategoryID"];
DataColumn child = ds.Tables["Products"].Columns["CategoryID"];
ForeignKeyConstraint fk =
    new ForeignKeyConstraint("FK_Product_CategoryID", parent, child);
fk.UpdateRule = Rule.Cascade;
fk.DeleteRule = Rule.SetNull;
ds.Tables["Products"].Constraints.Add(fk);
```

This constraint applies to the link between Categories.CategoryID and Products.CategoryID. There are four different ForeignKeyConstraints — use those that permit you to name the constraint.

Setting Update and Delete Constraints

In addition to defining that there is some type of constraint between parent and child tables, you can define what should happen when a column in the constraint is updated.

The previous example sets the update rule and the delete rule. These rules are used when an action occurs to a column (or row) within the parent table, and the rule is used to decide what should happen to the row(s) within the child table that could be affected. Four different rules can be applied through the Rule enumeration:

- ➤ Cascade — If the parent key has been updated, copy the new key value to all child records. If the parent record has been deleted, delete the child records also. This is the default option.

- ➤ None — Takes no action whatsoever. This option leaves orphaned rows within the child data table.

- ➤ SetDefault — Each child record affected has the foreign key column(s) set to its default value, if one has been defined.

- ➤ SetNull — All child rows have the key column(s) set to DBNull. (Following the naming convention that Microsoft uses, this should really be SetDBNull.)

> *Constraints are enforced only within a* DataSet *class if the* EnforceConstraints
> *property of the* DataSet *is* true.

This section has covered the main classes that make up the constituent parts of the DataSet class and has shown how to manually generate each of these classes in code. You can also define a DataTable, DataRow, DataColumn, DataRelation, and Constraint using the XML schema file(s) and the XSD tool that ships with .NET. The following section describes how to set up a simple schema and generate type-safe classes to access your data.

XML SCHEMAS: GENERATING CODE WITH XSD

XML is firmly entrenched in ADO.NET — indeed, the remoting format for passing data between objects is now XML. With the .NET runtime, it is possible to describe a DataTable class within an XML schema definition file (XSD). What's more, you can define an entire DataSet class, with a number of DataTable classes, and a set of relationships between these tables, and you can include various other details to fully describe the data.

When you have defined an XSD file, there is a tool in the runtime that will convert this schema to the corresponding data access class(es), such as the type-safe product DataTable class shown earlier. Let's start with a simple XSD file (Products.xsd) that describes the same information as the Products sample discussed earlier and then extend it to include some extra functionality:

Available for download on Wrox.com

```xml
<?xml version="1.0" encoding="utf-8" ?>
<xs:schema id="Products" targetNamespace="http://tempuri.org/XMLSchema1.xsd"
  xmlns:mstns="http://tempuri.org/XMLSchema1.xsd"
  xmlns:xs="http://www.w3.org/2001/XMLSchema"
  xmlns:msdata="urn:schemas-microsoft-com:xml-msdata">
  <xs:element name="Product">
    <xs:complexType>
      <xs:sequence>
        <xs:element name="ProductID" msdata:ReadOnly="true"
          msdata:AutoIncrement="true" type="xs:int" />
        <xs:element name="ProductName" type="xs:string" />
        <xs:element name="SupplierID" type="xs:int" minOccurs="0" />
        <xs:element name="CategoryID" type="xs:int" minOccurs="0" />
        <xs:element name="QuantityPerUnit" type="xs:string" minOccurs="0" />
        <xs:element name="UnitPrice" type="xs:decimal" minOccurs="0" />
        <xs:element name="UnitsInStock" type="xs:short" minOccurs="0" />
        <xs:element name="UnitsOnOrder" type="xs:short" minOccurs="0" />
        <xs:element name="ReorderLevel" type="xs:short" minOccurs="0" />
        <xs:element name="Discontinued" type="xs:boolean" />
      </xs:sequence>
    </xs:complexType>
  </xs:element>
</xs:schema>
```

code download Products.xsd

These options are covered in detail in Chapter 33; for now, this file basically defines a schema with the id attribute set to Products. A complex type called Product is defined, which contains a number of elements, one for each of the fields within the Products table.

These items map to data classes as follows. The Products schema maps to a class derived from DataSet. The Product complex type maps to a class derived from DataTable. Each subelement maps to a class derived from DataColumn. The collection of all columns maps to a class derived from DataRow.

Thankfully, there is a tool within the .NET Framework that produces the code for these classes with the help of the input XSD file. Because its sole job is to perform various functions on XSD files, the tool itself is called XSD.EXE.

Assuming that you saved the preceding file as Product.xsd, you would convert the file into code by issuing the following command in a command prompt:

```
xsd Product.xsd /d
```

This creates the file Product.cs.

Various switches can be used with XSD to alter the output generated. Some of the more commonly used switches are shown in the following table.

SWITCH	DESCRIPTION
/dataset (/d)	Enables you to generate classes derived from DataSet, DataTable, and DataRow.
/language:<language>	Permits you to choose which language the output file will be written in. C# is the default, but you can choose VB for a Visual Basic .NET file.
/namespace:<namespace>	Enables you to define the namespace that the generated code should reside within. The default is no namespace.

The following is an abridged version of the output from XSD for the Products schema. The output has been altered slightly to fit into a format appropriate for this book. To see the complete output, run XSD. EXE on the Products schema (or one of your own making) and look at the .cs file generated. The example includes the entire source code plus the Product.xsd file:

```
//--------------------------------------
// <autogenerated>
//      This code was generated by a tool.
//      Runtime Version:4.0.21006.1
//
//      Changes to this file may cause incorrect behavior and will be lost if
//      the code is regenerated.
// </autogenerated>
//--------------------------------------

//
// This source code was auto-generated by xsd, Version=4.0.21006.1
//

/// <summary>
///Represents a strongly typed in-memory cache of data.
///</summary>
[global::System.Serializable()]
[global::System.ComponentModel.DesignerCategoryAttribute("code")]
[global::System.ComponentModel.ToolboxItem(true)]
[global::System.Xml.Serialization.XmlSchemaProviderAttribute("GetTypedDataSetSchema")]
[global::System.Xml.Serialization.XmlRootAttribute("Products")]
[global::System.ComponentModel.Design.HelpKeywordAttribute("vs.data.DataSet")]
public partial class Products : global::System.Data.DataSet {
    private ProductDataTable tableProduct;

    private global::System.Data.SchemaSerializationMode _schemaSerializationMode =
        global::System.Data.SchemaSerializationMode.IncludeSchema;

    [global::System.Diagnostics.DebuggerNonUserCodeAttribute()]
    [global::System.CodeDom.Compiler.GeneratedCodeAttribute(
```

```
         "System.Data.Design.TypedDataSetGenerator", "4.0.0.0")]
     public Products() {
         this.BeginInit();
         this.InitClass();
         global::System.ComponentModel.CollectionChangeEventHandler
             schemaChangedHandler = new
             global::System.ComponentModel.CollectionChangeEventHandler(
             this.SchemaChanged);
         base.Tables.CollectionChanged += schemaChangedHandler;
         base.Relations.CollectionChanged += schemaChangedHandler;
         this.EndInit();
     }
}
```

code download product.cs

All private and protected members have been removed to concentrate on the public interface. The
`ProductDataTable` and `ProductRow` definitions show the positions of two nested classes, which will
be implemented next. You review the code for these classes after a brief explanation of the
`DataSet`-derived class.

The `Products()` constructor calls a private method, `InitClass()`, which constructs an instance of the
`DataTable`-derived class `ProductDataTable`, and adds the table to the `Tables` collection of the `DataSet`
class. The `Products` data table can be accessed by the following code:

```
DataSet ds = new Products();
DataTable products = ds.Tables["Products"];
```

Or, more simply by using the property `Product`, available on the derived `DataSet` object:

```
DataTable products = ds.Product;
```

Because the `Product` property is strongly typed, you could naturally use `ProductDataTable` rather than the
`DataTable` reference shown in the previous code.

The `ProductDataTable` class includes far more code (note this is an abridged version of the code):

Available for
download on
Wrox.com

```
[global::System.Serializable()]
[global::System.Xml.Serialization.XmlSchemaProviderAttribute("GetTypedTableSchema")]
public partial class ProductDataTable : global::System.Data.DataTable,
     global::System.Collections.IEnumerable {

         private global::System.Data.DataColumn columnProductID;
         private global::System.Data.DataColumn columnProductName;
         private global::System.Data.DataColumn columnSupplierID;
         private global::System.Data.DataColumn columnCategoryID;
         private global::System.Data.DataColumn columnQuantityPerUnit;
         private global::System.Data.DataColumn columnUnitPrice;
         private global::System.Data.DataColumn columnUnitsInStock;
         private global::System.Data.DataColumn columnUnitsOnOrder;
         private global::System.Data.DataColumn columnReorderLevel;
         private global::System.Data.DataColumn columnDiscontinued;

     [global::System.Diagnostics.DebuggerNonUserCodeAttribute()]
     [global::System.CodeDom.Compiler.GeneratedCodeAttribute(
         "System.Data.Design.TypedDataSetGenerator", "4.0.0.0")]
         public ProductDataTable() {
             this.TableName = "Product";
             this.BeginInit();
             this.InitClass();
             this.EndInit();
         }
```

code download product.cs

The `ProductDataTable` class, derived from `DataTable` and implementing the `IEnumerable` interface, defines a private `DataColumn` instance for each of the columns within the table. These are initialized again from the constructor by calling the private `InitClass()` member. Each column is used by the `DataRow` class (which is described shortly):

Available for download on Wrox.com

```
[global::System.Diagnostics.DebuggerNonUserCodeAttribute()]
[global::System.CodeDom.Compiler.GeneratedCodeAttribute(
    "System.Data.Design.TypedDataSetGenerator", "4.0.0.0")]
[global::System.ComponentModel.Browsable(false)]
public int Count {
    get {
        return this.Rows.Count;
    }
}

// Other row accessors removed for clarity — there is one for each column
```

code download product.cs

Adding rows to the table is taken care of by the two overloaded (and significantly different) `AddProductRow()` methods. The first takes an already constructed `DataRow` and returns a void. The second takes a set of values, one for each of the columns in the `DataTable`, constructs a new row, sets the values within this new row, adds the row to the `DataTable` object, and returns the row to the caller. Such widely different functions shouldn't really have the same name!

Available for download on Wrox.com

```
[global::System.Diagnostics.DebuggerNonUserCodeAttribute()]
[global::System.CodeDom.Compiler.GeneratedCodeAttribute(
    "System.Data.Design.TypedDataSetGenerator", "4.0.0.0")]
        public ProductRow AddProductRow(string ProductName, int SupplierID,
            int CategoryID, string QuantityPerUnit, decimal UnitPrice,
            short UnitsInStock, short UnitsOnOrder, short ReorderLevel,
            bool Discontinued) {
          ProductRow rowProductRow = ((ProductRow)(this.NewRow()));
          object[] columnValuesArray = new object[] {
                  null,
                  ProductName,
                  SupplierID,
                  CategoryID,
                  QuantityPerUnit,
                  UnitPrice,
                  UnitsInStock,
                  UnitsOnOrder,
                  ReorderLevel,
                  Discontinued};
          rowProductRow.ItemArray = columnValuesArray;
          this.Rows.Add(rowProductRow);
          return rowProductRow;
        }
```

code download product.cs

Just like the `InitClass()` member in the `DataSet`-derived class, which added the table into the `DataSet` class, the `InitClass()` member in `ProductDataTable` adds columns to the `DataTable` class. Each column's properties are set as appropriate, and the column is then appended to the columns collection:

Available for download on Wrox.com

```
[global::System.Diagnostics.DebuggerNonUserCodeAttribute()]
[global::System.CodeDom.Compiler.GeneratedCodeAttribute(
    "System.Data.Design.TypedDataSetGenerator", "4.0.0.0")]
        private void InitClass() {
            this.columnProductID = new
global::System.Data.DataColumn("ProductID",
                typeof(int), null, global::System.Data.MappingType.Element);
            base.Columns.Add(this.columnProductID);
```

```
            this.columnProductName = new global::System.Data.DataColumn(
                "ProductName", typeof(string), null,
                global::System.Data.MappingType.Element);
            base.Columns.Add(this.columnProductName);
            this.columnSupplierID = new global::System.Data.DataColumn(
                "SupplierID", typeof(int), null,
                global::System.Data.MappingType.Element);
            base.Columns.Add(this.columnSupplierID);
            this.columnCategoryID = new global::System.Data.DataColumn("CategoryID",
                typeof(int), null, global::System.Data.MappingType.Element);
            base.Columns.Add(this.columnCategoryID);
            this.columnQuantityPerUnit = new
                global::System.Data.DataColumn("QuantityPerUnit", typeof(string), null,
                global::System.Data.MappingType.Element);
            base.Columns.Add(this.columnQuantityPerUnit);
            this.columnUnitPrice = new global::System.Data.DataColumn("UnitPrice",
                typeof(decimal), null, global::System.Data.MappingType.Element);
            base.Columns.Add(this.columnUnitPrice);
            this.columnUnitsInStock = new global::System.Data.DataColumn("UnitsInStock",
                typeof(short), null, global::System.Data.MappingType.Element);
            base.Columns.Add(this.columnUnitsInStock);
            this.columnUnitsOnOrder = new global::System.Data.DataColumn("UnitsOnOrder",
                typeof(short), null, global::System.Data.MappingType.Element);
            base.Columns.Add(this.columnUnitsOnOrder);
            this.columnReorderLevel = new global::System.Data.DataColumn("ReorderLevel",
                typeof(short), null, global::System.Data.MappingType.Element);
            base.Columns.Add(this.columnReorderLevel);
            this.columnDiscontinued = new global::System.Data.DataColumn("Discontinued",
                typeof(bool), null, global::System.Data.MappingType.Element);
            base.Columns.Add(this.columnDiscontinued);
            this.columnProductID.AutoIncrement = true;
            this.columnProductID.AllowDBNull = false;
            this.columnProductID.ReadOnly = true;
            this.columnProductName.AllowDBNull = false;
            this.columnDiscontinued.AllowDBNull = false;
        }

        [global::System.Diagnostics.DebuggerNonUserCodeAttribute()]
        [global::System.CodeDom.Compiler.GeneratedCodeAttribute(
            "System.Data.Design.TypedDataSetGenerator", "4.0.0.0")]
        public ProductRow NewProductRow() {
            return ((ProductRow)(this.NewRow()));
        }
```

code download product.cs

`NewRowFromBuilder()` is called internally from the `DataTable` class's `NewRow()` method. Here, it creates a new strongly typed row. The `DataRowBuilder` instance is created by the `DataTable` class, and its members are accessible only within the `System.Data` assembly:

```
        [global::System.Diagnostics.DebuggerNonUserCodeAttribute()]
        [global::System.CodeDom.Compiler.GeneratedCodeAttribute(
            "System.Data.Design.TypedDataSetGenerator", "4.0.0.0")]
            protected override global::System.Data.DataRow NewRowFromBuilder(
                global::System.Data.DataRowBuilder builder) {
                return new ProductRow(builder);
            }
```

The last class to discuss is the `ProductRow` class, derived from `DataRow`. This class is used to provide type-safe access to all fields in the data table. It wraps the storage for a particular row, and provides members to read (and write) each of the fields in the table.

In addition, for each nullable field, there are functions to set the field to `null` and to check if the field is `null`. The following example shows the functions for the `SupplierID` column:

```
public partial class ProductRow : global::System.Data.DataRow {

        private ProductDataTable tableProduct;

        [global::System.Diagnostics.DebuggerNonUserCodeAttribute()]
        [global::System.CodeDom.Compiler.GeneratedCodeAttribute(
            "System.Data.Design.TypedDataSetGenerator", "4.0.0.0")]
        internal ProductRow(global::System.Data.DataRowBuilder rb) :
                base(rb) {
            this.tableProduct = ((ProductDataTable)(this.Table));
        }

        [global::System.Diagnostics.DebuggerNonUserCodeAttribute()]
        [global::System.CodeDom.Compiler.GeneratedCodeAttribute(
            "System.Data.Design.TypedDataSetGenerator", "4.0.0.0")]
        public int ProductID {
            get {
                return ((int)(this[this.tableProduct.ProductIDColumn]));
            }
            set {
                this[this.tableProduct.ProductIDColumn] = value;
            }
        }

    // Other column accessors/mutators removed for clarity

        [global::System.Diagnostics.DebuggerNonUserCodeAttribute()]
        [global::System.CodeDom.Compiler.GeneratedCodeAttribute(
            "System.Data.Design.TypedDataSetGenerator", "4.0.0.0")]
        public bool IsSupplierIDNull() {
            return this.IsNull(this.tableProduct.SupplierIDColumn);
        }

        [global::System.Diagnostics.DebuggerNonUserCodeAttribute()]
        [global::System.CodeDom.Compiler.GeneratedCodeAttribute(
            "System.Data.Design.TypedDataSetGenerator", "4.0.0.0")]
        public void SetSupplierIDNull() {
            this[this.tableProduct.SupplierIDColumn] = global::System.Convert.DBNull;
        }
    }
```

code download product.cs

The following code uses this class's output from the XSD tool to retrieve data from the `Products` table and display that data to the console:

```
using System;
using System.Data;
using System.Data.SqlClient;

public class XSD_DataSet
{
    public static void Main()
    {
        string source = "server=(local);" +
                        " integrated security=SSPI;" +
                        "database=northwind";
        string select = "SELECT * FROM Products";
        SqlConnection conn = new SqlConnection(source);
```

```
            SqlDataAdapter da = new SqlDataAdapter(select, conn);
            Products ds = new Products();
            da.Fill(ds, "Product");
            foreach(Products.ProductRow row in ds.Product )
            Console.WriteLine("'{0}' from {1}",
                                row.ProductID,
                                row.ProductName);
        }
    }
```

code download XSDDataSet.cs

The output of the XSD file contains a class derived from `DataSet`, `Products`, which is created and then filled by the use of the data adapter. The `foreach` statement uses the strongly typed `ProductRow` and also the `Product` property, which returns the `Product` data table.

To compile this example, issue the following commands:

```
xsd product.xsd /d
```

and

```
csc /recurse:*.cs
```

The first generates the `Products.cs` file from the `Products.XSD` schema, and then the `csc` command uses the `/recurse:*.cs` parameter to go through all files with the extension `.cs` and add these to the resulting assembly.

POPULATING A DATASET

After you have defined the schema of your data set, replete with `DataTable`, `DataColumn`, and `Constraint` classes, and whatever else is necessary, you need to be able to populate the `DataSet` class with some information. You have two main ways to read data from an external source and insert it into the `DataSet` class:

➤ Use a data adapter.

➤ Read XML into the `DataSet` class.

Populating a DataSet Class with a Data Adapter

The section on data rows briefly introduced the `SqlDataAdapter` class, as shown in the following code:

```
string select = "SELECT ContactName,CompanyName FROM Customers";
SqlConnection conn = new SqlConnection(source);
SqlDataAdapter da = new SqlDataAdapter(select, conn);
DataSet ds = new DataSet();
da.Fill(ds, "Customers");
```

The bold line shows the `SqlDataAdapter` class in use; the other data adapter classes are again virtually identical in functionality to the `Sql` equivalent.

To retrieve data into a `DataSet`, it is necessary to have some form of command that is executed to select that data. The command in question could be a SQL `SELECT` statement, a call to a stored procedure, or for the OLE DB provider, a `TableDirect` command. The preceding example uses one of the constructors available on `SqlDataAdapter` that converts the passed SQL `SELECT` statement into a `SqlCommand`, and issues this when the `Fill()` method is called on the adapter.

In the stored procedures example earlier in this chapter, the `INSERT`, `UPDATE`, and `DELETE` procedures were defined, but the `SELECT` procedure was not. That gap is filled in the next section, which also shows how to call a stored procedure from a `SqlDataAdapter` class to populate data in a `DataSet` class.

Using a Stored Procedure in a Data Adapter

The first step in this example is to define the stored procedure. The stored procedure to SELECT data is:

```
CREATE PROCEDURE RegionSelect AS
  SET NOCOUNT OFF
  SELECT * FROM Region
GO
```

code download StoredProcs.sql

You can type this stored procedure directly into the SQL Server Query Analyzer, or you can run the StoredProc.sql file that is provided for use by this example.

Next, you need to define the SqlCommand that executes this stored procedure. Again, the code is very simple, and most of it was already presented in the earlier section on issuing commands:

```
private static SqlCommand GenerateSelectCommand(SqlConnection conn)
{
    SqlCommand  aCommand = new SqlCommand("RegionSelect", conn);
    aCommand.CommandType = CommandType.StoredProcedure;
    aCommand.UpdatedRowSource = UpdateRowSource.None;
    return aCommand;
}
```

code download DataAdapter.cs

This method generates the SqlCommand that calls the RegionSelect procedure when executed. All that remains is to hook up this command to a SqlDataAdapter class and call the Fill() method:

```
DataSet ds = new DataSet();
// Create a data adapter to fill the DataSet
SqlDataAdapter da = new SqlDataAdapter();
// Set the data adapter's select command
da.SelectCommand = GenerateSelectCommand (conn);
da.Fill(ds, "Region");
```

code download DataAdapter.cs

Here, the SqlDataAdapter class is created, and the generated SqlCommand is then assigned to the SelectCommand property of the data adapter. Subsequently, Fill() is called, which will execute the stored procedure and insert all rows returned into the Region DataTable (which in this instance is generated by the runtime).

There is more to a data adapter than just selecting data by issuing a command, as discussed shortly in the "Persisting DataSet Changes" section.

Populating a DataSet from XML

In addition to generating the schema for a given DataSet, associated tables, and so on, a DataSet class can read and write data in native XML, such as a file on disk, a stream, or a text reader.

To load XML into a DataSet class, simply call one of the ReadXML() methods to read data from a disk file, as shown in this example:

```
DataSet ds = new DataSet();
ds.ReadXml(".\\MyData.xml");
```

The ReadXml() method attempts to load any inline schema information from the input XML. If a schema is found, the method uses this schema in the validation of any data loaded from that file. If no inline schema is found, the DataSet will extend its internal structure as data is loaded. This is similar to the behavior of Fill() in the previous example, which retrieves the data and constructs a DataTable based on the data selected.

PERSISTING DATASET CHANGES

After editing data within a `DataSet`, it is usually necessary to persist these changes. The most common example is selecting data from a database, displaying it to the user, and returning those updates to the database.

In a less "connected" application, changes might be persisted to an XML file, transported to a middle-tier application server, and then processed to update several data sources.

A `DataSet` class can be used for either of these examples; what's more, it's easy to do.

Updating with Data Adapters

In addition to the `SelectCommand` that a `SqlDataAdapter` most likely includes, you can also define an `InsertCommand`, `UpdateCommand`, and `DeleteCommand`. As the names imply, these objects are instances of the command object appropriate for your provider such as `SqlCommand` and `OleDbCommand`.

With this level of flexibility, you are free to tune the application by judicious use of stored procedures for frequently used commands (say `SELECT` and `INSERT`), and use straight SQL for less commonly used commands such as `DELETE`. In general, it is recommended to provide stored procedures for all database interaction because it is faster and easier to tune.

This example uses the stored procedure code from the "Calling Stored Procedures" section for inserting, updating, and deleting `Region` records, coupled with the `RegionSelect` procedure written previously, which produces an example that uses each of these commands to retrieve and update data in a `DataSet` class. The main body of code is shown in the following section.

Inserting a New Row

You can add a new row to a `DataTable` in two ways. The first way is to call the `NewRow()` method, which returns a blank row that you then populate and add to the `Rows` collection, as follows:

```
DataRow r = ds.Tables["Region"].NewRow();
r["RegionID"]=999;
r["RegionDescription"]="North West";
ds.Tables["Region"].Rows.Add(r);
```

The second way to add a new row would be to pass an array of data to the `Rows.Add()` method as shown in the following code:

```
DataRow r = ds.Tables["Region"].Rows.Add
            (new object [] { 999, "North West" });
```

Each new row within the `DataTable` will have its `RowState` set to `Added`. The example dumps out the records before each change is made to the database, so after adding a row (either way) to the `DataTable`, the rows will look something like the following. Note that the right-hand column shows the row's state:

```
New row pending inserting into database
  1   Eastern                                    Unchanged
  2   Western                                    Unchanged
  3   Northern                                   Unchanged
  4   Southern                                   Unchanged
  999 North West                                 Added
```

To update the database from the `DataAdapter`, call one of the `Update()` methods as shown here:

```
da.Update(ds, "Region");
```

For the new row within the `DataTable`, this executes the stored procedure (in this instance `RegionInsert`). The example then dumps the state of the data, so you can see that changes have been made to the database.

```
New row updated and new RegionID assigned by database
    1    Eastern                                        Unchanged
    2    Western                                        Unchanged
    3    Northern                                       Unchanged
    4    Southern                                       Unchanged
    5    North West                                     Unchanged
```

Look at the last row in the DataTable. The RegionID had been set in code to 999, but after executing the RegionInsert stored procedure, the value has been changed to 5. This is intentional — the database will often generate primary keys for you, and the updated data in the DataTable appears because the SqlCommand definition within the source code has the UpdatedRowSource property set to UpdateRowSource.OutputParameters:

```
SqlCommand aCommand = new SqlCommand("RegionInsert", conn);

aCommand.CommandType = CommandType.StoredProcedure;
aCommand.Parameters.Add(new SqlParameter("@RegionDescription",
                         SqlDbType.NChar,
                         50,
                         "RegionDescription"));
aCommand.Parameters.Add(new SqlParameter("@RegionID",
                         SqlDbType.Int,
                         0,
                         ParameterDirection.Output,
                         false,
                         0,
                         0,
                         "RegionID",   // Defines the SOURCE column
                         DataRowVersion.Default,
                         null));
aCommand.UpdatedRowSource = UpdateRowSource.OutputParameters;
```

code download DataAdapter2.cs

What this means is that whenever a data adapter issues this command, the output parameters should be mapped to the source of the row, which in this instance was a row in a DataTable. The flag states what data should be updated — the stored procedure has an output parameter that is mapped to the DataRow. The column it applies to is RegionID because this is defined within the command definition.

The following table shows the values for UpdateRowSource.

UPDATEROWSOURCE VALUE	DESCRIPTION
Both	A stored procedure might return output parameters and also a complete database record. Both of these data sources are used to update the source row.
FirstReturnedRecord	This implies that the command returns a single record, and that the contents of that record should be merged into the original source DataRow. This is useful where a given table has a number of default (or computed) columns because after an INSERT statement these need to be synchronized with the DataRow on the client. An example might be 'INSERT (columns) INTO (table) WITH (primarykey)', then 'SELECT (columns) FROM (table) WHERE (primarykey)'. The returned record would then be merged into the original row.
None	All data returned from the command is discarded.
OutputParameters	Any output parameters from the command are mapped onto the appropriate column(s) in the DataRow.

Updating an Existing Row

Updating an existing row within the `DataTable` is just a case of using the `DataRow` class's indexer with either a column name or column number, as shown in the following code:

```
r["RegionDescription"]="North West England";
r[1] = "North West England";
```

Both of these statements are equivalent (in this example):

```
Changed RegionID 5 description
   1   Eastern                                     Unchanged
   2   Western                                     Unchanged
   3   Northern                                    Unchanged
   4   Southern                                    Unchanged
   5   North West England                          Modified
```

Prior to updating the database, the row updated has its state set to `Modified` as shown.

Deleting a Row

Deleting a row is a matter of calling the `Delete()` method:

```
r.Delete();
```

A deleted row has its row state set to `Deleted`, but you cannot read columns from the deleted `DataRow` because they are no longer valid. When the adaptor's `Update()` method is called, all deleted rows will use the `DeleteCommand`, which in this instance executes the `RegionDelete` stored procedure.

Writing XML Output

As you have seen already, the `DataSet` class has great support for defining its schema in XML, and just as you can read data from an XML document, you can also write data to an XML document.

The `DataSet.WriteXml()` method enables you to output various parts of the data stored within the `DataSet`. You can elect to output just the data, or the data and the schema. The following code shows an example of both for the `Region` example shown earlier:

```
ds.WriteXml(".\\WithoutSchema.xml");
ds.WriteXml(".\\WithSchema.xml", XmlWriteMode.WriteSchema);
```

The first file, `WithoutSchema.xml`, is shown here:

```
<?xml version="1.0" standalone="yes"?>
<NewDataSet>
    <Region>
        <RegionID>1</RegionID>
        <RegionDescription>Eastern                   </RegionDescription>
    </Region>
    <Region>
        <RegionID>2</RegionID>
        <RegionDescription>Western                   </RegionDescription>
    </Region>
    <Region>
        <RegionID>3</RegionID>
        <RegionDescription>Northern                  </RegionDescription>
    </Region>
    <Region>
        <RegionID>4</RegionID>
        <RegionDescription>Southern                  </RegionDescription>
    </Region>
</NewDataSet>
```

code download WithoutSchema.xml

The closing tag on `RegionDescription` is over to the right of the page because the database column is defined as `NCHAR(50)`, which is a 50-character string padded with spaces.

The output produced in the `WithSchema.xml` file includes the XML schema for the `DataSet` as well as the data itself:

```xml
<?xml version="1.0" standalone="yes"?>
<NewDataSet>
    <xs:schema id="NewDataSet" xmlns=""
                xmlns:xs="http://www.w3.org/2001/XMLSchema"
                xmlns:msdata="urn:schemas-microsoft-com:xml-msdata">
        <xs:element name="NewDataSet" msdata:IsDataSet="true">
            <xs:complexType>
                <xs:choice maxOccurs="unbounded">
                    <xs:element name="Region">
                        <xs:complexType>
                            <xs:sequence>
                                <xs:element name="RegionID"
                                            msdata:AutoIncrement="true"
                                            msdata:AutoIncrementSeed="1"
                                            type="xs:int" />
                                <xs:element name="RegionDescription"
                                            type="xs:string" />
                            </xs:sequence>
                        </xs:complexType>
                    </xs:element>
                </xs:choice>
            </xs:complexType>
        </xs:element>
    </xs:schema>
    <Region>
        <RegionID>1</RegionID>
        <RegionDescription>Eastern                          </RegionDescription>
    </Region>
    <Region>
        <RegionID>2</RegionID>
        <RegionDescription>Western                          </RegionDescription>
    </Region>
    <Region>
        <RegionID>3</RegionID>
        <RegionDescription>Northern                         </RegionDescription>
    </Region>
    <Region>
        <RegionID>4</RegionID>
        <RegionDescription>Southern                         </RegionDescription>
    </Region>
</NewDataSet>
```

code download WithoutSchema.xml

Note the use in this file of the `msdata` schema, which defines extra attributes for columns within a `DataSet`, such as `AutoIncrement` and `AutoIncrementSeed` — these attributes correspond directly to the properties definable on a `DataColumn` class.

WORKING WITH ADO.NET

This section addresses some common scenarios when developing data access applications with ADO.NET.

Tiered Development

Producing an application that interacts with data is often done by splitting up the application into tiers. A common model is to have an application tier (the front end), a data services tier, and the database itself.

One of the difficulties with this model is deciding what data to transport between your tiers as well as figuring out the format in which the data should be transported. With ADO.NET, you will be pleased to learn that these wrinkles have been ironed out, and support for this style of architecture is part of the design.

One of the things that is much better in ADO.NET than OLE DB is the support for copying an entire record set. In .NET, it is easy to copy a `DataSet`:

```
DataSet source = {some dataset};
DataSet dest = source.Copy();
```

This creates an exact copy of the source `DataSet` — each `DataTable`, `DataColumn`, `DataRow`, and `Relation` will be copied, and all data will be in exactly the same state as it was in the source. If all you want to copy is the schema of the `DataSet`, you can use the following code:

```
DataSet source = {some dataset};
DataSet dest = source.Clone();
```

This again copies all tables, relations, and so on. However, each copied `DataTable` will be empty. This process really could not be more straightforward.

A common requirement when writing a tiered system, whether based on a Windows client application or the Web, is to be able to ship as little data as possible between tiers. This reduces the amount of resources consumed.

To cope with this requirement, the `DataSet` class has the `GetChanges()` method. This simple method performs a huge amount of work, and returns a `DataSet` with only the changed rows from the source data set. This is ideal for passing data between tiers because only a minimal set of data has to be passed along.

The following example shows how to generate a "changes" `DataSet`:

```
DataSet source = {some dataset};
DataSet dest = source.GetChanges();
```

Again, this is trivial. Under the hood, things are a little more interesting. There are two overloads of the `GetChanges()` method. One overload takes a value of the `DataRowState` enumeration, and returns only rows that correspond to that state (or states). `GetChanges()` simply calls `GetChanges(Deleted | Modified | Added)`, and first checks to ensure that there are some changes by calling `HasChanges()`. If no changes have been made, `null` is returned to the caller immediately.

The next operation is to clone the current `DataSet`. Once this is done, the new `DataSet` is set up to ignore constraint violations (`EnforceConstraints = false`), and then each changed row for every table is copied into the new `DataSet`.

When you have a `DataSet` that just contains changes, you can then move these off to the data services tier for processing. After the data has been updated in the database, the "changes" `DataSet` can be returned to the caller (for example, there might be some output parameters from the stored procedures that have updated values in the columns). These changes can then be merged into the original `DataSet` using the `Merge()` method. Figure 30-9 depicts this sequence of operations.

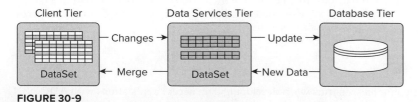

FIGURE 30-9

Key Generation with SQL Server

The `RegionInsert` stored procedure presented earlier in this chapter is one example of generating a primary key value on insertion into the database. The method for generating the key in this particular example is fairly crude and wouldn't scale well, so for a real application you should use some other strategy for generating keys.

Your first instinct might be to define an identity column and return the `@@IDENTITY` value from the stored procedure. The following stored procedure shows how this might be defined for the `Categories` table in the Northwind example database. Type this stored procedure into the SQL Query Analyzer or run the `StoredProcs.sql` file that is part of the code download:

Available for
download on
Wrox.com

```
CREATE PROCEDURE CategoryInsert(@CategoryName NVARCHAR(15),
                                @Description NTEXT,
                                @CategoryID INTEGER OUTPUT) AS
    SET NOCOUNT OFF
    INSERT INTO Categories (CategoryName, Description)
        VALUES(@CategoryName, @Description)
    SELECT @CategoryID = @@IDENTITY
GO
```

code download StoredProcs.sql

This inserts a new row into the `Category` table and returns the generated primary key to the caller (the value of the `CategoryID` column). You can test the procedure by typing the following in the SQL Query Analyzer:

```
DECLARE @CatID int;
EXECUTE CategoryInsert 'Pasties', 'Heaven Sent Food', @CatID OUTPUT;
PRINT @CatID;
```

When executed as a batch of commands, this inserts a new row into the `Categories` table and returns the identity of the new record, which is then displayed to the user.

Suppose that some months down the line, someone decides to add a simple audit trail, which will record all insertions and modifications made to the category name. In that case, you define a table similar to the one shown in Figure 30-10, which will record the old and new value of the category.

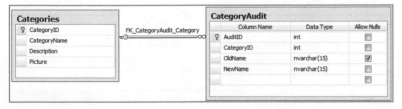

FIGURE 30-10

The script for this table is included in the `StoredProcs.sql` file. The `AuditID` column is defined as an `IDENTITY` column. You then construct a couple of database triggers that will record changes to the `CategoryName` field:

Available for
download on
Wrox.com

```
CREATE TRIGGER CategoryInsertTrigger
    ON Categories
    AFTER UPDATE
AS
    INSERT INTO CategoryAudit(CategoryID, OldName, NewName )
        SELECT old.CategoryID, old.CategoryName, new.CategoryName
        FROM Deleted AS old,
```

```
                 Categories AS new
        WHERE old.CategoryID = new.CategoryID;
  GO
```

code download StoredProcs.sql

If you are used to Oracle stored procedures, SQL Server doesn't exactly have the concept of OLD and NEW rows; instead, for an insert trigger there is an in-memory table called Inserted, and for deletes and updates the old rows are available within the Deleted table.

This trigger retrieves the CategoryID of the record(s) affected and stores this together with the old and new value of the CategoryName column.

Now, when you call your original stored procedure to insert a new CategoryID, you receive an identity value; however, this is no longer the identity value from the row inserted into the Categories table — it is now the new value generated for the row in the CategoryAudit table. Ouch!

To view the problem first-hand, open a copy of SQL Server Enterprise Manager, and view the contents of the Categories table (see Figure 30-11).

CategoryID	CategoryName	Description	Picture
1	Beverages	Soft drinks, coffees, teas, beers, and ales	<Binary data>
2	Condiments	Sweet and savory sauces, relishes, spreads, and seasonings	<Binary data>
3	Confections	Desserts, candies, and sweet breads	<Binary data>
4	Dairy Products	Cheeses	<Binary data>
5	Grains/Cereals	Breads, crackers, pasta, and cereal	<Binary data>
6	Meat/Poultry	Prepared meats	<Binary data>
7	Produce	Dried fruit and bean curd	<Binary data>
8	Seafood	Seaweed and fish	<Binary data>
NULL	NULL	NULL	NULL

FIGURE 30-11

This lists all the categories in the Northwind database.

The next identity value for the Categories table should be 9, so a new row can be inserted by executing the following code, to see what ID is returned:

```
DECLARE @CatID int;
EXECUTE CategoryInsert 'Pastries', 'Heaven Sent Food', @CatID OUTPUT;
PRINT @CatID;
```

The output value of this on a test PC was 1. If you look at the CategoryAudit table shown in Figure 30-12, you will find that this is the identity of the newly inserted audit record, not the identity of the category record created.

The problem lies in the way that @@IDENTITY actually works. It returns the LAST identity value created by your session, so as shown in Figure 30-12, it isn't completely reliable.

Results: Query(v...TA\NORTHWIND.MDF) ×

AuditID	CategoryID	OldName	NewName
1	9	NULL	Pastries

FIGURE 30-12

Two other identity functions can be used instead of @@IDENTITY, but neither is free from possible problems. The first, SCOPE_IDENTITY(), returns the last identity value created within the current *scope*. SQL Server defines scope as a stored procedure, trigger, or function. This may work most of the time, but if for some reason someone adds another INSERT statement to the stored procedure, you can receive this value rather than the one you expected.

The other identity function, IDENT_CURRENT(), returns the last identity value generated for a given table in any scope. For example, if two users were accessing SQL Server at exactly the same time, it might be possible to receive the other user's generated identity value.

As you might imagine, tracking down a problem of this nature is not easy. The moral of the story is to beware when using IDENTITY columns in SQL Server.

Naming Conventions

The following tips and conventions are not directly .NET-related. However, they are worth sharing and following, especially when naming constraints. Feel free to skip this section if you already have your own views on this subject.

Conventions for Database Tables

➤ **Always use singular names** — For example, `Product` rather than `Products`. This one is largely due to having to explain a database schema to customers; it is much better grammatically to say, "The `Product` table contains products" than "The `Products` table contains products." Check out the Northwind database to see an example of how not to do this.

➤ **Adopt some form of naming convention for the fields that go into a table** — Ours is `<Table>_Id` for the primary key of a table (assuming that the primary key is a single column), Name for the field considered to be the user-friendly name of the record, and Description for any textual information about the record itself. Having a good table convention means that you can look at virtually any table in the database and instinctively know what the fields are used for.

Conventions for Database Columns

➤ Use singular rather than plural names.

➤ Any columns that link to another table should be given the same name as the primary key of that table. For example, a link to the `Product` table would be `Product_Id`, and one to the `Sample` table `Sample_Id`. This is not always possible, especially if one table has multiple references to another. In that case, use your own judgment.

➤ Date fields should have a suffix of `_On`, as in `Modified_On` and `Created_On`. That makes it is easy to read some SQL output and infer what a column means just by its name.

➤ Fields that record activities from the user should be suffixed with `_By`, as in `Modified_By` and `Created_By`. Again, this aids comprehension.

Conventions for Constraints

➤ If possible, include in the name of the constraint the table and column name, as in `CK_<Table>_<Field>`. For example, use `CK_Person_Sex` for a check constraint on the `Sex` column of the `Person` table. A foreign key example would be `FK_Product_Supplier_Id`, for the foreign key relationship between product and supplier.

➤ Show the type of constraint with a prefix, such as `CK` for a check constraint or `FK` for a foreign key constraint. Feel free to be more specific, as in `CK_Person_Age_GT0` for a constraint on the age column indicating that the age should be greater than zero.

➤ If you have to trim the length of the constraint, do this on the table name part rather than the column name. When you get a constraint violation, it is usually easy to infer which table was in error, but sometimes not so easy to check which column caused the problem. Oracle has a 30-character limit on names, which is easy to surpass.

Stored Procedures

Just like the obsession many have developed over the past few years with putting a `C` in front of each and every class they declare (you know you have!), many SQL Server developers feel compelled to prefix every stored procedure with `sp_` or something similar. This is not a good idea.

SQL Server uses the `sp_` prefix for all (well, most) system stored procedures. So, you risk confusing your users into thinking that `sp_widget` is something that comes as standard with SQL Server. In addition, when looking for a stored procedure, SQL Server treats procedures with the `sp_` prefix differently from those without it.

If you use this prefix and do not qualify the database/owner of the stored procedure, SQL Server will look in the current scope and then jump into the master database and look up the stored procedure there. Without the sp_ prefix, your users would get an error a little earlier. What's worse, and also possible to do, is to create a local stored procedure (one within your database) that has the same name and parameters as a system stored procedure. Avoid this at all costs — if in doubt, do not prefix.

When calling stored procedures, always prefix them with the owner of the procedure, as in dbo. selectWidgets. This is slightly faster than not using the prefix, because SQL Server has less work to do to find the stored procedure. Something like this is not likely to have a huge impact on the execution speed of your application, but it is a tuning trick that is essentially available for free.

Above all, when naming entities, whether within the database or within code, *be consistent*.

SUMMARY

The subject of data access is a large one, especially in .NET, because there is an abundance of material to cover. This chapter has provided an outline of the main classes in the ADO.NET namespaces and has shown how to use the classes when manipulating data from a data source.

First, the Connection object was explored, using both SqlConnection (SQL Server–specific) and OleDbConnection (for any OLE DB data sources). The programming model for these two classes is so similar that one can normally be substituted for the other, and the code will continue to run.

This chapter also discussed how to use connections properly, so that these scarce resources could be closed as early as possible. All of the connection classes implement the IDisposable interface, called when the object is placed within a using clause. If there is one thing you should take away from this chapter, it is the importance of closing database connections as early as possible.

In addition, this chapter discussed database commands using examples that executed with no returned data, and examples that that called stored procedures with input and output parameters. It described various execute methods, including the ExecuteXmlReader() method available only on the SQL Server provider. This vastly simplifies the selection and manipulation of XML-based data.

The generic classes within the System.Data namespace were all described in detail, from the DataSet class through DataTable, DataColumn, DataRow, and on to relationships and constraints. The DataSet class is an excellent container of data, and various methods make it ideal for cross-tier data flow. The data within a DataSet is represented in XML for transport, and in addition, methods are available that pass a minimal amount of data between tiers. The ability to have many tables of data within a single DataSet can greatly increase its usability.

Having the schema stored within a DataSet is one thing, but .NET also includes the data adapter that, along with various Command objects, can be used to select data for a DataSet and subsequently update data in the data store. One of the beneficial aspects of a data adapter is that a distinct command can be defined for each of the four actions: SELECT, INSERT, UPDATE, and DELETE. The system can create a default set of commands based on database schema information and a SELECT statement. For the best performance, however, a set of stored procedures can be used, with the DataAdapter's commands defined appropriately to pass only the necessary information to these stored procedures.

The XSD tool (XSD.EXE) was described, using an example that showed how to work with classes based on an XML schema from within .NET. The classes produced are ready to be used within an application, and their automatic generation can save many hours of laborious typing.

Finally, this chapter discussed some best practices and naming conventions for database development.

Further information about accessing SQL Server databases is provided in Chapter 34, ".NET Programming with SQL Server."

31

ADO.NET Entity Framework

WHAT'S IN THIS CHAPTER?

➤ The ADO.NET Entity Framework

➤ Mapping between database tables and entity classes

➤ Creating entity classes and their features

➤ Object contexts

➤ Relationships

➤ Object queries

➤ Updates

➤ LINQ to Entities

The ADO.NET Entity Framework is an object-relational mapping framework that offers an abstraction of ADO.NET to get an object model based on the referential databases. This chapter gives information on the mappings between the database and the entity classes using the Conceptual Schema Definition Language (CSDL), Storage Schema Definition Language (SSDL), and the Mapping Schema Language (MSL). Different relationships between entities are covered, such as one Table-per-Hierarchy of objects, one Table-per-Type, and n-to-n relationships.

This chapter also describes different ways to access the database from the code directly with the Entity Client, using Entity SQL or helper methods that create Entity SQL, and using LINQ to Entities. Object tracking and how the data context holds change information for updating data is also shown.

 This chapter uses the Books, Formula1, and Northwind databases. You can download the Northwind database from msdn.microsoft.com; *the Books and Formula1 databases are included with the download of the code samples at* http://www.wrox.com.

OVERVIEW OF THE ADO.NET ENTITY FRAMEWORK

The ADO.NET Entity Framework provides a mapping from the relational database schema to objects. Relational databases and object-oriented languages define associations differently. For example, the Microsoft sample database Northwind contains the Customers and Orders tables. To access all the Orders rows for a customer, you need to do a SQL join statement. With object-oriented languages, it is more common to define a `Customer` and an `Order` class and access the orders of a customer by using an `Orders` property from the `Customer` class.

For object-relational mapping since .NET 1.0, it was possible to use the `DataSet` class and typed datasets. Datasets are very similar to the structure of a database containing `DataTable`, `DataRow`, `DataColumn`, and `DataRelation` classes instead of offering object-support. The ADO.NET Entity Framework gives support to directly define entity classes that are completely independent of a database structure and map them to tables and associations of the database. Using objects with the application, the application is shielded from changes in the database.

The ADO.NET Entity Framework makes use of Entity SQL to define entity-based queries to the store. LINQ to Entities makes it possible to use the LINQ syntax to query data. An object context keeps knowledge about entities that are changed, to have information when the entities should be written back to the store.

The namespaces that contain classes from the ADO.NET Entity Framework are listed in the following table.

NAMESPACE	DESCRIPTION
`System.Data`	This is a main namespace for ADO.NET. With the ADO.NET Entity Framework. This namespace contains exception classes related to entities — for example `MappingException` and `QueryException`.
`System.Data.Common`	This namespace contains classes shared by .NET data providers. The class `DbProviderServices` is an abstract base class that must be implemented by an ADO.NET Entity Framework provider.
`System.Data.Common.CommandTrees`	This namespace contains classes to build an expression tree.
`System.Data.Entity.Design`	This namespace contains classes used by the designer to create Entity Data Model (EDM) files.
`System.Data.EntityClient`	This namespace specifies classes for the .NET Framework Data Provider to access the Entity Framework. `EntityConnection`, `EntityCommand`, and `EntityDataReader` can be used to access the Entity Framework.
`System.Data.Objects`	This namespace contains classes to query and update databases. The class `ObjectContext` encapsulates the connection to the database and serves as a gateway for create, read, update, and delete methods. The class `ObjectQuery` represents a query against the store. `CompiledQuery` is a cached query.
`System.Data.Objects.DataClasses`	This namespace contains classes and interfaces required for entities.

ENTITY FRAMEWORK MAPPING

The ADO.NET Entity Framework offers several layers to map database tables to objects. You can start with a database schema and use a Visual Studio item template to create the complete mapping. You can also start designing entity classes with the designer and map it to the database where the tables and associations between the tables can have a very different structure.

The layers that need to be defined are as follows:

➤ *Logical* — This layer defines the relational data.

➤ *Conceptual* — This layer defines the .NET classes.

➤ *Mapping* — This layer defines the mapping from .NET classes to relational tables and associations.

Let's start with a simple database schema, as shown in Figure 31-1, with the tables Books and Authors, and an association table BookAuthors that maps the authors to books.

Logical Layer

The logical layer is defined by the Store Schema Definition Language (SSDL) and describes the structure of the database tables and their relations.

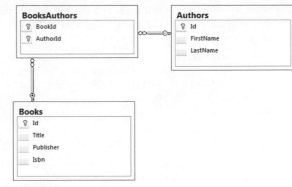

The following code uses SSDL to describe the three tables: Books, Authors, and BooksAuthors. The EntityContainer element describes all the tables with EntitySet elements, and associations with AssociationSet elements. The parts of a table

FIGURE 31-1

are defined with the EntityType element. With EntityType Books you can see the columns Id, Title, Publisher, and ISBN defined by the Property element. The Property element contains XML attributes to define the data type. The Key element defines the key of the table:

```xml
<edmx:StorageModels>
    <Schema Namespace="BooksModel.Store" Alias="Self" Provider="System.Data.SqlClient"
            ProviderManifestToken="2008"
            xmlns:store=
                "http://schemas.microsoft.com/ado/2007/12/edm/EntityStoreSchemaGenerator"
            xmlns="http://schemas.microsoft.com/ado/2009/02/edm/ssdl">
        <EntityContainer Name="BooksModelStoreContainer">
            <EntitySet Name="Authors" EntityType="BooksModel.Store.Authors" store:Type="Tables"
                    Schema="dbo" />
            <EntitySet Name="Books" EntityType="BooksModel.Store.Books" store:Type="Tables"
                    Schema="dbo" />
            <EntitySet Name="BooksAuthors" EntityType="BooksModel.Store.BooksAuthors"
                    store:Type="Tables" Schema="dbo" />
            <AssociationSet Name="FK_BooksAuthors_Authors"
                        Association="BooksModel.Store.FK_BooksAuthors_Authors">
                <End Role="Authors" EntitySet="Authors" />
                <End Role="BooksAuthors" EntitySet="BooksAuthors" />
            </AssociationSet>
            <AssociationSet Name="FK_BooksAuthors_Books"
                        Association="BooksModel.Store.FK_BooksAuthors_Books">
                <End Role="Books" EntitySet="Books" />
                <End Role="BooksAuthors" EntitySet="BooksAuthors" />
            </AssociationSet>
        </EntityContainer>
        <EntityType Name="Authors">
            <Key>
                <PropertyRef Name="Id" />
            </Key>
            <Property Name="Id" Type="int" Nullable="false" StoreGeneratedPattern="Identity" />
            <Property Name="FirstName" Type="nvarchar" Nullable="false" MaxLength="50" />
            <Property Name="LastName" Type="nvarchar" Nullable="false" MaxLength="50" />
        </EntityType>
        <EntityType Name="Books">
            <Key>
                <PropertyRef Name="Id" />
            </Key>
            <Property Name="Id" Type="int" Nullable="false" StoreGeneratedPattern="Identity" />
            <Property Name="Title" Type="nvarchar" Nullable="false" MaxLength="50" />
```

```
              <Property Name="Publisher" Type="nvarchar" Nullable="false" MaxLength="50" />
              <Property Name="Isbn" Type="nchar" MaxLength="18" />
            </EntityType>
            <EntityType Name="BooksAuthors">
              <Key>
                <PropertyRef Name="BookId" />
                <PropertyRef Name="AuthorId" />
              </Key>
              <Property Name="BookId" Type="int" Nullable="false" />
              <Property Name="AuthorId" Type="int" Nullable="false" />
            </EntityType>
            <Association Name="FK_BooksAuthors_Authors">
              <End Role="Authors" Type="BooksModel.Store.Authors" Multiplicity="1" />
              <End Role="BooksAuthors" Type="BooksModel.Store.BooksAuthors" Multiplicity="*" />
              <ReferentialConstraint>
                <Principal Role="Authors">
                  <PropertyRef Name="Id" />
                </Principal>
                <Dependent Role="BooksAuthors">
                  <PropertyRef Name="AuthorId" />
                </Dependent>
              </ReferentialConstraint>
            </Association>
            <Association Name="FK_BooksAuthors_Books">
              <End Role="Books" Type="BooksModel.Store.Books" Multiplicity="1" />
              <End Role="BooksAuthors" Type="BooksModel.Store.BooksAuthors" Multiplicity="*" />
              <ReferentialConstraint>
                <Principal Role="Books">
                  <PropertyRef Name="Id" />
                </Principal>
                <Dependent Role="BooksAuthors">
                  <PropertyRef Name="BookId" />
                </Dependent>
              </ReferentialConstraint>
            </Association>
          </Schema>
        </edmx:StorageModels>
```

code snippet BooksDemo/BooksModel.edmx

 The file BooksModel.edmx contains SSDL, CSDL, and MSL. You can open this file with an XML editor to see its contents.

Conceptual Layer

The conceptual layer defines .NET classes. This layer is created with the Conceptual Schema Definition Language (CSDL).

Figure 31-2 shows the entities `Author` and `Book` defined with the ADO.NET Entity Data Model Designer.

The following is the CSDL content that defines the entity types `Book` and `Author`. This was created from the Books database:

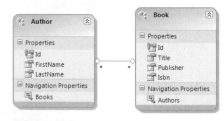

FIGURE 31-2

```
<edmx:ConceptualModels>
    <Schema Namespace="BooksModel" Alias="Self"
          xmlns:annotation="http://schemas.microsoft.com/ado/2009/02/edm/annotation"
          xmlns="http://schemas.microsoft.com/ado/2008/09/edm">
        <EntityContainer Name="BooksEntities" annotation:LazyLoadingEnabled="true">
          <EntitySet Name="Authors" EntityType="BooksModel.Author" />
```

```
        <EntitySet Name="Books" EntityType="BooksModel.Book" />
        <AssociationSet Name="BooksAuthors" Association="BooksModel.BooksAuthors">
          <End Role="Authors" EntitySet="Authors" />
          <End Role="Books" EntitySet="Books" />
        </AssociationSet>
      </EntityContainer>
      <EntityType Name="Author">
        <Key>
          <PropertyRef Name="Id" />
        </Key>
        <Property Name="Id" Type="Int32" Nullable="false"
                annotation:StoreGeneratedPattern="Identity" />
        <Property Name="FirstName" Type="String" Nullable="false" MaxLength="50"
                Unicode="true" FixedLength="false" />
        <Property Name="LastName" Type="String" Nullable="false" MaxLength="50"
                Unicode="true" FixedLength="false" />
        <NavigationProperty Name="Books" Relationship="BooksModel.BooksAuthors"
                        FromRole="Authors" ToRole="Books" />
      </EntityType>
      <EntityType Name="Book">
        <Key>
          <PropertyRef Name="Id" />
        </Key>
        <Property Name="Id" Type="Int32" Nullable="false"
                annotation:StoreGeneratedPattern="Identity" />
        <Property Name="Title" Type="String" Nullable="false" MaxLength="50" Unicode="true"
                FixedLength="false" />
        <Property Name="Publisher" Type="String" Nullable="false" MaxLength="50"
                Unicode="true" FixedLength="false" />
        <Property Name="Isbn" Type="String" MaxLength="18" Unicode="true"
                FixedLength="true" />
        <NavigationProperty Name="Authors" Relationship="BooksModel.BooksAuthors"
                        FromRole="Books" ToRole="Authors" />
      </EntityType>
      <Association Name="BooksAuthors">
        <End Role="Authors" Type="BooksModel.Author" Multiplicity="*" />
        <End Role="Books" Type="BooksModel.Book" Multiplicity="*" />
      </Association>
    </Schema>
  </edmx:ConceptualModels>
```

code snippet BooksDemo/BooksModel.edmx

The entity is defined by an `EntityType` element that contains `Key`, `Property`, and `NavigationProperty` elements to describe the properties of the created class. The `Property` element contains attributes to describe the name and type of the .NET properties of the classes that are generated by the designer. The `Association` element connects the types `Author` and `Book`. `Multiplicity="*"` means that one `Author` can write multiple `Books`, and one `Book` can be written by multiple `Authors`.

Mapping Layer

The mapping layer maps the entity type definition from the CSDL to the SSDL by using the Mapping Specification Language (MSL). The following specification includes a `Mapping` element that contains the `EntityTypeMapping` element to reference the `Book` type of the CSDL and defines the `MappingFragment` to reference the `Authors` table from the SSDL. The `ScalarProperty` maps the property of the .NET class with the `Name` attribute to the column of the database table with the `ColumnName` attribute:

```
<edmx:Mappings>
  <Mapping Space="C-S" xmlns="http://schemas.microsoft.com/ado/2008/09/mapping/cs">
    <EntityContainerMapping StorageEntityContainer="BooksModelStoreContainer"
                    CdmEntityContainer="BooksEntities">
```

```
<EntitySetMapping Name="Authors">
  <EntityTypeMapping TypeName="BooksModel.Author">
    <MappingFragment StoreEntitySet="Authors">
      <ScalarProperty Name="Id" ColumnName="Id" />
      <ScalarProperty Name="FirstName" ColumnName="FirstName" />
      <ScalarProperty Name="LastName" ColumnName="LastName" />
    </MappingFragment>
  </EntityTypeMapping>
</EntitySetMapping>
<EntitySetMapping Name="Books">
  <EntityTypeMapping TypeName="BooksModel.Book">
    <MappingFragment StoreEntitySet="Books">
      <ScalarProperty Name="Id" ColumnName="Id" />
      <ScalarProperty Name="Title" ColumnName="Title" />
      <ScalarProperty Name="Publisher" ColumnName="Publisher" />
      <ScalarProperty Name="Isbn" ColumnName="Isbn" />
    </MappingFragment>
  </EntityTypeMapping>
</EntitySetMapping>
<AssociationSetMapping Name="BooksAuthors" TypeName="BooksModel.BooksAuthors"
                       StoreEntitySet="BooksAuthors">
  <EndProperty Name="Authors">
    <ScalarProperty Name="Id" ColumnName="AuthorId" />
  </EndProperty>
  <EndProperty Name="Books">
    <ScalarProperty Name="Id" ColumnName="BookId" />
  </EndProperty>
</AssociationSetMapping>
      </EntityContainerMapping>
    </Mapping>
  </edmx:Mappings>
```

code snippet BooksDemo/BooksModel.edmx

ENTITY CLIENT

A low-level API to access the Entity Framework is in the namespace `System.Data.SqlClient`. This namespace contains an ADO.NET provider that accesses the database by using an Entity Data Model (EDM). This ADO.NET provider defines classes, as you know from Chapter 30, "Core ADO.NET." These classes derive from the base classes `DbConnection`, `DbCommand`, `DbParameter`, and `DbDataReader`. Here, the classes are known as `EntityConnection`, `EntityCommand`, `EntityParameter`, and `EntityDataReader`.

You can use these classes in the same way that we described in Chapter 30, except that a special connection string is required and Entity SQL is used instead of T-SQL to access the EDM.

The connection to the database is done with the `EntityConnection` that requires an entity connection string. This string is read from the configuration file with help of the `ConfigurationManager` class from the `System.Configuration` namespace. The `CreateCommand` method of the `EntityConnection` class returns an `EntityCommand`. The command text for the `EntityCommand` is assigned with the `CommandText` property and requires an Entity SQL command. `BooksEntities.Books` is made from the `EntityContainer` element in the `BooksEntities` CSDL definition, and the `Books` `EntitySet` gets all books from the Books table. `command.ExecuteReader` returns an `EntityDataReader` that reads row by row:

Available for download on Wrox.com

```
string connectionString = ConfigurationManager.ConnectionStrings["BooksEntities"].
                          ConnectionString;
var connection = new EntityConnection(connectionString);
connection.Open();

EntityCommand command = connection.CreateCommand();
command.CommandText = "[BooksEntities].[Books]";
```

```
EntityDataReader reader = command.ExecuteReader(
    CommandBehavior.CloseConnection | CommandBehavior.SequentialAccess);
while (reader.Read())
{
    Console.WriteLine("{0}, {1}", reader["Title"], reader["Publisher"]);
}
reader.Close();
```

code snippet BooksDemo/Program.cs

The code is done in the same way as in Chapter 30. The only real difference is the connection string and the Entity SQL statements; that's why we look at these now.

Connection String

With the earlier code snippet, the connection string is read from the configuration file. The connection string is required for EDM and is different from the normal ADO.NET connection string because mapping information is required. The mapping is defined with the keyword `metadata`. `metadata` requires three things: a delimited list of mapping files, `Provider` for the invariant provider name to access the data source, and a `Provider connection string` to assign the provider-dependent connection string.

The delimited list of mapping files references the files `BooksModel.csdl`, `BooksModel.ssdl`, and `BooksModel.msl`, which are contained within resources in the assembly as defined with the `res:` prefix. Within Visual Studio, the designer uses just one file, `BooksModel.edmx`, which contains CSDL, SSDL, and MSL. Setting the property Custom Tool to `EntityModelCodeGenerator` creates three files that are contained within resources.

Within the `connectionString` setting you can find the connection string to the database with the connection string setting. This part is the same as a simple ADO.NET connection string and depends on the provider that is set with the `provider` setting:

```
<connectionStrings>
  <add name="BooksEntities"
    connectionString="metadata=res://*/BooksModel.csdl|res://*/BooksModel.ssdl|
      res://*/BooksModel.msl;provider=System.Data.SqlClient;
      provider connection string=&quot;Data Source=(local);Initial Catalog=Books;
        Integrated Security=True;Pooling=False;MultipleActiveResultSets=True&quot;"
    providerName="System.Data.EntityClient" />
</connectionStrings>
```

 With the connection string you can also specify CSDL, SSDL, and MSL files that are not contained as a resource in the assembly. This is useful if you want to change the content of these files after deployment of the project.

Entity SQL

For querying data with the Entity Client, Entity SQL is used. Entity SQL enhances T-SQL by adding types. This syntax doesn't require joins because associations of entities can be used instead.

Here, just a few syntax options are shown that help you start with Entity SQL. In the MSDN documentation you can find the complete reference.

The previous example showed how Entity SQL uses definitions from the CSDL in the `EntityContainer` and `EntitySet` — for example, `BooksEntities.Books` to get all the books from the table Books because the `Books EntitySet` maps to the `Books EntitySet` in the SSDL.

Instead of retrieving all columns, you can also use the `Property` elements of an `EntityType`. This might look very similar to the T-SQL queries used in the previous chapter:

```
command.CommandText = "SELECT Books.Title, Books.Publisher FROM " +
                      "BooksEntities.Books";
```

code snippet BooksDemo/Program.cs

There's no `SELECT *` with Entity SQL. All the columns were retrieved earlier by requesting the `EntitySet`. Using `SELECT VALUE` you can also get all the columns, as is shown in the next snippet. It also uses a filter with WHERE that only gets specific publishers with the query. Pay attention that the `CommandText` specifies the parameter with the `@` character — however, the parameter that is added to the `Parameters` collection does not use the `@` character to write a value to the same parameter:

```
command.CommandText = "SELECT VALUE it FROM BooksEntities.Books AS it WHERE " +
                      "it.Publisher = @Publisher";
command.Parameters.AddWithValue("Publisher", "Wrox Press");
```

ENTITIES

Entity classes that are created with the designer and are created by CSDL typically derive from the base class `EntityObject`, as shown with the `Book` class in the code that follows.

The `Book` class derives from the base class `EntityObject` and defines properties for its data such as `Title` and `Publisher`. The set accessors of these properties fire change information in two different ways. One way is by invoking the methods `ReportPropertyChanging()` and `ReportPropertyChanged()` of the base class `EntityObject`. Invoking these methods uses the `INotifyPropertyChanging` and `INotifyPropertyChanged` interfaces to inform every client that registers with the events about these interfaces.

The other way is by using partial methods such as `OnTitleChanging()` and `OnTitleChanged()` that have no implementation by default, but can be implemented in custom extensions of this class. The `Authors` property uses the `RelationshipManager` class to return the `Books` for an author:

```
[EdmEntityTypeAttribute(NamespaceName="BooksModel", Name="Book")]
[Serializable()]
[DataContractAttribute(IsReference=true)]
public partial class Book : EntityObject
{
    public static Book CreateBook(int id, string title, string publisher)
    {
        Book book = new Book();
        book.Id = id;
        book.Title = title;
        book.Publisher = publisher;
        return book;
    }

    [EdmScalarPropertyAttribute(EntityKeyProperty=true, IsNullable=false)]
    [DataMemberAttribute()]
    public int Id
    {
        get
        {
            return _Id;
        }
        set
        {
            if (_Id != value)
            {
                OnIdChanging(value);
```

```
                    ReportPropertyChanging("Id");
                    _Id = StructuralObject.SetValidValue(value);
                    ReportPropertyChanged("Id");
                    OnIdChanged();
                }
            }
        }
        private int _Id;
        partial void OnIdChanging(int value);
        partial void OnIdChanged();

        [EdmScalarPropertyAttribute(EntityKeyProperty=false, IsNullable=false)]
        [DataMemberAttribute()]
        public string Title
        {
            get
            {
                return _Title;
            }
            set
            {
                OnTitleChanging(value);
                ReportPropertyChanging("Title");
                _Title = StructuralObject.SetValidValue(value, false);
                ReportPropertyChanged("Title");
                OnTitleChanged();
            }
        }
        private string _Title;
        partial void OnTitleChanging(string value);
        partial void OnTitleChanged();

        [EdmScalarPropertyAttribute(EntityKeyProperty=false, IsNullable=false)]
        [DataMemberAttribute()]
        public string Publisher
        {
            get
            {
                return _Publisher;
            }
            set
            {
                OnPublisherChanging(value);
                ReportPropertyChanging("Publisher");
                _Publisher = StructuralObject.SetValidValue(value, false);
                ReportPropertyChanged("Publisher");
                OnPublisherChanged();
            }
        }
        private string _Publisher;
        partial void OnPublisherChanging(string value);
        partial void OnPublisherChanged();

        [EdmScalarPropertyAttribute(EntityKeyProperty=false, IsNullable=true)]
        [DataMemberAttribute()]
        public string Isbn
        {
            get
            {
                return _Isbn;
            }
            set
```

```
            {
                OnIsbnChanging(value);
                ReportPropertyChanging("Isbn");
                _Isbn = StructuralObject.SetValidValue(value, true);
                ReportPropertyChanged("Isbn");
                OnIsbnChanged();
            }
        }
        private string _Isbn;
        partial void OnIsbnChanging(string value);
        partial void OnIsbnChanged();

        [XmlIgnoreAttribute()]
        [SoapIgnoreAttribute()]
        [DataMemberAttribute()]
        [EdmRelationshipNavigationPropertyAttribute("BooksModel", "BooksAuthors", "Authors")]
        public EntityCollection<Author> Authors
        {
            get
            {
                return ((IEntityWithRelationships)this).RelationshipManager.
                        GetRelatedCollection<Author>("BooksModel.BooksAuthors", "Authors");
            }
            set
            {
                if ((value != null))
                {
                    ((IEntityWithRelationships)this).RelationshipManager.
                      InitializeRelatedCollection<Author>("BooksModel.BooksAuthors",
                                                    "Authors", value);
                }
            }
        }
    }
}
```

code snippet BooksDemo/BooksModel.Designer.cs

The classes and interfaces important in regard to entity classes are explained in the following table. With the exception of `INotifyPropertyChanging` and `INotifyPropertyChanged`, the types are defined in the namespace `System.Data.Objects.DataClasses`.

CLASS OR INTERFACE	DESCRIPTION
StructuralObject	StructuralObject is the base class of the classes EntityObject and ComplexObject. This class implements the interfaces INotifyPropertyChanging and INotifyPropertyChanged.
INotifyPropertyChanging INotifyPropertyChanged	These interfaces define the PropertyChanging and PropertyChanged events to allow subscribing to information when the state of the object changes. Different from the other classes and interfaces here, these interfaces are defined in the namespace System.ComponentModel.
EntityObject	This class derives from StructuralObject and implements the interfaces IEntityWithKey, IEntityWithChangeTracker, and IEntityWithRelationships. EntityObject is a commonly used base class for objects mapped to database tables that contain a key and relationships to other objects.
ComplexObject	This class can be used as a base class for entity objects that do not have a key. It derives from StructuralObject but does not implement other interfaces as the EntityObject class does.

CLASS OR INTERFACE	DESCRIPTION
IEntityWithKey	This interface defines an EntityKey property that allows fast access to the object.
IEntityWithChangeTracker	This interface defines the method SetChangeTracker() where a change tracker that implements the interface IChangeTracker can be assigned to get information about state change from the object.
IEntityWithRelationships	This interface defines the read-only property RelationshipManager, which returns a RelationshipManager object that can be used to navigate between objects.

For an entity class, it's not necessary to derive from the base classes EntityObject or ComplexObject. Instead, an entity class can implement the required interfaces.

The Book entity class can easily be accessed by using the object context class BooksEntities. The Books property returns a collection of Book objects that can be iterated:

Available for
download on
Wrox.com

```
using (var data = new BooksEntities())
{
    foreach (var book in data.Books)
    {
        Console.WriteLine("{0}, {1}", book.Title, book.Publisher);
    }
}
```

code snippet BooksDemo/Program.cs

OBJECT CONTEXT

To retrieve data from the database, the ObjectContext class is needed. This class defines the mapping from the entity objects to the database. With core ADO.NET, you can compare this class to the data adapter that fills a DataSet.

The BooksEntities class created by the designer derives from the base class ObjectContext. This class adds constructors to pass a connection string. With the default constructor, the connection string is read from the configuration file. It is also possible to pass an already opened connection to the constructor in the form of an EntityConnection instance. If you pass a connection to the constructor that is not opened, the object context opens and closes the connection; if you pass an opened connection you also need to close it.

The created class defines Books and Authors properties, which return an ObjectSet<TEntity>. ObjectSet<TEntity> that is new with .NET 4 and derives from ObjectQuery<TEntity>:

Available for
download on
Wrox.com

```
public partial class BooksEntities : ObjectContext
{
    public BooksEntities() : base("name=BooksEntities", "BooksEntities")
    {
        this.ContextOptions.LazyLoadingEnabled = true;
        OnContextCreated();
    }

    public BooksEntities(string connectionString) : base(connectionString, "BooksEntities")
    {
        this.ContextOptions.LazyLoadingEnabled = true;
        OnContextCreated();
    }
```

```csharp
public BooksEntities(EntityConnection connection) : base(connection, "BooksEntities")
{
    this.ContextOptions.LazyLoadingEnabled = true;
    OnContextCreated();
}

partial void OnContextCreated();

public ObjectSet<Author> Authors
{
    get
    {
        if ((_Authors == null))
        {
            _Authors = base.CreateObjectSet<Author>("Authors");
        }
        return _Authors;
    }
}
private ObjectSet<Author> _Authors;

public ObjectSet<Book> Books
{
    get
    {
        if ((_Books == null))
        {
            _Books = base.CreateObjectSet<Book>("Books");
        }
        return _Books;
    }
}
private ObjectSet<Book> _Books;
}
```

code snippet BooksDemo/BooksModel.Designer.cs

The `ObjectContext` class provides several services to the caller:

➤ It keeps track of entity objects that are already retrieved. If the object is queried again, it is taken from the object context.

➤ It keeps state information about the entities. You can get information about added, modified, and deleted objects.

➤ You can update the entities from the object context to write the changes to the underlying store.

Methods and properties of the `ObjectContext` class are listed in the following table.

OBJECTCONTEXT METHODS AND PROPERTIES	DESCRIPTION
Connection	Returns a `DbConnection` object that is associated with the object context.
MetadataWorkspace	Returns a `MetadataWorkspace` object that can be used to read the metadata and mapping information.
QueryTimeout	With this property you can get and set the timeout value for the queries of the object context.
ObjectStateManager	This property returns an `ObjectStateManager`. The `ObjectStateManager` keeps track of entity objects retrieved and object changes in the object context.

OBJECTCONTEXT METHODS AND PROPERTIES	DESCRIPTION
CreateQuery()	This method returns an ObjectQuery to get data from the store. The Books and Authors properties shown earlier use this method to return an ObjectQuery.
GetObjectByKey() TryGetObjectByKey()	These methods return the object by the key either from the object state manager or the underlying store. GetObjectByKey() throws an exception of type ObjectNotFoundException if the key does not exist. TryGetObjectByKey() returns false.
AddObject()	This method adds a new entity object to the object context.
DeleteObject()	This method deletes an object from the object context.
Detach()	This method detaches an entity object from the object context, so it is no longer tracked if changes occur.
Attach() AttachTo()	The Attach() method attaches a detached object to the store. Attaching objects back to the object context requires that the entity object implements the interface IEntityWithKey. The AttachTo() method does not have the requirement for a key with the object, but it requires the entity set name where the entity object needs to be attached.
ApplyPropertyChanges()	If an object was detached from the object context, then the detached object is modified, and afterward the changes should be applied to the object within the object context, you can invoke the ApplyPropertyChanges() method to apply the changes. This is useful in a scenario where a detached object was returned from a Web service, changed from a client, and passed to the Web service in a modified way.
Refresh()	The data in the store can change while entity objects are stored inside the object context. To make a refresh from the store, the Refresh() method can be used. With this method you can pass a RefreshMode enumeration value. If the values for the objects are not the same between the store and the object context, passing the value ClientWins changes the data in the store. The value StoreWins changes the data in the object context.
SaveChanges()	Adding, modifying, and deleting objects from the object context does not change the object from the underlying store. Use the SaveChanges() method to persist the changes to the store.
AcceptAllChanges()	This method changes the state of the objects in the context to unmodified. SaveChanges() invokes this method implicitly.

RELATIONSHIPS

The entity types Book and Author are related to each other. A book is written by one or more authors, and an author can write one or more books. Relationships are based on the count of types they relate and the multiplicity. The ADO.NET Entity Framework supports several kinds of relationships, some of which are shown here, including Table-per-Hierarchy (TPH) and Table-per-Type (TPT). Multiplicity can be one-to-one, one-to-many, or many-to-many.

Table per Hierarchy

With TPH, there's one table in the database that corresponds to a hierarchy of entity classes. The database table Payments (see Figure 31-3) contains columns for a hierarchy of entity types. Some of the columns are common to all entities in the hierarchy, such as Id and Amount. The CreditCardNumber column is only used by a credit card payment.

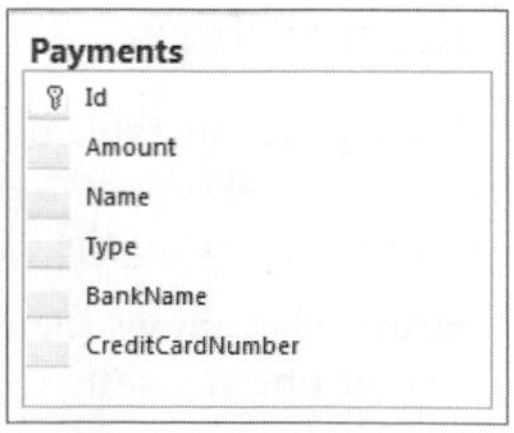

Payments
- Id
- Amount
- Name
- Type
- BankName
- CreditCardNumber

FIGURE 31-3

The entity classes that all map to the same `Payments` table are shown in Figure 31-4. `Payment` is an abstract base class to contain properties common for all types in the hierarchy. Concrete classes that derive from `Payment` are `CreditCardPayment`, `CashPayment`, and `ChequePayment`. `CreditCardPayment` has a `CreditCard` property in addition to the properties of the base class; `ChequePayment` has a `BankName` property.

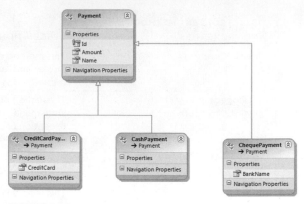

All this mapping can be defined with the designer. The mapping details can be configured with the Mapping Details window as shown in Figure 31-5. The selection of the type of the concrete class is done based on a `Condition` element as defined with the Maps to Payments

FIGURE 31-4

When Type = CREDIT. The type is selected based on the value of the `Type` column. Other options to select the type are also possible; for example, you can verify if a column is not null.

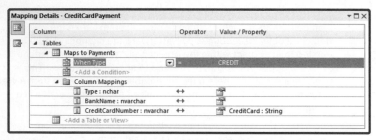

FIGURE 31-5

Now it's possible to iterate the data from the `Payments` table, and different types are returned based on the mapping:

```
using (var data = new PaymentsEntities())
{
    foreach (var p in data.Payments)
    {
        Console.WriteLine("{0}, {1} - {2:C}", p.GetType().Name, p.Name, p.Amount);
    }
}
```

code snippet PaymentsDemo/Program.cs

Running the application returns two `CashPayment` and one `CreditCardPayment` objects from the database:

```
CreditCardPayment, Gladstone - $22.00
CashPayment, Donald - $0.50
CashPayment, Scrooge - $80,000.00
```

Table per Type

With TPT, one table maps to one type. The Northwind database has a schema with the tables `Customers`, `Orders`, and `Order Details`. The `Orders` table has a relation with the `Customers` table with the foreign key `CustomerId`; the `Order Details` relates to the `Orders` table with the foreign key `OrderID`.

Figure 31-6 shows the entity types `Customer`, `Order`, and `Order_Detail`. `Customer` and `Order` have a zero or one-to-many relationship; `Order` to `Order_Detail` has a one-to-many relationship. There is a zero or one-to-many relationship with `Customer` and `Order` because the `CustomerID` with the `Order` table is defined as `Nullable` in the database schema.

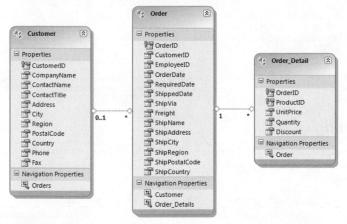

FIGURE 31-6

You access the customers and their orders with two iterations shown here. First the `Customer` objects are accessed, and the value of the `CompanyName` property is written to the console. Then all orders are accessed by using the `Orders` property of the `Customer` class. The related orders are lazy loaded to access the property because with the `ObjectContext` the `ContextOptions.LazyLoadingEnabled` property is set to `true`:

```
using (var data = new NorthwindEntities())
{
    foreach (Customer customer in data.Customers)
    {
        Console.WriteLine("{0}", customer.CompanyName);

        foreach (Order order in customer.Orders)
        {
            Console.WriteLine("\t{0} {1:d}", order.OrderID, order.OrderDate);
        }
    }
}
```

code snippet NorthwindDemo/Program.cs

Behind the scenes, the `RelationshipManager` class is used to access the relationship. The `RelationShipManager` instance can be accessed by casting the entity object to the interface `IEntityWithRelationships` as you can see in the designer-generated property `Orders` from the class `Customer`. This interface is explicitly implemented by the class `EntityObject`. The `RelationshipManager` property returns a `RelationshipManager` that is associated with the entity object at one end. The other end is defined by invoking the method `GetRelatedCollection()`. The first parameter `NorthwindModel. FK_Orders_Customers` is the name of the relationship: the second parameter `Orders` defines the name of the target role:

```
public EntityCollection<Order> Orders
{
    get
    {
        return ((IEntityWithRelationships)this).RelationshipManager.
            GetRelatedCollection<Order>("NorthwindModel.FK_Orders_Customers",
                                        "Orders");
    }
    set
```

```
            {
                if ((value != null))
                {
                    ((IEntityWithRelationships)this).RelationshipManager.
                        InitializeRelatedCollection<Order>(
                            "NorthwindModel.FK_Orders_Customers", "Orders", value);
                }
            }
        }
```

code snippet NorthwindDemo/NorthwindModel.Designer.cs

Lazy, Delayed, and Eager Loading

By default, relationships are lazy loaded on request when the property `LazyLoadingEnabled` from the `ContextOptions` is set to `true`. You have other options as well. Relationships can also be *eager loaded* or *delayed loaded*.

Eager loading means that the relationship is loaded at the same time the parent objects are loaded. The orders are loaded immediately after adding a call to the `Include()` method. It passes the relationship name with `ObjectSet<TEntity>`, as shown with the `Customers` property:

```
foreach (Customer customer in data.Customers.Include("Orders"))
{
    Console.WriteLine("{0}", customer.CompanyName);

    foreach (Order order in customer.Orders)
    {
        Console.WriteLine("\t{0} {1:d}", order.OrderID, order.OrderDate);
    }
}
```

Eager loading has the advantage that if all related objects are needed, then fewer requests to the database are done. Of course, if not all related objects are needed, lazy or delayed loading is preferred.

Delayed loading needs an explicit call to the `Load()` method of the `EntityCollection<T>` class. Using this method, the option `LazyLoadingEnabled` can be set to `false`. With the following code snippet, the orders are loaded with the `Load()` method if they are not loaded with the `IsLoaded` property:

```
if (!customer.Orders.IsLoaded)
    customer.Orders.Load();
```

One overload of the `Load()` method accepts a `MergeOption` enumeration. The possible values are explained in the following table.

MERGEOPTION VALUE	DESCRIPTION
AppendOnly	This is the default value. New entities are appended; existing entities in the object context are not modified.
NoTracking	The `ObjectStateManager` that tracks changes to entity objects is not modified.
OverwriteChanges	The current values of the entity objects are replaced with the values from the store.
PreserveChanges	The original values of the entity objects in the object context are replaced with the values from the store.

OBJECT QUERY

Querying objects is one of the services offered by the ADO.NET Entity Framework. Queries can be done using LINQ to Entities, Entity SQL, and Query Builder methods that create Entity SQL. LINQ to Entities is covered in the last section of this chapter; let's get into the other two options first.

The following sections of this book make use of a Formula1 database where you can see the entities created from the designer in Figure 31-7.

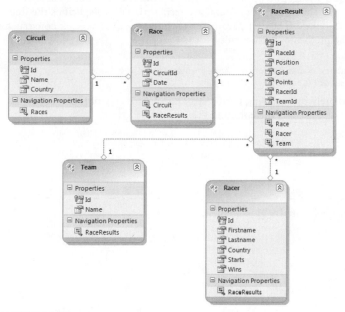

FIGURE 31-7

Queries can be defined with the `ObjectQuery<T>` class, or the class that derives from it: `ObjectSet<T>`. Let's start with a simple query to access all `Racer` entities. The `Racers` property of the generated `Formula1Entities` class returns a `ObjectSet<Racer>`:

```
using (Formula1Entities data = new Formula1Entities(connection))
{
    ObjectSet<Racer> racers = data.Racers;
    Console.WriteLine(racers.CommandText);
    Console.WriteLine(racers.ToTraceString());
}
```

code snippet Formula1Demo/Program.cs

The Entity SQL statement that is returned from the `CommandText` property is shown here:

```
[Formula1Entities].[Racers]
```

And this is the generated `SELECT` statement to retrieve the records from the database that is shown by the `ToTraceString()` method:

```
SELECT
[Extent1].[Id] AS [Id],
[Extent1].[Firstname] AS [Firstname],
[Extent1].[Lastname] AS [Lastname],
[Extent1].[Country] AS [Country],
[Extent1].[Starts] AS [Starts],
[Extent1].[Wins] AS [Wins]
FROM [dbo].[Racers] AS [Extent1]
```

Instead of accessing the `Racers` property from the object context, you can also create a query with the `CreateQuery()` method:

```
ObjectQuery<Racer> racers = data.CreateQuery<Racer>("[Formula1Entities].[Racers]");
```

This is similar to using the `Racers` property.

Now it would be interesting to filter the racers based on a condition. This can be done by using the `Where()` method of the `ObjectQuery<T>` class. `Where()` is one of the Query Builder methods that create Entity SQL. This method requires a predicate as a string, and optional parameters of type `ObjectParameter`. The predicate shown here specifies that only the racers from Brazil are returned. The `it` specifies the item of the result and Country is the column `Country`. The first parameter of the `ObjectParameter` constructor references the `@Country` parameter of the predicate, but doesn't list the `@` sign:

```
string country = "Brazil";
ObjectQuery<Racer> racers = data.Racers.Where("it.Country = @Country",
        new ObjectParameter("Country", country));
```

The magic behind `it` can be seen immediately by accessing the `CommandText` property of the query. With Entity SQL, `SELECT VALUE it` declares `it` to access the columns:

```
SELECT VALUE it
FROM (
[Formula1Entities].[Racers]
) AS it
WHERE
it.Country = @Country
```

The method `ToTraceString()` shows the generated SQL statement:

```
SELECT
[Extent1].[Id] AS [Id],
[Extent1].[Firstname] AS [Firstname],
[Extent1].[Lastname] AS [Lastname],
[Extent1].[Country] AS [Country],
[Extent1].[Starts] AS [Starts],
[Extent1].[Wins] AS [Wins]
FROM [dbo].[Racers] AS [Extent1]
WHERE [Extent1].[Country] = @Country
```

Of course, you can also specify the complete Entity SQL:

```
string country = "Brazil";
ObjectQuery<Racer> racers = data.CreateQuery<Racer>(
    "SELECT VALUE it FROM ([Formula1Entities].[Racers]) AS " +
    "it WHERE it.Country = @Country",
    new ObjectParameter("Country", country));
```

The class `ObjectQuery<T>` offers several Query Builder methods as explained in the following table. Many of these methods are very similar to the LINQ extension methods that you learned about in Chapter 11, "Language Integrated Query." An important difference with the methods here is that instead of parameters of type delegate or `Expression<T>`, the parameter type with `ObjectQuery<T>` is usually of type `string`.

OBJECTQUERY<T> QUERY BUILDER METHODS	DESCRIPTION
`Where()`	This method allows you to filter the results based on a condition.
`Distinct()`	This method creates a query with unique results.
`Except()`	This method returns the result without the items that meet the condition with the `except` filter.
`GroupBy()`	This method creates a new query to group entities based on a specified criteria.
`Include()`	With relations, you saw earlier that related items are delay loaded. It is required to invoke the `Load()` method of the `EntityCollection<T>` class to get related entities into the object context. Instead of using the `Load()` method, you can specify a query with the `Include()` method to eager fetch-related entities.

OBJECTQUERY<T> QUERY BUILDER METHODS	DESCRIPTION
OfType()	This method specifies to return only those entities of a specific type. This is very helpful with TPH relations.
OrderBy()	This method is for defining the sort order of the entities.
Select() SelectValue()	These methods return a projection of the results. Select() returns the result items in the form of a DbDataRecord; SelectValue() returns the values as scalars or complex types as defined by the generic parameter TResultType.
Skip() Top()	These methods are useful for paging. Skip a number of items with the Skip() method and take a specified number as defined by the Top() method.
Intersect() Union() UnionAll()	These methods are used to combine two queries. Intersect() returns a query containing only the results that are available in both of the queries. Union() combines the queries and returns the complete result without duplicates. UnionAll() also includes duplicates.

Let's get into one example on how to use these Query Builder methods. With the next code snippet, the racers are filtered with the Where() method to return only racers from the USA; the OrderBy() method specifies descending sort order first based on the number of wins and next on the number of starts. Finally, only the first three racers are in the result using the Top() method:

Available for download on Wrox.com

```
using (var data = new Formula1Entities())
{
    string country = "USA";
    ObjectQuery<Racer> racers = data.Racers.Where("it.Country = @Country",
        new ObjectParameter("Country", country))
        .OrderBy("it.Wins DESC, it.Starts DESC")
        .Top("3");
    foreach (var racer in racers)
    {
        Console.WriteLine("{0} {1}, wins: {2}, starts: {3}",
                racer.Firstname, racer.Lastname, racer.Wins, racer.Starts);
    }
}
```

code snippet Formula1Demo/Program.cs

This is the result from this query:

```
Mario Andretti, wins: 12, starts: 128
Dan Gurney, wins: 4, starts: 87
Phil Hill, wins: 3, starts: 48
```

UPDATES

Reading, searching, and filtering data from the store are just one part of the work that usually needs to be done with data-intensive applications. Writing changed data back to the store is the other part you need to know.

The sections that follow cover these topics:

➤ Object tracking

➤ Change information

➤ Attaching and detaching entities

➤ Storing entity changes

Object Tracking

To allow data read from the store to be modified and saved, the entities must be tracked after they are loaded. This also requires that the object context be aware if an entity has already been loaded from the store. If multiple queries are accessing the same records, the object context needs to return already loaded entities.

The `ObjectStateManager` is used by the object context to keep track of entities that are loaded into the context.

The following example demonstrates that indeed if two different queries are done that return the same record from the database, the state manager is aware of that and does not create a new entity. Instead, the same entity is returned. The `ObjectStateManager` instance that is associated with the object context can be accessed with the `ObjectStateManager` property. The `ObjectStateManager` class defines an event named `ObjectStateManagerChanged` that is invoked every time a new object is added or removed from the object context. Here, the method `ObjectStateManager_ObjectStateManagerChanged` is assigned to the event to get information about changes.

Two different queries are used to return an entity object. The first query gets the first racer from the country Austria with the last name Lauda. The second query asks for the racers from Austria, sorts the racers by the number of races won, and gets the first result. As a matter of fact, that's the same racer. To verify that the same entity object is returned, the method `Object.ReferenceEquals()` is used to verify whether the two object references indeed reference the same instance:

```csharp
private static void TrackingDemo()
{
    using (var data = new Formula1Entities())
    {
        data.ObjectStateManager.ObjectStateManagerChanged +=
            ObjectStateManager_ObjectStateManagerChanged;
        Racer niki1 = data.Racers.Where("it.Country='Austria' && it.Lastname='Lauda'").
                            First();
        Racer niki2 = data.Racers.Where("it.Country='Austria'").
                OrderBy("it.Wins DESC").First();
        if (Object.ReferenceEquals(niki1, niki2))
        {
            Console.WriteLine("the same object");
        }
    }
}

static void ObjectStateManager_ObjectStateManagerChanged(object sender,
        CollectionChangeEventArgs e)
{
    Console.WriteLine("Object State change — action: {0}", e.Action);
    Racer r = e.Element as Racer;
    if (r != null)
        Console.WriteLine("Racer {0}", r.Lastname);
}
```

code snippet Formula1Demo/Program.cs

Running the application, you can see that the event of the `ObjectStateManagerChanged` of the `ObjectStateManager` occurs only once, and the references niki1 and niki2 are indeed the same:

```
Object State change — action: Add
Racer Lauda
The same object
```

Change Information

The object context is also aware of changes with the entities. The following example adds and modifies a racer from the object context and gets information about the change. First, a new racer is added with the AddObject() method of the ObjectSet<T> class. This method adds a new entity with the EntityState. Added information. Next, a racer with the Lastname Alonso is queried. With this entity class, the Starts property is incremented and thus the entity is marked with the information EntityState.Modified. Behind the scenes, the ObjectStateManager is informed about a state change in the object based on the interface implementations INotifyPropertyChanged. This interface is implemented in the entity base class StructuralObject. The ObjectStateManager is attached to the PropertyChanged event, and this event is fired with every property change.

To get all added or modified entity objects, you can invoke the GetObjectStateEntries() method of the ObjectStateManager and pass an EntityState enumeration value as it is done here. This method returns a collection of ObjectStateEntry objects that keeps information about the entities. The helper method DisplayState iterates through this collection to give detail information.

You can also get state information about a single entity passing the EntityKey to the GetObjectStateEntry() method. The EntityKey property is available with entity objects implementing the interface IEntityWithKey, which is the case with the base class EntityObject. The ObjectStateEntry object returned offers the method GetModifiedProperties() where you can read all property values that have been changed, and also access the original and the current information about the properties with the OriginalValues and CurrentValues indexers:

Available for
download on
Wrox.com

```csharp
private static void ChangeInformation()
{
    using (var data = new Formula1Entities())
    {
        var jaime = new Racer
        {
            Firstname = "Jaime",
            Lastname = "Alguersuari",
            Country = "Spain",
            Starts = 0
        };
        data.Racers.AddObject(jaime);
        Racer fernando = data.Racers.Where("it.Lastname='Alonso'").First();
        fernando.Starts++;
        DisplayState(EntityState.Added.ToString(),
            data.ObjectStateManager.GetObjectStateEntries(EntityState.Added));
        DisplayState(EntityState.Modified.ToString(),
            data.ObjectStateManager.GetObjectStateEntries(EntityState.Modified));
        ObjectStateEntry stateOfFernando =
            data.ObjectStateManager.GetObjectStateEntry(fernando.EntityKey);
        Console.WriteLine("state of Fernando: {0}",
            stateOfFernando.State.ToString());
        foreach (string modifiedProp in stateOfFernando.GetModifiedProperties())
        {
            Console.WriteLine("modified: {0}", modifiedProp);
            Console.WriteLine("original: {0}",
                            stateOfFernando.OriginalValues[modifiedProp]);
            Console.WriteLine("current: {0}",
                            stateOfFernando.CurrentValues[modifiedProp]);
        }
    }
}
static void DisplayState(string state, IEnumerable<ObjectStateEntry> entries)
{
    foreach (var entry in entries)
    {
```

```
            var r = entry.Entity as Racer;
            if (r != null)
            {
                Console.WriteLine("{0}: {1}", state, r.Lastname);
            }
        }
    }
```

code snippet Formula1Demo/Program.cs

When you run the application, the added and modified racers are displayed, and the properties changed with their original and current values are shown:

```
Added: Alguersuari
Modified: Alonso
state of Fernando: Modified
modified: Starts
original: 138
current: 139
```

Attaching and Detaching Entities

When returning entity data to the caller, it might be important to detach the objects from the object context. This is necessary, for example, if an entity object is returned from a Web service. Here, if the entity object is changed on the client, the object context is not aware of the change.

With the sample code, the `Detach()` method of the `ObjectContext` detaches the entity named `fernando` and thus the object context is not aware of any change done on this entity. If a changed entity object is passed from the client application to the service, it can be attached again. Just attaching it to the object context might not be enough because it doesn't give the information that the object was modified. Instead, the original object must be available inside the object context. The original object can be accessed from the store by using the key with the method `GetObjectByKey()` or `TryGetObjectByKey()`. If the entity object is already inside the object context, the existing one is used; otherwise it is fetched newly from the database. Invoking the method `ApplyCurrentValues()` passes the modified entity object to the object context, and if there are changes, then the changes are done within the existing entity with the same key inside the object context, and the `EntityState` is set to `EntityState.Modified`. Remember that the method `ApplyCurrentValues()` requires the object to exist within the object context; otherwise the new entity object is added with `EntityState.Added`:

```
using (var data = new Formula1Entities())
{
    data.ObjectStateManager.ObjectStateManagerChanged +=
            ObjectStateManager_ObjectStateManagerChanged;
    ObjectQuery<Racer> racers = data.Racers.Where("it.Lastname='Alonso'");
    Racer fernando = racers.First();
    EntityKey key = fernando.EntityKey;
    data.Racers.Detach(fernando);

    // Racer is now detached and can be changed independent of the object context
    fernando.Starts++;
    Racer originalObject = data.GetObjectByKey(key) as Racer;
    data.Racers.ApplyCurrentValues(fernando);
}
```

code snippet Formula1Demo/Program.cs

Storing Entity Changes

Based on all the change information with the help of the `ObjectStateManager`, the added, deleted, and modified entity objects can be written to the store with the `SaveChanges()` method of the `ObjectContext` class. To verify changes within the object context, you can assign a handler method to the `SavingChanges` event of the `ObjectContext` class. This event is fired before the data is written to the store, so you can add some verification logic to see if the changes should be really done. `SaveChanges()` returns the number of entity objects that have been written.

What happens if the records in the database that are represented by the entity classes have been changed after reading the record? The answer depends on the `ConcurrencyMode` property that is set with the model. With every property of an entity object, you can configure the `ConcurrencyMode` to `Fixed` or `None`. The value `Fixed` means that the property is validated at write time to determine if the value was not changed in the meantime. `None` — which is the default — ignores any change. If some properties are configured to the `Fixed` mode, and data changed between reading and writing the entity objects, an `OptimisticConcurrencyException` occurs.

You can deal with this exception by invoking the `Refresh()` method to read the actual information from the database into the object context. This method accepts two refresh modes configured by a `RefreshMode` enumeration value: `ClientWins` or `StoreWins`. `StoreWins` means that the actual information is taken from the database and set to the current values of the entity objects. `ClientWins` means that the database information is set to the original values of the entity objects, and thus the database values will be overwritten with the next `SaveChanges`. The second parameter of the `Refresh()` method is either a collection of entity objects or a single entity object. You can decide the refresh behavior entity by entity:

Available for
download on
Wrox.com

```
private static void ChangeInformation()
{
    //...

        int changes = 0;
        try
        {
            changes += data.SaveChanges();
        }
        catch (OptimisticConcurrencyException ex)
        {
            data.Refresh(RefreshMode.ClientWins, ex.StateEntries);
            changes += data.SaveChanges();
        }
        Console.WriteLine("{0} entities changed", changes);
        //...
```

code snippet Formula1Demo/Program.cs

LINQ TO ENTITIES

In several chapters of this book, you've seen LINQ to Query objects, databases, and XML. Of course, LINQ is also available to query entities.

With LINQ to Entities, the source for the LINQ query is `ObjectQuery<T>`. Because `ObjectQuery<T>` implements the interface `IQueryable`, the extension methods selected for the query are defined with the class `Queryable` from the namespace `System.Linq`. The extension methods defined with this class have a parameter `Expression<T>`; that's why the compiler writes an expression tree to the assembly. You can read more about expression trees in Chapter 11. The expression tree is then resolved from the `ObjectQuery<T>` class to the SQL query.

You can use a simple LINQ query as shown here to return the racers that won more than 40 races:

Available for
download on
Wrox.com

```
using (var data = new Formula1Entities())
{
    var racers = from r in data.Racers
                 where r.Wins > 40
                 orderby r.Wins descending
                 select r;
```

```
        foreach (Racer r in racers)
        {
            Console.WriteLine("{0} {1}", r.Firstname, r.Lastname);
        }
    }
```

code snippet Formula1Demo/Program.cs

This is the result of accessing the Formula1 database:

```
Michael Schumacher
Alain Prost
Ayrton Senna
```

You can also define a LINQ query to access relations as shown here. Variable `r` references racers, variable `rr` references all race results. The filter is defined with the `where` clause to retrieve only racers from Switzerland who had a race position on the podium. To get the podium finishes, the result is grouped, and the podium count calculated. Sorting is done based on the podium finishes:

```
using (var data = new Formula1Entities())
{
    var query = from r in data.Racers
                from rr in r.RaceResults
                where rr.Position <= 3 && rr.Position >= 1 &&
                        r.Country == "Switzerland"
                group r by r.Id into g
                let podium = g.Count()
                orderby podium descending
                select new
                {
                    Racer = g.FirstOrDefault(),
                    Podiums = podium
                };
    foreach (var r in query)
    {
        Console.WriteLine("{0} {1} {2}", r.Racer.Firstname, r.Racer.Lastname,
                        r.Podiums);
    }
}
```

The names of three racers from Switzerland are returned when you run the application:

```
Clay Regazzoni 28
Jo Siffert 6
Rudi Fischer 2
```

SUMMARY

In this chapter, you've seen the features of the ADO.NET Entity Framework. The ADO.NET Entity Framework is based on mapping that is defined by CSDL, MSL, and SSDL — XML information that describes the entities, the mapping, and the database schema. Using this mapping technique, you can create different relation types to map entity classes to database tables.

You've seen how the object context keeps knowledge about entities retrieved and updated, and how the changes can be written to the store.

LINQ to Entities is just a facet of the ADO.NET Entity Framework that allows you to use the new query syntax to access entities.

32

Data Services

WHAT'S IN THIS CHAPTER?

- ➤ Overview of WCF Data Services
- ➤ WCF Data Services hosting with CLR objects
- ➤ HTTP client access to WCF Data Services
- ➤ URL queries to WCF Data Services
- ➤ WCF Data Services with the ADO.NET Entity Framework
- ➤ Using the WCF Data Services .NET Client Provider
- ➤ Tracking, Updates, and Batching

In the previous chapter you saw the ADO.NET Entity Framework used to easily create an object model to map to the database structures. The Entity Framework does not provide a way to get the objects across different tiers. This is where WCF Data Services come into play. WCF Data Services offers a WCF service to easily access data provided by an Entity Data Model or by simple CLR objects implementing the IQueryable<T> interface.

OVERVIEW

The ADO.NET Entity Framework offers mapping and creates entity classes representing databases. With the data context from the Entity Framework, the data context stays informed about changes to data so that it knows what should be updated. The Entity Framework does not help when creating solutions over multiple tiers.

Using WCF Data Services, you can use the Entity Framework (or a simple CLR object model) on the server side and send HTTP queries from the client to the service to retrieve and to update data. Figure 32-1 shows a typical scenario with a Windows client or a Web page using HTML and JavaScript to send an HTTP request to the server.

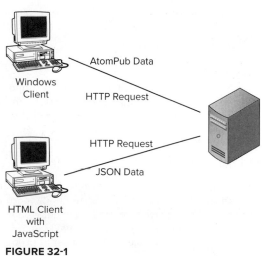

FIGURE 32-1

The returned information can be in AtomPub or JSON format. AtomPub is the Atom Publisher format based on XML. JSON (JavaScript Object Notation) is best accessed from JavaScript clients.

WCF Data Services makes use of WCF (Windows Communication Foundation) for the communication part and uses the WebHttpBinding.

 For more information about the Atom protocol you can read Chapter 47, "Syndication." Chapter 43, "Windows Communication Foundation," provides details about WCF.

With WCF Data Services you not only get features on the server and the capability to use HTTP Web requests with AtomPub or JSON, there's also a client-side part of WCF Data Services. For the client, there's a data service context and the possibility to create queries that are transformed in the AtomPub or JSON format. While the HTTP protocol is stateless, the data service context for the client is stateful. With this context the client can remember what entities are changed, added, or removed, and send a request with all the change information to the service.

Let's get into the details of WCF Data Services first by creating a simple service that is accessed from a client using HTTP Web requests.

CUSTOM HOSTING WITH CLR OBJECTS

The heart of WCF Data Services is the DataService<T> class that is the implementation of a WCF service. DataService<T> implements the interface IRequestHandler that is defined as follows. The attribute WebInvoke is specified to accept any URI parameters and any HTTP methods. With the parameter and return type, the method ProcessRequestForMessage() is very flexible. It accepts any stream and returns a Message. This is a requirement for the flexibility of data supported.

```
[ServiceContract]
public interface IRequestHandler
{
    [OperationContract]
    [WebInvoke(UriTemplate="*", Method="*")]
    Message ProcessRequestForMessage(Stream messageBody);
}
```

 The WCF attributes ServiceContract, OperationContract, *and* WebInvoke *are explained in Chapter 43.*

The .NET 4 version of WCF Data Services supports the AtomPub and JSON formats for sending and receiving requests. Let's start with a simple example by using a console application to host a service that offers a list of CLR objects. This service will then be used from a client application that directly sends HTTP requests to retrieve the data.

CLR Objects

The sample defines two entity classes: Category and Menu. These classes are simple data holders. The Menu contains Name, Price, and a reference to Category. To make the different instances uniquely identifiable by Data Services, the attribute DataServiceKey must be added to reference the unique identifier. This attribute is defined in the namespace System.Data.Services.Common. Instead of defining a single property as the identity, it is also possible to assign a list of properties for unique identification.

```csharp
[DataServiceKey("Id")]
public class Category
{
    public int Id { get; set; }
    public string Name { get; set; }

    public Category() { }
    public Category(int id, string name)
    {
        this.Id = id;
        this.Name = name;
    }
}
```

code snippet DataServicesHost/Category.cs

```csharp
[DataServiceKey("Id")]
public class Menu
{
    public int Id { get; set; }
    public string Name { get; set; }
    public decimal Price { get; set; }
    public Category Category { get; set; }

    public Menu() { }
    public Menu(int id, string name, decimal price, Category category)
    {
        this.Id = id;
        this.Name = name;
        this.Price = price;
        this.Category = category;
    }
}
```

code snippet DataServicesHost/Menu.cs

The class `MenuCard` manages the collections of `Menu` and `Category` items. It contains a list of `Menu` and `Category` items that can be iterated from the public `Menus` and `Categories` properties. This class implements a singleton pattern, so only one list of each exists.

```csharp
using System;
using System.Collections.Generic;
using System.Linq;
using System.Text;

namespace Wrox.ProCSharp.DataServices
{
    public class MenuCard
    {
        private static object sync = new object();
        private static MenuCard menuCard;
        public static MenuCard Instance
        {
            get
            {
                lock (sync)
                {
                    if (menuCard == null)
                        menuCard = new MenuCard();
                }
                return menuCard;
            }
```

```
        }

        private List<Category> categories;
        private List<Menu> menus;

        private MenuCard()
        {
            categories = new List<Category>
            {
                new Category(1, "Main"),
                new Category(2, "Appetizer")
            };

            menus = new List<Menu>() {
                new Menu(1, "Roasted Chicken", 22, categories[0]),
                new Menu(2, "Rack of Lamb", 32, categories[0]),
                new Menu(3, "Pork Tenderloin", 23, categories[0]),
                new Menu(4, "Fried Calamari", 9, categories[1])
            };
        }

        public IEnumerable<Menu> Menus
        {
            get
            {
                return menus;
            }
        }

        public IEnumerable<Category> Categories
        {
            get
            {
                return categories;
            }
        }
    }
}
```

code snippet DataServicesHost/MenuCard.cs

Data Model

Now it gets really interesting with the class MenuCardDataModel. This class defines what entities are offered from the data service by specifying properties that return IQueryable<T>. IQueryable<T> is used by the DataService<T> class to pass expressions for querying in object lists.

Available for download on Wrox.com

```
        public class MenuCardDataModel
        {
            public IQueryable<Menu> Menus
            {
                get
                {
                    return MenuCard.Instance.Menus.AsQueryable();
                }
            }

            public IQueryable<Category> Categories
            {
                get
                {
```

```
                    return MenuCard.Instance.Categories.AsQueryable();
            }
        }
    }
```

Data Service

The implementation of the data service `MenuDataService` derives from the base class `DataService<T>`. The generic parameter of the `DataService<T>` class is the class `MenuCardDataModel`, with the `Menus` and `Categories` properties returning `IQueryable<T>`.

In the `IntializeService()` method, you need to configure the entity and service operations access rules by using the `DataServiceConfiguration` class. You can pass * for the entity and operations access rules to allow access to every entity and operation. With the enumerations `EntitySetRights` and `ServiceOperationsRights`, you can specify if read and/or write access should be enabled. The `MaxProtocolVersion` property of the `DataServiceBehavior` defines what version of the AtomPub protocol should be supported. Version 2 is supported with .NET 4 and supports some additional features such as getting the number of items from a list.

```
using System.Data.Services;
using System.Data.Services.Common;
using System.Linq;
using System.ServiceModel.Web;

namespace Wrox.ProCSharp.DataServices
{
    public class MenuDataService : DataService<MenuCardDataModel>
    {
        public static void InitializeService(DataServiceConfiguration config)
        {
            config.SetEntitySetAccessRule("Menus", EntitySetRights.All);
            config.SetEntitySetAccessRule("Categories", EntitySetRights.All);
            config.SetServiceOperationAccessRule("*", ServiceOperationRights.All);

            config.DataServiceBehavior.MaxProtocolVersion = DataServiceProtocolVersion.V2;
        }
    }
}
```

Hosting the Service

Finally, you need a process to host the application. Later in this chapter, a Web application is used for hosting. You can also host the service in any application type that's supported by WCF; this can be a simple console application or Windows Service. This sample uses a console application that you easily can change to any other hosting type.

In the `Main()` method of the console application, a `DataServiceHost` is instantiated. `DataServiceHost` derives from the base class `ServiceHost` to offer WCF functionality. You can also use the `DataServiceHostFactory` for creating the `DataServiceHost`. Calling the `Open()` method, `DataServiceHost` instantiates an instance from the `MenuDataService` class for offering the service functionality. The address of the service is defined with `http://localhost:9000/Samples`.

```
using System;
using System.Data.Services;

namespace Wrox.ProCSharp.DataServices
```

```
    {
        class Program
        {
            static void Main()
            {
                DataServiceHost host = new DataServiceHost(typeof(MenuDataService),
                        new Uri[] { new Uri("http://localhost:9000/Samples ") });

                host.Open();

                Console.WriteLine("service running");
                Console.WriteLine("Press return to exit");
                Console.ReadLine();

                host.Close();
            }
        }
    }
```

code snippet DataServicesHost/Program.cs

Now you can start the executable and request the service with the links `http://localhost:9000/Samples/Menus` and `http://localhost:9000/Samples/Categories` from within Internet Explorer. To use Internet Explorer to see the data returned from the service, you need to deselect the option "Turn on feed reading view."

 To start a listener without elevated administrator rights, you need to configure the ACL for the port and the user with `netsh http add urlacl url=http://+:9000/Samples user=username listen=yes`. *Of course to change these administrative settings, elevated administrator rights are required.*

Additional Service Operations

Instead of offering just the properties from the data model, you can add additional service operations to the data service. In the sample code, you can see the method `GetMenusByName()`, which gets a request parameter from the client and returns all menus starting with the requested string with an `IQueryable<Menu>` collection. Such operations need to be added to the service operation access rules in the `InitalizeService()` method in case you do not offer all service operations using the *.

```
    public class MenuDataService : DataService<MenuCardDataModel>
    {
        public static void InitializeService(DataServiceConfiguration config)
        {
            config.SetEntitySetAccessRule("Menus", EntitySetRights.All);
            config.SetEntitySetAccessRule("Categories", EntitySetRights.All);
            config.SetServiceOperationAccessRule("GetMenusByName",
                                        ServiceOperationRights.All);

            config.DataServiceBehavior.MaxProtocolVersion = DataServiceProtocolVersion.V2;
        }

        [WebGet(UriTemplate="GetMenusByName?name={name}",
                BodyStyle=WebMessageBodyStyle.Bare)]
        public IQueryable<Menu> GetMenusByName(string name)
        {
            return (from m in CurrentDataSource.Menus
                    where m.Name.StartsWith(name)
                    select m).AsQueryable();
        }
    }
```

code snippet DataServicesHost/MenuDataService.cs

HTTP CLIENT APPLICATION

The client application can be a simple application to just send HTTP requests to the service and receive AtomPub or JSON responses. The first client application example is a WPF application that makes use of the `HttpWebRequest` class from the `System.Net` namespace.

Figure 32-2 shows the UI from the Visual Studio Designer. A `TextBox` named `textUrl` is used to enter the HTTP request with a default value of `http://localhost:9000/Samples/Menus`. The read-only `TextBox` named `textReturn` receives the answer from the service. You can also see a `CheckBox checkJSON`, where the response can be requested in the JSON format. The `Button` with the content Call Data Service has the `Click` event associated to the `OnRequest()` method.

In the implementation of the `OnRequest()` handler, an `HttpWebRequest` object is created with the `WebRequest.Create()` factory method. The HTTP request that is sent is defined by the `textUrl.Text` property. If the JSON checkbox is selected, the `Accept` property of the `HttpWebRequest` is set to `application/json`. This way, the data service returns a JSON response instead of the default AtomPub format. The request to the server is sent with the asynchronous method `BeginGetResponse`. When a response from the service is received, the method defined with the first parameter as a Lambda expression is invoked. The response is read from a stream associated with `HttpWebResponse`, converted to a `string`, and passed to the `textResult` TextBox.

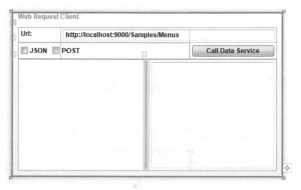

FIGURE 32-2

Available for
download on
Wrox.com

```csharp
private void OnRequest(object sender, RoutedEventArgs e)
{
    HttpWebRequest request = WebRequest.Create(textUrl.Text)
                                as HttpWebRequest;
    if (checkJSON.IsChecked == true)
    {
        request.Accept = "application/json";
    }

    request.BeginGetResponse((ar) =>
        {
            try
            {
                using (MemoryStream ms = new MemoryStream())
                {
                    const int bufferSize = 1024;
                    byte[] buffer = new byte[bufferSize];
                    HttpWebResponse response =
                        request.EndGetResponse(ar) as HttpWebResponse;

                    Stream responseStream = response.GetResponseStream();
                    int count;
                    while ((count = responseStream.Read(buffer, 0,
                                                bufferSize)) > 0)
                    {
                        ms.Write(buffer, 0, count);
                    }
                    responseStream.Close();
                    byte[] dataRead = ms.ToArray();
                    string data = UnicodeEncoding.ASCII.GetString(
```

```
                                    dataRead, 0, dataRead.Length);
                    Dispatcher.BeginInvoke(new Action<string>(s =>
                        {
                            textResult.Text = data;
                        }), data);
                    }
                }
                catch (WebException ex)
                {
                    Dispatcher.Invoke(new Action<string>(s =>
                        {
                            textResult.Text = s;
                        }), ex.Message);
                }

            }, null);
    }
```

code snippet WebRequestClient/WebRequestClient.xaml.cs

Now you can use several HTTP requests to the service and see the data returned. The running application is shown in Figure 32-3.

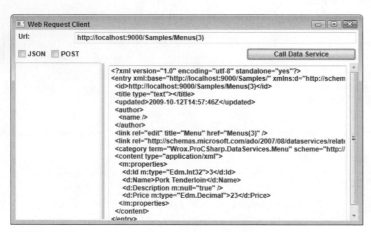

FIGURE 32-3

Using the request `http://localhost:9000/Samples/Menus(3)` to get the menu with the unique identifier 3, this AtomPub information is received:

```
<?xml version="1.0" encoding="utf-8" standalone="yes"?>
<entry xml:base="http://localhost:9000/Samples/"
       xmlns:d="http://schemas.microsoft.com/ado/2007/08/dataservices"
       xmlns:m="http://schemas.microsoft.com/ado/2007/08/dataservices/metadata"
       xmlns="http://www.w3.org/2005/Atom">
  <id>http://localhost:9000/Samples/Menus(3)</id>
  <title type="text"></title>
  <updated>2009-07-30T13:20:07Z</updated>
  <author>
    <name />
  </author>
  <link rel="edit" title="Menu" href="Menus(3)" />
  <link rel=
    "http://schemas.microsoft.com/ado/2007/08/dataservices/related/Category"
    type="application/atom+xml;type=entry" title="Category"
    href="Menus(3)/Category" />
```

```xml
<category term="Wrox.ProCSharp.DataServices.Menu"
  scheme="http://schemas.microsoft.com/ado/2007/08/dataservices/scheme" />
<content type="application/xml">
  <m:properties>
    <d:Id m:type="Edm.Int32">3</d:Id>
    <d:Name>Pork Tenderloin</d:Name>
    <d:Description m:null="true" />
    <d:Price m:type="Edm.Decimal">23</d:Price>
  </m:properties>
</content>
</entry>
```

If you select the JSON format, a response with the same information but a JSON representation that can be easily read from JavaScript is returned:

```json
{ "d" :
  { "__metadata":
    { "uri": "http://localhost:9000/Samples/Menus(3)",
      "type": "Wrox.ProCSharp.DataServices.Menu"
    },
    "Id": 3, "Name": "Pork Tenderloin", "Price": "23",
    "Category":
      { "__deferred":
        { "uri": "http://localhost:9000/Samples/Menus(3)/Category"
        }
      }
  }
}
```

Let's have a look at all the addressing options you have to build the query.

QUERIES WITH URLS

With the flexibility of the data services interface, you can request all objects from the service or get into specific objects and also values for specific properties.

 For better readability, in the following queries the address of the service `http://localhost:9000/Samples` *is omitted. This must be prefixed to all the queries.*

You've already seen that you can get a list of all entities in an entity set. The query

    Menus

returns all menu entities, while

    Categories

returns all category entities. According to the AtomPub protocol, the returned root element is `<feed>` and contains `<entry>` elements for every element. This query does not go across references; for example, getting all menus with `Menus` doesn't return the content of the category, only a reference to it. To get the category information within a menu, you can use the `$expand` query string:

    Menus?$expand=Category

Passing the primary key value inside brackets returns just a single entity. Here, the menu with identifier 3 is accessed. This requires the definition of the `DataServiceKey` attribute that was used earlier:

    Menus(3)

With a navigation property (using /), you can access a property of an entity:

    Menus(3)/Price

The same syntax works for relations, accessing properties from related entities:

```
Menus(3)/Category/Name
```

To get just the value without the surrounding XML content of an entity, you can use the `$value` query function:

```
Menus(3)/Category/Name/$value
```

Getting back to complete lists, you can get the number of entities in a list with `$count`. `$count` is only available with V2 of the AtomPub protocol.

```
Menus/$count
```

Getting just the first entities of a list is done with the top query string option `$top`:

```
Menus?$top=2
```

You can skip a number of entities with `$skip`. `$skip` and `$top` can be combined for implementing paging functionality.

```
Menus?$skip=2
```

Filtering entities can be performed with the `$filter` query string option and by using the logical operators `eq` (equal), `ne` (not equal), and `gt` (greater than), `ge` (greater than or equal to):

```
Menus?$filter=Category/Name eq 'Appetizer'
```

The result can also be sorted with the `$orderby` query string option:

```
Menus?$filter=Category/Name eq 'Appetizer'&orderby=Price desc
```

For only getting a projection, a subset of the available properties, `$select` can be used to specify the properties that should be accessed:

```
Menus?$select=Name, Price
```

USING WCF DATA SERVICES WITH THE ADO.NET ENTITY FRAMEWORK

Now that you've learned the basic concept of Data Services, passing AtomPub or JSON data across simple HTTP requests, let's get into a more complex example, using the ADO.NET Entity Framework for the data model, a Web application for hosting, and clients performing LINQ queries across a network that make use of classes from the `System.Data` `.Services.Client` namespace.

ASP.NET Hosting and EDM

First you have to create a new project. This time a Web Application project named `RestaurantDataServiceWeb` is used to host the service. The new data model is created with the help of the ADO.NET Entity Data Model (EDM) template and uses the tables Menus and Categories from a Restaurant database, as shown in Figure 32-4, to create the entity classes `Menu` and `Category`.

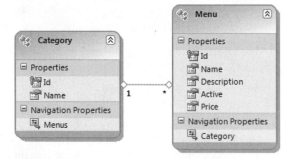

FIGURE 32-4

 Chapter 31, "ADO.NET Entity Framework," explains how to create and use ADO .NET Entity Data Models.

Now, use the Data Service template and create `RestaurantDataService.svc`. The `.svc` file contains the ASP.NET `ServiceHost` directive and uses the `DataServiceHostFactory` to instantiate the data service on request.

Available for
download on
Wrox.com

```
<%@ ServiceHost Language="C#" Factory="System.Data.Services.DataServiceHostFactory,
     System.Data.Services, Version=4.0.0.0, Culture=neutral,
     PublicKeyToken=b77a5c561934e089"
     Service="Wrox.ProCSharp.DataServices.RestaurantDataService" %>
```

code snippet RestaurantDataServiceWeb/RestaurantDataService.svc

With the code-behind, you need to change the template parameter of the `DataService<T>` class to reference the previously created entity data service context class, and change the entity set access rule and service operations access rule to allow access:

Available for
download on
Wrox.com

```csharp
using System.Data.Services;
using System.Data.Services.Common;

namespace Wrox.ProCSharp.DataServices
{
    public class RestaurantDataService : DataService<RestaurantEntities>
    {
        // This method is called only once to initialize service-wide policies.
        public static void InitializeService(DataServiceConfiguration config)
        {
            config.SetEntitySetAccessRule("Menus", EntitySetRights.All);
            config.SetEntitySetAccessRule("Categories", EntitySetRights.All);

            config.DataServiceBehavior.MaxProtocolVersion = DataServiceProtocolVersion.V2;
        }
    }
}
```

code snippet RestaurantDataServiceWeb/RestaurantDataService.svc.cs

Now, you can use a web browser to invoke queries as before to this data service; for example, you can use `http://localhost:13617/RestaurantDataService.svc/Menus` to receive the AtomPub of all menus from the database. Next, you create a client application that makes use of the client part of Data Services.

 With a large database you shouldn't return all the items with a query. Of course, the client can restrict the query to just request a certain limit of items. However, can you trust the client? With configuration options you can restrict limits on the server. For example, by setting `config.MaxResultsPerCollection` you can restrict the number of items that are returned from a collection to a maximum. You can also configure the maximum batch count, the maximum number of objects on an insert, and the maximum depth of objects in the tree. As an alternative, to allow any query you can also define service operations as was shown in the section "Additional Service Operations."

.NET Applications Using System.Data.Service.Client

Earlier in this chapter, you read how a .NET client application can be created that simply sends HTTP requests by using the `HttpWebRequest` class. The client part of Data Services, with the namespace `System.Data.Services.Client`, offers functionality for the client to build HTTP requests. The two most important classes with this namespace are `DataServiceContext` and `DataServiceQuery<TElement>`. `DataServiceContext` represents the state that is managed on the client. This state keeps track of objects that are loaded from the server as well as all the changes made on the client. `DataServiceQuery<TElement>` represents an HTTP query to a data service.

To call the data service, create a WPF application. Figure 32-5 shows the design view of the WPF application. The top row contains a `ComboBox` control, which is used to display all categories. The second row contains a `StackPanel` with four `Button` controls. The third row contains a `DataGrid` control to display the menus, and the fourth row contains a `TextBlock` element to display some status information.

To create a client proxy and entity classes to be used on the client, you need metadata information. The Data Service offers metadata by using the `$metadata` query string: `http://localhost:13617/RestaurantDataService.svc/$metadata`.

With this information a service reference can be added to the client application project to create a proxy class and entity classes. With the Restaurant data service, the class `RestaurantEntities` that derives from the base class `DataServiceContext` is created that can be used as a proxy. Entity classes `Menu` and `Category` to keep the data are created as well. The entity classes implement the interface `INotifyPropertyChanged`, which makes it easy to keep informed about changes from the UI.

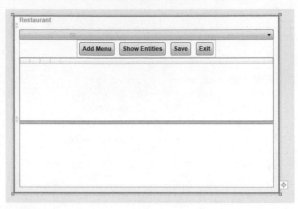

FIGURE 32-5

Data Service Context

Now you can use the data service context `RestaurantEntities` to send a query to the data service. A variable of the service context is defined in the code-behind of the WPF window, in the class `MainWindow`. To avoid conflict with the `Menu` class that's generated for the data service and the `Menu` control from WPF, a namespace alias is defined with the alias name R, for *Restaurant*, to reference the generated classes from the service reference.

```csharp
using System;
using System.Collections.Generic;
using System.Data.Services.Client;
using System.Linq;
using System.Text;
using System.Windows;
using System.Windows.Controls;
using R = Wrox.ProCSharp.DataServices.RestaurantService.RestaurantModel;

namespace Wrox.ProCSharp.DataServices
{
    public partial class MainWindow : Window
    {
        private R.RestaurantEntities data;
        private DataServiceCollection<R.Menu> trackedMenus;
```

code snippet ClientApp/MainWindow.xaml.cs

The instance of the `RestaurantEntities` is created in the constructor of the `MainWindow` class. The constructor of the data service context requires a link to the service root. This is defined within the application configuration file and accessed from the strongly typed settings.

```csharp
        public MainWindow()
        {
            Uri serviceRoot = new Uri(Properties.Settings.Default.RestaurantServiceURL);
            data = new R.RestaurantEntities(serviceRoot);
            data.SendingRequest += data_SendingRequest;

            InitializeComponent();
            this.DataContext = this;
        }
```

The content of the application configuration file used to reference the data service is shown here:

```xml
<?xml version="1.0" encoding="utf-8" ?>
<configuration>
    <configSections>
        <sectionGroup name="applicationSettings"
            type="System.Configuration.ApplicationSettingsGroup, System, Version=4.0.0.0,
                Culture=neutral, PublicKeyToken=b77a5c561934e089" >
            <section name="Wrox.ProCSharp.DataServices.Properties.Settings"
                type="System.Configuration.ClientSettingsSection, System, Version=4.0.0.0,
                    Culture=neutral, PublicKeyToken=b77a5c561934e089"
                    requirePermission="false" />
        </sectionGroup>
    </configSections>
    <applicationSettings>
        <Wrox.ProCSharp.DataServices.Properties.Settings>
            <setting name="RestaurantServiceURL" serializeAs="String">
                <value>http://localhost:13617/RestaurantDataService.svc</value>
            </setting>
        </Wrox.ProCSharp.DataServices.Properties.Settings>
    </applicationSettings>
</configuration>
```

code snippet ClientApp/app.config

With the `SendingRequest` event, the data service context invokes the handler every time a request is sent to the service. The method `data_sendingRequest()` is associated with the `SendingRequest` event and receives information about the request in the `SendingRequestEventArgs` argument. With `SendingRequestEventArgs`, you can access request and header information. The request method and URI retrieved from the `Method` and `RequestUri` properties is written to the *textStatus* control in the UI.

```csharp
void data_SendingRequest(object sender, SendingRequestEventArgs e)
{
    var sb = new StringBuilder();
    sb.AppendFormat("Method: {0}\n", e.Request.Method);
    sb.AppendFormat("Uri: {0}\n", e.Request.RequestUri.ToString());
    this.textStatus.Text = sb.ToString();
}
```

code snippet ClientApp/MainWindow.xaml.cs

The data service context `RestaurantEntities` allows you to retrieve entities from the service; tracks the entities that have been retrieved; allows you to add, delete, and change entities inside the data context; and keeps the state of the changes for sending update requests.

LINQ Query

The data service context implements a LINQ provider to convert LINQ requests to HTTP requests. The `Categories` property of the `MainWindow` class defines a LINQ query by using the data context to return all categories:

```csharp
public IEnumerable<R.Category> Categories
{
    get
    {
        return from c in data.Categories
               orderby c.Name
               select c;
    }
}
```

code snippet ClientApp/MainWindow.xaml.cs

The `ComboBox` in the XAML code defines a binding to this property to display all categories:

```
<ComboBox x:Name="comboCategories" Grid.Row="0"
        ItemsSource="{Binding Path=Categories}" SelectedIndex="0"
        SelectionChanged="OnCategorySelection">
    <ComboBox.ItemTemplate>
        <DataTemplate>
            <TextBlock Text="{Binding Path=Name}" />
        </DataTemplate>
    </ComboBox.ItemTemplate>
</ComboBox>
```

code snippet ClientApp/MainWindow.xaml

With the help of the `SendingRequest` event, it can easily be seen that the LINQ query to access all categories is converted to an HTTP `GET` Request with the following URI:

```
Method: GET
Uri: http://localhost:13617/RestaurantDataService.svc/Categories()?$orderby=Name
```

The `Categories` property of the `RestaurantEntities` class returns a `DataServiceQuery<Category>`. `DataServiceQuery<T>` implements `IQueryable`, and thus, the compiler creates expression trees from the LINQ query that are analyzed and converted to an HTTP `GET` request.

 LINQ queries are covered in Chapter 11, "Language Integrated Query."

You can also create a LINQ query to only get the menus from the category `Soups`:

```
var q = from m in data.Menus
        where m.Category.Name == "Soups"
        orderby m.Name
        select m;
```

This translates the URI `Menus()?$filter=Category/Name eq 'Soups'&$orderby=Name`.

The query can be expanded by using data service query options. For example, to include the relation and get all categories with the selected menus, add `AddQueryOption()` with `$expand` and the parameter value `Category`:

```
var q = from m in data.Menus.AddQueryOption("$expand", "Category")
        where m.Category.Name == "Soups"
        orderby m.Name
        select m;
```

This modifies the query to `Menus()?$filter=Category/Name eq 'Soups'&$orderby=Name&$expand=Category`.

The `DataServiceQuery<T>` class also offers the `Expand()` method for this particular query option:

```
var q = from m in data.Menus.Expand("Category")
        where m.Category.Name == "Soups"
        orderby m.Name
        select m;
```

Observable Collections

To keep the user interface informed about collection changes, Data Services contains the collection class `DataServiceCollection<T>`. This collection class is based on `ObservableCollection<T>`, which implements the interface `INotifyCollectionChanged`. WPF controls register with the event of this interface to keep informed about changes in the collection so that the UI can be updated immediately.

To create a `DataServiceCollection<T>` instance the class `DataServiceCollection` defines the static methods `Create()` and `CreateTracked()`. `Create()` creates a list that is independent of the data service context. `CreateTracked()` keeps track of the objects returned from the data service context so that you can take advantage of saving the objects by sending the changes to the service.

The `Menus` property invokes the `DataServiceCollection.CreateTracked<T>()` method to fill a `DataServiceCollection<R.Menu>` list named `trackedMenus` and returns this list. The retrieved entities that are defined by the LINQ query are associated with the data service context `data`.

```csharp
public IEnumerable<R.Menu> Menus
{
    get
    {
        if (trackedMenus == null)
            trackedMenus = DataServiceCollection.CreateTracked<R.Menu>(
                data,
                from m in data.Menus
                where m.CategoryId == (comboCategories.SelectedItem as R.Category).Id
                    && m.Active
                select m);
        return trackedMenus;
    }
}
```

code snippet ClientApp/MainWindow.xaml.cs

The `DataGrid` from the XAML code maps to the `Menus` property with the `Binding` markup extension:

```xml
<DataGrid Grid.Row="2" ItemsSource="{Binding Path=Menus}" AutoGenerateColumns="False">
    <DataGrid.Columns>
        <DataGridTextColumn Binding="{Binding Path=Name}" />
        <DataGridTextColumn Binding="{Binding Path=Description}" />
        <DataGridTextColumn Binding="{Binding Path=Price}" />
        <DataGridTextColumn Binding="{Binding Path=CategoryId}" />
    </DataGrid.Columns>
</DataGrid>
```

code snippet ClientApp/MainWindow.xaml

Using the `SelectionChanged` event from the `ComboBox` to select a new category, the menus are retrieved again with the newly selected category in the handler method `OnCategorySelection()`:

```csharp
private void OnCategorySelection(object sender, SelectionChangedEventArgs e)
{
    var selectedCategory = comboCategories.SelectedItem as R.Category;
    if (selectedCategory != null && trackedMenus != null)
    {
        trackedMenus.Clear();
        trackedMenus.Load(from m in data.Menus
                          where m.CategoryId == selectedCategory.Id
                          select m);
    }
}
```

code snippet ClientApp/MainWindow.xaml.cs

For more information about observable collections and the class `ObservableCollection<T>` please consult Chapter 10, "Collections."

Object Tracking

The data service context keeps track of all the objects that have been retrieved. You can get information about the objects by iterating through the return of the `Entities` property. `Entities` returns a read-only collection of `EntityDescriptor` objects. `EntityDescriptor` contains the entity itself that can be accessed via the `Entity` property, and also state information. The state of type `EntityStates` is an enumeration with the possible values `Added`, `Deleted`, `Detached`, `Modified`, and `Unchanged`. This information is used to keep track of changes and send a change request to the service.

To get information about the current entities associated with the data context, the handler method `OnShowEntities()` is associated with the `Click` event of the Show Entities button. Here, the `State`, `Identity`, and `Entity` properties are used to write status information to the UI.

Available for
download on
Wrox.com

```csharp
private void OnShowEntities(object sender, RoutedEventArgs e)
{
    var sb = new StringBuilder();
    foreach (var entity in data.Entities)
    {
        sb.AppendFormat("state = {0}, Uri = {1}, Element = {2}\n",
                        entity.State, entity.Identity, entity.Entity);
    }
    this.textStatus.Text = sb.ToString();
}
```

code snippet ClientApp/MainWindow.xaml.cs

Figure 32-6 shows the running application with information about the objects tracked.

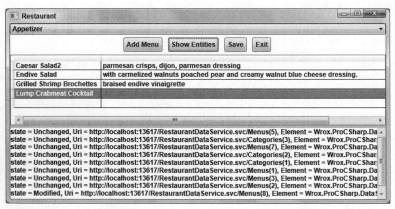

FIGURE 32-6

Adding, Modifying, and Deleting Entities

To add new entities to the data service context and thus send the new objects later to the data service, you can add entities to the data service context with the `AddObject()` method, or strongly typed variants such as `AddToMenus()` and `AddToCategories()`. You just have to fill the mandatory properties; otherwise, saving the state will not succeed. Adding new objects sets the state to `Added`.

The `DeleteObject()` method of the data service context sets the state of an object to `Deleted`.

If properties of an object are modified, the state changes from `Unchanged` to `Modified`.

Now you can invoke the method `SaveChanges()`, which sends HTTP `MERGE` requests to update entities, HTTP `DELETE` requests to delete entities, and HTTP `POST` requests to add new entities.

```
private void OnSave(object sender, RoutedEventArgs e)
{
    try
    {
        DataServiceResponse response = data.SaveChanges();
    }
    catch (DataServiceRequestException ex)
    {
        textStatus.Text = ex.ToString();
    }
}
```

code snippet ClientApp/MainWindow.xaml.cs

Operation Batching

Instead of sending DELETE and MODIFY requests for every entity in a collection, you can batch multiple change requests to a single network request. By default, every change is sent by using a single request when the SaveChanges() method is applied. Adding the parameter SaveChangesOptions.Batch to the SaveChanges() method combines all the change requests to a single network call with the $batch query option.

```
private void OnSave(object sender, RoutedEventArgs e)
{
    try
    {
        DataServiceResponse response = data.SaveChanges(SaveChangesOptions.Batch);
    }
    catch (DataServiceRequestException ex)
    {
        textStatus.Text = ex.ToString();
    }
}
```

code snippet ClientApp/MainWindow.xaml.cs

As the transferred data demonstrate, multiple HTTP headers are combined inside a single HTTP POST request and are split again on the server side. With the following HTTP POST request, you can see that the DELETE and MERGE requests are combined. The DELETE request deletes the menu with id 4; the MERGE request contains AtomPub information to update the menu with id 2.

```
POST /RestaurantDataService.svc/$batch HTTP/1.1
User-Agent: Microsoft WCF Data Services
DataServiceVersion: 1.0;NetFx
MaxDataServiceVersion: 2.0;NetFx
Accept: application/atom+xml,application/xml
Accept-Charset: UTF-8
Content-Type: multipart/mixed; boundary=batch_24448a55-e96f-4e88-853b-cdb5c1ddc8bd
Host: 127.0.0.1.:13617
Content-Length: 1742
Expect: 100-continue

--batch_24448a55-e96f-4e88-853b-cdb5c1ddc8bd
Content-Type: multipart/mixed;
boundary=changeset_8bc1382a-aceb-400b-9d19-dc2eec0e33b7

--changeset_8bc1382a-aceb-400b-9d19-dc2eec0e33b7
Content-Type: application/http
Content-Transfer-Encoding: binary

DELETE http://127.0.0.1.:13617/RestaurantDataService.svc/Menus(4) HTTP/1.1
```

```
Host: 127.0.0.1.:13617
Content-ID: 18

--changeset_8bc1382a-aceb-400b-9d19-dc2eec0e33b7
Content-Type: application/http
Content-Transfer-Encoding: binary

MERGE http://127.0.0.1.:13617/RestaurantDataService.svc/Menus(2) HTTP/1.1
Host: 127.0.0.1.:13617
Content-ID: 19
Content-Type: application/atom+xml;type=entry
Content-Length: 965

<?xml version="1.0" encoding="utf-8" standalone="yes"?>
<entry xmlns:d="http://schemas.microsoft.com/ado/2007/08/dataservices"
xmlsn:m="http://schemas.microsoft.com/ado/2007/08/dataservices/metadata"
xmlsn="http://www.w3.org/2005/Atom">
  <category scheme="http://schemas.microsoft.com/ado/2007/08/dataservices/scheme"
           term="RestaurantModel.Menu" />
  <title />
  <author>
    <name />
  </author>
  <updated>2009-08-01T19:17:43.4741882Z</updated>
  <id>http://127.0.0.1.:13617/RestaurantDataService.svc/Menus(2)</id>
  <content type="application/xml">
    <m:properties>
      <d:Active m:type="Edm.Boolean">true</d:Active>
      <d:Description>Lean and tender 8 oz. sirloin seasoned perfectly
                    with our own special seasonings and topped with seasoned
                    butter.
      </d:Description>
      <d:Id m:type="Edm.Int32">2</d:Id>
      <d:Name>Sirloin Steak</d:Name>
      <d:Price m:type="Edm.Decimal">44.0</d:Price>
    </m:properties>
  </content>
</entry>
--changeset_8bc1382a-aceb-400b-9d19-dc2eec0e33b7--
--batch_24448a55-e96f-4e88-853b-cdb5c1ddc8bd--
```

SUMMARY

In this chapter, you've seen the features of WCF Data Services. WCF Data Services brings the data model from the ADO.NET Entity Framework across multiple tiers. The technology that this is based on is WCF, by using connectionless, stateless communication sending AtomPub or JSON queries.

You've not only seen the server-side part of this technology but also the client-side part, where change information is tracked inside a data service context. The client-side part of WCF Data Services implements a LINQ provider, so you can create simple LINQ requests that are converted to HTTP GET/POST/PUT/DELETE requests.

33

Manipulating XML

WHAT'S IN THIS CHAPTER?

➤ XML standards

➤ XmlReader and XmlWriter

➤ XmlDocument

➤ XPathDocument

➤ XmlNavigator

➤ LINQ to XML

➤ Working with objects in the `System.Xml.Linq` namespace

➤ Querying XML documents using LINQ

➤ Using LINQ to SQL and LINQ to XML together

XML plays a significant role in the .NET Framework. Not only does the .NET Framework allow you to use XML in your application, but the .NET Framework itself uses XML for configuration files and source code documentation, as do SOAP, web services, and ADO.NET, to name just a few.

To accommodate this extensive use of XML, the .NET Framework includes the `System.Xml` namespace. This namespace is loaded with classes that can be used for the processing of XML, and many of these classes are discussed in this chapter.

This chapter discusses how to use the `XmlDocument` class, which is the implementation of the Document Object Model (DOM), as well as what .NET offers as a replacement for SAX (the `XmlReader` and `XmlWriter` classes). It also discusses the class implementations of XPath and XSLT and demonstrates how XML and ADO.NET work together, as well as how easy it is to transform one to the other. You also learn how you can serialize your objects to XML and create an object from (or deserialize) an XML document by using classes in the `System.Xml.Serialization` namespace. More to the point, you learn how you can incorporate XML into your C# applications.

You should note that the XML namespace allows you to get similar results in a number of different ways. It is impossible to include all these variations in one chapter, so while exploring one possible way of doing things, we'll try our best to mention alternative routes that will yield the same or similar results.

Because it's beyond the scope of this book to teach you XML from scratch, we assume that you are already somewhat familiar with XML. For example, you should be familiar with elements, attributes, and nodes, and you should also know what we mean when we refer to a *well-formed* document. You should also be familiar with SAX and DOM.

 If you want to learn more about XML, Wrox's Professional XML *(Wiley Publishing, 2007, ISBN 978-0471-77777-9) is a great place to start.*

In addition to general XML usage, the .NET Framework also includes the ability to work with XML by using LINQ to XML. One of the available web downloads, Chapter 56, "LINQ to SQL," takes a look at using LINQ to query SQL Server databases. This chapter takes a quick look at using LINQ to query your XML data sources instead.

The discussion begins with a brief overview of the current status of XML standards.

XML STANDARDS SUPPORT IN .NET

The World Wide Web Consortium (W3C) has developed a set of standards that give XML its power and potential. Without these standards, XML would not have the impact on the development world that it does. The W3C web site (www.w3.org) is a valuable source for all things XML.

The .NET Framework supports the following W3C standards:

➤ XML 1.0 (www.w3.org/TR/1998/REC-xml-19980210), including DTD support

➤ XML namespaces (www.w3.org/TR/REC-xml-names), both stream level and DOM

➤ XML schemas (www.w3.org/2001/XMLSchema)

➤ XPath expressions (www.w3.org/TR/xpath)

➤ XSLT transformations (www.w3.org/TR/xslt)

➤ DOM Level 1 Core (www.w3.org/TR/REC-DOM-Level-1)

➤ DOM Level 2 Core (www.w3.org/TR/DOM-Level-2-Core)

➤ SOAP 1.1 (www.w3.org/TR/SOAP)

The level of standards support will change as the framework matures and the W3C updates the recommended standards. Because of this, you need to make sure that you stay up to date with the standards and the level of support provided by Microsoft.

INTRODUCING THE SYSTEM.XML NAMESPACE

Support for processing XML is provided by the classes in the System.Xml namespace in .NET. This section looks (in no particular order) at some of the more important classes that the System.Xml namespace provides. The following table lists the main XML reader and writer classes.

CLASS NAME	DESCRIPTION
XmlReader	An abstract reader class that provides fast, noncached XML data. XmlReader is forward-only, like the SAX parser.
XmlWriter	An abstract writer class that provides fast, noncached XML data in stream or file format.
XmlTextReader	Extends XmlReader. Provides fast forward-only stream access to XML data.
XmlTextWriter	Extends XmlWriter. Fast forward-only generation of XML streams.

The following table lists some other useful classes for handling XML.

CLASS NAME	DESCRIPTION
XmlNode	An abstract class that represents a single node in an XML document. Base class for several classes in the XML namespace.
XmlDocument	Extends XmlNode. This is the W3C DOM implementation. It provides a tree representation in memory of an XML document, enabling navigation and editing.
XmlDataDocument	Extends XmlDocument. This is a document that can be loaded from XML data or from relational data in an ADO.NET DataSet. Allows the mixing of XML and relational data in the same view.
XmlResolver	An abstract class that resolves external XML-based resources such as DTD and schema references. Also used to process `<xsl:include>` and `<xsl:import>` elements.
XmlNodeList	A list of XmlNodes that can be iterated through.
XmlUrlResolver	Extends XmlResolver. Resolves external resources named by a uniform resource identifier (URI).

Many of the classes in the System.Xml namespace provide a means to manage XML documents and streams, whereas others (such as the XmlDataDocument class) provide a bridge between XML data stores and the relational data stored in DataSets.

> *The XML namespace is available to any language that is part of the .NET family. This means that all of the examples in this chapter could also be written in Visual Basic .NET, managed C++, and so on.*

USING SYSTEM.XML CLASSES

The following examples use books.xml as the source of data. You can download this file and the other code samples for this chapter from the Wrox web site (www.wrox.com), but it is also included in several examples in the .NET SDK. The books.xml file is a book catalog for an imaginary bookstore. It includes book information such as genre, author name, price, and ISBN number.

This is what the books.xml file looks like:

```
<?xml version='1.0'?>
<!--This file represents a fragment of a book store inventory database-->
<bookstore>
    <book genre="autobiography" publicationdate="1991" ISBN="1-861003-11-0">
        <title>The Autobiography of Benjamin Franklin</title>
        <author>
            <first-name>Benjamin</first-name>
            <last-name>Franklin</last-name>
        </author>
        <price>8.99</price>
    </book>
    <book genre="novel" publicationdate="1967" ISBN="0-201-63361-2">
        <title>The Confidence Man</title>
        <author>
            <first-name>Herman</first-name>
            <last-name>Melville</last-name>
        </author>
        <price>11.99</price>
    </book>
    <book genre="philosophy" publicationdate="1991" ISBN="1-861001-57-6">
        <title>The Gorgias</title>
```

```
        <author>
            <name>Plato</name>
        </author>
        <price>9.99</price>
    </book>
</bookstore>
```

code snippet books.xml

READING AND WRITING STREAMED XML

The `XmlReader` and `XmlWriter` classes will feel familiar if you have ever used SAX. `XmlReader`-based classes provide a very fast, forward-only, read-only cursor that streams the XML data for processing. Because it is a streaming model, the memory requirements are not very demanding. However, you don't have the navigation flexibility and the read or write capabilities that would be available from a DOM-based model. `XmlWriter`-based classes produce an XML document that conforms to the W3C's XML 1.0 Namespace Recommendations.

`XmlReader` and `XmlWriter` are both abstract classes. The following classes are derived from `XmlReader`:

➤   `XmlNodeReader`

➤   `XmlTextReader`

➤   `XmlValidatingReader`

The following classes are derived from `XmlWriter`:

➤   `XmlTextWriter`

➤   `XmlQueryOutput`

`XmlTextReader` and `XmlTextWriter` work with either a stream-based object from the `System.IO` namespace or `TextReader`/`TextWriter` objects. `XmlNodeReader` uses an `XmlNode` as its source instead of a stream. The `XmlValidatingReader` adds DTD and schema validation and therefore offers data validation. You look at these a bit more closely later in this chapter.

Using the XmlReader Class

`XmlReader` is a lot like SAX in the MSXML SDK. One of the biggest differences, however, is that whereas SAX is a *push* type of model (that is, it pushes data out to the application, and the developer has to be ready to accept it), the `XmlReader` is a *pull* model, where data is pulled into an application requesting it. This provides an easier and more intuitive programming model. Another advantage to this is that a pull model can be selective about the data that is sent to the application: if you don't want all of the data, you don't need to process it. In a push model, all of the XML data has to be processed by the application, whether it is needed or not.

The following is a very simple example of reading XML data, and later you will take a closer look at the `XmlReader` class. You'll find the code in the XmlReaderSample folder. Here is the code for reading in the `books.xml` document. As each node is read, the `NodeType` property is checked. If the node is a text node, the value is appended to the text box:

```
using System.Xml;

private void button3_Click(object sender, EventArgs e)
{
    richTextBox1.Clear();
    XmlReader rdr = XmlReader.Create("books.xml");
    while (rdr.Read())
    {
        if (rdr.NodeType == XmlNodeType.Text)
```

```
                    richTextBox1.AppendText(rdr.Value + "\r\n");
               }
          }
```

code download XMLReaderSample.sln

As previously discussed, XmlReader is an abstract class. So in order to use the XmlReader class directly, a Create static method has been added. The Create method returns an XmlReader object. The overload list for the Create method contains nine entries. In the preceding example, a string that represents the filename of the XmlDocument is passed in as a parameter. Stream-based objects and TextReader-based objects can also be passed in.

An XmlReaderSettings object can also be used. XmlReaderSettings specifies the features of the reader. For example, a schema can be used to validate the stream. Set the Schemas property to a valid XmlSchemaSet object, which is a cache of XSD schemas. Then the XsdValidate property on the XmlReaderSettings object can be set to true.

You can use several Ignore properties to control the way the reader processes certain nodes and values. These properties include IgnoreComments, IgnoreIdentityConstraints, IgnoreInlineSchema, IgnoreProcessingInstructions, IgnoreSchemaLocation, and IgnoreWhitespace. These properties can be used to strip certain items from the document.

Read Methods

Several ways exist to move through the document. As shown in the previous example, Read() takes you to the next node. You can then verify whether the node has a value (HasValue()) or, as you will see shortly, whether the node has any attributes (HasAttributes()). You can also use the ReadStartElement() method, which verifies whether the current node is the start element and then positions you on the next node. If you are not on the start element, an XmlException is raised. Calling this method is the same as calling the IsStartElement() method followed by a Read() method.

ReadElementString() is similar to ReadString(), except that you can optionally pass in the name of an element. If the next content node is not a start tag, or if the Name parameter does not match the current node Name, an exception is raised.

Here is an example of how ReadElementString() can be used. Notice that this example uses FileStreams, so you will need to make sure that you include the System.IO namespace via a using statement:

```
private void button6_Click(object sender, EventArgs e)
{
   richTextBox1.Clear();
        XmlReader rdr = XmlReader.Create("books.xml");
   while (!rdr.EOF)
   {
      //if we hit an element type, try and load it in the listbox
      if (rdr.MoveToContent() == XmlNodeType.Element && rdr.Name == "title")
      {
         richTextBox1.AppendText(rdr.ReadElementString() + "\r\n");
      }
      else
      {
         //otherwise move on
         rdr.Read();
      }
   }
}
```

code download XMLReaderSample.sln

In the `while` loop, you use `MoveToContent()` to find each node of type `XmlNodeType.Element` with the name `title`. You use the `EOF` property of the `XmlTextReader` as the loop condition. If the node is not of type `Element` or not named `title`, the `else` clause will issue a `Read()` method to move to the next node. When you find a node that matches the criteria, you add the result of a `ReadElementString()` to the list box. This should leave you with just the book titles in the list box. Note that you don't have to issue a `Read()` call after a successful `ReadElementString()` because `ReadElementString()` consumes the entire `Element` and positions you on the next node.

If you remove `&& rdr.Name=="title"` from the `if` clause, you will have to catch the `XmlException` when it is thrown. If you look at the data file, you will see that the first element that `MoveToContent()` will find is the `<bookstore>` element. Because it is an element, it will pass the check in the `if` statement. However, because it does not contain a simple text type, it will cause `ReadElementString()` to raise an `XmlException`. One way to work around this is to put the `ReadElementString()` call in a function of its own. Then, if the call to `ReadElementString()` fails inside this function, you can deal with the error and return to the calling function.

Go ahead and do this; call this new method `LoadTextBox()` and pass in the `XmlTextReader` as a parameter. This is what the `LoadTextBox()` method looks like with these changes:

```
private void LoadTextBox(XmlReader reader)
{
   try
   {
      richTextBox1.AppendText (reader.ReadElementString() + "\r\n");
   }
   // if an XmlException is raised, ignore it.
   catch(XmlException er){}
}
```

This section from the previous example:

```
if (tr.MoveToContent() == XmlNodeType.Element && tr.Name == "title")
{
   richTextBox1.AppendText(tr.ReadElementString() + "\r\n");
}
else
{
   //otherwise move on
   tr.Read();
}
```

will have to be changed to the following:

```
if (tr.MoveToContent() == XmlNodeType.Element)
{
   LoadTextBox(tr);
}
else
{
   //otherwise move on
   tr.Read();
}
```

After running this example, the results should be the same as before. What you are seeing is that there is more than one way to accomplish the same goal. This is where the flexibility of the classes in the `System.Xml` namespace starts to become apparent.

The `XmlReader` can also read strongly typed data. There are several `ReadElementContentAs` methods, such as `ReadElementContentAsDouble`, `ReadElementContentAsBoolean`, and so on. The following example shows how to read in the values as a decimal and do some math on the value. In this case, the value from the price element is increased by 25 percent:

```csharp
private void button5_Click(object sender, EventArgs e)
{
    richTextBox1.Clear();
    XmlReader rdr = XmlReader.Create("books.xml");
    while (rdr.Read())
    {
        if (rdr.NodeType == XmlNodeType.Element)
        {
            if (rdr.Name == "price")
            {
                decimal price = rdr.ReadElementContentAsDecimal();
                richTextBox1.AppendText("Current Price = " + price + "\r\n");
                price += price * (decimal).25;
                richTextBox1.AppendText("New Price = " + price + "\r\n\r\n");
            }
            else if(rdr.Name== "title")
                richTextBox1.AppendText(rdr.ReadElementContentAsString() + "\r\n");
        }
    }
}
```

code download XMLReaderSample.sln

If the value cannot be converted to a decimal value, a `FormatException` is raised. This is a much more efficient method than reading the value as a string and casting it to the proper data type.

Retrieving Attribute Data

As you play with the sample code, you might notice that when the nodes are read in, you don't see any attributes. This is because attributes are not considered part of a document's structure. When you are on an element node, you can check for the existence of attributes and optionally retrieve the attribute values.

For example, the `HasAttributes` property returns `true` if there are any attributes; otherwise, it returns `false`. The `AttributeCount` property tells you how many attributes there are, and the `GetAttribute()` method gets an attribute by name or by index. If you want to iterate through the attributes one at a time, you can use the `MoveToFirstAttribute()` and `MoveToNextAttribute()` methods.

The following is an example of iterating through the attributes of the `books.xml` document:

```csharp
private void button7_Click(object sender, EventArgs e)
{
    richTextBox1.Clear();
    XmlReader tr = XmlReader.Create("books.xml");
    //Read in node at a time
    while (tr.Read())
    {
        //check to see if it's a NodeType element
        if (tr.NodeType == XmlNodeType.Element)
        {
            //if it's an element, then let's look at the attributes.
            for (int i = 0; i < tr.AttributeCount; i++)
            {
                richTextBox1.AppendText(tr.GetAttribute(i) + "\r\n");
            }
        }
    }
}
```

code download XMLReaderSample.sln

This time you are looking for element nodes. When you find one, you loop through all of the attributes and, using the `GetAttribute()` method, you load the value of the attribute into the list box. In this example, those attributes would be `genre`, `publicationdate`, and `ISBN`.

Validating with XmlReader

Sometimes it's important to know not only that the document is well formed but also that it is valid. An `XmlReader` can validate the XML according to an XSD schema by using the `XmlReaderSettings` class. The XSD schema is added to the `XmlSchemaSet` that is exposed through the `Schemas` property. The `XsdValidate` property must also be set to `true`; the default for this property is `false`.

The following example demonstrates the use of the `XmlReaderSettings` class. The following is the XSD schema that will be used to validate the `books.xml` document:

Available for download on Wrox.com

```
<?xml version="1.0" encoding="utf-8"?>
<xs:schema attributeFormDefault="unqualified"
        elementFormDefault="qualified" xmlns:xs="http://www.w3.org/2001/XMLSchema">
  <xs:element name="bookstore">
    <xs:complexType>
      <xs:sequence>
        <xs:element maxOccurs="unbounded" name="book">
          <xs:complexType>
            <xs:sequence>
              <xs:element name="title" type="xs:string" />
              <xs:element name="author">
                <xs:complexType>
                  <xs:sequence>
                    <xs:element minOccurs="0" name="name"
                                              type="xs:string" />
                    <xs:element minOccurs="0" name="first-name"
                                              type="xs:string" />
                    <xs:element minOccurs="0" name="last-name"
                                              type="xs:string" />
                  </xs:sequence>
                </xs:complexType>
              </xs:element>
              <xs:element name="price" type="xs:decimal" />
            </xs:sequence>
            <xs:attribute name="genre" type="xs:string" use="required" />
            <!--<xs:attribute name="publicationdate"
                             type="xs:unsignedShort" use="required" />-->
            <xs:attribute name="ISBN" type="xs:string" use="required" />
          </xs:complexType>
        </xs:element>
      </xs:sequence>
    </xs:complexType>
  </xs:element>
</xs:schema>
```

code download books.xsd

This schema was generated from `books.xml` in Visual Studio. Notice that the `publicationdate` attribute has been commented out. This will cause the validation to fail.

The following is the code that uses the schema to validate the `books.xml` document:

Available for download on Wrox.com

```
private void button8_Click(object sender, EventArgs e)
{
    richTextBox1.Clear();
    XmlReaderSettings settings = new XmlReaderSettings();
    settings.Schemas.Add(null, "books.xsd");
```

```
    settings.ValidationType = ValidationType.Schema;
    settings.ValidationEventHandler +=
      new System.Xml.Schema.ValidationEventHandler(settings_ValidationEventHandler);
    XmlReader rdr = XmlReader.Create("books.xml", settings);
    while (rdr.Read())
    {
      if (rdr.NodeType == XmlNodeType.Text)
        richTextBox1.AppendText(rdr.Value + "\r\n");
    }
  }
```

code download XMLReaderSample.sln

After the `XmlReaderSettings` object setting is created, the schema `books.xsd` is added to the `XmlSchemaSet` object. The `Add` method for `XmlSchemaSet` has four overloads. One takes an `XmlSchema` object. The `XmlSchema` object can be used to create a schema on the fly, without having to create the schema file on disk. Another overload takes another `XmlSchemaSet` object as a parameter. Another takes two string values: the first is the target namespace and the other is the URL for the XSD document. If the target namespace parameter is null, the `targetNamespace` of the schema will be used. The last overload takes the `targetNamespace` as the first parameter as well, but it uses an `XmlReader`-based object to read in the schema. The `XmlSchemaSet` preprocesses the schema before the document to be validated is processed.

After the schema is referenced, the `XsdValidate` property is set to one of the `ValidationType` enumeration values. These valid values are `DTD`, `Schema`, or `None`. If the value selected is set to `None`, then no validation will occur.

Because the `XmlReader` object is being used, if there is a validation problem with the document, it will not be found until that attribute or element is read by the reader. When the validation failure does occur, an `XmlSchemaValidationException` is raised. This exception can be handled in a `catch` block; however, handling exceptions can make controlling the flow of the data difficult. To help with this, a `ValidationEvent` is available in the `XmlReaderSettings` class. This way, the validation failure can be handled without your having to use exception handling. The event is also raised by validation warnings, which do not raise an exception. The `ValidationEvent` passes in a `ValidationEventArgs` object that contains a `Severity` property. This property determines whether the event was raised by an error or a warning. If the event was raised by an error, the exception that caused the event to be raised is passed in as well. There is also a message property. In the example, the message is displayed in a `MessageBox`.

Using the XmlWriter Class

The `XmlWriter` class allows you write XML to a stream, a file, a `StringBuilder`, a `TextWriter`, or another `XmlWriter` object. Like `XmlTextReader`, it does so in a forward-only, noncached manner. `XmlWriter` is highly configurable, allowing you to specify such things as whether or not to indent content, the amount to indent, what quote character to use in attribute values, and whether namespaces are supported. Like the `XmlReader`, this configuration is done using an `XmlWriterSettings` object.

Here's a simple example that shows how the `XmlTextWriter` class can be used:

Available for
download on
Wrox.com

```
    private void button9_Click(object sender, EventArgs e)
    {
      XmlWriterSettings settings = new XmlWriterSettings();
      settings.Indent = true;
      settings.NewLineOnAttributes = true;
      XmlWriter writer = XmlWriter.Create("newbook.xml", settings);
      writer.WriteStartDocument();
      //Start creating elements and attributes
      writer.WriteStartElement("book");
      writer.WriteAttributeString("genre", "Mystery");
      writer.WriteAttributeString("publicationdate", "2001");
      writer.WriteAttributeString("ISBN", "123456789");
```

```
        writer.WriteElementString("title", "Case of the Missing Cookie");
        writer.WriteStartElement("author");
        writer.WriteElementString("name", "Cookie Monster");
        writer.WriteEndElement();
        writer.WriteElementString("price", "9.99");
        writer.WriteEndElement();
        writer.WriteEndDocument();
        //clean up
        writer.Flush();
        writer.Close();
    }
```

code download XMLReaderSample.sln

Here, you are writing to a new XML file called `newbook.xml`, adding the data for a new book. Note that `XmlWriter` will overwrite an existing file with a new one. You will look at inserting a new element or node into an existing document later in this chapter. You are instantiating the `XmlWriter` object by using the `Create` static method. In this example, a string representing a filename is passed as a parameter, along with an instance of an `XmlWriterSetting` class.

The `XmlWriterSettings` class has properties that control the way that the XML is generated. The `CheckedCharacters` property is a Boolean that will raise an exception if a character in the XML does not conform to the W3C XML 1.0 recommendation. The `Encoding` class sets the encoding used for the XML being generated; the default is Encoding.UTF8. The `Indent` property is a Boolean value that determines if elements should be indented. The `IndentChars` property is set to the character string that it is used to indent. The default is two spaces. The `NewLine` property is used to determine the characters for line breaks. In the preceding example, the `NewLineOnAttribute` is set to `true`. This will put each attribute in a separate line, which can make the XML generated a little easier to read.

`WriteStartDocument()` adds the document declaration. Now you start writing data. First comes the `book` element; next, you add the `genre`, `publicationdate`, and `ISBN` attributes. Then you write the `title`, `author`, and `price` elements. Note that the `author` element has a child element name.

When you click the button, you produce the `booknew.xml` file, which looks like this:

```
    <?xml version="1.0" encoding="utf-8"?>
    <book
      genre="Mystery"
      publicationdate="2001"
      ISBN="123456789">
      <title>Case of the Missing Cookie</title>
      <author>
        <name>Cookie Monster</name>
      </author>
      <price>9.99</price>
    </book>
```

The nesting of elements is controlled by paying attention to when you start and finish writing elements and attributes. You can see this when you add the `name` child element to the `authors` element. Note how the `WriteStartElement()` and `WriteEndElement()` method calls are arranged and how that arrangement produces the nested elements in the output file.

To go along with the `WriteElementString()` and `WriteAttributeString()` methods, there are several other specialized write methods. `WriteCData()` outputs a CData section (`<!CDATA[.]]>`), writing out the text it takes as a parameter. `WriteComment()` writes out a comment in proper XML format. `WriteChars()` writes out the contents of a `char` buffer. This works in a similar fashion to the `ReadChars()` method that you looked at earlier; they both use the same type of parameters. `WriteChars()` needs a buffer (an array of characters), the starting position for writing (an integer), and the number of characters to write (an integer).

Reading and writing XML using the `XmlReader`- and `XmlWriter`-based classes are surprisingly flexible and simple to do. Next, you'll learn how the DOM is implemented in the `System.Xml` namespace through the `XmlDocument` and `XmlNode` classes.

USING THE DOM IN .NET

The DOM implementation in .NET supports the W3C DOM Level 1 and Core DOM Level 2 specifications. The DOM is implemented through the `XmlNode` class, which is an abstract class that represents a node of an XML document.

There is also an `XmlNodeList` class, which is an ordered list of nodes. This is a live list of nodes, and any changes to any node are immediately reflected in the list. `XmlNodeList` supports indexed access or iterative access.

The `XmlNode` and `XmlNodeList` classes make up the core of the DOM implementation in the .NET Framework. The following table lists some of the classes that are based on `XmlNode`.

CLASS NAME	DESCRIPTION
XmlLinkedNode	Returns the node immediately before or after the current node. Adds `NextSibling` and `PreviousSibling` properties to `XmlNode`.
XmlDocument	Represents the entire document. Implements the DOM Level 1 and Level 2 specifications.
XmlDocumentFragment	Represents a fragment of the document tree.
XmlAttribute	Represents an attribute object of an `XmlElement` object.
XmlEntity	Represents a parsed or unparsed entity node.
XmlNotation	Contains a notation declared in a DTD or schema.

The following table lists classes that extend `XmlCharacterData`.

CLASS NAME	DESCRIPTION
XmlCDataSection	Represents a `CData` section of a document.
XmlComment	Represents an XML comment object.
XmlSignificantWhitespace	Represents a node with whitespace. Nodes are created only if the `PreserveWhiteSpace` flag is `true`.
XmlWhitespace	Represents whitespace in element content. Nodes are created only if the `PreserveWhiteSpace` flag is `true`.
XmlText	Represents the textual content of an element or attribute.

The following table lists classes that extend the `XmlLinkedNode`.

CLASS NAME	DESCRIPTION
XmlDeclaration	Represents the declaration node (`<?xml version='1.0'.>`).
XmlDocumentType	Represents data relating to the document type declaration.
XmlElement	Represents an XML element object.
XmlEntityReferenceNode	Represents an entity reference node.
XmlProcessingInstruction	Contains an XML processing instruction.

As you can see, .NET makes available a class to fit just about any XML type that you might encounter. Because of this, you end up with a very flexible and powerful tool set. This section won't look at every class in detail, but you will see several examples to give you an idea of what you can accomplish.

Using the XmlDocument Class

XmlDocument and its derived class XmlDataDocument (discussed later in this chapter) are the classes that you will be using to represent the DOM in .NET. Unlike XmlReader and XmlWriter, XmlDocument gives you read and write capabilities as well as random access to the DOM tree. XmlDocument resembles the DOM implementation in MSXML. If you have experience programming with MSXML, you will feel comfortable using XmlDocument.

This section introduces an example that creates an XmlDocument object, loads a document from disk, and loads a text box with data from the title elements. This is similar to one of the examples that you constructed in the "Using the XmlReader Class" section. The difference here is that you will be selecting the nodes you want to work with, instead of going through the entire document as in the XmlReader-based example.

Here is the code to create an XmlDocument object. Notice how simple it looks in comparison to the XmlReader example:

Available for
download on
Wrox.com

```
private void button1_Click(object sender, System.EventArgs e)
{
    //doc is declared at the module level
    //change path to match your path structure
    _doc.Load("books.xml");
    //get only the nodes that we want.
    XmlNodeList nodeLst = _doc.GetElementsByTagName("title");
    //iterate through the XmlNodeList
    textBox1.Text = "";
    foreach (XmlNode node in nodeLst)
    {
        textBox1.Text += node.OuterXml + "\r\n";
    }
}
```

code snippet frmXMLDOM.cs

Note that you also add the following declaration at the module level for the examples in this section:

```
private XmlDocument doc=new XmlDocument();
```

If this is all that you wanted to do, using the XmlReader would have been a much more efficient way to load the text box, because you just go through the document once and then you are finished with it. This is exactly the type of work that XmlReader was designed for. However, if you want to revisit a node, using XmlDocument is a better way.

Here is an example of using the XPath syntax to retrieve a set of nodes from the document:

Available for
download on
Wrox.com

```
private void button2_Click(object sender, EventArgs e)
{
    //doc is declared at the module level
    //change path to match your path structure
    doc.Load("books.xml");
    //get only the nodes that we want.
    XmlNodeList nodeLst = _doc.SelectNodes("/bookstore/book/title");
    textBox1.Text = "";
    //iterate through the XmlNodeList
    foreach (XmlNode node in nodeLst)
    {
        textBox1.Text += node.OuterXml + "\r\n";
    }
}
```

code snippet frmXMLDOM.cs

SelectNodes() returns a NodeList, or a collection of XmlNodes. The list contains only nodes that match the XPath statement passed in as the parameter SelectNodes. In this example, all you want to see are the title nodes. If you had made the call to SelectSingleNode, then you would have received a single node object that contained the first node in the XmlDocument that matched the XPath criteria.

A quick comment regarding the SelectSingleNode() method: This is an XPath implementation in the XmlDocument class. Both the SelectSingleNode() and SelectNodes() methods are defined in XmlNode, which XmlDocument is based on. SelectSingleNode() returns an XmlNode and SelectNodes() returns an XmlNodeList. However, the System.Xml.XPath namespace contains a richer XPath implementation, which you will look at in a later section.

Inserting Nodes

Earlier, you looked at an example using XmlTextWriter that created a new document. The limitation was that it would not insert a node into a current document. With the XmlDocument class, you can do just that. Change the button1_Click() event handler from the last example to the following:

Available for
download on
Wrox.com

```
private void button4_Click(object sender, System.EventArgs e)
{
    //change path to match your structure
    _doc.Load("books.xml");
    //create a new 'book' element
    XmlElement newBook = _doc.CreateElement("book");
    //set some attributes
    newBook.SetAttribute("genre", "Mystery");
    newBook.SetAttribute("publicationdate", "2001");
    newBook.SetAttribute("ISBN", "123456789");
    //create a new 'title' element
    XmlElement newTitle = _doc.CreateElement("title");
    newTitle.InnerText = "Case of the Missing Cookie";
    newBook.AppendChild(newTitle);
    //create new author element
    XmlElement newAuthor = _doc.CreateElement("author");
    newBook.AppendChild(newAuthor);
    //create new name element
    XmlElement newName = _doc.CreateElement("name");
    newName.InnerText = "Cookie Monster";
    newAuthor.AppendChild(newName);
    //create new price element
    XmlElement newPrice = _doc.CreateElement("price");
    newPrice.InnerText = "9.95";
    newBook.AppendChild(newPrice);
    //add to the current document
    _doc.DocumentElement.AppendChild(newBook);
    //write out the doc to disk
    XmlTextWriter tr = new XmlTextWriter("booksEdit.xml", null);
    tr.Formatting = Formatting.Indented;
    _doc.WriteContentTo(tr);
    tr.Close();
    //load listBox1 with all of the titles, including new one
    XmlNodeList nodeLst = _doc.GetElementsByTagName("title");
    textBox1.Text = "";
    foreach (XmlNode node in nodeLst)
    {
        textBox1.Text += node.OuterXml + "\r\n";
    }
}
```

code snippet frmXMLDOM.cs

After executing this code, you end up with the same functionality as in the previous example, but there is one additional book in the text box, *The Case of the Missing Cookie* (a soon-to-be classic). If you look closely at the code, you can see that this is actually a fairly simple process. The first thing that you do is create a new `book` element:

```
XmlElement newBook = doc.CreateElement("book");
```

`CreateElement()` has three overloads that allow you to specify the following:

➤ The element name

➤ The name and namespace URI

➤ The prefix, localname, and namespace

Once the element is created, you need to add attributes:

```
newBook.SetAttribute("genre","Mystery");
newBook.SetAttribute("publicationdate","2001");
newBook.SetAttribute("ISBN","123456789");
```

Now that you have the attributes created, you need to add the other elements of a book:

```
XmlElement newTitle = doc.CreateElement("title");
newTitle.InnerText = "The Case of the Missing Cookie";
newBook.AppendChild(newTitle);
```

Once again, you create a new `XmlElement`-based object (`newTitle`). Then you set the `InnerText` property to the title of our new classic and append the element as a child to the `book` element. You repeat this for the rest of the elements in this `book` element. Note that you add the `name` element as a child to the `author` element. This will give you the proper nesting relationship, as in the other `book` elements.

Finally, you append the `newBook` element to the `doc.DocumentElement` node. This is the same level as all of the other `book` elements. You have now updated an existing document with a new element.

The last thing to do is to write the new XML document to disk. In this example, you create a new `XmlTextWriter` and pass it to the `WriteContentTo()` method. `WriteContentTo()` and `WriteTo()` both take an `XmlTextWriter` as a parameter. `WriteContentTo()` saves the current node and all of its children to the `XmlTextWriter`, whereas `WriteTo()` just saves the current node. Because `doc` is an `XmlDocument`-based object, it represents the entire document and so that is what is saved. You could also use the `Save()` method. It will always save the entire document. `Save()` has four overloads. You can specify a string with the filename and path, a `Stream`-based object, a `TextWriter`-based object, or an `XmlWriter`-based object.

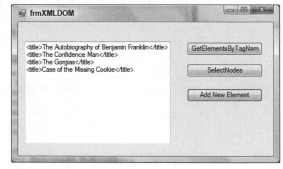

You also call the `Close()` method on `XmlTextWriter` to flush the internal buffers and close the file.

Figure 33-1 shows what you get when you run this example. Notice the new entry at the bottom of the list.

FIGURE 33-1

Earlier in the chapter, you saw how to create a document using the `XmlTextWriter` class. You can also use `XmlDocument`. Why would you use one in preference to the other? If the data that you want streamed to XML is available and ready to write, then the `XmlTextWriter` class is the best choice. However, if you need to build the XML document a little at a time, inserting nodes into various places, then creating the document with `XmlDocument` might be the better choice. You can accomplish this by changing the following line:

```
doc.Load("books.xml");
```

to this:

```
//create the declaration section
XmlDeclaration newDec = doc.CreateXmlDeclaration("1.0",null,null);
doc.AppendChild(newDec);
//create the new root element
XmlElement newRoot = doc.CreateElement("newBookstore");
doc.AppendChild(newRoot);
```

First, you create a new `XmlDeclaration`. The parameters are the version (always `1.0` for now), the encoding, and the standalone flag. The encoding parameter should be set to a string that is part of the `System.Text.Encoding` class if `null` is not used (`null` defaults to UTF-8). The standalone flag can be either `yes`, `no`, or `null`. If it is `null`, the attribute is not used and will not be included in the document.

The next element that is created will become the `DocumentElement`. In this case, it is called `newBookstore` so that you can see the difference. The rest of the code is the same as in the previous example and works in the same way. This is `booksEdit.xml`, which is generated from the following code:

```
<?xml version="1.0"?>
<newBookstore>
    <book genre="Mystery" publicationdate="2001" ISBN="123456789">
        <title>The Case of the Missing Cookie</title>
        <author>
            <name>C. Monster</name>
        </author>
        <price>9.95</price>
    </book>
</newBookstore>
```

You will want to use the `XmlDocument` class when you want to have random access to the document, or the `XmlReader`-based classes when you want a streaming-type model instead. Remember that there is a cost for the flexibility of the `XmlNode`-based `XmlDocument` class — memory requirements are higher and the performance of reading the document is not as good as when using `XmlReader`. There is another way to traverse an XML document: the `XPathNavigator`.

USING XPATHNAVIGATORS

An `XPathNavigator` is used to select, iterate through, and sometimes edit data from an XML document. An `XPathNavigator` can be created from an `XmlDocument` to allow editing capabilities or from an `XPathDocument` for read-only use. Because the `XPathDocument` is read-only, it performs very well. Unlike the `XmlReader`, the `XPathNavigator` is not a streaming model, so the same document can be used without having to re-read and parse.

The `XPathNavigaor` is part of the `System.Xml.XPath` namespace. XPath is a query language used to select specific nodes or elements from an XML document for processing.

The System.Xml.XPath Namespace

The `System.Xml.XPath` namespace is built for speed. It provides a read-only view of your XML documents, so there are no editing capabilities. Classes in this namespace are built to do fast iteration and selections on the XML document in a cursory fashion.

The following table lists the key classes in `System.Xml.XPath` and gives a short description of the purpose of each class.

CLASS NAME	DESCRIPTION
XPathDocument	Provides a view of the entire XML document. Read-only.
XPathNavigator	Provides the navigational capabilities to an XPathDocument.
XPathNodeIterator	Provides iteration capabilities to a node set.
XPathExpression	Represents a compiled XPath expression. Used by SelectNodes, SelectSingleNodes, Evaluate, and Matches.
XPathException	An XPath exception class.

XPathDocument

XPathDocument does not offer any of the functionality of the XmlDocument class. Its sole purpose is to create XPathNavigators. In fact, that is the only method available on the XPathDocument class (other than those provided by Object).

An XPathDocument can be created in a number of different ways. You can pass in an XmlReader, a filename of an XML document, or a Stream-based object to the constructor. This allows a great deal of flexibility. For example, you can use the XmlValidatingReader to validate the XML and then use that same object to create the XPathDocument.

XPathNavigator

XPathNavigator contains all of the methods for moving and selecting elements that you need. The following table lists some of the "move" methods defined in this class.

METHOD NAME	DESCRIPTION
MoveTo()	Takes XPathNavigator as a parameter. Moves the current position to be the same as that passed in to XPathNavigator.
MoveToAttribute()	Moves to the named attribute. Takes the attribute name and namespace as parameters.
MoveToFirstAttribute()	Moves to the first attribute in the current element. Returns true if successful.
MoveToNextAttribute()	Moves to the next attribute in the current element. Returns true if successful.
MoveToFirst()	Moves to the first sibling in the current node. Returns true if successful.
MoveToLast()	Moves to the last sibling in the current node. Returns true if successful.
MoveToNext()	Moves to the next sibling in the current node. Returns true if successful.
MoveToPrevious()	Moves to the previous sibling in the current node. Returns true if successful.
MoveToFirstChild()	Moves to the first child of the current element. Returns true if successful.
MoveToId()	Moves to the element with the ID supplied as a parameter. There needs to be a schema for the document, and the data type for the element must be of type ID.
MoveToParent()	Moves to the parent of the current node. Returns true if successful.
MoveToRoot()	Moves to the root node of the document.

To select a subset of the document, you can use one of the Select methods listed in the following table.

METHOD NAME	DESCRIPTION
Select()	Selects a node set using an XPath expression.
SelectAncestors()	Selects all the ancestors of the current node based on an XPath expression.
SelectChildren()	Selects all the children of the current node based on an XPath expression.
SelectDescendants()	Selects all of the descendants of the current node based on an XPath expression.
SelectSingleNode()	Selects one node based on an XPath expression.

If the `XPathNavigator` was created from an `XPathDocument`, it is read-only. If it is created from an `XmlDocument`, the `XPathNavigator` can be used to edit the document. This can be verified by checking the `CanEdit` property. If it is true, you can use one of the `Insert` methods. `InsertBefore` and `InsertAfter` will create a new node either before or after the current node. The source of the new node can be from an `XmlReader` or a string. Optionally, an `XmlWriter` can be returned and used to write the new node information.

Strongly typed values can be read from the nodes by using the `ValueAs` properties. Notice that this is different from `XmlReader`, which used `ReadValue` methods.

XPathNodeIterator

`XPathNodeIterator` can be thought of as the equivalent of a `NodeList` or a `NodeSet` in XPath. This object has two properties and three methods:

➤ `Clone()` — Creates a new copy of itself

➤ `Count` — Number of nodes in the `XPathNodeIterator` object

➤ `Current` — Returns an `XPathNavigator` pointing to the current node

➤ `CurrentPosition()` — Returns an integer with the current position

➤ `MoveNext()` — Moves to the next node that matches the XPath expression that created the `XPathNodeIterator`

The `XPathNodeIterator` is returned by the `XPathNavigator` `Select` methods. You use it to iterate over the set of nodes returned by a `Select` method of the `XPathNavigator`. Using the `MoveNext` method of the `XPathNodeIterator` does not change the location of the `XPathNavigator` that created it.

Using Classes from the XPath Namespace

The best way to see how these classes are used is to look at some code that iterates through the `books.xml` document. This will allow you to see how the navigation works. In order to use the examples, you first add a reference to the `System.Xml.Xsl` and `System.Xml.XPath` namespaces:

```
using System.Xml.XPath;
using System.Xml.Xsl;
```

For this example, you use the file `booksxpath.xml`. It is similar to the `books.xml` file that you have been using, except that there are a couple of extra books added. Here's the form code, which is part of the `XmlSample` project:

```
private void button1_Click(object sender, EventArgs e)
{
  //modify to match your path structure
  XPathDocument doc = new XPathDocument("books.xml");
  //create the XPath navigator
  XPathNavigator nav = ((IXPathNavigable)doc).CreateNavigator();
  //create the XPathNodeIterator of book nodes
  // that have genre attribute value of novel
  XPathNodeIterator iter = nav.Select("/bookstore/book[@genre='novel']");
  textBox1.Text = "";
  while (iter.MoveNext())
  {
    XPathNodeIterator newIter =
        iter.Current.SelectDescendants(XPathNodeType.Element, false);
    while (newIter.MoveNext())
    {
      textBox1.Text += newIter.Current.Name + ": " +
          newIter.Current.Value + "\r\n";
    }
  }
}
```

code snippet frmNavigator.cs

The first thing you do in the `button1_Click()` method is create the `XPathDocument` (called `doc`), passing in the file and path string of the document you want opened. The next line is where the `XPathNavigator` is created:

```
XPathNavigator nav = doc.CreateNavigator();
```

In the example, you can see that you use the `Select()` method to retrieve a set of nodes that all have `novel` as the value of the `genre` attribute. You then use the `MoveNext()` method to iterate through all of the novels in the book list.

To load the data into the list box, you use the `XPathNodeIterator.Current` property. This creates a new `XPathNavigator` object based on just the node that the `XPathNodeIterator` is pointing to. In this case, you are creating an `XPathNavigator` for one `book` node in the document.

The next loop takes this `XPathNavigator` and creates another `XPathNodeIterator` by issuing another type of select method, the `SelectDescendants()` method. This gives you an `XPathNodeIterator` of all of the child nodes and children of the child nodes of the `book` node.

Then, you do another `MoveNext()` loop on the `XPathNodeIterator` and load the text box with the element names and element values.

Figure 33-2 shows what the screen looks like after running the code. Note that novels are the only books listed now.

What if you wanted to add up the cost of these books? `XPathNavigator` includes the `Evaluate()` method for just this reason. `Evaluate()` has three overloads. The first one contains a string that is the XPath function call. The second overload uses the `XPathExpression` object as a parameter, and the third uses `XPathExpression` and an `XPathNodeIterator` as parameters. The following code is similar to the previous example, except that this time all of the nodes in the document are iterated through. The `Evaluate` method call at the end totals up the cost of all of the books:

FIGURE 33-2

```
private void button2_Click(object sender, EventArgs e)
{
    //modify to match your path structure
    XPathDocument doc = new XPathDocument("books.xml");
    //create the XPath navigator
    XPathNavigator nav = ((IXPathNavigable)doc).CreateNavigator();
    //create the XPathNodeIterator of book nodes
    XPathNodeIterator iter = nav.Select("/bookstore/book");
    textBox1.Text = "";
    while (iter.MoveNext())
    {
        XPathNodeIterator newIter =
            iter.Current.SelectDescendants(XPathNodeType.Element, false);
        while (newIter.MoveNext())
        {
            textBox1.Text += newIter.Current.Name + ": " + newIter.Current.Value +
                "\r\n";
        }
    }
    textBox1.Text += "=========================" + "\r\n";
    textBox1.Text += "Total Cost = " +
        nav.Evaluate("sum(/bookstore/book/price)");
}
```

code snippet frmNavigator.cs

This time, you see the total cost of the books evaluated in the text box (see Figure 33-3).

Now let's say that you need to add a node for discount. You can use the `InsertAfter` method to get this done fairly easily. Here is the code:

```csharp
private void button3_Click(object sender, EventArgs e)
{
  XmlDocument doc = new XmlDocument();
  doc.Load("books.xml");
  XPathNavigator nav = doc.CreateNavigator();

  if (nav.CanEdit)
  {
    XPathNodeIterator iter =
      nav.Select("/bookstore/book/price");
    while (iter.MoveNext())
    {
      iter.Current.InsertAfter("<disc>5</disc>");
    }
  }
  doc.Save("newbooks.xml");
}
```

FIGURE 33-3

code snippet frmNavigator.cs

Here, you add the `<disc>5</disc>` element after the price elements. First, all of the price nodes are selected. The `XPathNodeIterator` is used to iterate over the nodes, and the new node is inserted. The modified document is saved with a new name, `newbooks.xml`. The new version looks like the following:

```xml
<?xml version="1.0"?>
<!--This file represents a fragment of a book store inventory database-->
<bookstore>
  <book genre="autobiography" publicationdate="1991" ISBN="1-861003-11-0">
    <title>The Autobiography of Benjamin Franklin</title>
    <author>
      <first-name>Benjamin</first-name>
      <last-name>Franklin</last-name>
    </author>
    <price>8.99</price>
    <disc>5</disc>
  </book>
  <book genre="novel" publicationdate="1967" ISBN="0-201-63361-2">
    <title>The Confidence Man</title>
    <author>
      <first-name>Herman</first-name>
      <last-name>Melville</last-name>
    </author>
    <price>11.99</price>
    <disc>5</disc>
  </book>
  <book genre="philosophy" publicationdate="1991" ISBN="1-861001-57-6">
    <title>The Gorgias</title>
    <author>
      <name>Plato</name>
    </author>
    <price>9.99</price>
    <disc>5</disc>
  </book>
</bookstore>
```

Nodes can be inserted before or after a selected node. The nodes can also be changed, and they can be deleted. If you have changes that have to be done to large numbers of nodes, using the XPathNavigator created from an XmlDocument may be your best choice.

The System.Xml.Xsl Namespace

The System.Xml.Xsl namespace contains the classes that the .NET Framework uses to support XSL transforms. The contents of this namespace are available to any store whose classes implement the IXPathNavigable interface. In the .NET Framework, that would currently include XmlDocument, XmlDataDocument, and XPathDocument. Again, just as with XPath, use the store that makes the most sense. If you plan to create a custom store, such as one using the file system and you want to be able to do transforms, be sure to implement the IXPathNavigable interface in your class.

XSLT is based on a streaming pull model. Because of this, you can chain several transforms together. You could even apply a custom reader between transforms if needed. This allows a great deal of flexibility in design.

Transforming XML

The first example you will look at takes the books.xml document and transforms it into a simple HTML document for display, using the XSLT file books.xsl. (This code is in the XSLSample01 folder.) You will need to add the following using statements:

```
using System.IO;
using System.Xml.Xsl;
using System.Xml.XPath;
```

The following is the code to perform the transform:

Available for
download on
Wrox.com

```
private void button1_Click(object sender, EventArgs e)
{
    XslCompiledTransform trans = new XslCompiledTransform();
    trans.Load("books.xsl");
    trans.Transform("books.xml", "out.html");
    webBrowser1.Navigate(AppDomain.CurrentDomain.BaseDirectory + "out.html");
}
```

code download XslSample01.sln

A transform doesn't get any simpler than this. First, a new XmlCompiledTransform object is created. It loads the books.xsl transform document and then performs the transform. In this example, a string with the filename is used as the input. The output is out.html. This file is then loaded into the web browser control used on the form. Instead of using the filename books.xml as the input document, you can use an IXPathNavigable-based object. This would be any object that can create an XPathNavigator.

After the XmlCompiledTransform object is created and the stylesheet is loaded, the transform is performed. The Transform method can take just about any combination of IXPathNavigable objects, Streams, TextWriters, XmlWriters, and URIs as parameters. This allows a great deal of flexibility on transform flow. You can pass the output of one transform in as the input to the next transform.

XsltArgumentLists and XmlResolver objects are also included in the parameter options. We look at the XsltArgumentList object in the next section. XmlResolver-based objects are used to resolve items that are external to the current document. This could be things such as schemas, credentials, or, of course, stylesheets.

The books.xsl document is a fairly straightforward stylesheet. The document looks like this:

```
<xsl:stylesheet version="1.0"
 xmlns:xsl="http://www.w3.org/1999/XSL/Transform">
<xsl:template match="/">
    <html>
        <head>
            <title>Price List</title>
```

```
            </head>
            <body>
              <table>
                  <xsl:apply-templates/>
              </table>
            </body>
        </html>
         </xsl:template>
      <xsl:template match="bookstore">
          <xsl:apply-templates select="book"/>
      </xsl:template>
      <xsl:template match="book">
          <tr><td>
              <xsl:value-of select="title"/>
          </td><td>
              <xsl:value-of select="price"/>
          </td></tr>
      </xsl:template>
    </xsl:stylesheet>
```

Using XsltArgumentList

`XsltArgumentList` is a way that you can bind an object with methods to a namespace. Once this is done, you can invoke the methods during the transform. Here is an example:

Available for
download on
Wrox.com

```
private void button3_Click(object sender, EventArgs e)
{
    //new XPathDocument
    XPathDocument doc = new XPathDocument("books.xml");
    //new XslTransform
    XslCompiledTransform trans = new XslCompiledTransform();
    trans.Load("booksarg.xsl");
    //new XmlTextWriter since we are creating a new xml document
    XmlWriter xw = new XmlTextWriter("argSample.xml", null);
    //create the XslArgumentList and new BookUtils object
    XsltArgumentList argBook = new XsltArgumentList();
    BookUtils bu = new BookUtils();
    //this tells the argumentlist about BookUtils
    argBook.AddExtensionObject("urn:XslSample", bu);
    //new XPathNavigator
    XPathNavigator nav = doc.CreateNavigator();
    //do the transform
    trans.Transform(nav, argBook, xw);
    xw.Close();
    webBrowser1.Navigate(AppDomain.CurrentDomain.BaseDirectory + "argSample.xml");
}
```

code download XslSample01.sln

The following is the code for the `BooksUtil` class. This is the class that will be called from the transform:

Available for
download on
Wrox.com

```
class BookUtils
{
    public BookUtils() { }

    public string ShowText()
    {
      return "This came from the ShowText method!";
    }
}
```

code snippet BookUtils.cs

The following is what the output of the transform looks like; the output has been formatted for easier viewing (`argSample.xml`):

```
<books>
    <discbook>
        <booktitle>The Autobiography of Benjamin Franklin</booktitle>
        <showtext>This came from the ShowText method!</showtext>
    </discbook>
    <discbook>
        <booktitle>The Confidence Man</booktitle>
        <showtext>This came from the ShowText method!</showtext>
    </discbook>
    <discbook>
        <booktitle>The Gorgias</booktitle>
        <showtext>This came from the ShowText method!</showtext>
    </discbook>
    <discbook>
        <booktitle>The Great Cookie Caper</booktitle>
        <showtext>This came from the ShowText method!</showtext>
    </discbook>
    <discbook>
        <booktitle>A Really Great Book</booktitle>
        <showtext>This came from the ShowText method!</showtext>
    </discbook>
</books>
```

In this example, you define a new class, `BookUtils`. In this class, you have one rather useless method that returns the string `This came from the ShowText method!` In the `button3_Click()` event, you create the `XPathDocument` and `XslTransform` objects. In a previous example, you loaded the XML document and the transform document directly into the `XslCompiledTransform` object. This time, you will use the `XPathNavigator` to load the documents.

Next, you need to write the following:

```
XsltArgumentList argBook=new XsltArgumentList();
BookUtils bu=new BookUtils();
argBook.AddExtensionObject("urn:XslSample",bu);
```

This is where you create the `XsltArgumentList` object. You create an instance of the `BookUtils` object, and when you call the `AddExtensionObject()` method, you pass in a namespace for your extension and the object that you want to be able to call methods from. When you make the `Transform()` call, you pass in the `XsltArgumentList` (argBook), along with the `XPathNavigator` and the `XmlWriter` object you made.

The following is the `booksarg.xsl` document (based on `books.xsl`):

```
<xsl:stylesheet version="1.0" xmlns:xsl="http://www.w3.org/1999/XSL/Transform"
    xmlns:bookUtil="urn:XslSample">
<xsl:output method="xml" indent="yes"/>

<xsl:template match="/">
    <xsl:element name="books">
        <xsl:apply-templates/>
    </xsl:element>
</xsl:template>
<xsl:template match="bookstore">
    <xsl:apply-templates select="book"/>
</xsl:template>
<xsl:template match="book">
    <xsl:element name="discbook">
        <xsl:element name="booktitle">
            <xsl:value-of select="title"/>
        </xsl:element>
        <xsl:element name="showtext">
```

```
            <xsl:value-of select="bookUtil:ShowText()"/>
         </xsl:element>
      </xsl:element>
   </xsl:template>
</xsl:stylesheet>
```

The two important new lines are highlighted. First, you add the namespace that you created when you added the object to XsltArgumentList. Then, when you want to make the method call, you use standard XSLT namespace-prefixing syntax and make the method call.

Another way you could have accomplished this is with XSLT scripting. You can include C#, Visual Basic, and JavaScript code in the stylesheet. The great thing about this is that unlike current non-.NET implementations, the script is compiled at the XslTransform.Load() call; this way, you are executing already compiled scripts.

Go ahead and modify the previous XSLT file in this way. First, you add the script to the stylesheet. You can see the following changes in booksscript.xsl:

```
<xsl:stylesheet version="1.0" xmlns:xsl="http://www.w3.org/1999/XSL/Transform"
                xmlns:msxsl="urn:schemas-microsoft-com:xslt"
                xmlns:user="http://wrox.com">

   <msxsl:script language="C#" implements-prefix="user">

      string ShowText()
        {
            return "This came from the ShowText method!";

        }
   </msxsl:script>
   <xsl:output method="xml" indent="yes"/>
      <xsl:template match="/">
   <xsl:element name="books">
      <xsl:apply-templates/>
   </xsl:element>
      </xsl:template>
   <xsl:template match="bookstore">
      <xsl:apply-templates select="book"/>
   </xsl:template>
      <xsl:template match="book">
      <xsl:element name="discbook">
      <xsl:element name="booktitle">
         <xsl:value-of select="title"/>
      </xsl:element>
      <xsl:element name="showtext">
        <xsl:value-of select="user:ShowText()"/>
      </xsl:element>
    </xsl:element>
   </xsl:template>
</xsl:stylesheet>
```

Once again, the changes are highlighted. You set the scripting namespace, add the code (which was copied and pasted in from the Visual Studio .NET IDE), and make the call in the stylesheet. The output looks the same as that of the previous example.

Debugging XSLT

Visual Studio 2010 has the capability to debug transforms. You can actually step through a transform line by line, inspect variables, access the call stack, and set breakpoints just like you were debugging C# source code. You can debug a transform in two ways: by just using the stylesheet and input XML file or by running the application that the transform belongs to.

Debugging without the Application

When you first start creating the transforms, sometimes you don't really want to run through the entire application. You just want to get a stylesheet working. Visual Studio 2010 allows you to do this using the XSLT editor.

Load the `books.xsl` stylesheet into the Visual Studio 2010 XSLT editor. Set a breakpoint on the following line:

```
<xsl:value-of select="title"/>
```

Now, select the XML menu and then Debug XSLT. You will be asked for the input XML document. This is the XML that you will want transformed. Now under the default configuration the next thing you will see is in Figure 33-4.

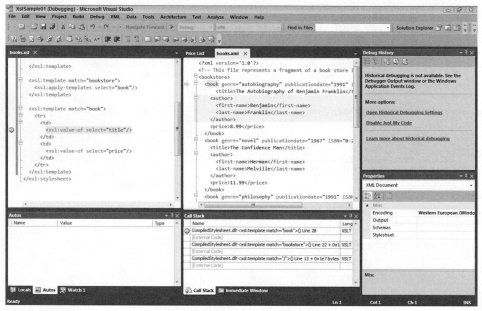

FIGURE 33-4

Now that the transform has been paused, you can explore almost all of the same debug information you can when debugging source code. Notice that the debugger is showing you the XSLT, the input document with the current element highlighted, and the output of the transform. Now you can step through the transform line by line. If your XSLT had any scripting, you could also set breakpoints in the scripts and have the same debugging experience.

Debugging with the Application

If you want to debug a transform and the application at the same time, then you will have to make one small change when you create the `XslCompiledTransform` object. The constructor has an overload that takes a Boolean as a parameter. This parameter is `enableDebug`. The default is false, which means that even if you have a breakpoint set in the transform, if you run the application code that calls the transform, it will not break. If you set the parameter to true, the debug information for the XSLT is generated and the breakpoint will be hit. Therefore, in the previous example, the line of code that created the `XslCompiledTransform` would change to this:

```
XslCompiledTransform trans = new XslCompiledTransform(true);
```

Now when the application is run in debug mode, even the XSLT will have debug information and you will again have the full Visual Studio debugging experience in your stylesheets.

To summarize, the key thing to keep in mind when performing transforms is to remember to use the proper XML data store. Use XPathDocument if you do not need editing capabilities, XmlDataDocument if you are getting your data from ADO.NET, and XmlDocument if you need to be able to edit the data. In each case, you are dealing with the same process.

XML AND ADO.NET

XML is the glue that binds ADO.NET to the rest of the world. ADO.NET was designed from the ground up to work within the XML environment. XML is used to transfer the data to and from the data store and the application or web page. Because ADO.NET uses XML as the transport in remoting scenarios, data can be exchanged with applications and systems that are not even aware of ADO.NET. Because of the importance of XML in ADO.NET, some powerful features in ADO.NET allow the reading and writing of XML documents. The System.Xml namespace also contains classes that can consume or utilize ADO.NET relational data.

The database that is used for the examples is from the AdventureWorksLT sample application. The sample database can be downloaded from codeplex.com/SqlServerSamples. Note that there are several versions of the AdventureWorks database. Most will work, but the LT version is the simplified version and is more than adequate for the purposes of this chapter.

Converting ADO.NET Data to XML

The first example uses ADO.NET, streams, and XML to pull some data from the database into a DataSet, load an XmlDocument object with the XML from the DataSet, and load the XML into a text box. To run the next few examples, you need to add the following using statements:

```
using System.Data;
using System.Xml;
using System.Data.SqlClient;
using System.IO;
```

The connection string is defined as a module-level variable:

```
string _connectString = "Server=.\\SQLExpress;
                         Database=adventureworkslt;Trusted_Connection=Yes";
```

The ADO.NET samples have a DataGrid object added to the forms. This will allow you to see the data in the ADO.NET DataSet because it is bound to the grid, as well as the data from the generated XML documents that you load in the text box. Here is the code for the first example. The first step in the examples is to create the standard ADO.NET objects to produce a DataSet object. After the data set has been created, it is bound to the grid.

```
private void button1_Click(object sender, EventArgs e)
{
    XmlDocument doc = new XmlDocument();
    DataSet ds = new DataSet("XMLProducts");
    SqlConnection conn = new SqlConnection(_connectString);
    SqlDataAdapter da = new SqlDataAdapter
                    ("SELECT Name, StandardCost FROM SalesLT.Product", conn);
    //fill the dataset
    da.Fill(ds, "Products");
    //load data into grid
    dataGridView1.DataSource = ds.Tables["Products"];
```

code snippet frmADOXML.cs

After you create the ADO.NET objects and bind to the grid, you instantiate a MemoryStream object, a StreamReader object, and a StreamWriter object. The StreamReader and StreamWriter objects will use the MemoryStream to move the XML around:

```
MemoryStream memStrm=new MemoryStream();
StreamReader strmRead=new StreamReader(memStrm);
StreamWriter strmWrite=new StreamWriter(memStrm);
```

You use a `MemoryStream` so that you don't have to write anything to disk; however, you could have used any object that was based on the `Stream` class, such as `FileStream`.

This next step is where the XML is generated. You call the `WriteXml()` method from the `DataSet` class. This method generates an XML document. `WriteXml()` has two overloads: one takes a string with the file path and name, and the other adds a mode parameter. This mode is an `XmlWriteMode` enumeration, with the following possible values:

➤   `IgnoreSchema`

➤   `WriteSchema`

➤   `DiffGram`

`IgnoreSchema` is used if you do not want `WriteXml()` to write an inline schema at the start of your XML file; use the `WriteSchema` parameter if you do want one. A DiffGram shows the data before and after an edit in a `DataSet`.

Available for
download on
Wrox.com

```
//write the xml from the dataset to the memory stream
ds.WriteXml(strmWrite, XmlWriteMode.IgnoreSchema);
memStrm.Seek(0, SeekOrigin.Begin);
//read from the memory stream to a XmlDocument object
doc.Load(strmRead);
//get all of the products elements
XmlNodeList nodeLst = doc.SelectNodes("//XMLProducts/Products");
textBox1.Text = "";

foreach (XmlNode node in nodeLst)
{
   textBox1.Text += node.InnerXml + "\r\n";
}
```

code snippet frmADOXML.cs

Figure 33-5 shows the data in the list as well as the bound data grid.

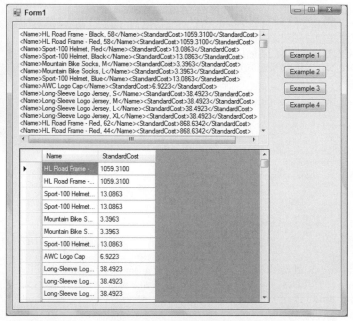

FIGURE 33-5

If you had wanted only the schema, you could have called `WriteXmlSchema()` instead of `WriteXml()`. This method has four overloads. One takes a string, which is the path and filename of the location where to write the XML document. The second overload uses an object that is based on the `XmlWriter` class. The third overload uses an object based on the `TextWriter` class. The fourth overload is derived from the `Stream` class.

In addition, if you wanted to persist the XML document to disk, you would have used something like this:

```
string file = "c:\\test\\product.xml";
ds.WriteXml(file);
```

This would give you a well-formed XML document on disk that could be read in by another stream or by a `DataSet` or used by another application or web site. Because no `XmlMode` parameter is specified, this `XmlDocument` would have the schema included. In this example, you use the stream as a parameter to the `XmlDocument.Load()` method.

You now have two views of the data, but more importantly, you can manipulate the data using two different models. You can use the `System.Data` namespace to use the data, or you can use the `System.Xml` namespace on the data. This can lead to some very flexible designs in your applications, because now you are not tied to just one object model to program with. This is the real power of the ADO.NET and `System.Xml` combination. You have multiple views of the same data and multiple ways to access the data.

The following example simplifies the process by eliminating the three streams and by using some of the ADO capabilities built into the `System.Xml` namespace. You will need to change the module-level line of code:

```
private XmlDocument doc = new XmlDocument();
```

to:

```
private XmlDataDocument doc;
```

You need this because you are now using the `XmlDataDocument`. Here is the code:

Available for
download on
Wrox.com

```
private void button3_Click(object sender, EventArgs e)
{
    XmlDataDocument doc;
    //create a dataset
    DataSet ds = new DataSet("XMLProducts");
    //connect to the northwind database and
    //select all of the rows from products table
    SqlConnection conn = new SqlConnection(_connectString);
    SqlDataAdapter da = new SqlDataAdapter
                        ("SELECT Name, StandardCost FROM SalesLT.Product", conn);
    //fill the dataset
    da.Fill(ds, "Products");
    ds.WriteXml("sample.xml", XmlWriteMode.WriteSchema);
    //load data into grid
    dataGridView1.DataSource = ds.Tables[0];
    doc = new XmlDataDocument(ds);
    //get all of the products elements
    XmlNodeList nodeLst = doc.GetElementsByTagName("Products");
    textBox1.Text = "";
    foreach (XmlNode node in nodeLst)
    {
        textBox1.Text += node.InnerXml + "\r\n";
    }
}
```

code snippet frmADOXML.cs

As you can see, the code to load the `DataSet` object into the XML document has been simplified. Instead of using the `XmlDocument` class, you are using the `XmlDataDocument` class. This class was built specifically for using data with a `DataSet` object.

The XmlDataDocument is based on the XmlDocument class, so it has all of the functionality that the XmlDocument class has. One of the main differences is the overloaded constructor that the XmlDataDocument has. Note the line of code that instantiates XmlDataDocument (doc):

```
doc = new XmlDataDocument(ds);
```

It passes in the DataSet object that you created, ds, as a parameter. This creates the XML document from the DataSet, and you do not have to use the Load() method. In fact, if you instantiate a new XmlDataDocument object without passing in a DataSet as the parameter, it will contain a DataSet with the name NewDataSet that has no DataTables in the tables collection. There is also a DataSet property, which you can set after an XmlDataDocument-based object is created.

Suppose that you add the following line of code after the DataSet.Fill() call:

```
ds.WriteXml("c:\\test\\sample.xml", XmlWriteMode.WriteSchema);
```

In this case, the following XML file, sample.xml, is produced in the folder c:\test:

```
<?xml version="1.0" standalone="yes"?>
<XMLProducts>
  <xs:schema id="XMLProducts" xmlns="" xmlns:xs="http://www.w3.org/2001/XMLSchema"
   xmlns:msdata="urn:schemas-microsoft-com:xml-msdata">
    <xs:element name="XMLProducts" msdata:IsDataSet="true"
     msdata:UseCurrentLocale="true">
      <xs:complexType>
        <xs:choice minOccurs="0" maxOccurs="unbounded">
          <xs:element name="Products">
            <xs:complexType>
              <xs:sequence>
                <xs:element name="Name" type="xs:string" minOccurs="0" />
                <xs:element name="StandardCost" type="xs:decimal" minOccurs="0" />
              </xs:sequence>
            </xs:complexType>
          </xs:element>
        </xs:choice>
      </xs:complexType>
    </xs:element>
  </xs:schema>
  <Products>
    <Name>HL Road Frame-Black, 58</Name>
    <StandardCost>1059.3100</StandardCost>
  </Products>
  <Products>
    <Name>HL Road Frame-Red, 58</Name>
    <StandardCost>1059.3100</StandardCost>
  </Products>
  <Products>
    <Name>Sport-100 Helmet, Red</Name>
    <StandardCost>13.0863</StandardCost>
  </Products>
</XMLProducts>
```

Only the first couple of Products elements are shown. The actual XML file would contain all of the products in the Products table of Northwind database.

Converting Relational Data

This looks simple enough for a single table, but what about relational data, such as multiple DataTables and Relations in the DataSet? It all still works the same way. Here is an example using two related tables:

```
private void button5_Click(object sender, EventArgs e)
{
    XmlDocument doc = new XmlDocument();
    DataSet ds = new DataSet("XMLProducts");
    SqlConnection conn = new SqlConnection(_connectString);
```

```
        SqlDataAdapter daProduct = new SqlDataAdapter
        ("SELECT Name, StandardCost, ProductCategoryID FROM SalesLT.Product", conn);
        SqlDataAdapter daCategory = new SqlDataAdapter
                ("SELECT ProductCategoryID, Name from SalesLT.ProductCategory", conn);
        //Fill DataSet from both SqlAdapters
        daProduct.Fill(ds, "Products");
        daCategory.Fill(ds, "Categories");
        //Add the relation
        ds.Relations.Add(ds.Tables["Categories"].Columns["ProductCategoryID"],
        ds.Tables["Products"].Columns["ProductCategoryID"]);
        //Write the Xml to a file so we can look at it later
        ds.WriteXml("Products.xml", XmlWriteMode.WriteSchema);
        //load data into grid
        dataGridView1.DataSource = ds.Tables[0];
        //create the XmlDataDocument
        doc = new XmlDataDocument(ds);
        //Select the productname elements and load them in the grid
        XmlNodeList nodeLst = doc.SelectNodes("//XMLProducts/Products");
        textBox1.Text = "";
        foreach (XmlNode node in nodeLst)
        {
          textBox1.Text += node.InnerXml + "\r\n";
        }
    }
```

code snippet frmADOXML.cs

In the sample you are creating, there are two `DataTable`s in the `XMLProducts` `DataSet`: `Products` and `Categories`. You create a new relation on the `ProductCategoryID` column in both tables.

By using the same `WriteXml()` method call that you did in the previous example, you will get the following XML file (`SuppProd.xml`):

```
<?xml version="1.0" standalone="yes"?>
<XMLProducts>
  <xs:schema id="XMLProducts" xmlns="" xmlns:xs="http://www.w3.org/2001/XMLSchema"
   xmlns:msdata="urn:schemas-microsoft-com:xml-msdata">
    <xs:element name="XMLProducts" msdata:IsDataSet="true"
     msdata:UseCurrentLocale="true">
      <xs:complexType>
        <xs:choice minOccurs="0" maxOccurs="unbounded">
          <xs:element name="Products">
            <xs:complexType>
              <xs:sequence>
                <xs:element name="Name" type="xs:string" minOccurs="0" />
                <xs:element name="StandardCost" type="xs:decimal" minOccurs="0" />
                <xs:element name="ProductCategoryID" type="xs:int" minOccurs="0" />
              </xs:sequence>
            </xs:complexType>
          </xs:element>
          <xs:element name="Categories">
            <xs:complexType>
              <xs:sequence>
                <xs:element name="ProductCategoryID" type="xs:int" minOccurs="0" />
                <xs:element name="Name" type="xs:string" minOccurs="0" />
              </xs:sequence>
            </xs:complexType>
          </xs:element>
        </xs:choice>
      </xs:complexType>
      <xs:unique name="Constraint1">
        <xs:selector xpath=".//Categories" />
```

```
         <xs:field xpath="ProductCategoryID" />
       </xs:unique>
       <xs:keyref name="Relation1" refer="Constraint1">
         <xs:selector xpath=".//Products" />
         <xs:field xpath="ProductCategoryID" />
       </xs:keyref>
     </xs:element>
   </xs:schema>
   <Products>
     <Name>HL Road Frame-Black, 58</Name>
     <StandardCost>1059.3100</StandardCost>
     <ProductCategoryID>18</ProductCategoryID>
   </Products>
   <Products>
     <Name>HL Road Frame-Red, 58</Name>
     <StandardCost>1059.3100</StandardCost>
     <ProductCategoryID>18</ProductCategoryID>
   </Products>
 </XMLProducts>
```

The schema includes both `DataTables` that were in the `DataSet`. In addition, the data includes all of the data from both tables. For the sake of brevity, only the first `Products` and `ProductCategory` records are shown here. As before, you could have saved just the schema or just the data by passing in the correct `XmlWriteMode` parameter.

Converting XML to ADO.NET Data

Suppose that you have an XML document that you would like to get into an ADO.NET `DataSet`. You would want to do this so that you could load the XML into a database, or perhaps bind the data to a .NET data control such as a `DataGrid`. This way, you could actually use the XML document as your data store and eliminate the overhead of the database altogether. If your data is reasonably small, this is an attractive possibility. Here is some code to get you started:

Available for
download on
Wrox.com

```csharp
private void button7_Click(object sender, EventArgs e)
{
    //create the DataSet
    DataSet ds = new DataSet("XMLProducts");

    //read in the xml document
    ds.ReadXml("Products.xml");

    //load data into grid
    dataGridView1.DataSource = ds.Tables[0];

    textBox1.Text = "";

    foreach (DataTable dt in ds.Tables)
    {
        textBox1.Text += dt.TableName + "\r\n";
        foreach (DataColumn col in dt.Columns)
        {
            textBox1.Text += "\t" + col.ColumnName + "-" + col.DataType.FullName + "\r\n";
        }
    }
}
```

code snippet frmADOXML.cs

It's that easy. In this example, you instantiate a new `DataSet` object. From there, you then call the `ReadXml()` method and you have XML in a `DataTable` in your `DataSet`. As with the `WriteXml()` methods,

`ReadXml()` has an `XmlReadMode` parameter. `ReadXml()` has a few more options in the `XmlReadMode`, as shown in the following table.

VALUE	DESCRIPTION
Auto	Sets the `XmlReadMode` to the most appropriate setting. If the data is in `DiffGram` format, `DiffGram` is selected. If a schema has already been read, or an inline schema is detected, then `ReadSchema` is selected. If no schema has been assigned to the `DataSet`, and none is detected inline, then `IgnoreSchema` is selected.
DiffGram	Reads in the `DiffGram` and applies the changes to the `DataSet`.
Fragment	Reads documents that contain XDR schema fragments, such as the type created by SQL Server.
IgnoreSchema	Ignores any inline schema that may be found. Reads data into the current `DataSet` schema. If data does not match `DataSet` schema, it is discarded.
InferSchema	Ignores any inline schema. Creates the schema based on data in the XML document. If a schema exists in the `DataSet`, that schema is used, and extended with additional columns and tables if needed. An exception is thrown if a column exists but is of a different data type.
ReadSchema	Reads the inline schema and loads the data. Will not overwrite a schema in the `DataSet` but will throw an exception if a table in the inline schema already exists in the `DataSet`.

There is also the `ReadXmlSchema()` method. This reads in a standalone schema and creates the tables, columns, and relations. You use this if your schema is not inline with your data. `ReadXmlSchema()` has the same four overloads: a string with filename and pathname, a `Stream`-based object, a `TextReader`-based object, and an `XmlReader`-based object.

To show that the data tables are being created properly, we iterate through the tables and columns and display the names in the text box. You can compare this to the database and see that all is well. The last `foreach` loops perform this task. Figure 33-6 shows the output.

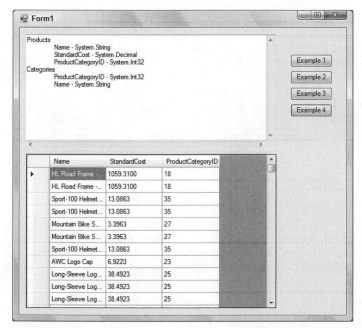

FIGURE 33-6

Looking at the list box, you can check that in the data tables that were created all the columns have the correct names and data types.

Something else you might want to note is that, because the previous two examples did not transfer any data to or from a database, no `SqlDataAdapter` or `SqlConnection` was defined. This shows the real flexibility of both the `System.Xml` namespace and ADO.NET: you can look at the same data in multiple formats. If you need to do a transform and show the data in HTML format, or if you need to bind the data to a grid, you can take the same data and, with just a method call, have it in the required format.

SERIALIZING OBJECTS IN XML

Serializing is the process of persisting an object to disk. Another part of your application, or even a separate application, can deserialize the object, and it will be in the same state it was in prior to serialization. The .NET Framework includes a couple of ways to do this.

This section looks at the `System.Xml.Serialization` namespace, which contains classes used to serialize objects into XML documents or streams. This means that an object's public properties and public fields are converted into XML elements, attributes, or both.

The most important class in the `System.Xml.Serialization` namespace is `XmlSerializer`. To serialize an object, you first need to instantiate an `XmlSerializer` object, specifying the type of the object to serialize. Then you need to instantiate a stream/writer object to write the file to a stream/document. The final step is to call the `Serialize()` method on the `XMLSerializer`, passing it the stream/writer object and the object to serialize.

Data that can be serialized can be primitive types, fields, arrays, and embedded XML in the form of `XmlElement` and `XmlAttribute` objects.

To deserialize an object from an XML document, you reverse the process in the previous example. You create a stream/reader and an `XmlSerializer` object and then pass the stream/reader to the `Deserialize()` method. This method returns the deserialized object, although it needs to be cast to the correct type.

> *The XML serializer cannot convert private data, only public data, and it cannot serialize object graphs. However, these should not be serious limitations; by carefully designing your classes, you should be able to easily avoid these issues. If you do need to be able to serialize public and private data as well as an object graph containing many nested objects, you will want to use the* `System.Runtime.Serialization` `.Formatters.Binary` *namespace.*

Some of the other tasks that you can accomplish with `System.Xml.Serialization` classes are:

➤ Determine if the data should be an attribute or element
➤ Specify the namespace
➤ Change the attribute or element name

The links between your object and the XML document are the custom C# attributes that annotate your classes. These attributes are what are used to inform the serializer how to write out the data. The `xsd.exe` tool, which is included with the .NET Framework, can help create these attributes for you. `xsd.exe` can do the following:

➤ Generate an XML schema from an XDR schema file
➤ Generate an XML schema from an XML file

➤ Generate DataSet classes from an XSD schema file

➤ Generate runtime classes that have the custom attributes for XmlSerialization

➤ Generate an XSD file from classes that you have already developed

➤ Limit which elements are created in code

➤ Determine which programming language the generated code should be in (C#, Visual Basic .NET, or JScript .NET)

➤ Create schemas from types in compiled assemblies

You should refer to the Framework documentation for details of command-line options for xsd.exe.

Despite these capabilities, you don't *have* to use xsd.exe to create the classes for serialization. The process is quite simple. The following is a simple application that serializes a class. At the beginning of the example, you have very simple code that creates a new Product object, pd, and fills it with some data:

Available for download on Wrox.com

```
private void button1_Click(object sender, EventArgs e)
{
    //new products object
    Product pd = new Product();
    //set some properties
    pd.ProductID = 200;
    pd.CategoryID = 100;
    pd.Discontinued = false;
    pd.ProductName = "Serialize Objects";
    pd.QuantityPerUnit = "6";
    pd.ReorderLevel = 1;
    pd.SupplierID = 1;
    pd.UnitPrice = 1000;
    pd.UnitsInStock = 10;
    pd.UnitsOnOrder = 0;

}
```

code snippet frmSerial.cs

The Serialize() method of the XmlSerializer class actually performs the serialization, and it has nine overloads. One of the parameters required is a stream to write the data to. It can be a Stream, TextWriter, or an XmlWriter parameter. In the example, you create a TextWriter-based object, tr. The next thing to do is to create the XmlSerializer-based object, sr. The XmlSerializer needs to know type information for the object that it is serializing, so you use the typeof keyword with the type that is to be serialized. After the sr object is created, you call the Serialize() method, passing in the tr (Stream-based object) and the object that you want serialized, in this case pd. Be sure to close the stream when you are finished with it:

Available for download on Wrox.com

```
//new TextWriter and XmlSerializer
TextWriter tr = new StreamWriter("serialprod.xml");
XmlSerializer sr = new XmlSerializer(typeof(Product));
//serialize object
sr.Serialize(tr, pd);
tr.Close();
webBrowser1.Navigate(AppDomain.CurrentDomain.BaseDirectory + "serialprod.xml");
```

code snippet frmSerial.cs

Next is the Product class, the class to be serialized. The only differences between this and any other class that you may write are the C# attributes that have been added. The XmlRootAttribute and XmlElementAttribute classes in the attributes inherit from the System.Attribute class. Don't confuse these attributes with the attributes in an XML document. A C# attribute is simply some declarative information that can be retrieved at runtime by the CLR (see Chapter 8, "Delegates, Lambdas, and Events," for more details). In this case, the attributes describe how the object should be serialized:

```
//class that will be serialized.
//attributes determine how object is serialized
[System.Xml.Serialization.XmlRootAttribute()]
  public class Product {
     private int prodId;
     private string prodName;
     private int suppId;
     private int catId;
     private string qtyPerUnit;
     private Decimal unitPrice;
     private short unitsInStock;
     private short unitsOnOrder;
     private short reorderLvl;
     private bool discont;
     private int disc;
     //added the Discount attribute
     [XmlAttributeAttribute(AttributeName="Discount")]
     public int Discount {
       get {return disc;}
       set {disc=value;}
     }
     [XmlElementAttribute()]
     public int  ProductID {
       get {return prodId;}
       set {prodId=value;}
     }
     [XmlElementAttribute()]
     public string ProductName {
       get {return prodName;}
       set {prodName=value;}
     }
     [XmlElementAttribute()]
     public int SupplierID {
       get {return suppId;}
       set {suppId=value;}
     }
     [XmlElementAttribute()]
     public int CategoryID {
       get {return catId;}
       set {catId=value;}
     }
     [XmlElementAttribute()]
     public string QuantityPerUnit {
       get {return qtyPerUnit;}
       set {qtyPerUnit=value;}
     }
     [XmlElementAttribute()]
     public Decimal UnitPrice {
       get {return unitPrice;}
       set {unitPrice=value;}
     }
     [XmlElementAttribute()]
     public short UnitsInStock {
       get {return unitsInStock;}
       set {unitsInStock=value;}
     }
     [XmlElementAttribute()]
     public short UnitsOnOrder {
       get {return unitsOnOrder;}
```

```
        set {unitsOnOrder=value;}
    }
    [XmlElementAttribute()]
    public short ReorderLevel {
        get {return reorderLvl;}
        set {reorderLvl=value;}
    }
    [XmlElementAttribute()]
    public bool Discontinued {
        get {return discont;}
        set {discont=value;}
    }
    public override string ToString()
    {
        StringBuilder outText = new StringBuilder();
        outText.Append(prodId);
        outText.Append(" ");
        outText.Append(prodName);
        outText.Append(" ");
        outText.Append(unitPrice);
        return outText.ToString();
    }
}
```

code snippet frmSerial.cs

The `XmlRootAttribute()` invocation in the attribute above the `Products` class definition identifies this class as a root element (in the XML file produced upon serialization). The attribute containing `XmlElementAttribute()` identifies that the member below the attribute represents an XML element.

You will also notice that the `ToString()` method has been overridden. This provides the string that the message box will show when you run the deserialize example.

If you look at the XML document created during serialization, you will see that it looks like any other XML document that you might have created, which is the point of the exercise:

```
<?xml version="1.0" encoding="utf-8"?>
<Products xmlns:xsi=http://www.w3.org/2001/XMLSchema-instance
    xmlns:xsd="http://www.w3.org/2001/XMLSchema"
    Discount="0">
    <ProductID>200</ProductID>
    <ProductName>Serialize Objects</ProductName>
    <SupplierID>1</SupplierID>
    <CategoryID>100</CategoryID>
    <QuantityPerUnit>6</QuantityPerUnit>
    <UnitPrice>1000</UnitPrice>
    <UnitsInStock>10</UnitsInStock>
    <UnitsOnOrder>0</UnitsOnOrder>
    <ReorderLevel>1</ReorderLevel>
    <Discontinued>false</Discontinued>
</Products>
```

There is nothing out of the ordinary here. You could use this any way that you would use an XML document. You could transform it and display it as HTML, load it into a `DataSet` using ADO.NET, load an `XmlDocument` with it, or, as you can see in the example, deserialize it and create an object in the same state that pd was in prior to serializing it (which is exactly what you're doing with the second button).

Next, you add another button event handler to deserialize a new `Products`-based object, `newPd`. This time you use a `FileStream` object to read in the XML:

```
private void button2_Click(object sender, EventArgs e)
{
    //create a reference to product type
```

```
Product newPd;
//new filestream to open serialized object
FileStream f = new FileStream("serialprod.xml", FileMode.Open);
```

Once again, you create a new `XmlSerializer`, passing in the type information of `Product`. You can then make the call to the `Deserialize()` method. Note that you still need to do an explicit cast when you create the `newPd` object. At this point, `newPd` is in exactly the same state that `pd` was:

```
//new serializer
XmlSerializer newSr = new XmlSerializer(typeof(Product));
//deserialize the object
newPd = (Product)newSr.Deserialize(f);
f.Close();
MessageBox.Show(newPd.ToString());
}
```

code snippet frmSerial.cs

The message box should show you the product ID, product name, and the unit price of the object you just deserialized. This comes from the `ToString()` override that you implemented in the `Product` class.

What about situations where you have derived classes and possibly properties that return an array? `XmlSerializer` has that covered as well. Here's a slightly more complex example that deals with these issues.

First, you define three new classes, `Product`, `BookProduct` (derived from `Product`), and `Inventory` (which contains both of the other classes). Notice that once again you have overridden the `ToString()` method. This time you're just going to list the items in the `Inventory` class:

```
public class BookProduct: Product
{
    private string isbnNum;
    public BookProduct() {}
    public string ISBN
    {
        get {return isbnNum;}
        set {isbnNum=value;}
    }
}

public class Inventory
{
    private Product[] stuff;
    public Inventory() {}
    //need to have an attribute entry for each data type
    [XmlArrayItem("Prod",typeof(Product)),
    XmlArrayItem("Book",typeof(BookProduct))]
    public Product[] InventoryItems
    {
        get {return stuff;}
        set {stuff=value;}
    }
    public override string ToString()
    {
        StringBuilder outText = new StringBuilder();
        foreach (Product prod in stuff)
        {
            outText.Append(prod.ProductName);
            outText.Append("\r\n");
        }
        return outText.ToString();
    }
}
```

code snippet frmSerial.cs

The Inventory class is the one of interest here. If you are to serialize this class, you need to insert an attribute containing XmlArrayItem constructors for each type that can be added to the array. You should note that XmlArrayItem is the name of the .NET attribute represented by the XmlArrayItemAttribute class.

The first parameter supplied to these constructors is what you would like the element name to be in the XML document that is created during serialization. If you leave off the ElementName parameter, the elements will be given the same name as the object type (Product and BookProduct in this case). The second parameter that must be specified is the type of the object.

There is also an XmlArrayAttribute class that you would use if the property were returning an array of objects or primitive types. Because you are returning different types in the array, you use XmlArrayItemAttribute, which allows the higher level of control.

In the button4_Click() event handler, you create a new Product object and a new BookProduct object (newProd and newBook). You add data to the various properties of each object, and add the objects to a Product array. You next create a new Inventory object and pass in the array as a parameter. You can then serialize the Inventory object to recreate it later:

```csharp
private void button4_Click(object sender, EventArgs e)
{
    //create the XmlAttributes object
    XmlAttributes attrs = new XmlAttributes();
    //add the types of the objects that will be serialized
    attrs.XmlElements.Add(new XmlElementAttribute("Book", typeof(BookProduct)));
    attrs.XmlElements.Add(new XmlElementAttribute("Product", typeof(Product)));
    XmlAttributeOverrides attrOver = new XmlAttributeOverrides();
    //add to the attributes collection
    attrOver.Add(typeof(Inventory), "InventoryItems", attrs);
    //create the Product and Book objects
    Product newProd = new Product();
    BookProduct newBook = new BookProduct();
    newProd.ProductID = 100;
    newProd.ProductName = "Product Thing";
    newProd.SupplierID = 10;
    newBook.ProductID = 101;
    newBook.ProductName = "How to Use Your New Product Thing";
    newBook.SupplierID = 10;
    newBook.ISBN = "123456789";
    Product[] addProd ={ newProd, newBook };
    Inventory inv = new Inventory();
    inv.InventoryItems = addProd;
    TextWriter tr = new StreamWriter("inventory.xml");
    XmlSerializer sr = new XmlSerializer(typeof(Inventory), attrOver);
    sr.Serialize(tr, inv);
    tr.Close();
    webBrowser1.Navigate(AppDomain.CurrentDomain.BaseDirectory + "inventory.xml");
}
```

code snippet frmSerial.cs

The XML document looks like this:

```xml
<?xml version="1.0" encoding="utf-8"?>
<Inventory xmlns:xsi="http://www.w3.org/2001/XMLSchema-instance"
 xmlns:xsd="http://www.w3.org/2001/XMLSchema">
  <Product Discount="0">
    <ProductID>100</ProductID>
    <ProductName>Product Thing</ProductName>
    <SupplierID>10</SupplierID>
    <CategoryID>0</CategoryID>
    <UnitPrice>0</UnitPrice>
```

```
    <Book Discount="0">
      <ProductID>101</ProductID>
      <ProductName>How to Use Your New Product Thing</ProductName>
      <SupplierID>10</SupplierID>
      <CategoryID>0</CategoryID>
      <UnitPrice>0</UnitPrice>
      <UnitsInStock>0</UnitsInStock>
      <UnitsOnOrder>0</UnitsOnOrder>
      <ReorderLevel>0</ReorderLevel>
      <Discontinued>false</Discontinued>
      <ISBN>123456789</ISBN>
    </Book>
  </Inventory>
```

As you can see, you get the same XML as you did with the earlier example. To deserialize this object
and recreate the `Inventory`-based object that you started out with, you need to create all of the same
`XmlAttributes`, `XmlElementAttribute`, and `XmlAttributeOverrides` objects that you created when you
serialized the object. After you do that, you can read in the XML and recreate the `Inventory` object just as
you did before. Here is the code to deserialize the `Inventory` object:

```
private void button2_Click(object sender, System.EventArgs e)
{
    //create the new XmlAttributes collection
    XmlAttributes attrs=new XmlAttributes();
    //add the type information to the elements collection
    attrs.XmlElements.Add(new XmlElementAttribute("Book",typeof(BookProduct)));
    attrs.XmlElements.Add(new XmlElementAttribute("Product",typeof(Product)));

    XmlAttributeOverrides attrOver=new XmlAttributeOverrides();
    //add to the Attributes collection
    attrOver.Add(typeof(Inventory),"InventoryItems",attrs);

    //need a new Inventory object to deserialize to
    Inventory newInv;

    //deserialize and load data into the listbox from deserialized object
    FileStream f=new FileStream(".\\.\\.\\inventory.xml",FileMode.Open);
    XmlSerializer newSr=new XmlSerializer(typeof(Inventory),attrOver);

    newInv=(Inventory)newSr.Deserialize(f);
    if(newInv!=null)
    {
        foreach(Product prod in newInv.InventoryItems)
        {
            listBox1.Items.Add(prod.ProductName);
        }
    }
    f.Close();
}
```

Note that the first few lines of code are identical to the code you used to serialize the object.

The `System.Xml.XmlSerialization` namespace provides a very powerful tool set for serializing objects to
XML. By serializing and deserializing objects to XML instead of to binary format, you are given the option
of doing something else with this XML, greatly adding to the flexibility of your designs.

LINQ TO XML AND .NET

With the introduction of LINQ to the .NET Framework, the focus was on easy access to the data that
you want to use in your applications. One of the main data stores in the application space is XML and,
therefore, it really was a natural evolution to create the LINQ to XML implementation.

Prior to the LINQ to XML release, working with XML using `System.Xml` was not an easy task. With the inclusion of `System.Xml.Linq`, you now find a series of capabilities that make the process of working with XML in your code much easier.

Many developers previously turned to the `XmlDocument` object to create XML within their application code. This object allows you to create XML documents that enable you to append elements, attributes, and other items in a hierarchical fashion. With LINQ to XML and the inclusion of the new `System.Xml.Linq` namespace, you will now find some new objects that make the creation of XML documents a much simpler process.

WORKING WITH DIFFERENT XML OBJECTS

In addition to the LINQ querying ability included in .NET 4, the .NET Framework includes XML objects that work so well they can stand on their own outside of LINQ. You can use these objects in place of working directly with the DOM in this release. Within the `System.Xml.Linq` namespace, you will find a series of LINQ to XML helper objects that make working with an XML document in memory much easier.

The following sections work through the objects that are available to you within this namespace.

 Many of the examples in this chapter use a file called `Hamlet.xml`. *You can find this file at* `http://metalab.unc.edu/bosak/xml/eg/shaks200.zip` *that includes all of Shakespeare's plays as XML files.*

XDocument

The `XDocument` is a replacement of the `XmlDocument` object from the pre-.NET 3.5 world; it is easier to work with in dealing with XML documents. The `XDocument` object works with the other new objects in this space, such as the `XNamespace`, `XComment`, `XElement`, and `XAttribute` objects.

One of the more important members of the `XDocument` object is the `Load()` method:

```
XDocument xdoc = XDocument.Load(@"C:\Hamlet.xml");
```

This operation will load the `Hamlet.xml` contents as an in-memory `XDocument` object. You can also pass a `TextReader` or `XmlReader` object into the `Load()` method. From here, you are able to programmatically work with the XML:

Available for download on Wrox.com

```
XDocument xdoc = XDocument.Load(@"C:\Hamlet.xml");
Console.WriteLine(xdoc.Root.Name.ToString());
Console.WriteLine(xdoc.Root.HasAttributes.ToString());
```

code download ConsoleApplication1.sln

This produces the following results:

```
PLAY
False
```

Another important member to be aware of is the `Save()` method, which, like the `Load()` method, allows you to save to a physical disk location or to a `TextWriter` or `XmlWriter` object:

```
XDocument xdoc = XDocument.Load(@"C:\Hamlet.xml");

xdoc.Save(@"C:\CopyOfHamlet.xml");
```

XElement

One object that you will work with frequently is the XElement object. With XElement objects, you can easily create single-element objects that are XML documents themselves, as well as fragments of XML. For instance, here is an example of writing an XML element with a corresponding value:

```
XElement xe = new XElement("Company", "Lipper");
Console.WriteLine(xe.ToString());
```

In the creation of a XElement object, you can define the name of the element as well as the value used in the element. In this case, the name of the element will be <Company>, and the value of the <Company> element will be Lipper. Running this in a console application with a System.Xml.Linq reference produces the following result:

```
<Company>Lipper</Company>
```

You can create an even more complete XML document using multiple XElement objects, as illustrated in the following example:

```
using System;
using System.Linq;
using System.Xml.Linq;

namespace ConsoleApplication1
{
    class Class1
    {
        static void Main()
        {
            XElement xe = new XElement("Company",
                new XElement("CompanyName", "Lipper"),
                new XElement("CompanyAddress",
                    new XElement("Address", "123 Main Street"),
                    new XElement("City", "St. Louis"),
                    new XElement("State", "MO"),
                    new XElement("Country", "USA")));

            Console.WriteLine(xe.ToString());

            Console.ReadLine();
        }
    }
}
```

code download ConsoleApplication1.sln

Running this application produces the results illustrated in Figure 33-7.

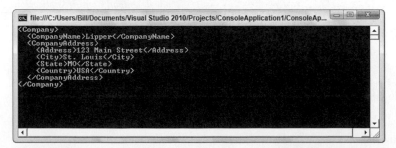

FIGURE 33-7

XNamespace

The XNamespace is an object that represents an XML namespace and is easily applied to elements within your document. For instance, you can take the previous example and easily apply a namespace to the root element:

```
using System;
using System.Linq;
using System.Xml.Linq;

namespace ConsoleApplication1
{
    class Class1
    {
        static void Main()
        {
            XNamespace ns = "http://www.lipperweb.com/ns/1";

            XElement xe = new XElement(ns + "Company",
                new XElement("CompanyName", "Lipper"),
                new XElement("CompanyAddress",
                    new XElement("Address", "123 Main Street"),
                    new XElement("City", "St. Louis"),
                    new XElement("State", "MO"),
                    new XElement("Country", "USA")));

            Console.WriteLine(xe.ToString());

            Console.ReadLine();
        }
    }
}
```

code download ConsoleApplication1.sln

In this case, an XNamespace object is created by assigning it a value of http://www.lipperweb.com/ns/1. From there, it is actually used in the root element <Company> with the instantiation of the XElement object:

```
XElement xe = new XElement(ns + "Company", // .
```

This produces the results illustrated in Figure 33-8.

FIGURE 33-8

In addition to dealing with only the root element, you can also apply namespaces to all your elements, as shown in the following example:

```
using System;
using System.Linq;
using System.Xml.Linq;

namespace ConsoleApplication1
```

```
    {
        class Class1
        {
            static void Main()
            {
                XNamespace ns1 = "http://www.lipperweb.com/ns/root";
                XNamespace ns2 = "http://www.lipperweb.com/ns/sub";

                XElement xe = new XElement(ns1 + "Company",
                    new XElement(ns2 + "CompanyName", "Lipper"),
                    new XElement(ns2 + "CompanyAddress",
                        new XElement(ns2 + "Address", "123 Main Street"),
                        new XElement(ns2 + "City", "St. Louis"),
                        new XElement(ns2 + "State", "MO"),
                        new XElement(ns2 + "Country", "USA"))));

                Console.WriteLine(xe.ToString());

                Console.ReadLine();
            }
        }
    }
```

code download ConsoleApplication1.sln

This produces the results shown in Figure 33-9.

FIGURE 33-9

In this case, you can see that the subnamespace was applied to everything you specified except for the `<Address>`, `<City>`, `<State>`, and the `<Country>` elements because they inherit from their parent, `<CompanyAddress>`, which has the namespace declaration.

XComment

The `XComment` object allows you to easily add XML comments to your XML documents. The following example shows the addition of a comment to the top of the document:

```
using System;
using System.Linq;
using System.Xml.Linq;

namespace ConsoleApplication1
{
    class Class1
    {
        static void Main(string[] args)
        {
            XDocument xdoc = new XDocument();

            XComment xc = new XComment("Here is a comment.");
```

Available for download on Wrox.com

```
                    xdoc.Add(xc);

                    XElement xe = new XElement("Company",
                        new XElement("CompanyName", "Lipper"),
                        new XElement("CompanyAddress",
                            new XComment("Here is another comment."),
                            new XElement("Address", "123 Main Street"),
                            new XElement("City", "St. Louis"),
                            new XElement("State", "MO"),
                            new XElement("Country", "USA")));
                    xdoc.Add(xe);

                    Console.WriteLine(xdoc.ToString());

                    Console.ReadLine();
                }
            }
        }
```

code download ConsoleApplication1.sln

Here, an `XDocument` object that contains two XML comments is written to the console, one at the top of the document and another within the `<CompanyAddress>` element. The output of this is presented in Figure 33-10.

FIGURE 33-10

XAttribute

In addition to elements, another important factor of XML is attributes. Adding and working with attributes is done through the use of the `XAttribute` object. The following example shows the addition of an attribute to the root `<Company>` node:

```
using System;
using System.Linq;
using System.Xml.Linq;

namespace ConsoleApplication1
{
    class Class1
    {
        static void Main()
        {
            XElement xe = new XElement("Company",
                new XAttribute("MyAttribute", "MyAttributeValue"),
                new XElement("CompanyName", "Lipper"),
                new XElement("CompanyAddress",
                    new XElement("Address", "123 Main Street"),
                    new XElement("City", "St. Louis"),
                    new XElement("State", "MO"),
```

```
                        new XElement("Country", "USA")));

            Console.WriteLine(xe.ToString());

            Console.ReadLine();
        }
    }
}
```

Here, the attribute `MyAttribute` with a value of `MyAttributeValue` is added to the root element of the XML document, producing the results shown in Figure 33-11.

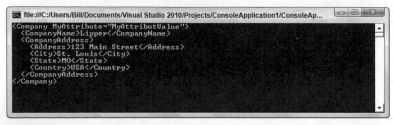

FIGURE 33-11

USING LINQ TO QUERY XML DOCUMENTS

Now that you can get your XML documents into an `XDocument` object and work with the various parts of this document, you can also use LINQ to XML to query your XML documents and work with the results.

Querying Static XML Documents

You will notice that querying a static XML document using LINQ to XML takes almost no work at all. The following example makes use of the `hamlet.xml` file and queries to get all the players (actors) that appear in the play. Each of these players is defined in the XML document with the `<PERSONA>` element:

```csharp
using System;
using System.Linq;
using System.Xml.Linq;

namespace ConsoleApplication1
{
    class Class1
    {
        static void Main(string[] args)
        {
            XDocument xdoc = XDocument.Load(@"C:\hamlet.xml");

            var query = from people in xdoc.Descendants("PERSONA")
                        select people.Value;

            Console.WriteLine("{0} Players Found", query.Count());
            Console.WriteLine();

            foreach (var item in query)
            {
                Console.WriteLine(item);
            }
```

```
        Console.ReadLine();
    }
  }
}
```

code download ConsoleApplication1.sln

In this case, an XDocument object loads up a physical XML file (hamlet.xml) and then performs a LINQ query over the contents of the document:

```
var query = from people in xdoc.Descendants("PERSONA")
            select people.Value;
```

The people object is a representation of all the <PERSONA> elements found in the document. Then the select statement gets at the values of these elements. From there, a Console .WriteLine() method is used to write out a count of all the players found using query.Count(). Next, each of the items is written to the screen in a foreach loop. The results you should see are presented here:

```
26 Players Found

CLAUDIUS, king of Denmark.
HAMLET, son to the late king, and nephew to the present king.
POLONIUS, lord chamberlain.
HORATIO, friend to Hamlet.
LAERTES, son to Polonius.
LUCIANUS, nephew to the king.
VOLTIMAND
CORNELIUS
ROSENCRANTZ
GUILDENSTERN
OSRIC
A Gentleman
A Priest.
MARCELLUS
BERNARDO
FRANCISCO, a soldier.
REYNALDO, servant to Polonius.
Players.
Two Clowns, grave-diggers.
FORTINBRAS, prince of Norway.
A Captain.
English Ambassadors.
GERTRUDE, queen of Denmark, and mother to Hamlet.
OPHELIA, daughter to Polonius.
Lords, Ladies, Officers, Soldiers, Sailors, Messengers, and other Attendants.
Ghost of Hamlet's Father.
```

Querying Dynamic XML Documents

A lot of dynamic XML documents are available on the Internet these days. You will find blog feeds, podcast feeds, and more that provide an XML document by sending a request to a specific URL endpoint. These feeds can be viewed either in the browser, through an RSS-aggregator, or as pure XML. This example shows you how to work with an RSS feed directly from your code.

```
using System;
using System.Linq;
using System.Xml.Linq;

namespace ConsoleApplication1
{
    class Class1
    {
```

```
static void Main()
{
    XDocument xdoc =
        XDocument.Load(@"http://geekswithblogs.net/evjen/Rss.aspx");

    var query = from rssFeed in xdoc.Descendants("channel")
                select new
                {
                    Title = rssFeed.Element("title").Value,
                    Description = rssFeed.Element("description").Value,
                    Link = rssFeed.Element("link").Value,
                };

    foreach (var item in query)
    {
        Console.WriteLine("TITLE: " + item.Title);
         Console.WriteLine("DESCRIPTION: " + item.Description);
         Console.WriteLine("LINK: " + item.Link);
    }

    Console.WriteLine();

    var queryPosts = from myPosts in xdoc.Descendants("item")
                     select new
                     {
                         Title = myPosts.Element("title").Value,
                         Published =
                             DateTime.Parse(
                               myPosts.Element("pubDate").Value),
                         Description =
                             myPosts.Element("description").Value,
                         Url = myPosts.Element("link").Value,
                         Comments = myPosts.Element("comments").Value
                     };

    foreach (var item in queryPosts)
    {
        Console.WriteLine(item.Title);
    }

    Console.ReadLine();
}
```

code download ConsoleApplication1.sln

Looking at this code, you can see that the Load() method of the XDocument object points to a URL where the XML is retrieved. The first query pulls out all the main subelements of the <channel> element in the feed and creates new objects called Title, Description, and Link to get at the values of these subelements.

From there, a foreach statement is run to iterate through all the items found in this query. The results are as follows:

```
TITLE: Bill Evjen's Blog
DESCRIPTION: Code, Life and Community
LINK: http://geekswithblogs.net/evjen/Default.aspx
```

The second query works through all the <item> elements and the various subelements it finds (these are all the blog entries found in the blog). Though a lot of the items found are rolled up into properties, in the foreach loop, only the Title property is used. You will see something similar to the following results from this query:

```
AJAX Control Toolkit Controls Grayed Out-HOW TO FIX
Welcome .NET 4.0!
Visual Studio
IIS 7.0 Rocks the House!
Word Issue-Couldn't Select Text
Microsoft Releases XML Schema Designer CTP1
Silverlight Book
Microsoft Tafiti as a beta
ReSharper on Visual Studio
Windows Vista Updates for Performance and Reliability Issues
First Review of Professional XML
Go to MIX07 for free!
Microsoft Surface and the Future of Home Computing?
Alas my friends-I'm *not* TechEd bound
```

MORE QUERY TECHNIQUES FOR XML DOCUMENTS

If you have been working with the XML document hamlet.xml, you will notice that it is quite large. So far, you've seen a couple of ways to query into the XML document in this chapter, but this next section takes a look at reading and writing to the XML document.

Reading from an XML Document

Earlier you saw just how easy it was to query into an XML document using the LINQ query statements, as shown here:

```
var query = from people in xdoc.Descendants("PERSONA")
            select people.Value;
```

This query returned all the players that were found in the document. Using the Element() method of the XDocument object, you can also get at specific values of the XML document that you are working with. For instance, the following XML fragment shows you how the title is represented in the hamlet.xml document:

```
<?xml version="1.0"?>

<PLAY>
    <TITLE>The Tragedy of Hamlet, Prince of Denmark</TITLE>

    <!-XML removed for clarity->

</PLAY>
```

As you can see, the <TITLE> element is a nested element of the <PLAY> element. You can easily get at the title by using the following bit of code in your console application:

```
XDocument xdoc = XDocument.Load(@"C:\hamlet.xml");

Console.WriteLine(xdoc.Element("PLAY").Element("TITLE").Value);
```

This bit of code will write out the title, The Tragedy of Hamlet, Prince of Denmark, to the console screen. In the code, you were able to work down the hierarchy of the XML document by using two Element() method calls — first calling the <PLAY> element and then the <TITLE> element found nested within the <PLAY> element.

Looking more at the hamlet.xml document, you will see a large list of players that are defined with the use of the <PERSONA> element:

```
<?xml version="1.0"?>

<PLAY>
```

```
<TITLE>The Tragedy of Hamlet, Prince of Denmark</TITLE>

<!--XML removed for clarity-->

<PERSONAE>
    <TITLE>Dramatis Personae</TITLE>

    <PERSONA>CLAUDIUS, king of Denmark.</PERSONA>
    <PERSONA>HAMLET, son to the late king,
     and nephew to the present king.</PERSONA>
    <PERSONA>POLONIUS, lord chamberlain.</PERSONA>
    <PERSONA>HORATIO, friend to Hamlet.</PERSONA>
    <PERSONA>LAERTES, son to Polonius.</PERSONA>
    <PERSONA>LUCIANUS, nephew to the king.</PERSONA>

    <!--XML removed for clarity-->

</PERSONAE>

</PLAY>
```

Now look at this C# query:

```
XDocument xdoc = XDocument.Load(@"C:\hamlet.xml");

Console.WriteLine(
    xdoc.Element("PLAY").Element("PERSONAE").Element("PERSONA").Value);
```

This bit of code starts at <PLAY>, works down to the <PERSONAE> element, and then makes use of the <PERSONA> element. However, using this will produce the following results:

```
CLAUDIUS, king of Denmark
```

The reason for this is that although there is a collection of <PERSONA> elements, you are dealing only with the first one that is encountered using the Element().Value call.

Writing to an XML Document

In addition to reading from an XML document, you can write to the document just as easily. For instance, if you wanted to change the name of the first player of the Hamlet play file, you could use the following code:

Available for download on Wrox.com

```
using System;
using System.Linq;
using System.Xml.Linq;

namespace ConsoleApplication1
{
    class Class1
    {
        static void Main()
        {
            XDocument xdoc = XDocument.Load(@"C:\hamlet.xml");

            xdoc.Element("PLAY").Element("PERSONAE").
                Element("PERSONA").SetValue("Bill Evjen, king of Denmark");

            Console.WriteLine(xdoc.Element("PLAY").
                Element("PERSONAE").Element("PERSONA").Value);

            Console.ReadLine();
        }
    }
}
```

code download ConsoleApplication1.sln

In this case, the first instance of the `<PERSONA>` element is overwritten with the value of `Bill Evjen, king of Denmark` using the `SetValue()` method of the `Element()` object. After the `SetValue()` is called and the value is applied to the XML document, the value is then retrieved using the same approach as before. When you run this bit of code, you can indeed see that the value of the first `<PERSONA>` element has been changed.

Another way to change the document (by adding items to it in this example) is to create the elements you want as `XElement` objects and then add them to the document:

```
using System;
using System.Linq;
using System.Xml.Linq;

namespace ConsoleApplication1
{
    class Class1
    {
        static void Main()
        {
            XDocument xdoc = XDocument.Load(@"C:\hamlet.xml");

            XElement xe = new XElement("PERSONA",
                "Bill Evjen, king of Denmark");

            xdoc.Element("PLAY").Element("PERSONAE").Add(xe);

            var query = from people in xdoc.Descendants("PERSONA")
                        select people.Value;

            Console.WriteLine("{0} Players Found", query.Count());
            Console.WriteLine();

            foreach (var item in query)
            {
                Console.WriteLine(item);
            }

            Console.ReadLine();
        }
    }
}
```

code download ConsoleApplication1.sln

In this case, an `XElement` document is created called `xe`. The construction of `xe` will give you the following XML output:

```
<PERSONA>Bill Evjen, king of Denmark</PERSONA>
```

Then using the `Element().Add()` method from the `XDocument` object, you are able to add the created element:

```
xdoc.Element("PLAY").Element("PERSONAE").Add(xe);
```

Now when you query all the players, you will find that instead of 26 as before, you now have 27 with the new one at the bottom of the list. In addition to `Add()`, you can also use `AddFirst()`, which will do what it says — add it to the beginning of the list instead of the end (which is the default).

SUMMARY

In this chapter, you explored many aspects of the `System.Xml` namespace of the .NET Framework. You looked at how to read and write XML documents using the very fast `XmlReader`- and `XmlWriter`-based classes. You looked at how the DOM is implemented in .NET and how to use the power of DOM. You saw that XML and ADO.NET are indeed very closely related. A `DataSet` and an XML document are just two different views of the same underlying architecture. In addition, you visited XPath, XSL transforms, and the debugging features added to Visual Studio.

Finally, you serialized objects to XML and were able to bring them back with just a couple of method calls.

XML will be an important part of your application development for years to come. The .NET Framework has made available a very rich and powerful toolset for working with XML.

This chapter also focused on using LINQ to XML and some of the options available to you in reading and writing from XML files and XML sources, whether the source is static or dynamic.

Using LINQ to XML, you are able to have a strongly typed set of operations for performing CRUD operations against your XML files and sources. However, you can still use your `XmlReader` and `XmlWriter` code along with the LINQ to XML capabilities.

This chapter also introduced the LINQ to XML helper objects of `XDocument`, `XElement`, `XNamespace`, `XAttribute`, and `XComment`. You will find these are outstanding objects that make working with XML easier than ever before.

34

.NET Programming with SQL Server

WHAT'S IN THIS CHAPTER?

- ➤ Hosting the .NET runtime with SQL Server
- ➤ Classes from the namespace `System.Data.SqlServer`
- ➤ Creating user-defined types and aggregates
- ➤ Stored procedures
- ➤ User-defined functions
- ➤ Triggers
- ➤ Using XML data types

SQL Server 2005 was the first version of this database product to host the .NET runtime. In fact, it was the first new version of Microsoft's SQL Server product in nearly six years. It allows running .NET assemblies in the SQL Server process. Furthermore, it enables you to create stored procedures, functions, and data types with .NET programming languages such as C# and Visual Basic.

> *This chapter requires a SQL Server edition hosting the CLR. This is possible with SQL Server 2005 or a later version. SQL Server 2005 and 2008 require .NET 3.5. So with the server-side projects of this chapter, the CLR version must be set to 3.5.*
>
> *The samples in this chapter use a newly created SqlServerSampleDB database that you can download with the code samples and the AdventureWorks database. The AdventureWorks database is a sample database from Microsoft that you can install as an optional component with SQL Server.*
>
> *SQL Server has many features that are not directly associated with the CLR, such as many T-SQL improvements, but they are not covered in this book. To get more information about these features, you can read Wrox's Professional Microsoft SQL Server 2008 Programming (Wiley Publishing, Inc., ISBN 978-0-470-25702-9).*

.NET RUNTIME HOST

SQL Server is a host of the .NET runtime. In versions prior to CLR 2.0, multiple hosts already existed to run .NET applications; for example, a host for Windows Forms and a host for ASP.NET. Internet Explorer is another runtime host that allows running Windows Forms controls.

SQL Server allows running a .NET assembly inside the SQL Server process, where it is possible to create stored procedures, functions, data types, and triggers with CLR code.

Every database that makes use of CLR code creates its own *application domain*. This guarantees that CLR code from one database doesn't have any influence on any other database.

 You can read more about application domains in Chapter 18, "Assemblies."

An important factor in programming for SQL Server is security. SQL Server as a .NET runtime host defines permission levels: safe, external, and unsafe.

Safe — With the safety level *safe*, only computational CLR classes can be used. The assembly is able to perform only local data access. The functionality of these classes is similar to a T-SQL stored procedure. The code access security defines that the only .NET permission is execution of CLR code.

External — With the safety level *external*, it is possible to access the network, file system, registry, or other databases with client-side ADO.NET.

Unsafe — The safety level *unsafe* means that everything can happen, because this safety level allows you to invoke native code. Assemblies with the unsafe permission level can be installed only by a database administrator.

With SQL Server 2008 you need to use a target framework set to version 2.0 because the assemblies from this version are trusted with SQL Server 2008.

To enable custom .NET code to be run within SQL Server, the CLR must be enabled with the `sp_configure` stored procedure:

```
sp_configure [clr enabled], 1
reconfigure
```

The attribute class `HostProtectionAttribute` in the namespace `System.Security.Permissions` is suited for protection of the hosting environment. With this attribute, it is possible to define whether a method uses shared state, exposes synchronization, or controls the hosting environment. Because such behavior is usually not needed within SQL Server code (and could influence the performance of the SQL Server), assemblies that have these settings applied are not allowed to be loaded in SQL Server with safe and external safety levels.

For using assemblies with SQL Server, the assembly can be installed with the CREATE ASSEMBLY command. With this command, the name of the assembly used in SQL Server, the path to the assembly, and the safety level can be applied:

```
CREATE ASSEMBLY mylibrary FROM c:/ProCSharp/SqlServer/Demo.dll
    WITH PERMISSION SET = SAFE
```

With Visual Studio 2010, the permission level of the generated assembly can be defined with the Database tab of the project properties, as shown in Figure 34-1.

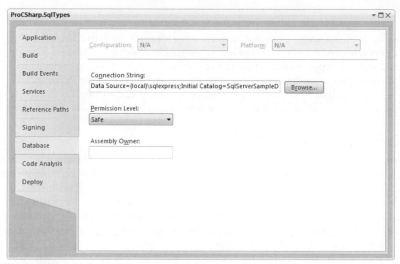

FIGURE 34-1

MICROSOFT.SQLSERVER.SERVER

Chapter 30, "Core ADO.NET," discusses classes from the namespace System.Data.SqlClient. This section discusses another namespace, the Microsoft.SqlServer.Server namespace. The Microsoft.SqlServer.Server namespace includes classes, interfaces, and enumerations specific to the .NET Framework. However, many of the System.Data.SqlClient classes are also needed within server-side code as you will see.

The following table lists the major classes from the Microsoft.SqlServer.Server namespace and their functionality.

CLASS	DESCRIPTION
SqlContext	Like an HTTP context, the SQL context is associated with the request of a client. With static members of the SqlContext class, SqlPipe, SqlTriggerContext, and WindowsIdentity can be accessed.
SqlPipe	With the SqlPipe class, results or information can be sent to the client. This class offers the methods ExecuteAndSend(), Send(), and SendResultsRow(). The Send() method has different overloads to either send a SqlDataReader, SqlDataRecord, or string.
SqlDataRecord	The SqlDataRecord represents a single row of data. This class is used in conjunction with SqlPipe to send or receive information from the client.
SqlTriggerContext	The SqlTriggerContext class is used within triggers. This class provides information about the trigger that was fired.

This namespace also includes several attribute classes: SqlProcedureAttribute, SqlFunctionAttribute, SqlUserDefinedAttribute, and SqlTriggerAttribute. These classes are used for deployment of stored procedures, functions, user-defined types, and triggers in SQL Server. When deploying from Visual Studio, it is required that you apply these attributes. When deploying the database objects using SQL statements, these attributes are not needed but they help, because some properties of these attributes influence the characteristics of the database objects.

You see these classes in action later in this chapter when writing stored procedures and user-defined functions is discussed, but first, the following section looks into creating user-defined types with C#.

USER-DEFINED TYPES

User-defined types (UDTs) can be used similarly to normal SQL Server data types to define the type of a column in a table. With older versions of SQL Server, it was already possible to define UDTs. Of course, these UDTs could be based only on SQL types, such as the ZIP type shown in the following code. The stored procedure sp_addtype allows you to create user-defined types. Here the user-defined type ZIP is based on the CHAR data type with a length of 5. NOT NULL specifies that NULL is not allowed with the ZIP data type. By using ZIP as a data type, it is no longer necessary to remember that it should be 5 char long and not null:

```
EXEC sp_addtype ZIP 'CHAR(5)', 'NOT NULL'
```

With SQL Server 2005 and later, UDTs can be defined with CLR classes. However, this feature is not meant to add object orientation to the database; for example, to create a Person class to have a Person data type. SQL Server is a relational data store, and this is still true with UDTs. You cannot create a class hierarchy of UDTs, and it is not possible to reference fields or properties of a UDT type with a SELECT statement. If properties of a person (for example, FirstName or LastName) must be accessed or a list of Person objects must be sorted (for example, by FirstName or LastName), it is still better to define columns for first name or last name inside a Persons table or to use the XML data type.

UDTs are meant for very simple data types. Before .NET, it was also possible to create custom data types; for example, the ZIP data type. With UDTs it is not possible to create a class hierarchy, and they are not meant to get complex data types to the database. One requirement of a UDT is that it must be convertible to a string, because the string representation is used to display the value.

How the data is stored within SQL Server can be defined: either an automatic mechanism can be used to store the data in a native format, or you can convert the data to a byte stream to define how the data should be stored.

Creating UDTs

In this example, you create a SqlCoordinate type representing the world coordinates longitude and latitude for easily defining the location of places, cities, and the like. To create CLR objects with Visual Studio, create a new Visual C# SQL CLR Database Project in the category Database Projects ⇨ SQL Server, and add a UDT by using the User-Defined Type template from the Solution Explorer. The name of the UDT should be SqlCoordinate.

With the template, the base functionality of a custom type is already defined:

```csharp
using System;
using System.Data;
using System.Data.SqlClient;
using System.Data.SqlTypes;
using Microsoft.SqlServer.Server;

[Serializable]
[Microsoft.SqlServer.Server.SqlUserDefinedType(Format.Native)]
public struct SqlCoordinate: INullable
{
    public override string ToString()
    {
        // Replace the following code with your code
        return "";
    }

    public bool IsNull
    {
        get
        {
```

```
            // Put your code here
            return m_Null;
        }
    }

    public static SqlCoordinate Null
    {
        get
        {
            SqlCoordinate h = new SqlCoordinate();
            h.m_Null = true;
            return h;
        }
    }

    public static SqlCoordinate Parse(SqlString s)
    {
        if (s.IsNull)
            return Null;
        SqlCoordinate u = new SqlCoordinate();
        // Put your code here
        return u;
    }

    // This is a place-holder method
    public string Method1()
    {
        //Insert method code here
        return "Hello";
    }

    // This is a place-holder static method
    public static SqlString Method2()
    {
        // Insert method code here
        return new SqlString("Hello");
    }

    // This is a placeholder field member
    public int var1;
    // Private member
    private bool m_Null;
}
```

Because this type can also be used directly from client code, it is a good idea to add a namespace, which is not done automatically.

The struct SqlCoordinate implements the interface INullable. The interface INullable is required for UDTs because database types can also be null. The attribute SqlUserDefinedType is used for automatic deployment with Visual Studio for UDTs. The argument Format.Native defines the serialization format to be used. Two serialization formats are possible: Format.Native and Format.UserDefined. Format .Native is the simple serialization format where the engine performs serialization and deserialization of instances. This serialization allows only value types (predefined and structs of value types). Reference types (which include the string type) require the UserDefined serialization format. With the SqlCoordinate struct, the data types to serialize are of type int and bool, which are value types.

Using Format.UserDefined requires the interface IBinarySerialize to be implemented. The IBinarySerialize interface provides custom implementation for user-defined types. Read() and Write() methods must be implemented for serialization of the data to a BinaryReader and a BinaryWriter.

```
namespace Wrox.ProCSharp.SqlServer

{
    [Serializable]
    [SqlUserDefinedType(Format.Native)]
    public struct SqlCoordinate: INullable
    {
        private int longitude;
        private int latitude;
        private bool isNull;
```

code snippet SqlTypes/SqlCoordinate.cs

The attribute `SqlUserDefinedType` allows setting several properties, which are shown in the following table.

SQLUSERDEFINEDTYPE ATTRIBUTE PROPERTY	DESCRIPTION
Format	The property `Format` defines how the data type is stored within SQL Server. Currently supported formats are `Format.Native` and `Format.UserDefined`.
IsByteOrdered	If the property `IsByteOrdered` is set to `true`, it is possible to create an index for the data type, and it can be used with `GROUP BY` and `ORDER BY` SQL statements. The disk representation will be used for binary comparisons. Each instance can have only one serialized representation, so binary comparisons can succeed. The default is `false`.
IsFixedLength	If the disk representation of all instances is of the same size, `IsFixedLength` can be set to `true`.
MaxByteSize	The maximum number of bytes needed to store the data is set with `MaxByteSize`. This property is specified only with a user-defined serialization.
Name	With the `Name` property, a different name of the type can be set. By default the name of the class is used.
ValidationMethodName	With the `ValidationMethodName` property a method name can be defined to validate instances when the deserialization takes place.

To represent the direction of the coordinate, the enumeration `Orientation` is defined:

```
public enum Orientation
{
    NorthEast,
    NorthWest,
    SouthEast,
    SouthWest
}
```

This enumeration can be used only within methods of the struct `SqlCoordinate`, not as a member field, because enumerations are not supported by the native serialization format although enums are based on number types. Future versions may support enums with the native format in SQL Server.

The struct `SqlCoordinate` specifies some constructors to initialize the `longitude`, `latitude`, and `isNull` variables. The variable `isNull` is set to `true` if no values are assigned to `longitude` and `latitude`, which is the case in the default constructor. A default constructor is needed with UDTs.

With the worldwide coordination system, longitude and latitude are defined with degrees, minutes, and seconds. Vienna, Austria has the coordinates 48° 14′ longitude and 16° 20′ latitude. (The symbols °, ′, and ″ represent degrees, minutes, and seconds, respectively.)

With the variables longitude and latitude, the longitude and latitude values are stored using seconds. The constructor with seven integer parameters converts degrees, minutes, and seconds to seconds, and sets the longitude and latitude to negative values if the coordinate is based in the South or West:

```
public SqlCoordinate(int longitude, int latitude)
{
    isNull = false;
    this.longitude = longitude;
    this.latitude = latitude;
}


public SqlCoordinate(int longitudeDegrees, int longitudeMinutes,
        int longitudeSeconds, int latitudeDegrees, int latitudeMinutes,
        int latitudeSeconds, Orientation orientation)
{
    isNull = false;
    this.longitude = longitudeSeconds + 60 * longitudeMinutes + 3600 *
        longitudeDegrees;
    this.latitude = latitudeSeconds + 60 * latitudeMinutes + 3600 *
        latitudeDegrees;
    switch (orientation)
    {
        case Orientation.SouthWest:
            longitude = -longitude;
            latitude = -latitude;
            break;
        case Orientation.SouthEast:
            longitude = -longitude;
            break;
        case Orientation.NorthWest:
            latitude = -latitude;
            break;
    }
}
```

The INullable interface defines the property IsNull, which must be implemented to support nullability. The static property Null is used to create an object that represents a null value. In the get accessor a SqlCoordinate object is created, and the isNull field is set to true:

```
public bool IsNull
{
    get
    {
        return isNull;
    }
}

public static SqlCoordinate Null
{
    get
    {
        return new SqlCoordinate { isNull = true };
    }
}
```

A UDT must be converted from and to a string. For conversion to a string, the ToString() method of the Object class must be overridden. The variables longitude and latitude are converted in the following code for a string representation to show the degrees, minutes, and seconds notation:

```
public override string ToString()
{
    if (this.isNull)
```

```
            return null;

        char northSouth = longitude > 0 ? 'N': 'S';
        char eastWest = latitude > 0 ? 'E': 'W';

        int longitudeDegrees = Math.Abs(longitude) / 3600;
        int remainingSeconds = Math.Abs(longitude) % 3600;
        int longitudeMinutes = remainingSeconds / 60;
        int longitudeSeconds = remainingSeconds % 60;

        int latitudeDegrees = Math.Abs(latitude) / 3600;
        remainingSeconds = Math.Abs(latitude) % 3600;
        int latitudeMinutes = remainingSeconds / 60;
        int latitudeSeconds = remainingSeconds % 60;

        return String.Format("{0}˚{1}'{2}\"{3},{4}˚{5}'{6}\"{7}",
            longitudeDegrees, longitudeMinutes, longitudeSeconds,
            northSouth, latitudeDegrees, latitudeMinutes,
            latitudeSeconds, eastWest);
    }
```

Conversion from a string happens with the `Parse()` method. The string that is entered from the user is represented in the `SqlString` parameter of the static method `Parse()`. First, the `Parse()` method checks if the string represents a null value, in which case the `Null` property is invoked to return an empty `SqlCoordinate` object. If the `SqlString s` does not represent a null value, the text of the string is converted to pass the longitude and latitude values to the `SqlCoordinate` constructor:

```
public static SqlCoordinate Parse(SqlString s)
{
    if (s.IsNull)
        return SqlCoordinate.Null;

    try
    {
        string[] coordinates = s.Value.Split(',');
        char[] separators = { '˚', '\'', '\"' };
        string[] longitudeVals = coordinates[0].Split(separators);
        string[] latitudeVals = coordinates[1].Split(separators);

        if (longitudeVals.Length != 4 && latitudeVals.Length != 4)
            throw new ArgumentException(
                "Argument has a wrong syntax. " +
                "This syntax is required: 37˚47\'0\"N,122˚26\'0\"W");

        Orientation orientation;
        if (longitudeVals[3] == "N" && latitudeVals[3] == "E")
            orientation = Orientation.NorthEast;
        else if (longitudeVals[3] == "S" && latitudeVals[3] == "W")
            orientation = Orientation.SouthWest;
        else if (longitudeVals[3] == "S" && latitudeVals[3] == "E")
            orientation = Orientation.SouthEast;
        else
            orientation = Orientation.NorthWest;

        return new SqlCoordinate(
            int.Parse(longitudeVals[0]), int.Parse(longitudeVals[1]),
            int.Parse(longitudeVals[2]),
            int.Parse(latitudeVals[0]), int.Parse(latitudeVals[1]),
            int.Parse(latitudeVals[2]), orientation);
    }
    catch (FormatException ex)
```

```
                    {
                        throw new ArgumentException(
                            "Argument has a wrong syntax. " +
                            "This syntax is required: 37'47\'0\"N,122'26\'0\"W",
                                ex.Message);
                    }
                }
            }
```

Using UDTs with SQL Server

After building the assembly, it can be deployed with SQL Server. Configuration of the UDT in SQL Server can be done either with Visual Studio 2010 using the Build Deploy Project menu or using these SQL commands:

```
CREATE ASSEMBLY SqlTypes FROM
'c:\ProCSharp\SqlServer\SqlTypes.dll'
CREATE TYPE Coordinate EXTERNAL NAME
[SqlTypes].[Wrox.ProCSharp.SqlServer.SqlCoordinate]
```

With `EXTERNAL NAME`, the name of the assembly as well as the name of the class, including the namespace, must be set.

Now it is possible to create a table called `Cities` that contains the data type `SqlCoordinate`, as shown in Figure 34-2. Fill the table with data as shown in Figure 34-3.

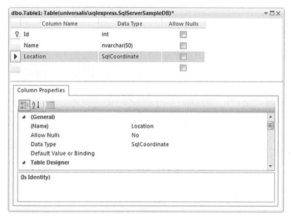

FIGURE 34-2

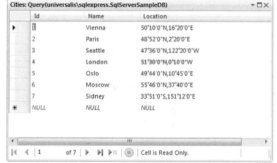

FIGURE 34-3

Using UDTs from Client-Side Code

The assembly of the UDT must be referenced to use the UDT from client-side code. Then it can be used like any other type on the client.

 Because the assembly containing the UDTs is used both from the client and from the SQL Server, it is a good idea to put UDTs in a separate assembly from the other SQL Server extensions such as stored procedures and functions.

In the sample code, the `SELECT` statement of the `SqlCommand` object references the columns of the `Cities` table that contains the `Location` column, which is of type `SqlCoordinate`. Calling the method

ToString() invokes the ToString() method of the SqlCoordinate class to display the coordinate value in a string format:

```
// UDTClient
using System;
using System.Data;
using System.Data.SqlClient;
using Wrox.ProCSharp.SqlServer;

class Program
{
    static void Main()
    {
        string connectionString =
            @"server=(local);database=ProCSharp;trusted_connection=true";
        var connection = new SqlConnection(connectionString);
        var command = connection.CreateCommand();
        command.CommandText = "SELECT Id, Name, Location FROM Cities";
        connection.Open();

        SqlDataReader reader =
                command.ExecuteReader(CommandBehavior.CloseConnection);
        while (reader.Read())
        {

            Console.WriteLine("{0,-10} {1}", reader[1].ToString(),
                    reader[2].ToString());
        }
        reader.Close();
    }
}
```

code snippet UDTClient/Program.cs

Of course, it is also possible to cast the returned object from the SqlDataReader to a SqlCoordinate type for using any other implemented methods of the Coordinate type:

```
SqlCoordinate coordinate = (SqlCoordinate)reader[2];
```

Running the application produces the following output:

```
Vienna      50°10'0"N,16°20'0"E
Paris       48°52'0"N,2°20'0"E
Seattle     47°36'0"N,122°20'0"W
London      51°30'0"N,0°10'0"W
Oslo        59°55'0"N,10°45'0"E
Moscow      55°46'0"N,37°40'0"E
Sydney      33°51'0"S,151°12'0"E
```

> *With all the great functionality of UDTs, you have to be aware of an important restriction. Before deploying a new version of a UDT, the existing version must be dropped. This is possible only if all columns using the type are removed. Don't plan on using UDTs for types that you change frequently.*

USER-DEFINED AGGREGATES

An aggregate is a function that returns a single value based on multiple rows. Examples of built-in aggregates are COUNT, AVG, and SUM:

➤ COUNT returns the record count of all selected records

➤ AVG returns the average of values from a column of selected rows

➤ SUM returns the sum of all values of a column

All built-in aggregates work only with built-in value types.

A simple usage of the built-in aggregate AVG is shown here to return the average unit price of all products from the AdventureWorks sample database by passing the ListPrice column to the AVG aggregate in the SELECT statement:

```
SELECT AVG(ListPrice) AS 'average list price'
FROM Production.Product
```

The result from the SELECT statement gives the average list price of all products:

```
average list price
438,6662
```

The SELECT statement returns just a single value that represents the average of all ListPrice column values. Aggregates can also work with groups. In the next example, the AVG aggregate is combined with the GROUP BY clause to return the average list price of every product line:

```
SELECT ProductLine, AVG(ListPrice) AS 'average list price'
FROM Production.Product
GROUP BY ProductLine
```

The average list price is now grouped by the product line:

```
ProductLine     average list price
NULL            16,8429
M               827,0639
R               965,3488
S               50,3988
T               840,7621
```

For custom value types, and if you want to do a specific calculation based on a selection of rows, you can create a user-defined aggregate.

Creating User-Defined Aggregates

To write a user-defined aggregate with CLR code, a simple class with the methods Init(), Accumulate(), Merge(), and Terminate() must be implemented. The functionality of these methods is shown in the following table.

METHOD	DESCRIPTION
Init()	The Init() method is invoked for every group of rows to be processed. In this method, initialization can be done for calculation of every row group.
Accumulate()	The Accumulate() method is invoked for every value in all groups. The parameter of this method must be of the correct type that is accumulated; this can also be the class of a user-defined type.
Merge()	The Merge() method is invoked when the result of one aggregation must be combined with another aggregation.
Terminate()	After the last row of every group is processed, the Terminate() method is invoked. Here, the result of the aggregate must be returned with the correct data type.

The code sample shows how to implement a simple user-defined aggregate to calculate the sum of all rows in every group. For deployment with Visual Studio, the attribute SqlUserDefinedAggregate is applied to the class SampleSum. As with the UDT, with user-defined aggregates the format for storing the aggregate must be defined with a value from the Format enumeration. Again, Format.Native is for using automatic serialization with blittable data types.

In the code sample, the variable `sum` is used for accumulation of all values of a group. In the `Init()` method, the variable `sum` is initialized for every new group to accumulate. The method `Accumulate()`, which is invoked for every value, adds the value of the parameter to the `sum` variable. With the `Merge()` method, one aggregated group is added to the current group. Finally, the method `Terminate()` returns the result of a group:

Available for download on Wrox.com

```csharp
[Serializable]
[SqlUserDefinedAggregate(Format.Native)]
public struct SampleSum
{
    private int sum;

    public void Init()
    {
        sum = 0;
    }

    public void Accumulate(SqlInt32 Value)
    {
        sum += Value.Value;
    }

    public void Merge(SampleSum Group)
    {
        sum += Group.sum;
    }

    public SqlInt32 Terminate()
    {
        return new SqlInt32(sum);
    }
}
```

code snippet SqlSamplesUsingAdventureWorks/SampleSum.cs

 You can use the Aggregate template from Visual Studio to create the core code for building the user-defined aggregate. The template from Visual Studio creates a struct that uses the `SqlString` *type as a parameter and return type with the* `Accumulate` *and* `Terminate` *methods. You can change the type to a type that represents the requirement of your aggregate. In the example, the* `SqlInt32` *type is used.*

Using User-Defined Aggregates

The user-defined aggregate can be deployed either with Visual Studio or with the `CREATE AGGREGATE` statement. Following the `CREATE AGGREGATE` is the name of the aggregate, the parameter (`@value int`), and the return type. `EXTERNAL NAME` requires the name of the assembly and the .NET type including the namespace:

```sql
CREATE AGGREGATE [SampleSum] (@value int) RETURNS [int] EXTERNAL NAME
                [Demo].[SampleSum]
```

After the user-defined aggregate has been installed, it can be used as shown in the following `SELECT` statement, where the number of ordered products is returned by joining the `Product` and `PurchaseOrderDetail` tables. For the user-defined aggregate, the `OrderQty` column of the Order `PurchaseOrderDetail` table is defined as an argument:

```
SELECT Purchasing.PurchaseOrderDetail.ProductID AS Id,
    Production.Product.Name AS Product,
    dbo.SampleSum(Purchasing.PurchaseOrderDetail.OrderQty) AS Sum
FROM Production.Product INNER JOIN
    Purchasing.PurchaseOrderDetail ON
    Purchasing.PurchaseOrderDetail.ProductID = Production.Product.ProductID
GROUP BY Purchasing.PurchaseOrderDetail.ProductID, Production.Product.Name
ORDER BY Id
```

An extract of the returned result that shows the number of orders for products by using the aggregate function SampleSum is presented here:

```
Id      Product              Sum
1       Adjustable Race      154
2       Bearing Ball         150
4       Headset Ball Bearings 153
317     LL Crankarm          44000
318     ML Crankarm          44000
319     HL Crankarm          71500
320     Chainring Bolts      375
321     Chainring Nut        375
322     Chainring            7440
```

STORED PROCEDURES

SQL Server allows the creation of stored procedures with C#. A stored procedure is a subroutine, and they are physically stored in the database. They definitely are not to be considered a replacement for T-SQL. T-SQL still has an advantage when the procedure is mainly data-driven.

Take a look at the T-SQL stored procedure GetCustomerOrders, which returns information from customer orders from the AdventureWorks database. This stored procedure returns orders from the customer that is specified with the parameter CustomerID:

```
CREATE PROCEDURE GetCustomerOrders
    (
    @CustomerID int
    )
AS
SELECT SalesOrderID, OrderDate, DueDate, ShipDate FROM Sales.SalesOrderHeader
    WHERE (CustomerID = @CustomerID)
    ORDER BY SalesOrderID
```

Creating Stored Procedures

As you can see in the following code listing, implementing the same stored procedure with C# has more complexity. The attribute SqlProcedure is used to mark a stored procedure for deployment. With the implementation, a SqlCommand object is created. With the constructor of the SqlConnection object, the string "Context Connection=true" is passed to use the connection that was already opened by the client calling the stored procedure. Very similarly to the code you saw in Chapter 30, the SQL SELECT statement is set and one parameter is added. The ExecuteReader() method returns a SqlDataReader object. This reader object is returned to the client by invoking the Send() method of the SqlPipe:

Available for
download on
Wrox.com

```
using System.Data;
using System.Data.SqlClient;
using Microsoft.SqlServer.Server;

public partial class StoredProcedures
{
    [SqlProcedure]
    public static void GetCustomerOrdersCLR(int customerId)
    {
        SqlConnection connection = new SqlConnection("Context Connection=true");
        connection.Open();
```

```
        SqlCommand command = new SqlCommand();
        command.Connection = connection;
        command.CommandText = "SELECT SalesOrderID, OrderDate, DueDate, " +
            "ShipDate " +
            "FROM Sales.SalesOrderHeader " +
            "WHERE (CustomerID = @CustomerID)" +
            "ORDER BY SalesOrderID";

        command.Parameters.Add("@CustomerID", SqlDbType.Int);
        command.Parameters["@CustomerID"].Value = customerId;

        SqlDataReader reader = command.ExecuteReader();
        SqlPipe pipe = SqlContext.Pipe;
        pipe.Send(reader);
        connection.Close();
    }
};
```

code snippet SqlSamplesUsingAdventureWorks/GetCustomerOrdersCLR.cs

CLR stored procedures are deployed to SQL Server either using Visual Studio or with the CREATE PROCEDURE statement. With this SQL statement, the parameters of the stored procedure are defined, as well as the name of the assembly, class, and method:

```
CREATE PROCEDURE GetCustomerOrdersCLR
(
    @CustomerID nchar(5)
)
AS EXTERNAL NAME Demo.StoredProcedures.GetCustomerOrdersCLR
```

Using Stored Procedures

The CLR stored procedure can be invoked just like a T-SQL stored procedure by using classes from the namespace System.Data.SqlClient. First, a SqlConnection object is created. The CreateCommand() method returns a SqlCommand object. With the command object, the name of the stored procedure GetCustomerOrdersCLR is set to the CommandText property. As with all stored procedures, the CommandType property must be set to CommandType.StoredProcedure. The method ExecuteReader() returns a SqlDataReader object to read record by record:

```
using System;
using System.Data;
using System.Data.SqlClient;

//...

        string connectionString =
            @"server=(local);database=AdventureWorks;trusted_connection=true";
        var connection = new SqlConnection(connectionString);
        SqlCommand command = connection.CreateCommand();
        command.CommandText = "GetCustomerOrdersCLR";
        command.CommandType = CommandType.StoredProcedure;
        var param = new SqlParameter("@customerId", 3);
        command.Parameters.Add(param);
        connection.Open();
        SqlDataReader reader =
                command.ExecuteReader(CommandBehavior.CloseConnection);
        while (reader.Read())
        {
            Console.WriteLine("{0} {1:d}", reader["SalesOrderID"], reader["OrderDate"]);
        }
        reader.Close();
```

code snippet UsingSP/Program.cs

The classes from the namespace `System.Data.SqlClient` *are discussed in Chapter 30.*

Invoking the stored procedure written with T-SQL or with C# is not different at all. The code for calling stored procedures is completely identical; from the caller code you don't know if the stored procedure is implemented with T-SQL or the CLR. An extract of the result shows the order dates for the customer with ID 3:

```
44124  9/1/2001
44791  12/1/2001
45568  3/1/2002
46377  6/1/2002
47439  9/1/2002
48378  12/1/2002
```

As you have seen, mainly data-driven stored procedures are better done with T-SQL. The code is a lot shorter. Writing stored procedures with the CLR has the advantage if you need some specific data-processing, for example, by using the .NET cryptography classes.

USER-DEFINED FUNCTIONS

User-defined functions are somewhat similar to stored procedures. The big difference is that user-defined functions can be invoked within SQL statements.

Creating User-Defined Functions

A CLR user-defined function can be defined with the attribute `SqlFunction`. The sample function `CalcHash()` converts the string that is passed to a hashed string. The MD5 algorithm that is used for hashing the string is implemented with the class `MD5CryptoServiceProvider` from the namespace `System.Security.Cryptography`. The `ComputeHash()` method computes the hash from the byte array input and returns a computed hash byte array. The hashed byte array is converted back to a `string` by using the `StringBuilder` class:

```csharp
using System.Data.SqlTypes;
using System.Security.Cryptography;
using System.Text;
using Microsoft.SqlServer.Server;

public partial class UserDefinedFunctions
{
    [SqlFunction]
    public static SqlString CalcHash(SqlString value)
    {
        byte[] source = ASCIIEncoding.ASCII.GetBytes(value.ToString());
        byte[] hash = new MD5CryptoServiceProvider().ComputeHash(source);

        var output = new StringBuilder(hash.Length);

        for (int i = 0; i < hash.Length - 1; i++)
        {
            output.Append(hash[i].ToString("X2"));
        }

        return new SqlString(output.ToString());
    }
}
```

code snippet SqlSamplesUsingAdventureWorks/CalcHash.cs

Using User-Defined Functions

A user-defined function can be deployed with SQL Server very similarly to the other .NET extensions: either with Visual Studio 2010 or with the CREATE FUNCTION statement:

```
CREATE FUNCTION CalcHash
(
    @value nvarchar
)
RETURNS nvarchar
AS EXTERNAL NAME Demo.UserDefinedFunctions.CalcHash
```

A sample usage of the CalcHash() function is shown with this SELECT statement, where the credit card number is accessed from the CreditCard table in the AdventureWorks database by returning just the hash code from the credit card number:

```
SELECT Sales.CreditCard.CardType AS [Card Type],
    dbo.CalcHash(Sales.CreditCard.CardNumber) AS [Hashed Card]
FROM Sales.CreditCard INNER JOIN Sales.ContactCreditCard ON
    Sales.CreditCard.CreditCardID = Sales.ContactCreditCard.CreditCardID
WHERE Sales.ContactCreditCard.ContactID = 11
```

The result returned shows the hashed credit card number for contact ID 11:

```
Card Type       Hashed Card
ColonialVoice 7482F7B4E613F71144A9B336A3B9F6
```

TRIGGERS

A *trigger* is a special kind of stored procedure invoked when a table is modified (for example, when a row is inserted, updated, or deleted). Triggers are associated with tables and the action that should activate them (for example, on insert/update/delete of rows).

With triggers, changes of rows can be cascaded through related tables or more complex data integrity can be enforced.

Within a trigger you have access to the current data of a row and the original data, so it is possible to reset the change to the earlier state. Triggers are automatically associated with the same transaction as the command that fires the trigger, so you get a correct transactional behavior.

The trigger uCreditCard that follows is part of the AdventureWorks sample database. This trigger is fired when a row in the CreditCard table is updated. With this trigger, the ModifiedDate column of the CreditCard table is updated to the current date. For accessing the data that is changed, the temporary table inserted is used:

```
CREATE TRIGGER [Sales].[uCreditCard] ON [Sales].[CreditCard]
AFTER UPDATE NOT FOR REPLICATION AS
BEGIN
    SET NOCOUNT ON;

    UPDATE [Sales].[CreditCard]
    SET [Sales].[CreditCard].[ModifiedDate] = GETDATE()
    FROM inserted
    WHERE inserted.[CreditCardID] = [Sales].[CreditCard].[CreditCardID];
END;
```

Creating Triggers Example

This example demonstrates implementing data integrity with triggers when new records are inserted into the Users table. To create a trigger with the CLR, a simple class must be defined that includes static methods that have the attribute SqlTrigger applied. The attribute SqlTrigger defines the table that is associated with the trigger and the event when the trigger should occur.

In this example, the associated table is `Person.Contact`, which is indicated by the `Target` property. The `Event` property defines when the trigger should occur; here, the event string is set to `FOR INSERT`, which means the trigger is started when a new row is inserted in the `Users` table.

The property `SqlContext.TriggerContext` returns the trigger context in an object of type `SqlTriggerContext`. The `SqlTriggerContext` class offers three properties:

➤   `ColumnsUpdated` returns a Boolean array to flag every column that was changed

➤   `EventData` contains the new and the original data of an update in XML format

➤   `TriggerAction` returns an enumeration of type `TriggerAction` to mark the reason for the trigger

The following code compares whether the `TriggerAction` of the trigger context is set to `TriggerAction.Insert` before continuing.

Triggers can access temporary tables; for example, in the following code listing the `INSERTED` table is accessed. With `INSERT`, `UPDATE`, and `DELETE` SQL statements, temporary tables are created. The `INSERT` statement creates an `INSERTED` table; the `DELETE` statement creates a `DELETED` table. With the `UPDATE` statement both `INSERTED` and `DELETED` tables are used. The temporary tables have the same columns as the table that is associated with the trigger. The SQL statement `SELECT Username, Email FROM INSERTED` is used to access username and e-mail, and to check the e-mail address for correct syntax. `SqlCommand.ExecuteRow()` returns a row represented in a `SqlDataRecord`. Username and e-mail are read from the data record. Using the regular expression class, `RegEx`, the expression used with the `IsMatch()` method checks if the e-mail address conforms to valid e-mail syntax. If it does not conform, an exception is thrown and the record is not inserted, because a rollback occurs with the transaction:

```
using System;
using System.Data.SqlClient;
using System.Text.RegularExpressions;
using Microsoft.SqlServer.Server;

public partial class Triggers
{
    [SqlTrigger(Name ="InsertContact", Target="Person.Contact",
        Event="FOR INSERT")]
    public static void InsertContact()
    {
        SqlTriggerContext triggerContext = SqlContext.TriggerContext;

        if (triggerContext.TriggerAction == TriggerAction.Insert)
        {
            var connection = new SqlConnection("Context Connection=true");
            var command = new SqlCommand();
            command.Connection = connection;
            command.CommandText = "SELECT EmailAddress FROM INSERTED";
            connection.Open();
            string email = (string)command.ExecuteScalar();
            connection.Close();

            if (!Regex.IsMatch(email,
                @"([\w-]+\.)*?[\w-]+@[\w-]+\.([\w-]+\.)*?[\w]+$"))
            {
                throw new FormatException("Invalid email");
            }
        }
    }
}
```

code snippet SqlSamplesUsingAdventureWorks/InsertContact.cs

Using Triggers

Using deployment of Visual Studio 2010, the trigger can be deployed to the database. You can use the CREATE TRIGGER command to create the trigger manually:

```
CREATE TRIGGER InsertContact ON Person.Contact
FOR INSERT
AS EXTERNAL NAME Demo.Triggers.InsertContact
```

Trying to insert rows into the Users table with an incorrect e-mail throws an exception, and the insert is not done.

XML DATA TYPE

One of the major programming features of SQL Server is the XML data type. With older versions of SQL Server, XML data is stored inside a string or a blob. Now XML is a supported data type that allows you to combine SQL queries with XQuery expressions to search within XML data. An XML data type can be used as a variable, a parameter, a column, or a return value from a UDF.

With Microsoft Office, it is possible to store Word and Excel documents as XML. Word and Excel also support using custom XML schemas, where only the content (and not the presentation) is stored with XML. The output of Office applications can be stored directly in SQL Server, where it is possible to search within this data. Of course, custom XML data can also be stored in SQL Server.

> *Don't use XML types for relational data. If you do a search for some of the elements and if the schema is clearly defined for the data, storing these elements in a relational fashion allows the data to be accessed faster. If the data is hierarchical and some elements are optional and may change over time, storing XML data has many advantages.*

Tables with XML Data

Creating tables with XML data is as simple as selecting the XML data type with a column. The following CREATE TABLE SQL command creates the Exams table with a column ID that is also the primary key, the column Number, and the column Info, which is of type XML:

```
CREATE TABLE [dbo].[Exams](
    [Id] [int] IDENTITY(1,1) NOT NULL,
    [Number] [nchar] (10) NOT NULL,
    [Info] [xml] NOT NULL,
    CONSTRAINT [PK_Exams] PRIMARY KEY CLUSTERED
    (
        [Id] ASC
    ) ON [PRIMARY]
) ON [PRIMARY]
```

For a simple test, the table is filled with this data:

```
INSERT INTO Exams values('70-502',
 '<Exam Number="70-502">
    <Title>TS: Microsoft .NET Framework 3.5, Windows Presentation Foundation
        Application Development
    </Title>
    <Certification Name="MCTS Windows Presentation Foundation Application Development"
        Status="Core" />
    <Certification Name="MCTS Web Applications" Status="Core" />
    <Certification Name="MCTS Distributed Applications" Status="Core" />
```

```
        <Course>6460</Course>
        <Topic>Creating a WPF Application</Topic>
        <Topic>Building User Interfaces</Topic>
        <Topic>Adding and Managing Content</Topic>
        <Topic>Binding to Data Sources</Topic>
        <Topic>Customizing Appearance</Topic>
        <Topic>Configuring and Deploying WPF Applications</Topic>
    </Exam>')

INSERT INTO Exams values('70-562',
 '<Exam Number="70-562">
        <Title>TS: Microsoft .NET Framework 3.5, ASP.NET Application Development</Title>
        <Certification Name="MCTS ASP.NET Applications" Status="Core" />
        <Course>2310</Course>
        <Course>6463</Course>
        <Topic>Configuring and Deploying Web Applications</Topic>
        <Topic>Consuming and Creating Server Controls</Topic>
        <Topic>Working with Data and Services</Topic>
        <Topic>Troubleshooting and Debugging Web Applications</Topic>
        <Topic>Working with ASP.NET AJAX and Client-Side Scripting</Topic>
        <Topic>Targeting Mobile Devices</Topic>
        <Topic>Programming Web Applications</Topic>
    </Exam>')

INSERT INTO Exams values('70-561',
 '<Exam Number="70-561">
        <Title>TS: Microsoft .NET Framework 3.5, ADO.NET Application Development</Title>
        <Certification Name="MCTS ADO.NET Applications" Status="Core" />
        <Course>2310</Course>
        <Course>6464</Course>
        <Topic>Connecting to Data Sources</Topic>
        <Topic>Selecting and Querying Data</Topic>
        <Topic>Modifying Data</Topic>
        <Topic>Synchronizing Data</Topic>
        <Topic>Working with Disconnected Data</Topic>
        <Topic>Object Relational Mapping by Using the Entity Framework</Topic>
    </Exam>')
```

Reading XML Values

You can read the XML data with ADO.NET using a `SqlDataReader` object. The `SqlDataReader` method `GetSqlXml()` returns a `SqlXml` object. The `SqlXml` class has a property `Value` that returns the complete XML representation and a `CreateReader()` method that returns an `XmlReader` object.

The `Read()` method of the `XmlReader` is repeated in a `while` loop to read node by node. With the output there's interest only in information about the value of the attribute `Number`, and the values of the elements `Title` and `Course`. The node to which the reader is positioned is compared with the corresponding XML element names, and the corresponding values are written to the console:

```
using System;
using System.Data;
using System.Data.SqlClient;
using System.Data.SqlTypes;
using System.Text;
using System.Xml;

    class Program
    {
        static void Main()
        {
            string connectionString =
```

```
            @"server=(local);database=ProCSharp;trusted_connection=true";
    var connection = new SqlConnection(connectionString);
    var command = connection.CreateCommand();
    command.CommandText = "SELECT Id, Number, Info FROM Exams";
    connection.Open();
    var reader = command.ExecuteReader(CommandBehavior.CloseConnection);
    while (reader.Read())
    {
        SqlXml xml = reader.GetSqlXml(2);

        XmlReader xmlReader = xml.CreateReader();

        StringBuilder courses = new StringBuilder("Course(s): ", 40);
        while (xmlReader.Read())
        {
            if (xmlReader.Name == "Exam" && xmlReaderIsStartElement())
            {
                Console.WriteLine("Exam: {0}", xmlReader.GetAttribute("Number"));
            }
            else if (xmlReader.Name == "Title" && xmlReader.IsStartElement())
            {
                Console.WriteLine("Title: {0}", xmlReader.ReadString());
            }
            else if (xmlReader.Name == "Course" && xmlReader.IsStartElement())
            {
                courses.AppendFormat("{0} ", xmlReader.ReadString());
            }
        }
        xmlReader.Close();
        Console.WriteLine(courses.ToString());
        Console.WriteLine();
    }
    reader.Close();
}
```

Running the application, you will get the output as shown:

```
Exam: 70-502
Title: TS: Microsoft .NET Framework 3.5, Windows Presentation Foundation Application Development
Course(s): 6460

Exam: 70-562
Title: TS: Microsoft .NET Framework 3.5, ASP.NET Application Development
Course(s): 2310 6463

Exam: 70-561
Title: TS: Microsoft .NET Framework 3.5, ADO.NET Application Development
Course(s): 2310 6464
```

Instead of using the `XmlReader` class, you can read the complete XML content into the `XmlDocument` class and parse the elements by using the DOM model. The method `SelectSingleNode()` requires an XPath expression and returns an `XmlNode` object. The XPath expression `//Exam` looks for the `Exam` XML element inside the complete XML tree. The `XmlNode` object returned can be used to read the children of the represented element. The value of the `Number` attribute is accessed to write the exam number to the console, then the `Title` element is accessed and the content of the `Title` element is written to the console, and the content of all `Course` elements is written to the console as well:

```
string connectionString =
        @"server=(local);database=SqlServerSampleDB;trusted_connection=true";
var connection = new SqlConnection(connectionString);
var command = connection.CreateCommand();
command.CommandText = "SELECT Id, Number, Info FROM Exams";
```

```
        connection.Open();
        var reader = command.ExecuteReader(CommandBehavior.CloseConnection);
        while (reader.Read())
        {
            SqlXml xml = reader.GetSqlXml(2);
            var doc = new XmlDocument();
            doc.LoadXml(xml.Value);

            XmlNode examNode = doc.SelectSingleNode("//Exam");
            Console.WriteLine("Exam: {0}", examNode.Attributes["Number"].Value);
            XmlNode titleNode = examNode.SelectSingleNode("./Title");
            Console.WriteLine("Title: {0}", titleNode.InnerText);
            Console.Write("Course(s): ");

            foreach (XmlNode courseNode in examNode.SelectNodes("./Course"))
            {
                Console.Write("{0} ", courseNode.InnerText);
            }
            Console.WriteLine();

        }
        reader.Close();
```

code snippet XmlSamples/Program.cs

 The `XmlReader` *and* `XmlDocument` *classes are discussed in Chapter 33, "Manipulating XML."*

With .NET 4 there's another option to access the XML column from the database. You can combine LINQ to SQL and LINQ to XML, which makes the programming code smaller.

You can use the ADO.NET Entity Framework designer by selecting the ADO.NET Entity Data Model template from the Data templates category. Name the file `ExamsModel.edmx` to create a mapping for the database SqlServerSampleDB. Select the Exams table and select the option to singularize object names. After you create the model with the wizard, a design surface, as shown in Figure 34-4, opens.

FIGURE 34-4

The data context class that is created by the designer has the name `ExamsEntities` and defines a property `Exams` to return all exam rows. Here a `foreach` statement is used to iterate through all records. Of course you can also define a LINQ query with a `where` expression if not all records are required. The `Exam` class defines the properties `Id`, `Number`, and `Info` according to the columns in the database table. The `Info` property is of type `string`. With the `XElement` class the string can be parsed and accessed by the LINQ to XML classes from the namespace `System.Xml.Linq`. Invoking the method `Element()` passing the name of the XML element `Exam` returns an `XElement` object that is then used to access the values of the attribute `Number` and the elements `Title` and `Course` in a much simpler way, as was done earlier with the `XmlDocument` class:

```
using System;
using System.Xml.Linq;

namespace Wrox.ProCSharp.SqlServer
{
```

```
class Program
{
    static void Main()
    {
        using (ExamsEntities data = new ExamsEntities())
        {
            foreach (Exam item in db.Exams)
            {
                XElement exam = XElement.Parse(item.Info);
                Console.WriteLine("Exam: {0}", exam.Attribute("Number").Value);
                Console.WriteLine("Title: {0}", exam.Element("Title").Value);
                Console.Write("Course(s): ");
                foreach (var course in exam.Elements("Course"))
                {
                    Console.Write("{0} ", course.Value);
                }
                Console.WriteLine();
            }
        }
    }
}
```

The ADO.NET Entity Framework and LINQ to XML are explained in Chapter 31, "ADO.NET Entity Framework," and Chapter 33, "Manipulating XML," respectively.

Querying the Data

Up until now, you haven't seen the really great features of the XML data type. SQL SELECT statements can be combined with XML XQuery.

A SELECT statement combined with an XQuery expression to read into the XML value is shown here:

```
SELECT [Id], [Number], [Info].query('/Exam/Course') AS Course FROM [Exams]
```

The XQuery expression /Exam/Course accesses the Course elements that are children of the Exam element. The result of this query returns the IDs, exam numbers, and courses:

```
1 70-502 <Course>6460</Course>
2 70-562 <Course>2310</Course><Course>6463</Course>
3 70-561 <Course>2310</Course><Course>6464</Course>
```

With an XQuery expression, you can create more complex statements to query data within the XML content of a cell. The next example converts the XML from the exam information to XML that lists information about courses:

```
SELECT [Info].query('
    for $course in /Exam/Course
    return
<Course>
    <Exam>{ data(/Exam[1]/@Number) }</Exam>
    <Number>{ data($course) }</Number>
</Course>')
AS Course
FROM [Exams]
WHERE Id=2
```

Here, just a single row is selected with SELECT [Info]. FROM Exams WHERE Id = 2. With the result of this SQL query, the for and return statements of an XQuery expression are used. for $course in /Exam/Course iterates through all Course elements. $course declares a variable that is set with every iteration (similar to a C# foreach statement). Following the return statement, the result of the query for every row is defined. The result for every course element is surrounded by the <Course> element. Embedded inside the <Course> element are <Exam> and <Number>. The text within the <Exam> element is defined with `data(/Exam[1]/@Number)`. `data()` is an XQuery function that returns the value of the node specified with the argument. The node `/Exam[1]` is used to access the first `<Exam>` element; `@Number` specifies the XML attribute `Number`. The text within the element `<Number>` is defined from the variable `$course`.

> *Contrary to C#, where the first element in a collection is accessed with an index of 0, with XPath the first element in a collection is accessed with an index of 1.*

The result of this query is shown here:

```
<Course>
  <Exam>70-562</Exam>
  <Number>2310</Number>
</Course>
<Course>
  <Exam>70-562</Exam>
  <Number>6463</Number>
</Course>
```

You can change the XQuery statement to also include a where clause for filtering XML elements. The following example only returns courses from the XML column if the course number has a value higher than 2562:

```
SELECT [Info].query('
  for $course in /Exam/Course
  where ($course > 2562)
  return
<Course>
  <Exam>{ data(/Exam[1]/@Number) }</Exam>
  <Number>{ data($course) }</Number>
</Course>')
AS Course
FROM [Exams]
WHERE Id=2
```

The result is reduced to just one course number:

```
<Course>
  <Exam>70-562</Exam>
  <Number>6463</Number>
</Course>
```

XQuery in SQL Server allows using several other XQuery functions for getting minimum, maximum, or summary values, working with strings, numbers, checking for positions within collections, and so on.

The next example shows the use of the `count()` function to get the number of `/Exam/Course` elements:

```
SELECT [Id], [Number], [Info].query('
  count(/Exam/Course)')
  AS "Course Count"
FROM [Exams]
```

The data returned displays the number of courses for the exams:

```
Id        Number        Course Count
1         70-502        1
2         70-562        2
3         70-561        2
```

XML Data Modification Language (XML DML)

XQuery, as it is defined by the W3C (http://www.w3c.org), allowed only querying of data when Microsoft implemented XQuery in SQL Server 2005. Because of this XQuery restriction, Microsoft defined an extension to XQuery that has the name XML Data Modification Language (XML DML).

Today the XQuery Update Facility 1.0 is a candidate recommendation since June 9, 2009. This recommendation was made by IBM, Oracle, and Red Hat, and is different from XML DML.

XML DML makes it possible to modify XML data with the following XQuery extensions: `insert`, `delete`, and `replace value of`.

This section looks at some examples to insert, delete, and modify XML contents within a cell.

You can use the `insert` keyword to insert some XML content within an XML column without replacing the complete XML cell. Here, `<Course>2555</Course>` is inserted as the last child element of the first `Exam` element:

```
UPDATE [Exams]
SET [Info].modify('
    insert <Course>2555</Course> as last into Exam[1]')
WHERE [Id]=3
```

XML content can be deleted with the `delete` keyword. Within the first `Exam` element, the last `Course` element is deleted. The last element is selected by using the `last()` function:

```
UPDATE [Exams]
SET [Info].modify('
    delete /Exam[1]/Course[last()]')
FROM [Exams] WHERE [Id]=3
```

It is also possible to change XML content. Here, the keyword `replace value of` is used. The expression `/Exam/Course[text() = 6463]` accesses only the child elements `Course` where the text content contains the string `6463`. From these elements, only the text content is accessed for replacement with the `text()` function. If only a single element is returned from the query, it is still required that you specify just one element for replacement. This is why explicitly the first text element returned is specified with `[1]`. `2599` specifies that the new course number is `2599`:

```
UPDATE [Exams]
SET [Info].modify('
    replace value of (/Exam/Course[text() = 6463]/text())[1] with 2599')
FROM [Exams]
```

XML Indexes

If some specific elements are often searched within the XML data, you can specify indexes within the XML data type. XML indexes must be distinguished as being a primary or a secondary XML index type. A primary XML index is created for the complete persisted representation of the XML value.

The following SQL command, `CREATE PRIMARY XML INDEX`, creates the index `idx_exams` on the `Info` column:

```
CREATE PRIMARY XML INDEX idx_exams on Exams (Info)
```

Primary indexes don't help if the query contains an XPath expression to directly access XML elements of the XML type. For XPath and XQuery expressions, XML secondary indexes can be used. If an XML secondary index is created, the primary index must already exist. With secondary indexes, these index types must be distinguished:

➤ `PATH` index

➤ `VALUE` index

➤ `PROPERTY` index

A `PATH` index is used if `exists()` or `query()` functions are used and XML elements are accessed with an XPath expression. Using the XPath expression `/Exam/Course`, it might be useful to do a `PATH` index:

```
CREATE XML INDEX idx_examNumbers on [Exams] (Info)
    USING XML INDEX idx_exams FOR PATH
```

The PROPERTY index is used if properties are fetched from elements with the value() function. The FOR PROPERTY statement with the index creation defines a PROPERTY index:

```
CREATE XML INDEX idx_examNumbers on [Exams] (Info)
    USING XML INDEX idx_exams FOR PROPERTY
```

If elements are searched through the tree with an XPath descendant-or-self axis expression, the best performance might be achieved with a VALUE index. The XPath expression //Certification searches all Certification elements with the descendant-or-self axis. The expression [@Name="MCTS ASP. NET Applications"] returns only the elements where the attribute Name has the value MCTS Web Applications:

```
SELECT [Info].query('/Exam/Title/text()') FROM [Exams]
    WHERE [Info].exist('//Certification[@Name="MCTS ASP.NET Applications"]') = 1
```

The result returned lists the titles of the exams that contain the requested certification:

```
TS: Microsoft .NET Framework 3.5, ASP.NET Application Development
```

The VALUE index is created with the FOR VALUE statement:

```
CREATE XML INDEX idx_examNumbers on [Exams] (Info)
    USING XML INDEX idx_exams FOR VALUE
```

Strongly Typed XML

The XML data type in SQL Server can also be strongly typed with XML schemas. With a strongly typed XML column, it is verified if the data conforms to the schema when XML data is inserted.

A XML schema can be created with the CREATE XML SCHEMA COLLECTION statement. The statement shown here creates a simple XML schema, CourseSchema. The schema defines the type CourseElt that contains a sequence of Number and Title, which are both of type string, and an element Any, which can be any type. Number and Title may occur only once. Because Any has the minOccurs attribute set to 0, and the maxOccurs attribute set to unbounded, this element is optional. This allows you to add any additional information to the CourseElt type in future versions, while the schema still remains valid. Finally, the element name Course is of type CourseElt:

```
CREATE XML SCHEMA COLLECTION CourseSchema AS
'<?xml version="1.0" encoding="UTF-8"?>
<xs:schema id="Courses" targetNamespace="http://thinktecture.com/Courses.xsd"
  elementFormDefault="qualified" xmlns="http://thinktecture.com/Courses.xsd"
  xmlns:mstns="http://thinktecture.com/Courses.xsd"
  xmlns:xs="http://www.w3.org/2001/XMLSchema">
    <xs:complexType name="CourseElt">
      <xs:sequence>
        <xs:element name="Number" type="xs:string" maxOccurs="1"
              minOccurs="1" />
        <xs:element name="Title" type="xs:string" maxOccurs="1"
              minOccurs="1" />
        <xs:element name="Any" type="xs:anyType"
            maxOccurs="unbounded" minOccurs="0" />
      </xs:sequence>
    </xs:complexType>
    <xs:element name="Course" type="CourseElt">
    </xs:element>
</xs:schema>'
```

With this schema, a valid XML looks like this:

```
<Course xmlns="http://thinktecture.com/Courses.xsd">
  <Number>2549</Number>
  <Title>Advanced Distributed Application Development with Visual Studio 2008
  </Title>
</Course>
```

With the Visual Studio Database project type, there's no support to add a schema to the database. This feature is not available from the GUI by Visual Studio 2010, but must be created manually. To create an XML schema with Visual Studio 2010, create a new Visual Studio project by using the Empty Project template. Add a new XML schema to the project. Then copy the XML syntax of the schema into the CREATE XML SCHEMA statement.

The XML schema can be assigned to a column by setting it with the XML data type:

```
CREATE TABLE [Courses]
(
    [Id] [int] IDENTITY(1,1) NOT NULL,
    [Course] [xml]([dbo].[CourseSchema]) NOT NULL
)
```

By creating the table with Visual Studio 2010 or with SQL Server Management Studio, the XML schema can be assigned to a column by setting the property XML schema namespace.

Now as you add data to the XML column, the schema is verified. If the XML does not satisfy the schema definition, a SqlException is thrown with an XML Validation error.

SUMMARY

This chapter discussed the new features of SQL Server as they relate to CLR functionality. The CLR is hosted by SQL Server, so it is possible to create user-defined types, aggregates, stored procedures, functions, and triggers with C#.

UDTs have some strict requirements in the .NET class for conversion to and from a string. How the data is stored internally in SQL Server depends on the format that is defined in the type. User-defined aggregates make it possible to do a custom accumulation using .NET classes. With stored procedures and functions, it is possible to make use of CLR classes for server-side code.

Using CLR with SQL Server doesn't mean that T-SQL is obsolete. You've seen that T-SQL has advantages because it requires less code if only data-intensive queries are done. CLR classes can have advantages in data-processing if .NET features such as cryptography come into play.

You've also had a glance into the XML data type of SQL Server to combine XQuery expressions with T-SQL statements.

This chapter concludes Part IV, "Data." Part V, "Presentation," gives details about defining the user interface of applications. With the user interface you have the options of working with WPF, Silverlight, Windows Forms, and ASP.NET.

PART V
Presentation

▶ **CHAPTER 35:** Core WPF

▶ **CHAPTER 36:** Business Applications with WPF

▶ **CHAPTER 37:** Creating Documents with WPF

▶ **CHAPTER 38:** Silverlight

▶ **CHAPTER 39:** Windows Forms

▶ **CHAPTER 40:** Core ASP.NET

▶ **CHAPTER 41:** ASP.NET Features

▶ **CHAPTER 42:** ASP.NET Dynamic Data and MVC

35

Core WPF

WHAT'S IN THIS CHAPTER?

➤ Shapes and geometry as the base drawing elements

➤ Scaling, rotating, and skewing with transformations

➤ Brushes to fill backgrounds

➤ WPF controls and their features

➤ Defining a layout with WPF panels

➤ Styles, templates, and resources

➤ Triggers and the Visual State Manager

➤ Animations

➤ 3-D

Windows Presentation Foundation (WPF) is a library to create the UI for smart client applications. This chapter gives you broad information on the important concepts of WPF. You can read about a large number of different controls and their categories, how to arrange the controls with panels, customize the appearance using styles, resources, and templates, add some dynamic behavior with triggers and animations, and get an introduction to 3-D with WPF.

OVERVIEW

One of the big features of WPF is that work can be easily separated between designers and developers. The outcome from the designer's work can directly be used by the developer. To make this possible, you need to understand *eXtensible Application Markup Language*, or *XAML*. You should read Chapter 27, "Core XAML" to get information on this XAML syntax.

The first topic of this chapter gives you an overview of the class hierarchy and categories of classes that are used with WPF, including additional information to understand the principles of XAML. WPF consists of several assemblies containing thousands of classes. So that you can navigate within this vast number of classes and find what you need, the overview explains the class hierarchy and namespaces in WPF.

Namespaces

Classes from Windows Forms and WPF can easily be confused. The Windows Forms classes are located in the `System.Windows.Forms` namespace, and the WPF classes are located inside the namespace `System.Windows` and subnamespaces thereof, with the exception of `System.Windows.Forms`. The `Button` class for Windows Forms has the full name `System.Windows.Forms.Button`, and the `Button` class for WPF has the full name `System.Windows.Controls.Button`. Windows Forms is covered in Chapter 39.

Namespaces and their functionality with WPF are described in the following table.

NAMESPACE	DESCRIPTION
System.Windows	This is the core namespace of WPF. Here you can find core classes from WPF such as the `Application` class; classes for dependency objects, `DependencyObject` and `DependencyProperty`; and the base class for all WPF elements, `FrameworkElement`.
System.Windows.Annotations	The classes from this namespace are used for user-created annotations and notes on application data that are stored separately from the document. The namespace `System.Windows.Annotations.Storage` contains classes for storing annotations.
System.Windows.Automation	This namespace can be used for automation of WPF applications. Several subnamespaces are available. `System.Windows.Automation.Peers` exposes WPF elements to automation — for example, `ButtonAutomationPeer` and `CheckBoxAutomationPeer`. The namespace `System.Windows.Automation.Provider` is needed if you create a custom automation provider.
System.Windows.Baml2006	This namespace is new with .NET 4 and contains the `Baml2006Reader` class, which is used to read binary markup language and produces XAML.
System.Windows.Controls	This is the namespace where you can find all the WPF controls, such as `Button`, `Border`, `Canvas`, `ComboBox`, `Expander`, `Slider`, `ToolTip`, `TreeView`, and the like. In the namespace `System.Windows.Controls.Primitives`, you can find classes to be used within complex controls — for example, `Popup`, `ScrollBar`, `StatusBar`, `TabPanel`, and so on.
System.Windows.Converters	This namespace contains classes for data conversion. Don't expect to find all converter classes in this namespace; core converter classes are defined in the namespace `System.Windows`.
System.Windows.Data	This namespace is used by WPF data binding. An important class in this namespace is the `Binding` class, which is used to define the binding between a WPF target element and a CLR source. Data binding is dealt with in Chapter 36, "Business Applications with WPF."
System.Windows.Documents	When working with documents, you can find many helpful classes in this namespace. `FixedDocument` and `FlowDocument` are content elements that can contain other elements from this namespace. With classes from the namespace `System.Windows.Documents.Serialization` you can write documents to disk. The classes from this namespace are explained in Chapter 37, "Creating Documents with WPF."
System.Windows.Ink	The Windows Tablet PC and Ultra Mobile PCs are being used more and more. With these PCs, ink can be used for user input. The namespace `System.Windows.Ink` contains classes to deal with ink input.
System.Windows.Input	This namespace contains several classes for command handling, keyboard inputs, working with a stylus, and so on.
System.Windows.Interop	For integration with Win32 and WPF, you can find classes in this namespace.

NAMESPACE	DESCRIPTION
System.Windows.Markup	Helper classes for XAML markup code are located in this namespace.
System.Windows.Media	To work with images, audio, and video content, you can use classes in this namespace.
System.Windows.Navigation	This namespace contains classes for navigation between windows.
System.Windows.Resources	This namespace contains supporting classes for resources.
System.Windows.Shapes	The core classes for the UI are located in the System.Windows.Shapes namespace: Line, Ellipse, Rectangle, and the like.
System.Windows.Threading	WPF elements are bound to a single thread. In the namespace System.Windows.Threading, you can find classes to deal with multiple threads — for example, the Dispatcher class belongs to this namespace.
System.Windows.Xps	XML Paper Specification (XPS) is a new document specification that is also supported by Microsoft Word. In the namespaces System.Windows.Xps, System.Windows.Xps.Packaging and System.Windows.Xps.Serialization, you can find classes to create and stream XPS documents.

Class Hierarchy

WPF consists of thousands of classes with a deep hierarchy. For help in understanding the relationship between the classes, see Figure 35-1. Some classes and their functionalities are described in the following table.

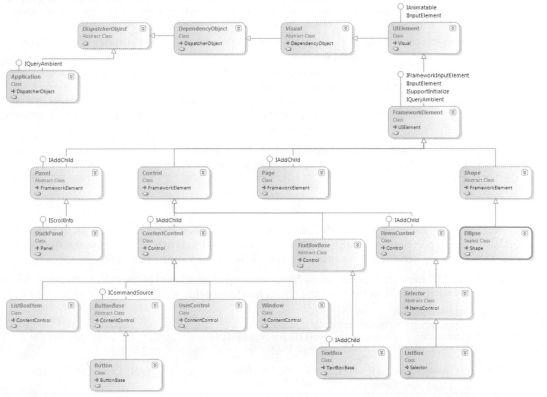

FIGURE 35-1

CLASS	DESCRIPTION
DispatcherObject	DispatcherObject is an abstract base class for classes that are bound to one thread. WPF controls require that methods and properties be invoked only from the creator thread. Classes that are derived from DispatcherObject have an associated Dispatcher object that can be used to switch the thread.
Application	In a WPF application, one instance of the Application class is created. This class implements a Singleton pattern for access to the application windows, resources, and properties.
DependencyObject	DependencyObject is the base class for all classes that support dependency properties. Dependency properties are discussed in Chapter 27, "Core XAML".
Visual	The base class for all visual elements is Visual. This class includes features for hit testing and transformation.
UIElement	The abstract base class for all WPF elements needing basic presentation features is UIElement. This class provides tunneling and bubbling events for mouse moves, drag and drop, and key clicks. It exposes virtual methods for rendering that can be overridden by derived classes, and it provides methods for layout. WPF does not use Window handles. You can consider this class equivalent to Window handles.
FrameworkElement	FrameworkElement is derived from the base class UIElement and implements the default behavior of the methods defined by the base class.
Shape	Shape is the base class for all shape elements — for example, Line, Ellipse, Polygon, and Rectangle.
Control	Control derives from FrameworkElement and is the base class for all user-interactive elements.
ContentControl	ContentControl is the base class for all controls that have a single content (for example, Label, Button). The default style of a content control may be limited, but it is possible to change the look by using templates.
ItemsControl	ItemsControl is the base class for all controls that contain a collection of items content (for example, ListBox, ComboBox).
Panel	The class Panel derives from FrameworkElement and is the abstract base class for all panels. This class has a Children property for all UI elements within the panel and defines methods for arranging the child controls. Classes that are derived from Panel define different behavior for how the children are organized — for example, WrapPanel, StackPanel, Canvas, and Grid.

As you can see, WPF classes have a really deep hierarchy. In this and the next chapters, you see classes of the core functionality, but it is not possible to cover all the features of WPF in this book.

SHAPES

Shapes are the core elements of WPF. With shapes you can draw 2-dimensional graphics using rectangles, lines, ellipses, paths, polygons, and polylines that are represented by classes derived from the abstract base class Shape. Shapes are defined in the namespace System.Windows.Shapes namespace.

The following XAML example draws a yellow face consisting of an ellipse for the face, two ellipses for the eyes, two ellipses for the pupils in the eyes, and a path for the mouth:

```
<Window x:Class="ShapesDemo.MainWindow"
        xmlns="http://schemas.microsoft.com/winfx/2006/xaml/presentation"
        xmlns:x="http://schemas.microsoft.com/winfx/2006/xaml"
        Title="Window1" Height="300" Width="300">
    <Canvas>
        <Ellipse Canvas.Left="10" Canvas.Top="10" Width="100" Height="100" Stroke="Blue"
            StrokeThickness="4" Fill="Yellow" />
        <Ellipse Canvas.Left="30" Canvas.Top="12" Width="60" Height="30">
```

```
        <Ellipse.Fill>
            <LinearGradientBrush StartPoint="0.5,0" EndPoint="0.5, 1">
                <GradientStop Offset="0.1" Color="DarkGreen" />
                <GradientStop Offset="0.7" Color="Transparent" />
            </LinearGradientBrush>
        </Ellipse.Fill>
    </Ellipse>
    <Ellipse Canvas.Left="30" Canvas.Top="35" Width="25" Height="20" Stroke="Blue"
        StrokeThickness="3" Fill="White" />
    <Ellipse Canvas.Left="40" Canvas.Top="43" Width="6" Height="5" Fill="Black" />

    <Ellipse Canvas.Left="65" Canvas.Top="35" Width="25" Height="20" Stroke="Blue"
        StrokeThickness="3" Fill="White" />
    <Ellipse Canvas.Left="75" Canvas.Top="43" Width="6" Height="5" Fill="Black" />
    <Path Name="mouth" Stroke="Blue" StrokeThickness="4"
        Data="M 40,74 Q 57,95 80,74 " />
    </Canvas>
</Window>
```

code snippet ShapesDemo/MainWindow.xaml

Figure 35-2 shows the result from the XAML code.

All these WPF elements can be accessed programmatically, even if they are buttons or shapes such as lines or rectangles. Setting the Name or x:Name property with the Path element to mouth allows you to access this element programmatically with the variable name mouth:

```
<Path Name="mouth" Stroke="Blue" StrokeThickness="4"
    Data="M 40,74 Q 57,95 80,74 " />
```

FIGURE 35-2

In the code-behind Data property of the Path element, mouth is set to a new geometry. For setting the path, the Path class supports PathGeometry with path markup syntax. The letter M defines the starting point for the path; the letter Q specifies a control point and an endpoint for a quadratic Bézier curve. Running the application, you see the window shown in Figure 35-3.

FIGURE 35-3

Available for
download on
Wrox.com

```
public MainWindow()
{
    InitializeComponent();
    mouth.Data = Geometry.Parse("M 40,92 Q 57,75 80,92");
}
```

code snippet ShapesDemo/MainWindow.xaml.cs

Following are the shapes available in the namespace System.Windows.Shapes.

SHAPE CLASS	DESCRIPTION
Line	You can draw a line from the coordinates X1.Y1 to X2.Y2.
Rectangle	With the Rectangle class, you can draw a rectangle by specifying Width and Height.
Ellipse	With the Ellipse class, you can draw an ellipse.
Path	You can use the Path class to draw a series of lines and curves. The Data property is a Geometry type. You can do the drawing by using classes that derive from the base class Geometry, or you can use the path markup syntax to define geometry.
Polygon	You can draw a closed shape formed by connected lines with the Polygon class. The polygon is defined by a series of Point objects assigned to the Points property.
Polyline	Similar to the Polygon class, you can draw connected lines with the Polyline. The difference is that the polyline does not need to be a closed shape.

GEOMETRY

One of the shapes, `Path`, uses `Geometry` for its drawing. `Geometry` elements can also be used in other places, for example with a `DrawingBrush`.

Geometry elements are very similar to shapes. Just as there are `Line`, `Ellipse`, and `Rectangle` shapes, there are also geometry elements for these drawings: `LineGeometry`, `EllipseGeometry`, and `RectangleGeometry`. There are big differences between shapes and geometries. A `Shape` is a `FrameworkElement` and can be used with any class that supports `UIElement` as its children. `FrameworkElement` derives from `UIElement`. Shapes participate with the layout system and render themselves. The `Geometry` class can't render itself and has fewer features and less overhead than `Shape`. The `Geometry` class derives from the `Freezable` base class and can be shared from multiple threads.

The `Path` class uses `Geometry` for its drawing. The geometry can be set with the `Data` property of the `Path`. Simple geometry elements that can be set are `EllipseGeometry` for drawing an ellipse, `LineGeometry` for drawing a line, and `RectangleGeometry` for drawing a rectangle. Combining multiple geometries, as is done in the next example, can be done with `CombinedGeometry`.

`CombinedGeometry` has the properties `Geometry1` and `Geometry2` and allows them to combine with `GeometryCombineMode` to form a `Union`, `Intersect`, `Xor`, and `Exclude`. `Union` merges the two geometries. With `Intersect`, only the area that is covered with both geometries is visible. `Xor` contrasts with `Intersect` to show the area that is covered by one of the geometries, but does not show the area covered by both. `Exclude` shows the area of the first geometry minus the area of the second geometry.

The following example combines an `EllipseGeometry` and a `RectangleGeometry` to form a union, as shown in Figure 35-4.

```
<Path Canvas.Top="0" Canvas.Left="250" Fill="Blue" Stroke="Black" >
    <Path.Data>
        <CombinedGeometry GeometryCombineMode="Union">
            <CombinedGeometry.Geometry1>
                <EllipseGeometry Center="80,60" RadiusX="80" RadiusY="40" />
            </CombinedGeometry.Geometry1>
            <CombinedGeometry.Geometry2>
                <RectangleGeometry Rect="30,60 105 50" />
            </CombinedGeometry.Geometry2>
        </CombinedGeometry>
    </Path.Data>
</Path>
```

code snippet GeometryDemo/MainWindow.xaml

Geometries can also be created by using segments. The geometry class `PathGeometry` uses segments for its drawing. The following code segment uses the `BezierSegment` and `LineSegment` elements to build one red and one green figure, as you can see in Figure 35-5. The first `BezierSegment` draws a Bézier curve between the points 70,40, which is the starting point of the figure, and 150,63 with control points 90,37 and 130,46. The following `LineSegment` uses the ending point of the Bézier curve and draws a line to 120,110:

FIGURE 35-4

```
<Path Canvas.Left="0" Canvas.Top="0" Fill="Red" Stroke="Blue"
        StrokeThickness="2.5">
    <Path.Data>
        <GeometryGroup>
            <PathGeometry>
                <PathGeometry.Figures>
                    <PathFigure StartPoint="70,40" IsClosed="True">
                        <PathFigure.Segments>
                            <BezierSegment Point1="90,37" Point2="130,46"
```

```
                                          Point3="150,63" />
                            <LineSegment Point="120,110" />
                            <BezierSegment Point1="100,95" Point2="70,90"
                                          Point3="45,91" />
                            <LineSegment Point="70,40" />
                        </PathFigure.Segments>
                    </PathFigure>
                </PathGeometry.Figures>
            </PathGeometry>
        </GeometryGroup>
    </Path.Data>
</Path>

<Path Canvas.Left="0" Canvas.Top="0" Fill="Green" Stroke="Blue"
    StrokeThickness="2.5">
    <Path.Data>
        <GeometryGroup>
            <PathGeometry>
                <PathGeometry.Figures>
                    <PathFigure StartPoint="160,70">
                        <PathFigure.Segments>
                            <BezierSegment Point1="175,85" Point2="200,99"
                                          Point3="215,100" />
                            <LineSegment Point="195,148" />
                            <BezierSegment Point1="174,150" Point2="142,140"
                                          Point3="129,115" />
                            <LineSegment Point="160,70" />
                        </PathFigure.Segments>
                    </PathFigure>
                </PathGeometry.Figures>
            </PathGeometry>
        </GeometryGroup>
    </Path.Data>
</Path>
```

Other than the `BezierSegment` and `LineSegment` elements, you can use `ArcSegment` to draw an elliptical arc between two points. With `PolyLineSegment` you can define a set of lines, `PolyBezierSegment` consists of multiple Bézier curves, `QuadraticBezierSegment` creates a quadratic Bézier curve, and `PolyQuadraticBezierSegment` consists of multiple quadratic Bézier curves.

FIGURE 35-5

A high performing drawing can be done with `StreamGeometry`. Programmatically, the figure can be defined by creating lines, Bézier curves, and arcs with members of the `StreamGeometryContext` class. With XAML, path markup syntax can be used. Path markup syntax can be used with the `Data` property of the `Path` class to define `StreamGeometry`. Special characters define how the points are connected. With the sample, `M` marks the start point, `L` is a line command to the point specified, and `Z` is the Close command to close the figure. Figure 35-6 shows the result of this drawing. The path markup syntax allows more commands such as horizontal lines (`H`), vertical lines (`V`), cubic Bézier curves (`C`), quadratic Bézier curves (`Q`), smooth cubic Bézier curves (`S`), smooth quadratic Bézier curves (`T`), and elliptical arcs (`A`):

FIGURE 35-6

```
<Path Canvas.Left="0" Canvas.Top="200" Fill="Yellow" Stroke="Blue"
    StrokeThickness="2.5"
    Data="M 120,5 L 128,80 L 220,50 L 160,130 L 190,220 L 100,150 L 80,230 L
         60,140 L0,110 L70,80 Z" StrokeLineJoin="Round">
</Path>
```

TRANSFORMATION

Because WPF is vector-based, you can resize every element. The vector-based graphics are now scaled, rotated, and skewed. Hit testing (for example with mouse moves and mouse clicks) is still working without the need for manual position calculation.

Adding the `ScaleTransform` element to the `LayoutTransform` property of the Canvas element, as shown, resizes the content of the complete canvas by 2 in the X and Y directions:

```
<Canvas.LayoutTransform>
  <ScaleTransform ScaleX="1.5" ScaleY="1.5" />
</Canvas.LayoutTransform>
```

code snippet TransformationDemo/MainWindow.xaml

Rotation can be done in a similar way as scaling. Using the `RotateTransform` element you can define the `Angle` for the rotation:

```
<Canvas.LayoutTransform>
  <RotateTransform Angle="40" />
</Canvas.LayoutTransform>
```

For skewing, you can use the `SkewTransform` element. With skewing you can assign angles for the X and Y directions:

```
<Canvas.LayoutTransform>
  <SkewTransform AngleX="20" AngleY="25" />
</Canvas.LayoutTransform>
```

To rotate and skew together, it is possible to define a `TransformGroup` that contains both `RotateTransform` and `SkewTransform`. It is also possible to define a `MatrixTransform` where the `Matrix` element specifies the properties `M11` and `M22` for stretch and `M12` and `M21` for skew:

```
<Canvas.LayoutTransform>
    <MatrixTransform>
        <MatrixTransform.Matrix>
            <Matrix M11="0.8" M22="1.6" M12="1.3" M21="0.4" />
        </MatrixTransform.Matrix>
    </MatrixTransform>
</Canvas.LayoutTransform>
```

Figure 35-7 shows the results of all the transformations. The figures are placed inside a `StackPanel`. Starting from the left side, the first figure is resized, the second figure rotated, the third figure skewed, and the fourth figure uses a matrix for its transformation. To see the difference more easily, the `Background` property of the `Canvas` elements are set to different colors.

FIGURE 35-7

BRUSHES

This section illustrates how to use the brushes that WPF offers for drawing backgrounds and foregrounds. This section will reference Figure 35-8, which shows the effects of using various brushes within a `Path` and the `Background` of `Button` elements, throughout.

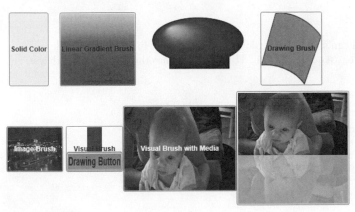

FIGURE 35-8

SolidColorBrush

The first button in Figure 35-8 uses the `SolidColorBrush`, which, by name, uses a solid color. The complete area is drawn with the same color.

You can define a solid color just by setting the `Background` attribute to a string that defines a solid color. The string is converted to a `SolidColorBrush` element with the help of the `BrushValueSerializer`:

```
<Button Height="30" Background="PapayaWhip">Solid Color</Button>
```

Of course, you will get the same effect by setting the `Background` child element and adding a `SolidColorBrush` element as its content. The first button in the application is using `PapayaWhip` as the solid background color:

```
<Button Content="Solid Color" Margin="10">
    <Button.Background>
        <SolidColorBrush Color="PapayaWhip" />
    </Button.Background>
</Button>
```

code snippet BrushesDemo/MainWindow.xaml

LinearGradientBrush

For a smooth color change, you can use the `LinearGradientBrush`, as shown with the second button. This brush defines the `StartPoint` and `EndPoint` properties. With this, you can assign 2-dimensional coordinates for the linear gradient. The default gradient is diagonal linear from `0,0` to `1,1`. By defining different values, the gradient can take different directions. For example, with a `StartPoint` of `0,0` and an `EndPoint` of `0,1`, you get a vertical gradient. The same `StartPoint` and an `EndPoint` value of `1,0` creates a horizontal gradient.

With the content of this brush, you can define the color values at the specified offsets with the `GradientStop` element. Between the stops, the colors are smoothed:

```
<Button Content="Linear Gradient Brush" Margin="10">
    <Button.Background>
        <LinearGradientBrush StartPoint="0,0" EndPoint="0,1">
```

```
                <GradientStop Offset="0" Color="LightGreen" />
                <GradientStop Offset="0.4" Color="Green" />
                <GradientStop Offset="1" Color="DarkGreen" />
            </LinearGradientBrush>
        </Button.Background>
    </Button>
```

RadialGradientBrush

With the RadialGradientBrush you can smooth the color in a radiant way. In Figure 35-8, the third element is a Path that uses RadialGradientBrush. This brush defines the color start with the GradientOrigin point:

```
<Canvas Width="200" Height="150">
    <Path Canvas.Top="0" Canvas.Left="20" Stroke="Black" >
        <Path.Fill>
            <RadialGradientBrush GradientOrigin="0.2,0.2">
                <GradientStop Offset="0" Color="LightBlue" />
                <GradientStop Offset="0.6" Color="Blue" />
                <GradientStop Offset="1.0" Color="DarkBlue" />
            </RadialGradientBrush>
        </Path.Fill>
        <Path.Data>
            <CombinedGeometry GeometryCombineMode="Union">
                <CombinedGeometry.Geometry1>
                    <EllipseGeometry Center="80,60" RadiusX="80"
                                     RadiusY="40" />
                </CombinedGeometry.Geometry1>
                <CombinedGeometry.Geometry2>
                    <RectangleGeometry Rect="30,60 105 50" />
                </CombinedGeometry.Geometry2>
            </CombinedGeometry>
        </Path.Data>
    </Path>
</Canvas>
```

DrawingBrush

The DrawingBrush allows you to define a drawing that is painted with the brush. The drawing that is shown with the brush is defined within a GeometryDrawing element. The GeometryGroup, which you can see within the Geometry property, consists of the Geometry elements that were discussed earlier in this chapter:

```
<Button Content="Drawing Brush" Margin="10" Padding="10">
    <Button.Background>
        <DrawingBrush>
            <DrawingBrush.Drawing>
                <GeometryDrawing Brush="Red">
                    <GeometryDrawing.Pen>
                        <Pen>
                            <Pen.Brush>
                                <SolidColorBrush>Blue</SolidColorBrush>
                            </Pen.Brush>
                        </Pen>
                    </GeometryDrawing.Pen>
                    <GeometryDrawing.Geometry>
                        <PathGeometry>
                            <PathGeometry.Figures>
                                <PathFigure StartPoint="70,40">
                                    <PathFigure.Segments>
```

```
                                    <BezierSegment Point1="90,37"
                                        Point2="130,46" Point3="150,63" />
                                    <LineSegment Point="120,110" />
                                    <BezierSegment Point1="100,95"
                                        Point2="70,90" Point3="45,91" />
                                    <LineSegment Point="70,40" />
                                </PathFigure.Segments>
                            </PathFigure>
                        </PathGeometry.Figures>
                    </PathGeometry>
                </GeometryDrawing.Geometry>
            </GeometryDrawing>
        </DrawingBrush.Drawing>
    </DrawingBrush>
</Button.Background>
</Button>
```

ImageBrush

To load an image into a brush, you can use the `ImageBrush` element. With this element, the image defined by the `ImageSource` property is displayed. The image can be accessed from the file system or from a resource within the assembly. In the example, the image is added as a resource to the assembly and referenced with the assembly and resource names:

```
<Button Content="Image Brush" Width="100" Height="80" Margin="5"
        Foreground="White">
    <Button.Background>
        <ImageBrush ImageSource="/BrushesDemo;component/Budapest.jpg" />
    </Button.Background>
</Button>
```

VisualBrush

The `VisualBrush` allows you to use other WPF elements in a brush. Here, you can add a WPF element to the `Visual` property. The sixth element in Figure 35-8 contains a `Rectangle` and a `Button`:

```
<Button Content="Visual Brush" Width="100" Height="80">
    <Button.Background>
        <VisualBrush>
            <VisualBrush.Visual>
                <StackPanel Background="White">
                    <Rectangle Width="25" Height="25" Fill="Blue" />
                    <Button Content="Drawing Button" Background="Red" />
                </StackPanel>
            </VisualBrush.Visual>
        </VisualBrush>
    </Button.Background>
</Button>
```

You can add any `UIElement` to the `VisualBrush`. One example is that you can play a video by using the `MediaElement`:

```
<Button Content="Visual Brush with Media" Width="200" Height="150"
        Foreground="White">
    <Button.Background>
        <VisualBrush>
            <VisualBrush.Visual>
                <MediaElement Source="./Stephanie.wmv" />
            </VisualBrush.Visual>
        </VisualBrush>
    </Button.Background>
</Button>
```

You can use the `VisualBrush` to create interesting effects such as reflection. The button shown here contains a `StackPanel` that itself contains a `MediaElement` playing a video and a `Border`. The `Border` contains a `Rectangle` that is filled with a `VisualBrush`. This brush defines an opacity value and a transformation. The `Visual` property is bound to the `Border` element. The transformation is done by setting the `RelativeTransform` property of the `VisualBrush`. This transformation uses relative coordinates. By setting `ScaleY` to -1, a reflection in the Y direction is done. `TranslateTransform` moves the transformation in the Y direction so that the reflection is below the original object. You can see the result in the eighth element in Figure 35-8.

 Data binding and the `Binding` *element that is used here are explained in detail in Chapter 36.*

```
<Button Width="200" Height="200" Foreground="White">
    <StackPanel>
        <MediaElement x:Name="reflected" Source="./Stephanie.wmv" />
        <Border Height="100">
            <Rectangle>
                <Rectangle.Fill>
                    <VisualBrush Opacity="0.35" Stretch="None"
                                 Visual="{Binding ElementName=reflected}">
                        <VisualBrush.RelativeTransform>
                            <TransformGroup>
                                <ScaleTransform ScaleX="1" ScaleY="-1" />
                                <TranslateTransform Y="1" />

                            </TransformGroup>
                        </VisualBrush.RelativeTransform>
                    </VisualBrush>
                </Rectangle.Fill>
            </Rectangle>
        </Border>
    </StackPanel>
</Button>
```

CONTROLS

You can use hundreds of controls with WPF. For a better understanding, the controls are categorized into these groups:

➤ Simple

➤ Content

➤ Headered content

➤ Items

➤ Headered items

➤ Decoration

Simple Controls

Simple controls are controls that don't have a `Content` property. With the `Button` class, you have seen that the `Button` can contain any shape, or any element you like. This is not possible with simple controls. The following table shows simple controls and their functionality.

SIMPLE CONTROL	DESCRIPTION
PasswordBox	This control is used to enter a password and has specific properties for password input, for example, `PasswordChar`, to define the character that should show up as the user enters the password, or `Password` to access the password entered. The `PasswordChanged` event is invoked as soon as the password is changed.
ScrollBar	This control contains a `Thumb` where the user can select a value. A scrollbar can be used, for example, if a document doesn't fit on the screen. Some controls contain scrollbars that show up if the content is too big.
ProgressBar	With this control, you can indicate the progress of a lengthy operation.
Slider	With this control, the user can select a range of values by moving a Thumb. `ScrollBar`, `ProgressBar`, and `Slider` are derived from the same base class, `RangeBase`.
TextBox	Used to display simple, unformatted text.
RichTextBox	Supports rich text with the help of the `FlowDocument` class. `RichTextBox` and `TextBox` are derived from the same base class, `TextBoxBase`.
Calendar	The `Calendar` control is new with .NET 4 — it displays a month, year, or decade. The user can select a date or range of dates.
DatePicker	The `DatePicker` is a control that opens a Calendar onscreen for date selection by the user.

 Although simple controls do not have a Content *property, you can completely customize the look of the control by defining a template. Templates are discussed later in this chapter.*

Content Controls

A `ContentControl` has a `Content` property, with which you can add any content to the control. The `Button` class derives from the base class `ContentControl`, so you can add any content to this control. In a previous example, you saw a `Canvas` control within the `Button`. Content controls are described in the following table.

CONTENTCONTROL CONTROLS	DESCRIPTION
Button RepeatButton ToggleButton CheckBoxRadioButton	The classes `Button`, `RepeatButton`, `ToggleButton`, and `GridViewColumnHeader` are derived from the same base class, `ButtonBase`. All buttons react to the `Click` event. The `RepeatButton` raises the `Click` event repeatedly until the button is released. `ToggleButton` is the base class for `CheckBox` and `RadioButton`. These buttons have an on and off state. The `CheckBox` can be selected and cleared by the user; the `RadioButton` can be selected by the user. Clearing the `RadioButton` must be done programmatically.
Label	The `Label` class represents the text label for a control. This class also has support for access keys, for example, a menu command.
Frame	The `Frame` control supports navigation. You can navigate to a page content with the `Navigate()` method. If the content is a Web page, then the Web browser control is used for display.
ListBoxItem	`ListBoxItem` is an item inside a `ListBox` control.
StatusBarItem	`StatusBarItem` is an item inside a `StatusBar` control.
ScrollViewer	The `ScrollViewer` control is a content control that includes scrollbars. You can put any content in this control; the scrollbars will show up as needed.
ToolTip	`ToolTip` creates a pop-up window to display additional information for a control.

continues

(continued)

CONTENTCONTROL CONTROLS	DESCRIPTION
UserControl	Using the class UserControl as a base class provides a simple way to create custom controls. However, the UserControl base class does not support templates.
Window	The Window class allows you to create windows and dialog boxes. With the Window class, you get a frame with minimize/maximize/close buttons and a system menu. When showing a dialog box, you can use the ShowDialog() method; the Show() method opens a window.
NavigationWindow	The NavigationWindow class derives from the Window class and supports content navigation.

Only a Frame control is contained within the Window of the following XAML code. The Source property is set to http://www.thinktecture.com, so the Frame control navigates to this web site, as you can see in Figure 35-9.

```xaml
<Window x:Class="FrameDemo.MainWindow"
        xmlns="http://schemas.microsoft.com/winfx/2006/xaml/presentation"
        xmlns:x="http://schemas.microsoft.com/winfx/2006/xaml"
        Title="Frame Demo" Height="240" Width="500">
    <Frame Source="http://www.thinktecture.com" />
</Window>
```

code snippet FrameDemo/MainWindow.xaml

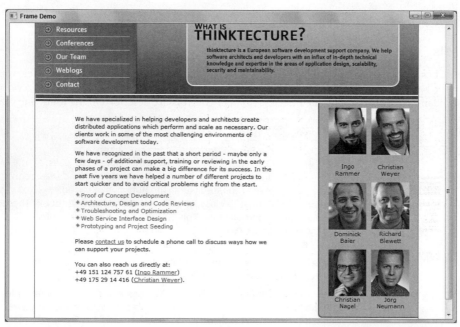

FIGURE 35-9

Headered Content Controls

Content controls with a header are derived from the base class HeaderedContentControl, which itself is derived from the base class ContentControl. The HeaderedContentControl class has a property Header to define the content of the header and HeaderTemplate for complete customization of the header. The controls that are derived from the base class HeaderedContentControl are listed in the following table.

HEADEREDCONTENTCONTROL	DESCRIPTION
Expander	With the Expander control, you can create an "advanced" mode with a dialog box that, by default, does not show all information but that can be expanded by the user to show more information. In the unexpanded mode, header information is shown. In expanded mode, the content is visible.
GroupBox	The GroupBox control provides a border and a header to group controls.
TabItem	TabItem controls are items within the class TabControl. The Header property of the TabItem defines the content of the header shown with the tabs of the TabControl.

A simple use of the Expander control is shown in the next example. The Expander control has the property Header set to Click for more. This text is displayed for expansion. The content of this control is shown only if the control is expanded. Figure 35-10 shows the application with a collapsed Expander control. Figure 35-11 shows the same application with an expanded Expander control:

```xml
<Window x:Class="ExpanderDemo.MainWindow"
        xmlns="http://schemas.microsoft.com/winfx/2006/xaml/presentation"
        xmlns:x="http://schemas.microsoft.com/winfx/2006/xaml"
        Title="Expander Demo" Height="240" Width="500">
    <StackPanel>
        <TextBlock>Short information</TextBlock>
        <Expander Header="Additional Information">
            <Border Height="200" Width="200" Background="Yellow">
                <TextBlock HorizontalAlignment="Center"
                  VerticalAlignment="Center">
                  More information here!
                </TextBlock>
            </Border>
        </Expander>
    </StackPanel>
</Window>
```

code snippet ExpanderDemo/MainWindow.xaml

To make the header text of the Expander *control change when the control is expanded, you can create a trigger. Triggers are explained later in this chapter.*

FIGURE 35-10

FIGURE 35-11

Items Controls

The `ItemsControl` class contains a list of items that can be accessed with the `Items` property. Classes that are derived from `ItemsControl` are shown in the following table.

ITEMSCONTROL	DESCRIPTION
Menu ContextMenu	The classes `Menu` and `ContextMenu` are derived from the abstract base class `MenuBase`. You can offer menus to the user by placing `MenuItem` elements in the items list and associating commands.
StatusBar	The `StatusBar` control is usually shown at the bottom of an application to give status information to the user. You can put `StatusBarItem` elements inside a `StatusBar` list.
TreeView	For a hierarchical display of items, you can use the `TreeView` control.
ListBox ComboBox TabControl	`ListBox`, `ComboBox`, and `TabControl` have the same abstract base class, `Selector`. This base class makes it possible to select items from a list. The `ListBox` displays the items from a list. The `ComboBox` has an additional `Button` control to display the items only if the button is clicked. With `TabControl`, content can be arranged in tabular form.
DataGrid	The `DataGrid` control is a customizable grid that displays data. This control is new with .NET 4 and is discussed in detail in the next chapter.

Headered Items Controls

`HeaderedItemsControl` is the base class of controls that include items but also has a header. The class `HeaderedItemsControl` is derived from `ItemsControl`.

Classes that are derived from `HeaderedItemsControl` are listed in the following table.

HEADEREDITEMSCONTROL	DESCRIPTION
MenuItem	The menu classes `Menu` and `ContextMenu` include items of the `MenuItem` type. Menu items can be connected to commands, as the `MenuItem` class implements the interface `ICommandSource`.
TreeViewItem	The `TreeView` class can include items of type `TreeViewItem`.
ToolBar	The `ToolBar` control is a container for a group of controls, usually `Button` and `Separator` elements. You can place the `ToolBar` inside a `ToolBarTray` that handles rearranging of `ToolBar` controls.

Decoration

Adding decorations to a single element is done with the `Decorator` class. `Decorator` is a base class that has derivations such as `Border`, `Viewbox`, and `BulletDecorator`. Theme elements such as `ButtonChrome` and `ListBoxChrome` are also decorators.

The following example demonstrates a `Border`, `Viewbox`, and `BulletDecorator`, as in Figure 35-12.

FIGURE 35-12

The `Border` class decorates the `Children` element by adding a border around it. You can define a brush and the thickness of the border, the background, the radius of the corner, and the padding of its children:

```
<Border BorderBrush="Violet" BorderThickness="5.5">
    <Label>Label with a border</Label>
</Border>
```

code snippet DecorationsDemo/MainWindow.xaml

The `Viewbox` stretches and scales its child to the available space. The `StretchDirection` and `Stretch` properties are specific to the functionality of the `Viewbox`. These properties allow setting if the child is stretched in both directions, and if the aspect ratio is preserved:

```
<Viewbox StretchDirection="Both" Stretch="Uniform">
    <Label>Label with a viewbox</Label>
</Viewbox>
```

The `BulletDecorator` class decorates its child with a bullet. The child can be any element (in this example, a `ComboBox`). Similarly, the bullet can also be any element. The example uses an `Image`, but you can use any `UIElement`:

```
<BulletDecorator>
    <BulletDecorator.Bullet>
        <Image Width="25" Height="25" Margin="5" HorizontalAlignment="Center"
               VerticalAlignment="Center"
               Source="/DecorationsDemo;component/images/apple1.jpg" />
    </BulletDecorator.Bullet>
    <BulletDecorator.Child>
        <ComboBox Margin="25,5,5,5" Width="120" HorizontalAlignment="Left">
            <ComboBoxItem>Granny Smith</ComboBoxItem>
            <ComboBoxItem>Gravenstein</ComboBoxItem>
            <ComboBoxItem>Golden Delicious</ComboBoxItem>
            <ComboBoxItem>Braeburn</ComboBoxItem>
        </ComboBox>
    </BulletDecorator.Child>
</BulletDecorator>
```

LAYOUT

To define the layout of the application, you can use a class that derives from the `Panel` base class. Several layout containers are available that are discussed here. A layout container needs to do two main tasks: measure and arrange. With measuring, the container asks its children for the preferred sizes. Because the complete size answered by the controls might not be available, the container next decides and arranges the size and positions of its children.

StackPanel

The `Window` can contain just a single element as content. If you want to have more than one element inside there, then you can use a `StackPanel` as a child of the `Window`, and add elements to the content of the `StackPanel`. The `StackPanel` is a simple container control that just shows one element after the other. The orientation of the `StackPanel` can be horizontal or vertical. The class `ToolBarPanel` is derived from `StackPanel`:

```
<Window x:Class="LayoutDemo.StackPanelWindow"
        xmlns="http://schemas.microsoft.com/winfx/2006/xaml/presentation"
        xmlns:x="http://schemas.microsoft.com/winfx/2006/xaml"
        Title="StackPanelWindow" Height="300" Width="300">
    <StackPanel Orientation="Vertical">
        <Label>Label</Label>
        <TextBox>TextBox</TextBox>
        <CheckBox>CheckBox</CheckBox>
        <CheckBox>CheckBox</CheckBox>
        <ListBox>
            <ListBoxItem>ListBoxItem One</ListBoxItem>
            <ListBoxItem>ListBoxItem Two</ListBoxItem>
```

```
        </ListBox>
        <Button>Button</Button>
    </StackPanel>
</Window>
```

code snippet LayoutDemo/StackPanelWindow.xaml

You can see the child controls of the StackPanel organized vertically in Figure 35-13.

WrapPanel

The WrapPanel positions the children from left to right, one after the other, as long as they fit into the line, and then continues with the next line. The orientation of the panel can be horizontal or vertical:

FIGURE 35-13

```
<Window x:Class="LayoutDemo.WrapPanelWindow"
        xmlns="http://schemas.microsoft.com/winfx/2006/xaml/presentation"
        xmlns:x="http://schemas.microsoft.com/winfx/2006/xaml"
        Title="WrapPanelWindow" Height="300" Width="300">
    <WrapPanel>
        <Button Width="100" Margin="5">Button</Button>
        <Button Width="100" Margin="5">Button</Button>
        <Button Width="100" Margin="5">Button</Button>
        <Button Width="100" Margin="5">Button</Button>
        <Button Width="100" Margin="5">Button</Button>
        <Button Width="100" Margin="5">Button</Button>
        <Button Width="100" Margin="5">Button</Button>
        <Button Width="100" Margin="5">Button</Button>
    </WrapPanel>
</Window>
```

code snippet LayoutDemo/WrapPanelWindow.xaml

Figure 35-14 shows the output of the panel. If you resize the application, then the buttons will be rearranged so that they fit into a line.

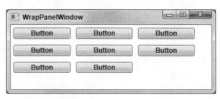

Canvas

Canvas is a panel that allows you to explicitly position controls. Canvas defines the attached properties Left, Right, Top, and Bottom that can be used by the children for positioning within the panel:

FIGURE 35-14

```
<Window x:Class="LayoutDemo.CanvasWindow"
        xmlns="http://schemas.microsoft.com/winfx/2006/xaml/presentation"
        xmlns:x="http://schemas.microsoft.com/winfx/2006/xaml"
        Title="CanvasWindow" Height="300" Width="300">
    <Canvas Background="LightBlue">
        <Label Canvas.Top="30" Canvas.Left="20">Enter here:</Label>
        <TextBox Canvas.Top="30" Canvas.Left="120" Width="100" />
        <Button Canvas.Top="70" Canvas.Left="130" Content="Click Me!" Padding="5" />
    </Canvas>
</Window>
```

code snippet LayoutDemo/CanvasWindow.xaml

Figure 35-15 shows the output of the Canvas panel with the positioned children Label, TextBox, and Button.

FIGURE 35-15   **FIGURE 35-16**

DockPanel

The DockPanel is very similar to the Windows Forms docking functionality. Here, you can specify the area where child controls should be arranged. DockPanel defines the attached property Dock, which you can set in the children of the controls to the values Left, Right, Top, and Bottom. Figure 35-16 shows the outcome of text blocks with borders that are arranged in the dock panel. For easier differentiation, different colors are specified for the various areas:

```xaml
<Window x:Class="LayoutDemo.DockPanelWindow"
        xmlns="http://schemas.microsoft.com/winfx/2006/xaml/presentation"
        xmlns:x="http://schemas.microsoft.com/winfx/2006/xaml"
        Title="DockPanelWindow" Height="300" Width="300">
    <DockPanel>
        <Border Height="25" Background="AliceBlue" DockPanel.Dock="Top">
            <TextBlock>Menu</TextBlock>
        </Border>
        <Border Height="25" Background="Aqua" DockPanel.Dock="Top">
            <TextBlock>Toolbar</TextBlock>
        </Border>
        <Border Height="30" Background="LightSteelBlue" DockPanel.Dock="Bottom">
            <TextBlock>Status</TextBlock>
        </Border>
        <Border Height="80" Background="Azure" DockPanel.Dock="Left">
            <TextBlock>Left Side</TextBlock>
        </Border>
        <Border Background="HotPink">
            <TextBlock>Remaining Part</TextBlock>
        </Border>
    </DockPanel>
</Window>
```

code snippet LayoutDemo/DockPanelWindow.xaml

Grid

Using the Grid, you can arrange your controls with rows and columns. For every column, you can specify a ColumnDefinition. For every row, you can specify a RowDefinition. The sample code lists two columns and three rows. With each column and row, you can specify the width or height. ColumnDefinition has a Width dependency property; RowDefinition has a Height dependency property. You can define the height and width in pixels, centimeters, inches, or points, or by setting it to Auto to determine the size depending on the content. The grid also allows star sizing, whereby the space for the rows and columns is calculated according to the available space and relative to other rows and columns. When providing the available space for a column, you can set the `Width` property to `*`. To have the size doubled for another column, you specify `2*`. The sample code, which defines two columns and three rows, doesn't define additional settings with the column and row definitions; the default is the star sizing.

The grid contains several `Label` and `TextBox` controls. Because the parent of these controls is a grid, you can set the attached properties `Column`, `ColumnSpan`, `Row`, and `RowSpan`:

```xml
<Window x:Class="LayoutDemo.GridWindow"
        xmlns="http://schemas.microsoft.com/winfx/2006/xaml/presentation"
        xmlns:x="http://schemas.microsoft.com/winfx/2006/xaml"
        Title="GridWindow" Height="300" Width="300">
    <Grid ShowGridLines="True">
        <Grid.ColumnDefinitions>
            <ColumnDefinition />
            <ColumnDefinition />
        </Grid.ColumnDefinitions>
        <Grid.RowDefinitions>
            <RowDefinition />
            <RowDefinition />
            <RowDefinition />
        </Grid.RowDefinitions>
        <Label Grid.Column="0" Grid.ColumnSpan="2" Grid.Row="0"
               VerticalAlignment="Center" HorizontalAlignment="Center" Content="Title" />
        <Label Grid.Column="0" Grid.Row="1" VerticalAlignment="Center"
               Content="Firstname:" Margin="10" />
        <TextBox Grid.Column="1" Grid.Row="1" Width="100" Height="30" />
        <Label Grid.Column="0" Grid.Row="2" VerticalAlignment="Center"
               Content="Lastname:" Margin="10" />
        <TextBox Grid.Column="1" Grid.Row="2" Width="100" Height="30" />
    </Grid>
</Window>
```

code snippet LayoutDemo/GridWindow.xaml

The outcome arranging controls in a grid is shown in Figure 35-17. For easier viewing of the columns and rows, the property `ShowGridLines` is set to `true`.

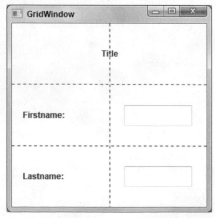

FIGURE 35-17

 For a grid where every cell has the same size, you can use the `UniformGrid` class.

STYLES AND RESOURCES

You can define the look and feel of the WPF elements by setting properties, such as FontSize and Background, with the Button element as shown:

```
<Button Width="150" FontSize="12" Background="AliceBlue" Content="Click Me!" />
```

code snippet StylesAndResources/MainWindow.xaml

Instead of defining the look and feel with every element, you can define styles that are stored with resources. To completely customize the look for controls, you can use templates and store them into resources.

Styles

The Style property of a control can be assigned to a Style element that has setters associated with it. A Setter element defines the Property and Value properties and sets a specified property to a value. Here, the Background, FontSize, and FontWeight properties are set. The Style is set to the TargetType Button, so that the properties of the Button can be directly accessed. If the TargetType of the style is not set, the properties can be accessed via Button.Background, Button.FontSize. This is especially important if properties of different element types need to be set:

```
<Button Width="150" Content="Click Me!">
    <Button.Style>
        <Style TargetType="Button">
            <Setter Property="Background" Value="Yellow" />
            <Setter Property="FontSize" Value="14" />
            <Setter Property="FontWeight" Value="Bold" />
        </Style>
    </Button.Style>
</Button>
```

code snippet StylesAndResources/MainWindow.xaml

Setting the Style directly with the Button element doesn't really help a lot in regard to style sharing. Styles can be put into resources. Within the resources you can assign styles to specific elements, assign a style to all elements of a type, or use a key for the style. To assign a style to all elements of a type, use the TargetType property of the Style and assign it to a Button by specifying the x:Type markup extension {x:Type Button}. For defining a style that needs to be referenced, x:Key must be set:

```
<Window.Resources>
    <Style TargetType="{x:Type Button}">
        <Setter Property="Background" Value="LemonChiffon" />
        <Setter Property="FontSize" Value="18" />
    </Style>
    <Style x:Key="ButtonStyle">
        <Setter Property="Button.Background" Value="Red" />
        <Setter Property="Button.Foreground" Value="White" />
        <Setter Property="Button.FontSize" Value="18" />
    </Style>
</Window.Resources>
```

In the following XAML code the first button — which doesn't have a style defined with the element properties — gets the style that is defined for the Button type. With the next button, the Style property is set with the StaticResource markup extension to {StaticResource ButtonStyle}, whereas ButtonStyle specifies the key value of the style resource defined earlier, so this button has a red background and a white foreground:

```
<Button Width="200" Content="Uses named style"
        Style="{StaticResource ButtonStyle}" Margin="3" />
```

Instead of setting the `Background` of a button to just a single value, you can also do more. You can set the `Background` property to a `LinearGradientBrush` with a gradient color definition as shown:

```
<Style x:Key="FancyButtonStyle">
    <Setter Property="Button.FontSize" Value="22" />
    <Setter Property="Button.Foreground" Value="White" />
    <Setter Property="Button.Background">
        <Setter.Value>
            <LinearGradientBrush StartPoint="0,0" EndPoint="0,1">
                <GradientStop Offset="0.0" Color="LightCyan" />
                <GradientStop Offset="0.14" Color="Cyan" />
                <GradientStop Offset="0.7" Color="DarkCyan" />
            </LinearGradientBrush>
        </Setter.Value>
    </Setter>
</Style>
```

The next button in this example has a fancy style with cyan applied as the linear gradient:

```
<Button Width="200" Content="Fancy button style"
        Style="{StaticResource FancyButtonStyle}" Margin="3" />
```

Styles offer a kind of inheritance. One style can be based on another one. The style `AnotherButtonStyle` is based on the style `FancyButtonStyle`. It uses all the settings defined by that style, and referenced by the `BasedOn` property, except the `Foreground` property — which is set to `LinearGradientBrush`:

```
<Style x:Key="AnotherButtonStyle" BasedOn="{StaticResource FancyButtonStyle}"
        TargetType="Button">
    <Setter Property="Foreground">
        <Setter.Value>
            <LinearGradientBrush>
                <GradientStop Offset="0.2" Color="White" />
                <GradientStop Offset="0.5" Color="LightYellow" />
                <GradientStop Offset="0.9" Color="Orange" />
            </LinearGradientBrush>
        </Setter.Value>
    </Setter>
</Style>
```

The last button has the `AnotherButtonStyle` applied:

```
<Button Width="200" Content="Style inheritance"
        Style="{StaticResource AnotherButtonStyle}" Margin="3" />
```

You can see the results of all these buttons styled in Figure 35-18.

FIGURE 35-18

Resources

As you have seen with the styles sample, usually styles are stored within resources. You can define any freezable element within a resource. For example, the brush created earlier for the background style of the button can itself be defined as a resource, so you can use it everywhere a brush is required.

The following example defines a `LinearGradientBrush` with the key name `MyGradientBrush` inside the `StackPanel` resources. `button1` assigns the `Background` property by using a `StaticResource` markup extension to the resource `MyGradientBrush`. Figure 35-19 shows the output from this XAML code:

```
<StackPanel x:Name="myContainer">
    <StackPanel.Resources>
        <LinearGradientBrush x:Key="MyGradientBrush" StartPoint="0,0"
                             EndPoint="0.3,1">
            <GradientStop Offset="0.0" Color="LightCyan" />
            <GradientStop Offset="0.14" Color="Cyan" />
            <GradientStop Offset="0.7" Color="DarkCyan" />
        </LinearGradientBrush>
    </StackPanel.Resources>
</StackPanel.Resources>
```

```
        <Button Width="200" Height="50" Foreground="White" Margin="5"
                Background="{StaticResource MyGradientBrush}" Content="Click Me!" />
    </StackPanel>
```

Here, the resources have been defined with the `StackPanel`. In the previous example, the resources were defined with the `Window` element. The base class `FrameworkElement` defines the property `Resources` of type `ResourceDictionary`. That's why resources can be defined with every class that is derived from the `FrameworkElement` — any WPF element.

FIGURE 35-19

Resources are searched hierarchically. If you define the resource with the `Window`, it applies to every child element of the `Window`. If the `Window` contains a `Grid`, and the `Grid` contains a `StackPanel`, and if you define the resource with the `StackPanel`, then the resource applies to every control within the `StackPanel`. If the `StackPanel` contains a `Button`, and you define the resource just with the `Button`, then this style is valid just for the button.

> *In regard to hierarchies, you need to pay attention if you use the `TargetType` without a `Key` for styles. If you define a resource with the `Canvas` element and set the `TargetType` for the style to apply to `TextBox` elements, then the style applies to all `TextBox` elements within the `Canvas`. The style even applies to `TextBox` elements that are contained in a `ListBox` when the `ListBox` is in the `Canvas`.*

If you need the same style for more than one window, then you can define the style with the application. In a Visual Studio WPF project, the file `App.xaml` is created for defining global resources of the application. The application styles are valid for every window of the application. Every element can access resources that are defined with the application. If resources are not found with the parent window, then the search for resources continues with the `Application`:

```
<Application x:Class="StylesAndResources.App"
             xmlns="http://schemas.microsoft.com/winfx/2006/xaml/presentation"
             xmlns:x="http://schemas.microsoft.com/winfx/2006/xaml"
             StartupUri="MainWindow.xaml">
    <Application.Resources>

    </Application.Resources>
</Application>
```

System Resources

There are also some system-wide resources for colors and fonts that are available for all applications. These resources are defined with the classes `SystemColors`, `SystemFonts`, and `SystemParameters`:

➤ With `SystemColors` you get the color settings for borders, controls, the desktop, and windows, such as `ActiveBorderColor`, `ControlBrush`, `DesktopColor`, `WindowColor`, `WindowBrush`, and so on.

➤ The class `SystemFonts` returns the settings for the fonts of the menu, status bar, and message box. These include `CaptionFont`, `DialogFont`, `MenuFont`, `MessageBoxFont`, `StatusFont`, and so on.

➤ The class `SystemParameters` gives you settings for sizes of menu buttons, cursors, icons, borders, captions, timing information, and keyboard settings, such as `BorderWidth`, `CaptionHeight`, `CaptionWidth`, `MenuButtonWidth`, `MenuPopupAnimation`, `MenuShowDelay`, `SmallIconHeight`, `SmallIconWidth`, and so on.

Accessing Resources from Code

To access resources from code-behind, the base class `FrameworkElement` implements the method `FindResource()`, so you can invoke the `FindResource()` method with every WPF object.

To do this, `button1` doesn't have a background specified, but the `Click` event is assigned to the method `button1_Click`:

```
<Button Name="button1" Width="220" Height="50" Margin="5" Click="button1_Click">
    Apply Resource Programmatically
</Button>
```

code snippet StylesAndResources/ResourceDemo.xaml

With the implementation of `button1_Click()`, the `FindResource()` method is used on the `Button` that was clicked. Then a search for the resource `MyGradientBrush` happens hierarchically, and the brush is applied to the `Background` property of the control. The resource `MyGradientBrush` was created previously in the resources of the `StackPanel`:

```
public void button1_Click(object sender, RoutedEventArgs e)
{
    Control ctrl = sender as Control;
    ctrl.Background = ctrl.FindResource("MyGradientBrush") as Brush;
}
```

code snippet StylesAndResources/ResourceDemo.xaml.cs

> If `FindResource()` *does not find the resource key, then an exception is thrown. If you don't know for sure if the resource is available, then you can use the method* `TryFindResource()` *instead.* `TryFindResource()` *returns* null *if the resource is not found.*

Dynamic Resources

With the `StaticResource` markup extension, resources are searched at load time. If the resource changes while the program is running, then you should use the `DynamicResource` markup extension instead.

The next example is using the same resource as defined previously. The earlier example used `StaticResource`. This button uses `DynamicResource` with the `DynamicResource` markup extension. The event handler of this button changes the resource programmatically. The handler method `button2_Click` is assigned to the `Click` event handler:

```
<Button Name="button2" Width="200" Height="50" Foreground="White" Margin="5"
        Background="{DynamicResource MyGradientBrush}" Content="Change Resource"
        Click="button2_Click" />
```

code snippet StylesAndResources/ResourceDemo.xaml

The implementation of `button2_Click()` clears the resources of the `StackPanel` and adds a new resource with the same name, `MyGradientBrush`. This new resource is very similar to the resource that is defined in XAML code; it just defines different colors:

```
private void button2_Click(object sender, RoutedEventArgs e)
{
    myContainer.Resources.Clear();
    var brush = new LinearGradientBrush
    {
        StartPoint = new Point(0, 0),
        EndPoint = new Point(0, 1)
    };

    brush.GradientStops = new GradientStopCollection()
```

```
        {
            new GradientStop(Colors.White, 0.0),
            new GradientStop(Colors.Yellow, 0.14),
            new GradientStop(Colors.YellowGreen, 0.7)
        };
        myContainer.Resources.Add("MyGradientBrush", brush);
    }
```

code snippet StylesAndResources/ResourceDemo.xaml.cs

When running the application, the resource changes dynamically by clicking the Change Resource button. Using the button with dynamic resource gets the dynamically created resource; the button with static resource looks the same as before.

 `DynamicResource` *requires more performance than* `StaticResource` *because the resource is always loaded when needed. Use* `DynamicResource` *only with resources where you expect changes during runtime.*

Resource Dictionaries

If the same resources are used with different applications, it's useful to put the resource in a resource dictionary. Using resource dictionaries, the files can be shared between multiple applications, or the resource dictionary can be put into an assembly and shared by the applications.

To share a resource dictionary in an assembly, create a library. A resource dictionary file, here `Dictionary1.xaml`, can be added to the assembly. The build action for this file must be set to `Resource` so that it is added as a resource to the assembly.

`Dictionary1.xaml` defines two resources: `LinearGradientBrush` with the `CyanGradientBrush` key, and a style for a `Button` that can be referenced with the `PinkButtonStyle` key:

```xml
<ResourceDictionary xmlns="http://schemas.microsoft.com/winfx/2006/xaml/presentation"
                    xmlns:x="http://schemas.microsoft.com/winfx/2006/xaml">
    <LinearGradientBrush x:Key="CyanGradientBrush" StartPoint="0,0" EndPoint="0.3,1">
        <GradientStop Offset="0.0" Color="LightCyan" />
        <GradientStop Offset="0.14" Color="Cyan" />
        <GradientStop Offset="0.7" Color="DarkCyan" />
    </LinearGradientBrush>

    <Style x:Key="PinkButtonStyle" TargetType="Button">
        <Setter Property="FontSize" Value="22" />
        <Setter Property="Foreground" Value="White" />
        <Setter Property="Background">
            <Setter.Value>
                <LinearGradientBrush StartPoint="0,0" EndPoint="0,1">
                    <GradientStop Offset="0.0" Color="Pink" />
                    <GradientStop Offset="0.3" Color="DeepPink" />
                    <GradientStop Offset="0.9" Color="DarkOrchid" />
                </LinearGradientBrush>
            </Setter.Value>
        </Setter>
    </Style>
</ResourceDictionary>
```

code snippet ResourcesLib/Dictionary1.xaml

With the target project, the library needs to be referenced, and the resource dictionary added to the dictionaries. You can use multiple resource dictionary files that can be added with the `MergedDictionaries` property of the `ResourceDictionary`. A list of resource dictionaries can be added to the merged dictionaries. With the `Source` property of `ResourceDictionary`, a dictionary can be referenced. For the reference, the pack URI syntax is used. The pack URI can be assigned as *absolute*, where the URI begins with `pack://`, or as *relative*, as it is used in this example. With relative syntax, the referenced assembly `ResourceLib`, which includes the dictionary, is first after the / followed by `;component`. `Component` means that the dictionary is included as a resource in the assembly. After that, the name of the dictionary file `Dictionary1.xaml` is added. If the dictionary is added into a subfolder, the folder name must be declared as well:

```xml
<Application x:Class="StylesAndResources.App"
             xmlns="http://schemas.microsoft.com/winfx/2006/xaml/presentation"
             xmlns:x="http://schemas.microsoft.com/winfx/2006/xaml"
             StartupUri="MainWindow.xaml">
    <Application.Resources>
        <ResourceDictionary>
            <ResourceDictionary.MergedDictionaries>
                <ResourceDictionary Source="/ResourceLib;component/Dictionary1.xaml" />
            </ResourceDictionary.MergedDictionaries>
        </ResourceDictionary>
    </Application.Resources>
</Application>
```

code snippet StylesAndResources/App.xaml

Now it is possible to use the resources from the referenced assembly in the same way as local resources:

```xml
<Button Width="300" Height="50" Style="{StaticResource PinkButtonStyle}"
        Content="Referenced Resource" />
```

code snippet StylesAndResources/ResourceDemo.xaml

TRIGGERS

With triggers you can change the look and feel of your controls dynamically because of some events or some property value changes. For example, when the user moves with the mouse over a button, the button can change its look. Usually, you need to do this with the C# code. With WPF, you can also do this with XAML, as long as only the UI is influenced.

There are several triggers with XAML. Property triggers are activated as soon as a property value changes. Multi-triggers are based on multiple property values. Event triggers fire when an event occurs. Data triggers happen when data that is bound is changed. In this section, property triggers, multi-triggers, and data triggers are discussed. Event triggers are explained later with animations.

Property Triggers

The `Style` class has a `Triggers` property where you can assign property triggers. The following example includes a `Button` element inside a `Grid` panel. With the `Window` resources, a default style for `Button` elements is defined. This style specifies that the `Background` is set to `LightBlue` and the `FontSize` to 17. This is the style of the `Button` elements when the application is started. Using triggers, the style of the controls change. The triggers are defined within the `Style.Triggers` element, using the `Trigger` element. One trigger is assigned to the property `IsMouseOver`; the other trigger is assigned to the property `IsPressed`. Both of these properties are defined with the `Button` class that the style applies to. If `IsMouseOver` has a value of `true`, then the trigger fires and sets the `Foreground` property to `Red` and the `FontSize` property to 22. If the `Button` is pressed, then the property `IsPressed` is `true`, and the second trigger fires and sets the `Foreground` property of the `TextBox` to `Yellow`.

If the `IsPressed` property is set to true, the `IsMouseOver` property will be true as well. Pressing the button also requires that the mouse is over the button. Pressing the button triggers it to fire and changes the properties accordingly. Here the order of triggers is important. If the `IsPressed` property trigger is moved before the `IsMouseOver` property trigger, the `IsMouseOver` property trigger overwrites the values that the first trigger set.

Available for
download on
Wrox.com

```xml
<Window x:Class="TriggerDemo.PropertyTriggerWindow"
        xmlns="http://schemas.microsoft.com/winfx/2006/xaml/presentation"
        xmlns:x="http://schemas.microsoft.com/winfx/2006/xaml"
        Title="PropertyTriggerWindow" Height="300" Width="300">
    <Window.Resources>
        <Style TargetType="Button">
            <Setter Property="Background" Value="LightBlue" />
            <Setter Property="FontSize" Value="17" />
            <Style.Triggers>
                <Trigger Property="IsMouseOver" Value="True">
                    <Setter Property="Foreground" Value="Red" />
                    <Setter Property="FontSize" Value="22" />
                </Trigger>
                <Trigger Property="IsPressed" Value="True">
                    <Setter Property="Foreground" Value="Yellow" />
                    <Setter Property="FontSize" Value="22" />
                </Trigger>
            </Style.Triggers>
        </Style>
    </Window.Resources>
    <Grid>
        <Button Width="200" Height="30" Content="Click me!" />
    </Grid>
</Window>
```

code snippet TriggerDemo/PropertyTriggerWindow.xaml

You don't need to reset the property values to the original values when the reason for the trigger is not valid anymore. For example, you don't need to define a trigger for IsMouseOver=true and IsMouseOver=false. As soon as the reason for the trigger is no longer valid, the changes made by the trigger action are reset to the original values automatically.

Figure 35-20 shows the trigger sample application, where on mouse focus the foreground and font size of the button are changed from their original values.

Click me!

FIGURE 35-20

When using property triggers, it is extremely easy to change the look of controls, fonts, colors, opacity, and the like. When the mouse moves over them, the keyboard sets the focus — not a single line of programming code is required.

The Trigger class defines the following properties to specify the trigger action.

TRIGGER PROPERTY	DESCRIPTION
Property Value	With property triggers, the Property and Value properties are used to specify when the trigger should fire, for example, Property="IsMouseOver" Value="True".
Setters	As soon as the trigger fires, you can use Setters to define a collection of Setter elements to change values for properties. The Setter class defines the properties Property, TargetName, and Value for the object properties to change.
EnterActions ExitActions	Instead of defining setters, you can define EnterActions and ExitActions. With both of these properties, you can define a collection of TriggerAction elements. EnterActions fires when the trigger starts (with a property trigger, when the Property/Value combination applies); ExitActions fires before it ends (just at the moment when the Property/Value combination no longer applies).Trigger actions that you can specify with these actions are derived from the base class TriggerAction, such as, SoundPlayerAction and BeginStoryboard. With SoundPlayerAction, you can start the playing of sound. BeginStoryboard is used with animation, which will be shown later in this chapter.

MultiTrigger

A property trigger fires when a value of a property changes. If you need to set a trigger because two or more properties have a specific value, you can use `MultiTrigger`.

`MultiTrigger` has a `Conditions` property where valid values of properties can be specified. It also has a `Setters` property, where the properties that need to be set can be specified. In the example, a style is defined for `TextBox` elements where the trigger applies if the `IsEnabled` property is `True` and the `Text` property has the `value` `Test`. If both apply, the `Foreground` property of the `TextBox` is set to `Red`:

Available for download on Wrox.com

```xml
<Window x:Class="TriggerDemo.MultiTriggerWindow"
        xmlns="http://schemas.microsoft.com/winfx/2006/xaml/presentation"
        xmlns:x="http://schemas.microsoft.com/winfx/2006/xaml"
        Title="MultiTriggerWindow" Height="300" Width="300">
    <Window.Resources>
        <Style TargetType="TextBox">
            <Style.Triggers>
                <MultiTrigger>
                    <MultiTrigger.Conditions>
                        <Condition Property="IsEnabled" Value="True" />
                        <Condition Property="Text" Value="Test" />
                    </MultiTrigger.Conditions>
                    <MultiTrigger.Setters>
                        <Setter Property="Foreground" Value="Red" />
                    </MultiTrigger.Setters>
                </MultiTrigger>
            </Style.Triggers>
        </Style>
    </Window.Resources>
    <Grid>
        <TextBox />
    </Grid>
</Window>
```

code snippet TriggerDemo/MultiTriggerWindow.xaml

Data Triggers

Data triggers fire if bound data to a control fulfills specific conditions. In the following example, a `Book` class is used that has different displays depending on the publisher of the book.

The `Book` class defines the properties `Title` and `Publisher` and has an overload of the `ToString()` method:

Available for download on Wrox.com

```csharp
public class Book
{
    public string Title { get; set; }
    public string Publisher { get; set; }

    public override string ToString()
    {
        return Title;
    }
}
```

code snippet TriggerDemo/Book.cs

In the XAML code, a style is defined for `ListBoxItem` elements. The style contains `DataTrigger` elements that are bound to the `Publisher` property of the class that is used with the items. If the value of the `Publisher` property is Wrox Press, the `Background` is set to `Red`. With the publishers Dummies and Sybex, the `Background` is set to `Yellow` and `LightBlue` accordingly:

```xml
<Window x:Class="TriggerDemo.DataTriggerWindow"
        xmlns="http://schemas.microsoft.com/winfx/2006/xaml/presentation"
        xmlns:x="http://schemas.microsoft.com/winfx/2006/xaml"
        Title="Data Trigger Window" Height="300" Width="300">
    <Window.Resources>
        <Style TargetType="ListBoxItem">
            <Style.Triggers>
                <DataTrigger Binding="{Binding Path=Publisher}" Value="Wrox Press">
                    <Setter Property="Background" Value="Red" />
                </DataTrigger>
                <DataTrigger Binding="{Binding Path=Publisher}" Value="Dummies">
                    <Setter Property="Background" Value="Yellow" />
                </DataTrigger>
                <DataTrigger Binding="{Binding Path=Publisher}" Value="Sybex">
                    <Setter Property="Background" Value="LightBlue" />
                </DataTrigger>
            </Style.Triggers>
        </Style>
    </Window.Resources>
    <Grid>
        <ListBox x:Name="list1" />
    </Grid>
</Window>
```

code snippet TriggerDemo/DataTriggerWindow.xaml

In the code-behind, the list with the name `list1` is initialized to contain several `Book` objects:

```csharp
public DataTriggerWindow()
{
    InitializeComponent();
    list1.Items.Add(new Book
        {
            Title = "Professional C# 4.0",
            Publisher = "Wrox Press"
        });
    list1.Items.Add(new Book
        {
            Title = "C# 2008 for Dummies",
            Publisher = "Dummies"
        });
    list1.Items.Add(new Book
        {
            Title = "Mastering Integrated HTML and CSS",
            Publisher = "Sybex"
        });
}
```

code snippet TriggerDemo/DataTriggerWindow.xaml.cs

Running the application, you can see in Figure 35-21 the `ListBoxItem` elements that are formatted according to the publisher value.

With `DataTrigger`, multiple properties must be set for `MultiDataTrigger` (similar to `Trigger` and `MultiTrigger`).

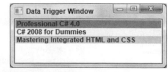

FIGURE 35-21

TEMPLATES

In this chapter, you have already seen that a `Button` control can have any content. The content can be simple text, but you can also add a `Canvas` element, which can contain shapes. You can add a `Grid`, or a video to the button. However, there is even more than that you can do with a button!

In WPF, the functionality of controls is completely separate from their look and feel. A button has a default look, but you can completely customize that look as you like with templates.

WPF gives you several template types that derive from the base class `FrameworkTemplate`.

TEMPLATE TYPE	DESCRIPTION
ControlTemplate	With a `ControlTemplate` you can specify the visual structure of a control and override the look.
ItemsPanelTemplate	For an `ItemsControl` you can specify the layout of its items by assigning an `ItemsPanelTemplate`. Each `ItemsControl` has a default `ItemsPanelTemplate`. For the `MenuItem`, it is a `WrapPanel`. The `StatusBar` uses a `DockPanel`, and the `ListBox` uses a `VirtualizingStackPanel`.
DataTemplate	`DataTemplates` are very useful for graphical representations of objects. Styling a `ListBox`, you will see that, by default, the items of the `ListBox` are shown according to the output of the `ToString()` method. By applying a `DataTemplate` you can override this behavior and define a custom presentation of the items.
HierarchicalDataTemplate	The `HierarchicalDataTemplate` is used for arranging a tree of objects. This control supports `HeaderedItemsControls`, such as `TreeViewItem` and `MenuItem`.

Control Templates

Previously in this chapter you've seen how the properties of a control can be styled. If setting simple properties of the controls doesn't give you the look you want, you can change the `Template` property. With the `Template` property, the complete look of the control can be customized.

The next example shows customizing buttons, and later, list boxes are customized step by step, so you can see the intermediate results of the changes.

The customization of the `Button` type is done in a separate resource dictionary file, `Styles.xaml`. Here, a style with the key name `RoundedGelButton` is defined.

The style `GelButton` sets the properties `Background`, `Height`, `Foreground`, and `Margin`, and the `Template`. The `Template` is the most interesting aspect with this style. The `Template` specifies a `Grid` with just one row and one column.

Inside this cell, you can find an ellipse with the name `GelBackground`. This ellipse has a linear gradient brush for the stroke. The stroke that surrounds the rectangle is very thin because the `StrokeThickness` is set to 0.5.

The second ellipse, `GelShine`, is a small ellipse where the size is defined by the `Margin` property and so is visible within the first ellipse. The stroke is transparent, so there is no line surrounding the ellipse. This ellipse uses a linear gradient fill brush, which goes from a light, partly transparent color to full transparency. This gives the ellipse a shimmering effect:

```xml
<ResourceDictionary xmlns="http://schemas.microsoft.com/winfx/2006/xaml/presentation"
                    xmlns:x="http://schemas.microsoft.com/winfx/2006/xaml">

    <Style x:Key="RoundedGelButton" TargetType="Button">
        <Setter Property="Width" Value="100" />
        <Setter Property="Height" Value="100" />
        <Setter Property="Foreground" Value="White" />
        <Setter Property="Template">
            <Setter.Value>
                <ControlTemplate TargetType="{x:Type Button}">
                    <Grid>
                        <Ellipse Name="GelBackground" StrokeThickness="0.5" Fill="Black">
                            <Ellipse.Stroke>
```

```
                            <LinearGradientBrush StartPoint="0,0" EndPoint="0,1">
                                <GradientStop Offset="0" Color="#ff7e7e7e" />
                                <GradientStop Offset="1" Color="Black" />
                            </LinearGradientBrush>
                        </Ellipse.Stroke>
                    </Ellipse>
                    <Ellipse Margin="15,5,15,50">
                        <Ellipse.Fill>
                            <LinearGradientBrush StartPoint="0,0" EndPoint="0,1">
                                <GradientStop Offset="0" Color="#aaffffff" />
                                <GradientStop Offset="1" Color="Transparent" />
                            </LinearGradientBrush>
                        </Ellipse.Fill>
                    </Ellipse>
                </Grid>
            </ControlTemplate>
        </Setter.Value>
    </Setter>
  </Style>
</ResourceDictionary>
```

code snippet TemplateDemo/Styles.xaml

From the `app.xaml` file, the resource dictionary is referenced as shown:

```
<Application x:Class="TemplateDemo.App"
             xmlns="http://schemas.microsoft.com/winfx/2006/xaml/presentation"
             xmlns:x="http://schemas.microsoft.com/winfx/2006/xaml"
             StartupUri="MainWindow.xaml">
    <Application.Resources>
        <ResourceDictionary Source="Styles.xaml" />
    </Application.Resources>
</Application>
```

code snippet TemplateDemo/App.xaml

Now a `Button` control can be associated with the style. The new look of the button is shown in Figure 35-22.

```
<Button Style="{StaticResource RoundedGelButton}" Content="Click Me!" /
```

The button now has a completely different look. However, the content that is defined with the button itself is missing. The template created previously must be extended to get the content of the `Button` into the new look. What needs to be added is a `ContentPresenter`. The `ContentPresenter` is the placeholder for the content of the control and defines the place where the content should be positioned. Here, the content is placed in the first row of the `Grid`, as are the `Ellipse` elements. The `Content` property of the `ContentPresenter` defines what the content should be. The content is set to a `TemplateBinding` markup expression. `TemplateBinding` binds the template parent, which is the `Button` element in this case. `{TempateBinding Content}` specifies that the value of the `Content` property of the `Button` control should be placed inside the placeholder as content. Figure 35-23 shows the result with the content shown:

FIGURE 35-22

```
            <Setter Property="Template">
                <Setter.Value>
                    <ControlTemplate TargetType="{x:Type Button}">
                        <Grid>
                            <Ellipse Name="GelBackground" StrokeThickness="0.5" Fill="Black">
                                <Ellipse.Stroke>
                                    <LinearGradientBrush StartPoint="0,0" EndPoint="0,1">
                                        <GradientStop Offset="0" Color="#ff7e7e7e" />
                                        <GradientStop Offset="1" Color="Black" />
                                    </LinearGradientBrush>
                                </Ellipse.Stroke>
                            </Ellipse>
                            <Ellipse Margin="15,5,15,50">
```

```
            <Ellipse.Fill>
                <LinearGradientBrush StartPoint="0,0" EndPoint="0,1">
                    <GradientStop Offset="0" Color="#aaffffff" />
                    <GradientStop Offset="1" Color="Transparent" />
                </LinearGradientBrush>
            </Ellipse.Fill>
        </Ellipse>
        <ContentPresenter Name="GelButtonContent"
                    VerticalAlignment="Center"
                    HorizontalAlignment="Center"
                    Content="{TemplateBinding Content}" />
    </Grid>
</ControlTemplate>
</Setter.Value>
```

code snippet TemplateDemo/StyledButtonWindow.xaml

Such a styled button now looks very fancy on the screen. There's still a problem: there is no action if the mouse is clicked or the mouse moves over the button. This isn't the typical feeling a user has with a button. This can be solved: with a template-styled button, you must have triggers for the button to appear differently in response to mouse moves and mouse clicks.

FIGURE 35-23

Using property triggers (discussed previously), this can be solved easily. The triggers just need to be added to the `Triggers` collection of the `ControlTemplate` as shown. Here, two triggers are defined. One property trigger is active when the `IsMouseOver` property of the button is true. Then the `Fill` property of the ellipse with the name `GelBackground` is changed to a `RadialGradientBrush` with values from `Lime` to `DarkGreen`. With the `IsPressed` property, other colors are specified for the `RadialGradientBrush`:

```
<ControlTemplate.Triggers>
    <Trigger Property="IsMouseOver" Value="True">
        <Setter Property="Ellipse.Fill" TargetName="GelBackground">
            <Setter.Value>
                <RadialGradientBrush>
                    <GradientStop Offset="0" Color="Lime" />
                    <GradientStop Offset="1" Color="DarkGreen" />
                </RadialGradientBrush>
            </Setter.Value>
        </Setter>
    </Trigger>
    <Trigger Property="IsPressed" Value="True">
        <Setter Property="Ellipse.Fill" TargetName="GelBackground">
            <Setter.Value>
                <RadialGradientBrush>
                    <GradientStop Offset="0" Color="#ffcc34" />
                    <GradientStop Offset="1" Color="#cc9900" />
                </RadialGradientBrush>
            </Setter.Value>
        </Setter>
    </Trigger>
</ControlTemplate.Triggers>
```

Now you can run the application and see a visual feedback from the button as soon as the mouse hovers over it or the mouse is clicked.

Data Templates

The content of `ContentControl` elements can be any content — not only WPF elements but also .NET objects. For example, an object of the `Country` type can be assigned to the content of a `Button` class. The `Country` class has been created to represent the name and flag with a path to an image. This class defines the `Name` and `ImagePath` properties, and it has an overridden `ToString()` method for a default string representation:

```csharp
public class Country
{
    public string Name { get; set; }
    public string ImagePath { get; set; }

    public override string ToString()
    {
        return Name;
    }
}
```

How does this content look within a `Button` or any other `ContentControl`? By default, the `ToString()` method is invoked, and the string representation of the object is shown. For a custom look you can also create a `DataTemplate` for the `Country` type.

Here, within the resources of the `Window`, a `DataTemplate` is created. This `DataTemplate` doesn't have a key assigned and thus is a default for the `Country`. `src` type — it is also the alias of the XML namespace referencing the .NET assembly and .NET namespace. Within the `DataTemplate` the main elements are a `TextBox` with the `Text` property bound to the `Name` property of the `Country`, and an `Image` with the `Source` property bound to the `ImagePath` property of the `Country`. The `Grid`, `Border`, and `Rectangle` elements define the layout and visual appearance:

```xml
<Window.Resources>
    <DataTemplate DataType="{x:Type src:Country}">
        <Grid>
            <Grid.ColumnDefinitions>
                <ColumnDefinition Width="Auto" />
                <ColumnDefinition Width="Auto" />
            </Grid.ColumnDefinitions>
            <Grid.RowDefinitions>
                <RowDefinition Height="60" />
            </Grid.RowDefinitions>
            <TextBlock FontSize="16" VerticalAlignment="Center" Margin="5"
                    Text="{Binding Name}" FontWeight="Bold" Grid.Column="0" />
            <Border Margin="4,0" Grid.Column="1" BorderThickness="2"
                    CornerRadius="4">
                <Border.BorderBrush>
                    <LinearGradientBrush StartPoint="0,0" EndPoint="0,1">
                        <GradientStop Offset="0" Color="#aaa" />
                        <GradientStop Offset="1" Color="#222" />
                    </LinearGradientBrush>
                </Border.BorderBrush>
                <Grid>
                    <Rectangle>
                        <Rectangle.Fill>
                            <LinearGradientBrush StartPoint="0,0" EndPoint="0,1">
                                <GradientStop Offset="0" Color="#444" />
                                <GradientStop Offset="1" Color="#fff" />
                            </LinearGradientBrush>
                        </Rectangle.Fill>
                    </Rectangle>
                    <Image Width="48" Margin="2,2,2,1"
                            Source="{Binding ImagePath}" />
                </Grid>
            </Border>
        </Grid>
    </DataTemplate>
</Window.Resources>
```

With the XAML code, a simple `Button` element with the name `button1` is defined:

```
<Button Grid.Row="1" x:Name="button1" Margin="10" />
```

Within the code-behind, a new `Country` object is instantiated that is assigned to the `Content` property of `button1`:

Available for
download on
Wrox.com

```
public StyledButtonWindow()
{
    InitializeComponent();
    button1.Content = new Country
                    {
                        Name = "Austria",
                        ImagePath = "images/Austria.bmp"
                    };
}
```

code snippet TemplateDemo/StyledButtonWindow.xaml.cs

After running the application, you can see that the `DataTemplate` is applied to the `Button` because `Country` data type has a default template, as shown in Figure 35-24.

Of course it is also possible to create a control template and use a data template from within.

FIGURE 35-24

Styling a ListBox

Changing a style of a button or a label is a simple task. How about changing the style of an element that contains a list of elements? For example, how about changing a `ListBox`? Again, a list box has behavior and a look. It can display a list of elements, and you can select one or more elements from the list. For the behavior, the `ListBox` class defines methods, properties, and events. The look of the `ListBox` is separate from its behavior. The `ListBox` element has a default look, but you can change this look by creating a template.

With a `ListBox` the `ControlTemplate` defines how the complete control looks, an `ItemTemplate` defines how an item looks, and a `DataTemplate` defines the type that might be within an item.

For filling a `ListBox` with some items, the static class `Countries` returns a list of a few countries that will be displayed:

Available for
download on
Wrox.com

```
public class Countries
{
    public static IEnumerable<Country> GetCountries()
    {
        return new List<Country>
        {
            new Country { Name = "Austria", ImagePath = "Images/Austria.bmp" },
            new Country { Name = "Germany", ImagePath = "Images/Germany.bmp" },
            new Country { Name = "Norway", ImagePath = "Images/Norway.bmp" },
            new Country { Name = "USA", ImagePath = "Images/USA.bmp" }
        };
    }
}
```

code snippet TemplateDemo/Countries.cs

Inside the code-behind file in the constructor of the `StyledListBoxWindow1` class, the `DataContext` property of the `StyledListBoxWindow1` instance is set to the list of countries that is returned from the method `Countries.GetCountries()`. (The `DataContext` property is a data binding feature discussed in the next chapter.)

```
public partial class StyledListBoxWindow1 : Window
{
    public StyledListBoxWindow1()
    {
        InitializeComponent();
        this.DataContext = Countries.GetCountries();
    }
}
```

code snippet TemplateDemo/StyledListBoxWindow1.xaml.cs

Within the XAML code, the `ListBox` named `countryList1` is defined. `countryList1` doesn't have a different style. It uses the default look from the `ListBox` element. The property `ItemsSource` is set to the `Binding` markup extension, which is used by data binding. From the code-behind, you have seen that the binding is done to an array of `Country` objects. Figure 35-25 shows the default look of the `ListBox`. By default, just the names of the countries returned by the `ToString()` method are displayed in a simple list:

```
<Window x:Class="TemplateDemo.StyledListBoxWindow1"
        xmlns="http://schemas.microsoft.com/winfx/2006/xaml/presentation"
        xmlns:x="http://schemas.microsoft.com/winfx/2006/xaml"
        xmlns:src="clr-namespace:TemplateDemo"
        Title="StyledListBoxWindow1" Height="300" Width="300">
    <Grid>
        <ListBox ItemsSource="{Binding}" Margin="10" />
    </Grid>
</Window>
```

code snippet TemplateDemo/StyledListBoxWindow1.xaml

ItemTemplate

The `Country` objects do have both the name and the flag in the object. Of course, you can also display both values in the list box. To do this, you need to define a template.

The `ListBox` element contains `ListBoxItem` elements. You can define the content for an item with the `ItemTemplate`. The style `ListBoxStyle1` defines an `ItemTemplate` with a value of a `DataTemplate`. A `DataTemplate` is used to bind data to elements. You can use the `Binding` markup extension with `DataTemplate` elements.

Austria
Germany
Norway
USA

FIGURE 35-25

The `DataTemplate` contains a grid with three columns. The first column contains the string `Country:`. The second column contains the name of the country. The third column contains the flag for the country. Because the country names have different lengths, but the view should be the same size for every country name, the `SharedSizeGroup` property is set with the second column definition. This shared size information for the column is used only because the property `Grid.IsSharedSizeScope` is also set.

After the column and row definitions, you can see two `TextBlock` elements. The first `TextBlock` element contains the text `Country:`. The second `TextBlock` element binds to the `Name` property that is defined in the `Country` class.

The content for the third column is a `Border` element containing a `Grid`. The `Grid` contains a `Rectangle` with a linear gradient brush and an `Image` element that is bound to the `ImagePath` property of the `Country` class. Figure 35-26 shows the countries in a `ListBox` with completely different output than before:

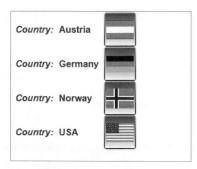

Country: Austria

Country: Germany

Country: Norway

Country: USA

FIGURE 35-26

```
<Style x:Key="ListBoxStyle1" TargetType="{x:Type ListBox}" >
    <Setter Property="ItemTemplate">
        <Setter.Value>
            <DataTemplate>
```

```
<Grid>
    <Grid.ColumnDefinitions>
        <ColumnDefinition Width="Auto" />
        <ColumnDefinition Width="*" SharedSizeGroup="MiddleColumn" />
        <ColumnDefinition Width="Auto" />
    </Grid.ColumnDefinitions>
    <Grid.RowDefinitions>
        <RowDefinition Height="60" />
    </Grid.RowDefinitions>
    <TextBlock FontSize="16" VerticalAlignment="Center" Margin="5"
            FontStyle="Italic" Grid.Column="0" Text="Country:" />
    <TextBlock FontSize="16" VerticalAlignment="Center" Margin="5"
            Text="{Binding Name}" FontWeight="Bold"
            Grid.Column="1" />
    <Border Margin="4,0" Grid.Column="2" BorderThickness="2"
            CornerRadius="4">
        <Border.BorderBrush>
            <LinearGradientBrush StartPoint="0,0" EndPoint="0,1">
                <GradientStop Offset="0" Color="#aaa" />
                <GradientStop Offset="1" Color="#222" />
            </LinearGradientBrush>
        </Border.BorderBrush>
        <Grid>
            <Rectangle>
                <Rectangle.Fill>
                    <LinearGradientBrush StartPoint="0,0"
                                        EndPoint="0,1">
                        <GradientStop Offset="0" Color="#444" />
                        <GradientStop Offset="1" Color="#fff" />
                    </LinearGradientBrush>
                </Rectangle.Fill>
            </Rectangle>
            <Image Width="48" Margin="2,2,2,1"
                    Source="{Binding ImagePath}" />
        </Grid>
    </Border>
</Grid>
                </DataTemplate>
            </Setter.Value>
        </Setter>
        <Setter Property="Grid.IsSharedSizeScope" Value="True" />
    </Style>
```

code snippet TemplateDemo/Styles.xaml

Control Templates for ListBox Elements

It is not necessary that a ListBox have items that follow vertically, one after the other. You can give the user a different view with the same functionality. The next style, ListBoxStyle2, defines a template in which the items are shown horizontally with a scrollbar.

In the previous example, only an ItemTemplate was created to define how the items should look in the default ListBox. Now, a template is created to define a different ListBox. The template contains a ControlTemplate element to define the elements of the ListBox. The element is now a ScrollViewer — a view with a scrollbar — that contains a StackPanel. As the items should now be listed horizontally, the Orientation of the StackPanel is set to Horizontal. The stack panel will contain the items that are defined with the ItemsTemplate. As a result, the IsItemsHost of the StackPanel element is set to true. IsItemsHost is a property that is available with every Panel element that can contain a list of items.

The ItemTemplate that defines the look for the items in the stack panel is taken from the style ListBoxStyle1 where ListBoxStyle2 is based.

Figure 35-27 shows the ListBox styled with ListBoxStyle2 where the scrollbar appears automatically when the view is too small to display all items in the list:

Available for download on Wrox.com

```xml
<Style x:Key="ListBoxStyle2" TargetType="{x:Type ListBox}"
        BasedOn="{StaticResource ListBoxStyle1}">
    <Setter Property="Template">
        <Setter.Value>
            <ControlTemplate TargetType="{x:Type ListBox}">
                <ScrollViewer HorizontalScrollBarVisibility="Auto">
                    <StackPanel Name="StackPanel1" IsItemsHost="True"
            Orientation="Horizontal" />
                </ScrollViewer>
            </ControlTemplate>
        </Setter.Value>
    </Setter>
    <Setter Property="VerticalAlignment" Value="Center" />
</Style>
```

code snippet TemplateDemo/Styles.xaml

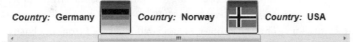

FIGURE 35-27

Certainly you see the advantages of separating the look of the controls from their behavior. You may already have many ideas about how you can display your items in a list that best fits the requirements of your application. Perhaps you just want to display as many items as will fit in the window, position them horizontally, and then continue to the next line vertically. That's where a WrapPanel comes in. And, of course, you can have a WrapPanel inside a template for a ListBox, as shown in ListBoxStyle3. Figure 35-28 shows the result of using the WrapPanel:

FIGURE 35-28

```xml
<Style x:Key="ListBoxStyle3" TargetType="{x:Type ListBox}">
    <Setter Property="Template">
        <Setter.Value>
            <ControlTemplate TargetType="{x:Type ListBox}">
                <ScrollViewer VerticalScrollBarVisibility="Auto"
                              HorizontalScrollBarVisibility="Disabled">
                    <WrapPanel IsItemsHost="True" />
                </ScrollViewer>
            </ControlTemplate>
        </Setter.Value>
    </Setter>
    <Setter Property="ItemTemplate">
        <Setter.Value>
            <DataTemplate>
                <Grid>
                    <Grid.ColumnDefinitions>
                        <ColumnDefinition Width="140" />
                    </Grid.ColumnDefinitions>
                    <Grid.RowDefinitions>
```

```
                        <RowDefinition Height="60" />
                        <RowDefinition Height="30" />
                    </Grid.RowDefinitions>
                    <Image Grid.Row="0" Width="48" Margin="2,2,2,1"
                            Source="{Binding ImagePath}" />
                    <TextBlock Grid.Row="1" FontSize="14"
                            HorizontalAlignment="Center" Margin="5"
                            Text="{Binding Name}" />
                </Grid>
            </DataTemplate>
        </Setter.Value>
    </Setter>
</Style>
```

ANIMATIONS

With animations you can make a smooth transition using moving elements, color changes, transforms, and so on. WPF makes it easy to create animations. You can animate the value of any dependency property. Different animation classes exist to animate the values of different properties, depending on their type.

The major elements of animations are as follows:

➤ **Timeline** — Defines how a value changes over time. Different kinds of timelines are available for changing different types of values. The base class for all timelines is `Timeline`. To animate a `double`, the class `DoubleAnimation` can be used. `Int32Animation` is the animation class for `int` values. `PointAnimation` is used to animate points, and `ColorAnimation` to animate colors.

➤ **Storyboard** — Used to combine animations. The `Storyboard` class itself is derived from the base class `TimelineGroup`, which derives from `Timeline`. With `DoubleAnimation` you can animate a double value; with `Storyboard` you combine all the animations that belong together.

➤ **Triggers** — Start and stop animations. You've seen property triggers previously. They fire when a property value changes. You can also create an event trigger. An event trigger fires when an event occurs.

 The namespace for animation classes is `System.Windows.Media.Animation`.

Timeline

A `Timeline` defines how a value changes over time. The first example animates the size of an ellipse. Here a `DoubleAnimation` timeline changes to a double value. The `Triggers` property of the `Ellipse` class is set to an `EventTrigger`. The event trigger is fired when the ellipse is loaded as defined with the `RoutedEvent` property of the `EventTrigger`. `BeginStoryboard` is a trigger action that begins the storyboard. With the storyboard, a `DoubleAnimation` element is used to animate the `Width` property of the `Ellipse` class. The animation changes the width of the ellipse from 100 to 300 within three seconds, and reverses the animation after three seconds. The animation `ColorAnimation` animates the color from the `ellipseBrush` which is used to fill the ellipse:

Available for
download on
Wrox.com

```
<Ellipse Height="50" Width="100">
    <Ellipse.Fill>
        <SolidColorBrush x:Name="ellipseBrush" Color="SteelBlue" />
    </Ellipse.Fill>
    <Ellipse.Triggers>
        <EventTrigger RoutedEvent="Ellipse.Loaded" >
            <EventTrigger.Actions>
                <BeginStoryboard>
                    <Storyboard Duration="00:00:06" RepeatBehavior="Forever">
                        <DoubleAnimation
                            Storyboard.TargetProperty="(Ellipse.Width)"
```

```
                                            Duration="0:0:3" AutoReverse="True"
                                                    FillBehavior="Stop"
                                                    RepeatBehavior="Forever"
                                            AccelerationRatio="0.9" DecelerationRatio="0.1"
                                                    From="100" To="300" />
                            <ColorAnimation Storyboard.TargetName="ellipseBrush"
                                    Storyboard.TargetProperty="(SolidColorBrush.Color)"
                                    Duration="0:0:3" AutoReverse="True"
                                    FillBehavior="Stop" RepeatBehavior="Forever"
                                            From="Yellow" To="Red" />
                        </Storyboard>
                    </BeginStoryboard>
                </EventTrigger.Actions>
            </EventTrigger>
        </Ellipse.Triggers>
    </Ellipse>
```

code snippet AnimationDemo/EllipseWindow.xaml

Figures 35-29 and 35-30 show two states from the animated ellipse.

Animations are far more than typical window-dressing animation that appears onscreen constantly and immediately. You can add animation to business applications that make the user interface more responsive.

FIGURE 35-29

The following example demonstrates a decent animation and also shows how the animation can be defined in a style. Within the `Window` resources you can see the style `AnimatedButtonStyle` for buttons. In the template, a rectangle-named outline is defined. This template has a thin stroke with the thickness set to 0.4.

FIGURE 35-30

The template defines a property trigger for the `IsMouseOver` property. The `EnterActions` property of this trigger applies as soon as the mouse is moved over the button. The action to start is `BeginStoryboard`. `BeginStoryboard` is a trigger action that can contain and thus start `Storyboard` elements. The `Storyboard` element defines a `DoubleAnimation` to animate a double value. The property value that is changed in this animation is the `Rectangle.StrokeThickness` of the `Rectangle` element with the name outline. The value is changed in a smooth way by 1.2, as the `By` property specifies, for a time length of 0.3 seconds as specified by the `Duration` property. At the end of the animation, the stroke thickness is reset to its original value because `AutoReverse="True"`. To summarize: as soon as the mouse moves over the button, the thickness of the outline is incremented by 1.2 for 0.3 seconds. Figure 35-31 shows the button without animation, and Figure 35-32 shows the button 0.3 seconds after the mouse moved over it. (It's just not possible to show the smooth animation and intermediate looks in a print medium.)

FIGURE 35-31

FIGURE 35-32

```
    <Window x:Class="AnimationDemo.ButtonAnimationWindow"
            xmlns="http://schemas.microsoft.com/winfx/2006/xaml/presentation"
            xmlns:x="http://schemas.microsoft.com/winfx/2006/xaml"
            Title="ButtonAnimationWindow" Height="300" Width="300">
        <Window.Resources>
            <Style x:Key="AnimatedButtonStyle" TargetType="{x:Type Button}">
                <Setter Property="Template">
                    <Setter.Value>
                        <ControlTemplate TargetType="{x:Type Button}">
                            <Grid>
                                <Rectangle Name="outline" RadiusX="9" RadiusY="9"
                                        Stroke="Black" Fill="{TemplateBinding Background}"
                                        StrokeThickness="1.6">
                                </Rectangle>
```

```
                        <ContentPresenter VerticalAlignment="Center"
                                    HorizontalAlignment="Center" />
                    </Grid>
                    <ControlTemplate.Triggers>
                        <Trigger Property="IsMouseOver" Value="True">
                            <Trigger.EnterActions>
                                <BeginStoryboard>
                                    <Storyboard>
                                        <DoubleAnimation Duration="0:0:0.3"
                                            AutoReverse="True"
                                            Storyboard.TargetProperty=
                                                "(Rectangle.StrokeThickness)"
                                            Storyboard.TargetName="outline"
                                            By="1.2" />
                                    </Storyboard>
                                </BeginStoryboard>
                            </Trigger.EnterActions>
                        </Trigger>
                    </ControlTemplate.Triggers>
                </ControlTemplate>
            </Setter.Value>
        </Setter>
    </Style>
</Window.Resources>
<Grid>
    <Button Style="{StaticResource AnimatedButtonStyle}" Width="200"
        Height="100" Content="Click Me!" />
</Grid>
</Window>
```

code snippet AnimationDemo/ButtonAnimationWindow.xaml

The following table lists things you can do with a timeline.

TIMELINE PROPERTIES	DESCRIPTION
AutoReverse	With the AutoReverse property, you can specify whether the value that is animated should return to the original value after the animation.
SpeedRatio	With SpeedRatio, you can transform the speed at which an animation moves. With this property, you can define the relation in regard to the parent. The default value is 1; setting the ratio to a smaller value makes the animation move slower; setting the value greater than 1 makes it move faster.
BeginTime	With BeginTime you can specify the timespan from the start of the trigger event until the moment the animation starts. You can specify days, hours, minutes, seconds, and fractions of seconds. This might not be real-time, depending on the speed ratio. For example, if the speed ratio is set to 2, and the beginning time is set to six seconds, the animation will start after three seconds.
AccelerationRatio DecelerationRatio	With an animation the values need not be changed in a linear way. You can specify an AccelerationRatio and DecelerationRatio to define the impact of acceleration and deceleration. The sum of both values must not be greater than 1.
Duration	With the Duration property, you specify the length of time for one iteration of the animation.
RepeatBehavior	Assigning a RepeatBehavior struct to the RepeatBehavior property lets you define how many times or how long the animation should be repeated.
FillBehavior	The FillBehavior property is important if the parent timeline has a different duration. For example, if the parent timeline is shorter than the duration of the actual animation, setting the FillBehavior to Stop means that the actual animation stops. If the parent timeline is longer than the duration of the actual animation, HoldEnd keeps the actual animation active before resetting it to its original value (if AutoReverse is set).

Depending on the type of `Timeline` class, more properties may be available. For example, with `DoubleAnimation` you can specify `From` and `To` properties for the start and end of the animation. An alternative is to specify the `By` property where the animation starts with the current value of the `Bound` property and is incremented by the value specified by `By`.

Non-Linear Animations

One way to define non-linear animations is by setting the speed of `AccelerationRatio` and `DecelerationRatio` animation in the beginning and at the end. .NET 4 has more flexible possibilities than that.

Several animation classes have an `EasingFunction` property. This property accepts an object that implements the interface `IEasingFunction`. With this interface an easing function object can define how the value should be animated over time. There are several easing functions available that create a non-linear animation. Examples of these are `ExponentialEase`, which uses an exponential formula for animations; `QuadraticEase`, `CubicEase`, `QuarticEase`, and `QuinticEase` with a power of 2, 3, 4, or 5; and `PowerEase` with a power level that is configurable. Of special interest are `SineEase`, which uses a sinus curve, `BounceEase`, which creates a bouncing effect, and `ElasticEase`, which resembles animation values of a spring oscillating back and forth.

Such an ease can be specified in XAML by adding the ease to the `EasingFunction` property of the animation as shown. Adding different ease functions you will see really interesting effects with the animation:

Available for
download on
Wrox.com

```
<DoubleAnimation
    Storyboard.TargetProperty="(Ellipse.Width)"
    Duration="0:0:3" AutoReverse="True"
        FillBehavior="Stop"
        RepeatBehavior="Forever"
        From="100" To="300">
    <DoubleAnimation.EasingFunction>
        <BounceEase EasingMode="EaseInOut" />
    </DoubleAnimation.EasingFunction>
</DoubleAnimation>
```

code snippet AnimationDemo/EllipseWindow.xaml

Event Triggers

Instead of having a property trigger, you can define an event trigger to start the animation. The property trigger fires when a property changes its value; the event trigger fires when an event occurs. Examples of such events are the `Load` event from a control, the `Click` event from the `Button`, and the `MouseMove` event.

The next example creates an animation for the face that was created earlier with shapes. It is now animated so the eye moves as soon as a `Click` event from a button is fired.

Inside the `Window` element, a `DockPanel` element is defined to arrange the face and buttons to control the animation. A `StackPanel` that contains three buttons is docked on top. The `Canvas` element that contains the face gets the remaining part of the `DockPanel`.

The first button is used to start the animation of the eye; the second button stops the animation. A third button is used to start another animation to resize the face.

The animation is defined within the `DockPanel.Triggers` section. Instead of a property trigger, an event trigger is used. The first event trigger is fired as soon as the `Click` event occurs with the `buttonBeginMoveEyes` button defined by the `RoutedEvent` and `SourceName` properties. The trigger action is defined by the `BeginStoryboard` element that starts the containing `Storyboard`. `BeginStoryboard` has a name defined, because a name is needed to control the storyboard with pause, continue, and stop actions. The `Storyboard` element contains four animations. The first two animate the left eye; the last two animate the right eye. The first and third animation changes the `Canvas.Left` position for the eyes, and the second and fourth animation changes `Canvas.Top`. The animations in x and y direction have different time values that make the eye movement very interesting using the defined repeated behavior.

The second event trigger is fired as soon as the `Click` event of the *buttonStopMoveEyes* button occurs. Here, the storyboard is stopped with the `StopStoryboard` element, which references the started storyboard *beginMoveEye*.

The third event trigger is fired by clicking the *buttonResize* button. With this animation the transformation of the `Canvas` element is changed. Because this animation doesn't run endlessly, there's no stop. This storyboard also makes use of the `EaseFunction` that was explained previously:

```xml
<Window x:Class="AnimationDemo.EventTriggerWindow"
        xmlns="http://schemas.microsoft.com/winfx/2006/xaml/presentation"
        xmlns:x="http://schemas.microsoft.com/winfx/2006/xaml"
        Title="EventTriggerWindow" Height="300" Width="300">
    <DockPanel>
        <DockPanel.Triggers>
            <EventTrigger RoutedEvent="Button.Click" SourceName="buttonBeginMoveEyes">
                <BeginStoryboard x:Name="beginMoveEyes">
                    <Storyboard>
                        <DoubleAnimation RepeatBehavior="Forever" DecelerationRatio=".8"
                                         AutoReverse="True" By="6" Duration="0:0:1"
                                         Storyboard.TargetName="eyeLeft"
                                         Storyboard.TargetProperty="(Canvas.Left)" />
                        <DoubleAnimation RepeatBehavior="Forever" AutoReverse="True"
                                         By="6" Duration="0:0:5"
                                         Storyboard.TargetName="eyeLeft"
                                         Storyboard.TargetProperty="(Canvas.Top)" />
                        <DoubleAnimation RepeatBehavior="Forever" DecelerationRatio=".8"
                                         AutoReverse="True" By="-6" Duration="0:0:3"
                                         Storyboard.TargetName="eyeRight"
                                         Storyboard.TargetProperty="(Canvas.Left)" />
                        <DoubleAnimation RepeatBehavior="Forever" AutoReverse="True"
                                         By="6" Duration="0:0:6"
                                         Storyboard.TargetName="eyeRight"
                                         Storyboard.TargetProperty="(Canvas.Top)" />
                    </Storyboard>
                </BeginStoryboard>
            </EventTrigger>
            <EventTrigger RoutedEvent="Button.Click" SourceName="buttonStopMoveEyes">
                <StopStoryboard BeginStoryboardName="beginMoveEyes" />
            </EventTrigger>
            <EventTrigger RoutedEvent="Button.Click" SourceName="buttonResize">
                <BeginStoryboard>
                    <Storyboard>
                        <DoubleAnimation RepeatBehavior="2" AutoReverse="True"
                            Storyboard.TargetName="scale1"
                            Storyboard.TargetProperty="(ScaleTransform.ScaleX)"
                            From="0.1" To="3" Duration="0:0:5">
                            <DoubleAnimation.EasingFunction>
                                <ElasticEase />
                            </DoubleAnimation.EasingFunction>
                        </DoubleAnimation>
                        <DoubleAnimation RepeatBehavior="2" AutoReverse="True"
                            Storyboard.TargetName="scale1"
                            Storyboard.TargetProperty="(ScaleTransform.ScaleY)"
                            From="0.1" To="3" Duration="0:0:5">
                            <DoubleAnimation.EasingFunction>
                                <BounceEase />
                            </DoubleAnimation.EasingFunction>
                        </DoubleAnimation>
                    </Storyboard>
```

```
                </BeginStoryboard>
            </EventTrigger>
    </DockPanel.Triggers>
    <StackPanel Orientation="Vertical" DockPanel.Dock="Top">
        <Button x:Name="buttonBeginMoveEyes" Content="Start Move Eyes" Margin="5" />
        <Button x:Name="buttonStopMoveEyes" Content="Stop Move Eyes" Margin="5" />
        <Button x:Name="buttonResize" Content="Resize" Margin="5" />
    </StackPanel>
    <Canvas>
        <Canvas.LayoutTransform>
            <ScaleTransform x:Name="scale1" ScaleX="1" ScaleY="1" />
        </Canvas.LayoutTransform>

        <Ellipse Canvas.Left="10" Canvas.Top="10" Width="100" Height="100"
                Stroke="Blue" StrokeThickness="4" Fill="Yellow" />
        <Ellipse Canvas.Left="30" Canvas.Top="12" Width="60" Height="30">
            <Ellipse.Fill>
                <LinearGradientBrush StartPoint="0.5,0" EndPoint="0.5, 1">
                    <GradientStop Offset="0.1" Color="DarkGreen" />
                    <GradientStop Offset="0.7" Color="Transparent" />
                </LinearGradientBrush>
            </Ellipse.Fill>
        </Ellipse>
        <Ellipse Canvas.Left="30" Canvas.Top="35" Width="25" Height="20"
                Stroke="Blue" StrokeThickness="3" Fill="White" />
        <Ellipse x:Name="eyeLeft" Canvas.Left="40" Canvas.Top="43" Width="6"
                Height="5" Fill="Black" />

        <Ellipse Canvas.Left="65" Canvas.Top="35" Width="25" Height="20"
                Stroke="Blue" StrokeThickness="3" Fill="White" />
        <Ellipse x:Name="eyeRight" Canvas.Left="75" Canvas.Top="43" Width="6"
                Height="5" Fill="Black" />
        <Path Name="mouth" Stroke="Blue" StrokeThickness="4"
            Data="M 40,74 Q 57,95 80,74 " />
    </Canvas>

    </DockPanel>
</Window>
```

code snippet AnimationDemo/EventTriggerWindow.xaml

Figure 35-33 shows the output after running the application.

Instead of starting and stopping the animation directly from event triggers in XAML, you can easily control the animation from code-behind. You just need to assign a name to the `Storyboard` and invoke the `Begin()`, `Stop()`, `Pause()`, and `Resume()` methods.

Keyframe Animations

With acceleration and deceleration ratio as well as the ease functions, you've seen how animations can be built in a non-linear fashion. If you need to specify several values for an animation, you can use keyframe animations. As with normal animations, keyframe animations are different animation types that exist to animate properties of different types.

FIGURE 35-33

`DoubleAnimationUsingKeyFrames` is the keyframe animation for double types. Other keyframe animation types are `Int32AnimationUsingKeyFrames`, `PointAnimationUsingKeyFrames`, `ColorAnimationUsingKeyFrames`, `SizeAnimationUsingKeyFrames`, and `ObjectAnimationUsingKeyFrames`.

The example XAML code animates the position of an ellipse by animating the X and Y values of a `TranslateTransform` element. The animation starts when the ellipse is loaded by defining an `EventTrigger` to the `RoutedEvent` `Ellipse.Loaded`. The event trigger starts a `Storyboard` with the `BeginStoryboard` element. The `Storyboard` contains two keyframe animations of `DoubleAnimationUsingKeyFrame` type. A keyframe animation consists of frame elements. The first keyframe animation uses a `LinearKeyFrame`, a `DiscreteDoubleKeyFrame`, and a `SplineDoubleKeyFrame`; the second animation is an `EasingDoubleKeyFrame`. The `LinearDoubleKeyFrame` makes a linear change of the value. The `KeyTime` property defines when in the animation the value of the Value property should be reached. Here, the `LinearDoubleKeyFrame` has three seconds to move the property X to the value 30. `DiscreteDoubleKeyFrame` makes an immediate change to the new value after four seconds. `SplineDoubleKeyFrame` uses a Bézier curve where two control points are specified by the `KeySpline` property. `EasingDoubleKeyFrame` is a new frame class with .NET 4 that supports setting an easing function such as `BounceEase` to control the animation value:

```xaml
<Canvas>
    <Ellipse Fill="Red" Canvas.Left="20" Canvas.Top="20" Width="25" Height="25">
        <Ellipse.RenderTransform>
            <TranslateTransform X="50" Y="50" x:Name="ellipseMove" />
        </Ellipse.RenderTransform>
        <Ellipse.Triggers>
            <EventTrigger RoutedEvent="Ellipse.Loaded">
                <BeginStoryboard>
                    <Storyboard>
                        <DoubleAnimationUsingKeyFrames Storyboard.TargetProperty="X"
                            Storyboard.TargetName="ellipseMove">
                            <LinearDoubleKeyFrame KeyTime="0:0:2" Value="30" />
                            <DiscreteDoubleKeyFrame KeyTime="0:0:4" Value="80" />
                            <SplineDoubleKeyFrame KeySpline="0.5,0.0 0.9,0.0"
                                KeyTime="0:0:10" Value="300" />
                            <LinearDoubleKeyFrame KeyTime="0:0:20" Value="150" />
                        </DoubleAnimationUsingKeyFrames>
                        <DoubleAnimationUsingKeyFrames Storyboard.TargetProperty="Y"
                            Storyboard.TargetName="ellipseMove">
                            <SplineDoubleKeyFrame KeySpline="0.5,0.0 0.9,0.0"
                                KeyTime="0:0:2" Value="50" />
                            <EasingDoubleKeyFrame KeyTime="0:0:20" Value="300">
                                <EasingDoubleKeyFrame.EasingFunction>
                                    <BounceEase />
                                </EasingDoubleKeyFrame.EasingFunction>
                            </EasingDoubleKeyFrame>
                        </DoubleAnimationUsingKeyFrames>
                    </Storyboard>
                </BeginStoryboard>
            </EventTrigger>
        </Ellipse.Triggers>
    </Ellipse>
</Canvas>
```

code snippet AnimationDemo/KeyFrameWindow.xaml

VISUAL STATE MANAGER

Since .NET 4, Visual State Manager offers an alternative way to control animations. Controls can have specific states. The *state* defines a look that is applied to controls when the state is reached. A state transition defines what happens when one state changes to another one.

With a data grid you can use Read, Selected, and Edit states to define different looks for a row, depending on user selection. MouseOver and IsPressed can be states as well that replace the triggers, which have been discussed earlier.

The example code displays different states of a baby and defines the states Sleeping, Playing, and Crying. The states are defined within the element VisualStateManager.VisualStateGroups. Here the states are defined within a Button element because they are needed only there. With the content, the Button defines a Border and an Image element that are named *border1* and *image1*. With VisualStateManager, a single VisualStateGroup named CommonStates is defined. This state group contains VisualState elements. Within a visual state a Storyboard is defined. With all the states the storyboard contains a ColorAnimation that changes the color of the border brush, and ObjectAnimationUsingKeyFrames. This keyframe animation just makes a one-time change to the Source property of the Image. The UriSource property requires a BitmapImage that is created and a filename that is stored within the project.

The VisualStateGroup also contains VisualTransition elements that define what should happen before a state changes. With VisualTransition you can specify both From and To values. With these you can create different transitions when the state changes from Sleeping to Crying as opposed to from Playing to Crying. In the example, only the To property is used, so this transition applies no matter what the previous state was. With the transitions, the Width property of the Button and the Thickness of the Border element are changed:

```xml
<Window x:Class="VisualStateDemo.MainWindow"
        xmlns="http://schemas.microsoft.com/winfx/2006/xaml/presentation"
        xmlns:x="http://schemas.microsoft.com/winfx/2006/xaml"
        Title="MainWindow" Height="240" Width="500">
  <DockPanel>
    <StackPanel Orientation="Vertical" DockPanel.Dock="Left">
      <Button Margin="5" Padding="3" Content="Sleeping" Click="OnSleeping" />
      <Button Margin="5" Padding="3" Content="Playing" Click="OnPlaying" />
      <Button Margin="5" Padding="5" Content="Crying" Click="OnCrying" />
    </StackPanel>
    <Grid>
      <Button Name="button1" Width="300" Height="200">
        <VisualStateManager.VisualStateGroups>
          <VisualStateGroup Name="CommonStates">
            <VisualState Name="Sleeping">
              <Storyboard>
                <ObjectAnimationUsingKeyFrames Duration="0:0:0"
                    Storyboard.TargetProperty="(Image.Source)"
                    Storyboard.TargetName="image1">
                  <DiscreteObjectKeyFrame KeyTime="0:0:0">
                    <DiscreteObjectKeyFrame.Value>
                      <BitmapImage
                          UriSource="Images/Sleeping.jpg" />
                    </DiscreteObjectKeyFrame.Value>
                  </DiscreteObjectKeyFrame>
                </ObjectAnimationUsingKeyFrames>
                <ColorAnimation To="LightBlue"
                    Storyboard.TargetProperty="(SolidColorBrush.Color)"
                    Storyboard.TargetName="brush1" Duration="0:0:5" />
              </Storyboard>
            </VisualState>
            <VisualState Name="Playing">
              <Storyboard>
                <ObjectAnimationUsingKeyFrames Duration="0:0:0"
                    Storyboard.TargetProperty="(Image.Source)"
                    Storyboard.TargetName="image1">
                  <DiscreteObjectKeyFrame KeyTime="0:0:0">
                    <DiscreteObjectKeyFrame.Value>
```

```xml
                    <BitmapImage
                        UriSource="Images/Playing.jpg" />
                </DiscreteObjectKeyFrame.Value>
            </DiscreteObjectKeyFrame>
        </ObjectAnimationUsingKeyFrames>
        <ColorAnimation To="Red"

            Storyboard.TargetProperty="(SolidColorBrush.Color)"
            Storyboard.TargetName="brush1" Duration="0:0:5" />
    </Storyboard>
</VisualState>
<VisualState Name="Crying">
    <Storyboard>
        <ObjectAnimationUsingKeyFrames Duration="0"
            Storyboard.TargetProperty="(Image.Source)"
            Storyboard.TargetName="image1">
            <DiscreteObjectKeyFrame KeyTime="0">
                <DiscreteObjectKeyFrame.Value>
                    <BitmapImage UriSource="Images/Crying.jpg" />
                </DiscreteObjectKeyFrame.Value>
            </DiscreteObjectKeyFrame>
        </ObjectAnimationUsingKeyFrames>
        <ColorAnimation To="LightBlue"
            Storyboard.TargetProperty="(SolidColorBrush.Color)"
            Storyboard.TargetName="brush1" Duration="0:0:5" />
    </Storyboard>
</VisualState>
<VisualStateGroup.Transitions>
    <VisualTransition To="Sleeping">
        <Storyboard>
            <DoubleAnimation By="50" AutoReverse="True"
                Storyboard.TargetProperty="Width"
                Storyboard.TargetName="button1"
                Duration="0:0:1.2">
                <DoubleAnimation.EasingFunction>
                    <BounceEase />
                </DoubleAnimation.EasingFunction>
            </DoubleAnimation>
        </Storyboard>
    </VisualTransition>
    <VisualTransition To="Crying">
        <Storyboard>
            <ThicknessAnimation Duration="0:0:2" By="100,100"
                AutoReverse="True"
                Storyboard.TargetProperty=
                    "(Border.BorderThickness)"
                Storyboard.TargetName="border1" />
        </Storyboard>
    </VisualTransition>
    <VisualTransition To="Playing">
        <Storyboard>
            <DoubleAnimation By="50" AutoReverse="True"
                Storyboard.TargetProperty="Width"
                Storyboard.TargetName="button1"
                Duration="0:0:1.2">
                <DoubleAnimation.EasingFunction>
                    <ElasticEase />
                </DoubleAnimation.EasingFunction>
            </DoubleAnimation>
        </Storyboard>
    </VisualTransition>
```

```
                  </VisualStateGroup.Transitions>
               </VisualStateGroup>
            </VisualStateManager.VisualStateGroups>

            <Border x:Name="border1" BorderThickness="12">
               <Border.BorderBrush>
                  <SolidColorBrush x:Name="brush1" Color="White" />
               </Border.BorderBrush>
               <Image x:Name="image1" />
            </Border>
         </Button>
      </Grid>
   </DockPanel>
</Window>
```

code snippet VisualStateDemo/MainWindow.xaml

With the `Click` events, the `Button` elements in the `StackPanel` handlers from code-behind are invoked. Within code-behind the `GoToElementState()` method of the `VisualStateManager` is invoked to change the *button1* object to a new state. The third argument of this method defines whether the transition changing to this state should be invoked:

```
private void OnSleeping(object sender, RoutedEventArgs e)
{
    VisualStateManager.GoToElementState(button1, "Sleeping", true);
}

private void OnPlaying(object sender, RoutedEventArgs e)
{
    VisualStateManager.GoToElementState(button1, "Playing", true);
}

private void OnCrying(object sender, RoutedEventArgs e)
{
    VisualStateManager.GoToElementState(button1, "Crying", true);
}
```

code snippet VisualStateDemo/MainWindow.xaml.cs

After running the application you can see the state changes as shown in Figure 35-34.

3-D

The last section in this large chapter gives you an introduction to the 3-D features of WPF. Here you'll find the information to get started.

FIGURE 35-34

 The namespace for 3-D with WPF is System.Windows.Media.Media3D.

To understand 3-D with WPF it is important to know the difference between the coordination systems. Figure 35-35 shows the WPF 3-D coordination system. The origin is placed in the center. The x-axis has positive values to the right and negative values to the left. The y-axis is vertical with positive values up and negative values down. The z-axis defines positive values in direction to the viewer.

The most important concepts that need to be known to understand 3-D with WPF are the model, camera, and lights. The model defines what is shown using triangles. The camera defines the point where and how we look at the model, and without a light the model is dark. The light defines how the complete scene is illuminated. This section gives you information on how to define the model, camera, and light with WPF and what different options you have here. Also, you will get the information on how the scene can be animated.

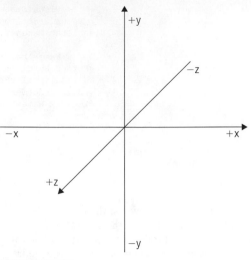

FIGURE 35-35

Model

This section creates a model that has the 3-D look of a book. A 3-D model is made up of triangles, so the simplest model is just one triangle. More complex models are made up from multiple triangles. Rectangles can be made up from two triangles. Balls are made up from a multiplicity of triangles. The more triangles used, the rounder the ball.

With the book model, each side is a rectangle, which could be made up from only two triangles. However, because the front cover has three different materials, six triangles are used.

A triangle is defined by the `Positions` property of the `MeshGeometry3D`. Here is just a part of the front side of the book. The `MeshGeometry3D` defines two triangles. You can count five coordinates for the points because the third point of the first triangle is also the first point of the second triangle. This can be done for optimization to reduce the size of the model. All the points use the same z coordinate, 0, and x/y coordinates 0 0, 10 0, 0 10, 10 10, and 10 0. The property `TriangleIndices` indicates the order of the positions. The first triangle is defined clockwise, the second triangle counterclockwise. With this property you define which side of the triangle is visible. One side of the triangle shows the color defined with the `Material` property of the `GeometryModel3D` class, and the other side shows the `BackMaterial` property.

The rendering surface for 3-D is `ModelVisual3D` that surrounds the models as shown:

```xml
<ModelVisual3D>
    <ModelVisual3D.Content>
        <Model3DGroup>

            <!-- front -->
            <GeometryModel3D>
                <GeometryModel3D.Geometry>
                    <MeshGeometry3D
                        Positions="0 0 0, 10 0 0, 0 10 0, 10 10 0, 10 0 0"
                        TriangleIndices="0, 1, 2, 2, 4, 3"
                    />
                </GeometryModel3D.Geometry>
```

code snippet 3DDemo/MainWindow.xaml

The `Material` property of the `GeometryModel` defines what material is used by the model. Depending on the viewpoint, the `Material` or `BackMaterial` property is important.

WPF offers different material types: `DiffuseMaterial`, `EmissiveMaterial`, and `SpecularMaterial`. The material will influence the look of the model together with the light that is used to illuminate the scene. `EmmisiveMaterial` and the color that is applied to the brush of the material is part of the calculations to define the light to show the model. SpecularMaterial adds illuminated highlight reflections when specular highlight reflections occur. The example code makes use of DiffuseMaterial and references a brush from the resource named mainCover:

```
<GeometryModel3D.Material>
    <DiffuseMaterial Brush="{StaticResource mainCover}" />
</GeometryModel3D.Material>
</GeometryModel3D>
```

The brush for the main cover is a VisualBrush. The VisualBrush has a Border with a Grid that consists of two Label elements. One Label element defines the text Professional C# 4 and is written to the cover:

```
<VisualBrush x:Key="mainCover">
    <VisualBrush.Visual>
        <Border Background="Red">
            <Grid>
                <Grid.RowDefinitions>
                    <RowDefinition Height="30" />
                    <RowDefinition Height="*" />
                </Grid.RowDefinitions>
                <Label Grid.Row="0" HorizontalAlignment="Center">
                    Professional C# 4</Label>
                <Label Grid.Row="1"></Label>
            </Grid>
        </Border>
    </VisualBrush.Visual>
</VisualBrush>
```

Because a brush is defined by a 2-D coordinate system and the model has a 3-D coordinate system, a translation between them needs to be done. This translation is done by the TextureCoordinates property of the MeshGeometry3D. The TextureCoordinates specify every point of the triangle and shows how it maps to 2-D. The first point 0 0 0 maps to 0 1, the second point 10 0 0 maps to 1 1, and so on. Be aware that y has a different direction in the 3-D and 2-D coordinate systems. Figure 35-36 shows the coordinate system for 2-D:

```
<MeshGeometry3D
    Positions="0 0 0, 10 0 0, 0 10 0, 10 10 0, 10 0 0"
    TriangleIndices="0, 1, 2, 2, 4, 3"
    TextureCoordinates="0 1, 1 1, 0 0, 1 0, 1 1"
    />
```

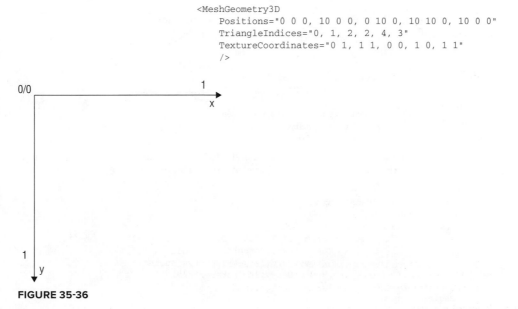

FIGURE 35-36

Cameras

A camera is needed with a 3-D model to see something. The example uses the `PerspectiveCamera` that has a position and a direction to look into. Changing the camera position to the left moves the model to the right and vice versa. Changing the y position of the camera, the model appears larger or smaller. With this camera, the further away the model is, the smaller it becomes:

```xml
<Viewport3D.Camera>
    <PerspectiveCamera Position="0,0,25" LookDirection="15,6,-50" />
</Viewport3D.Camera>
```

code snippet 3DDemo/MainWindow.xaml

WPF also has an `OrtographicCamera` that doesn't have a horizon on the scene, so the size of the element doesn't change if it is further away. With `MatrixCamera`, the behavior of the camera can be exactly specified.

Lights

Without a light it is dark. A 3-D scene requires a light to make the model visible. There are different lights that can be used. The `AmbientLight` lights the scene uniformly. `DirectionalLight` is a light that shines in one direction, similar to sunlight. `PointLight` has a position in space and lights in all directions. `SpotLight` has a position as well but uses a cone for its lighting.

The example code uses a `SpotLight` with a position, a direction, and cone angles:

```xml
<ModelVisual3D>
    <ModelVisual3D.Content>
        <SpotLight Color="White" InnerConeAngle="20" OuterConeAngle="60"
                   Direction="15,6,-50" Position="0,0,25" />
    </ModelVisual3D.Content>
</ModelVisual3D>
```

Rotation

To get a 3-D look from the model, it should be able to be rotated. For rotation, the `RotateTransform3D` element is used to define the center of the rotation and the rotation angle:

```xml
<Model3DGroup.Transform>
    <RotateTransform3D CenterX="0" CenterY="0" CenterZ="0">
        <RotateTransform3D.Rotation>
            <AxisAngleRotation3D x:Name="angle" Axis="-1,-1,-1"
                                 Angle="70" />
        </RotateTransform3D.Rotation>
    </RotateTransform3D>
</Model3DGroup.Transform>
```

To run a rotation from the completed model, an animation is started by an event trigger. The animation changes the `Angle` property of the `AxisAngleRotation3D` element continuously:

```xml
<Window.Triggers>
    <EventTrigger RoutedEvent=f"Window.Loaded">
        <BeginStoryboard>
            <Storyboard>
                <DoubleAnimation From="0" To="360" Duration="00:00:10"
                                 Storyboard.TargetName="angle"
                                 Storyboard.TargetProperty="Angle"
                                 RepeatBehavior="Forever" />
            </Storyboard>
        </BeginStoryboard>
    </EventTrigger>
</Window.Triggers>
```

After running the application, you will see the output in Figure 35-37.

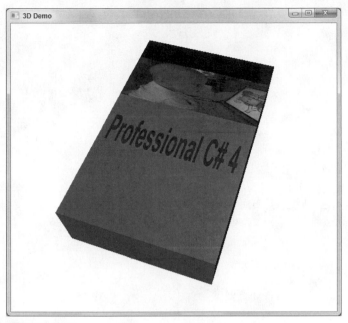

FIGURE 35-37

SUMMARY

In this chapter, you have taken a first tour through the many features of WPF. WPF makes it easy to separate work between developers and designers. All UI features can be created with XAML, and the functionality by using code-behind.

You have seen many controls and containers that are all based on vector-based graphics. Because of vector-based graphics, WPF elements can be scaled, sheared, and rotated. Because of the content flexibility of content controls, the event-handling mechanism is based on bubbling and tunneling events.

Different kinds of brushes are available to paint background and foreground of elements. You can use solid brushes, linear or radial gradient brushes, but also visual brushes to do reflections or show videos.

Styling and templates allow you to customize the look of controls. Triggers allow you to change properties of WPF elements dynamically. Animations can be done easily by animating a property value from a WPF control.

The next chapter continues with WPF showing data binding, commands, navigation, and several more features.

36

Business Applications with WPF

WHAT'S IN THIS CHAPTER?

➤ Data Binding to Elements, Objects, Lists, and XML

➤ Value Conversions and Validation

➤ Commanding

➤ Using the `TreeView` to display hierarchical data

➤ Displaying and Grouping data with the `DataGrid`

In the previous chapter you read about some of the core functionality of WPF. In this chapter the journey through WPF continues. Here you read about important aspects for creating complete applications, such as data binding and command handling, and about the new `DataGrid` control. Data binding is an important concept to bring data from .NET classes into the user interface, and allow the user to change data. Commanding allows mapping events from the UI to code. In contrast to the event model, this gives a better separation between XAML and code. The `TreeView` and `DataGrid` controls are UI controls to display bound data.

DATA BINDING

WPF data binding takes another huge step forward compared with previous technologies. Data binding gets data from .NET objects to the UI or the other way around. Simple objects can be bound to UI elements, lists of objects, and also XAML elements itself. With WPF data binding, the target can be any dependency property of a WPF element, and every property of a CLR object can be the source. Because a WPF element is implemented as a .NET class, every WPF element can be the source as well. See Figure 36-1 for the connection between the source and the target. The `Binding` object defines the connection.

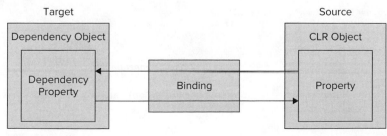

FIGURE 36-1

Binding supports several binding modes between the target and source. Binding can be *one-way,* where the source information goes to the target, but if the user changes information in the user interface, the source does not get updated. For updates to the source, *two-way* binding is required.

The following table shows the binding modes and their requirements.

BINDING MODE	DESCRIPTION
One-time	Binding goes from the source to the target and occurs only once when the application is started or the data context changes. Here, you get a snapshot of the data.
One-way	Binding goes from the source to the target. This is useful for read-only data, because it is not possible to change the data from the user interface. To get updates to the user interface, the source must implement the interface INotifyPropertyChanged.
Two-way	With two-way binding, the user can make changes to the data from the UI. Binding occurs in both directions — from the source to the target and from the target to the source. The source needs to implement read/write properties so that changes can be updated from the UI to the source.
One-way-to-source	With one-way-to-source binding, if the target property changes, the source object gets updated.

WPF data binding involves many facets beside the binding modes. This section gives you details on binding to XAML elements, binding to simple .NET objects, and binding to lists. Using change notifications, the UI is updated with changes in the bound objects. You will read about getting the data from object data providers and directly from the code. Multibinding and priority binding demonstrates different binding possibilities other than the default binding. You will also read about dynamically selecting data templates, and validation of binding values.

Let's start with the BooksDemo sample application.

BooksDemo Application

In this section, you create a new WPF application named BooksDemo to use throughout this chapter with data binding and commanding.

Change the XAML file MainWindow.xaml and add a DockPanel, a ListBox, a Hyperlink, and a TabControl:

```xml
<Window x:Class="Wrox.ProCSharp.WPF.MainWindow"
Insert IconMargin    [FILENAME]
        xmlns="http://schemas.microsoft.com/winfx/2006/xaml/presentation"
        xmlns:x="http://schemas.microsoft.com/winfx/2006/xaml"
        xmlns:local="clr-namespace:Wrox.ProCSharp.WPF"
        Title="Main Window" Height="400" Width="600">
    <DockPanel>
        <ListBox DockPanel.Dock="Left" Margin="5" MinWidth="120">
            <ListBoxItem>
                <Hyperlink Click=OnShowBook>Show Book</Hyperlink>
            </ListBoxItem>
        </ListBox>
        <TabControl Margin="5" x:Name="tabControl1">
        </TabControl>
    </DockPanel>
</Window>
```

code snippet BooksDemo/MainWindow.xaml

Now add a WPF user control named BookUC. This user control contains a DockPanel, a Grid with several rows and columns, a Label, and TextBox controls:

```xml
<UserControl x:Class="Wrox.ProCSharp.WPF.BookUC"
        xmlns="http://schemas.microsoft.com/winfx/2006/xaml/presentation"
        xmlns:x="http://schemas.microsoft.com/winfx/2006/xaml"
        xmlns:mc="http://schemas.openxmlformats.org/markup-compatibility/2006"
        xmlns:d="http://schemas.microsoft.com/expression/blend/2008"
        mc:Ignorable="d"
        d:DesignHeight="300" d:DesignWidth="300">
    <DockPanel>
        <Grid>
            <Grid.RowDefinitions>
                <RowDefinition />
                <RowDefinition />
                <RowDefinition />
                <RowDefinition />
            </Grid.RowDefinitions>
            <Grid.ColumnDefinitions>
                <ColumnDefinition Width="Auto" />
                <ColumnDefinition Width="*" />
            </Grid.ColumnDefinitions>
            <Label Content="Title" Grid.Row="0" Grid.Column="0" Margin="10,0,5,0"
                    HorizontalAlignment="Left" VerticalAlignment="Center" />
            <Label Content="Publisher" Grid.Row="1" Grid.Column="0"
                    Margin="10,0,5,0" HorizontalAlignment="Left"
                    VerticalAlignment="Center" />
            <Label Content="Isbn" Grid.Row="2" Grid.Column="0"
                    Margin="10,0,5,0" HorizontalAlignment="Left"
                    VerticalAlignment="Center" />
            <TextBox Grid.Row="0" Grid.Column="1" Margin="5" />
            <TextBox Grid.Row="1" Grid.Column="1" Margin="5" />
            <TextBox Grid.Row="2" Grid.Column="1" Margin="5" />
            <StackPanel Grid.Row="3" Grid.Column="0" Grid.ColumnSpan="2">
                <Button Content="Show Book" Margin="5" Click="OnShowBook" />
            </StackPanel>
        </Grid>
    </DockPanel>
</UserControl>
```

code snippet BooksDemo/BookUC.xaml

Within the `OnShowBook()` handler in the `MainWindow.xaml.cs`, create a new instance of the user control `BookUC` and add a new `TabItem` to the `TabControl`. Then change the `SelectedIndex` property of the `TabControl` to open the new tab:

```csharp
private void OnShowBook(object sender, RoutedEventArgs e)
{
    var bookUI = new BookUC();
    this.tabControl1.SelectedIndex =
        this.tabControl1.Items.Add(
            new TabItem { Header = "Book", Content = bookUI });
}
```

code snippet BooksDemo/MainWindow.xaml.cs

After building the project you can start the application and open the user control within the `TabControl` by clicking the hyperlink.

Binding with XAML

A WPF element can not only be the target for data binding, it can also be the source. You can bind the source property of one WPF element to the target of another WPF element.

In the following code example, data binding is used to resize the controls within the user control with a slider. Add a `StackPanel` control to the user control `BookUC` that contains a `Label` and a `Slider` control. The `Slider` control defines `Minimum` and `Maximum` values that define the scale, and an initial value of 1 is assigned to the `Value` property:

```
<DockPanel>
    <StackPanel DockPanel.Dock="Bottom" Orientation="Horizontal"
                HorizontalAlignment="Right">
        <Label Content="Resize" />
        <Slider x:Name="slider1" Value="1" Minimum="0.4" Maximum="3"
                Width="150" HorizontalAlignment="Right" />
    </StackPanel>
</DockPanel>
```

code snippet BooksDemo/BookUC.xaml

Set the `LayoutTransform` property of the `Grid` control and add a `ScaleTransform` element. With the `ScaleTransform` element, the `ScaleX` and `ScaleY` properties are data bound. Both properties are set with the `Binding` markup extension. In the `Binding` markup extension, the `ElementName` is set to `slider1` to reference the previously created `Slider` control. The `Path` property is set to the `Value` property to get the value of the slider:

```
<Grid>
    <Grid.LayoutTransform>
        <ScaleTransform x:Name="scale1"
            ScaleX="{Binding Path=Value, ElementName=slider1}"
            ScaleY="{Binding Path=Value, ElementName=slider1}" />
    </Grid.LayoutTransform>
```

When running the application, you can move the slider and thus resize the controls within the `Grid`, as you can see in Figures 36-2 and 36-3.

Instead of defining the binding information with XAML code, as was done in the preceding code with the `Binding` metadata extension, you can do it with code-behind. With code-behind you have to create a new `Binding` object and set the `Path` and `Source` properties. The `Source` property must be set to the source object; here, it is the WPF object `slider1`. The `Path` is set to a `PropertyPath` instance that is initialized with the name of the property of the source object, `Value`. With controls that derive from `FrameworkElement`, you can invoke the method `SetBinding()` to define the binding. However, `ScaleTransform` does not derive from `FrameworkElement` but from the `Freezable` base class instead. Use the helper class `BindingOperations` to bind such controls. The `SetBinding()` method of the `BindingOperations` class requires a `DependencyObject` — which is the `ScaleTransform` instance in the example. The `SetBinding()` method also requires the `dependency` property of the target be bound, and the `Binding` object.

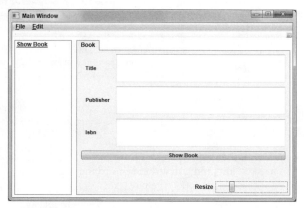

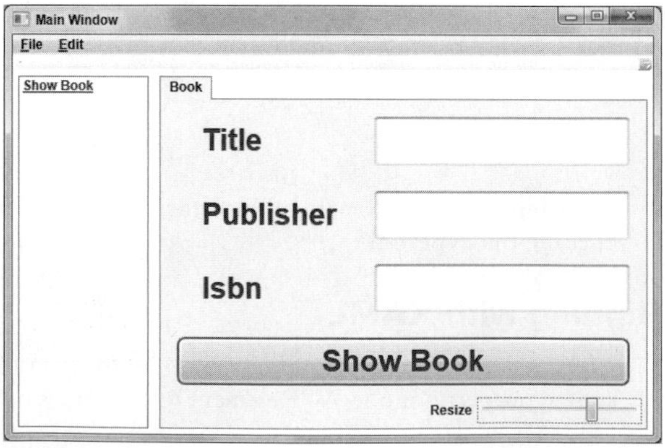

FIGURE 36-2

FIGURE 36-3

```
var binding = new Binding
{
    Path = new PropertyPath("Value"),
    Source = slider1
};
BindingOperations.SetBinding(scale1,
    ScaleTransform.ScaleXProperty, binding);
BindingOperations.SetBinding(scale1,
    ScaleTransform.ScaleYProperty, binding);
```

Remember that all classes that derive from DependencyObject *can have dependency properties. You can learn more about dependency properties in Chapter 27, "Core XAML."*

You can configure a number of binding options with the Binding class, as described in the following table.

BINDING CLASS MEMBERS	DESCRIPTION
Source	With the Source property, you define the source object for data binding.
RelativeSource	With RelativeSource, you can specify the source in relation to the target object. This is useful to display error messages when the source of the error comes from the same control.
ElementName	If the source is a WPF element, you can specify the source with the ElementName property.
Path	With the Path property, you specify the path to the source object. This can be the property of the source object, but indexers and properties of child elements are also supported.
XPath	With an XML data source, you can define an XPath query expression to get the data for binding.
Mode	The mode defines the direction for the binding. The Mode property is of type BindingMode. BindingMode is an enumeration with the following values: Default, OneTime, OneWay, TwoWay, and OneWayToSource. The default mode depends on the target: with a TextBox, two-way binding is the default; with a Label that is read-only, the default is one-way. OneTime means that the data is only init loaded from the source; OneWay updates from the source to the target. With TwoWay binding, changes from the WPF elements are written back to the source. OneWayToSource means that the data is never read but always written from the target to the source.
Converter	With the Converter property, you can specify a converter class that converts the data for the UI and back. The converter class must implement the interface IValueConverter, which defines the methods Convert() and ConvertBack(). You can pass parameters to the converter methods with the ConverterParameter property. The converter can be culture-sensitive; the culture can be set with the ConverterCulture property.
FallbackValue	With the FallbackValue property, you can define a default value that is used if binding doesn't return a value.
ValidationRules	With the ValidationRules property, you can define a collection of ValiationRule objects that are checked before the source is updated from the WPF target elements. The class ExceptionValidationRule is derived from the class ValidationRule and checks for exceptions.

Simple Object Binding

For binding to CLR objects, with the .NET classes you just have to define properties, as shown in the Book class example and the properties Title, Publisher, Isbn, and Authors. This class is in the Data folder of the BooksDemo project.

```csharp
using System.Collections.Generic;

namespace Wrox.ProCSharp.WPF.Data
{
    public class Book
    {
        public Book(string title, string publisher, string isbn,
                    params string[] authors)
        {
            this.Title = title;
            this.Publisher = publisher;
            this.Isbn = isbn;
            this.authors.AddRange(authors);
        }
        public Book()
            : this("unknown", "unknown", "unknown")
        {
        }
        public string Title { get; set; }
        public string Publisher { get; set; }
        public string Isbn { get; set; }

        private readonly List<string> authors = new List<string>();
        public string[] Authors
        {
            get
            {
                return authors.ToArray();
            }
        }

        public override string ToString()
        {
            return Title;
        }
    }
}
```

code snippet BooksDemo/Data/Book.cs

In the XAML code of the user control BookUC, several labels and TextBox controls are defined to display book information. Using Binding markup extensions, the TextBox controls are bound to the properties of the Book class. With the Binding markup extension, nothing more than the Path property is defined to bind it to the property of the Book class. There's no need to define a source because the source is defined by assigning the DataContext, as you can see in the code-behind that follows. The mode is defined by its default with the TextBox element, and this is two-way binding:

```xml
<TextBox Text="{Binding Path=Title}" Grid.Row="0" Grid.Column="1"
         Margin="5" />
<TextBox Text="{Binding Path=Publisher}" Grid.Row="1" Grid.Column="1"
         Margin="5" />
<TextBox Text="{Binding Path=Isbn}" Grid.Row="2" Grid.Column="1"
         Margin="5" />
```

code snippet BooksDemo//BookUC.xaml

With the code-behind, a new `Book` object is created, and the book is assigned to the `DataContext` property of the user control. `DataContext` is a dependency property that is defined with the base class `FrameworkElement`. Assigning the `DataContext` with the user control means that every element in the user control has a default binding to the same data context:

Available for download on Wrox.com

```csharp
private void OnShowBook(object sender, RoutedEventArgs e)
{
    var bookUI = new BookUC();
    bookUI.DataContext = new Book
    {
        Title = "Professional C# 2008",
        Publisher = "Wrox Press",
        Isbn = "978-0-470-19137-8"
    };
    this.tabControl1.SelectedIndex =
        this.tabControl1.Items.Add(
            new TabItem { Header = "Book", Content = bookUI });
}
```

code snippet BooksDemo/MainWindow.xaml.cs

After starting the application, you can see the bound data, as shown in Figure 36-4.

To see two-way binding in action (changes to the input of the WPF element are reflected inside the CLR object), the `Click` event handler of the button in the user control, the `OnShowBook()` method, is implemented. When implemented, a message box pops up to show the current title and ISBN number of the `book1` object. Figure 36-5 shows the output from the message box after a change to the input was made during runtime:

FIGURE 36-4

Available for download on Wrox.com

```csharp
private void OnShowBook(object
sender, RoutedEventArgs e)
{
    Book theBook = this.DataContext as Book;
    if (theBook != null)
        MessageBox.Show(theBook.Title, theBook.Isbn);
}
```

code snippet BooksDemo/BookUC.xaml.cs

Change Notification

With the current two-way binding, the data is read from the object and written back. However, if within the code the data is changed to the user interface, the UI does not receive the change information. You can easily verify this by adding a button to the user control and implementing the `Click` event handler `OnChangeBook()`. The book inside the data context gets changed but the user interface doesn't show the change:

Available for download on Wrox.com

FIGURE 36-5

```xaml
<StackPanel Grid.Row="3" Grid.Column="0" Grid.ColumnSpan="2"
            Orientation="Horizontal" HorizontalAlignment="Center">
    <Button Content="Show Book" Margin="5" Click="OnShowBook" />
    <Button Content="Change Book" Margin="5" Click="OnChangeBook" />
</StackPanel>
```

code snippet BooksDemo/BookUC.xaml

```
private void OnChangeBook(object sender, RoutedEventArgs e)
{
    Book theBook = this.DataContext as Book;
    if (theBook != null)
    {
        theBook.Title = "Professional C# 4 with .NET 4";
        theBook.Isbn = "978-0-470-50225-9";
    }
}
```

code snippet BooksDemo/BookUC.xaml.cs

To get change information to the user interface, the entity class must implement the interface
`INotifyPropertyChanged`. The `Book` class is modified to implement this interface. This interface
defines the `PropertyChanged` event, which also requires changing the implementation of the properties to
fire the event:

```
using System.ComponentModel;
using System.Collections.Generic;

namespace Wrox.ProCSharp.WPF.Data
{
    public class Book : INotifyPropertyChanged
    {
        public Book(string title, string publisher, string isbn,
                    params string[] authors)
        {
            this.title = title;
            this.publisher = publisher;
            this.isbn = isbn;
            this.authors.AddRange(authors);
        }
        public Book()
            : this("unknown", "unknown", "unknown")
        {
        }

        public event PropertyChangedEventHandler PropertyChanged;

        private string title;
        public string Title {
            get
            {
                return title;
            }
            set
            {
                title = value;
                if (PropertyChanged != null)
                    PropertyChanged(this, new
                        PropertyChangedEventArgs("Title"));
            }
        }
        private string publisher;
        public string Publisher
        {
            get
            {
                return publisher;
            }
            set
            {
```

```
                       publisher = value;
                       if (PropertyChanged != null)
                           PropertyChanged(this, new PropertyChangedEventArgs(
                                    "Publisher"));
                   }
               }
               private string isbn;
               public string Isbn {
                   get
                   {
                       return isbn;
                   }
                   set
                   {
                       isbn = value;
                       if (PropertyChanged != null)
                           PropertyChanged(this, new PropertyChangedEventArgs("Isbn"));
                   }
               }

               private readonly List<string> authors = new List<string>();
               public string[] Authors
               {
                   get
                   {
                       return authors.ToArray();
                   }
               }

               public override string ToString()
               {
                   return this.title;
               }
           }
       }
```

code snippet BooksDemo/Data/Book.cs

With this change, the application can be started again to verify that the user interface gets an update from the change in the event handler.

Object Data Provider

Instead of instantiating the object in code-behind, you can do this with XAML. To reference a class from code-behind within XAML, you have to reference the namespace with the namespace declarations in the XML root element. The XML attribute `xmlns:local="clr-namespace:Wrox.ProCsharp.WPF"` assigns the .NET namespace `Wrox.ProCSharp.WPF` to the XML namespace alias `local`.

One object of the `Book` class is now defined with the `Book` element inside the `DockPanel` resources. By assigning values to the XML attributes `Title`, `Publisher`, and `Isbn`, you set the values of the properties from the `Book` class. `x:Key="theBook"` defines the identifier for the resource so that you can reference the book object:

```xml
<UserControl x:Class="Wrox.ProCSharp.WPF.BookUC"
        xmlns="http://schemas.microsoft.com/winfx/2006/xaml/presentation"
        xmlns:x="http://schemas.microsoft.com/winfx/2006/xaml"
        xmlns:mc="http://schemas.openxmlformats.org/markup-compatibility/2006"
        xmlns:d="http://schemas.microsoft.com/expression/blend/2008"
        xmlns:local="clr-namespace:Wrox.ProCSharp.WPF.Data"
        mc:Ignorable="d"
```

```
                     d:DesignHeight="300" d:DesignWidth="300">
      <DockPanel>
          <DockPanel.Resources>
              <local:Book x:Key="theBook" Title="Professional C# 2010"
                          Publisher="Wrox Press" Isbn="978-0-470-50225-9" />
          </DockPanel.Resources>
```

code snippet BooksDemo/BookUC.xaml

 If the .NET namespace to reference is in a different assembly, you have to add the assembly to the XML declaration:

```
xmlns:sys="clr-namespace:System;assembly=mscorlib"
```

In the `TextBox` element, the `Source` is defined with the `Binding` markup extension that references the `theBook` resource:

```
      <TextBox Text="{Binding Path=Title,
                      Source={StaticResource theBook}}"
               Grid.Row="0" Grid.Column="1" Margin="5" />
      <TextBox Text="{Binding Path=Publisher,
                      Source={StaticResource theBook}}"
               Grid.Row="1" Grid.Column="1" Margin="5" />
      <TextBox Text="{Binding Path=Isbn,
                      Source={StaticResource theBook}}"
               Grid.Row="2" Grid.Column="1" Margin="5" />
```

Because all these `TextBox` elements are contained within the same control, it is possible to assign the `DataContext` property with a parent control and set the `Path` property with the `TextBox` binding elements. Because the `Path` property is a default, you can also reduce the `Binding` markup extension to the following code:

```
      <Grid x:Name="grid1" DataContext="{StaticResource theBook}">
      <!-- ... -->
          <TextBox Text="{Binding Title}" Grid.Row="0" Grid.Column="1"
                   Margin="5" />
          <TextBox Text="{Binding Publisher}" Grid.Row="1" Grid.Column="1"
                   Margin="5" />
          <TextBox Text="{Binding Isbn}" Grid.Row="2" Grid.Column="1"
                   Margin="5" />
```

Instead of defining the object instance directly within XAML code, you can define an object data provider that references a class to invoke a method. For use by the `ObjectDataProvider`, it's best to create a factory class that returns the object to display, as shown with the `BookFactory` class:

```
using System.Collections.Generic;

namespace Wrox.ProCSharp.WPF.Data
{
    public class BookFactory
    {
        private List<Book> books = new List<Book>();

        public BookFactory()
            {
            books.Add(new Book
            {
                Title = "Professional C# 2010",
                Publisher = "Wrox Press",
                Isbn = "978-0-470-50225-9"
            });
```

```
            }

        public Book GetTheBook()
        {
            return books[0];
        }
    }
}
```

The `ObjectDataProvider` element can be defined in the resources section. The XML attribute `ObjectType` defines the name of the class; with `MethodName` you specify the name of the method that is invoked to get the book object:

```xml
<DockPanel.Resources>
    <ObjectDataProvider x:Key="theBook" ObjectType="local:BookFactory"
                        MethodName="GetTheBook" />
</DockPanel.Resources>
```

The properties you can specify with the `ObjectDataProvider` class are listed in the following table.

OBJECTDATAPROVIDER	DESCRIPTION
`ObjectType`	The `ObjectType` property defines the type to create an instance.
`ConstructorParameters`	Using the `ConstructorParameters` collection, you can add parameters to the class to create an instance.
`MethodName`	The `MethodName` property defines the name of the method that is invoked by the object data provider.
`MethodParameters`	With the `MethodParameters` property, you can assign parameters to the method defined with the `MethodName` property.
`ObjectInstance`	With the `ObjectInstance` property, you can get and set the object that is used by the `ObjectDataProvider` class. For example, you can assign an existing object programmatically instead of defining the `ObjectType` so that an object is instantiated by `ObjectDataProvider`.
`Data`	With the `Data` property you can access the underlying object that Is used for data binding. If the `MethodName` is defined, with the `Data` property you can access the object that is returned from the method defined.

List Binding

Binding to a list is more frequently done than binding to simple objects. Binding to a list is very similar to binding to a simple object. You can assign the complete list to the `DataContext` from code-behind, or you can use an `ObjectDataProvider` that accesses an object factory that returns a list. With elements that support binding to a list (for example, a `ListBox`), the complete list is bound. With elements that support binding to just one object (for example, a `TextBox`), the current item is bound.

With the `BookFactory` class, now a list of `Book` objects is returned:

```csharp
public class BookFactory
{
    private List<Book> books = new List<Book>();

    public BookFactory()
    {
        books.Add(new Book("Professional C# 4 with .NET 4", "Wrox Press",
                  "978-0-470-50225-9", "Christian Nagel", "Bill Evjen",
                  "Jay Glynn", "Karli Watson", "Morgan Skinner"));
```

```
        books.Add(new Book("Professional C# 2008", "Wrox Press",
                            "978-0-470-19137-8", "Christian Nagel", "Bill Evjen",
                            "Jay Glynn", "Karli Watson", "Morgan Skinner"));
        books.Add(new Book("Beginning Visual C# 2010", "Wrox Press",
                            "978-0-470-50226-6", "Karli Watson", "Christian Nagel",
                            "Jacob Hammer Pedersen", "Jon D. Reid",
                            "Morgan Skinner", "Eric White"));
        books.Add(new Book("Windows 7 Secrets", "Wiley", "978-0-470-50841-1",
                            "Paul Thurrott", "Rafael Rivera"));
        books.Add(new Book("C# 2008 for Dummies", "For Dummies",
                            "978-0-470-19109-5", "Stephen Randy Davis",
                            "Chuck Sphar"));
    }

    public IEnumerable<Book> GetBooks()
    {
        return books;
    }
}
```

code snippet BooksDemo/Data/BookFactory.cs

To use the list, create a new `BooksUC` user control. The XAML code for this control contains `Label` and `TextBox` controls that display the values of a single book as well as a `ListBox` control that displays a book list. The `ObjectDataProvider` invokes the `GetBooks()` method of the `BookFactory`, and this provider is used to assign the `DataContext` of the `DockPanel`. The `DockPanel` has the bound `ListBox` and `TextBox` as its children.

Available for
download on
Wrox.com

```xml
<UserControl x:Class="Wrox.ProCSharp.WPF.BooksUC"
             xmlns="http://schemas.microsoft.com/winfx/2006/xaml/presentation"
             xmlns:x="http://schemas.microsoft.com/winfx/2006/xaml"
             xmlns:mc="http://schemas.openxmlformats.org/markup-compatibility/2006"
             xmlns:d="http://schemas.microsoft.com/expression/blend/2008"
             xmlns:local="clr-namespace:Wrox.ProCSharp.WPF.Data"
             mc:Ignorable="d"
             d:DesignHeight="300" d:DesignWidth="300">
    <UserControl.Resources>
        <ObjectDataProvider x:Key="books" ObjectType="local:BookFactory"
                            MethodName="GetBooks" />
    </UserControl.Resources>
    <DockPanel DataContext="{StaticResource books}">
        <ListBox DockPanel.Dock="Left" ItemsSource="{Binding}" Margin="5"
                MinWidth="120" />
        <Grid>
            <Grid.RowDefinitions>
                <RowDefinition />
                <RowDefinition />
                <RowDefinition />
                <RowDefinition />
            </Grid.RowDefinitions>
            <Grid.ColumnDefinitions>
                <ColumnDefinition Width="Auto" />
                <ColumnDefinition Width="*" />
            </Grid.ColumnDefinitions>
            <Label Content="Title" Grid.Row="0" Grid.Column="0" Margin="10,0,5,0"
                   HorizontalAlignment="Left" VerticalAlignment="Center" />
            <Label Content="Publisher" Grid.Row="1" Grid.Column="0"
                   Margin="10,0,5,0"
                   HorizontalAlignment="Left" VerticalAlignment="Center" />
            <Label Content="Isbn" Grid.Row="2" Grid.Column="0" Margin="10,0,5,0"
                   HorizontalAlignment="Left" VerticalAlignment="Center" />
            <TextBox Text="{Binding Title}" Grid.Row="0" Grid.Column="1"
```

```
                    Margin="5" />
        <TextBox Text="{Binding Publisher}" Grid.Row="1" Grid.Column="1"
                    Margin="5" />
        <TextBox Text="{Binding Isbn}" Grid.Row="2" Grid.Column="1"
                    Margin="5" />
    </Grid>
</DockPanel>
</UserControl>
```

code snippet BooksDemo/BooksUC.xaml

The new user control is started by adding a `Hyperlink` to `MainWindow.xaml`. It uses the `Click` event handler `OnShowBooks()` and the implementation of `OnShowBooks()` in the code-behind file `MainWindow.xaml.cs`:

Available for
download on
Wrox.com

```
<ListBox DockPanel.Dock="Left" Margin="5" MinWidth="120">
    <ListBoxItem>
        <Hyperlink Click="OnShowBook">Show Book</Hyperlink>
    </ListBoxItem>
    <ListBoxItem>
        <Hyperlink Click="OnShowBooks">Show Books</Hyperlink>
    </ListBoxItem>
</ListBox>
```

code snippet BooksDemo/BooksUC.xaml

Available for
download on
Wrox.com

```
private void OnShowBooks(object sender, RoutedEventArgs e)
{
    var booksUI = new BooksUC();
    this.tabControl1.SelectedIndex =
        this.tabControl1.Items.Add(
            new TabItem { Header="Books", Content=booksUI });

}
```

code snippet BooksDemo/BooksUC.xaml.cs

Because the `DockPanel` has the `Book` array assigned to the `DataContext`, and the `ListBox` is placed within the `DockPanel`, the `ListBox` shows all books with the default template, as illustrated in Figure 36-6.

For a more flexible layout of the `ListBox`, you have to define a template, as was discussed in the previous chapter for `ListBox` styling. The `ItemTemplate` of the `ListBox` defines a `DataTemplate` with a `Label` element. The content of the label is bound to the `Title`. The item template is repeated for every item in the list. Of course you can also add the item template to a style within resources:

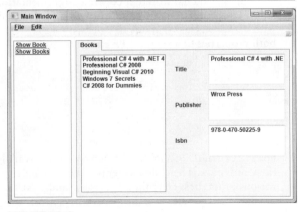

FIGURE 36-6

Available for
download on
Wrox.com

```
<ListBox DockPanel.Dock="Left" ItemsSource="{Binding}" Margin="5"
        MinWidth="120">
    <ListBox.ItemTemplate>
        <DataTemplate>
            <Label Content="{Binding Title}" />
        </DataTemplate>
    </ListBox.ItemTemplate>
</ListBox>
```

code snippet BooksDemo/BooksUC.xaml

Master Details Binding

Instead of just showing all the elements inside a list, you might want or need to show detail information about the selected item. It doesn't require a lot of work to do this. The `Label` and `TextBox` controls are already defined; currently they only show the first element in the list.

There's one important change you have to make to the `ListBox`. By default, the labels are bound to just the first element of the list. By setting the `ListBox` property `IsSynchronizedWithCurrentItem="True"`, the selection of the list box is set to the current item. In Figure 36-7 you can see the result; the selected item is shown in the detail section labels:

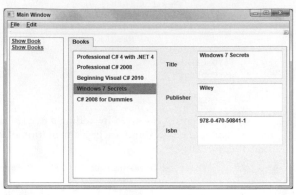

FIGURE 36-7

Available for download on Wrox.com

```xml
<ListBox DockPanel.Dock="Left" ItemsSource="{Binding}" Margin="5"
         MinWidth="120" IsSynchronizedWithCurrentItem="True">
    <ListBox.ItemTemplate>
        <DataTemplate>
            <Label Content="{Binding Title}" />
        </DataTemplate>
    </ListBox.ItemTemplate>
</ListBox>
```

code snippet BooksDemo/BooksUC.xaml

MultiBinding

`Binding` is one of the classes that can be used for data binding. `BindingBase` is the abstract base class of all bindings and has different concrete implementations. Besides `Binding`, there's also `MultiBinding` and `PriorityBinding`. `MultiBinding` allows you to bind one WPF element to multiple sources. For example, with a `Person` class that has `LastName` and `FirstName` properties, it is interesting to bind both properties to a single WPF element:

Available for download on Wrox.com

```csharp
public class Person
{
    public string FirstName { get; set; }
    public string LastName { get; set; }
}
```

code snippet MultiBindingDemo/Person.cs

For `MultiBinding`, a markup extension is not available — thus the binding must be specified with XAML element syntax. The child elements of `MultiBinding` are `Binding` elements that specify the binding to the various properties. Here the `FirstName` and `LastName` properties are used. The data context is set with the `Grid` element to reference the `person1` resource.

To connect the properties together, `MultiBinding` uses a `Converter` to convert multiple values to one. This converter uses a parameter that allows for different conversions based on the parameter:

Available for download on Wrox.com

```xml
<Window x:Class="Wrox.ProCSharp.WPF.MainWindow"
        xmlns="http://schemas.microsoft.com/winfx/2006/xaml/presentation"
        xmlns:x="http://schemas.microsoft.com/winfx/2006/xaml"
        xmlns:system="clr-namespace:System;assembly=mscorlib"
        xmlns:local="clr-namespace:Wrox.ProCSharp.WPF"
        Title="MainWindow" Height="240" Width="500">
    <Window.Resources>
        <local:Person x:Key="person1" FirstName="Tom" LastName="Turbo" />
```

```xml
            <local:PersonNameConverter x:Key="personNameConverter" />
        </Window.Resources>
        <Grid DataContext="{StaticResource person1}">
            <TextBox>
                <TextBox.Text>
                    <MultiBinding Converter="{StaticResource personNameConverter}" >
                        <MultiBinding.ConverterParameter>
                            <system:String>FirstLast</system:String>
                        </MultiBinding.ConverterParameter>
                        <Binding Path="FirstName" />
                        <Binding Path="LastName" />
                    </MultiBinding>
                </TextBox.Text>
            </TextBox>
        </Grid>
    </Window>
```

code snippet MultiBindingDemo/MainWindow.xaml

The multi-value converter implements the interface `IMultiValueConverter`. This interface defines two methods, `Convert()` and `ConvertBack()`. `Convert()` receives multiple values with the first argument from the data source and returns one value to the target. With the implementation, depending on whether the parameter has a value of `FirstLast` or `LastFirst`, the result is created differently:

```csharp
using System;
using System.Globalization;
using System.Windows.Data;

namespace Wrox.ProCSharp.WPF
{

    public class PersonNameConverter : IMultiValueConverter
    {
        public object Convert(object[] values, Type targetType, object parameter,
                              CultureInfo culture)
        {
            switch (parameter as string)
            {
                case "FirstLast":
                    return values[0] + " " + values[1];
                case "LastFirst":
                    return values[1] + ", " + values[0];
                default:
                    throw new ArgumentException(
                        String.Format("invalid argument {0}", parameter));
            }
        }

        public object[] ConvertBack(object value, Type[] targetTypes,
                                    object parameter, CultureInfo culture)
        {
            throw new NotSupportedException();
        }
    }
}
```

code snippet MultiBindingDemo/MainWindow.xaml.cs

Priority Binding

`PriorityBinding` makes it easy to bind to data that is not readily available. If you need time to get the result with `PriorityBinding`, you can inform the user about the progress so he knows to wait.

To illustrate priority binding, use the `PriorityBindingDemo` project to create the `Data` class. Accessing the `ProcessSomeData` property needs some time that is simulated by calling the `Thread.Sleep()` method:

```
public class Data
{
    public string ProcessSomeData
    {
        get
        {
            Thread.Sleep(8000);
            return "the final result is here";
        }
    }
}
```

code snippet PriorityBindingDemo/Data.cs

The `Information` class gives information to the user. The information from property `Info1` is returned immediately while `Info2` returns information after five seconds. With a real implementation, this class could be associated with the processing class to get an estimated timeframe for the user:

```
public class Information
{
    public string Info1
    {
        get
        {
            return "please wait...";
        }
    }
    public string Info2
    {
        get
        {
            Thread.Sleep(5000);
            return "please wait a little more";
        }
    }
}
```

code snippet PriorityBindingDemo/Information.cs

In the `MainWindow.xaml` file, the `Data` and `Information` classes are referenced and initiated within the resources of the `Window`:

```
<Window.Resources>
    <local:Data x:Key="data1" />
    <local:Information x:Key="info" />
</Window.Resources>
```

code snippet PriorityBindingDemo/MainWindow.xaml

`PriorityBinding` is done in place of normal binding within the `Content` property of a `Label`. `Priority Binding` consists of multiple `Binding` elements where all but the last one have the `IsAsync` property set to `True`. Because of this, if the first binding expression result is not immediately available, the binding process chooses the next one. The first binding references the `ProcessSomeData` property of the `Data` class that needs some time. Because of this, the next binding comes into play and references the `Info2` property of the Information class. `Info2` does not return a result immediately, and because `IsAsync` is set, the binding process does not wait but continues to the next binding. The last binding uses the `Info1` property and immediately returns a result. If it doesn't return a result immediately, you would wait for the result because `IsAsync` is set to the default, `False`:

```xml
<Label>
    <Label.Content>
        <PriorityBinding>
            <Binding Path="ProcessSomeData" Source="{StaticResource data1}"
                     IsAsync="True" />
            <Binding Path="Info2" Source="{StaticResource info}"
                     IsAsync="True" />
            <Binding Path="Info1" Source="{StaticResource info}"
                     IsAsync="False" />
        </PriorityBinding>
    </Label.Content>
</Label>
```

With the start of the application you can see the message please wait… in the user interface. After a few seconds the result from the Info2 property is returned as please wait a little more. It replaces the output from Info1. Finally, the result from ProcessSomeData replaces the output again.

Value Conversion

Let's get back to the BooksDemo application. The authors of the book are still missing in the user interface. If you bind the Authors property to a Label element, the ToString() method of the Array class is invoked, which returns the name of the type. One solution to this is to bind the Authors property to a ListBox. For the ListBox, you can define a template for a specific view. Another solution is to convert the string array returned by the Authors property to a string and use the string for binding.

The class StringArrayConverter converts a string array to a string. WPF converter classes must implement the interface IValueConverter from the namespace System.Windows.Data. This interface defines the methods Convert() and ConvertBack(). With the StringArrayConverter, the Convert() method converts the string array from the variable value to a string by using the String.Join() method. The separator parameter of the Join() is taken from the variable parameter received with the Convert() method.

 You can read more about the methods of the String *classes in Chapter 9, "Strings and Regular Expressions."*

Available for download on Wrox.com

```csharp
using System;
using System.Diagnostics.Contracts;
using System.Globalization;
using System.Windows.Data;

namespace Wrox.ProCSharp.WPF.Utilities
{
    [ValueConversion(typeof(string[]), typeof(string))]
    class StringArrayConverter : IValueConverter
    {
        public object Convert(object value, Type targetType, object parameter,
                              CultureInfo culture)
        {
            Contract.Requires(value is string[]);
            Contract.Requires(parameter is string);

            string[] stringCollection = (string[])value;
            string separator = (string)parameter;

            return String.Join(separator, stringCollection);
        }

        public object ConvertBack(object value, Type targetType, object parameter,
```

```
                                CultureInfo culture)
        {
            throw new NotImplementedException();
        }
    }
}
```

code snippet BooksDemo/Utilities/Information.cs

In the XAML code, the `StringArrayConverter` class can be declared as a resource for referencing it from the `Binding` markup extension:

```xml
<UserControl x:Class="Wrox.ProCSharp.WPF.BooksUC"
            xmlns="http://schemas.microsoft.com/winfx/2006/xaml/presentation"
            xmlns:x="http://schemas.microsoft.com/winfx/2006/xaml"
            xmlns:mc="http://schemas.openxmlformats.org/markup-compatibility/2006"
            xmlns:d="http://schemas.microsoft.com/expression/blend/2008"
            xmlns:local="clr-namespace:Wrox.ProCSharp.WPF.Data"
            xmlns:utils="clr-namespace:Wrox.ProCSharp.WPF.Utilities"
            mc:Ignorable="d"
            d:DesignHeight="300" d:DesignWidth="300">
    <UserControl.Resources>
        <utils:StringArrayConverter x:Key="stringArrayConverter" />
        <ObjectDataProvider x:Key="books" ObjectType="local:BookFactory"
                            MethodName="GetBooks" />
    </UserControl.Resources>
    <!--.-->
```

code snippet BooksDemo/BooksUC.xaml

For multiline output, a `TextBlock` element is declared with the `TextWrapping` property set to `Wrap` to make it possible to display multiple authors. In the `Binding` markup extension the `Path` is set to `Authors`, which is defined as a property returning a string array. The string array is converted from the resource `stringArrayConverter` as defined by the `Converter` property. The `Convert` method of the converter implementation receives the `ConverterParameter ', '` as input to separate the authors:

```xml
<TextBlock Text="{Binding Authors,
           Converter={StaticResource stringArrayConverter},
           ConverterParameter=', '}"
          Grid.Row="3" Grid.Column="1" Margin="5"
          VerticalAlignment="Center" TextWrapping="Wrap" />
```

Figure 36-8 shows the book details, including authors.

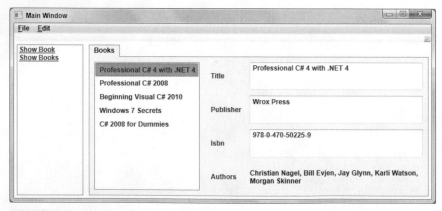

FIGURE 36-8

Adding List Items Dynamically

What if list items are added dynamically? The WPF element must be notified of elements added to the list.

In the XAML code of the WPF application, a `Button` element is added inside a `StackPanel`. The `Click` event is assigned to the method `OnAddBook()`:

Available for
download on
Wrox.com

```xml
<StackPanel Orientation="Horizontal" DockPanel.Dock="Bottom"
            HorizontalAlignment="Center">
    <Button Margin="5" Padding="4" Content="Add Book" Click="OnAddBook" />
</StackPanel>
```

code snippet BooksDemo/BooksUC.xaml

In the method `OnAddBook()`, a new `Book` object is added to the list. If you test the application with the `BookFactory` as it is implemented now, there's no notification to the WPF elements that a new object has been added to the list:

Available for
download on
Wrox.com

```csharp
private void OnAddBook(object sender, RoutedEventArgs e)
{
    ((this.FindResource("books") as ObjectDataProvider).Data as
        IList<Book>).Add(
            new Book(".NET 3.5 Wrox Box", "Wrox Press",
                "978-0470-38799-3"));
}
```

code snippet BooksDemo/BooksUC.xaml.cs

The object that is assigned to the `DataContext` must implement the interface `INotifyCollectionChanged`. This interface defines the `CollectionChanged` event that is used by the WPF application. Instead of implementing this interface on your own with a custom collection class, you can use the generic collection class `ObservableCollection<T>` that is defined with the namespace `System.Collections.ObjectModel` in the assembly `WindowsBase`. Now, as a new item is added to the collection, the new item immediately shows up in the `ListBox`:

Available for
download on
Wrox.com

```csharp
public class BookFactory
{
    private ObservableCollection<Book> books =
        new ObservableCollection<Book>();

    // ...

    public IEnumerable<Book> GetBooks()
    {
        return books;
    }
}
```

code snippet BooksDemo/Utilities/BookFactory.cs

Data Template Selector

In the previous chapter, you saw how controls can be customized with templates. You also saw how to create a data template that defines a display for specific data types. A data template selector can create different data templates dynamically for the same data type. A data template selector is implemented in a class that derives from the base class `DataTemplateSelector`.

Here a data template selector is implemented by selecting a different template based on the publisher. Within the user control resources these templates are defined. One template can be accessed by the key name `wroxTemplate`; the other template has the key name `dummiesTemplate`, and the third one `bookTemplate`:

```
<DataTemplate x:Key="wroxTemplate" DataType="{x:Type local:Book}">
    <Border Background="Red" Margin="10" Padding="10">
        <StackPanel>
            <Label Content="{Binding Title}" />
            <Label Content="{Binding Publisher}" />
        </StackPanel>
    </Border>
</DataTemplate>

<DataTemplate x:Key="dummiesTemplate" DataType="{x:Type local:Book}">
    <Border Background="Yellow" Margin="10" Padding="10">
        <StackPanel>
            <Label Content="{Binding Title}" />
            <Label Content="{Binding Publisher}" />
        </StackPanel>
    </Border>
</DataTemplate>

<DataTemplate x:Key="bookTemplate" DataType="{x:Type local:Book}">
    <Border Background="LightBlue" Margin="10" Padding="10">
        <StackPanel>
            <Label Content="{Binding Title}" />
            <Label Content="{Binding Publisher}" />
        </StackPanel>
    </Border>
</DataTemplate>
```

code snippet BooksDemo/BooksUC.xaml

For selecting the template, the class `BookDataTemplateSelector` overrides the method `SelectTemplate` from the base class `DataTemplateSelector`. The implementation selects the template based on the `Publisher` property from the `Book` class:

```
using System.Windows;
using System.Windows.Controls;
using Wrox.ProCSharp.WPF.Data;

namespace Wrox.ProCSharp.WPF.Utilities
{
    public class BookTemplateSelector : DataTemplateSelector
    {
        public override DataTemplate SelectTemplate(object item,
                                                    DependencyObject container)
        {
            if (item != null && item is Book)
            {
                var book = item as Book;
                switch (book.Publisher)
                {
                    case "Wrox Press":
                        return
                            (container as FrameworkElement).FindResource(
                                "wroxTemplate") as DataTemplate;
                    case "For Dummies":
                        return
                            (container as FrameworkElement).FindResource(
                                "dummiesTemplate") as DataTemplate;
                    default:
                        return
                            (container as FrameworkElement).FindResource(
                                "bookTemplate") as DataTemplate;
                }
            }
```

```
            return null;
        }
    }
}
```

code snippet BooksDemo/Utilities/BookTemplateSelector.cs

For accessing the class `BookDataTemplateSelector` from XAML code, the class is defined within the `Window` resources:

Available for download on Wrox.com

```
<src:BookDataTemplateSelector x:Key="bookTemplateSelector" />
```

code snippet BooksDemo/BooksUC.xaml

Now the selector class can be assigned to the `ItemTemplateSelector` property of the `ListBox`:

```
<ListBox DockPanel.Dock="Left" ItemsSource="{Binding}" Margin="5"
        MinWidth="120" IsSynchronizedWithCurrentItem="True"
        ItemTemplateSelector="{StaticResource bookTemplateSelector}">
```

When running the application, you can see different data templates based on the publisher, as shown in Figure 36-9.

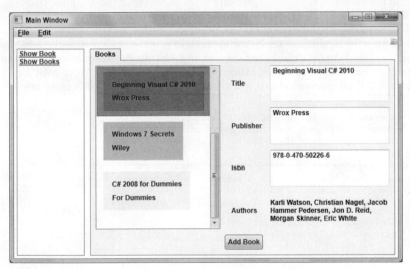

FIGURE 36-9

Binding to XML

WPF data binding has special support for binding to XML data. You can use `XmlDataProvider` as a data source and bind the elements by using XPath expressions. For a hierarchical display, you can use the `TreeView` control and create the view for the items by using the `HierarchicalDataTemplate`.

The following XML file containing `Book` elements is used as a source in the next examples:

Available for download on Wrox.com

```
<?xml version="1.0" encoding="utf-8" ?>
<Books>
  <Book isbn="978-0-470-12472-7">
    <Title>Professional C# 2008</Title>
    <Publisher>Wrox Press</Publisher>
    <Author>Christian Nagel</Author>
    <Author>Bill Evjen</Author>
    <Author>Jay Glynn</Author>
    <Author>Karli Watson</Author>
```

```
    <Author>Morgan Skinner</Author>
  </Book>
  <Book isbn="978-0-7645-4382-1">
    <Title>Beginning Visual C# 2008</Title>
    <Publisher>Wrox Press</Publisher>
    <Author>Karli Watson</Author>
    <Author>David Espinosa</Author>
    <Author>Zach Greenvoss</Author>
    <Author>Jacob Hammer Pedersen</Author>
    <Author>Christian Nagel</Author>
    <Author>John D. Reid</Author>
    <Author>Matthew Reynolds</Author>
    <Author>Morgan Skinner</Author>
    <Author>Eric White</Author>
  </Book>
</Books>
```

Similarly to defining an object data provider, you can define an XML data provider. Both `ObjectDataProvider` and `XmlDataProvider` are derived from the same base class, `DataSourceProvider`. With the `XmlDataProvider` in the example, the `Source` property is set to reference the XML file `books` `.xml`. The `XPath` property defines an XPath expression to reference the XML root element `Books`. The `Grid` element references the XML data source with the `DataContext` property. With the data context for the grid, all `Book` elements are required for a list binding, so the XPath expression is set to `Book`. Inside the grid, you can find the `ListBox` element that binds to the default data context and uses the `DataTemplate` to include the title in `TextBlock` elements as items of the `ListBox`. Inside the grid, you can also see three `Label` elements with data binding set to XPath expressions to display the title, publisher, and ISBN numbers:

```
<Window x:Class="XmlBindingDemo.MainWindow"
        xmlns="http://schemas.microsoft.com/winfx/2006/xaml/presentation"
        xmlns:x="http://schemas.microsoft.com/winfx/2006/xaml"
        Title="Main Window" Height="240" Width="500">
    <Window.Resources>
        <XmlDataProvider x:Key="books" Source="Books.xml" XPath="Books" />
        <DataTemplate x:Key="listTemplate">
            <TextBlock Text="{Binding XPath=Title}" />
        </DataTemplate>

        <Style x:Key="labelStyle" TargetType="{x:Type Label}">
            <Setter Property="Width" Value="190" />
            <Setter Property="Height" Value="40" />
            <Setter Property="Margin" Value="5" />
        </Style>
    </Window.Resources>

    <Grid DataContext="{Binding Source={StaticResource books}, XPath=Book}">
        <Grid.RowDefinitions>
            <RowDefinition />
            <RowDefinition />
            <RowDefinition />
            <RowDefinition />
        </Grid.RowDefinitions>
        <Grid.ColumnDefinitions>
            <ColumnDefinition />
            <ColumnDefinition />
        </Grid.ColumnDefinitions>
        <ListBox IsSynchronizedWithCurrentItem="True" Margin="5"
          Grid.Column="0" Grid.RowSpan="4" ItemsSource="{Binding}"
          ItemTemplate="{StaticResource listTemplate}" />

        <Label Style="{StaticResource labelStyle}" Content="{Binding XPath=Title}"
          Grid.Row="0" Grid.Column="1" />
```

```
                <Label Style="{StaticResource labelStyle}"
                  Content="{Binding XPath=Publisher}"
                  Grid.Row="1" Grid.Column="1" />
                <Label Style="{StaticResource labelStyle}"
                  Content="{Binding XPath=@isbn}"
                  Grid.Row="2" Grid.Column="1" />
          </Grid>
      </Window>
```

code snippet BooksDemo/MainWindow.xaml

Figure 36-10 shows the result of the XML binding.

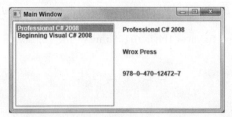

FIGURE 36-10

 If XML data should be shown hierarchically, you can use the `TreeView` *control.*

Binding Validation

Several options are available to validate data from the user before it is used with the .NET objects. These options are:

➤ Handling exceptions

➤ Data error information

➤ Custom validation rules

Handling Exceptions

One of the options demonstrated here is that the .NET class throws an exception if an invalid value is set as shown in the class `SomeData`. The property `Value1` accepts only values larger or equal to 5 and smaller than 12:

Available for
download on
Wrox.com

```
public class SomeData
{
    private int value1;
    public int Value1 {
      get
      {
          return value1;
      }
      set
      {
          if (value < 5 || value > 12)
              throw new ArgumentException(
                    "value must not be less than 5 or greater than 12");
          value1 = value;
      }
    }
}
```

code snippet ValidationDemo/SomeData.cs

In the constructor of the `MainWindow` class, a new object of the class `SomeData` is initialized and passed to the `DataContext` for data binding:

```
public partial class MainWindow: Window
{
    private SomeData p1 = new SomeData { Value1 = 11 };

    public MainWindow()
    {
        InitializeComponent();
        this.DataContext = p1;
    }
}
```

code snippet ValidationDemo/MainWindow.xaml.cs

The event handler method `OnShowValue` displays a message box to show the actual value of the `SomeData` instance:

```
private void OnShowValue(object sender, RoutedEventArgs e)
{
    MessageBox.Show(p1.Value1.ToString());
}
```

With simple data binding, here the `Text` property of a `TextBox` is bound to the `Value1` property. If you run the application now and try to change the value to one that is not valid, you can verify that the value never changed by clicking the Submit button. WPF catches and ignores the exception thrown by the set accessor of the property `Value1`:

```
<Label Margin="5" Grid.Row="0" Grid.Column="0" >Value1:</Label>
<TextBox Margin="5" Grid.Row="0" Grid.Column="1"
    Text="{Binding Path=Value1}" />
```

code snippet ValidationDemo/MainWindow.xaml

To display an error as soon as the context of the input field changes, you can set the `ValidatesOnException` property of the `Binding` markup extension to `True`. With an invalid value (as soon as the exception is thrown when the value should be set), the `TextBox` is surrounded by a red line, as shown in Figure 36-11.

```
<Label Margin="5" Grid.Row="0" Grid.Column="0" >Value1:</Label>
<TextBox Margin="5" Grid.Row="0" Grid.Column="1"
    Text="{Binding Path=Value1, ValidatesOnExceptions=True}" />
```

FIGURE 36-11

To return the error information in a different way to the user, you can assign the attached property `ErrorTemplate` that is defined by the `Validation` class to a template defining the UI for errors. The new template to mark the error is shown here with the key `validationTemplate`. The `ControlTemplate` puts a red exclamation point in front of the existing control content:

```
<ControlTemplate x:Key="validationTemplate">
    <DockPanel>
        <TextBlock Foreground="Red" FontSize="20">!</TextBlock>
        <AdornedElementPlaceholder/>
    </DockPanel>
</ControlTemplate>
```

Setting the `validationTemplate` with the `Validation.ErrorTemplate` attached property activates the template with the `TextBox`:

```
<Label Margin="5" Grid.Row="0" Grid.Column="0" >Value1:</Label>
<TextBox Margin="5" Grid.Row="0" Grid.Column="1"
    Text="{Binding Path=Value1, ValidatesOnExceptions=True}"
    Validation.ErrorTemplate="{StaticResource
validationTemplate}" />
```

The new look of the application is shown in Figure 36-12.

FIGURE 36-12

Another option for a custom error message is to register to the Error *event of the* Validation *class. Here the property* NotifyOnValidationError *must be set to true.*

The error information itself can be accessed from the Errors collection of the Validation class. To display the error information in the ToolTip of the TextBox you can create a property trigger as shown. The trigger is activated as soon as the HasError property of the Validation class is set to True. The trigger sets the ToolTip property of the TextBox:

```
<Style TargetType="{x:Type TextBox}">
    <Style.Triggers>
        <Trigger Property="Validation.HasError" Value="True">
            <Setter Property="ToolTip"
                    Value="{Binding RelativeSource=
                            {x:Static RelativeSource.Self},
                        Path=(Validation.Errors)[0].ErrorContent}" />
        </Trigger>
    </Style.Triggers>
</Style>
```

Data Error Information

Another way to deal with errors is if the .NET object implements the interface IDataErrorInfo.

The class SomeData is now changed to implement the interface IDataErrorInfo. This interface defines the property Error and an indexer with a string argument. With WPF validation during data binding, the indexer is called and the name of the property to validate is passed as the columnName argument. With the implementation the value is verified if it is valid, and an error string is passed otherwise. Here the validation is done on the property Value2 that is implemented by using the C# 3.0 simple property notation:

```
public class SomeData: IDataErrorInfo
{
    //...

    public int Value2 { get; set; }

    string IDataErrorInfo.Error
    {
        get
        {
            return null;
        }
    }

    string IDataErrorInfo.this[string columnName]
    {
        get
        {
            if (columnName == "Value2")
            {
                if (this.Value2 < 0 || this.Value2 > 80)
                    return "age must not be less than 0 or greater than 80";

            }
            return null;
        }
    }
}
```

code snippet ValidationDemo/SomeData.cs

With a .NET entity class, it would not be clear what an indexer would return; for example, what would you expect from an object of type Person calling an indexer? That's why it is best to do an explicit implementation of the interface IDataErrorInfo. This way this indexer can be accessed only by using the interface, and the .NET class could do a different implementation for other purposes.

If you set the property ValidatesOnDataErrors of the Binding class to true, the interface IDataErrorInfo is used during binding. Here, when the TextBox is changed, the binding mechanism invokes the indexer of the interface and passes Value2 to the columnName variable:

```
<Label Margin="5" Grid.Row="1" Grid.Column="0" >Value2:</Label>
<TextBox Margin="5" Grid.Row="1" Grid.Column="1"
    Text="{Binding Path=Value2, ValidatesOnDataErrors=True}" />
```

code snippet ValidationDemo/MainWindow.xaml

Custom Validation Rules

To get more control of the validation you can implement a custom validation rule. A class implementing a custom validation rule needs to derive from the base class ValidationRule. With the previous two examples, validation rules have been used as well. Two classes that derive from the abstract base class ValidationRule are DataErrorValidationRule and ExceptionValidationRule. DataErrorValidationRule is activated by setting the property ValidatesOnDataErrors and uses the interface IDataErrorInfo; ExceptionValidationRule deals with exceptions and is activated by setting the property ValidatesOnException.

Here a validation rule is implemented to verify for a regular expression. The class RegularExpressionValidationRule derives from the base class ValidationRule and overrides the abstract method Validate() that is defined by the base class. With the implementation, the RegEx class from the namespace System.Text.RegularExpressions is used to validate the expression defined by the Expression property:

```
public class RegularExpressionValidationRule: ValidationRule
{
    public string Expression { get; set; }
    public string ErrorMessage { get; set; }

    public override ValidationResult Validate(object value,
        CultureInfo cultureInfo)
    {
        ValidationResult result = null;
        if (value != null)
        {
            Regex regEx = new Regex(Expression);
            bool isMatch = regEx.IsMatch(value.ToString());
            result = new ValidationResult(isMatch, isMatch ?
                null: ErrorMessage);
        }
        return result;
    }
}
```

Regular expressions are explained in Chapter 9.

Instead of using the `Binding` markup extension, now the binding is done as a child of the `TextBox.Text` element. The bound object now defines an `Email` property that is implemented with the simple property syntax. The `UpdateSourceTrigger` property defines when the source should be updated. Possible options for updating the source are:

➤ When the property value changes — which is every character typed by the user

➤ When the focus is lost

➤ Explicitly

`ValidationRules` is a property of the `Binding` class that contains `ValidationRule` elements. Here the validation rule used is the custom class `RegularExpressionValidationRule`, where the `Expression` property is set to a regular expression that verifies if the input is a valid e-mail, and the `ErrorMessage` property that gives the error message in case the data entered to the `TextBox` is not valid:

```
<Label Margin="5" Grid.Row="2" Grid.Column="0">Email:</Label>
<TextBox Margin="5" Grid.Row="2" Grid.Column="1">
    <TextBox.Text>
        <Binding Path="Email" UpdateSourceTrigger="LostFocus">
            <Binding.ValidationRules>
                <src:RegularExpressionValidationRule
                    Expression="^([\w-\.]+)@((\[[0-9]{1,3}\.[0-9]{1,3}\.
                        [0-9]{1,3}\.)|(([\w-]+\.)+))([a-zA-Z]{2,4}|
                        [0-9]{1,3})(\]?)$"
                    ErrorMessage="Email is not valid" />
            </Binding.ValidationRules>
        </Binding>
    </TextBox.Text>
</TextBox>
```

COMMANDING

Commanding is a concept of WPF that creates a loose coupling between the source of an action (for example, a button) and the target that does the work (for example, a handler method). Events are strongly coupled (at least with XAML 2006). Compiling the XAML code that includes references to events requires that the code-behind have a handler implemented and available at compile time. With commands, the coupling is loose.

The action that is executed is defined by a command object. Commands implement the interface `ICommand`. Command classes that are used by WPF are `RoutedCommand` and a class that derives from it, `RoutedUICommand`. `RoutedUICommand` defines an additional text for the user interface that is not defined by `ICommand`. `ICommand` defines the methods `Execute()` and `CanExecute()`, which are executed on a target object.

The command source is an object that invokes the command. Command sources implement the interface `ICommandSource`. Examples of such command sources are button classes that derive from `ButtonBase`, `Hyperlink`, and `InputBinding`. `KeyBinding` and `MouseBinding` are examples of `InputBinding` derived classes. Command sources have a Command property where a command object implementing `ICommand` can be assigned. This fires the command when the control is used, such as with the click of a button.

The command target is an object that implements a handler to perform the action. With command binding, a mapping is defined to map the handler to a command. Command bindings define what handler is invoked on a command. Command bindings are defined by the `CommandBinding` property that is implemented in the `UIElement` class. Thus every class that derives from `UIElement` has the `CommandBinding` property. This makes the finding of the mapped handler a hierarchical process. For example, a button that is defined within a `StackPanel` that is inside a `ListBox` — which itself is inside a `Grid` — can fire a command. The handler is specified with command bindings somewhere up the tree — such as with command bindings of a `Window`.

Let's change the implementation of the BooksDemo project to use commands instead of the event model.

Defining Commands

.NET 4 gives you classes that return predefined commands. The `ApplicationCommands` class defines the static properties `New`, `Open`, `Close`, `Print`, `Cut`, `Copy`, `Paste`, and others. These properties return `RoutedUICommand` objects that can be used for a specific purpose. Other classes offering commands are `NavigationCommands` and `MediaCommands`. `NavigationCommands` gives you commands that are common for navigation such as `GoToPage`, `NextPage`, and `PreviousPage`. `MediaCommands` are useful for running a media player with `Play`, `Pause`, `Stop`, `Rewind`, and `Record`.

It's not hard to define custom commands that fulfill application domain–specific actions. For this, the `BooksCommands` class is created that returns a `RoutedUICommand` with the `ShowBooks` property. You can also assign an input gesture to a command, such as `KeyGesture` or `MouseGesture`. Here, a `KeyGesture` is assigned that defines the key B with the ALT modifier. An input gesture is a command source, so clicking the ALT-B key invokes the command:

Available for
download on
Wrox.com

```
public static class BooksCommands
{
    private static RoutedUICommand showBooks;
    public static ICommand ShowBooks
    {
        get
        {
            if (showBooks == null)
            {
                showBooks = new RoutedUICommand("Show Books", "ShowBooks",
                                            typeof(BooksCommands));
                showBook.InputGestures.Add(
                        new KeyGesture(Key.B, ModifierKeys.Alt));
            }
            return showBooks;
        }
    }
}
```

code snippet BooksDemo/BooksCommands.cs

Defining Command Sources

Every class that implements the `ICommandSource` interface can be a source of commands, such as `Button` and `MenuItem`. Inside the main window a `Menu` control is added as a child of the `DockPanel`. `MenuItem` elements are contained within the `Menu` control and the `Command` property is assigned to some predefined commands such as `ApplicationCommands.Close`, and the custom command `BooksCommands.ShowBooks`:

```
<DockPanel>
    <Menu DockPanel.Dock="Top">
        <MenuItem Header="_File">
            <MenuItem Header="_Show Books"
                    Command="local:BooksCommands.ShowBooks" />
            <Separator />
            <MenuItem Header="Exit" Command="ApplicationCommands.Close" />
        </MenuItem>
        <MenuItem Header="_Edit">
            <MenuItem Header="Undo" Command="ApplicationCommands.Undo" />
            <Separator />
            <MenuItem Header="Cut" Command="ApplicationCommands.Cut" />
            <MenuItem Header="Copy" Command="ApplicationCommands.Copy" />
            <MenuItem Header="Paste" Command="ApplicationCommands.Paste" />
        </MenuItem>
    </Menu>
```

code snippet BooksDemo/MainWindow.xaml

Command Bindings

Command bindings need to be added to connect them to handler methods. Here, the command bindings are defined within the `Window` element so these bindings are available to all elements within the window. When the command `ApplicationCommands.Close` is executed, the `OnClose()` method gets invoked. When the command `BooksCommands.ShowBooks` is executed, the `OnShowBooks()` method gets called:

```xml
<Window.CommandBindings>
    <CommandBinding Command="ApplicationCommands.Close" Executed="OnClose" />
    <CommandBinding Command="local:BooksCommands.ShowBooks"
                Executed="OnShowBooks" />
</Window.CommandBindings>
```

code snippet BooksDemo/MainWindow.xaml

With command binding you can also specify the `CanExecute` property, where a method is invoked to verify whether the command is available. For example, if a file is not changed, the `ApplicationCommands.Save` command could be unavailable.

The handler needs to be defined with an object parameter, for the sender, and `ExecutedRoutedEventArgs`, where information about the command can be accessed:

```csharp
private void OnClose(object sender, ExecutedRoutedEventArgs e)
{
    Application.Current.Shutdown();
}
```

code snippet BooksDemo/MainWindow.xaml.cs

> *You can also pass parameters with a command. You can do this by specifying the* `CommandParameter` *property with a command source, such as the* `MenuItem`. *You can access the parameter with the* `Parameter` *property of* `ExecutedRoutedEventArgs`.

Command bindings can also be defined by controls. The `TextBox` control defines bindings for `ApplicationCommands.Cut`, `ApplicationCommands.Copy`, `ApplicationCommands.Paste`, and `ApplicationCommands.Undo`. This way you only need to specify the command source and use the existing functionality within the `TextBox` control.

TREEVIEW

The `TreeView` control is a control to display hierarchical data. Binding to a `TreeView` is very similar to the binding you've seen with the `ListBox`. What's different is the hierarchical data display — a `HierarchicalDataTemplate` can be used.

The next example uses hierarchical displays and the new `DataGrid` control. The `Formula1` sample database is accessed with the ADO.NET Entity Framework. The mapping used is shown in Figure 36-13. The `Race` class contains information about the date of the race and is associated with the `Circuit` class. The `Circuit` class has information about the `Country` and the name of the race circuit. `Race` also has an association with `RaceResult`. A `RaceResult` contains information about the `Racer` and the `Team`.

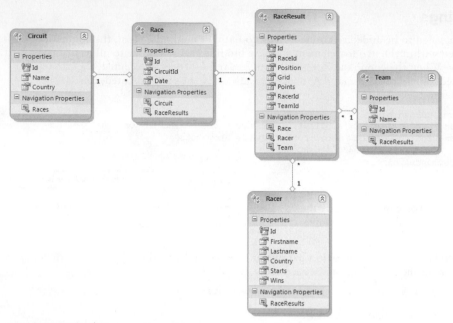

FIGURE 36-13

> The ADO.NET Entity Framework is covered in Chapter 31, "ADO.NET Entity Framework."

With the XAML code a `TreeView` is declared. `TreeView` derives from the base class `ItemsControl` where binding to a list can be done with the `ItemsSource` property. `ItemsSource` is bound to the data context. The data context is assigned in the code-behind, as you will see next. Of course, this could also be done with an `ObjectDataProvider`. To define a custom display for the hierarchical data, `HierarchicalDataTemplate` elements are defined. The data templates here are defined for specific data types with the `DataType` property. The first `HierarchicalDataTemplate` is the template for the `Championship` class and binds the `Year` property of this class to the `Text` property of a `TextBlock`. The `ItemsSource` property defines the binding for the data template itself to define the next level in the data hierarchy. If the `Races` property of the `Championship` class returns a collection, you bind the `ItemsSource` property directly to `Races`. However, because this property returns a `Lazy<T>` object, binding is done to `Races.Value`. The advantages of the `Lazy<T>` class are discussed later in this chapter.

The second `HierarchicalDataTemplate` element defines the template for the `F1Race` class and binds the `Country` and `Date` properties of this class. With the `Date` property a `StringFormat` is defined with the binding. The next level of the hierarchy is defined binding the `ItemsSource` to `Results.Value`.

The class `F1RaceResult` doesn't have a children collection, so the hierarchy stops here. For this data type, a normal `DataTemplate` is defined to bind `Position`, `Racer`, and `Car` properties:

```
<UserControl x:Class="Formula1Demo.TreeUC"
        xmlns="http://schemas.microsoft.com/winfx/2006/xaml/presentation"
        xmlns:x="http://schemas.microsoft.com/winfx/2006/xaml"
        xmlns:mc="http://schemas.openxmlformats.org/markup-compatibility/2006"
        xmlns:d="http://schemas.microsoft.com/expression/blend/2008"
        xmlns:local="clr-namespace:Formula1Demo"
        mc:Ignorable="d"
```

```xaml
                    d:DesignHeight="300" d:DesignWidth="300">
    <Grid>
        <TreeView ItemsSource="{Binding}" >
            <TreeView.Resources>
                <HierarchicalDataTemplate DataType="{x:Type local:Championship}"
                                          ItemsSource="{Binding Races.Value}">
                    <TextBlock Text="{Binding Year}" />
                </HierarchicalDataTemplate>

                <HierarchicalDataTemplate DataType="{x:Type local:F1Race}"
                                          ItemsSource="{Binding Results.Value}">
                    <StackPanel Orientation="Horizontal">
                        <TextBlock Text="{Binding Country}" Margin="5,0,5,0" />
                        <TextBlock Text="{Binding Path=Date, StringFormat=d }"
                                   Margin="5,0,5,0" />
                    </StackPanel>
                </HierarchicalDataTemplate>

                <DataTemplate DataType="{x:Type local:F1RaceResult}">
                    <StackPanel Orientation="Horizontal">
                        <TextBlock Text="{Binding Position}" Margin="5,0,5,0" />
                        <TextBlock Text="{Binding Racer}" Margin="5,0,0,0" />
                        <TextBlock Text=", " />
                        <TextBlock Text="{Binding Car}" />
                    </StackPanel>
                </DataTemplate>
            </TreeView.Resources>
        </TreeView>
    </Grid>
</UserControl>
```

code snippet Formula1Demo/TreeUC.xaml

Now for the code that fills the hierarchical control. In the code-behind file of the XAML code, `DataContext` is assigned to the `Years` property. The `Years` property uses a LINQ query, instead of the ADO.NET Entity Framework data context, to get all the years of the Formula-1 races in the database and to create a new `Championship` object for every year. With the instance of the `Championship` class, the `Year` property is set. This class also has a `Races` property to return the races of the year; however, this information is not yet filled in.

 LINQ is discussed in Chapter 11, "Language Integrated Query," and in Chapter 31.

Available for
download on
Wrox.com

```csharp
using System.Collections.Generic;
using System.Linq;
using System.Windows.Controls;

namespace Formula1Demo
{
    public partial class TreeUC : UserControl
    {
        private Formula1Entities data = new Formula1Entities();

        public TreeUC()
        {
            InitializeComponent();
            this.DataContext = Years;
        }
```

```
public IEnumerable<Championship> Years
{
    get
    {
        F1DataContext.Data = data;
        return (from r in data.Races
                orderby r.Date ascending
                select
                new Championship
                {
                    Year = r.Date.Year,
                }).Distinct();
    }
}
```

code snippet Formula1Demo/TreeUC.xaml.cs

The Championship class has a simple automatic property for the year. The Races property is of type Lazy<IEnumerable<F1Race>>. The Lazy<T> class is new with .NET 4 for lazy initialization. With a TreeView control, this class comes in very handy. If the data behind the tree is large and you do not want to load the full tree in advance, but only when a user makes a selection, lazy loading can be done. With the constructor of the Lazy<T> class, a delegate Func<IEnumerable<F1Race>> is used. With this delegate, IEnumerable<F1Race> needs to be returned. The implementation of the Lambda expression, assigned to the delegate, uses a LINQ query to create a list of F1Race objects that have the Date and Country property assigned:

Available for
download on
Wrox.com

```
public class Championship
{
    public int Year { get; set; }
    public Lazy<IEnumerable<F1Race>> Races
    {
        get
        {
            return new Lazy<IEnumerable<F1Race>>(() =>
            {
                return from r in F1DataContext.Data.Races
                       where r.Date.Year == Year
                       orderby r.Date
                       select new F1Race
                       {
                           Date = r.Date,
                           Country = r.Circuit.Country
                       };
            });
        }
    }
}
```

code snippet Formula1Demo/Championship.cs

The F1Race class again defines the Results property that uses the Lazy<T> type to return a list of F1RaceResult objects:

Available for
download on
Wrox.com

```
public class F1Race
{
    public string Country { get; set; }
    public DateTime Date { get; set; }
    public Lazy<IEnumerable<F1RaceResult>> Results
    {
        get
```

```
        {
            return new Lazy<IEnumerable<F1RaceResult>>(() =>
            {
                return from rr in F1DataContext.Data.RaceResults
                    where rr.Race.Date == this.Date
                    select new F1RaceResult
                    {
                        Position = rr.Position,
                        Racer = rr.Racer.Firstname + " " +
                            rr.Racer.Lastname,
                        Car = rr.Team.Name
                    };
            });
        }
    }
}
```

code snippet Formula1Demo/F1Race.cs

The final class of the hierarchy is `F1RaceResult`, which is a simple data holder for `Position`, `Racer`, and `Car`:

Available for
download on
Wrox.com

```
public class F1RaceResult
{
    public int Position { get; set; }
    public string Racer { get; set; }
    public string Car { get; set; }
}
```

code snippet Formula1Demo/Championship.cs

When you run the application, you can see at first all the years of the championships in the tree view. Because of binding, the next level is already accessed — every `Championship` object already has the `F1Race` objects associated. The user doesn't need to wait for the first level after the year or an open year with the default look of a small triangle. As you can see in Figure 36-14, the year 1984 is open. As soon as the user clicks on a year to see the second-level binding, the third level is done and the race results are retrieved.

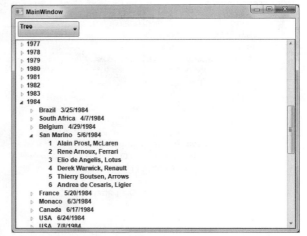

FIGURE 36-14

Of course you can also customize the `TreeView` control and define different styles for the complete template or the items in the view.

DATAGRID

Prior to .NET 4, a `DataGrid` control was missing with WPF. Now it's here! With the `DataGrid` control, information is displayed within rows and columns, and can also be edited.

The `DataGrid` control is an `ItemsControl` and defines the `ItemsSource` property that is bound to a collection. The XAML code of this user interface also defines two `RepeatButton` controls that are used for paging functionality. Instead of loading all the race information at once, paging is used so users can step through pages. In a simple scenario, only the `ItemsSource` property of the `DataGrid` needs to be assigned. By default, the `DataGrid` creates columns based on the properties of the bound data:

```xml
<UserControl x:Class="Formula1Demo.GridUC"
             xmlns="http://schemas.microsoft.com/winfx/2006/xaml/presentation"
             xmlns:x="http://schemas.microsoft.com/winfx/2006/xaml"
             xmlns:mc="http://schemas.openxmlformats.org/markup-compatibility/2006"
             xmlns:d="http://schemas.microsoft.com/expression/blend/2008"
             mc:Ignorable="d"
             d:DesignHeight="300" d:DesignWidth="300">
    <Grid>
        <Grid.RowDefinitions>
            <RepeatButton Margin="5" Click="OnPrevious">Previous</RepeatButton>
            <RepeatButton Margin="5" Click="OnNext">Next</RepeatButton>
        </Grid.RowDefinitions>
        <StackPanel Orientation="Horizontal" Grid.Row="0">
            <Button Click="OnPrevious">Previous</Button>
            <Button Click="OnNext">Next</Button>
        </StackPanel>
        <DataGrid Grid.Row="1" ItemsSource="{Binding}" />
    </Grid>
</UserControl>
```

code snippet Formula1Demo/GridUC.xaml

The code-behind uses the same `Formula1` database as the previous `TreeView` example. The `DataContext` of the `UserControl` is set to the `Races` property. This property returns `IEnumerable<object>`. Instead of assigning a strongly typed enumeration, an `object` is used to make it possible to create an anonymous class with the LINQ query. The LINQ query creates the anonymous class with `Year`, `Country`, `Position`, `Racer`, and `Car` properties and uses a compound to access `Races` and `RaceResults`. It also accesses other associations of `Races` to get country, racer, and team information. With the `Skip()` and `Take()` methods, paging functionality is implemented. The size of a page is fixed to 50 items, and the current page changes with the `OnNext()` and `OnPrevious()` handlers:

```csharp
using System.Collections.Generic;
using System.Linq;
using System.Windows;
using System.Windows.Controls;

namespace Formula1Demo
{
    public partial class GridUC : UserControl
    {
        private int currentPage = 0;
        private int pageSize = 50;
        private Formula1Entities data = new Formula1Entities();
        public GridUC()
        {
            InitializeComponent();
            this.DataContext = Races;
        }

        public IEnumerable<object> Races
        {
            get
            {
                return (from r in data.Races
                        from rr in r.RaceResults
                        orderby r.Date ascending
                        select new
                        {
                            Year = r.Date.Year,
```

```
                            Country = r.Circuit.Country,
                            Position = rr.Position,
                            Racer = rr.Racer.Firstname + " " + rr.Racer.Lastname,
                            Car = rr.Team.Name
                        }).Skip(currentPage * pageSize).Take(pageSize);
            }
        }


        private void OnPrevious(object sender, RoutedEventArgs e)
        {
            if (currentPage > 0)
            {
                currentPage--;
                this.DataContext = Races;
            }
        }

        private void OnNext(object sender, RoutedEventArgs e)
        {
            currentPage++;
            this.DataContext = Races;
        }
    }
}
```

code snippet Formula1Demo/GridUC.xaml.cs

Figure 36-15 shows the running application with the default grid styles and headers.

In the next `DataGrid` example, the grid is customized with custom columns and grouping.

Custom Columns

Setting the property `AutoGenerateColumns` of the `DataGrid` to `False` doesn't generate default columns. You can create custom columns with the `Columns` property. You can also specify elements that derive from `DataGridColumn`. Predefined classes exist that can be used. `DataGridTextColumn` can be used to read and edit text. `DataGridHyperlinkColumn` is for displaying hyperlinks. `DataGridCheckBoxColumn` displays a check box for Boolean data. For a list of items in a column you can use the

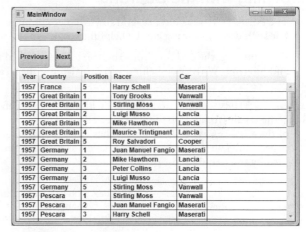

FIGURE 36-15

`DataGridComboBoxColumn`. More `DataGridColumn` types will be available in the future, but if you need a different representation now, you can use the `DataGridTemplateColumn` to define and bind any elements you want.

The example code uses `DataGridTextColumn` elements that are bound to the `Position` and `Racer` properties. The `Header` property is set to a string for display. Of course you can also use a template to define a complete custom header for the column:

```
<DataGrid ItemsSource="{Binding}" AutoGenerateColumns="False">
    <DataGrid.Columns>
        <DataGridTextColumn Binding="{Binding Position, Mode=OneWay}"
```

```
                                        Header="Position" />
                <DataGridTextColumn Binding="{Binding Racer, Mode=OneWay}"
                                        Header="Racer" />
        </DataGrid.Columns>
```

Row Details

When a row is selected, the `DataGrid` can display additional information for the row. This is done by specifying a `RowDetailsTemplate` with the `DataGrid`. A `DataTemplate` is assigned to the `RowDetailsTemplate` which contains several `TextBlock` elements that display the car and points:

```
        <DataGrid.RowDetailsTemplate>
            <DataTemplate>
                <StackPanel Orientation="Horizontal">
                    <TextBlock Text="Car:" Margin="5,0,0,0" />
                    <TextBlock Text="{Binding Car}" Margin="5,0,0,0" />
                    <TextBlock Text="Points:" Margin="5,0,0,0" />
                    <TextBlock Text="{Binding Points}" />
                </StackPanel>
            </DataTemplate>
        </DataGrid.RowDetailsTemplate>
```

Grouping with the DataGrid

The Formula-1 races have several rows that contain the same information, such as the year and the country. For such data, grouping can be helpful to organize the information for the user.

For grouping, the `CollectionViewSource` can be used in XAML code that supports grouping, sorting, and filtering. With code-behind you can also use the `ListCollectionView` class, which is used only by the `CollectionViewSource`.

`CollectionViewSource` is defined within a `Resources` collection. The source of `CollectionViewSource` is the result from an `ObjectDataProvider`. The `ObjectDataProvider` invokes the `GetRaces()` method of the `F1Races` type. This method has two `int` parameters that are assigned from the `MethodParameters` collection. The `CollectionViewSource` uses two descriptions for grouping, first by the `Year` property and then by the `Country` property:

```
        <Grid.Resources>
            <ObjectDataProvider x:Key="races" ObjectType="{x:Type local:F1Races}"
                            MethodName="GetRaces">
                <ObjectDataProvider.MethodParameters>
                    <sys:Int32>0</sys:Int32>
                    <sys:Int32>20</sys:Int32>
                </ObjectDataProvider.MethodParameters>
            </ObjectDataProvider>
            <CollectionViewSource x:Key="viewSource"
                            Source="{StaticResource races}">
                <CollectionViewSource.GroupDescriptions>
                    <PropertyGroupDescription PropertyName="Year" />
                    <PropertyGroupDescription PropertyName="Country" />
                </CollectionViewSource.GroupDescriptions>
            </CollectionViewSource>
        </Grid.Resources>
```

How the group is displayed is defined with the DataGrid GroupStyle property. With the GroupStyle element you need to customize the ContainerStyle as well as the HeaderTemplate and the complete panel. To dynamically select the GroupStyle and HeaderStyle, you can also write a container style selector and a header template selector. It is very similar in functionality to the data template selector you've seen earlier.

The GroupStyle in the example sets the ContainerStyle property of the GroupStyle. With this style the GroupItem is customized with a template. The GroupItem appears as the root element of a group when grouping is used. Displayed within the group is the name, using the Name property, and the number of items, using the ItemCount property. The third column of the Grid contains all the normal items using the ItemsPresenter. If the rows are grouped by country, the labels of the Name property would all have a different width, which doesn't look good. Therefore, the SharedSizeGroup property is set with the second column of the grid to make all items the same size. The shared size scope needs to be set with all elements that have the same size. This is done in the DataGrid setting Grid.IsSharedSizeScope="True":

```xml
<DataGrid.GroupStyle>
    <GroupStyle>
        <GroupStyle.ContainerStyle>
            <Style TargetType="{x:Type GroupItem}">
                <Setter Property="Template">
                    <Setter.Value>
                        <ControlTemplate >
                            <StackPanel Orientation="Horizontal" >
                                <Grid>
                                    <Grid.ColumnDefinitions>
                                        <ColumnDefinition
                                        SharedSizeGroup="LeftColumn"
                                        />
                                        <ColumnDefinition />
                                        <ColumnDefinition />
                                    </Grid.ColumnDefinitions>
                                    <Label Grid.Column="0"
                                      Background="Yellow"
                                      Content="{Binding Name}" />
                                    <Label Grid.Column="1"
                                      Content="{Binding ItemCount}"
                                    />
                                    <Grid Grid.Column="2"
                                      HorizontalAlignment="Center"
                                      VerticalAlignment="Center">
                                        <ItemsPresenter/>
                                    </Grid>
                                </Grid>
                            </StackPanel>
                        </ControlTemplate>
                    </Setter.Value>
                </Setter>
            </Style>
        </GroupStyle.ContainerStyle>
    </GroupStyle>
</DataGrid.GroupStyle>
```

The class F1Races that is used by the ObjectDataProvider uses LINQ to access the Formula1 database and returns a list of anonymous types with Year, Country, Position, Racer, Car, and Points properties. Again, the Skip() and Take() methods are used to access part of the data:

```csharp
using System.Collections.Generic;
using System.Linq;

namespace Formula1Demo
```

```
{
    public class F1Races
    {
        private int lastpageSearched = -1;
        private IEnumerable<object> cache = null;
        private Formula1Entities data = new Formula1Entities();

        public IEnumerable<object> GetRaces(int page, int pageSize)
        {
            if (lastpageSearched == page)
                return cache;
            lastpageSearched = page;

            var q = (from r in data.Races
                     from rr in r.RaceResults
                     orderby r.Date ascending
                     select new
                     {
                         Year = r.Date.Year,
                         Country = r.Circuit.Country,
                         Position = rr.Position,
                         Racer = rr.Racer.Firstname + " " + rr.Racer.Lastname,
                         Car = rr.Team.Name,
                         Points = rr.Points
                     }).Skip(page * pageSize).Take(pageSize);
            cache = q;
            return cache;
        }
    }
}
```

code snippet Formula1Demo/F1Races.cs

Now all that's left is for the user to set the page number and change the parameter of the `ObjectDataProvider`. In the user interface a `TextBox` and a `Button` are defined:

Available for download on Wrox.com

```xml
<StackPanel Orientation="Horizontal" Grid.Row="0">
    <TextBlock Margin="5" Padding="4"
               VerticalAlignment="Center">Page:</TextBlock>
    <TextBox Margin="5" Padding="4" VerticalAlignment="Center"
             x:Name="textPageNumber" Text="0" />
    <Button Click="OnGetPage">Get Page</Button>
</StackPanel>
```

code snippet Formula1Demo/GridGroupingUC.xaml

The `OnGetPage()` handler of the button in the code-behind accesses the `ObjectDataProvider` and changes the first parameter of the method. It then invokes the `Refresh` method so the `ObjectDataProvider` requests the new page:

Available for download on Wrox.com

```csharp
private void OnGetPage(object sender, RoutedEventArgs e)
{
    int page = int.Parse(textPageNumber.Text);
    var odp = (sender as FrameworkElement).FindResource("races")
                  as ObjectDataProvider;
    odp.MethodParameters[0] = page;
    odp.Refresh();
}
```

code snippet Formula1Demo/GridGroupingUC.xaml.cs

After running the application you can see grouping and row detail information, as shown in Figure 36-16.

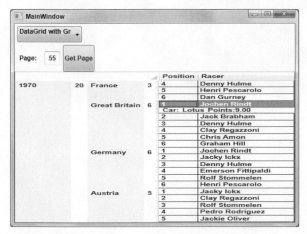

FIGURE 36-16

SUMMARY

This chapter covered some features of WPF that are extremely important for business applications.

WPF data binding gives a leap forward. You can bind any property of a .NET class to a property of a WPF element. The binding mode defines the direction of the binding. You can bind .NET objects and lists, and define a data template to create a default look for a .NET class with a data template.

Command binding makes it possible to map handler code to menus and toolbars. You've also seen how easy it is to copy and paste with WPF because a command handler for this technology is already included in the TextBox control.

The next chapter goes into another facet of WPF: documents with WPF.

37

Creating Documents with WPF

WHAT'S IN THIS CHAPTER?

➤ Creating flow documents

➤ Creating fixed documents

➤ Creating XPS documents

➤ Printing documents

Creating documents is a large part of WPF. The namespace `System.Windows.Documents` supports creating flow and fixed documents. This namespace contains elements with which you can have a rich Word-like experience with flow documents, and create WYSIWYG fixed documents.

Flow documents are geared towards screen reading; the content of the document is arranged based on the size of the window, and the flow of the document changes if the window is resized. *Fixed documents* are mainly used for printing and page-oriented content and the content is always arranged in the same way.

This chapter teaches you how to create and print flow and fixed documents, and covers the namespaces `System.Windows.Documents`, `System.Windows.Xps` and `System.IO.Packaging`.

TEXT ELEMENTS

To build the content of documents, you need document elements. The base class of these elements is `TextElement`. This class defines common properties for font settings, foreground and background, and text effects. `TextElement` is the base class for the classes `Block` and `Inline` whose functionality is explored in the following sections.

Fonts

An important aspect of text is the look of the text and thus the font. With the `TextElement`, the font can be specified with the properties `FontWeight`, `FontStyle`, `FontStretch`, `FontSize`, and `FontFamily`.

➤ Predefined `FontWeight` values are defined by the `FontWeights` class, which offers values such as `UltraLight`, `Light`, `Medium`, `Normal`, `Bold`, `UltraBold`, and `Heavy`.

➤ `FontStyle` values are defined by the `FontStyles` class that offers `Normal`, `Italic`, and `Oblique`.

➤ With `FontStretch` you can specify the degrees to stretch the font compared to the normal aspect ratio. `FrontStretch` defines predefined stretches that range from 50% (`UltraCondensed`) to 200% (`UltraExpanded`). Predefined values in between the range are `ExtraCondensed` (62.5%), `Condensed` (75%), `SemiCondensed` (87.5%), `Normal` (100%), `SemiExpanded` (112.5%), `Expanded` (125%), `ExtraExpanded` (150%)

➤ `FontSize` is of type `double` where you can specify the size of the font in device-independent units, inches, centimeters, and points.

➤ With `FontFamily` you define the name of the preferred font-family, e.g., `Arial` or `Times New Roman`. With this property you can specify a list of font family names so if one font is not available, the next one in the list is used. (If neither the selected font nor the alternate font are available, a flow document falls back to the default `MessageFontFamily`.) You can also reference a font family from a resource or use a URI to reference a font from a server. With fixed documents there's no fallback on a font not available because the font is available with the document.

To give you a feel for the look of different fonts, the following sample WPF application includes a `ListBox`. The `ListBox` defines an `ItemTemplate` for every item in the list. This template uses four `TextBlock` elements where the `FontFamily` is bound to the `Source` property of a `FontFamily` object. With different `TextBlock` elements `FontWeight` and `FontStyle` are set:

```xml
<ListBox ItemsSource="{Binding}">
    <ListBox.ItemTemplate>
        <DataTemplate>
            <StackPanel Orientation="Horizontal" >
                <TextBlock Margin="3, 0, 3, 0"
                    FontFamily="{Binding Path=Source}"
                    FontSize="18" Text="{Binding Path=Source}" />
                <TextBlock Margin="3, 0, 3, 0"
                    FontFamily="{Binding Path=Source}"
                    FontSize="18" FontStyle="Italic" Text="Italic" />
                <TextBlock Margin="3, 0, 3, 0"
                    FontFamily="{Binding Path=Source}"
                    FontSize="18" FontWeight="UltraBold"
                    Text="UltraBold" />
                <TextBlock Margin="3, 0, 3, 0"
                    FontFamily="{Binding Path=Source}"
                    FontSize="18" FontWeight="UltraLight"
                    Text="UltraLight" />
            </StackPanel>
        </DataTemplate>
    </ListBox.ItemTemplate>
</ListBox>
```

code snippet ShowFonts/ShowFontsWindow.xaml

In the code-behind, the data context is set to the result of the `SystemFontFamilies` property of the `System.Windows.Media.Font` class:

```csharp
public partial class ShowFontsWindow : Window
{
    public ShowFontsWindow()
    {
        InitializeComponent();

        this.DataContext = Fonts.SystemFontFamilies;
    }
}
```

code snippet ShowFonts/ShowFontsWindow.xaml.cs

Running the application, you get a large list of system font families with italic, bold, ultrabold, and ultralight characteristics, as shown in Figure 37-1.

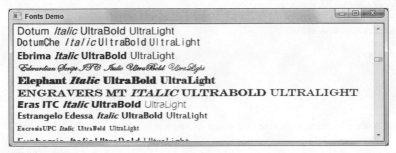

FIGURE 37-1

TextEffect

Next let's have a look into `TextEffect`, as it is also common to all document elements. `TextEffect` is defined in the namespace `System.Windows.Media` and derives from the base class `Animatable` that allows animation of text.

`TextEffect` allows you to animate a clipping region, the foreground brush, and a transformation. With the properties `PositionStart` and `PositionCount` you specify the position in the text the animation applies to.

For applying the text effects, the `TextEffects` property of a `Run` element is set. The `TextEffect` element specified within the property defines a foreground and a transformation. For the foreground, a `SolidColorBrush` with the name `brush1` is used that is animated with a `ColorAnimation` element. The transformation makes use of `ScaleTransformation` with the name `scale1` that is animated from two `DoubleAnimation` elements:

```xml
<TextBlock>
    <TextBlock.Triggers>
        <EventTrigger RoutedEvent="TextBlock.Loaded">
            <BeginStoryboard>
                <Storyboard>
                    <ColorAnimation AutoReverse="True" RepeatBehavior="Forever"
                                    From="Red" To="Yellow" Duration="0:0:3"
                                    Storyboard.TargetName="brush1"
                                    Storyboard.TargetProperty="Color" />
                    <DoubleAnimation AutoReverse="True"
                                    RepeatBehavior="Forever"
                                    From="0.2" To="12" Duration="0:0:6"
                                    Storyboard.TargetName="scale1"
                                    Storyboard.TargetProperty="ScaleX" />
                    <DoubleAnimation AutoReverse="True"
                                    RepeatBehavior="Forever"
                                    From="0.2" To="12" Duration="0:0:6"
                                    Storyboard.TargetName="scale1"
                                    Storyboard.TargetProperty="ScaleY" />
                </Storyboard>
            </BeginStoryboard>
        </EventTrigger>
    </TextBlock.Triggers>
    <Run FontFamily="Mangal">
        cn|elements
        <Run.TextEffects>
            <TextEffect PositionStart="0" PositionCount="30" >
```

```
            <TextEffect.Foreground>
                <SolidColorBrush x:Name="brush1" Color="Blue" />
            </TextEffect.Foreground>
            <TextEffect.Transform>
                <ScaleTransform x:Name="scale1" ScaleX="3" ScaleY="3" />
            </TextEffect.Transform>
          </TextEffect>
        </Run.TextEffects>
      </Run>
  </TextBlock>
```

code snippet TextEffectsDemo/MainWindow.xaml

Running the application, you can see the changes in size and color as shown in Figures 37-2 and 37-3.

 With pure XAML samples you can also use XAMLPad.exe to enter the code instead of creating an executable. This tool is part of the Windows SDK.

FIGURE 37-2

FIGURE 37-3

Inline

The base class for all inline flow content elements is Inline. You can use Inline elements within a paragraph of a flow document. Because within a paragraph one Inline element can be after another, the Inline class provides the PreviousInline and NextInline properties to navigate from one element to another. You can also get a collection of all peer inlines with SiblingInlines.

The Run element that was used earlier to write some text is an Inline element for formatted or unformatted text, but there are many more. A new line after a Run element can be done with the LineBreak element.

The Span element derives from the Inline class and allows grouping of Inline elements. Only Inline elements are allowed within the content of Span. The self-explanatory Bold, Hyperlink, Italic, and Underline classes all derive from Span and thus have the same functionality to allow Inline elements as its content, but act on these elements differently. The following XAML code demonstrates using Bold, Italic, Underline, and LineBreak, as shown in Figure 37-4.

```xaml
<Paragraph FontWeight="Normal">
    <Span>
        <Span>Normal</Span>
        <Bold>Bold</Bold>
        <Italic>Italic</Italic>
        <LineBreak />
        <Underline>Underline</Underline>
    </Span>
</Paragraph>
```

code snippet FlowDocumentsDemo/FlowDocument1.xaml

AnchoredBlock is an abstract class that derives from Inline and is used to anchor Block elements to flow content. Figure and Floater are concrete classes that derive from AnchoredBlock. Because these two inline elements become interesting in relation to blocks, these elements are discussed later in this chapter.

FIGURE 37-4

Another Inline element that maps UI elements that have been used in the previous chapters is InlineUIContainer. InlineUIContainer allows adding all UIElement objects (for example, a Button) to the document. The following code segment adds an InlineUIContainer with ComboBox, RadioButton, and TextBox elements to the document. The result is shown in Figure 37-5.

FIGURE 37-5

Of course you can also style the UI elements as shown in Chapter 35, "Core WPF."

```xaml
<Paragraph TextAlignment="Center" >
    <Span FontSize="36">
        <Italic>cn|elements</Italic>
    </Span>
    <LineBreak />
    <LineBreak />
    <InlineUIContainer>
        <Grid>
            <Grid.RowDefinitions>
                <RowDefinition />
                <RowDefinition />
            </Grid.RowDefinitions>
            <Grid.ColumnDefinitions>
                <ColumnDefinition />
                <ColumnDefinition />
            </Grid.ColumnDefinitions>
            <ComboBox Width="140"  Margin="3"  Grid.Row="0">
                <ComboBoxItem>Filet Mignon</ComboBoxItem>
                <ComboBoxItem>Rib Eye</ComboBoxItem>
                <ComboBoxItem>Sirloin</ComboBoxItem>
            </ComboBox>

            <StackPanel Grid.Row="0" Grid.RowSpan="2" Grid.Column="1">
                <RadioButton>Raw</RadioButton>
                <RadioButton>Medium</RadioButton>
                <RadioButton>Well done</RadioButton>
```

```
        </StackPanel>
        <TextBox Grid.Row="1" Grid.Column="0" Width="140"></TextBox>
    </Grid>
</InlineUIContainer>
</Paragraph>
```

code snippet FlowDocumentsDemo/FlowDocument2.xaml

Block

`Block` is an abstract base class for block-level elements. Blocks allow grouping elements contained to specific views. Common with all blocks are the properties `PreviousBlock`, `NextBlock`, and `SiblingBlocks` that allow you to navigate from block to block. Setting `BreakPageBefore` and `BreakColumnBefore` page and column breaks are done before the block starts. A `Block` also defines a border with the `BorderBrush` and `BorderThickness` properties.

Classes that derive from `Block` are `Paragraph`, `Section`, `List`, `Table`, and `BlockUIContainer`. `BlockUI Container` is similar to `InlineUIContainer` in that you can add elements that derive from `UIElement`.

`Paragraph` and `Section` are simple blocks where `Paragraph` contains inline elements; `Section` is used to group other `Block` elements. With the `Paragraph` block you can determine whether a page or column break is allowed within the paragraph or between paragraphs. `KeepTogether` can be used to disallow breaking within the paragraph; `KeepWithNext` tries to keep one paragraph and the next together. If a paragraph is broken by a page or column break, `MinWidowLines` defines the minimum number of lines that are placed after the break and `MinOrphanLines` defines the minimum number of lines before the break.

The `Paragraph` block also allows decorating the text within the paragraph with `TextDecoration` elements. Predefined text decorations are defined by `TextDecorations`: `Baseline`, `Overline`, `Strikethrough`, and `Underline`.

The following XAML code shows multiple `Paragraph` elements. One `Paragraph` element with a title follows another with the content belonging to this title. These two paragraphs are connected with the attribute `KeepWithNext`. It's also assured that the paragraph with the content is not broken by setting `KeepTogether` to `True`. The result is shown in Figure 37-6.

```
<FlowDocument xmlns="http://schemas.microsoft.com/winfx/2006/xaml/presentation"
              ColumnWidth="300" FontSize="16" FontFamily="Georgia">
    <Paragraph FontSize="36">
        <Run>Lyrics</Run>
    </Paragraph>

    <Paragraph TextIndent="10"  FontSize="24" KeepWithNext="True">
        <Bold>
            <Run>Mary had a little lamb</Run>
        </Bold>
    </Paragraph>

    <Paragraph KeepTogether="True">
        <Run>
            Mary had a little lamb,
        </Run>
        <LineBreak />
        <Run>
            little lamb, little lamb,
        </Run>
        <LineBreak />
        <Run>
            Mary had a little lamb,
        </Run>
        <LineBreak />
        <Run>
            whose fleece was white as snow.
        </Run>
```

```
                <LineBreak />
                <Run>
                    And everywhere that Mary went,
                </Run>
                <LineBreak />
                <Run>
                    Mary went, Mary went,
                </Run>
                <LineBreak />
                <Run>
                    and everywhere that Mary went,
                </Run>
                <LineBreak />
                <Run>
                    the lamb was sure to go.
                </Run>
        </Paragraph>

        <Paragraph TextIndent="10" FontSize="24" KeepWithNext="True">
            <Bold>
                <Run>Humpty Dumpty</Run>
            </Bold>
        </Paragraph>
        <Paragraph KeepTogether="True">
            <Run>Humpty dumpty sat on a wall</Run>
            <LineBreak />
            <Run>
                Humpty dumpty had a great fall</Run>
            <LineBreak />
            <Run>
                All the King's horses</Run>
            <LineBreak />
            <Run>
                And all the King's men</Run>
            <LineBreak />
            <Run>
                Couldn't put Humpty together again
            </Run>
        </Paragraph>
    </FlowDocument>
```

code snippet FlowDocumentsDemo/ParagraphDemo.xaml

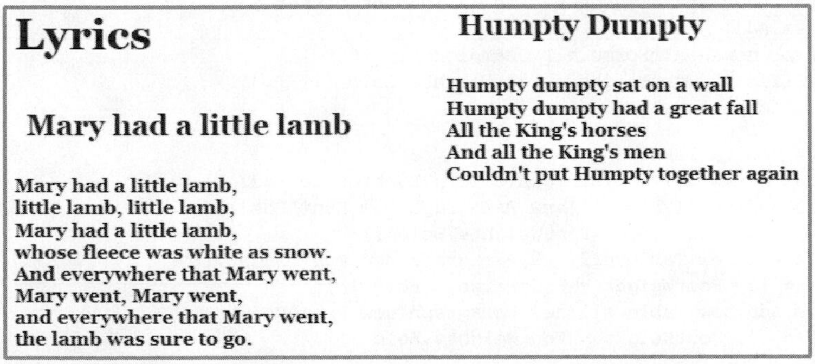

Lyrics

Mary had a little lamb

Mary had a little lamb,
little lamb, little lamb,
Mary had a little lamb,
whose fleece was white as snow.
And everywhere that Mary went,
Mary went, Mary went,
and everywhere that Mary went,
the lamb was sure to go.

Humpty Dumpty

Humpty dumpty sat on a wall
Humpty dumpty had a great fall
All the King's horses
And all the King's men
Couldn't put Humpty together again

FIGURE 37-6

Lists

The List class is used to create textual unordered or ordered lists. List defines the bullet style of its items by setting the MarkerStyle property. MarkerStyle is of type TextMarkerStyle and can be a number (Decimal), a letter (LowerLatin and UpperLatin), a roman numeral (LowerRoman and `UpperRoman`), or a graphic (`Disc`, `Circle`, `Square`, `Box`). `List` can only contain `ListItem` elements which in turn can only contain `Block` elements.

Defining the following list with XAML results in the output shown in Figure 37-7.

FIGURE 37-7

Available for
download on
Wrox.com

```xaml
<List MarkerStyle="Square">
    <ListItem>
        <Paragraph>Monday</Paragraph>
    </ListItem>
    <ListItem>
        <Paragraph>Tuesday</Paragraph>
    </ListItem>
    <ListItem>
        <Paragraph>Wednesday</Paragraph>
    </ListItem>
</List>
```

code snippet FlowDocumentsDemo/ListDemo.xaml

Tables

The `Table` class is very similar to the `Grid` class that was presented in Chapter 35 to define rows and columns. The following example demonstrates creating a `FlowDocument` with a `Table`. To create tables you can add `TableColumn` objects to the `Columns` property. With `TableColumn` you can specify the width and background.

The `Table` also contains `TableRowGroup` objects. The `TableRowGroup` has a `Rows` property where `TableRow` objects can be added. The `TableRow` class defines a `Cells` property where `TableCell` objects can be added. `TableCell` objects can contain any `Block` element. Here a `Paragraph` is used that contains the `Inline` element `Run`:

Available for
download on
Wrox.com

```csharp
var doc = new FlowDocument();
var t1 = new Table();
t1.Columns.Add(new TableColumn
    { Width = new GridLength(50, GridUnitType.Pixel) });
t1.Columns.Add(new TableColumn
    { Width = new GridLength(1, GridUnitType.Auto) });
t1.Columns.Add(new TableColumn
    { Width = new GridLength(1, GridUnitType.Auto) });

var titleRow = new TableRow();
titleRow.Background = new SolidColorBrush(Colors.LightBlue);
var titleCell = new TableCell
    { ColumnSpan = 3, TextAlignment = TextAlignment.Center };
titleCell.Blocks.Add(
    new Paragraph(new Run("Formula 1 Championship 2009")
        { FontSize=24, FontWeight = FontWeights.Bold }));
titleRow.Cells.Add(titleCell);

var headerRow = new TableRow
    { Background = new SolidColorBrush(Colors.LightGoldenrodYellow) };
headerRow.Cells.Add(new TableCell(new Paragraph(new Run("Pos"))
    { FontSize = 14, FontWeight=FontWeights.Bold}));
headerRow.Cells.Add(new TableCell(new Paragraph(new Run("Name"))
    { FontSize = 14, FontWeight = FontWeights.Bold }));
headerRow.Cells.Add(new TableCell(new Paragraph(new Run("Points"))
    { FontSize = 14, FontWeight = FontWeights.Bold }));

var row1 = new TableRow();
row1.Cells.Add(new TableCell(new Paragraph(new Run("1."))));
row1.Cells.Add(new TableCell(new Paragraph(
                            new Run("Jenson Button"))));
row1.Cells.Add(new TableCell(new Paragraph(new Run("95"))));

var row2 = new TableRow { Background =
```

```
                                new SolidColorBrush(Colors.LightGray)};
        row2.Cells.Add(new TableCell(new Paragraph(new Run("2."))));
        row2.Cells.Add(new TableCell(new Paragraph(new Run("Sebastian Vettel"))));
        row2.Cells.Add(new TableCell(new Paragraph(new Run("84"))));

        var row3 = new TableRow();
        row3.Cells.Add(new TableCell(new Paragraph(new Run("3."))));
        row3.Cells.Add(new TableCell(new Paragraph(
                                    new Run("Rubens Barrichello"))));
        row3.Cells.Add(new TableCell(new Paragraph(new Run("77"))));

        var rowGroup = new TableRowGroup();
        rowGroup.Rows.Add(titleRow);
        rowGroup.Rows.Add(headerRow);
        rowGroup.Rows.Add(row1);
        rowGroup.Rows.Add(row2);
        rowGroup.Rows.Add(row3);
        t1.RowGroups.Add(rowGroup);

        doc.Blocks.Add(t1);

        reader.Document = doc;
```

code snippet TableDemo/MainWindow.xaml

Running the application, you can see the nicely formatted table as shown in Figure 37-8.

Anchor to Blocks

Now that you've learned about the `Inline` and `Block` elements, you can combine the two by using the `Inline` elements of type `AnchoredBlock`. `AnchoredBlock` is an abstract base class with two concrete implementations, `Figure` and `Floater`.

Formula 1 Championship 2009		
Pos	Name	Points
1.	Jenson Button	95
2.	Sebastian Vettel	84
3.	Rubens Barrichello	77

FIGURE 37-8

The `Floater` displays its content parallel to the main content with the properties `HorizontalAlignment` and `Width`.

Starting from the earlier example, a new paragraph is added that contains a `Floater`. This `Floater` is aligned to the left and has a width of 160. As you can see in Figure 37-9, the next paragraph flows around it.

```
<Paragraph TextIndent="10" FontSize="24" KeepWithNext="True">
    <Bold>
        <Run>Mary had a little lamb</Run>
    </Bold>
</Paragraph>
<Paragraph>
    <Floater HorizontalAlignment="Left" Width="160">
        <Paragraph Background="LightGray">
            <Run>Sarah Josepha Hale</Run>
        </Paragraph>
    </Floater>
</Paragraph>
<Paragraph KeepTogether="True">
    <Run>
        Mary had a little lamb
    </Run>
    <LineBreak />
    <!-- ... -->
</Paragraph>
```

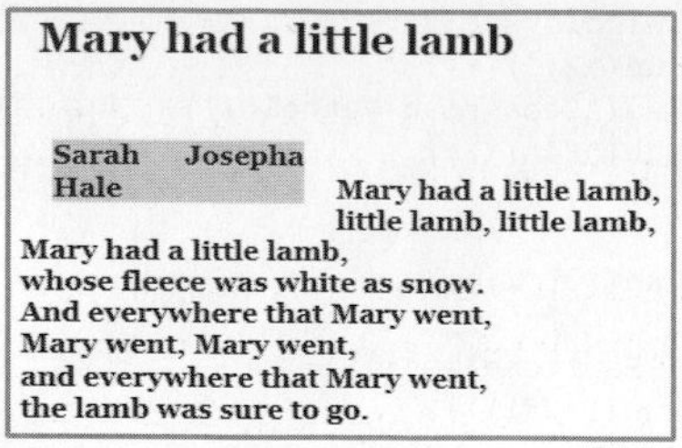

FIGURE 37-9

A `Figure` aligns horizontally and vertically and can be anchored to the page, content, a column, or a paragraph. The `Figure` in the following code is anchored to the page center but with a horizontal and vertical offset. The `WrapDirection` is set so that both left and right columns wrap around the figure. Figure 37-10 shows the result of the wrap:

```
<Paragraph>
    <Figure HorizontalAnchor="PageCenter" HorizontalOffset="20"
        VerticalAnchor="PageCenter" VerticalOffset="20" WrapDirection="Both" >
        <Paragraph Background="LightGray" FontSize="24">
            <Run>Lyrics Samples</Run>
        </Paragraph>
    </Figure>
</Paragraph>
```

FIGURE 37-10

`Floater` and `Figure` are both used to add content that is not in the main flow. Although these two features seem similar, the characteristics of these elements are quite different. The following table explains the differences between `Floater` and `Figure`.

CHARACTERISTICS	FLOATER	FIGURE
Position	A floater cannot be positioned. It is rendered where space is available.	A figure can be positioned with horizontal and vertical anchors. It can be docked relative to the page, content, column, or paragraph.
Width	A floater can be placed only within one column. If the width is set larger than the column size, it is ignored.	A figure can be sized across multiple columns. The width of a figure can be set to 0.5 pages or 2 columns.
Pagination	If a floater is larger than a column height, the floater breaks and paginates to the next column or page.	If a figure is larger than a column height, only the part of the figure that fits in the column is rendered; the other content is lost.

FLOW DOCUMENTS

With all the `Inline` and `Block` elements, now you know what should be put into a flow document. The class `FlowDocument` can contain `Block` elements, and the `Block` elements can contain `Block` or `Inline` elements, depending on the type of the `Block`.

A major functionality of the `FlowDocument` class is that it is used to break up the flow into multiple pages. This is done via the `IDocumentPaginatorSource` interface that is implemented by `FlowDocument`.

Other options with a `FlowDocument` are to set up the default font and foreground and background brushes, and to configure the page and column sizes.

The following XAML code for the `FlowDocument` defines a default font and font size, a column width, and also a ruler between columns:

```
<FlowDocument xmlns="http://schemas.microsoft.com/winfx/2006/xaml/presentation"
              ColumnWidth="300" FontSize="16" FontFamily="Georgia"
              ColumnRuleWidth="3" ColumnRuleBrush="Violet">
```

Now you just need a way to view the documents. The following list describes several viewers:

➤ `RichTextBox` — A simple viewer that also allows editing (as long as the `IsReadOnly` property is not set to `true`). The `RichTextBox` doesn't display the document with multiple columns but instead in scroll mode. This is similar to the Web layout in Microsoft Word. The scrollbar can be enabled by setting the `HorizontalScrollbarVisibility` to `ScrollbarVisibility.Auto`.

➤ `FlowDocumentsScrollViewer` — A reader that is meant only to read but not edit documents. This reader allows zooming into the document. There's also a toolbar with a slider for zooming that can be enabled with the property `IsToolbarEnabled`. Settings such as `CanIncreaseZoom`, `CanDecreaseZoom`, `MinZoom`, and `MaxZoom` allow setting the zoom features.

➤ `FlowDocumentPageViewer` — A viewer that paginates the document. With this viewer you not only have a toolbar to zoom into the document, but can also switch from page to page.

➤ `FlowDocumentReader` — A viewer that combines the functionality of `FlowDocumentScrollViewer` and `FlowDocumentPageViewer`. This viewer supports different viewing modes that can be set from the toolbar or with the property `ViewingMode` that is of type `FlowDocumentReaderViewingMode`. This enumeration has the possible values `Page`, `TwoPage`, and `Scroll`. The viewing modes can also be disabled according to your needs.

Figure 37-11 shows the previously created flow document with the `FlowDocumentReader` in `TwoPage` mode.

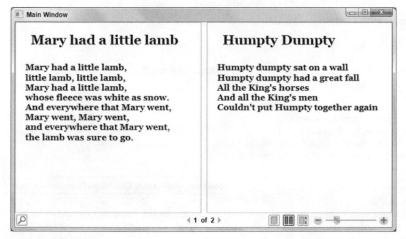

FIGURE 37-11

FIXED DOCUMENTS

Fixed documents always define the same look, the same pagination, and use the same fonts — no matter where the document is copied or used. WPF defines the class `FixedDocument` that can be used to create fixed documents, and the class `DocumentViewer` to view fixed documents.

This chapter uses a sample application to create a fixed document programmatically by requesting user input for a menu plan which is used to create a fixed document. Figure 37-12 shows the main user interface of this application, where the user can select a day with the `DatePicker` class, enter menus for a week in a `DataGrid`, and click the Create Doc button to create a new `FixedDocument`. This application uses `Page` objects that are navigated within a `NavigationWindow`. Clicking the Create Doc button navigates to a new page that contains the fixed document.

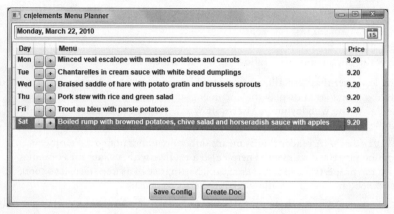

FIGURE 37-12

The event handler for the Create Doc button, `OnCreateDoc()`, navigates to a new page. To do this, the handler instantiates the new page, `DocumentPage`. This page includes a handler, `NavigationService_LoadCompleted()`, that is assigned to the `LoadCompleted` event of the `NavigationService`. Within this handler the new page can access the content that is passed to the page. Then the navigation is done by invoking the `Navigate()` method to `page2`. The new page receives the object `menus` that contain all the menu information that is needed to build up the fixed page. The `menus` variable is of type `ObservableCollection<MenuEntry>`:

```csharp
private void OnCreateDoc(object sender, RoutedEventArgs e)
{
    if (menus.Count == 0)
    {
        MessageBox.Show("Select a date first", "Menu Planner",
            MessageBoxButton.OK);
        return;
    }
    var page2 = new DocumentPage();
    NavigationService.LoadCompleted +=
        page2.NavigationService_LoadCompleted;
    NavigationService.Navigate(page2, menus);
}
```

code snippet CreateXps/MenuPlannerPage.xaml.cs

Within the `DocumentPage`, a `DocumentViewer` is used to give read access to the fixed document. The fixed document is created in the method `NavigationService_LoadCompleted`. With the event handler, the data that is passed from the first page is received with the `ExtraData` property of `NavigationEventArgs`.

The received `ObservableCollection<MenuEntry>` is assigned to the `menus` variable that is used to build up the fixed page:

```
internal void NavigationService_LoadCompleted(object sender,
                                              NavigationEventArgs e)
{
    menus = e.ExtraData as ObservableCollection<MenuEntry>;

    fixedDocument = new FixedDocument();
    var pageContent1 = new PageContent();
    fixedDocument.Pages.Add(pageContent1);
    var page1 = new FixedPage();
    pageContent1.Child = page1;
    page1.Children.Add(GetHeaderContent());
    page1.Children.Add(GetLogoContent());
    page1.Children.Add(GetDateContent());
    page1.Children.Add(GetMenuContent());

    viewer.Document = fixedDocument;

    NavigationService.LoadCompleted -= NavigationService_LoadCompleted;
}
```

code snippet CreateXps/DocumentPage.xaml.cs

Fixed documents are created with the `FixedDocument` class. The `FixedDocument` element only contains `PageContent` elements that are accessible via the `Pages` property. The `PageContent` elements must be added to the document in the order they should appear on the page. `PageContent` defines the content of a single page.

`PageContent` has a `Child` property such that a `FixedPage` can be associated with it. To the `FixedPage` you can add elements of type `UIElement` to the `Children` collection. This is where you can add all the elements you've learned about in the last two chapters, including a `TextBlock` element that itself can contain `Inline` and `Block` elements.

In the sample code, the children to the `FixedPage` are created with helper methods `GetHeaderContent()`, `GetLogoContent()`, `GetDateContent()`, and `GetMenuContent()`.

The method `GetHeaderContent()` creates a `TextBlock` that is returned. The `TextBlock` has the `Inline` element `Bold` added, which in turn has the `Run` element added. The `Run` element then contains the header text for the document. With `FixedPage.SetLeft()` and `FixedPage.SetTop()` the position of the `TextBox` within the fixed page is defined:

```
private UIElement GetHeaderContent()
{
    var text1 = new TextBlock();
    text1.FontFamily = new FontFamily("Mangal");
    text1.FontSize = 34;
    text1.HorizontalAlignment = HorizontalAlignment.Center;
    text1.Inlines.Add(new Bold(new Run("cn|elements")));
    FixedPage.SetLeft(text1, 170);
    FixedPage.SetTop(text1, 40);
    return text1;
}
```

The method `GetLogoContent()` adds a logo in the form of an `Ellipse` with a `RadialGradientBrush` to the fixed document:

```
private UIElement GetLogoContent()
{
    var ellipse = new Ellipse
    {
        Width = 90,
```

```
        Height = 40,
        Fill = new RadialGradientBrush(Colors.Yellow, Colors.DarkRed)
    };

    FixedPage.SetLeft(ellipse, 500);
    FixedPage.SetTop(ellipse, 50);
    return ellipse;
}
```

The method `GetDateContent()` accesses the `menus` collection to add a date range to the document:

```
private UIElement GetDateContent()
{
    string dateString = String.Format("{0:d} to {1:d}",
        menus[0].Day, menus[menus.Count - 1].Day);
    var text1 = new TextBlock
    {
        FontSize = 24,
        HorizontalAlignment = HorizontalAlignment.Center
    };
    text1.Inlines.Add(new Bold(new Run(dateString)));
    FixedPage.SetLeft(text1, 130);
    FixedPage.SetTop(text1, 90);
    return text1;
}
```

Finally the method `GetMenuContent()` creates and returns a `Grid` control. This grid contains columns and rows that contain the date, menu, and price information:

```
private UIElement GetMenuContent()
{
    var grid1 = new Grid { ShowGridLines = true };

    grid1.ColumnDefinitions.Add(new ColumnDefinition
                                { Width= new GridLength(50)});
    grid1.ColumnDefinitions.Add(new ColumnDefinition
                                { Width = new GridLength(300)});
    grid1.ColumnDefinitions.Add(new ColumnDefinition
                                { Width = new GridLength(70) });

    for (int i = 0; i < menus.Count; i++)
    {
        grid1.RowDefinitions.Add(new RowDefinition
                                { Height = new GridLength(40) });

        var t1 = new TextBlock(
            new Run(String.Format("{0:ddd}", menus[i].Day)));
        t1.VerticalAlignment = VerticalAlignment.Center;
        t1.Margin = new Thickness(5, 2, 5, 2);
        Grid.SetColumn(t1, 0);
        Grid.SetRow(t1, i);
        grid1.Children.Add(t1);

        var t2 = new TextBlock(new Run(menus[i].Menu));
        t2.VerticalAlignment = VerticalAlignment.Center;
        t2.Margin = new Thickness(5, 2, 5, 2);
        Grid.SetColumn(t2, 1);
        Grid.SetRow(t2, i);
        grid1.Children.Add(t2);

        var t3 = new TextBlock(new Run(menus[i].Price.ToString()));
        t3.VerticalAlignment = VerticalAlignment.Center;
        t3.Margin = new Thickness(5, 2, 5, 2);
        Grid.SetColumn(t3, 2);
```

```
            Grid.SetRow(t3, i);
            grid1.Children.Add(t3);
        }

        FixedPage.SetLeft(grid1, 100);
        FixedPage.SetTop(grid1, 140);
        return grid1;
    }
```

Run the application to see the created fixed document shown in Figure 37-13.

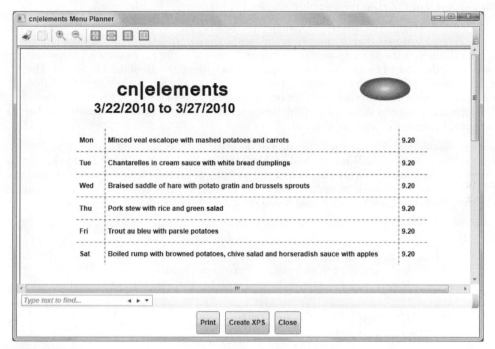

FIGURE 37-13

XPS DOCUMENTS

With Microsoft Word you can save a document as a PDF or XPS file. Since Word 2007 SP2 this feature is included with Microsoft Word. If you have Word 2007 but didn't install SP2 yet you can download the add-on for free. XPS is the *XML Paper Specification*, a subset of WPF. Windows includes an XPS reader.

.NET includes classes and interfaces to read and write XPS documents with the namespaces `System.Windows.Xps`, `System.Windows.Xps.Packaging`, and `System.IO.Packaging`.

XPS is packaged within the ZIP file format, so you can easily analyze an XPS document by renaming a file with an `.xps` extension to `.zip` and opening the archive..

An XPS file requires a specific structure in the zipped document that is defined by the XML Paper Specifications (which you can download from `http://www.microsoft.com/whdc/xps/xpsspec.mspx`). The structure is based on the Open Packaging Convention (OPC) that Word documents (OOXML or Office Open XML) are based on as well. Within such a file you can find different folders for metadata, resources (such as fonts and pictures), and the document itself. Within the document folder of an XPS document you can find the XAML code representing the XPS subset of XAML.

To create an XPS document, you use the `XpsDocument` class from the namespace `System.Windows` `.Xps.Packaging`. To use this class, you will need to reference the assembly `ReachFramework` as well. With this class you can add a thumbnail (`AddThumbnail()`) and fixed document sequences (`AddFixedDocumentSequence()`) to the document, as well as digitally sign the document. A fixed document sequence is written by using the interface `IXpsFixedDocumentSequenceWriter` that in turn uses an `IXpsFixedDocumentWriter` to write the document within the sequence.

If a `FixedDocument` already exists, there's an easier way to write the XPS document. Instead of adding every resource and every document page, you can use the class `XpsDocumentWriter` from the namespace `System.Windows.Xps`. For this class the assembly `System.Printing` must be referenced.

With the following code snippet you can see the handler to create the XPS document. First, a filename for the menu plan is created that uses a week number in addition to the name `menuplan`. The week number is calculated with the help of the `GregorianCalendar` class. Then the `SaveFileDialog` is opened to let the user overwrite the created filename and select the directory where the file should be stored. The `SaveFileDialog` class is defined in the namespace `Microsoft.Win32` and wraps the native file dialog. Then a new `XpsDocument` is created where the filename is passed to the constructor. Recall that the XPS file uses a ZIP format to compress the content. With the `CompressionOption` you can specify whether the compression should be optimized on time or space.

Next, an `XpsDocumentWriter` is created with the help of the static method `XpsDocument.` `CreateXpsDocumentWriter()`. The Write method of the `XpsDocumentWriter` is overloaded to accept different content or content parts to write the document. Examples of acceptable options with the `Write()` method are `FixedDocumentSequence`, `FixedDocument`, `FixedPage`, `string`, and a `DocumentPaginator`. In the sample code, only the `fixedDocument` that was created earlier is passed:

Available for
download on
Wrox.com

```csharp
private void OnCreateXPS(object sender, RoutedEventArgs e)
{
    var c = new GregorianCalendar();
    int weekNumber = c.GetWeekOfYear(menus[0].Day,
        CalendarWeekRule.FirstFourDayWeek, DayOfWeek.Monday);
    string fileName = String.Format("menuplan{0}", weekNumber);

    var dlg = new SaveFileDialog
    {
        FileName = fileName,
        DefaultExt = "xps",
        Filter = "XPS Documents|*.xps|All Files|*.*",
        AddExtension = true
    };

    if (dlg.ShowDialog() == true)
    {

        XpsDocument doc = new XpsDocument(dlg.FileName, FileAccess.Write,
                                 CompressionOption.Fast);
        XpsDocumentWriter writer = XpsDocument.CreateXpsDocumentWriter(doc);
        writer.Write(fixedDocument);
        doc.Close();

    }
}
```

code snippet CreateXps/DocumentPage.xaml.cs

By running the application to store the XPS document, you can view the document with an XPS viewer, as shown in Figure 37-14.

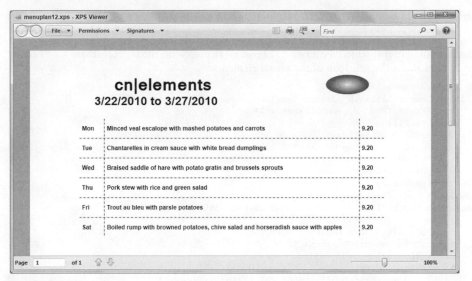

FIGURE 37-14

To one overload of the `Write()` method of the `XpsDocumentWriter` you can also pass a `Visual`, which is the base class of `UIElement`, and thus you can pass any `UIElement` to the writer to create an XPS document easily. This functionality will be used in the following printing example.

PRINTING

The simplest way to print a `FixedDocument` that is shown on the screen with the `DocumentViewer` is to invoke the `Print()` method of the `DocumentViewer` that has the document associated. This is all that needs to be done with the menu planner application in an `OnPrint()` handler. The `Print()` method of the `DocumentViewer` opens up the `PrintDialog` and sends the associated `FixedDocument` to the selected printer:

Available for
download on
Wrox.com

```
private void OnPrint(object sender, RoutedEventArgs e)
{
    viewer.Print();
}
```

code snippet CreateXps/DocumentPage.xaml.cs

Printing with the PrintDialog

If you want more control over the printing process, the `PrintDialog` can be instantiated, and the document printed with the `PrintDocument()` method. The `PrintDocument()` method requires a `DocumentPaginator` with the first argument. The `FixedDocument` returns a `DocumentPaginator` object with the `DocumentPaginator` property. The second argument defines the string that shows up with the current printer and in the printer dialogs for the print job:

Available for
download on
Wrox.com

```
var dlg = new PrintDialog();
if (dlg.ShowDialog() == true)
{
    dlg.PrintDocument(fixedDocument.DocumentPaginator, "Menu Plan");
}
```

code snippet CreateXps/DocumentPage.xaml.cs

Printing Visuals

It's also simple to create `UIElement` objects. The following XAML code defines an `Ellipse`, a `Rectangle`, and a `Button` that is visually represented with two `Ellipse` elements. With the `Button` there's a `Click` handler `OnPrint()` that starts the print job of the visual elements:

```xaml
<Canvas x:Name="canvas1">
    <Ellipse Canvas.Left="10" Canvas.Top="20" Width="180" Height="60"
            Stroke="Red" StrokeThickness="3" >
        <Ellipse.Fill>
            <RadialGradientBrush>
                <GradientStop Offset="0" Color="LightBlue" />
                <GradientStop Offset="1" Color="DarkBlue" />
            </RadialGradientBrush>
        </Ellipse.Fill>
    </Ellipse>
    <Rectangle Width="180" Height="90" Canvas.Left="50" Canvas.Top="50">
        <Rectangle.LayoutTransform>
            <RotateTransform Angle="30" />
        </Rectangle.LayoutTransform>
        <Rectangle.Fill>
            <LinearGradientBrush>
                <GradientStop Offset="0" Color="Aquamarine" />
                <GradientStop Offset="1" Color="ForestGreen" />
            </LinearGradientBrush>
        </Rectangle.Fill>
        <Rectangle.Stroke>
            <LinearGradientBrush>
                <GradientStop Offset="0" Color="LawnGreen" />
                <GradientStop Offset="1" Color="SeaGreen" />
            </LinearGradientBrush>
        </Rectangle.Stroke>
    </Rectangle>
    <Button Canvas.Left="90" Canvas.Top="190" Content="Print" Click="OnPrint">
        <Button.Template>
            <ControlTemplate TargetType="Button">
                <Grid>
                    <Grid.RowDefinitions>
                        <RowDefinition />
                        <RowDefinition />
                    </Grid.RowDefinitions>
                    <Ellipse Grid.Row="0" Grid.RowSpan="2" Width="60"
                            Height="40" Fill="Yellow" />
                    <Ellipse Grid.Row="0" Width="52" Height="20"
                            HorizontalAlignment="Center">
                        <Ellipse.Fill>
                            <LinearGradientBrush StartPoint="0.5,0"
                                                 EndPoint="0.5,1">
                                <GradientStop Color="White" Offset="0" />
                                <GradientStop Color="Transparent"
                                            Offset="0.9" />
                            </LinearGradientBrush>
                        </Ellipse.Fill>
                    </Ellipse>
                    <ContentPresenter Grid.Row="0" Grid.RowSpan="2"
                            HorizontalAlignment="Center"
                            VerticalAlignment="Center" />
                </Grid>

            </ControlTemplate>
```

```
            </Button.Template>
        </Button>
    </Canvas>
```

code snippet PrintingDemo/MainWindow.xaml

In the `OnPrint()` handler the print job can be started by invoking the `PrintVisual()` method of the `PrintDialog`. `PrintVisual()` accepts any object that derives from the base class `Visual`:

Available for
download on
Wrox.com

```
private void OnPrint(object sender, RoutedEventArgs e)
{
    PrintDialog dlg = new PrintDialog();
    if (dlg.ShowDialog() == true)
    {
        dlg.PrintVisual(canvas1, "Print Demo");

    }
}
```

code snippet PrintingDemo/MainWindow.xaml.cs

For programmatically printing without user intervention, the `PrintDialog` classes from the namespace `System.Printing` can be used to create a print job and adjust print settings. The class `LocalPrintServer` gives information about print queues and returns the default `PrintQueue` with the `DefaultPrintQueue` property. You can configure the print job with a `PrintTicket`. `PrintQueue.DefaultPrintTicket` returns a default `PrintTicket` that is associated with the queue. The `PrintQueue` method `GetPrintCapabilities()` returns the capabilities of a printer, and depending on the capabilities you can configure the `PrintTicket` as shown in the following code segment. After configuration of the print ticket is complete, the static method `PrintQueue.CreateXpsDocumentWriter()` returns an `XpsDocumentWriter` object. The `XpsDocumentWriter` class was used previously to create a XPS document. You can also use it to start a print job. The `Write()` method of the `XpsDocumentWriter` not only accepts a `Visual` or `FixedDocument` as the first argument but also a `PrintTicket` as the second argument. If a `PrintTicket` is passed with the second argument, the target of the writer is the printer that is associated with the ticket and thus the writer sends the print job to the printer.

```
LocalPrintServer printServer = new LocalPrintServer();

PrintQueue queue = printServer.DefaultPrintQueue;

PrintTicket ticket = queue.DefaultPrintTicket;
PrintCapabilities capabilities = queue.GetPrintCapabilities(ticket);
if (capabilities.DuplexingCapability.Contains(
        Duplexing.TwoSidedLongEdge))
    ticket.Duplexing = Duplexing.TwoSidedLongEdge;
if (capabilities.InputBinCapability.Contains(InputBin.AutoSelect))
    ticket.InputBin = InputBin.AutoSelect;
if (capabilities.MaxCopyCount > 3)
    ticket.CopyCount = 3;
if (capabilities.PageOrientationCapability.Contains(
    PageOrientation.Landscape))
    ticket.PageOrientation = PageOrientation.Landscape;
if (capabilities.PagesPerSheetCapability.Contains(2))
    ticket.PagesPerSheet = 2;
if (capabilities.StaplingCapability.Contains(
        Stapling.StapleBottomLeft))
    ticket.Stapling = Stapling.StapleBottomLeft;

XpsDocumentWriter writer = PrintQueue.CreateXpsDocumentWriter(queue);
writer.Write(canvas1, ticket);
```

SUMMARY

In this chapter you learned how WPF capabilities can be used with documents, how to create flow documents that adjust automatically depending on the screen sizes, and fixed documents that always look the same. You've also seen how to print documents and how to send visual elements to the printer.

The next chapter continues with the WPF technology and shows the capabilities of Silverlight.

38

Silverlight

WHAT'S IN THIS CHAPTER?

➤ Differences between WPF and Silverlight

➤ Creating Silverlight projects

➤ Navigation between pages

➤ Networking with System.Net, WCF, and data services

➤ Integration with the browser

In the last few chapters, you've read about creating WPF applications. Silverlight is a subset of WPF and offers applications running in a web browser. Since version 3.0, the applications can also run in a standalone fashion. The advantage of Silverlight is that you don't have to run it on a Windows operating system; it is also available on other platforms. All that's needed is an add-in in the browser that includes the Silverlight runtime. The Silverlight runtime contains a subset of the .NET Framework and a subset of WPF.

Before going through this chapter, you should be knowledgeable about XAML and WPF, as discussed in Chapters 27 and 35.

COMPARING WPF AND SILVERLIGHT

Silverlight and WPF are similar in many aspects, but there are also important differences. Silverlight consists of a core presentation framework (a subset of WPF), the .NET Framework for Silverlight (a subset of the .NET Framework), and installers and updaters. WPF applications run on a Windows system and require at least the .NET Client Profile. Silverlight uses a plugin model and is hosted in a web browser.

Silverlight is available for use with a wide range of browsers and operating systems. Beside Internet Explorer, Silverlight can also be used in Firefox, Safari, Opera, and Google Chrome. Not all of these browsers are supported yet. http://go.microsoft.com/fwlink/?LinkId=128526 contains a list of supported operating systems and browsers.

You can use Moonlight to run Silverlight applications on a Linux system. You can download Moonlight at `http://www.gomono.com/moonlight`*. Check this page for the current status of supported features with Moonlight.*

When you compile a WPF application, you get an executable assembly that contains XAML code in a binary form, named BAML, as a resource. With a Silverlight application, the compiler creates an XAP file that is a ZIP package containing the assembly and configuration.

In the .NET Framework for Silverlight, you will find the same classes as in the full .NET Framework but, of course, not all of them. Some classes are missing and also several methods and properties from classes that are available with Silverlight.

What's completely unavailable with Silverlight 3 that you have with WPF is support for flow and fixed documents (see Chapter 37, "Creating Documents with WPF") and 3-D (3-D is covered in Chapter 35, "Core WPF"). You can simulate 3-D with 2-D in Silverlight but, of course, this is completely different from the 3-D functionality of WPF. Interoperability to Windows Forms is not available either. In any case, it's better to write the UI new with XAML instead of integrating Windows Forms controls.

There are also some smaller differences that can be frustrating if you write applications both for WPF and Silverlight:

➤ **Mouse clicks and events** — In Silverlight, the right mouse click is always caught by the browser and doesn't get to the Silverlight control. That's why there's no right button down/up event. There's also no double-click event. Silverlight doesn't have events for the mouse wheel. When reading the properties of `RoutedEventArgs`, with Silverlight just the properties `Handled` and `OriginalSource` are used. This changes with Silverlight 4 with the right mouse click and mouse wheel support.

➤ **Brushes** — Silverlight doesn't have the `DrawingBrush`, `VisualBrush`, and `TileBrush` brushes. However, you have the `VideoBrush` brush available to add videos to the brush.

➤ **Fonts** — Because not all the fonts are available on all platforms, Silverlight is limited in the fonts it offers.

➤ **Controls** — Silverlight doesn't have `Menu`, `Toolbar`, `Window`, and `WebBrowser` controls. However, there are some controls that Silverlight has that are not available with WPF. Over time, these differences will disappear. `Calendar`, `DatePicker`, `DataGrid` controls first appeared in Silverlight and are now available with WPF as well. `AutoCompleteBox` and `NumericUpDown` are controls that are currently missing from WPF.

➤ **Networking** — To avoid blocking the UI thread, only asynchronous calls are available. With Silverlight 3, you're limited to the `BasicHttpBinding` and `PollingDuplexHttpBinding` with WCF. However, you can also use binary encoding.

➤ **File system access** — Silverlight 3 applications are not allowed to read and write anywhere from the client system. You can read and write from isolated storage. `IsolatedStorageFile` and `IsolatedStorageFileStream` are available. Isolated storage is covered in Chapter 29, "Manipulating Files and the Registry." On a running Silverlight control you can click the right mouse button to get into the Silverlight menu, where several tabs are available with information and configuration options. The Application Storage tab gives information about the applications using data with isolated storage, and you have control to remove it. You can compare this with cookies of web applications; just the quotas are very different between cookies and the isolated storage. With Silverlight 4 more control on the file system is available.

➤ **Browser integration** — Because Silverlight controls typically run within a web browser, integration with the browser is important. You can define .NET classes that can be called from JavaScript, and also call into HTML and JavaScript from Silverlight .NET code with classes from the namespace `System.Windows.Browser`.

➤ **Media** — This is an important aspect of web applications that has special support in Silverlight. With streaming, you can use features such as progressive downloading and smooth streaming, and add timeline markers to streams. With the DeepZoom technology and the `MultiScaleImage` control, you can create an impressive user experience, allowing users to zoom into large images that are built up from several image files. To create DeepZoom images, you use the DeepZoom composer, which creates the Silverlight code to use the `MultiScaleImage` control.

CREATING A SILVERLIGHT PROJECT

When creating a new Silverlight project with Visual Studio, you're asked if a Web project should be created as well (see Figure 38-1). The Web project contains test pages to test the Silverlight application and contains the binary files from the Silverlight project. With the Web project type, you can choose between an ASP.NET Web Application Project and an ASP.NET MVC Web Project. ASP.NET MVC is shown in Chapter 42.

The project that is created for this chapter is `SilverlightDemos`, with the Web project `SilverlightDemos.Web`. In the Visual Studio 2010 Web Project project settings is a tab labeled SilverlightApplications, which contains references to the Silverlight project in the solution and the path to the location that the binaries of the Silverlight project (the XAP file) should be copied to, usually the directory `ClientBin`.

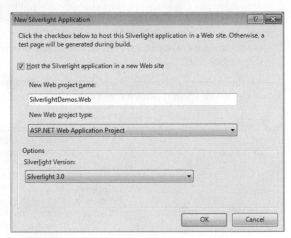

FIGURE 38-1

The HTML test page contains an `object` tag that references the binary of a Silverlight control with the `source` parameter. The parameter `minRuntimeVersion` defines what version of the Silverlight runtime is needed on the client system. If the client system doesn't have the Silverlight runtime installed, a hyperlink is specified with a default image from a Microsoft site, as shown in Figure 38-2, to inform the user about the Microsoft Silverlight installation. When this test page starts, the Silverlight control is loaded in the web browser.

FIGURE 38-2

```
<object data="data:application/x-silverlight-2,"
        type="application/x-silverlight-2" width="100%" height="100%">
    <param name="source" value="ClientBin/SilverlightDemos.xap"/>
    <param name="onError" value="onSilverlightError" />
    <param name="background" value="white" />
    <param name="minRuntimeVersion" value="3.0.40818.0" />
    <param name="autoUpgrade" value="true" />
    <a href="http://go.microsoft.com/fwlink/?LinkID=149156&v=3.0.40818.0"
       style="text-decoration:none">
      <img src="http://go.microsoft.com/fwlink/?LinkId=161376"
           alt="Get Microsoft Silverlight" style="border-style:none"/>
    </a>
</object>
```

code snippet SilverlightDemos.Web/SilverlightDemosTestPage.html

NAVIGATION

One difference between Silverlight and WPF projects is how navigation between pages is handled. Of course, in web applications, navigation between pages is a common task.

To see navigation in action, create a new Visual Studio 2010 project of type Silverlight Navigation Application, named EventRegistration. This project template contains predefined styles, a main page, and a few pages in the Views folder that are navigated to.

`MainPage.xaml` contains a `Frame` element. This element is prefixed with the `navigation` alias, which references the .NET namespace `System.Windows.Controls` in the assembly `System.Windows.Controls` `.Navigation`. Another alias that is used here is `uriMapper`, which references the .NET namespace `System` `.Windows.Navigation` in the same assembly. The `Frame` element is used as a parent of the different pages. The first page that is loaded is changed from the default to the `/Welcome` page by setting the `Source` property. The `UriMapper` class converts a URI to an object. So instead of specifying `/Views/Welcome.xaml` as the navigation source page, just `/Welcome` is enough and is translated to the `Welcome.xaml` file in the Views directory.

All the styles that are referenced here are defined as resources in the file `Styles.xaml` file. This file is added to the application resource files in the file `App.xaml`.

Available for download on Wrox.com

```xaml
<Border x:Name="ContentBorder" Style="{StaticResource ContentBorderStyle}">
    <navigation:Frame x:Name="ContentFrame"
                Style="{StaticResource ContentFrameStyle}"
                Source="/Welcome" Navigated="ContentFrame_Navigated"
                NavigationFailed="ContentFrame_NavigationFailed">
        <navigation:Frame.UriMapper>
          <uriMapper:UriMapper>
            <uriMapper:UriMapping Uri="" MappedUri="/Views/Home.xaml"/>
            <uriMapper:UriMapping Uri="/{pageName}"
                             MappedUri="/Views/{pageName}.xaml"/>
          </uriMapper:UriMapper>
        </navigation:Frame.UriMapper>
    </navigation:Frame>
</Border>
```

code snippet WCFRegistration/MainPage.xaml

`MainPage.xaml` contains a logo and application name section as well as `HyperlinkButton` controls to let the user navigate between the main pages of the application. The logo is specified with the resource `LogoIcon`, which is defined with a `Path` element in the file `Styles.xaml`. The style of the `HyperlinkButton` elements is also defined in the styles file. The `NavigateUri` property is set to a `Uri` that is mapped with the `UriMapper` definitions shown earlier.

```xaml
<Grid x:Name="NavigationGrid" Style="{StaticResource NavigationGridStyle}">
    <Border x:Name="BrandingBorder"
            Style="{StaticResource BrandingBorderStyle}">
        <StackPanel x:Name="BrandingStackPanel"
                Style="{StaticResource BrandingStackPanelStyle}">
            <ContentControl Style="{StaticResource LogoIcon}"/>
            <TextBlock x:Name="ApplicationNameTextBlock"
                    Style="{StaticResource ApplicationNameStyle}"
                    Text="CN innovation"/>
        </StackPanel>
    </Border>
    <Border x:Name="LinksBorder" Style="{StaticResource LinksBorderStyle}">
        <StackPanel x:Name="LinksStackPanel"
                Style="{StaticResource LinksStackPanelStyle}">
            <HyperlinkButton x:Name="Link1"
                    Style="{StaticResource LinkStyle}"
                    NavigateUri="/Home" TargetName="ContentFrame"
                    Content="home"/>
            <Rectangle x:Name="Divider1"
                    Style="{StaticResource DividerStyle}"/>
            <HyperlinkButton x:Name="Link2"
                    Style="{StaticResource LinkStyle}"
```

```
                                       NavigateUri="/About" TargetName="ContentFrame"
                                       Content="about"/>
                        </StackPanel>
                    </Border>
                </Grid>
```

The Welcome page is shown with loading the Silverlight control because it is referenced directly with the `Source` property from the `Frame` element. This `Page` just contains a `TextBlock` element with information about the application, which is contained within a `Border` element for defining some visual effects that is contained within a `Canvas` element for positioning.

```
<navigation:Page x:Class="Wrox.ProCSharp.Silverlight.Views.Welcome"
        xmlns="http://schemas.microsoft.com/winfx/2006/xaml/presentation"
        xmlns:x="http://schemas.microsoft.com/winfx/2006/xaml"
        xmlns:d="http://schemas.microsoft.com/expression/blend/2008"
        xmlns:mc="http://schemas.openxmlformats.org/markup-compatibility/2006"
        xmlns:navigation="clr-namespace:System.Windows.Controls;
                         assembly=System.Windows.Controls.Navigation"
        Title="Welcome Page">
    <Canvas x:Name="LayoutRoot">
        <Canvas.Resources>
            <!-- Storyboard Resources -->
        </Canvas.Resources>

        <Border x:Name="border1" Canvas.Left="0" Canvas.Top="0" Width="240"
                Height="80" CornerRadius="9">
            <Border.Effect>
                <DropShadowEffect ShadowDepth="7" BlurRadius="3"
                                Color="DarkGreen" />
            </Border.Effect>
            <Border.Background>
                <LinearGradientBrush StartPoint="0.5,0" EndPoint="0.5,1">
                    <GradientStop x:Name="gradient1" Offset="0"
                            Color="DarkGreen" />
                    <GradientStop x:Name="gradient2" Offset="0.4" Color="Green" />
                    <GradientStop x:Name="gradient3" Offset="0.7"
                            Color="MediumSeaGreen" />
                    <GradientStop x:Name="gradient4" Offset="0.9"
                            Color="LightGreen" />
                </LinearGradientBrush>
            </Border.Background>

            <TextBlock HorizontalAlignment="Center" VerticalAlignment="Center"
                    Text="Event Registration" FontFamily="Comic Sans MS"
                    FontSize="24" Foreground="Wheat" />
        </Border>
    </Canvas>
</navigation:Page>
```

code snippet WCFRegistration/Views/Welcome.xaml

Within the `Resources` section of the `Canvas` element, two `Storyboard` elements are defined to do an animation. This is very similar to the animations you saw in Chapter 35 for WPF. Minor differences can be detected between these technologies with animations; for example, the animations with Silverlight don't define the `AccelerationRatio` and `DecelerationRatio` properties you know from WPF. However, you can get the same features using key-frame animations or with ease functions. Ease functions were in Silverlight before they became available in WPF, which was extended in .NET 4 to include this feature.

```
<Canvas.Resources>
    <Storyboard x:Name="startStoryboard">
        <DoubleAnimation From="0" To="400" Duration="00:00:4"
```

```
                                 Storyboard.TargetName="border1"
                                 Storyboard.TargetProperty="(Canvas.Left)">
                    <DoubleAnimation.EasingFunction>
                        <CircleEase EasingMode="EaseIn" />
                    </DoubleAnimation.EasingFunction>
                </DoubleAnimation>
                <DoubleAnimation From="0" To="300" Duration="00:00:4"
                                 Storyboard.TargetName="border1"
                                 Storyboard.TargetProperty="(Canvas.Top)">
                    <DoubleAnimation.EasingFunction>
                        <BounceEase Bounces="4" EasingMode="EaseIn" />
                    </DoubleAnimation.EasingFunction>
                </DoubleAnimation>
            </Storyboard>
            <Storyboard x:Name="endStoryboard">
                <DoubleAnimation To="50" Duration="00:00:4"
                                 Storyboard.TargetName="border1"
                                 Storyboard.TargetProperty="(Canvas.Left)">
                    <DoubleAnimation.EasingFunction>
                        <CircleEase EasingMode="EaseOut" />
                    </DoubleAnimation.EasingFunction>
                </DoubleAnimation>
                <DoubleAnimation To="50" Duration="00:00:4"
                                 Storyboard.TargetName="border1"
                                 Storyboard.TargetProperty="(Canvas.Top)">
                    <DoubleAnimation.EasingFunction>
                        <ElasticEase EasingMode="EaseOut" Springiness="4"
                                     Oscillations="3" />
                    </DoubleAnimation.EasingFunction>
                </DoubleAnimation>
                <ColorAnimation Duration="00:00:4"
                                Storyboard.TargetName="gradient1"
                                Storyboard.TargetProperty="Color" To="DarkBlue" />
                <ColorAnimation Duration="00:00:4"
                                Storyboard.TargetName="gradient2"
                                Storyboard.TargetProperty="Color" To="Blue" />
                <ColorAnimation Duration="00:00:4"
                                Storyboard.TargetName="gradient3"
                                Storyboard.TargetProperty="Color"
                                To="MediumBlue" />
                <ColorAnimation Duration="00:00:4"
                                Storyboard.TargetName="gradient4"
                                Storyboard.TargetProperty="Color" To="LightBlue" />
                <DoubleAnimation Duration="00:00:4" BeginTime="00:00:2"
                                 Storyboard.TargetName="border1"
                                 Storyboard.TargetProperty="Width" To="500" />
                <DoubleAnimation Duration="00:00:4" BeginTime="00:00:2"
                                 Storyboard.TargetName="border1"
                                 Storyboard.TargetProperty="Height" To="300" />
            </Storyboard>
        </Canvas.Resources>
```

 Animations and ease functions are explained in Chapter 35, "Core WPF."

The first storyboard animation, startStoryboard, is started in the OnNavigateTo event handler by invoking the Begin() method. The Completed event of the first storyboard animation is set to a Lambda expression to start the second storyboard, endStoryboard, when the first is completed. When the second storyboard is completed, NavigationService.Navigate() is used to navigate to the Home page.

```
using System;
using System.Windows.Controls;
using System.Windows.Navigation;

namespace Wrox.ProCSharp.Silverlight.Views
{
    public partial class Welcome : Page
    {
        public Welcome()
        {
            InitializeComponent();
        }

        protected override void OnNavigatedTo(NavigationEventArgs e)
        {
            startStoryboard.Completed += (sender1, e1) =>
                {
                    endStoryboard.Completed += (sender2, e2) =>
                        NavigationService.Navigate(
                            new Uri("/Home", UriKind.Relative));
                    endStoryboard.Begin();
                };
            startStoryboard.Begin();
        }
    }
}
```

code snippet WCFRegistration/Views/Welcome.xaml.cs

When you run the application, you can see an animation and the hyperlink buttons, as shown in
Figure 38-3.

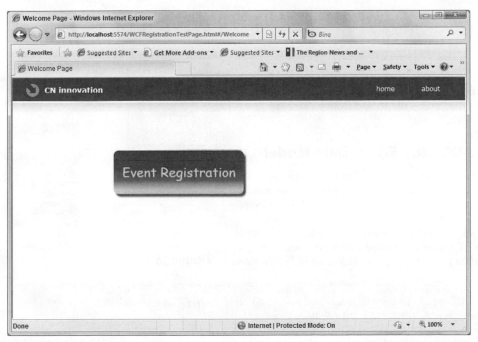

FIGURE 38-3

NETWORKING

With Silverlight, networking is in some ways the same as from the .NET Framework stack, but it is also different in important aspects. You have the socket classes `HttpRequest` and `WebClient` that you are familiar with from Chapter 24. WCF (Chapter 43) and WCF Data Services (Chapter 32) are available as well. However, only asynchronous methods are available to send and receive requests to and from the network. The UI thread shouldn't be blocked, as this can have a fatal effect for the user.

Before Silverlight 3.0, the only networking stack that could be used from Silverlight was the one that was offered by the browser. Since Silverlight 3.0, this is different; you can use a different HTTP stack as well.

One important restriction for applications running inside a browser on the client was that the client could only access networking services from the same server that the control came from. This has changed since Adobe's Flash technology, but the target server must support this. The Silverlight networking stack checks to see if a Silverlight Policy File named `clientaccesspolicy.xml` exists on the server. If such a file does not exist, Silverlight also accepts the file `crossdomain.xml`, which is the same file used with Adobe Flash. The second file is not checked if the first exists, and Silverlight doesn't use all entries from the `crossdomain.xml` file and requires that the entire domain be marked as public if this file is used.

A sample Silverlight Policy File, `clientaccesspolicy.xml`, is shown here. For the client domain www.cninnovation.com, access is granted to all subpaths. You can restrict the resources that the grant applies to, and also use an * for the domain URI to allow clients to come from anywhere.

```xml
<?xml version="1.0" encoding="utf-8"?>
<access-policy>
  <cross-domain-access>
    <policy>
      <allow-from http-request-headers="*">
        <domain uri="http://www.cninnovation.com"/>
      </allow-from>
      <grant-to>
        <resource path="/" include-subpaths="true"/>
      </grant-to>
    </policy>
  </cross-domain-access>
</access-policy>
```

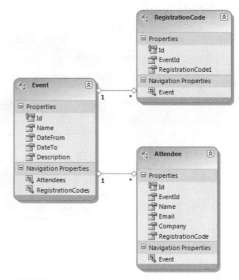

Let's look at an example that uses networking stacks from Silverlight. For this, an ADO.NET Entity Data Model is created first, to read and write to and from a database across the network.

Creating an ADO.NET Entity Data Model

The sample Silverlight control is used to write attendee registration information to a database. First, the user must select from a list of events before he can register for an event. The database `EventRegistration` defines three tables: Events, Attendees, and RegistrationCodes, which are mapped to the ADO.NET Entity Data Model entity classes `Event`, `Attendee`, and `RegistrationCode`, as shown in Figure 38-4.

FIGURE 38-4

> *You can read about how to create and use ADO.NET Entity Data Models in Chapter 31, "ADO.NET Entity Framework."*

Creating a WCF Service for Silverlight Clients

To access the generated entity classes, a WCF service is created. The contract for the service is defined by the interface `IRegistrationService`. This service contract defines the operations `GetEvents()` and `RegisterAttendee()`. `GetEvents()` accepts a date range for the event selection and returns an array of `Event` objects as defined by the Entity Data Model. The operation `RegisterAttendee()` requires an `Attendee` object as argument and returns `true` or `false`, depending on the success or failure of the registration.

```csharp
using System;
using System.ServiceModel;

namespace Wrox.ProCSharp.Silverlight.Web
{
    [ServiceContract]
    public interface IRegistrationService
    {
        [OperationContract]
        Event[] GetEvents(DateTime fromTime, DateTime toTime);

        [OperationContract]
        bool RegisterAttendee(Attendee attendee);
    }
}
```

code snippet SilverlightDemos.Web/IRegistrationService.cs

 You can read information on WCF and defining service contracts in Chapter 43, "Windows Communication Foundation."

The service contract is implemented with the class `RegistrationService`. The method `GetEvents()` uses a LINQ query that accesses the entity framework's data context to get all events from a specific timeframe and returns an array of `Event` objects. The method `RegisterAttendee()` first verifies that the registration code is valid and adds the `Attendee` object to the database with the `SaveChanges()` method of the data context.

```csharp
using System;
using System.Linq;
using System.ServiceModel.Activation;

namespace Wrox.ProCSharp.Silverlight.Web
{
    public class RegistrationService : IRegistrationService
    {
        public Event[] GetEvents(DateTime fromTime, DateTime toTime)
        {
            Event[] events = null;
            using (var data = new EventRegistrationEntities())
            {
                events = (from e in data.Events
                          where e.DateFrom >= fromTime && e.DateFrom <= toTime
                          select e).ToArray();

                foreach (var ev in events)
                {
                    data.Detach(ev);
                }
            }
            return events;
        }
```

```
public bool RegisterAttendee(Attendee attendee)
{
    using (EventRegistrationEntities data =
            new EventRegistrationEntities())
    {
        if ((from rc in data.RegistrationCodes
                where rc.RegistrationCode1 == attendee.RegistrationCode
                select rc).Count() < 1)
        {
            return false;
        }
        else
        {
            data.Attendees.AddObject(attendee);
            if (data.SaveChanges() == 1)
            {
                return true;
            }
            else
            {
                return false;
            }
        }
    }
}
```

code snippet SilverlightDemos.Web/RegistrationService.svc.cs

The default `BasicHttpBinding` that is used with WCF hosting in the ASP.NET web application is okay for use by Silverlight clients, and thus doesn't need any configuration. The only configuration needed to make it possible to add a service reference from Visual Studio is to allow the publishing of metadata with the HTTP GET protocol as shown.

Available for download on Wrox.com

```xml
<system.serviceModel>
  <behaviors>
    <serviceBehaviors>
      <behavior name="">
        <serviceMetadata httpGetEnabled="true" />
        <serviceDebug includeExceptionDetailInFaults="false" />
      </behavior>
    </serviceBehaviors>
  </behaviors>
</system.serviceModel>
```

code snippet SilverlightDemos.Web/Web.config

Starting with Silverlight 3, it is possible to configure a binary encoding with the HTTP transport. Silverlight 3 implements this encoding to allow for better performance. This custom binding is used by default if you add a Silverlight-enabled WCF Service.

Calling WCF Services

Before calling the service, a UI needs to be created. In the same Silverlight project as before, where the animation was done, the `Home.xaml` page is changed to include `ComboBox` and `TextBox` controls to allow entering information for an event and registering for the event. The design view of the application is shown in Figure 38-5.

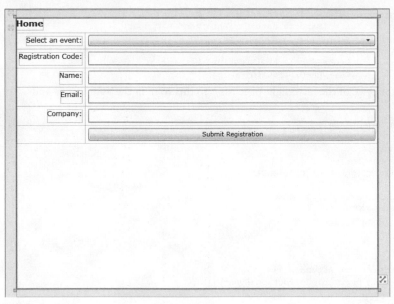

FIGURE 38-5

The `ComboBox` binds to the `EventList` property of the data context and uses a `DataTemplate` with two `TextBlock` elements that bind to the `Name` and `DateFrom` properties of the items.

Available for download on Wrox.com

```
<ComboBox x:Name="comboEvents"
          ItemsSource="{Binding Path=EventList, Mode=OneWay}"
          Grid.Row="0" Grid.Column="1" Margin="5"
          VerticalAlignment="Center">
    <ComboBox.ItemTemplate>
        <DataTemplate>
            <StackPanel Orientation="Vertical">
                <TextBlock Text="{Binding Path=Name}" />
                <TextBlock Text="{Binding Path=DateFrom}" />
            </StackPanel>
        </DataTemplate>
    </ComboBox.ItemTemplate>
</ComboBox>
```

code snippet WCFRegistration/Views/Home.xaml

For data input, the control uses several `TextBox` elements that bind to properties of the `Attendee` object that is returned by the `CurrentAttendee` property. With WPF, the default binding mode depends on the control where it is used; with Silverlight, the default binding mode is `OneWay` and thus needs to be changed for two-way bindings. The `Button` element has the handler method `OnRegistration()` associated to the `Click` event.

```
<TextBox Grid.Row="1" Grid.Column="1" Margin="5"
         Text="{Binding Path=CurrentAttendee.RegistrationCode,
                        Mode=TwoWay}" />
<TextBox Grid.Row="2" Grid.Column="1" Margin="5"
         Text="{Binding Path=CurrentAttendee.Name,
                        Mode=TwoWay}" />
<TextBox Grid.Row="3" Grid.Column="1" Margin="5"
         Text="{Binding Path=CurrentAttendee.Email,
                        Mode=TwoWay}" />
```

```
                    <TextBox Grid.Row="4" Grid.Column="1" Margin="5"
                           Text="{Binding Path=CurrentAttendee.Company,
                                     Mode=TwoWay}" />
                    <Button Grid.Row="5" Grid.Column="1"
                           Content="Submit Registration" Margin="5"
                           Click="OnRegistration" />
```

In the code-behind, the `DataContext` of the Silverlight page is set to this to map the `EventList` and `CurrentAttendee` properties.

```
using System.Collections.ObjectModel;
using System.Windows;
using System.Windows.Controls;
using System.Windows.Navigation;
using Wrox.ProCSharp.Silverlight.RegistrationService;

namespace Wrox.ProCSharp.Silverlight
{
    public partial class Home : Page
    {
        public Home()
        {
            CurrentAttendee = new Attendee();
            EventList = new ObservableCollection<Event>();
            InitializeComponent();

            this.DataContext = this;
        }

        public ObservableCollection<Event> EventList { get; private set; }
        public Attendee CurrentAttendee { get; private set; }
```

code snippet WCFRegistration/Views/Home.xaml.cs

By adding a service reference to the `RegistrationService`, only the asynchronous methods are created with the proxy class. This proxy class uses the async component pattern.

> *The async pattern and async component pattern are covered in Chapter 20, "Threads, Tasks, and Synchronization."*

The overridden method `OnNavigatedTo()` is invoked on navigation to the page. Here, the operation `GetEvents` of the WCF service is invoked by calling the method `GetEventsAsync()`. On completion of the asynchronous operation, the event `GetEventsCompleted` is fired. A Lambda expression is assigned to this event to add the returned events to the `eventList` collection. Because `eventList` is an `ObservableCollection<T>`, the user interface is updated about changes of this list.

```
        protected override void OnNavigatedTo(NavigationEventArgs e)
        {
            var client = new RegistrationServiceClient();
            client.GetEventsCompleted += (sender, e1) =>
                {
                    if (e1.Error != null)
                    {

                    }
                    else
                    {
                        foreach (var ev in e1.Result)
```

```
                              {
                                  EventList.Add(ev);
                              }
                          }
                      };
                  client.GetEventsAsync(DateTime.Today, DateTime.Today.AddMonths(2));
      }
```

The method `OnRegistration()` is invoked when the `Click` event of the Submit Registration button is fired. Here again, an asynchronous method is invoked: `RegisterAttendeeAsync()` to register the attendee. On completion of this method, `NavigationService.Navigate()` is used to navigate the user to a different page.

```
          private void OnRegistration(object sender, RoutedEventArgs e)
          {
              var client = new RegistrationServiceClient();
              CurrentAttendee.EventId = (comboEvents.SelectedItem as Event).Id;
              client.RegisterAttendeeCompleted += (sender1, e1) =>
                  {
                      if (e1.Error == null)
                      {
                          if (e1.Result)
                          {
                              NavigationService.Navigate(
                                  new Uri("/Success", UriKind.Relative));
                          }
                          else
                          {
                              NavigationService.Navigate(
                                  new Uri("/ErrorPage", UriKind.Relative));
                          }
                      }
                      else
                      {
                          // display error
                      }
                  };
              client.RegisterAttendeeAsync(CurrentAttendee);
          }
```

Now the Silverlight application can be started to invoke the WCF Web service.

Using WCF Data Services

Silverlight also gives you access to the client part of WCF Data Services. With this, you can use HTTP requests to retrieve and update data from the Silverlight control without the need to manually define service methods. Retrieving, updating, and adding new data can be done with simple HTTP requests.

 WCF Data Services is covered in Chapter 32, "Data Services."

To offer a service using WCF Data Services for the Silverlight application, a new WCF Data Service item named `EventRegistrationDataService` is added to the Web project. The implementation derives from `DataService<EventRegistrationEntities>`. The generic parameter for the base class `DataService<T>` is the entity data context that was created by the template for the ADO.NET Entity Framework. With `config.SetEntitySetAccessRule()`, access rules are defined to allow read and all access to the Events entity set and the Attendees entity set.

```csharp
using System.Collections.Generic;
using System.Data.Services;
using System.Data.Services.Common;
using System.Linq;
using System.ServiceModel.Web;

namespace Wrox.ProCSharp.Silverlight.Web
{
    public class EventRegistrationDataService :
            DataService<EventRegistrationEntities>
    {
        public static void InitializeService(DataServiceConfiguration config)
        {
            config.SetEntitySetAccessRule("Events", EntitySetRights.AllRead);
            config.SetEntitySetAccessRule("Attendees", EntitySetRights.All);
            config.SetServiceOperationAccessRule("AddAttendee",
                    ServiceOperationRights.All);
            config.DataServiceBehavior.MaxProtocolVersion =
                    DataServiceProtocolVersion.V2;
        }
```

code snippet SilverlightDemos.Web/EventRegistrationDataService.svc.cs

To make an operation available for registration of an attendee using WCF Data Services that is more complex than just adding a new record, the method `AddAttendee()` is added to the class `EventRegistrationDataService`. The `WebGet` attribute specifies that the method can be accessed with an `HTTP GET` request. For `POST`, `PUT`, or `DELETE` requests, the `WebInvoke` attribute can be used. Within the `InitializeService()` method, access is given to this operation with the method `SetServiceOperationAccessRule()`. `AddAttendee()` receives attendee information with separate parameters and first verifies that the `registrationCode` exists before writing the attendee to the `Attendees` table that is mapped from the Entity Data Model. Using separate parameters with this method instead of using an `Attendee` object is required to call this method with an `HTTP GET` request.

```csharp
[WebGet]
public bool AddAttendee(string name, string email, string company,
                        string registrationCode, int eventId)
{
    if ((from rc in this.CurrentDataSource.RegistrationCodes
         where rc.RegistrationCode1 == registrationCode
         select rc).Count() < 1)
    {
        return false;
    }
    else
    {
        var attendee = new Attendee {
            Name = name,
            Email = email,
            Company = company,
            RegistrationCode = registrationCode,
            EventId = eventId
        };
        this.CurrentDataSource.Attendees.AddObject(attendee);
        return !(this.CurrentDataSource.SaveChanges() < 1);
    }
}
```

Adding a service reference to the Silverlight control project `EventRegistration` makes it possible to use the WCF Data Services client classes to access the service. The method `OnNavigatedTo()` is now changed to use the generated proxy from the Data Services client instead of the pure WCF proxy used earlier.

EventRegistrationEntities is a class generated from adding the service reference and derives from DataServiceContext in the namespace System.Data.Services.Client. This class defines a context for the client to keep tracking and changing information and to create HTTP requests out of LINQ queries. A LINQ query is defined to get all the events from a specific date range. What's different here compared to WCF Data Services is that synchronous methods are not available, but this is to be expected. Calling the query as it is defined by the variable q results in a NotSupportedException. Instead, you must invoke the BeginExecute() method of the DataServiceQuery<T> class. This method uses the async pattern and accepts an AsyncCallback delegate as a first parameter. Here, a Lambda expression is passed to this delegate parameter, which is invoked as soon as the data is returned from the service. Calling EndExecute() retrieves the returned data and writes it to the ObservableCollection<T>.

Available for download on Wrox.com

```
protected override void OnNavigatedTo(NavigationEventArgs e)
{
    Uri serviceRoot =
            new Uri("EventRegistrationDataService.svc", UriKind.Relative);
    var data = new EventRegistrationEntities(serviceRoot);
    var q = from ev in data.Events
            where ev.DateFrom >= DateTime.Today &&
                    ev.DateFrom <= DateTime.Today.AddMonths(2)
            select ev;

    DataServiceQuery<Event> query = (DataServiceQuery<Event>)q;
    query.BeginExecute(ar =>
        {
            var query1 = ar.AsyncState as DataServiceQuery<Event>;
            var events = query1.EndExecute(ar);
            foreach (var ev in events)
            {
                EventList.Add(ev);
            }
        }, query);
}
```

code snippet EventRegistration/Home.xaml.cs

Calling the method AddAttendee() is done with the WebClient class from the System.Net namespace, shown next.

Using System.Net to Access the Service

As the AddAttendee method offered by the service can be directly accessed with an HTTP GET request, this request can easily be done with classes from the System.Net namespace such as WebClient or HttpWebRequest. Of course, with Silverlight only async methods are available. The WebClient class implements the async component pattern; the HttpWebRequest class implements the async pattern.

 The System.Net namespace is covered in Chapter 24, "Networking."

The changed implementation of the OnRegistration event handler method now makes use of the WebClient class. Calling the method DownloadStringAsync() starts the request passing the URL string to the method. With a GET request, all parameters are defined with the URL string. As soon as the data is returned from the services, the event DownloadStringCompleted is fired with the WebClient class. Here, a Lamba expression is created to parse the Boolean return value from the XML message. Depending on the result, navigation either goes to the Success or ErrorPage.

```csharp
private void OnRegistration(object sender, RoutedEventArgs e)
{
    CurrentAttendee.EventId = (comboEvents.SelectedItem as Event).Id;

    var client = new WebClient();
    client.DownloadStringCompleted += (sender1, e1) =>
        {
            if (e1.Error != null)
            {
                NavigationService.Navigate(
                        new Uri("/ErrorPage", UriKind.Relative));
            }

            bool result = bool.Parse(XElement.Parse(e1.Result).Value);
            if (result)
                NavigationService.Navigate(
                        new Uri("/Success", UriKind.Relative));
            else
                NavigationService.Navigate(
                        new Uri("/ErrorPage", UriKind.Relative));
        };
    Uri requestUri = new Uri(String.Format(
        "../../EventRegistrationDataService.svc/AddAttendee?name='{0}'" +
        "&email='{1}'&company='{2}'&registrationCode='{3}'&eventid={4}",
        CurrentAttendee.Name, CurrentAttendee.Email,
        CurrentAttendee.Company, CurrentAttendee.RegistrationCode,
        CurrentAttendee.EventId), UriKind.Relative);
    client.DownloadStringAsync(requestUri);
}
}
}
```

code snippet EventRegistration/Home.xaml.cs

When you run the application, you can register for an event.

Since version 3 of Silverlight, the Silverlight application does not have to use the networking stack from the browser. The networking stack from the browser is limited in the methods of the HTTP requests it can perform and returns only limited information on the response status codes. However, now it's possible to use a different networking stack that can be selected with the `WebRequestCreator` class from the `System.Net.Browser` namespace. The following code snippet changes the networking stack to `ClientHttp`. `BrowserHttp` is the second option in `WebRequestCreator`. This change switches the networking stack to use all the networking options you've seen.

```csharp
bool result = WebRequest.RegisterPrefix("http://", WebRequestCreator.ClientHttp);
```

BROWSER INTEGRATION

Integration with a web browser often is an important part of using Silverlight. Silverlight 1.0 could only be programmed using JavaScript. Luckily, this changed with Silverlight 2.0, but there are still many scenarios where you might want to control HTML and JavaScript code from within the Silverlight control or invoke .NET methods from JavaScript. Both are possible with the help of the namespace `System.Windows.Browser`.

To demonstrate this integration by using the existing web solution, the following example creates a new Silverlight project named `JavaScriptInterop`. This control is used to demonstrate both calling out to the HTML code from within the Silverlight control and to invoke .NET methods from JavaScript.

Calling out to JavaScript

To call into the HTML page from the Silverlight control, the HTML test page
`JavaScriptInteropTestPage.html` gets an HTML `Button` control with the name `button1`. This button
will be changed from within the Silverlight control.

Available for
download on
Wrox.com

```
<form id="form1" runat="server" style="height: 100%">
    <input id="button1" type="button" value="Click me!" />
```

code snippet SilverlightDemos.Web/JavaScripInteropTestPage.html

The XAML code from the Silverlight control has a `TextBox` and a `Button` control. The `TextBox` allows you
to enter text that will show up on the HTML button.

Available for
download on
Wrox.com

```
<TextBox Grid.Row="0" Grid.Column="0" x:Name="text1" Margin="5" />
<Button Grid.Row="0" Grid.Column="1" Content="Set value for HTML button"
        Click="OnChangeHtml" Margin="5" />
<TextBlock Grid.Row="1" Grid.Column="0" Grid.ColumnSpan="2" Margin="5"
           Text="" x:Name="text2" />
```

code snippet JavaScriptInterop/MainPage.xaml

In the handler of the `Click` event of the `Button`, the method `OnChangeHtml()`, the `button1` HTML element
is accessed by invoking the `GetElementById()` method of the `HtmlDocument`. If you're used to the DOM
model of HTML, the code here looks very similar. Using the `HtmlElement`, attributes from the HTML
element can be changed; for example, the value attribute can be changed to `text1.Text` to set it to the text
input from the user.

Available for
download on
Wrox.com

```
private void OnChangeHtml(object sender, RoutedEventArgs e)
{
    HtmlDocument doc = HtmlPage.Document;
    HtmlElement element = doc.GetElementById("button1");
    element.SetAttribute("value", text1.Text);
}
```

code snippet JavaScriptInterop/MainPage.xaml.cs

You can also add event handlers to HTML elements by invoking the `AttachEvent()` method on an
`HtmlElement`, as shown next. Here, the method `OnChangeHtmlButtonClick()` is assigned to the `onclick`
event of the HTML button `button1`.

```
public MainPage()
{
    InitializeComponent();
    HtmlDocument doc = HtmlPage.Document;
    HtmlElement element = doc.GetElementById("button1");
    element.AttachEvent("onclick", OnHtmlButtonClick);
}

private void OnHtmlButtonClick(object sender, HtmlEventArgs e)
{
    text2.Text = "HTML button onclick fired";
}
```

With the classes from the namespace `System.Windows.Browser`, you can access all the information from
HTML. `HtmlPage`, `HtmlDocument`, `HtmlWindow`, `HtmlPage`, and `HtmlObject` are the most important
classes for accessing browser information, cookies, elements from the page, and style sheets, and reading
and changing content. It also works the other way around; calling from JavaScript into Silverlight is
shown next.

JavaScript Calling Silverlight

To make a .NET method available from JavaScript, the attribute `ScriptableMember` must be applied. If you would like to make all members of a class available from JavaScript, you can apply the attribute `ScriptableType` instead. Here, the attribute `ScriptableMember` is applied to the method `ToUpper()`, which changes the input string to uppercase.

Available for
download on
Wrox.com

```
[ScriptableMember]
public string ToUpper(string s)
{
    return s.ToUpper();
}
```

code snippet JavaScriptInterop/MainPage.xaml.cs

The type containing scriptable members must be registered with the HTML page so that it can be found by scripting. This is done by invoking the `RegisterScriptableObject()` method from the `HtmlPage` class. The first argument of this method is a key name that is used by JavaScript to find the object. The second argument defines the instance that is used to access the scriptable members.

```
public MainPage()
{
    InitializeComponent();
    //...

    HtmlPage.RegisterScriptableObject("ScriptKey", this);
}
```

Now it is possible to access the .NET code from JavaScript. To find the scriptable object from JavaScript, the Silverlight control must be accessed. To make this easier, an id attribute is added to the `object` tag that references the Silverlight package. Also, text and button elements are added to the HTML code. The button has the JavaScript function `callDotnet()` assigned to the `onclick` event where the call to managed code happens.

Available for
download on
Wrox.com

```
<input id="text1" type="text" />
<input id="button2" type="button" value="Convert with a .NET method"
       onclick="callDotnet()" />
<div id="silverlightControlHost">
    <object id="plugin" data="data:application/x-silverlight-2,"
            type="application/x-silverlight-2"
        width="30%" height="30%">
        <param name="source" value="ClientBin/JavaScriptInterop.xap" />
        <param name="onError" value="onSilverlightError" />
        <param name="background" value="white" />
        <param name="minRuntimeVersion" value="3.0.40818.0" />
        <param name="autoUpgrade" value="true" />
        <a href="http://go.microsoft.com/fwlink/?LinkID=149156&v=3.0.40818.0"
           style="text-decoration: none">
            <img src="http://go.microsoft.com/fwlink/?LinkId=161376"
                alt="Get Microsoft Silverlight" style="border-style: none" />
        </a>
    </object>
</div>
```

code snippet SilverlightDemos.Web/JavaScripInteropTestPage.html

The JavaScript function `callDotnet()` uses the plugin identifier to find the Silverlight control with `getElementById()`. By using the `ScriptKey` defined earlier with the registration, the scriptable type can now be accessed. Using this scriptable type, the method `ToUpper()` is now available to change the input to uppercase.

```
function callDotnet() {
    var plugin = document.getElementById("plugin");
```

```
            var dotnet = plugin.content.ScriptKey;
            var input = document.getElementById("text1").value;
            var output = dotnet.ToUpper(input);
            document.getElementById("text1").value = output;
        }
```

If you don't plan to make your web site solely with Silverlight but want to mix in ASP.NET or HTML features and enhance it with Silverlight, the browser integration features come in very handy.

SILVERLIGHT OUT-OF-BROWSER APPLICATIONS

Since version 3 of Silverlight, Silverlight applications can also run out of browser. The application can be installed from a user without administrator privileges. However, the application is still restricted to a security sandbox and doesn't have full trust on the client system. What is the advantage of a Silverlight out-of-browser application compared to WPF? With Silverlight, it's not necessary to install the .NET Framework, only the Silverlight runtime that's installed with the browser plugin is necessary. Because this plugin is available on different platforms, out-of-browser applications can run on many more platforms than WPF applications.

With the Silverlight project settings of Visual Studio 2010, you can click the check box to enable running the application out of the browser and change out-of-browser settings as shown in Figure 38-6. With these settings, you can define application icons, title, description, and also if GPU acceleration should be used, which can be a great performance advantage with special graphics. By marking the check box for Show install menu, an installation option for the user is available on clicking the right mouse button on the Silverlight control.

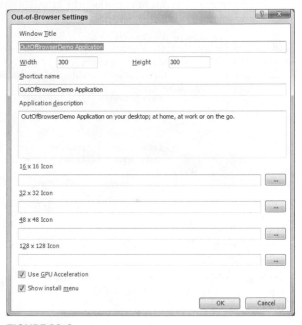

FIGURE 38-6

You can control installation and updates from the Silverlight application, as demonstrated next with the project `OutOfBrowserDemo` and a user interface that contains two `Button` and a `TextBlock` control. The first button, `installButton`, has the event handler method `OnInstall()` associated with it so that the user can install the application on the client system, and the button `updateButton` with the event handler `OnUpdate()` to check for available updates.

```
<Grid x:Name="LayoutRoot" Background="White">
    <Grid.RowDefinitions>
        <RowDefinition />
        <RowDefinition />
        <RowDefinition />
    </Grid.RowDefinitions>
    <Button x:Name="installButton" Grid.Row="0"
        Content="Install Out-of-Browser" Click="OnInstall" Margin="5" />
    <TextBlock x:Name="text1" Grid.Row="1" FontSize="24"
        HorizontalAlignment="Center" VerticalAlignment="Center" />
```

```
        <Button x:Name="updateButton" Grid.Row="2" Content="Check for Updates"
            Click="OnUpdate" Margin="5" />
    </Grid>
```

code snippet OutOfBrowserDemo/MainPage.xaml

The constructor `MainPage` checks whether the application is running out of browser or within the browser and sets the text of the `TextBlock` control accordingly. To check if the application is running out of browser, you can use the `IsRunningOutOfBrowser` property of the `Application` class. This class also provides information about the installation state of the application with the `InstallState` property. Possible values are `NotInstalled`, `Installing`, `Installed`, and `InstallFailed` with the `InstallState` enumeration. Using this information, the `installButton` and `updateButton` controls are visible or collapsed.

```
public MainPage()
{
    InitializeComponent();
    if (App.Current.IsRunningOutOfBrowser)
    {
        text1.Text = "running out of browser";
    }
    else
    {
        text1.Text = "running in the browser";
        updateButton.Visibility = Visibility.Collapsed;
    }
    if (App.Current.InstallState == InstallState.Installed)
    {
        installButton.Visibility = Visibility.Collapsed;
    }
}
```

code snippet OutOfBrowserDemo/MainPage.xaml.cs

The event handler `OnInstall()` is invoked by clicking the associated button. An installation happens just by invoking the `Install()` method of the `Application` class.

```
private void OnInstall(object sender, RoutedEventArgs e)
{
    if (App.Current.InstallState == InstallState.NotInstalled)
    {
        bool result = App.Current.Install();
        if (result)
            text1.Text = "installation successful";
    }
}
```

Checking for an update on the server can be done programmatically with the `Application` class as well. Here, the update is done in the event handler method `OnUpdate()`. `CheckAndDownloadUpdateAsync()` checks for an available update and installs the update. This is an asynchronous operation using the async component pattern that fires the event `CheckAndDownloadUpdateCompleted` on completion of the update. Success or error information is written in the handler of this event. After a successful update, the new version is available on the next start.

```
private void OnUpdate(object sender, RoutedEventArgs e)
{
    App.Current.CheckAndDownloadUpdateCompleted += (sender1, e1) =>
        {
            if (e1.Error != null)
            {
                text1.Text = e1.Error.Message;
            }
```

```
        else
        {
            if (e1.UpdateAvailable)
                text1.Text =
                    "Update successful and will be used with the next start";
        }
    };
    App.Current.CheckAndDownloadUpdateAsync();
}
```

Running the application — first in the browser — you can click the Install button, which opens the dialog shown in Figure 38-7. The user can choose to have an application shortcut available in the start menu and on the desktop. After installation, the application can also be started out of browser.

After you make some changes in the Silverlight project, you can check for updates by clicking the Update button. To get rid of the application, click the right mouse button to open the context menu and remove the application.

FIGURE 38-7

SUMMARY

In this chapter, you've seen the rich Silverlight framework, which includes a subset of the functionality of WPF applications and also some enhancements based on the functionality needed for applications running on the Web.

You've seen how to create Silverlight projects and how they differ from WPF, and how to integrate with the browser, run Silverlight applications out of the browser, and use networking features to access resources on the server.

In the next chapter, you read about a traditional technology for user interfaces: Windows Forms.

39

Windows Forms

WHAT'S IN THIS CHAPTER?

➤ The Form class

➤ The class hierarchy of Windows Forms

➤ The controls and components that are part of the System.Windows.Forms namespace

➤ Menus and toolbars

➤ Creating user controls

Web-based applications have taken off over the past several years and are fast becoming the standard. The ability to have all of your application logic reside on a centralized server is very appealing from an administrator's viewpoint. The downside of Web-based applications is that they typically don't provide a rich user experience. The .NET Framework has given developers the ability to create rich, smart client applications and eliminate the deployment problems and "DLL Hell" that existed before. Whether you choose to use Windows Forms or Windows Presentation Foundation (see Chapter 35, "Core WPF"), client applications are no longer difficult to develop or deploy.

Windows Forms will seem familiar if you are a Visual Basic developer. You create new forms (also known as windows or dialogs) in much the same way that you drag and drop controls from a toolbox onto the Form Designer. However, if your background is in the classic C style of Windows programming, where you create the message pump and monitor messages, or if you're an MFC programmer, you will find that you're able to get to the lower-level internals if you need to. You can override the window procedure and catch messages, but you might be surprised that you really won't need to very often.

CREATING A WINDOWS FORMS APPLICATION

In this example, you'll create a very simple Windows Forms application (the rest of the chapter uses a single example application, which can be found in the 03 MainExample folder in the download code zip file.). This first example does not use Visual Studio .NET. It has been entered in a text editor and compiled using the command-line compiler.

Available for download on Wrox.com

```
using System;
using System.Windows.Forms;
namespace NotepadForms
{
```

```
public class MyForm: System.Windows.Forms.Form
{
  public MyForm()
  {
  }
  [STAThread]
  static void Main()
  {
    Application.Run(new MyForm());
  }
}
```

code snippet 01 MyForm/NotepadForms.cs

When you compile and run this example, you will get a small blank form without a caption. The application is not terribly useful, but it serves to show a minimal implementation.

As you look at the code two items deserve attention. The first is the fact that you have used inheritance to create the MyForm class. The following line declares that MyForm is derived from the System.Windows .Forms.Form class:

```
public class MyForm: System.Windows.Forms.Form
```

The Form class is one of the main classes in the System.Windows.Forms namespace. The other section of code that you want to look at is:

```
[STAThread]
static void Main()
{
  Application.Run(new MyForm());
}
```

Main is the default entry point into any C# client application. Typically in larger applications, the Main() method would not be in a form, but instead would be in a separate class. In this case, you would set the startup class name in the project properties dialog box. Notice the attribute [STAThread]. This sets the COM threading model to single-threaded apartment (STA). The STA threading model is required for COM interop and is added by default to a Windows Forms project.

The Application.Run() method is responsible for starting the standard application message loop. ApplicationRun() has three overloads: the first takes no parameter, the second takes an ApplicationContext object as a parameter, and the one you see in the example takes a form object as a parameter. In the example, the MyForm object will become the main form of the application. This means that when this form is closed, the application ends. By using the ApplicationContext class, you can gain a little more control over when the main message loop ends and the application exits.

The Application class contains some very useful functionality. It provides a handful of static methods and properties for controlling the application's starting and stopping process and to gain access to the Windows messages that are being processed by the application. The following table lists some of the more useful of these methods and properties.

METHOD/PROPERTY	DESCRIPTION
CommonAppDataPath	The path for the data that is common for all users of the application. Typically, this is BasePath\Company Name\Product Name\Version, where BasePath is C:\Documents and Settings\username\ApplicationData. If it does not exist, the path will be created.
ExecutablePath	This is the path and filename of the executable file that starts the application.
LocalUserAppData Path	Similar to CommonAppDataPath with the exception that this property supports roaming.

METHOD/PROPERTY	DESCRIPTION
MessageLoop	Returns `true` if a message loop exists on the current thread; `false` otherwise.
StartupPath	Similar to `ExecutablePath`, except that the filename is not returned.
AddMessageFilter	Used to preprocess messages. By implementing an `IMessageFilter`-based object, the messages can be filtered from the message loop, or special processing can take place prior to the message being passed to the loop.
DoEvents	Similar to the Visual Basic `DoEvents` statement. Allows messages in the queue to be processed.
EnableVisualStyles	Enables XP visual styles for the various visual elements of the application. There are two overloads that will accept manifest information. One is a stream of the manifest, and the other is the full name and path of the location where the manifest exists.
Exit and ExitThread	`Exit` ends all currently running message loops and exits the application. `ExitThread` ends the message loop and closes all windows on the current thread.

Now, what does this sample application look like when it is generated in Visual Studio? The first thing to notice is that two files are created because Visual Studio takes advantage of the partial class feature of the Framework and separates all of the Designer-generated code into a separate file. Using the default name of Form1, the two files are Form1.cs and Form1.Designer.cs. (Unless you have the Show All Files option checked on the Project menu, you won't see Form1.Designer.cs in Solution Explorer.) Following is the code that Visual Studio generates for the two files. First is Form1.cs:

Available for download on Wrox.com

```
using System;
using System.Collections.Generic;
using System.ComponentModel;
using System.Data;
using System.Drawing;
using System.Linq;
using System.Text;
using System.Windows.Forms;
namespace VisualStudioForm
{
  public partial class Form1: Form
  {
    public Form1()
    {
      InitializeComponent();
    }
  }
}
```

code snippet Form1.cs

This is pretty simple, a handful of using statements and a simple constructor. Here is the code in Form1 .Designer.cs:

Available for download on Wrox.com

```
namespace VisualStudioForm
{
  partial class Form1
  {
    /// <summary>
    /// Required designer variable.
    /// </summary>
    private System.ComponentModel.IContainer components = null;
    /// <summary>
    /// Clean up any resources being used.
    /// </summary>
    /// <param name="disposing">true if managed resources
    /// should be disposed; otherwise, false.</param>
```

```
      protected override void Dispose(bool disposing)
      {
        if (disposing && (components != null))
        {
          components.Dispose();
        }
        base.Dispose(disposing);
      }
      #region Windows Form Designer generated code
      /// <summary>
      /// Required method for Designer support—do not modify
      /// the contents of this method with the code editor.
      /// </summary>
      private void InitializeComponent()
      {
        this.components =
       new System.ComponentModel.Container();
        this.AutoScaleMode =
         System.Windows.Forms.AutoScaleMode.Font;
        this.Text = "Form1";
      }
      #endregion
    }
  }
```

code snippet Form1.Designer.cs

The Designer file of a form should rarely be edited directly. The only exception is if there is any special processing that needs to take place in the `Dispose` method. The `InitializeComponent` method is discussed later in this chapter.

Looking at the code as a whole for this sample application, you can see it is much longer than the simple command-line example. There are several `using` statements at the start of the class; most are not necessary for this example. There is no penalty for keeping them there. The class `Form1` is derived from `System .Windows.Forms.Form` just like the earlier Notepad example, but things start to get different at this point. First, there is this line in the `Form1.Designer` file:

```
    private System.ComponentModel.IContainer components = null;
```

In the example, this line of code doesn't really do anything. When you add a component to a form, you can also add it to the `components` object, which is a container. The reason for adding to this container has to do with disposing of the form. The form class supports the `IDisposable` interface because it is implemented in the `Component` class. When a component is added to the `components` object, this container will make sure that the components are tracked properly and disposed of when the form is disposed of. You can see this if you look at the `Dispose` method in the code:

```
    protected override void Dispose(bool disposing)
    {
      if (disposing && (components != null))
      {
        components.Dispose();
      }
      base.Dispose(disposing);
    }
```

Here you can see that when the `Dispose` method is called, the `Dispose` method of the `components` object is also called, and because the `component` object contains the other components, they are also disposed of.

The constructor of the `Form1` class, which is in the `Form1.cs` file, looks like this:

```
    public Form1()
    {
      InitializeComponent();
    }
```

Notice the call to `InitializeComponent()`. `InitializeComponent()` is located in `Form1.Designer.cs` and does pretty much what it describes, and that is to initialize any controls that might have been added to the form. It also initializes the form properties. For this example, `InitializeComponent()` looks like the following:

```
private void InitializeComponent()
{
this.components = new System.ComponentModel.Container();
this.AutoScaleMode = System.Windows.Forms.AutoScaleMode.Font;
this.Text = "Form1";
}
```

As you can see, it is basic initialization code. This method is tied to the Designer in Visual Studio. When you make changes to the form by using the Designer, the changes are reflected in `InitializeComponent()`. If you make any type of code change in `InitializeComponent()`, the next time you make a change in the Designer, your changes will be lost. `InitializeComponent()` gets regenerated after each change in the Designer. If you need to add additional initialization code for the form or controls and components on the form, be sure to add it after `InitializeComponent()` is called. `InitializeComponent()` is also responsible for instantiating the controls so any call that references a control prior to `InitializeComponent()` will fail with a null reference exception.

To add a control or component to the form, press Ctrl+Alt+X or select Toolbox from the View menu in Visual Studio .NET to display the Toolbox. `Form1` should be in design mode. Right-click `Form1.cs` in Solution Explorer and select View Designer from the context menu. Select the Button control, and drag it to the form in the Designer. You can also double-click the control to add it to the form. Do the same with the `TextBox` control.

Now that you have added a `TextBox` control and a `Button` control to the form, `InitializeComponent()` expands to include the following code:

```
private void InitializeComponent()
{
  this.button1 = new System.Windows.Forms.Button();
  this.textBox1 = new System.Windows.Forms.TextBox();
  this.SuspendLayout();
  //
  // button1
  //
  this.button1.Location = new System.Drawing.Point(77, 137);
  this.button1.Name = "button1";
  this.button1.Size = new System.Drawing.Size(75, 23);
  this.button1.TabIndex = 0;
  this.button1.Text = "button1";
  this.button1.UseVisualStyleBackColor = true;
  //
  // textBox1
  //
  this.textBox1.Location = new System.Drawing.Point(67, 75);
  this.textBox1.Name = "textBox1";
  this.textBox1.Size = new System.Drawing.Size(100, 20);
  this.textBox1.TabIndex = 1;
  //
  // Form1
  //
  this.AutoScaleDimensions = new System.Drawing.SizeF(6F, 13F);
  this.AutoScaleMode = System.Windows.Forms.AutoScaleMode.Font;
  this.ClientSize = new System.Drawing.Size(284, 264);
  this.Controls.Add(this.textBox1);
  this.Controls.Add(this.button1);
  this.Name = "Form1";
  this.Text = "Form1";
  this.ResumeLayout(false);
  this.PerformLayout();
}
```

If you look at the first three lines of code in the method, you can see the `Button` and `TextBox` controls are instantiated. Notice the names given to the controls, `textBox1` and `button1`. By default, the Designer uses the name of the control and adds an integer value to the name. When you add another button, the Designer adds the name `button2`, and so on. Typically, you would change these names to suit your application. The next line is part of the `SuspendLayout` and `ResumeLayout` pair., `SuspendLayout()` temporarily suspends the layout events that take place when a control is first initialized. At the end of the method the `ResumeLayout()` method is called to set things back to normal. This process can be used to optimize form initialization by avoiding redrawing the screen while it is set up. In a complex form with many controls, the `InitializeComponent()` method can get quite large.

To change a property value of a control, either press F4 or select Properties Window from the View menu. The Properties window enables you to modify most of the properties for a control or component. When a change is made in the Properties window, the `InitializeComponent()` method is rewritten to reflect the new property value. For example, if the `Text` property is changed to `My Button` in the Properties window, `InitializeComponent()` will contain this code:

```
//
// button1
//
this.button1.Location = new System.Drawing.Point(77, 137);
this.button1.Name = "button1";
this.button1.Size = new System.Drawing.Size(75, 23);
this.button1.TabIndex = 0;
this.button1.Text = "My Button";
this.button1.UseVisualStyleBackColor = true;
```

 If you are using an editor other than Visual Studio .NET, you will want to include an `InitializeComponent()` type function in your designs. Keeping all of this initialization code in one spot will help keep the constructor cleaner, not to mention that if you have multiple constructors you can make sure that the initialization code is called from each constructor.

Class Hierarchy

The importance of understanding the hierarchy becomes apparent during the design and construction of custom controls. If your custom control is a derivative of a current control — for example, a text box with some added properties and methods — you will want to inherit from the text box control and then override and add the properties and methods to suit your needs. However, if you are creating a control that doesn't match up to any of the controls included with the .NET Framework, you will have to inherit from one of the three base control classes — `Control` or `ScrollableControl` if you need autoscrolling capabilities, and `ContainerControl` if your control needs to be a container of other controls.

The rest of this chapter is devoted to looking at many of these classes — how they work together and how they can be used to build professional-looking client applications.

CONTROL CLASS

The `System.Windows.Forms` namespace has one particular class that is the base class for virtually every control and form that is created. This class is the `System.Windows.Forms.Control` class. The `Control` class implements the core functionality to create the display that the user sees. The `Control` class is derived from the `System.ComponentModel.Component` class. The `Component` class provides the `Control` class with the necessary infrastructure that is required to be dropped on a design surface and to be contained by another object. The `Control` class provides a large list of functionality to the classes that are derived from it. The list is too long to itemize here, so this section looks at the more important items that are provided by the `Control` class. Later in the chapter, when you look at the specific controls based on the `Control` class, you will see the properties and methods in some sample code. The following subsections group the methods and properties by functionality, so related items can be looked at together.

Size and Location

The size and location of a control are determined by the properties `Height`, `Width`, `Top`, `Bottom`, `Left`, and `Right` along with the complementary properties `Size` and `Location`. The difference is that `Height`, `Width`, `Top`, `Bottom`, `Left`, and `Right` all take single integers as their value. `Size` takes a `Size` structure and `Location` takes a `Point` structure as their values. The `Size` and `Point` structures are a contained version of X,Y coordinates. `Point` generally relates to a location and `Size` is the height and width of an object. `Size` and `Point` are in the `System.Drawing` namespace. Both are very similar in that they provide an X,Y coordinate pair but also have overridden operators for easy comparison and conversion. You can, for example, add two `Size` structures together. In the case of the `Point` structure, the `Addition` operator is overridden so that you can add a `Size` structure to a `Point` and get a new `Point` in return. This has the effect of adding distance to a location and getting a new location. This is very handy if you have to dynamically create forms or controls.

The `Bounds` property returns a `Rectangle` object that represents the area of a control. This area includes scroll bars and title bars. `Rectangle` is also part of the `System.Drawing` namespace. The `ClientSize` property is a `Size` structure that represents the client area of the control, minus the scroll bars and title bar.

The `PointToClient` and `PointToScreen` methods are handy conversion methods that take a `Point` and return a `Point`. `PointToClient` takes a `Point` that represents screen coordinates and translates it to coordinates based on the current client object. This is handy for drag-and-drop actions. `PointToScreen` does just the opposite — it takes coordinates of a client object and translates them to screen coordinates. The `RectangleToScreen` and `ScreenToRectangle` methods perform the same functionality with `Rectangle` structures instead of `Points`.

The `Dock` property determines which edge of the parent control the control will be docked to. A `DockStyle` enumeration value is used as the property's value. This value can be `Top`, `Bottom`, `Right`, `Left`, `Fill`, or `None`. `Fill` sets the control's size to match the client area of the parent control.

The `Anchor` property anchors an edge of the control to the edge of the parent control. This is different from docking in that it does not set the edge to the parent control but sets the current distance from the edge so that it is constant. For example, if you anchor the right edge of the control to the right edge of the parent and the parent is resized, the right edge of the control will maintain the same distance from the parent's right edge. The `Anchor` property takes a value of the `AnchorStyles` enumeration. The values are `Top`, `Bottom`, `Left`, `Right`, and `None`. By setting the values, you can make the control resize dynamically with the parent as the parent is resized. This way, buttons and text boxes will not be cut off or hidden as the form is resized by the user.

The `Dock` and `Anchor` properties used in conjunction with the `Flow` and `Table` layout controls (discussed later in this chapter) enable you to create very sophisticated user windows. Window resizing can be difficult with complex forms with many controls. These tools help make that process much easier.

Appearance

Properties that relate to the appearance of the control are `BackColor` and `ForeColor`, which take a `System.Drawing.Color` object as a value. The `BackGroundImage` property takes an `Image`-based object as a value. The `System.Drawing.Image` class is an abstract class that is used as the base for the `Bitmap` and `Metafile` classes. The `BackgroundImageLayout` property uses the `ImageLayout` enumeration to set how the image is displayed on the control. Valid values are `Center`, `Tile`, `Stretch`, `Zoom`, and `None`.

The `Font` and `Text` properties deal with displaying the written word. In order to change the `Font` you will need to create a `Font` object. When you create the `Font` object, you specify the font name, size, and style.

User Interaction

User interaction is best described as the various events that a control creates and responds to. Some of the more common events are Click, DoubleClick, KeyDown, KeyPress, Validating, and Paint.

The Mouse events — Click, DoubleClick, MouseDown, MouseUp, MouseEnter, MouseLeave, and MouseHover — deal with the interaction of the mouse and the control. If you are handling both the Click and the DoubleClick events, every time you catch a DoubleClick event, the Click event is raised as well. This can result in undesired results if not handled properly. Also, Click and DoubleClick receive EventArgs as an argument, whereas the MouseDown and MouseUp events receive MouseEventArgs. The MouseEventArgs contain several pieces of useful information such as the button that was clicked, the number of times the button was clicked, the number of mouse wheel detents (notches in the mouse wheel), and the current X and Y coordinates of the mouse. If you have access to any of this information, you will have to handle either the MouseDown or MouseUp events, not the Click or DoubleClick events.

The keyboard events work in a similar fashion: The amount of information needed determines the event that is handled. For simple situations, the KeyPress event receives KeyPressEventArgs. This contains KeyChar, which is a char value that represents the key pressed. The Handled property is used to determine whether or not the event was handled. If you set the Handled property to true, the event is not passed on for default handling by the operating system. If you need more information about the key that was pressed, the KeyDown or KeyUp event is more appropriate to handle this. They both receive KeyEventArgs. Properties in KeyEventArgs include whether the Ctrl, Alt, or Shift key was pressed. The KeyCode property returns a Keys enumeration value that identifies the key that was pressed. Unlike the KeyPressEventArgs.KeyChar property, the KeyCode property tells you about every key on the keyboard, not just the alphanumeric keys. The KeyData property returns a Keys value and will also set the modifier. The modifiers are OR'd with the value. This tells you that the Shift key or the Ctrl key was pressed as well. The KeyValue property is the int value of the Keys enumeration. The Modifiers property contains a Keys value that represents the modifier keys that were pressed. If more than one has been selected, the values are OR'd together. The key events are raised in the following order:

1. KeyDown
2. KeyPress
3. KeyUp

The Validating, Validated, Enter, Leave, GotFocus, and LostFocus events all deal with a control gaining focus (or becoming active) or losing focus. This happens when the user tabs into a control or selects the control with the mouse. Enter, Leave, GotFocus, and LostFocus seem to be very similar in what they do. The GotFocus and LostFocus events are lower-level events that are tied to the WM_SETFOCUS and the WM_KILLFOCUS Windows messages. Generally, you should use the Enter and Leave events if possible. The Validating and Validated events are raised when the control is validating. These events receive CancelEventArgs. With this, you can cancel the following events by setting the Cancel property to true. If you have custom validation code, and validation fails, you can set Cancel to true and the control will not lose focus. Validating occurs during validation; Validated occurs after validation. The order in which these events are raised is:

1. Enter
2. GotFocus
3. Leave
4. Validating
5. Validated
6. LostFocus

Understanding the order of these events is important so that you don't inadvertently create a recursive situation. For example, trying to set the focus of a control from the control's LostFocus event creates a loop so the user would not be able to exit from your application.

Windows Functionality

The `System.Windows.Forms` namespace is one of the few namespaces that relies on Windows functionality. The `Control` class is a good example of that. If you were to do a disassembly of the `System.Windows` `.Forms.dll`, you would see a list of references to the `UnsafeNativeMethods` class. The .NET Framework uses this class to wrap many of the standard Win32 API calls. By using interop to the Win32 API, the look and feel of a standard Windows application can still be achieved with the `System.Windows.Forms` namespace.

Functionality that supports the interaction with Windows includes the `Handle` and `IsHandleCreated` properties. `Handle` returns an `IntPtr` that contains the HWND (windows handle) for the control. The window handle is an opaque value that uniquely identifies the window. A control can be considered a window, so it has a corresponding HWND. You can use the `Handle` property to call any number of Win32 API calls.

To gain access to the Windows messages, you can override the `WndProc` method. The `WndProc` method takes a `Message` object as a parameter. The `Message` object is a simple wrapper for a Windows message. It contains the `HWnd`, `LParam`, `WParam`, `Msg`, and `Result` properties. If you want to have the message processed by the system, you must make sure that you pass the message to the `base.WndProc(msg)` method. Failing to pass the message on to Windows can have drastic effects, as the normal event processing will no longer run and you'll most likely make your application fail spectacularly. If you want to handle the message, you don't want to pass the message on.

Miscellaneous Functionality

Some items that are a little more difficult to classify are the data-binding capabilities. The `BindingContext` property returns a `BindingManagerBase` object. The `DataBindings` collection maintains a `ControlBindingsCollection`, which is a collection of binding objects for the control. Data binding is discussed later in this chapter.

The `CompanyName`, `ProductName`, and `Product` versions provide data on the origination of the control and its current version.

The `Invalidate` method allows you to invalidate a region of the control for repainting. You can invalidate the entire control or specify a region or rectangle to invalidate. This causes a paint message to be sent to the control's `WndProc`. You also have the option to invalidate any child controls at the same time.

Dozens of other properties, methods, and events make up the `Control` class. This list represents some of the more commonly used ones and is meant to give you an idea of the functionality available.

STANDARD CONTROLS AND COMPONENTS

The previous section covered some of the common methods and properties for controls. This section looks at the various controls that ship with the .NET Framework and explains what each of them offers in added functionality.

This example is available in the `Chapter39Code` example in the download for the book.

Button

The `Button` class represents the simple command button and is derived from the `ButtonBase` class. The most common thing to do is to write code to handle the `Click` event of the button. The following code snippet implements an event handler for the `Click` event. When the button is clicked, a message box pops up that displays the button's name:

```
private void btnTest_Click(object sender, System.EventArgs e)
{
    MessageBox.Show(((Button)sender).Name + " was clicked.");
}
```

With the `PerformClick` method, you can simulate the `Click` event on a button without the user actually clicking the button, which could be useful when testing your UI. A window also has the notion of a default button, which is automatically clicked if the user presses the Enter key in that window. To identify the button as default, you set the `AcceptButton` property on the form that contains the button to the button object. Then, when the user presses the Enter key, the button `Click` event for the default button is raised. Figure 39-1 shows that the button with the caption Default is the default button (notice the dark border). You can also define a button as the `CancelButton` which indicates that this button will receive a click event if the user presses the `Escape` key.

FIGURE 39-1

Buttons can have images as well as text. Images are supplied by way of an `ImageList` object or the `Image` property. `ImageList` objects are exactly what they sound like: a list of images managed by a component placed on a form. They are explained in detail later in this chapter.

Both `Text` and `Image` have an `Align` property to align the text or image on the `Button`. The `Align` property takes a `ContentAlignment` enumeration value. The text or image can be aligned in combinations of left and right and top and bottom.

CheckBox

The `CheckBox` control is also derived from `ButtonBase` and is used to accept a two-state or three-state response from the user. If you set the `ThreeState` property to `true`, the `CheckBox`'s `CheckState` property can be one of the three `CheckState` enum values in the following table.

VALUE	DESCRIPTION
Checked	The check box has a check mark.
Unchecked	The check box does not have a check mark.
Indeterminate	In this state the check box becomes gray.

The `Indeterminate` state is useful if you need to convey to the user that an option has not been set. You can also check the `Checked` property if you want a Boolean value.

The `CheckedChanged` and `CheckStateChanged` events occur when the `CheckState` or `Checked` properties change. For a three-state check box, you need to attach to the `CheckStateChanged` event. Catching these events can be useful for setting other values based on the new state of the `CheckBox`. The example includes the following code to show the state of the three-state check box:

```
private void threeState_CheckStateChanged(object sender, EventArgs e)
{
    CheckBox cb = sender as CheckBox;

    if (null != cb)
        threeStateState.Text =
            string.Format("State is {0}", cb.CheckState);
}
```

code snippet 03 MainExample/ButtonExample.cs

As the state of the check box changes, a label is updated with the new state.

RadioButton

The last control derived from `ButtonBase` is the radio button. Radio buttons are generally used as a group. Sometimes referred to as option buttons, radio buttons allow the user to choose one of several options. When you have multiple `RadioButton` controls in the same container, only one at a time may be selected. So, if you have three options — for example, `Red`, `Green`, and `Blue` — if the `Red` option is selected and the user clicks the `Blue` option, `Red` is automatically deselected.

The Appearance property takes an Appearance enumeration value. This can be either Button or Normal. When you choose Normal, the radio button looks like a small circle with a label beside it. Selecting the button fills the circle; selecting another button deselects the currently selected button and makes the circle look empty. When you choose Button, the control looks like a standard button, but it works like a toggle — selected is the in position, and deselected is the normal, or out, position.

The CheckedAlign property determines where the circle is in relation to the label text. It could be on top of the label, on either side, or below it.

The CheckedChanged event is raised whenever the value of the Checked property changes. This way, you can perform other actions based on the new value of the control.

ComboBox, ListBox, and CheckedListBox

ComboBox, ListBox, and CheckedListBox are all derived from the ListControl class. This class provides some of the basic list management functionality. The most important aspects of using list controls are adding data to and selecting data from the list. Which list is used is generally determined by how the list is used and the type of data that is going to be in the list. If there is a need to have multiple selections or if the user needs to be able to see several items in the list at any time, the ListBox or CheckedListBox is the best choice. If only a single item is ever selected in the list at any time, a ComboBox may be a good choice.

Data must be added to a list box before it can be useful. You add data by adding objects to the ListBox .ObjectCollection. This collection is exposed by the list's Items property. Because the collection stores objects, any valid .NET type can be added to the list. In order to identify the items, two important properties need to be set. The first is the DisplayMember property. This setting tells the ListControl what property of your object should be displayed in the list. The other is ValueMember, which is the property of your object that you want to return as the value. If strings have been added to the list, by default the string value is used for both of these properties. The ListExample form in the sample application shows how data can be loaded into a list box. The example uses Vendor objects for the list data. The Vendor object contains just two properties: Name and Id. The DisplayMember property is set to the Name property. This tells the list control to display the value from the Name property in the list to the user.

Once the data is loaded in the list, the SelectedItem and SelectedIndex properties can be used to get at the data. The SelectedItem property returns the object that is currently selected. If the list is set to allow multiple selections, there is no guarantee which of the selected items will be returned. In this case, the SelectedItems collection should be used. This contains a list of all of the currently selected items in the list.

If the item at a specific index is needed, the Items property can be used to access the ListBox .ObjectCollection. Because this is a standard .NET collection class, the items in the collection can be accessed in the same way as any other collection class.

If DataBinding is used to populate the list, the SelectedValue property will return the property value of the selected object that was set to the ValueMember property. If Id is set to ValueMember, the SelectedValue will return the Id value from the selected item. In order to use ValueMember and SelectedValue the list must be loaded by way of the DataSource property. An ArrayList or any other IList-based collection must be loaded with the objects first, and then the list can be assigned to the DataSource property.

The Items property of the ComboBox returns ComboBox.ObjectCollection. A ComboBox is a combination of an edit control and a list box. You set the style of the ComboBox by passing a DropDownStyle enumeration value to the DropDownStyle property. The following table lists the various DropDownStyle values.

VALUE	DESCRIPTION
DropDown	The text portion of the combo box is editable, and users can enter a value. They can also click the arrow button to show the drop-down list of values.
DropDownList	The text portion is not editable. Users must make a selection from the list.
Simple	This is similar to DropDown except that the list is always visible.

If the values in the list are wide, you can change the width of the drop-down portion of the control with the `DropDownWidth` property. The `MaxDropDownItems` property sets the number of items to show when the drop-down portion of the list is displayed.

The `FindString` and `FindStringExact` methods are two other useful methods of the list controls. `FindString` finds the first string in the list that starts with the passed-in string. `FindString Exact` finds the first string that matches the passed-in string. Both return the index of the value that is found or `-1` if the value is not found. They can also take an integer that is the starting index to search from.

Lastly, the `CheckedListBox` control is similar to the `ListBox`; however, the `DisplayMember` and `ValueMember` properties do not show up in IntelliSense, nor do they display in the property grid. They are available on the actual control, but an attribute has been added to them to indicate that they are not used. This is not the case — you can use `DisplayMember` to determine what will show up on the user interface, or as an alternative, you can simply override the `ToString()` method on the objects you are adding into this list to display whatever you like onscreen.

The DataGridView Control

The `DataGrid` control that has been available from the initial release of .NET was functional, but it had many aspects that made it unsuitable for use in a commercial application — such as an inability to display images, drop-down controls, or lock columns, to name but a few. The control always felt half-completed, so many control vendors provided custom grid controls that overcame these deficiencies and also provided much more functionality.

.NET 2.0 introduced an additional `Grid` control — the `DataGridView`. This addressed many of the deficiencies of the original control, and added significant functionality that previously was available only with add-on products.

The `DataGridView` control has binding capabilities similar to the old `DataGrid`, so it can bind to an `Array`, `DataTable`, `DataView`, or `DataSet` class, or a component that implements either the `IListSource` or `IList` interface. It gives you a variety of views of the same data. In its simplest guise, data can be displayed (as in a `DataSet` class) by setting the `DataSource` and `DataMember` properties — note that this control is not a plugin replacement for the `DataGrid`, so the programmatic interface to it is entirely different from that of the `DataGrid`. This control also provides more complex capabilities, which are discussed in the course of this chapter.

In this section we use the Northwind sample database. If you don't already have it installed, please download the installer from the Web and create a database called Northwind in your SQL Server or SQL Express instance. You can find the installation scripts for Northwind at `http://msdn.microsoft.com/enus/library/ms143221.aspx`.

Displaying Tabular Data

Chapter 20, "Threads, Tasks, and Synchronization," introduced numerous ways of selecting data and reading it into a data table, although the data was displayed in a very basic fashion using `Console .WriteLine()`.

The following example demonstrates how to retrieve some data and display it in a `DataGridView` control. For this purpose, you will build a new application, `DisplayTabularData`, shown in Figure 39-2.

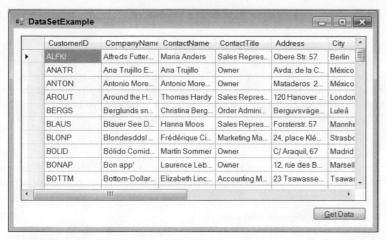

FIGURE 39-2

This simple application selects every record from the `Customer` table in the Northwind database and displays these records to the user in the `DataGridView` control. The following snippet shows the code for this example (excluding the form and control definition code):

```
using System;
using System.Configuration;
using System.Data;
using System.Data.Common;
using System.Data.SqlClient;
using System.Windows.Forms;

namespace DisplayTabularData
{
  partial class Form1: Form
  {
    public Form1()
    {
      InitializeComponent();
    }

    private void getData_Click(object sender, EventArgs e)
    {
      string customers = "SELECT * FROM Customers";

      using (SqlConnection con =
             new SqlConnection (ConfigurationManager.
               ConnectionStrings["northwind"].ConnectionString))
      {
        DataSet ds = new DataSet();

        SqlDataAdapter da = new SqlDataAdapter(customers, con);

        da.Fill(ds, "Customers");

        dataGridView.AutoGenerateColumns = true;
        dataGridView.DataSource = ds;
        dataGridView.DataMember = "Customers";
      }
    }
  }
}
```

The form consists of the getData button, which when clicked calls the getData_Click() method shown in the example code.

This constructs a SqlConnection object, using the ConnectionStrings property of the ConfigurationManager class. Subsequently, a data set is constructed and filled from the database table, using a DataAdapter object. The data is then displayed by the DataGridView control by setting the DataSource and DataMember properties. Note that the AutoGenerateColumns property is also set to true because this ensures that something is displayed to the user. If this flag is not specified, you need to create all the columns yourself.

Data Sources

The DataGridView control provides a flexible way to display data; in addition to setting the DataSource to a DataSet and the DataMember to the name of the table to display, the DataSource property can be set to any of the following sources:

➤ An array (the grid can bind to any one-dimensional array)

➤ DataTable

➤ DataView

➤ DataSet or DataViewManager

➤ Components that implement the IListSource interface

➤ Components that implement the IList interface

➤ Any generic collection class or object derived from a generic collection class

The following sections give an example of each of these data sources.

Displaying Data from an Array

At first glance, displaying data from an array seems to be easy. Create an array, fill it with some data, and set the DataSource property on the DataGridView control. Here's some example code:

```
string[] stuff = new string[] {"One", "Two", "Three"};
dataGridView.DataSource = stuff;
```

If the data source contains multiple possible candidate tables (such as when using a DataSet or DataViewManager), you need to also set the DataMember property.

You could replace the code in the previous example's getData_Click event handler with the preceding array code. The problem with this code is the resulting display (see Figure 39-3).

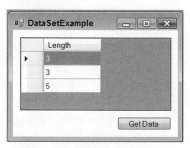

FIGURE 39-3

Instead of displaying the strings defined within the array, the grid displays the length of those strings. That's because when using an array as the source of data for a DataGridView control, the grid looks for the first public property of the object within the array and displays this value rather than the string value. The first (and only) public property of a string is its length, so that is what is displayed. The list of properties for any class can be obtained by using the GetProperties method of the TypeDescriptor class. This returns a collection of PropertyDescriptor objects, which can then be used when displaying data. The .NET PropertyGrid control uses this method when displaying arbitrary objects.

One way to rectify the problem with displaying strings in the DataGridView is to create a wrapper class:

```
protected class Item
{
    public Item(string text)
    {
        _text = text;
    }
```

```
public string Text
{
    get{return _text;}
}
private string _text;
}
```

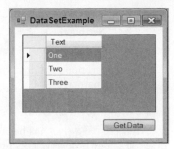

Figure 39-4 shows the output when an array of this `Item` class (which could just as well be a `struct` for all the processing that it does) is added to your data source array code.

DataTable

FIGURE 39-4

You can display a `DataTable` within a `DataGridView` control in two ways:

➤   If you have a standalone `DataTable`, simply set the `DataSource` property of the control to the table.

➤   If your `DataTable` is contained within a `DataSet`, you need to set the `DataSource` to the data set and the `DataMember` property should be set to the name of the `DataTable` within the data set.

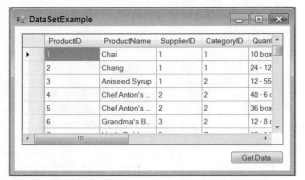

Figure 39-5 shows the result of running the `DataSourceDataTable` sample code.

The last column shows a check box instead of the more common edit control. The `DataGridView`

FIGURE 39-5

control, in the absence of any other information, will read the schema from the data source (which in this case is the `Products` table), and infer from the column types what control is to be displayed. Unlike the original `DataGrid` control, the `DataGridView` control has built-in support for image columns, buttons, and combo boxes.

The data in the database does not change when fields are altered in the data grid because the data is stored only locally on the client computer — there is no active connection to the database. Updating data in the database is discussed later in this chapter.

Displaying Data from a DataView

A `DataView` provides a means to filter and sort data within a `DataTable`. When data has been selected from the database, it is common to permit the user to sort that data, for example, by clicking on column headings. In addition, the user might want to filter the data to show only certain rows, such as all those that have been altered. A `DataView` can be filtered so that only selected rows are shown to the user; however, you cannot filter the columns from the `DataTable`.

 A `DataView` does not permit the filtering of columns, only rows.

To create a `DataView` based on an existing `DataTable`, use the following code:

```
DataView dv = new DataView(dataTable);
```

Once the DataView is created, further settings can be altered on it, which affect the data and operations permitted on that data when it is displayed within the data grid. For example:

➤   Setting `AllowEdit = false` disables all column edit functionality for rows.

➤   Setting `AllowNew = false` disables the new row functionality.

➤ Setting `AllowDelete = false` disables the delete row capability.

➤ Setting the `RowStateFilter` displays only rows of a given state.

➤ Setting the `RowFilter` enables you to filter rows.

The next section explains how to use the `RowStateFilter` setting; the other options are fairly self-explanatory.

Filtering Rows by Data

After the `DataView` has been created, the data displayed by that view can be altered by setting the `RowFilter` property. This property, typed as a string, is used as a means of filtering based on certain criteria defined by the value of the string. Its syntax is similar to a `WHERE` clause in regular SQL, but it is issued against data already selected from the database.

The following table shows some examples of filter clauses.

CLAUSE	DESCRIPTION
`UnitsInStock > 50`	Shows only those rows where the value in the `UnitsInStock` column is greater than 50.
`Client = 'Smith'`	Returns only the records for a given client.
`County LIKE 'C*'`	Returns all records where the `County` field begins with a C — in this example, the rows for Cornwall, Cumbria, Cheshire, and Cambridgeshire would be returned. The % character can be used as a single-character wildcard, whereas the * denotes a general wildcard that will match zero or more characters.

The runtime will do its best to coerce the data types used within the filter expression into the appropriate types for the source columns. For instance, it is perfectly legal to write `"UnitsInStock > '50'"` in the earlier example, even though the column is an integer. If an invalid filter string is provided, an `EvaluateException` will be thrown.

Filtering Rows on State

Each row within a `DataView` has a defined row state, which has one of the values shown in the following table. This state can also be used to filter the rows viewed by the user.

DATAVIEWROWSTATE	DESCRIPTION
`Added`	Lists all rows that have been newly created.
`CurrentRows`	Lists all rows except those that have been deleted.
`Deleted`	Lists all rows that were originally selected and have been deleted; does not show newly created rows that have been deleted.
`ModifiedCurrent`	Lists all rows that have been modified and shows the current value of each column.
`ModifiedOriginal`	Lists all rows that have been modified but shows the original value of the column and not the current value.
`OriginalRows`	Lists all rows that were originally selected from a data source. Does not include new rows. Shows the original values of the columns (that is, not the current values if changes have been made).
`Unchanged`	Lists all rows that have not changed in any way.

Figure 39-6 shows a grid that can have rows added, deleted, or amended, and a second grid that lists rows in one of the preceding states.

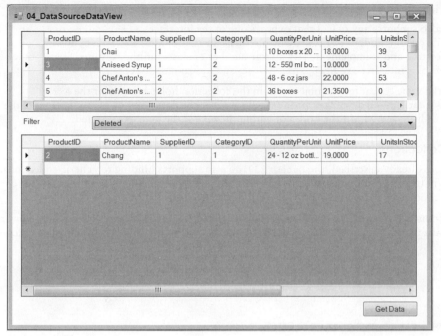

FIGURE 39-6

The filter not only applies to the visible rows but also to the state of the columns within those rows. This is evident when choosing the `ModifiedOriginal` or `ModifiedCurrent` selections. These states are based on the `DataRowVersion` enumeration. For example, when the user has updated a column in the row, the row will be displayed when either `ModifiedOriginal` or `ModifiedCurrent` is chosen; however, the actual value will be either the `Original` value selected from the database (if `ModifiedOriginal` is chosen) or the current value in the `DataColumn` (if `ModifiedCurrent` is chosen).

Sorting Rows

Apart from filtering data, you might also have to sort the data within a `DataView`. To sort data in ascending or descending order, simply click the column header in the `DataGridView` control (see Figure 39-7). The only trouble is that the control can sort by only one column, whereas the underlying `DataView` control can sort by multiple columns.

ProductID	ProductName	SupplierID ▲
1	Chai	1
3	Aniseed Syrup	1
4	Chef Anton's ...	2
5	Chef Anton's ...	2

FIGURE 39-7

When a column is sorted, either by clicking the header (as shown on the `SupplierId` column) or in code, the `DataGrid` displays an arrow bitmap to indicate which column the sort has been applied to.

To set the sort order on a column programmatically, use the `Sort` property of the `DataView`:

```
dataView.Sort = "ProductName";
dataView.Sort = "ProductName ASC, ProductID DESC";
```

The first line sorts the data based on the `ProductName` column, as shown in Figure 39-7. The second line sorts the data in ascending order, based on the `ProductName` column, then in descending order of `ProductID`.

The `DataView` supports both ascending (default) and descending sort orders on columns. If more than one column is sorted in code in the `DataView`, the `DataGridView` will cease to display any sort arrows.

Each column in the grid can be strongly typed, so its sort order is not based on the string representation of the column but instead is based on the data within that column. The upshot is that if there is a date column in the `DataGrid`, the user can sort numerically on the date rather than on the date string representation.

IListSource and IList Interfaces

The `DataGridView` also supports any object that exposes one of the interfaces `IListSource` or `IList`. `IListSource` has only one method, `GetList()`, which returns an `IList` interface. `IList`, however, is somewhat more interesting and is implemented by a large number of classes in the runtime. Some of the classes that implement this interface are `Array`, `ArrayList`, and `StringCollection`.

When using `IList`, the same caveat for the object within the collection holds true as for the `Array` implementation shown earlier — if a `StringCollection` is used as the data source for the `DataGrid`, the length of the strings is displayed within the grid, not within the text of the item as expected.

Displaying Generic Collections

In addition to the types already described, the `DataGridView` also supports binding to generic collections. The syntax is just as in the other examples already provided in this chapter — simply set the `DataSource` property to the collection, and the control will generate an appropriate display.

Once again, the columns displayed are based on the properties of the object — all public readable fields are displayed in the `DataGridView`. The following example shows the display for a list class defined as follows:

```csharp
class PersonList: List < Person >
{
}

class Person
{
    public Person( string name, Sex sex, DateTime dob )
    {
        _name = name;
        _sex = sex;
        _dateOfBirth = dob;
    }

    public string Name
    {
        get { return _name; }
        set { _name = value; }
    }

    public Sex Sex
    {
        get { return _sex; }
        set { _sex = value; }
    }

    public DateTime DateOfBirth
    {
        get { return _dateOfBirth; }
        set { _dateOfBirth = value; }
    }

    private string _name;
    private Sex _sex;
    private DateTime _dateOfBirth;
}

enum Sex
{
    Male,
    Female
}
```

code snippet 03 MainExample/Person.cs

The display shows several instances of the `Person` class that were constructed within the `PersonList` class. See Figure 39-8.

In some circumstances, it might be necessary to hide certain properties from the grid display — for this you can use the `Browsable` attribute as shown in the following code snippet. Any properties marked as non-browsable are not displayed in the property grid.

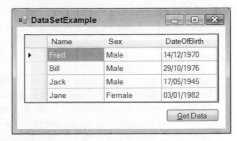

```
[Browsable(false)]
public bool IsEmployed
{
    .
    .
    .
}
```

FIGURE 39-8

The `DataGridView` uses this property to determine whether to display the property or hide it. In the absence of the attribute, the default is to display the property. If a property is read-only, the grid control will display the values from the object, but it will be read-only within the grid.

Any changes made in the grid view are reflected in the underlying objects — so, for example, if in the previous code the name of a person was changed within the user interface, the setter method for that property would be called.

DateTimePicker

The `DateTimePicker` allows users to select a date or time value (or both) in a number of different formats. You can display the `DateTime`-based value in any of the standard time and date formats. The Format property takes a `DateTimePickerFormat` enumeration that sets the format to `Long`, `Short`, `Time`, or `Custom`. If the `Format` property is set to `DateTimePickerFormat.Custom`, you can set the `CustomFormat` property to a string that represents the format.

There is both a `Text` property and a `Value` property. The `Text` property returns a text representation of the `DateTime` value, whereas the `Value` property returns the `DateTime` object. You can also set the maximum and minimum allowable date values with the `MinDate` and `MaxDate` properties.

When users click the down arrow, a calendar is displayed allowing the users to select a date in the calendar. Properties are available that allow you to change the appearance of the calendar by setting the title and month background colors as well as the foreground colors.

The `ShowUpDown` property determines whether an `UpDown` arrow is displayed on the control. The currently highlighted value can be changed by clicking the up or down arrow.

ErrorProvider

`ErrorProvider` is actually not a control but a component. When you drag a component to the Designer, it shows in the component tray under the Designer. The `ErrorProvider` flashes an icon next to a control when an error condition or validation failure exists. Suppose that you have a `TextBox` entry for an age and your business rules say that the age value cannot be greater than 65. If users try to enter an age greater than that, you must inform them that the age is greater than the allowable value and that they need to change the entered value. The check for a valid value takes place in the `Validated` event of the text box. If the validation fails, you call the `SetError` method, passing in the control that caused the error and a string that informs the user what the error is. An exclamation point icon starts flashing, indicating that an error has occurred, and when the user hovers over the icon the error text is displayed. Figure 39-9 shows the icon that is displayed when an invalid entry is made in the text box.

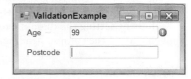

FIGURE 39-9

If the validation of a field fails you would then call the `SetIcon` method of the `ErrorProvider` object and pass through the control that failed validation and an appropriate error message. The error is displayed as a blinking icon next to the control that caused the validation error, and the error message is displayed as a tooltip. You can call `SetError` again with an empty error string to remove the error condition.

ImageList

An `ImageList` component is exactly what the name implies — a list of images. Typically, this component is used for holding a collection of images that are used as toolbar icons or icons in a `TreeView` control. Many controls have an `ImageList` property. The `ImageList` property typically comes with an `ImageIndex` property. The `ImageList` property is set to an instance of the `ImageList` component, and the `ImageIndex` property is set to the index in the `ImageList` that represents the image that should be displayed on the control. You add images to the `ImageList` component by using the `Add` method of the `ImageList.Images` property. The `Images` property returns an `ImageCollection`.

The two most commonly used properties are `ImageSize` and `ColorDepth`. `ImageSize` uses a `Size` structure as its value. The default value is 16 3 16, but it can be any value from 1 to 256. The `ColorDepth` uses a `ColorDepth` enumeration as its value. The color depth values go from 4-bit to 32-bit, with a default of `ColorDepth.Depth8Bit`.

Label

`Label`s are generally used to provide descriptive text to the user. The text might be related to other controls or the current system state. You usually see a label together with a text box. The label provides the user with a description of the type of data to be entered in the text box. The `Label` control is always read-only — the user cannot change the string value of the `Text` property. However, you can change the `Text` property in your code. The `UseMnemonic` property allows you to enable the access key functionality. When you precede a character in the `Text` property with the ampersand (`&`), that letter will appear underlined in the label control. Pressing the Alt key in combination with the underlined letter puts the focus on the next control in the tab order. If you wish to display an ampersand in the text, you need to escape the ampersand with another ampersand. For example, if the label text should be "Nuts & Bolts," set the property to "Nuts && Bolts." Because the `Label` control is read-only, it cannot gain focus; that's why focus is sent to the next control. Because of this, it is important to remember that if you enable mnemonics, you must be certain to set the tab order properly on your form.

The `AutoSize` property is a `Boolean` value that specifies whether the `Label` will resize itself based on the contents of the `Label`. This can be useful for multi-language applications where the length of the `Text` property can change based on the current language.

ListView

The `ListView` control enables you to display items in one of four different ways. You can display text with an optional large icon, text with an optional small icon, or text and small icons in a vertical list or in detail view, which allows you to display the item text plus any subitems in columns. If this sounds familiar, it should, because this is similar to the right-hand side of Windows Explorer. A `ListView` contains a collection of `ListViewItems`. `ListViewItems` allow you to set a `Text` property used for the display. `ListViewItem` has a property called `SubItems` that contains the text that appears in detail view.

The `ListView` control is one of the most flexible in the .NET Framework, and there are a multitude of options you can set to change the appearance of items. For example, you can emulate a checked list box simply by setting the `CheckBoxes` property to `True`. You can add images to items, alter the view, alter the behavior of the column headings to sort, and even group items into different groups.

PictureBox

The `PictureBox` control is used to display an image. The image can be a BMP, JPEG, GIF, PNG, metafile, or icon. The `SizeMode` property uses the `PictureBoxSizeMode` enumeration to determine how the image is sized and positioned in the control. The `SizeMode` property can be `AutoSize`, `CenterImage`, `Normal`, and `StretchImage`.

You can change the size of the display of the `PictureBox` by setting the `ClientSize` property. You load the `PictureBox` by first creating an `Image`-based object. For example, to load a JPEG file into a `PictureBox`, you would do the following:

```
Bitmap myJpeg = Bitmap.FromFile("whatever.png") as Bitmap;
pictureBox1.Image = myJpeg;
```

ProgressBar

The `ProgressBar` control is a visual clue to the status of a lengthy operation. It indicates to users that there is something going on and that they should wait. The `ProgressBar` control works by setting the `Minimum` and `Maximum` properties, which correspond to the progress indicator being all the way to the left (`Minimum`) or all the way to the right (`Maximum`). You set the `Step` property to determine the number that the value is incremented each time the `PerformStep` method is called. You can also use the `Increment` method and increment the value by the value passed in the method call. The `Value` property returns the current value of the `ProgressBar`.

TextBox, RichTextBox, and MaskedTextBox

The `TextBox` control is one of the most used controls in the toolbox. The `TextBox`, `RichTextBox`, and `MaskedTextBox` controls are all derived from `TextBoxBase`. `TextBoxBase` provides properties such as `MultiLine` and `Lines`. `MultiLine` is a `Boolean` value that allows the `TextBox` control to display text in more than one line. Each line in a text box is a part of an array of strings. This array is exposed through the `Lines` property. The `Text` property returns the entire text box contents as a single string. `TextLength` is the total length of the string that text would return. The `MaxLength` property will limit the length of the text to the specified amount.

`SelectedText`, `SelectionLength`, and `SelectionStart` all deal with the currently selected text in the text box. The selected text is highlighted when the control has focus.

The `TextBox` control adds a couple of interesting properties. `AcceptsReturn` is a Boolean value that will allow the `TextBox` to capture the Enter key. If the value is set to `false`, the Enter key clicks the default button on the form. When `AcceptsReturn` is set to `true`, pressing the Enter key creates a new line in the `TextBox`. `CharacterCasing` determines the casing of the text in the text box. The `CharacterCasing` enumeration contains three values, `Lower`, `Normal`, and `Upper`. `Lower` lowercases all text regardless of how it is entered, `Upper` renders all text in uppercase letters, and `Normal` displays the text as it is entered. The `PasswordChar` property takes a `char` that represents what is displayed to the users when they type text in the text box. This is typically used for entering passwords and PINs. The `text` property will return the actual text that was entered; only the display is affected by this property.

The `RichTextBox` is a text-editing control that can handle special formatting features. As the name implies, the `RichTextBox` control uses Rich Text Format (RTF) to handle the special formatting. You can make formatting changes by using the `Selection` properties: `SelectionFont`, `SelectionColor`, and `SelectionBullet`, and paragraph formatting with `SelectionIndent`, `SelectionRightIndent`, and `SelectionHangingIndent`. All of the `Selection` properties work in the same way. If a section of text is highlighted, a change to a `Selection` property affects the selected text. If no text is selected, the change takes effect with any text that is inserted to the right of the current insertion point.

The text of the control can be retrieved by using the `Text` property or the `Rtf` property. The `Text` property returns just the text of the control, whereas the `Rtf` property returns the formatted text.

The `LoadFile` method can load text from a file in a couple of different ways. It can use a string that represents the path and filename or it can use a stream object. You can also specify the `RichTextBoxStreamType`. The following table lists the values of `RichTextBoxStreamType`.

VALUE	DESCRIPTION
PlainText	No formatting information. In places that contained OLE objects, spaces are used.
RichNoOleObjs	Rich Text formatting, but spaces where the OLE objects would have been.
RichText	Formatted RTF with OLE objects in place.
TextTextOleObjs	Plain text with text replacing the OLE objects.
UnicodePlainText	Same as PlainText but Unicode encoded.

The SaveFile method works with the same parameters, saving the data from the control to a specified file. If a file by that name already exists, it will be overwritten. In the example, an RTF file is included as a resource in the application, and this text is loaded into the control when the form is loaded.

The MaskedTextBox has the ability to limit what the user may input into the control. It also allows for automatic formatting of the data entered. Several properties are used in order to validate or format the user's input. Mask is the property that contains the mask string, which is similar to a format string. The number of characters allowed, the data type of allowed characters, and the format of the data are all set using the Mask string. A MaskedTextProvider-based class can also provide the formatting and validation information needed. The MaskedTextProvider can only be set by passing it in on one of the constrictors.

Three different properties will return the text of the MaskedTextControl. The Text property returns the text of the control at the current moment. This could be different, depending on whether or not the control has focus, which depends on the value of the HidePromptOnLeave property. The prompt is a string that users see to guide them on what should be entered. The InputText property always returns just the text that the user entered. The OutputText property returns the text formatted according to the IncludeLiterals and IncludePrompt properties. If, for example, the mask is for a phone number, the Mask string might include parentheses and a couple of dashes. These would be the literal characters and would be included in the OutputText property if the IncludeLiteral property were set to true.

A couple of extra events also exist for the MaskedTextBox control. OutputTextChanged and InputTextChanged are raised when InputText or OutputText changes.

Panel

A Panel is simply a control that contains other controls. Grouping controls together and placing them in a panel makes it is a little easier to manage them. For example, you can disable all of the controls in the panel by disabling the panel. Because the Panel control is derived from ScrollableControl, you can also get the advantage of the AutoScroll property. If you have too many controls to display in the available area, place them in a Panel and set AutoScroll to true — now you can scroll through all of the controls.

Panels do not show a border by default, but by setting the BorderStyle property to something other than none, you can use the Panel to visually group related controls using borders. This makes the user interface more user-friendly.

Panel is the base class for the FlowLayoutPanel, TableLayoutPanel, TabPage, and SplitterPanel. Using these controls, you can create a very sophisticated and professional-looking form or window. The FlowLayoutPanel and TableLayoutPanel are especially useful for creating forms that resize properly.

FlowLayoutPanel and TableLayoutPanel

FlowLayoutPanel and TableLayoutPanel are recent additions to the .NET Framework. As the names suggest, the panels offer the capability to lay out a form using the same paradigm as a Web Form. FlowLayoutPanel is a container that allows the contained controls to flow in either the horizontal or vertical direction. Instead of flowing, it allows for the clipping of the controls. Flow direction is set using the FlowDirection property and the FlowDirection enumeration. The WrapContents property determines if controls flow to the next row or column when the form is resized or if the control is clipped.

`TableLayoutPanel` uses a grid structure to control the layout of controls. Any Windows Forms control can be a child of the `TableLayoutPanel`, including another `TableLayoutPanel`. This allows for a very flexible and dynamic window design. When a control is added to a `TableLayoutPanel`, four additional properties are added to the `Layout` category of the property page. They are `Column`, `ColumnSpan`, `Row`, and `RowSpan`. Much like an HTML table on a Web page, column and row spans can be set for each control. By default, the control will be centered in the cell of the table, but this can be changed by using the `Anchor` and `Dock` properties.

The default style of the rows and columns can be changed using `RowStyles` and `ColumnsStyles` collections. These collections contain `RowStyle` and `ColumnsStyle` objects, respectively. The `Style` objects have a common property, `SizeType`. `SizeType` uses the `SizeType` enumeration to determine how the column width or row height should be sized. Values include `AutoSize`, `Absolute`, and `Percent`. `AutoSize` shares the space with other peer controls. `Absolute` allows a set number of pixels for the size and `Percent` tells the control to size the column or width as a percentage of the parent control.

Rows, columns, and child controls can be added or removed at runtime. The `GrowStyle` property takes a `TableLayoutPanelGrowStyle` enumeration value that sets the table to add a column or a row, or stay a fixed size when a new control is added to a full table. If the value is `FixedSized`, an `ArgumentException` is thrown when there is an attempt to add another control. If a cell in the table is empty, the control will be placed in the empty cell. This property has an effect only when the table is full and a control is added.

The sample code includes a form containing both a flow layout panel and a table layout panel to show the effect of resizing the form on the controls within the panels.

SplitContainer

The `SplitContainer` control is really three controls in one. It has two panel controls with a bar or splitter between them. The user is able to move the bar and resize the panels. As the panels resize, the controls in the panels also can be resized. The best example of a `SplitContainer` is File Explorer. The left panel contains a `TreeView` of folders, and the right side contains a `ListView` of folder contents. When the user moves the mouse over the splitter bar, the cursor changes, showing that the bar can be moved. The `SplitContainer` can contain any control, including layout panels and other `SplitContainers`. This allows the creation of very complex and sophisticated forms.

The movement and position of the splitter bar can be controlled with the `SplitterDistance` and `SplitterIncrement` properties. The `SplitterDistance` property determines where the splitter starts in relation to the left or top of the control. The `SplitterIncrement` determines the number of pixels the splitter moves when being dragged. The panels can have their minimum size set with the `Panel1MinSize` and `Panel2MinSize` properties. These properties are also in pixels.

The `Splitter` control raises two events that relate to moving: the `SplitterMoving` event and the `SplitterMoved` event. One takes place during the move, and the other takes place after the move has happened. They both receive `SplitterEventArgs`. `SplitterEventArgs` contains properties for the X and Y coordinates of the upper-left corner of the `Splitter` (`SplitX` and `SplitY`) and the X and Y coordinates of the mouse pointer (X and Y).

The sample code includes a poor man's Windows Explorer, which uses a split container along with a tree view and list view to show directories and files.

TabControl and TabPages

`TabControl` allows you to group related controls onto a series of tab pages. `TabControl` manages the collection of `TabPages`. Several properties control the appearance of `TabControl`. The `Appearance` property uses the `TabAppearance` enumeration to determine what the tabs look like. The values are `FlatButtons`, `Buttons`, or `Normal`. The `Multiline` property is a `Boolean` that determines if more than one row of tabs is shown. If the `Multiline` property is set to `false` and there are more tabs than can fit in the display, arrows appear that allow the user to scroll and see the rest of the tabs.

The `TabPage` `Text` property is what is displayed on the tab. The `Text` property is a parameter in a constructor override as well.

Once you create a `TabPage` control, it is basically a container control in which you can place other controls. The Designer in Visual Studio .NET makes it easy to add `TabPage` controls to a `TabControl` control by using the collection editor. You can set the various properties as you add each page. Then you can drag the other child controls to each `TabPage` control.

You can determine the current tab by looking at the `SelectedTab` property. The `SelectedIndex` event is raised each time a new tab is selected. By listening to the `SelectedIndex` property and then confirming the current tab with `SelectedTab`, you can do special processing based on each tab. You could, for example, manage the data displayed for each tab.

ToolStrip

The `ToolStrip` control is a container control used to create toolbars, menu structures, and status bars. The `ToolStrip` is used directly for toolbars, and serves as the base class for the `MenuStrip` and `StatusStrip` controls.

When used as a toolbar, the `ToolStrip` control uses a set of controls based on the abstract `ToolStripItem` class. `ToolStripItem` adds the common display and layout functionality as well as managing most of the events used by the controls. `ToolStripItem` is derived from the `System.ComponentModel.Component` class and not from the `Control` class. `ToolStripItem`-based classes must be contained in a `ToolStrip`-based container.

`Image` and `Text` are probably the most common properties that will be set. Images can be set with either the `Image` property or by using the `ImageList` control and setting it to the `ImageList` property of the `ToolStrip` control. The `ImageIndex` property of the individual controls can then be set.

Formatting of the text on a `ToolStripItem` is handled with the `Font`, `TextAlign`, and `TextDirection` properties. `TextAlign` sets the alignment of the text in relation to the control. This can be any of the `ControlAlignment` enumeration values. The default is `MiddleRight`. The `TextDirection` property sets the orientation of the text. Values can be any of the `ToolStripTextDirection` enumeration values, which include `Horizontal`, `Inherit`, `Vertical270`, and `Vertical90`. `Vertical270` rotates the text 270 degrees, and `Vertical90` rotates the text 90 degrees.

The `DisplayStyle` property controls whether text, image, text and image, or nothing is displayed on the control. When `AutoSize` is set to `true`, the `ToolStripItem` will resize itself so that only the minimum amount of space is used.

The controls that are derived directly from `ToolStripItem` are listed in the following table.

TOOL STRIP ITEMS	DESCRIPTION
`ToolStripButton`	Represents a button that the user can select.
`ToolStripLabel`	Displays nonselectable text or images on the `ToolStrip`. The `ToolStripLabel` can also display one or more hyperlinks.
`ToolStripSeparator`	Used to separate and group other `ToolStripItems`. Items can be grouped according to functionality.
`ToolStripDropDownItem`	Displays drop-down items. Base class for `ToolStripDropDownButton`, `ToolStripMenuItem`, and `ToolStripSplitButton`.
`ToolStripControlHost`	Hosts other non–`ToolStripItem`-derived controls on a `ToolStrip`. Base class for `ToolStripComboBox`, `ToolStripProgressBar`, and `ToolStripTextBox`.

The last two items in the list, `ToolStripDropDownItem` and `ToolStripControlHost`, deserve a little more discussion. `ToolStripDropDownItem` is the base class for `ToolStripMenuItems`, which are used to build the menu structure. `ToolStripMenuItems` are added to `MenuStrip` controls. As mentioned earlier, `MenuStrips` are derived from `ToolStrip` controls. This is important when it comes time to manipulate or extend menu items. Because toolbars and menus are derived from the same classes, creating a framework for managing and executing commands is much easier.

`ToolStripControlHost` can be used to host other controls that do not derive from `ToolStripItem`. Remember that the only controls that can be directly hosted by a `ToolStrip` are those that are derived from `ToolStripItem`.

MenuStrip

The `MenuStrip` control is the container for the menu structure of an application. As mentioned earlier, `MenuStrip` is derived from the `ToolStrip` class. The menu system is built by adding `ToolStripMenu` objects to the `MenuStrip`. You can do this in code or in the Designer of Visual Studio. Drag a `MenuStrip` control onto a form in the Designer and the `MenuStrip` will allow the entry of the menu text directly on the menu items.

The `MenuStrip` control has only a couple of additional properties. `GripStyle` uses the `ToolStripGripStyle` enumeration to set the grip as visible or hidden. The `MdiWindowListItem` property takes or returns a `ToolStripMenuItem`. This `ToolStripMenuItem` is the menu that shows all open windows in an MDI application.

ContextMenuStrip

To show a context menu, or a menu displayed when the user right-clicks the mouse, the `ContextMenuStrip` class is used. Like `MenuStrip`, `ContextMenuStrip` is a container for `ToolStripMenuItems` objects. However, it is derived from `ToolStripDropDownMenu`. A `ContextMenu` is created the same way as a `MenuStrip`. `ToolStripMenuItems` are added, and the `Click` event of each item is defined to perform a specific task. Context menus are assigned to specific controls. This is done by setting the `ContextMenuStrip` property of the control. When the user right-clicks the control, the menu is displayed.

ToolStripMenuItem

`ToolStripMenuItem` is the class that builds the menu structures. Each `ToolStripMenuItem` object represents a single menu choice on the menu system. Each `ToolStripMenuItem` has a `ToolStripItemCollection` that maintains the child menus. This functionality is inherited from `ToolStripDropDownItem`.

Because `ToolStripMenuItem` is derived from `ToolStripItem`, all of the same formatting properties apply. Images appear as small icons to the right of the menu text. Menu items can have check marks show up next to them with the `Checked` and `CheckState` properties.

Shortcut keys can be assigned to each menu item. They are generally two key chords such as Ctrl+C (common shortcut for Copy). When a shortcut key is assigned, it can optionally be displayed on the menu by setting the `ShowShortCutKey` property to `true`.

To be useful, the menu item has to do something when the user clicks it or uses the defined shortcut keys. The most common way is to handle the `Click` event. If the `Checked` property is being used, the `CheckStateChanged` and `CheckedChanged` events can be used to determine a change in the checked state.

ToolStripManager

Menu and toolbar structures can become large and cumbersome to manage. The `ToolStripManager` class provides the ability to create smaller, more manageable pieces of a menu or toolbar structure and then combine them when needed. An example of this is a form that has several different controls on it.

Each control must display a context menu. Several menu choices will be available for all of the controls, but each control will also have a couple of unique menu choices. The common choices can be defined on one `ContextMenuStrip`. Each of the unique menu items can be predefined or created at runtime. For each control that needs a context menu assigned to it, the common menu is cloned and the unique choices are merged with the common menu using the `ToolStripManager.Merge` method. The resulting menu is assigned to the `ContextMenuStrip` property of the control.

ToolStripContainer

The `ToolStripContainer` control is used for docking of `ToolStrip`-based controls. When you add a `ToolStripContainer` and set the `Docked` property to `Fill`, a `ToolStripPanel` is added to each side of the form, and a `ToolStripContainerPanel` is added to middle of the form. Any `ToolStrip` (`ToolStrip`, `MenuStrip`, or `StatusStrip`) can be added to any of the `ToolStripPanels`. The user can move a `ToolStrip` by grabbing it and dragging it to either side or bottom of the form. If you set the `Visible` property to false on any of the `ToolStripPanels`, a `ToolStrip` can no longer be placed in the panel. The `ToolStripContainerPanel` in the center of the form can be used to place the other controls the form may need.

FORMS

Earlier in this chapter, you learned how to create a simple Windows application. The example contained one class derived from the `System.Windows.Forms.Form` class. According to the .NET Framework documentation, "a Form is a representation of any window in your application." If you come from a Visual Basic background, the term "form" will seem familiar. If your background is C++ using MFC, you're probably used to calling a form a window, dialog box, or maybe a frame. Regardless, the form is the basic means of interacting with the user. Earlier, the chapter covered some of the more common and useful properties, methods, and events of the `Control` class, and because the `Form` class is a descendant of the `Control` class, all of the same properties, methods, and events exist in the `Form` class. The `Form` class adds considerable functionality to what the `Control` class provides, and that's what this section discusses.

Form Class

A Windows client application can contain one form or hundreds of forms. The forms can be an SDI-based (Single Document Interface) or MDI-based (Multiple Document Interface) application. Regardless, the `System.Windows.Forms.Form` class is the heart of the Windows client. The `Form` class is derived from `ContainerControl`, which is derived from `ScrollableControl`, which is derived from `Control`. Because of this, you can assume that a form is capable of being a container for other controls, is capable of scrolling when the contained controls do not fit the client area, and has many of the same properties, methods, and events that other controls have. This also makes the `Form` class rather complex. This section looks at much of that functionality.

Form Instantiation and Destruction

The process of form creation is important to understand. What you want to do depends on where you write the initialization code. For instantiation, the events occur in the following order:

- ➤ Constructor
- ➤ Load
- ➤ Activated
- ➤ Closing
- ➤ Closed
- ➤ Deactivate

The first three events are of concern during initialization. The type of initialization you want to do could determine which event you hook into. The constructor of a class occurs during the object instantiation. The Load event occurs after object instantiation, but just before the form becomes visible. The difference between this and the constructor is the viability of the form. When the Load event is raised, the form exists but isn't visible. During constructor execution, the form is in the process of coming into existence. The Activated event occurs when the form becomes visible and current.

This order can be altered slightly in one particular situation. If during the constructor execution of the form, the Visible property is set to true or the Show method is called (which sets the Visible property to true), the Load event fires immediately. Because this also makes the form visible and current, the Activate event is also raised. If there is code after the Visible property has been set, it will execute. So, the startup event might look something like this:

➤ Constructor, up to Visible = true

➤ Load

➤ Activate

➤ Constructor, after Visible = true

This could potentially lead to some unexpected results. From a best practices standpoint, it would seem that doing as much initialization as possible in the constructor might be a good idea.

Now what happens when the form is closed? The Closing event gives you the opportunity to cancel the process. The Closing event receives CancelEventArgs as a parameter. This has a Cancel property that, if set to true, cancels the event and the form remains open. The Closing event happens as the form is being closed, whereas the Closed event happens after the form has been closed. Both allow you to do any cleanup that might have to be done. Notice that the Deactivate event occurs after the form has been closed. This is another potential source of difficult-to-find bugs. Be sure that you don't have anything in Deactivate that could keep the form from being properly garbage collected. For example, setting a reference to another object would cause the form to remain alive.

If you call the Application.Exit() method and you have one or more forms currently open, the Closing and Closed events will not be raised. This is an important consideration if you have open files or database connections that you were going to clean up. The Dispose method is called, so perhaps another best practice would be to put most of your cleanup code in the Dispose method.

Some properties that relate to the startup of a form are StartPosition, ShowInTaskbar, and TopMost. StartPosition can be any of the FormStartPosition enumeration values. They are:

➤ CenterParent — The form is centered in the client area of the parent form.

➤ CenterScreen — The form is centered in the current display.

➤ Manual — The form's location is based on the values in the Location property.

➤ WindowsDefaultBounds — The form is located at the default Windows position and uses the default size.

➤ WindowsDefaultLocation — The Windows default location is used, but the size is based on the Size property.

The ShowInTaskbar property determines if the form should be available in the taskbar. This is relevant only if the form is a child form and you only want the parent form to show in the taskbar. The TopMost property tells the form to start in the topmost position in the Z-order of the application. This is true even if the form does not immediately have focus.

In order for users to interact with the application, they must be able to see the form. The Show and ShowDialog methods accomplish this. The Show method just makes the form visible to the user. The following code segment demonstrates how to create a form and show it to the user. Assume that the form you want to display is called MyFormClass.

```
MyFormClass myForm = new MyFormClass();
myForm.Show();
```

That's the simple way. The one drawback to this is that there isn't any notification back to the calling code that myForm is finished and has been exited (unless you hook up the Closing or Closed events on the form). Sometimes this isn't a big deal, and the Show method will work fine. If you do need some type of notification, ShowDialog is a better option.

When the Show method is called, the code that follows the Show method is executed immediately. When ShowDialog is called, the calling code is blocked and will wait until the form that ShowDialog called is closed. Not only will the calling code be blocked, but the form will optionally return a DialogResult value. The DialogResult enumeration is a list of identifiers that describe the reason the dialog is closed. These include OK, Cancel, Yes, No, and several others. In order for the form to return a DialogResult, the form's DialogResult property must be set or the DialogResult property on one of the form's buttons must be set.

For example, suppose that part of application asks for the phone number of a client. The form has a text box for the phone number and two buttons; one is labeled OK and the other is labeled Cancel. If you set the DialogResult of the OK button to DialogResult.OK and the DialogResult property on the Cancel button to DialogResult.Cancel, then when either of these buttons is selected, the form becomes invisible and returns to the calling form the appropriate DialogResult value. Now notice that the form is not destroyed; the Visible property is just set to false. That's because you still must get values from the form. For this example, you need to get a phone number. By creating a property on the form for the phone number, the parent form can now get the value and call the Close method on the form. This is what the code for the child form looks like:

```
namespace FormsSample.DialogSample
{
    partial class Phone: Form
    {
        public Phone()
        {
            InitializeComponent();
            btnOK.DialogResult = DialogResult.OK;
            btnCancel.DialogResult = DialogResult.Cancel;
        }

        public string PhoneNumber
        {
            get { return textBox1.Text; }
            set { textBox1.Text = value; }
        }
    }
}
```

The first thing to notice is that there is no code to handle the click events of the buttons. Because the DialogResult property is set for each of the buttons, the form disappears after either the OK or Cancel button is clicked. The only property added is the PhoneNumber property. The following code shows the method in the parent form that calls the Phone dialog:

```
Phone frm = new Phone();
frm.ShowDialog();
if (frm.DialogResult == DialogResult.OK)
{
    label1.Text = "Phone number is " + frm.PhoneNumber;
}
else if (frm.DialogResult == DialogResult.Cancel)
{
    label1.Text = "Form was canceled. ";
}
frm.Close();
```

This looks simple enough. Create the new Phone object (frm). When the frm.ShowDialog() method is called, the code in this method will stop and wait for the Phone form to return. You can then check the

`DialogResult` property of the `Phone` form. Because it has not been destroyed yet, just made invisible, you can still access the public properties, one of them being the `PhoneNumber` property. Once you get the data you need, you can call the `Close` method on the form.

Within the dialog you can validate the controls before the form closes, so in this example you might want to validate the format of the phone number (and update the `Enabled` state of the `OK` button accordingly).

Appearance

The first thing that the user sees is the form for the application. It should be first and foremost functional. If the application doesn't solve a business problem, it really doesn't matter how it looks. This is not to say that the form and application's overall GUI design should not be pleasing to the eye. Simple things like color combinations, font sizing, and window sizing can make an application much more attractive for the user.

Sometimes you don't want the user to have access to the system menu. This is the menu that appears when you click the icon on the top-left corner of a window. Generally, it has such items as `Restore`, `Minimize`, `Maximize`, and `Close`. The `ControlBox` property allows you to set the visibility of the system menu. You can also set the visibility of the `Maximize` and `Minimize` buttons with the `MaximizeBox` and `MinimizeBox` properties. If you remove all of the buttons and then set the `Text` property to an empty string (`""`), the title bar disappears completely.

If you set the `Icon` property of a form and you don't set the `ControlBox` property to `false`, the icon will appear in the top-left corner of the form. It's common to set this to the `app.ico`. This makes each form's icon the same as the application icon.

The `FormBorderStyle` property sets the type of border that appears around the form. This uses the `FormBorderStyle` enumeration. The values can be as follows:

- ➤ Fixed3D
- ➤ FixedDialog
- ➤ FixedSingle
- ➤ FixedToolWindow
- ➤ None
- ➤ Sizable
- ➤ SizableToolWindow

Most of these are self-explanatory, with the exception of the two tool window borders. A `Tool` window will not appear in the taskbar, regardless of how `ShowInTaskBar` is set. Also a `Tool` window will not show in the list of windows when the user presses Alt+Tab. The default setting is `Sizable`.

Unless a requirement dictates otherwise, colors for most GUI elements should be set to system colors, not to specific colors. This way, if some users like to have all of their buttons green with purple text, the application will follow along with the same colors. To set a control to use a specific system color, you must call the `FromKnownColor` method of the `System.Drawing.Color` class. The `FromKnownColor` method takes a `KnownColor` enumeration value. Many colors are defined in the enumeration, as well as the various GUI element colors, such as `Control`, `ActiveBorder`, and `Desktop`. So, for example, if the `Background` color of the form should always match the `Desktop` color, the code would look like this:

```
myForm.BackColor = Color.FromKnownColor(KnownColor.Desktop);
```

Now if users change the color of their desktops, the background of the form changes as well. This is a nice, friendly touch to add to an application. Users might pick out some strange color combinations for their desktops, but it is their choice.

Windows XP introduced a feature called visual styles. Visual styles change the way buttons, text boxes, menus, and other controls look and react when either the mouse pointer is hovering or the mouse button is clicked. You can enable visual styles for your application by calling the `Application.EnableVisualStyles` method.

This method has to be called before any type of GUI is instantiated. Because of this, it is generally called in the Main method, as demonstrated in this example:

```
[STAThread]
static void Main()
{
   Application.EnableVisualStyles();
   Application.Run(new Form1());
}
```

This code allows the various controls that support visual styles to take advantage of them. Because of an issue with the EnableVisualStyles method, you might have to add an Application. DoEvents() method right after the call to EnableVisualStyles. This should resolve the problem if icons on toolbars begin to disappear at runtime. Also, EnableVisualStyles is available in .NET Framework 1.1 only.

You have to accomplish one more task pertaining to the controls. Most controls expose the FlatStyle property, which takes a FlatStyle enumeration as its value. This property can take one of four different values:

➤   Flat — The control has a flat appearance with no 3D outline.

➤   Popup — Similar to flat, except that when the mouse pointer hovers over the control, it appears in 3D.

➤   Standard — The control appears in 3D.

➤   System — The look of the control is controlled by the operating system.

To enable visual styles, the control's FlatStyle property should be set to FlatStyle.System. The application will now take on the XP look and feel and will support XP themes.

Multiple Document Interface

MDI-type applications are used when you have an application that can show either multiple instances of the same type of form, such as a text editor that can show multiple editor windows at the same time, or one in which different forms are contained in some way, such as Microsoft Access. With Access, you can have query windows, design windows, and table windows all open at the same time. The windows never leave the boundaries of the main Access application.

The project that contains the examples for this chapter is an MDI application. The form MainForm in the project is the MDI parent form. Setting the IsMdiContainer to true will make any form an MDI parent form. If you have the form in the Designer, you'll notice that the background turns a dark gray color. This is to let you know that this is an MDI parent form. You can still add controls to the form, but it is generally not recommended.

For a child form to behave like an MDI child, it needs to have a link to the parent form. This is done by setting the MdiParent property of the child form to the parent form. In the example, all children forms are created using the ShowMdiChild method. This method takes a reference to the child form that is to be shown. After setting the MdiParent property to this, which is referencing the MainForm form, the form is displayed.

One of the issues with MDI applications is that there may be several child forms open at any given time. A reference to the current active child can be retrieved by using the ActiveMdiChild property on the parent form. This is demonstrated on the Current Active menu choice on the Window menu. This choice will show a message box with the form's name and text value.

The child forms can be arranged by calling the LayoutMdi method. The LayoutMdi method takes an MdiLayout enumeration value as a parameter. The possible values include Cascade, TileHorizontal, and TileVertical.

Creating Your Own User Controls

In addition to using the built-in controls, it is also possible to create your own custom controls and then reuse these in your own applications. There are two types of custom controls — those derived from the UserControl base class and those derived from Control. A UserControl is the simplest type to create, as you can compose one from the other controls in the toolbox. Typically, you'll write a custom control only when the built-in controls cannot be used to do what you want. Entire books have been written on the creation of custom controls, so here we'll concentrate on user controls.

In this section, you'll build the user control shown in Figure 39-10, which includes an error provider validator, and exposes its fields for reuse. The code for this example is available in the 02 UserControl folder of the chapter downloads.

FIGURE 39-10

To begin you need to construct a new user control, which can be done from the Solution Explorer or the project menu. Once it is created, you'll have a class that derives from UserControl and can then drag and drop other controls onto the design surface. In this example you use a set of label controls and a set of text boxes to replicate the functionality shown in Figure 39-10.

Once the UI has been laid out, you want to define anchor behavior for the controls. This is important to do as it permits the user control to resize properly when its size is changed. In the example control, each of the text boxes has had its alignment set to Left + Top + Right, and a small space on the right of the list boxes has been provided, which will show any validation errors.

In addition to the text boxes, an ErrorProvider object has been added to the control so that validation errors can be shown while the user tabs around the control. The first two address fields and the postcode have validation errors assigned, so they are mandatory.

Once you are happy with the design and implementation of your control, you can simply compile it, and it will be displayed within the tool palette in Visual Studio. You can then reuse that control in any application that needs it.

SUMMARY

This chapter has given you the basics for building Windows-based client applications. It explained many of the basic controls by discussing the hierarchy of the Windows.Forms namespace and examining the various properties and methods of the controls.

The chapter also showed you how to create a basic user control. The power and flexibility of creating your own controls cannot be emphasized enough. By creating your own toolbox of custom controls, Windows-based client applications will become easier to develop and to test because you will be reusing the same tested components over and over again.

40

Core ASP.NET

WHAT'S IN THIS CHAPTER?

➤ Introduction to ASP.NET

➤ Creating ASP.NET Web Forms

➤ Binding data with ADO.NET

➤ Configuring applications

If you are new to the world of C# and .NET, you might wonder why a chapter on ASP.NET has been included in this book. It's a whole new language, right? Well, not really. In fact, as you will see, you can use C# to create ASP.NET pages.

ASP.NET is part of the .NET Framework and is a technology that allows for the dynamic creation of documents on a web server when they are requested via HTTP. This mostly means HTML and XHTML documents, although it is equally possible to create XML documents, cascading style sheet (CSS) files, images, PDF documents, or anything else that supports MIME types.

In some ways, ASP.NET is similar to many other technologies — such as PHP, ASP, or ColdFusion. There is, however, one key difference: ASP.NET, as its name suggests, has been designed to be fully integrated with the .NET Framework, part of which includes support for C#.

Perhaps you are familiar with Active Server Pages (ASP) technology, which enables you to create dynamic content. If you are, you will probably know that programming in this technology used scripting languages such as VBScript or JScript. The result was not always perfect, at least not for those of us used to "proper," compiled programming languages, and it certainly resulted in a loss of performance.

One major difference related to the use of more advanced programming languages is the provision of a complete server-side object model for use at runtime. ASP.NET provides access to all the controls on a page as objects, in a rich environment. On the server side, you also have access to other .NET classes, allowing for the integration of many useful services. Controls used on a page expose a lot of functionality; in fact, you can do almost as much as with Windows Forms classes, which provide plenty of flexibility. For this reason, ASP.NET pages that generate HTML content are often called *Web Forms*.

This chapter takes a more detailed look at ASP.NET, including how it works, what you can do with it, and how C# fits in.

ASP.NET INTRODUCTION

ASP.NET works with Internet Information Services (IIS) to deliver content in response to HTTP requests. ASP.NET pages are found in .aspx files. Figure 40-1 illustrates the technology's basic architecture.

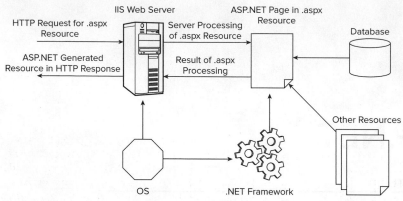

FIGURE 40-1

How ASP.NET Files are Processed

During ASP.NET processing, you have access to all .NET classes, custom components created in C# or other languages, databases, and so on. In fact, you have as much power as you would have running a C# application; using C# in ASP.NET is, in effect, running a C# application.

An ASP.NET file can contain any of the following:

➤ Processing instructions for the server

➤ Code in C#, Visual Basic .NET, JScript .NET, or any other language that the .NET Framework supports

➤ Content in whatever form is appropriate for the generated resource, such as HTML

➤ Client-side script code, such as JavaScript

➤ Embedded ASP.NET server controls

So, in fact, you could have an ASP.NET file as simple as this:

```
Hello!
```

This would simply result in an HTML page being returned (as HTML is the default output of ASP.NET pages) containing just this text.

As you will see later in this chapter, it is also possible to split certain portions of the code into other files, which can provide a more logical structure.

Web Sites and Web Applications

In ASP.NET it is possible to create both "web sites" and "web applications". These two terms both mean that you supply a collection of ASP.NET, C#, and other files, but the way that they are processed is subtly different.

In a *web site*, any code that you supply is dynamically compiled as and when it is required. This generally means that code is compiled the first time that the site is accessed. The .cs files for a web site are stored on the web server, which means that you can make changes by uploading new versions of these files, which will trigger a recompile the next time the site is accessed.

Conversely, *web applications* are compiled before being deployed to a web server, and don't include .cs files. Instead, a pre-compiled assembly is deployed to the server along with ASP.NET pages.

In general, most ASP.NET programmers tend to prefer the web application model, and there are some technologies (such as MVC) that will only work with web applications. Web sites are mainly useful in the development stage, where quick changes to code may be required and a full deployment may not be desirable.

State Management in ASP.NET

One of the key properties of ASP.NET pages is that they are effectively stateless. By default, no information is stored on the server between user requests (although there are methods for doing this, as you will see later in this chapter). At first glance, this seems a little strange because state management is something that seems essential for user-friendly interactive sessions. However, ASP.NET provides a workaround to this problem, such that session management becomes almost transparent.

In short, information such as the state of controls on a Web Form (including data entered in text boxes or selections from drop-down lists) is stored in a hidden *viewstate* field that is part of the page generated by the server and passed to the user. Subsequent actions, such as triggering events that require server-side processing, such as submitting form data, result in this information being sent back to the server; this is known as a *postback* operation. On the server, this information is used to repopulate the page object model allowing you to operate on it as if the changes had been made locally.

You will see this in action shortly and examine the details.

ASP.NET WEB FORMS

As mentioned earlier, much of the functionality in ASP.NET is achieved using Web Forms. Before long, you will dive in and create a simple Web Form to give you a starting point to explore this technology. First, however, this section reviews some key points pertinent to Web Form design.

Note that some ASP.NET developers simply use a text editor such as Notepad to create files. We wouldn't advocate this ourselves because the benefits you get via an IDE, such as Visual Studio or Web Developer Express are substantial, but it's worth mentioning because it is a possibility. If you do take this route, you have a great deal of flexibility as to which parts of a web application you put where. This enables you, for example, to combine all your code in one file. You can achieve this by enclosing code in <script> elements, using two attributes on the opening <script> tag:

```
<script language="c#" runat="server">
    // Server-side code goes here.
</script>
```

The runat="server" attribute here is crucial because it instructs the ASP.NET engine to execute this code on the server rather than sending it to the client, thus giving you access to the rich environment hinted at earlier. You can place your functions, event handlers, and so on in server-side script blocks.

If you omit the runat="server" attribute, you are effectively providing client-side code, which will fail if it uses any of the server-side style coding that is discussed in this chapter. You can, however, use <script> elements to supply client-side script in languages such as JavaScript. For example:

```
<script language="JavaScript" type="text/JavaScript">
    // Client-side code goes here; you can also use "vbscript".
</script>
```

 Note that the type *attribute here is optional, but necessary if you want to comply with HTML and XHTML standards.*

It may seem strange that the facility to add JavaScript code to your pages is included with ASP.NET. However, JavaScript allows you to add dynamic client-side behavior to your web pages and can be very useful. This is especially true for Ajax programming, as you will see in Chapter 41, "ASP.NET Features."

It is possible to create ASP.NET files in Visual Studio, which is great for you, as you are already familiar with this environment for C# programming. However, the default project setup for web applications in this environment has a slightly more complex structure than a single .aspx file. This isn't a problem for you, however, and does make things a bit more logical (more programmer-like and less web developer–like). For this reason, you will use Visual Studio throughout this chapter for your ASP.NET programming (instead of Notepad).

The .aspx files can also include code in blocks enclosed by <% and %> tags. However, function definitions and variable declarations cannot go here. Instead, you can insert code that is executed as soon as the block is reached, which is useful when outputting simple HTML content. This behavior is similar to that of old-style ASP pages, with one important difference — the code is compiled, not interpreted. This results in far better performance.

Now it's time for an example. In Visual Studio, you create a new web site by using the File ⇨ New ⇨ Web Site . . . menu option or a web application through the File ⇨ New ⇨ Project . . . menu option by selecting a web application template. In either case, from the dialog box that appears, select the Visual C# language type and the specific template you want. For web sites, you have an additional choice to make. Visual Studio can create web sites in a number of different locations:

➤ On your local IIS web server

➤ On your local disk, configured to use the built-in Visual Web Developer web server

➤ At any location accessible via FTP

➤ On a remote web server that supports Front Page Server Extensions

The latter two choices use remote servers so you are left with the first two choices. In general, IIS is the best place to install ASP.NET web sites because it is likely to be closest to the configuration required when you deploy a web site. The alternative, using the built-in web server, is fine for testing but has certain limitations:

➤ Only the local computer can see the web site.

➤ Access to services such as SMTP is restricted.

➤ The security model is different from IIS — the application runs in the context of the current user rather than in an ASP.NET-specific account.

This last point requires clarification because security is very important when it comes to accessing databases or anything else that requires authentication. By default, web applications running on IIS do so in an account called ASPNET on IIS5 web servers, or in an account called NT AUTHORITY\NETWORK SERVICE on IIS6 and above. This is configurable if you are using IIS, but not if you use the built-in web server.

For the purposes of illustration, however, and because you may not have IIS installed on your computer, you can use the built-in web server. You aren't worried about security at this stage, so you can go with simplicity.

Web applications don't prompt you to choose a location like web sites do. Instead, web sites must be deployed to web servers in a separate step — although for testing they will use the VWD web server.

Create a new ASP.NET web site called PCSWebSite1 using the File System option and the Empty Web Site template, at C:\ProCSharp\Chapter40, as shown in Figure 40-2.

FIGURE 40-2

 Note that the ASP.NET Web Site template is not used here in order to keep things simple for the first example. The ASP.NET Web Site template includes techniques such as Master Pages, which you won't examine until the next chapter.

After a few moments, Visual Studio .NET should have set up the following:

➤ `PCSWebSite1`, a new solution containing the C# web site PCSWebSite1

➤ `Web.config`, a configuration file for the web application

Next you need to add a web page. You can do this through the Website ➪ Add New Item . . . menu option. Select the Web Form template and leave the rest of the settings unchanged (with a file name of `Default.aspx` and the "Place code in separate file" option selected), and then click Add. This adds the following:

FIGURE 40-3

➤ `Default.aspx`, the first ASP.NET page in the web application

➤ `Default.aspx.cs`, a "code-behind" class file for `Default.aspx`

You can see all this in the Solution Explorer, as shown in Figure 40-3.

You can view `.aspx` files in design or source (HTML) view. This is the same as for Windows Forms (as discussed in Chapter 39, "Windows Forms"). The initial view in Visual Studio is either the design or source view for `Default.aspx` (you can toggle between the views or view them together in a split view using the buttons in the bottom left). The design view is shown in Figure 40-4.

FIGURE 40-4

Underneath the (currently empty) form, you can see where in the HTML for the form the cursor is currently positioned. Here the cursor is in a `<div>` element inside a `<form>` element inside the `<body>` element of the page. The `<form>` element is displayed as `<form#form1>` to identify the element by its `id` attribute, which you will see shortly. The `<div>` element is also labeled in the design view.

The source view for the page shows you the code generated inside the `.aspx` file:

```
<%@ Page Language="C#" AutoEventWireup="true" CodeFile="Default.aspx.cs"
    Inherits="_Default" %>
<!DOCTYPE html PUBLIC "-//W3C//DTD XHTML 1.0 Transitional//EN"
    "http://www.w3.org/TR/xhtml1/DTD/xhtml1-transitional.dtd">
<html xmlns="http://www.w3.org/1999/xhtml">
<head runat="server">
  <title></title>
</head>
<body>
  <form id="form1" runat="server">
    <div>
    </div>
  </form>
</body>
</html>
```

code snippet PCSWebSite1/Default.aspx

If you know any HTML syntax, then this will look familiar to you. You are presented with the basic code required for an HTML page following the XHTML schema, with a few extra bits of code. The most important extra is the `<form>` element, which has an `id` attribute of `form1`. This element will contain your ASP.NET code. The most important thing to note here is the `runat` attribute. Just as with the server-side code blocks you saw at the start of this section, this is set to `server`, meaning that the processing of the form will take place on the server. If you don't include this reference, then no server-side processing will be performed, and the form won't do anything. There can be only one server-side `<form>` element in an ASP.NET page.

The other interesting thing about this code is the `<%@ Page %>` tag at the top. This tag defines page characteristics that are important to you as a C# web developer. There is a `Language` attribute that specifies that you will use C# throughout your page, as you saw earlier with `<script>` blocks. (The default for ASP. NET pages is Visual Basic .NET, although this can be changed using a `Web.config` file, which you will see later in this chapter.) The other three attributes — `AutoEventWireup`, `CodeFile`, and `Inherits` — are used to associate the Web Form with a class in a code-behind code file, in this case the partial class `_Default` in the file `Default.aspx.cs`. This leads straight into a necessary discussion about the ASP.NET code model.

The ASP.NET Code Model

In ASP.NET, a combination of layout (HTML) code, ASP.NET controls, and C# code is used to generate the HTML that users see. The layout and ASP.NET code are stored in an `.aspx` file, such as the one you looked at in the preceding section. The C# code that you add to customize the behavior of the form is contained either in the `.aspx` file or, as in the preceding example, in a separate `.aspx.cs` file, which is usually referred to as the "code-behind" file.

In a web site project, when an ASP.NET Web Form is processed — typically when a user requests the page, although sites can be precompiled — several things happen:

➤   The ASP.NET process examines the page and determines what objects must be created to instantiate the page object model.

➤   A base class for the page is dynamically created, including members for the controls on the page as well as event handlers for these controls (such as button click events).

➤   Additional code contained in the `.aspx` page is combined with this base class to complete the object model.

➤ The complete code is compiled and cached ready to process subsequent requests.

➤ HTML is generated and returned to the user.

In web applications the process is similar, although no dynamic compilation is required as web applications are precompiled by definition.

The code-behind file generated for you in the PCSWebSite1 web site for `Default.aspx` is initially very sparse. First, you see the default set of namespace references that you are likely to use in ASP.NET web pages:

Available for download on Wrox.com

```
using System;
using System.Collections.Generic;
using System.Linq;
using System.Web;
using System.Web.UI;
using System.Web.UI.WebControls;
```

code snippet PCSWebSite1/Default.aspx.cs

Below these references, you see an almost completely empty partial class definition for `Default_aspx`:

```
public partial class _Default : System.Web.UI.Page
{
    protected void Page_Load(object sender, EventArgs e)
    {
    }
}
```

Here, the `Page_Load()` event handler can be used to add any code that is required when the page is loaded. As you add more event handlers, and so on, this class file will become increasingly full of code. Note that you don't see the code that wires up this event handler to the page — event handlers are inferred by the ASP. NET runtime, as noted earlier. This is due to the `AutoEventWireUp` attribute — setting this to `false` will mean that you will need to associate the event handlers in your code with events on your own.

This class is a partial class definition because the process outlined earlier requires it. When the page is precompiled, a separate partial class definition is created from the ASP.NET code for your page. This includes all the controls you have added to the page. At design time, the compiler infers this partial class definition, which allows you to use IntelliSense in your code-behind to reference controls on your page.

ASP.NET Server Controls

Your generated code doesn't do very much yet, so next you need to add some content. You can do this in Visual Studio using the Web Form designer, which supports drag-and-drop in just the same way as the Windows Forms designer.

You can add three types of server controls to your ASP.NET pages:

➤ **HTML server controls** — These controls mimic HTML elements, which will be familiar to HTML developers.

➤ **Web server controls** — This is a new set of controls, some of which have the same functionality as HTML controls. These controls have a common naming scheme for properties and other elements to ease development, and provide consistency with analogous Windows Forms controls. There are also some completely new and very powerful controls, as you will see later. Several types of web server controls exist, including the standard ones such as buttons, validation controls for validating user input, login controls to simplify user management, and more complicated controls for dealing with data sources.

➤ **Custom and user controls** — These controls are defined by the developer and can be created in a number of ways, as discussed in Chapter 41.

The next section lists many of the frequently used web server controls, along with usage notes. Some additional controls are examined in the next chapter. HTML controls are not covered in this book. These controls don't do anything more than the web server controls, and the web server controls provide a richer environment for developers more familiar with programming than with HTML design. If you learn how to use the web server controls, then you will have all the information you require to use HTML server controls. For more information, check out Professional ASP.NET 4 *(Wiley Publishing, Inc., 2010, ISBN 978-0470-50220-4).*

Adding Web Server Controls

You can add a couple of web server controls to the PCSWebSite1 web site that you created in the last section. All web server controls are used in the following XML element-type form:

```
<asp:controlName runat="server" attribute="value">Contents</asp:controlName>
```

In the preceding code, `controlName` is the name of the ASP.NET server control, `attribute="value"` is one or more attribute specifications, and `Contents` specifies the control content, if any. Some controls allow properties to be set using attributes and control element content, such as `Label` (used for simple text display), where `Text` can be specified in either way. Other controls might use an element containment scheme to define their hierarchy — for example `Table` (which defines a table), which can contain `TableRow` elements in order to specify table rows declaratively.

Because the syntax for controls is based on XML (although the controls may be used embedded in non-XML code such as HTML), it is an error to omit the closing tags and `/>` for empty elements, or to overlap controls.

Finally, you once again see the `runat="server"` attribute on the web server controls. It is just as essential here as it is elsewhere, and it is a common mistake to skip this attribute. If you do, your Web Forms won't work.

Adding Web Server Controls In Source View

This first example is simple. Change the HTML source view for `Default.aspx` as follows:

```
<%@ Page Language="C#" AutoEventWireup="true" CodeFile="Default.aspx.cs"
    Inherits="_Default" %>
<!DOCTYPE html PUBLIC "-//W3C//DTD XHTML 1.1//EN"
"http://www.w3.org/TR/xhtml11/DTD/xhtml11.dtd">
<html xmlns="http://www.w3.org/1999/xhtml">
<head runat="server">
  <title></title>
</head>
<body>
  <form id="form1" runat="server">
    <div>
       <asp:Label runat="server" ID="resultLabel" /><br />
       <asp:Button runat="server" ID="triggerButton" Text="Click Me" />
    </div>
  </form>
</body>
</html>
```

code snippet PCSWebSite1/Default.aspx

Here you have added two Web Form controls: a label and a button.

Note that as you do this, Visual Studio .NET IntelliSense predicts your code entry, just as in the C# code editor. Also, if you edit your code in split view and synchronize the views, the element that you are editing in the source pane will be highlighted in the design pane.

Going back to the design screen, you can see that your controls have been added and named using their ID attributes (the ID attribute is often known as the *identifier* of a control). As with Windows Forms, you have full access to properties, events, and so on through the Properties window and get instant feedback in code or design whenever you make changes.

You can also use the CSS Properties window and other style windows to style your controls. However, unless you are familiar with CSS, you will probably want to leave this technique alone for now and concentrate on the functionality of the controls.

Any server controls you add will automatically become part of the object model for the form that you are building. This is an instant bonus for Windows Forms developers — the similarities are beginning to emerge!

Adding an Event Handler

To make this application do something, you can add an event handler for clicking the button. Here you can either enter a method name in the Properties window for the button or just double-click the button to get the default event handler. If you double-click the button, you will automatically add an event-handling method as follows:

**Available for
download on
Wrox.com**

```
protected void triggerButton_Click(object sender, EventArgs e)
{
}
```

code snippet PCSWebSite1/Default.aspx.cs

This is hooked up to the button by some code added to the source of Default.aspx:

```
<div>
  <asp:Label Runat="server" ID="resultLabel" /><br />
  <asp:Button Runat="server" ID="triggerButton" Text="Click Me"
    onclick="triggerButton_Click" />
</div>
```

Here, the onclick attribute lets the ASP.NET runtime know to wire up the click event of the button to the triggerButton_Click() method when it generates the code model for the form.

Modify the code in triggerButton_Click() as follows (note that the label control type is inferred from the ASP.NET code so that you can use it directly from the code-behind):

```
protected void triggerButton_Click(object sender, EventArgs e)
{
    resultLabel.Text = "Button clicked!";
}
```

Running the Project

Now you're ready to make it go. There is no need to build the project; you simply need to make sure everything is saved and then point a web browser at the location of the web site. If you had used IIS, this would be simple because you would know the URL to point at. However, because you are using the built-in web server for this example, you need to start things running. The quickest way to do this is to press Ctrl+F5, which will start the server and open a browser pointing at the required URL.

When the built-in web server is running, an icon will appear in your system tray. By double-clicking this icon, you can see what the web server is doing, and stop it if required (see Figure 40-5).

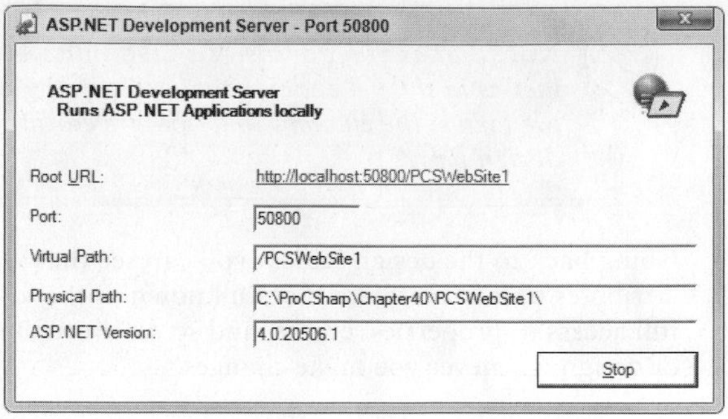

In Figure 40-5, you can see the port that the web server is running on and the URL required to see the web site you have created.

The browser that has opened should display the Click Me button on a web page. Before you press the button, take a quick look at the code received by the browser by selecting Page ⇨ View Source (in IE7). The `<form>` section should look something like this:

FIGURE 40-5

```html
<form method="post" action="Default.aspx" id="form1">
  <div>
    <input type="hidden" name="__VIEWSTATE" id="__VIEWSTATE"
      value="/wEPDwUKLTE2MjY5MTY1NWRkzNjRYstdlOK5KcJ9a8/X3pYTHvM=" />
  </div>
  <div>
    <input type="hidden" name="__EVENTVALIDATION" id="__EVENTVALIDATION"
      value="/wEWAgK39qTFBwLHpP+yC4rCCl22/GGMaFwD0l7nokvyFZ8Q" />
  </div>
  <div>
    <span id="resultLabel"></span><br />
    <input type="submit" name="triggerButton" value="Click Me"
      id="triggerButton" />
  </div>
</form>
```

The web server controls have generated straight HTML: `<span>` and `<input>` for `<asp:Label>` and `<asp:Button>`, respectively. There is also an `<input type="hidden">` field with the name `__VIEWSTATE`. This encapsulates the state of the form, as mentioned earlier. This information is used when the form is posted back to the server to re-create the user interface, so that the server can keep track of changes and so on. Note that the `<form>` element has been configured for this; it will post data back to `Default.aspx` (specified in `action`) via an HTTP POST operation (specified in `method`). It has also been assigned the name `form1`.

Changes to the Source HTML when the Button is Clicked

After clicking the button and seeing the text appear, check out the source HTML again (spacing has been added for clarity):

```html
<form method="post" action="Default.aspx" id="form1">
  <div>
    <input type="hidden" name="__VIEWSTATE" id="__VIEWSTATE"
      value="/wEPDwUKLTE2MjY5MTY1NQ9kFgICAw9kFgICAQ8PFgIeBFRleHQFD0J1dHR
            vbiBjbGlja2VkIWRkZExUtMwuSlVTrzMtG7wrmj98tVn7" />
  </div>
  <div>
    <input type="hidden" name="__EVENTVALIDATION" id="__EVENTVALIDATION"
      value="/wEWAgKTpL7LBALHpP+yC0Ymqe9SgScfB2yHTGjnlQKtbudV" />
  </div>
  <div>
    <span id="resultLabel">Button clicked!</span><br />
    <input type="submit" name="triggerButton" value="Click Me"
      id="triggerButton" />
  </div>
</form>
```

This time, the value of the view state contains more information because the HTML result relies on more than the default output from the ASP.NET page. In complex forms this can be a very long string indeed, but you shouldn't complain because so much is done for you behind the scenes. You can almost forget about state management, keeping field values between posts, and so on. Where the length of the view state string becomes a problem, you can disable the view state for controls that do not need to retain state information. You can also do this for entire pages if you want, which can be useful if the page does not ever need to retain state between postbacks to improve performance.

 For more on view state, see Chapter 41.

To convince yourself that you don't need to perform any compilation for web sites manually, try changing the text "Button clicked!" in `Default.aspx.cs` to something else, saving the file, and clicking the button again. The text on the web page should change appropriately.

The Control Palette

This section takes a quick look at some of the available controls before you put more of them together into a full, and more interesting, application. Figure 40-6 shows the toolbox that you see when editing ASP.NET pages.

Note that the following control descriptions discuss properties; in all cases, the corresponding attribute for use in ASP.NET code is identically named. This section isn't an attempt to provide a complete reference, so instead, we focus on only the most frequently used controls and properties. The controls you see in this chapter are in the Standard, Data, and Validation categories. The Navigation, Login, Web Parts, and AJAX Extensions categories are covered in Chapter 41. The Reporting controls to be presented on web pages, which enable reporting information, including Crystal Reports, are not covered in this book.

FIGURE 40-6

Standard Web Server Controls

Almost all the web server controls (in this and other categories) inherit from `System.Web.UI.WebControls.WebControl`, which in turn inherits from `System.Web.UI.Control`. Those that don't use this inheritance instead derive either directly from `Control` or from a more specialized base class that derives (eventually) from `Control`. As a result, the web server controls have many common properties and events that you can use as required. There are quite a few of these, so we won't attempt to cover them all, just as with the properties and events of the web server controls themselves.

Many of the frequently used inherited properties are those that deal with display style. This can be controlled simply, using properties such as `ForeColor`, `BackColor`, `Font`, and so on, but can also be controlled using CSS classes. To use CSS styling, you set the string property `CssClass` to the name of a CSS class in a separate file. You can use the CSS Properties window along with the style management windows to assist you with CSS control styling. Other notable properties include `Width` and `Height` to size a control, `AccessKey` and `TabIndex` to ease user interaction, and `Enabled` to set whether the control's functionality is activated in the Web Form.

Some controls can contain other controls, building up a control hierarchy on a page. You can get access to the controls contained by a given control using its `Controls` property, or to the container of a control via the `Parent` property.

You are likely to use the inherited `Load` event most often, to perform initialization on a control, and `PreRender` to perform last-minute modifications before HTML is output by the control.

Plenty more events and properties exist, and you see many of these in more detail in the next chapter. In particular, Chapter 41 deals with more advanced styling and skinning techniques. The following table describes the standard web server controls in more detail.

CONTROL	DESCRIPTION
Label	Simple text display; use the `Text` property to set and programmatically modify displayed text.
TextBox	Provides a text box that users can edit. Use the `Text` property to access the entered data, and the `TextChanged` event to act on selection changes on postback. If automatic postback is required (as opposed to using a button), then set the `AutoPostBack` property to `true`.
Button	Adds a standard button for the user to click. Use the `Text` property for text on the button, and the `Click` event to respond to clicks (server postback is automatic). You can also use the `Command` event to respond to clicks, which gives access to additional `CommandName` and `CommandArgument` properties on receipt.
LinkButton	Identical to `Button`, but displays the button as a hyperlink.
ImageButton	Displays an image that doubles as a clickable button. Properties and events are inherited from `Button` and `Image`.
HyperLink	Adds an HTML hyperlink. Set the destination with `NavigateUrl` and the text to display with `Text`. You can also use `ImageUrl` to specify an image for the link and `Target` to specify the browser window to use. This control has no nonstandard events, so use a `LinkButton` instead if additional processing is required when the link is followed.
DynamicHyperLink	Used to render an HTML hyperlink to a predefined location in a dynamic data web site. Dynamic data web sites are covered in Chapter 42, "ASP.NET MVC."
DropDownList	Allows the user to select one of a list of choices, either by choosing it directly from a list or by typing the first letter or two. Use the `Items` property to set the item list (this is a `ListItemCollection` class containing `ListItem` objects) and the `SelectedItem` and `SelectedIndex` properties to determine what is selected. The `SelectedIndexChanged` event can be used to determine whether the selection has changed, and this control also has an `AutoPostBack` property so that this selection change will trigger a postback operation.
ListBox	Allows the user to make one or more selections from a list. Set `SelectionMode` to `Multiple` or `Single` to specify if only one or multiple items can be selected at the same time, and `Rows` to determine how many items to display. Other properties and events are the same as for `DropDownList`.
CheckBox	Displays a box that can be checked or unchecked. The state is stored in the Boolean property `Checked`, and the text associated with the check box in `Text`. The `AutoPostBack` property can be used to initiate automatic postback and the `CheckedChanged` event to act on changes.
CheckBoxList	Creates a group of check boxes. Properties and events are identical to other list controls, such as `DropDownList`.
RadioButton	Displays a button that can be turned on or off. Generally, these are grouped such that only one in the group is active at any time. Use the `GroupName` property to link `RadioButton` controls into a group. Other properties and events are as per `CheckBox`.
RadioButtonList	Creates a group of radio buttons where only one button in the group can be selected at a time. Properties and events are the same for other list controls, such as `DropDownList`.
Image	Displays an image. Use `ImageUrl` for the image reference, and `AlternateText` to provide text if the image fails to load.
ImageMap	Like `Image`, but it allows you to specify specific actions to trigger if users click one or more hotspots in the image. The action to take can either be a postback or a redirection to another URL. Hotspots are supplied by embedded controls that derive from `HotSpot`, such as `RectangleHotSpot` and `CircleHotSpot`.

CONTROL	DESCRIPTION
Table	Specifies a table. Use this in conjunction with `TableRow` and `TableCell` at design time, or programmatically assign rows using the `Rows` property of type `TableRowCollection`. You can also use this property for runtime modifications. This control has several styling properties unique to tables, as do `TableRow` and `TableCell`.
BulletedList	Formats a list of items as a bulleted list. Unlike the other list controls, this one has a `Click` event that you can use to determine what item a user has clicked during a post-back. Other properties and events are the same as for `DropDownList`.
HiddenField	Used to provide a hidden field, to store nondisplayed values for any reason. These can be very useful to store settings that would otherwise need an alternative storage mechanism to function. Use the `Value` property to access the stored value.
Literal	Performs the same function as `Label`, but has no styling properties because it derives from `Control`, not `WebControl`. You set the text to display for this control with the `Text` property.
Calendar	Allows the user to select a date from a graphical calendar display. This control has many style-related properties, but essential functionality can be achieved using the `SelectedDate` and `VisibleDate` properties (of type `System.DateTime`) to get access to the date selected by the user and the month to display (which will always contain `VisibleDate`). The key event to hook up to is `SelectionChanged`. Postback from this control is automatic.
AdRotator	Displays several images in succession, with a different one displayed after each server round trip. Use the `AdvertisementFile` property to specify the XML file describing the possible images, and the `AdCreated` event to perform processing before each image is sent back. You can also use the `Target` property to name a window to open when an image is clicked.
FileUpload	This control presents the user with a text box and a Browse button, such that a file to be uploaded can be selected. After the user has done this, you can look at the `HasFile` property to determine if a file has been selected, and then use the `SaveAs()` method from code-behind to perform the file upload.
Wizard	An advanced control used to simplify the common task of getting several pages of user input in one go. You can add multiple steps to a wizard, which can be presented to a user sequentially or nonsequentially, and rely on this control to maintain state and so on.
Xml	A more complicated text display control, used for displaying XML content, which may be transformed using an XSLT style sheet. The XML content is set using one of the `Document`, `DocumentContent`, or `DocumentSource` properties (depending on the format of the original XML), and the XSLT style sheet (optional) using either `Transform` or `TransformSource`.
MultiView	A control that contains one or more `View` controls, where only one `View` is rendered at a time. The currently displayed view is specified using `ActiveViewIndex`, and you can detect if the view changes (perhaps because a Next link on the currently displayed view is clicked) with the `ActiveViewChanged` event.
Panel	Adds a container for other controls. You can use `HorizontalAlign` and `Wrap` to specify how the contents are arranged.
PlaceHolder	This control doesn't render any output but can be handy for grouping other controls together, or for adding controls programmatically to a given location. Contained controls can be accessed using the `Controls` property.
View	A container for controls, much like `PlaceHolder`, but designed for use as a child of `MultiView`. You can tell if a given `View` is being displayed using `Visible`, or use the `Activate` and `Deactivate` events to detect changes in activation state.

continues

(continued)

CONTROL	DESCRIPTION
Substitution	Specifies a section of a web page that isn't cached along with other output. This is an advanced topic related to ASP.NET caching behavior, which you won't be looking at in this book.
Localize	Exactly like `Literal`, but enables text to be localized by using project resources to specify the text to display for various locales.

Data Web Server Controls

The data web server controls are divided into three types:

➤ **Data source controls** (`SqlDataSource`, `AccessDataSource`, `LinqDataSource`, `EntityDataSource`, `ObjectDataSource`, `XmlDataSource`, and `SiteMapDataSource`)

➤ **Data display controls** (`GridView`, `DataList`, `DetailsView`, `FormView`, `ListView`, `Repeater`, and `DataPager`)

➤ **Dynamic data controls** (`DynamicControl` and `DynamicDataManager`)

In general, you will place one of the (nonvisual) data source controls on a page to link to a data source; and then you will add a data display control that binds to a data source control to display that data. Some of the more advanced data display controls, such as `GridView`, also allow you to edit data.

All the data source controls derive from either `System.Web.UI.DataSource` or `System.Web.UI.HierarchicalDataSource`. These classes expose methods such as `GetView()` or `GetHierarchicalView()` to give access to internal data views and skinning capabilities.

The following table describes the various data source controls. Note that there is less detail about properties in this section than in others — mainly because configuration of these controls is best done graphically or through wizards. Later in this chapter, you will see some of these controls in action.

CONTROL	DESCRIPTION
SqlDataSource	Acts as a conduit for data stored in a SQL Server database. By placing this control on a page, you can manipulate SQL Server data using a data display control. You will see this control in action later in this chapter.
AccessDataSource	Like `SqlDataSource`, but it works with data stored in a Microsoft Access database.
LinqDataSource	This control allows you to manipulate objects in a LINQ-enabled data model.
EntityDataSource	This control allows you to manipulate ADO.NET Entity Data Model objects.
ObjectDataSource	This control allows you to manipulate data stored in objects that you have created, which may be grouped in a collection class. This can be a very quick way to expose custom object models to an ASP.NET page.
XmlDataSource	Enables you to bind to XML data. This works well in binding to, for example, a `TreeView` control (one of the Navigation controls). You can also transform XML data using an XSL style sheet using this control if desired.
SiteMapDataSource	Allows binding to hierarchical site map data. See the section on navigation web server controls in Chapter 41 for more information.

The following table displays the data display controls. Several of these are available to suit various needs. Some are more fully functional than others, but often you can go with simplicity (for example, when you don't need to be able to edit data items).

CONTROL	DESCRIPTION
GridView	Displays multiple data items (such as rows in a database) in the form of rows, where each row has columns reflecting data fields. By manipulating the properties of this control, you can select, sort, and edit data items.
DataList	Displays multiple data items where you can supply templates for each item to display data fields in any way you choose. As with GridView, you can select, sort, and edit data items.
DetailsView	Displays a single data item in tabular form, with each row of the table relating to a data field. This control enables you to add, edit, and delete data items.
FormView	Displays a single data item using a template. As with DetailsView, this control enables you to add, edit, and delete data items.
ListView	Like DataList, but with support for pagination using DataPager and more template capabilities.
Repeater	Like DataList, but without selecting or editing capabilities.
DataPager	Allows pagination of ListView controls.
Chart	Displays data in a chart, such as a bar chart or pie chart. This control is examined in the next chapter.

The dynamic data controls are covered in Chapter 42.

Validation Web Server Controls

Validation controls provide a method of validating user input without (in most cases) your having to write any code at all. Whenever postback is initiated, each validation control checks the control it is validating and changes its IsValid property accordingly. If this property is false, then the user input for the validated control has failed validation. The page containing all the controls also has an IsValid property — if any of the validation controls has its version of this property set to false, then this will be false also. You can check this property from your server-side code and act on it.

Validation controls also have another function. Not only do they validate controls at runtime; they can also output helpful hints to users. Simply setting the ErrorMessage property to the text you want means users will see it when they attempt to postback invalid data.

The text stored in ErrorMessage may be output at the point where the validation control is located, or at a separate point, along with the messages from all other validation controls on a page. This latter behavior is achieved using the ValidationSummary control, which displays all error messages along with additional text as required.

On browsers that support it, these controls even generate client-side JavaScript functions to streamline their validation behavior. This means that in some cases postback won't even occur, because the validation controls can prevent this under certain circumstances and output error messages without involving the server.

All validation controls inherit from BaseValidator and thus share several important properties. Perhaps the most important is the ErrorMessage property discussed earlier in this section, with the ControlToValidate property coming in a close second. This property specifies the programmatic ID of the control that is being validated. Another important property is Display, which determines whether to place text at the validation summary position (if set to none), or at the validator position. You also have the choice to make space for the error message even when it is not being displayed (set Display to Static) or to dynamically allocate space when required, which might shift page contents around slightly (set Display to Dynamic). The following table describes the validation controls.

CONTROL	DESCRIPTION
RequiredFieldValidator	Used to check if the user has entered data in a control such as TextBox.
CompareValidator	Used to check that data entered fulfills simple requirements, by use of an operator set using the Operator property and a ValueToCompare property to validate against. Operator can be Equal, GreaterThan, GreaterThanEqual, LessThan, LessThanEqual, NotEqual, and DataTypeCheck. DataTypeCheck simply compares the data type of ValueToCompare with the data in the control to be validated. ValueToCompare is a string property but is interpreted as different data types based on its contents. To further control the comparison, you can set the Type property to Currency, Date, Double, Integer, or String.
RangeValidator	Validates that data in the control falls between MaximumValue and MinimumValue property values. Has a Type property similar to CompareValidator.
RegularExpressionValidator	Validates the contents of a field based on a regular expression stored in ValidationExpression. This can be useful for known sequences such as ZIP codes, phone numbers, IP numbers, and so on.
CustomValidator	Used to validate data in a control using a custom function. ClientValidationFunction is used to specify a client-side function used to validate a control (which means, unfortunately, that you can't use C#). This function should return a Boolean value indicating whether validation was successful. Alternatively, you can use the ServerValidate event to specify a server-side function to use for validation. This function is a bool type event handler that receives a string containing the data to validate, instead of an EventArgs parameter. Returns true if validation succeeds, otherwise false.
DynamicValidator	This validation control is used to provide business logic validation for dynamic data sites, and is covered in Chapter 42.
ValidationSummary	Displays validation errors for all validation controls that have an ErrorMessage set. The display can be formatted by setting the DisplayMode (BulletList, List, or SingleParagraph) and HeaderText properties. The display can be disabled by setting ShowSummary to false, and displayed in a pop-up message box by setting ShowMessageBox to true.

Server Control Event-Booking Example

In this example, you create the framework for a web application, a meeting room booking tool. (As with the other examples in this book, you can download the sample application and code from the Wrox web site at www.wrox.com.) At first, you will include only the front end and simple event processing; later, you will extend this example with ADO.NET and data binding to include server-side business logic.

The Web Form you are going to create contains fields for username, event name, meeting room, and attendees, along with a calendar to select a date (you are assuming for the purposes of this example that you are dealing with all-day events). You will include validation controls for all fields except the calendar, which you will validate on the server side, and provide a default date in case none has been entered.

For user interface (UI) testing, you will also have a Label control on the form that you can use to display submission results.

For starters, create a new empty web site in Visual Studio .NET in the `C:\ProCSharp\Chapter40\` directory, and call it PCSWebSite2. Next, add a new Web Form using the default settings and modify the code in the generated `Default.aspx` file as follows:

```
<%@ Page Language="C#" AutoEventWireup="true" CodeFile="Default.aspx.cs"
   Inherits="_Default" %>
<!DOCTYPE html PUBLIC "-//W3C//DTD XHTML 1.1//EN"
   "http://www.w3.org/TR/xhtml11/DTD/xhtml11.dtd">
<html xmlns="http://www.w3.org/1999/xhtml">
<head runat="server">
  <title>Meeting Room Booker</title>
</head>
<body>
  <form id="form1" runat="server">
    <div>
      <h1 style="text-align: center;">
        Enter details and set a day to initiate an event.
      </h1>
    </div>
```

code snippet PCSWebSite2/Default.aspx

After the title of the page (which is enclosed in HTML `<h1>` tags to get large, title-style text), the main body of the form is enclosed in an HTML `<table>`. You could use a web server control table, but this introduces unnecessary complexity because you are using a table purely for formatting the display, not to be a dynamic UI element. This is an important point to bear in mind when designing Web Forms — don't add web server controls unnecessarily. The table is divided into three columns: the first column holds simple text labels; the second column holds UI fields corresponding to the text labels (along with validation controls for these); and the third column contains a calendar control for date selection, which spans four rows. The fifth row contains a submission button spanning all columns, and the sixth row contains a `ValidationSummary` control to display error messages, when required (all the other validation controls have `Display="None"`, because they will use this summary for display). Beneath the table is a simple label that you can use to display results for now, before you add database access later:

```
<div style="text-align: center;">
  <table style="text-align: left; border-color: #000000;
    border-width: 2px; background-color: #fff99e;" cellspacing="0"
    cellpadding="8" rules="none" width="540">
    <tr>
      <td valign="top">
        Your Name:</td>
      <td valign="top">
        <asp:TextBox ID="nameBox" Runat="server" Width="160px" />
        <asp:RequiredFieldValidator ID="validateName" Runat="server"
          ErrorMessage="You must enter a name."
          ControlToValidate="nameBox" Display="None" />
      </td>
      <td valign="middle" rowspan="4">
        <asp:Calendar ID="calendar" Runat="server" BackColor="White" />
      </td>
    </tr>
    <tr>
      <td valign="top">
        Event Name:</td>
      <td valign="top">
        <asp:TextBox ID="eventBox" Runat="server" Width="160px" />
        <asp:RequiredFieldValidator ID="validateEvent" Runat="server"
```

```
            ErrorMessage="You must enter an event name."
            ControlToValidate="eventBox" Display="None" />
      </td>
   </tr>
```

Most of the ASP.NET code in this file is remarkably simple, and much can be learned simply by reading through it. Of particular note in this code is the way in which list items are attached to the controls for selecting a meeting room and multiple attendees for the event:

```
<tr>
   <td valign="top">
      Meeting Room:</td>
   <td valign="top">
      <asp:DropDownList ID="roomList" Runat="server" Width="160px">
         <asp:ListItem Value="1">The Happy Room</asp:ListItem>
         <asp:ListItem Value="2">The Angry Room</asp:ListItem>
         <asp:ListItem Value="3">The Depressing
            Room</asp:ListItem>
         <asp:ListItem Value="4">The Funked Out
            Room</asp:ListItem>
      </asp:DropDownList>
      <asp:RequiredFieldValidator ID="validateRoom" Runat="server"
         ErrorMessage="You must select a room."
         ControlToValidate="roomList" Display="None" />
   </td>
</tr>
<tr>
   <td valign="top">
      Attendees:</td>
   <td valign="top">
      <asp:ListBox ID="attendeeList" Runat="server" Width="160px"
         SelectionMode="Multiple" Rows="6">
         <asp:ListItem Value="1">Bill Gates</asp:ListItem>
         <asp:ListItem Value="2">Monica Lewinsky</asp:ListItem>
         <asp:ListItem Value="3">Vincent Price</asp:ListItem>
         <asp:ListItem Value="4">Vlad the Impaler</asp:ListItem>
         <asp:ListItem Value="5">Iggy Pop</asp:ListItem>
         <asp:ListItem Value="6">William
            Shakespeare</asp:ListItem>
      </asp:ListBox>
```

Here you are associating `ListItem` objects with the two web server controls. These objects are not web server controls in their own right (they simply inherit from `System.Object`), which is why you don't need to use `Runat="server"` on them. When the page is processed, the `<asp:ListItem>` entries are used to create `ListItem` objects, which are added to the `Items` collection of their parent list control. This makes it easier for you to initialize lists than to write code for this yourself (you would need to create a `ListItemCollection` object, add `ListItem` objects, and then pass the collection to the list control). Of course, you can still do all this programmatically if you want.

```
            <asp:RequiredFieldValidator ID="validateAttendees" Runat="server"
               ErrorMessage="You must have at least one attendee."
               ControlToValidate="attendeeList" Display="None" />
         </td>
      </tr>
      <tr>
         <td align="center" colspan="3">
            <asp:Button ID="submitButton" Runat="server" Width="100%"
               Text="Submit meeting room request" />
         </td>
      </tr>
      <tr>
```

```
                <td align="center" colspan="3">
                  <asp:ValidationSummary ID="validationSummary" Runat="server"
                    HeaderText="Before submitting your request:" />
                </td>
              </tr>
            </table>
          </div>
          <div>
            <p>
              Results:
              <asp:Label Runat="server" ID="resultLabel" Text="None." />
            </p>
          </div>
        </form>
      </body>
    </html>
```

In design view, the form you have created looks like Figure 40-7. This is a fully functioning UI, which maintains its own state between server requests, and validates user input. Considering the brevity of the preceding code, this is quite something. In fact, it leaves you with very little to do, at least for this example; you just need to specify the button click event for the submission button.

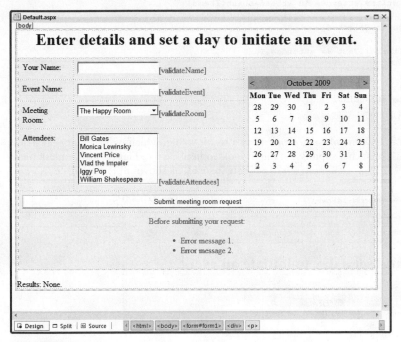

FIGURE 40-7

Actually, that's not quite true. So far, you have no validation for the calendar control. All you need to do is give it an initial value. You can do this in the `Page_Load()` event handler for your page in the code-behind file:

```
protected void Page_Load(object sender, EventArgs e)
{
    if (!this.IsPostBack)
    {
```

```
            calendar.SelectedDate = DateTime.Now;
        }
    }
```

code snippet PCSWebSite2/Default.aspx.cs

Here you just select today's date as a starting point. Note that you first check to see if `Page_Load()` is being called as the result of a postback operation, by checking the `IsPostBack` property of the page. If a postback is in progress, this property will be `true` and you leave the selected date alone (you don't want to lose the user's selection, after all).

To add the button click handler, simply double-click the button and add the following code:

```
protected void submitButton_Click(object sender, EventArgs e)
{
    if (this.IsValid)
    {
        resultLabel.Text = roomList.SelectedItem.Text +
            " has been booked on " +
            calendar.SelectedDate.ToLongDateString() +
            " by " + nameBox.Text + " for " +
            eventBox.Text + " event. ";
        foreach (ListItem attendee in attendeeList.Items)
        {
            if (attendee.Selected)
            {
                resultLabel.Text += attendee.Text + ", ";
            }
        }
        resultLabel.Text += " and " + nameBox.Text +
            " will be attending.";
    }
}
```

Here you just set the `resultLabel` control `Text` property to a result string, which will then appear below the main table. In IE, the result of such a submission might look something like Figure 40-8, unless there are errors, in which case the `ValidationSummary` will activate instead, as shown in Figure 40-9.

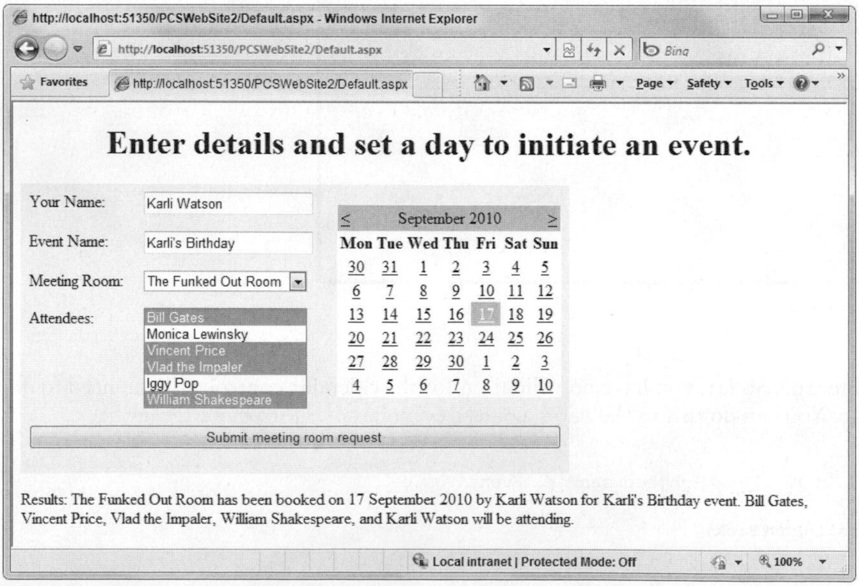

FIGURE 40-8

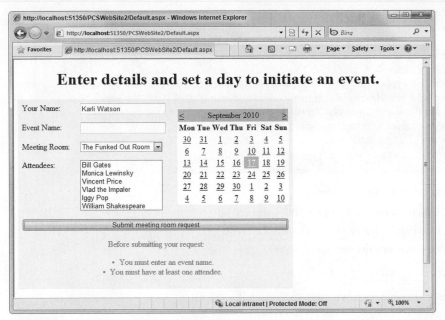

FIGURE 40-9

ADO.NET AND DATA BINDING

The web site you created in the previous section is perfectly functional, but it contains only static data. In addition, the event-booking process does not include persisting event data. To solve both of these problems, you can make use of ADO.NET to access data stored in a database, so that you can store and retrieve event data along with the lists of rooms and attendees.

Data binding makes the process of retrieving data even easier. Controls such as list boxes (and some of the more specialized controls you'll look at a bit later) come enabled for this technique. They can be bound to any object that exposes an IEnumerable, ICollection, or IListSource interface, as well as any of the data source web server controls.

In this section, you start by updating your event-booking application to be data-aware, and then move on to take a look at some of the other results you can achieve with data binding, using some of the other data-aware web controls.

Updating the Event-Booking Application

To keep things separate from the last example, create a new empty web site called PCSWebSite3 in the directory C:\ProCSharp\Chapter40\ and copy the code from the PCSWebSite2 application created earlier into the new application. Before you start on your new code, take a look at the database you will be accessing.

The Database

For the purposes of this example, you will use a Microsoft SQL Server Express database called MeetingRoomBooker.mdf, which is part of the downloadable code for this book. For an enterprise-scale application, it makes more sense to use a full SQL Server database, but the techniques involved are practically identical, and SQL Server Express makes life a bit easier for testing. The code will also be identical.

If you are adding your own version of this database, you will need to add a new database to a folder called App_Data in the web site. This is one of several "special" folders that can exist in an ASP.NET web site; you can add by selecting Website ⇨ Add ASP.NET Folder ⇨ App_Data. To add a new database to this folder, right-click the new App_Data folder, select Add New Item, then select the SQL Server Database option. Name the new database MeetingRoomBooker and click Add. This will also configure a data connection in the Server Explorer window ready for you to use. Next, you can add the tables required as shown in the next sections and supply your own data. Alternatively, to use the downloadable database with your own code, simply copy it to the App_Data *directory for your web site.*

The database provided contains three tables:

➤ Attendees, which contains a list of possible event attendees

➤ Rooms, which contains a list of possible rooms for events

➤ Events, which contains a list of booked events

Attendees

The Attendees table contains the columns shown in the following table.

COLUMN	TYPE	NOTES
ID	Identity, primary key	Attendee identification number
Name	varchar, required, 50 chars	Name of attendee
Email	varchar, optional, 50 chars	E-mail address of attendee

The supplied database includes entries for 20 attendees, all with their own (fictional) e-mail addresses. You can envision that in a more developed application, e-mails could automatically be sent to attendees when a booking is made, but this is left to you as an optional exercise using techniques found elsewhere in this book.

Rooms

The Rooms table contains the columns shown in the following table.

COLUMN	TYPE	NOTES
ID	Identity, primary key	Room identification number
Room	varchar, required, 50 chars	Name of room

Twenty records are supplied in the database.

Events

The Events table contains the columns shown in the following table.

COLUMN	TYPE	NOTES
ID	Identity, primary key	Event identification number
Name	varchar, required, 255 chars	Name of event
Room	int, required	ID of room for event
AttendeeList	text, required	List of attendee names
EventDate	datetime, required	Date of event

A few events are supplied in the downloadable database.

Binding to the Database

The two controls you are going to bind to data are `attendeeList` and `roomList`. Before you do this, you need to add `SqlDataSource` web server controls that map to the tables you want to access in the `MeetingRoomBooker.mdf` database. The quickest way to do this is to drag them from the toolbox onto the `Default.aspx` Web Form and configure them via the Configuration Wizard. Figure 40-10 shows how to access this wizard for a `SqlDataSource` control.

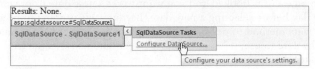

FIGURE 40-10

From the first page of the data source Configuration Wizard, you need to select the connection to the database created earlier. Next, choose to save the connection string as `MRBConnectionString`; then choose to select * (all fields) from the `Attendees` table in the database.

After completing the wizard, change the `ID` of the `SqlDataSource` control to `MRBAttendeeData`. You also need to add and configure two more `SqlDataSource` controls to obtain data from the `Rooms` and `Events` tables, with `ID` values of `MRBRoomData` and `MRBEventData` respectively. For these subsequent controls, you can use the saved `MRBConnectionString` for your connection.

After you've added these data sources, you will see in the code for the form that the syntax is very simple:

Available for
download on
Wrox.com

```
<asp:SqlDataSource ID="MRBAttendeeData" runat="server"
  ConnectionString="<%$ ConnectionStrings:MRBConnectionString %>"
  SelectCommand="SELECT * FROM [Attendees]"></asp:SqlDataSource>
<asp:SqlDataSource ID="MRBRoomData" runat="server"
  ConnectionString="<%$ ConnectionStrings:MRBConnectionString %>"
  SelectCommand="SELECT * FROM [Rooms]"></asp:SqlDataSource>
<asp:SqlDataSource ID="MRBEventData" runat="server"
  ConnectionString="<%$ ConnectionStrings:MRBConnectionString %>"
  SelectCommand="SELECT * FROM [Events]"></asp:SqlDataSource>
```

code snippet PCSWebSite3/Default.aspx

The definition of the connection string in use is found in the `web.config` file, which we look at in more detail later in this chapter.

Next, you need to set the data-binding properties of the `roomList` and `attendeeList` controls. For `roomList` the settings required are as follows:

- ➤ `DataSourceID` — `MRBRoomData`
- ➤ `DataTextField` — `Room`
- ➤ `DataValueField` — `ID`

And, similarly, for `attendeeList`:

- ➤ `DataSourceID` — `MRBAttendeeData`
- ➤ `DataTextField` — `Name`
- ➤ `DataValueField` — `ID`

You can also remove the existing hard-coded list items from the code for these controls.

Running the application now will result in the full attendee and room data being available from your data-bound controls. You will use the `MRBEventData` control shortly.

Customizing the Calendar Control

Before adding events to the database, you need to modify your calendar display. It would be nice to display all days where a booking has previously been made in a different color, and prevent such days from being selectable. This requires that you modify the way you set dates in the calendar and the way day cells are displayed.

You will start with date selection. You need to check for dates where events are booked in three places, and modify the selection accordingly: 1) when you set the initial date in Page_Load(), 2) when the user attempts to select a date from the calendar, and 3) when an event is booked and you want to set a new date to prevent the user from booking two events on the same day before selecting a new date. Because this is going to be a common feature, you might as well create a private method to perform this calculation. This method should accept a trial date as a parameter and return the date to use, which will either be the same date as the trial date, or the next available day after the trial date.

Before adding this method, you need to give your code access to data in the Events table. You can use the MRBEventData control to do this because this control is capable of populating a DataView. To facilitate this, add the following private member and property (you may also require a namespace import for System.Data for this code to work):

```
private DataView eventData;
private DataView EventData
{
    get
    {
        if (eventData == null)
        {
            eventData =
                MRBEventData.Select(new DataSourceSelectArguments())
                as DataView;
        }
        return eventData;
    }
    set
    {
        eventData = value;
    }
}
```

code snippet PCSWebSite3/Default.aspx.cs

The EventData property populates the eventData member with data as it is required, with the results cached for subsequent use. Here you use the SqlDataSource.Select() method to obtain a DataView.

Next, add this method, GetFreeDate(), to the code-behind file:

```
private DateTime GetFreeDate(DateTime trialDate)
{
    if (EventData.Count > 0)
    {
        DateTime testDate;
        bool trialDateOK = false;
        while (!trialDateOK)
        {
            trialDateOK = true;
            foreach (DataRowView testRow in EventData)
            {
                testDate = (DateTime)testRow["EventDate"];
                if (testDate.Date == trialDate.Date)
                {
                    trialDateOK = false;
```

```
                    trialDate = trialDate.AddDays(1);
                }
            }
        }
    }
    return trialDate;
}
```

This simple code uses the `EventData DataView` to extract event data. First, you check for the trivial case where no events have been booked, in which case you can just confirm the trial date by returning it. Next, you iterate through the dates in the `Event` table, comparing them with the trial date. If you find a match, add one day to the trial date and perform another search.

Extracting the date from the `DataTable` is remarkably simple:

```
testDate = (System.DateTime)testRow["EventDate"];
```

Casting the column data into `System.DateTime` works fine.

The first place you will use `GetFreeDate()`, then, is back in `Page_Load()`. This simply means making a minor modification to the code that sets the calendar `SelectedDate` property:

```
if (!this.IsPostBack)
{
    DateTime trialDate = DateTime.Now;
    calendar.SelectedDate = GetFreeDate(trialDate);
}
```

Next, you need to respond to date selection on the calendar. To do this, simply add an event handler for the `SelectionChanged` event of the calendar, and force the date to be checked against existing events. Double-click the calendar in the Designer and add this code:

```
protected void calendar_SelectionChanged(object sender, EventArgs e)
{
    DateTime trialDate = calendar.SelectedDate;
    calendar.SelectedDate = GetFreeDate(trialDate);
}
```

The code here is practically identical to that in `Page_Load()`.

The third place that you must perform this check is in response to the pressed booking button. We will come back to this shortly, as you have several changes to make here.

Next, you need to color the day cells of the calendar to signify existing events. To do this, you add an event handler for the `DayRender` event of the `calendar` object. This event is raised each time an individual day is rendered, and gives you access to the `cell` object being displayed and the date of this cell through the `Cell` and `Date` properties of the `DayRenderEventArgs` parameter you receive in the handler function. You simply compare the date of the cell being rendered to the dates in the `eventTable` object and color the cell using the `Cell.BackColor` property if there is a match:

```
protected void calendar_DayRender(object sender, DayRenderEventArgs e)
{
    if (EventData.Count > 0)
    {
        DateTime testDate;
        foreach (DataRowView testRow in EventData)
        {
            testDate = (DateTime)testRow["EventDate"];
            if (testDate.Date == e.Day.Date)
            {
                e.Cell.BackColor = System.Drawing.Color.Red;
            }
        }
    }
}
```

Here you are using red, which will give you a display along the lines of Figure 40-11, in which June 12, 15, and 22 (2010) all contain events.

With the addition of the date-selection logic, it is now impossible to select a day that is shown in red. If you attempt it, a later date is selected instead (for example, selecting June 15 results in the selection of June 16).

Adding Events to the Database

The `submitButton_Click()` event handler currently assembles a string from the event characteristics and displays it in the `resultLabel` control. To add an event to the database, you simply reformat the string created in a SQL `INSERT` query and execute it.

≤		June 2010				≥
Mon	**Tue**	**Wed**	**Thu**	**Fri**	**Sat**	**Sun**
31	1	2	3	4	5	6
7	8	9	10	11	12	13
14	15	16	17	18	19	20
21	22	23	24	25	26	27
28	29	30	1	2	3	4
5	6	7	8	9	10	11

FIGURE 40-11

 Note that in the development environment that you are using, you don't have to worry too much about security. Adding a SQL Server 2008 Express database via a web site solution and configuring `SqlDataSource` controls to use it will automatically give you a connection string that you can use to write to the database. In more advanced situations, you might want to access resources using other accounts — for example, a domain account used to access a SQL Server instance elsewhere on a network. The capability to do this (via impersonation, COM+ Services, or other means) exists in ASP.NET, but is beyond the scope of this chapter. In most cases, configuring the connection string appropriately is as complicated as things need to get.

Much of the following code will therefore look familiar:

```
protected void submitButton_Click(object sender, EventArgs e)
{
    if (this.IsValid)
    {
        System.Text.StringBuilder sb = new System.Text.StringBuilder();
        foreach (ListItem attendee in attendeeList.Items)
        {
            if (attendee.Selected)
            {
                sb.AppendFormat("{0} ({1}), ", attendee.Text, attendee.Value);
            }
        }
        sb.AppendFormat(" and {0}", nameBox.Text);
        string attendees = sb.ToString();
        try
        {
            System.Data.SqlClient.SqlConnection conn =
                new System.Data.SqlClient.SqlConnection(
                    ConfigurationManager.ConnectionStrings[
                    "MRBConnectionString"].ConnectionString);
            System.Data.SqlClient.SqlCommand insertCommand =
                new System.Data.SqlClient.SqlCommand("INSERT INTO [Events] "
                    + "(Name, Room, AttendeeList, EventDate) VALUES (@Name, "
                    + "@Room, @AttendeeList, @EventDate)", conn);
            insertCommand.Parameters.Add(
                "Name", SqlDbType.VarChar, 255).Value = eventBox.Text;
            insertCommand.Parameters.Add(
                "Room", SqlDbType.Int, 4).Value = roomList.SelectedValue;
            insertCommand.Parameters.Add(
                "AttendeeList", SqlDbType.Text, 16).Value = attendees;
            insertCommand.Parameters.Add(
                "EventDate", SqlDbType.DateTime, 8).Value =
                calendar.SelectedDate;
```

The most interesting thing here is how you access the connection string you created earlier, using the following syntax:

```
ConfigurationManager.ConnectionStrings["MRBConnectionString"].ConnectionString
```

The `ConfigurationManager` class (which requires a namespace import for `System.Configuration`) gives you access to all assorted configuration information, all stored in the `Web.config` configuration file for your web application. You will look at this in more detail later in this chapter.

After you have created your SQL command, you can use it to insert the new event:

```
conn.Open();
int queryResult = insertCommand.ExecuteNonQuery();
conn.Close();
```

`ExecuteNonQuery()` returns an integer representing how many table rows were affected by the query. If this is equal to 1, your insertion was successful. If so, put a success message in `resultLabel`, clear `EventData` because it is now out of date, and change the calendar selection to a new, free date. Because `GetFreeDate()` involves using `EventData`, and the `EventData` property automatically refreshes itself if it has no data, the stored event data will be refreshed:

```
if (queryResult == 1)
{
    resultLabel.Text = "Event Added.";
    EventData = null;
    calendar.SelectedDate =
        GetFreeDate(calendar.SelectedDate.AddDays(1));
}
```

If `ExecuteNonQuery()` returns a number other than 1, you know that there has been a problem. The code in this example throws an exception if a number other than 1 is returned. This exception is caught by the general catch block for the database access code.

This catch block simply displays a general failure notification in `resultLabel`:

```
        else
        {
            throw new System.Data.DataException("Unknown data error.");
        }
    }
    catch
    {
        resultLabel.Text = "Event not added due to DB access "
                            + "problem.";
    }
    }
}
```

This completes your data-aware version of the event-booking application.

More on Data Binding

As mentioned earlier in this chapter, the available web server controls include several that deal with data display (`GridView`, `DataList`, `DetailsView`, `FormView`, and `Repeater`). These are all extremely useful when it comes to outputting data to a web page because they perform many tasks automatically that would otherwise require a fair amount of coding.

First, you will look at how easy using these controls can be, by adding an event list display to the bottom of the display of `PCSWebSite3`.

Drag a `GridView` control from the toolbox to the bottom of `Default.aspx`, and select the `MRBEventData` data source you added earlier for it, as shown in Figure 40-12.

Next, click Refresh Schema, and that's all you need to do to display a list of events under the form — try viewing the web site now and you should see the events, as shown in Figure 40-13.

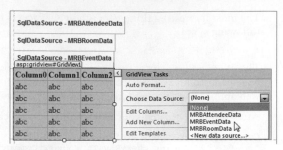

FIGURE 40-12

ID	Name	Room	AttendeeList	EventDate
1	My Birthday	4	Iggy Pop (5), Sean Connery (7), Albert Einstein (10), George Clooney (14), Jules Verne (18), Robin Hood (20), and Karli Watson	17/09/2010 00:00:00
2	Dinner	1	Bill Gates (1), Monika Lewinsky (2), and Bruce Lee	05/08/2010 00:00:00
3	Discussion of darkness	6	Vlad the Impaler (4), Myra Hindley (13), and Beelzebub	29/10/2010 00:00:00
4	Christmas with Pals	9	Dr Frank N Furter (11), Bobby Davro (15), John F Kennedy (16), Stephen King (19), and Karli Watson	25/12/2010 00:00:00
5	Escape	17	Monika Lewinsky (2), Stephen King (19), and Spartacus	10/05/2010 00:00:00
6	Planetary Conquest	14	Bill Gates (1), Albert Einstein (10), Dr Frank N Furter (11), Bobby Davro (15), and Darth Vader	15/06/2010 00:00:00
7	Homecoming Celebration	7	William Shakespeare (6), Christopher Columbus (12), Robin Hood (20), and Ulysses	22/06/2010 00:00:00
8	Dalek Reunion Ball	12	Roger Moore (8), George Clooney (14), Bobby Davro (15), and Davros	12/06/2010 00:00:00
9	Romantic meal for two	13	George Clooney (14), and Donna Watson	29/03/2010 00:00:00

FIGURE 40-13

You can also make one further modification in `submitButton_Click()` to ensure that this data is updated when new records are added:

```
if (queryResult == 1)
{
    resultLabel.Text = "Event Added.";
    EventData = null;
    calendar.SelectedDate =
        GetFreeDate(calendar.SelectedDate.AddDays(1));
    GridView1.DataBind();
}
```

All data-bindable controls support this method, which is normally called by the form if you call the top-level (`this`) `DataBind()` method.

You probably noticed in Figure 40-13 that the date/time display for the `EventDate` field is a little messy. Because you are looking at dates only, the time is always 00:00:00 AM — information that isn't really necessary to display. In the next sections, you see how this date information can be displayed in a more user-friendly fashion in the context of a `ListView` control. As you might expect, the `DataGrid` control contains many properties that you can use to format the displayed data, but I'll leave these for you to discover.

Data Display with Templates

Many of the data display controls allow you to use templates to format data for display. Templates, in an ASP.NET sense, are parameterized sections of HTML that are used as elements of output in certain controls. They enable you to customize exactly how data is output to the browser, and can result in professional-looking displays without too much effort.

Several templates are available to customize various aspects of list behavior. One of the most important templates is `<ItemTemplate>`, which is used in the display of each data item in a list for `Repeater`, `DataList`, and `ListView` controls. You declare this template (and all the others) inside the control declaration. For example:

```
<asp:DataList Runat="server" ... >
  <ItemTemplate>
    ...
  </ItemTemplate>
</asp:DataList>
```

Within template declarations, you will normally want to output sections of HTML along with parameters from the data that is bound to the control. You can use a special syntax to output such parameters:

```
<%# expression %>
```

The *expression* placeholder might be simply an expression binding the parameter to a page or control property, but is more likely to consist of an `Eval()` or `Bind()` expression. These functions can be used to output data from a table bound to a control simply by specifying the column. The following syntax is used for `Eval()`:

```
<%# Eval("ColumnName") %>
```

An optional second parameter allows you to format the data returned, which has syntax identical to string formatting expressions used elsewhere. This can be used, for example, to format date strings into a more readable format — something that was lacking in the earlier example.

The `Bind()` expression is identical but allows you to insert data into attributes of server controls. For example:

```
<asp:Label RunAt="server" ID="ColumnDisplay" Text='<%# Bind("ColumnName") %>' />
```

Note that because double quotes are used in the `Bind()` parameter, single quotes are required to enclose the attribute value.

The following table provides a list of available templates and when they are used.

TEMPLATE	APPLIES TO	DESCRIPTION
`<ItemTemplate>`	`DataList`, `Repeater`, `ListView`	Used for list items
`<HeaderTemplate>`	`DataList`, `DetailsView`, `FormView`, `Repeater`	Used for output before item(s)
`<FooterTemplate>`	`DataList`, `DetailsView`, `FormView`, `Repeater`	Used for output after item(s)
`<LayoutTemplate>`	`ListView`	Used to specify output surrounding items
`<SeparatorTemplate>`	`DataList`, `Repeater`	Used between items in list
`<ItemSeparatorTemplate>`	`ListView`	Used between items in list
`<AlternatingItemTemplate>`	`DataList`, `ListView`	Used for alternate items; can aid visibility
`<SelectedItemTemplate>`	`DataList`, `ListView`	Used for selected items in the list
`<EditItemTemplate>`	`DataList`, `FormView`, `ListView`	Used for items being edited
`<InsertItemTemplate>`	`FormView`, `ListView`	Used for items being inserted

continues

(continued)

TEMPLATE	APPLIES TO	DESCRIPTION
`<EmptyDataTemplate>`	`GridView`, `DetailsView`, `FormView`, `ListView`	Used to display empty items — for example, when no records are available in a `GridView`
`<PagerTemplate>`	`GridView`, `DetailsView`, `FormView`	Used to format pagination
`<GroupTemplate>`	`ListView`	Used to specify the output surrounding groups of items
`<GroupSeparatorTemplate>`	`ListView`	Used between groups of items
`<EmptyItemTemplate>`	`ListView`	When using item groups, used to supply output for empty items in a group. This template is used when there are not enough items in a group to fill the group.

The easiest way to understand how to use these is through an example.

Using Templates

You will extend the table at the top of the `Default.aspx` page of `PCSWebSite3` to contain a `ListView` displaying each of the events stored in the database. You will make these events selectable such that details of any event can be displayed by clicking on its name, in a `FormView` control.

First, you need to create new data sources for the data-bound controls. It is good practice (and strongly recommended) to have a separate data source for each data-bound control.

The `SqlDataSource` control required for the `ListView` control, `MRBEventData2`, is similar to `MRBEventData`, except that it needs to return only `Name` and `ID` data. The required code is as follows:

```
<asp:SqlDataSource ID="MRBEventData2" Runat="server"
  SelectCommand="SELECT [ID], [Name] FROM [Events]"
  ConnectionString="<%$ ConnectionStrings:MRBConnectionString %>">
</asp:SqlDataSource>
```

The data source for the `FormView` control, `MRBEventDetailData`, is more complicated, although you can build it easily enough through the data source Configuration Wizard. This data source uses the selected item of the `ListView` control, which you will call `EventList`, to get only the selected item data. This is achieved using a parameter in the SQL query, as follows:

```
<asp:SqlDataSource ID="MRBEventDetailData" Runat="server"
  SelectCommand="SELECT dbo.Events.Name, dbo.Rooms.Room,
                 dbo.Events.AttendeeList, dbo.Events.EventDate
                 FROM dbo.Events INNER JOIN dbo.Rooms
                 ON dbo.Events.ID = dbo.Rooms.ID WHERE dbo.Events.ID = @ID"
  ConnectionString="<%$ ConnectionStrings:MRBConnectionString %>">
  <SelectParameters>
    <asp:ControlParameter Name="ID" DefaultValue="-1" ControlID="EventList"
      PropertyName="SelectedValue" />
  </SelectParameters>
</asp:SqlDataSource>
```

Here, the `ID` parameter results in a value being inserted in place of `@ID` in the select query. The `ControlParameter` entry takes this value from the `SelectedValue` property of `EventList`, or uses –1 if there is no selected item. At first glance, this syntax seems a little odd, but it is very flexible, and after you've generated a few of these using the wizard, you won't have any trouble assembling your own.

Next, you need to add the `ListView` and `FormView` controls. The changes to the code in `Default.aspx` in the `PCSWebSite3` project are shown in the following code:

```
<tr>
  <td align="center" colspan="3">
    <asp:ValidationSummary ID="validationSummary" Runat="server"
      HeaderText="Before submitting your request:" />
  </td>
</tr>
<tr>
  <td align="left" colspan="3" style="width: 40%;">
    <table cellspacing="4" style="width: 100%;">
      <tr>
        <td colspan="2" style="text-align: center;">
          <h2>Event details</h2>
        </td>
      </tr>
      <tr>
        <td style="width: 40%; background-color: #ccffcc;"
          valign="top">
          <asp:ListView ID="EventList" runat="server"
            DataSourceID="MRBEventData2" DataKeyNames="ID"
            OnSelectedIndexChanged="EventList_SelectedIndexChanged">
            <LayoutTemplate>
              <ul>
                <asp:PlaceHolder ID="itemPlaceholder"
                  runat="server" />
              </ul>
            </LayoutTemplate>
            <ItemTemplate>
              <li>
                <asp:LinkButton Text='<%# Bind("Name") %>'
                  runat="server" ID="NameLink" CommandName="Select"
                  CommandArgument='<%# Bind("ID") %>'
                  CausesValidation="false" />
              </li>
            </ItemTemplate>
            <SelectedItemTemplate>
              <li>
                <b><%# Eval("Name") %></b>
              </li>
            </SelectedItemTemplate>
          </asp:ListView>
        </td>
        <td valign="top">
          <asp:FormView ID="FormView1" Runat="server"
            DataSourceID="MRBEventDetailData">
            <ItemTemplate>
              <h3><%# Eval("Name") %></h3>
              <b>Date:</b>
              <%# Eval("EventDate", "{0:D}") %>
              <br />
              <b>Room:</b>
              <%# Eval("Room") %>
              <br />
              <b>Attendees:</b>
              <%# Eval("AttendeeList") %>
            </ItemTemplate>
          </asp:FormView>
        </td>
      </tr>
    </table>
  </td>
</tr>
</table>
```

Here you have added a new table row containing a table with a `ListView` control in one column and a `FormView` control in the other.

The `ListView` uses `<LayoutTemplate>` to output a bulleted list and `<ItemTemplate>` and `<SelectedItemTemplate>` to display event details as list items. In `<LayoutTemplate>`, a container element for items is specified with a `PlaceHolder` control that has the `ID="itemPlaceholder"` attribute. To facilitate selection, you raise a `Select` command from the event name link rendered in `<ItemTemplate>`, which automatically changes the selection. You also use the `OnSelectedIndexChanged` event, triggered when the `Select` command changes the selection, to ensure that the list display updates itself to display the selected item in a different style. The event handler for this is shown in the following code:

```
protected void EventList_SelectedIndexChanged(object sender, EventArgs e)
{
    EventList.DataBind();
}
```

You also need to ensure new events are added to the list:

```
if (queryResult == 1)
{
    resultLabel.Text = "Event Added.";
    EventData = null;
    calendar.SelectedDate =
        GetFreeDate(calendar.SelectedDate.AddDays(1));
    GridView1.DataBind();
    EventList.DataBind();
}
```

Now selectable event details are available in the table, as shown in Figure 40-14.

There is *much* more that you can do with templates and data-bound controls in general, enough in fact to fill a whole book. However, this should be enough to get you started with your experimentation.

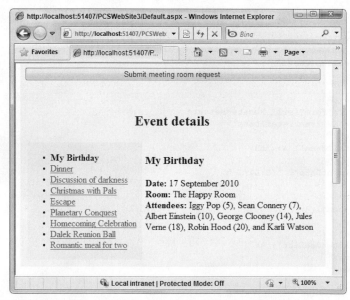

FIGURE 40-14

APPLICATION CONFIGURATION

Throughout this chapter, we have alluded to the existence of a conceptual application containing web pages and configuration settings. This is an important concept to grasp, especially when configuring your web site for multiple concurrent users.

A few notes on terminology and application lifetime are necessary here. An *application* is defined as all files in your project, and is configured by the web.config file. An Application object is created when an application is started for the first time, which will be when the first HTTP request arrives. Also at this time, the Application_Start event is triggered and a pool of HttpApplication instances is created. Each incoming request receives one of these instances, which performs request processing. Note that this means HttpApplication objects do not need to cope with concurrent access, unlike the global Application object. When all HttpApplication instances finish their work, the Application_End event fires and the application terminates, destroying the Application object.

The event handlers for the events mentioned earlier (along with handlers for all other events discussed in this chapter) can be defined in a global.asax file, which you can add to any web site project (it is listed as Global Application Class in the templates that you see when you add a new item to a web application). The generated file contains blanks for you to fill in; for example:

```
void Application_Start(Object sender, EventArgs e)
{
    // Code that runs on application startup
}
```

When an individual user accesses the web application, a *session* is started. Similar to the application, this involves the creation of a user-specific Session object, along with the triggering of a Session_Start event. Within a session, individual *requests* trigger Application_BeginRequest and Application_EndRequest events. These can occur several times during the scope of a session as different resources within the application are accessed. Individual sessions can be terminated manually, or will time out if no further requests are received. Session termination triggers a Session_End event and the destruction of the Session object.

Against the background of this process, you can do several things to streamline your application. If all instances of your application use a single, resource-heavy object, for example, then you might consider instantiating it at the application level. This can improve performance and reduce memory usage with multiple users because in most requests no such instantiation will be required.

Another technique you can use is to store session-level information for use by individual users across requests. This might include user-specific information that is extracted from a data store when the user first connects (in the Session_Start() event handler), and is made available until the session is terminated (through a timeout or user request).

These techniques are beyond the scope of this book — and you might want to consult *Professional ASP.NET 4: in C# and VB* (Wiley Publishing, Inc., 2010, ISBN 978-0470-502204) for details — but it helps to have a broad understanding of the processes.

Finally, you need to look at web.config files. A web site will usually have one of these in its root directory (although it is not created for you by default), and may have additional ones in subdirectories to configure directory-specific settings (such as security). The PCSWebSite3 web site developed in this chapter received an auto-generated Web.config file when you added a stored database connection string, which you can see in the file:

```
<connectionStrings>
  <add name="MRBConnectionString"
    connectionString="Data Source=.\SQLEXPRESS;
    AttachDbFilename=|DataDirectory|\MeetingRoomBooker.mdf;
    Integrated Security=True;User Instance=True"
    providerName="System.Data.SqlClient" />
</connectionStrings>
```

If you ran the project in debug mode, then you will also see some additional settings in the `web.config` file.

You can edit `web.config` files manually, but you can also configure web sites (and their underlying configuration files) using a tool that is accessible on the web site menu in Visual Studio, under ASP.NET Configuration. The display for this tool is shown in Figure 40-15.

As you can see from the figure, this tool lets you configure a number of settings, including security. You will see much more of this tool in the next chapter.

FIGURE 40-15

SUMMARY

This chapter has provided an overview of web application creation with ASP.NET. You have seen how you can use C# in combination with web server controls to provide a truly rich development environment. You have developed an event-booking sample application which illustrates many of the techniques available, such as the variety of server controls that exist, and data binding with ADO.NET.

Specifically, you have seen the following:

➤ An introduction to ASP.NET and how it fits in with .NET development in general

➤ How the basic syntax of ASP.NET works, how state management is achieved, and how to integrate C# code with ASP.NET pages

➤ How to create an ASP.NET web application using Visual Studio, and what options exist for hosting and testing web sites

➤ A summary of the web controls available to ASP.NET developers, and how they work together to deliver dynamic and/or data-driven content

➤ How to work with event handlers to both detect and act on user interaction with controls and customize controls via page and rendering events

➤ How to bind data to web controls, and format the data displayed using templates and data-binding expressions

➤ How to put all this together to build a meeting room booker application

With this information, you are already at a point where you could assemble powerful web applications of your own. However, we've only scratched the surface of what's possible. So, before you put down this book and dive into your own web development, we recommend that you keep reading. In Chapter 41, you expand your knowledge of ASP.NET by looking at some more important web topics, including master pages, skinning, and personalization. And trust us — the results are worth it!

41

ASP.NET Features

WHAT'S IN THIS CHAPTER?

➤ User and custom controls

➤ Master pages

➤ Site navigation

➤ Security

➤ Themes

➤ Web Parts

➤ ASP.NET AJAX

In this chapter you look at some of the techniques that ASP.NET supplies to enhance your web sites and applications. These techniques make it easier for you to create web sites and applications, make it possible for you to add advanced functionality, and improve the user experience.

Sometimes the built-in web controls, however powerful, don't quite match up with your requirements for a specific project. In the first part of this chapter, you examine the options available to control developers and assemble some simple user controls of your own. You also look at the basics of more advanced control construction.

Next, you look at master pages, a technique that enables you to provide templates for your web sites. Using master pages you can implement complex layouts on web pages throughout a web site with a great deal of code reuse. You also see how you can use the navigation web server controls in combination with a master page to provide consistent navigation across a web site.

Site navigation can be made user-specific, such that only certain users (those that are registered with the site, or site administrators, say) can access certain sections. You also look at site security and how to log in to web sites — something that is made extremely easy via the login web server controls.

After that, you look at some more advanced techniques, namely, providing and choosing themes for web sites, and how to use Web Parts to enable your users to dynamically personalize web pages by positioning and customizing controls on a page.

Finally, in the largest section of this chapter, you look at ASP.NET AJAX. This technology is a powerful way to enhance the user experience. It enables web sites and applications to become more responsive by updating sections of a page independently, as well as streamlining the process of adding client-side functionality.

Throughout much of this chapter, you will refer to a large example web site that includes all the techniques that you have seen in this and the previous chapter. This web site, PCSDemoSite, is available for download (along with the other code for this chapter) at www.wrox.com. The relevant sections of code are examined as necessary, and the additional code (mostly dummy content or simple code you have already seen) is left for you to examine at your convenience.

USER AND CUSTOM CONTROLS

Sometimes, a given control doesn't quite work as you would like it to, or perhaps one section of code, intended for reuse on several pages, is too complex in the hands of multiple developers. In such cases, there is a strong argument for building your own controls.

The .NET Framework provides an ideal setting for the creation of custom controls, using simple programming techniques. Every aspect of ASP.NET server controls is exposed for you to customize, including such capabilities as templating and client-side scripting. However, there is no need to write code for all these eventualities; simpler controls can be a lot easier to create.

In addition, the dynamic discovery of assemblies that is inherent in a .NET system makes installation of web sites and applications on a new web server as simple as copying the directory structure containing your code. To make use of the controls you have created, you simply copy the assemblies containing those controls along with the rest of the code. You can even place frequently used controls in an assembly located in the global assembly cache (GAC) on the web server, so that all web sites and applications on the server have access to them.

This chapter discusses two different kinds of controls:

➤ **User controls** and how to convert existing ASP.NET pages into controls

➤ **Custom controls** and how to group the functionality of several controls, extend existing controls, and create new controls from scratch

User controls are illustrated with a simple control that displays a card suit (club, diamond, heart, or spade), so that you can embed it in other ASP.NET pages with ease. We won't go into too much depth for custom controls, although we show you the basic principles and direct you to more information beyond this book.

User Controls

User controls are controls that you create using ASP.NET code, just as you use in standard ASP.NET web pages. The difference is that after you have created a user control you can reuse it in multiple ASP.NET pages.

For example, say that you have created a page that displays some information from a database, perhaps information about an order. Instead of creating a fixed page that does this, you can to place the relevant code into a user control, and then insert that control into as many different web pages as you want.

In addition, you can define properties and methods for user controls. For example, you can specify a property for the background color for displaying your database table in a web page, or a method to re-run a database query to check for changes.

To start, you create a simple user control.

A Simple User Control

In Visual Studio, create a new empty web site called `PCSUserCWebApp1` in the directory `C:\ProCSharp\Chapter41`. After the web site has been generated, select the Website ⇨ Add New Item ... menu option and add a Web User Control called `PCSUserC1.ascx`.

The files added to your project, with the extensions `.ascx` and `.ascx.cs`, work in a very similar way to the `.aspx` files that you have seen already. The `.ascx` file contains your ASP.NET code and looks very similar to a normal `.aspx` file. The `.ascx.cs` file is your code-behind file, which defines custom code for the user control, much in the same way that forms are extended by `.aspx.cs` files.

The `.ascx` files can be viewed in Design or Source view, just like `.aspx` files. Looking at the file in Source view reveals an important difference: there is no HTML code present, and in particular no `<form>` element. This is because user controls are inserted inside ASP.NET forms in other files and so don't need a `<form>` tag of their own. The generated code is as follows:

Available for download on Wrox.com

```
<%@ Control Language="C#" AutoEventWireup="true" CodeFile="PCSUserC1.ascx.cs"
    Inherits="PCSUserC1" %>
```

code snippet PCSUserCWebApp1/PCSUserC1.ascx

This is very similar to the `<%@ Page %>` directive generated in `.aspx` files, except that `Control` is specified rather than `Page`. The `CodeFile` attribute specifies the code-behind file and `Inherits` specifies the class defined in the code-behind file from which the page inherits. The code in the `.ascx.cs` file contains, as in auto-generated `.aspx.cs` files, a class definition that is empty apart from a `Page_Load()` event handler method.

Your simple control will be one that displays a graphic corresponding to one of the four standard suits in cards (club, diamond, heart, or spade). The graphics required for this were shipped as part of a previous version of Visual Studio; you can find them in the downloadable code for this chapter, in the `CardSuitImages` directory, with the filenames `CLUB.BMP`, `DIAMOND.BMP`, `HEART.BMP`, and `SPADE.BMP`. Copy these files into a new `Images` subdirectory of your project's directory, so that you can use them in a moment. If you do not have access to this download, you can use any images you like for this example because they are not important to the functionality of the code.

> *Note that unlike earlier versions of Visual Studio, changes you make to the web site structure outside of Visual Studio are automatically reflected in the IDE. You have to hit the refresh button in the Solution Explorer window, but you should see the new `Images` directory and bitmap files appear automatically.*

Adding Content to the Control

Now add some code to your new control. In the HTML view of `PCSUserC1.ascx`, add the following:

```
<%@ Control Language="C#" AutoEventWireup="true" CodeFile="PCSUserC1.ascx.cs"
    Inherits="PCSUserC1" %>
<table cellspacing="4">
  <tr valign="middle">
    <td>
      <asp:Image Runat="server" ID="suitPic" ImageURL="~/Images/club.bmp"/>
    </td>
```

```
      <td>
        <asp:Label Runat="server" ID="suitLabel">Club</asp:Label>
      </td>
    </tr>
  </table>
```

This defines a default state for your control, which is a picture of a club along with a label. The ~ in the path to the image means "start at the root directory of the web site." Before you add functionality, you will test this default by adding this control to a web page, so before continuing, add a new web page called `Default` `.aspx` to the web site.

To use a custom control in an `.aspx` file, you first need to specify how you will refer to it, that is, the name of the tag that will represent the control in your HTML. To do this, you use the `<%@ Register %>` directive at the top of the code in `Default.aspx`, as follows:

```
<%@ Register TagPrefix="pcs" TagName="UserC1" Src="PCSUserC1.ascx" %>
```

code snippet PCSUserCWebApp1/Default.aspx

The `TagPrefix` and `TagName` attributes specify the tag name to use (in the form `<TagPrefix:TagName>`), and you use the `Src` attribute to point to the file containing your user control. Now you can use the control by replacing the existing `<form>` element in the file with code as follows adding the following element:

```
<form id="Form1" method="post" runat="server">
  <div>
    <pcs:UserC1 Runat="server" ID="myUserControl"/>
  </div>
</form>
```

This is all you need to do to test your user control. Figure 41-1 shows the results of running this code.

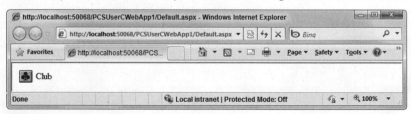

FIGURE 41-1

As it stands, this control groups two existing controls, an image and a label, in a table layout. Therefore, it falls into the category of a composite control.

Adding a Suit Property

To gain control over the displayed suit, you can use an attribute on the `<PCS:UserC1>` element. Attributes on user control elements are automatically mapped to properties on user controls, so all you have to do to make this work is add a property to the code behind your control, `PCSUserC1.ascx.cs`. Call this property `Suit`, and let it take any suit value. To make it easier for you to represent the state of the control, you define an enumeration to hold the four suit names. The best way to do this is to add an `App_Code` directory to your web site, and then add a `.cs` file called `Suit.cs` in this directory. `App_Code` is another "special" directory, like `App_Data`, whose functionality is defined for you — in this case it holds additional code files for your web site. You can add this directory by right-clicking the web site in Solution Explorer and clicking Add ASP.NET Folder ⇨ App_Code. When you have done this, add `Suit.cs` with code as follows:

```
using System;

public enum Suit
{
    Club, Diamond, Heart, Spade
}
```

code snippet PCSUserCWebApp1/App_Code/Suit.cs

The `PCSUserC1` class needs a member variable to hold the suit type, `currentSuit`:

```
public partial class PCSUserC1 : System.Web.UI.UserControl
{
    protected Suit currentSuit;
```

code snippet PCSUserCWebApp1/PCSUserC1.ascx.cs

And a property to access this member variable, `Suit`:

```
public Suit Suit
{
    get
    {
        return currentSuit;
    }
    set
    {
        currentSuit = value;
        suitPic.ImageUrl = "~/Images/" + currentSuit.ToString() + ".bmp";
        suitLabel.Text = currentSuit.ToString();
    }
}
```

The `set` accessor here sets the URL of the image to one of the files you copied earlier, and the text displayed to the suit name.

Accessing the New Property

Next, you must add code to `Default.aspx` so that you can access this new property. You could simply specify the suit using the property you have just added (if you compile the project the options will even appear in IntelliSense for you):

```
<PCS:UserC1 Runat="server" id="myUserControl" Suit="diamond"/>
```

code snippet PCSUserCWebApp1/Default.aspx

The ASP.NET processor is intelligent enough to get the correct enumeration item from the string provided. To make things a bit more interesting and interactive, though, you will use a radio button list to select a suit:

```
<form id="form1" runat="server">
  <div>
    <pcs:UserC1 id="myUserControl" runat="server" />
    <asp:RadioButtonList Runat="server" ID="suitList" AutoPostBack="True">
      <asp:ListItem Value="Club" Selected="True">Club</asp:ListItem>
      <asp:ListItem Value="Diamond">Diamond</asp:ListItem>
      <asp:ListItem Value="Heart">Heart</asp:ListItem>
      <asp:ListItem Value="Spade">Spade</asp:ListItem>
    </asp:RadioButtonList>
  </div>
</form>
```

You also need to add an event handler for the `SelectedIndexChanged` event of the list, which you can do simply by double-clicking the radio button list control in Design view.

> *Note that you have set the* `AutoPostBack` *property of this list to* `True`, *because the* `suitList_SelectedIndexChanged()` *event handler won't be executed on the server unless a postback is in operation, and this control doesn't trigger a postback by default.*

The `suitList_SelectedIndexChanged()` method requires the following code in `Default.aspx.cs`:

Available for
download on
Wrox.com

```
public partial class Default
{
    protected void suitList_SelectedIndexChanged(object sender, EventArgs e)
    {
        myUserControl.Suit = (Suit)Enum.Parse(typeof(Suit),
                                    suitList.SelectedItem.Value);
    }
}
```

code snippet PCSUserCWebApp1/Default.aspx.cs

You know that the `Value` attributes on the `<ListItem>` elements represent valid values for the suit enumeration you defined earlier, so you simply parse these as enumeration types and use them as values of the `Suit` property of your user control. You cast the returned object type to `Suit` using simple casing syntax, because this cannot be achieved implicitly.

Now you can change the suit when you run your web site (see Figure 41-2).

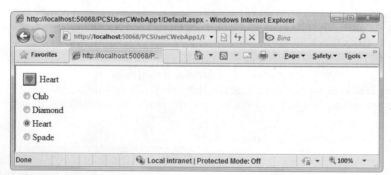

FIGURE 41-2

Now that you have created your user control, you can use it in any other web page simply by using the `<%@ Register %>` directive and the two source code files (`PCSUserC1.ascx` and `PCSUserC1.ascx.cs`) you have created for the control.

User Controls in PCSDemoSite

In PCSDemoSite, the meeting room booker web site from the previous chapter has been converted into a user control for ease of reuse. To see the control, you have to log in to the site as User1, with password User1!!, and navigate to the Meeting Room Booker page, as shown in Figure 41-3. (You learn how the logging-in system works later in this chapter, in the "Security" section.)

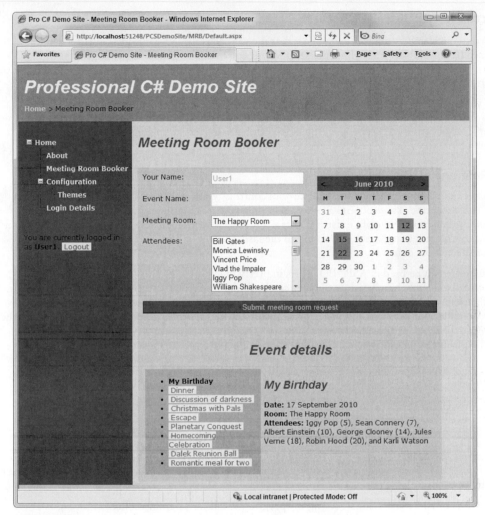

FIGURE 41-3

Apart from the obvious change in style, which is achieved by themes, as you see later in this chapter, the major modifications are as follows:

➤   The username is automatically taken from user details.

➤   There is no extra data display at the bottom of the page, and corresponding `DataBind()` calls are removed from the code behind.

➤   There is no result label beneath the control — the user gets enough feedback by seeing events added to the calendar and event list, without being told that event addition was successful.

➤   The page containing the user control uses navigation controls and a master page.

The code modifications to achieve all this are remarkably simple. You won't look at them here, but you will come back to this control later in this chapter.

Custom Controls

Custom controls go a step beyond user controls in that they are entirely self-contained in C# assemblies, requiring no separate ASP.NET code. This means that you don't need to go through the process of assembling a user interface (UI) in an `.ascx` file. Instead, you have complete control over what is written to the output stream, that is, the exact HTML generated by your control.

In general, it will take longer to develop custom controls than user controls because the syntax is more complex, and you often have to write significantly more code to get results. A user control may be as simple as a few other controls grouped together, as you have seen, whereas a custom control can do just about anything short of making you a cup of coffee.

Creating and Referencing Custom Controls

To get the most customizable behavior for your custom controls, you can derive a class from `System.Web.UI.WebControls.WebControl`. If you do this, you are creating a full custom control. Or, you can extend the functionality of an existing control, creating a derived custom control. Finally, you can group existing controls together, much as you did in the last section but with a more logical structure, to create a composite custom control.

Whatever you create can be used in ASP.NET pages in pretty much the same way. All you need to do is place the generated assembly in a location where it can be found by the web site or application that uses it, and register the element names to use with the `<%@ Register %>` directive. For this location, you have two options: you can either put the assembly in the bin directory of the web site or application, or place it in the GAC if you want all web sites and applications on the server to have access to it. Or, if you are just using a user control on a single web site, you can just put the `.cs` file for the control in the `App_Code` directory for the site.

The `<%@ Register %>` directive takes a slightly different syntax for custom controls:

```
<%@ Register TagPrefix="PCS" Namespace="PCSCustomWebControls"
             Assembly="PCSCustomWebControls"%>
```

You use the `TagPrefix` option in the same way as before, but you don't use the `TagName` or `Src` attributes. This is because the custom control assembly you use may contain several custom controls, and each of these will be named by its class, so `TagName` is redundant. Plus, because you can use the dynamic discovery capabilities of the .NET Framework to find your assembly, you simply have to name it and the namespace in it that contains your controls.

In the previous line of code, you are instructing the program to use an assembly called `PCSCustomWebControls.dll` with controls in the `PCSCustomWebControls` namespace, and use the tag prefix `PCS`. If you have a control called `Control1` in this namespace, you could use it with the ASP.NET code:

```
<PCS:Control1 Runat="server" ID="MyControl1"/>
```

The `Assembly` attribute of the `<%@ Register %>` directive is optional — if you have custom controls in the `App_Code` directory of your site, you can omit this, and the web site will look at code here for controls. One thing though — the `Namespace` attribute is *not* optional. You must include a namespace in code files for custom controls, or the ASP.NET runtime will not be able to find them.

With custom controls, it is also possible to reproduce some of the control nesting behavior that exists in list controls, for example the way that you can nest `<asp:ListItem>` controls inside a list control to populate the list control:

```
<asp:DropDownList ID="roomList" Runat="server" Width="160px">
    <asp:ListItem Value="1">The Happy Room</asp:ListItem>
    <asp:ListItem Value="2">The Angry Room</asp:ListItem>
    <asp:ListItem Value="3">The Depressing Room</asp:ListItem>
    <asp:ListItem Value="4">The Funked Out Room</asp:ListItem>
</asp:DropDownList>
```

You can create controls that should be interpreted as being children of other controls in a very similar way to this. This is one of the more advanced techniques that you won't be looking at in this book.

Custom Control Sample

Now it's time to put some of this theory into practice. You will use a single web site called `PCSCustomCWebSite1` in the `C:\ProCSharp\Chapter41\` directory (made using the empty web site template), with a custom control in its `App_Code` directory to illustrate a simple custom control. The control here will be a multicolored version of the existing `Label` control, with the ability to cycle through a set of colors for each letter in its text.

The code for the control, `RainbowLabel`, in the file `App_Code\RainbowLabel.cs`, starts with the following `using` statements:

Available for download on Wrox.com

```
using System.Drawing;
using System.Web.UI;
using System.Web.UI.WebControls;
```

code snippet PCSCustomCWebSite1/RainbowLabel.cs

The `System.Drawing` namespace is required for the `Color` enumeration, and the `Web` namespaces for the ASP.NET control references. The class maintains an array of colors to use for letters in its text in a private `Color` array called `colors`:

```
namespace PCSCustomWebControls
{
    public class RainbowLabel : Label
    {
        private Color[] colors = new Color[] {Color.Red,
                                              Color.Orange,
                                              Color.Yellow,
                                              Color.GreenYellow,
                                              Color.Blue,
                                              Color.Indigo,
                                              Color.Violet};
```

Also notice that the namespace `PCSCustomWebControls` is used to contain the control. As discussed earlier, this is necessary so that web pages can reference the control correctly.

To enable color cycling, you also store an integer offset value in a private `offset` property:

```
        private int offset
        {
            get
            {
                object rawOffset = ViewState["_offset"];
                if (rawOffset != null)
                {
                    return (int)rawOffset;
                }
                else
                {
                    ViewState["_offset"] = 0;
                    return 0;
                }
            }
            set
            {
                ViewState["_offset"] = value;
            }
        }
```

Note that this property isn't as simple as just storing a value in a member field. This is due to the way ASP.NET maintains state, as discussed in the previous chapter. Controls are instantiated on each postback operation, so to store values you must make use of view state. This is easy to access — you simply use the `ViewState` collection, which can store any object that is serializable. Otherwise, `offset` would revert to its initial value between each postback.

To modify `offset`, you use a method called `Cycle()`:

```
public void Cycle()
{
    offset = ++offset;
}
```

This simply increments the value stored in the view state for `offset`.

Finally, you come to perhaps the most important method override for any custom control — `Render()`. This is where you output HTML, and as such it can be a very complicated method to implement. If you were to take into account all the browsers that may view your controls, and all the variables that could affect rendering, this method could get very big. Fortunately, for this example, it's quite simple:

```
protected override void Render(HtmlTextWriter output)
{
    string text = Text;
    for (int pos = 0; pos < text.Length; pos++)
    {
        int rgb = colors[(pos + offset) % colors.Length].ToArgb()
                                                    & 0xFFFFFF;
        output.Write(string.Format(
            "<font color=\"#{0:X6}\">{1}</font>", rgb, text[pos]));
    }
}
```

This method gives you access to the output stream to display your control content. There are only two cases where you don't need to implement this method:

➤   When you are designing a control that has no visual representation (usually known as a component)

➤   When you are deriving from an existing control and don't need to change its display characteristics

Custom controls can also expose custom methods, raise custom events, and respond to child controls (if any). In the case of `RainbowLabel`, you don't have to worry about any of this.

Next, you need to add a web page, `Default.aspx`, and add code to view the control and provide access to `Cycle()`, as follows:

```
<%@ Register TagPrefix="pcs" Namespace="PCSCustomWebControls" %>

...

<form id="form1" runat="server">
  <div>
    <pcs:RainbowLabel runat="server" ID="rainbowLabel1"
      Text="Multicolored label!" />
    <asp:Button Runat="server" ID="cycleButton" Text="Cycle colors"
      OnClick="cycleButton_Click" />
  </div>
</form>
```

code snippet PCSCustomCWebSite1/Default.aspx

The required code in `Default.aspx.cs` is simply this:

```
protected void cycleButton_Click(object sender, EventArgs e)
{
    rainbowLabel1.Cycle();
}
```

code snippet PCSCustomCWebSite1/Default.aspx.cs

Now you can view the sample and cycle the colors in the sample text, as shown in Figure 41-4.

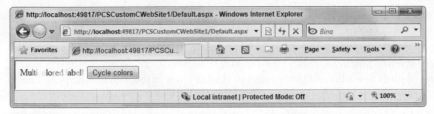

FIGURE 41-4

You can do a lot more with custom controls; indeed, the possibilities are practically limitless, but you will have to experiment with these possibilities on your own.

MASTER PAGES

Master pages provide an excellent way to make your web sites easier to design. Putting all (or at least most) of your page layout in a single file allows you to concentrate on the more important things for the individual web pages of your site.

Master pages are created in files with the extension .master, and can be added via the Website ⇨ Add New Item ... menu item, like any other site content. At first glance, the code generated for a master page is much like that for a standard .aspx page:

```
<%@ Master Language="C#" AutoEventWireup="true"
  CodeFile="MyMasterPage.master.cs" Inherits="MyMasterPage" %>
<!DOCTYPE html PUBLIC "-//W3C//DTD XHTML 1.0 Transitional//EN"
  "http://www.w3.org/TR/xhtml1/DTD/xhtml1-transitional.dtd">
<html xmlns="http://www.w3.org/1999/xhtml">
<head runat="server">
  <title></title>
  <asp:ContentPlaceHolder id="head" runat="server">
  </asp:ContentPlaceHolder>
</head>
<body>
  <form id="form1" runat="server">
    <div>
      <asp:ContentPlaceHolder ID="ContentPlaceHolder1" Runat="server">
      </asp:ContentPlaceHolder>
    </div>
  </form>
</body>
</html>
```

The differences are:

➤ A `<%@ Master %>` directive is used instead of a `<%@ Page %>` directive, although the attributes are the same.

➤ A `ContentPlaceHolder` control with an `ID` of head is placed in the page header.

➤ A `ContentPlaceHolder` control with an `ID` of `ContentPlaceHolder1` is placed in the page body.

The `ContentPlaceHolder` controls are what make master pages so useful. You can have any number of these on a page, and they are used by `.aspx` pages using the master page to "plug in" content. You can put default content inside a `ContentPlaceHolder` control, but `.aspx` pages can override this content.

For an `.aspx` page to use a master page, you need to modify the `<%@ Page %>` directive as follows:

```
<%@ Page Language="C#" AutoEventWireup="true" CodeFile="Default.aspx.cs"
  Inherits="_Default" MasterPageFile="~/MyMasterPage.master"
  Title="Page Title" %>
```

Here you have added two new attributes: a `MasterPageFile` attribute saying which master page to use and a `Title` attribute that sets the content of the `<title>` element in the master page.

Or, when you add an `.aspx` page to a web site that contains master pages, you can choose to select a master page. The Add New Item Wizard contains a "Select master page" check box, and if you select this option, the next page of the wizard gives you a list of master pages to choose from in the web application. The generated code for the page will then include the MasterPageFile attribute as previously described.

The `.aspx` page doesn't have to contain any other code, if you want to use the default master page content. Also, you must not include a `Form` control, because a page may only have one of these and there is one in the master page.

`.aspx` pages that use a master page can contain no root-level content other than directives, script elements, and `Content` controls. You can have as many `Content` controls as you like, where each one inserts content into one of the `ContentPlaceHolder` controls in the master page. The only thing to look out for is to make sure that the `ContentPlaceHolderID` attribute of the `Content` control matches the `ID` of the `ContentPlaceHolder` control where you want to insert content. So, to add content into the master page shown earlier, you would simply need the following in the `.aspx` file:

```
<%@ Page Language="C#" MasterPageFile="~/MyMasterPage.master"
  AutoEventWireup="true" CodeFile="Default.aspx.cs" Inherits="_Default"
  Title="Untitled Page" %>

<asp:Content ID="Content1" ContentPlaceHolderID="head" Runat="Server">
</asp:Content>
<asp:Content ID="Content2" ContentPlaceHolderID="ContentPlaceHolder1"
  runat="Server">
  Custom content!
</asp:Content>
```

The true power of master pages comes when you surround the `ContentPlaceHolder` controls in your master pages with other content, such as navigation controls, site logos, and HTML. You can supply multiple `ContentPlaceHolder` controls for main content, sidebar content, footer text, and so on.

You can omit `Content` controls on a page if you do not wish to supply content for a specific `ContentPlaceHolder`. For example, you can remove the `Content1` control from the preceding code without affecting the resultant display.

Accessing Master Page Content from Web Pages

When you add a master page to a web page, you will sometimes need to access the master page from code in your web page. To do this, you can use the `Page.Master` property, which will return a reference to the master page in the form of a `MasterPage` object. You can cast this to the type of the master page as defined by the master page file (for the example in the previous section, this class would be called `MyMasterPage`). After you have this reference, you can access any public members of the master page class.

Also, you can use the `MasterPage.FindControl()` method to locate controls on the master page by their identifier. This enables you to manipulate content on the master page that is outside of content placeholders.

One typical use of this might be if you define a master page that is used for a standard form, with a submit button. You can locate the submit button in the child page and add an event handler for the submit button in the master page. In this way, you can provide, for example, custom validation logic in response to a form submission.

Nested Master Pages

The "Select master page" option is also available when you create a new master page. By using this option, you can create a *nested* master page that is based on a parent master page. For example, you can create a master page called MyNestedMasterPage that uses MyMasterPage as follows:

```
<%@ Master Language="C#" MasterPageFile="~/MyMasterPage.master"
  AutoEventWireup="false" CodeFile="MyNestedMasterPage.master.cs"
  Inherits="MyNestedMasterPage" %>

<asp:Content ID="Content1" ContentPlaceHolderID="head" Runat="Server">
  <!--Disabled for child controls.-->
</asp:Content>
<asp:Content ID="Content2" ContentPlaceHolderID="ContentPlaceHolder1"
  Runat="Server">
  First nested place holder:
  <asp:ContentPlaceHolder ID="NestedContentPlaceHolder1" runat="server">

  </asp:ContentPlaceHolder>
  <br />
  <br />
  Second nested place holder:
  <asp:ContentPlaceHolder ID="NestedContentPlaceHolder2" runat="server">

  </asp:ContentPlaceHolder>
</asp:Content>
```

Pages that use this master page would supply content for NestedContentPlaceHolder1 and NestedContentPlaceHolder2, but would not have direct access to the ContentPlaceHolder controls specified in MyMasterPage. In this example, MyNestedMasterPage fixes the content for the head control and supplies a template for the ContentPlaceHolder1 control.

By creating a family of nested master pages, you can provide alternate layouts for pages while leaving some aspects of the base master pages untouched. For example, the root master page might include navigation and basic layout, and nested master pages could provide layouts with different amounts of columns. You could then use the nested master pages in the pages of your site and quickly switch between these alternate layouts on different pages.

Master Pages in PCSDemoSite

In PCSDemoSite, the single master page MasterPage.master (the default name for a master page) is used, with code as follows:

```
<%@ Master Language="C#" AutoEventWireup="true"
CodeFile="MasterPage.master.cs"
  Inherits="MasterPage" %>
<!DOCTYPE html PUBLIC "-//W3C//DTD XHTML 1.1//EN"
  "http://www.w3.org/TR/xhtml11/DTD/xhtml11.dtd">
<html xmlns="http://www.w3.org/1999/xhtml">
<head runat="server">
  <link rel="stylesheet" href="StyleSheet.css" type="text/css" />
  <title></title>
</head>
<body>
  <form id="form1" runat="server">
    <div id="header">
      <h1><asp:literal ID="Literal1" runat="server"
        text="<%$ AppSettings:SiteTitle %>" /></h1>
      <asp:SiteMapPath ID="SiteMapPath1" Runat="server"
        CssClass="breadcrumb" />
    </div>
```

```
      <div id="nav">
        <div class="navTree">
          <asp:TreeView ID="TreeView1" runat="server"
            DataSourceID="SiteMapDataSource1" ShowLines="True" />
        </div>
        <br />
        <br />
        <asp:LoginView ID="LoginView1" Runat="server">
          <LoggedInTemplate>
            You are currently logged in as
            <b><asp:LoginName ID="LoginName1" Runat="server" /></b>.
            <asp:LoginStatus ID="LoginStatus1" Runat="server" />
          </LoggedInTemplate>
        </asp:LoginView>
      </div>
      <div id="body">
        <asp:ContentPlaceHolder ID="ContentPlaceHolder1" Runat="server" />
      </div>
    </form>
    <asp:SiteMapDataSource ID="SiteMapDataSource1" Runat="server" />
  </body>
</html>
```

code snippet PCSDemoSite/MasterPage.master

Many of the controls here are ones that you haven't looked at yet, and you will come back to those shortly. The important things to note here are the `<div>` elements that hold the various content sections (header, navigation bar, and body), and the use of `<%$ AppSettings:SiteTitle %>` to obtain the site title from the `web.config` file:

```
<appSettings>
  <add key="SiteTitle" value="Professional C# Demo Site"/>
</appSettings>
```

code snippet PCSDemoSite/web.config

There is also a style sheet link to `StyleSheet.css`:

```
<link rel="stylesheet" href="StyleSheet.css" type="text/css" />
```

This CSS style sheet contains the basic layout information for the `<div>` elements on this page, as well as for a section of the meeting room booker control. Note that none of the style information in this file includes colors, fonts, and so on. This is achieved by style sheets within themes, which you see later in this chapter. The only information here is layout information, such as `<div>` sizes.

> Note that web site best practices have been adhered to in this chapter whenever possible. Using CSS for layout rather than tables is fast becoming the industry standard for web site layout and is well worth learning about. In the preceding code, # symbols are used to format `<div>` elements with specific `id` attributes, whereas `.mrbEventList` will format an HTML element with a specific `class` attribute.

SITE NAVIGATION

The three navigation web server controls, `SiteMapPath`, `Menu`, and `TreeView`, can work with an XML site map that you provide for your web site, or a site map provided in a different format if you implement an alternative site map provider. When you have created such a data source, these navigation web server controls are able to automatically generate location and navigation information for users.

You see an example XML site map later in this section.

You can also use a `TreeView` control to display other structured data, but it really comes into its own with site maps, and gives you an alternative view of navigation information.

The navigation web server controls are shown in the following table.

CONTROL	DESCRIPTION
SiteMapPath	Displays breadcrumb-style information, allowing users to see where they are in the structure of a site and navigate to parent areas. You can supply various templates, such as `NodeStyle` and `CurrentNodeStyle`, to customize the appearance of the breadcrumb trail.
Menu	Links to site map information via a `SiteMapDataSource` control, and enables a view of the complete site structure. The appearance of this control can be customized by templates.
TreeView	Allows the display of hierarchical data, such as a table of contents, in a tree structure. Tree nodes are stored in a `Nodes` property, with the selected node stored in `SelectedNode`. Several events allow for server-side processing of user interaction, including `SelectedNodeChanged` and `TreeNodeCollapsed`. This control is typically data-bound.

Adding a Site Map File

To provide a site map XML file for your site, you can add a site map file (`.sitemap`) using the Website ⇨ Add New Item ... menu item. You link to site maps via providers. The default XML provider looks for a file called `Web.sitemap` in the root of your site, so unless you are going to use a different provider, you should accept the default filename supplied.

A site map XML file contains a root `<siteMap>` element containing a single `<siteMapNode>` element, which in turn can contain any number of nested `<siteMapNode>` elements.

Each `<siteMapNode>` element uses the attributes shown in the following table.

ATTRIBUTE	DESCRIPTION
Title	Page title, used as the text for links in site map displays
url	Page location, used as the hyperlink location in site map displays
Roles	The user roles that are allowed to see this site map entry in menus and so on
description	Optional text used for tooltip pop-ups for site map displays

When a site has a `Web.sitemap` file, adding a breadcrumb trail is as simple as putting the following code on your page:

```
<asp:SiteMapPath ID="SiteMapPath1" Runat="server" />
```

This will use the default provider and the current URL location to format a list of links to parent pages.

Adding a menu or tree view menu requires a `SiteMapDataSource` control, but again this can be very simple:

```
<asp:SiteMapDataSource ID="SiteMapDataSource1" Runat="server" />
```

When using a custom provider, the only difference is that you can supply the provider ID via a `SiteMapProvider` attribute. You can also remove upper levels of the menu data (such as the root `Home` item) using `StartingNodeOffset`; remove just the top-level link using `ShowStartingNode="False"`; start from the current location using `StartFromCurrentNode="True"`; and override the root node using `StartingNodeUrl`.

The data from this data source is consumed by `Menu` and `TreeView` controls simply by setting their `DataSourceID` to the ID of the `SiteMapDataSource`. Both controls include numerous styling properties and can be themed, as you see later in this chapter.

Navigating in PCSDemoSite

The site map for PCSDemoSite is as follows:

```xml
<?xml version="1.0" encoding="utf-8" ?>
<siteMap>
  <siteMapNode url="~/Default.aspx" title="Home">
    <siteMapNode url="~/About/Default.aspx" title="About" />
    <siteMapNode url="~/MRB/Default.aspx" title="Meeting Room Booker"
      roles="RegisteredUser,SiteAdministrator" />
    <siteMapNode url="~/Configuration/Default.aspx" title="Configuration"
      roles="RegisteredUser,SiteAdministrator">
      <siteMapNode url="~/Configuration/Themes/Default.aspx" title="Themes"
        roles="RegisteredUser,SiteAdministrator"/>
    </siteMapNode>
    <siteMapNode url="~/Users/Default.aspx" title="User Area"
      roles="SiteAdministrator" />
    <siteMapNode url="~/Login.aspx" title="Login Details" />
  </siteMapNode>
</siteMap>
```

code snippet PCSDemoSite/Web.sitemap

The PCSDemoSite web site uses a custom provider to obtain information from `Web.sitemap` — which is necessary because the default provider ignores the `roles` attributes. The provider is defined in the `web.config` file for the web site as follows:

```xml
<siteMap defaultProvider="CustomProvider">
  <providers>
    <add name="CustomProvider"
      type="System.Web.XmlSiteMapProvider"
      siteMapFile="Web.sitemap" securityTrimmingEnabled="true" />
  </providers>
</siteMap>
```

code snippet PCSDemoSite/web.config

The only difference between this and the default provider is the addition of `securityTrimmingEnabled="true"`, which instructs the provider to supply data for just those nodes that this current user is allowed to see. This visibility is determined by the role membership of the user, as you see in the next section.

The `MasterPage.master` page in PCSDemoSite includes `SiteMapPath` and `TreeView` navigation displays along with a data source, as follows:

```aspx
<div id="header">
  <h1><asp:literal ID="Literal1" runat="server"
    text="<%$ AppSettings:SiteTitle %>" /></h1>
  <asp:SiteMapPath ID="SiteMapPath1" Runat="server"
    CssClass="breadcrumb" />
</div>
<div id="nav">
  <div class="navTree">
    <asp:TreeView ID="TreeView1" runat="server"
      DataSourceID="SiteMapDataSource1" ShowLines="True" />
  </div>
  <br />
  <br />
```

```
      <asp:LoginView ID="LoginView1" Runat="server">
        <LoggedInTemplate>
          You are currently logged in as
          <b><asp:LoginName ID="LoginName1" Runat="server" /></b>.
          <asp:LoginStatus ID="LoginStatus1" Runat="server" />
        </LoggedInTemplate>
      </asp:LoginView>
    </div>
    <div id="body">
      <asp:ContentPlaceHolder ID="ContentPlaceHolder1" Runat="server" />
    </div>
  </form>
  <asp:SiteMapDataSource ID="SiteMapDataSource1" Runat="server" />
```

code snippet PCSDemoSite/MasterPage.master

The only point to note here is that CSS classes are supplied for both `SiteMapPath` and `TreeView`, to facilitate theming (discussed later in this chapter).

SECURITY

Security and user management have often been seen as quite complicated to implement in web sites, and with good reason. You have to consider a number of factors, including:

➤ What sort of user management system will I implement? Will users map to Windows user accounts, or will I implement something independent?

➤ How do I implement a login system?

➤ Do I let users register on the site; if so, how?

➤ How do I let some users see and do only some things, while supplying other users with additional privileges?

➤ What happens in the case of forgotten passwords?

With ASP.NET, you have a whole suite of tools at your disposal for dealing with questions such as these, and it can in fact take only a matter of minutes to implement a user system on your site. You have three types of authentication at your disposal:

➤ Windows Authentication, whereby users have Windows accounts, typically used with intranet sites or Wide Area Network (WAN) portals

➤ Forms Authentication, whereby the web site maintains its own list of users and handles its own authentication

➤ Microsoft Live ID Authentication (formerly known as Passport authentication), whereby Microsoft provides a centralized authentication service for you to use

A full discussion of security in ASP.NET would take up at least a full chapter, but we provide a brief look in this section to give you an idea of how things work. You concentrate on Forms Authentication here, because it is the most versatile system and very quick to get up and running.

The quickest way to implement Forms Authentication is via the web site ASP.NET Configuration tool, which you saw briefly in the previous chapter. This tool has a Security tab, and on it a Security Setup Wizard. This wizard lets you choose an authentication type, add roles, add users, and secure areas of your site.

Adding Forms Authentication Using the Security Setup Wizard

For the purposes of this explanation, create a new empty web site called `PCSAuthenticationDemo` in the directory `C:\ProCSharp\Chapter41\`. After you create the site, configure security using the following example steps:

1. Open the web site ASP.NET Configuration tool.

2. Navigate to the Security tab.

3. Click the "Use the security Setup Wizard to configure the security step by step" link.

4. Click Next in Step 1 of the wizard after reading the information there.

5. In Step 2 of the wizard, select "From the internet" to select Forms Authentication and click Next.

6. Click Next again after confirming that you will be using the default "Advanced provider settings" provider to store security information.

This provider information is configurable via the Provider tab, where you can choose to store information elsewhere, such as in an SQL Server database, but the default SQL Server Express database is fine for illustrative purposes.

7. Check the "Enable roles for this Web site" option and click Next.

8. Add two roles, Administrator and User, and click Next.

9. Add two user accounts, also called Administrator and User. Note that the default security rules for passwords (defined in `machine.config`) are quite strong; there is a seven-character minimum, including at least one symbol character and a mix of uppercase and lowercase.

In the downloadable code for this chapter, the password for both the User and Administrator account is Pa$$w0rd.

10. Click Next, and then Next again, skipping the Add New Access Rules page.

By default, all users and roles will have access to all areas of your site. From the Add New Access Rules page you can restrict areas by role, by user, or for anonymous users. You can do this for each directory in your site because this is achieved via web.config *files in directories, as you will see shortly.*

11. Click Finish.

12. On the main page for the Security tab, click Manage users.

13. Click Edit Roles for each user in turn, and add the Administrator user to both roles and the User user to just the User role.

After you have done all this, you are pretty much there. You have a user system in place, as well as roles and users.

To illustrate what this makes possible, you have to add a few controls to your web site to make things work. The example code in the following sections assumes that the web site is configured with the User and Administrator roles and users as described in this section.

Implementing a Login System

If you open `web.config` after running the security wizard you will see that it has been modified with the following content:

```
<roleManager enabled="true" />
```

and:

```
<authentication mode="Forms" />
```

This doesn't seem like a lot for the work that you have put in, but remember that a lot of information is stored in an SQL Server Express database, which you can see in the `App_Data` directory (you may need to click the refresh button in the Solution Explorer to see this file), called `ASPNETDB.MDF`. You can inspect the data that has been stored in this file using any standard database management tool, including Visual Studio. You can even add users and roles directly to this database, if you are careful.

By default, logging in is achieved via a page called `Login.aspx` in the root of your web site. If users attempt to navigate to a location that they don't have permission to access, they will automatically be redirected to this page and returned to the desired location after successfully logging in.

Add two Web Forms called `Default.aspx` and `Login.aspx` to the PCSAuthenticationDemo site and drag a `Login` control onto the `Login.aspx` form from the toolbox.

This is all you need to do to enable users to log in to your web site. Open the site in a browser, and navigate to `Login.aspx` (you have to do this manually for now as you haven't restricted access to `Default.aspx`). Enter the details for a user you added in the Security Setup Wizard, as shown in Figure 41-5.

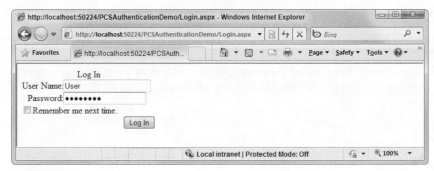

FIGURE 41-5

After you have logged in, you will be sent to `Default.aspx`, currently a blank page.

Login Web Server Controls

The Login section of the toolbox contains several controls, as shown in the following table.

CONTROL	DESCRIPTION
Login	As you have seen, this control allows users to log in to your web site. Most of the properties of this control are for styling the supplied template. You can also use `DestinationPageUrl` to force redirection to a specific location after logging in, and `VisibleWhenLoggedIn` to determine whether the control is visible to logged-in users. And, you can use various text properties such as `CreateUserText` to output helpful messages to users.
LoginView	This control enables you to display content that varies depending on whether users are logged in, or what roles users are in. You can put content in `<AnonymousTemplate>` and `<LoggedInTemplate>`, as well as `<RoleGroups>` to control the output of this control.
PasswordRecovery	This control enables users to have their password mailed to them, and it can use the password recovery question defined for a user. Again, most properties are for display formatting, but there are properties such as `MailDefinition-Subject` for configuring the e-mail to be sent to the user's address, and `SuccessPageUrl` to redirect the users after they have requested a password.
LoginStatus	This control displays a Login or Logout link, with customizable text and images, to users depending on whether they are logged in.

continues

(continued)

CONTROL	DESCRIPTION
LoginName	This control outputs the username for the currently logged-in user.
CreateUserWizard	This control displays a form that users can use to register with your site and to be added to the user list. As with other login controls, there are a large number of properties relating to layout formatting, but the default is perfectly serviceable.
ChangePassword	This control enables users to change their passwords. There are three fields, for the old password, the new password, and the confirmation. There are many styling properties.

You see some of these in action in the "Security in PCSDemoSite" section.

Securing Directories

One final thing to discuss is how to restrict access to directories. You can do this via the Site Configuration tool, as noted earlier, but it's actually quite easy to do this yourself.

Add a directory to PCSAuthenticationDemo called SecureDirectory, as well as a Default.aspx web page in this directory, and a new web.config file. Replace the contents of web.config with the following:

```xml
<?xml version="1.0" ?>
<configuration>
  <system.web>
    <authorization>
      <deny users="?" />
      <allow roles="Administrator" />
      <deny roles="User" />
    </authorization>
  </system.web>
</configuration>
```

code snippet PCSAuthenticationDemo/SecureDirectory/web.config

The <authorization> element can contain one or more <deny> or <allow> elements representing permission rules, each of which can have a users or roles attribute saying what the rule applies to. The rules are applied from top to bottom, so more specific rules should generally be near the top if the membership of rules overlaps. In this example, ? refers to anonymous users, who will be denied access to this directory, along with users in the User role. Note that users in both the User and Administrator roles will be allowed access only if the <allow> rule shown here comes before the <deny> rule for the User role — all of a user's roles are taken into account, but the rule order still applies.

Now when you log in to the web site and try to navigate to SecureDirectory/Default.aspx, you will be permitted only if you are in the Admin role. Other users, or users that are not authenticated, will be redirected to the login page.

Security in PCSDemoSite

The PCSDemoSite site uses the Login control that you have already seen, as well as a LoginView control, a LoginStatus control, a LoginName control, a PasswordRecovery control, and a ChangePassword control.

One difference is that a Guest role is included, and one consequence of this is that guest users should not be able to change their password — an ideal use for LoginView, as illustrated by Login.aspx:

```
<asp:Content ID="Content1" ContentPlaceHolderID="ContentPlaceHolder1"
  Runat="server">
  <h2>Login Page</h2>
```

```
            <asp:LoginView ID="LoginView1" Runat="server">
              <RoleGroups>
                <asp:RoleGroup Roles="Guest">
                  <ContentTemplate>
                    You are currently logged in as <b>
                    <asp:LoginName ID="LoginName1" Runat="server" /></b>.
                    <br />
                    <br />
                    <asp:LoginStatus ID="LoginStatus1" Runat="server" />
                  </ContentTemplate>
                </asp:RoleGroup>
                <asp:RoleGroup Roles="RegisteredUser,SiteAdministrator">
                  <ContentTemplate>
                    You are currently logged in as <b>
                    <asp:LoginName ID="LoginName2" Runat="server" /></b>.
                    <br />
                    <br />
                    <asp:ChangePassword ID="ChangePassword1" Runat="server">
                    </asp:ChangePassword>
                    <br />
                    <br />
                    <asp:LoginStatus ID="LoginStatus2" Runat="server" />
                  </ContentTemplate>
                </asp:RoleGroup>
              </RoleGroups>
              <AnonymousTemplate>
                <asp:Login ID="Login1" Runat="server">
                </asp:Login>
                <asp:PasswordRecovery ID="PasswordRecovery1" Runat="Server" />
              </AnonymousTemplate>
            </asp:LoginView>
          </asp:Content>
```

code snippet PCSAuthenticationDemo/Login.aspx

The view here displays one of several pages:

➤ For anonymous users a `Login` and a `PasswordRecovery` control are shown.

➤ For `Guest` users `LoginName` and `LoginStatus` controls are shown, giving the logged-in username and the facility to log out if required.

➤ For `RegisteredUser` and `SiteAdministrator` users `LoginName`, `LoginStatus`, and `ChangePassword` controls are shown.

The site also includes various `web.config` files in various directories to limit access, and the navigation is also restricted by role.

 Note that the configured users for the site are shown on the About page, or you can add your own. The users in the base site (and their passwords) are User1 (User1!!), Admin (Admin!!), and Guest (Guest!!).

One point to note here is that although the root of the site denies anonymous users, the Themes directory (described in the next section) overrides this setting by permitting anonymous users. This is necessary because without this, anonymous users would see a themeless site, because the theme files would not be accessible. In addition, the full security specification in the root `web.config` file is as follows:

```
          <location path="StyleSheet.css">
            <system.web>
              <authorization>
                <allow users="?"/>
              </authorization>
```

```
      </system.web>
    </location>
    <system.web>
      <authorization>
        <deny users="?" />
      </authorization>
      ...
    </system.web>
```

Here a `<location>` element is used to override the default setting for a specific file specified using a `path` attribute, in this case for the file `StyleSheet.css`. `<location>` elements can be used to apply any `<system.web>` settings to specific files or directories, and can be used to centralize all directory-specific settings in one place, if desired (as an alternative to multiple `web.config` files). In the preceding code, permission is given for anonymous users to access the root style sheet for the web site, which is necessary because this file defines the layout of the `<div>` elements in the master page. Without this, the HTML shown on the login page for anonymous users would be difficult to read.

Another point to note is in the code-behind file for the meeting room booker user control, in the `Page_Load()` event handler:

Available for download on Wrox.com

```
void Page_Load(object sender, EventArgs e)
{
    if (!this.IsPostBack)
    {
        nameBox.Text = Context.User.Identity.Name;
        DateTime trialDate = DateTime.Now;
        calendar.SelectedDate = GetFreeDate(trialDate);
    }
}
```

Here the username is extracted from the current context. Note that in your code-behind files you will probably also use `Context.User.IsInRole()` frequently to check access.

THEMES

By combining ASP.NET pages with master pages and CSS style sheets, you can go a long way in separating form and function, whereby the look and feel of your pages are defined separately from their operation. With themes you can take this a step further and dynamically apply this look and feel from one of several themes that you supply yourself.

A theme consists of the following:

➤ A name for the theme

➤ An optional CSS style sheet

➤ Skin (`.skin`) files allowing individual control types to be styled

These can be applied to pages in two different ways — with Theme or `StyleSheetTheme` attributes:

➤ **Theme** — All skin properties are applied to controls, overriding any properties that the controls on the page may already have.

➤ **StyleSheetTheme** — Existing control properties take precedence over properties defined in skin files.

CSS style sheets work in the same way whichever method is used because they are applied in the standard CSS way.

Applying Themes to Pages

You can apply a theme to a page in several ways, declaratively or programmatically. The simplest declarative way to apply a theme is via the `<%@ Page %>` directive, using the `Theme` or `StyleSheetTheme` attribute:

```
<%@ Page Theme="myTheme" ... %>
```

or:

```
<%@ Page StyleSheetTheme="myTheme" ... %>
```

Here `myTheme` is the name defined for the theme.

Alternatively, you can specify a theme to use for all pages in a site, using an entry in the `web.config` file for your web site:

```
<configuration>
  <system.web>
    <pages Theme="myTheme" />
  </system.web>
</configuration>
```

Again, you can use `Theme` or `StyleSheetTheme` here. You can also be more specific by using `<location>` elements to override this setting for individual pages or directories, in the same way as this element was used in the previous section for security information.

Programmatically, you can apply themes in the code-behind file for a page. There is only one place where you are allowed to do this — in the `Page_PreInit()` event handler, which is triggered very early on in the lifecycle of the page. In this event, you simply have to set the `Page.Theme` or `Page.StyleSheetTheme` property to the name of the theme you want to apply, for example:

```
protected override void OnPreInit(EventArgs e)
{
    Page.Theme = "myTheme";
}
```

Because you are using code to do this, you can dynamically apply a theme file from a selection of themes. This technique is used in the "Themes in PCSDemoSite" section.

Defining Themes

Themes are defined in yet another of the "special" directories in ASP.NET — in this case `App_Themes`. The `App_Themes` directory can contain any number of subdirectories, one per theme, where the name of the subdirectory defines the name of the theme.

Defining a theme involves putting the required files for the theme in the theme subdirectory. For CSS style sheets, you don't have to worry about the filename; the theme system simply looks for a file with a `.css` extension. Similarly, `.skin` files can have any filename, although it is recommended that you use multiple `.skin` files, one for each control type you want to skin, and each named after the control it skins.

Skin files contain server control definitions in exactly the same format as you would use in standard ASP.NET pages. The difference is that the controls in skin files are never added to your page; they are simply used to extract properties. A definition for a button skin, typically placed in a file called `Button.skin`, might be as follows:

```
<asp:Button Runat="server" BackColor="#444499" BorderColor="#000000"
    ForeColor="#ccccff" />
```

This skin is actually taken from the `DefaultTheme` theme in PCSDemoSite, and is responsible for the look of the button on the Meeting Room Booker page you saw earlier in this chapter.

When you create a skin for a control type in this way you don't use an `ID` property.

Themes in PCSDemoSite

The PCSDemoSite web site includes three themes that you can select on the `/Configuration/Themes/` `Default.aspx` page — as long as you are logged in as a member of either the `RegisteredUser` or `SiteAdministrator` role. This page is shown in Figure 41-6.

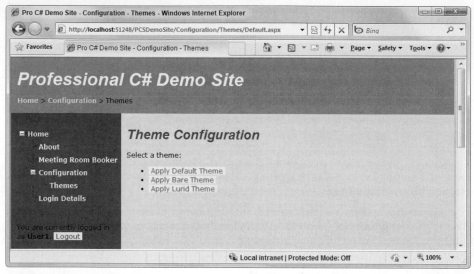

FIGURE 41-6

The theme in use here is `DefaultTheme`, but you can select from the other options on this page. Figure 41-7 shows the `BareTheme` theme.

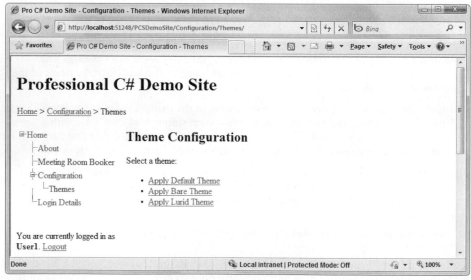

FIGURE 41-7

This sort of theme is useful in, for example, printable versions of web pages. The BareTheme directory actually consists of no files at all — the only file in use here is the root StyleSheet.css style sheet.

The demo site also contains a third theme, called LuridTheme. This brightly colored and difficult-to-read theme is just a bit of fun, really, but it does show how the look of a site can be dramatically changed using themes. On a more serious note, themes similar to this can be used to provide high-contrast or large-text versions of web sites for accessibility purposes.

In PCSDemoSite, the currently selected theme is stored in session state, so the theme is maintained when you navigate around the site. The code-behind file for /Configuration/Themes/Default.aspx is as follows:

Available for download on Wrox.com

```csharp
public partial class _Default : MyPageBase
{
    private void ApplyTheme(string themeName)
    {
        if (Session["SessionTheme"] != null)
        {
            Session.Remove("SessionTheme");
        }
        Session.Add("SessionTheme", themeName);
        Response.Redirect("~/Configuration/Themes", true);
    }

    void applyDefaultTheme_Click(object sender, EventArgs e)
    {
        ApplyTheme("DefaultTheme");
    }

    void applyBareTheme_Click(object sender, EventArgs e)
    {
        ApplyTheme("BareTheme");
    }

    void applyLuridTheme_Click(object sender, EventArgs e)
    {
        ApplyTheme("LuridTheme");
    }
}
```

code snippet PCSDemoSite/Configuration/Themes/Default.aspx.cs

The key functionality here is in ApplyTheme(), which puts the name of the selected theme into session state, using the key SessionTheme. It also checks to see if there is already an entry here, and if so, removes it.

As mentioned earlier, themes must be applied in the Page_PreInit() event handler. This isn't accessible from the master page that all pages use, so if you want to apply a selected theme to all pages, you are left with two options:

➤ Override the Page_PreInit() event handler in all pages where you want themes to be applied.

➤ Provide a common base class for all pages where you want themes to be applied, and override the Page_PreInit() event handler in this base class.

PCSDemoSite uses the second option, with a common page base class provided in Code/MyPageBase.cs:

Available for download on Wrox.com

```csharp
public class MyPageBase : Page
{
    protected override void OnPreInit(EventArgs e)
    {
        // theming
        if (Session["SessionTheme"] != null)
        {
```

```
        Page.Theme = Session["SessionTheme"] as string;
    }
    else
    {
        Page.Theme = "DefaultTheme";
    }

    // base call
    base.OnPreInit(e);
    }
}
```

code snippet PCSDemoSite/App_Code/MyPageBase.cs

This event handler checks the session state for an entry in `SessionTheme` and applies the selected theme if there is one; otherwise `DefaultTheme` is used.

Note also that this class inherits from the usual page base class `Page`. This is necessary because, otherwise, the page wouldn't function as an ASP.NET web page.

For this to work, it is also necessary to specify this base class for all web pages. There are several ways of doing this, the most obvious being either in the `<@ Page %>` directive for a page or in the code behind a page. The former strategy is fine for simple pages but precludes the use of custom code behind for a page, as the page will no longer use the code in its own code-behind file. The other alternative is to change the class that the page inherits from in the code-behind file. By default, new pages inherit from `Page`, but you can change this. In the code-behind file for the theme selection page shown earlier, you may have noticed the following code:

Available for download on Wrox.com

```
public partial class _Default : MyPageBase
{
    ...
}
```

code snippet PCSDemoSite/Configuration/Themes/Default.aspx.cs

Here `MyPageBase` is specified as the base of the `Default` class, and thus the method override in `MyPageBase.cs` is used.

WEB PARTS

ASP.NET contains a group of server controls known as Web Parts, which are designed to enable users to personalize web pages. You may have seen this in action, for example, in SharePoint-based web sites or on the My MSN home page: `http://my.msn.com/`. When you use Web Parts, the resulting functionality is as follows:

➤   Users are presented with a default page layout that you supply. This layout consists of a number of component Web Parts, each of which has a title and content.

➤   Users can change the position of the Web Parts on a page.

➤   Users can customize the appearance of Web Parts on a page or remove them from the page completely.

➤   Users can be supplied with a catalog of Web Parts that they can add to the page.

➤   Users can export Web Parts from a page, and then import them on a different page or site.

➤   Connections can exist between Web Parts. For example, the content displayed in a Web Part could be a graphical representation of the content displayed in another Web Part.

➤   Any changes that users make persist between site visits.

ASP.NET supplies a complete framework for implanting Web Parts functionality, including management and editing controls.

The use of Web Parts is a complex topic, and this section does not describe all available functionality or list all the properties and methods that the Web Part components supply. However, you do see enough to get a flavor of Web Parts and to understand the basic functionality that is possible.

Web Parts Application Components

The Web Parts section of the toolbox contains 13 controls, as described in the following table. The table also introduces some of the key concepts for Web Parts pages.

CONTROL	DESCRIPTION
WebPartManager	Every page that uses Web Parts must have one (and only one) instance of the WebPartManager control. You can place it on a master page if you wish, although if you do you should use the master page only when you want to use Web Parts on a page. This control is responsible for the majority of Web Parts functionality, which it supplies without much intervention. You may not need to do much more than place it on a web page, depending on the functionality you require. For more advanced functionality, you can use the large number of properties and events that this control exposes.
ProxyWebPartManager	If you place the WebPartManager control on a master page, it can be difficult to configure it on individual pages — and impossible to do so declaratively. This is particularly relevant for the definition of static connections between Web Parts. The ProxyWebPartManager control enables you to define static connections declaratively on a web page, which circumvents the problem of not being able to have two WebPartManager controls on the same page.
WebPartZone	The WebPartZone control is used to define a region of a page that can contain Web Parts. You will typically use more than one of these controls on a page. For example, you might use three of them in a three-column layout on a page. Users can move Web Parts between WebPartZone regions or reposition them within a single WebPartZone.
CatalogZone	The CatalogZone control enables users to add Web Parts to a page. This control contains controls that derive from CatalogPart, of which three are supplied for you — the next three entries in this table describe these controls. Whether the CatalogZone control and the controls it contains are visible depends on the current display mode set by WebPartManager.
DeclarativeCatalogPart	The DeclarativeCatalogPart control enables you to define Web Part controls inline. These controls will then be available to the user through the CatalogZone control.
PageCatalogPart	Users can remove (close) Web Parts that are displayed on a page. To retrieve them, the PageCatalogPart control provides a list of closed Web Parts that can be replaced on the page.
ImportCatalogPart	The ImportCatalogPart control enables Web Parts that have been exported from a page to be imported to another page through the CatalogPart interface.
EditorZone	The EditorZone control contains controls that enable users to edit various aspects of Web Part display and behavior, depending on what controls it contains. It can contain controls that derive from EditorPart, including the four that are listed in the next four rows of this table. As with CatalogZone, the display of this control depends on the current display mode.
AppearanceEditorPart	This control enables users to modify the look and size of Web Part controls, as well as to hide them.

continues

(continued)

CONTROL	DESCRIPTION
`BehaviorEditorPart`	This control enables users to configure the behavior of Web Parts by using a variety of properties that control, for example, whether a Web Part can be closed or what URL the title of a Web Part links to.
`LayoutEditorPart`	This control enables users to change layout properties of a Web Part, such as what zone it is contained in and whether it is displayed in a minimized state.
`PropertyGridEditorPart`	This is the most general Web Part editor control that enables you to define properties that can be edited for custom Web Part controls. Users can then edit these properties.
`ConnectionsZone`	This control enables users to create connections between Web Parts that expose connection functionality. Unlike `CatalogZone` and `EditorZone`, there are no controls to place inside this control. The user interface that this control generates depends on the controls on the page that are available for connections. The visibility of this control is dependent on the display mode.

You may notice that this list of controls does not include any Web Parts. This is because you create these yourself. Any control that you put into a `WebPartZone` region automatically becomes a Web Part — including (most importantly) user controls. By using user controls, you can group together other controls to provide the user interface and functionality of a Web Part control.

Web Parts Example

To illustrate the functionality of Web Parts, you can look at another of the example web sites in the downloadable code for this chapter, called PCSWebParts. This example uses the same security database as the PCSAuthenticationDemo example. It has two users with usernames of User and Administrator and a password of Pa$$w0rd for both. You can log in as a user, manipulate the Web Parts on the page, log out, log in as the other user, and manipulate the Web Parts in a completely different way. The personalization for both users is retained between site visits.

After you have logged in to the site, the initial display (with user logged in) is as shown in Figure 41-8.

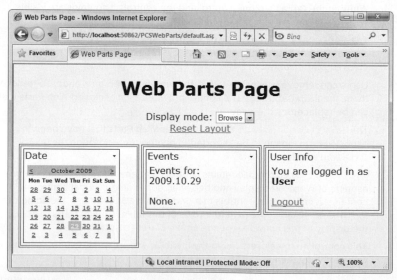

FIGURE 41-8

➤ A WebPartManager control (which doesn't have a visual component).

➤ Three WebPartZone controls.

➤ Three Web Parts (Date, Events, and User Info); one in each WebPartZone. Two of the Web Parts are connected by a static connection — if you change the date in Date, the date displayed in Events updates.

➤ A drop-down list for changing the display mode. This list doesn't contain all the possible display modes, just the available ones. The available modes are obtained from the WebPartManager control, as you see shortly. The modes listed are:

➤ Browse — This mode is the default and allows you to view and use Web Parts. In this mode, each Web Part can be minimized or closed by using the drop-down menu accessible in the top right of each Web Part.

➤ Design — In this mode, you can reposition Web Parts.

➤ Edit — In this mode, you can edit Web Part properties. An additional item in the drop-down menu for each Web Part becomes available: Edit.

➤ Catalog — In this mode, you can add new Web Parts to the page.

➤ A link to reset the Web Part layout to the default (for the current user only).

➤ An EditorZone control (visible only in Edit mode).

➤ A CatalogZone control (visible only in Catalog mode).

➤ One additional Web Part in the catalog that you can add to the page.

Each of the Web Parts is defined in a user control.

Web Parts in Action

To illustrate how layout can be changed, use the drop-down list to change the display mode to Design. You will notice that each WebPartZone is then labeled with an ID value (LeftZone, CenterZone, and RightZone, respectively). You will also be able to move Web Parts simply by dragging their titles — and will even see visual feedback as you drag. This is illustrated in Figure 41-9, which shows the Date Web Part being moved.

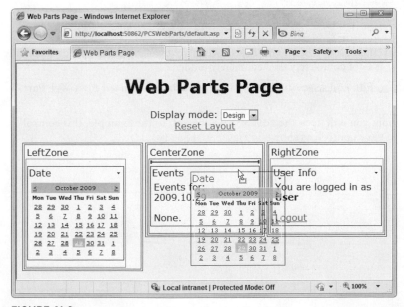

FIGURE 41-9

Next, try adding a new Web Part from the catalog. Change the display mode to Catalog, and you will notice that the `CatalogZone` control becomes visible at the bottom of the page. Click the Declarative Catalog link, and you will be able to add a `Links` control to the page, as shown in Figure 41-10.

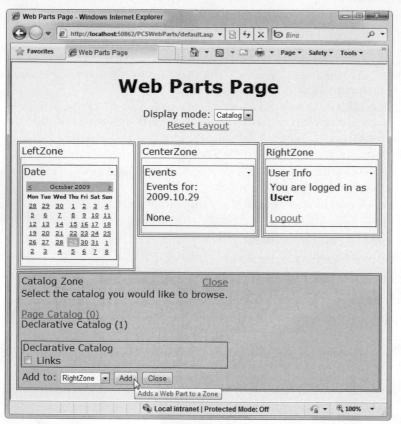

FIGURE 41-10

Notice that there is also a Page Catalog link here. If you close a Web Part by using the drop-down menu for the part, you will find it here — it's not completely deleted, merely hidden.

Next, change the display mode to Edit and select the Edit item from the drop-down list for a Web Part, as shown in Figure 41-11.

When you select this menu option, you will open the `EditorZone` control. In the example, this control contains an `AppearanceEditorPart` control, as shown in Figure 41-12.

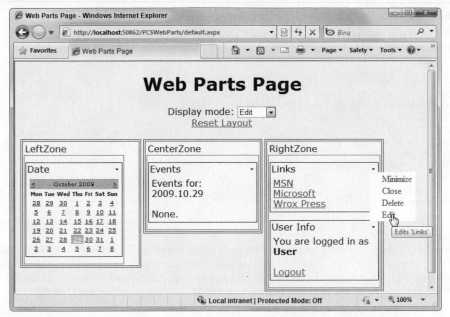

FIGURE 41-11

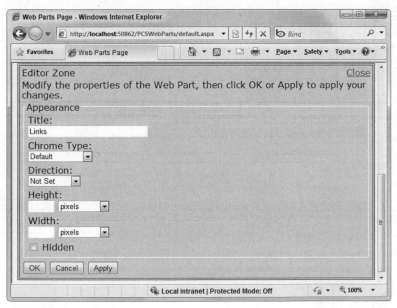

FIGURE 41-12

You can edit and apply property values for Web Parts by using this interface.

After making changes, confirm that they are stored for the user by logging off and logging in as a different user, and then switching back to the first user.

Web Part Host Page Code

Now, you might think that this functionality requires quite a lot of code. In fact, the code in this example is remarkably simple. Look at the code for the Web Parts page. The `<form>` element starts with a `WebPartManager` control:

```
<form id="form1" runat="server">
  <asp:WebPartManager ID="WebPartManager1" runat="server"
    OnDisplayModeChanged="WebPartManager1_DisplayModeChanged">
    <StaticConnections>
      <asp:WebPartConnection ID="dateConnection"
        ConsumerConnectionPointID="DateConsumer"
        ConsumerID="EventListControl1"
        ProviderConnectionPointID="DateProvider"
        ProviderID="DateSelectorControl1" />
    </StaticConnections>
  </asp:WebPartManager>
```

code snippet PCSWebParts/Default.aspx

There is an event handler for the `DisplayModeChanged` event of this control, which is used to show or hide the editor `<div>` at the bottom of the page. There is also a specification for a static connection between the Date and Events Web Parts. This is achieved by defining named endpoints for the connection in the two user controls for these Web Parts and referring to those endpoints here. You see the code for this shortly.

Next, the title, display mode changer, and reset link are defined:

```
<div class="mainDiv">
  <h1>Web Parts Page</h1>
  Display mode:
  <asp:DropDownList ID="displayMode" runat="server" AutoPostBack="True"
    OnSelectedIndexChanged="displayMode_SelectedIndexChanged" />
  <br />
  <asp:LinkButton runat="server" ID="resetButton" Text="Reset Layout"
    OnClick="resetButton_Click" />
  <br />
  <br />
```

The display mode drop-down list is populated in the `Page_Load()` event handler by using the `WebPartManager1.SupportedDisplayModes` property. The reset button uses the `WebPartManager1.Personalization.ResetPersonalizationState()` method to reset the personalization state for the current user.

Next come the three `WebPartZone` controls, each of which contains a user control that is loaded as a Web Part:

```
<div class="innerDiv">
  <div class="zoneDiv">
    <asp:WebPartZone ID="LeftZone" runat="server">
      <ZoneTemplate>
        <uc1:DateSelectorControl ID="DateSelectorControl1" runat="server"
          title="Date" />
      </ZoneTemplate>
    </asp:WebPartZone>
  </div>
  <div class="zoneDiv">
    <asp:WebPartZone ID="CenterZone" runat="server">
      <ZoneTemplate>
        <uc2:EventListControl ID="EventListControl1" runat="server"
          title="Events" />
      </ZoneTemplate>
    </asp:WebPartZone>
  </div>
```

```
        <div class="zoneDiv">
          <asp:WebPartZone ID="RightZone" runat="server">
            <ZoneTemplate>
              <uc4:UserInfo ID="UserInfo1" runat="server" title="User Info" />
            </ZoneTemplate>
          </asp:WebPartZone>
        </div>
```

And finally you have the `EditorZone` and `CatalogZone` controls, containing an `AppearanceEditor` control and `PageCatalogPart` and `DeclarativeCatalogPart` controls, respectively:

```
        <asp:PlaceHolder runat="server" ID="editorPH" Visible="false">
          <div class="footerDiv">
            <asp:EditorZone ID="EditorZone1" runat="server">
              <ZoneTemplate>
                <asp:AppearanceEditorPart ID="AppearanceEditorPart1"
                  runat="server" />
              </ZoneTemplate>
            </asp:EditorZone>
            <asp:CatalogZone ID="CatalogZone1" runat="server">
              <ZoneTemplate>
                <asp:PageCatalogPart ID="PageCatalogPart1" runat="server" />
                <asp:DeclarativeCatalogPart ID="DeclarativeCatalogPart1"
                  runat="server">
                  <WebPartsTemplate>
                    <uc3:LinksControl ID="LinksControl1" runat="server"
                      title="Links" />
                  </WebPartsTemplate>
                </asp:DeclarativeCatalogPart>
              </ZoneTemplate>
            </asp:CatalogZone>
          </div>
        </asp:PlaceHolder>
      </div>
    </div>
  </form>
```

The `DeclarativeCatalogPart` control contains a fourth user control, which is the `Links` control that users can add to the page.

Web Part Code

The code for the Web Parts is equally simple. The Links Web part, for example, simply contains the following code:

Available for download on Wrox.com

```
<%@ Control Language="C#" AutoEventWireup="true"
CodeFile="LinksControl.ascx.cs"
  Inherits="LinksControl" %>
<a href="http://www.msn.com/">MSN</a>
<br />
<a href="http://www.microsoft.com/">Microsoft</a>
<br />
<a href="http://www.wrox.com/">Wrox Press</a>
```

code snippet PCSWebParts/LinksControl.ascx

No additional markup is required to make this user control work as a Web Part. The only point to note here is that the `<uc3:LinksControl>` element for the user control (as used in `Default.aspx`) has a `title` attribute — even though the user control doesn't have a `Title` property. This attribute is used by the `DeclarativeCatalogPart` control to infer a title to display for the Web Part (which you can edit at runtime with the `AppearanceEditorPart`).

Connecting Controls

The connection between the Date and Events controls is achieved by passing an interface reference from `DateSelectorControl` to `EventListControl` (the two user control classes used by these Web Parts):

```
public interface IDateProvider
{
    SelectedDatesCollection SelectedDates
    {
        get;
    }
}
```

code snippet PCSWebParts/App_Code/IDateProvider.cs

`DateSelectorControl` supports this interface, and so can pass an instance of `IDateProvider` by using `this`. The reference is passed by an endpoint method in `DateSelectorControl`, which is decorated with the `ConnectionProvider` attribute:

```
[ConnectionProvider("Date Provider", "DateProvider")]
public IDateProvider ProvideDate()
{
    return this;
}
```

code snippet PCSWebParts/DateSelectorControl.ascx.cs

This is all that is required to mark a Web Part as a provider control. You can then reference the provider by its endpoint ID, in this case `DateProvider`.

To consume a provider, you use the `ConnectionConsumer` attribute to decorate a consumer method in `EventListControl`:

```
[ConnectionConsumer("Date Consumer", "DateConsumer")]
public void GetDate(IDateProvider provider)
{
    this.provider = provider;
    IsConnected = true;
    SetDateLabel();
}
```

code snippet PCSWebParts/EventListControl.ascx.cs

This method stores a reference to the `IDateProvider` interface passed, sets a flag, and changes the label text in the control.

There is not a lot more to look at in this example. There are a few minor cosmetic sections of code, and details for the event handlers in `Page_Load()`, but nothing that you really need to see here. You can investigate further by examining the downloadable code for this chapter.

There is, however, a whole lot more to Web Parts than this. The Web Parts framework is extremely powerful and richly featured. Whole books are devoted to the subject. Hopefully, though, this section has enabled you to get an insight into Web Parts and has demystified some of their functionality.

ASP.NET AJAX

Web application programming is subject to continuous change and improvement. If you spend much time on the Internet, you may have noticed that more recent web sites are significantly better, in terms of usability, than older web sites. Many of today's best web sites provide rich user interfaces that feel almost as responsive as Windows applications. They achieve this by using client-side processing, primarily through JavaScript code, and increasingly through a technology known as Ajax.

Ajax is not a new technology. Rather, it is a combination of standards that makes it possible to realize the rich potential functionality of current web browsers.

Perhaps the key defining feature of Ajax-enabled web applications is the ability for the web browser to communicate with the web server in out-of-band operations; this is known as asynchronous, or partial-page, postbacks. In practice, this means that the user can interact with server-side functionality and data without needing a full-page refresh. For example, when a link is followed to move to the second page of data in a table, Ajax makes it possible to refresh just the table's content rather than the entire web page. This means that there is less traffic required across the Internet, which leads to a more responsive web application.

You will be using Microsoft's implementation of Ajax in the code, known as ASP.NET AJAX. This implementation takes the Ajax model and applies it to the ASP.NET Framework. ASP.NET AJAX provides a number of server controls and client-side techniques that are specifically targeted at ASP.NET developers and that enable you to add Ajax functionality to your web applications with surprisingly little effort.

This section introduces you to:

> ➤ Ajax and the technologies that make Ajax possible.

> ➤ ASP.NET AJAX and its component parts, as well as the functionality that ASP.NET AJAX offers.

> ➤ How to use ASP.NET AJAX in your web applications, by using both server-side and client-side code. This coverage forms the largest part of this section.

WHAT IS AJAX?

Ajax lets you enhance the user interfaces of web applications by means of asynchronous postbacks and dynamic client-side web page manipulation. The term Ajax was invented by Jesse James Garrett and is shorthand for Asynchronous JavaScript and XML.

 Note that Ajax is not an acronym, which is why it is not capitalized as AJAX. However, it is capitalized in the product name ASP.NET AJAX, which is Microsoft's implementation of Ajax, as you will see in the next section of this chapter.

By definition, Ajax involves both JavaScript and XML. However, Ajax programming requires the use of other technologies as well, which are described in the following table.

TECHNOLOGY	DESCRIPTION
HTML/XHTML	HTML (Hypertext Markup Language) is the presentation and layout language used by web browsers to render information in a graphical user interface. You have already seen how HTML achieves this functionality and how ASP.NET generates HTML code. Extensible HTML (XHTML) is a stricter definition of HTML that uses XML structure.
CSS	CSS (cascading style sheets) is a means by which HTML elements can be styled according to rules defined in a separate style sheet. This enables you to apply styles simultaneously to multiple HTML elements and to swap styles to change the way a web page looks without HTML modifications. CSS includes both layout and style information, so you can also use CSS to position HTML elements on a page.
DOM	The DOM (Document Object Model) is a means of representing and manipulating (X)HTML code in a hierarchical structure. This enables you to access, for example, "the second column of the third row in table x" in a web page, rather than having to locate this element using more primitive text processing.

continues

(continued)

TECHNOLOGY	DESCRIPTION
JavaScript	JavaScript is a client-side scripting technology that enables you to execute code inside a web browser. The syntax of JavaScript is similar to other C-based languages, including C#, and provides variables, functions, branching code, looping statements, and other familiar programming elements. However, unlike C#, JavaScript is not strongly typed, and debugging JavaScript code can be difficult. In terms of Ajax programming, JavaScript is a key technology because it allows dynamic modifications to web pages by way of DOM manipulation — among other functionality.
XML	XML, as you have seen throughout this book, is a platform-neutral way to mark up data and is crucial to Ajax both as a way to manipulate data and as a language for communication between the client and the server.
XMLHttpRequest	Since Internet Explorer 5, browsers have supported the XMLHttpRequest API as a means of performing asynchronous communication between the client and server. This was originally introduced by Microsoft as a technology to access e-mail stored in an Exchange server over the Internet, in a product known as Outlook Web Access. Since then, it has become the standard way to perform asynchronous communications in web applications, and is a core technology of Ajax-enabled web applications. Microsoft's implementation of this API is known as XMLHTTP, which communicates over what is often called the XMLHTTP protocol.

Ajax also requires server-side code to handle partial-page postbacks as well as full-page postbacks. This can include both event handlers for server-control events and Web services. Figure 41-13 shows how these technologies fit together in the Ajax web browser model, in contrast to the "traditional" web browser model.

Prior to Ajax, the first four technologies listed in the preceding table (HTML, CSS, the DOM, and JavaScript) were used to create what was known as Dynamic HTML (DHTML) web applications. These applications were notable for two reasons: they provided a much better user interface, and they generally worked on only one type of web browser.

"Traditional" Web Browser Model

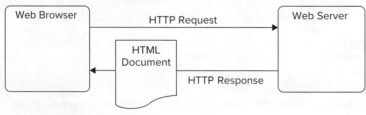

Ajax Web Browser Model

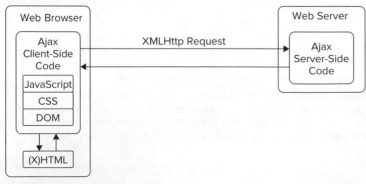

FIGURE 41-13

Since DHTML, standards have improved, along with the level of adherence to standards in web browsers. However, there are still differences, and an Ajax solution must take these differences into account. This has meant that most developers have been quite slow to implement Ajax solutions. Only with the advent of more abstracted Ajax frameworks (such as ASP.NET AJAX) has Ajax-enabled web site creation really become a viable option for enterprise-level development.

What Is ASP.NET AJAX?

ASP.NET AJAX is Microsoft's implementation of the Ajax framework and is specifically targeted at ASP. NET developers. It is part of the core ASP.NET functionality. It is also available for use with previous versions of ASP.NET from the web site `http://ajax.asp.net`. This web site also has documentation, forums, and sample code that you may find useful for whichever version of ASP.NET you are using.

ASP.NET AJAX provides the following functionality:

➤ A server-side framework that enables ASP.NET web pages to respond to partial-page postback operations

➤ ASP.NET server controls that make the implementation of Ajax functionality easy

➤ An HTTP handler that enables ASP.NET Web services to communicate with client-side code by using JavaScript Object Notation (JSON) serialization in partial-page postback operations

➤ Web services that enable client-side code to gain access to ASP.NET application services, including authentication and personalization services

➤ A web site template for creating ASP.NET AJAX-enabled web applications

➤ A client-side JavaScript library that provides a number of enhancements to JavaScript syntax as well as code to simplify the implementation of Ajax functionality

These server controls and the server-side framework that makes them possible are collectively known as the ASP.NET Extensions. The client-side part of ASP.NET AJAX is known as the AJAX Library.

There are several additional downloads that you can obtain from `http://ajax.asp.net`, including the following important ones:

➤ **ASP.NET AJAX Control Toolkit** — This download contains additional server controls that have been created by the developer community. These controls are shared-source controls that you can inspect and modify as you see fit.

➤ **Microsoft AJAX Library 3.5** — This download contains the JavaScript client-side framework that is used by ASP.NET AJAX to implement Ajax functionality. You will not need this if you are developing ASP.NET AJAX applications. Instead, this download is intended to be used with other languages, for example PHP, to implement Ajax functionality using the same codebase as ASP.NET AJAX. This is beyond the scope of this chapter.

 There is also a preview download for the next version of ASP.NET AJAX available on the web site. This download is not covered in this chapter.

Together these downloads provide you with a richly featured framework that you can use to add Ajax functionality to your ASP.NET web applications. In the following sections, you learn more about what is contained in the various component parts of ASP.NET AJAX.

Core Functionality

The core functionality of ASP.NET AJAX is divided into two parts, the AJAX Extensions and the AJAX Library.

AJAX Extensions

ASP.NET AJAX functionality is contained in two assemblies that are installed in the GAC:

➤ `System.Web.Extensions.dll` — This assembly contains the ASP.NET AJAX functionality, including the AJAX Extensions and the AJAX Library JavaScript files, which are available through the `ScriptManager` component (which is described shortly).

➤ `System.Web.Extensions.Design.dll` — This assembly contains ASP.NET Designer components for the AJAX Extensions server controls. This is used by the ASP.NET Designer in Visual Studio or Visual web developer.

Much of the AJAX Extensions component of ASP.NET AJAX is concerned with enabling partial-page postbacks and JSON serialization for Web services. This includes various HTTP handler components and extensions to the existing ASP.NET Framework. All this functionality can be configured through the `web.config` file for a web site. There are also classes and attributes that you can use for additional configuration. However, most of this configuration is transparent, and you will rarely need to change the defaults.

Your main interaction with AJAX Extensions will be using server controls to add Ajax functionality to your web applications. There are several of these, which you can use to enhance your applications in various ways. The following table shows a selection of the server-side components. You see these components in action later in this chapter.

CONTROL	DESCRIPTION
ScriptManager	This control is central to ASP.NET AJAX functionality and is required on every page that uses partial-page postbacks. Its main purpose is to manage client-side references to the AJAX Library JavaScript files, which are served from the ASP.NET AJAX assembly. The AJAX Library is used extensively by the AJAX Extensions server controls, which all generate their own client-side code.
	This control is also responsible for the configuration of Web services that you intend to access from client-side code. By supplying Web service information to the `ScriptManager` control, you can generate client-side and server-side classes to manage asynchronous communication with Web services transparently.
	You can also use the `ScriptManager` control to maintain references to your own JavaScript files.
UpdatePanel	The `UpdatePanel` control is an extremely useful one and is perhaps the ASP.NET AJAX control that you will use most often. This control acts like a standard ASP.NET placeholder and can contain any other controls. More important, it also marks a section of a page as a region that can be updated independently of the rest of the page, in a partial-page postback.
	Any controls contained by an `UpdatePanel` control that cause a postback (a `Button` control, for example) will not cause full-page postbacks. Instead, they cause partial-page postbacks that will update only the contents of the `UpdatePanel`.
	In many situations, this control is all you need to implement Ajax functionality. For example, you can place a `GridView` control in an `UpdatePanel` control, and any pagination, sorting, and other postback functionality of the control will take place in a partial-page postback.
UpdateProgress	This control enables you to provide feedback to users when a partial page postback is in progress. You can supply a template for this control that will be displayed when an `UpdatePanel` is updating. For example, you could use a floating `<div>` control to display a message such as "Updating..." so that the user is aware that the application is busy. Note that partial-page postbacks do not interfere with the rest of a web page, which will remain responsive.

CONTROL	DESCRIPTION
Timer	The ASP.NET AJAX `Timer` control is a useful way to cause an `UpdatePanel` to update periodically. You can configure this control to trigger postbacks at regular intervals. If this control is contained in an `UpdatePanel` control, then the `UpdatePanel` will be updated every time the `Timer` control is triggered. This control also has an associated event so that you can carry out periodic server-side processing.
AsyncPostBackTrigger	You can use this control to trigger `UpdatePanel` updates from controls that aren't contained in the `UpdatePanel`. For example, you can enable a drop-down list elsewhere on a web page to cause an `UpdatePanel` containing a `GridView` control to update.

The AJAX Extensions also include the `ExtenderControl` abstract base class for extending existing ASP. NET server controls. This is used, for example, by various classes in the ASP.NET AJAX Control Toolkit, as you will see shortly.

AJAX Library

The AJAX Library consists of JavaScript files that are used by client-side code in ASP.NET AJAX-enabled web applications. There is a lot of functionality included in these JavaScript files, some of which is general code that enhances the JavaScript language and some of which is specific to Ajax functionality. The AJAX Library contains layers of functionality that are built on top of each other, as shown in the following table.

LAYER	DESCRIPTION
Browser compatibility	The lowest-level code in the AJAX Library consists of code that maps various JavaScript functionality according to the client web browser. This is necessary because there are differences in the implementation of JavaScript in different browsers. By providing this layer, JavaScript code in other layers does not have to worry about browser compatibility, and you can write browser-neutral code that will work in all client environments.
Core services	This layer contains the enhancements to the JavaScript language, in particular OOP functionality. By using the code in this layer you can define namespaces, classes, derived classes, and interfaces using JavaScript script files. This is of particular interest to C# developers, because it makes writing JavaScript code much more like writing .NET code (by using C# and encouraging reusability).
Base class library	The client base class library (BCL) includes many JavaScript classes that provide low-level functionality to classes further down the AJAX Library hierarchy. Most of these classes are not intended to be used directly.
Networking	Classes in the networking layer enable client-side code to call server-side code asynchronously. This layer includes the basic framework for making a call to a URL and responding to the result in a callback function. For the most part, this is also functionality that you will not use directly; instead, you will use classes that wrap this functionality. This layer also contains classes for JSON serialization and deserialization. You will find most of the networking classes on the client-side `Sys. Net` namespace.
User interface	This layer contains classes that abstract user interface elements such as HTML elements and DOM events. You can use the properties and methods of this layer to write language-neutral JavaScript code to manipulate web pages from the client. User interface classes are contained in the `Sys.UI` namespace.
Controls	The final layer of the AJAX Library contains the highest-level code, which provides Ajax behaviors and server control functionality. This includes dynamically generated code that you can use, for example, to call Web services from client-side JavaScript code.

You can use the AJAX Library to extend and customize the behavior of ASP.NET AJAX-enabled web applications, but it is important to note that you don't have to. You can go a long way without using any additional JavaScript in your applications — it becomes a requirement only when you require more advanced functionality. If you do write additional client-side code, however, you will find that it is much easier with the functionality that the AJAX Library offers.

ASP.NET AJAX Control Toolkit

The AJAX Control Toolkit is a collection of additional server controls, including extender controls, that have been written by the ASP.NET AJAX community. Extender controls are controls that enable you to add functionality to an existing ASP.NET server control, typically by associating a client-side behavior with it. For example, one of the extenders in the AJAX Control Toolkit extends the `TextBox` control by placing "watermark" text in the `TextBox`, which appears when the user hasn't yet added any content to the text box. This extender control is implemented in a server control called `TextBoxWatermark`.

You can use the AJAX Control Toolkit to add quite a lot more functionality to your sites, beyond what is in the core download. These controls are also interesting simply to browse and will probably give you plenty of ideas about enhancing your web applications. However, because the AJAX Control Toolkit is separate from the core download, you should not expect the same level of support for these controls.

ASP.NET AJAX Web Site Example

Now that you have seen the component parts of ASP.NET AJAX, it is time to start looking at how to use them to enhance your web sites. In this section, you see how web applications that use ASP.NET AJAX work, and how to use the various aspects of functionality that ASP.NET AJAX includes. You start by examining a simple application, and then add functionality in subsequent sections.

The ASP.NET Web Site template includes all the ASP.NET AJAX core functionality. You can also use the AJAX Control Toolkit Web Site template (after it is installed) to include controls from the AJAX Control Toolkit. For the purposes of this example, you can create a new web site that uses the empty web site template in the `C:\ProCSharp\Chapter41` directory, called `PCSAjaxWebSite1`.

Add a web form called `Default.aspx` and modify its code as follows:

```
<%@ Page Language="C#" AutoEventWireup="true" CodeFile="Default.aspx.cs"
    Inherits="_Default" %>

<!DOCTYPE html PUBLIC "-//W3C//DTD XHTML 1.0 Transitional//EN"
  "http://www.w3.org/TR/xhtml1/DTD/xhtml1-transitional.dtd">
<html xmlns="http://www.w3.org/1999/xhtml">
<head runat="server">
  <title>Pro C# ASP.NET AJAX Sample</title>
</head>
<body>
  <form id="form1" runat="server">
    <asp:ScriptManager ID="ScriptManager1" runat="server" />
    <div>
      <h1>Pro C# ASP.NET AJAX Sample</h1>
      This sample obtains a list of primes up to a maximum value.
      <br />
      Maximum:
      <asp:TextBox runat="server" id="MaxValue" Text="2500" />
      <br />
      Result:
      <asp:UpdatePanel runat="server" ID="ResultPanel">
        <ContentTemplate>
          <asp:Button runat="server" ID="GoButton" Text="Calculate " />
          <br />
```

```
                  <asp:Label runat="server" ID="ResultLabel" />
                  <br />
                  <small>
                     Panel render time: <% =DateTime.Now.ToLongTimeString() %>
                  </small>
                </ContentTemplate>
            </asp:UpdatePanel>
            <asp:UpdateProgress runat="server" ID="UpdateProgress1">
                <ProgressTemplate>
                <div style="position: absolute; left: 100px; top: 200px;
                     padding: 40px 60px 40px 60px; background-color: lightyellow;
                     border: black 1px solid; font-weight: bold; font-size: larger;
                     filter: alpha(opacity=80);">Updating.</div>
                </ProgressTemplate>
            </asp:UpdateProgress>
            <small>Page render time: <% =DateTime.Now.ToLongTimeString() %></small>
        </div>
    </form>
  </body>
</html>
```

code snippet PCSAjaxWebSite1/Default.aspx

Switch to design view (note that the ASP.NET AJAX controls such as `UpdatePanel` and `UpdateProgress` have visual designer components), and double-click the Calculate button to add an event handler. Modify the code as follows:

Available for
download on
Wrox.com

```
protected void GoButton_Click(object sender, EventArgs e)
{
    int maxValue = 0;
    System.Text.StringBuilder resultText = new System.Text.StringBuilder();
    if (int.TryParse(MaxValue.Text, out maxValue))
    {
        for (int trial = 2; trial <= maxValue; trial++)
        {
            bool isPrime = true;
            for (int divisor = 2; divisor <= Math.Sqrt(trial); divisor++)
            {
                if (trial % divisor == 0)
                {
                    isPrime = false;
                    break;
                }
            }
            if (isPrime)
            {
                resultText.AppendFormat("{0} ", trial);
            }
        }
    }
    else
    {
        resultText.Append("Unable to parse maximum value.");
    }
    ResultLabel.Text = resultText.ToString();
}
```

code snippet PCSAjaxWebSite1/Default.aspx.cs

Save your modifications and press F5 to run the project. If prompted, enable debugging in `web.config`.

When the web page appears as shown in Figure 41-14, note that the two render times shown are the same.

Click the Calculate button to display prime numbers less than or equal to 2500. Unless you are running on a slow machine, this should be almost instantaneous. Note that the render times are now different — only the one in the `UpdatePanel` has changed.

Finally, add some zeros to the maximum value to introduce a processing delay (about three more should be enough on a fast PC) and click the Calculate button again. This time, before the result is displayed, note that the `UpdateProgress`

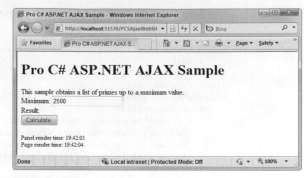

FIGURE 41-14

control displays a partially transparent feedback message, as shown in Figure 41-15.

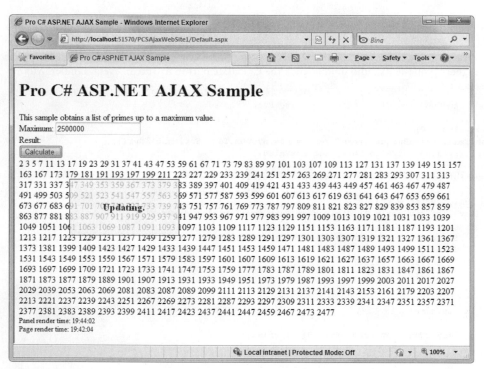

FIGURE 41-15

While the application updates, the page remains responsive. You can, for example, scroll through the page.

 Note that when the update completes, the scroll position of the browser is set to the point it was at before you clicked Calculate. In most cases, when partial-page updates are quick to execute, this is great for usability.

Close the browser to return to Visual Studio.

ASP.NET AJAX-Enabled Web Site Configuration

Most of the configuration required for ASP.NET AJAX is supplied for you by default, and you only really need to add to `web.config` if you want to change these defaults. For example, you can add a `<system.web.extensions>` section to provide additional configuration. Most of the configuration that you can add with this section concerns Web services and is contained in an element called `<webServices>`, which in turn is placed in a `<scripting>` element. First, you can add a section to enable access to the ASP.NET authentication service through a Web service (you can choose to enforce SSL here if you wish):

```
<system.web.extensions>
  <scripting>
    <webServices>
      <authenticationService enabled="true" requireSSL="true"/>
```

Next, you can enable and configure access to ASP.NET personalization functionality through the profile Web service:

```
<profileService enabled="true"
  readAccessProperties="propertyname1,propertyname2"
  writeAccessProperties="propertyname1,propertyname2" />
```

The last Web service-related setting is for enabling and configuring access to ASP.NET role functionality through the role Web service:

```
      <roleService enabled="true"/>
    </webServices>
```

Finally, the `<system.web.extensions>` section can contain an element that enables you to configure compression and caching for asynchronous communications:

```
      <scriptResourceHandler enableCompression="true" enableCaching="true" />
    </scripting>
  </system.web.extensions>
```

Additional Configuration for the AJAX Control Toolkit

To use the controls in the AJAX Control Toolkit, you can add the following configuration to `web.config`:

```
<controls>
  ...
  <add namespace="AjaxControlToolkit" assembly="AjaxControlToolkit"
    tagPrefix="ajaxToolkit"/>
</controls>
```

This maps the toolkit controls to the `ajaxToolkit` tag prefix. These controls are contained in the `AjaxControlToolkit.dll` assembly, which should be in the `/bin` directory for the web application.

Alternatively, you could register the controls individually on web pages using the `<%@ Register %>` directive:

```
<%@ Register Assembly="AjaxControlToolkit" Namespace="AjaxControlToolkit"
  TagPrefix="ajaxToolkit" %>
```

Adding ASP.NET AJAX Functionality

The first step in adding Ajax functionality to a web site is to add a `ScriptManager` control to your web pages. Next, you add server controls such as `UpdatePanel` controls to enable partial-page rendering and dynamic controls such as those supplied in the AJAX Control Toolkit to add usability and glitz to your application. You may also add client-side code, and you can use the AJAX Library for further assistance in customizing and enhancing the functionality of your application.

In this section, you learn about the functionality you can add using server controls. Later in this chapter you look at client-side techniques.

The ScriptManager Control

As mentioned earlier in the chapter, the `ScriptManager` control must be included on all pages that use partial-page postbacks and several other aspects of ASP.NET AJAX functionality.

 A great way to ensure that all the pages in your web application contain the `ScriptManager` *control is to add this control to the master page (or master pages) that your application uses.*

As well as enabling ASP.NET AJAX functionality, you can also use properties to configure this control. The simplest of these properties is `EnablePartialRendering`, which is `true` by default. If you set this property to `false`, you will disable all asynchronous postback processing, such as that provided by `UpdatePanel` controls. This can be useful, for example, if you want to compare your AJAX-enabled web site with a traditional web site; perhaps if you are giving a demonstration to a manager.

You can use the `ScriptManager` control for several reasons, such as in the following common situations:

➤ To determine whether server-side code is being called as a result of a partial-page postback

➤ To add references to additional client-side JavaScript files

➤ To reference Web services

➤ To return error messages to the client

These configuration options are covered in the following sections.

Detect Partial-Page Postbacks

The `ScriptManager` control includes a Boolean property called `IsInAsyncPostBack`. You can use this property in server-side code to detect whether a partial-page postback is in progress. Note that the `ScriptManager` for a page may actually be on a master page. Rather than accessing this control through the master page, you can obtain a reference to the current `ScriptManager` instance by using the static `GetCurrent()` method, for example:

```
ScriptManager scriptManager = ScriptManager.GetCurrent(this);
if (scriptManager != null && scriptManager.IsInAsyncPostBack)
{
    // Code to execute for partial-page postbacks.
}
```

You must pass a reference to a `Page` control to the `GetCurrent()` method. For example, if you use this method in a `Page_Load()` event handler for an ASP.NET web page, you can use `this` as your `Page` reference. Also, remember to check for a `null` reference to avoid exceptions.

Client-Side JavaScript References

Rather than adding code to the HTML page header, or in `<script>` elements on the page, you can use the `Scripts` property of the `ScriptManager` class. This centralizes your script references and makes it easier to maintain them. You can do this declaratively by adding a child `<Scripts>` element to the `<UpdatePanel>` control element, and then adding `<asp:ScriptReference>` child control elements to `<Scripts>`. You use the `Path` property of a `ScriptReference` control to reference a custom script.

The following sample shows how to add references to a custom script file called `MyScript.js` in the root folder of the web application:

```
<asp:ScriptManager runat="server" ID="ScriptManager1">
  <Scripts>
    <asp:ScriptReference Path="~/MyScript.js" />
  </Scripts>
</asp:ScriptManager>
```

Web Service References

To access Web services from client-side JavaScript code, ASP.NET AJAX must generate a proxy class. To control this behavior, you use the `Services` property of the `ScriptManager` class. As with `Scripts`, you can specify this property declaratively, this time with a `<Services>` element. You add `<asp:ServiceReference>` controls to this element. For each `ServiceReference` object in the `Services` property, you specify the path to the Web service by using the `Path` property.

The `ServiceReference` class also has a property called `InlineScript`, which defaults to `false`. When this property is `false`, client-side code obtains a proxy class to call the Web service by requesting it from the server. To enhance performance (particularly if you use a lot of Web services on a page), you can set `InlineScript` to `true`. This causes the proxy class to be defined in the client-script for the page.

ASP.NET Web services use a file extension of `.asmx`. Without wanting to get into too much detail in this chapter, to add a reference to a Web service called `MyService.asmx` in the root folder of a web application, you would use code as follows:

```
<asp:ScriptManager runat="server" ID="ScriptManager1">
  <Services>
    <asp:ServiceReference Path="~/MyService.asmx" />
  </Services>
</asp:ScriptManager>
```

You can only add references to local Web services (that is, Web services in the same web application as the calling code) in this way. You can call remote Web services indirectly via local web methods.

Later in this chapter you see how to make asynchronous web method calls from client-side JavaScript code that uses proxy classes generated in this way.

Client-Side Error Messages

If an exception is thrown as part of a partial-page postback, the default behavior is to place the error message contained in the exception into a client-side JavaScript alert message box. You can customize the message that is displayed by handling the `AsyncPostBackError` event of the `ScriptManager` instance. In the event handler, you can use the `AsyncPostBackErrorEventArgs.Exception` property to access the exception that is thrown and the `ScriptManager.AsyncPostBackErrorMessage` property to set the message that is displayed to the client. You might do this to hide the exception details from users.

If you want to override the default behavior and display a message in a different way, you must handle the `endRequest` event of the client-side `PageRequestManager` object by using JavaScript. This is described later in this chapter.

Using UpdatePanel Controls

The `UpdatePanel` control is perhaps the control that you will use most often when you write ASP.NET AJAX-enabled web applications. This control, as you have seen in the simple example earlier in the chapter, enables you to wrap a portion of a web page so that it is capable of participating in a partial-page postback operation. To do this, you add an `UpdatePanel` control to the page and fill its child `<ContentTemplate>` element with the controls that you want it to contain:

```
<asp:UpdatePanel runat="Server" ID="UpdatePanel1">
  <ContentTemplate>
    ...
  </ContentTemplate>
</asp:UpdatePanel>
```

The contents of the `<ContentTemplate>` template are rendered in either a `<div>` or `<span>` element according to the value of the `RenderMode` property of the `UpdatePanel`. The default value of this property is `Block`, which will result in a `<div>` element. To use a `<span>` element, set `RenderMode` to `Inline`.

Multiple UpdatePanel Controls on a Single Web Page

You can include any number of `UpdatePanel` controls on a page. If a postback is caused by a control that is contained in the `<ContentTemplate>` of any `UpdatePanel` on the page, a partial-page postback will occur instead of a full-page postback. This will cause all the `UpdatePanel` controls to update according to the value of their `UpdateMode` property. The default value of this property is `Always`, which means that the `UpdatePanel` will update for a partial-page postback operation on the page, even if this operation occurs in a different `UpdatePanel` control. If you set this property to `Conditional`, the `UpdatePanel` updates only when a control that it contains causes a partial-page postback or when a trigger that you have defined occurs. Triggers are covered shortly.

If you have set `UpdateMode` to `Conditional`, you can also set the `ChildrenAsTriggers` property to `false` to prevent controls that are contained by the `UpdatePanel` from triggering an update of the panel. Note, though, that in this case these controls still trigger a partial-page update, which may result in other `UpdatePanel` controls on the page being updated. For example, this will update controls that have an `UpdateMode` property value of `Always`. This is illustrated in the following code:

```
<asp:UpdatePanel runat="Server" ID="UpdatePanel1" UpdateMode="Conditional"
  ChildrenAsTriggers="false">
  <ContentTemplate>
    <asp:Button runat="Server" ID="Button1" Text="Click Me" />
    <small>Panel 1 render time: <% =DateTime.Now.ToLongTimeString() %></small>
  </ContentTemplate>
</asp:UpdatePanel>
<asp:UpdatePanel runat="Server" ID="UpdatePanel2">
  <ContentTemplate>
    <small>Panel 2 render time: <% =DateTime.Now.ToLongTimeString() %></small>
  </ContentTemplate>
</asp:UpdatePanel>
<small>Page render time: <% =DateTime.Now.ToLongTimeString() %></small>
```

In this code, the `UpdatePanel2` control has an `UpdateMode` property of `Always`; the default value. When the button is clicked, it will cause a partial-page postback, but only `UpdatePanel2` will be updated. Visually, you will notice that only the "Panel 2 render time" label is updated.

Server-Side UpdatePanel Updates

Sometimes when you have multiple `UpdatePanel` controls on a page, you might decide not to update one of them unless certain conditions are met. In this case, you would configure the `UpdateMode` property of the panel to `Conditional` as shown in the previous section and possibly also set the `ChildrenAsTriggers` property to `false`. Then, in your server-side event-handler code for one of the controls on the page that causes a partial-page update, you would (conditionally) call the `Update()` method of the `UpdatePanel`. For example:

```
protected void Button1_Click(object sender, EventArgs e)
{
    if (TestSomeCondition())
    {
        UpdatePanel1.Update();
    }
}
```

UpdatePanel Triggers

You can cause an `UpdatePanel` control to be updated by a control elsewhere on the web page by adding triggers to the `Triggers` property of the control. A trigger is an association between an event of a control elsewhere on the page and the `UpdatePanel` control. All controls have default events (for example, the default event of a `Button` control is `Click`), so specifying the name of an event is optional. There are two types of triggers that you can add, represented by the following two classes:

➤　　`AsyncPostBackTrigger` — This class causes the `UpdatePanel` to update when the specified event of the specified control is triggered.

➤　　`PostBackTrigger` — This class causes a full-page update to be triggered when the specified event of the specified control is triggered.

You will mostly use `AsyncPostBackTrigger`, but `PostBackTrigger` can be useful if you want a control inside an `UpdatePanel` to trigger a full-page postback.

Both of these trigger classes have two properties: `ControlID`, which specifies the control that causes the trigger by its identifier, and `EventName`, which specifies the name of the event for the control that is linked to the trigger.

To extend an earlier example, consider the following code:

```
<asp:UpdatePanel runat="Server" ID="UpdatePanel1" UpdateMode="Conditional"
  ChildrenAsTriggers="false">
  <Triggers>
    <asp:AsyncPostBackTrigger ControlID="Button2" />
  </Triggers>
  <ContentTemplate>
    <asp:Button runat="Server" ID="Button1" Text="Click Me" />
    <small>Panel 1 render time: <% =DateTime.Now.ToLongTimeString() %></small>
  </ContentTemplate>
</asp:UpdatePanel>
<asp:UpdatePanel runat="Server" ID="UpdatePanel2">
  <ContentTemplate>
    <asp:Button runat="Server" ID="Button2" Text="Click Me" />
    <small>Panel 2 render time: <% =DateTime.Now.ToLongTimeString() %></small>
  </ContentTemplate>
</asp:UpdatePanel>
<small>Page render time: <% =DateTime.Now.ToLongTimeString() %></small>
```

The new `Button` control, `Button2`, is specified as a trigger in the `UpdatePanel1`. When this button is clicked, both `UpdatePanel1` and `UpdatePanel2` will be updated: `UpdatePanel1` because of the trigger, and `UpdatePanel2` because it uses the default `UpdateMode` value of `Always`.

Using UpdateProgress

The `UpdateProgress` control, as you saw in the earlier example, enables you to display a progress message to the user while a partial-page postback is in operation. You use the `ProgressTemplate` property to supply an `ITemplate` for the progress display. You will typically use the `<ProgressTemplate>` child element of the control to do this.

You can place multiple `UpdateProgress` controls on a page by using the `AssociatedUpdatePanelID` property to associate the control with a specific `UpdatePanel`. If this is not set (the default), the `UpdateProgress` template will be displayed for any partial-page postback, regardless of which `UpdatePanel` causes it.

When a partial-page postback occurs, there is a delay before the `UpdateProgress` template is displayed. This delay is configurable through the `DisplayAfter` property, which is an `int` property that specifies the delay in milliseconds. The default is 500 milliseconds.

Finally, you can use the Boolean `DynamicLayout` property to specify whether space is allocated for the template before it is displayed. For the default value of `true` for this property, space on the page is dynamically allocated, which may result in other controls being moved out of the way for an inline progress template display. If you set this property to `false`, space will be allocated for the template before it is displayed, so the layout of other controls on the page will not change. You will set this property according to the effect you want to achieve when displaying progress. For a progress template that is positioned by using absolute coordinates, as in the earlier example, you should leave this property set to the default value.

Using Extender Controls

The core ASP.NET AJAX download includes a class called `ExtenderControl`. The purpose of this control is to enable you to extend (that is, add functionality to) other ASP.NET server controls. This is used extensively in the AJAX Control Toolkit to great effect, and you can use the ASP.NET AJAX Server Control Extender project template to create your own extended controls. `ExtenderControl` controls all work in a similar way — you place them on a page, associate them with target controls, and add further configuration. The extender then emits client-side code to add functionality.

To see this in action in a simple example, create a new empty web site called `PCSExtenderDemo` in the `C:\ProCSharp\Chapter41` directory, add the AJAX Control Toolkit assembly to the bin directory of the web site, and then add the following code to a new web form called `Default.aspx`:

```
<%@ Page Language="C#" AutoEventWireup="true" CodeFile="Default.aspx.cs"
    Inherits="_Default" %>
<%@ Register Assembly="AjaxControlToolkit" Namespace="AjaxControlToolkit"
    TagPrefix="ajaxToolkit" %>

<!DOCTYPE html PUBLIC "-//W3C//DTD XHTML 1.0 Transitional//EN"
 "http://www.w3.org/TR/xhtml1/DTD/xhtml1-transitional.dtd">
<html xmlns="http://www.w3.org/1999/xhtml">
<head runat="server">
  <title>Color Selector</title>
</head>
<body>
  <form id="form1" runat="server">
    <asp:ScriptManager ID="ScriptManager1" runat="server" />
    <div>
      <asp:UpdatePanel runat="server" ID="updatePanel1">
        <ContentTemplate>
          <span style="display: inline-block; padding: 2px;">
            My favorite color is:
          </span>
          <asp:Label runat="server" ID="favoriteColorLabel" Text="green"
            style="color: #00dd00; display: inline-block; padding: 2px;
                   width: 70px; font-weight: bold;" />
          <ajaxToolkit:DropDownExtender runat="server" ID="dropDownExtender1"
            TargetControlID="favoriteColorLabel"
            DropDownControlID="colDropDown" />
          <asp:Panel ID="colDropDown" runat="server"
            Style="display: none; visibility: hidden; width: 60px;
                   padding: 8px; border: double 4px black;
                   background-color: #ffffdd; font-weight: bold;">
            <asp:LinkButton runat="server" ID="OptionRed" Text="red"
              OnClick="OnSelect" style="color: #ff0000;" /><br />
            <asp:LinkButton runat="server" ID="OptionOrange" Text="orange"
              OnClick="OnSelect" style="color: #dd7700;" /><br />
            <asp:LinkButton runat="server" ID="OptionYellow" Text="yellow"
              OnClick="OnSelect" style="color: #dddd00;" /><br />
            <asp:LinkButton runat="server" ID="OptionGreen" Text="green"
              OnClick="OnSelect" style="color: #00dd00;" /><br />
            <asp:LinkButton runat="server" ID="OptionBlue" Text="blue"
              OnClick="OnSelect" style="color: #0000dd;" /><br />
            <asp:LinkButton runat="server" ID="OptionPurple" Text="purple"
              OnClick="OnSelect" style="color: #dd00ff;" />
          </asp:Panel>
        </ContentTemplate>
      </asp:UpdatePanel>
    </div>
  </form>
</body>
</html>
```

code snippet PCSExtenderDemo/Default.aspx

You also need to add the following event handler to the code behind this file:

Available for download on Wrox.com

```
protected void OnSelect(object sender, EventArgs e)
{
    favoriteColorLabel.Text = ((LinkButton)sender).Text;
    favoriteColorLabel.Style["color"] = ((LinkButton)sender).Style["color"];
}
```

code snippet PCSExtenderDemo/Default.aspx.cs

In the browser, not very much is visible at first, and the extender seems to have no effect. This is shown in Figure 41-16.

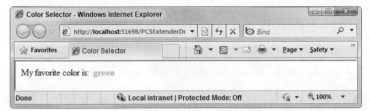

FIGURE 41-16

However, when you hover over the text that reads "green," a drop-down dynamically appears. If you click this drop-down, a list appears, as shown in Figure 41-17.

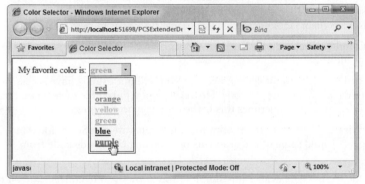

FIGURE 41-17

When you click one of the links in the drop-down list, the text changes accordingly (after a partial-page postback operation).

There are two important points to note about this simple example:

➤ It was extremely easy to associate the extender with target controls.

➤ The drop-down list was styled using custom code — meaning that you can place whatever content you like in the list. This simple extender is a great way to add functionality to your web applications, and it is very simple to use.

The extenders that are contained in the AJAX Control Toolkit are continually being added to and updated, so check `http://www.asp.net/ajax/AjaxControlToolkit/Samples/` regularly. This web page includes live demonstrations of all the current extenders so that you can see them in action.

In addition to the extender controls that are supplied by the AJAX Control Toolkit, you can create your own. To create an effective extender, you must use the AJAX Library.

Using the AJAX Library

There is a great deal of functionality available in the AJAX Library that you can use to further enhance your web applications. However, to do this you need at least a working knowledge of JavaScript. In this section, you see some of this functionality, although this is not an exhaustive tutorial.

The basic principles behind the use of the AJAX Library are much the same as for adding any type of client-side script to a web application. You will still use the core JavaScript language, and you will still interact with the DOM. However, there are many areas where the AJAX Library makes things easier for you. This section explains many of these areas and provides a foundation that you can build on with further experimentation and study of the online AJAX Library documentation.

The techniques covered in this section are illustrated in the `PCSLibraryDemo` project, which is referred to throughout the rest of this chapter.

Adding JavaScript to a Web Page

The first thing you need to know is how to add client-side JavaScript to a web page. You have three options here:

> ➤ Add JavaScript inline in ASP.NET web pages by using the `<script>` element.
> ➤ Add JavaScript to separate JavaScript files with the extension `.js` and reference these files from `<script>` elements or (preferably) by using the `<Scripts>` child element of the `ScriptManager` control.
> ➤ Generate JavaScript from server-side code, such as code behind or custom extender controls.

Each of these techniques has its own benefits. For prototyping code, there is no substitute for inline code because it is so quick and easy to use. You will also find it easy to associate client-side event handlers of HTML elements and server controls with client-side functions, because everything is in the same file.

Having separate files is good for reusability, because you may create your own library of classes much like the existing AJAX Library JavaScript files.

Generating code from code-behind can be tricky to implement because you will not usually have access to IntelliSense for JavaScript programming when you use C# code. However, you will be able to generate code dynamically in response to application state, and sometimes this is the only way to do things.

The extenders that you can create with the AJAX Control Toolkit include a separate JavaScript file that you use to define behaviors, which gets around some of the problems of exposing client-side code from the server.

In this chapter, you use the inline code technique, because it is simplest and allows you to concentrate on the JavaScript functionality.

Global Utility Functions

One of the features supplied by the AJAX Library that you will use most often is the set of global functions that wrap other functionality. These include the following:

> ➤ `$get()` — This function enables you to get a reference to a DOM element by supplying its client-side `id` value as a parameter, with an optional second parameter to specify the parent element to search in.
> ➤ `$create()` — This function enables you to create objects and perform initialization at the same time. You can supply between one and five parameters to this function. The first parameter is the type you want to instantiate, which will typically be a type defined by the AJAX Library. The other parameters enable you to specify initial property values, event handlers, references to other components, and the DOM element that the object is attached to, respectively.
> ➤ `$addHandler()` — This function provides a shorthand for adding an event handler to an object.

There are more global functions, but these are the ones you will use most often. `$create()` in particular is a very useful way to reduce the amount of code required to create and initialize an object.

Using the AJAX Library JavaScript OOP Extensions

The AJAX Library includes an enhanced framework for defining types that uses an OOP-based system that maps closely to .NET Framework techniques. You can create namespaces, add types to namespaces, add constructors, methods, properties, and events to types, and even use inheritance and interfaces in type definitions.

In this section, you see how to implement the basics of this functionality, but you won't look at events and interfaces here. These constructs are beyond the scope of this chapter.

Defining Namespaces

To define a namespace, you use the `Type.registerNamespace()` function, for example:

```
Type.registerNamespace("ProCSharp");
```

After you have registered a namespace you can add types to it.

Defining Classes

Defining a class is a three-stage process. First, you define the constructor. Next, you add properties and methods. Finally, you register the class.

To define a constructor, you define a function using a namespace and class name, for example:

```
ProCSharp.Shape = function(color, scaleFactor) {
  this._color = color;
  this._scaleFactor = scaleFactor;
}
```

This constructor takes two parameters and uses them to set local fields (note that you do not have to explicitly define these fields — you just have to set their values).

To add properties and methods, you assign them to the `prototype` property of the class as follows:

```
ProCSharp.Shape.prototype = {

  get_Color : function() {
    return this._color;
  },

  set_Color : function(color) {
    this._color = color;
  },

  get_ScaleFactor : function() {
    return this._scaleFactor;
  },

  set_ScaleFactor : function(scaleFactor) {
    this._scaleFactor = scaleFactor;
  }

}
```

This code defines two properties by their get and set accessors.

To register a class, you call its `registerClass()` function:

```
ProCSharp.Shape.registerClass('ProCSharp.Shape');
```

Inheritance

You derive a class in much the same way as creating a class but with some slight differences. You use the `initializeBase()` function to initialize the base class in the constructor, passing parameters in the form of an array:

```
ProCSharp.Circle = function(color, scaleFactor, diameter) {
  ProCSharp.Circle.initializeBase(this, [color, scaleFactor]);
  this._diameter = diameter;
}
```

You define properties and methods in the same way as before:

```
ProCSharp.Circle.prototype = {

  get_Diameter : function() {
    return this._diameter;
  },

  set_Diameter : function(diameter) {
    this._diameter = diameter;
  },

  get_Area : function() {
    return Math.PI * Math.pow((this._diameter * this._scaleFactor) / 2, 2);
  },

  describe : function() {
    var description = "This is a " + this._color + " circle with an area of "
      + this.get_Area();
    alert(description);
  }
}
```

When you register the class, you provide the base class type as a second parameter:

```
ProCSharp.Circle.registerClass('ProCSharp.Circle', ProCSharp.Shape);
```

You can implement interfaces by passing them as additional parameters, although, to keep things simple, you won't see details of that here.

Using User-Defined Types

After you have defined classes in this way, you can instantiate and use them with simple syntax. For example:

```
var myCircle = new ProCSharp.Circle('red', 1.0, 4.4);
myCircle.describe();
```

This code would result in a JavaScript alert box, as shown in Figure 41-18.

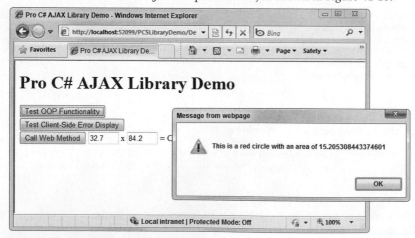

FIGURE 41-18

If you want to test this, run the `PCSLibraryDemo` project and click the Test OOP Functionality button.

The PageRequestManager and Application Objects

Among the most useful classes that the AJAX Library provides are the `PageRequestManager` and `Application` classes. You will find `PageRequestManager` in the `Sys.WebForms` namespace and `Application` in the `Sys` namespace. The important thing about these classes is that they expose several events that you can attach JavaScript event handlers to. These events occur at particularly interesting points in the lifecycle of a page (for `Application`) or partial-page postback (for `PageRequestManager`) and enable you to perform operations at these critical times.

The AJAX Library defines event handlers in a similar way to event handlers in the .NET Framework. Every event handler has a similar signature, with two parameters. The first parameter is a reference to the object that generated the event. The second parameter is an instance of the `Sys.EventArgs` class or an instance of a class that derives from this class. Many of the events exposed by `PageRequestManager` and `Application` include specialized event argument classes that you can use to determine more information about the event. The following table lists these events in the order they will occur in a page that is loaded, triggers a partial-page postback, and is then closed.

EVENT	DESCRIPTION
`Application.init`	This event is the first to occur in the lifecycle of a page. It is raised after all the JavaScript files have been loaded but before any objects in the application have been created.
`Application.load`	This event fires after the objects in the application have loaded and been initialized. You will often use an event handler attached to this event to perform actions when the page is first loaded. You can also provide an implementation for a function called `pageLoad()` on a page, which is automatically defined as an event handler for this event. It sends event arguments by using a `Sys.ApplicationLoadEventArgs` object, which includes the `isPartialLoad` property that you can use to determine if a partial-page postback has occurred. Access this property with the `get_isPartialLoad()` accessor.
`PageRequestManager.initializeRequest`	This event occurs before a partial-page postback, before the request object is created. You can use the `Sys.WebForms.InitializeRequestEventArgs` event argument properties to access the element that triggered the postback (`postBackElement`) and the underlying request object (`request`).
`PageRequestManager.beginRequest`	This event occurs before a partial-page postback, after the request object is created. You can use the `Sys.WebForms.BeginRequestEventArgs` event argument properties to access the element that triggered the postback (`postBackElement`) and the underlying request object (`request`).
`PageRequestManager.pageLoading`	This event is raised after a partial-page postback, before any subsequent processing occurs. This processing can include `<div>` elements that will be deleted or updated, which you can reference through the `Sys.WebForms.PageLoadingEventArgs` object by using the `panelsDeleting` and `panelsUpdating` properties.

continues

(continued)

EVENT	DESCRIPTION
`PageRequestManager.pageLoaded`	This event is raised after a partial-page postback, after `UpdatePanel` controls have been processed. This processing can include `<div>` elements that have been created or updated, which you can reference through the `Sys.WebForms.PageLoadedEventArgs` object by using the `panelsCreated` and `panelsUpdated` properties.
`PageRequestManager.endRequest`	This event occurs after the processing of a partial-page postback has completed. The `Sys.WebForms.EndRequestEventArgs` object passed to the event handler enables you to detect and process server-side errors (by using the `error` and `errorHandled` properties) as well as to access the response object through `response`.
`Application.unload`	This event is raised just before the objects in the application are disposed, which gives you a chance to perform final actions or clean up if necessary.

You can add an event handler to an event of the `Application` object by using the static `add_xxx()` functions, for example:

```
Sys.Application.add_load(LoadHandler);

function LoadHandler(sender, args)
{
   // Event handler code.
}
```

The process is similar for `PageRequestManager`, but you must use the `get_instance()` function to obtain an instance of the current object, for example:

```
Sys.WebForms.PageRequestManager.getInstance().add_beginRequest(
   BeginRequestHandler);

function BeginRequestHandler(sender, args)
{
   // Event handler code.
}
```

In the `PCSLibraryDemo` application, an event handler is added to the `PageRequestManager.endRequest` event. This event handler responds to server-side processing errors and displays an error message in a `<span>` element with an `id` of `errorDisplay`. To test this method, click the Test Client-Side Error Display button, as shown in Figure 41-19.

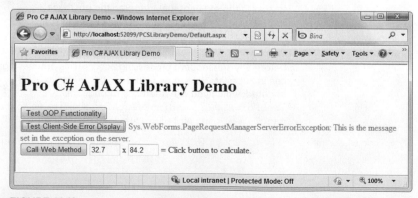

FIGURE 41-19

The code that achieves this is:

```
Sys.WebForms.PageRequestManager.getInstance().add_endRequest(
  EndRequestHandler);

function EndRequestHandler(sender, args)
{
  if (args.get_error() != undefined)
  {
    var errorMessage = args.get_error().message;
    args.set_errorHandled(true);
    $get('errorDisplay').innerHTML = errorMessage;
  }
}
```

Note that the `errorHandled` property of the `EndRequestEventArgs` object is set to `true`. This prevents the default behavior, which is to display the error message in a dialog box, by using the JavaScript `alert()` function.

The error itself is generated by throwing an exception on the server as follows:

```
protected void testErrorDisplay_Click(object sender, EventArgs e)
{
    throw new ApplicationException(
        "This is the message set in the exception on the server.");
}
```

There are many other situations when you will want to use event handling techniques to act on the `Application` and `PageRequestManager` events.

JavaScript Debugging

In the past, JavaScript has had a reputation of being difficult to debug. However, this has been addressed in the latest version of Visual Studio. You can now add breakpoints and step through JavaScript code just like C# code. You can also interrogate object state in break mode, change property values, and so on. The IntelliSense that is available when you write JavaScript code is also vastly improved in the latest version of Visual Studio.

However, there will still be times when you will want to add debug and trace code to report information as code is executed. For example, you might want to use the JavaScript `alert()` function to show information in dialog boxes.

There are also some third-party tools that you can use to add a client-side UI for debugging. These include:

➤ **Fiddler** — This tool, which you can obtain from `www.fiddlertool.com`, enables you to log all HTTP traffic between your computer and a web application — including partial-page postbacks. There are also additional tools that you can use to look at what occurs during the processing of web pages in more detail.

➤ **Nikhil's Web Development Helper** — This tool, available at `http://projects.nikhilk.net/WebDevHelper`, can also log HTTP traffic. In addition, this tool contains a number of utilities specifically aimed at ASP.NET and ASP.NET AJAX development, for example, the ability to examine view state and to execute immediate JavaScript code. This latter feature is particularly useful to test objects that you may have created on the client. The Web Development Helper also displays extended error information when JavaScript errors occur, which makes it easier to track down bugs in JavaScript code.

The AJAX Library also provides the `Sys.Debug` class, which you can use to add some extra debugging features to your application. One of the most useful features of this class is the `Sys.Debug.traceDump()` function, which enables you to analyze objects. One way to use this function is to place a `textarea` control on your web page with an `id` attribute of `TraceConsole`. Then, all output from `Debug` will be sent to this control. For example, you can use the `traceDump()` method to output information about the `Application` object to the console:

```
Sys.Application.add_load(LoadHandler);

function LoadHandler(sender, args)
{
    Sys.Debug.traceDump(sender);
}
```

This results in output along the lines of the following:

```
traceDump {Sys._Application}
    _updating: false
    _id: null
    _disposing: false
    _creatingComponents: false
    _disposableObjects {Array}
    _components {Object}
    _createdComponents {Array}
    _secondPassComponents {Array}
    _loadHandlerDelegate: null
    _events {Sys.EventHandlerList}
        _list {Object}
            load {Array}
                [0] {Function}
    _initialized: true
    _initializing: true
```

You can see all the properties of this object in this output. This technique can be extremely useful for ASP.NET AJAX development.

Making Asynchronous Web Method Calls

One of the most powerful features of ASP.NET AJAX is the ability to call web methods from client-side script. This gives you access to data, server-side processing, and all manner of other functionality.

You will not be looking at web methods in this book until Chapter 43, "Windows Communication Foundation," so we will save the details until then and cover the basics here. Put simply, a *web method* is a method that you can expose from a Web service that enables you to access remote resources over the Internet. In ASP.NET AJAX, you can also expose web methods as static methods of server-side web page code-behind code. You can use parameters and return values in web methods just as you do in other method types.

In ASP.NET AJAX, web methods are called asynchronously. You pass parameters to a web method and define a callback function, which is called when the web method call completes. You use this callback function to process the web method response. You can also provide an alternative callback function to call in the event of a call failure.

In the `PCSLibraryDemo` application, you can see a web method call being performed by clicking the Call Web Method button, as shown in Figure 41-20.

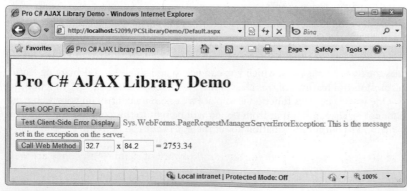

FIGURE 41-20

Before you can use a web method from client-side script, you must generate a client-side proxy class to perform the communication. The easiest way to do this is simply to reference the URL of the Web service that contains the web method in the `ScriptManager` control:

```
<asp:ScriptManager ID="ScriptManager1" runat="server">
  <Services>
    <asp:ServiceReference Path="~/SimpleService.asmx" />
  </Services>
</asp:ScriptManager>
```

ASP.NET Web services use the extension `.asmx`, as shown in this code. To use a client-side proxy to access a web method in a Web service, you must apply the `System.Web.Script.Services.ScriptService` attribute to the Web service.

For web methods in the code behind for the web page, you do not need this attribute, or this reference in `ScriptManager`, but you must use static methods and apply the `System.Web.Services.WebMethod` attribute to the methods.

After you have generated a client-side stub, you can access the web method by its name, which is defined as a function of a class with the same name as the Web service. In `PCSLibraryDemo`, the `SimpleService.asmx` Web service has a web method called `Multiply()`, which multiplies two double parameters. When you call this method from client-side code, you pass the two parameters required by the method (obtained from HTML `<input>` elements in the example) and can pass one or two callback function references. If you pass one reference, this is the callback function that is used when the call returns a success result. If you pass two references, the second one is the callback function that is used for web method failure.

In `PCSLibraryDemo`, a single callback function is used, which takes the result of the web method call and assigns it to the `<span>` with the `id` of `webMethodResult`:

```
function callWebMethod()
{
  SimpleService.Multiply(parseFloat($get('xParam').value),
    parseFloat($get('yParam').value), multiplyCallBack);
}

function multiplyCallBack(result)
{
  $get('webMethodResult').innerHTML = result;
}
```

This method is a very simple one but illustrates the ease with which you can call Web services asynchronously from client-side code.

ASP.NET Application Services

ASP.NET AJAX includes three specialized Web services that you can use to access ASP.NET application services. These services are accessed through the following client-side classes:

➤ `Sys.Services.AuthenticationService` — This service includes methods to log in or log out a user or determine whether a user is logged in.

➤ `Sys.Services.ProfileService` — This service enables you to get and set profile properties for the currently logged-on user. The profile properties are configured in the `web.config` file for the application.

➤ `Sys.Services.RoleService` — This service enables you to determine role membership for the currently logged-on user.

Used properly, these classes enable you to implement extremely responsive user interfaces that include authorization, profile, and membership functionality.

These services are beyond the scope of this chapter, but you should be aware of them — plus they are well worth investigating.

SUMMARY

In this chapter you looked at several advanced techniques for creating ASP.NET pages and web sites, and you saw these techniques in action in a demonstration web site called PCSDemoSite. You also learned how you can use ASP.NET AJAX to enhance ASP.NET web sites. ASP.NET AJAX contains a wealth of functionality that makes web sites far more responsive and dynamic and can provide a much better user experience.

First, you learned how to create reusable ASP.NET server controls by using C#. You saw how to create simple user controls from existing ASP.NET pages, as well as how to create custom controls from scratch. You also saw how the meeting room booker sample from the previous chapter can be reformatted as a user control.

You then looked at master pages, and how to provide a template for the pages of your web site, which is another way to reuse code and simplify development. In PCSDemoSite, in the downloadable code for this chapter, you saw a master page that included navigation web server controls to enable users to move around the site. The PCSDemoSite sample also laid the framework for themes, which are an excellent way to separate functionality from design and can be a powerful accessibility technique.

You also took a brief look at security and how you can implement forms-based authentication on your web sites with minimal effort.

Next, you investigated Web Parts and how to use the Web Parts server controls to put together a basic application that illustrated some of the possibilities that this technology offers.

In the last part of this chapter, you learned about ASP.NET AJAX. You saw what Ajax is, and how to use Microsoft's implementation of Ajax, ASP.NET AJAX. This included both the server-side techniques for creating ASP.NET AJAX-enabled web sites and applications, and client-side techniques implemented by using the AJAX Library.

We hope that this chapter has given you an appetite for creating web sites with ASP.NET, and in particular for using the exciting new capabilities that ASP.NET AJAX offers. Ajax has blossomed across the Web, and ASP.NET AJAX is an excellent way to integrate Ajax functionality with ASP.NET applications. This product is also very well supported, and the community-based releases, such as the AJAX Control Toolkit, provide you with even more great functionality that you are free to use in your applications.

Even though you may find yourself having to learn the JavaScript language you never thought you would need, the end result is well worth the effort. By using ASP.NET AJAX you will make far better, more functional, and more dynamic web sites than you could with ASP.NET alone. And with the latest release of Visual Studio you have tools that make ASP.NET AJAX much easier to use. The most recent version of ASP.NET AJAX includes much more functionality than there was space to cover in this chapter, such as client-side templates and live data binding. It is well worth researching these advances (and more) by keeping an eye on developer blogs and the http://www.asp.net web site.

In the next chapter you will look at some of the latest techniques for structuring ASP.NET web sites and applications — dynamic data sites and the MVC framework — as well as an enabling technology, ASP.NET routing.

42

ASP.NET Dynamic Data and MVC

WHAT'S IN THIS CHAPTER?

➤ Using routing to implement URLs

➤ Building web sites with dynamic data

➤ Building web applications with ASP.NET MVC

In the previous two chapters, you have learned about how to use ASP.NET to create web sites, and how to add advanced functionality to streamline those web sites. In this chapter, you will look at frameworks that you can use to both accelerate the creation of web sites and include best-practice techniques to make the best sites possible.

There are currently two of these frameworks that ship with ASP.NET as part of .NET 4, both of which have grown from years of research by Microsoft and the ASP.NET development community. These are:

➤ Dynamic data

➤ ASP.NET MVC (Model-View-Controller)

The first of these, dynamic data, enables you to build a web site from preexisting data that you have in a database. The wizards that VS supplies make it possible to generate dynamic data web sites very quickly, which you can then go on to customize to get the look and feel you want. Advanced template capabilities are included in dynamic data web sites so that you can get up and running quickly. Dynamic data isn't suitable for all types of web sites, but for many types — including e-commerce sites and data manipulation sites — it provides a perfect starting point for development.

MVC is a framework for creating all sorts of sites that has emerged from a desire for both a cleaner separation of user interface and business logic and the ability to unit test that business logic independently. This aspect is becoming more important as the world moves toward test-driven development (TDD) models. Traditionally, ASP.NET web sites have been hard to test along these lines, as some way of directly interacting with web pages is required. Separating design and functionality makes things much easier.

There are other advantages of MVC, as you will see later in this chapter, and it leads to very clean, easy to understand code that is perfect for enterprise-level web site development and makes unit testing much simpler.

Both dynamic data and MVC make use of another methodology that was introduced in .NET 3.5, routing. This makes it possible for URLs to be simplified and to include additional information, and is the first thing you will look at in this chapter. After routing, this chapter moves on to dynamic data and MVC in turn, with a final section about how to combine these technologies.

 Both dynamic data and MVC are large subjects to cover and would require multiple chapters to cover in depth. This chapter gives a general overview of using these frameworks, which will hopefully give you enough information to get started before finding more in-depth resources if you want to use them in more depth.

ROUTING

ASP.NET routing is a technology that enables you to assign sensible, human-readable URLs to web pages. Essentially, this means that the URL for a web page that a user sees in the address bar of a browser doesn't necessarily match the physical location of a web page. Instead, the URL will include information that your web site can use to map to a page that you define, and can pass parameters to that page.

At first glance, this may seem a little counterintuitive. Why wouldn't you want users to see the address of a web page? Surely not exposing this information will make it more difficult to locate resources. In fact, as you will see in this section, mapping URLs can make it much easier for users, and it has several other benefits as well.

As an example, consider the following URL:

```
http://www.myecommercesite.com/products/kites/reddragon
```

Without knowing anything about the web site that uses this URL, you can probably take a good guess at what you'd find on the page. From the words in the URL, you would expect to see a product page for a kite called "Red Dragon."

The advantages of this type of URL are as follows:

➤ Users can see at a glance what pages are.

➤ URLs are easy for users to remember, even without creating bookmarks.

➤ Users can modify URLs manually to navigate (for example, a user might replace the last section of the above URL with `/products/balloons`).

➤ Search engine results are optimized for these descriptive URLs, so the page ranking will be higher.

There are essentially two ways to implement URLs of this form. You can either create a page for every possible URL, or you can use a framework that maps URLs to pages that can display data for multiple URLs. This first possibility is worth mentioning, as it isn't necessarily out of the question — it is possible to create static HTML sites that are generated from back-end data. However, this requires a fair amount of maintenance and, in most situations, can be more trouble than it's worth. Now that the tools have matured the second scenario is more practical.

In fact, ASP.NET has included the capability to use URLs like this for some time, although "URL rewriting" (as it was known in earlier versions of ASP.NET) required an in-depth knowledge of the ASP .NET architecture and could be quite tricky to implement. With the advent of ASP.NET routing, things have become much easier.

In this section, you will look at the following:

➤ **Query string parameters** — Before looking at routing specifically, it is worth understanding the case for including additional data in URLs in more detail. Query string parameters provide an alternative way of doing this, and have existed since the very beginnings of the web. However, while simpler than routing, they do not include all of the advantages.

➤ **Defining routes** — ASP.NET routing requires you to define the routes that are available in your web site so that they can be used.

➤ **Using route parameters** — Once a route has been detected in a URL, the target page can make use of routing parameters.

The downloadable code for this chapter includes a simple solution called `PCSRoutingDemo` that will be referred to from this section to illustrate the techniques.

Query String Parameters

While surfing the web, you've probably noticed that a lot of web pages include information in their URLs in addition to their location. For example, in an e-commerce web site, you might see a URL that looks a little like the following:

```
http://www.myecommercesite.com/products.aspx?id=4
```

In this URL the target page is `products.aspx`, but after the identifier for this page, you can see additional information in the form of a query string. The `?` character indicates the start of the query string, and the remainder of the URL consists of a name/value pair, with an equals character (`=`) separating the name (`id`) from the value (`4`). In fact, URLs can contain several query string name/value pairs, separated by `&` symbols.

When users navigate to an ASP.NET page with a query string (perhaps by clicking on a link that you have rendered from database data), you can write code to render the page accordingly. In this example, you might use the value of the `id` query string parameter to extract data from a database, for a product with the corresponding ID. This means that you don't have to create a page for every product in your database; you can, instead, create a single page that can show the details for any product.

In practice, ASP.NET pages receive query string information in the form of a `NameValueCollection` object. This is passed in the `QueryString` property of the `HttpRequest` object that is available in code-behind through the inherited `Request` property. The query string collection is indexed by name and index, so to get the value of the `id` query string parameter shown above, you could use either of the following lines of code:

```
string idValue = Request.QueryString[0];
```

or:

```
string idValue = Request.QueryString["id"];
```

Note that all query string values are passed as strings, so to get an integer value for `id` you'd need to parse the value.

The use of query string parameters is illustrated in the PCSRoutingDemo web site for this chapter. If you view the web site in a browser and click the "Navigation with query string" link, you will see the query string parameters displayed, as shown in Figure 42-1.

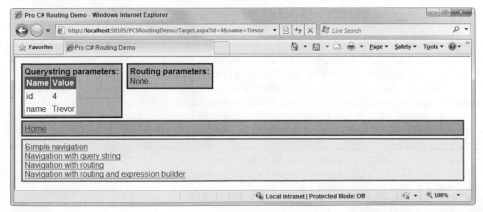

FIGURE 42-1

The code that displays these values is in the code-behind for the master page and is as follows:

```
if (Request.QueryString.Count == 0)
{
    this.NoQuerystringLabel.Text = "None.";
}
else
{
    GridView1.DataSource = from string key in Request.QueryString.Keys
                           select
                               new
                               {
                                   Name = key,
                                   Value = Request.QueryString[key]
                               };
    GridView1.DataBind();
}
```

code snippet PCSRoutingDemo/MasterPage.master.cs

Here, the collection of query string parameters is transformed into a collection of objects with `Name` and `Value` properties that can be data bound to a `GridView` control and displayed.

This method of passing data with query string parameters is well established and extremely useful, but ASP.NET routing achieves the same results in a much neater way, with all of the advantages.

Defining Routes

In order to use ASP.NET routing, you need to configure the routes that are available in your web site. Once you have done this, typically in the `HttpApplication.Application_Start` event handler, users will be able to use those routes and your web site can make use of the parameters passed.

A route definition consists of the following:

➤ A name for the route (which can be omitted)

➤ A URL pattern for the route, including parameter specifications where required

➤ A handler for the route, which determines which target URL the route is mapped to

➤ An optional collection of default values to use for route parameters if they are not included in the URL

➤ An optional collection of constraints for parameters, which are used to determine if a route is valid

As you might expect, ASP.NET includes classes that make it easy to specify all of this.

An ASP.NET web site maintains a collection of route specifications that are checked when a URL is requested to see if there is a match. This collection is accessible in your code through the static `RouteTable.Routes` property. This property is a collection of routes defined by an optional name and an object that derives from the abstract `RouteBase` class. Unless you want to create your own class to represent a route, you can add instances of the `Route` class to this collection.

The `Route` class has a number of constructors that you can use to define a route, the simplest of which includes a path and a route handler. The path is specified as a string, with parameters included and delimited with curly braces. The route handler is an object that implements the `IRouteHandler` interface, such as the system-defined `PageRouteHandler` class. When instantiating `PageRouteHandler` you specify a target page path, and, optionally, whether to check the physical path for authorization with the ASP.NET security model (more on this later). The simplest way to add a route is, therefore, as follows:

```
RouteTable.Routes.Add("RouteName",
                new Route("path/{pathparameter}",
                    new PageRouteHandler("target.aspx")));
```

Here, a route called `RouteName` is added to the route definitions. This route matches URLs of the form:

```
http://<domain>/path/{pathparameter}
```

Any matching URLs will be mapped to the `target.aspx` file.

For example, if a user requested the following URL:

```
http://<domain>/path/oranges
```

The web site would detect this as a matching URL for the `RouteName` route, and the user would be redirected to the `target.aspx` page. If the code for this page requested the value of the `pathparameter` parameter, it would receive the value `oranges`.

In the sample PCSRoutingDemo web site for this chapter, you can see a route in action by clicking the "Navigation with routing" link, which results in the display shown in Figure 42-2.

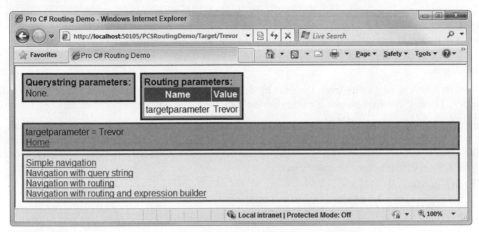

FIGURE 42-2

This route is defined in `Global.cs` in `App_Code` (the code-behind file used for `Global.asax`) as follows:

```
RouteTable.Routes.Add("TestRoute",
                new Route("Target/{targetparameter}",
                        new PageRouteHandler("~/Target.aspx")));
```

code snippet PCSRoutingDemo/App_Code/Global.cs

You'll see how the parameter is rendered on the page shortly.

Route Authorization

Since there are effectively two URLs taking part in routing — the one requested by the user and the one that is used for the physical file location that generates the page — ASP.NET authorization can take place in two places. The default behavior is to check both of these URLs to determine whether the user has access to the page. You can override this in the constructor for `PageRouteHandler` with a second parameter as follows:

```
RouteTable.Routes.Add("RouteName",
                new Route("path/{pathparameter}",
                        new PageRouteHandler("~/target.aspx", false)));
```

If you do this, then only the requested URL will be checked for authorization, not the physical URL. By doing this, you can place the physical URL in a location that is not directly accessible to the user, which can be useful if you want to prevent direct navigation to that URL.

Default Parameter Values

The default behavior for routes is that all parameters must be specified in order to match the requested URL to a route path. In the preceding example, this means that the following URL is invalid:

```
http://<domain>/path
```

However, you can if you wish specify default values for route parameters, in which case this URL would be valid and the default value for `pathparameter` would be used.

To do this, you supply a `RouteValueDictionary` collection, which is a collection of name/value pairs of route parameters and default values. You can pass this collection to the `Route` constructor; for example:

```
RouteTable.Routes.Add("RouteName",
                new Route("path/{pathparameter}",
                        new RouteValueDictionary
                        {
                            { "pathparameter", "defaultValue" }
                        },
                        new PageRouteHandler("~/target.aspx")));
```

In this code a default value of `defaultvalue` is specified for the `pathparameter` parameter, which will be used if no value is matched in the URL.

Parameter Constraints

Route parameters will accept any value from the user by default, but sometimes you might want to restrict the allowed values. Then, if the user passes a value that isn't allowed, the path will not match.

Parameter constraints are also defined with a `RouteValueDictionary` collection, in this case containing a collection of name/value pairs of route parameters and constraints. A constraint can either be a regular expression or an object that implements the `IRouteConstraint` interface. As with defaults, constraints can be specified in the `Route` constructor, for example:

```
RouteTable.Routes.Add("RouteName",
                new Route("path/{pathparameter}",
                        new RouteValueDictionary
                        {
                            { "pathparameter", "yes" }
                        },
                        new RouteValueDictionary
                        {
                            { "pathparameter", "yes|no" }
                        },
                        new PageRouteHandler("~/target.aspx")));
```

Here, only the values `yes` and `no` are valid values for `pathparameter`. If a different value is specified the route won't be matched.

Route Order and Data Tokens

When you define routes, the order in which you add them to the `RouteTable.Routes` collection is important. This is because ASP.NET will attempt to match URLs to routes in the order that they appear in the collection. If no match is found after looking at all the routes, then the URL is used directly. If a single match is found, then that route is used. If more than one route matches the URL, then the first one is used.

This can be used to good effect in combination with constraints. For example, you could add two routes, the first being the constrained route shown in the previous section, and the second as follows:

```
RouteTable.Routes.Add("RouteName",
                new Route("path/{pathparameter}",
                        new PageRouteHandler("~/alternatetarget.aspx")));
```

This would mean that a URL containing a `pathparameter` value of `yes` or `no` would map to `target` `.aspx` as before, but if any other parameter value was passed, then the URL would map instead to `alternatetarget.aspx`, rather than returning a 404 not found error.

However, if these two routes were added in reverse order, then all values of `pathparameter` would result in a call to `alternatetarget.aspx`, as this route would always provide a match before the constrained route was checked.

If you have two routes that map to the same URL, you may want to determine which route was matched. To do so, you can include additional data that is passed to the page as a data token. Data tokens are supplied with another `RouteValueDictionary` collection, containing a collection of name/value pairs of route parameters and data tokens. For example:

```
RouteTable.Routes.Add("RouteName",
                new Route("path/{pathparameter}",
                      new RouteValueDictionary
                      {
                          { "pathparameter", "yes" }
                      },
                      new RouteValueDictionary
                      {
                          { "pathparameter", "yes|no" }
                      },
                      new RouteValueDictionary
                      {
                          { "customdatatoken", "yesnomatch" }
                      },
                      new PageRouteHandler("~/target.aspx")));
```

If this route is matched a data token called `customdatatoken` with a string value of `yesnomatch` is passed to the target URL, so that pages can identify that this route was used.

You can pass whatever data you like as a data token for a parameter, so this is only one example of how you might use it.

Using Route Parameters

Reading and using parameter values that are passed to pages through ASP.NET routing is very similar to doing the same for query string parameters. Instead of using `Request.QueryString`, you use `Page.RouteData`, which is populated by ASP.NET when your page is loaded. This contains all of the information you need to extract route parameters or data tokens.

Parameter values are also available for use in ASP.NET markup, through expression builders and data query parameter values.

RouteData Values

The route parameters are available in code through the `Page.RouteData.Values` property, which is another instance of the `RouteValueDictionary` class. Similarly, data tokens are available through `Page.RouteData.DataTokens`. In the example web site, values are extracted from the `Values` property and displayed through a `DataGrid` with the following code:

Available for download on Wrox.com

```
if (Page.RouteData.Values.Count == 0)
{
    this.NoRoutingLabel.Text = "None.";
}
else
{
    GridView2.DataSource = from entry in Page.RouteData.Values
                           select
                                new
                                {
                                    Name = entry.Key,
                                    Value = entry.Value
                                };
    GridView2.DataBind();
}
```

code snippet PCSRoutingDemo/MasterPage.master.cs

Alternatively, you can extract parameters by name as they are indexed in the collection; for example:

```
string parameterValue = Page.RouteData.Values["pathparameter"] as string;
```

Expression Builders

There are two expression builders that you can use in ASP.NET markup files to extract and use route parameter values: `RouteValue` and `RouteUrl`.

`RouteValue` can be used inline to output the value of a parameter, as follows:

```
<%$ RouteValue:parameterName %>
```

For example, in the PCSRoutingDemo web site, the `Target.aspx` file includes the following line of markup code:

```
targetparameter = <asp:Label runat="server"
                     Text="<%$ RouteValue:targetparameter %>" />
```

code snippet PCSRoutingDemo/Target.aspx

This sets the `Text` property of a `Label` control to the value of the `targetparameter` parameter.

`RouteUrl` is used to construct URLs to match a route. This is a great feature when you are putting links in your ASP.NET code, as a URL created in this way will change if the route definition ever changes. To use this expression builder, you use markup inline as follows:

```
<%$ RouteUrl:parameterName=parameterValue %>
```

You can include more than one parameter by separating name/value pairs with commas. The expression builder will attempt to match the parameters you specify to a route by the names of the parameters you use. In some cases, you might have more than one route that uses the same parameters, in which case you can identify the specific route to use by name as follows:

```
<%$ RouteUrl:parameterName=parameterValue,routename=routeName %>
```

In PCSRoutingDemo, there are two separate links in the master page, one of which uses this expression builder:

```
<asp:HyperLink ID="HyperLink3" runat="server" NavigateUrl="~/Target/Trevor"
  >Navigation with routing</asp:HyperLink>

<asp:HyperLink ID="HyperLink4" runat="server"
  NavigateUrl="<%$ RouteUrl:targetparameter=Reginald,routename=TestRoute %>"
  >Navigation with routing and expression builder</asp:HyperLink>
```

code snippet PCSRoutingDemo/MasterPage.master

The second version of this link shows the best way to include links in your markup, as it allows you to change the route specification later, as noted above.

Data Query Parameters

Another way to use route parameters in your code is to supply them directly to data queries. This technique enables you to fetch data from a database directly from markup code, rather than having to extract parameter values and use them in the code-behind.

To do this, you use an `<asp:routeparameter>` in the parameters for a query. For example, you could use the following in an `<asp:sqldatasource>` data source:

```
<asp:sqldatasource id="SqlDataSource1" runat="server"
    connectionstring="<%$ ConnectionStrings:ProductDatabase %>"
    selectcommand="SELECT ProductName,ProductId,ProductDescription FROM Products
             WHERE ProductName = @productname"
  <selectparameters>
    <asp:routeparameter name="productname" RouteKey="productnameparameter" />
  </selectparameters>
</asp:sqldatasource>
```

This code extracts the value from a route parameter called `productnameparameter` and passes this value to the `@productname` parameter in a SQL query.

DYNAMIC DATA

If you think about data-driven web sites (which these days includes most web sites), you will probably realize that a lot of their functionality is very similar. Such a web site is likely to include one or more of the following concepts:

➤ Render HTML that is shaped dynamically based on data in an underlying data source (such as a database table or individual database row)

➤ Include pages in a site map that map directly or indirectly to entries in a data source (such as a database table)

➤ Have a structure that relates directly or indirectly to the structure of the underlying data source (a section of the site may map to a database table, such as About or Products, for example)

➤ Allow modification to the underlying data source that will be reflected on pages

If you wanted to build a data-driven site, you would probably use fairly standardized code to achieve the above. You might bind ASP.NET elements such as tables of data directly to a database table, or you might include an intermediate layer of data objects to represent data in the database and bind to those. You have seen a lot of the code you would use for that in earlier chapters.

However, because this situation is so common, there is an alternative. You could instead use a framework that provides a lot of the code for you to save yourself a lot of tedious coding. ASP.NET dynamic data is just such a framework, and it makes creating a data-driven web site much easier. As well as giving you the code outlined above (referred to in dynamic data web sites as *scaffolding*), dynamic data web sites provide a lot of additional functionality, as you will see shortly.

In this section, you will see how to create a dynamic data site and look at some of the features that it offers.

Creating Dynamic Data Web Sites

The best way to get a taste of what dynamic data web sites have to offer is to build one in Visual Studio, which is a surprisingly simple thing to do. In order to create a dynamic data web site you need to have some source data. You can use whatever data you like, but if you want you can use the sample data that is included in the downloadable code for this chapter. This data is a SQL Server Express database with the filename `MagicShop .mdf`. Figure 42-3 shows the tables that are included in this database.

The `MagicShop.mdf` database represents a simple structure that you could use in an e-commerce web site. The types of and relationships between data will serve to illustrate how dynamic data sites work.

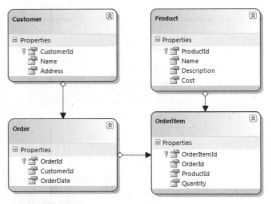

FIGURE 42-3

Choosing a Data Access Model

When you create a dynamic data site through the File ➪ New ➪ Web Site... menu item, you will notice that there are two templates available:

➤ Dynamic Data Linq to SQL Web Site

➤ Dynamic Data Entities Web Site

These two templates are identical, apart from the way your data will be accessed: through LINQ to SQL or the ADO.NET Entity Framework, respectively. Which of these templates you choose depends entirely on personal preference. The core functionality of a dynamic data web site is the same for both templates.

The downloadable code for this chapter includes two web sites, PCSDynamicDataDemoLinq and PCSDynamic DataDemoEntities, that contain uncustomized versions of sites that use the MagicShop.mdf database.

Adding a Data Source

Once you have created a site using either of the templates that are available, the next thing to do is to add a data source. This means adding a new item to your project, using either the LINQ to SQL classes or ADO.NET Entity Model template (either of which should be added to the App_Code directory of a web site as a best practice). Before you do that, you may also want to add a local copy of your database to the App_Data directory of your web site, unless you are using a remote data source.

If you are using the MagicShop.mdf database as a test, then depending on the site template you are using, you can do the following (after adding the database to the App_Data directory):

➤ For LINQ to SQL, add LINQ to SQL classes with the filename MagicShop.dbml, and then once the file is added, add all tables from the MagicShop.mdf database to the designer.

➤ For ADO.NET Entities, add an entity model called MagicShop.edmx, and in the Add New Item Wizard, use the default settings and add entities for all tables in the database.

Configuring Scaffolding

There is one more step to perform before the initial build of your dynamic data web site is complete. You must configure your data model for scaffolding in the Global.asax file for the web site. Apart from differences in explanatory comments, this file is identical in both site template types. If you inspect the file, you will see that scaffolding for the web site is configured through a model, which is defined at the application level as follows:

```
private static MetaModel s_defaultModel = new MetaModel();
public static MetaModel DefaultModel
{
    get
    {
        return s_defaultModel;
    }
}
```

The Global.asax file accesses this model in the RegisterRoutes() method, called in the Application_ Start() handler. This method also configures dynamic data routing in the web site, which you'll look at later in this chapter. The method contains the following commented-out line of code (split over two lines here for clarity):

```
//DefaultModel.RegisterContext(typeof(YourDataContextType),
//    new ContextConfiguration() { ScaffoldAllTables = false });
```

Configuring the model simply requires you to uncomment this code and supply the appropriate data context type for your data model. You can also change the ScaffoldAllTables property to true initially to instruct the model to provide scaffolding for all available tables. Later, you may want to revert this change, as you will probably want a finer degree of control over exactly what scaffolding is created (including what data is visible in the site, what is editable, and so on), as you will see later in this chapter.

The following code is required for a LINQ to SQL site accessing the MagicShop.mdf database with the LINQ to SQL classes as described in the previous section:

```
DefaultModel.RegisterContext(typeof(MagicShopDataContext),
    new ContextConfiguration() { ScaffoldAllTables = true });
```

Available for download on Wrox.com

code snippet PCSDynamicDataDemoLinq/Global.asax

For the ADO.NET Entities version of this site, the code is as follows:

```
DefaultModel.RegisterContext(typeof(MagicShopModel.MagicShopEntities),
    new ContextConfiguration() { ScaffoldAllTables = true });
```

code snippet PCSDynamicDataDemoEntities/Global.asax

Exploring the Result

At this point, everything is in place to test the default dynamic data web sites. The end result is identical regardless of which template you use. If you look at `Default.aspx` in a browser, the display appears as shown in Figure 42-4.

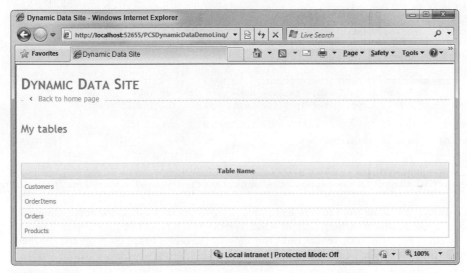

FIGURE 42-4

This page shows a list of links to each of the tables in the database along with some additional information, defined in the `Default.aspx` page as follows:

```
<%@ Page Language="C#" MasterPageFile="~/Site.master" CodeFile="Default.aspx.cs"
        Inherits="_Default" %>

<asp:Content ID="headContent" ContentPlaceHolderID="head" Runat="Server">
</asp:Content>

<asp:Content ID="Content1" ContentPlaceHolderID="ContentPlaceHolder1"
  Runat="Server">
  <asp:ScriptManagerProxy ID="ScriptManagerProxy1" runat="server" />

  <h2 class="DDSubHeader">My tables</h2>

  <br /><br />

  <asp:GridView ID="Menu1" runat="server" AutoGenerateColumns="false"
    CssClass="DDGridView" RowStyle-CssClass="td" HeaderStyle-CssClass="th"
    CellPadding="6">
    <Columns>
      <asp:TemplateField HeaderText="Table Name" SortExpression="TableName">
        <ItemTemplate>
          <asp:DynamicHyperLink ID="HyperLink1" runat="server"><%#
            Eval("DisplayName") %></asp:DynamicHyperLink>
```

```
          </ItemTemplate>
        </asp:TemplateField>
      </Columns>
    </asp:GridView>
  </asp:Content>
```

code snippet PCSDynamicDataDemoEntities/Default.aspx and PCSDynamicDataDemoLinq/Default.aspx

A lot of the display code is contained in the master page and the CSS file for the web site, which won't be listed here to save space. The important section of the preceding code is the `GridView` control, which contains a `DynamicHyperLink` control that renders the link to a table. Data is bound to the `GridView` control from code-behind as follows (reformatted slightly for clarity):

```
protected void Page_Load(object sender, EventArgs e)
{
    System.Collections.IList visibleTables =
        ASP.global_asax.DefaultModel.VisibleTables;
    if (visibleTables.Count == 0)
    {
        throw new InvalidOperationException(
            "There are no accessible tables. Make sure that at least one data"
            + " model is registered in Global.asax and scaffolding is enabled"
            + " or implement custom pages.");
    }
    Menu1.DataSource = visibleTables;
    Menu1.DataBind();
}
```

code snippets PCSDynamicDataDemoEntities/Default.aspx.cs and PCSDynamicDataDemoLinq/Default.aspx.cs

This extracts the list of visible tables from the model (in this case, all the tables, because scaffolding is provided for all of them as discussed earlier), each of which is described by a `MetaTable` object. The `DynamicHyperLink` controls intelligently render links to pages for the tables based on properties of these objects. For example, the link for the Customers table is as follows:

```
/PCSDynamicDataDemoLinq/Customers/List.aspx
```

Obviously, the web site has no such page defined; instead, routing is used as described in the first part of this chapter to generate content for this link. If you click on the link, you'll see a listing page for the Customers table, as shown in Figure 42-5.

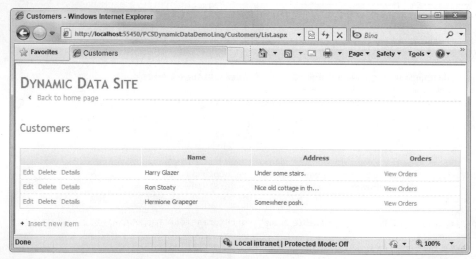

FIGURE 42-5

This page is generated from templates, which are stored in the code for the site and are discussed in the next section. You can use the links on this page to inspect, edit, insert, and delete records, as well as to traverse associations between tables. The View Orders link for each customer will display any orders for that particular customer — on a page that includes a drop-down list of customers that you can use to view orders for different customers if you want to.

If you click on Edit for a customer, you will see an edit customer view as shown in Figure 42-6.

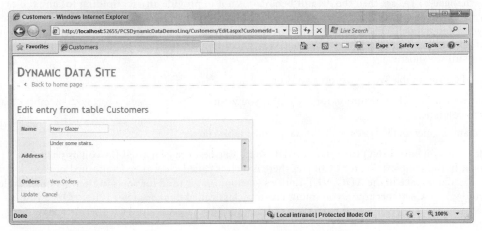

FIGURE 42-6

The template system used by a dynamic data web site enables you to customize what is shown for each column in a table according to what data type it is. Or you can make further customizations that are unique to columns that you specify; you really do have a lot of flexibility here.

> *The ID values used in the* `MagicShop.mdf` *database are stored as integer values. It is also common for databases to use GUID ID values (using the* `uniqueidentifier` *SQL type). These are currently not handled perfectly by dynamic data web sites and, although workarounds are possible, there is currently no ideal solution.*

What you have seen in this section is that, even with the default settings, dynamic data can get you up and running very quickly. Now, you may think that this ease of use comes at a cost, namely flexibility. In fact, this is not the case. Using some very simple techniques, you can completely customize how dynamic data web sites work, as you will see in the next section.

Customizing Dynamic Data Web Sites

There are a number of ways in which you can customize dynamic data web sites to get exactly the effect you want. These range from simply modifying the HTML and CSS for the templates to customizing the way in which data is rendered though code and attribute modifications. In this section, you'll look at a few of these, starting with how to customize scaffolding — which, among other things, can affect the visibility of primary key values as noted in the previous section.

Controlling Scaffolding

In the sample dynamic data web sites you have seen so far in this chapter, scaffolding was configured automatically for all tables (and all columns of those tables). This was achieved by setting the

`ScaffoldAllTables` property of the `ContextConfiguration` for the sites to `true`, as illustrated in this code for the LINQ to SQL site:

```
DefaultModel.RegisterContext(typeof(MagicShopDataContext),
    new ContextConfiguration() { ScaffoldAllTables = true });
```

code snippet PCSDynamicDataDemoLinq/Global.asax

If the value is changed to `false`, then the default behavior is not to provide any scaffolding for any tables or columns. In order to instruct the dynamic data framework to scaffold a table of column, you must provide metadata in your data model. This metadata will then be read by the dynamic data runtime, and scaffolding will be generated for you. Metadata can also provide information for other things — such as validation logic — as you will see shortly.

To supply metadata for a table, you must do two things:

➤ Create a metadata class definition for each table you want to supply metadata for, with members that map to columns.

➤ Associate the metadata classes with the data model table classes.

All data model items, in both LINQ to SQL and ADO.NET Entities, are generated for you as partial class definitions. In the sample code, for example, there is a class called `Customer` (contained in the `MagicShopModel` namespace in the ADO.NET Entities version) that is used for rows in the Customer table. To supply metadata for Customer rows, you might create a class called `CustomerMetadata`. Once you have done that, you can supply a second partial class definition for `Customer` and use the `MetadataType` attribute to link the classes together.

In the .NET Framework, metadata is supported through *data annotations*. As such it should come as no surprise that the `MetadataType` attribute, along with other metadata attributes, is found in the `System.ComponentModel.DataAnnotations` namespace. The `MetadataType` attribute uses a `Type` parameter to specify the metadata type. The two attributes that control scaffolding are `ScaffoldTable` and `ScaffoldColumn`. Both of these attributes have a Boolean parameter to specify whether scaffolding will be generated for a table or column.

The following code shows an example of how this is achieved:

```
using System.ComponentModel.DataAnnotations;

...

[MetadataType(typeof(CustomerMetadata))]
public partial class Customer { }
```

code snippets PCSDynamicDataDemoEntities/App_Code/Customer.cs and PCSDynamicDataDemoLinq/App_Code/Customer.cs

```
using System.ComponentModel.DataAnnotations;

...

[ScaffoldTable(true)]
public class CustomerMetadata
{
    [ScaffoldColumn(false)]
    public object Address { get; set; }
}
```

code snippets PCSDynamicDataDemoEntities/App_Code/CustomerMetadata.cs and PCSDynamicDataDemoLinq/App_Code/CustomerMetadata.cs

Here, the `ScaffoldTable` attribute specifies that scaffolding will be generated for the Customer table, and the `ScaffoldColumn` attribute is used to ensure that the `Address` column will have no scaffolding. Note that columns are represented by object type properties, regardless of the type. You just have to ensure that the name of the property matches the name of the column.

The code shown here can be used with the example web sites introduced in the previous section to hide the addresses of customers.

Customizing Templates

As mentioned earlier in the chapter, dynamic data is generated through a system of templates. There are page templates that are used for laying out controls within different types of list and details pages, and field templates for displaying different data types in display, edit, and foreign key selection modes.

All of these templates are located in the DynamicData subfolder of a dynamic data web site, which has the nested subfolders described in the following table.

Dynamic Data Template Directories

DIRECTORY	DESCRIPTION
Content	This folder contains images that are used in other templates as well as the template for pagination (which is applied automatically when lists of data are long).
CustomPages	Use this directory if you want to supply custom pages.
EntityTemplates	This directory contains user control templates that are used for displaying a single row of data on a page, in either view, edit, or insert mode.
FieldTemplates	This directory contains user control templates that are used to display individual column data.
Filters	This directory contains user control templates that are used to display filters for foreign key relationships. In the default code, these are drop-down lists. For example, the list page for Orders includes a filter to display only those orders that are associated with a particular user.
PageTemplates	This directory contains the main templates that are used to display single or multiple rows of data in various modes of operation. The body of these pages uses the user control templates from the other directories to build its content.

It is worth digging into these templates and their code-behind to see how everything fits together. For example, text columns are displayed using two field templates in the FieldTemplates directory. The first of these, Text.ascx, is as follows:

```
<asp:Literal runat="server" ID="Literal1" Text="<%# FieldValueString %>" />
```

This code is fairly self-explanatory — it simply outputs the text value of a column in a Literal control. If, though, the column is in an editable mode, Text_Edit.ascx is used instead:

```
<asp:TextBox ID="TextBox1" runat="server" Text='<%# FieldValueEditString %>'
  CssClass="DDTextBox"></asp:TextBox>

<asp:RequiredFieldValidator runat="server" ID="RequiredFieldValidator1"
  CssClass="DDControl" ControlToValidate="TextBox1" Display="Dynamic"
  Enabled="false" />
<asp:RegularExpressionValidator runat="server" ID="RegularExpressionValidator1"
  CssClass="DDControl" ControlToValidate="TextBox1" Display="Dynamic"
  Enabled="false" />
<asp:DynamicValidator runat="server" ID="DynamicValidator1" CssClass="DDControl"
  ControlToValidate="TextBox1" Display="Dynamic" />
```

A TextBox control is used here to render the control so that it is editable, and a combination of the three validation controls is used to provide validation functionality if required. Exactly how these validation controls work is determined by the data model and its associated metadata. Non-nullable columns, for example, will result in the RequiredFieldValidator being active. The DynamicValidator control is used in conjunction with metadata attributes, for example, StringLength, which you can use to set the maximum permitted length of a string.

Configuring Routing

One of the most important concepts to grasp when dealing with dynamic data sites is that pages are generated according to *actions*. An action is a way of defining what a page should do in response to, for example, the user clicking on a particular link. There are four page actions that are defined for you by default: List, Details, Edit, and Insert.

Each of the page templates defined for a dynamic data site (which are also known as *views*) can function differently according to what action is currently being performed. The routing configuration for the web site associates actions with views, and each route can optionally be constrained by the tables that it should apply to. For example, you might create a new view that is intended for listing customers. That view might function differently from the default List.aspx view. To create the new view, you must configure routing so that the correct view will be used.

The default routing for a dynamic data web site is configured in Global.asax as follows:

```
routes.Add(new DynamicDataRoute("{table}/{action}.aspx")
{
    Constraints = new RouteValueDictionary(
        new { action = "List|Details|Edit|Insert" }),
    Model = DefaultModel
});
```

code snippet PCSDynamicDataDemoEntities/Global.asax and PCSDynamicDataDemoLinq/Global.asax

This uses the routing framework described earlier in the chapter, although here routes use the DynamicDataRoute type. This class derives from Route and provides specialized functionality for dealing with actions, views, and tables.

You will notice in this code that this route includes the name of a table and the name of an action — where the value of the action is constrained to the four predefined page action types. To take the example of using a different view for listing customers, you might add the following route (before the existing one, or that one would take precedence):

```
routes.Add(new DynamicDataRoute("Customers/List.aspx")
{
    Table = "Customers",
    Action = PageAction.List,
    ViewName = "ListCustomers",
    Model = DefaultModel
});
```

This route associates the /Customers/List.aspx URL with the view ListCustomers.aspx, and so for this code to work, you must supply a file of this name in the PageTemplates directory. You can also see that the Table and Action properties are specified here, as they are not available in the URL any more. The way the dynamic data routing works is that {table} and {action} routing parameters are used to populate the Table and Action properties, and in this URL these parameters are not present.

You can build up as complex a system of routing as you wish in this manner, providing specialized pages for tables and actions as you see fit. You can also make use of the ListDetails.aspx view, which is a master-detail view of data that enables row selection and inline editing. To use this view, you can supply alternative routes, or simply uncomment the following routes that the dynamic data site template provides:

```
//routes.Add(new DynamicDataRoute("{table}/ListDetails.aspx")
//{
//    Action = PageAction.List,
//    ViewName = "ListDetails",
//    Model = DefaultModel
//});
```

```
//routes.Add(new DynamicDataRoute("{table}/ListDetails.aspx")
//{
//    Action = PageAction.Details,
//    ViewName = "ListDetails",
//    Model = DefaultModel
//});
```

These routes will cause the `ListDetails.aspx` view to be used whenever the List or Details page actions are used. The Edit and Insert page actions are then not required, since (as mentioned earlier) editing capabilities are provided inline. An example of this is shown in Figure 42-7.

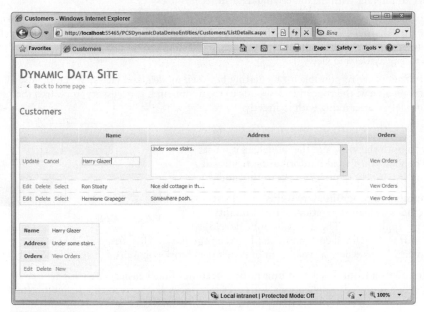

FIGURE 42-7

Further Development

This section has really only scratched the surface of what is possible with dynamic data. By combining custom code with the framework provided, you will find that the possibilities are vast. Having the framework in place can drastically reduce the work you have to do to access data, while leaving you free to concentrate on the rest of your web site. There are many resources available that dig much deeper into what is possible, but hopefully this section has given you enough information to make a start and explained what the benefits and possibilities are.

MVC

As web site development continues to evolve, new and exciting ways to do things continually appear. One of the most recent (and most exciting) developments is the Model-View-Controller architectural pattern for web sites. This is not a new pattern — in fact the concept is at least 30 years old. However, it hasn't been used in web sites for very long, and (more importantly in the context of this chapter) has only been integrated with the .NET Framework with .NET 4. The version included in .NET 4 is ASP.NET MVC 2, a name that alludes to the fact that ASP.NET MVC has been around for a little while, although it was a separate download before .NET 4.

Before looking at the ASP.NET-specific implementation of MVC, though, it's worth taking a step back to describe what MVC actually means, and why it is useful. In this section you will look at:

➤ What MVC is

➤ What ASP.NET MVC is

➤ How to build and customize ASP.NET MVC-based web sites

What Is MVC?

MVC is a way of programming that involves breaking your code into three distinct parts: models, views, and controllers. This is not a web-specific idea, and can be applied to any system that involves user interaction. The definition of these terms is as follows:

➤ **Model** — A *model* refers to code that represents the data or state of an application. Note that this doesn't include data storage, which if included is the job of, for example, a database. However, it does encapsulate all manipulation of data, including business logic such as validation rules. It also includes the code necessary to interact with the underlying data store, if one exists.

➤ **View** — A *view* is the user interface that exposes the model to the user and allows the user to perform operations on the model. There is not necessarily a one-to-one relationship between views and models; a given model may be visualized through multiple views. Any changes to models should be reflected through changes in any associated views.

➤ **Controller** — *Controllers* are responsible for mediating between models and views. When the user performs an action on a view, the controller responds to the action and, if necessary, forwards the action on to the model by interacting with it directly.

The relationship between these three parts are shown in Figure 42-8.

The controller has access to both the view and the model, as it must mediate between them. The view must render information from and reflect changes in the model, so it also requires access to the model.

There are numerous advantages to programming in this way. First, and most obviously, it provides a clean separation of functionality between distinct units of an application. These may even be developed independently, assuming that well-defined contracts exist between the parts. This means that MVC applications are perfect in situations where a large team of developers works on a project simultaneously.

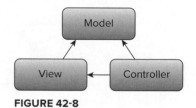

FIGURE 42-8

Another advantage that follows on from this is that unit testing becomes much easier, as each part can be unit tested independently when required. Applications with user interfaces are notoriously difficult to test, as it is often difficult or impossible to design tests that precisely mimic what a user will do, and automation of a user interface can be a major challenge. Since MVC defines exactly what actions a user may perform via controllers, you can be sure that if those controllers are tested adequately you won't run into any surprises. After all, the view can only interact with the controller in the same way as any other client code can interact with the controller, including test code.

The main disadvantage of MVC is that there is an increase in complexity and, potentially, more code to be written. For small-scale applications, this may not be desirable, and it certainly will increase development time. It may also make it more difficult to make use of all the features provided by the overarching technology being used for the application. For example, when this technology is used with ASP.NET, as you will see, event-based user interaction and view state are not usable.

What Is ASP.NET MVC?

ASP.NET MVC applies the principles of MVC to the ASP.NET development environment. This means that ASP.NET pages and controls are used as views, .NET classes are used for controllers, and a data framework such as LINQ to SQL or the ADO.NET Entity Framework is used for the model.

You could, if you wanted, stop reading right now and start writing MVC web sites using ASP.NET. However, what is particularly exciting with .NET 4 is that a full implementation of the MVC pattern is included for you, with plenty of supporting classes that handle a lot of the plumbing (to connect things) and scaffolding (to reduce repetitive or boilerplate code) for you. This is the ASP.NET MVC 2 Framework.

The best way to see what is on offer here is to dive straight in and build an application (or inspect the version in the downloadable code for this chapter).

A Simple ASP.NET MVC Application

In this section, you will build an ASP.NET MVC application using the `MagicShop.mdf` database introduced earlier in this chapter. Along the way, you will walk through the code responsible for models, views, and controllers and see how it all fits together, before adding some additional customizations.

Creating the Application

To get started, create a new project in Visual Studio via the File ⇨ New ⇨ Project . . . menu item. Select the ASP.NET MVC 2 Web Application template, call the project PCSMVCMagicShop, and save it in the `C:\ProCSharp\Chapter42` directory. You will be prompted as to whether to create a unit test application at the same time, but for now deselect that option (unit testing is beyond the scope of this chapter).

 Note that there is no template for ASP.NET MVC if you use the File ⇨ New ⇨ Web Site ... menu item. ASP.NET MVC applications must be web applications, not web sites, as they require sites to be fully compiled before deployment in order to work. This is because of the interconnectedness of the modules that make up an ASP.NET MVC application and the way in which views are dynamically generated.

Inspecting the Application

When the wizard has completed, you will notice that a fair number of directories and files have been created for you. These are described in the following table.

ITEM	DESCRIPTION
Content directory	This directory, like the Content directory for a dynamic data web site, is intended for images and other miscellaneous resources that are used by the application. Initially, it contains the CSS file used by the web application, `Site.css`.
Controllers directory	This directory contains the controller classes used by the site. The template includes two controllers to get you started, `HomeController` and `AccountController`.
Models directory	This directory, initially empty, is where you should put your models. For example, you could add LINQ to SQL classes, ADO.NET Entity Framework classes, or whatever custom classes you see fit here.
Scripts directory	This directory contains any script files, such as JavaScript files, used by the application. You will find a fair amount of JavaScript files here by default, including those required for the Microsoft jquery and AJAX libraries.
Views directory	This directory contains the views for the application, which are ASP.NET Web Forms and user controls. Each controller has its own views subdirectory, so you will see content in Home and Account directories by default. You will also see a Shared directory that includes general purpose views and master pages, including `Site .Master`, which is the default master page for the site. There is also a `Web.config` file in this directory, which is configured to prevent direct access to the view files.
Global.asax	The `Global.asax` file (and its code-behind file) included in the application root sets up routing as described earlier in this chapter. ASP.NET MVC defines extension methods on the `RouteCollection` class to make it easier to add routes in the way it requires.
Web.config	This configuration file references all of the additional resources required by ASP.NET MVC, including the required assemblies. It also configures the HTTP handler that is used to dynamically generate views according to the routing path requested, and (due to the project template) configures forms-based authentication.

At this point, you can run the application and see what's there. There's a perfectly functional home page with an About page and a registration/log on system. However, it's easier to learn about how everything works if you work through modifying what is there.

Adding a Model

The order in which you add model, view, and controller code will vary according to what you want to achieve. Typically, though, you will start with a model, particularly if you want to access data in a database. By starting with a model, you then have access to strongly typed model classes from the outset, and the ASP .NET MVC wizards will be able to use the model type information to automatically generate a lot of the scaffolding code you require.

In this example, you will use the `MagicShop.mdf` database introduced earlier in the chapter. Because the sample code is a web application rather than a web site, you cannot simply copy this file to the App_Data directory. Instead, you must add it to the App_Data directory by right-clicking on the directory and selecting the Add ➪ Existing Item . . . menu item, then browsing to the database file and clicking Add. Or, if you prefer, you can build a database in place through Visual Studio, connect to a different database, or select an entirely different data source.

Once you have a data source in place, you can add a model using whatever technique you prefer. This includes using LINQ to SQL classes, an ADO.NET Entity Data Model, or custom classes that you design from scratch. Whichever method you use, you should place the code in the Models folder of the application. For simplicity, add an ADO.NET Entity Data Model with the name `MagicShop` by right-clicking on the Models directory and selecting the Add ➪ New Item . . . menu item. This template is located in the Data templates section. Since a data source exists, most of the default settings in the wizard will already be configured for you, so all you have to do is to select the tables to model (all of them).

After adding your model code, you must build the solution before proceeding in order to make the subsequent wizards aware of your new code.

Adding a Controller

To add a controller for your new model, you use the ASP .NET MVC Add Controller Wizard. You access this wizard by right-clicking on the Controllers folder and selecting the Add New Controller menu item.

Add a controller for the products in the MagicShop database with the name ProductsController, as shown in Figure 42-9, ensuring that the check box is checked as shown.

FIGURE 42-9

The controller that is added contains several methods, each of which returns an `ActionResult`. These methods encapsulate operations that users (or other code) can perform, and each is exposed through a URL through routing (see the section "URL Operation Routing" for more details). The methods added by the wizard are shown in the following table.

METHOD	DESCRIPTION
Index()	This is the default operation for the controller, which views will use if no other method is specified; for example, when a view is first displayed. For the products controller, you want this to display a list of products.
Create()	There are two methods added for creating new items. The first, which takes no parameters, is used when a request to add a new item is triggered, perhaps with an "Add new item" link. The second is responsible for actually adding an item.
Details()	This method is responsible for displaying a detail view of a single item.
Edit()	The two edit methods are similar to the two create methods. The first takes a single ID value and will trigger editing for a specific, existing item. The second takes an ID and a second parameter that specifies the values to change.

Note that none of the methods that are added for you are implemented. Implementation is your responsibility, and you will see how this is done in subsequent sections.

Adding an Index Operation

The simplest controller method to implement is the `Index()` method. All this method needs to do is to return a view based on a collection of items. This requires a reference to the model in the code, and code to obtain and return the view, as follows:

```csharp
using PCSMVCMagicShop.Models;

namespace PCSMVCMagicShop.Controllers
{
    public class ProductsController : Controller
    {
        private MagicShopEntities entities = new MagicShopEntities();

        public ActionResult Index()
        {
            return View(entities.Products.ToList());
        }

        ...
    }
}
```

code snippet PCSMVCMagicShop/Controllers/ProductsController.cs

What this code is doing is instructing the ASP.NET MVC framework to construct a view for a collection of `Product` items, or, more specifically, for an `IEnumerable<Product>` instance. In order for this to work, you have to create a suitable view.

Adding a Products View

Luckily, adding a view isn't nearly as tricky as it might sound. In fact, ASP.NET MVC includes a wizard that is capable of creating many simple views for you.

To use this wizard, you right-click on the method that returns the view and select Add View from the context menu, as shown in Figure 42-10.

This brings up the Add View Wizard, which you should customize for the view you want to add. In this case, you can leave the View name with the default value of Index, but you should select a strongly typed view for the data model class type, and change the View content to List, as shown in Figure 42-11.

```csharp
public class ProductsController : Controller
{
    private MagicShopEntities entities = new MagicShopEntities();
    //
    // GET: /Products/

    public ActionResult Index()
    {
        return View(entities.Products.ToList());
    }
    //
    // GET: /Prod
```

Add View...	Ctrl+M, Ctrl+V
Go To View	Ctrl+M, Ctrl+G
Refactor	►
Organize Usings	►

FIGURE 42-10

FIGURE 42-11

This wizard adds a new folder to the Views folder called Products and a Web Form called Index.aspx. The code added to the view is as follows:

```
<%@ Page Title="" Language="C#" MasterPageFile="~/Views/Shared/Site.Master"
  Inherits="System.Web.Mvc.ViewPage<IEnumerable<PCSMVCMagicShop.Models.Product>>" %>

<asp:Content ID="Content1" ContentPlaceHolderID="TitleContent" runat="server">
  Index
</asp:Content>
<asp:Content ID="Content2" ContentPlaceHolderID="MainContent" runat="server">
  <h2>
    Index</h2>
  <table>
    <tr>
      <th>
      </th>
      <th>
        ProductId
      </th>
      <th>
        Name
      </th>
      <th>
        Description
      </th>
      <th>
        Cost
      </th>
    </tr>
    <% foreach (var item in Model)
       { %>
    <tr>
      <td>
        <%= Html.ActionLink("Edit", "Edit", new { id=item.ProductId }) %>
        |
        <%= Html.ActionLink("Details", "Details", new { id=item.ProductId })%>
      </td>
      <td>
        <%= Html.Encode(item.ProductId) %>
      </td>
      <td>
        <%= Html.Encode(item.Name) %>
      </td>
      <td>
        <%= Html.Encode(item.Description) %>
      </td>
      <td>
        <%= Html.Encode(String.Format("{0:F}", item.Cost)) %>
      </td>
    </tr>
    <% } %>
  </table>
  <p>
    <%= Html.ActionLink("Create New", "Create") %>
  </p>
</asp:Content>
```

code snippet PCSMVCMagicShop/Views/Products/Index.aspx

There is no code-behind file for this view; instead, it inherits the ASP.NET MVC generic base class `ViewPage<>`, located in the `System.Web.Mvc` namespace. The generic parameter used is, as you might have guessed, `IEnumerable<Product>`.

This code is fairly self-explanatory, but some features are worthy of mention. First, note that the Web Form uses the site master page, and that the content regions are populated for you. Next, notice that the ASP.NET MVC framework has used the model type information to intelligently populate the view according to the properties available, including a looping structure to output information for multiple items. Finally, note that several helper methods are used to output model information and to add action links. An action link is a link that calls a controller method by navigating to an appropriate URL (more on this in the "URL Operation Routing" section).

You are free to edit this view as you see fit. For example, in this application you don't really need to expose the `ProductId` values, so you can remove the following sections:

```
<th>
   ProductId
</th>
```

and:

```
<td>
   <%= Html.Encode(item.ProductId) %>
</td>
```

Don't worry, this won't break anything.

Testing View Products Functionality

Now it's time to test that things are working. Build the application and run it (enabling debugging when prompted). You haven't yet added any code to provide a link to the new view, but that's not a problem as all of the plumbing is in place. When you see the home page, manually edit the URL by adding `Products` to the end and navigate to the page. The display should be updated as shown in Figure 42-12.

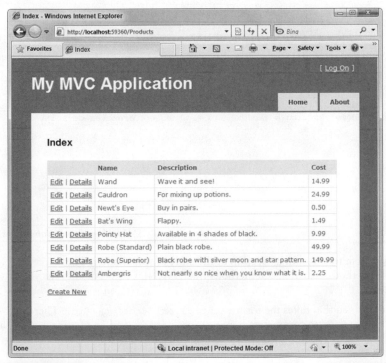

FIGURE 42-12

Our list view is now implemented, with a minimum of effort.

Note that none of the links provided are yet active. If you try to click on the first Details link, for example, the page will navigate to `http://localhost:59360/Products/Details/1` and receive the following error message:

```
The view 'Details' or its master was not found. The following locations were searched:
~/Views/Products/Details.aspx
~/Views/Products/Details.ascx
~/Views/Shared/Details.aspx
~/Views/Shared/Details.ascx
```

What is happening here is that the view exposes a URL that maps to the `Details()` method in `ProductsController`, which you haven't yet configured. You can put a breakpoint in this method and refresh the page to confirm this if you like. This method currently returns an `ActionResult` using a call to `View()` with no parameters, which has no associated view defined, hence the error.

Customizing ASP.NET MVC Applications

You now have a functioning ASP.NET MVC application, although you certainly wouldn't call it "fully" functioning. At the moment, you have created a simple list view for products, but as you saw at the end of the previous section, there are other views required in order to make things work properly. Also, navigating to a list of products by manually entering a URL is hardly a good way to navigate through a web site, so that needs fixing, too.

In this section, you will look in a little more detail at how URLs are mapped to controller operations, and then modify the PCSMVCMagicShop web application to add additional functionality for the Products page.

URL Operation Routing

Earlier, it was noted that the `Global.asax` file in your application configures routing. The contents of the code-behind for this file are as follows:

```csharp
public class MvcApplication : System.Web.HttpApplication
{
    public static void RegisterRoutes(RouteCollection routes)
    {
        routes.IgnoreRoute("{resource}.axd/{*pathInfo}");

        routes.MapRoute(
            "Default",                                          // Route name
            "{controller}/{action}/{id}",                       // URL with parameters
            new { controller = "Home", action = "Index", id = "" } // Parameter defaults
        );
    }

    protected void Application_Start()
    {
        RegisterRoutes(RouteTable.Routes);
    }
}
```

code snippet PCSMVCMagicShop/Global.asax.cs

Much of this should look familiar from the "Routing" section at the start of this chapter. The `IgnoreRoute()` and `MapRoute()` methods are extension methods that ASP.NET MVC defines for you to make it easier to customize routes.

You can see a single default route defined that takes the form `{controller}/{action}/{id}`. There are also default values provided for the three route parameters `controller`, `action`, and `id` of `Home`, `Index`, as well as an empty string. For the `/Products` route you entered to get to the products list, these parameters were set to `Products`, `Index`, and an empty string.

At this point, hopefully, things should click into place. Prior to testing you added a controller called `ProductsController`, which had a method called `Index()`, which at the time was described as being the default controller method. Now you can deduce what actually happened when you entered the URL:

1. The routing system interpreted the URL entered and assigned values to `controller`, `action`, and `id` as noted above.
2. ASP.NET MVC searched for — and found — a controller for Products (note that the URL didn't need to be `/ProductsController`, the `Controller` suffix is added automatically).
3. ASP.NET MVC searched for — and, again, found — an action called `Index`, which is the `Index()` method in `ProductsController`.
4. When calling `Index()`, ASP.NET MVC searched for — and, you guessed it, found — a view in the Products view folder capable of displaying a collection of `Product` objects.
5. ASP.NET rendered the view.

Similarly, when you subsequently attempted to view the details for an item, the appropriate method (`Details()`) was located after interpreting the URL route `/Products/Details/1`. The final parameter here was passed to the `Details()` method as an argument, although at this point things fell to pieces a bit as that method is not yet implemented and no view was available.

This routing behavior, and the way that URLs are mapped directly to controller methods, is central to understanding ASP.NET MVC. It means that you have a direct route from a given URL into your code, and what you do in that code is, of course, entirely up to you. The "simple" operations, such as listing products and so on, are therefore just the start of what is possible; you can write any action you can conceive of in the same way.

However, you must also consider other implications of this. You are in effect exposing your code, and the parameters passed to your code, directly to users. This means that defensive coding is essential, as who knows what parameters your methods might receive from people typing URLs manually.

Action Links

Now that you know how URLs are mapped to actions, it's worth looking at how to include links in your application. You could just hard-code a link in your site, for example, the following to get to the Products page you added:

```
<asp:HyperLink runat="server" NavigateUrl="~/Products">Products</asp:HyperLink>
```

However, this link makes assumptions about the site's structure that aren't necessarily permanent. If at some point you were to change the routing specification this link would break.

Earlier in the chapter, you saw how the ASP.NET Routing system allows links to be dynamically generated according to routing parameters. Similarly, ASP.NET MVC allows links to be generated according to the controller, action, and additional values you want to use, as well as the text you want to display. This is achieved through the `Html.ActionLink()` extension method, which has a number of overloads, depending on what you want to achieve.

For example, if you look in the `Site.Master` master page file in the Views\Shared folder, you will see the following code that defines the menu for the site:

**Available for
download on
Wrox.com**

```
<div id="menucontainer">
  <ul id="menu">
    <li><%= Html.ActionLink("Home", "Index", "Home")%></li>
    <li><%= Html.ActionLink("About", "About", "Home")%></li>
  </ul>
</div>
```

code snippet PCSMVCMagicShop/Views/Shared/Site.Master

The overload used here has three string parameters, `linkText`, `actionName`, and `controllerName`. The first parameter specifies the text to display, and the other two specify the action and controller to use. The first of the calls in the previous code snippet, for example, maps to the `Index()` method in the `HomeController` controller class.

When rendered with the default routing settings, these `ActionLink()` calls output the following HTML:

```
<div id="menucontainer">
  <ul id="menu">
    <li><a href="/">Home</a></li>
    <li><a href="/Home/About">About</a></li>
  </ul>
</div>
```

Given what you know about how the URLs map to controller methods, and how the defaults are set up for routing in `Global.asax`, this makes perfect sense. And the beauty is, you don't have to work these links out for yourself or rewrite them if routing changes.

To add a link to the product list page in the same way, add the following code to master page:

```
<div id="menucontainer">
  <ul id="menu">
    <li><%= Html.ActionLink("Home", "Index", "Home")%></li>
    <li><%= Html.ActionLink("About", "About", "Home")%></li>
    <li><%= Html.ActionLink("Products", "Index", "Products")%></li>
  </ul>
</div>
```

code snippet PCSMVCMagicShop/Views/Shared/Site.Master

The various overloads of `ActionLink()` enable you to do other things, such as pass parameters to a controller method. For example, in the product list view you created, the edit item link is rendered with the following code:

```
<%= Html.ActionLink("Edit", "Edit", new { id=item.ProductId }) %>
```

code snippet PCSMVCMagicShop/Views/Products/Index.aspx

This overload uses `linkText`, `actionName`, and `routeValues` parameters (the controller name defaults to the current controller). In this case, a single route value of `id` is used, which maps to the `id` parameter of the `Edit` method in `ProductsController`. This call renders links, as shown in the following example HTML:

```
<a href="/Products/Edit/1">Edit</a>
```

Viewing Items with Details()

The `Details()` action method in `ProductsController` is requested when a user clicks the Details link in the application. This results in the method being executed with the product ID passed as a parameter. All you need to do is to locate the requested product and, if it exists, return a new view, as follows:

```
public ActionResult Details(int id)
{
    var product = (from e in entities.Products
                   where e.ProductId == id
                   select e).FirstOrDefault();

    if (product != null)
    {
        return View(product);
    }
    else
    {
        return RedirectToAction("Index");
    }
}
```

The `RedirectToAction()` method is used if no product is located and does exactly what its name suggests — it redirects the user to another view, in this case the Index view.

To add the new view, right-click on the `Details()` method and, as before, click the Add View . . . menu item. This time, create a strongly typed view for the `Product` class with Details view content, as shown in Figure 42-13.

Now when you run the application, you will be able to navigate to the products list through the Products menu item added in the previous section and view the details for any item, as shown in Figure 42-14.

FIGURE 42-13

FIGURE 42-14

If you manually edit the URL to an ID for a nonexistent product, you will be redirected to the product listing.

Adding Items with Create()

There are two actions associated with creating new items, which are currently defined in code as follows:

Available for
download on
Wrox.com

```
public ActionResult Create()
{
    return View();
}
```

```
        [AcceptVerbs(HttpVerbs.Post)]
        public ActionResult Create(FormCollection collection)
        {
            try
            {
                // TODO: Add insert logic here

                return RedirectToAction("Index");
            }
            catch
            {
                return View();
            }
        }
```

code snippet PCSMVCMagicShop/Controllers/ProductsController.cs

The first of these, which has no parameters, simply redirects to the create view, which you can add in the same way as other views (remembering the View content value to Create in the Add View Wizard). The second is used to actually create a new item in the data source, and you have to implement it yourself.

Note that the second Create() overload includes an AcceptVerbs attribute. This restricts the HTTP verb used to POST, which makes sense as you will typically want to submit more information when creating an item than you could reasonably include in a URL for a GET request.

The view that you created for the first Create() method includes the following auto-generated code:

```
<asp:Content ID="Content2" ContentPlaceHolderID="MainContent" runat="server">
  <h2>
    Create</h2>
  <%= Html.ValidationSummary(
    "Create was unsuccessful. Please correct the errors and try again.") %>
  <% using (Html.BeginForm())
     {%>
<fieldset>
  <legend>Fields</legend>
  <p>
    <label for="ProductId">
      ProductId:</label>
    <%= Html.TextBox("ProductId") %>
    <%= Html.ValidationMessage("ProductId", "*") %>
  </p>
  <p>
    <label for="Name">
      Name:</label>
    <%= Html.TextBox("Name") %>
    <%= Html.ValidationMessage("Name", "*") %>
  </p>
  <p>
    <label for="Description">
      Description:</label>
    <%= Html.TextBox("Description") %>
    <%= Html.ValidationMessage("Description", "*") %>
  </p>
  <p>
    <label for="Cost">
      Cost:</label>
    <%= Html.TextBox("Cost") %>
    <%= Html.ValidationMessage("Cost", "*") %>
  </p>
```

```
        <p>
          <input type="submit" value="Create" />
        </p>
      </fieldset>
    <% } %>
    <div>
      <%=Html.ActionLink("Back to List", "Index") %>
    </div>
</asp:Content>
```

code snippet PCSMVCMagicShop/Views/Products/Create.aspx

Several helper methods are included here to create and edit the form, and again you can see how the data model has been interrogated to extract information for the fields to use and the validation required. The form itself is contained in the following code block:

```
using (Html.BeginForm())
{
    ...
}
```

This helper method creates a form that is submitted using a standard HTML `<input type="submit" />` control, which results in the form values being passed to the action method. You then have access to these values so that you can add a new item.

You can delete the following section of code to remove the text box for the product ID, since this is auto-generated:

```
        <p>
          <label for="ProductId">
            ProductId:</label>
          <%= Html.TextBox("ProductId") %>
          <%= Html.ValidationMessage("ProductId", "*") %>
        </p>
```

The code required to add an item is as follows:

```
        [AcceptVerbs(HttpVerbs.Post)]
        public ActionResult Create([Bind(Exclude = "ProductId")] Product productToCreate)
        {
            try
            {
                if (!ModelState.IsValid)
                {
                    return View();
                }

                entities.AddToProducts(productToCreate);
                entities.SaveChanges();
                return RedirectToAction("Index");
            }
            catch
            {
                return View();
            }
        }
```

code snippet PCSMVCMagicShop/Controllers/ProductsController.cs

There are several points to note about this code. First, note that you can change the method signature to accept a strongly-typed `Product` value. This is easier than working through a collection of form values, but to facilitate it you need to exclude the `ProductId` field, since it won't be passed. The `Bind` attribute achieves this.

Next, note that a property called `ModelState.IsValid` is used to check that the model passed to the method is valid, and if not the method simply returns the create view with no parameters. If this happens, the validation summary and validation errors will be displayed, as shown in Figure 42-15.

FIGURE 42-15

If there are no errors, the new item is added through the ADO.NET Entity Framework-defined `AddToProducts()` method, and the page redirects to the list view as follows:

```
entities.AddToProducts(productToCreate);
entities.SaveChanges();
return RedirectToAction("Index");
```

An important point to note here is that the validation can be controlled through data annotations, introduced earlier in the chapter. Most of the default validation comes automatically from the constraints on data in the database, but you may want to modify this behavior. For example, you could limit the number of characters for a product name with the following two classes:

```
using System.ComponentModel.DataAnnotations;

namespace PCSMVCMagicShop.Models
{
    [MetadataType(typeof(ProductMetadata))]
    public partial class Product
    {
    }
}
```

code snippet PCSMVCMagicShop/Models/Product.cs

```
using System.ComponentModel.DataAnnotations;

namespace PCSMVCMagicShop.Models
{
    public class ProductMetadata
    {
        [StringLength(20)]
        public object Name { get; set; }
    }
}
```

code snippet PCSMVCMagicShop/Models/ProductMetadata.cs

This will validate the data, as shown in Figure 42-16.

Obviously the code you need to use in the controller comes down to the model you are using, and this option may not always be available, but it can be very useful in the right circumstances.

You will also probably want to edit the view created to provide more meaningful text, but the

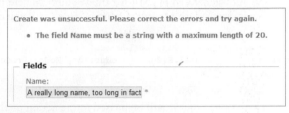

FIGURE 42-16

skeleton created is suitable for most needs. In this example, you'd probably want to change the form's title and validation messages, as well as providing a bit more space for the item description.

Editing Items with Edit()

Editing items uses very similar code to creating new items. Rather than working through how to do this, let's just take a look at the code in the controller:

```
public ActionResult Edit(int id)
{
    var productToEdit = (from p in entities.Products
                         where p.ProductId == id
                         select p).First();

    return View(productToEdit);
}


[AcceptVerbs(HttpVerbs.Post)]
public ActionResult Edit(Product productToEdit)
{
    try
    {
        var originalProduct = (from p in entities.Products
                               where p.ProductId == productToEdit.ProductId
                               select p).First();

        if (!ModelState.IsValid)
        {
            return View(originalProduct);
        }

        entities.ApplyCurrentValues(originalProduct.EntityKey.EntitySetName,
                                    productToEdit);
        entities.SaveChanges();

        return RedirectToAction("Index");
    }
```

```
        catch
        {
            return View();
        }
    }
```

This time, both `Edit()` method overloads need implementing. The first obtains a `Product` item from an ID value, and the second updates an item, using standard ADO.NET Entity Framework code.

Note that this time you require the product ID in the second `Create()` overload, so you can't just remove the auto-generated HTML for the `ProductId` field in the edit view as you did in the details and create views. Instead, to prevent it from being edited, you can include it as a hidden field as follows:

```
<fieldset>
  <legend>Fields</legend>
  <%= Html.Hidden("ProductId", Model.ProductId) %>
```

This ensures that it will be passed to the action method correctly.

Further Development

As with dynamic data web sites, this chapter has only included a brief introduction to ASP.NET MVC. There is plenty more that is worth looking into, including:

➤ Adding your own actions

➤ Custom action return types

➤ Unit testing controllers

➤ Custom HTML helper methods

And much more. If you are interested in learning more, your first point of call should be the ASP.NET MVC web site at `http://asp.net/mvc`, which contains tutorials, samples, and everything you need to dig deeper into this exciting new technology. There are also plenty of other great resources on the internet, including Scott Guthrie's blog at `http://weblogs.asp.net/scottgu/`. Scott has also written a great book for Wrox, *Professional ASP.NET MVC 1.0* (ISBN: 0470384611), with fellow expert ASP.NET MVC authors Rob Conery, Scott Hanselman, and Phil Haack. While this only covers version 1.0 of ASP.NET MVC, it is well worth a look, and I expect an updated version for ASP.NET MVC 2 before too long.

SUMMARY

In this chapter, you have completed your grand tour of ASP.NET by looking at some of the latest additions to the language and tools built on the framework that make it such an exciting way to develop for the web.

You started by looking at how routing can make friendly URLs much easier to implement, and how to control that routing to tweak URL mapping in exactly the way you want.

Next, you saw how to create dynamic data web sites that provide seamless integration of your data with a powerful front-end ASP.NET UI. This technology provides so much code for you by default that at times it feels like your web sites write themselves. You saw how two different data access methodologies, LINQ to SQL and the ADO.NET Entity Framework, are both supported by dynamic data sites, and how to customize scaffolding to make sites work just the way you want.

Finally, you explored the latest (and perhaps greatest) web technology to make use of ASP.NET, the ASP .NET MVC 2 framework. You saw how this provides you with a robust structure to work with, ideal for large-scale applications that require proper unit testing. You saw how easy it is to provide advanced capabilities with the minimum of effort, and how the logical structure and separation of functionality that this framework provides makes code easy to understand and easy to maintain.

In the next chapter, you'll look at Windows Communication Foundation, which enables you to make remote calls across application boundaries in a flexible, secure way. This underpins a lot of web development, as you will often want to pull in data from disparate sources for your web applications rather than including in-place databases as you have been doing in this chapter.

PART VI
Communication

▶ **CHAPTER 43:** Windows Communication Foundation

▶ **CHAPTER 44:** Windows Workflow Foundation 4

▶ **CHAPTER 45:** Peer-to-Peer Networking

▶ **CHAPTER 46:** Message Queuing

▶ **CHAPTER 47:** Syndication

43

Windows Communication Foundation

WHAT'S IN THIS CHAPTER?

- ➤ WCF overview
- ➤ A simple service and client
- ➤ Service, Operation, Data, and Message Contracts
- ➤ Implementing a Service
- ➤ Using Binding for Communication
- ➤ Different Hosting Options for Services
- ➤ Creating Clients with a Service Reference and Programmatically
- ➤ Duplex communication

Previous to .NET 3.0, several communication technologies were required in a single enterprise solution. For platform-independent communication, ASP.NET Web services were used. For more advanced Web services — technologies such as reliability, platform-independent security, and atomic transactions — Web Services Enhancements added a complexity layer to ASP.NET Web services. If the communication needed to be faster, and both the client and service were .NET applications, .NET Remoting was the technology of choice. .NET Enterprise Services with its automatic transaction support, by default, used the DCOM protocol, which was even faster than .NET Remoting. DCOM was also the only protocol to allow the passing of transactions. All of these technologies have different programming models that require many skills from the developer.

.NET Framework 3.0 introduced a new communication technology that includes all the features from these predecessors and combines them into one programming model: Windows Communication Foundation (WCF).

WCF OVERVIEW

WCF combines the functionality from ASP.NET Web services, .NET Remoting, Message Queuing, and Enterprise Services. What you get from WCF is:

➤ **Hosting for components and services** — Just as you can use custom hosts with .NET Remoting and Web Service Enhancements (WSE), you can host a WCF service in the ASP.NET runtime, a Windows service, a COM+ process, or just a Windows Forms application for peer-to-peer computing.

➤ **Declarative behavior** — Instead of the requirement to derive from a base class (this requirement exists with .NET Remoting and Enterprise Services), attributes can be used to define the services. This is similar to Web services developed with ASP.NET.

➤ **Communication channels** — Although NET Remoting is very flexible for changing the communication channel, WCF is a good alternative because it offers the same flexibility. WCF offers multiple channels to communicate using HTTP, TCP, or an IPC channel. Custom channels using different transport protocols can be created as well.

➤ **Security infrastructure** — For implementing platform-independent Web services, a standardized security environment must be used. The proposed standards are implemented with WSE 3.0, and this continues with WCF.

➤ **Extensibility** — .NET Remoting has a rich extensibility story. It is not only possible to create custom channels, formatters, and proxies, but also to inject functionality inside the message flow on the client and on the server. WCF offers similar extensibilities; however, here the extensions are created by using SOAP headers.

➤ **Support of previous technologies** — Instead of rewriting a distributed solution completely to use WCF, WCF can be integrated with existing technologies. WCF offers a channel that can communicate with serviced components using DCOM. Web services that have been developed with ASP.NET can be integrated with WCF as well.

The final goal is to send and receive messages between a client and a service across processes or different systems, across a local network, or across the Internet. This should be done, if required, in a platform-independent way and as fast as possible. From a distant view, the service offers an endpoint that is described by a contract, binding, and an address. The contract defines the operations offered by the service, binding gives information about the protocol and encoding, and the address is the location of the service. The client needs a compatible endpoint to access the service.

Figure 43-1 shows the components that participate with a WCF communication.

The client invokes a method on the proxy. The proxy offers methods as defined by the service but converts the method call to a message and transfers the message to the channel. The channel has a client-side part and a server-side part that communicate across a networking protocol. From the channel, the message is passed to the dispatcher, which converts the message to a method call that is invoked with the service.

WCF supports several communication protocols. For platform-independent communication, Web services standards are supported. For communication between .NET applications, faster communication protocols with less overhead can be used.

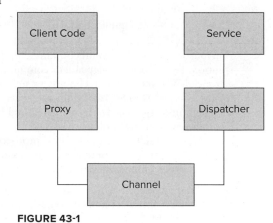

FIGURE 43-1

The following sections look at the functionality of core services used for platform-independent communication:

➤ SOAP — a platform-independent protocol that is the foundation of several Web service specifications to support security, transactions, reliability

➤ WSDL (Web Services Description Language) — offers metadata to describe a service

➤ REST (Representational State Transfer) — used with RESTful web services to communicate across HTTP

➤ JSON (JavaScript Object Notation) — allows easy use from within JavaScript clients.

SOAP

For platform-independent communication, the SOAP protocol can be used and is directly supported from WCF. SOAP originally was shorthand for Simple Object Access Protocol (SOAP), but since SOAP 1.2 this is no longer the case. SOAP no longer is an object access protocol, because, instead, messages are sent that can be defined by an XML schema.

A service receives a SOAP message from a client and returns a SOAP response message. A SOAP message consists of an envelope, which contains a header and a body:

```
<s:Envelope xmlns:a="http://www.w3.org/2005/08/addressing"
    xmlns:s="http://www.w3.org/2003/05/soap-envelope">
  <s:Header>
  </s:Header>
  <s:Body>
    <ReserveRoom xmlns="http://www.wrox.com/ProCSharp/2010">
      <roomReservation
          xmlns:d4p1="http://schemas.datacontract.org/2009/10/Wrox.ProCSharp.WCF"
          xmlns:i="http://www.w3.org/2001/XMLSchema-instance">
        <d4p1:RoomName>Hawelka</d4p1:RoomName>
        <d4p1:StartDate>2010-06-21T08:00:00</d4p1:StartDate>
        <d4p1:EndDate>2010-06-21T14:00:00</d4p1:EndDate>
        <d4p1:Contact>Georg Danzer</d4p1:Contact>
        <d4p1:Event>White Horses</d4p1:Event>
      </roomReservation>
    </ReserveRoom>
  </s:Body>
</s:Envelope>
```

The header is optional and can contain information about addressing, security, and transactions. The body contains the message data.

WSDL

A Web Services Description Language (WSDL) document describes the operations and messages of the service. WSDL defines metadata of the service that can be used to create a proxy for the client application.

The WSDL contains this information:

➤ **Types** for the messages that are described using an XML schema.

➤ **Messages** that are sent to and from the service. Parts of the messages are the types that are defined with an XML schema.

➤ **Port types** map to service contracts and list operations that are defined with the service contract. Operations contain messages; for example, an input and an output message as used with a request and response sequence.

➤ **Binding** information that contains the operations listed with the port types and that defines the SOAP variant used.

➤ **Service** information that maps port types to endpoint addresses.

 With WCF, WSDL information is offered by MEX (Metadata Exchange) endpoints.

REST

WCF also offers communication by using REST. This is not really a protocol but defines several principles for using services to access resources. A RESTful web service is a simple service based on the HTTP protocol and REST principles. The principles are defined by three categories: a service can be accessed with a simple URI, supports MIME types, and uses different HTTP methods. With the support of MIME types, different data formats can be returned from the service such as plain XML, JSON, or AtomPub. The GET method of a HTTP request returns data from the service. Other methods that are used are PUT, POST, and DELETE. The PUT method is used to make an update on the service side, POST creates a new resource, and DELETE deletes a resource.

REST allows the sending of smaller requests to services than is possible with SOAP. If transactions, secure messages, (secure communication is still possible, for example. via HTTPS), and the reliability that is offered by SOAP are not needed, a REST-architected service can reduce overhead.

With the REST architecture, the service is always stateless, and the response from the service can be cached.

JSON

Instead of sending SOAP messages, accessing services from JavaScript can best be done by using JSON. .NET includes a data contract serializer to create objects with the JSON notation.

JSON has less overhead than SOAP because it is not XML but is optimized for JavaScript clients. This makes it extremely useful from Ajax clients. Ajax is discussed in Chapter 41, "ASP.NET Features." JSON does not provide the reliability, security, and transaction features that can be sent with the SOAP header, but these are features usually not needed by JavaScript clients.

SIMPLE SERVICE AND CLIENT

Before going into the details of WCF, let's start with a simple service. The service is used to reserve meeting rooms.

For a backing store of room reservations, a simple SQL Server database with the table RoomReservations is used. You can download the database from www.wrox.com together with the sample code of this chapter.

Create an empty solution with the name RoomReservation, and add a new Component Library project with the name RoomReservationData to the solution. The first project that is implemented contains just the code to access the database. Because the ADO.NET Entity Framework makes the database access code much simpler, this .NET 4 technology is used here.

 Chapter 31 gives you the details of the ADO.NET Entity Framework.

Add a new item, ADO.NET Entity Data Model, and name it RoomReservationModel.edmx. After selecting the RoomReservations database, select the RoomReservations table to create an entity data model. After its creation, you can see the RoomReservation entity in the Designer, as shown in figure 43-2.

This designer creates an entity class, RoomReservation, which contains properties for every column of the table, and the class RoomReservationsEneities. RoomReservationsEntities connects to the database and registers with the entity classes to be notified of all changes.

FIGURE 43-2

To read and write data to and from the database using the ADO.NET Entity Framework, add the class `RoomReservationData`. The method `ReserveRoom()` writes a room reservation to the database. The method `GetReservations()` returns an array of room reservations from a specified date range.

```csharp
using System;
using System.Collections.Generic;
using System.Linq;

namespace Wrox.ProCSharp.WCF
{
    public class RoomReservationData
    {
        public void ReserveRoom(RoomReservation roomReservation)
        {
            using (var data = new RoomReservationsEntities())
            {
                data.RoomReservations.AddObject(roomReservation);
                data.SaveChanges();
            }
        }

        public RoomReservation[] GetReservations(DateTime fromDate,
                                                 DateTime toDate)
        {
            using (var data = new RoomReservationsEntities())
            {
                return (from r in data.RoomReservations
                        where r.StartDate > fromDate && r.EndDate < toDate
                        select r).ToArray();
            }
        }
    }
}
```

code snippet RoomReservationData/RoomReservationData.cs

Now start creating the service.

Service Contract

Add a new project of type WCF Service Library to the solution, and name the project `RoomReservationService`. Rename the generated files `IService1.cs` to `IRoomService.cs` and `Service1.cs` to `RoomReservationService.cs`, and change the namespace within the generated files to `Wrox.ProCSharp.WCF.Service`. The assembly `RoomReservationData` needs to be referenced to have the entity types and the `RoomReservationData` class available.

The operations offered by the service can be defined by an interface. The interface `IRoomService` defines the methods `ReserveRoom` and `GetRoomReservations`. The service contract is defined with the attribute `ServiceContract`. The operations defined by the service have the attribute `OperationContract` applied.

```csharp
using System;
using System.ServiceModel;

namespace Wrox.ProCSharp.WCF
{
    [ServiceContract()]
    public interface IRoomService
    {
        [OperationContract]
        bool ReserveRoom(RoomReservation roomReservation);
```

```
        [OperationContract]
        RoomReservation[] GetRoomReservations(DateTime fromDate, DateTime toDate);
    }
}
```

code snippet RoomReservationService/IRoomService.cs

Service Implementation

The service class `RoomReservationService` implements the interface `IRoomService`. The service is implemented just by invoking the appropriate methods of the `RoomReservationData` class:

Available for download on Wrox.com

```csharp
using System;
using System.Linq;

namespace Wrox.ProCSharp.WCF
{
    public class RoomReservationService : IRoomService
    {
        public bool ReserveRoom(RoomReservation roomReservation)
        {
            var data = new RoomReservationData();
            data.ReserveRoom(roomReservation);
            return true;
        }

        public RoomReservation[] GetRoomReservations(DateTime fromDate, DateTime toDate)
        {
            var data = new RoomReservationData();
            return data.GetReservations(fromDate, toDate);
        }
    }
}
```

code snippet RoomReservationService/RoomReservationService.cs

WCF Service Host and WCF Test Client

The WCF Service Library project template creates an application configuration file named `App.config` that you need to adapt to the new class and interface names. The `service` element references the service type `RoomReservationService`, including the namespace; the contract interface needs to be defined with the `endpoint` element.

Available for download on Wrox.com

```xml
<?xml version="1.0" encoding="utf-8" ?>
<configuration>
  <system.web>
    <compilation debug="true" />
  </system.web>
  <!-- When deploying the service library project, the content of the config file must be added
  to the host's app.config file. System.Configuration does not support config files for
  libraries. -->
  <system.serviceModel>
    <services>
      <service name="Wrox.ProCSharp.WCF.RoomReservationService">
        <host>
          <baseAddresses>
            <add baseAddress =
                "http://localhost:8732/Design_Time_Addresses/RoomReservationService/Service1/"
            />
```

```
          </baseAddresses>
        </host>
        <!-- Service Endpoints -->
        <!-- Unless fully qualified, address is relative to base address supplied above -->
        <endpoint address ="" binding="wsHttpBinding"
                  contract="Wrox.ProCSharp.WCF.IRoomService">
          <!--
              Upon deployment, the following identity element should be removed or replaced to
              reflect the identity under which the deployed service runs.  If removed, WCF will
              infer an appropriate identity automatically.
          -->
          <identity>
            <dns value="localhost"/>
          </identity>
        </endpoint>
        <!-- Metadata Endpoints -->
        <!-- The Metadata Exchange endpoint is used by the service to describe itself to
             clients. -->
        <!-- This endpoint does not use a secure binding and should be secured or removed
             before deployment -->
        <endpoint address="mex" binding="mexHttpBinding" contract="IMetadataExchange"/>
      </service>
    </services>
    <behaviors>
      <serviceBehaviors>
        <behavior>
          <!-- To avoid disclosing metadata information,
          set the value below to false and remove the metadata endpoint above before
          deployment -->
          <serviceMetadata httpGetEnabled="True"/>
          <!-- To receive exception details in faults for debugging purposes,
          set the value below to true.  Set to false before deployment
          to avoid disclosing exception information -->
          <serviceDebug includeExceptionDetailInFaults="False" />
        </behavior>
      </serviceBehaviors>
    </behaviors>
  </system.serviceModel>
</configuration>
```

code snippet RoomReservationService/App.config

 The service address `http://localhost:8732/Design_Time_Addresses` *has an access control list (ACL) associated with it that allows the interactive user to create a listener port. By default, a non-administrative user is not allowed to open ports in listening mode. You can view the ACLs with the command-line utility* `netsh http show urlacl`, *and add new entries with* `netsh http add urlacl url=http://+:8080/ MyURI user=someUser`.

Starting this library from Visual Studio 2010 starts the WCF Service Host, which appears as an icon in the notification area of the taskbar. Clicking this icon opens the WCF Service Host window (see Figure 43-3), where you can see the status of the service. The project properties of a WCF library application include the tab WCF options, where you can select whether the WCF service host should be started when running a project from the same solution. By default, this option is turned on. Also, with the Debug configuration of the project properties, you will find the command-line argument `/client: "WcfTestClient.exe"` defined. With this option, the WCF Service host starts the WCF Test Client (see Figure 43-4), which you can use to test the application. When you double-click an operation, input fields appear on the right side of the application that you can fill to send data to the service. When you click the XML tab, you can see the SOAP messages that have been sent and received.

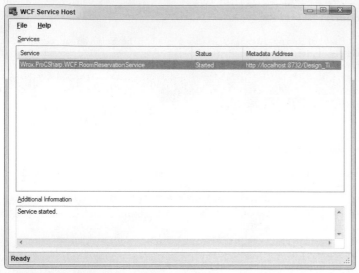

FIGURE 43-3

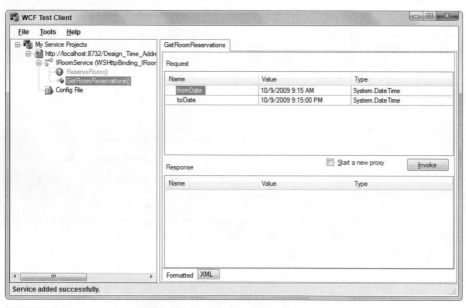

FIGURE 43-4

Custom Service Host

WCF allows services to run in any host. You can create a Windows Forms or Windows Presentation Foundation (WPF) application for peer-to-peer services, or you can create a Windows service, or host the service with Windows Activation Services (WAS). A console application is also good to demonstrate a simple host.

With the service host, you must reference the library `RoomReservationService`. The service is started by instantiating and opening an object of type `ServiceHost`. This class is defined in the namespace `System.ServiceModel`. The `RoomReservationService` class that implements the service is defined in the constructor. Invoking the `Open()` method starts the listener channel of the service — the service is ready to listen for requests. The `Close()` method stops the channel.

```csharp
using System;
using System.ServiceModel;

namespace Wrox.ProCSharp.WCF
{
    class Program
    {
        internal static ServiceHost myServiceHost = null;

        internal static void StartService()
        {
            myServiceHost = new ServiceHost(typeof(RoomReservationService));
            myServiceHost.Open();
        }

        internal static void StopService()
        {
            if (myServiceHost.State != CommunicationState.Closed)
                myServiceHost.Close();
        }

        static void Main()
        {
            StartService();

            Console.WriteLine("Server is running. Press return to exit");
            Console.ReadLine();

            StopService();
        }
    }
}
```

code snippet RoomReservationServiceHost/Program.cs

For the WCF configuration, you need to copy the application configuration file that was created with the service library to the host application. You can edit this configuration file with the WCF Service Configuration Editor (see Figure 43-5).

Using the custom service host, you can deselect the WCF option to start the WCF Service Host in the project settings of the WCF library.

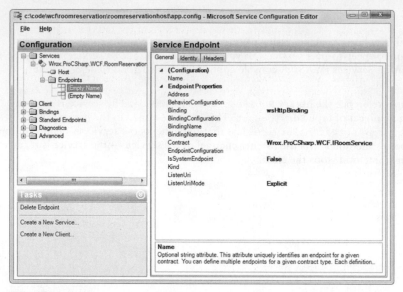

FIGURE 43-5

WCF Client

For the client, WCF is flexible again in what application type can be used. The client can be a simple console application as well. However, for reserving rooms, create a WPF application with controls, as shown in Figure 43-6.

Because the service offers a MEX endpoint with the binding `mexHttpBinding`, and metadata access is enabled with the behavior configuration, you can add a service reference from Visual Studio. When you add a service reference, the dialog shown in Figure 43-7 pops up. When you click the Discover button, you can find services within the same solution.

Enter the link to the service, and set the service reference name to `RoomReservationService`. The service reference name defines the namespace of the generated proxy class.

FIGURE 43-6

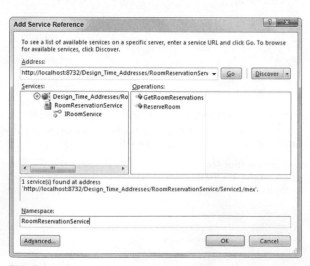

FIGURE 43-7

Adding a service reference adds references to the assemblies `System.Runtime.Serialization` and `System.ServiceModel` and a configuration file containing the binding information and the endpoint address to the service.

From the data contract the class `RoomReservation` is generated. This class contains all `[DataMember]` elements of the contract. The class `RoomServiceClient` is the proxy for the client that contains methods that are defined by the service contract. Using this client, you can send a room reservation to the running service.

Available for download on Wrox.com

```csharp
private void OnReserveRoom(object sender, RoutedEventArgs e)
{
    var reservation = new RoomReservation()
    {
        RoomName = textRoom.Text,
        Event = textEvent.Text,
        Contact = textContact.Text,
        StartDate = DateTime.Parse(textStartTime.Text),
        EndDate = DateTime.Parse(textEndTime.Text)
    };

    var client = new RoomServiceClient();
    bool reserved = client.ReserveRoom(reservation);
    client.Close();
    if (reserved)
        MessageBox.Show("reservation ok");
}
```

code snippet RoomReservationClient/MainWindow.xaml.cs

By running both the service and the client, you can add room reservations to the database. With the settings of the `RoomReservation` solution, you can configure multiple startup projects, which should be `RoomReservationClient` and `RoomReservationHost` in this case.

Diagnostics

When running a client and service application, it can be very helpful to know what's happening behind the scenes. For this, WCF makes use of a trace source that just needs to be configured. You can configure tracing using the Service Configuration Editor, selecting Diagnostics, and enabling Tracing and Message Logging. Setting the trace level of the trace sources to Verbose produces very detailed information. This configuration change adds trace sources and listeners to the application configuration file as shown here:

Available for download on Wrox.com

```xml
<?xml version="1.0" encoding="utf-8" ?>
<configuration>
  <system.diagnostics>
    <sources>
      <source name="System.ServiceModel.MessageLogging" switchValue="Verbose,ActivityTracing">
        <listeners>
          <add type="System.Diagnostics.DefaultTraceListener" name="Default">
            <filter type="" />
          </add>
          <add name="ServiceModelMessageLoggingListener">
            <filter type="" />
          </add>
        </listeners>
      </source>
      <source name="System.ServiceModel" switchValue="Verbose,ActivityTracing"
        propagateActivity="true">
        <listeners>
          <add type="System.Diagnostics.DefaultTraceListener" name="Default">
            <filter type="" />
          </add>
          <add name="ServiceModelTraceListener">
            <filter type="" />
          </add>
```

```
          </listeners>
        </source>
      </sources>
      <sharedListeners>
        <add initializeData="c:\code\wcf\roomreservation\roomreservationhost\app_messages.svclog"
          type="System.Diagnostics.XmlWriterTraceListener, System, Version=4.0.0.0,
                Culture=neutral, PublicKeyToken=b77a5c561934e089"
          name="ServiceModelMessageLoggingListener" traceOutputOptions="Timestamp">
          <filter type="" />
        </add>
        <add initializeData="c:\code\wcf\roomreservation\roomreservationhost\app_tracelog.svclog"
          type="System.Diagnostics.XmlWriterTraceListener, System, Version=4.0.0.0,
                Culture=neutral, PublicKeyToken=b77a5c561934e089"
          name="ServiceModelTraceListener" traceOutputOptions="Timestamp">
          <filter type="" />
        </add>
      </sharedListeners>
      <trace autoflush="true" />
    </system.diagnostics>
    <!-- -->
```

code snippet RoomReservationHost/App.config

> *The implementation of the WCF classes uses the trace sources named* System
> .ServiceModel *and* System.ServiceModel.MessageLogging *for writing trace
> messages. You can read more about tracing and configuring trace sources and listeners
> in Chapter 19, "Instrumentation."*

When you start the application, the trace files soon get large with verbose trace settings. To analyze
the information from the XML log file, the .NET SDK includes the Service Trace Viewer tool,
svctraceviewer.exe. Figure 43-8 shows the view from this tool after selecting the trace and message log
files. With the default configuration, you can see several messages exchanged; many of them are related to
security. Depending on your security needs, you can choose other configuration options.

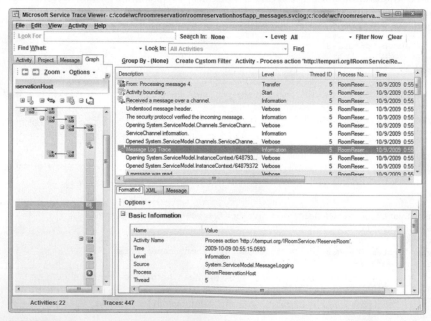

FIGURE 43-8

The following sections discuss the details and different options of WCF.

CONTRACTS

A contract defines what functionality a service offers and what functionality can be used by the client. The contract can be completely independent of the implementation of the service.

The contracts defined by WCF can be grouped into three different contract types: data, service, and message. The contracts can be specified by using .NET attributes:

➤ **Data contract** — The data contract defines the data received by and returned from the service. The classes used for sending and receiving messages have data contract attributes associated with them.

➤ **Service contract** — The service contract is used to define the WSDL that describes the service. This contract is defined with interfaces or classes.

➤ **Message contract** — If complete control over the SOAP message is needed, a message contract can specify what data should go into the SOAP header and what belongs in the SOAP body.

The following sections explore these contract types further and discuss versioning issues that should be thought about when defining the contracts.

Data Contract

With the data contract, CLR types are mapped to XML schemas. The data contract is different from other .NET serialization mechanisms: with runtime serialization, all fields are serialized (including private fields); with XML serialization, only the public fields and properties are serialized. The data contract requires explicit marking of the fields that should be serialized with the `DataMember` attribute. This attribute can be used regardless of whether the field is private or public, or if it is applied to a property.

```
[DataContract(Namespace="http://www.thinktecture.com/SampleServices/2010")]
public class RoomReservation
{
    [DataMember] public string Room { get; set; }
    [DataMember] public DateTime StartDate { get; set; }
    [DataMember] public DateTime EndDate { get; set; }
    [DataMember] public string ContactName { get; set; }
    [DataMember] public string EventName { get; set; }
}
```

To be platform-independent, and provide the option to change data with new versions without breaking older clients and services, using data contracts is the best way to define which data should be sent. However, you can also use XML serialization and runtime serialization. XML serialization is the mechanism used by ASP.NET Web services; .NET Remoting uses runtime serialization.

With the attribute `DataMember`, you can specify the properties described in the following table.

DATAMEMBER PROPERTY	DESCRIPTION
Name	By default, the serialized element has the same name as the field or property where the `[DataMember]` attribute is applied. You can change the name with the `Name` property.
Order	The `Order` property defines the serialization order of the data members.
IsRequired	With the `IsRequired` property, you can specify that the element must be received with serialization. This property can be used for versioning.
	If you add members to an existing contract, the contract is not broken because, by default, the fields are optional (`IsRequired=false`). You can break an existing contract by setting `IsRequired` to true.
EmitDefaultValue	The property `EmitDefaultValue` defines whether the member should be serialized if it has the default value. If `EmitDefaultValue` is set to true, the member is not serialized if it has the default value for the type.

Versioning

When you create a new version of a data contract, pay attention to what kind of change it is and act accordingly if old and new clients and old and new services should be supported simultaneously.

When defining a contract, you should add XML namespace information with the `Namespace` property of the `DataContractAttribute`. This namespace should be changed if a new version of the data contract is created that breaks compatibility. If just optional members are added, the contract is not broken — this is a compatible change. Old clients can still send a message to the new service because the additional data is not needed. New clients can send messages to an old service because the old service just ignores the additional data.

Removing fields or adding required fields breaks the contract. Here, you should also change the XML namespace. The name of the namespace can include the year and the month, for example, `http://thinktecture.com/SampleServices/2009/10`. Every time a breaking change is done, the namespace is changed; for example, by changing the year and month to the actual value.

Service Contract

The service contract defines the operations the service can perform. The attribute `ServiceContract` is used with interfaces or classes to define a service contract. The methods that are offered by the service have the attribute `OperationContract` applied, as you can see with the interface `IRoomService`:

```
[ServiceContract]
public interface IRoomService
{
    [OperationContract]
    bool ReserveRoom(RoomReservation roomReservation);
}
```

The possible properties that you can set with the `ServiceContract` attribute are described in the following table.

SERVICECONTRACT PROPERTY	DESCRIPTION
`ConfigurationName`	This property defines the name of the service configuration in a configuration file.
`CallbackContract`	When the service is used for duplex messaging, the property `CallbackContract` defines the contract that is implemented in the client.
`Name`	The `Name` property defines the name for the `<portType>` element in the WSDL.
`Namespace`	The `Namespace` property defines the XML namespace for the `<portType>` element in the WSDL.
`SessionMode`	With the `SessionMode` property, you can define whether sessions are required for calling operations of this contract. The possible values `Allowed`, `NotAllowed`, and `Required` are defined with the `SessionMode` enumeration.
`ProtectionLevel`	The `ProtectionLevel` property defines whether the binding must support protecting the communication. Possible values defined by the `ProtectionLevel` enumeration are `None`, `Sign`, and `EncryptAndSign`.

With the `OperationContract`, you can specify properties, as shown in the following table.

OPERATIONCONTRACT PROPERTY	DESCRIPTION
Action	WCF uses the `Action` of the SOAP request to map it to the appropriate method. The default value for the `Action` is a combination of the contract XML namespace, the name of the contract, and the name of the operation. If the message is a response message, `Response` is added to the `Action` string. You can override the `Action` value by specifying the `Action` property. If you assign the value "*", the service operation handles all messages.
ReplyAction	Whereas `Action` sets the `Action` name of the incoming SOAP request, `ReplyAction` sets the `Action` name of the reply message.
AsyncPattern	If the operation is implemented by using an asynchronous pattern, set the `AsyncPattern` property to `true`. The async pattern is discussed in Chapter 20, "Threads, Tasks, and Synchronization."
IsInitiating IsTerminating	If the contract consists of a sequence of operations, the initiating operation should have the `IsInitiating` property assigned to it; the last operation of the sequence needs the `IsTerminating` property assigned. The initiating operation starts a new session; the server closes the session with the terminating operation.
IsOneWay	With the `IsOneWay` property set, the client does not wait for a reply message. Callers of a one-way operation have no direct way to detect a failure after sending the request message.
Name	The default name of the operation is the name of the method the operation contract is assigned to. You can change the name of the operation by applying the `Name` property.
ProtectionLevel	With the `ProtectionLevel` property, you define whether the message should be signed or encrypted and signed.

With the service contract, you can also define the requirements that the service has from the transport with the attribute [DeliveryRequirements]. The property RequireOrderedDelivery defines that the messages sent must arrive in the same order. With the property QueuedDeliveryRequirements, you can define that the message should be sent in a disconnected mode, for example, by using Message Queuing (covered in Chapter 46).

Message Contract

A message contract is used if complete control over the SOAP message is needed. With the message contract, you can specify what part of the message should go into the SOAP header and what belongs in the SOAP body. The following example shows a message contract for the class ProcessPersonRequestMessage. The message contract is specified with the attribute MessageContract. The header and body of the SOAP message are specified with the attributes MessageHeader and MessageBodyMember. By specifying the Position property, you can define the element order within the body. You can also specify the protection level for header and body fields.

```
[MessageContract]
public class ProcessPersonRequestMessage
{
    [MessageHeader]
    public int employeeId;

    [MessageBodyMember(Position=0)]
    public Person person;
}
```

The class `ProcessPersonRequestMessage` is used with the service contract that is defined with the interface `IProcessPerson`:

```
[ServiceContract]
public interface IProcessPerson
{
    [OperationContract]
    public PersonResponseMessage ProcessPerson(
        ProcessPersonRequestMessage message);
}
```

Another contract that is important in regard to WCF services is the fault contract. This contract is discussed in the next section with Error Handling.

SERVICE IMPLEMENTATION

The implementation of the service can be marked with the attribute `ServiceBehavior`, as shown with the class `RoomReservationService`:

```
[ServiceBehavior]
public class RoomReservationService: IRoomService
{
    public bool ReserveRoom(RoomReservation roomReservation)
    {
    // implementation
    }
}
```

The attribute `ServiceBehavior` is used to describe behavior as is offered by WCF services to intercept the code for required functionality, as shown in the following table.

SERVICEBEHAVIOR PROPERTY	DESCRIPTION
TransactionAutoCompleteOn SessionClose	When the current session is finished without error, the transaction is automatically committed. This is similar to the `AutoComplete` attribute, which is discussed with Enterprise Services in Chapter 51 (this is a downloadable chapter).
TransactionIsolationLevel	To define the isolation level of the transaction within the service, the property `TransactionIsolationLevel` can be set to one value of the `IsolationLevel` enumeration. You can read information about transaction information levels in Chapter 23, "System.Transactions."
ReleaseServiceInstanceOn TransactionComplete	When the transaction is finished, the instance of the service is recycled.
AutomaticSessionShutdown	If the session should not be closed when the client closes the connection, you can set the property `AutomaticSessionShutdown` to `false`. By default, the session is closed.
InstanceContextMode	With the property `InstanceContextMode`, you can define whether stateful or stateless objects should be used. The default setting is `InstanceContextMode.PerCall` to create a new object with every method call. Other possible settings are `PerSession` and `Single`. With both of these settings, stateful objects are used. However, with `PerSession` a new object is created for every client. `Single` allows the same object to be shared with multiple clients.

SERVICEBEHAVIOR PROPERTY	DESCRIPTION
ConcurrencyMode	Because stateful objects can be used by multiple clients (or multiple threads of a single client), you must pay attention to concurrency issues with such object types. If the property ConcurrencyMode is set to Multiple, multiple threads can access the object, and you must deal with synchronization. If you set the option to Single, only one thread accesses the object at a time. Here, you don't have to do synchronization; however, scalability problems can occur with a higher number of clients. The value Reentrant means that only a thread coming back from a callout might access the object. For stateless objects, this setting has no meaning, because new objects are instantiated with every method call and thus no state is shared.
UseSynchronizationContext	With Windows Forms and WPF, members of controls can be invoked only from the creator thread. If the service is hosted in a Windows application, and the service methods invoke control members, set the UseSynchronizationContext to true. This way, the service runs in a thread defined by the SynchronizationContext.
IncludeExceptionDetailInFaults	With .NET, errors show up as exceptions. SOAP defines that a SOAP fault is returned to the client in case the server has a problem. For security reasons, it's not a good idea to return details of server-side exceptions to the client. Thus, by default, exceptions are converted to unknown faults. To return specific faults, throw an exception of type FaultException. For debugging purposes, it can be helpful to return the real exception information. This is the case when changing the setting of IncludeExceptionDetailIn Faults to true. Here a FaultException<TDetail> is thrown where the original exception contains the detail information.
MaxItemsInObjectGraph	With the property MaxItemsInObjectGraph, you can limit the number of objects that are serialized. The default limitation might be too low if you serialize a tree of objects.
ValidateMustUnderstand	The property ValidateMustUnderstand set to true means that the SOAP headers must be understood (which is the default).

To demonstrate a service behavior, the interface IStateService defines a service contract with two operations to set and get state. With a stateful service contract, a session is needed. That's why the SessionMode property of the service contract is set to SessionMode.Required. The service contract also defines methods to initiate and close the session by applying the IsInitiating and IsTerminating properties to the operation contract:

```
[ServiceContract(SessionMode=SessionMode.Required)]
public interface IStateService
{
    [OperationContract(IsInitiating=true)]
    void Init(int i);

    [OperationContract]
    void SetState(int i);

    [OperationContract]
    int GetState();
```

```
    [OperationContract(IsTerminating=true)]
    void Close();
}
```

The service contract is implemented by the class `StateService`. The service implementation defines the `InstanceContextMode.PerSession` to keep state with the instance:

```
[ServiceBehavior(InstanceContextMode=InstanceContextMode.PerSession)]
public class StateService: IStateService
{
    int i = 0;

    public void Init(int i)
    {
        this.i = i;
    }

    public void SetState(int i)
    {
        this.i = i;
    }

    public int GetState()
    {
        return i;
    }

    public void Close()
    {
    }
}
```

Now the binding to the address and protocol must be defined. Here, the `basicHttpBinding` is assigned to the endpoint of the service:

```xml
<?xml version="1.0" encoding="utf-8" ?>
<configuration>
  <system.serviceModel>
    <services>
      <service behaviorConfiguration="StateServiceSample.Service1Behavior"
        name="Wrox.ProCSharp.WCF.StateService">
        <endpoint address="" binding="basicHttpBinding"
            bindingConfiguration=""
            contract="Wrox.ProCSharp.WCF.IStateService">
        </endpoint>
        <endpoint address="mex" binding="mexHttpBinding"
            contract="IMetadataExchange" />
        <host>
          <baseAddresses>
            <add baseAddress="http://localhost:8731/Design_Time_Addresses/
                           StateServiceSample/Service1/" />
          </baseAddresses>
        </host>
      </service>
    </services>
    <behaviors>
      <serviceBehaviors>
        <behavior name="StateServiceSample.Service1Behavior">
          <serviceMetadata httpGetEnabled="True"/>
```

```
                    <serviceDebug includeExceptionDetailInFaults="False" />
                 </behavior>
              </serviceBehaviors>
           </behaviors>
        </system.serviceModel>
     </configuration>
```

If you start the service host with the defined configuration, an exception of type `InvalidOperationException` is thrown. The error message with the exception gives this error message: "Contract requires Session, but Binding 'BasicHttpBinding' doesn't support it or isn't configured properly to support it."

Not all bindings support all services. Because the service contract requires a session with the attribute `[ServiceContract(SessionMode=SessionMode.Required)]`, the host fails because the configured binding does not support sessions.

As soon as you change the configuration to a binding that supports sessions (for example, the `wsHttpBinding`), the server starts successfully:

```
<endpoint address="" binding="wsHttpBinding"
    bindingConfiguration=""
    contract="Wrox.ProCSharp.WCF.IStateService">
</endpoint>
```

Creating a Client Programmatically

Now a client application can be created. In the previous example, the client application was created by adding a service reference. Instead of adding a service reference, you can directly access the assembly containing the contract interface and use the `ChannelFactory<TChannel>` class to instantiate the channel to connect to the service.

The constructor of the class `ChannelFactory<TChannel>` accepts the binding configuration and endpoint address. The binding must be compatible with the binding defined with the service host, and the address defined with the `EndpointAddress` class references the URI of the running service.

The `CreateChannel()` method creates a channel to connect to the service. Then, you can invoke methods of the service, and you can see that the service instance holds state until the `Close()` method that has the `IsTerminating` operation behavior assigned is invoked:

```
using System;
using System.ServiceModel;

namespace Wrox.ProCSharp.WCF
{
    class Program
    {
        static void Main()
        {
            var binding = new WSHttpBinding();
            var address = new EndpointAddress("http://localhost:8731/" +
                "Design_Time_Addresses/StateServiceSample/Service1/");

            var factory = new ChannelFactory<IStateService>(binding, address);

            IStateService channel = factory.CreateChannel();
            channel.Init(1);
            Console.WriteLine(channel.GetState());
            channel.SetState(2);
```

```
            Console.WriteLine(channel.GetState());
            channel.Close();

            factory.Close();
        }
    }
}
```

code snippet StateClient/program.cs

With the implementation of the service, you can apply the properties in the following table to the service methods, with the attribute `OperationBehavior`.

OPERATIONBEHAVIOR PROPERTY	DESCRIPTION
AutoDisposeParameters	By default, all disposable parameters are automatically disposed. If the parameters should not be disposed, you can set the property `AutoDisposeParameters` to false. Then the sender is responsible for disposing the parameters.
Impersonation	With the `Impersonation` property, the caller can be impersonated and the method runs with the identity of the caller.
ReleaseInstanceMode	The `InstanceContextMode` defines the lifetime of the object instance with the service behavior setting. With the operation behavior setting, you can override the setting based on the operation. The `ReleaseInstanceMode` defines an instance release mode with the enumeration `ReleaseInstanceMode`. The value `None` uses the instance context mode setting. With the values `BeforeCall`, `AfterCall`, and `BeforeAndAfterCall` you can define recycle times with the operation.
TransactionScopeRequired	With the property `TransactionScopeRequired`, you can specify if a transaction is required with the operation. If a transaction is required, and the caller already flows a transaction, the same transaction is used. If the caller doesn't flow a transaction, a new transaction is created.
TransactionAutoComplete	The `TransactionAutoComplete` property specifies whether the transaction should complete automatically. If the `TransactionAutoComplete` property is set to true, the transaction is aborted if an exception is thrown. The transaction is committed if it is the root transaction and no exception is thrown.

Error Handling

By default, the detailed exception information that occurs in the service is not returned to the client application. The reason for this behavior is security. You wouldn't want to give detailed exception information to a third party by using your service. Instead, the exception should be logged on the service (which you can do with tracing and event logging), and an error with useful information should be returned to the caller.

You can return SOAP faults by throwing a `FaultException`. Throwing a `FaultException` creates an untyped SOAP fault. The preferred way of returning errors is to generate a strongly typed SOAP fault.

The information that should be passed with a strongly typed SOAP fault is defined with a data contract, as shown with the `StateFault` class:

```
[DataContract]
public class StateFault
{
    [DataMember]
```

```
    public int BadState { get; set; }
}
```

code snippet StateServiceSample/IStateService.cs

The type of the SOAP fault must be defined by using the `FaultContractAttribute` with the operation contract:

```
[FaultContract(typeof(StateFault))]
[OperationContract]
void SetState(int i);
```

With the implementation, a `FaultException<TDetail>` is thrown. With the constructor, you can assign a new `TDetail` object, which is a `StateFault` in the example. In addition, error information within a `FaultReason` can be assigned to the constructor. `FaultReason` supports error information in multiple languages.

Available for download on Wrox.com

```
public void SetState(int i)
{
    if (i == -1)
    {
        FaultReasonText[] text = new FaultReasonText[2];
        text[0] = new FaultReasonText("Sample Error",
            new CultureInfo("en"));
        text[1] = new FaultReasonText("Beispiel Fehler",
            new CultureInfo("de"));
        FaultReason reason = new FaultReason(text);

        throw new FaultException<StateFault>(
            new StateFault() { BadState = i }, reason);
    }
    else
    {
        this.i = i;
    }
}
```

code snippet StateServiceSample/StateService.cs

With the client application, exceptions of type `FaultException<StateFault>` can be caught. The reason for the exception is defined by the `Message` property; the `StateFault` is accessed with the `Detail` property:

Available for download on Wrox.com

```
try
{
    channel.SetState(-1);
}
catch (FaultException<StateFault> ex)
{
    Console.WriteLine(ex.Message);
    StateFault detail = ex.Detail;
    Console.WriteLine(detail.BadState);
}
```

code snippet StateServiceClient/Program.cs

In addition to catching the strongly typed SOAP faults, the client application can also catch exceptions of the base class of `FaultException<Detail>`: `FaultException` and `CommunicationException`. By catching `CommunicationException`, you can also catch other exceptions related to the WCF communication.

BINDING

A binding describes how a service wants to communicate. With binding, you can specify the following features:

➤ Transport protocol

➤ Security

➤ Encoding format

➤ Transaction flow

➤ Reliability

➤ Shape change

➤ Transport upgrade

A binding is composed of multiple binding elements that describe all binding requirements. You can create a custom binding or use one of the predefined bindings that are shown in the following table.

STANDARD BINDING	DESCRIPTION
BasicHttpBinding	BasicHttpBinding is the binding for the broadest interoperability, the first-generation Web services. Transport protocols used are HTTP or HTTPS; security is available only from the transport protocol.
WSHttpBinding	WSHttpBinding is the binding for the next-generation Web services, platforms that implement SOAP extensions for security, reliability, and transactions. The transports used are HTTP or HTTPS; for security the WS-Security specification is implemented; transactions are supported, as has been described, with the WS-Coordination, WS-AtomicTransaction, and WS-BusinessActivity specifications; reliable messaging is supported with an implementation of WS-ReliableMessaging. WS-Profile also supports MTOM (Message Transmission Optimization Protocol) encoding for sending attachments. You can find specifications for the WS-* standards at http://www.oasis-open.org.
WS2007HttpBinding	WS2007HttpBinding derives from the base class WSHttpBinding and supports security, reliability, and transaction specifications defined by OASIS (Organization for the Advancement of Structured Information Standards).
WSHttpContextBinding	WSHttpContextBinding derives from the base class WSHttpBinding and adds support for a context without using cookies. This binding adds a ContextBindingElement to exchange context information.
WebHttpBinding	This binding is used for services that are exposed through HTTP requests instead of SOAP requests. This is useful for scripting clients — for example, ASP.NET AJAX.
WSFederationHttpBinding	WSFederationHttpBinding is a secure and interoperable binding that supports sharing identities across multiple systems for authentication and authorization.
WSDualHttpBinding	The binding WSDualHttpBinding, in contrast to WSHttpBinding, supports duplex messaging.
NetTcpBinding	All standard bindings prefixed with the name Net use a binary encoding used for communication between .NET applications. This encoding is faster than the text encoding with WSxxx bindings. The binding NetTcpBinding uses the TCP/IP protocol.
NetTcpContextBinding	Similar to WSHttpContextBinding, NetTcpContextBinding adds a ContextBindingElement to exchange context with the SOAP header.
NetPeerTcpBinding	NetPeerTcpBinding provides a binding for peer-to-peer communication.

STANDARD BINDING	DESCRIPTION
NetNamedPipeBinding	NetNamedPipeBinding is optimized for communication between different processes on the same system.
NetMsmqBinding	The binding NetMsmqBinding brings queued communication to WCF. Here, the messages are sent to the message queue.
MsmqIntegrationBinding	MsmqIntegrationBinding is the binding for existing applications that uses message queuing. In contrast, the binding NetMsmqBinding requires WCF applications both on the client and server.
CustomBinding	With a CustomBinding the transport protocol and security requirements can be completely customized.

Depending on the binding, different features are supported. The bindings starting with WS are platform-independent, supporting Web services specifications. Bindings that start with the name Net use binary formatting for high-performance communication between .NET applications. Other features are support of sessions, reliable sessions, transactions, and duplex communication; the following table lists the bindings supporting these features.

FEATURE	BINDING
Sessions	WSHttpBinding, WSDualHttpBinding, WsFederationHttpBinding, NetTcpBinding, NetNamedPipeBinding
Reliable Sessions	WSHttpBinding, WSDualHttpBinding, WsFederationHttpBinding, NetTcpBinding
Transactions	WSHttpBinding, WSDualHttpBinding, WSFederationHttpBinding, NetTcpBinding, NetNamedPipeBinding, NetMsmqBinding, MsmqIntegrationBinding
Duplex Communication	WsDualHttpBinding, NetTcpBinding, NetNamedPipeBinding, NetPeerTcpBinding

Along with defining the binding, the service must define an endpoint. The endpoint is dependent on the contract, the address of the service, and the binding. In the following code sample, a ServiceHost object is instantiated, and the address http://localhost:8080/RoomReservation, a WsHttpBinding instance, and the contract are added to an endpoint of the service:

```
static ServiceHost host;

static void StartService()
{
    var baseAddress = new Uri("http://localhost:8080/RoomReservation");
    host = new ServiceHost(
        typeof(RoomReservationService));

    var binding1 = new WSHttpBinding();
    host.AddServiceEndpoint(typeof(IRoomService), binding1, baseAddress);
    host.Open();
}
```

In addition to defining the binding programmatically, you can define it with the application configuration file. The configuration for WCF is placed inside the element <system.serviceModel>. The <service> element defines the services offered. Similarly, as you've seen in the code, the service needs an endpoint, and the endpoint contains address, binding, and contract information. The default binding configuration of wsHttpBinding is modified with the bindingConfiguration XML attribute that references the binding configuration wsHttpConfig1. This is the binding configuration you can find inside the <bindings> section, which is used to change the wsHttpBinding configuration to enable reliableSession.

```xml
<?xml version="1.0" encoding="utf-8" ?>
<configuration>
  <system.serviceModel>
    <services>
      <service name="Wrox.ProCSharp.WCF.RoomReservationService">
        <endpoint address=" http://localhost:8080/RoomReservation"
            contract="Wrox.ProCSharp.WCF.IRoomService"
            binding="wsHttpBinding" bindingConfiguration="wsHttpBinding" />
      </service>
    </services>
    <bindings>
      <wsHttpBinding>
        <binding name="wsHttpBinding">
          <reliableSession enabled="true" />
        </binding>
      </wsHttpBinding>
    </bindings>
  </system.serviceModel>
</configuration>
```

HOSTING

WCF is very flexible when you are choosing a host to run the service. The host can be a Windows service, a COM+ application, WAS (Windows Activation Services) or IIS, a Windows application, or just a simple console application. When creating a custom host with Windows Forms or WPF, you can easily create a peer-to-peer solution.

Custom Hosting

Let's start with a custom host. The sample code shows hosting of a service within a console application; however, in other custom host types, such as Windows services or Windows applications, you can program the service in the same way.

In the `Main()` method, a `ServiceHost` instance is created. After the `ServiceHost` instance is created, the application configuration file is read to define the bindings. You can also define the bindings programmatically, as shown earlier. Next, the `Open()` method of the `ServiceHost` class is invoked, so the service accepts client calls. With a console application, you need to be careful not to close the main thread until the service should be closed. Here, the user is asked to "press return" to exit the service. When the user does this, the `Close()` method is called to actually end the service:

```csharp
using System;
using System.ServiceModel;

public class Program
{
    public static void Main()
    {
        using (var serviceHost = new ServiceHost())
        {
            serviceHost.Open();

            Console.WriteLine("The service started. Press return to exit");
            Console.ReadLine();

            serviceHost.Close();
        }
    }
}
```

To abort the service host, you can invoke the `Abort()` method of the `ServiceHost` class. To get the current state of the service, the `State` property returns a value defined by the `CommunicationState` enumeration. Possible values are `Created`, `Opening`, `Opened`, `Closing`, `Closed`, and `Faulted`.

> *If you start the service from within a Windows Forms or WPF application and the service code invokes methods of Windows controls, you must be sure that only the control's creator thread is allowed to access the methods and properties of the control. With WCF, this behavior can be achieved easily by setting the* `UseSynchronizationContext` *property of the attribute* `[ServiceBehavior]`.

WAS Hosting

With WAS (Windows Activation Services) hosting, you get the features from the WAS worker process such as automatic activation of the service, health monitoring, and process recycling.

To use WAS hosting, you just need to create a web site and a `.svc` file with the `ServiceHost` declaration that includes the language and the name of the service class. The code shown here is using the class `Service1`. In addition, you must specify the file that contains the service class. This class is implemented in the same way that you saw earlier when defining a WCF service library.

```
<%@ServiceHost language="C#" Service="Service1" CodeBehind="Service1.svc.cs" %>
```

If you use a WCF service library that should be available from WAS hosting, you can create a `.svc` file that just contains a reference to the class:

```
<%@ ServiceHost Service="Wrox.ProCSharp.WCF.Services.RoomReservationService" %>
```

Since the introduction of Windows Vista and Windows Server 2008, WAS allows defining .NET TCP and Message Queue bindings. If you are using the previous edition, IIS 6 or IIS 5.1, which is available with Windows Server 2003 and Windows XP, activation from a `.svc` file can be done only with an HTTP binding.

> *You can also add a WCF service to Enterprise Service components. This is discussed in Chapter 51.*

Preconfigured Host Classes

To reduce the configuration necessities, WCF also offers some hosting classes with preconfigured bindings. One example is located in the assembly `System.ServiceModel.Web` in the namespace `System.ServiceModel.Web` with the class `WebServiceHost`. This class creates a default endpoint for HTTP and HTTPS base addresses if a default endpoint is not configured with the `WebHttpBinding`. Also, this class adds the `WebHttpBehavior` if another behavior is not defined. With this behavior, simple HTTP `GET` and `POST`, `PUT`, `DELETE` (with the `WebInvoke` attribute) operations can be done without additional setup.

Available for
download on
Wrox.com

```
Uri baseAddress = new Uri("http://localhost:8000/RoomReservation");
var host = new WebServiceHost(typeof(RoomReservationService), baseAddress);
host.Open();

Console.WriteLine("service running");
Console.WriteLine("Press return to exit...");
Console.ReadLine();

if (host.State == CommunicationState.Opened)
    host.Close();
```

code snippet RoomReservationWebServiceHost/Program.cs

To use a simple HTTP GET request to receive the reservations, the method GetRoomReservation needs a WebGet attribute to map the method parameters to the input from the GET request. In the following code, a UriTemplate is defined that requires Reservations to be added to the base address followed by From and To parameters. The From and To parameters in turn are mapped to the fromDate and toDate variables.

```
[WebGet(UriTemplate="Reservations?From={fromDate}&To={toDate}")]
public RoomReservation[] GetRoomReservations(DateTime fromDate, DateTime toDate)
{
    var data = new RoomReservationData();
    return data.GetReservations(fromDate, toDate);
}
```

code snippet RoomReservationService/RoomReservationService.cs

Now the service can be invoked with a simple request as shown. All the reservations for the specified time frame are returned.

```
http://localhost:8000/RoomReservation/Reservations?From=2010/1/1&To=2010/8/1
```

 System.Data.Services.DataServiceHost *is another class with preconfigured features. This class derives itself from* WebServiceHost *and offers data services that are discussed in Chapter 32, "Data Services."*

CLIENTS

A client application needs a proxy to access a service. There are three ways to create a proxy for the client:

➤ **Visual Studio Add Service Reference** — This utility creates a proxy class from the metadata of the service.

➤ **ServiceModel Metadata Utility tool (Svcutil.exe)** — You can create a proxy class with the Svcutil utility. This utility reads metadata from the service to create the proxy class.

➤ **ChannelFactory class** — This class is used by the proxy generated from Svcutil; however, it can also be used to create a proxy programmatically.

Adding a service reference from Visual Studio requires accessing a WSDL document. The WSDL document is created by a MEX endpoint that needs to be configured with the service. With the following configuration, the endpoint with the relative address mex uses the mexHttpBinding and implements the contract IMetadataExchange. To access the metadata with an HTTP GET request, the behaviorConfiguration MexServiceBehavior is configured.

```
<?xml version="1.0" encoding="utf-8" ?>
<configuration>
  <system.serviceModel>
    <services>
      <service behaviorConfiguration=" MexServiceBehavior "
        name="Wrox.ProCSharp.WCF.RoomReservationService">
        <endpoint address="Test" binding="wsHttpBinding"
            contract="Wrox.ProCSharp.WCF.IRoomService" />
        <endpoint address="mex" binding="mexHttpBinding"
            contract="IMetadataExchange" />
        <host>
          <baseAddresses>
            <add baseAddress=
                "http://localhost:8732/Design_Time_Addresses/RoomReservationService/" />
          <baseAddresses>
        </host>
      </service>
```

```
      </services>
      <behaviors>
        <serviceBehaviors>
          <behavior name="MexServiceBehavior">
            <! — To avoid disclosing metadata information,
            set the value below to false and remove the metadata endpoint above
            before deployment — >
            <serviceMetadata httpGetEnabled="True"/>
          </behavior>
        </serviceBehaviors>
      </behaviors>
    </system.serviceModel>
  </configuration>
```

Similar to the Add service reference from Visual Studio, the `Svcutil` utility needs metadata to create the proxy class. The `Svcutil` utility can create a proxy from the MEX metadata endpoint, the metadata of the assembly, or WSDL and XSD documentation:

```
svcutil http://localhost:8080/RoomReservation?wsdl /language:C# /out:proxy.cs
svcutil CourseRegistration.dll
svcutil CourseRegistration.wsdl CourseRegistration.xsd
```

After the proxy class is generated, it just needs to be instantiated from the client code, the methods need to be called, and finally the `Close()` method must be invoked:

```
var client = new RoomServiceClient();
client.RegisterForCourse(roomReservation);
client.Close();
```

The generated proxy class derives from the base class `ClientBase<TChannel>` that wraps the `Channel Factory<TChannel>` class. Instead of using a generated proxy class, you can use the `ChannelFactory<TChannel>` class directly. The constructor requires the binding and endpoint address; next, you can create the channel and invoke methods as defined by the service contract. Finally, the factory must be closed:

```
var binding = new WsHttpBinding();
var address = new EndpointAddress("http://localhost:8080/RoomService");

var factory = new ChannelFactory<IStateService>(binding, address);

IRoomService channel = factory.CreateChannel();
channel.ReserveRoom(roomReservation);

//.
factory.Close();
```

The `ChannelFactory<TChannel>` class has several properties and methods, as shown in the following table.

CHANNELFACTORY MEMBERS	DESCRIPTION
Credentials	Credentials is a read-only property to access the ClientCredentials object that is assigned to the channel for authentication with the service. The credentials can be set with the endpoint.
Endpoint	Endpoint is a read-only property to access the ServiceEndpoint that is associated with the channel. The endpoint can be assigned in the constructor.
State	The State property is of type CommunicationState and returns the current state of the channel. CommunicationState is an enumeration with the values Created, Opening, Opened, Closing, Closed, and Faulted.
Open()	The Open() method is used to open the channel.
Close()	The Close() method closes the channel.
Opening Opened Closing Closed Faulted	You can assign event handlers to get informed about state changes of the channel. Events are fired before and after the channel is opened, before and after the channel is closed, and in case of a fault.

DUPLEX COMMUNICATION

The next sample application shows how a duplex communication can be done between the client and the service. The client starts the connection to the service. After the client connects to the service, the service can call back into the client.

For duplex communication, a contract must be specified that is implemented in the client. Here the contract for the client is defined by the interface IMyMessageCallback. The method implemented by the client is OnCallback(). The operation has the operation contract setting IsOneWay=true applied. This way, the service doesn't wait until the method is successfully invoked on the client. By default, the service instance can be invoked from only one thread (see the ConcurrencyMode property of the service behavior, which is, by default, set to ConcurrencyMode.Single).

If the service implementation now does a callback to the client and waits to get an answer from the client, the thread getting the reply from the client must wait until it gets a lock to the service object. Because the service object is already locked by the request to the client, a deadlock occurs. WCF detects the deadlock and throws an exception. To avoid this situation, you can change the ConcurrencyMode property to the value Multiple or Reentrant. With the setting Multiple, multiple threads can access the instance concurrently. Here, you must implement locking on your own. With the setting Reentrant, the service instance stays single-threaded, but allows answers from callback requests to reenter the context. Instead of changing the concurrency mode, you can specify the IsOneWay property with the operation contract. This way, the caller does not wait for a reply. Of course, this setting is possible only if return values are not expected.

The contract of the service is defined by the interface IMyMessage. The callback contract is mapped to the service contract with the CallbackContract property of the service contract definition:

Available for download on Wrox.com

```csharp
public interface IMyMessageCallback
{
    [OperationContract(IsOneWay=true)]
    void OnCallback(string message);
}

[ServiceContract(CallbackContract=typeof(IMyMessageCallback))]
public interface IMyMessage
{
    [OperationContract]
    void MessageToServer(string message);
}
```

code snippet MessageService/IMyMessage.cs

The class MessageService implements the service contract IMyMessage. The service writes the message from the client to the console. To access the callback contract, you can use the OperationContext class. OperationContext.Current returns the OperationContext that is associated with the current request from the client. With the OperationContext, you can access session information, message headers and properties, and, in the case of a duplex communication, the callback channel. The generic method GetCallbackChannel() returns the channel to the client instance. This channel can then be used to send a message to the client by invoking the method OnCallback(), which is defined with the callback interface IMyMessageCallback. To demonstrate that it is also possible to use the callback channel from the service independently of the completion of the method, a new thread that receives the callback channel is created. The new thread sends messages to the client by using the callback channel.

Available for download on Wrox.com

```csharp
public class MessageService: IMyMessage
{
    public void MessageToServer(string message)
    {
        Console.WriteLine("message from the client: {0}", message);
        IMyMessageCallback callback =
            OperationContext.Current.
```

```
                        GetCallbackChannel<IMyMessageCallback>();

            callback.OnCallback("message from the server");

            new Thread(ThreadCallback).Start(callback);
        }

        private void ThreadCallback(object callback)
        {
            IMyMessageCallback messageCallback = callback as IMyMessageCallback;
            for (int i = 0; i < 10; i++)
            {
                messageCallback.OnCallback("message " + i.ToString());
                Thread.Sleep(1000);
            }
        }
    }
```

code snippet MessageService/MessageService.cs

Hosting the service is the same as it was with the previous samples, so it is not shown here. However, for duplex communication, you must configure a binding that supports a duplex channel. One of the bindings supporting a duplex channel is `wsDualHttpBinding`, which is configured in the application's configuration file:

Available for download on Wrox.com

```xml
<?xml version="1.0" encoding="utf-8" ?>
<configuration>
  <system.serviceModel>
    <services>
      <service name="Wrox.ProCSharp.WCF.MessageService">
        <endpoint contract="Wrox.ProCSharp.WCF.IMyMessage"
            binding="wsDualHttpBinding"/>
        <host>
          <baseAddresses>
            <add baseAddress="http://localhost:8732/Service1" />
          </baseAddresses>
        </host>
      </service>
    </services>
  </system.serviceModel>
</configuration>
```

code snippet MessageService/app.config

With the client application, the callback contract must be implemented as shown here with the class `ClientCallback` that implements the interface `IMyMessageCallback`:

Available for download on Wrox.com

```csharp
class ClientCallback: IMyMessageCallback
{
    public void OnCallback(string message)
    {
        Console.WriteLine("message from the server: {0}", message);
    }
}
```

code snippet MessageClient/Program.cs

With a duplex channel, you cannot use the `ChannelFactory` to initiate the connection to the service as was done previously. To create a duplex channel, you can use the `DuplexChannelFactory` class. This class has a constructor with one more parameter in addition to the binding and address configuration. This parameter specifies an `InstanceContext` that wraps one instance of the `ClientCallback` class. When passing this instance to the factory, the service can invoke the object across the channel. The client just needs to keep the connection open. If the connection is closed, the service cannot send messages across it.

```
var binding = new WSDualHttpBinding();
var address = new EndpointAddress("http://localhost:8732/Service1");

ClientCallback clientCallback = new ClientCallback();
InstanceContext context = new InstanceContext(clientCallback);

DuplexChannelFactory<IMyMessage> factory =
    new DuplexChannelFactory<IMyMessage>(context, binding, address);

IMyMessage messageChannel = factory.CreateChannel();

messageChannel.MessageToServer("From the client");
```

Duplex communication is achieved by starting the service host and the client application.

SUMMARY

In this chapter, you learned how to use Windows Communication Foundation for communication between a client and a server. WCF is platform-independent like ASP.NET Web services, but it offers features similar to .NET Remoting, Enterprise Services, and Message Queuing.

WCF has a heavy focus on contracts to make it easier to isolate developing clients and services, and to support platform independence. It defines three different contract types: service contracts, data contracts, and message contracts. You can use several attributes to define the behavior of the service and its operations.

You saw how to create clients from the metadata offered by the service and also by using the .NET interface contract. You learned the features of different binding options. WCF offers not only bindings for platform independence but also bindings for fast communication between .NET applications. You've seen how to create custom hosts and also make use of the WAS host. You saw how duplex communication is achieved by defining a callback interface, applying a service contract, and implementing a callback contract in the client application.

The next few chapters continue with WCF features. In Chapter 44 you learn about Windows Workflow Foundation and how WCF is used to communicate with workflow instances. Chapter 46 explains how disconnected Message Queuing features can be used with WCF bindings. Chapter 47 is about the syndication features of WCF. And in Chapter 51 (available as a download), you learn how to integrate Enterprise Services with WCF.

44

Windows Workflow Foundation 4

WHAT'S IN THIS CHAPTER?

➤ The different types of workflows that can be created

➤ A description of some of the built-in activities

➤ How to create custom activities

➤ Overview of a workflow

This chapter presents an overview of the Windows Workflow Foundation 4 (referred to as Workflow 4 throughout the rest of this chapter), which provides a model to define and execute processes using a set of building blocks called *activities*. WF provides a Designer that, by default, is hosted within Visual Studio, and that allows you to drag and drop activities from the toolbox onto the design surface to create a workflow template.

This template can then be executed in a number of different ways, which we explain throughout the chapter. As a workflow executes, it may need to access the outside world, and there are a couple of methods that are typically used that allow you to do this. In addition, a workflow may need to save and restore its state, for example, when a long wait is needed.

A workflow is constructed from a number of activities, and these activities are executed at runtime. An activity might send an e-mail, update a row in a database, or execute a transaction on a back-end system. There are a number of built-in activities that can be used for general-purpose work, and you can also create your own custom activities and plug these into the workflow as necessary.

With Visual Studio 2010, there are now effectively two versions of Workflow — the 3.*x* version, which shipped with the .NET Framework 3, and version 4, which ships with the .NET Framework 4. This chapter concentrates on the latest version of Workflow — for details of the previous version see Chapter 57, "Windows Workflow Foundation 3.0," which is available online.

While there is broad feature parity between the versions, there are many subtle differences. If you are using Workflow for the first time, we urge you to use the latest version; however, if you have already used version 3.*x*, there are some tips in Chapter 57 to assist you in moving to Workflow 4.

We begin with the canonical example that everyone uses when faced with a new technology — Hello World.

HELLO WORLD

Visual Studio 2010 contains built-in support for creating workflow projects for both the 3.*x* and version 4 of the frameworks, and when you open the New Project dialog you will see a list of workflow project types, as shown in Figure 44-1.

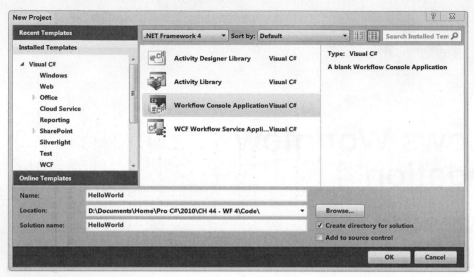

FIGURE 44-1

Ensure that you select .NET Framework 4 from the version combo box, and then choose Workflow Console Application from the available templates. This will construct a simple console application that includes a workflow template and also a main program, which executes this template.

Next, drag a `WriteLine` activity from the toolbox onto the design surface so that you have a workflow that looks like the one shown in Figure 44-2.

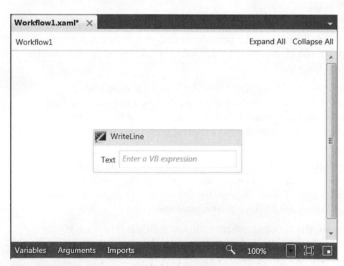

FIGURE 44-2

The `WriteLine` activity includes a `Text` property that you can set either on the design surface itself by simply entering text inline, or by displaying the property grid. Later in this chapter, we show you how to define your custom activities to use this same behavior.

The `Text` property is not just a simple string — it's actually defined as an argument type that can use an expression as its source. Expressions are evaluated at runtime to yield a result, and it is this textual result that is used as the input to the `WriteLine` activity. To enter a simple text expression, you must use double quotation marks — so if you are following along with this in Visual Studio, type "Hello World" into the `Text` property. If you omit the quotation marks, you will receive a compiler error, as without quotation marks this is not a legal expression.

If you build and run the program, you will see the output text on the console. When the program executes, an instance of the workflow is created in the `Main` method, which uses a static method of the `WorkflowInvoker` class to execute the instance. The code for this example is available in the 01_HelloWorld solution.

The `WorkflowInvoker` class is new to Workflow 4, and it lets you synchronously invoke a workflow. There are two other methods of workflow execution that execute workflows asynchronously, which you'll see later in this chapter. Synchronous execution was possible in Workflow 3.*x* but was somewhat more difficult to set up, and there was a lot more overhead.

The synchronous nature of `WorkflowInvoker` makes it ideal for running short-lived workflows in response to some UI action — you could use a workflow here to enable or disable some elements of the UI. While it was possible to do this in Workflow 3.*x*, it was also more difficult to synchronously execute a given workflow instance.

ACTIVITIES

Everything in a workflow is an activity, including the workflow itself. The workflow is a specific type of activity that typically allows other activities to be defined within it — this is known as a composite activity, and you'll see other composite activities later in this chapter. An activity is just a class that ultimately derives from the abstract `Activity` class.

The class hierarchy is somewhat deeper than that defined for Workflow 3.*x*, and the main classes are defined in Figure 44-3.

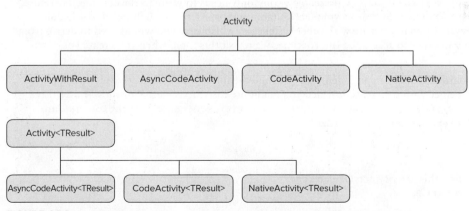

FIGURE 44-3

The `Activity` class is the root for all workflow activities and typically you will derive custom activities from the second tier. To create a simple activity like the `WriteLine` activity previously mentioned, you would derive from `CodeActivity`, as this class has just enough functionality for your write line clone to function. Activities that execute and return some form of a result should derive from the `ActivityWithResult` class — and note that it is preferable to use the generic `Activity<TResult>` class here as that provides a strongly typed `Result` property.

Deciding which base class to derive from can be the main battle when constructing custom activities, and we show you examples in this chapter to assist with choosing the right base class.

In order for an activity to do something, it will typically override the `Execute()` method, which has a number of different signatures depending on the base class chosen. These signatures are shown in the following table.

BASE CLASS	EXECUTE METHOD
`AsyncCodeActivity`	`IAsyncResult BeginExecute(AsyncCodeActivityContext, AsyncCallback, object)`
	`void EndExecute(AsyncCodeActivityContext, IAsyncResult)`
`CodeActivity`	`void Execute (CodeActivityContext)`
`NativeActivity`	`void Execute (NativeActivityContext)`
`AsyncCodeActivity<TResult>`	`IAsyncResult BeginExecute(AsyncCodeActivityContext, AsyncCallback, object)`
	`TResult EndExecute(AsyncCodeActivityContext, IAsyncResult)`
`CodeActivity<TResult>`	`TResult Execute (CodeActivityContext)`
`NativeActivity<TResult>`	`void Execute (NativeActivityContext)`

Here you may notice that the parameter(s) passed into the `Execute` methods differ in that there are type-specific execution context parameters used. In Workflow 3.x, there was a single class used (the `ActivityExecutionContext`); however, in Workflow 4 we use different contexts for different classes of activity.

The main difference is that the `CodeActivityContext` (and by derivation the `AsyncCodeActivityContext`) has a limited set of functionality compared with the `NativeActivityContext`. This means that activities deriving from `CodeActivity` and `AsyncCodeActivity` can do far less with their container. As an example, the `WriteLine` activity presented earlier only needs to write to the console. Therefore, it doesn't need access to its runtime environment. A more complex activity might need to schedule other child activities or communicate with other systems, in which case you would need to derive from `NativeActivity` in order to access the full runtime. We revisit this topic when you create your own custom activities.

Numerous standard activities are provided with WF, and the following sections provide examples of some of these together with scenarios in which you might use these activities. Workflow 4 uses three main assemblies: `System.Activities.dll`, `System.Activities.Core.Presentation.dll`, an `System.Activities.Presentation.dll`.

If Activity

As its name implies, this activity acts like an `If-Else` statement in C#.

When you drop an `If` onto the design surface, you will see an activity, as displayed in Figure 44-4. The `If` is a composite activity that contains two child activities that are dropped into the Then and Else portions of the screen.

FIGURE 44-4

The If activity shown in Figure 44-4 also includes a glyph indicating that the Condition property needs to be defined. This condition is evaluated when the activity is executed; if it returns True, the Then branch will execute, otherwise the Else branch will be called.

The Condition property is an expression that evaluates to a Boolean value, so you can include any expression here that is valid.

Workflow 4 includes an expression engine that uses Visual Basic syntax. This might seem strange to a C# programmer, as VB is significantly different from C#. Unfortunately, that is the way it is at the moment, so to use the built-in activities you'll have to learn enough VB to get by. Just remember to be extremely verbose and leave off any semicolons and you'll be OK.

An expression can reference any variables defined in the workflow and also access many static classes available in the .NET framework. So you could, for example, define an expression based on the Environment.Is64BitOperatingSystem value, if that was crucial to some part of your workflow. Naturally, you can define arguments that are passed into the workflow and that can then be evaluated by an expression inside an If activity. We'll cover arguments and variables later in the chapter.

InvokeMethod Activity

This is one of the most useful activities in the box, as it allows you to execute code that already exists and effectively wrap that code within the execution semantics of a workflow.

It's typical to have a lot of preexisting code, and this activity allows you to call that code directly from within a workflow.

There are two ways that you can use InvokeMethod to call code; which method you use depends on whether you wish to call a static method or an instance method. If you're calling a static method, you need to define the TargetType and the MethodName parameters. However if you're calling an instance method, then the TargetObject and MethodName properties are used, and in this instance the TargetObject could be created inline, or it could be a variable defined somewhere within the workflow itself. The example code in the 02_ParallelExecution sample shows both modes of using the InvokeMethod activity.

If you need to pass arguments to the method you're invoking, you can define these using the Parameters collection. The order of the parameters in the collection must match the order of the parameters to the method. In addition, there is a Result property that is set to the return value of the function call. You can bind this to a variable within the workflow in order to use the value as appropriate.

Parallel Activity

The Parallel activity is rather poorly named because, at first sight, you might think that on a multiprocessor machine this activity would schedule its children in true parallel; however, that isn't the case apart from some special circumstances.

After you drop a Parallel activity onto the design surface, you can then drop in other subordinate activities, as shown in Figure 44-5.

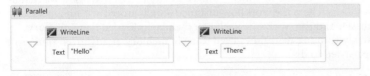

FIGURE 44-5

These child activities can be singular activities, as in Figure 44-5, or they can form a composite activity, such as a Sequence or another Parallel activity.

At runtime, the `Parallel` activity schedules each immediate child for execution. The underlying runtime execution engine will then schedule these children in a FIFO (first in, first out) manner, thereby providing the illusion of parallel execution; however, they run only on a single thread.

To include true parallel execution, the activities you drop into the `Parallel` activity must be derived from the `AsyncCodeActivity` class. The sample code in `02_ParallelExecution` includes an example that shows how to asynchronously process code within two branches of a `Parallel` activity. Figure 44-6 shows the use of two `InvokeMethod` activities within a `Parallel` activity.

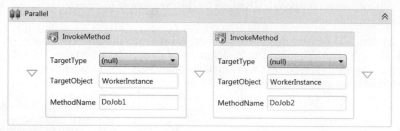

FIGURE 44-6

The `InvokeMethod` activities used here call two simple methods, `DoJob1` and `DoJob2`, which sleep for two and three seconds, respectively. In order to run these methods asynchronously, there is one final change that is needed. The `InvokeMethod` activity has a Boolean `RunAsynchronously` property that defaults to `False`. Setting this in the UI to `True` then calls the target method asynchronously, thereby allowing the `Parallel` activity to execute more than one activity at the same time. With a uni-processor machine, two threads will execute, giving the illusion of simultaneous execution; however, on a multiprocessor machine, these threads may well be scheduled on different cores, thereby providing true parallel execution. If you are creating your own activities, it is worthwhile creating these as asynchronous activities, as then the end user can get the benefits of true parallel execution.

Delay Activity

Business processes often need to wait for a period before completing. Consider using a workflow for expense approval. Your workflow might send an e-mail to your immediate manager asking him or her to approve your expense claim. The workflow then enters a waiting state where it waits for approval (or, horror of horrors, rejection); but it would also be nice to define a timeout so that if no response is returned within, say, one day, the expense claim is then routed to the next manager up the chain of command.

The `Delay` activity can form part of this scenario (the other part is the `Pick` activity defined in the next section). Its job is to wait for a predefined time before continuing execution of the workflow.

The `Delay` activity contains a `Duration` property, which can be set to a discrete `TimeSpan` value, but, as it is defined as an expression, this value could be linked to a variable within the workflow or computed from some other values as required.

When a workflow is executed, it enters an `Idle` state in which it runs a `Delay` activity. Workflows that are idle are candidates for persistence — this is where the workflow instance data is stored within a persistent medium (such as a SQL Server database), and the workflow itself can then be unloaded from memory. This conserves system resources, as only running workflows need to be in memory at any given time. Any workflows that are delayed will be persisted to disk.

Pick Activity

A common programming construct is to wait for one of a set of possible events — one example of this is the `WaitAny` method of the `WaitHandle` class in the `System.Threading` namespace. The `Pick` activity is the way to do this in a workflow because it can define any number of branches, and each branch can wait for a trigger action to occur before running. Once a trigger has been fired, the other activities within that branch execute.

As a concrete example, consider the expense claims procedure outlined in the previous section. Here, we'll have a Pick activity with three branches — one to deal with accepted claims, one to deal with rejected claims, and a third to deal with a timeout.

The example is available in the 03_PickDemo code in the download. This contains a sample workflow consisting of a Pick activity and three branches. When it is run, you are prompted to accept or reject the claim. If 10 seconds or more elapses, it'll close this prompt and run the delay branch instead.

In the example, the DisplayPrompt activity is used as the first activity in the workflow. This calls a method defined on an interface that would prompt the manager for approval or rejection. Because this functionality is defined as an interface, the prompt could be an e-mail, an IM message, or any other manner of notifying your manager that an expense claim needs to be processed. The workflow then executes the Pick, which awaits input from this external interface (either an approval or a rejection) and also waits on a delay.

When the pick executes, it effectively queues a wait on the first activity in each branch, and when one event is triggered, this cancels all other waiting events and then processes the rest of the branch where the event was raised. So, in the instance where the expense report is approved, the WaitForAccept activity completes and then the next action is to write out a confirmation message. If, however, your manager rejects the claim, the WaitForReject activity completes, and in the example this then outputs a rejection message.

Lastly, if neither the WaitForAccept nor WaitForReject activities completes, the WaitForTimeout ultimately completes after its delay expires, and the expense report could then be routed to another manager — potentially looking up that person in Active Directory. In the example, a dialog is displayed to the user when the DisplayPrompt activity is executed, so if the delay executes, you also need to close the dialog, which is the purpose of the activity named ClosePrompt in Figure 44-7.

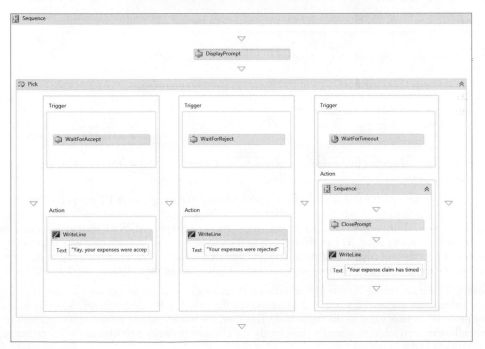

FIGURE 44-7

Some concepts used in that example have not been covered yet — such as how to write custom activities or waiting on external events; however, we cover these topics later in the chapter.

CUSTOM ACTIVITIES

So far, you have used activities that are defined within the `System.Activities` namespace. In this section, you learn how to create custom activities and extend these activities to provide a good user experience at both design time and runtime.

To begin, you create a `DebugWrite` activity that can be used to output a line of text to the console in debug builds. Although this is a trivial example, it will be expanded to show the full gamut of options available for custom activities using this example. When creating custom activities, you can simply construct a class within a workflow project; however, it is preferable to construct your custom activities inside a separate assembly, because the Visual Studio design-time environment (and specifically workflow projects) will load activities from your assemblies and can lock the assembly that you are trying to update. For this reason, you should create a simple class library project to construct your custom activities within. The code for this example is available in the `04_CustomActivities` project.

A simple activity, such as the `DebugWrite` activity, will be derived directly from the `CodeActivity` base class. The following code shows a constructed activity class and defines a `Message` property that is displayed when the activity is executed:

Available for download on Wrox.com

```
using System;
using System.Activities;
using System.Diagnostics;

namespace Activities
{
    public class DebugWrite : CodeActivity
    {
        [Description("The message output to the debug stream")]
        public InArgument<string> Message { get; set; }

        protected override void Execute(CodeActivityContext context)
        {
            Debug.WriteLine(Message.Get(context));
        }
    }
}
```

code download 04_CustomActivities

When a `CodeActivity` is scheduled for execution, its `Execute` method is called — this is where the activity actually needs to do something.

In the example, we have defined the `Message` property, which looks like a regular .NET property; however, its usage inside the `Execute` method may be unfamiliar. One of the many changes made in Workflow 4 is where state data is stored. Within Workflow 3.*x*, it was common to use standard .NET properties and store activity data within the activity itself. The problem with that method was that this storage was effectively opaque to the workflow runtime engine, and so in order to persist a workflow, it was necessary to perform binary persistence on all constructed activities in order to faithfully restore their data.

With Workflow 4, all data is stored outside of the individual activities — so the model here is that in order to get the value of an argument, you ask the context for the value, and in order to set the value of an argument, you provide the new value to the context. In this way, the workflow engine can track changes to state as the workflow executes and potentially stores only the changes between persistence points rather than the entire workflow data.

The [Description] attribute defined on the Message property is used within the property grid in Visual Studio to provide extra information about the property, as shown in Figure 44-8.

FIGURE 44-8

As it stands, the activity is perfectly usable; however, there are several areas that should be addressed to make this more user-friendly. As you have seen with activities such as the Pick earlier in the chapter, an activity may have some mandatory properties that, when not defined, produce an error glyph on the design surface. To get the same behavior from your activity, you need to extend the code.

Activity Validation

When an activity is placed on the design surface, the Designer will look in two places for validation information. The simplest form of validation is to add a [RequiredArgument] attribute to the argument property. If the argument is not defined, the exclamation mark glyph is shown to the right of the activity name, as in Figure 44-9.

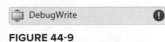

FIGURE 44-9

If you hover over the glyph, a tooltip is displayed that states "Value for a required activity argument 'Message' was not supplied." This is a compilation error, so you need to define a value for this argument before you can execute your application.

In the case where there are multiple properties that may be related, you can override the CacheMetadata method to add on some extra validation code. This method is called prior to the activity being executed; within it you can check that mandatory arguments are defined and optionally add extra metadata to the passed argument. You can also add extra validation errors (or warnings) by calling one of the AddValidationError overrides on the CodeActivityMetadata object passed to the CacheMetadata method.

Now that you have completed the activity validation, the next thing to do is to change the rendering behavior of the activity, as the current Designer experience is provided for you, and it could stand to be made more interesting.

Designers

When an activity is rendered onscreen, it is typical to associate a designer with the activity. The job of the designer is to provide the on-screen representation of that activity, and in Workflow 4 this representation is done in XAML. If you haven't used XAML before we recommend looking at Chapter 35, "Core WPF," before continuing.

The design-time experience for an activity is typically created in a separate assembly from the activity itself, as this design experience is unnecessary at runtime. Visual Studio includes an Activity Designer Library project type that is an ideal starting point, as when you create a project using this template you're provided with a default activity designer that you can then alter as appropriate.

Within the XAML for your designer, you can provide anything you wish — including animations, if you so desire. Less is usually more when it comes to user interfaces, and we suggest looking at the preexisting activities in order to get a feel for what is appropriate.

First, we'll create a simple designer and associate this with the DebugWrite activity. The code that follows shows the template created for you when you add an activity designer to your project (or when you construct a new activity designer library project). Again, this code is available in the 04_CustomActivities solution.

```
<sap:ActivityDesigner x:Class="Activities.Presentation.DebugWriteDesigner"
    xmlns="http://schemas.microsoft.com/winfx/2006/xaml/presentation"
    xmlns:x="http://schemas.microsoft.com/winfx/2006/xaml"
```

```
    xmlns:sap="clr-namespace:System.Activities.Presentation;
             assembly=System.Activities.Presentation"
    xmlns:sapv="clr-namespace:System.Activities.Presentation.View;
             assembly=System.Activities.Presentation">
  <Grid>

  </Grid>
</sap:ActivityDesigner>
```

code download 04_CustomActivities

The XAML created simply constructs a grid and also includes some imported namespaces, which may be needed by your activity. Obviously, there is little content within the template, so to begin we add in a label and a text box that will be used to define the message.

```
<Grid>
    <Grid.ColumnDefinitions>
        <ColumnDefinition Width="Auto"/>
        <ColumnDefinition Width="*"/>
    </Grid.ColumnDefinitions>
    <TextBlock Text="Message" Margin="0,0,5,0"/>
    <TextBox Text="{Binding Path=ModelItem.Message, Mode=TwoWay}"
        Grid.Column="1"/>
</Grid>
```

The XAML here constructs a binding between the `Message` property of the activity and the text box. Within the designer XAML, you can always reference the activity being designed by using the `ModelItem` reference.

In order to associate the designer defined above with the `DebugWrite` activity, you also need to alter the activity and add on a `Designer` attribute (you can also implement the `IRegisterMetadata` interface but we don't cover that further in this chapter).

```
[Designer("Activities.Presentation.DebugWriteDesigner, Activities.Presentation")]
public class DebugWrite : CodeActivity
{
    ...
}
```

Here, we've used the `[Designer]` attribute to define the link between the designer and the activity. It's good practice to use the string version of this attribute, as that ensures that there is no reference to the design assembly within the activity assembly.

Now when you use an instance of the `DebugWrite` activity within Visual Studio, you'll see something like Figure 44-10.

The problem with this, however, is the `Message` property — it's not showing the value defined within the property grid, and if you try to set a value by typing it into the text box, you'll receive an exception. The reason is that you're trying to bind a simple text value to an

FIGURE 44-10

`InArgument<string>` type, and in order to do that, you need to use another couple of built-in classes that come with Workflow 4 — the `ExpressionTextBox` and the `ArgumentToExpressionConverter`. The full XAML for the designer is now as follows. We have added boldface to the lines that have been added or modified.

```
<sap:ActivityDesigner x:Class="Activities.Presentation.DebugWriteDesigner"
    xmlns="http://schemas.microsoft.com/winfx/2006/xaml/presentation"
    xmlns:x="http://schemas.microsoft.com/winfx/2006/xaml"
    xmlns:sap="clr-namespace:System.Activities.Presentation;
        assembly=System.Activities.Presentation"
    xmlns:sapv="clr-namespace:System.Activities.Presentation.View;
        assembly=System.Activities.Presentation"
    xmlns:sadc="clr-namespace:System.Activities.Presentation.Converters;
```

```
            assembly=System.Activities.Presentation"
        >
    <sap:ActivityDesigner.Resources>
        <sadc:ArgumentToExpressionConverter x:Key="argConverter"/>
    </sap:ActivityDesigner.Resources>
    <Grid>
        <Grid.ColumnDefinitions>
            <ColumnDefinition Width="Auto"/>
            <ColumnDefinition Width="*"/>
        </Grid.ColumnDefinitions>
        <TextBlock Text="Message" Margin="0,0,5,0" />
        <sapv:ExpressionTextBox Grid.Column="1"
            Expression="{Binding Path=ModelItem.Message, Mode=TwoWay,
                        Converter={StaticResource argConverter},
                        ConverterParameter=In}"
            OwnerActivity="{Binding ModelItem}"/>
    </Grid>
</sap:ActivityDesigner>
```

code download 04_CustomActivitiesFirst

We have included a new namespace in the file — the `System.Activities.Presentation.View`. This includes the converter used to convert between an expression onscreen and the `Message` property of the activity — this is the `ArgumentToExpressionConverter`, which has been added to the resources of the XAML file.

Then we replaced the standard `TextBox` control with an `ExpressionTextBox`. This control is used to permit the user to enter expressions as well as simple text, so the `DebugWrite` activity could include an expression combining many values from the running workflow, rather than just a simple text string. With those changes in place, the activity behaves much more like the built-in activities.

Custom Composite Activities

A common requirement with activities is to create a composite activity — that is, an activity that contains other child activities. You have already seen examples, such as the `Pick` activity and the `Parallel` activity. The execution of a composite activity is entirely up to the programmer — you could, for example, have a random activity that only schedules one of its children, or an activity that bypasses some children based on the current day of the week. The simplest execution pattern would be to execute all children, but as the developer you can decide how child activities are executed and also when your activity is complete.

The first type of composite activity we create is a "retry" activity. It is quite common to try an operation, and if it fails, retry it a number of times before having it fail. The pseudo-code for this activity is as follows:

```
int iterationCount = 0;
bool looping = true;
while ( looping )
{
  try
  {
    // Execute the activity here
    looping = false;
  }
  catch (Exception ex)
  {
    iterationCount += 1;
    if ( iterationCount >= maxRetries )
      rethrow;
  }
}
```

What we would like to do is replicate the preceding code as an activity and insert the activity we wish to execute where the comment is placed. You might consider doing this all within the Execute method of a custom activity. However, there is another way — you can code the whole lot using other activities. What we need to do is create a custom activity that contains a "hole" into which the end user can place the activity that will be retried, and then a maximum retry count property. The code that follows shows how this can be done.

```csharp
public class Retry : Activity
{
    public Activity Body { get; set; }

    [RequiredArgument]
    public InArgument<int> NumberOfRetries { get; set; }

    public Retry()
    {
        Variable<int> iterationCount =
            new Variable<int> ( "iterationCount", 0 );
        Variable<bool> looping = new Variable<bool> ( "looping", true );

        this.Implementation = () =>
        {
            return new While
            {
                Variables = { iterationCount, looping },
                Condition = new VariableValue<bool>
                    { Variable = looping },
                Body = new TryCatch
                {
                    Try = new Sequence
                    {
                        Activities =
                        {
                            this.Body,
                            new Assign
                            {
                                To = new OutArgument<bool> ( looping ),
                                Value = new InArgument<bool>
                                    { Expression = false }
                            }
                        }
                    },
                    Catches =
                    {
                        new Catch<Exception>
                        {
                            Action = new ActivityAction<Exception>
                            {
                                Handler = new Sequence
                                {
                                    Activities =
                                    {
                                        new Assign
                                        {
                                            To = new OutArgument<int>
                                                (iterationCount) ,
                                            Value = new InArgument<int>
                            (ctx => iterationCount.Get(ctx) + 1)
                                        },
                                        new If
                                        {
                                            Condition = new InArgument<bool>
                                                (env=>iterationCount.Get(env)
```

```
                                            >= NumberOfRetries.Get(env)),
                            Then = new Rethrow()
                          }
                        }
                      }
                    }
                  }
                }
              }
            };
          };
        }
      }
```

code download 04_CustomActivities

Phew!

First, we've defined a Body property of type Activity — this will be the activity that is executed within the retry loop. Then we've defined the RetryCount property, which is used to define the number of times the operation will be tried.

This custom activity derives directly from the Activity class and provides the implementation as a function. When a workflow is executed that contains this activity, it will effectively execute the function, which provides a runtime execution path similar to the pseudo-code defined earlier. Within the constructor, we create the local variables used by the activity and then construct a set of activities that matches the pseudo-code. The code for this example is also available in the 04_CustomActivities solution.

From the preceding, you'll also be able to infer that we can create workflows without XAML — there is no design experience (that is, you can't drag and drop activities to generate code); however, if code is what you prefer, then there's no reason not to use it instead of XAML.

Now that you have the custom composite activity, you'll also need to define a designer. What's needed here is an activity that has a placeholder into which you can drop another activity. If you look at other standard activities, there are several that exhibit a similar behavior, such as the If and Pick activities. Ideally, you would like the activity to work in a similar manner to the built-in activities, so it's time to look at their implementations.

If you use Reflector to poke around inside the workflow libraries, you'll find a distinct lack of any designer XAML. This is because it's been compiled into the assemblies as a set of resources. You can use Reflector to look at these resources, but first you need to download the BAML viewer add-on. This decompiles the binary BAML format and produces text, so you can use it to view the XAML used by the standard activities. To find the BAML viewer, search for "Reflector BAML viewer" online, and you'll soon find it.

When you have the add-in loaded in Reflector, load up the System .Activities.Presentation assembly, and then click the BAML Viewer item on the Tools menu. This will then present you with a list of all the BAML resources in the currently loaded assemblies, and you can then look at an appropriate sample in order to see some sample XAML.

FIGURE 44-11

I used this method to learn about the XAML that was used for the built-in activities, and this helped me to construct the example for the Retry activity shown in Figure 44-11.

The key to this activity is the WorkflowItemPresenter class, which is used in the XAML to define the placeholder for the child activity. This is defined as follows:

```
<sap:WorkflowItemPresenter IsDefaultContainer="True"
    AllowedItemType="{x:Type sa:Activity}"
    HintText="Drop an activity here" MinWidth="100" MinHeight="60"
    Item="{Binding Path=ModelItem.Body, Mode=TwoWay}"
    Grid.Column="1" Grid.Row="1" Margin="2">
```

This control is bound to the `Body` property of the `Retry` activity, and the `HintText` defines the help text shown when no child activity has been added to the control. The XAML also includes some styles that are used to show the expanded or contracted version of the designer — this ensures that the activity works the same way as the built-in activities. All of the code and XAML for this example is available in the `04_CustomActivities` solution.

WORKFLOWS

Up to this point, the chapter has concentrated on activities but has not discussed workflows. A workflow is simply a list of activities, and indeed a workflow itself is just another type of activity. Using this model simplifies the runtime engine, because the engine just needs to know how to execute one type of object — that being anything derived from the `Activity` class.

You've already seen the `WorkflowExecutor` class, which can be used to execute a workflow, but as mentioned at the time, this is only one of the ways that a workflow can be executed. There are three different options for executing workflows, and each has different capabilities. Before getting into the other methods of executing workflows, we must delve into arguments and variables.

Arguments and Variables

A workflow can be considered a program, and one of the facets of any programming language is the ability to create variables, and pass arguments into and out of that program. Naturally, Workflow 4 supports both constructs, and in this section we show you how you can define both arguments and variables.

To begin with, let's assume that the workflow is processing an insurance policy, so a likely argument to pass to the workflow would be the policy ID. In order to define an argument to a workflow, you need to go into the Designer and click on the Arguments button on the bottom left. This brings up a list of arguments defined for the workflow, as shown in Figure 44-12, and here you can also add your own.

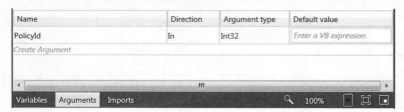

Name	Direction	Argument type	Default value
PolicyId	In	Int32	*Enter a VB expression*
Create Argument			

Variables | **Arguments** | Imports   🔍 100%

FIGURE 44-12

To define an argument, you need to specify the Name, Direction (which can be `In`, `Out`, or `InOut`) and the data type for that argument. You can optionally specify a default value, which will be used if the argument is not provided.

The direction of the argument is used to define whether the argument is expected as an input to the workflow, as an output from the workflow, or in the case of the `InOut` direction, as both an input and output.

In the first section of this chapter, we described using the `WorkflowInvoker` class to execute a workflow. There are several overrides of the `Invoke` method that can be used to pass arguments into the workflow. They are passed as a dictionary of name/value pairs, where the name must match the argument's name exactly — this match is case sensitive. The code below is used to pass a `PolicyId` value into a workflow — the code for this example is available in the `05_ArgsAndVars` solution.

```
Dictionary<string, object> parms = new Dictionary<string, object>();
parms.Add("PolicyId", 123);

WorkflowInvoker.Invoke(new PolicyFlow(), parms);
```

code download 05_ArgsAndVars

This will then invoke the workflow and pass the `PolicyId` from the dictionary to the named parameter. If you supply a name in the dictionary for which an argument does not exist, then an `ArgumentException` will be thrown. Conversely, if you don't supply the value for an `In` argument, no exception is thrown. we feel that this is the wrong way around — we would expect an argument exception to be thrown for any `In` arguments that were not defined and would prefer no exception to be thrown if we passed in too many arguments.

When a workflow completes, you may wish to retrieve output arguments. In order to do this, there is a specific override of the `WorkflowInvoker.Invoke` method that returns a dictionary. This dictionary will contain just the `Out` or `InOut` arguments.

Within the workflow, you may then wish to define variables. This wasn't easy to do in XAML workflows in Workflow 3.*x*, however in Workflow 4 this has been addressed and you can easily define parameters in the XAML.

As in any programming language, workflow variables have the notion of scope. You can define "globally" scoped variables by defining them on the root activity of the workflow. These variables are available by all activities within the workflow, and their lifetime is tied to that of the workflow.

You can also define variables on individual activities, and in this case these variables are only available to the activity that the variable is defined on and also children of that activity. Once an activity has completed, its variables go out of scope and are no longer accessible.

WorkflowApplication

While `WorkflowInvoker` is a useful class for synchronous execution of workflows, you might need to have long-running workflows that may persist to a database and need to be rehydrated at some point in the future. If that's the case then you might wish to use the `WorkflowApplication` class.

The `WorkflowApplication` class is similar to the `WorkflowRuntime` class that existed in Workflow 3 in that it allows you to run a workflow and also respond to events that occur on that workflow instance. Probably the simplest program you can write to use the `WorkflowApplication` class is shown here:

```
WorkflowApplication app = new WorkflowApplication(new Workflow1());

ManualResetEvent finished = new ManualResetEvent(false);

app.Completed = (completedArgs) => { finished.Set(); };

app.Run();

finished.WaitOne();
```

code download 06_WorkflowApplication

This constructs a workflow application instance and then hooks up to the `Completed` delegate of that instance in order to set a manual reset event. The `Run` method is called to start the workflow execution, and lastly the code waits for the event to be triggered.

This shows one of the main differences between `WorkflowExecutor` and `WorkflowApplication` — the latter is asynchronous. When you call `Run`, the system uses a thread pool thread to execute the workflow rather than the calling thread. Thus, you need some form of synchronization in order to ensure that the application hosting the workflow doesn't exit before the workflow completes.

A typical long-running workflow may have many periods when it is dormant — the execution behavior for most workflows can best be described as periods of episodic execution. There is typically some work done at the start of the workflow, then it waits on some input or a delay, and once this input has been received it processes up to the next wait state.

So, when a workflow is dormant it would be ideal to unload it from memory and only reload it when an event triggers the workflow to continue. In order to do this, we need to add an `InstanceStore` object to the `WorkflowApplication` and also make some other minor alterations to the preceding code. There is one implementation of the abstract `InstanceStore` class in the framework — the `SqlWorkflowInstanceStore`. In order to use this class, you first need a database, and the scripts for this can be found by default in the `C:\Windows\Microsoft.NET\Framework\v4.0.21006\SQL\en` directory. Note that the version number is subject to change.

You'll find a number of SQL files in this directory, but the two you need are `SqlWorkflowInstanceStoreSchema.sql` and `SqlWorkflowInstanceStoreLogic.sql`. You can run these against an existing database or create an entirely new database as appropriate, and you can use a full SQL server installation or a SQL Express installation.

Once you have a database, you need to make some alterations to the hosting code. First, you need to construct an instance of the `SqlWorkflowInstanceStore` and then add this to the workflow application:

```
SqlWorkflowInstanceStore store = new SqlWorkflowInstanceStore
    (ConfigurationManager.ConnectionStrings["db"].ConnectionString);

AutoResetEvent finished = new AutoResetEvent(false);

WorkflowApplication app = new WorkflowApplication(new Workflow1());
app.Completed = (e) => { finished.Set(); };
app.PersistableIdle = (e) => { return PersistableIdleAction.Unload; };
app.InstanceStore = store;

app.Run();

finished.WaitOne();
```

code download 06_WorkflowApplication

The emboldened lines are those added to the previous example. You'll also notice that we've added an event handler to the `PersistableIdle` delegate on the workflow application. When a workflow executes, it runs as many activities as it can, until there is no more work to do. At that point, it transitions to an `Idle` state, and an idle workflow is a candidate for persistence. The `PersistableIdle` delegate is used to determine what should happen to an idle workflow. The default is to do nothing; however, you can also specify `PersistableIdleAction.Persist`, which will take a copy of the workflow and store that in the database but still leave the workflow in memory, or you can specify `PersistableIdleAction.Unload`, which will persist and then unload the workflow.

It is also possible to request persistence of a workflow by using the `Persist` activity, and indeed as a custom activity writer you can also request persistence if you have derived from `NativeActivity` by calling the `RequestPersist` method of the `NativeActivityContext`.

We now have a problem — we have the ability to unload a workflow from memory and store it in the persistence store, but as yet we've not described how to go about retrieving it from the store and getting it to execute again.

Bookmarks

The traditional use of a bookmark is to mark a page in a book, so you can resume reading from the same point. In the context of a workflow, a bookmark specifies a place where you would like to resume running that workflow, and bookmarks are typically used when you're waiting for external input.

As an example, you might be writing an application that deals with insurance quotes. An end user might go online to produce a quotation, and as you can imagine, there would be a workflow associated with that quotation. The quotation might only be valid for 30 days, so you would like to invalidate the quote after that point. Similarly, you might request proof of a no claims discount, and cancel the policy if that proof didn't arrive within a specified time. This workflow then has a number of periods of execution, and other times when it is dormant and could be unloaded from memory. Before being unloaded, however, it is necessary to define a point in the workflow where processing can be resumed, and this is where bookmarks are used.

To define a bookmark, you need a custom activity that derives from `NativeActivity`. You can then create a bookmark within the `Execute` method, and when the bookmark has been resumed your code will continue. The example activity below defines a simplistic `Task` activity that creates a bookmark, and on resumption at the point of that bookmark, the activity completes.

```
public class Task : NativeActivity<Boolean>
{
    [RequiredArgument]
    public InArgument<string> TaskName { get; set; }

    protected override bool CanInduceIdle
    {
        get { return true; }
    }

    protected override void Execute(NativeActivityContext context)
    {
        context.CreateBookmark(TaskName.Get(context),
            new BookmarkCallback(OnTaskComplete));
    }

    private void OnTaskComplete(NativeActivityContext context,
        Bookmark bookmark, object state)
    {
        bool taskOK = Convert.ToBoolean(state);

        this.Result.Set(context, taskOK);
    }
}
```

code download 06_WorkflowApplication

The call to `CreateBookmark` passes the name of the bookmark and also a callback function. This callback will be executed when the bookmark is resumed. The callback itself is passed an arbitrary object, which in this case is a `Boolean`, as we've decided that each task should report success or failure, and we can then use this to decide on the next steps in the workflow. There's nothing to stop you from passing any object into the workflow — it could be a complex type with many fields.

So that's the activity written — we now need to alter the hosting code so as to resume at the point of the bookmarks. But there's another problem — how does the hosting code know that a workflow has created a bookmark? If it's the host's responsibility to resume from the bookmark, it needs to know that one exists.

The `Task` we've created above really needs to do some more work — telling the outside world that a task has been created. In a production system, this would typically result in an entry being stored in a queue table, and this queue would be presented to the call center staff as a job list.

Communicating with the host is the subject of the next section, "Extensions."

Extensions

An extension is simply a class or interface that is added to the runtime context of a workflow application. In Workflow 3.*x* these were called Services, however that clashed with WCF Services, so these have been renamed *extensions* in Workflow 4.

You will typically define an interface for your extensions and then provide a runtime implementation of this interface. Your activities will simply call the interface, and this allows the implementation to change as necessary. A good example of an extension is something that sends an e-mail. You could create a `SendEmail` activity that would call the extension within its `Execute` method, and then you could define an SMTP based e-mail extension or an Exchange-based outlook extension to actually send the e-mail at runtime. Your activity wouldn't need to be changed to use any e-mail provider — you can just plug in a new one by altering the application configuration file.

For the task sample, we need an extension that will be notified when the `Task` activity is about to wait at its bookmark. This could write the name of the bookmark and other pertinent information into a database so that a task queue could then be presented to the user. We'll use the following interface to define this extension:

```
public interface ITaskExtension
{
    void ExecuteTask(string taskName);
}
```

The task activity can then be updated to notify the task extension that it's executing by modifying the `Execute` method as follows:

```
protected override void Execute(NativeActivityContext context)
{
    context.CreateBookmark(TaskName.Get(context),
        new BookmarkCallback(OnTaskComplete));
    context.GetExtension<ITaskExtension>().
        ExecuteTask(TaskName.Get(context));
}
```

The context object passed to the `Execute` method is queried for the `ITaskExtension` interface and then the code calls the `ExecuteTask` method. The `WorkflowApplication` maintains a collection of extensions, so you can create a class that implements this extension interface, which can then be used to maintain the list of tasks. You could then construct and execute a new workflow, and each task would then notify the extension when it was executed. Some other process might look at the task list and present this to the end user.

To keep things simple in the sample code, we've created just one workflow instance. This instance contains a `Task` activity followed by an `If`, which outputs a message according to whether the user accepts or rejects the task.

Putting It All Together

Now you can run, persist, and unload a workflow, and also deliver events into that workflow via bookmarks; the last part is reloading the workflow. When using `WorkflowApplication`, you can call `Load` and pass through the unique ID of the workflow. Every workflow has a unique ID that can be retrieved from the `WorkflowApplication` object by calling the `Id` property. So, in pseudo-code, our workflow-hosting application is as follows:

```
WorkflowApplication app = BuildApplication();
Guid id = app.Id;
app.Run();
// Wait for a while until a task is created, then reload the workflow
app = BuildApplication();
app.Load(id);
app.ResumeBookmark()
```

The sample code provided is a little more complex than the preceding, as it also includes an implementation of the `ITaskExtension` interface, but the code follows the earlier pattern. You may notice two calls to the `BuildApplication` method. This is one we've used in the code to construct a `WorkflowApplication` instance and to set up all required properties, such as the `InstanceStore` and the delegates for `Completed` and `PersistableIdle`. After the first call, we execute the `Run` method. This begins execution of a new instance of the workflow.

The second time the application is loaded is after a persistence point, so by that point the workflow has been unloaded, hence, the application instance is also essentially dead. We then construct a new `WorkflowApplication` instance, but instead of calling `Run`, we call the `Load` method, which uses the persistence provider to load up an existing instance from the database. This instance is then resumed by calling the `ResumeBookmark` function.

If you run the example, you'll see a prompt onscreen. While that prompt is there the workflow is persisted and unloaded, and you can check this by running SQL Server Management Studio and executing the command shown in Figure 44-13.

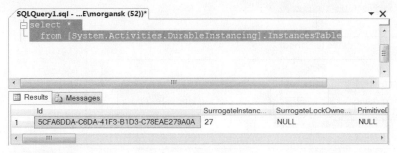

FIGURE 44-13

Workflow instances are stored within the `InstancesTable` of the `System.Activities.DurableInstancing` schema. The entry shown in Figure 44-13 is the persisted instance of the workflow running on my machine.

When we continue the workflow it will eventually complete, and at that point the workflow will be deleted from the instances table, as there's an option on the instance store exposed as the `InstanceCompletionAction`, which by default is set to be `DeleteAll`. This ensures that any data stored in the database for a given workflow instance will be deleted once that workflow completes. This is a sensible default, as once a workflow completes you would normally not expect any data to hang around. You can change this option when you define the instance store by setting the instance completion action to `DeleteNothing`.

If you now continue running the test application and then retry the SQL command from Figure 44-13, you should notice that the workflow instance has been deleted.

WorkflowServiceHost

A long way back in this chapter we mentioned that there were three ways to host workflows — the last is by using the `WorkflowServiceHost` class which exposes a workflow through WCF. One of the major areas that Workflow is destined to be used for is as the back-end to WCF services. If you think about what a typical WCF service does, it's usually a bunch of related methods that are typically called in some sort of order. The main problem here is that you could call these methods in any order, and usually you need to define the ordering so that, for example, the order details are not uploaded before the order itself.

With Workflow you can easily expose WCF services that also have a notion of method ordering. The main classes you'll use here are the `Receive` and the `Send` activities. In the code for this example (which is available in the `07_WorkflowsAsServices` solution), the scenario used is an estate agent (a Realtor if you're in the United States) who wishes to upload information about a property to a web site.

The first call to the service will construct a new workflow instance, and this call will return a unique ID that is used in subsequent calls to the service. We'll then use this unique ID in subsequent calls, as this will identify which workflow instance on the server we wish to communicate with. Workflow uses a facility called "correlation" to map an incoming request to a workflow instance. Here, we're using message-based correlation to link a property of the incoming message with an existing workflow instance. The workflow we'll use for this example is outlined in Figure 44-14.

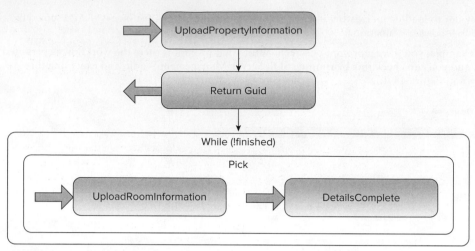

FIGURE 44-14

Defining the WorkflowServiceHost

The workflow begins in a `Receive` activity which defines the initial service operation of UploadPropertyInformation. The data received from the service call is stored within the workflow and a `Guid` is then returned to the caller by the `Send` activity. This `Guid` uniquely defines this workflow instance and is used when calling back to that instance in the other operations.

Once these initial two activities have completed, the workflow then runs a `While` activity within which there is a `Pick` activity with two branches. The first branch has a `Receive` activity with an operation named UploadRoomInformation and the second has a `Receive` activity with an operation named DetailsComplete.

The code shown in the following snippet is used to host the workflow. It makes use of the `WorkflowServiceHost` class, which is very similar to the `ServiceHost` class available with WCF.

Available for
download on
Wrox.com

```
string baseAddress = "http://localhost:8080/PropertyService";

using (WorkflowServiceHost host =
    new WorkflowServiceHost(GetPropertyWorkflow(), new Uri(baseAddress)))
{
    host.AddServiceEndpoint(XName.Get("IProperty", ns),
        new BasicHttpBinding(), baseAddress);

    ServiceMetadataBehavior smb = new ServiceMetadataBehavior();
    smb.HttpGetEnabled = true;
    host.Description.Behaviors.Add(smb);
    try
    {
        host.Open();

        Console.WriteLine("Service host is open for business...");
        Console.ReadLine();
    }
    finally
    {
        host.Close();
    }
}
```

code download 07_WorkflowsAsServices

Here, an instance of the `WorkflowServiceHost` class is constructed, and the workflow it exposes is provided by the `GetPropertyWorkflow` method call. You can use a code based workflow, as we have done with this example, or an XAML-based workflow. We then add an endpoint and specify a basic HTTP binding, and then enable metadata publishing so that a client can point `svcutil.exe` at this endpoint to download the service definition. Once that's done, it is simply a matter of calling `Open` on the service host class, and we're then ready to receive incoming calls.

Ensuring That a Workflow Can Be Created

The first activity within the workflow is a `Receive`, and it has been defined with the `CanCreateInstance` property set to `True`. This is important, as it notifies the host that, if a caller calls this operation, a new workflow instance will be constructed based on that call. What is happening under the covers is that the `WorkflowServiceHost` is probing the workflow definition looking for `Receive` activities, and it will construct a service contract based on these activities. It's also looking for any such activities with `True` set for `CanCreateInstance`, as then it knows what to do when it receives a message.

The sample code contains a client application that creates a new workflow instance by calling `UploadPropertyInformation`; it then uploads information about three rooms using the `UploadRoomInformation` operation, and finally it calls `DetailsComplete`. This sets the `Finished` flag used by the `While` activity, and this completes that workflow.

The workflow code is fairly complex, as there's a lot going on under the covers. Knowing how it works, though, is instructive, so we'll go through some of it here.

The first activity within the workflow is defined as follows:

```
Variable<string> address = new Variable<string>();
Variable<string> owner = new Variable<string>();
Variable<double> askingPrice = new Variable<double>();

// Initial receive - this kicks off the workflow
Receive receive = new Receive
{
    CanCreateInstance = true,
    OperationName = "UploadPropertyInformation",
    ServiceContractName = XName.Get("IProperty", ns),
    Content = new ReceiveParametersContent
    {
        Parameters =
        {
            {"address", new OutArgument<string>(address)},
            {"owner", new OutArgument<string>(owner)},
            {"askingPrice", new OutArgument<double>(askingPrice)}
        }
    }
};
```

This `Receive` has the `CanCreateInstance` flag set to `true`, and it defines both operation and service contract names. The `ServiceContractName` includes a namespace (in the example set to `http://pro-csharp/`) so as to uniquely identify this service. The `Content` property defines what is expected to be passed up from the client when the operation is called — in this instance we're passing up address, owner, and asking price values. The service operation is completely defined here by this code — and the metadata exported uses this code to construct the operation definition.

The arguments received from this operation are bound to variables defined by the workflow. This is how we pass arguments from the outside world into a workflow hosted by WCF.

Inside the workflow, we then create the unique ID that will be used when calling back to this workflow instance. In order to do this, we need to define a workflow variable and assign its value — in the code that follows, we've used an `Assign` activity to do this.

```
return new Sequence
{
    Variables = { propertyId, operationHandle, finished,
                  address, owner, askingPrice },
    Activities =
    {
        receive,
        new WriteLine { Text = "Assigning a unique ID" },
        new Assign<Guid>
        {
            To = new OutArgument<Guid> (propertyId),
            Value = new InArgument<Guid> (Guid.NewGuid())
        },
        new SendReply
        {
            Request = receive,
            Content = SendContent.Create
                (new InArgument<Guid> (env => propertyId.Get(env))),
            CorrelationInitializers =
            {
                new QueryCorrelationInitializer
                {
                    CorrelationHandle = operationHandle,
                    MessageQuerySet = extractGuid
                }
            }
        }
        // Other activities omitted for clarity
    }
};
```

Next, the `SendReply` activity is used to respond to the caller with the `Guid` defined by the workflow. This part is fairly complex.

The `SendReply` activity is linked to the initial `Receive` activity by setting its `Request` property to the receive activity instance. The return value of the operation is defined by the `Content` property. There are three types of responses that can be returned from an operation — a discrete value, such as a `Guid` used here, a set of parameters defined by a dictionary of name/value pairs, or a message type. The `SendContent` class is a helper that constructs the appropriate object for you.

The last part is the most complex. The `CorrelationInitializers` property is effectively used to extract a correlation token from the current message and use this in subsequent calls to the workflow to uniquely identify the workflow. The `MessageQuerySet` is used to do the extraction and is defined as shown below for this outgoing message. Once the query has been defined, it is then linked with a handle value. This handle is used by any other activity wishing to be part of the same correlation group.

```
MessageQuerySet extractGuid = new MessageQuerySet
{
    { "PropertyId",
      new XPathMessageQuery ( "sm:body()/ser:guid", messageContext ) }
};
```

This query uses XPath (otherwise known as voodoo magic) to extract data from the message being sent back to the client. Here, it is reading the `body` element and, within that, looking for the value of the `guid` element within the message.

Awaiting Events with Pick

So, we've constructed a new workflow instance and replied to the caller with a unique operation ID. The next part is to await further data from the client, which is done with two further `Receive` activities. The first of these corresponds to the `UploadRoomInformation` operation.

```
Variable<string> roomName = new Variable<string>();
Variable<double> width = new Variable<double>();
Variable<double> depth = new Variable<double>();

// Receive room information
Receive receiveRoomInfo = new Receive
{
    OperationName = "UploadRoomInformation",
    ServiceContractName = XName.Get("IProperty", ns),
    CorrelatesWith = operationHandle,
    CorrelatesOn = extractGuidFromUploadRoomInformation,
    Content = new ReceiveParametersContent
    {
        Parameters =
        {
            {"propertyId", new OutArgument<Guid>()},
            {"roomName", new OutArgument<string>(roomName)},
            {"width", new OutArgument<double>(width)},
            {"depth", new OutArgument<double>(depth)},
        }
    }
};
```

The variables initially defined are used to record the data passed from the client to the workflow. Again the `Receive` activity specifies both the `OperationName` and the `ServiceContractName` so that metadata can be generated for this operation. The `CorrelatesWith` value is critical here, as it links the different operations of the workflow together. In the `SendReply` activity, we created this handle so that we could reference it with these later operations. Without this handle, it would not be possible to work out which workflow instance an incoming message is for.

The `CorrelatesOn` property defines what is extracted from the incoming message in order to verify that the message is for this workflow instance. Again, a `MessageQuerySet` is used, which in this case extracts the unique ID from the incoming message:

```
MessageQuerySet extractGuidFromUploadRoomInformation =
    new MessageQuerySet
    {
        { "PropertyId",
          new XPathMessageQuery
          ( @"sm:body()/local:UploadRoomInformation/local:propertyId",
            messageContext ) }
    };
```

Here, the XPath is looking for the `propertyId` element within the `UploadRoomInformation` call.

The last part of this `Receive` defines what happens with the incoming parameters passed to the service operation. Here, I'm expecting the unique `propertyId`, a room name and dimensions. This data is extracted into variables, and in the example code we simply output it to the console. In a real application, you would obviously use this data to update a database or something similar.

The last `Receive` activity is used to await the `DetailsComplete` message from the client. It follows a similar pattern to the other receive activities in that it defines the service contract name and operation name, uses the same correlation handle as the initial `Send` and the `Receive` used for the `UploadRoomInformation` operation, and it uses a `MessageQuerySet` in order to retrieve the unique property ID from the incoming message.

With those activities in place, the rest of the workflow is a `While` loop that contains the `Pick` activity and its branches:

```
new While
{
    Condition = ExpressionServices.Convert<bool>
        (env => !finished.Get(env)),
    Body = new Pick
```

```
    {
        Branches =
        {
            new PickBranch
            {
                Variables = { roomName, width, depth },
                Trigger = receiveRoomInfo,
                Action = new WriteLine { Text = "Room Info Received"},
            },
            new PickBranch
            {
                Trigger = receiveDetailsComplete,
                Action = new Sequence
                {
                    Activities =
                    {
                        new Assign<bool>
                        {
                            To = new OutArgument<bool>(finished),
                            Value = new InArgument<bool>(true)
                        },
                        new WriteLine { Text = "Finished" }
                    }
                }
            }
        }
    }
}
```

Here, the `While` defines a `Condition` that evaluates the value of the `finished` variable. The `Condition` property is defined as an `Activity<bool>`, so the `ExpressionServices` helper class is used to convert the variable expression into an activity.

The `Pick` contains two branches, and the `Trigger` activity of each branch is what we are waiting for in order to execute the `Action` activity. Building workflows in code is somewhat long-winded; however, we believe it's easier to see what is going on when you are learning Workflow 4 than using XAML-based workflows. You might disagree!

Hosting the Designer

Often one wishes to save the best till last. We'd rather not break with tradition, so that's what we've done with this chapter. The Workflow Designer that is used within Visual Studio can also be hosted within your own application, allowing your end users to create their own workflows without a copy of Visual Studio in sight. This is, we believe, the best feature of Workflow 4 by far. Traditional application extension mechanisms always require some form of developer — either to write an extension DLL and plug it into the system somewhere, or by writing macros or scripts. Windows Workflow allows end users to customize an application simply by dragging and dropping activities onto a design surface.

Rehosting the designer in Workflow 3.*x* was not for the faint-hearted; however, in Workflow 4 it becomes almost trivial. The Designer itself is a WPF control, so we'll use a WPF project as the main application. The code for this example is available in the `08_DesignerRehosting` project.

The first thing we need to do is to include the workflow assemblies, and then we need to define the main window XAML. We always use the Model-View-ViewModel (MVVM) pattern when constructing WPF user interfaces, as it simplifies the coding and also ensures that we can drape different XAML over the same view model if necessary. The XAML for the main window is as follows:

```
<Window x:Class="HostApp.MainWindow"
        xmlns="http://schemas.microsoft.com/winfx/2006/xaml/presentation"
        xmlns:x="http://schemas.microsoft.com/winfx/2006/xaml"
        Title="MainWindow">
```

```
<Grid>
    <Grid.RowDefinitions>
        <RowDefinition Height="Auto"/>
        <RowDefinition Height="*"/>
    </Grid.RowDefinitions>
    <Menu IsMainMenu="True">
        <MenuItem Header="_File">
            <MenuItem Header="_New" Command="{Binding New}"/>
            <MenuItem Header="_Open" Command="{Binding Open}"/>
            <MenuItem Header="_Save" Command="{Binding Save}"/>
            <Separator/>
            <MenuItem Header="_Exit" Command="{Binding Exit}"/>
        </MenuItem>
        <MenuItem Header="Workflow">
            <MenuItem Header="_Run" Command="{Binding Run}"/>
        </MenuItem>
    </Menu>
    <Grid Grid.Row="1">
        <Grid.ColumnDefinitions>
            <ColumnDefinition Width="*"/>
            <ColumnDefinition Width="4*"/>
            <ColumnDefinition Width="*"/>
        </Grid.ColumnDefinitions>
        <ContentControl Content="{Binding Toolbox}" />
        <ContentControl Content="{Binding DesignerView}"
            Grid.Column="1"/>
        <ContentControl Content="{Binding PropertyInspectorView}"
            Grid.Column="2"/>
    </Grid>
</Grid>
</Window>
```

code download 08_DesignerRehosting

It is a fairly simple layout with a main menu and then a grid that defines placeholders for the toolbox, designer, and property grid. You'll notice that everything is bound, including the commands.

The `ViewModel` we've created consists of properties for each of the main UI elements — those being the Toolbox, Designer, and Property Grid. In addition to these properties there are also properties for each command, such as New, Save, and Exit.

```
public class ViewModel : BaseViewModel
{
    public ViewModel()
    {
        // Ensure all designers are registered for inbuilt activities
        new DesignerMetadata().Register();
    }

    public void InitializeViewModel(Activity root)
    {
        _designer = new WorkflowDesigner();
        _designer.Load(root);

        this.OnPropertyChanged("DesignerView");
        this.OnPropertyChanged("PropertyInspectorView");
    }

    public UIElement DesignerView
    {
        get { return _designer.View; }
    }
```

```
        public UIElement ProperttInspectorView
        {
            get { return _designer.PropertyInspectorView; }
        }

        private WorkflowDesigner _designer;
    }
```

To begin, the `ViewModel` class derives from `BaseViewModel` — this base class is one that we use every time we construct a view model, as it provides an implementation of `INotifyPropertyChanged`. It comes from a set of snippets written by Josh Twist and available on `www.thejoyofcode.com`.

The constructor ensures that the metadata for all of the built-in activities is registered — without this call, none of the type specific designers will show up on the user interface. Within the `InitializeViewModel` method, we then construct an instance of the Workflow Designer and load an activity into it. The `WorkflowDesigner` class is curious in that once you've loaded one workflow into it, you cannot load another, so here we re-create this class whenever a new workflow is created.

The last thing that the `InitializeViewModel` method does is to call the property change notification function to indicate to the user interface that both the `DesignerView` and `PropertyInspectorView` are updated. As the UI is bound to these properties, they will be requeried and will load the new values from the new Workflow Designer instance.

The next part of the user interface that needs to be created is the toolbox. In Workflow 3.*x* you had to construct this control yourself; however, in Workflow 4 there is a `ToolboxControl`, which is trivially easy to use.

```
    public UIElement Toolbox
    {
        get
        {
            if (null == _toolbox)
            {
                _toolbox = new ToolboxControl();

                ToolboxCategory cat = new ToolboxCategory
                    ("Standard Activities");
                cat.Add(new ToolboxItemWrapper(typeof(Sequence),
                    "Sequence"));
                cat.Add(new ToolboxItemWrapper(typeof(Assign), "Assign"));
                _toolbox.Categories.Add(cat);

                ToolboxCategory custom = new ToolboxCategory
                    ("Custom Activities");
                custom.Add(new ToolboxItemWrapper(typeof(Message),
                    "MessageBox"));
                _toolbox.Categories.Add(custom);
            }

            return _toolbox;
        }
    }
```

Here, we construct the toolbox control, then add two toolbox items to the first category and one toolbox item to a second category. The `ToolboxItemWrapper` class is used to simplify the code needed to add a given activity to the toolbox.

With that code in place, we have a functioning application — well almost. All we need to do now is wire up the `ViewModel` with the XAML. This is done in the constructor for the main window.

```
    public MainWindow()
    {
        InitializeComponent();

        ViewModel vm = new ViewModel();
```

```
            vm.InitializeViewModel(new Sequence());

            this.DataContext = vm;
    }
```

Here, we construct the view model, and, by default, add in a `Sequence` activity so that something is displayed onscreen when the application runs. Figure 44-15 shows what the screen looks like if you run the application at this point.

FIGURE 44-15

The only part missing now is some commands. We use a `DelegateCommand` class to write `ICommand`-based commands for WPF, as then we find the code in the view model is easy to understand. The commands are fairly trivial to implement, as is evident by the `New` command shown here:

```
    public ICommand New
    {
        get
        {
            return new DelegateCommand(unused =>
            {
                InitializeViewModel(new Sequence());
            });
        }
    }
```

This command is bound to the New menu item, so when that is clicked the delegate is executed, and in this instance that simply calls the `InitializeViewModel` method with a new `Sequence` activity. Because this method also raises the property change notification for the designer and the property grid, these are updated, too.

The `Open` command is a little more involved but not much:

```
    public ICommand Open
    {
        get
        {
            return new DelegateCommand(unused =>
```

```
            {
                OpenFileDialog ofn = new OpenFileDialog();
                ofn.Title = "Open Workflow";
                ofn.Filter = "Workflows (*.xaml)|*.xaml";
                ofn.CheckFileExists = true;
                ofn.CheckPathExists = true;

                if (true == ofn.ShowDialog())
                    InitializeViewModel(ofn.FileName);
            });
        }
    }
```

Here, we've used another override of `InitializeViewModel`, which in this instance takes a filename rather than an activity. We've not shown this code, but it is available in the code download. This command displays an `OpenFileDialog`, and when one is chosen it loads the workflow into the Designer. There is a corresponding `Save` command, which calls the `WorkflowDesigner.Save` method to store the workflow XAML on disk.

The last section of code in the view model is the Run command. It wouldn't be much good designing workflows without being able to execute them, so we've included this facility in the view model as well. It's fairly trivial — the Designer includes a `Text` property, which is the XAML representation of the activities within the workflow. All we need to do is convert this into an `Activity` and then execute that using the `WorkflowInvoker` class.

```
    public ICommand Run
    {
        get
        {
            return new DelegateCommand(unused =>
            {
                Activity root = _designer.Context.Services.
                    GetService<ModelService>().Root.
                    GetCurrentValue() as Activity;

                WorkflowInvoker.Invoke(root);
            },
            unused => { return !HasErrors; }
            );
        }
    }


    public bool HasErrors
    {
        get { return (0 != _errorCount); }
    }

    public void ShowValidationErrors(IList<ValidationErrorInfo> errors)
    {
        _errorCount = errors.Count;
        OnPropertyChanged("HasErrors");
    }

    private int _errorCount;
```

I have had to butcher the preceding code to fit it into the space on the page, as the first line of the delegate command that retrieves the root activity from the designer is long to say the least. All we then have to do is use the `WorkflowInvoker.Invoke` method to execute the workflow.

The command infrastructure within WPF includes a way to disable commands if they cannot be accessed, and that's the second Lambda function on the `DelegateCommand`. This function returns the value of `HasErrors`, a Boolean property that has been added to the view model. This property indicates whether any validation errors have been found within the workflow, as the view model implements the `IValidationErrorService`, which is notified whenever the valid state of the workflow changes.

You could extend the sample to expose this list of validation errors on the user interface as necessary — and you will probably want to add in some more activities to the toolbox, as you won't get far with just three activities.

SUMMARY

Windows Workflow will produce a radical change in the way that applications are constructed. You can now surface complex parts of an application as activities and permit users to alter the processing of the system simply by dragging and dropping activities into a workflow.

There is almost no application that you could not apply workflow to — from the simplest command-line tool to the most complex system containing many hundreds of modules. Where before you might have needed a developer to write an extension module for a system, it is now possible to provide a simple and extensible customization mechanism that almost anyone can use. As an application vendor, you would have provided the custom activities that interacted with your system, and you would also have provided the code in the application that called the workflow(s), but you can now leave it up to your customers to define what they want to happen when an event occurs in the application.

Workflow 3.*x* has now been largely superseded by Workflow 4, and if you are planning on using workflow for the first time, we would recommend starting this new version and bypassing Workflow 3.*x* entirely.

45

Peer-to-Peer Networking

WHAT'S IN THIS CHAPTER?

➤ An overview of P2P

➤ The Microsoft Windows Peer-to-Peer Networking platform, including PNRP and PNM

➤ Building P2P applications with the .NET Framework

Peer-to-peer networking, often referred to as P2P, is perhaps one of the most useful and yet misunderstood technologies to emerge in recent years. When people think of P2P they usually think of one thing: sharing music files, often illegally. This is because file-sharing applications such as BitTorrent have risen in popularity at a staggering rate, and these applications use P2P technology to work.

Although P2P is used in file-sharing applications, that doesn't mean it doesn't have other applications. Indeed, as you see in this chapter, P2P can be used for a vast array of applications, and is becoming more and more important in the interconnected world in which we live. You learn about this in the first part of this chapter, when you look at an overview of P2P technologies.

Microsoft has not been oblivious to the emergence of P2P, and has been developing its own tools and technologies to use it. You can use the Microsoft Windows Peer-to-Peer Networking platform as a communication framework for P2P applications. This platform includes the important components Peer Name Resolution Protocol (PNRP) and People Near Me (PNM). Also, version 3.5 of the .NET Framework introduced a new namespace, `System.Net.PeerToPeer`, and several new types and features that you can use to build P2P applications yourself with minimal effort.

PEER-TO-PEER NETWORKING OVERVIEW

Peer-to-peer networking is an alternative approach to network communication. To understand how P2P differs from the "standard" approach to network communication it is helpful to take a step backward and look at client-server communications. Client-server communications are ubiquitous in networked applications today.

Client-Server Architecture

Traditionally, you interact with applications over a network (including the Internet) using a client-server architecture. Web sites are a great example of this. When you look at a web site you send a request over the Internet to a web server, which then returns the information that you require. If you want to download a file, you do so directly from the web server.

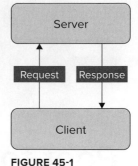

Similarly, desktop applications that include local or wide area network connectivity will typically connect to a single server, for example, a database server or a server that hosts other services.

This simple form of client-server architecture is illustrated in Figure 45-1.

There is nothing inherently wrong with the client-server architecture, and indeed in many cases it will be exactly what you want. However, there is a scalability problem. Figure 45-2 shows how the client-server architecture scales with additional clients.

FIGURE 45-1

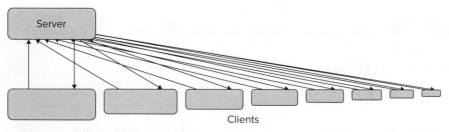

FIGURE 45-2

With every client that is added an increased load is placed on the server, which must communicate with each client. To return to the web site example, this increased communication load is how web sites collapse. When there is too much traffic the server simply becomes unresponsive.

There are of course scaling options that you can implement to mitigate this situation. You can *scale up* by increasing the power and resources available to the server, or you can *scale out* by adding additional servers. Scaling up is of course limited by the technology available and the cost of better hardware. Scaling out is potentially more flexible, but requires an additional infrastructure layer to ensure that clients either communicate with individual servers or maintain session state independent of the server with which they are communicating. Plenty of solutions are available for this, such as web or server farm products.

P2P Architecture

The peer-to-peer approach is completely different from either the scaling up or scaling out approach. With P2P, instead of focusing on and attempting to streamline the communication between the server and its clients, you instead look at ways in which clients can communicate with each other.

Say, for example, that the web site that clients are communicating with is www.wrox.com. In our imaginary scenario, Wrox has announced that a new version of this book is to be released on the wrox.com web site and will be free to download to anyone who wants it; however, it will be removed after one day. Before the book becomes available on the web site you might imagine that an awful lot of people will be looking at the web site and refreshing their browsers, waiting for the file to appear. When the file is available, everyone will try to download it at the same time, and more than likely the wrox.com web server will collapse under the strain.

You could use P2P technology to prevent this web server collapse. Instead of sending the file directly from the server to all the clients, you send the file to just a few clients. A few of the remaining clients then download the file from the clients that already have it, a few more clients download it from those second-level clients, and so on. In fact, this process is made even faster by splitting the file into chunks and dividing these chunks among clients, some of whom download it directly from the server, and some whom download chunks from other clients. This is how file-sharing technologies such as BitTorrent work, and is illustrated in Figure 45-3.

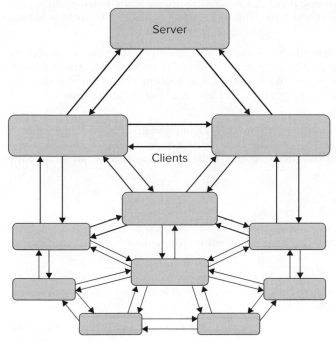

FIGURE 45-3

P2P Architectural Challenges

There are still problems to solve in the file-sharing architecture discussed here. For a start, how do clients detect that other clients exist, and how do they locate chunks of the file that other clients might have? Also, how can you ensure optimal communication between clients that may be separated by entire continents?

Every client participating in a P2P network application must be able to perform the following operations to overcome these problems:

➤ It must be able to *discover* other clients.

➤ It must be able to *connect* to other clients.

➤ It must be able to *communicate* with other clients.

The discovery problem has two obvious solutions. You can either keep a list of the clients on the server so clients can obtain this list and contact other clients (known as *peers*), or you can use an infrastructure (for example PNRP, covered in the next section) that enables clients to find each other directly. Most file-sharing systems use the "list on a server" solution by using servers known as *trackers*. Also, in file-sharing systems any client may act as a server as shown in Figure 45-3, by declaring that it has a file available and registering it with a tracker. In fact, a pure P2P network needs no servers at all, just peers.

The connection problem is a more subtle one, and concerns the overall structure of the networks used by a P2P application. If you have one group of clients, all of which can communicate with one another, the topology of the connections between these clients can become extremely complex. You can often improve performance by having more than one group of clients, each of which consists of connections between clients in that group, but not to clients in other groups. If you can make these groups locale-based you will get an additional performance boost, because clients can communicate with each other with fewer hops between networked computers.

Communication is perhaps a problem of lesser importance, because communication protocols such as TCP/IP are well established and can be reused here. There is, however, scope for improvement in both high-level technologies (for example, you can use WCF services and therefore all the functionality that WCF offers) and low-level protocols (such as multicast protocols to send data to multiple endpoints simultaneously).

Discovery, connection, and communication are central to any P2P implementation. The implementation you look at in this chapter is to use the `System.Net.PeerToPeer` types with PNM for discovery and PNRP for connection. As you see in subsequent sections, these technologies cover all three of these operations.

P2P Terminology

In the previous sections you were introduced to the concept of a *peer,* which is how clients are referred to in a P2P network. The word "client" makes no sense in a P2P network because there is not necessarily a server to be a client of.

Groups of peers that are connected to each other are known by the interchangeable terms *meshes, clouds,* or *graphs*. A given group can be said to be *well-connected* if at least one of the following statements applies:

➤ There is a connection path between every pair of peers, so that every peer can connect to any other peer as required.

➤ There are a relatively small number of connections to traverse between any pair of peers.

➤ Removing a peer will not prevent other peers from connecting to each other.

Note that this does not mean that every peer must be able to connect to every other peer directly. In fact, if you analyze a network mathematically you will find that peers need to connect only to a relatively small number of other peers for these conditions to be met.

Another P2P concept to be aware of is *flooding*. Flooding is the way in which a single piece of data may be propagated through a network to all peers, or of querying other nodes in a network to locate a specific piece of data. In unstructured P2P networks this is a fairly random process of contacting nearest neighbor peers, which in turn contact their nearest neighbors, and so on until every peer in the network is contacted. It is also possible to create structured P2P networks such that there are well-defined pathways for queries and data flow among peers.

P2P Solutions

When you have an infrastructure for P2P you can start to develop not just improved versions of client-server applications, but entirely new applications. P2P is particularly suited to the following classes of applications:

➤ Content distribution applications, including the file-sharing applications discussed earlier

➤ Collaboration applications, such as desktop sharing and shared whiteboard applications

➤ Multi-user communication applications that allow users to communicate and exchange data directly rather than through a server

➤ Distributed processing applications, as an alternative to supercomputing applications that process enormous amounts of data

➤ Web 2.0 applications that combine some or all the above in dynamic, next-generation web applications

MICROSOFT WINDOWS PEER-TO-PEER NETWORKING

The Microsoft Windows Peer-to-Peer Networking platform is Microsoft's implementation of P2P technology. It is part of Windows XP SP2, Windows Vista, and Windows 7, and is also available as an add-on for Windows XP SP1. It includes two technologies that you can use when creating .NET P2P applications:

➤ The Peer Name Resolution Protocol (PNRP), which is used to publish and resolve peer addresses

➤ The People Near Me server, which is used to locate local peers (currently for Vista and Windows 7 only)

In this section you learn about these technologies.

Peer Name Resolution Protocol (PNRP)

You can of course use any protocol at your disposal to implement a P2P application, but if you are working in a Microsoft Windows environment (and, let's face it, if you're reading this book you probably are) it makes sense to at least consider PNRP. There have been two versions of PNRP released to date. PNRP version 1 was included in Windows XP SP2, Windows XP Professional x64 Edition, and Windows XP SP1 with the Advanced Networking Pack for Windows XP. PNRP version 2 was released with Windows Vista, and was made available to Windows XP SP2 users through a separate download (see KB920342 at `support.microsoft.com/kb/920342`). Windows 7 also uses version 2. Version 1 and version 2 of PNRP are not compatible, and this chapter covers only version 2.

In itself, PNRP doesn't give you everything you need to create a P2P application. Rather, it is one of the underlying technologies that you use to resolve peer addresses. PNRP enables a client to register an endpoint (known as a *peer name*) that is automatically circulated among peers in a cloud. This peer name is encapsulated in a PNRP ID. A peer that discovers the PNRP ID is able to use PNRP to resolve it to the actual peer name, and can then communicate directly with the associated client.

For example, you might define a peer name that represents a WCF service endpoint. You could use PNRP to register this peer name in a cloud as a PNRP ID. A peer running a suitable client application that uses a discovery mechanism that can identify peer names for the service you are exposing might then discover this PNRP ID. Once discovered, the peer would use PNRP to locate the endpoint of the WCF service and then use that service.

An important point is that PNRP makes no assumptions about what a peer name actually represents. It is up to peers to decide how to use them when discovered. The information a peer receives from PNRP when resolving a PNRP ID includes the IPv6 (and usually also the IPv4) address of the publisher of the ID, along with a port number and optionally a small amount of additional data. Unless the peer knows what the peer name means it is unlikely to be able to do anything useful with this information.

PNRP IDs

PNRP IDs are 256-bit identifiers. The low-order 128 bits are used to uniquely identify a particular peer, and the high-order 128 bits identify a peer name. The high-order 128 bits are a hashed combination of a hashed public key from the publishing peer and a string of up to 149 characters that identifies the peer name. The hashed public key (known as the *authority*) combined with this string (the *classifier*) are together referred to as the P2P ID. It is also possible to use a value of 0 instead of a hashed public key, in which case the peer name is said to be *unsecured* (as opposed to *secured* peer names, which use a public key).

The structure of a PNRP ID is illustrated in Figure 45-4.

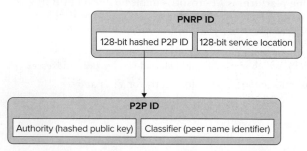

FIGURE 45-4

The PNRP service on a peer is responsible for maintaining a list of PNRP IDs, including the ones that it publishes as well as a cached list of those it has obtained by PNRP service instances elsewhere in the cloud. When a peer attempts to resolve a PNRP ID, the PNRP service either uses a cached copy of the endpoint to resolve the peer that published the PNRP or it asks its neighbors if they can resolve it. Eventually a connection to the publishing peer is made and the PNRP service can resolve the PNRP ID.

Note that all this happens without you having to intervene in any way. All you have to do is ensure that peers know what to do with peer names after they have resolved them using their local PNRP service.

Peers can use PNRP to locate PNRP IDs that match a particular P2P ID. You can use this to implement a very basic form of discovery for unsecured peer names. This is because if several peers expose an unsecured peer name that uses the same classifier, the P2P ID will be the same. Of course, because any peer can use an unsecured peer name you have no guarantee that the endpoint you connect to will be the sort of endpoint you expect, so this is only really a viable solution for discovery over a local network.

PNRP Clouds

In the preceding discussion you learned how PNRP registers and resolves peer names in clouds. A cloud is maintained by a *seed server,* which can be any server running the PNRP service that maintains a record of at least one peer. Two types of clouds are available to the PNRP service:

➤ **Link local** — These clouds consist of the computers attached to a local network. A PC may be connected to more than one link local cloud if it has multiple network adapters.

➤ **Global** — This cloud consists of computers connected to the Internet by default, although it is also possible to define a private global cloud. The difference is that Microsoft maintains the seed server for the global Internet cloud, whereas if you define a private global cloud you must use your own seed server. If you use your own seed server you must ensure that all peers connect to it by configuring policy settings.

In past releases of PNRP there was a third type of cloud, site local. *This is no longer used and is not covered in this chapter.*

You can discover what clouds you are connected to with the following command:

```
netsh p2p pnrp cloud show list
```

A typical result is shown in Figure 45-5.

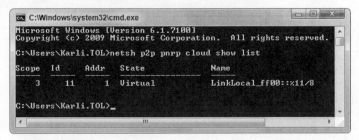

FIGURE 45-5

Figure 45-5 shows that a single cloud is available, and that it is a link local cloud. You can tell this from both the name and the `Scope` value, which is 3 for link local clouds and 1 for global clouds. To connect to a global cloud you must have a global IPv6 address. The computer used to generate Figure 45-5 does not have one, which is why only a local cloud is available.

Clouds may be in one of the following states:

➤ **Active** — If the state of a cloud is `active`, you can use it to publish and resolve peer names.

➤ **Alone** — If the peer you are querying the cloud from is not connected to any other peers, it will have a state of `alone`.

➤ **No Net** — If the peer is not connected to a network, the cloud state may change from `active` to `no net`.

➤ **Synchronizing** — Clouds will be in the `synchronizing` state when the peer is connecting to them. This state will change to another state extremely quickly because this connection does not take long, so you will probably never see a cloud in this state.

➤ **Virtual** — The PNRP service connects to clouds only as required by peer name registration and resolution. If a cloud connection has been inactive for more than 15 minutes it may enter the `virtual` state.

 If you experience network connectivity problems you should check your firewall in case it is preventing local network traffic over the UDP ports 3540 or 1900. UDP port 3540 is used by PNRP, and UDP port 1900 is used by the Simple Service Discovery Protocol (SSDP), which in turn is used by the PNRP service (as well as UPnP devices).

PNRP in Windows 7

With Windows 7, PNRP makes use of a new component called the *Distributed Routing Table (DRT)*. This component is responsible for determining the structure of the keys used by PNRP, the default implementation of which is the PNRP ID previously described. By using the DRT API it is possible to define an alternative key scheme, but the keys must be 256-bit integer values (just like PNRP IDs). This means that you can use any scheme you want, but you are then responsible for the generation and security of the keys. By using this component you can create new cloud topologies beyond the scope of PNRP, and indeed, beyond the scope of this chapter as this is an advanced technique.

Windows 7 also introduces a new way of connecting to other users for the Remote Assistance application: Easy Connect. This connection option uses PNRP to locate users to connect to. Once a session is created, through Easy Connect or by other means (for example an e-mail invitation), users can share their desktops and assist each other through the Remote Assistance interface.

People Near Me

PNRP, as you saw in the previous section, is used to locate peers. This is obviously important as an enabling technology when you consider the discovery/connection/ communication process of a P2P application, but in itself is not a complete implementation of any of these stages. The People Near Me service is an implementation of the discovery stage, and enables you to locate peers that are signed in to the Windows People Near Me service in your local area (that is, in a link local cloud that you are connected to).

You may have come across this service because it is built into Vista and Windows 7, and is used in the Windows Meeting Space application, which you can use for sharing applications among peers. You can configure this service through the Change People Near Me settings control panel item (you can navigate to this quickly by typing "people" in the Start menu search box). This control panel item displays the dialog box shown in Figure 45-6.

FIGURE 45-6

After you have signed in, the service is available to any application that is built to use the PNM service.

At the time of writing, PNM is available only on the Windows Vista family of operating systems (and it has been removed from Windows 7). However, it is possible that future service packs or additional downloads may make it available on Windows XP.

BUILDING P2P APPLICATIONS

Now that you have learned what P2P networking is and what technologies are available to .NET developers to implement P2P applications, it's time to look at how you can build them. From the preceding discussion you know that you will be using PNRP to publish, distribute, and resolve peer names, so the first thing you look at here is how to achieve that using .NET. Next you look at how to use PNM as a framework for a P2P application. This can be advantageous because if you use PNM you do not have to implement your own discovery mechanisms.

To examine these subjects you need to learn about the classes in the following namespaces:

- ➤ `System.Net.PeerToPeer`
- ➤ `System.Net.PeerToPeer.Collaboration`

To use these classes you must have a reference to the `System.Net.dll` assembly.

System.Net.PeerToPeer

The classes in the `System.Net.PeerToPeer` namespace encapsulate the API for PNRP and enable you to interact with the PNRP service. You will use these classes for two main tasks:

➤ Registering peer names

➤ Resolving peer names

In the following sections, all the types referred to come from the `System.Net.PeerToPeer` namespace unless otherwise specified.

Registering Peer Names

To register a peer name you must carry out the following steps:

1. Create a secured or unsecured peer name with a specified classifier.

2. Configure a registration for the peer name, providing as much of the following optional information as you choose:

➤ A TCP port number

➤ The cloud or clouds with which to register the peer name (if unspecified, PNRP will register the peer name in all available clouds)

➤ A comment of up to 39 characters

➤ Up to 4,096 bytes of additional data

➤ Whether to generate endpoints for the peer name automatically (the default behavior, where endpoints will be generated from the IP address or addresses of the peer and, if specified, the port number)

➤ A collection of endpoints

3. Use the peer name registration to register the peer name with the local PNRP service.

After Step 3 the peer name will be available to all peers in the selected cloud (or clouds). Peer registration continues until it is explicitly stopped, or until the process that registered the peer name is terminated.

To create a peer name you use the `PeerName` class. You create an instance of this class from a string representation of a P2P ID in the form `authority.classifier` or from a classifier string and a `PeerNameType`. You can use `PeerNameType.Secured` or `PeerNameType.Unsecured`. For example:

```
PeerName pn = new PeerName("Peer classifier", PeerNameType.Secured);
```

Because an unsecured peer name uses an authority value of 0, the following lines of code are equivalent:

```
PeerName pn = new PeerName("Peer classifier", PeerNameType.Unsecured);

PeerName pn = new PeerName("0.Peer classifier");
```

After you have a `PeerName` instance you can use it along with a port number to initialize a `PeerNameRegistration` object:

```
PeerNameRegistration pnr = new PeerNameRegistration(pn, 8080);
```

Alternatively, you can set the `PeerName` and (optionally) the `Port` properties on a `PeerNameRegistration` object created using its default parameter. You can also specify a `Cloud` instance as a third parameter of the `PeerNameRegistration` constructor, or through the `Cloud` property. You can obtain a `Cloud` instance from the cloud name or by using one of the following static members of `Cloud`:

➤ `Cloud.Global` — This static property obtains a reference to the global cloud. This may be a private global cloud depending on peer policy configuration.

➤ `Cloud.AllLinkLocal` — This static field gets a cloud that contains all the link local clouds available to the peer.

➤ `Cloud.Available` — This static field gets a cloud that contains all the clouds that are available to the peer, which includes link local clouds and (if available) the global cloud.

When created, you can set the `Comment` and `Data` properties if you want. Be aware of the limitations of these properties, though. You will receive a `PeerToPeerException` if you try to set `Comment` to a `string` greater than 39 Unicode characters or an `ArgumentOutOfRangeException` if you try to set `Data` to a `byte[]` greater than 4,096 bytes. You can also add endpoints by using the `EndPointCollection` property. This property is a `System.Net.IPEndPointCollection` collection of `System.Net.IPEndPoint` objects. If you use the `EndPointCollection` property you might also want to set the `UseAutoEndPointSelection` property to `false` to prevent automatic generation of endpoints.

When you are ready to register the peer name you can call the `PeerNameRegistration.Start()` method. To remove a peer name registration from the PNRP service you use the `PeerNameRegistration.Stop()` method.

The following code registers a secured peer name with a comment:

```
PeerName pn = new PeerName("Peer classifier", PeerNameType.Unsecured);
PeerNameRegistration pnr = new PeerNameRegistration(pn, 8080);
pnr.Comment = "Get pizza here";
pnr.Start();
```

Resolving Peer Names

To resolve a peer name you must carry out the following steps:

1. Generate a peer name from a known P2P ID or a P2P ID obtained through a discovery technique.

2. Use a resolver to resolve the peer name and obtain a collection of peer name records. You can limit the resolver to a particular cloud and/or a maximum number of results to return.

3. For any peer name records that you obtain, obtain peer name, endpoint, comment, and additional data information as required.

This process starts with a `PeerName` object similar to a peer name registration. The difference here is that you use a peer name that is registered by one or more remote peers. The simplest way to get a list of active peers in your link local cloud is for each peer to register an unsecured peer name with the same classifier and to use the same peer name in the resolving phase. However, this is not a recommended strategy for global clouds because unsecured peer names are easily spoofed.

To resolve peer names you use the `PeerNameResolver` class. When you have an instance of this class you can choose to resolve peer names synchronously by using the `Resolve()` method, or asynchronously using the `ResolveAsync()` method.

You can call the `Resolve()` method with a single `PeerName` parameter, but you can also pass an optional `Cloud` instance to resolve in, an `int` maximum number of peers to return, or both. This method returns a `PeerNameRecordCollection` instance, which is a collection of `PeerNameRecord` objects. For example, the following code resolves an unsecured peer name in all link local clouds and returns a maximum of 5 results:

```
PeerName pn = new PeerName("0.Peer classifier");
PeerNameResolver pnres = new PeerNameResolver();
PeerNameRecordCollection pnrc = pnres.Resolve(pn, Cloud.AllLinkLocal, 5);
```

The `ResolveAsync()` method uses a standard asynchronous method call pattern. You pass a unique `userState` object to the method and listen for `ResolveProgressChanged` events for peers being found and the `ResolveCompleted` event when the method terminates. You can cancel a pending asynchronous request with the `ResolveAsyncCancel()` method.

Event handlers for the `ResolveProgressChanged` event use the `ResolveProgressChangedEventArgs` event arguments parameter, which derives from the standard `System.ComponentModel.ProgressChangedEventArgs` class. You can use the `PeerNameRecord` property of the event argument object you receive in the event handler to get a reference to the peer name record that was found.

Similarly, the `ResolveCompleted` event requires an event handler that uses a parameter of type `ResolveCompletedEventArgs`, which derives from `AsyncCompletedEventArgs`. This type includes a `PeerNameRecordCollection` parameter you can use to obtain a complete list of the peer name records that were found.

The following code shows an implementation of event handlers for these events:

```
private pnres_ResolveProgressChanged(object sender,
    ResolveProgressChangedEventArgs e)
{
    // Use e.ProgressPercentage (inherited from base event args)
    // Process PeerNameRecord from e.PeerNameRecord
}

private pnres_ResolveCompleted(object sender,
    ResolveCompletedEventArgs e)
{
    // Test for e.IsCancelled and e.Error (inherited from base event args)
    // Process PeerNameRecordCollection from e.PeerNameRecordCollection
}
```

After you have one or more `PeerNameRecord` objects you can proceed to process them. This `PeerNameRecord` class exposes `Comment` and `Data` properties to examine the comment and data set in the peer name registration (if any), a `PeerName` property to get the `PeerName` object for the peer name record, and, most importantly, an `EndPointCollection` property. As with `PeerNameRegistration`, this property is a `System.Net.IPEndPointCollection` collection of `System.Net.IPEndPoint` objects. You can use these objects to connect to endpoints exposed by the peer in any way you want.

Code Access Security in System.Net.PeerToPeer

The `System.Net.PeerToPeer` namespace also includes the following two classes that you can use with Code Access Security (CAS). See Chapter 21, "Security" for more details.

> ➤ `PnrpPermission`, which inherits from `CodeAccessPermission`
> ➤ `PnrpPermissionAttribute`, which inherits from `CodeAccessSecurityAttribute`

You can use these classes to provide permissions functionality for PNRP access in the usual CAS way.

Sample Application

The downloadable code for this chapter includes a sample P2P application (P2PSample) that uses the concepts and namespace introduced in this section. It is a WPF application that uses a WCF service for a peer endpoint.

The application is configured with an application configuration file, in which you can specify the name of the peer and a port to listen on as follows:

```
<?xml version="1.0" encoding="utf-8" ?>
<configuration>
  <appSettings>
    <add key="username" value="Karli" />
    <add key="port" value="8731" />
  </appSettings>
</configuration>
```

code snippet App.config

After you have built the application you can test it either by copying it to other computers in your local network and running all instances, or by running multiple instances on one computer. If you choose the latter option you must remember to change the port used for each instance by changing individual config files (copy the contents of the `Debug` directory on your local computer and edit each config file in turn). The results will be clearer in both ways of testing this application if you also change the username for each instance.

When the peer applications are running, you can use the Refresh button to obtain a list of peers asynchronously. When you have located a peer you can send a default message by clicking the Message button for the peer.

Figure 45-7 shows this application in action with three instances running on one machine. In the figure, one peer has just messaged another and this has resulted in a dialog box.

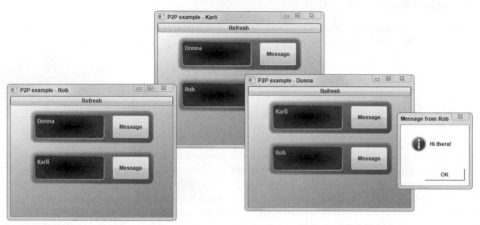

FIGURE 45-7

Most of the work in this application takes place in the `Window_Loaded()` event handler for the `Window1` window. This method starts by loading configuration information and setting the window title with the username:

Available for download on Wrox.com

```
private void Window_Loaded(object sender, RoutedEventArgs e)
{
    // Get configuration from app.config
    string port = ConfigurationManager.AppSettings["port"];
    string username = ConfigurationManager.AppSettings["username"];
    string machineName = Environment.MachineName;
    string serviceUrl = null;

    // Set window title
    this.Title = string.Format("P2P example — {0}", username);
```

code snippet Window1.xaml.cs

Next the peer host address is used along with the configured port to determine the endpoint on which to host the WCF service. The service will use `NetTcpBinding` binding, so the URL of the endpoint uses the `net.tcp` protocol:

```
    // Get service url using IPv4 address and port from config file
    foreach (IPAddress address in Dns.GetHostAddresses(Dns.GetHostName()))
    {
        if (address.AddressFamily ==
            System.Net.Sockets.AddressFamily.InterNetwork)
        {
            serviceUrl = string.Format("net.tcp://{0}:{1}/P2PService",
                address, port);
```

```
                    break;
            }
        }
```

The endpoint URL is validated, and then the WCF service is registered and started:

```
// Check for null address
if (serviceUrl == null)
{
    // Display error and shutdown
    MessageBox.Show(this, "Unable to determine WCF endpoint.",
        "Networking Error", MessageBoxButton.OK, MessageBoxImage.Stop);
    Application.Current.Shutdown();
}

// Register and start WCF service.
localService = new P2PService(this, username);
host = new ServiceHost(localService, new Uri(serviceUrl));
NetTcpBinding binding = new NetTcpBinding();
binding.Security.Mode = SecurityMode.None;
host.AddServiceEndpoint(typeof(IP2PService), binding, serviceUrl);
try
{
    host.Open();
}
catch (AddressAlreadyInUseException)
{
    // Display error and shutdown
    MessageBox.Show(this, "Cannot start listening, port in use.",
        "WCF Error", MessageBoxButton.OK, MessageBoxImage.Stop);
    Application.Current.Shutdown();
}
```

A singleton instance of the service class is used to enable easy communication between the host app and the service (for sending and receiving messages). Also, note that security is disabled in the binding configuration for simplicity.

Next, the `System.Net.PeerToPeer` namespace classes are used to register a peer name:

```
// Create peer name
peerName = new PeerName("P2P Sample", PeerNameType.Unsecured);

// Prepare peer name registration in link local clouds
peerNameRegistration = new PeerNameRegistration(peerName, int.Parse(port));
peerNameRegistration.Cloud = Cloud.AllLinkLocal;

// Start registration
peerNameRegistration.Start();
}
```

When the Refresh button is clicked the `RefreshButton_Click()` event handler uses `PeerNameResolver.ResolveAsync()` to get peers asynchronously:

```
private void RefreshButton_Click(object sender, RoutedEventArgs e)
{
    // Create resolver and add event handlers
    PeerNameResolver resolver = new PeerNameResolver();
    resolver.ResolveProgressChanged +=
        new EventHandler<ResolveProgressChangedEventArgs>(
            resolver_ResolveProgressChanged);
    resolver.ResolveCompleted +=
        new EventHandler<ResolveCompletedEventArgs>(
            resolver_ResolveCompleted);

    // Prepare for new peers
```

```
        PeerList.Items.Clear();
        RefreshButton.IsEnabled = false;

        // Resolve unsecured peers asynchronously
        resolver.ResolveAsync(new PeerName("0.P2P Sample"), 1);
    }
```

The remainder of the code is responsible for displaying and communicating with peers, and you can explore it at your leisure.

Exposing WCF endpoints through P2P clouds is a great way of locating services within an enterprise, as well as being an excellent way to communicate between peers, as in this example.

System.Net.PeerToPeer.Collaboration

The classes in the `System.Net.PeerToPeer.Collaboration` namespace provide a framework you can use to create applications that use the People Near Me service and the P2P collaboration API. As mentioned earlier, at the time of writing this is only possible if you are using Windows Vista or Windows 7.

You can use the classes in this namespace to interact with peers and applications in a number of ways, including

➤ Signing in and signing out

➤ Discovering peers

➤ Managing contacts and detecting peer presence

You can also use the classes in this namespace to invite other users to join an application, and to exchange data between users and applications. However, to do this you need to create your own PNM-capable applications, which is beyond the scope of this chapter.

In the following sections, all the types referred to come from the `System.Net.PeerToPeer.Collaboration` namespace unless otherwise specified.

Signing In and Signing Out

One of the most important classes in the `System.Net.PeerToPeer.Collaboration` namespace is the `PeerCollaboration` class. This is a static class that exposes numerous static methods that you can use for various purposes, as you will see in this and subsequent sections. You can use two of the methods it exposes, `SignIn()` and `SignOut()`, to (unsurprisingly) sign in and sign out of the People Near Me service. Both of these methods take a single parameter of type `PeerScope`, which can be one of the following values:

➤ `PeerScope.None` — If you use this value, `SignIn()` and `SignOut()` will have no effect.

➤ `PeerScope.NearMe` — This will sign you in to or out of the link local clouds.

➤ `PeerScope.Internet` — This will sign you in to or out of the global cloud (which may be necessary to connect to a contact who is not currently on your local subnet).

➤ `PeerScope.All` — This will sign you in to or out of all available clouds.

If necessary, calling `SignIn()` will cause the People Near Me configuration dialog to be displayed.

When a peer is signed in you can use the `PeerCollaboration.LocalPresenceInfo` property to a value of type `PeerPresenceInfo`. This enables standard IM functionality, such as setting your status to away. You can set the `PeerPresenceInfo.DescriptiveText` property to a Unicode string of up to 255 characters, and the `PeerPresenceInfo.PresenceStatus` property to a value from the `PeerPresenceStatus` enumeration. The values that you can use for this enumeration are as follows:

➤ `PeerPresenceStatus.Away` — The peer is away.

➤ `PeerPresenceStatus.BeRightBack` — The peer is away, but will be back soon.

> ➤ PeerPresenceStatus.Busy — The peer is busy.
>
> ➤ PeerPresenceStatus.Idle — The peer isn't active.
>
> ➤ PeerPresenceStatus.Offline — The peer is offline.
>
> ➤ PeerPresenceStatus.Online — The peer is online and available.
>
> ➤ PeerPresenceStatus.OnThePhone — The peer is busy with a phone call.
>
> ➤ PeerPresenceStatus.OutToLunch — The peer is away, but will be back after lunch.

Discovering Peers

You can obtain a list of peers near you if you are logged in to the link local cloud. You do this by using the `PeerCollaboration.GetPeersNearMe()` method. This returns a `PeerNearMeCollection` object containing `PeerNearMe` objects.

You can use the `Nickname` property of `PeerNearMe` to obtain the name of a peer, `IsOnline`, to determine whether the peer is online, and (for lower-level operations) the `PeerEndpoints` property to determine endpoints related to the peer. `PeerEndPoints` is also necessary if you want to find out the online status of a `PeerNearMe`. You can pass an endpoint to the `GetPresenceInfo()` method to obtain a `PeerPresenceInfo` object, as described in the previous section.

Managing Contacts and Detecting Peer Presence

Contacts are a way in which you can remember peers. You can add a peer discovered through the People Near Me service and from then onward you can connect to them whenever you are both online. You can connect to a contact through link local or global clouds (assuming you have IPv6 connectivity to the Internet).

You can add a contact from a peer that you have discovered by calling the `PeerNearMe.AddToContactManager()` method. When you call this method you can choose to associate a display name, nickname, and e-mail address with the contact. Typically, though, you will manage contacts by using the `ContactManager` class.

However you manipulate contacts, you will be dealing with `PeerContact` objects. `PeerContact`, like `PeerNearMe`, inherits from the abstract `Peer` base class. `PeerContact` has more properties and methods than `PeerNearMe`. `PeerContact` includes `DisplayName` and `EmailAddress` properties that further describe a PNM peer, for example. Another difference between these two types is that `PeerContact` has a more explicit relationship with the `System.Net.PeerToPeer.PeerName` class. You can get a `PeerName` from a `PeerContact` through the `PeerContact.PeerName` property. After you have done this you can proceed to use techniques you looked at earlier to communicate with any endpoints the `PeerName` exposes.

Information about the local peer is also accessible through the `ContactManager` class, through the static `ContactManager.LocalContact` property. This gets you a `PeerContact` property with details of the local peer.

You can add `PeerNearMe` objects to the local list of contacts by using either the `ContactManager.CreateContact()` or `CreateContactAsync()` method, or `PeerName` objects by using the `GetContact()` method. You can remove contacts represented by a `PeerNearMe` or `PeerName` object with the `DeleteContact()` method.

Finally, there are events that you can handle to respond to changes to contacts. For example, you can use the `PresenceChanged` event to respond to changes of presence for any contacts known by the `ContactManager`.

Sample Application

There is a second sample application in the downloadable code for this chapter that illustrates the use of classes in the `System.Net.PeerToPeer.Collaboration` namespace. This application is similar to the other example, but much simpler. You need two computers that can both sign in to the PNM server to see this application in action, because it enumerates and displays PNM peers from the local subnet.

When you run the application with at least one peer available for discovery the display will be similar to Figure 45-8.

The code is structured in the same way as the previous example, so if you've read through that code you should be familiar with this code. This time there is not much work to do in the `Window_Loaded()` event handler except sign in, because there is no WCF service to initialize or peer name registration to achieve:

FIGURE 45-8

```
private void Window_Loaded(object sender, RoutedEventArgs e)
{
    // Sign in to PNM
    PeerCollaboration.SignIn(PeerScope.NearMe);
```

To make things look a little nicer, though, `ContactManager.LocalContact.Nickname` is used to format the window title:

```
    // Get local peer name to display
    this.Title = string.Format("PNMSample — {0}",
        ContactManager.LocalContact.Nickname);
}
```

In `Window_Closing()` the local peer is automatically signed out of PNM:

```
private void Window_Closing(object sender,
    System.ComponentModel.CancelEventArgs e)
{
    // Sign out of PNM
    PeerCollaboration.SignOut(PeerScope.NearMe);
}
```

Most of the work is done in the `RefreshButton_Click()` event handler. This uses the `PeerCollaboration.GetPeersNearMe()` method to obtain a list of peers and add those peers to the display using the `PeerEntry` class defined in the project, or display a failure message if none are found:

```
private void RefreshButton_Click(object sender, RoutedEventArgs e)
{
    // Get local peers
    PeerNearMeCollection peersNearMe = PeerCollaboration.GetPeersNearMe();

    // Prepare for new peers
    PeerList.Items.Clear();

    // Examine peers
    foreach (PeerNearMe peerNearMe in peersNearMe)
    {
        PeerList.Items.Add(
            new PeerEntry
            {
                PeerNearMe = peerNearMe,
                PresenceStatus = peerNearMe.GetPresenceInfo(
                    peerNearMe.PeerEndPoints[0]).PresenceStatus,
                DisplayString = peerNearMe.Nickname
            });
    }

    // Add failure message if necessary
    if (PeerList.Items.Count == 0)
    {
        PeerList.Items.Add(
            new PeerEntry
            {
```

```
            DisplayString = "No peers found."
        });
    }
}
```

As you can see from this example, interacting with the PNM service is made very simple by the classes you have learned about.

SUMMARY

This chapter demonstrated how to implement peer-to-peer functionality in your applications by using the P2P classes in .NET 4.

You have looked at the types of solutions that P2P makes possible and how these solutions are structured, how to use PNRP and PNM, and how to use the types in the `System.Net.PeerToPeer` and `System.Net.PeerToPeer.Collaboration` namespaces. You also saw the extremely useful technique of exposing WCF services as P2P endpoints.

If you are interested in developing P2P applications, it is well worth investigating PNM further. It is also worth looking at the peer channel, by which WCF services can broadcast communications among multiple clients simultaneously.

In the next chapter you look at Message Queuing.

46

Message Queuing

WHAT'S IN THIS CHAPTER?

➤ Message Queuing overview

➤ Message Queuing architecture

➤ Message Queuing administrative tools

➤ Programming Message Queuing

➤ Course order sample application

➤ Message Queuing with WCF

`System.Messaging` is a namespace that includes classes for reading and writing messages with the Message Queuing facility of the Windows operating system. Messaging can be used in a disconnected scenario where the client and server needn't be running at the same time.

This chapter gives you information about the architecture and usage scenarios of Message Queuing, and then you dive into the classes from the `System.Messaging` namespace to create queues, and send and receive messages. You will see how to deal with getting answers from the server with acknowledgement and response queues, and also how to use message queuing with a WCF message queuing binding.

OVERVIEW

Before diving into programming Message Queuing in the rest of this chapter, this section discusses the basic concepts of messaging and compares it to synchronous and asynchronous programming. With synchronous programming, when a method is invoked, the caller has to wait until the method is completed. With asynchronous programming, the calling thread starts the method that runs concurrently. Asynchronous programming can be done with delegates, class libraries that already support asynchronous methods (for example, Web service proxies, `System.Net`, and `System.IO` classes), or by using custom threads (see Chapter 20, "Threads, Tasks, and Synchronization"). With both synchronous and asynchronous programming, the client and the server must be running at the same time.

Although Message Queuing operates asynchronously, because the client (sender) does not wait for the server (receiver) to read the data sent to it, there is a crucial difference between Message Queuing and asynchronous programming: Message Queuing can be done in a disconnected environment. At the time data is sent, the receiver can be offline. Later, when the receiver goes online, it receives the data without intervention from the sending application.

You can compare connected and disconnected programming with talking to someone on the phone and sending an e-mail. When talking to someone on the phone, both participants must be connected at the same time; the communication is synchronous. With an e-mail, the sender isn't sure when the e-mail will be dealt with. People using this technology are working in a disconnected mode. Of course the e-mail may never be dealt with — it may be ignored. That's in the nature of disconnected communication. To avoid this problem, it is possible to ask for a reply to confirm that the e-mail has been read. If the answer doesn't arrive within a time limit, you may be required to deal with this "exception." This is also possible with Message Queuing.

You can think of Message Queuing as e-mail for application-to-application communication, instead of person-to-person communication. Message Queuing offers a lot of features that are not available with mailing services, such as guaranteed delivery, transactions, confirmations, express mode using memory, and so on. As you see in the next section, Message Queuing has a lot of features useful for communication between applications.

With Message Queuing, you can send, receive, and route messages in a connected or disconnected environment. Figure 46-1 shows a very simple way of using messages. The sender sends messages to the message queue, and the receiver receives messages from the queue.

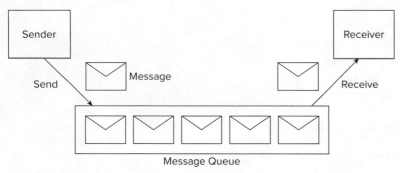

FIGURE 46-1

When to Use Message Queuing

One case in which Message Queuing is useful is when the client application is often disconnected from the network, for example, when a salesperson is visiting a customer onsite. The salesperson can enter order data directly at the customer's site. The application sends a message for each order to the message queue that is located on the client's system (see Figure 46-2). As soon as the salesperson is back in the office, the order is automatically transferred from the message queue of the client system to the message queue of the target system, where the message is processed.

In addition to using a laptop, the salesperson could use a Pocket Windows device where Message Queuing is available.

Message Queuing can also be useful in a connected environment. Imagine an e-commerce site (see Figure 46-3) where the server is fully loaded with order transactions at certain times, for example, early evening and weekends, but the load is low at nighttime. A solution would be to buy a faster server or to add additional servers to the system so that the peaks can be handled. But there's a cheaper solution: flatten the peak loads by moving transactions from the times with higher loads to the times with lower loads. In this scheme, orders are sent to the message queue, and the receiving side reads the orders at the rates that are useful for the database system. The load of the system is now flattened over time so that the server dealing with the transactions can be less expensive than an upgrade of the database server(s).

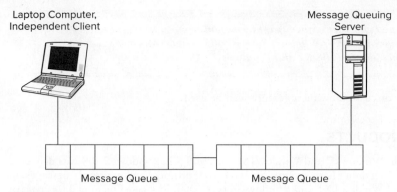

FIGURE 46-2

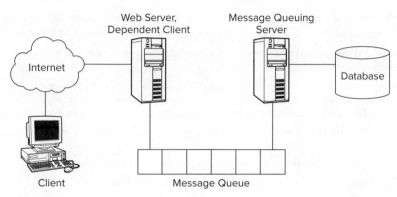

FIGURE 46-3

Message Queuing Features

Message Queuing is part of the Windows operating system. The main features of this service are:

➤ Messages can be sent in a disconnected environment. It is not necessary for the sending and receiving applications to run at the same time.

➤ With express mode, messages can be sent very quickly. Express-mode messages are just stored in memory.

➤ For a recoverable mechanism, messages can be sent using guaranteed delivery. Recoverable messages are stored within files. They are delivered even in cases when the server reboots.

➤ Message queues can be secured with access-control lists to define which users can send or receive messages from a queue. Messages can also be encrypted to avoid network sniffers reading them. Messages can be sent with priorities so that high-priority items are handled faster.

➤ Message Queuing 3.0 supports sending multicast messages.

Message Queuing 4.0 supports *poison messages*. A poison message is one that isn't getting resolved. You can define a *poison queue* where unresolved messages are moved. For example, if the job after reading the message from the normal queue was to insert it into the database, but the message did not get into the database and thus this job failed, it would get sent to the poison queue. It is someone's job to handle the poison queue — and that person should deal with the message in a way that resolves it.

➤ Message Queuing 5.0 supports more secure authentication algorithms and can handle a larger number of queues. (Message Queuing 4.0 had performance problems with several thousand queues.)

> *Because Message Queuing is part of the operating system, you cannot install Message Queuing 5.0 on a Windows XP or Windows Server 2003 system. Message Queuing 5.0 is part of Windows Server 2008 R2 and Windows 7.*

The remainder of this chapter discusses how these features can be used.

MESSAGE QUEUING PRODUCTS

Message Queuing 5.0 is part of Windows 7 and Windows Server 2008 R2. Windows 2000 was delivered with Message Queuing 2.0, which didn't have support for the HTTP protocol and multicast messages. Message Queuing 3.0 is part of Windows XP and Windows Server 2003. Message Queuing 4.0 is part of Windows Vista and Windows Server 2008.

When you use the link "Turn Windows Features on or off" in Configuring Programs and Features of Windows 7, there is a separate section for Message Queuing options. With this section, you can select these components:

➤ **Microsoft Message Queue (MSMQ) Server Core** — The Core subcomponent is required for base functionality with Message Queuing.

➤ **Active Directory Domain Services Integration** — With the Active Directory Domain Services Integration, message queue names are written to the Active Directory. With this option, it is possible to find queues with the Active Directory integration, and to secure queues with Windows users and groups.

➤ **MSMQ HTTP Support** — MSMQ HTTP Support allows you to send and receive messages using the HTTP protocol.

➤ **Triggers** — With triggers, applications can be instantiated on the arrival of a new message.

➤ **Multicast Support** — With multicasting, a message can be sent to a group of servers.

➤ **MSMQ DCOM Proxy** — With the DCOM proxy, a system can connect to a remote server by using the DCOM API.

When Message Queuing is installed, the Message Queuing service (see Figure 46-4) must be started. This service reads and writes messages and communicates with other Message Queuing servers to route messages across the network.

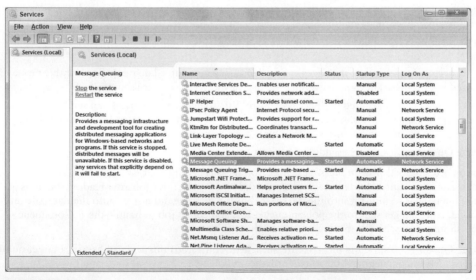

FIGURE 46-4

MESSAGE QUEUING ARCHITECTURE

With Message Queuing, messages are written to and read from a message queue. Messages and message queues have several attributes that must be further elaborated.

Messages

A message is sent to a message queue. The message includes a body containing the data that is sent and a label that is the title of the message. Any information can be put into the body of the message. With .NET, several formatters convert data to be put into the body. In addition to the label and the body, the message includes more information about the sender, timeout configuration, transaction ID, or priority.

Message queues have several types of messages:

A *normal message* is sent by an application.

An *acknowledgment message* reports the status of a normal message. Acknowledgment messages are sent to administration queues to report success or failure when sending normal messages.

Response messages are sent by receiving applications when the original sender requires some special answer.

A *report message* is generated by the Message Queuing system. Test messages and route-tracking messages belong to this category.

A message can have a priority that defines the order in which the messages will be read from the queue. The messages are sorted in the queue according to their priority, so the next message read in the queue is the one with the highest priority.

Messages have two delivery modes: *express* and *recoverable*. Express messages are delivered very quickly because memory is used only for the message store. Recoverable messages are stored in files at every step along the route until the message is delivered. This way, delivery of the message is assured, even with a computer reboot or network failure.

Transactional messages are a special version of recoverable messages. With transactional messaging, it is guaranteed that messages arrive only once and in the same order that they were sent. Priorities cannot be used with transactional messages.

Message Queue

A message queue is a storage bin for messages. Messages that are stored on disk can be found in the `<windir>\system32\msmq\storage` directory.

Public or private queues are usually used for sending messages, but other queue types also exist:

A *public queue* is published in the Active Directory. Information about these queues is replicated across Active Directory domains. You can use browse and search features to get information about these queues. A public queue can be accessed without knowing the name of the computer where it is placed. It is also possible to move such a queue from one system to another without the client knowing it. It's not possible to create public queues in a Workgroup environment because the Active Directory is needed. The Active Directory is discussed in online Chapter 52, "Directory Services."

Private queues are not published in the Active Directory. These queues can be accessed only when the full pathname to the queue is known. Private queues can be used in a Workgroup environment.

Journal queues are used to keep copies of messages after they have been received or sent. Enabling journaling for a public or private queue automatically creates a journal queue. With journal queues, two different queue types are possible: source journaling and target journaling. *Source journaling* is turned on with the properties of a message; journal messages are stored with the source system. *Target journaling* is turned on with the properties of a queue; these messages are stored in the journal queue of the target system.

Dead-letter queues store messages if a message doesn't arrive at the target system before a specific timeout is reached. Contrary to synchronous programming where errors are immediately detected, errors must be dealt with differently using Message Queuing. The dead-letter queue can be checked for messages that didn't arrive.

Administration queues contain acknowledgments for messages sent. The sender can specify an administration queue from which it receives notification of whether the message was sent successfully.

A *response queue* is used if more than a simple acknowledgment is needed as an answer from the receiving side. The receiving application can send response messages back to the original sender.

A *report queue* is used for test messages. Report queues can be created by changing the type (or category) of a public or private queue to the predefined ID `{55EE8F33-CCE9-11CF-B108-0020AFD61CE9}`. Report queues are useful as a testing tool to track messages on their route.

System queues are private and are used by the Message Queuing system. These queues are used for administrative messages, storing of notification messages, and to guarantee the correct order of transactional messages.

MESSAGE QUEUING ADMINISTRATIVE TOOLS

Before looking at how to deal with Message Queuing programmatically, this section looks at the administrative tools that are part of the Windows operating system to create and manage queues and messages.

 The tools shown here are not used only with Message Queuing. The Message Queuing features of these tools are available only if Message Queuing is installed.

Creating Message Queues

Message queues can be created with the Computer Management MMC snap-in. On a Windows 7 system, you can start the Computer Management MMC snap-in with the Start ➪ Control Panel ➪ Administrative Tools ➪ Computer Management menu. In the tree view pane, Message Queuing is located below the Services and Applications entry. By selecting Private Queues or Public Queues, new queues can be created from the Action menu (see Figure 46-5). Public queues are available only if Message Queuing is configured in Active Directory mode.

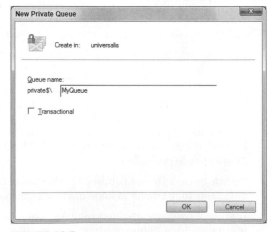

FIGURE 46-5

Message Queue Properties

After a queue is created, you can modify the queue's properties with the Computer Management snap-in by selecting the queue in the tree pane and selecting the Action Properties menu (see Figure 46-6).

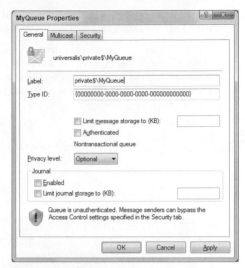

Several options can be configured:

➤ The label is the name of the queue that can be used to search for the queue.

➤ The type ID, which is by default, set to {00000000–0000–0000–0000–000000000000} to map multiple queues to a single category or type. Report queues use a specific type ID, as discussed earlier. A type ID is a universal unique ID (UUID) or GUID.

FIGURE 46-6

 Custom type identifiers can be created with the uuidgen.exe *or* guidgen.exe *utilities.* uuidgen.exe *is a command-line utility used to create unique IDs, and* guidgen.exe *is a graphical version to create UUIDs.*

➤ The maximum size of all messages of a queue can be limited to avoid filling up the disk.

➤ When checked, the Authenticated option allows only authenticated users to write and read messages to and from the queue.

➤ With the Privacy Level option, the content of the message can be encrypted. The possible values to set are None, Optional, or Body. None means that no encrypted messages are accepted, Body accepts only encrypted messages, and the default Optional value accepts both.

➤ Target journaling can be configured with the Journal settings. With this option, copies of the messages received are stored in the journal. The maximum size of disk space that is occupied can be configured for the journal messages of a queue. When the maximum size is reached, target journaling is ceased.

➤ With the configuration option Multicast, you can define a multicast IP address for the queue. The same multicast IP address can be used with different nodes in the network, so that a message sent to a single address is received with multiple queues.

PROGRAMMING MESSAGE QUEUING

Now that you understand the architecture of Message Queuing, you can look into the programming. In the next sections, you see how to create and control queues, and how to send and receive messages.

You also build a small course order application that consists of a sending and a receiving part.

Creating a Message Queue

You've already seen how to create message queues with the Computer Management utility. Message queues can be created programmatically with the Create() method of the MessageQueue class.

With the Create() method, the path of the new queue must be passed. The path consists of the host name where the queue is located and the name of the queue. In the following example, the queue

MyNewPublicQueue is created on the local host. To create a private queue, the pathname must include Private$; for example, \Private$\MyNewPrivateQueue.

After the Create() method is invoked, properties of the queue can be changed. For example, using the Label property, the label of the queue is set to Demo Queue. The sample program writes the path of the queue and the format name to the console. The format name is automatically created with a UUID that can be used to access the queue without the name of the server:

```csharp
using System;
using System.Messaging;

namespace Wrox.ProCSharp.Messaging
{
    class Program
    {
        static void Main()
        {
            using (var queue = MessageQueue.Create(@".\MyNewPublicQueue"))
            {
                queue.Label = "Demo Queue";
                Console.WriteLine("Queue created:");
                Console.WriteLine("Path: {0}", queue.Path);
                Console.WriteLine("FormatName: {0}", queue.FormatName);
            }
        }
    }
}
```

code snippet CreateMessageQueue/Program.cs

 Administrative privileges are required to create a queue. Usually, you cannot expect the user of your application to have administrative privileges. That's why queues usually are created with installation programs. Later in this chapter, you see how message queues can be created with the MessageQueueInstaller *class.*

Finding a Queue

The pathname and the format name can be used to identify queues. To find queues, you must differentiate between public and private queues. Public queues are published in the Active Directory. For these queues, it is not necessary to know the system where they are located. Private queues can be found only if the name of the system where the queue is located is known.

You can find public queues in the Active Directory domain by searching for the queue's label, category, or format name. You can also get all queues on a machine. The class MessageQueue has static methods to search for queues: GetPublicQueuesByLabel(), GetPublicQueuesByCategory(), and GetPublicQueuesByMachine(). The method GetPublicQueues() returns an array of all public queues in the domain:

```csharp
using System;
using System.Messaging;

namespace Wrox.ProCSharp.Messaging
{
    class Program
    {
```

```
        static void Main()
        {
            foreach (var queue in MessageQueue.GetPublicQueues())
            {
                Console.WriteLine(queue.Path);
            }
        }
    }
}
```

The method `GetPublicQueues()` is overloaded. One version allows passing an instance of the `MessageQueueCriteria` class. With this class, you can search for queues created or modified before or after a certain time, and you can also look for a category, label, or machine name.

Private queues can be searched with the static method `GetPrivateQueuesByMachine()`. This method returns all private queues from a specific system.

Opening Known Queues

If the name of the queue is known, it is not necessary to search for it. Queues can be opened by using the path or format name. They both can be set in the constructor of the `MessageQueue` class.

Pathname

The path specifies the machine name and the queue name to open the queue. This code example opens the queue `MyPublicQueue` on the local host. To be sure that the queue exists, you use the static method `MessageQueue.Exists()`:

```
using System;
using System.Messaging;

namespace Wrox.ProCSharp.Messaging
{
    class Program
    {
        static void Main()
        {
            if (MessageQueue.Exists(@".\MyPublicQueue"))
            {
                var queue = new MessageQueue(@".\MyPublicQueue");
                //.
            }
            else
            {
                Console.WriteLine("Queue .\MyPublicQueue not existing");
            }
        }
    }
}
```

Depending on the queue type, different identifiers are required when queues are opened. The following table shows the syntax of the queue name for specific types.

QUEUE TYPE	SYNTAX
Public queue	MachineName\QueueName
Private queue	MachineName\Private$\QueueName
Journal queue	MachineName\QueueName\Journal$
Machine journal queue	MachineName\Journal$
Machine dead-letter queue	MachineName\DeadLetter$
Machine transactional dead-letter queue	MachineName\XactDeadLetter$

When you use the pathname to open public queues, it is necessary to pass the machine name. If the machine name is not known, the format name can be used instead. The pathname for private queues can be used only on the local system. The format name must be used to access private queues remotely.

Format Name

Instead of the pathname, you can use the format name to open a queue. The format name is used for searching the queue in the Active Directory to get the host where the queue is located. In a disconnected environment where the queue cannot be reached at the time the message is sent, it is necessary to use the format name:

```
MessageQueue queue = new MessageQueue(
    @"FormatName:PUBLIC=09816AFF-3608-4c5d-B892-69754BA151FF");
```

The format name has some different uses. It can be used to open private queues and to specify a protocol that should be used:

➤ To access a private queue, the string that has to be passed to the constructor is `FormatName:PRIVATE=MachineGUID\QueueNumber`. The queue number for private queues is generated when the queue is created. You can see the queue numbers in the `<windows>\System32\msmq\storage\lqs` directory.

➤ With `FormatName:DIRECT=Protocol:MachineAddress\QueueName`, you can specify the protocol that should be used to send the message. The HTTP protocol is supported since Message Queuing 3.0.

➤ `FormatName:DIRECT=OS:MachineName\QueueName` is another way to specify a queue using the format name. This way you don't have to specify the protocol but still can use the machine name with the format name.

Sending a Message

You can use the `Send` method of the `MessageQueue` class to send a message to the queue. The object passed as an argument of the `Send()` method is serialized to the associated queue. The `Send()` method is overloaded so that a label and a `MessageQueueTransaction` object can be passed. Transactional behavior of Message Queuing is discussed later.

The code example first checks if the queue exists. If it doesn't exist, a queue is created. Then the queue is opened and the message `Sample Message` is sent to the queue using the `Send()` method.

The pathname specifies a dot (just like a period) for the server name, which is the local system. Pathnames to private queues work only locally:

Available for download on Wrox.com

```
using System;
using System.Messaging;

namespace Wrox.ProCSharp.Messaging
{
    class Program
    {
        static void Main()
        {
```

```
        try
        {
            if (!MessageQueue.Exists(@".\Private$\MyPrivateQueue"))
            {
                MessageQueue.Create(@".\Private$\MyPrivateQueue");
            }
            var queue = new MessageQueue(@".\Private$\MyPrivateQueue");

            queue.Send("Sample Message", "Label");
        }
        catch (MessageQueueException ex)
        {
            Console.WriteLine(ex.Message);
        }
    }
  }
}
```

code snippet SendMessage/Program.cs

Figure 46-7 shows the Computer Management admin tool where you can see the message that arrived in the queue.

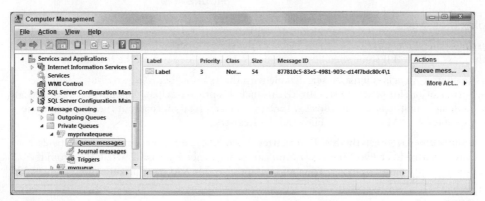

FIGURE 46-7

By opening the message and selecting the Body tab (see Figure 46-8) of the dialog box, you can see that the message was formatted using XML. Determining how the message is formatted is the function of the formatter that's associated with the message queue.

Message Formatter

The format in which messages are transferred to the queue depends on the formatter. The MessageQueue class has a Formatter property through which a formatter can be assigned. The default formatter, XmlMessageFormatter, will format the message in XML syntax as shown in the previous example.

FIGURE 46-8

A message formatter implements the interface `IMessageFormatter`. Three message formatters are available with the namespace `System.Messaging`:

➤ The `XmlMessageFormatter` is the default formatter. It serializes objects using XML. See Chapter 33, "Manipulating XML," for more on XML formatting.

➤ With the `BinaryMessageFormatter`, messages are serialized in a binary format. These messages are shorter than the messages formatted using XML.

➤ The `ActiveXMessageFormatter` is a binary formatter so that messages can be read or written with COM objects. Using this formatter, it is possible to write a message to the queue with a .NET class and to read the message from the queue with a COM object or vice versa.

The sample message shown in Figure 46-8 with XML is formatted with the `BinaryMessageFormatter` in Figure 46-9.

FIGURE 46-9

Sending Complex Messages

Instead of passing strings, it is possible to pass objects to the `Send()` method of the `MessageQueue` class. The type of the class must fulfill some specific requirements, but they depend on the formatter.

For the binary formatter, the class must be serializable with the `[Serializable]` attribute. With the .NET runtime serialization, all fields are serialized (this includes private fields). Custom serialization can be defined by implementing the interface `ISerializable`. You can read more about the .NET runtime serialization in Chapter 29, "Manipulating Files and the Registry."

XML serialization takes place with the XML formatter. With XML serialization, all public fields and properties are serialized. The XML serialization can be influenced by using attributes from the `System.Xml.Serialization` namespace. You can read more about XML serialization in Chapter 33.

Receiving Messages

To read messages, again, you can use the `MessageQueue` class. With the `Receive()` method, a single message is read and removed from the queue. If messages are sent with different priorities, the message with the highest priority is read. Reading messages with the same priority may mean that the first message sent is not the first message read because the order of messages across the network is not guaranteed. For a guaranteed order, you should use transactional message queues.

In the following example, a message is read from the private queue `MyPrivateQueue`. Previously, a simple string was passed to the message. When you read a message using the `XmlMessageFormatter`, you have to pass the types of the objects that are read to the constructor of the formatter. In the example, the type `System.String` is passed to the argument array of the `XmlMessageFormatter` constructor. This constructor allows either a `String` array that contains the types as strings to be passed or a `Type` array.

The message is read with the `Receive()` method, and then the message body is written to the console:

```
using System;
using System.Messaging;

namespace Wrox.ProCSharp.Messaging
{
    class Program
    {
```

```
        static void Main()
        {
            var queue = new MessageQueue(@".\Private$\MyPrivateQueue");
            queue.Formatter = new XmlMessageFormatter(
                    new string[] {"System.String"});

            Message message = queue.Receive();
            Console.WriteLine(message.Body);
        }
    }
}
```

code snippet SendMessage/Program.cs

The Receive() message behaves synchronously and waits until a message is in the queue if there is none.

Enumerating Messages

Instead of reading message by message with the Receive() method, you can use an enumerator to walk through all messages. The MessageQueue class implements the interface IEnumerable and thus can be used with a foreach statement. Here, the messages are not removed from the queue, but you get just a peek at the messages to get their content:

```
var queue = new MessageQueue(@".\Private$\MyPrivateQueue");
queue.Formatter = new XmlMessageFormatter(
        new string[] {"System.String"});

foreach (Message message in queue)
{
    Console.WriteLine(message.Body);
}
```

Instead of using the IEnumerable interface, the class MessageEnumerator can be used. MessageEnumerator implements the interface IEnumerator, but has some more features. With the IEnumerable interface, the messages are not removed from the queue. The method RemoveCurrent() of the MessageEnumerator removes the message from the current cursor position of the enumerator.

In the example, the MessageQueue method GetMessageEnumerator() is used to access the MessageEnumerator. The MoveNext() method takes a peek message by message with the MessageEnumerator. The MoveNext() method is overloaded to allow a time span as an argument. This is one of the big advantages when using this enumerator. Here, the thread can wait until a message arrives in the queue, but only for the specified time span. The Current property, which is defined by the IEnumerator interface, returns a reference to a message:

```
var queue = new MessageQueue(@".\Private$\MyPrivateQueue");
queue.Formatter = new XmlMessageFormatter(
        new string[] {"System.String"});

using (MessageEnumerator messages = queue.GetMessageEnumerator())
{
    while (messages.MoveNext(TimeSpan.FromMinutes(30)))
    {
        Message message = messages.Current;
        Console.WriteLine(message.Body);
    }
}
```

Asynchronous Read

The Receive method of the MessageQueue class waits until a message from the queue can be read. To avoid blocking the thread, a timeout can be specified in an overloaded version of the Receive method. To read the message from the queue after the timeout, Receive() must be invoked again. Instead of polling for messages, the asynchronous method `BeginReceive()` can be called. Before starting the asynchronous read with `BeginReceive()`, the event `ReceiveCompleted` should be set. The `ReceiveCompleted` event requires a `ReceiveCompletedEventHandler` delegate that references the method that is invoked when a message arrives in the queue and can be read. In the example, the method `MessageArrived` is passed to the `ReceivedCompletedEventHandler` delegate:

Available for
download on
Wrox.com

```
var queue = new MessageQueue(@".\Private$\MyPrivateQueue");
queue.Formatter = new XmlMessageFormatter(
        new string[] {"System.String"});

queue.ReceiveCompleted += MessageArrived;
queue.BeginReceive();
// thread does not wait
```

code snippet ReceiveMessageAsync/Program.cs

The handler method `MessageArrived` requires two parameters. The first parameter is the origin of the event, the `MessageQueue`. The second parameter is of type `ReceiveCompletedEventArgs` that contains the message and the asynchronous result. In the example, the method `EndReceive()` from the queue is invoked to get the result of the asynchronous method, the message:

```
public static void MessageArrived(object source, ReceiveCompletedEventArgs e)
{
    MessageQueue queue = (MessageQueue)source;
    Message message = queue.EndReceive(e.AsyncResult);
    Console.WriteLine(message.Body);
}
```

If the message should not be removed from the queue, the `BeginPeek()` and `EndPeek()` methods can be used with asynchronous I/O.

COURSE ORDER APPLICATION

To demonstrate the use of Message Queuing, in this section you create a sample solution to order courses. The sample solution is made up of three assemblies:

➤ A component library (`CourseOrder`) that includes entity classes for the messages that are sent and received in the queue

➤ A WPF application (`CourseOrderSender`) that sends messages to the message queue

➤ A WPF application (`CourseOrderReceiver`) that receives messages from the message queue

Course Order Class Library

Both the sending and the receiving application need the order information. For this reason, the entity classes are put into a separate assembly. The `CourseOrder` assembly includes three entity classes: `CourseOrder`, `Course`, and `Customer`. With the sample application, not all properties are implemented as they would be in a real application, but just enough properties to show the concept.

In the file `Course.cs`, the class `Course` is defined. This class has just one property for the title of the course:

Available for
download on
Wrox.com

```
namespace Wrox.ProCSharp.Messaging
{
    public class Course
    {
        public string Title { get; set; }
    }
}
```

code snippet CourseOrder/Course

The file `Customer.cs` includes the class `Customer`, which includes properties for the company and contact names:

Available for download on Wrox.com

```
namespace Wrox.ProCSharp.Messaging
{
    public class Customer
    {
        public string Company { get; set; }
        public string Contact { get; set; }
    }
}
```

code snippet CourseOrder/Customer.cs

The class `CourseOrder` in the file `CourseOrder.cs` maps a customer and a course inside an order and defines whether the order is high priority. This class also defines the name of the queue that is set to a format name of a public queue. The format name is used to send the message, even if the queue cannot be reached currently. You can get the format name by using the Computer Management snap-in to read the ID of the message queue. If you don't have access to an Active Directory to create a public queue, you can easily change the code to use a private queue.

Available for download on Wrox.com

```
namespace Wrox.ProCSharp.Messaging
{
    public class CourseOrder
    {
        public const string CourseOrderQueueName =
    "FormatName:Public=D99CE5F3-4282-4a97-93EE-E9558B15EB13";

        public Customer Customer { get; set; }
        public Course Course { get; set; }
    }
}
```

code snippet CourseOrder/CourseOrder.cs

Course Order Message Sender

The second part of the solution is a Windows application called `CourseOrderSender`. With this application, course orders are sent to the message queue. The assemblies `System.Messaging` and `CourseOrder` must be referenced.

The user interface of this application is shown in Figure 46-10. The items of the combo box `comboBoxCourses` include several courses such as Advanced .NET Programming, Programming with LINQ, and Distributed Application Development using WCF.

When the Submit the Order button is clicked, the handler method `buttonSubmit_Click()` is invoked. With this method, a `CourseOrder` object is created and filled with the content from the `TextBox` and `ComboBox` controls. Then a `MessageQueue` instance is created to open a public queue with a format name. With the `Send()` method, the `CourseOrder` object is passed to serialize it with the default `XmlMessageFormatter` and to write it to the queue:

FIGURE 46-10

Available for download on Wrox.com

```
private void buttonSubmit_Click(object sender, RoutedEventArgs e)
{
    try
    {
        var order = new CourseOrder();
```

```
        order.Course = new Course()
        {
            Title = comboBoxCourses.SelectedItem.ToString()
        };
        order.Customer = new Customer()
        {
            Company = textCompany.Text,
            Contact = textContact.Text
        };

        using (var queue = new MessageQueue(CourseOrder.CourseOrderQueueName))
        {
            queue.Send(order, String.Format("Course Order {{0}}",
                    order.Customer.Company));
        }
        MessageBox.Show("Course Order submitted", "Course Order",
                MessageBoxButton.OK, MessageBoxImage.Information);
    }
    catch (MessageQueueException ex)
    {
        MessageBox.Show(ex.Message, "Course Order Error",
                MessageBoxButton.OK, MessageBoxImage.Error);
    }
}
```

code snippet CourseOrderSender/CourseOrderWindow.xaml.cs

Sending Priority and Recoverable Messages

Messages can be prioritized by setting the `Priority` property of the `Message` class. If messages are specially configured, a `Message` object must be created where the body of the message is passed in the constructor.

In the example, the priority is set to `MessagePriority.High` if the `checkBoxPriority` check box is checked. `MessagePriority` is an enumeration that allows you to set values from `Lowest` (0) to `Highest` (7). The default value, `Normal`, has a priority value of 3.

To make the message recoverable, the property `Recoverable` is set to `true`:

```
private void buttonSubmit_Click(object sender, RoutedEventArgs e)
{
    try
    {
        var order = new CourseOrder
        {
            Course = new Course
            {
                Title = comboBoxCourses.Text
            },
            Customer = new Customer
            {
                Company = textCompany.Text,
                Contact = textContact.Text
            }
        };

        using (var queue = new MessageQueue(CourseOrder.CourseOrderQueueName))
        using (var message = new Message(order))
        {
            if (checkBoxPriority.IsChecked == true)
            {
                message.Priority = MessagePriority.High;
            }
```

```
                    message.Recoverable = true;
                    queue.Send(message,  String.Format("Course Order {{{0}}}",
                        order.Customer.Company));
                }
            MessageBox.Show("Course Order submitted");
        }
        catch (MessageQueueException ex)
        {
            MessageBox.Show(ex.Message, "Course Order Error",
                MessageBoxButton.OK, MessageBoxImage.Error);
        }
    }
```

code snippet CourseOrderSender/CourseOrderWindow.xaml.cs

By running the application, you can add course orders to the message queue (see Figure 46-11).

FIGURE 46-11

FIGURE 46-12

Course Order Message Receiver

The design view of the Course Order receiving application that reads messages from the queue is shown in Figure 46-12. This application displays labels of every order in the `listOrders` list box. When an order is selected, the content of the order is displayed with the controls on the right side of the application.

In the constructor of the `Window` class `CourseOrderReceiverWindow`, the `MessageQueue` object is created that references the same queue that was used with the sending application. For reading messages, the `XmlMessageFormatter` with the types that are read is associated with the queue using the `Formatter` property.

To display the available messages in the list, a new task is created that peeks at messages in the background. The task's main method is `PeekMessages`.

 You can read more about tasks in Chapter 20.

Available for
download on
Wrox.com

```
using System;
using System.Messaging;
using System.Threading;
using System.Windows;
using System.Windows.Controls;
```

```
using System.Windows.Threading;

namespace Wrox.ProCSharp.Messaging
{
    public partial class CourseOrderReceiverWindow: Window
    {
        private MessageQueue orderQueue;

        public CourseOrderReceiverWindow()
        {
            InitializeComponent();

            string queueName = CourseOrder.CourseOrderQueueName;
            orderQueue = new MessageQueue(queueName);
            orderQueue.Formatter = new XmlMessageFormatter(
                new Type[]
                {
                    typeof(CourseOrder),
                    typeof(Customer),
                    typeof(Course)
                });

            // start the task that fills the ListBox with orders
            Task t1 = new Task(PeekMessages);
            t1.Start();
        }
```

code snippet CourseOrderReceiver/CourseOrderReceiverWindow.xaml.cs

The task's main method, `PeekMessages()`, uses the enumerator of the message queue to display all messages. Within the `while` loop, the `messagesEnumerator` checks to see if there is a new message in the queue. If there is no message in the queue, the thread waits three hours for the next message to arrive before it exits.

To display every message from the queue in the list box, the thread cannot directly write the text to the list box, but needs to forward the call to the list box's creator thread. Because WPF controls are bound to a single thread, only the creator thread is allowed to access methods and properties. The `Dispatcher` `.Invoke()` method forwards the request to the creator thread:

```
        private void PeekMessages()
        {
            using (MessageEnumerator messagesEnumerator =
                orderQueue.GetMessageEnumerator2())
            {
                while (messagesEnumerator.MoveNext(TimeSpan.FromHours(3)))
                {
                    var labelId = new LabelIdMapping()
                    {
                        Id = messagesEnumerator.Current.Id,
                        Label = messagesEnumerator.Current.Label
                    };
                    Dispatcher.Invoke(DispatcherPriority.Normal,
                            new Action<LabelIdMapping>(AddListItem),
                            labelId);
                }
            }
            MessageBox.Show("No orders in the last 3 hours. Exiting thread",
                "Course Order Receiver", MessageBoxButton.OK,
                MessageBoxImage.Information);
        }
```

```
private void AddListItem(LabelIdMapping labelIdMapping)
{
    listOrders.Items.Add(labelIdMapping);
}
```

The `ListBox` control contains elements of the `LabelIdMapping` class. This class is used to display the labels of the messages in the list box, but to keep the ID of the message hidden. The ID of the message can be used to read the message at a later time:

```
private class LabelIdMapping
{
    public string Label { get; set; }
    public string Id { get; set; }

    public override string ToString()
    {
        return Label;
    }
}
```

The `ListBox` control has the `SelectedIndexChanged` event associated with the method `listOrders_SelectionChanged()`. This method gets the `LabelIdMapping` object from the current selection, and uses the ID to peek at the message once more with the `PeekById()` method. Then the content of the message is displayed in the `TextBox` control. Because by default the priority of the message is not read, the property `MessageReadPropertyFilter` must be set to receive the `Priority`:

```
private void listOrders_SelectionChanged(object sender,
    RoutedEventArgs e)
{
    LabelIdMapping labelId = listOrders.SelectedItem as LabelIdMapping;
    if (labelId == null)
        return;

    orderQueue.MessageReadPropertyFilter.Priority = true;
    Message message = orderQueue.PeekById(labelId.Id);

    CourseOrder order = message.Body as CourseOrder;
    if (order != null)
    {
        textCourse.Text = order.Course.Title;
        textCompany.Text = order.Customer.Company;
        textContact.Text = order.Customer.Contact;
        buttonProcessOrder.IsEnabled = true;

        if (message.Priority > MessagePriority.Normal)
        {
            labelPriority.Visibility = Visibility.Visible;
        }
        else
        {
            labelPriority.Visibility = Visibility.Hidden;
        }
    }
    else
    {
        MessageBox.Show("The selected item is not a course order",
            "Course Order Receiver", MessageBoxButton.OK,
            MessageBoxImage.Warning);
    }
}
```

When the Process Order button is clicked, the handler method `OnProcessOrder()` is invoked. Here again, the currently selected message from the list box is referenced, and the message is removed from the queue by calling the method `ReceiveById()`:

```
private void buttonProcessOrder_Click(object sender, RoutedEventArgs e)
{
    LabelIdMapping labelId = listOrders.SelectedItem as LabelIdMapping;
    Message message = orderQueue.ReceiveById(labelId.Id);

    listOrders.Items.Remove(labelId);
    listOrders.SelectedIndex = -1;
    buttonProcessOrder.IsEnabled = false;
    textCompany.Text = string.Empty;
    textContact.Text = string.Empty;
    textCourse.Text = string.Empty;

    MessageBox.Show("Course order processed", "Course Order Receiver",
        MessageBoxButton.OK, MessageBoxImage.Information);
    }
  }
}
```

Figure 46-13 shows the running receiving application that lists three orders in the queue, and one order is currently selected.

RECEIVING RESULTS

With the current version of the sample application, the sending application never knows if the message is ever dealt with. To get results from the receiver, acknowledgment queues or response queues can be used.

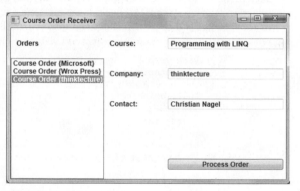

FIGURE 46-13

Acknowledgment Queues

With an acknowledgment queue, the sending application can get information about the status of the message. With acknowledgments, you can define if you would like to receive an answer, if everything went okay, or if something went wrong. For example, acknowledgments can be sent when the message reaches the destination queue or when the message is read, or if it didn't reach the destination queue or was not read before a timeout elapsed.

In the example, the `AdministrationQueue` of the `Message` class is set to the `CourseOrderAck` queue, which must be created similar to a normal queue. This queue is just used the other way around: the original sender receives acknowledgments. The `AcknowledgeType` property is set to `AcknowledgeTypes.FullReceive` to get an acknowledgment when the message is read:

```
Message message = new Message(order);

message.AdministrationQueue = new MessageQueue(@".\CourseOrderAck");
message.AcknowledgeType = AcknowledgeTypes.FullReceive;

queue.Send(message, String.Format("Course Order {{0}}",
    order.Customer.Company);

string id = message.Id;
```

The *correlation ID* is used to determine what acknowledgment message belongs to which message sent. Every message that is sent has an ID, and the acknowledgment message that is sent in response to that message holds the ID of the originating message as its correlation ID. The messages from the acknowledgment queue can be read using `MessageQueue.ReceiveByCorrelationId()` to receive the associated acknowledgment.

Instead of using acknowledgments, the dead-letter queue can be used for messages that didn't arrive at their destination. With the `UseDeadLetterQueue` property of the `Message` class set to `true`, the message is copied to the dead-letter queue if it didn't arrive at the target queue before the timeout was reached.

Timeouts can be set with the `Message` properties `TimeToReachQueue` and `TimeToBeReceived`.

Response Queues

If more information than an acknowledgment is needed from the receiving application, a response queue can be used. A response queue is like a normal queue, but the original sender uses the queue as a receiver and the original receiver uses the response queue as a sender.

The sender must assign the response queue with the `ResponseQueue` property of the `Message` class. The sample code here shows how the receiver uses the response queue to return a response message. With the response message `responseMessage`, the property `CorrelationId` is set to the ID of the original message. This way the client application knows to which message the answer belongs. This is similar to acknowledgment queues. The response message is sent with the `Send()` method of the `MessageQueue` object that is returned from the `ResponseQueue` property:

```
public void ReceiveMessage(Message message)
{
    Message responseMessage = new Message("response");
    responseMessage.CorrelationId = message.Id;

    message.ResponseQueue.Send(responseMessage);
}
```

TRANSACTIONAL QUEUES

With recoverable messages, it is not guaranteed that the messages will arrive in order and just once. Failures on the network can cause messages to arrive multiple times; this happens also if both the sender and receiver have multiple network protocols installed that are used by Message Queuing.

Transactional queues can be used when these guarantees are required:

➤ Messages arrive in the same order they have been sent.

➤ Messages arrive only once.

With transactional queues, a single transaction doesn't span the sending and receiving of messages. The nature of Message Queuing is that the time between send and receive can be quite long. In contrast, transactions should be short. With Message Queuing, the first transaction is used to send the message into the queue, the second transaction forwards the message on the network, and the third transaction is used to receive the messages.

The next example shows how to create a transactional message queue and how to send messages using a transaction.

A transactional message queue is created by passing `true` with the second parameter of the `MessageQueue.Create()` method.

If you want to write multiple messages to a queue within a single transaction, you have to instantiate a `MessageQueueTransaction` object and invoke the `Begin()` method. When you are finished with sending all messages that belong to the transaction, the `Commit()` method of the `MessageQueueTransaction` object must be called. To cancel a transaction (and have no messages written to the queue), the `Abort()` method must be called, as you can see within the `catch` block:

```
using System;
using System.Messaging;

namespace Wrox.ProCSharp.Messaging
{
    class Program
    {
        static void Main()
        {
            if (!MessageQueue.Exists(@".\MyTransactionalQueue"))
            {
                MessageQueue.Create(@".\MyTransactionalQueue", true);
            }

            var queue = new MessageQueue(@".\MyTransactionalQueue");
            var transaction = new MessageQueueTransaction();

            try
            {
                transaction.Begin();
                queue.Send("a", transaction);
                queue.Send("b", transaction);
                queue.Send("c", transaction);
                transaction.Commit();
            }
            catch
            {
                transaction.Abort();
            }
        }
    }
}
```

MESSAGE QUEUING WITH WCF

Chapter 43, "Windows Communication Foundation," covers the architecture and core features of WCF. With WCF, you can configure a Message Queuing binding that makes use of the Windows Message Queuing architecture. With this, WCF offers an abstraction layer to Message Queuing. Figure 46-14 explains the architecture using a simple picture. The client application invokes a method of a WCF proxy to send a message to the queue. The message is created by the proxy. For the client developer, there's no need to know that a message is sent to the queue. The client developer just invokes a method of the proxy. The proxy abstracts dealing with the classes from the `System.Messaging` namespace and sends a message to the queue. The MSMQ listener channel on the service side reads messages from the queue, converts them to method calls, and invokes the method calls with the service.

Next, the Course Ordering application gets converted to make use of Message Queuing from a WCF viewpoint. With this solution, the three projects done earlier are modified, and one more assembly is added that includes the contract of the WCF service:

➤ The component library (`CourseOrder`) includes entity classes for the messages that

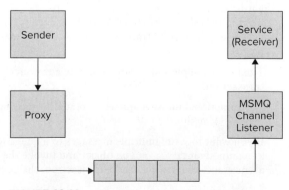

FIGURE 46-14

are sent across the wire. These entity classes are modified to fulfill the data contract for serialization with WCF.

➤ A new library is added (`CourseOrderService`) that defines the contract offered by the service.

➤ The WPF sender application (`CourseOrderSender`) is modified to not send messages but instead invoke methods of a WCF proxy.

➤ The WPF receiving application (`CourseOrderReceiver`) is modified to make use of the WCF service that implements the contract.

Entity Classes with a Data Contract

In the library `CourseOrder`, the classes `Course`, `Customer`, and `CourseOrder` are modified to apply the data contract with the attributes `[DataContract]` and `[DataMember]`. For using these attributes, you have to reference the assembly `System.Runtime.Serialization` and import the namespace `System.Runtime.Serialization`:

```
using System.Runtime.Serialization;

namespace Wrox.ProCSharp.Messaging
{
    [DataContract]
    public class Course
    {
        [DataMember]
        public string Title { get; set; }
    }
}
```

code snippet CourseOrder/Course.cs

The `Customer` class requires the data contract attributes as well:

```
[DataContract]
public class Customer
{
    [DataMember]
    public string Company { get; set; }

    [DataMember]
    public string Contact { get; set; }
}
```

code snippet CourseOrder/Customer.cs

With the class `CourseOrder`, not only the data contract attributes are added, but an override of the `ToString()` method as well to have a default string representation of these objects:

```
[DataContract]
public class CourseOrder
{
    [DataMember]
    public Customer Customer { get; set; }

    [DataMember]
    public Course Course { get; set; }
```

```
            public override string ToString()
            {
                return String.Format("Course Order {{{0}}}", Customer.Company);
            }
        }
```

WCF Service Contract

To offer the service with a WCF service contract, add a WCF service library with the name
CourseOrderServiceContract. The contract is defined by the interface ICourseOrderService.
This contract needs the attribute [ServiceContract]. If you want to restrict using this interface only
with message queues, you can apply the [DeliveryRequirements] attribute and assign the property
QueuedDeliveryRequirements. Possible values of the enumeration QueuedDeliveryRequirementsMode
are Required, Allowed, and NotAllowed. The method AddCourseOrder() is offered by the service.
Methods used by Message Queuing can only have input parameters. Because the sender and receiver
can run independent of each other, the sender cannot expect an immediate result. With the attribute
[OperationContract], the IsOneWay property is set. The caller of this operation does not wait for an
answer from the service:

```
using System.ServiceModel;

namespace Wrox.ProCSharp.Messaging
{
    [ServiceContract]
    [DeliveryRequirements(
        QueuedDeliveryRequirements=QueuedDeliveryRequirementsMode.Required)]
    public interface ICourseOrderService
    {
        [OperationContract(IsOneWay = true)]
        void AddCourseOrder(CourseOrder courseOrder);
    }
}
```

 You can use acknowledgment and response queues to get answers to the client.

WCF Message Receiver Application

The WPF application CourseOrderReceiver is now modified to implement the WCF service and
receive the messages. References to the assembly System.ServiceModel and the WCF contract assembly
CourseOrderServiceContract are required.

The class CourseOrderService implements the interface ICourseOrderService. With the
implementation, the event CourseOrderAdded is fired. The WPF application will register to this event to
receive CourseOrder objects.

Because WPF controls are bound to a single thread, the property UseSynchronizationContext is set with
the [ServiceBehavior] attribute. This is a feature of the WCF runtime to pass the method call invocation
to the thread that is defined by the synchronization context of the WPF application:

```
using System.ServiceModel;

namespace Wrox.ProCSharp.Messaging
{
    [ServiceBehavior(UseSynchronizationContext=true)]
```

```
public class CourseOrderService: ICourseOrderService
{
    public static event EventHandler<CourseOrderEventArgs>
        CourseOrderAdded;

    public void AddCourseOrder(CourseOrder courseOrder)
    {
        if (CourseOrderAdded != null)
            CourseOrderAdded(this, new CourseOrderEventArgs(courseOrder));
    }
}

public class CourseOrderEventArgs : EventArgs
{
    public CourseOrderEventArgs(CourseOrder courseOrder)
    {
        this.CourseOrder = courseOrder;
    }
    public CourseOrder CourseOrder { get; private set; }
}
```

code snippet CourseOrderReceiver/CourseOrderService.cs

 Chapter 20 explains the synchronization context.

With the constructor of the class `CourseReceiverWindow`, a `ServiceHost` object is instantiated and opened to start the listener. The binding of the listener will be done in the application configuration file.

In the constructor, the event `CourseOrderAdded` of the `CourseOrderService` is subscribed. Because the only thing that happens here is adding the received `CourseOrder` object to a collection, a simple Lambda expression is used.

 Lambda expressions are explained in Chapter 8, "Delegates, Lambdas, and Events."

The collection class that is used here is `ObservableCollection<T>` from the namespace `System.Collections.ObjectModel`. This collection class implements the interface `INotifyCollectionChanged`, and thus the WPF controls bound to the collection are informed about dynamic changes to the list:

```
using System;
using System.Collections.ObjectModel;
using System.ServiceModel;
using System.Windows;

namespace Wrox.ProCSharp.Messaging
{
    public partial class CourseOrderReceiverWindow: Window
    {
        private ObservableCollection<CourseOrder> courseOrders =
            new ObservableCollection<CourseOrder>();

        public CourseOrderReceiverWindow()
        {
            InitializeComponent();
```

```
CourseOrderService.CourseOrderAdded += (sender, e) =
    {
        courseOrders.Add(e.CourseOrder);
        buttonProcessOrder.IsEnabled = true;
    }

    var host = new ServiceHost(typeof(CourseOrderService));
    try
    {
        host.Open();
    }
    catch (Exception ex)
    {
        Console.WriteLine(ex.Message);
    }

    this.DataContext = courseOrders;
}
```

code snippet CourseOrderReceiver/CourseOrderReceiverWindow.xaml.cs

The WPF elements in the XAML code now make use of data binding. The `ListBox` is bound to the data context, and the single-item controls are bound to properties of the current item of the data context:

```
<ListBox Grid.Row="1" x:Name="listOrders" ItemsSource="{Binding}"
         IsSynchronizedWithCurrentItem="true" />

<!-- ... -->

<TextBox x:Name="textCourse" Grid.Row="0" Grid.Column="1"
    Text="{Binding Path=Course.Title}" />
<TextBox x:Name="textCompany" Grid.Row="1" Grid.Column="1"
    Text="{Binding Path=Customer.Company}" />
<TextBox x:Name="textContact" Grid.Row="2" Grid.Column="1"
    Text="{Binding Path=Customer.Contact}" />
```

code snippet CourseOrderReceiver/CourseOrderReceiverWindow.xaml

The application configuration file defines the `netMsmqBinding`. For reliable messaging, transactional queues are required. To receive and send messages to non-transactional queues, the `exactlyOnce` property must be set to `false`.

> `netMsmqBinding` *is the binding to be used if both the receiver and the sender application are WCF applications. If one of these applications is using the* `System`
> `.Messaging` *API to send or receive messages, or is an older COM application, you can use* `msmqIntegrationBinding`.

```
<?xml version="1.0" encoding="utf-8" ?>
<configuration>
  <system.serviceModel>
    <bindings>
      <netMsmqBinding>
        <binding name="NonTransactionalQueueBinding" exactlyOnce="false">
          <security mode="None" />
        </binding>
      </netMsmqBinding>
    </bindings>
    <services>
      <service name="Wrox.ProCSharp.Messaging.CourseOrderService">
```

```
        <endpoint address="net.msmq://localhost/private/courseorder"
          binding="netMsmqBinding"
          bindingConfiguration="NonTransactionalQueueBinding"
          name="OrderQueueEP"
          contract="Wrox.ProCSharp.Messaging.ICourseOrderService" />
      </service>
    </services>
  </system.serviceModel>
</configuration>
```

The Click event handler of the buttonProcessOrder button removes the selected course order from the collection class:

```
private void buttonProcessOrder_Click(object sender, RoutedEventArgs e)
{
    CourseOrder courseOrder = listOrders.SelectedItem as CourseOrder;
    courseOrders.Remove(courseOrder);
    listOrders.SelectedIndex = -1;
    buttonProcessOrder.IsEnabled = false;

    MessageBox.Show("Course order processed", "Course Order Receiver",
        MessageBoxButton.OK, MessageBoxImage.Information);

}
```

code snippet CourseOrderReceiver/CourseOrderReceiverWindow.xaml.cs

WCF Message Sender Application

The sending application is modified to make use of a WCF proxy class. For the contract of the service, the assembly CourseOrderServiceContract is referenced, and the assembly System.ServiceModel is required for use of the WCF classes.

In the Click event handler of the buttonSubmit control, the ChannelFactory class returns a proxy. The proxy sends a message to the queue by invoking the method AddCourseOrder():

```
private void buttonSubmit_Click(object sender, RoutedEventArgs e)
{
    try
    {
        var order = new CourseOrder
        {
            Course = new Course()
            {
                Title = comboCourses.Text
            },
            Customer = new Customer()
            {
                Company = textCompany.Text,
                Contact = textContact.Text
            }
        };

        var factory = new ChannelFactory<ICourseOrderService>("queueEndpoint");
        ICourseOrderService proxy = factory.CreateChannel();
        proxy.AddCourseOrder(order);
        factory.Close();

        MessageBox.Show("Course order submitted", "Course Order",
            MessageBoxButton.OK, MessageBoxImage.Information);
    }
    catch (Exception ex)
```

```
            {
                MessageBox.Show(ex.Message, "Course Order Error",
                    MessageBoxButton.OK, MessageBoxImage.Error);
            }
        }
```

code snippet CourseOrderSender/CourseOrderWindow.xaml.cs

The application configuration file defines the client part of the WCF connection. Again, the netMsmqBinding is used:

```xml
<?xml version="1.0" encoding="utf-8" ?>
<configuration>
    <system.serviceModel>
        <bindings>
            <netMsmqBinding>
                <binding name="nonTransactionalQueueBinding"
                    exactlyOnce="false">
                    <security mode="None" />
                </binding>
            </netMsmqBinding>
        </bindings>
        <client>
            <endpoint address="net.msmq://localhost/private/courseorder"
                binding="netMsmqBinding"
                bindingConfiguration="nonTransactionalQueueBinding"
                contract="Wrox.ProCSharp.Messaging.ICourseOrderService"
                name="queueEndpoint" />
        </client>
    </system.serviceModel>
</configuration>
```

code snippet CourseOrderSender/app.config

When you start the application now, it works in a similar way as before. There is no longer a need to use classes of the System.Messaging namespace to send and receive messages. Instead, you write the application in a similar way as using TCP or HTTP channels with WCF.

However, to create message queues and to purge messages, you still need the MessageQueue class. WCF is only an abstraction to send and receive messages.

> *If you need to have a* System.Messaging *application to communicate with a WCF application, you can do so by using the* msmqIntegrationBinding *instead of the* netMsmqBinding. *This binding uses the message format that is used with COM and* System.Messaging.

MESSAGE QUEUE INSTALLATION

Message queues can be created with the MessageQueue.Create() method. However, the user running an application usually doesn't have the administrative privileges that are required to create message queues.

Usually, message queues are created with an installation program, using the class MessageQueueInstaller. If an installer class is part of an application, the command-line utility installutil.exe (or a Windows Installation Package) invokes the Install() method of the installer.

Visual Studio has special support for using the MessageQueueInstaller with Windows Forms applications. If a MessageQueue component is dropped from the toolbox onto the form, the smart tag of the component allows you to add an installer with the menu entry Add Installer. The MessageQueueInstaller object can be configured with the properties editor to define transactional queues, journal queues, the type of the formatter, the base priority, and so on.

 Installers are discussed in Chapter 17, "Deployment."

SUMMARY

In this chapter, you've seen how Message Queuing can be used. Message Queuing is an important technology that offers not only asynchronous, but also disconnected communication. The sender and receiver can be running at different times, which makes Message Queuing an option for smart clients and also useful to distribute the load on the server over time.

The most important classes with Message Queuing are `Message` and `MessageQueue`. The `MessageQueue` class allows sending, receiving, and peeking at messages, and the `Message` class defines the content that is sent.

WCF offers an abstraction to Message Queuing. You can use the concepts offered by WCF to send messages by calling methods of a proxy and to receive messages by implementing a service.

The next chapter dives into Directory Services, how and when to use these hierarchical data stores, and different ways to connect to this service.

47

Syndication

WHAT'S IN THIS CHAPTER?

➤ `System.ServiceModel.Syndication`
➤ Syndication Reader
➤ Syndication Feeds

Do you have some structured data to offer, data that changes from time to time? With many web sites, Really Simple Syndication (RSS) or Atom (another syndication format) allow you to subscribe with feed readers. RSS is an XML format that allows syndicate information. RSS became very popular with blogs. This XML information makes it easy to subscribe to using RSS readers.

Nowadays, RSS is not only used with blogs but with many different data sources, such as online news magazines. Any data that changes from time to time is offered by RSS or by its successor protocol Atom. Microsoft Internet Explorer and Microsoft Outlook include RSS and Atom readers that are integrated into the product.

Windows Communication Foundation (WCF) includes an extension for syndication features in the namespace `System.ServiceModel.Syndication`. This namespace provides classes that can be used to both read and write RSS and Atom feeds.

This chapter shows you how to create syndication readers, as well as how data can be offered.

OVERVIEW OF SYSTEM.SERVICEMODEL.SYNDICATION

For syndication you can use the namespace `System.ServiceModel.Syndication`, which offers classes for syndication in an RSS or Atom format.

With the release of RSS version 2.0, RSS is now the shorthand notation for Really Simple Syndication. In earlier versions, it had the name Resource Description Framework (RDF) Site Summary and Rich Site Summary. The first version of RDF was created by Netscape to describe content of its portal site. It became successful when the *New York Times* began offering its readers subscriptions to RSS news feeds in 2002.

The Atom syndication format was designed to be the successor for RSS and is a proposed standard with RFC 4287: www.ietf.org/rfc/rfc4287.txt. The major difference between RSS and Atom is in the content that can be defined with an item. With RSS, the description element can contain simple text or HTML content in which the reading application does not care about this content. Atom requires that you define a specific type for the content with a type attribute, and it also allows you to have XML content with defined namespaces.

Figure 47-1 shows the logo that is used by RSS and Atom feeds. If a site shows this logo, then an RSS or Atom feed is offered.

FIGURE 47-1

The following table lists classes and elements that allow you to create a syndication feed. These classes are independent of the syndication type, RSS or Atom.

CLASS	DESCRIPTION
SyndicationFeed	SyndicationFeed represents the top-level element of a feed. With Atom, the top-level element is <feed>; RSS defines <rss> as the top-level element.
	With the static method Load(), a feed can be read using an XmlReader.
	Properties of this class such as Authors, Categories, Contributors, Copyright, Description, ImageUrl, Links, Title, and Items allow you to define child elements.
SyndicationPerson	SyndicationPerson represents a person with Name, Email, and Uri that can be assigned to the Authors and Contributors collection.
SyndicationItem	A feed consists of multiple items. Some of the properties of an item are Authors, Contributors, Copyright, and Content.
SyndicationLink	SyndicationLink represents a link within a feed or an item. This class defines the properties Title and Uri.
SyndicationCategory	A feed can group Items Into categories. The keyword of a category can be set to the Name and Label properties of SyndicationCategory.
SyndicationContent	SyndicationContent is an abstract base class that describes the content of an item. Content can be of type HTML, plain text, XHTML, XML, or a URL, described with the concrete classes TextSyndicationContent, UrlSyndicationContent, and XmlSyndicationContent.
SyndicationElementExtension	With an extension element, you can add additional content. The SyndicationElementExtension can be used to add information to a feed, a category, a person, a link, and an item.

To format a feed to the RSS and Atom formats, you can use classes that derive from SyndicationFeedFormatter and SyndicationItemFormatter. With .NET 4, the formatters for feeds are Atom10FeedFormatter and Rss20FeedFormatter, and for items are Atom10ItemFormatter and Rss20ItemFormatter.

READING SYNDICATION FEEDS SAMPLE

The first sample is a Syndication Reader application with a user interface developed with Windows Presentation Format (WPF). The user interface of the WPF application is shown in Figure 47-2.

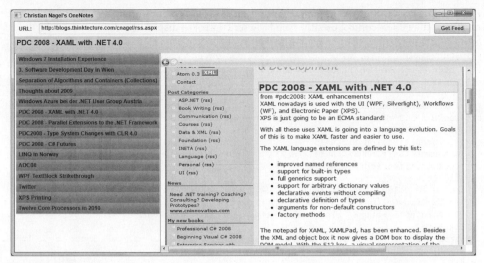

FIGURE 47-2

To use the Syndication API, the assembly `System.ServiceModel` is referenced with the application. The `OnGetFeed()` event handler method is set to the `Click` event of the button showing the Get Feed text. The code needed to read the application is really simple. First, the XML content from the RSS feed is read into the `XmlReader` class from the `System.Xml` namespace. `Rss20FeedFormatter` accepts an `XmlReader` with the `ReadFrom()` method. For data binding, the `Feed` property that returns a `SyndicationFeed` is assigned to the `DataContext` of the `Window`, and the `Feed.Items` property that returns `IEnumerable<SyndicationItem>` is assigned to the `DataContext` of a `DockPanel` container:

```csharp
private void OnGetFeed(object sender, RoutedEventArgs e)
{
    try
    {
        using (var reader = XmlReader.Create(textUrl.Text))
        {
            var formatter = new Rss20FeedFormatter();
            formatter.ReadFrom(reader);
            this.DataContext = formatter.Feed;
            this.feedContent.DataContext = formatter.Feed.Items;
        }
    }
    catch (WebException ex)
    {
        MessageBox.Show(ex.Message, "Syndication Reader");
    }
}
```

code snippet SyndicationReader/SyndicationReader.xaml.cs

The XAML code that defines the user interface is shown next. The `Title` property of the `Window` class is bound to the `Title.Text` property of the `SyndicationFeed` to display the title of the feed.

In the XAML code, a `DockPanel` named `heading`, which contains a `Label` bound to `Title.Text` and a `Label` bound to `Description.Text`, is defined. Because these labels are contained within the `DockPanel` named `feedContent`, and `feedContent` is bound to the `Feed.Items` property, these labels give title and description information about the current selected item.

A list of items is displayed in a `ListBox` that uses an `ItemTemplate` to bind a label to the `Title`.

The `DockPanel` named `content` contains a `Frame` element that binds the `Source` property to the first link of an item. With that setting, the `Frame` control uses the web browser control to display the content from the link:

```xml
<Window x:Class="Wrox.ProCSharp.Syndication.SyndicationReaderWindow"
    xmlns="http://schemas.microsoft.com/winfx/2006/xaml/presentation"
    xmlns:x="http://schemas.microsoft.com/winfx/2006/xaml"
    Title="{Binding Path=Title.Text}" Height="300" Width="450">

    <DockPanel x:Name="feedContent">
        <Grid DockPanel.Dock="Top">
            <Grid.ColumnDefinitions>
                <ColumnDefinition Width="50" />
                <ColumnDefinition Width="*" />
                <ColumnDefinition Width="90" />
            </Grid.ColumnDefinitions>
            <Label Grid.Column="0" Margin="5">URL:</Label>
            <TextBox Grid.Column="1" x:Name="textUrl" MinWidth="150"
                    Margin="5">http://blogs.thinktecture.com/cnagel/rss.aspx
            </TextBox>
            <Button Grid.Column="2" Margin="5" MinWidth="80"
                    Click="OnGetFeed">Get Feed</Button>
        </Grid>
        <StackPanel Orientation="Vertical" Background="LightGreen"
                DockPanel.Dock="Top" x:Name="heading">
            <Label DockPanel.Dock="Top" Content="{Binding Path=Title.Text}"
                    FontSize="16" />
            <Label DockPanel.Dock="Top" Content="{Binding Path=Description.Text}" />
        </StackPanel>
        <ListBox DockPanel.Dock="Left" ItemsSource="{Binding}"
                Style="{StaticResource listTitleStyle}"
                IsSynchronizedWithCurrentItem="True"
                HorizontalContentAlignment="Stretch" />
        <DockPanel x:Name="content" >
            <Label DockPanel.Dock="Top" Content="{Binding Path=Description.Text}" />
            <Frame Source="{Binding Path=Links[0].Uri}" />
        </DockPanel>
    </DockPanel>
</Window>
```

code snippet SyndicationReader/SyndicationReader.xaml

OFFERING SYNDICATION FEEDS SAMPLE

Reading syndication feeds is one scenario in which the Syndication API can be used. Another is to offer a syndication feed to RSS and Atom clients.

For this, Visual Studio 2010 offers the Syndication Service Library template, which you can use to start with. This template defines a reference to the `System.ServiceModel` library, and adds an application configuration file to define a WCF endpoint.

To offer data for the syndication feed, the ADO.NET Entity Framework is helpful. In the sample application, the Formula-1 database is used, which you can download from the Wrox web site at www.wrox.com with the sample applications for the book. The ADO.NET Entity Data Model item with the name `Formula1Model.edmx` is added to the project. Here, the tables Racers, RaceResults, Races, and Circuits are mapped to entity classes `Racer`, `RaceResult`, `Race`, and `Circuit`, as shown in Figure 47-3.

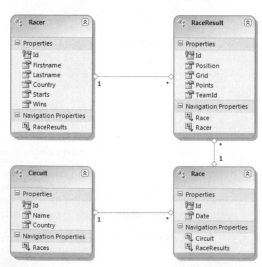

FIGURE 47-3

Check out Chapter 31, "ADO.NET Entity Framework," for more information.

The project template creates a file `IService1.cs` that contains the contract of the WCF service. The interface contains the `CreateFeed()` method, which returns a `SyndicationFeedFormatter`. Because `SyndicationFeedFormatter` is an abstract class, and the real types returned are either `Atom10FeedFormatter` or `Rss20FeedFormatter`, these types are listed with the `ServiceKnownTypeAttribute`, so the type is known for serialization.

The attribute `WebGet` defines that the operation can be called from a simple HTTP GET request that can be used to request syndication feeds. `WebMessageBodyStyle.Bare` defines that the result (the XML from the syndication feed) is sent as it is without adding an XML wrapper element around it:

Available for download on Wrox.com

```csharp
using System.ServiceModel;
using System.ServiceModel.Syndication;
using System.ServiceModel.Web;

namespace Wrox.ProCSharp.Syndication
{
    [ServiceContract]
    [ServiceKnownType(typeof(Atom10FeedFormatter))]
    [ServiceKnownType(typeof(Rss20FeedFormatter))]
    public interface IFormula1Feed
    {
        [OperationContract]
        [WebGet(UriTemplate = "*", BodyStyle = WebMessageBodyStyle.Bare)]
        SyndicationFeedFormatter CreateFeed();
    }
}
```

code snippet SyndicationService/IFormula1Feed.cs

The implementation of the service is done in the class `Formula1Feed`. Here, a `SyndicationFeed` item is created, and various properties of this class such as `Generator`, `Language`, `Title`, `Categories`, and `Authors` are assigned. The `Items` property is filled from a LINQ query that requests the winners of Formula-1 races of the requested date. The select clause of this query creates a new anonymous type that is filled with a few properties which then is used by a `Select()` method to create a `SyndicationItem` for every winner. With `SyndicationItem`, the `Title` property is assigned to plain text containing the country of the race. The `Content` property is filled with the help of LINQ to XML. `XElement` classes are used to create XHTML code that can be interpreted by the browser. This content shows the date of the race, the country, and the name of the winner.

Depending on the query string to request the syndication, the `SyndicationFeed` is formatted with the `Atom10FeedFormatter` or the `Rss20FeedFormatter`:

Available for download on Wrox.com

```csharp
using System;
using System.Linq;
using System.ServiceModel.Syndication;
using System.ServiceModel.Web;
using System.Xml.Linq;

namespace Wrox.ProCSharp.Syndication
{
    public class Formula1Feed: IFormula1Feed
    {
        public SyndicationFeedFormatter CreateFeed()
        {
            DateTime fromDate = DateTime.Today - TimeSpan.FromDays(365);
            DateTime toDate = DateTime.Today;
```

```
string from = WebOperationContext.Current.IncomingRequest.UriTemplateMatch
    .QueryParameters["from"];
string to = WebOperationContext.Current.IncomingRequest.UriTempateMatch
    .QueryParameters["to"];

if (from != null && to != null)
{
    try
    {
        fromDate = DateTime.Parse(from);
        toDate = DateTime.Parse(to);
    }
    catch (FormatException)
    {
        // keep the default dates
    }
}

// Create a new Syndication Feed.
var feed = new SyndicationFeed();
feed.Generator = "Pro C# 4.0 Sample Feed Generator";
feed.Language = "en-us";
feed.LastUpdatedTime = new DateTimeOffset(DateTime.Now);
feed.Title = SyndicationContent.CreatePlaintextContent(
            "Formula1 results");
feed.Categories.Add(new SyndicationCategory("Formula1"));
feed.Authors.Add(new SyndicationPerson("web@christiannagel.com",
        "Christian Nagel", "http://www.christiannagel.com"));
feed.Description = SyndicationContent.CreatePlaintextContent(
        "Sample Formula 1");
using (var data = new Formula1Entities())
{
    var races = (from racer in data.Racers
                from raceResult in racer.RaceResults
                where raceResult.Race.Date > fromDate &&
                    raceResult.Race.Date < toDate &&
                    raceResult.Position == 1
                orderby raceResult.Race.Date
                select new
                {
                    Country = raceResult.Race.Circuit.Country,
                    Date = raceResult.Race.Date,
                    Winner = racer.Firstname + " " + racer.Lastname
                }).ToArray();

    feed.Items = races.Select(race =>
        {
            return new SyndicationItem
            {
                Title = SyndicationContent.CreatePlaintextContent(
                        String.Format("G.P. {0}", race.Country)),
                Content = SyndicationContent.CreateXhtmlContent(
                        new XElement("p",
                            new XElement("h3", String.Format("{0}, {1}",
                                race.Country,
                                race.Date.ToShortDateString())),
                            new XElement("b", String.Format("Winner: {0}",
                                race.Winner))).ToString())
            };
        });

    // Return ATOM or RSS based on query string
```

```
// rss -> http://localhost:8732/Design_Time_Addresses/SyndicationService/
//      Feed1/
// atom -> http://localhost:8732/Design_Time_Addresses/SyndicationService/
//      Feed1/?format=atom
        string query = WebOperationContext.Current.IncomingRequest.
            UriTemplateMatch.QueryParameters["format"];
        SyndicationFeedFormatter formatter = null;
        if (query == "atom")
        {
            formatter = new Atom10FeedFormatter(feed);
        }
        else
        {
            formatter = new Rss20FeedFormatter(feed);
        }
        return formatter;
    }
  }
 }
}
```

code snippet SyndicationService/Formula1Feed.cs

When you start the service from within Visual Studio 2010, the WCF Service Host starts up to host the service, and you can see the feed result with the URL parameter `?from=1970/1/1&to=1971/1/1` formatted in Internet Explorer, as shown in Figure 47-4.

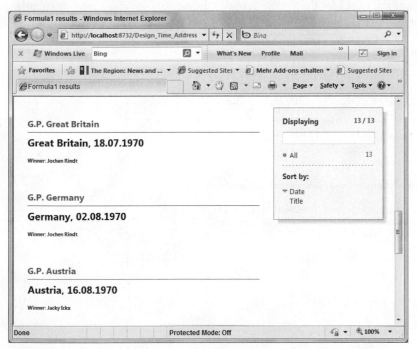

FIGURE 47-4

With the default request to the service, the RSS feed is returned. An extract of the RSS feed with the `rss` root element follows. With RSS, the `Title` property is translated to the `title` element, and the `Description` property goes to the `description` element. The `Authors` property of the `SyndicationFeed` that contains `SyndicationPerson` uses the e-mail address to create the `managingEditor` element. With RSS, the content of the `item`'s description element is encoded:

```xml
<?xml version="1.0" encoding="utf-8"?>
<rss version="2.0" xmlns:a10="http://www.w3.org/2005/Atom">
  <channel>
    <title>Formula1 results</title>
    <description>Sample Formula 1</description>
    <language>en-us</language>
    <managingEditor>web@christiannagel.com</managingEditor>
    <lastBuildDate>Sat, 25 Jul 2009 11:25:31+0200</lastBuildDate>
    <category>Formula1</category>
    <generator>Pro C# 4.0 Sample Feed Generator</generator>
    <item>
      <title>G.P. South Africa</title>
      <description>&lt;p&gt;&#xD; &lt;h3&gt;South Africa, 07.03.1970&lt;/h3&gt;
          &#xD;&lt;b&gt;Winner: Jack Brabham&lt;/b&gt;&#xD;&lt;/p&gt;

      </description>
    </item>
    <item>
      <!-- -->
  </channel>
</rss>
```

An Atom-formatted feed is returned with the query `?from=1970/1/1&to=1971/1/1&format=atom` with the result shown. The root element now is the `feed` element; the `Description` property turns into a `subtitle` element; and the values for the `Author` property are now shown completely differently from the RSS feed shown earlier. Atom allows the content to be unencoded. You can easily find the XHTML elements:

```xml
<feed xml:lang="en-us" xmlns="http://www.w3.org/2005/Atom">
  <title type="text">Formula1 results</title>
  <subtitle type="text">Sample Formula 1</subtitle>
  <id>uuid:c19284e7-aa40-4bc2-9be8-f1960b0f747e;id=1</id>
  <updated>2009-07-25T11:44:01+02:00</updated>
  <category term="Formula1"/>
  <author>
    <name>Christian Nagel</name>
    <uri>http://www.christiannagel.com</uri>
    <email>web@christiannagel.com</email>
  </author>
  <generator>Pro C# 4.0 Sample Feed Generator</generator>
  <entry>
    <id>uuid:c19284e7-aa40-4bc2-9be8-f1960b0f747e;id=2</id>
    <title type="text">G.P. South Africa</title>
    <updated>2009-07-25T09:44:05Z</updated>
    <content type="xhtml">
      <p><h3>South Africa, 07.03.1970</h3><b>Winner: Jack Brabham</b></p>
    </content>
  </entry>
  <!-- -->
</feed>
```

SUMMARY

In this chapter, you have seen how the classes from the `System.ServiceModel.Syndication` namespace can be used to create an application that receives a feed, as well as an application that offers a feed. The syndication API supports RSS 2.0 and Atom 1.0. As syndication standards emerge, new formatters will be available. You have seen that the SyndicationXXX classes are independent of the format that is generated.

The concrete implementation of the abstract class `SyndicationFeedFormatter` defines what properties are used and how they are translated to the specific format.

This chapter concludes the communication part of the book. You've read about communication technologies to directly use sockets, and abstraction layers that are offered. Windows Communication Foundation is a technology that has been discussed in several chapters. With Message Queuing (Chapter 46, "Message Queuing"), WCF offers a disconnected communication model.

There's still more to read. The appendices cover the Windows API code pack, a .NET extension to Windows 7 and Windows Server 2008 R2, and guidelines for developing applications on these platforms.

APPENDIX

Guidelines for Windows 7 and Windows Server 2008 R2

WHAT'S IN THIS APPENDIX?

➤ The Windows API Code Pack

➤ Restart Manager

➤ User account control

➤ Windows 7 directory structure

➤ Command links and task dialogs

➤ The taskbar and Jump List

This appendix gives you the information you need to know about developing applications for Windows 7 and Windows Server 2008 R2, and how you can use new Windows features from .NET applications.

 This appendix targets features important for developers. It does not cover features useful for a Windows 7 user or a Windows Server 2008 administrator.

If your applications are not targeting Windows Vista or higher, you should be aware that while WPF, WCF, WF, and LINQ are also available for Windows XP, this is not the case with the topics covered here. Also, some of the features are only available with Windows 7. If you're still targeting Windows XP, you should be aware of issues running your applications on Windows 7 and you should have a special focus on user account control and directory changes.

OVERVIEW

The Windows API has many new calls that expose new functionality available with Windows 7 and Windows Server 2008 R2; however, as of the .NET 4 release many of these calls are not available from the .NET Framework. The *Windows API Code Pack* helps here as it contains .NET classes that wrap native API calls to make them available from a .NET library. You can use this library within your .NET applications. You can download the Windows API Code Pack from `http://code.msdn .microsoft.com/WindowsAPICodePack`. This toolkit is used with most samples in this appendix. You can either use the libraries that come with this toolkit or copy the source code to your application. Typically, the classes from this toolkit are a thin wrapper around the Windows API.

Another toolkit you can use to target applications for the Windows platform is the *Windows Software Logo Kit*. On the Microsoft downloads page, you can find the Windows 7 Client Software Logo program documentation and toolkit that contains information about what's necessary for an application to get the Windows 7 software logo. Even if you're not interested in receiving a logo for your application, this documentation and toolkit is still interesting, as it explains what is required for an application to be considered well-behaved on the Windows operating system.

What are the requirements to receive a logo for an application? Here's a short list of the requirements; you can get many more details in the Windows 7 Client Software Logo document.

➤ The application may not contain spyware or malware. Of course, that's a requirement that should be fulfilled with every application. Interestingly, this is verified for logo compliance.

➤ Windows resource protected files may not be replaced.

➤ Errors must be reported with Windows Error Reporting (WER).

➤ The application must cleanly install and uninstall. Read chapter 17, "Deployment," for information on creating installation programs. The application should not force a reboot with the installation.

➤ The application should install to the correct folders. User data should not be written to the application folders. In the "Directory Structure" section of this appendix you can read how to find the correct folders for application and user data.

➤ Files and drivers must be digitally signed. Read Chapter 21, "Security," for information how to sign applications.

➤ 64-bit systems must be supported. This means that 16-bit code is not allowed. It's okay to run 32-bit applications on 64-bit. With .NET applications, you can set the platform configuration to Any CPU, x86, x64, or Itanium. Any CPU lets your application run with 32 bits on a 32-bit platform and with 64 bits on a 64-bit platform. When you set the configuration to Any CPU, you may not directly wrap native code with platform invoke in the assembly. Using native code restricts you to the native-code native API calls that are used, and thus Any CPU will not work on both versions.

➤ Version check with the installation must be done to check if the operating system has a minimum version required, but it's not allowed to check for a specific version.

➤ User account control guidelines must be followed. This is discussed in detail in this appendix.

➤ The applications may not block shutdown. You can use the Restart Manager to return the application to a working state after a reboot or failure. This is discussed in the section "Application Recovery."

➤ Multiuser sessions must be supported. Different users on one system should be able to use the application. This requirement is because of the fast user switching facility of Windows.

APPLICATION RECOVERY

Maybe you've already seen that some applications recover to a previous state if they crash or the system is rebooted. Such applications (for example, Microsoft Office and Visual Studio) make use of the *Application Recovery and Restart* (ARR) API that has been part of the Windows API since Windows Vista.

An application can register with the Restart Manager, and if the application crashes or becomes unresponsive (after running for at least 60 seconds), Windows Error Reporting (WER) restarts the application. An application can also register for recovery so that if the application hangs, it is recovered.

To see this in action, this example shows the creation of a simple WPF editor. This application registers for a restart and recovery if it fails. For reading and writing files, the class `CurrentFile` defines the `IsDirty` and `Content` properties, and `Load()` and `Save()` methods. The application makes use of tracing to write verbose messages to a trace listener so that you can retrace the events from the application.

Tracing is discussed in Chapter 19, "Instrumentation."

Available for download on Wrox.com

```csharp
using System;
using System.Diagnostics;
using System.IO;

namespace Wrox.ProCSharp.Windows7
{
    public class CurrentFile
    {
        public bool IsDirty { get; set; }
        public string Content { get; set; }

        public void Load(string fileName)
        {
            App.Source.TraceEvent(TraceEventType.Verbose, 0,
                                String.Format("begin Load {0}", fileName));
            Content = File.ReadAllText(fileName);
            IsDirty = false;
            App.Source.TraceEvent(TraceEventType.Verbose, 0,
                                String.Format("end Load {0}", fileName));
        }

        public void Save(string fileName)
        {
            App.Source.TraceEvent(TraceEventType.Verbose, 0,
                                String.Format("begin Save {0}", fileName));
            File.WriteAllText(fileName, Content);
            IsDirty = false;
            App.Source.TraceEvent(TraceEventType.Verbose, 0,
                                String.Format("end Save {0}", fileName));
        }
    }
}
```

code snippet EditorDemo/CurrentFile.cs

If the application is restarted because of a crash, the `/restart:[filename]` command-line argument is passed to the executable. To retrieve command-line information, the `OnStartup()` handler method is assigned to the `Startup` event of the `App` class. With the second argument, which is of type `StartupEventArgs`, the command-line arguments can be retrieved. With the `/restart:` argument, the following filename is assigned to the `RestartPath` property. The `App` class also contains the `TraceSource` object, which is used for tracing.

Available for download on Wrox.com

```csharp
using System;
using System.Diagnostics;
using System.Windows;

namespace Wrox.ProCSharp.Windows7
{
    public partial class App : Application
    {
        public static TraceSource Source = new TraceSource("RestartDemo");

        private void OnStartup(object sender, StartupEventArgs e)
```

```
        {
            Source.TraceEvent(TraceEventType.Verbose, 0,
                            "RestartDemo begin OnStartup");

            foreach (var arg in e.Args)
            {
                Source.TraceEvent(TraceEventType.Verbose, 0,
                                String.Format("argument {0}", arg));
                if (arg.StartsWith("/restart:",
                                StringComparison.InvariantCultureIgnoreCase))
                {
                    Source.TraceEvent(TraceEventType.Verbose, 0,
                                    "/restart: argument found");
                    RestartPath = arg.Substring(9);
                    Source.TraceEvent(TraceEventType.Verbose, 0,
                                    String.Format("RestartPath: {0}",
                                                RestartPath));
                }
            }
        }
        public string RestartPath { get; private set; }
    }
}
```

code snippet EditorDemo/App.xaml.cs

The main window (see Figure A-1) just contains a `TextBox` for editing the text in the middle area, a `TextBlock` control in the bottom area for status messages, and a `Menu` control.

The constructor of the `MainWindow` class checks to see if the application was started from a recovery, by checking the `RestartPath` property from the `App` class. If the application was started because of a recovery, the filename assigned to the `RestartPath` property is used to load this file and assign it to the `DataContext` of the `TextBox`. If the application was started normally, a new filename for recovery is created.

FIGURE A-1

Inside the constructor, a `DispatcherTimer` is also created that fires after 60 seconds. This is used to inform the user that the application can only recover from a crash after running for at least 60 seconds.

The most important calls in this scenario are the helper methods `RegisterForRestart()` and `RegisterForRecovery()`, which are called to register with the Restart Manager.

```
using System;
using System.Diagnostics;
using System.Threading;
using System.Windows;
using System.Windows.Controls;
using System.Windows.Input;
using System.Windows.Threading;
using Microsoft.WindowsAPICodePack.ApplicationServices;

namespace Wrox.ProCSharp.Windows7
{
    public partial class MainWindow : Window
    {
        private DispatcherTimer minuteTimer;
```

```
private CurrentFile currentFile = new CurrentFile();
private string tempPath;

public MainWindow()
{
    InitializeComponent();
    if ((Application.Current as App).RestartPath != null)
    {
        tempPath = (Application.Current as App).RestartPath;
        currentFile.Load(tempPath);
        App.Source.TraceEvent(TraceEventType.Verbose, 0,
            String.Format("Application recovered data from the file {0}",
                    tempPath));
    }
    else
    {
        string tempFileName = String.Format("{0}.txt", Guid.NewGuid());
        tempPath = System.IO.Path.Combine(Environment.GetFolderPath(
                    Environment.SpecialFolder.LocalApplicationData),
                    tempFileName);
        App.Source.TraceEvent(TraceEventType.Verbose, 0,
            String.Format("Normal start with temp-filename {0}",
                    tempPath));
    }
    this.text1.DataContext = currentFile;

    minuteTimer = new DispatcherTimer(TimeSpan.FromSeconds(60),
        DispatcherPriority.Normal, On60Seconds,
        Dispatcher.CurrentDispatcher);
    minuteTimer.Start();

    RegisterForRestart();
    RegisterForRecovery();
}
```

code snippet EditorDemo/MainWindow.xaml.cs

The application is only restarted if it runs for at least 60 seconds. This makes sense, as it's better not to restart applications that crash within the first 60 seconds; the user probably will not have lost too much data within that time. When testing this feature, you always need to wait for 1 minute before crashing the application.

To mark that the content has changed, the IsDirty property of the *currentFile* is set with the handler of the TextChanged event of the TextBox control:

```
private void OnTextChanged(object sender, TextChangedEventArgs e)
{
    if (!currentFile.IsDirty)
    {
        currentFile.IsDirty = true;
        textStatus.Text += String.Format("{0:T}: Set IsDirty\n",
                                DateTime.Now);
    }
}
```

The handler method of the DispatcherTimer class, On60Seconds(), writes status information to the TextBlock *textStatus*, noting that the 60-second limit has gone by and it's now possible to crash the application for recovery.

```
private void On60Seconds(object sender, EventArgs e)
{
    this.textStatus.Text += String.Format("{0:T}: Application can crash " +
                                "now\n", DateTime.Now);
    minuteTimer.Stop();
}
```

The method `RegisterForRestart()` invokes the `RegisterForApplicationRestart()` method of the `ApplicationRestartRecoveryManager` class. `ApplicationRestartRecoveryManager` is defined in the namespace `Microsoft.WindowsAPICodePack.ApplicationServices`. The method `RegisterForApplicationRestart()` wraps the Windows API call `RegisterApplicationRestart()` function. With this method, you can define the command-line arguments that should be used to restart the application and the cases when the application should not be restarted. In this example, it is defined that the application should not be restarted on a reboot or on installation of a patch. You can also specify that the application should not restart on an application crash and on application hang.

```
private void RegisterForRestart()
{
    var settings = new RestartSettings(
        String.Format("/restart:{0}", tempPath),
        RestartRestrictions.NotOnReboot | RestartRestrictions.NotOnPatch);
    ApplicationRestartRecoveryManager.RegisterForApplicationRestart(
        settings);
    textStatus.Text += String.Format("{0:T}: Registered for restart\n",
                            DateTime.Now);
    App.Source.TraceEvent(TraceEventType.Verbose, 0,
                    "Registered for restart");
}
```

Within the Windows API Code Pack, the Windows API call is defined to be invoked by using P/Invoke:

```
[DllImport("kernel32.dll")]
[PreserveSig]
internal static extern HRESULT RegisterApplicationRestart(
    [MarshalAs(UnmanagedType.BStr)] string commandLineArgs,
    RestartRestrictions flags);
```

 P/Invoke is discussed in Chapter 26, "Interop."

With this facility, if the application crashes or hangs, it is restarted. With the Restart Manager, you can also define a handler method that is invoked before the application is stopped because of a crash or a hang. This is done by invoking the `RegisterForApplicationRecovery()` method of the `ApplicationRestartRecoveryManager` class. This method wraps the Windows API function `RegisterApplicationRecoveryCallback()`. `RegisterForApplicationRecovery()` can be configured with an object of type `RecoverySettings`. With `RecoverySettings`, you assign an object of type `RecoveryData` and a recovery ping interval. This ping interval is defined in 100 ns units, and the callback method must give progress information to the recovery manager within that time span. By default, with a value of 0 the time interval is 5 seconds. The maximum value that can be set is 5 minutes. With `RecoveryData` you specify the method that is invoked by the Restart Manager to do the recovery, and an argument that is passed to that method:

```
private void RegisterForRecovery()
{
    var settings = new RecoverySettings(new RecoveryData(
                                    DoRecovery, tempPath), 0);
    ApplicationRestartRecoveryManager.RegisterForApplicationRecovery(
            settings);
```

```
textStatus.Text += String.Format("{0:T}: Registered for recovery\n",
                            DateTime.Now);
App.Source.TraceEvent(TraceEventType.Verbose, 0,
                        "Registered for recovery");
}
```

`DoRecovery()` is the callback method that is defined by the `RegisterForApplicationRecovery()` method call and is invoked by WER. Within the handler, the Recovery Manager is informed that recovery is in progress by calling the method `ApplicationRecoveryInProgress()`. This method returns `true` if the user canceled the recovery. You can verify user cancellation during the recovery to stop the recovery in case it was canceled by the user. Here, the content of the `TextBox` is written to the temporary file that is used when restarting the application. At the end of the recovery process, the Restart Manager is informed of its success by invoking `ApplicationRecoveryFinished()`.

```
private int DoRecovery(object state)
{
    App.Source.TraceEvent(TraceEventType.Verbose, 0, "begin Recovery");
    this.tempPath = (string)state;
    bool canceled = ApplicationRestartRecoveryManager.
                        ApplicationRecoveryInProgress();
    if (canceled)
    {
        textStatus.Text += String.Format(
            "{0:T}: Recovery canceled, shutting down\n", DateTime.Now);
        App.Source.TraceEvent(TraceEventType.Verbose, 0,
            "end Recovery with cancel");
        ApplicationRestartRecoveryManager.ApplicationRecoveryFinished(
            false);
        return 0;
    }
    SaveFile(tempPath);

    App.Source.TraceEvent(TraceEventType.Verbose, 0, "end Recovery");
    ApplicationRestartRecoveryManager.ApplicationRecoveryFinished(true);
    return 0;
}
```

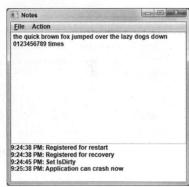

With all this in place, you can run the application, as shown in Figure A-2. The `TextBlock` on the bottom gives status information such as when registering for restart and recovery happened, and after 60 seconds, information that the application can now crash.

Selecting the menu Action ⇨ Crash invokes the handler method `OnCrash()`, which does a fast fail. The method `Environment.FailFast()` can be used to terminate a process in a fast way. This method writes an application event log and creates a dump of the application before the process is terminated. Only `CriticalFinalizerObject` objects are executed. Try-finally blocks and finalizers are not executed.

FIGURE A-2

```
private void OnCrash(object sender, ExecutedRoutedEventArgs e)
{
    Environment.FailFast("RestartDemo stopped from Menu command");
}
```

After crashing, the application is restarted and you can see the dialog shown in Figure A-3.

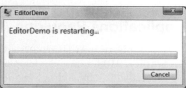

FIGURE A-3

USER ACCOUNT CONTROL

As a developer, *user account control* (UAC) is one of the features you can see immediately with Windows Vista: every time an administrative task is done, a dialog pops up asking for admin rights. In Windows 7, you can now configure this feature, as shown in Figure A-4. The default setting is to provide no notifications if admin changes are required from applications that are part of the operating system.

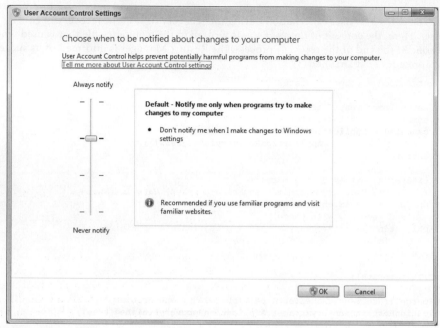

FIGURE A-4

What's the purpose behind the hassle of these dialogs? Although Windows guidelines have always mentioned that applications should not require admin privileges if it's not really necessary, many applications still need to run with the administrator account. For example, a normal user is not allowed to write data to the program files directory; administrative privileges are required. Because many applications don't run without administrative privileges as the developers didn't follow the guidelines, many users log in to the system with an Administrator account. By using the Administrator account on daily work you can unintentionally install Trojan horse programs.

Windows Vista and later versions avoid this problem because the Administrator, by default, doesn't have administrative privileges. The process has two security tokens associated with it, one with normal user privileges and one with admin privileges (for the case where the login is done to the Administrator account). With applications that require administrative privileges, the user can elevate the application to run with Administrator rights. This is either be done from the context menu Run as Administrator option, or the Compatibility Properties of an application can be configured to always require administrator privileges to run it. This setting adds application compatibility flags to the registry at `HKCU\Software\Microsoft\Windows NT\CurrentVersion\AppCompatFlags\Layers` with a value for `RUNASADMIN`.

Applications Requiring Admin Privileges

For applications that require administrative privileges, you can also add an application manifest. Visual Studio 2010 has an item template to add an application manifest to an application. Such a manifest can be created either by adding a manifest file to an existing application or by embedding a Win32 resource file within the assembly. In the Application tab of the Project Properties, you can select the manifest file of the application that's included as a native resource.

An application manifest is an XML file similar to the application configuration file. While the application configuration file has the file extension `.config`, the manifest ends with `.manifest`. The name of the file must be set to the name of the application, including the .exe file extension followed by `.manifest`. Visual Studio renames and copies the `app.manifest` file just as it does an application configuration file. The manifest file contains XML data, as shown here. The root element is `<assembly>`, which contains the child element `<trustInfo>`. The administrator requirement is defined with the `level` attribute of the `<requestedExecutionLevel>` element.

```xml
<?xml version="1.0" encoding="utf-8"?>
<asmv1:assembly manifestVersion="1.0" xmlns="urn:schemas-microsoft-com:asm.v1"
    xmlns:asmv1="urn:schemas-microsoft-com:asm.v1"
    xmlns:asmv2="urn:schemas-microsoft-com:asm.v2"
    xmlns:xsi="http://www.w3.org/2001/XMLSchema-instance">
  <assemblyIdentity version="1.0.0.0" name="MyApplication.app"/>
  <trustInfo xmlns="urn:schemas-microsoft-com:asm.v2">
    <security>
      <requestedPrivileges xmlns="urn:schemas-microsoft-com:asm.v3">
        <requestedExecutionLevel level="requireAdministrator" uiAccess="false" />
      </requestedPrivileges>
    </security>
  </trustInfo>
</asmv1:assembly>
```

code snippet AdminRightsRequired/app.manifest

When starting the application this way, you get an elevation prompt where the user is asked if he or she trusts the application to run with administrative privileges.

With the `requestedExecutionLevel` setting, you can specify the values `requireAdministrator`, `highestAvailable`, and `asInvoker`. The value `highestAvailable` means that the application gets the privileges the user has — but only after getting the consent from the user. The value `requireAdministrator` requires Administrator privileges. If the user is not logged on to the system as Administrator, a login dialog appears where the user can log in as Administrator for the application. The value `asInvoker` means that the application is running with the security token of the user.

The `uiAccess` attribute specifies if the application requires input to a higher-privilege-level window on the desktop. For example, an onscreen keyboard needs to drive input to other windows on the desktop, so the setting should be set to `true` for the application to display the onscreen keyboard. Non-UI-accessible applications should have this attribute set to `false`.

> *Another way to get admin privileges to an application is to write a Windows service. Because UAC applies to interactive processes only, a Windows service can get admin privileges. You can also write an unprivileged Windows application to communicate with the privileged Windows service by using WCF or another communication technology.*
>
> *Windows services are covered in Chapter 25, "Windows Services." WCF is covered in Chapter 43, "Windows Communication Foundation."*

Shield Icon

If an application or a task from an application requires administrative privileges, the user is informed by an easily recognizable shield icon. The shield icon is attached to the controls that require elevation. The user expects to see an elevation prompt when clicking on an item with a shield. Figures A-5 and A-6 show the shield in use. The Task Manager requires elevation to see processes from all users. Within User Accounts, adding or removing user accounts requires elevation as well as setting up parental controls.

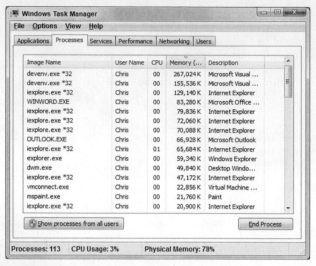

FIGURE A-5

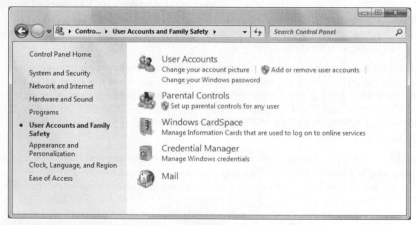

FIGURE A-6

You can create shield icons in your application by using the new command link control that is shown later in this appendix.

When the user clicks a control with a shield icon, an elevation prompt is shown. Elevation prompts are different, depending on the type of application that is elevated. The system differentiates between applications that are delivered with Windows (with the default setting of Windows 7, this prompt is not shown at all), applications that contain a certificate, and applications without a certificate. Of course, for applications without a certificate the prompt is shown with a special emphasis by highlighting it in color and marking the unknown publisher in bold.

DIRECTORY STRUCTURE

The directory structure of Windows changed with Windows Vista and that new structure continues with Windows 7. There's no longer a directory `c:\Documents and Settings\<username>`. It has been replaced by the new folder `c:\Users\<username>`. Windows XP defines the subdirectory `My Documents` for storing user-specific data. Windows 7 defines `c:\Users\<username>\Documents`.

If you just follow the simple rule not to use hard-coded path values with the program, it doesn't matter where the real folders are located. The folders differ with different Windows languages anyway. For special folders, use the `Environment` class and the `SpecialFolder` enumeration:

```
string folder = Environment.GetFolderPath(Environment.SpecialFolder.Personal);
```

Some of the folders defined by the `SpecialFolder` enumeration are described in the following table.

CONTENT	SPECIALFOLDER ENUMERATION	WINDOWS 7 DEFAULT DIRECTORY
User-specific documents	`Personal`	`C:\Users\<User>\Documents`
User-specific data for roaming users	`ApplicationData`	`C:\Users\<User>\AppData\Roaming`
User-specific data that is local to a system	`LocalApplicationData`	`C:\Users\<User>\Appdata\Local`
Program files	`ProgramFiles`	`C:\Program Files`
Program files that are shared among different programs	`CommonProgramFiles`	`C:\Program Files\Common Files`
Application data common to all users	`CommonApplicationData`	`C:\ProgramData`

 At logoff, the content of roaming directories is copied to the server, so if the user logs on to a different system, the same content is copied and is, thus, available on all systems accessed by the user.

With the special folders, you must be careful that a normal user doesn't have write access to the program files directory. You can write user-specific data from the application to `LocalApplicationData`, or for roaming users, to `ApplicationData`. Data that should be shared among different users can be written to `CommonApplicationData`.

NEW CONTROLS AND DIALOGS

Windows Vista and Windows 7 deliver several new controls. The command link control is an extension to the `Button` control and is used in combination with several other controls. The task dialog is a next-generation `MessageBox`, and for opening and saving files, new dialogs are available as well.

Command Link

Command link controls are an extension of the Windows `Button` control. Command links contain an optional icon and note text. This control is often used in task dialogs and wizards and gives much more information than button controls with OK and Cancel content.

With .NET applications, you can create command link controls by using the Windows API Code Pack. If you add the project Microsoft.WindowsAPICodePack.Shell to your solution, you can add a Windows Forms `CommandLink` controls from the toolbox to your Windows Forms application. The class `CommandLink` derives from the `System.Windows.Forms.Button` class. A command link is an extension of the native Windows `Button` and defines additional Windows messages and a new style to configure the `Button`. The wrapper class `CommandLink` sends the Windows messages `BCM_SETNOTE` and `BCM_SETSHIELD` and sets the style `BS_COMMANDLINK`. The public methods and properties offered in addition to the members of the `Button` class are `NoteText` and `ShieldIcon`.

The following code segment creates a new command link control that sets the `NoteText` and `ShieldIcon`. Figure A-7 shows the configured command link during runtime.

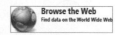

FIGURE A-7

Available for download on Wrox.com

```
this.commandLink1 =
new Microsoft.WindowsAPICodePack.Controls.
                             WindowsForms.CommandLink();
this.commandLink1.FlatStyle =
System.Windows.Forms.FlatStyle.System;
this.commandLink1.Location = new System.Drawing.Point(44, 54);
this.commandLink1.Name = "commandLink1";
this.commandLink1.NoteText = "Clicking this command requires " +
                             "admin rights";
this.commandLink1.ShieldIcon = true;
this.commandLink1.Size = new System.Drawing.Size(193, 121);
this.commandLink1.TabIndex = 0;
this.commandLink1.Text = "Give access to this computer";
this.commandLink1.UseVisualStyleBackColor = true;
this.commandLink1.Click += new System.EventHandler(
                             this.OnClickCommandLink);
```

code snippet WindowsFormsCommandLink/Form1.Designer.cs

For WPF, the command link is redefined as a WPF user control. This control is located in the namespace `Microsoft.WindowsAPICodePack.Controls.WindowsPresentationFoundation` with the name `CommandLink`. The `Icon` property allows you to specify an `IconSource`, the `Link` property, the value of the main text, and the `Note` property, the value of the additional text. Figure A-8 shows the result of this command link.

FIGURE A-8

Available for download on Wrox.com

```
<shell:CommandLink Icon="Images/Globe.ico" x:Name="commandLink1"
                   Link="Browse the Web"
                   Note="Find data on the World Wide Web"
                   Click="OnBrowse" Margin="5" Height="57"
                   VerticalAlignment="Top"
                   HorizontalAlignment="Center" />
```

code snippet WPFCommandLink/MainWindow.xaml

Task Dialog

The task dialog is a next-generation dialog that replaces the old message box. The task dialog is part of the new common controls. The Windows API defines the functions `TaskDialog` and `TaskDialogIndirect` to create task dialogs. `TaskDialog` allows you to create simple dialogs; `TaskDialogIndirect` is used to create more complex dialogs that contain command link controls and expanded content.

With the Windows API Code Pack, the native API call to `TaskDialogIndirect()` is wrapped with P/Invoke:

```
[DllImport(CommonDllNames.ComCtl32, CharSet = CharSet.Auto,
    SetLastError = true)]
internal static extern HRESULT TaskDialogIndirect(
    [In] TaskDialogNativeMethods.TASKDIALOGCONFIG pTaskConfig,
    [Out] out int pnButton,
    [Out] out int pnRadioButton,
    [MarshalAs(UnmanagedType.Bool)][Out]
            out bool pVerificationFlagChecked);
```

The first parameter of `TaskDialogIndirect()` is defined as a `TASKDIALOGCONFIG` class that maps to the same structure of the native API call:

```
                [StructLayout(LayoutKind.Sequential, CharSet = CharSet.Auto, Pack = 4)]
                internal class TASKDIALOGCONFIG
                {
                    internal uint cbSize;
                    internal IntPtr hwndParent;
                    internal IntPtr hInstance;
                    internal TASKDIALOG_FLAGS dwFlags;
                    internal TASKDIALOG_COMMON_BUTTON_FLAGS dwCommonButtons;
                    [MarshalAs(UnmanagedType.LPWStr)]
                    internal string pszWindowTitle;
                    internal TASKDIALOGCONFIG_ICON_UNION MainIcon;
                            // NOTE: 32-bit union field, holds pszMainIcon as well
                    [MarshalAs(UnmanagedType.LPWStr)]
                    internal string pszMainInstruction;
                    [MarshalAs(UnmanagedType.LPWStr)]
                    internal string pszContent;
                    internal uint cButtons;
                    internal IntPtr pButtons;              // Ptr to TASKDIALOG_BUTTON structs
                    internal int nDefaultButton;
                    internal uint cRadioButtons;
                    internal IntPtr pRadioButtons;         // Ptr to TASKDIALOG_BUTTON structs
                    internal int nDefaultRadioButton;
                    [MarshalAs(UnmanagedType.LPWStr)]
                    internal string pszVerificationText;
                    [MarshalAs(UnmanagedType.LPWStr)]
                    internal string pszExpandedInformation;
                    [MarshalAs(UnmanagedType.LPWStr)]
                    internal string pszExpandedControlText;
                    [MarshalAs(UnmanagedType.LPWStr)]
                    internal string pszCollapsedControlText;
                    internal TASKDIALOGCONFIG_ICON_UNION FooterIcon;
                            // NOTE: 32-bit union field, holds pszFooterIcon as well
                    [MarshalAs(UnmanagedType.LPWStr)]
                    internal string pszFooter;
                    internal PFTASKDIALOGCALLBACK pfCallback;
                    internal IntPtr lpCallbackData;
                    internal uint cxWidth;
                }
```

To use the new version of the common controls with a WPF application, an application manifest with the reference to version 6 of the common controls library must be added:

```xml
<?xml version="1.0" encoding="utf-8"?>
<asmv1:assembly manifestVersion="1.0" xmlns="urn:schemas-microsoft-com:asm.v1"
            xmlns:asmv1="urn:schemas-microsoft-com:asm.v1"
            xmlns:asmv2="urn:schemas-microsoft-com:asm.v2"
            xmlns:xsi="http://www.w3.org/2001/XMLSchema-instance">
    <assemblyIdentity version="1.0.0.0" name="MyApplication.app"/>
    <dependency>
      <dependentAssembly>
        <assemblyIdentity type="win32"
                        name="Microsoft.Windows.Common-Controls"
                        version="6.0.0.0"
                        processorArchitecture="*"
                        publicKeyToken="6595b64144ccf1df"
                        language="*" />
      </dependentAssembly>
    </dependency>
</asmv1:assembly>
```

code snippet TaskDialogDemo/app.manifest

The public class from the Windows API Code Pack used to show task dialogs is `TaskDialog`. To display a simple dialog, only the static method `Show()` must be invoked. The simple dialog is shown in Figure A-9.

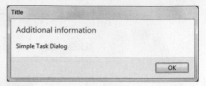

FIGURE A-9

Available for download on Wrox.com

```
TaskDialog.Show("Simple Task Dialog",
"Additional Information", "Title");
```

code snippet TaskDialogDemo/MainWindow.xaml.cs

For more features of the `TaskDialog` class, you can set the `Caption`, `Text`, `StandardButtons`, and `MainIcon` properties. You can see the result in Figure A-10.

```
var dlg1 = new TaskDialog();
dlg1.Caption = "Title";
dlg1.Text = "Some Information";
dlg1.StandardButtons =
TaskDialogStandardButtons.Ok |
                TaskDialogStandardButtons.Cancel;
dlg1.Icon = TaskDialogStandardIcon.Information;
dlg1.Show();
```

FIGURE A-10

With the task dialog, you can set the shield icon that was first shown with command links. Also, you can expand it by setting the `ExpansionMode` property. With the enumeration `TaskDialogExpandedInformationLocation`, you can specify that either the content or the footer should be expanded. Figure A-11 shows the task dialog in collapsed mode.

```
var dlg2 = new TaskDialog();
dlg2.Caption = "Title";
dlg2.Text = "Some Information";
dlg2.StandardButtons = TaskDialogStandardButtons.Yes |
                TaskDialogStandardButtons.No;
dlg2.Icon = TaskDialogStandardIcon.Shield;
dlg2.DetailsExpandedText = "Additional Text";
dlg2.DetailsExpandedLabel = "Less Information";
dlg2.DetailsCollapsedLabel = "More Information";
dlg2.ExpansionMode = TaskDialogExpandedDetailsLocation.ExpandContent;
dlg2.FooterText = "Footer Information";
dlg2.FooterIcon = TaskDialogStandardIcon.Information;
dlg2.Show();
```

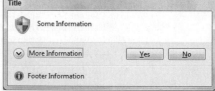

FIGURE A-11

A task dialog can also contain other controls. In the following code snippet, a task dialog is created that contains two radio buttons, a command link, and a progress control. You've already seen command links in the previous section, and indeed, command links are used very frequently within task dialogs. Figure A-12 shows the task dialog with the controls in the content area. Of course, you can also combine the expansion mode with controls.

```
var radio1 = new TaskDialogRadioButton();
radio1.Name = "radio1";
radio1.Text = "One";
var radio2 = new TaskDialogRadioButton();
radio2.Name = "radio2";
radio2.Text = "Two";
```

FIGURE A-12

```
        var commandLink = new TaskDialogCommandLink();
        commandLink.Name = "link1";
        commandLink.ShowElevationIcon = true;
        commandLink.Text = "Information";
        commandLink.Instruction = "Sample Command Link";
        var progress = new TaskDialogProgressBar();
        progress.Name = "progress";
        progress.State = TaskDialogProgressBarState.Marquee;

        var dlg3 = new TaskDialog();
        dlg3.Caption = "Title";
        dlg3.InstructionText = "Sample Task Dialog";

        dlg3.Controls.Add(radio1);
        dlg3.Controls.Add(radio2);
        dlg3.Controls.Add(commandLink);
        dlg3.Controls.Add(progress);
        dlg3.StandardButtons = TaskDialogStandardButtons.Ok;
        dlg3.Show();
```

Taskbar and Jump List

Windows 7 has a new taskbar. In the taskbar, you see not only the running applications, but also fast access icons. The user can pin most-often-used applications for fast access. When you hover over an item of the taskbar, you can see a preview of the currently running application. The item can also have visual state so the user can receive feedback from the items on the taskbar. Did you copy some large files using Explorer? You can see progress information on the Explorer item. Progress information is shown with the visual state. Another feature of the taskbar is the Jump List. Clicking the right mouse key on a taskbar button opens the Jump List. This list can be customized per application. With Microsoft Outlook, you can go directly to the Inbox, Calendar, Contacts, and Tasks or create a new e-mail. With Microsoft Word, you can open the recent documents.

The capability to add all these features to WPF applications is included with the .NET Framework 4 in the namespace System. Windows.Shell.

The sample application shown in this section lets you plays videos, gives you visual feedback on the taskbar button as to whether the video is running or stopped, and allows you to start and stop a video directly from the taskbar. The main window of the application consists of a grid with two rows, as shown in Figure A-13. The first row contains a ComboBox to display available videos, and two buttons to start and stop the player. The second row contains a MediaElement for playing the videos.

FIGURE A-13

The XAML code of the user interface is shown below. The buttons are associated with the commands MediaCommands.Play and MediaCommands.Stop, which map to the handler methods OnPlay() and OnStop(). With the MediaElement the property LoadedBehavior is set to Manual so that the player doesn't start immediately on loading the video.

```
<Window.CommandBindings>
    <CommandBinding Command="MediaCommands.Play" Executed="OnPlay" />
    <CommandBinding Command="MediaCommands.Stop" Executed="OnStop" />
</Window.CommandBindings>
<Grid>
```

```
<Grid.RowDefinitions>
    <RowDefinition Height="Auto" />
    <RowDefinition Height="*" />
</Grid.RowDefinitions>
<StackPanel Grid.Row="0" Orientation="Horizontal"
            HorizontalAlignment="Left">
    <ComboBox x:Name="comboVideos" ItemsSource="{Binding}" Width="220"
              Margin="5" IsSynchronizedWithCurrentItem="True" />
    <Button x:Name="buttonPlay" Content="Play" Margin="5" Padding="4"
            Command="MediaCommands.Play" />
    <Button x:Name="buttonStop" Content="Stop" Margin="5" Padding="4"
            Command="MediaCommands.Stop" />
</StackPanel>
<MediaElement x:Name="player" Grid.Row="1" LoadedBehavior="Manual"
        Margin="5"
        Source="{Binding ElementName=comboVideos, Path=SelectedValue}" />
</Grid>
```

code snippet TaskbarDemo/MainWindow.xaml

To configure the taskbar item, the namespace `System.Windows.Shell` contains a dependency property for the `Window` class to add taskbar information. The `TaskbarItemInfo` property can contain a `TaskbarItemInfo` element. With `TaskbarItemInfo`, you can set the `Description` property, which is shown as tooltip information. With the properties `ProgressState` and `ProgressValue`, feedback can be given on a current state of the application. `ProgressState` is of type `TaskbarItemProgressState`, which defines the enumeration values `None`, `Intermediate`, `Normal`, `Error`, and `Paused`. Depending on the value of this setting, progress indicators are shown on the taskbar item. The `Overlay` property allows you to define an image that is displayed over the icon in the taskbar. This property will be set from code-behind.

The taskbar item can contain a `ThumbButtonInfoCollection`, which is assigned to the `TumbButtonInfos` property of the `TaskbarItemInfo`. Here, you can add buttons of type `ThumbButtonInfo`, which are displayed in the preview of the application. The sample contains two `ThumbButtonInfo` elements, which have `Command` set to the same commands as the play and stop `Button` elements created previously. With these buttons, you can control the application in the same way as with the other `Button` elements in the application. The image for the buttons in the taskbar is taken from resources with the keys `StartImage` and `StopImage`.

```
<Window.TaskbarItemInfo>
    <TaskbarItemInfo x:Name="taskBarItem" Description="Sample Application">
        <TaskbarItemInfo.ThumbButtonInfos>
            <ThumbButtonInfo IsEnabled="True" Command="MediaCommands.Play"
                             CommandTarget="{Binding ElementName=buttonPlay}"
                             Description="Play"
                             ImageSource="{StaticResource StartImage}" />
            <ThumbButtonInfo IsEnabled="True" Command="MediaCommands.Stop"
                             CommandTarget="{Binding ElementName=buttonStop}"
                             Description="Stop"
                             ImageSource="{StaticResource StopImage}" />
        </TaskbarItemInfo.ThumbButtonInfos>
    </TaskbarItemInfo>
</Window.TaskbarItemInfo>
```

 Dependency properties are explained in Chapter 27, "Core XAML."

The images referenced from the `ThumbButtonInfo` elements are defined within the `Resources` section of the `Window`. One image is made up from a light green ellipse, the other image from two orange-red lines.

```xml
<Window.Resources>
    <DrawingImage x:Key="StopImage">
        <DrawingImage.Drawing>
            <DrawingGroup>
                <DrawingGroup.Children>
                    <GeometryDrawing>
                        <GeometryDrawing.Pen>
                            <Pen Thickness="5" Brush="OrangeRed" />
                        </GeometryDrawing.Pen>
                        <GeometryDrawing.Geometry>
                            <GeometryGroup>
                                <LineGeometry StartPoint="0,0"
                                              EndPoint="20,20" />
                                <LineGeometry StartPoint="0,20"
                                              EndPoint="20,0" />
                            </GeometryGroup>
                        </GeometryDrawing.Geometry>
                    </GeometryDrawing>
                </DrawingGroup.Children>
            </DrawingGroup>
        </DrawingImage.Drawing>
    </DrawingImage>
    <DrawingImage x:Key="StartImage">
        <DrawingImage.Drawing>
            <DrawingGroup>
                <DrawingGroup.Children>
                    <GeometryDrawing Brush="LightGreen">
                        <GeometryDrawing.Geometry>
                            <EllipseGeometry RadiusX="20" RadiusY="20"
                                             Center="20,20" />
                        </GeometryDrawing.Geometry>
                    </GeometryDrawing>
                </DrawingGroup.Children>
            </DrawingGroup>
        </DrawingImage.Drawing>
    </DrawingImage>
</Window.Resources>
```

In the code-behind, all videos from the special My Videos folder are assigned to the `DataContext` to the `Window` object, and thus, because the `ComboBox` is data-bound, listed in the `ComboBox`. In the `OnPlay()` and `OnStop()` event handlers, the `Play()` and `Stop()` methods of the `MediaElement` are invoked. To give visual feedback to the taskbar item, as well on playing and stopping a video, image resources are accessed and assigned to the `Overlay` property of the `TaskbarItemInfo` element.

```csharp
using System;
using System.Collections.Generic;
using System.IO;
using System.Text;
using System.Windows;
using System.Windows.Input;
using System.Windows.Media;
using System.Windows.Shell;

namespace Wrox.ProCSharp.Windows7
{
    public partial class MainWindow : Window
    {
        public MainWindow()
        {
            InitializeComponent();
            string videos = Environment.GetFolderPath(
                                Environment.SpecialFolder.MyVideos);
```

```
        this.DataContext = Directory.EnumerateFiles(videos);
    }

    private void OnPlay(object sender, ExecutedRoutedEventArgs e)
    {
        object image = TryFindResource("StartImage");
        if (image is ImageSource)
            taskBarItem.Overlay = image as ImageSource;
        player.Play();
    }

    private void OnStop(object sender, ExecutedRoutedEventArgs e)
    {
        object image = TryFindResource("StopImage");
        if (image is ImageSource)
            taskBarItem.Overlay = image as ImageSource;
        player.Stop();
    }
  }
}
```

code snippet TaskbarDemo/MainWindow.xaml.cs

Now you can run the application, start and stop the video from the taskbar, and see visual feedback, as shown in Figure A-14.

Customizing the Jump List is done by adding a JumpList to the application class. This can either be done in code by invoking the static method JumpList.SetJumpList() or by adding JumpList elements as a child of the Application element.

FIGURE A-14

The sample code creates the Jump List in the code-behind. JumpList. SetJumpList() requires as the first argument the object of the application, which is returned from the Application.Current property. The second argument requires an object of type JumpList. The *jumpList* is created with a JumpList constructor passing JumpItem elements and two Boolean values. By default, a Jump List contains frequent and recent items. Setting the Boolean values, you can influence this default behavior. The items you can add to a JumpList derive from the base class JumpItem. The classes available are JumpTask and JumpPath. With JumpTask, you can define a program that should be started when the user selects this item from the Jump List. JumpTask defines the properties that are needed to start the application and give information to the user, which are CustomCategory, Title, Description, ApplicationPath, IconResourcePath, WorkingDirectory, and Arguments. With the JumpTask that is defined in the code snippet, notepad.exe is started and initialized with the readme.txt document. With a JumpPath item, you can define a file that should be listed in the Jump List to start the application from the file. JumpPath defines a Path property for assigning the filename. Using a JumpPath item requires that the file extension be registered with the application. Otherwise, the registration of the items is rejected. To find the reasons for items being rejected, you can register a handler to the JumpItemsRejected event. Here, you can get a list of the rejected items (RejectedItems) and the reasons for them (RejectedReasons).

```
        var jumpItems = new List<JumpTask>();
        var workingDirectory = Environment.CurrentDirectory;
        var windowsDirectory = Environment.GetFolderPath(
                                Environment.SpecialFolder.Windows);
        var notepadPath = System.IO.Path.Combine(windowsDirectory,
                                    "Notepad.exe");

        jumpItems.Add(new JumpTask
        {
            CustomCategory="Read Me",
            Title="Read Me",
            Description="Open read me in Notepad.",
```

```
                    ApplicationPath=notepadPath,
                    IconResourcePath=notepadPath,
                    WorkingDirectory=workingDirectory,
                    Arguments="readme.txt"
            });

            var jumpList = new JumpList(jumpItems, true, true);
            jumpList.JumpItemsRejected += (sender1, e1) =>
                {
                    var sb = new StringBuilder();
                    for (int i = 0; i < e1.RejectedItems.Count; i++)
                    {
                        if (e1.RejectedItems[i] is JumpPath)
                            sb.Append((e1.RejectedItems[i] as JumpPath).Path);
                        if (e1.RejectedItems[i] is JumpTask)
                            sb.Append((e1.RejectedItems[i] as JumpTask).
                                        ApplicationPath);
                        sb.Append(e1.RejectionReasons[i]);
                        sb.AppendLine();
                    }
                    MessageBox.Show(sb.ToString());
                };

            JumpList.SetJumpList(Application.Current, jumpList);
```

When you run the application and click the right mouse button, you see the Jump List, as shown in Figure A-15.

FIGURE A-15

To use the taskbar and Jump List from Windows Forms applications, you can use extensions defined in the Windows API Code Pack.

SUMMARY

In this appendix, you saw various features available in Windows 7 and Windows Server 2008 R2 that are important for the development of applications.

Microsoft has defined guidelines for many years that state that non-administrative applications should not require administrative privileges. Because many applications have failed to comply with that requirement, the operating system is now strict about UAC. The user must explicitly elevate admin rights to applications. You saw how this affects applications.

This appendix covered several dialogs that were introduced in Windows Vista for better user interaction. These include the new task dialog that replaces the message box, and the command link extension to the button control. New with Windows 7 are the taskbar items and Jump Lists.

More features that are available only since Windows Vista and Windows Server 2008 are covered in other chapters:

➤ Chapter 19, "Instrumentation," discusses the event logging facility, Event Tracing for Windows (ETW).

➤ Chapter 21, "Security," gives you information about Cryptography Next Generation (CNG), the Crypto API.

➤ Chapter 23, "System.Transactions," gives you information about file-based and registry-based transactions.

➤ Chapter 43, "Windows Communication Foundation," uses Windows Activation Services (WAS) to host a WCF service.

INDEX

Symbols

\', 35
\ ", 35
\\, 35
\0, 35
\a, 35
\b, 35
\f, 35
\n, 35
\r, 35
\t, 35
\w, 35
{ }. *See* curly braces
==. *See* comparison operators
; *See* semicolons
'. *See* single quotation mark
". *See* double quotation marks
&
  address operator, 152, 319
  bitwise AND, 152, 157, 172, 319, 336
*
  escape sequence (regular expression), 221
  indirection operator, 152, 319
  multiplication, 157, 167, 168, 319
+
  addition operator, 151, 164, 165
  escape sequence (regular expression), 221
  string concatenation operator, 151
( ) (cast operator), 152, 172
. (regular expression escape sequence), 221
: : (namespace alias qualifier), 47, 152
/, % (division operator), 151, 152, 153, 157
| (bitwise OR), 152, 157, 172, 319, 336
/*...*/ (multiline comments), 25, 53
?
  escape sequence (regular expression), 221
  operator, 123
?: (conditional (ternary) operator), 152, 154, 157, 223, 224
?? (null coalescing operator), 123, 152, 156–157
-> (pointer member access operator), 323–324
(preprocessor directives), 55–58, 387

$ (regular expression escape sequence), 221
^ (regular expression escape sequence), 221
// (single-line comments), 25, 53
/// (XML documentation), 53
[ ] index operator, 152, 172
@ symbol
  identifiers and, 59
  string literals and, 37, 220
  verbatim strings and, 219

A

abstract (modifier), 100
abstract classes, 93
abstract functions, 93
AccelerationRatio, 1022
AcceptAllChanges(), 873
AcceptChanges(), 837, 838
AcceptSocket(), 672, 679
access control entries (ACE), 559, 805
access control lists. See ACLs
access modifiers, for properties, 73
AccessDataSource, 1162
accessing array elements, 130–131
Account class, 124, 125
Account property (ServiceProcessInstaller class), 681
Accumulate(), 125, 126, 965, 966
AccumulateSimple(), 124, 125
ACE (access control entries), 559, 805
ACID (*atomicity, consistency, isolation, durability*), 607, 635
acknowledgment messages, 1361
acknowledgment queues, 1376–1377
ACLs (access control lists), 558–561, 568
  adding/removing, from file, 805–806
  COM interop and, 802
  discretionary, 559
  programming, 568
  reading
    from directory, 803–804
    from file, 802–803
  system, 559

action links, 1267–1268
Action⟨T⟩, 190, 759
Active Directory Domain Services Integration, 1360, 1361
Active Directory domains, 1361, 1364
active phase (transactions), 606
Active Server Pages (ASP) technology, 1149
Active Template Library. *See* ATL
ActiveX controls
  server-side controls *v.*, 18
  Windows Controls *v.*, 19
ActiveX Data Objects. *See* ADO
activities (Workflow 4), 1309, 1311–1322. *See also* workflows; *specific activities*
  class hierarchy, 1311
  custom, 1316–1322
  custom composite, 1319–1322
  designers for, 1317–1319
  Retry, 1319, 1320, 1321, 1322
  workflows as, 1311
Activity Designer Library, 381, 1317
Activity Library, 381
activity validation, 1317
Activity⟨TResult⟩, 1311
ActivityWithResult, 1311, 1312
Add(), 51, 54, 108, 109, 226, 229, 236, 246, 252, 255, 263, 264, 265
Add New Project dialog box, 385
Add Service Reference (Visual Studio), 1304, 1305
AddDocument(), 114, 238, 244
AddDocumentToPriorityNode(), 244
AddHandler(), 738
$addHandler(), 1234
adding pointers, 322
add-ins, 747. *See also* MEF; parts
  MAF and, 747–748
  as parts, 749
addition operator (+), 151, 164, 165
AddLast(), 110, 112, 113, 242, 244, 265
AddMessageFilter, 1119
AddObject(), 873, 881, 900
AddRange(), 229, 230
AddRef(), 696, 705, 709, 713
AddRemoveProgramsIcon, 414
address operator (&), 152, 319
AddStudent(), 608, 612, 613, 618
AddToAmount(), 86, 87
AddWithValue(), 826, 830
administration queues, 1363
administration tool (for Windows Services), 668
administrative privileges, UAC and, 1404–1405
ADO (ActiveX Data Objects), 817–818
ADO.NET, 817–860
  ADO *v.*, 817–818
  commands and, 825–829

connection strings and, 821–822
data binding and, 1169–1180
data reader and, 832–834
database connections, 820–821, 822–824
database development
  key generation with SQL Server, 857–858
  naming conventions, 859–860
  tiered development, 856–857
database-specific classes, 819
disconnected record set, 817, 818, 819
namespaces, 818
object model, 817, 835–844
overview, 817–820
shared classes, 818–819
stored procedures
  calling, 829–832
  naming conventions, 859–860
transactions, 824–825
  System.Transactions *v.*, 609–610
  transaction scope, 824–825
XML and, 844, 927–934
  converting ADO.NET data to XML, 927–932
  converting XML to ADO.NET data, 932–934
XML schemas and, 844–850
ADO.NET Entity Data Model. *See* EDM
ADO.NET Entity Data Model Designer, 864
ADO.NET Entity Framework, 294, 861–884
  ambient transactions and, 635
  classes, 818
  entity classes, 868–871
  Entity Client, 866–867
  Entity SQL, 862, 867–868
  LINQ to Entities and, 883–884
  LINQ to SQL and, 293
  mapping, 862–866
  object contexts, 871–873
  object queries, 876–879
  overview of, 861–862
  relationships, 873–876
  updates and, 879–884
  WCF Data Services with, 885–886, 894–895
ADOXML.cs (code snippet), 927, 928, 929, 931, 932
AdRotator, 1161
ADSI COM, 695
Advanced Encryption Standard (AES), 554, 557
AdvCalculator, 752
AdvCalculator/Calculator.cs, 753
AdventureWorks database, 955, 965, 967, 970
  SqlSamplesUsingAdventureWorks/CalcHash.cs, 969
  SqlSamplesUsingAdventureWorks/ GetCustomerOrdersCLR.cs, 968
  SqlSamplesUsingAdventureWorks/InsertContact.cs, 971
  SqlSamplesUsingAdventureWorks/SampleSum.cs, 966

AdventureWorksLT sample application, 927
AES (Advanced Encryption Standard), 554, 557
AesCryptoServiceProvider, 554, 557, 558
Aggregate(), 276, 286
aggregate operators (query operator category), 276, 286–287
Aggregate template, 966
AggregateCatalog, 768
aggregates, 964–965
  built-in, 964–965
  user-defined, 964–967, 980
Ajax, 1218–1221. *See also* ASP.NET AJAX
alert (escape sequence), 35
Alice/Bob/Eve (encryption example), 553
All (quantifier operator), 276
'all or nothing' characteristic, of transactions, 605
AllowDirectoryBrowsing, 418
AllowPartiallyTrustedCallers, 565
AllowReadAccess, 418
AllowRecomposition, 763, 767
AllowScriptSourceAccess, 418
AllowWriteAccess, 418
AltDirectorySeparatorChar, 775
‹AlternatingItemTemplate›, 1177
ambient transactions, 618–624, 635
  multithreading with, 621–624
  nested scopes with, 620–621
AnalyzeType(), 343, 344
Ancestors(), 293
anchor to blocks, 1083–1084
AnchoredBlock, 1083
And(), 258, 259
AnimationDemo/ButtonAnimationWindow.xaml, 1022
AnimationDemo/EllipseWindow.xaml, 1021, 1023
AnimationDemo/EventTriggerWindow.xaml, 1025
AnimationDemo/KeyFrameWindow.xaml, 1026
animations (WPF), 1020–1029
  elements of, 1020
  event triggers, 1020, 1023–1025
  keyframe, 1025–1026
  non-linear, 1023
  Timeline, 1020–1023
  Visual State Manager and, 1026–1029
anonymous functions. *See* anonymous methods;
  Lambda expressions
anonymous methods, 196
  delegates with, 196–197
  dynamic programming (C#) and, 295
anonymous types, 79
AnonymousMethods/Program.cs, 196–197
AnotherButtonStyle, 1004
Any (quantifier operator), 276
apartment models. *See* MTAs; STAs
APIs
  reading/writing XAML and, 744

Sandbox API, 562, 565–566
Windows API Code Pack, 1397–1398, 1402, 1407, 1408, 1410, 1415
AppDomain class, 441, 442, 444
AppDomainHost/Program.cs, 566
AppearanceEditorPart, 1211
AppendFormat(), 211, 212, 214, 215
AppendOnly, 876
application (ASP.NET), 1181. *See also* web applications
application cache (ClickOnce files), 421
Application class
  ASP.NET AJAX Library, 1237
  System.Windows.Forms, 1118–1119
  WPF, 986
application configuration (ASP.NET), 1181–1182
application deployment. *See* deployment
application domains, 11–13
  assemblies and, 441–444
  CLR and, 956
  virtual memory and, 12–13
application manifest, 419, 420–421
Application object, 1181
application recovery (Restart Manager), 1398–1403
Application Recovery and Restart (ARR), 1398
Application.init, 1237
Application.load, 1237
ApplicationProtection, 418
ApplicationRestartRecoveryManager, 1402, 1403
application-to-application e-mail communication, 1358. *See also* Message Queuing
Application.unload, 1238
ApplyPropertyChanges(), 873
AppMappings, 418
AppServices/SampleRoleProvider.cs, 550
AppServices/web.config, 551
AppSupport, 409–410
App.xaml, 595, 1005, 1013, 1098
ArcSegment, 989
ArgsExample.cs, 49
ArgumentException, 244, 246, 352, 353, 362
ArgumentNullException, 353
arguments, workflows and, 1322–1323
arithmetic, on pointers, 322–323
arithmetic operators, 151
ARR (Application Recovery and Restart), 1398
Array class, 129, 134–139, 149
array covariance, 139
array initializers, 130, 132, 133, 228
Array.Copy(), 136, 228
ArrayList, 108, 225, 228, 230, 264, 265, 288
arrays, 129–140
  bit, 258–260
  copying, 135–136
  creating, 134–135
  DataGridView control and, 1130–1131

arrays *(continued)*
  declaring, 129
  elements
        accessing, 130–131
        sorting, 136–139
  on heap, 329
  indexers and, 130–131
  initializing, 130, 132, 133, 228
  jagged, 133–134
  multidimensional, 132–133
  as parameters, 139–140
  reference types and, 131–132
  simple, 129–132
  on stack, 329–330
  stack-based, 329–331
  syntax, pointers and, 331
  tuples *v.*, 147–149
ArraySegmentSample/Program.cs, 140
ArraySegment⟨T⟩, 140
as operator, 152, 155
ASCII format, 785, 791, 794, 795, 796
AsEnumerable, 276
ASP (Active Server Pages) technology, 1149
AsParallel(), 289, 290
ASP.NET
  application configuration, 1181–1182
  application services, AJAX and, 1241
  architecture, 1150
  code model, 1154–1155
  code-behind feature, 18
  controls. *See* ASP.NET server controls
  core, 1149–1183
  CSS and, 1149
  dynamic data. *See* dynamic data
  features, 17–18, 1185–1242
  files
        components, 1150
        processing, 1150
  IIS and, 409, 1150
  introduction, 1150–1151
  localization with, 591–593
  master pages, 1195–1198
  MVC, 1243, 1259–1274
  PCSDemoSite. *See* PCSDemoSite
  Professional ASP.NET4: in C# and VB, 247, 1156,
        1181
  role-based security and, 547
  routing, 1244–1251
  sandboxing and, 561
  security and, 1201–1206
  server controls. *See* ASP.NET server controls
  site navigation, 1198–1201
  state management in, 1151
  themes, 1206–1210
  web applications, 1150–1151
  Web Forms. *See* Web Forms

  Web Parts, 1210–1218
  web sites, 1150–1151
ASP.NET AJAX, 1218–1241, 1242
  Ajax and, 1218–1221
  AJAX Extensions, 1222–1223
  AJAX Library, 1223–1224
  ASP.NET application services and, 1241
  asynchronous web method calls and, 1240–1241
  configuration, 1227
  defined, 1221
  downloads for, 1221
  functionality, 1221–1224
        adding to web site, 1227–1233
  JavaScript debugging and, 1239–1240
  JSON and, 1221, 1222
  web site example, 1224–1226
ASP.NET AJAX Control Toolkit, 1224, 1227
ASP.NET AJAX Extensions, 1222–1223
ASP.NET AJAX Library, 1223–1224
  adding JavaScript to web page, 1234
  global utility functions, 1234
  JavaScript OOP extensions, 1235–1236
  layers of, 1223
  PCSLibraryDemo project, 1234–1241
ASP.NET AJAX Server Control, 380
ASP.NET AJAX Server Control Extender, 380, 1232
ASP.NET AJAX-enabled web site configuration, 1227
ASP.NET MVC, 1243, 1259–1274. *See also* dynamic
        data; routing
  dynamic data and, 1243
  MVC *v.*, 1260
  Web.config, 1261
ASP.NET MVC 2 Web Application, 380, 1261
ASP.NET MVC applications
  customizing, 1266–1274
  MagicShop.mdf database, 1261–1274
        action links, 1267–1268
        controller added to, 1262–1263
        creating, 1261
        customizing, 1266–1274
        index operation added to, 1263
        inspecting, 1261–1262
        model added to, 1262
        products view added to, 1263–1266
        URL operation routing, 1266–1267
        viewing items with details, 1268–1269
ASP.NET server controls, 1155–1169. *See also* custom
        controls; user controls; Web Parts; web server
        controls
  event-booking example, 1164–1175
  HTML, 1155
  project type, 380
ASP.NET Web Application (project type), 380
ASP.NET Web Site template, 1153, 1224
assemblies, 431–459. *See also* shared assemblies
  application domains and, 441–444

attributes, 436–438
binding to, 453–454
creating, 435–441
defined, 431–432
delayed signing of, 449–450
demanding permissions programmatically, 564–565
dynamic, creating/loading, 438–441
features of, 432, 458–459
ildasm tool and, 14, 297, 434, 435, 448, 449
manifests, 14, 433
metadata and, 14, 15
modules *v.*, 435–436
namespaces *v.*, 46, 434
overview, 14–15
private, 14–15, 434, 447, 448, 452, 453, 454, 459
references to, 450–451
satellite, 434, 579, 581, 588, 590, 594, 597, 598, 603
shared. *See* shared assemblies
structure of, 432–433
versions
    binding to, 456–457
    programmatically getting, 455–456
    version numbers, 455
viewing, 434–435
assembly: prefix, 437
Assembly class, 344–345
AssemblyA/Program.cs, 442
AssemblyCompany, 437
AssemblyCopyright, 437
AssemblyCulture, 437
AssemblyDefaultAlias, 437
AssemblyDescription, 437
AssemblyFileVersion, 437
Assembly.GetTypes(), 344
AssemblyInfo.cs, 384, 436, 455, 581
AssemblyInformationalVersion, 437
AssemblyProduct, 437
AssemblyTitle, 437
AssemblyTrademark, 437
AssemblyVersion, 437
assignment operators, 152, 157
asymmetric key algorithms, 554
asymmetric keys, 552–554
async pattern. *See* asynchronous component pattern; asynchronous event pattern
AsyncCodeActivity, 1311, 1312, 1314
AsyncCodeActivity‹TResult›, 1311, 1312
AsyncComponent/AsyncComponent.cs, 540
AsyncComponent/Program.cs, 543
AsyncDelegate/Program.cs, 492, 493, 494, 522
asynchronous callbacks, 494–495, 534
asynchronous component pattern, 539–543, 1106
asynchronous delegates, 492–495, 496, 522
asynchronous event pattern, 534–543, 1106, 1109, 1293

asynchronous page requests (WebRequest class), 642–643
asynchronous programming. *See also* WebRequest/WebResponse classes
Message Queuing *v.*, 1357–1358
WebRequest and, 535
WebResponse and, 535
asynchronous web method calls, 1240–1241
AsyncPattern (OperationContract property), 1293
AsyncPostBackTrigger, 1223
@ symbol
    identifiers and, 59
    string literals and, 37, 220
    verbatim strings and, 219
ATL (Active Template Library), 90, 379, 418, 702, 721
ATL library, 90
ATL Project Wizard, 702, 718
Atom format, 886, 1387, 1388, 1390, 1394
Atom10FeedFormatter, 1388
Atom10ItemFormatter, 1388
atomicity, 607
atomicity, consistency, isolation, durability. See ACID
AtomPub, 885, 886, 889, 891, 892, 893, 894, 895, 901, 902, 1282
Attach(), 873
attached properties, 739–741
AttachedPropertyDemo/MainWindow.xaml, 740, 741
AttachedPropertyDemo/MyAttachedProperty Provider.cs, 740
attaching/detaching entities, 882
AttachTo(), 873
attribute parameters, 336–337
AttributedModelServices, 751, 767
attributes. *See also* custom attributes; *specific attributes*
    assembly, 436–438
    COP interop, 716–717
    IDL and, 13
    .NET Framework and, 13
    properties as (XAML), 730–731
AttributeTargets enumeration, 335
AttributeUsage attribute, 335–336
authentication/authorization, 545–552
    client application services and, 548–552
    Forms Authentication, 548, 551, 1201, 1202
    identity/principal and, 545–547
    Microsoft Live ID Authentication, 1201
    role-based security, 547–548, 568
        code access security *v.*, 11
        declarative, 547–548
    WebRequest class and, 642
    Windows Authentication, 820, 1201
AuthenticationServices/app.config, 552
authenticode signature, 416, 445
Author (project property), 414
authorization, 545. *See also* authentication/ authorization

Authors table, 863
AutoComplete attribute, 610, 1294
AutoDisposeParameters, 1298
auto-implemented properties, 74
AutoLog, 675
automatic fallback, for resources, 590
automatic transactions, 610, 611, 636, 1279
AutomaticSessionShutdown, 1294
AutoReverse, 1022
Autos window, 399
AVERAGE, 964, 965
Average(), 276, 286

B

Background property, 1003
background threads, 497–498
BackgroundWorker, 535–539
BackgroundWorkersSample/Window1.xaml.cs, 536,
    537, 538
backslash, escape sequences and, 35, 221
backspace (escape sequence), 35
backward compatibility, pointers and, 317
BAML (Binary Application Markup Language), 595,
    597, 728, 744, 1096
   LocBaml tool, 597–598
   Viewer, 1321
Baml2006Reader, 744, 984
bank account example, 101–104
BankAccounts.cs, 102
Bar(), 127, 128
Barrier class, 529–530
BarrierSample/Program.cs, 529
base class library (ASP.NET AJAX Library layer), 1223
base classes (.NET base classes). *See also specific base*
       classes
   casting base classes to derived classes, 177–178
   comprehensiveness of, 16
base keyword, 96
base.‹MethodName›() syntax, 93
BaseType (System.Type), 341
BaseValidator, 1163
BasicHttpBinding, 1300
BasicWebClient.sln, 638
batching (data service context), 901–902
beatlesClone, 136
BeginEdit(), 837, 838, 839
BeginExecute(), 1109
BeginGetResponse(), 642, 643
BeginInvoke(), 493
Beginning Regular Expressions (Wiley), 218
BeginTime, 1022
BehaviorEditorPart, 1212
Berkeley sockets interface, 637
Bézier curves, 989

BezierSegment, 989
BigClassPart1.cs, 81, 82
BigClassPart2.cs, 81, 82
BigEndianUnicode, 795
Binary Application Markup Language. *See* BAML
binary code reuse, generics and, 109
binary operators, 156, 167, 172, 319
BinaryFileReader (sample application), 791–793
BinaryFileReader.sln, 792, 793
BinaryReader, 788, 794
BinaryWriter, 788
binding. *See also* data binding
   to assemblies, 453–454
   to assembly versions, 456
   early, 21, 698
   late, 433, 698, 715
   method binding, 698
   WCF and, 1300–1302
Binding elements, 994, 1044, 1048, 1050, 1300
binding validation (WPF), 1057–1061
bit arrays, 258–260
bit vectors, 260–262
BitArraySample/Program.cs, 258, 260
BitVector32, 260–262
bitwise AND (&), 152, 157, 172, 319, 336
bitwise binary, 172
bitwise OR (|), 152, 157, 172, 319, 336
bitwise unary, 172
bitwise XOR, 157
blittable data types, 701
Block (base class), 1080
Block elements, 1080–1081
block scope, 308
BlockingCollection‹T›, 263
blocks, curly braces and, 25, 38
Bob/Alice/Eve (encryption example), 553
Book class, 868, 1010, 1040, 1042, 1043, 1054
book model (3-D with WPF), 1030–1033
bookmarks, workflows and, 1324–1325
BookOfTheDay (Windows Forms localization),
    584–590
BookOfTheDay/BookOfTheDayForm.cs, 589, 590
BookOfTheDay/BookOfTheDayForm.resx, 587
BookOfTheDay/Demo.BookOfTheDayForm.
    Designer.cs, 586
BookOfTheDay/Program.cs, 589
Books table, 861, 863, 866, 867
BooksAuthors table, 863
BooksDemo application (WPF), 1036–1037
   adding list items dynamically, 1053
   binding to XML, 1055–1057
   command bindings, 1063
   commanding, 1061–1063
       defining command sources, 1062
       defining commands, 1062

data template selector, 1053–1055
value conversion, 1051–1052
BooksDemo/BooksModel.Designer.cs, 870, 872
BooksDemo/BooksModel.edmx, 864, 865, 866
BooksDemo/Program.cs, 867, 868, 871
BooksModel.edmx, 864, 865, 866, 867
books.xml, 905–906
  booksxpath.xml and, 919
  code for reading in, 906–907
  iterating through attributes of, 909–910
  XSD schema and, 910–911
  XslSample01.sln and, 922, 923
booksxpath.xml, 919
books.xsd, 910, 911
BookUtils, 923, 924
bool (value type), 35
Boolean AND, 157
Boolean OR, 157
Border class, 998
boxing, 108, 111, 161, 178–179
break statements, 39, 43–44
breakpoints, 398–399
browser compatibility (ASP.NET AJAX Library layer),
  1223
browser integration (Silverlight), 1110–1113
  calling out to JavaScript, 1111
  JavaScript calling Silverlight, 1112–1113
Browser.sln, 644, 647–649
brushes (WPF), 991–994
BrushesDemo/MainWindow.xaml, 991
BSTR, 698, 701, 706
BubbleDemo/MainWindow.xaml, 736, 737
BubbleSorter, 190–193
BubbleSorter/BubbleSorter.cs, 192
BubbleSorter/Employee.cs, 192
BubbleSorter/Program.cs, 193
bubble-sorting algorithm, 191
bubbling events, 201, 736–739
buffer, 789
buffered streams, 788–789
BufferedStream, 788, 789
Build - Publish menu, 411
Build Deploy Project menu, 963
building. *See also* compilation
  compiling *v.*, 394–395
  making *v.*, 394
  strings, 207, 209–212
  WF applications (in Visual Studio 2010), 405–406
Building table, 841
built-in aggregates, 964–965
built-in controls (Windows Forms), 1125–1140
BulletDecorator, 998, 999
BulletedList, 1161
business applications (WPF), 1035–1073. *See also*
  BooksDemo application; Formula-1 sample database

commanding, 1061–1063
data binding, 1035–1051
DataGrid control, 1067–1073
TreeView control, 1063–1067
validation, 1057–1061
value conversion, 1051–1057
Button class
  Windows Forms, 984
  WPF, 984, 995
Button control, 1160
Button element, 728, 729, 730, 731
  styles and, 1003–1004
ButtonBase, 995
ButtonChrome, 998
buttons, 1125–1126. *See also* command link controls
byte, 33
byte code
  Java, 4
  markers, 794

C

‹c›, 53
C#, Visual Basic, C++/CLI, and F# (online Chapter 53),
  7, 726
C (currency format), 52, 213
C# (programming language)
  ASP.NET applications with, 17–19
  case sensitivity, 61, 73
  compilation process in, 4
  core/fundamentals, 23–64
  dynamic capabilities of, 295
  flow control, 37–44
  guidelines, 58–64
  .NET base classes and, 16
  .NET enterprise architecture and, 20–21
  .NET Framework *v.*, 3–4
  object-oriented programming and, 3
  significance of, 3
  strong data typing and, 157
  syntax, 25–26
C++ (programming language). *See also* Visual C++ 2010
  ATL library, 90
  Chapter 53 (*C#, Visual Basic, C++/CLI, and F#*) and,
    7, 726
  exception handling, 13
  exceptions and, 351
  header files, 47
  interoperability and, 7
  managed, 6, 8
  memory leaks, 10
  multiple inheritance, 90
  preprocessor directives and, 55
  pure virtual function, 93
  templates, 107

C++ (programming language) *(continued)*
  unmanaged, 6, 11
  using namespace statement, 25
Cab Projects, 412
CAB size (project property), 416
CalcHash(), 969, 970
CalcTax(), 302
Calculator property, 751, 764
CalculatorContract, 754
CalculatorContract/ICalculatorExtension.cs, 754
CalculatorExtension, 742
CalculatorUtils/ExportAttribute.cs, 762
CalculatorUtils/ISpeedCapabilities.cs, 762
Calendar control, 995, 1161, 1172–1174
callbacks, asynchronous, 494–495, 534
calling base versions of functions, 93
calling constructors from other constructors, 77–78
CallingConvention, 724
CallSite, 299, 300
CallSiteBinder, 299, 300
camel casing, 61
cameras (3-D with WPF), 1030, 1032
Cancel(), 290
CancelEdit(), 837, 839
cancellation framework, 290–291, 507–510
CancellationSamples/Program.cs, 508, 510
CancellationToken, 290, 291, 507, 508, 509
CanGoBackChanged(), 650
CanGoForwardChanged(), 650
CanHandlePowerEvent, 675
CanHandleSessionChangeEvent, 675
CanPauseAndContinue, 675, 685
CanShutdown, 685
CanStop, 685
Canvas panel, 1000–1001, 1005
captures (regular expressions), 223–224
CarDealer, 200, 201, 202, 203, 204
CardSpace, Windows, 404
carriage return (escape sequence), 35
cascading style sheets. *See* CSS
case sensitivity
  C#, 61, 73
  format strings and, 52
  identifiers and, 58
  IL, 9
  Visual Basic.NET and, 61, 62
casing schemes, 60–61
cast operator [( )], 152, 172
casting, 172
  base classes to derived classes, 177–178
  boxing and, 108, 111, 161, 178–179
  classes to other classes, 176–178
  Currency to float, 173–174
  Currency to ulong, 180
  danger of, 159
  explicit, 159–161, 172–173

  float to Currency, 175–176
  float to long, 179
  float to uint, 175
  generics and, 113
  implicit, 158–159
  multiple, 179–182
  nullable types, 159, 160–161
  pointers to integer types, 320–321
  pointers to other pointers, 321
  QueryInterface() and, 698
  type safety and, 157
  types, 158–161
  uint to float, 174
  unboxing and, 108, 111, 161, 178–179
  user-defined, 172–182
Cast‹TResult›, 276
catalogs (MEF), 748, 749, 767–769
CatalogZone, 1211
catch blocks, 353–354, 355–359
catching
  exceptions, 353–359
  user-defined exceptions, 363–364
Categories table, 843, 857, 858
Category class, 886, 887, 894
CategoryCount, 479
CategoryResourceFile, 479
CCOMDemo, 705
CCW (COM callable wrapper), 713, 716, 718, 719, 726
Certificate Manager, 568
certificates, 567–568
Certificates MMC snap-in, 568
change information, 881–882
ChangePassword, 1204
ChangeRejectedException, 751
ChannelFactory, 1297, 1304, 1305, 1307, 1383
Chaos (isolation level), 625
char (data type), 35
character escape sequences, 35, 221, 318
CharSet, 724
Chart control, 1163
check boxes (dialog box), 424
CheckBox control, 1126, 1160
CheckBoxList, 1160
CheckBoxRadioButton, 995
CheckedListBox, 1127–1128
checked/unchecked operators, 152, 154–155
Circle(), 145
clashes, variable scope, 29–31
class hierarchy
  exceptions, 352, 353
  Windows Forms, 1122
  WPF, 985–986
class ID. *See* CLSID
Class Library (project type), 379, 380, 387
class members, 66

data members, 66–67. *See also* constants; events; fields
function members, 67. *See also* constructors; finalizers; indexers; methods; operators; properties
pointers to, 324–325
Class View window, 392–393
classes. *See also* base classes; class hierarchy; derived classes; Object class; structs
  abstract, 93
  casting classes to classes, 176–178
  event logging, 477–478
  exception, 352–353
    user-defined, 362–369
  generic, 110–118
  hierarchies and, 113
  instances, objects and, 185
  language interoperability and, 7
  members. *See* class members
  naming conventions, 60–63
  new keyword and, 66
  operator overloading and, 166
  partial, 82–83
  performance monitoring, 483
  pointers to, 324
  sealed, 94
  static, 84
  structs *v.*, 65–66, 81–82, 90
  for Windows Services, 670
  in WPF, 983, 984, 985–986
ClassInterface attribute, 717
Clear(), 478
Click event, 200, 206, 736, 737
ClickOnce technology, 408, 419–422
  application cache, 421
  application security, 421–422
  certificates and, 567
  limitations, 420
  manifest files, 419, 420
    properties/settings, 420–421
  publishing applications, 420
  Windows Installer *v.*, 420
client applications, WCF and, 1304–1305
client console application (Socket class), 663–664
Client Software Logo document (Windows 7), 1398
ClientApp/app.config, 897
Client/App.config, 457, 458
ClientApp/MainWindow.xaml.cs, 896, 897, 899, 900, 901
ClientAuthenticationMembershipProvider, 551, 552
Client/Program.cs, 449, 455
ClientRoleProvider, 551
client-server architecture, 1340
ClientWinForms, 409
  installers for, 413–417
  xcopy deployment and, 410
ClientWinFormsSetup, 413, 416

ClientWPF, 409
Clone(), 135, 136
Close(), 82, 315, 810, 823. *See also* Dispose()
closing database connections, 822–824, 860
Cloud property, static members of, 1347–1348
Cloud Services, 381
clouds
  defined, 1342
  link local, 1344
  PNRP, 1344–1345
  site local, 1345
  states, 1345
  WCF endpoints and, 1348, 1349, 1352
  well-connected, 1342
CLR (Common Language Runtime, .NET runtime)
  application domains and, 956
  classes, encryption and, 969, 980
  code access permissions and, 562–563
  deploying, 409
  DLR and, 295
  garbage collection and, 312
  inlining and, 74
  managed code and, 4, 6, 8, 10, 15, 16
  .NET Framework and, 4
  objects, binding to, 1040–1041
  orphaned objects and, 32
  SQL Server and, 955–980
    as CLR host, 956–957
  stored procedures, 967–969
  triggers and, 970–972
  user-defined functions, 969–970
  versions
    filenames and, 409
    installing/using multiple versions, 458
CLR objects, hosting with, 886–890
CLS (Common Language Specification), 9–10
CLSID (class ID), 699, 715, 716, 718
cng (Cryptography Next Generation), 553
coalescing operator. *See* null coalescing operator
‹code›, 53
code access permissions, CLR and, 562–563
code access security, 11, 561–567
  custom attributes and, 334
  permissions and, 562–567
  pointers and, 318
  role-based security *v.*, 11
  security transparency level 2, 561, 562
  in System.Net.PeertoPeer, 1349
code bloat, generics and, 109–110
code contracts, 461–466
  for interfaces, 465–466
  invariants, 465
  postconditions, 464
  preconditions, 463–464
code model, ASP.NET, 1154–1155
code snippets. *See specific code snippets*

CodeAccessPermission, 567, 1349
CodeAccessSecurityAttribute, 1349
CodeActivity, 1311, 1316
CodeActivity‹TResult›, 1311, 1312
‹codeBase›, 453–454
code-behind feature (ASP.NET), 18
CodeContractsSamples/IPerson.cs, 465
CodeContractsSamples/PersonContract.cs, 466
CodeContractsSamples/Program.cs, 463, 464, 465
CodeDriver, 438, 439, 443, 444
CodeDriverInAppDomain, 443, 444
CodeIntro/Program.cs, 729
CodePlex web site, 295
coerce value callback, 734–735
CoerceValue(), 734
cold calling, 362
ColdCallFileFormatException, 363, 364, 365, 366, 368
ColdCallFileReader, 363, 364, 365, 366
collection initializers, 228–229
collection interfaces/types, 225–226
CollectionChangedEventManager, 204
collections, 225–266
  concurrent, 262–264
  foreach loop and, 43
  generic collection classes. *See* generic collection classes
  observable, 256–258, 898–899
  performance and, 264–266
  read-only, 236
  type conversions and, 235–236
  XAML and, 731–732
Color.DateTime, 77
ColumnDefinition, 1001
COM
  apartment models. *See* MTAs; STAs
  data types and, 698
  errors and, 700
  event-handling architecture, 701
  exception handling, 13
  IDL, 13
  interfaces and, 697–698. *See also* interfaces
  metadata and, 696
  method binding and, 698
  .NET Framework *v.*, 6, 695–701
  reference counts, 10, 696
  registration, 698–699, 718
  type library and, 696
  WebBrowser control and, 643
COM+
  hosting model, transactions (System.EnterpriseServices) and, 611
  .NET Framework and, 6
COM callable wrapper (CCW), 713, 716, 718, 719, 726
COM client application, 713, 718–719, 721
COM components
  connection points added to, 710–712

creating, 702–707
RCW and, 707–709
COM interop, 6, 16, 22, 695–726
  ACLs and, 802
  attributes, 716–717
COM objects, releasing, 708–709
COM servers, 714
  with dynamic language extensions, 709
  IDispatch interface and, 698, 709
CombinedGeometry, 988
ComboBox, 998, 1127–1128
COMClient/COMClient.cpp, 719, 721
COMClient/stdafx.cpp, 721
COMClient/stdafx.h, 721
COMDemo.cpp, 706, 712
command bindings, 1063, 1073
command link controls, 1407–1408
command prompt (Visual Studio 2010), 24
commanding (WPF), 1061–1063
  defining command sources, 1062
  defining commands, 1062
commands (ADO.NET), 825–829. *See also* stored procedures
  executing, 826–829
  stored procedures as, 825
CommandType enumeration, 826
comments, 53–55
  internal, 53
  multiline, 25, 53
  single-line, 25, 53
  XML, 53–55
Commit(), 627, 679, 680
committable transactions, 612–614
CommittableTransaction, 611, 613, 617, 625
committing phase (transactions), 606
Common Language Runtime. *See* CLR
Common Language Specification. *See* CLS
Common Type System. *See* CTS
CommonAppDataPath, 1118
CommonObjectSecurity, 559
communication, P2P and, 1341, 1342
Compact Framework, 407, 408
Compare(), 137, 138, 208, 226
CompareOrdinal(), 208
CompareValidator, 1164
comparing objects for equality. *See also* Equals()
  reference types, 162–163
  value types, 163
comparison operators, 151, 152, 163
  overloading, 164, 170–171
  overriding, 163
compilation
  building *v.*, 394–395
  conditional, 56–57, 396
  JIT, 4

options (for C# files), 50–51
process, 4, 21–22
CompileAndRun(), 438, 440, 443
Compile_Click(), 440, 444
Complete(), 616, 618, 619
CompletionMethod, 539, 540, 541
ComplexObject, 870, 871
Component Services MMC snap-in, 616
ComponentInstaller class, 680, 682
ComposablePart, 748, 765, 767
composite activities, 1319–1322
CompositionContainer class, 751, 764, 765, 767, 768
compound from clause, 278, 283
compound from query, 288
compression (project property), 416
ComputeHash(), 969
Computer Management MMC snap-in, 1362
COMServer/COMDemo.cpp, 707, 712
COMServer/COMDemo.h, 706, 712
COMServer/COMServer.idl, 703, 711
COMServer.idl, 696
ComVisible attribute, 716
Concat(), 208
conceptual layer, 862, 864–865
Conceptual Schema Definition Language. *See* CSDL
ConcurrencyMode, 1295
concurrent collections, 262–264
    cancellation framework and, 507
    multiple threads and, 264
ConcurrentBag‹T›, 263
ConcurrentDictionary‹TKey, TValue›, 263
ConcurrentQueue‹T›, 262–263
ConcurrentSample/Program.cs, 263–264
ConcurrentStack‹T›, 263
ConcurrentXXX, 263
Condition (project property), 418
Conditional attribute, #if and, 57
conditional compilation, 56–57, 396
conditional (ternary) operator (?:), 152, 154, 157, 223, 224
conditional statements, 37–40. *See also* if statements; switch statements
config.MaxResultsPerCollection, 895
confirm installation (dialog box), 424
connection, P2P and, 1341, 1342
connection point objects (CPOs), 701
connection points
    COM component and, 710–712
    .NET component and, 720
Connection String Example.txt, 821
connection strings
    ADO.NET, 821–822
    EDM and, 867
ConnectionsZone, 1212
consistency (ACID), 607. *See also* ACID

Console Application (project type), 379, 381, 397, 405, 662, 1310
ConsoleApplication1.sln, 943, 944, 945, 946, 947, 949, 950, 952, 953
Console.ReadLine(), 51
Console.Write(), 51
Console.WriteLine(), 51
const keyword, 31, 66, 78
constants, 31, 66–67
    advantages of, 31
    readonly fields *v.*, 78
Constraint class, 818
constraints
    data, 842–844
    delete, 843–844
    generic classes with, 114–116
    generic methods with, 125–126
    naming conventions, 859
    update, 843–844
constructor initializer, 77–78
constructors, 67, 74–78
    calling constructors from other constructors, 77–78
    of derived classes, 94–98
    finalizers *v.*, 67
    in hierarchy, 96–97
    with parameters, in hierarchy, 97–98
    static, 75–77
    StreamReader and, 794–795
    for structs, 82
    XAML and, 732
    zero-parameter, 76, 82
Consumer class, 200, 202, 203, 205
contacts, peers and, 1353
containers (MEF), 748, 749, 765–767
    export providers and, 765–767
    in MEF architecture, 748, 749
Contains(), 240
Contains (quantifier operator), 276
content controls (WPF), 995–996
Content directory, 1261
ContentControl class, 986, 995, 996
ContentPlaceHolder controls, 1196
ContextMenu class, 998
ContextMenuStrip control, 1141
continuation tasks, 502–503
Continue(), 690
continue statement, 44
Contract class, 462
contracts. *See also specific contracts*
    MEF and, 749, 754–755
    WCF and, 1291–1294
contra-variance, 118–123
Control class
    FrameworkElement, 986
    System.Windows.Forms, 1122–1125

control templates, 1012–1014
  for ListBox elements, 1018–1020
controllers (MVC framework), 1260. *See also* MVC
Controllers directory, 1261
controlling threads, 499
controls
  Web Parts, 1211–1212
  Windows Forms, 1122–1125
      appearance properties, 1123
      built-in, 1125–1140
      custom, 1147
      miscellaneous functionality, 1125
      size/location properties, 1123
      user controls, 1147
      user interaction and, 1124
      Windows functionality, 1125
  WPF, 994–999. *See also* templates
      content, 995–996
      decoration, 998–999
      headered content, 996–997
      headered item, 998
      item, 998
      simple, 994–995
controls layer (ASP.NET AJAX Library), 1223
ControlTemplate, 1012
conventions. *See* guidelines; naming conventions; usage
      conventions
conversion operators (query operator category), 276,
      287–288
Conversion Wizard (Visual Studio 2010), 376
conversions. *See* casting
ConvertAll‹TOutput›(), 25, 236
converting ADO.NET data to XML, 927–932
converting XML to ADO.NET data, 932–934
coordinate system (3-D with WPF), 1029–1030
Copy(), 780
Copy Web Tool, 408, 411
copying/moving/deleting files, 780–783
CopyTo(), 208, 226, 774, 780, 798
core services (ASP.NET AJAX Library layer), 1223
correlation, 472–475
COUNT, 964, 965
Count (), 276, 280, 286
Count Length, 258
Count property, 237, 240
Course Order (sample application), 1370–1384
  acknowledgment queues and, 1376–1377
  class library, 1370–1371
  entity classes with data contract, 1379–1380
  message receiver, 1373–1376
  message sender, 1371–1373
  sending priority/recoverable messages, 1372–1373
  WCF and, 1378–1384
      message receiver application, 1380–1383
      message sender application, 1383–1384
      service contract, 1380

CourseAttendees, 607
CourseDates, 607
CourseManagement structure, 607
CourseOrder, 1370. *See also* Course Order
CourseOrderReceiver, 1379
CourseOrderSender, 1379
CourseOrderService, 1379
Courses table, 607
covariance, 118–120
  array covariance, 139
CPOs (connection point objects), 701
Create(), 146, 290, 1262
  FileInfo/DirectoryInfo classes and, 774
  MagicShop.mdf and, 1269–1273
$create(), 1234
CREATE AGGREGATE, 966
CREATE ASSEMBLY, 956, 963
CREATE FUNCTION, 970
CREATE PRIMARY XML INDEX, 978
CREATE PROCEDURE, 968
CREATE TABLE, 972
CREATE TRIGGER, 857, 970, 972
CREATE XML SCHEMA COLLECTION,
      979, 980
CreateEventSource(), 478
CreateFileTransacted(), 565, 632, 633, 634
CreateFromConfiguration(), 300, 301, 302
CreateFromFile(), 800
CreateHardLink(), 723, 724
CreateHardLinkTransacted(), 632
CreateInstance(), 134, 135
CreateKeys(), 555, 556
CreateMask(), 260, 261
CreateQuery(), 873, 877
CreateQuery‹T›(), 294
CreateResource/Program.cs, 580
CreateSection(), 260, 261
CreateService(), 693
CreateSubKey(), 810
CreateSymbolicLinkTransacted(), 632
CreateText(), 774
CreateUserWizard, 1204
CreateXps/DocumentPage.xaml.cs, 1087, 1090, 1091
CreateXps/MenuPlannerPage.xaml.cs, 1086
CreationTime, 773
Cross(), 145
CRUD operations, 954. *See also* LINQ to XML
cryptography. *See* encryption
Cryptography Next Generation (cng), 553
CryptoKeySecurity, 559
CryptoStream, 557, 558
Crystal Reports Application, 381
csc command, 24
CSDL (Conceptual Schema Definition Language), 861,
      864, 865, 866, 867, 868, 884
CSharpCodeProvider, 438, 439, 440

CSS (cascading style sheets), 1198
  Ajax and, 1219, 1220
  ASP.NET and, 1149
  Content directory and, 1261
  control styling, 1159
  dynamic data web sites and, 1254, 1255
  Properties window, 1157, 1159
  tables *v.*, 1198
  themes and, 1206, 1207
  Visual Studio 2010 and, 375
CTS (Common Type System), 9
CTS types, 33–35
  bool type and, 35
  decimal type and, 34
  floating-point types and, 34
  integer types and, 33
  reference types (predefined) and, 35–37
CultureAndRegionInfoBuilder, 601–603
CultureDemo/MainWindow.xaml.cs, 574, 576
CultureInvariant, 220
cultures
  in action, 574–577
  custom, 601–603
  date formatting and, *573–574*
  invariant, 571
  neutral, 571
  number formatting and, 572–573
  regions and, 570–574
  sorting orders and, 578–579
  specific, 571
  strong names and, 445
curly braces { }
  blocks and, 25, 38
  if statement and, 38, 39
  markup extensions and, 741, 742
Currency (struct)
  Currency to float, 173–174
  Currency to ulong, 180
  float to Currency, 175–176
currency format (C), 52, 213
CurrencyStruct, 327, 328, 329
Current property (Transaction class), 611
CurrentAccounts.cs, 104–105
CurrentChangedEventManager, 204
CurrentChangingEventManager, 204
CurrentCulture, 571–572, 588
CurrentFile, 1398, 1399
CurrentUICulture, 571–572, 588
Custom Actions editor, 424–426
custom activities, 1316–1322
custom attributes, 334–340
  assembly, 436–438
  code access security and, 334
  defined, 333
  parameters and, 336–337
  preprocessor directives and, 55

WhatsNewAttributes (example), 337–340, 345–349
  writing, 334–337
custom composite activities, 1319–1322
custom controls (ASP.NET), 1155, 1192–1195
custom controls (Windows Forms), 1147
custom cultures, 601–603
custom hosting
  with CLR objects, 886–890
  WCF and, 1302–1303
custom installation packages. *See* installation packages
custom interfaces, 697
custom .NET classes, XAML and, 729–730
custom resource managers, 626–632
custom resource messages, 590
custom resource readers, 598–600, 603
custom service hosts (WCF), 1287
CustomBinding, 1301
CustomCultures/app.manifest, 603
CustomCultures/Program.cs, 602
customer information (dialog box), 424
Customers table (Northwind database), 832–833,
    874, 875
customizing dynamic data web sites, 1255–1259
CustomResource/Program.cs, 631
CustomResource/ResourceManager.cs, 630
CustomResource/Transactional.cs, 627
CustomValidator, 1164

D

D (decimal format), 52, 213
DACL (discretionary access control list), 559
daemon processes, 17
data access (ADO.NET), 817–860. *See also* ADO.NET
  classes/interfaces for, 818–820
  data reader and, 832–834
data adapters
  ambient transactions and, 635
  DataSet class and, 850–854
  stored procedures in, 851
data annotations, 1256
data binding
  ASP.NET and, 1169–1180
  VisualBrush and, 994
  WPF, 1035–1051
    to CLR objects, 1040–1045
    command binding, 1063, 1073
    to lists, 1045–1047
    master detail, 1048
    multibinding, 1048–1049
    priority, 1049–1051
    validation, 1057–1061
    to XAML, 1037–1039
    to XML, 1055–1057
data columns, 836–837
data constraints, 842–844

data contracts, 1291
data display controls, 1162, 1175–1178
  with templates, 1176–1178
Data Encryption Standard (DES), 554
data members, 66–67. *See also* constants; events; fields
Data property
  BitVector member, 260
  System.Exception, 359
data providers. *See also* export providers
  LINQ, 293–294
  LINQ to SQL, 818
  namespaces and, 818
  ODBC, 818
  OLE DB, 818, 832, 834, 850
  in same assembly, 832
  SQL Server, 818, 832, 834, 860
  TableDirect and, 826
data query parameters, route parameters and, 1250
data reader, 832–834
data rows, 837–839
data service context, 886, 896–897, 902
  adding/modifying/deleting entities, 900–901
  DataServiceContext, 895, 896, 1109
  object tracking and, 900
  operation batching and, 901–902
Data Services. *See* WCF Data Services
data source controls, 1162
data tables, 835–836
  objects in, 835
  schemas, 835
      generation, 839–840
data template selector, 1053–1055
data templates, 1014–1016
data tokens, route order and, 1248–1249
data triggers, 1010–1011
data types, 31–33. *See also* reference types; value types
  blittable, 701
  COM and, 698
  data columns and, 836
  IL and, 8
  nonblittable, 701
  reference types/value types comparison, 8, 32–33
  SQL Server, 818
  XAML and, 731
data web server controls, 1162–1163
  data display controls, 1162, 1175–1178
  data source controls, 1162
DataAdapter2.cs, 853
DataAdapter.cs, 851
Database (project type), 980
database columns naming conventions, 859
database connection strings
  format of, 821
  managing, 821–822
database connections, 820–821, 822–824
  closing, 822–824, 860

efficient usage of
  try...catch...finally blocks, 822–823
  using clause, 823–824, 860
database development (ADO.NET)
  key generation with SQL Server, 857–858
  naming conventions and, 859–860
  tiered development, 856–857
DatabaseResourceManager, 600–601
DatabaseResourceReader, 598–600
DatabaseResourceReaderClient/Program.cs, 601
*DatabaseResourceReader/DatabaseResourceManager
  .cs*, 600
*DatabaseResourceReader/DatabaseResourceReader
  .cs*, 598
DatabaseResourceReader/DatabaseResourceSet.cs, 600
DatabaseResourceSet, 600
database-specific classes (ADO.NET), 819
DataBind(), 1176, 1191
data-bound controls, 1171, 1178, 1180
DataChangedEventManager, 204
DataColumn, 818, 836, 837, 860
  properties, 837
DataColumnMapping, 819
DataGrid control, 998, 1067–1073
  custom columns, 1069–1070
  grouping with, 1070–1073
  row details, 1070
DataGridView control, 1128–1135
  arrays and, 1130–1131
  data sources and, 1130
  DataTable and, 1131
  DataView and, 1131–1133
  generic collections and, 1134–1135
  IList and, 1134
  IListSource and, 1134
  tabular data and, 1128–1130
DataLib/Formula1.cs, 269–270
DataLib/Racer.cs, 268–269
DataLib/Student.cs, 608
DataLib/StudentData.cs, 608, 613
DataLib/Team.cs, 269
DataList, 1163, 1175
DataPager, 1163
DataReaderExample.cs, 832–833
DataReaderSql.cs, 834
DataRelation, 818
DataRelationships.cs, 841
DataRow, 818, 860
  version values, 837
DataRowState enumeration, 838, 860
DataServiceBehavior, 889
DataServiceConfiguration, 889
DataServiceContext, 895, 896, 1109. *See also* data
  service context
DataServiceHost, 889, 890, 1304
DataServiceHostFactory, 889, 895

DataServiceKey, 886, 887, 893
DataServiceQuery‹TElement›, 895
DataServicesHost/Category.cs, 887
DataServicesHost/MenuCard.cs, 888
DataServicesHost/MenuCardDataModel.cs, 889
DataServicesHost/Menu.cs, 887
DataServicesHost/MenuDataService.cs, 889, 890
DataServicesHost/Program.cs, 890
DataService‹T›, 886, 888, 889, 895, 1107
DataSet class, 818, 835, 860
  data relationships, 840–842
  EnforceConstraints property, 844, 856
  persisting DataSet changes, 852–855
  populating
      with data adapter, 850–851
      from XML, 851
  purpose of, 835
  updating with data adapters, 852–854
  writing XML output, 854–855
DataTable, 818, 860
  DataGridView control and, 1131
  deleting rows, 854
  foreign key constraints, 842–843
  inserting rows, 852–853
  primary key restraints, 842
  updating rows, 854
DataTableMapping, 819
DataTemplate, 1012
DataView, DataGridView control and, 1131–1133
date formatting, cultures and, 573–574
DatePicker control, 995
Dateservice.cs, 410
DateTime constructors, 79
DateTimeFormatInfo, 572, 573
DateTimePicker, 1135
DbCommand, 822, 866
DbConnection, 819, 822, 866, 872
DbDataReader, 822, 866
DbParameter, 866
DbProviderFactories class, 822
DCOM protocol, 1279, 1280, 1360
dead-letter queues, 1363
deadlocks, 513–514, 543, 1306
DEBUG preprocessor symbol, 397
debugging
  stepping between languages, 7, 8
  Visual Studio 2010, 375, 398–401
      breakpoints, 398–399
      debugger symbols, 396
      design-time debugging, 374, 388
      exceptions, 400–401
      release builds, 395–396
      watches, 375, 399–400
  XSLT, 925–927
DebugWrite, 1316, 1317, 1318, 1319
DecelerationRatio, 1022

decimal, 34
decimal format (D), 52, 213
declarative programming, 19
  WPF and, 19
declarative role-based security, 547–548
DeclarativeCatalogPart, 1211
decoration controls (WPF), 998–999
DecorationsDemo/MainWindow.xaml, 999
Decorator class, 998
decrement operator (--), 151, 153, 154
deep comparison, 170
DeepCopy(), 630
default keyword, 113, 114
DefaultDocument, 418
deferred query execution, 272, 273–275
#define, 55–56
Delay activity, 1314
delayed loading (of relationships), 876
delayed signing (of assemblies), 449–450
delegate concatenation/removal operators, 152
delegate inference, 186
delegate keyword, 701
delegates, 183–197. *See also* events; Lambda
    expressions
  anonymous methods and, 196–197
  asynchronous, 492–495, 496, 522
  BubbleSorter example, 190–193
  declaring, 184–185
  defining, 184–185
  events and, 183, 184, 200
  generic methods with, 126
  instance of, 185, 187
  Lambda expressions and, 183, 197
  multicast, 193–196
  simple example, 188–190
  using, 185–188
DELETE, 819, 826, 830, 850, 852, 860, 971
Delete(), 478, 774, 780
delete constraints, 843–844
DeleteEventSource(), 478
DeleteObject(), 873, 900
DeleteSubKey(), 810
DeleteSubKeyTree(), 810
DeleteValue(), 810
deleting/moving/copying files, 780–783
DelimitedListTraceListener, 470, 471, 472
delivery modes (messages), 1361
demanding permissions programmatically,
    564–565
DemandPermissionDemo/DemandPermissions.cs, 564
DemoLib/AssemblyInfo.cs, 730
DemoLib/Person.cs, 729
DemoSolution, 385, 389
dependency properties, 732–736, 739
  attached properties *v.*, 739
  coerce value callback and, 734–735

dependency properties (*continued*)
  creating, 733–734
  taskbar and, 1412
  value changed callbacks and, 735–736
DependencyObject, 986
DependencyObjectDemo/MyDependencyObject.cs,
  733, 734, 735, 736, 739
dependent transactions, 616–618
DependentClone(), 612, 617, 623
DependentServices, 685
DependentTransaction, 611, 616, 623, 636
deployment (application deployment), 407–427
  ClickOnce technology, 408, 419–422
  of CLR, 409
  Copy Web Tool and, 408, 411
  options, 408, 409–410
  planning for, 407–409
  requirements, 408–409
  xcopy, 408, 410–411, 412, 452
deployment manifest, 419, 420–421
deployment projects, 408, 412
Dequeue(), 236, 237, 238, 265
dereference operator. *See* indirection operator
derived classes
  base classes to derived classes (casting), 177–178
  constructors of, 94–98
derived interfaces, 104–105
DeriveKeyMaterial(), 557
DES (Data Encryption Standard), 554
Descendants(), 293
Description (project property), 414
Deserialize(), 934, 938
design view editor, 374, 388
Design View window, 388–391
design-by-contracts, 461. *See also* code contracts
Designer rehosting, 1332–1337
designers (for activities), 1317–1319
design-time debugging, 374, 388
destruction/instantiation, of forms, 1142–1145
destructors, 313–314
  as finalizers, 313
  IDisposable and, 315–317
Detach(), 873, 882
detaching/attaching entities, 882
Details(), 1262, 1268
DetailsView, 1163, 1175
DetectNewerInstalledVersion, 414
DHTML (Dynamic HTML), 18, 1220, 1221
dialog boxes, for projects, 424
dictionaries (hash tables, maps), 248–254
  GetHashCode() and, 84, 147, 162, 170, 248, 249,
    250, 251, 284
  key type, 248–250
  lookup and, 253–254
  sorted, 254

DictionarySample/Employee.cs, 252
DictionarySample/EmployeeId.cs, 251
DictionarySample/Program.cs, 252
Dictionary‹TKey, TValue›, 248, 250, 252, 266, 287
Dictionary.xaml, 1007
DiffuseMaterial, 1030
digital certificates. *See* certificates
dimension (rank), 132, 134, 136
Dimensions class, 80, 81
directories
  folders *v.*, 772
  reading ACLs from directory, 803–804
Directory class, 772, 773, 780
directory structure (Windows 7), 1406–1407
DirectoryCatalog, 751, 753, 767, 768
DirectoryInfo, 772, 774, 776, 778, 779, 783, 784, 787,
  804, 808
  methods, 774
  properties, 773–774
DirectoryName (FileInfo), 773
DirectorySeparatorChar, 775
DirectoryServicesPermission, 562, 563
dirty reads, 625, 626
disconnected record set, 817, 818, 819
discount application (shopping cart application),
  300–302
discovering peers, 1353
discovery, P2P and, 1341–1342
discretionary access control list (DACL), 559
dispatch interfaces, 697
DispatcherObject, 986
DispatcherTimer, 487, 488, 533, 1400, 1401
DispId attribute, 717
Display(), 118
DisplayAllDocuments(), 115
DisplayAllNodes(), 245
DisplayFile(), 792, 797, 798
DisplayFolderList(), 778, 779, 780, 783
displaying output as HTML page (WebBrowser
  control), 643
DisplayName
  ServiceController class, 685
  ServiceInstaller class, 682
DisplayTabularData application, 1128–1130
DisplayTree(), 292
DisplayTypeInfo(), 347
Dispose(), 82, 100, 101, 141, 314, 315, 316, 317, 357,
  618, 619, 823
Distinct(), 276, 283, 878
Distributed Routing Table (DRT), 1345–1346
Distributed Transaction Coordinator (DTC), 611, 616
distributing code, with certificates, 567–568
Divide(), 146, 147
division operator, 157
division operator (/, %), 151, 152, 153, 157

"DLL Hell," 21, 459
DllImport, 100, 317, 633, 723, 724
  extern modifier, 100
  properties/fields, 724
DLR (Dynamic Language Runtime), 295, 305
  CLR and, 295
  open-source version of, 295
  ScriptRuntime, 300–302
  Silverlight and, 295
Dns class, 655
DNS names. *See* IP addresses
DnsLookup example, 655–656
DNSLookupResolver, 655
DnsPermission, 562
DockPanel, 1001
Document Object Model. *See* DOM
document window (Visual Studio), 376, 398, 402, 405
DocumentManager class, 238
DocumentManager/Document.cs, 115
DocumentManager/DocumentManager.cs, 114, 115
DocumentManager/Program.cs, 116
DocumentManager‹T›, 114, 115, 116
documents (WPF), 1075–1094
  anchor to blocks, 1083–1084
  Block elements, 1080–1081
  fixed documents, 1075, 1086–1089
  flow documents, 1075, 1085
  fonts, 1075–1077
  Inline elements, 1078–1080
  lists, 1081–1082
  printing, 1091–1093
  tables, 1082–1083
  text elements, 1075–1084
  TextEffect, 1077–1078
  XPS documents, 1089–1091
DocumentViewer, 1086, 1091
DoEvents, 1119
DoLongTask(), 540, 541
DOM (Document Object Model), 903, 1219. *See also*
    XmlDataDocument; XmlDocument
  Ajax and, 1219
  Level 1/Level 2, W3C and, 904, 913
  .NET Framework and, 913–917
  XmlNode and, 905, 906, 913, 915, 917, 928, 974
  XmlNodeList and, 905, 913, 914, 915
DomainTest/Program.cs, 442, 443
DotnetClient/Program.cs, 708, 712
DotnetServer/DotnetServer.cs, 714, 717, 720
double, 34
double quotation marks (")
  escape sequence for, 35
  string literals and, 37
DoubleMain.cs, 48–49
do...while loops, 42
DownloadData(), 639, 642
DownloadFile(), 638

downloading files (with WebClient class), 638–639
DrawingBrush, 992–993
drive information, reading, 800–802
DriveInfo class, 772, 800, 801
DriveViewer.sln, 801
DropDownList, 1160
DRT (Distributed Routing Table), 1345–1346
DSA algorithm, 554
DTC (Distributed Transaction Coordinator), 611, 616
dual interfaces, 697–698
duplex communication, 1301, 1306–1308
durability (ACID), 607. *See also* ACID
Duration (Timeline property), 1022
DWORDs, 320
dynamic data (ASP.NET), 1243, 1251–1259, 1274.
    See also ASP.NET MVC; routing
  ASP.NET MVC and, 1243
  controls, 1162, 1163
  templates, 1251, 1257
      directories, 1257
      Dynamic Data Entities Web Site, 380, 1251
      Dynamic Data Linq to SQL Web Site, 380, 1251
dynamic data web sites
  creation, 1251–1255
      adding data source, 1252
      choosing data access model, 1251–1252
      configuring scaffolding, 1252–1253
  CSS and, 1254, 1255
  customizing, 1255–1259
  DynamicValidator and, 1164
  LINQ to SQL and, 1251, 1252, 1256, 1260, 1261,
      1262, 1274
Dynamic HTML (DHTML), 18, 1220, 1221
dynamic keyword
  COM binder and, 709
  Foo property and, 755
  reflection and, 754
dynamic language extensions, 295–305
  COM servers with, 709
  DLR ScriptRuntime and, 300–302
Dynamic Language Runtime. *See* DLR
dynamic programming, 295, 305
dynamic resources (WPF), 1005–1006
dynamic type, 296–300, 305
  behind the scenes, 297–300
  IL and, 297–299
  limitations of, 297
DynamicAssembly/CodeDriver.cs, 438–440, 444
DynamicAssembly/CodeDriverInApp
    Domain.cs, 444
DynamicAssembly/DynamicAssemblyWindow.xaml
    .cs, 440, 444
DynamicClass, 297, 298
DynamicDotnetClient/Program.cs, 709
DynamicHyperLink, 1160
DynamicObject, 302–304

DynamicPartitionerForArray‹TSource›, 290
Dynamic/Program.cs, 296, 303
DynamicResource, 1006, 1007
DynamicValidator, 1164, 1257

E

eager loading (of relationships), 876
early binding, 21, 698
ease functions, 1023, 1025, 1099, 1100
EasingDoubleKeyFrame, 1026
Easy Connect, 1346
ECDiffieHellman, 554, 556, 557, 558
ECDiffieHellmanCng, 554, 557, 558
ECDSA algorithm, 554–555
echo service, 661
EDI (Electronic Data Interchange), 19
Edit(), 1262, 1273–1274
‹EditItemTemplate›, 1177
editor application (WPF example), 1398–1403
  EditorDemo/App.xaml.cs, 1400
  EditorDemo/CurrentFile.cs, 1399
  EditorDemo/MainWindow.xaml.cs, 1401
  tracing and, 1399
editors, Visual Studio 2010, 422–427
EditorZone, 1211
EDM (Entity Data Model), 862, 866, 885, 975, 1102,
  1162, 1262, 1282, 1390
  ASP.NET hosting and, 894–895
  Designer, 864
  Silverlight networking example, 1102
E/e (scientific (exponential) format), 52, 213
Eiffel programming language, 461
Electronic Data Interchange (EDI), 19
element operators (query operator category), 276
ElementAt, 276
ElementAtOrDefault, 276
Elements(), 293
#elif, 56–57
Ellipse class, 987
EllipseGeometry, 988
#else, 56–57
else if statements, 38
else statements, 37, 38. *See also* if statements
ElseIf.cs, 38
e-mail for application-to-application communication,
  1358. *See also* Message Queuing
EmissiveMaterial, 1030
Empty(), 276, 288, 289
‹EmptyDataTemplate›, 1178
‹EmptyItemTemplate›, 1178
EnableVisualStyles, 1119
Encoding.ASCII class, 661
encryption, 552–558, 568
  CLR classes and, 969, 980

signature and, 554–556
System.Security.Cryptography classes, 553, 554, 555,
  556, 969
WCF and, 545
EndEdit(), 837, 838, 839
EndExecute(), 1109
EndGetResponse(), 642
#endif, 56–57
EndInvoke(), 494
EndOfStreamException, 353
#endregion, 57, 387, 1120
EnforceConstraints property, 844, 856
enlist methods (Transaction class), 611
EnlistDurable(), 611, 626
EnlistPromotableSinglePhase(), 611
EnlistVolatile(), 611, 626
Enqueue(), 236, 237, 238, 262, 263, 265
Ensures(), 464, 465
EnsuresOnThrow‹TException›, 464
Enterprise Manager (SQL Server), 858
Enterprise Services (online Chapter 51), 609,
  610–611
  AutoComplete attribute and, 610, 1294
  automatic transactions, 610, 611, 636, 1279
  WCF and, 1303, 1308
entity classes (ADO.NET Entity Framework), 868–871
  attaching/detaching, 882
  classes/interfaces and, 870–871
  LINQ to Entities, 883–884
  relationships, 873–876
  storing changes, 882–883
Entity Client, 866–867
Entity Data Model. *See* EDM
Entity Framework. *See* ADO.NET Entity Framework
Entity SQL, 862, 867–868
EntityCommand, 862, 866
EntityConnection, 862, 866, 871
EntityDataReader, 862, 866, 867
EntityDataSource, 1162
EntityObject, 868, 870, 871, 875, 881
EntityParameter, 866
Entries property, 477
EntryPoint, 724
Enumerable class, 272, 273, 275, 288, 289, 291, 294.
  See also extension methods; query operators
EnumerableSample/Program.cs, 277, 279, 281,
  283, 287
enumerations, 44–45, 140–146. *See also specific
  enumerations*
  foreach statement and, 140, 141
  naming conventions, 60–63
enumerators, yield return and, 145–146
Enum.Parse(), 45
EnvironmentPermission, 562
equality

comparing reference types for equality, 162–163
comparing value types for equality, 163
Equals(), 84–85. *See also* comparison operators
  ReferenceEquals() and, 84, 162, 163
  static, 162
  virtual, 162
#error, 57
Error Reporting. *See* Windows Error Reporting
ErrorProvider component, 1135–1136
errors, 351. *See also* exceptions
  COM and, 700
  StateService sample and, 1298–1299
escape sequences, 35, 218, 221
Eve/Bob/Alice (encryption example), 553
event bubbling. *See* events
event keyword, 701
event listener, 202–203
Event Log service, 668
event logging, 461, 475–483, 692–693
  architecture, 476–477
  classes, 477–478
  message resource files, 479–483
  writing event log entries, 479
event manager classes, 204
event publisher, 200–201
event source, 478–479
event triggers, 1020, 1023–1025
Event Viewer, 461, 475, 476, 477, 479, 482, 483
event-based asynchronous component, 539–543
event-based asynchronous pattern, 534–543, 1106,
  1109, 1293
event-booking example (ASP.NET server control),
  1164–1169
  updating, 1169–1175
EventHandler‹T›, 201, 202
event-handling architecture (COM), 701
EventLog class, 475, 477–479, 482
  members, 477–478
EventLogDemo/EventLogDemoMessages.mc, 481
EventLogDemo/Program.cs, 478, 479, 483
EventLogEntry, 477
EventLogInstaller, 475
EventLogPermission, 562
EventLogTraceListener, 470, 475, 477
EventManager, 738
EventRegistration (Silverlight Navigation Application),
  1097
  creation, 1097
  navigation, 1097–1101
  tables, 1102
EventRegistrationDataService, 1107, 1108
EventRegistration/Home.xaml.cs, 1109, 1110
events, 67, 184, 200–205. *See also* delegates; Lambda
  expressions
  bubbling, 201, 736–739

delegates and, 183, 184, 200
.NET Framework and, 701
synchronization and, 526–529
tunneling, 201, 736–739
weak, 203–205
EventSample/Calculator.cs, 528
EventSample/Program.cs, 526, 527, 529
EventSourceCreationData, 478–479
EventsSample/CarDealer.cs, 200
EventsSample/Consumer.cs, 202
EventsSample/Program.cs, 202
EventTypeFilter, 472
Everything (permission set), 564
‹example›, 53
Except(), 276, 283, 878
‹exception›, 53
exception classes, 352–353
  user-defined, 362–369
exception handling, 351
exceptions, 13, 351–369
  C++ and, 351
  catching, 353–359
  class hierarchy for, 352, 353
  debugging and, 400–401
  exceptional circumstances for, 355, 356, 359
  nested try blocks and, 360–362
  .NET Framework and, 700
  One() and, 195
  performance and, 351
  throwing, 354
  unhandled, 360
  user-defined, throwing, 364–367
ExecutablePath, 1118
Execute(), 1061, 1312
ExecuteCommand(), 690
ExecuteNonQuery(), 826–827, 830, 832
ExecutePermissions, 418
ExecuteReader(), 826, 827, 832, 833
ExecuteReaderExample.cs, 827, 828, 829
ExecuteScalar(), 826, 828, 832
ExecuteXmlReader(), 826, 828–829, 860
Execution (permission set), 563
execution process (.NET Framework), 21–22
Exists(), 463
Exists property, 773
Exit, 1119
ExitThread, 1119
Expander control, 997
ExpanderDemo/MainWindow.xaml, 997
ExpandoObject, 304, 741
explicit casting, 159–161, 172–173. *See also*
  user-defined casts
ExplicitCapture, 220
exponential format (E/e), 52, 213
Export attribute, 748, 750, 754, 757, 759, 762

export providers, 765–767
  containers and, 765–767
  purpose of, 765
exports (MEF), 749, 755–762
  exported metadata, 760–762
  exported properties/methods, 759–760
express delivery mode (messages), 1361
Expression Blend, 727
expression builders, route parameters and, 1250
Expression class, 200, 292
Expression Design, 727
expression trees, 291–293
Expression‹T›, 200, 291, 292, 293
ExpressionTreeSample/Program.cs, 291
extender controls, 1232–1233
ExtenderControl, 1223, 1232–1233
Extensible Application Markup Language.
    See XAML
Extensible Markup Language. *See* XML
extension methods, 86–87
  dynamic type and, 297
  LINQ, 272–273
  MEF implementation and, 748, 751, 764, 765
  this keyword and, 87, 272
Extension property, 773
extensions, workflows and, 1325–1326
extern (modifier), 100
external (safety level), 956

F

F (fixed-point format), 52, 213
F# (programming language)
  Chapter 53 (C#, *Visual Basic, C++/CLI, and F#*) and,
    7, 726
  tuples and, 146
fall-through behavior, 39, 40
FancyButtonStyle, 1004
fat-client applications, 19
Fiddler tool, 1239
FieldName attribute, 334, 335, 336
fields (member variables), 29, 66
  /local variables, scope clashes for, 30–31
  structs and, 81
  underscore and, 73
  usage guidelines, 64
FIFO (first in, first out), 236, 266
Figure, Floater *v.*, 1084
file: identifier, 638
File object, 784, 803
FILE protocol, 653
file system. *See also* files
  exploring/managing, 771–780
  file manipulation. *See* files
  registry *v.*, 806, 807
File System editor, 415, 418, 422, 424, 425

File Types editor, 423
FileAccess enumeration, 789
FileAccessControl/Program.cs, 560
FileDialogPermission, 563
FileInfo, 772, 774, 777, 778, 779, 780, 787, 790
  methods, 774
  properties, 773–774
FileIOPermission, 562, 563, 564, 724
FileMode enumeration, 789
FileNotFound, 362, 363, 364
FileProperties (sample application), 775–780
FilePropertiesAndMovement (sample application),
    780–783
FilePropertiesAndMovement.sln, 781, 782, 783
FileProperties.sln, 777, 778, 779, 780
files. *See also* file system
  ACLs
    adding/removing ACLs from files, 805–806
    reading ACLs from file, 802–803
  folders and, 772
  mapped-memory files, 799–800
  moving/copying/deleting files, 780–783
  reading/writing to files, 784–787
    binary files, 789–793
    text files, 793–799
  security, 771, 802, 814
FileSecurity class, 559, 560, 803, 805
FileShare enumeration, 789
FileStream, 365, 559, 634, 787
  in hierarchy of stream-related classes, 788
  reading/writing to binary files with, 789–793
FileStreamSecurity, 559
FileSystemAccessRule class, 560, 561, 569, 803, 804,
    805
FileSystemInfo, 772, 774
FileSystemTransactions/IKernelTransaction.cs, 634
FileSystemTransactions/NativeMethods.cs, 633
FileSystemTransactions/SafeTransactionHandle.cs, 633
FileSystemTransactions/TransactedFile.cs, 635
FileSystemWatcher, 768
FileUpload, 1161
FillBehavior, 1022
filtering operators (query operator category), 275,
    277–278
filters, 467, 471–472
Finalize(), 85, 313, 314
finalizers, 67. *See also* constructors; destructors
  constructors *v.*, 67
  as destructors, 313
finally blocks, 13, 353–355
Find(), 232, 233, 242
FindIndex(), 232, 233
FindLast(), 232, 233, 242
FindLastIndex(), 232, 233
FindResource(), 1006
finished (dialog box), 424

Finnish sorting (example), 578
First (element operator), 276
first C# program, 23–25
first in, first out (FIFO), 236, 266
First.cs, 24
FirstOrDefault, 276
fixed documents, 1075, 1086–1089
fixed keyword, 324, 328
FixedDocument class, 1086, 1087
fixed-point format (F), 52, 213
flags (DataRowState enumeration), 838
float, 34
  casting
        Currency to float, 173–174
        float to Currency, 175–176
        float to long, 179
        float to uint, 175
        uint to float, 174
Floater, Figure *v.*, 1084
floating-point types, 34. *See also* double; float
flooding, 1342
flow control, 37–44
flow documents, 1075, 1085
FlowDocument class, 1085
FlowDocumentDemo/FlowDocument1.xaml, 1079
FlowDocumentDemo/FlowDocument2.xaml, 1080
FlowDocumentDemo/ListDemo.xaml, 1082
FlowDocumentDemo/ParagraphDemo.xaml, 1081
FlowDocumentPageViewer, 1085
FlowDocumentReader, 1085
FlowDocumentsScrollViewer, 1085
FlowLayoutPanel, 1138–1139
folders
  defined, 772
  directories *v.*, 772
  .NET classes for. *See* Directory class; DirectoryInfo
folding editor feature, 386–388
FontFamily, 1075, 1076
fonts, 1075–1077
FontSize, 1003, 1075, 1076
FontStretch, 1075, 1076
FontStyle, 1075, 1076
FontWeight, 1075, 1076
Foo(), 126, 127, 128, 272, 473, 474
Foo property, 754, 755
‹FooterTemplate›, 1177
for loops, 40–42
  nested, 41–42
  Parallel.For() and, 504–506
ForAll(), 463, 464
foreach loops, 43
  enumerations and, 140, 141
  IEnumerable/IEnumerator interfaces and, 140–141
  Parallel.ForEach() and, 506–507
foreign key constraints (DataTable), 842–843

ForeignKeyConstraint, 842, 843
Form class, 1142. *See also* forms
form feed (escape sequence), 35
Form1.cs, 389, 1119, 1120, 1121
Form1.cs (code snippet), 1119
Form1.Designer.cs, 389, 1119, 1120, 1121
Form1.Designer.cs (code snippet), 1120
Format(), 198, 208
format specifiers, 52, 213
format strings, 52, 212–217
FormatException, 359, 360, 365
FormattableVector, 216–217
FormBorderStyle, 1145
forms (Windows Forms), 1142–1146. *See also* Windows
  Forms
  appearance, 1145–1146
  Form class and, 1142
  instantiation/destruction, 1142–1145
Forms Authentication, 548, 551, 1201, 1202
Formula-1 champions
  collections and, 227–229
  LINQ queries and, 267–286
  sets and, 255
Formula1 class, 269
Formula-1 sample database
  Syndication Feeds sample, 1390–1394
  WPF, 1063–1073
        custom columns, 1069–1070
        DataGrid control, 1067–1069
        grouping with DataGrid control, 1070–1073
        mapping for, 1063–1064
        row details, 1070
        TreeView control, 1063–1067
Formula1Demo/Program.cs, 877, 879, 880, 882,
    883, 884
FormView, 1163, 1175, 1178–1179
Frame control, 995, 996
FrameDemo/MainWindow.xaml, 996
FrameworkElement, 986, 1006
freeing unmanaged resources, 312–313
frmADOXML.cs, 927, 928, 929, 931, 932
frmNavigator.cs, 919, 920, 921
frmSerial.cs, 935, 937, 938, 939, 940, 941
frmXMLDOM.cs, 914, 915
from clause, compound, 278, 283
from query, compound, 288
FuelEconomy/FuelCalculatorExtension.cs, 758
FuelEconomy/FuelEconomyUC.xaml.cs, 758
FullName property, 773
FullTrust (permission set), 563
fully qualified name, 46
Func‹T›, 190, 759
function members, 67. *See also* constructors; finalizers;
    indexers; methods; operators; properties
functions

functions (*continued*)
 abstract, 93
 anonymous. *See* anonymous methods; Lambda
  expressions
 calling base versions of functions, 93
 methods *v.*, 67
 pure virtual, 93

G

G (general format), 52, 213
GAC (global assembly cache), 15, 446–447
gacuil.exe, 446–447, 456, 457
GameMoves, 145, 146
garbage collection, 10–11, 311–312
 CLR and, 312
 freeing unmanaged resources and, 312–313
 memory management and, 303, 696
GC class, 312, 317
general format (G), 52, 213
generation operators (query operator category), 276,
  288–289
generic classes, 110–118, 225–226
 constraints, 114–116
 creating, 110–113
 default values, 114
 features, 113–118
 generic types and, 107
 inheritance and, 117
 keywords and, 113, 114
 static members of, 117–118
generic collection classes, 108. *See also* collections
 DataGridView control and, 1134–1135
 IEnumerable⟨T⟩ and, 112, 125, 226
 non-generic collection classes and, 108,
  225, 732
 ObservableCollection⟨T⟩. *See* ObservableCollection⟨T⟩
 System.Collections.Generic and, 108, 109, 578
 XAML and, 732
generic interfaces, 118–123
 contra-variance with, 118–123
 covariance with, 119–120
generic methods, 123–128
 with constraints, 125–126
 with delegates, 126
 specialization, 126–128
generic types
 generic classes and, 107
 naming guidelines for, 110
 null and, 113, 114
GenericConsumer, 95, 96, 97, 98
GenericMethods/Account.cs, 124, 125
GenericMethods/Algorithm.cs, 125, 126
GenericMethods/IAccount.cs, 125
GenericMethods/Program.cs, 124, 126, 127

GenericPrincipal, 546
generics, 107–128
 binary code reuse and, 109
 casting and, 113
 code bloat and, 109–110
 default keyword and, 114
 naming guidelines, 110
 overview, 107–110
 performance and, 108
 type safety and, 107, 109
 XAML and, 728, 732, 744
geometries (WPF), 988–989
GeometryDemo/MainWindow.xaml, 988
GeometryDrawing, 992
GeometryGroup, 992
Get(), 258
$get(), 1234
get accessor, 732, 733
GetAccessControl(), 559, 560, 803, 804, 805, 810
GetAssemblies(), 444
GetAStringDemo/Currency.cs, 187
GetAStringDemo/Program.cs, 185–186
GetChampions(), 269, 278, 284
GetChanges(), 856
GetChildRows(), 839, 841
GetConstructor(), GetConstructors(), 342
GetConstructorChampions(), 270, 282
GetCustomAttributes(), 345, 348
GetCustomerOrdersCLR, 968
GetDatabaseConnection.txt, 822, 827
GetDefaultMembers(), 342
GetDirectories(), 774, 778, 783
GetDocument(), 114, 238, 245
GetDrives(), 801
GetEnumerator(), 110, 111, 112, 113, 118, 134, 140,
  141, 142, 143, 144, 226
GetEvent(), GetEvents(), 342
GetField(), GetFields(), 342
GetFileNames(), 814
GetFiles(), 774, 778, 783
GetFileSystemInfo(), 774
GetFormat(), 572
GetHashCode(), 84, 147, 162, 170, 248, 249, 250,
  251, 284
GetHostByAddress(), 655
GetInvocationList(), 196, 201
GetManifestResourceNames(), 581
GetMember(), GetMembers(), 342
GetMenusByName(), 890
GetMethod(), GetMethods(), 342
GetNextTextElement(), 570
GetObjectByKey(), 873, 882
GetParentRows(), 841, 842
GetProperty(), GetProperties(), 342
GetQuoteOfTheDay(), 447, 449

GetResponse(), 640, 641, 642, 652
GetSubKeyNames(), 810
GetTextElementEnumerator(), 570
GetTransactedFileStream(), 634
GetType(), 85, 340
GetUI(), 754, 757, 766
GetValue(), 134, 628, 629, 733, 739, 810
GetValueKind(), 810
GetValueNames(), 810
global assembly cache. *See* GAC
Global Assembly Cache Viewer, 448
global clouds, 1344
global utility functions (ASP.NET AJAX Library), 1234
Global.asax, 1261
globalization. *See also* localization
  cultures and regions. *See* cultures
  defined, 569
  sorting orders and, 578–579
  Unicode issues, 570
globally unique identifier. *See* GUID
GoBack(), 649
GoForward(), 649
GoHome(), 649
GoldAccount, 103, 104
goto statements, 39, 40, 43
Graphics with GDI+ (online Chapter 48), 77
graphs. *See* clouds
GregorianCalendar, 569, 576, 1090
Grid, 1001–1002
GridView, 1163, 1175
GroupBox control, 997
GroupBy, 276
GroupBy(), 280, 281, 878
grouping operators (query operator category), 276,
    280–281
GroupJoin operator, 276
groups (regular expressions), 223–224
‹GroupSeparatorTemplate›, 1178
‹GroupTemplate›, 1178
GUID (globally unique identifier), 621
Guid attribute, 716
guidelines
  C# programming, 58–64
  usage
      fields, 64
      methods/properties, 64
  Windows 7/Windows Server 2008, 1397–1415
guidgen.exe utility, 704, 716, 1363

H

Hamlet.xml, 943, 948, 949, 951, 952, 953
hand-coded schema, 839–840
handlers (service program), 669
hash algorithms, 554

hash tables. *See* dictionaries
HashSet‹T›, 255, 265, 266
Hashtable, 584
header files (C++), 47
headered content controls (WPF), 996–997
headered item controls (WPF), 998
HeaderedContentControl, 996–997
HeaderTemplate, 996
‹HeaderTemplate›, 1177
heaps (managed heaps)
  arrays on, 329
  defined, 8, 32, 309
  garbage collection and, 311–312
  memory allocation on, 309–311
  reference data types and, 8, 32, 309–311
  structs and, 80, 87
Hello World examples
  HelloCollection, 142, 143
  Workflow 4, 1310–1311
HelpLink (System.Exception), 359
hexadecimal format (X), 52, 213
hexadecimal values, char and, 35
HiddenField, 1161
hiding methods, 92–93
HierarchicalDataTemplate, 1012
hierarchies. *See also* class hierarchy
  classes and, 113
  constructors in, 96–97
  constructors with parameters in, 97–98
  CTS and, 9
  file system. *See* file system
  registry, 806. *See also* registry
  resources (WPF) and, 1005
  stream-related classes, 787–788
  task, 502–503
  WebRequest/WebResponse classes, 652–653
highCostMinutesUsed, 95
HisBaseClass, 92, 93
hives, registry, 807
HKEY_CLASSES_ROOT, 422, 718, 807
HKEY_CURRENT_CONF, 807
HKEY_CURRENT_USER, 422, 467, 807, 808
HKEY_DYN_DATA, 807
HKEY_LOCAL_MACHINE, 422, 476, 477, 679, 807,
    808, 809
HKEY_LOCAL_
    MACHINESystemCurrentControlSetServices, 679
HKEY_PERFORMANCE_DATA, 807
HKEY_USERS, 422, 807
host classes, preconfigured, 1303–1304
host names. *See* IP addresses
hosting
  with CLR objects, 886–890
  DLR ScriptRuntime, 300–302
  WCF and, 1302–1304

hosting (*continued*)
   Workflow Designer, 1332–1337
   workflows, 1327–1332
HostProtectionAttribute, 956
HTML (Hypertext Markup Language), 1219
HTML page output (WebBrowser control), 643
HTML server controls (ASP.NET), 1155
http: identifier, 638
HTTP client application (Data Services), 891–893
HTTP protocol, 637, 638, 640, 641, 642, 652, 656, 657, 658
https: identifier, 638
HTTPS protocol, 653
HttpWebRequest, 495, 641, 652, 891, 895, 1109
HttpWebResponse, 641, 652, 891
Hungarian notation, 60, 102
Hyperlink control, 1160
Hypertext Markup Language. *See* HTML

I

IAccount interface, 125, 126
IANA (Internet Assigned Numbers Authority), 658
IAsyncResult, 493, 494, 495, 642, 643, 1312
IBankAccount, 101–102, 103, 104
ICalculator interface, 749, 750, 751, 759, 762, 764, 765
ICalculatorExtension, 754, 757, 758, 763, 765, 767
ICloneable, 135
ICollection‹T›, 118, 226, 232, 236, 255
IComparable interface, 118, 136, 137, 138, 139, 149, 234
IComparable‹Racer›, 268
IComparable‹T›, 118, 227, 234
IComparer interface, 137, 138, 139, 149
IComparer‹T›, 137, 226, 234
ICompletedEvents, 701, 710, 711
IConnectionPoint, 701, 713
IConnectionPointContainer, 701, 711, 713
identifiers
   case sensitivity of, 58
   keywords as, 58–59
   rules for, 58–59
identity, principal and, 545–547
IDENTITY columns, 857, 858
IdentityReference, 559
IDictionary‹TKey, TValue›, 226
IDispatch, 697, 698, 705, 707, 709, 721
IDisplay‹T›, 121
IDisposable (System.IDisposable), 100, 101, 313, 314–315
   database connections and, 823, 824, 860
   destructors and, 315–317
   freeing unmanaged resources with, 314–317
IDL (Interface Definition Language)
   attributes and, 13

COMServer.idl, 696
   files, 696, 703, 705, 714
IEnlistmentNotification, 626–627, 636
IEntityWithChangeTracker, 870, 871
IEntityWithKey, 870, 871, 873, 881
IEntityWithRelationships, 870, 871, 875, 876
IEnumerable, 43, 112, 140–141
IEnumerable‹out T›, 117, 118
IEnumerable‹T›, 112, 125, 226
IEnumerable‹TSource›, 270, 273, 279, 280, 289, 294
IEnumeration‹T›, 761
IEnumerator, 112, 131, 140–141
IEnumerator‹out T›, 118
IEnumerator‹T›, 112, 141
IEqualityComparer, 148, 149
IEqualityComparer‹T›, 148, 226, 250, 284
IExtensibleObject‹T›, 118
#if, 56–57. *See also* Conditional attribute
If activity, 1312–1313
if statements, 37–39
if...else construction, 37, 154. *See also* conditional operator
IFormattable interface, 84, 207, 212, 214, 215, 216, 227, 231, 268, 339, 349
IgnoreCase, 220
IgnorePatternWhitespace, 220
IIdentity interface, 546, 568
IIndex‹T›, 120
IIS (Internet Information Server)
   Administrator tool, 411, 419
   ASP.NET and, 409, 1150, 1152, 1157
   properties, 418, 419
   WCF hosting and, 1302, 1303
   World Wide Web Publishing Service, 668
IJW (It Just Works), 726
IKernelTransaction, 633, 634
IL (Microsoft Intermediate Language), 4, 6–13
   advantages of, 4
   case sensitivity, 9
   dynamic type and, 297–299
   features of, 6–13
   generics and, 107
   interfaces and, 7
   Java byte code *v.*, 4
   language interoperability and, 5–6, 7–8
   .NET Framework and, 6
   object-oriented programming and, 7
   performance improvement and, 4–5
   platform independence and, 4
   strong data typing and, 8–13, 157
   type safety and, 11, 12
ildasm tool, 14, 297, 434, 435, 448, 449, 581, 588
IList, 226, 230, 276
   DataGridView control and, 1134
IListSource, DataGridView control and, 1134

IList‹T›, 226, 230, 236, 290
ILookup‹TKey, TValue›, 226
Image control, 1160
ImageBrush, 993
ImageButton, 1160
ImageList component, 1136
ImageMap, 1160
IMath interface, 697, 704, 706, 707, 708, 715, 717, 719
immutable, strings as, 36, 70, 209
implementation inheritance, 89, 90–98
implicit casting, 158–159. *See also* user-defined casts
implicit permissions, 566–567
ImplicitPermissions/Program.cs, 567
Import attribute, 748, 750, 751, 759, 765, 767
import statement (Java), 25
ImportCatalogPart, 1211
ImportMany attribute, 761, 763
imports (MEF), 749, 762–765
in keyword, 120
Include(), 876, 878
‹include›, 53
IncludeExceptionDetailInFaults, 1295
Increment(), 487, 520
increment operator (++), 151, 153, 154
Index(), 1262, 1263, 1267, 1268
Index (project property), 418
index operator [ ], 152, 172
indexers, 67
    array elements and, 130–131
indexes, XML, 978–979
IndexOf(), 208, 232, 233
IndexOfAny(), 208
IndexOutOfRangeException, 131, 354, 355,
        356, 357, 358, 359, 360
indirection operator (*), 152, 319
InDoubt(), 627
inheritance, 89–105
    generic classes and, 117
    implementation inheritance, 89, 90–98
    interface inheritance, 89, 101
    multiple (C++), 90
    multiple interface inheritance, 90, 105
    private (C++), 90
    structs and, 82, 90
    types, 89–90
Init(), 965, 966
initialization
    of arrays, 130, 132, 133, 228
    of variables, 27
InitializeComponent(), 390, 391, 586, 675, 1122
InitializePerformanceCounts(), 486, 487
InitializeService(), 889, 890, 1108
InitializeViewModel(), 1334, 1335, 1336
Inline (base class), 1078
inline comments, 53
Inline elements, 1078–1080

inlining, 74
InnerException (System.Exception), 359, 362
INotifyPropertyChanged, 868, 870, 881, 896, 1036,
        1042, 1334
INotifyPropertyChanging, 868, 870
In/Out (attributes), 717
input string, 219
INSERT, 819, 860, 971
Insert(), 208, 230
inserting nodes (XmlDocument class), 915–917
‹InsertTemplate›, 1177
Install(), 679, 680, 683
InstallAllUsers, 414
installation address (dialog box), 424
installation folder (dialog box), 424
installation packages, creating, 413
    for client applications, 413–417
installation program (Quote service), 679–683
Installer class, 680
installer project types (Visual Studio 2010),
        408, 412
installutil.exe, 680, 682–683
instance, of delegate, 185, 187
instance field, 31
InstanceContextMode, 1294
instantiation/destruction, of forms, 1142–1145
instrumentation, 461–489
    code contracts, 461–466
    event logging, 475–483
    performance monitoring, 483–489
    tracing, 467–475
insurance policy example, 1322
int, 33
integer types
    implicit conversions, 158–159
    predefined, 33
    user-defined. *See* enumerations
integrity, strong names and, 446
IntelliSense, 44, 60, 115, 374, 375, 388, 709, 1128,
        1155, 1157, 1189, 1234, 1239
Interface Definition Language. *See* IDL
interface inheritance, 89, 101
interface references, 104
interfaces, 100–105. *See also specific interfaces*
    code contracts for, 465–466
    COM and, 697–698
    custom, 697
    defining/implementing, 101–104
    derived, 104–105
    dispatch, 697
    dual, 697–698
    generic, 118–123
    Hungarian notation and, 102
    IL and, 7
    .NET Framework and, 697–698
    object-oriented programming and, 100

InterfaceType attribute, 717
Interlocked class, 520
Interlocked.CompareExchange(), 520
Interlocked.Increment(), 520
Intermediate Language. *See* IL
internal (modifier), 66, 99
internal comments, 53. *See also* comments
Internet (permission set), 564
Internet Assigned Numbers Authority. *See* IANA
Internet Explorer
  add-ins and, 747
  instances (WebBrowser control), 645
Internet Information Server. *See* IIS
Internet Protocol version 4. *See* IPv4
Internet Security Zone, 421
interop. *See* COM interop
interoperability. *See* language interoperability
Intersect(), 276, 283, 879
InvalidOperationException, 122, 123, 160, 237
invariant cultures, 571
invariants, 465
InvokeMember(), 440
InvokeMethod activity, 1313
IOperation interface, 749, 750, 754, 762
IP addresses (DNS names, host names), 654–656
  defined, 654
  .NET classes for, 654–655
IPAddress class, 654–655
IPartImportsSatisfiedNotification, 763
IPerson interface, 465, 466
IPHostEntry class, 655, 656
IPrinciple interface, 546, 547, 568
IProducerConsumerCollection‹T›, 226
IPv4 (Internet Protocol version 4), 654
IPv6 (Internet Protocol version 6), 654
IQueryable‹T›, 294, 883, 888, 889, 898
IRequestHandler, 886
IResourceReader, 584
IResourceWriter, 584
IronPython, 295, 300, 301, 302
IronRuby, 295, 300
is operator, 152, 155
IsApplication, 419
IsBackground, 498
IsDocumentAvailable, 238
ISet‹T›, 226, 255
isolated storage, 806, 810–814
  access types for, 810–811
  IsolatedStoragePermission, 563
IsolatedStorageFilePermission, 563
isolation (ACID), 607. *See also* ACID
isolation level (transactions), 624–626, 824–825
IsolationLevel property, 611, 625, 626, 1294
IsSubsetOf(), 255
IsSupersetOf(), 255

IStructuralComparable, 147–149
IStructuralEquatable, 147–149
ISupportErrorInfo, 700
It Just Works (IJW), 726
item controls (WPF), 998
ItemsControl class, 986
‹ItemSeparatorTemplate›, 1177
ItemsPanelTemplate, 1012
ItemTemplate, 1017–1018
‹ItemTemplate›, 1177
iterator blocks, 142, 145
ITransferBankAccount, 104
IUnknown, 7, 696, 697, 698, 705, 707, 713, 717, 722
IValidationErrorService, 1337
IWelcome, 702, 705, 707, 711, 715, 722

J

jagged arrays, 133–134
Java
  disadvantages of, 4
  exception handling, 13
  garbage collection, 11
  import statement, 25
  interoperability and, 7
  Java byte code, 4
  syntax, 25, 42
  types, 33
JavaScript
  Ajax and, 1220
  browser integration. *See* browser integration
  debugging, AJAX and, 1239–1240
  dynamic programming and, 295
  OOP extensions, 1235–1236
  ScriptRuntime and, 300
  Web Forms and, 18
  Windows Forms and, 21
JavaScript Object Notation. *See* JSON
JavaScriptInterop, 1110
JavaScriptInterop/MainPage.xaml, 1111, 1112
JIT (Just-in-Time) compilation, 4
Join(), 208
Join (operator), 276, 282–283
join operators (query operator category), 276, 282–283
journal queues, 1361–1362
JSON (JavaScript Object Notation), 1281, 1282
  ASP.NET AJAX and, 1221, 1222
  SOAP *v.*, 1282
  WCF and, 1282
  WCF Data Services and, 886, 891, 893, 894, 902
Jump Lists, 1411, 1414–1415
jump statements, 43–44. *See also* break statements;
    continue statement; goto statements; return statement
  anonymous methods and, 197
Just-in-Time compilation. *See* JIT compilation

K

KeepAlive property, 641
key exchange, secure transfer and, 556–558
key generation, with SQL Server, 857–858
key type, 248–250
keyframe animations, 1025–1026
KeyNotFoundException, 247, 253
keys, registry, 807
keywords. *See also specific keywords*
  generic classes and, 113, 114
  as identifiers, 58–59
  list of, 58–59, 62–63
  modifiers and, 99–100
  names and, 62–63
Keywords (project property), 414

L

Label class, 995
Label control, 1136, 1160
Lambda expressions, 126, 197–200. *See also* delegates;
    events
  delegates and, 183, 197
  dynamic type and, 297
  Expression class and, 200, 292
  Expression‹T› and, 290, 291, 292, 293
  multiple code lines and, 198–199
  parameters and, 198
  variables outside of, 199
LambdaExpressions/Program.cs, 198
language extensions, dynamic, 295–305
language independence
  .NET Framework, 7, 13
  Visual Studio, 385
Language Integrated Query. *See* LINQ
language interoperability, 5–6. *See also* COM interop
  defined, 7
  IL and, 5–6, 7–8
  strong data typing and, 8–9, 157
language specifications, 60. *See also* CLS; usage
    conventions
Large Object Heap, 312
Last (element operator), 276
last in, first out (LIFO), 240, 266
LastAccessTime, 774
LastIndexOf(), 208, 232
LastIndexOfAny(), 208
LastModifiedAttribute, 338, 347, 348
LastOrDefault, 276
LastWriteTime, 774
late binding, 433, 698, 715
Launch Conditions editor, 426–427
layered/modular approach, to network
    communication, 657

layout containers(WPF), 999–1002
LayoutDemo/CanvasWindow.xaml, 1000
LayoutDemo/DockPanelWindow.xaml, 1001
LayoutDemo/GridWindow.xaml, 1002
LayoutDemo/StackPanelWindow.xaml, 1000
LayoutDemo/WrapPanelWindow.xaml, 1000
LayoutEditorPart, 1212
‹LayoutTemplate›, 1177
lazy loading
  of parts (add-ins), 764–765
  of relationships, 876
Lazy‹T, TMetadata›, 761
left-hand side (lhs), 167
Length property (FileInfo), 774
lhs (left-hand side), 167
library assembly (WhatsNewAttributes), 338–339
license agreement (dialog box), 424
LIFO (last in, first out), 240, 266
lights (3-D with WPF), 1030, 1032
#line, 57–58
Line class, 987
LinearGradientBrush, 731, 991–992, 1004
LineGeometry, 988
LineSegment, 989
link local clouds, 1344
LinkButton control, 1160
linked lists, 241–246
LinkedList, 110, 111, 112
LinkedListNode, 110, 111
LinkedListNode‹T›, 112, 242
LinkedListObjects/LinkedListNode.cs, 110, 111
LinkedListSample/Document.cs, 242
LinkedListSample/LinkedList.cs, 113
LinkedListSample/LinkedListNode.cs, 112
LinkedListSample/PriorityDocumentManager.cs, 244
LinkedListSample/Program.cs, 113, 246
LinkedList‹T›, 110, 112, 113, 241, 242, 265
LinkLabel control, 645
LINQ (Language Integrated Query), 267–294. *See also*
    Parallel LINQ; queries
  extension methods, 272–273
  overview, 267–268
  providers, 293–294
  WCF Data Services and, 897–898, 902
LINQ to Amazon, 294
LINQ to Entities, 883–884
LINQ to Flickr, 294
LINQ to LDAP, 294
LINQ to MySQL, 294
LINQ to Objects, 288, 291, 294
LINQ to SharePoint, 294
LINQ to SQL, 293, 294
  Chapter 56 (online), 904
  Dynamic Data LINQ to SQL Web Application,
    380, 1251

LINQ to SQL (*continued*)
dynamic data sites and, 1251, 1252, 1256, 1260,
    1261, 1262, 1274
LINQ to XML and, 975
provider classes, 818
System.Data.Linq.SqlClient, 818
LINQ to XML, 293, 954
CRUD operations and, 954
helper objects, 943–948, 954
LINQ to SQL and, 975
.NET Framework and, 942–943
querying dynamic XML documents, 949–951
querying static XML documents, 948–949
LinqDataSource, 1162
LINQIntro/Program.cs, 271
Linux, 17
‹list›, 53
list binding (WPF), 1045–1047
List class, 1081
ListBox control, 638, 641, 998, 1127–1128, 1160
ListBox elements
control templates for, 1018–1020
styling of, 1016–1017
ListBoxChrome, 998
ListBoxItem, 995
lists, 226–236, 1081–1082
binding to, 1045–1047
creating, 228–236
elements in
    accessing, 230–231
    adding, 229
    inserting, 230
    removing, 231–232
    searching, 232–233
    sorting, 234–235
linked, 241–246
sorted, 246–247
ListSamples/Program.cs, 229
ListSamples/RacerComparer.cs, 234–235
ListSamples/Racer.cs, 227–228
List‹T› class, 108, 109, 225, 226
ListView control, 1136, 1163, 1178–1179
Literal control, 1161
Load(), 344
LoadFrom(), 344
loading assemblies, dynamically, 438–441
local variable scope, 29–31
localhost, 664
LocalIntranet (permission set), 563
localization, 569–603
ASP.NET and, 591–593
BookOfTheDay and, 584–590
defined, 569
resource dictionaries and, 594–598
resource files and, 579–584

satellite assemblies and, 434, 579, 581, 588, 590, 594,
    597, 598, 603
System.Resources and, 569, 580, 584, 603
Uid attributes and, 594, 596–597
Visual Studio 2010 and, 584–591
Windows Forms application and, 584–591
WPF and, 593–598
Localization (project property), 414
Localize control, 1162
LocalUserAppDataPath, 1118
LocBaml tool, 597–598
lock statement, 238, 515–520
Log property, 477
LogDisplayName property, 477
logical layer, 862, 863–864
logical operators, 151
Login, 1203
login web server controls, 1203–1204
login.cs, 821
LoginName, 1204
LoginStatus, 1203
LoginView, 1203
logos for applications (requirements), 1398
LogVisits, 419
long, 33
LongTask(), 539, 541
lookup, dictionaries and, 253–254
LookupSample/Program.cs, 254
Lookup‹TKey, TElement›, 246, 253, 287
LookUpWhatsNew assembly, 34, 337, 345
LookUpWhatsNew.cs, 346
loops, 40–43. *See also* do...while loops; for loops;
    foreach loops; while loops
Parallel.For() and, 504–506
Parallel.ForEach() and, 506–507
LostFocusEventManager, 204
lower-level network protocols, 656–657

M

MachineName, 477, 685
MAF (Managed Add-in Framework), 747–748. *See also*
    MEF
Chapter 50 (*Managed Add-in Framework*), 561, 748, 769
MEF *v.*, 747–748
sandboxing and, 561
mage.exe, 420
mageUI.exe, 420
MagicShop.mdf database, 1251–1255, 1261–1274
ASP.NET MVC application, 1261–1274
Create() and, 1269–1273
data access model for, 1251–1252
data source added to, 1252
Edit() and, 1273–1274
ID values in, 1255
scaffolding and, 1252–1253

MailMessage, 657, 658
Main(), 24, 26, 48–50
    multiple, 48–49
    passing arguments to, 49–50
    threads and, 492
main function (service program), 669
MainWindow, 1400
making, 394. *See also* building; compilation
Managed Add-in Framework. *See* MAF
managed C++, 6, 8
managed code, 4, 6, 8, 10, 15, 16
Managed Extensibility Framework. *See* MEF
managed heaps. *See* heaps
Managed Resources Editor, 582, 594
managed types, 320
manifests
    assembly, 14, 433
    ClickOnce applications, 419, 420
            properties/settings, 420–421
ManufacturedDataSet.cs, 840, 842
ManufactureProductDataTable(), 840
Manufacturer (project property), 414
ManufacturerURL, 414
many-to-many relationship, 873
mapped-memory files, 799–800
MappedMemoryFiles.sln, 800
mapping layer, 862, 865–866
Mapping Schema Language. *See* MSL
maps. *See* dictionaries
markup extensions, 741–744
    curly braces and, 741, 742
    custom, 742–743
    XAML-defined, 744
MarkupExtension, 742
MarkupExtensionDemo/CalculatorExtension.cs, 743
MarkupExtensionDemo/MainWindow.xaml,
    741, 743
MarshalByRefObject, 444, 566, 772, 788
marshaling, 7, 12, 696, 701, 772
Marshal.ReleaseComObject(), 708, 709
MaskedTextBox control, 1137–1138
MaskedTextProvider, 1138
master details binding, 1048
master pages, 1195–1198
    accessing, from web pages, 1196
    nested, 1197
    in PCSDemoSite, 1197–1198
matches (regular expressions), 219, 223–224
MathClient.cs, 51
MathLibrary.cs, 50
MathLibrary.xml, 54–55
MathOperations class, 188, 189, 190, 193, 194
MathTest.cs, 68–69
Max(), 276, 286
MaxItemsInObjectGraph, 1295
mc.exe, 481

MD5 algorithm, 554, 969
MD5CryptoServiceProvider, 969
MDAC versions, 409, 427
MDI (multiple document interface) applications, 78,
    1141, 1142, 1146
MediaElement, 993, 994
MeetingRoomBooker.mdf, 1169–1171
MEF (Managed Extensibility Framework), 747–769.
    See also MAF
    architecture, 747–754
    catalogs and, 748, 749, 767–769
    categories of, 748
    containers and, 748, 749, 765–767
    contracts and, 749, 754–755
    export providers and, 765–767
    exports and, 749, 755–762
    extension methods and, 748, 751, 764, 765
    imports and, 749, 762–765
    MAF *v.*, 747–748
member access operator, 152
member variables. *See* fields
members (of classes), 66
    data members, 66–67
    function members, 67
MembershipProvider, 549
MemberwiseClone(), 85
memory
    access, with pointers, 317–325. *See also* pointers
    allocation. *See also* heaps; stacks
            on heap, 309–311
            on stack, 308–311
    freeing. *See* garbage collection
memory leaks, 10
memory management, 307–332. *See also* garbage
    collection
    garbage collection and, 307, 696
    under the hood, 307
memory type safety, 13, 22
MemoryStream, 787, 788
Menu class, 886, 887, 894, 998
Menu control (navigation web server control), 1199
menu planner application, 1086–1089
MenuBase, 998
MenuCard, 887, 888
MenuCardDataModel, 888, 889
MenuDataService, 889, 890
MenuItem, 998
MenuStrip control, 1141
Merge(), 856, 965, 966
Merge Module Projects, 412
MergeOption enumeration, 876
meshes, 1342. *See also* clouds
Message class, 1372, 1376, 1377, 1385. *See also*
    messages
message contracts, 1293–1294
Message property (System.Exception), 359

message queues, 1361–1362
  acknowledgment, 1376–1377
  creating, 1362
  finding, 1364–1365
  installation, 1384
  opening, 1365–1366
  poison, 1359
  properties, 1363
  transactional, 1377–1378, 1382, 1385
  types of, 1361–1362
Message Queuing, 1357–1385
  administrative tools, 1362–1363
  architecture, 1361–1362
  asynchronous programming *v.*, 1357–1358
  Course Order (sample application), 1370–1384
  e-mail and, 1358
  features of, 1359–1360
  overview, 1357–1360
  products, 1360
  programming, 1363–1370
  reasons for using, 1358–1359
  synchronous programming *v.*, 1357–1358, 1362
  triggers and, 1360
  with WCF, 1378–1385
message resource files, 479–483
message text files, 480
MessageLoop, 1119
MessageQueue, 1363, 1364, 1365, 1385. *See also* message queues
MessageQueue.Create(), 1363, 1377, 1384
MessageQueueInstaller, 1364, 1384
MessageQueuePermission, 563
MessageResourceFile, 479
messages (Message Queuing), 1361
  delivery modes, 1361
  priority, 1372–1373
  receiving, 1368–1370
  recoverable, 1372–1373
  sending, 1366–1368
  types of, 1361
Messages Compiler, 481
meta-characters, 220, 221, 223
metadata
  assemblies and, 14, 15
  COM and, 696
  exports (MEF) and, 760–761
  .NET Framework and, 696
Metadata Exchange (MEX) endpoints, 1281, 1288, 1304, 1305
Metadata property, 761
MetadataWorkspace, 872
method binding, 698
method overloading, 65, 72, 98, 168, 181
methods, 67–72
  anonymous, 196

delegates with, 196–197
  dynamic programming (C#) and, 295
  declaring, 67–68
  exports (MEF) and, 759–760
  extension, 86–87
  functions *v.*, 67
  generic, 123–128
  hiding, 92–93
  invoking, 68–69
  naming conventions, 60–63
  for Object class, 84–86
  overriding, 91–92
  parameters passed into, 69–70
  properties *v.*, 64
  sealed, 94
  System.Type, 341–342
  usage guidelines, 64
  virtual, 91–92
MEX (Metadata Exchange) endpoints, 1281, 1288, 1304, 1305
MFC (Microsoft Foundation Classes), 379, 712, 1117, 1142
Microsoft Foundation Classes (MFC), 379, 712, 1117, 1142
Microsoft Intermediate Language. *See* IL
Microsoft Live ID Authentication, 1201
Microsoft Management Console snap-in. *See* MMC snap-in
Microsoft Message Queue (MSMQ) Server Core, 1360
Microsoft Visual Studio 2010. *See* Visual Studio 2010
Microsoft Windows Peer-to-Peer Networking platform, 1343–1346
  PNRP, 1339, 1343–1346, 1355
Microsoft.CSharp, 438
Microsoft.SqlServer.Server, 957
Microsoft.Win32 namespace, 771, 806, 808
Microsoft.Win32.SafeHandles, 726
Min(), 276, 286
MMC (Microsoft Management Console) snap-in
  Certificates, 568
  Component Services, 616
  Computer Management, 1362
  Services, 616, 669, 683
model (MVC framework), 1260. *See also* MVC
models (3-D with WPF), 1030–1031
Models directory, 1261
Model-View-Controller. *See* MVC
modifiers, 99–100. *See also* keywords
  list of, 99, 100
  visibility, 66, 99
ModifyAccessControl(), 560
modular/layered approach, to network communication, 657
modules, 435–436. *See also* assemblies
Money class, 85, 86

Monitor class, 521
Mono project, 4
Moonlight, 1096
MortimerPhones.cs, 95
MouseMove, 736
"move" methods (XPathNavigator class), 918
MoveNext(), 141, 142, 143, 146
MoveTo(), 774, 780, 918
MoveToAttribute(), 918
MoveToFirst(), 918
MoveToFirstAttribute(), 909, 918
MoveToFirstChild(), 918
MoveToId(), 918
MoveToLast(), 918
MoveToNext(), 918
MoveToNextAttribute(), 909, 918
MoveToParent(), 918
MoveToPrevious(), 918
MoveToRoot(), 918
moving/copying/deleting files, 780–783
msbuild command, 596
MSBuild tasks, 450, 728
MSDeploy Publish option, 411
MSDN documentation
    Entity SQL and, 867
    escape sequences in, 221
    message text files, 480
    Visual Studio 2010 and, 375
MSL (Mapping Schema Language), 861, 864, 865, 867, 884
MSMQ DCOM proxy, 1360
MSMQ HTTP Support, 1360
MSMQ (Microsoft Message Queue) Server Core, 1360
MsmqIntegrationBinding, 1301
MSXML, 906, 914
MTAs (multithreaded apartments), 501, 699–700, 710, 718
multibinding, 1048–1049
multicast delegates, 193–196
Multicast Support, 1360. *See also* Message Queuing
MulticastDelegates/MathOperations.cs, 194
MulticastDelegates/Program.cs, 193
MulticastDelegateWithIteration/Program.cs, 195
multidimensional arrays, 132–133
Multiline, 220
multiline comments, 25, 53
multiple casting, 179–182
multiple catch blocks, 355–359
multiple code lines, Lambda expressions and, 198–199
multiple document interface (MDI) applications, 78, 1141, 1142, 1146
multiple inheritance (C++), 90
multiple interface inheritance, 90, 105
multiple Main() methods, 48–49
multiplication (*), 157, 167, 168, 319
multithreaded apartments. *See* MTAs

multithreading, with ambient transactions, 621–624
MultithreadingAmbientTx/Program.cs, 622
MultiTrigger, 1010
MultiView control, 1161
MusicTitles, 144
mutex (mutual exclusion), 523–524, 559
mutual exclusion. *See* mutex
MVC (Model-View-Controller), 1260. *See also* ASP. NET MVC
myArray, 130, 131
MyAttachedPropertyProvider, 739, 740
MyBase, 177, 178
MyDerived, 177
MyForm/NotepadForms.cs, 1118
MyGradientBrush, 1004, 1006
MyGroovyMethod(), 92, 93
MyThread, 497

N

N (number format), 52, 213
Name property
    FileInfo or DirectoryInfo, 774
    RegistryKey, 810
named arguments, 71
Named Pipes, 799
namespace alias qualifier (: :), 47, 152
namespace aliases, using keyword and, 47–48
namespaces, 17, 25, 45–46. *See also specific namespaces*
    ADO.NET, 818
    assemblies *v.*, 46, 434
    C++ header files and, 47
    names for, 61
    using keyword and, 25, 46–47
    in WPF, 984–985
naming conventions, 60–63
    case sensitivity
        C#, 61, 73
        format strings and, 52
        identifiers and, 58
        IL, 9
    casing schemes, 60
    constraints, 859
    database columns, 859
    database tables, 859
    generic types, 110
    name styles, 61
    namespace names, 61
    stored procedures, 859–860
native image generator, 451–452, 459
Native Runtime Optimization Service, 452
NativeActivity, 1311, 1312, 1324, 1325
NativeActivity‹TResult›, 1311, 1312
NativeMethods.RegisterServiceCtrlHandler[Ex](), 676
NativeMethods.StartServiceCtrlDispatcher(), 676
NativeObjectSecurity, 559

Navigate(), 644, 645
navigation web server controls, 1198–1201
NavigationWindow class, 996
Navigator.cs (code snippet), 919, 920, 921
nested for loops, 41–42
nested master pages, 1197
nested namespaces, 46
nested partial classes, 83
nested scopes, with ambient transactions, 620–621
nested try blocks, 360–362
NestedFor.cs, 42
.NET applications
  configuration, 452–454
  System.Data.Service.Client and, 895–902
.NET base classes. *See* base classes
.NET component (from COM client)
  COM client application, 718–719
  connection points added to, 720
  creating, 713–714
  type library for, 714–716
.NET enterprise architecture, C# and, 20–21
.NET Framework. *See also* .NET Framework 4
  architecture, 3–22
  attributes and, 13
  C# *v.*, 3–4
  code-based security and, 11
  COM+ and, 6
  COM *v.*, 6, 695–701
  compilation process and, 4, 21–22
  DOM and, 913–917
  errors and, 351. *See also* exceptions
  events and, 701. *See also* events
  exceptions and. *See* exceptions
  execution process and, 21–22
  IL and, 6
  interfaces and, 697–698. *See also* interfaces
  language independence, 7, 13
  LINQ to XML and, 942–943
  metadata and, 696
  method binding and, 698
  Mono project and, 4
  network communication and, 637–665
  P2P applications with, 1346–1355
  platform independence, 4
  usage conventions and, 60
  Visual Basic 2010 and, 5
  Visual C++ 2010 and, 5–6
  XML and, 903, 904, 942–943
.NET Framework 4. *See also* base classes; contra-variance; covariance; parallel programming; tuples
  base classes and, 16
  cancellation framework, 290–291, 507–510
  covariance/contra-variance and, 118
  DLR and, 295, 305

DynamicPartitionerForArray‹TSource› and, 290
HashSet‹T› and, 255
IProducerConsumerCollection‹T› and, 226
ISet‹T› and, 226
IStructuralComparable and, 147–149
IStructuralEquatable and, 147–149
LINQ providers and, 293–294
Managed Extensibility Framework. *See* MEF
mapped-memory files and, 799–800
multi-targeting, Visual Studio 2010 and, 375, 403–404
parallel programming and, 15
ParallelEnumerable and, 289
SortedSet‹T› and, 255
StaticPartitionerForArray‹TSource› and, 290
System.Collections.Concurrent and, 225, 262, 290
tuples and, 129, 146
WebBrowser control and. *See* WebBrowser control
Zip() and, 276, 284–285
.NET Framework for Silverlight, 1095, 1096. *See also* Silverlight
.NET programming, with SQL Server, 955–980
.NET Reflector, 435, 823, 1321
.NET Remoting, 13, 20, 566, 1279, 1280, 1291, 1308
.NET resource files. *See* resource files
.NET runtime. *See* CLR
net.exe utility, 683, 684
NetMsmqBinding, 1301
netMsmqBinding, 1301, 1382, 1383, 1384
NetNamedPipeBinding, 1301
NetPeerTcpBinding, 1300
NetTcpBinding, 1300, 1301, 1350, 1351
NetTcpContextBinding, 1300
network communication, 637–665. *See also* peer-to-peer networking
  client-server architecture, 1340
  modular/layered approach to, 657
  .NET Framework and, 637
  performance counters and, 484
network protocols. *See also* HTTP protocol; TCP
  lower-level, 656–657
  WCF and, 637
NetworkCredential, 642
networking (ASP.NET AJAX Library layer), 1223
networking example (Silverlight), 1102–1110
  ADO.NET Entity Data Model, 1102
  calling WCF Services, 1104–1107
  System.Net and, 1109–1110
  using WCF Data Services, 1107–1109
  WCF service for Silverlight clients, 1103–1104
NetworkStream class, 656, 787
neutral cultures, 571
Nevermore60Customer, 95, 96, 97, 98
new keyword, 27, 32
  classes/structs and, 66

hiding methods and, 92, 105
 as modifier, 100, 105
 var keyword and, 79
New Project dialog box, 379, 381, 403, 405,
 413, 1310
newline (escape sequence), 35
ngen.exe, 451–452, 459
Nikhil's Web Development Helper, 1239
node insertion (XmlDocument class), 915–917
NodeType property, 906
nonblittable data types, 701
non-CLS-compliant code, 10
nondeterministic destruction, 823
non-generic collection classes, 108, 225, 732. *See also*
 generic collection classes
non-linear animations, 1023
nonrepeatable reads, 625, 626
Norm(), 216, 217
normal messages, 1361
Northwind database, 820
 Categories table, 843, 857, 858
 Customers table, 832–833, 874, 875
 database connections and, 820–821
 Order Details table, 874, 875
 Orders table, 874, 875
 Products table, 839, 842, 843, 844
 Region table, 829–831
 stored procedures and, 829–832
NorthwindDemo/NorthwindModel.Designer.cs, 876
NorthwindDemo/Program.cs, 875
Not(), 258, 259
Nothing (permission set), 563
NoTracking, 876
NotSupportedException, 141, 143, 236
NT Services. *See* Windows Services
null
 escape sequence for, 35
 generic types and, 113, 114
null coalescing operator (??), 123, 152, 156–157
nullable types, 123
 casting, 159, 160–161
 operators and, 156
Nullable‹T›, 121, 122, 123
NullExtension (x:Null), 744
NullReferenceException, 132
number format (N), 52, 213
number formatting, cultures and, 572–573
NumberAndDateFormatting/Program.cs, 573
numeric indexers, 834

object binding (WPF), 1040–1045
Object Browser window, 393
Object class (System.Object), 84

methods, 84–86
 object keyword and, 91
object contexts, 871–873
object creation operator, 152
object keyword, 91
object model (ADO.NET), 817, 835–844
object queries, 876–879
object tracking, 880, 900
object type (reference type)
 System.Object and, 35
 uses for, 36
ObjectContext class, 871–873
 CreateQuery‹T›() of, 294
 methods, 872–873
 properties, 872–873
 System.Data.Objects and, 862
ObjectDataSource, 1162
object-oriented programming. *See also* classes;
 CTS types; data types; inheritance; interfaces;
 overriding; usage conventions
 C# and, 3
 CTS and, 9
 goto statement and, 43
 IL and, 7
 interfaces and, 100
 online information (Chapter 53) for, 7
 refactoring and, 401–403, 406, 695
 usage conventions and, 60, 64
ObjectQuery‹T›, 294, 877, 878, 883
 Query Builder methods, 876, 878–879
object-relational mapping, 861, 862. *See also* ADO.NET
 Entity Framework
objects (as instances of classes), 185
ObjectSecurity, 559
ObjectSet‹T›, 871, 876, 877, 881
ObjectStateManager, 872, 876, 880, 881, 882
observable collections, 256–258, 898–899
ObservableCollectionSample/Program.cs, 257
ObservableCollection‹T›, 256–258, 266, 728, 732, 737,
 898, 899, 1053, 1106, 1109, 1381
ODBC provider classes, 818
ODBCCommand, 819
ODBCCommandBuilder, 819
ODBCConnection, 819
ODBCDataAdapter, 819
ODBCDataReader, 819
ODBCParameter, 819
ODBCTransaction, 819
ODP.NET, 818
Offering Syndication Feeds (sample), 1390–1394
Office (project type), 381
Office Open XML (OOXML), 1089
OfType(), 278, 879
OfType‹TResult›, 275
OLE DB provider, 832, 834, 850

OLE DB provider classes, 818
OLE/COM Object Viewer, 714
OleDbCommand, 819, 826, 832, 833, 852
OleDbCommandBuilder, 819
OleDbConnection, 819
OleDbDataAdapter, 819
OleDbDataReader, 819, 832, 833, 834
OleDbParameter, 819
OleDbTransaction, 819
oleview32.exe, 714
OnCustomCommand(), 676, 678
One(), 195
one-dimensional arrays, 132
one-to-many relationship, 873, 874, 875
OnOuterButtonClick(), 736, 737
OnPause(), 676, 678, 690
OnPowerEvent(), 676, 678
OnShutdown(), 678
OnStart(), 676, 677, 678, 679, 690
OnStartUp(), 1399
OnStop(), 676, 678, 690
OOP extensions, JavaScript, 1235–1236
OOXML (Office Open XML), 1089
OPC (Open Packaging Convention), 1089
Open(), 364, 365, 773, 774
Open Packaging Convention (OPC), 1089
OpenRead(), 638, 774
open-source DLR, 295
OpenSubKey(), 810
OpenText(), 774
OpenWrite(), 639, 774
Operate(), 749, 751, 760
operation batching (data service context),
    901–902
OperationBehavior property, 1298
OperationContract, 882, 1292–1293
Operations/Operations2.cs, 761
Operations/Operations.cs, 759, 760, 762
operator overloading, 37, 67, 163–172
  classes and, 166
  operators (list) for, 171–172
  string concatenation and, 208
  Vector Struct example, 165–171
operator precedence, 157
operators, 67, 151–157. *See also* query operators;
    specific operators
  as, 152, 155
  arithmetic, 151
  assignment, 152
  binary, 156, 167, 172, 319
  cast, 152
  checked, 152, 154–155
  comparison, 151, 152, 163, 164
  conditional (ternary), 152, 154, 157, 223, 224
  decrement, 151, 153, 154

  delegate concatenation/removal, 152
  increment, 151, 153, 154
  indexing, 152
  is, 152, 155
  list of, 151–152
  logical, 151
  member access, 152
  namespace alias qualifier, 152
  null coalescing, 123, 152, 156–157
  nullable types and, 156
  object creation, 152
  overflow exception control, 152
  parentheses and, 157
  primary, 154, 157
  relational, 157
  shortcuts, 153–154
  sizeof, 152, 155–156, 323
  string concatenation, 151
  type information, 152
  typeof, 45, 152, 156, 340
  unary, 156, 157, 172, 319
  unchecked, 152, 154–155
  workings of, 164–165
optional arguments, 71
optional attribute parameters, 337
Or(), 258, 259
Oracle .NET Developer site, 818
Order Details table, 874, 875
OrderBy(), 275, 279, 280, 291, 879
OrderByDescending(), 273, 275, 279
Orders table, 874, 875
orphaned objects, 32
/out, 50
out keyword, 71, 119
out parameters, 71
Out/In (attributes), 717
out-of-browser Silverlight applications,
    1113–1115
OutOfBrowserDemo/MainPage.xaml, 1114
OutOfBrowserDemo/MainPage.xaml.cs, 1114
output filename, 416
outsourcing translations, 591
overflow checking, 154, 155, 176
overflow exception control, checked/unchecked
    operators, 152, 154–155
OverflowException, 154, 353, 354, 362
overloading. *See* method overloading; operator
    overloading
override (keyword/modifier), 91, 100, 105
overriding
  comparison operator, 163
  Equals(), 162
  methods, 91–92
  ToString(), 36, 82, 85
OverwriteChanges, 876

P

P (percentage format), 52, 213
P2P. *See* peer-to-peer networking
package files (project property), 416
PadLeft(), 208, 292
PadRight(), 208
PageCatalogPart, 1211
PageRequestManager, 1229, 1237–1238
PageRequestManager.beginRequest, 1237
PageRequestManager.endRequest, 1238
PageRequestManager.initializeRequest, 1237
PageRequestManager.pageLoaded, 1238
PageRequestManager.pageLoading, 1237
‹PagerTemplate›, 1178
paging, 285–286
Panel class, 986, 999
Panel control, 1138, 1161
Parallel activity, 1313–1314
Parallel class, 504–507
Parallel LINQ, 289–291
   cancellation framework and, 507
   threading issues and, 510
parallel programming, 15
ParallelEnumerable, 289
ParallelEnumerable class, 289, 290
Parallel.For(), 504–506
   cancellation of, 507–509
   for loop *v.*, 504
Parallel.ForEach(), 506–507
Parallel.Invoke(), 507
ParallelLinqSample/Program.cs, 289
ParallelQuery‹TSource›, 289, 290
ParallelSamples/Program.cs, 504, 506, 507
‹param›, 53
ParameterizedThreadStart, 495, 496, 497
ParameterResourceFile, 479
parameters
   arrays as, 139–140
   and constructors, in hierarchy, 97–98
   for custom attributes, 336–337
   Lambda expressions and, 198
   out, 71
   passed to methods, 69–70
   ref, 70
   zero-parameter constructor, 76, 82
ParameterTest.cs, 69–70
‹paramref›, 53
Parent (DirectoryInfo), 773
parentheses, operator precedence and, 157
Parse(), 744
ParseCombiningCharacters(), 570
partial classes, 82–83
partial keyword, 82, 83
Partitioner class, 290

partitioning operators (query operator category), 276, 285–286
parts (add-ins), 748, 749
   lazy loading of, 764–765
   loading of, 748
Pascal casing, 60–61
passing arguments to Main(), 49–50
passing data to threads, 496–497
PasswordBox, 995
PasswordRecovery, 1203
Path class, 772, 775, 987
PATH index, 978
PathGeometry, 988
PathSeparator, 775
pattern, 219
Payments table, 873, 874
PaymentsDemo/Program.cs, 874
PCSAjaxWebSite, 1224–1226
PCSAuthenticationDemo, 1201–1205
   Forms Authentication and, 1201–1202
   login system and, 1202–1203
   PCSWebParts and, 1212
   securing directories, 1204
PCSCustomCWebSite1 (custom control), 1193–1195
PCSDemoSite
   master pages in, 1197–1198
   navigating in, 1200–1201
   security in, 1204–1206
   site map file added to, 1199–1200
   themes in, 1208–1210
   user controls in, 1190–1191
PCSDynamicDataDemoEntities, 1252–1258
PCSDynamicDataDemoLinq web site, 1252–1258
PCSLibraryDemo project, 1234–1241
PCSRoutingDemo, 1245–1250
PCSUserCWebApp1 (user control), 1187–1190
PCSWebParts, 1212–1218
   in action, 1213–1215
   controls for, 1213
   Date/Events controls, 1218
   host page code, 1216–1217
   PCSAuthenticationDemo and, 1212
   Web Part code, 1217
PCSWebSite1 (ASP.NET), 1152–1158
   creating, 1152–1153
   running, 1157–1158
   web page added to, 1153
   web server controls added to, 1156–1157
PCSWebsite2 (event-booking example), 1164–1169
PCSWebSite3, 1169–1175
   Calendar control and, 1172–1174
   FormView control and, 1178–1179
   ListView control and, 1178–1179

PCSWebSite3 (*continued*)
  MeetingRoomBooker.mdf, 1169–1171
        binding to, 1171
        events added to, 1174–1175
        tables, 1170
  templates and, 1178–1180
Peek(), 237, 240
Peer Name Resolution Protocol (PNRP), 1339,
        1343–1346, 1355
  clouds, 1344–1345
  IDs, 1344
  in Windows 7, 1345–1346
peer names
  defined, 1343
  registering, 1347–1348
  resolving, 1348–1349
peer presence, 1352, 1353
PeerCollaboration class, 1352
PeerPresenceStatus enumeration, 1352–1353
peers, 1342
  contacts and, 1353
  defined, 1341, 1342
  discovering, 1353
  groups of, 1342. *See also* clouds
  signing in/signing out, 1352
PeerScope, 1352
peer-to-peer networking (P2P), 1339–1355
  architecture, 1340–1342
        challenges, 1341–1342
        client-server architecture *v.*, 1340–1341
  communication and, 1341, 1342
  connection and, 1341, 1342
  discovery and, 1341–1342
  Microsoft Windows Peer-to-Peer Networking
        platform, 1343–1346
  overview, 1339–1343
  PNM. *See* People Near Me
  PNRP and, 1339, 1343–1346, 1355
  sample applications, 1346–1355
  solutions, 1342–1343
  System.Net.PeertoPeer, 1347–1352
  System.Net.PeertoPeer.Collaboration, 1352–1355
  terminology, 1342
Peer-to-Peer Networking platform (Microsoft
        Windows), 1343–1346
People Near Me (PNM), 1339, 1346
  signing in/signing out, 1352–1353
percentage format (P), 52, 213
perfmon.exe. *See* Performance Monitor
performance
  collection classes and, 264–266
  exceptions and, 351
  garbage collection and, 311–312
  generics and, 108
  IL and, 4–5

pointers and, 317, 329–332
processes and, 12
performance counter builder, 484–486
performance counts, 461, 484, 485, 486, 487, 488
Performance Monitor (perfmon.exe), 375, 461, 478,
        488–489, 692
performance monitoring, 483–489
PerformanceCounter, 483
PerformanceCounter components, 486–489
PerformanceCounterCategory, 483, 484, 485,
        486, 487
PerformanceCounterDemo/MainWindow.xaml.cs, 485,
        486, 487
PerformanceCounterInstaller, 483
Perl, 217, 218. *See also* regular expressions
‹permission›, 53
permission sets, 563–564
permissions, 562–567
  code access, CLR and, 562–563
  demanding permissions programmatically, 564–565
  implicit, 566–567
  Sandbox API and, 562, 565–566
PersonComparer, 138
phantom reads, 625, 626
PhoneCustomer class, 66
Pick activity, 1314–1316, 1321, 1328, 1330, 1331
PictureBox control, 1136–1137
pin buttons, 394
pinning/unpinning windows, 394
p/invoke. *See* platform invoke
P/Invoke Interop Assistant, 723
pinvoke.net, 723
PInvokeSample/NativeMethods.cs, 725
PlaceHolder, 1161
platform independence (.NET), 4
platform invoke (p/invoke), 16, 632, 722–726, 799,
        1398, 1402, 1408
PLINQ Execution Engine, 15
pluggable controls, 652
PNM. *See* People Near Me
PNRP. *See* Peer Name Resolution Protocol
PnrpPermission, 1349
PnrpPermissionAttribute, 1349
pointer member access operator (->), 323–324
PointerPlayground, 325–329
PointerPlayground/Program.cs, 326
PointerPlayground.sln, 327
pointers, 8, 11, 12, 32
  adding, 322
  arithmetic operations on, 322–323
  array syntax and, 331
  backward compatibility and, 317
  casting
        between pointer types, 321
        pointers to integer types, 320–321

to class members, 324–325
to classes, 324
code access security and, 318
example (PointerPlayground), 325–329
memory access with, 317–325
performance and, 317, 329–332
QuickArray example, 331–332
reasons for, 317
reference types and, 317
to structs, 323–324
subtracting, 323
syntax, 319–320
type safety and, 8, 318
unsafe code and, 317–319
void, 321
poison messages, 1359
poison queue, 1359
polling, 493
PolyBezierSegment, 989
Polygon class, 987
Polyline class, 987
PolyLineSegment, 989
PolyQuadraticBezierSegment, 989
Pop(), 240, 241, 263, 265
POP protocol, 656
POST, 639, 656
PostBuildEvent, 414
postconditions, 464
postfix/prefix, 153
#pragma, 58
PreBuildEvent, 414
precedence, operator, 157
preconditions, 463–464
preconfigured host classes, 1303–1304
predefined integer types, 33
predefined reference types, 35–37
predefined value types, 33–35
prefix/postfix, 153
Prepare(), 627
preparing phase (transactions), 606
preprocessor directives, 55–58, 387. *See also* custom
    attributes
prerequisites URL, 416
PreserveChanges, 876
PreviewMouseMove, 736
primary key constraints (DataTable), 842
primary operators, 154, 157
principal, identity and, 545–547
PrintDialog, 1091
printing, 1091–1093
    with PrintDialog, 1091
    visuals, 1092–1093
    with WebBrowser control, 651
PrintingDemo/MainWindow.xaml.cs, 1093
PrintingPermission, 563
priority, thread, 498–499

priority binding, 1049–1051
priority messages, 1372–1373
priority node, 242, 244, 245
PriorityDocumentManager, 243, 244, 246
private (modifier), 66, 99
private assemblies, 14–15, 434, 447, 448, 452, 453, 454,
    459. *See also* shared assemblies
private inheritance (C++), 90
private queues, 1361
private/public keys, 552–554
‹probing›, 454
Process class, 643
ProcessAndDisplayNumber(), 189, 190, 194, 195
ProcessDocuments, 238, 239
processes. *See also* application domains
    code isolation and, 11–12
    performance and, 12
    security and, 12
ProcessRequestForMessage(), 886
ProductCode, 414
product.cs, 846, 847, 848, 849
ProductDataTable, 846–847
ProductName (project property), 414
ProductRow class, 848–849
Products table, 839, 842, 843, 844
Products.xsd, 844
Professional ASP.NET4: in C# and VB (Wiley
    Publishing), 247, 1156, 1181
Professional Microsoft SQL Server 2008 Programming
    (Wiley Publishing), 955
Professional XML (Wiley Publishing), 904
ProgId attribute, 716
progress (dialog box), 424
ProgressBar, 995
ProgressBar control, 1137
ProgressChangedEventArgs, 538, 1349
projection operators (query operator category), 275
projects (Visual Studio 2010). *See* Visual
    Studio 2010
promotable transactions, 614–616
properties, 67, 72–74. *See also specific properties*
    access modifiers for, 73
    attached, 739–741
    as attributes (XAML), 730–731
    auto-implemented, 74
    dependency, 732–736, 739
    as elements (XAML), 731
    exports (MEF) and, 759–760
    methods *v.*, 64
    project, 414–415
    read-only, 73
    System.Exception, 359–360
    System.Type, 340–341
    usage guidelines, 64
    virtual, 91–92
    write-only, 73

Properties editor, 675
Properties window, 391–392
Property (project property), 419
PROPERTY index, 978
property triggers, 1008–1009, 1014
PropertyChangedEventManager, 204
PropertyGridEditorPart, 1212
protected (modifier), 66, 99
protected internal (modifier), 66, 99
protocol stack, 657
providers. *See* data providers
proxy servers, WebRequest and, 642
ProxyWebPartManager, 1211
public (modifier), 66, 99
public keys
  assembly manifests and, 433, 446, 448
  public/private key pairs, 552–554
  strong names and, 445
  Trusted Application Deployment and, 421
public queues, 1361
publisher policy files, 453, 457–458
publishing ClickOnce applications, 420
publishing web sites, 408, 411
pure virtual function, 93. *See also* abstract functions
Push(), 240, 263, 265
Python, 295, 300, 302, 305

Q

QuadraticBezierSegment, 989
quantifier operators (query operator category), 276
queries
  to dynamic XML documents, 949–951
  LINQ queries
    deferred query execution, 272, 273–275
    Formula-1 champions and, 267–286
  to static XML documents, 948–949
  URL queries to WCF Data Services, 893–894
  to XML data types, 976–977
Query Analyzer, 851, 857
Query Builder methods, 876, 878–879
query operators
  aggregate operators, 276, 286–287
  conversion operators, 276, 287–288
  element operators, 276
  filtering operators, 275, 277–278
  generation operators, 276, 288–289
  grouping operators, 276, 280–281
  join operators, 276, 282–283
  list of, 275–276
  partitioning operators, 276, 285–286
  projection operators, 275
  quantifier operators, 276
  set operators, 276, 283–284
  sorting operators, 275, 279–280
query string parameters, 1245–1246

Queryable class, 294
Queryable⟨T⟩, 291
querying objects, 876–879
QueryInterface(), 698, 702, 705, 708, 713, 719
QueryTimeout, 872
queues. *See also* message queues
  collections and, 236–240
  poison, 1359
QueueSample/Document.cs, 237
QueueSample/DocumentManager.cs, 238
QueueSample/ProcessDocuments.cs, 239
QueueSample/Program.cs, 239
Queue⟨T⟩ class, 28, 237, 240, 262, 265
QuickArray, 331–332
QuickSort algorithm, 136
Quote service (application example), 670–692
  client, 670, 673–675
    QuoteClient, 670, 673–675
  completed application, 692
  creating functionality for, 671–673
  event logging, 692, 693
  overview, 670
  QuoteService (Windows Service program), 670, 675–683
    configuration in registry, 679
    creating, 675–676
    handler methods, 678
    installation program, 679–683
    main function, 676–677
    monitoring/controlling, 683–691
    service start, 677–678
    ServiceBase class, 676
  server, 670
    QuoteServer, 670
    socket server, 670, 671, 677
  TestQuoteServer, 673
  troubleshooting, 692
QuoteClient/MainWindow.xaml.cs, 674
QuoteServer/QuoteServer.cs, 671
QuoteService/Program.cs, 677
QuoteService/ProjectInstaller.cs, 680
QuoteService/ProjectInstaller.Designer.cs, 681
QuoteService/QuoteService.cs, 677

R

/r switch, 50, 51
race conditions, 15, 510–513
Racer class, 227, 267–269
RacerComparer, 234, 235
RAD (Rapid Application Development), 406
RadialGradientBrush, 992
radio buttons (dialog box), 424
RadioButton controls, 1126–1127, 1160
RadioButtonList, 1160
Range(), 276, 288, 289

ranges
  bool type, 35
  decimal type, 34
  floating-point types, 34
  integer types, 33
RangeValidator, 1164
rank (dimension), 132, 134, 136
Rapid Application Development (RAD), 406
rc.exe, 482
RCW (runtime callable wrapper), 702, 707–709, 710, 712, 726
RDF (Resource Description Framework), 1387. *See also* RSS
read me (dialog box), 424
read methods (XmlReader), 907–909
ReadAllByes(), 785, 786
ReadAllLines(), 785, 786
ReadAllText(), 785, 786
ReadCommitted (isolation level), 625, 825
ReadElementString(), 907, 908
ReaderWriterLockSlim, 530–533
ReaderWriterSample/Program.cs, 532
ReadFileIntoStringCollection(), 798
reading ACLs
  from directory, 803–804
  from file, 802–803
reading drive information, 800–802
reading from streams, 787
reading from XML documents, 951–952
reading XAML, 744–745
ReadingACLsFromDirector.cs, 804
ReadingACLs.sln, 803
ReadingFiles.sln, 785
reading/writing
  to files, 784–787
      binary files, 789–793
      text files, 793–799
  to isolated storage, 810–814
  to registry, 806–810
read-only collections, 236
readonly fields, 77, 78–79
read-only properties, 73
ReadSettings(), 811, 813
ReadUncommitted (isolation level), 625, 825
ReadWriteText (sample application), 797–799
ReadWriteText.sln, 797, 798
ReadXML(), 851, 932, 933
ReadXMLSchema(), 933
Really Simple Syndication. *See* RSS
Receive activity, 1327, 1328, 1329
receiving messages, 1368–1370
recoverable delivery mode (messages), 1361
recoverable messages, 1372–1373
Rectangle class, 987
RectangleCollection class, 120
RectangleGeometry, 988

RedirectToAction(), 1269
ref keyword, 70
ref parameters, 70
refactoring, 401–403, 406, 695
/reference, 50
reference counts, 10, 696
reference types, 309–311
  arrays and, 131–132
  defined, 8
  memory management and, 309–311
  object type. *See* object type
  pointers and, 317
  predefined, 35–37
  string type. *See* string type
  value types *v.*, 8, 32–33
ReferenceEquals(), 84, 162, 163
references (to assemblies), 450–451
referent, 317
reflection, 15, 333–349
  capabilities of, 333
  defined, 333
  dynamic keyword and, 754
  InvokeMember() and, 440
  System.Type and, 85, 156, 340–342
  TypeView example, 342–344
ReflectionModelServices, 748
ReflectionPermission, 563
Reflector (.NET Reflector), 435, 823, 1321
Refresh(), 649, 767, 873, 883
RefreshButton_Click(), 1351, 1354
REG_BINARY, 808
REG_DWORD, 808
regedit, 679, 806–808
regedt32, 806
RegexOptions enumeration, 220
#region, 57, 387, 1120
Region table (Northwind database), 829–831
RegionInfo, 571
RegionInsert stored procedure, 853, 857
regions, 570–574. *See also* cultures
register user (dialog box), 424
RegisterAttached(), 739
registering peer names, 1347–1348
registration, COM, 698–699, 718
RegistrationService, 1103, 1106
registry, 806–810
  classes, 808–810
  file system *v.*, 806, 807
  reading/writing to, 806–810
Registry class, 806, 808
Registry editor, 422
registry hives, 807
registry keys, 807
RegistryKey, 806
  methods, 810
  properties, 810

RegistryPermission, 563
REG_SZ, 808
regular expressions, 217–224
   Beginning Regular Expressions and, 218
   captures and, 223–224
   escape sequences, 218, 221
   groups and, 223–224
   matches and, 219, 223–224
   strings and, 218
RegularExpressionsPlayaround, 219–223
RegularExpressionsPlayaround.cs, 219
RegularExpressionValidator, 1164
rehosting Designer. *See* Designer rehosting
relational operators, 157
relationships (ADO.NET Entity Framework),
   873–876
Release(), 525, 696, 705, 708, 709, 713
release builds, debugging and, 395–396
ReleaseInstanceMode, 1298
ReleaseServiceInstanceOnTransactionComplete,
   1294
releasing COM objects, 708–709
reloading workflows, 1326
‹remarks›, 54
remoting services. *See* .NET Remoting
RemoveHandler(), 738
RemovePreviousVersions, 414
RemoveRange(), 232
Repeat(), 276, 288, 289
RepeatableRead (isolation level), 625, 825
RepeatBehavior, 1022
RepeatButton, 995
Repeater, 1163, 1175
Replace(), 208, 209, 210, 211, 212
report messages, 1361
report queues, 1363
Reports Application, 381
Representational State Transfer (REST), 1281, 1282
request, 1181
RequiredFieldValidator, 1164, 1257
RequireFileIOPermissionsDemo/
   RequirePermissionsDemo.cs, 565
Requires(), 463
Reset(), 141
Resolve(), 655
resolving peer names, 1348–1349
Resource Compiler, 482
Resource Description Framework (RDF), 1387.
   See also RSS
resource dictionaries
  localization and, 594–598
  XAML, 594–598
Resource File Generator, 579–580
resource files (.NET resource files). *See also* message
   resource files

automatic fallback for, 590
  creating, 579
  custom, 590
  localization and, 579–584
  outsourcing translations with, 591
  System.Resources and, 569, 580, 584, 603
  using, 581–584
  WPF and, 594
Resource Localization Editor, Windows, 591
resource managers, 606
  custom, 626–632
  IEnlistmentNotification methods and,
    626–627
  transaction classes and, 626
resource readers, 598–600, 603
ResourceDemo/Demo.Designer.cs, 584
ResourceDemo/Program.cs, 582
ResourceDictionary, 1005, 1007, 1008
ResourceHolder.cs, 316
ResourceManager, 584
resources, transactional, 627–632
resources (WPF), 1004–1008
  accessing, from code, 1006
  dynamic, 1006–1007
  hierarchies and, 1005
  styles and, 1004
  system-wide, 1005
ResourceSet, 584
ResourcesLib/Dictionary1.xaml, 1007
Resources/Wrox.ProCSharp.Localization.
   MyResources.txt, 579
ResourceWriter, 580, 584
response messages, 1361
response queues, 1363, 1377
REST (Representational State Transfer),
   1281, 1282
Restart Manager, 1398–1403
RestaurantDataServiceWeb/RestaurantDataService.
   svc.cs, 895
RestaurantEntities, 896, 897, 898
results, from tasks, 503–504
ResXFileRef, 584
ResXGen, 580
ResXResourceReader, 584
ResXResourceSet, 584
ResXResourceWriter, 584
Retry activity, 1319, 1320, 1321, 1322
return statement, 44
‹returns›, 54
Reverse(), 144, 145, 235, 275
rhs (right-hand side), 167
RichTextBox control, 793, 995, 1137–1138
RichTextBox viewer, 1085
RichTextBoxStreamType, 1137, 1138
right-hand side (rhs), 167

RightToLeft, 220
Rijandel, 554
role-based security, 547–548, 568
  ASP.NET and, 547
  code access security *v.*, 11
  declarative, 547–548
RoleBasedSecurity/Program.cs, 548
Rollback(), 611, 627, 679, 680
Room table, 841
RoomReservation service (WCF), 1282–1290
  custom service host, 1287
  diagnostics, 1289–1290
  implementation, 1284, 1294
  service contract, 1283–1284
  WCF client, 1288–1289
  WCF Service Host, 1284–1286
  WCF Test Client, 1284–1286
Root property (DirectoryInfo), 774
RotateTransform, 990
rotating, 990
rotation (3-D with WPF), 1032
round-robin scheduling principle, 498, 499
route authorization, 1247
route order, 1248–1249
route parameters, 1249–1250
RouteData values, 1249
routing (ASP.NET), 1244–1251
  configuring, 1258–1259
  default parameter values, 1247–1248
  defining routes, 1246–1249
  parameter constraints, 1248
  PCSRoutingDemo, 1245–1250
  query string parameters, 1245–1246
  URL operation, 1266–1267
RowDefinition, 1001
RSA algorithm, 554
RSACryptoServiceProvider, 554
RSS (Really Simple Syndication), 1387,
    1389, 1390, 1393, 1394. *See also*
      Atom format
  Atom and, 1387, 1388
  dynamic XML documents and, 949–950
  logo, 1388
Rss20FeedFormatter, 1388
Rss20ItemFormatter, 1388
Ruby, 295
Rule enumeration, 843–844
Run(), 238
RunPostBuildEvent, 414
runtime callable wrapper. *See* RCW
runtime schema generation, 839
runtime serialization, 1291, 1368

S

SACL (system access control list), 559
safe (safety level), 956
SAFEARRAY, 701
safe-critical code, 561
SafeHandle class, 632, 726
SalesSpyFoundException, 363, 366, 367, 368
Sample1/Person.cs, 131
Sample1/Program.cs (arrays), 132, 133, 134, 135, 136
SampleRoleProvider, 550
Sandbox API, 561, 562, 565–566
satellite assemblies, 434, 579, 581, 588, 590, 594, 597,
    598, 603
SaveChanges(), 873, 882, 900, 901, 1103
SaveFile(), 797
SaverAccount, 103, 104
SaveSettings(), 811
SAX, 903, 904, 906. *See also* XmlReader; XmlWriter
sbyte, 33
scaffolding, 1251, 1252–1253
  controlling, 1255–1257
  defined, 1251
scalar, 165, 167, 168, 170
ScaleTransform, 990
scaling, 990
sc.exe utility, 683, 684
schemas (data tables), 835
  generation, 839–840
  hand-coded, 839–840
  XML, 844–850
scientific format (E/e), 52, 213
SCM. *See* Service Control Manager
scope
  local variable, 29–31
  transaction scope, 824–825
ScopeBad.cs, 30
scope.Complete(), 824
Scope.cs, 29
ScopeTest2.cs, 30
ScriptEngine, 300, 301, 302
ScriptManager, 1222, 1228–1229
ScriptRuntime (DLR), 300–302
Scripts directory, 1261
ScriptScope, 301, 302
ScriptSource, 301, 302
ScrollBar control, 995
ScrollViewer, 995
sealed (keyword/modifier), 94, 100
sealed classes, 94
sealed methods, 94
SearchPath, 415
secure transfer, key exchange and, 556–558
SecureTransfer/Program.cs, 556

security, 545–568. *See also* ACLs; authentication/
    authorization; code access security
  ASP.NET and, 1201–1206
  ClickOnce applications and, 421–422
  encryption and, 552–558, 568
  files and, 771, 802, 814
  in PCSDemoSite, 1204–1206
  processes and, 12
  SQL programming and, 956
Security Setup Wizard, 1201–1203
security transparency level 2, 561, 562
security-critical code, 561
SecurityException, 548, 564, 565
SecurityPermission, 563
‹see›, 54
‹seealso›, 54
seed server, 1344
SELECT, 819, 828, 833, 850, 860
Select(), 273, 275, 277, 279, 281, 289, 290, 291, 879,
    918, 920, 1172, 1391
SelectAncestors(), 918
SelectChildren(), 918
SelectDescendants(), 918, 920
‹SelectedItemTemplate›, 1177
SelectMany(), 275, 278, 279
SelectSingleNode(), 915, 918, 974
SelectValue(), 879
SelfPlacingWindow sample, 811, 812, 813, 814
Semaphore, 524–525
Semaphore/Program.cs, 524
SemaphoreSlim, 524–525
semicolons (;)
  C# and, 25
  Lambda expressions and, 198
  preprocessor directives and, 56
Send activity, 1327
sending messages, 1366–1368
‹SeparatorTemplate›, 1177
Serial.cs (code snippet), 935, 937, 938, 939, 940, 941
Serializable (isolation level), 625, 825
serialization
  defined, 771, 934
  runtime, 1291, 1368
  XML and, 934–942, 1291, 1368
Serialize(), 934, 935, 942
server console application (Socket class), 662–663
server control event-booking example, 1164–1169
  updating, 1169–1175
server controls. *See* ASP.NET server controls
Server Explorer, 476, 484, 486, 683, 684
Server Explorer window, 393–394, 1170
server-side controls, 18
service behavior, 1294–1295
service configuration program, 668, 670
service contracts, 1291, 1292–1293
Service Control Manager (SCM), 669

ServiceBase class and, 676
service control programs, 668, 670
service implementation (WCF), 1294–1299
service programs, 668–669
Service Trace Viewer tool, 474, 1290
ServiceBase class, 670, 676
ServiceBehavior properties, 1294–1295
ServiceCommandCallback(), 676
ServiceContract attribute, 886, 1292–1293
ServiceControl/app.manifest, 691
ServiceController class, 670, 693
  custom service controller and, 684–692
  methods, 690
  properties, 685
ServiceControllerInfo, 685, 686, 687, 688, 689, 690
ServiceControllerPermission, 563
ServiceControl/ServiceControllerInfo.cs, 686
ServiceControl/ServiceControlWindow.xaml, 689
ServiceControl/ServiceControlWindow.xaml.cs,
  688, 691
ServiceHost, 889, 895, 1287, 1301, 1303, 1328, 1381
ServiceInstaller class, 670, 679, 680, 682, 693
  properties, 682
ServiceInstallerDialog, 682
service-main function, 669
ServiceMainCallback(), 676, 677
ServiceModel Metadata Utility tool, 1304, 1305,
  1329
ServiceName, 675, 682, 685
ServiceProcessInstaller class, 670, 679, 680, 681,
  682, 693
services. *See* Windows Services
Services MMC snap-in, 616, 669, 683
ServicesDependentOn, 682, 685
Services.exe, 677
ServicesToRun, 676, 677
ServiceType, 685
session, 1181
Set(), 258, 259
set accessor, 732, 733
set operators (query operator category), 276, 283–284
Set Service Login dialog box, 682
SetAccessControl(), 560, 805, 810
SetAll(), 258, 259
SetLastError, 724
sets, 255–256
SetSample/Program.cs, 255
Setup Projects, 412
Setup Wizard, 412
SetValue(), 134, 135, 628, 629, 733, 739, 809, 810, 953
SHA algorithms, 554
Shakespeare's plays, as XML files, 943
shallow comparison, 170
Shape class, 986
ShapeDisplay class, 121
shapes (WPF), 986–987. *See also specific shapes*

ShapesDemo/MainWindow.xaml, 987
shared assemblies, 15, 434, 445–454
  binding to, 453–454
  creating, 447
  GAC and, 15, 446–875
  installing, 448
  publisher policy files and, 457–458
  references to, 450–451
  removing, 451
  strong names and, 15, 445–448
  using, 448–449
  versioning and, 454–458
shared classes (ADO.NET), 818–819
SharedDemo/SharedDemo.cs, 447
shield icons, 1405–1406
shopping cart application (discount application),
    300–302
short, 33
ShowFonts/ShowFontsWindow.xaml, 1076
sign assemblies, 567
signatures
  delayed signing of assemblies, 449–450
  ECDSA algorithm and, 554–556
SignIn(), 1352
signing in/signing out (PNM), 1352–1353
SigningDemo/Program.cs, 555
SignOut(), 1352
Silverlight, 1095–1115
  browser integration, 1110–1113
      calling out to JavaScript, 1111
      JavaScript calling Silverlight, 1112–1113
  DLR and, 295
  .NET Framework for, 1095, 1096
  networking, 1102
  networking example, 1102–1110
      ADO.NET Entity Data Model, 1102
      calling WCF Services, 1104–1107
      System.Net and, 1109–1110
      using WCF Data Services, 1107–1109
      WCF service for Silverlight clients, 1103–1104
  out-of-browser applications, 1113–1115
  projects
      creating, 1097
      navigation between pages, 1097–1101
  sandboxing and, 561
  WPF *v.*, 1095–1097
  XAML and, 727, 728, 745
Silverlight Application (project type), 380
Silverlight Class Library, 380
Silverlight Navigation Application, 380, 1097. *See also*
    EventRegistration
SilverlightDemos, 1097
SilverlightDemos.Web, 1097
  SilverlightDemos.Web/EventRegistrationDataService
    .svc.cs, 1108
  SilverlightDemos.Web/IRegistrationService.cs, 1103

SilverlightDemos.Web/JavaScripInteropTestPage.
    html, 1111, 1112
SilverlightDemos.Web/RegistrationService.svc.cs, 1104
SilverlightDemos.Web/SilverlightDemosTestPage.
    html, 1097
SilverlightDemos.Web/Web.config, 1104
simple arrays, 129–132
simple controls (WPF), 994–995
Simple Object Access Protocol. *See* SOAP
Simple Service Discovery Protocol (SSDP), 1345
Simple TCP/IP Services, 668, 671
SimpleCalculator, 749, 755, 759, 768
SimpleCalculator/Calculator.cs, 750, 760, 761, 762
SimpleCalculator/Operation.cs, 750
SimpleContract/ICalculator.cs, 749
SimpleContract/IOperation.cs, 749
SimpleCurrency2/Program.cs, 181
SimpleCurrency/Program.cs, 173–174
SimpleDelegate/MathOperations.cs, 188
SimpleDelegate/Program.cs, 189
SimpleExceptions.cs, 356–357
SimpleHost/Program.cs, 751
Single (element operator), 276
single quotation mark ('), escape sequence for, 35
SingleLine, 220
single-line comments, 25, 53
SingleOrDefault, 276
single-threaded apartments. *See* STAs
sink object, 701, 720, 721–722
site local clouds, 1345
site map XML file (.sitemap), 1199–1200
site navigation (ASP.NET), 1198–1201
.sitemap. *See* site map XML file
SiteMapDataSource, 1162
SiteMapPath, 1199
sizeof operator, 152, 155–156, 323
skewing, 990
SkewTransform, 990
Skip(), 276, 285, 879, 1068, 1071
SkipVerification (permission set), 563
SkipWhile(), 276, 286
Sleep(), 492, 499, 1050
Slider control, 995
smart client applications, 21, 380, 407,
    409, 983, 1117, 1385
Smart Device Cab Projects, 412
"smart pointer" class, 718, 719
SMTP, 652, 653, 656, 657, 658
SmtpClient class, 656, 657–658
sn - k mykey.snk, 447, 449
Snapshot (isolation level), 625
SOAP (Simple Object Access Protocol), 1281
Socket class, 656, 661–665
  client console application and, 663–664
  server console application and, 662–663
socket server (for Quote service), 670, 671, 677

SocketPermission, 563
SolicitColdCall, 362, 363, 365, 367, 369
SolicitColdCall.cs, 365, 367
SolidColorBrush, 991
Solution Explorer, 384, 385, 386
Solution Property Pages dialog box, 413
solutions
  defined, 383
  projects *v.*, 383–386
SomeMethod(), 316
sort(), 136, 190, 191, 234, 235, 271
sorted dictionaries, 254
sorted lists, 246–247
SortedDictionary‹TKey, TValue›, 254, 265, 266
SortedListSample/Program.cs, 247
SortedList‹TKey, TValue›, 246, 247, 254, 265, 266
SortedSet‹string›, 256
SortedSet‹T›, 255, 265, 266
sorting
  array elements, 136–139
  cultures and, 578–579
  elements (in lists), 234–235
  Finnish sort example, 578
sorting operators (query operator category), 275,
    279–280
SortingDemo/Program.cs, 578
SortingSample/Person.cs, 137, 138
SortingSample/Program.cs, 136, 137, 138, 139
source journaling, 1362
Source property
  EventLog class, 478
  System.Exception, 359
SourceExists(), 478
SourceFilter, 472
sp_ prefix, 859
special folders, 1407
SpecialFolder enumeration, 1407
Specialization/Program.cs, 127
specializations, generic methods and, 126–128
specific cultures, 571
SpecularMaterial, 1030
SpeedExport, 761, 762
SpeedExportAttribute, 761
SpeedRatio, 1022
SpinLock struct, 522
splash (dialog box), 424
Split(), 208
SplitContainer control, 1139
SQL Server, 955–980. *See also* T-SQL
  AdventureWorks database and, 955, 965, 967, 970
  CLR and, 955–980
  Configuration Manager, 669
  data types, 818
  Enterprise Manager, 858
  key generation with, 857–858

as .NET runtime host, 956–957
Professional Microsoft SQL Server 2008
    Programming, 955
provider, 832, 834, 860
provider classes, 818
Query Analyzer, 851, 857
security and, 956
stored procedures, 967–969
System.Data.Sql, 818, 822
System.Data.SqlClient, 818, 822, 866, 957,
    968, 969
System.Data.SqlTypes, 818
UDTs with, 963
user-defined functions and, 969–970
XML data types and, 972–980
SQLClientPermission, 563
SqlCommand, 495, 599, 819, 852, 963, 967, 968
SqlCommandBuilder, 819
SqlConnection, 819
SqlContext, 957, 968, 971
SqlCoordinate, 958–964
SqlDataAdapter, 819
SqlDataReader, 819
SqlDataRecord, 957, 971
SqlDataSource, 1162
SqlFunctionAttribute, 957
SqlParameter, 819
SqlPipe, 957, 967, 968
SqlProcedureAttribute, 957
SqlSamplesUsingAdventureWorks/CalcHash.cs, 969
SqlSamplesUsingAdventureWorks/
    GetCustomerOrdersCLR.cs, 968
SqlSamplesUsingAdventureWorks/InsertContact.cs,
    971
SqlSamplesUsingAdventureWorks/SampleSum.cs, 966
SqlTransaction, 819
SqlTrigger, 970
SqlTriggerAttribute, 957
SqlTriggerContext, 957, 971
SqlTypes/SqlCoordinate.cs, 960
SqlUserDefinedAttribute, 957
SqlUserDefinedType, 960
square brackets [ ]
  escape sequences and, 221
  pointers and, 330
SSDL (Storage Schema Definition Language), 861, 863,
    864, 865, 867, 884
SSDP (Simple Service Discovery Protocol), 1345
stack pointer, 308, 309, 310, 320
stackalloc command, 329–330
stack-based arrays, 329–331
StackOverflowException, 352, 353
StackPanel, 999–1000
stacks, 240–241
  as LIFO containers, 240

memory allocation on, 308–311
value types and, 8, 32, 308–309
StackSample/Program.cs, 241
Stack‹T›, 240, 265
StackTrace (System.Exception), 359
Start(), 16, 184, 238, 239
starting tasks, 501–502
StartType property (ServiceInstaller class), 682
StartupPath, 1119
STAs (single-threaded apartments), 699, 710, 718, 719
state management, in ASP.NET, 1151
StateService class, 1296
StateService sample (WCF), 1295–1299
    client application and, 1297–1298
    error handling, 129–1299
static (modifier/keyword), 84, 100
static classes, 84
static constructors, 75–77
static Equals(), 162
static members, of generic classes, 117–118
StaticClass, 297, 298
StaticDemo‹T›, 117, 118
StaticExtension (x:Static), 744
StaticPartitionerForArray‹TSource›, 290
StaticResource, 1006, 1007
StaticResourceExtension, 741, 742
Status (ServiceController class), 685
StatusBarItem, 995
stepping between languages, 7, 8
Stop(), 649
Storage Schema Definition Language. *See* SSDL
stored procedures
    calling, 829–832
        returns nothing, 829–831
        returns output parameters, 831–832
    CLR, 967–969
    as commands, 825
    in data adapter, 851
    naming conventions, 859–860
    sp_ prefix and, 859
    SQL Server and, 967–969
    triggers as, 970–972
    T-SQL, 956, 967–969
StoredProcedure, 826
StoredProcs.cs, 830, 831
StoredProcs.sql, 830, 831, 851, 857, 858
storing entity changes, 882–883
Stream class, 787
StreamReader class, 365, 366, 639, 660, 662
    constructors and, 794–795
    in hierarchy of stream-related classes, 788
    new options, 794
    ReadWriteText sample, 797–799
streams, 353, 774, 787–788
    buffered, 788–789

EndOfStreamException and, 353
    reading from, 787
    stream-related classes (hierarchy), 787–788
    writing to, 787
StreamWriter class, 787
    constructing, 796–797
    in hierarchy of stream-related classes, 788
    ReadWriteText sample, 797–799
String class (System.String), 35, 208–209
    methods (list), 208
string concatenation, 208
string concatenation operator (+), 151
string type (reference type), 35, 36–37
StringBuilder (System.Text.StringBuilder), 207, 210–212
    members, 211–212
    methods, 212
    properties, 210, 211
StringCollection, 230, 797
StringEncoder.cs, 209
StringExample.cs, 36
String.Format(), 86
StringInfo, 570
strings, 207–217
    building, 207, 209–212
    format, 52, 212–217
    formatting process (diagram), 215
    as immutable, 36, 70, 209
    regular expressions and, 218. *See also* regular
        expressions
    Unicode characters and, 37
strong data typing, 8–13
    C# and, 157
    IL and, 8–13, 157
    language interoperability and, 8–9, 157
    XML data types, 979–980
strong name tool, 447
strong names, 15, 445–448
    creating, 447–448
    culture and, 445
    integrity with, 446
strongly typed XML, 979–980. *See also* strong data
        typing
StronglyTypedResourceBuilder, 583, 584
StructLayout attributes, 334
structs, 80–82
    classes *v.*, 65–66, 81–82, 90
    constructors for, 82
    fields and, 81
    inheritance and, 82, 90
    managed heaps and, 80, 87
    new keyword and, 66
    pointers to, 323–324
    as value types, 81
StructuralComparison/Person.cs, 147–148
StructuralComparison/Program.cs, 148, 149

StructuralObject, 870, 881
structure scope, 308
Students table, 607
Style class, 1008
styles (WPF elements), 1003–1004. *See also* resources
    Button element and, 1003–1004
    resources and, 1004
StylesAndResources/App.xaml, 1003, 1005, 1008
StylesAndResources/MainWindow.xaml, 1003, 1005
StylesAndResources/ResourceDemo.xaml, 1006,
    1007, 1008
StyleSheetTheme, 1206
Subject (project property), 415
SubKeyCount, 810
Subset(), 144
Substitution control, 1162
Substring(), 208, 222
subtracting pointers, 323
SUM, 964, 965
Sum(), 276, 286
‹summary›, 54
SumOfSegments(), 140
supporting windows (Visual Studio 2010), 374
SupportPhone, 415
SupportsWhatsNewAttribute, 338, 339, 345
SupportURL, 415
svctraceviewer.exe, 474, 1290
svcutil.exe, 1304, 1305, 1329
Swap‹T› (), 124
switch statements, 39–40
    default keyword and, 114
switches (trace switches), 467, 469
symmetric key algorithms, 554
symmetric keys, 552–554
synchronization, 317, 514–533
SynchronizationSamples/Job.cs, 515, 519
SynchronizationSamples/Program.cs, 516, 521
SynchronizationSamples/SharedState.cs, 515, 518,
    519, 520
synchronous programming
    asynchronous programming *v.*, 1357
    Message Queuing *v.*, 1357–1358, 1362
syndication, 1387–1395
    API, 1389, 1390, 1394
    Atom format and, 886, 1387, 1388, 1390, 1394
    RSS and, 949–950, 1387, 1388, 1389, 1390,
        1393, 1394
    System.SeviceModel.Syndication, 1387–1388,
        1391, 1394
    WCF and, 1387
Syndication Feeds (sample), 1390–1394
Syndication Reader (sample), 1388–1390
Syndication Service Library template, 1390
SyndicationCategory, 1388
SyndicationContent, 1388
SyndicationElementExtension, 1388

SyndicationFeed, 1388
SyndicationFeedFormatter, 1388
SyndicationItem, 1388
SyndicationItemFormatter, 1388
SyndicationLink, 1388
SyndicationPerson, 1388
SyndicationReader/SyndicationReader.xaml, 1390
*SyndicationReader/SyndicationReader.xaml
    .cs*, 1389
SyndicationService/IFormula1Feed.cs, 1391, 1393
syntax
    array, pointers and, 331
    base.‹MethodName›(), 93
    C#, 25–26
    Java, 25, 42
    pointers, 319–320
    XAML, 728–732
sysglobl, 601, 602
Sys.Services.AuthenticationService, 1241
Sys.Services.ProfileService, 1241
Sys.Services.RoleService, 1241
system access control list (SACL), 559
system queues, 1363
System.Activities, 744, 1316
System.Activities.Core.Presentation.dll, 1312
System.Activities.Debugger, 744
System.Activities.dll, 1312
System.Activities.DurableInstancing, 1327
System.Activities.Presentation.dll, 1312
System.Activities.Presentation.View, 1319
System.Activities.Statements, 728
System.ApplicationException, 353
System.Attribute, 334
System.Boolean, 35
System.Byte, 33
System.Char, 35
System.Collections, 108
System.Collections.ArrayList, 108
System.Collections.Concurrent, 225, 262, 290
System.Collections.Generic, 108, 109, 578
System.Collections.Specialized, 797
SystemColors, 1005
System.ComponentModel, 536, 586, 731, 870
System.ComponentModel.Composition, 747, 750, 765
System.Configuration.Install.Installer, 680
System.Convert, 176, 357
System.Core, 253, 273, 294
System.Data namespace, 818, 842, 860, 862
    shared classes in, 818
System.Data.Common, 818, 819, 862, 1129
System.Data.Common.CommandTrees, 862
System.Data.dll assembly, 832
System.Data.EntityClient, 818, 862
System.Data.Entity.Design, 862
System.Data.Linq.SqlClient, 818
System.Data.Objects, 862, 870

System.Data.Objects.DataClasses, 862, 870
System.Data.Odbc, 818
System.Data.OleDb, 818, 832
System.Data.ProviderBase, 818
System.Data.Services.Client, 894, 896, 1109
  DataServiceContext and, 895, 896, 1109
  .NET applications and, 896–902
System.Data.Services.Common, 886
System.Data.Services.DataServiceHost, 1304
System.Data.Sql, 818, 822
System.Data.SqlClient, 818, 822, 866, 957, 968, 969
System.Data.SqlTypes, 818
System.DateTime, 77, 79, 170, 212
System.Decimal, 34
System.Delegate, 185, 193
System.Diagnostics, 375, 461, 643
System.Diagnostics.Contracts, 461, 492, 1051
System.DirectoryServices, 562, 695
System.Double, 34
System.Drawing, 77
System.Drawing.Rectangle, 68
System.Dynamic, 295
System.EnterpriseServices transactions, 609, 610–611.
  See also transactions
System.Enum, 45, 85
System.Exception, 352, 357, 358, 362, 364
  properties, 359–360
SystemFonts, 1005
System.FormatException, 358, 365
System.GC.Collect(), 312
System.GC.SuppressFinalize(), 317
System.Globalization namespace, 569–570, 578, 601.
  See also globalization
System.IDisposable. See IDisposable
System.Int16, 33
System.Int32, 33
System.Int64, 33
System.IntPtr, 317
System.IO, 637, 638, 639, 658, 659
  classes in, 771
  stream-related classes (hierarchy) in, 787–788
System.IO.FileSystemWatcher, 768
System.IO.MemoryMappedFiles, 799
System.IO.MemoryStream, 787, 788
System.IO.Stream, 787
System.Linq, 253, 272, 273, 287, 289, 294
System.MarshalByRefObject, 444, 566, 772, 788
System.MulticastDelegate, 185, 193
System.Net, 637, 638, 640, 642, 665
System.Net.dll, 1346
System.Net.PeertoPeer, 1347–1352
System.Net.PeertoPeer.Collaboration, 1352–1355
System.Net.Sockets
  classes, 656
  networking and, 637, 656
System.Net.Sockets.NetworkStream, 787

System.Object, 84, 87, 89. See also Object class
SystemParameters, 1005
System.Reflection, 344, 437, 455, 698
System.Resources, 569, 580, 584, 603. See also
  localization
System.Resources.Tools, 584
System.Runtime.CompilerServices, 295, 299
System.Runtime.InteropServices, 437, 708, 716, 726
System.Runtime.Serialization, 771, 1289, 1379
System.Runtime.Serialization.Formatters.Binary,
  639, 924
System.Sbyte, 33
System.Security.AccessControl, 559, 802, 803, 804
System.Security.Cryptography classes, 553, 554, 555,
  556, 969. See also encryption
System.Security.Permissions, 564, 956
System.ServiceProcess, 670, 676, 679, 684, 685
System.ServiceProcess.NativeMethods, 676
System.ServiceProcess.ServiceController, 683. See also
  ServiceController class
System.SeviceModel.Syndication, 1387–1388, 1391,
  1394. See also syndication
System.Single, 34
System.String, 35, 208–209. See also String class
System.SystemException, 352–353
System.Text, 207, 210, 343, 346
System.Text.RegularExpressions, 207, 218, 219, 222
System.Text.StringBuilder. See StringBuilder
System.Threading, 184, 434, 533, 543, 546, 578, 1314
System.Threading.Tasks, 501
System.Threading.Thread, 184
System.Transactions, 605–636. See also transactions
System.Type, 85, 156
  methods, 341–342
  properties, 340–341
  reflection and, 85, 156, 340–342
System.UInt16, 33
System.UInt32, 33
System.UInt64, 33
System.ValueType, 82, 84, 90, 163, 178
System.Web.UI.WebControls.WebControl, 18, 1192
system-wide resources (WPF), 1005
System.Windows, 19, 203, 984
System.Windows.Annotations, 984
System.Windows.Automation, 984
System.Windows.Bam12006, 984
System.Windows.Browser, 1096, 1110
System.Windows.Controls, 984
System.Windows.Converters, 984
System.Windows.Data, 984
System.Windows.Documents, 984
System.Windows.Forms, 777, 784, 793, 801,
  1118–1119
System.Windows.Forms.PropertyGrid, 392
System.Windows.Ink, 984
System.Windows.Input, 984

System.Windows.Interop, 984
System.Windows.Markup, 728, 744, 985
System.Windows.Media, 985
System.Windows.Media.Animation, 1020
System.Windows.Media.Media3D, 1029
System.Windows.Navigation, 985
System.Windows.Resources, 985
System.Windows.Shapes, 985, 986
System.Windows.Threading, 985
System.Windows.Xps, 985
System.Xaml, 728, 744
System.Xml namespace, 829, 903, 904–905
System.Xml.Linq, 293, 903, 943, 944, 975
System.Xml.Serialization, 903, 934, 936, 1368
System.Xml.XPath, 917–922
System.Xml.Xsl, 922–927

T

tab character (escape sequence), 35
TabControl, 998, 1139–1140
TabItem control, 997
Table class, 1082
Table control, 1161
table per hierarchy (TPH), 873–874, 879
table per type (TPT), 874–876
TableDemo/MainWindow.xaml, 1083
TableDirect, 826, 850
TableLayoutPanel, 1138–1139
TableRow, 1082
tables, 1082–1083
    CSS stylesheets *v.*, 1198
    naming conventions, 859
    XML data types and, 972–973
TabPages, 1139–1140
tags, XML, 53–54
Take(), 263, 276, 279, 285, 1068, 1071
TakesAWhile(), 492
TakesAWhileCompleted(), 494
TakesAWhileDelegate, 492, 494, 495
TakeWhile, 276
target journaling, 1362
TargetPlatform (project property), 415
TargetSite (System.Exception), 359
TargetType, 1005
task dialog, 1408–1411, 1415
Task Parallel Library, 15
taskbar (Windows 7), 1411–1415
TaskbarDemo/MainWindow.xaml, 1412
TaskbarDemo/MainWindow.xaml.cs, 1414
TaskCanceledException, 510
TaskDialogDemo/app.manifest, 1409
TaskDialogDemo/MainWindow.xaml.cs, 1410
TaskFactory, 475, 501, 502, 509, 527, 530
tasks, 501–504

cancellation of, 507, 509–510
continuation, 502–503
defined, 501
hierarchies, 502–503
results from, 503–504
starting, 501–502
TaskSamples/Program.cs, 501, 502, 503
TaskWithResult, 503, 504
TCP (Transmission Control Protocol), 637, 658
    classes, 658–660
    UDP *v.*, 660
TcpClient class, 656, 673
TCP/IP, 637
TCP/IP Services, Simple, 668, 671
TcpListener class, 656, 658, 659, 660
TcpReceive application, 658–660
TcpSend application, 658–660
TDD (test-driven development) models, 1243
Team class, 269
TemperatureCalculatorExtension, 757
TemperatureConversion user control, 755, 757
TemperatureConversion/
    TemperatureCalculatorExtension.cs, 757
TemperatureConversion/TemperatureConversion.xaml
    .cs, 756
TemplateDemo/App.xaml, 1013
TemplateDemo/Countries.cs, 1016
TemplateDemo/Country.cs, 1015
TemplateDemo/StyledButtonWindow.xaml, 1014,
    1015, 1016
TemplateDemo/StyledListBoxWindow1.xaml
    .cs, 1017
TemplateDemo/Styles.xaml, 1013, 1018, 1019
templates (C++), 107. *See also* generics
templates (WPF), 995, 1011–1020
    control templates, 1012–1014
    types, 1012
Terminate(), 965, 966
ternary operator. *See* conditional operator
test-driven development (TDD) models, 1243
TestQuoteServer/Program.cs, 673
/t:exe, 50
Text (CommandType), 826
text boxes (dialog box), 424
text editor (Visual Studio 2010), 373–374
text elements, 1075–1084
TextBox control, 643, 645, 651, 659, 995,
    1137–1138, 1160
TextEffect, 1077–1078
TextEffectsDemo/MainWindow.xaml, 1078
TextWriterTraceListener, 470
TheBigClass, 81, 82
Theme attribute, 1206
themes (ASP.NET), 1206–1210
    applying to pages, 1207

defining, 1207
in PCSDemoSite, 1208–1210
ThenBy(), 279, 280, 281
ThenByDescending(), 275, 279
thick-client applications, 19
this keyword
  constructors and, 78, 96
  extension methods and, 87, 272
  instance field and, 31
  member fields and, 75
Thread class, 495–499
thread pools, 492, 499–501
thread priority, 498–499
ThreadingIssues/Program.cs, 513
ThreadingIssues/SampleTask.cs, 511, 512, 513, 514
ThreadPoolSamples/Program.cs, 500
threads, 184, 238, 317, 491–543. *See also*
    synchronization
  background, 497–498
  concurrent collections and, 264
  controlling, 499
  dependent transactions and, 617
  guidelines for, 543
  issues with, 510–514
  Main() and, 492
  MTAs and, 501, 699–700, 710, 718
  overview of, 492
  Parallel class and, 504–507
  passing data to, 496–497
  reasons for, 491
  safety. *See* lock statement
  STAs and, 699, 710, 718, 719
  tasks and, 501–504
  Windows Services and, 13
ThreadSamples/Program.cs, 496, 497, 498
Thread.Sleep(), 492, 499, 1050
ThreadStart, 238, 495
3-D book model, 1030–1033
3-D with WPF, 1029–1033
3DDemo/MainWindow.xaml, 1030, 1032
three-dimensional arrays, 133
throwing an exception, 354
throwing user-defined exceptions, 364–367
TicTacToe game, 145
tiered development, 856–857
time quantum, 498
Timeline, 1020–1023
TimeOfDay enum, 44, 45
Timer classes, 533–534
Timer control (ASP.NET AJAX), 1223
timers, 533–534
TimerSample/Program.cs, 534
Title (project property), 415
tlbexp utility, 714, 726
tlbimp utility, 707, 726

/t:library, 50
/t:module, 50
ToArray(), 274
ToArray (conversion operator), 276
ToDictionary, 276
ToEnumerable(), 274
ToggleButton, 995
ToList, 276
ToLongDateString(), 573, 574
ToLookup(), 253, 254, 276, 288
ToLower(), 208
ToolBar control, 998
ToolBarPanel, 999
ToolStrip control, 1140–1141
ToolStripButton, 1140
ToolStripContainer control, 1142
ToolStripControlHost, 1140–1141
ToolStripDropDownItem, 1140–1141
ToolStripLabel, 1140
ToolStripManager, 1141–1142
ToolStripMenuItem, 1141
ToolStripSeparator, 1140
ToolTip, 995
Top(), 879
ToString(), 33, 36, 84, 85–86, 212, 214, 215,
    227, 251
  IFormattable and, 214
  overriding, 36, 82, 85
  StringBuilder and, 212
ToUpper(), 208, 216, 227
TPH. *See* table per hierarchy
TPT. *See* table per type
trace listeners, 467, 470–471
TRACE preprocessor symbol, 397
trace sources, 467, 468–469
trace switches, 467, 469
trace viewer, 473
Trace Viewer tool, Service, 474, 1290
TraceFilter, 467, 472
TraceListener, 470
TraceListenerCollection, 467
TraceSource class, 468, 1399
tracing, 461, 467–475
  architecture, 467
  classes for, 467
  correlation and, 472–475
  editor application and, 1399
  filters and, 471–472
  WCF and, 1289–1290
TracingDemo/App.config, 469, 470, 471, 472, 473
TracingDemo/Program.cs, 468, 469, 473
trackers, 1342
traditional transactions, 609–611. *See also*
    transactions
TransactedFile, 634, 635

Transaction class
  methods, 611–612
  properties, 611–612
transaction manager, 606
transactional queues, 1377–1378, 1382, 1385
transactional resources, 627–632
TransactionAutoComplete, 1298
TransactionAutoCompleteOnSessionClose, 1294
TransactionCompleted event, 612, 618
TransactionInformation property, 611
TransactionIsolationLevel, 1294
transactions (System.Transactions), 605–636
  ACID properties and, 607, 635
  ADO.NET transactions *v.*, 609–610. *See also* ADO
    .NET
  'all or nothing' characteristic of, 605
  ambient, 618–624, 635
        multithreading with, 621–624
        nested scopes with, 620–621
  automatic, 610, 611, 636, 1279
  committable, 612–614
  components of, 606
  dependent, 616–618
  isolation level and, 624–626, 824–825
  overview, 605–606
  phases of, 606
  promotable, 614–616
  System.EnterpriseServices transactions *v.*, 609,
    610–611
  transaction scope, 824–825
  with Windows 7/ Windows Serve 2008, 632–635
TransactionSamples/Program.cs, 614, 615, 617, 619,
    620
TransactionScope, 618, 619, 620, 625, 635, 824
TransactionScopeOption, 620, 621, 626
TransactionScopeRequired, 1298
TransformationDemo/MainWindow.xaml, 990
transformations (WPF), 990
TransformGroup, 990
transforms, 922–927
  debugging, 925–927
  transforming XML, XsltArgumentList, 923–925
  XML data store and, 927
TranslateTransform, 994
Transmission Control Protocol. *See* TCP
transparent code, 561
TreeView control, 998, 1063–1067, 1199
TreeViewItem, 998
Trigger class, 1009
TriggerDemo/Book.cs, 1010
TriggerDemo/DataTriggerWindow.xaml, 1011
TriggerDemo/MultiTriggerWindow.xaml, 1010
TriggerDemo/PropertyTriggerWindow.xaml,
    1009
triggers, 970–972. *See also specific triggers*

event, 1020, 1023–1025
  Expander control and, 997
  Message Queueing and, 1360
  WPF, 1008–1111
TrimExcess(), 228, 237
Trust Manager, 422
Trusted Application Deployment, 421
Trusted Publishers, 568
Trusted Root Certification Authorities, 568
try blocks, 314, 353–355
  nested, 360–362
try...catch...finally blocks, database connections and,
    822–823
TryFindResource(), 1006
TryGetMember(), 303
TryGetObjectByKey(), 873, 882
TryGetValue(), 247, 253, 263
TryInvokeMember(), 303
TrySetMember(), 303
T-SQL. *See also* Entity SQL
  Entity SQL and, 866, 867, 868
  stored procedures, 956, 967–969
  XQuery expressions and, 980
tunneling events, 201, 736–739
tuples, 129, 146–149, 226, 503, 504, 529
  arrays *v.*, 147–149
  F# and, 146
  TaskWithResult and, 503, 504
TuplesSample/Program.cs, 146
/t:winexe, 50
Two(), 195
two-dimensional arrays, 132, 133
Type class. *See* System.Type
type conversions, 158–161. *See also* casting
  collections and, 235–236
  explicit, 159–161
  implicit, 158–159
  type safety and, 157
type converters, 731
type inference, 28
type information operator, 152
type library
  COM and, 696
  for .NET component, 714–716
type safety. *See also* strong data typing
  generics and, 107, 109
  IL and, 11, 12, 157
  memory type safety, 13, 22
  pointers and, 8, 318
  type conversions and, 157
  unsafe code, operators, 152
TypeCatalog, 768
TypeConverter, 730, 731
TypeExtension (x:Type), 744
typeof operator, 45, 152, 156, 340

types. *See* CTS types; data types; generic types;
      reference types; value types
TypeView example, 342–344

U

UAC (user account control), 1397, 1398, 1404–1406,
      1415
   administrative privileges and, 1404–1405
   shield icons and, 1405–1406
uCreditCard, 970
UDP (User Datagram Protocol), 660
   class for, 661
   ports, 1345
   TCP *v.*, 660
UdpClient class, 656, 661
UDTClient/Program.cs, 964
UDTs (user-defined types)
   from client-side code, 963–964
   creating, 958–963
   restriction for, 964
   with SQL Server, 963
Uid attributes, 594, 596–597
UIElement, 986, 999
uint, 33
   casting
            float to uint, 175
            uint to float, 174
UIPermission, 563
ulong, 33
unary operators, 156, 157, 172, 319
unboxing, 108, 111, 161, 178–179
unchecked operator. *See* checked/unchecked operators
#undef, 55–56
UnderlyingSystemType (System.Type), 341
underscore
   fields and, 61, 73
   identifiers and, 58, 59
   joining names with, 60
UnexpectedException, 363, 366, 367, 368
unhandled exceptions, 360
Unicode characters
   char and, 35
   identifiers and, 59
   strings and, 37
   System.Globalization and, 570
   Unicode-based formats, 794, 795, 797, 798
Uniform Resource Identifiers. *See* URIs
Uniform Resource Locators. *See* URLs
UniformGrid, 1002
Uninstall(), 679, 680, 683
Union(), 276, 283, 879
UnionAll(), 879
UniqueConstraint, 842, 843
universal unique ID (UUID), 703, 1363, 1364

UNIX, 17, 59, 217
unmanaged C++, 6, 11
unmanaged resources
   freeing, 312–313
   working with, 307
unmanaged types, 320
unpinning/pinning windows, 394
unsafe (safety level), 956
unsafe code
   anonymous methods and, 197
   operators and, 152
   pointers and, 317–319. *See also* pointers
unsafe keyword, 318–319
Unspecified (isolation level), 625
UPDATE, 819, 826, 830, 838, 850, 860, 971
update constraints, 843–844
UpdatePanel controls, 1222, 1229–1231
UpdateProgress control, 1222, 1231
UpdateRowSource, 832, 853
updates (ADO.NET Entity Framework),
      879–884
   attaching/detaching entities, 882
   change information, 881–882
   object tracking, 880
   storing entity changes, 882–883
Upgrade Wizard (Visual Studio 2010), 376
UpgradeCode, 415
UploadData(), 639
UploadFile(), 639
uploading files (with WebClient class), 639–640
Uri class, 653–654
UriBuilder class, 653–654
URIs (Uniform Resource Identifiers)
   defined, 638
   utility classes and, 653–654
URL operation routing, 1266–1267
URL queries, to WCF Data Services, 893–894
URLs (Uniform Resource Locators), 638
usage conventions, 59–64. *See also* naming
      conventions
user account control. *See* UAC
user controls
   ASP.NET, 1155, 1186–1191
   Windows Forms, 1147
User Datagram Protocol. *See* UDP
user interaction, controls and, 1124
user interface (ASP.NET AJAX Library layer), 1223
User Interface editor, 423–424
user interfaces, Windows Forms and, 21
UserControl class, 996
user-defined aggregates, 964–967, 980
   creating, 965–966
   using, 966–967
user-defined casts, 172–182
user-defined exception classes, 362–369

user-defined exceptions
  catching, 363–364
  throwing, 364–367
user-defined functions, 969–970
user-defined integer types. *See* enumerations
user-defined types. *See* UDTs
UseSynchronizationContext, 1295
ushort, 33
using clause, 823–824, 860
using keyword
  aliases and, 47
  namespaces and, 25, 46–47
using namespace statement (C++), 25
using System statement, 47
UsingSP/Program.cs, 968
UTF7, 794, 795
UTF8 encoding, 794, 795, 796, 811, 812
UTF32, 794, 795
Utilities class, 612
Utilities/Utilities.cs, 612
UUID (universal unique ID), 703,
    1363, 1364
uuidgen.exe utility, 1363

V

ValidateMustUnderstand, 1295
validation
  activity validation, 1317
  web server controls, 1163–1164
  WPF and, 1057–1061
  with XmlReader, 910–911
ValidationSummary, 1163, 1164, 1165, 1168
‹value›, 54
value changed callbacks, 735–736
value conversion (WPF), 1051–1057
VALUE index, 978
value types, 308–309
  defined, 8
  memory management and, 307–309
  predefined, 33–35
  reference types *v.*, 8, 32–33
  stack and, 8, 32, 308–309
  structs as, 81
ValueCount, 810
var keyword
  dynamic programming (C#) and, 295
  dynamic type and, 296
  new keyword and, 79
  type inference and, 28
Var.cs, 28
variable scope, 29–31
variables
  declaring, 26–31
  initialization of, 27
  naming conventions, 60–63

  outside of Lambda expressions, 199
  workflows and, 1322–1323
Variance/IDisplay.cs, 121
Variance/IIndex.cs, 119
Variance/Program.cs, 120, 121
Variance/RectangleCollection.cs, 120
Variance/Rectangle.cs, 119
Variance/Shape.cs, 119
Variance/ShapeDisplay.cs, 121
VARIANT, 698, 701
Vector class, 32, 337, 339, 341
Vector Struct (operator overloading example),
    165–171. *See also* FormattableVector
VectorAsCollection sample, 337, 339
vector-based WPF, 990
VectorClass assembly (WhatsNewAttributes), 337,
    339–340
VectorEnumerator, 340, 349
vectors
  adding, 165–166
  bit vectors, 260–262
  comparing, 170–171
  multiplying, 168–169
VectorStruct solution, 166
VectorStructMoreOverloads.sln, 168
Version (project property), 415
versioning
  data contracts and, 1292
  shared assemblies and, 454–458
versions
  assemblies
    binding to, 456–457
    programmatically getting, 455–456
    version numbers, 455
  CLR
    filenames and, 409
    installing/using multiple versions, 458
vertical tab (escape sequence), 35
View (container for controls), 1161
view (MVC framework), 1260. *See also* MVC
Viewbox, 998, 999
viewing assemblies, 434–435
Views directory, 1261
virtual (modifier), 100
virtual address space. *See* virtual memory
virtual addressing, 308
virtual Equals(), 162
virtual keyword, 91, 93
virtual memory (virtual address space), 11, 308
  allocation
    on heap, 309–311
    on stack, 308–311
  application domains and, 12–13
  processes and, 11–12
virtual methods, 91–92
virtual properties, 91–92

virtual table (vtable), 697, 698
VirtualDirectory, 419
visibility modifiers, 66, 99
Visual Basic 6, 5, 8, 16, 18, 19
    COM component creation and, 702
    MTAs and, 700
Visual Basic 2010
    CLS-compliant code and, 9
    .NET Framework and, 5
Visual Basic.NET, 5, 61, 62, 100
Visual C++ 2010, .NET Framework and, 5–6
Visual class, 986
Visual InterDev, 18
Visual State Manager, 1026–1029
Visual Studio 2010, 373–406
    Add Service Reference, 1304, 1305
    add-ins and, 747
    Aggregate template, 966
    Build Deploy Project menu, 963
    Class View window, 392–393
    code contracts and, 462
    command prompt, 24
    compiling
        from within environment, 374–375
        unsafe code, 319
    Conversion Wizard, 376
    debugging in, 375, 398–401
    deployment and, 407–427. See also deployment
    design view editor, 374, 388
    Design View window, 388–391
    document window, 376, 398, 402, 405
    editors, 422–427
    features, 373–375
    folding editor feature, 386–388
    installer project types, 408, 412
    IntelliSense, 44, 60, 115, 374, 375, 388, 709, 1128,
        1155, 1157, 1189, 1234, 1239
    language independence, 385
    localization and, 584–591
    MSDN documentation and, 375
    multi-targeting .NET Framework 4 with, 375,
        403–404
    Object Browser window, 393
    projects
        building, 394–398
        coding, 386–394
        creating, 378–386
        deployment, 408, 412
        dialog boxes for, 424
        files in, 382–383
        setup, 412
        solutions v., 383–386
        types, 379–381
    Properties window, 391–392
    refactoring with, 401–403
    Server Explorer, 476, 484, 486, 683, 684

    Server Explorer window, 393–394, 1170
    supporting windows, 374
    text editor, 373–374
    Upgrade Wizard, 376
    Visual Studio 2010 and, 375
    WF applications in, 405–406
    WPF applications in, 404–405
VisualBrush, 993–994
visuals, printing, 1092–1093
VisualStateDemo/MainWindow.xaml, 1029
VisualStateGroups, 1027, 1028, 1029
void pointers, 321
voltage levels, 657
VolumeSeparatorChar, 775
vtable (virtual table), 697, 698

W

W3C (World Wide Web Consortium)
    DOM Level 1,DOM Level 2, 904, 913
    XML 1.0 namespace recommendations, 906, 912
    XML standards support (in .NET), 904
    XmlDocument, 905
    XQuery and, 977
W3SVC service registry configuration, 679
wait handles, 493–494, 495, 522–523
WaitAny(), 522, 527, 1314
WaitHandle class, 515, 522, 526, 527, 1314
#warning, 57
WAS (Windows Activation Services), 1287, 1302, 1303,
    1308
watches, 375, 399–400
WCF (Windows Communication Foundation),
    20, 1279–1308. See also Message Queuing;
    syndication; WCF Data Services; Workflow 4
    binding and, 1300–1302
    client applications and, 1304–1305
    components in, 1280
    contracts and, 1291–1294
    Course Order application and, 1378–1384
    custom service hosts, 1287
    encryption and, 545
    features of, 1280
    hosting and, 1302–1304
    IIS and, 1302, 1303
    JSON and, 1282
    mapped-memory files and. See mapped-memory files
    markup extensions and, 744
    Message Queuing with, 1378–1385
    network protocols and, 637
    overview, 1279–1282
    REST and, 1281, 1282
    service implementation, 1294–1299
    simple service and client (RoomReservation service),
        1282–1290
    SOAP and, 1281
    StateService sample, 1295–1299

WCF (Windows Communication Foundation)
  (*continued*)
  syndication and, 1387
  tracing and, 1289–1290
  WCF Data Services and, 886, 889
  WSDL and, 1281, 1290, 1291, 1292, 1304, 1305
WCF Data Services, 885–902
  ADO.NET Entity Framework and, 885–886, 894–895
  data service context, 886, 896–897, 902
      adding/modifying/deleting entities, 900–901
      DataServiceContext, 895, 896, 1109
      object tracking and, 900
      operation batching and, 901–902
  hosting with CLR objects, 886–890
  HTTP client application, 891–893
  LINQ queries and, 897–898, 902
  networking example. *See* networking example
  observable collections and, 898–899
  overview of, 885–886
  URL queries to, 893–894
  WCF and, 886, 889
WCF Service Application, 381
WCF Service Host, 1284–1286, 1287, 1393
WCF Service Library, 381, 1283, 1284, 1303, 1380
WCF Test Client, 1284–1286
WCFRegistration/MainPage.xaml, 1098
WCFRegistration/Views/Home.xaml, 1105, 1106
WCFRegistration/Views/Welcome.xaml, 1099
WCFRegistration/Views/Welcome.xaml.cs, 1101
weak events, 203–205
WeakEventsSample/Consumer.cs, 205
WeakEventsSample/Program.cs, 205
WeakEventsSample/WeakCarInfoEventManager.cs,
  204
web applications (ASP.NET), 1150–1151
  Copy Web Tool and, 411
  defined, 1181
  security, 1201–1206
  xcopy and, 411
Web Forms (ASP.NET), 18, 1149, 1151–1154
  Windows Forms *v.*, 19
web method calls, asynchronous, 1240–1241
web methods, 1240
Web Parts, 1210–1218
  controls, 1211–1212
  functionality of, 1210
  PCSWebParts example, 1212–1218
web server controls (ASP.NET), 18, 1155
  data web server controls, 1162–1163
  dynamic data controls, 1162, 1163
  list of, 1160–1162
  login, 1203–1204
  navigation, 1198–1201
  validation web server controls, 1163–1164
Web Setup Projects, 412
web sites

ASP.NET, 1150–1151
  navigation, 1198–1201
  security, 1201–1206
  publishing, 408, 411
WebApplication/MultiLanguage.aspx, 592
WebApplication/Web.config, 592
WebBrowser control, 637, 643–652
  COM and, 643
  displaying code of requested page with, 651–652
  examples
      browsing inside applications, 643–645
      displaying output as HTML page, 643
      IE-type features for application, 645–650
      launching Internet Explorer instances, 645
  printing with, 651
WebClient class, 638–640
  asynchronous event pattern and, 535
  downloading files with, 638–639
  uploading files with, 639–640
WebClient project, 409
Web.config (ASP.NET MVC), 1261
WebHttpBinding, 1300
WebInvoke, 886
WebPartManager, 1211
WebPartZone, 1211
WebPermission, 563
WebRequestClient/WebRequestClient.xaml.cs, 892
WebRequest/WebResponse classes, 640–643, 665.
      See also HttpWebRequest; HttpWebResponse
  asynchronous page requests and, 642–643
  asynchronous programming and, 535
  authentication and, 642
  hierarchy of, 652–653
  proxy servers and, 642
welcome (dialog box), 424
well-connected clouds, 1342
WER (Windows Error Reporting), 567, 1398
WF. *See* Workflow 4
WhatsNewAttributes, 337–340, 345–349
  completion of, 345–349
  library assembly, 338–339
  VectorClass assembly, 337, 339–340
WhatsNewAttributes.cs, 339
WhatsNewChecker, 346
Where(), 272, 273, 275, 277, 279, 281, 289, 290, 291,
      294, 878, 879
where clause, 115, 116, 125, 277, 278, 280, 283, 289
where T: class, 116
where T: Foo, 116
where T: IFoo, 116
where T: new(), 116
where T: struct, 116, 122
where T1: T2, 116
while loops, 42
Wiley Publishing
  Beginning Regular Expressions, 218

Professional ASP.NET4: in C# and VB, 247, 1156, 1181
Professional Microsoft SQL Server 2008 Programming, 955
Professional XML, 904
WinCV utility, 16
Window class, 996
Window element, 1005
Window_Loaded(), 1350, 1354
Windows 7
   Client Software Logo document, 1398
   command link controls, 1407–1408
   directory structure, 1406–1407
   Easy Connect, 1346
   guidelines, 1397–1415
   Jump Lists, 1411, 1414–1415
   Message Queuing. *See* Message Queuing
   PNRP in, 1345–1346
   taskbar, 1411–1415
   transactions with, 632–635
   UAC, 1397, 1398, 1404–1406, 1415
Windows Activation Services (WAS), 1287, 1302, 1303, 1308
Windows API Code Pack, 1397–1398, 1402, 1407, 1408, 1410, 1415
Windows Authentication, 820, 1201
Windows CardSpace, 404
Windows Communication Foundation. *See* WCF
Windows Controls, 19
Windows Error Reporting (WER), 567, 1398
Windows Forms, 19, 1117–1147
   applications
      localization and, 584–591
      MDI-type, 78, 1141, 1142, 1146
      project template, 380
      simple example, 1117–1122, 1142
   class hierarchy, 1122
   Control class, 1122–1125. *See also* controls
   Form class, 1142
   forms, 1142–1146
   performance counters and, 486
   user interfaces and, 21
   Web Forms *v.*, 19
Windows Forms Control Library, 379, 380
Windows Forms Designer, 585, 586, 589, 591
Windows functionality, controls and, 1125
Windows Installer technology, 408, 412. *See also* installation packages
   ClickOnce *v.*, 420
   SDK, 412
   Visual Studio 2010 installer project types and, 408, 412
Windows Presentation Foundation. *See* WPF
Windows Resource Localization Editor, 591
Windows Search, 668
Windows Server 2008

   guidelines, 1397–1415. *See also* Windows 7
   Message Queuing. *See* Message Queuing
   transactions with, 632–635
Windows Services (formerly NT Services), 20, 381, 667–693
   administration tool, 668
   architecture, 668–670
   classes for, 670
   creating functionality for, 671
   defined, 667–668
   event logging, 692–693
   HKEY_LOCAL_MACHINESystemCurrentControl SetServices and, 679
   installer classes (class diagram), 679
   MMC snap-in, 616, 669, 683
   performance counters and, 484, 486
   Quote service. *See* Quote service
   threads and, 679
   troubleshooting, 692
   xcopy installation and, 670
Windows socket API functions, 637
Windows Software Logo Kit, 1398
Windows Workflow Foundation 3.0 (online Chapter 57), 1309
Windows Workflow Foundation 4. *See* Workflow 4
Windows1.xaml.cs, 301
Windows7Transactions/Program.cs, 638
WindowsFormsCommandLink/Form1.Designer.cs, 1408
Windows-integrated security, 820
WindowsPrincipal/Program.cs, 546
winres.exe, 591
WithCancellation(), 290
WithDegreeOfParallelism(), 290
WithExecutionMode(), 290
WithoutSchema.xml, 854, 855
Wizard control, 1161
Workflow 4 (WF/ Windows Workflow Foundation 4), 20, 1309–1337
   applications, in Visual Studio 2010, 405–406
   Designer rehosting, 1332–1337
   Hello World example, 1310–1311
   markup extensions and, 744
   XAML and, 727, 728, 744, 745
Workflow Console Application, 381, 405, 1310
Workflow Designer. *See* Designer rehosting
WorkflowApplication class, 1323–1327
WorkflowExecutor, 1322, 1323
WorkflowInvoker, 1311, 1322, 1323, 1336
workflows, 1322–1332. *See also* activities
   as activities, 1311
   arguments and, 1322–1323
   bookmarks and, 1324–1325
   defined, 1311
   extensions and, 1325–1326
   hosting, 1327
   reloading, 1326

WorkflowServiceHost, 1327–1332
WorkflowXamlServices, 744
World Wide Web Consortium. *See* W3C
World Wide Web Publishing Service, 668
WPF (Windows Presentation Foundation), 19.
    See also Silverlight
  applications, in Visual Studio 2010, 404–405
  business application features, 1035–1073. *See also*
      BooksDemo application; Formula-1 sample
      database
          commanding, 1061–1063
          data binding, 1035–1051
          DataGrid control, 1067–1073
          TreeView control, 1063–1067
          validation, 1057–1061
          value conversion, 1051–1057
  class hierarchy, 985–986
  classes in, 983, 984, 985–986
  core, 983–1033
  dependency properties, XAML and, 732–736
  documents and, 1075–1094. *See also* documents
  features
          animations, 1020–1029
          brushes, 991–994
          controls, 994–999
          geometries, 988–989
          layout containers, 999–1002
          resources, 1004–1008
          shapes, 986–987
          styles, 1003–1004
          templates, 995, 1011–1020
          3-D features, 1029–1033
          transformations, 990
          triggers, 1008–1111
  localization and, 593–598
  markup extensions and, 744
  namespaces in, 984–985
  .NET resources and, 594
  overview, 983–985
  performance counters and, 486
  Silverlight *v.*, 1095–1097
  trace sources and, 467
  type converters, XML attributes and, 731
  vector-based, 990
  weak event pattern and, 204
  XAML and, 19, 727, 728, 731, 732, 734, 736, 738,
      744, 745, 983
WPF Application (project type), 380
WPF Browser Application (project type), 380
WPF Custom Control Library, 380
WPF editor application, 1398–1403
  EditorDemo/App.xaml.cs, 1400
  EditorDemo/CurrentFile.cs, 1399
  EditorDemo/MainWindow.xaml.cs, 1401
  tracing and, 1399

WPF User Control Library, 380, 755
WPF User Controls, 755, 757, 762
WPFApplicationUsingResources/MainWindow.xaml,
    593, 594
WPFApplicationUsingXAMLDictionaries/
    AssemblyInfo.cs, 595
WPFApplicationUsingXAMLDictionaries/
    LocalizationStrings.xaml, 595
WPFApplicationUsingXAMLDictionaries/
    MainWindow.xaml, 596
WPFApplicationUsingXAMLDictionaries/
    WPFApplicationUsingXAMLDictionaries.csproj,
    595
WPFCalculator, 762, 765
WPFCalculator/CalculatorExtensionImport.cs, 763
WPFCalculator/CalculatorImport.cs, 764
WPFCalculator/MainWindow.xaml.cs, 764, 765,
    766, 768
WPFCommandLink/MainWindow.xaml, 1408
WrapPanel, 1000, 1019
WriteAllBytes(), 786
WriteAllLines(), 786, 787
WriteAllText(), 786
WriteAttributeInfo(), 348
WriteEntry(), 478, 479, 483
WriteEvent(), 478, 479, 483
write-only properties, 73
WriteXml(), 854, 928, 929, 931, 932
writing custom attributes, 334–337
writing event log entries, 479
writing to files, 784–787
  binary files, 789–793
  text files, 793–799
writing to isolated storage, 810–814
writing to registry, 806–810
writing to streams, 787
writing to XML documents, 952–953
writing XAML, 744–1173
WroxDynamicObject, 303, 304
WS2007HttpBinding, 1300
WSDL (Web Services Description Language), 1281,
    1290, 1291, 1292, 1304, 1305
WSDualHttpBinding, 1300
WSFederationHttpBinding, 1300
WSHttpBinding, 1300
WSHttpContextBinding, 1300

X

X (hexadecimal format), 52, 213
XAML (Extensible Application Markup Language),
    727–745
  attached properties and, 739–741
  bubbling events and, 201, 736–739
  collections and, 731–732

constructors and, 732
custom .NET classes and, 3–4
data binding with, 1037–1039
data types and, 5
dependency properties and, 732–736, 739
generic collection classes and, 732
generics and, 728, 732, 744
markup extensions and, 741–744
overview, 727–728
reading, 744–745
Silverlight and, 727, 728, 745
syntax, 728–732
        elements map to .NET objects, 728–729
        properties as attributes, 730–731
        properties as elements, 731
tools for creating, 727
tunneling events and, 201, 736–739
WF and, 727, 728, 744, 745
WPF and, 19, 727, 728, 731, 732, 734, 736, 738, 744,
        745, 983
writing, 744–745
XAML resource dictionaries, 594–598
XAML view (document window), 405
XamlDebuggerXmlReader, 744
XAML-defined markup extensions, 744
XAMLIntro/App.xaml, 729
XAMLIntro/MainWindow.xaml, 729, 730
XamlObjectWriter, 744
XAMLPad.exe tool, 1078
XamlReader, 728, 744
XamlServices, 744
XAMLSyntax/MainWindow.xaml, 730, 731, 732
XamlWriter, 728, 744
XamlXmlWriter, 744
x:Array, 732, 744
XAttribute, 947–948
XComment, 946–947
xcopy deployment, 408, 410–411, 412, 452
xcopy installation, 15, 670
XDocument, 943
XElement, 944
XML (Extensible Markup Language), 903–954
  ADO.NET and, 844, 927–934
        converting ADO.NET data to XML, 927–932
        converting XML to ADO.NET data, 932–934
  Ajax and, 1220
  attributes, type converters (WPF) and, 731
  binding to, 1055–1057
  documentation, 53–55
  LINQ to XML, 293, 942–943, 954
        CRUD operations, 954
        helper objects, 943–948, 954
        querying dynamic XML documents, 949–951
        querying static XML documents, 948–949
  .NET Framework and, 903, 904, 942–943

objects, 943–948
Professional XML, 904
RSS and. *See* RSS
schemas (XSD), 844–850
serializing objects in, 934–942, 1291, 1368
Shakespeare's plays in, 943
standards, .NET and, 904
System.XML namespace, 904–905
tags, 53–54
Xml (text display control), 1161
XML Data Modification Language (XML DML),
        977–978
XML data store, transforms and, 927
XML data types, 972–980
  querying, 976–977
  reading values, 973–976
  strongly typed, 979–980
  XML DML and, 977–978
XML DML. *See* XML Data Modification Language
XML documents
  querying
        dynamic XML documents, 949–951
        static XML documents, 948–949
  reading from, 951–952
  writing to, 952–953
XML indexes, 978–979
XML Paper Specification. *See* XPS
XML serialization, 934–942, 1291, 1368
XML Web Services, 18–19, 21, 373
XmlAttribute, 913, 934
XmlAttributeOverrides, 940, 941, 942
XmlAttributes, 940, 941, 942
XmlCDataSection, 913
XmlComment, 913
XmlDataDocument, 905, 914, 922, 927, 929,
        930, 931
XmlDataSource, 1162
XmlDeclaration, 913, 917
XmlDocument, 471, 905, 914–917
XmlDocumentFragment, 913
XmlDocumentType, 913
XMLDOM.cs (code snippet), 914, 915
XmlElement, 913, 915, 916, 917, 934
XmlEntity, 913
XmlEntityReferenceNode, 913
XMLHttpRequest, 1220
XmlLinkedNode, 913
XmlNode, 905, 906, 915, 917, 928, 974
XmlNodeList, 905, 913, 914, 915
XmlNotation, 913
XmlnsDefinition, 730
XmlProcessingInstruction, 913
XmlQueryOutput, 906
XmlReader, 904, 906–911
  read methods, 907–909

XmlReader (*continued*)
   retrieving attribute data, 909–910
   validating with, 910–911
XMLReaderSample.sln, 907, 909, 911, 912
XmlResolver, 905, 922
XmlSamples/Program.cs, 975
XmlSerializer, 934, 938, 941
XmlSignificantWhitespace, 913
XmlText, 913
XmlTextReader, 813, 814, 904, 906, 908, 911
XmlTextWriter, 811, 812, 904, 906, 911, 916, 923
XmlUrlResolver, 905
XmlValidatingReader, 906, 918
XmlWhitespace, 913
XmlWriter, 904, 911–913
XmlWriterSettings, 911, 912
XmlWriterTraceListener, 470, 471, 472, 473,
   474, 1290
XNamespace, 945–946
x:Null, 744
Xor(), 258, 260
XPath, 917. *See also* System.Xml.XPath
XPathDocument, 918
XPathNavigator class, 918
   "move" methods in, 918
   Select methods in, 918
XPathNavigators, 471, 917–922
XPathNodeIterator, 918–919, 920, 921
XPS (XML Paper Specification), 1089
XPS documents, 1089–1091
XpsDocument, 1090

XpsDocumentWriter, 1090, 1091, 1092, 1093
XQuery, 977
XQuery Update Facility 1.0, 978
XSD (XML schema definition file), 844–850
XSD tool (XSD.EXE), 844, 845, 849, 860
XSDDataSet.cs, 850
XslSample01.sln, 922, 923
XSLT, 903, 904, 922
   debugging, 925–927
   editor, 926
   style sheet, 1161
   System.Xml.Xsl, 922–927
x:Static, 744
x:Type, 744
x:TypeArguments, 732
x:Uid attributes, 594, 596–597

Y

yield break, 142, 145, 146
yield return, 142, 144, 145–146, 273, 289
yield statement, 110, 111, 142–146
YieldDemo/GameMoves.cs, 145–146
YieldDemo/Program.cs, 142, 144, 146

Z

zero impact installation, 15. *See also* xcopy installation
zero-parameter constructor, 76, 82
Zip(), 276, 284–285

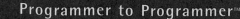